DOD'S
PARLIAMENTARY
COMPANION
2000

Dod's Parliamentary Companion 2000

168th Year

ONE HUNDRED AND EIGHTY FIRST EDITION

*The Fifteenth Parliament of HM Queen Elizabeth II
elected May 1, 1997*

1832

Dod's Parliamentary Companion
First published in 1832

Published by
Vacher Dod Publishing Ltd
PO Box 3700, Westminster, London SW1E 5NP
Telephone: 020 7828 7256
Fax: 020 7828 7269
Editorial enquiries: 01932 860288
E-mail: politics@vacherdod.co.uk
Websites: www.vacherdod.co.uk
www.politicallinks.co.uk

Publisher
Andrew Cox

Chairman
Arthur Kerswill

Editor
Michael Bedford

Contributing Editors
Elizabeth Gunn, Janet Eaton, Rohan Bolton (Europe)

IT and Production
Eddie Green, Alf Gatward, Roy Hodgkinson

Listings Manager
Gordon Collier

Subscriptions
Jo Wass

Dod on Disk
Oliver Cox

ISBN 0 905702 28 X   ISSN 0070-7007

Database typesetting by Vacher Dod Publishing Limited
Printed in Great Britain by The Cromwell Press, Trowbridge, Wiltshire

CONTENTS

The Keys to the House

The latest Parliamentary Publications can be ordered directly from the number below. Orders received by 3pm despatched same day.

FOREWORD

H OUSE OF C OMMONS
L ONDON SW1A 0AA

It is no exaggeration to say that *Dod's Parliamentary Companion* is an integral part of British political life. What changes there have been since it first appeared in 1832 – a massively expanded franchise, dramatic changes in the types of legislation that pass through Parliament, and the establishment of new representative bodies for the EU, Scotland, Wales and Northern Ireland.

Throughout momentous changes, Dod's has been consistently invaluable to MPs and their staff, as well as those well beyond Westminster. I have used it many times, and thoroughly recommend it as the first port of call for any query about the workings of Parliament.

The Rt Hon. Charles Kennedy, MP

There's more than just books at the Parliamentary Bookshop

Here, you'll find the full range of publications on parliamentary activity. But more than that you will find help, information, pictures, videos, CDs and much much more.

Run by House of Commons staff, the shop offers a service to keep enquirers not only fully informed about documents from the current session of Parliament, but also to provide ready access to material from previous sessions.

Among the range of documents available are:

- Commons and Lords Hansard.
- Bills.
- Standing Committee Hansard.
- Select Committees reports.
- Command Papers including State Papers, White Papers, Green Papers, Reports of Royal Commissions.
- Acts of Parliament and Statutory Instruments.
- Citizens Charter documents.
- Parliamentary Office of Science and Technology reports.

Professional organisations can be provided with special facilities for their couriers, allowing them to collect urgently needed publications. They may also place a Standing Order for documentation relating to special topics, to receive it as soon as it is published. Customers account facilities are, of course, available upon request.

THE PARLIAMENTARY BOOKSHOP

12 Bridge Street, Parliament Square, London SW1A 2JX
Tel: 020 7219 3890 Fax: 020 7219 3866

Introduction

Elections in Scotland and Wales

If 1998 was the year of referendums, 1999 was the year of elections. On 6 May the elections to the Scottish Parliament and the National Assembly for Wales took place – the third occasion on which Scotland and Wales had gone to the polls in just over two years. The elections combined the traditional first past the post system and a form of proportional representation called the Additional Member System. Each voter cast two votes, one vote for a constituency member, based on the Westminster parliament constituencies. The second went towards the election of 'top-up' members for each of the regions used in the European Parliament elections. These seats ensure that each party's representation reflects its overall share of the vote. In both countries the Labour Party came first but failed to obtain an overall majority of votes or seats and the national parties (SNP and Plaid Cymru) came second. The Liberal Democrats won more first past the post seats than the Conservatives but due to the operation of the top-up system came fourth, behind the Conservatives, in both elections. The Greens and the Scottish Socialist Party each won one of the regional top-up seats in Scotland. The biggest disappointment was generally agreed to be the turnout, which was around 57 per cent in Scotland and 46 per cent in Wales.

The ceremonial opening of the National Assembly for Wales was on 26 May and the State Opening of the Scottish Parliament was on 1 July, the date on which the two bodies assumed their full powers.

European Parliament Elections

The European Parliament elections on 10 June also recorded the lowest national turnout ever, with a national average for Great Britain of around 23 per cent. Overall the Conservatives came out best with just under 36 per cent of the vote (8.3 per cent of the electorate) and took 39 seats under the controversial new proportional representation system. Labour took 28 per cent of the vote (6.5 per cent of the electorate) and won 29 seats. The Liberal Democrats took just under 13 per cent of the vote and won 10 seats. The UK Independence Party won three seats on 7 per cent of the vote and the Greens two seats on just over 6 per cent of the vote, both parties gaining their first seats in a national election. The SNP took two seats in Scotland and Plaid Cymru two seats in Wales.

By-elections

The first by-election of 1999 appeared to be triggered when on 19 March Fiona Jones MP was convicted at Nottingham Crown Court of having made a false declaration of election expenses. The Speaker declared her Newark seat vacant under the provisions of the 1983 Representation of the People Act. The conviction was set aside on appeal in a judgement given on 15 April. It appeared, however, that there was no provision in law for the disqualification, which had been automatically applied, to be annulled. The Speaker referred the matter back to the High Court, which ruled on 29 April that Fiona Jones was entitled to resume her seat.

The untimely death on 9 May of Derek Fatchett, the Foreign Office minister who was the Labour member for Leeds Central, resulted in the first by-election in nearly 18 months, which must be something of a modern record. The government moved the writ for the by-election with unusual speed, to enable it to fall on 10 June, the same day as the European Parliament elections. The result was a win for the Labour candidate, Hilary Benn, but with a very substantially reduced majority on a turnout of around 20 per cent, one of the lowest by-election turnouts in modern times.

A by-election in Eddisbury was triggered when Sir Alastair Goodlad applied for the Chiltern Hundreds on 28 June on his appointment as High Commissioner to Australia. On a turnout of 51 per cent the Conservatives held the seat with a very slightly increased majority, a swing in their favour of less than 1 per cent.

George Robertson, the Secretary of State for Defence, left the Commons in August on his elevation to the peerage before he went on to his new post as Secretary-General of NATO. The resulting by-election at Hamilton South was held on 23 September, as was that to fill the vacancy created by the death of Roger Stott, the long-serving member for Wigan who died in August. Both by-elections were triggered under the procedures of the rarely used Recess Elections Act. In Hamilton South the Labour candidate, Bill Tynan, was run an unexpectedly close second by the SNP candidate. In Wigan, where the turnout was just over 25 per cent, the Labour candidate Neil Turner had an easy win.

On 25 November the by-election in Kensington and Chelsea to fill the vacancy created by the death of Alan Clark saw the return to the Commons of the Conservative candidate, Michael Portillo in an easy victory, though turnout, at just under 30 per cent, was again very low.

House of Lords
Perhaps the most unusual election of the year took place in the autumn in Westminster itself. The Lords had accepted a compromise whereby in exchange for passing the bill abolishing the rights of hereditary peers to sit and vote in the Lords, 92 hereditary peers would retain their places in the 'transitional' House. The various groups of hereditaries were elected by their peers in November. The House of Lords bill received the royal assent on the very last day of the session, but its passage had been easier than many had predicted. The much reduced House met for the first time at the State Opening on 17 November.

These changes are invariably described as 'Phase One' of Lords reform. Before the bill began its progress through the Lords, the government published a White Paper on options for Phase Two.

It announced at the same time the establishment of a Royal Commission to bring forward proposals for further reform. The Commission, chaired by Lord Wakeham, who has been the Leader of both Houses, reported on 20 January 2000. It proposed a chamber of around 550 members, of whom between 65 and 195 would be elected by the nations and regions of the UK for a 15-year term. The remainder would be appointed by a new statutorily independent appointments commission, with a duty to create a second chamber which was 'broadly representative of British society'. It also recommended a number of enhancements to the 'scrutiny' functions of the reformed chamber, but no significant changes to its formal powers.

During 1999 we recorded the deaths of 48 peers and the creation of 49 new life peers; 22 life peerages and three hereditary peerages became extinct.

Northern Ireland Assembly

The elections to the new Northern Ireland Assembly had taken place in 1998, but the process of 'rolling devolution' in Northern Ireland was impeded for much of 1999 by difficulties in negotiations over the 'peace process'. Several deadlines came and went, and then, after almost a week of intensive negotiations at the end of June another deadline passed without a final settlement being reached. Yet another deadline was set and the new Assembly met on 15 July to nominate ministers to the new 'inclusive' executive. Due to the boycott of the proceedings by the Ulster Unionists the process was nullified. The situation remained under review over the summer, and the independent peace negotiator and former US senator George Mitchell returned to the province to try to mediate. At the end of November a compromise was announced, and the first Order transferring powers from Westminster to the new Assembly was passed on 30 November.

House of Commons

At Westminster the Modernisation Committee of the House of Commons has continued to press forward with its programme of reform. When the House returned in January 1999, it began its experiment with earlier sittings on Thursdays, which now begin at 11.30 am rather than 2.30 pm. This experiment has continued into the present session. The latest innovation to be proposed by the Committee is the establishment of a 'parallel chamber', which sits in the Grand Committee Room off Westminster Hall.

This new forum began its sittings at the end of November 1999 and is meeting in the first instance three times a week, mainly to consider private members' business and Select Committee reports. It has taken over the current Wednesday morning sittings from the Chamber, and additionally has a Tuesday and Thursday sitting to consider private members' adjournment debates, government adjournment debates and select committee reports. If the experiment proves a success, it is possible the range of business considered there might be enlarged.

The essential feature of this second chamber (or 'the House sitting in Westminster Hall' as it is supposed to become known) is that it will proceed by consensus. The body will take no votes, and make no decisions other than by unanimity.

Cabinet and Opposition reshuffles

In June, immediately following the European Parliament elections, Leader of the Opposition William Hague had a sweeping reshuffle, in which Norman Fowler, Michael Howard, Peter Lilley, Gillian Shephard and Nicholas Lyell left his front bench team. The new arrivals were Angela Browning (returning to the front bench), Edward Garnier, Andrew Lansley and Theresa May.

As a result of the establishment of the new executives in Scotland and Wales, the Prime Minister had to replace both his Scottish and Welsh Secretaries of State. In May Donald Dewar was succeeded as Secretary of State for Scotland by John Reid. In July Alun Michael was replaced as Secretary of State for Wales by Paul Murphy.

The long-anticipated cabinet reshuffle took place in October, triggered by Lord Robertson of Port Ellen leaving the government to take up his post as Secretary-General of NATO. He was replaced by Geoffrey Hoon. Frank Dobson resigned as Secretary of State for Health, to be replaced by Alan Milburn. Mr Dobson is seeking the Labour Party's candidacy for the election of the first mayor of London under the Greater London Authority Act (the elections take place on 4 May 2000). Jack Cunningham also left the government and was replaced as Chancellor of the Duchy of Lancaster by Mo Mowlam, the former Secretary of State for Northern Ireland. She was in turn replaced by Peter Mandelson, returning to the Cabinet after an absence of 10 months. Andrew Smith entered the Cabinet for the first time as Chief Secretary to the Treasury.

The Queen's Speech
The second session of this Parliament ended on 11 November. The State Opening of the third session took place on 17 November. The Queen's Speech announced a very heavy legislative programme, including the Freedom of Information bill, proposals to change the right of access to trial by jury in England and Wales, major transport legislation including the establishment of a Strategic Rail Authority, a bill to change the status of the Post Office, more social security reform, legislation on standards in health and social services, new anti-terrorism legislation, sweeping reform of local authority powers and organisation, the creation of a 'right to roam' and the establishment of an Electoral Commission.

New Liberal Democrat Leader
In January 1999 the leader of the Liberal Democrats, Paddy Ashdown, surprised everyone, including it seemed his own party, by announcing that he was stepping down from its leadership. He resigned formally on 11 June the day after the European parliamentary election. The party had the largest theoretical field of candidates since the 1930s, having 46 MPs eligible. The candidates were: Jackie Ballard, Malcolm Bruce, Simon Hughes, Charles Kennedy and David Rendel. In the election all members of the party were entitled to vote. The result was declared on 9 August: Charles Kennedy was the winner with 56 per cent of the votes.

Acknowledgements
The editor would like to thank Charles Kennedy for writing the foreword to this edition, and express his gratitude to all advisers and contributors both inside and outside the Palace of Westminster for their invaluable help.

Michael Bedford, *Editor*
January 2000

New Year Honours 2000

The Queen's New Year Honours List published on December 31st 1999 included the following:

LIFE PEERS

Baroness
Sally, Lady Greengross, OBE

Barons
Sir John Birt
The Rt Hon. Sir Leon Brittan, QC
Joel Goodman Joffe Esq, CBE
Adam Hafejee Patel Esq
Sir Charles Powell, KCMG

KNIGHT BACHELOR

Peter Nevile Wake Jennings, CVO, lately Serjeant at Arms, House of Commons

---

Public Information

HOUSE OF LORDS   Enquiries about aspects of the work of the House of Lords may be directed to The Clerk, Journal and Information Office, House of Lords, London SW1A 0PW (Tel: 020 7219 3107). During the Session a telephone service is available between 10 am and 6 pm Monday to Thursday, and between 10 am and 4 pm on Friday. During the recess the service is available from 10 am until 1 pm and from 2 pm until 4 pm on weekdays (excepting bank holidays and the day following bank holidays). Information about the House can also be found on the Internet. The Parliamentary home page URL is http://www.parliament.uk

HOUSE OF COMMONS   Enquiries about aspects of the work and history of the House of Commons may be addressed to the House of Commons Information Office at the House and telephone enquiries are answered on 020 7219 4272. The Office also compiles the *Weekly Information Bulletin*, containing the work of the House and its Committees, published on Saturdays; and a series of 68 free Factsheets, a list of which can be had on request. These are on the Internet at www.parliament.uk

RECORDS OF BOTH HOUSES   Enquiries about the records of both Houses, 1497 to date, and the history of Parliament, are answered on 020 7219 3074. Documents may be seen in the Record Office Search Room on application to the Clerk of the Records, Record Office, House of Lords, London SW1A 0PW.

Letters to Members of Parliament

The normal method of sending letters to Members of Parliament is by payment through the Post, addressed to the Member at the House of Commons, London SW1A 0AA. For callers, one unstamped letter will be accepted for delivery by hand on sitting days, and on non-sitting days only stamped letters are accepted.

Bulk postage of unstamped letters under one cover is not accepted. Letters must be individually stamped at the second class rate.

For further information telephone the Postmaster: Tel: 020 7219 4642.

Addenda

Opposition Spokesmen (see p 451)

Front Bench Spokesmen

Agriculture, Fisheries and Food	**Malcolm Moss** replaces Patrick Nicholls
Northern Ireland	**John M Taylor** replaces Malcolm Moss
Social Security	**Jacqui Lait** replaces Michael Trend

Opposition Whips' responsibilities

Education and Employment; Defence; Agriculture	**Geoffrey Clifton-Brown**
Environment, Transport and the Regions; Scotland	**Peter Atkinson**
Social Security; Culture, Media and Sport	**John Randall**

Conservative Party (see p 740)

Principal private secretary to chairman	**Graham Brady** replaces Robert Syms

The Queen's Speech

Her Majesty the Queen, accompanied by HRH the Duke of Edinburgh, went in state to the Palace of Westminster and opened the new Session of Parliament on November 17, 1999. The following is the text of the Queen's speech.

My Lords and Members of the House of Commons

This is my Government's third legislative programme. It aims to build on my Government's programme of reform as they seek to modernise the country and its institutions to meet the challenges of the new Millennium.

My Government's aim is to promote fairness and enterprise, providing people with real opportunities to liberate their potential. They will focus on continued modernising of our economy, the promotion of enterprise, reform of the welfare system, protection of the public, and the development of a safe transport system.

The central economic objectives of my Government are high and stable levels of economic growth and employment. More people are in work in Britain today than ever before, with employment up by 700,000, and long term unemployment has halved.

My Government are helping people back into work. The New Deal has helped 145,000 young people into employment.

My Government have introduced a national minimum wage and a new 10p starting rate of tax. They have reformed National Insurance and from next April will cut the basic rate of income tax. The new Working Families Tax Credit, introduced in October, is raising incomes of working families.

My Government will continue to manage the public finances prudently, in accordance with the Code for Fiscal Stability and the two fiscal rules.

The new system of monetary policy-making ensures that interest rate decisions are taken in the best long-term interests of the economy. As a result, long-term interest rates are around their lowest level for almost thirty years. Inflation is historically low and expected to meet my Government's target of 2½ per cent.

My Government will continue to work with others to promote economic reform in Europe. They will work for more open markets, greater economic growth and new job creation.

To prepare Britain as a dynamic, knowledge-based economy my Government will introduce a Bill to promote electronic commerce and electronic government, improving our ability to compete in the digital marketplace.

Financial services lie at the heart of a modern economy. The financial services industry accounts for 7 per cent of our national income, employing over 1 million people. With the new Financial Services Authority, my Government are determined to maintain and advance the UK's position, and the Bill introduced last Session will be carried over to this.

As part of my Government's drive to address inappropriate and over-complex regulation, legislation will be introduced to increase the effectiveness of the power to remove regulatory burdens.

My Government will introduce a Bill to enable the Post Office to improve its services and to compete more effectively in UK and overseas markets.

To put the consumer first, cut prices and make utility regulation more transparent and accountable, a Bill will be introduced to modernise the utility regulation system.

Legislation will be introduced to assist the rescue of viable businesses in short term difficulties, and improve the procedure for disqualifying unfit company directors.

My Government believe a stronger and fairer society strengthens our economy. They will continue to give young people and the long-term unemployed the opportunity to learn new skills and fulfil their potential.

Education remains my Government's number one priority. My Government will continue to implement policies to reward good teaching, reduce infant class sizes, and continue the drive to build on the improvements in literacy and numeracy already achieved.

Having focused change upon primary and secondary education, a Bill will now be introduced to establish a new Learning and Skills Council to improve standards for Post 16 education and training.

As part of my Government's drive against social exclusion, a Bill will be introduced to improve the help available to young people leaving local authority care.

To build on my Government's modernisation of the welfare system, a Bill will be introduced to reform child support so that money gets to children more speedily and effectively. It will introduce further pension reforms, including the State Second Pension which will give more help to low earners, carers and long term disabled people with broken work records. And it will reinforce people's obligations to society by linking benefit entitlement to compliance with community sentences.

Legislation will be introduced to improve the education of children with Special Educational Needs. My Government are determined to promote fairness of opportunity for disabled people building on the establishment of a Disability Rights Commission.

Members of the House of Commons
Estimates for the public service will be laid before you.

My Lords and Members of the House of Commons
My Government's ten year programme of modernisation for health and social care will provide faster, more convenient services to help improve the country's health.

As part of this programme, a Bill will be introduced to improve standards and stamp out abuse in social services, in private and voluntary healthcare, and in childcare.

My Government are determined to reduce crime and improve public protection. A Bill will be introduced to extend the use of mandatory drug testing in the criminal justice system. It will reform the probation services in England and Wales, create a new Children and Family Court Advisory Service, and prevent unsuitable people from working with children.

A Bill will be introduced to give the courts themselves the power to decide whether certain defendants should be tried by jury or by magistrates.

The Bill to equalise the age of consent, and strengthen the protection of young people from abuse of trust, will be re-introduced.

My Government are determined to combat terrorism. A Bill will be introduced to modernise and make permanent the powers available to respond to all forms of terrorism.

A Bill will be introduced to ensure that the interception of communications, and the use of other intrusive techniques, continues to be regulated for the protection both of the rights of individuals and of society as a whole.

The report into the murder of Stephen Lawrence raised profound issues for our multi-racial society. A Bill will be introduced which will make it unlawful for public bodies to racially discriminate, implementing one of the report's key recommendations.

A Bill will be introduced to give people greater access to the countryside and to improve protection for wildlife. And my Government will continue their leading role in protecting the global climate.

My Government are committed to creating a modern integrated and safe transport system, providing more choice for the travelling public. Following the recent tragedy at Paddington my Government will ensure that rail safety is a top priority. A Bill will be re-introduced to establish a Strategic Rail Authority. It will contain measures to improve bus services and reduce road congestion. It will include measures for National Air Traffic Services to separate safety regulation from operational matters, and deliver major investment in the next generation technology.

My Government will bring forward a Bill to introduce the latest accounting methods to improve value for money in Whitehall and generate more investment in public infrastructure and front line services.

A Bill will be brought forward to allow firms to incorporate with limited liability whilst organising themselves as partnerships.

A Bill will be introduced to modernise the powers and duties of trustees.

My Lords and Members of the House of Commons
In Northern Ireland, my Government will continue to work closely with the political parties and the Irish Government to secure the full implementation of the Good Friday Agreement. A Bill will be presented to implement proposals from the Independent Commission on Policing, following the completion of consultation.

My Government are committed to making devolution in Scotland and Wales work and to continue the process of decentralising Government in the interests of all the people in the United Kingdom.

A Bill will be introduced to set up an Electoral Commission to regulate the funding and spending of political parties and organisations. My Government will also bring forward a Bill to reform our electoral procedures to make it easier for people to participate in elections.

My Government are committed to further long-term reform of the House of Lords and will look forward to the recommendations of the Royal Commission on the Reform of the House of Lords.

A Bill will be brought forward to reform local government to make it more innovative and accountable.

My Government will introduce a Bill on Freedom of Information. It will give everyone the right of access to information held across the public sector for the first time.

My Government will continue to provide greater openness by publishing legislation in draft for public scrutiny. This will include Bills enabling the United Kingdom to ratify the International Criminal Court, promoting more efficient water use and leasehold reform as well as commonhold for flat owners.

Other measures will be laid before you.

The Duke of Edinburgh and I look forward to receiving a State Visit by Her Majesty Queen Margrethe of Denmark and Prince Henrik in February next year.

We also look forward to our visit to Australia in March.

My Government will work towards a new partnership between Britain and the Overseas Territories. They will take forward the offer of British Citizenship to the people of the Territories.

My Government will take a leading role with our partners to shape the future development of the European Union. They will promote the enlargement of the Union, support co-operation in the fight against cross-border crime and work to improve the effectiveness of the European Union's Foreign and Security Policy and its development programmes.

My Government will ensure that NATO remains the foundation of Britain's defence and security. They will seek to continue the work of adapting the Alliance to meet the challenges and opportunities of the new century.

A Bill will be introduced to reform aspects of the armed forces' system for administering discipline.

My Government will seek to modernise the United Nations. They will work to make the Security Council more effective and more representative.

Over the coming year, which is the 10th anniversary of the United Nations Convention on the Rights of the Child, my Government will build on their work to strengthen protection for children. My Government will take further measures to meet its target of abolishing child poverty in 20 years. It will play an active part in the Council of Europe Conference against Racism.

My Government believe this is a substantial programme of work, addressing their priorities and helping the country to meet the challenges of the new millennium.

My Lords and Members of the House of Commons
I pray that the blessing of Almighty God may rest upon your counsels.

Parliamentary Summary, Legislation and Party Conferences 1999

1998–99 SESSION

JANUARY

Both Houses returned from the Christmas recess on Monday *January 11*. MPs heard a Statement on the National Health Service from Mr Frank Dobson, Secretary of State for Health, in which he paid tribute to the way the service was coping with the "recent sharp rise in the number of people falling ill"; for the Opposition Miss Ann Widdecombe asked what was new in the statement? She argued that Labour's obsession with waiting list reductions had made the current crisis far worse by distorting priorities. The House then approved the **Rating (Valuation) Bill** at second reading by 268 votes to 30.

On *January 12* the Commons debated and approved the **Local Government Bill** at second reading by 334 votes to 170. In the Upper House Lord Kingsland initiated a debate on a European Communities Committee report on parliamentary scrutiny of the third pillar, to which the Government minister responded by saying that "no major point in the report has not been favourably accepted", which according to Lord Kingsland would result in significant improvements in the scrutiny of inter-governmental matters.

At prime minister's question time on *January 13* Mr Hague attacked the Government's handling of the health service. Initiating a short debate on select committees Mr Andrew Mackinlay said he wanted to canvass cultural changes in the House so that the aspiration to chair a select committee was viewed similarly to the aspiration to be a minister. He was strongly supported in a short debate by several speakers including Mr Derek Foster, former Chief Whip who deprecated the fact that the House had become the "Prime Minister's poodle" with Labour members crawling their way into office instead of kicking their way in, and argued that the Whips should not be involved in selecting select committee members. This was also the second Opposition Day with two Liberal Democrat motions being debated: the first on Government Information was defeated by 42 votes to 331, and the second on the UK role in Europe by 42 votes to 281. The House of Lords debated Aids in Africa and then leisure activities.

On *January 14* MPs held their annual debate on Public Accounts Committee Reports, of which Mr David Davis, chairman of the Committee stated their had been 67 in the previous year "more than in any equivalent period in our 137 year history".

On *January 19* MPs debated the **Greater London Authority Bill** in committee with an opposition amendment seeking to clarify the role of the proposed deputy mayor defeated by 120 votes to 371.

Monday *January 20* was the 3rd Opposition Day, with Miss Ann Widdecombe introducing a motion which among other things expressed dismay that Mr Dobson, Secretary of State for Health, should deny that rationing took place within the NHS; the motion was defeated by 169 votes to 336. There followed a second Opposition motion on dividend tax credits which again after debate and defeated by 166 votes to 336.

The Government published its White Paper and Bill on reform of the House of Lords on *January 20*. Baroness Jay, Leader of the House of Lords, stated that the Government's proposals would remove a "fundamental anachronism as we reach the new millennium": they were first, to remove hereditary peers from the House; second, to reform arrangements for the nomination of life peers; and third, to establish a Royal Commission to consider long term reform. Responding Lord Strathclyde said there was a "deep sense of disquiet and regret in the House" about what had been announced, and continued: "The most depressing aspect of the announcement is that we have seen no clear vision of the future of this House". In the Commons Dr Liam Fox from the Opposition front-bench said that the Government's clear intention was to remove the hereditary peers then "kick the whole subject into the long grass", and that the real objective was to strengthen the Executive at the expense of Parliament; "it is out with the ermine and in with the straitjackets". Following the Statement in the Lords peers debated the significance for the British economy of the introduction of the euro on a motion moved by Lord Taverne.

On *January 21* the **Road Traffic (NHS Charges) Bill** was debated and passed at third reading by 228 votes to 24, with Liberal Democrat MPs continuing to press their opposition to the Bill which in their view had no logic because it singled out victims of only one source of accidents for charges.

On Monday *January 25* the Home Secretary, Mr Jack Straw, introduced the **Sexual Offences (Amendment) Bill** at second reading saying that it dealt with the widely shared concerns about the need to protect vulnerable young people and also provided for the lowering of the age of consent (on a free vote) to the same age for boys as for girls. The Bill was approved by 313 votes to 130. The **Tax Credits Bill** was debated and accepted at second reading on *January 26* by 320 votes to 160. In the Upper House the Earl of Onslow moved the rejection of an Order made under the Registration of Political Parties Act, the effect of which was to restrict the freedom of candidates at certain elections describing their party in various ways, such as "Independent Labour"; he withdrew his motion because he had been asked to do so by the Chief Whip on the grounds that the House of Lords did not vote against statutory orders.

On *January 27* Mr Hague raised the subject of terrorist mutilations in Northern Ireland at prime minister's question time, and this was followed by an opposition motion (this being the 4th Opposition Day) on the same subject, with Conservatives arguing that further release of paramilitary prisoners should be suspended, but their motion was defeated by 141 votes to 343. A second Conservative motion on the London Underground was then debated and defeated by 130 votes to 335.

On Thursday *January 28* the House of Commons met at 11.30am, with questions to the Treasury being the first item on the agenda. MPs later debated social security, while peers defeated the government by 88 votes to 77 on a motion moved by Lord Ackner to delete from the **Access to Justice Bill** a clause relating to audience rights.

FEBRUARY

On Monday *February 1* the House of Commons began a two-day second reading debate on the **House of Lords Bill.** The Conservative Opposition moved an amendment which rejected the Bill because it: "fails to address the role of the second chamber, its relationship to this House and its long-term composition and hence, rather than improving the governance of the UK by establishing a sustainable, balanced and effective constitution, it merely adds to the

incoherence of HM Government's piecemeal constitutional changes". During the debate Dr Liam Fox speaking from the Opposition front-bench said: "This is not about whether we will defend the rights of hereditary peers; we have accepted that those rights in the House of Lords are to end. The argument is about how we wish the House of Lords to be constituted". The former Tory Prime Minister, Sir Edward Heath, said that he believed with conviction that the time had come to end the rights of hereditary peers in politics, but Mr John Major said: "The Government are tearing apart – piece by piece, act by act – the most sophisticated constitution with little real understanding of what they are doing". The Conservative amendment was defeated by 383 votes to 137, after which the Bill was approved at second reading by 381 votes to 135.

The 5th Opposition Day on *February 3* saw two debates. First, a motion criticising the Government for having failed pensioners was debated and defeated by 327 votes to 185; then a motion regretting the Government's decisions on large scale planning development in the countryside was defeated by 164 votes to 320. On the same day peers debated the National Health Service. On *February 4* MPs debated police finances and then local government finance, with the Government gaining their usual comfortable majorities in both divisions.

On Monday *February 8* MPs debated the **Social Security Contributions (Transfer of . Functions Etc.) Bill** which transferred the Contributions Agency from the Department of Social Security to the Inland Revenue; this was opposed by the Conservative opposition on the grounds that it would facilitate the ending of the contributory principle but approved on division by 132 votes to 322. The following day the Commons approved at second reading the **Employment Relations Bill** by 395 votes to 135; according to Mr Byers, Secretary of State for Trade and Industry, the Bill would "promote the best of modern employment relationships in all our companies, encourage a culture of fairness and trust in the workplace coupled with rights and responsibilities", but for the Opposition, Mr John Redwood, said that "all the Government do, as they watch manufacturing retreat, is make it dearer and dearer to make things in Britain", adding: "We believe that having a job is more important than giving new rights to trade unions".

Peers debated the **Health Bill** at second reading, after which they heard a grisly tale of student discomfort when Lord Tope introduced a short debate on university accommodation, a subject taken up by Mr Phil Willis the next day, *February 10,* at a morning adjournment debate in the Commons. Later at prime minister's question time both Mr Hague and Mr Ashdown took up the Foreign Affairs Select Committee report which criticised the Foreign Office for its handling of arms sales to forces in Sierra Leone by Sandline International, with Mr Blair saying he did not accept the severe criticisms made by the Committee. Mr David Drew then introduced a ten minute rule bill on poverty and social exclusion, but Mr Eric Forth opposed the motion to approve the Bill saying that it was nothing but a "series of gestures", and that MPs ought to take themselves more seriously. Later in committee of the whole House MPs debated the **Sexual Offences (Amendment) Bill;** Sir Norman Fowler spoke against the inclusion in the Bill of the clause lowering the age of consent for males from 18 to 16, but this was approved by 330 votes to 126. Among the majority was Mr Shaun Woodward who spoke from the Conservative benches in support of lowering the age of consent.

On the same day Peers debated the arts and then homeless young people. On *February 11* the Government was defeated in the House of Lords by 182 votes to 111 on an amendment to the **Access to Justice Bill** moved by the retired Law Lord, Lord Lloyd of Berwick, which inserted a statement of purpose concerned with possible sources of discrimination in relation to the work of the proposed Criminal Defence Service and Community Legal Service.

On *February 11* MPs debated Orders relating to spending in Scotland, with the Scottish Office minister, Mr Henry McLeish saying that it "was challenging and exciting to think that this is the last time the House will be called upon to consider the detailed public spending plans for Scotland".

On Monday *February 15* the House of Commons commenced the committee stage of the **House of Lords Bill**. An amendment moved from the Conservative front-bench by Sir Patrick Cormack to allow hereditary peers to retain membership but not voting rights was defeated by 332 votes to 131. The following day, *February 16,* Mrs Eleanor Laing moved an amendment embodying the so-called Weatherill proposal to retain some 90 hereditary peers chosen by their colleagues. This was opposed by the Government, and defeated by 51 votes to 269 because ministers wanted the amendment added

in the Lords rather than the Commons, so that if the opposition to the Bill became intractable the amendment could be withdrawn. Following this the House of Commons went into recess for the remainder of the week.

On *February 16* peers continued work on the **Access to Justice Bill** and inflicted a further defeat on the Government in voting by 189 votes to 134 in support of an amendment moved from the Liberal Democrat front-bench by Lord Thomas of Gresford to prevent the proposed Criminal Defence Service employing salaried lawyers.

On *February 17* Lord Lester of Herne Hill introduced a debate on the separation of powers in the House of Lords between the judicial, legislative and executive branches, with a particular focus on the office of Lord Chancellor. He argued that the varied role served by the Lord Chancellor was no longer appropriate, and further that serving law lords should no longer play an active role as legislators. The Lord Chancellor argued that his office stood at a critical cusp in the separation of powers, and that it should remain as a buffer between the judiciary and the Executive, and that although the Human Rights Act would bring differences they were of degree not of kind.

On Monday *February 22* Mr Jack Straw, Home Secretary, introduced the second reading of the **Immigration and Asylum Bill**, which he said represented the most fundamental reform of immigration and asylum law for decades, and would give the UK "a modern, flexible and streamlined system capable of dealing with the ever-growing pressures and demands placed upon it". For the Opposition Sir Norman Fowler moved an amendment critical of the Government for not holding an independent inquiry before introducing the Bill and critical of the Bill because it failed "to create a situation whereby only genuine asylum applicants will be given permission to settle in this country" The amendment was defeated on division by 135 votes to 346 and then the Liberal Democrats mustered 38 votes against the second reading, which was however comfortably carried.

The House of Lords held a two day debate on the White Paper on reform of their House on *February 22-23.* Baroness Jay leading for the Government said she really had nothing new to say beyond what had been said in the three previous debates held on the same subject since last October, but Lord Strathclyde said the debate was an opportunity for the Government to explain its vision for the future, which so far had been sadly lacking. Lord Strathclyde as Conservative leader moved an amendment to the Government motion which urged the Royal Commission to set as an objective an increase in the independence of Parliament and specifically to reject the proposal in the White Paper to consider reducing the powers of the House. During the debate almost 100 speeches were made though only five from the Labour backbenches, a matter criticised by some Conservatives, though Labour spokesmen reiterated that little new could be said on the subject. The Conservative amendment was carried by 193 votes to 2.

On *February 23* the Prime Minister made a Statement to the Commons on British policy on economic and monetary union, indicating that the Government was authorising expenditure to prepare for a changeover to the euro, and arguing that if joining was best for British employment and trade, then the Government would let the people decide in a referendum; this was therefore a change of gear, not a change of policy. But Mr Hague described the action as unnecessary, expensive and time-consuming, while Mr Ashdown said the Government had crossed the Rubicon, a fact which he greatly welcomed. Sir Edward Heath said that Mr Blair had been "absolutely right in everything he said", while both Mr Kenneth Clarke and Mr Michael Heseltine gave support to Mr Blair. Following this MPs debated the **Welfare Reform and Pensions Bill** at second reading, and after defeating a Conservative amendment carried the Bill by 318 votes to 180.

Mr Jack Straw, Home Secretary, made a Statement to Parliament on *February 24* on the inquiry into the death of Stephen Lawrence. This had concluded that the original murder inquiry had been "marred by a combination of professional incompetence, institutional racism and a failure of leadership by senior officers", which had subsequently not been uncovered by a flawed police review. The report then made some 70 recommendations to combat the institutional racism it had uncovered. Mr Straw said the report should serve as a "watershed in our attitudes to racism". Later MPs gave a third reading by 344 votes to 89 to the **Social Security Contributions Bill.**

The House of Commons debated Welsh Affairs on *February 25* with many speeches looking forward to the elections to the Welsh Assembly, due just over two months later. Mr Dafydd Wigley clashed heatedly with the Secretary of State for Wales, Mr Alun Michael,

on the subject of obtaining matching funds from the Treasury to take full benefit of funds available through the European Union.

On *February 26* the Minister of State at the Home Office, Mr Paul Boateng made a further Statement on the Lawrence Report, explaining why distribution of volume two was being suspended because this contained the addresses of various witnesses, information which it had not been intended to place in the public domain, a "serious and regrettable error". The House also debated and passed at second reading two private member's bills that day.

MARCH
On Monday *March 1* MPs debated and passed at third reading by 281 votes to 82 the **Sexual Offences (Amendment) Bill.** In the Upper House Lord Patten initiated a short debate on achieving greater openness in the appointment of the judiciary, with particular reference to the increased constitutional role of the judiciary in the light of recent legislation. Lord Neill of Bladen said he was a "sceptic, both as to the perceived mischief and as to the suggested remedy". In reply the Lord Chancellor said he saw "no reason why adjudicating on legislation that might be called "constitutional" – I have to say that I find the expression very imprecise – should require any change in the way judges are appointed".

March 2 was the 6th Opposition Day with a motion on Sierra Leone being debated and defeated by 171 votes to 336; and one deploring the "bureaucratic burdens being placed on schools" defeated by 172 votes to 334.

At prime minister's question time on *March 3* the independent MP Martin Bell asked Mr Blair whether he would consider "allowing backbenchers more freedom to speak their minds and to vote with their consciences, so that this place might become rather more the free Parliament of a free people, and rather less a rubber stamp assembly?" Mr Blair replied that he believed the Government was "perfectly entitled to put through our programme" and that "what is important is that we do deliver that programme". The Commons then considered the **House of Lords Bill** for a third day in committee, voting down by 125 to 322 a Conservative amendment to introduce a "sunset" clause to the Bill, with the Government arguing that this was unnecessary because it had every intention of bringing in a stage two reform at an early date. A further amendment to ensure that hereditary peers who left the House of Lords were placed on electoral registers by the end of the same session was defeated by 125 votes to 315.

On *March 4* MPs continued with a fourth committee day on the Bill, with Conservative amendments the effect of which would have been to limit membership of the House to working life peers being voted down by 104 votes to 288. Meanwhile in the upper House on *March 3* peers debated public service broadcasting on a motion moved by Lord Bragg, with many peers praising the quality of BBC programmes.

On Friday *March 5* MPs debated the **Fur Farming (Prohibition) Bill** introduced by Maria Eagle, agreeing to the closure after three and a half hours debate by 127 votes to 4, and then approving the Bill at second reading.

On Monday *March 8* Mr Michael Meacher, Minister for the Environment, made a Statement announcing that the Government had decided to create a statutory right to roam over "four million acres of mountain, moor, heath and down"; legislation would however have to await the availability of parliamentary time. Mrs Gillian Shepherd speaking for the Opposition said that she strongly supported a right to roam, but that this should be based on voluntary co-operation set within a secure legal framework. The House then held a five and a half hour debate on women on a motion for the adjournment moved by Ms Tessa Jowell who said: "Today is the 73rd international women's day – a day to mark what women do, want and achieve". Peers also debated women in a debate initiated by Baroness Uddin.

March 9 was Budget Day. In a 69 minute speech Gordon Brown, Chancellor of the Exchequer, announced various tax cuts, including a one pence cut in the main rate of corporation tax to 30 pence and a 10p tax rate for small business, and he gave advance notice of a cut in basic rate income tax by one penny to 22 pence. The net effect of the tax changes would be a cut of £4 billion, and various public spending increases were also announced. In his immediate response Mr Hague said that the most interesting thing about the speech was what the Chancellor did not say, such as the fact that previously announced tax increases taking effect this year would total over £7 billion. For the Liberal Democrats Mr Ashdown said the Chancellor had had the opportunity to do big things in this budget but instead had followed a scatter-gun approach and done quite a number of small things.

Debate on the Budget continued in the House of Commons on *March 10* and *11*, and resumed on Monday *March 15*, when the debate ended with ten divisions spread over two hours, the Government of course having a comfortable majority in all of them. At prime minister's question time on *March 10* Mr Hague attacked the Government for allegedly hiding the scale of increase in national insurance for self-employed people. Mr Ashdown criticised the Government for having as its real priority undercutting the Tories on income tax and so wrong-footing them rather than spending more on education. On *March 10* in the House of Lords Lord McIntosh of Haringey became the first front-bencher in recent times to answer all four starred (oral) questions, the maximum allowed in the House, on the same day.

At report stage of the **Disability Rights Commission Bill** on *March 11* the Government was defeated by 112 votes to 81 on an amendment moved by Baroness Blatch to extend the remit of the proposed Disability Rights Commission, in particular by requiring it to give advice to government agencies. Later that day in the Lords Baroness Blatch moved a prayer against the draft Code of Practice on School Admissions, which she said had brought despair to staff in schools, but Baroness Blackstone replying for the Government said the new code should not place onerous burdens on schools, while Lord Russell said the whole area was one on which delicate compromises had been reached, and though it remained a matter of great concern, this was not the time for throwing stones. Baroness Blatch withdrew her prayer.

On *March 12* the Minister for Agriculture, Mr Nick Brown, made a Statement to the House on negotiations in which he had been involved on reforming the Common Agriculture Policy, proposals which Mr Tim Yeo from the Opposition front-bench described as a "not satisfactory no-win deal".

On Monday *March 15* the House of Lords debated the **Health Bill** at report stage, the Government suffering a defeat when peers voted 120 to 117 to give health professionals a say in the setting up of Primary Care Trusts.

On Tuesday *March 16* the Prime Minister made a Statement on the resignation of the entire European Commission, following what he described as a "damning report" from the Committee of Independent Experts set up to investigate allegations of fraud and mismanagement. Mr Blair said this presented an opportunity to "push through root and branch reform of the

Commission". Mr Hague in his response said the work of the Commission should be cut back with more being done by national governments, but Mr Blair said it would be wrong to "use this event as an excuse to indulge the anti-Europeanism of the current Conservative party".

Later that day Mrs Margaret Beckett, Leader of the House of Commons, introduced the third reading of the **House of Lords Bill,** saying that further reform of the Upper House may be possible within the lifetime of the current Parliament, but that "even stage one of reform will be better than what we have today". This was because: "we will have the emergence of a House of Lords all of whose members will have earned their place on the basis of their contribution to our public life", and she concluded by saying that "The Government believe the removal of the hereditary peerage is a prize worth securing in its own right". From the Opposition front-bench Dr Liam Fox, commenting on the so-called Weatherill amendments, said the Government "intend to accept a major change to the Bill in the Chamber that they say has no democratic legitimacy, but have refused amendments to do the same thing in the House of Commons". Sir Nicholas Lyell said the Bill left the House of Lords "as little more than a destructive totem to Labour's manifesto pledges". Mr Mark Fisher emphasised that when the Bill returned to the Commons, assuming the Weatherill amendment had been added, it would be a very different Bill and would require fresh consideration. Sir Patrick Cormack too drew attention to the oddity that the Bill would come back from the Lords "wholly re-written", and he continued: "What the Government are seeking to do, by removing the hereditary peers without telling us in any detail what they have in mind for constitutional reform, is to place the institution of parliament in jeopardy". The third reading was carried by 340 votes to 132.

On *March 17* Mr Steven Webb from the Liberal Democrat benches moved an amendment declining to give the **Tax Credits Bill** a third reading because "the proposed working families tax credit represented a highly inefficient way of spending public money"; this was defeated by 164 votes to 295, following which the Bill was on division accorded its third reading. On the same day peers debated Parliament and Democracy on a motion moved by Lord Waddington.

March 18 was the 7th Opposition day with Conservative motions on policing and roads being debated.

In the Lords the Government were again defeated on the **Health Bill** when peers voted 161 to 113 to extend the remit of the proposed Commission for Health Improvement to regulate the private sector.

On Friday *March 19* Mr Andrew Robathan introduced his **Referendums Bill** the purpose of which was to introduce rules based on the Nairne Committee report to make referendums fair. After four hours' debate, and while the Government minister was speaking, Mr Robathan moved a closure motion which was carried by 129 votes to 5, following which the House voted 128 to 0 for the Bill to be given a second reading.

Monday *March 22* was the 8th Opposition day, and was allocated to the Liberal Democrats. Their first motion criticised the Government for not improving the funding of local services, and was defeated by 40 votes to 309, while their second, which dealt with the trade dispute between the US and the EU over bananas, was defeated by 39 votes to 314. Peers debated a report from their Procedure Committee which included a recommendation to make Thursday the general debate day (rather than Wednesday); this was supported by the Government but opposed by Baroness Young who argued that if the change were made Thursday "would be seen as a kind of afterthought, or a dead day, when it was not necessary for most of your Lordships to be present". On division Baroness Young carried her amendment by 225 to 87. The House then debated a report from its European Communities Committee on the future financing of the EU.

On *March 23* MPs heard a Statement from the Prime Minister announcing that armed action by Nato in Kosovo was imminent. He acknowledged this would not bring a quick end to the suffering of the Kosovars, but argued that the consequences of not acting were likely to be even more serious for human life and for peace in the long term, and reiterated that the clear objective of action was to curb Milosevic's ability to engage in repression. Mr Hague was in basic agreement with the Prime Minister, but Sir Peter Tapsell said it was almost certain that air strikes alone would not achieve the objectives, and that the Prime Minister should not use weasel words to the British people. Mr Tony Benn said this was a grave statement because it amounted to a declaration of war against a member state of the UN which had the right of self-defence, though other speakers from both sides of the House supported the Prime Minister's views. Later that day MPs considered the **Local Government Bill** at report stage until just after midnight when the Leader of the House announced that a guillotine on the Bill would be brought in the following day. The allocation of time motion was duly accepted on *March 24* by 332 votes to 162, after which the House immediately proceeded to complete work on the Bill which was given a third reading by 319 votes to 170. At 9.00pm the Deputy Prime Minister, Mr John Prescott, announced that British aircraft had participated in a NATO attack on targets in the Federal Republic of Yugoslavia. Mr Douglas Hogg said there was dismay in the House because "we have gone to war without there being a sufficient national interest, without there being a clear understanding of the strategic and political objectives, without there being a proper exit strategy, and without the authority of the House", but Mr Bruce George said that the House overwhelmingly supported the Government in this matter.

Meanwhile on *March 23* in the House of Lords the Government suffered a defeat on the **Youth Justice and Criminal Evidence Bill** when Lord Windlesham moved an amendment to make it discretionary rather than mandatory for magistrates courts to refer young first offenders to youth offender panels.

On *March 24* peers debated marriage on a motion moved by Lord Northbourne who said that as a country we were facing a social revolution because marriage was facing a sharp decline in popularity. Lord Griffiths of Fforestfach said this was a debate about the public interest not about peers' private views, and that the evidence overwhelmingly showed that marriage scores consistently ahead of other family forms on all kinds of indicators. Later that day peers also debated persistent juvenile offenders.

On *March 25* peers voted by 113 to 86 to support an amendment moved by Baroness Mashon of Ilton, and resisted by the Government, to amend the **Health Bill** to facilitate and encourage "out of area" specialist treatment. The House of Commons debated Kosovo on a motion for the adjournment on *March 25* with the Foreign Secretary, Robin Cook, saying NATO had no alternative but to initiate air strikes, and most speeches reflecting majority support for the Government, though some MPs expressed their strong misgivings and opposition to the Government's actions. Mr Tony Benn tried but failed to force a vote against the motion for the adjournment.

On Friday *March 26* MPs debated Mr Gordon Prentice's **Right to Roam Bill** as first business, but at 2.30pm the debate stood adjourned with no second reading having been granted.

The Prime Minister made a Statement on *March 29* on the meeting of the European Council held in Berlin. This had considered the Kosovo crisis, and also the Agenda 2000 package of negotiations for enlargement of the European Union. Mr Hague while expressing support for the action in Kosovo said that the summit had left a largely unreformed agricultural policy, a disgraced Commission still in place and enlargement more distant rather than nearer. The House then debated the Stephen Lawrence Inquiry, with Mr Straw as Home Secretary saying that he was taking personal responsibility for the delivery of the detailed action plan setting out the Government's response to the report.

Peers began a two-day second reading debate on the **House of Lords Bill** on *March 29*. For the Opposition Lord Strathclyde questioned whether the Bill wasn't more about marginalising rather than modernising the House. Baroness Young described the Bill as constitutional vandalism; Lord Kennet said the interim House would be no more democratic than the present House, and Lord Stoddart of Swindon said the Government wanted a less effective second chamber, a poodle to the House of Commons. Lord Cobbold moved an amendment stating that "this House regrets that the Bill radically alters the historic composition of the House of Lords for party political advantage, without consultation or consensus on the successor House's role and composition and without making it more democratic". Some 180 speeches later at 2.55am on *March 31* peers voted by 192 votes to 126 in support of Lord Cobbold's amendment.

In the Commons Mr Jack Cunningham, Minister for the Cabinet Office, made a Statement on *March 30* on the modernisation of government, which he described as "the most radical programme of public service reform for a generation". On *March 30* and *31* MPs debated further the **Employment Relations Bill** which was then given a third reading by 328 votes to 124.

On *March 31* both Houses heard a Statement in which the Secretary of State for International development, Ms Clare Short, explained the steps being taken to make relief available to the Kosovo refugees. In response Mr Alan Clark said that the £500,000 of food supplies she had announced was slightly less than the cost of a single cruise missile, some 50 of which were being dumped on Yugoslavia every night. Later that day both Houses adjourned for the Easter recess.

APRIL

The House of Lords reassembled after the Easter recess on *April 12*, and debated at second reading two Bills, the **Tax Credits Bill** and then the **Local Government Bill**. On the latter Bill the Government spokesman, Lord Whitty, said that 80 per cent of local government expenditure was now provided by the national taxpayer and this justified central government powers, but that this was not a centralising Bill.

When the Commons returned on *April 13* MPs heard another Statement from the Prime Minister on Kosovo in which he said the objectives of the operation remained exactly as before. In answer to a question about reports from Belgrade suggesting that the NATO action was the best possible recruiting sergeant for Milosevic, Mr Blair said it was worth remembering that the only reports that are heard in the UK are those made by reporters who depend on the Serbian Government to allow them to stay.

The House then debated the **Health Bill** at second reading, with a Conservative amendment making sweeping criticisms of the Bill being rejected by 127 votes to 368.

Peers debated the **Sexual Offences (Amendment) Bill** at second reading on *April 13*, with Baroness Young moving a hostile motion, which she explained she felt free to do because this was not a manifesto bill, and in the Commons it had been subject to a free vote, and therefore the House was constitutionally entitled to reject the Bill at second reading. After a seven-and-a-half hour debate in a midnight vote the Bill was rejected by 222 to 146.

On *April 14* the Deputy Prime Minister, Mr John Prescott, answered questions on behalf of the Prime Minister who was abroad, but his preference for giving answers to questions different from those that had been asked resulted in periodic uproar. Replying to a question from Mr Alan Beith about class sizes being larger than when Labour took office, he said the Government was keeping to its targets, and when pressed said that was the only answer he would give. When asked by Sir Michael Spicer to give a guarantee that the withholding tax would not be introduced in the UK, he replied: "As Secretary of State for the Environment, I constantly have to deal with the disastrous poll tax" and said nothing whatsoever about the withholding tax.

The House then debated the **Access to Justice Bill** at second reading, approving this by 335 votes to 156, after defeating a hostile Conservative amendment.

The following day, *April 15*, MPs debated and gave an unopposed second reading to the **Youth Justice and Criminal Evidence Bill**, while peers debated the Stephen Lawrence Inquiry report, with Lord Imbert, former Commissioner of the Metropolitan Police, making his maiden speech.

On *April 16* Mr Simon Burns secured a second reading for his **Football (Offences and Disorder) Bill**, the purpose of which he explained was to "strengthen and tighten existing powers in legislation already in operation".

Madam Speaker made a Statement on *April 19* explaining that she had asked the Attorney-General on behalf of the House to seek an authoritative declaration from the High Court on the construction of the 1983 Representation of the People Act following the success of the appeal made by Fiona Jones, Member for Newark, against her conviction under the Act which had resulted in the declaration that her seat was vacant.

The House then debated Kosovo. During the speech of the Foreign Secretary, Robin Cook, Tony Benn intervened to ask why the House was not invited to endorse the policy rather than being treated as a sort of press conference; Mr Cook replied that this was the traditional way of handling such a matter when the leadership of the other main parties in the House was in agreement with the Government. However some members made speeches critical of the conduct of the war: Mr Alan Clark described it as "clumsy, wasteful and shambolic". Others criticised the strategy, with Sir Peter Tapsell declaring that "the making of war must be judged by results and not by intentions, however admirable these might be". At the end of the debate 11 MPs voted against the adjournment, but with no MPs voting in the other lobby, and fewer than 40 having taken part in the division, Madam Speaker declared the question not decided in the affirmative.

The second reading debate of the **Finance Bill** took place on *April 20*, with Mr David Heathcoat-Amory for the Opposition moving an amendment declaring that the Bill imposed further hidden taxes on many groups in society. This was defeated by 132 votes to 341, and the Bill then granted a second reading by 304 votes to 164.

Peers commenced the committee stage of the **House of Lords Bill** that day, with Lord Strathclyde opening proceedings by making a plea to the Government to stay its hand and seek a consensus, but Baroness Jay for the Government merely congratulated him on "another attempt to delay progress on this Bill". An amendment moved by Lord Mackay of Drumadoon inserting a clause saying: "The purpose of this Act is to create a more legitimate and more democratic House of Lords" was withdrawn after being resisted by the Government on the grounds that it was not necessary. During debate Lord Longford said: "It would be an appalling tragedy were we to have an elected Chamber. What should we have here then? We should have the dregs of politics-people who could not get into the European Parliament. That is the last thing we want. We want a highly-qualified, high-minded House".

Lord Cranborne said he was unclear why a nominated Chamber was considered any more legitimate than a hereditary Chamber, and reminisced about the "good and the great" who had implored him with requests for a peerage and said that, although if granted one they would sit on the cross-benches, they could nevertheless be relied upon to support the Conservatives, and though such people were not given peerages, he did fear for the great temptations to which Prime Ministers were subjected!

April 21 was taken as the 9th Opposition day, with Conservative motions on the road haulage industry and on British livestock farming being debated and rejected. Peers also debated two motions that day, one on human embryos and cloning, the other on hedgerows. Before doing so however Lord Stanley of Alderley asked a private notice question on the power of the National Assembly for Wales to revoke beef on the bone regulations, a subject upon which he claimed the Government had changed its mind since the House had debated amendments on this point during the passage of the Wales Act. Some peers felt the House had been misled on this matter and responded by voting against a purely procedural motion (to set up a select committee).

On *April 22* MPs debated and gave an unopposed second reading to the **Disability Rights Commission Bill**, and on *April 23* Mr Mark Oaten secured a second reading for his **Adoption (Intercountry Aspects) Bill.**

On Monday *April 26* the main debate in the House of Commons was on defence equipment, but this was preceded by a Statement from Mr Jack Straw, Home Secretary, on two bomb explosions on successive Saturdays in London which he said appeared to have been racially motivated.

On *April 27* when MPs debated fuel duty increases while considering the **Finance Bill**, Mr Alan Milburn, Chief Secretary to the Treasury, said the increases were necessary to meet targets on greenhouse gas emissions, but Mr Francis Maude for the Opposition said British fuel prices were now the highest in Europe; an Opposition amendment was defeated by 305 votes to 177.

Peers debated the **House of Lords Bill** dealing with amendments on Scottish peers representation, on the nature of the writ of summons, and the possibility of peers retaining sitting but not voting rights. Shortly after 1.00am the House voted on an amendment moved by Earl Ferrers to "leave out ("a") and insert ("an")" before "hereditary peer"; by 63 votes to 31 the House decided to stick with ("a").

On *April 28* MPs continued their work on the **Finance Bill**, and on *April 29* debated two Conservative opposition motions on this the 10th Opposition day; the first concerned housing and the green belt, the second industry and employment.

On the same day peers continued work on the **House of Lords Bill** with debates on sundry proposals, such as keeping hereditary peers over the age of 75, or those who were members of the Privy Council, and allowing hereditary peers still to correspond with ministers on a privileged basis.

On *April 30* Madam Speaker made a further Statement on the position of Fiona Jones, member for Newark, saying that the high court had now declared that she was entitled to resume her seat.

The House then spent the day dealing with the **Protection of Children Bill** sponsored by Debra Shipley; from the Conservative benches Mr Philip Hammond called for a report on the working of the Bill after twelve months' operation, but the Government minister, John Hutton, said it would be unwise to write this into the Bill, which was later granted an unopposed third reading.

MAY
On Tuesday *May 4* MPs debated the **Greater London Authority Bill** at report stage, completing work on this Bill the following day. Meanwhile peers dealt with the **Tax Credits Bill**, with the Government suffering two defeats. First a Liberal Democrat amendment giving small employers the right to opt out of paying the

working families tax credit, which Baroness Hollis for the Government said would potentially exclude 70 per cent of employers, was carried by 161 votes to 121. Second an amendment moved by the Tory peer Lord Higgins concerned with the mechanism for paying tax credit to lone parents was carried by 150 votes to 103.

The following day, *May 5*, peers debated the 50th Anniversary of the Council of Europe on a motion moved by the Liberal Democrat leader in the House, Lord Rodgers of Quarry Bank.

Frank Dobson, Secretary of State for Health, initiated a debate on London's health service on a motion for the adjournment on *May 6*, while peers debated Kosovo, with most speakers supporting the Government action, but some including the Earl of Lauderdale, who introduced an amendment (but withdrew it), regretting that the attack took place without clear sanction in international law or by resolution of the UN security council.

Peers met again on Friday *May 7* to debate the Schengen Accord and UK border controls on a motion moved by Lord Wallace of Saltaire. In the Commons MPs completed work on James Clapison's **Breeding and Sale of Dogs (Welfare) Bill** which sought to tighten controls on inspection and regulation of dog breeding kennels ("puppy farms") giving the Bill an unopposed third reading.

On Monday *May 10* the Foreign Secretary, Mr Robin Cook, paid tribute to Mr Derek Fatchett,a fellow Foreign Office minister, who had died suddenly at the week-end. He then made a Statement on Kosovo outlining the agreement reached between NATO and Russia, and also dealing with the accidental destruction of the Chinese embassy in Belgrade.

The **Northern Ireland (Location of Victims Remains) Bill** was then debated at second reading by MPs. Introducing this measure Mr Adam Ingram, Minister of State at the Northern Ireland Office, said its purpose was to ensure that any information given to help locate remains was not used in subsequent criminal prosecutions. The Conservative front-bench spokesman, Mr Malcolm Moss, said that the Bill was odious and that his party deeply deplored the necessity for it, but the Opposition would not oppose the Bill, which was granted a second reading by 289 votes to 10.

In the Lords peers debated the **Employment Relations Bill** at second reading.

May 11 was the 11th Opposition day. A Conservative motion on Pensions was debated first, then Dr Liam Fox introduced a motion

calling on the Government to address the imbalances and tensions introduced within the UK by the establishment of devolved bodies, with much of the debate focusing on conflicting interpretations of the results of the Scottish and Welsh elections to devolved bodies held the previous week.

Peers further debated the **House of Lords Bill** in committee on *May 11*, with the Weatherill amendment providing for the continued membership in the so-called transitional House of 92 peers by succession being agreed. This was described by Lord Irvine of Lairg, the Lord Chancellor, as representing an "inspired way forward by consensus towards major constitutional change". Lord Cranborne said the amendment made a "bad bill better", but Lord Richard said it "made a good bill worse" and was a "somewhat grubby compromise". For the Liberal Democrats Lord Rodgers of Quarry Bank said he opposed the amendment, and that if it was considered desirable for some hereditary peers to remain in the House they should be given life peerages to enable them to do so. Labour and Conservative as well as Cross-bench peers combined to give the amendment a huge majority – it was approved by 352 votes to 32. On *May 13* peers spent a fifth committee day on the Bill, debating amendments dealing with rural and religious representation, and one moved by Lord Archer of Weston-super-Mare to impose an attendance criterion for life peers; none were accepted.

On Wednesday *May 12* the House of Lords debated a motion moved by Lord Hayhoe calling attention to the case for an independent statutory commission for the conduct of referendums.

The 12th Opposition day in the Commons on *May 13* was devoted to two Liberal Democrat motions. The first, which was rejected by 38 votes to 300, concerned Europe's ban on hormonally modified beef from America and the threat of trade retaliation from America under World Trade Organisation rules. The second motion, moved by Mr David Heath, expressed regret at the "failure of the disunited Conservative Parliamentary Party at Westminster and the antipathetic and complacent Conservative group in the European Parliament" to provide proper checks on the executive in relation to EU policy.

This motion was unusual for apparently targeting the Opposition rather than the Government, and prompted the Conservative party to put down an amendment moved by Mr

Michael Ancram which noted "with contempt that the Liberal Democratic Party considers it to be a constructive use of specially allocated opposition time to indulge in a petty and vindictive attack on Her Majesty's Opposition rather than to challenge the executive and hold it to account; and points out that, in so doing, a Party whose record of attendance and willingness to sacrifice principle for party advantage shows that it has no constitutional claim to the position and privileges which are rightly accorded to opposition parties in the parliamentary system".

During the debate Mr Tony Benn said parliament was becoming less and less relevant to policy-making and to checking the executive, and added: "If I ever left parliament it would be to devote more time to politics, because it is very difficult to be in the House and have any political role". Mrs Virginia Bottomley said that almost all her time in Parliament had been spent in government office, but that in the last two years she had been appalled at the "use of patronage, the culture of the control freak, the manipulation of the media and the abuse of the House of Commons".

Replying from the Conservative front bench Sir Patrick Cormack described the Liberal Democrats as providing " a shoddy performance by a rather third-rate crew". Ms Joyce Quinn for the Government said she had never seen a motion like this. She and Labour members abstained in the division, allowing the Conservative amendment to be carried against the Liberal Democrats by 137 votes to 36, though the vote took place only because Conservative members stood as tellers for the Liberal Democrats!

On Friday May 14 MPs spent the whole day debating the **Fur Farming (Prohibition) Bill,** but without completing work on this private member's bill.

On Monday May 17 the House of Commons sat though the night until after 5.00am debating the **Welfare Reform and Pensions Bill**, and encountering a good deal of opposition from their own back-benchers. Peers again debated the **House of Lords Bill**, considering among other matters whether their House should have a change of name, and whether some alternative to the Weatherill arrangement might be viable, before voting against the Government's wishes to adjourn at 11.15pm by 145 votes to 136.

The following day Lord Irvine, Lord Chancellor, deplored this "high-order profligacy" with parliamentary time, resulting –

so he alleged – from the action of "busloads of hereditaries". Earl Ferrers responded by saying that Lord Irvine "does not do himself or his office great credit when he speaks in those terms".

Debate continued on this Bill on May 18 with further amendments dealing with proposed "sunset" arrangements for the provisional House, and the privileges that may still be accorded to excluded hereditary peers. During the debate Lord Irvine said that he regarded life peers as representatives of the country, while hereditary peers were representatives of the hereditary peerage. Peers also debated the **Northern Ireland (Location of Victims' Remains) Bill** at second reading and the **Tax Credits Bill** at report stage.

On May 18 the Commons once more debated Kosovo, with Mr George Robertson, Secretary of State for Defence concluding the debate by saying "We will assuredly defeat Milosevic".

At prime minister's question time on May 19 Mr Blair defended his record in the House by saying that he had "answered more parliamentary questions in my first two years than my predecessor answered in his last two years. I have spent more time at prime ministers questions than he did. I have made double the number of statements to the House on which I can be questioned". That day was taken as the 13th Opposition day, with a Conservative motion on European Union Fraud and another on NHS personnel being debated.

On May 19 Lord Monson asked about the Government's view of the "West Lothian Question"; Lord Sewell replied that the future development of regional government in England, the adjustment of the number of Members representing Scottish seats in the Commons, and the development of Westminster procedures would together provide "as much of an answer as the Question requires".

On May 20 the Commons agreed by 377 votes to 145 to an allocation of time order for the **Welfare Reform and Pensions Bill,** following which Dr Roger Berry from the Labour back benches moved a series of amendments concerned with entitlement to incapacity benefits, which were rejected by the House by 310 votes to 270, a Government majority of only 40. In answer to a question from Lord Ackner, the Lord Chancellor told the House of Lords that the Human Rights Act 1998 would be brought into force on October 2, 2000, and that such delay was necessary because of the vast amount of work that needed to be done to implement what he described as "undoubtedly the flagship of the present administration".

The following day, *May 21*, the House of Lords debated at second reading and approved two private members' bills originating in their House, while the House of Commons completed work on Mr Andrew Hunter's **Road Traffic (Vehicle Testing) Bill.**

On Monday *May 24* Mr Jack Straw, Home Secretary, made a Statement to the House on the draft Freedom of Information Bill being published that day for extensive consultation with public, Parliament and the select committee on Public Administration. Sir Norman Fowler said that the Government had in some respects retreated from the position adopted in their White Paper, and Mr Alan Beith said that the "mice had got at the Bill" while it was hidden in the Home Office.

Following this Mrs Margaret Beckett, Leader of the House, spoke as chairman of the Modernisation Committee in recommending to the House the adoption of a proposal to introduce sittings of the House in Westminster Hall as an experiment in the following session. This would she said give more time for back-bench initiated debates and for debates on select committee reports.

From the Opposition front-bench Sir George Young said he had been initially doubtful about this proposal but that as he heard evidence of how this had worked elsewhere, and analysed the problems the House faced, he had become persuaded that this was worth a try because it would help the House "to patrol better the frontier between it and the executive". The proposal was agreed by 145 votes to 36.

On *May 25* MPs held a wide ranging debate in advance of the six-monthly European Council meeting, with internal reform of the EU being discussed as well as the EU response to the Kosovo crisis, and EU enlargement.

Peers that day debated further the **House of Lords Bill** on re-commitment debating in particular the implementation of the Weatherill amendment and accepting that the procedures for elections should be written into the Standing Orders of the House rather than the Bill itself.

The forthcoming European Parliament elections were clearly in the minds of MPs at Prime Ministers question time in *May 26*, with Mr Hague attacking the Prime Minister for saying one thing in Parliament and another in EU meetings and for talking about the past rather than looking to the future.

The House then heard a Statement on Kosovo from Mr George Robertson, Secretary of State for Defence, who said that two months on in the air campaign he was pleased to say that it was working.

Mrs Marion Roe introduced a report from the Administration Committee concerning tourist access to the Palace of Westminster during the summer recess. Various domestic matters were then dealt with such as allowances for Members' travel to National Parliaments and EU institutions, financial assistance to opposition parties, and the quorum for select committees. Later that day the Commons rose for the Whitsun recess.

On the following day, *May 27,* the House of Lords considered a report on genetic modification in agriculture which Lord Shore of Stepney described as admirably lucid, balanced, impartial, responsible and timely, before also rising for the recess.

JUNE

The House of Lords returned from the recess on Monday *June 7*. During exchanges following a question asked by Lord Chalfont on a new report into the Chinook helicopter disaster in 1994, some peers expressed their unease at the official verdict placing blame on the pilots involved, with Lord Fitt commenting: "Does the Minister accept that over a number of years there have been many miscarriages of justice in these islands? Time and time again such cases have been brought to the Court of Appeal, where it has been decided that those who were against the original decisions have been found to be right." Lord Gilbert replying for the Government said he and other ministers had "crawled over the evidence with very great care" and reached the conclusion that the findings of the inquiry were "totally justified".

The House then spent the day on the committee stage of the **Employment Relations Bill.**

The House of Commons returned on Tuesday *June 8* and heard a Statement from the Prime Minister on Kosovo and the European Council in Cologne, in which he reported the acceptance by the Serb Parliament of the NATO peace plan, though he also indicated continued difficulties in securing Milosevic's acquiescence with the plan. A ten-minute rule Bill making it illegal to import meat from any country whose animal welfare standards were not as high as in the UK was then introduced by Mr Tony Baldry, and accepted by 173 votes to 0, after which the House debated and approved at second reading without a division the **Pollution Prevention and Control Bill**.

On *June 9* MPs debated constitutional reform with special reference to England on a motion moved by Mr James Gray, who in introducing the debate said the recent select committee on Procedure report entitled "The Procedural Consequences of Devolution" failed to mention the English question. One matter of concern was the fact that Scottish members of the UK Parliament could vote on everything to do with England, while English members could not vote on much to do with Scotland. Many Conservatives referred to those with seats in two parliaments as "double-troughers".

Later the House debated the White Paper on House of Lords reform. For the Government Mrs Margaret Beckett said the future of the House of Lords should be considered quite separately from that of the House of Commons, but for the Conservatives Liam Fox said it would be quite wrong to deal with one chamber in isolation. Again strong views were expressed both in favour of an elected second chamber and against having a chamber any part of which was elected. Summing up the debate for the Government Mr Paddy Tipping said there was not much sign of a consensus, but equally it was not much good the Conservatives saying they would not start from here because in fact they would not have started at all.

The following day, *June 10*, the Commons debated defence in the world, an appropriate title for the debate according to Mr George Robertson, Secretary of State for Defence, because the security of our country could be guaranteed only by linking it to the security of our continent and the wider world.

On Friday, *June 11*, both Houses debated private members' bills.

On Monday *June 14* Tony Benn sponsored his son, Hilary Benn, who took his seat in the House for the first time following Labour's victory in the Leeds Central by-election. The House then debated the **Health Bill** at report stage, until 10.00pm when the Leader of the House, Mrs Margaret Beckett, announced that a guillotine motion would be brought in the following day.

On *June 15*, a timetable motion dealing with both this Bill and the **Immigration and Asylum Bill** was debated and accepted by 325 votes to 145, with the House then dealing with both Bills, passing the **Health Bill** at third reading by 372 votes to 112. Earlier the House had heard a Statement from Mr John Prescott concerned with the future of London Underground in which he said £7 billion would be spent in a public private partnership to modernise the Underground, on which he said he personally often travelled.

Peers commenced the report stage of the **House of Lords Bill** on *June 15*, debating amendments on a possible referendum on the reform, and on various complex methods of composing the house, including one allowing all existing peers by succession to retain their seats but to have their votes weighted to give parity between the main parties. During the debate Lord Williams of Mostyn said that if this was accepted actuarially speaking the last hereditary peer in the House would die in 2068.

At prime minister's question time on *June 16* Mr Hague asked Mr Blair if he was still in favour of proportional representation after the experience of the European Parliament elections. The Prime Minister replied that Government policy had not changed, to which Mr Hague retorted that Mr Blair was "afraid to argue the case for the few things that he actually believes in". MPs then completed work on the **Immigration and Asylum Bill,** which received its third reading just after midnight by 310 votes to 41.

In the Lords the Government was defeated on the **Employment Relations Bill** when by 98 votes to 78 peers supported an amendment moved by Baroness Miller of Hendon who argued that the Bill introduced a "closed shop through the back door", and that protection should be offered to employees who negotiate pay beyond that agreed in a collective agreement.

The Commons once more debated Kosovo on *June 17* with Mr Robin Cook, Foreign Secretary, speaking of NATO's military campaign as having secured its objectives, a view endorsed by Mr John Maple in his maiden appearance as shadow Foreign Secretary, though others, including Sir John Stanley, asked "whether this appalling humanitarian disaster in Kosovo could have been averted".

Peers that day accepted the overturning of all three amendments they had carried against the Government's wishes to the **Health Bill**.

On *June 18* peers debated a private member's bill introduced by Lord Willoughby de Broke called the **European Community Legislation (Impact) Bill**, during which Lord Pearson of Rannoch cited a 50-page directive on condoms, which he said contained "unbelievable detail"; he asked what on earth was wrong with the British condom industry before this directive appeared? In the Commons Mr Chris Smith, Secretary of State for Culture, Media and Sport, introduced a debate on tourism, which he said was a vital industry contributing £53 billion annually to earnings in the economy and supporting at least 1.7 million jobs.

On Monday *June 21* the Prime Minister made a Statement on the outcome of the G8 summit on Kosovo. In this he referred to the atrocities being uncovered since Milosevic "caved in", saying that: "if ever justification was needed for the military campaign, the whole world has seen it now", but also urging the Serbian people to recognise that the future was now in their own hands as far as rebuilding their country was concerned. The House then debated and accepted without a division the second reading of the **Food Standards Bill** which Mr Nick Brown, Minister for Agriculture, Fisheries and Food said would provide a new framework for food standard and food safety based on openness, transparency and the best science.

On *June 22* Mr David Davis introduced a ten-minute rule bill entitled Parliamentary Control of the Executive, which among other things would require the agreement of a departmental select committee before a departmental estimate was approved. Among the co-sponsors of his Bill were former Conservative ministers Mr Douglas Hogg and Mr Eric Forth. Later the House debated the **Access to Justice Bill** at report stage with Mr Robert Marshall-Andrews tabling an amendment calling for the retention of legal aid for the disabled and less well off in personal injuries cases, which was defeated by 291 votes to 173, having received backing from some 21 Labour MPs.

Peers debated the **House of Lords Bill** again, with Lord Strathclyde, Leader of the Opposition in the House, expressing his surprise and pleasure at the Lord Chancellor's acceptance of an amendment providing for by-elections to fill places that may be caused by the deaths of hereditary peers elected to the House. Later an amendment to establish an appointments commission was carried against the Government by 231 votes to 189.

The Conservatives chose proportional representation as the subject for debate in the Commons on *June 23*, the first part of the 14th Opposition day. Their motion, which was defeated by 143 votes to 365, asserted that in the light of recent experience proportional representation would not be an appropriate basis for elections to the House, and urged the Government to resolve uncertainty by aban-

doning its earlier commitment to hold a referendum.

Two Liberal Democrat motions were debated on *June 24*, the 15th Opposition day, the first on widows was defeated by 37 votes to 274, while the second on supermarkets ended without any division taking place.

On Friday *June 25* Mr Ian McCartney, Minister of State at the Department for Trade and Industry, introduced a debate on innovation and enterprise, much of which focused on whether tax was actually falling or rising.

On Monday *June 28* Mr Straw, Home Secretary, made a Statement on Wormwood Scrubs prison in which he said a "destructive, unco-operative and self-seeking attitude" had been found among a minority of staff, and that because of this he would require a "radical overhaul of Wormwood Scrubs, its culture and its working practices". The House then debated the **Financial Services and Markets Bill** which was given an unopposed second reading.

June 29 was the 16th Opposition day with the newly appointed shadow home secretary, Miss Ann Widdecombe moving a motion critical of the Government's handling of "the current crisis in issuing passports", which was defeated by 165 votes to 351. After this Mr John Redwood moved a motion critical of the way the Government was handling transport congestion, instancing in particular the M4 bus lane and the circle line on the London Underground; this was defeated by 137 votes to 350.

Peers that day debated the **Immigration and Asylum Bill** at second reading, introduced by Lord Williams of Mostyn, with Lord Russell saying it was the "skill of a great advocate to make the best of a very weak brief".

The Deputy Prime Minister, Mr John Prescott, took prime minister's question time on *June 30* with Sir George Young, Shadow Leader of the House, standing in for Mr Hague. The whole House offered its good wishes to the Prime Minister who had decided to stay in Northern Ireland seeking agreement between the conflicting parties in the province. MPs then debated the **Disability Rights Bill** at report stage and then gave it an unopposed third reading.

Peers spent a third day on report stage of the **House of Lords Bill**, with the Government suffering a further defeat, by 283 votes to 177, on an amendment moved by Lord Mancroft designed to write into the Bill a ban on peers created during a parliament from voting on any measure to extend the life of that parliament. The Government was successful in securing defeats for other amendments concerned with disqualifying from membership of the Lords any members of devolved parliaments, and the nomenclature of members.

JULY

On *July 1* MPs debated the armed forces on a government motion for the adjournment. Later Mr Tony McWalter introduced a short debate on the teaching of philosophy in which he deplored the marginalisation of the subject; he received some encouragement from the minister who replied, Mr Charles Clarke, who revealed that he had been to observe the teaching of philosophy in his local school, and that the Government was "strongly committed to the contribution that philosophy and thinking can make to our education system". Peers began their day by hearing tributes to a former Leader of their House, Viscount Whitelaw, who had died that morning.

On Friday *July 2* the Commons debated drugs on a government motion for the adjournment. Mr Paul Flynn said he felt like addressing his colleagues as "right hon and hon drug users" because of the hypocrisy of seeing Members "with a glass of whisky in one hand, a cigarette in the other, and a packet of paracetemol in their top pocket, denouncing young people for using drugs".

On Monday *July 5* the Prime Minister made a Statement reporting progress on the Good Friday Agreement, but acknowledging that the question of decommissioning remained a serious stumbling block. Among those who responded, including the former Prime Minister John Major and former Secretaries of State, support and good will was expressed towards Mr Blair's endeavours.

The House of Commons then debated the **Finance Bill**, continuing with this the following day, *July 6*, when the Bill was given a third reading by 326 votes to 149.

Earlier that day Mr Frank Dobson, Secretary of State for Health, made a Statement introducing a White Paper entitled "Saving Lives: Our Healthier Nation", in which he referred to "Conservative Members who represent areas where people are comfortably off and pretty healthy". Mrs Virginia Bottomley responded by suggesting his policy was "to make the sick healthy by making the healthy sick", and to support her case she referred to people in healthy areas being starved of resources. This charge Mr Dobson denied arguing that "every part of the country is getting more in real terms this year than last year".

Meanwhile in the Lords the detention of General Pinochet was the subject of a debate which drew a sharply critical speech from Baroness Thatcher who said our reputation as a nation had been sullied by the arrest and detention of the former head of the Chilean Government.

At prime minister's question time the following day, *July 7*, Mr Hague said that 200,000 more people were now waiting to see a consultant than in 1997, but Mr Blair said waiting lists had fallen by 62,000 since he became prime minister. The Foreign Secretary, Mr Robin Cook, then made a Statement announcing that diplomatic relations with Libya were being resumed.

Two Conservative motions were debated on this the 17th Opposition day, the first drawing attention to the difficulties in the dairy industry, and the second deploring the reduction in choice and diversity in education. Peers spent a further committee day on the **Greater London Authority Bill**.

On *July 8* Mr Stephen Byers, Secretary of State for Trade and Industry, made a Statement on the Government's "careful and balanced policy" for the future of the Post Office, which would he said give more commercial freedom, though Mrs Angela Browning from the Opposition front bench said what was needed was total privatisation.

The House then debated the **Youth Justice and Criminal Evidence Bill** at report stage before according it an unopposed third reading. Peers debated various private members' bills on *July 9*, but for the Commons this was a "constituency Friday".

On Monday *July 12* Madam Speaker made a Statement offering guidance to the House on the admissibility of questions to the Secretaries of State for Scotland and Wales in which she underlined the fundamental rule that questions must relate to matters for which ministers in the Commons carry responsibility. That day was taken as the 2nd Estimates Day with debates on select committee reports on school inspections and on transport taking place. The House also agreed to a report from its Committee on Standards and Privileges suspending Mr Ernie Ross from the House for ten sitting days because of his premature disclosure of a Foreign Affairs select committee report to the Foreign Office.

The following day, *July 13*, the Committee Chairman, Mr Donald Anderson, made a brief personal statement apologising to the House for disclosing certain aspects of the report on Sierra Leone to a Foreign Office official in advance of publication.

The House then took the **Northern Ireland Bill** through all its stages under a tight guillotine motion agreeing to a second reading by 312 votes to 19. Mo Mowlam, Secretary of State for Northern Ireland, said that the Bill assisted what was the "best chance for peace" by allowing devolved institutions to start work in advance of decommissioning, but it included a "fail-safe mechanism" to ensure that if undertakings on decommissioning of weapons were not met the devolved institutions would be suspended.

Mr Nick Brown, Minister for Agriculture, Fisheries and Food, made a Statement on *July 14* saying that he was very pleased to inform the House that from August 1 it would be possible to export boneless beef from cattle born after August 1996 throughout the European Union. The House then completed work on the **Pollution Prevention and Control Bill** and the **Commonwealth Development Corporation Bill,** both of which were given unopposed third readings.

The main business in the Lords was the consideration of Commons amendments to the **Access to Justice Bill**, with peers voting by 141 to 85 to insist on their amendment preventing the proposed Criminal Defence Service from employing its own lawyers which the Commons wished to delete.

July 15 was the 18th Opposition day, with two motions being moved from the Conservative front-bench, the first on motorists and the second on the post office.

On Friday *July 16* MPs debated policing in London with Mr Jack Straw, Home Secretary, looking forward very positively to the establishment of the Metropolitan Police Authority under the Greater London Authority Bill. During the debate Mr Greenway referred to a personal experience of crime in London and mentioned the skin colour of those who perpetrated the crime, to the evident anger of some Labour MPs.

On Monday *July 19* the House of Commons debated the **Railways Bill** at second reading. Introducing this Mr John Prescott, Secretary of State for the Environment, Transport and the Regions, said the Bill was about "providing a more punctual, reliable, accountable railway system as part of an integrated transport system". The Government proposed that the Bill be sent to the relevant departmental select committee for scrutiny before enactment in the following session, but the Opposition put down an amendment opposing this, which was defeated by 123 votes to 330, after which the Bill was given a second reading by 329 votes to 121. One

Conservative suggested that the reference of the Bill to the select committee was part of a deal whereby the select committee chairman would then refrain from criticising the Bill, but this was immediately denied.

July 20 was the 19th Opposition day, with two Conservative motions, one on health care and one on energy tax being debated.

Prime minister's question time on *July 21* was the last occasion on which Mr Paddy Ashdown spoke as Leader of the Liberal Democrats, asking a question on Kosovo. Mr Blair paid tribute to him, referring to "the tremendous contribution he has made to British politics in the past few years, not least on Kosovo and Bosnia, where he was well ahead of the rest of us and right long before the rest of us".

MPs then debated Lords' reasons for disagreeing to Commons amendments to the **Access to Justice Bill**, and passed a number of Government amendments in lieu of the Lords amendment, thus preserving the right of the proposed Criminal Defence Service to employ its own salaried lawyers. MPs then debated Lords amendments to the **Employment Relations Bill**, deleting on division an amendment made against government advice concerned with the rights of those employees who negotiate their own employment contracts.

The same Bill was made subject to an allocation of time order the following day, *July 22*, along with the **Food Standards Bill**, with the latter being passed at third reading later that day without a division. Peers debated a report from their Procedure Committee setting out rules for the election of the so-called Weatherill peers. The debate revealed differences of view between those who saw such peers as providing a continuing representation of hereditary peers, and those who saw them as providing a desirable element of continuity in the working House through its transitional period.

Lord Bledisloe moved an amendment seeking to enlarge the electorate for those to be elected as party peers to include life as well as hereditary peers, thus making the electorate the same as that for the 15 to be elected as office-holders, but this was rejected by 146 votes to 229. The House thus approved a new Standing Order "in implementation of the House of Lords Act 1999" some months before the Bill by that name was to reach the Statute Book, and well before the House of Commons approved the crucial amendments to which the new standing order related!

On Friday *July 23* the House of Commons completed work on two private members' bills, the **Criminal Cases Review (Insanity) Bill**, introduced by Lord Ackner, and the **Mental Health (Amendment)(Scotland) Bill**, introduced by Mr Eric Clarke, but at 2.30pm as the titles of 52 other private members' bills were read out they were greeted with the word "Object" and accordingly fell.

Both Houses began the final week before the recess by considering the amendments made to various Bills by the other House. The Lords accepted without divisions, though not without further debate the deletion of several of their earlier amendments as the **Access to Justice Bill**, the **Youth Justice and Criminal Evidence Bill**, the **Pollution Prevention and Control Bill** and the **Employment Relations Bill** were all further debated.

The following day, *July 27*, peers defeated the Government twice on matters related to the **House of Lords Bill**. First a motion moved by Lord Mayhew of Twysden to refer to the Privileges Committee of the House the question of the effect of the Bill on peers' writs of summons was supported by 353 to 203, and second a motion moved by Lord Gray asking the Privileges Committee to consider the effect of the Bill on the 1706 Treaty of Union with Scotland, in particular the provision guaranteeing 16 seats to representative peers of Scotland, was carried by 275 votes to 185.

That same day Mr Jack Straw, Home Secretary, made a Statement outlining a draft Bill on the funding of political parities which he said was being published then, but would not be introduced until the following session. Two Labour MPs made personal statements admitting that they had been involved in the leak of a report from the Social Security select committee; one resigned from the select committee and the other from his post as PPS to the Chancellor.

At the end of business a brief adjournment debate was initiated by Mr Peter Bradley on reform of the Commons, in which he called for much bolder reform than had yet taken place. The Commons then rose for the summer recess.

Peers continued work on the **Immigration and Asylum Bill** on *July 28*, and spent a ninth committee day on the **Greater London Authority Bill** on *July 29*. They then debated at second reading the **Food Standards Bill** on Friday *July 30*, before also rising for the recess.

SEPTEMBER

The Liberal Democrat conference was held at Harrogate from *September 19* to *23*. It was notable for a farewell speech from Mr Paddy Ashdown, and the first conference speech as leader of the party from Mr Charles Kennedy. This indicated that he intended broadly to follow the strategy of his predecessor in co-operating with Labour at Westminster.

The Labour Party conference was held at Bournemouth from *September 26* to *October 1*. Mr Blair said the foundations of "New Britain" were being laid; the class war was over, but giving every one equal access to knowledge and opportunity had only just begun. The 21st century "would not be about the battle between capitalism and socialism, but the battle between the forces of progress and the forces of conservatism".

When the Conservatives met at Blackpool between *October 4* and *October 7*, Mr Hague launched a new policy document entitled "The Common Sense Revolution". He described the Government as "the most two-faced, interfering, over-regulating, bossy, intolerant, arrogant and crony-run in our history" and concluded: "Come with me and I will give you back your country".

OCTOBER

The House of Lords returned on Monday *October 11*. Their first item of business after questions was to hear a Statement on railway safety from Lord Macdonald of Tradeston. This followed the railway accident the previous week near Paddington station, which he reported had resulted in thirty confirmed dead, twenty-nine seriously injured, and others still unaccounted for.

Later the House had its first report stage day – sitting until almost 2.30am – on the **Welfare Reform and Pensions Bill,** with peers defeating the government by 145 votes to 137 on an amendment, moved by Lord Higgins, to allow more flexibility in the time at which people with stakeholder pensions would be required to take their annuity.

On *October 12* peers again defeated the Government, this time by 213 votes to 117, introducing a provision backed by Liberal Democrats and Conservatives to the **Greater London Authority Bill,** to allow for impeachment of the mayor if at least 19 of the 25 members of the London assembly voted for this.

Peers returned to the **Welfare Reform and Pensions Bill** on *October 13* with the Government going down to a record number of six defeats in a single day. First peers voted 193 to 114 to extend the bereavement allowance from 26 weeks to two years; next despite protest from Lord Higgins the Government insisted on another vote to determine the outcome on a

Government amendment to make the bereavement allowance applicable for one year, which was rejected by 164 votes to 185.

Lord Ashley of Stoke, a Labour peer and veteran campaigner for the disabled, then moved three amendments deleting various clauses in the Bill, all of which were carried on division with substantial help from Labour peers. First by 251 votes to 95 the House accepted the removal of a clause limiting incapacity benefit to people who had been in recent employment; next by 198 votes to 90 the deletion of a clause means-testing incapacity benefit for people on pension income; and finally by 119 votes to 81 a clause which would have abolished the severe disablement allowance.

The sixth defeat of the day came when Lord Higgins moved an amendment deleting proposals to alter the tax arrangements for "service companies", on the grounds that these were at best half-baked, and furthermore had not yet had any consideration in the Commons.

Peers heard a Statement from the Leader of the House, Baroness Jay, on *October 14*, explaining that from the commencement of the year 2000, Acts of Parliament would be printed on archival paper, not vellum, at a saving of approximately £30,000 a year. When Lord Peston suggested Acts should be placed on CD-ROM, he was told the life of archival paper is about 500 years, but "the life of a CD-ROM has yet to be tested in this context".

The House then continued with the **Greater London Authority Bill**, while on three days that week peers had also been considering the **Food Standards Bill** in Grand Committee meeting parallel to the main chamber.

On Friday *October 15* the House debated a motion moved by the Archbishop of Canterbury on the role of religion in the promotion of international order. Dr Carey argued that more could be done to use religion to help forestall conflict, and many other speakers indicated a little of how they thought this might be done.

On Monday *October 18* the House of Lords began the report stage of the **Immigration and Asylum Bill**, and on Tuesday *October 19* continued with the **Greater London Authority Bill**. On the latter day the House of Commons returned from the recess. The Prime Minister made a Statement on the meeting of the European Council in Finland which had especially addressed the area of justice and home affairs. Mr Hague accused Mr Blair of being carried along on a tide to a single European state, but Mr Blair in response said this was not so and

accused the Conservative party of becoming "a single-issue anti-European pressure group controlled by Thatcherite right-wingers".

The House next debated the Office for National Statistics, on a motion moved by Mr Giles Radice, who stressed the importance of statistics being free of political interference. Then Dr Tony Wright introduced a debate on the work of the Parliamentary Ombudsman, saying that it was a pity only members of the relevant select committee appeared to be present, and that an annual debate should be held as is the case with reports of the Public Accounts Committee.

One of the morning adjournment debates on *October 20* concerned the differential between prices for cars in the UK and elsewhere in the EU, with Mr Martin O'Neill calling for a stop to "rip-off Britain in car showrooms". Mr Peter Mandelson answered questions for the first time as Secretary of State for Northern Ireland, and urged the paramilitaries on both sides to complete the journey along the road to peace which they had been travelling for some time, especially in relation to decommissioning.

At prime minister's question time Mr Hague challenged Mr Blair over the question of police numbers, alleging that the Home Secretary had misled the public in statements made at the Labour Party conference. This was the 20th Opposition day and was given over to Liberal Democrat motions. The first concerned food and farming and was opened by the party leader, Mr Charles Kennedy who called for more support for farmers in this the worst crisis to hit their industry since the 1930s. From the Conservative front-bench Mr Tim Yeo was also very critical of the Government but in the division the Liberal Democrats lacked Conservative support and their motion was lost by 50 votes to 326.

The second motion concerned transport safety, and was defeated by 46 votes to 329. Peers debated a motion moved by the Duke of Montrose to refer the **House of Lords Bill** to the Examiners. He argued that the Bill was hybrid in respect of clause one, but Lord Elton opposed the motion because "hybrid procedure is about protecting individual rights when they are threatened by a piece of legislation which treats others of the same class differently", and Lord Brightman said that it was "as plain as a pikestaff that it is not hybrid". The motion was defeated by 85 votes to 214.

Later when the House was considering the **Immigration and Asylum Bill** the Bishop of Southwark introduced an amendment to delay a plan to replace cash benefits for asylum seekers with vouchers until such time as the Home Office has met its six-month target for processing appeals. In his speech the Bishop said the Home Office computer was in his diocese and stories he heard made him doubtful about the timescale being met. His amendment was carried by 161 votes to 116.

On *October 21* the Home Secretary, Mr Jack Straw, made a Statement saying that he was referring five cases connected with the archive of the KGB defector Vasili Mitrokhin for possible prosecution. Miss Widdecombe challenged Mr Straw as to when he first heard of allegations against some of those involved. The main Commons debate concerned the procedural consequences of devolution. During this Sir George Young, from the Opposition front bench, called for Bills affecting England to be considered only by English MPs, but this was rejected by Mrs Margaret Beckett speaking for the Government who said that it would be rare for a bill to be classified as applying only to England.

On Monday *October 25* the House of Commons approved the establishment of a parallel chamber in Westminster Hall as well as the continuation of the experiment in Thursday morning sittings. The House also approved the carrying forward into the following session of the **Financial Services and Markets Bill**, with the Conservative front bench supporting the Government in this move, but with some, notably Mr Eric Forth, objecting on the grounds that the discipline imposed by the one-session rule was desirable, and that if the door was once opened to carry forward bills the Government "would want to walk through it with ever greater frequency".

On *October 26* a record number of 752 peers attended their House for the third reading debate on the **House of Lords Bill**. After a brief interruption at the commencement of proceedings (when the heir to a hereditary peer leapt onto the woolsack), peers considered various amendments including one moved by Earl Ferrers which would have introduced elections allowing life peers to choose 400 of their number to remain in the House; this was rejected by 186 votes to 238. A further amendment moved by Lord Tebbit to delay implementation of the Bill until after the next election, on the grounds that peers did not have a vote at the previous election, was rejected by 238 votes to 154. Eventually just after 11.00pm the motion that "the Bill do now pass" was carried by 221 votes to 81. In the Commons Jack Straw faced attack from the Opposition for a catalogue of alleged Home Office misdeeds.

At prime minister's question time on *October 27* Mr Hague attacked Mr Blair over the handling of the beef crisis, suggesting that the Government should ban French meat after allegations that sewage had been fed to their cattle, but Mr Blair said he would not engage in any tit-for-tat trade war. Later MPs debated a report from the Joint Select Committee on Parliamentary Privilege, agreeing with the committee that part of the Defamation Act 1996 should be repealed to limit the ability of Members to waive parliamentary privilege for personal reasons.

On the same day the House of Lords voted 166 to 107 in support of an amendment moved by Baroness Strange to the **Welfare Reform and Pensions Bill** the effect of which was to allow widows of servicemen who remarry to keep their service pensions.

On *October 28* MPs debated agriculture on a government motion for the adjournment, and on Friday *October 29* broadcasting was the subject of another Government adjournment debate. That day in the House of Lords just after 1.00pm the Clerk of the Parliaments read out the names of those 15 hereditary peers who had been successful in the ballot for office holders, thereby retaining their seats in the House.

NOVEMBER

On Monday *November 1* the House of Commons voted by 121 to 53 to overturn the recommendation backed by the Government (as a "modest piece of modernisation") that vellum should no longer be used to record Acts of Parliament. Peers completed work on the **Greater London Authority Bill** with the Government winning five divisions. Lord Chalfont introduced a debate on the 1994 Chinook helicopter crash during the dinner hour, with twelve other peers speaking before the Government minister, Baroness Symons of Vernham Dean, refuted the need for any further inquiry.

On *November 2* peers dealt with the **Immigration and Asylum** Bill at third reading, while in the Commons the second part of the Opposition's 14th day was taken with a debate initiated by Mr John Redwood on planning.

On *November 3* the Commons considered Lords amendments to the **Welfare Reform and Pensions Bill**, with the Government facing substantial criticism from Labour back bench MPs, over 50 of whom voted with the Opposition in resisting ministers demands to overturn Lords amendments. Dr Roger Berry said that this was a sad day for Labour because benefits would be reduced for disabled people unable to work, and that despite Government concessions at least 310,000 people would be worse off.

The following day, *November 4*, the Commons rejected by 306 votes to 151 the Lords amendment to the **Greater London Authority Bill** which had provided for the possible impeachment of the mayor. Peers that day debated a report from their select committee on Monetary Policy, introduced by Lord Peston.

On *November 5* the results of the election for the 75 hereditary peers representing party groups in the continuing House of Lords were announced by the Clerk of the Parliaments in the chamber of the House.

On Monday *November 8* the House of Commons continued considering Lords amendments to the **Greater London Authority Bill**, first voting by 304 to 150 in support of a guillotine motion to allow proceedings to be completed that day; on this Mr John Redwood said the fact that the Government had put down over 800 amendments to their own Bill meant that ministers were re-writing it as they went along, and a self-respecting government would start again on the Bill.

Peers considered Commons amendments to the **Welfare Reform and Pensions Bill**, and by 153 votes to 140 decided again to oppose the Government in seeking protection for the pensions of widows of servicemen who die in the line of duty and who subsequently re-marry, but this time excluding those who were themselves already of pensionable age. Lord Ashley of Stoke then moved that the House should insist on the substance of its amendments concerning incapacity benefit, arguing that although the Government had come some way towards the House, this was not far enough; his view prevailed by 260 votes to 127.

The following day, *November 9*, the Bill returned to the Commons where MPs voted by 361 to 178 to reject the Lords amendment on servicemen's widows, and by 314 to 234 to reject the amendment on incapacity benefit. Speaking on the latter amendment the Secretary of State for Social Security, Mr Alistair Darling, drew attention to the concessions already made and said: "the time has come for the Lords to accept that the will of the elected chamber must take precedence". Mr Gerald Kaufman said: "Anyone who votes against the Government tonight will be voting for the House of Lords to prevail over the House of Commons", but from the Liberal Democrat benches Steven Webb said

that to vote for the amendment would not be an expression of subservience to the House of Lords but an expression of the will of the House of Commons. Dr Roger Berry said the Bill without the Lords amendment would leave many disabled people who are unable to work without incapacity benefit or with reduced benefit, and concluded by quoting in agreement from Baroness Kennedy, a Labour peer, who in the Lords the previous day had said: "I believe in welfare reform, but I also believe in welfare".

On the same day the Commons debated a guillotine motion on the **Immigration and Asylum Bill**, with Mr Stunnell for the Liberal Democrats saying the guillotine was unnecessary and rebuking the Government for the mis-management that had resulted in "days of slack business last week", while Miss Ann Widdecombe from the Conservative front bench deplored the fact that the guillotine left very little time to debate over 300 new government amendments to the Bill, saying that this was "an arrogant motion of an arrogant and incompetent Government". After the guillotine was approved, by 339 votes to 175, the amendment inserted by the Lords to delay replacing cash benefits with vouchers was rejected by 331 votes to 60, the minority being made up of Liberal Democrats and a few Labour MPs.

That same evening an unusual adjournment debate took place with some 50 MPs listening to Mr Tony Benn speak on the relationship between the Executive and the Legislature. He emphasised that MPs were legislators and had to take responsibility for the legislation that Parliament enacted: he had not himself voted that day "against the Government" but "for disabled people", and those who voted "for the Government" were not actually voting for the Government but for the changes introduced in this Bill. He drew attention to an early day motion he had tabled which invited all members to speak and vote more freely in the House and in so doing assert their historic role as elected representatives.

Earlier that day Mr Gordon Brown, the Chancellor of the Exchequer, had made his pre-budget Statement in which he emphasised enterprise, fairness and stability, along with the fall in public borrowing that had taken place since 1997, and his determination to keep to a low inflation target and "not relax our discipline". For the Opposition Mr Francis Maude said the Chancellor claimed to be prudent, but he was prudent with the truth, and that in reality taxes were rising faster than elsewhere in Europe.

On *November 10* the House of Commons debated Lords amendments to the **House of Lords Bill**, agreeing the "Weatherill" amendment by 438 votes to 22. During the debate Mr Mark Fisher questioned the legal basis of the elections that had already taken place in the House of Lords, given that the Bill with this crucial amendment had not yet been considered by the Commons. The House then rejected the amendment to include provision in the Bill for an appointments commission by 353 votes to 133.

On Thursday *November 11* the final day of the session peers held their last debate on the **House of Lords Bill** amidst some procedural confusion, but the deletion by the Commons of the amendment on an appointments commission was accepted without a division. In moving the adjournment Baroness Jay, as Leader of the House, said: "We should today look back as well as forwards and respectfully acknowledge that in this House hereditary peers have served honourably".

Lord Strathclyde said that "this House has inflicted no evil in its history and much good has been done by it", and went on to comment that the past session had been the most difficult he had experienced, but he continued: "this is not a time for recrimination but for resolution that we who stay will be worthy in every way of those who go, that we shall not rest in the battle to achieve genuine and lasting reform and we shall practise the virtues of modesty, courtesy and a willingness to listen as much as we talk".

Lord Rodgers of Quarry Bank, the Liberal Democrat leader in the House, spoke of the sense of "anticipated bereavement" which had been particularly strong in the last restless, uncomfortable and difficult days. Meanwhile the Commons voted on a procedural motion to adjourn the House while awaiting the message that the House of Lords had given assent to the Bill, then following a Commission giving Royal Assent to the Bill, the Lord Chancellor read the prorogation speech at 5.00pm, and the session duly ended. Some 653 hereditary peers ceased to be members of Parliament.

1999-2000 SESSION

The Queen's Speech opening the new session of Parliament was delivered on *November 17*. Dr Jack Cunningham moved the Loyal Address in reply, speaking of the delights of his constituency, Copeland in the Lake District, and the benefits that the Government was bringing to his constituents. Mr Ivan Lewis seconded the motion.

The Leader of the Opposition, Mr William Hague, in a speech full of humour poked fun at the Deputy Prime Minister, likening him to an ageing Soviet leader in times past who gradually had his powers removed. He then accused the Prime Minister of finding it difficult to tell the truth. Mr Blair responded by saying that: "New Labour was working", though "the Conservatives would reverse the work we have done". For the Liberal Democrats Mr Charles Kennedy said the Speech was disappointing and a Government with so large a majority should be more ambitious.

On *November 18* the debate focused on the environment, transport and the countryside, with Mr Prescott denying that the Government was anti-motorist and Mr Heseltine supporting the Government's plans for elected mayors as a way of encouraging people of the "right calibre" to enter local government, though he and others ridiculed the contortions going on within the Labour party over its choice of candidate as mayor of London.

On Friday *November 19* the House debated trade, industry and social security. On Monday *November 22* Mr Peter Mandelson made a Statement on political progress in Northern Ireland; in this he announced his intention to call a meeting of the Assembly the following week, and – assuming ministers were nominated to the new Executive – transfer of powers would take place immediately afterwards. The Conservatives expressed support; Mr John Major said this was a "justifiable gamble" which he "wholly supported". For the Democratic Unionists Mr John Taylor said this was a "jump into the dark", but Mr David Trimble of the Ulster Unionists said: "we have a basis on which we can proceed to both devolution and decommissioning".

MPs then debated foreign affairs and defence with Mr Robin Cook, Foreign Secretary, saying that the good health of the Atlantic alliance had been demonstrated during the Kosovo conflict, and criticising the Russians for the scale of the military conflict in Chechnya. Mr John Maples for the Opposition said the Government's handling of European affairs had been characterised by surrender. Mr Donald Anderson, the Labour back bench chairman of the Foreign Affairs select committee, said that he was concerned that the foreign affairs content of the Speech "appeared to be an afterthought".

On *November 23* the debate dealt with home affairs, education and employment. From the Conservative front bench Miss Widdecombe accused Mr Straw of topping the year's league of incompetence with "all his ministerial bungles".

On *November 24* at prime minister's question time the two party leaders clashed sharply, disagreeing whether tax was rising or falling, a theme continued in the debate that day which concerned the economy. The Queen's Speech debate concluded with a Conservative amendment being defeated by 149 votes to 381.

In the House of Lords the four-day debate on the Speech ended on *November 24* with the Conservative opposition pressing their amendment to the Loyal Address to a division; this deplored "the incoherence and lack of vision" of the proposed legislation. Baroness Jay questioned the procedure, asking: "what is the point of making a political point to a constitutional monarch?" Despite their three-line whip the Conservatives were defeated by 168 votes to 164 in the new 670-strong House.

On *November 25* the House of Commons held its annual debate on reports from the Public Accounts Committee, and then on *November 26* debated Government support for the arts on a motion for the adjournment. Peers debated two reports from their European Communities Committee on the *25th*.

On Monday *November 29* Mr Jack Straw, Home Secretary, made a Statement on the Government's crime reduction strategy in which he said recorded crime had risen at an annual rate of around 5 per cent throughout the century, but had fallen by 19 per cent over the past five years. Some police forces had been much more successful in reducing crime than others, as figures published that day indicated. Tough prison sentences, many more CCT cameras and an expansion of the DNA database were all planned. Mr Michael Howard said that nearly all the proposals announced built on measures that he had introduced as Home Secretary before 1997.

The House then debated the **Electronic Communications Bill** at second reading, voting by 128 to 319 against an Opposition amendment which said that the Bill introduced a "completely unnecessary element of regulation in the supervision of electronic commerce". On Tuesday *November 30* Dr Phyllis Starkey introduced the first ever debate in the Commons parallel Chamber in Westminster Hall. Her subject was Palestinian refugees, and this was followed by debates on RAF Fairford, children and tobacco products and pensions mis-selling in a three-hour sitting, to be repeated experimentally on three days a week.

Later Mr Nick Brown, Minister for Agriculture, Fisheries and Food, announced the lifting of the ban on beef on the bone, to the evident pleasure of many MPs. Mr Jack Straw then introduced the second reading of the **Representation of the People Bill** which he said was concerned with modernising electoral procedures. An Opposition amendment criticising the Government for haste on the Bill and seeking more consultation was defeated by 143 votes to 332.

DECEMBER
On *December 1* the Prime Minister announced that the Queen had made the Order devolving power to the Northern Ireland Assembly from midnight. Mr Chris Smith then made a Statement about Wembley Stadium in which he cast serious doubt about the viability of the new stadium design for international athletics events. The debate that followed was on the European Union in advance of the Helsinki summit. Mr Robin Cook said that widening the Union and making its institutions more effective were the Government's aims, but for the Opposition Mr John Maples said this Government had "given away a great deal and got nothing in return, not even goodwill". In Westminster Hall that morning Mr Paddy Ashdown had made his first ever speech as a back bencher; in this he was sharply critical of policy towards the Balkans, saying that having fought a war there we were now in danger of losing the peace. Peers debated the countryside on a motion moved by Earl Ferrers, who began his speech by saying that hereditary peers who are in the House have more legitimacy than anyone else: "we have been elected. Everyone else has been appointed". Replying Lord Haskel said he was not sure of the legitimacy of the electoral college which elected Earl Ferrers!

On *December 2* MPs debated the report of the Royal Commission on long term care, while in the Upper House Lord Forsyth of Drumlean moved an address seeking leave to introduce a Bill to amend the Act of Settlement to allow a Roman Catholic, or someone married to a Catholic, to ascend the Throne. Lord St John of Fawsley opposed the motion, arguing that it was in part incorrect, and on division it was defeated by 14 votes to 65. Peers then debated at second reading the **Criminal Justice (Mode of Trial) Bill** with many peers expressing strong criticism of the Bill.

On Monday *December 6* Mr Straw made a Statement on increases in fees for passports, saying these were necessary in order to fund an investment programme to speed up processing applications, but Miss Widdecombe said his announcement would convince "the average applicant that the spirit of Ebenezer Scrooge lives on in the Home Office". MPs then debated the **Government Resources and Accounts Bill** which the Conservatives opposed with an amendment which said that it gave "unfettered discretion to the Treasury"; their amendment was defeated by 140 votes to 327.

Mr Straw was in action again when on *December 7* when he introduced the second reading of the **Freedom of Information Bill.** This would for the first time, he said, give the public the right to know, and it would transform the culture in which government operated. Other speakers were critical of the restrictions and exceptions contained within the Bill. Mr Robert Maclennan for the Liberal Democrats said he was baffled and mystified by the extent to which the draft Bill had been watered down. Dr Tony Wright, Labour chairman of the Public Administration select committee, said this was a historic Bill which had already been improved since it was first published in draft form, but it was capable of further improvement.

Peers debated enlargement of the EU that day, and then on the following day, *December 8* peers debated the state of British universities. In the Commons this was the 1st Opposition day with debate on a Conservative motion condemning the Government for its mishandling of the future of the London Underground. One of the morning debates in Westminster Hall concerned the scrutiny of European legislation, and indicated that difficulties still arose over the precise practical remit of varying committees engaged in this area.

The following day, *December 9,* the first Government initiated debate in Westminster Hall took place, on the subject of the White Paper on modernising government. The debate in the main chamber that day was on the World Trade Organisation following its recent Seattle conference, with Mr Stephen Byers, Secretary of State for Trade and Industry saying that Britain would be pressing for the modernisation and reform of the WTO after the collapse of the Seattle talks. Prior to that Mr Nick Brown made a Statement on the refusal by the French Government to lift its ban on British beef, which was greeted with anger around the House, with Conservative members criticising the Government for failing to take a tougher line at an earlier stage. In the Lords peers voted by 122 to 76 to allow former members of the House certain privileges, including the right to sit on the steps of the throne,

at least for an experimental period. However given that no car parking privileges were included Lord Boston of Faversham, Lord Chairman of Committees, didn't foresee much demand for the use of "club rights".

In a Statement on the recent Helsinki summit on Monday *December 13* the Prime Minister said "the main issue was the enlargement of the European Union, which the Government strongly support"; he went on to say that in addition to the six countries with whom negotiations had already commenced, the European Council decided to open negotiations with six more. On Russia he said that "business as usual was not possible while human rights were being comprehensively abused in Chechnya. Mr Hague in response said "Labour in Europe is not working" and accused the Government of being "experts in tactical ineptitude".

The House then debated fisheries in advance of the December quota fixing meeting of the European Council. A Conservative amendment to the Government motion calling for the devolution of power to national, regional and local levels was defeated by 131 votes to 347. During the debate the Father of the House,

Sir Edward Heath, revealed that he had once caught over 146lb of cod in a single day, a national record! He went on to say that when he negotiated British entry to the Community his Government had secured a 12-mile fishing limit exclusive to our fishermen; that was what had been asked for and it had been renewed up to at least 2002, though it was now necessary to limit catches. He criticised the Conservative amendment saying it led him to conclude that the party leadership now wished to leave the Community. Later fifteen back bench members had the opportunity to pursue varied constituency matters in the recess adjournment debate.

In the Upper House Lord Peyton of Yeovil asked about staff working at 10 Downing Street, and was told the number had risen by half – to 199 – since the election; Lord Lipsey, drawing on his own experience as a former employee there, commented: "the amazing thing about No 10 is not that the staff is so big, but that it is so small".

On *December 14* the Commons debated the **Terrorism Bill** which would repeal but in part re-enact the Prevention of Terrorism Act. Introducing the measure Mr Straw, Home Secretary, said it would be used in situations where demonstrations turned ugly, but some of his back bench colleagues suggested the Bill could lead to the outlawing of campaigning groups such as Greenpeace, and that Mr Straw himself had undergone a "Damascene conversion" since his time in opposition when he had opposed the Prevention of Terrorism Act.

Miss Ann Widdecombe said the Conservatives would not oppose the Bill, but the Liberal Democrats forced a division on a motion seeking to refer the Bill to a Special Standing Committee; this was lost by 47 votes to 262. Peers debated the **Race Relations (Amendment) Bill** at second reading that day.

At prime minister's questions on *December 15* Mr Hague took up the theme that 1999 was supposed to be the year of delivery for the Government, but as far as police numbers, hospital waiting lists and tax levels were concerned this had not been so; he suggested Mr Blair's new year resolution should be "to keep the promises he has been breaking over the past year". Mrs Margaret Beckett, Lord President of the Council, made a Statement on preparations for the millennium bug problems, saying that over £400 million had been spent making sure that computers in government departments were Year 2000 compliant, and that a special official unit would monitor any difficulties over the new year period.

The House then debated the **Representation of the People Bill** in committee, with Mr Simon Hughes arguing that the voting age should be reduced from 18 to 16, the age at which people were "old enough to marry, have children, fight, work and pay tax". Mr Mike O'Brien, Parliamentary Under-Secretary at the Home Office, asked Mr Hughes to withdraw his amendment and allow the matter to be considered by the Home Affairs select committee, but Mr Hughes declined, whereupon the amendment was defeated by 434 votes to 36. The continued applicability of the Salisbury Convention exercised the minds of peers at question time in their House, with the Leader of the House, Baroness Jay, saying that "the convention had nothing to do with the strength of the parties in either House and everything to do with the relationship between the two Houses".

Lord Denham, former Tory Chief Whip in the House, said that Labour had taken a "lot of convincing" that the convention applied to them when they were in opposition, and Lord Hooson from the Liberal Democrat benches said the conditions that necessitated the convention coming into being still existed, but Lord Strathclyde, Conservative leader in the House, said the time had come to re-examine the convention. The following day, *December 16*, the argument over whether taxes were rising or falling led to further sharp exchanges at Treasury question time in the Commons.

Later Mr Straw made a Statement saying he would study the ruling of the European Court of Human Rights concerning the trial of the two children convicted of murdering the two-year-old boy, James Bulger, but that the judgement had not overturned the guilty verdict or in any way exonerated the two youths.

Later the House debated select committee reports on this the first Estimates Day. Mrs Gwyneth Dunwoody, chairman of the Transport committee said the Government had responded complacently to a report made by her committee on aviation safety. A report from the Scottish Affairs committee on inward and outward investment was also debated. The House of Lords debated the **Armed Forces Discipline Bill** in committee that day, following which the House adjourned for the Christmas recess, with the customary short speeches of reflection and thanks being made from all sides. The Chief Whip, Lord Carter, welcomed Lord Craig of Radley as the new Convenor of the Cross Bench peers following the retirement of Lord Weatherill from this role.

On Monday *December 20* Mr John Prescott introduced the second reading of the **Transport Bill,** a wide-ranging measure authorising congestion taxes, creating a Strategic Rail Authority "to plug the loopholes in the last Government's rail legislation", and privatising in part the national air traffic control services. Among back bench speakers was the former Labour transport minister, Mr Gavin Strang, who argued that air traffic control should not be privatised. The Bill was given a second reading by 358 votes to 163.

On *December 21* MPs heard from Mr George Foulkes, Parliamentary Under-Secretary for International Development, about British help to the people of Venezuela following the recent floods which Mr Foulkes said had directly affected at least 150,000 people. Mr Jack Straw then made a Statement about millennium preparations, emphasising police readiness to cope with large scale celebrations in city centres. Following this the House debated public expenditure on a government motion, to which the Conservative Opposition put down an amendment focusing on the increased "burden of taxation". The amendment was defeated by 125 votes to 306. The House then rose for the Christmas recess.

Public Legislation 1998-99

[A * sign indicates legislation introduced by a private member whose name is then given immediately after the title of the Act. The letters *HL* after an Act indicate legislation introduced into the House of Lords. The dates given are the dates on which Royal Assent was attained].

Access to Justice Act, 1999 *HL* (July 27, 1999)
Replaces the existing legal aid scheme; establishes a Legal Services Commission which will be required to maintain and develop a Community Legal Service and a Criminal Defence Service; amends the law on conditional fee arrangements; replaces the Lord Chancellor's Advisory Committee on Legal Education and Conduct with a Legal Services Consultative Panel; reforms the system for appeals in civil and family cases; provides for changes to the organisation and management of magistrates courts.

*Adoption (Intercountry Aspects) Act, 1999 *Mark Oaten Esq* (July 27, 1999)
Provides for the ratification of the 1993 Hague Convention on the Protection of Children and Co-operation in respect of Intercountry adoption; makes various provisions designed to regulate adoption and to prevent trafficking in children; clarifies responsibilities of both central and local government bodies in relation to intercountry adoption; provides that children lawfully adopted from overseas have the same legal status as children adopted within the UK.

Appropriation Act, 1999 (July 15, 1999)
[Introduced as Consolidated Fund Appropriation Bill]
Prescribes how expenditure is appropriated in order to finance specific public services.

*Breeding and Sale of Dogs (Welfare) Act, 1999 *James Clappison Esq* (June 30, 1999)
Makes provision for new rules in relation to commercial breeding establishments, including the licensing and inspecting of premises; places restrictions on the ages at which bitches are used for breeding and the number of permissible litters; provides for local authorities to charge appropriate fees for licensing and provides for increased penalties including imprisonment for operating un-licensed establishments.

Commonwealth Development Corporation Act, 1999 *HL* (July 27, 1999)
Provides for the Commonwealth Development Corporation to be converted from a statutory corporation to a public limited company; retains for the Government an entrenched role in the Corporation; provides for financial restructuring of the Corporation and for continued Government financial assistance until conversion takes place.

*Company and Business Names (Chamber of Commerce Etc) Act, 1999 *Andrew Lansley Esq* (July 27, 1999)
Provides for the Secretary of State to give approval for the use of the words "chamber of commerce" and to consult with the British Chamber of Commerce or the Scottish Chamber of Commerce when considering applications by organisations for such approval.

Consolidated Fund (No 2) Act, 1998 (December 12, 1998)
Gives parliamentary authority for sums to be issued out of the Consolidated Fund to meet the Government's expenditure requirements.

Consolidated Fund Act, 1999 (March 23, 1999)
Gives parliamentary authority for sums to be issued out of the Consolidated Fund to meet the Government's expenditure requirements.

Contracts (Rights of Third Parties) Act, 1999 *HL* (November 11, 1999)
Implements recommendations made by the Law Commission establishing the right of third parties to enforce a term of a contract; restricts the right of contracting parties to alter a contract in ways that change a third party's entitlement without that third party's consent.

*Criminal Cases Review (Insanity) Act, 1999 *HL Lord Ackner* (July 27, 1999)
Makes provision for verdicts of guilty but insane to be referred to and reviewed by the Court of Appeal.

Disability Rights Commission Act, 1999 (July 27, 1999)
Establishes a Disability Rights Commission, with the duty to work towards the elimination of discrimination against disabled people, and to promote the equalisation of opportunities for disabled people; provides for the Commission to undertake formal investigations to determine whether discrimination has taken place; provides that the Commission can assist individuals with legal support where they seek redress for discrimination; requires the Secretary of State to consult the Commission about adjustments to the small employer threshold.

Employment Relations Act, 1999 (July 27, 1999)
Makes various provisions to ensure fair treatment in relation to recruitment and employment; provides for the prohibition of the compilation of black lists for use in recruitment; provides for part-time employees to be treated in accordance with the European Part Time Work Directive; prohibits the waiving of unfair dismissal rights in fixed term contracts; authorises the Secretary of State to make funding available to promote partnerships at work.

European Parliamentary Elections Act, 1999 (January 14, 1999)
Amends the European Parliamentary Elections Act 1978; specifies the number of Members of the European Parliament to be returned for each constituent part of the UK; establishes that the electoral system to be used requiring voters to cast a single vote for either a registered party or an individual candidate; makes provision for the allocation of seats according to the number of votes cast; provides that the electoral system in Northern Ireland will remain a single transferable vote system.

Finance Act, 1999 (July 27, 1999)
Reforms corporation tax, introducing new lower rates; introduces a new lower starting rate for income tax; makes various provisions for the improvement of investment; provides tax relief for companies seconding staff to education institutions; introduces a children's tax credit.

Food Standards, 1999. (November 11, 1999)
Establishes a Food Standards Agency with duties to ensure food safety and consumer protection; requires the Agency to provide policy advice to ministers and other public bodies; empowers the Agency to commission and carry out research into food safety; requires the Agency to monitor food law enforcement and to be an enforcement authority; provides for the Agency to be accountable to ministers and to devolved authorities in Scotland, Wales and Northern Ireland.

*Football (Offences and Disorder) Act, 1999 *Simon Burns Esq* (July 27, 1999)
Amends existing legislation to strengthen powers to curb disorderly behaviour in connection with football; tightens the existing law in relation to international banning orders served in consequence of football related offences.

Greater London Authority Act, 1999 (November 11, 1999)
Establishes the Greater London Authority, and provides for elections for the mayor of London and the London Assembly; defines the powers and functions of the mayor and of the Assembly; establishes the Metropolitan Police Authority and the London Fire and Emergency Planning Authority. Specifies that elections for the post of mayor will be by first-past-the-post if only two candidates stand, and by supplementary vote if three or more candidates stand, and that Assembly members will be elected by the additional member system.

Health Act, 1999 (June 30, 1999)
Abolishes GP fund-holding; amends the National Health Service Act 1977 to make provision for the establishment of new statutory bodies in England and Wales to be known as Primary Care Trusts; amends the National Health Service and Community Care Act 1990 in relation to NHS Trusts; places a new statutory duty of quality on NHS Trusts and Primary Care Trusts; establishes a new statutory

body for England and Wales to be known as the Commission for Health Improvement; creates new duties of partnership between NHS bodies and local authorities; makes new provisions for tackling fraud within the NHS; provides for regulation in relation to pharmaceutical prices and profit margins; makes further provision for the regulation of health care professions.

House of Lords Act, 1999 (November 11, 1999)
Provides for the removal from the House of Lords of hereditary peers; makes provision for up to 92 hereditary peers at any time to remain members of the House of Lords.

Immigration and Asylum Act, 1999 (November 11, 1999)
Provides for changes in the operation of existing immigration controls; provides new civil penalties in relation to clandestine entry to the UK; introduces a greater judicial element for immigration detainees; introduces a new asylum appeal procedure for persons lawfully present when an application is made; reinstates a right of appeal for those refused a visa for family visits; provides for the regulation of immigration advisers; makes new provision for asylum seekers in need separate from the main benefits system; extends the powers of immigration officers; places new powers and responsibilities on marriage registrars.

Local Government Act, 1999 (July 27, 1999)
Imposes new duties on local authorities to provide best value to their communities; provides for new external audit checks on performance plans and management systems; provides for national performance indicators; abolishes compulsory competitive tendering; replaces powers to cap council tax with reserve powers designed to be invoked with greater flexibility.

*Mental Health (Amendment)(Scotland) Act, **1999** *Eric Clarke Esq* (November 11, 1999)
Enables hospital managers in Scotland to release funds committed to their care on behalf of a patient when that patient is released into care in the community.

Northern Ireland (Location of Victims Remains) Act, 1999 (May 26, 1999)
Makes provision in connection with the location of the remains of victims killed before 10th April 1998 in unlawful acts of violence committed by proscribed organisations.

Pollution Prevention and Control Act, 1999 *HL* (July 27, 1999)
Provides for the implementation of European Council directives on integrated pollution control; provides for the Secretary of State to make new regulations for integrated pollution control; provides for transfer of functions to devolved authorities.

*Protection of Children Act, 1999 *Ms Debra Shipley* (July 15, 1999)
Provides for the Department of Health's listing of individuals considered unsuitable for work with children to be placed on a statutory basis, with appropriate rights of appeal; requires regulated childcare organisations to check the names of potential employees.

Rating (Valuation) Act, 1999 (May 26, 1999)
Makes provision concerning the valuation of properties for national non-domestic rates, requiring valuers to assume a reasonable state of repair in properties.

Road Traffic (NHS Charges) Act, 1999 (March 10, 1999)
Makes provision concerning the recovery from insurers and certain other persons of charges in connection with the treatment of road traffic casualties in national health service and certain other hospitals.

*Road Traffic (Vehicle Testing) Act, 1999 *Andrew Hunter Esq* (June 30, 1999)
Makes further provision for the testing of motor vehicles for the purposes of Part II of the Road Traffic Act 1988.

Scottish Enterprise Act, 1999 (May 26, 1999)
Increases the financial limit set in Section 25(2) of the Enterprise and New Towns (Scotland) Act 1990; removes the power given to the Secretary of State to increase the limit further by statutory instrument.

Social Security Contributions (Transfer of Functions, Etc) Act, 1999 *HL* (February 25, 1999)
Transfers the Contributions Agency from the Department of Social Security to the Inland Revenue; provides for the transfer of policy responsibility for National Insurance Contributions to the Inland Revenue; makes further provision consequent upon these transfers in relation to appeals.

Tax Credits Act, 1999 (June 30, 1999)
Provides for the conversion of existing benefits to tax credits to be administered by the Inland Revenue; makes various related provisions for disabled persons tax credit.

Trustee Delegation Act, 1999 *HL* (July 15, 1999)
Implements a Law Commission report relating to the delegation by individual trustees of their trust responsibilities and provides further protection for beneficiaries.

Water Industry Act, 1999 (June 30, 1999)
Makes further provisions as to charges in respect of the supply of water and the provision of sewerage services.

Welfare Reform and Pensions Act, 1999 (November 11, 1999)
Makes provision to amend existing law in relation to social security in various ways designed to assist people into employment; alters the system of support for disabled people, including adjustments to benefit entitlement; amends bereavement benefit and widows benefit; provides for pension rights to be shared at the time of divorce; establishes a framework for new stakeholder pensions, makes other provisions for connected purposes.

Youth Justice and Criminal Evidence Act, 1999 *HL* (July 27, 1999)
Introduces the new sentence of referral to a youth offender panel for young people convicted for a first time; provides greater protection for complainants in cases of rape and certain other serious sexual offences; provides clearer protection for witnesses in certain circumstances.

Departmental Select Committee Reports 1998-99

Excluding special reports

AGRICULTURE
1st   MAFF/Intervention Board Departmental Report 1998 and Comprehensive
        Spending Review, *HC 125*
2nd   CAP Reform: Rural Development, *HC 61*
3rd   The UK Pig Industry, *HC 87*
4th   The UK Pig Industry: Government Response, *HC 367*
5th   Badgers and Bovine Tuberculosis, *HC 233*
6th   Genetically Modified Organisms, *HC 427*
7th   Outcome of the CAP Negotiations, *HC 442*
8th   Sea Fishing, *HC 141*
9th   MAFF/Intervention Board Departmental Report 1999, *HC582*

CULTURE, MEDIA AND SPORT
1st   The Heritage Lottery Fund, *HC 195*
2nd   The Preservation of HMS Cavalier, *HC 196*
3rd   Back to the Dome, *HC 21*
4th   Staging International Sporting Events, *HC 124*
5th   The Performing Rights Society, *HC 468*
6th   The DCMs and its Quangos, *HC 506*

DEFENCE
1st   Strategic Defence Review: Territorial Army Restructuring, *HC 70*
2nd   The Appointment of the New Head of Defence Export Services, *HC 147*
3rd   The Future of NATO: The Washington Summit, *HC 39*
4th   The Draft Visiting Forces and International Headquarters Order 1999, *HC 399*
5th   Security of Supply and the Future of Royal Ordnance Factory Bishopston, *HC 274*
6th   The Reserves Call-out Order 1999, *HC 860*
7th   The Strategic Defence Review: Defence Medical Services, *HC 447*
8th   Major Procurement Projects Survey, *HC 544*
9th   Defence Research, *HC 616*

EDUCATION AND EMPLOYMENT
1st   Active Labour Market Policies and their Delivery: Lessons From Australia,
        HC 163
2nd   Part-Time Working, HC 346
3rd   Highly Able Children, *HC 22*
4th   The Work of OFSTED, *HC 62*
5th   The Role of School Governors, *HC 509*
6th   The One Service Pilots, *HC 412*
7th   The Performance and Future of the Employment Service, *HC 197*
8th   Access for All? A Survey of Post-16 Participation, *HC 57*
9th   Opportunities for Disabled People, *HC 111*

ENVIRONMENT, TRANSPORT AND REGIONAL AFFAIRS
1st   Railway Safety, *HC 30*
2nd   Millennium Compliance in the Transport Industry, *HC 90*
3rd   The Future of National Air Traffic Services, *HC 122*
4th   The Countryside Agency, *HC 6*
5th   Regional Eurostar Services, *HC 89*
6th   The Maritime and Coastguard Agency, *HC 31*

NORTHERN IRELAND AFFAIRS
1st   Public Expenditure in Northern Ireland: Special Needs Education, *HC 33*
2nd   Electricity Supplies in Northern Ireland: Impact of the 26 December 1998 Storm, *HC 227*
3rd   Impact in Northern Ireland of Cross-Border Road Fuel Price Differentials, *HC 334*
4th   The Operation of the Fair Employment (Northern Ireland) Act 1989: Ten Years On, *HC 95*

PUBLIC ADMINISTRATION
1st   Report of the Parliamentary Ombudsman for 1997-98, *HC 136*
2nd   Annual Report of the Health Service Ombudsman for 1997-98, *HC 54*
3rd   Freedom of Information Draft Bill, *HC 570*
4th   Ministerial Accountability and Parliamentary Questions, *HC 821*
5th   Freedom of Information Draft Bill: The Committee's Response to the Home Office
        Reply, *HC 925*
6th   Quangos, *HC 209*

SCIENCE AND TECHNOLOGY
1st   Scientific Advisory System: Genetically Modified Foods, *HC 286*
2nd   The National Endowment for Science, Technology and the Arts, *HC 472*
3rd   Scientific Advisory System: Mobile Phones and Health, *HC 489*
4th   The Regulation of the Biotechnology Industry, *HC 535*

SCOTTISH AFFAIRS
1st   Inward/Outward Investment in Scotland, *HC 84*
2nd   Tourism in Scotland, *HC 85*

SOCIAL SECURITY
1st   Tax and Benefits: Implementation of Tax Credits, *HC 29*
2nd   Family Credit Fraud, *HC 217*
3rd   Disability Living Allowance, *HC 63*
4th   Child Benefit, *HC 114*
5th   Pension on Divorce: Parts III and IV of the Welfare Reform and Pensions Bill,
        HC 304
6th   War Pensions Agency Business Plan 1999-2000, *HC 377*
7th   The One Service Pilots, *HC 412*
8th   The Modernisation of Social Security Appeals, *HC 581*
9th   Social Security Implications of Parental Leave, *HC 543*
10th   The 1999 Child Support White paper, *HC 798*

TRADE AND INDUSTRY
1st   Vehicle Pricing, *HC 64*
2nd   Strategic Export Controls, *HC 65*
3rd   Multilateral Agreement on Investment, *HC 112*
4th   Draft Limited Liability Partnership Bill, *HC 59*
5th   Telephone Numbering, *HC 139*
6th   Ethical Trading, *HC 235*
7th   Building Confidence in Electronic Commerce: The Government's Proposals. *HC 187*
8th   Trade Marks, Fakes and Consumers, *HC 380*
9th   Impact on Industry of the Climate Change Levy, *HC 678*
10th   Electronic Commerce, *HC 648*
11th   The Horizon Project, *HC 550*
12th   The 1999 Post Office White Paper, *HC 94*
13th   Small Business and Enterprise, *HC 330*
14th   Draft Electronic Communications Bill, *HC 862*

TREASURY

WELSH AFFAIRS

The Royal Family

THE REIGNING SOVEREIGN

ELIZABETH the Second, by the GRACE OF GOD, OF THE UNITED KINGDOM OF GREAT BRITAIN AND NORTHERN IRELAND, AND OF HER OTHER REALMS AND TERRITORIES QUEEN, HEAD OF THE COMMONWEALTH, DEFENDER OF THE FAITH.

HER MAJESTY ELIZABETH ALEXANDRA MARY, elder Daughter of His late Majesty King George the Sixth and Lady Elizabeth Angela Marguerite Bowes-Lyon (*HM Queen Elizabeth The Queen Mother*), daughter of Claude, 14th Earl of Strathmore and Kinghorne, KG, KT, GCVO.

HER MAJESTY was born on April 21, 1926. She married on November 20, 1947, HRH The Prince Philip, Duke of Edinburgh, KG, KT, OM, GBE, AC, QSO, PC. She ascended the Throne February 6, 1952, was proclaimed Queen February 8, 1952, and crowned at Westminster Abbey June 2, 1953. It was declared in Council April 9, 1952, that she and her children shall be styled and known as the House and Family of Windsor; and further February 8, 1960, that her descendants, other than descendants enjoying the style, title or attribute of HRH and the titular dignity of Prince or Princess, and female descendants who marry, and their descendants shall bear the name Mountbatten-Windsor.

Residences: Buckingham Palace, London SW1A 1AA; Windsor Castle, Berkshire SL4 1NJ; Balmoral Castle, Aberdeenshire AB35 5TB; Sandringham House, Norfolk PE35 6EN.

Issue: **WALES (Prince of), HRH THE PRINCE CHARLES PHILIP ARTHUR GEORGE,** Earl of Chester, Duke of Cornwall and Rothesay, Earl of Carrick and Baron of Renfrew, Lord of the Isles and Great Steward of Scotland, Knight of the Most Noble Order of the Garter, Knight of the Most Ancient and Most Noble Order of the Thistle, Knight Grand Cross of the Most Honourable Order of the Bath, Knight of the Order of Australia, Queen's Service Order (New Zealand), Aide-de-Camp. Invested as Prince of Wales and Earl of Chester at Caernarvon Castle July 1, 1969. Born November 14, 1948; m. July 29, 1981, Lady Diana Spencer (marriage dissolved 1996 and who died August 31, 1997), y.d. of 8th Earl Spencer. *Issue:* Prince William Arthur Philip Louis, b. June 21, 1982, Prince Henry Charles Albert David, b. September 15, 1984. *Residences:* Highgrove, Doughton, Tetbury, Gloucestershire GL8 8TN; St James's Palace, London SW1A 1BS. *Office:* St James's Palace, London SW1A 1BA.

YORK (Duke of), HRH THE PRINCE ANDREW ALBERT CHRISTIAN EDWARD, Earl of Inverness, Baron Killyleagh, CVO. Born February 19, 1960: m. July 23, 1986, Miss Sarah Margaret Ferguson. *Issue:* Princess Beatrice Elizabeth Mary, b. August 8, 1988; Princess Eugenie Victoria Helena, b. March 23, 1990 (marriage dissolved 1996). *Residence:* Sunninghill Park, Ascot, Berkshire SL5 7TH. *Office:* Buckingham Palace, London SW1A 1AA.

WESSEX (Earl of), HRH THE PRINCE EDWARD ANTONY RICHARD LOUIS, CVO. Born March 10, 1964; m. June 19, 1999, Miss Sophie Helen Rhys-Jones. *Residence and Office:* Bagshot Park, Bagshot, Surrey GU19 5PL.

HRH PRINCESS ANNE ELIZABETH ALICE LOUISE, THE PRINCESS ROYAL, Lady of the Most Noble Order of the Garter, GCVO. Born August 15, 1950; m. 1st, Nov. 14, 1973, Capt. Mark Anthony Peter Phillips, CVO. *Issue:* Peter Mark Andrew Phillips, b. Nov. 15, 1977, Zara Anne Elizabeth Phillips, b. May 15, 1981 (marriage dissolved 1992); m. 2nd, Dec. 12, 1992, Commodore Timothy Laurence, MVO, RN. *Residence:* Gatcombe Park, Minchinhampton, Stroud, Gloucestershire GL6 9AT; *Office:* Buckingham Palace, London SW1A 1AA.

HER MAJESTY QUEEN ELIZABETH THE QUEEN MOTHER

LADY ELIZABETH ANGELA MARGUERITE BOWES-LYON, daughter of Claude, 14th Earl of Strathmore and Kinghorne, KG, KT, GCVO, GBE. Born Aug. 4, 1900; married, April 26, 1923, His Majesty King George the Sixth, who died Feb. 6, 1952. Lady of The Most Noble Order of the Garter, Dame Grand Cross of the Victorian Order and of the Order of the British Empire; Lady of the Most Ancient and Most Noble Order of the Thistle; has the Royal Victorian Chain; Dame Grand Cross of the Order of St. John of Jerusalem. *Residences:* Clarence House, St. James's Palace, London SW1A 1BA; Royal Lodge, The Great Park, Windsor, Berkshire; Birkhall, Ballater, Aberdeenshire; Castle of Mey, Caithness.

SISTER OF HER MAJESTY

HRH THE PRINCESS MARGARET ROSE, Countess of Snowdon, CI, GCVO, DJStJ. Received the Insignia of the Royal Victorian Chain 1990. B. August 21, 1930; m. May 6, 1960, Antony Armstrong-Jones, 1st Earl of Snowdon, GCVO, Grand Cross of the Order of the Netherlands Lion (marriage dissolved 1978). *Residence:* Kensington Palace, London W8 4PU.

Issue: DAVID ALBERT CHARLES ARMSTRONG-JONES, Viscount Linley. Born Nov. 3, 1961; m. Oct. 8, 1993, Hon. Serena Alleyne Stanhope. *Issue:* Charles Patrick Inigo Armstrong-Jones, b. July 1, 1999.

Issue: Lady SARAH FRANCES ELIZABETH ARMSTRONG-JONES. Born May 1, 1964; m. July 14, 1994, Daniel St George Chatto. *Issue:* Samuel David Benedict Chatto, b. July 28, 1996 and Arthur Robert Nathaniel Chatto, b. Feb. 5, 1999.

SONS OF HRH THE LATE PRINCE HENRY WILLIAM FREDERICK ALBERT, DUKE OF GLOUCESTER (DIED JUNE 10, 1974) AND HRH PRINCESS ALICE, DUCHESS OF GLOUCESTER

HRH Prince WILLIAM HENRY ANDREW FREDERICK, b. Dec. 18, 1941; died Aug. 28, 1972.

HRH Prince RICHARD ALEXANDER WALTER GEORGE, GCVO, **Duke of Gloucester,** b. Aug. 26, 1944; m. July 8, 1972, Birgitte Eva van Deurs, GCVO. *Issue:* Alexander Patrick Gregers Richard, Earl of Ulster, b. Oct. 24, 1974, Davina Elizabeth Alice Benedikte, Lady Davina Windsor, b. Nov. 19, 1977 and Rose Victoria Birgitte Louise, Lady Rose Windsor, b. March 1, 1980. *Residence:* Kensington Palace, London W8 4PU.

SONS AND DAUGHTER OF HRH THE LATE PRINCE GEORGE EDWARD ALEXANDER EDMOND, **DUKE OF KENT** (KILLED ON ACTIVE SERVICE 1942) AND HRH THE LATE PRINCESS MARINA, **DUCHESS OF KENT** (Uncle and Aunt of Her Majesty)

HRH Prince EDWARD GEORGE NICHOLAS PAUL PATRICK, KG, GCMG, GCVO, ADC, **Duke of Kent,** b. Oct. 9, 1935; m. June 8, 1961, Miss Katharine Lucy Mary Worsley, GCVO. *Issue:* George Philip Nicholas, Earl of St. Andrews, b. June 26, 1962; m. Jan. 8, 1988, Mrs Sylvana Tomaselli. *Issue:* Edward Edmund Maximillian George, Lord Downpatrick, b. Dec. 2, 1988 and Lady Marina-Charlotte Alexandra Katharine Helen Windsor, b. Sept. 13, 1992; and Lady Amelia Sophia Theodora Mary Margaret Windsor, b. Aug. 24, 1995; and Lord Nicholas Charles Edward Jonathan Windsor, b. July 25, 1970 and Lady Helen Marina Lucy Windsor, b. April 28, 1964; m. July 18, 1992, Timothy Verner Taylor. *Issue:* Columbus George Donald Taylor, b. Aug. 6, 1994 and Cassius Edward Taylor, b. Dec. 26, 1996. *Residence:* York House, St. James's Palace, London SW1 1BQ.

HRH Prince MICHAEL GEORGE CHARLES FRANKLIN, KCVO, b. July 4, 1942; m. June 30, 1978, Baroness Marie-Christine von Reibnitz, formerly Mrs. Thomas Troubridge. *Issue:* Frederick Michael George David Louis, Lord Frederick Windsor, b. April 6, 1979 and Gabriella Marina Alexandra Ophelia, Lady Gabriella Windsor, b. April 23, 1981. *Residences:* Kensington Palace, London W8 4PU; Nether Lypiatt Manor, Stroud, Gloucestershire GL6 7LS.

HRH Princess ALEXANDRA HELENE ELIZABETH OLGA CHRISTABEL, GCVO, b. Dec. 25, 1936; m. April 24, 1963, The Rt Hon. Sir Angus James Bruce Ogilvy KCVO. *Issue:* James Robert Bruce Ogilvy, b. Feb. 29, 1964, m. July 30, 1988 Miss Julia Caroline Rawlinson. *Issue:* Flora Alexandra Ogilvy, b. Dec. 15, 1994; Marina Victoria Alexandra, Mrs Paul Mowatt, b. July 31, 1966; m. Feb. 2, 1990 Paul Julian Mowatt (marriage dissolved 1997). *Issue:* Zenouska May Mowatt, b. May 26, 1990 and Christian Alexander Mowatt, b. June 4, 1993. *Residence:* Thatched House Lodge, Richmond, Surrey; *Office:* Buckingham Palace, London SW1A 1AA.

SONS OF HRH THE LATE PRINCESS (VICTORIA ALEXANDRA ALICE) MARY THE PRINCESS ROYAL (Aunt of Her Majesty)

GEORGE HENRY HUBERT (Lascelles), 7th Earl of Harewood, b. Feb. 7, 1923; m. 1st. 1949 Maria Donata (marriage dissolved 1967) (three sons); m. 2nd 1967 Patricia Elizabeth, d. of Charles Tuckwell (one son and one stepson).

Hon. GERALD DAVID LASCELLES, b. Aug. 21, 1924, died Feb. 27, 1998; m. 1st 1952, Angela d. of C. S. Dowding, and has issue, Henry Ulick, b. May 19, 1953 (marriage dissolved 1978); m. 2nd Nov. 17, 1978, Elizabeth Evelyn Collingwood.

The Royal Family

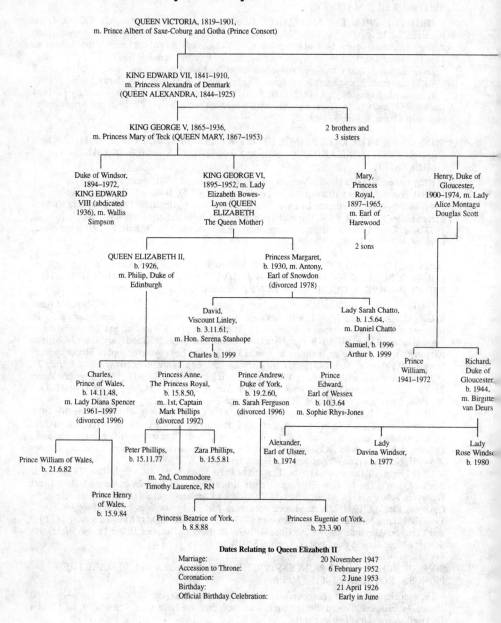

QUEEN VICTORIA, 1819–1901,
m. Prince Albert of Saxe-Coburg and Gotha (Prince Consort)

KING EDWARD VII, 1841–1910,
m. Princess Alexandra of Denmark
(QUEEN ALEXANDRA, 1844–1925)

KING GEORGE V, 1865–1936,
m. Princess Mary of Teck (QUEEN MARY, 1867–1953)

2 brothers and
3 sisters

Duke of Windsor,
1894–1972,
KING EDWARD
VIII (abdicated
1936), m. Wallis
Simpson

KING GEORGE VI,
1895–1952, m. Lady
Elizabeth Bowes-
Lyon (QUEEN
ELIZABETH
The Queen Mother)

Mary,
Princess
Royal,
1897–1965,
m. Earl of
Harewood

Henry, Duke of
Gloucester,
1900–1974, m. Lady
Alice Montagu
Douglas Scott

2 sons

QUEEN ELIZABETH II,
b. 1926,
m. Philip, Duke of
Edinburgh

Princess Margaret,
b. 1930, m. Antony,
Earl of Snowdon
(divorced 1978)

David,
Viscount Linley,
b. 3.11.61,
m. Hon. Serena Stanhope

Charles b. 1999

Lady Sarah Chatto,
b. 1.5.64,
m. Daniel Chatto

Samuel, b. 1996
Arthur b. 1999

Prince
William,
1941–1972

Richard,
Duke of
Gloucester,
b. 1944,
m. Birgitte
van Deurs

Charles,
Prince of Wales,
b. 14.11.48,
m. Lady Diana Spencer
1961–1997
(divorced 1996)

Princess Anne,
The Princess Royal,
b. 15.8.50,
m. 1st, Captain
Mark Phillips
(divorced 1992)

Prince Andrew,
Duke of York,
b. 19.2.60,
m. Sarah Ferguson
(divorced 1996)

Prince
Edward,
Earl of Wessex
b. 10.3.64
m. Sophie Rhys-Jones

Prince William of Wales,
b. 21.6.82

Peter Phillips,
b. 15.11.77

Zara Phillips,
b. 15.5.81

Alexander,
Earl of Ulster,
b. 1974

Lady
Davina Windsor,
b. 1977

Lady
Rose Windsor
b. 1980

m. 2nd, Commodore
Timothy Laurence, RN

Prince Henry
of Wales,
b. 15.9.84

Princess Beatrice of York,
b. 8.8.88

Princess Eugenie of York,
b. 23.3.90

Dates Relating to Queen Elizabeth II

Marriage:	20 November 1947
Accession to Throne:	6 February 1952
Coronation:	2 June 1953
Birthday:	21 April 1926
Official Birthday Celebration:	Early in June

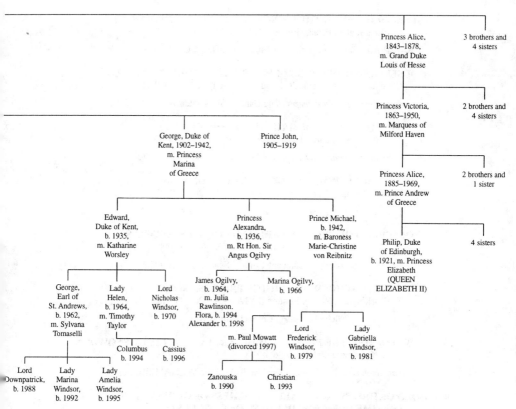

Princess Alice, 1843–1878, m. Grand Duke Louis of Hesse — 3 brothers and 4 sisters

Princess Victoria, 1863–1950, m. Marquess of Milford Haven — 2 brothers and 4 sisters

Princess Alice, 1885–1969, m. Prince Andrew of Greece — 2 brothers and 1 sister

George, Duke of Kent, 1902–1942, m. Princess Marina of Greece

Prince John, 1905–1919

Edward, Duke of Kent, b. 1935, m. Katharine Worsley

Princess Alexandra, b. 1936, m. Rt Hon. Sir Angus Ogilvy

Prince Michael, b. 1942, m. Baroness Marie-Christine von Reibnitz

Philip, Duke of Edinburgh, b. 1921, m. Princess Elizabeth (QUEEN ELIZABETH II) — 4 sisters

George, Earl of St. Andrews, b. 1962, m. Sylvana Tomaselli

Lady Helen, b. 1964, m. Timothy Taylor

Lord Nicholas Windsor, b. 1970

James Ogilvy, b. 1964, m. Julia Rawlinson. Flora, b. 1994 Alexander b. 1998

Marina Ogilvy, b. 1966

m. Paul Mowatt (divorced 1997)

Lord Frederick Windsor, b. 1979

Lady Gabriella Windsor, b. 1981

Columbus b. 1994

Cassius b. 1996

Zanouska b. 1990

Christian b. 1993

Lord Downpatrick, b. 1988

Lady Marina Windsor, b. 1992

Lady Amelia Windsor, b. 1995

In the Order of Succession the sons of the Sovereign and their descendants have precedence over the daughters. The daughters and their descendants have precedence over collateral lines.

Order of Succession to the Throne

1 The Prince of Wales
2 Prince William of Wales
3 Prince Henry of Wales
4 The Duke of York
5 Princess Beatrice of York
6 Princess Eugenie of York
7 The Earl of Wessex
8 The Princess Royal
9 Mr Peter Phillips
10 Miss Zara Phillips
11 The Princess Margaret, Countess of Snowdon
12 Viscount Linley
13 Hon. Charles Armstrong-Jones
14 Lady Sarah Chatto
15 Master Samuel Chatto
16 Master Arthur Chatto
17 The Duke of Gloucester
18 Earl of Ulster
19 Lady Davina Windsor
20 Lady Rose Windsor
21 The Duke of Kent
22 Lord Downpatrick
23 Lady Marina Charlotte Windsor
24 Lady Amelia Windsor
25 Lord Nicholas Windsor
26 Lady Helen Taylor
27 Master Columbus Taylor
28 Master Cassius Taylor
29 Lord Frederick Windsor
30 Lady Gabriella Windsor
31 Princess Alexandra, The Hon. Lady Ogilvy
32 Mr James Ogilvy
33 Master Alexander Ogilvy
34 Miss Flora Ogilvy
35 Mrs Paul Mowatt
36 Master Christian Mowatt
37 Miss Zenouska Mowatt
38 The Earl of Harewood

HER MAJESTY'S HOUSEHOLD
Buckingham Palace, London SW1A 1AA 020 7930 4832

Private Secretary to HM The Queen: The Rt Hon Sir Robin Janvrin, KCVO, CB

HOUSEHOLD OF HRH THE PRINCE PHILIP, DUKE OF EDINBURGH
Buckingham Palace, London SW1A 1AA 020 7930 4832

Private Secretary: Brigadier Miles Hunt-Davis, CVO, CBE

HOUSEHOLD OF HM QUEEN ELIZABETH THE QUEEN MOTHER
Clarence House, St James's, London SW1A 1BA 020 7930 3141

Private Secretary and Comptroller: Captain Sir Alastair Aird, GCVO

HOUSEHOLD OF HRH THE PRINCE OF WALES
St James's Palace, London SW1A 1BS 020 7930 4832

Private Secretary and Treasurer: Stephen Lamport, Esq, CVO

HOUSEHOLD OF HRH THE DUKE OF YORK
Buckingham Palace, London SW1A 1AA 020 7930 4832

Private Secretary and Treasurer: Captain Neil Blair, LVO, RN

HOUSEHOLD OF TRH THE EARL AND COUNTESS OF WESSEX
Bagshot Park, Bagshot, Surrey GU19 5PL 01276 700843

Private Secretary: Lieutenant-Colonel Sean O'Dwyer, LVO

HOUSEHOLD OF HRH THE PRINCESS ROYAL
Buckingham Palace, London SW1A 1AA 020 7930 4832

Private Secretary: Colonel Timothy Earl

HOUSEHOLD OF HRH THE PRINCESS MARGARET COUNTESS OF SNOWDON
Kensington Palace, London W8 4PU 020 7930 3141

Private Secretary and Comptroller: The Rt Hon the Viscount Ullswater

HOUSEHOLD OF HRH PRINCESS ALICE, DUCHESS OF GLOUCESTER AND TRH THE DUKE AND DUCHESS OF GLOUCESTER
Kensington Palace, London W8 4PU 020 7937 6374

Private Secretary, Comptroller and Equerry: Major Nicholas Barne, LVO

HOUSEHOLD OF TRH THE DUKE AND DUCHESS OF KENT
St James's Palace, London SW1A 1BQ 020 7930 4872

Private Secretary: Nicolas Adamson, Esq, OBE

HOUSEHOLD OF TRH PRINCE AND PRINCESS MICHAEL OF KENT
Kensington Palace, London W8 4PU 020 7938 3519

Private Secretary: Nicholas Chance, Esq

HOUSEHOLD OF HRH PRINCESS ALEXANDRA, THE HONOURABLE LADY OGILVY
Buckingham Palace, London SW1A 1AA 020 7930 1860

Private Secretary: Captain Neil Blair, LVO, RN

HOUSE OF LORDS

PEERS' BIOGRAPHIES

The style Rt Hon. signifies that a peer is a member of the Privy Council

A

ABERDARE (4th Baron, UK), Morys George Lyndhurst Bruce; cr. 1873; PC 1974; KBE 1984; DL

Son of 3rd Baron, GBE. Born June 16, 1919. Succeeded his father 1957; educated Winchester; New College, Oxford (MA); Hon. LLD, University of Wales 1985. Married 1946, Maud Helen Sarah, daughter of late Sir John Dashwood, 10th Bt, CVO, of West Wycombe Park, Bucks (4 sons). *Armed Forces:* Major, Welsh Guards 1939–46. *Councils, Public Bodies:* DL, Dyfed 1985. *Career:* Chairman: Albany Life Assurance Co Ltd 1975–92, Metlife (UK) Ltd 1986–92. *House of Lords:* Minister of State, Department of Health and Social Security 1970–74; Minister without Portfolio 1974; Chairman of Committees, House of Lords 1976–92; A Deputy Speaker of the House of Lords 1976–; A Deputy Chairman of Committees 1992–; An elected hereditary peer 1999–. *Select Committees:* Chairman, Select Committee on Broadcasting 1978–92. *Other:* President, Welsh National Council of YMCAs; Former President, National Association of Leagues of Hospital Friends; President: Kidney Research Unit for Wales Foundation, The Queen's Club 1993–96. *Trusts, etc:* Chairman, The Football Trust 1979–98. *Honours:* Prior for Wales, Order of St John 1957–88; Bailiff Grand Cross, Order of St John 1974; PC 1974; KBE 1984. *Publications: The Story of Tennis* (1959); *The Willis Faber Book of Tennis and Rackets* (1980). *Recreations:* Real tennis. *Sportsclubs:* All England Lawn Tennis, Jesters, Queens. *Clubs:* Lansdowne, MCC, Boodle's. *Heir:* His son, Hon. Alastair John Lyndhurst Bruce, born May 2, 1947. A Conservative. *Address:* The Rt Hon. the Lord Aberdare, KBE, DL, 32 Elthiron Road, London, SW6 4BW *Tel:* 020 7736 0825 *Tel:* House of Lords 020 7219 6925.

ACKNER (Life Baron, UK), Desmond James Conrad Ackner; cr. 1986; PC 1980; Kt 1971

Son of late Dr Conrad Ackner. Born September 18, 1920; educated Highgate School; Clare College, Cambridge (MA); Hon. Fellow, Clare College 1984. Married August 24, 1946, Joan, daughter of late John Evans, JP and widow of K. B. Spence (1 son 2 daughters). *Armed Forces:* Served in RA 1941–42; Admiralty Naval Law branch 1942–45. *Career:* Called to Bar, Middle Temple 1945; QC 1961; Recorder of Swindon 1962–71; Judge of Courts of Appeal, Jersey and Guernsey 1967–71; Member, General Council of the Bar 1957–61, 1963–70, Treasurer 1964–66, Vice-Chairman 1966–68, Chairman 1968–70; Judge of High Court of Justice, Queen's Bench Division 1971–80; A Lord Justice of Appeal 1980–86; A Lord of Appeal in Ordinary 1986–92. *Select Committees:* Member, House of Lords Select Committees on: Murder and Life Imprisonment 1988–89; Science and Technology Subcommittee on Digital Images as Evidence 1997–98. *Other:* President, Senate of the Four Inns of Court 1983–84; Deputy Treasurer, Middle Temple 1983, Treasurer 1984; President, Society of Sussex Downsmen 1993–96, Vice-President 1996–. *Miscellaneous:* Member, British Council 1991–; President, Arbitration Appeal Panel of the Securities and Futures Authority 1993–; Appeal Commissioner, Personal Investment Authority 1994–; Director, City Disputes Panel 1994–98. *Honours:* Kt 1971; PC 1980. *Special Interests:* Law, Alternative Dispute Resolutions. *Recreations:* Gardening, swimming, theatre. *Name, Style and Title:* Raised to the peerage as Baron Ackner, of Sutton in the County of West Sussex 1986. A Cross-Bencher. *Address:* The Rt Hon. the Lord Ackner, House of Lords, London, SW1A 0PW *Tel:* 020 7219 3295; 4 Pump Court, Temple, London, EC4Y 7AN *Tel:* 020 7353 2656; Browns House, Sutton, near Pulborough, West Sussex *Tel:* 01798 869206.

ADDINGTON (6th Baron, UK), Dominic Bryce Hubbard; cr. 1887

Son of 5th Baron. Born August 24, 1963. Succeeded his father 1982; educated The Hewett School, Norwich; Aberdeen University (MA Hons 1988). *House of Lords:* An elected hereditary peer 1999–. *Spokesman:* Party Spokesman on Disability 1994–. *Other:* Vice-President, British Dyslexia Association. *Trusts, etc:* With Apex Trust as fund raiser 1990–. *Special Interests:* Education, Environment, Prison Reform. *Recreations:* Rugby football. *Clubs:* National Liberal. *Heir:* His brother, Hon. Michael Walter Leslie Hubbard, born July 6, 1965. A Liberal Democrat. *Address:* The Lord Addington, 9–11 Chalk Hill Road, Norwich, NR1 1SL.

AHMED (Life Baron, UK), Nazir Ahmed; cr. 1998

Son of late Haji Sain Mohammed and Rashem Bibi. Born April 24, 1957; educated Sheffield Hallam University (BA Public Administration). Married, Sakina Bibi (2 sons 1 daughter). *Trades Union:* Member, USDAW. *Councils, Public Bodies:* Councillor, Rotherham Metropolitan Borough Council 1990–; JP. *Career:* Company Director; Business Development Manager, Kilnhurst Business Park; Non-Executive Chairman, Halal World Plc. *All-Party:* Chairman, All-Party Libyan Country Group 1999–; Member, All-Party: Human Rights Group, University Group, America Country Group, Pakistan Country Group, Tunisia Country Group. *International Bodies:* Member: IPU, CPA. *International Bodies (General):* Member, Kashmir Policy Group; Patron: Kashmiri Journalist Association Mirpur, Jammu and Kashmir Human Rights Commission, Mirpur Friendship Association. *Party Groups (General):* Chairman, South Yorkshire Labour Party; Vice-Chairman, South Yorkshire Euro-constituency Party. *Other:* Founder, British Muslim Councillors Forum; Patron: Kashmiri and Pakistani Professional Association, British Mujjaj Association, Young Pakistani Doctors' Association. *Special Interests:* Human Rights, Kashmiri Right of Self Determination. *Recreations:* Volleyball. *Name, Style and Title:* Raised to the peerage as Baron Ahmed, of Rotherham in the County of South Yorkshire 1998. Labour. *Address:* The Lord Ahmed, House of Lords, London, SW1A 0PW.

ALDERDICE (Life Baron, UK), John Thomas Alderdice; cr. 1996

Son of Reverend David Alderdice and Annie Margaret Helena, née Shields. Born March 28, 1955; educated Ballymena Academy; Queen's University, Belfast (MB, BCh, BAO); Hon. Fellow, Royal College of Physicians of Ireland Hon. Professor, Faculty of Medicine University of San Marcos Peru. Married July 30, 1977, Joan Margaret Hill (2 sons 1 daughter). *Councils, Public Bodies:* Councillor, Belfast City Council 1989–97; Member, Belfast Education and Library Board 1993–97. *Career:* Consultant Psychotherapist, Eastern Health and Social Services Board 1988–; Hon. Lecturer, Faculty of Medicine, Queen's University, Belfast 1991–99, Senior Lecturer 1999–; Executive Medical Director, South and East Belfast Health and Social Services Trust 1993–97. *All-Party:* Vice-Chairman, All-Party Mental Health Group 1998–. *International Bodies:* Associate Member, British-Irish Inter-Parliamentary Body; Member, Commonwealth Parliamentary Association. *Party Groups (General):* Executive Committee, Alliance Party 1984–98, Chairman, Policy Committee 1985–87; Vice-Chairman, Alliance Party March 1987-October 1987, Party Leader 1987–98; Executive Committee, European Liberal Democrat and Reform Party 1987–, Treasurer 1995–99, Vice-President 1999–; Candidate (NI) in European Parliament Election 1989; Leader, Alliance Delegation at Inter-Party and Inter-Governmental Talks on the Future of Northern Ireland 1991–98; Vice-President, Liberal International 1992–99, Bureau Member 1996–; Chairman, Liberal International Human Rights Committee 1999–. *Other:* Member: British Medical Association, Northern Ireland Institute of Human Relations, Association for Psychoanalytic Psychotherapy. *Trusts, etc:* Trustee, Ulster Museum 1993–97. *Miscellaneous:* Leader, Alliance Delegation, Forum for Peace and Reconciliation, Dublin Castle 1994–97; Member, Northern Ireland Forum 1996–98; Leader, Alliance Delegation to Northern Ireland Multiparty Talks 1996–98; Elected to the Northern Ireland Assembly (as one of the members for Belfast East) 1998–; Speaker of the Northern Ireland Assembly 1998–. Fellow: Ulster Medical Society, Royal

Academy of Medicine of Ireland, Royal College of Physicians of Ireland, FRCPsych; Hon. Fellow, Royal College of Physicians of Ireland 1997. *Publications:* Various professional articles on Eating Disorders, Psychotherapy and Ethics, many political papers and articles. *Special Interests:* Northern Ireland, Psychoanalysis and Political Conflict Resolution, Mental Health. *Recreations:* Reading, music, gastronomy. *Clubs:* National Liberal, Ulster Reform (Belfast). *Name, Style and Title:* Raised to the peerage as Baron Alderdice, of Knock in the City of Belfast 1996. A Liberal Democrat. *Address:* The Lord Alderdice, 55 Knock Road, Belfast, BT5 6LB *Tel:* 028 9079 3097; Parliament Buildings, Stormont, Belfast, BT4 3XX *E-Mail:* alderdicej@parliament.uk.

ALDINGTON (1st Baron, UK), Toby Austin Richard William Low; cr. 1962; (Life) Baron Low (UK) 1999; KCMG 1957; PC 1954; CBE (Mil) 1945; DSO 1941; TD 1950; DL

Son of late Colonel Stuart Low, DSO. Born May 25, 1914; educated Winchester; New College, Oxford (BA, MA); Hon. Fellow, New College, Oxford 1976. Married 1947, Mrs Felicite Ann Araminta Bowman, daughter of late Sir Harold MacMichael, GCMG, DSO (1 son 2 daughters). *Armed Forces:* Joined the Rangers KRRC as a Territorial, served in the Middle East, Italy, appointed Brigadier General Staff of 5th Corps of the 8th Army 1944; Hon. Col, 268 LAA Regt RA (TA) 1947–59. *Councils, Public Bodies:* DL, Kent 1973. *Career:* Barrister (Middle Temple) 1939; Chairman, Grindlays Bank Ltd 1963–76; Chairman, General Electric Co. Ltd 1964–68, Deputy Chairman 1968–84; Chairman: Sun Alliance and London Insurance Ltd 1971–1985, National Nuclear Corporation 1973–1980, Westland plc 1977–85. *House of Commons:* MP (Conservative) for Blackpool North 1945–62; Parliamentary Secretary to Ministry of Supply 1951–54; Minister of State, Board of Trade 1954–57. *Select Committees (Commons):* Chairman, House of Commons Select Committee on Nationalised Industries 1957–61. *Select Committees:* Chairman: House of Lords Select Committee on Overseas Trade 1984–85, Sub-Committee A House of Lords European Communities Select Committee 1989–92. *Party Groups (General):* Deputy Chairman, Conservative Party Organisation 1959–63. *Other:* Warden, Winchester College 1979–87, Fellow 1972–87; Chairman, Leeds Castle Foundation 1984–94. *Trusts, etc:* Brain Research Trust: Chairman 1972–87, President 1987–; Kent Foundation: Member 1986–, Chairman 1986–94. *Miscellaneous:* Chairman: Institute of Neurology Management Committee 1962–86, Port of London Authority 1971–77, General Advisory Council BBC 1971–78, Governing Bodies Association 1983–89, Independent Schools Joint Council 1986–89; President, British Standards Institution 1986–89. *Honours:* DSO 1941; CBE (Mil) 1945; TD 1950; PC 1954; KCMG 1957. *Recreations:* Golf, gardening. *Sportsclubs:* Royal St George's GC, Royal and Ancient GC. *Clubs:* Carlton. *Heir:* His son, Hon. Charles Harold Stuart Low, born June 22, 1948. *Name, Style and Title:* Created a life peer as Baron Low, of Bispham in the County of Lancashire 1999. A Conservative. *Address:* The Rt Hon. the Lord Aldington, KCMG, CBE, DSO, TD, DL, Knoll Farm, Aldington, Ashford, Kent, TN25 7BY *Tel:* 01233 720292.

ALEXANDER OF WEEDON (Life Baron, UK), Robert Scott Alexander; cr. 1988; QC 1973

Son of late Samuel James Alexander and Hannah May Alexander. Born September 5, 1936; educated Brighton College; King's College, Cambridge (MA); Hon. LLD, Universities of: Sheffield 1991, Buckingham 1992, Keele 1993, Exeter 1994. Married 3rd, 1985, Marie Anderson (2 sons 1 daughter from 1st marriage). *Career:* Called to the Bar, Middle Temple 1961, Bencher 1979; QC (NSW Australia) 1983; Vice-Chairman, Bar Council 1984–85, Chairman 1985–86; Judge of the Courts of Appeal of Jersey and Guernsey 1985–88; Chairman: Panel on Takeovers and Mergers 1987–89, National Westminster Bank plc 1989–99; Non-Executive Director: RTZ Corporation plc 1991–96, International Stock Exchange of the UK and Republic of Ireland 1991–93; Deputy Chairman, Securities and Investments Board 1994–96; Member, Government's Panel on Sustainable Development 1994–. *Chancellor:* Chancellor, University of Exeter 1998–. *Select Committees:* Chairman: Delegated Powers Scrutiny Committee, House of Lords 1995–97, Select Committee on Delegated Powers and Deregulation 1997–. *Other:* Governor, Wycombe Abbey School 1986–92; Chairman, Council of Justice; Chairman, Foundation Board, Royal Shakespeare Company. *Trusts, etc:* Trustee, National Gallery 1986–93; Chairman, Trustees of Crisis 1988–96. *Miscellaneous:* Member, Independent Commission on Voting Reform 1998; Chairman, Inquiry into Tonnage Tax 1999.

Publications: The Voice of the People: A Constitution for Tomorrow, 1997. *Special Interests:* Law, Legal Profession, City, Arts. *Recreations:* Tennis, theatre, gardening. *Clubs:* Garrick. *Name, Style and Title:* Raised to the peerage as Baron Alexander of Weedon, of Newcastle-under-Lyme in the County of Staffordshire 1988. A Conservative. *Address:* The Lord Alexander of Weedon, QC, House of Lords, London, SW1A 0PW *Tel:* 020 7219 3000.

ALLEN OF ABBEYDALE (Life Baron, UK), Philip Allen; cr. 1976; GCB 1970

Son of late Arthur Allen. Born July 8, 1912; educated King Edward VII School, Sheffield; Queens' College, Cambridge (MA); Hon. Fellow: Queens' College, Cambridge, Royal Holloway and Bedford New College. Married 1938, Marjorie Brenda, daughter of late T. J. C. Coe. *Career:* Entered Home Office 1934; Served in Offices of War Cabinet 1943–44; Deputy Secretary, Ministry of Housing and Local Government 1955–60; Deputy Under-Secretary of State, Home Office 1960–62; Second Secretary, H.M. Treasury 1963–66; Permanent Under-Secretary of State, Home Office 1966–72; Chief Counting Officer, EEC Referendum 1975. *Select Committees:* Chairman, Select Committee on a Bill of Rights 1977–78. *Other:* Chairman, Council of Royal Holloway and Bedford New College, University of London 1985–92, Visitor 1992–97; Chairman: National Council of Social Service 1973–77, MENCAP 1982–88. *Miscellaneous:* Chairman, Occupational Pensions Board 1973–78; Member: Security Commission 1973–91, Royal Commission on Standards of Conduct in Public Life, Royal Commission on Compensation for Personal Injury, Tribunal of Inquiry into Crown Agents; Chairman, Gaming Board 1977–85. *Honours:* CB 1954; KCB 1964; GCB 1970. *Name, Style and Title:* Raised to the peerage as Baron Allen of Abbeydale, of the City of Sheffield 1976. A Cross-Bencher. *Address:* The Lord Allen of Abbeydale, GCB, Holly Lodge, Middle Hill, Englefield Green, Surrey, TW20 0JP *Tel:* 01784 432291.

ALLENBY OF MEGIDDO (3rd Viscount, UK), Michael Jaffray Hynman Allenby; cr. 1919

Son of 2nd Viscount. Born April 20, 1931. Succeeded his father 1984; educated Eton; RMA, Sandhurst. Married July 29, 1965, Sara Margaret, daughter of Lieutenant-Colonel Peter Milner Wiggin, of Newbury, Berkshire (1 son). *Armed Forces:* Commissioned August 3, 1951, 11th Hussars as 2nd Lieutenant; Served Malaya and Cyprus, as ADC to Governor 1956–58; Brigade Major, 51 Brigade, Hong Kong 1967–70; Commanded The Royal Yeomanry (TA) 1974–77; GSO1 Instructor, Nigerian Staff College, Kaduna, Nigeria 1977–79. *Career:* Director, Quickrest Ltd 1987–91. *House of Lords:* A Deputy Speaker of the House of Lords; A Deputy Chairman of Committees 1997–; An elected hereditary peer 1999–. *Select Committees:* Member, Select Committee on House of Lords' Offices 1997–. *All-Party:* Member, All-Party: Defence Group, Racing and Bloodstock Group, Animal Welfare Group. *Other:* Chairman, The International League for The Protection of Horses 1997–99, Vice-President 1999–. *Special Interests:* Defence, Animal Welfare. *Recreations:* Horses, sailing. *Clubs:* Naval and Military. *Heir:* His son, Hon. Henry Jaffray Hynman Allenby, born July 29, 1968. A Cross-Bencher. *Address:* The Viscount Allenby of Megiddo, House of Lords, London, SW1A 0PW.

ALLI (Life Baron, UK), Waheed Alli; cr. 1998

Born November 16, 1964; educated Norbury Manor School, South London. *Career:* Director, Atomic TV Poland 1992–98; Joint Managing Director, Planet 24 Television; Managing Director, Planet 24 Products Ltd; Director: Deep Silver Television Limited, Entertainment Reports Ltd, Yemeyah Ltd, Music Publishing Ltd, Impossible TV Ltd, International Classical Music Awards, Planet 24 Ltd, Animation Distribution Company Ltd, Doomsday II Ltd, Fleetwillow Ltd, Enrapture Ltd, Planet 24 Services Ltd, Planet Wild Productions Ltd, Planet World Ltd, 24 Hour Productions Ltd, Charles Parsons Productions Ltd, G104.9 FM Ltd, More 105.4 FM Ltd, Regional Radio Scotland Ltd, Crystal FM Ltd, Planet Hat Trick Ltd, Carlton Television 1999–; Managing Director, Carlton Productions 1999–. *Other:* Member: Panel 2000, Creative Industries Task Force, Board of the Teacher Training Agency. *Name, Style and Title:* Raised to the peerage as Baron Alli, of Norbury in the London Borough of Croydon 1998. Labour. *Address:* The Lord Alli, House of Lords, London, SW1A 0PW.

ALTON OF LIVERPOOL (Life Baron, UK), David Patrick Paul Alton; cr. 1997

Son of late Frederick Alton, car worker with Ford Motor Company, and Bridget Mulroe. Born March 15, 1951; educated Edmund Campion School, Hornchurch; Christ's College of Education, Liverpool; St Andrews University. Married 1988, Elizabeth Bell (3 sons 1 daughter). *Councils, Public Bodies:* Elected at 21 as a city councillor to Liverpool City Council 1972–80; Councillor, Merseyside County Council 1973–77, Chairman, Housing Committee and Deputy Leader of the Council 1978. *Career:* Teacher 1972–74, then with children with special needs 1974–79; Local Government 1972–80, including Deputy Leader of Liverpool City Council; Professor of Citizenship, Liverpool John Moores University 1997–. *House of Commons:* Contested Liverpool Edge Hill February and October 1974; MP for Liverpool Edge Hill 1979–83, and for Liverpool Mossley Hill 1983–97; Elected as youngest Member of Parliament in March 1979 by-election for Edge Hill Constituency of Liverpool; Served for six days until dissolution and re-elected in General Election; Parliamentary Chairman, Council for Education in the Commonwealth 1983–87. *Whip (Commons):* Liberal Chief Whip 1985–87. *Spokesman (Commons):* Former Liberal Spokesman in Parliament on Home Affairs and Environment; Alliance Spokesman, Northern Ireland 1987–88. *Select Committees (Commons):* Member, Select Committees on: Environment, Privileges 1994–96. *All-Party Committees (Commons):* Chairman: All-Party Friends of Croatia 1991–95, All-Party Street Children Committee 1992–97; Former Vice-Chairman, All-Party Anti-Drugs Committee. *All-Party:* Secretary, All-Party Ukraine Group; Treasurer, All-Party: Mines Advisory Group, Pro-life Group, CAFOD Group 1998–, Landmine Eradication Group 1999–; Member, Central Asia Country Group, Citizenship Group. *International Bodies (General):* Member, IPU. *Party Groups (General):* Former National President, National League of Young Liberals; Chairman: Liberal Policy Committee 1981–83, Candidates Committee 1984–87, Liberal Democrat Campaign on Law and Order 1993. *Other:* President, Liverpool Old People's Hostels Association; Western Care Association Sponsor, Jubilee Campaign; National Vice-President, LIFE; Vice-President, Liverpool YMCA; Member, Royal Society for the Protection of Birds; Founder member: Jubilee Campaign 1987, Epiphany Group 1989, Movement for Christian Democracy 1990; President, Liverpool Branch, NSPCC; Chairman: Merseyside Council for Voluntary Service, Liverpool Royal Hospital Forget-Me-Not Cancer Appeal; Member, Wavertree Society; Unremunerated Director, The Catholic Central Library. *Trusts, etc:* Trustee of the Charity, Crisis; Patron, Belfast Trust. *Miscellaneous:* Visiting Fellowship, St Andrews University (School of Philosophy and Public Affairs and St Mary's College). *Publications: What Kind of Country,* 1987; *Whose Choice Anyway – the Right to Life,* 1988; *Faith in Britain,* 1991; *Signs of Contradiction,* 1996; *Life After Death,* 1997; *Citizen Virtues,* 1998. *Special Interests:* Abortion, Environment, Housing, Inner Cities, Refugees, Human Rights, Northern Ireland, Citizenship. *Recreations:* Walking, reading, theatre. *Name, Style and Title:* Raised to the peerage as Baron Alton of Liverpool, of Mossley Hill in the County of Merseyside 1997. A Cross-Bencher. *Address:* The Lord Alton of Liverpool, House of Lords, London, SW1A 0PW *E-Mail:* d.alton@livjm.ac.uk.

AMOS (Life Baroness, UK), Valerie Ann Amos; cr. 1997

Daughter of Michael and Eunice Amos. Born March 13, 1954; educated Townley Grammar School for Girls; University of Warwick (BA Sociology); University of Birmingham (MA Cultural Studies); University of East Anglia (doctoral research); Hon. Professor, Thames Valley University; Doctor of Letters, University of Staffordshire. *Career:* With London Boroughs: Lambeth 1981–82, Camden 1983–85; Hackney 1985–89, Head of Training, Head of Management Services; Chief Executive, Equal Opportunities Commission 1989–94; Director, Amos Fraser Bernard 1995–98. *Whip:* A Baroness in Waiting (Government Whip) 1998–. *Spokesman:* Spokesperson on: Social Security 1998–, International Development 1998–, Women's Issues 1998–. *Select Committees:* Co-opted Member, Select Committee on European Communities Sub-Committee F (Social Affairs, Education and Home Affairs) 1997–98. *Other:* Council Member, Institute of Employment Studies 1993–98; Chairman, Board of Governors, Royal College of Nursing Institute 1994–98; Director, Hampstead Theatre 1995–98. *Trusts, etc:* Deputy Chairman, Runnymede Trust 1990–98; Trustee, Institute of Public Policy Research 1994–98; Non-Executive Director, UCLH Trust; Chairman, Afiya Trust 1996–98; Trustee: VSO 1997–98, Project Hope 1997–98. *Name, Style and Title:* Raised to the peerage as Baroness Amos, of Brondesbury in the London Borough of Brent 1997. Labour. *Address:* The Baroness Amos, House of Lords, London, SW1A 0PW *Tel:* 020 7219 4120 *E-Mail:* amosv@parliament.uk.

AMPTHILL (4th Baron, UK), Geoffrey Denis Erskine Russell; cr. 1881; CBE 1986; PC 1995

Son of 3rd Baron, CBE. Born October 15, 1921. Succeeded his father 1973; educated Stowe. Married 1st, 1946, Susan Mary, daughter of late Hon. Charles Winn (2 sons 1 daughter and 1 son deceased) (marriage dissolved 1971), married 2nd, 1972, Elisabeth Anne Marie, daughter of late Claude Henri Gustave Mallon (marriage dissolved 1987). *Armed Forces:* Irish Guards 1941–46, Captain 1944. *Career:* General Manager, Fortnum & Mason 1947–51; Chairman, New Providence Hotel Co. Ltd; Managing Director, theatre owning and producing companies 1953–71; Director, Dualvest plc 1980–1987; Director, United Newspapers plc 1981–96, Deputy Chairman 1991–96; Director, Express Newspapers plc 1985–98, Deputy Chairman 1989–98; Chairman, London's Helicopter Emergency Service 1992–97. *House of Lords:* Deputy Chairman of Committees, House of Lords 1980–92, 1997–, Chairman 1992–94; A Deputy Speaker of the House of Lords 1982–; An elected hereditary peer 1999–. *Select Committees:* Member or Chairman, Select Committees on Offices, Finance and Administration 1979–94; Chairman, Refreshment Sub-Committee 1980–92; Chairman, Select Committees on: Channel Tunnel Bill 1987–88, Rail Link Bill 1996; Member, Delegated Powers and Deregulation 1997–. *Other:* Formerly Director, Leeds Castle Foundation. *Honours:* CBE 1986; PC 1995. *Heir:* His son, Hon. David Whitney Erskine Russell, born May 27, 1947. A Cross-Bencher. *Address:* The Rt Hon. the Lord Ampthill, CBE, 6 North Court, Great Peter Street, London, SW1P 3LL *Tel:* 020 7233 0133 *Fax:* 020 7233 0122.

ANELAY OF ST JOHNS (Life Baroness, UK) Joyce Anne Anelay; cr. 1996; DBE 1995

Daughter of late Stanley Charles Clarke and of Annette Marjorie Clarke. Born July 17, 1947; educated Merryhills Primary School, Enfield; Enfield County School; Bristol University (BA Hons History); London University Institute of Education (CertEd); Brunel University (MA Public and Social Administration); Hon. DSocSci, Brunel 1997. Married 1970, Richard Alfred Anelay, QC. *Councils, Public Bodies:* JP, NW Surrey 1985–97. *Career:* Teacher, St David's School, Ashford, Middlesex 1969–74. *Whip:* An Opposition Whip 1997–98. *Spokesman:* An Opposition Spokeswoman on: Agriculture 1997–98, Culture, Media and Sport December 1998–, Social Security December 1998–99. *Select Committees:* Co-opted Member, Select Committee on European Communities Sub-Committee E (Law and Institutions) 1997–; Member, Select Committee on Procedure 1997–. *All-Party:* Hon. Treasurer, All-Party British-Saudi Arabian Group; Member, All-Party British-American Group. *Party Groups (General):* Chairman, SE Area Conservative Womens' Committee 1987–90; Member, National Union Executive Committee of the Conservative Party 1987–97, Vice-Chairman, SE Area Executive Committee 1990–93; Chairman, Women's National Committee 1993–96, Vice-President, National Union 1996–97. *Other:* Voluntary Adviser, Woking Citizens' Advice Bureau 1976–85, Chairman 1988–93, President 1996–; Chairman, Governors, Hermitage First and Middle Schools 1981–88. *Miscellaneous:* Member: Social Security Appeal Tribunal 1983–96, Social Security Advisory Committee for Great Britain and Northern Ireland 1989–96, Women's National Commission 1991–94, Child Support Appeal Tribunal 1993–96. *Honours:* OBE 1990; DBE 1995. FRSA. *Special Interests:* Social Security, Home Affairs. *Recreations:* Golf, reading. *Sportsclubs:* Woking Golf. *Name, Style and Title:* Raised to the peerage as Baroness Anelay of St Johns, of St Johns in the County of Surrey 1996. A Conservative. *Address:* The Baroness Anelay of St Johns, DBE, House of Lords, London, SW1A 0PW *E-Mail:* anelayj@parliament.uk.

ANNAN (Life Baron, UK), Noel Gilroy Annan; cr. 1965; OBE (Mil) 1946

Son of late James Gilroy Annan, Company Director. Born December 25, 1916; educated Stowe; King's College, Cambridge; Fellow, King's College, Cambridge 1944–56, 1966–; Hon. Degrees: Essex, York Ontario, New York, Pennsylvania, London. Married 1950, Gabriele, daughter of Louis Ferdinand Ullstein (2 daughters). *Armed Forces:* Military Intelligence Directorate, War Office 1940–44; Staff College, Camberley 1942; G III I, 9 Armoured Division 1943; GSO II, Joint Intelligence Staff, War Cabinet Offices 1943–44; Intelligence Staff, SHAEF 1944–45; Political Division, British Control Commission Germany (GSO I) 1945–46. *Career:* University Lecturer in Politics, Cambridge 1948; Provost: King's College 1956–66, University College, London 1966–78; Vice-Chancellor, University of London 1978–81. *Select Committees:* Chairman, Committee on the Future of Broadcasting 1974–77. *Other:* Director, Royal Opera House, Covent Garden 1967–78; Chairman, National Gallery 1980–85; President, The London Library 1981–96. *Trusts, etc:* Trustee: British Museum 1963–78, National Gallery 1978–1985. *Miscellaneous:* Chairman, Departmental Committee on Teaching of Russian in Schools 1960; Member, Public Schools Commission 1966–70. *Honours:* OBE (Mil) 1946; Commander of the Royal Order of King George of the Hellenes (Greece) 1962. Fellow, Royal Historical Society. *Publications:* Author of *Leslie Stephen*, 1951 (revised edition 1984); *The Curious Strength of Positivism in English Political Thought*, 1959; *Roxburgh of Stowe*, 1966; *Our Age*, 1990; *Changing Enemies*, 1995; *The Dons*, 1999. *Clubs:* Brooks's. *Name, Style and Title:* Raised to the peerage as Baron Annan, of Royal Burgh of Annan, in the County of Dumfries 1965. A Cross-Bencher. *Address:* The Lord Annan, OBE, 45 Ranelagh Grove, London, SW1W 8PB *Tel:* 020 7730 4930.

ARCHER OF SANDWELL (Life Baron, UK), Peter Kingsley Archer; cr. 1992; PC 1977; QC 1971

Son of late Cyril Kingsley Archer and May Archer. Born November 20, 1926; educated Wednesbury Boys' High School; London School of Economics; University College, London. Married August 7, 1954, Margaret Irene, daughter of late Sydney John Smith (1 son). *Career:* Called to the Bar, Gray's Inn 1952, Bencher 1974, Recorder 1981–. *House of Commons:* MP (Labour) for Rowley Regis and Tipton 1966–74; PPS to Attorney-General 1967–70; MP (Labour) for Warley West 1974–92; Solicitor General 1974–79; Member, Shadow Cabinet 1981–87. *Spokesman (Commons):* Opposition Front Bench Spokesman on: Legal Affairs 1979–82, Trade, Prices and Consumer Protection 1982–83, Northern Ireland 1983–87. *Spokesman:* An Opposition Spokesman on Foreign Affairs 1992–97. *Select Committees:* Member, Select Committees on: the Scrutiny of Delegated Powers, Delegated Powers and Deregulation 1997–, Parliamentary Privilege (Joint Committee), Chairman, Select Committee on Freedom of Information Bill. *All-Party:* Member, All-Party Human Rights Group. *International Bodies (General):* Chairman, Esperanto Parliamentary Group. *Party Groups (General):* Chairman, Society of Labour Lawyers 1971–74, 1980–93; President, Fabian Society 1993–; Joint President, Society of Labour Lawyers 1993–; Member, Labour Party Departmental Committees for: Home Affairs, Foreign Affairs, Defence. *Other:* Chairman, Amnesty International (British Section) 1971–74; President: Methodist Homes for the Aged 1993–, World Disarmament Campaign 1994–. *Trusts, etc:* President, One World Trust. *Miscellaneous:* Chairman: Council on Tribunals 1992–99, Enemy Property Compensation Panel, Member, Intelligence and Security Committee. *Honours:* PC 1977. Freeman: Metropolitan Borough of Sandwell, State of Maryland. *Publications:* Author of: *The Queen's Courts*; *Communism and the Law*; *The International Protection of Human Rights*; *Freedom at Stake* (co-author); *Purpose in Socialism*; Editor, *Social Welfare and the Citizen*; Editor, *More Law Reform Now*. *Special Interests:* Human Rights, Law Reform, Northern Ireland, World Government, Conservation, Third World. *Recreations:* Music, writing, fly fishing. *Name, Style and Title:* Raised to the peerage as Baron Archer of Sandwell, of Sandwell in the County of West Midlands 1992. Labour. *Address:* The Rt Hon. the Lord Archer of Sandwell, QC, 7 Old School Court, Staines Road, Wraysbury, Staines, Middlesex, TW19 5BP.

ARCHER OF WESTON-SUPER-MARE (Life Baron, UK), Jeffrey Howard Archer; cr. 1992

Son of late William Archer and of Lola Archer. Born April 15, 1940; educated Wellington School, Somerset; Brasenose College, Oxford. Married 1966, Mary Doreen (Dr Mary Archer), daughter of late Harold Norman Weeden (2 sons). *Councils, Public Bodies:* Councillor, GLC for Havering 1966–70. *Career:* Athletics Blues 1963–65; Gymnastics Blue 1963; Represented Great Britain in athletics 1966; Author, Playright and Auctioneer. *House of Commons:* MP (Conservative) for Louth 1969–74. *Party Groups (General).* Deputy Chairman, Conservative Party 1985–86. *Publications:* Plays: *Beyond Reasonable Doubt*, 1987; *Exclusive*, 1990; Author of: *Not a Penny More, Not a Penny Less*, 1975; *Shall We Tell the President?* 1977; *Kane and Abel*, 1979; *A Quiver Full of Arrows (short stories)*, 1980; *The Prodigal Daughter*, 1982; *First Among Equals*, 1984; *A Matter of Honour*, 1986; *A Twist in the Tale* (short stories) 1988; *As the Crow Flies*, 1991; *Honour Among Thieves*, 1993; *Twelve Red Herrings (short stories)*, 1994; *The Fourth Estate*, 1996; *Collected Short Stories*, 1997; *The Eleventh Commandment*, 1998. *Recreations:* Theatre, cricket, auctioneering, art. *Sportsclubs:* President, Somerset AAA 1973–99; Vice-President, Cambridge City RFU; President, World Snooker Association. *Clubs:* MCC. *Name, Style and Title:* Raised to the peerage as Baron Archer of Weston-super-Mare, of Mark in the County of Somerset 1992. *Address:* The Lord Archer of Weston-super-Mare, The Penthouse, 93 Albert Embankment, London, SE1 7TY; The Old Vicarage, Grantchester, Cambridge, CB3 9ND.

ARMSTRONG OF ILMINSTER (Life Baron, UK), Robert Temple Armstrong; cr. 1988; GCB 1983; CVO 1975

Son of Sir Thomas Armstrong, Musician (died 1994), and Hester Muriel Armstrong, née Draper (died 1982). Born March 30, 1927; educated Dragon School; Eton (King's Scholar); Christ Church, Oxford (Scholar) (2nd Class Classical Mods 1947, 2nd Class Literae Humaniores 1949); Fellow, Eton College 1979–94; Hon. LLD, University of Hull 1994. Married 1st, 1953, Serena Mary Benedicta, daughter of late Sir Roger Chance, 3rd Bt, MC (2 daughters) (marriage dissolved 1985, she died 1994), married 2nd, 1985, (Mary) Patricia, daughter of late C. Carlow. *Career:* Assistant Principal, HM Treasury 1950–55; Private Secretary to: Rt Hon. Reginald Maudling, MP when Economic Secretary to the Treasury 1953–54, Rt Hon. R. A. Butler, CH, MP when Chancellor of the Exchequer 1954–55; Principal, Treasury 1955–57; Secretary, Radcliffe Committee on Working of Monetary System 1957–59; Returned to Treasury as Principal 1959–64; Secretary, Armitage Committee on Pay of Postmen 1964; Assistant Secretary: Cabinet Office 1964–66, Treasury 1967–68; Principal Private Secretary to Rt Hon. Roy Jenkins, MP when Chancellor of the Exchequer 1968; Under-Secretary (Home Finance), Treasury 1968–70; Principal Private Secretary to Prime Minister 1970–75; Deputy Under-Secretary of State, Home Office 1975–77; Permanent Under-Secretary of State, Home Office 1977–79; Secretary of the Cabinet 1979–87; Head of the Home Civil Service 1981–87; Director various companies 1988; Director, Royal Opera House 1988–93; Chairman: Biotechnology Investments Ltd 1989–, Bristol and West plc (formerly Building Society) 1993–97; Forensic Investigative Associates plc 1997–. *Chancellor:* Chancellor, University of Hull 1994–. *Other:* Director, Royal Academy of Music. *Trusts, etc:* Member: Rhodes Trust 1975–97, Pilgrim Trust 1987–; Chairman: Board of Trustees, V & A Museum 1988–98, Hestercombe Gardens Trust 1996–, Royal Academy of Music Foundation. *Honours:* CB 1974; CVO 1975; KCB 1978; GCB 1983; Hon. Student, Christ Church, Oxford 1985; Hon. Bencher, Inner Temple 1985. Freeman, City of London. Honorary Member, Salters' Company. *Recreations:* music. *Clubs:* Brooks's, Garrick. *Name, Style and Title:* Raised to the peerage as Baron Armstrong of Ilminster, of Ashill in the County of Somerset 1988. A Cross-Bencher. *Address:* The Lord Armstrong of Ilminster, GCB, CVO, House of Lords, London, SW1A 0PW.

ARRAN (9th Earl of, I), Arthur Desmond Colquhoun Gore; cr. 1762; 9th Viscount Sudley and Baron Saunders (I) 1758; 5th Baron Sudley (UK) 1884; 11th Bt of Castle Gore (I) 1662

Son of 8th Earl. Born July 14, 1938. Succeeded his father 1983. Sits as Baron Sudley; educated Eton; Balliol College, Oxford (MA Hons English Literature). Married September 28, 1974, Eleanor, daughter of late Bernard Van Cutsem and Lady Margaret Fortescue (2 daughters). *Armed Forces:* Served Grenadier Guards, National Service, Commissioned. *Career:* Assistant Manager *Daily Mail* 1972–73; Managing Director, Clark Nelson 1973–74; Assistant General Manager, *Daily Express* and *Sunday Express* June-November 1974; Director, Waterstone & Co Ltd 1984–87; Parliamentary Consultant to the Waste Industry 1995–; Non-Executive Director: HMV (EMI) 1995–98, SWEL (the Economy and Inward Investment of the West Country), Bonham's (Auctioneers) 1998; Azerbaijan Real Estate Holdings 1998. *House of Lords:* Parliamentary Under-Secretary of State for: The Armed Forces, Ministry of Defence 1989–92, Northern Ireland Office 1992–94, Department of the Environment January-July 1994; An elected hereditary peer 1999–. *Whip:* A Lord in Waiting (Government Whip) 1987–89; Captain of the Queen's Bodyguard of the Yeomen of the Guard (Government Deputy Chief Whip in the House of Lords) July 1994-January 1995. *Spokesman:* Spokesman for: The Home Office, DES and DHSS 1987–89, Department of the Environment 1988–89. *Other:* Co-Chairman, Children's Country Holidays Fund. *Special Interests:* Media, Charity, Sport, Foreign Affairs. *Recreations:* Tennis, golf, croquet, shooting and gardening. *Clubs:* Turf, Beefsteak, Pratt's, White's, Annabels. *Heir:* Heir to his Irish honours, his kinsman, Paul Annesley Gore, CMG, CVO, born February 28, 1921; Heir to the barony of Sudley, none. A Conservative. *Address:* The Earl of Arran, House of Lords, London, SW1A 0PW.

ASHLEY OF STOKE (Life Baron, UK), Jack Ashley; cr. 1992; CH 1975; PC 1979

Son of late Jack Ashley. Born December 6, 1922; educated St Patrick's Elementary School, Widnes; Ruskin College, Oxford; Gonville and Caius College, Cambridge (President of Union); Twelve Hon. Degrees. Married December 15, 1951, Pauline, daughter of C. A. Crispin (3 daughters). *Trades Union:* Shop steward convenor 1946. *Councils, Public Bodies:* Councillor, Widnes Borough Council 1945. *Career:* Labourer and crane driver 1935–46; BBC Radio Producer 1951–57; Commonwealth Fund Fellow 1955; BBC Senior Television Producer 1957–66. *House of Commons:* MP (Labour) for Stoke-on-Trent South 1966–92; PPS: to Secretary of State for Economic Affairs 1967–70, to Secretary of State for Health and Social Security 1974–79. *All-Party Committees (Commons):* Chairman, All-Party Lords and Commons Disablement Group 1969–. *Chancellor:* Chancellor, Staffordshire University 1993–. *All-Party:* Joint Vice-Chairman, All-Party: Doctor Assisted Dying Group 1998–, Voice Group 1999–. *Party Groups (General):* Member, Labour Party National Executive Committee 1976–78. *Other:* Member, General Advisory Council, BBC 1967–69; President: Royal College of Speech and Language Therapists 1995–, Royal National Institute for Deaf, Defeating Deafness. *Honours:* CH 1975; PC 1979. *Publications:* Author of: *Journey into Silence* (autobiography) 1973; *Acts of Defiance*, 1992. *Special Interests:* Disability, Health, Medical Drugs, Poverty, Disadvantaged, Hong Kong, China. *Sportsclubs:* Patron, Widnes Rugby League Club. *Name, Style and Title:* Raised to the peerage as Baron Ashley of Stoke, of Widnes in the County of Cheshire 1992. Labour. *Address:* The Rt Hon. the Lord Ashley of Stoke, CH, House of Lords, London, SW1A 0PW.

ASHTON OF UPHOLLAND (Life Baroness, UK), Catherine Margaret Ashton; cr. 1999

Daughter of late Harold and Clare Ashton. Born March 20, 1956; educated Upholland Grammar School; Bedford College, London University (BSc 1977). Married, Peter Jon, son of Michael and Pippa Kellner (1 son, 1 daughter, 1 step-son, 2 stepdaughters). *Councils, Public Bodies:* Chairman, East and North Herts Health Authority. *Career:* Administrative Officer, CND 1977–79; The Coverdale Organisation 1979–81; Central Council for Education and Training in Social Work 1981–83; Director of Community Development and Public Affairs, Business in the Community 1983–89; Public Policy Adviser 1989–, seconded by London First to Home Office 1998–99. *Other:* Parent Governor, Bernards Heath Infants and Spencer Junior Schools; Advisory Board Member, "Can Do" Network; Director, ERA (Economic and Regional Analysis). *Special Interests:* Policy Implementation. *Recreations:* Swimming, theatre, "retail therapy". *Clubs:* Royal Commonwealth Society. *Name, Style and Title:* Raised to the peerage as Baroness Ashton of Upholland, of St Albans in the County of Hertfordshire 1999. Labour. *Address:* The Baroness Ashton of Upholland, House of Lords, London, SW1A 0PW; East and North Herts Health Authority, Charter House, Parkway, Welwyn Garden City *Tel:* 01707 390855.

ASTOR (4th Viscount, UK), William Waldorf Astor; cr. 1917; 4th Baron Astor (UK) 1916

Son of 3rd Viscount and Hon. Sarah Katharine Elinor Norton, daughter of 6th Baron Grantley. Born December 27, 1951. Succeeded his father 1966; educated Eton. Married January 14, 1976, Mrs Annabel Sheffield, daughter of Timothy Jones (2 sons 1 daughter). *Career:* Citibank, New York 1970–72; Observer, USA 1972; Westminster Press 1973–74; Director: UK and US Property and Investment Companies 1974–84, Blakeney Hotels and Cliveden Hotels 1984–90; Director: Chorion Plc 1996–, Prestbury Plc 1996–, Jupiter European Investment Trust 1996–. *House of Lords:* Parliamentary Under-Secretary of State: Department of Social Security 1993–94, Department of National Heritage 1994–95; An elected hereditary peer 1999–. *Whip:* A Lord in Waiting (Government Whip) 1990–93. *Spokesman:* Spokesman for: Department of Environment 1990–91, Home Office 1991–92, Department of National Heritage 1992–93; An Opposition Spokesman for: Home Office 1997–, Education and Employment (Employment) 1999–. *All-Party:* Member, All-Party: Racing Group, Media Group. *Trusts, etc:* Trustee, Stanley Spencer Gallery, Cookham. *Clubs:* White's, Turf. *Heir:* His son, Hon. William Waldorf Astor, born January 18, 1979. A Conservative. *Address:* The Viscount Astor, Ginge Manor, Nr Wantage, Oxfordshire, OX12 8QT *Tel:* 01235 833228.

ASTOR OF HEVER (3rd Baron, UK), John Jacob Astor; cr. 1956; DL

Son of 2nd Baron, and late Lady Irene Haig, daughter of Field Marshal 1st Earl Haig, KT, GCB, OM, GCVO, KCIE. Born June 16, 1946. Succeeded his father 1984; educated Eton. Married 1st, July 18, 1970, Fiona, daughter of late Captain Roger Harvey (3 daughters) (marriage dissolved 1990), married 2nd, 1990, Hon. Elizabeth Mackintosh, daughter of 2nd Viscount Mackintosh of Halifax, OBE, BEM (1 son 1 daughter). *Armed Forces:* Lieutenant, The Life Guards 1966–70. *Councils, Public Bodies:* DL Kent 1996–. *Career:* Managing Director: Honon et Cie 1982–, Astor France SARL 1989–; President, Astor Enterprises Inc. 1986–. *House of Lords:* An elected hereditary peer 1999–. *Whip:* An Opposition Whip (Health/Social Security) December 1998–. *Select Committees:* Member: Select Committee on Selection, Personal Bills Committee, Finance and Staff Sub-Committee. *All-Party:* Secretary, Anglo-Swiss Parliamentary Association 1992–; Treasurer, British-South Africa Parliamentary Group 1994–; Joint Treasurer, All-Party Franco-British Parliamentary Relations Group; Joint Secretary, All-Party Motor Group 1998–. *Party Groups:* Member of Executive, Association of Conservative Peers 1996–98. *Other:* President, Sevenoaks Westminster Patrons Club 1991–; Governor, Cobham Hall School 1992–96; Patron, Kent Association of Youth Clubs 1994–; President: Earl Haig Branch, Royal British Legion 1994–, Kent Federation of Amenity Societies 1995–, Motorsport Industry Association 1995–, RoSPA 1996–99, RoSPA Advanced Drivers Association 1997–, CPRE Kent. *Trusts, etc:* Trustee: Astor of Hever Trust 1986–, Astor Foundation 1988–, Rochester

Cathedral Trust 1988–; Patron, Edenbridge Music and Arts Trust 1989–; Trustee, Canterbury Cathedral Trust 1992–; Patron, Bridge Trust 1993–. *Honours:* Chairman, Council of the Order of St John for Kent 1987–97. Member, Goldsmiths' Company. *Special Interests:* France, Motor Industry, Defence. *Clubs:* White's, Riviera Golf (France). *Heir:* His son, Hon. Charles Gavin John Astor, born November 10, 1990. A Conservative. *Address:* The Lord Astor of Hever, DL, Frenchstreet House, Westerham, Kent, TN16 1PW *Tel:* 01959 562783 *E-Mail:* astorjj@parliament.uk.

ATTENBOROUGH (Life Baron, UK), Richard Samuel Attenborough; cr. 1993; Kt 1976; CBE 1967

Son of late Frederick Attenborough. Born August 29, 1923; educated Wyggeston Grammar School, Leicester; Leverhulme scholarship to Royal Academy of Dramatic Art; Hon. DLitt, Leicester 1970; Hon. DCL, Newcastle 1974; Hon. DLitt, Kent 1981; Hon. LLD, Dickinson, Penn. 1983; Hon. DLitt, Sussex 1987; Fellow, Kings College, London 1993; Hon. Fellow, University of Wales 1997; Hon. DLit, American International University, London 1994. Married 1945, Sheila Sim (1 son 2 daughters). *Armed Forces:* Served RAF 1943–46. *Career:* Actor, producer and director; Appeared in a number of pro-ductions on the London stage including: *Brighton Rock* 1943, *The Mousetrap* 1952–54, *The Rape of the Belt* 1957–58; Film appearances include: *In Which We Serve, Brighton Rock, London Belongs to Me, The Guinea Pig, Morning Departure, The Ship That Died of Shame, I'm Alright Jack, The League of Gentlemen, The Angry Silence* (also co-produced), *The Dock Brief, The Great Escape, Seance On a Wet Afternoon* (also produced, BAFTA Award), *Guns at Batasi* (BAFTA Award), *The Flight of the Phoenix, The Sand Pebbles* (Hollywood Golden Globe), *Dr Dolittle* (Hollywood Golden Globe), *10 Rillington Place, The Chess Players, Jurassic Park, Miracle on 34th Street, Lost World, Elizabeth I*; Produced: *Whistle Down the Wind, The L-Shaped Room*; Directed: *Young Winston* (Hollywood Golden Globe), *A Bridge Too Far, Magic, A Chorus Line*; Produced and directed: *Oh! What a Lovely War* (BAFTA Award, Hollywood Golden Globe), *Gandhi* (8 Oscars, 5 BAFTA Awards, 5 Hollywood Golden Globes), *Cry Freedom, Chaplin, Shadowlands* (BAFTA Award); *In Love and War, Grey Owl*; Chairman, Capital Radio 1972–92, Life President 1992–; Chairman: Goldcrest Films and Television Ltd 1982–87, Channel Four Television 1987–92, Deputy Chairman 1980–86. *Chancellor:* Pro-Chancellor, Sussex University 1970–, Chancellor 1998–. *Other:* Member: British Actors' Equity Council 1949–73, Cinematograph Films Council 1967–73; Chairman, BAFTA 1969–70, Vice-President 1971–94; Member, Arts Council of Great Britain 1970–73; Chairman, Royal Academy of Dramatic Art 1970–, Mem. Council 1963–; President, Muscular Dystrophy Group of Great Britain 1971–, Vice-President 1962–71; Director, Young Vic 1976–82; Chairman: Duke of York's Theatre 1979–92, British Film Institute 1981–92; Patron, Kingsley Hall Community Centre 1982–; Chairman, Committee of Inquiry into Arts and Disabled People 1983–85; President: The Gandhi Foundation 1983–, British Film Year 1984–86, Brighton Festival 1984–95; Chairman, British Screen Advisory Council 1987–96, Hon. President 1996; Patron, Goodwill Ambassador for Unicef 1987–; Chairman, European Script Fund 1988–96, Hon. President 1996–; President, Combined Theatrical Charities Appeals Council 1988–, Chairman 1964–88; President, Arts for Health 1989–; President, Gardner Centre for the Arts, Sussex University 1990–, Patron 1969–90; Patron, Richard Attenborough Centre for Disability and the Arts, Leicester University 1990–; President, National Film and TV School 1997–, Governor 1970–81. *Awards Granted: Evening Standard* Film Award, 40 years service to British Cinema 1983; Martin Luther King Jr Peace Prize 1983; European Film Awards Award of Merit for Humanitarianism in Film Making 1988; Shakespeare Prize for Outstanding Contribution to European Culture 1992; Praemium Imperiale 1998. *Trusts, etc:* President, The Actors' Charitable Trust 1988–, Chairman 1956–88; Trustee: Help a London Child 1975–, Tate Gallery 1976–82 and 1994–96; Chairman, UK Trustees Waterford-Kamhlaba School Swaziland 1976–, Governor 1987–; Trustee: Motability 1977–, Tate Foundation 1986–. *Honours:* CBE 1967; Kt 1976; Padma Bhushan, India 1983; Commandeur, Ordre des Arts et des Lettres, France 1985; Chevalier, Legion d'Honneur, France 1988. Fellow: BAFTA 1983, BFI 1992. Freeman, City of Leicester 1990. *Publications: In Search of Gandhi,* 1982; *Richard Attenborough's Chorus Line* (with Diana Carter) 1986; *Cry Freedom, A Pictorial Record,* 1987. *Special Interests:* Arts, Education, Disability, Underdeveloped Countries. *Recreations:* Collecting paintings and sculpture, listening to music, watching football and reading the newspapers. *Sportsclubs:* Director, Chelsea Football Club 1969–82, Life Vice-President 1993–. *Clubs:* Garrick, Beefsteak. *Name, Style and Title:* Raised to the peerage as Baron Attenborough, of Richmond upon Thames in the London Borough of Richmond upon Thames 1993. Labour. *Address:* The Lord Attenborough, CBE, Old Friars, Richmond Green, Richmond upon Thames, Surrey, TW9 1NH *Tel:* 020 8940 7234.

ATTLEE (3rd Earl, UK), John Richard Attlee; cr. 1955; Viscount Prestwood

Son of 2nd Earl. Born October 3, 1956. Succeeded his father 1991; educated Stowe. Married July 31, 1993, Celia Jane, daughter of Dexter Plummer, of Bishop's Stortford, Hertfordshire. *Armed Forces:* Major, Territorial Army, Officer Commanding 150 Recovery Company, REME (V) 1998–. *Career:* President, The Heavy Transport Association 1994–; British Direct Aid: In-Country Director (Rwanda) 1995–96. *House of Lords:* An elected hereditary peer 1999–. *Whip:* An Opposition Whip 1997–99. *Spokesman:* An Opposition Spokesman for: Defence June-Oct 1997, Environment, Transport and the Regions (Transport) June-Oct 1997, Northern Ireland June-Oct 1997, December 1998-June 1999, Defence 1998–, Trade and Industry 1998–99, Transport 1999–. *All-Party:* Treasurer, All-Party Defence Study Group 1995–97. *Trusts, etc:* Trustee, Attlee Foundation. *Special Interests:* Engineering, Defence, Transport, Overseas Aid and Development. *Heir:* None. A Conservative. *Address:* The Earl Attlee, House of Lords, London, SW1A 0PW *E-Mail:* attleej@parliament.uk.

AVEBURY (4th Baron, UK), Eric Reginald Lubbock; cr. 1900; 7th Bt of Lamas (UK) 1806

Son of late Hon. Maurice Lubbock, youngest son of 1st Baron, PC, DL, and late Hon. Mary Katharine Adelaide Stanley, daughter of 5th Baron Stanley of Alderley, KCMG, DL. Born September 29, 1928. Succeeded his cousin 1971; educated Upper Canada College, Toronto; Harrow; Balliol College, Oxford (BA). Married 1953, Kina Maria, daughter of late Count Joseph O'Kelly de Gallagh, KM (2 sons 1 daughter) (marriage dissolved 1983), married 2nd, 1985, Lindsay Stewart (1 son). *Armed Forces:* Second Lieutenant, Welsh Guards 1949–51. *Career:* With Rolls-Royce (Aero-engine division) 1951–53; Production Engineering Ltd (Management consultant) 1955–60; Charterhouse Group 1960–62; Director, C.L. Projects Ltd. *House of Commons:* MP (Liberal) for Orpington 1962–70. *Whip (Commons):* A former Whip. *Select Committees (Commons):* Member: Commons Select Committee on Science and Technology 1968–70. Select Committee on Members' Interests 1969. *House of Lords:* An elected hereditary peer 1999–. *Spokesman:* Spokesman on: Race Relations and Immigration 1971–83, Foreign and Commonwealth Affairs 1998–. *All-Party:* Chairman, All-Party Lords and Commons Parliamentary Human Rights Group 1976–97. *Other:* President: Fluoridation Society 1972–84, Conservation Society 1973–81, London Bach Society, Steinitz Bach Players 1984–98; Patron: Angulinala, Buddhist Prison Chaplaincy 1990–, Kurdish Human Rights Project 1993–, British Campaign for East Timor 1994–. *Miscellaneous:* Member: Speaker's Conference on Electoral Law 1963–65, Royal Commission on Standards of Conduct in Public Life 1975–76. MInstMechE; FBCS; CEng. *Publications: The Energy Crisis – Growth, Stability or Collapse*, 1973; *Alcohol – Politics and Practicalities*, 1981; *Authority and Accountability*, 1986; *Desolated and Profaned*, 1992; *A Desolation called Peace*, 1993; *Iran: The Subjection of Women*, 1995; *Iran: State of Terror*, 1996. *Heir:* His son, Hon. Lyulph Ambrose Jonathan Lubbock, born June 15, 1954. A Liberal Democrat. *Address:* The Lord Avebury, 26 Flodden Road, London, SE5 9LH *Tel:* 020 7274 4617 *Fax:* 020 7738 7864 *E-Mail:* ericavebury@compuserve.com.

B

BACH (Life Baron, UK), William Stephen Goulden Bach; cr. 1998

Son of late Stephen Bach, CBE, and late Joan Bach. Born December 25, 1946; educated Westminster School; New College, Oxford (BA). Married 1984, Caroline Jones (1 daughter plus 2 children from previous marriage). *Trades Union:* Member, TGWU 1977–. *Councils, Public Bodies:* Leicester City Council: Councillor 1976–87, Chair, Personnel Committee 1979–81, Chair, Finance Committee 1981–83, Chief Whip, Labour Group 1981–83, Chair, Environmental Health Committee 1984–85; Councillor, Lutterworth Town Council 1991–99; Mayor, Lutterworth 1993–94; Harborough District Council: Councillor 1995–99, Chair, Contracts Services Committee 1995–97. *Career:* Barrister; Tenant Barristers' Chambers 1975–, Head of Chambers 1996–; Served on a number of circuit and local court and bar committees over many years. *Whip:* A Lord in

Waiting (Government Whip) 1999–. *Select Committees:* Member, European Communities Sub Committee E (Laws and Institutions) 1998–99. *All-Party:* A spokesman: Home Office 1999–, Department for Education and Employment 1999–, Lord Chancellor's Department 1999–. *Party Groups (General):* Executive Committee Member, Society of Labour Lawyers; Elected Member, Labour Party: National Policy Forum 1998–99, Economic Policy Commission 1998–99; Member: Co-operative Party, Fabian Society; Chair and Co-Founder, Society of Labour Lawyers, East Midlands; Chair: Harborough District Labour Party 1989–95, Northants and Blaby Euro Constituency GC 1992–99. *Other:* Council Member, Leicester University 1980–. *Miscellaneous:* Contested (Labour): Gainsborough 1979, Sherwood 1983 and 1987 General Elections. *Special Interests:* Crime and Criminal Justice, Local Government, USA Affairs, Sport. *Recreations:* Playing and watching football and cricket, supporting Leicester City FC, American crime writing. *Sportsclubs:* Leicester City FC, Leicestershire CCC; Founder Member and President, Walcote Cricket Club. *Name, Style and Title:* Raised to the peerage as Baron Bach, of Lutterworth in the County of Leicestershire 1998. Labour. *Address:* The Lord Bach, House of Lords, London, SW1A 0PW *Tel:* 020 7222 2597 *Tel:* 0116–252 7710.

BAGRI (Life Baron, UK), Raj Kumar Bagri; cr. 1997; CBE 1995

Son of late Sohan Lal Bagri. Born August 24, 1930; Hon. Dsc. The City University London 1999. Married 1954, Usha Maheshwary (1 son 1 daughter). *Career:* Founder and Chairman, Metdist Group 1970–; Chairman, The London Metal Exchange Limited 1993–, Director 1983, Vice-Chairman 1990. *Other:* Member: Advisory Committee of The Prince's Youth Business Trust, Governing Body of School of Oriental and African Studies; Chairman, Bagri Foundation. *Trusts, etc:* Chairman, Trustees of The Rajiv Gandhi (UK) Foundation; Trustee, Sangam. *Honours:* CBE 1995. *Recreations:* Fine art, classical music, antiques. *Clubs:* MCC. *Name, Style and Title:* Raised to the peerage as Baron Bagri, of Regent's Park in the City of Westminster 1997. A Conservative. *Address:* The Lord Bagri, CBE, 80 Cannon Street, London, EC4N 6EJ.

BAKER OF DORKING (Life Baron, UK), Kenneth Wilfred Baker; cr. 1997; CH 1992; PC 1984

Son of late Wilfred Michael Baker, OBE. Born November 3, 1934; educated St Paul's School; Magdalen College, Oxford (Secretary of Union); Hon. Degree, Richmond College, The American University in London. Married 1963, Mary Elizabeth Gray-Muir (1 son 2 daughters). *Armed Forces:* National Service 1953–55 (Lieutenant in Gunners). *Councils, Public Bodies:* Councillor, Twickenham Borough Council 1960–62. *House of Commons:* Contested Poplar 1964, Acton 1966; MP (Conservative) for Acton 1968–70, St Marylebone 1970–83 and for Mole Valley June 1983–97; PPS to Minister of State, Department of Employment 1970–72; Parliamentary Secretary, Civil Service Department 1972–74; Minister of State for Industry and Information Technology 1981–84; Minister for Local Government 1984–85; Secretary of State: for The Environment 1985–86, for Education and Science 1986–89; Chancellor of the Duchy of Lancaster 1989–90; Secretary of State for the Home Department 1990–92. *Backbench Committees (Commons):* Member, Executive of 1922 Committee 1975–81. *Party Groups (General):* Chairman, Conservative Party 1989–90. *Other:* Chairman: Hansard Society 1978–81, Museum of British History 1995–. *Honours:* PC 1984; CH 1992. *Publications:* Author of: *London Lines; I Have No Gun But I Can Spit; The Faber Book of English History in Verse; Unauthorised Versions: Poems and their Parodies; The Faber Book of Conservatism; The Turbulent Years: My Life in Politics,* 1993; *The Prime Ministers – An Irreverent Political History in Cartoons,* 1995; *Kings and Queens: An Irreverent Cartoon History of the British Monarchy,* 1996; *The Faber Book of War Poetry,* 1996. *Special Interests:* Education, History, Information Technology. *Recreations:* Collecting books, collecting political cartoons. *Clubs:* Carlton, Athenaeum, Garrick. *Name, Style and Title:* Raised to the peerage as Baron Baker of Dorking, of Iford in the County of East Sussex 1997. A Conservative. *Address:* The Rt Hon. the Lord Baker of Dorking, CH, House of Lords, London, SW1A 0PW.

BALDWIN OF BEWDLEY (4th Earl, UK), Edward Alfred Alexander Baldwin; cr. 1937; Viscount Corvedale

Son of 3rd Earl and late Joan Elspeth, née Tomes. Born January 3, 1938. Succeeded his father 1976; educated Eton; Trinity College, Cambridge (MA, CertEd). Married 1970, Sarah, daughter of Evan James (3 sons). *Armed Forces:* National Service 1956–58, 2nd Lieutenant, Intelligence Corps 1957–58. *Career:* Schoolmaster 1970–77; Education Officer 1978–87. *House of Lords:* An elected hereditary peer 1999–. *All-Party:* Joint Chairman, Parliamentary Group for Alternative and Complementary Medicine 1992–; Committee Member, Parliamentary Food and Health Forum. *Miscellaneous:* Chairman, British Acupuncture Accreditation Board 1990–98; Former Member, Research Council for Complementary Medicine. *Special Interests:* Complementary Medicine, Environment, Education. *Recreations:* Mountains, tennis, music. *Clubs:* MCC. *Heir:* His son, Viscount Corvedale, born December 28, 1973. A Cross-Bencher. *Address:* The Earl Baldwin of Bewdley, Manor Farm House, Godstow Road, Upper Wolvercote, Oxford, OX2 8AJ *Tel:* 01865 552683 *Fax:* 01865 552683.

BARBER (Life Baron, UK), Anthony Perrinott Lysberg Barber; cr. 1974; PC 1963; TD; DL

Son of late John Barber, CBE, Company director of Doncaster. Born July 4, 1920; educated Retford Grammar School; Oriel College, Oxford (MA); Hon. Fellow, Oriel College 1973. Married 1st, September 5, 1950, Jean Patricia (died 1983), daughter of Milton Asquith (2 daughters), married 2nd, September 8, 1989, Mrs Rosemary Surgenor, daughter of late Canon Youens. *Armed Forces:* Served 1939–45, Commissioned Army, seconded RAF pilot (mentioned in despatches) (P.O.W. 1942–45) (Germany). *Councils, Public Bodies:* DL, West Yorkshire 1987. *Career:* Called to the Bar 1948; Chairman, Standard Chartered Bank plc. 1974–87; Director, BP 1979–88. *House of Commons:* MP (Conservative) for: Doncaster 1951–64, Altrincham and Sale 1965–74; PPS, Air Ministry 1952; PPS to Rt Hon. Harold Macmillan, Prime Minister 1958; Economic Secretary to the Treasury 1959–62; Financial Secretary to Treasury 1962–63; Minister of Health and member of the Cabinet 1963–64; Chancellor of the Duchy of Lancaster and member of the Cabinet June-July 1970; Chancellor of the Exchequer 1970–74. *Whip (Commons):* Government Whip 1955; Lord Commnr., H.M. Treasury 1957–58. *Party Groups (General):* Chairman, Conservative Party 1967–70. *Other:* Member, Falkland Islands Enquiry (Franks Committee) 1982; British Member, Eminent Persons Group on South Africa 1986; Chairman, RAF Benevolent Fund 1991–96. *Clubs:* Carlton, RAF. *Name, Style and Title:* Raised to the peerage as Baron Barber, of Wentbridge in the County of West Yorkshire 1974. A Conservative. *Address:* The Rt Hon. the Lord Barber, TD, DL, House of Lords, London, SW1A 0PW.

BARBER OF TEWKESBURY (Life Baron, UK), Derek Coates Barber; cr. 1992; Kt 1984

Son of late Thomas Smith-Barber. Born June 17, 1918; educated Royal Agricultural College, Cirencester; Hon. DSc, Bradford University 1986. Married 1st, (dissolved 1981), married 2nd, 1983, Rosemary Jennifer, daughter of late Lieutenant-Commander Randolph Brougham Pearson, RN. *Armed Forces:* Served in Second World War (invalided). *Councils, Public Bodies:* Councillor, Cheltenham Rural District Council 1948–52. *Career:* Farmer in Gloucestershire; Various posts, Ministry of Agriculture, Fisheries and Food 1946–72; Environment consultant to Humberts, Chartered Surveyors 1972–93. *Select Committees:* Member, House of Lords Select Committees on: European Communities, Sub-Committee D (Food and Agriculture) 1993–96, Sustainable Development 1994–95. *All-Party:* Member, All-Party: Conservation Group, Rural Economy Group, Forestry Group. *Other:* Chairman, Royal Society for the Protection of Birds 1976–81, Vice-President 1981–, President 1990–91; President, Gloucestershire Naturalists' Society 1981–; Vice-President, Ornithological Society of the Middle East 1987–97; President: Royal Agricultural Society of England 1991–92, British Pig Association 1995–97. *Awards Granted:* Bledisloe Gold Medal for distinguished service to UK agriculture 1967; RSPB Gold Medal 1982; RASE Gold Medal for services to agriculture 1991; Massey-Ferguson Award for Services to agriculture. *Trusts, etc:* Council Member, British Trust for Ornithology 1987–90; President: Rare Breeds Survival Trust 1991–95 and 1997–99, The Hawk and Owl Trust 1991–96. *Miscellaneous:* Chairman: BBC Central Agricultural Advisory Committee 1974–80,

Countryside Commission 1981–91; Member, Ordnance Survey Advisory Board 1982–85; Chairman: Booker Countryside Advisory Board 1990–96, The National Forest Advisory Board 1991–94. *Honours:* Kt 1984. Hon. Fellow, Royal Agricultural Society of England 1986; Fellow: Royal Agricultural Societies (FRAgS) 1991, Institute of Agricultural Management (FIAgrM) 1992. *Publications:* Joint Author of books on agriculture as well as contributing to journals on farming and wildlife. *Special Interests:* Farming, Forestry, Environment. *Recreations:* Birds, farming. *Clubs:* Farmers'. *Name, Style and Title:* Raised to the peerage as Baron Barber of Tewkesbury, of Gotherington in the County of Gloucestershire 1992. A Cross-Bencher. *Address:* The Lord Barber of Tewkesbury, Chough House, Gretton Road, Gotherington, Gloucestershire, GL52 4QU *Tel:* 01242 673908.

BARKER (Life Baroness, UK); Elizabeth Jean Barker; cr. 1999

Born January 31, 1961; educated Dalziel High School, Motherwell, Lanarkshire, Scotland; Broadway School, Oldham, Lancashire; University of Southampton (BSc(SocSci) Honours, Upper Second Class in Psychology). *Trades Union:* Member, ACCTS. *Career:* Age Concern England; Project Co-ordinator, Opportunities for Volunteering Programme 1983–88, Grants Officer 1988–92, Field Officer based in London 1992–; Management Consultant to Age Concern organisations in eight London Boroughs. *Party Groups (General):* Joined Liberal Party 1979; Member, Union of Liberal Students 1979–83, President 1982–83; Member: Liberal Party National Executive 1982–83, Liberator Collective which produces *Liberator* magazine 1983–96, Liberal Assembly Committee 1984–, Federal Policy Committee 1997–; Chair, Liberal Democrat Federal Conference Committee 1997–; Member: The Future of Social Services Policy Working Group, Freedom and Fairness for Women Policy Working Group. *Trusts, etc:* Trustee, Andy Lawson Memorial Fund. *Special Interests:* Health, Social Services, Ageing, Poverty, Civil Liberties, Governance of the UK. *Name, Style and Title:* Raised to the peerage as Baroness Barker, of Anagach in Highland 1999. A Liberal Democrat. *Address:* The Baroness Barker, c/o Liberal Democrat Whips Office, House of Lords, London, SW1A 0PW.

BARNETT (Life Baron, UK), Joel Barnett; cr. 1983; PC 1975

Son of late Louis and Ettie Barnett. Born October 14, 1923; educated Elementary school; Manchester Central High School; Correspondence course, qualified as Accountant; Hon. LLD, Strathclyde University 1983; Hon. Fellow, Birkbeck College, London University. Married 1949, Lilian Goldstone (1 daughter). *Armed Forces:* RASC 1939–45. *Councils, Public Bodies:* Councillor, Prestwich Council 1956–59; JP, Manchester Bench 1960. *Career:* Accountant; Senior Partner, J. C. Allen & Co (now Hacker Young) until 1974; Vice-Chairman, BBC 1986–93; Chairman, British Screen Finance Ltd 1986–97; Member, International Advisory Board of Unisys Inc. 1989–96; Chairman: Education Broadcasting Services Trust Ltd 1993–, Origin (UK) Ltd 1996–, Mercury Recycling Ltd 1996–, Helping Hands plc 1997–98. *House of Commons:* Contested (Labour) Runcorn 1959; MP (Labour) for Heywood and Royton 1964–83; Chief Secretary to the Treasury 1974–79; Member of Cabinet, February 1977–79. *Spokesman (Commons):* Official Opposition Spokesman on Financial and Economic matters 1970–74. *Select Committees (Commons):* Member, Public Accounts Committee 1966–71, Chairman 1979–83. *Backbench Committees (Commons):* Member, Public Expenditure Committee 1971–74. *All-Party Committees (Commons):* Former Chairman, Parliamentary Labour Party Economic, Finance and Taxation Group 1967–70, 1972–74. *Spokesman:* Official Front Bench Spokesman on Treasury Affairs in House of Lords 1983–86. *Select Committees:* Chairman, Sub-Committee A of European Communities Select Committee (Economic and Financial Affairs, Trade and External Relations) 1995–97, 1997–98; Member, Select Committees on: European Communities 1997–, Monetary Policy of the Bank of England 1998–. *Party Groups (General):* Member, Fabian Society. *Other:* Chairman, Hansard Society 1984–90; President, Royal Institute of Public Administration (RIPA) 1988–91; Chairman, Mansfield 2010 1993–97. *Trusts, etc:* Trustee: Victoria and Albert Museum 1983–97, Open University Foundation 1995–. *Miscellaneous:* Chairman, Building Society Ombudsman Council 1986–96. *Honours:* PC 1975. FACCA. *Publications: Inside the Treasury,* 1982. *Recreations:* Walking, reading, theatre, good food, watching Manchester United. *Name, Style and Title:* Raised to the peerage as Baron Barnett, of Heywood and Royton in Greater Manchester 1983. Labour. *Address:* The Rt Hon. the Lord Barnett, 7 Hillingdon Road, Whitefield, Manchester, M45 7QQ; House of Lords, London, SW1A 0PW *Tel:* House of Lords 020 7219 5440.

BASSAM OF BRIGHTON (Life Baron, UK), (John) Steven Bassam; cr. 1997

Son of late Sydney Stevens and of Enid Bassam. Born June 11, 1953; educated Secondary Modern School; University of Sussex (BA); University of Kent (MA). *Trades Union:* Member, UNISON. *Councils, Public Bodies:* Councillor, Brighton and Hove Council 1983, subsequently Deputy Leader of Labour Group, Leader of Unitary Council 1996–99; Head of Environmental Health and Consumer Issues, Local Government Association 1997–99. *Career:* Social Worker, East Sussex County Council 1976–77; Legal Adviser, North Lewisham Law Centre 1979–88; Former Consultant Advisor, KPMG Capital. *House of Lords:* Parliamentary Under-Secretary of State, Home Office 1999–. *All-Party:* Member, All-Party: Business Services Group, Town Centres Group.

Miscellaneous: Contested Brighton Kemptown (Lab) 1987. *Recreations:* Cricket, walking. *Sportsclubs:* Preston Village Cricket Club. *Name, Style and Title:* Raised to the peerage as Baron Bassam of Brighton, of Brighton in the County of East Sussex 1997. Labour. *Address:* The Lord Bassam of Brighton, House of Lords, London, SW1A 0PW; Longstone, 25 Church Place, Brighton, BN2 5JN.

BATH AND WELLS (77th Bishop of), James Lawton Thompson

Son of Bernard and Marjorie Thompson. Born August 11, 1936; educated Dean Close School, Cheltenham; Emmanuel College, Cambridge (MA 1971); Hon. Fellow, Queen Mary College, London 1986; Hon. DLitt, East London Polytechnic 1989; Hon. Fellow, Emmanuel College, Cambridge 1992; Hon. DD, Exeter 1995; Hon. DLitt, Bath 1998. Married 1965, Sally Patricia Stallworthy (1 son 1 daughter). *Armed Forces:* Second Lieutenant, 3rd Royal Tank Regiment 1959–61. *Career:* Deacon 1966; Curate, East Ham 1966–68; Chaplain, Cuddesdon College, Oxford 1968–71; Rector of Thamesmead and Ecumenical Team Leader 1971–78; Suffragan, then Area, Bishop of Stepney 1978–91; Chairman: London Diocesan Board for Social Responsibility 1978–96, Committee for Relations with People of Other Faiths, British Council of Churches 1983–89; Member, House of Bishops, General Synod of the Church of England 1983–; Chairman, Urban Studies Centre, then Urban Learning Foundation 1985–91; Co-Chairman, Interfaith Network (UK) 1987–92; Chairman: Church at Work, London 1989–91, Social Policy Committee, Board of Social Responsibility 1990–97; Bishop of Bath and Wells 1991–; Took his seat in the House of Lords 1997. *Other:* Member, NFU; Chairman: Tower Hamlets Association for Racial Justice, Auschwitz Exhibition 1983, The Children's Society 1997–; President, Royal Bath and West of England Show 1997–98; Co-President, English Churches Housing Group. *Awards Granted:* (Jointly) Sir Sigmund Sternberg Award for Christian-Jewish Relations 1987; Founding Society Award 1995. *Miscellaneous:* Visitor, Wadham College, Oxford 1992. FCA 1959. *Publications: Halfway: Reflections in Midlife,* 1986; *The Lord's Song,* 1990; *Stepney Calling,* 1991; *Why God?,* 1997. *Recreations:* Riding, painting, sport. *Clubs:* Farmers'. *Address:* The Rt Rev. the Lord Bishop of Bath and Wells, The Palace, Wells, Somerset, BA5 2PD *Tel:* 01749 672341 *E-Mail:* bishop@bathwells.anglican.org.

BAUER (Life Baron, UK), Peter Thomas Bauer; cr. 1983

Son of late Aladar Bauer. Born November 6, 1915; educated Scolae Piae, Budapest, Hungary; Gonville and Caius College, Cambridge (MA). *Career:* Fellow, Gonville and Caius College 1946–60, 1968–; Smuts Reader, Cambridge University 1956–60; Professor of Economics, London School of Economics (University of London) 1960–1983, Emeritus Professor 1983–. *Publications:* Author of several books and articles on economic subjects. *Clubs:* Garrick, Beefsteak. *Name, Style and Title:* Raised to the peerage as Baron Bauer, of Market Ward in the City of Cambridge 1983. A Conservative. *Address:* Professor The Lord Bauer, House of Lords, London, SW1A 0PW.

BEAUMONT OF WHITLEY (Life Baron, UK), Timothy Wentworth Beaumont; cr. 1967

Son of late Major Michael Wentworth Beaumont, TD, DL, MP and Hon. Faith Pease, daughter of 1st Baron Gainford, PC, DL. Born November 22, 1928; educated Gordonstoun; Christ Church, Oxford (MA); Westcott House, Cambridge. Married June 13, 1955, Mary Rose, daughter of Lieutenant-Colonel Charles Edward Wauchope, MC (1 son 2 daughters and 1 son deceased). *Trades Union:* Member, NUJ 1970–80. *Career:* Ordained 1955; Assistant Chaplain, Hong Kong Cathedral 1955–57; Vicar of Christchurch, Kowloon Tong, Hong Kong 1957–59; Owner of various periodicals including: *Time & Tide*, 1960–62, *New Christian*, 1965–70; Chairman, Studio Vista Ltd. (book publishers) 1963–68; Member, Parliamentary Assembly Council of Europe and Western European Union 1974–78; Leader, British Liberal Delegation 1977–78; Vice-Chairman, Council of Europe Liberal Group 1977–78; Vicar of St Philip's and St Luke's churches, Kew 1986–91; Joint Organiser, Southwark Diocese Spiritual Direction Course 1994–96. *Spokesman:* Liberal Party Spokesman on the Arts, Education, the Environment 1983–86; Liberal Democrat Party Spokesman on Conservation and Countryside 1993–99. *Select Committees:* Member, Select Committee on Sustainable Development 1994–95; Co-opted Member, Select Committee on European Communities Sub-Committee C (Environment, Public Health and Consumer Protection) 1997–; Member, Ecclesiastical Committee 1997–. *All-Party:* Former Treasurer, All-Party Family Farms Group, Secretary 1998–; Joint Secretary, All-Party Jubilee 2000 Coalition Group 1998–; Joint Vice-Chairman, All-Party Overseas Territories Group. *Party Groups (General):* Hon. Treasurer, Liberal Party 1965–66; Chairman, Liberal Party 1967–68, President 1969–70; Editor, *New Outlook* 1972–74; Chairman: Liberal Party Education Panel 1972–74, Liberal Party General Election Committee 1974; Co-ordinator, The Green Alliance 1978–80; Director of Policy Promotion, Liberal Party 1980–82; Member, Liberal Democrat Party National Policy Committee 1992–95. *Other:* Chairman, Institute of Research into Mental Retardation 1972–74; President, British Federation of Film Societies 1974–79. *Publications:* Author of *Where shall I put my Cross? exercising Christian responsibility in politics*, 1987; *The End of the Yellow Brick Road: Ways and Means to the Sustainable Society*, 1997. *Special Interests:* Ecological Economics, Poverty, Environment. *Name, Style and Title:* Raised to the peerage as Baron Beaumont of Whitley, of Child's Hill in the County of Greater London 1967. Green Party. *Address:* The Lord Beaumont of Whitley, 40 Elms Road, London, SW4 9EX *Tel:* Home: 020 7498 8664; House of Lords, London, SW1A 0PW *Tel:* House of Lords 020 7219 3121.

BELL (Life Baron, UK), Timothy John Leigh Bell; cr. 1998; Kt 1990

Son of Arthur and Greta Bell. Born October 18, 1941; educated Queen Elizabeth's Grammar School, Barnet, Herts. Married 1988, Virginia Wallis Hornbrook (1 son 1 daughter). *Career:* ABC Television 1959–61; Colman Prentis and Varley 1961–63; Hobson Bates 1963–66; Geers Gross 1966–70; Managing Director, Saatchi and Saatchi 1970–75; Chairman and Managing Director, Saatchi and Saatchi Compton 1975–85; Group Chief Executive, Lowe Howard-Spink Campbell Ewald 1985–87; Deputy Chairman, Lowe Hoard-Spink and Bell 1987–89; Chairman, Lowe Bell Communications 1987–; Director, Centre for Policy Studies 1989–92; Chairman, Chime Communications plc 1994–. *Other:* Member: Public Relations Committee, Greater London Fund for the Blind 1979–86, Council, Royal Opera House 1982–85; Chairman, Charity Projects 1984–93, President 1993–; Member: Public Affairs, World Wide Fund for Nature 1985–88, Council, School of Communication Arts 1985–87. *Miscellaneous:* Governor, British Film Institute 1983–86; Special Adviser: to Chairman, National Coal Board 1984–86, to South Bank Board 1985–86. *Honours:* Kt 1990. *Name, Style and Title:* Raised to the peerage as Baron Bell, of Belgravia in the City of Westminster 1998. A Conservative. *Address:* The Lord Bell, Office: 7 Hertford Street, London, W1Y 7DY.

BELLWIN (Life Baron, UK), Irwin Norman Bellow; cr. 1979; DL

Son of late Abraham Bellow. Born February 7, 1923; educated Leeds Grammar School; Leeds University (LLB). Married November 15, 1948, Doreen Barbara, daughter of Myer Saperia (1 son 2 daughters). *Councils, Public Bodies:* Councillor, Leeds City Council 1965–79; JP, City of Leeds 1969; Leader of Leeds City Council 1975–79; DL, West Yorkshire 1991–. *House of Lords:* Parliamentary Under-Secretary of State at Department of the Environment 1979–83; Minister of State for Local Government at Department of the Environment 1983–1984. *Other:* Former Vice-President, International New Towns Association; Vice-Chairman, Board of Governors, Leeds Grammar School. *Trusts, etc:* Chairman, North Hull Housing Action Trust 1993–99. *Miscellaneous:* Member, Commission for the New Towns 1985–95; Vice-Chairman, Association of Metropolitan Authorities 1976–79. Past Master, Guild of World Traders in London 1990. *Recreations:* Golf (President Moor Allerton Golf Club, Leeds). *Name, Style and Title:* Raised to the peerage as Baron Bellwin, of the City of Leeds 1979. A Conservative. *Address:* The Lord Bellwin, DL, Woodside Lodge, Ling Lane, Scarcroft, Leeds, West Yorkshire, LS14 3HX.

BELSTEAD (2nd Baron, UK), John Julian Ganzoni; cr. 1938; (Life) Baron Ganzoni (UK) 1999; 2nd Bt of Ipswich (UK) 1929; PC 1983

Son of 1st Baron, DL. Born September 30, 1932. Succeeded his father 1958; educated Eton; Christ Church, Oxford. *Councils, Public Bodies:* JP for Borough of Ipswich 1962; DL, Suffolk 1979–94, Lord Lieutenant 1994–; Chairman, The Parole Board 1992–97. *House of Lords:* Parliamentary Under-Secretary of State: Department of Education and Science 1970–1973, Northern Ireland Office 1973–74, Home Office 1979–82; Minister of State: Foreign and Commonwealth Office 1982–83, Ministry of Agriculture, Fisheries and Food 1983–87, Department of Environment 1987–88; Deputy Leader of House of Lords 1983–87; Lord Privy Seal and Leader of the House of Lords 1987–90; Paymaster General and Deputy to the Secretary of State for Northern Ireland 1990–92. *Spokesman:* Government Spokesman on: Trade and Industry 1982–84, Employment 1984–85, Arts and Civil Service 1985–87. *Other:* Chairman, Association of Governing Bodies of Public Schools 1974–79. *Honours:* PC 1983. *Sportsclubs:* All England Lawn Tennis. *Clubs:* MCC, Boodle's. *Heir:* None. *Name, Style and Title:* Created a life peer as Baron Ganzoni, of Ipswich in the County of Suffolk 1999. A Conservative. *Address:* The Rt Hon. the Lord Belstead, House of Lords, London, SW1A 0PW.

BIFFEN (Life Baron, UK) (William) John Biffen; cr. 1997; PC 1979; DL

Son of late Victor W. Biffen. Born November 3, 1930; educated Dr Morgan's Grammar School, Bridgwater; Jesus College, Cambridge (BA). Married November 2, 1979, Mrs Sarah Wood, daughter of J. A. C. Drew (1 step son 1 step daughter). *Councils, Public Bodies:* DL, Shropshire 1993–. *Career:* Tube Investments Ltd. 1953–60; Economist Intelligence Unit 1960–61; Member Board: Glynwed International 1987–, Rockware Group 1988–91, J. Bibby & Sons 1988–97; Barlow International plc 1997–. *House of Commons:* Contested (Conservative) Coventry East 1959; MP (Conservative) for Oswestry By-election 1961–83 and for Shropshire North 1983–97; Chief Secretary to the Treasury 1979–81; Secretary of State for Trade 1981–82; Lord President of the Council 1982–83; Leader of the House of Commons 1982–87; Lord Privy Seal 1983–87. *Party Groups (General):* Vice-Chairman, Federation of University Conservative and Unionist Associations. *Honours:* PC 1979. *Publications:* Author of *Inside the House of Commons*, 1989. *Name, Style and Title:* Raised to the peerage as Baron Biffen, of Tanat in the County of Shropshire 1997. A Conservative. *Address:* The Rt Hon. the Lord Biffen, DL, House of Lords, London, SW1A 0PW.

BINGHAM OF CORNHILL (Life Baron, UK), Thomas Henry Bingham; cr. 1996; Kt 1980; PC 1986

Son of late Dr Thomas Bingham and Dr Catherine Bingham. Born October 13, 1933; educated Sedbergh; Balliol College, Oxford (MA, Gibbs Scholar in Modern History 1956); Hon. Fellow, Balliol College, Oxford 1989; Presentation Fellow, King's College, London 1992; Fellow, Queen Mary and Westfield College, London 1993; Hon. Bencher, Inn of Court, Northern Ireland 1993; Hon. LLD, Birmingham 1993; Hon. DCL, Oxford 1994; Hon. DU, Essex 1997; Hon. Fellow: University College, London 1997, College of Estate Management 1997, Nuffield College 1998; Hon. LLD: Wales 1998, London 1998, Glamorgan 1999. Married 1963, Elizabeth, daughter of late Peter Loxley (2 sons 1 daughter). *Armed Forces:* 2nd Lieutenant, Royal Ulster Rifles 1952–54; London Irish Rifles (TA) 1954–59. *Career:* Called to the Bar, Gray's Inn 1959, Bencher 1979; Standing Junior Counsel to Department of Employment 1968–72; QC 1972; A Recorder of the Crown Court 1975–80; Leader, Investigation into the supply of petroleum products to Rhodesia 1977–78; Judge of the High Court of Justice, Queen's Bench Division and Judge of the Commercial Court 1980–86; A Lord Justice of Appeal 1986–92; Chairman: King's Fund Working Parties into Statutory Registration of Osteopaths and Chiropractors 1989–93, Inquiry into the Supervision of the Bank of Credit and Commerce 1991–92; Interceptions Commissioner 1992–94; Master of the Rolls 1992–96; Lord Chief Justice of England 1996–; Member, Lord Chancellor's Law Reform Committee. *Other:* Governor, Sedbergh 1978–88; Chairman, Council of Legal Education 1982–86; Fellow, Winchester 1983–93; Governor, Atlantic College 1984–89; Visitor, Balliol College, Oxford 1986–; Advisory Council, Centre for Commercial Law Studies, Queen Mary and Westfield College, London University 1989–92; Visitor, Royal Postgraduate Medical School 1989–99; Advisory Council on Public Records 1992–96; President, British Records Association 1992–96; Visitor, Nuffield College, Oxford 1992–96; Royal Commission of Historical Manuscripts 1994–; Visitor: Darwin College, Cambridge 1996, Templeton College, Oxford 1996–. *Trusts, etc:* Trustee, Pilgrim Trust 1991–; Magna Carta Trust 1992–96. *Publications:* Assistant Editor, *Chitty on Contracts* (22nd edition), 1961. *Clubs:* Athenaeum. *Name, Style and Title:* Raised to the peerage as Baron Bingham of Cornhill, of Boughrood in the County of Powys 1996. A Cross-Bencher. *Address:* The Rt Hon. the Lord Bingham of Cornhill, Royal Courts of Justice, Strand, London, WC2A 2LL.

BIRMINGHAM (7th Bishop of), Mark Santer

Son of late Rev. Canon Eric Arthur Robert Santer and late Phyllis Clare Barlow. Born December 29, 1936; educated Marlborough; Queens' College, Cambridge; Westcott House, Cambridge; Hon. Fellow: Clare College, Cambridge 1987, Queens' College, Cambridge 1991; Hon. DD, University of Birmingham 1998; DD, Lambeth 1999. Married 1st, 1964, Henriette Cornelia Weststrate (died August 8, 1994) (1 son 2 daughters); married 2nd, 1997, Sabine Boehmig Bird. *Career:* Deacon 1963; Assistant Curate, Cuddesdon 1963–67; Tutor, Cuddesdon Theological College 1963–67; Priest 1964; Fellow and Dean of Clare College, Cambridge 1967–72; University Assistant Lecturer in Divinity 1968–72; Principal, Westcott House, Cambridge 1973–81; Hon. Canon, Winchester Cathedral 1978–81; Bishop of Kensington 1981–87; Co-Chairman, Anglican Roman Catholic International Commission 1983–; Bishop of Birmingham 1987–; Took his seat in the House of Lords 1994. *Other:* Member, Council of NACRO 1985–; Chairman, NACRO Young Offenders' Committee 1987–97. *Miscellaneous:* Chairman, Anglian-Roman Catholic International Commission 1983–98. *Publications:* (contributor) *The Phenomenon of Christian Belief*, 1970; (jointly) *Documents in Early Christian Thought*, 1975; *Their Lord and Ours*, 1982; (contributor) *The Church and the State*, 1984; (contributor) *Dropping the Bomb*, 1985; (contributor) *Reconciling Memories*, 1988, 1998. *Address:* The Rt Rev. the Lord Bishop of Birmingham, Bishop's Croft, Old Church Road, Harborne, Birmingham, B17 0BG *Tel:* 0121–427 1163 *Fax:* 0121–426 1322.

BLACKBURN (7th Bishop of), Alan David Chesters

Son of Herbert and Catherine Chesters. Born August 26, 1937; educated Elland Grammar School, West Yorkshire; St Chad's College, University of Durham (BA Modern History); St Catherine's College, Oxford (BA Theology, MA). Married 1975, Jennie Garrett (1 son). *Career:* Curate of St Anne's, Wandsworth 1962–66; Chaplain and Head of Religious Education, Tiffin School, Kingston-upon-Thames 1966–72; Director of Education and Rector of Brancepeth, Diocese of Durham 1972–84; Honorary Canon, Durham Cathedral 1975–84; Member. General Synod of the Church of England 1975, Standing Committee 1985–89, 1990–95; A Church Commissioner 1982–98, Member, Board of Governors 1984–89, 1992–98; Archdeacon of Halifax 1985–89; Bishop of Blackburn 1989–; Chairman, Higher Education Funding Council for England Church Colleges Committee 1993–99; President, Woodard Corporation 1994–99; Member: The Countryside Agency 1994–; The Countryside Commission 1995–99, Took his seat in the House of Lords 1995. *Other:* Chairman, Governors of The University College of St Martin's, Lancaster 1990–; President, Relate Lancashire 1997; Governor, Elmslie School, Blackpool; Member, Corporation Board, Blackburn College. *Special Interests:* Education, Countryside, Transport. *Recreations:* Railways, hill walking, reading. *Address:* The Rt Rev. the Lord Bishop of Blackburn, Bishop's House, Ribchester Road, Blackburn, Lancashire, BB1 9EF.

BLACKSTONE (Life Baroness, UK), Tessa Ann Vosper Blackstone; cr. 1987

Daughter of late Geoffrey Blackstone, CBE, GM, and of Joanna (née Vosper). Born September 27, 1942; educated Ware Grammar School; LSE (BScSoc, PhD); Hon. Doctorates: Bradford University 1990, Bristol Polytechnic 1991, Middlesex University 1993, Aberdeen University 1994, St Andrew's University 1995; Hon. Fellow, LSE 1995; Hon. Doctorates: Strathclyde University 1996, Leeds Metropolitan University 1996; Fellow, Birbeck College 1997; Hon. Degree, l'Université Paris Dauphine. Married 1963, Tom Evans (1 son 1 daughter) (marriage dissolved 1975, he died 1985). *Career:* Associate Lecturer, Enfield College 1965–66; Assistant Lecturer then Lecturer, Department of Social Administration, LSE 1966–75; Fellow, Centre for Studies in Social Policy 1972–74; Adviser, Central Policy Review Staff, Cabinet Office 1975–78; Professor of Educational Administration, University of London Institute of Education 1978–83; Deputy Education Officer (Resources), Inner London Education Authority 1983–86; Fellow, Policy Studies Institute 1987; Master, Birkbeck College, University of London October 1987–97. *House of Lords:* Minister of State, Department for Education and Employment (Minister for Education and Employment) (Lords) 1997–. *Spokesman:* Opposition Spokesman on: Education and Science 1988–96, Treasury Matters 1990–91; Principal Opposition Spokesman on Education and Science 1990–92; Opposition Spokesman on Trade and Industry 1992–96; Principal Opposition Spokesman on Foreign Affairs 1992–97. *Other:* Chairman and Founder Member, Institute for Public Policy Research 1988–97; Member of Board, Royal Opera House 1987–97, Chairman, Ballet Board 1991–97. *Trusts, etc:* Member, Board of Trustees, The Natural History Museum 1992–97. *Miscellaneous:* Chairman, General Advisory Council of BBC 1987–91. *Publications:* Author of: *A Fair Start*, 1971; (with William Plowden) *Inside the Think Tank: Advising the Cabinet* 1971–84, 1988; *Prison and Penal Reform*, 1982; *The Academic Labour Market*, 1974 (co-author); (with Paul Lodge) *Educational Policy and Educational Inequality*, 1982; (with Jo Mortimore) *Disadvantage and Education*, 1982; (with Gareth Williams) *Response to Adversity*, 1983; (with Bhiku Parekh, Peter Sanders) *Race Relations in Britain*, 1998. *Special Interests:* Education, Social Policy, Foreign Affairs, Arts. *Recreations:* Tennis, walking, ballet, opera, cinema. *Name, Style and Title:* Raised to the peerage as Baroness Blackstone, of Stoke Newington in the County of Greater London 1987. Labour. *Address:* The Baroness Blackstone, Department for Education and Employment, Sanctuary Buildings, Great Smith Street, London, SW1P 3BT *Tel:* 020 7925 6242 *Fax:* 020 7925 5011.

BLACKWELL (Life Baron, UK), Norman Roy Blackwell; cr. 1997

Son of Albert and Frances Blackwell. Born July 29, 1952; educated Latymer Upper School, Hammersmith; Royal Academy of Music (Junior Exhibitioner); Trinity College, Cambridge (MA); Wharton Business School, University of Pennsylvania (AM, MBA, PhD 1976). Married 1974, Brenda Clucas (3 sons 2 daughters). *Career:* Plessey Company 1976–78; Partner, McKinsey & Co 1978–95, Partner 1984; Special Adviser, Prime Minister's Policy Unit 1986–87, Head 1995–97; Director, Group Development, NatWest Group 1997–. *Recreations:* Classical music, walking. *Clubs:* Carlton, Royal Automobile. *Name, Style and Title:* Raised to the peerage as Baron Blackwell, of Woodcote in the County of Surrey 1997. A Conservative. *Address:* The Lord Blackwell, House of Lords, London, SW1A 0PW *Tel:* 020 7726 1000.

BLAKE (Life Baron, UK), Robert Norman William Blake; cr. 1971; FBA 1967

Son of late William Joseph Blake, of Brundall, Norfolk and late Norah Lindley, née Daynes. Born December 23, 1916; educated King Edward VI School, Norwich; Magdalen College, Oxford; Hon. Student, Christ Church, Oxford 1977; Hon. Fellow: The Queen's College, Oxford 1987, Pembroke College, Cambridge 1992. Married August 22, 1953, Patricia Mary, eldest daughter of Thomas Richard Waters, of Great Plumstead, Norfolk and Cicelie Bowyer Howlett (3 daughters). *Armed Forces:* Served Royal Artillery 1939–46 (despatches 1944). *Councils, Public Bodies:* Councillor (Conservative), Oxford City Council 1957–64; JP, Oxford City 1964–85. *Career:* Student and Tutor in Politics, Christ Church, Oxford 1947–68; Provost, The Queen's College, Oxford 1968–87; A Pro Vice-Chancellor of Oxford 1971–87; A Director of Channel Four Television 1983–87. *Party Groups:* Member, Association of Conservative Peers 1971–. *Other:* High Steward, Westminster Abbey 1989–99. *Trusts, etc:* Trustee, British Museum 1978–88, Rhodes Trustee 1971–87, Beit Trustee 1973–99, Chairman 1983. *Miscellaneous:* Member, Royal Commission on Historical Manuscripts 1975, Chairman 1982–89. Fellow, British Academy 1967. Member: Dyers' Company 1947–, Prime Warden 1976–77. *Publications:* Author of several books including: *The Unknown Prime Minister, Bonar Law,* 1955; *Disraeli,* 1966; *The Conservative Party from Peel to Churchill,* 1970 (re-issued as *Peel to Thatcher,* 1985 and *Peel to Major,* 1997); *A History of Rhodesia,* 1977; *The Decline of Power 1915–64,* 1985. *Special Interests:* Electoral Reform, Education, Foreign Affairs. *Clubs:* Vincent's (Oxford), United Oxford and Cambridge University, Brooks's, Beefsteak, Pratt's, Norfolk (Norwich). *Name, Style and Title:* Raised to the peerage as Baron Blake, of Braydeston in the County of Norfolk 1971. A Conservative. *Address:* The Lord Blake, Riverview House, Brundall, Norfolk, NR13 5LA *Tel:* 01603 712133.

BLAKER (Life Baron, UK), Peter Allan Renshaw Blaker; cr. 1994; PC 1983; KCMG 1983

Son of late Cedric Blaker, CBE, MC, ED and Louisa Douglas Chapple. Born October 4, 1922; educated Shrewsbury; Toronto University (BA 1st Class Classics); New College, Oxford (MA 1st Class Jurisprudence). Married October 24, 1953, Jennifer, daughter of late Sir Pierson Dixon, GCMG, CB (1 son 2 daughters). *Armed Forces:* Served with Argyll and Sutherland Highlanders of Canada 1942–46 (wounded; Captain). *Career:* Admitted a Solicitor 1948; Called to the Bar, Lincoln's Inn 1952; HM Foreign Service 1953–64, serving in Cambodia, Canada, the UN and London; Private Secretary to the Minister of State, Foreign Office 1962–64, attended the signing of the Nuclear Test Ban Treaty, Moscow 1963; Chairman, Royal Ordnance Factories 1972–74. *House of Commons:* MP (Conservative), Blackpool South 1964–92; PPS to Chancellor of the Exchequer 1970–72; Parliamentary Under-Secretary of State: Army, Ministry of Defence 1972–74, Foreign and Commonwealth Office 1974; Minister of State: FCO 1979–81, Armed Forces, MoD 1981–83. *Whip (Commons):* An Opposition Whip 1966–67. *Select Committees (Commons):* Member: Select Committee on Conduct of Members 1976–77, Public Accounts Commission 1987–92. *Backbench Committees (Commons):* Joint Secretary: Conservative Parliamentary Foreign Affairs Committee 1965–66, Trade Committee 1967–70, Executive Committee of 1922 Committee 1967–70; Vice-Chairman, Conservative Foreign and Commonwealth Affairs Committee 1974–79, Chairman 1983–92.

All-Party Committees (Commons): Vice-Chairman, All-Party Tourism Committee 1974–79; Chairman, Hong Kong Parliamentary Group 1970–72, 1983–92; Member, Exec Committee British-American Parliamentary Group 1975–79. *International Bodies (Commons):* Hon. Secretary, Franco-British Parliamentary Relations Committee 1975–79. *Party Groups (General):* Vice-President, Conservative Foreign and Commonwealth Council 1983–92, Patron 1992–. *Other:* Chairman of Governors, Welbeck College 1972–74; Member of Council: Royal Institute for International Affairs (Chatham House) 1977–79, 1986–90; Freedom Association 1984–97. *Trusts, etc:* Trustee, Institute for Negotiation and Conciliation 1984–92. *Miscellaneous:* Vice-Chairman, Peace Through NATO 1983–93; Member, Intelligence and Security Committee 1996–97. *Honours:* PC 1983; KCMG 1983. *Publications:* Author of: *Coping with the Soviet Union*, 1977; *Small is Dangerous: micro states in a macro world*, 1984. *Special Interests:* Foreign Affairs, Commonwealth, Defence, Tourism. *Recreations:* Opera, tennis, sailing. *Name, Style and Title:* Raised to the peerage as Baron Blaker, of Blackpool in the County of Lancashire and of Lindfield in the County of West Sussex 1994. A Conservative. *Address:* The Rt Hon. the Lord Blaker, KCMG, House of Lords, London, SW1A 0PW.

BLATCH (Life Baroness, UK), Emily May Blatch; cr. 1987; CBE 1983; PC 1993

Daughter of late Stephen and Sarah Triggs. Born July 24, 1937; educated Prenton Girls School, Birkenhead; Rotarian Paul Harris Fellow 1992; Hon. LLD, Teesside University 1997. Married September 7, 1963, John Richard, AFC, son of George Henry Blatch (1 son 1 twin son and daughter and 1 son deceased). *Armed Forces:* Women's Royal Air Force, Air Traffic Control 1955–59. *Councils, Public Bodies:* Leader, Cambridgeshire County Council 1981–85; Member, Peterborough Development Corporation 1984–88. *Career:* Air Traffic Control (Civilian) 1959–63. *House of Lords:* Parliamentary Under-Secretary of State, Department of Environment 1990–91; Minister of State (Heritage) 1991–92; Minister of State: Department for Education 1992–94, Home Office 1994–97; Shadow Minister for Education 1997–. *Whip:* A Baroness in Waiting (Government Whip) January–September 1990. *Spokesman:* A Spokeswoman on Education and Employment 1998–. *Party Groups:* Member, Association of Conservative Peers. *Other:* Member, European Economic and Social Committee 1986–87; President, National Benevolent Institute 1988–; National Vice-President, Alzheimers Disease Society; Patron: Macmillan Nurses, Cathedral Camps; Member, Air League Council. *Trusts, etc:* Trustee: Dorman Museum, RAF Museum. *Honours:* CBE 1983; PC 1993. FRSA 1985. *Special Interests:* Local Government Management, Education, Anglo-American Relations. *Recreations:* Family, music, theatre. *Clubs:* Royal Air Force. *Name, Style and Title:* Raised to the peerage as Baroness Blatch, of Hinchingbrooke, in the County of Cambridgeshire 1987. A Conservative. *Address:* The Rt Hon. the Baroness Blatch, CBE, House of Lords, London, SW1A 0PW.

BLEASE (Life Baron, UK), William John Blease; cr. 1978

Son of late William John Blease. Born May 28, 1914; educated Public Elementary School; Technical College, Belfast; Hon. DLitt, New University of Ulster 1972; Hon. LLD, Queen's University Belfast 1982. Married July 14, 1939, Sarah Evelyn (died November 25, 1995), daughter of William J. Caldwell (3 sons 1 daughter). *Trades Union:* Divisional Councillor, Union Shop Workers 1948–59; Northern Ireland Officer, Irish Congress of Trade Unions 1959–75. *Councils, Public Bodies:* JP, County Borough of Belfast 1974–. *Career:* Apprentice to Provision Trade 1930; Branch Manager Co-op. 1939. *Whip:* An Opposition Whip 1979–84. *Spokesman:* Formerly Opposition Spokesman on Northern Ireland Affairs 1979–83. *All-Party:* Member, All-Party Groups on: Ageism, Children, Energy Studies, Maritime Affairs. *International Bodies:* Member, British-Irish Inter-Parliamentary Body 1990–. *Other:* President, Northern Ireland Hospice 1980–85, Vice-President 1985–95, Patron 1995–; Member, Board of Governors, St MacNissi's College 1981–91; President: Northern Ireland Care and Resettlement of Offenders (NICRO) 1982–84, Northern Ireland Festival of Youth Society 1982–84, Belfast East Group for Disabled 1983–88; Patron, Northern Ireland Widows' Association 1985–90; Member, Board of Co-operative Development Agency Northern Ireland 1987–91, Patron 1991–; President, Belfast Housing Aid 1988–95; Member of Management Board, Rathgael Child Care and Youth Treatment Centre 1989–93; Patron, Action Cancer 1994–; Joint President, Northern Ireland Forum on Industrial Relations (NIFIR) 1994–; Hon. President, Institute of Management (Belfast

Branch) 1995–. *Awards Granted:* Awarded New Ireland University Peace Trophy 1971. *Trusts, etc:* Trustee, Belfast Charitable Trust for Integrated Education 1984–88; Member, Board of Trustees, TSB Foundation (Northern Ireland) 1986–94. *Miscellaneous:* Northern Ireland Economic Council 1964–75; Member, Independent Broadcasting Authority 1974–79; Research Fellow, New University of Ulster (NUU) 1976–78; Member, Standing Commission on Human Rights 1977–79; Appointed Rapporteur to EEC on Cross Border Communications Study on Londonderry-Donegal 1978–79; Chairman, Community Service Order Committee 1979–80. Elected Fellow, British Institute of Management 1981. *Name, Style and Title:* Raised to the peerage as Baron Blease, of Cromac in the City of Belfast 1978. Labour. *Address:* The Lord Blease, House of Lords, London, SW1A 0PW.

BLEDISLOE (3rd Viscount, UK), Christopher Hiley Ludlow Bathurst; cr. 1935; 3rd Baron Bledisloe (UK) 1918; QC 1978

Son of 2nd Viscount, QC. Born June 24, 1934. Succeeded his father 1979; educated Eton; Trinity College, Oxford. Married 1962, Elizabeth Mary, daughter of late Sir Edward Thompson (2 sons 1 daughter) (marriage dissolved 1986). *Armed Forces:* 2nd Lieutenant, 11th Hussars (PAO) 1954–55. *Career:* Called to Bar Gray's Inn 1959; QC 1978; Director, Portsmouth & Sunderland Newspapers plc. *House of Lords:* An elected hereditary peer 1999–. *Trusts, etc:* Trustee, Equitas. *Clubs:* Garrick. *Heir:* His son, Hon. Rupert Edward Ludlow Bathurst, born March 13, 1964. A Cross-Bencher. *Address:* The Viscount Bledisloe, QC, Lydney Park, Gloucestershire, GL15 6BT *Tel:* 01594 842566; Fountain Court, Temple, London, EC4Y 9DH *Tel:* 020 7583 3335; 44 Sussex Street, London, SW1V 4RH *Tel:* 020 7630 6300.

BLOOD (Life Baroness, UK), May Blood; cr. 1999; MBE

Daughter of late William and Mary Blood. Born May 26, 1938; educated Donegall Road Primary, Belfast; Linfield Secondary, Belfast; Hon. Doctorate. *Trades Union:* Member, TGWU. *Career:* Cutting Supervisor, Blackstaff Mill 1952–90; Community Worker, Gt Shankill Partnership 1990–. *Miscellaneous:* Member: Independent Industrial Tribunals, Labour Relations Agency. *Honours:* MBE. *Special Interests:* Women's Issues, Low Pay, Working Class Issues, Family, Children. *Recreations:* Reading, gardening. *Name, Style and Title:* Raised to the peerage as Baroness Blood, of Blackwatertown in the County of Armagh 1999. A Cross-Bencher. *Address:* The Baroness Blood, MBE, 7 Blackmountain Place, Belfast, BT13 3TT *Tel:* 028 9032 6514; Alessie Centre, 60 Shankhill Road, Belfast, BT13 2BD *Tel:* 028 9087 4000 *Fax:* 028 9087 4009.

BLYTH OF ROWINGTON (Life Baron, UK), James Blyth; cr. 1995; Kt 1985

Son of Daniel and Jane Blyth. Born May 8, 1940; educated Spiers School; Glasgow University (MA); Hon. LLD, Nottingham University 1992; Hon. Fellow, London Business School 1997. Married 1967, Pamela Anne Campbell Dixon (1 daughter and 1 son deceased). *Career:* Mobil Oil Company 1963–69; General Foods Ltd 1969–71; Mars Ltd 1971–74; General Manager: Lucas Batteries Ltd 1974–77, Lucas Aerospace Ltd 1977–81; Head of Defence Sales, Ministry of Defence 1981–85; Non-executive Director, Imperial Group plc 1984–86; Managing Director, Plessey Electronic Systems 1985–86; Chief Executive, The Plessey Co plc 1986–87; Non-executive Director, Cadbury-Schweppes plc 1986–90; Director and Chief Executive, The Boots Company plc 1987–, Deputy Chairman 1994–98, Chairman 1998–; Non-executive Director: British Aerospace 1990–94, Anixter Inc 1995–; Director: NatWest Group 1998–, Diaoeo 1999–. *Other:* Governor, London Business School 1987–96. *Miscellaneous:* Chairman, Advisory panel on Citizen's Charter 1991–97. *Honours:* Kt 1985. FRAeS. Liveryman, Coachmakers' and Coach Harness Makers' Company. *Recreations:* Skiing, tennis, paintings, theatre. *Sportsclubs:* The Queen's Club. *Clubs:* East India, Devonshire, Sports and Public Schools, Royal Automobile. *Name, Style and Title:* Raised to the peerage as Baron Blyth of Rowington, of Rowington in the County of Warwickshire 1995. A Conservative. *Address:* The Lord Blyth of Rowington, The Boots Company plc., Nottingham, NG2 3AA *E-Mail:* chairmans.office@boots-plc.com.

BOARDMAN (Life Baron, UK), Thomas Gray Boardman; cr. 1980; MC 1944; TD 1952; DL

Son of late John Clayton Boardman and late Janet Boardman (née Houston). Born January 12, 1919; educated Bromsgrove; Hon. LLD, University of Nottingham 1987; Hon. DCL, The City University 1988; Companionship of Leicester Polytechnic (now De Montfort University) 1990. Married 1948, Norah Mary Deirdre, daughter of late Hubert Gough and widow of John Chaworth-Musters (2 sons 1 daughter). *Armed Forces:* Served Northants Yeomanry 1939–45, 1947–56, Commanding 1954–56. *Councils, Public Bodies:* DL, Northants 1977–; High Sheriff, Northants 1979; One of HM Lieutenants for the City of London 1979–. *Career:* Qualified as a Solicitor 1947; Director, Chamberlain Phipps Ltd 1958–72, Chairman 1968–72; Director, Allied Breweries Ltd 1968–72, 1974–77, Vice-Chairman 1975–76; Director, Steetley plc 1975–83, Chairman 1978–83; Director, National Westminster Bank plc 1979, Chairman 1983–89; Director, MEPC plc 1980–89; Chairman, Committee of London and Scottish Banks 1987–89; Advisory Board, L.E.K. 1990–97; Chairman, Heron International NV 1993–95. *House of Commons:* MP (Conservative): Leicester South West 1967–74, Leicester South February-September 1974; Minister for Industry, Department of Trade and Industry 1972–74; Chief Secretary to Treasury 1974. *Backbench Committees (Commons):* Member, 1922 Executive 1968–72, 1974; Chairman, Trade Committee 1970–72. *Select Committees:* Member, Sub-Committee A of House of Lords Select Committee on European Communities 1991–94, Co-opted Member 1997–. *Party Groups:* Member, Executive Association of Conservative Peers 1981–84, 1991–95. *Party Groups (General):* Honorary Treasurer, Conservative Party 1981–82. *Other:* President, Association of British Chambers of Commerce 1977–80. *Trusts, etc:* Chairman, Appeal for Prince's Youth Business Trust (PYBT) 1987–90, Trustee 1989–93. *Honours:* MC 1944; TD 1952. Freeman, City of London. *Special Interests:* Finance, Trade and Industry. *Recreations:* Riding, hunting. *Clubs:* Cavalry and Guards. *Name, Style and Title:* Raised to the peerage as Baron Boardman, of Welford in the County of Northampton 1980. A Conservative. *Address:* The Lord Boardman, MC, TD, DL, The Manor House, Welford, Northampton, NN6 6HX *Tel:* 01858 575235; 29 Tufton Court, Tufton Street, London, SW1P 3QH *Tel:* 020 7222 6793.

BORRIE (Life Baron, UK), Gordon (Johnson) Borrie; cr. 1995; Kt 1982; QC 1986

Son of Stanley Borrie. Born March 13, 1931; educated John Bright Grammar School, Llandudno; University of Manchester (LLB, LLM); Hon. LLD: City of London Polytechnic 1989, Manchester University 1990, Hull University 1991, Dundee University 1993, Nottingham Trent University 1996, University of the West of England 1997. Married 1960, Dorene, daughter of Herbert Toland, of Toronto, Canada. *Armed Forces:* National Service with Army Legal Services, HQ British Commonwealth Forces in Korea 1952–54. *Career:* Barrister-at-Law and Harmsworth Scholar of the Middle Temple; Called to the Bar, Middle Temple 1952, Bencher 1980; Practiced as a barrister in London 1954–57; Lecturer and later Senior Lecturer, College of Law 1957–64; University of Birmingham: Senior Lecturer in Law 1965–68, Professor of English Law and Director, Institute of Judicial Administration 1969–76, Dean of Faculty of Law 1974–76, Hon. Professor of Law 1989–; Member: Parole Board for England and Wales 1971–74, CNAA Legal Studies Board 1971–76; Member, Equal Opportunities Commission 1975–76; Director General of Fair Trading 1976–92; Director: Woolwich Building Society 1992–, Three Valleys Water 1992–, Chairman, Commission on Social Justice 1992–94; Director: Mirror Group 1993–99, TeleWest 1994–, General Utilities 1998–. *Select Committees:* Member: European Communities Committee 1997–, Select Committee on European Communities Sub-Committee E (Law and Institutions) 1996–. *Other:* Governor, Birmingham College of Commerce 1966–70; Member: Circuit Advisory Committee, Birmingham Group of Courts 1972–74, Council, Consumers' Association 1972–75, Consumer Protection Advisory Committee 1973–76; Vice-President, Institute of Trading Standards Administration 1985–92 and 1997–, President 1992–97; Patron, Public Concern at Work; Jubilee Patron, MIND; Access to Justice Advisory Board, NSPCC. *Miscellaneous:* Contested (Labour): Croydon North East 1955, Ilford South 1959 General Elections. *Honours:* Kt 1982. Fellow: Chartered Institute of Arbitrators, Royal Society of Arts. *Publications: Commercial Law,* 1962; *The Consumer, Society and the Law,* 1963 (with Professor A. L. Diamond); *Law of Contempt,* 1973 (with N. V. Lowe); *The Development of Consumer Law and Policy* (Hamlyn Lectures) 1984. *Recreations:* Gastronomy, playing the piano, travel. *Clubs:* Garrick, Reform. *Name, Style and Title:* Raised to the peerage as Baron Borrie, of Abbots Morton in the County of Hereford and Worcester 1995. Labour. *Address:* The Lord Borrie, QC, Manor Farm, Abbots Morton, Worcestershire, WR7 4NA *Tel:* 01386 792330; 4 Brick Court, Temple, London, EC4Y 9AD *Tel:* 020 7353 4434.

BOSTON OF FAVERSHAM (Life Baron, UK), Terence George Boston; cr. 1976; QC 1981

Son of late George Thomas and Kate Boston. Born March 21, 1930; educated Woolwich Polytechnic School; King's College, University of London. Married April 3, 1962, Margaret Joyce, eldest daughter of late R. H. J. Head and of late Mrs E. M. Winters, and step-daughter of late H. F. Winters, all of Melbourne, Australia. *Armed Forces:* Commissioned RAF; National Service 1950–52. *Career:* BBC News Sub-editor 1957–60; Senior Producer, Current Affairs 1960–64; Called to the Bar, Inner Temple 1960; UK Delegate, UN General Assembly 1976–78; Chairman: TVS Entertainment plc 1980–90, TVS Television Ltd 1986–90, TVS Music Ltd 1983–90. *House of Commons:* MP (Labour) for Kent, Faversham division 1964–70; PPS: to Minister of Public Building and Works 1964–66, to Minister of Power 1966–68, to Minister of Transport 1968–69. *Whip (Commons):* Assistant Government Whip 1969–70. *Select Committees (Commons):* Member, Speaker's Conference on Electoral Law 1965–68. *House of Lords:* Minister of State, Home Office 1979; Deputy Chairman of Committees, House of Lords 1991–92; Principal Deputy Chairman of Committees 1992–94, Chairman of Committees 1994–97, 1997–; A Deputy Speaker of the House of Lords. *Spokesman:* Opposition Spokesman: Home Office Affairs 1979–84, Defence 1984–86. *Select Committees:* Member, Select Committee on Bill of Rights 1977–78; Member: Joint Select Committee on Statutory Instruments 1986–92, Select Committee on the Committee work of the House of Lords 1991–92; Chairman: Select Committee on the European Communities 1992–94, Select Committee on House of Lords' Offices 1994–97, 1997–; and other Domestic Select Committees of the House of Lords. *Party Groups (General):* Member: National Committee Young Socialists (then Labour League of Youth) 1949–51, Executive Committee, International Union of Socialist Youth 1950. *Publications:* Joint Author of *Do We Needs A Bill of Rights?*. *Recreations:* Fell-walking, opera. *Name, Style and Title:* Raised to the peerage as Baron Boston of Faversham, of Faversham in the County of Kent 1976. A Cross-Bencher. *Address:* The Lord Boston of Faversham, QC, House of Lords, London, SW1A 0PW.

BOWNESS (Life Baron, UK), Peter (Spencer) Bowness; cr. 1996; Kt 1987; CBE 1981; DL

Son of Hubert and Doreen Bowness. Born May 19, 1943; educated Whitgift School, Croydon. Married 1st, 1969 (1 daughter) (marriage dissolved), married 2nd, 1984, Mrs Patricia Jane Cook (1 step son). *Armed Forces:* Hon. Colonel, 151 (Greater London) Transport Regiment, Royal Corps of Transport (Volunteers) 1988–93. *Councils, Public Bodies:* Councillor, London Borough of Croydon 1968–, Leader 1976–94, Mayor 1979–80; Deputy Chairman, Association of Metropolitan Authorities 1978–80; Chairman, London Boroughs Association 1978–94; DL, Greater London 1981–; Member: Audit Commission 1983–95, London Residuary Body 1985–93, National Training Task Force 1989–92. *Career:* Admitted Solicitor 1966; Partner, Weightman Sadler, Solicitors, Purley, Surrey 1970–. *Spokesman:* An Opposition Spokesman on Environment, Transport and the Regions (Local Government) 1997–98. *Select Committees:* Chairman, Joint Committee on Draft Local Government (Organisation and Standards) Bill 1999. *All-Party:* Member, All-Party: London Group, Consumer Affairs and Trading Standards Group, Town Centre Management Group. *International Bodies (General):* Member: UK Delegation to Congress of Regional and Local Authorities of Europe (Council of Europe) 1990–98, UK Delegation to the Committee of the Regions of the EU (COR) 1994–98; Member of the Bureau and of Transport and Telecommunications Commission and of Institutional Affairs Commission (COR) 1994–98; Vice-President, European Peoples Party Group COR 1994–98. *Other:* Governor, Whitgift Foundation 1982–96; Member, Royal Society for the Protection of Birds. *Honours:* CBE 1981; Kt 1987. Freeman, City of London 1984. *Special Interests:* Local Government, Europe. *Recreations:* Travel, theatre. *Name, Style and Title:* Raised to the peerage as Baron Bowness, of Warlingham in the County of Surrey and of Croydon in the London Borough of Croydon 1996. A Conservative. *Address:* The Lord Bowness, CBE, DL, 1/2 The Exchange, Purley Road, Purley, Surrey, CR2 2YY *Tel:* 020 8660 6455 (Office) *Tel:* 01883 624546 (Home) *E-Mail:* bowness@globalnet.co.uk.

BRABAZON OF TARA (3rd Baron, UK), Ivon Anthony Moore-Brabazon; cr. 1942; DL

Son of 2nd Baron, CBE. Born December 20, 1946. Succeeded his father 1974; educated Harrow. Married September 8, 1979, Harriet Frances, daughter of Mervyn Peter de Courcy Hamilton, of Salisbury, Rhodesia (1 son 1 daughter). *Councils, Public Bodies:* DL, Isle of Wight 1993–. *Career:* Member, Stock Exchange 1972–84; Director: Aurigny Aviation Holdings Ltd, Exxtor Group CI Ltd. *House of Lords:* Parliamentary Under-Secretary of State, Department of Transport 1986–89; Minister of State: Foreign and Commonwealth Office 1989–90, Department of Transport 1990–92; An elected hereditary peer 1999–. *Whip:* A Lord in Waiting (Government Whip) 1984–86. *Spokesman:* House of Lords Spokesman on: Transport 1984–85, Trade and Industry, Treasury and Energy 1985–86; Opposition Spokesman on Environment, Transport and the Regions (Transport) 1998–. *Select Committees:* Member: House of Lords European Communities Sub-Committee B 1993–97, Select Committee on the Public Service 1996–97, Select Committee on House of Lords' Offices 1997–. *All-Party:* Member, All-Party London Group. *Other:* President, United Kingdom Warehousing Association 1992–; Deputy Chairman, Foundation for Sport and the Arts 1992–; Council Member, Shipwrecked Mariners' Society 1993–; President, Natural Gas Vehicles Association 1995–97; Deputy President, Institute of the Motor Industry 1997–98, President 1998–; President, British International Freight Association 1997–98. *Trusts, etc:* Trustee, Medical Commission on Accident Prevention. *Miscellaneous:* Director, Parliamentary Council for Transport Safety. Fellow, Institute of the Motor Industry 1997–. *Special Interests:* Transport. *Recreations:* Sailing, golf. *Clubs:* White's, Royal Yacht Squadron (Cowes). *Heir:* His son, Hon. Benjamin Ralph Moore-Brabazon, born March 15, 1983. A Conservative. *Address:* The Lord Brabazon of Tara, DL, House of Lords, London, SW1A 0PW *E-Mail:* brabazoni@parliament.uk.

BRADFORD (8th Bishop of), David James Smith

Son of Stanley and Gwendolen Smith. Born July 14, 1935; educated Hertford Grammar School; King's College, London. Married 1961, Mary Hunter Moult (1 son 1 daughter). *Armed Forces:* National Service, Royal Artillery 1953–55. *Career:* Assistant Curate: All Saints, Gosforth 1959–62, St Francis, High Heaton 1962–64, Long Benton 1964–68; Vicar: Longhirst with Hebron 1968–75, St Mary, Monkseaton 1975–81; Archdeacon of Lindisfarne 1981–87; Vicar, Felton 1982–83; Bishop Suffragan of Maidstone 1987–92; Bishop to HM Forces 1990–92; Bishop of Bradford 1992–; Took his seat in the House of Lords 1997. Fellow, King's College London 1999. *Recreations:* Fell-walking, reading novels. *Clubs:* Bradford. *Address:* The Rt Rev. the Lord Bishop of Bradford, Bishopscroft, Ashwell Road, Bradford, West Yorkshire, BD9 4AU *Tel:* 01274 545414 *Fax:* 01274 544831 *E-Mail:* bishbrad@nildram.co.uk.

BRADSHAW (Life Baron, UK), William Peter Bradshaw; cr. 1999

Son of late Leonard Charles and Ivy Doris Bradshaw. Born September 9, 1936; educated Slough Grammar School; University of Reading (BA 1957, MA 1960). Married November 30, 1957, Jill, daughter of James and Florence Hayward (1 son 1 daughter). *Armed Forces:* National Service 1957–59. *Councils, Public Bodies:* Councillor, Oxfordshire County Council 1993; Member, Thames Valley Police Authority 1993–95 and 1997–, Vice-Chairman 1999. *Career:* Management Trainee, British Rail Western Region 1959; Various Appointments, London and West of England Division; Division Manager, Liverpool 1973; Chief Operating Manager, London Midland Region Crewe 1976; Deputy General Manager, LM Region 1977; Chief Operations Manager, BR Headquarters 1978; Director, Policy Unit 1980; General Manager, Western Region BR 1983–85; Professor of Transport Management, University of Salford 1986–92; Chairman, Ulsterbus and Citybus Ltd Belfast 1987–93; Special Adviser to Transport Select Committee of the House of Commons 1992–97. *Trusts, etc:* Trustee, Oxford Preservation Trust. FCIT. *Publications:* Many chapters and articles on transport issues. *Special Interests:* Transport, Environment, Planning, Police. *Recreations:* Growing hardy perennial plants, playing member of a brass band. *Clubs:* National Liberal. *Name, Style and Title:* Raised to the peerage as Baron Bradshaw, of Wallingford in the County of Oxfordshire 1999. A Liberal Democrat. *Address:* Professor The Lord Bradshaw, House of Lords, London, SW1A 0PW.

BRAGG (Life Baron, UK), Melvyn Bragg; cr. 1998

Son of Stanley and Mary Ethel Bragg. Born October 6, 1939; educated Nelson-Thomlinson Grammar School, Wigton; Wadham College, Oxford (MA); Hon. DLitt, Liverpool 1986; Hon. Fellow, Lancashire Polytechnic 1987; Domus Fellow, St Catherine's College, Oxford 1990; Hon. DLitt, Lancaster 1990; Hon. LLD, St Andrews 1993; Hon. DCL, Northumbria 1994; Hon. Fellow: Wadham College, Oxford 1995, University of Wales, Cardiff 1996; Hon. DLitt, South Bank University, London 1997. Married 1st, 1961, Marie-Elisabeth Roche (deceased) (1 daughter); married 2nd, 1973, Catherine Mary Haste (1 son 1 daughter). *Career:* BBC Radio and TV Producer 1961–67; Novelist 1964–; Writer and Broadcaster 1967–; Presenter, BBC TV series: *2nd House* 1973–77, *Read All About It* 1976–77; Presenter and Editor: *The South Bank Show* for ITV 1978–, *Start the Week* for Radio 4 1988–98; Controller of Arts, London Weekend Television 1990–, Head of Arts 1982–90; Chairman, Border Television 1990–95, Deputy Chairman 1985–90; Governor, London School of Economics 1997; *In Our Time* for Radio 4 1998–. *Chancellor:* Chancellor, Leeds University 1999–. *Other:* Member, Arts Council; Chairman, Literature Panel of Arts Council 1977–80; President: Cumbrians for Peace 1982–, Northern Arts 1983–87, National Campaign for the Arts 1986–. *Awards Granted:* RTS Gold Medal; John Llewllyn-Rhys Memorial Award; PEN Awards for Fiction; Richard Dimbleby Award for Outstanding Contribution to Television 1987; Ivor Novello Award for Best Musical *The Hired Man* 1985; Numerous prizes for *The South Bank Show* including a record three Prix Italia's; TRIC Award: Radio Programme of the Year for *Start the Week* 1990, Radio Personality of the Year for *Start the Week* 1991. Fellow: Royal Society of Literature, Royal Television Society. *Publications: For Want of a Nail,* 1965; *The Second Inheritance,* 1966; *Without a City Wall,* 1968; *The Hired Man,* 1969; *A Place in England,* 1970; *The Nerve,* 1971; *Josh Lawton,* 1972; *The Silken Net,* 1974; *A Christmas Child,* 1976; *Speak for England,* 1976; *Mardi Gras,* (musical) 1976; *Orion,* (TV play) 1977; *Autumn Manoeuvres,* 1978; *Kingdom Come,* 1980; *Love and Glory,* 1983; *Land of the Lakes,* 1983; *Laurence Olivier,* 1984; *The Hired Man,* (musical) 1984; *The Maid of Buttermere,* 1987; *Rich: The Life of Richard Burton,* 1988; *A Time to Dance,* 1990; *Crystal Rooms,* 1992; *King Lear in New York,* (play) 1992; *The Seventh Seal: a study of Ingmar Bergman,* 1993; *Credo,* 1996; *On Giants' Shoulders,* 1998; *The Soldier's Return,* 1999; Screenplays: *Isadora; Jesus Christ Superstar, Clouds of Glory* (with Ken Russell). *Recreations:* Walking, books. *Clubs:* Garrick. *Name, Style and Title:* Raised to the peerage as Baron Bragg, of Wigton in the County of Cumbria 1998. Labour. *Address:* The Lord Bragg, 12 Hampstead Hill Gardens, London, NW3 2PL.

BRAMALL (Life Baron, UK), Edwin Noel Westby Bramall; cr. 1987; KG 1990; GCB (Mil) 1979; OBE (Mil) 1965; MC 1945

Son of late Major Edmund Haselden Bramall and late Katharine Bridget Bramall, née Westby. Born December 18, 1923; educated Eton; Army Staff College; Imperial Defence College. Married 1949, Dorothy Avril Wentworth, daughter of late Brigadier Henry Albemarle Vernon, DSO (1 son 1 daughter). *Armed Forces:* Commissioned into KRRC 1943; Served in North West Europe 1944–45; Occupation of Japan 1946–47; Instructor, School of Infantry 1949–51; PSC 1952; Middle East 1953–58; Instructor, Army Staff College 1958–61; On staff of Lord Mountbatten with special responsibilty for reorgan-isation of MOD 1963–64; CO, 2 Green Jackets KRRC, Malaysia, during Indonesian confrontation 1965–66; Commander, 5th Airportable BDE 1967–69; IDC 1970; GOC, 1st Division BAOR 1971–73; Lt Gen. 1973; Commander, British Forces, Hong Kong 1973–76; Colonel Commandant, 3rd Battalion Royal Green Jackets 1973–84; General 1976; Commander-in-Chief, UK Land Forces 1976–78; Colonel, 2nd Goorkas 1976–86; Vice-Chief of Defence Staff (Personnel and Logistics) 1978–79; Chief of the General Staff 1979–82; ADC (General) 1979–82; Field Marshal 1982; Chief of the Defence Staff 1982–85. *Councils, Public Bodies:* Lord Lieutenant, Greater London 1986–98; JP 1986. *Other:* Vice-President, SSAFA 1985–; President: Greater London TAVRA 1986–98, Gurkha Brigade Association 1987–97, London Playing Fields Society 1990–, Greater London Association of Disabled People, Age Concern Greater London, Not Forgotten Association. *Trusts, etc:* Trustee, Imperial War Museum 1983–, Chairman 1990–98. *Miscellaneous:* Member, Council of Radley College 1985–. *Honours:* MC 1945; OBE (Mil) 1965; GCB (Mil) 1979; KG 1990. Freeman, City of London. Hon. Member, The Skinner's Company. *Publications:* Co-Author: *The Chiefs – The Story of the UK Chiefs of Staff. Special Interests:* Defence, Hong Kong, Foreign Affairs, Education.

Recreations: Cricket, painting, shooting, travel. *Sportsclubs:* I Zingari, Free Foresters. *Clubs:* Travellers', Army and Navy, Pratt's, MCC (President 1988–89). *Name, Style and Title:* Raised to the peerage as Baron Bramall, of Bushfield in the County of Hampshire 1987. A Cross-Bencher. *Address:* Field Marshal The Lord Bramall, KG, GCB, OBE, MC, JP, House of Lords, London, SW1A 0PW.

BRETT (Life Baron, UK), William Henry Brett; cr. 1999

Son of late William and Mary Brett. Born March 6, 1942; educated Radcliffe Secondary Technical College. Married 1st, 1961, Jean Valerie (marriage dissolved 1986) (1 son 1 daughter); married 2nd, 1994, Janet Winters (2 daughters). *Trades Union:* Member: APEX 1960–99, IPMS 1974–. *Councils, Public Bodies:* Councillor, London Borough of Lewisham 1964–68. *Career:* Various Administrative Positions, British Rail 1958–64; Administrative Assistant, Transport Salaried Staffs Association 1965–67; North West Organiser, National Union of Bank Employees 1966–68; Divisional Officer, Association of Scientific Technical and Managerial Staffs 1968–74; Institution of Professionals, Managers and Specialists: Assistant General Secretary 1980–89, General Secretary 1989–99; Member: Executive Committee, Public Services International 1989–99, General Council, Trades Union Congress 1989–99; Member, Governing Body, International Labour Organisation (Geneva) 1992–; Vice-Chairman, ILO 1993–; Chair, Worker Group, ILO 1993–. FRSA. *Publications: International Labour in the 21st Century,* 1994. *Special Interests:* Human Rights, Development, Economics, Labour Issues. *Recreations:* Reading, walking. *Clubs:* Lydd War Memorial Institute. *Name, Style and Title:* Raised to the peerage as Baron Brett, of Lydd in the County of Kent 1999. Labour. *Address:* The Lord Brett, Sycamore House, 2 Mill Road, Lydd, Romney Marsh, Kent, TN29 9EP *Tel:* 01797 321597 *Fax:* 01797 322148 *E-Mail:* brett4571@aol.com.

BRIDGE OF HARWICH (Life Baron, UK), Nigel Cyprian Bridge; cr. 1980; PC 1975; Kt 1968

Son of late Commander C. D. C. Bridge, RN. Born February 26, 1917; educated Marlborough; Hon. Fellow: American College of Trial Lawyers 1984, Wolfson College, Cambridge 1989. Married 1944, Margaret Swinbank (1 son 2 daughters). *Armed Forces:* Army Service 1940–46, Commissioned KRRC 1941. *Career:* Called to the Bar, Inner Temple 1947, Bencher 1964, Treasurer 1986; Junior Counsel to Treasury (Common Law) 1964–68; Judge of High Court, Queen's Bench Division 1968–75; Presiding Judge, Western Circuit 1972–74; A Lord Justice of Appeal 1975–80; A Lord of Appeal in Ordinary 1980–92. *Select Committees:* Chairman, Ecclesiastical Committee (Joint Committee of both Houses of Parliament) 1981–92. *Miscellaneous:* Member, Security Commission 1977–85, Chairman 1982–85; Chairman, Church of England Synodical Government Review 1993–97. *Honours:* Kt 1968; PC 1975. *Name, Style and Title:* Raised to the peerage as Baron Bridge of Harwich, of Harwich in the County of Essex 1980. A Cross-Bencher. *Address:* The Rt Hon. the Lord Bridge of Harwich, House of Lords, London, SW1A 0PW.

BRIDGEMAN (3rd Viscount, UK), Robin John Orlando Bridgeman; cr. 1929

Son of late Brigadier Hon. Geoffrey Bridgeman, MC, FRCS, second son of 1st Viscount, PC. Born December 5, 1930. Succeeded his uncle 1982; educated Eton. Married 1966, Victoria Harriet Lucy Turton (4 sons). *Armed Forces:* 2nd Lieutenant, The Rifle Brigade 1950–51. *Career:* Chartered Accountant; Partner, Henderson Crosthwaite and Co., Stockbrokers 1973–86; Director: Guinness Mahon and Co. Ltd 1988–90, Nestor-BNA plc 1988–. *House of Lords:* An elected hereditary peer 1999–. *Whip:* An Opposition Whip (Home Office, Legal Affairs, Treasury) December 1998–. *Select Committees:* Former Member: Joint Committee on Statutory Instruments, European Communities, Sub-Committee C (Environment, Public Health and Consumer Protection). *Other:* Chairman, Friends of Lambeth Palace Library; Treasurer, New England Company. *Trusts, etc:* Special Trustee, Hammersmith and Queen Charlotte's Hospital Authority; Treasurer, Florence Nightingale Aid in Sickness Trust. CA. *Special Interests:* Health, Social Services, Environment, Local Government. *Recreations:* Gardening, music, shooting, skiing. *Clubs:* Beefsteak, MCC, Pitt. *Heir:* His son, Hon. William Orlando Caspar Bridgeman, born August 15, 1968. A Conservative. *Address:* The Viscount Bridgeman, 19 Chepstow Road, London, W2 5BP *Tel:* 020 7727 4065.

BRIDGES (2nd Baron, UK), Thomas Edward Bridges; cr. 1957; GCMG 1988

Son of 1st Baron, KG, PC, GCB, GCVO, MC, and late Hon. Katharine Dianthe Farrer, daughter of 2nd Baron Farrer. Born November 27, 1927. Succeeded his father 1969; educated Eton; New College, Oxford (MA). Married 1953, Rachel Mary, daughter of late Sir Henry Noel Bunbury, KCB, of Ewell, Surrey (2 sons 1 daughter). *Armed Forces:* Commissioned in Royal Signals 1946–48. *Career:* Entered HM Foreign Service 1951; Served in Bonn, Berlin, Rio de Janeiro, Athens and Moscow, Private Secretary (Overseas Affairs) to the Prime Minister 1972–74; Minister (Commercial) at British Embassy, Washington, DC 1976–79; Deputy Secretary, Foreign and Commonwealth Office 1979–82; HM Ambassador to Italy 1983–87; Independent Board Member, Securities and Futures Authority Ltd 1989–97. *House of Lords:* An elected hereditary peer 1999–. *Select Committees:* Member, Select Committee on the European Communities 1988–92, 1994–98. *Other:* Chairman, UK National Committee for UNICEF 1989–97; Chairman, British-Italian Society 1991–97, Hon. Vice-President 1998–; President, Dolmetsch Foundation. *Trusts, etc:* Trustee, Rayne Foundation. FRSA. *Clubs:* Athenaeum. *Heir:* His son, Hon. Mark Thomas Bridges, born July 25, 1954. A Cross-Bencher. *Address:* The Lord Bridges, GCMG, 56 Church Street, Orford, Woodbridge, Suffolk, IP12 2NT.

BRIGGS (Life Baron, UK), Asa Briggs; cr. 1976

Son of late William Walker Briggs. Born May 7, 1921; educated Keighley Grammar School; Sidney Sussex College, Cambridge (MA). Married 1955, Susan Anne Banwell (2 sons 2 daughters). *Career:* Professor of Modern History, Leeds University 1955–61; Professor of History, University of Sussex 1961–76; Vice-Chancellor, University of Sussex 1967–76; Provost, Worcester College, Oxford 1976–91. *Chancellor:* Chancellor, Open University 1979–94. *Other:* President: Social History Society, Victorian Society. *Trusts, etc:* Trustee, Glyndebourne Arts Trust 1966–91; Member, Civic Trust 1976–86. *Miscellaneous:* Chairman: Committee on Nursing 1970–72, Advisory Board Redundant Churches 1983–88, Commonwealth of Learning Board 1988–93. Fellow, British Academy; American Academy of Arts and Sciences. Member, Spectacle Makers Company. *Publications:* Author of various historical works including six volumes on history of British Broadcasting. *Special Interests:* Education, Social Policy. *Recreations:* Travel. *Clubs:* Beefsteak, United Oxford and Cambridge University. *Name, Style and Title:* Raised to the peerage as Baron Briggs, of Lewes in the County of East Sussex 1976. A Cross-Bencher. *Address:* The Lord Briggs, The Caprons, Keere Street, Lewes, East Sussex, BN7 1TY *Tel:* 01273 474704.

BRIGHTMAN (Life Baron, UK), John Anson Brightman; cr. 1982; Kt 1970; PC 1979

Son of late William Henry Brightman. Born June 20, 1911; educated Marlborough; St John's College, Cambridge; Honorary Fellow, St John's College, Cambridge 1982. Married 1945, Roxane, daughter of Gerasimo Ambatielo (1 son). *Armed Forces:* Able seaman, merchant navy 1939–40; RNVR (Lieutenant-Commander) 1940–46; Anti-submarine warfare base, Tobermory; North Atlantic and Mediterranean convoys; Royal Naval Staff College, Greenwich; Assistant Naval Attaché, Ankara; Staff, South East Asia Command. *Career:* Called to the Bar, Lincoln's Inn 1932; Member, General Council of the Bar 1956–60, 1966–70; QC 1961; Bencher of Lincoln's Inn 1966; Attorney General of the Duchy of Lancaster 1969–70; Judge of the High Court of Justice, Chancery Division 1970–79; Judge of National Industrial Relations Court 1971–74; Lord Justice of Court of Appeal 1979–82; A Lord of Appeal in Ordinary 1982–86. *Select Committees:* Chairman: Select Committee on Parochial and Small Charities 1983–84, Joint Committee on Consolidation Bills 1983–86, Select Committee on Infant Life Preservation 1986–88, Select Committee on Bristol Urban Development 1988, Select Committee on Spitalfields Market 1989, Select Committee on British Waterways 1991–92, Special Standing Committee on Property Law 1994, Special Public Bill Committee on Private International Law 1995, Special Public Bill Committee on Family Homes and Domestic Violence 1995; Member, Ecclesiastical Committee 1997–. *All-Party:* Member, Parliamentary All-Party: Maritime Group, Arts and Heritage Group, Children Group. *Other:* Chairman, Tancred's

Foundation 1982–96. *Miscellaneous:* Member, Tax Law Review Committee's Working Party on Parliamentary Procedures for the enactment of Rewritten Tax Law 1996. *Honours:* Kt 1970; PC 1979. FRGS 1993. *Publications: Historical Sites in Franz Josef Land,* 1997. *Special Interests:* Charity Law, Abortion, High Arctic. *Recreations:* Arctic travel, cross country skiing, mountain trekking. *Sportsclubs:* Bar Yacht. *Name, Style and Title:* Raised to the peerage as Baron Brightman, of Ibthorpe in the County of Hampshire 1982. A Cross-Bencher. *Address:* The Rt Hon. the Lord Brightman, 30 Onslow Gardens, London, SW7 3AH *Tel:* 020 7584 8488 *Fax:* 020 7584 8488; House of Lords, London, SW1A 0PW *Tel:* House of Lords 020 7219 2034; Ibthorpe, Nr Hurstbourne Tarrant, Hampshire, SP11 0BY *Tel:* 01264 736280 *Fax:* 01264 736280.

BRIGSTOCKE (Life Baroness, UK), Heather Renwick Brigstocke; cr. 1990

Daughter of late Squadron-Leader J. R. Brown, DFC and Mrs. M. J. C. Brown. Born September 2, 1929; educated Abbey School, Reading; Girton College, Cambridge (MA). Married August 16, 1952, Geoffrey Brigstocke (died 1974), son of Charles Reginald Brigstocke, CB and Dora Brigstocke (3 sons 1 daughter). *Career:* Classics Mistress, Francis Holland School, London SW1 1951–53; Part-time Classics Mistress, Godolphin and Latymer School 1954–60; Part-time Latin Teacher, National Cathedral School, Washington DC 1962–64; Headmistress, Francis Holland School London NW1 1965–74; High Mistress, St. Paul's Girl's School 1974–89; Non-Executive Director, London Weekend Television 1982–90, Member, Programme Advisory Board 1990–93; Independent National Director, Times Newspapers Holdings 1990–; Hon. Bencher, The Inner Temple 1992–; Non exec director, Burberry's 1993–96; Associate director, Great Universal Stores 1993–96. *Select Committees:* Former Member, House of Lords Library Sub-Committee. *Other:* Council Member, London House for Overseas Graduates 1965–, Vice-Chairman 1975–80; Council Member, Middlesex Hospital Medical School 1971–80; Committee Member, The Automobile Association 1975–90; Governor, Wellington College 1975–87; President, Bishop Creighton House Settlement, Fulham 1977–; Council Member, Royal Holloway College 1977–85; Governor, The Royal Ballet School 1977–92; Council Member, The City University 1978–83; President, Girls' Schools Association 1980–81; Governor, Forest School 1982–90; Council Member, Royal Society of Arts 1983–87; Member, Council, St George's House, Windsor 1984–90; Governor, Museum of London 1986–92; Chairman: Autistic Care and Training Development Appeal 1990, Geffrye Museum 1990–; Governor: Gordonstoun School 1991–93, Imperial College of Science, Technology and Medicine 1991–; Member, European Cultural Foundation (UK Committee) 1992–; Chairman, Landau Forte City Technology College, Derby 1993–, Governor 1992–; Chairman, English Speaking Union 1993–; Vice-President, City and Guilds of London Institute 1993–98. *Trusts, etc:* Trustee: National Gallery 1975–82, Kennedy Memorial Trust 1980–85, City Technology Colleges Trust 1987–; Chairman: Thames LWT Telethon Trust 1990, The Menerva Educational Trust 1991–93; Council Member, National Literacy Trust 1993–; Trustee, The Great Britain Sasakawa Foundation 1994–. *Miscellaneous:* Non-Executive Director, Health Education Authority 1989–98; Member, Modern Foreign Languages Working Group 1989–90; Commissioner, Museums and Galleries Commission 1992–. *Special Interests:* Education, Health, Broadcasting, Museums and Galleries. *Name, Style and Title:* Raised to the peerage as Baroness Brigstocke, of Kensington in the Royal Borough of Kensington and Chelsea 1990. A Conservative. *Address:* The Baroness Brigstocke, House of Lords, London, SW1A 0PW *Tel:* House of Lords 020 7219 3000.

BRISTOL (54th Bishop of), Barry Rogerson

Son of late Eric Rogerson, and of Olive Rogerson. Born July 25, 1936; educated Magnus Grammar School, Newark, Notts; University of Leeds (BA); Wells Theological College; Hon. LLD, Bristol. Married December 28, 1961, Olga, daughter of late Wilfred Gibson, and of May Gibson (2 daughters). *Armed Forces:* National Service, RAF (Radar) 1955–57. *Career:* Bank Clerk, Midland Bank 1952–57; Deaconed; Curate, St. Hilda with St. Thomas, South Shields (diocese of Durham; priested 1963) 1962–65; Curate, St. Nicholas, Bishopwearmouth 1965–67; Lecturer, Lichfield Theological College 1967–71; Vice-Principal 1971–72; Lecturer, Salisbury and Wells Theological College 1972–75; Team Rector, St. Thomas, Wednesfield (diocese of Lichfield) 1975–79; Chairman, Melanesian Mission 1979–; Honorary Canon, Lichfield Cathedral 1979–85;

Suffragan Bishop of Wolverhampton 1979–85; Bishop of Bristol 1985–; Chairman, Advisory Board of Ministry, General Synod of Church of England 1987–93; Member, World Council of Churches Faith and Order Commission 1987–98 and Central Committee 1991–; Took his seat in the House of Lords 1990; President, Churches Together in Britain and Ireland (CTBI) 1999–. *Special Interests:* Homeless, Housing, Vocational Education. *Recreations:* Cinema, stained glass, photography, sailing. *Clubs:* Commonwealth Trust. *Address:* The Rt Rev. the Lord Bishop of Bristol, Bishop's House, Clifton Hill, Clifton, Bristol, BS8 1BW *Tel:* 0117–973 0222 *Fax:* 0117–923 9670.

BROOKE OF ALVERTHORPE (Life Baron, UK), Clive Brooke; cr. 1997

Son of John and Mary Brooke. Born June 21, 1942; educated Thornes House School, Wakefield. Married 1967, Lorna Hopkin Roberts. *Trades Union:* Member, Public and Commercial Services Union (PCS). *Career:* Inland Revenue Staff Federation: Assistant Secretary 1964–82, Deputy General Secretary 1982–88, General Secretary 1988–95; Joint General Secretary, Public Services Tax and Commerce Union 1996–98; Member, TUC: General Council 1989–96, Executive Committee 1993–96. *Select Committees:* Member, Select Committee on European Communities Sub-Committee B (Energy, Industry and Transport). *Backbench Committees:* Member, Labour Departmental Committees for: Defence, Home Affairs, Education and Employment, Cabinet Office. *All-Party:* Member, All-Party: Socially Responsible Investment Group, Defence Study Group, Rail Freight Group, Further Education Group. *International Bodies:* Member: IPA, CPA. *Party Groups (General):* Member: Labour Party, Fabian Society. *Other:* Patron: Learning Through Life Foundation, Community Initiatives Foundation; Council Member, Institute for Employment Studies; Chairman, Unions 21. *Trusts, etc:* Trustee: Community Service Volunteers 1989–, Duke of Edinburgh's Study Conference 1993–, Institute for Public Policy Research, London Dorchester Committee Trust. *Miscellaneous:* Member: House of Commons Speaker's Commission on Citizenship 1988, Pensions Compensation Board 1996–, Council of Churches for Britain and Ireland Enquiry into Unemployment and the Future of Work 1995–97. FRSA. *Special Interests:* Employment, Education, Community Care. *Recreations:* Travel, community services, politics, church affairs, reading, walking. *Name, Style and Title:* Raised to the peerage as Baron Brooke of Alverthorpe, of Alverthorpe in the County of West Yorkshire 1997. Labour. *Address:* The Lord Brooke of Alverthorpe, House of Lords, London, SW1A 0PW *Tel:* 020 7219 5353.

BROOKE OF YSTRADFELLTE (Life Baroness, UK), Barbara Muriel Brooke; cr. 1964; DBE 1960

Daughter of late Rev. Canon A. A. Mathews. Born January 14, 1908; educated Queen Anne's School, Caversham, Berkshire; Gloucester Training College of Domestic Science; Hon. Fellow, Westfield College. Married April 22, 1933, Henry Brooke, PC, CH (later Baron Brooke of Cumnor) (died March 29, 1984), son of late L. Leslie Brooke, Artist (2 sons 2 daughters). *Councils, Public Bodies:* Councillor, Hampstead Borough Council 1948–65. *Party Groups (General):* Vice-Chairman, Conservative and Unionist Party 1954–64. *Other:* Member, North West Metropolitan Regional Hospital Board 1954–66; Chairman: Executive Committee, Queen's Institute of District Nursing 1961–71, Governors of Godolphin and Latymer Girls School Hammersmith 1961–78; Member, Management Committee King Edward's Hospital Fund for London 1966–71. *Name, Style and Title:* Raised to the peerage as Baroness Brooke of Ystradfellte, of Ystradfellte in the County of Brecknock 1964. A Conservative. *Address:* The Baroness Brooke of Ystradfellte, DBE, Romans' Halt, Mildenhall, Marlborough, Wiltshire, SN8 2LX.

BROOKEBOROUGH (3rd Viscount, UK), Alan Henry Brooke; cr. 1952; 7th Bt of Cole Brooke (UK) 1822; DL

Son of 2nd Viscount, PC. Born June 30, 1952. Succeeded his father 1987; educated Harrow; Millfield; Royal Agricultural College, Cirencester. Married April 12, 1980, Janet Elizabeth, daughter of J. P. Cooke, of Doagh, Co Antrim. *Armed Forces:* Commission, 17th/21st Lancers 1971; Transferred to: Ulster Defence Regiment 1977, Royal Irish Regiment 1992; Lieutenant-Colonel 1993; Hon. Colonel, 4th/5th Battalion, The Royal Irish Rangers 1997–. *Councils, Public Bodies:* DL, Co. Fermanagh 1987–; High Sheriff, Co. Fermanagh 1995. *Career:* Executive Director, Green Park Health Care Trust 1993–; Chairman, Basel International (Jersey); A Personal Lord in Waiting to HM The Queen 1997–. *House of Lords:* An elected hereditary peer 1999–. *Select Committees:* Member, Select Committee on European Communities: Sub-Committee D (Agriculture and Food) 1989–93, 1994–97; Sub-Committee B (Energy, Industry and Transport) 1998–. *All-Party:* Member, All-Party Defence Study Group. *Other:* Vice-President, Somme Association 1990–; President, Army Benevolent Fund, Northern Ireland 1995–. *Trusts, etc:* Fellow, Industry and Parliament Trust. *Special Interests:* Northern Ireland, Agriculture, Tourism, Defence, Health. *Recreations:* Shooting, fishing, gardening. *Clubs:* Cavalry and Guards. *Heir:* His brother, Hon. Christopher Arthur Brooke, born May 16, 1954. A Cross-Bencher. *Address:* The Viscount Brookeborough, DL, Colebrooke, Brookeborough, Enniskillen, Co. Fermanagh, BT94 4DW *Tel:* 01365 53402.

BROOKES (Life Baron, UK), Raymond (Percival) Brookes; cr. 1976; Kt 1971

Son of late William Brookes. Born April 10, 1909; educated Kenrick Technical College, West Bromwich. Married 1937, Florence Sharman (1 son). *Career:* Group Chairman and Chief Executive, Guest, Keen & Nettlefolds Ltd. 1965–74, now Life President. *Other:* President, Society of Motor Manufacturers and Traders Ltd. 1974–75; Member, Court of Governors, University of Birmingham 1966–75; A Vice-President, Engineering Employers' Federation 1967–75. *Honours:* Kt 1971. *Name, Style and Title:* Raised to the peerage as Baron Brookes, of West Bromwich in the County of West Midlands 1976. A Cross-Bencher. *Address:* The Lord Brookes, Mallards, Santon, Isle of Man, IM4 1EH.

BROOKMAN (Life Baron, UK), David Keith Brookman; cr. 1998

Son of George Henry Brookman, MM and Blodwin Brookman. Born January 3, 1937; educated Nantyglo Grammar School, Gwent. Married 1958, Patricia Worthington (3 daughters). *Trades Union:* Member: Educational Advisory Committee for Wales 1976–82, Trades Union Congress 1992–99; Chairman, Trades Union Congress: Steel Committee (UK) 1998–99, European Coal and Steel Committee (ECCC) 1992–; President, Trades Union Congress: International Metal Workers (IMF), Iron and Steel Non-Ferrous Department 1992–99. *Armed Forces:* National Service, RAF 1955–57. *Career:* Crane Driver, Richard Thomas and Baldwin, Ebbw Vale 1953–55, 1957–73; Iron and Steel Trades Confederation: Organiser 1973–85, Assistant General Secretary 1985–93, General Secretary 1993–99; Board Member, British Steel (Industry) 1993–. *International Bodies (General):* Honorary Secretary, International Metalworkers' Federation (British Section) 1993–; President, International Metalworkers' Federation, Iron, Steel and Non-Ferrous Metals Department 1993–99. *Party Groups (General):* Labour Party: Member: Executive Committee, Wales 1982–85, National Constitutional Committee 1987–91, NEC 1991–92. *Other:* Governor, Gwent College of Higher Education 1980–84. *Trusts, etc:* Trustee, Julian Melchett Trust 1985–95. *Miscellaneous:* Member: Joint Industrial Council for Slag Industry 1985–93, British Steel Joint Accident Prevention Advisory Committee 1985–93, British Steel Advisory Committee on Education and Training 1986–93, Executive Council, European Metalworkers Federation 1985–95; Member, National T.U. Steel Co-ordinating Committee 1991–, Chairman 1993–; Member, European Coal and Steel Community Consultative Committee 1993–; Joint Secretary: British Steel Strip Trade Board 1993–98, British Steel Joint Standing Committee 1993–98, British Steel European Works Council 1996–. *Recreations:* Cricket, rugby, reading, keep-fit, golf. *Clubs:* Reform. *Name, Style and Title:* Raised to the peerage as Baron Brookman, of Ebbw Vale in the County of Gwent 1998. Labour. *Address:* The Lord Brookman, 4 Bassett Close, Redbourn, Hertfordshire, AL3 2JY *Tel:* 01582 792066 (Home).

BROOKS OF TREMORFA (Life Baron, UK), John Edward Brooks; cr. 1979; DL

Son of Edward George Brooks. Born April 12, 1927; educated Elementary schools; Coleg Harlech. Married 1st, 1948 (1 son 1 daughter) (marriage dissolved 1956), married 2nd, 1958, Margaret, daughter of Donald Pringle (2 sons). *Councils, Public Bodies:* Councillor, South Glamorgan County Council 1973–93, Leader 1973–77, 1986–92, Chairman 1981–82; Member, Cardiff Bay Development Corporation 1987–, currently Deputy Chairman; DL, South Glamorgan 1994–. *Spokesman:* Opposition Defence Spokesman 1980–81. *Select Committees:* Former Member, Joint Committee on Statutory Instruments. *Party Groups (General):* Secretary, Cardiff South East Labour Party 1966–; Parliamentary Agent to Rt Hon. James Callaghan MP in General Elections of 1970 and 1979; Chairman, Labour Party, Wales 1978–79. *Other:* Steward, British Boxing Board of Control 1986–, Vice-Chairman 1999–; Chairman: Welsh Sports Hall of Fame 1988–, Sportsmatch Wales 1992–. *Miscellaneous:* Contested Barry (Labour) February and October 1974 General Elections. *Recreations:* Reading, most sports. *Name, Style and Title:* Raised to the peerage as Baron Brooks of Tremorfa, of Tremorfa in the County of Glamorgan 1979. Labour. *Address:* The Lord Brooks of Tremorfa, DL, 46 Kennerleigh Road, Rumney, Cardiff, CF3 9BJ *Tel:* 01222 791848.

BROUGHAM AND VAUX (5th Baron, UK), Michael John Brougham; cr. 1860; CBE 1995

Son of 4th Baron. Born August 2, 1938. Succeeded his father 1967; educated Lycée Jaccard, Lausanne; Millfield School; Northampton Institute of Agriculture. Married 1st, 1963, Olivia Susan, daughter of Rear-Admiral Gordon T. S. Gray, CB, DSC (1 daughter) (marriage dissolved 1967); married 2nd, January 17, 1969, Catherine, daughter of late W. Gulliver (1 son) (marriage dissolved 1981 and who died 1986). *House of Lords:* A Deputy Chairman of Committees, House of Lords 1993–97, 1997–; A Deputy Speaker House of Lords 1995–; An elected hereditary peer 1999–. *Select Committees:* Member, Select Committees on: House of Lords' Offices 1997–, Hybrid Instruments, Procedure. *Other:* President, Royal Society for the Prevention of Accidents 1986–89; Chairman: The Tax Payers' Society 1989–91, European Secure Vehicle Alliance 1992–; President, National Health Safety Groups Council 1994–. *Special Interests:* Road Safety, Transport, Motor Industry, Aviation. *Recreations:* Photography, bridge, shooting. *Heir:* His son, Hon. Charles William Brougham, born November 9, 1971. A Conservative. *Address:* The Lord Brougham and Vaux, CBE, 11 Westminster Gardens, Marsham Street, London, SW1P 4JA.

BROWNE-WILKINSON (Life Baron, UK), Nicolas Christopher Henry Browne-Wilkinson; cr. 1991; Kt 1977; PC 1983

Son of late Canon A. R. Browne-Wilkinson. Born March 30, 1930; educated Lancing; Magdalen College, Oxford (BA); Hon. Fellow: St Edward Hall, Oxford 1987, Magdalen College, Oxford 1993. Married 1st, 1955, Ursula de Lacy Bacon (died 1987) (3 sons 2 daughters), married 2nd, 1990, Mrs Hilary Tuckwell. *Career:* Called to the Bar, Lincoln's Inn 1953, Bencher 1977; Junior Counsel: to Registrar of Restrictive Trading Agreements 1964–66, to Attorney-General in Charity Matters 1966–72, in bankruptcy to Department of Trade and Industry 1966–72; QC 1972; A Judge of the Courts of Appeal of Jersey and Guernsey 1976–77; A Judge of the High Court, Chancery Division 1977–83; President, Employment Appeal Tribunal 1981–83; A Lord Justice of Appeal 1983–85; President, Senate of the Inns of Court and the Bar 1984–86; Vice-Chancellor of the Supreme Court 1985–91; A Lord of Appeal in Ordinary 1991–; Senior Law Lord 1998–. *Recreations:* Gardening, music. *Name, Style and Title:* Raised to the peerage as Baron Browne-Wilkinson, of Camden in the London Borough of Camden 1991. A Cross-Bencher. *Address:* The Rt Hon. the Lord Browne-Wilkinson, House of Lords, London, SW1A 0PW.

BRUCE OF DONINGTON (Life Baron, UK), Donald William Trevor Bruce; cr. 1974

Son of late W. T. Bruce. Born October 3, 1912; educated The Grammar School, Donington, Lincolnshire. Married 1st, 1939, Joan, daughter of H. C. Butcher (1 son 2 daughters and 1 daughter deceased) (marriage dissolved 1980), married 2nd, 1981, Mrs Cyrena Shaw Heard. *Armed Forces:* Served Royal Signals 1939; Major 1942; General Staff 1943–45. *Career:* Chartered Accountant; Economist; Member, European Parliament 1975–79. *House of Commons:* MP (Labour), Portsmouth North Division 1945–50; PPS to Minister of Health 1945–50. *Select Committees (Commons):* Member, Select Committee on Public Accounts 1949–50. *Spokesman:* Opposition Spokesman on: Trade and Industry 1985–88, The Treasury 1979–85, 1988–90. *Select Committees:* Member: House of Lords Select Committee on the European Community 1982–97, Select Committee on House of Lords' Offices 1997–. FCA. *Special Interests:* Finance, Industry, Economic Policy, European Union. *Recreations:* Swimming. *Name, Style and Title:* Raised to the peerage as Baron Bruce of Donington, of Rickmansworth in the County of Hertfordshire 1974. Labour. *Address:* The Lord Bruce of Donington, 2 Bloomsbury Street, London, WC1B 3ST *Tel:* 020 7413 5100.

BULLOCK (Life Baron, UK), Alan Louis Charles Bullock; cr. 1976; Kt 1972; FBA 1967

Son of late Rev. Frank Bullock. Born December 13, 1914; educated Bradford Grammar School; Wadham College, Oxford; Hon. DLitt: Bradford, Reading, Newfoundland, Leicester, Sussex. Married 1940, Hilda, daughter of Edwin Handy (3 sons 1 daughter and 1 daughter deceased). *Career:* Fellow, Dean and Tutor in Modern History, New College Oxford 1945–52; Founding Master, St. Catherine's College, Oxford 1960–80; Vice-Chancellor, Oxford University 1969–73. *Other:* Foreign Member, American Academy of Arts and Sciences; Chairman, Friends of the Ashmolean Museum. *Miscellaneous:* Chairman, National Advisory Council on the Training and Supply of Teachers 1963–65. *Honours:* Kt 1972; Chevalier, Legion D'Honneur (France) 1970; Commander's Cross of the Order of Merit (Germany) 1995. FBA 1967. *Publications:* Author of: *Hitler, A Study in Tyranny; The Liberal Tradition; The Life and Times of Ernest Bevin; Hitler and Stalin: Parallel Lives*, and other Works. *Name, Style and Title:* Raised to the peerage as Baron Bullock, of Leafield in the County of Oxfordshire 1976. A Cross-Bencher. *Address:* The Lord Bullock, St. Catherine's College, Oxford, OX1 3UJ.

BURLISON (Life Baron, UK), Thomas Henry Burlison; cr. 1997; DL

Son of Robert and Georgina Burlison. Born May 23, 1936; educated Edmondsley, Co. Durham. Married 1981, Valerie Stephenson (2 sons 1 daughter). *Trades Union:* Member, GMB. *Armed Forces:* RAF 1959–61. *Councils, Public Bodies:* DL, Tyne and Wear 1997–. *Career:* Panel Beater 1951–57; Professional Footballer 1953–65; General and Municipal Workers' Union, then General, Municipal, Boilermakers and Allied Trades Union, later GMB: Regional Officer 1965–78, Regional Secretary 1978–91, Deputy General Secretary 1991–. *Whip:* A Lord in Waiting (Government Whip) 1999–. *Spokesman:* A Spokesman on: Cabinet Office 1999–, Defence 1999–, Home Office 1999–. *Party Groups (General):* Treasurer, Labour Party 1992–96. *Miscellaneous:* Honorary President, Hartlepool United F.C. *Recreations:* Gardening. *Name, Style and Title:* Raised to the peerage as Baron Burlison, of Rowlands Gill in the County of Tyne and Wear 1997. Labour. *Address:* The Lord Burlison, DL, High Point, West Highhorse Close, Rowlands Gill, Tyne and Wear, NE39 1AL.

BURNHAM (6th Baron, UK), Hugh John Frederick Lawson; cr. 1903; 6th Bt of Hall Barn and Peterborough Court (UK) 1892

Son of Major-General 4th Baron, CB, DSO, MC, TD, DL. Born August 15, 1931. Succeeded his brother 1993; educated Eton; Balliol College, Oxford (MA). Married 1955, Hilary, youngest daughter of late Alan Hunter, of Huntingtowerfield House, Almondbank, Perthshire (1 son 2 daughters). *Armed Forces:* Late Scots Guards. *Career: Daily Telegraph* 1954–86, Deputy Managing Director 1984–86. *House of Lords:* A Deputy Speaker 1995–; A Deputy Chairman of Committees 1995–; An elected hereditary peer 1999–. *Whip:* Opposition Deputy Chief Whip 1997–. *Spokesman:* Opposition Spokesman on Defence 1997–. *Select Committees:* Member: Hybrid Instruments Committee 1996–, Select Committee on Procedure 1997–. *All-Party:* Member, All-Party Racing and Bloodstock Group 1993–. *Other:* Director General, King George's Fund for Sailors 1988–93; A Younger Brother of Trinity House 1998. *Miscellaneous:* Provincial Grand Master, Buckinghamshire Freemasons. *Special Interests:* Freemasonry. *Recreations:* Horse racing, shooting, sailing. *Clubs:* Pratt's, Royal Yacht Squadron (Cowes), Royal Ocean Racing. *Heir:* His son, Hon. Harry Frederick Alan Lawson, born February 22, 1968. A Conservative. *Address:* The Lord Burnham, Woodlands Farm, Burnham Road, Beaconsfield, Buckinghamshire, HP9 2SF.

BURNS (Life Baron, UK), Terence Burns; cr. 1998; GCB 1995; Kt 1983

Son of Patrick and Doris Burns. Born March 13, 1944; educated Houghton-le-Spring Grammar School; University of Manchester (BA Hons Economics); Hon. Degrees: University of Manchester, University of Sunderland, University of Durham. Married 1969, Anne Elizabeth Powell (1 son 2 daughters). *Career:* London Business School: Research posts 1965–70, Lecturer in Economics 1970–74, Senior Lecturer 1974–79, Director, LBS Centre for Economic Forecasting 1976–79, Professor of Economics 1979, Fellow 1989; Member, HM Treasury Academic Panel 1976–79; Chief Economic Adviser to the Treasury and Head of the Government Economic Service 1980–91; Visiting Fellow, Nuffield College, Oxford 1989–97; Permanent Secretary, HM Treasury 1991–98; Visiting Professor, Durham University 1995–; Non-Executive Director, Legal and General Assurance Society Ltd 1999–. *Select Committees:* Member, Select Committee on Monetary Policy of the Bank of England 1998–. *Other:* Vice-President: Society of Business Economists 1985–, Royal Economic Society 1992–; Board Member, Manchester Business School 1992–; Non-executive Director, Queens Park Rangers FC. *Honours:* Kt 1983; GCB 1995. *Publications: The Interpretation and Use of Economic Predictions (Proceedings of the Royal Society,* London, A 407), 1986; *The UK Government's Financial Strategy (Keynes and Economic Policy),* 1988; Recent Lectures: *Change and the Treasury* (Durham Business School Lecture), 1994; *The Management of Economic Policy* (Eleanor Rathbone Memorial Lecture at University of Manchester), 1995; *Managing the Nation's Economy – the Conduct of Monetary and Fiscal Policy* (South Bank University Annual Lecture), 1995; *Preparing the Treasury for the Election* (The Frank Stacey Memorial Lecture), 1997. *Recreations:* Watching football, music, golf. *Sportsclubs:* Ealing Golf, Royal St George's Golf; President, Civil Service Golf Society. *Clubs:* Reform. *Name, Style and Title:* Raised to the peerage as Baron Burns, of Pitshanger in the London Borough of Ealing 1998. A Cross-Bencher. *Address:* The Lord Burns, GCB, House of Lords, London, SW1A 0PW *E-Mail:* burnst@parliament.uk.

BUSCOMBE (Life Baroness, UK), Peta Jane Buscombe; cr. 1998

Born March 12, 1954; educated Hinchley Wood School, Hinchley Wood, Surrey; Rosebery Grammar School, Epsom, Surrey; Inns of Court School of Law. Married 1980, Philip John Buscombe (twin sons, 1 daughter). *Councils, Public Bodies:* Councillor, South Oxfordshire District Council 1995–99. *Career:* Former Corporate Lawyer; Barrister-at-Law; Called to the Bar, Inner Temple 1977. *Spokesman:* Opposition Spokeswoman for: Law Officers and Lord Chancellor's Department 1999–, Social Security 1999–, Trade and Industry 1999–. *International Bodies:* Member, IPU. *Party Groups (General):* A Vice-Chairman, The Conservative Party 1997–99; President, Slough Conservative Association 1997–. *Miscellaneous:* Contested (Conservative) Slough 1997 General Election. *Special Interests:* Education, Law and Order, Trade and Industry. *Recreations:* Gardening, boating, swimming, tennis, theatre, cinema. *Sportsclubs:* Rock Sailing. *Clubs:* Carlton, Sloane. *Name, Style and Title:* Raised to the peerage as Baroness Buscombe, of Goring in the County of Oxfordshire 1998. A Conservative. *Address:* The Baroness Buscombe, House of Lords, London, SW1A 0PW *E-Mail:* buscombep@parliament.uk.

BUTLER OF BROCKWELL (Life Baron, UK), (Frederick Edward) Robin Butler; cr. 1998; GCB 1992; CVO 1986

Son of late Bernard Butler and of Nora Butler. Born January 3, 1938; educated Harrow School; University College, Oxford (BA Lit. Hum. 1961, MA) ; Hon. Degrees: Cranfield University, Exeter University, Aston University, London University. Married 1962, Gillian Lois Galley (1 son 2 daughters). *Career:* Joined HM Treasury 1961; Private Secretary to Financial Secretary to Treasury 1964–65; Secretary, Budget Committee 1965–69; Seconded to Cabinet Office as Member, Central Policy Review Staff 1971–72; Private Secretary: to Rt Hon. Edward Heath, MP 1972–74, to Rt Hon. Harold Wilson, MP 1974–75; Returned to HM Treasury as Assistant Secretary, General Expenditure Intelligence Division 1975; Under Secretary, General Expenditure Policy Group 1977–80; Principal Establishment Officer 1980–82; Principal Private Secretary to Rt Hon. Margaret Thatcher 1982–85; Second Permanent Secretary, Public Expenditure, HM Treasury 1985–87; Secretary of the Cabinet and Head of the Home Civil Service 1988–98; Master, University College, Oxford 1998–. *Other:* Governor, Harrow School 1975–91, Chairman of Governors 1988–91; Chairman of Governors, Dulwich College 1997–. *Miscellaneous:* Member, Royal Commission on the Reform of the House of Lords 1999. *Honours:* CVO 1986; KCB 1988; GCB 1992. Hon. Member, The Salters' Company. *Recreations:* Competitive games. *Sportsclubs:* President, Oxford University Rugby Football Member: Royal Lytham and St Anne's Golf, Fritford Heath Golf, St Enodoc Golf, Dulwich and Sydenham Hill Golf. *Clubs:* Athenaeum, Brooks's, Beefsteak, Anglo-Belgian, MCC. *Name, Style and Title:* Raised to the peerage as Baron Butler of Brockwell, of Herne Hill in the London Borough of Lambeth 1998. *Address:* The Lord Butler of Brockwell, GCB, CVO, University College, Oxford, OX1 4BH.

BUTTERFIELD (Life Baron, UK), William John Hughes Butterfield; cr. 1988; Kt 1978; OBE 1953

Son of late William Hughes Butterfield. Born March 28, 1920; educated Solihull School; Exeter College, Oxford; John Hopkins Medical School, Baltimore, USA; Professorial Fellow, Downing College, Cambridge 1975–78; Hon. LLD, Nottingham University; Hon. MD, Keio University, Tokyo; Hon. DSc, Chinese University of Hong Kong' Hon. LLD, University of Bristol; Hon. DSc: Johns Hopkins University, USA, Florida International University, USA; Fellow, UMDS (United Medical and Dental Schools of Guy's and St Thomas's); Hon. LLD, London; Hon. DSc, London. Married 1st, 1946, Ann Sanders (died 1948) (1 son); married 2nd, 1950, Isabel-Ann Foster Kennedy (2 sons 1 daughter). *Armed Forces:* Major, RAMC 1947–49. *Career:* Member, Scientific Staff, Medical Research Council 1946–58; Professor of Experimental Medicine, Guy's Hospital 1958–70; Examiner in Medicine, Oxford University 1960–66; Vice-Chancellor, Nottingham University 1970–75; Regius Professor of Physic, University of Cambridge 1975–87; Master of Downing College, Cambridge 1978–87; Vice-Chancellor, Cambridge University 1983–85. *Select Committees:* Former Member: Select Committee on Science and Technology, Sub-Committee 1 (Medical Research and NHS Reforms) 1994–97; European Communities Committee, Sub-Committee C (Environment, Public Health and Education). *Other:* Visitor, King Edward's Hospital Fund 1964–71; Member, Council, European Association for Study of Diabetes 1968–71; Chairman, Croucher Foundation in Hong Kong 1989–; President, The British Universities Sports Association; Patron, GB-Sasakawa Foundation. *Trusts, etc:* Chairman: Jardine Educational Trust in Hong Kong 1984–93, HPRT (Health Promotion Research Trust). *Miscellaneous:* Chairman: East Midlands Economic Planning Council 1974–75, Medicines Commission 1976–81. *Honours:* Kt 1978. Fellow, New York Academy of Medicine 1988; FRCP; Fellow, New York Academy of Science. Freeman, City of London. Emeritus Assistant, Worshipful Society of Apothecaries. *Publications:* Author of several medical books and contributor to official reports on diabetes and health care. *Special Interests:* Medicine, Research, Education, Hong Kong, Oman. *Recreations:* Tennis, cricket, conversation. *Sportsclubs:* OUHC, OURFC, OUCC, President: CURUFC. *Clubs:* Athenaeum, MCC. *Name, Style and Title:* Raised to the peerage as Baron Butterfield, of Stechford in the County of West Midlands 1988. A Conservative. *Address:* The Lord Butterfield, OBE, FRCP, 39 Clarendon Street, Cambridge, CB1 1JX *Tel:* 01223 328854.

BUTTERWORTH (Life Baron, UK), John Blackstock Butterworth; cr. 1985; CBE 1982; DL

Son of late John William Butterworth. Born March 13, 1918; educated Queen Elizabeth's Grammar School, Mansfield; The Queen's College, Oxford (MA); Hon. DCL (Sierra Leone); Hon. DSc (Aston); Hon. LLD (Warwick). Married 1948, Doris Crawford Elder (1 son 2 daughters). *Armed Forces:* Served Royal Artillery 1939–46. *Councils, Public Bodies:* JP: Oxford 1962–63, Coventry 1963–88; DL, West Midlands 1974–. *Career:* New College, Oxford: Fellow 1946–63, Bursar 1956–63; Barrister-at-law, Lincolns Inn 1947; First Vice-Chancellor, University of Warwick 1963–85; Hon. Bencher, Lincolns Inn 1988. *Select Committees:* Frequent Member: Sub-Committees of Select Committee on Science and Technology, Sub-Committee A of Select Committee on European Communities. *All-Party:* Member, All-Party: Children Group, Northern Cyprus Country Group. *Other:* Governor, Royal Shakespeare Theatre 1964–, Honorary Emeritus Governor 1999–; Chairman, Inter-University Council for Higher Education Overseas 1968–77; Board Member, British Council 1981–85; Member, Foundation for Science and Technology 1989–, Chairman 1990–97, President 1997–. *Trusts, etc:* Managing Trustee, Nuffield Foundation 1964–85, Ordinary Trustee 1985–. *Miscellaneous:* Member: Royal Commission on Working of Tribunals of Inquiry (Act) 1921 1966, Inter-governmental Committee on Law of Contempt in relation to Tribunals of Inquiry 1968, Committee on University Efficiency 1986; Croham Committee on the Review of the UGC 1987. *Honours:* CBE 1982. *Special Interests:* Education, Industry, Industrial Relations, Overseas Aid and Development. *Name, Style and Title:* Raised to the peerage as Baron Butterworth, of Warwick in the County of Warwickshire 1985. A Conservative. *Address:* The Lord Butterworth, CBE, DL, The Barn, Barton, Guiting Power, Gloucestershire, GL54 5US *Tel:* 01451 850297 *Fax:* 01451 850108; 727 Nell Gwynn House, Sloane Avenue, London, SW3 3AX *Tel:* 020 7581 4838 *Fax:* 020 7823 9388.

BUXTON OF ALSA (Life Baron, UK), Aubrey Leland Oakes Buxton; cr. 1978; KCVO 1996; MC 1943

Son of late Leland Wilberforce Buxton. Born July 15, 1918; educated Ampleforth; Trinity College, Cambridge. Married 1st, 1946, Pamela, (died 1983), daughter of late Sir Henry Birkin, 3rd Bt (2 sons 4 daughters), married 2nd, July 16, 1988, Mrs Kathleen Peterson, of Maine, USA. *Armed Forces:* Served RA 1939–45; In Burma 1942–45. *Councils, Public Bodies:* High Sheriff, Essex 1972; DL, Essex 1975–85. *Career:* Extra Equerry to HRH the Duke of Edinburgh 1964–97; Member, Countryside Commission 1968–72; Member, Royal Commission on Pollution 1970–75; Chairman: Independent Television News Ltd 1980–86, Oxford Scientific Films Ltd 1982–86; Member, Nature Conservancy Council 1984–86; Chairman: Anglia Television Group 1986–88, Survival Anglia 1986–92. *Other:* Treasurer, Zoological Society 1976–83; President, Falkland Islands Foundation 1990–96. *Trusts, etc:* A Trustee of the British Museum (Natural History) 1971–73; British Trustee, World Wildlife Fund; Trustee, Wildfowl Trust. *Honours:* MC 1943; KCVO 1996. *Recreations:* Travel, natural history, painting, sport. *Clubs:* White's. *Name, Style and Title:* Raised to the peerage as Baron Buxton of Alsa, of Stiffkey in the County of Norfolk 1978. A Conservative. *Address:* The Lord Buxton of Alsa, KCVO, MC, Old Hall Farm, Stiffkey, Norfolk, NR23 1QJ *Tel:* 01328 830351.

BYFORD (Life Baroness, UK), Hazel Byford; cr. 1996; DBE 1994

Daughter of late Sir Cyril Osborne, Conservative MP for Louth 1945–69, and Lady Osborne. Born January 14, 1941; educated St Leonard's School, St Andrews; Moulton Agricultural College, Northampton. Married 1962, C. Barrie Byford (1 daughter and 1 son deceased). *Career:* Farmer. *Whip:* An Opposition Whip 1997–98. *Spokesman:* Opposition Spokesman on: Agriculture December 1998–, Environment, Transport and the Regions (Rural Affairs) December 1998–. *Party Groups (General):* Chairman, National Committee, Conservative Women 1990–93; Vice-President, National Union of Conservative and Unionist Associations 1993–95, President 1996–97. *Other:* WRVS Leicestershire 1961–96, County Organiser 1972–76; Member: CLA, NFU. *Miscellaneous:* Member: Transport Users' Consultative Committee 1989–94, Rail Users' Consultative Committee 1994–95. *Honours:* DBE 1994. *Recreations:* Golf, reading, bridge. *Clubs:* Farmers'. *Name, Style and Title:* Raised to the peerage as Baroness Byford, of Rothley in the County of Leicestershire 1996. A Conservative. *Address:* The Baroness Byford, DBE, House of Lords, London, SW1A 0PW *E-Mail:* byfordh@Parliament.uk.

C

CAITHNESS (20th Earl of, S), Malcolm Ian Sinclair; cr. 1455; Lord Berriedale; 15th Bt of Canisbay (NS) 1631; PC 1990

Son of 19th Earl, CVO, CBE, DSO. Born November 3, 1948. Succeeded his father 1965; educated Marlborough; Royal Agricultural College, Cirencester. Married January 9, 1975, Diana Caroline Coke (died January 8, 1994) (1 son 1 daughter). *Career:* Savills 1972–78; Brown and Mumford 1978–80; Director of various companies 1980–84; Director: Victoria Soames Ltd, Residential Property Consultants, and other companies. *House of Lords:* Parliamentary Under-Secretary of State, Department of Transport 1985–86; Minister of State: Home Office 1986–88, Department of Environment 1988–89; Paymaster General and Treasury Minister 1989–90; Minister of State: Foreign and Commonwealth Office 1990–92, for Aviation and Shipping, Department of Transport 1992–94; An elected hereditary peer 1999–. *Whip:* A Lord in Waiting (Government Whip) 1984–85. *Spokesman:* A Government Spokesman for DHSS 1984–85; A Government Spokesman on Scotland 1984–86. *Select Committees:* Member, Select Committee on House of Lords' Offices 1997–. *Honours:* PC 1990. FRICS. *Heir:* His son, Lord Berriedale, born March 26, 1981. A Conservative. *Address:* The Rt Hon. the Earl of Caithness, House of Lords, London, SW1A 0PW.

CALLAGHAN OF CARDIFF (Life Baron, UK), Leonard James Callaghan; cr. 1987; KG 1987; PC 1964

Son of late James Callaghan, RN, and Charlotte (née Cundy). Born March 27, 1912; educated Portsmouth Northern Secondary School; Hon. Life Fellow, Nuffield College 1967; Hon. LLD, University of Wales 1976; Hon. Bencher, Inner Temple 1976; Hon. Fellow, University College of Cardiff 1978 (now University of Wales, Cardiff); Hon. LLD: Sardar Patel University Gujarat, India 1978, University of Birmingham 1981; Hon. Fellow, Portsmouth University 1981; Hon. PhD, Meisei University, Tokyo 1984; Hon. LLD, University of Sussex 1988; Hon. Fellow, University College, Swansea 1992; Hon. LLD: University of Westminster 1993, Open University 1996, University of Liverpool 1996. Married 1938, Audrey Elizabeth Moulton (1 son 2 daughters). *Trades Union:* Member, GMBU; Hon. Member, NUM (South Wales); Life Member, IRSF. *Armed Forces:* Served with Royal Navy during World War II. *Career:* Inland Revenue 1929–36; Assistant Secretary, Inland Revenue Staff Federation 1936–50; Consultant to Police Federations of England, Wales and Scotland 1955–64. *House of Commons:* MP (Labour) for South Cardiff 1945–50, for Cardiff South East 1950–83, and for Cardiff South and Penarth 1983–87; Parliamentary Secretary, Ministry of Transport 1947–50; Parliamentary and Financial Secretary to the Admiralty 1950–51; Chancellor of the Exchequer 1964–67;

Secretary of State for the Home Department from 1967–1970; Foreign and Commonwealth Secretary 1974–76; Prime Minister and First Lord of the Treasury 1976–79; Leader of the Opposition 1979–80. *International Bodies (General):* Member, The Interaction Council. *Party Groups (General):* Member, National Executive Labour Party 1957–80, Treasurer 1967–76, Chairman 1973. *Other:* Chairman, Advisory Committee on Protection of the Sea 1952–63, President 1963–; President: United Kingdom Pilots Association 1963–76, International Maritime Pilots Association 1971–76, University College of Swansea (now University of Wales, Swansea) 1986–95; Joint President, Royal Institute of International Affairs (Chatham House); President, Cardiff Community Housing Association. *Awards Granted:* Hubert H. Humphrey International Award 1978. *Trusts, etc:* Member: Trust House Charity Foundation, British Museum Development Trust Council, Cambridge Commonwealth Trust, Pegasus Trust, Inner Temple. *Miscellaneous:* Visiting Fellow, Nuffield College, Oxford 1956–67. *Honours:* PC 1964; Grand Cross First Class of the Order of Merit of the Federal Republic of Germany 1979; KG 1987; Order of the Nile, Egypt. Hon. Freeman: City of Cardiff 1975, City of Sheffield 1979, City of Portsmouth 1991, City of Swansea 1993. *Publications:* Author of: *A House Divided: the dilemma of Northern Ireland,* 1973; *Time and Chance* (autobiography) 1987. *Special Interests:* Agriculture, Farming. *Clubs:* Athenaeum. *Name, Style and Title:* Raised to the peerage as Baron Callaghan of Cardiff, of the City of Cardiff in the County of South Glamorgan 1987. Labour. *Address:* The Rt Hon. the Lord Callaghan of Cardiff, KG, House of Lords, London, SW1A 0PW *Tel:* 020 7219 5802.

CAMERON OF LOCHBROOM (Life Baron, UK), Kenneth John Cameron; cr. 1984; QC (Scot) 1972; PC 1984

Son of late Hon. Lord Cameron, KT, DSC. Born June 11, 1931; educated The Edinburgh Academy; Corpus Christi, Oxford (MA); Edinburgh University (LLB). Married August 8, 1964, Jean Pamela, daughter of late Colonel Granville Murray, RA (2 daughters). *Armed Forces:* Served RNVR 1950–62; Commissioned 1951. *Career:* Called to the Bar 1958; QC (Scot) 1972; Advocate Depute 1981–84; Senator, College of Justice in Scotland 1989–. *House of Lords:* Lord Advocate 1984–89. *Miscellaneous:* President, Pensions Appeal Tribunal (Scotland) 1976–84; Chairman, Royal Fine Art Commission for Scotland 1995–. *Special Interests:* Law, Local Government, Arts. *Recreations:* Fishing, music, sailing. *Clubs:* Scottish Arts (Edinburgh), New (Edinburgh). *Name, Style and Title:* Raised to the peerage as Baron Cameron of Lochbroom, of Lochbroom in the District of Ross and Cromarty 1984. A Cross-Bencher. *Address:* The Rt Hon. the Lord Cameron of Lochbroom, Court of Session, Parliament Square, Edinburgh, EH1 1RF *Tel:* 0131–225 2595.

CAMPBELL OF ALLOWAY (Life Baron, UK), Alan Robertson Campbell; cr. 1981; ERD 1996; QC 1965

Son of late John Kenneth Campbell and Juliet Pinner. Born May 24, 1917; educated Aldenham; Ecole des Sciences Politiques, Paris; Trinity Hall, Cambridge (MA). Married 1957, Vivien, daughter of late Commander A. H. de Kantzow, DSO, RN. *Armed Forces:* Second Lieutenant (Royal Artillery Supplementary Reserve), BEF 1939–40; PoW Colditz 1940–45. *Career:* QC 1965; Bencher of the Inner Temple 1972; Recorder of the Crown Court 1976–89. *Select Committees:* Member: House of Lords Committee for Privileges 1982–, House of Lords Select Committee on Murder and Life Imprisonment 1988–89. *All-Party:* Member, All-Party Defence Study Group. *Party Groups:* Member, Association of Conservative Peers. *International Bodies (General):* Consultant to Council of Europe on Industrial Espionage 1965–74. *Party Groups (General):* Chairman, Legal Research Committee of Society of Conservative Lawyers 1968–80; Co-Patron, Inns of Court School of Law Conservatives 1996–. *Other:* Member, Management Committee of UK Association for European Law 1975–89; Vice-President, Association des Juristes Franco-Britanniques 1989–91; President, Colditz Association 1978–. *Miscellaneous:* Member: Law Advisory Panel of British Council 1974–79, Scottish Peers' Association. *Honours:* ERD 1996. *Publications:* (with Lord Wilberforce) *Restrictive Trade Practices and Monopolies,* 1956, 2nd edn 1966, Supplements 1 and 2 1965; *Restrictive Trading Agreements in the Common Market,* 1964, Supplement 1965; *Common Market Law,* vols 1 and 2 1969, vol 3 1973, Supplement 1975; *Industrial Relations Act,* 1971; *EC Competition Law,* 1980; *Trade Unions and the Individual,* 1980. *Special Interests:* Industrial Relations, European Union, Restrictive Trade

Practices and Monopolies, Constitutional Affairs. *Clubs:* Beefsteak, Carlton, Pratt's. *Name, Style and Title:* Raised to the peerage as Baron Campbell of Alloway, of Ayr in the District of Kyle and Carrick 1981. A Conservative. *Address:* The Lord Campbell of Alloway, ERD, QC, 2 King's Bench Walk, Temple, London, EC4 7DE.

CAMPBELL OF CROY (Life Baron, UK), Gordon Thomas Calthrop Campbell; cr. 1974; PC 1970; MC 1944 and Bar 1945; DL

Son of late Major-General J. A. Campbell, DSO and Bar. Born June 8, 1921, educated Wellington. Married 1949, Nicola, daughter of late G. S. Madan (2 sons 1 daughter). *Armed Forces:* Served Regular Army 1939–46; Major, 15th Scottish Division 1942 (MC 1944 and Bar 1945); Wounded and disabled 1945. *Councils, Public Bodies:* DL, Nairn 1985–; Vice-Lord Lieutenant of Nairn 1988–. *Career:* HM Foreign Service 1946–57; Foreign Office 1946–49; UK Permanent Mission UN 1949–52; Private Secretary to the Secretary to the Cabinet 1954–56; British Embassy, Vienna 1956–57; Partner, Holme Rose Farms and Estate; Consultant to Chevron Corporation 1975–94; Chairman, Stoic Insurance Services 1980–93; Director, Alliance and Leicester Building Society 1985–92, Chairman of its Scottish Board to 1994; In retirement, lecturing to the Armed Forces in the UK and abroad on World War II battles. *House of Commons:* MP (Conservative), Moray and Nairn 1959–74; Under-Secretary of State for Scotland 1963–64; Secretary of State for Scotland 1970–74. *Whip (Commons):* Assistant Government Whip 1961–62; A Lord Commissioner of HM Treasury and Scottish Whip 1962–63. *Spokesman (Commons):* Opposition Front Bench Spokesman on: Defence 1966–68, Scotland (Shadow Cabinet) 1969–70. *Spokesman:* Opposition Front Bench Spokesman on many subjects 1975–79. *Select Committees:* Member, and co-opted to its sub-committees at other times, Select Committee on the European Communities 1975–93; Co-opted to Sub-Committee, Select Committee on Science and Technology 1989–92; Member, Select Committee on Delegated Powers 1993–95. *All-Party:* Vice-President, Parliamentary Maritime Group 1985–; Member, All-Party: Energy Group, Media Group, Disablement Group, Environment Group, Consumer Affairs Group, British-Austrian Country Group. *Other:* Vice-President and Acting Chairman, Advisory Committee on Pollution of the Sea 1980–82, Chairman 1987–89; Chairman for Scotland of the International Year of Disabled People 1981; Office-bearer in several disabled organisations; President, Anglo-Austrian Society 1991–. *Trusts, etc:* Trustee, Thomson Foundation 1980–. *Miscellaneous:* Chairman, Scottish Council of Independent Schools 1976–80. *Honours:* PC 1970; Gold Grand Cross With Star (Austria). First Fellow, Nuffield Provincial Hospitals Trust, Queen Elizabeth The Queen Mother Fellowship 1980. *Publications: Disablement in the UK, Problems and Prospects*, 1981. *Special Interests:* Foreign Affairs, Defence, Environment, Consumer Affairs. *Recreations:* Music, natural history. *Name, Style and Title:* Raised to the peerage as Baron Campbell of Croy, of Croy in the County of Nairn 1974. A Conservative. *Address:* The Rt Hon. the Lord Campbell of Croy, MC, DL, Holme Rose, Cawdor, Nairnshire, IV12 5XT *Tel:* 01667 493223; House of Lords, London, SW1A 0PW *Tel:* 020 7219 5353 *Fax:* 020 7219 5979.

CANTERBURY (103rd Archbishop of), George Leonard Carey; PC 1991

Son of late George and Ruby Carey. Born November 13, 1935; educated Bifrons School, Barking; King's College, London (PhD); London College of Divinity (ALCD, BD (Hons), MTh). Married June 25, 1960, Eileen Harmsworth, daughter of Douglas Cunningham Hood, of Dagenham, Essex (2 sons 2 daughters). *Career:* Curate of St Mary's, Islington 1962–66; Lecturer: Oakhill Theological College 1966–70, St John's College, Nottingham; Occasional teacher at Nottingham University 1970–75; Vicar of St Nicholas Church, Durham 1975–82; Principal, Trinity Theological College, Bristol 1982–87; Bishop of Bath and Wells 1987–91; Archbishop of Canterbury 1991–; Entered the House of Lords 1991. *Publications: I Believe in Man*, 1975; *God Incarnate*, 1976; *The Great Acquittal*, (jointly) 1980; *The Meeting of the Waters*, 1985; *The Church in the Market Place*, 1984; *The Gate of Glory*, 1986; *The Message of the Bible*, 1986; *The Great God Robbery*, 1989; *I Believe*, 1991; *Sharing a Vision*, 1993; *Spiritual Journey*, 1994; *My Journey, Your Journey*, (jointly) 1996; *Canterbury Letters to the Future*, 1998. *Recreations:* Family life, music, poetry, reading, walking. *Clubs:* Athenaeum, Nobodies. *Address:* The Most Rev. and Rt Hon. the Lord Archbishop of Canterbury, Lambeth Palace, London, SE1 7JU *Tel:* 020 7928 8282; Old Palace, Canterbury, Kent, CT1 2EE.

CARLILE OF BERRIEW (Life Baron, UK), Alexander Charles Carlile; cr. 1999; QC 1984

Son of Dr Erwin Falik. Born February 12, 1948; educated Epsom College; King's College, University of London; Council of Legal Education. Married October 19, 1968, Frances, daughter of Michael Soley (3 daughters). *Career:* Called to the Bar by Gray's Inn 1970, Bencher 1992–; QC 1984; Recorder of the Crown Court; Deputy High Court Judge; Honorary Recorder of the City of Hereford 1986–. *House of Commons:* Contested (Liberal Democrat) Flint East, February 1974 and 1979; MP (Lib) for Montgomery 1983–88, (Lib Dem) 1988–97. *Spokesman (Commons):* Liberal Spokesman on Home Affairs, Law 1985–88; Former Alliance Spokesman on Legal Affairs 1987; SLD Spokesman on Foreign Affairs 1988–89; Liberal Democrat Spokesman on: Legal Affairs 1989–90, Trade and Industry 1990–92, Wales 1992–97, Employment 1992–94, Health 1994–95, Justice, Home Affairs and Immigration 1995–97. *Select Committees (Commons):* Member, Select Committee on Welsh Affairs 1992–97. *All-Party Committees (Commons):* Member, All Party: UN Parliamentary Group, Barristers' Group. *Party Groups (General):* Chairman, Welsh Liberal Party 1980–82; Leader, Welsh Liberal Democrat Party 1992–97; President, Liberal Democrats Wales 1997–99. *Other:* Patron, National Depression Campaign. *Trusts, etc:* Fellow and Trustee, Industry and Parliament Trust; Trustee: Nuffield Trust, Hope House Childrens' Hospice; Council Member and Trustee, NACRO. *Miscellaneous:* Lay Member, General Medical Council 1989–99; Member, Advisory Council on Public Records 1989–95. Fellow, Institute of Advanced Legal Studies. *Publications:* Various Articles. *Special Interests:* Home Affairs, Agriculture, Legal Affairs, United Nations, Central and Eastern Europe, Arts, Wales, Mental Health, Medical Profession. *Recreations:* Family, politics, theatre, food, Association Football. *Clubs:* Athenaeum. *Name, Style and Title:* Raised to the peerage as Baron Carlile of Berriew, of Berriew in the County of Powys 1999. A Liberal Democrat. *Address:* The Lord Carlile of Berriew, QC, 9–12 Bell Yard, London, WC2A 2LF *E-Mail:* accqc@compuserve.com.

CARLISLE (65th Bishop of), Ian Harland

Son of late Canon Samuel James Harland and of Brenda Gwendolyn Harland. Born December 19, 1932; educated Dragon School, Oxford; Haileybury; Peterhouse, Cambridge (MA); Wycliffe Hall, Oxford. Married 1967, Susan Hinman (1 son 3 daughters). *Councils, Public Bodies:* Councillor, Wortley Rural District Council 1969–73. *Career:* Teacher, Sunningdale School 1956–58; Curate, Melton Mowbray 1960–63; Vicar: Oughtibridge, Sheffield 1963–72, St Cuthbert's, Fir Vale, Sheffield 1972–75; Priest-in-charge, All Saints, Brightside 1973–75; Rural Dean of Ecclesfield 1973–75; Vicar of Rotherham 1975–79; Proctor in Convocation 1975–85; Rural Dean of Rotherham 1976–79; Archdeacon of Doncaster 1979–85; Bishop Suffragan of Lancaster 1985–89; Bishop of Carlisle 1989–; Took his seat in the House of Lords 1996. *All-Party:* Member, Parliamentary Middle Way Group. *Recreations:* Politics, sport. *Clubs:* Farmers'. *Address:* The Rt Rev. the Lord Bishop of Carlisle, Rose Castle, Dalston, Carlisle, Cumbria, CA5 7BZ *Tel:* 016974 76274 *E-Mail:* bishcarl@carlisle-c-of-e.org.

CARLISLE OF BUCKLOW (Life Baron, UK), Mark Carlisle; cr. 1987; PC 1979; QC 1971; DL

Son of late Philip and Mary Carlisle. Born July 7, 1929; educated Radley; Manchester University. Married 1959, Sandra Joyce Des Voeux (1 daughter). *Armed Forces:* Served as 2nd Lieutenant, Royal Army Education Corps 1948–50. *Councils, Public Bodies:* DL, Cheshire 1983–. *Career:* Called to the Bar Gray's Inn 1953, Entrance Scholar Junior; Northern Circuit; Practised in Manchester from February 1954; Member of Bar Council 1966–70; QC 1971; Recorder 1976–98; Chairman, Criminal Injuries Compensation Board 1989–; A Judge of the Courts of Appeal of Jersey and Guernsey 1990–99; Chairman, Manchester and London Investment Trust plc 1997–. *House of Commons:* Contested (Conservative) St. Helens 1958; MP (Conservative) for Runcorn 1964–83; Under-Secretary of State, Home Office 1970–72; Minister of State, Home Office 1972–74; Secretary of State for Education and Science 1979–81; MP (Conservative) for Warrington South 1983–87. *Backbench Committees (Commons):* Joint Hon. Secretary, Conservative Party Home Affairs

Committee 1966–69; Chairman, Conservative Home Affairs Committee 1983–87. *International Bodies (General):* Hon. Treasurer, Commonwealth Parliamentary Association 1982–85, Vice-Chairman (UK Branch) 1985–87. *Party Groups (General):* Chairman: Federation of University Conservative and Union Associations 1953–54, Society of Conservative Lawyers 1996–. *Trusts, etc:* Trustee, The Foundation for Children with Leukaemia; Chairman, The Drugwatch Trust. *Miscellaneous:* Member: Home Office Advisory Council on the Penal System 1966–70, BBC Advisory Council 1975–79; Chairman: Parole Review Committee 1987–88, Review Committee into the Parole System in England and Wales 1988, Prime Minister's Advisory Committee on Business Appointments for Crown Servants 1988–1998, Prime Minister's Advisory Committee on Business Appointments 1988–98, Commonwealth Observer Group to the Elections in Lesotho 1993. *Honours:* PC 1979. *Special Interests:* Penal Affairs and Policy, Education, Law, Human Rights. *Recreations:* Golf. *Clubs:* Garrick, St James' (Manchester). *Name, Style and Title:* Raised to the peerage as Baron Carlisle of Bucklow, of Mobberley in the County of Cheshire 1987. A Conservative. *Address:* The Rt Hon. the Lord Carlisle of Bucklow, QC, DL, 3 Holt Gardens, Blakeley Lane, Mobberley, Cheshire, WA16 7LH; Office: Queen Elizabeth Buildings, Temple, London, EC4Y 9BS *Tel:* 020 7583 5766.

CARMICHAEL OF KELVINGROVE (Life Baron, UK), Neil George Carmichael; cr 1983

Son of late James Carmichael; educated Estbank Academy; Royal College of Science and Technology, Glasgow. Married 1948, Catherine McIntosh Rankin (1 daughter) (marriage dissolved). *Councils, Public Bodies:* A Glasgow City Councillor 1962–63. *Career:* Employed by Gas Board in Planning Department. *House of Commons:* MP (Labour) for Glasgow Woodside 1962–74; Joint Parliamentary Under-Secretary, Ministry of Transport 1967–1969; Joint Parliamentary Secretary, Ministry of Technology 1969–70; MP (Labour) for Glasgow Kelvingrove 1974–83; Under-Secretary of State: Department of Environment 1974–75, Department of Industry 1975–1976. *Select Committees (Commons):* Member, Select Committee on Nationalised Industries 1976. *Spokesman:* Opposition Front Bench Spokesman on: Transport 1987–97, Scotland 1987–97. *Name, Style and Title:* Raised to the peerage as Baron Carmichael of Kelvingrove, of Camlachie in the District of the City of Glasgow 1983. Labour. *Address:* The Lord Carmichael of Kelvingrove, 53 Partickhill Road, Glasgow, G11 5AB.

CARNARVON (7th Earl of, GB), Henry George Reginald Molyneux Herbert; cr. 1793; Baron Porchester (GB) 1780; KCVO 1982; KBE 1976; DL

Son of 6th Earl. Born January 19, 1924. Succeeded his father 1987; educated Eton; Royal Agricultural College, Cirencester (McClelland Gold Medal); Hon. Fellow, Portsmouth Polytechnic 1976; Hon. DSc, Reading University 1980. Married 1956, Jean Margaret, MBE, eldest daughter of late Hon. Oliver Wallop, of Big Horn, Sheridan, Wyoming, USA (2 sons 1 daughter). *Armed Forces:* Lieutenant, Royal Horse Guards 1943–47; Hon. Colonel, Hampshire Fortress Regiment Royal Engineers (TA) 1963–67. *Councils, Public Bodies:* Councillor, Hampshire County Council 1954–65, County Alderman 1965–74; Member: Hampshire Agricultural Executive 1955–65, Andover Town Development Committee 1960–65, Basingstoke Town Development Committee 1960–74;

DL, Hants 1965–; Chairman, New Hampshire County Council 1974–77. *Career:* Racing Manager to Her Majesty the Queen 1969–; Chairman: Newbury Racecourse plc 1985–98, Serplan 1989–. *House of Lords:* An elected hereditary peer 1999–. *Select Committees:* Chairman, House of Lords Select Committee on the Croydon Tramlink Bill November 1992-January 1993; Member, Joint Select Committee on Draft Local Government (Organisation and Standards) Bill 1999. *All-Party:* Chairman, All-Party London Group. *Other:* Verderer of the New Forest 1961–65; Chairman, Thoroughbred Breeders' Association 1964–66, President 1969–74, 1986–91; President: Amateur Riders Association 1970–76, Hampshire Association for the Care of the Blind (Sight-Concern Hampshire) 1975–. *Trusts, etc:* Chairman, Basingstoke Sports Trust 1970–82, President 1983–86; President, Hampshire and the Isle of Wight Naturalists Trusts 1987–; Chairman, North Hampshire Hospital Fund. *Miscellaneous:* Member, Nature Conservancy 1953–66; Chairman and founding member, Game Research Association 1960–67, became Game Conservancy 1967, Vice-President 1967; Member, Sports Council, Chairman, Planning Committee 1965–70, Member, Forestry Commission 1967–70; Chairman, South East Economic Planning Council 1971–79; Vice-Chairman, County Councils Association 1972–79; Chairman: Agricultural Research Council 1978–83, Standing Conference on Countryside Sports 1978–; London and South East Regional Planning Conference 1989–; Member: Horseracing Betting Levy Board, National Stud Advisory Panel.

Honours: KBE 1976; KCVO 1982. *Publications: A Study of Exmoor,* 1977 *Second Chamber,* (Joint Publication) 1995. *Special Interests:* Horse Racing. *Recreations:* Gardening. *Sportsclubs:* Member, Jockey Club 1964–; Member, Hampshire Cricket Club 1966–, President 1966–68; Hon. Member, South Wales Hunts Cricket Club. *Clubs:* White's, Portland. *Heir:* His son, Lord Porchester, born November 10, 1958. A Cross-Bencher. *Address:* The Earl of Carnarvon, KCVO, KBE, DL, Milford Lake House, Burghclere, Newbury, Berkshire, RG15 9EL *Tel:* 01635 253387.

CARNEGY OF LOUR (Life Baroness, UK), Elizabeth Patricia Carnegy of Lour; cr. 1982; DL

Daughter of late Lieutenant-Colonel U. E. C. Carnegy of Lour, DSO, MC, DL, and of late Violet Carnegy, MBE. Born April 28, 1925; educated Downham School, Essex; Hon. LLD: University of Dundee 1991, University of St Andrews 1997; Hon. DrUniv, Open University 1998. *Councils, Public Bodies:* Co-opted Education Committee, Angus County Council 1967–75; Honorary Sheriff 1969–84; Councillor, Tayside Regional Council 1974–82; Convener, Education Committee 1976–82; DL, Angus 1988–; Chairman, Tayside Committee on Medical Research Ethics 1990–93. *Career:* Farmer 1956–89. *Select Committees:* Member: House of Lords European Communities Select Committee 1993–96, Sub-committee D (Agriculture and Food) 1990–93, Sub-committee E (Law and Institutions) 1993–97. *All-Party:* Member, All-Party: Universities Parliamentary Group, Children Group, Children in Scotland Group. *Party Groups:* Member, Association of Conservative Peers, Vice-Chairman 1990–94. *Other:* Served Cavendish Laboratory, Cambridge 1943–46; Girl Guides Association: Training Advisor, Scotland 1958–62, Commonwealth HQ 1963–65, President for Scotland 1979–89; Formerly Member, Visiting Committee Noranside Borstal Institution; Member, Council and Finance Committee of Open University 1984–96; Honorary President, Scottish Library Association 1989–92, Honorary Member 1996–; Member of Court, St Andrews University 1991–96. *Trusts, etc:* Member, Administration Council, Royal Jubilee Trusts 1984–88. *Miscellaneous:* Chairman, Working Party on Professional Training in Community Education Scotland 1975–77; Commissioner, Manpower Services Commission 1979–82; Member, Scottish Council for Tertiary Education 1979–84; Chairman, Manpower Services Commission Committee for Scotland 1980–83; Member, Scottish Economic Council 1980–93; Former Chairman, Scottish Council for Education 1981–88; Hon. Fellow, Scottish Community Education Council 1993. FRSA; Hon. Fellow, Scottish Community Education Council. *Special Interests:* Education, European Union, Local Government, Scottish Affairs, Agriculture, Countryside, Medical Research Ethics, Constitution, Health Service, Social Security. *Clubs:* Lansdowne, New (Edinburgh). *Name, Style and Title:* Raised to the peerage as Baroness Carnegy of Lour, of Lour in the District of Angus 1982. A Conservative. *Address:* The Baroness Carnegy of Lour, DL, Lour, Forfar, Angus, DD8 2 LR *Tel:* 01307 820237.

CARR OF HADLEY (Life Baron, UK), (Leonard) Robert Carr; cr. 1976; PC 1963

Son of late Ralph Edward Carr. Born November 11, 1916; educated Westminster School; Gonville and Caius College, Cambridge (MA); Fellow, Imperial College 1985. Married 1943, Joan Kathleen, daughter of Dr E. W. Twining, MRCP (2 daughters and 1 son deceased). *Career:* Director, John Dale Ltd 1948–55, Chairman 1958–63, 1965–70; Member, London Board Scottish Union and National Insurance Co. 1958–63; Director, S. Hoffnung & Co. 1958–63, 1965–70, 1974–80; Deputy Chairman, Metal Closures Group Ltd 1960–63, 1965–70, Director 1965–70; Director, Securicor Ltd and Security Services Ltd 1961–63, 1965–70, 1974–85; Member, Norwich Union Insurance Group (London Advisory Board) 1965–70, 1974–76; Director, SGB Group Ltd 1974–86; Member of Council, CBI 1976–78; Director, Prudential Assurance Co. 1976–85, Chairman 1980–85; Chairman, CBI Education and Training Committee 1977–82; Director, Cadbury Schweppes Ltd 1979–87; Director, Prudential Corporation 1979–89, Chairman 1980–85; Chairman, CBI Special Programme Unit 1981–84; Chairman, Business in the Community 1984–87; Advisory Director: P. A. Strategy Partners 1985–87, Lek Partnership 1987–95. *House of Commons:* MP (Conservative) for: Mitcham 1950–74, Sutton Carshalton 1974–76; PPS to Rt Hon. Anthony Eden as: Secretary of State for Foreign Affairs 1951–55, Prime Minister 1955; Parliamentary Secretary, Ministry of Labour 1955–58; Secretary for Technical Co-operation 1963–64; Secretary of State for Employment 1970–72; Lord President of the Council and Leader of the House of Commons 1972; Home Secretary 1972–74.

Spokesman (Commons): Opposition Spokesman on: Aviation 1965–67, Labour 1967–70, Treasury 1974–75. *Select Committees (Commons):* Member, Select Committee on Estimates and Chairman of its Sub-Committee B 1959–63. *Backbench Committees (Commons):* Chairman, Conservative Backbench Committees on: Aviation 1965–67, Labour 1967–70. *Spokesman:* Opposition Spokesman on Economics, Industrial and Home Affairs 1976–79. *Select Committees:* Member, House of Lords Select Committee on the European Communities 1990–93. *Other:* Governor: St Mary's Hospital 1954–55, 1958–63, Imperial College of Science and Technology 1959–63, 1976–87; Vice-President, Birmingham Settlement; Vice-President, CORDA (Coronary Artery Disease Research Association). *Honours:* PC 1963. Fellow, Institute of Metallurgists 1957; Companion: British Institute of Management, Institute of Personel Management. *Publications: One Nation,* 1950 (jointly); *Change is our Ally,* 1954 (jointly); *The Responsible Society,* 1958 (jointly); *One Europe,* 1965 (jointly). *Recreations:* Lawn tennis, music, gardening. *Sportsclubs:* President, Surrey County Cricket Club 1985–86; Vice-President, All England Lawn Tennis Club 1990–. *Clubs:* Brooks's, MCC. *Name, Style and Title:* Raised to the peerage as Baron Carr of Hadley, of Monken Hadley in the County of Greater London 1976. A Conservative. *Address:* The Rt Hon. the Lord Carr of Hadley, 14 North Court, Great Peter Street, London, SW1P 3LL.

CARRINGTON (6th Baron, I), Peter Alexander Rupert Carington; cr. 1796; 6th Baron Carrington (GB) 1797; (Life) Baron Carington of Upton (UK) 1999; KG 1985; GCMG 1988; CH 1983; MC 1945; PC 1959; DL

Son of 5th Baron, DL, and late Hon. Sybil Marion Colville, daughter of 2nd Viscount Colville of Culross. Born June 6, 1919. Succeeded his father 1938; educated Eton; RMC, Sandhurst; Fellow, Eton College 1966–81; Hon. LLD: Cambridge 1981, Leeds 1981; Hon. Fellow, St Antony's College, Oxford 1982; Hon. Dr. of Laws: University of Philippines 1982, University of South Carolina 1983; Hon. LLD, Aberdeen 1985; DUniv, Essex 1983; Hon. Dr. of Laws, Harvard 1986; Hon. DSc, Cranfield 1988; Hon. Dr. of Laws: Reading 1989, Sussex 1989, DUniv, Buckingham 1989; Nottingham 1993, Birmingham 1993, Newcastle 1998. Married April 25, 1942, Iona, daughter of late Lieutenant-Colonel Sir Francis McClean, AFC, of Huntercombe Place, Henley-on-Thames (1 son 2 daughters). *Armed Forces:* Major, Grenadier Guards, served North West Europe 1940–46. *Councils, Public Bodies:* JP, Bucks 1948; DL, Bucks 1951. *Career:* UK High Commissioner in Australia 1956–59; Chairman, GEC 1983–84; Hon. Bencher of the Middle Temple 1983–; Secretary-General, NATO 1984–88; Chairman, Christies International plc 1988–93; Director, The Telegraph plc 1990–96; Chairman, EC Peace Conference on Yugoslavia 1991–92. *Chancellor:* Chancellor, University of Reading 1992–. *House of Lords:* Joint Parliamentary Secretary, Ministry of Agriculture and Fisheries 1951–54; Parliamentary Secretary, Ministry of Defence 1954–56; First Lord of the Admiralty 1959–63; Minister without Portfolio and Leader of the House of Lords October 1963-October 1964; Leader of Opposition, House of Lords 1964–70, 1974–79; Secretary of State for Defence 1970–74; Minister of Aviation Supply 1971–74; Secretary of State for: Energy January-February 1974, Foreign and Commonwealth Affairs 1979–82. *Whip:* Opposition Whip, House of Lords 1947–51. *Party Groups (General):* Chairman, Conservative Party 1972–74. *Other:* President, The Pilgrims 1983–; Elder Brother, Trinity House 1984; President, VSO 1993–98. *Trusts, etc:* Trustee, Cambridge Commonwealth Trust 1982–; Chairman of Trustees, Victoria and Albert Museum 1983–88; Trustee, Winston Churchill Memorial Trust. *Miscellaneous:* Chancellor of the Order of St Michael and St George 1984–94; Chancellor of the Most Noble Order of the Garter 1994–. *Honours:* MC 1945; PC 1959; CH 1983; KG 1985; GCMG 1988. *Publications:* Author of *Reflect on Things Past* (autobiography) 1988. *Clubs:* Pratt's, White's. *Heir:* His son, Hon. Rupert Francis John Carington, born December 2, 1948. *Name, Style and Title:* Created a life peer as Baron Carington of Upton, of Upton in the County of Nottinghamshire 1999. A Conservative. *Address:* The Rt Hon. the Lord Carrington, KG, GCMG, CH, MC, DL, The Manor House, Bledlow, Princes Risborough, Buckinghamshire, HP27 9PB *Tel:* 01844 343499; 32A Ovington Square, London, SW3 1LR *Tel:* 020 7584 1476 *Fax:* 020 7823 9051.

CARTER (Life Baron, UK), Denis Victor Carter; cr. 1987; PC 1997

Son of late Albert and Annie Carter. Born January 17, 1932; educated Xaverian College, Brighton; East Sussex College of Agriculture; Essex College of Agriculture (Queens Prize of the Royal Agricultural Society of England and Fream Memorial Prize); Worcester College, Oxford (BLitt 1976); Hon. Doctorate, University of Essex. Married August 3, 1957, Teresa Mary, daughter of late Cecil and Elsie Greengoe (1 daughter and 1 son deceased). *Armed Forces:* National Service, Egypt 1950–52. *Councils, Public Bodies:* Member, Northfield Committee of enquiry into ownership and occupancy of agricultural land 1977–79; JP 1966–70. *Career:* Audit Clerk 1949–50, 1953; Farmworker 1953–54; Agricultural education 1954–57; Founder and Director, Agricultural Accounting and Management Co. (AKC Ltd) 1957–97; Director: United Oilseeds Marketing Ltd 1972–97, W.E. and D.T. Cave Ltd 1976–97; Partner, Drayton Farms 1976–97; Executive Producer, Link Television programme for people with disabilities 1988–97. *House of Lords:* A Deputy Chairman of Committees 1997–; A Deputy Speaker 1999–. *Whip:* Opposition Whip 1987–92; Deputy Opposition Chief Whip 1990–92; Captain of the Honourable Corps of the Gentlemen at Arms (Government Chief Whip) 1997–. *Spokesman:* Spokesman on: Agriculture 1987–97, Social Security 1988–97, Health (Community Care) 1989–97. *Select Committees:* Member: House of Lords Select Committee on European Communities, Sub-Committee D 1987–92, Select Committee on House of Lords' Offices 1997–, Select Committee on House of Lords' Procedure 1997–. *All-Party:* Member: All-Party Disablement Group, All-Party Football Group, All-Party Cricket Group. *Other:* Member, Council of Royal Agricultural Society of England 1994–97. *Trusts, etc:* Trustee: Farmers' Club 1985–97, Rural Housing Trust 1991–97, John Arlott Memorial Trust 1993–97. *Miscellaneous:* Contested (Labour) Basingstoke 1970; MAFF Senior Research Fellowship in Agricultural Marketing, Oxford 1970–72; Member, Central Council for Agricultural and Horticultural Co-operation 1977–80; Chairman: BBC Central Agricultural Advisory Committee 1985–89, UK Co-operative Council 1993–97. *Honours:* PC 1997. Fellow, Institute of Agricultural Management 1992–; Fellow in Business Administration, Royal Agricultural College Fellow, Royal Agricultural Societies. *Special Interests:* Agriculture, Rural Affairs, Disability, Community Care, Health, Football. *Recreations:* Walking, reading, supporting Southampton FC. *Clubs:* Farmers' (Chairman 1982). *Name, Style and Title:* Raised to the peerage as Baron Carter, of Devizes in the County of Wiltshire 1987. Labour. *Address:* The Rt Hon. the Lord Carter, House of Lords, London, SW1A 0PW *Tel:* 020 7219 3131.

CARVER (Life Baron, UK), Richard Michael Power Carver; cr. 1977; GCB (Mil) 1970; CBE (Mil) 1945; DSO 1943 and Bar 1943; MC 1941

Son of late Harold Power Carver and Anne Carver (née Wellesley). Born April 24, 1915; educated Winchester; RMC, Sandhurst; DLitt (Hon), Southampton University 1991. Married November 22, 1947, Edith, daughter of late Lieutenant-Colonel Sir Henry Lowry-Corry, MC (2 sons 2 daughters). *Armed Forces:* Comd., 4th Armd Bde 1944–47; Deputy Chief of Staff, E. Africa 1954–55; Chief of Staff, E. Africa 1955–56; Director Army Plans 1958–59; Comd, 6th Bde 1960–62; GOC, 3rd Divn 1962–64; Director, Army Staff Duties 1964–66; Comd, Far East Land Forces 1966–67; Commander-in-Chief, Far East 1967–69; GOC in C, Southern Command 1969–71; Chief of General Staff 1971–73; Chief of Defence Staff 1973–76; Field Marshal 1973. *Select Committees:* Member, House of Lords Select Committee on Science and Technology 1985–92. *Other:* Vice-Councillor, Cancer Research Campaign. *Honours:* MC 1941; DSO and Bar 1943; CBE (Mil) 1945; GCB (Mil) 1970. *Publications:* Author of: *El Alamein*, 1962; *Tobruk*, 1964; *Harding of Petherton*, 1978; *The Apostles of Mobility*, 1979; *War Since 1945*, 1980; *A Policy for Peace*, 1982; *The Seven Ages of the British Army*, 1984; *Dilemmas of the Desert War*, 1986; *Twentieth Century Warriors*, 1987; *Out of Step*, 1989; *Tightrope Walking*, 1992; *Britain's Army in the Twentieth Century*, 1998; *The National Army Museum Book of the Boer War*, 1999; Editor: *The War Lords*, 1976; *Letters of A Victorian Army Officer: Edward Wellesley: 1840–1854*, 1995. *Special Interests:* Defence, Science and Technology. *Recreations:* Gardening. *Clubs:* Anglo-Belgian, Cavalry and Guards. *Name, Style and Title:* Raised to the peerage as Baron Carver, of Shackleford in the County of Surrey 1977. A Cross-Bencher. *Address:* Field Marshal The Lord Carver, GCB (Mil), CBE (Mil), DSO, MC, Wood End House, Wickham, Nr Fareham, Hampshire, PO17 6JZ *Tel:* 01329 832143.

CASTLE OF BLACKBURN (Life Baroness, UK), Barbara Anne Castle; cr. 1990; PC 1964

Daughter of late Frank and Annie Betts. Born October 6, 1910; educated Bradford Girls' Grammar School; St. Hugh's College, Oxford (BA); Hon. Fellow, St. Hugh's College, Oxford 1966; Hon. DTech: Bradford University 1968, Loughborough University 1969; Hon. Fellow: Bradford and Ilkley Community College 1985, UMIST 1991; Hon. LLD, Lancaster University 1991; Hon. Fellow: Humberside Polytechnic 1991, York University 1992; Hon. LLD: University of Manchester 1993, Cambridge University 1998; Hon. DLitt, De Montfort University 1998; Hon. DU, University of North London. Married 1944, Edward Cyril Castle (later created life peer as Baron Castle, died 1979). *Councils, Public Bodies:* Elected to St. Pancras Borough Council 1937; Member, Metropolitan Water Board 1940–45. *Career:* Assistant Editor, *Town and County Councillor* 1936–40; Administrative Officer, Ministry of Food 1941–44; Housing Correspondent and Forces Adviser, Daily Mirror 1944–45; MEP (Labour) for: Greater Manchester North, European Parliament 1979–84, Greater Manchester West 1984–89; Leader, British Labour Group 1979–85; Vice-Chairman, Socialist Group, European Parliament 1979–86. *House of Commons:* MP (Labour) for: Blackburn 1945–50, Blackburn East 1950–55, Blackburn 1955–79; Minister of Overseas Development 1964–65; Minister of Transport 1965–68; First Secretary of State and Secretary of State for Employment and Productivity 1968–70; Secretary of State for Social Services 1974–76. *Party Groups (General):* Member, National Executive Committee of Labour Party 1950–85; Vice-Chairman, Labour Party 1957–58, Chairman 1958–59. *Miscellaneous:* Co-Chairman, Women's National Commission 1975–76. *Honours:* PC 1964; Cross of Order of Merit of the Federal Republic of Germany 1990. Freeman, City of Bradford 1997. *Publications:* Author of: The Castle Diaries, (two volumes) 1980 and 1984; Sylvia and Christabel Pankhurst 1987; The Castle Diaries 1964–76, (paperback) 1990; Fighting all the Way, 1993. *Recreations:* Poetry, walking. *Name, Style and Title:* Raised to the peerage as Baroness Castle of Blackburn, of Ibstone in the County of Buckinghamshire 1990. Labour. *Address:* The Rt Hon. the Baroness Castle of Blackburn, House of Lords, London, SW1A 0PW.

CAVENDISH OF FURNESS (Life Baron, UK), Richard Hugh Cavendish; cr. 1990; DL

Son of late Captain Richard Edward Osborne Cavendish, DL. Born November 2, 1941; educated Eton. Married 1970, Grania Mary, daughter of Brigadier Toby St. George Caulfeild, CBE (1 son 2 daughters). *Councils, Public Bodies:* Councillor, Cumbria County Council 1985–90; High Sheriff of Cumbria 1978; DL, Cumbria 1988. *Career:* International merchanting and banking in London 1961–71; Chairman, Holker Estate Group of Companies 1971–; Director, UK Nirex Ltd 1993–99. *Whip:* A Lord in Waiting (Government Whip) 1990–92. *Select Committees:* Member, House of Lords Select Committee on the Croydon Tramlink Bill 1992–93. *All-Party:* Member, All-Party: Racing and Bloodstock Industries Committee, Arts and Heritage Group. *Party Groups:* Member, Association of Conservative Peers. *Party Groups (General):* Chairman, Morecambe and Lonsdale Conservative Association 1975–78. *Other:* Chairman of Governors, St. Anne's School, Windermere 1983–89; Chairman, Lancashire and Cumbria Foundation for Medical Research 1994–. *Miscellaneous:* Commissioner for the Historic Buildings and Monuments Commission (English Heritage) 1992–98. Fellow, Royal Society of Arts 1988. Liveryman, Fishmongers' Company. *Special Interests:* Education, Environment, Local Issues, Industry, Foreign Affairs, Drug and Alcohol Rehabilitation, Agriculture, Forestry. *Recreations:* Gardening, National Hunt racing, shooting, reading, travel. *Clubs:* Brooks's, White's, Pratt's, Beefsteak. *Name, Style and Title:* Raised to the peerage as Baron Cavendish of Furness, of Cartmel in the County of Cumbria 1990. A Conservative. *Address:* The Lord Cavendish of Furness, DL, Holker Hall, Cark-in-Cartmel, Cumbria, LA11 7PL *Tel:* 01539 558220 *Tel:* Office: 01539 558123 *Fax:* 01539 558776 *E-Mail:* cavendish@holker.co.uk.

CHADLINGTON (Life Baron, UK), Peter Selwyn Gummer; cr. 1996

Son of late Canon Selwyn Gummer and late Sybille (née Mason). Born August 24, 1942; educated King's School, Rochester, Kent; Selwyn College, Cambridge (BA, MA). Married 1982, Lucy Rachel, daughter of A. Ponsonby Dudley-Hill (1 son 3 daughters). *Career:* Portsmouth and Sunderland Newspaper Group Ltd 1964–65; Viyella International 1965–66; Hodgkinson and Partners 1966–67; Industrial and Commercial Finance Corporation 1967–74; Chairman, Shandwick plc 1974–; Non-Executive Director: CIA Group plc 1990–94, Halifax Building Society 1994–. *Other:* Chairman, Royal Opera House 1996–97. *Trusts, etc:* Chairman, Understanding Industry Trust 1991–95. *Miscellaneous:* Member: NHS Policy Board 1991–95, Arts Council of England 1991–96; Chairman, National Lottery Advisory Board for Arts and Film 1994–96. FRSA; FIPR. Freeman, City of London. *Publications:* Various articles and booklets on public relations. *Recreations:* Opera, rugby, cricket. *Clubs:* Garrick, MCC, Carlton. *Name, Style and Title:* Raised to the peerage as Baron Chadlington, of Dean in the County of Oxfordshire 1996. A Conservative. *Address:* The Lord Chadlington, 61 Grosvenor Street, London, W1X 9DA *Tel:* 020 7408 2232.

CHALFONT (Life Baron, UK), Alun Arthur Gwynne Jones; cr. 1964; PC 1964; OBE (Mil) 1961; MC 1957

Son of late Arthur Gwynne Jones, of Llantarnam, Gwent. Born December 5, 1919; educated West Monmouth School; School of Slavonic Studies, University of London. Married November 6, 1948, Mona, daughter of late Harry Douglas Mitchell (1 daughter deceased). *Armed Forces:* Commissioned as 2nd Lieutenant in South Wales Borderers 1940; Served in Burma and afterwards in Cyprus, Malaya and East Africa; Has held various intelligence appointments; Graduate of: Army Staff College 1950, Joint Service Staff College 1958; Resigned commission as Brevet Lieutenant-Colonel in 1961 upon appointment as Defence Correspondent of *The Times*; Hon. Colonel, University of Wales Officer Training Corps 1992–95. *Career:* Director: Shandwick plc 1979–94, IBM (UK) 1983–90, Lazard Bros & Co Ltd 1983–91; Chairman, Vickers Shipbuilding and Engineering Ltd 1987–95; Deputy Chairman, Independent Broadcasting Authority 1989–90; Chairman, Radio Authority 1991–95; Chairman, Marlborough Stirling 1994–; Director, Television Corporation 1996–; Chairman, Southern Mining Corp 1997–99. *House of Lords:* Minister of State for Foreign Affairs 1964–70. *Spokesman:* Opposition Spokesman on Defence and Foreign Affairs 1970–73. *All-Party:* President, House of Lords All-Party Defence Group. *International Bodies (General):* President: Hispanic and Luso Brazilian Council 1972–79, European Atlantic Group 1983–90. *Other:* President: Llangollen International Music Festival 1978–87, RNID 1980–87, Freedom in Sport 1982–88; Member: Royal Academy of Morocco, Pilgrims Society. *Honours:* MC 1957; OBE (Mil) 1961; PC 1964; Grand Officer, Order of the Southern Cross (Brazil) 1976. FRSA. Freeman, City of London. Member, Paviors' Company. *Publications:* Author of several books including: *The Great Commanders*, 1973; *Montgomery of Alamein*, 1976; *Waterloo: A Battle of Three Armies*, 1979; *Star Wars*, 1985; *Defence of the Realm*, 1987; *By God's Will*, 1989. *Special Interests:* Defence, Foreign Affairs. *Recreations:* Music. *Sportsclubs:* London Welsh RFC, Llanelli RFC. *Clubs:* MCC, Garrick, City Livery. *Name, Style and Title:* Raised to the peerage as Baron Chalfont, of Llantarnam, in the County of Monmouth 1964. A Cross-Bencher. *Address:* The Rt Hon. the Lord Chalfont, OBE, MC, House of Lords, London, SW1A 0PW.

CHALKER OF WALLASEY (Life Baroness, UK), Lynda Chalker; cr. 1992; PC 1987

Daughter of late Sidney Henry James Bates, and late Marjorie Kathleen Randell. Born April 29, 1942; educated Roedean; Heidelberg University; London University; Central London Polytechnic; Hon. Degrees: John Moores University, Bradford, Warwick, Liverpool, Westminster, East London, Cranfield. Married 1st 1967, Eric Robert Chalker (marriage dissolved 1973), married 2nd, December 10, 1981, Clive Landa. *Armed Forces:* Hon. Colonel, Royal Logistic Corps (156 Transport Regiment NW). *Career:* Formerly executive director, International Market Research company; Independent Consultant on Africa and Development 1997–. *House of Commons:* MP (Conservative) for Wallasey February 1974–92; Parliamentary Under-Secretary of State,

Department of Health and Social Security 1979–82; Parliamentary Under-Secretary of State, Department of Transport 1982–83, Minister of State 1983–86; Minister of State, Foreign and Commonwealth Office with special responsibility for: Europe, International trade, Economic relations, Personnel 1986–89, Sub-Saharan Africa and The Commonwealth 1986–97; Deputy to Foreign Secretary 1987–97. *Spokesman (Commons):* Opposition spokesman on Social Services 1976–79. *Select Committees (Commons):* Member, Select Committee on Immigration and Race Relations 1974–75. *Backbench Committees (Commons):* Member, Health and Social Security Committee 1974–76. *House of Lords:* Minister of Overseas Development and Minister for Africa and Commonwealth in Foreign and Commonwealth Office 1989–97. *All-Party:* Member, All-Party British-Ukrainian Country Group 1999–. *Party Groups (General):* National Vice-Chairman, Young Conservatives 1970–71. *Other:* President and Chairman, Board of Management of London School of Hygiene and Tropical Medicine. *Miscellaneous:* Member, BBC Advisory Committee 1974–79. *Honours:* PC 1987. Fellow, Royal Statistical Society. *Publications:* Author of: *Police in Retreat*, 1968; *Unhappy Families*, 1972; *We're Richer than We Think*, 1978; *Africa – Turning the Tide*, 1989. *Special Interests:* Voluntary Sector, European Co-operation, Africa, Overseas Aid and Development, Trade, Transport. *Recreations:* Theatre, cooking, gardening, jazz. *Name, Style and Title:* Raised to the peerage as Baroness Chalker of Wallasey, of Leigh-on-Sea in the County of Essex 1992. A Conservative. *Address:* The Rt Hon. the Baroness Chalker of Wallasey, House of Lords, London, SW1A 0PW *Tel:* House of Lords 020 7219 3000.

CHAPPLE (Life Baron, UK), Francis Joseph Chapple; cr. 1985

Son of late Frank Chapple. Born 1921; educated Elementary School. Married 1944, Joan (died 1994), daughter of James Nicholls (2 sons). *Trades Union:* Member, Electrical Trade Union 1937–83; Shop Steward and Branch Official; General Secretary, Electrical, Electronic, Telecommunication and Plumbing Union 1966–84; Member, General Council of the TUC 1971–83, Chairman 1982–83, Gold Badge of Congress 1983. *Select Committees:* Member, Select Committee on Sustainable Development 1994–95. *Miscellaneous:* Member: Royal Commission on Environmental Pollution 1973–77, Horserace Totalisator Board 1976–90, NEDC 1979–83. *Publications:* Sparks Fly (autobiography) 1984. *Name, Style and Title:* Raised to the peerage as Baron Chapple, of Hoxton in Greater London 1985. A Cross-Bencher. *Address:* The Lord Chapple, House of Lords, London, SW1A 0PW.

CHICHESTER (77th Bishop of), Eric Waldram Kemp; DD

Son of late Tom and Florence Kemp. Born April 27, 1915; educated Brigg Grammar School; Exeter College, Oxford (MA); St Stephen's House, Oxford (DD); Hon. DLitt, University of Sussex; Hon. DD, Berne. Married 1953, Leslie Patricia, daughter of late Rt Rev. K. E. Kirk (1 son 4 daughters). *Career:* Curate of St Luke, Southampton 1939–41; Librarian, Pusey House, Oxford 1941–46; Chaplain, Christ Church, Oxford 1943–46; Chaplain, Fellow and Lecturer at Exeter College, Oxford 1946–69; Proctor in Convocation 1949–69; Prebendary of Caistor in Lincoln Cathedral 1954–; Chaplain to HM Queen 1967–69; Dean of Worcester 1969–74; Bishop of Chichester 1974–; Took his seat in the House of Lords November 1979. *Miscellaneous:* Chanoine d'Honeur (Honorary Canon), Chartres Cathedral 1998. FRHistS. *Publications: Canonization and Authority in the Western Church*, 1948; *Norman Powell Williams*, 1954; *An Introduction to Canon Law in the Church of England*, 1957; *The Life and Letters of Kenneth Escott Kirk, Bishop of Oxford 1937–1954*, 1959; *Counsel and Consent: Aspects of the Government of the Church*, 1961; *The Anglican Methodist Conversations*, 1964; (Editor) *Man: Fallen and Free*, 1969; *Square Words in a Round World*, 1980. *Recreations:* Music, history. *Clubs:* National Liberal (President 1994–). *Address:* The Rt Rev. the Lord Bishop of Chichester, DD, The Palace, Chichester, West Sussex, PO19 1PY *Tel:* 01243 782161 *Fax:* 01243 531332.

CHILVER (Life Baron, UK), Amos Henry Chilver; cr. 1987; Kt 1978; FRS 1982

Son of late Amos Henry Chilver. Born October 30, 1926; educated Southend High School; Bristol University; Fellow, Corpus Christi College, Cambridge 1958–61. Married 1959, Claudia, only daughter of late Sir Wilfrid Grigson, CSI (3 sons 2 daughters). *Councils, Public Bodies:* Chairman, Milton Keynes Development Corporation 1983–92. *Career:* Railway Engineer 1947–48; Research Assistant, then Assistant Lecturer, then Lecturer, Bristol University 1948–54; Demonstrator then Lecturer, Cambridge University 1954–61; Professor Civil Engineering, UCL 1961–69; Vice-Chancellor, Cranfield Institute of Technology 1970–89; Chairman, English China Clays plc 1989–95; Non-executive Director: ICI 1990–93, Zeneca 1993–95; Chairman, RJB Mining 1993–97. *Miscellaneous:* Chairman, Universities Funding Council 1988–91. *Special Interests:* Education, Industry, Environment. *Clubs:* Athenaeum, United Oxford and Cambridge University. *Name, Style and Title:* Raised to the peerage as Baron Chilver, of Cranfield in the County of Bedfordshire 1987. A Conservative. *Address:* The Lord Chilver, FRS, English China Clays plc, 125 Wood Street, London, EC2V 7AQ *Tel:* 020 7696 9229.

CHITNIS (Life Baron, UK), Pratap Chidamber Chitnis; cr. 1977

Son of late Dr Chidamber N. Chitnis. Born May 1, 1936; educated Stonyhurst College; University of Birmingham (BA Hons); University of Kansas (MA). Married October 24, 1964, Anne, daughter of F. M. Brand (1 son deceased). *Career:* Administration Assistant, National Coal Board 1958–59; Secretary, The Joseph Rowntree Social Service Trust 1969–75, Chief Executive and Director, 1975–88; Member, Community Relations Commission 1970–77; Member, BBC Asian Programme Advice Committee 1972–77, Chairman 1979–83; Chairman, Refugee Action 1981–86; Chairman, British Refugee Council 1986–89. *Party Groups (General):* Liberal Party Organisation: Local Government Officer 1960–62, Agent, Orpington By-election 1962, Training Officer 1962–64, Press Officer 1964–66; Head, Liberal Party Organisation 1966–69. *Name, Style and Title:* Raised to the peerage as Baron Chitnis, of Ryedale in the County of North Yorkshire 1977. A Cross-Bencher. *Address:* The Lord Chitnis, House of Lords, London, SW1A 0PW.

CHOLMONDELEY (7th Marquess of, UK), David George Philip Cholmondeley; cr. 1815; 10th Earl of Cholmondeley (E) 1706; 7th Earl of Rocksavage (UK) 1815; 10th Viscount Malpas (E) 1706; 11th Viscount Cholmondeley (I) 1661; 10th Baron Cholmondeley (E) 1689; 10th Baron Newburgh (GB) 1716; 10th Baron Newborough (I) 1715; DL

Son of 6th Marquess, GCVO, MC, DL. Born June 27, 1960. Succeeded his father 1990; educated Eton; Sorbonne. *Councils, Public Bodies:* DL, Cheshire 1992. *Career:* A film maker; A Page of Honour to HM The Queen 1974–76; Joint Hereditary Lord Great Chamberlain of England (acting for the reign of Queen Elizabeth II) since 1990. *Recreations:* Music, tennis, travel. *Clubs:* White's, Vanderbilt, Champney's, Cercle de l'Union Interallée (Paris). *Heir:* His kinsman, Charles George Cholmondeley, born March 18, 1959. A Cross-Bencher. *Address:* The Most Hon. the Marquess of Cholmondeley, DL, Office: 10 St. James's Place, London, SW1A 1PE *Tel:* 020 7408 0418; House of Lords, London, SW1A 0PW; Cholmondeley Castle, Malpas, Cheshire, SY14 8AH.

CHRISTOPHER (Life Baron, UK), Anthony (Tony) Martin Grosvenor Christopher; cr. 1998; CBE 1984

Son of George and Helen Christopher. Born April 25, 1925; educated Cheltenham Grammar School; Westminster College of Commerce. Married 1962, Adela Joy Thompson. *Trades Union:* Member, TUC General Council 1976–89, Chairman 1988–89; Member, TUC Committees: Economic Committee 1977–89, Education Committee 1977–85, International Committee 1982–89, Finance and General Purposes Committee 1983–89, Education and Training Committee 1985–86, Employment and Organisation Committees 1985–89. *Armed Forces:* RAF 1944–48. *Career:* Articled Pupil, Agricultural Valuers, Gloucester 1941–44; Inland Revenue 1948–57; Inland Revenue Staff Federation: Assistant Secretary 1957–60, Assistant General Secretary 1960–74, Joint General Secretary 1975, General Secretary 1976–88; Chairman, TU Fund Managers Ltd 1983, Director 1981–; Industrial and Public Affairs Consultant 1988–. *Select Committees:* Member, Select Committee on European Communities Sub-Committee D (Agriculture, Fisheries and Food) 1999–. *International Bodies (General):* Members' Auditor, International Confederation of Free Trades Unions 1984–. *Trusts, etc:* Trustee: NACRO 1956–98, Trades Union Unit Trust Charitable Trust 1981–, Commonwealth Trades Union Council Charitable Trust 1985–89, Save The Children Fund 1985–90; Trustee, Institute for Public Policy Research 1989–94, Treasurer 1990–94. *Miscellaneous:* Member, Council, NACRO 1956–98, Chairman 1973–98; Director, Civil Service Building Society 1958–87, Chairman 1978–87; Member: Inner London Probation and After-care Committee 1966–79, Tax Reform Committee 1974–70, Royal Commission on Distribution of Income and Wealth 1978–79, Independent Broadcasting Authority 1978–83; Chairman, Tyre Industry Economic Development Council 1983–86; Member: Council of Institute of Manpower Studies 1984–89, Economic and Social Research Council 1985–88; Vice-President, Building Societies Association 1985–90; Director, Birmingham Midshires Building Society 1987–88; Member: General Medical Council 1989–94, Audit Commission 1989–95, Broadcasting Complaints Commission 1989–97; Former member of several other committees, inquiries and working parties. *Honours:* CBE 1984. FRSA 1989. *Publications: Policy for Poverty,* 1970 (jointly); *The Wealth Report,* 1979 (jointly); *The Wealth Report 2,* 1982 (jointly). *Special Interests:* Agriculture, Financial Services, Pensions, Penal Affairs and Policy, Economics, Industry. *Recreations:* Gardening. *Clubs:* Beefsteak, Wig and Pen, Royal Automobile. *Name, Style and Title:* Raised to the peerage as Baron Christopher, of Leckhampton in the County of Gloucestershire 1998. Labour. *Address:* The Lord Christopher, CBE, TU Fund Managers Ltd, Congress House, Great Russell Street, London, WC1B 3LQ.

CLARK OF KEMPSTON (Life Baron, UK), William Gibson Haig Clark; cr. 1992; Kt 1980; PC 1990

Son of late Hugh Clark. Born October 18, 1917; educated London. Married August 28, 1944, Irene Dorothy, daughter of F. D. Rands (2 sons and 1 son and 1 daughter deceased). *Armed Forces:* Served in Army in UK and India 1941–46, Major. *Councils, Public Bodies:* Councillor, Wandsworth Borough Council 1949–53; Vice-Chairman, Finance Committee 1949–52. *House of Commons:* Contested (Conservative) Northampton in 1955 General Election; MP (Conservative) for: Nottingham South 1959–66, Surrey East 1970–74, Croydon South 1974–92. *Spokesman (Commons):* Front Bench Spokesman on Trade, Finance and Economics 1964–66. *Select Committees (Commons):* Chairman, Select Committee on Tax Credits 1972–73. *Backbench Committees (Commons):* Chairman, Conservative Back Bench Finance Committee 1979–92. *Select Committees:* Former Member, Procedure Committee. *All-Party:* Member (former Chairman), All-Party British-Austrian Country Group. *Party Groups (General):* Chairman: Clapham Conservative Association 1949–52, Mid-Bedforshire Conservative Association 1956–59; Joint Treasurer, Conservative Party 1974–75; Deputy Chairman, Conservative Party 1975–77. *Other:* Hon. National Director, £2 million Carrington Appeal 1967; Chairman, Anglo-Austrian Society 1983–98, Patron 1998–; President, The City Group for Smaller Companies (Cisco) 1993–98. *Trusts, etc:* Fellow, Industry and Parliament Trust; Trustee, Carlton Club. *Honours:* Order of the Golden Fleece (Austria) 1989; PC 1990; Grand Decoration of Honour in Gold with Star (Austria) 1994. Member, Chartered Association of Certified Accountants 1941. Freeman, City of London. *Special Interests:* Finance, Industry, Trade and Industry, Housing, Cane Sugar, Insurance. *Recreations:* Reading. *Clubs:* Buck's, Carlton. *Name, Style and Title:* Raised to the peerage as Baron Clark of Kempston, of Kempston in the County of Bedfordshire 1992. A Conservative. *Address:* The Rt Hon. the Lord Clark of Kempston, The Clock House, Box End, Bedford, MK43 8RT *Tel:* 01234 852361; 3 Barton Street, London, SW1P 3NG *Tel:* 020 7222 5759.

CLARKE OF HAMPSTEAD (Life Baron, UK), Anthony James Clarke; cr. 1998; CBE 1998

Son of Henry Walter and Elizabeth Clarke. Born April 17, 1932; educated New End Primary School, Hampstead; St Dominics Roman Catholic School, Kentish Town; Ruskin College, Oxford. Married 1954, Josephine Ena Turner (1 son and 1 daughter). *Trades Union:* UPW: Committee Member 1953, Branch Secretary 1962–69; Member: London Trades Council 1965–69 (EC Member 1967–68), TUC Disputes Panel 1972–93, TUC SE Regional Council 1974–79, London Council of Post Office Unions 1975–79, Midlands Council of Post Office Unions 1975–79. *Armed Forces:* National Service, Royal Signals 1950–52; TA and Army Emergency Reserve 1952–68. *Councils, Public Bodies:* Councillor, London Borough of Camden 1971–78. *Career:* Post Office: Telegraph Boy, Postman, Postman Higher Grade (Sorter); Full-time Trade Union Officer, UPW 1979–93; Editor, UPW journal (*The Post*) 1979; Deputy General Secretary, UPW 1981–93. *International Bodies (General):* Organiser and Lecturer, Postal and Telegraph International (PTTI) in Malaysia and India. *Party Groups (General):* Member: Hampstead Labour Party 1954–86, Executive Committee, Labour Friends of Israel 1972–, Labour Party National Executive Committee 1983, St Albans Labour Party 1986–98, Chair, The Labour Party 1992–93; Governor, Westminster Foundation for Democracy 1992–98. *Other:* Governor, Quentin Kynaston Comprehensive School (ILEA) 1973–78; Executive Committee Member, Camden Committee for Community Relations 1974–81; Chairman, Camden Council of Social Services 1978–87; Management Committee Member: Hampstead Old Peoples' Homes, Newstead Old Peoples' Home. *Trusts, etc:* Trustee, Post Office Pension Funds 1991–97; Founder Member and Trustee, One World Action. *Miscellaneous:* Contested (Labour) Camden Hampstead February and October 1974 General Elections. *Honours:* Knight of St Gregory (Papal Order) 1994; CBE 1998. *Special Interests:* Overseas Aid and Development, Industrial Relations. *Recreations:* Arsenal FC, *The Archers*, reading. *Name, Style and Title:* Raised to the peerage as Baron Clarke of Hampstead, of Hampstead in the London Borough of Camden 1998. Labour. *Address:* The Lord Clarke of Hampstead, CBE, House of Lords, London, SW1A 0PW.

CLEDWYN OF PENRHOS (Life Baron, UK), Cledwyn Hughes; cr. 1979; PC 1966; CH 1977

Son of late Rev. Henry David Hughes, Presbyterian Minister, and Emily Hughes. Born September 14, 1916; educated Holyhead Grammar School; University College of Wales, Aberystwyth; Law Society; Hon. LLD: University of Wales 1970, University of Sheffield 1992, University of Glamorgan 1996; Fellow: University of Wales, Aberystwyth, Trinity College, Carmarthen. Married June 19, 1949, Jean Beatrice, only daughter of Captain Jesse Hughes, of Holyhead (1 son 1 daughter). *Armed Forces:* Served RAF (Flight/Lieutenant 1940–46). *Councils, Public Bodies:* Alderman, Anglesey County Council 1973. *Career:* Solicitor, qualified 1940 admitted January 1946; Consultant and Former Partner, T. R. Evans, Hughes & Co, Holyhead; Acting Clerk, Holyhead UDC to 1949; Anglesey County Council 1946–53. *House of Commons:* MP (Labour) Anglesey 1951–79; Minister of State, Commonwealth Relations 1964–1966; Secretary of State for Wales 1966–68; Minister of Agriculture, Fisheries and Food 1968–70. *Spokesman (Commons):* Opposition Spokesman on Housing and Local Government 1959–64; Opposition Spokesman on Agriculture 1970–72. *Select Committees (Commons):* Member: Estimates Committee 1955–58, Public Accounts Committee 1958–64, Privileges Committee 1974–79. *Party Groups (Commons):* Chairman, Parliamentary Labour Party 1974–79. *Chancellor:* Pro-Chancellor, University of Wales 1985–95. *House of Lords:* Deputy Leader of the Opposition 1981–82; Leader of the Opposition 1982–92. *Spokesman:* Opposition Spokesman on: Agriculture, The Civil Service 1983–88, Foreign Affairs, Welsh Affairs 1983–92. *Select Committees:* Chairman, Select Committee on Agriculture, Food and Consumer Affairs 1980–82; Member, Select Committee on Privileges. *Party Groups (General):* Member of Labour Party since 1938; Vice-Chairman, Parliamentary Labour Party 1974–75, Chairman 1975–79. *Other:* President: University College of Wales, Aberstwyth 1976–84, University of Wales, Bangor 1995–. *Miscellaneous:* Visited St Helena 1958; Represented British Government at Kenya Republic celebrations 1964; Leader, UK delegation to The Gambia Independence celebrations 1965; Hon. Freeman: Borough of Beaumaris 1972, Isle of Anglesey 1976; Leader, UK delegation to Russia 1977; Prime Minister's Envoy to Southern Africa 1978; Chairman, Welsh Committee on Economic Affairs 1982–84; President, Assembly of Welsh Counties 1990–; Member, Political Honours Scrutiny Committee 1992–. *Honours:* PC 1966; CH 1977.

Publications: Problems of St Helena, 1958. *Special Interests:* Welsh Literature, Welsh Sport. *Clubs:* Travellers'. *Name, Style and Title:* Raised to the peerage as Baron Cledwyn of Penrhos, of Holyhead in the Isle of Anglesey 1979. Labour. *Address:* The Rt Hon. the Lord Cledwyn of Penrhos, CH, Penmorfa, Trearddur, Holyhead, Gwynedd *Tel:* 01407 860544; House of Lords, London, SW1A 0PW *Tel:* House of Lords 020 7219 3236.

CLEMENT-JONES (Life Baron, UK), Timothy Francis Clement-Jones; cr. 1998; CBE 1988

Son of late Maurice Llewelyn Clement-Jones. Born October 26, 1949; educated Haileybury; Trinity College, Cambridge (Degree in Economics (Part 1) and Law (Part 2). Married 1st, June 14, 1973, Dr Vicky Clement-Jones (died 1987); married 2nd, July 15, 1994, Jean Whiteside (1 son). *Career:* Solicitor; Founding Partner, Independent Corporate Mentoring (ICM); Director, Political Context Ltd; Head of Legal Services, London Weekend Television 1980–83; Legal Director, Grand Metropolitan Retailing 1984–86; Group Company Secretary and Legal Adviser, Kingfisher plc 1986–95; Chairman, Environmental Context Ltd. *Spokesman:* Liberal Democrat Spokesman on Health 1998–. *All-Party:* Member, All-Party: Cancer Group, Kidney Group, Retail Group. *Party Groups (General):* Chairman: Association of Liberal Lawyers 1981–86, Liberal Democrat Party Federal Finance Committee 1991–; Director, Liberal Democrat Campaign for the European Parliamentary Elections 1994; Member, Liberal Democrat National Executive. *Other:* Former Chairman and Director, Crime Concern; Former Member, Council of the London Lighthouse; Former Director, Brixton City Challenge. *Trusts, etc:* Trustee: Cancer BACUP, Lambeth Crime Prevention Trust. *Honours:* CBE 1988. *Recreations:* Travelling, eating, talking, reading, walking. *Clubs:* Royal Automobile, National Liberal. *Name, Style and Title:* Raised to the peerage as Baron Clement-Jones, of Clapham in the London Borough of Lambeth 1998. A Liberal Democrat. *Address:* The Lord Clement-Jones, CBE, House of Lords, London, SW1A 0PW.

CLINTON-DAVIS (Life Baron, UK), Stanley Clinton Clinton-Davis; cr. 1990; PC 1998

Son of Sidney and Lily Davis. Born December 6, 1928; educated Hackney Down School, Mercer's School; King's College, London University (LLB 1950); Fellow, Queen Mary and Westfield College; Holds an Hon. Doctorate at the Polytechnic University of Bucharest; Hon. ACA Degree. Married 1954, Frances Jane, daughter of late Dr Marcus Gerschon Lucas, of Birmingham (1 son 3 daughters). *Councils, Public Bodies:* Councillor, London Borough of Hackney 1959, Mayor 1968. *Career:* Admitted solicitor 1953; President, UN Selection Committee for the Sasakawa Environment Project 1989–97; Consultant on European law and affairs with S. J. Berwin & Co. solicitors 1989–. *House of Commons:* Contested (Labour): Portsmouth, Langstone in 1955, Yarmouth in 1959 and 1964 General Elections; MP (Labour) for Hackney Central 1970–83; Parliamentary Under-Secretary of State, Department of Trade 1974–79. *Spokesman (Commons):* Opposition Spokesman on: Trade, prices and consumer protection 1979–81, Foreign affairs 1981–83. *All-Party Committees (Commons):* Secretary, PLP Anglo-Chilean Group 1972–74. *House of Lords:* Minister of State, Department of Trade and Industry (Minister for Trade) 1997–98. *Spokesman:* Opposition Spokesman on Transport in the House of Lords 1990–97; Supporting Spokesman on: Trade and Industry 1990–96, Foreign Affairs 1990–97. *All-Party:* Member, All-Party: Environment Group, Transport Group. *International Bodies:* Member, Council of Europe and WEU. *International Bodies (General):* Member, Royal Institute for International Affairs. *Party Groups (General):* Member, Executive Council, National Association of Labour Student Organisations 1949–50; Joint President, Society of Labour Lawyers. *Other:* President, Hackney Branch, Multiple Sclerosis Society; Patron, Hackney Association for the Disabled; President, UK Pilots (Marine); President: Institute of Travel Management, British Airline Pilots Association, Aviation Environment Federation; Vice-President, Chartered Institute of Environmental Health; Chairman, Europe 21. *Awards Granted:* Awarded first medal by Eurogroup for Animal Welfare 1988. *Trusts, etc:* Trustee, Bernt Carlsson Trust 1989–. *Miscellaneous:* Member, Commission of the European Communities 1985–89; Chair, Advisory Committee on Pollution of the Sea 1984–85, 1989–97; Member: Council of Justice, Council of British Maritime League 1989–; Chair, Refugee Council 1989–97; Former President, Association of Municipal Authorities (AMA); Member, Advisory Panel of CIS Environ Trust. *Honours:* Honoured with Grand Cross, Order of Leopold II (Belgium) for services to the EC 1990; PC 1998. Fellow, Chartered Institution of Water and Environmental Management. *Publications:* Joint Author of a Report in a British Parliamentary Delegation in 1982, *Good Neighbours? Nicaragua, Central America and the United States. Special Interests:* Transport, Environment, Foreign Affairs, Law, Civil Liberties. *Recreations:* Association football, golf, political biographies. *Sportsclubs:* Hendon Golf Club. *Clubs:* Royal Overseas League. *Name, Style and Title:* Raised to the peerage as Baron Clinton-Davis, of Hackney in the London Borough of Hackney 1990. Labour. *Address:* The Rt Hon. the Lord Clinton-Davis, House of Lords, London, SW1A 0PW.

CLYDE (Life Baron, UK), James John Clyde; cr. 1996; PC 1996

Son of late Rt Hon. Lord Clyde. Born January 29, 1932; educated Edinburgh Academy; Corpus Christi College, Oxford (BA); Edinburgh University (LLB); DUniv, Heriot-Watt 1991; DLitt, Napier University 1995; Hon. Fellow Corpus Christi College, Oxford 1996 DUniv, Edinburgh University 1997. Married 1963, Ann Clunie Hoblyn (2 sons). *Armed Forces:* National Service 1954–56. *Career:* Called to the Scottish Bar 1959; QC (Scot) 1971; Advocate-Depute 1973–74; Chancellor to the Bishop of Argyll and the Isles 1972–85; A Judge of the Courts of Appeal of Jersey and Guernsey 1979–85; A Senator of the College of Justice in Scotland 1985–96; A Lord of Appeal in Ordinary 1996–; Elected as Honorary Master of the Bench of the Middle Temple 1996. *Select Committees:* Chairman, Joint Select Committee on Consolidation of Bills 1998–. *Other:* Director, Edinburgh Academy 1979–88; Vice-President, Royal Blind Asylum and School 1987–; Hon. President, Scottish Young Lawyers' Association 1988–97; Governor, Napier Polytechnic 1989–93; Chairman, Governors, St George's School for Girls 1989–97; Assessor to the Chancellor of Edinburgh University and Vice-Chairman of Court 1989–97. *Trusts, etc:* Trustee: St Mary's Music School 1976–92, National Library of Scotland 1977–93; Chairman, Special Trustees of St Mary's Hospital, Paddington 1997–99. *Miscellaneous:* Contested (Conservative) Dundee East 1974; Chairman: Medical Appeal Tribunal 1974–85, Committee of Investigation for Scotland on Agricultural Marketing 1984–85, Scottish Valuation Advisory Council 1987–96, Member 1972–96, European Institute 1990–97, Orkney Children Inquiry 1991–92. *Honours:* PC 1996. *Publications:* (Ed. jointly) *Armour on Valuation,* 3rd ed. 1961, 5th ed. 1985. *Recreations:* Music, gardening. *Clubs:* New (Edinburgh). *Name, Style and Title:* Raised to the peerage as Baron Clyde, of Briglands in Perthshire and Kinross 1996. A Cross-Bencher. *Address:* The Rt Hon. the Lord Clyde, 12 Dublin Street, Edinburgh, EH1 3PP *Tel:* 0131–556 7114; House of Lords, London, SW1A 0PW.

COCKFIELD (Life Baron, UK), Francis Arthur Cockfield; cr. 1978; Kt 1973; PC 1982

Son of Lieutenant Charles Francis Cockfield, killed in the battle of the Somme 1916. Born September 28, 1916; educated Dover Grammar School; London School of Economics (LLB, BSc Economics); Hon. Fellow, LSE 1972–; Hon. Doctor, University Surrey 1989; Hon. LLD: Fordham (New York) 1989, Sheffield University 1990. Married 1970, Aileen Monica Mudie (died April 3, 1992). *Career:* Called to the Bar, Inner Temple, 1942; HM Customs and Excise 1933; Estate Duty Office 1935; Secretaries' Office Board of Inland Revenue 1938, Assistant Secretary 1945; Director, Statistics and Intelligence 1945–52; Commissioner of Inland Revenue 1951–52; Finance Director, Boots Pure Drug Co. 1953–61, Managing Director and Chairman of Executive Committee 1961–67 (retired); Member, NEDC 1962–64, 1982–83; Adviser on Taxation Policy to Chancellor of the Exchequer 1970–73; Chairman, Price Commission 1973–77; Vice-President, Commission of the European Communities 1985–89; Adviser, Peat Marwick McLintock 1989–93. *House of Lords:* Minister of State, Treasury, June 1979–82; Secretary of State for Trade 1982–1983; Chancellor of the Duchy of Lancaster 1983–84. *Spokesman:* Government Spokesman on Trade and Industry and for the Treasury 1983–84. *Other:* Member, County Governors, Nottingham University 1963–67. *Honours:* Kt 1974; PC 1982; Grand Cross, Order of Leopold II (Belgium). President, The Royal Statistical Society 1968–69. *Publications: The European Union: Creating the Single Market,* 1994. *Name, Style and Title:* Raised to the peerage as Baron Cockfield, of Dover in the County of Kent 1978. A Conservative. *Address:* The Rt Hon. the Lord Cockfield, House of Lords, London, SW1A 0PW.

COCKS OF HARTCLIFFE (Life Baron, UK), Michael Francis Lovell Cocks; cr 1987; PC 1976

Son of late Dr H. F. Lovell Cocks. Born August 19, 1929; educated Bristol University. Married 1st, 1954, Janet Macfarlane (2 sons 2 daughters), married 2nd, 1979, Valerie Davis. *Career:* Various posts in education from 1954; Lecturer, Bristol Polytechnic 1968. *House of Commons:* Contested (Labour): Bristol West 1959, South Gloucestershire 1964, 1966; MP (Labour) for Bristol South 1970–87. *Whip (Commons):* Parliamentary Secretary to HM Treasury (Chief Whip) April 1976–79. *House of Lords:* A Deputy Speaker of the House of Lords 1990–; A Deputy Chairman of Committees 1997–. *Party Groups (General):* President, Bristol Borough Labour Party 1961–63. *Miscellaneous:* Vice-Chairman, BBC 1993–98. *Name, Style and Title:* Raised to the peerage as Baron Cocks of Hartcliffe, of Chinnor in the County of Oxfordshire 1987. Labour. *Address:* The Rt Hon. the Lord Cocks of Hartcliffe, House of Lords, London, SW1A 0PW.

COGGAN (Life Baron, UK), Frederick Donald Coggan; cr. 1980; PC 1961; MA; DD

Son of late Cornish Arthur Coggan, company director. Born October 9, 1909; educated Merchant Taylors' School; St John's College, Cambridge (MA 1st Class Oriental Languages); Wycliffe Hall, Oxford; Hon. DD: Leeds 1958, Cambridge 1962, Aberdeen 1963, Tokyo 1963, Saskatoon 1963, Huron 1963, Hull 1963; HHD, Westminster Choir College, Princeton 1966; Hon. DLitt, Lancaster 1967; STD, Gen Theol Seminary, NY 1967; Hon. DD, Manchester 1972; Hon. LLD, Liverpool 1972; Hon. DCL, Kent 1975; DUniv, York 1975; Hon. DD: Moravian Theol Seminary 1976, Virginia Theol Seminary 1979. Married October 17, 1935, Jean Braithwaite, daughter of Dr. Loudon Strain (2 daughters). *Career:* Assistant Lecturer in Semitic Languages and Literature at Manchester University 1931–34; Ordained Deacon 1934, Priest 1935; Curate of St Mary's, Islington 1934–37; Professor of New Testament, Wycliffe College Toronto 1937–44; Principal, London College of Divinity 1944–56; Bishop of Bradford 1956–61; Took his seat in the House of Lords 1961; Archbishop of York 1961–74; Prelate Order of St John of Jerusalem 1967–91; Archbishop of Canterbury 1974–80; Chairman, Executive Committee, Council of Christians and Jews 1983–87. *Chancellor:* Pro-Chancellor, Universities of: York 1962–74, Hull 1968–74. *Other:* President, Society for Old Testament Studies 1967–68; Chairman, College of Preachers to 1980; First Life President, Church Army 1981. *Honours:* PC 1961; Received the Royal Victorian Chain 1980. Freeman, City of Canterbury 1976. *Publications:* Author of: *A People's Heritage; The Ministry of the Word; The Glory of God; Stewards of Grace; Five Makers of the New Testament; Christian Priorities; The Prayers of the New Testament; Sinews of Faith; Word and World; Convictions; On Preaching; The Heart of Christian Faith,* 1978; *Sure Foundation; Mission to the World,* 1982; *Paul: Portrait of a Revolutionary,* 1984; *The Sacrament of the Word,* 1987; *Cuthbert Bardsley – Bishop, Pastor, Evangelist,* 1989; *God of Hope,* 1991; *Voice from the Cross,* 1993; *The Servant Son: Jesus Then and Now,* 1995; *A New Day for Preaching,* 1996; *Meet Paul,* 1998; *Psalms 1–72,* 1998; *Psalms 73–150,* 1999. *Recreations:* Reading, travel, tapestry. *Clubs:* Athenaeum, Grillion's. *Name, Style and Title:* Raised to the peerage as Baron Coggan, of Canterbury and Sissinghurst in the County of Kent 1980. A Cross-Bencher. *Address:* The Rt Rev. and Rt Hon. the Lord Coggan, MA, DD, 28 Lions Hall, St Swithun Street, Winchester, Hampshire, SO23 9HW *Tel:* 01962 864289.

COLVILLE OF CULROSS (4th Viscount, UK), John Mark Alexander Colville; cr. 1902; 13th Lord Colville of Culross (S) 1604; 4th Baron Colville of Culross (UK) 1885; QC 1978

Son of 3rd Viscount, DL. Born July 19, 1933. Succeeded his father, who was killed on active service, 1945; educated Rugby; New College, Oxford (BA 1957, MA 1963); Hon. Fellow, New College, Oxford 1997; Hon. DCL, University of East Anglia 1998. Married 1st, 1958, Mary Elizabeth Webb-Bowen (4 sons) (marriage dissolved 1973), married 2nd, 1974, Margaret Birgitta, Viscountess Davidson, daughter of late Major-General C. H. Norton, CB, CBE, DSO (1 son). *Armed Forces:* Lieutenant, Grenadier Guards (RARO). *Career:* Barrister-at-Law, Lincoln's Inn 1960; QC 1978; UK Representative, UN Commission on Human Rights 1980–83; Special Rapporteur on Guatemala 1983–87; Chairman, Mental Health Act Commission 1983–87; Bencher 1986; Chairman, Parole Board for England and Wales 1988–92; Recorder 1990–93; Judge, South Eastern Circuit 1993–99; Member, UN Human Rights Committee 1996–. *House of Lords:* Minister of State,

Home Office 1972–74; An elected hereditary peer 1999–. *Select Committees:* Member, Joint Select Committee on Consolidation of Bills 1998–. *Miscellaneous:* Member, Queen's Bodyguard for Scotland, Royal Company of Archers. *Heir:* His son, Hon. Charles Mark Townshend Colville, Master of Colville, born September 5, 1959. A Cross-Bencher. *Address:* The Viscount Colville of Culross, QC, The Manor House, West Lexham, Kings Lynn, Norfolk, PE32 2QN.

COLWYN (3rd Baron, UK), (Ian) Anthony Hamilton-Smith; cr. 1917; 3rd Bt of Colwyn Bay (UK) 1912; CBE 1989

Son of 2nd Baron. Born January 1, 1942. Succeeded his father 1966; educated Cheltenham College; St Bartholomew's Hospital and Royal Dental Hospital, University of London (BDS (University of London 1966, LDS, RCS (England) 1966). Married 1st, May 30, 1964, Sonia Jane, daughter of Peter H. G. Morgan, of Upton-on-Severn, Worcestershire (1 son 1 daughter) (marriage dissolved 1977), married 2nd, 1977, Nicola Jeanne, daughter of Arthur Tyers, of Sunbury-on-Thames (2 daughters). *Trades Union:* Member, Musicians' Union. *Career:* Dental Practice; Chairman, Dental Protection Ltd. 1995–; Non-Executive Director: Medical Protection Society, Project Hope; Bandleader, Lord Colwyn Organisation. *House of Lords:* An elected hereditary peer 1999–.
Select Committees: Member, Select Committees on: Medical Ethics 1993–97, House of Lords' Offices 1997–; Chairman, Refreshment Sub-Committee 1997–. *All-Party:* President, Parliamentary All-Party Group on Alternative and Complementary Medicine 1989–; Joint Chair, All-Party Jazz Group; Member, All-Party: Arts and Heritage Group, Cycling Group, Breast Cancer Group, AIDS Group, Food and Health Group, Rugby Union Group, Skin Group, Pharmaceutical Industry Group, Kidney Group. *Party Groups (General):* Member, Conservative Medical Society. *Other:* President: Natural Medicines Society 1988–, Huntington's Disease Association 1991–98, Society for Advancement of Anaesthesia in Dentistry 1993–98, Arterial Health Foundation 1993–, Metropolitan Branch, British Dental Association 1994–95; Council Member, Medical Protection Society 1994–. *Trusts, etc:* Member, Eastman Research Institute Trust. Member, Royal Society of Medicine. *Publications:* Various articles on Anaesthesia in Dentistry. *Special Interests:* Broadcasting, Health, Alternative Medicine, Arts. *Recreations:* Bandleader, music, riparian pursuits. *Sportsclubs:* Cheltenham Rugby, Colwyn Bay Rugby. *Heir:* His son, Hon. Craig Peter Hamilton-Smith, born October 13, 1968. A Conservative. *Address:* The Lord Colwyn, CBE, 53 Wimpole Street, London, W1M 7DF *Tel:* 020 7935 6809 *E-Mail:* colwyna@parliament.uk.

CONSTANTINE OF STANMORE (Life Baron, UK), Theodore Constantine; cr. 1981; Kt 1964; CBE 1956; AE 1945; DL

Son of late Leonard Constantine. Born March 15, 1910; educated Acton College, London. Married May 2, 1935, Sylvia Mary (died September 11, 1990), daughter of late Wallace Legge-Pointing (1 son 1 daughter). *Armed Forces:* Served Royal Auxiliary Air Force, Fighter Command 1939–45 (Air Efficiency Award 1945). *Councils, Public Bodies:* High Sheriff, Greater London 1967; DL, Greater London 1967. *Career:* Secretary to Managing Director, Calders Ltd 1926–28; Personal Assistant to Managing Director, Pedestros Ltd 1928–31; Adminstration Manager, A.T. Betts & Co Ltd 1931–34; General Manager, Allen and Hanburys (Acoustic Division) 1934–39; Director, Allen and Hanburys (Acoustics) Ltd 1945–50; Chief Executive, Bonochord Ltd 1950–63; Deputy Chairman, Henry C. Stephens Ltd 1964–66; Chairman: Waterman Pen Co. Ltd 1966–68, Anscon Ltd 1966–, London Private Health Group plc 1981–85, Health Care Services plc 1985; Director, Stratstone Ltd 1985–92. *Party Groups (General):* Chairman, National Union Conservative Party 1968, President 1980; Work for Conservative party as constituency Chairman, area Chairman, Member National Executive Committee, Policy Committee, National Advisory Committee on publicity. *Trusts, etc:* Trustee, Sir John Wolstenholme Charity 1962–89. *Honours:* AE 1945; CBE 1956; Kt 1964. Freeman, City of London 1949. Master, Worshipful Company of Coachmakers 1975. *Recreations:* Reading, walking, watching motor racing. *Clubs:* Carlton. *Name, Style and Title:* Raised to the peerage as Baron Constantine of Stanmore, of Stanmore in Greater London 1981. A Conservative. *Address:* The Lord Constantine of Stanmore, CBE, AE, DL, House of Lords, London, SW1A 0PW.

COOKE OF ISLANDREAGH (Life Baron, UK), Victor Alexander Cooke; cr. 1992; OBE 1981

Son of Victor and Alice Cooke. Born October 18, 1920; educated Marlborough College; Trinity College, Cambridge (MA). Married 1951, Alison Sheila Casement (2 sons 1 daughter). *Armed Forces:* Engineer Officer, Royal Navy 1940–46. *Councils, Public Bodies:* DL, Co. Antrim 1970–96. *Career:* Henry R. Ayton Ltd, Belfast 1946–89, Chairman 1970–89; Chairman: Belfast Savings Bank 1963, Springvale EPS 1964–; Chairman, Harland & Wolff Ltd 1980–81, Director 1970–87; Director, Northern Ireland Airports 1970–85; Senator, Parliament of Northern Ireland 1960–68. *Miscellaneous:* Member, Northern Ireland Economic Council 1974–78; A Belfast Harbour Commissioner 1968–79; A Commissioner of Irish Lights 1983–96, Chairman 1990–92. CEng; FIMechE. *Special Interests:* Manufacturing Industries, Energy, Maritime Affairs. *Recreations:* Sailing, shooting. *Name, Style and Title:* Raised to the peerage as Baron Cooke of Islandreagh, of Islandreagh in the County of Antrim 1992. A Ulster Unionist/Cross-Bencher. *Address:* The Lord Cooke of Islandreagh, OBE, House of Lords, London, SW1A 0PW.

COOKE OF THORNDON (Life Baron, UK), Robin (Brunskill) Cooke; cr. 1996; KBE 1986; Kt 1977; PC 1977

Son of late Hon. Philip Brunskill Cooke, MC, Judge of the Supreme Court of New Zealand, and of Valmai Digby Gore. Born May 9, 1926; educated Wanganui Collegiate School; Victoria University College, Wellington (LLM); Clare College, Cambridge; Gonville and Caius College, Cambridge (MA, PhD); Hon. Fellow, Gonville and Caius College, Cambridge 1982; Hon. LLD: Victoria University of Wellington 1989, Cambridge University 1990; Hon. DCL, Oxford University 1991. Married 1952, Phyllis Annette Miller (3 sons). *Career:* Travelling Scholarship in Law, New Zealand 1950; Fellow, Gonville and Caius College, Cambridge 1952–56; Called to the Bar, Inner Temple 1954; Hon. Bencher 1985; Practised at New Zealand Bar 1955–72; QC 1964; Chairman, Commission of Inquiry into Housing 1970–71; Judge of the Supreme Court 1972; President, Court of Appeal of: Western Samoa 1982, 1994, 1995, Cook Islands 1981, 1982; Appointed a Judge of the Supreme Court of Fiji and sat at its inaugural session in November 1995; Administrator, Government of New Zealand for periods in 1986, 1992, 1993 and 1995; Judge, Court of Appeal of New Zealand 1976–86, President 1986–96; Member, Advisory Board, Centre for Independence of Judges and Lawyers 1989; Commission Member representing New Zealand, International Commission of Jurists 1993–; A Lord of Appeal 1996–; Overseas Judge: Court of Final Appeal of Hong Kong 1997–, Court of Appeal Kiribati 1999–. *Other:* Special Status Member, The American Law Institute 1993–; Life Member, Lawasia; Patron, Wellington Cricket Association, New Zealand. *Awards Granted:* Yorke Prize, University of Cambridge 1954. *Miscellaneous:* Visiting Fellow, All Souls, Oxford 1990; Hon. Fellow, New Zealand Legal Research Foundation 1993–; Distinguished Visiting Fellow, Victoria University of Wellington 1998–. *Honours:* PC 1977; Kt 1977; KBE 1986. *Publications: Portrait of a Profession* (Centennial Book of New Zealand Law Society), 1969 (editor); *The Laws of New Zealand,* Editor-in-Chief 1990–; Sultan Azlan Shah Lecture, Malaysia 1990; Peter Allan Memorial Lecture, Hong Kong 1994; *Turning Points of the Common Law* (Hamlyn Lectures), 1996; Has contributed many articles in law journals and papers at international law conferences. *Recreations:* Theatre, cricket, *The Times* crossword. *Sportsclubs:* Wellington Golf (NZ). *Clubs:* United Oxford and Cambridge University, Wellington (NZ). *Name, Style and Title:* Raised to the peerage as Baron Cooke of Thorndon, of Wellington in New Zealand and of Cambridge in the County of Cambridgeshire 1996. A Cross-Bencher. *Address:* The Rt Hon. the Lord Cooke of Thorndon, KBE, 4 Homewood Crescent, Karori, Wellington, New Zealand; Lords of Appeal Corridor, House of Lords, London, SW1A 0PW.

Dod *on* Disk
The Vacher Dod Parliamentary Database – configured for PC or Network

For further details please telephone the Westminster Office

020 7828 7256

COPE OF BERKELEY (Life Baron, UK), John Ambrose Cope; cr. 1997; Kt 1991; PC 1988

Son of late George Cope, MC, FRIBA. Born May 13, 1937; educated Oakham School, Rutland. Married March 29, 1969, Djemila Payne (2 daughters). *Armed Forces:* National Service (Commissioned RA) 1955–57, subsequently TA. *Career:* Chartered Accountant; Worked for the Conservative Party, Westminster 1965–70. *House of Commons:* MP (Conservative) for Gloucestershire South 1974–83 and for Northavon 1983–97; Minister of State for: Employment with special responsibility for Small Firms 1987–89, Northern Ireland Office 1989–90; Paymaster General, HM Treasury 1992–94. *Whip (Commons):* Government Whip 1979–1981; Lord Commissioner to the Treasury 1981–83; Treasurer, Her Majesty's Household and Deputy Chief Whip 1983–87. *Spokesman:* Opposition Spokesman on: Northern Ireland 1997–, the Home Office 1998–. *International Bodies (General):* Member, UK Parliamentary Delegation to Council of Europe and Western European Union 1995–97. *Party Groups (General):* Conservative Party: Deputy Chairman 1990–92, Hon. Joint Treasurer 1991–92. *Other:* Commissioner, Royal Hospital Chelsea 1992–94; Deputy Chairman, Small Business Bureau; Chairman, Horse and Pony Taxation Committee; Patron, Friends of Spafford Children's Centre of Jerusalem; President, Dyrham Park Appeal. *Trusts, etc:* Patron, The Vigilant Trust. *Honours:* PC 1988; Knighted 1991. *Special Interests:* Aerospace, Agriculture, Small Businesses. *Clubs:* Carlton, Beefsteak, Tudor House (Chipping Sodbury). *Name, Style and Title:* Raised to the peerage as Baron Cope of Berkeley, of Berkeley in the County of Gloucestershire 1997. A Conservative. *Address:* The Rt Hon. the Lord Cope of Berkeley, House of Lords, London, SW1A 0PW *E-Mail:* john.cope@email.tory.org.uk.

COURTOWN (9th Earl of, I), James Patrick Montagu Burgoyne Winthrop Stopford; cr. 1762; Viscount Stopford; 9th Baron Courtown (I) 1758; 8th Baron Saltersford (GB) 1796

Son of 8th Earl, OBE, TD. Born March 19, 1954. Succeeded his father 1975. Sits as Baron Saltersford; educated Eton; Berkshire College of Agriculture; Royal Agricultural College, Cirencester. Married July 6, 1985, Elisabeth, daughter of I. R. Dunnett, of Broad Campden, Gloucestershire (1 son 1 daughter). *Career:* Land Agent: Bruton Knowles, Gloucester 1987–90, John German, Shrewsbury 1990–93. *House of Lords:* An elected hereditary peer 1999–. *Whip:* A Lord-in-Waiting (Government Whip) 1995–97; An Opposition Whip 1997–. *Spokesman:* Former Government Spokesman for the Home Office, Scotland and Transport. *Select Committees:* Member, Select Committee on Bodmin Moor Commons Bill 1994. *All-Party:* Member, All-Party: Forestry Group, Anglo-Swiss Group; Chairman, All-Party Ski Group 1999–. ARICS. *Special Interests:* Agriculture, Environment, Property. *Recreations:* Fishing, shooting, skiing. *Heir:* His son, Viscount Stopford, born March 30, 1988. A Conservative. *Address:* The Earl of Courtown, House of Lords, London, SW1A 0PW.

COWDREY OF TONBRIDGE (Life Baron, UK), Michael Colin Cowdrey; cr. 1997; Kt 1992; CBE 1972

Son of Ernest and Kathleen Cowdrey. Born December 24, 1932; educated Tonbridge; Brasenose College, Oxford; Hon. Fellow, Durham University. Married 1st, 1956, Penelope Susan Chiesman (3 sons 1 daughter) (marriage dissolved 1985); married 2nd, 1985, Lady Herries of Terregles, daughter of 16th Duke of Norfolk, KG. *Armed Forces:* RAF, National Service. *Career:* A cricketer; 117 appearances for England 1954–75, Captain on 23 occasions, 11 Overseas Tours, 107 centuries in first-class cricket, of which 22 were Test centuries, on retirement in 1975, held record for most runs and most catches in Test matches; Chairman: International Cricket Conference 1986–87, International Cricket Council 1989–93; Director, Bilton plc; Consultant, Barclays Bank plc. *Trusts, etc:* Member, Council of Winston Churchill Memorial Trust 1969–88. *Honours:* CBE 1972; Kt 1992. Freeman, City of London 1962. Master, Skinners' Company 1985. *Publications: Cricket Today,* 1961; *Time for Reflection,* 1962; *Tackle Cricket This Way, 1969;* The Incomparable Game, 1970; MCC: The Autobiography of a Cricketer, 1976. *Recreations:* Golf. *Sportsclubs:* President, Lords Taverners; West Sussex Golf Club, Kent County Cricket Club, I Zingari. *Clubs:* MCC, Boodle's, Royal and Ancient Golf. *Name, Style and Title:* Raised to the peerage as Baron Cowdrey of Tonbridge, of Tonbridge in the County of Kent 1997. A Conservative. *Address:* The Lord Cowdrey of Tonbridge, CBE, Angmering Park, Littlehampton, West Sussex, BN16 4EX *Tel:* 01903 871423.

COX (Life Baroness, UK), Caroline Anne Cox; cr. 1983

Daughter of late Robert John McNeill Love, FRCS, FACS, and late Dorothy Ida Borland. Born July 6, 1937; educated Channing School; London University (external student, (BSc(Soc), MSc(Econ); London Hospital (SRN); Hon. Doctorate of Philosophy, Polish University in London 1988; Hon. PhD, Southern Utah University 1991; Hon. Fellow: City and Guilds of London Institute 1991, Westminster University 1992; CNAA Hon. LLD 1992; Hon. Doctorate, University of Yerevan, Armenia 1995; Hon. DSS, Queen's University, Belfast 1996; Hon. DUniv, University of Surrey 1995; Hon. DU, University of Central England 1997. Married January 10, 1959, Dr Murray Newall Cox (died June 28, 1997), son of Rev. Roland Cox (2 sons 1 daughter). *Career:* Staff Nurse, Edgware General Hospital 1960; Lecturer, Senior Lecturer and Principal Lecturer, Polytechnic of North London 1969–74; Head, Department of Sociology 1975–77; Director, Nursing Education Research Unit, Chelsea College, University of London 1977–84; Fellow, Royal College of Nursing, Vice-President, 1990–. *Chancellor:* Chancellor, Bournemouth University 1992–. *House of Lords:* A Deputy Speaker of the House of Lords 1986–; A Deputy Chairman of Committees 1986–. *Whip:* A Baroness in Waiting (Government Whip) April-August 1985. *All-Party:* Member, All-Party: British Armenian Parliamentary Group, Human Rights Group; Joint Vice-Chairman, All-Party Research and Development in Fertility and Contraception Group 1998–; Secretary, All-Party Social Development in Europe Group 1999–. *Other:* Member, Council of the Freedom Association; Chairman, Parental Alliance for Choice in Education; Council of Management, St Christopher's Hospice 1986–92; President: Christian Solidarity Worldwide, Standing Conference on Women's Organisations, Institute of Administrative Management, Christian Broadcasting Council 1996–98; Vice-President, Girl Guides Association; Patron: Medical Aid for Poland Fund, Physicians for Human Rights, UK, UK-USSR Medical Exchange Programme; Non-executive Director: Andrei Sakarov Foundation; Board of Management, Christian Solidarity Worldwide; President, Girls' Brigade of England and Wales. *Awards Granted:* Wilberforce Award 1995. *Trusts, etc:* President, Tushinskaya Children's Hospital Trust; Trustee: MERLIN (Medical Emergency Relief International, Siberian Medical University, Smith and Nephew Foundation until 1998, Lambeth Health Care Trust. *Honours:* Commander Cross of the Order of Merit of the Republic of Poland 1990. SRN; FRCN; Hon. FRCS 1997. *Publications:* Former Co-editor, International Journal of Nursing Studies; Author of numerous publications on education and health care, including: *A Sociology of Medical Practice*, (edited jointly) 1975; *The Right to Learn*, 1982; *Sociology: A Guide for Nurses, Midwives and Health Visitors*, 1983; Editor, *Trajectories of Despair: Misdiagnosis and Maltreatment of Soviet Orphans*, 1991; Co-author with John Eibner (CSI): *Ethnic Cleansing in Progress: War in Nagorno Karabakh*, 1993; *Made to Care: The Case for Residential and Village Communities for People with a Mental Handicap*, (jointly) 1995. *Special Interests:* Human Rights, Humanitarian Aid, Education, Health, Nursing. *Recreations:* Squash, campanology, hill walking. *Sportsclubs:* Axis Squash, Northwood. *Clubs:* Royal Over-Seas League. *Name, Style and Title:* Raised to the peerage as Baroness Cox, of Queensbury in Greater London 1983. A Conservative. *Address:* The Baroness Cox, House of Lords, London, SW1A 0PW *Tel:* 020 8204 7336 *Fax:* 020 8204 5661 *E-Mail:* cox@ertnet.demon.co.uk.

CRAIG OF RADLEY (Life Baron, UK), David Brownrigg Craig; cr. 1991; GCB (Mil) 1984; OBE (Mil) 1967

Son of late Major Francis Brownrigg Craig and Hannah Olivia (Olive) Craig. Born September 17, 1929; educated Radley College; Lincoln College, Oxford (MA); Hon. Fellow, Lincoln College, Oxford 1984; Hon. DSc, Cranfield Institute of Technology 1988. Married March 12, 1955, June, daughter of late Charles James Derenburg (1 son 1 daughter). *Armed Forces:* Commissioned into RAF 1951; Served as Qualified Flying Instructor on Meteors and as Hunter Pilot in Fighter Command; CO, No. 35 Squadron 1963–65; Military Assistant to Chief of the Defence Staff 1965–68; Group Captain 1968; Station CO, RAF College, Cranwell 1968–70; ADC to HM The Queen 1969–71; Director, Plans and Operations, HQ Far East Command 1970–71; OC, RAF Akrotiri (Cyprus) 1972–73; Assistant Chief of Air Staff (Operations) Ministry of Defence 1975–78; Air Officer Commanding No 1 Group 1978–80; Vice-Chief of Air Staff 1980–82; Air Officer Commanding-in-Chief Strike Command and Commander-in-Chief UK Air Forces 1982–85; Chief of the Air Staff 1985–88;

Air ADC to HM The Queen 1985–88; Marshal of the Royal Air Force 1988; Chief of the Defence Staff 1988–91. *House of Lords:* Convenor of the Cross-Bench Peers December 1999–. *Select Committees:* Member, Select Committee on Science and Technology 1993–98. *All-Party:* Member, Parliamentary All-Party: Defence Group, Aerospace Group. *Honours:* OBE (Mil) 1967; CB 1978; KCB 1981; GCB (Mil) 1984. FRAeS. *Special Interests:* Defence. *Recreations:* Golf, fishing, shooting, woodwork. *Clubs:* Royal Air Force. *Name, Style and Title:* Raised to the peerage as Baron Craig of Radley, of Helhoughton in the County of Norfolk 1991. A Cross-Bencher. *Address:* Marshal of the Royal Air Force The Lord Craig of Radley, GCB (Mil), OBE (Mil), House of Lords, London, SW1A 0PW *E-Mail:* craigd@parliament.uk.

CRAIGAVON (3rd Viscount, UK), Janric Fraser Craig; cr. 1927; 3rd Bt of Craigavon (UK) 1918

Son of 2nd Viscount. Born June 9, 1944. Succeeded his father 1974; educated Eton; London University (BA, BSc). *Career:* A Chartered Accountant. *House of Lords:* An elected hereditary peer 1999–. *Select Committees:* Member, Hybrid Instruments Committee .1993–97. *All-Party:* Vice-Chairman, British Parliamentary Group on Population, Development and Reproductive Health; Officer, All-Party Parliamentary Groups for Austria, Denmark, Finland, Iceland and Sweden; Treasurer, All-Party: Pro-Choice Group 1998–, Cycling Group. *Other:* Member, Executive Committee Anglo-Austrian Society. *Trusts, etc:* Former Trustee now Advisor, Progress Educational Trust. *Honours:* Commander of the Order of the Lion (Finland) 1998. *Heir:* None. A Cross-Bencher. *Address:* The Viscount Craigavon, 54 Westminster Mansions, 1 Little Smith Street, London, SW1P 3DQ *Tel:* 020 7222 1949.

CRANBORNE (Viscount, E), Robert Michael James Gascoyne-Cecil; cr. 1604; (Life) Baron Gascoyne-Cecil 1999; PC 1994; DL

Son of 6th Marquess of Salisbury. Born September 30, 1946; educated Eton; Christ Church, Oxford. Married 1970, Hannah Ann, daughter of late Lieutenant-Colonel William Joseph Stirling of Keir (2 sons 3 daughters). *Councils, Public Bodies:* DL, Dorset 1987–. *House of Commons:* MP (Conservative) for Dorset South 1979–87. *House of Lords:* Parliamentary Under-Secretary of State for Defence, Ministry of Defence 1992–94; Lord Privy Seal and Leader of the House of Lords 1994–97; Member, Shadow Cabinet 1997–98; Leader of the Opposition in the House of Lords 1997–98. *Spokesman:* An Opposition Spokesman on the Public Service 1997–98. *Miscellaneous:* Holds courtesy title of Viscount Cranborne (E) 1604; Heir to marquessate; Summoned to the Upper House in his father's barony of Cecil, of Essendon in the County of Rutland, by a Writ in Acceleration 1992. *Honours:* PC 1994. *Clubs:* White's, Pratt's, Beefsteak. *Heir:* His son, Hon. Robert Edward William Gascoyne-Cecil, born December 18, 1970. *Name, Style and Title:* Created a life peer as Baron Gascoyne-Cecil, of Essendon in the County of Rutland 1999. A Conservative. *Address:* The Rt Hon. the Viscount Cranborne, DL, House of Lords, London, SW1A 0PW.

CRATHORNE (2nd Baron, UK), Charles James Dugdale; cr. 1959; 2nd Bt of Crathorne (UK) 1945

Son of 1st Baron, PC, TD. Born September 12, 1939. Succeeded his father 1977; educated Eton; Trinity College, Cambridge. Married January 8, 1970, Sylvia Mary, daughter of late Brigadier Arthur Montgomery, OBE, TD (1 son 2 daughters). *Councils, Public Bodies:* DL, County of Cleveland 1983–96; DL, County of North Yorkshire 1996–98, Lord Lieutenant 1999–; JP. *Career:* Impressionist Painting department, Sotheby & Co. 1963–66; Assistant to President, Parke-Bernet Galleries, New York 1966–69; Independent Fine Art Consultancy, James Dugdale & Associates 1969–; Lecture tours to the USA 1969–; Director, Blakeney Hotels Ltd 1979–96; Lecture series *Aspects of England*, in Metropolitan Museum, New York 1981; Australian Bicentennial Lecture Tour 1988; Director: Woodhouse Securities Ltd 1988–, Cliveden plc 1996–99, Cliveden Ltd 1999–. *House of Lords:* An elected hereditary peer 1999–. *All-Party:* Hon. Secretary, All-Party Parliamentary Arts and Heritage Group 1981–; Hon. Secretary, All-Party Photography Group 1997–.

Party Groups (General): Member, Conservative Advisory Group on Arts and Heritage 1988–99. *Other:* Council, RSA 1982–88; Editorial Board of the House Magazine 1983–; Member, University Court of the University of Leeds 1985–97; Executive Committee, Georgian Group 1985–, Chairman 1990–99; Governor, Queen Margarets School York Ltd. 1986–99; President: Yarm Civic Society 1987–, Cleveland Family History Society 1988–, Cleveland Sea Cadets 1988–; Hambleton District of CPRE 1988–; Patron, Cleveland Community Foundation 1990–; Deputy Chairman, Joint Committee of National Amenity Societies 1993–96, Chairman 1996–99; President, Cleveland and North Yorkshire Magistrates' Association 1997–; Vice-President: The Public Monuments and Sculpture Association 1997–, Yorkshire and Humberside TAVRA 1999–; President, North Yorkshire County Scout Council 1999–; Patron, British Red Cross North Yorkshire Branch 1999–. *Trusts, etc:* Trustee, Georgian Theatre Royal, Richmond, Yorkshire 1970–; Trustee, Captain Cook Birthplace Museum Trust 1978–, Chairman 1993–; Yorkshire Regional Committee, National Trust 1988–94; Vice-President, Cleveland Wildlife Trust 1989–; Patron, Attingham Trust for the Study of the British Country House 1990–; Trustee, National Heritage Memorial Fund 1992–95. *Honours:* KStJ 1999. FRSA 1972. *Publications:* Author of articles in The Connoisseur and Apollo; Author of: *Edouard Vuillard*, 1967; *Cliveden, the Place and the People*, 1995; *The Royal Crescent Book of Bath*, 1998; Co-Author of: *Tennant's Stalk*, 1973; *A Present from Crathorne*, 1989; Co-Photographer *Parliament in Pictures*, 1999. *Special Interests:* Visual and Performing Arts, Country Houses. *Recreations:* Photography, collecting, fishing, shooting, travel with the family, jazz. *Heir:* His son, Hon. Thomas Arthur John Dugdale, born September 30, 1977. A Conservative. *Address:* The Lord Crathorne, Crathorne House, Yarm, North Yorkshire, TS15 0AT *Tel:* 01642 700431 *Fax:* 01642 700632; House of Lords, London, SW1A 0PW *Tel:* 020 7219 5224 *Tel:* Office: 020 7730 5420.

CRAWFORD (29th Earl of, S), cr. 1398, AND BALCARRES (12th Earl of, S), cr. 1651; Robert Alexander Lindsay; Lord Lindsay of Crawford before 1143. Lord Lindsay (S) 1633; Lord Balniel (S) 1651; 5th Baron Wigan (UK) 1826; (Life) Baron Balniel (UK) 1974; KT 1996; PC 1972; DL

Son of 28th Earl, KT, GBE. Born March 5, 1927. Succeeded his father 1975; educated Eton; Trinity College, Cambridge. Married 1949, Ruth Beatrice, daughter of Leo Meyer-Bechtler, of Zurich (2 sons 2 daughters). *Armed Forces:* Served with Grenadier Guards 1945–48. *Councils, Public Bodies:* DL, Fife. *Career:* A Director, National Westminster Bank 1975–89; Vice-Chairman, Sun Alliance & London Insurance 1975–91; First Commissioner of the Crown Estate 1980–85; Chairman, Royal Commission on the Ancient and Historical Monuments of Scotland 1985–95; Chairman, Board of the National Library of Scotland 1991–; Lord Chamberlain to HM Queen Elizabeth the Queen Mother 1992–. *House of Commons:* MP (Conservative) for: Hertford 1955–74, Welwyn and Hatfield March-October 1974; PPS: to Financial Secretary to The Treasury 1955–56, to Minister of Housing and Local Government 1956–59; Minister of State for Defence 1970–72, Minister of State, Foreign and Commonwealth Affairs 1972–74. *Spokesman (Commons):* Principal Opposition Front Bench Spokesman on Health and Social Security 1967–70. *Miscellaneous:* Premier Earl of Scotland on Union Roll; Head of the House of Lindsay. *Honours:* PC 1972; KT 1996. *Heir:* His son, Lord Balniel, born November 24, 1958. *Name, Style and Title:* Created a life peer as Baron Balniel, of Pitcorthie in the County of Fife 1974. A Conservative. *Address:* The Rt Hon. the Earl of Crawford and Balcarres, KT, DL, House of Lords, London, SW1A 0PW.

CRAWLEY (Life Baroness, UK), Christine Mary Crawley; cr. 1998

Born January 1, 1950; educated Notre Dame Catholic Secondary Girls School, Plymouth; Digby Stuart Training College, Roehampton. Married (1 son 2 daughters). *Trades Union:* Member: MSF, UNISON. *Councils, Public Bodies:* Former Town and District Councillor in South Oxfordshire. *Career:* Former Teacher and Youth Theatre Leader; MEP for Birmingham East 1984–99: Member, Women's Rights Committee 1984–99, Chair 1989–94; Member, Civil Liberties and Internal Affairs Committee 1992–99; Substitute, Regional Policy Committee 1997–99; Member: US Delegation 1997–99, Russia Delegation 1997–99; Chair, Women's National Commission. *Select Committees:* Member, European Select Committee. *Party Groups (General):* Member: Fabian Society, Co-operative Party, Labour Movement in Europe; Deputy Leader, EP Labour Party in charge of links with the Labour Government in UK 1994–98; Member, Socialist Group Bureau in European Parliament. *Other:* Member, Amnesty International. *Miscellaneous:* Contested Staffordshire South East 1983 General Election; Chair, Regional Cultural Consortium – West Midlands. Fellow, Royal Society of Arts. *Publications:* Contributions to a number of publications including *Changing States – Labour Agenda for Europe*; Articles on women's rights and equality policy. *Special Interests:* Women's Rights, Equal Opportunities, Economics and Monetary Union, European Union. *Recreations:* Latin American literature, amateur dramatics, attending local football matches in Birmingham. *Name, Style and Title:* Raised to the peerage as Baroness Crawley, of Edgbaston in the County of West Midlands 1998. Labour. *Address:* The Baroness Crawley, House of Lords, London, SW1A 0PW *E-Mail:* ccrawley@enterprise.net.

CRICKHOWELL (Life Baron, UK), Roger Nicholas Edwards; cr. 1987; PC 1979

Son of late Ralph Edwards, CBE, FSA. Born February 25, 1934; educated Westminster School; Trinity College, Cambridge; Hon. Fellow, Cardiff University of Wales. Married 1963, Ankaret, daughter of late W. J. Healing (1 son 2 daughters). *Armed Forces:* National Service, (Second Lieutenant) Royal Welch Fusiliers; Lieutenant, TA. *Career:* Member of Lloyds 1963–; Chairman: ITnet Holdings Ltd, HTV Group Ltd; Director, Anglesey Mining plc; Former Director: William Brandts Ltd and Associated Companies, A. L. Sturge Holdings Ltd, PA International & Sturge Underwriting Agency Ltd, Associated British Ports Holdings plc, Globtik Tankers Ltd; Chairman: National Rivers Authority Advisory Committee 1988–89, National Rivers Authority 1989–96. *House of Commons:* MP (Conservative) for Pembroke 1970–87; Secretary of State for Wales, May 1979–87. *Other:* Member, Committee of the AA 1988–98; President: Cardiff University of Wales 1988–98, South East Wales Arts Association 1988–94. *Trusts, etc:* Chairman, Cardiff Bay Opera House Trust 1993–97. *Honours:* PC 1979. Member, Fishmongers' Company. *Publications: Opera House Lottery – Zaha Hadid and The Cardiff Bay Project*, 1997; *Westminster, Wales and Water*, 1999. *Special Interests:* Environment, Economic Policy, Urban Policies, Arts. *Clubs:* Brooks's, Cardiff and County (Cardiff). *Name, Style and Title:* Raised to the peerage as Baron Crickhowell, of Pont Esgob in the Black Mountains and County of Powys 1987. A Conservative. *Address:* The Rt Hon. the Lord Crickhowell, 4 Henning St, London, SW11 3DA; Pont Esgob Mill, Fforest Coalpit, Nr Abergavenny, Gwent, NP7 7LS.

CROHAM (Life Baron, UK), Douglas Albert Vivian Allen; cr. 1978; GCB 1973

Son of Albert John Allen (killed in action 1918). Born December 15, 1917; educated Wallington County Grammar School for Boys; London School of Economics; Hon. DSocSc, Southampton University. Married August 16, 1941, Sybil Eileen, (died September 18, 1994), daughter of late John Marco Allegro (2 sons 1 daughter). *Trades Union:* Member, First Division Association (FDA). *Armed Forces:* Served Royal Artillery 1940–45. *Career:* Joined Home Civil Service, Board of Trade 1939; Treasury 1948, Assistant Secretary 1949–58; Under-Secretary, Ministry of Health 1958–60; Treasury 1960–64, Third Secretary 1962; Department of Economic Affairs 1964–68, Permanent Secretary 1966–68; Permanent Secretary, Treasury 1968–74; Permanent Secretary, Civil Service Department and Head of Home Civil Service 1974–77; Chairman: British National Oil Corporation 1982–86, Guinness Peat Group plc 1982–87, Trinity Insurance Ltd 1987–92. *Select Committees:* Member, Select Committee on the Public Service 1996–97. *Other:* President, Institute for Fiscal Studies 1978–92; Chairman, Anglo-German Foundation 1982–98; President, British Institute of Energy Economics 1986–94; Vice-President, Anglo-German Association; Governor: London School of Economics, Wallington County Grammar School. *Miscellaneous:* Member, Institute of Directors; Companion, Institute of Management. *Honours:* CB 1963; KCB 1967; GCB 1973. Fellow, Royal Society of Arts. *Special Interests:* Finance, Economic Policy, Energy. *Recreations:* Woodwork, Bridge. *Clubs:* Reform, Civil Service. *Name, Style and Title:* Raised to the peerage as Baron Croham, of the London Borough of Croydon 1978. A Cross-Bencher. *Address:* The Lord Croham, GCB, 9 Manor Way, South Croydon, Surrey, CR2 7BT *Tel:* 020 8688 0496.

CUCKNEY (Life Baron, UK), John (Graham) Cuckney; cr. 1995; Kt 1978

Son of late Air Vice-Marshal E. J. Cuckney, CB, CBE, DSC and Bar, and Lilian (née Williams). Born July 12, 1925; educated Shrewsbury; St Andrews University (MA); Hon. DSc, Bath 1991; Hon. LLD, St Andrews 1993. Married 2nd, 1960, Muriel, daughter of late Walter Scott Boyd. *Armed Forces:* War service with Royal Northumberland Fusiliers, King's African Rifles, followed by attachment to War Office (Civil Assistant General Staff) until 1957. *Career:* Director, Lazard Brothers & Co. 1964–70, 1988–90; Independent Member, Railway Policy Review Committee 1966–67; Chairman, Mersey Docks and Harbour Board 1970–72; Chief Executive (Second Permanent Secretary), Property Services Agency, DoE 1972–74; Senior Crown Agent and Chairman, Crown Agents for Overseas Governments and Administrations 1974–78; Chairman: International Military Services (an MoD company) 1974–85, EDC for Building 1976–80, Port of London Authority 1977–79, Thomas Cook Group Ltd 1978–88; Director, Midland Bank plc 1978–88; Council, British Executive Service Overseas 1981–84; Chairman: Brooke Bond Group plc 1981–84, International Maritime Bureau of International Chamber of Commerce 1981–85, John Brown plc 1983–86, Westland Group 1985–89; Deputy Chairman, TI Group plc 1985–90; Chairman, Royal Insurance Holdings plc 1985–94; Director: Brixton Estate plc 1985–96, SBAC 1986–89; Chairman: 3i Group plc 1987–92, Understanding Industry Trust 1988–91; NEDC Working Party on European Public Purchasing 1990–92; Vice-Chairman, Glaxo Wellcome plc 1990–95; Adviser to the Secretary of State for Social Security on the Maxwell pensions affair and founder Chairman of the Maxwell Pensioners' Trust 1992–95; Controller, ROH Development Land Trust 1993–96; Chairman, The Orion Publishing Group Ltd 1994–97. *Select Committees:* Member, Select Committee on Science and Technology Sub-Committee II on the Innovation Exploitation Barrier 1996–97; Member, Select Committee on the Public Service 1996–97. *Other:* Governor, Centre for International Briefing, Farnham Castle 1974–84; Elder Brother of Trinity House 1980–; Vice-President, Liverpool School of Tropical Medicine 1985–93. *Trusts, etc:* Trustee, RAF Museum 1987–99. *Honours:* Kt 1978. Freeman, City of London 1977. *Special Interests:* City, Economic Policy. *Clubs:* Athenaeum. *Name, Style and Title:* Raised to the peerage as Baron Cuckney, of Millbank in the City of Westminster 1995. A Conservative. *Address:* The Lord Cuckney, House of Lords, London, SW1A 0PW.

CUMBERLEGE (Life Baroness, UK), Julia Frances Cumberlege; cr. 1990; CBE 1985; DL

Daughter of late Dr. L. U. Camm. Born January 27, 1943; educated Convent of the Sacred Heart, Tunbridge Wells; DUniv: Surrey University 1990, Brighton University 1994. Married 1961, Patrick Cumberlege (3 sons). *Councils, Public Bodies:* Chairman, Brighton Health Authority 1981–88; Councillor, Lewes District Council 1966–79, Leader 1977–78; Councillor, East Sussex County Council 1974–85, Chairman, Social Services Committee 1979–82; Chairman, South West Thames Regional Health Authority 1988–92; JP, East Sussex 1973–85; DL, East Sussex 1986–; Vice-Lord Lieutenant 1992. *Career:* Executive Director, MJM Healthcare Solutions 1997–. *House of Lords:* Joint Parliamentary Under-Secretary of State, Department of Health 1992–97. *Spokesman:* An Opposition Spokeswoman on Health 1997. *All-Party:* Member, All-Party AIDS and HIV Group; Joint Vice-Chairman, All-Party CAFOD Group 1999–. *Other:* Vice-President: Royal College of Nursing 1989–, Pre-School Playgroups Association 1989–91; Council Member: Brighton Polytechnic 1987–89, St George's Medical School 1988–92; Governor, Chailey Heritage School and Hospital 1982–88, Patron 1996–; President: Age Concern Sussex 1993–, Sussex Care for the Carers 1996–. *Trusts, etc:* Trustee, Chailey Heritage. *Miscellaneous:* Council Member, National Association of Health Authorities 1982–88, Vice-Chairman 1984–87, Chairman 1987–88; Member, Press Council 1984–90; Chairman, Review of Community Nursing for England 1985; Member: DHSS Expert Advisory Group on AIDS 1987–89, NHS Policy Board for England 1989–; Council Member, UK Central Council for Nursing, Midwifery and Health Visiting 1989–92; Chairman, Review of Maternity Services for England 1993. *Honours:* CBE 1985. Fellow, Royal Society of Arts 1989. *Special Interests:* Local Government, Health Service, Media, Education. *Recreations:* Other people's gardens, bicycling. *Clubs:* Royal Society of Medicine. *Name, Style and Title:* Raised to the peerage as Baroness Cumberlege, of Newick in the County of East Sussex 1990. A Conservative. *Address:* The Baroness Cumberlege, CBE, DL, Snells Cottage, The Green, Newick, Lewes, East Sussex, BN8 4LA *Tel:* 01825 722154 *E-Mail:* cumberlegej@parliament.uk.

CURRIE OF MARYLEBONE (Life Baron, UK), David Anthony Currie; cr. 1996

Son of Kennedy and Marjorie Currie. Born December 9, 1946; educated Battersea Grammar School; University of Manchester (BSc 1st Class Maths); University of Birmingham (MSoc Sci Econs); University of London (PhD Economics); Hon. Fellow, Queen Mary and Westfield College, University of London 1997; DLitt, University of Glasgow 1998. Married 1st, 1975, Shaziye Gazioglu (2 sons) (marriage dissolved 1992); married 2nd, 1995, Angela Mary Piers Dumas. *Career:* Economist, Hoare Govett 1971–72; Lecturer, Reader and Professor of Economics, Queen Mary College, University of London 1972–88; Visiting Scholar, International Monetary Fund 1987; London Business School: Professor of Economics 1988–, Research Dean 1989–92, Governor 1989–95, Deputy Principal 1992–95, Deputy Dean, External Relations 1999–; Director, Joseph Rowntree Reform Trust 1991–; International Schools of Business Management 1992–95; Visiting Professor, European University Institute 1992–95; Director, Charter 88 1994–98. *Other:* Member, Royal Economic Society. *Miscellaneous:* Research Fellow, Centre for Economic Policy Research 1983–; Houblon-Norman Resident Fellow, Bank of England 1985–86; Member: Retail Price Index Advisory Committee 1992–95, Treasury's Panel of Independent Forecasters 1992–95, Management Board OFGEM. FRSA. *Publications: Advances in Monetary Economics*, 1985; *The Operation and Regulation of Financial Markets* (with Charles Goodhart and David Llewellyn), 1986; *Macroeconomic Interactions Between North and South* (with David Vines), 1988; *Rules, Reputation and Macroeconomic Policy Co-ordination* (with Paul Levine), 1993; *EMUs Problems in the Transition to a Single European Currency* (with John Whitley), 1995; *North-South Linkages and International Macroeconomic Policy* (with David Vines), 1995; *The Pros and Cons of EMU*, 1997; *Will the Euro Work?*, 1998; Articles in journals. *Special Interests:* Economic Policy, Education, Constitutional Reform. *Recreations:* Music, literature, swimming. *Name, Style and Title:* Raised to the peerage as Baron Currie of Marylebone, of Marylebone in the City of Westminster 1996. Labour. *Address:* Professor The Lord Currie of Marylebone, London Business School, Sussex Place, London, NW1 4SA *Tel:* 020 7262 5050 *E-Mail:* dcurrie@lbs.ac.uk.

D

DACRE OF GLANTON (Life Baron, UK), Hugh Redwald Trevor-Roper; cr. 1979

Son of late Dr Bertie W. E. Trevor-Roper. Born January 15, 1914; educated Charterhouse School; Christ Church, Oxford. Married October 4, 1954, Lady Alexandra Howard-Johnston (died August 15, 1997), daughter of Field Marshal 1st Earl Haig, KT, GCB, OM. *Armed Forces:* Served in Army Intelligence Corps (Major) 1939–45. *Career:* Student of Christ Church, Oxford 1946–57; Regius Professor of Modern History, Oxford 1957–80; Director, Times Newspapers Ltd 1974–88; Master of Peterhouse, Cambridge 1980–87. *Miscellaneous:* Junior Research Fellow, Merton College, Oxford 1937. *Publications:* Author of several works including: *Archbishop Laud*; *The Last Days of Hitler*; *The Rise of Christian Europe*; *Religion, The Reformation and Social Change*; *Princes and Artists*; *A Hidden Life*; *Renaissance Essays*; *Catholics, Anglicans and Puritans*; *From Counter-Reformation to Glorious Revolution. Clubs:* Beefsteak, Garrick. *Name, Style and Title:* Raised to the peerage as Baron Dacre of Glanton, of Glanton in the County of Northumberland 1979. A Conservative. *Address:* The Lord Dacre of Glanton, The Old Rectory, Didcot, Oxon, OX11 7EB.

Dod *on* Disk
The Vacher Dod Parliamentary Database
that will run on your PC or Network
For further details please telephone the Westminster Office
020 7828 7256

DAHRENDORF (Life Baron, UK), Ralf Dahrendorf; cr. 1993; KBE 1982; FBA 1977

Son of late Gustav Dahrendorf and of Lina Dahrendorf. Born May 1, 1929; educated in Hamburg and Berlin; Postgraduate studies at London School of Economics 1952–54 (Leverhulme Research Scholar 1953–54, PhD 1956); Hon. Fellow, London School of Economics 1970; Fellow, St Antony's College, Oxford 1976; Holder of twenty-five Honorary Degrees from Universities in Great Britain, Ireland, Belgium, Italy, Malta, the United States, Canada, Argentina, Israel and France. Married 1980, Mrs Ellen de Kadt (née Krug). *Career:* Fellow at Center for Advanced Study in the Behavioural Sciences, Palo Alto, USA 1957–58; Professor of Sociology: Hamburg 1957–60, Tubingen 1960–64, Konstanz 1966–69; Parliamentary Secretary of State, Federal German Ministry of Foreign Affairs 1969–70; Member, EEC, Brussels 1970–74; Director, London School of Economics 1974–84, Governor 1986–; Professor of Social Science, Konstanz University 1984–86; Non-Exec Director, Glaxo Holdings plc 1984–92; Visiting Professor at several European and North American Universities; Visiting Scholar, Russell Sage Foundation, New York 1986–87; Warden, St Antony's College, Oxford 1987–97; Chairman, Newspaper Publishing plc 1992–93; Non-Executive Director, Bank Gesellschaft Berlin 1996–. *Select Committees:* Member, Select Committee on Delegated Powers and Deregulation 1997–; Co-opted Member, Select Committee on European Communities Sub-Committee A (Economic and Financial Affairs, Trade and External Relations) 1997–99. *All-Party:* Member, All-Party London Group. *Other:* Chairman, Council for Charitable Support 1995–. *Trusts, etc:* Trustee, Ford Foundation 1976–88. *Miscellaneous:* Adopted British nationality 1988; Member: Hansard Society Commission on Electoral Reform 1975–76, Royal Commission on Legal Services 1976–79, Committee to Review Functioning of Financial Institutions 1977–80. *Honours:* Holder of decorations from Senegal, Germany, Luxembourg, Austria, Belgium and Spain; KBE 1982. FBA 1977; FRSA 1977; Hon. FRCS 1982. Freeman, City of London 1998. *Publications:* Author of several works on philosophy, sociology and politics, including: *Marx in Perspective*, 1953; *Class and Class Conflict*, 1959; *Society and Democracy in Germany*, 1966; *Essays on the Theory of Society*, 1968; *The New Liberty*, 1975; *On Britain*, 1982; *Law and Order*, 1985; *The Modern Social Conflict*, 1988; *Reflections on the Revolution in Europe*, 1990; *A History of the London School of Economics and Political Science 1895–1995*, 1995; *After 1989*, 1997; many of which have been translated into several European and Asian languages. *Clubs:* Reform, Garrick. *Name, Style and Title:* Raised to the peerage as Baron Dahrendorf, of Clare Market in the City of Westminster 1993. A Liberal Democrat. *Address:* The Lord Dahrendorf, KBE, FBA, Bankgesellschaft Berlin (UK) plc, 1 Crown Court, Cheapside, London, EC2V 6JP *Tel:* 020 7572 6100 *Fax:* 020 7572 6256.

DARCY DE KNAYTH (Baroness, 18th in line, E), Davina Marcia Ingrams; cr. 1332; DBE 1996

Daughter of 17th Baron (Viscount Clive), son of 4th Earl of Powis. Born July 10, 1938. Succeeded her father, who was killed in action, March 1943; educated St. Mary's School, Wantage, Oxfordshire; Italy; Sorbonne, Paris. Married 1960, Rupert George Ingrams (died in a motor accident, 1964), son of late Leonard Ingrams (1 son 2 daughters). *House of Lords:* An elected hereditary peer 1999–. *Select Committees:* Member: House of Lords European Committees Sub-Committee C 1985–88, House of Lords Select Committee on murder and life imprisonment 1988–89. *All-Party:* Member, All-Party: Children Group, Disablement Group, Drug Misuse Group, Ageing Group, Media Group, Water Group, Tibet Country Group, Heritage Group, Aids Group, Epilepsy Group. *Other:* President, SKILL (National Bureau for Students with Disabilities); Member, Joint Committee on Mobility for Disabled People (JCMDP); Member, IPSEA (Independent Panel on Special Education Advice); Council Member, Grange Centre for People with Disabilities; President, Windsor and Maidenhead District Sports Association for Disabled People. *Miscellaneous:* Former Member, Independent Broadcasting Authority General Advisory Council. *Special Interests:* Disability. *Honours:* DBE 1996. *Recreations:* Theatre, cinema. *Sportsclubs:* Stoke Paraplegic Athletics, Windsor and Maidenhead District Sports Association for Disabled People. *Heir:* Her son, Hon. Caspar David Ingrams, born January 5, 1962. A Cross-Bencher. *Address:* The Baroness Darcy de Knayth, DBE, Camley Corner, Stubbings, Maidenhead, Berkshire, SL6 6QW *Tel:* 01628 822935.

DAVID (Life Baroness, UK), Nora Ratcliff David; cr. 1978

Daughter of late George Blockley Blakesley, JP. Born September 23, 1913; educated Ashby-De-La-Zouch Girls' Grammar School; St. Felix School, Southwold; Newnham College, Cambridge (MA); Hon. Fellow: Newnham College, Cambridge 1986, Anglia Polytechnic University 1989; Hon. DLitt, Staffordshire University 1995. Married August 18, 1935, Richard William David, CBE, MA (died April 25, 1993), son of late Rev. Frederick Paul David (2 sons 2 daughters). *Councils, Public Bodies:* Councillor: Cambridge City Council 1964–67, 1968–74, Cambridgeshire County Council 1974–78; Member of Board, Peterborough Development Corporation 1976–78; JP, Cambridge City 1965–. *Whip:* Baroness-in-Waiting (Government Whip)

November 1978–79; Opposition Whip 1979–85; Opposition Deputy Chief Whip 1983–87. *Spokesman:* Spokesman for Education 1979–85; Opposition Spokesman on: the Environment 1985–87, Education 1987–97. *Select Committees:* Member: Select Committee on European Communities 1990–94, Sub-Committee on Social and Consumer Affairs 1989–94, Sub-Committee on Agriculture 1993–97. *All-Party:* Member, All-Party Groups on: Children, Parenting, Arts and Heritage, The Environment, Penal Affairs. *Special Interests:* Education, Environment, Home Affairs, Children. *Recreations:* Walking, swimming, theatre, travel. *Name, Style and Title:* Raised to the peerage as Baroness David, of Romsey in the City of Cambridge 1978. Labour. *Address:* The Baroness David, 50 Highsett, Cambridge, CB2 1NZ *Tel:* 01223 350376; Cove, New Polzeath, Cornwall, PL27 6UF *Tel:* 01208 863310; House of Lords, London, SW1A 0PW *Tel:* House of Lords 020 7219 3159.

DAVIES OF COITY (Life Baron, UK), (David) Garfield Davies; cr. 1997; CBE 1996

Son of David and Lizzie Davies. Born June 24, 1935; educated Heolgam Secondary Modern School; Bridgend Technical College (part-time). Married 1960, Marian Jones (4 daughters). *Trades Union:* Member, TUC General Council 1986–97, Chairman, International Committee 1992–94; Spokesperson on International Affairs 1994–97; Member: Executive Board, International Confederation of Free Trade Unions 1992–97, Executive Committee, European Trade Union Confederation 1992–97; Governor, Birmingham College of Food, Tourism and Creative Studies. *Armed Forces:* RAF 1956–58. *Councils, Public Bodies:* Parish and District Councillor 1963–69; JP 1972–79. *Career:* Junior Operative, Electrial Apprentice and Electrician, British Steel Corporation, Port Talbot 1950–69; USDAW: Area Organiser, Ipswich 1969–73, Deputy Division Officer, London/Ipswich 1973–78, National Officer, Manchester 1978–85, General Secretary 1986–97. *International Bodies (General):* Member: IPU, CPU, British-American Parliamentary Group. *Miscellaneous:* Member, Employment Appeal Tribunal. *Special Interests:* Health Service, Education, Industrial Relations. *Honours:* CBE 1996. *Recreations:* Most sport, swimming, jogging, family, reading, golf. *Sportsclubs:* Lancashire CCC, Stockport County AFC. *Clubs:* Reform. *Name, Style and Title:* Raised to the peerage as Baron Davies of Coity, of Penybont in the County of Mid Glamorgan 1997. Labour. *Address:* The Lord Davies of Coity, CBE, 64 Dairyground Road, Bramhall, Stockport, Cheshire, SK7 2QW *Tel:* 0161–439 9548.

DAVIES OF OLDHAM (Life Baron, UK), Bryan Davies; cr. 1997

Son of George and Beryl Davies. Born November 9, 1939; educated Redditch High School, Worcs; University College, London (BA Hons History); Institute of Education (PGCE Education (Distinction); London School of Economics (BSc Economics); Honorary Doctorate, Middlesex University 1996. Married 1963, Monica Shearing (2 sons 1 daughter). *Trades Union:* Divisional Executive Officer, NATFHE 1967–74; Member, TGWU 1979–. *Career:* Teacher, Latymer School 1962–65; Lecturer, Middlesex Polytechnic, Enfield 1965–74; Secretary, Parliamentary Labour Party and Shadow Cabinet 1979–92. *House of Commons:* Contested Norfolk Central 1966 and Newport West 1983; MP (Labour) for Enfield North 1974–1979 and for Oldham Central and Royton

1992–97. *Whip (Commons):* Assistant Government Whip 1978–79. *Spokesman (Commons):* Opposition Spokesman on: Education 1993–95, Education and Employment 1995–97. *Select Committees (Commons):* Member, Select Committees on: Public Expenditure 1975–79, Overseas Development 1975–79,

National Heritage 1992–93. *Backbench Committees (Commons):* Secretary, Parliamentary Labour Party Education Committee 1992–93; Former Chairman, Parliamentary Labour Party National Heritage Committee. *Backbench Committees:* Member, Education, Transport and Economic Affairs Committees 1997–. *Other:* President, Royal Society for the Prevention of Accidents (RoSPA) 1999–. *Miscellaneous:* Member, Medical Research Council 1977–79; Chairman, Further Education Funding Council 1998–. *Special Interests:* Economic Policy, Employment, Training, Education, Arts, Transport. *Recreations:* Sport, literature. *Name, Style and Title:* Raised to the peerage as Baron Davies of Oldham, of Broxbourne in the County of Hertfordshire 1997. Labour. *Address:* The Lord Davies of Oldham, House of Lords, London, SW1A 0PW *Tel.* 020 7219 4103 *Fax:* 01992 300166.

DEAN OF HARPTREE (Life Baron, UK), (Arthur) Paul Dean; cr. 1993; Kt 1985; PC 1991

Son of late Arthur Percival Dean and of Jessie Margaret Dean. Born September 14, 1924; educated Ellesmere College, Shropshire; Exeter College, Oxford (MA, BLitt). Married 1st, 1957, Doris Ellen Webb (died 1979), married 2nd, April 8, 1980, Mrs Peggy Parker. *Armed Forces:* Served War of 1939–45, Captain, Welsh Guards, ADC to Commander, 1st British Corps in Germany. *Career:* Farmer 1950–56; Resident Tutor, Swinton Conservative College 1957; Conservative Research Department 1957–64, Assistant Director 1962–64; Member, Commonwealth Parliamentary Association, UK Branch Executive Committee 1975–92; Former Director: Charterhouse Pensions Ltd, Watney, Mann and Truman Holdings Ltd, Grand Metropolitan Brewing, Foods, Leisure and Retailing Ltd. *House of Commons:* Contested (Conservative) Pontefract 1962 By-Election; MP (Conservative): Somerset North 1964–83, Woodspring 1983–92; Parliamentary Under-Secretary of State, Department of Health and Social Security 1970–74; Deputy Chairman of Ways and Means and Deputy Speaker 1982–92. *Spokesman (Commons):* A Front Bench Spokesman on Health and Social Security 1969–70. *Select Committees (Commons):* Member: House of Commons Select Services Committee 1979–82, House of Commons Chairman's Panel 1979–82. *Backbench Committees (Commons):* Chairman, Conservative Parliamentary Health and Social Security Committee 1979–82. *House of Lords:* A Deputy Speaker of the House of Lords 1995–; A Deputy Chairman of Committees 1997–. *Select Committees:* Member, Select Committees on: Procedure 1995, Delegated Legislation 1995–97, Delegated Powers and Deregulation 1997–. *Party Groups:* Member Executive Committee, Association of Conservative Peers 1995–. *Honours:* Kt 1985; PC 1991. *Special Interests:* Constitutional Affairs, Health, Social Security. *Recreations:* Fishing, walking, gardening. *Clubs:* United Oxford and Cambridge University. *Name, Style and Title:* Raised to the peerage as Baron Dean of Harptree, of Wedmore in the County of Somerset 1993. A Conservative. *Address:* The Rt Hon. the Lord Dean of Harptree, Archer's Wyck, Knightcott, Banwell, Weston-Super-Mare, BS24 6HS; House of Lords, London, SW1A 0PW.

DEAN OF THORNTON-LE-FYLDE (Life Baroness, UK), Brenda McDowall; cr. 1993; PC 1998

Daughter of Hugh and Lillian Dean. Born April 29, 1943; educated St Andrew's Junior School, Eccles; Stretford High School for Girls; Hon. MA, Salford 1986; Hon. Fellow, Lancashire Polytechnic 1991; Hon. Degree, City University, London 1993; Hon. MA, South Bank University, London 1995; Hon. LLB, De Montfort University, Leicester 1998. Married 1988, Keith Desmond McDowall, CBE (2 step-daughters). *Trades Union:* Member, TUC General Council 1985–92. *Career:* Administrative Secretary, SOGAT 1959–72; Assistant Secretary, SOGAT Manchester Branch 1972–76, Secretary 1976–83; Member, National Executive Council 1977–83; President, SOGAT '82 1983–85, General-Secretary 1985–91; Deputy General Secretary, Graphical, Paper and Media Union 1991–92. *Whip:* An Opposition Whip 1996–97. *Spokesman:* An Opposition Spokesperson on: Employment 1994–96, National Heritage 1996–97. *Select Committees:* Co-opted Member, Select Committee on European Communities Sub-Committee B (Energy, Industry and Transport) 1995–97, 1997–98. *All-Party:* Member, All-Party Consumer Affairs Group; Member and Director, EURIM. *Other:* Council Member: Association for Business Sponsorship of the Arts 1990–96; City University 1991–; Governor, Ditchley Foundation 1992–; Member, Board of Council, London School of Economics 1994–; Member of Council, Open University 1995–. *Trusts, etc:* Non-Executive Board Member, University College London Hospitals NHS Trust 1993–98; Trustee: Industry and Parliament Trust, Inveresk plc Pension Fund 1996–. *Miscellaneous:* Co-Chairman, Women's National

Commission 1985–87; Member: Printing and Publishing Training Board 1974–82, Supplementary Benefits Commission 1976–80, Price Commission 1977–79, Occupational Pensions Board 1983–87, General Advisory Council, BBC 1984–88, NEDC 1989–92, Employment Appeal Tribunal 1991–93; Member, Independent Committee for Supervision of Telephone Information Services 1991–93, Chairman 1993–; Non-Executive Director, Inveresk plc 1993–96; Member: Armed Forces Pay Review Body 1993–94, Press Complaints Commission 1993–98, Broadcasting Complaints Commission 1993–94; Non-Executive Director: Chamberlain Phipps plc 1994–, Takecare plc 1995–98; Chairman, Housing Corporation 1997–; Member, Royal Commission on the Reform of the House of Lords 1999. *Honours:* PC 1998. FRSA. *Special Interests:* Industry, Media, Arts Sponsorship, Women's Issues, Telecommunications, Pensions, Housing. *Recreations:* Sailing, family, theatre, cooking. *Sportsclubs:* Royal Cornwall Yacht. *Clubs:* Reform. *Name, Style and Title:* Raised to the peerage as Baroness Dean of Thornton-le-Fylde, of Eccles in the County of Greater Manchester 1993. Labour. *Address:* The Rt Hon. the Baroness Dean of Thornton-le-Fylde, House of Lords, London, SW1A 0PW.

DEARING (Life Baron, UK), Ronald Ernest Dearing; cr. 1998; Kt 1984; CB 1979

Son of late E. H. A. Dearing. Born July 27, 1930; educated Doncaster Grammar School; Hull University (BSc Economics); London Business School (Sloan Fellow); Hon. DSc, Hull 1986; Hon. DCL: Durham 1992, Northumbria 1993; Hon. LLD, Notingham 1993; Hon. Dr hc, Humberside 1993; Hon. FTCL 1993; Hon. Fellow, Institute of Education 1995; DUniv, Open University 1995; Hon. DLitt: Brighton, Exeter, Strathclyde; Hon. DTech, Staffordshire. Married 1954, Margaret Patricia Riley (2 daughters). *Armed Forces:* RAF 1949–51. *Career:* Ministry of Labour and National Service 1946–49; Ministry of Power 1949–62; HM Treasury 1962–64; Ministry of Power, Ministry of Technology, Department of Trade and Industry 1965–72; Regional Director, Northern Region, DTI 1972–74; Under-Secretary, DTI later Department of Industry 1972–75, Deputy Secretary 1975–80; Deputy Chairman, Post Office Corporation 1980–81, Chairman 1981–87; Chairman: CNAA 1987–88, County Durham Development Company 1987–90; Non-Executive Director: Whitbread Company plc 1987–90, Prudential plc 1987–91 IMI plc 1988–95, British Coal 1988–91, English Estates 1988–90; Chairman: Polytechnics and Colleges Funding Council 1988–93, Northern Development Company 1990–94; Non-Executive Director, Ericsson Ltd 1991–94; Chairman: Universities' Funding Council 1991–93, High Education Funding Council for England 1992–93, Camelot Group 1993–95, School Curriculum and Assessment Authority 1993–96; Non Executive Director, SDX plc 1995–98; Chairman: National Committee of Enquiry into Higher Education 1996–97, Write Away 1996–; University for Industry 1999–. *Chancellor:* Chancellor, Nottingham University 1993–. *Other:* Member: Council Industrial Society 1985–98, Governing Council London Business School 1985–89; Chairman, Accounting Standards Review Committee 1987–88; Member, Council, Durham University 1988–91; Chairman: Financial Reporting Council 1989–94, London Education Business Partnership 1989–92, Northern Sinfonia Appeals Committee 1993–94; President, Institute of Direct Marketing 1994–; Member, Council Melbourne University 1997–. *Awards Granted:* Gold Medal of British Institute of Management 1994. *Honours:* CB 1979; Kt 1984. Hon. FEng 1992. Freeman, City of London 1982. *Publications: The National Curriculum and its Assessment*, 1993; *Review of Qualifications for 16–19 Year Olds*, 1996. *Recreations:* Gardening, DIY. *Clubs:* Athenaeum. *Name, Style and Title:* Raised to the peerage as Baron Dearing, of Kingston upon Hull in the County of the East Riding of Yorkshire 1998. A Cross-Bencher. *Address:* The Lord Dearing, CB, c/o UFI, 31 St James, London, SW1Y 4JR.

DEEDES (Life Baron, UK), William Francis Deedes; cr. 1986; KBE 1999; PC 1962; MC 1944; DL

Son of late William Herbert Deedes. Born June 1, 1913; educated Harrow; Hon. DCL, University of Kent. Married November 21, 1942, Evelyn Hilary Branfoot (1 son 3 daughters and 1 son deceased). *Armed Forces:* Served with 12th KRRC 1939–44. *Councils, Public Bodies:* DL, Kent 1962. *Career:* Journalist with the *Morning Post* and *Daily Telegraph* 1931–; Editor, *The Daily Telegraph* 1974–86. *House of Commons:* MP (Conservative) for Ashford 1950–74; Parliamentary Secretary, Ministry of Housing and Local Government 1954–55; Parliamentary Under-Secretary of State, Home Office 1955–57; Minister without Portfolio 1962–64. *Select Committees (Commons):* Member, Select Committee on Race Relations and Immigration, Deputy Chairman 1968–70, Chairman 1970–74. *Party Groups (Commons):* Chairman, One Nation Group 1970–74. *Other:* Trustee: CARE International UK, African Medical and Research Foundation (AmREF); Member, Mines Advisory

Group (MAE). *Honours:* MC 1944; PC 1962; KBE 1999. *Publications: The Drugs Epidemic,* 1970. *Special Interests:* Race Relations, Agriculture, Media, Home Office Affairs, Overseas Aid and Development. *Recreations:* Golf. *Clubs:* Carlton, Beefsteak, Royal and Ancient (St Andrews). *Name, Style and Title:* Raised to the peerage as Baron Deedes, of Aldington in the County of Kent 1986. A Conservative. *Address:* The Rt Hon. the Lord Deedes, KBE, MC, DL, New Hayters, Aldington, Kent, TN25 7DT *Tel:* 01233 720269 *Tel:* Office: 020 7538 5000.

DELACOURT-SMITH OF ALTERYN (Life Baroness, UK), Margaret Delacourt-Smith; cr. 1974

Daughter of late F. J. Hando, of Newport, Monmouth. Born April 5, 1916; educated Newport High School for Girls; St Anne's College, Oxford (MA). Married 1st, 1939, Charles Smith, later Baron Delacourt-Smith, PC (died 1972) (1 son 2 daughters); married 2nd, 1978, Professor Charles Blackton. *Name, Style and Title:* Raised to the peerage as Baroness Delacourt-Smith of Alteryn, of Alteryn in the County of Gwent 1974. Labour. *Address:* The Baroness Delacourt-Smith of Alteryn, House of Lords, London, SW1A 0PW.

DENHAM (2nd Baron, UK), Bertram Stanley Mitford Bowyer; cr. 1937; 10th Bt of Denham (E) 1660; 2nd Bt of Weston Underwood (UK) 1933; PC 1981; KBE 1991

Son of 1st Baron, MC. Born October 3, 1927. Succeeded his father 1948; educated Eton; King's College, Cambridge (BA EngLit). Married February 14, 1956, Jean, eldest daughter of late Kenneth McCorquodale, MC, TD, of Essex (3 sons 1 daughter). *House of Lords:* An elected hereditary peer 1999–. *Whip:* Lord in Waiting (Government Whip) 1961–64, 1970–71; Opposition Whip 1964–70; Deputy Chief Whip and Captain Yeomen of the Guard 1972–74; Opposition Deputy Chief Whip 1974–78; Opposition Chief Whip 1978–79; Government Chief Whip and Captain of the Honourable Corps of Gentlemen at Arms 1979–91. *Miscellaneous:* Member, Countryside Commission 1993–99; A Extra Lord in Waiting to HM The Queen 1998–. *Honours:* PC 1981; KBE 1991. *Publications:* Author of: *The Man Who Lost His Shadow,* 1979; *Two Thyrdes,* 1983; *Foxhunt,* 1988; *Black Rod,* 1997. *Clubs:* White's, Pratt's, Garrick, Beefsteak. *Heir:* His son, Hon. Richard Grenville George Bowyer, born February 8, 1959. A Conservative. *Address:* The Rt Hon. the Lord Denham, KBE, The Laundry Cottage, Weston Underwood, Olney, Buckinghamshire, MK46 5JZ *Tel:* 01234 711535.

DENTON OF WAKEFIELD (Life Baroness, UK), Jean Denton; cr. 1991; CBE 1990

Daughter of late Charles and Kathleen Moss. Born December 29, 1935; educated Rothwell Grammar School; London School of Economics (BSc Econ); Hon. DLitt, Bradford University 1993; Hon. Doctor of Humanities, King's College, Pennsylvania 1994. *Councils, Public Bodies:* Deputy Chairman, Black Country Development Corporation 1987–92. *Career:* Procter and Gamble 1959–61; EIU 1961–64; IPC 1964–66; Racing/rally driver 1969–72; Managing Director, Herondrive 1980–85; External Affairs Director, Austin-Rover 1985–86; Director, Ordnance Survey 1985–88; Director: British Nuclear Fuels 1987–92, Burson-Marsteller 1987–92, London and Edinburgh Insurance Group 1989–92; Director, Triplex Lloyd plc 1990–92; Director: Eureka! 1991–92, North West Television 1991–92; Managing Director, Burson-Marstellar Europe 1997–. *House of Lords:* Parliamentary Under-Secretary of State: for Consumer Affairs and Small Firms, Department of Trade and Industry 1992–93, at Department of Environment 1993–94, at Northern Ireland Office (Minister for Economy, Agriculture and Women's Issues) 1994–97. *Whip:* A Baroness in Waiting (Government Whip) 1991–92. *Spokesman:* An Opposition Spokeswoman on: Northern Ireland 1997, Trade and Industry 1997, 1998–. *All-Party:* Secretary, All-Party Sex Equality Group. *Party Groups (General):* President, Wakefield Conservative Association 1994–. *Other:* President: FORUM UK 1989–, Women on the Move against Cancer 1979–; Governor, LSE 1982–92. *Trusts, etc:* Trustee, Brooklands Museum 1987–89. *Miscellaneous:* Director, Interim Advisory Committee on School Teachers' Pay and Conditions 1989, 1990, 1991; Director, NHS Policy Board 1991–92; Co-Chairman, Women's National Commission 1992–95. FCIM. *Special Interests:* Motor Industry, Retail Industry, Transport, Northern Ireland, Women's Issues. *Recreations:* Talking Shop, USA. *Sportsclubs:* British Women's Racing Drivers. *Name, Style and Title:* Raised to the peerage as Baroness Denton of Wakefield, of Wakefield in the County of West Yorkshire 1991. A Conservative. *Address:* The Baroness Denton of Wakefield, CBE, House of Lords, London, SW1A 0PW *Tel:* House of Lords 020 7219 3000.

DERBY (6th Bishop of), Jonathan Sansbury Bailey

Son of late Walter Bailey, and of Audrey Sansbury Bailey. Born February 24, 1940; educated Quarry Bank High School, Liverpool; Trinity College, Cambridge (MA). Married 1965, Rev Susan Bennett-Jones (3 sons). *Career:* Assistant Curate: Sutton, St Helens, Lancashire 1965–68, St Paul, Warrington 1968–71; Warden, Marrick Priory 1971–76; Vicar of Wetherby, West Yorkshire 1976–82; Archdeacon of Southend and Bishop's Officer for Industry and Commerce, Diocese of Chelmsford 1982–92; Suffragan Bishop of Dunwich 1992–95; Bishop of Derby 1995–; Clerk of the Closet to HM the Queen 1996–; Took his seat in the House of Lords 1999. *Recreations:* Theatre, music, beekeeping, carpentry. *Clubs:* United Oxford and Cambridge University. *Address:* The Rt Rev. the Lord Bishop of Derby, Bishop's Office, Derby Church House, Full Street, Derby, DE1 3DR *Tel:* 01332 346744 *Fax:* 01332 295810.

DESAI (Life Baron, UK), Meghnad Jagdishchandra Desai; cr. 1991

Son of late Jagdishchandra and Mandakini Desai. Born July 10, 1940; educated University of Bombay (BA, MA); University of Pennsylvania (PhD); Hon. DSc, University of Kingston 1992; Hon. DUniv: University of Middlesex 1993, University of East London 1994; Hon. DPhil, London Guildhall University 1996. Married June 27, 1970, Gail Graham, daughter of late George Ambler Wilson, CBE (1 son 2 daughters) (separated 1995). *Trades Union:* Member, AUT. *Councils, Public Bodies:* Chair, Management Committee, City Roads. *Career:* Associate specialist, Department of Agricultural Economics, University of California, Berkeley, California 1963–65; London School of Economics: Lecturer in Economics 1965–77, Senior Lecturer 1977–80, Reader 1980–83, Professor 1983–, Convenor, Economics Department 1987–90, Head, Development Studies Institute 1990–95, Director, Centre for the Study of Global Governance 1992–. *Whip:* Opposition Whip 1991–94. *Spokesman:* Opposition Spokesman on: Health 1991–93, Treasury and Economic Affairs 1992–93. *Select Committees:* Member: Science and Technology 1993–94, European Affairs Sub Committee A 1995–97; Co-opted Member, Select Committee on European Communities Sub-Committee A (Economic and Financial Affairs, Trade and External Relations) 1997–. *International Bodies:* Member, Executive Committee, IPU British Group 1995–. *Other:* Member: One World Action; Association of University Teachers. *Trusts, etc:* Member: Sir Ernest Cassel Trust, Tribune Newspaper; Chair of Trustees, Training for Life. *Miscellaneous:* Member, Marshall Aid Commission until 1998. FRSA. *Publications:* Author of several publications on economics. *Special Interests:* Economic Policy, Education, Development. *Recreations:* Reading, writing, cricket. *Clubs:* Reform. *Name, Style and Title:* Raised to peerage as Baron Desai, of St Clement Danes in the City of Westminster 1991. Labour. *Address:* Professor The Lord Desai, London School of Economics, Houghton Street, Aldwych, London, WC2A 2AE *Tel:* 020 7955 7489; 606 Collingwood House, Dolphin Square, London, SW1V 3NF *Tel:* 020 7798 8673 *E-Mail:* m.desai@lse.ac.uk.

DHOLAKIA (Life Baron, UK), Navnit Dholakia; cr. 1997; OBE 1992; DL

Son of Permananddas Mulji Dholakia and Shantabai Permananddas Dholakia. Born March 4, 1937; educated Indian Public Schools in Moshi, Arusha, Tabora and Morogoro in Tanzania; Institute of Science, Bhavnager, Gujarat, India; Brighton Technical College. Married 1967, Ann McLuskie (2 daughters). *Councils, Public Bodies:* Councillor, County Borough of Brighton 1961–64; JP 1978; Member, Sussex Police Authority 1991–94; DL, West Sussex 1999–. *Career:* Medical Laboratory Technician, Southlands Hospital, Shoreham-by-Sea 1960–66; Development Officer, National Committee for Commonwealth Immigrants 1966–68; Senior Development Officer, Community Relations Commission 1968–74, Principal Officer and Secretary 1974–76; Principal Fieldwork, Administration and Liaison Officer, Commission for Racial Equality 1976–78, Principal Officer, Management 1978–81, Head, Administration of Justice Section 1984–94; Member, Police Complaints Authority 1994–98. *Whip:* Liberal Democrat Party Whip October 1998–. *Spokesman:* A Liberal Democrat Spokesman on Home Affairs October 1998–. *Select Committees:* Co-opted Member, European Communities Sub-Committee F (Social Affairs, Education and Home Affairs) 1997–.

All-Party: Joint Vice-Chairman, All-Party Police Group 1998–. *Party Groups (General):* Chairman: Brighton Young Liberals 1959–62, Brighton Liberal Association 1962–64; Secretary, Race and Community Relations Panel, Liberal Party 1969–74; Member, Federal Policy and Federal Executive Committee of the Liberal Democrats 1996–97. *Other:* Member, Lord Hunt's Committee on Immigration and Youth Service 1967–69; Secretary, Race and Community Relations Panel, Liberal Party 1969–74; Member, Board of Visitors, HM Prison Lewes 1978–95; Council Member, National Association of Care and Resettlement of Offenders 1984–, Chairman 1998–; Member, Home Office Inter-departmental Committee on Racial Attacks and Harassment 1987–92; Chairman, Race Issues Advisory Committee of the National Association of Care and Resettlement of Offenders 1989–; Member, Ethnic Minority Advisory Committee of the Judicial Studies Board 1992–96; Council Member: The Howard League of Penal Reform 1992–, Save The Children Fund; Editorial Board, The Howard Journal of Criminology 1993–; Member: Lord Carlisle's Committee on Parole Systems Review, Home Secretary's Race Forum 1999–; Vice Chairman, Policy Research Institute on Aging and Ethnicity. *Trusts, etc:* Trustee, Mental Health Foundation 1997–. *Miscellaneous:* Member, Governing Body, Commonwealth Institute 1999–. *Honours:* OBE 1992. *Publications:* Various articles on criminal justice matters. *Recreations:* Photography, travel, gardening, cooking exotic dishes. *Name, Style and Title:* Raised to the peerage as Baron Dholakia, of Waltham Brooks in the County of West Sussex 1997. A Liberal Democrat. *Address:* The Lord Dholakia, OBE, DL, 76 Penland Road, Haywards Heath, West Sussex, RH16 1PH *Tel:* 01444 450065 *Fax:* 01444 450065.

DIAMOND (Life Baron, UK), John Diamond; cr. 1970; PC 1965

Son of late Rev. Solomon Diamond, a minister. Born April 30, 1907; educated Leeds Grammar School; Hon. LLD, Leeds 1978. Married (2 sons 2 daughters). *Career:* Practised as Chartered Accountant from 1931–64 Managing Director, Capital and Provincial News Theatres 1951–57. *House of Commons:* MP (Labour): Manchester, Blackley division 1945–51, Gloucester 1957–70; PPS to Minister of Works 1946; Chief Secretary to the Treasury 1964–68; Chief Secretary to the Treasury (inside the Cabinet) 1968–70. *House of Lords:* Principal Deputy Chairman Committees, House of Lords 1974. *Party Groups (General):* Hon. Treasurer, Fabian Society 1950–64; Trustee, Social Democratic Party 1981–82; Leader of SDP in the House of Lords 1982–88. *Other:* Council Member, London Philharmonic Orchestra 1972–74. *Trusts, etc:* Director, Sadler's Wells Trust 1957–64; Chairman of Trustees, Industry and Parliament Trust 1977–82. *Miscellaneous:* Member, General Nursing Council (Chairman of Financial and General Purposes Committee) 1947–53; Hon. Treasurer, The European Movement 1973–74; Chairman, Royal Commission on Distribution of Income and Wealth 1974–79; Chairman, Civil Service Advisory Committee on Business Appointments 1975–88. FCA. *Publications: Public Expenditure in Practice,* 1975; Co-author *Socialism The British Way,* 1948. *Recreations:* Music, gardening, classical languages. *Name, Style and Title:* Raised to the peerage as Baron Diamond, of the City of Gloucester 1970. Labour. *Address:* The Rt Hon. the Lord Diamond, Aynhoe, Doggetts Wood Lane, Chalfont St. Giles, Buckinghamshire, HP8 4TH *Tel:* 01494 763229.

DIXON (Life Baron, UK), Donald Dixon; cr. 1997; PC 1996; DL

Son of late Albert Dixon, shipyard worker. Born March 6, 1929; educated Ellison Street Elementary School, Jarrow. Married Doreen Morad (1 son 1 daughter). *Trades Union:* Member, GMWU and Branch Secretary. *Armed Forces:* Royal Engineers 1947–49. *Councils, Public Bodies:* Councillor, South Tyneside 1963–81; DL, Tyne and Wear 1997–. *Career:* Previously shipyard worker. *House of Commons:* MP (Labour) for Jarrow May 1979–97. *Whip (Commons):* Opposition Deputy Chief Whip 1987–96. *Select Committees (Commons):* Former Member, Select Committees on: Finance and Services, Selection, Catering, Employment Sub-Committee. *Backbench Committees (Commons):* Former Chairman, Parliamentary Labour Party Shipbuilding Group; Former Secretary, Parliamentary Labour Party Trade Union Group. *Select Committees:* Member, House of Lords' Offices Committee. *All-Party:* Member, All-Party: Maritime Group, Rail Freight Group, Defence Group, Employment Group. *Party Groups (General):* Joined Labour Party 1950; Former Chairman, Northern Group Labour MPs; Member, Local Co-operative Group. *Honours:* PC 1996. Freeman: Jarrow 1972, South Tyne 1997. *Special Interests:* Trade Unions, Ships and Shipbuilding,

Maritime Affairs, Housing, Transport, Social Services. *Recreations:* Football, reading, boxing. *Clubs:* Jarrow Ex-Servicemen's, Jarrow Labour. *Name, Style and Title:* Raised to the peerage as Baron Dixon, of Jarrow in the County of Tyne and Wear 1997. Labour. *Address:* The Rt Hon. the Lord Dixon, DL, 1 Hillcrest, Jarrow, Tyne and Wear, NE32 4DP *Tel:* 0191–489 7635.

DIXON-SMITH (Life Baron, UK), Robert William Dixon-Smith; cr. 1993; DL

Son of late Dixon and Alice Winifred Smith. Born September 30, 1934; educated Oundle; Writtle Agricultural College, Essex; Honorary Doctorate, Anglia Polytechnic University; Fellow, Writtle College. Married February 13, 1960, Georgina Janet, daughter of George and Kathleen Cook (1 son 1 daughter). *Armed Forces:* Second Lieutenant, King's Dragoon Guards (National Service) 1956–57. *Councils, Public Bodies:* Councillor, Essex County Council 1965–93, Chairman 1986–89; DL, Essex 1986. *Career:* Farmer. *Spokesman:* An Opposition Spokesman on Environment, Transport and the Regions (Local Government) December 1998–. *Select Committees:* Member, Select Committees on: Science and Technology 1994–97, European Communities 1994–97. *All-Party:* Member, All-Party London Group. *Other:* Governor, Writtle Agricultural College 1967–94, Chairman 1973–85; Chairman, Governors of Anglia Polytechnic University 1993–94 (formerly Anglia Polytechnic), Governor 1973–. *Miscellaneous:* Member, Association of County Councils 1983–93, Chairman 1992–93. Liveryman, Farmers' Company 1990. *Special Interests:* Agriculture, Environment, Transport. *Recreations:* Country sports, golf. *Name, Style and Title:* Raised to the peerage as Baron Dixon-Smith, of Bocking in the County of Essex 1993. A Conservative. *Address:* The Lord Dixon-Smith, DL, Home: Lyons Hall, Braintree, Essex, CM7 9SH *Tel:* 01376 326834; Office: Houchins, Coggeshall, Colchester, Essex, CO6 1RT *Tel:* 01376 561448.

DONALDSON OF LYMINGTON (Life Baron, UK), John Francis Donaldson; cr. 1988; Kt 1966; PC 1979

Son of late Malcolm Donaldson, FRCS, FRCOG. Born October 6, 1920; educated Charterhouse; Trinity College, Cambridge (MA 1949, MA (Oxon) 1982); Hon. Fellow, Trinity College, Cambridge 1983; Hon. DU, Essex 1983; Hon. LLD: Sheffield 1984, Nottingham Trent University 1992, Southampton 1998. Married 1945, Dorothy Mary (Dame Mary Donaldson, GBE), daughter of late Reginald George Gale Warwick (1 son 2 daughters). *Armed Forces:* Commissioned, Royal Signals 1941; Served with: Guards Armoured Divisional Signals in UK and North West Europe 1942–45, Military Government, Schleswig-Holstein 1945–46. *Councils, Public Bodies:* Councillor, Croydon Borough Council 1949–53. *Career:* Called to Bar, Middle Temple 1946; Harmsworth Law Scholar 1946; Bencher 1966; Member, General Council of the Bar 1956–61; QC 1961; Judge of the High Court, Queen's Bench Division 1966–79; President, National Industrial Relations Court 1971–74; A Lord Justice of Appeal 1979–82; Master of the Rolls 1982–92. *All-Party:* Member, All-Party Maritime Group. *Other:* Hon. Member, Association of Average Adjusters 1966, Chairman 1981; President, British Maritime Law Association 1979–95, Vice-President 1969–78; President, British Insurance Law Association 1979–81, Deputy President 1978–79; Governor, Sutton's Hospital in Charterhouse 1981–84; Visitor: UCL 1982–92, Nuffield College, Oxford 1982–92, London Business School 1986–92; President, Council, Inns of Court 1987–90; Hon. Life Member, The Law Society 1994. *Miscellaneous:* Chairman: Financial Law Panel 1993–, Inquiry into pollution from merchant shipping 1993–94, Lord Donaldson's Assessment (Derbyshire) 1995; Member, Review of: Salvage and Intervention Command and Control 1997–98, Four Year Strategy for HM Coastguard 1999. *Honours:* Kt 1966; PC 1979. Fellow, Chartered Institute of Arbitrators 1980, President 1980–83. Freeman, Drapers Company. *Special Interests:* Law and the Administration of Justice, Maritime Safety. *Recreations:* Sailing. *Sportsclubs:* Royal Lymington Yacht. *Clubs:* Royal Cruising. *Name, Style and Title:* Raised to the peerage as Baron Donaldson of Lymington, of Lymington in the County of Hampshire 1988. A Cross-Bencher. *Address:* The Rt Hon. the Lord Donaldson of Lymington, House of Lords, London, SW1A 0PW *Tel:* Home: 020 7588 6610.

DONOUGHUE (Life Baron, UK), Bernard Donoughue; cr. 1985

Son of late Thomas Joseph Donoughue. Born September 8, 1934; educated Campbell Secondary Modern School, Northampton; Northampton Grammar School; Lincoln College and Nuffield College, Oxford (MA, DPhil); Harvard University, USA; Hon. Fellow, Lincoln College, Oxford; Hon. LLD, Leicester; Hon. Fellow, LSE. Married November 26, 1959, Carol Ruth Goodman (2 sons 2 daughters) (marriage dissolved 1989). *Trades Union:* Member, GMBW. *Career:* Editorial Staff, *The Economist* 1959–60; Senior Research Officer, Political and Economic Planning Institute 1960–63; Senior Lecturer, London School of Economics 1963–74; Senior Policy Adviser to the Prime Minister 1974–79; Development Director, Economist Intelligence Unit 1979–81; Assistant Editor, *The Times* 1981–82; Head of Research and Investment Policy, Grieveson Grant and Co. 1982–86; Head of International Research and Director, Kleinwort Grieveson Securities Ltd 1986–88; Executive Vice-Chairman, LBI 1988–91; Director, Towcester Racecourse Ltd 1992–97. *House of Lords:* Parliamentary Secretary (Lords), Ministry of Agriculture, Fisheries and Food (Minister for Farming and the Food Industry) 1997–99. *Spokesman:* Opposition Spokesman on: Energy 1991–92, Treasury Affairs 1991–92, National Heritage 1992–97. *All-Party:* Member, All-Party Groups on: London, Arts and Heritage, Racing and Bloodstock. *Other:* Chairman Executive, London Symphony Orchestra 1979–91, Patron 1989–95; Member, LSE Court of Governors 1997; Consultant Member, House Industry Confederation 1999–. *Trusts, etc:* Member, Dorneywood Trust. *Miscellaneous:* Member: Sports Council 1965–71, Commission of Enquiry into Association Football 1966–68, London Arts Board 1992–97. FRHS. *Publications:* Author of books on history and politics including: *Trade Unions in a Changing Society*, 1963; *British Politics and the American Revolution*, 1964; *The People into Parliament*, 1966; *Herbert Morrison*, 1973; *Prime Minister*, 1987. *Special Interests:* Arts, Finance, Sport. *Recreations:* Music, theatre, sport. *Sportsclubs:* Houses of Parliament Cricket Club. *Clubs:* Pratts', Farmers', 1795. *Name, Style and Title:* Raised to the peerage as Baron Donoughue, of Ashton in the County of Northamptonshire 1985. Labour. *Address:* The Lord Donoughue, House of Lords, London, SW1A 0PW *Tel:* Home: 020 7730 7332 *E-Mail:* parlsecl@sec.maff.gov.uk.

DORMAND OF EASINGTON (Life Baron, UK), John Donkin Dormand; cr. 1987

Son of late Bernard and Mary Dormand. Born August 27, 1919; educated Bede College, Durham; Loughborough College; St Peter's College, Oxford; Harvard University; Hon. Fellow, St Peter's College, Oxford. Married December 26, 1963, Mrs Doris Robinson, daughter of Thomas Pearson (1 step-son 1 step-daughter). *Trades Union:* Member: APEX (GMB), NUT. *Career:* Teacher 1940–48; Education Adviser 1948–52, 1959–63; Education Officer, NCB 1957–59; Education Officer, Easington Rural District Council 1963–70. *House of Commons:* MP (Labour) for Easington 1970–87. *Whip (Commons):* Assistant Government Whip 1974; A Lord Commissioner of HM Treasury 1974–79; Opposition Whip 1979–81. *All-Party Committees (Commons):* Vice-Chairman, Commons and Lords All-Party Group on Tourism; Hon. Secretary, Humanist Group. *House of Lords:* Labour Peers' Representative on Parliamentary Committee (Shadow Cabinet) 1994–97. *Select Committees:* Former Member: Select Committee on Committee Structure of House of Lords June-December 1991; House of Lords Liaison Committee 1992–97, Procedure Committee. *All-Party:* Vice-Chairman, All-Party British-Philippines Country Group 1999–. *Party Groups (General):* Chairman, Parliamentary Labour Party 1981–87. *Special Interests:* Education, Coal Industry, Regional Policy, Local Government, Tourism, Film Industry. *Recreations:* Music, sport, films. *Clubs:* Peterlee Labour, Easington Workmen's. *Name, Style and Title:* Raised to the peerage as Baron Dormand of Easington, of Easington in the County of Durham 1987. Labour. *Address:* The Lord Dormand of Easington, House of Lords, London, SW1A 0PW *Tel:* House of Lords 020 7219 5419.

DUBS (Life Baron, UK), Alfred Dubs; cr. 1994

Born December 5, 1932 in Prague, Czech Republic; educated London School of Economics (BSc Econ). Married (1 son 1 daughter). *Trades Union:* Member, TGWU. *Councils, Public Bodies:* Councillor, Westminster City Council 1971–78; Chairman, Westminster Community Relations Council 1972–77; Member, Kensington, Chelsea and Westminster Area Health Authority 1975–78; Non-Executive Director, Pathfinder NHS Trust 1995–97. *Career:* Formerly a local government officer; Director, Refugee Council 1988–95; Member, Broadcasting Standards Council 1988–94, Deputy Chairman 1994–97. *House of Commons:* Contested (Labour): Cities of London and Westminster 1970, Hertfordshire South February and October 1974, Battersea 1987 and 1992 General Elections; MP (Labour) for: Battersea South 1979–83, Battersea 1983–87. *Spokesman (Commons):* Opposition Front Bench Spokesman on Home Affairs 1983–87. *Select Committees (Commons):* Member: Home Affairs Select Committee 1981–83, Sub-Committee on Race Relations and Immigration 1981–83. *House of Lords:* Parliamentary Under-Secretary of State, Northern Ireland Office (Minister for Environment and Agriculture) 1997–99. *Whip:* An Opposition Whip 1995–97. *Spokesman:* An Opposition Spokesman on: The Environment (Health and Safety) 1996–97, Energy 1996–97. *Select Committees:* Member, Select Committees on: Relations between Central and Local Government 1995–96, European Community 1996–97. *Party Groups (General):* Member, The Co-operative Party; Chairman, Fabian Society 1993–94. *Other:* Chairman, Liberty 1990–92. *Trusts, etc:* Trustee: Action Aid 1989–97, Immigration Advisory Service 1992–97. *Publications: Lobbying: An Insider's Guide to the Parliamentary Process,* 1989. *Special Interests:* Civil Liberties, Penal Reform, Race Relations, Immigration, Health Service, Ireland, Human Rights. *Recreations:* Walking in the Lake District. *Name, Style and Title:* Raised to the peerage as Baron Dubs, of Battersea in the London Borough of Wandsworth 1994. Labour. *Address:* The Lord Dubs, House of Lords, London, SW1A 0PW.

DUNDEE (12th Earl of, S), Alexander Henry Scrymgeour; cr. 1660; Viscount Dudhope (S) 1641; Lord Scrymgeour (S) 1641; Lord Inverkeithing (S) 1660; Baron Glassary (UK) 1954

Son of 11th Earl, PC, DL. Born June 5, 1949. Succeeded his father 1983; educated Eton; St Andrews University. Married July 19, 1979, Siobhan Mary, daughter of David Llewellyn (1 son 3 daughters). *House of Lords:* An elected hereditary peer 1999–. *Whip:* Lord in Waiting (Government Whip) 1986–89. *Select Committees:* Member, Select Committee on European Communities Sub-Committee F (Social Affairs, Education and Home Affairs) 1997–. *All-Party:* Co-Chairman, All-Party Social Development in Europe Group 1999–. *International Bodies (General):* Substitute, UK Delegation to Council of Europe and Western European Union; Representative, UK Delegation to Organisation for Security and Co-operation in Europe. *Miscellaneous:* Hereditary Royal Standard Bearer for Scotland; Page of Honour to HM The Queen 1964–65; Contested (Conservative) Hamilton By-election 1978. *Clubs:* White's, New (Edinburgh). *Heir:* His son, Lord Scrymgeour, born June 20, 1982. A Conservative. *Address:* The Earl of Dundee, Farm Office, Birkhill, Cupar, Fife, KY15 4QP *Tel:* 01826 24200.

DUNN (Life Baroness, UK), Lydia Dunn; cr. 1990; DBE 1989

Daughter of late Yen Chuen Yih Dunn and Bessie Dunn. Born February 29, 1940; educated St Paul's Convent School, Hong Kong; College of the Holy Names, Oakland, California; University of California, Berkeley, California; Hon. LLD: Chinese University of Hong Kong 1984, Hong Kong University 1991, University of British Columbia, Canada 1991, University of Leeds 1994; Hon. DSc, University of Buckingham 1995. Married April 2, 1988, Michael Thomas, CMG, QC. *Career:* Member, Legislative Council, Hong Kong 1976–88, Senior Member 1985–88; Director: John Swire & Sons (HK) Ltd 1978–, Mass Transit Railway Corporation 1979–85; Chairman: Special Committee on Land Supply 1981–83, Prince Philip Dental Hospital 1981–87; Director, Hong Kong & Shanghai Banking Corporation Ltd 1981–96, Deputy Chairman 1992–96; Director: Swire Pacific Ltd 1981–, Kowloon Canton Railway Corporation 1982–84; Member, Hong Kong Executive Council 1982–95, Senior Member 1988–95; Chairman, Hong Kong Trade Development Council 1983–91; Deputy Chairman, Executive Committee, Commonwealth Parliamentary Association, Hong Kong Branch 1985–88; Director, Cathay Pacific Airways Ltd 1985–97; Director, HSBC Holdings plc 1990,

Non-Executive Deputy Chairman 1992–; Director: Volvo AB 1991–93, Christies International plc 1996–98; Executive Director, John Swire & Sons Ltd 1996–; Director, The General Electric Company plc 1997–; Adviser to Board, Cathay Pacific Airways Ltd 1997–; Christies Fine Art Limited 1998–. *Other:* Member: General Committee, Federation of Hong Kong Industries 1978–83, World Wildlife Fund Hong Kong 1982–85, Hong Kong/Japan Business Co-operation Committee 1983–87, Hong Kong/US Economic Co-operation Committee 1984–93, The International Council of the Asia Society 1986–96, Hong Kong Association, United Kingdom 1991, Council United World College of The Atlantic. *Awards Granted:* Prime Minister of Japan's Trade Award 1987; *To Peace and Commerce* Award, USA Secretary of Commerce 1988. *Trusts, etc:* Industry Committee of the Animal Health Trust 1996–. *Miscellaneous:* Member: Governing Body Commonwealth Institute 1999–; Executive Council Hong Kong 1982–95. *Honours:* OBE 1978; CBE 1983; DBE 1989. Fellow: Institute of Directors 1989–, The Royal Society for the Encouragement of Arts, Manufacturers and Commerce 1989–. *Publications: In the Kingdom of the Blind,* published by Trade Policy Research Centre 1983. *Recreations:* Art, antiques. *Clubs:* Hong Kong, Hong Kong Jockey. *Name, Style and Title:* Raised to the peerage as Baroness Dunn, of Hong Kong Island in Hong Kong and of Knightsbridge in the Royal Borough of Kensington and Chelsea 1990. A Cross-Bencher. *Address:* The Baroness Dunn, DBE, John Swire and Sons Ltd, Swire House, 59 Buckingham Gate, London, SW1E 6AJ *Tel:* 020 7834 7717.

DURHAM (93rd Bishop of), Anthony Michael Arnold Turnbull

Son of late George and late Adeline Turnbull. Born December 27, 1935; educated Ilkley Grammar School; Keble College, Oxford (MA); St John's College, Durham (Dip. Theology); DLitt (Hon. Causa). Married 1963, Brenda Susan Merchant (1 son 2 daughters). *Career:* Deacon 1960; Priest 1961; Curate: Middleton 1960–61, Luton 1961–65; Domestic Chaplain to Archbishop of York 1965–69; Rector of Heslington and Chaplain to York University 1969–76; Member, General Synod of the Church of England 1970–75, 1987–; Chief Secretary, Church Army 1976–84; Examining Chaplain to the Bishop of Norwich 1982–84; Archdeacon of Rochester, also Canon Residentiary of Rochester Cathedral and Chairman Diocesan Board for Mission and Unity 1984–88; Bishop of Rochester 1988–94; Member, Board of Church Commissioners 1989–98, Vice-Chairman, Central Board of Finance, C of E 1990–98; Member, Archbishop's Commission on Cathedrals 1992–94; Bishop of Durham 1994–; Took his seat in the House of Lords 1994; Chairman, Archbishop's Commission on Organisation of C of E 1994–95; Visitor, University of Durham; Member, Archbishops' Council, Chairman, Ministry Division. *Other:* Chairman: College of Preachers 1990–98, Bible Reading Fellowship 1990–94, Partnership for World Mission 1991–94; Member, Court of Governors, University of Greenwich 1992–94. *Publications:* Author of: *God's Front Line,* 1979; *Parish Evangelism,* 1980; *Learning to Pray,* 1981. *Special Interests:* Housing, Employment, Overseas Aid and Development. *Recreations:* Cricket, family life. *Sportsclubs:* Member, Durham CCC. *Clubs:* Athenaeum, MCC. *Address:* The Rt Rev. the Lord Bishop of Durham, Auckland Castle, Bishop Auckland, Co. Durham, DL14 7NR *Tel:* 01388 602576 *E-Mail:* bishop.of.durham@durham.anglican.org.

E

EAMES (Life Baron, UK), Robert Henry Alexander Eames; cr. 1995

Son of William and Mary Eames. Born April 27, 1937; educated Belfast Royal Academy; Methodist College, Belfast; Queen's University, Belfast (LLB (Hons), PhD); Trinity College, Dublin; Hon. LLD: Queen's University 1989, Trinity College, Dublin 1992; Hon. DLitt, Greenwich University School of Theology 1993; Hon. DD, Cambridge 1994; Hon. LLD, Lancaster University 1994; Hon. DD, Aberdeen University 1997; Hon. DD, Exeter University 1999. Married 1966, Ann Christine Daly (2 sons). *Career:* Research Scholar and Tutor, Faculty of Laws, Queen's University 1960–63; Curate Assistant, Bangor Parish Church 1963–66; Rector of St Dorothea's, Belfast 1966–74; Examining Chaplain to the Bishop of Down 1973; Rector of St Mark's, Dundela 1974–75; Bishop of Derry and Raphoe 1975–80; Bishop of Down and Dromore 1980–86; Archbishop of Armagh and Primate of All Ireland 1986–; Select Preacher, Oxford University 1987; Chairman: Commission on Communion and Women in the Episcopate 1988–, Commission on Inter-Anglican Relations 1988–; Select Preacher, University of Cambridge 1990; Chairman, Inter-Anglican Theological and Doctrinal Commission 1991; Select Preacher, University of Edinburgh 1993; Chairman, Inter-Anglican Finance Committee 1997–. *International Bodies (General):* Member, Anglican International Consultative Council. *Other:* Governor, Church Army 1985–; Chairman: Board of Governors, Royal School, Armagh, Armagh Observatory and Planetarium. *Publications:* Author of: *A Form of Worship for Teenagers*, 1965; *The Quiet Revolution – Irish Disestablishment*, 1970; *Through Suffering*, 1973; *Thinking through Lent*, 1978; *Through Lent*, 1984; *Chains to be Broken*, 1992. *Special Interests:* Northern Ireland, Social Issues, Community Care. *Recreations:* Sailing, Rugby Union. *Clubs:* Kildare Street and University (Dublin). *Name, Style and Title:* Raised to the peerage as Baron Eames, of Armagh in the County of Armagh 1995. A Cross-Bencher. *Address:* The Most Rev. the Lord Eames, Lord Archbishop of Armagh and Primate of All Ireland, The See House, Cathedral Close, Armagh, Co. Armagh, BT61 7EE *Tel:* 01861 522851 *Fax:* 01861 527823.

EATWELL (Life Baron, UK), John Leonard Eatwell; cr. 1992

Son of late Harold Jack Eatwell, and late Mary Eatwell. Born February 2, 1945; educated Headlands Grammar School, Swindon; Queens' College, Cambridge (BA 1967, MA 1971); Harvard University (PhD 1975). Married April 24, 1970, Hélène, daughter of Georges Seppain (2 sons 1 daughter). *Trades Union:* Member, Association of University Teachers. *Career:* Teaching Fellow, Graduate School of Arts and Sciences, Harvard University 1968–69; Research Fellow, Queens' College, Cambridge 1969–70; Fellow of Trinity College, Cambridge 1970–96; Assistant Lecturer, Faculty of Economics and Politics, Cambridge University 1975–77, Lecturer 1977–; Visiting Professor of Economics, New School for Social Research, New York 1982–96; Economic Adviser to Rt Hon. Neil Kinnock MP, Leader of the Labour Party 1985–92; Trustee and Secretary, Institute for Public Policy Research 1988–97, Chairman 1997–; Chairman, Extemporary Dance Theatre 1990; Non-executive Director: Anglia Television Group Ltd 1994–, Cambridge Econometrics Ltd 1996–; Director, Securities and Futures Authority 1997–; President, Queens' College, Cambridge 1997–; Chairman, British Screen 1997–; Member, Board of Directors of the Royal Opera House and Chairman, Royal Ballet 1998–. *Spokesman:* An Opposition Spokesman on: Trade and Industry 1992–96, Treasury and Economic Affairs 1992–93; Principal Opposition Spokesman on Treasury and Economic Affairs 1993–97. *Other:* Chairman, Crusaid, the national fundraiser for AIDS 1993–. *Trusts, etc:* Governor, Contemporary Dance Trust 1991–95; Director, Arts Theatre Trust, Cambridge 1991–98. *Publications: An Introduction to Modern Economics* (with Joan Robinson), 1973; *Whatever happened to Britain?*, 1982; *Keynes's Economics and the Theory of Value and Distribution*, (edited with Murray Milgate), 1983; *The New Palgrave: A Dictionary of Economics*, (edited with Murray Milgate and Peter Newman), 4 vols, 1987; *The New Palgrave Dictionary of Money and Finance*, (edited with Murry Milgate and Peter Newman), 3 vols, 1992; Articles in scientific journals and other collected works. *Special Interests:* Economics, Trade and Industry, Arts. *Recreations:* Classical and contemporary dance, rugby union football. *Sportsclubs:* Lords and Commons RUFC. *Name, Style and Title:* Raised to the peerage as Baron Eatwell, of Stratton St Margaret in the County of Wiltshire 1992. Labour. *Address:* The Lord Eatwell, The President's Lodge, Queens' College, Cambridge, CB3 9ET *Tel:* 01223 335532 *Fax:* 01223 335555 *E-Mail:* president@quns.cam.ac.uk.

ECCLES OF MOULTON (Life Baroness, UK), Diana Catherine Eccles; cr. 1990; DL

Daughter of late Raymond and Margaret Sturge. Born October 4, 1933; educated St. James's School, West Malvern; Open University (BA); Hon. DCL, Durham 1995. Married January 29, 1955, Hon. John Dawson Eccles (Now 2nd Viscount Eccles, CBE) (1 son 3 daughters). *Councils, Public Bodies:* Member, Teesside Urban Development Corporation 1987–98; Chairman: Ealing District Health Authority 1988–93, Ealing, Hammersmith and Hounslow Health Authority 1993–; DL, North Yorkshire 1998–. *Career:* Voluntary work, Middlesbrough Community Council 1955–58; Partner in graphic design business 1963–77; Member, North Eastern Electricity Board 1974–85; Vice-Chairman, National Council for Voluntary Organisations 1981–87; Lay Member, Durham

University Council 1981–, Vice-Chairman 1985–; Chairman, Tyne Tees Television Programme Consultative Council 1982–84; Member: Advisory Council on Energy Conservation (Department of Energy) 1982–84, Widdicombe Inquiry into Local Government 1985–86, Home Office Advisory Panel on Licences for Experimental Community Radio 1985–86, British Rail Eastern Board 1986–92; Director: Tyne Tees Television 1986–94, J. Sainsbury plc 1986–95, Yorkshire Electricity Group plc 1990–97; Member, Unrelated Live Transplant Regulatory Authority 1990–99; Director: National and Provincial Building Society 1991–96, Times Newspapers Holdings Ltd 1998–, Opera North 1998–. *Trusts, etc:* Trustee, Charities Aid Foundation 1982–89; Member: York Minster Trust Fund, British Heart Foundation. *Name, Style and Title:* Raised to the peerage as Baroness Eccles of Moulton, of Moulton in the County of North Yorkshire 1990. A Conservative. *Address:* The Viscountess Eccles, Lady Eccles of Moulton, DL, 6 Barton Street, London, SW1P 3NG *Tel:* 020 7222 7559; Moulton Hall, Richmond, North Yorkshire, DL10 6QH *Tel:* 01325 377227.

EDEN OF WINTON (Life Baron, UK), John Benedict Eden; cr 1983; 9th Bt of West Auckland (E) 1672; 7th Bt of Maryland (GB) 1776; PC 1972

Son of Sir Timothy Eden, 8th and 6th Bt. Born September 15, 1925; educated Eton; St Paul's School, USA. Married 1st, January 28, 1958, Belinda Jane, daughter of late Sir John Pascoe (2 sons 2 daughters) (marriage dissolved 1974), married 2nd, 1977, Margaret Ann, Viscountess Strathallan, daughter of late Robin Gordon. *Armed Forces:* Served British and Indian Armies 1943–47; Lieutenant, Rifle Brigade, seconded to 2nd King Edward's Own Goorkha Rifles and the Gilgit Scouts. *Career:* Former Chairman of various plcs; Chairman, Lady Eden's School Ltd; Member, Timken Company International Advisory Board. *House of Commons:* MP (Conservative) for Bournemouth West 1954–83; Minister of State, Ministry of Technology June-October 1970; Minister for Industry 1970–72; Minister of Posts and Telecommunications 1972–74. *Spokesman (Commons):* Former opposition Spokesman on Defence (RAF) and Power. *Select Committees (Commons):* Member, Trade and Industry Sub-Committee of the House of Commons Expenditure Committee 1974–76; Chairman: House of Commons Select Committee European Legislation etc. 1976–79, House of Commons Select Committee on Home Affairs 1981–83. *Backbench Committees (Commons):* Former Officer: Conservative Party Committee for Defence, Conservative Party Committee for Power, 1922 Committee. *All-Party Committees (Commons):* Former Member, All-Party Privileges Group. *International Bodies (Commons):* Former Member: WEU, NATO Parliamentarians, Council of Europe. *Party Groups (General):* Hon. Life Vice-President, Association of Conservative Clubs Ltd. *Other:* President, Independent Schools Association 1969–71; Chairman, The British Lebanese Association 1990–98; Vice-President, International Tree Foundation to 1998. *Trusts, etc:* Chairman, The Royal Armouries Board of Trustees 1986–94. *Honours:* PC 1972. Hon. Freeman: Annapolis, Maryland, USA 1976, Bournemouth 1984. *Clubs:* Boodle's, Pratt's. *Heir:* To the baronetcies, his son, Hon. Robert Frederick Calvert Eden, born April 30, 1964. *Name, Style and Title:* Raised to the peerage as Baron Eden of Winton, of Rushyford in the County of Durham 1983. A Conservative. *Address:* The Rt Hon. the Lord Eden of Winton, 41 Victoria Road, London, W8 5RH *E-Mail:* lordeden@clara.net.

ELDER (Life Baron, UK), Thomas Murray Elder; cr. 1999

Born May 9, 1950; educated Kirkcaldy High School; Edinburgh University (MA Economic History). *Career:* Bank of England 1972–80; Labour Party Scotland 1984–92, General Secretary 1988–92; Chief of Staff to Rt Hon. John Smith, MP 1992–94; Special Adviser, Scottish Office 1997–99. *Recreations:* Walking, reading, opera. *Name, Style and Title:* Raised to the peerage as Baron Elder, of Kirkcaldy in Fife 1999. Labour. *Address:* The Lord Elder, House of Lords, London, SW1A 0PW.

ELIS-THOMAS (Life Baron, UK), Dafydd Elis Elis-Thomas; cr. 1992

Born October 18, 1946; educated Ysgol Dyffryn Conwy; University College of Wales (PhD). Married 1st, 1970, Elen M. Williams (3 sons) (marriage dissolved), married 2nd, December 29, 1993, Mair Parry Jones. *Career:* Tutor in Welsh Studies, Coleg Harlech 1971–74; Has subsequently taught at: The University College of North Wales, Bangor, Aberystwyth, Cardiff, The Open University; Has been a broadcaster on BBC Wales, HTV, S4C, Radio Wales; Consultant to: S4C, The Welsh Development Agency, The Rural Initiative Programme, The Assembly of European Regions, The Government of Catalonia; Chairman, Screen Wales; Director and Deputy Chairman, Cynefin Environmental; Director and Chairman, New Media Agency; Director: Oriel Mostyn, National Botanical Gardens, MFM Marcher. *House of Commons:* MP (Plaid Cymru) for: Meirionnydd 1974–83, Meirionnydd Nant Conwy 1974–92. *Select Committees (Commons):* Member, first Select Committee of House of Commons on Education, Science and the Arts 1979–83; Former Member of other select and standing committees. *Select Committees:* Member: Select Committee on European Communities 1997–98, Select Committee on European Communities Sub-Committee C (Environment, Public Health and Consumer Protection) 1997–98. *Party Groups (General):* President, Plaid Cymru 1984–91. *Other:* President, Hay-on-Wye Literature Festival; Vice-President: Ramblers Association in Wales, Snowdonia National Park Society, Abbeyfield. *Trusts, etc:* Trustee: Big Issue Foundation, Theatr Bara Caws; Patron, Prince of Wales Trust – Bro; Member, Wales Committee of National Trust. *Miscellaneous:* Member: Welsh Arts Council, Welsh Film Council, Welsh Film Board, BBC General Consultative Council; Chairman, Welsh Language Board 1993–96, 1996–99; Fellow, International Centre for Intercultural Studies, Institute of Education, London; AM for the Constituency of Meirionnydd Nant Conwy since May 6, 1999 (contested the seat as Dafydd Elis-Thomas); Elected Presiding Officer (The Speaker) of the Welsh Assembly May 1999–. *Recreations:* Welsh literature and art, music, theatre, films, hill and mountain walking, swimming, jogging. *Name, Style and Title:* Raised to the peerage as Baron Elis-Thomas, of Nant Conwy in the County of Gwynnedd 1992. A Cross-Bencher. *Address:* The Lord Elis-Thomas, AM, 3 Lon Warfield, Caernarfon, Gwynedd, LL55 1LA.

ELLES (Life Baroness, UK), Diana Louie Elles; cr. 1972

Daughter of late Colonel Stewart Newcombe, DSO. Born July 19, 1921; educated Private Schools, London, Paris, Florence; London University (BA Hons). Married August 14, 1945, Neil Patrick Moncrieff Elles (1 son 1 daughter). *Armed Forces:* Served in WAAF 1941–45; Flight Officer 1944. *Career:* Barrister-at-Law, Lincoln's Inn, 1956; Voluntary Care Committee Worker, Kennington 1956–72; UK delegate, United Nations General Assembly 1972; Member, UN Sub-Commission for Prevention of Discrimination and Protection of Minorities 1973–74; International Chairman, European Union of Women 1973–79; UK delegate to European Parliament 1973–75; UN Special Rapporteur on Human Rights 1975–79; Member for Thames Valley in the European Parliament 1979–89; Vice-President, European Parliament 1982–1987; Group Spokesman, Political Affairs Northern Ireland 1980–1987; Chairman, European Parliament Legal Affairs Committee 1987–89. *Spokesman:* Opposition Spokesman in House of Lords 1975–79. *Select Committees:* Member: House of Lords European Communities Select Committee 1989–94, Ad Hoc Sub-Committee on 1996 Inter-Governmental Conference 1995–97, Sub-Committee E on Law and Institutions 1994–97, Co-opted Member 1997–. *Party Groups (General):* Chairman, Conservative Party International Office 1973–78. *Other:* Council Member, Royal Institute of International Affairs 1977–86; Governor, British Institute Florence 1986–96, Chairman, Board of Governors 1994–96, Life Governor 1996–; Governor, Reading University 1986–96. *Trusts, etc:* Trustee: Industry and Parliament Trust 1985–96, Caldecott Community 1990–97. *Honours:* Hon. Bencher, Lincoln's Inn 1993. *Publications: UN Human Rights of Non-Citizens*, 1984; *Legal Issues of the Maastricht Treaty*, 1995; *European and World Trade Law*, 1996; *Procedural Aspects of Competition Law*, 1975; articles on EC law. *Name, Style and Title:* Raised to the peerage as Baroness Elles, of the City of Westminster 1972. A Conservative. *Address:* The Baroness Elles, 75 Ashley Gardens, London, SW1P 1HG *Tel:* House of Lords 020 7219 3149; Villa Fontana, Ponte del Giglio, Lucca, Italy.

ELLIOTT OF MORPETH (Life Baron, UK), Robert William Elliott; cr. 1985; Kt 1974; DL

Son of late Richard Elliott. Born December 11, 1920; educated Edward VI Grammar School, Morpeth. Married June 16, 1956, Catherine Jane Morpeth (1 son 4 daughters inc twins). *Councils, Public Bodies:* DL, Northumberland 1985. *Career:* Chairman, Newcastle and Gateshead Water Company 1983–93; Non-Executive Director, T. Cowie 1987–95; Chairman, United Artists Communications (North East) 1995–; Vice-Chairman, Lyonaisse UK; Former Chairman, Metro Radio Group; Former Director: Port of Tyne Authority, Ferguson Industrial Holdings plc, Corporate Trade Finance plc, Sino French Holdings (Hong Kong). *House of Commons:* Contested (Conservative): Morpeth by-election 1954, General Election 1955; MP (Conservative) for Newcastle upon Tyne North 1957–83; PPS to: Joint Parliamentary Secretaries, Ministry of Transport and Civil Aviation 1958–59, Under-Secretary, Home Office 1959–60, Minister of State, Home Office 1960–61, Secretary for Technical Co-operation 1961–63. *Whip (Commons):* Assistant Government Whip 1963–64; Opposition Whip 1964; Comptroller of HM Household June-September 1970. *Select Committees (Commons):* Chairman, Commons Select Committee on Agriculture, Fisheries and Food 1980–83. *House of Lords:* A Deputy Speaker of the House of Lords 1992–; A Deputy Chairman of Committees 1997–. *All-Party:* Member, All-Party Cable and Satellite Group 1997–. *Party Groups (General):* Vice-Chairman, Conservative Party Organisation 1970–74. *Other:* President, Water Companies Association 1975–92; Chairman, Tyneside Save The Children. *Special Interests:* Regional Policy. *Recreations:* Country life, family. *Clubs:* Northern Counties (Newcastle-upon-Tyne). *Name, Style and Title:* Raised to the peerage as Baron Elliott of Morpeth, of Morpeth in the County of Northumberland and of the City of Newcastle-upon-Tyne 1985. A Conservative. *Address:* The Lord Elliott of Morpeth, DL, No 3 Apartment, Hindley Hall, Stocksfield, Northumberland, NE43 7RY *Tel:* 01434 684777 *Tel:* 020 7730 7619.

ELTON (2nd Baron, UK), Rodney Elton; cr. 1934; TD 1970

Son of 1st Baron. Born March 2, 1930. Succeeded his father 1973; educated Eton; New College, Oxford (MA). Married 1st, 1958, Anne Frances, daughter of late Brigadier R. A. G. Tilney, CBE, DSO, TD, DL (1 son 3 daughters) (marriage dissolved 1979), married 2nd, August 24, 1979, Richenda, CVO, daughter of late Sir Hugh Gurney, KCMG, MVO. *Armed Forces:* Late 2nd Lieutenant, The Queens Bays; Late Captain, Queen's Own Warwickshire and Worcestershire Yeomanry; Late Major, Leicestershire and Derbyshire Yeomanry. *Career:* Farming 1957–73; Assistant Mastership (History), Loughborough Grammar School 1962–67; Assistant Mastership (History), Fairham Comprehensive School for Boys 1967–69; Lecturer, Bishop Lonsdale College of Education 1969–72; Director: Overseas Exhibitions Ltd 1977–79, Building Trades Exhibition Ltd 1977–79; Director and Deputy Chairman, Andry Montgomery Ltd 1987–; Licencesd Lay Minister, Church of England 1998–. *House of Lords:* Parliamentary Under-Secretary of State for Northern Ireland 1979–81; Parliamentary Under-Secretary of State: Department of Health and Social Security September 1981–82, Home Office 1982–84; Minister of State: Home Office 1984–85, Department of the Environment 1985–86; A Deputy Chairman of Committees 1997–; A Deputy Speaker 1999–; An elected hereditary peer 1999–. *Whip:* Opposition Whip in House of Lords, March 1974–76. *Spokesman:* An Opposition Spokesman 1976–79. *Select Committees:* Member, Select Committee on the Scrutiny of Delegated Powers 1994–97. *All-Party:* Member, Parliamentary All-Party: Penal Affairs Group, British American Group, British Norwegian Group. *Party Groups:* Deputy Chairman, Association of Conservative Peers 1988–93. *Other:* Chairman, Intermediate Treatment Fund 1990–93; Vice-President, Institute of Trading Standards Administration. *Trusts, etc:* Trustee: The Airey Neave Trust 1991–96, City Parochial Foundation and Trust for London 1991–97; Chairman, DIVERT Trust 1993–99, President 1999–. *Miscellaneous:* Contested (Conservative) Loughborough division of Leicestershire 1966 and 1970 General Elections; Member, Boyd Commission (South Rhodesia Independence Elections) 1979; Chairman, Financial Intermediaries Managers & Brokers Regulatory Association 1987–90; Member, Panel on Takeovers and Mergers 1988–90; Chairman, Inquiry into Discipline in Schools (The Elton Report) 1988; Chairman, Quality and Standards Committee, City and Guilds of London Institute 1999–. *Honours:* TD 1970. *Special Interests:* Juvenile Justice. *Recreations:* Painting. *Clubs:* Beefsteak, Pratt's, Cavalry and Guards. *Heir:* His son, Hon. Edward Paget Elton, born May 28, 1966. A Conservative. *Address:* The Lord Elton, TD, House of Lords, London, SW1A 0PW.

ELYSTAN-MORGAN (Life Baron, UK), Dafydd Elystan Elystan-Morgan; cr. 1981

Son of late Dewi Morgan, Journalist. Born December 7, 1932; educated Ardwyn Grammar School; University of Wales, Aberystwyth LLB(Hons.). Married November 14, 1959, Alwen, daughter of late William Roberts (1 son 1 daughter). *Career:* Called to the Bar 1971 (Gray's Inn); Formerly partner in North Wales firm of solicitors 1958–68; Recorder of the Wales and Chester Circuit 1983–1987; Judge of the Wales and Chester Circuit 1987–. *House of Commons:* MP (Labour) for Cardigan 1966–74; Joint Under-Secretary of State, Home Office April 1968–70. *Spokesman (Commons):* Deputy Opposition Spokesman: Home Affairs 1970–72, Welsh Affairs 1972–74. *Spokesman:* Opposition Spokesman on Home Affairs and Legal Affairs 1983–87. *Party Groups (General):* Chairman, Welsh Parliamentary Party 1964, 1974. *Miscellaneous:* President, Association of Welsh Local Authorities 1970–74. *Name, Style and Title:* Raised to the peerage as Baron Elystan-Morgan, of Aberteifi in the County of Dyfed 1981. A Cross-Bencher. *Address:* His Honour Judge The Lord Elystan-Morgan, Carreg Afon, Dolau, Bow Street, Dyfed.

EMERTON (Life Baroness, UK), Audrey Caroline Emerton; cr. 1997; DBE 1989; DL

Daughter of late George Emerton, and of Lily Emerton. Born September 10, 1935; educated Tunbridge Wells Grammar School; St George's Hospital; Battersea College of Technology; Hon. DCL, Kent University 1989; Hon. DUniv, University of Central England in Birmingham 1997; Hon. DSc, University of Brighton 1997. *Councils, Public Bodies:* DL, Kent 1992–. *Career:* Senior Tutor, St George's Hospital, London SW1 1965–68; County Nursing Officer, St John Ambulance, Kent 1967–85, County Commissioner 1985–88; Principal Nursing Officer, Education, Bromley Hospital Management Committee 1968–70; Chief Nursing Officer, Tunbridge Wells and Leybourne Hospital Management Committee 1970–73; Regional Nursing Officer, SE Thames RHA 1973–91; Chief Nursing Officer, St John Ambulance 1988–96, Chairman, Medical Board 1993–96; Vice-Chairman, Brighton Health Care NHS Trust 1993–94, Chairman 1994–; Chief Officer, Care in the Community, St John Ambulance 1996–; Chief Commander, St John Ambulance 1998–. *Other:* President, Association of Nurse Administrators 1979–82; Chairman, English National Board for Nursing, Midwifery and Health Visiting 1983–85; Chairman, United Kingdom Central Council for Nursing, Midwifery and Health Visiting 1985–93; Hon. Vice-President, Royal College of Nursing 1994–; Member, Court of the University of Sussex 1996–98; Lay Member, General Medical Council 1996–. *Trusts, etc:* Trustee, Kent Community Housing Trust 1993–98. *Honours:* CStJ 1978; DBE 1989; DStJ 1993. Fellow, Royal Society of Arts; Member, Royal Society of Medicine. *Name, Style and Title:* Raised to the peerage as Baroness Emerton, of Tunbridge Wells in the County of Kent and of Clerkenwell in the London Borough of Islington 1997. A Cross-Bencher. *Address:* The Baroness Emerton, DBE, DL, St John Ambulance HQ, 1 Grosvenor Crescent, London, SW1X 7EF.

EMSLIE (Life Baron, UK), George Carlyle Emslie; cr. 1980; MBE (Mil) 1946; PC 1972

Son of late Alexander Emslie, Insurance Manager, Glasgow. Born December 6, 1919; educated The High School of Glasgow; Glasgow University (MA, LLB); Hon. LLD, Glasgow 1973. Married October 2, 1942, Lilias Ann Mailer (died January 7, 1998), daughter of late Robert Hannington (3 sons). *Armed Forces:* Served with Argyll & Sutherland Highlanders in Middle East, Italy and Greece and as Brigade Major 1939–45. *Career:* Advocate 1948; Advocate Depute 1955; QC (Scotland) 1957; Sheriff of Perth and Angus 1963–66; Dean of the Faculty of Advocates 1965–70; Senator (Lord Emslie) of the College of Justice 1970–72; Lord Justice-General and Lord President of the Court of Session 1972–89. *Trusts, etc:* Trustee, National Library of Scotland 1965–, Vice-Chairman 1975–. *Miscellaneous:* Member, Scottish Committee, Council on Tribunals 1962–70; Chairman, Scottish Agricultural Wages Board 1969–73. *Honours:* MBE (Mil) 1946; PC 1972; Hon. Bencher: Inner Temple 1974, Inn of Court, Northern Ireland. FRSE 1987. *Recreations:* Golf, walking. *Clubs:* New (Edinburgh). *Name, Style and Title:* Raised to the peerage as Baron Emslie, of Potterton in the district of Gordon 1980. A Cross-Bencher. *Address:* The Rt Hon. the Lord Emslie, MBE, LLB, FRSE, 47 Heriot Row, Edinburgh, EH3 6EX *Tel:* 0131-225 3657.

ERROLL (24th Earl of, S), Merlin Sereld Victor Gilbert Hay; cr. 1452. 25th Lord Hay (S) 1429, 24th Lord Slains (S) 1452; 12th Bt of Moncreiffe of that Ilk (NS) 1685; 28th Hereditary Lord High Constable of Scotland, 1314; 32nd Chief of The Hays since 1160 (Celtic Title) Mac Garadh Mhor

Son of Sir Iain Moncreiffe of that Ilk, 11th Bt and Diana Denyse, Countess of Erroll (23rd in line). Born April 20, 1948. Succeeded his mother to the earldom 1978 and his father to the baronetcy 1985; educated Eton; Trinity College, Cambridge. Married 1982, Isabelle Jacqueline Laline, daughter of late Major Thomas Astell, MC (changed surname from Hohler and assumed name and arms of Astell by Royal Licence 1978), and of late Mrs Astell, of Wolverton Park, Basingstoke, Hampshire (2 sons 2 daughters). *Armed Forces:* TA 1975–90; Hon. Colonel, RMPTA 1992–97. *Career:* Hayway Partners (Marketing) 1991–; Computer Consultant until 1993; Group Director Applications and Development, Girovend Holdings plc 1993–94; Chairman, CRC Ltd 1995–. *House of Lords:* An elected hereditary peer 1999–. *Select Committees:* Member, Library and Computers Sub-Committee. *All-Party:* Member, Scottish Peers Association. *Miscellaneous:* Page to the Lord Lyon 1956; Lieutenant, Atholl Highlanders 1974; Member, Queens Body Guard for Scotland, Royal Company of Archers. *Honours:* OStJ 1977. Freeman, City of London. Member, Court of Assistant of Fishmongers' Company, Fifth and Renter Warden 1998–. *Special Interests:* Defence, Technology, Scotland, Environment. *Recreations:* Skiing, climbing. *Clubs:* White's, Pratt's, Puffin's (Edinburgh). *Heir:* His son, Lord Hay, born August 8, 1984. A Cross-Bencher. *Address:* The Earl of Erroll, Woodbury Hall, Everton, Sandy, Bedfordshire, SG19 2HR *Tel:* 01767 650251.

ERROLL OF HALE (1st Baron, UK), Frederick James Erroll; cr. 1964; (Life) Baron Erroll of Kilmun (UK) 1999; PC 1960; TD 1945

Son of late George Murison Erroll of Glasgow. Born May 27, 1914; educated Oundle; Trinity College, Cambridge (Hons.). Married, Elizabeth, daughter of Mr and Mrs Sowton Barrow, of Exmouth. *Armed Forces:* Commissioned in 4th County of London Yeomanry (TA) 1939; Transferred to Tank Division Ministry of Supply 1941; To Italy, India and Burma as Technical Adviser on Armoured Fighting Vehicles to 1945; Colonel 1945. *Career:* Chairman: Bowater Corporation plc 1973–84, Whessoe plc 1970–87; Chairman, Consolidated Gold Fields plc 1976–83, President 1983–89. *House of Commons:* MP (Conservative) for Altrincham and Sale division of Cheshire from 1945–1964; Parliamentary Secretary, Ministry of Supply 1955–1956; Board of Trade 1956–58; Economic Secretary, Treasury 1958–59; Minister of State, Board of Trade 1959–61; President of the Board of Trade 1961–63; Minister of Power 1963–1964. *Spokesman:* Opposition Front Bench Spokesman on Economic and Trade Affairs 1965–70. *Select Committees:* Member, House of Lords Select Committee on Science and Technology 1985–91. *Other:* President, London Chamber of Commerce 1966–69, Vice-President 1969–; President: Canning House 1969–73; Electrical Research Association 1971–73, British Executive Services Overseas 1972–85; Chairman, Automobile Association 1974–86, Vice-President 1986–; Vice-President, Institute of Marketing 1983–92; President, World Travel Market 1986–96. *Miscellaneous:* Member, National Economic Development Council 1962–63; Deputy Chairman, Decimal Currency Board 1966–71; Chairman, Liquor Licensing Committee 1970–72; Chairman, Council of Institute of Directors 1973–76, President 1976–84, Chancellor 1984–87. *Honours:* PC 1960; TD 1945. FIEE; FIMechE; CEng. *Clubs:* Carlton. *Heir:* None. *Name, Style and Title:* Created a life peer as Baron Erroll of Kilmun, of Kilmun in Argyll and Bute 1999. A Conservative. *Address:* The Rt Hon. the Lord Erroll of Hale, TD, House of Lords, London, SW1A 0PW.

EVANS OF PARKSIDE (Life Baron, UK), John Evans; cr. 1997

Son of late James and Margaret Evans. Born October 19, 1930; educated Jarrow Central School. Married June 6, 1959, Joan, daughter of late Thomas Slater (2 sons 1 daughter). *Trades Union:* Joined AEU 1951. *Armed Forces:* Royal Engineers 1949–50. *Councils, Public Bodies:* Hebburn Urban District Council: Councillor 1962–74, Chairman 1972–73, Leader 1969–74; Councillor, South Tyneside Metropolitan District Council 1973–74. *Career:* Tyneside Shipyard Worker. *House of Commons:* MP (Labour) for Newton 1974–83 and for St. Helens North 1983–97; PPS to Leader of Opposition 1980–83; Shadow Employment Minister 1983–87. *Whip (Commons):* Labour Whip 1978–1979; Opposition Whip 1979–80. *Select Committees (Commons):* Member, Select Committee on Standards and Privileges 1995–97. *International Bodies (General):* UK Member, European Parliament 1975–78; Chairman, European Parliament Policy and Transport Committee 1976–78. *Party Groups (General):* Joined Labour Party 1954; Political Secretary, National Union of Labour and Socialist Clubs; Member, National Executive Committee of the Labour Party 1982–96; Labour Party: Vice-Chairman 1990–91, Chairman 1991–92. Freeman, Metropolitan Borough of St Helens 1997. *Special Interests:* Employment, Energy, Transport, Manufacturing Industries, Industrial Relations, Licensed Trade. *Recreations:* Gardening, watching Rugby League and Association Football. *Name, Style and Title:* Raised to the peerage as Baron Evans of Parkside, of St Helens in the County of Merseyside 1997. Labour. *Address:* The Lord Evans of Parkside, 6 Kirkby Road, Culcheth, Warrington, Cheshire, WA3 4BS.

EVANS OF WATFORD (Life Baron, UK), David Charles Evans; cr. 1998

Son of Arthur Charles Evans and Phyllis Connie Evans. Born November 30, 1942; educated Watford College of Technology. Married May 7, 1966, June Scaldwell (1 son 1 daughter). *Trades Union:* GPMU. *Career:* Apprentice Printer, Stone and Cox Ltd 1957; Has worked for various printers as Sales Executive and Sales Director; Chairman, Centurion Press Group and subsidiary companies in the United Kingdom, The Netherlands and the USA; Chairman: Personnel Publications Ltd, Indigo Publishing Ltd. *Other:* Life Governor, Imperial Cancer Research Fund; Chairman, CT Spiral Scanner Appeal, Watford Hospital. *Miscellaneous:* Assisted in the creation of the One World group (now One World Action); Lecturer, on a voluntary basis, for the Postal Telegraph and Telephone International in trade union studies and media public relations. Fellow: Chartered Institute of Marketing, Institute of Directors. Member, Worshipful Company of Marketors. *Special Interests:* Industrial Relations, Current Affairs, Education, Voluntary Sector. *Recreations:* Theatre, the arts, reading. *Clubs:* Mortons. *Name, Style and Title:* Raised to the peerage as Baron Evans of Watford, of Chipperfield in the County of Hertfordshire 1998. Labour. *Address:* The Lord Evans of Watford, House of Lords, London, SW1A 0PW *Tel:* 01923 891001 (Office) *E-Mail:* lordevans@centurion.co.uk.

EWING OF KIRKFORD (Life Baron, UK), Harry Ewing; cr. 1992; DL

Son of late William Ewing. Born January 20, 1931; educated Beath High School, Cowdenbeath; Hon. DU, University of Stirling 1998. Married July 10, 1954, Margaret, daughter of John Greenhill (1 son 1 daughter). *Trades Union:* Active Trade Unionist, AUEW, Member No. 1 District Council 1958–61; Holder of various offices within Union of Post Office Workers 1962–71. *Armed Forces:* RAF 1949–51. *Councils, Public Bodies:* DL, Fife 1995–. *House of Commons:* Contested (Labour) East Fife in 1970 General Election; MP (Labour) for: Stirling and Falkirk 1971–74, Stirling, Falkirk and Grangemouth 1974–83, Falkirk East 1983–92; Parliamentary Under-Secretary of State, Scottish Office (with special responsibility for Devolution matters) 1974–79. *Spokesman (Commons):* Opposition Front Bench Spokesman on: Scotland 1979–84, Trade and Industry 1984–85, Scotland 1985–87. *Spokesman:* An Opposition Spokesman on: Scottish Office Affairs 1992–96, Transport 1993–96, Energy 1994–95. *International Bodies (General):* Member: Council of Europe 1987–92, Western European Union 1987–92. *Party Groups (General):* Has held many local and national positions in the Co-operative Movement. *Other:* Chairman, Scottish Disability Foundation 1992–;

Non-executive Director, Kirkcaldy Acute Hospitals NHS Trust 1994–96; Chairman, Fife Healthcare NHS Trust 1996–98. *Miscellaneous:* Joint Chairman, Scottish Constitutional Convention 1990–96; Chairman, Ewing Enquiry into the availability of housing for wheelchair disabled in Scotland November 1993, report published April 1994. *Special Interests:* Health, Social Services. *Recreations:* Gardening, bowls. *Name, Style and Title:* Raised to the peerage as Baron Ewing of Kirkford, of Cowdenbeath in the District of Dunfermline 1992. Labour. *Address:* The Lord Ewing of Kirkford, DL, Gowanbank, 45 Glenlyon Road, Leven, Fife, KY8 4AA *Tel:* 01333 426123.

EZRA (Life Baron, UK), Derek Ezra; cr. 1983; Kt 1974; MBE (Mil) 1945

Son of late David Ezra. Born February 23, 1919; educated Monmouth School; Magdalene College, Cambridge. Married 1950, Julia Elizabeth Wilkins. *Armed Forces:* Army Service 1939–47. *Career:* Various positions in Marketing Department, National Coal Board 1947–60; Director General of Marketing, NCB 1960–65, Board Member 1965–67, Deputy Chairman 1967–71; Chairman: NCB 1971–82, Energy and Technical Services Group plc, AHS-Emstar plc, Sheffield Heat & Power Ltd; Director, Aran Energy plc; Chairman, Throgmorton Trust 1985–90; Director: Solvay SA 1979–89, Redland plc 1981–89; Member, International Advisory Board: Banca del Lavoro 1981–, Creditanstalt Bankverein 1981–91; Member: Advisory Board, Petrofina SA 1981–90, Advisory Committee, Energy International SA 1975–90. *Spokesman:* Former Liberal Democrat spokesman on economic affairs in the House of Lords; Spokesman on: Energy 1998–, Rural Affairs 1999–. *Select Committees:* Member, Select Committee on Monetary Policy of the Bank of England 1998–. *Other:* Former President, Coal Industry Society. *Miscellaneous:* Former President, British Standards Institution; President, Institute of Trading Standards Administration 1987–92; Former President, Keep Britain Tidy Group; Patron (Past President), Neighbourhood Energy Action; President, Combustion Engineering Association. *Honours:* MBE (Mil) 1945; Kt 1974. *Publications: Coal and Energy*, 1978; *The Energy Debate*, 1983. *Name, Style and Title:* Raised to the peerage as Baron Ezra, of Horsham in the County of West Sussex 1983. A Liberal Democrat. *Address:* The Lord Ezra, MBE, House of Lords, London, SW1A 0PW *Tel:* House of Lords 020 7219 3180.

F

FALCONER OF THOROTON (Life Baron, UK), Charles Leslie Falconer; cr. 1997; QC 1991

Son of John Leslie Falconer and of late Anne Mansel Falconer. Born November 19, 1951; educated Trinity College, Glenalmond; Queens' College, Cambridge. Married 1985, Marianna Catherine Thoroton, daughter of Sir David Hildyard, KCMG, DFC (3 sons 1 daughter). *Career:* Called to the Bar, Inner Temple 1974; QC 1991. *House of Lords:* Solicitor General 1997–98; Minister of State, Cabinet Office 1998–. *Miscellaneous:* Elected Master, Bench of the Inner Temple 1997. *Name, Style and Title:* Raised to the peerage as Baron Falconer of Thoroton, of Thoroton in the County of Nottinghamshire 1997. Labour. *Address:* The Lord Falconer of Thoroton, QC, Cabinet Office, 70 Whitehall, London, SW1A 2AS.

FALKENDER (Life Baroness, UK), Marcia Matilda Falkender; cr. 1974; CBE 1970

Daughter of late Harry Field. Born March 10, 1932; educated Northampton High School for Girls; Queen Mary College, London University (BA Hons, History). Married December 1, 1955, George Edmund Charles Williams (marriage dissolved 1961). *Career:* Secretary to General Secretary Labour Party HQ 1955–56; Private Secretary to Rt Hon. Harold Wilson 1956–64; Political Secretary to Rt Hon. Harold Wilson and head of his Political Office 1964–76; Columnist, *Mail on Sunday* 1983–88; Local Director, Cheltenham and Gloucester Building Society, Peckham; Director: South London Investment Mortgage Corporation 1986–91, Canvasback Productions 1988–91, Regent (GM) Laboratories 1996–. *All-Party:* Member, Breast Cancer All-Party Committee.

Other: Lay Governor, Queen Mary and Westfield College, London University 1987–93. *Trusts, etc:* Formerly President, UN Unifem,UK Trust; Trustee: The Silver Trust 1986–, Women Aid. *Miscellaneous:* Member: Film Industry Working Party 1975, British Screen Advisory Council 1985–, Film Industry Action Committee 1977–. *Publications: Inside No. 10*, 1972; *Perspective on Downing Street*, 1983. *Special Interests:* Exports, Health, Breast Cancer, British Film Industry. *Recreations:* Films. *Clubs:* Reform. *Name, Style and Title:* Raised to the peerage as Baroness Falkender, of West Haddon in the County of Northamptonshire 1974. Labour. *Address:* The Baroness Falkender, CBE, 3 Wyndham Mews, Upper Montagu Street, London, W1H 1RS *Tel:* 020 7402 8570 *Fax:* 020 7402 3407.

FALKLAND (15th Viscount of, S), Lucius Edward William Plantagenet Cary; cr. 1620; Lord Cary

Son of 14th Viscount. Born May 8, 1935. Succeeded his father 1984; educated Wellington College. Married 1st, 1962, Caroline, daughter of late Lieutenant-Commander Gerald Butler, DSC, RN (1 son 2 daughters and 1 daughter deceased) (marriage dissolved 1990), married 2nd, September 12, 1990, Nicole, daughter of late Milburn Mackey (1 son). *Armed Forces:* Late 2nd Lieutenant, 8th Hussars. *Career:* Formerly: Journalist, Theatrical agent, Chartered shipbroker; Chief executive, C. T. Bowring Trading (Holdings) Ltd; Marketing consultant 1980–. *House of Lords:* An elected hereditary peer 1999–. *Whip:* Liberal Democrat Deputy Whip 1988–. *Spokesman:* Party Spokesman on: National Heritage 1995–97, Culture, Media and Sport 1997–. *Select Committees:* Member: House of Lords Select Committee on Overseas Trade 1984–85, Select Committee on House of Lords' Offices 1997–. *Miscellaneous:* Chairman, Motorcycle Industry Theft Action Group 1991–. *Special Interests:* Developing World, Film Industry, Alcohol and Drug Addiction, Transport, Motorcycle Industry. *Recreations:* Golf, cinema, motorcycling. *Sportsclubs:* Sunningdale Golf. *Clubs:* Brooks's. *Heir:* His son, Hon. Lucius Alexander Plantagenet Cary, Master of Falkland, born February 1, 1963. A Liberal Democrat. *Address:* The Viscount of Falkland, House of Lords, London, SW1A 0PW *Tel:* House of Lords 020 7219 3230.

FANSHAWE OF RICHMOND (Life Baron, UK), Anthony Henry Fanshawe Royle; cr. 1983; KCMG 1974

Son of late Sir Lancelot Royle, KBE. Born March 27, 1927; educated Harrow; RMA, Sandhurst. Married 1957, Shirley, daughter of late J. R. Worthington (2 daughters). *Armed Forces:* Captain, The Life Guards 1945–48; 21st Special Air Service Regiment (TA) 1948–51. *Career:* Director, Brooke Bond Liebig plc 1974–84; Director, Wilkinson Sword Ltd 1974–86, Chairman 1980–83; Director, Sedgwick Group 1984–, Chairman 1993–97; Director: Westland Group plc 1985–94, TI Group plc 1990–, Xerox UK Ltd 1988–, Pratt & Whitney Europe Advisory Board 1993–. *House of Commons:* Contested (Conservative): St Pancras North 1955, Torrington 1958; MP (Conservative) for Richmond 1959–83; PPS to: Secretary of State for Air 1960–62, Minister of Aviation 1962–64; Member, UK Delegation to Council of Europe and WEU 1965; Parliamentary Under-Secretary of State for Foreign and Commonwealth Affairs 1970–74. *Whip (Commons):* Opposition Whip 1967–70. *Select Committees (Commons):* Chairman, Select Committee on Broadcasting 1979–83; Member, Select Committee on Foreign Affairs 1979–83. *Backbench Committees (Commons):* Vice-Chairman, Conservative Foreign Affairs Committee 1965–67. *All-Party Committees (Commons):* Chairman, All-Party Anglo-Hong Kong Committee 1962–70. *Party Groups (General):* Vice-Chairman, Conservative Party Organisation 1979–84; Chairman, Conservative Party International Office 1979–84. *Trusts, etc:* Trustee, National Army Museum 1975–. *Honours:* KCMG 1974; Most Esteemed Family Order of the State of Brunei (1st Class) 1974. *Special Interests:* Foreign Affairs, Defence, Arts, Aviation. *Clubs:* Brooks's, White's, Pratt's. *Name, Style and Title:* Raised to the peerage as Baron Fanshawe of Richmond, of South Cerney in the County of Gloucestershire 1983. A Conservative. *Address:* The Lord Fanshawe of Richmond, KCMG, The Chapter Manor, South Cerney, Gloucestershire, GL7 5TN.

FARRINGTON OF RIBBLETON (Life Baroness, UK), Josephine Farrington; cr. 1994

Daughter of late Ernest Joseph Cayless, and of Dorothy Cayless. Born June 29, 1940. Married April 16, 1960, Michael James Farrington, son of Leonard James Farrington (3 sons). *Councils, Public Bodies:* Councillor: Preston Borough Council 1973–76, Lancashire County Council 1977–; Chairman, Education Committee 1981–91; Chairman of County Council 1992–93. *Career:* Member, Council of Europe Standing Conference of Local and Regional Authorities 1981–94 and of new Congress; Chairman, Culture, Education, Media and Sport Committee 1988–94; International observer at local elections in Poland, Ukraine and Albania; Member, Committee of the Regions – EU; Chairman, Education and Training 1994; Currently Chairman, Association of County Councils; Service as: Education Spokesperson, Chairman of Policy Committee, Labour Group Deputy and Leader; Has served on Burnham Primary and Secondary and Further Education Committees; Member, National Advisory Body for Public Sector Higher Education. *Whip:* An Opposition Whip 1995–97; A Baroness in Waiting (Government Whip) 1997–. *Spokesman:* A Spokeswoman on: Environment, Transport and the Regions 1997–, Northern Ireland 1997–. *Awards Granted:* UK Woman of Europe 1994. *Recreations:* Reading. *Name, Style and Title:* Raised to the peerage as Baroness Farrington of Ribbleton, of Fulwood in the County of Lancashire 1994. Labour. *Address:* The Baroness Farrington of Ribbleton, House of Lords, London, SW1A 0PW.

FAULKNER OF WORCESTER (Life Baron, UK), Richard Oliver Faulkner; cr. 1999

Son of late Harold and Mabel Faulkner. Born March 22, 1946; educated Merchant Taylors' School, Northwood; Worcester College, Oxford (MA, PPE). Married 1968, Susan, daughter of Donald Heyes (2 daughters). *Trades Union:* Member: RMT, NUJ. *Councils, Public Bodies:* Councillor, Merton Borough Council 1971–78. *Career:* Research Assistant and Journalist, Labour Party 1967–69; Public Relations Officer, Construction Industry Training Board 1969–70; Editor, *Steel News* 1971; Account Director, F J Lyons (Public Relations) Ltd 1971–73; Director, PPR International 1973–76; Government Relations Adviser: Fyffes Group 1973–99, Railway Trade Unions 1975–76, C A Parsons & Co 1976–77, Pool Promoters Association 1977–99, British Railways Board 1977–97, Prudential Assurance 1978–88; Co-Founder, Parliamentary Journal *The House Magazine*; Communications Adviser to Leader of the Opposition and Labour Party (unpaid) in general elections 1987, 1992, 1997; Government Relations Adviser: IPU 1988–90, Southampton City Council 1989–91, CAMRA 1989, Barclays de Zoete Wedd 1990–92, Standard Life Assurance 1990–; Communications Adviser to the Bishop at Lambeth 1990; Government Relations Adviser: South Glamorgan County Council 1991–96, Cardiff Bay Development Corporation 1993–98, Littlewoods Organisation 1994–99, Deputy Chairman, Citigate Westminster 1997–99 (Joint Managing Director, Westminster Communications Group 1989–97); Director, Cardiff Millennium Stadium plc 1997–; Strategy Adviser: Cardiff County Council 1999–, Littlewoods Leisure 1999–, Financial Services Authority 1999–, Inception Group plc 1999–. *All-Party:* Member, All-Party: American Country Group, Argentina Country Group, Arts and Heritage Group, Caribbean Country Group, Cyprus Country Group, Film Industry Group, Football Group, Future of Europe Group, Greyhound Racing Group, Human Rights Group, Norway Country Group, Penal Affairs Group, Rail Freight Group, Railways Group, Smoking and Health Group, Sports Group, University Group, Waterways Group. *International Bodies:* Member, CPA IPU. *Other:* Member: Football League Enquiry into Membership Schemes 1984, Sports Council 1986–88, Anti-hooliganism Committee 1987–90, Women's Football Association 1988–91; Chairman, Sports Grounds Initiative 1995–; Director, Brighton and Hove Albion Football Club 1997–; Former Director, Wimbledon and Crystal Palace Football Clubs; Vice-Chairman, Transport 2000 Ltd 1986–; Chairman, Worcester College Appeal Campaign 1996–; Vice-Chairman, Football Task Force 1997–99; Patron, Roy Castle Lung Cancer Foundation 1999–; Member, Court of University of Luton 1999–. *Trusts, etc:* Foundation Trustee, Football Trust 1979–82, Secretary 1983–86, First Deputy Chairman 1986–98. *Miscellaneous:* Contested (Labour) Devizes 1970, February 1974, Monmouth October 1974, Huddersfield West 1979. MIPR. *Special Interests:* Transport, Sport, Human Rights. *Recreations:* Travelling by railway, collecting Lloyd George memorabilia, tinplate trains, watching Association Football. *Clubs:* Reform. *Name, Style and Title:* Raised to the peerage as Baron Faulkner of Worcester, of Wimbledon in the London Borough of Merton 1999. Labour. *Address:* The Lord Faulkner of Worcester, 14 Great College Street, London, SW1 3RX *Tel:* 020 7799 3171 *Fax:* 020 7799 3451 *Tel:* 020 7219 8503 (Voice Mail) *E-Mail:* faulknerro@parliament.uk; rofaulkner@msn.com.

FELDMAN (Life Baron, UK), Basil Feldman; cr. 1996; Kt 1982

Son of late Philip and Tilly Feldman. Born September 23, 1926; educated Grocers' School; SE London Technical College. Married 1952, Gita Julius (2 sons 1 daughter). *Career:* Chairman, Martlet Services Group Ltd 1973–81; Member, Post Office Users' National Council 1978–81; Chairman, The Clothing Little Neddy 1978–85; Underwriting Member of Lloyds 1979–97; Chairman: Solport Ltd 1980–85, Better Made in Britain 1983–; A Director, The Young Entrepreneurs Fund 1985–94; Member, English Tourist Board 1986–96; Chairman: The Quality Mark 1987–92, Shopping Hours Reform Council 1988–94, Better Business Opportunities 1990–, Market Opportunities Advisory Group, Department of Trade and Industry 1991–93. *All-Party:* Member, All-Party: London Group, Town Centre Management Issues Group, Clothing and Textiles Group, Advertising Group. *Party Groups (General):* Deputy Chairman, National Union of Conservative and Unionist Associations, Greater London Area 1975–78, Chairman 1978–81, President 1981–85, Vice President 1985–; Vice Chairman, National Union of the Conservative Party 1982–85, Chairman 1985–86, Vice-President 1986–; Member, National Union Executive Committee 1975–, Chairman 1991–96; Joint National Chairman, Conservative Party's Impact 80s Campaign 1982–87; Vice-President, Greater London Young Conservatives 1975–77; Has held various other posts within the Conservative Party including Party Treasurer 1996–. *Other:* Governor, Sports Aid Foundation 1990–; Founder/Chairman, The London Arts Season 1993–96; Chairman: The Festival of Arts and Culture 1995, Conservative National Golf Tournament Charitable Settlement. *Miscellaneous:* Adopted Member: GLC Housing Management Committee 1973–77, GLC Arts Board 1976–81. *Honours:* Kt 1982. FRSA 1987. Freeman, City of London 1983. *Publications:* Several publications, booklets and pamphlets for the Conservative Party; *Constituency Campaigning*, 1977; *Some Thoughts on Job Creation*, (for NEDO) 1984. *Special Interests:* Industry, Arts, Construction Industry, Retail Industry, Import Substitution, Tourism, Sport. *Recreations:* Golf, tennis, theatre, opera, travel. *Clubs:* Carlton. *Name, Style and Title:* Raised to the peerage as Baron Feldman, of Frognal in the London Borough of Camden 1996. A Conservative. *Address:* The Lord Feldman, House of Lords, London, SW1A OPW.

FELLOWES (Life Baron, UK), Robert Fellowes; cr. 1999; GCB 1998; GCVO 1996; PC 1990; QSO 1999

Son of late Sir William Fellowes, KCVO and Lady Fellowes. Born December 11, 1941; educated Eton. Married April 20, 1978, Lady Jane Spencer, daughter of 8th Earl Spencer, LVO, and Hon. Mrs Shand Kydd (1 son 2 daughters). *Armed Forces:* Short Service Commission, Scots Guards 1960–63. *Career:* Director, Allen Harvey & Ross Ltd 1968–77; Assistant Private Secretary to HM The Queen 1977–86, Deputy Private Secretary 1986–90, Private Secretary 1990–99; Vice-Chairman, Barclays Private Banking 1999–; Director, South African Breweries 1999–. *Honours:* LVO 1983; CB 1987; KCVO 1989; PC 1990; KCB 1991; GCVO 1996; GCB 1998; QSO 1999. Liveryman, Goldsmith's Company. *Recreations:* Golf, watching cricket, reading, shooting. *Clubs:* White's, Pratt's, MCC, Royal Overseas League. *Name, Style and Title:* Raised to the peerage as Baron Fellowes, of Shotesham in the County of Norfolk 1999. A Cross-Bencher. *Address:* The Rt Hon. the Lord Fellowes, GCB, GCVO, QSO, House of Lords, London, SW1A 0PW.

FERRERS (13th Earl, GB), Robert Washington Shirley; cr. 1711; Viscount Tamworth; 19th Bt of Staunton Harold (E) 1611; PC 1982; DL

Son of 12th Earl. Born June 8, 1929. Succeeded his father 1954; educated Winchester College; Magdalene College, Cambridge (MA); Fellow, Winchester College 1988–, Sub-Warden 1998–. Married July 21, 1951, Annabel Mary, daughter of late Brigadier W. G. Carr, CVO, DSO, of Ditchingham Hall, Norfolk (2 sons 3 daughters). *Armed Forces:* Coldstream Guards, Malaya 1949. *Councils, Public Bodies:* DL, Norfolk 1983. *Career:* Trustee, East Anglian Trustee Savings Bank 1957–74; Trustee, Trustee Savings Bank of Eastern England 1975–79, Chairman 1977–79; Member, Central Board Trustee Savings Bank 1977–79; Director: Central Trustee Savings Bank Ltd 1978–79, TSB Trustcard Ltd 1978–79; Director, Norwich Union Insurance

Group 1975–79, 1983–88; Director, Economic Forestry Group plc 1985–88. *House of Lords:* Parliamentary Secretary to Ministry of Agriculture, Fisheries and Food 1974; Member, Armitage Committee on Political Activities of Civil Servants 1976; Joint Deputy Leader of the Opposition, House of Lords 1976–79; Minister of State, Ministry of Agriculture, Fisheries and Food 1979–83; Deputy Leader of the House of Lords 1979–83; Minister of State, Home Office 1988–94; Deputy Leader of the House of Lords 1988–97; Minister of State, Department of Trade and Industry (Minister for Small Firms and Consumer Affairs) 1994–95; Minister of State, Department of the Environment (Minister for the Environment and Countryside) 1995–97; An elected hereditary peer 1999–. *Whip:* Opposition Whip, House of Lords 1964–67; A Lord in Waiting (Government Whip) 1962–64, 1971–74. *Other:* Member, Council of Hurstpierpoint College 1959–68; High Steward, Norwich Cathedral 1979–; Member, Council of Food from Britain 1985–88. *Trusts, etc:* Director, The Chatham Historic Dockyard Trust 1984–88. *Miscellaneous:* Chairman: Royal Commission on Historical Monuments (England) 1984–88, British Agricultural Export Council 1984–88. *Honours:* PC 1982. *Recreations:* Shooting, music, travel. *Clubs:* Beefsteak. *Heir:* His son, Viscount Tamworth, born December 29, 1952. A Conservative. *Address:* The Rt Hon. the Earl Ferrers, DL, Ditchingham Hall, Bungay, Suffolk, NR35 2LE *Tel:* 01508 482250.

FILKIN (Life Baron, UK), David Geoffrey Nigel Filkin; cr. 1999; CBE 1997

Son of late Donald Geoffrey and Winifred Filkin. Born July 1, 1944; educated King Edward VI School, Birmingham; Clare College, Cambridge (MA History); Manchester University (DipTP); Birmingham University (post graduate study). Married 1974, Elizabeth Tompkins (3 daughters) (marriage dissolved 1994). *Career:* Teacher on VSO, Ghana 1966–67; Town Planner, Redditch Development Corporation (New Town) 1969–72; Manager, Brent Housing Aid Centre, London Borough of Brent 1972–75; Deputy Chief Executive, Merseyside Improved Housing 1975–79; Borough Housing Officer, Ellesmere Port and Neston Borough Council 1979–82; Director of Housing, London Borough of Greenwich 1982–88; Chief Executive, Reading Borough Council 1988–91; Secretary, Association of District Councils 1991–97; Local Government Adviser to Joseph Rowntree Foundation 1997–; Director, New Local Government Network 1997–; Policy Analyst and Writer 1997–. *Honours:* CBE 1997. *Publications: Best Value for the Public; Political Leadership of Best Value; Partnerships for Best Value; Modernising Local Government; Starting to Modernise; Achieving Best Value. Special Interests:* Policy Development, Policy Implementation, West Africa, Southern Africa. *Recreations:* Music, walking, swimming, singing, church. *Name, Style and Title:* Raised to the peerage as Baron Filkin, of Pimlico in the City of Westminster 1999. Labour. *Address:* The Lord Filkin, CBE, House of Lords, London, SW1A 0PW *E-Mail:* gfilkin1@aol.com.

FISHER OF REDNAL (Life Baroness, UK), Doris Mary Fisher; cr. 1974

Daughter of late Frederick Satchwell, BEM. Born September 13, 1919; educated Birmingham Schools; Fircroft College; Hon. Doctor, University of Central England, Birmingham 1998. Married July 1, 1939, Joseph Fisher (died 1978) (2 daughters). *Councils, Public Bodies:* Councillor, Birmingham City Council for 15 years; Past Chairman of its Housing Committee; JP 1961; Formerly Member, Warrington New Town Development Corporation; Member, New Towns Staff Commission 1976–79. *Career:* Member, European Parliament 1975–79. *House of Commons:* MP (Labour) for Birmingham, Ladywood division 1970–74. *Whip:* Opposition Whip 1983–84. *Spokesman:* Opposition Spokesman on the Environment 1983–84. *Party Groups (General):* National President, Women's Co-op Guild 1961–62. *Other:* Chairman, Baskerville Special School 1981–89; Warden, Birmingham Assay Office 1981–89; President, Birmingham Royal Institute of Blind 1982–; Member, Hallmarking Council 1989–94; President, Motability Midlands 1989–95; Governor, Hunters Hill Special School, Bromsgrove; President, The British Fluoridation Society 1993–; Midland Area Chairman: NSPCC 1993–, Macmillan Nurses 1995–; Patron, St Basil's Young Homeless, Birmingham. Formerly Member, General Medical Council. *Special Interests:* Housing, Local Government. *Recreations:* Swimming. *Name, Style and Title:* Raised to the peerage as Baroness Fisher of Rednal, of Rednal in the City of Birmingham 1974. Labour. *Address:* The Baroness Fisher of Rednal, 60 Jacoby Place, Priory Road, Edgbaston, Birmingham, B5 7UW.

FITT (Life Baron, UK), Gerard Fitt; cr. 1983

Son of late George Fitt. Born April 9, 1926; educated in Belfast. Married November 5, 1947, Susan (died January 23, 1996), daughter of James Doherty (5 daughters and 1 daughter deceased). *Councils, Public Bodies:* Councillor, Dock Ward, Belfast Corporation 1958. *Career:* Merchant Seaman 1941–53; Member (Irish Labour) Parliament of Northern Ireland, Dock Division of Belfast 1962–72; Member (SDLP), North Belfast, Northern Ireland Assembly 1973–75; Deputy Chief Executive of the Northern Ireland Executive 1974. *House of Commons:* MP for Belfast West as: Republican Labour 1966–70, SDLP 1970–79, Socialist 1979–83. *Name, Style and Title:* Raised to the peerage as Baron Fitt, of Bell's Hill in the County of Down 1983. An Independent Socialist. *Address:* The Lord Fitt, House of Lords, London, SW1A 0PW.

FLATHER (Life Baroness, UK), Shreela Flather; cr. 1990; DL

Daughter of Aftab and Krishna Rai; educated University College, London (LLB); Hon. DUniv, Open University 1994. Married, Gary Denis Flather, OBE, QC, son of late Denis Flather and Joan Flather (2 sons). *Councils, Public Bodies:* JP 1971–90 (Crown Supplemental List); Councillor, Royal Borough of Windsor and Maidenhead 1976–91, Deputy Mayor 1985–86, Mayor 1986–87; DL, Berkshire 1994–. *Career:* Called to the Bar, Inner Temple 1962; Infant teacher, ILEA 1965–67; Teacher of English as second language, Altwood Comprehensive School, Maidenhead 1968–74; Teacher of English as second language, Broadmoor Hospital 1974–78; Member, Committee of Management, Servite Houses Ltd 1987–94; UK Member, Economic and Social Committee European Community 1987–90; Director, Meridian Broadcasting (MAI) Ltd 1990–; Chairman, Alcohol Education and Research Council 1995–; Director: Marie Stopes International 1996–, Cable Corporation 1997–; Fellow, University College, London. *Select Committees:* Former Member: European Communities Sub-Committee C, Select Committee on Medical Ethics. *All-Party:* Vice-Chairman, Indo-British Parliamentary Group; Treasurer, Population and Development Group; Vice-Chairman, All-Party Sri Lanka Country Group 1999–; Member, All-Party Charities and the Voluntary Sector Group. *Party Groups (General):* Member, Conservative Women's National Committee 1978–88; Member, Anglo-Asian Conservative Society 1979–83. *Other:* Vice-Chairman, The Refugee Council 1991–94; President: League of Friends of Broadmoor Hospital 1991–98, Community Council for Berkshire 1991–98; Chairman: Ethics Committee Broadmoor Hospital 1992–97, Street Children Charities 1992–94; Governor, Commonwealth Institute 1993–98; Joint President, Family Planning Association 1995–98; President, Alumni Association of University College London 1998–; Vice-President, Carers National Association. *Awards Granted:* Asian of the Year 1996 (*Asian Who's Who*). *Trusts, etc:* Trustee: Hillingdon Hospital 1990–98, Rajiv Gandhi (UK) Foundation 1993–; Member, Council of the Winston Churchill Memorial Trust 1993–; Member, Council of St George's House, Windsor Castle 1996–. *Miscellaneous:* Founder Member and Vice-Chairman, Maidenhead Community Relations Council 1970; Member, West Metropolitan Conciliation Committee Race Relations Board 1973–78; Member, Committee of Inquiry (Rampton later Swann Committee) into education of children from ethnic minority groups 1979–85; Member: Commission for Racial Equality 1980–86, Board of Visitors, Holloway Prison 1981–83, Police Complaints Board 1982–85, HRH The Duke of Edinburgh's Inquiry into British Housing 1984–85, Lord Chancellor's Legal Aid Advisory Committee 1985–88, Social Security Advisory Committee 1987–90, Broadmoor Hospital Board 1987–89, Berkshire FPC 1987–89; Member, BBC South and East Regional Advisory Council 1987–89; President, Cambs. Chilterns and Thames Rent Assessment Panel 1983–97 A Vice-President, Building Societies Association 1988–90; Vice-President: Association of District Councils 1990–97 Commonwealth Countries League 1990–, Association of Metropolitan Authorities 1991–97 LWT Programme Advisory Board 1990–93; Resigned the Conservative Whip December 1998, rejoined November 1999. FRSA. *Special Interests:* Race Relations, European Union. *Recreations:* Reading, cinema, travel. *Name, Style and Title:* Raised to the peerage as Baroness Flather, of Windsor and Maidenhead in the Royal County of Berkshire 1990. A Conservative. *Address:* The Baroness Flather, JP, DL, FRSA, Triveni, Ascot Road, Maidenhead, Berkshire, SL6 2HT *Tel:* 01628 625408.

FLOWERS (Life Baron, UK), Brian Hilton Flowers; cr. 1979; Kt 1969; FRS 1961

Son of late Rev. Harold Joseph Flowers. Born September 13, 1924; educated Bishop Gore Grammar School, Swansea; Gonville and Caius College, Cambridge (MA); University of Birmingham (DSc); Hon MA, Oxon 1956; Hon DSc: Sussex 1968, Wales 1972, Manchester 1973, Leicester 1973, Liverpool 1974, Bristol 1982; Hon DEng, Nova Scotia 1983; Hon ScD, Dublin, 1984; Hon LLD, Dundee 1985; Hon DSc, Oxford 1985; Hon Fellow, UMIST 1985; Hon LLD, Glasgow 1987; Hon DSc, NUI 1990; Hon LLD, Manchester 1995; Hon DSc: Reading 1996, London 1996; Hon Fellow: Royal Holloway, London University 1996, University of Wales, Swansea 1996. Married October 26, 1951, Mary Frances, eldest daughter of late Sir Leonard F. Behrens, CBE (2 step-sons). *Career:* Anglo-Canadian Atomic Energy Project (Tube Alloys) 1944–46; Research in nuclear physics and atomic energy at Atomic Energy Research Establishment, Harwell 1946–50; Department of Mathematical Physics, University of Birmingham 1950–52; Head of Theoretical Physics Division, AERE, Harwell 1952–58; Professor of Theoretical Physics, University of Manchester 1958–61; Langworthy Professor of Physics, University of Manchester 1961–72; Chairman, Science Research Council 1967–73; Rector, Imperial College, University of London 1973–85; Vice-Chancellor, London University 1985–90. *Chancellor:* Chancellor, University of Manchester 1994–. *Select Committees:* Member, House of Lords Select Committee on Science and Technology 1980–93, 1994–97, Chairman 1989–93. *All-Party:* President, All-Party Parliamentary and Scientific Committee 1993–97. *Other:* Chairman: Computer Board for Universities and Research Council 1966–70, Member, Atomic Energy Authority 1971–81; President, Institute of Physics 1972–74; Chairman, Royal Commission on Environmental Pollution 1973–76; President: European Science Foundation 1974–80, National Society for Clean Air 1977–79; Chairman: Commission on Energy and the Environment 1978–81, University of London Working Party on future of medical and dental teaching resources 1979–80, Committee of Vice-Chancellors and Principals for 1983–85; Member of Council, Academia Europaea 1988–91; Member of Council and Vice-Chairman, Royal Postgraduate Medical School 1990–97; Member of Management Board, London School of Hygiene and Tropical Medicine 1991–95, Chairman 1994–95; Governor, Middlesex University 1992–; Chairman, Committee of Enquiry into the Academic Year 1992–93. *Trusts, etc:* Managing Trustee, Nuffield Foundation 1982–98, Chairman 1987–98. *Miscellaneous:* Vice-Chairman, Parliamentary Office of Science and Technology (POST) 1998–. *Honours:* Kt 1969; Officier de la Légion d'Honneur (France), 1981. FRS 1961. *Publications: Properties of Matter* (with E. Mendoza), 1970; *An Introduction to Numerical Methods C++*, 1995; Contributions to scientific periodicals on scientific structure of atomic nucleus, nuclear reations, science policy, energy and the environment. *Special Interests:* Higher Education, Science and Technology, Environment. *Recreations:* Music, walking, gardening, computing. *Name, Style and Title:* Raised to the peerage as Baron Flowers, of Queen's Gate in the City of Westminster 1979. A Cross-Bencher. *Address:* The Lord Flowers, FRS, 53 Athenaeum Road, London, N20 9AL *Tel:* 020 8446 5993 *E-Mail:* fofqg@clumsies.demon.co.uk.

FOOKES (Life Baroness, UK), Janet Evelyn Fookes; cr. 1997; DBE 1989

Daughter of late Lewis Aylmer Fookes, retired company director, and late Evelyn Margery (née Holmes). Born February 21, 1936; educated Hastings and St. Leonards Ladies' College; Hastings High School for Girls; Royal Holloway College, London University (BA Hons); DLitt, University of Plymouth (hc); Hon. Fellow, Royal Holloway College. *Councils, Public Bodies:* County Borough of Hastings: Councillor 1960–61, 1963–70, Chairman, Education Committee 1967–70; Member, Council of Stonham Housing Association 1980–92. *Career:* School Teacher 1958–70. *House of Commons:* MP (Conservative) for Merton and Morden 1970–74, and for Plymouth Drake 1974–97; Deputy Speaker and Second Deputy Chairman of Ways and Means 1992–97; Sponsored as Private Member's Bill: Sexual Offences Act 1985, Dangerous Dogs Act 1989. *Select Committees (Commons):* Chairman, Education, Arts and Home Office Sub-Committee of the Expenditure Committee 1975–79; Member: Speaker's Panel of Chairmen 1976–97, Select Committee on Home Affairs 1983–92. *Backbench Committees (Commons):* Secretary, Education Committee 1971–75. *All-Party Committees (Commons):* All-Party Mental Health Group: Secretary 1979–85, Vice-Chairman 1985–92; Chairman (former Secretary), Parliamentary Group for Animal Welfare 1985–92. *Other:* Council of RSPCA: Member 1973–92, Chairman 1979–81, Vice-Chairman 1981–83; Member: Council of SSAFA 1980–98, Commonwealth War Graves Commission 1987–97, Council of Management, College of St Mark and St John 1989–, Royal Horticultural Society, National Art Collections Fund. *Trusts, etc:* Fellow, Industry and Parliament Trust. *Honours:* DBE 1989. *Special Interests:* Penal Affairs and Policy, Mental Health, Defence, Animal Welfare, Equal Opportunities, Housing. *Recreations:* Keep fit exercises, swimming, gardening, theatre, Yoga. *Sportsclubs:* Westminster Gymnasium. *Name, Style and Title:* Raised to the peerage as Baroness Fookes, of Plymouth in the County of Devon 1997. A Conservative. *Address:* The Baroness Fookes, DBE, House of Lords, London, SW1A 0PW.

FORSYTH OF DRUMLEAN (Life Baron, UK), Michael Bruce Forsyth; cr. 1999; Kt 1997; PC 1995

Son of John T. Forsyth. Born October 16, 1954; educated Arbroath High School; St Andrews University (MA). Married 1977, Susan Jane, daughter of John B. Clough (1 son 2 daughters). *Councils, Public Bodies:* Councillor, Westminster City Council 1978–83. *Career:* Former Company Director; Director, Robert Fleming & Co Ltd 1997–. *House of Commons:* MP (Conservative) for Stirling 1983–97; PPS to the Foreign Secretary 1986–87; Parliamentary Under-Secretary of State, Scottish Office 1987–90; Minister of State at: Scottish Office with responsibility for Health, Education, Social Work and Sport 1990–92, Department of Employment 1992–94, Home Office 1994–95; Secretary of State for Scotland 1995–97. *Select Committees (Commons):* Member, Select Committee on Scottish Affairs. *Backbench Committees (Commons):* Member, Conservative Party Environment Committee. *Party Groups (General):* Founder and President, St Andrews University Conservative Association 1973–76; Member, Executive Committee National Union of Conservative and Unionist Associations 1975–77; Chairman: Federation of Conservative Students 1976–77, Scottish Conservative Party 1989–90. *Other:* Patron, Craighalbent Centre for Children with motor impairments. *Awards Granted:* Highland Park/*The Spectator* Parliamentarian of the Year 1996; Member to Watch 1993. *Miscellaneous:* Vice-President, Students' Representative Council, St Andrew's University 1974–75. *Honours:* PC 1995; Kt 1997. *Publications:* Various Pamphlets on Privatisation and Local Government. *Special Interests:* Local Government, Privatisation, Economics, Health Care, Mental Handicap, Environment. *Recreations:* Mountaineering, photography, gardening, fishing. *Name, Style and Title:* Raised to the peerage as Baron Forsyth of Drumlean, of Drumlean in Stirling 1999. A Conservative. *Address:* The Rt Hon. the Lord Forsyth of Drumlean, House of Lords, London, SW1A 0PW.

FORTE (Life Baron, UK), Charles Forte; cr. 1982; Kt 1970

Son of late Rocco Giovanni Forte. Born November 26, 1908; educated Alloa Academy; Dumfries College; Mamiani, Rome. Married 1943, Irene Chierico (1 son 5 daughters). *Career:* Former Honorary Consul-General for the Republic of San Marino; Chief Executive, Forte plc 1971–78, Deputy Chairman 1970–78, Executive Chairman 1979–92, President 1992–96; Member, London Tourist Board. *Publications: Forte* (autobiography). *Clubs:* Carlton, Royal Thames Yacht. *Name, Style and Title:* Raised to the peerage as Baron Forte, of Ripley in the County of Surrey 1982. A Conservative. *Address:* The Lord Forte, House of Lords, London, SW1A 0PW *Tel:* 020 7235 6244.

FOSTER OF THAMES BANK (Life Baron, UK), Norman Robert Foster; cr. 1999; OM 1997; Kt 1990

Son of late Robert and Lily Foster. Born June 1, 1935; educated Burnage Grammar School; University of Manchester School of Architecture (DipArch, CertTP 1961); Yale University School of Architecture (MArch); Henry Fellowship and Guest Fellow, Jonathan Edward College, Yale School of Architecture; Hon. LittD, University of East Anglia 1980; Hon. DSc, Bath University 1986; Hon. Dr hc, Royal College of Art 1991; Hon. Degree: University of Valencia, Spain 1992, University of Humberside 1992, University of Manchester 1993; Hon. Fellow, Kent Institute of Art and Design 1994; Hon. Dr hc, Technical University of Eindhoven 1996; Hon. DLitt, Oxford University 1996; Hon. DLit, University of London 1996. (4 sons 1 daughter). *Armed Forces:* National Service, Royal Air Force 1953–55. *Career:* Private Practice, Team Four 1963–67; Foster Associate, later Foster and Partners (Chairman) 1967–;

Collaboration with Richard Buckminster Fuller 1968–83; RIBA Visiting Board of Education and External Examiner 1971–73; Vice-President, Architectural Association 1974; Consultant Architect to University of East Anglia 1978–87; Trustee, Architecture Foundation 1991–99; Hon. Professor, University of Buenos Aires 1997; Visiting Professor, Urban Research, Bartlett School of Architecture, London 1998. *Other:* Member, The Norman Foster Foundation; Council Member: Architectural Association, London 1969–71, Royal College of Art, London 1981. *Awards Granted:* RIBA Silver Medal; Heywood Medal; Builders Association Scholarship; Manchester Society of Architects Bronze Medal; Walpamur Design Prize; Batsford Essay Prize; RIBA Royal Gold Medal 1983; Japan Design Foundation Award 1987; Gorsse Kunstpreis Award, Akademie der Kunst, Berlin 1989; The Chicago Architecture Award 1990; Academie d'Architecture, France Gold Medal 1991; Mies van der Rohe Pavilion Award 1991; Arnold W Brunner Memorial Prize, American Academy and Institute of Arts and Letters 1992; American Institute of Atechitects Gold Medal 1994; Universidad Internacional 'Menendez Pelayo' Santander, Spain Gold Medal 1995; MIPIM Man of the Year Award 1996; The 'Building' Award Construction Personality of the Year Award 1996; Premi a la millor tasca de promoció international de Barcelona Award 1997; Chartered Society of Designers Silver Medal 1997; Prince Phillip Designers Prize 1997; Berliner Zeitung Kulturpreis 1998; German-British Forum Special Prize 1998; Pritzker Architecture Prize – 21st Laureate 1999. *Honours:* Kt 1990; Officer of the Order of the Arts and Letters – Ministry of Culture, France 1994; Order of North Rhine Westphalia 1995; OM 1997; Commander's Cross of the Order of Merit of the Federal Republic of Germany 1999. RIBA 1965; FCSD 1975; IBM Fellow Aspen Conf 1980; RA 1983; Hon. BDA 1983: Hon. FAIA 1980; Member, International Academy of Atechitecture, Sofia, Bulgaria 1988; RDI 1988; Member, French Order of Architects 1989; Associate, Academie Royale de Belgique 1990; Hon. Fellow, Kent Institute of Art and Design 1994; Member, Department of Architecture Akademie der Künste 1994; Foreign Member, Royal Academy of Fine Arts Sweden 1995; Hon.FEng 1995; Member, European Academy of Sciences and Art 1996; Foreign Hon. Member, American Academy of Arts and Sciences 1996. *Publications: Buildings and Projects: Foster Associates Volumes 1, 2, 3, 4,* 1989–96; *Norman Foster Sketches,* 1992; *Sir Norman Foster* 1997; *Norman Foster: Selected and Current Works,* 1997; *Rebuilding The Reichstag,* 1999. *Recreations:* Flying, skiing, running. *Clubs:* Athenaeum, The China Club, Hong Kong. *Name, Style and Title:* Raised to the peerage as Baron Foster of Thames Bank, of Reddish in the County of Greater Manchester 1999. *Address:* The Lord Foster of Thames Bank, OM, Foster and Partners, Riverside Three, 22 Hester Road, London, SW11 4AN *Tel:* 020 7738 0455 *Fax:* 020 7738 1107/8 *E-Mail:* enquiries@fosterandpartners.com.

FRASER OF CARMYLLIE (Life Baron, UK), Peter Lovat Fraser; cr. 1989; PC 1989; QC (Scot) 1982

Son of late George Robson Fraser, Church of Scotland Minister. Born May 29, 1945; educated Loretto; Gonville and Caius College, Cambridge (BA Hons, LLM Hons); Edinburgh University; Hon. Professor of Law, Dundee University; Hon. Bencher of Lincoln's Inn 1989. Married July 26, 1969, Fiona Macdonald Mair (1 son 2 daughters). *Career:* Advocate 1969–; Lecturer in Constitutional Law, Heriot Watt University 1972–74; Standing Junior Counsel in Scotland to Foreign and Commonwealth Office 1979; Solicitor General for Scotland 1982–89; Chairman, International Petroleum Exchange 1999–. *House of Commons:* Contested (Conservative) Aberdeen North October 1974 General Election; MP (Conservative) for: Angus South 1979–83, Angus East 1983–87; PPS to the Rt Hon. George Younger MP, Secretary of State for Scotland 1981–82. *Select Committees (Commons):* Member, Select Committee Scottish Affairs 1979. *House of Lords:* Lord Advocate 1989–92; Minister of State: Scottish Office 1992–95, Department of Trade and Industry 1995–97; Deputy Leader of the Opposition 1997–98. *Spokesman:* An Opposition Spokesman on Trade and Industry 1997–98. *Select Committees:* Member, Select Committee on House of Lords' Offices 1997–98. *All-Party:* Joint Vice-Chairman, All-Party Scottish Children Group 1998–; Member, All-Party British-Ukrainian Country Group 1999–. *Party Groups (General):* Chairman, Scottish Conservative Lawyers Reform Group 1976. *Trusts, etc:* Fellow, Industry and Parliament Trust. *Recreations:* Skiing, golf. *Name, Style and Title:* Raised to the peerage as Baron Fraser of Carmyllie, of Carmyllie in the District of Angus 1989. A Conservative. *Address:* The Rt Hon. the Lord Fraser of Carmyllie, QC, Slade House, Carmyllie, by Arbroath, Angus, DD11 2RE.

FREEMAN (Life Baron, UK), Roger Norman Freeman; cr. 1997; PC 1993

Son of Norman James Freeman, CBE. Born May 27, 1942; educated Whitgift School; Balliol College, Oxford. Married February 15, 1969, Jennifer Margaret, daughter of M. W. Watson of Sale (1 son 1 daughter). *Career:* Managing Director, Bow Publications Ltd 1968–69; Executive Director, Lehman Bros 1969–86; Director, Martini & Rossi UK Ltd and Baltic Leasing Group plc to May 1986; Partner, Pricewaterhouse Cooper, Corporate Finance Division. *House of Commons:* Contested Don Valley 1979; MP (Conservative) for Kettering 1983–97; Parliamentary Under-Secretary of State: for the Armed Forces 1986–88, at the Department of Health 1988–90; Minister of State for: Public Transport, Department of Transport 1990–94, Defence Procurement, Ministry of Defence 1994–95; Chancellor of the Duchy of Lancaster and Cabinet Minister for Public Service 1995–97. *Select Committees (Commons):* Member, Select Committee on Treasury and Civil Service 1984–86. *Party Groups (General):* President, Oxford University Conservative Association 1964; Treasurer, Bow Group 1967–68; Chief Financial Officer, Conservative Central Office 1984–86; Vice-Chairman, Conservative Party July-December 1997; Special Adviser on Candidates, Conservative Party December 1997–. *Other:* President, Council of the Territorial Auxiliary and Volunteer Reserve Associations 1999–. *Honours:* PC 1993. Fellow, Institute of Chartered Accountants, England and Wales. *Clubs:* Carlton, Kennel, Institute of Directors. *Name, Style and Title:* Raised to the peerage as Baron Freeman, of Dingley in the County of Northamptonshire 1997. A Conservative. *Address:* The Rt Hon. the Lord Freeman, House of Lords, London, SW1A 0PW.

FREYBERG (3rd Baron, UK), Valerian Bernard Freyberg; cr. 1951

Son of Colonel 2nd Baron, OBE, MC, and Ivry Perronelle Katharine, daughter of Cyril Harrower Guild. Born December 15, 1970. Succeeded his father 1993; educated Eton; Camberwell College of Arts. *Career:* Sculptor. *House of Lords:* An elected hereditary peer 1999–. *Select Committees:* Former Member, House of Lords Library and Computers Sub-Committee until 1999. *All-Party:* Member, All-Party: Heritage Group, Media Group, Cycling Group; Co-Chairman, All-Party Design and Innovation Group 1999–. *Special Interests:* Visual Arts. *Recreations:* Beekeeping, music. *Heir:* None. A Cross-Bencher. *Address:* The Lord Freyberg, Munstead House, Godalming, Surrey, GU8 4AR *E-Mail:* freybergv@parliament.uk.

G

GALE (Life Baroness, UK), Anita Gale; cr. 1999

Daughter of late Arthur Gale, coalminer and late Lilian Gale, housewife. Born November 28, 1940; educated Treherbert Secondary Modern School; Pontypridd Technical College; University College Cardiff (BSc Econ). Married 1959, Morcom Holmes (marriage dissolved 1983) (2 daughters). *Trades Union:* Shop Steward, Tailors and Garment Workers' Union 1966–69; Chair, National Union of Labour Organisers 1988–92; Labour Organiser/Equalities Officer, branch of GMB, Branch Chair 1992–99. *Career:* Sewing machinist, clothing factory 1956–57; Shop assistant 1957–59; Sewing machinist 1965–69; Women's Officer and Assistant Organiser, Wales Labour Party 1976–84; General Secretary, Wales Labour Party 1984–99. *Other:* Member: Ramblers Association, Christian Socialist Movement. *Recreations:* Swimming, walking, gardening. *Name, Style and Title:* Raised to the peerage as Baroness Gale, of Blaenrhondda in the County of Mid Glamorgan 1999. Labour. *Address:* The Baroness Gale, 52 Kensington Drive, Porth, Rhondda, CF39 9NN *Tel:* 01443 686752.

GALLACHER (Life Baron, UK), John Gallacher; cr. 1983

Son of late William Gallacher. Born May 7, 1920; educated St Patrick's High School, Dumbarton; Co-operative College, Loughborough 1946–48. Married June 28, 1947, Freda Vivian, daughter of late Alfred Chittenden (1 son). *Trades Union:* Member, National Association of Co-operative Officials. *Armed Forces:* RAF 1940–45. *Career:* Chartered Secretary; President, Enfield Highway Co-operative Society 1954–68; Secretary, International Co-operative Alliance 1964–68; Sectional Secretary, Co-operative Union 1968–73; Parliamentary Secretary, Co-operative Union 1973–83. *Whip:* Opposition Whip 1985–92. *Spokesman:* Opposition Front Bench Spokesman on Agriculture, Food, Forestry and Fisheries 1987–97. *Select Committees:* Chairman, Sub-Committee on Common Agricultural Policy and Fisheries 1984–87; Co-opted Member, Select Committee on European Communities Sub-Committee D (Agriculture, Fisheries and Food) 1997–. *International Bodies (General):* Member, Economic and Social Committee of the European Communities 1978–82. *Party Groups (General):* Member, Co-operative Party. *Other:* President, Institute of Meat 1983–86. Hon. Freeman, The Worshipful Company of Butchers. *Special Interests:* European Union. *Name, Style and Title:* Raised to the peerage as Baron Gallacher, of Enfield in Greater London 1983. Labour. *Address:* The Lord Gallacher, House of Lords, London, SW1A 0PW.

GARDNER OF PARKES (Life Baroness, UK), Rachel Trixie Anne Gardner; cr. 1981

Daughter of late Hon. J. J. Gregory McGirr and late Rachel McGirr, OBE, LC. Born July 17, 1927; educated Monte Sant Angelo College, North Sydney; East Sydney Technical College; University of Sydney (BDS 1954); Cordon Bleu de Paris (Diplome 1956); DU, Middlesex 1997. Married 1956, Kevin Anthony, son of late George Gardner and of late Rita Gardner, of Sydney, Australia (3 daughters). *Councils, Public Bodies:* Councillor, Westminster City Council 1968–78; Lady Mayoress of Westminster 1987–88; Member, Westminster, Kensington & Chelsea Area Health Authority 1974–81; JP, North Westminster 1971–97 Councillor, GLC for: Havering 1970–73, Enfield-Southgate 1977–86; Vice-Chairman, North East Thames Regional Health Authority 1990–94. *Career:* Came to UK 1954; Dentist in General Practice 1955–90; British Chairman, European Union of Women 1978–82; UK representative on the UN Status of Women Commission 1982–88; Director: Gateway Building Society 1987–88, Woolwich Building Society 1988–93; Chairman (UK), Plan International 1989–; Chairman, Royal Free Hampstead NHS Trust 1994–97. *House of Lords:* A Deputy Chairman of Committees 1999–; A Deputy Speaker 1999–. *All-Party:* Joint Chairman, All-Party Osteoporosis Group 1996–; Vice-Chairman, All-Party Aids Group 1996–98; Member: All-Party Kidney Group, Primary Care and Public Health Group. *International Bodies:* Elected Member, Executive of Inter-Parliamentary Union to 1997. *Other:* Governor: National Heart Hospital 1974–90, Eastman Dental Hospital 1971–80; Hon. President, War Widows' Association of Great Britain 1984–87; President, British Fluoridation Society 1990–93; Chairman, The Cook Society 1996. *Trusts, etc:* Chairman, Suzy Lamplugh Trust 1993–96. *Miscellaneous:* Member, Inner London Executive Council NHS 1966–71; Standing Dental Advisory Committee for England and Wales 1968–76; Contested (Conservative) Blackburn 1970, North Cornwall February 1974 General Elections; Chairman, London Canal's Consultative Committee 1970–73; Member, Inland Waterways Amenity Advisory Council 1971–74; Member, Industrial Tribunal Panel for London 1974–97; Department of Employment's Advisory Committee on Women's Employment 1980–89; North Thames Gas Consumer Council 1980–82; Elected to General Dental Council 1984–86, 1987–91; Member, London Electricity Board 1984–90; Trustee, Parliamentary Advisory Council on Transport Safety 1992–98; Vice-President, National House Building Council 1992–. Former Fellow, Institute of Directors. Freeman, City of London 1992. *Special Interests:* Transport, Housing, Health, Planning, Energy. *Recreations:* Family life, gardening, needlework, travel. *Name, Style and Title:* Raised to the peerage as Baroness Gardner of Parkes, of Southgate in Greater London and of Parkes in the State of New South Wales and Commonwealth of Australia 1981. A Conservative. *Address:* The Baroness Gardner of Parkes, House of Lords, London, SW1A 0PW *E-Mail:* gardnert@parliament.uk.

GAREL-JONES (Life Baron, UK), (William Armand Thomas) Tristan Garel-Jones; cr. 1997; PC 1992

Son of Bernard Garel-Jones. Born February 28, 1941; educated The Kings School, Canterbury; Madrid University. Married 1966, Catalina Garrigues (4 sons 1 daughter). *Career:* In business on the Continent 1960–70; Merchant banker 1971–74; Managing Director, Warburg Dillon Read. *House of Commons:* Personal Assistant to Michael Roberts, MP at Cardiff North in February 1970 General Election; Contested Caernarvon February 1974, and Watford October 1974 General Elections; Personal Assistant to Rt Hon. Lord Thorneycroft 1978–79; MP (Conservative) for Watford 1979–97; PPS to Barney Hayhoe, MP, as Minister of State, Civil Service Department March 1981–82; Minister of State, Foreign and Commonwealth Office 1990–93. *Whip (Commons):* Assistant Government Whip March 1982–83; Lord Commissioner of the Treasury 1983–86; Vice-Chamberlain, HM Household 1986–88; Comptroller, HM Household 1988–89; Treasurer, HM Household (Deputy Chief Whip) 1989–90. *Honours:* PC 1992. *Recreations:* Book collecting. *Clubs:* Beefsteak. *Name, Style and Title:* Raised to the peerage as Baron Garel-Jones, of Watford in the County of Hertfordshire 1997. A Conservative. *Address:* The Rt Hon. the Lord Garel-Jones, House of Lords, London, SW1A 0PW.

GAVRON (Life Baron, UK), Robert Gavron; cr. 1999; CBE 1990

Son of Nathaniel and Leah Gavron. Born September 13, 1930; educated Leighton Park School; St Peter's College, Oxford (MA); Hon. Fellow, St Peter's College, Oxford 1992; Hon. PhD, Thames Valley University 1997. Married 1st, 1955, Hannah Fyvel (died 1965) (2 Sons); Married 2nd, 1967, Nicolette Coates (2 daughters) (marriage dissolved 1987); Married 3rd, Katharine Gardiner (née Macnair). *Armed Forces:* RAF, National Service 1949–50. *Career:* Called to the Bar 1955; Founded St Ives Group 1964, Director 1964–98, Chairman 1964–93; Director: Octopus Publishing plc 1975–87, Electra Management plc 1981–92; Proprietor, The Carcanet Press Ltd 1983–; Chairman: Folio Society Ltd 1982–, National Gallery Publications Ltd 1996–98, Guardian Media Group plc 1997–. *Other:* Chairman, Open College of the Arts 1991–96; Director, Royal Opera House 1992–98; Governor, LSE 1997–. *Trusts, etc:* Trustee: National Gallery 1994–, Scott Trust 1997–; Chairman of Trustees, Robert Gavron Charitable Trust. *Honours:* CBE 1990. Hon. Fellow: Royal College of Art 1990, Royal Society of Literature 1996. *Publications:* (jointly) *The Entrepreneurial Society*, 1998. *Clubs:* Groucho, MCC. *Name, Style and Title:* Raised to the peerage as Baron Gavron, of Highgate in the London Borough of Camden 1999. Labour. *Address:* The Lord Gavron, CBE, 44 Eagle Street, London, WC1R 4FS *Tel:* 020 7400 4300.

GEDDES (3rd Baron, UK), Euan Michael Ross Geddes; cr. 1942

Son of 2nd Baron, KBE, DL. Born September 3, 1937. Succeeded his father 1975; educated Rugby; Gonville and Caius College, Cambridge (MA); Harvard Business School; Hon. FTCL. Married 1st, May 7, 1966, Gillian (died 1995), daughter of late William Arthur Butler (1 son 1 daughter), married 2nd, 1996, Susan Margaret Hunter, daughter of late George Harold Carter. *Armed Forces:* Royal Navy 1956–58; Lieutenant-Commander, RNR (Rtd). *Career:* Chairman: Trinity College London, Parasol Portrait Photography Ltd, Director: Pacific Chartered Capital Management Limited, Trinity College of Music and other Companies. *House of Lords:* An elected hereditary peer 1999–. *Select Committees:* Member: House of Lords European Select Committee 1994–, Sub-Committee A 1985–90; Member, Sub-Committee B 1990–94, 1995–, Chairman 1996–; Member, Science and Technology Sub-Committee 1 1990–92. *Backbench Committees:* Member, Executive of Association of Conservative Peers 1999–. *Special Interests:* Shipping, Anglo-Chinese Relations, Hong Kong, South East Asia, Immigration, Energy, Transport, Industry. *Recreations:* Golf, music, bridge, gardening, skiing. *Sportsclubs:* Aldeburgh Golf, Hong Kong Golf. *Clubs:* Brooks's, Hong Kong, Noblemen and Gentlemen's Catch. *Heir:* His son, Hon. James George Neil Geddes, born September 10, 1969. A Conservative. *Address:* The Lord Geddes, House of Lords, London, SW1A 0PW *Tel:* 01379 388001.

GERAINT (Life Baron, UK), Geraint Wyn Howells; cr. 1992

Son of late David and Mary Howells. Born April 15, 1925; educated Ardwyn Grammar School, Aberystwyth. Married September 7, 1957, Mary Olwen Hughes, daughter of M. A. Griffiths (2 daughters). *Career:* Farmer; Vice-Chairman, British Wool Marketing Board 1971–83; Chairman, Wool Producers of Wales 1977–87. *House of Commons:* MP (Liberal) for: Cardigan 1974–83, Ceredigion and Pembroke North 1983–92 (Liberal Democrat 1989–92). *Spokesman (Commons):* Spokesman on Welsh Affairs 1985–87, Agriculture 1987–92. *Select Committees (Commons):* Former member, Select Committee on House of Commons Services. *House of Lords:* A Deputy Speaker of the House of Lords; A Deputy Chairman of Committees 1997–.
Spokesman: Spokesman on Welsh Rural Affairs. *Other:* Past President, Royal Welsh Show, Builth Wells, Powys; Chairman, Bronglais Hospital Cancer Appeal Fund, Aberystwyth. *Miscellaneous:* A Extra Lord in Waiting to HM The Queen 1998–. FRAgS. *Special Interests:* Agriculture, Wales, Devolution of Power, Language and Culture, Rural Affairs, Third World. *Recreations:* Rugby, walking. *Sportsclubs:* London Welsh RFC Ltd, Aberstwyth Football Club. *Clubs:* National Liberal, St David's (London), London Welsh. *Name, Style and Title:* Raised to the peerage as Baron Geraint, of Ponterwyd in the County of Dyfed 1992. A Liberal Democrat. *Address:* The Lord Geraint, Glennydd, Ponterwyd, Sir Aberteifi, SY23 3LB *Tel:* 01970 85258.

GIBSON (Life Baron, UK), Richard Patrick Tallentyre Gibson; cr. 1975

Son of late Thornely Carbutt Gibson. Born February 5, 1916; educated Eton; Magdalen College, Oxford; Hon. Fellow, Magdalen College, Oxford; Hon. Degrees: Sussex University, Reading University, Keele University. Married July 14, 1945, Elisabeth Dione, daughter of late Hon. Clive Pearson (4 sons). *Armed Forces:* Served Middlesex Yeomanry 1939–46 (North Africa 1940–41; POW 1941–43; Special Operations Executive 1943–45); Political Intelligence Department, Foreign Office 1945–46. *Career:* London Stock Exchange 1937; Director, Whitehall Securities Corporation 1948–60; Director, S. Pearson & Son 1960–88, Chairman 1978–83; Chairman, Pearson Longman 1967–79; Director, Whitehall Securities Corporation 1973–83. *All-Party:* Member, All-Party Arts and Heritage Group. *Other:* Chairman, Arts Council of Great Britain 1972–77. *Trusts, etc:* Chairman, National Trust 1977–86. *Special Interests:* Arts, Heritage, Environment, Media. *Recreations:* Architecture, music, gardening. *Clubs:* Brooks's, Garrick. *Name, Style and Title:* Raised to the peerage as Baron Gibson, of Penn's Rocks in the County of East Sussex 1975. A Cross-Bencher. *Address:* The Lord Gibson, Penn's Rocks, Groombridge, East Sussex, TN3 9PA.

GIBSON-WATT (Life Baron, UK), James David Gibson-Watt; cr 1979; PC 1974; MC 1943 and 2 Bars

Son of late Major James Miller Gibson-Watt, DL, JP. Born September 11, 1918; educated Eton; Trinity College, Cambridge (BA). Married 1942, Diana, daughter of late Sir Charles Hambro, KBE, MC (2 sons 2 daughters and 1 son deceased). *Armed Forces:* Major, Welsh Guards during 2nd World War. *Councils, Public Bodies:* DL, Powys 1968–97. *House of Commons:* MP (Conservative) for Hereford 1956–74; Minister of State, Welsh Office 1970–74. *Whip (Commons):* A Lord Commissioner of the Treasury 1959–61. *Other:* Chairman, Council of Royal Welsh Agricultural Society 1977–93; Chairman, Timber Growers United Kingdom 1987–90, currently Hon. President. *Miscellaneous:* Member, Historic Buildings Council, Wales 1975–80; A Forestry Commissioner 1976–86; Chairman, Council on Tribunals 1980–86. *Honours:* MC 1943; PC 1974. *Recreations:* Fishing, forestry. *Clubs:* Boodle's, Army and Navy. *Name, Style and Title:* Raised to the peerage as Baron Gibson-Watt, of the Wye in the District of Radnor 1979. A Conservative. *Address:* The Rt Hon. the Lord Gibson-Watt, MC, Doldowlod, Llandrindod Wells, Powys, LD1 6HF *Tel:* 01597 89208.

GILBERT (Life Baron, UK), John (William) Gilbert; cr. 1997; PC 1978

Son of Stanley Gilbert. Born April 5, 1927; educated Merchant Taylors' School, Northwood, Middlesex; St John's College, Oxford; New York University (PhD); Hon. LLD, Wake Forest (S. Carolina) 1983. Married 1963, Jean Ross Skinner (2 daughters from previous marriage). *Trades Union:* Member, GMB 1951–. *Armed Forces:* 1st Lieutenant, Royal Navy 1946–48. *Career:* Chartered Accountant (Canada). *House of Commons:* Contested: Ludlow 1966, Dudley 1968; MP for: Dudley 1970–74, Dudley East 1974–97; Financial Secretary to the Treasury 1974–75; Minister for Transport 1975–76; Minister of State for Defence 1976–79. *Select Committees (Commons):* Member, Select Committees on: Expenditure 1970–74, Corporation Tax 1973; Defence 1979–87, Trade and Industry 1987–92. *House of Lords:* Minister of State for Defence Procurement, Ministry of Defence 1997–99. *Miscellaneous:* Member, Committee on Intelligence and Security 1994–97. *Honours:* PC 1978. FRGS. *Special Interests:* Defence, Foreign Affairs, Economic Policy, Conservation, Transport, Amnesty International. *Clubs:* Reform. *Name, Style and Title:* Raised to the peerage as Baron Gilbert, of Dudley in the County of West Midlands 1997. Labour. *Address:* The Rt Hon. the Lord Gilbert, House of Lords, London, SW1A 0PW.

GILMOUR OF CRAIGMILLAR (Life Baron, UK), Ian Hedworth John Little Gilmour; cr. 1992; 3rd Bt of Liberton and Craigmillar (UK) 1926; PC 1973

Son of Sir John Little Gilmour, 2nd Bt. Born July 8, 1926. Succeeded his father 1977; educated Eton; Balliol College, Oxford; Hon. DU, Essex 1995. Married 1951, Lady Caroline Margaret Montagu-Douglas-Scott, youngest daughter of 8th Duke of Buccleuch and Queensberry, KT, GCVO, PC (4 sons 1 daughter). *Armed Forces:* Served with Grenadier Guards 1944–47; 2nd Lieutenant 1945. *Career:* Called to the Bar, Inner Temple 1952; Editor, *The Spectator* 1954–59; Chairman, Conservative Research Department 1974–75. *House of Commons:* MP (Conservative) for: Norfolk Central 1962–74, Chesham and Amersham 1974–92; PPS to Rt Hon. Quintin Hogg, MP 1963–64; Parliamentary Under-Secretary of State for the Army, Ministry of Defence 1970–71; Minister of State for: Defence Procurement 1971–72, Defence 1972–74; Secretary of State for Defence 1974; Lord Privy Seal 1979–81. *Select Committees (Commons):* Member, Committee on Estimates 1965–70. *Honours:* PC 1973. *Publications:* Author of: *The Body Politic*, 1969; *Inside Right: A Study of Conservatism*, 1977; *Britain Can Work*, 1983; *Riot, Risings and Revolution*, 1992; *Dancing with Dogma*, 1992; *Whatever Happened to the Tories*, (with Mark Garnett) 1997. *Clubs:* Pratt's, White's, MCC. *Heir:* (to baronetcy) His son, Hon. David Robert Gilmour, born November 14, 1952. *Name, Style and Title:* Raised to the peerage as Baron Gilmour of Craigmillar, of Craigmillar in the District of the City of Edinburgh 1992. A Conservative. *Address:* The Rt Hon. the Lord Gilmour of Craigmillar, The Ferry House, Park Road, Old Isleworth, Middlesex, TW7 6BD *Tel:* 020 8560 6769.

GLADWIN OF CLEE (Life Baron, UK), Derek Oliver Gladwin; cr. 1994; CBE 1979

Son of late Albert and Ethel Gladwin. Born June 6, 1930; educated Carr Lane Junior School, Grimsby; Wintringham Grammar School; Ruskin College, Oxford (MA); London School of Economics; Hon MA (Oxon 1978). Married 1956, Ruth Ann Pinion (1 son). *Councils, Public Bodies:* JP, Surrey 1969. *Career:* British Railways, Grimsby 1946–52; Fishing industry, Grimsby 1952–56; General and Municipal Workers' Union: Regional Officer 1956–63, National Industrial Officer 1963–70, Regional Secretary (Southern Region) 1970–90; Board Member: Post Office 1972–94, British Aerospace 1977–91; Member, Employment Appeal Tribunal 1992–. *Whip:* An Opposition Whip 1995–97. *Select Committees:* Member, Select Committees on: Broadcasting 1995–97, Procedure 1997–. *All-Party:* Member, All-Party Committee on Arts and Heritage 1995–; Vice-Chairman, All-Party Croatia Country Group 1999–. *International Bodies:* Member, NATO Parliamentary Assembly 1997. *Party Groups (General):* Chairman, Labour Party Conference Arrangements Committee 1974–90.

Other: Chairman, Governing Council, Ruskin College, Oxford 1979–99; Governor, Kingston University 1998–; President, Holiday Care Service 1998–. *Trusts, etc:* Trustee, British Diabetic Association 1995–. *Miscellaneous:* Visiting Fellow, Nuffield College, Oxford (MA) 1978–86; Member, Armed Forces Pay Review Body 1998–. *Honours:* OBE 1977; CBE 1979. *Special Interests:* Industrial Relations, Employment Law, Tourism, Industry. *Name, Style and Title:* Raised to the peerage as Baron Gladwin of Clee, of Great Grimsby in the County of Humberside 1994. Labour. *Address:* The Lord Gladwin of Clee, CBE, 2 Friars Rise, Woking, Surrey, GU22 7JL *Tel:* 01483 714591.

GLENAMARA (Life Baron, UK), Edward Watson Short; cr. 1977; PC 1964; CH 1976

Son of late Charles Short. Born December 17, 1912; educated Bede College, Durham; Hon. DCL: Durham University; Newcastle University; Hon. DLitt; CNAA; Hon. Dr, Open University; Hon. Fellow: Northumbria University, Portsmouth University, North London University. Married 1941, Jennie, daughter of Thomas Sewell, of Newcastle-upon-Tyne (1 son 1 daughter). *Armed Forces:* Served 1939–45 War as Captain, DLI. *Councils, Public Bodies:* Former Councillor, Newcastle City Council, Leader of Labour Group 1948. *Career:* Chairman, Cable and Wireless Ltd 1976–80. *House of Commons:* MP (Labour) for Newcastle-upon-Tyne Central 1951–76; Postmaster General 1966–68; Secretary of State for Education and Science 1968–70; Lord President of the Council and Leader of the House of Commons 1974-April 1976. *Whip (Commons):* Opposition Assistant Whip 1955; Deputy Opposition Chief Whip 1962; Parliamentary Secretary to the Treasury and Chief Whip, October 1964–66. *Spokesman (Commons):* Opposition Spokesman on Education 1970–72. *Chancellor:* Chancellor, University of Northumbria at Newcastle upon Tyne 1984–. *Select Committees:* Member: Privileges Committee 1985–, Ecclesiastical Committee 1997–. *Party Groups (General):* Deputy Leader Labour Party April 1972-December 1976. *Other:* President, Finchale Abbey Training College for the Disabled 1985–. *Honours:* PC 1964; CH 1976. Fellow, College of Preceptors. *Publications: The Story of the Durham Light Infantry; The Infantry Instructor; Education in a Changing World; Birth to Five; I Knew my Place; Whip to Wilson. Recreations:* Painting. *Name, Style and Title:* Raised to the peerage as Baron Glenamara, of Glenridding in the County of Cumbria 1977. Labour. *Address:* The Rt Hon. the Lord Glenamara, CH, House of Lords, London, SW1A 0PW.

GLENARTHUR (4th Baron, UK), Simon Mark Arthur; cr. 1918; 4th Bt of Carlung (UK) 1903; DL

Son of 3rd Baron, OBE, DL. Born October 7, 1944. Succeeded his father 1976; educated Eton. Married November 12, 1969, Susan, daughter of Commander H. W. Barry, RN (1 son 1 daughter). *Armed Forces:* Commissioned 10th Royal Hussars (PWO) 1963; ADC to High Commissioner, Aden 1964–65; Captain 1970; Major 1973; Retired 1975; Major, The Royal Hussars TAVR 1976–80. *Councils, Public Bodies:* DL, Aberdeenshire 1988. *Career:* Captain, British Airways Helicopters Ltd 1976–82; Director: Aberdeen and Texas Corporate Finance Ltd 1977–82, ABTEX Computer Systems Ltd 1979–82; Senior Executive Hanson plc 1989–96; Deputy Chairman, Hanson Pacific Ltd 1994–98; Director, Whirly Bird Services Ltd 1995–; Consultant, British Aerospace 1989–; President, National Council for Civil Protection 1991–; Chairman, British Helicopter Advisory Board 1992–; Director, Lewis Group plc 1993–94; Consultant, Chevron UK Ltd 1994–97; Director, Millennium Chemicals Inc 1996–; Consultant: Hanson plc 1996–99, Imperial Tobacco Group plc 1996–98; Chairman: European Helicopter Association 1996–, International Federation of Helicopter Associations 1997–. *House of Lords:* Parliamentary Under-Secretary of State, DHSS 1983–85; Parliamentary Under-Secretary of State, Home Office 1985–86; Minister of State: Scottish Office 1986–87, Foreign and Commonwealth Office 1987–89; An elected hereditary peer 1999–. *Whip:* A Lord in Waiting (Government Whip) 1982–83. *Spokesman:* Government Spokesman for: the Treasury 1982–85, Home Office, Employment and Industry 1982–83; A Government Spokesman on Defence 1983–89. *Other:* Council Member, The Air League 1994–. *Trusts, etc:* Chairman, St Mary's Hospital, Paddington, NHS Trust 1991–98; Scottish Patron, The Butler Trust 1994–. *Miscellaneous:* Member (Brigadier) of the Queen's Bodyguard for Scotland (Royal Company of Archers). Member, Chartered Institute of Transport 1978, Fellow 1999; Fellow, Royal Aeronautical Society 1992. Freeman, City of London 1996. Freeman, Guild of Air Pilots and Air Navigators 1992, Liveryman 1996. *Special Interests:* Aviation, Foreign Affairs, Defence, Penal Affairs and Policy, Health, Scotland. *Recreations:* Field sports, gardening, choral singing, photography, barometers. *Clubs:* Cavalry and Guards, Pratt's, White's. *Heir:* His son, Hon. Edward Alexander Arthur, born April 9, 1973. A Conservative. *Address:* The Lord Glenarthur, DL, PO Box 11012, Banchory, Kincardineshire, AB31 6ZJ *Tel:* 01330 844467 *Fax:* 01330 844465 *E-Mail:* glenarth@rsc.co.uk; glenarthurs@parliament.uk.

GLENTORAN (3rd Baron, UK), (Thomas) Robin Valerian Dixon; cr. 1939; 5th Bt of Ballymenoch (UK) 1903; CBE 1992; DL

Son of 2nd Baron, PC, KBE, and late Lady Diana Wellesley, daughter of 3rd Earl Cowley. Born April 21, 1935. Succeeded his father 1995; educated Eton; University of Grenoble, France. Married 1st, January 12, 1959, Rona, daughter of Captain George Cecil Colville, CBE, RN, of The Hill House, Bishop's Waltham, Hants (3 sons) (marriage dissolved 1975), married 2nd, January 2, 1979, Alwyn, daughter of Hubert Mason, of Donaghadee, Co. Down (marriage dissolved 1988), married 3rd, January 3, 1990, Mrs Margaret Rainey. *Armed Forces:* Grenadier Guards 1954–66, retired as Major. *Councils, Public Bodies:* DL, Co. Antrim 1995. *Career:* Managing Director, Redland (NI) Ltd 1971–95, Chairman 1995–98; Chairman, Roofing Industry Alliance 1997–. *House of Lords:* An elected hereditary peer 1999–. *Spokesman:* An Opposition Spokesman for Northern Ireland 1999–. *All-Party:* Member, All-Party Defence Group. *International Bodies:* Associate Member, British/Irish Parliamentary Body. *Other:* Member, The Sports Council for Northern Ireland 1980–87; Founder Chairman, The Ulster Games Foundation 1983–90; Commissioner, Irish Lighthouse Service 1986–; President, British Bobsleigh Association 1987–; Chairman, Northern Ireland Tall Ships Council 1987; Regional Chairman, The British Field Sports Society 1990–; Chairman: Positively Belfast 1992–96, Growing a Green Economy (reporting to Minister for the Environment, Northern Ireland Office) 1993–95; Member, The Millennium Commission 1994–; Chairman, Northern Ireland Classic Gold Promotions 1996–; Hon. President: Chartered Institute of Marketing, Northern Ireland 1996–, The Institute of Roofing 1996–; Member, Countryside Alliance. *Miscellaneous:* Won Olympic Gold Medal (Bobsleigh) 1964. *Honours:* MBE 1969; CBE 1992. Liveryman, Worshipful Company of Tylers and Bricklayers. *Special Interests:* Sport, Environment, Northern Ireland, Army, Maritime Affairs. *Recreations:* Sailing, golf, travel, music, arts. *Sportsclubs:* Royal Portrush Golf, Aloha Golf, Irish Cruising, Soto Grande Golf Club. *Clubs:* Royal Cruising, Kildare Street and University, Dublin, Carlton, Royal Yacht Squadron (Cowes). *Heir:* His son, Hon. Daniel George Dixon, born July 26, 1959. A Conservative. *Address:* The Lord Glentoran, CBE, DL, Drumadarragh House, Ballyclare, Co. Antrim, BT39 0TA *Tel:* 019603 40222; 17 Redcliffe Street, London, SW10 9DR *Tel:* 020 7370 7190 *Fax:* 020 7341 0023 *E-Mail:* tg@glentoran.demon.co.uk.

GLOUCESTER (39th Bishop of), David Edward Bentley

Son of William and Florence Bentley. Born August 7, 1935; educated Great Yarmouth Grammar School; University of Leeds (BA English); Westcott House, Cambridge. Married 1962, Clarice Lahmers (2 sons 2 daughters). *Armed Forces:* Second Lieutenant, 5th Regiment, Royal Horse Artillery. *Career:* Deacon 1960; Priest 1961; Curate: St Ambrose, Bristol 1960–62, Holy Trinity with St Mary, Guildford 1962–66; Rector: Headley, Bordon 1966–73, Esher 1973–86; Rural Dean of Emly 1977–82; Chairman: Guildford Diocesan House of Clergy 1977–86, Guildford Diocesan Council of Social Responsibility 1980–86; Hon. Canon, Guildford Cathedral 1980; Member, various church committees on recruitment and selection 1987–; Warden, Community of All Hallows, Ditchingham 1989–93; Bishop of Gloucester 1993–; Took his seat in the House of Lords 1998. *Recreations:* Music, cricket, theatre. *Sportsclubs:* Vice President, Gloucestershire CCC. *Clubs:* MCC. *Address:* The Rt Rev. the Lord Bishop of Gloucester, Bishopscourt, Pitt Street, Gloucester, GL1 2BQ *Tel:* 01452 524598 *E-Mail:* bshpglos@star.co.uk.

GOFF OF CHIEVELEY (Life Baron, UK), Robert Lionel Archibald Goff; cr. 1986; Kt 1975; PC 1982; FBA 1987

Son of late Lieutenant Colonel L. T. Goff. Born November 12, 1926; educated Eton; New College, Oxford (MA 1953, DCL 1972); Hon. Fellow: Lincoln College, Oxford 1983, New College, Oxford 1986; Hon. LLD: Buckingham University, London University, Bristol University; Hon. DLitt: City University, Reading University. Married 1953, Sarah, daughter of Captain G. R. Cousins, DSC, RN (1 son 2 daughters and 1 son deceased). *Armed Forces:* Served Scots Guards 1945–48. *Career:* Fellow and Tutor, Lincoln College, Oxford 1951–55; Called to Bar, Inner Temple 1951; Bencher 1975; QC 1967; In practice at the Bar 1956–75; Member, General Council of the Bar 1971–74; A Recorder 1974–75; Judge of the High Court, Queen's Bench Division 1975–82; Judge i/c Commercial Court 1979–81; A Lord Justice of Appeal 1982–86; A Lord of Appeal in Ordinary 1986–98; Second Senior Law Lord 1994–96; Senior Law Lord 1996–98. *Select Committees:* Chairman, Sub-Committee E, House of Lords Select Committee on European Communities 1986–88. *Other:* Chairman, Council of Legal Education 1975–82; President, Chartered Institute of Arbitrators 1986–91; Chairman, Court of London University 1986–91; President, New College Society; High Steward, Oxford University; Chairman: British Institute of International and Comparative Law, Oxford Institute of European and Comparative Law. *Honours:* Kt 1975; PC 1982. FBA 1987. *Publications:* Joint Author (with Professor Gareth Jones, QC, FBA) *The Law of Restitution. Name, Style and Title:* Raised to the peerage as Baron Goff of Chieveley, of Chieveley in the Royal County of Berkshire 1986. A Cross-Bencher. *Address:* The Rt Hon. the Lord Goff of Chieveley, FBA, House of Lords, London, SW1A 0PW.

GOLDSMITH (Life Baron, UK), Peter Henry Goldsmith; cr. 1999; QC 1987

Son of late Sydney Elland Goldsmith, and of Myra Goldsmith. Born January 5, 1950; educated Quarry Bank High School, Liverpool; Gonville and Caius College, Cambridge (MA); University College, London (LLM 1972). Married December 22, 1974, Joy, daughter of Alan and Joan Elterman (3 sons 1 daughter). *Career:* Called to the Bar 1972; In Practice 1972–; QC 1987; A Recorder 1991–; Chairman, Bar of England and Wales 1995; Member, Paris Bar (Avocat a la Cour) 1997. *Other:* Executive Committee Member, Great Britain China Centre 1996–; Council Member, Public Concern at Work 1996–99. *Miscellaneous:* Chairman, Bar Council International Relations Committee 1996–; Member, Financial Reporting Review Panel 1995–, Chairman 1997–; Chairman, IBA Standing Committee on Globalisation 1996–98; Founder and Chairman, Bar Bono Unit 1996–; Co-Chairman, IBA Human Rights Institute 1998–; Various Offices held in International Law Organizations. *Name, Style and Title:* Raised to the peerage as Baron Goldsmith, of Allerton in the County of Merseyside 1999. Labour. *Address:* The Lord Goldsmith, QC, House of Lords, London, SW1A 0PW; Fountain Court Chambers, Fountain Court, Temple, London, EC4 *Tel:* 020 7583 3335 *Fax:* 020 7353 0329 *E-Mail:* PHgoldsmith_QC@compuserve.com.

GOODHART (Life Baron), William (Howard) Goodhart; cr. 1997; Kt 1989; QC 1979

Son of late Professor Arthur Goodhart, Hon. KBE, QC, FBA. Born January 18, 1933; educated Eton; Trinity College, Cambridge (Scholar, MA); Harvard Law School (Commonwealth Fund Fellow, LLM). Married May 21, 1966, Hon. Celia McClare Herbert, daughter of 2nd Baron Hemingford (1 son 2 daughters). *Armed Forces:* Second Lieutenant, Oxford and Bucks Light Infantry 1951–53 (National Service). *Career:* Called to the Bar, Lincoln's Inn 1957, Bencher 1986–; Director, Bar Mutual Indemnity Fund Ltd 1988–97. *Select Committees:* Co-opted Member, Select Committee on European Communities Sub-Committee E 1997–; Member, Select Committees on: Delegated Powers and Deregulation 1998–, European Communities 1998–, Freedom of Information Bill 1999–. *International Bodies (General):* Member, International Commission of Jurists 1993–, Executive Committee 1995–; Committee Officer, Human Rights Institute 1995–. *Party Groups (General):* Chairman: SDP Council Arrangements Committee 1982–88, Liberal Democrat Conference Committee 1988–91, Liberal Democrat Lawyers Association 1988–91; Member, Liberal Democrat Policy

Committee 1988, Vice-Chairman 1995–97. *Other:* Justice: Member of Council 1972–, Vice-Chairman, Executive Committee 1978–88, Chairman, Executive Committee 1988–94; Member: Trust Law Committee 1994–, Tax Law Review Committee 1994–. *Trusts, etc:* Trustee, Airey Neave Trust 1999–. *Miscellaneous:* Contested: Kensington (SDP) 1983, (SDP/Alliance) 1987, (Lib Dem) July 1988, Oxford West and Abingdon (Lib Dem) 1992; Member: Council of Legal Education 1986–92, Conveyancing Standing Committee, Law Commission 1987–89; Has led reporting missions on human rights to Hong Kong 1991, Kashmir 1993, Israel and the West Bank 1994, Kenya 1996 and Sri Lanka 1997; Member, Committee on Standards in Public Life (The Neill Committee) 1997–. *Honours:* Kt 1989. *Publications: Specific Performance,* 1986 (2nd ed. 1996) (with Professor Gareth Jones); Has contributed to *Halsbury's Laws of England*; also articles in legal journals. *Special Interests:* Human Rights. *Recreations:* Walking, skiing. *Clubs:* Brooks's, Century Association (New York). *Name, Style and Title:* Raised to the peerage as Baron Goodhart, of Youlbury in the County of Oxfordshire 1997. A Liberal Democrat. *Address:* The Lord Goodhart, QC, 11 Clarence Terrace, London, NW1 4RD *Tel:* 020 7262 1319 *Fax:* 020 7723 5851; Youlbury House, Boars Hill, Oxford, OX1 5HH *Tel:* 01865 735477.

GORDON OF STRATHBLANE (Life Baron, UK), James Stuart Gordon; cr. 1997; CBE 1984

Son of James and Elsie Gordon (née Riach). Born May 17, 1936; educated St Aloysius' College, Glasgow; Glasgow University (MA Hons); Hon. DLitt, Glasgow Caledonian 1994; DUniv, Glasgow University 1997. Married, 1971, Margaret Anne Stevenson (2 sons 1 daughter). *Career:* Political Editor, STV 1965–73; Chief Executive, Radio Clyde 1973–96; Chief Executive, Scottish Radio Holdings 1991–96, Chairman 1996–; Vice-Chairman, Melody Radio 1991–97; Director: Clydeport Holdings 1992–98, Johnston Press plc 1996–, AIM Trust plc 1996–; Chairman, Scottish Tourist Board 1998–. *Other:* Member, Scottish Development Agency 1981–90; Chairman, Scottish Exhibition Centre 1983–89; Member: Court of University of Glasgow 1984–97, Committee of Enquiry into Teachers' Pay and Conditions 1986, Scottish Advisory Board, BP 1990–; Member, Scottish Tourist Board 1997–, Chairman 1998–; Chair, Advisory Group on Listed Events 1997–98; Board Member, British Tourist Authority 1999–. *Miscellaneous:* Contested East Renfrewshire (Lab) 1964 General Election; Member, Committee on Funding of the SBC 1998–99. *Honours:* CBE 1984. *Recreations:* Skiing, walking, genealogy, golf. *Sportsclubs:* Buchanan Castle Golf, Prestwick Golf. *Clubs:* New (Edinburgh), Glasgow Art. *Name, Style and Title:* Raised to the peerage as Baron Gordon of Strathblane, of Deil's Craig in Stirling 1997. Labour. *Address:* The Lord Gordon of Strathblane, CBE, Deil's Craig, Strathblane, Glasgow, G63 9ET *Tel:* 0141–565 2202 *Fax:* 0141–565 2322 *E-Mail:* james.gordon@srh.co.uk.

GOSCHEN (4th Viscount, UK), Giles John Harry Goschen; cr. 1900

Son of 3rd Viscount, KBE. Born November 16, 1965. Succeeded his father 1977; educated Eton. Married February 23, 1991, Sarah Penelope, daughter of late Alan Horsnail (1 daughter). *Career:* Deutsche Bank 1997–. *House of Lords:* Parliamentary Under-Secretary of State, Department of Transport 1994–97; An elected hereditary peer 1999–. *Whip:* A Lord in Waiting (Government Whip) 1992–94. *Spokesman:* A Government Spokesman for Environment, Employment, Social Security, Transport and Trade and Industry 1992–94; An Opposition Spokesman on Environment, Transport and the Regions (Transport) 1997. *Clubs:* Air Squadron, Pratt's. *Heir:* None. A Conservative. *Address:* The Viscount Goschen, House of Lords, London, SW1A 0PW.

GOUDIE (Life Baroness, UK), Mary Teresa Goudie; cr. 1998

Daughter of Martin and Hannah Brick. Born September 2, 1946; educated Our Lady of The Visitation, Greenford; Our Lady of St Anselm, Hayes. Married 1969, James Goudie, QC (2 sons). *Trades Union:* Member: APEX, GMB. *Councils, Public Bodies:* Councillor, London Borough of Brent 1971–78, Chairman, Housing and Planning Committees, Deputy Whip. *Career:* Assistant Director, Brent People's Housing Association 1980–87; Director: The Hansard Society for Parliamentary Government 1985–89, *The House Magazine* (weekly journal of the Houses of Parliament and the Parliamentary Information Unit) 1989–90; Public Affairs Manager, World Wide Fund for Nature (UK) 1990–95; Independent Public Affairs Consultant 1995–. *Select Committees:* Co-opted Member – European Select Committee, Sub-Committee E, Law and Institutions. *All-Party:* Secretary, All-Party Children's Group; Member, All-Party: Rail Freight Group, Parliamentary Homlessness and Housing Group. *International Bodies (General):* Member: Labour Movement in Europe, Inter-Parliamentary Union, British-American Parliamentary Group. *Party Groups (General):* Member, The Labour Party 1964–; Secretary, Labour Solidarity Campaign 1980–84; Member: Society of Labour Lawyers, Fabian Society, Smith Institute. *Other:* Chairman, Family Courts' Consortium; Patron: Grandparents' Federation, Neighbourhood Care, St John's Wood and Maida Vale; Member: Executive of the Industry Forum Scotland, Centre for Scottish Public Policy, The Council of The Historic Gardens Foundation, CSV Development Board, London Zoo Fundraising Committee. *Trusts, etc:* Trustee, Tower Hamlets Old People's Trust. *Special Interests:* Europe, Scotland, Housing, Regional Development, Children, Charity Law, Machinery of Government. *Recreations:* Family, travelling, gardening, food and wine, art. *Clubs:* Reform. *Name, Style and Title:* Raised to the peerage as Baroness Goudie, of Roundwood in the London Borough of Brent 1998. Labour. *Address:* The Baroness Goudie, House of Lords, London, SW1A 0PW.

GOULD OF POTTERNEWTON (Life Baroness, UK), Joyce Brenda Gould; cr. 1993

Daughter of late Sydney and Fanny Manson. Born October 29, 1932; educated Roundhay High School for Girls; Bradford Technical College; Hon. Degree, Bradford University 1997. Married 1952, Kevin Gould (1 daughter) (separated). *Trades Union:* Member: TGWU, GMW. *Career:* Pharmaceutical Dispenser 1952–65; Organiser, Pioneer Women 1965; Clerical Worker 1966–69; Worked for the Labour Party 1969–93; Assistant Regional Organiser 1969–75; Secretary, National Joint Committee of Working Women's Organisations 1975–85; Assistant National Agent and Chief Women's Officer 1975–85; Director of Organisation, Labour Party 1985–93. *Whip:* An Opposition Whip 1994–97; A Baroness in Waiting (Government Whip) (Social Security, Health and Women) May-December 1997. *Spokesman:* Opposition Spokesperson on: Citizen's Charter 1994–96, Women 1996–97. *Select Committees:* Former Member: Select Committee on Finance and Staffing, European Select Committee, Sub-Committee C (Environmental Affairs). *Backbench Committees:* Vice-Chairperson, Labour Party Departmental Committee for Women; Member, Labour Party Departmental Committees for: Health, Social Security. *All-Party:* Chair, All-Party Pro-Choice Group 1998–; Vice-Chair, All-Party Constitutional Affairs Group; Executive Member, All-Party Population, Development and Reproduction Group; Member, All-Party: Human Rights Group, Sex Equality Group, Electoral Reform Group, Czech/Slovak Group, Disablement Group, Tibet Group, Breast Cancer Group; Secretary, All-Party Children Group 1998–; Treasurer, All-Party Epilepsy Group 1999–. *International Bodies (General):* Vice-President, Socialist International Women 1978–85; Member: Council of Europe and Education and Cultural Committee 1993–95, WEU and Parliamentary and Public Relations Committee, CPA, IPU. *Party Groups (General):* Member: Labour Party 1951–, Regional Women's Advisory Committee, National Labour Women's Committee, Plant Committee on Electoral Systems; Chair, Computing for Labour; Member: Fabian Society, Labour Electoral Reform Association, Bevan Society, Labour Heritage, Arts for Labour. *Other:* Secretary: National Joint Committee of Working Women, Yorkshire National Council for Civil Liberties; Committee Member, Campaign Against Racial Discrimination; Executive Member, Joint Committee Against Racism; Member, Management Committee, Grand Theatre, Leeds; School Governor; Vice-President: Population Concern, Action for Dysphasic Adults; President: British Epilepsy Association 1998–, Full Franchise; Vice-Chair, Parliament and Industry Trust Dinner Club; Member: Fawcett Society, Hansard Society, Howard League, Yorkshire Society; Council Member, Constitution Unit. *Trusts, etc:* Chair and Trustee, Mary MacArthur Holiday Trust;

Trustee and Director: Diarama Arts, Studio Upstairs, Yigol Allon Trust; Trustee and Fellow, Industry and Parliamentary Trust. *Miscellaneous:* Executive Member, Women's National Commission; Member: Department of Employment Women's Advisory Committee, Home Office Committee on Electoral Matters, Commission on Conduct of Referendums, Independent Commission on Electoral System 1997–98. *Publications:* Include *Women and Health* (editor); pamphlets on Feminism, Socialism and Sexism, Women's Right to Work, Violence in Society; articles and reports on Women's Rights, Electoral systems – their practices and procedures. *Special Interests:* Women's Equality, Constitutional Affairs, Electoral Affairs, Race Relations, Population and Development, Disabled. *Recreations:* Theatre, cinema, reading. *Name, Style and Title:* Raised to the peerage as Baroness Gould of Potternewton, of Leeds in the County of West Yorkshire 1993. Labour. *Address:* The Baroness Gould of Potternewton, Flat 1, 5 Foulser Road, London, SW17 8UE *Tel:* 020 8672 0641 *Fax:* 020 8672 0641; 6 St Johns Mews, Bristol Road, Brighton, BN2 1BN *Tel:* 01273 607474.

GRABINER (Life Baron, UK), Anthony Stephen Grabiner; cr. 1999; QC 1981

Son of late Ralph and Freda Grabiner (née Cohen). Born March 21, 1945; educated Central Foundation Boys' Grammar School, London EC2; LSE; University of London (LLB 1st Class Hons 1966, LLM Distinction 1967); Lincoln's Inn (Hardwicke Scholar 1966, Droop Scholar 1968). Married 1983, Jane, daughter of Dr Benjamin Portnoy, TD, JP, MD, PhD, FRCP, of Hale, Cheshire (3 sons 1 daughter). *Career:* Called to the Bar 1968; Standing Junior Counsel to Department of Trade, Export Credits Guarantee Department 1976–71; Junior Counsel to the Crown 1978–81; QC 1981; Bencher 1989; Recorder of the Crown Court 1990; Deputy High Court Judge 1994–. *Other:* Member, Court of Governors, LSE 1991–, Vice-Chairman 1993–98, Chairman 1998–. QC, 1981; LLM, 1967. *Publications:* Edited jointly, *Sutton and Shannon on Contract*, 7th edition 1970; Contributor, *Banking Documents to Encyclopedia of Forms and Precedents*, 5th edition 1986. *Special Interests:* Law Reform, Commercial and Intellectual Property Law, Higher Education. *Recreations:* Golf, theatre, reading. *Sportsclubs:* Hendon Golf. *Clubs:* Garrick, Royal Automobile, MCC. *Name, Style and Title:* Raised to the peerage as Baron Grabiner, of Aldwych in the City of Westminster 1999. Labour. *Address:* The Lord Grabiner, QC, 1 Essex Court, Temple, London, EC4Y 9AR *Tel:* 020 7583 2000 *Fax:* 020 7583 0118; House of Lords, London, SW1A 0PW *E-Mail:* jhuxley@oneessexcourt.co.uk.

GRAHAM OF EDMONTON (Life Baron, UK), Thomas Edward Graham; cr. 1983; PC 1998

Son of Thomas Edward Graham. Born March 26, 1925; educated Elementary School; WEA Co-operative College; Open University (BA); Hon. Degree of Master of Open University 1989. Married 1950, Margaret Golding (2 sons). *Trades Union:* Member, National Association of Co-operative Officials. *Armed Forces:* Corporal, Royal Marines 1943–46. *Councils, Public Bodies:* Former Labour Leader, Enfield Council; Chairman, Housing and Redevelopment Committee 1961–68. *Career:* Various posts within the Co-operative Movement 1939–74. *House of Commons:* Contested (Labour and Co-operative) Enfield West in 1966; MP (Labour and Co-operative) for Enfield, Edmonton 1974–83; PPS to Minister of State, Department of Prices and Consumer Affairs 1974–76. *Whip (Commons):* Lord Commissioner of the Treasury 1976–79. *Spokesman (Commons):* Spokesman on the Environment 1981–83. *House of Lords:* A Deputy Speaker of the House of Lords; A Deputy Chairman of Committees 1997–. *Whip:* Opposition Whip 1983–90, Opposition Chief Whip in the Lords 1990–97. *Spokesman:* Opposition Front Bench Spokesman on the Environment, Northern Ireland and Defence 1983–90; Former Opposition Spokesman on National Heritage (Tourism). *Select Committees:* Former Member of several select committees including Privileges, Procedure and Selection. *Backbench Committees:* Member, Refreshments Committee 1990–. *All-Party:* Hon. Secretary, All-Party: Retail Industry Group, Welfare of Mobile Home Owners Group; Member, All-Party British-Austrian Country Group. *Party Groups:* Chair, Labour Peers Group. *Party Groups (General):* Member, Co-operative Party. *Other:* President, Institute of Meat. *Honours:* PC 1998. Fellow: Institute of British Management, Royal Society of Arts. Freeman, Worshipful Company of Butchers. *Special Interests:* Local Government, Consumer Affairs, Environment. *Name, Style and Title:* Raised to the peerage as Baron Graham of Edmonton, of Edmonton in Greater London 1983. Labour. *Address:* The Rt Hon. the Lord Graham of Edmonton, 2 Clerks Piece, Loughton, Essex, IG10 1NR; House of Lords, London, SW1A 0PW *Tel:* House of Lords 020 7219 6704.

GRAY OF CONTIN (Life Baron, UK), James Hector Northey Hamish Gray; cr. 1983; PC 1982

Son of late James Northey Gray, JP, and late Mrs M. E. Gray. Born June 28, 1927; educated Inverness Royal Academy. Married September 11, 1953, Judith W. Brydon, BSc (2 sons 1 daughter). *Armed Forces:* Served Queens Own Cameron Highlanders 1945–48. *Councils, Public Bodies:* Served Highland Chamber of Commerce 1963–70; Inverness Town Council 1965–70; DL, Lochaber, Inverness, Badenoch and Strathspey 1989–96, Vice-Lord Lieutenant 1994–96; Lord Lieutenant of Inverness 1996–; JP 1996–. *Career:* Company Director 1950–70; Business and Parliamentary Consultant 1987–; Non-Executive Director 1995–. *House of Commons:* MP (Conservative) Ross and Cromarty 1970–83; Successfully piloted Education Scotland (Mentally Handicapped) Bill through Parliament 1974; Minister of State for Energy 1979–83. *Whip (Commons):* Assistant Government Whip 1971–73; Lord Commissioner of the Treasury 1973–74; Opposition Whip 1974–75. *Spokesman (Commons):* Opposition Spokesman on Energy 1975–79. *Select Committees (Commons):* Former member, Select Committee on Scottish Affairs 1970–71. *House of Lords:* Minister of State, Scottish Office 1983–86. *Spokesman:* A Government Spokesman in the House of Lords on Employment 1983–84; Principal Government Spokesman on Energy 1984–86. *Select Committees:* Member, Select Committees on: Channel Tunnel 1986–87, Relations between Central and Local Government 1995–96. *All-Party:* Member: Parliamentary Group for Energy Studies 1986–, Parliamentary Cricket Group 1994–, Parliamentary Group for Scottish Opera 1996–. *International Bodies (General):* President, British Romanian Chamber of Commerce 1999–. *Other:* Hon. President: National Charities, Energy Action Scotland 1987–97; Hon. Vice-President: Neighbourhood Energy Action 1987–98, National Energy Action 1987–98. *Honours:* PC 1982. *Recreations:* Golf, cricket, walking, gardening, reading. *Name, Style and Title:* Raised to the peerage as Baron Gray of Contin, of Contin in the District of Ross and Cromarty 1983. A Conservative. *Address:* The Rt Hon. the Lord Gray of Contin, House of Lords, London, SW1A 0PW.

GREENE OF HARROW WEALD (Life Baron, UK), Sidney Francis Greene; cr. 1974; Kt 1970; CBE 1966

Son of late Frank Greene. Born February 12, 1910; educated elementary schools. Married 1936, Masel Elizabeth Carter (3 daughters). *Trades Union:* General Secretary, National Union of Railwaymen 1957–75; Member, General Council of TUC 1957–75. *Councils, Public Bodies:* JP, London 1941–65. *Career:* Joined Railway Service 1924; A director, Bank of England 1970–78. *Miscellaneous:* Member, National Economic Development Council 1962–75. *Name, Style and Title:* Raised to the peerage as Baron Greene of Harrow Weald, of Harrow in the County of Greater London 1974. Labour. *Address:* The Lord Greene of Harrow Weald, CBE, 26 Kynaston Wood, Boxtree Road, Harrow Weald, Middlesex, HA3 6UA.

GREENHILL OF HARROW (Life Baron, UK), Denis Arthur Greenhill; cr. 1974; GCMG 1972; OBE (Mil) 1941

Son of James and Susie Greenhill. Born November 7, 1913; educated Bishops Stortford College, Herts; Christ Church, Oxford (Hon. Student). Married June 4, 1941, Angela, daughter of late William McCulloch (1 son and 1 son deceased). *Armed Forces:* Royal Engineers 1939–45. *Career:* Apprentice, London North Eastern Railway 1935–39; Diplomatic Service, Sofia, Washington, NATO delegation Paris, Singapore 1946–73; Permanent Under-Secretary, Foreign and Commonwealth Office 1969–73; Government Director, British Petroleum 1973–78; Director, Leyland International 1977–82; Director, S. G. Warburg & Co. 1974–86, Adviser 1986–95; Director: BAT Industries 1974–83, Hawker Siddeley Group 1974–84, Clerical Medical Association 1974–86, Wellcome Foundation 1974–85. *Select Committees:* Member, House of Lords Select Committee on Overseas Trade 1985; Member, European Select Committee and Sub-Committee 1985–87; Former Chairman, House of Lords Select Committee on King's Cross Private Bill. *All-Party:* Chairman, All-Party Overseas Development Group 1989–91. *Other:* Governor, BUPA 1978–84; Chairman, King's College Hospital Medical School 1976–83; Member, Rayne Foundation; Former Chairman of the Governing Body, School of Oriental and African Studies, London University 1978–85; Governor, Wellington

College 1974–83; President: Royal Society of Asian Affairs 1976–84, Anglo-Finnish Society 1981–84. *Miscellaneous:* Governor, BBC 1973–78; Member, Security Commission. *Honours:* OBE (Mil) 1941; CMG 1960; KCMG 1967; GCMG 1972; Grand Cross Order of the Finnish Lion 1984. Fellow, King's College, London. *Publications:* Author of *More by Accident* (memoir) 1992. *Clubs:* Travellers'. *Name, Style and Title:* Raised to the peerage as Baron Greenhill of Harrow, of the Royal Borough of Kensington and Chelsea 1974. A Cross-Bencher. *Address:* The Lord Greenhill of Harrow, GCMG, OBE, 25 Hamilton House, Vicarage Gate, London, W8 4HL *Tel:* 020 7937 8362.

GREENWAY (4th Baron, UK), Ambrose Charles Drexel Greenway; cr. 1927; 4th Bt of Stanbridge Earls (UK) 1919

Son of 3rd Baron. Born May 21, 1941. Succeeded his father 1975; educated Winchester. Married October 26, 1985, Mrs Rosalynne Peta Schenk, daughter of late Lieutenant-Colonel Peter Fradgley. *Career:* Marine Photographer. *House of Lords:* An elected hereditary peer 1999–. *Other:* Younger Brother, Trinity House 1987; Chairman, The Marine Society 1994–; Vice-President, Sail Training Association 1995–. *Publications: Soviet Merchant Ships*, 1976; *Comecon Merchant Ships*, 1978; *A Century of Cross-Channel Passenger Ferries*, 1981; *A Century of North Sea Passenger Steamers*, 1986. *Special Interests:* Shipping, Marine Industry. *Recreations:* Sailing. *Clubs:* House of Lords Yacht. *Heir:* His brother, Hon. Mervyn Stephen Kelvynge Greenway, born August 19, 1942. A Cross-Bencher. *Address:* The Lord Greenway, House of Lords, London, SW1A 0PW.

GREGSON (Life Baron, UK), John Gregson; cr. 1975; DL

Son of late John Gregson. Born January 29, 1924; Hon. Doctor, Open University; Hon. DSc, University of Aston; Hon. DTech, Brunel University; Hon. DSc, Cranfield. *Councils, Public Bodies:* DL, County of Greater Manchester 1979. *Career:* Joined Fairey Engineering 1939, Board Member 1966, Managing Director 1978–94, retired as Non-Executive Director, Fairey Holding 1994; Non-Executive Director: British Steel plc 1976–94, Otto-Simon Carves Ltd 1995, Innvotech Ltd. *Select Committees:* Member, House of Lords Select Committees on: Science and Technology 1980–97, Sustainable Development 1994–97. *All-Party:* Past President, Parliamentary and Scientific Committee 1986–89. *Party Groups (General):* President, Labour Finance and Industry Group. *Other:* Former Vice-President, Association of Metropolitan Authorities; Member, National Rivers Authority 1991–95; Member Council, University of Manchester Institute of Science and Technology; President, Defence Manufacturers Association 1984–; Chairman, Waste Management Industry Training and Advisory Board; Member, Court of: UMIST, University of Manchester. Hon. Fellow: Royal Academy of Engineering, Institute of Civil Engineers 1987; AMCT; CIMgt. *Recreations:* Mountaineering, ski-ing, sailing, gardening. *Name, Style and Title:* Raised to the peerage as Baron Gregson, of Stockport in the County of Greater Manchester 1975. Labour. *Address:* The Lord Gregson, DL, 12 Rosemont Road, Richmond, Surrey, TW10 6QL.

GRIFFITHS (Life Baron, UK), William Hugh Griffiths; cr. 1985; Kt 1971; MC 1944; PC 1980

Son of late Sir Hugh Griffiths, CBE. Born September 26, 1923; educated Charterhouse; St John's College, Cambridge. Married 1949, Evelyn Krefting (died March 1998) (1 son 3 daughters). *Armed Forces:* Commissioned Welsh Guards 1942. *Career:* Called to the Bar, Inner Temple 1949; QC 1964; Recorder of: Margate 1962–64, Cambridge 1964–70; A Judge of the High Court of Justice, Queen's Bench Division 1971–80; A Lord Justice of Appeal 1980–85; A Lord of Appeal in Ordinary 1985–93. *Other:* President, Bar Association for Commerce, Finance and Industry. *Miscellaneous:* Chairman, Security Commission 1985–92. *Honours:* MC 1944; Kt 1971; PC 1980. *Clubs:* Garrick, MCC, Royal and Ancient (St Andrews). *Name, Style and Title:* Raised to the peerage as Baron Griffiths, of Govilon in the County of Gwent 1985. A Cross-Bencher. *Address:* The Rt Hon. the Lord Griffiths, MC, House of Lords, London, SW1A 0PW.

GRIFFITHS OF FFORESTFACH (Life Baron, UK), Brian Griffiths; cr. 1991

Son of Ivor Winston and Phyllis Griffiths. Born December 27, 1941; educated Dynevor Grammar School; London School of Economics. Married September 18, 1965, Rachel Jane, daughter of Howard and Ruth Jones (1 son 2 daughters). *Career:* Lecturer, London School of Economics 1965–76; Professor of Banking and Director of Centre, Banking and International Finance The City University 1977–82; Dean, Business School The City University 1983–85; Director, Bank of England 1983–85; Head, Prime Minister's Policy Unit and Special Adviser to The Rt Hon. Margaret Thatcher MP 1985–90; Director: Thorn EMI 1990–96, Herman Miller Inc. 1991–, Times Newspapers Ltd 1991–; Chairman, Schools Examinations and Assessment Council 1991–93; International Adviser, Goldman Sachs 1991–; Vice-Chairman, Goldman Sachs (Europe); Director: Servicemaster 1992–, HTV 1992–93, Telewest 1995–98; Chairman: Trillium 1998–, Westminster Health Care 1999–. Freeman, City of London. *Publications:* Author of several books on economics including: *The Creation of Wealth*, 1984; *Morality and the Market Place*, 1989. *Special Interests:* Economic Policy, Education, Broadcasting, Social Policy. *Clubs:* Garrick. *Name, Style and Title:* Raised to the peerage as Baron Griffiths of Fforestfach, of Fforestfach in the County of West Glamorgan 1991. A Conservative. *Address:* The Lord Griffiths of Fforestfach, House of Lords, London, SW1A 0PW.

GUILDFORD (8th Bishop of), John Warren Gladwin

Son of Thomas and Muriel Gladwin. Born May 30, 1942; educated Hertford Grammar School; Churchill College, Cambridge (BA History and Theology, MA 1969); St John's College, Durham (DipTheol). Married 1981, Lydia Elizabeth Adam. *Career:* Assistant Curate, St John the Baptist, Kirkheaton, Huddersfield 1967–71; Tutor, St John's College, Durham and Hon. Chaplain to Students, St Nicholas Church, Durham 1971–77; Director, Shaftesbury Project on Christian Involvement in Society 1977–82; Secretary, General Synod Board for Social Responsibility 1982–88; Prebendary, St Paul's Cathedral 1984–88; Provost of Sheffield 1988–94; Member, General Synod of the Church of England 1990–; Bishop of Guildford 1994–; Took his seat in the House of Lords 1999. *Other:* President, Church's National Housing Coalition; Chairman, Board of Christian Aid; Member, Archbishop's Council. *Publications: God's People in God's World*, 1979; *The Good of the People*, 1988; *Love and Liberty*, 1998. *Recreations:* Gardening, travel. *Address:* The Rt Rev. the Lord Bishop of Guildford, Willow Grange, Woking Road, Guildford, Surrey, GU4 7QS *Tel:* 01483 590500 *Fax:* 01483 590501 *E-Mail:* bishop.john@cofeguildford.org.uk; mary.morris@cofeguildford.org.uk (Secretary).

H

HABGOOD (Life Baron, UK), John Stapylton Habgood; cr. 1995; PC 1983

Son of late Arthur Henry Habgood, DSO, MB, BCH, and late Vera Chetwynd-Stapylton. Born June 23, 1927; educated Eton; King's College, Cambridge (MA, PhD); Cuddesdon Theological College, Oxford; Hon. DD: Durham 1975, Cambridge 1984; Fellow, King's College, Cambridge, Hon. Fellow from 1985; Hon. DD: Aberdeen 1988, Huron 1990, Hull 1991; Hon. DHum, York, Pennsylvania 1995; Hon. DD: Oxford 1996, Manchester 1996; Hon. DUniv, York 1996. Married 1961, Rosalie Mary Anne, daughter of late E. L. Boston (2 sons 2 daughters). *Career:* Demonstrator in Pharmacology, Cambridge University 1950–53; Curate, St Mary Abbots, Kensington 1954–56; Vice-Principal, Westcott House, Cambridge 1956–62; Rector, St John's Church, Jedburgh 1962–67; Principal, Queen's College, Birmingham 1967–73; Bishop of Durham 1973–83; Took his seat in the House of Lords 1973; Archbishop of York 1983–95. *Chancellor:* Pro-Chancellor, University of York 1985–90. *Select Committees:* Member, Select Committee on Medical Ethics 1993–94. *International Bodies (General):* Member, World Council of Churches 1983–91. *Other:* Patron, National Family Mediation 1990–; Vice-President, Population Concern 1991–. *Miscellaneous:* Chairman, UK Xenotransplantation Interim Regulatory Authority 1997–; Member, Round Table on Sustainable

Development 1997–99. *Honours:* PC 1983. *Publications:* Author of: *Religion and Science,* 1964; *A Working Faith,* 1980; *Church and Nation in a Secular Age,* 1983; *Confessions of a Conservative Liberal,* 1988; *Making Sense,* 1993; *Faith and Uncertainty,* 1997; *Being A Person,* 1998; *Varieties of Unbelief,* 2000. *Special Interests:* Science, Medicine, Ethics. *Recreations:* Travel, DIY, Painting. *Clubs:* Athenaeum. *Name, Style and Title:* Raised to the peerage as Baron Habgood, of Calverton in the County of Buckinghamshire 1995. A Cross-Bencher. *Address:* The Rt Rev. and Rt Hon. the Lord Habgood, 18 The Mount, Malton, North Yorkshire, YO17 7ND.

HAILSHAM OF ST MARYLEBONE (Life Baron, UK), Quintin McGarel Hogg; cr. 1970; KG 1988; PC 1956; CH 1974; FRS 1973

Son of 1st Viscount, PC, KC whom he succeeded in 1950; disclaimed the viscountcy and barony of Hailsham for life, under the provisions of the Peerage Act 1963. Born October 9, 1907; educated Eton; Christ Church, Oxford (MA) (President of the Union 1929); Fellow, All Souls College 1931; Hon. DCL: Newcastle, New Brunswick, Westminster College, Fulton, Missouri, Oxford, Sussex, Ulster; Hon. LLD: Cambridge 1964, Delhi 1973; Hon. degree, Buckingham University 1992. Married 1st, November 12, 1932, Natalie Sullivan (marriage dissolved 1943, she died 1987), married 2nd, April 18, 1944, Mary Evelyn (died 1978), daughter of late Richard Martin (2 sons 3 daughters), married 3rd, March 1, 1986, Deirdre (died December 22, 1998), daughter of late Captain Peter Shannon, and of Mrs Margaret Briscoe. *Armed Forces:* Served overseas with Rifle Brigade 1939–45. *Career:* Called to the Bar, Lincoln's Inn 1932; QC 1953, Bencher 1956, Treasurer 1975; Editor, *Halsbury's Laws of England,* 4th edition 1972–98. *House of Commons:* MP (Conservative) for: Oxford City 1938–50, St. Marylebone 1963–70; Joint Parliamentary Under-Secretary of State for Air April-July 1945; Minister with responsibility for: Sport 1962–64; Unemployment in the North East 1963–64; Higher Education December 1963-February 1964; Secretary of State for Education and Science April-October 1964. *House of Lords:* First Lord of the Admiralty 1956–57; Minister of Education January-September 1957; Deputy Leader of the House of Lords 1957–60, Leader 1960–63; Lord President of the Council 1957–59, 1960–64; Minister for Science and Technology 1959–64; Lord High Chancellor 1970–74, 1979–87; A Deputy Speaker of the House of Lords. *Party Groups (General):* Chairman, Conservative Party 1957–59. *Honours:* PC 1956; CH 1974; KG 1988. FRS 1973. *Publications:* Author of: *The Law of Arbitration* 1935; *One Year's Work* 1944; *The Law and Employers' Liability* 1944; *The Times We Live In* 1944; *Making Peace* 1945; *The Left was never Right* 1945; *The Purpose of Parliament* 1946; *Care for Conservatism* 1947; *The Law of Monopolies, Restrictive Practices and Resale Price Maintenance* 1956; *The Conservative Case* 1959; *Interdependence* 1961; *Science and Politics* 1963; *The Devil's Own Song* 1968; *The Door Wherein I Went* 1975; *Elective Dictatorship* 1976; *The Dilemma of Democracy* 1978; *Hamlyn Revisited: the British legal system (Hamlyn Lectures)* 1978; *A Sparrow's Flight* (memoirs) 1990; *On the Constitution* 1992; *Values: Collapse and Cure* 1994. *Recreations:* In recent years, reading and study, formerly mountaineering and walking. *Clubs:* Carlton, Alpine, MCC. *Heir:* To disclaimed viscountcy, his son, Rt Hon. Douglas Martin Hogg, QC, MP, born February 5, 1945 (*qv*). *Name, Style and Title:* Raised to the peerage as Baron Hailsham of St Marylebone, of Herstmonceux in the County of Sussex 1970. A Conservative. *Address:* The Rt Hon. the Lord Hailsham of St Marylebone, KG, CH, FRS, The Corner House, Heathview Gardens, London, SW15 3SZ.

HAMBRO (Life Baron, UK), Charles Eric Alexander Hambro; cr. 1994

Son of late Sir Charles Hambro, KBE, MC. Born July 24, 1930; educated Eton. Married 1st, July 1, 1954, Rose Evelyn, daughter of Sir Richard Cotterell, 5th Bt, CBE (2 sons 1 daughter) (marriage dissolved 1976), married 2nd, July 2, 1976, Cherry Felicity, daughter of late Sir John Huggins, GCMG, MC. *Armed Forces:* Served Coldstream Guards 1949–51. *Career:* Joined Hambros Bank Ltd 1952: Managing Director 1957, Deputy Chairman 1965, Chairman 1972–83; Chairman, Hambros plc 1983–97; Director, Guardian Royal Exchange Assurance 1968, Chairman 1988–99; Director: Peninsula and Oriental Steamship Company 1987–, Taylor Woodrow 1984–97, General Oriental Investments, San Paolo Bank Holdings 1989–98. *Party Groups (General):* Senior Hon. Treasurer, Conservative Party 1993–97. *Other:* Chairman, Royal National

Pension Fund for Nurses 1968. *Trusts, etc:* Trustee, The British Museum 1984–94. Liveryman, Fishmongers' Company. *Recreations:* Shooting, golf. *Clubs:* White's, MCC. *Name, Style and Title:* Raised to the peerage as Baron Hambro, of Dixton and Dumbleton in the County of Gloucestershire 1994. A Conservative. *Address:* The Lord Hambro, Dixton Manor, Gotherington, Cheltenham, Gloucestershire, GL52 4RB *Tel:* 01242 672011; 21st Floor, LTC Building, 58–72 Upper Ground, London, SE1 9PA *Tel:* 020 7321 4189.

HAMLYN (Life Baron, UK), Paul Bertrand Hamlyn; cr. 1998; CBE 1993

Second son of late Professor Richard Hamburger and Mrs L Hamburger (née Hamburg). Born February 12, 1926; educated St Christopher's School, Letchworth, Herts; Hon. DLitt: Keele 1988, Warwick 1991. Married 1st, 1952, 1952, Eileen Margaret (Bobbie), daughter of Colonel Richard Watson (1 son 1 daughter) (marriage dissolved 1969); married 2nd, 1970, Mrs Helen Guest. *Career:* Publisher and Company Director; Founded: Books for Pleasure 1949, Prints for Pleasure 1960, Records for Pleasure and Golden Pleasure Books (jointly with Golden Press Inc. New York) 1961, Music for Pleasure (jointly with EMI) 1965, Hamlyn Publishing Group 1968, which he re-purchased from Reed International 1986; Director, IPC 1965–70; Chairman, IPC Books controlling Hamlyn Publishing Group 1965–70; Joint Managing Director, News International Ltd 1970–71; Chairman: Octopus Books 1971, Mandarin Offset (formerly Mandarin Publishers) Hong Kong 1971–97; Founder and Chairman, Octopus Publishing Group 1971–97; Director: News International Ltd 1971–86, Reed Book Publishing 1971–97, Octopus Books International BV (Holland) 1973–86, Octopus Books Ltd 1979–91, TV am 1981–83, Reed International Books 1983–97, Michelin House Development 1985–; Chairman, Heinemann Publishers (Oxford) Ltd (formerly Heinemann Group) 1985–97; Director: Bibendum Restaurant 1986–, Reed International 1987–97, Brandchart 1987–, Chateau de Bagnols 1988–, Michelin House Investment Co 1989–, Reed Elsevier 1993–98. *Chancellor:* Chancellor, Thames Valley University 1993–99. *Awards Granted:* Albert Medal, RSA 1993. *Trusts, etc:* Chairman, Trustees, Public Policy Centre 1985–87. *Honours:* CBE 1993. Hon. FRCSI (Dublin) 1993. *Name, Style and Title:* Raised to the peerage as Baron Hamlyn, of Edgeworth in the County of Gloucestershire 1998. Labour. *Address:* The Lord Hamlyn, CBE, 18 Queen Anne's Gate, London, SW1H 9AA *Tel:* 020 7227 3500.

HAMWEE (Life Baroness, UK), Sally Rachel Hamwee; cr. 1991

Daughter of late Alec and Dorothy Hamwee. Born January 12, 1947; educated Manchester High School for Girls; Girton College, Cambridge. *Councils, Public Bodies:* Councillor, London Borough of Richmond upon Thames 1978–98; Chairman, Planning Committee 1983–87; Vice-Chairman, Policy and Resources Committee 1987–91; Chairman, London Planning Advisory Committee 1986–94. *Career:* Admitted Solicitor 1972; Currently partner, Clintons Solicitors. *Spokesman:* Liberal Democrat Spokesman on: Local Government 1991–98, Housing and Planning 1993–98, Local Government and Planning 1998–; Principal Spokesman on Environment, Transport and the Regions 1999–. *Select Committees:* Member, House of Lords Select Committee on Relations between Central and Local Government 1995–96. *All-Party:* Member, All-Party: Housing and Homelessness Group, London Group, Children Group, Parenting Group, Building Societies Group. *Party Groups (General):* Past President, ALDC (Liberal Democrat Councillors' and Campaigners' Association); Member: National Executive, Liberal Party 1987–88, Federal Executive, Liberal Democrats 1989–91, Federal Policy Committee 1996–98. *Other:* Member of Council, Parents for Children 1977–86; Legal adviser, The Simon Community 1980–; Member of Council, Refuge (formerly Chiswick Family Rescue) 1991–; Chair, Xfm Ltd 1996–98; Member of Council, Family Policy Studies Centre; President, Town and Country Planning Association; Member, Joseph Rowntree Foundation Inquiry, Planning for Housing; Member, Advisory Council, London First. *Special Interests:* Local Government, Planning, London, Arts, Media, Housing. *Name, Style and Title:* Raised to the peerage as Baroness Hamwee, of Richmond upon Thames in the London Borough of Richmond upon Thames 1991. A Liberal Democrat. *Address:* The Baroness Hamwee, 101A Mortlake High Street, London, SW14 8HQ *Tel:* 020 8878 1380 *E-Mail:* sallyhamwee@cix.co.uk.

HANHAM (Life Baroness, UK), Joan Brownlow Hanham; cr. 1999; CBE 1997

Daughter of late Alfred and Mary Spark (née Mitchell). Born September 23, 1939; educated Hillcourt School, Dublin. Married 1964, Dr Iain William Ferguson Hanham, FRCP, FRCR (1 son 1 daughter). *Councils, Public Bodies:* Royal Borough of Kensington and Chelsea: Councillor 1970–, Mayor 1983–84, Chairman: Town Planning Committee 1984–86, Social Services Committee 1987–89, Policy and Resources Committee 1989–, Leader of the Council 1989–; Chairman, Policy Committee, London Boroughs Association 1991–95; JP: City of London Commission 1984, Inner London Family Proceedings Court 1992. *Other:* Director, London First 1996–; Governor: Sir John Cass Foundation 1996–, Sir John Cass primary School 1997–. *Trusts, etc:* Trustee: Commonwealth Institute 1991–, Children's Hospital Trust; Patron, Kensington Housing Trust (Appeal). *Miscellaneous:* Member, Mental Health Act Commission 1983–90; Non-Executive Member, North West Thames Regional Health Authority 1983–94; Non-Executive Director, Chelsea and Westminster Health Care NHS Trust 1994–. *Honours:* CBE 1997. Freeman, City of London 1984. *Special Interests:* Local Government, Health, Justice, Environment. *Recreations:* Music, travel. *Clubs:* Hurlingham. *Name, Style and Title:* Raised to the peerage as Baroness Hanham, of Kensington in the Royal Borough of Kensington and Chelsea 1999. A Conservative. *Address:* Councillor The Baroness Hanham, CBE, The Town Hall, Hornton Street, London, W8 7NX *Tel:* 020 7937 8692 *Fax:* 020 7361 3105.

HANNINGFIELD (Life Baron, UK), Paul Edward Winston White; cr. 1998; DL

Son of Edward Ernest William White and Irene Joyce Gertrude White (née Williamson. Born September 16, 1940; educated King Edward VI Grammar School, Chelmsford; Nuffield Scholarship for Agriculture (research in USA specialising in marketing in farming). *Councils, Public Bodies:* DL Essex; Essex County Council: Councillor, Stock Area 1970–, various positions from 1973–98 including Chairman of Education Committee, Chairman 1989–92, Leader of the Council 1998–99, Conservative Group Leader. *Career:* A Farmer. *International Bodies (General):* President, Assembly of European Regions Sub-Commission 1990–; Conservative Group Leader, Committee of the Regions, Member 1994–. *Party Groups (General):* Member, Chelmsford Conservative Party Executive 1962–; Chairman: Conservative Party (Stock Area) 1968–75, Conservative Party Eastern Area Local Government Advisory Committee 1995–98, Conservative Party National Local Government Advisory Committee, Conservative Councillors Association Steering Committee; Board Member, Conservative Party representing local government; Member, Conservative Party National Union Executive. *Other:* Member, National Executive, NFU 1965; Association of County Councils: Member 1981–97, Chairman of Education Committee 1989–93, Conservative Leader 1995–97. Chairman: Council of Local Education Authorities (CLEA) 1990–92; Eastern Region Further Education Funding Council 1992–97; Deputy Chairman and Conservative Group Leader, Local Government Association. *Miscellaneous:* Chairman, Chelmsford Young Farmers 1962; Member, Court of Essex University; Governor, Brentwood School, Essex. *Publications:* Several contributions to local government journals. *Recreations:* Botany, current affairs, travel, food and wine. *Name, Style and Title:* Raised to the peerage as Baron Hanningfield, of Chelmsford in the County of Essex 1998. A Conservative. *Address:* The Lord Hanningfield, DL, House of Lords, London, SW1A 0PW.

HANSON (Life Baron, UK), James Edward Hanson; cr. 1983; Kt 1976

Son of late Robert Hanson, CBE. Born January 20, 1922; Hon. LLD, Leeds 1984; Hon. DBA, Huddersfield 1991; Hon. Fellow: St Peter's College, Oxford 1996, Royal College of Radiologists 1998. Married 1959, Geraldine Kaelin (2 sons 1 step-daughter). *Armed Forces:* Served Duke of Wellington's Regiment (TA) 1939–46. *Career:* Chairman, Hanson plc 1965–97, Chairman Emeritus 1997–; Chairman, Hanson Transport Group Ltd 1965–96, Director 1997–; Former Chairman, Trident Television Ltd 1972–76, 1984–85, Director 1970–85. *Other:* Member, Court of Patrons, Royal College of Surgeons of England 1991. *Honours:* Kt 1976. Hon. Liveryman, Worshipful Company of Saddlers. *Special Intérests:* Industry. *Clubs:* Brooks's, Huddersfield Borough, The Brook (New York), Toronto (Canada). *Name, Style and Title:* Raised to the peerage as Baron Hanson, of Edgerton in the County of West Yorkshire 1983. A Conservative. *Address:* The Lord Hanson, 1 Grosvenor Place, London, SW1X 7JH *Tel:* 020 7245 6996.

HARDIE (Life Baron, UK), Andrew Rutherford Hardie; cr 1997; PC 1997; QC (Scot) 1985

Son of Andrew Rutherford and Elizabeth Currie Hardie. Born January 8, 1946; educated St Mungo's Primary School, Alloa; St Modan's High School, Stirling; Edinburgh University (MA, LLB Hons). Married 1971, Catherine Storrar Elgin (2 sons 1 daughter). *Career:* Solicitor 1971; Member, Faculty of Advocates 1973; Advocate Depute 1979–83; Treasurer, Faculty of Advocates 1989–94, Dean 1994–97. *House of Lords:* Lord Advocate 1997–; Lord Advocate, Scottish Executive 1999–. *Honours:* PC 1997. *Special Interests:* Childcare. *Recreations:* Cricket. *Clubs:* Caledonian. *Name, Style and Title:* Raised to the peerage as Baron Hardie, of Blackford in the City of Edinburgh 1997. Labour. *Address:* The Rt Hon. the Lord Hardie, QC, Lord Advocate's Department, 25 Chambers Street, Edinburgh, EH1 1LA *Tel:* 0131–226 2626.

HARDY OF WATH (Life Baron, UK), Peter Hardy; cr. 1997; DL

Son of late Lawrence Hardy, Miner – Underground Official. Born July 17, 1931; educated Wath-upon-Dearne Grammar School, South Yorkshire; Westminster College, London; Sheffield University; University of Leeds; College of Preceptors. Married July 28, 1954, Margaret Ann, daughter of C. A. Brookes, of Canada (2 sons). *Trades Union:* Sponsored by NACODS 1983–97; Hon. Life Member, UNISON. *Armed Forces:* RAF 1949–51 and Reserve service. *Councils, Public Bodies:* Councillor, Wath-upon-Dearne Urban District Council 1960–70, Chairman 1968; DL, South Yorkshire 1997–. *Career:* Teacher, South Yorkshire 1953–70; Head of Department 1960–70. *House of Commons:* Contested Scarborough and Whitby 1964 and Sheffield Hallam 1966; MP (Labour) for Rother Valley 1970–83 and for Wentworth 1983–97; Sponsored: The Badgers Act 1973, The Conservation of Wild Creatures and Wild Plants Act 1975, The Protection of Birds (Amendment) Act 1976, The Education (Northern Ireland) Act 1978; PPS: to Secretary of State for the Environment 1974–76, to Foreign and Commonwealth Secretary 1976–79. *Select Committees (Commons):* Member, Ecclesiastical Committee 1991–97. *Backbench Committees (Commons):* Chairman, Parliamentary Labour Party Energy Committee 1974–92. *All-Party Committees (Commons):* Vice-Chairman, All-Party Conservation Group 1973–97; Hon. Secretary, All-Party Group for Energy Studies 1992–97. *International Bodies (Commons):* Member, Delegation to Council of Europe and Western European Union 1976–97, Leader, Labour Delegation 1983–96; Vice-Chairman, Socialist Group of Council of Europe 1983–96; Chairman, Environment Committee 1986–90; Rapporteur Defence Committee WEU and for several Council of Europe Committees. *House of Lords:* Sponsor, Waste Minimisation Bill 1998. *Select Committees:* Member: Ecclesiastical Committee 1997–, Select Committee on Statutory Instruments (Joint Committee) 1999–. *Backbench Committees:* Chairman, Labour Party Departmental Committee for Defence; Member, Home Office Committee. *All-Party:* Vice-Chairman, All-Party Conservation Group 1997–; Hon. Secretary, All-Party Group for Energy Studies 1997–; Member, All-Party: Defence Studies Group, Family Farms Group. *International Bodies (General):* Vice-Chairman, Socialist Group WEU 1979–83; Leader, Labour delegation to Council of Europe and WEU 1983–95; Vice-Chairman, Socialist Group of Council of Europe 1983–95; Chairman, Council of Europe Committee on Environment 1986–89; Leader, Labour delegation to OSCE 1990–97; Rapporteur, Committee on Environment and Committee on Defence (WEU); Hon. Member, Parliamentary Assembly of Council of Europe 1997–. *Other:* Member: Council of RSPB 1985–89, Central Executive NSPCC 1986–94; Vice-President, The South Yorkshire Foundation; Hon. Member, The Kennel Club 1992; Member, Board of Landscape Foundation; President, South Yorkshire, North Derbyshire and Peak District Branch, CPRE; President, Air Training Corps Squadron, Rotherham. *Awards Granted:* Green Ribbon Award for Services to Conservation 1997. *Trusts, etc:* Patron, Yorkshire Wildlife Trust; Fellow, Industry and Parliament Trust. *Miscellaneous:* Defence attachment with RAF 1992; Involved in campaign to improve hedgerow protection for fifteen years. *Special Interests:* Energy, Wildlife, Conservation, Foreign Affairs, Home Affairs, Defence. *Recreations:* Wildlife observation, dogs, occasionally judging dogs. *Clubs:* Kennel. *Name, Style and Title:* Raised to the peerage as Baron Hardy of Wath, of Wath upon Dearne in the County of South Yorkshire 1997. Labour. *Address:* The Lord Hardy of Wath, DL, House of Lords, London, SW1A 0PW.

HARMAR-NICHOLLS (Life Baron, UK), Harmar Harmar-Nicholls; cr. 1974; 1st Bt of Darlaston (UK) 1960

Son of late Charles Nicholls, of Walsall, Staffs. Born November 1, 1912; educated Queen Mary's Grammar School, Walsall. Married 1940, Dorothy, daughter of James Edwards (2 daughters). *Armed Forces:* Served with Royal Engineers 1943–46 (India and Burma). *Career:* Director: J. & H. Nicholls Paints Ltd, Nicholls & Hennessy Hotels Ltd; Chairman, Radio Luxembourg (London) Ltd; MEP (Conservative) for Greater Manchester South in the European Parliament, June 1979–84. *House of Commons:* MP (Conservative) for Peterborough 1950–74; PPS to Assistant Postmaster-General 1951; Parliamentary Secretary to: Ministry of Agriculture, Fisheries & Food 1955–57, Ministry of Works 1957–60. *All-Party:* Member, All-Party British-Austrian Country Group. *Other:* President: Federation of Wholesale and Industrial Distributors, Association of Conference Executives. *Trusts, etc:* Chairman, Malvern Festival Theatre Trust Ltd. *Clubs:* St. Stephen's Constitutional. *Heir:* To Baronetcy, none. *Name, Style and Title:* Raised to the peerage as Baron Harmar-Nicholls, of Peterborough in the County of Cambridgeshire 1974. A Conservative. *Address:* The Lord Harmar-Nicholls, Abbeylands, Weston, Stafford, ST18 0HX *Tel:* 01889 270252.

HARRIS OF GREENWICH (Life Baron, UK), John Henry Harris; cr. 1974; PC 1998

Son of late Alfred George Harris. Born April 5, 1930; educated Pinner County Grammar School, Middlesex. Married 1st, September 1, 1952, Patricia Margaret Alstrom (1 son 1 daughter) (marriage dissolved 1982), married 2nd, March 25, 1983, Angela Smith. *Armed Forces:* National Service in the Directorate of Army Legal Services, The War Office. *Councils, Public Bodies:* Councillor, Harlow Council (Essex) 1957–63, Chairman 1960–61. *Career:* A director of companies; Journalist on newspapers in Bournemouth, Leicester, Glasgow and London; Personal Assistant to Rt Hon. Hugh Gaitskell as Leader of the Opposition 1960–62; Special Assistant to: Foreign Secretary 1964–66, Home Secretary 1966–67, Chancellor of the Exchequer 1967–70; Staff of *The Economist* 1970–74; Member, Executive Committee Britain in Europe Referendum Campaign 1975, Joint Chairman, Publicity Committee; Chairman, Parole Board for England and Wales 1979–82. *House of Lords:* Minister of State, Home Office 1974–79. *Whip:* Liberal Democrat Chief Whip 1994–. *Spokesman:* SDP Spokesman on Home Affairs 1983–88; Liberal Democrat Spokesman on Home Affairs 1988–94. *Select Committees:* Member, House of Lords Select Committees on: Murder and Life Imprisonment 1988–89, The Public Services 1996–97, House of Lords' Offices 1997–. *All-Party:* Member, All-Party Penal Reform Group (jointly with House of Commons). *Party Groups (General):* Director of Publicity, Labour Party 1962–64. *Other:* President, National Association of Senior Probation Officers 1983–93. *Trusts, etc:* Trustee, The Police Foundation, Chairman, Executive Committee. *Honours:* PC 1998. *Special Interests:* Criminal Justice. *Sportsclubs:* Member: Kent CCC, Durham CCC. *Clubs:* MCC, Reform. *Name, Style and Title:* Raised to the peerage as Baron Harris of Greenwich, of Greenwich in the County of Greater London 1974. A Liberal Democrat. *Address:* The Rt Hon. the Lord Harris of Greenwich, House of Lords, London, SW1A 0PW.

HARRIS OF HARINGEY (Life Baron, UK), Jonathan Toby Harris; cr. 1998

Son of Professor Harry Harris, FRS and of Mrs Muriel Harris. Born October 11, 1953; educated Haberdashers' Aske's School, Elstree; Trinity College, Cambridge (Natural Sciences and Economics) (President of the Union 1974). Married 1979, Ann Sarah Herbert (2 sons). *Trades Union:* Member, MSF. *Councils, Public Bodies:* London Borough of Haringey: Member 1978–, Chair, Social Services Committee 1982–87, Leader of the Council 1987–99; Member: London Ambulance Service NHS Trust 1998–, London Pension Fund Authority 1998–, Metropolitan Police Committee 1998–. *Career:* Economics Division, Bank of England 1975–79; Member, Electricity Consumers' Council 1979–86, Director 1983; Director, Association of Community Health Councils for England and Wales 1987–98. *International Bodies (General):* Committee of the Regions of EU: Member 1994–98, Alternate Member 1998–. *Party Groups (General):* Chair: Cambridge University

Labour Club 1973, Young Fabian Group 1976–77, Hornsey Labour Party 1978, 1979, 1980; Member: Labour Party National Policy Forum 1992–, Labour Party Local Government Committee 1993–. *Other:* Governor, National Institute for Social Work 1986–94; Board Member, London First 1993–; Executive Council Member, RNIB 1993–94; Member, Court of Middlesex University 1995–. *Trusts, etc:* Trustee: Evening Standard Blitz Memorial Appeal 1995–, Help for Health Trust 1995–, The Learning Agency 1996–; Chair, English National Stadium Trust 1997–. *Miscellaneous:* Deputy Chair, National Fuel Poverty Forum 1981–86; Deputy Chair, AMA 1991, Chair, Social Services Committee 1986–93; Member: London Drug Policy Forum 1990–, National Nursery Examination Board 1992–94, Home Office Advisory Council on Race Relations 1992–97; Chair, Association of London Authorities 1993–95, Deputy Chair 1990–93, Chair, Social Services Committee 1984–88; Chair: Local Government Anti-Poverty Unit 1994–97, Association of London Government 1995–; Member, Joint London Advisory Panel 1996–. FRSA. Freeman, City of London 1998. *Publications: Why Vote Labour?,* (with Nick Butler and Neil Kinnock) 1979; Contributor to *Economics of Prosperity,* 1980; *Energy and Social Policy,* (edited with Jonathan Bradshaw) 1983; Contributor to *Rationing in Action,* 1993; Contributor to *Whistleblowing in the Health Service: accountability, law and professional practice,* 1994. *Recreations:* Reading, walking. *Name, Style and Title:* Raised to the peerage as Baron Harris of Haringey, of Hornsey in the London Borough of Haringey 1998. Labour. *Address:* The Lord Harris of Haringey, 4 Beatrice Road, London, N4 4PD.

HARRIS OF HIGH CROSS (Life Baron, UK), Ralph Harris; cr. 1979

Son of late W. H. Harris. Born December 10, 1924; educated Tottenham Grammar School; Queens' College, Cambridge (Foundation Scholar); DSc honoris causa, Buckingham University 1984. Married November 5, 1949, Jose Jeffery (1 daughter and 2 sons deceased). *Career:* Lecturer, St Andrew's University 1949–56; Leader writer, Glasgow Herald 1956; General Director, Institute of Economic Affairs 1957–87, Chairman, Institute of Economic Affairs 1987–89, A director, Times Newspapers Holdings Ltd 1988–; Chairman, Bruges Group 1989–91; Founder President, Institute of Economic Affairs 1990–; Joint Chairman, International Centre for Research into Economic Transformation (Moscow) 1990–. *Other:* Member, Political Economy Club; Chairman, FOREST 1989–; President, Mont Pelerin Society 1982–84. *Trusts, etc:* Trustee: Wincott Foundation, McWhirter Foundation, Centre for Research into Communist Economies 1984–. *Miscellaneous:* Contested: Kirkcaldy (Liberal Unionist) 1951, Edinburgh Central (Conservative) 1955. *Publications:* Author of (with Arthur Seldon) several publications including: *Advertising in a Free Society*; *Hire Purchase in a Free Society*; *Choice in Welfare*; *Over-ruled on Welfare*; *Not from Benevolence*; *End of Government*; *Morality and Markets*; *Challenge of a Radical Reactionary*; *Beyond the Welfare State*; *No Prime Minister!*. *Special Interests:* European Union, Economic Policy, Social Policy, Russia, Eastern Europe. *Recreations:* Word processing, reading, sea swimming. *Name, Style and Title:* Raised to the peerage as Baron Harris of High Cross, of Tottenham in the County of Greater London 1979. A Cross-Bencher. *Address:* The Lord Harris of High Cross, 5 Catley Close, Wood Street, Barnet, Hertfordshire, EN5 4SN *Tel:* 020 8449 6212.

HARRIS OF PECKHAM (Life Baron, UK), Philip (Charles) Harris; cr. 1996; Kt 1985

Son of Charles Harris, MC and Ruth Harris. Born September 15, 1942; educated Streatham Grammar School; Hon. Fellow: Oriel College, Oxford 1989, United Medical and Dental Schools of Guy's and St Thomas' Hospital 1992, Goldsmith's College, Lewisham 1995. Married 1960, Pauline Norma Chumley (3 sons 1 daughter). *Career:* Chairman, Harris Queensway plc 1964–88, Chief Executive 1987–88; Non-executive director: Great Universal Stores 1986–, Fisons plc 1986–94; Chairman: Harris Ventures Ltd 1988–, C. W. Harris Properties 1988–97; Non-executive director, Molyneux Estates 1990–95; Chairman, Carpetright plc 1993–. *Party Groups (General):* Deputy Chairman, Conservative Party Treasurers 1993. *Other:* Member, British Show Jumping Association 1974; Member, United Medical and Dental Schools of Guy's and St Thomas's Hospitals 1984–, Governor 1983–; Member, Court of Patrons, Royal College of Gynaecologists 1984–; University of London Court 1990–94, Council Member 1994–96. *Awards Granted:* Hambro Business Man of the Year 1983. *Trusts, etc:* Chairman, Guy's and Lewisham NHS Trust 1991–93; Deputy Chairman,

Lewisham NHS Trust 1991–97. *Honours:* Kt 1985. Hon. Fellow, Royal College of Radiologists 1993. Freeman, City of London 1992. *Recreations:* Football, cricket, show jumping, tennis. *Name, Style and Title:* Raised to the peerage of Baron Harris of Peckham, of Peckham in the London Borough of Southwark 1996. A Conservative. *Address:* The Lord Harris of Peckham, Harris Ventures Limited, Philip Harris House, 1A Spur Road, Orpington, Kent, BR6 0AR *Tel:* 01689 875135 *Fax:* 01689 870781.

HARRIS OF RICHMOND (Life Baroness, UK), Angela Felicity Harris; cr. 1999; DL

Daughter of late Rev. G H Hamilton Richards and Eva Richards. Born January 4, 1944; educated Canon Slade Grammar School, Bolton; Ealing Hotel and Catering College. Married 1976, John Philip Roger Harris, son of Philip and Margaret Harris (1 son from previous marriage). *Councils, Public Bodies:* Councillor, Richmond Town Council 1978–81, 1991–99, Mayor 1993–94; Councillor, Richmondshire District Council 1979–89, Chair 1987–88; Councillor, North Yorkshire County Council 1981–, Chair 1991–92; DL, North Yorkshire; JP 1982–98; Non-Executive Director, Northallerton NHS Trust 1990–97; Deputy Chairman, National Association of Police Authorities 1997–; Member, Service Authority of National Crime Squad and Police Negotiating Board. *Other:* Patron, Hospice Homecare, Northallerton; Member: Trauma International, Lister House (Royal British Legion). *Miscellaneous:* A Liberal Democrat candidate in European Elections 1999. *Special Interests:* Police. *Recreations:* Music, political biographies, novels of Lindsey Davis. *Name, Style and Title:* Raised to the peerage as Baroness Harris of Richmond, of Richmond in the County of North Yorkshire 1999. A Liberal Democrat. *Address:* The Baroness Harris of Richmond, DL, House of Lords, London, SW1A 0PW.

HARRISON (Life Baron, UK), Lyndon Henry Arthur Harrison; cr. 1999

Son of late Charles and Edith Harrison. Born September 28, 1947; educated Oxford School; Warwick University (BA Hons); Sussex University (MA); Keele University (MA). Married October 25, 1980, Hilary Plank (1 son 1 daughter). *Trades Union:* Member, GMB. *Councils, Public Bodies:* Former Councillor, Cheshire County Council, Chairman: Libraries Committee 1982, 1984–89, Tourism Committee 1985–89, Further Education Committee 1984–89. *Career:* Research Officer, UMIST Union, Manchester 1975–78; Union Manager, North East Wales Institute, Clwyd 1978–89; MEP for Cheshire West 1989–94, and for Cheshire West and Wirral 1994–99; Vice-Chair, Rules of Procedure 1989–92; Substitute, Youth and Education Committee 1989–92; Member: Mashreq Delegation 1989–92, Regional Policy and Planning Committee 1989–94; Substitute, United States Delegation 1989–94; Secretary, European Parliamentary Labour Party 1991–94; Member: Economic and Monetary Affairs Committee 1992–99, Delegation for ASEAN, South-East Asia and Republic of Korea 1992–99, Monetary Affairs Sub-committee 1994–99; Substitute, Transport and Tourism Committee 1994–99; EPLP-DTI Link Person 1999; Former Socialist Spokesman on: Monetary Affairs Sub-Committee, ASEAN and Korea Delegation; Former Vice-President: Tourism Intergroup, Small and Medium-sized Enterprises (SME) Intergroup, Maritime Intergroup. *Miscellaneous:* Deputy Chairman, North West Tourist Board 1986–89; Vice-President, Association of County Councils 1990–97. *Special Interests:* Small Business, Tourism, Monetary Union, Children. *Recreations:* Chess, the arts, sport. *Name, Style and Title:* Raised to the peerage as Baron Harrison, of Chester in the County of Cheshire 1999. Labour. *Address:* The Lord Harrison, 3 Newton Lane, Hoole, Chester, Cheshire, CH2 3RB *Tel:* 01244 343428.

Dod *on* Disk

The Vacher Dod Parliamentary Database – configured for PC or Network

For further details please telephone the Westminster Office

020 7828 7256

HARTWELL (Life Baron, UK), William Michael Berry; cr. 1968; 3rd Bt of Long Cross (UK) 1921; MBE (Mil) 1944; TD

Son of 1st Viscount Camrose, DL. Born May 18, 1911. Succeeded his brother to viscountcy, barony, and baronetcy 1995; disclaimed the viscountcy and barony of Camrose for life on March 9, 1995 under the provisions of the Peerage Act, 1963; educated Eton; Christ Church, Oxford (MA). Married January 7, 1936, Lady Pamela Margaret Elizabeth Smith (died 1982), younger daughter of 1st Earl of Birkenhead, PC, GCSI, KC (2 sons 2 daughters). *Armed Forces:* Second Lieutenant, (City of London Yeomanry) Light Anti-Aircraft Regiment, RA (TA) 1938; Served War of 1939–45 (despatches twice, MBE); Captain and Major 1940, Lieutenant-Colonel 1944. *Career:* Editor, *Sunday Mail*, Glasgow 1934–35; Managing Editor, *Financial Times* 1937–39; Chairman, Amalgamated Press Ltd 1954–59; Chairman and Editor-in-Chief: *The Daily Telegraph* 1954–87, *The Sunday Telegraph* 1961–87; Director, The Daily Telegraph (later The Telegraph plc) 1946–95. *Publications: Party Choice*, 1948; *William Camrose, Giant of Fleet Street*, 1992. *Clubs:* White's, Beefsteak, Royal Yacht Squadron (Cowes). *Heir:* To disclaimed viscountcy and barony, his son, Hon. Adrian Michael Berry, born June 15, 1937. *Name, Style and Title:* Raised to the peerage as Baron Hartwell, of Peterborough Court in the City of London 1968. A Cross-Bencher. *Address:* The Lord Hartwell, MBE, TD, 18 Cowley Street, London, SW1H 0BH *Tel:* 020 7222 4673; Office: 36 Broadway, London, SW1H 0BH *Tel:* 020 7222 3833; Oving House, Whitchurch, Nr Aylesbury, Bucks, HP22 4HN *Tel:* 01296 641307.

HASKEL (Life Baron, UK), Simon Haskel; cr. 1993

Son of late Isaac and Julia Haskel. Born October 8, 1934; educated Sedbergh School; Salford College of Advanced Technology (now Salford University). Married June 24, 1962, Carole, daughter of Wilbur Lewis, and late Frances Lewis, of New York (1 son 1 daughter). *Armed Forces:* National Service Commission, Royal Artillery 1959. *Career:* Joined Perrotts Ltd 1961; Chairman, Perrotts Group plc and associated companies 1973–97. *Whip:* An Opposition Whip 1994–97; A Lord in Waiting (Government Whip) 1997–98. *Spokesman:* An Opposition Spokesman on Trade and Industry 1994–97; A Spokesman on: Social Security 1997–98, Trade and Industry 1997–98, the Treasury 1997–98. *Select Committees:* Member, Select Committees on: Science and Technology 1994–97, Science and Technology Sub-Committee II (Science and Society) 1999–. *All-Party:* Co-Chairman, Parliamentary Manufacturing and Industry Group 1996–97. *Party Groups (General):* Joined Labour Party 1968; Founder Member, Labour Party Industry 1972 Group, Secretary 1976–81; Secretary, Labour Finance and Industry Group 1982–90, Chairman 1990–96. *Other:* Vice-Chairman, Institute of Jewish Affairs 1993–; Chairman, Thames Concerts Society 1982–90. *Trusts, etc:* Trustee, Lord and Lady Haskel Charitable Foundation. *Miscellaneous:* Member, Joint Committee on Financial Services and Regulation Bill. *Special Interests:* Trade and Industry, Science and Technology. *Recreations:* Music, cycling. *Sportsclubs:* Cyclists' Touring, Tandem. *Clubs:* Reform. *Name, Style and Title:* Raised to the peerage as Baron Haskel, of Higher Broughton in the County of Greater Manchester 1993. Labour. *Address:* The Lord Haskel, House of Lords, London, SW1A 0PW *E-Mail:* haskel@compuserve.com.

HASKINS (Life Baron, UK), Christopher Robin Haskins; cr. 1998

Son of Robin and Margaret Haskins. Born May 30, 1937; educated St Columba's College, Dublin; Trinity College, Dublin (BA); Hon. LLB, Hull University. Married 1959, Gilda Horsley (3 sons 2 daughters). *Councils, Public Bodies:* Member, Board of "Yorkshire Forward" Regional Development Agency. *Career:* Ford Motor Company, Dagenham 1960–62; Northern Foods 1962–, Chairman 1986–. *All-Party:* Member, All-Party: Consumer Affairs and Trading Standards Group, Irish in Britain Group, Ireland in Schools Group. *International Bodies (General):* Member: Aspen Institute, Italia. *Trusts, etc:* Trustee: Runnymede Trust 1989–, Demos 1993–, Civil Liberties Trust 1997–, Legal Assistance Trust 1998–. *Miscellaneous:* Member: Commission for Social Justice 1992–94, UK Round Table on Sustainable Development 1995–97, Hampel Committee on Corporate Governance 1996–97, New Deal Task Force 1997–; Chairman, Better Regulation Task Force 1997–. *Special Interests:* Europe. *Name, Style and Title:* Raised to the peerage as Baron Haskins, of Skidby in the County of the East Riding of Yorkshire 1998. Labour. *Address:* The Lord Haskins, Quarryside Farm, Skidby, Nr Cottingham, East Yorkshire, HU16 5TG *Tel:* 01482 842692.

HASLAM (Life Baron, UK), Robert Haslam; cr. 1990; Kt 1985

Son of late Percy and Mary Haslam. Born February 4, 1923; educated Bolton School; Birmingham University; Hon. DEng, Birmingham University; Hon. DTech, Brunel University. Married 1st, June 5, 1947, Joyce (died March 29, 1995), daughter of late Frederick Quin (2 sons), married 2nd, July 20, 1996, Elizabeth, daughter of late William Norman Pitt, of Hampton, Middlesex, and widow of Hon. Michael David Sieff, CBE. *Career:* Mining Engineer: Manchester Collieries 1944, National Coal Board 1947; Personnel Director, ICI Nobel Division 1960; Commercial Director, ICI Plastics Division 1963, Deputy Chairman 1966; Deputy Chairman, ICI Fibres 1969, Chairman 1971; Director, Main Board ICI plc 1974, Deputy Chairman 1980–83; Chairman, ICI Americas Inc. 1978–81; Director: Imperial Metal Industries Ltd. 1975–77, AECI 1978–79; Non-Exec Director, Cable and Wireless 1982–83; Chairman: Tate and Lyle plc 1983–86, British Steel plc 1983–86; Chairman, Nationalised Industries Chairmen's Group 1985–86; Member, NEDC 1985–89; Director, Bank of England 1985–93; Advisory Director, Unilever plc 1986–93; Chairman: British Coal Corporation 1986–90, Bechtel Ltd 1991–94, Wasserstein Perella & Co Ltd 1991–99, British Occupational Health Research Foundation 1991–, Michael Sieff Foundation 1995–. *Select Committees:* Member: Sub-Committee A of European Communities Committee 1993–97, Select Committee on European Communities 1997–99, Select Committee on European Communities Sub-Committee B (Energy, Industry and Transport) 1997–. *Other:* Chairman: Council, Manchester Business School 1985–90, Governors of Bolton School 1990–97. Freeman, City of London 1985. *Special Interests:* Energy, Finance, Industry, Industrial Relations, Environment. *Recreations:* Golf, travel. *Sportsclubs:* Wentworth Golf. *Name, Style and Title:* Raised to the peerage as Baron Haslam, of Bolton in the County of Greater Manchester 1990. A Conservative. *Address:* The Lord Haslam, Tokeneke Lodge, East Drive, Virginia Water, Surrey, GU25 4JY *Tel:* 01344 842553.

HATTERSLEY (Life Baron, UK), Roy Sydney George Hattersley; cr. 1997; PC 1975

Son of late Frederick Roy Hattersley. Born December 28, 1932; educated Sheffield City Grammar School; University of Hull (BSc Economics). Married 1956, Molly Loughran. *Trades Union:* Member, NUJ. *Councils, Public Bodies:* Councillor, Sheffield City Council 1957–65. *House of Commons:* Contested Sutton Coldfield in 1959; MP (Labour) for Birmingham Sparkbrook 1964–97; PPS to Minister of Pensions October 1964-February 1967; Parliamentary Secretary, Ministry of Labour March 1967-March 1968; Parliamentary Under-Secretary of State, Department of Employment and Productivity March 1968-August 1969; Minister of Defence for Administration August 1969–70; Minister of State, Foreign and Commonwealth Affairs 1974–76; Secretary of State for Prices and Consumer Protection September 1976–79; Deputy Leader, Labour Party 1983–92. *Spokesman (Commons):* Opposition Spokesman on: Defence 1972, Education and Science 1972–74; Principal Opposition Front Bench Spokesman on: the Environment May 1979-December 1980, Home Affairs Dec 1980–83, Treasury and Economic Affairs October 1983–87, Home Affairs June 1987–92. *Party Groups (General):* Joined Labour Party 1949. *Honours:* PC 1975. *Publications:* Author of: *Nelson*, 1974; *Goodbye to Yorkshire*, (essays) 1976; *Politics Apart*, 1982; *Press Gang*, 1983; *A Yorkshire Boyhood*, 1983; *Endpiece Revisited*, (essays) 1985; *Choose Freedom: the future for Democratic Socialism*, 1987; *Economic Priorities for a Labour Government*, 1987; *The Maker's Mark* (novel), 1990; *In that Quiet Earth*, (novel) 1991; *Between Ourselves*, (essays) 1993; *Who Goes Home? Scenes from a Political Life*, 1995; *Fifty Years On*, 1997. *Recreations:* Writing, watching football and cricket. *Clubs:* Garrick. *Name, Style and Title:* Raised to the peerage as Baron Hattersley, of Sparkbrook in the County of West Midlands 1997. Labour. *Address:* The Rt Hon. the Lord Hattersley, House of Lords, London, SW1A 0PW.

HAYHOE (Life Baron, UK), Bernard (Barney) John Hayhoe; cr. 1992; Kt 1987; PC 1985

Son of late Frank and Catherine Hayhoe. Born August 8, 1925; educated State schools; Croydon and Borough Polytechnics. Married 1962, Ann Gascoigne, daughter of late Bernard W. Thornton (2 sons 1 daughter). *Career:* Tool Room Apprentice 1941–44; Technical and Engineering appointments in Ministry of Supply and Ministry of Aviation 1944–63; Associate Director, Ariel Foundation 1963–65; Head of Research Section, Conservative Research Department 1965–70; Director: Portman Building Society 1987–96, Abbott Laboratories Inc. 1989–96. *House of Commons:* MP (Conservative) for: Heston and Isleworth 1970–74, Brentford and Isleworth 1974–92; PPS to Lord President of the Council and Leader of the House of Commons 1972–74; Parliamentary Under-Secretary of State for Defence (Army) 1979–81; Minister of State: Civil Service Department January–November 1981, Treasury 1981–85; Minister of State for Health, DHSS 1985–86. *Spokesman (Commons):* An Opposition Spokesman on Employment 1974–79. *Select Committees (Commons):* Member, Select Committees on: Race Relations and Immigration 1971–73, Defence 1987–92. *Backbench Committees (Commons):* Joint Hon. Secretary, Conservative Parliamentary Employment Committee 1970–73, Vice-Chairman 1973–76. *Select Committees:* Member, Select Committee on the Public Service 1997–98. *Party Groups:* Member, Association of Conservative Peers Executive Committee 1995–98. *Party Groups (General):* Joint Secretary, Conservative Group for Europe 1970, Vice-Chairman 1973–76; Chairman, The Hansard Society 1991–94. *Other:* Governor, Birkbeck College 1976–79; President, Help The Hospices 1992–98. *Trusts, etc:* Chairman, The Guys and St Thomas' NHS Trust 1993–95; Trustee: The Tablet Trust 1991–, British Brain and Spine Foundation 1992–, Liver Research Trust 1994–. *Honours:* PC 1985; Kt 1987. CEng; FIMechE. *Clubs:* Garrick. *Name, Style and Title:* Raised to the peerage as Baron Hayhoe, of Isleworth in the London Borough of Hounslow 1992. A Conservative. *Address:* The Rt Hon. the Lord Hayhoe, 20 Wool Road, London, SW20 0HW *Tel:* 020 8947 0037.

HAYMAN (Life Baroness, UK), Helene (Valerie) Hayman; cr. 1996

Daughter of late Maurice and Maude Middleweek. Born March 26, 1949; educated Wolverhampton Girls' High School; Newnham College, Cambridge (MA) (President of Union 1969); Hon. Fellow, University of North London 1995; Hon. Doctorate, Middlesex University 1996. Married August 30, 1974, Martin Heathcote, son of Ronald and Rosemary Hayman (4 sons). *Councils, Public Bodies:* Member, Bloomsbury Health Authority 1985–88; Vice-Chairman: Bloomsbury Health Authority 1988–90, Bloomsbury and Islington Health Authority 1991–92. *Career:* With Shelter, National Campaign for the Homeless 1969–71; Social Services Department, London Borough of Camden 1971–74; Deputy Director, National Council for One Parent Families 1974; Member, Royal College of Gynaecologists Ethics Committee 1982–97; Member, University College London/University College Hospital Committee on Ethics of Clinical Investigation 1987–97, Vice Chairman 1990–97; Member, Council, University College, London 1992–97; Chairman, Whittington Hospital NHS Trust 1992–97. *House of Commons:* Contested (Labour) Wolverhampton South West, February 1974; MP (Labour) for Welwyn and Hatfield, October 1974–79. *House of Lords:* Parliamentary Under-Secretary of State: Department of the Environment, Transport and the Regions (Minister for Roads) 1997–98, Department of Health 1998–99; Minister of State, Ministry of Agriculture, Fisheries and Food 1999–. *Spokesman:* An Opposition Spokeswoman on Health 1996–97; A Spokeswoman on: Environment, Transport and the Regions 1997–98, Health 1998–99, Agriculture 1999–. *Special Interests:* Health, Education. *Name, Style and Title:* Raised to the peerage as Baroness Hayman, of Dartmouth Park in the London Borough of Camden 1996. Labour. *Address:* The Baroness Hayman, House of Lords, London, SW1A 0PW.

HEALEY (Life Baron, UK), Denis Winston Healey; cr. 1992; PC 1964; CH 1979; MBE (Mil) 1945

Son of late William Healey. Born August 30, 1917; educated Bradford Grammar School; Balliol College, Oxford (BA, MA); Hon. Fellow, Balliol College, Oxford 1979; Hon. DLitt, Bradford University 1990; Hon. Degree: Sussex University, Leeds University; Hon. Fellow, Birkbeck College 1999. Married December 21, 1945, Edna May, daughter of Edward Edmunds, of Coleford, Gloucestershire (1 son 2 daughters). *Armed Forces:* Served North Africa and Italy in Second World War (mentioned in despatches, MBE), Major RE. *House of Commons:* Contested (Labour) Pudsey and Otley 1945 General Election; MP (Labour) for: South East Leeds 1952–55, Leeds East 1955–92; Member, Shadow Cabinet 1959–64, 1970–74, 1979–87; Secretary of State for Defence 1964–70; Chancellor of the Exchequer 1974–79. *Spokesman (Commons):* Opposition Spokesman on Foreign Affairs 1983–87. *Party Groups (General):* Secretary, International Department, Labour Party 1945–52; Member, Labour Party National Exec Committee 1970–75; Deputy Leader, Labour Party 1980–83. *Miscellaneous:* Chairman, IMF Interim Committee 1977–79. *Honours:* MBE (Mil) 1945; PC 1964; CH 1979; Grand Cross of Order of Merit (Germany) 1979. Freeman, City of Leeds 1991. *Publications:* Author of several political works and Fabian essays as well as: *Healey's Eye*, 1980; *The Time of My Life*, (autobiography) 1989; *When Shrimps Learn to Whistle* (essays), 1990; *My Secret Planet* (anthology) 1992; *Denis Healey's Yorkshire Dales*, 1995. *Special Interests:* Foreign Affairs, Defence, Arts. *Recreations:* Music, painting photography, gardening. *Name, Style and Title:* Raised to the peerage as Baron Healey, of Riddlesden in the County of West Yorkshire 1992. Labour. *Address:* The Rt Hon. the Lord Healey, CH, MBE, House of Lords, London, SW1A 0PW.

HENDERSON OF BROMPTON (Life Baron, UK), Peter Gordon Henderson; cr. 1984; KCB 1975

Son of late James Alexander Leo Henderson. Born September 16, 1922; educated Stowe; Magdalen College, Oxford. Married September 2, 1950, Susan Mary, daughter of R. C. G. Dartford, MC (2 sons 2 daughters). *Armed Forces:* Served Scots Guards 1942–44. *Career:* Clerk, House of Lords 1954–60; Seconded to HM Treasury as Secretary to Leader and Chief Whip, House of Lords 1960–63; Reading Clerk and Clerk of Public Bills 1964–74; Member, Committee on preparation of legislation 1973–74; Clerk Assistant 1974; Clerk of the Parliaments 1974–83. *Other:* President: The New Bridge 1987, Progress 1992; Vice-President, Population Concern. *Trusts, etc:* President, John Hunt Award Trust 1986. *Honours:* KCB 1975. *Name, Style and Title:* Raised to the peerage as Baron Henderson of Brompton, of Brompton in the Royal Borough of Kensington and Chelsea and of Brough in the County of Cumbria 1984. A Cross-Bencher. The Lord Henderson of Brompton died on January 13, 2000.

HENLEY (8th Baron, I), Oliver Michael Robert Eden; cr. 1799; 6th Baron Northington (UK) 1885

Son of 7th Baron. Born November 22, 1953. Succeeded his father 1977. Sits as Baron Northington; educated Dragon School, Oxford; Clifton College; Durham University. Married October 11, 1984, Caroline Patricia, daughter of late Alan Sharp, of Mackney, Oxfordshire (3 sons 1 daughter). *Councils, Public Bodies:* County Councillor, Cumbria 1986–89. *Career:* Called to the Bar, Middle Temple 1977. *House of Lords:* Joint Parliamentary Under-Secretary of State: Department of Social Security 1989–93, Department of Employment 1993–94; Ministry of Defence 1994–95; Minister of State, Department of Education and Employment 1995–97; A Deputy Speaker 1999–; A Deputy Chairman of Committees 1999–; An elected hereditary peer 1999–. *Whip:* A Lord in Waiting (Government Whip and Spokesman for Health) February–July 1989; Opposition Chief Whip in the House of Lords December 1998–. *Spokesman:* An Opposition Spokesman for: Defence 1997, Education and Employment 1997, Treasury 1997–98, Home Affairs 1997–98, Constitutional Affairs December 1998–June 1999, Cabinet Office June 1999–. *Select Committees:* Member, Select Committee on Selection 1999–. *Party Groups (General):* Chairman, Penrith and the Border Conservative Association 1987–89, President 1989–94. *Miscellaneous:* President, Cumbria Association of Local Councils 1981–89. *Clubs:* Brooks's, Pratt's. *Heir:* His son, Hon. John Michael Oliver Eden, born June 30, 1988. A Conservative. *Address:* The Lord Henley, Scaleby Castle, Carlisle, Cumbria, CA6 4LN *E-Mail:* henleyo@parliament.uk.

HEREFORD (103rd Bishop of), John Keith Oliver

Son of Walter and Ivy Oliver. Born April 14, 1935; educated Westminster School; Gonville and Caius College, Cambridge (MA, MLitt); Westcott House. Married 1961, Meriel Moore (2 sons 1 daughter). *Career:* Assistant Curate, Hilborough Group of Parishes, Norfolk 1964–68; Chaplain and Assistant Master, Eton College 1968–72; Team Rector: South Molton Group of Parishes, Devon 1973–82, Parish of Central Exeter 1982–85; Archdeacon of Sherborne 1985–90; Bishop of Hereford 1990– ; Chairman, Advisory Board of Ministry 1993–; Took his seat in the House of Lords 1997. *Spokesman:* Spokesman for the Bench of Bishops on Environmental, Agricultural and Transport Issues. *Other:* Chairman, West Midlands Churches' Forum; President, Herefordshire CPRE. *Trusts, etc:* Trustee, Eveson Charitable Trust; President, River Wye Preservation Trust. *Publications: The Church and Social Order,* 1968; Contributions to: *Theology, Crucible. Special Interests:* Transport, Environment. *Recreations:* Railways, music, architecture, motorcycling. *Sportsclubs:* Worcester Cricket Club. *Clubs:* United Oxford and Cambridge University. *Address:* The Rt Rev. the Lord Bishop of Hereford, Bishop's House, The Palace, Hereford, HR4 9BN.

HIGGINS (Life Baron, UK), Terence Langley Higgins; cr. 1997; KBE 1993; PC 1979; DL

Son of late Reginald and Rose Higgins. Born January 18, 1928; educated Alleyn's School, Dulwich; Gonville and Caius College, Cambridge (MA); Yale University, USA. Married September 30, 1961, HE Judge Rosalyn Higgins, DBE, QC (Member of the International Court of Justice), daughter of Lewis Cohen (1 son 1 daughter). *Armed Forces:* Served in the RAF 1946–48. *Councils, Public Bodies:* DL, West Sussex 1988. *Career:* New Zealand Shipping Co., in UK and New Zealand 1948–55; British Olympic Team 1948, 1952; Commonwealth Games Team 1950; Former President, Cambridge Union 1958; Economic Specialist, Unilever Ltd 1958–64; Economic Consultant, Lex Services Group plc 1975–; Director: Warne Wright Group 1976–84, Lex Service Group 1980–92; First Choice Holidays plc (formerly Owners Abroad plc) 1991–97; Chairman and Trustee, Lex Services Pension Fund 1994–. *House of Commons:* MP (Conservative) for Worthing 1964–97; Minister of State, Treasury 1970–72; Financial Secretary, Treasury 1972–74. *Spokesman (Commons):* Conservative Opposition Front Bench Spokesman on Treasury and Economic Affairs 1967–70; Opposition Spokesman on: Treasury and Economic Affairs 1974, Trade 1974–76. *Select Committees (Commons):* Member, Select Committee on Treasury and Civil Service 1971–92, Chairman 1984–92; Chairman, Select Committee on Procedure (Finance) 1981–82; Chairman, House of Commons Liaison Committee 1984–97; Chairman, Public Accounts Commission 1996–97, Member 1984–97. *Backbench Committees (Commons):* Secretary, Conservative Parliamentary Finance Committee 1965–67; Chairman: Conservative Sport and Recreation Committee 1979–82, Conservative Transport Committee 1979–92; Member, 1922 Executive Committee 1980–97. *Spokesman:* Principal Opposition Spokesman for Social Security 1997–; Opposition Spokesman for the Treasury 1997–99. *Party Groups (General):* Former Treasurer, Cambridge University Conservative Association. *Other:* Governor: Dulwich College 1980–95, National Institute Economic Social Research 1988–, Alleyn's School, Dulwich 1995–99. *Trusts, etc:* Trustee, Industry and Parliament Trust 1987–92. *Miscellaneous:* Council, Royal Institute of International Affairs 1980–85; Council, Institute of Advanced Motorists 1980–97, Fellow 1997. *Honours:* PC 1979; KBE 1993. Freeman, Worthing 1997. *Special Interests:* Finance, Transport, Sport, Social Security. *Recreations:* Golf. *Sportsclubs:* Royal Blackheath Golf, Worthing Golf, Koninklijke Haagsche Golf. *Clubs:* Hawk's (Cambridge), Reform, Yale Club of London. *Name, Style and Title:* Raised to the peerage as Baron Higgins, of Worthing in the County of West Sussex 1997. A Conservative. *Address:* The Rt Hon. the Lord Higgins, KBE, DL, House of Lords, London, SW1A 0PW *E-Mail:* higginst@parliament.uk.

HILL-NORTON (Life Baron, UK), Peter John Hill-Norton; cr. 1979; GCB (Mil) 1970; KCB 1967

Son of late Captain Martin John Norton and late Mrs M. B. Gooch. Born February 8, 1915; educated Royal Naval Colleges, Dartmouth and Greenwich. Married July 30, 1936, Margaret Eileen, daughter of late C. A. Linstow (1 son 1 daughter). *Armed Forces:* Served War 1939–45, Arctic Convoys and NW Approaches; Commander 1948; Captain 1952; Naval Attaché, Argentina, Uruguay and Paraguay 1953–55; Commanded: HMS Decoy 1956–57, HMS Ark Royal 1959–61; Second Sea Lord and Chief of Naval Personnel January-August 1967; Vice-Chief of Naval Staff 1967–68; Commander-in-Chief, Far East 1969–70; First Sea Lord 1970–71; Chief of Defence Staff 1971–73; Chairman, NATO Military Committee 1974–77. *All-Party:* Member, All-Party Defence Study Group. *Other:* Friends of Osborne House. Freeman, City of London 1973. Liveryman, Worshipful Company of Shipwrights. *Publications:* Author of: *No Soft Options*, 1978; *Sea Power*, 1982. *Special Interests:* Defence, UFOs. *Honours:* CB 1964; KCB 1967; GCB (Mil) 1970. *Recreations:* Shooting, gardening. *Clubs:* Army and Navy, Royal Navy of 1765. *Name, Style and Title:* Raised to the peerage as Baron Hill-Norton, of South Nutfield in the County of Surrey 1979. A Cross-Bencher. *Address:* Admiral of the Fleet The Lord Hill-Norton, GCB, Cass Cottage, Hyde, Fordingbridge, Hampshire, SP6 2QH.

HILTON OF EGGARDON (Life Baroness, UK), Jennifer Hilton; cr. 1991; QPM 1989

Daughter of late John Robert Hilton, CMG, and of Margaret Frances Hilton. Born January 12, 1936; educated Bedales School, Hampshire; Manchester University (MA, BA (Hons) Psychology); London University (Diplomas: Criminology, History of Art). *Career:* Joined Metropolitan Police as Constable 1956; Sergeant 1961; Inspector 1965; Served Stepney, King's Cross, East Ham Islington, Cannon Row, Hammersmith; Manchester University (Police Scholarship) 1967–71; National Police Staff College, directing staff (Psychology and Management Studies); Chief Inspector 1973–74; Metropolitan Police Management Services (Research on Recruitment and Wastage) 1975–76; Superintendent/Chief Superintendent, Airport, Battersea and Chiswick Divisions (responsible for policing Brentford Football 1979–83) 1977–83; Senior Command Course, National Staff College 1979; New Scotland Yard, responsible for Traffic and Forward Planning 1983–84; Promoted to Commander at New Scotland Yard 1984, responsible for Courts, Obscene Publications, Neighbourhood Policing, Uniform Department, Planning and Projects, and Police Regulations; North West London, responsible for Complaints/Discipline, Personnel, Community Relations 1987–88; Peel Centre, Hendon, responsible for all Metropolitan Police Training 1988–90; Retired 1990; Member of: ACPOs Executive Committee, Equal Opportunities, Extended Interview Panel, Various Home Office Committees. *Whip:* Opposition Whip 1991–95. *Spokesman:* An Opposition Spokesman on: the Environment 1991–97, Home Affairs 1994–97. *Select Committees:* Member, Environment Sub-Committee of European Communities Committee 1991–95, Chairman 1995–97; Member: Science and Technology Select Committee 1992–95, Select Committee on European Communities 1997–; Chairman: Select Committee on European Communities Sub-Committee C (Environment, Public Health and Consumer Protection) 1997–99, Advisory Panel on Works of Art. *Honours:* QPM 1989. *Publications:* Author of: *The Gentle Arm of the Law*, 1967 (with S. M. Hunt); *Individual Development and Social Experience*, 1974. *Special Interests:* Environment, Race Relations, Criminal Justice. *Recreations:* Gardening, travel, art. *Name, Style and Title:* Raised to the peerage as Baroness Hilton of Eggardon, of Eggardon in the County of Dorset 1991. Labour. *Address:* The Baroness Hilton of Eggardon, QPM, House of Lords, London, SW1A 0PW.

HOBHOUSE OF WOODBOROUGH (Life Baron, UK), John Stewart Hobhouse; cr. 1998; Kt 1982; PC 1993

Born January 31, 1932; educated Christ Church, Oxford (BCL 1955, MA 1958). Married 1959, Susannah Roskill (2 sons 1 daughter). *Career:* Called to the Bar, Inner Temple 1955; QC 1973; A Judge of the High Court, Queen's Bench Division 1982–93; A Lord Justice of Appeal 1993–98; A Lord of Appeal in Ordinary 1998–. *Honours:* Kt 1982; PC 1993. *Name, Style and Title:* Raised to the peerage as Baron Hobhouse of Woodborough, of Woodborough in the County of Wiltshire 1998. A Cross-Bencher. *Address:* The Rt Hon. the Lord Hobhouse of Woodborough, House of Lords, London, SW1A 0PW.

HOFFMANN (Life Baron, UK), Leonard Hubert Hoffmann; cr. 1995; Kt 1985; PC 1992

Son of B. W. Hoffmann and G. Hoffmann. Born May 8, 1934; educated South African College School, Cape Town; University of Cape Town (BA); The Queen's College, Oxford (Rhodes Scholar, MA, BCL, Vinerian Law Scholar); Hon. Fellow, The Queen's College, Oxford 1992; Hon. DCL: City University 1992, University of the West of England 1995. Married 1957, Gillian Lorna Sterner (2 daughters). *Career:* Advocate of Supreme Court of South Africa 1958–60; Stowell Civil Law Fellow, University College, Oxford 1961–73; Called to the Bar, Gray's Inn 1964; Bencher 1984; Member, Royal Commission on Gambling 1976–78; QC 1977; A Judge of the Courts of Appeal of Jersey and Guernsey 1980–85; Member, Council of Legal Education 1983–92, Chairman 1989–92; A Judge of the High Court of Justice, Chancery Division 1985–92; A Lord Justice of Appeal 1992–95; A Lord of Appeal in Ordinary 1995–. *Select Committees:* Member, Select Committee on European Committees; Chairman, Select Committee on European Communities Sub-Committee E (Law and Institutions) 1997–. *Other:* President, British-German Jurists Association 1991–; Director, English National Opera 1985–90, 1991–94. *Honours:* Kt 1985; PC 1992. *Publications:* Author of *The South African Law of Evidence*, 1963. *Name, Style and Title:* Raised to the peerage as Baron Hoffmann, of Chedworth in the County of Gloucestershire 1995. A Cross-Bencher. *Address:* The Rt Hon. the Lord Hoffmann, House of Lords, London, SW1A 0PW; Surrey Lodge, 23 Keats Grove, London, NW3 2RS.

HOGG (Life Baroness, UK), Sarah Elizabeth Mary Hogg; cr. 1995

Daughter of late Baron Boyd-Carpenter. Born May 14, 1946; educated St Mary's Convent, Ascot; Lady Margaret Hall, Oxford (1st class PPE); Hon. MA, Open University 1987; Hon. DLitt, Loughborough University 1992; Fellow, Eton College 1996–; Hon. Fellow, Lady Margaret Hall, Oxford. Married 1968, Rt Hon. Douglas Martin Hogg, QC, MP (*qv*), son of Rt Hon. Baron Hailsham of St Marylebone (*qv*) (1 son 1 daughter). *Career:* On staff of *The Economist* 1967–81, Literary Editor 1970–77, Economics Editor 1977–81; Economics Editor, *The Sunday Times* 1981–82; Presenter, Channel 4 News 1982–83; Economics Editor and Deputy Executive Editor, Finance and Industry, *The Times* 1984–86; Assistant Editor and Business and City Editor, *The Independent* 1986–89; Economics Editor, *The Daily Telegraph* and *The Sunday Telegraph* 1989–90; Head, Prime Minister's Policy Unit 1990–95; Director: London Broadcasting Company 1982–90, Royal National Theatre 1988–91; London Economics 1995–96, Chairman 1997–99; Foreign and Colonial Smaller Companies Trust 1995–, Chairman 1997–99; NPI 1996–; International Advisory Board, National Westminster Bank 1995–98; Advisory Board, Bankinter 1995–98; Director: The Energy Group 1996–98, GKN 1996–, 3i 1997–, Scottish Eastern Investment Trust 1998–99, Martin Currie Portfolio Trust 1999–, P&O 1999–. *Select Committees:* Member, House of Lords Select Committee for Science and Technology 1996–. *Other:* Governor, Centre for Economic Policy Research 1985–92; Council Member: The Royal Economic Society 1996–, The Institute for Fiscal Studies 1996–, The Hansard Society for Parliamentary Government 1996–, The Lincolnshire Foundation 1996–98. *Awards Granted:* Wincott Foundation Financial Journalist of the Year 1985. *Trusts, etc:* Trustee, St Mary's School, Ascot. *Publications:* (with Jonathan Hill) *Too Close to Call*, 1995. *Name, Style and Title:* Raised to the peerage as Baroness Hogg, of Kettlethorpe in the County of Lincolnshire 1995. A Conservative. *Address:* The Baroness Hogg, House of Lords, London, SW1A 0PW *Tel:* 020 7219 5417 *E-Mail:* hoggs@parliament.uk.

HOGG OF CUMBERNAULD (Life Baron, UK), Norman Hogg; cr. 1997

Son of late Norman Hogg, CBE, DL, LLD, JP and late Mary Hogg. Born March 12, 1938; educated Causewayend School; Ruthrieston Secondary School, Aberdeen; Hon LLD, University of Aberdeen 1999. Married March 28, 1964, Elizabeth McCall, daughter of late John Christie. *Career:* Local Government Officer, Aberdeen Corporation 1953–67; District Officer, Scottish District, National and Local Government Officers Association 1967–79. *House of Commons:* MP (Labour) for Dunbartonshire East 1979–83 and for Cumbernauld and Kilsyth 1983–97. *Whip (Commons):* Scottish Labour Whip 1982–83; Opposition Deputy Chief Whip November 1983–87. *Spokesman (Commons):* Front Bench Spokesman on Scottish Affairs 1987–88. *Select Committees (Commons):* Member, Select Committees on: Scottish Affairs 1979–82, Speaker's Panel of Chairmen's 1989–97, Public Accounts 1991–92, Standing Orders Committee 1996–97. *Party Groups*

(Commons): Chairman, Scottish Parliamentary Labour Group 1981–82. *Other:* Member, Transport Users Consultative Committee for Scotland 1977–79; Hon. President, YMCA Scotland 1998–. *Miscellaneous:* Appointed Lord High Commissioner to the 1998 and 1999 General Assembly of the Church of Scotland 1997. *Special Interests:* Public Transport, Local Government, Constitutional Affairs. *Name, Style and Title:* Raised to the peerage as Baron Hogg of Cumbernauld, of Cumbernauld in North Lanarkshire 1997. Labour. *Address:* The Lord Hogg of Cumbernauld, House of Lords, London, SW1A 0PW *E-Mail:* normanhoggl@compuserve.com.

HOLDERNESS (Life Baron, UK), Richard Frederick Wood; cr. 1979; PC 1959; DL

Son of 1st Earl of Halifax, KG, PC, OM, GCMG, GCSI, GCIE, TD, and late Lady Dorothy Onslow, CI, DCVO, daughter of 4th Earl of Onslow, PC, GCMG. Born October 5, 1920; educated Eton; New College, Oxford; Hon. LLD: Sheffield University 1962, Leeds University 1978, Hull University 1982. Married April 15, 1947, Diana, daughter of late Colonel E. O. Kellett, DSO, MP and Hon. Mrs William McGowan (1 son 1 daughter). *Armed Forces:* Lieutenant, 60th Rifles 1941–43 (wounded); Hon. Colonel: Queen's Royal Rifles 1962, 4th Battalion, Royal Green Jackets 1967–89. *Councils, Public Bodies:* DL, Humberside 1968. *Career:* Director: Hargreaves Group of Companies until 1986, Lloyds Bank, Yorkshire and Humberside 1980–89; Chairman: Disablement Services Authority 1987–91, Advisory Group on Rehabilitation, Department of Health 1991–96, Wilton 65 Publishing. *House of Commons:* MP (Conservative) for Bridlington 1950–79; PPS to Viscount Amory 1951–55; Joint Parliamentary Secretary to Minister of Pensions and National Insurance 1955–58; Parliamentary Secretary to Minister of Labour 1958–59; Minister of Power 1959–63; Minister of Pensions and National Insurance 1963–64; Ministry for Overseas Development 1970–74. *Select Committees (Commons):* Has served on several Select Committees since 1979, including Committee on Channel Tunnel Bill 1983. *Select Committees:* Member, Ecclesiastical Committee 1994–97. *Other:* President, Queen Elizabeth's Foundation for Disabled People 1983–96. *Honours:* PC 1959. *Recreations:* Gardening, reading. *Name, Style and Title:* Raised to the peerage as Baron Holderness, of Bishop Wilton in the County of Humberside 1979. A Conservative. *Address:* The Rt Hon. the Lord Holderness, DL, Flat Top House, Bishop Wilton, York, YO42 1RY *Tel:* 01759 368266; 43 Lennox Gardens, London, SW1X 0DF *Tel:* 020 7225 2151.

HOLLICK (Life Baron, UK), Clive Richard Hollick; cr. 1991

Son of late Leslie Hollick, and of Olive Hollick. Born May 20, 1945; educated Taunton's School, Southampton; Nottingham University; Hon. LLD, University of Nottingham 1993. Married August 27, 1977, Susan, daughter of HE Ulric Cross (3 daughters). *Armed Forces:* University Air Squadron. *Career:* Joined Hambros Bank 1967, Director 1973–; Managing Director, MAI plc 1974–96; Director, Mills and Allen Ltd. 1975–89; Chairman, Shepperton Studios Ltd. 1976–84; Member, National Bus Company 1984–91; Director: Logica plc 1987–91, Avenir Havas Media SA (France) 1988–92, National Opinion Polls Ltd. 1989–97, Satellite Information Services 1990–94; Chairman, Meridian Broadcasting 1991–96; Director, British Aerospace 1992–97; Member, Financial Law Panel 1993–97; Director, Anglia Television 1994–97; Member, Commission on Public Policy and British Business 1995–97; Director, United Broadcasting and Entertainment Ltd 1995–; Chief Executive, United News and Media plc 1996–; Special Adviser to President of the Board of Trade 1997–; Director, Express Newspapers plc 1998–. *Select Committees:* Member, Science and Technology Sub-Committee I, Information Superhighway 1995–96. *Other:* Governor, London School of Economics and Political Science 1997–. *Trusts, etc:* Founding Trustee, Institute for Public Policy Research 1988. *Special Interests:* Business, Economic Policy, Constitutional Affairs, Transport. *Recreations:* Reading, countryside, cinema, theatre, tennis. *Name, Style and Title:* Raised to the peerage as Baron Hollick, of Notting Hill in the Royal Borough of Kensington and Chelsea 1991. Labour. *Address:* The Lord Hollick, United News and Media plc, Ludgate House, 245 Blackfriars Road, London, SE1 9UY.

HOLLIS OF HEIGHAM (Life Baroness, UK), Patricia Lesley Hollis; cr. 1990; PC 1999; DL

Daughter of late H. L. G. Wells, of Norwich. Born May 24, 1941; educated Plympton Grammar School; Cambridge University (BA, MA); University of California and Columbia University, New York (Harkness Fellow 1962–64); Nuffield College, Oxford (MA, DPhil); Hon. DLitt, Anglia Polytechnic University. Married September 18, 1965, Professor James Martin Hollis, FBA (died February 27, 1998), son of Hugh Mark Noel Hollis, of Oxted, Surrey (2 sons). *Trades Union:* Member, AUT. *Councils, Public Bodies:* Councillor, Norwich City Council 1968–91, Leader 1983–88; Councillor, Norfolk County Council 1981–85; Member: East Anglian Planning Council 1975–79, Regional Health Authority 1979–83; DL, Norfolk 1994–. *Career:* Lecturer, then Reader and former Dean, University of East Anglia; Founder-director, Radio Broadland 1983–97. *House of Lords:* Parliamentary Under-Secretary of State, Department of Social Security 1997–. *Whip:* Opposition Whip 1990–95. *Spokesman:* Opposition Spokesman on Environment and Social Security 1990–97. *Other:* Patron: Chatterbox, Norwich, Fightback, Suffolk, Norfolk Millenium Carers, Norfolk Rural Art. *Trusts, etc:* Patron, St Martin's Housing Trust. *Miscellaneous:* Contested (Labour) Great Yarmouth 1974, 1979 General Elections; National Commissioner, English Heritage 1988–91; Member, Press Council 1988–90; Former Vice-President: Association of District Councils, Association of Metropolitan Authorities, Environmental Health Officers, National Federation of Housing Associations. *Honours:* PC 1999. Fellow, Royal Historical Society. *Publications:* Author of: *The Pauper Press*, 1970; *Class and Class Conflict 1815–50*, 1973; *Pressure from Without*, 1974; *Women in Public, 1850–1900*, 1979; *Robert Lowry, Radical and Chartist*, 1979; *Ladies Elect: women in English Local Government 1865–1914*, 1987; *Jennie Lee: a Life*, 1997. *Special Interests:* Local Government, Education, Media, Heritage, Health. *Recreations:* Boating, singing, domesticity. *Name, Style and Title:* Raised to the peerage as Baroness Hollis of Heigham, of Heigham in the City of Norwich 1990. Labour. *Address:* The Rt Hon. the Baroness Hollis of Heigham, DL, 30 Park Lane, Norwich, Norfolk, NR2 3EE *Tel:* 01603 621990.

HOLME OF CHELTENHAM (Life Baron, UK), Richard Gordon Holme; cr. 1990; CBE 1983

Son of late Jack Richard Holme. Born May 27, 1936; educated Royal Masonic School, Bushey, Hertfordshire; St. John's College, Oxford; Hon. Fellow, St John's College, Oxford. Married 1958, Kay Mary, daughter of V. T. Powell, FRCS (2 sons 2 daughters). *Armed Forces:* Commissioned, 10th Gurkha Rifles 1954. *Career:* Marketing Trainee and Manager, Unilever 1959–63; Marketing Director, Penguin Books Ltd. 1963–65; Chairman, BPC Publishing 1967–69; Executive Vice-President, CRM Inc 1970–74; Chairman: Threadneedle Publishing Group 1988–, Hollis Directories 1989–, DPR Publishing Ltd 1993–, Brassey's Ltd 1995–98; Director, RTZ Corporation plc (now Riotinto plc) 1995–98; CRA Ltd (now Riotinto Ltd) 1996–98; Deputy Chairman, Independent Television Commission 1999–; Chairman, Broadcasting Standards Commission 1999–. *Chancellor:* Chancellor, Greenwich University 1998–. *Spokesman:* Liberal Democrat Spokesman on Northern Ireland 1991–99. *Party Groups (General):* President, The Liberal Party 1980–81; Vice-Chairman, Policy Committee, Liberal Democrat Party 1989–. *Other:* Chairman, English College Foundation in Prague 1991–; Board Member, Campaign for Oxford 1990–; Council Member, Cheltenham Ladies College 1994–, Chairman, College Council 1998–. *Miscellaneous:* Contested (Liberal): East Grinstead 1964 and By-election 1965, Braintree 1974, Cheltenham 1983, 1987; Director, National Committee for Electoral Reform 1975–85; Member of Council, The Hansard Society 1979–, Vice-Chairman 1990–; Chairman: Constitutional Reform Centre 1985–, ICC Recruitment Commission 1999–. *Special Interests:* Constitutional Reform, Industry, Environment, Foreign Affairs, Broadcasting. *Honours:* CBE 1983. *Recreations:* Walking, opera, collecting books. *Clubs:* Brooks's, Reform. *Name, Style and Title:* Raised to the peerage as Baron Holme of Cheltenham, of Cheltenham in the County of Gloucestershire 1990. A Liberal Democrat. *Address:* The Lord Holme of Cheltenham, CBE, House of Lords, London, SW1A 0PW.

HOME (15th Earl of, S), David Alexander Cospatrick Douglas-Home; cr. 1604; Lord Dunglass; 20th Lord Home (S) 1473; 5th Baron Douglas (UK) 1875; CVO 1997; CBE 1991

Son of 14th Earl, KT, PC, DL, who disclaimed the earldom for life on October 23, 1963 under the provisions of the Peerage Act, October 1963, and who was subsequently raised to the peerage as a life peer as Baron Home of the Hirsel 1974. Born November 20, 1943. Succeeded his father 1995; educated Eton; Christ Church, Oxford (BA 1966). Married 1972, Jane Margaret, younger daughter of Colonel John Francis Williams-Wynne, CBE, DSO, of Peniarth, Tywyn, Gwynedd (1 son 2 daughters). *Career:* Director, Douglas and Angus Estates 1966–, Chairman 1995–; Director: Morgan Grenfell & Co. Ltd. 1974–99, Arab-British Chamber of Commerce 1975–84; Director, Morgan Grenfell (Asia) Ltd. 1978–82, Deputy Chairman 1979–82; Director: Arab Bank Investment Co. 1979–87, Agricultural Mortgage Corporation plc 1979–93; Director, Tandem Group plc (formerly EFG plc) 1981–96, Chairman 1993–96; Chairman: Morgan Grenfell Export Services 1984–98 (name changed to Deutsche Export Services Ltd from July 1998–), Morgan Grenfell (Scotland) 1986–98 (named changed to Deutsche (Scotland) Limited from August 1998–), Committee for Middle East Trade 1986–92, Morgan Grenfell International Ltd 1987–98; Director: Deutsche Morgan Grenfell Hong Kong Ltd (name changed May 1996 from Morgan Grenfell Asia (Hong Kong) Ltd) 1989–99, Deutsche Morgan Grenfell Asia Holdings Pte Ltd (name changed May 1996 from Morgan Grenfell Asia Holdings Pte Ltd) 1989–99, K & N Kenanga Holdings Bhd 1993–99; Non-Executive Director, Grosvenor Estate Holdings 1993–; Director: Kenanga DMG Futures Sdn Bhd 1995–99 (name changed to Kenanga Deutsche Futures Sdn Bhd from September 1998–), Deutsche Morgan Grenfell Group plc 1996–99; Chairman, Coutts and Company 1999–. *House of Lords:* An elected hereditary peer 1999–. *Spokesman:* Opposition Front Bench Spokesman on: Trade 1997–98, the Treasury 1997–98. *Other:* Governor: Ditchley Foundation 1977–, Commonwealth Institute 1988–98; Council Member: Royal Agricultural Society of England 1990–, Glenalmond College 1995–. *Trusts, etc:* Trustee, Grosvenor Estate 1993–. *Miscellaneous:* Member, Export Guarantee Advisory Council, ECGD 1988–93. *Honours:* CBE 1991; CVO 1997. Fellow, Chartered Institute of Bankers 1999–. *Special Interests:* Foreign Affairs, Scottish Affairs, Industry, Agriculture. *Recreations:* Outdoor sports. *Clubs:* Turf, Caledonian Westminster Business. *Heir:* His son, Lord Dunglass, born November 30, 1987. A Conservative. *Address:* The Earl of Home, CVO, CBE, 99 Dovehouse Street, London, SW3 6JZ *Tel:* 020 7352 9060; The Hirsel, Coldstream, Berwickshire, TD12 4LP *Tel:* 01890 882345; Castlemains, Douglas, Lanarkshire, ML11 0RX *Tel:* 01555 851241.

HOOPER (Life Baroness, UK), Gloria Dorothy Hooper; cr. 1985

Daughter of late Frederick Hooper. Born May 25, 1939; educated La Sainte Union Convent; The Royal Ballet School; University of Southampton (BA Hons Law); Universidad Central, Ecuador (Rotary Foundation Fellow). *Career:* Assistant to Chief Registrar, John Lewis Partnership; Editor, Current Law, Sweet & Maxwell, Law Publishers; Information Officer, Winchester City Council; Assistant Solicitor, Taylor and Humbert; Legal Adviser, Slater Walker France S.A.; Partner, Taylor Garrett 1974–84; Member, European Parliament (Conservative) for Liverpool 1979–84; Vice-Chairman, European Parliament's Committee on Environment, Public Health and Consumer Protection; Deputy Chief Whip, European Democratic Group; Member, Delegation to Council of Europe and Western European Union 1992–97. *House of Lords:* Parliamentary Under-Secretary of State, Department of: Education and Science 1987–88, Energy 1988–89, Health 1989–92; A Deputy Speaker of the House of Lords 1993–; A Deputy Chairman of Committees 1993–; PPS (Lords) to Rt Hon. William Hague, MP, as Leader of the Opposition 1999–. *Whip:* A Baroness in Waiting (Government Whip) 1985–87. *All-Party:* Member, All-Party Groups on: Ecuador, Latin America, Colombia, Argentina, Energy; Peers' London Group; Co-Chairman, All-Party Primary Care and Public Health Group 1998–; Member, All-Party Overseas Territories Group. *Party Groups:* Member, Association of Conservative Peers. *International Bodies (General):* Member: IPU, CPA. *Other:* Member, The Law Society; General Governor, British Nutrition Foundation; President: British Educational Equipment and Supplies Association, Canning House (Hispanic and Luso Brazilian Council), Waste Watch, European Foundation For Heritage Skills. *Trusts, etc:* Trustee/Governor: English Speaking Union, Royal Academy of Dancing, Centre for International Briefing, Royal Ballet, Centre for Global Energy Studies, National Museums and Galleries of Merseyside; Fellow and Trustee, Industry and Parliament Trust. *Honours:* Order of Francisco de Miranda (Venezuela). Fellow: Royal Geographical Society, RSA. *Special Interests:* European Union, Latin America, Inner Cities. *Recreations:* Theatre, travel. *Name, Style and Title:* Raised to the peerage as Baroness Hooper, of Liverpool and St James's in the City of Westminster 1985. A Conservative. *Address:* The Baroness Hooper, House of Lords, London, SW1A 0PW.

HOOSON (Life Baron, UK), Hugh Emlyn Hooson; cr. 1979; QC 1960

Son of late Hugh Hooson, farmer and Elsie Hooson. Born March 26, 1925; educated Denbigh Grammar School; University College of Wales, Aberystwyth; Hon. Professorial Fellow, University of Wales Aberystwyth 1971–. Married 1950, Shirley Margaret Wynne, daughter of late Sir George Hamer, CBE (2 daughters). *Armed Forces:* Royal Navy 1943–46. *Career:* Called to the Bar, Gray's Inn 1949; Deputy Chairman, Flintshire Quarter Sessions 1960–72; Deputy Chairman, Merioneth Quarter Sessions 1960–67, Chairman 1967–72; Bencher, Gray's Inn 1968; Recorder of Merthyr Tydfil 1971; Recorder of Swansea July 1971; Elected Leader of Wales and Chester Circuit 1971–74; Vice-Treasurer, Gray's Inn 1985, Treasurer 1986; Non-executive Director, Laura Ashley plc 1985–95, Chairman: Severn River Crossing plc 1991–, Laura Ashley plc 1995–96. *House of Commons:* MP (Liberal) for Montgomeryshire 1962–79. *Spokesman (Commons):* Spokesman for Defence, Foreign Affairs, Home Affairs, Legal Affairs, Agriculture and Welsh Affairs 1962–79. *All-Party Committees (Commons):* Chairman, All-Party Parliamentary Group for World Government 1966–70. *International Bodies (Commons):* British Delegate to the Atlantic Assembly (formerly NATO Parliamentarians) 1962–79; Raporteur, Working Party on East-West Relations 1974–79; Vice-Chairman, Political Committee of North Atlantic Assembly 1975–79. *Spokesman:* Liberal Democrat Spokesman on Welsh Affairs 1996–98; Former Spokesman on Legal Affairs, Agriculture and European Affairs. *International Bodies (General):* European and International Affairs. *Party Groups (General):* Leader, Welsh Liberal Party 1966–79; President, Welsh Liberal Party 1983–86. *Other:* President: Royal National Eisteddfod of Wales, Newtown 1965, Llangollen International Eisteddfod 1987–93, Wales International 1995–. *Trusts, etc:* Chairman, Trustees of Laura Ashley Foundation 1986–97. *Special Interests:* Law, Constitutional Affairs, Agriculture, Defence, Wales, Europe, International Affairs. *Recreations:* Music, theatre, reading, walking, farming. *Name, Style and Title:* Raised to the peerage as Baron Hooson, of Montgomery in the County of Powys and Colomendy in the County of Clwyd 1979. A Liberal Democrat. *Address:* The Lord Hooson, QC, Summerfield Park, Llanidloes, Powys *Tel:* 01686 412298; House of Lords, London, SW1A 0PW *Tel:* House of Lords 020 7219 5226.

HOPE OF CRAIGHEAD (Life Baron, UK), James Arthur David Hope; cr. 1995; PC 1989

Son of late Arthur Henry Cecil Hope, OBE, WS. Born June 27, 1938; educated Edinburgh Academy; Rugby School; St John's College, Cambridge (Scholarship 1956, BA 1962, MA 1978); Edinburgh University (LLB 1965); Hon. LLD: Aberdeen 1991, Strathclyde 1993, Edinburgh 1995. Married 1966, Katharine Mary, daughter of late W. Mark Kerr, WS, of Edinburgh (twin sons 1 daughter). *Armed Forces:* National Service, Seaforth Highlanders 1957–59. *Career:* Admitted Faculty of Advocates 1965; Standing Junior Counsel in Scotland to Board of Inland Revenue 1974–78; Advocate-Depute 1978–82; QC (Scotland) 1978; Legal Chairman, Pensions Appeal Tribunal 1985–86; Chairman, Medical Appeal Tribunals 1985–86; Dean, Faculty of Advocates 1986–89; Lord Justice General of Scotland and Lord President of the Court of Session 1989–96; Hon. Bencher: Gray's Inn 1989, Inn of Court of Northern Ireland 1995; A Lord of Appeal in Ordinary 1996–. *Chancellor:* Chancellor, Strathclyde University 1998–. *Select Committees:* Member, Select Committee on European Communities, Chairman, Sub-Committee E (Law and Institutions) 1998–. *Other:* President, The Stair Society 1993–; Member, Canadian Bar Association 1987; Council Member, Commonwealth Magistrates' and Judges' Association 1998–. *Trusts, etc:* Board of Trustees, National Library of Scotland 1989–1996. *Honours:* PC 1989. *Publications:* (edited jointly) *Gloag and Henderson's Introduction to the Law of Scotland; Armour on Value for Rating;* (with A. G. M. Duncan *The Rent (Scotland) Act, 1984,* 1986; (contributor) *Stair Memorial Encyclopaedia of Scots Law. Recreations:* Walking, ornithology, music. *Clubs:* New (Edinburgh). *Name, Style and Title:* Raised to the peerage as Baron Hope of Craighead, of Bamff in the District of Perth and Kinross 1995. A Cross-Bencher. *Address:* The Rt Hon. the Lord Hope of Craighead, 34 India Street, Edinburgh, EH3 6HB *Tel:* 0131–225 8245 *Fax:* 0131–225 8245; Law Lords Corridor, House of Lords, London, SW1A 0PW *Tel:* 020 7219 3202 *Fax:* 020 7219 3202 *E-Mail:* craighead@dial.pipex.com.

HOWE (7th Earl, UK), Frederick Richard Penn Curzon; cr. 1821; 8th Viscount Curzon (UK) 1802; 9th Baron Howe (GB) 1788; 8th Baron Curzon (GB) 1794

Son of late Commander Chambré George William Penn Curzon, RN, grandson of 3rd Earl, GCVO, CB, and of late Mrs Jane Victoria Curzon (née Fergusson). Born January 29, 1951. Succeeded his kinsman 1984; educated Rugby; Christ Church, Oxford (MA Hons. Literae Humaniores). Married March 26, 1983, Elizabeth Helen, DL, daughter of Captain Burleigh Edward St Lawrence Stuart (1 son 3 daughters). *Career:* Arable and Dairy Farmer; Director: Adam & Company plc 1987–90, Provident Life Association Ltd 1988–91; Barclays Bank plc 1973–87, Senior Manager 1984–87. *House of Lords:* Parliamentary Secretary, Ministry of Agriculture, Fisheries and Food 1992–95; Parliamentary Under-Secretary of State, Ministry of Defence 1995–97; An elected hereditary peer 1999–. *Whip:* A Lord in Waiting (Government Whip) 1991–92. *Spokesman:* An Opposition Spokesman on: Defence May-October 1997, Health October 1997–. *All-Party:* Member, All-Party: Penal Affairs Group, Defence Study Group. *Other:* Governor, King William IV Naval Foundation 1984–; Vice-President, National Society for Epilepsy 1984–86, President 1986–; President: Chilterns Branch RNLI 1985–, South Bucks Association for the Disabled 1984–; Member, RNLI Committee of Management 1997–; Chairman, LAPADA 1999–. *Trusts, etc:* Governor, The Trident Trust 1985–. *Miscellaneous:* President, CPRE (Penn Country Branch) 1986–92. Associate, Chartered Institute of Bankers 1976–. *Special Interests:* Agriculture, Penal Affairs and Policy, Finance. *Recreations:* Gardening, music, writing. *Heir:* His son, Viscount Curzon, born October 22, 1994. A Conservative. *Address:* The Earl Howe, House of Lords, London, SW1A 0PW *E-Mail:* howef@parliament.uk.

HOWE OF ABERAVON (Life Baron, UK), (Richard Edward) Geoffrey Howe; cr. 1992; PC 1972; CH 1996; Kt 1970; QC 1965

Son of late Benjamin Edward Howe, of Port Talbot, Glamorgan. Born December 20, 1926; educated Winchester; Trinity Hall, Cambridge (Scholar, MA, LLB) ; Hon. LLD, Wales 1988; Hon. Fellow, Trinity Hall, Cambridge 1992, Rede Memorial Lecturer 1994; Hon. DCL, City University 1994; Hon. Fellow: University of Wales, Swansea 1996, Cardiff University 1998. Married August 29, 1953, Elspeth Rosamund, CBE, daughter of late Philip Morton Shand (1 son 2 daughters). *Armed Forces:* Lieutenant, Royal Signals 1945–48; Seconded to E African Signals 1947–48. *Career:* Called to the Bar, Middle Temple 1952, Bencher 1969, Reader 1993; Deputy Chairman, Glamorgan Quarter Sessions 1966–70; Director: AGB Research Group 1974–79, Sun Alliance and Insurance Group 1974–79, EMI Ltd 1976–79, BICC plc 1991–97, Glaxo Wellcome 1991–96; Chairman, Framlington Russian Investment Fund 1994–; Special Adviser on European and International Affairs to law firm of Jones, Day, Reavis and Pogue; International Advisory Councils of: J. P. Morgan & Co., Stanford University's Institute for International Studies; Visitor at the School of Oriental and African Studies, University of London 1991–; Fuji International European Advisory Board 1996–; Carlyle European Advisory Board 1996–. *House of Commons:* Contested (Conservative) Aberavon in 1955 and 1959 General Elections; MP (Conservative) for: Bebington 1964–66, Reigate 1970–74, Surrey East 1974–92; Solicitor-General 1970–72; Minister for Trade and Consumer Affairs, Department of Trade and Industry 1972–74; Chancellor of the Exchequer 1979–83; Secretary of State for Foreign and Commonwealth Affairs 1983–89; Lord President of the Council, Leader of the House of Commons and Deputy Prime Minister 1989–90. *Spokesman (Commons):* Opposition Spokesman on: Social Services 1974–75, Treasury and Economic Affairs 1975–79. *All-Party:* A Vice-President, All-Party British-American Country Group; Joint Vice-Chairman, All-Party British-Ukrainian Country Group 1999–. *International Bodies (General):* Chairman, Interim Committee International Monetary Fund 1982–83. *Party Groups (General):* Chairman: Cambridge University Conservative Association 1951, Bow Group 1955; Managing Director, Crossbow 1957–60, Editor 1960–62. *Other:* Member, General Council of the Bar 1957–61; Visitor, School of Oriental and African Studies 1991–; President: Great Britain-China Centre 1992–, The Academy of Experts 1996–. *Awards Granted:* Joseph Bech Memorial Prize, Luxembourg 1993. *Trusts, etc:* Trustee, Thomson Foundation 1991–. *Miscellaneous:* President, Consumers' Association 1993–. *Honours:* Kt 1970; PC 1972; Grand Cross of the Order of Merit of the Federal Republic of Germany 1992; CH 1996. Freeman, Borough of Port Talbot 1992. *Publications:* Author of: *Conflict of Loyalty*, 1994; Various political pamphlets for the Bow Group and Conservative Political Centre. *Clubs:* Athenaeum, Garrick. *Name, Style and Title:* Raised to the peerage as Baron Howe of Aberavon, of Tandridge in the County of Surrey 1992. A Conservative. *Address:* The Rt Hon. the Lord Howe of Aberavon, CH, QC, House of Lords, London, SW1A 0PW *Tel:* 020 7236 0137.

HOWELL OF GUILDFORD (Life Baron, UK), David Arthur Russell Howell; cr. 1997; PC 1979

Son of late Arthur Howell, retired Army Officer and Businessman. Born January 18, 1936; educated Eton; King's College, Cambridge (Graduated First Class Honours 1959 (MA). Married August 10, 1967, Davina Wallace (1 son 2 daughters). *Armed Forces:* Second Lieutenant, 2nd Btn Coldstream Guards 1954–56. *Career:* Treasury 1959–60; Leader writer, *Daily Telegraph* 1960–64; Director: Monks Investment Trust plc, John Laing (Investment) plc; Advisory Director, Warburg, Dillon, Read. *House of Commons:* Contested (Conservative) Dudley 1964; MP (Conservative) for Guildford 1966–97; Parliamentary Secretary, Civil Service Department 1970–72; Parliamentary Under-Secretary of State at: Department of Employment 1971–72, Northern Ireland Office March-November 1972; Minister of State at: Northern Ireland Office 1972–74, Department of Energy 1974; Secretary of State for: Energy 1979–81, Transport 1981–83. *Whip (Commons):* Lord Commissioner of the Treasury 1970–71. *Select Committees (Commons):* Chairman, Select Committee on Foreign Affairs 1987–97; Former Member, Select Committee on Liaison. *Backbench Committees (Commons):* Former Chairman, The One Nation Group of Conservative MPs. *Select Committees:* Member: Select Committee on European Communities Sub-Committee B (Energy, Industry and Transport), Select Committee on European Communities 1999–. *International Bodies (General):* Member, Trilateral Commission. *Party Groups (General):* Chairman, Bow Group 1962; Editor, "Crossbow" 1962–64; Director, Conservative Political Centre 1964–66. *Other:* Member: Royal Institute of International Affairs (Chatham House), Development Council, Shakespeare Globe Theatre. *Miscellaneous:* Visiting Fellow, Nuffield College, Oxford; Chairman, UK-Japan 21st Century Group. *Honours:* PC 1979. Liveryman, Clothworkers' Company. *Publications:* Author of: (jointly) *Principles in Practice*, 1960; *The Conservative Opportunity*, 1965; *Freedom and Capital*, 1981; *Blind Victory: a study in income, wealth and power*, 1986. *Special Interests:* Economics, International Finance, Energy, Oil, Foreign Affairs. *Recreations:* Writing, travel, golf, do-it-yourself. *Clubs:* Buck's. *Name, Style and Title:* Raised to the peerage as Baron Howell of Guildford, of Penton Mewsey in the County of Hampshire 1997. A Conservative. *Address:* The Rt Hon. the Lord Howell of Guildford, House of Lords, London, SW1A 0PW *Tel:* (Business) 020 7568 2157.

HOWELLS OF ST DAVIDS (Life Baroness, UK), Rosalind Patricia-Anne Howells; cr 1999; OBE 1993

Born January 10, 1931; educated St Joseph's Convent, Grenada; South West London College; City University, Washington DC; Hon. DUniv, Greenwich 1998. Married 1955, John Charles Howells (2 daughters). *Career:* Former Community and Equal Opportunities Worker, with Moonshot Youth Club, Community Industry, then to Greenwich Racial Equality Council as Equal Opportunities Director until retirement. *Other:* Chair, Lewisham Racial Equality Council; Ex-Chair: Charlton Consortium, Carnival Liaison Committee, Greater London Action on Race Equality; Director, Smithville Associates; President, Grenada Convent Past Pupils Association; Patron: Grenada Arts Council, Mediation Service; Member, Court of Governors, University of Greenwich; Former Vice-Chair, London Voluntary Services Council; Has served on various committees including: Advisory Committee to the Home Secretary, Commonwealth Countries League, Greenwich Police/Community Consultative Group. *Awards Granted:* Hansib Publications Award; The Voice Newspaper Community Award. *Trusts, etc:* Trustee: West Indian Standing Conference, Museum of Ethnic Arts, Women of the Year Committee, Stephen Lawrence Charitable Trust, City Parochial Foundation. *Miscellaneous:* Has been an active campaigner for justice in the field of race relations: The New Cross Fire, Roland Adams Campaign, Stephen Lawrence Family Campaign, SUS Campaign. *Honours:* OBE 1993. *Special Interests:* Community Relations. *Recreations:* Food, music of all kinds, cricket, football. *Name, Style and Title:* Raised to the peerage as Baroness Howells of St Davids, of Charlton in the London Borough of Greenwich 1999. Labour. *Address:* The Baroness Howells of St Davids, OBE, House of Lords, London, SW1A 0PW *Tel:* 020 8852 9808 *Fax:* 020 8297 1975.

HOWIE OF TROON (Life Baron, UK), William Howie; cr. 1978

Son of late Peter Howie. Born March 2, 1924; educated Marr College, Troon; Royal Technical College, Glasgow; Hon. DSc, City University; Hon. LLD, Strathclyde. Married March 24, 1951, Mairi, daughter of late John Sanderson (2 daughters 2 sons). *Trades Union:* Life Member, NUJ. *Career:* Civil Engineer; Journalist and Publisher; Director, Internal Relations of Thomas Telford Ltd 1976–95; Parliamentary Adviser to Society of Telecom Engineers. *House of Commons:* MP (Labour) for Luton 1963–70. *Chancellor:* Pro-Chancellor, City University 1984–91. *Select Committees:* Member of House of Lords Select Committees on: Science and Technology 1992–95, the European Communities 1995–97; Co-opted Member, Select Committee on European Communities Sub-Committee B (Energy, Industry and Transport) 1997–98; Member, Select Committee on Science and Technology Sub-Committee II (Science and Society) 1999–. *Other:* Member: Council of Institution of Civil Engineers 1965–68, Council of City University 1968–91; Vice-President, Periodical Publishers Association. *Trusts, etc:* Fellow, Industry and Parliamentary Trust. *Miscellaneous:* Member, Committee of Inquiry into Engineering Profession 1977–79. Fellow, Institution of Civil Engineers; Member, Society of Engineers and Scientists (France). *Special Interests:* Construction Industry, Professional Engineers, Higher Education. *Name, Style and Title:* Raised to the peerage as Baron Howie of Troon, of Troon, Kyle and Carrick 1978. Labour. *Address:* The Lord Howie of Troon, 34 Temple Fortune Lane, London, NW11 7UL *Tel:* 020 8455 0492.

HOYLE (Life Baron, UK), (Eric) Douglas (Harvey) Hoyle; cr. 1997

Son of late William Hoyle. Born February 17, 1930; educated Adlington School; Horwich Technical College. Married December 20, 1952, Pauline (died 1991), daughter of William Spencer (1 son). *Trades Union:* Vice-President, ASTMS 1972–74, President 1977–81, Vice-President 1981–85, President 1985–88; Merged with TASS 1988; Joint President, MSF 1988–90, President 1990–91. *Councils, Public Bodies:* JP 1958; Former Member, North West Regional Health Authority. *Career:* British Rail 1945–51; AEI 1951–53; Sales Engineer, C. Weston Ltd, Salford 1953–74; Chairman, Warrington Rugby League plc 1999–. *House of Commons:* Contested Clitheroe 1964; MP for: Nelson and Colne 1974–79, Warrington 1981–83, Warrington North 1983–97. *Select Committees (Commons):* Member, Select Committees on: Trade and Industry 1984–92, Privileges 1994–95, Standards and Privileges 1995–96. *Backbench Committees (Commons):* Member, Backbench Committee on Home Policy 1983–84; Chairman, Parliamentary Labour Party's Trade and Industry Committee 1987–92. *Party Groups (Commons):* Member, Labour Party National Executive 1978–82, 1983–85; Chairman, Parliamentary Labour Party 1992–97. *Whip:* A Lord in Waiting (Government Whip) 1997–99. *Spokesman:* A Spokesman on: Defence 1997–99, Home Office 1997–99, Agriculture 1997–99. *All-Party:* Member, All-Party Defence Study Group 1999–. *Special Interests:* Trade, Employment, Industrial Relations, Health, Immigration, Arts. *Recreations:* Cricket, theatre, cinema, sport. *Sportsclubs:* President: Chorley Rugby League Club 1989–96, Warrington Rugby League Supporters Club 1990–, Adlington Cricket Club 1994–. *Name, Style and Title:* Raised to the peerage as Baron Hoyle, of Warrington in the County of Cheshire 1997. Labour. *Address:* The Lord Hoyle, JP, 30 Ashfield Road, Anderton, Nr Chorley, Lancashire, PR6 9PN; House of Lords, London, SW1A 0PW.

HUGHES OF WOODSIDE (Life Baron, UK), Robert Hughes; cr. 1997

Born January 31, 1932; educated Robert Gordon's College, Aberdeen; Benoni High School, Transvaal; Pietermaritzburgh Technical College, Natal. Married 1957, Ina Margaret Miller (2 sons 3 daughters). *Trades Union:* Member, AEF. *Councils, Public Bodies:* Councillor, Aberdeen Town Council 1962–71; Former Member, North East Scotland Regional Hospital Board. *Career:* Emigrated to South Africa 1947; Returned UK 1954; Draughtsman. *House of Commons:* Contested North Angus and Mearns 1959; MP (Labour) for Aberdeen North 1970–97; Parliamentary Under-Secretary of State, Scottish Office March 1974–75; Piloted the Rating (Disabled Persons) Act 1978 to Statute as Private Members Bill. *Spokesman (Commons):* Front Bench Opposition Spokesman on Transport November 1981–83; Opposition Spokesman on: Agriculture,

Fisheries and Food 1983–84, Transport 1984–88. *Select Committees (Commons):* Member, Select Committee on Scottish Affairs 1992–97, Chairman 1981. *Party Groups (Commons):* Vice-Chairman, Tribune Group of MPs 1984–85. *Party Groups (General):* Chairman, Aberdeen City Labour Party 1963–69. *Other:* Founder Member, CND; Vice-Chairman, Anti-Apartheid Movement 1976, Chairman 1977–94; Chairman, Action for Southern Africa (ACTSA) 1994–. *Miscellaneous:* Member, General Medical Council 1976–81. *Special Interests:* Anti-Apartheid Work, Agriculture, Fishing Industry, Transport, Health Service, Overseas Aid and Development. *Recreations:* Fishing, golf. *Name, Style and Title:* Raised to the peerage as Baron Hughes of Woodside, of Woodside in the City of Aberdeen 1997. Labour. *Address:* The Lord Hughes of Woodside, House of Lords, London, SW1A 0PW.

HUNT OF KINGS HEATH (Life Baron, UK), Philip Alexander Hunt; cr. 1997; OBE 1993

Son of late Rev. Philip Hunt and Muriel Hunt. Born May 19, 1949; educated City of Oxford High School; Oxford School; Leeds University (BA). Married 1st (dissolved) (1 daughter); married 2nd, 1988, Selina Ruth Stewart (3 sons 1 daughter). *Trades Union:* Member, Unison. *Councils, Public Bodies:* Councillor, Oxford City Council 1973–79; Member, Oxfordshire Area Health Authority 1975–77; Councillor, Birmingham City Council 1980–82. *Career:* Oxford Regional Hospital Board 1972–74; Nuffield Orthopaedic Centre 1974–75; Secretary, Edgware/Hendon Community Health Council 1975–78; National Association of Health Authorities: Assistant Secretary 1978–79, Assistant Director 1979–84, Director 1984–90; Director, National Association of Health Authorities and Trusts 1990–96; Chief Executive, NHS Confederation 1996–97. *House of Lords:* Parliamentary Under-Secretary of State, Department of Health 1999–. *Whip:* A Lord in Waiting (Government Whip) 1998–99. *Spokesman:* A Spokesman on: Education and Employment 1998–99, Health 1998–. *Select Committees:* Member, Joint Select Committee on Consolidation of Bills 1998–. *All-Party:* Co-Chair, All-Party Primary Care and Public Health Group 1997–98; Vice-Chair, All-Party Group on AIDS 1997–98. *International Bodies (General):* Council, International Hospital Federation 1986–91. *Other:* Council, Association for Public Health 1992, Co-Chairman 1994–98; President, Family Planning Association 1997–98. *Honours:* OBE 1993. *Special Interests:* Devolution, Transport, Environment. *Recreations:* Cycling, swimming, supporting Birmingham City FC, music. *Sportsclubs:* Warwickshire CCC. *Name, Style and Title:* Raised to the peerage as Baron Hunt of Kings Heath, of Birmingham in the County of West Midlands 1997. Labour. *Address:* The Lord Hunt of Kings Heath, OBE, 31 Ashfield Avenue, Kings Heath, Birmingham, B14 7AT *Tel:* 0121–449 1615.

HUNT OF TANWORTH (Life Baron, UK), John Joseph Benedict Hunt; cr. 1980; GCB 1977

Son of late Major A. L. Hunt. Born October 23, 1919; educated Downside; Magdalene College, Cambridge; Hon. Fellow, Magdalene College, Cambridge 1977. Married 1st, 1941, Hon. Magdalen Robinson (died 1971), daughter of 1st Baron Robinson (2 sons and 1 daughter deceased), married 2nd, 1973, Lady Madeleine Frances, daughter of late Sir William Hume, CMG, FRCP, and widow of Sir John Charles, KCB, FRCP. *Armed Forces:* Served Royal Naval Volunteer Reserve 1940–45. *Career:* Entered Home Civil Service 1946; Dominions Office 1946; Private Secretary to Parliamentary Under-Secretary 1947; Second Secretary, UK High Commission Ceylon 1948–50; Private Secretary to Secretary of Cabinet and Permanent Secretary to Treasury and Head of Civil Service 1956–58; Assistant Secretary, Commonwealth Relations Office 1958; Cabinet Office 1960; HM Treasury 1962–67; Deputy Secretary 1968; First Civil Service Commissioner, Civil Service Department 1968–71; Third Secretary, Treasury 1971–72; Second Permanent Secretary, Cabinet Office 1972–73; Secretary of the Cabinet 1973–79; Chairman, Banque Nationale de Paris plc 1980–97; Director, IBM (UK) Ltd 1980–90; Advisory Director, Unilever 1980–90; Director, Prudential Corporation plc 1980–92, Chairman: Disasters Emergency Committee 1981–89, Inquiry into Cable Expansion and Broadcasting Policy 1982, Tablet Publishing Co. Ltd 1984–96, Director 1984–, Prudential Corporation plc 1985–90, European Policy Forum 1992–98, Council 1992–. *Select Committees:* Member, Sub-Committee A of House of Lords European Communities Committee 1992–95, Chairman 1993–97; Member, House of Lords European Communities Committee 1993–96; Chairman, House of Lords Select

Committee on Central and Local Government Relations 1995–96. *Other:* Chairman, Ditchley Foundation 1983–91; President, The Local Government Association 1997–. *Honours:* CB 1968; KCB 1973; GCB 1977; Officier, Légion d'Honneur (France) 1987; Knight Commander with Star of the Order of Pius IX 1997. *Recreations:* Gardening. *Name, Style and Title:* Raised to the peerage as Baron Hunt of Tanworth, of Stratford-on-Avon in the County of Warwickshire 1980. A Cross-Bencher. *Address:* The Lord Hunt of Tanworth, GCB, 8 Wool Road, London, SW20 0HW *Tel:* 020 8947 7640 *Fax:* 020 8947 4879.

HUNT OF WIRRAL (Life Baron, UK), David James Fletcher Hunt; cr. 1997; MBE 1973; PC 1990

Son of late Alan Nathaniel Hunt, OBE, Shipping Agent and late Jessie Edna Ellis Hunt. Born May 21, 1942; educated Liverpool College; Montpellier University, France; Bristol University; Guildford College of Law (LLB). Married June 2, 1973, Paddy, daughter of late Roger and Margery Orchard (2 sons 2 daughters). *Career:* Solicitor; Senior Partner, Beachcroft Wansbroughs; Director, BET Omnibus Services Ltd 1980–81. *House of Commons:* Contested Bristol South in 1970 and Kingswood in 1974; MP (Conservative) for Wirral 1976–83 and for Wirral West 1983–97; PPS: to Secretary of State for Trade 1979–81, to Secretary of State for Defence 1981; Parliamentary Under-Secretary of State, Department of Energy 1984–87; Minister of State, Department of the Environment (Minister for Local Government and Inner Cities) 1989–90; Secretary of State: for Wales 1990–93, for Employment 1993–94; Chancellor of the Duchy of Lancaster and Minister for Public Service and Science 1994–95. *Whip (Commons):* Assistant Government Whip 1981–83; Lord Commissioner of the Treasury 1983–84; Treasurer of Her Majesty's Household and Deputy Government Chief Whip 1987–89. *Spokesman (Commons):* Spokesman for Shipping and Shipbuilding 1977–79. *Select Committees (Commons):* Former Member, Select Committees on: House of Commons Services 1987–89, Public Service 1995–97. *Backbench Committees (Commons):* Chairman, Conservative Shipping and Shipbuilding Committee 1977–79. *All-Party Committees (Commons):* Vice-Chairman, All-Party Parliamentary Youth Lobby 1978–79; Vice-Chairman, Conservative Group for Europe 1978–81, Chairman 1981–82. *Select Committees:* Member, Offices Committee 1999–, European Communities Committee, Sub-Committee E, Law and Institutions 1999–. *All-Party:* President, All-Party Occupational Health and Safety Group. *Party Groups (General):* Chairman, Bristol University Conservative Association 1964–65; National Vice-Chairman, Federation of Conservative Students 1965–66; Chairman: Bristol City CPC 1965–68, Bristol Federation of Young Conservatives; Member: General Purposes Committee, National Union Executive 1967–76, 1983–89; Vice-Chairman, Bristol Conservative Association 1970; Chairman, National Young Conservatives 1972–73; Vice-Chairman, National Union 1974–76; Vice-President, European Conservative and Christian Democratic Youth Community; Vice-Chairman, Conservative Party 1983–84; President, Tory Reform Group 1991–. *Other:* Member, Government Advisory Committee on Pop Festivals; Governor, European Youth Foundation at Strasbourg 1972–75. *Miscellaneous:* Chairman, British Youth Council 1971–74; Member, South West Economic Planning Council 1972–76; Chairman, National Youth Study Group on Young People and Politics; President, British Youth Council 1978–80. *Honours:* MBE 1973; PC 1990. *Recreations:* Cricket, walking. *Clubs:* Hurlingham. *Name, Style and Title:* Raised to the peerage as Baron Hunt of Wirral, of Wirral in the County of Merseyside 1997. A Conservative. *Address:* The Rt Hon. the Lord Hunt of Wirral, MBE, Senior Partner, Beachcroft Wansbroughs, 100 Fetter Lane, London, EC4A 1BN *E-Mail:* lordhunt@bwlaw.co.uk.

HURD OF WESTWELL (Life Baron, UK), Douglas Richard Hurd; cr. 1997; CH 1996; CBE 1974; PC 1982

Son of late Baron Hurd (Life Peer). Born March 8, 1930; educated Eton; Trinity College, Cambridge (President, Cambridge Union 1952). Married 1st, November 10, 1960, Tatiana, daughter of Arthur Benedict Eyre, MBE (3 sons) (marriage dissolved 1982), married 2nd, May 7, 1982, Judith, daughter of Sidney Smart (1 son 1 daughter). *Armed Forces:* 2nd Lieutenant, Royal Artillery 1948–49. *Career:* HM Foreign Service, Peking; UN, Rome 1952–66; Conservative Research Department 1966–68; Deputy Chairman, Natwest Markets 1995–98; Chairman, British Invisibles 1997–; Deputy Chairman, Coutts & Co 1998–. *House of Commons:* MP (Conservative) for Mid Oxon 1974–83 and for Witney 1983–97; Political Secretary to the Rt Hon. Edward Heath, MBE, MP 1968–74; Minister of State for: Foreign and Commonwealth Office 1979–83,

Home Office 1983–84; Secretary of State for: Northern Ireland 1984–85, The Home Department 1985–89, Foreign and Commonwealth Affairs 1989–95; Contested Leadership of the Conservative Party November 1990. *Spokesman (Commons):* Opposition Spokesman on Europe 1976–79. *Trusts, etc:* Trustee, Prayer Book Society 1989–; Chairman, Prison Reform Trust 1997–. *Miscellaneous:* Member: The Constitutional Commission 1998–99, Royal Commission on the Reform of the House of Lords 1999; High Steward, Westminster Abbey 1999–. *Honours:* CBE 1974; PC 1982; CH 1996. *Publications: The Arrow War*, 1967; *Truth Game*, 1972; *Vote to Kill*, 1975; *An End to Promises*, 1979; (with Andrew Osmond): *Send Him Victorious*, 1968; *The Smile on the Face of the Tiger*, 1969; *Scotch on the Rocks*, 1971; *War Without Frontiers*, 1982; (with Stephen Lamport) *Palace of Enchantments*, 1985; *The Search for Peace*, 1997; *The Shape of Ice*, 1998; *Ten Minutes to Turn the Devil*, 1999. *Recreations:* Writing novels. *Clubs:* Beefsteak, Travellers', Pratt's. *Name, Style and Title:* Raised to the peerage as Baron Hurd of Westwell, of Westwell in the County of Oxfordshire 1997. A Conservative. *Address:* The Rt Hon. the Lord Hurd of Westwell, CH, CBE, House of Lords, London, SW1A 0PW *Tel:* 020 7219 3000.

HUSSEY OF NORTH BRADLEY (Life Baron, UK) Marmaduke James Hussey; cr. 1996

Son of late Eric Robert James Husssey, CMG, and of Mrs Christine Hussey. Born August 29, 1923; educated Rugby; Trinity College, Oxford (Scholar, MA); Hon. Fellow, Trinity College, Oxford 1989. Married April 25, 1959, Lady Susan Waldegrave, DCVO, daughter of 12th Earl Waldegrave, KG, GCVO, TD, DL (1 son 1 daughter). *Armed Forces:* Served World War II, with Grenadier Guards in Italy (wounded). *Career:* Associated Newspapers 1949, Director 1964; Managing Director, Harmsworth Publications 1967–70; Thomson Organisation Executive Board 1971; Chief Executive and Managing Director, Times Newspapers Ltd 1971–80, Director 1982–86; Director, Colonial Mutual Group 1982–96; Joint Chairman, Great Western Radio 1985–86; Director, William Collins plc 1985–89, MAID plc 1996–; Chairman: Ruffer Investment Management 1996–, Casweb Ltd. *Select Committees:* Member: Select Committee on European Communities 1997–, Select Committee on European Communities Sub-Committee A (Economic and Financial Affairs, Trade and External Relations) 1997–. *Other:* Member: Board of British Council 1983–96, Government Working Party on Artificial Limb and Appliance Centres in England 1984–86; Chairman: Royal Marsden Hospital 1985–98, BBC 1986–96; Member, Management and Education Committees, King Edward's Hospital Fund for London 1987–; President, Royal Bath and West of England Society 1990–91; Chairman, King's Fund London Committee 1996; President, Iris Fund for Prevention of Blindness 1998–. *Trusts, etc:* Trustee: Rhodes Trust 1972–91, Royal Academic Trust 1988–97. *Clubs:* Brooks's. *Name, Style and Title:* Raised to the peerage as Baron Hussey of North Bradley, of North Bradley in the County of Wiltshire 1996. A Cross-Bencher. *Address:* The Lord Hussey of North Bradley, Flat 15, 45–47 Courtfield Road, London, SW7 4DB *Tel:* 020 7370 1414; Waldegrave House, Chewton Mendip, near Bath, Somerset, BA3 4PD *Tel:* 01761 241289.

HUTCHINSON OF LULLINGTON (Life Baron, UK), Jeremy Nicolas Hutchinson; cr. 1978; QC 1961

Son of late St John Hutchinson, KC. Born March 28, 1915; educated Stowe; Magdalen College, Oxford (MA). Married 1st, 1940, Dame Peggy Ashcroft, DBE (1 son 1 daughter) (marriage dissolved 1966, she died 1991), married 2nd, 1966, June Osborn. *Armed Forces:* RNVR 1939–46. *Career:* Called to the Bar, Middle Temple 1939; QC 1961; Bencher 1963; Recorder of Bath 1962–72; Recorder of Crown Court 1973–76; Professor of Law, Royal Academy of Arts 1988–. *Spokesman:* Liberal Democrat Spokesman on the Arts, Penal Affairs 1983–92. *Trusts, etc:* Trustee, Tate Gallery 1977–80, Chairman 1980–84. *Miscellaneous:* Member: Committee on Immigration Appeals 1966–68, Committee on Identification Procedures 1974–76; Vice-Chairman, Arts Council of Great Britain 1976–78. *Clubs:* MCC. *Name, Style and Title:* Raised to the peerage as Baron Hutchinson of Lullington, of Lullington in the County of East Sussex 1978. A Liberal Democrat. *Address:* The Lord Hutchinson of Lullington, QC, House of Lords, London, SW1A 0PW.

HUTTON (Life Baron, UK), James Brian Edward Hutton; cr. 1997; PC 1988; Kt 1988

Son of late James and Mabel Hutton. Born June 29, 1931; educated Shrewsbury; Balliol College, Oxford (1st Class Final School of Jurisprudence); Queen's University, Belfast; Hon. Fellow, Balliol College, Oxford 1988; Hon. Bencher: Inner Temple 1988, King's Inn, Dublin 1988; Hon. LLD, Queen's University, Belfast 1992. Married, Mary Gillian, daughter of late J R W Murland (2 daughters). *Career:* Called to Northern Ireland Bar 1954; Junior Counsel to Attorney-General for Northern Ireland 1969; QC (NI) 1970; Called to English Bar 1972; Legal Adviser to Ministry of Home Affairs (NI) 1973; Senior Crown Counsel in NI 1973–79; Member, Joint Law Enforcement Commission 1974; Bencher, Inn of Court of Northern Ireland 1974; Judge of the High Court of Justice (NI) 1979–88; Lord Chief Justice of Northern Ireland 1988–97; Lord of Appeal in Ordinary 1997–. *Other:* President, Northern Ireland Association for Mental Health 1983–90. *Miscellaneous:* Deputy Chairman, Boundary Commission (NI) 1985–88. *Honours:* PC 1988; Kt 1988. *Name, Style and Title:* Raised to the peerage as Baron Hutton, of Bresagh in the County of Down 1997. A Cross-Bencher. *Address:* The Rt Hon. the Lord Hutton, House of Lords, London, SW1A 0PW.

HYLTON (5th Baron, UK), Raymond Hervey Jolliffe; cr. 1866; 5th Bt of Merstham (UK) 1821

Son of 4th Baron. Born June 13, 1932. Succeeded his father 1967; educated Eton; Trinity College, Oxford (MA); Hon. DSc, Southampton University 1994. Married June 29, 1966, Joanna, daughter of late Andrew de Bertodano (4 sons 1 daughter). *Armed Forces:* National Service, commissioned Coldstream Guards. *Councils, Public Bodies:* DL, Somerset 1975–90; Councillor, Frome RDC 1968–72. *House of Lords:* Private Members Bills: Sexual Offences (Amendment) Bill, Overseas Domestic Workers (Protection) Bill; An elected hereditary peer 1999–. *All-Party:* Member, All-Party Lords and Commons Committees on: Penal Affairs, Human Rights. *International Bodies (General):* Chairman, MICOM – Moldova Initiatives Committee of Management 1994. *Other:* Associated in various capacities since 1962 with: Abbeyfield Society, Catholic Housing Aid Society, The London Housing Aid Centre, National Federation of Housing Associations, Age Concern, L'Arche Ltd, Royal MENCAP, Foundation for Alternatives, Christian College for Adult Education, Mendip Wansdyke Local Enterprise Group, Hugh of Witham Foundation, Action around Bethlehem Children with Disability (ABCD); President, Northern Ireland Association for Care and Resettlement of Offenders 1988–. *Trusts, etc:* Associated in various capacities since 1962 with: Housing Associations Charitable Trust, Acorn Christian Healing Trust; Chairman, St Francis and St Sergius Trust Fund (for the churches in Russia) 1993–. *Miscellaneous:* Attaché, Governor-General of Canada 1960–62. ARICS 1960. *Special Interests:* Northern Ireland, Housing, British-Irish Relations, Human Rights, Prisons, Penal Affairs and Policy, Middle East, Europe, Former Soviet Union, Conflict Resolution. *Clubs:* Lansdowne. *Heir:* His son, Hon. William Henry Martin Jolliffe, born April 1, 1967. A Cross-Bencher. *Address:* The Lord Hylton, House of Lords, London, SW1A 0PW *Tel:* Messages: 020 7219 5353 *Fax:* 020 7219 5979.

HYLTON-FOSTER (Life Baroness, UK), Audrey Pellew Hylton-Foster; cr. 1965; DBE 1990

Daughter of late 1st Viscount Ruffside, PC, DL, Speaker of the House of Commons 1943–51 and late Viscountess Ruffside. Born May 19, 1908; educated St George's, Ascot; Ivy House, Wimbledon. Married December 22, 1931, Rt Hon. Sir Harry Hylton-Foster, QC, MP (died 1965), Speaker of the House of Commons 1959–65, son of late H. B. H. Hylton-Foster. *House of Lords:* Former Member of all Sub-Committees of the House of Lords in past position of Convenor of the Cross-Bench Peers. *Party Groups (General):* Member, Cross-Bench Parliamentary Group 1965–; Convenor, Cross Bench Peers 1974–95. *Other:* Director, Chelsea Division, County of London Branch, British Red Cross Society 1950–60; President, County of London Branch, BRCS 1960–74; Member, Executive Committee BRCS 1966–76; President and Chairman, The London Branch BRCS 1974–83; Member, Council of BRCS 1977–81, Patron, London Branch; Member, National BRCS HQ consultative panel 1984; President, Prevention of Blindness Research Fund 1965–76, Patron 1976–.

Awards Granted: BRCS Badge of Honour. *Honours:* DBE 1990. *Special Interests:* Social Welfare, Environment. *Recreations:* Fishing, gardening. *Name, Style and Title:* Raised to the peerage as Baroness Hylton-Foster, of the City of Westminster 1965. A Cross-Bencher. *Address:* The Baroness Hylton-Foster, DBE, The Coach House, Tanhurst, Leith Hill, Holmbury St. Mary, Dorking, Surrey, RH5 6LU *Tel:* 01306 711975; 54 Cranmer Court, Whitehead's Grove, London, SW3 3HW *Tel:* 020 7584 2889 *Tel:* House of Lords 020 7219 3209.

I

IMBERT (Life Baron, UK), Peter (Michael) Imbert; cr. 1999; Kt 1988; QPM 1980

Son of late William Henry Imbert, and of Frances May (née Hodge). Born April 27, 1933; educated Harvey's Grammar School, Folkestone; Holborn College of Law, Languages and Commerce; Hon. DLitt, Reading University 1987. Married 1956, Iris Dove (1 son 2 daughters). *Councils, Public Bodies:* DL, Greater London 1994–98, Lord Lieutenant 1998–; JP 1998. *Career:* Joined Metropolitan Police 1953; Metropolitan Police Anti-Terrorist Squad 1973–75; Police negotiator at Balcombe Street siege December 1975; Assistant Chief Constable, Surrey Constabulary 1976, Deputy Chief Constable 1977; Chief Constable, Thames Valley Police 1979–85; Secretary, National Crime Committee-ACPO Council 1980–83, Chairman 1983–85; Deputy Commissioner, Metropolitan Police 1985–87, Commissioner 1987–93; Leader, International Criminal Justice Delegation to Russia 1993; Visiting International Fellow, Australian Police Staff College 1994 and 1997; Has lectured on terrorism and siege situations in UK, Europe, Australia and Canada; Non-Executive Director: Securicor Goup 1993–, Camelot Group 1994–; Non-Executive Chairman, Retainagroup 1995–; Chairman, Capital Eye Security 1997–. *Other:* President, Richmond Horse Show 1993–; Governor, Harvey's Grammar School 1994–. *Trusts, etc:* Trustee, Queen Elizabeth Foundation of St Catharine's 1988–; Chairman, Surrey CCC Youth Trust 1993–96. *Miscellaneous:* Member: General Advisory Council, BBC 1980–87, Criminal Justice Consultative Committee 1992–93, Ministerial Advisory Group, Royal Parks 1993–, Public Policy Committee, RAC 1993–, Mental Health Foundation, Committee of Inquiry into Care in the Community for the Severely Mentally Ill 1994. *Honours:* QPM 1980; Kt 1988. CIMgt (CBIM 1982). *Recreations:* Bridge, golf, grandchildren. *Name, Style and Title:* Raised to the peerage as Baron Imbert, of New Romney in the County of Kent 1999. *Address:* The Lord Imbert, QPM, The Lieutenancy Office, 18th Floor, City Hall, PO Box 240, Victoria Street, London, SW1E 6QP.

INGE (Life Baron, UK), Peter (Anthony) Inge; cr. 1997; GCB (Mil) 1992; DL

Son of late Raymond and Grace Inge. Born August 5, 1935; educated Summer Fields; Wrekin College; RMA, Sandhurst; Hon. DCL, University of Newcastle upon Tyne. Married 1960, Letitia Marion Beryl, daughter of late Trevor Thornton-Berry (2 daughters). *Armed Forces:* Regular Army Officer with Service of 43 years; Commissioned Green Howards 1956; Served Hong Kong, Malaya, Germany, Libya and UK; ADC to GOC, 4 Division 1960–61; Adjutant, 1 Green Howards 1963–64; Student, Staff College 1966; Ministry of Defence 1967–69; Company Commander, 1 Green Howards 1969–70; Student, Joint Services Staff College 1971; BM, 11 Armoured Brigade 1972; Instructor, Staff College 1973–74; CO, 1 Green Howards 1974–76; Commandant, Junior Division, Staff College 1977–79; Commander, Task Force C/4 Armoured Brigade 1980–81; Chief of Staff, HQ 1 (BR) Corps 1982–83; Colonel, The Green Howards 1982–94; GOC, NE District and Commander 2nd Infantry Division 1984–86; Director General, Logistic Policy (Army), Ministry of Defence 1986–87; Commander, 1st (Br) Corps 1987–89; Colonel Commandant, Royal Military Police 1987–92; Commander, Northern Army Group and C-in-C, BAOR 1989–92; ADC General to HM The Queen 1991–94; Chief of the General Staff 1992–94; Field Marshal 1994; Chief of the Defence Staff 1994–97; Constable, HM Tower of London 1996–. *Councils, Public Bodies:* DL, North Yorkshire 1994. *All-Party:* Member, All-Party: Defence Group, Britain-Nepal Group. *International Bodies (General):* Member, International Institute of Strategic Studies. *Other:* Commissioner: Royal Hospital, Chelsea,

Royal Armouries; Deputy Chairman, Historic Royal Palaces. *Trusts, etc:* Chairman, Windsor Leadership Trust; St George's House. *Honours:* KCB 1988; GCB 1992. Freeman, City of London. Liveryman, Fan Makers' Company. *Special Interests:* Defence. *Recreations:* Cricket, walking, music, reading. *Clubs:* Boodle's, Beefsteak, Army and Navy, MCC. *Name, Style and Title:* Raised to the peerage as Baron Inge, of Richmond in the County of North Yorkshire 1997. A Cross-Bencher. *Address:* Field Marshal The Lord Inge, GCB, DL, House of Lords, London, SW1A 0PW.

INGLEWOOD (2nd Baron, UK), (William) Richard Fletcher-Vane; cr. 1964; DL

Son of 1st Baron, TD, DL. Born July 31, 1951. Succeeded his father 1989; educated Eton; Trinity College, Cambridge (MA); Cumbria College of Agriculture and Forestry. Married August 29, 1986, Cressida, daughter of late Desmond Pemberton-Pigott, CMG (1 son 2 daughters). *Councils, Public Bodies:* Member, Lake District Special Planning Board 1984–90; Chairman, Development Control Committee 1985–89; Member, North West Water Authority 1987–89; DL, Cumbria 1993. *Career:* Called to the Bar, Lincoln's Inn 1975; MEP (Conservative) for Cumbria and Lancashire North 1989–94; British Conservative Group spokesman, Legal Affairs Committee, European Parliament 1989–94, 1999–; Chief Whip, British Conservative Section of EPP Group 1994; Elected a Conservative MEP for the North West Region 1999–. *House of Lords:* Parliamentary Under-Secretary of State, Department of National Heritage 1995–97; An elected hereditary peer 1999–. *Whip:* A Lord in Waiting (Government Whip) 1994–95; Captain of HM Bodyguard of the Yeomen of the Guard (Government Deputy Chief Whip) January-July 1995. *Spokesman:* An Opposition Spokesman: on National Heritage 1997, on Culture, Media and Sport 1997–98. *Miscellaneous:* Contested (Conservative), Houghton and Washington 1983 General Election; Contested (Conservative), Durham 1984 European Election. ARICS. Liveryman, Skinners' Company. *Special Interests:* Rural Affairs, Agriculture, Environment, Europe, Local Government, Regional Policy, Legal Affairs, Media, Arts. *Clubs:* Travellers', Pratt's. *Heir:* His son, Hon. Henry William Frederick Fletcher-Vane, born December 24, 1990. A Conservative. *Address:* The Lord Inglewood, MEP, ARICS, DL, Hutton-in-the-Forest, Penrith, Cumbria, CA11 9TH *Tel:* 017684 84500 *Fax:* 017684 84571.

INGROW (Life Baron, UK), John Aked Taylor; cr. 1983. Kt 1972; OBE 1960; TD 1951

Son of late Percy Taylor. Born August 15, 1917; educated Shrewsbury School; Hon. D, University of Bradford 1990. Married October 11, 1949, Barbara Mary (died July 11, 1998), daughter of Percy Wright Stirk (2 daughters). *Armed Forces:* Served Overseas in 1939–45 War, DWR and Royal Signals (Major). *Councils, Public Bodies:* Councillor, Keighley Town Council 1946–67; JP, Keighley 1949; Mayor, Keighley 1956–57; DL, West Yorks 1971–76; Vice Lord-Lieutenant, West Yorks 1976–85; Lord-Lieutenant, West Yorks 1985–92. *Career:* Chairman and Managing Director, Timothy Taylor & Co. Ltd 1954–95, Life President 1995–; General Commissioner of Income Taxes 1965–92. *Party Groups (General):* Chairman: Keighley Conservative Association 1952–56, 1957–67, Yorkshire Area Conservatives 1966–71, Executive Committee, National Union 1971–76. *Other:* Member, Magistrates' Association Council 1957–86, Hon. Treasurer 1976–86; Member, Court of University of Leeds 1986–. *Honours:* TD 1951; OBE 1960; Kt 1972; KStJ 1986. *Name, Style and Title:* Raised to the peerage as Baron Ingrow, of Keighley in the County of West Yorkshire 1983. A Conservative. *Address:* The Lord Ingrow, OBE, TD, Fieldhead, Keighley, West Yorkshire, BD20 6LP *Tel:* 01535 603895.

Dod *on* Disk

The Vacher Dod Parliamentary Database

that will run on your PC or Network

For further details please telephone the Westminster Office

020 7828 7256

IRVINE OF LAIRG (Life Baron, UK), Alexander Andrew Mackay Irvine; cr. 1987; PC 1997; QC 1978

Son of Alexander and Margaret Christina Irvine. Born June 23, 1940; educated Inverness Royal Academy, Hutchesons' Boys' Grammar School, Glasgow; Glasgow University (MA, LLB); Christ's College, Cambridge (Scholar, BA, LLB); Hon. Fellow, Christ's College, Cambridge 1996; Hon. LLD, Glasgow 1997. Married 1974, Alison Mary, youngest daughter of Dr James Shaw McNair, MD and Agnes McNair, MA (2 sons). *Career:* University Lecturer, London School of Economics 1965–69; Called to the Bar, Inner Temple 1967; QC 1978; Head, 11 King's Bench Walk Chambers 1981–97; Bencher of the Inner Temple, 1985; Recorder 1985–88; Deputy High Court Judge 1987–97; Hon. Bencher, Inn of Court of Northern Ireland 1998. *House of Lords:* Shadow Lord Chancellor 1992–97; Lord Chancellor 1997–. *Spokesman:* Shadow Spokesman on Legal Affairs and Home Affairs 1987–92. *Select Committees:* Member, Select Committees on: House of Lords' Offices 1997–, Procedure 1997–. *International Bodies:* Joint President: British-American Parliamentary Group, CPA, IPU. *International Bodies (General):* Vice-Patron, World Federation of Mental Health. *Other:* President, Magistrates Association; Chairman, Glasgow 2001 Committee; Member, Committee of the Slade School of Fine Art 1990–. *Awards Granted:* George and Thomas Hutcheson Award 1998. *Trusts, etc:* Foundation Trustee, Whitechapel Art Gallery 1990–97; Trustee: John Smith Memorial Trust 1992–97, Hunterian Collection 1997–; Joint President, Industry and Parliament Trust. *Miscellaneous:* Contested (Labour) Hendon North, General Election 1970; Church Commissioner. *Honours:* PC 1997. Hon. Fellow, Society for Advanced Legal Studies; Fellow, US College of Trial Lawyers 1998–. *Special Interests:* Legal Affairs, Home Affairs, Constitutional Affairs. *Recreations:* Collecting paintings, travel, reading, cinema and theatre. *Clubs:* Garrick. *Name, Style and Title:* Raised to the peerage as Baron Irvine of Lairg, of Lairg in the District of Sutherland 1987. Labour. *Address:* The Rt Hon. the Lord Irvine of Lairg, House of Lords, London, SW1A 0PW.

ISLWYN (Life Baron, UK), Royston John (Roy) Hughes; cr. 1997; DL

Son of late John Hughes, Miner. Born June 9, 1925; educated Ruskin College, Oxford. Married June 10, 1957, Marion, daughter of John Appleyard, of Scarborough (3 daughters). *Trades Union:* Has held numerous offices in TGWU from 1959; Chairman, Parliamentary Group TGWU 1968–69, 1979–82. *Armed Forces:* Served 2nd Btn, Welch Regiment. *Councils, Public Bodies:* Coventry City Councillor 1962–66; DL, Gwent 1992–. *House of Commons:* MP (Labour) for Newport 1966–83 and for Newport East 1983–97. *Spokesman (Commons):* Front Bench Spokesman on Welsh Affairs 1984–88. *Select Committees (Commons):* Member, Speaker's Panel of Chairmen 1990–97. *Backbench Committees (Commons):* Chairman: Parliamentary Labour Party Sports Group 1974–84, Parliamentary Labour Party Steel Group 1977–97. *All-Party Committees (Commons):* Joint Chairman: All-Party Roads Group 1982–97, All-Party Motors Group 1987–97, All-Party Rugby Union Group 1993–97. *All-Party:* Member, All-Party Road Passenger Transport Group. *International Bodies (General):* Member, Executive British Group, Inter Parliamentary Union 1986–92, Treasurer 1991; Member, Council of Europe 1990–97. *Party Groups (General):* Secretary, Coventry Borough Labour Party 1962–66; Chairman, Welsh Parliamentary Party 1969–70. *Miscellaneous:* Chairman, Welsh Grand Committee 1982–84, 1990–97; Spokesman, Pensioners' Convention 1998–. *Special Interests:* Steel, Motor Industry, Sport, Road Programme, International Affairs. *Recreations:* Rugby, soccer, cricket, gardening. *Sportsclubs:* Vice-President: Crawshay's (Wales) Rugby XV 1991–, Glamorgan County Cricket Club. *Name, Style and Title:* Raised to the peerage as Baron Islwyn, of Casnewydd in the County of Gwent 1997. Labour. *Address:* The Lord Islwyn, DL, Chapel Field, Chapel Lane, Abergavenny, Gwent, NP7 7BT *Tel:* 01873 856502.

J

JACOBS (Life Baron, UK), (David) Anthony Jacobs; cr. 1997; Kt 1988

Son of Ridley and Ella Jacobs. Born November 1931; educated Clifton College; London University (BCom). Married 1954, Evelyn Felicity Patchett (1 son 1 daughter). *Career:* Chairman: Nig Securities Group 1957–72, Tricoville Group 1961–90, 1992–94, British School of Motoring 1973–90. *Party Groups (General):* Joint Treasurer, Liberal Party 1984–87; Vice-President, Social and Liberal Democrats 1988, Member, Federal Executive 1988. *Other:* Chairman, Board of Governors, Haifa University, Israel. *Miscellaneous:* Crown Estate Paving Commissioner. *Honours:* Kt 1988. FCA. *Recreations:* Golf, reading, theatre, opera, travel. *Sportsclubs:* Coombe Hill Golf (Surrey). *Name, Style and Title:* Raised to the peerage as Baron Jacobs, of Belgravia in the City of Westminster 1997. A Liberal Democrat. *Address:* The Lord Jacobs, FCA, 9 Nottingham Terrace, London, NW1 4QB *Tel:* 020 7486 6323.

JAMES OF HOLLAND PARK (Life Baroness, UK), Phyllis Dorothy James; cr. 1991; OBE 1983

Daughter of late Sydney and Dorothy James. Born August 3, 1920; educated Cambridge High School for Girls; Associate Fellow, Downing College, Cambridge 1986; Hon. degree, Doctor of Letters, University of Buckingham 1992; Hon. degree, Doctor of Literature, University of London 1993; Hon. degree, Doctor of Letters: University of Hertfordshire 1994, University of Glasgow 1995; Doctor of the University of Essex 1996; Hon. Fellow, St Hilda's College, Oxford 1996; Hon. DLitt, Durham 1998; Hon. Doctor of Letters, University of Portsmouth 1999. Married August 8, 1941, Connor Bantry White (died 1964) (2 daughters). *Councils, Public Bodies:* JP, Willesden and Inner London 1979–84. *Career:* Administrator, National Health Service 1949–68; Civil Servant: appointed Principal, Home Office 1968, Police Department 1968–72, Criminal Policy Department 1972–79; A Governor, BBC 1988–93; Member, Arts Council 1988–92, Chairman, Literature Advisory Panel 1988–92; Board Member, British Council 1988–93. *Other:* Chairman: Booker Panel of Judges 1987, Society of Authors 1984–86; President, Society of Authors 1997–; Member, Liturgical Commission, Church of England; Vice-President, Prayer Book Society. *Honours:* OBE 1983. Fellow, Royal Society of Literature 1987; FRSA. *Publications:* Author (as P.D. James) of: *Cover her Face*, 1962; *A Mind to Murder*, 1963; *Unnatural Causes*, 1967; *Shroud for a Nightingale*, 1971; *The Maul and the Pear Tree* (with T.A. Critchley), 1971; *An Unsuitable Job for a Woman*, 1972; *The Black Tower*, 1975; *Death of an Expert Witness*, 1977; *Innocent Blood*, 1980; *The Skull Beneath the Skin*, 1982; *A Taste for Death*, 1986; *Devices and Desires*, 1989; *The Children of Men*, 1992; *Original Sin*, 1994; *A Certain Justice*, 1997; *Time to be in Earnest*, 1999. *Special Interests:* Literature, Arts, Criminal Justice, Broadcasting. *Recreations:* Reading, exploring churches, walking by the sea. *Clubs:* Detection. *Name, Style and Title:* Raised to the peerage as Baroness James of Holland Park, of Southwold in the County of Suffolk 1991. A Conservative. *Address:* The Baroness James of Holland Park, OBE, c/o Greene and Heaton Ltd, 37 Goldhawk Road, London, W12 8QQ.

JANNER OF BRAUNSTONE (Life Baron, UK), Greville Ewan Janner; cr. 1997; QC 1971

Son of late Baron Janner (Life Peer) and Lady Janner, CBE. Born July 11, 1928; educated St Paul's School; Trinity Hall, Cambridge (MA); Harvard Post-Graduate Law School, USA; Hon. PhD, Haifa University; Hon. LLD, De Montfort University. Married July 6, 1955, Myra Sheink, of Melbourne, Australia (died 1996) (1 son 2 daughters). *Trades Union:* Member, NUJ (London Freelance Branch); Hon. Member, NUM, Leicester. *Armed Forces:* National Service 1946–48, RA, BAOR, War Crimes Investigator. *Career:* Former President, Cambridge Union; Barrister-at-Law; QC 1971; Non-executive director, Ladbroke plc 1986–95; Chairman, JSB Group and Effective Presentational Skills 1987–97; President, REACH (Retired Executives' Action Clearing House) 1989–. *House of Commons:* Contested Wimbledon 1955; MP (Labour) for Leicester North-West 1970–74, and for Leicester West 1974–97. *Select Committees (Commons):* Member, Select

Committee on Employment 1983–96, Chairman 1992–96; Member, Select Committee on Liaison 1992–96. *All-Party Committees (Commons):* Former Vice-Chairman, All-Party Parliamentary Committee for release of Jews in the former Soviet Union; Former Chairman, All-Party Industrial Safety Group; President, Inter-Parliamentary Council Against Anti-Semitism 1991–; Chairman, All-Party Parliamentary Magic Group 1991–97; Former Vice-Chairman: British-India Group, British-Israel Group 1991–97, All-Party British Southern Africa Group 1995–97; Former Treasurer, All-Party British Romania Group; Former Secretary: All-Party British Lithuanian Group, All-Party Spanish Group, All-Party War Crimes Group; Co-Chairman, All-Party Employment Group 1996–97. *Select Committees:* Member, Joint Select Committee on Consolidation of Bills 1998–. *Party Groups (General):* Former Chairman, Cambridge University Labour Club; International Secretary, National Association of Labour Students 1952. *Other:* President: Board of Deputies of British Jews 1979–85, Commonwealth Jewish Council 1982–; Hon. Vice-President, World Jewish Congress 1991–; Founder and President, Maimonides Foundation 1995–; Vice-President: Association of Jewish Ex-Servicemen, Association for Jewish Youth. *Trusts, etc:* Chairman: Holocaust Educational Trust, Lord Forte Charitable Trust. Fellow, Institute of Personnel Management and Development. Freeman, City of London. *Publications:* Author of many books including: *Janner's Complete Speechmaker* (6th Edition); *One Hand Alone Cannot Clap*, 1998. *Special Interests:* Employment Law, Industrial Relations, Jewish Causes, Human Rights, Consumer Protection, Commonwealth, India, Middle East. *Recreations:* Swimming, member of the Magic Circle and International Brotherhood of Magicians, languages. *Name, Style and Title:* Raised to the peerage as Baron Janner of Braunstone, of Leicester in the County of Leicestershire 1997. Labour. *Address:* The Lord Janner of Braunstone, QC, House of Lords, London, SW1A 0PW.

JAUNCEY OF TULLICHETTLE (Life Baron, UK), Charles Eliot Jauncey; cr. 1988; PC 1988

Son of late Captain John Henry Jauncey, DSO, RN. Born May 8, 1925; educated Radley; Christ Church, Oxford; Glasgow University. Married 1st, 1948, Jean, daughter of late Admiral Sir Angus Cunninghame Graham of Gartmore, KBE, CB (2 sons 1 daughter) (marriage dissolved 1969), married 2nd, 1973, Elizabeth, widow of Major John Ballingal, MC (marriage dissolved 1977), married 3rd, 1977, Camilla, daughter of late Lieutenant-Colonel Charles Cathcart, DSO (1 daughter). *Armed Forces:* Served in War 1943–46, Sub-Lieutenant RNVR. *Career:* Advocate, Scottish Bar 1949; Standing Junior Counsel to Admiralty 1954; QC (Scotland) 1963; Kintyre Pursuivant of Arms 1955–71; Sheriff Principal of Fife and Kinross 1971–74; Judge of the Courts of Appeal of Jersey and Guernsey 1972–79; A Senator of the College of Justice in Scotland 1979–88; A Lord of Appeal in Ordinary 1988–96. *Miscellaneous:* Member: Queen's Body Guard for Scotland, Royal Company of Archers 1951, Historic Buildings Council for Scotland 1972–92. *Honours:* PC 1998. *Recreations:* Shooting, fishing, genealogy, bicycling. *Clubs:* Royal (Perth). *Name, Style and Title:* Raised to the peerage as Baron Jauncey of Tullichettle, of Comrie in the District of Perth and Kinross 1988. A Cross-Bencher. *Address:* The Rt Hon. the Lord Jauncey of Tullichettle, Tullichettle, Comrie, Crieff, Perthshire, PH6 2HU.

JAY OF PADDINGTON (Life Baroness, UK), Margaret Ann Jay; cr. 1992; PC 1998

Daughter of Rt Hon. Baron Callaghan of Cardiff, KG (*qv*). Born November 18, 1939; educated Blackheath High School; Somerville College, Oxford (BA Politics, Philosophy and Economics). Married 1st, 1961, Hon. Peter Jay, son of late Baron Jay, PC (1 son 2 daughters) (marriage dissolved 1986), married 2nd, 1994, Professor Michael W. Adler. *Trades Union:* Member, NUJ. *Councils, Public Bodies:* Member, Kensington and Chelsea and Westminster Health Authority 1993–97; Former Member, Central Research and Development Committee for the NHS. *Career:* Various production posts with BBC Television in current affairs and further education 1965–77; A Former Reporter for: BBC Television's *Panorama*, Thames Television's *This Week*; Founder Director, The National AIDS Trust 1988–92; Non-Executive Director: Carlton Television to 1997, Scottish Power to 1997. *House of Lords:* Minister of State, Department of Health 1997–98; Deputy Leader, House of Lords 1997–98; Lord Privy Seal, Leader of the House of Lords and Minister for Women 1998–. *Whip:* An Opposition Whip 1992–95. *Spokesman:* An Opposition Spokesman on Health 1992–97, Principal Opposition Spokesman 1995–97. *Select Committees:* Member: House of Lords Select Committee on Medical Ethics 1993–94, Select Committee on House of Lords' Offices 1997–. *All-Party:* Vice-Chairman, All-Party Parliamentary Group on AIDS. *Other:* Former Chairman: National Association of League of Hospital Friends, North Thames Regional Committee for Research and Development in the NHS;

Former Member of Council, The Overseas Development Institute; Former Governor, South Bank University; Former Member, Governing Board: Queen Charlotte's Maternity Hospital, Chelsea Hospital for Women. *Trusts, etc:* Trustee, International Crisis Group; Patron, Help the Aged ReAction Trust and Progress – The Campaign for Research into Human Reproduction. *Honours:* PC 1998. *Publications: How Rich Can We Get?*, 1972; *Battered – The Story of Child Abuse* (joint author), 1986. *Special Interests:* Health, Overseas Aid and Development, Media, Broadcasting. *Name, Style and Title:* Raised to the peerage as Baroness Jay of Paddington, of Paddington in the City of Westminster 1992. Labour. *Address:* The Rt Hon. the Baroness Jay of Paddington, House of Lords, London, SW1A 0PW.

JEGER (Life Baroness, UK), Lena May Jeger; cr. 1979

Daughter of late Charles and Alice Chivers, of Yorkley, Gloucestershire. Born November 19, 1915; educated Southgate County School; Birkbeck College (BA (London). Married 1948, Dr Santo Jeger (died 1953), formerly MP for Holborn and St Pancras South. *Councils, Public Bodies:* Labour representative for Holborn and St. Pancras South on the LCC 1951–54; Councillor, St Pancras Borough Council 1945–59. *Career:* Formerly employed at the Ministry of Information and Foreign Office; Assistant editor in Moscow of *British Ally*, a newspaper published by the British Government for issue in the Soviet Union; Staff writer on *The Guardian* 1959–64; UK representative on the Status of Women Commission of UN 1967; Member, Consultative Assembly of the Council of Europe and of Western European Union 1969–71. *House of Commons:* MP (Labour) for Holborn and St Pancras South 1953–59, 1964–79; Chairman, Government's Working Party on Sewage Disposal 1969–70. *Spokesman:* Opposition Spokesman on: Health 1983–86, Social Security 1983–90. *Party Groups (General):* Member, National Executive Committee of the Labour Party 1960–61, 1968–80; Chairman, Labour Party 1979–80. *Name, Style and Title:* Raised to the peerage as Baroness Jeger, of St Pancras in the County of Greater London 1979. Labour. *Address:* The Baroness Jeger, 9 Cumberland Terrace, Regents Park, London, NW1 4HS.

JELLICOE (2nd Earl, UK), George Patrick John Rushworth Jellicoe; cr. 1925; Viscount Brocas; Viscount Jellicoe (UK) 1918; (Life) Baron Jellicoe of Southampton (UK) 1999; KBE 1986; DSO 1942; MC 1944; PC 1963; FRS 1990

Son of Admiral of the Fleet 1st Earl, GCB, OM, GCVO. Born April 4, 1918. Succeeded his father 1935; educated Winchester; Trinity College, Cambridge (Exhibitioner, 1st Class Hons History); Hon. Degrees: Kings College, London, Southampton University, University of Southampton, Long Island, USA. Married 1st, 1944, Patricia Christine, daughter of late Jeremiah O'Kane, of Vancouver (2 sons 2 daughters) (marriage dissolved 1966), married 2nd, 1966, Philippa, daughter of late Philip Dunne (1 son 2 daughters). *Armed Forces:* Served in Middle East 1941–45 (despatches thrice, DSO, MC), No 8 Commando, Coldstream Guards, SAS and SBS, Lieutenant-Colonel. *Career:* HM Foreign Service 1947–58, serving in Washington, Brussels and Baghdad (Deputy Secretary General, The Baghdad Pact); Chairman: Greece Fund 1988–94, European Capital 1991–95; Director, Tate & Lyle plc 1973–93, Chairman 1978–83; Director, Sothebys 1973–93; Chairman: Davy Corporation 1985–90, Booker Tate 1988–91; Director: Smiths Industries 1973–86, S. G. Warburg 1964–70, 1973–88, Morgan Crucible 1974–88; President, East European Trade Council, Chairman 1986–90; Chairman, British Overseas Trade Board 1983–86. *Chancellor:* Chancellor, Southampton University 1984–95. *House of Lords:* Joint Parliamentary Secretary, Ministry of Housing and Local Government 1961–62; Minister of State, Home Office 1962–63; First Lord of the Admiralty 1963–64; Minister of Defence for the Royal Navy April-October 1964; Deputy Leader of Opposition in the House of Lords 1967–70; Lord Privy Seal, Leader of the House of Lords and Minister for the Civil Service Department 1970–73. *Whip:* A Lord in Waiting (Government Whip) January-June 1961. *Select Committees:* Former Chairman, Select Committee on Committees. *All-Party:* President, Parliamentary and Scientific Committee 1980–83; Patron, All-Party AIDS Group; Member, All-Party British-Ukrainian Country Group 1999–. *Other:* Chairman, Council, King's College, London 1977–84; President, London Chamber of Commerce and Industry 1979–82; Chairman, Medical Research Council 1982–90; President: British Heart Foundation 1992–95, Royal Geographical Society 1993–97, The Geographical Club 1993–97, SAS Regimental Association 1996–. *Trusts, etc:* President, Kennet and Avon Canal Trust 1987–94.

Honours: DSO 1942; MC 1944; PC 1963; KBE 1986; French Legion d'Honneur; Croix de Guerre; Greek Order of Honour; Greek War Cross. Hon. Fellow, Royal Scottish Geographical Society 1997; FRS. Freeman, City of Athens. Member, Mercers' Company. *Special Interests:* Foreign Affairs, Education, Environment, Arts. *Recreations:* Skiing, travel. *Sportsclubs:* Ski Club of Great Britain. *Clubs:* Brooks's, Special Forces. *Heir:* His son, Viscount Brocas, born August 29, 1950. *Name, Style and Title:* Created a life peer as Baron Jellicoe of Southampton, of Southampton in the County of Hampshire 1999. A Conservative. *Address:* The Rt Hon. the Earl Jellicoe, KBE, DSO, MC, FRS, Tidcombe Manor, Tidcombe, Nr Marlborough, Wiltshire, SN8 3SL *Tel:* 01264 731225 *Fax:* 01264 731418; 97 Onslow Square, London, SW7 3LU *Tel:* 020 7584 1551.

JENKIN OF RODING (Life Baron, UK), Charles Patrick Fleeming Jenkin; cr. 1987; PC 1973

Son of late Charles Jenkin, Industrial Chemist. Born September 7, 1926; educated Clifton College; Jesus College, Cambridge; Fellow, Queen Mary and Westfield College 1991–; Hon. LLD, South Bank University, London 1995. Married 1952, Alison Monica, daughter of late Captain P. S. Graham, RN (2 sons 2 daughters). *Armed Forces:* Served in the Cameron Highlanders, including service abroad 1945–48. *Councils, Public Bodies:* Councillor, Hornsey Borough Council 1960–63. *Career:* Went to the Middle Temple as a Harmsworth Scholar; Called to the Bar 1952; A Barrister, practised at the Bar 1952–57; Employed by The Distillers Co. Ltd 1957–70; Adviser, Andersen Consulting, Management Consultants 1985–96; Member, UK Advisory Board, National Economic Research Associates Inc. 1985–; Chairman, Target Finland Ltd 1987–96; Director, Friends Provident Life Office, Chairman 1988–98; Member, Supervisory Board, Achmea Holding NV (Netherlands) 1992–98; UK Co-Chairman, UK-Japan 2000 Group 1986–90; Board Member 1990–99; Non-Executive Director, Crystalate Holdings plc 1987–90, Chairman 1988–90; Chairman, Lamco Paper Sales Ltd 1987–93; Adviser, Sumitomo Trust and Banking Co. Ltd 1989–; Member, International Advisory Board, Marsh and McLennan Group of Companies (US) 1993–99; Adviser, Thames Estuary Airport Co. Ltd. 1992–; Senior Vice-President, World Congress on Urban Growth and the Environment (Hong Kong) 1992–94. *House of Commons:* MP (Conservative) for Wanstead and Woodford 1964–87; Financial Secretary to the Treasury 1970–72; Chief Secretary to the Treasury 1972–74; Mininster for Energy 1974; Secretary of State for: Social Services 1979–81, Industry September 1981–83, the Environment 1983–85. *Spokesman (Commons):* Opposition Spokesman on Treasury, Trade and Economic Affairs October 1965; An Opposition Front Bench Spokesman for the Treasury 1967–70; Member, Shadow Cabinet and Opposition Spokesman on: Energy 1974–76, Social Services 1976–79. *Backbench Committees (Commons):* Vice-Chairman, Conservative Parliamentary Trade and Power Committee 1966. *All-Party Committees (Commons):* Member, All-Party Anglo-Japanese Parliamentary Group 1970–; Founder Chairman, All-Party Chemical Industry Group 1985–. *Select Committees:* Member: House of Lords Offices Committee and Finance and Staffing Sub-Committee 1991–94, House of Lords Select Committee on Sustainable Development 1994–95, Select Committee on Science and Technology 1997–; Chairman, Select Committee on Science and Technology Sub-Committee II (Science and Society) 1999–. *All-Party:* Member, House of Lords All-Party Group on London 1995–. *Party Groups:* Executive Committee Member, ACP. *International Bodies (General):* Member: CPA, IPU. *Party Groups (General):* Member, Bow Group from 1951; President: Conservative Greater London Area Education Committee 1967–80, Conservative Greater London Area CPC Committee 1981–83, National CPC Committee 1982–85; Vice-President, Greater London Area Conservatives 1987–89, President 1989–93; President, Saffron Walden Constituency Conservative Association 1994–. *Other:* Member, London Council of Social Service 1963–67; Governor, Westfield College (London University) 1964–70; President, Old Cliftonian Society 1987–89; Council Member, Guide Dogs for the Blind Association 1987–97; Council Member, UK Council for Economic and Environmental Development 1987–; Vice-President: National Association of Local Councils 1987–97; Association of Metropolitan Authorities 1987–97; President, British Urban Regeneration Association 1990–96; Chairman, Visual Handicap Group 1991–98; Council Member, Imperial Cancer Research Fund 1991–93, Deputy Chairman 1994–97; President: London Boroughs Association 1993–95, Clifton College, Bristol 1993–99; Member, International Advisory Board, Nijenrode University (Netherlands) 1994–99; Joint President, Association of London Government 1995–; Vice-President, Foundation for Science and Technology 1996–97, Chairman 1997–; Vice-President, Local Government Association 1997–. *Trusts, etc:* Chairman, Westfield College Trust 1989–; Patron: Stort Trust 1991–, Redbridge Community Trust 1992–95, St Clare Hospice

Trust 1992–; Chairman, Forest Healthcare NHS Trust 1992–97; Trustee: Monteverdi Choir and Orchestra 1992–, Conservative Agents Superannuation Fund 1992–; Patron, London North-East Community Foundation 1995–. *Honours:* PC 1973. Freeman, City of London 1985; Hon. Freeman, London Borough of Redbridge 1988. *Special Interests:* Economic Policy, Industry, Technology, Health, Disabled, Urban Policies, Housing, Planning, Financial Services. *Recreations:* Gardening, DIY, bricklaying, sailing, music. *Clubs:* West Essex Conservative Club. *Name, Style and Title:* Raised to the peerage as Baron Jenkin of Roding, of Wanstead and Woodford in Greater London 1987. A Conservative. *Address:* The Rt Hon. the Lord Jenkin of Roding, House of Lords, London, SW1A 0PW *Tel:* 020 7219 6966 *Fax:* 020 7219 0759 *E-Mail:* jenkinp@parliament.uk.

JENKINS OF HILLHEAD (Life Baron, UK), Roy Harris Jenkins; cr. 1987; OM 1993; PC 1964

Son of late Arthur Jenkins, MP for Pontypool 1935–46. Born November 11, 1920; educated Abersychan Grammar School; Balliol College, Oxford; Hon. Fellow, Balliol College, Oxford 1968; Hon. LLD: Leeds 1971, Harvard 1972; Hon. Fellow, Berkeley College, Yale 1972; Hon. DLitt, Glasgow 1972; Hon. DCL, Oxford 1973; Hon. LLD: Pennsylvania 1973, Dundee 1973, Loughborough 1975; Hon. DLitt, City 1976; Hon. DSc, Aston 1977; DUniv: Keele 1977, Essex 1978; Hon. LLD: Bath 1978, Michigan 1978; Hon. DLitt: Warwick 1978, Reading 1979; DUniv, Open 1979; Hon. DPhil, Katholieke University, Leuven 1979; Hon. doctorates: Urbino 1979, Trinity College, Dublin 1979; Hon. LLD: Wales 1979, Bristol 1980, Georgetown 1988; Hon. Fellow, St. Antony's College, Oxford 1988; Hon. doctorates: West Virginia 1992, Kent 1992, Glamorgan 1994, Bologna, 1994; Hon. Fellow: University of Wales, Cardiff 1995, University of Wales, Newport 1996, Sofia (Bulgaria) 1998. Married 1945, Dame (Mary) Jennifer, DBE, daughter of late Sir Parker Morris (2 sons 1 daughter). *Armed Forces:* Served War of 1939–45; RA 1942–46; Captain 1944–46. *Career:* Member, Staff of Industrial and Commercial Finance Corporation Ltd 1946–48; Director, Financial Operations, John Lewis Partnership 1962–64; Director, Morgan Grenfell Holdings Ltd 1981–82; President, European Commission 1977–81; Chairman, Independent Commission on the Voting System 1998. *House of Commons:* Contested (Labour) Solihull division of Warwickshire at General Election 1945; MP (Labour): Central Southwark 1948–50, Stechford, Birmingham 1950–76; PPS to Secretary of State for Commonwealth Relations 1949–50; Minister of Aviation 1964–65; Home Secretary 1965–67; Chancellor of the Exchequer 1967–70; Home Secretary 1974–76; MP (SDP) Glasgow Hillhead 1983–87. *Spokesman (Commons):* Senior Spokesman of the Social Democrat Party 1983. *Chancellor:* Chancellor, Oxford University 1987–. *Spokesman:* Treasury Spokesman for the Alliance 1987. *Party Groups:* Leader, Liberal Democrat Peers 1988–97. *Party Groups (General):* Chairman, Oxford University Democratic Socialist Club; Member, Executive Committee of Fabian Society 1949–61; Chairman, Fabian Society 1957–58; Deputy Leader, Labour Party 1970–72; Member, Joint Leadership Social Democratic Party 1981–82; Elected Leader July 1982–June 83. *Other:* Secretary and Librarian, Oxford Union Society; Member, Committee of Management, Society of Authors 1956–60; President, Royal Society of Literature 1988–. *Awards Granted:* Charlemagne Prize 1972; Robert Schuman Prize 1972; Prix Bentinck 1978. *Trusts, etc:* Trustee, Pilgrim Trust 1973–98. *Miscellaneous:* Governor, British Film Institute 1955–58; President, UWIST 1975–81. *Honours:* PC 1964; Order of European Merit (Luxemburg) 1976; Grand Cross, Order of Charles III (Spain) 1980; Order of Merit (Italy) 1990; Ordem do Infante Dom Henrique of Portugal 1993; OM 1993. Hon. Foreign Member, American Academic Arts and Sciences 1973; Honorary Fellow, British Academy 1993. Freeman, City of Brussels 1980. Liveryman, Goldsmiths' Company 1965. *Publications:* (editor) *Purpose and Policy* (a volume of the Prime Minister's Speeches), 1947; *Mr Attlee: An Interim Biography,* 1948; *Pursuit of Progress,* 1953; *Mr Balfour's Poodle,* 1954; *Sir Charles Dilke: A Victorian Tragedy,* 1958; *The Labour Case* (Penguin Special), 1959; *Asquith,* 1964; *Essays and Speeches,* 1967; *Afternoon on the Potomac,* 1972; *What Matters Now,* 1972; *Nine Men of Power,* 1975; *Partnership of Principle,* 1985; *Truman,* 1986; *Baldwin,* 1987; *Gallery of Twentieth Century Portraits,* 1988; *European Diary,* 1989; *A Life at the Centre,* 1991; *Portraits and Miniatures,* 1993; *Gladstone,* 1995; *The Chancellors,* 1998. *Clubs:* Athenaeum, Beefsteak, Brooks's, Pratt's, Reform, United Oxford and Cambridge University. *Name, Style and Title:* Raised to the peerage as Baron Jenkins of Hillhead, of Pontypool in the County of Gwent 1987. A Liberal Democrat. *Address:* The Rt Hon. the Lord Jenkins of Hillhead, OM, 2 Kensington Park Gardens, London, W11 3HB; St Amand's House, East Hendred, Oxfordshire, OX12 8LF *E-Mail:* Macphersong@parliament.uk.

JENKINS OF PUTNEY (Life Baron, UK), Hugh Gater Jenkins; cr. 1981

Son of late Joseph Walter Jenkins, Dairyman and late Florence Gater. Born July 27, 1908; educated Enfield Grammar School. Married 1st, 1936, Marie (died 1989), daughter of late Squadron-Leader Ernest Crosbie, RAF, married 2nd, 1991, Helena Maria (died January 31, 1994), daughter of late Nicholas Pavlidis, of Athens. *Trades Union:* Trade Unionist since 1930; Member: Prudential Staff Union 1930–40, MSF 1947–, Actors Equity 1948–. *Armed Forces:* Flight-Lieutenant, Royal Air Force during World War II *Councils, Public Bodies:* London County Councillor 1958–64, Member, Town Planning Committee. *Career:* Prudential Assurance Company 1930–40, Assistant-Superintendent 1935–40; Research and Publicity Officer, National Union of Bank Employees 1946–50; Former Editor, *The Bank Officer;* Assistant General Secretary, Actors' Equity to 1964. *House of Commons:* Contested (Labour) Enfield West 1950, Mitcham 1955; MP (Labour) for Wandsworth, Putney division October 15, 1964–79; Minister for the Arts 1974–76. *Spokesman (Commons):* Spokesman for the Arts 1973–74. *Select Committees (Commons):* Former Member, Public Accounts Committee. *All-Party Committees (Commons):* Member, Joint Parliamentary Committee on Theatre Censorship. *Party Groups (Commons):* Member, Tribune Group. *International Bodies (Commons):* Member: CPA, IPU. *Spokesman:* Spokesman on the Arts 1981–83. *All-Party:* Member, All-Party Ageing Group. *International Bodies (General):* Member, British-American Security Information Committee. *Party Groups (General):* Joined Labour Party 1933; Member, London Labour Party Executive Committee; Chairman, Victory For Socialism; Vice-Chairman, Labour Action For Peace. *Other:* Former Chairman, now Vice-President, Campaign for Nuclear Disarmament. *Trusts, etc:* President, Theatres Trust. *Miscellaneous:* President, Theatres Advisory Council; Former Member: The Arts Council, The National Theatre Board. *Publications: The Culture Gap,* 1980; *Rank and File,* 1981; As well as radio plays (BBC Radio Four), various pamphlets and contributions to journals and newspapers. *Special Interests:* Disarmament, Arts, Trade Unions, Media, Nuclear Disarmament. *Recreations:* Avoiding retirement, writing, listening, talking, viewing, reading, concert and theatre-going. *Name, Style and Title:* Raised to the peerage as Baron Jenkins of Putney, of Wandsworth in Greater London 1981. Labour. *Address:* The Lord Jenkins of Putney, House of Lords, London, SW1A 0PW *Tel:* House of Lords 020 7219 6706 *Tel:* 020 8788 0371.

JOHNSTON OF ROCKPORT (Life Baron, UK), Charles Collier Johnston; cr. 1987; Kt 1973; TD 1945

Son of Captain Charles Moore Johnston (killed, Somme, 1916) and late Muriel Florence Mellon. Born March 4, 1915; educated Tonbridge. Married 1st, June 15, 1939, Audrey Boyes, only daughter of late Edgar Monk (2 sons), married 2nd, September 1, 1981, Mrs Yvonne Shearman, daughter of late Reginald and Dora Marley. *Armed Forces:* Commissioned 1938, Territorial; RA 1939–46; Retired as Major. *Career:* Managing Director, Standtex International Ltd 1948–76, Chairman 1951–77; Chairman: Thames & Kennet Marina Ltd 1982–94, James Burn International 1986–, Standtex Holdings Ltd 1983. *Party Groups (General):* Chairman, Macclesfield Constituency Conservative Association 1961–65; Hon. Treasurer, North West Conservatives, Member, Conservative Board of Finance 1965–71; Chairman, North West Area Conservatives 1971–76; A Vice-President, National Union of Conservative and Unionist Associations, Executive Committee 1965–87, Chairman 1976–81, President 1986–87; Joint Hon. Treasurer, Conservative Party 1984–87; National Chairman, Conservative Friends of Israel 1983–86. *Miscellaneous:* An official observer at 1980 elections, Zimbabwe (Boyd Commission). *Honours:* Kt 1973. *Recreations:* Gardening, Spectator Sports. *Name, Style and Title:* Raised to the peerage as Baron Johnston of Rockport, of Caversham in the Royal County of Berkshire 1987. A Conservative. *Address:* The Lord Johnston of Rockport, TD, The Dower House, Marston, Devizes, Wiltshire, SN10 5SN *Tel:* 01380 725782 *Tel:* 020 7730 3557.

JOPLING (Life Baron, UK), (Thomas) Michael Jopling; cr. 1997; PC 1979; DL

Son of late Mark Jopling. Born December 10, 1930; educated Cheltenham College; King's College, Newcastle-upon-Tyne (BSc Agriculture); Hon. DCL, Newcastle 1992. Married April 1958, Gail, daughter of late Ernest Dickinson, of Harrogate (2 sons). *Councils, Public Bodies:* Councillor, Thirsk Rural District Council for six years; DL: Cumbria 1991–97, North Yorkshire 1998–. *Career:* Farmer, farms 500 acres. *House of Commons:* Contested (Conservative) Wakefield at 1959 General Election; MP (Conservative) for Westmorland 1964–83 and for Westmorland and Lonsdale 1983–97; Sponsored Private Member's Bill on Parish Councils 1969; PPS to the Minister of Agriculture, Fisheries and Food June 1970–71; Shadow Cabinet 1975–76;

Minister of Agriculture, Fisheries and Food 1983–87; Sponsored Private Member's Bills on: Children's Seat Belts 1990, Antarctica 1994. *Whip (Commons):* Assistant Whip 1971–73; Lord Commissioner of the Treasury 1973–74; Parliamentary Secretary to the Treasury and Chief Whip 1979–83. *Spokesman (Commons):* Front Bench Spokesman on Agriculture 1974–79. *Select Committees (Commons):* Member, Select Committees on; Agriculture 1966–68, Science and Technology 1969–70, Foreign Affairs 1987–97, Privileges 1991–92; Chairman, Select Committee on Sittings of the House (Jopling Report) 1991–92. *Backbench Committees (Commons):* Joint Secretary, Conservative Parliamentary Agricultural Committee 1966–70. *All-Party Committees (Commons):* Vice-Chairman, British-American Parliamentary Group 1983–86, Hon. Secretary 1987–; Vice-Chairman, All-Party Landmines Group 1996–. *Select Committees:* Co-opted Member, Select Committee on European Communities Sub-Committee D (Agriculture, Fisheries and Food). *All-Party:* Vice-Chairman, All-Party Landmine Eradication Group 1999–. *Party Groups:* Committee Member, Association of Conservative Peers 1997–. *International Bodies (General):* Executive Committee, UK Branch of CPA 1974–79, 1987–97, Vice-Chairman 1977–78 Executive, CPA HQ 1988–89; UK Delegate, North Atlantic Assembly 1987–97; Leader of UK Delegation, OSCE Parliamentary Assembly 1991–97. *Other:* Member, National Council of NFU 1962–65; President, Auto Cycle Union 1990–. *Trusts, etc:* Fellow, Industry and Parliament Trust. *Honours:* PC 1979. Member, Farmers Company. *Clubs:* Beefsteak, Buck's, Royal Automobile. *Name, Style and Title:* Raised to the peerage as Baron Jopling, of Ainderby Quernhow in the County of North Yorkshire 1997. A Conservative. *Address:* The Rt Hon. the Lord Jopling, DL, Ainderby Hall, Thirsk, North Yorkshire, YO7 4HZ.

JUDD (Life Baron, UK), Frank Ashcroft Judd; cr. 1991

Son of late Charles Judd, CBE, and late Helen Judd, JP. Born March 28, 1935; educated City of London School; London School of Economics (BSc Economics); Hon. DLitt: Bradford University 1987, Portsmouth University 1997; Hon. Fellow: Portsmouth University, Selly Oak Colleges; Hon. LLD, Greenwich University 1999. Married 1961, Christine Elizabeth Willington (2 daughters). *Trades Union:* Member: MSF, GMB. *Armed Forces:* Short Service Commission, RAF 1957–59. *Career:* General Secretary, International Voluntary Service 1960–66; Associate Director, International Defence and Aid Fund for Southern Africa 1979–80; Director, Voluntary Service Overseas 1980–85; Director, Oxfam 1985–91; Chairman, International Council of

Voluntary Agencies 1985–90; Professional Consultant on international affairs, UN, global institutions, arms control, environmental and development issues and community relations to The Forbes Trust, Saferworld and De Montfort University; Non-Executive Director, Portsmouth Harbour Renaissance. *House of Commons:* Contested (Labour): Sutton and Cheam 1959 General Election, Portsmouth West 1964 General Election; MP (Labour) for: Portsmouth West 1966–74, Portsmouth North 1974–79; PPS to: Minister of Housing 1967–70, Leader of Opposition 1970–72; Parliamentary Under-Secretary of State (Navy) Ministry of Defence 1974–76; Minister of State: Overseas Development 1976–77, Foreign and Commonwealth Office 1977–79. *Spokesman (Commons):* Opposition Defence Spokesman (Navy) 1972–74. *Select Committees (Commons):* Member: Public Accounts Committee 1966–69, Parliamentary Select Committee on Overseas Development 1969–74. *All-Party Committees (Commons):* Former Member: UN Group, Foreign Affairs Group, Overseas Development Group. *International Bodies (Commons):* Member, Parliamentary Delegation to Council of Europe and WEU 1969–72. *Spokesman:* An Opposition Spokesman on Foreign Affairs 1991–92; Principal Opposition Spokesman on: Development and Co-operation 1992–97, Education 1992–94; An Opposition Spokesman on Defence 1995–97. *Select Committees:* Co-opted Member, Select Committee on European Communities Sub-

Committee C (Environment, Public Health and Consumer Protection) 1997–. *All-Party:* Vice-Chair, All-Party Defence Group; Member, Charities and the Voluntary Sector Group; Chair, European Atlantic Group 1997–. *International Bodies:* Member, Parliamentary Delegation to Council of Europe and WEU 1997–. *Party Groups (General):* Member, Labour Party since 1951; Member, Fabian Society, former Chair; Member, Christian Socialist Movement. *Other:* President, YMCA (England); Governor: London School of Economics, Lancaster University, Vice-President, Intermediate Technology Group; Member: Royal Institute for International Affairs, Oxfam Association. *Trusts, etc:* Trustee: Overseas Development Institute, Global Education Trust, Beryl Le Poer Power Trust (Royal Institute of International Affairs); Trustee, International Alert, Chair 1997–; Member, North West Regional Committee of the National Trust. *Miscellaneous:* Member: Commission on Global Governance, World Health Organisation Task Force on Health and Development, British Council, Justice Goldstone's Task Force on Human Responsibilities in the New Millennium, Vice-President, Council for National Parks. FRSA. Freeman, City of Portsmouth 1995. *Publications:* Author of: (jointly) *Radical Future*, 1967; *Purpose in Socialism*, 1973; Also various articles on current affairs. *Special Interests:* Foreign Affairs, Third World, Defence, Education, Refugees, Migration, Race Relations, Penal Affairs and Policy. *Recreations:* Walking, family holidays. *Clubs:* Commonwealth Trust. *Name, Style and Title:* Raised to the peerage as Baron Judd, of Portsea in the County of Hampshire 1991. Labour. *Address:* The Lord Judd, House of Lords, London, SW1A 0PW.

K

KEITH OF CASTLEACRE (Life Baron, UK), Kenneth Alexander Keith; cr.1980; Kt 1969

Son of late Edward Charles Keith of Dereham, Norfolk. Born August 30, 1916; educated Rugby. Married 1st, 1946, Lady Ariel Olivia Winifred Baird, CVO, 2nd daughter of 1st Viscount Stonehaven, PC, GCMG, DSO, DL, and Ethel Sydney, Countess of Kintore (11th in line) (1 son 1 daughter) (marriage dissolved 1958), married 2nd, 1962, Mrs Nancy Hayward, of New York (marriage dissolved 1972, she died 1990), married 3rd, 1973, Mrs Marie Hanbury, of Burley-on-the-Hill, Rutland. *Armed Forces:* 2nd Lieutenant, Welsh Guards 1939; Lieutenant-Colonel 1945; Served in North Africa, Italy, France and Germany; (despatches, Croix de Guerre with Silver Star). *Career:* Trained as a chartered accountant; Merchant Banker; Assistant to Director General, Political Intelligence Department, Foreign Office 1945–46; Director: Philip Hill and Partners 1947–51, Eagle Star Insurance Co. 1955–75; Vice-Chairman, BEA 1964–71; Member, NEDC 1964–71; Chairman, Economic Planning Council for East Anglia 1965–70; Director, National Provincial Bank 1967–69; Chairman, Hill Samuel Group Ltd 1970–80; Director, British Airways 1971–72; Chairman, Philip Hill Investment Trust Ltd 1972–87; Chairman and Chief Executive, Rolls-Royce Ltd 1972–80; Member, CBI/NEDC Liaison Committee 1974–78, Vice-Chairman, Beecham Group Ltd 1974–87, Director, Standard Telephones & Cables Ltd 1977–89, Member, National Defence Industries Council to January 1980; Chairman, Standard Telephones & Cables Ltd 1985–1989; Chairman, Beecham Group Ltd 1986–87; Member: SBAC, Defence Industries Council. *Other:* Vice-President, Engineering Employers' Federation to January 1980; Governor, National Institute of Economic and Social Research; President, British Standards Institute 1989–94. Hon. Companion, Royal Aeronautical Society 1979. *Recreations:* Shooting, golf. *Clubs:* White's, Links (New York). *Name, Style and Title:* Raised to the peerage as Baron Keith of Castleacre, of Swaffham in the County of Norfolk 1980. A Conservative. *Address:* The Lord Keith of Castleacre, 9 Eaton Square, London, SW1W 9DB *Tel:* 020 7730 4000; The Wicken House, Castle Acre, Norfolk, PE32 2BP *Tel:* 01760 755225.

KEITH OF KINKEL (Life Baron, UK), Henry Shanks Keith; cr. 1977; PC 1976; GBE 1997

Son of late Rt Hon. Baron Keith of Avonholm. Born February 7, 1922; educated Edinburgh Academy; Magdalen College, Oxford (MA); Edinburgh University (LLB); Hon. Fellow, Magdalen College, Oxford 1978. Married 1955, Alison Hope Alan Brown, MA, JP (4 sons 1 daughter). *Armed Forces:* Served Second World War Scots Guards (mentioned in despatches). *Career:* Advocate, Scottish Bar 1950; Barrister, Gray's Inn 1951; QC (Scot) 1962; Sheriff, Roxburgh, Berwick and Selkirk 1970–71; Senator, College of Justice in Scotland with judicial title of Lord Keith 1971–77; Bencher, Gray's Inn 1976; Deputy Chairman, Parliamentary Boundary Commission for Scotland 1976; A Lord of Appeal in Ordinary 1977–96; Chairman, Committee on the Powers of the Revenue Departments 1980–84. *Honours:* PC 1976; GBE 1997. *Clubs:* Flyfishers'. *Name, Style and Title:* Raised to the peerage as Baron Keith of Kinkel, of Strathtummel in the District of Perth and Kinross 1977. A Cross-Bencher. *Address:* The Rt Hon. the Lord Keith of Kinkel, GBE, House of Lords, London, SW1A 0PW.

KELVEDON (Life Baron, UK), (Henry) Paul Guinness Channon; cr. 1997; PC 1980

Son of late Sir Henry Channon MP. Born October 9, 1935; educated Eton; Christ Church, Oxford. Married 1963, Mrs Ingrid Olivia Georgia Guinness, daughter of late Major Guy Wyndham, MC (1 son 1 daughter, 1 daughter deceased). *Armed Forces:* 2nd Lieutenant, Royal Horse Guards (The Blues) 1955–56. *House of Commons:* MP (Conservative) for Southend West 1959–97; PPS: to Minister of Power 1959–60, to Home Secretary 1960–62, to First Secretary of State July 1962, to Foreign Secretary 1963–64; Joint Parliamentary Secretary to the Minister of Housing and Local Government June-October 1970; Joint Parliamentary Under-Secretary of State, Department of the Environment 1970–72; Minister of State for Northern Ireland 1972; Minister for Housing and Construction 1972–74; Minister of State, Civil Service Department 1979–81; Minister for: The Arts 1981–83, Trade 1983–86; Secretary of State for: Trade and Industry 1986–87, Transport 1987–89. *Spokesman (Commons):* Opposition Spokesman on: Arts and Amenities 1967–70, Price and Consumer Affairs February-November 1974, The Environment 1974–75. *Select Committees (Commons):* Member, Select Committee on National Heritage 1992–93; Chairman, Select Committee on Finance and Services 1992–97; Member, Select Committee on Liaison 1993–97; Chairman, Select Committee on Transport 1993–97; Former Member, Procedure Committee. *International Bodies (General):* Deputy Leader, Conservative Group on Council of Europe 1976–79. *Miscellaneous:* Chairman, British Association for Central and Eastern Europe 1992–. *Honours:* PC 1980. *Clubs:* White's, Buck's. *Name, Style and Title:* Raised to the peerage as Baron Kelvedon, of Ongar in the County of Essex 1997. A Conservative. *Address:* The Rt Hon. the Lord Kelvedon, House of Lords, London, SW1A 0PW.

KENNEDY OF THE SHAWS (Life Baroness, UK), Helena Ann Kennedy; cr. 1997; QC 1991

Daughter of late Joshua Kennedy and of Mary Kennedy. Born May 12, 1950; educated Holyrood Secondary School, Glasgow; Council of Legal Education; Hon. LLD: Strathclyde 1992, Teesside 1993, Keele 1994, Lancaster 1994, Leeds Metropolitan 1995, Bristol 1997, Wolverhampton 1997, Open University 1997, Abertay Dundee 1997, Tavistock Centre under auspices of University of East London 1997, Derby 1998. Partner 1977–84, Roger Iain Mitchell (1 son); married 1986, Dr Iain Louis Hutchison (1 son 1 daughter). *Career:* Called to the Bar, Gray's Inn 1972; Established Chambers at: Garden Court 1974, Tooks Court 1984, Doughty Street 1990. *Chancellor:* Chancellor, Oxford Brookes University 1994–. *Other:* Member: National Board, Women's Legal Defence Fund 1989–91, Council, Howard League for Penal Reform 1989–, Bar Council 1990–93, Committee, Association of Women Barristers 1991–92, Hampstead Theatre Board. *Awards Granted:* Women's Network Award for her work on women and justice 1992; UK Woman of Europe Award 1995; Making a World of Difference Award from the National Federation of Women's Institutes for her work on equal rights 1996; The Times Newspaper (Joint) Lifetime Achievement Award 1997. *Miscellaneous:* Board Member, City Limits Magazine 1982–84; Chairman, Haldane Society 1983–86, Vice-President 1986–; Broadcaster: First female moderator, Hypotheticals (Granada) on surrogate motherhood and artificial insemination; Presenter: Heart of the Matter, BBC 1987, Putting Women in the Picture, BBC2 1987, Time Gentlemen Please, BBC Scotland 1994; Has also presented many other television programmes;

Board Member: New Statesman 1990–96, Counsel Magazine 1990–; Chairman, Charter '88 1992–97; Chairman, Standing Committee for Youth Justice, NACRO 1993–; British Council's Law Advisory Committee; Advisory Board, International Centre for Prison Studies; Advisor on Steering Group, University College London's Diploma in Forensic Psycho-Therapy; Chair, London International Festival of Theatre; Chairman, British Council 1998–. Fellow, Royal Society of Arts; Hon. Fellow, Institute of Advanced Legal Studies 1997. *Publications:* (Jointly) *The Bar on Trial*, 1978; (Jointly) *Child Abuse Within the Family*, 1984; (Jointly) *Balancing Acts*, 1989; *Eve was Framed*, 1992; Leader of enquiry into health, environmental and safety aspects of Atomic Weapons Establishment *Secrecy Versus Safety*, 1994; Author of *Learning Works* Official report for the FEFC on widening participation in Further Education, 1997; *Inquiry into Violence in Penal Institutions for Young People*, report published 1995; Lectures; Has contributed articles on law, civil liberties and women. *Recreations:* Theatre, spending time with family and friends. *Name, Style and Title:* Raised to the peerage as Baroness Kennedy of The Shaws, of Cathcart in the City of Glasgow 1997. Labour. *Address:* The Baroness Kennedy of The Shaws, QC, c/o Hilary Hard, 12 Athelstan Close, Harold Wood, Essex, RM3 0QJ.

KILPATRICK OF KINCRAIG (Life Baron, UK), Robert Kilpatrick; cr. 1996; Kt 1986; CBE 1979

Son of late Robert Kilpatrick. Born July 29, 1926; educated Buckhaven High School; Edinburgh University (MB, ChB (Hons) 1949, MD 1960) (Ettles Scholar, Leslie Gold Medallist); Dr hc Edinburgh 1987; Hon. LLD, Dundee 1992; Hon. DSc: Hull 1994, Leicester 1994; Hon. LLD, Sheffield 1995. Married 1950, Elizabeth Gibson Page Forbes (2 sons 1 daughter). *Career:* Medical Registrar, Edinburgh 1951–54; University of Sheffield: Lecturer 1955–66, Professor of Clinical Pharmacology and Therapeutics 1966–75, Dean, Faculty of Medicine 1971–74; Member, General Medical Council 1972–76, 1979–, President 1989–95; Chairman, Society of Endocrinology 1975–78; Professor and Head of Department of Clinical Pharmacology and Therapeutics, University of Leicester 1975–83; Chairman, Advisory Committee on Pesticides 1975–87; Dean, Faculty of Medicine, University of Leicester 1975–89, Professor of Medicine, University of Leicester 1984–89; President, British Medical Association 1997–98. *Honours:* CBE 1979; Kt 1986. FRCP (Ed) 1963; FRCP 1975; FRCPGlas 1991; Hon. FRCS, 1995; Hon. FRCP, Dublin 1995; Hon. FRCS, Edinburgh 1996; Hon. RC Path. 1996. *Publications:* Several articles in medical and scientific journals. *Special Interests:* Health, Education, Professional Self-Regulation. *Recreations:* Golf. *Clubs:* Royal and Ancient (St Andrews), New (Edinburgh). *Name, Style and Title:* Raised to the peerage as Baron Kilpatrick of Kincraig, of Dysart in the District of Kirkcaldy 1996. A Cross-Bencher. *Address:* The Lord Kilpatrick of Kincraig, CBE, 12 Wester Coates Gardens, Edinburgh, EH12 5LT.

KIMBALL (Life Baron, UK), Marcus Richard Kimball; cr. 1985; Kt 1981; DL

Son of late Major Lawrence Kimball. Born October 18, 1928; educated Eton; Trinity College, Cambridge. Married March 15, 1956, June Mary, eldest daughter of Montagu Fenwick, of Great Stukeley Hall, Huntingdon (2 daughters). *Armed Forces:* Captain, Leicestershire and Derbyshire Yeomanry (TA). *Councils, Public Bodies:* Member, Rutland County Council 1955; DL, Leicestershire 1984. *Career:* Director, The Royal Trust Bank 1970–93; Elected to the Council of Lloyd's of London 1982–90; Chairman, South East Assured Tenancies plc 1989–96; Chairman, British Greyhound Racing Fund Ltd 1993–96. *House of Commons:* Contested (Conservative) Derby South 1955; MP (Conservative) for Gainsborough 1956–83. *Party Groups (General):* Chairman, East Midlands Area Young Conservatives 1954–58. *Other:* Privy Council Representative, Royal College of Veterinary Surgeons 1969–82; Chairman: British Field Sports Society 1966–82, Firearms Consultation Committee 1989–94; President: National Light Horse Breeding Society 1990–, Olympia International Show Jumping Championship 1991–; President, British Field Sports Society 1996–98, Deputy President 1998–. *Trusts, etc:* Chairman, University of Cambridge Veterinary School Trust 1989–97. Hon. Associate, Royal College of Veterinary Surgeons 1982. *Special Interests:* Finance, Agriculture. *Recreations:* Fishing, hunting, shooting. *Clubs:* White's, Pratt's. *Name, Style and Title:* Raised to the peerage as Baron Kimball, of Easton in the County of Leicestershire 1985. A Conservative. *Address:* The Lord Kimball, DL, Great Easton Manor, Market Harborough, Leicestershire, LE16 8TB *Tel:* 01536 770333 *Fax:* 01536 770453.

KING OF WARTNABY (Life Baron, UK), John Leonard King; cr. 1983; Kt 1979

Son of late Albert John King; Hon. Dr Hum., Gardner-Webb College (USA) 1980; Hon. Dr of Science, Cranfield Institute of Technology; Hon. City and Guilds Insignia Award in Technology. Married 1st, 1941, Lorna Sykes (died 1969) (3 sons 1 daughter), married 2nd, 1970, Hon. Isabel Monckton, daughter of 8th Viscount Galway, PC, GCMG, DSO, OBE, DL. *Career:* Founded: Whitehouse Industries Ltd 1945, Ferrybridge Industries Ltd; Chairman, Pollard Ball & Roller Bearing Co Ltd 1961–69; Babcock International Group plc (firstly Babcock and Wilcox Ltd, secondly Babcock International plc, thirdly FKI Babcock plc and fourthly Babcock International Group plc) 1970–, President 1994–; Dennis Motor Holdings Ltd 1970–72; NEDC Finance Committee, Review Board for Government Contracts 1975–78; SKF (UK) Ltd 1976–89; British Nuclear Associates Ltd 1978–89; British Airways 1981–93, President 1993–; Formerly Director: RJ Dick Inc (USA), Dick Corporation (USA); Deputy Chairman and Chairman, NEB 1979–81; Deputy Chairman, National Nuclear Corp. 1981–89; Deputy Chairman, Royal Ordnance plc 1985–88; Director: Shorts Bros 1989–, Sabena World Airlines 1990, The Telegraph plc 1990–, York Trust 1990–, Norman Broadbent International Ltd 1990–, Wide Range Engineering Services 1992–; Formerly Director, First Union Corp. (USA); Director, Wide Range Engineering Services Ltd 1992–, Chairman, Aerostructures Hamble Ltd 1992–; Director: The Spectator (1828) Ltd 1993–, Gartland Whalley and Barker Holdings Ltd 1995–, Gartland Whalley and Barker Group 1995–; Member: Advisory Committee, Optima Fund Management LP, USA, Advisory Council, Westinghouse Electric Europe. *Other:* Chairman, British Olympics Appeal Committee 1975–78; MacMillan Appeal for Continuing Care (Cancer Relief) 1977–78; Alexandra Rose Day 1980–85; Committee Member, Ranfurly Library Service; MFH Badsworth Foxhounds 1949–58; Duke of Rutlands Foxhounds (Belvoir) 1958–72, Chairman 1972–; President: Brooklands Club, British Show Jumping Association. *Trusts, etc:* Trustee: Royal Opera House Trust, Liver Research Unit, Blenheim Foundation; Advisory Council, Prince's Youth Business Trust. *Honours:* Kt 1979; Commander of the Royal Order of the Polar Star (Sweden) 1983. ARAeS 1982 (President Heathrow Branch); FCIT 1982; FBIM; Companion, Royal Aeronautical Society 1985–87. Freedom, City of London 1984. *Clubs:* White's, Pratt's, The Brook (New York). *Name, Style and Title:* Raised to the peerage as Baron King of Wartnaby, of Wartnaby in the County of Leicestershire 1983. A Conservative. *Address:* The Lord King of Wartnaby, Wartnaby, Melton Mowbray, Leicestershire, LE14 3HY.

KING OF WEST BROMWICH (Life Baron, UK), Tarsem King; cr. 1999

Son of Ujagar Singh, and Dalip Kaur. Born April 24, 1937; educated Khalsa High School, Dosanjh, Kalan, Punjab, India; Punjab University, India (BA Exam); National Foundry College, Wolverhampton (Diploma in Foundry Technology and Management); Aston University, Birmingham (Post Graduate Diploma in Management Studies); Teacher Training College, Wolverhampton (Teachers' Certificate); Essex University (MSc Statistics and Operational Research). Married 1957, Mrs Mohinder Kaur, daughter of Gurdev Singh and Satwant Kaur (1 son). *Councils, Public Bodies:* Councillor, Sandwell Metropolitan Borough Council 1979–, Deputy Mayor, 1982–83, Deputy Leader 1992–97, Leader 1997–; JP, West Bromwich 1987–. *Career:* Laboratory Assistant, Coneygre Foundry 1960–62; Foundry Trainee, Birmid Group of Companies 1964–65; Teacher, Churchfields School, West Bromwich 1968–74; Deputy Head, Mathematics Department, Great Barr School, Birmingham 1974–90; Managing Director, Sandwell Polybags Ltd 1990–. *Party Groups (General):* National Policy Forum Member, West Midlands Constituency Labour Party; Co-operative Party Sponsored Councillor; Secretary, West Bromwich Ward Branch Labour Party; Treasurer: Sandwell Local Government Committee, Birmingham West Euro CLP; Executive Member, West Bromwich East GC; Member, SEA. *Other:* Member: Sandwell and District West Indian Community Association, Black Country Joint Advisory Group, Black Country Consortium; Vice-Chair: Faith in Sandwell Organisation, Governing Body of King George V Primary School; Non-Executive Director, Sandwell Health Authority Audit Committee; Director, Smethwick Asian Sheltered and Residential Association; Vice-President, West Bromwich and District YMCA. *Trusts, etc:* Member, South Staffs Water Disconnections Charitable Trust. *Miscellaneous:* Represents Sandwell in: West Midlands Local Goverment Association, West Midlands Regional Chamber, West Midlands Joint Committee. MSc; CEd; DipFTM; DMS; MBIM. *Special Interests:* Local Government, Education, Small Businesses. *Recreations:* Reading, music. *Name, Style and Title:* Raised to the peerage as Baron King of West Bromwich, of West Bromwich in the County of West Midlands 1999. Labour. *Address:* Councillor The Lord King of West Bromwich, Sandwell MBC, Leader's Office, Sandwell Council House, PO Box 2374, Oldbury, West Midlands, B69 3DE *Tel:* 0121–569 3045 *Fax:* 0121–569 3051; 27 Roebuck Lane, West Bromwich, B70 6QP.

KINGSDOWN (Life Baron, UK), Robert (Robin) Leigh-Pemberton; cr. 1993; KG 1994; PC 1987

Son of late Robert Douglas Leigh-Pemberton, MBE, MC. Born January 5, 1927; educated St Peter's Court, Broadstairs; Eton; Trinity College, Oxford (MA); Hon. DCL, Kent 1983; Hon. Fellow, Trinity College, Oxford 1984; Hon. DLitt: City 1988, Loughborough 1990. Married 1953, Rosemary Davina, OBE, daughter of late Lieutenant-Colonel D. W. A. W. Forbes, MC and late Dowager Marchioness of Exeter (4 sons and 1 son deceased). *Armed Forces:* Served Grenadier Guards 1945–48; Hon. Colonel: Kent and Sharpshooters Yeomanry Squadron 1979–92, 265 (Kent and County of London Yeomanry) Signal Squadron (V) 1979–92, 5th Volunteer Battalion, The Queen's Regiment 1987–93. *Councils, Public Bodies:* Councillor, Kent County Council 1961–77, Chairman 1972–75; JP, Kent 1961–75; DL, Kent 1970–72, Vice-Lord-Lieutenant 1972–82, Lord Lieutenant 1982–. *Career:* Called to Bar, Inner Temple 1954, Hon. Bencher 1983; Director, National Westminster Bank 1972–83, Deputy Chairman 1974–77, Chairman 1977–83; Director, Birmid Qualcast 1966–83, Chairman 1975–77; Director, University Life Assurance Society 1967–78; Member, South East Planning Council 1972–74; Director, Redland Ltd 1972–83; Member: Prime Minister's Committee on Local Government Rules of Conduct 1973–74, Medway Ports Authority 1974–76, Committee on Police Pay 1977–79; Director, Equitable Life Assurance Society 1979–83; Member, National Economic Development Council 1982–92, Governor, Bank of England 1983–93; Non-Executive Director: Hambros plc 1993–98, Glaxo Wellcome plc 1993–96, Redland plc 1993–98, Foreign and Colonial Investment Trust 1993–98. *Chancellor:* Pro-Chancellor, University of Kent 1977–83. *Other:* Seneschal, Canterbury Cathedral 1983–; Governor, Ditchley Foundation 1987–. *Trusts, etc:* Trustee, Glyndebourne Arts Trust 1977–83. *Honours:* PC 1987; KG 1994. FRSA 1977; FBIM 1977. Liveryman, Mercers' Company. *Recreations:* Country life, The Arts. *Sportsclubs:* Kent County Cricket, Royal St George Golf (Sandwich). *Clubs:* Brooks's, Cavalry and Guards. *Name, Style and Title:* Raised to the peerage as Baron Kingsdown, of Pemberton in the County of Lancashire 1993. A Cross-Bencher. *Address:* The Rt Hon. the Lord Kingsdown, KG, Lieutenancy Office, County Hall, Maidstone, Kent, ME14 1XQ *E-Mail:* gill.herriot@kent.gov.uk.

KINGSLAND (Life Baron, UK), Christopher James Prout; cr. 1994; PC 1994; Kt 1990; TD 1987; QC 1988; DL

Son of late Frank Yabsley Prout, MC and Bar, and of Doris Lucy Prout (née Osborne). Born January 1, 1942; educated Sevenoaks School; Manchester University (BA); The Queen's College, Oxford (Scholar, BPhil, DPhil). *Armed Forces:* TA Officer (Major); OU OTC 1966–74; 16/5 The Queen's Royal Lancers 1974–82; 3rd Armoured Division 1982–88; RARO 1988–. *Councils, Public Bodies:* DL, Shropshire 1997–. *Career:* English Speaking Union Fellow, Columbia University, New York 1963–64; Leverhulme Fellow and Lecturer in Law, Sussex University 1969–79; Staff Member, IBRD (UN) Washington DC 1966–69; Barrister-at-Law, Called to the Bar Middle Temple 1972, QC 1988, Bencher 1996. *House of Lords:* Shadow Lord Chancellor 1997–. *Select Committees:* Chairman, Select Committee on European Communities Sub-Committee F 1996–97. *All-Party:* Member, All-Party Bloodstock and Racing Group 1997–. *Other:* President, Shropshire and West Midlands Agricultural Show 1993. *Awards Granted:* Grande Medaille de la Ville de Paris 1988; Schuman Medal 1995. *Miscellaneous:* MEP (Conservative) for Shropshire and Stafford 1979–94; Deputy Whip, European Democratic Group (EDG) 1979–82; Chief Whip, EDG 1983–87; Chairman, Parliamentary Committee, Legal Affairs 1987; Leader, Conservative MEPs 1987–94; Chairman and Leader, EDG 1987–92; Vice-Chairman, European People's Party Parliamentary Group 1992–94; Contested Herefordshire and Shropshire in 1994 European Elections. *Honours:* TD 1987; Kt 1990; PC 1994. Master, Shrewsbury Drapers Company 1995. *Publications: Market Socialism in Yugoslavia,* 1985; (contributed) Vols 8, 51 and 52, *Halsbury's Law of England* (4th ed.); Miscellaneous lectures, pamphlets, chapters and articles. *Recreations:* Boating, gardening, musical comedy, the turf. *Clubs:* Pratt's, Beefsteak, Royal Ocean Racing, Royal Yacht Squadron (Cowes). *Name, Style and Title:* Raised to the peerage as Baron Kingsland, of Shrewsbury in the County of Shropshire 1994. A Conservative. *Address:* The Rt Hon. the Lord Kingsland, TD, QC, DL, 4 Breams Buildings, London, EC4A 1AQ *Tel:* 020 7353 5835.

KIRKHAM (Life Baron, UK), Graham Kirkham; cr. 1999; Kt 1995

Son of Tom and Elsie Kirkham. Born December 14, 1944; educated Maltby Grammar School; Hon. Member, Emmanuel College, Cambridge 1995 Hon. Doctorate, Bradford University 1997. Married 1965, Pauline Fisher (1 son and 1 daughter). *Career:* Executive Chairman, DFS Furniture, Founded Company in 1969, Listed on UK Stock Exchange 1993. *Party Groups (General):* Chairman, Conservative Party Treasurers 1997. *Other:* Member: Duke of Edinburgh's Award Scheme, Duke of Edinburgh's International Award Scheme, Chairman, Joint Funding Board; Member, Blue Cross; Patron, War on Cancer. *Trusts, etc:* Trustee, Outward Bound Trust; Member: Animal Health Trust (Hon. Fellow 1997), The Prince's Youth Business Trust. *Honours:* Kt 1995.

Name, Style and Title: Raised to the peerage as Baron Kirkham, of Old Cantley in the County of South Yorkshire 1999. A Conservative. *Address:* The Lord Kirkham, DFS Furniture Co Ltd, Bentley Moor Lane, Adwick-le-Street, Doncaster, DN6 7BD.

KIRKHILL (Life Baron, UK), John Farquharson Smith; cr. 1975

Son of late Alexander Findlay Smith and Ann Farquharson. Born May 7, 1930; Hon. LLD, Aberdeen University 1974. Married 1965, Frances Mary Walker Reid. *Career:* Lord Provost, Aberdeen 1971–75; Chairman, North of Scotland Hydro-Electric Board 1979–82. *House of Lords:* Minister of State, Scottish Office 1975–78. *International Bodies (General):* Member, Assemblies of the Council of Europe and of WEU 1987–; Chairman, Legal Affairs and Human Rights Committee of the Parliamentary Assembly of the Council of Europe 1991–95. *Name, Style and Title:* Raised to the peerage as Baron Kirkhill, in the District of the City of Aberdeen 1975. Labour. *Address:* The Lord Kirkhill, 3 Rubislaw Den North, Aberdeen, AB15 4AL.

KNIGHT OF COLLINGTREE (Life Baroness, UK), Joan Christabel Jill Knight; cr. 1997; DBE 1985

Daughter of late A. E. Christie. Born July 9, 1927; educated King Edward Grammar School, Birmingham; Hon. DSc, Aston University 1998. Married June 14, 1947, James Montague Knight (died 1986) (2 sons). *Councils, Public Bodies:* Councillor, Northampton County Borough Council 1956–66. *Career:* Director: Computeach International Ltd, Heckett Multiserv plc. *House of Commons:* Contested Northampton 1959 and 1964; MP (Conservative) for Birmingham Edgbaston 1966–97. *Select Committees (Commons):* Member, Select Committees on: Parliamentary Race Relations and Immigration 1969–72, Home Affairs 1980–83, 1992–97, Privileges 1994–97, Standards and Privileges 1995–97. *Backbench Committees (Commons):* Chairman: Conservative Backbench Health and Social Services Committee 1982–96, Conservative Backbench Health Committee 1996–97; Hon. Secretary, 1922 Committee 1983–87, Vice-Chairman 1987–97. *All-Party Committees (Commons):* Chairman, Lords and Commons All-Party Family and Child Protection Group 1975–97. *International Bodies (General):* Council of Europe 1977–88, 1999–; Chairman: WEU Relations with Parliaments Committee 1984–88, 1999–, British IPU 1994–97. *Other:* National Chairman, Lifeline 1974–84; Vice-President, Townswomen's Guilds 1989–95. *Honours:* MBE (New Year's Honours) 1964; DBE 1985. *Publications: About the House,* 1995. *Special Interests:* Health, Social Security, Childcare, Industry, Council of Europe and Western European Union. *Recreations:* Antique collecting, tapestry work, singing, theatre, cooking. *Name, Style and Title:* Raised to the peerage as Baroness Knight of Collingtree, of Collingtree in the County of Northamptonshire 1997. A Conservative. *Address:* The Baroness Knight of Collingtree, DBE, House of Lords, London, SW1A 0PW.

KNIGHTS (Life Baron, UK), Philip Douglas Knights; cr. 1987; Kt 1980; CBE 1976; QPM 1964; DL

Son of late Thomas James Knights, market gardener and late Ethel Ginn, schoolteacher. Born October 3, 1920; educated East Grinstead County School; King's School, Grantham; Police Staff College; Hon. DSc, Aston University 1996. Married June 23, 1945, Jean, daughter of late James Burman. *Armed Forces:* RAF 1943–45. *Councils, Public Bodies:* DL, West Midlands 1985. *Career:* Police Cadet, Lincolnshire Constabulary 1937; Constable 1940; Police Sergeant, Lincolnshire 1946; Seconded to the Home Office in 1946; Superintendent 1955; Chief Superintendent 1957; Assistant Chief Constable, Birmingham 1959; Deputy Commandant, Police Staff College, Bramshill 1962–66; Deputy Chief Constable, Birmingham 1970; Chief Constable, Sheffield and Rotherham Constabulary 1972, responsible for Police Force of the newly created County of South Yorkshire 1974; Chief Constable, West Midlands Police 1975–85; Member, Departmental Committee, chaired by Lord Devlin, which reported in 1976 on Identification Procedures; Formerly Adviser, Police and Fire Committee of the Association of Municipal Authorities; Vice-President, Association of Metropolitan Authorities. *Other:* Past President, Association of Chief Police Officers; Member: Council of Aston University 1985–98, Council of Cambridge Institute of Criminology 1986–. *Trusts, etc:* Trustee, Police Foundation 1979–98. *Honours:* QPM 1964; OBE 1971; CBE 1976; Kt 1980. Companion, British Institute of Management 1977. *Special Interests:* Law and Order, Police, Inner Cities, Local Government. *Recreations:* Gardening, reading, travel, sport. *Sportsclubs:* Vice-President, Warwickshire County Cricket Club. *Clubs:* Royal Over-Seas League. *Name, Style and Title:* Raised to the peerage as Baron Knights, of Edgbaston in the County of West Midlands 1987. A Cross-Bencher. *Address:* The Lord Knights, CBE, QPM, CIMgt, DL, 11 Antringham Gardens, Edgbaston, Birmingham, B15 3QL *Tel:* 0121–455 0057.

L

LAING OF DUNPHAIL (Life Baron, UK), Hector Laing; cr. 1991; Kt 1978

Son of late Hector Laing and Margaret Norris Grant. Born May 12, 1923; educated Loretto School; Jesus College, Cambridge; Hon. Doctorates: Stirling University 1984, Heriot-Watt University 1986; Hon. Fellow, Jesus College, Cambridge 1988. Married April 1, 1950, Marian Clare, daughter of late Major-General Sir John Laurie, 6th Bt, CBE, DSO (3 sons). *Armed Forces:* Served Scots Guards 1942–47 Captain (American Bronze Star, mentioned in despatches). *Career:* Director, McVitie and Price 1947, Chairman 1963; Director, United Biscuits 1953, Managing Director 1964; Chairman, United Biscuits (Holdings) plc 1972–90, Life President 1990–; Director, Bank of England 1973–91; Chairman: Food and Drink Industries Council 1977–79, City and Industrial Liaison Council 1985–90; Director: Grocery Manufacturers of America 1984–90, Exxon Corporation Inc 1984–94. *Party Groups (General):* Joint Treasurer, Conservative Party 1988–93. *Other:* Governor, Wycombe Abbey School 1981–93; Chairman, Scottish Business in the Community 1982–90; President, Goodwill 1983–92; Joint Chairman, The Per Cent Club 1986–90; Chairman, Business in the Community 1987–92; President, The Weston Spirit 1989–95; Member, Advisory Board, Phillips Son and Neale 1990–93; President, Trident 1992–95. *Trusts, etc:* Chairman of Trustees, The Lambeth Fund 1983–; Trustee, Royal Botanic Gardens Kew Foundation 1990–. *Recreations:* Walking, gardening. *Clubs:* White's, Boodle's. *Name, Style and Title:* Raised to the peerage as Baron Laing of Dunphail, of Dunphail in the County of Moray 1991. A Conservative. *Address:* The Lord Laing of Dunphail, High Meadows, Gerrards Cross, Buckinghamshire, SL9 8ST *Tel:* 01753 882437.

LAIRD (Life Baron, UK), John Dunn Laird; cr. 1999

Son of late Dr Norman D Laird, OBE, MP, and of Councillor Mrs Margaret Laird. Born April 23, 1944; educated Royal Belfast Academical Institution. Married, Caroline Ethel, daughter of William and Mary Ferguson of Derrygonnelly, Co Fermanagh (1 son 1 daughter). *Career:* Bank Official 1963–67; Bank Inspector 1967–68; Computer Programmer 1968–73; PR Consultant 1973–76; Chairman, John Laird Public Relations 1976–; Visiting Professor of Public Relations, University of Ulster. *Party Groups (General):* Member, Ulster Unionist Party. *Other:* Member, Ulster Orchestra Board; Governor, Royal Belfast Academical Institution. *Miscellaneous:* MP for St Annes, Belfast, Northern Ireland Parliament 1970–73; Member for West Belfast: Northern Ireland Assembly 1973–75, Northern Ireland Convention 1975–76. Fellow, Institute of Public Relations 1991. *Publications:* Videos: *Trolley Bus Day in Belfast,* 1992, *Swansong of Steam in Ulster,* 1994, *Twilight of Steam in Ulster* 1995. *Special Interests:* Transport. *Recreations:* Local history, railways, cricket. *Name, Style and Title:* Raised to the peerage as Baron Laird, of Artigarvan in the County of Tyrone 1999. A Cross-Bencher/Ulster Unionist. *Address:* The Lord Laird, 104 Holywood Road, Belfast, BT4 1ND *Tel:* 028 9047 1282 *Fax:* 028 9065 6022.

LAMING (Life Baron, UK), William Herbert Laming; cr. 1998; Kt 1996; CBE 1985; DL

Son of William and Lillian Laming. Born July 19, 1936; educated University of Durham (Applied Social Sciences); Rainer House; LSE; Hon. DSc, University of Hertfordshire 1997; Hon. DSc, University of Durham 1999. Married July 21, 1962, Aileen Margaret Pollard. *Councils, Public Bodies:* DL, Hertfordshire 1999–. *Career:* Nottingham Probation Service: Probation Officer 1961–66, Senior Probation Officer 1966–68; Assistant Chief Probation Officer, Nottingham City and County Probation Service 1968–71; Hertfordshire County Council Social Services: Deputy Director 1971–75, Director 1975–91; Chief Inspector, Social Services Inspectorate, Department of Health 1991–98. *All-Party:* Joint Vice-Chairman, All-Party Voice Group 1999–. *Other:* President, Association of Directors of Social Services 1982–83. *Honours:* CBE 1985; Kt 1996. Freeman, City of London 1996. *Publications: Lessons from America: the balance of services in social care,* 1985. *Name, Style and Title:* Raised to the peerage as Baron Laming, of Tewin in the County of Hertfordshire 1998. A Cross-Bencher. *Address:* The Lord Laming, CBE, DL, 1 Firs Walk, Tewin Wood, Welwyn, Hertfordshire, AL6 0NY *Tel:* 01438 798574.

LAMONT OF LERWICK (Life Baron, UK), Norman Stewart Hughson Lamont; cr. 1998; PC 1986

Son of late Daniel Lamont. Born May 8, 1942; educated Loretto School (Scholar); Fitzwilliam College, Cambridge (BA 1965) (President of Union 1964). Married September 18, 1971, Rosemary, daughter of Lieutenant-Colonel Peter White (1 son 1 daughter). *Career:* N. M. Rothschild & Sons Ltd 1968–79, Director 1993–95; Director, Balli plc 1995–; Adviser, The Monsanto Company; Chairman: Indonesia Fund, East European Food Fund, Archipelago Fund; Director: Jupiter European Investment Trust, Taiwan Investment Trust; Adviser, Board of the Philippine Investment Company. *House of Commons:* Contested Kingston-upon-Hull East 1970 General Election; MP (Conservative) for Kingston-upon-Thames 1972–97; PPS to Norman St John Stevas, MP, as Minister for the Arts 1974; Parliamentary Under-Secretary of State, Department of Energy 1979–81; Minister of State, Department of Trade and Industry 1981–85; Minister for Defence Procurement, Ministry of Defence 1985–86; Financial Secretary to HM Treasury 1986–89; Chief Secretary to HM Treasury 1989–90; Chancellor of the Exchequer 1990–93; Contested Harrogate and Knaresborough 1997 General Election. *Spokesman (Commons):* Opposition Spokesman on: Prices and Consumer Affairs 1975–76, Industry 1976–79. *Backbench Committees (Commons):* Secretary, Conservative Parliamentary Finance Commiittee 1974. *Party Groups (General):* Chairman, Bow Group 1971–72. *Honours:* PC 1986. *Publications: Sovereign Britain,* 1995. *Special Interests:* Economics, Industrial Policy, Foreign Affairs. *Recreations:* Reading, the countryside, ornithology. *Clubs:* Garrick, Beefsteak. *Name, Style and Title:* Raised to the peerage as Baron Lamont of Lerwick, of Lerwick in the Shetland Islands 1998. A Conservative. *Address:* The Lord Lamont of Lerwick, Balli Group plc, 5 Stanhope Gate, London, SW1Y 5LA.

LANE (Life Baron, UK), Geoffrey Dawson Lane; cr. 1979; PC 1974; Kt 1966; AFC 1943

Son of late Percy Albert Lane and late Mary Lane (née Dawson). Born July 17, 1918; educated Shrewsbury; Trinity College, Cambridge (1st Class Hons Classical Tripos and Law Tripos Parts 1 and 2); Hon. DCL, Cambridge; Hon. Fellow, Trinity College, Cambridge. Married January 25, 1944, Jan, daughter of Donald Macdonald (1 son). *Armed Forces:* Served in RAF 1939–45. *Career:* Called to the Bar, Gray's Inn 1946; QC 1962; Bencher 1966; Recorder of Bedford 1963–66; A Judge of the High Court of Justice, Queen's Bench Division 1966–74; A Lord Justice of Appeal 1974–79; A Lord of Appeal in Ordinary 1979–80; Lord Chief Justice of England 1980–92; Elected an Honorary Master of the Bench of the Inner Temple July 1980. *Trusts, etc:* Former Member, Prison Reform Trust. *Name, Style and Title:* Raised to the peerage as Baron Lane, of St Ippollitts in the County of Hertfordshire 1979. A Cross-Bencher. *Address:* The Rt Hon. the Lord Lane, AFC, c/o Child & Co., 1 Fleet Street, London, EC4Y 1BD.

LANE OF HORSELL (Life Baron, UK), Peter Stewart Lane; cr. 1990; Kt 1984

Son of late Leonard George Lane. Born January 29, 1925; educated Sherborne. Married, Doris Florence Botsford (died 1969) (2 daughters). *Armed Forces:* Sub-Lieutenant, RNVR 1943–46. *Councils, Public Bodies:* JP, Surrey. *Career:* Senior Partner, BDO Binder Hamlyn, Chartered Accountants 1979–92; Chairman, Brent International 1985–95; Deputy Chairman, More O'Ferrall 1985–97; Deputy Chairman, Automated Security (Holdings) 1992–94, Chairman 1994–96; Director, Attwoods 1992–94, Chairman 1994. *Select Committees:* Member, Select Committees on: the Public Service 1996–; House of Lords' Offices 1997–98. *All-Party:* Joint Vice-Chairman, All-Party Ageing and Older People Group 1998–. *Party Groups (General):* National Union of Conservative Associations: Vice-President 1984–, Chairman 1983–84, Chairman Executive Committee 1986–91. *Trusts, etc:* Governor, Nuffield Nursing Homes Trust 1985–96, Chairman 1993–96; Trustee, Chatham Historic Dockyard Trust 1992–. FCA. Freeman, City of London. *Publications: Maw on Corporate Governance*, 1994 (jointly). *Clubs:* Boodle's, MCC, Beefsteak. *Name, Style and Title:* Raised to the peerage as Baron Lane of Horsell, of Woking in the County of Surrey 1990. A Conservative. *Address:* The Lord Lane of Horsell, Rossmore, Pond Road, Woking, Surrey, GU22 0JY.

LANG OF MONKTON (Life Baron, UK), Ian Bruce Lang; cr. 1997; PC 1990; DL

Son of late James Lang, DSC. Born June 27, 1940; educated Lathallan School, Montrose; Rugby School; Sidney Sussex College, Cambridge (BA Hons). Married 1971, Sandra Montgomerie (2 daughters). *Councils, Public Bodies:* DL, Ayrshire and Arran 1998–. *Career:* Non-Executive Director: CGU plc, Marsh and Mclennan Companies Inc, and other companies. *House of Commons:* Contested Ayrshire Central 1970 and Glasgow Pollok in February 1974 General Elections; MP (Conservative) for Galloway 1979–83 and for Galloway and Upper Nithsdale 1983–97; Parliamentary Under-Secretary of State: at Department of Employment 1986, at Scottish Office 1986–87; Minister of State, Scottish Office 1987–90; Secretary of State for Scotland 1990–95; President of the Board of Trade and Secretary of State for Trade and Industry 1995–97. *Whip (Commons):* Assistant Government Whip 1981–83; Lord Commissioner of HM Treasury 1983–86. *Select Committees (Commons):* Member, Select Committee on Scottish Affairs 1979–81. *Party Groups (General):* Hon. President, Scottish Young Conservatives 1982–84; Vice-Chairman, Scottish Conservative Party 1983–87. *Other:* A Governor, Rugby School 1997–; President, The Association for the Protection of Rural Scotland 1998–. *Miscellaneous:* Member, Queen's Bodyguard for Scotland, Royal Company of Archers 1974. *Honours:* Officer of the Order of St John 1974; PC 1990. *Name, Style and Title:* Raised to the peerage as Baron Lang of Monkton, of Merrick and the Rhinns of Kells in Dumfries and Galloway 1997. A Conservative. *Address:* The Rt Hon. the Lord Lang of Monkton, DL, House of Lords, London, SW1A 0PW.

LAWSON OF BLABY (Life Baron, UK), Nigel Lawson; cr. 1992; PC 1981

Son of late Ralph Lawson and late Elisabeth Lawson (née Davis). Born March 11, 1932; educated Westminster School; Christ Church, Oxford (Scholar, first class hons PPE); Hon. Student, Christ Church, Oxford 1996. Married 1st, 1955, Vanessa Mary Salmon (1 son 2 daughters and 1 daughter deceased) (marriage dissolved 1980, she died 1985), married 2nd, 1980, Thérèse Mary Maclear (1 son 1 daughter). *Armed Forces:* Served Royal Navy 1954–56. *Career:* A former journalist; Member, editorial staff, *Financial Times* 1956–60; City Editor, *Sunday Telegraph* 1961–63; Special Assistant to Rt Hon. Sir Alec Douglas-Home, KT, MP then Prime Minister 1963–64; *Financial Times* columnist and BBC broadcaster 1965; Editor, *The Spectator* 1966–70; Chairman, Central Europe Trust (CET) 1990–; Director, Barclays Bank plc 1990–98. *House of Commons:* Contested (Conservative) Eton and Slough in 1970 General Election; MP (Conservative) for Blaby February 1974–92; Financial Secretary to the Treasury 1979–81; Secretary of State for Energy 1981–83; Chancellor of the Exchequer 1983–89. *Whip (Commons):* An Opposition Whip 1976–77. *Spokesman (Commons):* Opposition Spokesman on Treasury and Economic Affairs 1977–79. *Miscellaneous:* President, British Insititute of Energy Economics 1995–. *Honours:* PC 1981. *Publications:* Author of: *The Power Game* (jointly with late Lord Bruce-Gardyne), 1976; *The View from Number 11: Memoirs of a Tory Radical*, 1992; *The Nigel Lawson Diet Book* (jointly with Thérèse Lawson), 1996. *Clubs:* Garrick, Pratt's. *Name, Style and Title:* Raised to the peerage as Baron Lawson of Blaby, of Newnham in the County of Northamptonshire 1992. A Conservative. *Address:* The Rt Hon. the Lord Lawson of Blaby, House of Lords, London, SW1A 0PW.

LEA OF CRONDALL (Life Baron, UK), David Edward Lea; cr. 1999; OBE 1978

Son of late Edward and Lilian Lea. Born November 2, 1937; educated Farnham Grammar School; Christ's College, Cambridge (MA 1961). *Trades Union:* Member, T&GWU 1962–. *Armed Forces:* National Service, Royal Horse Artillery 1955–57. *Career:* Economist Intelligence Unit 1961–63; Trades Union Congress: Research/Economic Department 1964–67, Assistant Secretary, Economic and Social Affairs 1968–70, Head, Economic and Social Affairs 1970–77, Secretary, Economic Department 1970–77, Assistant General Secretary 1978–99. *Other:* Committee Member, Tilford Bach Society; Chair, Farnham Roads Action. *Trusts, etc:* Trustee, Employment Policy Institute. *Miscellaneous:* Member: DTI Inward Investment Mission in Japan 1974, Channel Tunnel Advisory Committee 1974–75, Bullock Committee on Industrial Democracy 1975–77, Royal Commission on the Distribution of Income and Wealth 1975–79, Delors Committee on Economic and Social Concepts in the Community 1977–79, Energy Commission 1977–79, UN Commission on Transnational Corporations 1977–82, NEDC Committee on Finance for Industry 1978–82, Led TUC Mission to Study Employment and Technology in the USA 1980; Chair, ETUC Economic Committee 1980–90; Member, Franco-British Council 1982–99; Governor, National Institute of Economic and Social Research; Editorial Board Member, New Economy (IPPR) 1991–99; Member, Retail Prices Index Advisory Committee 1985–99; Secretary, TUC National Energy Review Body 1986–88; Member: Kreisky Commission on Employment Issues in Europe 1987–89, Tripartite Mission EU, Japan 1990, European TUC Executive Committee and Steering Group 1991–99, European Social Dialogue Joint Steering Committee 1992–, UK Delegation Earth Summit, Rio 1992; Secretary, TUC Task Force on Representation at Work 1994–; Member, Round Table on Sustainable Development 1995–99; Vice-President, ETUC 1997–98; Chair, Sub-Group on Sustainable Business – A Stakeholder Approach 1997–98; Member: Trade Union and Sustainable Development Advisory Committee 1998–99, Advisory Committee on Vehicle Emissions 1998–99, EU High Level Group on Benchmarking 1998–99, Treasury Advisory Committee on EMU 1998–99. *Honours:* OBE 1968. *Publications: Trade Unionism*, 1966; *Industrial Democracy*, 1974; *Trade Unions and Multinational Companies. Recreations:* Music, theatre, skiing, theatre. *Clubs:* Bourne Club, Farnham. *Name, Style and Title:* Raised to the peerage as Baron Lea of Crondall, of Crondall in the County of Hampshire 1999. Labour. *Address:* The Lord Lea of Crondall, OBE, South Court, Crondall, Nr Farnham, Surrey, GU10 5QF *Tel:* 01252 850711 *Fax:* 01252 850711; 17 Ormonde Mansions, 106 Southampton Row, London, WC1B 4BP *Tel:* 020 7405 6237 *E-Mail:* lead@parliament.uk.

LESTER OF HERNE HILL (Life Baron, UK), Anthony Paul Lester; cr. 1993; QC 1975; QC (NI) 1984

Son of late Harry Lester, and of Kate Lester. Born July 3, 1936; educated City of London School; Trinity College, Cambridge (MA); Harvard Law School (LLM); Hon. DUniv, The Open University; Hon. DLitt: University of Ulster, University of South Bank; Hon. Life Fellow, University College London 1998. Married 1971, Catherine Elizabeth Debora Wassey (1 son 1 daughter). *Armed Forces:* 2nd Lieutenant, Royal Artillery 1955–57 (National Service). *Career:* Called to Bar, Lincoln's Inn 1963; Bencher 1985; Called to Bar of Northern Ireland 1984; Irish Bar 1983; Special Adviser to: Home Secretary 1974–76, Special Adviser to Standing Advisory Commission on Human Rights in Northern Ireland 1975–77; Hon. Visiting Professor, University College London 1983–; A Recorder of the Crown Court 1987–93. *Select Committees:* Member, House of Lords Procedure Committee 1995–97; Member, European Communities Select Committee Sub-Committees on: Law and Institutions 1995–97, 1996 Inter-Governmental Conference 1995–97; Member, Select Committee on European Communities Sub-Committee F (Social Affairs, Education and Home Affairs) 1997–. *Party Groups (General):* A founder member of the Social Democrat Party; President, Liberal Democrat Lawyers' Association. *Other:* President, Interights (The International Centre for the Legal Protection of Human Rights) 1991–; Governor, British Institute of Human Rights; Board of Governors, James Allen's Girls' School 1987–93; Member, Executive Committee and Council of Justice; Executive Committee, European Roma Rights Center, Co-Chair 1998–; Member, Board of Directors, Salzburg Seminar; Governor, Westminster School 1998–. *Awards Granted:* Liberty Human Rights Lawyer of the Year Award 1997. Member, American Law Institute 1985–; Hon. Fellow, Society for Advanced Legal Studies 1998–. *Publications:* Author of: *Justice in the American South,* (Amnesty International) 1964; *Shawcross and Beaumont on Air Law,* 3rd edition 1964, (co-editor); *Race and Law,* 1972 (jointly); Numerous articles on human rights law and constitutional reform; Contributor to other legal publications; Editor-in-Chief, *Butterworths Human Rights Cases*; Member, Editorial Board of *Public Law*; Consultant Editor and Contributor, *Halsbury's Laws of England,* 4th edition, reissued 1996, title on 'Constitutional Law and Human Rights'; Co-editor, *Butterworths Human Rights Law and Practice,* 1999. *Special Interests:* Human Rights, Constitutional Reform, Law Reform, Equality and Non-Discrimination, Media, European Political Integration. *Recreations:* Walking, golf, sailing, watercolours. *Name, Style and Title:* Raised to the peerage as Baron Lester of Herne Hill, of Herne Hill in the London Borough of Southwark 1993. A Liberal Democrat. *Address:* The Lord Lester of Herne Hill, QC, Odysseus Trust, 18–20 Outer Temple, 222 Strand, London, WC2 1BA *E-Mail:* lestera@parliament.uk.

LEVENE OF PORTSOKEN (Life Baron, UK), Peter Keith Levene; cr. 1997; KBE 1989)

Son of late Maurice and Rose Levene. Born December 8, 1941; educated City of London School; Manchester University (BA Econ); Fellow, Queen Mary and Westfield College 1995; Hon. DSc, City University 1998. Married 1966, Wendy Fraiman (2 sons 1 daughter). *Armed Forces:* Hon. Col. Comdt, Royal Logistic Corps 1993–. *Councils, Public Bodies:* Member (Candlewick Ward), Court of Common Council, City of London 1983–84, Alderman (Portsoken Ward) 1984–; JP, City of London 1984–; Sheriff, City of London 1995–96; Lord Mayor of London 1998–99. *Career:* Joined United Scientific Holdings 1963, Managing Director 1968–85, Chairman 1982–85; Member, SE Asia Trade Advisory Group 1979–83; Council Member, Defence Manufacturers' Association 1982–85, Chairman 1984–85; Personal Adviser to the Secretary of State for Defence 1984; Chief of Defence Procurement, Ministry of Defence 1985–91; UK National Armaments Director 1988–91; Chairman, European National Armaments Directors 1989–90; Special Adviser to Secretary of State for the Environment 1991–92, Chairman, Docklands Light Railway Ltd 1991–94; Deputy Chairman, Wasserstein Perella & Co Ltd 1991–94; Special Adviser to Chancellor of the Exchequer on Competition and Purchasing 1992; Member, Citizen's Charter Advisory Panel 1992–93; Personal Adviser to the President of the Board of Trade 1992–95; Adviser to the Prime Minister on Efficiency and Effectiveness 1992–97; Chairman and Chief Executive, Canary Wharf Ltd 1993–96; Senior Adviser, Morgan Stanley & Co Ltd 1996–98; Chairman: Bankers Trust International plc 1998–99, Investment Banking Europe Deutsche Bank 1999–. *Chancellor:* Chancellor, City University 1998–99. *Other:* Governor, City of London School for Girls 1984–85; Member, Board of Management, London Homes for the Elderly 1984–93, Chairman 1990–93; Governor, City of London School 1986–. *Trusts, etc:* Chairman, Bevis Marks Trust. *Honours:* KBE 1989; OStJ 1996; Commandeur, Ordre National du Merite (France) 1996; Knight Commander Order of Merit (Germany) 1998; Middle Cross Order of Merit (Hungary) 1999. CIMgt; FCIT; FCIPS. Liveryman, Carmen's Company 1984–, Master 1992–93; Liveryman, Information Technologists 1992–. *Recreations:* Ski-ing, watching football, travel. *Clubs:* Guildhall, City Livery, Royal Automobile. *Name, Style and Title:* Raised to the peerage as Baron Levene of Portsoken, of Portsoken in the City of London 1997. A Cross-Bencher. *Address:* The Lord Levene of Portsoken, KBE, House of Lords, London, SW1A 0PW *E-Mail:* levenep@ms.com.

LEVY (Life Baron, UK), Michael Abraham Levy; cr. 1997

Son of Samuel and Annie Levy. Born July 11, 1944; educated Fleetwood Primary School (Head Boy); Hackney Downs Grammar School; Honorary Doctorate, Middlesex University 1999. Married 1967, Gilda Altbach (1 son 1 daughter). *Career:* Lubbock Fine (Chartered Accountants) 1961–66; Principal, M. Levy & Co. 1966–69; Partner, Wagner Prager Levy & Partners 1969–73; Chairman, Magnet Group of Companies 1973–88; Vice-Chairman: Phonographic Performance Ltd 1979–84, British Phonographic Industry Ltd 1984–87; Chairman: D & J Securities Ltd 1988–92, M & G Records Ltd 1992–97, Chase Music Ltd (formerly M & G Music Ltd) 1992–, Wireart Ltd 1992–. *Other:* National Campaign Chairman, United Joint Israel Appeal 1982–85, Vice-President 1994–; Member, World Board of Governors of the Jewish Agency 1990–95; Governor, Jewish Free School 1990–95, Hon. President 1995–; Chairman, Jewish Care 1991–97, President 1998–; World Chairman, Youth Aliyah Committee of Jewish Agency Board of Governors 1991–95; Chairman: Chief Rabbinate Awards for Excellence 1992–, Foundation for Education 1993–, Jewish Care Community Foundation 1995–; Member: World Commission on Israel-Diaspora Relations 1995–, International Board of Governors of the Peres Centre for Peace 1997–; Patron, Ben Uri Art Society 1997–; Member: Advisory Council to the Foreign Policy Centre 1997–, Foreign and Commonwealth Office Panel 2000 1998–; President, Community Service Volunteers 1998–; Member, National Council for Voluntary Organisations Advisory Committee. *Awards Granted:* B'nai B'rith First Lodge Award 1994; Friends of the Hebrew University of Jerusalem Scopus Award 1998. *Trusts, etc:* Member, Keren Hayesod World Board of Trustees 1991–95; Patron, Prostate Cancer Charitable Trust 1997–; Trustee, Holocaust Education Trust 1998–; Patron, Friends of Israel Educational Trust 1998–. *Miscellaneous:* Chairman, British Music Industry Awards Committee 1992–95; Patron, British Music Industry Awards 1995–. FCA 1966. *Special Interests:* Voluntary Sector, Social Welfare, Education. *Recreations:* Tennis, swimming. *Name, Style and Title:* Raised to the peerage as Baron Levy, of Mill Hill in the London Borough of Barnet 1997. Labour. *Address:* The Lord Levy, House of Lords, London, SW1A 0PW *E-Mail:* ml@lmalvy.demon.co.uk.

LEWIS OF NEWNHAM (Life Baron, UK), Jack Lewis; cr. 1989; Kt 1982; FRS 1973; Hon. MRSC

Son of late Robert Lewis. Born February 13, 1928; educated Barrow Grammar School; University of London (BSc 1949, DSc 1961); University of Nottingham (PhD 1952); University of Mancherster (MSc 1964); Cambridge University (MA 1970, ScD 1977); Hon. Fellow, Sidney Sussex College, Fellow 1970–77; DHon, Causa Rennes 1980; DUniv, Open 1982; Hon. DSc: East Anglia 1983, Nottingham 1983, Keele 1984, Birmingham 1988, Leicester 1988, Waterloo Canada 1988, Manchester 1990, University of Wales 1990; Hon. Fellowships: UCL 1990, UMIST 1990; Hon. DSc: Sheffield 1992, Cranfield Institute of Technology 1993; DUniv, Kingston 1993; Hon. Fellowship, Central Lancashire 1993; Hon. DSc: Edinburgh 1994, Bath 1995, Durham 1996, Hong Kong 1998, National University of Ireland 1999. Married 1951, Elfreida Mabel, daughter of Frank Lamb (1 son 1 daughter). *Career:* Lecturer: University of Sheffield 1954–56, Imperial College, London 1956–57; Lecturer/Reader, University College, London 1957–61; Professor of Chemistry: University of Manchester 1961–67, University College, London 1967–70, University of Cambridge 1970–95; Member, Cambridge University 1970–; First Warden, Robinson College, University of Cambridge 1975–; Member, Council of SERC 1979–84; Member, Council, Royal Society 1982–84, 1996–98, Vice-President 1983–84; Chairman, Visiting Committee, Cranfield Institute of Technology 1982–92; Chairman, Royal Commission on Environmental Pollution 1986–92; President, Royal Society of Chemistry 1986–88; Science Representative for UK on NATO Science Committee 1986–98; Director, The BOC Foundation 1990–; Member, Council, Royal Society of Chemistry 1992–95, 1996–98; President, National Society for Clean Air and Environmental Protection 1993–95; Chairman, ESART Board 1998–. *Select Committees:* Member: Science and Technology Sub-Committee II 1990–91, 1995–97, European Communities Sub-Committee F 1991–92, Science and Technology Sub-Committee I 1992–93, European Communities Sub-Committee C 1993–95 (Chairman), European Communities Sub-Committee B 1995–97; Co-opted Member, Select Committee on European Communities: Sub-Committee B (Energy, Industry and Transport) 1997–, Sub-Committee C 1997 . *Other:* Patron, Student Community Action Development Unit 1985–; Foreign Member: American Academy of Arts and Sciences 1983, American Philosophical Society 1994, Accademia Nazionale dei Lincei, Italy 1995, Polish Academy of Arts and Sciences 1996–; Hon. Member, Society of Chemical Industry 1996; Chairman, The Leys School Governors 1997–; President, Arthritis Research Campaign 1998–; Hon. Member, Royal Society of Chemistry. *Trusts, etc:* Chairman, Executive Committee of the Cambridge Overseas Trust 1988–; Trustee: Kennedy Memorial Trust 1989–99, Croucher Foundation 1989–98. *Miscellaneous:* Hon. President, Environmental Industries Commission 1996–; Chairman, Standing Committee on Structural Safety 1998–. *Honours:* Kt; Chevalier dans l'Ordre des Palmes Académiques; Commander Cross of the Order of Merit of the Republic of Poland. Fellow, Indian National Science Academy 1985; Foreign Associate, National Academy of Sciences, USA 1987; Foreign Fellow, Bangladesh Academy of Sciences 1992; FRSA. *Publications:* Some 850 papers and review articles. *Special Interests:* Education, Environment. *Recreations:* Music, walking. *Clubs:* Royal Over-Seas League, United Oxford and Cambridge University. *Name, Style and Title:* Raised to the peerage as Baron Lewis of Newnham, of Newnham in the County of Cambridgeshire 1989. A Cross-Bencher. *Address:* Professor The Lord Lewis of Newnham, FRS, Robinson College, Grange Road, Cambridge, CB3 9AN *Tel:* 01223 339120 *E-Mail:* jl219@cam.ac.uk.

LICHFIELD (97th Bishop of), Keith Norman Sutton

Son of late Norman and Irene Sutton. Born June 23, 1934; educated Battersea Grammar School; Jesus College, Cambridge; Ridley Hall, Cambridge; Hon. D University Keele 1992; Hon. DLit, Wolverhampton 1994. Married June 8, 1963, Edith Mary Jean, daughter of Dr Henry and late Mrs Anne Geldard (3 sons 1 daughter). *Career:* Curate, St Andrew's, Plymouth 1959–62; Chaplain, St John's College, Cambridge 1962–67; Tutor and Chaplain, Bishop Tucker College, Mukono, Uganda 1968–73; Principal, Ridley Hall, Cambridge 1973–78; Suffragan Bishop of Kingston-upon-Thames 1978–84; Governing Body Member, St John's College, Durham 1986–94; President, Queen's College, Birmingham 1986–94; Diocesan Bishop of Lichfield 1984–;
Entered the House of Lords 1989; Chairman: General Synod Board for Mission and Unity 1989–91, General Synod Board of Mission 1991–94; Episcopal Visitor, Simon of Cyrene Theological Institute, London 1992–. *Publications: The People of God*, (SPCK) 1984; Articles in: *The Times, The Guardian, Church Times* etc. *Special Interests:* Foreign Affairs, Africa, Overseas Aid and Development, Inner Cities. *Recreations:* Russian literature, walking, Baroque music. *Address:* The Rt Rev. the Lord Bishop of Lichfield, Bishop's House, 22 The Close, Lichfield, Staffordshire, WS13 7LG *Tel:* 01543 306000 *Fax:* 01543 306009.

LINCOLN (70th Bishop of), Robert Maynard Hardy

Son of Harold and Monica Hardy. Born October 5, 1936; educated Queen Elizabeth Grammar School, Wakefield; Clare College, Cambridge (MA); Fellow and Chaplain, Selwyn College, Cambridge 1965–72, Hon. Fellow 1986; Hon. DD, University of Hull 1993. Married 1970, Isobel Mary, daughter of Charles and Ella Burch (2 sons 1 daughter). *Career:* Deacon 1962; Priest 1963; Assistant Curate, All Saints and Martyrs, Langley, Manchester 1962–65; Vicar of All Saints, Borehamwood 1972–75; Priest-in-charge, Apsley Guise 1975; Course Director, St Albans Diocese Ministerial Training Scheme 1975; Incumbent of United Benefice of Apsley Guise with Husborne Crawley and Ridgmont 1980; Bishop of Suffragan of Maidstone 1980–86; Bishop to HM
Prisons 1985–; Bishop of Lincoln 1987–; Entered the House of Lords 1993. *Recreations:* Walking, gardening, reading. *Address:* The Rt Rev. the Lord Bishop of Lincoln, Bishop's House, Eastgate, Lincoln, LN2 1QQ *Tel:* 01522 534701 *E-Mail:* bishlincoln@claranet.co.uk.

LINDSAY (16th Earl of, S), James Randolph Lindesay-Bethune; cr. 1633; Viscount Garnock (S) 1703; Lord Lindsay of the Byres (S) 1445; Lord Parbroath (S) 1633; Lord Kilbirnie, Kingsburn and Drumry (S) 1703

Son of 15th Earl and Hon. Mary-Clare Douglas Scott Montagu, daughter of 2nd Baron Montagu of Beaulieu, KCIE, CSI, DL. Born November 19, 1955. Succeeded his father 1989; educated Eton; Edinburgh University (MA (Hons); University of California, Davis. Married March 2, 1982, Diana Mary, daughter of Major Nigel Chamberlayne-Macdonald, LVO, OBE (2 sons 3 daughters inc. twins). *Career:* Vice-President, International Tree Foundation 1993–95, President 1995–; Chairman, Assured British Meat Ltd (ABM) 1997–; Deputy Chairman, Scottish Salmon Growers Association Ltd (SSGA) 1997–98; Chairman 1998–; Board Member, Cairngorms Partnership 1998–; Non-Executive Director, UA Group plc 1998–; Chairman: UA Properties Ltd 1999–,
UA Forestry Ltd 1999–. *House of Lords:* Parliamentary Under-Secretary of State, Scottish Office 1995–97; An elected hereditary peer 1999–. *Whip:* A Lord-in-Waiting (Government Whip) January–July 1995. *Spokesman:* An Opposition Spokesman on Agriculture, Fisheries and Food, Environment, Transport and the Regions (Green Issues) June-October 1997. *Select Committees:* Member: European Communities Sub-Committee C (Environment and Social Affairs) 1993–95, 1997–98, Select Committee on Sustainable Development 1994–95. *International Bodies:* Inter-Parliamentary Union Committee on Environment 1993–95, Vice-Chairman 1994–95. *Other:* Chairman: Landscape Foundation 1992–95, RSPB Scotland 1998–; Council Member, RSPB (UK) 1998–. *Awards Granted:* Winner of Green Ribbon Political Award 1995. *Trusts, etc:* Member, Advisory Panel, Railway Heritage Trust 1990–. *Miscellaneous:* Member: Advisory Council World Resource Foundation 1994–99, Secretary of State's Advisory Group on Sustainable Development 1998–99, UK Round Table on Sustainable Development Sub-Group: Sustainability – Devolved and Regional Dimensions 1998–99, ScottishPower Environment Forum 1998–. Hon. Fellow, Institute of Wastes Management (IWM) 1998–. *Publications: Garden Ornament,* 1989 (co-author); *Trellis,* 1991. *Special Interests:* Environment, Transport, Energy, Waste Management. *Clubs:* New (Edinburgh). *Heir:* His son, Viscount Garnock, born December 30, 1990. A Conservative. *Address:* The Earl of Lindsay, Lahill, Upper Largo, Fife, KY8 6JE *Tel:* 01333 360251.

LINKLATER OF BUTTERSTONE (Life Baroness, UK), Veronica Linklater; cr. 1997

Daughter of Lieutenant-Colonel Archibald Michael Lyle, OBE, JP, DL and late Hon. Elizabeth Sinclair, daughter of 1st Viscount Thurso, KT, PC, CMG. Born April 15, 1943; educated Cranborne Chase School; University of Sussex; University of London (DipSoc). Married 1967, Magnus Duncan Linklater, son of late Eric Robert Linklater, CBE, TD (2 sons 1 daughter). *Career:* Social Worker (Childcare Officer); Social Administrator. *All-Party:* Secretary, The Scottish Peers Association. *Other:* Founder and Chairman, The New School, Butterstone Ltd; President, The Society of Friends of Dunkeld Cathedral; Patron, The Airborne Initiative (Scotland) Ltd; Member, The Beattie Committee on post-school provision for young people with special needs
1998–99; Vice-Chairman, Pushkin Prizes, Scotland. *Trusts, etc:* Member: The Butler Trust, The Esmée Fairbairn Charitable Trust, The Maggie Keswick Jencks Cancer Caring Trust, The Sutherland Trust. *Miscellaneous:* Contested (Lib Dem) Perth and Kinross By-election 1995. *Special Interests:* Education, Youth Affairs, Penal Affairs and Policy. *Recreations:* Music, theatre, gardening. *Name, Style and Title:* Raised to the peerage as Baroness Linklater of Butterstone, of Riemore in Perth and Kinross 1997. A Liberal Democrat. *Address:* The Baroness Linklater of Butterstone, 5 Drummond Place, Edinburgh, EH3 6PH *Tel:* 0131–557 5705.

Dod *on* Disk

The Vacher Dod Parliamentary Database – configured for PC or Network

For further details please telephone the Westminster Office

020 7828 7256

LIPSEY (Life Baron, UK), David Lawrence Lipsey; cr. 1999

Son of late Lawrence Lipsey, and of Penlope Lipsey. Born April 21, 1948; educated Bryanston School; Magdalen College, Oxford (PPE 1st Class Hons 1970). Married 1982 (1 daughter, 2 step-sons). *Career:* Research Assistant, GMWU 1970–72; Political Adviser to Rt Hon. Anthony Crosland (in Opposition, DoE and FCO) 1972–77; Adviser to 10 Downing Street 1977–79; Journalist, *New Society* 1979–80, Editor 1986–88; Journalist, then Economics Editor, *Sunday Times* 1980–86; Founder/Deputy Editor, *Sunday Correspondent* 1985–90; Associate (Acting Deputy Editor) *Times* 1990–92; Journalist, Political Editor, Public Policy Editor, *Economist* 1992–99; Public Interest Director, Personal Investment Authority; Non-Executive Director, The Tote; Member of Council, Advertising Standards Authority; Director, Political Quarterly; International Advisory Board, Angus Reid Group. *Party Groups (General):* Secretary, Streatham Labour Party 1970–72; Chair, Fabian Society 1982–83. *Other:* Advisory Council: Constitution Unit, Centre for Research into Election and Social Trends. *Miscellaneous:* Member: Jenkins Commission on Electoral Reform 1998; Royal Commission on Long-term Care of the Elderly 1998–99, Davies Panel on BBC Licence Fee 1999. *Publications: Labour and Land,* 1972; *The Socialist Agenda,* Editor 1981; *The Name of the Rose,* 1992. *Special Interests:* Horse Racing, Financial Regulation, Electoral Reform, Broadcasting, Machinery of Government, Psephology. *Recreations:* Golf, racing, opera, swimming. *Name, Style and Title:* Raised to the peerage as Baron Lipsey, of Tooting Bec in the London Borough of Wandsworth 1999. Labour. *Address:* The Lord Lipsey, 94 Drewstead Road, London, SW16 1AG *Tel:* 020 8677 7446 *Fax:* 020 8677 7446 *E-Mail:* david.lipsey@btinernet.com.

LISTOWEL (6th Earl of, I), Francis Michael Hare; cr. 1822; 6th Viscount Ennismore and Listowel (I) 1816; 6th Baron Ennismore (I) 1800; 4th Baron Hare (UK) 1869

Son of 5th Earl, PC, GCMG. Born June 28, 1964. Succeeded his father 1997. Sits as Baron Hare; educated Westminster School; Queen Mary and Westfield College, University of London. *House of Lords:* An elected hereditary peer 1999–. *Special Interests:* Young Under-privileged, Small Farmers, Hereditary Peers. *Recreations:* Singing, music, art. *Clubs:* Reform. *Heir:* His brother, Hon. Timothy Patrick Hare, born February 23, 1966. A Cross-Bencher. *Address:* The Earl of Listowel, House of Lords, London, SW1A 0PW.

LIVERPOOL (5th Earl of, UK), Edward Peter Bertram Savile Foljambe; cr. 1905; Viscount Hawkesbury; 5th Baron Hawkesbury (UK) 1893

Son of Captain Peter George William Savile Foljambe (killed in action 1944), grandson of 1st Earl, PC, DL. Born November 14, 1944. Succeeded his great-uncle 1969; educated Shrewsbury; Perugia University, Italy. Married 1st, January 29, 1970, Lady Juliana Noel, daughter of 5th Earl of Gainsborough (*qv*) (2 sons) (marriage dissolved 1994), married 2nd, May 26, 1995, Comtesse Marie-Ange de Pierredon, eldest daughter of Comte Géraud Michel de Pierredon. *Career:* Managing Director, Melbourns Brewery Ltd, Stamford, Lincolnshire 1971–76, Joint Chairman and Managing Director 1977–87; Director: Hilstone Developments Ltd 1986–91, Hart Hambleton plc 1986–92, Rutland Properties Ltd 1987–, J. W. Cameron & Co. Ltd 1987–91; Chairman and Managing Director, Maxador Ltd 1987–. *House of Lords:* An elected hereditary peer 1999–. *Recreations:* Flying, golf, shooting. *Clubs:* Turf, Pratt's, Air Squadron. *Heir:* His son, Viscount Hawkesbury, born March 25, 1972. A Conservative. *Address:* The Earl of Liverpool, House of Lords, London, SW1A 0PW.

LLOYD OF BERWICK (Life Baron, UK), Anthony John Leslie Lloyd; cr. 1993; Kt 1978; PC 1984; DL

Son of late Edward John Boydell Lloyd. Born May 9, 1929; educated Eton; Trinity College, Cambridge (1st class Classical Tripos Part I, 1st class with distinction Law Tripos Part II); Choate Fellow, Harvard 1952; Fellow: Peterhouse 1953, Eton 1974–86; Hon. Fellow, Peterhouse 1981. Married 1960, Jane Helen Violet, daughter of C. W. Shelford, of Chailey Place, Lewes, East Sussex. *Armed Forces:* Served Coldstream Guards (National Service) 1948. *Councils, Public Bodies:* DL, East Sussex 1983–. *Career:* Called to Bar, Inner Temple 1955; QC 1967; Bencher 1976; Attorney-General to HRH The Prince of Wales 1969–77; Judge of the High Court of Justice, Queen's Bench Division 1978–84; A Lord Justice of Appeal 1984–93; Vice-Chairman, Security Commission 1985–92, Chairman 1992–; A Lord of Appeal in Ordinary 1993–98. *Other:* Director, Royal Academy of Music 1979–98; Vice-President, Corporation of the Sons of the Clergy 1996–. *Trusts, etc:* Trustee, Glyndebourne Arts Trust 1973–, Chairman 1975–94. *Honours:* Kt 1978; PC 1984. Hon. FRAM 1985. Hon. Member, Salters' Company 1988–, Second Warden 1998. *Recreations:* Music, carpentry. *Clubs:* Brooks's. *Name, Style and Title:* Raised to the peerage as Baron Lloyd of Berwick, of Ludlay in the County of East Sussex 1993. A Cross-Bencher. *Address:* The Rt Hon. the Lord Lloyd of Berwick, DL, House of Lords, London, SW1A 0PW.

LLOYD OF HIGHBURY (Life Baroness, UK), June Kathleen Lloyd; cr. 1996; DBE 1990

Daughter of late Arthur Cresswell Lloyd, MBE, and late Lucy Bevan Lloyd. Born January 1, 1928; educated Royal School, Bath; Bristol University (MD); Durham University (DPH); Hon. DSc: Bristol 1991, Birmingham 1993. *Career:* Junior hospital appointments in Bristol, Oxford and Newcastle 1951–57; Resident Fellow and Lecturer on Child Health, University of Birmingham 1958–65; Senior Lecturer, Reader in Paediatrics, Institute of Child Health 1965–73; Professor of Paediatrics, London University 1973–75; Professor of Child Health, St George's Medical School, London University 1975–85; Visiting Examiner in Paediatrics in Universities in the UK and abroad; Nuffield Professor of Child Health, British Postgraduate Medical Federation, London University 1985–92, currently Emeritus Professor; Past Chairman, Department of Health Advisory Committee on Gene Therapy. *International Bodies (General):* Member of Paediatric Associations in: Finland, France, Switzerland, Germany, USA, Sri Lanka, Australia. *Other:* Member, Royal College of Physicians, London 1982–85, 1986–88; President, British Paediatric Association 1988–91. *Honours:* DBE 1990. *Publications:* Several articles in scientific journals. *Recreations:* Cooking, gardening, walking. *Name, Style and Title:* Raised to the peerage as Baroness Lloyd of Highbury, of Highbury in the London Borough of Islington 1996. A Cross-Bencher. *Address:* The Baroness Lloyd of Highbury, DBE, House of Lords, London, SW1A 0PW.

LLOYD-WEBBER (Life Baron, UK), Andrew Lloyd Webber; cr. 1997; Kt 1992

Son of late William Southcombe Lloyd Webber, CBE, FRCM, FRCO, and Jean Hermione Johnstone. Born March 22, 1948; educated Westminster School; Magdalen College, Oxford; Royal College of Music. Married 1st, 1971, Sarah Jane Tudor (1 son 1 daughter) (marriage dissolved 1983), married 2nd, 1984, Sarah Brightman (marriage dissolved 1990), married 3rd, 1991, Madeleine Astrid Gurdon (2 sons, 1 daughter). *Career:* Composer: Variations (based on A minor Caprice No 24 by Paganini) 1977, symphonic version 1986, Joseph and the Amazing Technicolour Dreamcoat (with lyrics by Timothy Rice) 1968, Jesus Christ Superstar (with lyrics by Timothy Rice) 1970, Gumshoe (film score) 1971, The Odessa File (film score) 1974, Jeeves (with lyrics by Alan Ayckbourn) 1975, Evita (with lyrics by Timothy Rice) 1976, Tell Me On a Sunday 1980, Cats (with lyrics by T. S. Eliot) 1981, Starlight Express 1984, Requiem Mass 1985, The Phantom of the Opera (with lyrics by Charles Hart and Richard Stilgoe) 1986, Aspects of Love (with lyrics by Don Black and Charles Hart) 1989, Sunset Boulevard (with lyrics by Don Black and Christopher Hampton) 1993, By Jeeves (with lyrics by Alan Ayckbourn) 1996, Whistle Down The Wind (with lyrics by Jim Steinman) 1996, Evita (film score) 1996. *Awards Granted:* Star on the Hollywood Walk of Fame 1993; The American Society of Composers, Authors and Publishers Triple Play Award 'First recipient'; Tony Awards; Drama Desk Awards; Grammy Awards; Five Laurence Olivier Awards; Praemium Imperial Award for Music 1995;

Richard Rodger's Award for contributions/excellence to/in Musical Theatre 1996; Oscar and Golden Globe for best original song "You must love me' from Evita the movie. *Trusts, etc:* Member, Open Churches Trust. *Honours:* Kt 1992. FRCM 1988. *Publications: Evita,* (with Tim Rice); *Cats the book of the musical,* 1981; *Joseph and the Amazing Technicolor Dreamcoat,* 1982; *The Complete Phantom of the Opera,* 1987; *The Complete Aspects of Love,* 1989; *Sunset Boulevard: From Movie to Musical,* 1993. *Special Interests:* Art, Architecture. *Recreations:* Architecture, art, food and wine. *Clubs:* Marc's. *Name, Style and Title:* Raised to the peerage as Baron Lloyd-Webber, of Sydmonton in the County of Hampshire 1997. A Conservative. *Address:* The Lord Lloyd-Webber, 22 Tower Street, London, WC2H 9NS.

LOCKWOOD (Life Baroness, UK), Betty Lockwood; cr. 1978; DL

Daughter of late Arthur Lockwood. Born January 22, 1924; educated East Borough Girls School, Dewsbury; Ruskin College, Oxford; Hon. DLitt, Bradford 1981; Hon. Dr of Law, Strathclyde University 1985; Hon. Fellow: UMIST 1986, Birkbeck College, University of London 1987. Married 1978, Lieutenant-Colonel Cedric Hall (died 1988). *Councils, Public Bodies:* Member, Leeds Development Corporation 1988–95; DL, West Yorkshire 1987. *Career:* Assistant Agent, Reading Labour Party 1948–50; Secretary-Agent, Gillingham Labour Party 1950–52; Yorkshire Regional Women's Officer, Labour Party 1952–67; Chief Woman Officer and Assistant National Agent, Labour Party 1967–75; Chairman, Equal Opportunities Commission 1975–83; Chairman, European Advisory Committee on Equal Opportunities for Women and Men 1982–83; Member, Council of Advertising Standards Authority 1983–92; Member, Council of Europe and WEU 1992–94. *Chancellor:* Pro-Chancellor, University of Bradford 1987–97, Chancellor 1997–. *House of Lords:* A Deputy Speaker of the House of Lords 1990–; A Deputy Chairman of Committees 1997–. *Select Committees:* Member, House of Lords Select Committees: Science and Technology 1983–89, European Communities 1985–93; Chairman, Sub-Committee on Social and Community Affairs 1990–93. *All-Party:* Executive Committee Member, All-Party Population, Development and Reproductive Health Group 1983–; Deputy President, Parliamentary and Scientific Committee 1992–99; Co-Chairman, Parliamentary University Group 1995–99. *Other:* President, Birkbeck College, University of London 1983–89; Member of Council: University of Bradford 1983–, University of Leeds 1985–91; President, Hillcroft College 1987–94; Chairman, National Coal Mining Museum for England 1995–. *Trusts, etc:* Fellow, Industry and Parliament Trust. Hon. Fellow: UMIST 1986, Birkbeck College 1987. *Special Interests:* Sex Equality, Education, Industrial Training, Training, Industry. *Recreations:* Enjoying the Yorkshire Dales. *Clubs:* Soroptimist International. *Name, Style and Title:* Raised to the peerage as Baroness Lockwood, of Dewsbury in the County of West Yorkshire 1978. Labour. *Address:* The Baroness Lockwood, DL, 6 Sycamore Drive, Addingham, Nr Ilkley, West Yorkshire, LS29 0NY *Tel:* 01943 831098.

LOFTHOUSE OF PONTEFRACT (Life Baron, UK), Geoffrey Lofthouse; cr. 1997; Kt 1997

Son of late Ernest Lofthouse. Born December 18, 1925; educated Featherstone Primary and Secondary Schools; Leeds University (day release). Married April 20, 1946, Sarah, daughter of Joesh Thomas Onions (died 1985) (1 daughter). *Trades Union:* Member, NUM. *Councils, Public Bodies:* Appointed Magistrate 1970; Pontefract Borough Council: Councillor 1962–74, Leader of Council, Chairman: Building, Town Planning and Streets Committees; Deputy Chairman: Housing Committee, Finance Committee, Member, All Council Committees; Mayor of Pontefract 1967–68; Wakefield Metropolitan District Council: Councillor 1973–79, First Chairman, Chairman, Housing Committee, Member Committees on: Education, Finance, Policy and Resources. *Career:* Personnel Manager, NCB Fryston 1970–78. *House of Commons:* MP (Labour) for Pontefract and Castleford 1978 By-election–97; First Deputy Chairman, Ways and Means 1992–97. *Select Committees (Commons):* Former Member, Select Committee on Energy. *House of Lords:* A Deputy Chairman of Committees 1999–. *All-Party:* Chairman, All-Party Rugby League Group. *Party Groups (General):* Vice-President, Wakefield District Labour Party. *Other:* Member: Division Education Executive Committee, All Governing/Managing Bodies of Pontefract Schools; Chairman: Primary Schools' Managers, Pontefract Carleton High School Governing Body; Patron, Heartlink. *Honours:* Knighted 1995. Fellow,

Institute of Personnel Development 1984–. *Publications: A Very Miner MP* (Autobiography), 1986 *From Coal Sack to Woolsack*(Autobiography), 1999. *Special Interests:* Housing, Industrial Relations, Energy, Local Government, Human Rights. *Recreations:* Rugby League and cricket. *Sportsclubs:* Vice-President, Featherstone Rovers RLFC; President, British Amateur Rugby League Association; Vice-Chairman, Policy Making Board of Rugby Football League. *Name, Style and Title:* Raised to the peerage as Baron Lofthouse of Pontefract, of Pontefract in the County of West Yorkshire 1997. Labour. *Address:* The Lord Lofthouse of Pontefract, 67 Carleton Crest, Pontefract, West Yorkshire, WF8 2QR *Tel:* 01977 704275.

LONDON (132nd Bishop of), Richard John Carew Chartres; PC 1996

Son of late Richard Chartres and of Charlotte Chartres. Born July 11, 1947; educated Hertford Grammar School; Trinity College, Cambridge (MA); Cuddesdon Theological College, Oxford; Lincoln Theological College (BD (Lambeth); Hon. DD: London, City, Brunel Universities; Hon. DLitt, Guildhall London. Married 1982, Caroline Mary McLintock (2 sons 2 daughters). *Career:* Deacon 1973; Priest 1974; Assistant Curate, St Andrew's, Bedford 1973–75; Bishop's Domestic Chaplain, St Albans 1975–80; Archbishop of Canterbury's Chaplain 1980–84; Vicar, St Stephen with St John, Westminster 1984–92; Director of Ordinands for the London Area 1985–92; Gresham Professor of Divinity 1986–92; Area Bishop of Stepney 1992–95; Prelate of the Most Excellent Order of the British Empire 1995–; Bishop of London 1995–; Took his seat in the House of Lords 1996; Dean of HM Chapels Royal 1996–. *Other:* Member: The Court of the City University, The Ecclesiological Society; Chairman, Church Heritage Forum; Bencher of the Middle Temple; Ecclesiastical Patron, The Prayer Book Society; Chaplain to the Order of St John. *Trusts, etc:* Member: St Ethelburga's Centre for Reconciliation and Peace, St Catherine's Foundation, St Andrew's Trust. FSA, 1999. Freeman, City of London. Liveryman, Merchant Taylors' Company; Hon. Freeman, Weavers' Company. *Publications: A Brief History of Gresham College*, 1997. *Special Interests:* London, Environment. *Recreations:* Family. *Clubs:* Garrick. *Address:* The Rt Rev. and Rt Hon. the Lord Bishop of London, The Old Deanery, Dean's Court, London, EC4V 5AA *Tel:* 020 7248 6233.

LONGFORD (7th Earl of, I), Francis Aungier Pakenham; cr. 1785; Baron Longford (I) 1756; 6th Baron Silchester (UK) 1821; 1st Baron Pakenham (UK) 1945; (Life) Baron Pakenham of Cowley (UK) 1999; KG 1971; PC 1948

Son of 5th Earl, KP, MVO, and late Lady Mary Julia Child Villiers, daughter of 7th Earl of Jersey, PC, GCB, GCMG. Born December 5, 1905. Succeeded his brother 1961. Sits as Baron Pakenham; educated Eton; New College, Oxford (MA 1934, 1st class in Modern Greats). Married November 3, 1931, Elizabeth, CBE, daughter of late N. B. Harman, FRCS, of Harley Street, London, W1 (4 sons 3 daughters and 1 daughter deceased). *Armed Forces:* Served with Oxford and Bucks. Yeomanry (TA) May 1939-May 1940; Member, Oxford Home Guard 1940–45. *Career:* Former Tutor, Christ Church, Oxford, Member, Governing Body; Member, Conservative Party Economic Research Department 1930–32; Chief Assistant to Sir William Beveridge 1941–44; Chairman, National Bank Ltd 1955–63; Chairman, National Youth Employment Council 1968–71; Chairman, Sidgwick and Jackson Ltd Publishers 1970–80. *House of Lords:* A Lord in Waiting to HM King George VI 1945–46; Parliamentary Under-Secretary of State for War 1946–47; Chancellor of the Duchy of Lancaster 1947–48; Minister of Civil Aviation 1948–51; First Lord of the Admiralty May-October 1951; Lord Privy Seal 1964–65, 1966–68; Leader of the House of Lords 1964–68; Secretary of State for the Colonies December 1965-April 1966. *Party Groups (General):* Joined Labour Party 1936. *Other:* Joint Founder, New Bridge for Ex-Prisoners 1956. *Honours:* PC 1948; KG 1971. *Publications:* Author of several books including: *A History of the House of Lords*, 1988; *Suffering and Hope*, 1990; *Punishment and the Punished*, 1991; *Prisoner or Patient*, 1992; *Young Offenders*, 1993; *Avowed Intent* (memoir), 1994. *Heir:* His son, Thomas Frank Dermot Pakenham, born August 14, 1933. *Name, Style and Title:* Created a life peer as Baron Pakenham of Cowley, of Cowley in the County of Oxfordshire 1999. Labour. *Address:* The Rt Hon. the Earl of Longford, KG, Bernhurst, Hurst Green, East Sussex, TN19 7QN *Tel:* 01580 860248; 18 Chesil Court, Chelsea Manor Street, London, SW3 5QP.

LOVELL-DAVIS (Life Baron, UK), Peter Lovell Lovell-Davis; cr. 1974

Son of late William Lovell-Davis, Accountant. Born July 8, 1924; educated King Edward VI Grammar School, Stratford-upon-Avon; Jesus College, Oxford (MA). Married July 29, 1950, Jean, daughter of late Peter Foster Graham (1 son 1 daughter). *Armed Forces:* RAF Flight/Lieutenant Pilot 1943–47. *Councils, Public Bodies:* Member, Islington District Health Authority 1982–85. *Career:* Managing Director, Central Press Features Ltd; Director of other newspaper and printing companies 1950–70; Chairman: Features Syndicate Ltd, Davis and Harrison Visual Productions Ltd 1970–74; Member, London Consortium 1977–87; Board Member, Commonwealth Development Corporation 1978–84; Chairman, Lee Cooper Licensing Services Ltd 1983–90; Chairman, Pettifor, Morrow and Associates 1986–99. *House of Lords:* Parliamentary Under-Secretary of State for Energy 1975–76. *Whip:* A Lord in Waiting (Government Whip) 1974–75. *Spokesman:* Spokesman for Energy 1974–76. *Select Committees:* Former Member, Select Committee on European Communities; Former Chairman, Sub-Committee Report on Energy Conservation. *Party Groups (General):* Voluntary Adviser on publicity to the Labour Party and Government Departments 1962–74. *Other:* Vice-President, Youth Hostels Association 1977–. *Trusts, etc:* Trustee: Academic Centre of the Whittington Hospital, Highgate 1980–, The Museum of the Port of London and Docklands 1985–98. *Special Interests:* Health, European Union, Media, Energy. *Recreations:* Aviation, bird-watching, industrial archaeology, inland waterways, walking, music. *Name, Style and Title:* Raised to the peerage as Baron Lovell-Davis, of Highgate in the County of Greater London 1974. Labour. *Address:* The Lord Lovell-Davis, 80 North Road, Highgate, London, N6 4AA *Tel:* 020 8348 3919; Office: Pettifor Morrow and Associates Ltd, 17 Harwood Road, London, SW6 4QP *Tel:* 020 7384 1344 *E-Mail:* ploved@dircon.co.uk.

LUCAS OF CRUDWELL (11th Baron, E) cr. 1663, and DINGWALL (de facto 8th Lord, 14th but for the attainder) (S) 1609; Ralph Matthew Palmer

Son of late Major Hon. Robert Jocelyn Palmer, MC, and Anne Rosemary, Baroness Lucas of Crudwell (10th in line). Born June 7, 1951. Succeeded his mother 1991; educated Eton; Balliol College, Oxford (BA Hons Physics). Married 1st 1978, Clarissa Marie, daughter of George Vivian Lockett, TD, and Alice Jeannine Lockett, of Stratford St Mary, Colchester, Essex (1 son 1 daughter) (marriage dissolved 1995), married 2nd, 1995, Amanda Atha. *Career:* Articles with various firms now part of Arthur Andersen 1972–76; With S. G. Warburg & Co. Ltd 1976–88; Director of various companies. *House of Lords:* An elected hereditary peer 1999–. *Whip:* A Lord in Waiting (Government Whip) 1994–97. *Spokesman:* A Spokesman for: the Department of Education 1994–95, Department of Social Security and the Welsh Office 1994–97, the Ministry of Agriculture, Fisheries and Food and Department of the Environment 1995–97; An Opposition Spokesman on: Agriculture, Fisheries and Food 1997, Constitutional Affairs, Scotland and Wales (Wales) 1997, Environment, Transport and the Regions (Environment) 1997, International Development 1997–98. *Miscellaneous:* A Co-heir to the Barony of Butler. FCA. Liveryman, Mercers' Company. *Special Interests:* Education, Trade and Industry, Finance. *Heir:* His son, Hon. Lewis Edward Palmer, born December 7, 1987. A Conservative. *Address:* The Lord Lucas of Crudwell and Dingwall, House of Lords, London, SW1A 0PW *Tel:* 020 7219 4177 *E-Mail:* lucas@dingwall.demon.co.uk.

Dod *on* Disk

The Vacher Dod Parliamentary Database
that will run on your PC or Network

For further details please telephone the Westminster Office

020 7828 7256

LUDFORD (Life Baroness, UK), Sarah Ann Ludford; cr. 1997

Daughter of Joseph Campbell Ludford and Valerie Kathleen Ludford (née Skinner). Born March 14, 1951; educated Portsmouth High School for Girls; London School of Economics (BSc (Econ) International History, MSc (Econ) European Studies); Inns of Court School of Law. Married, Stephen Hitchins. *Councils, Public Bodies:* Councillor, London Borough of Islington 1991–. *Career:* Department of the Environment 1972–73; Independent Broadcasting Authority 1973–75; Called to the Bar 1979; European Commission, Brussels 1977–78 and 1979–85; Lloyds of London 1985–87; American Express Europe 1987–90; Freelance European Consultant 1990–; Elected a Liberal Democrat MEP for the London Region 1999–. *Spokesman:* A Spokesman on Foreign and Commonwealth Affairs 1998–. *International Bodies (General):* Member: European Movement Management Board, European Liberal Democrat and Reform Party (ELDR). *Party Groups (General):* Vice-Chair, Liberal Democrat Federal Policy Committee. *Miscellaneous:* Member, Royal Institute of International Affairs (Chatham House); Contested (Lib Dem) European Elections: Hampshire East and Wight 1984, London Central 1989 and 1994, Islington North 1992, Islington South and Finsbury 1997. *Special Interests:* Europe, Local Government, Social Issues, Health, Economic Policy. *Recreations:* Theatre, ballet, gardening. *Clubs:* National Liberal. *Name, Style and Title:* Raised to the peerage as Baroness Ludford, of Clerkenwell in the London Borough of Islington 1997. A Liberal Democrat. *Address:* The Baroness Ludford, MEP, 70 St Peter's Street, London, N1 8JS.

LUKE (3rd Baron, UK), Arthur Charles St John Lawson Johnston; cr. 1929; DL

Son of 2nd Baron, KCVO, TD, DL. Born January 13, 1933. Succeeded his father 1996; educated Eton; Trinity College, Cambridge (BA). Married 1st, August 6, 1959, Silvia Maria, daughter of H.E. Don Honorio Roigt, former Argentine Ambassador to The Netherlands (1 son 2 daughters) (marriage dissolved 1971), married 2nd, 1971, Sarah Louise, daughter of Richard Hearne, OBE (1 son). *Councils, Public Bodies:* A County Councillor for Bedfordshire 1965–70; High Sheriff, Bedfordshire 1969–70; DL, Bedfordshire 1989. *Career:* Fine Art Dealer. *House of Lords:* An elected hereditary peer 1999–. *Whip:* An Opposition Whip 1997–. *Spokesman:* Spokesman for: Agriculture, Culture, Media and Sport. *All-Party:* Member, All-Party: Charities and the Voluntary Sector Group, Defence Study Group, Motor Group. *Other:* President, National Association of Warehouse-keepers 1962–78; Member, Court of Corporation of Sons of the Clergy 1980–; Commander, St John's Ambulance Brigade, Bedfordshire 1983–90; President, International Association of Book Keepers 1997–. *Honours:* KStJ. Freeman, City of London. Junior Warden, Drapers' Company 1993, Member of Court 1993–, Second Master Warden 1999–. *Special Interests:* Art, Heritage, Church Affairs, Military History, River Thames, Tourism, Defence. *Recreations:* Watching cricket, shooting, fishing, watching motor sports. *Clubs:* MCC. *Heir:* His son, Hon. Ian James St John Lawson Johnston, born October 4, 1963. A Conservative. *Address:* The Lord Luke, Odell Manor, Bedfordshire, MK43 7BB *Tel:* 01234 720416 *Fax:* 01234 721311 *Tel:* House of Lords: 020 7219 3703 *E-Mail:* rupes@currantbun.com.

LYELL (3rd Baron, UK), Charles Lyell; cr. 1914; 3rd Bt of Kinnordy (UK) 1894; DL

Son of 2nd Baron, VC. Born March 27, 1939. Succeeded his father, who was killed in action, 1943; educated Eton; Christ Church, Oxford. *Armed Forces:* 2nd Lieutenant Scots Guards 1957–59. *Councils, Public Bodies:* DL, Angus 1988. *Career:* Chartered Accountant. *House of Lords:* Parliamentary Under-Secretary of State for Northern Ireland 1984–89; A Deputy Speaker of the House of Lords; A Deputy Chairman of Committees 1997–; An elected hereditary peer 1999–. *Whip:* Opposition Whip 1974–79; A Lord in Waiting (Government Whip) 1979–1984. *Spokesman:* A Government Spokesman on: Health and Social Security, The Treasury 1982, Scotland 1982–84, Foreign Office Affairs 1983–84. *All-Party:* Treasurer, Anglo-Swiss Parliamentary Group 1978–85. *International Bodies (General):* Member: North Atlantic Assembly 1973–79, UK Delegation to North Atlantic Assembly 1994–. *Miscellaneous:* Member, Queen's Bodyguard for Scotland, Royal Company of Archers. *Sportsclubs:* Chairman, Lords and Commons Ski Club 1990–93. *Clubs:* Turf, White's. *Heir:* None. A Conservative. *Address:* The Lord Lyell, DL, 20 Petersham Mews, London, SW7 5NR *Tel:* 020 7584 9419; Kinnordy, Kirriemuir *Tel:* 01575 72848; Angus, DD8 5ER.

M

McALPINE OF WEST GREEN (Life Baron, UK), Robert Alistair McAlpine; cr. 1984

Son of late Baron McAlpine of Moffat (Life Peer). Born May 14, 1942; educated Stowe. Married 1st, 1964, Sarah Alexandra Baron (2 daughters) (marriage dissolved 1979), married 2nd, 1980, Romilly, daughter of A. T. Hobbs, of Cranleigh, Surrey (1 daughter). *Career:* Joined Sir Robert McAlpine and Sons Ltd 1958, Director 1963–95; Treasurer, European League for Economic Co-operation 1974–75, Vice-President 1975–; Director, ICA 1972–73; Member, Arts Council of GB 1981–82. *Party Groups (General):* Hon. Treasurer, European Democratic Union 1978–88; Hon. Treasurer, Conservative and Unionist Party 1975–90, jointly 1981–90, Deputy Chairman 1979–83. *Other:* Vice-President, Friends Ashmolean Museum 1969–; Greater London Arts Association 1971–77; Vice-Chairman, Contemporary Arts Society 1973–80; President, British Waterfowl Association 1978–81, Patron since 1981; Member: Friends of V & A Museum 1976–, Council, English Stage Co. 1973–75; Governor: Polytechnic of the South Bank 1981–82, Stowe School 1981–83; President, Medical College of St. Bartholomew's Hospital 1993–. *Trusts, etc:* Trustee, Royal Opera House Trust 1974–80. *Miscellaneous:* Chairman, The Referendum Movement 1997. *Publications: The Servant,* 1992; *Journal of a Collector,* 1994; *Letters to a Young Politician,* 1995; *Once a Jolly Bagman,* 1997; *The New Machiavelli,* 1997; *Collecting and Display,* 1998; *Bagman to Swagman,* 1999. *Recreations:* The arts, horticulture, aviculture, agriculture. *Clubs:* Garrick, Pratt's. *Name, Style and Title:* Raised to the peerage as Baron McAlpine of West Green, of West Green in the County of Hampshire 1984. An Independent Conservative. *Address:* The Lord McAlpine of West Green, Sir Robert McAlpine & Sons Ltd, 40 Bernard Street, London, WC1N 1LE.

MACAULAY OF BRAGAR (Life Baron, UK), Donald Macaulay; cr. 1989; QC (Scot) 1975

Son of late John and Henrietta Macaulay, of Bragar, Isle of Lewis. Born November 14, 1933; educated Elgin Street Primary School, Clydebank; Cumbernauld Primary School; Hermitage School, Helensburgh; Clydebank High School; University of Glasgow (MA, LLB). Married March 26, 1962, Mary, daughter of Murdo Morrison, of Bragar (2 daughters). *Armed Forces:* National Service, RASC 1958–60. *Councils, Public Bodies:* Member, Bryden Committee on Identification following Devlin Report. *Career:* Solicitor 1960–62; Called to Scottish Bar 1963; Advocate Depute (Crown Prosecutor) 1967–70, 1973–74; Standing Junior Counsel to Highlands and Islands Development Board; Chairman, SACRO 1993–96; Chairman, Supreme Court Legal Aid Committee; Member, Central Legal Aid Committee both during 1970s; Member, Criminal Injuries Compensation Board; Scottish Chairman, Committee for Abolition of Paybeds in NHS; Founder Member and former Chairman, Advocates' Criminal Law Group. *Spokesman:* Former Opposition Spokesman on Scottish Legal Affairs. *Select Committees:* Member, Select Committees on: Computers, Crofting. *Miscellaneous:* Contested (Labour) Inverness 1970 General Election. *Special Interests:* Scottish Law, Education, Local Government, Sport, Theatre. *Recreations:* Art, music, theatre, football, golf, running. *Sportsclubs:* Royal Musselburgh Golf. *Clubs:* Edinburgh Press, College Club, University of Glasgow. *Name, Style and Title:* Raised to the peerage as Baron Macaulay of Bragar, of Bragar in the County of Ross and Cromarty 1989. Labour. *Address:* The Lord Macaulay of Bragar, QC, Belmont, 2 South Morton Street, Edinburgh, EH15 2NB *Tel:* 0131–669 6419; Advocates' Library, Parliament House, Edinburgh *E-Mail:* macaulayd@parliament.uk.

McCARTHY (Life Baron, UK), William Edward John McCarthy; cr. 1976

Son of Edward McCarthy. Born July 30, 1925; educated Ruskin College; Merton College, Oxford; Nuffield College, Oxford (MA, DPhil). Married January 18, 1956, Margaret, daughter of Percy and Anne Godfrey. *Trades Union:* Member, Association of University Teachers. *Career:* Research Director, Royal Commission on Trade Union & Employers Associations 1965–68; Fellow, Nuffield College 1969–; Chairman, Railway National Staff Tribunal 1974–85; Member, ACAS Arbitrational Panel 1975–; Associate Fellow, Templeton College 1980–; Member, Civil Service Arbitration Tribunal 1994–; Formerly Special Commissioner, Equal Opportunities Commission; Member, TUC's Independent Review Committee; Chairman, TUC Working Party on new National Daily; Former Director, Harland and Wolff, Belfast. *Spokesman:* Front Bench Spokesman on Employment 1979–97. *Select Committees:* Member, Select Committee on Unemployment 1980–82. *All-Party:* Member, Parliamentary Arts and Heritage Group; Vice-Chairman, All-Party Parliamentary Friends of Music Group 1992–; Member, All-Party: Poverty Group, Adult Education Group. *Party Groups:* Member, Labour Peers Trade and Industry Group. *Party Groups (General):* Member: Labour Party Job Creation Group, Labour Party Education and Employment Group, Labour Party Culture, Media and Sport Committee. *Other:* Member, Society for Theatre Research. *Miscellaneous:* Research Fellow, Nuffield College 1959–63. Fellow, Institute of Personnel and Development 1989. *Publications:* Numerous books and articles on industrial relations and labour economics. *Recreations:* Theatre, ballet, gardening, theatrical history, opera. *Clubs:* Reform. *Name, Style and Title:* Raised to the peerage as Baron McCarthy, of Headington in the City of Oxford 1976. Labour. *Address:* The Lord McCarthy, Nuffield College, Oxford, OX1 1NF *Tel:* 01865 278554; House of Lords, London, SW1A 0PW *Tel:* House of Lords 020 7219 3214.

McCLUSKEY (Life Baron, UK), John Herbert McCluskey; cr. 1976

Son of late Francis John McCluskey and Margaret McCluskey (née Doonan). Born June 12, 1929; educated St Bede's College, Manchester; Holy Cross Academy, Edinburgh; Edinburgh University (Harry Dalgety Bursar 1948, Vans Dunlop Scholar); Hon. LLD, Dundee 1989. Married December 28, 1956, Ruth, daughter of Aaron Friedland (2 sons 1 daughter). *Armed Forces:* Royal Air Force 1952–54 (Sword of Honour, Spitalgate OCTU 1953). *Career:* Admitted to Faculty of Advocates 1955; QC (Scot) 1967; Sheriff Principal of Dumfries and Galloway 1973–74; Senator of the College of Justice in Scotland 1984–; Reith Lecturer 1986. *House of Lords:* Solicitor-General for Scotland 1974–79. *Spokesman:* Opposition Spokesman on Scottish Legal Affairs 1979–84. *International Bodies (General):* Vice-Chairman: International Bar Association, IBA Human Rights Institute. *Other:* Chairman: Scottish Association for Mental Health 1985–94, Fairbridge in Scotland 1995–97. *Trusts, etc:* Chair, John Smith Memorial Trust. *Publications:* Law, Justice and Democracy, 1987; *Criminal Appeals*, 1992. *Special Interests:* Mental Health. *Recreations:* Tennis, swimming. *Sportsclubs:* Edinburgh Sports. *Clubs:* Royal Air Force, Edinburgh University Staff. *Name, Style and Title:* Raised to the peerage as Baron McCluskey, of Churchhill in the District of the City of Edinburgh 1976. A Cross-Bencher. *Address:* The Lord McCluskey, Parliament House, Edinburgh, EH1 1RQ *Tel:* 0131–225 2595.

McCOLL OF DULWICH (Life Baron, UK), Ian McColl; cr. 1989; CBE 1997

Son of late Frederick and Winifred McColl. Born January 6, 1933; educated Hutchesons' Grammar School, Glasgow; St Paul's School, London (Foundation Scholarship in Classics); University of London (MS). Married 1960, Dr Jean Lennox, daughter of late Arthur James McNair, FRCS, FRCOG (1 son 2 daughters). *Career:* Consultant surgeon and Sub Dean, St Bartholomew's Hospital 1967–71; Professor and Director of Surgery, Guy's Hospital 1971–98; Professor of Surgery, University of London 1971–; Consultant Surgeon to the Army 1980–98; Chairman, Government Working Party on Artificial Limbs and Wheelchair Service 1984–86; Vice-Chairman, Disablement Services Authority 1987–91; Chairman, Department of Surgery of the United Medical Schools of Guy's and St Thomas' Hospital 1988–92. *House of Lords:* PPS (Lords) to the Prime Minister 1994–97; A Deputy Speaker of the House of Lords 1994–97, 1998–; A Deputy

Chairman of Committees 1994–97, 1998–. *Spokesman:* Opposition Spokesman on Health 1997–. *Select Committees:* Former Member, House of Lords Select Committees on: European Communities, Sub-Committee F (Environment), Medical Ethics 1993–94. *Backbench Committees:* Member, Backbench Committee on Disablement. *International Bodies:* Member, Executive Committee, CPA UK Branch 1999–. *International Bodies (General):* Member, International Board of Mercy Ships. *Other:* Governor-at-large for England, Board of Governors, American College of Surgeons 1982–86; President, Mildmay Mission Hospital 1985–; Member of Council, Royal College of Surgeons 1986–94; President: Society of Minimally Invasive Surgery 1991–94, National Association of Limbless Disabled 1992–, Vice-President, John Groom's Association for Disabled People 1992–; President: The Hospital Saving Association 1994–, Association of Endoscopic Surgery of Great Britain and Ireland, Leprosy Mission 1996–. *Awards Granted:* George and Thomas Hutchesons Award 2000. *Miscellaneous:* Research Fellow, Harvard Medical School 1967. *Honours:* CBE 1997. FRCS; FRCSE; FACS. Master, Worshipful Company of Barbers. *Publications: Intestinal Absorption in Man,* 1976; *NHS Data Book,* 1984; *Government Report on Artificial Limb and Appliance Centre Service,* 1986; As well as articles in medical journals. *Special Interests:* Disability, Higher Education, Health Service, Forestry, Medicine, Health. *Recreations:* Forestry. *Sportsclubs:* Palace of Westminster. *Clubs:* Royal College of Surgeons. *Name, Style and Title:* Raised to the peerage as Baron McColl of Dulwich, of Bermondsey in the London Borough of Southwark 1989. A Conservative. *Address:* Professor The Lord McColl of Dulwich, CBE, House of Lords, London, SW1A 0PW *E-Mail:* mccolli@parliament.uk.

McCONNELL (Life Baron, UK), Robert William Brian McConnell; cr. 1995; PC (NI) 1964

Son of late Alfred McConnell. Born November 25, 1922; educated Sedbergh School; Queen's University, Belfast (BA, LLB). Married 1951, Sylvia Elizabeth Joyce Agnew (2 sons 1 daughter). *Career:* Called to the Bar of Northern Ireland 1948; MP (U) for South Antrim in the Northern Ireland Parliament 1951–68; Deputy Chairman, Ways and Means 1962; Held various posts in the Government and Parliament of Northern Ireland 1963–68; Parliamentary Secretary to Ministry of Health and Local Government 1963–64; Minister of Home Affairs 1964–66; Minister of State, Ministry of Development 1966–67; Leader of the House of Commons 1967–68; President, Industrial Court of Northern Ireland 1968–81; Social Security (formerly National Insurance) Commissioner for Northern Ireland 1968–87. *Select Committees:* Former Member, European Select Committee and Sub-Committee A. *Other:* President, European Movement in Northern Ireland 1992–95, Vice-Chairman 1987–92. *Honours:* PC (NI) 1964. Freeman, City of London 1971. *Clubs:* Ulster Reform (Belfast), Farmers'. *Name, Style and Title:* Raised to the peerage as Baron McConnell, of Lisburn in the County of Antrim 1995. A Ulster Unionist – sits as a Cross-Bencher. *Address:* The Rt Hon. the Lord McConnell, 50A Glenavy Road, Knocknadona, Lisburn, Co. Antrim, BT28 3UT *Tel:* 01846 663432.

MACDONALD OF TRADESTON (Life Baron, UK), Angus John Macdonald; cr. 1998; CBE 1997; PC 1999

Son of Colin and Jean Macdonald. Born August 20, 1940; educated Allan Glen's School, Glasgow; DUniv, Stirling 1992; DLit: Napier 1997, Robert Gordon 1998. Married 1963, Theresa McQuaid (2 daughters). *Career:* Marine Fitter 1955–63; Circulation Manager, *Tribune* 1964–65; Feature Writer, *The Scotsman* 1965–67; Granada Television: Reporter, Editor and Executive Producer, *World in Action* 1967–75, Successively Head of Current Affairs, Regional Programmes, Features 1975–82, Programme Presenter: ITV, Channel 4; Chairman: Scottish Media Group plc 1996–97 (Director of Programmes 1985–90, Managing Director 1990–96), Taylor and Francis plc 1997–98; Board Member, Bank of Scotland. *House of Lords:* Parliamentary Under-Secretary of State, Scottish Office (Minister of Business and Industry) 1998–99; Minister of State for Transport, Department of the Environment, Transport and the Regions (Minister for Transport) 1999–. *Spokesman:* Spokesman on the Scottish Office 1998–99. *Other:* Chairman: Edinburgh International Television Festival 1976, ITV Broadcasting Board 1992–94, Edinburgh Film Festival 1994–96; Member, Press and Broadcasting Advisory Committee, Ministry of Defence 1994–95; Vice-President, Royal Television Society 1994–98; Chairman, Cairngorms Partnership 1997–98; Board Member: Scottish Enterprise,

British Film Institute. *Awards Granted:* BAFTA Award, Best Factual Television (*World in Action*) 1973; BAFTA Scotland Lifetime Achievement Award 1997–; Scottish Business Elite 'Corporate Leader of the Year' and 'Chairman of the Year' 1997. *Honours:* CBE 1997; PC 1999. *Publications: The Documentary Idea and Television Today,* 1977; *Camera: Victorian eyewitness,* 1979. *Clubs:* Royal Automobile, Groucho. *Name, Style and Title:* Raised to the peerage as Baron Macdonald of Tradeston, of Tradeston in the County of Glasgow 1998. Labour. *Address:* The Rt Hon. the Lord Macdonald of Tradeston, CBE, House of Lords, London, SW1A 0PW.

MACFARLANE OF BEARSDEN (Life Baron, UK), Norman (Somerville) Macfarlane; cr. 1991; KT 1996; Kt 1983; DL

Son of late Daniel Robertson Macfarlane. Born March 5, 1926; educated High School of Glasgow; Hon. LLD: Strathclyde 1986, Glasgow 1988; Hon. DUniv (Stirling) 1992; Hon. Dr. hc (Edinburgh) 1992; Hon. Fellow, Glasgow School of Art 1993; Hon. LLD: Glasgow Caledonian 1993, Aberdeen University 1995. Married 1953, Marguerite Campbell (1 son 4 daughters). *Armed Forces:* Served in Palestine with RA 1945–47. *Councils, Public Bodies:* DL, Dumbartonshire 1993. *Career:* Founded N. S. Macfarlane & Co. Ltd. 1949, becoming Macfarlane Group (Clansman) plc 1973, Managing Director 1973–90, Chairman 1973–98, Honorary Life President 1998; Member, Council CBI Scotland 1975–81; Underwriting Member, Lloyd's 1978–; Member, Board of Scottish Development Agency 1979–87; Member, Royal Fine Art Commission for Scotland 1980–82; Director, Clydesdale Bank plc 1980–96, Deputy Chairman 1993–96; Director, General Accident Fire & Life Assurance Corporation 1984–96; Chairman, United Distillers UK plc 1989–96, Hon. Life President 1996–; Joint Deputy Chairman, Guinness plc 1989–92, Chairman 1987–89; Lord High Commissioner to the General Assembly of the Church of Scotland 1992, 1993 and 1997. *Other:* President: Stationers Association of Great Britain and Ireland 1965, Royal Glasgow Institute of the Fine Arts 1976–87; Director, Scottish National Orchestra 1977–82; Member, Court of the University of Glasgow 1979–87; Vice-Chairman, Scottish Ballet 1983–87; Hon. President, Chas Rennie McIntosh Society 1988–; President, High School of Glasgow 1992–; Patron, Scottish Licensed Trade Association (SLTA) 1992; Regent, Royal College of Surgeons of Edinburgh 1997–. *Trusts, etc:* Trustee: National Heritage Memorial Fund 1984–97, National Galleries of Scotland 1986–97. *Honours:* Kt 1983; KT 1996. Hon. FRIAS 1984; Hon. RSA 1987; Hon. RGI 1987; Hon. SCOTVEC 1991; Hon. FRCPS (Glasgow) 1992. *Sportsclubs:* Glasgow Golf. *Clubs:* Royal Scottish Automobile (Glasgow). *Name, Style and Title:* Raised to the peerage as Baron Macfarlane of Bearsden, in the District of Bearsden and Milngavie 1991. A Conservative. *Address:* The Lord Macfarlane of Bearsden, KT, DL, FRSE, Macfarlane Group (Clansman) plc, 21 Newton Place, Glasgow, G3 7PY.

McFARLANE OF LLANDAFF (Life Baroness, UK), Jean Kennedy McFarlane; cr. 1979

Daughter of late Dr James McFarlane, FDS, RCS. Born April 1, 1926; educated Howell's School, Llandaff; Bedford and Birkbeck Colleges, University of London (MA, BSc(Soc), HV Tut Cert); Hon. MSc, Manchester; Hon. DSc, Ulster. *Career:* Staff Nurse, St. Bartholomew's Hospital, London 1950–51; Health Visitor, Cardiff City 1953–59; Tutor, Royal College of Nursing, London 1960–62; Education Officer, Royal College of Nursing, Birmingham 1962–66; Research Project Leader, Royal College of Nursing, London 1967–69; Director of Education, Royal College of Nursing, London 1969–71; Senior Lecturer in Nursing, University of Manchester 1971–74; Professor and Head of Department of Nursing, University of Manchester 1974–88; Member: General Synod, Church of England 1990–, General Synod Review of Synodical Government Group 1993–. *Select Committees:* Member, House of Lords Select Committees on: Priorities in Medical Research 1987–88, Medical Ethics 1993–97. *Miscellaneous:* Member: Royal Commission on NHS 1976–79, Commonwealth War Graves Commission 1983–88. FRCN; SRN; SCM. *Special Interests:* Health, Education. *Name, Style and Title:* Raised to the peerage as Baroness McFarlane of Llandaff, of Llandaff in the County of South Glamorgan 1979. A Cross-Bencher. *Address:* The Baroness McFarlane of Llandaff, 5 Dovercourt Avenue, Heaton Mersey, Stockport, SK4 3QB *Tel:* 0161–432 8367.

McINTOSH OF HARINGEY (Life Baron, UK), Andrew Robert McIntosh; cr. 1983

Son of late Professor Albert William McIntosh, OBE, and late Jenny McIntosh (née Britton). Born April 30, 1933; educated Royal Grammar School, High Wycombe; Jesus College, Oxford; Ohio State University. Married May 15, 1962, Mrs Naomi Ellen Kelly, daughter of late Tom Sargant, OBE, and Marie Cerny (née Hlouskova) (2 sons). *Councils, Public Bodies:* Councillor: Borough of Hornsey 1963–64, London Borough of Haringey 1964–68; Councillor, Greater London Council 1973–83, Leader of the Opposition 1980–81. *Career:* Editor, Journal of Market Research Society 1963–67; Managing Director, IFF Research Ltd 1965–81, Chairman 1981–88, Deputy Chairman 1988–97; Chairman, Market Research Society 1972–73, President 1995–98; Principal (Honorary), Working Men's College, London 1988–97. *House of Lords:* Deputy Leader of the Opposition 1992–97; A Deputy Chairman of Committees 1997–; A Deputy Speaker 1999–. *Whip:* Captain of HM Bodyguard of the Yeomen of the Guard (Deputy Chief Whip) 1997–. *Spokesman:* Opposition Spokesman on: Education and Science 1985–87, The Environment 1987–92, Home Affairs 1992–97; A Spokesman on: Legal Affairs 1997–98, the Treasury 1997–, Trade and Industry 1998–. *Party Groups (General):* Chairman, Fabian Society 1985–86. *Miscellaneous:* Chairman, Association for Neighbourhood Councils 1974–80. *Recreations:* Cooking, reading, music. *Name, Style and Title:* Raised to the peerage as Baron McIntosh of Haringey, of Haringey in the County of Greater London 1983. Labour. *Address:* The Lord McIntosh of Haringey, 27 Hurst Avenue, London, N6 5TX *Tel:* 020 8340 1496 *Fax:* 020 8348 4641; House of Lords, London, SW1A 0PW *Tel:* House of Lords 020 7219 3126/6782.

McINTOSH OF HUDNALL (Life Baroness, UK), Genista Mary McIntosh; cr. 1999

Daughter of late Geoffrey Tandy, and of Maire Tandy. Born September 23, 1946; educated Hemel Hempstead Grammar School; University of York (BA Philosophy and Sociology 1968); Hon. DUniv, University of York 1998. Married 1971, Neil Scott Wishart McIntosh, son of William and Mary McIntosh (1 son 1 daughter) (marriage dissolved 1990). *Career:* Press Secretary, York Festival of Arts 1968–69; Royal Shakespeare Company: Casting Director 1972–77, Planning Controller 1977–84, Senior Administrator 1986–90, Associate Producer 1990; Executive Director, Royal National Theatre 1990-January 1997 and October 1997–; Chief Executive, Royal Opera House, Covent Garden 1997; Board Member: English Stage Company, The Roundhouse Trust, Young Vic Theatre. *Trusts, etc:* Trustee, National Endowment for Science, Technology and Arts; Member, Peggy Ramsay Foundation. *Miscellaneous:* Member, British Council Drama and Dance Advisory Committee. FRSA. *Special Interests:* Arts, Public Health, Prison Reform. *Recreations:* Gardening, music. *Name, Style and Title:* Raised to the peerage as Baroness McIntosh of Hudnall, of Hampstead in the London Borough of Camden 1999. Labour. *Address:* The Baroness McIntosh of Hudnall, Royal National Theatre, Upper Ground, London, SE1 9PX *Tel:* 020 7452 3347 *Fax:* 020 7452 3350.

MACKAY OF ARDBRECKNISH (Life Baron, UK), John Jackson MacKay; cr. 1991; PC 1996; DL

Son of late Jackson MacKay. Born November 15, 1938; educated Dunoon and Campbeltown Grammar Schools; Glasgow University; Jordanhill College of Education. Married 1961, Sheena, daughter of late James Wagner (2 sons 1 daughter). *Councils, Public Bodies:* Councillor, Oban Town Council and Burgh Treasurer 1969–74; Member, Argyll Water Board 1970–74; JP, City of Glasgow; DL, City of Glasgow 1997. *Career:* Principal mathematics teacher, Oban High School 1972–79; Chief Executive, Scottish Conservative Central Office 1987–90; Chairman, Sea Fish Industry Authority 1990–93. *House of Commons:* Contested (Conservative): Western Isles in February 1974, Argyll in October 1974 General Elections; MP (Conservative): Argyll 1979–83, Argyll and Bute 1983–87; Parliamentary Under-Secretary of State, Scottish Office 1982–87. *House of Lords:* Parliamentary Under-Secretary of State, Department of Transport January-July 1994; Minister of State, Department of Social Security 1994–97; Deputy Leader of the Opposition December 1998–. *Whip:* A Lord in Waiting (Government Whip) 1993–94. *Spokesman:* An Opposition Spokesman for: Treasury 1997–98,

Constitutional Affairs (Scotland) 1997–, Education and Employment (Employment) December 1998-June 1999, Cabinet Office June 1999–, Trade and Industry June 1999–. *Select Committees:* Former Member: Select Committee on the European Communities, Sub-Committee B of EC Committee, Delegated Powers Scrutiny Committee; Member, Select Committee on House of Lords' Offices 1998–. *Awards Granted:* Channel 4 and House Award 'Peer of 1998' 1999. *Honours:* PC 1996. *Recreations:* Fishing, sailing. *Clubs:* Royal Scottish Automobile (Glasgow). *Name, Style and Title:* Raised to the peerage as Baron MacKay of Ardbrecknish, of Tayvallich in the District of Argyll and Bute 1991. A Conservative. *Address:* The Rt Hon. the Lord MacKay of Ardbrecknish, DL, Innishail, 51 Springkell Drive, Pollokshields, Glasgow, G41 4EZ *E-Mail:* mackayj@parliament.uk.

MACKAY OF CLASHFERN (Life Baron, UK), James Peter Hymers Mackay; cr. 1979; KT 1997; PC 1979

Son of late James Mackay, Railwayman. Born July 2, 1927; educated George Heriot's School; Edinburgh University; Trinity College, Cambridge; Hon. Fellow: Trinity College, Cambridge, Girton College, Cambridge. Married 1958, Elizabeth Gunn Hymers (1 son 2 daughters). *Career:* Lecturer in Mathematics, St Andrews 1948–50; Advocate 1955; QC (Scotland) 1965; Sheriff Principal, Renfrew and Argyll 1972–74; Vice-Dean, Faculty of Advocates 1973–76, Dean of Faculty 1976–79; Director, Stenhouse Holdings Ltd 1976–78; Part-time Member, Scottish Law Commission 1976–79; Member, Insurance Brokers' Registration Council 1978–79; Senator of the College of Justice in Scotland 1984–85; Lord of Appeal in Ordinary 1985–87; Editor, *Halsbury's Laws of England* 1998–. *Chancellor:* Chancellor, Heriot-Watt University 1991–. *House of Lords:* Lord Advocate 1979–84; Lord High Chancellor 1987–97. *Spokesman:* Government Spokesman on Legal Affairs in Scotland 1983–84. *Miscellaneous:* Chairman, The Constitutional Commission 1998–99. *Honours:* PC 1979; KT 1997. Hon. Fellow: Royal College of Surgeons of Edinburgh 1989, Royal Society of Edinburgh, RICE, Royal College of Physics Edinburgh 1990, Royal College of Obstetrics and gynecology. *Clubs:* New (Edinburgh). *Name, Style and Title:* Raised to the peerage as Baron Mackay of Clashfern, of Eddrachillis in the District of Sutherland 1979. A Conservative. *Address:* The Rt Hon. the Lord Mackay of Clashfern, KT, House of Lords, London, SW1A 0PW *Tel:* 020 7219 3000.

MACKAY OF DRUMADOON (Life Baron, UK), Donald Sage Mackay; cr. 1995; PC 1996; QC (Scot) 1987

Son of late Rev. Donald George Mackintosh Mackay and late Jean Margaret Mackay. Born January 30, 1946; educated George Watson's Boys' College, Edinburgh; University of Edinburgh (LLB 1966, LLM 1968); University of Virginia (LLM 1969). Married 1979, Lesley Ann Waugh (1 son 2 daughters). *Career:* Law apprentice 1969–71; Solicitor with Allan McDougall & Co., SSC, Edinburgh 1971–76; Called to the Scottish Bar 1976; Advocate Depute 1982–85; Member, Criminal Injuries Compensation Board 1989–95; Solicitor-General for Scotland 1995. *House of Lords:* Lord Advocate 1995–97. *Spokesman:* A Government Spokesman on Legal Affairs and for the Home and Scottish Offices 1995–97; An Opposition Spokesman on: Constitutional Affairs, Scotland 1997–, Home Affairs 1997–, Lord Advocate's Department 1997–. *All-Party:* Member, All-Party Saudi Arabia Country Group. *Honours:* PC 1996. *Recreations:* Golf, gardening, Isle of Arran. *Clubs:* Western (Glasgow). *Name, Style and Title:* Raised to the peerage as Baron Mackay of Drumadoon, of Blackwaterfoot in the District of Cunninghame 1995. A Conservative. *Address:* The Rt Hon. the Lord Mackay of Drumadoon, QC, Advocates Library, Parliament House, Edinburgh, EH1 1RF *Tel:* 0131-226 5071 *Fax:* 0131-225 3642; 39 Hermitage Gardens, Edinburgh, EH10 6AZ *Tel:* 0131-447 1412 *Fax:* 0131-447 9863.

MACKENZIE OF CULKEIN (Life Baron, UK), Hector Uisdean MacKenzie; cr. 1999

Son of late George MacKenzie, principal lighthouse keeper, and late Williamina Budge MacKenzie (née Sutherland). Born February 25, 1940; educated Isle of Erraid Public School, Argyll; Aird Public School, Isle of Lewisl Nicholson Institute, Stornoway; Portree High School, Skye; Leverndale School of Nursing, Glasgow; West Cumberland School of Nursing, Whitehaven. Married March 2, 1961, Anna, daughter of late George and Sarah Morrison (1 son 3 daughters) (marriage dissolved 1991). *Trades Union:* Member, UNISON. *Armed Forces:* Sergeant, 1st Cadet Btn Queen's Own Cameron Highlanders. *Career:* Student Nurse, Leverndale Hospital 1958–61; Assistant Lighthouse Keeper, Clyde Lighthouses Trust 1961–64; West Cumberland Hospital: Student Nurse 1964–66, Staff Nurse 1966–69; Confederation of Health Service Employees: Assistant Regional Secretary 1969, Regional Secretary, Yorkshire and East Midlands 1970–74, National Officer 1974–83, Assistant General Secretary 1983–87, General Secretary 1987–93; Associate General Secretary, UNISON 1993–; Company Secretary, UIA Insurance ltd 1996–; President, TUC 1998–99; Senior Vice-President, TUC 1999–2000. *International Bodies (General):* First Substitute Member, World Executive of Public Services International 1987–2000. *Party Groups (General):* Member: Labour Party Policy Forum, Labour Party Policy Commission on Health. *Other:* Governor Member, RNLI; Hon. Secretary, Wallington Branch, RNLI; Governor Member, Marine Society; Member, RSPB. *Awards Granted:* Lindsay Robertson Gold Medal for Nurse of the Year 1966. *Trusts, etc:* Member, National Trust for Scotland. RGN; RMN. *Publications:* Various articles in Nursing and Specialist Health Service Press. *Special Interests:* Health, Nursing, Defence, Aviation, Maritime Affairs, Land Reform. *Recreations:* Reading, Celtic music, shinty, aviation. *Clubs:* St Elpheges, Wallington. *Name, Style and Title:* Raised to the peerage as Baron MacKenzie of Culkein, of Assynt in Highland 1999. Labour. *Address:* The Lord MacKenzie of Culkein, Unison Centre, 1 Mabledon Place, London, WC1H 9AJ *Tel:* 020 7388 2366 *Fax:* 020 7383 7218; House of Lords, London, SW1A 0PW.

MACKENZIE OF FRAMWELLGATE (Life Baron, UK), Brian Mackenzie; cr. 1998; OBE 1998

Son of Frederick Mackenzie and Lucy Mackenzie (née Ward). Born March 21, 1943; educated Eastbourne Boys' School, Darlington; London University (LLB Hons); FBI National Academy, Quantico, USA (Graduate). Married March 6, 1965, Jean Seed (2 Sons). *Trades Union:* Former Member: Police Federation of England and Wales, Police Superintendents' Association; Member, National Association of Retired Police Officers (NARPO). *Career:* Former Chief Superintendent, Durham Constabulary. *Party Groups:* Chair, Labour Home Affairs Committee. *International Bodies (General):* Member: FBI National Academy Associates, International Association of Chiefs of Police. *Other:* President, Association of Police Superintendents of England and Wales 1995–98; Patron, Kid Scape. *Miscellaneous:* Honorary Billetmaster, City of Durham. *Honours:* OBE 1998. *Special Interests:* Police, Home Affairs, Legal Affairs. *Recreations:* Herpetology, after-dinner speaking, swimming, fitness, singing. *Clubs:* Dunelm, Durham City. *Name, Style and Title:* Raised to the peerage as Baron Mackenzie of Framwellgate, of Durham in the County of Durham 1998. Labour. *Address:* The Lord Mackenzie of Framwellgate, OBE, House of Lords, London, SW1A 0PW *E-Mail:* mackenzieb@parliament.uk.

MACKENZIE-STUART (Life Baron, UK), Alexander John Mackenzie Stuart; cr. 1988

Son of late Professor A. Mackenzie Stuart, KC. Born November 18, 1924; educated Fettes College, Edinburgh; Sidney Sussex College, Cambridge; Edinburgh University; Honorary Doctorates: Stirling University, Exeter University, Edinburgh University, Glasgow University, Aberdeen University, Cambridge University, Birmingham University; Honorary Bencher: Middle Temple 1978, King's Inn, Dublin 1984. Married 1952, Anne Burtholme, daughter of late J. S. L. Millar, WS, of Edinburgh (4 daughters). *Armed Forces:* Served Royal Engineers 1942–47. *Career:* Admitted Faculty of Advocates 1951; Standing Junior Counsel to: Scottish Home Department 1956–57, Inland Revenue in Scotland 1957–63; Governor, Fettes College 1962–72; QC (Scotland) 1963; Sheriff-Principal, Aberdeen, Kincardine and Banff 1971–72; A Senator of the College of Justice in Scotland 1972; President, Court of Justice, European Communities at Luxembourg 1984–1988; Judge of the Court of Justice 1973–84; President,

British Academy of Experts 1989–92; President, European Movement, Scottish Division. *Awards Granted:* Awarded 1989 Prix Bech for Services to Europe. FRSE. *Clubs:* Athenaeum, New (Edinburgh). *Name, Style and Title:* Raised to the peerage as Baron Mackenzie-Stuart, of Dean in the District of the City of Edinburgh 1988. A Cross-Bencher. *Address:* The Lord Mackenzie-Stuart, 7 Randolph Cliff, Edinburgh, EH3 7TZ *Tel:* 0131–225 1089; Le Garidel, Gravières, 07140, Les Vans, France *Tel:* 04.75.37.35.29.

MACKIE OF BENSHIE (Life Baron, UK), George Yull Mackie; cr. 1974; CBE 1971; DSO 1944; DFC 1944

Son of late Maitland Mackie, OBE, LLD, of North Ythsie, Tarves. Born July 10, 1919; educated Aberdeen Grammar School; Aberdeen University; Hon. LLD, Dundee University 1982. Married 1st, 1944, Lindsay (died 1985), daughter of Isabella Sharp, OBE, and late Alexander Sharp, Advocate, of Aberdeen (3 daughters and 1 son deceased), married 2nd, 1988, Mrs Jacqueline Lane, daughter of late Colonel Marcel Rauch, and widow of Andrew Lane. *Armed Forces:* Served with RAF 1940–46; Squadron-Leader 1944; DSO 1944; DFC 1944; Air Staff 1944–45. *Career:* Farming in Angus for 45 years; Formerly Chairman: Perth and Angus Fruit Growers Ltd, Caithness Glass Ltd; Rector, Dundee University 1980–83; Member Council of Europe and WEU 1986. *House of Commons:* MP (Liberal) Caithness and Sutherland 1964–66. *Whip (Commons):* Scottish Whip 1964–66. *Spokesman (Commons):* Spokesman on Economic Affairs 1964–66. *Spokesman:* Former Liberal Democrat Party Spokesman on Agriculture and currently on Scottish Affairs. *Select Committees:* Member, European Communities Committee: Sub-Committee D 1975–95, Sub-Committee C 1998–. *All-Party:* Vice-Chairman, All-Party Fruit Industry Group 1999–. *International Bodies:* Executive Committee Member, IPU British Group; Member, CPA. *Party Groups (General):* Former Chairman, Scottish Liberal Party; President, Scottish Liberal Party 1983–88. *Other:* Member, Scottish Farmers Union. *Honours:* DSO 1944; DFC 1944; CBE 1971. *Special Interests:* Agriculture. *Recreations:* Golf, social life. *Clubs:* Garrick, Farmers', Royal Air Force. *Name, Style and Title:* Raised to the peerage as Baron Mackie of Benshie, of Kirriemuir in the County of Angus 1974. A Liberal Democrat. *Address:* The Lord Mackie of Benshie, CBE, DSO, DFC, Benshie Cottage, Oathlaw, By Forfar, Angus, DD8 3PQ *Tel:* 01307 850376; House of Lords, London, SW1A 0PW *Tel:* House of Lords 020 7219 3179.

MACLAURIN OF KNEBWORTH (Life Baron, UK), Ian Charter MacLaurin; cr. 1996; Kt 1989; DL

Son of late Arthur George and Evelina Florence MacLaurin. Born March 30, 1937; educated Malvern College; Hon. DPhil, Stirling 1987; Hon. LLD, University of Hertfordshire; Hon. Fellow, University of Wales. Married 1961, Ann Margaret Collar (died May 28, 1999) (1 son 2 daughters). *Armed Forces:* National Service, RAF Flight Command 1956–58. *Councils, Public Bodies:* DL, Hertfordshire 1992–. *Career:* Tesco plc: Joined 1959, Director 1970, Managing Director 1973–85, Deputy Chairman 1983–85, Chairman 1985–97; Director, Enterprise Oil 1984–90; Non-Executive Director: National Westminster Bank plc 1990–96, Gleneagles Hotels plc 1992–97, Vodafone Group plc 1997– (Chairman 1998–), Whitbread plc 1997–. *Chancellor:* Chancellor, University of Hertfordshire 1996–. *Other:* Chairman, Food Policy Group, Retail Consortium 1980–84; Committee Member, MCC 1986–; President, Institute of Grocery Distribution 1989–92; Governor and Member of Council, Malvern College. *Trusts, etc:* Trustee, Royal Opera House Trust 1992. *Miscellaneous:* Former Chairman, UK Sports Council, resigned 1997; Chairman, England and Wales Cricket Board (formerly Test and County Cricket Board) 1996–. *Honours:* Kt 1989. FRSA 1986; FIM 1987; Hon. FCGI 1992. Freeman, City of London 1981. Liveryman, The Carmen's Company 1982–. *Recreations:* Golf. *Sportsclubs:* President, Brocket Hall Golf. *Clubs:* MCC, Harry's Bar. *Name, Style and Title:* Raised to the peerage as Baron MacLaurin of Knebworth, of Knebworth in the County of Hertfordshire 1996. A Conservative. *Address:* The Lord MacLaurin of Knebworth, DL, 14 Great College Street, London, SW1P 3RX *Tel:* 020 7233 2203 *Fax:* 020 7233 0438.

MACLEHOSE OF BEOCH (Life Baron, UK), (Crawford) Murray MacLehose; cr. 1982; KT 1983; GBE 1977; KCMG 1971; KCVO 1975; DL

Son of late H. A. MacLehose, Printer. Born October 16, 1917; educated Rugby; Balliol College, Oxford; Hon. Fellow, School of Oriental and African Studies; Hon. LLD: Strathclyde, York, Hong Kong. Married 1947, Margaret Noel, daughter of late Sir Charles Dunlop, TD (2 daughters). *Armed Forces:* RNVR 1942–45. *Councils, Public Bodies:* DL, Ayr and Arran 1983–. *Career:* Joined Foreign Service 1947; Acting Consul 1947; Served Hankow 1948; Prague 1951 (First Secretary (Commercial) and Consul); Seconded to Commonwealth Relations Office, served: Wellington, New Zealand 1954, Paris 1957–59; Counsellor, seconded to Hong Kong Government as Political Advisor 1959–62; Foreign Office 1963; Principal Private Secretary to Secretary of State 1965–67; Ambassador to; Vietnam 1967–69, Denmark 1969–71; Governor and Commander-in-Chief, Hong Kong 1971–82; Former Chairman, Victoria League for Commonwealth Friendship; Director: National Westminster Bank plc 1982–88, Pacific Investment Trust plc 1985–91. *Chancellor:* Chancellor: Hong Kong University 1971–82, Chinese University of Hong Kong 1971–82. *Other:* Chairman: Margaret Blackwood Housing Association 1982–90, School of Oriental and African Studies 1984–90; Former President, Great Britain-China Centre, A Vice-President 1992–. *Honours:* MBE (Military) 1945; CMG 1964; KCMG 1971; KStJ 1972; KCVO 1975; GBE 1977; KT 1983. *Special Interests:* Far East, Europe. *Recreations:* Farming. *Clubs:* Athenaeum. *Name, Style and Title:* Raised to the peerage as Baron MacLehose of Beoch, of Maybole in the District of Kyle and Carrick, and of Victoria in Hong Kong 1982. A Cross-Bencher. *Address:* The Lord MacLehose of Beoch, KT, GBE, KCMG, KCVO, DL, Beoch, Maybole, Ayrshire, KA19 8EN *Tel:* 01655 883114.

McNALLY (Life Baron, UK), Tom McNally; cr. 1995

Son of late John and Elizabeth McNally. Born February 20, 1943; educated College of St Joseph, Blackpool; University College, London (BSc Economics) (President, Students Union 1965–66); Fellow, University College, London 1995. Married 1st, 1970, Eileen Powell (marriage dissolved 1990), married 2nd, 1990, Juliet Lamy Hutchinson (2 sons 1 daughter). *Trades Union:* Vice-President, National Union of Students 1966–67. *Career:* Political Adviser to: Secretary of State for Foreign and Commonwealth Affairs 1974–76, Prime Minister 1976–79; Public Affairs Adviser, GEC 1983–84; Director-General, Retail Consortium, Director, British Retailers Association 1985–87; Head of Public Affairs, Hill & Knowlton 1987–93; Head of Public Affairs, Shandwick 1993–96, Vice-Chairman 1996–. *House of Commons:* MP (Labour 1979–81, SDP 1981–83) for Stockport South; Contested (SDP) Stockport in 1983 General Election. *Spokesman (Commons):* SDP Spokesman on Education and Sport 1981–83. *Select Committees (Commons):* Member, Select Committee on Trade and Industry 1979–83. *Spokesman:* Spokesman on: Broadcasting and Trade and Industry 1996–97, Home Affairs 1998–. *Select Committees:* Member: Select Committee on Public Service 1996–97; Select Committee on Freedom of Information 1999. *All-Party:* Member, All-Party Sport Group. *Party Groups (General):* Assistant General Secretary, The Fabian Society 1966–67; Labour Party Researcher 1967–68; International Secretary, Labour Party 1969–74. *Other:* Member, Institute of Public Relations (MIPR); President, British Radio and Electronic Equipment Manufacturers Association (BREMA). *Special Interests:* Trade and Industry, Broadcasting, Retail Industry, Tourism, Leisure Industries, Foreign Affairs. *Recreations:* Playing and watching sport, reading political biographies. *Clubs:* National Liberal. *Name, Style and Title:* Raised to the peerage as Baron McNally, of Blackpool in the County of Lancashire 1995. A Liberal Democrat. *Address:* The Lord McNally, House of Lords, London, SW1A 0PW *E-Mail:* tmcnally@shandwick.com.

Dod *on* Disk

The Vacher Dod Parliamentary Database – configured for PC or Network

For further details please telephone the Westminster Office

020 7828 7256

MADDOCK (Life Baroness, UK), Diana Maddock; cr. 1997

Daughter of late Reginald Derbyshire, former Senior Scientific Officer, AERE, Harwell, and of Margaret Evans. Born May 19, 1945; educated Shenstone Training College; Portsmouth Polytechnic (CertEd, Postgraduate linguistics diploma). Married July 23, 1966, Robert Frank Maddock (2 daughters). *Councils, Public Bodies:* Portswood Ward, Southampton City Council: Councillor 1984–93, Leader, Liberal Democrat Group. *Career:* Teacher: Weston Park Girls' School, Southampton 1966–69, Extra-Mural Department, Stockholm University 1969–72, Sholing Girls' School, Southampton 1972–73, Anglo-Continental School of English, Bournemouth 1973–76, Greylands School of English (part time) 1990–91. *House of Commons:* Contested Southampton Test in 1992 General Election; MP (Liberal Democrat) for Christchurch By-election 1993–97; Sponsored as Private Member's Bill, Home Energy Conservation Act 1995. *Spokesman (Commons):* Liberal Democrat Spokeswoman on: Housing, Women's Issues and Family Policy 1994–97. *All-Party Committees (Commons):* Former Vice-Chair: All-Party Parliamentary Warm Homes Group, Homelessness and Housing Need Group. *Spokesman:* Liberal Democrat Spokesperson on Housing 1998–. *All-Party:* Vice-Chair, All-Party Electoral Reform Group; Treasurer, Homelessness and Housing Need Group; Member, All-Party: Park Homes Group, Building Societies Group, Scandinavia Group. *Party Groups (General):* President, Liberal Democrat Party 1998–. *Other:* Former Chairman, Governors, St Denys First School; President, National Housing Forum 1997–; Vice-President, National Housing Federation 1997–; President, Dorset Victim Support 1997–; Board Member, Western Challenge Housing Association 1997–99; Member, Board of Corporation, Brockenhurst College. *Miscellaneous:* Member, Standing Committees for: Finance Bill 1994, Housing Bill 1996. *Special Interests:* Education, Local Government, Housing, Environment. *Recreations:* Theatre, music, reading, travel. *Clubs:* National Liberal. *Name, Style and Title:* Raised to the peerage as Baroness Maddock, of Christchurch in the County of Dorset 1997. A Liberal Democrat. *Address:* The Baroness Maddock, House of Lords, London, SW1A 0PW.

MALLALIEU (Life Baroness, UK), Ann Mallalieu; cr. 1991; QC 1988

Daughter of late Sir William Mallalieu and Lady Mallalieu. Born November 27, 1945; educated Holton Park Girls' Grammar School; Newnham College, Cambridge (MA, LLM); Hon. Fellow, Newnham College, Cambridge 1992. Married 1979, Timothy Felix Harold Cassel, QC, son of His Honour Sir Harold Cassel, 3rd Bt, TD, QC (2 daughters). *Career:* Called to the Bar, Inner Temple 1970; Elected Member, General Council of the Bar 1973–75; A Recorder 1985–94; Bencher 1992. *Spokesman:* An Opposition Spokesman on: Home Affairs 1992–97, Legal Affairs 1992–97. *Select Committees:* Member, Joint Select Committee on Consolidation of Bills 1998–. *All-Party:* Member, All-Party Penal Affairs Group. *Party Groups (General):* Member, Society of Labour Lawyers; Chairman, Leave Country Sports Alone Labour Support Campaign. *Other:* President, Countryside Alliance May 1998–. *Trusts, etc:* Chairman, Suzy Lamplugh Trust 1996–. *Miscellaneous:* Chairman, Council of the Ombudsman for Corporate Estate Agents 1993–. *Special Interests:* Law, Home Affairs, Agriculture, Environment. *Recreations:* Hunting, poetry, sheep, fishing. *Name, Style and Title:* Raised to the peerage as Baroness Mallalieu, of Studdridge in the County of Buckinghamshire 1991. Labour. *Address:* The Baroness Mallalieu, QC, House of Lords, London, SW1A 0PW.

MANCHESTER (10th Bishop of), Christopher John Mayfield

Son of Dr Roger Mayfield and Muriel Mayfield. Born December 18, 1935; educated Sedbergh School; Gonville and Caius College, Cambridge (MA 1961); Linacre House, Oxford (DipTheology); Cranfield Institute of Technology (MSc 1993). Married 1962, Caroline Ann Roberts (2 sons 1 daughter). *Armed Forces:* Served as Commissioned Officer, Education Branch, RAF 1957–61. *Career:* Deacon 1963; Priest 1964; Curate of St Martin-in-the-Bull Ring, Birmingham 1963–67; Lecturer at St Martin's, Birmingham 1967–71; Chaplain at Children's Hospital, Birmingham 1967–71; Vicar of: Luton 1971–80, East Hyde 1971–76; Rural Dean of Luton 1974–79; Archdeacon of Bedford 1979–85; Bishop Suffragan of Wolverhampton 1985–93; Bishop of Manchester 1993–; Took his seat in the House of Lords 1998. *Recreations:* Marriage, evangelism, walking. *Address:* The Rt Rev. the Lord Bishop of Manchester, Bishopscourt, Bury New Road, Manchester, M7 4LE *Tel:* 0161–792 2096.

MANCROFT (3rd Baron, UK), Benjamin Lloyd Stormont Mancroft; cr. 1937; 3rd Bt of Mancroft (UK) 1932

Son of 2nd Baron, KBE, TD and of late Diana, only daughter of late Lieutenant-Colonel Horace Lloyd, DSO. Born May 16, 1957. Succeeded his father 1987; educated Eton. Married September 20, 1990, Emma, eldest daughter of Thomas and Gabriel Peart (2 sons 1 daughter). *Career:* Chairman: Inter Lotto (UK) Ltd 1995–, Scratch-n-Win Lotteries Ltd 1995. *House of Lords:* An elected hereditary peer 1999–. *Select Committees:* Member, Select Committee on Broadcasting 1992–94. *All-Party:* Member, All-Party Committee on Drug Misuse 1988–, Vice-Chairman 1997–; Hon. Secretary, Racing and Bloodstock Industries Committee 1992–97. *Party Groups:* Member, Executive Association of Conservative Peers 1989–94, 1999–. *Party Groups (General):* Member, Executive of National Union of Conservative Associations 1989–94. *Other:* Joint Master, Vale of White Horse Fox Hounds 1987–89; Chairman, Addiction Recovery Foundation 1989–; Director, Phoenix House Housing Association 1991–, Vice-Chairman 1992–96; Deputy Chairman, British Field Sports Society 1992–97; Chairman, Drug and Alcohol Foundation 1994–; President, Alliance of Independent Retailers 1996–; Director, Countryside Alliance 1997–. *Trusts, etc:* Patron, Sick Dentists' Trust 1991–; Board Member, Mentor Foundation; Patron, Osteopathic Centre for Children. *Special Interests:* Drug Addiction, Alcoholism, Rural Affairs. *Recreations:* Hunting, stalking, shooting, fishing. *Clubs:* Pratt's. *Heir:* His son, Hon. Arthur Louis Stormont Mancroft, born May 3, 1995. A Conservative. *Address:* The Lord Mancroft, House of Lords, London, SW1A 0PW; Office: Chichester House, 37 Brixton Road, Kennington Park, London, SW9 6DZ.

MAR (Countess of, 31st in line, S), Margaret of Mar; cr. 1114, precedence 1404; Lady Garioch (24th in line, S) 1320

Daughter of 30th Earl. Born September 19, 1940. Succeeded her father 1975; educated Kenya High School for Girls, Nairobi; Lewes County Grammar School for Girls. Married 1st, 1959, Edwin Noel Artiss (1 daughter) (marriage dissolved 1976), married 2nd, 1976, John Salton (marriage dissolved 1981), married 3rd, 1982, John Jenkin, MA, (Cantab) FRCO, LRAM, ARCM. *Career:* Civil Service Clerical Officer 1959–63; PO/BT Sales Superintendent 1969–82. *House of Lords:* A Deputy Chairman of Committees 1997–; A Deputy Speaker 1999–; An elected hereditary peer 1999–. *Select Committees:* Co-opted Member, Select Committee on European Communities Sub-Committee C (Environment, Public Health and Consumer Protection) 1997–. *Other:* Lay Governor, The King's School, Gloucester 1984–87; Patron, Dispensing Doctors Association 1985–96; Lay Member, Immigration Appeal Tribunal 1985–; Member, English Advisory Committee for Telecommunications 1985–86; Patron, Worcester Branch National Back Pain Association 1987–89; President, Avanti 1987–89; Chairman, Employer-led Endorsed Care Training Steering Committee 1988–; Patron, Worcestershire Mobile Disabled Group 1989–; President, Elderly Accommodation Counsel 1993–; Member, British Red Cross 1994–; Patron, Gulf Veterans' Association 1995–; Member, OP Information Network 1995–; Chairman, Environmental Medicine Foundation 1996–; Member, Specialist Cheesemakers Association. *Awards Granted:* Laurent Perrier/Country Life Parliamentarian of the Year 1996; BBC Wildlife Magazine Green Ribbon Award 1997; Spectator 'Peer of the Year' 1997. *Miscellaneous:* Holder of the Premier Earldom of Scotland; Recognised in the surname "of Mar" by warrant of the Court of the Lord Lyon 1967, when she abandoned her second Christian name of Alison. *Special Interests:* Adult Education, Unemployment, Health Service, Social Security, Agriculture, Environment. *Recreations:* Gardening, goat keeping, reading. *Heir:* Her daughter, Lady Susan Helen of Mar, Mistress of Mar, born May 31, 1963. A Cross-Bencher. *Address:* The Countess of Mar, St Michael's Farm, Great Witley, Worcester, WR6 6JB *Tel:* 01299 896608.

MARLESFORD (Life Baron, UK), Mark Shuldham Schreiber; cr. 1991; DL

Son of late John Shuldham Schreiber, AE, DL. Born September 11, 1931; educated Eton; Trinity College, Cambridge. Married 1969, Gabriella Federica, daughter of Count Teodoro Veglio di Castelletto d'Uzzone (2 daughters). *Armed Forces:* National Service, Coldstream Guards, 2nd Lieutenant 1950–51. *Councils, Public Bodies:* Councillor, East Suffolk County Council 1968–70; DL, Suffolk 1991–. *Career:* Fisons Ltd 1957–63; Conservative Research Department 1963–70; Special Adviser to HM Government 1970–74; Special Adviser to Leader of the Opposition 1974–75; Editorial consultant, *The Economist* 1974–91; Member: Countryside Commission 1980–92, Rural Development Commission 1985–93; Director, Eastern Group plc 1990–96; Adviser to Mitsubishi Corporation International NV 1990–; An independent national director of Times Newspaper Holdings 1991–; Adviser to Board of John Swire and Sons Ltd 1992–; Chairman, Council for the Protection of Rural England 1993–98. *All-Party:* Member, All-Party: Defence Study Group, Arts and Heritage Group, China Country Group, Hong Kong Country Group. *Other:* President: Suffolk ACRE 1995–, Suffolk Preservation Society 1997–. *Special Interests:* Hong Kong, China, Conservation. *Recreations:* Planting trees and hedges, collecting minerals. *Clubs:* Pratt's. *Name, Style and Title:* Raised to the peerage as Baron Marlesford, of Marlesford in the County of Suffolk 1991. A Conservative. *Address:* The Lord Marlesford, DL, Marlesford Hall, Woodbridge, Suffolk, IP13 0AU *E-Mail:* marlesford@parliament.uk.

MARSH (Life Baron, UK), Richard (William) Marsh; cr. 1981; PC 1966; Kt 1976

Son of late William Marsh. Born March 14, 1928; educated Jennings School, Swindon; Ruskin College, Oxford. Married 1st, 1950, Evelyn Mary Andrews (2 sons) (marriage dissolved 1973); married 2nd, 1973, Caroline Dutton (died 1975); married 3rd, June 25, 1979, Hon. Felicity McFadzean, daughter of late Lord McFadzean of Kelvinside. *Trades Union:* Health Services Officer, National Union of Public Employees 1951–59. *Career:* Chairman: British Rail Board 1970–75, Newspaper Publishers Association 1975–, Allied Investments Ltd 1977–81, British Iron and Steel Consumers Council 1977–82, Strategy International Ltd 1978–84; Director, European Board Imperial Life of Canada 1980–; Chairman: Lee Cooper Group plc 1982–88, Mannington Management Services Ltd 1981–; Deputy Chairman, TV-AM Ltd 1981, Chairman 1982; Chairman, China & Eastern Investment Co. 1987–96; Executive Chairman: Laurentian Holding Company, Laurentian Life 1989–95; Chairman, British Industry Committee on South Africa Ltd 1989–95; Chairman, British Income and Growth Trust Ltd 1993–; Director, Imperial Life of Canada (Canada) 1995–. *House of Commons:* MP (Labour) for Greenwich 1959–70; Parliamentary Secretary, Ministry of Labour 1964–65; Joint Parliamentary Secretary, Ministry of Technology 1965–66; Minister of Power 1966–68; Minister of Transport 1968–70. *Select Committees:* Member, Select Committee on: European Communities 1997–, European Communities Sub-Committee B (Energy, Industry and Transport) 1997–. *All-Party:* Member, All-Party Insurance and Financial Services Group. *Trusts, etc:* Chairman, Special Trustees of Guy's Hospital 1982–96. *Honours:* PC 1966; Kt 1976. FCIT, FInstD; FInstM. *Special Interests:* Industry, Economic Policy, Financial Services, Far East. *Name, Style and Title:* Raised to the peerage as Baron Marsh, of Mannington in the County of Wiltshire 1981. A Cross-Bencher. *Address:* The Rt Hon. the Lord Marsh, House of Lords, London, SW1A 0PW.

MARSHALL OF KNIGHTSBRIDGE (Life Baron, UK), Colin Marsh Marshall; cr. 1998; Kt 1987

Son of Marsh and Florence Marshall. Born November 16, 1933; educated University College School, Hampstead; Hon. Dr of Humane Letters, Suffolk University, Boston, USA 1984; Hon. LLD, University of Bath 1989; Hon. DSc, University of Buckingham 1990; Hon. LLD, American University in London, Richmond College 1993; Hon. LLD, University of Lancaster 1997; Hon. DSc, Cranfield University 1997; Hon. Dr of Civil Laws, University of Durham 1997. Married 1958, Janet Cracknell (1 daughter). *Career:* Orient Steam Navigation Co 1951–58; Hertz Corporation in USA, Canada, Mexico, UK, Netherlands, Belgium 1958–64; Avis Inc 1964–79: President and Chief Operating Officer, New York 1975–76, President and Chief Executive Officer 1976–79; Norton Simon Inc 1979–81; Sears Holdings Ltd 1981–83; Director: British Airways Helicopters Limited 1983–86,

BEA Airtours Limited 1983–87; Chairman, British Airways Associated Companies Limited 1983–97; British Airways 1983–: Chief Exective 1983–95, Deputy Chairman 1989–93, Chairman 1993–; Chairman: British Caledonian Airways Limited 1988–91, British Caledonian Group plc 1988–97; Director: Grand Metropolitan plc 1988–95, Sabena World Airlines 1989–90, Midland Bank plc 1989–94, IBM United Kingdom Holdings Limited 1990–95, HSBC Holdings 1992–, US Air Group Inc 1993–96, US Air 1993–96, Qantas Airways Limited 1993–96, HSBC Holdings plc 1993–, New York Stock Exchange 1994–, MCI Communications Corporation 1997–; Deputy Chairman, British Telecommunications plc 1996–; Chairman: Inchcape plc 1996–, Invensys plc 1998–. *All-Party:* Member, All-Party London Group. *Other:* Member, British Tourist Authority 1986–1993; Vice-Chairman, World Travel and Tourism Council 1990–; Governor, Ashridge Management College 1991–99; President, Chartered Institute of Marketing 1991–96; Chairman: International Advisory Board British American Business Council 1994–96, London First Centre 1994–98; President: CBI 1996–98, Commonwealth Youth Exchange Council 1998–; Chairman, London Development Partnership 1998–; Chairman, Britain in Europe 1999–. *Trusts, etc:* Trustee, RAF Museum. *Honours:* Kt 1987. FCIT; FCIM. Freeman, City of London. Liveryman: Company of Information Technologists, Guild of Airline Pilots and Navigators. *Recreations:* Tennis. *Clubs:* Queen's, Royal Automobile. *Name, Style and Title:* Raised to the peerage as Baron Marshall of Knightsbridge, of Knightsbridge in the City of Westminster 1998. A Cross-Bencher. *Address:* The Lord Marshall of Knightsbridge, Chairman, British Airways plc, Berkeley Square House, Berkeley Square, London, W1X 6BA.

MASHAM OF ILTON (Life Baroness, UK), Susan Lilian Primrose Cunliffe-Lister; cr. 1970; DL

Daughter of late Major Sir Ronald Sinclair, 8th Bt, TD, DL. Born April 14, 1935; educated Heathfield School, Ascot; London Polytechnic; Hon. MA: Open University 1981, York University 1985; Hon. LLM, Leeds University 1988; Hon. Fellowship, Bradford and Ilkley Community College 1988; Hon. DSc, University of Ulster 1990; Hon. DLitt, Keele University 1993; Hon. LLD, University of Teesside. Married December 8, 1959, Lord Masham, now 2nd Earl of Swinton (*qv*) (1 son 1 daughter both adopted). *Councils, Public Bodies:* Member: Peterlee and Newton Aycliffe Corporation 1973–85; Yorkshire Regional Health Authority 1982–90; DL, North Yorkshire 1991–; Member, North Yorkshire Family Health Service Authority 1990–96. *Career:* Has made career in voluntary social work. *Select Committees:* Member, Select Committee on Science and Technology Sub-Committee on Resistance to Anti-Microbial Agents 1997–. *All-Party:* Vice-Chairman: All-Party Drug Misuse Committee 1984–, All-Party Aids Committee; Member: All-Party Penal Affairs Group 1975–, All-Party Children's Group, All-Party Disablement Committee 1970–; Member, All-Party Groups on: Alcohol Misuse, Breast Cancer, Food and Health Forum, Skin, Epilepsy. *Other:* President, North Yorkshire Red Cross 1963–88, Patron 1989–; President: Chartered Society of Physiotherapy 1975–82; Papworth and Enham Village Settlements 1973–85; Chairman, Board of Directors of Phoenix House 1986–92, Patron 1992–; Director, Association for Prevention of Addiction (APA); President: League of Friends of Harrogate Hospitals, Institute of Welfare Officers; Board Member, Visitors for Young Offenders Institution, Wetherby 1963–94; Council Member, London Lighthouse; Director, Association for Prevention of Addiction; Member/Governor, Ditchley Foundation 1980–; Advisory Council, National Listening Library; President: Yorkshire Association for Disabled 1963–98, Spinal Injuries Association 1982–, The Psoriasis Association, The Registration Council of Scientists in Health Care; Vice-President: Disabled Drivers Association, Action for Dysphasic Adults (DIA), Hospital Saving Association, Association of Occupational Therapists, British Sports Association for the Disabled, College of Occupational Therapists, Haemophilia Society, British Wheelchair Sports Foundation, Mildmay Mission Hospital, National Association of Citizens Advice Bureaux, Ponies of Britain, Riding for the Disabled Association; Patron: Yorkshire Faculty of General Practitioners, Disablement Income Group, Alert – Information on Euthanasia, Church Action on Disability, PHAB (Physically Handicapped and Able Bodied), Tacade. *Trusts, etc:* Council Member, Winston Churchill Trust 1980–; Patron: International Spinal Research Trust, Northern Counties Trust for People Living with HIV/AIDS; Chairman, Stonham Memorial Trust. *Miscellaneous:* Chairman: Home Office Crime Prevention Working Group on Young People and Alcohol 1987, Howard League Inquiry into Girls in Prison. Hon. Fellowship: RCGP 1981, Chartered Society of Physiotherapy 1996. Freedom, Borough of Harrogate 1989. *Publications: The World Walks By. Special Interests:* Health, Disability, Penal Affairs and Policy, Drug Abuse. *Recreations:* Breeding Highland ponies, gardening, swimming. *Name, Style and Title:* Raised to the peerage as Baroness Masham of Ilton, of Masham in the North Riding of the County of Yorkshire 1970. A Cross-Bencher. *Address:* The Countess of Swinton, Baroness Masham of Ilton, DL, Dykes Hill House, Masham, Nr Ripon, North Yorkshire, HG4 4NS *Tel:* 01765 689241 *Fax:* 01765 689596; 46 Westminster Gardens, Marsham Street, London, SW1P 4JG *Tel:* 020 7834 0700.

MASON OF BARNSLEY (Life Baron, UK), Roy Mason; cr. 1987; PC 1968; DL

Son of late Joseph Mason, miner. Born April 18, 1924; educated Carlton and Royston Elementary Schools; London School of Economics (TUC Scholarship); DUniv, Hallam University, Sheffield. Married October 20, 1945, Marjorie, daughter of Ernest Sowden, of Royston, West Yorkshire (2 daughters). *Trades Union:* Member, Yorkshire Miners' Council 1949–53; Chairman, Parliamentary Triple Alliance of Miners, Railway and Steel Union MPs 1979–80. *Armed Forces:* Flight Sergeant, Air Force Cadets, Royston Flight, Barnsley. *Councils, Public Bodies:* DL, South Yorkshire 1992–. *Career:* Coal Miner 1938–53; Member, Council of Europe and Western European Union 1973. *House of Commons:* Labour candidate for Bridlington 1951–53; MP

(Labour) for: Barnsley 1953–83, Barnsley Central 1983–87; Minister of State (Shipping), Board of Trade 1964–67; Minister of Defence Equipment 1967–1968; Postmaster General April–June 1968; Minister of Power 1968–69; President, Board of Trade 1969–70; Secretary of State for: Defence 1974–76, Northern Ireland 1976–79. *Spokesman (Commons):* Opposition Spokesman on Defence and Post Office Affairs 1960–64; Principal Opposition Spokesman on Board of Trade Affairs 1970–74; Principal Opposition Spokesman on Agriculture, Fisheries and Food 1979–81. *Party Groups (Commons):* Chairman: Yorkshire Group of Labour MPs 1970–74, 1981–84, Miners' Group of MPs 1973–74, 1980–81. *International Bodies (Commons):* Member, Council of Europe 1970–71. *All-Party:* Vice-Chairman, All-Party Lords and Commons Defence Study Group; Joint Treasurer, All-Party War Crimes Group. *Other:* President, Yorkshire Salmon and Trout Association, Member, National Council; President, Yorkshire Water Colour Society; Vice-President, South Yorkshire Foundation (Charity); Chairman, Barnsley Business and Innovation Centre Ltd; Member, National Council of The Scouts Association. *Trusts, etc:* Chairman, Prince's Youth Business Trust, South Yorkshire. *Miscellaneous:* Member: National Rivers Authority Advisory Committee 1988, National Rivers Authority 1989–92; President, Lords and Commons Pipe and Cigar Club. *Honours:* PC 1968. *Publications: Paying the Price* (Autobiography), 1999. *Special Interests:* Coal Industry, Human Rights, Northern Ireland, Defence, Anti-Pollution Matters. *Recreations:* Fly-fishing, golf, tie designing (cravatology), specialist philately. *Sportsclubs:* President, Lords and Commons Fly Fishing Club. *Name, Style and Title:* Raised to the peerage as Baron Mason of Barnsley, of Barnsley in South Yorkshire 1987. Labour. *Address:* The Rt Hon. the Lord Mason of Barnsley, DL, 12 Victoria Avenue, Barnsley, South Yorkshire, S70 2BH.

MASSEY OF DARWEN (Life Baroness, UK), Doreen Elizabeth Massey; cr. 1999

Daughter of late Jack and Mary Ann Hall (née Sharrock). Born September 5, 1938; educated Darwen Grammar School; Birmingham University (BA Hons French 1961, DipEd 1962); London University (MA Health Education 1985). Married February 26, 1966, Dr Leslie Massey, son of James and Annie Massey (2 sons 1 daughter). *Trades Union:* Former Member: NUT, MSF. *Career:* Graduate Service Overseas, Gabon 1962–63; Teacher: South Hackney School 1964–67; Springside School, Philadelphia 1967–69; Running Community Playgroup 1970–77, Teacher/Head of Year/Senior Teacher, Walsingham School, London 1979–83; Adviser in Personal, Social and Health Education, Inner London Education Authority 1983–85; Director

of Training, Family Planning Association 1981–89; Director of Young People's Programme, Health Education Authority 1985–87; Director, FPA 1989–94; Independent Consultant in Health Education 1994–. *Other:* School Governor; Member: Advisory Council on Alcohol and Drug Education, Book Advisory Centres, Family Planning Association, Opera North, English National Opera, Royal Shakespeare Company, Sex Education Forum. FRSA. *Publications: Teaching About HIV/AIDS,* 1988; *Sex Education Factpack,* co-author 1988; *Sex Education: Why, What and How,* 1988; *The Sex Education Source Book,* editor 1995; *Womens' Guide Encyclopaedia,* 1996; articles on health education in a variety of journals. *Special Interests:* Education, Health, International Development. *Recreations:* Theatre, opera, reading, walking, yoga, travel, sports. *Name, Style and Title:* Raised to the peerage as Baroness Massey of Darwen, of Darwen in the County of Lancashire 1999. Labour. *Address:* The Baroness Massey of Darwen, 66 Lessar Avenue, London, SW4 9HQ *Tel:* 020 8673 5436 *Fax:* 020 8673 7734 *E-Mail:* dem@healthskills.demon.co.uk.

MAYHEW OF TWYSDEN (Life Baron, UK), Patrick Barnabas Burke Mayhew; cr. 1997; Kt 1983; PC 1986; QC 1972

Son of late A. G. H. Mayhew, MC, and the late Sheila Mayhew (née Roche). Born September 11, 1929; educated Tonbridge; Balliol College, Oxford (MA). Married April 15, 1963, Jean Elizabeth, OBE, daughter of John Gurney (4 sons). *Armed Forces:* Served in 4th/7th Royal Dragoon Guards National Service; Army Emergency Reserve (Captain). *Career:* Called to the Bar by Middle Temple 1955; QC 1972; Bencher 1976. *House of Commons:* Contested (Conservative) Camberwell-Dulwich 1970; MP (Conservative) for Tunbridge Wells 1974–97; Parliamentary Under Secretary of State, Department of Employment 1979–81; Minister of State, Home Office 1981–83; Solicitor-General 1983–87; Attorney General 1987–92; Secretary of State for Northern Ireland 1992–97. *Select Committees (Commons):* Former Member, Select Committees on: Violence in Marriage 1976, Conduct of Members 1976. *Backbench Committees (Commons):* Executive, 1922 Committee 1976–79; Vice-Chairman, Conservative Home Affairs Committee 1976–79. *Select Committees:* Member, Select Committees on: Deregulation and Devolved Legislation 1997–, Parliamentary Privilege (Joint Committee) 1997–99. *All-Party:* Chairman, All-Party Fruit Industry Group 1999–. *Party Groups:* Executive Member, Association Conservative Peers 1998–. *Trusts, etc:* President, The Airey Neave Trust 1997–. *Honours:* Knighted 1983; PC 1986. Liveryman, Worshipful Company of Skinners 1954–. *Clubs:* Pratt's, Beefsteak, Garrick. *Name, Style and Title:* Raised to the peerage as Baron Mayhew of Twysden, of Kilndown in the County of Kent 1997. A Conservative. *Address:* The Rt Hon. the Lord Mayhew of Twysden, QC, House of Lords, London, SW1A 0PW.

MERLYN-REES (Life Baron, UK), Merlyn Merlyn-Rees; cr. 1992; PC 1974

Son of late L. D. Rees. Born December 18, 1920; educated Elementary schools in South Wales; Harrow Weald Grammar School; Goldsmiths' College (President, Students' Union 1940); London School of Economics (BSc Economics, MSc Economics); Hon. LLD, Wales 1987; Fellow, Polytechnic of Wales 1989; Hon. LLD, Leeds 1992. Married December 26, 1949, Colleen Faith, daughter of H. F. Cleveley, of Kenton, Middlesex (3 sons). *Armed Forces:* Served RAF 1941–46; Demobilised as Squadron-Leader. *Councils, Public Bodies:* Member, Committee to examine Section 2 of Official Secrets Act 1971; Member, Franks' Committee of Enquiry on Falkland Islands 1982. *Career:* Economics and History teacher, Harrow Weald Grammar School 1949–60; Lecturer in Economics, Luton College of Technology 1962–63. *House of Commons:* Contested (Labour) Harrow East in: General Elections 1955, 1959, By-election 1959; MP (Labour) for: Leeds South1963–83, Morley and South Leeds 1983–92; PPS to Chancellor of the Exchequer 1964–65; Parliamentary Under-Secretary of State: Ministry of Defence, for the Army 1965–66, for the Royal Air Force 1966–68, Home Office 1968–70; Member, Shadow Cabinet 1972–74; Secretary of State for Northern Ireland 1974–76; Home Secretary 1976–79. *Spokesman (Commons):* Opposition Front Bench Spokesman for Northern Ireland 1972; Principal Front Bench Spokesman on: Home Affairs 1979–80, Energy 1980–82, Industry and Employment Co-ordination 1982–83. *Chancellor:* Chancellor, University of Glamorgan 1993–. *Select Committees:* Member, Select Committees on: the Civil Service 1996–97, Delegated Powers and Deregulation 1997–, Public Service 1997–, Parliamentary Privilege (Joint Committee) 1997–. *International Bodies (General):* Member: CPA, IPU, British American Parliamentary Group. *Party Groups (General):* Organiser, Festival of Labour 1960–62. *Miscellaneous:* Assumed the surname of Merlyn-Rees in lieu of his patronymic 1992; President, Video Standards Council 1990–. *Honours:* PC 1974. *Publications:* Author of: *The Public Sector in the Mixed Economy,* 1973; *Northern Ireland: A Personal Perspective,* 1985. *Special Interests:* Housing, Education, Penal Reform. *Recreations:* Reading, theatre. *Name, Style and Title:* Raised to the peerage as Baron Merlyn-Rees, of Morley and South Leeds in the County of West Yorkshire and of Cilfynydd in the County of Mid Glamorgan 1992. Labour. *Address:* The Rt Hon. the Lord Merlyn-Rees, House of Lords, London, SW1A 0PW.

METHUEN (7th Baron, UK), Robert Alexander Holt Methuen; cr. 1838

Son of 5th Baron. Born July 22, 1931. Succeeded his brother 1994; educated Shrewsbury; Trinity College, Cambridge. Married 1st, May 10, 1958, Mary Catherine Jane, daughter of late Venerable Charles Hooper, Archdeacon of Ipswich (2 daughters) (marriage dissolved 1993), married 2nd, January 8, 1994, Margrit Andrea, daughter of Friedrich Karl Ernst Hadwiger, of Vienna, Austria. *Career:* Design Engineer, Westinghouse Brake and Signal Company 1957–67; Computer Systems Engineer: IBM UK Ltd 1968–75, Rolls-Royce plc 1975–94; Retired. *House of Lords:* A Deputy Chairman of Committees 1999–; An elected hereditary peer 1999–. *Spokesman:* Spokesman for Transport. *Select Committees:* Member: European Communities Sub-Committee B (Energy, Industry and Transport) 1995–, Channel Tunnel Rail Link 1996, Administration and Works Sub-Committee 1997–. *Heir:* His kinsman, James Paul Archibald Methuen-Campbell, born October 25, 1952. A Liberal Democrat. *Address:* The Lord Methuen, House of Lords, London, SW1A 0PW.

MILLER OF CHILTHORNE DOMER (Life Baroness, UK), Susan Elisabeth Miller; cr. 1998

Daughter of Frederick Oliver Meddows Taylor and Norah Langham. Born January 1, 1954; educated Sidcot School, Winscombe, Somerset; Oxford Polytechnic. Married April 12, 1980 (marriage dissolved 1998) (2 daughters). *Councils, Public Bodies:* Councillor, Chilthorne Domer Parish Council 1987; Councillor, South Somerset District Council 1991–, Leader 1996–98; Councillor, Somerset County Council 1997–. *Career:* In publishing: David & Charles, Weidenfeld & Nicolson, Penguin Books 1975–79; Bookshop Owner 1979–89. *Spokesman:* Liberal Democrat Spokesman on Agriculture and Rural Affairs 1999–. *Select Committees:* Member, European Communities Sub Committee D (Agriculture, Fisheries and Food). *All-Party:* Member, All-Party: National Parks Group, Rail Freight Group. *Miscellaneous:* Member: Local Government Association Europe and International Panel, Rural Commission Steering Group. *Recreations:* Walking, reading, friends. *Name, Style and Title:* Raised to the peerage as Baroness Miller of Chilthorne Domer, of Chilthorne Domer in the County of Somerset 1998. A Liberal Democrat. *Address:* The Baroness Miller of Chilthorne Domer, House of Lords, London, SW1A 0PW *E-Mail:* millers@parliament.uk.

MILLER OF HENDON (Life Baroness, UK), Doreen Miller; cr. 1993; MBE 1989

Daughter of Bernard and Hetty Feldman. Born June 13, 1933; educated Brondesbury and Kilburn High School; London School of Economics. Married September 1, 1955, Henry Lewis Miller, son of Ben and Eva Miller (3 sons). *Councils, Public Bodies:* JP, Brent 1971; Chairman, Barnet Family Health Services Authority 1990–94. *Whip:* A Baroness in Waiting (Government Whip) 1994–97; An Opposition Whip 1997–99. *Spokesman:* Spokeswoman on: Health 1995–97, Education and Employment 1996–97, Trade and Industry 1996–97, Office of Public Service 1996, Environment 1996–97; An Opposition Spokeswoman on Environment, Transport and the Regions, DTI 1997–. *Party Groups (General):* Greater London Area Conservative and Unionist Associations: Joint Treasurer 1990–93, Chairman 1993–96, President 1996–98; Member, Conservative Board of Finance and its Training and Fund Raising Sub-Committees 1990–93; President, Hampstead and Highgate Womens' Committee 1993–96; Member, Conservative Womens' National and General Purposes Committees 1993–96, Patron 1996–; President, Greenwich and Woolwich Conservative Association 1996–; Patron: Eltham and Woolwich Conservative Association 1996–, Hackney North Conservative Association 1996–, North Thanet Conservative Association 1996–. *Other:* National Chairman and Executive Director, 300 Group 1985–88; Chairman, Women into Public Life Campaign 1986–92; Human Rights Adviser, Soroptomist International 1987–90; Chairman, National Association of Leagues of Hospital and Community Friends 1997–. *Trusts, etc:* Patron, Minerva Educational Trust. *Miscellaneous:* Contested (Conservative): London South Inner, European Parliamentary elections 1984, ILEA 1986; Non-Executive Director, Crown Agents 1990–94; Member, Monopolies and Mergers Commission 1992–93. *Honours:* MBE, 1989. Fellow, Institute of Marketing; FRSA. *Special Interests:* Women's Issues, Health, Law and Order, Small Businesses. *Recreations:* Reading, football, politics. *Clubs:* Carlton, St. Stephen's Constitutional. *Name, Style and Title:* Raised to the peerage as Baroness Miller of Hendon, of Gore in the London Borough of Barnet 1993. A Conservative. *Address:* The Baroness Miller of Hendon, MBE, House of Lords, London, SW1A 0PW *Tel:* 020 7219 3164 *E-Mail:* hlmillerandco@compuserve.com.

MILLETT (Life Baron, UK), Peter Julian Millett; cr. 1998; Kt 1986; PC 1994

Son of late Denis Millett and Adele Millett. Born June 23, 1932; educated Harrow; Trinity Hall, Cambridge (Scholar, MA); Hon. Fellow, Trinity Hall, Cambridge. Married 1959, Ann Mireille, daughter of late David Harris (2 sons and 1 son deceased). *Armed Forces:* Flying Officer, RAF, National Service 1955–57. *Career:* Called to the Bar: Middle Temple 1955, Lincoln's Inn 1959 (Bencher 1960), Singapore 1976, Hong Kong 1979; At Chancery Bar 1958–86; Examiner and Lecturer in Practical Conveyancing, Council of Legal Education 1962–76; Junior Counsel to Department of Trade and Industry in Chancery matters 1967–73; Member, General Council of the Bar 1971–75; Outside Member, Law Commission on working party on co-ownership of the matrimonial home 1972–73; QC 1973; Member, Department of Trade Insolvency Law Review Committee 1977–82; A Judge of the High Court of Justice 1986–94; A Lord Justice of Appeal 1994–98; A Lord of Appeal in Ordinary 1998–. *Other:* President, West London Synagogue of British Jews 1991–95. *Honours:* Kt 1986; PC 1994. *Publications:* Has contributed to several legal publications including *Halsbury's Law of England*; Editor in Chief, *Encyclopaedia of Forms and Precedents. Recreations:* Philately, bridge, *The Times* crossword. *Clubs:* Home House. *Name, Style and Title:* Raised to the peerage as Baron Millett, of St Marylebone in the City of Westminster 1998. A Cross-Bencher. *Address:* The Rt Hon. the Lord Millett, House of Lords, London, SW1A 0PW.

MILNER OF LEEDS (2nd Baron, UK), Arthur James Michael Milner; cr. 1951; AE 1952

Son of 1st Baron, PC, MC, TD, DL. Born September 12, 1923. Succeeded his father 1967; educated Oundle; Trinity Hall, Cambridge (MA). Married 1951, Sheila Margaret, daughter of late Gerald Hartley (1 son 1 daughter and 1 daughter deceased). *Armed Forces:* RAF short course, Trinity Hall, Cambridge 1942; RAF 1942–46, Flight-Lieutenant; 609 (West Riding) Squadron, RAuxAF 1947–52, Flight-Lieutenant. *Career:* Admitted Solicitor 1951; Former Partner, Milners Curry & Gaskell; Consultant, Gregory Rowcliffe and Milners 1988–. *House of Lords:* An elected hereditary peer 1999–. *Whip:* Opposition Whip 1971–74. *Select Committees:* Member: Joint Committee on Consolidation Bills 1982–92, Select Committee on Channel Rail Link Bill 1996, Several Private Bill Committees 1990–93. *Other:* Member, Pilgrims Society. Member, Clothworkers' Company. *Clubs:* Royal Air Force. *Heir:* His son, Hon. Richard James Milner, born May 16, 1959. Labour. *Address:* The Lord Milner of Leeds, AE, 2 The Inner Court, Old Church Street, London, SW3 5BY *Tel:* 020 7352 7588; 1 Bedford Row, London, WC1R 4BZ *Tel:* 020 7242 0631.

MISHCON (Life Baron, UK), Victor Mishcon; cr. 1978; DL

Son of late Rabbi Arnold Mishcon. Born August 14, 1915; educated City of London School; Hon. LLD, Birmingham University 1991; Hon. Fellow, University College, London 1993. Married 1976, Joan Estelle Monty (2 sons 1 daughter by former marriage). *Armed Forces:* Served HM Forces during Second World War. *Councils, Public Bodies:* Councillor, Lambeth Borough Council 1945–49, Chairman, Finance Committee; Councillor, LCC 1946–65. Chairman of Council 1954–55, Former Chairman of several of its committees; Councillor, GLC, Chairman, General Purposes Committe; Member, ILEA 1964–67; DL, Greater London 1954. *Career:* A Solicitor, Former Senior Partner and now Consultant to Mishcon De Reya; Member: National Theatre Board 1965–90, South Bank Theatre Board 1966–67; Vice-President, Board of Deputies of British Jews 1967–73; Vice-Chairman, Council of Christians and Jews 1976–77; Former Member, various Government Committees. *Spokesman:* Principal Opposition Spokesman on: Home Affairs 1983–90, Legal Affairs 1990–93. *Select Committees:* Former Member: Standing Joint Committee with the Commons on Consolidation of Bills, Select Committee on Procedure 1981–83, Select Committee on Medical Ethics 1983. *All-Party:* Vice-Chairman, Solicitors All-Party Parliamentary Group. *Miscellaneous:* Contested (Labour): North West Leeds 1950, Bath 1951, Gravesend 1955, 1959 General Elections. *Honours:* Commander, Royal Swedish Order of North Star 1954; Star of Ethiopia 1954; QC (Hon) 1992; Star of Jordan 1995. *Name, Style and Title:* Raised to the peerage as Baron Mishcon, of Lambeth in the County of Greater London 1978. Labour. *Address:* The Lord Mishcon, QC, DL, 21 Southampton Row, London, WC1B 5HS.

MOLLOY (Life Baron, UK), William John Molloy; cr. 1981

Son of late William John Molloy. Born October 26, 1918; educated St Thomas's Council School, Swansea; Swansea College, University of Wales; Hon. Fellow, Swansea College, University Wales 1986. Married 1945, Eva Mary (died 1980), daughter of Henry Lewis (1 daughter). *Armed Forces:* TA 1938; Served Field Company Royal Engineers 1939–46. *Councils, Public Bodies:* Leader, Fulham Borough Council 1956–66. *Career:* Foreign Office, Whitley Council Departmental Staff-Side Chairman 1946–52; Trade Union Lecturer; Former Editor *Civil Service Review*; Member, Assemblies Council of Europe (Chairman, Health Services Committee) and Western European Union 1969–73; Member, European Parliament 1975–78; Member, Executive Committee IPU; Member, CPA. *House of Commons:* MP (Labour) Ealing North 1964–79; PPS to Minister of Post and Telecommunications 1969–70. *Backbench Committees (Commons):* Member, Commons Estimates Committee 1968–70. *All-Party Committees (Commons):* Vice-Chairman and Founder, Parliamentary Labour Party European Affairs Group. *Other:* Patron, Metropolitan Area Royal British Legion; National Vice-President, Royal British Legion; Vice-President, Greenford Branch Royal British Legion; Elected to RGS Council 1981. Fellow: Royal Geographical Society, World Association Arts and Sciences (elected 1985); Hon. Associate, British Vetinerary Association 1988. *Special Interests:* Health Service, Foreign Affairs, Commonwealth, Commerce, Industry. *Recreations:* Music, collecting dictionaries. *Name, Style and Title:* Raised to the peerage as Baron Molloy, of Ealing in Greater London 1981. Labour. *Address:* The Lord Molloy, 2A Uneeda Drive, Greenford, Middlesex, UB6 8QB; House of Lords, London, SW1A 0PW *Tel:* House of Lords 020 7219 6710.

MOLYNEAUX OF KILLEAD (Life Baron, UK), James Henry Molyneaux; cr. 1997; KBE 1996; PC 1983

Son of late William Molyneaux, Seacash, Killead, Co. Antrim. Born August 27, 1920; educated Aldergrove School, Co. Antrim. *Armed Forces:* RAF 1941–46. *Councils, Public Bodies:* JP, Co. Antrim 1957–86; Antrim County Councillor 1964–73. *House of Commons:* MP (UUP) for Antrim South 1970–83 and for Lagan Valley 1983–97. *Spokesman (Commons):* Spokesman, Treasury 1995–97. *Select Committees (Commons):* Member, Chairmen's Panel 1996–97. *Spokesman:* Spokesman on Northern Ireland. *Party Groups (General):* Hon. Secretary, South Antrim Unionist Association 1964–70; Former Chairman, Antrim division Unionist Association; Leader: United Ulster Unionist Coalition 1974–77, Ulster Unionist Parliamentary Party 1974–95, Ulster Unionist Party 1979–95. *Other:* Vice-Chairman, Eastern Special Care Hospital Committee 1966–73; Chairman: Antrim Mental Health Branch 1967–70, Crumlin Branch, Royal British Legion; Sovereign Grand Master, British Commonwealth Royal Black Institution; A Vice-President, Federation of Economic Development Authorities. *Honours:* PC 1983; KBE 1996. *Special Interests:* Constitutional Affairs, Mental Health, Local Government. *Name, Style and Title:* Raised to the peerage as Baron Molyneaux of Killead, of Killead in the County of Antrim 1997. A Ulster Unionist/Cross-Bencher. *Address:* The Rt Hon. the Lord Molyneaux of Killead, KBE, House of Lords, London, SW1A 0PW.

MONRO OF LANGHOLM (Life Baron, UK), Hector Seymour Peter Monro; cr. 1997; Kt 1981; PC 1995; AE 1953; DL

Son of late Captain Alastair Monro, Queens Own Cameron Highlanders. Born October 4, 1922; educated Canford School; King's College, Cambridge. Married 1st, March 4, 1949, Elizabeth Anne (died May 20, 1994), daughter of Major H. Welch (2 sons), married 2nd, December 23, 1994, Mrs Doris Kaestner, of Baltimore, Maryland, USA. *Armed Forces:* Served RAF 1941–46; RAuxAF 1947–54; Hon. Air Commodore 1982–2000; Hon. Inspector General RAuxAF 1989–2000. *Councils, Public Bodies:* Councillor, Dumfries County Council 1952–67; DL, Dumfriesshire 1973. *House of Commons:* Member for Dumfries since October 15, 1964–97; Parliamentary Under-Secretary of State: for Scotland 1971–74, at Department of Environment and Minister for Sport 1979–81; Joint Parliamentary Under-Secretary of State, Scottish Office 1992–95. *Whip (Commons):* Conservative Whip January 1967–70; Lord Commissioner of Treasury and Government Whip 1970–71.

Spokesman (Commons): Opposition Spokesman on: Scottish Affairs 1974–75 Sport 1974–79. *Select Committees (Commons):* Member, Select Committees on: Scottish Affairs 1983–87, Procedure 1983–87, Defence 1987. *Backbench Committees (Commons):* Vice-Chairman, Conservative Agriculture Committee 1983–87; Chairman: Scottish Conservative Committee 1983–92, Conservative Sports Committee 1984–87. *Party Groups (General):* Chairman, Dumfriesshire Conservative Association 1958–63. *Other:* Chairman, Dumfries and Galloway Police Committee; Area Executive, NFU; Member, Nature Conservancy Council 1982–91; President: Auto Cycle Union 1983–90, National Small-bore Rifle Association 1987–92. *Miscellaneous:* Member, Queen's Bodyguard for Scotland, Royal Company of Archers. *Honours:* AE 1953; Knighted 1981; PC 1995. FRAGS. *Special Interests:* Scotland, Agriculture, Aviation, Defence, Sport, Recreation, Heritage. *Recreations:* Sport, flying, shooting, music. *Sportsclubs:* Scottish Rugby Union: Member 1957–77, Vice-President 1975, President 1976–77. *Clubs:* MCC, Royal Scottish Automobile (Glasgow), Royal Air Force, Royal and Ancient (St Andrews). *Name, Style and Title:* Raised to the peerage as Baron Monro of Langholm, of Westerkirk in Dumfries and Galloway 1997. A Conservative. *Address:* The Rt Hon. the Lord Monro of Langholm, AE, DL, Williamwood, Kirtlebridge, Lockerbie, Dumfries, DG11 3LU.

MONSON (11th Baron, GB), John Monson; cr. 1728; 15th Bt of Carlton (E) 1611

Son of 10th Baron. Born May 3, 1932. Succeeded his father 1958; educated Eton; Trinity College, Cambridge (BA). Married 1955, Emma, daughter of late Anthony Devas, ARA (3 sons). *House of Lords:* An elected hereditary peer 1999–. *Other:* President, Society for Individual Freedom. *Heir:* His son, Hon. Nicholas John Monson, born October 19, 1955. A Cross-Bencher. *Address:* The Lord Monson, The Manor House, South Carlton, Nr Lincoln, LN1 2RN *Tel:* 01522 730263.

MONTAGU OF BEAULIEU (3rd Baron, UK), Edward John Barrington Douglas-Scott-Montagu; cr. 1885

Son of 2nd Baron, KCIE, CSI, DL. Born October 20, 1926. Succeeded his father 1929; educated St Peter's Court, Broadstairs; Ridley College; St Catharines, Ontario; Eton; New College, Oxford; Hon. DTech. Married 1st, April 11, 1959, Belinda Crossley (1 son 1 daughter) (marriage dissolved 1974), married 2nd, 1974, Fiona Herbert (1 son). *Armed Forces:* Lieutenant, Grenadier Guards 1945–48. *Career:* Founded Montagu Motor Museum 1952, which became the National Motor Museum 1972; Founder and Editor, *Veteran and Vintage Magazine* 1956–79; President, Fédération Internationale des Voitures Anciennes 1980–83; Development Commissioner 1980–84; First Chairman, Historic Buildings and Monuments Commission (English Heritage) 1984–92; Chairman: Report on Britain's Historic Buildings: A Policy for their Future Use, English Tourist Board's Committee of Enquiry publishing Britain's Zoos. *House of Lords:* An elected hereditary peer 1999–. *All-Party:* Member, All-Party: Arts and Heritage Group, Tourism Group. *Other:* President: Southern Tourist Board, Tourism Society, United Kingdom Vineyards Association; Chancellor, Wine Guild UK; First President: Historic Houses Association 1973–78, European Union of Historic Houses Associations 1978–81; President: Museums Association 1982–84, Federation of British Historic Vehicle Clubs 1988–, Historic Commercial Vehicle Society, Disabled Drivers Motor Club President, Millennium Institute of Journalists. FRSA; FMA; Hon. RICS; FMI; FIMI; FIPR. *Publications:* Author of: *More Equal than Others*; *Jaguar: A Biography*; *Daimler Century*, 1995, and many other motoring books; Author of books on Motoring History and Historic Houses. *Special Interests:* Heritage, Museums and Galleries, Road Transport, Tourism. *Recreations:* Water and field sports. *Sportsclubs:* Commodore, Beaulieu River Sailing Club. *Clubs:* Vice-Commodore, House of Lords Yacht. *Heir:* His son, Hon. Ralph Douglas-Scott-Montagu, born March 13, 1961. A Conservative. *Address:* The Lord Montagu of Beaulieu, Palace House, Beaulieu, Brockenhurst, Hampshire, SO42 7ZN *Tel:* 01590 612345 *Fax:* 01590 612623; Flat 11, Wyndham House, Bryanston Square, London, W1H 7FJ *Tel:* 020 7262 2603 *Fax:* 020 7724 3262.

MONTROSE (8th Duke of, S), James Graham; cr. 1707; Marquess of Montrose (S) 1644; Marquess of Graham and Buchanan (S) 1707; Earl of Montrose (S) 1505; Earl of Kincardine (S) 1707; Earl Graham (GB) 1722; Viscount Dundaff (S) 1707; Lord Graham (S) 1445; Lord Aberuthven, Mugdock and Fintrie (S) 1707; Baron Graham (GB) 1722; 12th Bt of Braco (NS) 1625

Son of 7th Duke and late Isobel Veronica, daughter of late Lieutenant-Colonel Thomas Sellar, CMG, DSO. Born April 6, 1935. Succeeded his father 1992; educated Loretto. Married 1970, Catherine Elizabeth MacDonnell, daughter of late Captain Norman Andrew Thomson Young, of Ottawa, Canada (2 sons 1 daughter). *Councils, Public Bodies:* Chairman, Buchanan Community Council 1982–93. *House of Lords:* An elected hereditary peer 1999–. *All-Party:* Member, All-Party: Energy Studies Group, Scottish Opera Group; Treasurer, Scottish Peers Association. *Other:* Member: Council of Scottish National Farmers Union 1981–90, Royal Scottish Pipers Society, Royal Highland and Agricultural Society, President 1997–98. *Miscellaneous:* Member, Queen's Bodyguard for Scotland (Royal Company of Archers) 1965–, Brigadier 1986–; Hereditary Sheriff, Dunbartonshire; Vice-Chairman, Secretary of State's Working Party for Loch Lomond and the Trossachs. *Honours:* OStJ 1978. *Special Interests:* Europe, Agriculture, Rural Affairs. *Heir:* His son, Marquess of Graham, born August 16, 1973. A Conservative. *Address:* His Grace the Duke of Montrose, Auchmar, Drymen, Glasgow, G63 0AG.

MOORE OF LOWER MARSH (Life Baron, UK), John Edward Michael Moore; cr. 1992; PC 1986

Son of late Edward Moore. Born November 26, 1937; educated Licensed Victuallers' School, Slough; London School of Economics (BSc Econ). Married June 23, 1962, Sheila Sarah Tillotson (2 sons 1 daughter). *Armed Forces:* National Service with Royal Sussex Regiment in Korea 1955–57, Commissioned. *Councils, Public Bodies:* Councillor, London Borough of Merton 1971–74. *Career:* Resident in USA 1961–65, Democratic Precinct Captain 1962, Ward Chairman, Evanston, Illinois 1964; Chairman, Dean Witter (International) Ltd 1975–79, Director 1968–79; Advisory Board Member, Marvin and Palmer Inc. 1989–; Director, Monitor Inc. 1990–, Chairman, European Executive Committee; Member, Advisory Board, Sir Alexander Gibb & Co. 1990–95; Chairman, Credit Suisse Asset Management 1992–; Director: Swiss American NY Inc 1992–96, GTECH 1993–, Blue Circle Industries plc 1993–, Camelot Holdings plc 1993–98; Director, Rolls-Royce plc 1994–, Deputy Chairman 1996–; Supervisory Board Member, ITT Automotive Europe GMBH, Germany 1994–97; Director: Central European Growth Fund Ltd 1995–, BEA (NY) 1996–98, TIG Holdings Inc (NY) 1997–99, PCP (Zurich) 1999–. *House of Commons:* MP (Conservative) Croydon Central February 1974–92; Parliamentary Under-Secretary of State for Energy 1979–83; Economic Secretary to the Treasury June-October 1983; Financial Secretary to the Treasury 1983–86; Secretary of State for: Transport 1986–87, Social Services 1987–88, Social Security 1988–89. *Party Groups (General):* Chairman, Conservative Association, LSE 1958; Chairman, Stepney Green Conservative Association 1968; Vice-Chairman, Conservative Party with responsibility for Youth 1975–79. *Other:* President, Student Union, LSE 1959–60; Member, Court of Governors, LSE 1977–; Council Member, Institute of Directors 1991–99. *Trusts, etc:* Chairman, Energy Savings Trust 1992–95, President 1995–. *Honours:* PC 1986. *Clubs:* Royal Automobile, Institute of Directors. *Name, Style and Title:* Raised to the peerage as Baron Moore of Lower Marsh, of Lower Marsh in the London Borough of Lambeth 1992. A Conservative. *Address:* The Rt Hon. the Lord Moore of Lower Marsh, House of Lords, London, SW1A 0PW.

MOORE OF WOLVERCOTE (Life Baron, UK), Philip Brian Cecil Moore; cr. 1986; GCB 1985; GCVO 1983; CMG 1966; PC 1977; QSO 1986

Son of late Cecil Moore, ICS. Born April 6, 1921; educated Dragon School; Cheltenham College; Brasenose College, Oxford (Classical Exhibitioner 1940); Hon. Fellow, Brasenose College, Oxford. Married 1945, Joan Ursula, daughter of Captain M. E. Greenop, late DCLI (2 daughters). *Armed Forces:* RAF Bomber Command, POW 1942–45. *Career:* Entered Home Civil Service 1947; Assistant Private Secretary to First Lord of the Admiralty 1950–51; Principal Private Secretary 1957–58; Deputy UK Commissioner and Deputy British High Commissioner, Singapore 1961–65; Chief of Public Relations, Ministry of Defence 1965–66; Assistant Private Secretary to HM The Queen 1966–72, Deputy Private Secretary 1972–77, Private Secretary 1977–86; A Permanent Lord-in-Waiting to HM The Queen 1990–. *Honours:* CMG 1966; CB 1973; KCVO 1976; PC 1977; KCB 1980; GCVO 1983; GCB 1985; QSO 1986. *Special Interests:* Foreign Affairs, Commonwealth, Defence, Church Affairs. *Recreations:* Golf, shooting, fishing. *Clubs:* Athenaeum, MCC. *Name, Style and Title:* Raised to the peerage as Baron Moore of Wolvercote, of Wolvercote in the City of Oxford 1986. A Cross-Bencher. *Address:* The Rt Hon. the Lord Moore of Wolvercote, GCB, GCVO, CMG, QSO, Hampton Court Palace, East Molesey, Surrey, KT8 9AU *Tel:* 020 7943 4695.

MORAN (2nd Baron, UK), (Richard) John McMoran Wilson; cr. 1943; KCMG 1981

Son of 1st Baron, MC, MD, FRCP, and late Dorothy, MBE, daughter of late Samuel Dufton. Born September 22, 1924. Succeeded his father 1977; educated Eton; King's College, Cambridge. Married 1948, Shirley Rowntree, daughter of George James Harris, MC, of Bossall Hall, York (2 sons 1 daughter). *Armed Forces:* Served RNVR 1943–45; Ordinary Seaman, HMS Belfast 1943; Sub-Lieutenant, Motor Torpedo Boats and HM Destroyer Oribi 1944–45. *Career:* Foreign Office 1945; Served in Ankara, Tel Aviv, Rio de Janeiro, Washington and South Africa; Head of West African Department, Foreign Office 1968–73; Concurrently non-resident Ambassador to Chad 1970–73; Ambassador to: Hungary 1973–76, Portugal 1976–81; High Commissioner to Canada 1981–84. *House of Lords:* An elected hereditary peer 1999–. *Select Committees:* Member: Industry Sub-Committee of European Communities Committee 1984–86, Environmental Sub-Committee of European Communities Committee 1986–91, Sub-Committee of the Science and Technology Committee on the Scientific Base of the Nature Conservancy Council 1990, Agriculture Sub-Committee of European Communities Committee 1991–95, Sub-Committee of the Science and Technology Committee on Fish Stocks 1995, Sub-Committee on the 1996 Inter-Governmental Conference 1995–97; Co-opted Member, Select Committee on European Communities Sub-Committee D (Agriculture, Fisheries and Food) 1997–. *All-Party:* Chairman, All-Party Conservation Group of both Houses of Parliament. *Other:* Chairman, Wildlife and Countryside Link 1990–95; Council Member, RSPB 1992–94, Vice-President 1996–97; President, Welsh Salmon and Trout Angling Association 1988–95; Chairman, Salmon and Trout Association 1997–. *Trusts, etc:* Vice-Chairman, Atlantic Salmon Trust 1988–95; President, Radnorshire Wildlife Trust 1994–. *Miscellaneous:* Chairman, National Rivers Authority Regional Fisheries Advisory Committee for the Welsh Region 1989–94. *Honours:* CMG 1970; KCMG 1981; Grand Cross Order of the Infante, Portugal 1978. *Publications:* Author of: *C.B. – A Life of Sir Henry Campbell-Bannerman*, 1973 (Whitbread Award for Biography); *Fairfax*, 1985. *Recreations:* Fly-fishing, bird-watching. *Clubs:* Flyfishers' (President 1987–88). *Heir:* His son, Hon. James McMoran Wilson, born August 6, 1952. A Cross-Bencher. *Address:* The Lord Moran, KCMG, House of Lords, London, SW1A 0PW.

MORRIS OF CASTLEMORRIS (Life Baron, UK), Brian Robert Morris; cr. 1990

Son of late Capt. William Robert Morris and of Ellen Elizabeth Morris (née Shelley). Born December 4, 1930; educated Cardiff High School; Worcester College, Oxford (MA, DPhil); Hon. LittD, Sheffield 1991; Hon. LLD, Wales 1992. Married 1955, Sandra, daughter of late Percival Samuel James (1 son 1 daughter). *Trades Union:* Member, AUT 1954–91. *Armed Forces:* Served, Welch Regiment, National Service 1949–51; TA 1951–56. *Career:* Fellow, Shakespeare Institute, University of Birmingham 1956–58; Assistant Lecturer, Reading University 1958–60, Lecturer 1960–65; General Editor, New Mermaid Dramatists 1964–86; Lecturer, York University 1965–67, Senior Lecturer 1967–71; Member, Archbishops' Council on Evangelism 1971–75; Professor of English Literature, Sheffield University 1971–80; General Editor, New Arden Shakespeare 1974–82; Member, Museum and Galleries Commission 1975, Chairman 1985–90, Member, Yr Academi Gymreig 1979–; Council Member, Poetry Society 1980–90, Vice-President 1990–; Director, British Library Board 1980–91; Council Member, National Library of Wales 1981–91; Member: Welsh Arts Council 1983–86, Welsh Advisory Committee, British Council 1983–91; Vice-President, Council for National Parks 1985–; Member, Anthony Panizzi Foundation 1987–91; Broadcaster, scriptwriter and presenter of television programmes. *Whip:* Opposition Whip 1990–92; Deputy Opposition Chief Whip, House of Lords 1992–97. *Spokesman:* An Opposition Spokesman on: Home Office matters 1990–92, Citizen's Charter 1992–94, National Heritage 1992–96, Welsh Affairs 1992–97, Northern Ireland 1994–97, Principal Spokesman on: Education 1994–97, Education and Employment 1994–97; Former Front Bench Spokesman on: Arts and Heritage, Libraries, Broadcasting, Energy and Science. *Select Committees:* Member, Select Committees on: Liaison 1997–, Offices, Advisory Panel on Works of Art. *All-Party:* Member, All-Party Parliamentary: Hospice Group 1997–, Arts and Heritage Group 1997–, Adult Education Group 1997–, Universities Group 1997–. *Other:* Member, Council of Yorkshire Arts Association 1973–81; Vice-President, Museums Association 1985–88; Principal, St. David's University College, Lampeter and Pro-Vice-Chancellor of the University of Wales 1980–91; Chairman of Council, The Prince of Wales's Institute of Architecture 1993–97; President, Brontë Society 1996–; Vice-President: Prayer Book Society 1990–, The Arkwright Society 1992–; Director, Middleton Botanic Garden (now known as the Botanic Garden of Wales) 1994–97; Member, Advisory Board of the Botanic Garden of Wales 1997–. *Trusts, etc:* Trustee, National Portrait Gallery 1977–, Vice-Chairman of Trustees 1993–; Trustee, National Heritage Memorial Fund 1980–91; President, Welsh Historic Gardens Trust 1990–; Trustee: Museum of Empire and Commonwealth Trust 1991–, Campaign for the Protection of Rural Wales 1991–, National Heritage 1993–. Freeman, Fulton County, Georgia, USA. *Publications:* Author/editor of several books on poetry as well as plays, also contributor to journals. *Recreations:* Music, mountains, museums. *Clubs:* Athenaeum. *Name, Style and Title:* Raised to the peerage as Baron Morris of Castlemorris, of St. Dogmaels in the County of Dyfed 1990. Labour. *Address:* The Lord Morris of Castlemorris, The Old Hall, Foolow, Eyam, Hope Valley, Derbyshire, S32 5QR *Tel:* 01433 631186 *Fax:* 01433 631186.

MORRIS OF MANCHESTER (Life Baron, UK), Alfred Morris; cr. 1997; QSO 1989; AO 1991; PC 1979

Son of late George Henry Morris and late Jessie Morris (née Murphy). Born March 23, 1928; educated Manchester Elementary School; Matriculated by means of evening school tuition; Ruskin College, Oxford 1949–50; St Catherine's College, Oxford 1950–53 (MA); Department of Education, University of Manchester 1953–54 (DipEd); Hon. Fellow, Manchester Metropolitan University 1990; Hon. MA, University of Salford 1997; Hon. LLD, University of Manchester 1998. Married September 30, 1950, Irene, daughter of Abel and Esther Jones (2 sons 2 daughters). *Trades Union:* Member, GMB. *Armed Forces:* Served in the army, mainly in the Middle East 1946–48. *Career:* Manchester Schoolteacher and Lecturer 1954–56; Industrial Relations Officer, Electricity Supply Industry 1956–64. *House of Commons:* Contested Liverpool, Garston 1951 and Manchester Wythenshawe 1959; MP (Labour/Co-operative) for Manchester Wythenshawe 1964–97; PPS: to Minister of Agriculture, Fisheries and Food 1964–1967, to Leader of the House of Commons 1968–70; Parliamentary Under-Secretary of State, Department of Health and Social Security with special responsibility for the Disabled 1974–79; UK's first Minister for Disabled People; Promoted three Acts of Parliament as Private Member: Chronically Sick and Disabled Persons Act 1970,

Food and Drugs (Milk) Act 1970, Police Act 1972. *Spokesman (Commons):* Opposition Front Bench Spokesman on the Social Services 1970–74; Principal Opposition Front Bench Spokesman for the Disabled 1979–92. *Select Committees (Commons):* Member, Select Committee on Privileges 1994–97. *All-Party Committees (Commons):* Chairman, Parliamentary and Scientific Committee 1988–91. *International Bodies (Commons):* Treasurer, IPU British Group 1968–74; Joint-Treasurer, British-American Parliamentary Group 1983–97; Chairman, ANZAC Group of MPs and Peers 1972–97, President 1997. *International Bodies:* Member, Executive Committee, CPA UK Branch 1999–. *International Bodies (General):* British representative, UN advisory Council on the International Year of Disabled People; Chairman, World Planning Group appointed to draft *Charter for the 1980's* for disabled people world-wide; Life Patron, Rehabilitation International. *Party Groups (General):* Joined Labour Party 1944; Former National Chairman, Labour League of Youth; Chairman, Parliamentary Cooperative Group 1970–71, 1983–85; President, Co-operative Congress 1995–96. *Other:* Member, General Advisory Council, BBC 1968–74, 1983–97; Vice-President, Rehab UK 1995–; President: Society of Chiropodists and Pediatrists 1997; Haemophilia Society 1999–. *Awards Granted:* First-ever recipient, Field Marshal Lord Harding Award for outstanding services to disabled people 1971; Louis Braille Memorial Award of the National Federation of the Blind for distinguished services to blind people 1971; Paul Harris Fellow, Rotary International; Earl of Snowdon Award for expanding the rights of disabled people 1997; Automobile Association Award for work of immeasurable value to disabled road users 1998. *Trusts, etc:* Chairman, Managing Trustees, Parliamentary Contributory Pension Scheme and House of Commons Members' Fund 1983–97; Trustee of many charities for disabled people. *Honours:* PC 1979; Queen's Service Order (QSO) awarded by Government of New Zealand 1989; Order of Australia (AO) 1991. Hon. Associate, British Veterinary Association. *Publications: Human Relations in Industry,* 1963; *The Growth of Parliamentary Scrutiny by Committee,* 1971; *VAT: A Tax on the Consumer,* 1972; Contributor to numerous books on the problems and needs of disabled people. *Special Interests:* Disability, Co-operative Movement, Regional Development, Airport Policy, Science and Technology. *Recreations:* Tennis, gardening, chess, snooker. *Name, Style and Title:* Raised to the peeerage as Baron Morris of Manchester, of Manchester in the County of Greater Manchester 1997. Labour. *Address:* The Rt Hon. the Lord Morris of Manchester, AO, QSO, 20 Hitherwood Drive, London, SE19 1XB.

MOWBRAY (26th Baron, E), Charles Edward Stourton; cr. 1283; 27th Baron SEGRAVE (E) 1283; 23rd Baron STOURTON (E) 1448; CBE 1982

Son of 25th Baron, MC, Premier Baron of England. Born March 11, 1923. Succeeded his father 1965; educated Ampleforth; Christ Church, Oxford. Married 1st, June 28, 1952, Hon. Jane de Yarburgh-Bateson (died April 2, 1998), daughter of 5th Baron Deramore (2 sons); married 2nd, February 1999, Joan, Lady Holland, daughter of late Captain Herbert Edmund Street, 20th Hussars, and widow of Sir Guy Holland, 3rd Bt. *Armed Forces:* Served as Lieutenant, 2nd Armoured Battalion Grenadier Guards 1943–45; Wounded in France 1944; Invalided. *Councils, Public Bodies:* Councillor, Niddesdale RDC 1954–61. *Career:* Director, Securicor (Scotland) Ltd 1964–70; Chairman, Government Picture Buying Committee 1972–74; Director: EIRC Holdings Ltd (Jersey), EIRC (Ghana) Ltd, GDC (Ghana) Ltd 1980, EIRC Canada Inc. 1980–, Ghadeco (UK) Ltd 1986–; Chairman, Thames Estuary Airport Company Ltd 1993–; Member, Parliamentary Delegation to Bicentennial Celebrations in Washington DC. *House of Lords:* An elected hereditary peer 1999–. *Whip:* Opposition Whip in House of Lords 1967–70, 1974–78; Deputy Chief Opposition Whip in House of Lords 1978–79; A Lord in Waiting (Government Whip) 1970–74, 1979–80. *Spokesman:* Spokesman for Department of the Environment 1970–74; Spokesman for Departments of Environment and Transport and Arts 1979–80. *Select Committees:* Member, House of Lords Select Committee for Privileges 1992–97. *Other:* President, British Association Constantian Order of St George; Patron, Normandy Veterans Association Tayside and Mearns Branch; Chairman, British Legion – Brechin Branch. *Awards Granted:* Recipient, 1976 Bicentennial Year Award of Baronial Order of Magna Carta (USA). *Trusts, etc:* Trustee, College of Arms Trust 1975–. *Honours:* CBE 1982; Knight of Sovereign and Military Order of Malta; Bailiff Grand Cross of Justice – Constantian Order of St George. *Clubs:* Turf, White's, Pratt's. *Heir:* His son, Hon. Edward William Stephen Stourton, born April 17, 1953. A Conservative. *Address:* The Lord Mowbray and Stourton, CBE, 23 Warwick Square, London, SW1V 2AB; Marcus, By Forfar, Angus, DD8 3QH *Tel:* 01307 850219.

MOYNIHAN (4th Baron, UK), Colin Berkeley Moynihan; cr. 1929; 4th Bt of Carr Manor (UK) 1922

Son of 2nd Baron, OBE, TD. Born September 13, 1955. Succeeded his half-brother (who died in 1991) in 1997; educated Monmouth School (Music Scholar); University College, Oxford (BA, PPE 1977, MA 1982) (President of the Union). Married 1992, Gaynor-Louise, daughter of Paul Metcalf (2 sons 1 daughter). *Career:* Personal Assistant to Chairman, Tate and Lyle Ltd 1978–80; Manager, Tate and Lyle Agribusiness 1980–82; Chief Executive, Ridgways Tea and Coffee Merchants 1982–83, Chairman 1983–87; Chairman, CMA Consultants 1993–; Managing Director, Independent Power Corporation plc 1996–. *House of Commons:* MP (Conservative) for Lewisham East 1983–92; Chairman, Trade and Industry Standing Committee 1983–87; PPS: to Minister of Health 1985, to Paymaster-General 1985–87; Parliamentary Under-Secretary of State: at Department of Environment (Minister for Sport) 1987–90, at Department of Energy 1990–92. *Backbench Committees (Commons):* Secretary, Conservative Foreign and Commonwealth Affairs Committee 1983–85. *All-Party Committees (Commons):* Chairman, All-Party Parliamentary Group on Afghanistan 1986. *House of Lords:* An elected hereditary peer 1999–. *Spokesman:* Senior Opposition Spokesman on Foreign and Commonwealth Affairs 1997–. *Party Groups (General):* Member, The Bow Group 1978–92. *Other:* Governor, Sports Aid Foundation (London and South East) 1980–82. *Awards Granted:* Oxford Double Blue, Rowing and Boxing 1976 and 1977; World Gold Medal for Lightweight Rowing, International Rowing Federation 1978; Olympic Silver Medal for Rowing 1980; World Silver Medal for Rowing 1981. *Miscellaneous:* Member, Sports Council 1982–85; The succession to the barony was in dispute between 1991 and 1997, when the present baron was recognised as the lawful holder of the peerage by decision of the House of Lords. Freeman, City of London 1978. Liveryman, Worshipful Company of Haberdashers 1981. *Special Interests:* Foreign Affairs, Trade and Industry, Sport, Inner Cities, Refugees, Overseas Aid and Development. *Recreations:* Reading, sport, music. *Sportsclubs:* London Rowing, Leander Rowing. *Clubs:* Brooks's, Commonwealth Trust, Vincent's (Oxford). *Heir:* His son, Hon. Nicholas Ewan Berkeley Moynihan, born March 31, 1994. A Conservative. *Address:* The Lord Moynihan, House of Lords, London, SW1A 0PW *E-Mail:* cma@dircon.co.uk.

MOYOLA (Life Baron, UK), James Dawson Chichester-Clark; cr. 1971; PC (NI) 1966; DL

Son of late Captain James Jackson Chichester-Clark, DSO, RN. Born February 12, 1923; educated Eton. Married March 14, 1959, Mrs Moyra Maud Haughton, daughter of late Brigadier Arthur De Burgh Morris, CBE, DSO (1 stepson 2 daughters). *Armed Forces:* Served Irish Guards 1942–60; Wounded Anzio 1944; ADC to Governor-General of Canada 1947–49; Staff College, Camberley 1956; Retired from Irish Guards as Major 1960. *Councils, Public Bodies:* DL, Co Londonderry 1954. *Career:* MP (UU) for South Londonderry, Northern Ireland Parliament 1960; Assistant Whip 1963; Chief Whip 1963–66; Leader of House and Chief Whip 1966–67; Minister of Agriculture 1967–69; Prime Minister of Northern Ireland 1969–71. *Honours:* PC (NI) 1966. *Special Interests:* Agriculture, Northern Ireland. *Recreations:* Fishing, gardening, dendrology, shooting. *Name, Style and Title:* Raised to the peerage as Baron Moyola, of Castledawson in the County of Londonderry 1971. A Conservative. *Address:* The Rt Hon. the Lord Moyola, DL, Moyola Park, Castledawson, Co. Londonderry, BT45 8ED.

MURRAY OF EPPING FOREST (Life Baron, UK), Lionel Murray; cr. 1985; PC 1976; OBE 1966

Born August 2, 1922; educated State Schools; Queen Mary College, University of London; New College, Oxford; Hon. Fellow, New College, Oxford 1975; Hon. DSc: Aston 1977, Salford 1978; Hon. LLD, St Andrews 1979; Hon. Fellow, Sheffield 1979; Hon. LLD, Leeds 1985; Hon. Fellow, Queen Mary and Westfield College, London 1992. Married September 22, 1945, Heather Woolf (2 sons 2 daughters). *Armed Forces:* Wartime service with King's Shropshire Light Infantry. *Career:* TUC 1947–84, General Secretary 1973–84. *Other:* Vice-Chairman, NCH Action for Children; President, Friends of Epping Forest; Vice-President: Wesley's Chapel, National Youth Theatre; Patron, St Clare's Hospice. *Trusts, etc:* President, Friends of Ironbridge Museum Trust: Trustee: NUMAST, ADAPT; Patron, Winged Fellowship Trust. *Honours:* OBE 1966; PC 1976. *Special Interests:* Children, Homeless, Disability. *Recreations:* Theatre, music, looking at Epping Forest. *Name, Style and Title:* Raised to the peerage as Baron Murray of Epping Forest, of Telford in the County of Shropshire 1985. Labour. *Address:* The Rt Hon. the Lord Murray of Epping Forest, OBE, 29 The Crescent, Loughton, Essex, IG10 4PY *Tel:* Home: 020 8508 4425.

MURTON OF LINDISFARNE (Life Baron, UK), (Henry) Oscar Murton; cr. 1979; PC 1976; OBE (Mil) 1946; TD 1947 (and Clasp 1951)

Son of late H. E. C. Murton, of Hexham, Northumberland. Born May 8, 1914; educated Uppingham. Married 1st, May 1939, Constance Frances (died 1977), eldest daughter of late F. O. Connell, of Low Fell, Co. Durham (1 son and 1 daughter deceased 1986), married 2nd, April 1979, Pauline Teresa, youngest daughter of late Thomas Keenan, JP, of Johannesburg. *Armed Forces:* Commissioned TA 1934 in Royal Northumberland Fusiliers; Army Staff College, Camberley 1939, tsc; General Staff 1939–46; A Lieutenant-Colonel. *Councils, Public Bodies:* Councillor, Poole Borough Council 1961–64; Member, Herrison (Dorchester) Hospital Management Committee until 1974; JP, Borough of Poole 1963, latterly Supplemental List Inner London. *Career:* Managing Director, Private Limited Company with Department Stores NE England 1949–57. *House of Commons:* MP (Conservative) for Poole 1964–79; Introduced Highways (Amendment) Act 1965, PPS to Minister of Local Government and Development 1970–71; Deputy Chairman, Ways and Means 1973–76; Chairman, Ways and Means and the Deputy Speaker House of Commons 1976–79. *Whip (Commons):* Assistant Government Whip 1971; Lord Commissioner, Treasury 1972–73. *Select Committees (Commons):* Member, Panel of Chairmen of Standing Committees 1970–71. *Backbench Committees (Commons):* Secretary and later Vice-Chairman, Conservative Parliamentary Committee Housing Local Government and Land 1964–70; Chairman, Conservative Parliamentary Committee Public Building and Works 1970. *House of Lords:* A Deputy Chairman of Committees House of Lords 1981–; A Deputy Speaker since 1983; Introduced Access to Neighbouring Land Act 1992. *Select Committees:* Member, Joint Select Committee of Lords and Commons on Private Bill Procedure 1987–88. *All-Party:* Member, All-Party Defence Study Group. *Party Groups (General):* President, Poole Conservative Association 1983–95. *Other:* Chancellor, Primrose League 1983–88. *Honours:* OBE (Mil) 1946; PC 1976. Freeman, City of London. Freeman, Wax Chandlers Company; Past-Master, Clockmakers Company. *Special Interests:* Defence. *Recreations:* Sailing, painting. *Name, Style and Title:* Raised to the peerage as Baron Murton of Lindisfarne, of Hexham in the County of Northumberland 1979. A Conservative. *Address:* The Rt Hon. the Lord Murton of Lindisfarne, OBE, TD, 49 Carlisle Mansions, Carlisle Place, London, SW1P 1HY *Tel:* 020 7834 8226.

MUSTILL (Life Baron, UK), Michael John Mustill; cr. 1992; PC 1985; Kt 1978

Son of late Clement William and Marion Mustill. Born May 10, 1931; educated Oundle; St John's College, Cambridge (LLD 1992). Married 1st, 1960, Beryl Davies (marriage dissolved 1983), married 2nd, 1991, Mrs Caroline Phillips (2 sons 1 step-daughter). *Armed Forces:* Served Royal Artillery 1949–51. *Career:* Called to the Bar, Gray's Inn 1955; Bencher 1976; QC 1968; Deputy Chairman, Hampshire Quarter Sessions 1971; Chairman, Civil Service Appeal Tribunal 1971–78; A Recorder of the Crown Court 1972–78; Judge of the High Court, Queen's Bench Division 1978–85; Presiding Judge, NE Circuit 1981–84; Chairman: Judicial Studies Board 1985–89, Departmental Committee on Law of

Arbitration 1985–90; A Lord Justice of Appeal 1985–92; A Lord of Appeal in Ordinary 1992–97. *Select Committees:* Member, House of Lords Select Committee on Medical Ethics 1993–. *Honours:* Kt 1978; PC 1985. FBA. *Publications:* Author of several legal works as well as articles in legal journals. *Name, Style and Title:* Raised to the peerage as Baron Mustill, of Pateley Bridge in the County of North Yorkshire 1992. A Cross-Bencher. *Address:* The Rt Hon. the Lord Mustill, Essex Court Chambers, 24 Lincoln's Inn Fields, London, WC2A 3ED.

N

NASEBY (Life Baron, UK), Michael Wolfgang Laurence Morris; cr. 1997; PC 1994

Son of late C. L. Morris, FRIBA. Born November 25, 1936; educated Bedford School; St Catharine's College, Cambridge (MA 1960). Married September 3, 1960, Ann, daughter of late Percy Appleby (2 sons 1 daughter). *Armed Forces:* National Service Pilot (RAF and NATO wings). *Councils, Public Bodies:* London Borough of Islington: Councillor 1968–74, Leader 1969–71, Alderman 1971–74. *Career:* Marketing Manager, Reckitt and Colman Group 1960–64; Director: Service Advertising 1964–71, Benton & Bowles Ltd 1971–81. *House of Commons:* Contested Islington North 1966; MP (Conservative) for Northampton South 1974–97; PPS to Minister of State, Northern Ireland 1979–81; Chairman, Ways and Means and Deputy Speaker 1992–97. *Select Committees (Commons):* Member, Select Committees on: Public Accounts 1979–92, Energy 1982–85, Speakers Panel of Chairmen 1985–92. *Backbench Committees (Commons):* Secretary, Conservative Environment Committee 1978–79; Vice-Chairman, Conservative Energy Committee 1981–92; Joint Founder with late Lord Ennals of Parliamentary Food and Health Committee. *All-Party Committees (Commons):* Former Chairman, Committees on: British-Sri Lanka, British-Malaysia, British-Singapore, British-Burma; Former Vice-Chairman, British Indonesia Committee; Former Treasurer, British Thai and ASEAN Committee. *All-Party:* Joint Chairman, All-Party Sri Lanka Country Group 1999–. *International Bodies (General):* Member, Council of Europe and Western European Union 1983–91. *Other:* Chairman, Progressive Supranuclear Palsy Charity; Chairman of Governors, Bedford School. *Trusts, etc:* Chairman, Northamptonshire Victoria County History Trust. *Honours:* PC 1994. *Publications: Helping The Exporter,* 1967; *Marketing Below The Line* (joint author), 1970; *The Disaster of Direct Labour,* 1978. *Special Interests:* Energy, Health Service, Food and Nutrition, Exports, South East Asia, Marketing, Parliamentary Procedure, National Lottery. *Recreations:* Golf (Past Captain Parliamentary Golfing Society), cricket, tennis, shooting, forestry, budgerigars. *Sportsclubs:* John O'Gaunt Golf, Port Stanley Golf, All England Lawn Tennis, Royal St George's Golf, Lords Taverners, Northamptonshire County Cricket (Committee). *Clubs:* Carlton, Northampton Town and Country, MCC. *Name, Style and Title:* Raised to the peerage as Baron Naseby, of Sandy in the County of Bedfordshire 1997. A Conservative. *Address:* The Rt Hon. the Lord Naseby, Caesar's Camp, Sandy, Bedfordshire, SG19 2AD.

NEILL OF BLADEN (Life Baron, UK), Francis Patrick Neill; cr. 1997; Kt 1983; QC 1966

Son of late Sir Thomas Neill, JP, and late Lady (Annie) Neill. Born August 8, 1926; educated Highgate School; Magdalen College, Oxford (BA, MA); All Souls College, Oxford (BCL); Hon. LLD, Hull 1978; Hon. DCL, Oxford 1987; Hon. Fellow, Magdalen College, Oxford 1988; Hon. LLD, Buckingham 1994; Hon. Fellow, All Souls College 1995. Married 1954, Caroline Susan, daughter of late Sir Piers Debenham, 2nd Bt (4 sons 2 daughters). *Armed Forces:* Served Rifle Brigade 1944–47 (Captain); GSO III (Training) British Troops, Egypt 1947. *Career:* Fellow, All Souls, Oxford 1950–77, Sub-Warden 1972–74, Warden 1977–95; Called to the Bar, Gray's Inn 1951, QC 1966, Bencher 1971, Vice-Treasurer 1989, Treasurer 1990; Lecturer in Air Law, LSE 1955–58; Member, Bar Council 1967–71, Vice-Chairman 1973–74, Chairman 1974–75; Chairman, Senate of the Inns of Court and the Bar 1974–75; A Recorder of the Crown Court 1975–78; A Judge of the Courts of Appeal of Jersey and Guernsey 1977–94; Chairman: Press Council 1978–83, Council for the Securities Industry 1978–85; Chairman, Justice – All Souls Committee for Review of Administrative Law 1978–87; Hon. Professor of Legal Ethics, Birmingham University 1983–84; Vice-Chancellor, Oxford University 1985–89;

Chairman, DTI Committee of Inquiry into Regulatory Arrangements at Lloyd's 1986–87; Vice-Chairman, Committee of Vice-Chancellors and Principals of the Universities of the United Kingdom 1987–90; Independent National Director, Times Newspaper Holdings 1988–97; Chairman: Feltrum Loss Review Committee at Lloyd's 1991–92, Committee on Standards in Public Life 1997–; Visitor, Buckingham University 1997–. *Honours:* Kt 1983. *Publications: Administrative Justice: some necessary reforms,* 1988. *Recreations:* Music, forestry. *Clubs:* Athenaeum, Garrick, Beefsteak. *Name, Style and Title:* Raised to the peerage as Baron Neill of Bladen, of Briantspuddle in the County of Dorset 1997. A Cross-Bencher. *Address:* The Lord Neill of Bladen, QC, 1 Hare Court, Temple, London, EC4Y 7BE.

NEWBY (Life Baron, UK), Richard Mark Newby; cr 1997; OBE 1990

Son of Frank and Kathleen Newby. Born February 14, 1953; educated Rothwell Grammar School; St Catherine's College, Oxford (MA). Married 1978, Ailsa Ballantyne Thomson (2 sons). *Career:* HM Customs and Excise: Administration Trainee 1974; Private Secretary to Permanent Secretary 1977–79; Principal, Planning Unit 1979–81; Secretary, SDP Parliamentary Committee 1981; Joined SDP Headquarters staff 1981; National Secretary, SDP 1983–88, Executive 1988–90; Director, Corporate Affairs, Rosehaugh plc 1991; Director, Matrix Communications Consultancy Ltd 1992–; Chair: Reform Publications Ltd 1993–, Centre for Reform Management Committee; Director, Flagship Group Ltd 1999–; Chief of Staff to Charles Kennedy, MP 1999–. *Spokesman:* A Liberal Democrat Spokesman for: Trade and Industry 1998–, The Treasury 1998–. *Select Committees:* Member, Select Committee on Monetary Policy of the Bank of England 1998–. *Party Groups (General):* Deputy Chairman, Liberal Democrat General Election Team 1995–97. *Trusts, etc:* Trustee, Allachy Trust. *Honours:* OBE 1990. *Recreations:* Football. *Clubs:* Reform, MCC. *Name, Style and Title:* Raised to the peerage as Baron Newby, of Rothwell in the County of West Yorkshire 1997. A Liberal Democrat. *Address:* The Lord Newby, OBE, 4 Rockwells Gardens, Dulwich Wood Park, London, SE19 1HW *Tel:* 020 8244 5675.

NEWTON OF BRAINTREE (Life Baron, UK), Antony Harold Newton; cr. 1997; OBE 1972; PC 1988

Son of late Harold Newton. Born August 29, 1937; educated Friend's School, Saffron Walden; Trinity College, Oxford. Married 1st, August 25, 1962, Janet, daughter of Philip Huxley (2 daughters) (marriage dissolved 1986), married 2nd, September 26, 1986, Patricia, widow of John Gilthorpe (1 step-son 2 step-daughters). *Career:* President, Oxford Union Society 1959; Debating tour in US 1960; Conservative Research Department 1961–74; Head, Economic Section 1965–70; Assistant Director 1970–74. *House of Commons:* Contested Sheffield Brightside 1970; MP (Conservative) for Braintree 1974–97; Parliamentary Under-Secretary of State, Department of Health and Social Security 1982–84; Minister for the Disabled 1983; Minister of State for Social Security and the Disabled 1983–86; Minister for Health 1986–88; Chancellor of the Duchy of Lancaster (Minister of Trade and Industry) 1988–89; Secretary of State for Social Security 1989–92; Lord President of the Council and Leader of the House of Commons 1992–97. *Whip (Commons):* Assistant Government Whip 1979–81; Lord Commissioner of the Treasury 1981–82. *Select Committees (Commons):* Chairman, Select Committee on Broadcasting 1992–97; Member: Select Committee on Finance and Services 1992–97, Public Accounts Commission 1992–97, House of Commons Commission 1992–97; Chairman, Select Committees on: Privileges 1994–95, Standards and Privileges 1995–97. *Backbench Committees (Commons):* Secretary, Conservative Health and Social Services Committee 1977–79. *Party Groups (General):* President, Oxford University Conservative Association 1958; Secretary, Bow Group 1962–64. *Honours:* OBE 1972; PC 1988. *Special Interests:* Tax, Social Security, Pensions, Disability, Health, Social Services. *Name, Style and Title:* Raised to the peerage as Baron Newton of Braintree, of Coggeshall in the County of Essex 1997. A Conservative. *Address:* The Rt Hon. the Lord Newton of Braintree, OBE, House of Lords, London, SW1A 0PW.

NICHOLLS OF BIRKENHEAD (Life Baron, UK), Donald James Nicholls; cr. 1994; Kt 1983; PC 1986

Son of late William Greenhow Nicholls. Born January 25, 1933; educated Birkenhead School; Liverpool University (LLB 1st class hons); Trinity Hall, Cambridge (BA 1st class hons, with distinction, part II Law Tripos, LLB 1st class hons with distinction); Hon. Fellow, Trinity Hall, Cambridge 1986; Hon. LLD, Liverpool University 1987. Married 1960, Jennifer Mary, daughter of late W. E. C. Thomas, MB, BCh, MRCOG, JP (2 sons 1 daughter). *Career:* Called to the Bar, Middle Temple 1958; Bencher 1981, Treasurer 1997; In practice, Chancery Bar 1958–83; QC 1974; Judge of the High Court of Justice, Chancery Division 1983–86; A Lord Justice of Appeal 1986–91; Vice-Chancellor of the Supreme Court 1991–94; A Lord of Appeal in Ordinary 1994–; Member, Senate of Inns of Court and the Bar 1974–76; Chairman, Lord Chancellor's Advisory Committee on Legal Education and Conduct 1996–97. *Select Committees:* Chairman, Select Committee on Parliamentary Privilege (Joint Committee) 1997–99. *Other:* President, Birkenhead School 1986–. *Honours:* Kt 1983; PC 1986. *Recreations:* Walking, history, music. *Clubs:* Athenaeum (Trustee). *Name, Style and Title:* Raised to the peerage as Baron Nicholls of Birkenhead, of Stoke D'Abernon in the County of Surrey 1994. A Cross-Bencher. *Address:* The Rt Hon. the Lord Nicholls of Birkenhead, House of Lords, London, SW1A 0PW.

NICHOLSON OF WINTERBOURNE (Life Baroness, UK), Emma Harriet Nicholson; cr. 1997

Daughter of late Sir Godfrey Nicholson, 1st and last Bt and late Lady Katharine Lindsay, daughter of 27th Earl of Crawford, KT, PC. Born October 16, 1941; educated Portsdown Lodge School, Bexhill; St Mary's, Wantage; The Royal Academy of Music (LRAM, ARCM); Hon. Doctorate, University of North London. Married May 9, 1987, Sir Michael Harris Caine (died March 20, 1999), son of late Sir Sidney Caine, KCMG (2 step-children and 1 ward/foster son). *Career:* Computer Software Developer, Teacher and Systems Engineer, ICL 1961–64; Computer Consultant, John Tyzack and Partners 1967–69; General Management and Computer Consultant, McLintock Mann and Whinney Murray 1969–74; Joined the Save the Children Fund 1974, Director of Fundraising 1977–85; Director, Nicholson Productions Ltd; Visiting Fellow, St Antony's College, Oxford 1995–96, Senior Associate Member 1997–98, 1998–99; Elected a Liberal Democrat MEP for the South East Region 1999–. *House of Commons:* Contested Blyth 1979: MP for Devon West and Torridge 1987–97; Resigned from the Conservative Party December 1995 and joined the Liberal Democrats; PPS to Michael Jack, MP, as Minister of State: at Home Office 1992–93, at Ministry of Agriculture, Fisheries and Food 1993–95, at The Treasury 1995. *Spokesman (Commons):* Liberal Democrat Spokesman on Overseas Development and Human Rights 1996–97. *Select Committees (Commons):* Member, Select Committee on Employment 1990–91. *Backbench Committees (Commons):* Secretary, then Chairman, Conservative Party Environment Committee 1990–91. *All-Party Committees (Commons):* Former Chairman, All-Party Parliamentary Groups on: Kuwait, Iraq, Oman; Former Deputy Chairman, All-Party Anglo-Iranian Group; Former Treasurer: British Caribbean All-Party Group, All-Party Group for Saudi Arabia, All-Party Group for Romanian Children; Former Secretary, All-Party Syria and Jordan Group; Former Member, All-Party Lebanon Group; Former Vice-Chairman, The European Movement. *Party Groups (Commons):* Former Treasurer, Positive European Group (Conservative). *Spokesman:* Member, Liberal Democrat Foreign Affairs Team; Front Bench Spokesperson on Data Protection 1998. *International Bodies (General):* Treasurer, Positive European Group; Alternate Member, UK Delegation to WEU and Council of Europe 1990–92; Former Member, European Union of Women; Official Observer, Commonwealth Secretariat team for Zambian General Election 1991. *Party Groups (General):* Vice-Chairman, Conservative Party with special responsibility for women 1983–87; Member, Liberal Democrat Parliamentary Foreign Affairs Team 1996. *Other:* Vice-Moderator, Movement for Ordination of Women 1991–93; Member, Executive Board of Medical Research Council 1991–94; Former Director, Shelter; Chairman: The Amar Appeal, The Iraqi Humanitarian Relief Committee, Blind in Business, The AMAR International Charitable Foundation; President: Hatherleigh and District Save the Children, Devon Help the Aged Committee, The Chartered Society of Psychotherapy (Devon), Plymouth and West Devon Talking Cassette Newspapers; Board Member, HOST (Hosting for Overseas Students); Vice-President: The National Association for Maternal and Child Welfare, The Association of District Councils,

The Small Farmers' Association, The Duke of Edinburgh's Award (Devon), LEPRA, Mary Hare Grammar School for the Deaf, The Little Foundation; Governor, Queen's College, Taunton; Patron: The International Committee for a Free Iraq, Orphan Aid to Romania, The British Deaf Accord, The National Deaf, Blind and Rubella Association, Womens' Engineering Society, Womens' Business Association, Sauvez Les Enfants (France), AMANA (Society to Promote Study of Islam), Opera South West, Cities in Schools; Vice-Patron: The Child Psychotherapy Trust, The Missing Persons Helpline; Member: The Council of Arab-British Understanding, The Royal Association in Aid of Deaf People 150th Appeal Committee, The Editorial Panel of 300 Group, The Royal Academy of Music Appeal Committee, Officer of a great many other organisations; Council Member: The Hansard Society, PITCOM; Co-Chairman, UNA Advisory Group UNESCO, International Year of the Disabled, Chairman, UNA 1998–. *Trusts, etc:* Trustee: The Covent Garden Cancer Research Trust, The Little Foundation, The Motor Neurone Disease Association; Trustee and Vice-Patron, ADAPT (Access for Disabled People to Arts Premises Today); Member: The Prince of Wales Advisory Trust on Disability, Manningford Trust; Fellow: Industry and Parliament Trust, Federal Trust for Education and Research; Chairman, Emily Trust Appeal Committee 1993–95. *Miscellaneous:* Member: European Standing Committee A, Standing Committee on Statutory Instruments; Liberal Democrat Prospective European Parliament Candidate for the South-East Region 1999. LRAM; ARCM; FRSA. Freeman, Worshipful Company of Information Technologists. *Publications: Why Does the West Forget?*, 1993; *Secret Society – Inside and Outside the Conservative Party*, 1996; as well as various articles and pamphlets. *Special Interests:* European Union, Information Technology, Human Rights, Education, Health, Foreign Affairs, Intellectual Property, Farming, Defence, Iraq, Iran, Kuwait, Islamic World, Children, Refugees/Displaced People, Freedom of Information. *Recreations:* Music, chess, walking, reading. *Clubs:* Reform, The National Liberal Club. *Name, Style and Title:* Raised to the peerage as Baroness Nicholson of Winterbourne, of Winterbourne in the Royal County of Berkshire 1997. A Liberal Democrat. *Address:* The Baroness Nicholson of Winterbourne, MEP, House of Lords, London, SW1A 0PW.

NICKSON (Life Baron, UK), David Wigley Nickson; cr. 1994; KBE 1987

Son of late Geoffrey Wigley Nickson and of late Janet Mary Dobie. Born November 27, 1929; educated Eton; RMA, Sandhurst; DUniversity: Stirling University 1986, Napier University 1991, Paisley University 1992; Hon. Dr., Glasgow Caledonian University 1993. Married 1952, Helen Louise Cockcraft (3 daughters). *Armed Forces:* Commissioned Coldstream Guards 1949–54. *Councils, Public Bodies:* DL, Stirling and Falkirk 1982–97, Vice-Lieutenant 1997–. *Career:* Joined William Collins Sons & Co. Ltd publishers 1954, Director 1961–85, Joint Managing Director 1967, Vice-Chairman 1976–83, Group Managing Director 1979–82; Director, Scottish United Investors plc 1970–83; Director, General Accident Fire and Life Assurance Corporation plc 1971–98, Deputy Chairman 1993–98; Member, Scottish Committee, Design Council 1978–81; Chairman, CBI in Scotland 1979–81; Member, Scottish Economic Council 1980–95; Director, Clydesdale Bank plc 1981–89, 1990–98, Deputy Chairman 1990–91, Chairman 1991–98; Director, Scottish & Newcastle Breweries plc 1981–95, Deputy Chairman 1982–83, Chairman 1983–89; Chairman, Pan Books Ltd 1982; Director, Radio Clyde plc 1982–85; Chairman, Countryside Commission for Scotland 1983–85; Director, Edinburgh Investment Trust plc 1983–94; Member, NEDC 1985–88; President, CBI 1986–88; Director, Hambro's plc 1989–98; Chairman, Senior Salaries Review Body 1989–95; Director, National Australia Bank Ltd 1991–96. *Chancellor:* Chancellor, Glasgow Caledonian University 1993–. *Other:* Vice-Chairman, Association of Scottish District Salmon Fishery Boards 1989–92, President 1996–; Chairman, Scottish Advisory Committee, Imperial Cancer Research Fund 1994–, Life Governor. *Trusts, etc:* Atlantic Salmon Trust: Member, Council of Management 1982–, Chairman 1989–95, Vice-President 1995–; Trustee: Prince's Youth Business Trust 1987–90, Game Conservancy 1988–91, Princess Royal's Trust for Carers 1990–94. *Miscellaneous:* Brigadier, Queen's Body Guard for Scotland, The Royal Company of Archers; Chairman, Secretary of State for Scotland's Scottish Salmon Strategy Task Force 1996–; Independent Adviser, Secretary of State for Scotland's Appointments Committee 1996–99. *Honours:* CBE 1981; KBE 1987. CIMgt; FRSE 1987. Freeman, City of London. Hon. Freeman, Fishmongers' Company 1999–. *Recreations:* Fishing, shooting, birdwatching. *Clubs:* Boodle's, MCC, Flyfishers'. *Name, Style and Title:* Raised to the peerage as Baron Nickson, of Renagour in the District of Stirling 1994. A Cross-Bencher. *Address:* The Lord Nickson, KBE, House of Lords, London, SW1A 0PW.

NICOL (Life Baroness, UK), Olive Mary Wendy Nicol; cr. 1982

Daughter of late James and Harriet Rowe-Hunter. Born March 21, 1923; edu-
cated Cahir School, Ireland. Married December 18, 1947, Alexander Douglas
Ian, CBE, son of late Alexander Nicol (2 sons 1 daughter). *Councils, Public
Bodies:* JP, Cambridge Bench 1972–86; Cambridge City Council 1972–82,
Deputy Mayor 1974, Chairman, Environment Committee 1978–82. *Career:*
Inland Revenue 1942–44; Admiralty 1944–48; United Charities 1967–86;
Supplementary Benefits Tribunal 1976–78; Co-operative Board 1976–85,
President 1981–85 Careers Service Consultative Panel 1978–81. *House of
Lords:* Member, Opposition Front Bench Environment Team with responsibil-
ity for Green issues 1983–92; A Deputy Speaker, House of Lords 1995–; A
Deputy Chairman of Committees 1997–. *Whip:* Opposition Whip 1983–87; Opposition Deputy Chief
Whip 1987–89. *Spokesman:* Opposition Spokesman on Energy 1988–89. *Select Committees:* Member,
Select Committees on: European Communities 1986–91, Science and Technology 1990–93, Environment
and Social Affairs Sub-Committee of EC Committee 1993–95, Sustainable Development 1994–95;
Member, Ecclesiastical Committee 1990–96; Member, Select Committees on: House of Lords' Offices
1997–, Offices Library and Computers Sub-Committee, Science and Technology Sub-Committee on
Management of Nuclear Waste 1998–99. *All-Party:* Chairman, All-Party Retail Group; Vice-Chair, All-
Party: Conservation Group, Parliamentary Environment Group; Vice-President, All-Party Arts and
Heritage Group; Member, All-Party: Forestry Group, Water Group, Skin Group, Animal Welfare Group,
Food and Health Group, Norwegian Group. *Party Groups:* Member, Labour Party Departmental
Committees for: Agriculture, Environment. *Party Groups (General):* Member of the Co-operative Party.
Other: Various School Governing Bodies and other public service areas, including Granta Housing
Association; Council Member, RSPB 1989–94; Vice-President: Marine Conservation Society, War
Widows' Association, RSPB, Council for National Parks. *Miscellaneous:* Member, Lord Chancellors
Advisory Committee 1982–88; Vice-President: Council for National Parks 1995–, Association of
Municipal Authorities, Association of District Councils; Board Member, Parliamentary Office of Science
and Technology (POST) 1998–. FRGS 1990. *Special Interests:* Commerce, Conservation, Environment,
Energy, Forestry. *Recreations:* Reading, walking, gardening. *Name, Style and Title:* Raised to the peerage
as Baroness Nicol, of Newnham in the County of Cambridge 1982. Labour. *Address:* The Baroness Nicol,
39 Granchester Road, Newnham, Cambridge, CB3 9ED *Tel:* 01223 323733; House of Lords, London,
SW1A 0PW *Tel:* House of Lords 020 7219 6705.

NOLAN (Life Baron, UK), Michael Patrick Nolan; cr. 1994; Kt 1982; PC 1991

Son of James Thomas Nolan. Born September 10, 1928; educated Ampleforth;
Wadham College, Oxford; Hon. Fellow, Wadham College, Oxford 1992; DU:
Essex University 1995, Surrey University 1995; Hon. LLD: Buckingham
University 1998, Exeter University 1998. Married 1953, Margaret, daughter of
Alfred Noyes, CBE (1 son 4 daughters). *Armed Forces:* Served Royal Artillery
1947–49; TA 1949–55. *Career:* Called to the Bar, Middle Temple 1953;
Bencher 1975; QC 1968; Member, Bar Council 1973–74; Member, Sandilands
Committee on Inflation Accounting 1973–75; Called to the Bar, Northern
Ireland 1974; QC (Northern Ireland) 1974; Member, Senate of Inns of Court
and Bar 1974–81, Treasurer 1977–79; A Recorder of the Crown Court
1975–82; Judge, High Court of Justice, Queen's Bench Division 1982–91; Presiding Judge, Western
Circuit 1985–88; A Lord Justice of Appeal 1991–94; A Lord of Appeal in Ordinary 1994–98; Chairman,
Committee on Standards in Public Life 1994–97. *Chancellor:* Chancellor, Essex University 1997–.
Other: Member, Governing Body, Convent of the Sacred Heart, Woldingham 1973–83; Chairman,
Board of Institute of Advanced Legal Studies 1994–. *Honours:* Kt 1982; PC 1991. *Clubs:* Army and
Navy, MCC, Boodle's. *Name, Style and Title:* Raised to the peerage as Baron Nolan, of Brasted in the
County of Kent 1994. A Cross-Bencher. *Address:* The Rt Hon. the Lord Nolan, House of Lords, London,
SW1A 0PW.

NORFOLK (17th Duke of, E), Miles Francis Stapleton Fitzalan-Howard; cr. 1483; Earl of Arundel (E) 1139/1289; Earl of Surrey (E) 1483; Earl of Norfolk (E) 1644; Baron Beaumont (E) 1309; Baron Maltravers (E) 1330; Baron FitzAlan, Clun, and Oswaldestre (E) 1627; Baron Howard of Glossop (UK) 1869; KG 1983; GCVO 1986; CB (Mil) 1966; CBE (Mil) 1960; MC 1944; DL

Son of 3rd Baron Howard of Glossop, MBE, great grandson of 13th Duke, KG, and Mona Josephine Tempest, OBE, Baroness Beaumont (11th in line). Born July 21, 1915. Succeeded his mother 1971, his father 1972 and his cousin to the dukedom in 1975; educated Ampleforth; Christ Church, Oxford (MA); Hon. Fellow, St Edmund's College, Cambridge 1983–. Married July 4, 1949, Anne Mary Theresa, CBE, daughter of late Wing Commander Gerald Constable-Maxwell, MC, DFC, AFC (2 sons 3 daughters). *Armed Forces:* 2nd Lieutenant, Grenadier Guards 1937; Served War of 1939–45 France, North Africa, Sicily, Italy (despatches, MC), NW Europe; Appointed Head, British Military Mission to Russian Forces in Germany 1957; Commanded 70 Brigade KAR 1961–63; GOC, 1 Division 1963–65, Major-General; Director: Management and Support Intelligence MoD 1965–66, Service Intelligence MoD 1966–67; Retired 1967. *Councils, Public Bodies:* DL, West Sussex, 1977. *Career:* Chairman, Arundel Castle Trustees Ltd; Former Director, Robert Fleming Holdings Ltd. *Other:* President, Building Societies Association 1982–86. *Miscellaneous:* Earl Marshal and Hereditary Marshal and Chief Butler of England; Premier Duke and Earl of England. *Honours:* CBE (Mil) 1960; CB 1966; Knight of the Sovereign Order of Malta; Knight Grand Cross of the Order of Pius IX 1977; KG 1983; Hon. Student, Christ Church, Oxford 1983–; Hon. Bencher, Inner Temple 1984; GCVO 1986. Prime Warden, Fishmongers' Livery Co. 1985–86. *Heir:* His son, Earl of Arundel and Surrey, born December 2, 1956. A Conservative. *Address:* Major-General His Grace the Duke of Norfolk, KG, GCVO, CB, CBE, MC, DL, Arundel Castle, Arundel, West Sussex, BN18 9AB; Carlton Towers, Goole, Yorkshire, DN14 9LZ; Bacres House, Hambleden, Henley-on-Thames, Oxfordshire, RG9 6RY; 61 Clabon Mews, London, SW1X 0EQ *Tel:* 020 7584 3430.

NORTHBOURNE (5th Baron, UK), Christopher George Walter James; cr. 1884; 6th Bt of Langley Hall (GB) 1791; DL

Son of 4th Baron. Born February 18, 1926. Succeeded his father 1982; educated Eton; Magdalen College, Oxford (MA). Married 1959, Marie Sygne, daughter of Henri Claudel, of Chatou-sur-Seine, France (3 sons 1 daughter). *Councils, Public Bodies:* DL Kent 1996–. *Career:* Farmer and Businessman in the UK and Overseas; Chairman, Betteshanger Farms Ltd. *House of Lords:* An elected hereditary peer 1999–. *Spokesman:* Independent Spokesman on Education and Children especially disadvantaged and excluded children. *Select Committees:* Former Member, Select Committee on European Communities Sub-Committees C and D. *All-Party:* Member: All-Party Parliamentary Group for Children, All-Party Parliamentary Group on Parenting, All-Party Rural Group. *International Bodies:* Member, Anglo French Parliamentary Group. *Other:* Deputy Chairman, Toynbee Hall; Chairman: Parenting Support Forum, Stepney Childrens Fund; Governor, Wye College. *Trusts, etc:* Trustee, Caldecott Community/Toynbee Hall. FRICS. *Special Interests:* Agriculture, Horticulture, Education, Disadvantaged and Excluded Children, Family. *Recreations:* Painting, sailing, gardening. *Clubs:* Brooks's, Royal Yacht Squadron (Cowes), House of Lords Yacht Club. *Heir:* His son, Hon. Charles Walter Henri James, born June 14, 1960. A Cross-Bencher. *Address:* The Lord Northbourne, DL, 11 Eaton Place, London, SW1X 8BN *Tel:* 020 7235 6790 *Tel:* Office 020 7235 6224 *Fax:* Office 020 7235 6224; Coldharbour, Northbourne, Deal, Kent, CT14 0LP *Tel:* 01304 611277 *Fax:* 01304 611128.

NORTHBROOK (6th Baron, UK), Francis Thomas Baring; cr. 1866; 8th Bt of The City of London (GB) 1793

Son of 5th Baron. Born February 21, 1954. Succeeded his father 1990; educated Winchester; Bristol University (BA). Married 1987, Amelia, eldest daughter of Dr Reginald Taylor, of Hursley, Winchester (3 daughters). *Career:* Trainee Accountant, Dixon Wilson & Co. 1976–80; Baring Bros & Co. Ltd 1981–89; Senior Investment Manager, Taylor Young Investment Management Ltd 1990–93; Investment Fund Manager, Smith and Williamson 1993–95; Managing Director, Cabincity Ltd 1995–; Director, Mars Asset Management 1996–. *House of Lords:* An elected hereditary peer 1999–. *Whip:* An Opposition Whip 1999–. *Trusts, etc:* Trustee, Winchester Medical Trust. *Special Interests:* City, Agriculture, Foreign Affairs. *Recreations:* Cricket, Skiing, Shooting. *Clubs:* White's. *Heir:* To barony, none. Heir to baronetcy, his kinsman, Peter Baring, born September 12, 1939. A Conservative. *Address:* The Lord Northbrook, House of Lords, London, SW1A 0PW.

NORTHESK (14th Earl of, S), David John MacRae Carnegie; cr. 1647; 14th Lord Rosehill and Inglismaldie (S) 1639

Son of 13th Earl. Born November 3, 1954. Succeeded his father 1994; educated Eton; University College, London. Married 1979, Jacqueline, daughter of David Reid, of Sintra, Portugal (1 son 3 daughters). *Career:* Landowner; Estate manager; Company director. *House of Lords:* An elected hereditary peer 1999–. *Whip:* An Opposition Whip 1999–. *Select Committees:* Member, Select Committee on House of Lords' Offices 1997–. *Special Interests:* Agriculture, Conservation, Heritage. *Heir:* His son, Lord Rosehill, born November 16, 1980. A Conservative. *Address:* The Earl of Northesk, House of Lords, London, SW1A 0PW.

NORTHFIELD (Life Baron, UK), (William) Donald Chapman; cr. 1975

Son of late W. H. Chapman. Born November 25, 1923; educated Barnsley Grammar School; Emmanuel College, Cambridge (MA Hons. Econ, Senior Scholar); G. Gibbon Fellow, Nuffield College, Oxford 1971–73. *Councils, Public Bodies:* Cambridge City Councillor 1945–47; Chairman: HM Development Commissioners 1974–80, Telford Development Corporation 1975–87, Northfield Committee of Enquiry into Ownership and Occupancy of Agricultural land 1977–79. *Career:* A Company director; Special Adviser to ECC Commission on Environmental Policy 1981–85; Chairman, Consortium Developments Ltd 1986–92; Director, Wembley Stadium plc 1985–88. *House of Commons:* MP (Labour) for Birmingham Northfield 1951–70. *Select Committees (Commons):* Chairman, Procedure Committee 1966–69. *Party Groups (General):* General Secretary, Fabian Society 1949–53; Formerly Hon. Secretary, Cambridge Trades Council and Labour Party. *Other:* A Vice-President, Federation of Economic Development Authorities. *Recreations:* Swimming, travel. *Name, Style and Title:* Raised to the peerage as Baron Northfield, of Telford in the County of Shropshire 1975. Labour. *Address:* The Lord Northfield, House of Lords, London, SW1A 0PW.

NORTON OF LOUTH (Life Baron, UK), Philip Norton; cr. 1998

Youngest son of late George E. Norton, and of Ena D. Norton. Born March 5, 1951; educated King Edward VI Grammar School, Louth; University of Sheffield (BA, PhD) (Nalgo Prize); University of Pennsylvania (MA) (Thouron Scholar). *Councils, Public Bodies:* Chairman, Standards Committee, Kingston-upon-Hull City Council 1999–. *Career:* University of Hull: Lecturer 1977–82, Senior Lecturer 1982–84, Reader 1984–86, Professor of Government 1986–, Director, Centre of Legislative Studies 1992–. *Select Committees:* Member, Select Committee on European Communities Sub-Committee E (Law and Institutions) 1999–. *Other:* Council Member, Hansard Society 1977–; Executive Committee Member: Study of Parliament Group 1981–93, Political Studies Association 1983–89; Member, Society and Politics Research Development Group, Economic and Social Research Council 1987–90; Associate Editor, *Political Studies* 1987–93; Governor, King Edward VI Grammar School 1988–, Warden 1990–93; President: British Politics Group (USA) 1988–90, Politics Association 1993–; Co-chair, Research Committee of Legislative Specialists, International Political Science Association 1994–; Editor, *The Journal of Legislative Studies* 1995–; Chairman,

Commission to Strengthen Parliament 1999–. FRSA 1995. *Publications:* Author or editor: *Dissension in the House of Commons 1945–74*, 1975; *Conservative Dissidents*, 1978; *Dissension in the House of Commons 1974–79*, 1980; *The Commons in Perspective*, 1981; *Conservatives and Conservatism*, (co-author) 1981; *The Constitution in Flux*, 1982; *Law and Order and British Politics*, 1984; *The British Polity*, 1984 (3rd edition 1993); *Parliament in the 1980s*, 1985; *The Political Science of British Politics*, (joint editor) 1986; *Legislature*, 1990; *Parliaments in Western Europe*, 1990; *New Directions in British Politics?*, 1991; *Politics UK*, (with others) 1990 (4th edition 1997); *Parliamentary Questions*, (joint editor) 1993; *Back from Westminster*, (joint author) 1993; *Does Parliament Matter?*, 1993; *National Parliaments and the European Union*, 1996; *The New Parliaments of Central and Eastern Europe*, (joint editor) 1996; *The Conservative Party*, 1996; *Legislatures and Legislators*, 1998; *Governments and Parliaments in Western Europe*, 1998; *Parliaments and Pressure Groups in Western Europe*, 1998; *Parliaments in Asia*, 1999. *Special Interests:* Constitutional Affairs, Parliamentary Affairs, Legislatures, British Politics, American Politics. *Recreations:* Table-tennis, walking, writing. *Clubs:* Royal Overseas League, Royal Commonwealth Society. *Name, Style and Title:* Raised to the peerage as Baron Norton of Louth, of Louth in the County of Lincolnshire 1998. A Conservative. *Address:* Professor The Lord Norton of Louth, Department of Politics, University of Hull, HU6 7RX *Tel:* 01482 465863 *Fax:* 01482 466208 *E-Mail:* p.norton@pol-as.hull.ac.uk.

O

O'CATHAIN (Life Baroness, UK), Detta O'Cathain; cr. 1991; OBE 1983

Daughter of late Caoimhghin and Margaret O'Cathain. Born February 3, 1938; educated Laurel Hill, Limerick; University College, Dublin (BA Economics, English and French). Married June 4, 1968, William Ernest John Bishop, son of late William and Clara Bishop. *Career:* Assistant Economist, Aer Lingus 1959–66; Group Economist, Tarmac 1966–69; Economic Adviser to Chairman, Rootes Motors/Chrysler 1969–72; Senior Economist, Carrington Viyella 1972; Economic Adviser, British Leyland 1973–74; Director, Market Planning 1974–76; Corporate Planning Executive, Unigate plc 1976–81; Head of Strategic Planning, Milk Marketing Board 1981–83; Director and General Manager 1984–85; Managing Director 1985–88; Managing Director, Barbican Centre 1990–95; Non-executive director: Midland Bank plc 1984–93, Tesco plc 1985–, Sears plc 1987–94, British Airways plc 1993–, BET plc 1994–96, Thistle Hotels plc 1996–, South East Water plc 1997–. *Select Committees:* Former Member: Public Service Select Committee 1996–97, European Communities Committee – Sub-Committee A; Member, Select Committee on Monetary Policy of the Bank of England 1998– Member, Select Committee on European Communities Sub Committee B (Energy, Industry and Transport) 1998–. *All-Party:* Member, All-Party London Group. *Other:* Member, Council of Industrial Society 1986–92; Past President, Agricultural Section of the British Association for the Advancement of Science; Former Member: Design Council, Engineering Council; President, Chartered Institute of Marketing 1998–. *Honours:* OBE 1983; Commander: Royal Norwegian Order 1993, Order of the Lion of Finland 1994. Fellow: Royal Society of Arts 1986, Chartered Institute of Marketing 1987. Freeman, City of London. *Special Interests:* Arts, Agriculture, Industry, Commerce, Banking, Retail Industry, Disabled, Economic Policy. *Recreations:* Music, reading, swimming, walking, gardening. *Name, Style and Title:* Raised to the peerage as Baroness O'Cathain, of The Barbican in the City of London 1991. A Conservative. *Address:* The Baroness O'Cathain, OBE, Eglantine, Tower House Gardens, Arundel, West Sussex, BN18 9RU *Tel:* 01903 883775; 121 Shakespeare Tower, Barbican, London, EC2Y 8DR *Tel:* 020 7638 6443 *E-Mail:* ocathaind@parliament.uk.

Dod *on* Disk
The Vacher Dod Parliamentary Database – configured for PC or Network
For further details please telephone the Westminster Office
020 7828 7256

OLIVER OF AYLMERTON (Life Baron, UK), Peter Raymond Oliver; cr. 1986; Kt 1974; PC 1980

Son of late David Thomas Oliver, LLM, LLD. Born March 7, 1921; educated Leys School, Cambridge; Trinity Hall, Cambridge (Scholar). Married 1st, July 4, 1945, Mary Chichester (died September 6, 1985), daughter of late Sir Eric Keightley Rideal, MBE, FRS (1 son 1 daughter), married 2nd, January 6, 1987, Wendy Anne, widow of I. L. Lloyd Jones. *Armed Forces:* Military Service, 12th Battalion RTR 1941–45. *Career:* Called to the Bar, Lincoln's Inn 1948; QC 1965; Bencher, Lincoln's Inn 1973; Judge of the High Court 1974–80; Member, Restrictive Practices Court 1976–80; Chairman, Review Body on Chancery Division 1979–81; Lord Justice of Appeal 1980–86; A Lord of Appeal in Ordinary 1986–92. *Select Committees:* Chairman, Sub-Committee E (Law and Institutions) of Select Committee on the European Communities 1989–91. *Honours:* Kt 1974; PC 1980. *Recreations:* Gardening, music. *Name, Style and Title:* Raised to the peerage as Baron Oliver of Aylmerton, of Aylmerton in the County of Norfolk 1986. A Cross-Bencher. *Address:* The Rt Hon. the Lord Oliver of Aylmerton, House of Lords, London, SW1A 0PW.

O'NEILL OF BENGARVE (Life Baroness, UK), Onora Sylvia O'Neill; cr. 1999; CBE 1995; FBA 1993

Daughter of late Hon. Sir Con O'Neill, GCMG and Lady Garvey, neé Pritchard and widow of Sir Terence Garvey, KCMG. Born August 23, 1941; educated St Paul's Girls' School; Somerville College, Oxford (BA, MA); Harvard University (PhD); Hon. Fellow, Somerville College, Oxford 1993; Hon. DLitt, University of East Anglia 1995; Hon. Degree, University of Essex 1996; Hon. LLD, Nottingham 1999. Married January 19, 1963, Edward John Nell, son of late J E Nell, of Riverside, Illinois, USA (2 sons) (marriage dissolved 1976). *Career:* Assistant, then Associate Professor, Barnard College, Columbia University 1970–77; University of Essex: Lecturer 1977–78, Senior Lecturer 1978–83, Reader 1983–87, Professor of Philosophy 1987–92; Principal, Newnham College, Cambridge 1992–. *International Bodies (General):* Fellow, Wissenschaftskolleg, Berlin 1989–90; Foreign Hon. Member, American Academy of Arts and Sciences 1993; Fellow, Academic Advisory Board 1996–. *Other:* Chairman, Nuffield Foundation 1998–. *Miscellaneous:* President, Aristotelian Society 1988–89; Member, Animal Procedures Committee 1990–94; Member, Nuffield Council on Bioethics 1991–98, Chairman 1996–98; Member, Human Genetics Advisory Commission 1996–. *Honours:* CBE 1995. FBA 1993. *Publications:* Author of: *Acting on Principle*, 1976, *Faces of Hunger*, 1986; *Constructions of Reason*, 1989, *Towards Justice and Virtue*, 1996; Numerous articles on philosophy in learned journals. *Name, Style and Title:* Raised to the peerage as Baroness O'Neill of Bengarve, of The Braid in the County of Antrim 1999. A Cross-Bencher. *Address:* The Baroness O'Neill of Bengarve, CBE, FBA, Newnham College, Cambridge, CB3 9DF *Tel:* 01223 335821.

ONSLOW (7th Earl of, UK), Michael William Coplestone Dillon Onslow; cr. 1801; Viscount Cranley; 10th Baron Onslow (GB) 1716; Baron Cranley (GB) 1776; 11th Bt of West Clandon (E) 1660

Son of 6th Earl, KBE, MC, TD. Born February 28, 1938. Succeeded his father 1971; educated Eton; Sorbonne. Married 1964, Robin Lindsay, daughter of Major Robert Lee Bullard, of Atlanta, Georgia, USA (1 son 2 daughters). *Career:* A Farmer. *House of Lords:* An elected hereditary peer 1999–. *Clubs:* Beefsteak, White's. *Heir:* His son, Viscount Cranley, born June 16, 1967. A Conservative. *Address:* The Earl of Onslow, Temple Court, Clandon Park, Guildford, Surrey, GU4 7RQ.

ONSLOW OF WOKING (Life Baron, UK), Cranley Gordon Douglas Onslow; cr. 1997; KCMG 1993; PC 1988

Son of late F. R. D. Onslow. Born June 8, 1926; educated Harrow; Oriel College, Oxford; Geneva University. Married May 7, 1955, Lady June Hay, daughter of 14th Earl of Kinnoull (1 son 3 daughters). *Armed Forces:* Served Royal Armoured Corps (Lieutenant 7th Hussars) 1944–48. *Councils, Public Bodies:* Councillor, Kent County Council 1961–64. *Career:* HM Foreign Service 1951–60, serving in Burma 1953–56. *House of Commons:* MP (Conservative) for Woking 1964–97; Parliamentary Under-Secretary of State, Aerospace and Shipping, Department of Trade and Industry 1972–74; Minister of State, Foreign and Commonwealth Office April 1982-June 1983. *Spokesman (Commons):* Opposition Spokesman on: Health and Social Security 1974–75, Defence 1975–76. *Select Committees (Commons):* Chairman, Select Committee on Defence 1981–82; Member, Select Committees on: Trade and Industry 1992–97, Privileges 1994–97. *Backbench Committees (Commons):* Chairman, 1922 Committee 1984–92. *Honours:* PC 1988; KCMG 1993. *Special Interests:* Aviation, Defence, Conservation. *Recreations:* Fishing, shooting. *Clubs:* Beefsteak, Travellers'. *Name, Style and Title:* Raised to the peerage as Baron Onslow of Woking, of Woking in the County of Surrey 1997. A Conservative. *Address:* The Rt Hon. the Lord Onslow of Woking, KCMG, House of Lords, London, SW1A 0PW.

OPPENHEIM-BARNES (Life Baroness, UK), Sally Oppenheim-Barnes; cr. 1989; PC 1979

Daughter of late Mark Viner. Born July 26, 1930; educated Sheffield High School; Lowther College, North Wales. Married 1st, 1949, Henry (died 1980), son of A. L. Oppenheim (1 son 2 daughters), married 2nd, July 5, 1984, John Barnes. *Career:* A Non-Executive Director, The Boots Co. plc 1981–93; Chairman, National Consumer Council 1987–89; Director, Fleming High Income Trust plc 1989–97; Non-Executive Director, HFC Bank plc 1990–98; Former Vice-President, South Wales and West Fire Liaison Panel. *House of Commons:* MP (Conservative) for Gloucester 1970–87; Member of the Shadow Cabinet 1975–79; Minister of State for Consumer Affairs 1979–82. *Spokesman (Commons):* Opposition Spokesman on Prices and Consumer Protection 1974–79. *Party Groups (General):* President, Conservative Club of Gloucester 1970. *Other:* Former National Vice-President, National Mobile Homes Residents' Association; Vice-President, National Union of Townswomen's Guilds 1973–79; Former Vice-President, Western Centre of Public Health Inspectors. *Honours:* PC 1979. *Recreations:* Bridge, tennis. *Sportsclubs:* Vanderbilt Racquet Club. *Name, Style and Title:* Raised to the peerage as Baroness Oppenheim-Barnes, of Gloucester in the County of Gloucestershire 1989. A Conservative. *Address:* The Rt Hon. the Baroness Oppenheim-Barnes, Quietways, The Highlands, Painswick, Gloucestershire, GL6 6SL.

ORME (Life Baron, UK), Stanley Orme; cr. 1997; PC 1974

Son of Sherwood Orme. Born April 5, 1923; educated Elementary school; Part-time Technical; NCLC; WEA; Hon. DSc, University of Salford 1985. Married 1951, Irene Mary, daughter of Vernon F. Harris. *Trades Union:* Member, AEEU. *Armed Forces:* Served in RAF 1942–47, Warrant Officer, Air-Bomber Navigator. *Councils, Public Bodies:* Councillor, Sale Borough Council 1958–64. *Career:* Skilled Engineer. *House of Commons:* Contested Stockport South 1959; MP (Labour) for Salford West 1964–83 and for Salford East 1983–97; Minister of State: for Northern Ireland 1974–76, for Department of Health and Social Security April-September 1976; Minister for Social Security and Member of the Cabinet 1976–79. *Spokesman (Commons):* Principal Opposition Front Bench Spokesman on: Health and Social Security 1979–80, Industry 1980–83, Energy 1983–87. *Select Committees (Commons):* Former Member, Select Committees on: House of Commons Services, Trade and Industry 1992–93, Privileges 1994–96; Standards in Public Life 1995–96. *All-Party Committees (Commons):* Chairman, All-Party Cricket Group 1994–97; Vice-Chairman, All-Party Football Group 1994–97; Former Chairman, AEEU Parliamentary Group. *International Bodies (General):* Member: IPU, CPA. *Party Groups (General):* Joined Labour Party 1944; Chairman, AEEU Parliamentary Group of Labour Members 1976–96; Chairman, Parliamentary Labour Party 1987–92. *Other:* Hon. President, The Lotteries Council. *Honours:* PC 1974. *Recreations:* Walking, jazz, opera, reading American literature, supporting Manchester United Football Club and Lancashire County Cricket Club. *Name, Style and Title:* Raised to the peerage as Baron Orme, of Salford in the County of Greater Manchester 1997. Labour. *Address:* The Rt Hon. the Lord Orme, 8 Northwood Grove, Sale, Cheshire, M33 3DZ.

OWEN (Life Baron, UK), David Anthony Llewellyn Owen; cr. 1992; PC 1976; CH 1994

Son of late Dr John Owen, General Practitioner. Born July 2, 1938; educated Bradfield College; Sidney Sussex College, Cambridge (MA, BChir); St Thomas's Hospital, London (MB). Married 1968, Deborah, daughter of late Kyril Schabert, of New York, USA (2 sons 1 daughter). *Career:* Various house appointments, St Thomas's Hospital 1962–64; Neurological and Psychiatric Registrar 1964–66; Non-Executive Director: New Crane Publishing 1992–, Coats Viyella 1994–; Executive Chairman, Middlesex Holdings plc 1995–; Director: Center for International Health and Cooperation 1995–, Abbott Laboratories 1996–, New Europe 1999–. *House of Commons:* Contested (Labour) Torrington in 1964 General Election; MP (Labour) for Plymouth Sutton 1966–74; MP for Plymouth Devonport 1974–92 (Labour 1974–81, SDP 1981–92); PPS to Minister of Defence (Administration) 1966–68; Parliamentary Under-Secretary of State for Defence (Royal Navy) 1968–70; Parliamentary Under-Secretary of State, Department of Health and Social Security 1974, Minister of State 1974–76; Minister of State, Foreign Office 1976–77; Secretary of State for Foreign and Commonwealth Affairs 1977–79. *Spokesman (Commons):* Opposition Spokesman on Defence 1970–72; Principal Opposition Spokesman on Energy 1979–80. *Chancellor:* Chancellor, University of Liverpool 1996–. *Party Groups (General):* One of the founders of the Social Democratic Party, Formally launched March 26 1981; Chairman, Parliamentary Committee 1981–82; Deputy Leader of the Party 1982–83, Leader 1983–87, Resigned over merger with Liberal Party; Re-elected SDP Leader 1988–92. *Other:* Patron, Social Market Foundation; Chairman, Humanitas. *Miscellaneous:* Research Fellow, Medical Unit 1966–68; Member: Palme Commission on Disarmament and Security Issues 1980–89, Independent Commission on International Humanitarian Issues 1983–88; EU Co-Chairman, International Conference on former Yugoslavia 1992–95, Carnegie Commission on Preventing Deadly Conflict 1994–. *Honours:* PC 1976; CH 1994. *Publications:* Author of: *A Unified Health Service*, 1968; *The Politics of Defence*, 1972; *In Sickness and in Health*, 1976; *Human Rights*, 1978; *Face the Future*, 1981; *A Future that will Work*, 1984; *A United Kingdom*, 1986; *Personally Speaking* (to Kenneth Harris), 1987; *Our NHS*, 1988; *Time to Declare* (autobiography) 1991; *Seven Ages* (an anthology of poetry) 1992; *Balkan Odyssey*, 1995. *Special Interests:* International affairs (foreign and defence). *Recreations:* Sailing. *Name, Style and Title:* Raised to the peerage as Baron Owen, of the City of Plymouth 1992. An An Independent Social Democrat/Sits as a Cross-Bencher. *Address:* The Rt Hon. the Lord Owen, CH, House of Lords, London, SW1A 0PW; 78 Narrow Street, London, E14 8BP *Tel:* 020 7987 5441 *E-Mail:* lordowen@nildram.co.uk.

OXBURGH (Life Baron, UK), Ernest Ronald Oxburgh; cr. 1999; KBE 1992; FRS 1978

Son of Ernest Oxburgh and Violet Oxburgh (née Bugden). Born November 2, 1934; educated Liverpool Institute; Oxford University (BA 1957, MA 1960); Princeton University, USA (PhD 1960); Hon. Fellow: Trinity Hall, Cambridge 1982, University College, Oxford 1983, St Edmund Hall, Oxford 1986; DSc (*hc*): Paris 1986, Leicester 1990, Loughborough 1991; Hon. Fellow, Queen's College Cambridge 1992; DSc (*hc*): Edinburgh 1994, Birmingham 1996, Liverpool 1996. Married, Ursula Mary Brown (1 son 2 daughter). *Career:* Departmental Demonstrator, Oxford University 1960–61, Lecturer in Geology 1962–78; Fellow, St Edmund Hall, Oxford 1964–78, Emeritus Fellow 1978; Visiting Professor: California Institute of Technology 1967–68, Stanford and Cornell Universities 1973–74; Cambridge University: Professor of Mineralogy and Petrology 1978–91, Head of Department of Earth Sciences 1980–88, Fellow of Trinity Hall 1978–82, President, Queens' College 1982–89, Professorial Fellow 1989–91; Chief Scientific Adviser, Ministry of Defence 1988–93; Rector, Imperial College of Science, Technology and Medicine 1993–. *Select Committees:* Member, Select Committee on Science and Technology 1999–. *Other:* President, European Union of Geosciences 1985–87; Member, National Committee of Inquiry into Higher Education (Dearing Committee) 1996–97; Member of Geological and Scientific Academies and Societies in USA, Germany, Austria and Venezuela. *Awards Granted:* Bigsby Medal, Geological Society 1979. *Trusts, etc:* Council Member, Winston Churchill Memorial Trust 1995–; Trustee, Natural History Museum 1993, Chairman of Trustees 1999–. *Honours:* KBE 1992; Officier, Ordre des Palmes Académiques (France) 1995. FRS 1978. *Publications:* Has contributed to several geological, defence and scientific journals. *Clubs:* Athenaeum. *Name, Style and Title:* Raised to the peerage as Baron Oxburgh, of Liverpool in the County of Merseyside 1999. *Address:* The Lord Oxburgh, KBE, FRS, Rector, Imperial College of Science, Technology and Medicine, Exhibition Road, London, SW7 2AZ *E-Mail:* rector@ic.ac.uk.

OXFORD (41st Bishop of), Richard Douglas Harries; DD

Son of late Brigadier W. D. J. Harries, CBE. Born June 2, 1936; educated Wellington College; RMA, Sandhurst; Selwyn College, Cambridge (MA 1965); Cuddesdon College, Oxford; Hon. DD, University of London; Hon. Fellow, Selwyn College Cambridge. Married 1963, Josephine Bottomley, MB, BChir, DCH (1 son 1 daughter). *Armed Forces:* Lieutenant, Royal Corps of Signals 1955–58. *Career:* Curate, Hampstead Parish Church 1963–69; Chaplain, Westfield College 1966–69; Lecturer, Wells Theological College 1969–72; Vicar, All Saints, Fulham 1972–81; Dean, King's College, London 1981–87; Bishop of Oxford 1987–; Took his seat in the House of Lords December 1993. *House of Lords:* Convenor of Bench of Bishops. *Select Committees:* Member, Select Committee on House of Lords' Offices 1997–. *International Bodies (General):* Member, Anglican Consultative Council; Consultant, Anglican Peace and Justice Network. *Other:* General Ordination examiner in Christian Ethics 1972–76; Director, Post Ordination Training, Kensington Jurisdiction 1973–79; Chairman, Southwark Ordination Course 1982–87; President, Johnson Society 1988–89. *Miscellaneous:* Vice-Chairman: Council for Christian Action 1979–87, Council for Arms Control 1982–87; Member, Home Office Advisory Committee for reform of sexual offences law 1981–85; Chairman: Board of Social Responsibility for the Church of England, Council of Christians and Jews; Board Member, Christian Aid; Member, Royal Commission on the Reform of the House of Lords 1999. Fellow: King's College, London, Royal Society of Literature. *Publications:* Author of: *Prayers of Hope*, 1975; *Turning to Prayer*, 1978; *Prayers of Grief and Glory*, 1979; *Being a Christian*, 1981; *Should Christians Support Guerillas?* 1982; *The Authority of Divine Love*, 1983; *Praying Round the Clock*, 1983; *Prayer and the Pursuit of Happiness*, 1985; *Morning Has Broken*, 1985; *Christianity and War in a Nuclear Age*, 1986; *C. S. Lewis: the man and his God*, 1987; *Christ is Risen*, 1988; *Is There a Gospel for the Rich*, 1992; *Art and the Beauty of God*, 1993; *The Real God: A Response to Anthony Freeman*, 1994; *Questioning Belief*, 1995; *A Gallery of Reflections – The Nativity in Art*, 1995; *Two Cheers For Secularism*, (ed. with Sidney Brichto) 1998 Has edited and contributed to other Christian publications as well as articles in the press and periodicals. *Special Interests:* Overseas Aid and Development, Poverty, Housing, Business Ethics, Arts, Arms Control, Moral Issues. *Recreations:* Theatre, literature, sport. *Address:* The Rt Rev. the Lord Bishop of Oxford, FKC, DD, FRSL, Diocesan Church House, North Hinksey, Oxford, OX2 0NB *Tel:* 01865 208222 *E-Mail:* bishopoxon@oxford.anglican.org.

OXFUIRD (13th Viscount of, S), George Hubbard Makgill; cr. 1651; Lord Makgill of Cousland; 13th Bt of Cranston Riddell (NS) 1627; CBE 1997

Son of late Squadron-Leader Richard James Robert Haldane Makgill, AFC. Born January 7, 1934. Succeeded his uncle 1986; educated Wanganui Collegiate School, Wanganui, New Zealand. Married 1st, 1967, Alison Campbell, daughter of late Niels Jensen, of Randers, Denmark (3 sons) (marriage dissolved 1977), married 2nd,, 1980, Venita Cunitia Mary, daughter of Major C. A. Steward, of Crondall, Hampshire (1 son). *Armed Forces:* Royal Air Force 1954; Commission G. D. Branch. *Career:* Department of Civil Engineering, Wellington, New Zealand 1952; Ford Motor Company 1958, Lansing Ltd 1964; Export Area Manager 1976; External Affairs Manager, Lansing Linde Ltd 1988–93. *House of Lords:* A Deputy Speaker of the House of Lords 1990–; A Deputy Chairman of Committees 1990–; An elected hereditary peer 1999–. *Select Committees:* Former Member: Joint Committee on Statutory Instruments, Personal Bills Committee 1992–94, Offices Committee 1995–97; Member, Hybrid Bills Committee 1996–. *All-Party:* Member, All-Party: Defence Study Group, Motor Industry Group. *Party Groups:* Member, Executive of the Association of Conservative Peers 1991–; Deputy Chairman 1993–98. *Other:* President: World Travel Market Council, Institute of Supervision and Management. *Trusts, etc:* Member, Understanding Industry Trust. *Miscellaneous:* Committee for British Postal Equipment Exports 1967. *Honours:* CBE 1997. MIMH. *Special Interests:* Industry, Exports. *Recreations:* Fishing, gardening, racing, shooting. *Clubs:* Caledonian. *Heir:* His son, Hon. Ian Arthur Alexander Makgill, Master of Oxfuird, born October 14, 1969. A Conservative. *Address:* The Viscount of Oxfuird, CBE, House of Lords, London, SW1A 0PW.

P

PALMER (4th Baron, UK), Adrian Bailie Nottage Palmer; cr. 1933; 4th Bt of Grosvenor Crescent (UK) 1916

Son of late Colonel Hon. Sir Gordon Palmer, KCVO, OBE, TD, youngest son of 2nd Baron. Born October 8, 1951. Succeeded his uncle 1990; educated Eton; Edinburgh University. Married 1977, Cornelia Dorothy Katharine, daughter of Rohan Wadham, DFC, of Newmarket, Suffolk (2 sons 1 daughter). *Career:* Served as an apprentice with Huntley and Palmers Ltd; Sales manager in Southern Belgium and Luxembourg for three years; Scottish Representative to the European Landowning Organisation 1986–92; A Farmer. *House of Lords:* An elected hereditary peer 1999–. *Select Committees:* Member: Advisory Panel on Works of Art, Refreshment Committee. *Other:* Vice-Chairman, Historic Houses Association for Scotland 1993–94, Chairman 1994–99; Member: Executive Council of Historic Houses Association 1981–99, Council of Scottish Landowners Federation 1986–92; Secretary, Royal Caledonian Hunt 1989–; President, Palm Tree Silk Co (St Lucia). *Trusts, etc:* Chairman, Country Sports Defence Trust 1994–. *Miscellaneous:* Member, Queen's Bodyguard for Scotland (The Royal Company of Archers) 1990–96. *Special Interests:* Agriculture, Environment, Heritage, Media. *Recreations:* Hunting, shooting, gardening. *Clubs:* New (Edinburgh), MCC. *Heir:* His son, Hon. Hugo Bailie Rohan Palmer, born December 5, 1980. A Cross-Bencher. *Address:* The Lord Palmer, Manderston, Duns, Berwickshire, TD11 3PP *Tel:* 01361 883450 *Fax:* 01361 882010 *E-Mail:* palmer@manderston.demon.co.uk.

PALUMBO (Life Baron, UK), Peter Garth Palumbo; cr. 1991

Son of late Rudolph Palumbo and of Elsie Palumbo. Born July 20, 1935; educated Eton; Worcester College, Oxford (MA); Hon. DLitt, Portsmouth University 1993. Married 1st, 1959, Denia (died 1986), daughter of late Major Lionel Wigram (1 son 2 daughters), married 2nd, 1986, Hayat, daughter of late Kamel Morowa (1 son 2 daughters). *Chancellor:* Chancellor, University of Portsmouth 1992–. *Other:* Governor, London School of Economics and Political Science 1976–94; Chairman: Tate Gallery Foundation 1986–87, Serpentine Gallery 1994–; Member of Council, Royal Albert Hall 1995–99; Governor, The Royal Shakespeare Theatre 1995–. *Trusts, etc:* Trustee: Mies van der Rohe Archive 1977–, Tate Gallery 1978–85, Whitechapel Arts Gallery Foundation 1981–87; Trustee and Hon. Treasurer, Writers and Scholars Educational Trust 1984–99; Chairman, Painshill Park Trust Appeal 1986–96; Trustee: The Natural History Museum 1994–, The Design Museum 1995–. *Miscellaneous:* Chairman, Arts Council of Great Britain 1989–94. *Honours:* National Order of the Southern Cross (Federal Republic of Brazil). Hon. FRIBA; Hon. FFB 1994; Hon. FIStructE 1994. Liveryman, Salters' Company. *Recreations:* Music, travel, gardening, reading. *Clubs:* White's, Pratt's, Athenaeum, Knickerbocker (New York), Garrick. *Name, Style and Title:* Raised to the peerage as Baron Palumbo, of Walbrook in the City of London 1991. A Conservative. *Address:* The Lord Palumbo, Bagnor Manor, Bagnor, Newbury, Berkshire, RG20 8AG *Tel:* 01635 40930; Office:, Vestry House, Laurence Poutney Hill, London, EC4R 0EH *Tel:* 020 7626 9236.

PARK OF MONMOUTH (Life Baroness, UK), Daphne Margaret Sybil Désirée Park; cr. 1990; CMG 1971; OBE 1960

Daughter of late John Alexander and Doreen Gwynneth Park. Born September 1, 1921; educated Rosa Bassett School, Streatham; Somerville College, Oxford (BA Modern Languages); Newnham College, Cambridge (CCK Russian); Hon. LLD: Bristol 1988, Mount Holyoke College 1993. *Armed Forces:* Served WTS (FANY) 1943–48; Allied Commission, Austria 1946–48. *Councils, Public Bodies:* Member, Sheffield Development Corporation Board 1989–92. *Career:* Entered Foreign Office 1948; Member, UK delegation to NATO 1952; Second Secretary, British Embassy, Moscow 1954–56; FO 1956–59; Consul and First Secretary, Leopoldville 1959–61; FO 1961–63; High Commission, Lusaka 1964–67; FO 1967–69; Consul-General, Hanoi 1969–70; Hon. Research

Fellow, University of Kent 1971–72; Chargé d'Affaires a.i. British Embassy, Ulan Bator, Mongolia April–June 1972; FCO 1973–79; Principal, Somerville College, Oxford 1980–89; Governor, BBC 1982–87; Member, British Library Board 1983–89; Chairman, Lord Chancellor's Advisory Committee on Legal Aid 1984–90; Pro-Vice Chancellor, University of Oxford 1985–89; Chairman, Royal Commission on the Historical Monuments of England 1989–94. *Select Committees:* Member, European Communities Sub-Committee C (Environment, Public Health and Education) 1994–97. *All-Party:* Member, All-Party Defence Study Group 1992–; Member, All-Party Group on Ageing 1991–93, Joint Vice-Chairman 1992; Member, All-Party European Atlantic Group. *Other:* Member, Royal Asiatic Society; Governor, Ditchley Foundation; Member, Forum UK 1994–96; President, Society for the Promotion of the Training of Women 1994–. *Trusts, etc:* Director, Zoo Development Trust 1989–90; Trustee: Jardine Educational Trust to 1998, Royal Armouries Development Trust 1991–92, Great Britain-Sasakawa Foundation 1994–, Lucy Faithfull Travel Scholarship Fund. Fellow: Chatham House (RIIA), RSA. *Special Interests:* Higher Education, Foreign Affairs, Defence, Heritage, Northern Ireland. *Honours:* OBE 1960; CMG 1971. *Recreations:* Good talk, politics and difficult places. *Clubs:* Naval and Military, Commonwealth Trust, Special Forces, United Oxford and Cambridge University. *Name, Style and Title:* Raised to the peerage as Baroness Park of Monmouth, of Broadway in the County of Hereford and Worcester 1990. A Conservative. *Address:* The Baroness Park of Monmouth, CMG, OBE, House of Lords, London, SW1A 0PW.

PARKINSON (Life Baron, UK), Cecil Edward Parkinson; cr. 1992; PC 1981

Son of Sydney Parkinson. Born September 1, 1931; educated Royal Grammar School, Lancaster; Emmanuel College, Cambridge (MA). Married 1957, Ann Mary, DL, daughter of late F. A. Jarvis, MC, of Harpenden, Herts. (3 daughters). *Career:* Chartered Accountant; Company director. *House of Commons:* MP (Conservative) for: Enfield West 1970–74, Hertfordshire South 1974–83, Hertsmere 1983–92; PPS to Minister for Aerospace and Shipping, Department of Trade and Industry 1972–74; Minister for Trade, Department of Trade 1979–81; Paymaster General 1981–83; Chancellor, Duchy of Lancaster 1982–83; Secretary of State for: Trade and Industry June-October 1983, Energy 1987–89, Transport 1989–90; Member, Shadow Cabinet 1997–98. *Whip (Commons):* An Assistant Whip 1974; An Opposition Whip 1974–79. *Spokesman (Commons):* Spokesman on Trade 1976–79. *Backbench Committees (Commons):* Secretary, Conservative Parliamentary Finance Committee 1971–72. *All-Party Committees (Commons):* Chairman, Anglo-Swiss Parliamentary Group 1979–82. *Party Groups (General):* Chairman, Conservative Party 1981–83 and 1997–98. *Publications: Right at the Centre: An Autobiography,* 1992. *Recreations:* Reading, golf, skiing. *Clubs:* Beefsteak, Garrick, Pratt's, Hawks (Cambridge). *Name, Style and Title:* Raised to the peerage as Baron Parkinson, of Carnforth in the County of Lancashire 1992. A Conservative. *Address:* The Rt Hon. the Lord Parkinson, House of Lords, London, SW1A 0PW.

PARRY (Life Baron, UK), Gordon Samuel David Parry; cr. 1975; DL

Son of late Rev. Thomas Lewis Parry. Born November 30, 1925; educated Trinity College, Carmarthen; University of Liverpool; Hon. Fellow: James Cook University, Australia, Trinity College, Carmarthen, University of Glamorgan; Awarded Hon. Doctorate of Education, Swansea Institute of Higher Education 1992; Fellow, Pembrokeshire College 1996. Married August 4, 1948, Glenys Catherine, daughter of Jack Leslie Incledon (1 daughter). *Trades Union:* Member, NUT 1945. *Councils, Public Bodies:* Councillor, Neyland (Dyfed) Urban District Council 1948–65; DL, Dyfed 1993–. *Career:* Assistant Teacher at: Coronation School, Pembroke Dock 1945–46, Llanstadwell Voluntary School 1946–47, Haverfordwest Voluntary School 1947, Neyland Board School 1946–52; Housemaster, County Secretary School, Haverfordwest 1952–62; Institute of Education, Liverpool University 1962–63; Housemaster, Haverfordwest 1963–67; Warden, Pembrokeshire Teachers' Centre 1967–76; President, Milford Docks Co.; Chairman: Milford Leisure Co. 1984–, Taylor Plan Services 1988–97; Director, Seacon 1990–97; Chairman, Clean World International 1991–; Director, Marriott UK 1997–98. *Other:* President: Wales Spastics Society, Pembrokeshire Spastics Society, Pembrokeshire Multiple Sclerosis Society; Member, Council until end 1972, Open University and Chairman of its Education Committee; Vice-President, Mentally Handicapped Society for Wales; Chairman: Keep Wales Tidy Campaign's Consultative Committee, Commonwealth Games 1982 Appeal

Committee for Wales; President, British Institute of Cleaning Science; Chairman, Tidy Britain Group and the Beautiful Britain Campaign 1985–91; President: Tidy Britain Group 1991–97, HOPE (Hyperbaric Oxygen Pembrokeshire Endeavour), Cor Meibion DeCymme South Wales Male Choir 1997–, Neyland Ladies Choir 1997–. *Miscellaneous:* Member: Welsh Independent TV Authority, Welsh Independent Broadcasting Authority, General Advisory Council, IBA, Welsh Development Agency, Welsh Arts Council, Schools Council for Wales; Chairman, The Wales Tourist Board; Member, British Tourist Authority 1978–84; Chairman, British Cleaning Council; Member: Board of British Rail, Western Region 1982–83, BBC Advisory Council and of its Council for Wales. Fellow: Tourism Society, Royal Society of Arts, British Institute of Cleaning Science, Hotel and Catering and Institutional Management Association; Hon. Fellow, Institute of Wastes Management. Hon. Freedom: Niagara, New York, USA 1981; Dallas, Texas, USA 1982; Macon, Georgia, USA 1985; Myrtle Beach, North Carolina, USA 1985; Burgess (Hon. Freeman), Guild of Freemen of Haverford West, Pembrokeshire 1998. *Publications: A Legacy For Life,* 1996. *Special Interests:* Tourism, Wales, North American Matters, Australia. *Recreations:* Watching the Welsh Rugby XV win, travelling, reading and writing. *Sportsclubs:* Neyland Yacht Club, Neyland RFC. *Name, Style and Title:* Raised to the peerage as Baron Parry, of Neyland in the County of Dyfed 1975. Labour. *Address:* The Lord Parry, DL, Willowmead, 52 Portlion, Llangwm, Pembrokeshire, Dyfed, SA62 4JT *Tel:* 01646 600667 *Tel:* Office: 01437 751294.

PATEL (Life Baron, UK), Narendra Babubhai Patel; cr. 1999; Kt 1997

Son of Babubhai and Lalita Patel. Born May 11, 1938; educated Government Secondary School, Dar Es Salaam, Tanzania; Harrow High School; St Andrews University; Hon. DSc; Hon. Degrees from: Australia, South Africa, USA, Canada, India, Sri Lanka, Finland, Argentina, Italy, Germany. Married 1970, Helen Dally. *Career:* Consultant Obstetrician, Ninewells Hospital, Dundee. *International Bodies (General):* Member, International Federation of Obstetrician and Gynaecologists; Member, European Board, College of Obstetricians and Gynaecologists. *Other:* Past President, Royal College of Obstetricians; Past Chairman, Academy of Medical Royal Colleges. *Honours:* Kt 1997. Hon. FRCS (Eng); Hon. FRCS (Edinburgh); Hon. FRCP (Edinburgh); Hon. FRCP (Glasgow); Hon. FRCAnest; MBClB; FACOG; FSOGC; FRCOG; PRACOG; PSLCOG; PSACOG; PFCOG. *Publications:* Author of publications in the areas of Maternal/Fetal medicine, epidemiology, obstetrics, gynaecology, etc. *Name, Style and Title:* Raised to the peerage as Baron Patel, of Dunkeld in Perth and Kinross 1999. A Cross-Bencher. *Address:* The Lord Patel, House of Lords, London, SW1A 0PW *E-Mail:* npatel@sol.co.uk.

PATTEN (Life Baron, UK), John Haggitt Charles Patten; cr. 1997; PC 1990

Son of late Jack Patten. Born July 17, 1945; educated Wimbledon College; Sidney Sussex College, Cambridge (MA, PhD); Hon. Fellow, Harris Manchester College, Oxford. Married July 4, 1978, Louise Alexandra Virginia Charlotte, daughter of late John Rowe (1 daughter). *Councils, Public Bodies:* Oxford City Councillor 1973–76. *Career:* University Teacher, University of Oxford 1969–79; Fellow and Tutor, Hertford College, Oxford 1972–81; Supernumerary Fellow, Hertford College 1981–94; Editor (with Lord Blake) *The Conservative Opportunity;* Investment Banker and Company Director. *House of Commons:* MP (Conservative) for Oxford 1979–83 and for Oxford West and Abingdon 1983–97; PPS to the Ministers of State at the Home Office 1980; Parliamentary Under-Secretary of State for: Northern Ireland 1981–83, Health 1983–85; Minister of State for: Housing, Urban Affairs and Construction, Department of Environment 1985–87, Home Office 1987–92; Secretary of State for Education 1992–94. *Honours:* PC 1990. Liveryman, Drapers' Company. *Publications:* Author of: *Things to Come: The Tories in the 21st Century,* 1995. *Recreations:* Talking with my wife and daughter. *Name, Style and Title:* Raised to the peerage as Baron Patten, of Wincanton in the County of Somerset 1997. A Conservative. *Address:* The Rt Hon. the Lord Patten, House of Lords, London, SW1A 0PW.

PAUL (Life Baron, UK), Swraj Paul; cr. 1996

Son of late Payare Paul and of Mongwati Paul. Born February 18, 1931; educated Punjab University (BSc); Massachusetts Institute of Technology (BSc, MSc Mechanical Engineering); Hon. PhD, American College of Switzerland, Leysin 1986; Hon. DSc Economics, University of Hull 1992; Hon. Doctor of Humane Letters, Chapman University, California, USA 1996. Married 1956, Aruna Vij (3 sons 1 daughter and 1 daughter deceased). *Career:* Partner in family firm in India, Apeejay Surrendra Group 1953; Came to the UK in 1966, establishing first business Natural Gas Tubes Ltd; Caparo Group Ltd formed in 1978; Chairman: Caparo Group Ltd 1978–; Caparo Industries plc 1981–; Caparo Inc. USA 1988–. *Chancellor:* Pro-Chancellor, Thames Valley University 1998–; Chancellor, University of Wolverhampton 1999–. *Select Committees:* Member, Select Committees on: European Communities Sub-Committee B (Energy, Industry and Transport) 1997–, Monetary Policy of the Bank of England 1998–. *All-Party:* Member, All-Party Parliamentary Manufacturing and Industry Group. *International Bodies:* Member, Parliamentarians for Global Action. *Other:* Past President, BISPA (British Iron and Steel Producers Association) 1994–95; Vice-President, Engineering Employers Federation. *Awards Granted:* Corporate Leadership Award, MIT 1987. *Trusts, etc:* Founder and Chairman, Ambika Paul Foundation. *Honours:* Padma Bhushan (Government of India) 1983. Freeman, City of London 1998. *Publications: Indira Gandhi,* 1984, 2nd ed. 1985; *Beyond Boundaries,* 1998. *Sportsclubs:* Royal Calcutta Turf, Royal Calcutta Golf, Cricket of India (Bombay). *Clubs:* MCC, Royal Automobile. *Name, Style and Title:* Raised to the peerage as Baron Paul, of Marylebone in the City of Westminster 1996. Labour. *Address:* The Lord Paul, Caparo Group Ltd, Caparo House, 103 Baker Street, London, W1M 1FD *Tel:* 020 7486 1417.

PEARSON OF RANNOCH (Life Baron, UK), Malcolm Everard MacLaren Pearson; cr. 1990

Son of late Colonel John MacLaren Pearson. Born July 20, 1942; educated Eton; Hon. LLD from CNAA 1992. Married 1st, 1965, Francesca Frua, daughter of late Giuseppe Frua de Angeli and Umberta Nasi (1 daughter) (marriage dissolved 1970); married 2nd, 1977, Hon. Mary Charteris, daughter of Baron Charteris of Amisfield (*qv*) (2 daughters) (marriage dissolved 1995); married 3rd, 1997, Caroline, daughter of Major Hugh Launcelot St Vincent Rose. *Career:* Founded Pearson Webb Springbett (PWS) Group of reinsurance brokers 1964, currently Chairman. *Select Committees:* Member, House of Lords Select Committee on the European Communities and Sub-Committee on Social Affairs and the Environment 1992–96. *Other:* Hon. President, RESCARE (The National Society for Mentally Handicapped People in Residential Care) 1994–; Patron, British Society of Chinese Herbal Medicine Practitioners. *Trusts, etc:* Founded Rannoch Trust 1984. *Miscellaneous:* Member, Council for National Academic Awards 1983–93, Hon. Treasurer 1986–93. *Special Interests:* Europe, Mental Handicap, Scottish Highlands, Education. *Recreations:* Stalking, shooting, fishing, golf. *Sportsclubs:* Swinley Forest Golf. *Clubs:* White's. *Name, Style and Title:* Raised to the peerage as Baron Pearson of Rannoch, of Bridge of Gaur in the District of Perth and Kinross 1990. A Conservative. *Address:* The Lord Pearson of Rannoch, House of Lords, London, SW1A 0PW; Office: PWS Holdings plc, 52 Minories, London, EC3N 1JJ *Tel:* 020 7480 6622.

PEEL (3rd Earl, UK), William James Robert Peel; cr. 1929. 4th Viscount Peel (UK) 1895; Viscount Clanfield (UK) 1929; 8th Bt of Drayton Manor (GB) 1800; DL

Son of 2nd Earl. Born October 3, 1947. Succeeded his father 1969; educated Ampleforth College; Tours University, France; Royal Agricultural College, Cirencester. Married 1st, March 28, 1973, Veronica Naomi, daughter of Major Alastair Timpson, MC (1 son 1 daughter) (marriage dissolved 1987), married 2nd, April 15, 1989, Hon. Mrs. Charlotte Hambro, daughter of late Lord Soames, CH, GCMG, GCVO, CBE, PC, and of Lady Soames, of Castle Mill House, Odiham, Hants (1 daughter). *Councils, Public Bodies:* DL, North Yorkshire 1998–. *House of Lords:* An elected hereditary peer 1999–. *Other:* Former member, Yorkshire Dales National Parks Committee; Chairman, North of England Grouse Research Project 1979–96; Member, The Moorland Association Executive Committee 1988–; President, Gun Trade Association. *Trusts, etc:* President,

Yorkshire Wildlife Trust. *Miscellaneous:* Chairman, The Game Conservancy; Council Member, Nature Conservancy Council 1989–95. Member, Council of the Duchy of Cornwall 1993–; Lord Warden of the Stannaries, Duchy of Cornwall 1994–; Vice-Chairman, Standing Committee on Country Sports. *Recreations:* Shooting, cricket, photography, ornithology. *Clubs:* White's. *Heir:* His son, Viscount Clanfield, born September 16, 1976. A Conservative. *Address:* The Earl Peel, DL, Kilgram Grange, Jervaulx, Ripon, North Yorkshire, HF4 4PQ *Tel:* 01677 460212 *Fax:* 01677 460008.

PERRY OF SOUTHWARK (Life Baroness, UK), Pauline Perry; cr. 1991

Daughter of late John and Elizabeth Welch. Born October 15, 1931; educated Wolverhampton Girls' High School; Girton College, Cambridge (MA); Hon. LLD, University of Bath 1991; Hon. Fellow, Sunderland University 1991; Hon. DLitt, Sussex University 1992; Hon. DEd, University of Wolverhampton 1994; Hon. LLD: Aberdeen University 1994, South Bank University 1994; Hon. Fellow, Girton College, Cambridge 1994; DUniv. Surrey 1995; Hon. Fellow: Nene College 1995, City and Guilds of London Institute 1999. Married July 26, 1952, George Perry, son of late Percy and Edith Perry (3 sons 1 daughter). *Career:* University lecturer, journalist and teacher 1952–70; Has worked in USA, Canada and at Universities of Exeter and Oxford; HM Inspector, Department of Education and Science 1970–74; Staff Inspector, HM Inspectorate, responsible for: teacher training 1975–78 higher education 1978–81; Chief Inspector, HM Inspectorate, responsible for advice to Ministers on general higher education, research, LEA finance, teacher training and international relations 1981–86; Vice-Chancellor and Chief Executive, South Bank University (formerly South Bank Polytechnic) 1987–93; Chairman, South Bank University Enterprises Ltd 1989–93; Member, Board of Directors, Greater London Enterprise 1990–91; Director, South Bank Arts Centre 1991–94; President, Lucy Cavendish College, Cambridge University 1994–; Member, Economic and Social Research Council. *Select Committees:* Member, House of Lords Select Committees on: Science and Technology 1992–97, Scrutiny of Delegated Powers 1993–97, Relations between Central and Local Government 1995–96, Delegated Powers and Deregulation 1997–. *All-Party:* Co-Chairman, Parliamentary Universities Group. *Party Groups:* Member, Association of Conservative Peers. *International Bodies:* Member, IPU. *International Bodies (General):* Chair, DTI Export Group for Education and Training 1993–98; Member, Overseas Projects Board, DTI 1993–98. *Other:* Rector's Warden, Southwark Cathedral 1990–94; Member of the Court, Bath University 1991–98; Vice-President, City and Guilds of London Institute 1994–99; Member, Board of Patrons of the Royal Society Appeal 1996–; Chairman, Friends of Southwark Cathedral 1996–; A Governor, English Speaking Union of the Commonwealth 1997–; Governor (Board Member), English Speaking Union 1997–; Member: British-Thai Business Group, Partnership Korea, Indo-British Partnership. *Trusts, etc:* Member: Cambridge Foundation, Alzheimer's Research Trust, Southwark Cathedral Millennium Project. *Miscellaneous:* Member: British Council's Committee on International Co-operation in Higher Education 1987–96, Economic and Social Research Council 1988–91; Academic Adviser, Home Office, Police Training Council 1990–92; Chairman, DTI Committee for Education and Training Exports 1993–98; Member, Citizen's Charter Advisory Panel 1993–97; Chairman, Charter Mark Judging Panel 1997–. Hon. Fellow: College of Preceptors 1987, Royal Society of Arts 1988; City and Guilds London Institute 1999; Member, Institute of Directors; Companion, Institute of Management. Freedom, City of London 1991. Liveryman, Worshipful Company of Bakers. *Publications:* Has published three books, chapters in nine other books and a wide variety of articles in educational journals and in the national press, and has participated in international seminars and study visits on education. *Special Interests:* Education, International Affairs. *Recreations:* Gardening, walking, listening to music, French countryside, food and literature. *Clubs:* Institute of Directors. *Name, Style and Title:* Raised to the peerage as Baroness Perry of Southwark, of Charlbury in the County of Oxfordshire 1991. A Conservative. *Address:* The Baroness Perry of Southwark, Lucy Cavendish College, Lady Margaret Road, Cambridge, CB3 0BU *Tel:* Office: 01223 332192 *E-Mail:* pp204@cam.ac.uk.

PERRY OF WALTON (Life Baron, UK), Walter Laing Macdonald Perry; cr. 1979; Kt 1974; OBE 1957; FRS 1985

Son of late Fletcher Perry. Born June 16, 1921; educated Ayr Academy; Dundee High School; University of St Andrews (MB, ChB 1943, MD 1948, DSc 1958); Fellow: Open University, University College, London; Holder of ten Hon. Degrees from Universities in UK, Asia, Australia, Canada and USA. Married 1st, 1946, Anne Elizabeth Grant (3 sons) (marriage dissolved 1971), married 2nd, 1971, Catherine Hilda, daughter of late Ambrose Crawley (2 sons 1 daughter). *Armed Forces:* Medical Officer, RAF 1946–47. *Career:* Medical Officer, Colonial Medical Service, Nigeria 1944–46; Member of Staff, Medical Research Council 1947–52; Director, Department of Biological Standards, National Institute for Medical Research 1952–58; Professor of Pharmacology, University of Edinburgh 1958–68, Vice-Principal 1967–68; Vice-Chancellor, The Open University 1969–81; Formerly Senior Consultant to United Nations University; President, Videotel International; Member, Board of Editors Encyclopaedia Britannica; Hon. Director, International Centre for Distance Learning. *Spokesman:* SDP Spokesman on Education, Health and Social Security 1983–91. *Select Committees:* Member, Select Committees on: Science and Technology 1985–90, 1992–97, 1997–, Science and Technology Sub-Committee II (Science and Society) 1999–. *Party Groups:* Deputy Leader, Social Democratic Peers 1981–83, 1988–89. *Other:* President, Research Defence Society. *Honours:* Kt 1974; OBE 1957. FRS; FRCP; FRCPE; FRSE. *Publications: Open University,* 1976. *Recreations:* Music, golf. *Clubs:* Scottish Arts (Edinburgh). *Name, Style and Title:* Raised to the peerage as Baron Perry of Walton, of Walton in the County of Buckinghamshire 1979. A Liberal Democrat. *Address:* The Lord Perry of Walton, OBE, FRS, The Open University, 10 Drumsheugh Gardens, Edinburgh, EH3 7QJ *Tel:* 0131–226 3851; Glenholm, 2 Cramond Road South, Davidson's Mains, Edinburgh, EH4 6AD *Tel:* 0131–336 3666.

PESTON (Life Baron, UK), Maurice Harry Peston; cr. 1987

Son of late Abraham and Yetta Peston. Born March 19, 1931; educated Belle Vue High School, Bradford; Hackney Downs School; London School of Economics (BSc Economics); Princeton; Hon. DEd, University of East London 1984; Hon. Fellow: Portsmouth University 1987, Queen Mary and Westfield College 1992, London School of Economics 1995. Married 1958, Helen Conroy (2 sons 1 daughter). *Career:* Scientific and Senior Scientific Officer, Army Operations Research Group 1954–57; Assistant Lecturer, Lecturer, Reader in Economics, LSE 1957–65; Economic Adviser, HM Treasury 1962–64; Professor of Economics, Queen Mary College 1965–88, Emeritus Professor 1988–; Editor, Applied Economics 1972–; Special Adviser to Secretary of State for: Education and Science 1974–75, Prices 1976–79; Chairman: Pools Panel 1991–94, National Foundation for Education Research 1991–97, Office of Health Economics 1991–. *Chancellor:* Pro-Chancellor, Gyosei International College. *Spokesman:* Opposition Spokesman on: Energy 1987–97, Education and Science 1987–97, Treasury 1990–92, Trade and Industry 1992–97. *Select Committees:* Chairman, Select Committee on Monetary Policy of the Bank of England 1998–. *Other:* Member, Council Royal Pharmaceutical Society of Great Britain 1986–96. *Miscellaneous:* Member, CNNA 1967–73, Chairman, Economics Board; Member, SSRC 1976–79, Chairman, Economics Board. Hon. Member, Royal Pharmaceutical Society of Great Britain 1996. *Publications: Elementary Matrices for Economics,* 1969; *Public Goods and the Public Sector,* 1972; *Theory of Macroeconomic Policy,* 1974; *Whatever Happened to Macroeconomics?,* 1980; *The British Economy,* 1982. *Name, Style and Title:* Raised to the peerage as Baron Peston, of Mile End in Greater London 1987. Labour. *Address:* The Lord Peston, House of Lords, London, SW1A 0PW *E-Mail:* pestonhh@parliament.uk.

Dod *on* Disk

The Vacher Dod Parliamentary Database – configured for PC or Network

For further details please telephone the Westminster Office

020 7828 7256

PEYTON OF YEOVIL (Life Baron, UK), John Wynne William Peyton; cr. 1983; PC 1970

Son of late Ivor Eliot Peyton. Born February 13, 1919; educated Eton; Trinity College, Oxford. Married 1st, 1947, Diana, daughter of late Douglas Clinch (1 son 1 daughter and 1 son deceased) (marriage dissolved 1966), married 2nd, July 27, 1966, Mrs Mary Cobbold, daughter of late Colonel Hon. Humphrey Wyndham, MC. *Armed Forces:* Served 1939–45 with 15/19 Hussars (POW Germany). *Career:* Called to the Bar, Inner Temple June 1945; Chairman, Texas Instruments 1974–90; Non-Executive Chairman, British Alcan Aluminium 1987–91, President 1991–97. *House of Commons:* Contested (Conservative) Bristol Central 1950; MP (Conservative) for Yeovil 1951–1983; Parliamentary Secretary to Ministry of Power 1962–64; Minister of Transport June–October 1970; Minister of Transport Industries 1970–74. *Other:* Treasurer, The Zoological Society of London 1984–91. *Honours:* PC 1970. *Publications: Without Benefit of Laundry,* 1997. *Clubs:* Boodle's, Pratt's, Beefsteak. *Name, Style and Title:* Raised to the peerage as Baron Peyton of Yeovil, of Yeovil in the County of Somerset 1983. A Conservative. *Address:* The Rt Hon. the Lord Peyton of Yeovil, 6 Temple West Mews, West Square, London, SE11 4TJ *Tel:* 020 7582 3611; The Old Malt House, Hinton St George, Somerset, TA17 8SE *Tel:* 01460 73618.

PHILLIPS OF SUDBURY (Life Baron, UK), Andrew Wyndham Phillips; cr. 1998; OBE 1996

Born March 15, 1939; educated Uppingham; Trinity Hall, Cambridge (Hons Economics and Law). Married 1968, Penelope Ann Bennett (1 son 2 daughters). *Career:* Solicitor 1964; Established own practice, Bates, Wells & Braithwaite 1970; Director of several commercial companies including Dalehead Food Holdings; Chairman, Gough Hotels; Freelance Journalist and Broadcaster (including the Jimmy Young Show). *Party Groups (General):* Member, Society of Liberal Democrat Lawyers 1996–. *Other:* Governor, Contemporary Applied Arts; Co-Founder and Chairman, Legal Action Group 1971; Initiated: Lawyers in the Community Scheme 1987, Solicitors Pro Bono Group 1996; Chairman, Citizenship Foundation 1989–; Member: Charter 88 from inception until 1994, National Lottery Charities Board 1994–96. *Miscellaneous:* Contested: Harwich (Lab) 1970, expelled as Lab candidate for North Norfolk 1973, Saffron Walden By-election (Lib) 1977 and General Election (Lib) 1979, North East Essex Euro-election (Lib) 1979, Gainsborough (Lib/All) 1983. *Honours:* OBE 1996. *Publications:* Author: *The Living Law, Charitable Status – A Practical Handbook, Justice Beyond Reach;* Co-author: *Charity Investment – Law and Practice.* Name, Style and Title: Raised to the peerage as Baron Phillips of Sudbury, of Sudbury in the County of Suffolk 1998. A Liberal Democrat. *Address:* The Lord Phillips of Sudbury, OBE, House of Lords, London, SW1A 0PW.

PHILLIPS OF WORTH MATRAVERS (Life Baron, UK), Nicholas Addison Phillips; cr. 1999; Kt 1987; PC 1995

Born January 21, 1938; educated Bryanston School; King's College, Cambridge (MA); Hon. LLD, Exeter 1998. Married 1972, Christylle Marie-Thérèse Rouffiac (née Doreau) (2 daughters and 1 step-son 1 step-daughter). *Armed Forces:* National Service with Royal Navy, commissioned RNVR 1956–58. *Career:* Called to the Bar, Middle Temple (Harmsworth Scholar) 1962; In practice at the Bar 1962–87; Junior Counsel to the Ministry of Defence and to Treasury in Admiralty matters 1973–78; QC 1978; Member, Panel of Wreck Commissioners 1979; A Recorder 1982–87; A Judge of the High Court of Justice (Queen's Bench Division) 1987–95; Chairman, Law Advisory Committee, British Council 1991–97; Chairman, Council of Legal Education 1992–97; Vice-President, British Maritime Law Association 1993–; Lord Justice of Appeal 1995–98; A Lord of Appeal in Ordinary 1999–. *Other:* Governor, Bryanston School 1975–, Chairman of Governors 1981–. *Honours:* Kt 1987; PC 1995. *Recreations:* Sea, mountains. *Clubs:* Brooks's. *Name, Style and Title:* Raised to the peerage as Baron Phillips of Worth Matravers, of Belsize Park in the London Borough of Camden 1999. A Cross-Bencher. *Address:* The Rt Hon. the Lord Phillips of Worth Matravers, House of Lords, London, SW1A 0PW.

PIKE (Life Baroness, UK), Irene Mervyn Pike; cr. 1974; DBE 1981

Daughter of late Samuel Pike, and late Alice Goodhead, of Okehampton, Devon. Born September 16, 1918; educated Hunmanby Hall, East Yorks; Reading University (BA). *Armed Forces:* Served in WAAF 1941–46. *Career:* Managing Director, Clokie and Co. Ltd 1946–60; Director, Watts, Blake, Bearne 1964–89. *House of Commons:* Contested (Conservative): Pontefract (Yorkshire) 1951, Leek (Staffordshire) 1955; MP (Conservative) for Melton 1956–74; Assistant Postmaster-General 1959–63; Joint Parliamentary Under-Secretary of State, Home Office 1963–64. *Other:* National Chairman, WRVS 1974–81. *Miscellaneous:* Chairman, Broadcasting Complaints Commission 1981–85. *Honours:* DBE 1981. *Recreations:* Gardening, reading, walking. *Name, Style and Title:* Raised to the peerage as Baroness Pike, of Melton in the County of Leicestershire 1974. A Conservative. *Address:* The Baroness Pike, DBE, Hownam, Nr Kelso, Roxburgh, TD5 8AL.

PILKINGTON OF OXENFORD (Life Baron, UK), Peter Pilkington; cr. 1996

Son of late Frank and Doris Pilkington. Born September 5, 1933; educated Dame Allans School, Newcastle upon Tyne; Jesus College, Cambridge (MA). Married 1966, Helen (died December 1, 1997), daughter of Charles Wilson (2 daughters). *Trades Union:* Member, National Association of Head Teachers. *Career:* Schoolmaster, Tanganyika 1955–57; Ordained 1959; Curate in Bakewell, Derbyshire 1959–62; Schoolmaster, Eton College 1962–75, Master in College 1965–75; Headmaster, The King's School, Canterbury 1975–86; High Master, St Paul's School 1986–92; Hon. Canon of Canterbury Cathedral 1975–90, currently Canon Emeritus; Member, Parole Board 1990–95; Chairman, Broadcasting Complaints Commission 1992–96. *Spokesman:* An Opposition Spokesman on Education and Employment 1997–98. *Select Committees:* Co-opted Member, Select Committee on European Communities Sub-Committee F (Social Affairs, Education and Home Affairs) 1997–; Member, Ecclesiastical Committee 1997–. *Clubs:* Beefsteak, Garrick. *Name, Style and Title:* Raised to the peerage as Baron Pilkington of Oxenford, of West Dowlish in the County of Somerset 1996. A Conservative. *Address:* The Rev. Canon the Lord Pilkington of Oxenford, Oxenford House, Nr Ilminster, Somerset, TA19 OPP *Tel:* 01460 52813.

PITKEATHLEY (Life Baroness, UK), Jill Elizabeth Pitkeathley; cr. 1997; OBE 1993

Daughter of Roland and May Bisson. Born January 4, 1940; educated Ladies' College, Guernsey; Bristol University (BA Economics). Married 1961, W. Pitkeathley (1 son 1 daughter) (marriage dissolved 1978). *Career:* Social Worker 1961–68; Voluntary Service Co-ordinator, West Berkshire Health Authority 1970–83; National Consumer Council 1983–86; Director, National Council for Carers 1986 until merger with Association of Carers 1988; Adviser to Griffith's Review of Community Care 1986–88; Chief Executive, Carers National Association 1988–98; Vice-President, Community Council for Berkshire 1990–98, President 1998–. *Other:* Patron: Bracknell CVS, National Centre for Volunteering, National Institute for Social Work. *Miscellaneous:* Chair, New Opportunities Fund 1998–. *Honours:* OBE 1993. Hon. RCGP. *Publications: When I Went Home*, 1978; *Mobilising Voluntary Resources*, 1984; *Supporting Volunteers*, 1985; *It's my duty, isn't it?*, 1989; *Age Gap Relationships*, 1996 (with David Emerson); *Only Child*, 1994 (with David Emerson). *Recreations:* Gardening, grand-children, writing. *Name, Style and Title:* Raised to the peerage as Baroness Pitkeathley, of Caversham in the Royal County of Berkshire 1997. Labour. *Address:* The Baroness Pitkeathley, OBE, House of Lords, London, SW1A 0PW *E-Mail:* pitkeathleyj@parliament.uk.

PLANT OF HIGHFIELD (Life Baron, UK), Raymond Plant; cr. 1992

Son of late Stanley Plant and of Marjorie Plant. Born March 19, 1945; educated Havelock School, Grimsby; King's College, London (BA); Hull University (PhD); Hon. DLitt: Hull University, London Guildhall; Hon. ACA Degree. Married 1967, Katherine Sylvia, daughter of late Jack Dixon and of Jessie Dixon, of Grimsby (3 sons). *Career:* Lecturer, then Senior Lecturer in Philosophy, University of Manchester 1967–79; Has lectured on philosophy in several universities 1981–91; Professor of Politics, University of Southampton 1979–94; Master, St Catherine's College, Oxford 1994–. *Chancellor:* Pro-Chancellor, Southampton University 1996–. *Spokesman:* An Opposition Spokesman on Home Affairs 1992–96. *Select Committees:* Member, House of Lords Select Committee on Relations between Central and Local Government 1995–96. *Party Groups (General):* Chairman, Labour Party Commission on Electoral Systems 1991–. *Other:* President, National Council for Voluntary Organisations (NCVO) 1998–. FRSA 1992. *Publications:* A contributor to *The Times*; Author of: *Hegel*, 1974; *Community and Ideology*, 1974; *Political Philosophy and Social Welfare*, 1981; *Philosophy, Politics and Citizenship*, 1984; *Conservative Capitalism in Britain and the United States: a critical appraisal*, 1988; *Modern Political Thought*, 1991. *Recreations:* Music, opera, reading. *Name, Style and Title:* Raised to the peerage as Baron Plant of Highfield, of Weelsby in the County of Humberside 1992. Labour. *Address:* Professor The Lord Plant of Highfield, Master's Lodgings, St Catherine's College, Oxford, OX1 3UJ.

PLATT OF WRITTLE (Life Baroness, UK), Beryl Catherine Platt; cr. 1981; CBE 1978; DL

Daughter of late Ernest and Dorothy Myatt. Born April 18, 1923; educated Westcliff High School for Girls; Girton College, Cambridge (MA); Hon. DSc: City University, University of Salford, Cranfield University; Hon. DEng, Bradford University; Hon. Fellow, Polytechnic of Wales; Hon. Doctorate, Brunel University 1986; Hon. LLD, Cambridge University 1988; Hon. Fellow: Girton College, Cambridge 1988, Manchester Polytechnic 1989, UMIST 1992; Hon. DSc, Nottingham Trent University 1992; Hon. DTech, University of Loughborough 1993; Hon. DUniv: Open University, University of Essex, University Middlesex 1993, University of Westminster 1997. Married October 22, 1949, Stewart Sydney, son of late Sydney Rowland Platt (1 son 1 daughter). *Councils, Public Bodies:* Councillor, Chelmsford RDC 1959–74; Elected to Essex County Council 1965, Alderman 1969–74; Vice-Chairman, Education Committee 1969–71, Chairman 1971–80; Vice-Chairman, County Council 1980–83; DL, County of Essex 1983. *Career:* Technical Assistant: Hawker Aircraft 1943–46, British European Airways 1946–49. *Chancellor:* First Chancellor, Middlesex University 1993–. *Select Committees:* Member, House of Lords Select Committees on: Murder and Life Imprisonment 1988–89, Science and Technology 1982–85, 1990–94, 1996–, Relations between Central and Local Government 1995–96; Science and Technology Sub-Committee II (Science and Society) 1999–. *All-Party:* Vice-President, The Parliamentary Scientific Committee 1996–. *Party Groups:* Member, Association of Conservative Peers. *Other:* Member of Court, Essex University, from its establishment until 1999; Member of Court, City University 1969–78; Member: Burnham Further Education Salary Negotiation Committee 1975–80, Cambridge University Appointment Board 1975–79, Royal Aeronautical Society Education Committee 1975–77, 1990–93; President, Chelmsford Engineering Society 1979–80; Member, Council of RSA 1983–88; Vice-President, UMIST 1985–92 Member, Court Brunel University 1985–92; President: Cambridge University Engineers' Association 1987–, Association of Science Education 1988; Member, Committee on the Public Understanding of Science 1990–93; President, National Society for Clean Air 1991–93; Member, Meteorological Advisory Committee 1992–, Chairman 1995–; Member, Foundation for Science and Technology 1989–, Member of Council 1991–97; Member, Court of Cranfield University 1989–; President: Pipeline Industries Guild 1994–96, Essex Association of Local Councils; Patron: Women into Science and Engineering 1995, Women in Banking and Finance, and local charities. *Awards Granted:* City and Guilds of London Insignia Award 1988. *Trusts, etc:* Trustee, Homerton College 1970–81. *Miscellaneous:* Member: CNAA 1973–79, TEC 1973–82, Training and Education for the RAF Advisory Committee 1976–79, ACC Education Committee from its establishment to 1980, CLEA 1976–80, Council NFER 1975–77, City and Guilds of London Institute Council 1974–95; Vice-Chairman, London Regional Advisory Council for Technological Education 1975–81; Member, Engineering Council 1981–90; Chairman, Equal Opportunities

Commission 1983–88; Member, Careers Research Advisory Council 1983–93; Board Member, British Gas 1988–94; Vice-President, Association of County Councils 1992–98; Member, Engineering Training Authority 1990–92. *Honours:* CBE 1978. Hon. FIMechE; Hon. FInst of Training and Development; Hon. Fellowship,: Royal Aeronautical Society 1994, Royal College of Preceptors 1986; Fellow, Fellowship of Engineering (FEng) (now Royal Academy of Engineering) 1987; European Engineer (EurIng) 1987; Hon. Fellow: Girton College 1988, Women's Engineering Society 1989, Smallpiece Trust 1989; Fellow, Institution of Gas Engineers 1990; Hon. Fellow: Institute of Civil Engineers 1991, Institute of Structural Engineers 1991; Companion: Institute of Energy, Institute of Personnel Development 1995. Freeman, City of London 1988. Liveryman, Worshipful Company of Engineers 1988, Assistant to the Court 1996. *Special Interests:* Education, Women's Opportunities in Engineering, Local Government. *Recreations:* Reading, swimming for pleasure, cookery. *Clubs:* United Oxford and Cambridge University. *Name, Style and Title:* Raised to the peerage as Baroness Platt of Writtle, of Writtle in the County of Essex 1981. A Conservative. *Address:* The Baroness Platt of Writtle, CBE, DL, House of Lords, London, SW1A 0PW.

PLOWDEN (Life Baron, UK), Edwin Noel Plowden; cr. 1959; GBE 1987; KCB 1951

Son of late Roger H. Plowden. Born January 6, 1907; educated Switzerland; Pembroke College, Cambridge; Hon. Fellow, Pembroke College, Cambridge 1958; Hon. DSc: Pennsylvania State University 1958, University of Aston 1972; Hon. LLD, Loughborough University of Technology 1976. Married 1933, Dame Bridget Horatia, DBE, JP, daughter of late Admiral Sir Herbert Richmond, KCB (2 sons 1 daughter and 1 daughter deceased). *Career:* Temporary Civil Servant, Ministry of Economic Warfare 1939–40; Ministry of Aircraft Production 1940–46; Chief Executive and Member, Aircraft Supply Council 1945–46; Director, Commercial Union Assurance Co. Ltd 1946–78; Cabinet Office 1947; Treasury, as Chief Planning Officer and Chairman, Economic Planning Board 1947–53; Vice-Chairman, Temporary Council Committee NATO 1951–52; Chairman Designate, UK Atomic Energy Authority 1953–54, Chairman 1954–59; Chairman, Committee of Enquiry, Treasury Control of Public Expenditure 1959–61; Director, National Westminster Bank Ltd 1960–77; Chairman, Committee of Enquiry, Organization of Representational Services Overseas 1963–64; Chairman, Committee of Enquiry, Aircraft Industry 1964–65; Chairman, London Graduate School of Business Studies 1964–76, President 1976–90; Chairman, Standing Advisory Committee on Pay of Higher Civil Service 1968–70; Member, Civil Service College Advisory Council 1970–76; Chairman: Committee of Enquiry into Structure of Electricity Supply Industry 1974–75, Enquiry into CBI's Aims and Organisation 1974–75, Police Complaints Board 1976–80, CBI Companies Committee 1976–80, Equity Capital for Industry Ltd 1976–83; Member, Ford European Advisory Council 1976–83; Chairman, Tube Investments Ltd 1963–76, President 1976–90; Deputy Chairman, Committee of Inquiry on the Police 1977–79; Vice-Chairman, CBI Presidents Committee 1977–80; Member, Top Salaries Review Body 1977–81, Chairman 1981–89; Chairman, Police Negotiating Board 1979–82; Member, International Advisory Board Southeast Bank NA Miami 1982–86. *Miscellaneous:* Visiting Fellow, Nuffield College 1956–64. *Honours:* KBE 1946; KCB 1951; GBE 1987. *Publications: An Industrialist in the Treasury: the post war years. Clubs:* Brooks's. *Name, Style and Title:* Raised to the peerage as Baron Plowden, of Plowden in the County of Salop 1959. A Cross-Bencher. *Address:* The Lord Plowden, GBE, KCB, Martels Manor, Dunmow, Essex, CM6 1NB *Tel:* 01371 872141.

PLUMB (Life Baron, UK), Charles Henry Plumb; cr. 1987; Kt 1973; DL

Son of late Charles Plumb. Born March 27, 1925; educated King Edward VI School, Nuneaton; Hon. Fellow, Wye College 1995; Hon. DSc: Silsoe College of Technology, De Montfort University; Hon. LLD, University of Warwick. Married 1947, Marjorie Dorothy, daughter of Thomas Victor Dunn (1 son 2 daughters). *Councils, Public Bodies:* DL, Warwick 1977. *Career:* Member, Council, NFU 1959, Vice-President 1964–65, Deputy President 1966–69, President 1970–79; Member, Duke of Northumberland's Committee of Enquiry, Foot and Mouth Disease 1967–68; President, Comité des Organisations Professionnelles Agricoles de la CEE (COPA) 1975–77; Chairman, British Agricultural Council 1975–79; Non-Executive Director, Lloyds Bank, United Biscuits, Fisons 1979–94; MEP (Conservative) for Cotswolds 1979–99; Chairman, EP Agricultural Committee 1979–82; Chairman (Conservative) EDG, EP 1982–87, 1994–99; President:

European Parliament 1987–89, EU-ACP Joint Assembly 1994–99; Chairman, International Policy Council on Agriculture, Food and Trade; Chairman, Agricultural Mortgage Corporation 1994–95. *Chancellor:* Chancellor, Coventry University. *Other:* Member Council, NFU 1959, Vice-President 1964–65, Deputy President 1966–69, President 1970–79; President, Royal Agricultural Society of England 1977; Deputy to HRH The Prince of Wales 1978. *Trusts, etc:* Member, Henry Plumb Trust. *Honours:* Kt 1973; Grosses Verdienstkreuz des Verdienstordens der Bundesrepublik Deutschland 1976; Ordén de Merito, Portugal 1987; Order of Merit, Luxembourg 1988; Grand Cross of the Order of Civil Merit, Spain 1989; Knight Commander's Cross of the Order of Merit, Federal Republic of Germany 1990; Grand Order of the Phoenix, Greece 1997. Court Member, Farmers' Company; Hon. Liveryman, Worshipful Company of Fruiterers. *Clubs:* St Stephen's Constitutional. *Name, Style and Title:* Raised to the peerage as Baron Plumb, of Coleshill in the County of Warwickshire 1987. A Conservative. *Address:* The Lord Plumb, DL, The Dairy Farm, Maxstoke, Coleshill, Warwickshire, B46 2QJ *Tel:* 01675 463133 *Fax:* 01675 464156 *E-Mail:* hp@wertwyn.demon.co.uk.

PLUMMER OF ST MARYLEBONE (Life Baron, UK), (Arthur) Desmond (Herne) Plummer; cr. 1981; Kt 1971; TD 1950; DL

Son of late Arthur Herne and Janet Plummer, née McCormick. Born May 25, 1914; educated Hurstpierpoint College; College of Estate Management; Hon. FFAS 1966. Married 1941, Pat (died December 20, 1998), daughter of late Albert Holloway (1 daughter). *Armed Forces:* Served Royal Engineers 1939–46. *Councils, Public Bodies:* Councillor, St Marylebone Borough Council 1952–65, Mayor 1958–59; London County Council for St Marylebone 1960–65; Inner London Education Authority 1964–76; Greater London Council for: Cities of London and Westminster 1964–73, St Marylebone 1973–76; Leader of GLC Opposition 1966–67, 1973–74; Leader of Council 1967–73; JP 1958; DL, Greater London 1970. *Career:* Executive Committee British Section of International Union of Local Authorities 1967–74; Deputy Chairman, National Employers' Mutual General Insurance Association 1973–86; Chairman, National Stud 1975–82; Chairman, National Employers' Life Assurance Association 1983–88; Chairman, Portman Building Society 1983–90, President 1990–. *All-Party:* Member, All-Party: Racing and Bloodstock Industries Committee, London Group, Rugby Union Group, Parliamentary Sports Group, Building Societies Group. *Party Groups:* Member, Association of Conservative Peers. *Other:* President, Metropolitan Association of Building Societies 1983–89; Member Court, University of London 1967–77. *Miscellaneous:* Member: South Bank Theatre Board 1964–74, Standing Conference on South East Planning 1967–74, Transport Co-ordinating Council for London 1967–69, Local Authority Conditions of Service Advisory Board 1967–71; Chairman, Horserace Betting Levy Board 1974–82. *Honours:* Kt 1971; KStJ 1986. FRSA; FRICS; Hon. FFAS. The Worshipful Company of Tin Plate Workers Alias Wireworkers of London. *Publications: Time For Change in Greater London,* 1958; *Report to London,* 1970. *Sportsclubs:* Otter Swimming Club. *Clubs:* Carlton, MCC, Royal Automobile. *Name, Style and Title:* Raised to the peerage as Baron Plummer of St Marylebone, of the City of Westminster 1981. A Conservative. *Address:* The Lord Plummer of St Marylebone, TD, DL, 4 The Lane, Marlborough Place, London, NW8 0PN *E-Mail:* plumerne@clara.co.uk.

PORTER OF LUDDENHAM (Life Baron, UK), George Porter; cr. 1990; OM 1989; Kt 1972; FRS 1960

Son of late John and Alice Porter. Born December 6, 1920; educated Thorne Grammar School; Leeds University (BSc); Emmanuel College, Cambridge (MA, PhD, ScD); Fellow, Emmanuel College 1952–54; Research Professor and Fellow, Imperial College, London 1987–; Hon. Doctorates of 34 universities in UK and abroad, including: DSc Oxford, DSc London, LLD Cambridge. Married August 12, 1949, Stella Jean, daughter of late Colonel George Brooke (2 sons). *Armed Forces:* Served RNVR, Radar Officer 1941–45. *Career:* Demonstrator in Physical Chemistry, Cambridge University 1949–52; Assistant Director of Research in Physical Chemistry, Cambridge University; Assistant Director, British Rayon Research Association 1954–55; Professor of Physical Chemistry, Firth Professor and Head of Department of Chemistry, Sheffield University 1955–66; Director, The Royal Institution 1966–87, Emeritus Professor 1988–; President, Royal Society 1985–90;

Chairman, Centre for Photomolecular Sciences, Imperial College, London 1986–. *Chancellor:* Chancellor, Leicester University 1986–95. *Select Committees:* Member, House of Lords Select Committee on Science and Technology 1990–94, 1995–99. *Awards Granted:* Nobel Prize (joint) for Chemistry 1967; Royal Society: Davy Medal 1971, Rumford Medal 1978; Royal Society of Chemistry: Faraday Medal 1981, Copley Medal 1992. *Honours:* Kt 1972; OM 1989. FRS 1960. Master, Salters' Company 1993–94. *Publications:* Author of: *Chemistry for the Modern World*, 1962; *Chemistry in Microtime*, 1997; as well as scientific papers for Royal Society, Faraday Society etc. *Special Interests:* Education, Science. *Recreations:* Sailing. *Clubs:* Athenaeum. *Name, Style and Title:* Raised to the peerage as Baron Porter of Luddenham, of Luddenham in the County of Kent 1990. A Cross-Bencher. *Address:* Professor The Lord Porter of Luddenham, OM, FRS, Departments of Chemistry and Biochemistry, Imperial College, London, SW7 2AY *Tel:* 020 7594 5785 *E-Mail:* gporter@ic.ac.uk.

PORTSMOUTH (Bishop of), Kenneth William Stevenson

Son of Frederik and Margrete Stevenson. Born November 9, 1949; educated Edinburgh Academy; Edinburgh University (MA 1970); Southampton University (PhD 1975); Manchester University (DD 1987). Married 1970, Sarah Glover (1 son 3 daughters). *Career:* Ordained Deacon 1973; Priest 1974–; Assistant Curate, Grantham with Manthorpe 1973–76; Lecturer, Boston 1976–80; Part-time Lecturer, Lincoln Theological College 1975–80; Chaplain and Lecturer, Manchester University 1980–86; Team Vicar 1980–82; Team Rector, Whitworth, Manchester 1982–86; Visiting Professor, University of Notre Dame, Indiana 1983; Rector, Holy Trinity and St Mary's, Guildford 1986–95; Secretary, Anglo-Nordic Baltic Theological Conference, 1986–97

Member: Church of England Liturgical Commission 1986–96, Faith and Order Advisory Group 1991–96, Church of England Doctrine Commission 1996–; Bishop of Portsmouth 1995–; Chairman, Anglo-Nordic-Baltic Theological Conference 1997–; Took his seat in the House of Lords 1999. Fellow, Royal Historical Society 1990. *Publications:* include: *Nuptial Blessing*, 1982; *Eucharist and Offering*, 1986; *Jerusalem Revisited*, 1988; *The First Rites*, 1989; *Covenant of Grace Renewed*, 1994; *The Mystery of the Eucharist in the Anglican Tradition*, (with H. R. McAdoo) 1995; *The Mystery of Baptism in the Anglican Tradition*, 1998; *All the Company of Heaven*, 1998; Contributor to: *Theology, Scottish Journal of Theology, La Maison Dieu;* Reviewer in: *Theology, Journal of Theological Studies; Church Times. Recreations:* Historical biographies, thrillers, walking, butterflies, piano, horn. *Address:* The Rt Rev. the Lord Bishop of Portsmouth, Bishopgrove, 26 Osborn Road, Fareham, Hampshire, PO16 7DQ *Tel:* 01329 280247 *Fax:* 01329 231538 *E-Mail:* bishports@clara.co.uk.

PRASHAR (Life Baroness, UK), Usha Kumari Prashar; cr. 1999; CBE 1994

Daughter of late Naurhia and Durga Prashar. Born June 29, 1948; educated Duchess Gloucester School, Nairobi, Kenya; Wakefield Girls' High School, Wakefield, Yorkshire; University of Leeds (BA Hons 1970); University of Glasgow (DipSocAdmin 1971); Hon. Fellow, Goldsmith's College, University of London; Hon. LLD: De Montfort University 1994, South Bank University 1994, Greenwich University, Leeds Metropolitan University. Married July 21, 1973, Vijay Kumar Sharma. *Career:* Conciliation Officer, Race Relations Board 1971–75; Director, Runnymede Trust 1976–84; Fellow, Policy Studies Institute 1984–86; Director, National Council of Voluntary Organisations 1986–91; Part-time Civil Service Commissioner 1991–96; Chairman, Parole Board of England and Wales 1997–. *Other:* Patron: Sickle Cell Society 1986–, Elfrida Rathbone Society 1988–; Hon. Vice-President, Council for Overseas Student Affairs 1986–; Governor, De Montfort University 1996–. *Miscellaneous:* Member: Arts Council of Great Britain 1979–81, Study Commission on the Family 1980–83, Social Security Advisory Committee 1980–83, Executive Committee, Child Poverty Action Group 1984–85, London Food Commission 1984–90, BBC Educational Broadcasting Council 1987–89, Solicitor's Complaints Bureau 1989–90, Royal Commission on Criminal Justice 1991–93, Lord Chancellor's Advisory Committee on Legal Education and Conduct 1991–97, Board of Energy Saving Trust 1992–98, Arts Council of England 1994–97; Non-Executive Director, Channel Four 1992–; Deputy Chairman, National Literacy Trust 1992–. *Honours:* CBE 1994. FRSA. *Publications:* Has contributed to several publications on health and race relations. *Recreations:* Golf, music, art, reading. *Sportsclubs:* Foxhills Golf Club. *Clubs:* Reform, Royal Commonwealth Society. *Name, Style and Title:* Raised to the peerage as Baroness Prashar, of Runnymede in the County of Surrey 1999. A Cross-Bencher. *Address:* The Baroness Prashar, CBE, Parole Board, Abell House, John Islip Street, London, SW1P 4LH *Tel:* 020 7217 5484 *Fax:* 020 7217 5793.

PRENTICE (Life Baron, UK), Reginald (Ernest) Prentice; cr. 1992; Kt 1987; PC 1966

Son of late Ernest and Elizabeth Prentice. Born July 16, 1923; educated Whitgift School; London School of Economics (BSc Economics). Married 1948, Joan, daughter of Rosa Godwin (1 daughter). *Trades Union:* Member of staff, TGWU 1950–57. *Armed Forces:* Served RA 1942–46; Commissioned 1943; Served Italy and Austria 1944–46. *Councils, Public Bodies:* Alderman, GLC 1970–71; JP, Croydon 1961. *Career:* Temporary civil servant 1940–42; Company Director and Consultant; Director, EW Fact plc; Consultant, Aid-Call plc. *House of Commons:* MP (Labour): East Ham North 1957–74, Newham North East 1974–77; Resigned from Labour Party and joined Conservative Party 1977; MP (Conservative): Newham North East 1977–79, Daventry 1979–87; Minister of State, Department of Education and Science 1964–66; Minister of Public Building and Works 1966–67; Minister of Overseas Development 1967–69, 1975–76; Secretary of State for Education and Science 1974–75; Minister of State for Social Security, DHSS 1979–81. *Spokesman (Commons):* Opposition Spokesman on Employment 1972–74. *Party Groups (General):* Member, Executive Committee, National Union of Conservative Associations 1988–90; President, Devizes Constituency Conservative Association. *Honours:* PC 1966; Kt 1987. *Publications:* Author of: (jointly) *Social Welfare and the Citizen,* 1957; *Right Turn,* 1978. *Special Interests:* Industrial Relations, Foreign Affairs. *Recreations:* Walking. *Name, Style and Title:* Raised to the peerage as Baron Prentice, of Daventry in the County of Northamptonshire 1992. A Conservative. *Address:* The Rt Hon. the Lord Prentice, Wansdyke, Church Lane, Mildenhall, Marlborough, Wiltshire, SN8 2LU.

PRIOR (Life Baron, UK), James Michael Leathes Prior; cr. 1987; PC 1970

Son of late Charles Bolingbroke Leathes Prior, JP. Born October 11, 1927; educated Charterhouse; Pembroke College, Cambridge; Hon. Fellow, Pembroke College, Cambridge; Hon. Doctorate: Anglia Polytechnic University, Stafford University. Married January 30, 1954, Jane Primrose Gifford, daughter of late Air Vice-Marshal O. G. W. G. Lywood, CB, CBE (3 sons 1 daughter). *Armed Forces:* Commissioned in Army 1946; Served in India and Germany. *Career:* Farmer and Land Agent 1950; Chairman: The General Electric Company plc 1984–98, Allders Ltd 1984–94; Director, United Biscuits plc 1990–94; Member: Tenneco Europe Ltd (Advisory Committee) to 1998, American International (Advisory Council); Chairman: East Anglia Radio plc 1992–95, African Cargo Handling Ltd 1998–. *House of Commons:* MP (Conservative) for: Lowestoft 1959–83, Waveney 1983–87; PPS to the: President of the Board of Trade 1962–63, Minister of Power 1963–64, Leader of the Opposition 1965–70; Minister of Agriculture, Fisheries and Food 1970–72; Lord President and Leader of the House 1972–74; Secretary of State for: Employment 1979–81, Northern Ireland 1981–1984. *Spokesman (Commons):* Conservative Spokesman on Employment 1974–79. *Chancellor:* Chancellor, Anglia Polytechnic University 1993–99. *International Bodies (General):* Chairman, Arab-British Chamber of Commerce 1996–. *Party Groups (General):* Vice-Chairman, Conservative Party 1965, Deputy Chairman 1972–74. *Other:* Chairman: Royal Veterinary College 1990–99, Wishing Well Appeal (Great Ormond Street Childrens' Hospital). *Trusts, etc:* Chairman: Industry and Parliament Trust 1990–94, NAC Rural Housing Trust 1990–99, London Playing Fields Society 1998–; Chairman, Special Trustees, Wishing Well Appeal (Great Ormond Street Childrens' Hospital). *Miscellaneous:* Chairman: Council for Industry and Higher Education 1985–92, Archbishops' Commission on Rural Areas. *Honours:* PC 1970. *Publications:* Author of *A Balance of Power,* 1986. *Clubs:* Garrick, MCC. *Name, Style and Title:* Raised to the peerage as Baron Prior, of Brampton in the County of Suffolk 1987. A Conservative. *Address:* The Rt Hon. the Lord Prior, House of Lords, London, SW1A 0PW.

PRYS-DAVIES (Life Baron, UK), Gwilym Prys-Davies; cr 1982

Son of late William Davies. Born December 8, 1923; educated Tywyn School, Gwynedd; University College of Wales, Aberystwyth; Hon. Fellow: University College of Wales, Aberystwyth, Trinity College, Carmarthen, University of Wales Institute, Cardiff; Hon. LLD (Wales). Married August 30, 1951, Llinos, daughter of Abraham and Olwen Evans (3 daughters). *Career:* Solicitor; Consultant and formerly Partner, Morgan Bruce & Hardwickes, Cardiff and Pontypridd; Chairman, Welsh Hospitals Board 1968–74; Special Adviser to Secretary of State for Wales 1974–78; Member, Economic and Social Committee, EEC 1978–82. *Spokesman:* Opposition Front Bench Spokesman on: Health 1983–87, Welsh Office 1987–97, Northern Ireland 1982–93. *Select Committees:* Member, House of Lords Select Committees on: Murder and Life Imprisonment 1988–89, Parochial Charities (Neighbourhood Trusts Bill and the Small Charities Bill) 1983–84, Relations between Central and Local Government 1995–96; Member: Joint Committee on Statutory Instruments 1993–99; Select Committee on Delegated Powers and Deregulation 1999–. *International Bodies:* Member, British-Irish Parliamentary Body 1990–97. *Other:* President, University of Wales, Swansea 1997–. *Name, Style and Title:* Raised to the peerage as Baron Prys-Davies, of Llanegryn in the County of Gwynedd 1982. Labour. *Address:* The Lord Prys-Davies, Lluest, 78 Church Road, Tonteg, Pontypridd, Mid Glamorgan, CF38 1EN *Tel:* 01443 202462 *Tel:* Office: 01443 402233.

PUTTNAM (Life Baron, UK), David (Terence) Puttnam; cr. 1997; Kt 1995; CBE 1983

Son of late Leonard and Marie Puttnam. Born February 25, 1941; educated Minchenden Grammar School, London; City and Guilds 1958–62; Hon. LLD, Bristol 1983; Hon. DLitt, Leicester 1986; Hon. Fellow, Manchester 1990; Hon. LittD, Leeds 1992; Hon. DLitt: Sunderland 1992, Bradford 1993; Hon. Doctorate, Humberside 1996; Hon. DLitt: Westminster 1997, The University of Kent at Canterbury 1998; Hon. DMus, Royal Scottish Academy of Music and Drama 1998; Hon. Dlitt, Imperial College of Science, Technology and Medicine 1999; Diploma of Fellowship, City and Guilds Institute 1999. Married 1961, Patricia Jones (1 son 1 daughter). *Trades Union:* Member, BECTU. *Career:* Advertising 1958–66; Photography 1966–68; Film Production 1968–; Producer of films including: *Bugsy Malone*, 1976 (four BAFTA Awards), *Midnight Express*, 1978 (two Academy Awards, three BAFTA Awards), *Chariots of Fire*, 1981 (four Academy Awards, three BAFTA Awards including awards for best film), *Local Hero*, 1982 (two BAFTA Awards); *The Killing Fields*, 1984 (three Academy Awards, seven nominations: eight BAFTA Awards including Best Film); *The Mission*, 1986 (Palme D'Or, Cannes, one Academy Award, seven nominations; three BAFTA Awards); *Memphis Belle*, 1990, as well as several others; Chairman, Enigma Productions Ltd 1978–; Director: National Film Finance Corporation 1980–85, Anglia Television Group 1982–99; Chairman and Chief Executive Officer, Columbia Pictures 1986–88; Village Roadshow plc 1988–. *Chancellor:* Chancellor, University of Sunderland. *All-Party:* Member, All-Party: Education Group, Media Group. *Other:* Governor, National Film and Television School 1974–, Chairman 1988–96; Vice-President, BAFTA 1993–; Chairman, National Museum of Photography, Film and Television 1996–97; Member, Court of Governors: The London School of Economics 1997–, The London Institute 1997–; Member, Academic Board Bristol University. *Awards Granted:* Michael Balcon Award for outstanding contribution to British Film Industry, BAFTA 1982; Benjamin Franklin Award, RSA 1996; The Crystal Award presented by The World Economic Forum 1997. *Trusts, etc:* Trustee: Tate Gallery 1986–93, Science Museum 1996–. *Miscellaneous:* Visiting Professor, Bristol University 1983–97; Visiting Lecturer, London School of Economics 1997–; President, CPRE 1985–92, Vice-President 1997–; Member: British Screen Advisory Council 1988, British Film Commission 1992–, Arts Council Lottery Panel 1995–97; Vice-President, Royal Geographical Society 1997–; Member, Government's Education Standards Task Force; Chairman, National Endowment for Science, Technology and Arts. *Honours:* CBE 1983; Officier de l'Ordre des Arts and des Lettres (France) 1992; Kt 1995. FRGS; FRSA; FRPS; BFI; FCGI. *Publications: The Third Age of Broadcasting* (ed. Brian Wenham), 1982; *Rural England* (David Puttnam and Derrik Mercer), 1988; *A Submission to the EC Think Tank on Audio-Visual Policy*, 1994; *The Creative Imagination* in 'What Needs to Change' (ed. Giles Radice), 1996; *The Undeclared War*, 1997. *Recreations:* Reading, cinema. *Clubs:* Chelsea Arts, MCC, Athenaeum. *Name, Style and Title:* Raised to the peerage as Baron Puttnam, of Queensgate in the Royal Borough of Kensington and Chelsea 1997. Labour. *Address:* The Lord Puttnam, CBE, Enigma Productions Ltd, 29a Tufton Street, London, SW1P 3QL *Tel:* 020 7222 5757 *Fax:* 020 7222 5858 *E-Mail:* lordputtnam@hotmail.com.

PYM (Life Baron, UK), Francis Leslie Pym; cr. 1987; PC 1970; MC 1945; DL

Son of late Leslie Ruthven Pym, JP, MP, and late Iris Rosalind (née Orde). Born February 13, 1922; educated Eton; Magdalene College, Cambridge; Hon. Fellow, Magdalene College, Cambridge 1979. Married June 25, 1949, Valerie Fortune, daughter of late F. J. H. Daglish (2 sons 2 daughters). *Armed Forces:* Captain, 9th Lancers; Served in Africa and Italy, MC 1945. *Councils, Public Bodies:* Councillor, Herefordshire County Council 1958–61; DL, Cambridgeshire 1973–. *Career:* Director, Christie Brockbank Shipton Ltd; Chairman, Diamond Cable Communications. *House of Commons:* Contested (Conservative) Rhondda West 1959; MP (Conservative) for: Cambridgeshire 1961–83, Cambridgeshire South East 1983–87; PPS to the Chancellor of the Exchequer 1962; Secretary of State for Northern Ireland 1973–74; Secretary of State for Defence 1979–1981; Chancellor of the Duchy of Lancaster, Paymaster General and Leader of the House of Commons 1981; Lord President of the Council and Leader of the House of Commons 1981–82; Secretary of State for Foreign and Commonwealth Affairs 1982–83. *Whip (Commons):* Assistant Government Whip 1962; Opposition Whip 1964–67; Deputy Chief Whip for the Opposition 1967–70; Parliamentary Secretary to the Treasury and Government Chief Whip 1970–73. *Spokesman (Commons):* Opposition Spokesman on: Northern Ireland and Agriculture 1974, Agriculture, Fisheries and Food 1974–76, House of Commons Affairs and on Devolution 1976–78, Foreign and Commonwealth Affairs 1978–79. *Other:* Member, Liverpool University Council 1949–53; President, Atlantic Treaty Association 1985–88; Chairman, English Speaking Union 1987–92. *Trusts, etc:* Chairman, The St Andrew's (Ecumenical) Trust. *Honours:* PC 1970. *Publications: The Politics of Consent,* 1984; *Sentimental Journey,* 1998. *Special Interests:* Foreign Affairs, Defence, Rural Affairs, Parliamentary Affairs. *Recreations:* Gardens, touching life at many points. *Clubs:* Buck's. *Name, Style and Title:* Raised to the peerage as Baron Pym, of Sandy in the County of Bedfordshire 1987. A Conservative. *Address:* The Rt Hon. the Lord Pym, MC, DL, Everton Park, Sandy, Bedfordshire, SG19 2DE.

Q

QUINTON (Life Baron, UK), Anthony Meredith Quinton; cr. 1983; FBA 1977

Son of late Surgeon-Captain Richard Frith Quinton, RN. Born March 25, 1925; educated Stowe School; Christ Church, Oxford; Hon DHum Lit, New York University USA; Hon DHum, Ball State University USA. Married August 2, 1952, Marcelle, daughter of late Maurice Wegier, of New York (1 son 1 daughter). *Armed Forces:* Served RAF 1943–46; Flying Officer and Navigator. *Career:* Delegate, Oxford University Press 1970–76; Fellow: All Souls College, Oxford 1949–55, New College 1955–78, Winchester College 1970–85; President, Trinity College, Oxford 1978–87; Fellow, Member, Arts Council 1979–81; Chairman, British Library Board 1985–90; Emeritus Fellow, New College, Oxford; Former Vice-Chairman, Encyclopaedia Britannica Board of Editors. *Other:* Governor, Stowe School 1963–84, Chairman of Governors 1969–75; President: Aristotelian Society 1975–76, Royal Institute of Philosophy 1990–; Chairman, Kennedy Memorial Foundation 1990–95. *Trusts, etc:* Wolfson Foundation; Radcliffe Trusts. *Honours:* Order of Leopold II (Belgium) 1984; FBA. *Publications: Political Philosophy* (editor) 1967; *The Nature of Things,* 1973; *Utilitarian Ethics,* 1973, 1990; *The Politics of Imperfection,* 1978; *Francis Bacon,* 1980; *Thoughts and Thinkers,* 1982; *From Wodehouse to Wittgenstein,* 1998. *Special Interests:* Education, Arts, Media. *Clubs:* Garrick, Beefsteak, Brooks's. *Name, Style and Title:* Raised to the peerage as Baron Quinton, of Holywell in the City of Oxford and County of Oxfordshire 1983. A Conservative. *Address:* The Lord Quinton, FBA, A11 Albany, Piccadilly, London, W1V 9RD *Tel:* 020 7287 8686.

QUIRK (Life Baron, UK), Charles Randolph Quirk; cr. 1994; Kt 1985; CBE 1976; FBA 1975

Son of late Thomas and Amy Randolph Quirk. Born July 12, 1920; educated Douglas High School, Isle of Man; University College, London (MA, PhD, DLitt); Yale University; Hon. LLD, DLitt, DSc. from universities in the United Kingdom, USA and Europe; Jubilee Medal, Institute of Linguistics 1973; Foreign Fellow, Royal Belgian Academy of Science 1975; Hon. Fellow: Imperial College 1985, Queen Mary College 1986, Goldsmiths' College 1987; Foreign Fellow, Royal Swedish Academy 1987; Member, Academia Europaea 1988; Hon. Fellow, King's College 1990; Foreign Fellow: Finnish Academy of Science 1991, American Academy of Arts and Sciences 1995. Married 1st, 1946, Jean, daughter of Ellis Gauntlett Williams (2 sons) (marriage dissolved 1979, she died 1995), married 2nd, 1984, Gabriele, daughter of Judge Helmut Stein. *Armed Forces:* Served RAF 1940–45. *Career:* Lecturer in English, University College, London 1947–54; Commonwealth Fund Fellow, Yale University and University of Michigan 1951–52; Reader in English Language and Literature, University of Durham 1954–58, Professor 1958–60 and at University of London 1960–68; Quain Professor of English Language and Literature, University College, London 1968–81; Chairman, Committee of Enquiry in Speech Therapy Services 1969–72; Member of Senate, University of London 1970–85; Governor, British Institute of Recorded Sound 1975–80; Member, BBC Archives Committee 1975–81; Vice-Chancellor, University of London 1981–85; President, Institute of Linguistics 1982–86; Member, Board of British Council 1983–91; Chairman, Anglo-Spanish Foundation 1983–85; Chairman, British Library Advisory Committee 1984–97; Member, RADA Council 1985–; President, British Academy 1985–89; Trustee, City Technology Colleges 1986–98; President, College of Speech Therapists 1987–91; Trustee, Wolfson Foundation 1987–; Royal Commissioner, 1851 Exhibition 1987–95; President, North of England Educational Conference 1989. *Select Committees:* Member, Select Committee on Science and Technology Sub-Committee II (Science and Society) 1999–. *Other:* Member: Linguistic Society of America, Modern Language Association. *Awards Granted:* Jubilee Medal, Institute of Linguistics 1973. *Honours:* CBE 1975; Kt 1985. FBA 1975. *Publications:* Author of several works on the English Language (jointly with others); Solely: *The Concessive Relation in Old English Poetry*, 1954; *Essays on the English Language – Medieval and Modern*, 1968; *The English Language and Images of Matter*, 1972; *The Linguist and the English Language*, 1974; *Style and Communication in the English Language*, 1984; *Words at Work – Lectures on Textual Structures*, 1986; *Grammatical and Lexical Variance in English*, 1995; Has contributed to conference proceedings and learned journals. *Special Interests:* Education, Public Communication, Health, Speech Pathology, Broadcasting, Media. *Clubs:* Athenaeum. *Name, Style and Title:* Raised to the peerage as Baron Quirk, of Bloomsbury in the London Borough of Camden 1994. A Cross-Bencher. *Address:* Professor The Lord Quirk, CBE, FBA, University College London, Gower Street, London, WC1E 6BT *Tel:* 020 7387 7050.

R

RAMSAY OF CARTVALE (Life Baroness, UK), Meta Ramsay; cr. 1996

Daughter of Alexander Ramsay and Sheila Ramsay (née Jackson). Born July 12, 1936; educated Battlefield Primary School; Hutchesons' Girls' Grammar School, Glasgow; Glasgow University (MA, MEd); Graduate Institute for International Affairs, Geneva; Hon. DLitt, University of Bradford. *Trades Union:* Member, GMB. *Councils, Public Bodies:* Member, Lewisham Community Health Council 1992–94. *Career:* HM Diplomatic Service 1969–91; Foreign Policy Adviser to late Rt Hon. John Smith, MP, Leader of the Labour Party 1992–94; Special Adviser to Rt Hon. John Cunningham, MP, Shadow Secretary of State for Trade and Industry 1994–95. *Whip:* A Baroness in Waiting (Government Whip) December 1997–. *Spokesman:* A Spokeswoman on: Culture, Media and Sport 1997–98, Health 1997–98, Scotland 1997–, Foreign Affairs and Europe 1998–. *Select Committees:* Member: Select Committee on European Communities 1997, Select Committee on European Communities Sub-Committee F (Social Affairs, Education and Home Affairs) 1997. *International Bodies:* Member, British Delegation to the Parliamentary Assembly of OSCE 1997. *Party Groups (General):* Member: Labour Party, Fabian Society, Co-operative Party, Labour Finance and Industry Group, Labour Movement in Europe. *Other:* President, Scottish Union of Students 1959–60;

Chair, Atlantic Council of the United Kingdom 1997; Member: RIIA, Institute for Jewish Policy Research, 300 Group; Chair, Board of Governors, Fairlawn Primary School, Forest Hill, South London. *Miscellaneous:* Honorary Visiting Research Fellow in Peace Studies, Bradford University; Member, Intelligence and Security Committee 1997. FRSA. *Recreations:* Theatre, opera, ballet. *Clubs:* University Women's, Reform, Royal Scottish Automobile (Glasgow). *Name, Style and Title:* Raised to the peerage as Baroness Ramsay of Cartvale, of Langside in the City of Glasgow 1996. Labour. *Address:* The Baroness Ramsay of Cartvale, House of Lords, London, SW1A 0PW.

RANDALL OF ST BUDEAUX (Life Baron, UK), Stuart Jeffrey Randall; cr. 1997

Son of late Charles Randall. Born June 22, 1938; educated University of Wales, Cardiff. Married August 22, 1963, Gillian Michael (3 daughters). *Career:* Electrical fitter apprentice, HM Dockyard, Devonport 1953–58; Systems engineer: English Electric Computers, Radio Corporation of America, USA 1963–66; Project leader, Marconi Automation 1966–68; Consultant, Inter-Bank Research Organisation 1968–71; Manager: British Steel Corporation 1971–76, British Leyland 1976–80; Consultant, Nexos Office Systems 1980–82; Manager, Plessey Communications Systems Ltd 1982–83. *House of Commons:* Contested Worcestershire South October 1974; Contested Midlands West European Election 1979; MP (Labour) for Hull West 1983–97; PPS to the Rt Hon. Roy Hattersley, as Deputy Leader of the Labour Party and Shadow Chancellor of the Exchequer 1984–85. *Spokesman (Commons):* Opposition Front Bench Spokesman on: Agriculture 1985–87, Home Affairs 1987–92. *Select Committees:* Member, Select Committee on European Communities Sub-Committee A (Economic and Financial Affairs, Trade and External Relations) 1997–. *Special Interests:* Information Technology. *Recreations:* Sailing, walking, flying. *Name, Style and Title:* Raised to the peerage as Baron Randall of St Budeaux, of St Budeaux in the County of Devon 1997. Labour. *Address:* The Lord Randall of St Budeaux, House of Lords, London, SW1A 0PW.

RAWLINGS (Life Baroness, UK), Patricia Elizabeth Rawlings; cr. 1994

Daughter of late Louis Rawlings and of Mary Rawlings (née Boas de Winter). Born January 27, 1939; educated Oak Hall, Haslemere, Surrey; Le Manoir, Lausanne, Switzerland; Florence University; University College, London (BA Hons); London School of Economics (Postgraduate diploma (International Relations); Hon. DLitt, University of Buckingham. Married 1962, Sir David Wolfson (created Baron Wolfson of Sunningdale, *qv*) (marriage dissolved 1967). *Career:* Director: California Dress Company 1969–82, Rheims and Laurent, French Fine Art Auctioneers 1969–71; Member, Peace through NATO Council 1985–88; Member, British Video Classification Council 1986–89; Special Adviser, Department of the Environment 1987–88; MEP (Conservative) for Essex South West 1989–94; Group Deputy Whip; Former Spokesman, EP Committee on Youth, Education, the Arts and Broadcasting; Former Vice-President, Delegation for Relations with Albania, Bulgaria and Romania; Former Member, Delegation for Relations with USA; Board Member, British Association for Central and Eastern Europe 1994–. *Whip:* An Opposition Whip 1997–98. *Spokesman:* An Opposition Spokeswoman on: Culture, Media and Sport 1997–98, Foreign and Commonwealth Affairs December 1998–, International Development December 1998–. *Party Groups (General):* Member, Conservative Women's National Committee 1983–88. *Other:* Member, LCC Children's Care Committee 1959–61; Member, British Red Cross Society 1964–, Chairman Appeals, London Branch (National Badge of Honour 1981), Hon. Vice-President 1988–; Director, English Chamber Orchestra and Music Society 1980–; Member, British Council 1997–; Council Member: RIIA, NACF, IISS; Chairman of Council, King's College, London. *Awards Granted:* British Red Cross National Badge of Honour 1987. *Miscellaneous:* Contested (Conservative): Sheffield Central 1983, Doncaster Central 1987 General Elections; Contested Essex West and Hertfordshire East in 1994 European Parliamentary Elections. *Honours:* Order of the Rose (Silver) Bulgaria 1991; Grand Official, Order of the Southern Cross, Republic of Brazil 1997. *Special Interests:* International Affairs, Culture, Heritage, Broadcasting. *Recreations:* Music, art, architecture, gardening, travel, skiing, golf. *Clubs:* Grillions, Royal West Norfolk, Queen's. *Name, Style and Title:* Raised to the peerage as Baroness Rawlings, of Burnham Westgate in the County of Norfolk 1994. A Conservative. *Address:* The Baroness Rawlings, House of Lords, London, SW1A 0PW.

RAWLINSON OF EWELL (Life Baron, UK), Peter Anthony Grayson Rawlinson; cr. 1978; Kt 1962; PC 1964; QC 1959; QC (NI) 1972

Son of late Lieutenant-Colonel A. R. Rawlinson, OBE. Born June 26, 1919; educated Downside; Christ's College, Cambridge (Exhibitioner 1938); Hon. Fellow, Christ's College, Cambridge 1981. Married 1st, 1940, Haidee Kavanagh (3 daughters) (marriage dissolved and annulled by Sacred Rota, Rome 1954), married 2nd, 1954, Elaine, daughter of late Vincent Dominguez of Newport, RI, USA (2 sons 1 daughter). *Armed Forces:* Irish Guards, Major, mentioned in despatches 1939–46. *Career:* Called to the Bar, Inner Temple 1946; Queens Counsel 1959; Bencher, Inner Temple 1962, Treasurer 1984; Recorder, Salisbury 1960–62; Chairman of the Bar 1975–76; Leader, Western Circuit 1975–82; Recorder, Kingston-upon-Thames 1975; President, Senate of Inns of Court and the Bar 1986–87. *House of Commons:* MP (Conservative) for Epsom and Ewell 1955–78; Solicitor General 1962–64; Attorney General 1970–74. *Spokesman (Commons):* Conservative Spokesman on Law 1967–70. *Select Committees:* Member, Select Committee on Euthanasia. *Other:* President, Senate of Inns of Court and the Bar 1986–87. *Honours:* Kt 1962; PC 1964. Hon. Member, Americans' Bar Association; Hon. Fellow, American College Trial Lawyers. *Publications:* Author of: *War Poems and Poetry,* 1943; *Public Duty and Personal Faith – the example of Thomas More,* 1978; *A Price Too High* (autobiography) 1989; *The Jesuit Factor,* 1990; *The Colombia Syndicate* (novel) 1991; *Hatred and Contempt* (novel) 1992; *His Brother's Keeper* (novel) 1993; *Indictment for Murder,* (novel) 1994; *The Caverel Claim,* (novel) 1998. *Recreations:* Painting. *Clubs:* White's, MCC, Royal Automobile (Vice-President). *Name, Style and Title:* Raised to the peerage as Baron Rawlinson of Ewell, of Ewell in the County of Surrey 1978. A Conservative. *Address:* The Rt Hon. the Lord Rawlinson of Ewell, QC, House of Lords, London, SW1A 0PW.

RAYNE (Life Baron, UK), Max Rayne; cr. 1976; Kt 1969

Son of late Phillip and Deborah Rayne. Born February 8, 1918; educated Central Foundation School, London; University College, London; Hon. Fellow: Darwin College, Cambridge 1966, University College, London 1966; Hon. LLD, London 1968; Hon. Fellow: London School of Economics 1974, King's College Hospital Medical School 1980, University College, Oxford 1982, King's College, London 1983, Westminster School 1989, United Medical and Dental Schools of Guy's and St. Thomas's Hospitals 1992. Married 1st, 1941, Margaret Marco (1 son 2 daughters) (marriage dissolved 1960), married 2nd, 1965, Lady Jane Vane-Tempest-Stewart, daughter of 8th Marquess of Londonderry, DL (2 sons 2 daughters). *Armed Forces:* Served RAF 1940–45. *Career:* Chairman, London Merchant Securities 1960–; Deputy Chairman, British Lion Films 1967–72; Director, Housing Corporation (1974) Ltd 1974–78 Chairman, Westpool Investment Trust 1980–; Non-executive Director, First Leisure Corporation plc 1995–99, Deputy Chairman 1984–92, Chairman 1992–95. *Other:* Governor: St Thomas's Hospital 1962–74, Royal Ballet School 1966–79, Yehudi Menuhin School 1966–87, Malvern College 1966–, Centre for Environmental Studies 1967–73; Member: General Council, King Edward VII's Hospital Fund for London 1966–98, Council, St Thomas's Hospital Medical School 1965–82, Council of Governors, United Medical Schools of Guy's and St Thomas' Hospitals 1982–89; Hon. Vice-President, Jewish Care 1966–; Chairman, National Theatre Board 1971–88; Founder Patron, The Rayne Foundation 1962–; Vice-President, Yehudi Menuhin School 1987–; RADA Council 1973–; Founder Member, Motability 1979–96 (Life Vice-President 1996). *Trusts, etc:* Special Trustee, St Thomas's Hospital 1974–92; Chairman, London Festival Ballet Trust 1967–75. *Honours:* Kt 1969; Officier, Legion d'Honneur 1987; Chevalier 1973. Hon. Fellow: Royal College of Psychiatrists 1977, Royal College of Physicians 1992. *Name, Style and Title:* Raised to the peerage as Baron Rayne, of Prince's Meadow in the County of Greater London 1976. A Cross-Bencher. *Address:* The Lord Rayne, 33 Robert Adam Street, London, W1M 5AH *Tel:* 020 7935 3555.

RAZZALL (Life Baron, UK), Edward Timothy Razzall; cr. 1997; CBE 1993

Son of Leonard Humphrey Razzall. Born June 12, 1943; educated St Paul's School; Worcester College, Oxford (BA). Married 1982, Deirdre Bourke (1 son 1 daughter from previous marriage). *Councils, Public Bodies:* Councillor, Mortlake Ward, London Borough of Richmond 1974–; Deputy Leader, Richmond Council 1983–96. *Career:* Teaching Associate, North Western University, Chicago 1965–66; Frere Cholmeley Bischoff, solicitors 1966–96, Partner 1973–96; Partner, Argonaut Associates 1996–; Director, Cala plc 1973–99; Chairman, Abaco Investments plc 1974–90; Director: Star Mining Corporation NL 1993–, Milner Estates plc 1994–; Chairman, C&B Publishing plc 1997–. *Spokesman:* Liberal Democrat Spokesman on Trade and Industry 1998–. *Select Committees:* Member, Joint Select Committee on Consolidation of Bills 1998–. *Party Groups (General):* Treasurer: Liberal Party 1986–87, Liberal Democrats 1987–; President, Association of Liberal Democrat Councillors 1990–95; Chairman, Liberal Democrats General Election Campaign 1999–. *Honours:* CBE 1993. *Recreations:* Sport, food and wine. *Clubs:* National Liberal, MCC. *Name, Style and Title:* Raised to the peerage as Baron Razzall, of Mortlake in the London Borough of Richmond 1997. A Liberal Democrat. *Address:* The Lord Razzall, CBE, House of Lords, London, SW1A 0PW *Tel:* 020 7976 1233.

REA (3rd Baron, UK), John Nicolas Rea; cr. 1937; 3rd Bt of Eskdale (UK) 1935

Son of late Hon. James Russell Rea, Barrister-at-law, second son of 1st Baron. Born June 6, 1928. Succeeded his uncle 1981; educated Dartington Hall School; Belmont Hill School, Massachusetts, USA; Dauntsey's School; Christ's College, Cambridge University (MA, MD); UCH Medical School (DObst, DCH, DPH). Married 1st, March 24, 1951, Elizabeth, daughter of late William Hensman Robinson (4 sons 2 daughters) (marriage dissolved 1991), married 2nd, December 16, 1991, Judith Mary, daughter of late Norman Powell. *Trades Union:* Member, MSF. *Armed Forces:* Acting Sergeant, Suffolk Regiment, National Service 1946–48. *Career:* Junior Hospital Posts 1954–57; Research Fellow in Paediatrics in Ibadan and Lagos, Nigeria 1962–65; Lecturer in Social Medicine at St Thomas' Hospital Medical School 1966–68; General Medical Practitioner in Kentish Town NW5 1957–62, 1968–93. *House of Lords:* An elected hereditary peer 1999–. *Spokesman:* An Opposition Spokesman on Health and International Development 1992–97. *Select Committees:* Member, Select Committee on Science and Technology 1987–88, 1997–. *All-Party:* Chairman, All-Party Parliamentary Food and Health Forum 1992–; Member, All Party: Parliamentary Human Rights Group 1993–, Population and Development Group 1985–, Drugs Misuse Group 1985–. *International Bodies:* Member: IPU, CPA. *Trusts, etc:* Member: Action Research, Healthlink Worldwide, Back Care, Mary Ward Centre, Medicinal Cannabis Centre. FRCGP. *Publications:* Papers in Medical Journals. *Special Interests:* Health, Food and Nutrition, Third World, Arms Control, Human Rights. *Recreations:* Music (bassoon), outdoor activities. *Clubs:* Royal Society of Medicine. *Heir:* His son, Hon. Matthew James Rea, born March 28, 1956. Labour. *Address:* The Lord Rea, 11 Anson Road, London, N7 0RB *Tel:* 020 7607 0546 *Fax:* 020 7687 1219 *Tel:* Office: 020 7267 4411.

REAY (14th Lord, S), Hugh William Mackay; cr. 1628; 14th Bt of Far (NS) 1627; 7th Baron Mackay Van Ophemert (Netherlands) 1822

Son of 13th Lord. Born July 19, 1937. Succeeded his father 1963; educated Eton; Christ Church, Oxford. Married 1st, September 14, 1964, Hon. Annabel Therese Fraser, daughter of 15th Lord Lovat, DSO, MC, TD, DL (2 sons 1 daughter) (marriage dissolved 1978), married 2nd, June 20, 1980, Hon. Victoria Isabella Warrender, daughter of 1st Baron Bruntisfield, MC (2 daughters). *Career:* Member: European Parliament 1973–79, Council of Europe and WEU 1979–86. *House of Lords:* Joint Parliamentary Under-Secretary of State, Department of Trade and Industry 1991–92; An elected hereditary peer 1999–. *Whip:* A Lord in Waiting (Government Whip) 1989–91. *Spokesman:* Former Spokesman for Department of Environment, Home Office, Foreign and Commonwealth Office and Ministry of Defence and Welsh Office. *Select Committees:* Member, European Select Committee 1993–97, 1997–; Chairman, Select Committee on European Communities Sub-Committee D (Agriculture, Fisheries and Food) 1997–. *Miscellaneous:* Chief of Clan Mackay. *Heir:* His son, Hon. Aeneas Simon Mackay, Master of Reay, born March 20, 1965. A Conservative. *Address:* The Lord Reay, House of Lords, London, SW1A 0PW.

REES (Life Baron, UK), Peter Wynford Innes Rees; cr. 1987; PC 1983; QC 1969

Son of late Major-General T. W. Rees, IA. Born December 9, 1926; educated Stowe; Christ Church, Oxford. Married December 15, 1969, Mrs Anthea Wendell, daughter of late Major H. J. M. Hyslop. *Armed Forces:* Served with Scots Guards 1945–48. *Career:* Called to the Bar, Inner Temple 1953; Practised Oxford Circuit, Bencher, Inner Temple 1976; Chairman and Director of companies. *House of Commons:* Contested (Conservative): Abertillery 1964, 1965, Liverpool, West Derby 1966 General Elections; MP (Conservative) for: Dover 1970–74, Dover and Deal 1974–83, Dover 1983–87; PPS to Solicitor General 1972–73; Minister of State, HM Treasury 1979–81; Minister for Trade 1981–83; Chief Secretary, HM Treasury 1983–85. *Miscellaneous:* Member: Court and Council of the Museum of Wales until 1997, Museums and Galleries Commission 1988–97. *Honours:* PC 1983. Liveryman, Clockmakers Company. *Clubs:* Boodle's, Beefsteak, White's, Pratt's. *Name, Style and Title:* Raised to the peerage as Baron Rees, of Goytre in the County of Gwent 1987. A Conservative. *Address:* The Rt Hon. the Lord Rees, QC, Goytre Hall, Nantyderry, Abergavenny, Gwent, NP7 9DL; 39 Headfort Place, London, SW1X 7DE.

REES-MOGG (Life Baron, UK), William Rees-Mogg; cr. 1988; Kt 1981

Son of late Edmund Fletcher Rees-Mogg. Born July 14, 1928; educated Charterhouse; Balliol College, Oxford; Hon. LLD, Bath. Married 1962, Gillian, daughter of late T. R. Morris (2 sons 3 daughters). *Armed Forces:* RAF (National Service) 1946–48. *Councils, Public Bodies:* High Sheriff, Somerset 1978. *Career: Financial Times* 1952–60, Chief Leader Writer 1955–60, Assistant Editor 1957–60; *Sunday Times* City Editor 1960–61, Political and Economic Editor 1961–63, Deputy Editor 1964–67; Editor, *The Times* 1967–81; Member, Executive Board Times Newspapers 1968–81; Director, *The Times* Ltd 1968–81; Vice-Chairman, Board of Governors BBC 1981–86; Chairman and Proprietor, Pickering and Chatto (Publishers) Ltd 1981–; Chairman, Arts Council of Great Britain 1982–89; Chairman, Sidgwick and Jackson Ltd 1985–88; Director, M & G 1988–92; Chairman, Broadcasting Standards Council 1988–93; Chairman: American Trading Company Ltd 1992–, International Business Communications plc (now IBC Group plc) 1993–99, Fleet Street Publications Ltd 1995–; Director: General Electric Company 1981–97, J. Rothschild Investment Management Ltd 1987–96, St James's Place Capital plc 1990–96, The Private Bank and Trust Company 1993–, Private Financial Holdings Ltd 1995–, Value Realisation Trust plc 1996–99. *Party Groups (General):* Vice-Chairman, Conservative Party's National Advisory Committee on Political Education 1961–63. *Miscellaneous:* Contested (Conservative) Chester-le-Street, Co. Durham: 1956 (By-election), General Election 1959; Visiting Fellow, Nuffield College, Oxford 1968–72. *Honours:* Kt 1981. *Recreations:* Collecting. *Clubs:* Garrick. *Name, Style and Title:* Raised to the the peerage as Baron Rees-Mogg, of Hinton Blewitt in the County of Avon 1988. A Cross-Bencher. *Address:* The Lord Rees-Mogg, 17 Pall Mall, London, SW1Y 5NB *Tel:* Office: 020 7242 2241.

RENDELL OF BABERGH (Life Baroness, UK), Ruth Barbara Rendell; cr. 1997; CBE 1996

Daughter of Arthur and Ebba Grasemann. Born February 17, 1930; Hon. DLitt: University of Bowling Green (Ohio), University of Essex, University of East Anglia; Hon. MLitt, University of East London. Married 1950, Donald Rendell (marriage dissolved 1975), re-married 1977, Donald Rendell (died March 21, 1999) (1 son). *Career:* Author and crime novelist 1964–. *Awards Granted:* Arts Council National Book Award for Genre Fiction, 1981; *Sunday Times* Award for Literary Excellence, 1990; Crime Writers' Association Gold Dagger (4 times) and Diamond Dagger; Mystery Writers of America three Edgar Allan Poe Awards. *Honours:* CBE 1996. FRSL. *Publications: From Doon with Death,* 1964; *To Fear a Painted Devil,* 1965; *Vanity Dies Hard,* 1966; *A New Lease of Death,* 1967; *Wolf to the Slaughter,* 1967; *The Secret House of Death,* 1968; *The Best Man to Die,* 1969; *A Guilty Thing Surprised,* 1970; *One Across Two Down,* 1971; *No More Dying Then,* 1972; *Some Die and Some Lie,* 1973; *The Face of Trespass,* 1974; *Shake Hands for Ever,* 1975; *A Demon in my View,* 1976; *A Judgement in Stone,* 1977; *A Sleeping Life,* 1978; *Make Death Love Me,* 1979; *The Lake of Darkness,* 1980; *Put on by Cunning,* 1981; *Master of the Moor,* 1982; *The Speaker of Mandarin,* 1983;

The Killing Doll, 1984; *The Tree of Hands*, 1984; *An Unkindness of Ravens*, 1985; *Live Flesh*, 1986; *Heartstones*, 1987; *Talking to Strange Men*, 1987; (Editor) *A Warning to the Curious – The Ghost Stories of M. R. James*, 1987; *The Veiled One*, 1988; *The Bridesmaid*, 1989; *Ruth Rendell's Suffolk*, 1989; (with Colin Ward) *Undermining the Central Line*, 1989; *Going Wrong*, 1990, *Kissing the Gunner's Daughter*, 1992; *The Crocodile Bird*, 1993; *Simisola*, 1994; (Editor) *The Reason Why*, 1995; Short Stories: *The Fallen Curtain*, 1976; *Means of Evil*, 1979; *The Fever Tree*, 1982; *The New Girl Friend*, 1985; *Collected Short Stories*, 1987; *The Copper Peacock*, 1991; *Blood Linen*, 1995; As Barbara Vine: *A Dark-Adapted Eye*, 1986; *A Fatal Inversion*, 1987; *The House of Stairs*, 1988; *Gallowglass*, 1990; *King Solomon's Carpet*, 1991; *Asta's Book*, 1993; *No Night is Too Long*, 1994; *The Brimstone Wedding*, 1996; *Road Rage*, 1997; *The Chimney Sweeper's Boy*, 1998. *Recreations:* Reading, walking, opera. *Clubs:* Groucho. *Name, Style and Title:* Raised to the peerage as Baroness Rendell of Babergh, of Aldeburgh in the County of Suffolk 1997. Labour. *Address:* The Baroness Rendell of Babergh, CBE, House of Lords, London, SW1A 0PW; 11 Maida Avenue, Little Venice, London, W2 1SR.

RENFREW OF KAIMSTHORN (Life Baron, UK), (Andrew) Colin Renfrew; cr. 1991; FBA 1980

Son of late Archibald and Helena Renfrew. Born July 25, 1937; educated St Albans School; St John's College, Cambridge (Exhibitioner, BA 1st class hons Archaeology and Anthropology, MA, PhD, ScD); British School of Archaeology, Athens; Hon. DLitt, Sheffield 1987; Hon. Doctorate, Athens 1991; Hon. DLitt, Southampton 1995. Married 1965, Jane Margaret, daughter of Ven. Walter Ewbank (2 sons 1 daughter). *Armed Forces:* National Service with RAF 1956–58. *Career:* University of Sheffield: Lecturer in Prehistory and Archaeology 1965–70, Senior Lecturer 1970–72, Reader 1972; Professor of Archaeology, Southampton University 1972–81; Visiting Lecturer, University of California 1967; Has lectured on archaeology in numerous British and American Universities; Has excavated in Greece and the United Kingdom; Chairman, Hampshire Archaeological Committee 1974–81; Member: Ancient Monuments Board for England 1974–84, Royal Commission for Historical Monuments (England) 1977–87; Disney Professor of Archaeology, Cambridge University 1981–; A Vice-President, Royal Archaeological Institute 1982–85; Member: Historical Buildings and Monuments Commission for England 1984–86, Ancient Monuments Advisory Committee 1984–, UK National Commission for UNESCO 1984–86; Master, Jesus College, Cambridge 1986–97, Fellow 1986–; Director, McDonald Institute for Archaeological Research 1990–; A Trustee, British Museum 1991–. *Select Committees:* Member, House of Lords European Communities Select Committee, Sub-Committee A 1993–96; Chairman, Library and Computing Sub-Committee 1995–; Member, Select Committee on House of Lords' Offices 1995–. *Miscellaneous:* Contested (Conservative) Sheffield Brightside 1968 By-Election; Board Member, Parliamentary Office of Science and Technology (POST) 1997–98. FSA; FSA (Scotland); FBA 1980. Freeman, City of London. *Publications:* Author of: *The Emergence of Civilisation*, 1972; *The Explanation of Culture Change*, 1973 (editor); *Before Civilisation*, 1973; *British Prehistory, a New Outline*, 1974 (editor); *Investigations in Orkney*, 1979; *Problems in European Prehistory*, 1979; *An Island Polity*, 1982; *Approaches to Social Archaeology*, 1984; *The Prehistory of Orkney*, 1985; *The Archaeology of Cult*, 1985; *Archaeology and Language*, 1987; *The Cycladic Spirit*, 1991; Has also collaborated with other authors on archaeological subjects, as well as contributions to archaeological journals. *Special Interests:* National Heritage, Arts, Museums and Galleries, Education, Foreign Affairs. *Recreations:* Contemporary Art. *Clubs:* Athenaeum, United Oxford and Cambridge University. *Name, Style and Title:* Raised to the peerage as Baron Renfrew of Kaimsthorn, of Hurlet in the District of Renfrew 1991. A Conservative. *Address:* Professor The Lord Renfrew of Kaimsthorn, FBA, FSA, McDonald Institute for Archaeological Research, Downing Street, Cambridge, CB2 3ER *Tel:* 01223 333521.

RENNARD (Life Baron, UK), Christopher John Rennard; cr. 1999; MBE 1989

Son of late Cecil and Jean Rennard. Born July 8, 1960; educated Liverpool Blue Coat School; Liverpool University (BA Hons 1982). Married 1989, Ann McTegart. *Trades Union:* Member, GMBATU. *Career:* Liberal Party Agent, Liverpool, Mossley Hill 1982–84; Liberal Party Regional Agent, East Midlands 1984–88; Social and Liberal Democrats Election Co-Ordinator 1988–89; Liberal Democrats Organiser, Parliamentary by-elections since 1989, and Target Seat Campaign for General Election 1997. *International Bodies (General):* Member: IPU, CPA. *Other:* Member, Amnesty International. *Honours:* MBE 1989. *Publications: Winning Local Elections,* 1988; *The Campaign Manual,* 1995. *Recreations:* Cooking, wine, France. *Name, Style and Title:* Raised to the peerage as Baron Rennard, of Wavertree in the County of Merseyside 1999. A Liberal Democrat. *Address:* The Lord Rennard, MBE, Liberal Democrat Party, 4 Cowley Street, London, SW1P 3NB *Tel:* 020 7222 7999 *Fax:* 020 7233 3140 *E-Mail:* chrisrennard@cix.

RENTON (Life Baron, UK), David Lockhart-Mure Renton; cr. 1979; PC 1962; KBE 1964; QC 1954; TD; DL

Son of late Dr Maurice Waugh Renton, MD, CM, DPH. Born August 12, 1908; educated Oundle; University College, Oxford (MA, BCL); Hon. Fellow, University College, Oxford 1990–. Married July 17, 1947, Claire Cicely (died 1986), daughter of late Walter Duncan (3 daughters). *Armed Forces:* Major RA; Served 1939–45 (overseas 1942–45). *Councils, Public Bodies:* DL: Huntingdonshire 1962, Huntingdonshire and Peterborough 1964, Cambridgeshire 1974. *Career:* Called to the Bar, Lincoln's Inn 1933; QC 1954; Bencher of Lincoln's Inn 1962; Treasurer 1979; Recorder: Rochester 1963–68, Guildford 1968–71. *House of Commons:* MP for Huntingdonshire 1945–79 (National Liberal 1945–50, National Liberal and Conservative 1951–66, Conservative 1966–79); Parliamentary Secretary: Ministry of Fuel and Power December 1955–57, Ministry of Power 1957–58; Joint Parliamentary Under-Secretary of State, Home Office 1958–61; Minister of State 1961–62. *Select Committees (Commons):* Member, House of Commons Committee of Privileges 1974–79; Chairman, House of Commons Standing Orders Revision Committee 1963, 1970. *Backbench Committees (Commons):* Chairman, Conservative Transport Committee 1953–55. *Party Groups (Commons):* Chairman, Conservative Transport 1953–55. *House of Lords:* A Deputy Speaker House of Lords 1982–88. *Select Committees:* Member, Committee for Privileges 1975–99. *All-Party:* Joint President, All-Party Arts and Heritage Group 1992–. *International Bodies (General):* Delegate to Council of Europe 1951 and 1952. *Party Groups (General):* Patron, Huntingdon Conservative Association. *Other:* President, Conservation Society 1971–72; Chairman, MENCAP 1978–82, President 1982–88; President, Statute Law Society 1980–; Patron: National Law Library, Design and Manufacture for Disability, Greater London Association for the Disabled, Ravenswood Foundation, Royal British Legion, Huntingdonshire. *Miscellaneous:* Royal Commission on the Constitution 1971–74; Chairman, Committee on Preparation of Legislation 1973–75; Vice-Chairman, Council of Legal Education 1968–73; President, National Council for Civil Protection 1980–91. *Honours:* PC 1962; KBE 1964; TD. *Publications:* Various Legal and Political Articles; Various Obituaries. *Special Interests:* Drafting of Legislation, Mental Handicap, Environment, Law and Order, Trade Union Law, Devolution, European Legislation. *Recreations:* Gardening, outdoor sports and games. *Clubs:* Carlton, Pratt's. *Name, Style and Title:* Raised to the peerage as Baron Renton, of Huntingdon in the County of Cambridgeshire 1979. A Conservative. *Address:* The Rt Hon. the Lord Renton, KBE, QC, TD, DL, 16 Old Buildings, Lincoln's Inn, London, WC2A 3TL *Tel:* 020 7242 8986; Moat House, Abbots Ripton, Huntingdon, Cambridgeshire, PE17 2PE *Tel:* 01487 773227.

Dod *on* Disk

The Vacher Dod Parliamentary Database – configured for PC or Network

For further details please telephone the Westminster Office

020 7828 7256

RENTON OF MOUNT HARRY (Life Baron, UK), (Ronald) Timothy Renton; cr. 1997; PC 1989

Son of late R. K. D. Renton, CBE. Born May 28, 1932; educated Eton (Kings Scholar); Magdalen College, Oxford (Roberts Gawen Scholar) (MA 1st Class Modern History). Married April 2, 1960, Alice, daughter of late Sir James Fergusson, 8th Bt of Kilkerran (2 sons 3 daughters). *Trades Union:* Member, APEX 1977–90. *Career:* C. Tennant Sons & Co. Ltd, Canada 1957–62; Managing Director, Tennant Trading Ltd 1964–71; Director: Silvermines Ltd 1966–84, ANZ Banking Group Ltd 1969–76, J. H. Vavasseur & Co. Ltd 1971–74; Director, Fleming Continental European Investment Trust 1992–, Chairman 1999–. *House of Commons:* Contested (Conservative) Sheffield Park 1970; MP (Conservative) for Sussex Mid 1974–97; PPS: to Chief Secretary to the Treasury 1979–81, to Secretary of State for Trade January–May 1981, to Chancellor of the Exchequer, Rt Hon. Sir Geoffrey Howe, QC, MP January–June 1983; Parliamentary Under-Secretary of State, at Foreign and Commonwealth Office 1984–85; Minister of State: at Foreign and Commonwealth Office 1985–87, at Home Office 1987–89; Parliamentary Secretary to HM Treasury and Government Chief Whip 1989–90; Minister of State, Privy Council Office (Minister for the Arts) 1990–92. *Whip (Commons):* Government Chief Whip 1989–90. *Select Committees (Commons):* Member, Select Committees on: Nationalised Industries 1974–79, National Heritage 1995–97. *Backbench Committees (Commons):* Vice-Chairman, Conservative Parliamentary Trade Committee 1974–79; Chairman, Conservative Parliamentary Employment Committee 1981–82; President, Conservative Foreign and Commonwealth Council 1982–84. *All-Party Committees (Commons):* Chairman, All-Party Hong Kong Group 1992–97. *Select Committees:* Member, Select Committee on European Communities 1997–. *Party Groups (General):* President, Conservative Trade Unionists 1980–84. *Other:* President, Roedean School 1997–. *Trusts, etc:* Fellow, Industry and Parliament Trust. *Miscellaneous:* Member, Know How Fund Advisory Board 1992–; Vice-Chairman, British Council 1992–97, Board Member 1997–99; Chairman: Outside Art Archive and Collection 1993–; Sussex Downs Conservation Board 1997–. *Honours:* PC 1989. *Publications:* Author of: *The Dangerous Edge*, 1994; *Hostage to Fortune*, 1997; Articles published in journals and newspapers. *Special Interests:* Arts, Privatisation, Financial Institutions, Conservation. *Recreations:* Writing, mucking about in boats, arguing about operatic tenors, touring France on a bicycle. *Clubs:* Garrick. *Name, Style and Title:* Raised to the peerage as Baron Renton of Mount Harry, of Offham in the County of East Sussex 1997. A Conservative. *Address:* The Rt Hon. the Lord Renton of Mount Harry, House of Lords, London, SW1A 0PW *E-Mail:* rentont@parliament.uk.

RENWICK OF CLIFTON (Life Baron, UK), Robin William Renwick; cr. 1997; KCMG 1988

Son of late Richard Renwick and of Clarice Renwick. Born December 13, 1937; educated St Paul's School; Jesus College, Cambridge; University of Paris (Sorbonne); Hon. Fellow, Jesus College 1992; Hon. DLitt: University of the Witwatersrand 1990, College of William and Mary (USA) 1993, Oglethorpe University 1995. Married 1965, Annie Colette Giudicelli (1 son 1 daughter). *Armed Forces:* Army Service 1956–58. *Career:* Entered Foreign Service 1963; Dakar 1963–64; FO 1964–66; New Delhi 1966–70; Private Secretary to Minister of State, FCO 1970–72; First Secretary, Paris 1972–76; Counsellor, Cabinet Office 1976–78; Rhodesia Department, FCO 1978–80; Political Adviser to Governor of Rhodesia 1980; Head of Chancery, Washington 1981–84; Assistant Under-Secretary of State, FCO 1984–87; Ambassador to: South Africa 1987–91, USA 1991–95; Deputy Chairman, Robert Fleming Holdings Ltd 1999–; Chairman: Fluor Daniel 1996–, Robert Fleming Inc 1998–; Director: Compagnie Financiere Richemont AG 1995–, British Airways plc 1996–, Liberty International 1996–, Fluor Corporation 1997–, Canal Plus 1997–, Billiton plc 1997–, South African Breweries 1999–. *All-Party:* Member, All-Party Defence Group. *Trusts, etc:* Trustee, The Economist 1996–. *Miscellaneous:* Visiting Fellow, Center for International Affairs, Harvard University 1980–81. *Honours:* CMG 1980; KCMG 1988. FRSA. *Publications: Economic Sanctions*, 1981; *Fighting with Allies*, 1996; *Unconventional Diplomacy*, 1997. *Recreations:* Tennis, trout fishing. *Clubs:* Brooks's, Hurlingham, Travellers'. *Name, Style and Title:* Raised to the peerage as Baron Renwick of Clifton, of Chelsea in the Royal Borough of Kensington and Chelsea 1997. Labour. *Address:* The Lord Renwick of Clifton, KCMG, Robert Fleming & Co Ltd, 25 Copthall Avenue, London, EC2R 7DR.

RICHARD (Life Baron, UK), Ivor Seward Richard; cr. 1990; PC 1993; QC 1971

Son of Seward Thomas Richard. Born May 30, 1932; educated St. Michael's School, Bryn, Llanelly; Cheltenham College; Pembroke College, Oxford (Wightwick Scholar, BA (Jurisprudence) 1953); Hon. Fellow, Pembroke College, Oxford 1981. Married 1st, 1956, Geraldine, daughter of Alfred Moore (1 son) (marriage dissolved 1962), married 2nd, June 2, 1962, Alison Mary, daughter of J. Imrie (1 son 1 daughter) (marriage dissolved), married 3rd, September 1, 1989, Janet, daughter of John Jones (1 son). *Career.* Called to the Bar, Inner Temple 1955; Bencher 1985; Practised in London 1955–74; QC 1971; UK Permanent Representative to UN 1974–79; Member, EEC Commission 1981–85; Chairman, World Trade Centre Wales Ltd 1985–97. *House of Commons:* Contested (Labour) South Kensington General Election 1959; MP (Labour) Barons Court 1964–74; PPS to Secretary of State for Defence 1966–67; Parliamentary Under-Secretary of State (Army) Ministry of Defence 1969–70. *Spokesman (Commons):* Opposition Spokesman, Broadcasting, Posts and Telecommunications 1970–71; Deputy Spokesman on Foreign Affairs 1971–74. *House of Lords:* Leader of the Opposition in the House of Lords 1992–97; Lord Privy Seal and Leader of the House of Lords 1997–98. *Spokesman:* An Opposition Spokesman on: Home Office affairs 1990–92, The Civil Service 1992–97, European Affairs 1992–97, The Treasury and Economic Affairs 1992–93. *Select Committees:* Former Member, Select Committees on: House of Lords' Offices 1997–98, Finance and Staff Sub-Committee, Liaison, Privileges, Procedure, Selection. *Honours:* PC 1993. *Publications:* Author of: *Europe or the Open Sea*, 1971 (jointly); *We, the British*, 1983; as well as articles in political journals. *Recreations:* Music, talking. *Name, Style and Title:* Raised to the peerage as Baron Richard, of Ammanford in the County of Dyfed 1990. Labour. *Address:* The Rt Hon. the Lord Richard, QC, House of Lords, London, SW1A 0PW.

RICHARDSON (Life Baron, UK), John Samuel Richardson; cr. 1979; 1st Bt of Eccleshall (UK) 1963; Kt 1960; LVO 1943; MD; FRCP

Son of late John Watson Richardson, solicitor, killed in action 1917. Born June 16, 1910; educated Charterhouse; Trinity College, Cambridge; St Thomas's Hospital (MB, BChir, MD, MRCP); Hon. Fellow: Kings College, London, Trinity College, Cambridge; Hon. DCL, Newcastle; Hon. LLD: Nottingham, Liverpool; Hon. DSc: NUI, Hull. Married 1933, Sybil Angela Stephanie, daughter of late A. R. Trist, of Stanmore (2 daughters). *Armed Forces:* RAMC, medical specialist – Major and Lieutenant-Colonel August 1939-November 1945. *Career:* Qualified 1935; Junior posts at St Thomas's Hospital until 1939; Deputy, Medical Unit at St Thomas's Hospital 1945–47, Physician 1947–75; Consulting Physician for Metropolitan Police 1957–80; Consulting Physician to Army 1964–75; President, International Society for Internal Medicine 1966–70; Chairman, Joint Consultants Committee 1967–72; President: Royal Society of Medicine 1969–71, BMA 1970–71, GMC 1973–80. *International Bodies (General):* President, International Society for Internal Medicine. *Awards Granted:* Gold Medal, BMA 1982. *Honours:* LVO 1943; Kt 1960; Hon. Bencher, Gray's Inn; CStJ. FRCP; FRCPE; Hon. FRCPI; Hon. FRCS; Hon. FRCPSG; Hon. FRCPsych; Hon. FRPharm Soc. Member: Cutlers, Society of Apothecaries. *Publications: The Practice of Medicine*, 2nd ed. 1960; *Connective Tissue Disorders*, 1963. *Recreations:* Living in the country. *Heir:* To baronetcy, none. *Name, Style and Title:* Raised to the peerage as Baron Richardson, of Lee in the County of Devon 1979. A Cross-Bencher. *Address:* The Lord Richardson, LVO, FRCP, Windcutter, Lee, Nr Ilfracombe, Devon, EX34 8LW *Tel:* 01271 863198.

RICHARDSON OF CALOW (Life Baroness, UK), Kathleen Margaret Richardson; cr. 1998; OBE 1994

Daughter of Francis William and Margaret Fountain. Born February 24, 1938; educated St Helena School, Chesterfield; Stockwell College; Wesley Deaconess College; Wesley House, Cambridge; Hon. BLitt, Bradford University; Hon. LLD, Liverpool University. Married 1964, Ian David Godfrey Richardson (3 daughters). *Career:* Moderator, Free Churches Council; President, Churches Together In England; First Woman President of the Methodist Conference. *Honours:* OBE 1994. *Special Interests:* Church Affairs. *Recreations:* Reading, needlework. *Name, Style and Title:* Raised to the peerage as Baroness Richardson of Calow, of Calow in the County of Derbyshire 1998. A Cross-Bencher. *Address:* The Reverend Baroness Richardson of Calow, OBE, House of Lords, London, SW1A 0PW.

RICHARDSON OF DUNTISBOURNE (Life Baron, UK), Gordon William Humphreys Richardson, cr. 1983; KG 1983; MBE (Mil) 1944; PC 1976; TD 1979; DL

Son of late John Robert and Nellie Richardson. Born November 25, 1915; educated Nottingham High School; Gonville and Caius College, Cambridge (MA, LLB); Hon. LLD, Cambridge; Hon. Fellow: Wolfson College, Cambridge, Gonville and Caius College, Cambridge; Hon. DSc: City University, Aston University; Hon. DCL, University of East Anglia. Married January 18, 1941, Margaret Alison, elder daughter of late Very Rev. Hugh Richard Lawrie Sheppard, Canon and Precentor of St Paul's Cathedral (1 son 1 daughter). *Armed Forces:* Commissioned South Notts Hussars Yeomanry 1939; Staff College, Camberley 1941; Served until 1946. *Councils, Public Bodies:* One of HM Lieutenants, City of London 1974–; DL, Gloucestershire 1983–. *Career:* Called to the Bar, Gray's Inn 1946; Member, Bar Council 1951–55; With Industrial & Commercial Finance Corporation 1957; Director, J. Henry Schroder & Co Ltd 1957, Deputy Chairman 1960–62, Chairman 1962–72; Member, Company Law Amendment Committee 1959–62; Chairman: Committee on Turnover Taxation 1963–64, Schroders Ltd 1966–73; Director, Bank of England 1967–83, Governor 1973–83; Chairman, Schroders Incorporated 1968–73; Member, NEDC 1971–73, 1980–83; Chairman, Industrial Development Advisory Board 1972–73; Director, Bank for International Settlements 1973–93, Vice-Chairman 1985–88, 1991–93; Member, Morgan Stanley Advisory Board 1984–; Chairman, Morgan Stanley International Incorporated 1986–95; Chairman, International Advisory Board Chemical Bank, New York 1986–96; Vice-Chairman, The Chase Manhattan Corporation International Advisory Council 1996–98, Member 1998–. *Other:* High Steward, Westminster Cathedral 1985–89; Deputy High Steward, University of Cambridge 1982–. *Trusts, etc:* Trustee, Pilgrim Trust, Chairman 1984–89. *Honours:* MBE 1944; PC 1976; TD 1979; KG 1983; Hon. Bencher, Gray's Inn. Freeman, City of London 1975. Liveryman, Mercers' Company. *Clubs:* Athenaeum, Brooks's, Pratt's. *Name, Style and Title:* Raised to the peerage as Baron Richardson of Duntisbourne, of Duntisbourne in the County of Gloucestershire 1983. A Cross-Bencher. *Address:* The Rt Hon. the Lord Richardson of Duntisbourne, KG, MBE, TD, DL, c/o Morgan Stanley UK Group, 25 Cabot Square, Canary Wharf, London, E14 4QA *E-Mail:* lordgr@ms.com; gaffg@ms.com.

RIX (Life Baron, UK), Brian (Norman Roger) Rix; cr. 1992; Kt 1986; CBE 1977; DL

Son of late Herbert and Fanny Rix. Born January 27, 1924; educated Bootham School, York; Hon. MA: Hull University 1981, Open University 1983; Hon. Dr, University Essex 1984; Hon. Fellow, Humberside College of Higher Education (now Lincolnshire and Humberside University) 1984; Hon. LLD, Manchester University 1986; Hon. DSc, Nottingham University 1987; Hon. LLD: Dundee University 1994, Exeter University 1997. Married 1949, Elspet Jeans, daughter of late James MacGregor-Gray (Elspet Gray, actress) (2 sons 2 daughters). *Trades Union:* Life Member, British Actors' Equity Association. *Armed Forces:* Served in RAF and as Bevin Boy. *Councils, Public Bodies:* DL, Greater London 1987–88, 1997–, Vice-Lord-Lieutenant 1988–97. *Career:* Actor 1942–; Actor Manager 1947–77 (mostly at the Whitehall Theatre and Garrick Theatre, London). *Chancellor:* Chancellor, University of East London. *Select Committees:* Co-opted Member, Select Committee on European Communities Sub-Committee F (Social Affairs, Education and Home Affairs) 1997–. *All-Party:* Member, All-Party Disablement Group; Hon. Secretary, All-Party Charities and Voluntary Sector Group. *Other:* Chairman, Friends of Normansfield 1973–; Secretary-General, MENCAP (Royal Society for Mentally Handicapped Children and Adults) 1980–87, Chairman 1988–98, President 1998–; Founder and Governor, Mencap City Foundation 1984, Chairman 1988–; Chairman: Libertas Group of Charities 1988–, Mencap City Insurance Services (now MCIS Ltd) 1993–; Life Vice-President, Radio Society of Great Britain. *Trusts, etc:* Chairman, Family Charities Ethical Trust Advisory Panel 1994–. *Miscellaneous:* Member, Arts Council 1986–93; Chairman: Drama Panel 1986–93, Monitoring Committee, Arts and Disabled People 1988–93, Independent Development Council for People with Mental Handicap 1981–86. *Honours:* CBE 1977; Kt 1986. Hon. FRSM, Hon. FRCPsch. *Publications:* Author of: *My Farce from My Elbow* (autobiography) 1975; *Farce about Face* (autobiography) 1989; *Tour de Farce* (history of theatre touring) 1992; *Life in the Farce Lane,* 1995 (history of farce); Editor and Contributor, *Gullible's Travels* 1996. *Special Interests:* Arts, Disability, Theatre, Voluntary Sector, Charities, Cricket. *Recreations:* Cricket, amateur radio, gardening. *Sportsclubs:* Yorkshire County Cricket. *Clubs:* Garrick, MCC. *Name, Style and Title:* Raised to the peerage as Baron Rix, of Whitehall in the City of Westminster and of Hornsea in Yorkshire 1992. A Cross-Bencher. *Address:* The Lord Rix, CBE, DL, 8 Ellerton Road, Wimbledon Common, London, SW20 0EP *Tel:* 020 8879 7748.

ROBERTS OF CONWY (Life Baron, UK), (Ieuan) Wyn (Pritchard) Roberts; cr. 1997; Kt 1990; PC 1991

Son of late Rev. Evan Pritchard Roberts. Born July 10, 1930; educated Beaumaris County School; Harrow School; University College, Oxford (MA); Hon. Fellow, University of Wales, Bangor and Aberystwyth. Married 1956, Enid Grace Williams (3 sons). *Armed Forces:* Intelligence Corps 1948–49. *Career:* Sub-Editor, *Liverpool Daily Post* 1952–54; News Assistant, BBC 1954–57; Executive: TWW Ltd 1957–68, Harlech TV Ltd 1968–69. *House of Commons:* MP (Conservative) for Conwy 1970–97; PPS to Secretary of State for Wales 1970–74; Parliamentary Under-Secretary of State, Welsh Office 1979–87; Minister of State, Welsh Office 1987–94. *Spokesman (Commons):* Conservative Spokesman on Welsh Affairs 1974–79. *Select Committees (Commons):* Member, Select Committee on Welsh Affairs 1994–97. *Spokesman:* Front Bench Spokesman on Welsh Affairs 1997–. *International Bodies:* Life Member, CPA. *Party Groups (General):* President, Welsh Conservative Clubs. *Other:* Member, Royal National Eisteddfod Gorsedd of Bards; President, University of Wales College of Medicine. *Honours:* Knighted 1990; PC 1991. *Special Interests:* Education, Health, Training, Tourism, Small Businesses, Transport, Economics, Conservation. *Recreations:* Fishing, walking. *Clubs:* Savile, Cardiff and County (Cardiff). *Name, Style and Title:* Raised to the peerage as Baron Roberts of Conwy, of Talyfan in the County of Gwynedd 1997. A Conservative. *Address:* The Rt Hon. the Lord Roberts of Conwy, House of Lords, London, SW1A 0PW *E-Mail:* lordwyn@aol.com.uk.

ROBERTSON OF PORT ELLEN (Life Baron, UK), George Islay MacNeill Robertson; cr. 1999; PC 1997

Son of George P. Robertson, Police Inspector, and late Marion Robertson. Born April 12, 1946; educated Dunoon Grammar School, Argyll; University of Dundee (MA Honours 1968). Married June 1, 1970, Sandra, daughter of James U. Wallace (2 sons 1 daughter). *Career:* Research Assistant, Tayside Study, Economics Group 1968–69; Scottish Organiser, GMWU 1969–78; Governor, Scottish Police College 1974–78; Board Member, Scottish Development Agency 1976–78; Secretary-General, North Atlantic Treaty Organisation (NATO) 1999–. *House of Commons:* MP (Lab) for Hamilton from By-election May 1978–1997, and for Hamilton South from May 1, 1997-August 24, 1999; PPS to Secretary of State for Social Services February-May 1979; Shadow Secretary of State for Scotland 1993–97; Secretary of State for Defence 1997–99. *Spokesman (Commons):* Opposition Front Bench Spokesman on: Scotland 1979–80, Defence 1980–81, Foreign and Commonwealth Affairs 1981–93, European and Community Affairs 1985–93. *Backbench Committees (Commons):* Member, Labour Party Departmental Committees for: Defence 1997–99, Foreign and Commonwealth Affairs 1997–99, Northern Ireland 1997–99. *All-Party Committees (Commons):* Chairman, British-German Country Group 1992–94; Co-Chairman, British Parliamentary Lighting Group 1984–94; Vice-Chairman, All-Party America Country Group until 1999. *Party Groups (Commons):* Chairman, Scottish Labour Party 1977–78. *House of Lords:* Secretary of State for Defence August-October 1999. *International Bodies (General):* Member, Steering Committee, British German Königswinter Committee 1985–92; Joint Vice-Chairman, British-American Parliamentary Group 1996–99. *Other:* Council, Royal Institute of International Affairs 1985–91; Vice-President, Raleigh International 1984–; Chairman, Seatbelt Survivors Club; Governor, Ditchley Foundation 1990–; Council, British Executive Service Overseas 1991–97; Vice-Chairman, Westminster Foundation for Democracy 1992–94. *Trusts, etc:* Fellow, Industry and Parliament Trust. *Miscellaneous:* Vice-Chairman, British Council 1985–94. *Honours:* Commanders Cross of the Order of Merit (Federal Republic of Germany) 1991; PC 1997. FRSA, 1999. *Special Interests:* Foreign Affairs, Car Safety, Defence, Industrial Relations, Lighting, Scotland, European Union. *Recreations:* Photography, golf. *Name, Style and Title:* Raised to the peerage as Baron Robertson of Port Ellen, of Islay in Argyll and Bute 1999. Labour. *Address:* The Rt Hon. the Lord Robertson of Port Ellen, House of Lords, London, SW1A 0PW.

ROCHESTER (106th Bishop of), Michael Nazir-Ali

Son of James and Patience Nazir-Ali. Born August 19, 1949; educated St Paul's School and St Patrick's College, Karachi; University of Karachi (BA Economics and Sociology 1970); Fitzwilliam College and Ridley Hall, Cambridge (MLitt 1976); St Edmund Hall, Oxford (BLitt 1974, MLitt 1981); Australian College of Theology, University of New South Wales (PhD) with Centre for World Religions, Harvard 1983; Fellow, St Edmund Hall, Oxford 1998–. Married 1972, Valerie Cree (2 sons). *Career:* Assistant: Christ Church, Cambridge 1970–72, St Ebbe's, Oxford 1972–74; Burney Lecturer in Islam, Cambridge 1973–74; Assistant Curate, Holy Sepulchre Cambridge 1974–76; Tutorial Supervisor in Theology, University of Cambridge 1974–76; Tutor, then Senior Tutor, Karachi Theological College 1976–81; Associate Priest, Holy Trinity Cathedral, Karachi 1976–79; Priest-in-Charge, St Andrew's, Akhtar Colony, Karachi 1979–81; Provost of Lahore Cathedral 1981–84; Bishop of Raiwind, Pakistan 1984–86; Assistant to Archbishop of Canterbury, Co-ordinator of Studies and Editor for the Lambeth Conference 1986–89; Director-in-Residence, Oxford Centre for Mission Studies 1986–89; Member, Board of Christian Aid 1987–96; Secretary, Archbishop's Commission on Communion and Women in the Episcopate (Eames' Commission) 1988–; General Secretary, Church Missionary Society 1989–94; Member, Anglican-Roman Catholic International Commission 1991–; Member, Board of Mission of the General Synod of the Church of England 1991–; Chairman, Church of England Mission Theology Advisory Group 1992–; Canon Theologian, Leicester Cathedral 1992–94; Bishop of Rochester 1994–; Visiting Professor, University of Greenwich 1996–; Took his seat in the House of Lords 1999. *International Bodies (General):* World Council of Chruches. *Awards Granted:* Oxford Society Award for Graduate Studies 1972–73. *Trusts, etc:* Trustee: Traidcraft 1986–89, Mission Enterprise–1994, Trinity College Bristol 1996–, Church of England Newspaper 1998–; Adviser to: Diocesan Trust 1994–, Layton Rahimtoola Trust 1999–. *Miscellaneous:* Member, Human Fertilisation and Embryology Authority 1998–, Chairman, Ethics Committee 1998–. *Publications: Islam: a Christian perspective,* 1983; *Frontiers in Muslim-Christian Encounter,* 1987; *Martyrs and Magistrates: toleration and trial in Islam,* 1989; *From Everywhere to Everywhere: a World-View of Christian Mission,* 1990; *Mission and Dialogue,* 1995; *The Mystery of Faith,* 1995; *Citizens and Exiles: Christian Faith in a plural world,* 1998; Has edited various Lambeth Conference papers and reports as well as contributing articles for journals. *Special Interests:* Sufism, Middle Eastern History and Politics. *Recreations:* Cricket, hockey, detective novels, humour and poetry, writing fiction and poetry, table-tennis, Persian poetry. *Clubs:* Nikaean. *Address:* The Rt Rev. the Lord Bishop of Rochester, Bishopscourt, Rochester, Kent, ME1 1TS *Tel:* 01634 842721 *E-Mail:* bchaplain@clara.net.

RODGER OF EARLSFERRY (Life Baron, UK), Alan Ferguson Rodger; cr. 1992; PC 1992; QC (Scot) 1985; FBA 1991

Son of late Professor Thomas Ferguson Rodger and Jean Margaret Smith Chalmers. Born September 18, 1944; educated Kelvinside Academy, Glasgow; Glasgow University (MA, LLB); New College, Oxford (MA, DPhil, DCL); Fellow, New College, Oxford 1970–72; Hon. LLD, Glasgow University 1995. *Career:* Member, Faculty of Advocates 1974, Clerk of Faculty 1976–79; QC (Scot) 1985; Advocate Depute 1985–88; Home Advocate Depute 1986–88; Maccabaean Lecturer, British Academy 1991; Solicitor-General for Scotland 1989–92; A Senator of the College of Justice 1995–96; Lord Justice General and President of the Court of Session in Scotland 1996–. *House of Lords:* Lord Advocate 1992–95. *Other:* Hon. Member, Society of Public Teachers of Law. *Miscellaneous:* Junior Research Fellow, Balliol College, Oxford 1969–70; Member, Mental Welfare Commission for Scotland 1981–84. *Honours:* Hon. Bencher, Lincoln's Inn 1992. FBA 1991; FRSE 1992. *Publications:* Author of several publications and articles on legal matters. *Recreations:* Walking. *Clubs:* Athenaeum. *Name, Style and Title:* Raised to the peerage as Baron Rodger of Earlsferry, of Earlsferry in the District of North East Fife 1992. A Cross-Bencher. *Address:* The Rt Hon. the Lord Rodger of Earlsferry, FBA, House of Lords, London, SW1A 0PW.

RODGERS OF QUARRY BANK (Life Baron, UK), William Thomas Rodgers; cr. 1992; PC 1975

Son of William and Gertrude Rodgers. Born October 28, 1928; educated Sudley Road Council School; Quarry Bank High School, Liverpool; Magdalen College, Oxford. Married 1955, Silvia, daughter of Hirsch Szulman (3 daughters). *Armed Forces:* National Service 1947–48. *Councils, Public Bodies:* Borough Councillor, St Marylebone 1958–62. *Career:* Director-General, Royal Institute of British Architects 1987–94; Chairman, Advertising Standards Authority 1995–. *House of Commons:* Contested (Labour) Bristol West 1957; MP (Labour) Stockton-on-Tees 1962–74; Parliamentary Under-Secretary of State: Department of Economic Affairs 1964–67, Foreign Office 1967–68; Leader, UK Delegation to the Council of Europe and WEU 1967–68; Minister of State: Board of Trade 1968–69, Treasury 1969–70; Chairman, Expenditure Committee on Trade and Industry 1971–74; MP (Labour) Teeside, Stockton 1974–81; Minister of State, Ministry of Defence 1974–76; Secretary of State for Transport 1976–79; Elected to Shadow Cabinet (Labour) 1979 and 1980; MP (SDP) Teeside, Stockton 1981–83; Contested: (SDP) Stockton North 1983, (SDP/Alliance) Milton Keynes 1987. *Spokesman (Commons):* Opposition (Shadow) Defence Secretary 1979–80. *Spokesman:* Liberal Democrat Spokesman on Home Office Affairs 1994–97. *Select Committees:* Former Member: Sub-Committee on Declaration and Registration of Interests, Select Committee on the Public Service. *Party Groups:* Leader, Liberal Democrat Peers 1998–. *Party Groups (General):* General Secretary, Fabian Society 1953–60; A joint founder, Social Democratic Party 1981, Vice-President 1982–87. Hon. FRIBA; Hon. FIStructE. *Publications: Hugh Gaitskell 1906–1963,* (editor) 1964; *The People into Parliament,* (jointly) 1966; *The Politics of Change,* 1982; *Government and Industry,* (editor) 1986. *Clubs:* Garrick. *Name, Style and Title:* Raised to the peerage as Baron Rodgers of Quarry Bank, of Kentish Town in the London Borough of Camden 1992. A Liberal Democrat. *Address:* The Rt Hon. the Lord Rodgers of Quarry Bank, 43 North Road, London, N6 4BE *Tel:* 020 8341 2434.

ROGAN (Life Baron, UK), Dennis Robert David Rogan; cr. 1999

Son of late Robert Henderson Rogan. Born June 30, 1942; educated The Wallace High School; Belfast Institute of Technology; The Open University (BA). Married August 7, 1968, Lorna Elizabeth, daughter of late John Colgan (2 sons). *Councils, Public Bodies:* Chairman, Lisburn Unit of Management Health Board 1984–85. *Career:* Moygashel Ltd 1960–69; William Ewart & Sons Ltd 1969–72; Lamont Holdings plc 1972–78; Dennis Rogan Assoc 1978–, currently Managing Director; Associated Processors Ltd 1985–, currently Chairman; Communications Ltd 1996–, currently Chairman; Northern Ireland Events Company 1996–, currently Director. *Party Groups (General):* Chairman: Ulster Young Unionist Council 1968–69, South Belfast Constituency Association 1992–96, Ulster Unionist Party 1996–. *Special Interests:* Northern Ireland, Trade and Industry, Defence. *Recreations:* Rugby football, oriental carpets, gardening. *Name, Style and Title:* Raised to the peerage as Baron Rogan, of Lower Iveagh in the County of Down 1999. A Cross-Bencher. *Address:* The Lord Rogan, 31 Notting Hill, Malone Road, Belfast, BT9 5NS *Tel:* 028 9066 2468; House of Lords, London, SW1A 0PW.

ROGERS OF RIVERSIDE (Life Baron, UK), Richard George Rogers; cr. 1996; Kt 1991

Son of Dada Geiringer and Nino Rogers. Born July 23, 1933; educated Architectural Association (AA Dipl); Yale University (MArch, Fulbright, Edward D. Stone and Yale Scholar); RIBA; Hon. Doctorate, Royal College of Art, London; Hon. Member, Bund Deutscher Architekten 1989; Hon. Doctorate: University of Westminster 1992, Bath University 1994, South Bank University 1996; Hon. Professor, Thames Valley University 1997. Married 1st, 1961, Su Brumwell (3 sons); married 2nd, 1973, Ruth Elias (2 sons). *Career:* Team 4 1963–67; Richard & Su Rogers 1968–70; Piano + Rogers 1970–78; Visiting Professor to Yale and UCL 1978; Chairman, Richard Rogers Architects Ltd 1978–; Gave the BBC Reith Lectures entitled 'Cities for a Small Planet' 1995; Has been involved in masterplans for many city centres, including Shanghai, Berlin, Palma and London; Has designed buildings including: the Centre Georges Pompidou in Paris (with Renzo Piano),

Lloyds of London, the European Court of Human Rights in Strasbourg, Kabuki-Cho Tower in Tokyo, Channel 4 Headquarters in London, Millennium Experience, Greenwich, Law Courts, Bordeaux; Current projects include: National Assembly of Wales, Cardiff, Barajas Airport, Madrid, Terminal 5, Heathrow Airport, London. *All-Party:* Member, All-Party: Architecture and Planning Group, Conservation Group. *Other:* Director, River Cafe; Member, United Nations Architects' Committee. *Awards Granted:* BSC Award 1975; RIBA Regional Awards (Commendation) 1975; Financial Times Industrial Architecture Award 1975, Architecture at Work Award (Commendation) 1983; Royal Gold Medal for Architecture 1985; Friend of Barcelona 1997; Thomas Jefferson Memorial Foundation Medal in Architecture 1999. *Trusts, etc:* Chairman: Board of Trustees, Tate Gallery 1984–88, National Tenants Resource Centre 1991–, Architecture Foundation 1991–. *Miscellaneous:* Vice-Chairman, Arts Council of England 1994–96; Chairman, Government's Urban Task Force 1997–99. *Honours:* Kt 1991; Chevalier de la Legion d'Honneur (France); Officier des Arts et des Lettres 1995. Hon. Fellow: Royal Academy of Art, The Hague, American Institute of Architects, Tokyo Society of Architects and Building Engineers 1996; Fellow, Royal Society for the Arts 1996; Academician, International Academy of Architecture; Royal Academician, Royal Academy of London. *Publications: Richard Rogers + Architects,* 1985; *A + U: Richard Rogers 1978–88,* 1988; *Architecture: A Modern View,* 1990; (jointly) *A New London,* 1992; *Richard Rogers,* 1995; *Cities for a Small Planet,* 1997; *Towards an Urban Renaissance (Urban Task Force),* 1999. *Special Interests:* Sustainable Built Environment, Arts. *Recreations:* Friends, food, art, architecture, travel. *Name, Style and Title:* Raised to the peerage as Baron Rogers of Riverside, of Chelsea in the Royal Borough of Kensington and Chelsea 1996. Labour. *Address:* The Lord Rogers of Riverside, Thames Wharf, Rainville Road, London, W6 9HA *Tel:* 020 7385 1235 *Fax:* 020 7385 8409 *E-Mail:* jo.m@richardrogers.co.uk.

ROLL OF IPSDEN (Life Baron, UK), Eric Roll; cr. 1977; KCMG 1962; CB 1956

Son of late Mathias Roll, Banker. Born December 1, 1907; educated on the Continent; University of Birmingham; Hon. DSc, Hull 1967; Hon. DSocSci, Birmingham 1967; Hon. LLD, Southampton 1974; Hon. Fellow, LSE. Married 1934, Winifred (died January 28, 1998), daughter of late Elliott Taylor (2 daughters). *Career:* Professor of Economics, University College, Hull 1935–46; Entered Civil Service 1941; Under-Secretary, Treasury 1948; Deputy Head, UK delegation to NATO 1952; Under-Secretary, Ministry of Agriculture, Fisheries and Food 1953–57; Executive Director, International Sugar Council 1957–59; Economic Minister and Head of UK Treasury delegation Washington and UK Executive Director International Monetary Fund and World Bank 1963–64; Permanent Under-Secretary of State, Department of Economic Affairs 1964–66; Hon. Chairman, Book Development Council 1967–; Director: Times Newspapers Ltd 1967–80, Bank of England 1968–77; Chairman (later Joint Chairman), S. G. Warburg & Co. Ltd 1974–86; Director, Times Newspapers Holdings Ltd 1980–83; President, S. G. Warburg Group plc 1986–95; Senior Advisor, Warburg Dillon Read 1995–. *Chancellor:* Chancellor, University of Southampton 1974–84. *Select Committees:* Former Member, Subcommittee A of Select Committee on European Community; Member, Select Committee on Monetary Policy of the Bank of England 1999–. *Trusts, etc:* Chairman, Daiwa Anglo-Japanese Foundation. *Honours:* CMG 1947; CB 1956; KCMG 1962; Grosses Goldene Ehrenzeichen Mit Stern (Austria) 1979; First Class Order of the Dannebrog (Denmark) 1981; Officer Legion D'Honneur (France) 1984; Order of the Sacred Treasure (First Class) (Japan) 1993. *Publications: An Early Experiment in Industrial Organisation,* 1930; *Spotlight on Germany,* 1933; *About Money,* 1935; *Crowded Hours,* 1985; *A History of Economic Thought,* 1995 (fifth edition); *Where Did We Go Wrong?,* 1996. *Special Interests:* Economics, Finance. *Recreations:* Reading, music. *Clubs:* Brooks's. *Name, Style and Title:* Raised to the peerage as Baron Roll of Ipsden, of Ipsden in the County of Oxfordshire 1977. A Cross-Bencher. *Address:* The Lord Roll of Ipsden, KCMG, CB, Warburg Dillon Read, 1 Finsbury Avenue, London, EC2M 2PP.

Dod *on* Disk
The Vacher Dod Parliamentary Database – configured for PC or Network
For further details please telephone the Westminster Office
020 7828 7256

ROSSLYN (7th Earl of, UK), Peter St Clair-Erskine; cr. 1801; 7th Baron Loughborough (GB) 1795; 11th Bt of Alva (NS) 1666

Son of 6th Earl. Born March 31, 1958. Succeeded his father 1977; educated Eton; Bristol University. Married 1982, Helen, daughter of C. R. Watters, of Christ's Hospital, Sussex (2 sons 2 daughters). *Career:* Metropolitan Police 1980–. *House of Lords:* An elected hereditary peer 1999–. *Trusts, etc:* Trustee, Dunimarle Museum. *Recreations:* Church music, piano, opera. *Clubs:* White's. *Heir:* His son, Lord Loughborough, born May 28, 1986. A Cross-Bencher. *Address:* The Earl of Rosslyn, House of Lords, London, SW1A 0PW.

ROTHERWICK (3rd Baron, UK), (Herbert) Robin Cayzer; cr. 1939; 3rd Bt of Tylney (UK) 1924

Son of 2nd Baron. Born March 12, 1954. Succeeded his father 1996; educated Harrow; RMA, Sandhurst; Royal Agricultural College, Cirencester (Diploma in Agriculture). Married 1982, Sara Jane, only daughter of Robert James McAlpine, of Swettenham Hall, Tarporley, Cheshire (2 sons 1 daughter) (marriage dissolved 1994). *Armed Forces:* Former Acting Captain, The Life Guards. *Career:* Aviation, Agriculture and Conservation. *House of Lords:* An elected hereditary peer 1999–. *All-Party:* Member, All-Party: Motorcycling Group, Defence Group. *Other:* Member, Executive Committee of the Popular Flying Association; President, General Aviation Awareness Council. *Miscellaneous:* Heir presumptive to baronetcy of his kinsman Sir James Cayzer, 5th Bt of Gartmore. *Special Interests:* Defence, Aviation, Agriculture. *Recreations:* Aviation, equitation, conservation. *Clubs:* White's. *Heir:* His son, Hon. Herbert Robin Cayzer, born July 10, 1989. A Conservative. *Address:* The Lord Rotherwick, Cornbury Park, Charlbury, Oxford, OX7 3EH *E-Mail:* rr@cpark.co.uk.

RUNCIE (Life Baron, UK), Robert Alexander Kennedy Runcie; cr. 1991; MC 1945; PC 1980

Son of late Robert Dalziel Runcie and late Ann Edna Runcie, née Benson. Born October 2, 1921; educated Merchant Taylor's School, Crosby; Brasenose College, Oxford; Westcott House, Cambridge (MA, DD); Hon. DD: Oxford 1980, Cambridge 1981; Hon. DLitt: Keele 1981, Liverpool 1983; Hon. DCL, West Indies 1984; Hon. DD: Yale 1989, London 1990; Hon. DLitt, Hertfordshire 1991. Married 1957, Angela Rosalind, daughter of late J. W. Cecil Turner, MC (1 son 1 daughter). *Armed Forces:* Served Scots Guards 1939–45 (MC). *Career:* Ordained Deacon 1950; Priest in the Diocese of Newcastle 1951; Chaplain, Westcott House, Cambridge 1953–54, Vice-Principal 1954–56; Fellow, Dean and Tutor, Trinity Hall, Cambridge 1956–60; Vicar of Cuddesdon and Principal of Cuddesdon Theological College, Oxford 1960–69; Bishop of St Albans 1970–80; Took his seat in the House of Lords 1973; Chairman, BBC and IBA Central Religious Advisory Committee 1973–79; Archbishop of Canterbury 1980–91. *Honours:* PC 1980; Elected an Honorary Master of the Bench of Gray's Inn 1980; Invested with the Royal Victorian Chain 1991. Freeman: St Albans 1980, City of London 1981, City of Canterbury 1984. Hon. Liveryman: Merchant Taylors' Company, Grocers' Company, Butchers' Company. *Publications:* Author of: *Cathedral and City: St Albans Ancient and Modern* (editor) 1978; *Windows onto God*, 1983; *Seasons of the Spirit*, 1983; *One Light for One World*, 1988; *Authority in Crisis? An Anglican response*, 1988; *The Unity We Seek*, 1989. *Recreations:* Travelling, reading Mediterranean history, opera. *Clubs:* Athenaeum, Cavalry and Guards, MCC. *Name, Style and Title:* Raised to the peerage as Baron Runcie, of Cuddesdon in the County of Oxfordshire 1991. A Cross-Bencher. *Address:* The Rt Rev. and Rt Hon. the Lord Runcie, MC, 26A Jennings Road, St Albans, Hertfordshire, AL1 4PD.

RUSSELL (5th Earl, UK), Conrad Sebastian Robert Russell; cr. 1861; Viscount Amberley; FBA 1991

Son of 3rd Earl, OM, FRS. Born April 15, 1937. Succeeded his half-brother 1987; educated Eton; Merton College, Oxford. Married 1962, Elizabeth, daughter of Horace Sanders, of Chippenham, Wiltshire (2 sons). *Career:* Lecturer in History, Bedford College, London 1960–74; Reader in History, Bedford College 1974–79; Professor of History, Yale University, USA 1979–84; Astor Professor of British History, University College, London 1984–89; Professor of History, King's College London 1990–. *House of Lords:* An elected hereditary peer 1999–. *Spokesman:* Liberal Democrat Spokesman on Social Security 1990–. *All-Party:* Treasurer, All-Party Parliamentary Homelessness Group to 1997; Vice-Chairman, All-Party Parliamentary Refugees Group. *Awards Granted:* Highland Park/*Spectator:* Peer of the Year Award 1996. *Miscellaneous:* President of the Electoral Reform Society 1997–. FBA. *Publications:* Author of: *The Crisis of Parliaments: English History 1509–1660,* 1971; *Parliaments and English Politics 1621–1629,* 1979; *The Causes of the English Civil War,* 1990; *The Fall of the British Monarchies,* 1991; *An Intelligent Person's Guide to Liberalism,* 1999. *Heir:* His son, Viscount Amberley, born September 12, 1968. A Liberal Democrat. *Address:* Professor The Earl Russell, FBA, Dept of History, King's College, Strand, London, WC2R 2LS.

RUSSELL-JOHNSTON (Life Baron, UK), David Russell Russell-Johnston; cr. 1997; Kt 1985

Son of late David Knox Johnston. Born July 28, 1932; educated Carbost Public School, Isle of Skye; Portree Secondary School, Skye; Edinburgh University (MA Hons History); Moray House College of Education. Married 1967, Joan Graham, daughter of Donald Menzies (3 sons). *Armed Forces:* Commissioned into Intelligence Corps (National Service) 1958. *Career:* History Teacher, Liberton Secretary School Edinburgh 1961–63. *House of Commons:* MP for Inverness 1964–83 and for Inverness, Nairn and Lochaber 1983–97. *Spokesman (Commons):* Liberal Spokesman on: Scotland 1985–87, Foreign and Commonwealth Affairs 1970–75, 1979–85, 1987–88, EEC 1986–88; Alliance Spokesman on Scotland and EEC affairs 1987–88; SLD Spokesman on Foreign and Commonwealth Affairs 1988–89; Liberal Democrat Spokesman on: European Community Affairs 1988, Europe Affairs and East-West relations 1989–94, Central and Eastern Europe 1994–97. *Select Committees (Commons):* Member, Select Committee on Privileges 1988–92. *Backbench Committees (Commons):* Secretary: Falkland Islands Backbench Committee 1977–87, Hong Kong, Backbench Committee 1980–87. *All-Party Committees (Commons):* Former Vice-Chairman, All-Party Bosnian Group. *International Bodies (General):* Member: UK Delegation to European Parliament 1973–75, 1976–79, WEU and Representative to Council of Europe 1984–86, 1987–; President: Council of Europe Liberal, Democratic and Reform Group 1994–99, Sub-Committee on Youth and Sport 1992–94; Vice-President: European Liberal, Democratic and Reform Parties 1990–92, Liberal International 1994–; President, Committee on Culture and Education 1995–99; Vice-President, WEU Defence Committee; Vice Chairman: WEU Parliamentary and Public Relations Committee, WEU Liberal, Democratic and Reformers' Group; President, Parliamentary Assembly of the Council of Europe. *Party Groups (General):* President, Edinburgh University Liberal Club 1956–57, Vice-President 1960–61; Member, Scottish Liberal Party Executive 1961–; Research Assistant, Scottish Liberal Party 1963–64; Vice-Chairman, Scottish Liberal Party 1965–70, Chairman 1970–74, Leader 1974–88; President, Scottish Liberal Democrats 1988–94; Deputy Leader: SLD 1988–89, Liberal Democrats 1989–92. *Other:* Member, Governing Body, Know How Fund for Poland; Vice-Chairman, Westminster Foundation for Democracy; Parliamentary Spokesman, Scottish National Federation for the Welfare of the Blind 1967–; Parliamentary Representative, RNIB 1977. *Miscellaneous:* Member, Royal Commission on Local Government in Scotland 1966–69. *Honours:* Knighted 1985. *Publications: Highland Development; To Be A Liberal; Scottish Liberal Party Speeches,* (2 vols). *Special Interests:* Foreign Affairs, Commonwealth, European Union, East-West Relations, Scottish Affairs, Human Rights, Blind People, Light Rail Transport. *Recreations:* Reading, photography, shinty (Vice-Chief, Camanachd Association 1987–90). *Name, Style and Title:* Raised to the peerage as Baron Russell-Johnston, of Minginish in Highland 1997. A Liberal Democrat. *Address:* The Lord Russell-Johnston, House of Lords, London, SW1A 0PW.

RYDER OF EATON HASTINGS (Life Baron, UK), Sydney Thomas Franklin Ryder; cr. 1975; Kt 1972

Son of late John Ryder. Born September 16, 1916; educated Ealing County Grammar School. Married 1950, Eileen, daughter of William Dodds (1 son 1 daughter). *Career:* Editor *Stock Exchange Gazette* 1950–60; Joint Managing Director 1960–61, Managing Director, Kelly Iliffe Holdings & Associated Press Ltd 1961–63; Director, IPC 1963–70; Chief Executive, Reed International 1963, Chairman and Chief Executive 1968–75; President, National Materials Handling Centre 1970–77; Board Member, British Gas Corporation 1973–78; Member, National Economic Development Council 1975–77; Chairman, National Enterprise Board 1975–77. *Other:* Vice-President, Royal Society for the Prevention of Accidents. Formerly Fellow and Deputy Chairman, British Institute of Management. *Name, Style and Title:* Raised to the peerage as Baron Ryder of Eaton Hastings, of Eaton Hastings in the County of Oxfordshire 1975. A Cross-Bencher. *Address:* The Lord Ryder of Eaton Hastings, Eaton House, Curly Hill, Ilkley, West Yorkshire.

RYDER OF WARSAW (Life Baroness, UK), Sue Ryder; cr. 1979; CMG 1976; OBE 1957

Daughter of late Charles Ryder. Born July 3, 1923; educated Benenden School, Kent; Hon. LLD: Liverpool University 1973, Exeter University 1980, London University 1981; Hon. Degree of Doctor of Letters, Reading University 1982; Hon. Degree of Doctor of Laws, Leeds University 1984; Hon. Doctorate of Civil Law, Kent University 1986; Hon. Degree of Doctor of Law, Cambridge University 1989; Hon. Degree of Essex University 1993; Hon. Fellow, Liverpool John Moores University 1998. Married April 5, 1959, Group-Captain Leonard Cheshire, VC, OM, DSO, DFC (created a life peer as Baron Cheshire, 1991, died July 31, 1992) (1 son 1 daughter). *Armed Forces:* Served war of 1939–45 with FANY and Special Operations Executive. *Other:* Founder and Social Worker, Sue Ryder Foundation for the Sick and Disabled of all age groups; Co-founder, Ryder Cheshire Foundation; Founder, International Sue Ryder Foundation for the Relief of Suffering of all Age Groups. *Trusts, etc:* President, Leonard Cheshire; Trustee: National Memorial Arboretum, The Depaul Trust. *Honours:* OBE 1957; Polonia Restituta (Poland) 1965; Medal of Yugoslav Flag with Gold Wreath and Diploma by Marshall Tito 1971; Golden Order of Merit – Polish People's Republic 1976; CMG 1976; Polish Order of the Smile 1981; Pro Ecclesia et Pontifice Award 1982; Commander's Cross of the Order of Polonia Restituta 1992; Order of Merit from the President of Poland 1992; Silver Cross of the Czech Parachutists 1996; Polish Humanitarian Award 1996; Ecclesiae Populoque Servitium Praestanti, awarded by Cardinal Glemp of Poland 1996. *Publications:* Author of: *And The Morrow Is Theirs*, 1975; *Child Of My Love*, 1986 (new edition 1997). *Special Interests:* Architecture, Building. *Recreations:* Listening to classical music while driving trucks and other vehicles. *Clubs:* SOE. *Name, Style and Title:* Raised to the peerage as Baroness Ryder of Warsaw, of Warsaw in Poland and of Cavendish in the County of Suffolk 1979. A Cross-Bencher. *Address:* The Baroness Ryder of Warsaw, CMG, OBE, PO Box 5259, Sue Ryder Home, Cavendish, Sudbury, Suffolk, CO10 8AN *Tel:* 01787 280653 *Fax:* 01787 280548.

RYDER OF WENSUM (Life Baron, UK), Richard Ryder; cr. 1997; PC 1990; OBE 1981

Son of Stephen Ryder, DL, farmer. Born February 4, 1949; educated Radley; Magdalene College, Cambridge. Married 1981, Caroline, MBE, daughter of late Sir David Stephens, KCB, CVO (1 daughter, 1 son deceased). *Career:* Former journalist; Partner in family business in Suffolk; Political Secretary to Rt Hon. Mrs Margaret Thatcher 1975–81; Chairman, Eastern Counties Radio 1997–. *House of Commons:* Contested Gateshead East February and October 1974; MP (Conservative) for Norfolk Mid 1983–97; Former PPS to Financial Secretary to the Treasury; PPS to Foreign Secretary 1983–86; Parliamentary Secretary, Ministry of Agriculture, Fisheries and Food 1988–89; Economic Secretary, HM Treasury 1989–90; Paymaster-General July-November 1990. *Whip (Commons):* Government Whip 1986–88; Parliamentary Secretary to HM Treasury and Government Chief Whip 1990–95. *Backbench Committees (Commons):* Chairman, Conservative Foreign and Commonwealth Council 1984–89. *Other:* Former Vice-Chairman, Eastern Region Council for Sport and Recreation. *Honours:* OBE 1981; PC 1990. *Name, Style and Title:* Raised to the peerage as Baron Ryder of Wensum, of Wensum in the County of Norfolk 1997. A Conservative. *Address:* The Rt Hon. the Lord Ryder of Wensum, OBE, House of Lords, London, SW1A 0PW.

S

SAATCHI (Life Baron, UK), Maurice Saatchi; cr. 1996

Son of Nathan and Daisy Saatchi. Born June 21, 1946; educated London School of Economics (BSc Economics 1st Class). Married 1984, Josephine Hart (1 son 1 step-son). *Career:* Co-Founder, Saatchi & Saatchi 1970, Chairman 1985–94; Partner, M & C Saatchi Agency 1995–. *Spokesman:* Opposition Spokesman for the Treasury 1999–. *Other:* Governor, London School of Economics; Council Member, Royal College of Art. *Name, Style and Title:* Raised to the peerage as Baron Saatchi, of Staplefield in the County of West Sussex 1996. A Conservative. *Address:* The Lord Saatchi, M & C Saatchi Agency, 36 Golden Square, London, W1R 4EE *Tel:* 020 7543 4500 *E-Mail:* maurices@mcsaatchi.com.

SAINSBURY OF PRESTON CANDOVER (Life Baron, UK), John Davan Sainsbury; cr. 1989; KG 1992; Kt 1980

Son of late Lord Sainsbury (Life Peer). Born November 2, 1927; educated Stowe; Worcester College, Oxford; Hon. Fellow, Worcester College, Oxford 1982; Hon. DSc Economics (London) 1985; Hon. DLitt, South Bank University 1992; Hon. LLD, Bristol University 1993. Married 1963, Anya, daughter of George and Ada Eltenton (2 sons 1 daughter). *Armed Forces:* Served Life Guards 1945–48. *Career:* Joined J. Sainsbury 1950 in buying departments, Director 1958, Vice-Chairman 1967, Chairman and Chief Executive 1969–92, President 1992–; Director, Royal Opera House, Covent Garden 1969–85, Chairman 1987–91; Director, The Economist 1972–80; Joint Hon. Treasurer, European Movement 1972–75; Member of Council, British Retail Consortium 1975–79, President 1993–97; President's Committee CBI 1982–84. *Other:* Governor, Royal Ballet School 1965–76, 1987–91; Chairman, Council of Friends of Covent Garden 1969–81; Chairman, Royal Ballet Governors 1995–, Governor 1987–; Chairman, Benesh Institute of Choreology 1986–87; Member, Contemporary Arts Society 1958–, Hon. Secretary 1965–71, Vice-Chairman 1971–74, Vice-President 1984; Associate, Victoria and Albert Museum 1976–85; President, Sparsholt College, Hampshire 1993–. *Awards Granted:* Awarded the Albert Medal, Royal Society of Arts 1989. *Trusts, etc:* Director, Royal Opera House Trust 1974–84, 1987–; Chairman, Trustees of Dulwich Picture Gallery 1994–; Trustee: National Gallery 1976–83, Westminster Abbey Trust 1977–83, Tate Gallery 1982–83, Rhodes Trust 1984–98. *Honours:* Kt 1980; Honorary Bencher, Inner Temple 1985; KG 1992. Fellow, Institute of Grocery Distribution 1973–; Hon. FRIBA 1993. *Special Interests:* Commerce, Arts. *Clubs:* Garrick, Beefsteak. *Name, Style and Title:* Raised to the peerage as Baron Sainsbury of Preston Candover, of Preston Candover in the County of Hampshire 1989. A Conservative. *Address:* The Lord Sainsbury of Preston Candover, KG, Stamford House, Stamford Street, London, SE1 9LL *Tel:* 020 7695 6663 *E-Mail:* Offjds@tao.j-sainsbury.co.uk.

SAINSBURY OF TURVILLE (Life Baron, UK), David John Sainsbury; cr 1997

Son of Sir Robert Sainsbury. Born October 24, 1940; educated King's College, Cambridge (BA); Columbia University, New York (MBA); Hon. DSc, Salford 1989; Hon. FEng 1994; Hon. LLD (Cantab) 1997. Married 1973, Susan Carole Reid (3 daughters). *Career:* Joined J. Sainsbury plc 1963: Finance Director 1973–90, Deputy Chairman 1988–92, Chairman and Chief Executive 1992–98. *House of Lords:* Parliamentary Under-Secretary of State, Department of Trade and Industry (Minister for Science) 1998–. *Other:* Member, Committee of Review of the Post Office (Carter Committee) 1975–77; Member, Governing Body, London Business School 1985, Chairman 1991–98. *Trusts, etc:* Trustee, Social Democratic Party 1982–90. *Miscellaneous:* Visiting Fellow, Nuffield College, Oxford 1987–95. *Publications: Government and Industry: a new partnership*, 1981; *Wealth Creation and Jobs*, (with Christopher Smallwood) 1987. *Name, Style and Title:* Raised to the peerage as Baron Sainsbury of Turville, of Turville in the County of Buckinghamshire 1997. Labour. *Address:* The Lord Sainsbury of Turville, House of Lords, London, SW1A 0PW *Tel:* 020 7215 5624.

ST ALBANS (Bishop of), Christopher William Herbert

Son of Walter Meredith Herbert and Hilda Lucy Dibben. Born January 7, 1944; educated Monmouth School; St David's College, Lampeter (BA); Bristol University (PGCE); Wells Theological College; currently studying for MPhil at Leicester University. Married 1968, Janet Elizabeth Turner (2 sons). *Career:* Assistant Curate, Tupsley, Hereford 1967–71; Assistant Master, Bishop's School, Hereford 1967–71; Diocese of Hereford: Adviser in Religious Education 1971–76, Director of Education 1976–81; Vicar, St Thomas on The Bourne, Farnham, Surrey 1981–90; Archdeacon of Dorking 1990 95; Director of Postordination Training, Diocese of Guildford 1984–90; Hon. Canon of Guildford 1990–95; Bishop of St Albans 1995–; Took his seat in the House of Lords 1999–. FRSA. *Publications: The New Creation,* 1971; *A Place to Dream,* 1976; *St Paul's: A Place to Dream,* 1981; *The Edge of Wonder,* 1981; *Listening to Children,* 1983; *On the Road,* 1984; *Be Thou My Vision,* 1985; *This Most Amazing Day,* 1986; *The Question of Jesus,* 1987; *Alive to God,* 1987; *Ways into Prayer,* 1987; *Help in your Bereavement,* 1988; *Prayers for Children,* 1993; *Pocket Prayers,* 1993; *The Prayer Garden,* 1994; *Words of Comfort,* 1994; *Pocket Prayers for Children,* 1999. *Special Interests:* Education, National Health Service (Hospital Chaplaincy). *Recreations:* Walking, cycling, gardening, reading, art history of fifteenth century northern Europe. *Address:* The Rt Rev. the Lord Bishop of St Albans, Abbey Gate House, St Albans, Hertfordshire, AL3 4HD *Tel:* 01727 853305.

ST JOHN OF BLETSO (21st Baron, E), Anthony Tudor St John; cr. 1558; 18th Bt of Bletso (E) 1660

Son of 20th Baron, TD. Born May 16, 1957. Succeeded his father 1978; educated Diocesan College, Capetown; University of Capetown (BSocSc 1977, BA (Law) 1979, BProc (Law) 1982, LLM (London University) 1983). Married September 16, 1994, Dr Helen Jane Westlake, daughter of Michael Westlake, of Monkshill, Monkton Combe, Bath (2 sons). *Career:* Solicitor; Attorney in South Africa 1983–85; Oil Analyst/Stockbroker, County Natwest 1985–88; Consultant to Merrill Lynch 1988–; Chairman, Eurotrust International 1993–; Business Development Director, Globex 1997–. *House of Lords:* An elected hereditary peer 1999–. *Select Committees:* Former Member, Select Committee A – Trade, Finance and Foreign Affairs; Co-opted Member, Select Committee on European Communities Sub-Committee A (Economic and Financial Affairs, Trade and External Relations) 1997–; Member, Library and Computers Sub-Committee 1998–. *All-Party:* Member, All-Party: South Africa Group, Human Rights Group, Motorcycle Group. *Trusts, etc:* Trustee: TVE (Television for the Environment), TUSK, SAN Foundation. *Miscellaneous:* A Extra Lord in Waiting to HM The Queen 1998–. *Special Interests:* Environment, Foreign Affairs, South Africa, Human Rights, Finance, Legal Affairs. *Recreations:* Ski-ing, golf, windsurfing, tennis. *Sportsclubs:* Wisley Golf. *Clubs:* Hurlingham. *Heir:* His son, Hon. Oliver Beauchamp St John, born July 11, 1995. A Cross-Bencher. *Address:* The Lord St John of Bletso, House of Lords, London, SW1A 0PW; Woodlands, Llanishen, Nr Chepstow, Gwent, NP6 6QQ *E-Mail:* asj@enterprise.net.

ST JOHN OF FAWSLEY (Life Baron, UK), Norman Anthony Francis St John-Stevas; cr. 1987; PC 1979

Son of late Stephen S. Stevas and late Kitty St John-O'Connor. Born May 18, 1929; educated Ratcliffe College, Leicester; Fitzwilliam College, Cambridge (MA, 1st Class Hons Law 1950, Yorke Prize 1957) (President, Cambridge Union 1950); Christ Church, Oxford (BCL 1954); Yale University (Blackstone and Harmsworth Scholar 1952); Fellow, Yale Law School 1960. *Career:* An author and barrister; Called to the Bar, Middle Temple 1952; Tutored in jurisprudence: King's College, London, Christ Church and Merton, Oxford 1953–57; Political correspondent, *The Economist* 1959; Editor, *Dublin Review* 1961; Chairman, Royal Fine Arts Commission July 1985–; Master of Emmanuel College, Cambridge 1991–. *House of Commons:* Contested (Conservative) Dagenham General Election 1951; MP (Conservative) for Chelmsford 1964–87; Chancellor of the Duchy of Lancaster and Leader of the House of Commons 1979–1981.

Spokesman (Commons): Conservative Spokesman on Education and the Arts 1975–79. Fellow, Royal Society of Literature 1966. *Publications:* include *Obscenity and the Law,* 1956; *Walter Bagehot,* 1959; *Life, Death and the Law,* 1961; *The Right to Life,* 1963; *The Collected Works of Walter Bagehot,* in fifteen volumes 1965–86; *The Agonising Choice,* 1971. *Clubs:* Garrick, White's, Pratt's. *Name, Style and Title:* Raised to the peerage as Baron St John of Fawsley, of Preston Capes in the County of Northamptonshire 1987. A Conservative. *Address:* The Rt Hon. the Lord St John of Fawsley, The Old Rectory, Preston Capes, Daventry, Northamptonshire, NN11 6TE.

SALISBURY (77th Bishop of), David Staffurth Stancliffe

Son of late Very Rev. Michael Staffurth Stancliffe. Born October 1, 1942; educated Westminster School; Trinity College, Oxford (MA); Cuddesdon Theological College; DLitt, Portsmouth University 1993. Married 1965, Sarah Loveday Smith (1 son 2 daughters). *Career:* Assistant Curate, St Bartholomew's, Armley, Leeds 1967–70; Chaplain to Clifton College, Bristol 1970–77; Canon Residentiary of Portsmouth Cathedral, Diocesan Director of Ordinands and Lay Ministry Adviser 1977–82; Provost of Portsmouth 1982–93; Member, General Synod 1985–; Member, Liturgical Commission 1986, Chairman 1993–; Member, Cathedral's Fabric Commission 1991–; Bishop of Salisbury 1993–; Took his seat in the House of Lords 1998. *Other:* President, Council of Marlborough College 1994–. *Recreations:* Old music, Italy. *Address:* The Rt Rev. the Lord Bishop of Salisbury, South Canonry, 71 The Close, Salisbury, Wiltshire, SP1 2ER *Tel:* 01722 334031 *E-Mail:* dsarum@eluk.co.uk.

SALTOUN OF ABERNETHY (Lady, 20th in line, S), Flora Marjory Fraser; cr. 1445

Daughter of 19th Lord, MC. Born October 18, 1930. Succeeded her father 1979; educated St Mary's School, Wantage. Married October 6, 1956, Captain Alexander Ramsay of Mar, DL, only son of late Admiral Hon. Sir Alexander Ramsay, GCVO, KCB, DSO, and Lady Patricia Ramsay, CI (3 daughters). *House of Lords:* An elected hereditary peer 1999–. *Awards Granted:* Cordon Bleu Diploma in Cookery 1950. *Miscellaneous:* Member, Standing Council of Scottish Chiefs; Chief of the Name of Fraser. *Special Interests:* Scottish Affairs, Defence. *Heir:* Her daughter, Hon. Katharine Ingrid Mary Isabel Fraser (Hon. Mrs. Mark Nicolson), born October 11, 1957. A Cross-Bencher. *Address:* The Lady Saltoun of Abernethy, House of Lords, London, SW1A 0PW.

SANDBERG (Life Baron, UK), Michael Graham Ruddock Sandberg; cr. 1997; Kt 1986; CBE 1982

Son of Gerald and Ethel Sandberg. Born May 31, 1927; educated St Edward's School, Oxford; Hon. LLD, Hong Kong 1984. Married 1954, Carmel Mary Donnelly (2 sons 2 daughters). *Armed Forces:* 6th Lancers (Indian Army) and First King's Dragoon Guards 1945. *Career:* Joined Hong Kong and Shanghai Banking Corporation 1949, Chairman 1977–86. *Select Committees:* Member, Select Committee on European Communities Sub-Committee B (Energy, Industry and Transport) 1999–. *Other:* Member, Executive Council, Hong Kong 1978–86; Treasurer, University of Hong Kong 1977–86. *Honours:* OBE 1977; CBE 1982; Kt 1986. FCIB; FRSA 1983. Freeman, City of London. Liveryman, Clockmakers' Company. *Recreations:* Horse racing, bridge, cricket, horology. *Sportsclubs:* President, Surrey County Cricket Club 1988. *Clubs:* Cavalry and Guards, Portland, White's, MCC. *Name, Style and Title:* Raised to the peerage as Baron Sandberg, of Passfield in the County of Hampshire 1997. A Liberal Democrat. *Address:* The Lord Sandberg, CBE, 100 Piccadilly, London, W1V 9FN.

SANDERSON OF BOWDEN (Life Baron, UK), Charles Russell Sanderson; cr. 1985; Kt 1981; DL

Son of late Charles Plummer Sanderson. Born April 30, 1933; educated St Mary's School, Melrose; Glenalmond College; Bradford Technical College; Scottish College of Textiles. Married July 5, 1958, Elizabeth, daughter of late Donald Alfred Macaulay, of Skipton, Yorks (1 son 2 daughters and 1 son deceased). *Armed Forces:* Commissioned Royal Signals 1952. *Councils, Public Bodies:* DL, Roxburgh, Ettrick and Lauderdale 1990–. *Career:* Partner, Charles P. Sanderson, Wool and Yarn Merchants 1958–87; Director: Johnston of Elgin 1980–87, Illingworth Morris 1982–87; Chairman: Edinburgh Financial Trust plc 1983–87, Shires Investment plc 1983–87; Director, Clydesdale Bank plc 1986–87, 1994–, Deputy Chairman 1996–99, Chairman 1999–; Chairman, Hawick Cashmere Co. 1991–; Director, Scottish Mortgage and Trust plc 1991–, Chairman 1993–; Director: Woolcombers plc 1992–95, Edinburgh Woollen Mills 1992–97, United Auctions Ltd 1992–99, Watson-Philip plc 1993–99, Morrison Construction 1995–. *House of Lords:* Minister of State, Scottish Office 1987–90. *Party Groups:* Vice-Chairman, Scottish Peers Association 1996, Chairman 1998–. *Party Groups (General):* President, Scottish Conservative and Unionist Association 1977–79; Vice-President, National Union of Conservative and Unionist Associations 1979–81; Chairman, National Union Executive Committee 1981–86; Chairman, Scottish Conservative Party 1990–93. *Other:* Chairman, Eildon Housing Association 1976–82; Member, Scottish Council of Independent Schools 1984–87; Chairman, Council of Glenalmond College 1994–; Member of Court, Napier University, Edinburgh 1994–. *Honours:* Kt 1981. Liveryman, The Worshipful Company of Framework Knitters. *Special Interests:* Industry, Textile Industry, Small Businesses, Scottish Affairs, Housing, Transport. *Recreations:* Golf, fishing. *Sportsclubs:* Hon. Company of Edinburgh Golfers. *Clubs:* Caledonian. *Name, Style and Title:* Raised to the peerage as Baron Sanderson of Bowden, of Melrose in the District of Ettrick and Lauderdale 1985. A Conservative. *Address:* The Lord Sanderson of Bowden, DL, Becketts Field, Bowden, Melrose, Borders, TD6 0ST *Tel:* 01835 822736; Office: The Square, Bowden, Melrose, Borders, TD6 0ST *Tel:* 01835 822271 *Fax:* 01835 823272.

SANDWICH (11th Earl of, E), John Edward Hollister Montagu; cr. 1660; Viscount Hinchingbrooke and Baron Montagu

Son of Victor Montagu, 10th Earl, formerly Viscount Hinchingbrooke MP, who disclaimed the earldom and other honours for life on July 24, 1964 under the terms of the Peerage Act, 1963. Born April 11, 1943. Succeeded his father 1995; educated Eton; Trinity College, Cambridge (MA); OU Course in European Studies 1973. Married July 1, 1968, (Susan) Caroline, daughter of late Canon Perceval Hayman, of Rogate, Sussex (2 sons 1 daughter). *Career:* Assistant Editor, The Bodley Head 1966–68; Editor, India Tourism Development Corporation 1968–69; Christian Aid: Information Officer 1974–85, Research Officer 1985–86; Joint owner/administrator, Mapperton Estate, Dorset 1982–; Consultant, CARE Britain 1987–93; Editor, Save the Children 1990–92. *House of Lords:* An elected hereditary peer 1999–. *All-Party:* Member, All-Party: Tibet Group, Sudan Group, Nepal Group, India Group, Overseas Development Group, Refugees Group, South Africa Group, Human Rights Group. *Other:* Governor, Beaminster School, Dorset 1996–; Council, Anti-Slavery International 1997–; Vice-President, Worldaware 1997–; Board, Christian Aid 1999. *Trusts, etc:* Managing Trustee, St Francis School, Dorset 1987–92; TSW Telethon Trustee 1987–93; Trustee, Britain-Afghanistan Trust 1994–98. *Publications:* Author or Editor of: *The Book of the World*, 1971; *Prospects for Africa*, 1988; *Prospects for Africa's Children*, 1990; *Children at Crisis Point*, 1992; *Hinch: A Celebration*, (with Andrew Best) 1997. *Special Interests:* Overseas Aid and Development, International Affairs, National Heritage. *Recreations:* Walking, tennis, sailing, ski-ing. *Heir:* His son, Viscount Hinchingbrooke, born December 5, 1969. A Cross-Bencher. *Address:* The Earl of Sandwich, House of Lords, London, SW1A 0PW.

SAVILLE OF NEWDIGATE (Life Baron, UK), Mark Oliver Saville; cr. 1997; Kt 1985; PC 1994

Son of Kenneth and Olivia Saville. Born March 20, 1936; educated Rye Grammar School; Brasenose College, Oxford (BA, BCL); Hon. LLD, Guildhall University 1997; Hon. Fellow, Brasenose College, Oxford 1998. Married 1961, Jill Gray (2 sons). *Armed Forces:* Second Lieutenant, Royal Sussex Regiment 1954–56. *Career:* Oxford University 1956–60, Vinerian Scholar 1960; Called to the Bar, Middle Temple 1962, Bencher 1963; QC 1975; Judge of the High Court, Queen's Bench Division 1985–93; A Lord Justice of Appeal 1994–97; A Lord of Appeal in Ordinary 1997–. *Select Committees:* Member, Joint Select Committee on Consolidation of Bills 1998–. *Honours:* Kt 1985; PC 1994. *Recreations:* Sailing, flying. *Name, Style and Title:* Raised to the peerage as Baron Saville of Newdigate, of Newdigate in the County of Surrey 1997. A Cross-Bencher. *Address:* The Rt Hon. the Lord Saville of Newdigate, House of Lords, London, SW1A 0PW.

SAWYER (Life Baron, UK), Lawrence Sawyer; cr. 1998

Born May 12, 1943. *Trades Union:* Member, UNISON. *Career:* Former Deputy General Secretary: NUPE, Unison; General Secretary, The Labour Party 1994–98; Non-Executive Director, Reed Executive 1999–. *Party Groups (General):* Labour Party: Member, National Executive 1982–94, Party Chairman 1992. *Miscellaneous:* Board Member, Investors in People UK 1999–. *Name, Style and Title:* Raised to the peerage as Baron Sawyer, of Darlington in the County of Durham 1998. Labour. *Address:* The Lord Sawyer, House of Lords, London, SW1A 0PW.

SCANLON (Life Baron, UK), Hugh Parr Scanlon; cr. 1979

Son of late Hugh Scanlon. Born October 26, 1913; educated Stretford Elementary School; National Council of Labour Colleges (NCLC); Hon. DCL, Kent University 1988. Married 1943, Nora Markey (2 daughters). *Trades Union:* Divisional Organiser, AEU Manchester 1947–63; Member, Executive Council 1963–67; President, Amalgamated Union of Engineering Workers 1968–78; Member, TUC General Council 1968–78; President, European Metal Workers Federation 1974–78. *Miscellaneous:* Member, British Gas Corporation 1976–82; Chairman, Engineering Industry Training Board 1975–82. *Recreations:* Golf, gardening. *Name, Style and Title:* Raised to the peerage as Baron Scanlon, of Davyhulme in the County of Greater Manchester 1979. Labour. *Address:* The Lord Scanlon, 23 Seven Stones Drive, Broadstairs, Kent, CT10 1TW.

SCARMAN (Life Baron, UK), Leslie George Scarman; cr. 1977; PC 1972; Kt 1961; OBE (Mil) 1944

Son of late George Charles Scarman, Lloyds Underwriter. Born July 29, 1911; educated Radley College; Brasenose College, Oxford; Hon. LLD: Exeter 1965, Glasgow 1969, London 1971, Keele 1972, Freiburg 1973, Warwick 1974, Bristol 1976, Manchester 1977, Kent 1981, Wales 1985, QUB 1990, Dundee 1990. Married 1947, Ruth, daughter of late Clement Wright, ICS (1 adopted son). *Armed Forces:* RAFVR 1940–45. *Career:* Called to the Bar, Middle Temple 1936; QC 1957; Judge of the High Court of Justice, Probate, Divorce and Admiralty Division 1961–72; Chairman, Law Commission 1965–72; Lord Justice of Appeal 1972–77; President, Senate of Inns of Court and Bar 1976–79; Lord of Appeal in Ordinary 1977–86. *Chancellor:* Chancellor, University of Warwick 1977–89. *Other:* Member, Charter 88. *Honours:* OBE (Mil) 1944; Order of Battle Merit (Russia) 1945; Kt 1961; PC 1972. *Publications: English Law: The New Dimension*, 1974. *Special Interests:* Law Reform, Constitutional Reform, Homeless, Human Rights, Education. *Recreations:* History, music, walking. *Clubs:* Royal Air Force. *Name, Style and Title:* Raised to the peerage as Baron Scarman, of Quatt in the county of Shropshire 1977. A Cross-Bencher. *Address:* The Rt Hon. the Lord Scarman, OBE, House of Lords, London, SW1A 0PW *Tel:* House of Lords 020 7219 3202.

SCOTLAND OF ASTHAL (Life Baroness, UK), Patricia Janet Scotland; cr. 1997; QC 1991

Educated University of London (LLB). Married 1985, Richard Mawhinney (2 sons). *Career:* Called to the Bar 1997; Member, Antigua Bar. *House of Lords:* Parliamentary Under-Secretary of State, Foreign and Commonwealth Office 1999–. *Miscellaneous:* Former Member, Commission for Racial Equality; Member, Millenium Commission 1994–. *Name, Style and Title:* Raised to the peerage as Baroness Scotland of Asthal, of Asthal in the County of Oxfordshire 1997. Labour. *Address:* The Baroness Scotland of Asthal, QC, 1 Gray's Inn Square, London, WC1R 5AG.

SECCOMBE (Life Baroness, UK), Joan Anna Dalziel Seccombe; cr. 1991; DBE 1984

Daughter of late Robert John Owen, and of Olive Barlow Owen. Born May 3, 1930; educated St Martin's, Solihull. Married July 15, 1950, Henry Laurence, son of late Herbert Stanley Seccombe (2 sons). *Councils, Public Bodies:* JP, Solihull 1968–, Chairman of Bench 1981–84; Councillor, West Midlands County Council 1977–81, Chairman, Trading Standards Committee 1979–81. *Whip:* An Opposition Whip (Education, Environment, Northern Ireland) 1997–. *Select Committees:* Member, House of Lords Committees on: Offices 1992–94, 1998–, Broadcasting 1994–97, Personal Bills 1994–97; Member, Sub-Committees on: Administration and Works 1992–94, Finance and Staff 1994–97. *All-Party:* Member All-Party: Skin Group, Consumer Affairs and Trading Standards Group. *Party Groups (General):* Chairman, West Midlands Conservative Women's Committee 1975–78; Chairman, Conservative Women's National Committee 1981–84; Chairman, National Union of Conservative and Unionist Associations 1987–88, Vice-Chairman 1984–87, Member of Executive 1975–97; Chairman, Conservative Party Annual Conference, Blackpool 1987; Vice-Chairman, Conservative Party with special responsibility for Women 1987–97. *Other:* A Vice-President, Institute of Trading Standards Administration 1992–; Governor, Nuffield Hospitals 1988–, Deputy Chairman 1993–. *Trusts, etc:* Chairman, Trustees of Nuffield Hospitals Pension Scheme. *Miscellaneous:* Chairman, Lord Chancellor's Advisory Committee 1975–93; Member, Heart of England Tourist Board 1977–81, Chairman, Marketing Sub-committee 1979–81; Member, Women's National Commission 1984–90. *Honours:* DBE, 1984. *Special Interests:* Women's Issues, Family. *Recreations:* Golf, ski-ing, embroidery. *Sportsclubs:* President, St Enedoc Golf Club. *Name, Style and Title:* Raised to the peerage as Baroness Seccombe, of Kineton in the County of Warwickshire 1991. A Conservative. *Address:* The Baroness Seccombe, DBE, JP, Linden Cottage, The Green, Little Kineton, Warwickshire, CV35 0DJ *Tel:* 01926 640562 *Fax:* 01926 640308.

SEFTON OF GARSTON (Life Baron, UK), William Henry Sefton; cr. 1978

Son of late George Sefton. Born August 5, 1915; educated Duncombe Road School, Liverpool. Married 1940, Phyllis Kerr. *Councils, Public Bodies:* Joined Liverpool City Council 1953, Leader 1964; Chairman and Leader, Merseyside County Council 1974–77; Chairman, Runcorn Development Corporation 1974–81; Chairman, North West Economic Planning Council 1975–89. *Select Committees:* Member, House of Lords Select Committee on Relations between Central and Local Government 1995–96. *Name, Style and Title:* Raised to the peerage as Baron Sefton of Garston, of Garston in the County of Merseyside 1978. Labour. *Address:* The Lord Sefton of Garston, House of Lords, London, SW1A 0PW.

SELBORNE (4th Earl of, UK), John Roundell Palmer; cr. 1882; Viscount Wolmer; 4th Baron Selborne (UK) 1872; KBE 1987; FRS 1991; DL

Son of Captain Viscount Wolmer (died on active service 1942), son of 3rd Earl, PC, CH. Born March 24, 1940. Succeeded his grandfather 1971; educated Eton; Christ Church, Oxford; Hon. LLD, Bristol 1989; Hon. DSc: Cranfield 1991, East Anglia 1996, Southampton 1996. Married 1969, Joanna Van Antwerp, daughter of Evan James (3 sons 1 daughter). *Councils, Public Bodies:* DL, Hampshire 1982. *Career:* Member, Apple and Pear Development Council 1969–73; Chairman: Hops Marketing Board 1978–82, Agricultural and Food Research Council 1982–89; Chairman, Joint Nature Conservation Committee 1991–97; Member, NEDC Food Sector Group 1991–92; Member, Royal Commission on Environmental Pollution 1993–98; Director: Lloyd's Bank Plc 1994–95, Lloyds TSB Group Plc 1995–. *Chancellor:* Chancellor, Southampton University 1996–. *House of Lords:* An elected hereditary peer 1999–. *Select Committees:* Chairman, Sub-Committee D, European Communities Select Committee 1991–93; Member, Select Committee on Science and Technology 1992–97, Chairman 1993–97; Co-opted Member, Select Committee on European Communities Sub-Committee (Environment, Public House and Consumer Protection) 1998; Member, Select Committee on Science and Technology Sub-Committee I (Non-Food Crops) 1999. *All-Party:* President, Parliamentary and Scientific Committee 1997–. *Other:* President: Royal Agricultural Society of England 1987–88, Royal Institute of Public Health and Hygiene 1991–97; A Vice-President, Foundation for Science and Technology; President, Royal Geographical Society (with the Institute of British Geographers) 1997–. *Honours:* KBE 1987. FRS 1991. Master, Mercers' Company 1989. *Special Interests:* Science, Agriculture, Education, Conservation. *Clubs:* Brooks's, Farmers'. *Heir:* His son, Viscount Wolmer, born September 1, 1971. A Conservative. *Address:* The Earl of Selborne, KBE, FRS, DL, Temple Manor, Selborne, Alton, Hampshire, GU34 3LR.

SELKIRK OF DOUGLAS (Life Baron, UK), James Alexander Douglas-Hamilton; cr. 1997; PC 1996; QC (Scot) 1996

Son of 14th Duke of Hamilton and Brandon, KT, PC, GCVO, AFC, DL, and Lady Elizabeth Percy, OBE, DL, daughter of 8th Duke of Northumberland, KG, CBE, MVO. Born July 31, 1942; educated Eton; Balliol College, Oxford (MA Modern History) (Oxford Boxing Blue 1961, President, Oxford Union Society Summer 1964); Edinburgh University (LLB Scots Law). Married August 24, 1974, Hon. Susan Buchan, daughter of 2nd Baron Tweedsmuir, CBE, and late Baroness Tweedsmuir of Belhelvie, PC (4 sons including twins). *Armed Forces:* Captain, Cameronians RARO 1961–66; Captain, 2nd Btn Lowland Volunteers, TAVR 1971–73; Hon. Air Commodore No 2 (City of Edinburgh), Maritime Headquarters Unit 1994. *Councils, Public Bodies:* Councillor: Murrayfield-Cramond Ward 1972–74, Murrayfield District 1974. *Career:* Scots Advocate and Interim Procurator Fiscal Depute at Scottish Bar 1968–72; QC 1996. *House of Commons:* MP (Conservative) for Edinburgh West 1974–97; PPS to Rt Hon. Malcolm Rifkind: as Minister of State, Foreign Office 1983–85, as Secretary of State for Scotland 1986–87; Parliamentary Under-Secretary of State, Scottish Office: Minister for Home Affairs and Environment 1987–92, Minister for Education and Housing 1992–95; Minister of State (Minister for Health and Home Affairs) 1995–97. *Whip (Commons):* Scottish Conservative Whip 1976–79; Government Whip and Lord Commissioner of the Treasury 1979–81. *Select Committees (Commons):* Member, Select Committee on Scottish Affairs 1981–83. *Backbench Committees (Commons):* Former Secretary, Conservative Party Committee for Constitutional Affairs. *All-Party Committees (Commons):* Chairman, Scottish All-Party Penal Affairs Group 1983–85; Former Secretary, All-Party: Nepal Group, Malta Group. *International Bodies (General):* President, International Rescue Corps 1995–. *Party Groups (General):* President, Oxford University Conservative Association Winter 1963. *Other:* Hon. President, Scottish Boxing Association 1975–98; President: Royal Commonweath Society in Scotland 1979–87, Scottish National Council, UN Association 1981–87. *Trusts, etc:* Trustee, Selkirk Charitable Trust. *Miscellaneous:* Disclaimed the Earldom of Selkirk, November 1994; Member, Royal Company of Archers, the Queen's Bodyguard for Scotland; Contested Edinburgh West constituency, MSP for the Region of Lothians since May 6, 1999 (contested the seat as Lord James Douglas-Hamilton); Scottish Parliament: Member, Parliamentary Bureau 1999–; Business Manager (Chief Whip of the Conservative Group) 1999–. *Honours:* PC 1996. *Publications:* Author of:

Motive for a Mission: The Story Behind Hess's Flight to Britain, 1971; *The Air Battle for Malta: The Diaries of a Fighter Pilot*, 1981; *Roof of the World: Man's First Flight over Everest*, 1983; *The Truth About Rudolph Hess*, 1993. *Special Interests:* Foreign Affairs, Defence, Scottish Affairs, Law Reform, Conservation, Arts, Housing, Health, Education, Local Government, Environment, Heritage. *Recreations:* Golf, boxing, forestry, debating, history. *Clubs:* Pratt's, New (Edinburgh). *Heir:* Heir to disclaimed Earldom, his son, Hon. John Andrew Douglas-Hamilton, Master of Selkirk, born February 8, 1978. *Name, Style and Title:* Raised to the peerage as Baron Selkirk of Douglas, of Cramond in the City of Edinburgh 1997. A Conservative. *Address:* The Rt Hon. the Lord Selkirk of Douglas, MSP, House of Lords, London, SW1A 0PW.

SELSDON (3rd Baron, UK), Malcolm McEacharn Mitchell-Thomson; cr. 1932; 4th Bt of Polmood (UK) 1900

Son of 2nd Baron, DSC. Born October 27, 1937. Succeeded his father 1963; educated Winchester. Married 1st, 1965, Patricia Anne Smith (1 son) (marriage dissolved), married 2nd, 1995, Gabrielle, daughter of Richard G. Williams. *Armed Forces:* Served in the Royal Navy 1956–58, Sub-Lieutenant RNR. *Career:* Merchant Banker, Midland Bank Group, Public Finance Adviser 1979–90; Delegate, Council of Europe and Western European Union 1972–78; Member, British Overseas Trade Board 1983–86; Chairman, Committee for Middle East Trade (COMET) 1979–86; Member, East European Trade Council 1983–87. *House of Lords:* An elected hereditary peer 1999–. *Other:* President, British Exporters' Association 1992–. *Miscellaneous:* Chairman, Greater London and South East Council for Sport and Recreation 1977–83. *Special Interests:* Trade and Industry, Foreign Affairs, Defence, Economic Policy. *Recreations:* Ski-ing, sailing, tennis, lawn tennis. *Clubs:* MCC. *Heir:* His son, Hon. Callum Malcolm McEacharn Mitchell-Thomson, born November 7, 1969. A Conservative. *Address:* The Lord Selsdon, House of Lords, London, SW1A 0PW.

SEROTA (Life Baroness, UK), Beatrice Serota; cr. 1967; DBE 1992

Daughter of Alexander Katz. Born October 15, 1919; educated John Howard School; London School of Economics (BSc Economics); Hon. DLitt, Loughborough; Hon. Fellow, LSE. Married December 27, 1942, Stanley Serota, BSc (Engineering), FICE (1 son 1 daughter). *Councils, Public Bodies:* JP, Inner London Area; Councillor, Hampstead Borough Council 1945–49; Councillor, LCC for Brixton 1954–65, Chairman, Children's Committee 1958–65; Councillor, GLC for Lambeth 1964–67; Chief Whip (GLC) and Vice-Chairman, Inner London Education Committee 1964–67; Member: Longford Committee on Crime – a Challenge to us all 1964, Latey Committee on Age of Majority 1965–66, Seebohm Committee on Organization of the Local Authority Personal Social Services 1966–68. *Career:* Assistant Principal, Ministry of Fuel and Power 1941–46; Member: Advisory Council on Child Care and Central Training Council in Child Care 1958–68, Advisory Council on Treatment of Offenders 1960–64, Royal Commission on Penal System 1964–66; Member, Advisory Council on the Penal System 1966–78, Chairman 1976–78; Member, Community Relations Commission 1971–77; Founder Chairman, Commission for Local Administration in England, Local Commissioner for Greater London and the South-East (Local Government Ombudsman) 1974–82; Member, BBC Complaints Commission 1975–77; Governor, BBC 1977–82. *House of Lords:* Minister of State (Health), Department of Health and Social Security 1969–70; A Deputy Speaker, House of Lords 1985–; A Deputy Chairman of Committees 1985–; Principal Deputy Chairman of Committees 1986–92. *Whip:* Baroness-in-waiting (Government Whip) 1968–69. *Spokesman:* Opposition Spokesperson on Health 1970–73. *Select Committees:* Member, Select Committee on Sport and Leisure 1972–73; Chairman, House of Lords Select Committee on the European Communities 1986–92; Member, Select Committee on the Public Service 1996–97. *All-Party:* Member, All-Party Parliamentary Committees on: Children, Ageing. *Honours:* DBE 1992. *Recreations:* Gardening, needlepoint, collecting shells. *Name, Style and Title:* Raised to the peerage as Baroness Serota, of Hampstead in Greater London 1967. Labour. *Address:* The Baroness Serota, DBE, The Coach House, 15 Lyndhurst Terrace, London, NW3 5QA.

SEWEL (Life Baron, UK), John Buttifant Sewel; cr. 1996; CBE 1984

Son of late Leonard Sewel, and of Hilda Ivy Sewel. Born January 15, 1946; educated Hanson Boys' Grammar School, Bradford; Durham University (BA); University College, Swansea (MSc Economics); Aberdeen University (PhD). Married, 2nd, 1987, Leonora Mary Harding (1 son 1 daughter from previous marriage). *Councils, Public Bodies:* Councillor, Aberdeen City Council 1974–84, Leader 1977–80. *Career:* From 1969, successively Research Fellow, Lecturer, Senior Lecturer, Professor, University of Aberdeen; Dean, Faculty of Economic and Social Sciences 1989–94; Vice-Principal and Dean, Faculty of Social Sciences and Law, University of Aberdeen 1995–97; Professor and Vice Principal, University of Aberdeen 1999–. *House of Lords:* Parliamentary Under-Secretary of State, Scottish Office (Minister for Agriculture, the Environment and Fisheries) 1997–99. *Spokesman:* An Opposition Spokesman on Scotland 1996–97. *Miscellaneous:* President, Convention of Scottish Local Authorities 1982–84; Member: Accounts Commission for Scotland 1987–97, Scottish Constitutional Commission 1994–95. *Publications:* Books and learned articles mainly on politics and development in Scotland. *Special Interests:* Scotland, Local Government, Public Finance. *Recreations:* Hill walking, skiing. *Name, Style and Title:* Raised to the peerage as Baron Sewel, of Gilcomstoun in the District of the City of Aberdeen 1996. Labour. *Address:* The Lord Sewel, CBE, Birklands, Raemoir, Banchory, Kincardineshire, AB31 3QU *Tel:* 01330 844545.

SHARMAN (Life Baron, UK), Colin Morven Sharman; cr. 1999; OBE 1979

Son of Colonel Terence John Sharman. Born February 19, 1943; educated Bishops Wordsworth School, Salisbury, Wiltshire; Hon. Doctorate, Cranfield School of Management 1998. Married 1966, Angela Timmins (1 son 1 daughter). *Career:* Qualified as a Chartered Accountant 1965; Joined Peat Marwick Mitchell, later KPMG Peat Marwick, then KPMG 1966; Manager, Frankfurt Office 1970–72 and The Hague 1972–81; Partner 1973; Senior Partner (National Marketing and Industry Groups) 1987–90; UK Senior Partner 1994–98; Chairman, KPMG International 1998–99; Director: UKAEA, AEA Technology; Chairman: Le Gavroche Ltd, Aegis Group Plc. *Other:* Member: Council, CBI, Appeal Committee, Golden Jubilee Appeal, National Association of Almshouses, Industry Society. *Miscellaneous:* Companion, British Institute of Management; Member: Council of the CBI, Industrial Society, Association of Business Sponsorship of the Arts, Advisory Board of the George Washington Institute for Management, Hon. Member, Securities Institute; Chairman: Audit Committee, DTI Foresight Crime Prevention Panel. *Honours:* OBE 1979. FCA; CIMgt. Liveryman, Company of Gunmakers 1992. *Recreations:* Shooting, sailing, opera, food and wine. *Sportsclubs:* Bembridge Sailing. *Clubs:* Flyfishers', Reform. *Name, Style and Title:* Raised to the peerage as Baron Sharman, of Redlynch in the County of Wiltshire 1999. A Liberal Democrat. *Address:* The Lord Sharman, OBE, KPMG, 8 Salisbury Square, London, EC4Y 8BB.

SHARP OF GUILDFORD (Life Baroness, UK), Margaret Lucy Sharp; cr. 1998

Daughter of Osmund Hailstone and Sydney Mary Ellen Hailstone. Born November 21, 1938; educated Tonbridge Girls' Grammar School; Newnham College, Cambridge. Married March 24, 1962. *Trades Union:* Member, Association of University Teachers. *Career:* Assistant Principal, Board of Trade and Industry 1960–63; Lecturer, LSE 1964–72; Economic Advisor, NEDO 1977–81; University of Sussex: Research Fellow 1981–84, Senior Research Fellow 1984–92, Director, ESRC Research Centre 1992–99. *Select Committees:* Member, Select Committee on European Communities Sub Committee A (Economic and Financial Affairs, Trade and External Relations) 1998–. *Party Groups (General):* Founder Member: Social Democrat Party 1981, Liberal Democrats 1988; Member, Liberal Democrat Federal Policy Committee 1992–, Vice-Chair 1995–96, 1998–99. *Other:* Governor, Stoke Hill School, Guildford; Local Council Member, Guildford High School; Executive Committee Member, Save British Science 1988–97; Editorial Board Member, *Political Quarterly* 1987–97; Member: Charter 88, Howard League. *Miscellaneous:* Contested Guildford Constituency: for SDP/All 1983 and 1987, for Lib Dems 1992 and 1997. Fellow, Royal Economic Society.

Publications: The State, the Enterprise and the Individual, 1974; *Europe and the New Technologies*, (editor) 1985; *Managing Change in British Industry*, (with G. Shepherd) 1986; *Strategies for New Technologies*, (editor with P. Holmes) 1987; *Technology and the Future of Europe*, (editor with C. Freeman and W. Walker) 1992; *Technology Policy in the European Union*, (with J. Peterson) 1998; plus numerous articles, book chapters etc in learned journals on issues relating to science and technology policy. *Special Interests:* Economic Policy, Industrial Issues, Science and Technology, Higher Education. *Recreations:* Reading, walking, theatre and concert going. *Name, Style and Title:* Raised to the peerage as Baroness Sharp of Guildford, of Guildford in the County of Surrey 1998. A Liberal Democrat. *Address:* The Baroness Sharp of Guildford, House of Lords, London, SW1A 0PW *E-Mail:* m.l.sharp@sussex.ac.uk.

SHARPLES (Life Baroness, UK), Pamela Sharples; cr. 1973

Daughter of late Lieutenant-Commander K. W. Newall, RN (Retired). Born February 11, 1923; educated Southover Manor, Lewes; Florence. Married 1st, July 12, 1946, Major Richard C. Sharples, OBE, MC (later Sir Richard Sharples, KCMG, OBE, MC, Governor of Bermuda, assassinated 1973) (2 sons 2 daughters), married 2nd, August 13, 1977, Patrick D. de Laszlo (died 1980), married 3rd, December 24, 1983, Robert Douglas Swan (died 1995). *Armed Forces:* WAAF 1941–46. *Career:* Director, TVS 1982–93; A Former Publican. *All-Party:* Member, All-Party: Golf Parliamentary Group, Defence Parliamentary Group, Arts and Heritage Parliamentary Group. *Trusts, etc:* Member, Wessex Medical Trust 1997–. *Miscellaneous:* Member, Review Body on Armed Services Pay 1979–81. *Special Interests:* Small Businesses, Cheque-Book Journalism, Prisoners' Wives, Pet Quarantine. *Recreations:* Tennis, golf, walking, gardening, fishing. *Sportsclubs:* Royal Cape Golf, Rushmoor Golf. *Clubs:* Mid-Ocean Bermuda. *Name, Style and Title:* Raised to the peerage as Baroness Sharples, of Chawton in the County of Hampshire 1973. A Conservative. *Address:* The Baroness Sharples, Well Cottage, Higher Coombe, Shaftesbury, Dorset, SP7 9LR *Tel:* 01747 852971; 60 Westminster Gardens, London, SW1P 4JG *Tel:* 020 7821 1875.

SHAW OF NORTHSTEAD (Life Baron, UK), Michael Norman Shaw; cr. 1994; Kt 1982; DL

Son of late Norman Shaw, FCA. Born October 9, 1920; educated Sedbergh. Married April 25, 1951, Joan Mary Louise, daughter of late Sir Alfred Mowat, DSO, OBE, MC, DL, 2nd and last Bt (3 sons). *Councils, Public Bodies:* JP, Dewsbury 1953; DL, West Yorkshire 1977. *Career:* Chartered Accountant; Member, UK Delegation to the European Parliament 1974–79. *House of Commons:* MP (Conservative) for: Brighouse and Spenborough 1960 (By-election)–1964, Scarborough and Whitby 1966–74, Scarborough 1974–92; PPS to: Minister of Labour 1962–63, Secretary of State for Trade and Industry 1970–72, Chancellor of the Duchy of Lancaster 1972–74. *Select Committees (Commons):* Former Member: House of Commons Public Accounts and Selection Committees, Speaker's Panel of Chairmen. *Select Committees:* Co-opted Member, Select Committee on European Communities Sub-Committee A (Economic and Financial Affairs, Trade and External Relations) 1997–. *All-Party:* Member, All-Party British-Austrian Country Group. *Honours:* Kt 1982. ACA 1945; FCA 1952. *Recreations:* Golf, opera, music. *Clubs:* Carlton. *Name, Style and Title:* Raised to the peerage as Baron Shaw of Northstead, of Liversedge in the County of West Yorkshire 1994. A Conservative. *Address:* The Lord Shaw of Northstead, DL, Duxbury Hall, Liversedge, West Yorkshire, WF15 7NR *Tel:* 01924 402270.

SHAWCROSS (Life Baron, UK), Hartley William Shawcross; cr. 1959; GBE 1974; PC 1946; Kt 1945; QC 1939

Son of late John Shawcross, MA. Born February 4, 1902; educated Dulwich College; Geneva University; Hon. LLD: Bristol, Liverpool, Sussex, Hull, Columbia USA, Michigan USA, Lehigh USA, New Brunswick Canada, London 1978 Universities. Married 1st, May 24, 1929, Alberta (died 1943), daughter of late W. Shyvers, married 2nd, September 21, 1944, Joan (died 1974), daughter of late Hume Mather (2 sons 1 daughter). *Career:* Called to the Bar, Gray's Inn 1925; Bencher 1939; Chairman, Enemy Aliens' Tribunal 1939–40; Regional Commissioner 1940–45; Chief Prosecutor for UK before International Military Tribunal, Nuremberg 1945–46; Director: Shell Petroleum Co. 1958, Shell Transport and Trading Co. 1962–72; Recorder of Salford 1942–45; Chairman: General Council of the Bar 1952–57, Medical Research Council 1961–65, Royal Commission on the Press 1962, Upjohn Ltd 1967–76; Special Adviser, Morgan Guaranty Trust Co. of New York 1968–93; Former Director: EMI Ltd, Hawker-Siddeley Group Ltd, Caffyns Ltd, Morgan et Cie SA, Morgan et Cie International SA; Director, Times Newspapers Ltd 1968–74; Chairman: City Panel on Take Overs and Mergers 1968–80, Thames Television Ltd 1970–74, European Enterprises Development SA 1970–78, The Press Council 1974–78, London and Continental Bank Ltd 1974–80; Consultant to public companies. *House of Commons:* MP (Labour) for St Helens 1945–58; Attorney-General 1945–51; President, Board of Trade April-October 1951 with Cabinet rank. *Chancellor:* Chancellor, University of Sussex 1965–86. *Other:* Chairman of Governors, Dulwich College and Alleyn's School 1958–72; Member, Court of London University 1956–78; Chairman, International Chamber of Commerce Committee on Unethical Practices. *Honours:* Kt 1945; PC 1946; GBE 1974. Hon. Fellow: Royal College of Obstetricians and Gynaecologists 1978, Royal College of Surgeons 1980. *Publications: Life Sentence* (Autobiography), 1994. *Special Interests:* City, Foreign Affairs. *Recreations:* Sailing. *Clubs:* Pratt's, Garrick, Royal Yacht Squadron (Cowes). *Name, Style and Title:* Raised to the peerage as Baron Shawcross, of Friston in the County of Sussex 1959. A Cross-Bencher. *Address:* The Rt Hon. the Lord Shawcross, GBE, QC, Friston Place, East Dean, Nr Eastbourne, East Sussex, BN20 0AH *Tel:* 01323 422206; Office: 60 Victoria Embankment, London, EC4Y 0JP *Tel:* 020 7325 5127.

SHEPHERD (2nd Baron, UK), Malcolm Newton Shepherd; cr. 1946; (Life) Baron Shepherd of Spalding (UK) 1999; PC 1965

Son of 1st Baron, PC. Born September 27, 1918. Succeeded his father 1954; educated Friends' School, Saffron Walden. Married November 15, 1941, Allison (died February 3, 1998), daughter of late Patrick Redmond, of Edinburgh (2 sons). *Armed Forces:* Served as Lieutenant, RASC 1939–45 war in North Africa, Sicily and Italy. *Career:* Deputy Chairman, Sterling Group of Companies 1976–86; Director, Sun Hung Kai Securities 1977–86; Chairman, National Bus Co. 1979–84; President, Centre European De L'Enterprise Publique 1985–; Member of Council, European Security Forum 1990–; Chairman: Cheque Point International Ltd, Ceko Banka Cheque Point Prague. *House of Lords:* Minister of State for Foreign and Commonwealth Affairs 1967–70; Deputy Leader Opposition 1970–74; Lord Privy Seal and Leader of House of Lords 1974–76. *Whip:* Opposition Whip 1959–64; Opposition Chief Whip 1964; Captain of the Gentlemen-at-Arms and Government Chief Whip in the House of Lords 1964–67. *Select Committees:* Former Member, Select Committee Channel Tunnel; Chairman: Lords Select Committee on Procedure 1976, European Communities Sub-Committee on Energy and Transport Research 1986–90; Former Member: European Communities Sub-Committee A (Finance and Economics Affairs) 1990–97, Delegated Powers Scrutiny Committee, House of Lords. *Other:* President, Institute of Road Transport Engineers 1987–. *Miscellaneous:* Chairman, Civil Service Pay Research Unit Board 1978–81; Chairman: Medical Research Council 1978–82, Packaging Council 1978–82. *Honours:* PC 1965. FCIT 1986; FIRTE 1986. *Recreations:* Golf. *Heir:* His son, Hon. Graeme George Shepherd, born January 6, 1949. *Name, Style and Title:* Created a life peer as Baron Shepherd of Spalding, of Spalding in the County of Lincolnshire 1999. Labour. *Address:* The Rt Hon. the Lord Shepherd, 29 Kennington Palace Court, London, SE11 5UL.

SHEPPARD OF DIDGEMERE (Life Baron, UK), Allen John George Sheppard; cr. 1994; KCVO 1998; Kt 1990

Son of late John Sheppard and of Lily Sheppard. Born December 25, 1932; educated Ilford County School; London School of Economics (BSc Econ); Hon. doctorates: International Management Centre 1989, Brunel University 1994, South Bank University 1994, University of East London 1997, Westminster University 1998, Middlesex University 1999. Married 1st, 1959, Peggy Jones (marriage dissolved 1980), married 2nd, 1980, Mary Stewart. *Career:* Ford Motor Company 1958–68; Rootes/Chrysler 1968–71; British Leyland 1971–75; Grand Metropolitan plc 1975–96, Group Managing Director 1982–86, Chief Executive 1986–93, Chairman 1987–96; Chairman: UBM Group 1981–85, Mallinson-Denny Group 1985–87; Director, Meyer International plc 1989–92, Deputy Chairman 1992–94; Non-executive Director, Bowater plc 1994–95; Non-executive Chairman: Bright Reasons Group plc 1995–96, Group Trust plc 1995–96, McBride plc 1995–, Unipart Group 1996–; Non-executive Chairman, GB Railways plc 1996–; Director, High-Point Rendel Group plc 1997–; Non-executive Chairman, Vizual Business Tools Ltd 1999–; Director: Gladstone plc 1999–, Pet-Check Ltd 1999–. *Select Committees:* Member, House of Lords' Offices Committee, Finance and Staff Sub-Committee. *All-Party:* Member, All-Party London Group. *Party Groups (General):* Member, Board of Management, Conservative Party 1993–98. *Other:* Governor, London School of Economics 1989–; Deputy Chairman, International Business Leaders' Forum 1990–96; Chairman: Advisory Board, British-American Chamber of Commerce 1991–94, London First 1992–; Board of Governors, Blue Cross; Director, London Development Partnership; Member, Executive Committee, Animal Health Trust; Vice-President: United Response, Brewers and Licensed Retailers Association, Business in the Community 1994–. *Awards Granted:* Institute of Management Gold Medal 1993; Marketing Society International Hall of Fame Award 1994; British-American Chamber of Commerce Trans-Atlantic Business Award 1995. *Trusts, etc:* Board of Trustees, Prince's Youth Business Trust 1990–94; Chairman, Administrative Council, Prince of Wales' Trusts 1995–; Board of Governors, Animal Health Trust. *Miscellaneous:* Part-time Member, British Rail Board 1985–90. *Honours:* Kt 1990; KCVO 1998. FCMA; FCIS; ATII; FRSA. *Publications:* Author of: *Your Business Matters*, 1958; *Maximum Leadership*, 1995. *Recreations:* Gardens, reading, red setter dogs. *Name, Style and Title:* Raised to the peerage as Baron Sheppard of Didgemere, of Roydon in the County of Essex 1994. A Conservative. *Address:* The Lord Sheppard of Didgemere, KCVO, House of Lords, London, SW1A 0PW.

SHEPPARD OF LIVERPOOL (Life Baron, UK), David Stuart Sheppard; cr. 1998

Son of late Stuart Morton Winter Sheppard and late Barbara Sheppard. Born March 6, 1929; educated Sherborne School; Trinity Hall, Cambridge (MA); Ridley Hall Theological College; Hon. LLD, Liverpool 1981; Hon. DTech, Liverpool Polytechnic 1987; Hon. DD: Cambridge 1991, Exeter University 1998; Hon. DU, The Open University 1999; Hon. DD, Birmingham University 1999. Married 1957, Grace Isaac (1 daughter). *Armed Forces:* 2nd Lieut, Royal Sussex Regiment, National Service 1947–49. *Career:* Assistant Curate, St Mary's, Islington 1955–57; Warden, Mayflower Family Centre, Canning Town 1957–69; Chairman, Evangelical Urban Training Project 1968–75; Bishop Suffragan of Woolwich 1969–75; Bishop of Liverpool 1975–97; Chairman Area Manpower Board, Manpower Services Commission 1976–83; A Lord Spiritual 1980–97; National President, Family Service Units 1987–97; Chairman: Central Religious Advisory Committee for BBC and IBA 1989–93, General Synod Board for Social Responsibility 1991–96, Churches' Enquiry in to Unemployment and the Failure of Work 1995–97. *Miscellaneous:* Cricket: Cambridge University 1950–52, Captain 1952, Sussex 1947–62, Captain 1953, England (played 22 times) 1950–63, Captain 1954. Freeman, City of Liverpool 1995 (jointly with late Archbishop Derek Worlock). *Publications: Parson's Pitch*, 1964; *Built as a City*, 1974; *Bias to the Poor*, 1983; *Better Together*, 1988 (with late Archbishop Derek Worlock); *Christ in the Wilderness*, 1990 (with late Archbishop Derek Worlock); *With Hope in our Hearts*, 1994 (with late Archbishop Derek Worlock). *Special Interests:* Urban Policies, Race Relations, Unemployment, Future of Work, Youth Work. *Recreations:* Family, reading, music, painting, visiting gardens, following cricket. *Sportsclubs:* Vice-President: Sussex County Cricket Club, Lancashire County Cricket Club. *Clubs:* MCC. *Name, Style and Title:* Raised to the peerage as Baron Sheppard of Liverpool, of West Kirby in the County of Merseyside 1998. Labour. *Address:* The Rt Rev. the Lord Sheppard of Liverpool, Ambledown, 11 Melloncroft Drive, West Kirby, Merseyside, CH48 2JA.

SHORE OF STEPNEY (Life Baron, UK), Peter David Shore; cr. 1997; PC 1967

Born May 20, 1924; educated Quarry Bank Grammar School, Liverpool; King's College, Cambridge; Hon. Fellow, Queen Mary and Westfield College London. Married 1948, Elizabeth Catherine Wrong (Dr Elizabeth Catherine Shore, CB) (1 son 2 daughters, and 1 son deceased). *Trades Union:* Member, TGWU. *Armed Forces:* Flying Officer, RAF 1943–46. *Career:* Head of Research Department, Labour Party 1959–64. *House of Commons:* Contested (Labour): St Ives, Cornwall 1950, Halifax 1959; MP (Labour) for Stepney 1964–74, for Stepney and Poplar 1974–83, and for Bethnal Green and Stepney 1983–97; PPS to the Prime Minister 1965–1966; Joint Parliamentary Secretary, Ministry of Technology 1966–1967; Joint Parliamentary Under-Secretary, Department of Economic Affairs 1967; Secretary of State for Economic Affairs 1967–1969; Minister without Portfolio October 1969–70; Deputy Leader of the House of Commons 1969–70; Secretary of State for: Trade 1974–1976, The Environment 1976–1979; Shadow Leader of the House of Commons 1984–87. *Spokesman (Commons):* Member, Shadow Cabinet and Opposition Spokesman on Europe 1971–74; Principal Opposition Front Bench Spokesman on: Foreign and Commonwealth Affairs 1979–1980, Treasury and Economic Affairs 1980–83; Shadow Leader of the House and Opposition Front Bench Spokesman on Trade and Industry 1983–84. *Select Committees (Commons):* Member, Select Committees on: Foreign Affairs 1989–97, Privileges 1994–97, Standards in Public Life 1994–97; Former Member, House of Commons Commission. *Party Groups (General):* Joined Labour Party 1948; Member, Fabian Society. *Honours:* PC 1967. *Publications:* Author of: *Entitled to Know*, 1966; *Leading the Left*, 1993. *Special Interests:* Europe (Anti-Federalist), Unemployment, Race Relations, Home Affairs, Middle East. *Recreations:* Reading, swimming. *Name, Style and Title:* Raised to the peerage as Baron Shore of Stepney, of Stepney in the London Borough of Tower Hamlets 1997. Labour. *Address:* The Rt Hon. the Lord Shore of Stepney, 23 Dryburgh Road, London, SW15 1BN.

SHREWSBURY (22nd Earl of, E), cr. 1442, AND WATERFORD (22nd Earl of, I), cr. 1446; Charles Henry John Benedict Crofton Chetwynd Chetwynd-Talbot; Earl Talbot and Viscount Ingestre (GB) 1784; Baron Talbot (GB) 1733; DL

Son of 21st Earl. Born December 18, 1952. Succeeded his father 1980; educated Harrow; Hon. LLD, Wolverhampton University 1994. Married 1974, Deborah, daughter of Noel Hutchinson (2 sons 1 daughter). *Councils, Public Bodies:* DL, Staffordshire 1994–. *Career:* Landowner and Farmer; Joint Deputy Chairman, Britannia Building Society 1987–92; Director, Richmount Enterprise Zone Trust 1988–94; Chairman, Firearms Consultative Committee 1994–99; President and National Executive Director, British Institute of Innkeeping 1996–98; Director: PMI Limited 1996–98, Banafix Limited 1996–98, Minibusplus 1997–. *Chancellor:* Chancellor, Wolverhampton University 1993–99. *House of Lords:* An elected hereditary peer 1999–. *Other:* President, Building Societies Association 1993–97. *Miscellaneous:* Premier Earl on Rolls of both England and Ireland; Hereditary Lord High Steward of Ireland. Member: Worshipful Company of Blacksmiths, Worshipful Company of Weavers. *Special Interests:* Transport, Agriculture, Environment, Construction Industry, Property, West Midlands, Mineral Extraction. *Recreations:* Shooting, fishing. *Clubs:* Farmers'. *Heir:* His son, Viscount Ingestre, born January 11, 1978. A Cross-Bencher. *Address:* The Earl of Shrewsbury and Waterford, DL, Wanfield Hall, Kingstone, Uttoxeter, Staffordshire, ST14 8QT *Tel:* 01889 500275 *E-Mail:* eof@wanfield.u-net.com.

SIEFF OF BRIMPTON (Life Baron, UK), Marcus Joseph Sieff; cr. 1980; Kt 1971; OBE (Mil) 1944

Son of late Baron Sieff (Life Baron). Born July 2, 1913; educated Manchester Grammar; St Paul's; Corpus Christi College, Cambridge (MA); Hon. LLD, St Andrew's University 1983; Hon. Dr, Babson College, Massachusetts 1984; Hon. DLitt, Reading 1986; D, University of Stirling 1986; Hon. LLD, Leicester University 1988. Married 1st, 1937, Rosalie Fromson (1 son) (marriage dissolved 1947), married 2nd, 1951, Elsie Florence Gosen (marriage dissolved 1953), married 3rd, 1956, Brenda Mary Beith (1 daughter) (marriage dissolved 1962), married 4th, 1963, Mrs Pauline Lily Moretzki (died February 28, 1997), daughter of Friedrich Spatz (1 daughter). *Armed Forces:* Served with Royal Artillery 1939–45. *Career:* Joined Marks and Spencer plc 1935, Assistant Managing Director 1963, Vice-Chairman 1965,

Joint Managing Director 1967, Deputy Chairman 1971, Chairman and Managing Director 1972–84, President 1984, Hon. President 1985; Chairman, First International Bank of Israel Financial Trust Ltd 1983–94. *Other:* President, Anglo-Israel Chamber of Commerce 1975. *Awards Granted:* Hambro Award, Businessman of the Year 1976. *Trusts, etc:* A Trustee, National Portrait Gallery 1986–92. *Miscellaneous:* Member, BNEC 1965–71, Chairman, Export Committee for Israel 1965–68. *Honours:* Hon. Master, Bench of the Inner Temple 1987. Hon. FRCS 1984. *Name, Style and Title:* Raised to the peerage as Baron Sieff of Brimpton, of Brimpton in the Royal County of Berkshire 1980. A Conservative. *Address:* The Lord Sieff of Brimpton, OBE.

SIMON (3rd Viscount, UK), Jan David Simon; cr. 1940

Son of 2nd Viscount, CMG. Born July 20, 1940. Succeeded his father 1993; educated Westminster School; School of Navigation, University of Southampton; Sydney Technical College. Married 1969, Mary Elizabeth, daughter of late John Joseph Burns, of Sydney, New South Wales (1 daughter). *House of Lords:* A Deputy Chairman of Committees 1998–; A Deputy Speaker 1999–; An elected hereditary peer 1999–. *Select Committees:* Member, Select Committees on: Dangerous Dogs (Amendment) Bill 1995–96, London Local Authorities Bill 1998, House of Lords Procedure 1999–. *All-Party:* Member: All-Party Disablement Group, Parliamentary Maritime Group, PACTS, CSA Monitoring Group. *Special Interests:* Disability, Motor Industry, Police, Road Safety, Science and Technology, Aviation. *Clubs:* Oriental. *Heir:* None. Labour. *Address:* The Viscount Simon, House of Lords, London, SW1A 0PW.

SIMON OF GLAISDALE (Life Baron, UK), Jocelyn Edward Salis Simon; cr. 1971; PC 1961; Kt 1959; DL

Son of late Frank Cecil Simon. Born January 15, 1911; educated Gresham's School, Holt; Trinity Hall, Cambridge (LLD); Docteur-en-Droit Hon, Laval University, Quebec. Married 1st, 1934, Gwendolen Helen (died 1937), daughter of E. J. Evans, married 2nd, 1948, Fay Elizabeth Leicester, daughter of Brigadier H. G. A. Pearson (3 sons). *Armed Forces:* Served War World II; Commissioned Royal Tank Regiment 1939; Madagascar 1942 (despatches); Burma 1944. *Councils, Public Bodies:* DL, North Yorkshire 1973–. *Career:* Called to the Bar, Middle Temple 1934; Bencher 1958; KC 1951; President, Probate, Divorce and Admiralty Division of High Court of Justice 1962–71; Lord of Appeal in Ordinary 1971–77. *House of Commons:* MP (Conservative) for Middlesbrough West 1951–62; Joint Parliamentary Under-Secretary, Home Office 1957–58; Financial Secretary, HM Treasury 1958–59; Solicitor-General 1959–62. *Party Groups (Commons):* Member, One-Nation Group. *Select Committees:* Former Chairman, Joint Select Committee on Consolidation Bill. *Other:* Elder Brother, Trinity House. *Miscellaneous:* Member, Royal Commission on Law relating to Mental Illness and Mental Deficiency 1954–57. *Honours:* Kt 1959; PC 1961. *Name, Style and Title:* Raised to the peerage as Baron Simon of Glaisdale, of Glaisdale in the North Riding of the County of Yorkshire 1971. A Cross-Bencher. *Address:* The Rt Hon. the Lord Simon of Glaisdale, DL, House of Lords, London, SW1A 0PW.

SIMON OF HIGHBURY (Life Baron, UK), David Alec Gwyn Simon; cr. 1997; Kt 1995; CBE 1991

Son of late Roger Simon. Born July 24, 1939; educated Christ's Hospital, Horsham; Gonville and Caius College, Cambridge (MA Hons); INSEAD (MBA); Hon. DSc Economics, Hull 1990; Hon. DU, North London 1995; Hon. DSc Economics, Bath 1997. Married 1st, 1964, Hanne Mohn (2 sons) (marriage dissolved 1987); married 2nd, 1992, Sarah Roderick Smith. *Career:* Joined The British Petrolum Co plc 1961; Marketing Co-ordinator, European Region 1975–80; Director, BP Oil UK and Chairman, National Benzole Company 1980–82; Managing Director, BP Oil International 1982–85: Managing Director 1986–95; Chief Operating Officer 1990–92; Deputy Chairman 1990–95; Chief Group Executive 1992–95; Chairman 1995–97; Non-executive Director, Grand Metropolitan plc 1989–97; Member, Advisory Board, Deutsche Bank 1991–97; Non-executive Director, RTZ Corporation plc 1995–97; Member, International Advisory Council, Allianz AG Holding 1993–97. *House of Lords:* Minister of State, at both the Treasury and Department of Trade and Industry (Minister for Trade and Competitiveness in Europe) 1997–99. *Spokesman:* Spokesman for

Department of Trade and Industry 1997–99. *Miscellaneous:* Member: Sports Council 1988–92, 1994–95, President's Committee, CBI 1992–97, European Round Table 1993–97, Vice-Chairman 1995–97, European Union Competitive Advisory Group 1995–, International Council, INSEAD; Adviser, European Commission President 1999–. *Honours:* CBE 1991; Kt 1995. Liveryman: Tallow Chandlers, Carmen. *Recreations:* Golf, books, music. *Sportsclubs:* Highgate Golf, Royal West Norfolk Golf, Hunstanton Golf. *Clubs:* Brooks's, Athenaeum. *Name, Style and Title:* Raised to the peerage as Baron Simon of Highbury, of Canonbury in the London Borough of Islington 1997. Labour. *Address:* The Lord Simon of Highbury, CBE, House of Lords, London, SW1A 0PW.

SIMPSON OF DUNKELD (Life Baron, UK), George Simpson; cr. 1997

Son of late William and Elizabeth Simpson. Born July 2, 1942; educated Morgan Academy, Dundee; Dundee Institute of Technology; Hon. Degrees: Warwick University, Abertay University, Aston University. Married 1964, Eva Chalmers (1 son 1 daughter). *Career:* Senior Accountant, Gas Industry, Scotland 1962–69; Central Audit Manager, British Leyland 1969–73; Financial Controller, Leyland Bus and Truck Division 1973–76; Director of Accounting, Leyland Cars 1976–78; Finance and Systems Director, Leyland Trucks 1978–80; Managing Director: Coventry Climax Ltd 1980–83, Freight Rover Ltd 1983–86; Chief Executive Officer, Leyland DAF 1986–88; Rover Group: Managing Director 1989–91, Chief Executive 1991–92, Chairman 1991–94; Deputy Chief Executive, British Aerospace 1992–94, Director 1990–94; Chairman, Ballast Nedam Construction Ltd 1992–94; Member, Supervisory Board and Non-Executive Director: Pilkington plc 1992–99, Northern Venture Capital 1992–, Pro Share 1992–94; Chairman, Arlington Securities 1993–94; Chief Executive, Lucas Industries plc 1994–96; Non-Executive Director, ICI plc 1995–; Chief Executive, General Electric Company plc 1996–; Non-Executive Director, Nestlé SA 1999–. *International Bodies (General):* Governor, Economic Forum; Member, European Round Table. *Other:* Member, Executive Committee, Society of Motor Manufacturers and Traders 1986–, Vice-President 1986–95, President 1995–96. ACIS; FCCA; FIMI; FCIT. Liveryman, Worshipful Company of Coachmakers. *Recreations:* Golf, squash, watching rugby. *Sportsclubs:* Royal Birkdale, Gleneagles Golf, New Zealand Golf, Kenilworth Rugby Football. *Name, Style and Title:* Raised to the peerage as Baron Simpson of Dunkeld, of Dunkeld in Perth and Kinross 1997. Labour. *Address:* The Lord Simpson of Dunkeld, General Electric Company plc, 1 Bruton Street, London, W1X 8AQ *Tel:* 020 7493 8484.

SKELMERSDALE (7th Baron, UK), Roger Bootle-Wilbraham; cr. 1828

Son of Brigadier 6th Baron, DSO, MC and late Ann Quilter. Born April 2, 1945. Succeeded his father 1973; educated Eton; Lord Wandsworth College, Odiham, Hampshire; Somerset Farm Institute; Hadlow College of Agriculture and Horticulture. Married February 5, 1972, Christine Joan, daughter of Roy Morgan, of Evercreech, Somerset (1 son 1 daughter). *Career:* Horticulturist; Managing Director, Broadleigh Nurseries Ltd 1973–81, Director 1991–; Parliamentary Affairs Adviser 1992–. *House of Lords:* Parliamentary Under-Secretary of State: Department of the Environment 1986–87, Department of Health and Social Security 1987–88, Department of Social Security 1988–89, Northern Ireland Office 1989–90; A Deputy Chairman of Committees, House of Lords 1991–95, 1997–; A Deputy Speaker of the House of Lords 1994–; An elected hereditary peer 1999–. *Whip:* A Lord in Waiting (Government Whip) 1981–86. *Spokesman:* At various times a Former Government Spokesman on: Environment, Transport, Foreign Affairs, Energy, Agriculture, Post Office. *Select Committees:* Member: Sub-Committee F of European Select Committee (Environment) 1975–81, Sub-Committee B European Energy Transport and Industry; Co-opted Member, Select Committee on European Communities Sub-Committee B (Energy, Industry and Transport) 1997–; Member, Joint Committee on Statutory Instruments 1998–. *All-Party:* Member, All-Party Bridge Group. *Other:* Vice-Chairman, Co-En-Co (Council for Environmental Conservation) 1979–81; President, British Naturalists Association 1979–95; Governor, Castle School, Taunton 1992–96; Chairman of Council, The Stroke Association 1993–; President, Somerset Opera 1980–. *Trusts, etc:* President, Somerset Trust for Nature Conservation 1980–. Fellow, Linnaen Society. Liveryman, Worshipful Company of Gardeners. *Special Interests:* Horticulture, Post Office, Energy, Environment, Privatised Utilities. *Recreations:* Bridge, gardening, reading, walking. *Heir:* His son, Hon. Andrew Bootle-Wilbraham, born August 9, 1977. A Conservative. *Address:* The Lord Skelmersdale, House of Lords, London, SW1A 0PW *Tel:* House of Lords 020 7219 3224.

SKIDELSKY (Life Baron, UK), Robert Jacob Alexander Skidelsky; cr. 1991; FBA 1994

Son of late Boris Skidelsky and Galia, née Sapelkin. Born April 25, 1939; educated Brighton College; Jesus College, Oxford; Hon. DLitt, University of Buckingham; Hon. Fellow, Jesus College, Oxford 1997. Married 1970, Augusta, daughter of late Humphrey Hope and of Elisabeth Hope (2 sons 1 daughter). *Career:* Associate Professor, School of Advanced International Studies, Johns Hopkins University, Washington DC 1970–76; Head of the Department of History, Philosophy and European Studies, Polytechnic of North London 1976–78; Professor of International Studies, Warwick University 1978–90; Professor of Political Economy 1990–; Member, School Examinations and Assessment Council 1992–93. *Spokesman:* Opposition Spokesman on: Culture, Media and Sport 1997–98, the Treasury 1998–99. *Select Committees:* Member, House of Lords Select Committees on: The European Communities 1991–94, Sustainable Development 1994–97. *All-Party:* Member: European Parliamentary Intercultural Committee, British-Hong Kong All-Party Group, Parliamentary University Group. *International Bodies:* Member, Inter-Parliamentary Union. *Other:* Chairman: Social Market Foundation 1991–, Hands Off Reading Campaign 1994–97; Governor: Portsmouth University 1994–97, Brighton College 1998–. *Awards Granted:* Wolfson Prize for History 1992. *Trusts, etc:* Chairman, Charleston Trust 1987–92; Trustee, Humanitas 1991. *Miscellaneous:* Research Fellow, Nuffield College, Oxford 1965–68; Member, Lord Chancellor's Advisory Council on Public Records 1987–92. Fellow: Royal Historical Society 1973, Royal Society of Literature 1978, British Academy 1994. Freeman, Knocksville, Tennessee, USA 1998. *Publications:* Author of several works including: *Politicians and the Slump,* 1967; *English Progressive Schools,* 1969; *Oswald Mosley,* 1975; *John Maynard Keynes,* Vol. 1, 1983; *John Maynard Keynes,* Vol. 2, 1992; *The World After Communism,* 1995. *Special Interests:* Education, Economic Policy, Europe, Transition Economies, Hong Kong, Arts. *Recreations:* Opera, listening to music, tennis, table tennis, good conversation. *Name, Style and Title:* Raised to the peerage as Baron Skidelsky, of Tilton in the County of East Sussex 1991. A Conservative. *Address:* Professor The Lord Skidelsky, Tilton House, Firle, East Sussex, BN8 6LL.

SLIM (2nd Viscount, UK), John Douglas Slim; cr. 1960; OBE (Mil) 1973; DL

Son of Field Marshal 1st Viscount, KG, GCB, GCMG, GCVO, GBE, DSO, MC. Born July 20, 1927. Succeeded his father 1970; educated Prince of Wales Royal Indian Military College, Dehra Dun. Married July 18, 1958, Elisabeth, daughter of late Arthur Rawdon Spinney, CBE (2 sons 1 daughter). *Armed Forces:* Served: Indian Army 6th Gurkha Rifles 1944, Argyll and Sutherland Highlanders 1948, Special Air Service; Staff College Camberley 1961; Joint Services Staff College 1964; Retired from Army 1972. *Councils, Public Bodies:* DL, Greater London 1988. *Career:* Deputy Chairman, Peek plc; Director, Trailfinders Ltd, and other companies. *House of Lords:* An elected hereditary peer 1999–. *Select Committees:* Member, Select Committee on House of Lords' Offices 1997–. *All-Party:* Member: All-Party Defence Study Group, Parliamentary and Scientific Committee. *Other:* President, Burma Star Association 1971; Vice-President: Britain-Australia Society, Arab-British Chamber of Commerce 1977–96. Fellow, Royal Geographical Society 1983. *Honours:* OBE (Mil) 1973; Master, The Clothworkers' Company 1995–96. *Clubs:* White's, Special Forces. *Heir:* His son, Hon. Mark William Rawdon Slim, born February 13, 1960. A Cross-Bencher. *Address:* The Viscount Slim, OBE, DL, House of Lords, London, SW1A 0PW.

SLYNN OF HADLEY (Life Baron, UK), Gordon Slynn; cr. 1992; PC 1992; Kt 1976

Son of late John Slynn and of Edith Slynn. Born February 17, 1930; educated Sandbach School, Cheshire; Goldsmiths' College; Trinity College, Cambridge (Senior Scholar, MA, LLM); Hon. LLD: Birmingham 1983, Buckingham 1983, Exeter 1985; Hon. DCL, Durham 1989; Hon. LLD, University of Technology, Sydney 1991; Hon. Fellow: St Andrew's College, University of Sydney 1991, John Moore's University, Liverpool 1992; Hon. LLD: Bristol Polytechnic CNAA 1992, Sussex 1992; Hon. DCL, City 1994; Hon. DU, University Museo Social, Buenos Aires 1994; Hon. Fellow, Goldsmiths' College 1994; Hon. LLD: Staffordshire 1994, Saarlandes 1994, Stetson USA 1994, Pace NY 1995, Kingston 1996, Pondicherry (India) 1997; Fellow, Kings College, London 1997.

Married 1962, Odile Marie Henriette Boutin. *Armed Forces:* Commissioned RAF 1951–54. *Career:* Called to the Bar, Gray's Inn 1956, Bencher 1970, Treasurer 1988; Junior Counsel, Ministry of Labour 1967–68; Junior Counsel to the Treasury (Common Law) 1968–74; Recorder of Hereford 1971; A Recorder and Hon. Recorder of Hereford 1972–76; QC 1974; Leading Counsel to the Treasury 1974–76; A Judge of the High Court of Justice, Queen's Bench Division 1976–81; President, Employment Appeal Tribunal 1978–81; An Advocate-General of the Court of Justice of the European Communities 1981–88, Visiting Professor in Law: University of Durham 1981–88, Cornell University 1983, King's College, London 1985–90, 1995–, National University of India 1992–; Judge 1988–91; A Lord of Appeal in Ordinary 1992–. *Select Committees:* Member, European Communities Select Committee 1992–97; Chairman: Sub-Committee E 1992–95, Select Committee on Public Service 1996–97. *International Bodies (General):* Chairman, Executive Council, International Law Association 1988–; Hon. Vice-President, Union Internationale des Avocats. *Other:* Visitor, Mansfield College, Oxford. *Miscellaneous:* Deputy Chief Steward of Hereford 1977–78, Chief Steward 1978–. *Honours:* Kt 1976; PC 1992. FCIArb; FKC. Freeman, City of Hereford. Master, Broderers' Company 1994–95. *Publications:* Has contributed to *Halsbury's Laws of England* as well as lectures published in legal journals. *Clubs:* Beefsteak, Garrick, Athenaeum. *Name, Style and Title:* Raised to the peerage as Baron Slynn of Hadley, of Eggington in the County of Bedfordshire 1992. A Cross-Bencher. *Address:* The Rt Hon. the Lord Slynn of Hadley, House of Lords, London, SW1A 0PW.

SMITH OF CLIFTON (Life Baron, UK), Trevor Arthur Smith; cr. 1997; Kt 1996

Son of late Arthur Smith, and of Vera Smith. Born June 14, 1937; educated LSE (BSc Economics 1958); Hon. LLD: Dublin 1992, Hull 1993, Belfast 1995, NUI 1996; Hon. DHL, Alabama 1998. Married 1st, 1960, Brenda Eustace (2 sons) (marriage dissolved 1973); married 2nd, 1979, Julia Bullock (1 daughter). *Councils, Public Bodies:* Member, Tower Hamlets District Health Authority 1987–91. *Career:* Schoolteacher, LCC 1958–59; Temporary Assistant Lecturer, Exeter University 1959–60; Research Officer, Acton Society Trust 1960–62; Lecturer in Politics, Hull University 1962–67; Visiting Associate Professor, California State University, Los Angeles 1969; Queen Mary College, later Queen Mary and Westfield College, London: Head of Department 1972–85, Dean of Social Studies 1979–82, Pro-Principal 1983–87, Lecturer, Senior Lecturer, Professor in Political Studies 1983–91, Senior Pro-Principal 1987–89, Senior Vice-Principal 1989–91; Director: Job Ownership Ltd 1978–85, New Society Ltd 1986–88; Member, Senate, London University 1987–91; Director, Statesman and Nation Publishing Company Ltd 1988–90, Chairman 1990; Director, Gerald Duckworth & Co 1990–95; Vice-Chancellor and Hon. Professor, University of Ulster 1991–99; Visiting Professor of Politics, University of York 1999–. *Party Groups (General):* Member, Liberal Party Executive 1958–59. *Other:* Governor: St John Cass and Redcoats School 1979–94, University of Haifa 1985–91; Chairman, Political Studies Association of UK 1988–89, Vice-President 1989–91 and 1993–, President 1991–93; Vice-Chairman, Board of Governors, Princess Alexandra and Newnham College of Nursing and Midwifery 1990–91; Deputy President, Institute of Citizenship Studies 1992–; Member, UK Socrates Council 1993–, Chairman 1996–99; Member: Administrative Board, International Association of Universities 1995–96, Editorial Board, Government and Opposition 1995–, Board, A Taste of Ulster 1996–99. *Trusts, etc:* Trustee, Joseph Rowntree Reform Trust 1975–, Chairman 1987–99; Trustee: Acton Society Trust 1975–87, Employment Institute 1987–92; President, Belfast Civic Trust 1995–99. *Honours:* Kt 1996. FRHistS; CIMgt (CBIM 1992); FICPD. *Publications: Training Managers*, 1962 (with M. Argyle); *Town Councillors*, 1964 (with A. M. Rees); *Town and County Hall*, 1966; *Anti-Politics: consensus and reform*, 1972; *The Politics of the Corporate Economy*, 1979; *The Fixers*, 1996 (with A. Young); Author of various articles and papers and book reviews and broadcasts. *Recreations:* Water colour painting. *Clubs:* Reform. *Name, Style and Title:* Raised to the peerage as Baron Smith of Clifton, of Mountsandel in the County of Londonderry 1997. A Liberal Democrat. *Address:* Professor The Lord Smith of Clifton, House of Lords, London, SW1A OPW *Tel:* 020 7219 5353 *Fax:* 020 7219 5979 *E-Mail:* sirtas@cocoon.co.uk.

SMITH OF GILMOREHILL (Life Baroness, UK), Elizabeth Margaret Smith; cr. 1995; DL

Daughter of late Frederick William Moncrieff Bennett, and of late Elizabeth Waters Irvine Shanks. Born June 4, 1940; educated Hutchesons' Girls' Grammar School, Glasgow; University of Glasgow (MA); Hon. LLD, University of Glasgow. Married July 5, 1967, Rt Hon. John Smith, MP (died May 12, 1994), Member for Lanarkshire North 1970–83 and for Monklands East 1983–94, Leader of the Labour Party 1992–94, son of late Archibald Smith (3 daughters). *Councils, Public Bodies:* DL, City of Edinburgh 1996. *Chancellor:* Chancellor, Birbeck College. *Spokesman:* Opposition Spokeswoman on National Heritage (Tourism) 1996–97. *Backbench Committees:* Member, Labour Party Departmental Committee for Foreign Affairs. *All-Party:* Member: Scottish Opera All-Party Group, British-Russia All-Party Group. *International Bodies:* Executive Committee Member, IPU British Group. *International Bodies (General):* Member: Britain-Russia Centre, British Association for Central and Eastern Europe. *Other:* Member: British Heart Foundation, English Speaking Union, Russo-British Chamber of Commerce, Centre for European Reform; President, Scottish Opera; Chairman, Edinburgh Festival Fringe; Board Member, Edinburgh International Festival. *Trusts, etc:* Member: Future of Europe Trust, John Smith Memorial Trust, Know How Fund Advisory Board; Trustee, Hakluyt Foundation. *Miscellaneous:* Member: Press Complaints Commission 1995–, BP Scottish Advisory Board. *Special Interests:* Arts, Russia, Former Soviet Union. *Name, Style and Title:* Raised to the peerage as Baroness Smith of Gilmorehill, of Gilmorehill in the District of the City of Glasgow, 1995. Labour. *Address:* The Baroness Smith of Gilmorehill, DL, House of Lords, London, SW1A 0PW.

SMITH OF LEIGH (Life Baron, UK), Peter Richard Charles Smith; cr. 1999

Son of Ronald and Kathleen Smith; educated London School of Economics (BSc Economics 1967); Garnett College, London University (CertEd(FE) 1969); Salford University (MSc Urban Studies 1983). Married January 5, 1968, Joy Lesley, daughter of James and Dorothy Booth (1 daughter). *Trades Union:* Member, NATFHE. *Councils, Public Bodies:* Wigan Metropolitan Borough Council: Councillor 1978–, Chairman, Finance Committee 1982–91, Leader of Council 1991–. *Career:* Lecturer, Walbrook College, London 1969–74; Lecturer, Manchester College of Art and Technology 1974–91, part-time 1991–. *Miscellaneous:* Member: Association of Metropolitan Authorities Policy Committee 1991–97, Local Government Association Policy and Strategy Committee 1997–; Vice-Chair, Special Interest Group for Municipal Authorities 1997–; Member, Improvement and Development Agency 1999–; Chair, North West Regional Assembly 1999–. *Special Interests:* Local Government, Regionalism, Airport Policy. *Recreations:* Gardening, sport, jazz. *Clubs:* Hindley Green Labour. *Name, Style and Title:* Raised to the peerage as Baron Smith of Leigh, of Wigan in the County of Greater Manchester 1999. Labour. *Address:* The Lord Smith of Leigh, Town Hall, Library Street, Wigan, WN1 1YN *Tel:* 01942 827001 *Fax:* 01942 827365; Mysevin, Old Hall Mill Lane, Atherton, Manchester, M46 0RG *Tel:* 01942 676127 *Fax:* 01942 676127 *E-Mail:* leader@wiganmbc.gov.uk.

SNOWDON (1st Earl of, UK), Antony Charles Robert Armstrong-Jones; cr. 1961; Viscount Linley; (Life) Baron Armstrong-Jones (UK) 1999; GCVO 1969

Son of late Ronald Owen Lloyd Armstrong-Jones, MBE, QC, DL, and late Anne, Countess of Rosse. Born March 7, 1930; educated Eton; Jesus College, Cambridge; Hon. LLD: Bradford University 1989, Bath University 1989, Portsmouth University 1993. Married 1st, May 6, 1960, HRH The Princess Margaret, CI, GCVO (1 son 1 daughter) (marriage dissolved 1978), married 2nd, December 15, 1978, Mrs Lucy Lindsay-Hogg (1 daughter). *Trades Union:* Member, NUJ. *Career:* Constable of Caernarfon Castle, Wales 1963–; Artistic Adviser to the: *Sunday Times* and Sunday Times Publications Ltd 1962–90, *Daily Telegraph* Magazine 1990–95; Consultative Adviser to the Design Council, London 1962–87; Editorial Adviser to Design Magazine 1962–87; President for England, International Year for Disabled People 1981; Public Appearances 1991; Television Films: 'Don't Count the Candles' 1968 (2 Hollywood EMMY Awards); 'Love of a Kind' 1969; 'Born To Be Small' 1971 (Chicago Hugo Awards); 'Happy Being Happy' 1973; 'Mary Kingsley' 1975; 'Burke and Wills' 1975; 'Peter, Tina and Steve' 1977; 'Snowdon on Camera' (BAFTA nomination) 1981; Exhibitions: Photocall 1957, Assignments 1972, Serendipity 1989; Designer of: Snowdon Aviary for London Zoo 1965 (Listed Grade II* starred 1998), Mobile chair for disabled people (The Chairmobile) 1972. *Other:* President: Contemporary Art Society for Wales, Welsh Theatre Company; Member of

Council, National Fund for Research into Crippling Diseases; Patron: National Youth Theatre 1962–87, Metropolitan Union of YMCAs, British Water Ski Federation, Welsh National Rowing Club, Physically Handicapped and Able Bodied, Circle of Guide Dog Owners; Started Snowdon award scheme for further education of disabled students 1981; Patron: Polio Plus 1988, British Disabled Water Ski Association; Provost, Royal College of Art. *Trusts, etc:* President, Civic Trust for Wales. *Miscellaneous:* Member, Prince of Wales Advisory Group on Disability. *Honours:* GCVO 1969. Senior Fellow, Royal College of Art 1986; Fellow: Manchester College of Art and Design; Chartered Society of Designers (London), Royal Photographic Society (London), Royal Society of Arts; FRSA, RDI. *Publications: Malta* (in collaboration with Sacheverell Sitwell) 1958; *London,* 1958; *Assignments,* 1972; *A View of Venice,* 1972; *Integrating the disabled -The Snowdon Report,* 1976; *Inchcape Review,* 1977; *Personal View,* 1979; *Private View* (in collaboration with John Russell and Bryan Robertson) 1965; *Pride of the Shires* (with John Oaksey) 1979; *Tasmania Essay,* 1981; *Sittings,* 1983; *Israel – A First View,* 1986; *My Wales* (with Viscount Tonypandy), 1986; *Stills,* 1987; *Personal Appearances,* 1992; *Wild Flowers,* 1995; *Snowdon On Stage,* 1996; *Wild Fruit,* 1997; *London Sight Unseen,* 1999. *Special Interests:* Art and Design. *Recreations:* Photography. *Sportsclubs:* Leander (Henley-on-Thames), Hawks. *Clubs:* Buck's. *Heir:* His son, Viscount Linley, born November 3, 1961. *Name, Style and Title:* Created a life peer as Baron Armstrong-Jones, of Nymans in the County of West Sussex 1999. A Cross-Bencher. *Address:* The Earl of Snowdon, GCVO, 22 Launceston Place, London, W8 5RL.

SOULSBY OF SWAFFHAM PRIOR (Life Baron, UK), Ernest Jackson Lawson Soulsby; cr. 1990

Son of late William George Lawson Soulsby. Born June 23, 1926; educated Queen Elizabeth Grammar School, Penrith; Edinburgh University (DVSM, PhD); Cambridge University (MA); Hon. AM, University of Pennsylvania 1975; Hon. DSc, University of Pennsylvania 1984; Hon. DVMS, University of Edinburgh 1991; Hon. DVM, University of Leon 1993; Emeritus Fellow, Wolfson College, Cambridge 1993–; Hon. DSc, University of Peradeniya, Sri Lanka. Married 1st 1950, Margaret Macdonald (1 son 1 daughter), married 2nd, 1962, Georgina Elizabeth Annette Williams. *Career:* Veterinary Officer, City of Edinburgh 1949–52; Lecturer in Clinical Parasitology, Bristol University 1952–54; University Lecturer in Animal Pathology, University of Cambridge 1954–63; Professor of Parasitology, University of Pennsylvania 1964–78; Professor of Animal Pathology, University of Cambridge 1978–93, Emeritus Professor 1993–; Ford Foundation Visiting Professor, University of Ibadan 1964; Member, EEC Advisory Committee on Veterinary Training 1981–86; Expert Advisor to several UN Agencies and overseas governments 1963–; Member, Veterinary Advisory Committee Horserace Betting Levy Board 1984, Chairman 1985–; Member, Agriculture and Food Research Council 1984–88; Chairman, Animal Research Grants Board 1986–89; Member, Home Office Animal Procedures Committee 1987–95; Chairman, Ethics Committee, British Veterinary Association 1994–. *Select Committees:* Former Member: Select Committee River Calder (Welbeck Site) Bill, Sub-Committee F of European Communities 1990–92, Sub-Committee II, Select Committee for Science and Technology 1993–97, Select Committee for Science and Technology 1995; Chairman, Sub-Committee I of Select Committee for Science and Technology 1997–. *All-Party:* Member, Parliamentary and Scientific Committee; Member, All-Party Group on Animal Welfare, Hon. Secretary 1997–; Member: All-Party Group on The Environment, All-Party Group for Chemical Industry, All-Party Parliamentary University Group. *Other:* Council Member, Royal College of Veterinary Surgeons 1978–92, President 1984, Senior Vice-President 1985; Hon. Member, Parasitology Societies in Germany, Mexico, Argentina, UK and USA; Corresponding Member, Academic Royale de Médicine de Belgique; President, Pet Advisory Committee 1996–; Patron, Veterinary Benevolent Fund. *Awards Granted:* R. N. Chaudhury Gold Medal, Calcutta School of Tropical Medicine 1976; Behring-Bilharz Prize, Cairo 1977; Ludwig-Schunk Prize, Justus Liebig University, Germany 1979; Mussemmeir Medal, Humboldt University, Berlin 1991. FRCVS; Hon. Fellow, Royal Society of Medicine 1996. Freeman, City of London. Member, Worshipful Company of Farriers. *Publications:* Include: *Textbook of Veterinary Clinical Parasitology,* 1965; *Biology of Parasites,* 1966; *Reaction of the Host to Parasitism,* 1968; *Immune Response to Parasitic Infections,* 1987; *Zoonoses,* 1998; As well as other works, articles in journals of parasitology, immunology and pathology. *Special Interests:* Higher Education, Environment, Agriculture, Animal Welfare, Foreign Affairs. *Recreations:* Gardening, travel. *Clubs:* Farmers', United Oxford and Cambridge University. *Name, Style and Title:* Raised to the peerage as Baron Soulsby of Swaffham Prior, of Swaffham Prior in the County of Cambridgeshire 1990. A Conservative. *Address:* The Lord Soulsby of Swaffham Prior, House of Lords, London, SW1A 0PW.

SOUTHWARK (9th Bishop of), Thomas Frederick Butler

Son of late Thomas and Elsie Butler. Born March 5, 1940; educated King Edward's Grammar School, Fiveways, Birmingham; University of Leeds (BSc 1st Class Hons, MSc, PhD); Hon. LLD: Leicester University, De Montfort University; Hon. DSc, Loughborough University. Married 1964, Barbara Joan Clark (1 son 1 daughter). *Career:* College of the Resurrection, Mirfield 1962–64; Curate: St Augustine's, Wisbech 1964–66, St Saviour's, Folkestone 1966–68; Lecturer and Chaplain, University of Zambia 1968–73; Acting Dean of Holy Cross Cathedral, Lusaka, Zambia 1973; Chaplain to University of Kent at Canterbury 1973–80; Six Preacher, Canterbury Cathedral 1979–84; Archdeacon of Northolt 1980–85; Area Bishop of Willesden 1985–91; Bishop of Leicester 1991–98; Chairman, Board of Mission, General Synod of the Church of England 1995–; Took his seat in the House of Lords 1996; Bishop of Southwark 1998–. *Select Committees:* Former Member, Select Committee on Science and Technology Sub-Committee on Digital Images as Evidence. *Publications: Just Mission* (with B. J. Butler); *Just Spirituality in a World of Faiths* (with B. J. Butler). *Special Interests:* Science, Technology, Education, Development. *Recreations:* Reading, mountain walking, marathon running. *Address:* The Rt Rev. the Lord Bishop of Southwark, Bishop's House, 38 Tooting Bec Gardens, Streatham, London, SW16 1QZ *Tel:* 020 8769 3256 *Fax:* 020 8769 4126 *E-Mail:* bishops.house@dswark.org.uk.

STALLARD (Life Baron, UK), Albert William Stallard; cr. 1983

Son of late Frederick and Agnes Stallard. Born November 5, 1921; educated Low Waters School; Hamilton Academy. Married July 29, 1944, Julia, daughter of W. C. Murphy (1 son 1 daughter). *Trades Union:* Member, AUEW (AUEW Order of Merit 1968). *Councils, Public Bodies:* Councillor, St Pancras 1953–59, Alderman 1962–65; Councillor, Camden 1965–71, Alderman 1971–78. *Career:* Precision Engineer 1937–65; Technical Training Officer 1965–70. *House of Commons:* MP (Labour) for: St Pancras North 1970–1974, St Pancras North division of Camden 1974–1983; PPS to: Minister of Agriculture 1974–75, Minister of Housing 1975–76. *Whip (Commons):* An Assistant Government Whip 1976–78, Lord Commissioner HM Treasury 1978–79. *All-Party Committees (Commons):* Joint Chairman, All-Party Pensioners Group 1975–83; Chairman, All-Party CHAR Group 1975–83. *Spokesman:* A former Opposition Front Bench Spokesman on Environment and on Social Security. *All-Party:* Chairman, All-Party Group on Ageing Issues 1990–98; Secretary, All-Party Group for Housing and Homeless 1992–; Co-Chairman, All-Party Ageing and Older People Group 1998–. *Other:* Vice-President, Camden Association for Mental Health; Chairman and Member, Camden Town Disablement Advisory Committee 1951–. *Miscellaneous:* Formerly Member, Institution of Training Officers. *Special Interests:* Education, Social Services, Health, Housing, Northern Ireland, Cyprus. *Recreations:* Photography, chess, reading. *Name, Style and Title:* Raised to the peerage as Baron Stallard, of St Pancras in the London Borough of Camden 1983. Labour. *Address:* The Lord Stallard, Flat 2, 2 Belmont Street, Chalk Farm Road, London, NW1 8HH; House of Lords, London, SW1A 0PW *Tel:* House of Lords 020 7219 3225.

STEEL OF AIKWOOD (Life Baron, UK), David Martin Scott Steel; cr. 1997; KBE 1990; PC 1977

Son of Very Rev. Dr David Steel, Moderator of the General Assembly of the Church of Scotland 1974–75. Born March 31, 1938; educated Prince of Wales School, Nairobi; George Watson's College; Edinburgh University (MA 1960, LLB 1962); DUniv Stirling 1991; Hon. DLitt, Buckingham 1994; DUniv, Heriot Watt University, Edinburgh 1996; Hon. LLD, University of Edinburgh 1997. Married October 26, 1962, Judith, daughter of W. D. MacGregor, CBE, of Dunblane, Perthshire (2 sons 1 daughter). *Councils, Public Bodies:* DL, Roxburgh, Ettrick and Lauderdale 1990. *Career:* Broadcaster; Journalist; President, Edinburgh University Students' Representative Council 1961; BBC Television interviewer in Scotland 1964–65; Rector, University of Edinburgh 1982–85. *House of Commons:* Contested (Liberal) Roxburgh, Selkirk and Peebles October 1964; MP (Liberal) for Roxburgh, Selkirk and Peebles 1965 By-election–83, and for Tweeddale, Ettrick and Lauderdale 1983–97 (as Liberal Democrat 1988–97); Sponsor, Abortion Act 1967. *Whip (Commons):*

Liberal Chief Whip 1970–74. *Spokesman (Commons):* Liberal Democrat Convenor and Spokesman on Foreign Affairs and Overseas Development 1989–94. *Party Groups:* Deputy Leader, Liberal Democrat Peers 1997–99. *International Bodies (General):* President, Liberal International 1992–94. *Party Groups (General):* President, Edinburgh University Liberal Club 1960, Assistant Secretary, Scottish Liberal Party 1962–64; Leader, Liberal Party 1976–88; Joint Founder, Social and Liberal Democrats 1988. *Other:* Past President, Anti-Apartheid Movement in GB; Chairman, Scottish Advisory Council of Shelter 1968–72; Vice-President, Countryside Alliance 1998–99. *Miscellaneous:* Visiting Fellow, Yale University 1987; MSP for the Region of Lothians since May 6, 1999 (stood as Sir David Steel); Elected Presiding Officer of the Scottish Parliament May 1999–. *Honours:* PC 1977; KBE 1990; Commander's Cross of the Order of Merit (Germany) 1992. Freeman: Tweeddale 1987, Ettrick and Lauderdale 1989. *Publications:* Author of: *No Entry, A House Divided; Partners in One Nation*, (editor); *David Steel's Border Country; Mary Stuart's Scotland* (with Judy Steel); *Against Goliath*, 1989. *Recreations:* Angling, classic car rallying. *Clubs:* National Liberal, Galashiels Liberal. *Name, Style and Title:* Raised to the Peerage as Baron Steel of Aikwood, of Ettrick Forest in The Scottish Borders 1997. A Liberal Democrat. *Address:* The Rt Hon. the Lord Steel of Aikwood, KBE, DL, MSP, Scottish Parliament, Edinburgh, EH99 1SP.

STERLING OF PLAISTOW (Life Baron, UK), Jeffrey Maurice Sterling; cr. 1991; Kt 1985; CBE 1977

Son of late Harry and Alice Sterling. Born December 27, 1934; educated Reigate Grammar School; Preston Manor County School; Guildhall School of Music; Hon. D (Business Administration), Nottingham Trent University 1995; Hon. DCL, Durham University 1996. Married June 14, 1985, Dorothy Ann, daughter of Ronald Smith (1 daughter). *Armed Forces:* Honorary Captain, Royal Naval Reserve 1991. *Career:* Paul Schweder and Co. (Stock Exchange) 1955–57; G. Eberstadt & Co. 1957–62; Financial Director, General Guarantee Corporation 1962–64; Managing Director, Gula Investments Ltd 1964–69; Chairman, Sterling Guarantee Trust plc 1969, merging with P & O 1985; Board Member, British Airways 1979–82; Chairman, The Peninsular and Oriental Steam Navigation Company 1983–; Special Adviser to: Secretary of State for Industry 1982–83, Secretary of State for Trade and Industry 1983–90; President, General Council of British Shipping 1990–91; President, European Community Shipowners' Associations 1992–94. *Other:* Chairman, Organisation Committee, World ORT Union 1969–73, Member: Executive 1966–, Technical Services 1974–; Vice-President, British ORT 1978–; Deputy Chairman and Hon. Treasurer, London Celebrations Committee, Queen's Silver Jubilee 1975–83; Chairman, Young Vic Company 1975–83; Chairman, Motability 1994–, Vice-Chairman 1977–94, Chairman of Executive 1977–; Chairman of Governors, Royal Ballet School 1983–; Governor, Royal Ballet 1986–; Elder Brother, Trinity House 1991. *Honours:* Kt 1985; CBE 1977; KStJ 1998. Hon. Fellow: Institute of Marine Engineers 1991, Institute of Chartered Shipbrokers 1992; Hon. Member, Royal Institute of Chartered Surveyors 1993; Fellow, Incorporated Society of Valuers and Auctioneers 1995; Hon. Fellow, Royal Institute of Naval Architects 1997. Freeman, City of London. *Special Interests:* Shipping, Construction Industry, Economics, Disability, Arts, Music. *Recreations:* Music, swimming, tennis. *Clubs:* Carlton, Garrick, Hurlingham. *Name, Style and Title:* Raised to the peerage as Baron Sterling of Plaistow, of Pall Mall in the City of Westminster 1991. A Conservative. *Address:* The Lord Sterling of Plaistow, CBE, The Peninsular and Oriental Steam Navigation Company Ltd., 79 Pall Mall, London, SW1Y 5EJ *Tel:* 020 7930 4343.

STERN (Life Baroness, UK) Vivien Helen Stern; cr. 1999; CBE 1992

Daughter of Frederick Stern and Renate Mills. Born September 25, 1941; educated Kent College, Pembury, Kent; Bristol University (BA, MLitt, CertEd); Hon. LLD: Bristol 1990, Oxford Brookes 1996; Hon. Fellow, LSE 1996. *Career:* Lecturer in Education 1970; Community Relations Commission 1970–77; Director, NACRO 1977–96; Visiting Fellow, Nuffield College Oxford 1984–91; Secretary-General, Penal Reform International 1989–; Senior Research Fellow, International Centre for Prison Studies, King's College London. *Other:* Patron, Clean Break; Board Member: Association for Prevention of Torture, Geneva 1993–, Eisenhower Foundation, Washington 1993–. *Trusts, etc:* Patron, Prisoners Education Trust. *Miscellaneous:* Member: Special Programmes Board, Manpower Services Commission 1980–82, Youth Training Board 1982–88,

General Advisory Council, IBA 1982–87, Committee on the Prison Disciplinary System 1984–85, Advisory Council, PSI 1993–96, Law Advisory Council, British Council 1995–. *Honours:* CBE 1992. *Publications: Bricks of Shame,* 1987; *Imprisoned by Our Prisons,* 1989; *Deprived of their Liberty, a report for Caribbean Rights,* 1990; *The Future of the Voluntary Sector and the Pressure Groups in Prison after Woolf,* 1994; *A Sin Against the Future: imprisonment in the world,* 1998. *Special Interests:* Criminal Justice, Foreign Affairs, Human Rights, International Development. *Name, Style and Title:* Raised to the peerage as Baroness Stern, of Vauxhall in the London Borough of Lambeth 1999. A Cross-Bencher. *Address:* The Baroness Stern, CBE, International Centre for Prison Studies, School of Law, King's College London, 8th Floor, 75–79 York Road, London, SE1 7AW *Tel:* 020 7401 2559 *Fax:* 020 7401 2577 *E-Mail:* vivien.stern@kcl.ac.uk.

STEVENS OF LUDGATE (Life Baron, UK), David Robert Stevens; cr. 1987

Son of late A. Edwin Stevens, CBE and of Kathleen James. Born May 26, 1936; educated Stowe; Sidney Sussex College, Cambridge; Hon. Fellow, Sidney Sussex College, Cambridge. Married 1st, May 1961, Patricia Rose (1 son 1 daughter) (marriage dissolved 1971), married 2nd, 1977, Mrs Melissa Sadoff (died February 19, 1989), daughter of M. Milicevic, married 3rd, January 20, 1990, Mrs Meriza Giori, daughter of Mr and Mrs Dzienciolsky. *Armed Forces:* Second Lieutenant, Royal Artillery, National Service 1954–56. *Career:* Management Trainee, Elliot Automation 1959; Hill Samuel Securities 1959–68; Drayton Group 1968–74; Chairman: City and Foreign (Renamed in 1987 Alexander Proudfoot) 1976–95, Drayton Far East 1976–93, English and International 1976–89, Consolidated Venture 1979–93, Drayton Consolidated 1980–92, Drayton Japan 1980–88; Chairman and Chief Executive, MIM Britannia Ltd (formerly Montagu Investment Management Ltd) 1980–89, Chairman only 1989–93; Chairman, United Newspapers plc 1981–95, United News and Media plc 1995–99, Director 1974–; Chairman, Express Newspapers plc 1985–98; Deputy Chairman, Britannia Arrow Holdings plc 1987–89; Chairman: Invesco MIM plc (formerly Britannia Arrow Holdings) 1989–93, Premier Asset Mangement 1997–, Express National Newspapers Limited 1998–99, The Personal Number Company 1998–. *Miscellaneous:* Chairman, EDC for Civil Engineering 1984–86. *Honours:* Grand Official Order of the Southern Cross (Brazil). *Recreations:* Gardening, golf. *Sportsclubs:* Sunningdale Golf, Swinley Forest Golf. *Clubs:* White's. *Name, Style and Title:* Raised to the peerage as Baron Stevens of Ludgate, of Ludgate in the City of London 1987. A Conservative. *Address:* The Lord Stevens of Ludgate, 22 Cheyne Gardens, London, SW3 5QT.

STEVENSON OF CODDENHAM (Life Baron, UK), Henry Dennistoun Stevenson; cr. 1999; Kt 1998; CBE 1981

Son of late Alexander and Sylvia Stevenson (née Ingleby). Born July 19, 1945; educated Trinity College, Glenalmond; King's College, Cambridge (MA). Married 1972, Charlotte Susan, daughter of late Air Commodore Hon. Sir Peter Vanneck, GBE, CB, AFC, AE, DL (4 sons). *Career:* Chairman, SRU Group of Companies 1972–96; Director: National Building Agency 1977–81, British Technology Group 1979–89, Tyne Tees Television 1982–87; Director, Pearson plc 1986–97, Chairman 1997–; Director, Manpower Inc (formerly Blue Arrow) 1988–; Chairman, Sinfonia 21; Director: Thames Television plc 1991–93, J Rothschild Assurance plc 1991–97, J Rothschild Assurance Holdings plc 1991–, English Partnerships 1993–; Chairman, AerFi Group plc (formerly GPA Group plc) 1993–; Director: BSkyB Group plc 1994–, Cloaca Maxima Ltd 1996–, Lazard Brothers 1997–, Whitehall Trust Ltd 1997–, St James's Place Capital 1997–, The Economist Newspapers Ltd 1998–, Glyndebourne Productions Ltd 1998–; Chairman, Halifax plc 1999–. *Other:* Chairman, National Association of Youth Clubs 1973–81; Governor: London Business School 1999–, London School of Economics 1966–. *Trusts, etc:* Member, Administrative Council, Royal Jubilee Trusts 1978–80; Chairman, Trustees, Tate Gallery 1988–98; Member, Tate Gallery Foundation 1998. *Miscellaneous:* Chairman: Government Working Party on role of voluntary movements and youth in the environment 1971, Newton Aycliffe and Peterlee New Town Development Corporation 1971–80, Independent Advisory Committee on Pop Festivals 1972–76; Director, National Building Agency 1977–81; Adviser on Agricultural Marketing to the Minister of Agriculture 1979–83; Director, London Docklands Development Corporation 1981–88; Chairman, Intermediate Technology Development Group 1983–90;

Member: Panel on Takeovers and Mergers 1992–, Board, British Council 1996–; Hon. Member, The Royal Society of Musicians of Great Britain 1998–. *Honours:* CBE 1981; Kt 1998. *Publications: Stevenson Commission Information and Communications Technology in UK Schools Report,* 1997. *Clubs:* Brooks's, MCC. *Name, Style and Title:* Raised to the peerage as Baron Stevenson of Coddenham, of Coddenham in the County of Suffolk 1999. A Cross-Bencher. *Address:* The Lord Stevenson of Coddenham, CBE, 68 Pall Mall, London, SW1Y 5ES *Tel:* 020 7976 2870 *Fax:* 020 7976 2875 *E-Mail:* dennis@maxima.demon.co.uk.

STEWARTBY (Life Baron, UK), (Bernard Harold) Ian (Halley) Stewart; cr. 1992; Kt 1991; PC 1989; RD 1972; FBA 1981

Son of Professor Harold Stewart, CBE, MD, DL, KStJ, FRSE. Born August 10, 1935; educated Haileybury; Jesus College, Cambridge (MA, DLitt 1978); Hon. Fellow, Jesus College, Cambridge 1994. Married October 8, 1966, Deborah Charlotte, JP, daughter of Hon. William Buchan (now 3rd Baron Tweedsmuir, *qv*) (1 son 2 daughters). *Armed Forces:* Served RNVR 1954–56; Lieutenant-Commander RNR. *Career:* Brown Shipley & Co. Ltd 1960–83, Director 1971–83; Chairman, The Throgmorton Trust plc 1990–; Deputy Chairman, Standard Chartered plc 1993–; Director, Securities and Investments Board 1993–97; Deputy Chairman: Amlin plc (formerly Angerstein Underwriting Trust plc) 1995–, Portman Building Society 1999–. *House of Commons:* Contested (Conservative) North Hammersmith 1970 General Election; MP (Conservative) for: Hitchin 1974–83, Hertfordshire North 1983–92; PPS to Chancellor of the Exchequer 1979–83; Parliamentary Under-Secretary of State (Procurement) Ministry of Defence January–October 1983; Economic Secretary to the Treasury 1983–87; Minister of State: Armed Forces, MoD 1987–88, Northern Ireland Office 1988–89. *Spokesman (Commons):* Opposition Spokesman on the Banking Bill 1978–79. *Select Committees (Commons):* Member, Public Expenditure Committee 1977–79; Member, Public Accounts Committee 1991–92. *Backbench Committees (Commons):* Secretary, Conservative Parliamentary Finance Committee 1977–79. *Party Groups (General):* Chairman, Bow Group Economic Standing Committee 1978–83. *Other:* Life Governor, Haileybury 1977; County Vice-President, St John's Ambulance Brigade for Hertfordshire 1978–; Director, British Numismatic Society 1965–75. *Awards Granted:* Royal Numismatic Society Medal 1996. *Trusts, etc:* Trustee, Sir Halley Stewart Trust 1978–. *Miscellaneous:* Chairman, Treasure Valuation Committee 1996–. *Honours:* RD 1972; PC 1989; Kt 1991; KStJ 1992. FSA (Council Member 1974–76); FBA 1981; FRSE 1986. *Publications:* Author of: *The Scottish Coinage,* 1955 (revised edition 1967); *Scottish Mints,* 1971; (jointly) *Studies in Numismatic Method,* 1983; (jointly) *Coinage in Tenth Century England,* 1989. *Special Interests:* Financial Markets, Tax, Charities, Foreign Affairs, Defence. *Recreations:* Archaeology, tennis. *Clubs:* New (Edinburgh), MCC, Hawks (Cambridge), Royal Automobile. *Name, Style and Title:* Raised to the peerage as Baron Stewartby, of Portmoak in the District of Perth and Kinross 1992. A Conservative. *Address:* The Rt Hon. the Lord Stewartby, RD, FBA, House of Lords, London, SW1A 0PW.

STEYN (Life Baron, UK), Johan van Zyl Steyn; cr. 1995; Kt 1985; PC 1992

Born August 15, 1932; educated Jan van Riebeeck School, Cape Town, South Africa; University of Stellenbosch (BA, LLB); University College, Oxford (MA); Hon. LLD, Queen Mary and Westfield College, London; Hon. LLD, UAE. Married Susan Lewis (2 sons and 2 daughters from previous marriage; 1 step-son and 1 step-daughter). *Career:* Cape Province Rhodes Scholar 1955; Commenced practice at the South African Bar 1958, English Bar 1973; QC 1979; Bencher, Lincoln's Inn 1985; Judge of the High Court, Queen's Bench Division 1985–91; Chairman, Race Relations Committee of the Bar 1987–88; A Presiding Judge, Northern Circuit 1989–91; President, British Insurance Law Association 1992–94; A Lord Justice of Appeal 1992–95; Chairman, Advisory Council, Centre for Commercial Law Studies, Queen Mary and Westfield College, London 1993–94; Chairman, Lord Chancellor's Advisory Committee on Legal Aid and Conduct 1994–96; A Lord of Appeal in Ordinary 1995–. *Honours:* Kt 1985; PC 1992. Hon. Member, American Law Institute. *Name, Style and Title:* Raised to the peerage as Baron Steyn, of Swafield in the County of Norfolk 1995. A Cross-Bencher. *Address:* The Rt Hon. the Lord Steyn, House of Lords, London, SW1A 0PW.

STODART OF LEASTON (Life Baron, UK), (James) Anthony Stodart; cr. 1981; PC 1974

Son of late Colonel Thomas Stodart, CIE. Born June 6, 1916; educated Wellington. Married September 12, 1940, Hazel Jean (died March 18, 1995), daughter of late Ronald James Usher. *Career:* Farmer since 1934; Executive Committee, East Lothian NFU 1948–51; Chairman, Agricultural Credit Corporation 1975–87; Chairman: Committee of Enquiry into Local Government in Scotland 1980, Manpower Review of Veterinary Profession in UK 1984–85. *House of Commons:* Contested: (Liberal) Berwick and East Lothian 1950, (Conservative) Midlothian and Peebles 1951, 1955; MP (Conservative) for Edinburgh West 1959–74; Joint Under-Secretary of State for Scotland 1963–1964; Parliamentary Secretary, Ministry of Agriculture, Fisheries and Food 1970–72, Minister of State 1972–74. *Spokesman (Commons):* Spokesman on Agriculture and Scottish Affairs 1966–69. *Backbench Committees (Commons):* Vice-Chairman, Conservative Agricultural Committee 1962–63, 1964–65, 1966–70. *Other:* Hon. President, Edinburgh University Agricultural Society 1952. *Special Interests:* Agriculture, Fishing Industry, Local Government. *Honours:* PC 1974; *Recreations:* Music, vintage films. *Sportsclubs:* Hon. Company of Edinburgh Golfers. *Clubs:* Cavalry and Guards, New (Edinburgh). *Name, Style and Title:* Raised to the peerage as Baron Stodart of Leaston, of Humbie in the District of East Lothian 1981. *Address:* The Rt Hon. the Lord Stodart of Leaston, Lorimers, North Berwick, East Lothian, EH39 4NG *Tel:* 01620 892457; Leaston, Humbie, East Lothian, EH36 5PD *Tel:* 01875 833213.

STODDART OF SWINDON (Life Baron, UK), David Leonard Stoddart; cr. 1983

Son of late Arthur L. Stoddart, Coal Miner. Born May 4, 1926; educated St Clement Danes and Henley Grammar Schools. Married 2nd, June 24, 1961, Jennifer, daughter of late L. Percival-Alwyn (2 sons) (1 daughter by previous marriage). *Trades Union:* Trade Unions: EETPU 1953, NALGO 1951–70. *Councils, Public Bodies:* Councillor, Reading County Borough Council 1954–72; Leader of Labour Group on Council 1962–70; Served at various times as Chairman of Housing, Transport and Finance Committees and as a member of various Boards inc. Thames Valley Water Board and Police Authority. *Career:* Power Station Clerical Worker 1951–70. *House of Commons:* Contested (Labour) Newbury 1959, 1964; MP (Labour) for Swindon 1970–83; PPS to Minister for Housing and Construction 1974–75. *Whip (Commons):* Assistant Government Whip from January 26, 1975-November 17, 1977; Lord Commissioner of the Treasury April 1976-November 1977. *Spokesman (Commons):* Junior Opposition Front Bench Spokesman on Industry 1982–83. *Select Committees (Commons):* Former Member, House of Commons Select Committee on Nationalised Industries; Member, Select Committee on Energy 1980–82. *Whip:* Opposition Whip in House of Lords 1983–88. *Spokesman:* Opposition Front Bench Spokesman in House of Lords on Energy 1983–88. *All-Party:* Member, All-Party Family Farms Group. *Other:* Member, Court and Council of Reading University; Treasurer, Anzac Group 1985–; Chairman, Campaign for an Independent Britain 1989–. *Miscellaneous:* Member, National Joint Council for the Electricity Supply Industry 1967–70. *Special Interests:* Commonwealth, Economic Policy, Energy, European Union, Housing, Industry, Local Government, Transport. *Name, Style and Title:* Raised to the peerage as Baron Stoddart of Swindon, of Reading in the Royal County of Berkshire 1983. Labour. *Address:* The Lord Stoddart of Swindon, 'Sintra', 37A Bath Road, Reading, Berkshire, RG1 6HL *Tel:* 0118–957 6726.

STOKES (Life Baron, UK), Donald Gresham Stokes; cr. 1969; Kt 1965; TD 1945; DL; FEng

Son of late Harry Potts Stokes. Born March 22, 1914; educated Blundell's School; Harris Institute of Technology, Preston; Hon. DSc, University of Southampton; Hon. LLD, University of Lancaster 1967; Hon. Fellow, Keble College, Oxford 1968; Hon. Degree in Technology, University of Technology, Loughborough 1968; Hon. Degree of Doctor of Science, University of Salford 1971. Married 1939, Laura Elizabeth Courteney (died April 1, 1995), daughter of late Frederick C. Lamb (1 son). *Armed Forces:* Served War 1939–45, REME, Lieutenant-Colonel. *Councils, Public Bodies:* DL, Lancs 1968. *Career:* Commenced Student Apprenticeship, Leyland Motors Ltd 1930; Re-joined Leyland as Exports Manager 1946, General Sales and Service Manager 1950, Director 1954; Managing Director, The Leyland Motor Corporation 1963, Chairman 1967. Chairman and

Chief Executive: British Leyland (UK) Ltd, British Leyland International and subsidiary companies 1968–75; President, British Leyland Limited 1975–79; Consultant to Leyland Vehicles Ltd 1979–81; Director, District Bank Limited 1964–69; President, Motor Industry Research Association 1966; Chairman, Electronics Committee of the NEDC 1966–68; Director, London Weekend Television Limited 1967–71; Deputy Chairman, Industrial Reorganisation Corporation 1969–71; Director, National Westminster Bank 1969–81; Member, CBI Council; President, EDC for the Motor Manufacturing Industry 1969–; Chairman, British Arabian Advisory Co. Ltd 1977–85; Chairman, Two Counties Radio Ltd 1979–84, 1990–, President 1994–; Director: GWR Group 1990–94, Opus Public Relations Ltd 1979–84, KBH Communications Ltd 1985–96; Chairman, Jack Barclay Ltd 1980–90; Director, Scottish and Universal Investments Ltd 1980–92; Chairman: Dovercourt Motor Co. Ltd 1980–90, Dutton-Forshaw Motor Group Ltd 1981–91, Beherman Auto-Transports NV (Belgium) 1982–89. *Other:* President: SMMT Council 1961–2, The Institution of Mechanical Engineers 1972, The University of Manchester Institute of Science and Technology 1968–76. *Trusts, etc:* Chairman, Nuffield Trust for the Forces of the Crown 1971–96. *Honours:* TD 1945; Kt 1965; Officier de l'Ordre de la Couronne (Belgium) 1964; Commandeur de l'Ordre de Leopold II (Belgium) 1972. FEng; FIMechE; MSAE; FIMI; FCIT; FICE; FIRTE; Fellow, Institute of Road Transport Engineers 1968, President 1982. President, Worshipful Company of Carmen. *Sportsclubs:* Commodore, Royal Motor Yacht Club, Poole 1979–81. *Clubs:* Army and Navy. *Name, Style and Title:* Raised to the peerage as Baron Stokes, of Leyland in the County Palatine of Lancaster 1969. A Cross-Bencher. *Address:* The Lord Stokes, TD, DL, Branksome Cliff, Westminster Road, Poole, Dorset, BH13 6JW *Tel:* 01202 763088.

STONE OF BLACKHEATH (Life Baron, UK), Andrew Zelig Stone; cr. 1997

Son of Sydney and Louise Stone. Born September 7, 1942; educated Cardiff High School; Hon. LLD, Oxford Brookes 1998. Married 1973, Vivienne Wendy Lee (1 son 2 daughters). *Career:* Marks and Spencer plc: Management Trainee 1966, Merchandise Manager 1973, Personal Assistant to Chairman 1978–80, Divisional Director 1986, Menswear 1986, Children's Wear 1990, Director 1990–, Joint Managing Director 1994–2000. *Other:* Chairman, British Overseas Trade Board for Israel 1991–. *Trusts, etc:* Trustee, Jewish Association of Business Ethics. *Miscellaneous:* Governor, Weizmann Institute Foundation 1993–; Patron, Interalia Institute of Arts and Science; Council Member, Arts and Business; Member, National Advisory Committee for Creative and Cultural Education; President, British Overseas Trade Board for Israel. FRSA. *Special Interests:* Middle East, Arts, Science, Conflict Resolution. *Recreations:* Reading, walking, thinking. *Name, Style and Title:* Raised to the peerage as Baron Stone of Blackheath, of Blackheath in the London Borough of Greenwich 1997. Labour. *Address:* The Lord Stone of Blackheath, House of Lords, London, SWIA OPW *Tel:* 020 7935 4422 *E-Mail:* lord.stoneofb@marks_and_spencer.com.

STRABOLGI (11th Baron, E), David Montague de Burgh Kenworthy; cr. 1318

Son of 10th Baron and Doris Whitley, only child of late Sir Frederick Whitley-Thomson, MP. Born November 1, 1914. Succeeded his father 1953. A Co-heir to the baronies of Cobham and Burgh; educated Gresham's School, Holt; Chelsea School of Art. Married June 3, 1961, Doreen Margaret, daughter of late Alexander Morgan, of Ashton-under-Lyne. *Armed Forces:* Served BEF 1939–40; MEF 1940–45, Lieutenant-Colonel, RAOC. *Career:* Member, Parliamentary delegations to: Russia 1954, France 1981, 1983, 1985; Director, Bolton Building Society 1958–74, 1979–87, Deputy Chairman 1983–85, Chairman 1986–87; Member, British Section Franco-British Council 1981–98; President, Franco-British Society 1999. *House of Lords:* PPS to the Rt Hon. Lord Shackleton, KG, Lord Privy Seal and the Leader of the House of Lords 1969–70; A Deputy Speaker House of Lords and Deputy Chairman of Committees 1986–; An Extra Lord in Waiting to HM The Queen 1998–; An elected hereditary peer 1999–. *Whip:* Opposition Whip 1970–74; Captain of the Yeomen of the Guard and Deputy Chief Whip, House of Lords 1974–79. *Spokesman:* Opposition Front Bench Spokesman on the Arts 1979–85. *Select Committees:* Member: Select Committee for Privileges 1987–, Joint Committee (with Commons) on Consolidation Bills 1987–97, 1998–, Personal Bills Committee 1987–97, Ecclesiastical Committee 1991–97, 1997–, Select Committee on Procedure of the House 1993–97, 1998–. *All-Party:* Hon. Treasurer, Franco-British Parliamentary Relations Committee 1991–96;

Member, All-Party Arts and Amenities Group. *Party Groups (General):* Vice-Chairman, Labour Party Films Group 1968–70. *Honours:* Officier de la Légion d'Honneur 1981. Freeman, City of London. *Special Interests:* Environment, National Heritage, France. *Recreations:* French Literature. *Clubs:* Reform. *Heir:* Heir presumptive, his nephew, Andrew David Whitley Kenworthy, born February 11, 1967. Labour. *Address:* The Lord Strabolgi, House of Lords, London, SW1A 0PW.

STRANGE (Baroness, 16th in line, E), Jean Cherry Drummond of Megginch; cr. 1628

Daughter of 15th Baron and late Violet Margaret Florence, daughter of late Sir Robert Buchanan-Jardine, 2nd Bt. Born December 17, 1928; educated Oxenfoord Castle School; St Andrews University (MA); Cambridge University. Married June 2, 1952, Captain Humphrey ap Evans, MC, who assumed the name of Drummond of Megginch by decree of the Lord Lyon, 1966, son of Major J. J. P. Evans, MBE, MC, DL (3 sons 3 daughters). *House of Lords:* An elected hereditary peer 1999–. *All-Party:* Member, All-Party Parliamentary Defence Group, visiting: Cyprus, Northern Ireland, Belize in 1989, Falkland Islands in 1990, Northern Ireland in 1992, 1996; Member, All-Party: Children's Group, Maritime Group, Complementary Medicine Group, Tibetan Group. *Party Groups:* Member, Executive Committee Association of Conservative Peers 1991–94. *International Bodies:* Member, Parliamentary Delegation, Bangladesh 1990; Delegate, Inter-Parliamentary Union Conference, Ottawa 1993; Member, Parliamentary Delegation, Bulgaria 1998; Member: IPU, CPA. *Party Groups (General):* Chairman, Glencarse Junior Unionists 1947–52. *Other:* President, War Widows Association of Great Britain 1990–; Member: Age Concern, Scottish Peers Association. *Miscellaneous:* The barony was in abeyance from 1982–86, when terminated in favour of the present peer. FSA (Scotland); Hon. FIMarE. *Publications: Love from Belinda; Lalage in Love; Creatures Great and Small; Love is For Ever; The Remarkable Life of Victoria Drummond – Marine Engineer. Special Interests:* Defence, Foreign Affairs, Children, Countryside, Arts. *Heir:* Her son, Major Hon. Adam Humphrey Drummond yr of Megginch, born April 20, 1953. A Cross-Bencher. *Address:* The Baroness Strange, Megginch Castle, Errol, Perthshire, PH2 7SW *Tel:* 01821 642222.

STRATHCLYDE (2nd Baron, UK), Thomas Galloway Dunlop du Roy de Blicquy Galbraith; cr. 1955; PC 1995

Son of late Hon. Sir Thomas Galloway Dunlop Galbraith, KBE, MP, eldest son of 1st Baron, PC. Born February 22, 1960. Succeeded his grandfather 1985; educated Wellington; University of East Anglia; University of Aix-en-Provence. Married June 27, 1992, Jane, daughter of John Skinner, of Chenies, Buckinghamshire (3 daughters). *Career:* Lloyd's Insurance Broker; Bain Clarkson Ltd 1982–88. *House of Lords:* Parliamentary Under-Secretary of State: Department of Employment (Minister for Tourism) 1989–90, Department of Environment July-Sept 1990, Scottish Office (Minister for Agriculture and Fisheries) 1990–92; Joint Parliamentary Under-Secretary of State, Department of Environment 1992–93; Joint Parliamentary Under-Secretary of State for Consumer Affairs and Small Firms, Department of Trade and Industry 1993–94, Minister of State January-July 1994; Member, Shadow Cabinet 1997–; A Former Deputy Speaker of the House of Lords; A Former Deputy Chairman of Committees; Leader of the Opposition in the House of Lords December 1998–; An elected hereditary peer 1999–. *Whip:* A Lord in Waiting (Government Whip) 1988–89; Captain of the Honourable Corps of the Gentlemen-at-Arms (Government Chief Whip) 1994–97; Opposition Chief Whip in the House of Lords 1997–98. *Spokesman:* Government Spokesman for DTI, Treasury and Scotland 1988–89; Opposition Spokesman on Constitutional Affairs December 1998–. *Select Committees:* Member, Select Committee on House of Lords' Offices 1997–. *Miscellaneous:* Contested (Conservative) European Elections for Merseyside East 1984; Chairman, Commission on the Future Structure of the Scottish Conservative and Unionist Party. *Honours:* PC 1995. *Clubs:* Carlton. *Heir:* His brother, Hon. Charles William du Roy de Blicquy Galbraith, born May 20, 1962. A Conservative. *Address:* The Rt Hon. the Lord Strathclyde, House of Lords, London, SW1A 0PW *Tel:* House of Lords 020 7219 5353.

SWINFEN (3rd Baron, UK), Roger Mynors Swinfen Eady; cr. 1919

Son of 2nd Baron. Born December 14, 1938. Succeeded his father 1977; educated Westminster; RMA, Sandhurst. Married 1962, Patricia Anne, daughter of late Frank Blackmore (1 son 3 daughters). *Armed Forces:* Lieutenant, The Royal Scots (The Royal Regiment). *Councils, Public Bodies:* JP, Kent 1983–85. *House of Lords:* An elected hereditary peer 1999–. *Select Committees:* Member: Select Committee on Greater Manchester Bill 1979, House of Lords European Communities Sub-Committee C 1990–94. *All-Party:* Member, All-Party: Disablement Group, Bangladesh Group. *Other:* President, South East Region British Sports Association for the Disabled; Patron: Disablement Income Group 1988–, 1 in 8 Group 1996, Labrador Rescue South East 1996; Hon. President, Britain Bangladesh Friendship Association. *Trusts, etc:* Fellow, Industry and Parliament Trust 1983–. *Miscellaneous:* Chairman, Parliamentary Working Party on Video Violence and Children 1982–85; Member, Direct Mail Services Standards Board 1983–97. ARICS 1970. Liveryman, Worshipfull Company of Drapers. *Special Interests:* Disability. *Recreations:* Gardening, painting, reading history. *Heir:* His son, Hon. Charles Roger Peregrine Swinfen Eady, born March 8, 1971. A Conservative. *Address:* The Lord Swinfen, House of Lords, London, SW1A 0PW.

SYMONS OF VERNHAM DEAN (Life Baroness, UK), Elizabeth Conway Symons; cr. 1996

Daughter of Ernest Vize Symons, CB, and Elizabeth Megan Symons. Born April 14, 1951; educated Putney High School for Girls; Girton College, Cambridge (MA). *Career:* Research, Girton College, Cambridge 1972–74; Administration Trainee, Department of the Environment 1974–77; Inland Revenue Staff Federation: Assistant Secretary 1977–78, Deputy General Secretary 1978–89; General Secretary, Association of First Division Civil Servants 1989–97. *House of Lords:* Parliamentary Under-Secretary of State, Foreign and Commonwealth Office 1997–99; Minister of State for Defence Procurement, Ministry of Defence 1999–. *Other:* Former Member: General Council, TUC, Council, RIPA, Governor, Polytechnic of North London 1989–94; Member: Executive Council, Campaign for Freedom of Information 1989–97, Hansard Society Council 1992–97, Advisory Council, Civil Service College 1992–97; Governor, London Business School 1993–97; Member: Council, Industrial Society 1994–97, Council, Open University 1994–97. *Miscellaneous:* Hon. Associate, National Council of Women 1989; Member, Employment Appeal Tribunal 1995–97. FRSA. *Recreations:* Reading, gardening. *Name, Style and Title:* Raised to the peerage as Baroness Symons of Vernham Dean, of Vernham Dean in the County of Hampshire 1996. Labour. *Address:* The Baroness Symons of Vernham Dean, House of Lords, London, SW1A 0PW.

T

TANLAW (Life Baron, UK), Simon Brooke Mackay; cr. 1971

Son of late 2nd Earl of Inchcape. Born March 30, 1934; educated Eton; Trinity College, Cambridge (MA 1966); Hon. DUniversity, University of Buckingham 1983. Married 1st, April 1, 1959, Joanna Susan, daughter of late Major J. S. Hirsch (1 son 2 daughters and 1 son deceased), married 2nd, May 5, 1976, Rina Siew Yong, daughter of late Tiong Cha Tan (1 son 1 daughter). *Armed Forces:* Served as 2nd Lieutenant, XII Royal Lancers, Malaya. *Career:* Worked in Inchcape Group of Companies India and Far East 1960–66, Managing Director 1967–71, Director 1971–92; Chairman and Managing Director, Fandstan Group of Companies 1973–; Member, Executive Committee of the Great Britain-China Centre 1981–88. *Select Committees:* Member, European Communities Committee Sub-Committee F (Energy Transport, Research and Technology) 1980–83. *All-Party:* Chairman, Parliamentary Liaison Group for Alternative Energy Strategies 1981–83; Member, All-Party Group for Energy Studies; Chairman, All-Party Astronomy and Space Environment Group (APASEG) 1999–. *Other:* Chairman, Building Committee, University College at Buckingham 1973–77, Council of Management 1973–; Member, Court of Governors, London School of Economics 1980–96; President, Sarawak Association 1973–75, 1997–; Hon. Treasurer, Scottish Peers Association 1979–86.

Miscellaneous: Contested Galloway 1959, 1960 and 1964 as Liberal candidate; Member, Lord Chancellor's Inner London Advisory Committee on Justices of the Peace 1972–83. Fellow, British Horological Institute. Member: Worshipful Company of Fishmongers, Worshipful Company of Clockmakers. *Publications:* In the *Horological Journal: The Case for a British Astro-Physical Masterclock, Spacetime and Horology GMT or UTC for the Millennium?. Special Interests:* Time, Space. *Recreations:* Fishing, horology. *Clubs:* White's, Oriental, Puffin's (Edinburgh). *Name, Style and Title:* Raised to the peerage as Baron Tanlaw, of Tanlawhill in the County of Dumfries 1971. A Cross-Bencher. *Address:* The Lord Tanlaw, 31 Brompton Square, London, SW3 2AE; Tanlawhill, Eskdalemuir, by Langholm, Dumfriesshire, DG13 0PQ.

TAVERNE (Life Baron, UK), Dick Taverne; cr. 1996; QC 1965

Son of late Dr N. J. M. Taverne and of Mrs L. V. Taverne. Born October 18, 1928; educated Charterhouse; Balliol College, Oxford (First in Greats). Married 1955, Janice, daughter of late Dr Hennessey (2 daughters). *Career:* Called to the Bar, Middle Temple 1954; QC 1965; Director, Institute for Fiscal Studies 1970–79, Director-General 1979–81, Chairman 1981–83; Director, Axa Equity and Law 1972–, Chairman 1997–; Director, BOC Group 1975–95; Member, International Independent Review Body to review workings of the European Commission 1979; Chairman, Public Policy Centre 1983–87; Director, PRIMA Europe Ltd 1987–, Chairman 1991–93, President 1993–98; Chairman, OLIM Investment Trust 1989–99; Deputy Chairman, Central European Growth Fund. *House of Commons:* Contested Wandsworth, Putney (Labour) 1959 General Election; MP (Labour) for Lincoln, March 1962-October 1972, resigned; Parliamentary Under-Secretary of State, Home Office 1966–68; Minister of State, HM Treasury 1968–69; Financial Secretary, HM Treasury 1969–70; MP (Democratic Labour) for Lincoln, March 1973-September 1974; Contested (SDP): Southwark, Peckham, October 1982, Dulwich 1983. *Select Committees (Commons):* Chairman, Public Expenditure Sub-Committee 1971–72. *Spokesman:* Liberal Democrat Spokesman on Treasury Issues 1998–. *Party Groups (General):* Member: National Committee, Social Democratic Party 1981–87; Federal Policy Committee, Liberal Democrats 1989–90. *Other:* Chairman: Council of Alcohol and Drug Abuse Prevention and Treatment Ltd, Advisory Board of Oxford Centre for the Environment, Ethics and Society. *Publications: The Future of the Left: Lincoln and after*, 1974; *The Pension Time Bomb in Europe*, 1995; *Pensions in Europe*, 1997; *Tax and the Euro*, 1999. *Special Interests:* European Union, Pensions, Welfare, Corporate Governance, Science and Technology, Crime and Drugs, Tax, Economic Policy. *Recreations:* Sailing. *Sportsclubs:* Cruising Association. *Name, Style and Title:* Raised to the peerage as Baron Taverne, of Pimlico in the City of Westminster 1996. A Liberal Democrat. *Address:* The Lord Taverne, QC, 60 Cambridge Street, London, SW1V 4QQ.

TAYLOR OF BLACKBURN (Life Baron, UK), Thomas Taylor; cr. 1978; CBE 1974; FRGS; DL

Son of James Taylor. Born June 10, 1929; educated Mill Hill Council School; Blakey Moor Elementary School; Hon. LLD, Lancaster 1996. Married September 23, 1950, Kathleen, daughter of John Edward Nurton (1 son). *Councils, Public Bodies:* Councillor, Blackburn Council 1954–76, Leader of Council until 1976; JP, Blackburn 1960; DL, Lancashire 1994–. *Career:* Former Deputy Director, Central Lancashire Family and Community Project; Chairman: Bygone Times Ltd, Grove Properties Ltd, Canatxx Energy Ventures Limited, Chameleon Educational Systems Limited; Director of other companies; Consultant, Shorrock Security Systems Ltd; Adviser: BAe, BAe Sema, EDS, Omega Investment Research Limited. *Chancellor:* Deputy Pro-Chancellor, University of Lancaster 1961–95. *Select Committees:* Member: Select Committee on Science and Technology 1987–92, House of Lords' Offices Committee 1993–97. *Party Groups:* Member, Labour North West Group. *International Bodies:* Member, CPA 1978–. *Other:* Past President, Association of Education Committees; Member of Council, University of Lancaster 1961–95; President, Free Church Council 1962–63; Chairman, Electricity Consumers Council for North West 1977–80; Member, Norweb Board; Vice-President, The Association of Lancastrians in London. *Trusts, etc:* Patron, Lancashire Wildlife Trust. *Miscellaneous:* Past Chairman of several Government Committees of Enquiry. *Honours:* OBE 1969; CBE 1974. FRGS 1994. Freeman, Borough of Blackburn 1992. *Special Interests:* Education,

North West, Railways, Commonwealth, Energy, Local Government. *Recreations:* Gardening, radio, books, music. *Name, Style and Title:* Raised to the peerage as Baron Taylor of Blackburn, of Blackburn in the County of Lancaster 1978. Labour. *Address:* The Lord Taylor of Blackburn, CBE, JP, DL, 9 Woodview, Cherry Tree, Blackburn, Lancashire, BB2 5LL *Tel:* 01254 209571; House of Lords, London, SW1A 0PW *Tel:* House of Lords 020 7219 5130.

TAYLOR OF GRYFE (Life Baron, UK), Thomas Johnston Taylor; cr. 1968; DL

Son of late John Taylor. Born April 27, 1912; educated Bellahouston Academy, Glasgow; Hon. LLD, Strathclyde 1974. Married 1943, Isobel Wands (2 daughters). *Councils, Public Bodies:* DL, Renfrewshire 1970. *Career:* Former President, Scottish Co-operative Wholesale Society; Executive Committee, Scottish Council (Development & Industry); Former Chairman: Forestry Commission, Economic Forestry Group; Former Director, British Railways Board; Director: British Railways Property Board, Scottish Metropolitan Property Co. Ltd, Whiteways, Laidlaw & Co; Former Chairman, Morgan Grenfell (Scotland) Ltd; Member, Advisory Board Morgan Grenfell Ltd. *All-Party:* Chairman, All-Party Forestry Group (both Houses) –1999; Treasurer, Anglo-Belize Parliamentary Group. *Other:* Chairman, Scottish Peers Association 1989–91. *Trusts, etc:* Chairman, Edith and Isaac Wolfson (Scotland) Trust 1972–90; Trustee, Dulverton Trust 1980–. *Honours:* Commanders Cross of the Order of Merit of the Federal Republic of Germany. Fellow: Royal Society (Edinburgh), Royal Society of Arts. *Special Interests:* Finance, Industry, Forestry, Transport. *Recreations:* Golf, theatre. *Clubs:* Caledonian, Royal and Ancient (St Andrews). *Name, Style and Title:* Raised to the peerage as Baron Taylor of Gryfe, of Bridge of Weir in the County of Renfrewshire 1968. Labour. *Address:* The Lord Taylor of Gryfe, DL, Glentyan, 33 Seagate, Kingsbarns, Fife, KY16 8SR *Tel:* 01334 880430.

TAYLOR OF WARWICK (Life Baron, UK), John David Beckett Taylor; cr. 1996

Son of late Derief Taylor, professional cricketer, and Mrs Enid Taylor, nurse. Born September 21, 1952; educated Moseley Church of England School, Birmingham; Moseley Grammar School (Head Pupil); University of Keele (BA Hons Law); Gray's Inn, Inns of Court School of Law. Married, 1981, Dr Katherine Taylor, BSc, MD (1 son 2 daughters). *Trades Union:* Member, NUJ. *Councils, Public Bodies:* Councillor, Solihull Borough Council 1986–91; Member: North West Thames Regional Health Authority 1992–93, Greater London Further Education Funding Council 1992–95. *Career:* Barrister-at-Law, called Gray's Inn 1978; Television and radio presenter, writer and company director 1992. *House of Lords:* Introduced the Criminal Evidence (Amendment) Bill on February 10, 1997, which came into force March 1997 as the Criminal Evidence (Amendment) Act 1997. *All-Party:* Member, European Informations Market Broadcasting Committee (EURIM) 1996–; Member, All-Party: Trade and Industry Committee, Retail Industry Group, British American Parliamentary Group, British South Africa Parliamentary Group. *Party Groups:* Member, Association of Conservative Peers. *International Bodies:* Member, Commonwealth Parliamentary Association. *Other:* Life Patron, West Indian Senior Citizens Association (WISCA); Patron, Parents Need Children Adoption Charity; Executive Committee Member, Sickle Cell Anaemia Relief Charity; Member: Royal Television Society, Radio Academy; Vice-President, National Small Business Bureau; President, African Caribbean Westminster Business Initiative; Barker, Variety Club of Great Britain. *Awards Granted:* Gray's Inn Advocacy Prize 1978. *Trusts, etc:* Member, Industry and Parliament Trust. *Miscellaneous:* Contested (Conservative) Cheltenham 1992 General Election; Member, Institute of Directors; Vice-President, British Board of Film Classification 1998–. *Special Interests:* Law, Broadcasting, Film. *Recreations:* Singing, sport – especially soccer and cricket, spending time with my family. *Sportsclubs:* Aston Villa Football Club; President, Ilford Town Football Club. *Name, Style and Title:* Raised to the peerage as Baron Taylor of Warwick, of Warwick in the County of Warwickshire 1996. A Conservative. *Address:* The Lord Taylor of Warwick, House of Lords, London, SW1A 0PW.

TEBBIT (Life Baron, UK), Norman Beresford Tebbit; cr. 1992; CH 1987; PC 1981

Son of late Leonard Albert Tebbit. Born March 29, 1931; educated Edmonton County Grammar School. Married September 29, 1956, Margaret Elizabeth, daughter of S. Daines (2 sons 1 daughter). *Trades Union:* Member, BALPA. *Armed Forces:* RAF Pilot, 1949–51, Commissioned; Served RAuxAF 604 Squadron 1952–55. *Career:* Journalist 1947–49; Publicist and Publisher 1951–53; Airline Pilot 1953–70; Assistant Director of Information, National Federation of Building Trades Employers 1975–79; A Political Commentator on Sky Television's Target programme 1989–98; Columnist: *Sun* newspaper 1995–97, *The Mail on Sunday* 1997–; Company Director: Sears Holdings plc 1987–99, British Telecom 1987–96, BET 1987–96, Spectator (1828) Ltd 1989–, Onix Ltd 1990–92. *House of Commons:* Prospective Parliamentary candidate (Conservative) South West Islington 1967–69; MP (Conservative) for: Epping 1970–74, Chingford 1974–92; PPS to Minister of State, Department of Employment 1972–73; Parliamentary Under-Secretary of State, Department of Trade 1979–81; Minister of State for Industry January-September 1981; Secretary of State for Employment 1981–83; Secretary of State for Trade and Industry and President of the Board of Trade 1983–85; Chancellor of the Duchy of Lancaster 1985–87. *Select Committees (Commons):* Former Member, Select Committee on Science and Technology. *Backbench Committees (Commons):* Former Member, several Conservative Parliamentary committees including: Aviation, Housing, Industry. *Party Groups (General):* Held various offices in: YC organisation 1946–55, Hemel Hempstead Conservative Association 1960–67; Chairman, Conservative Party 1985–87. *Other:* Chairman: The Nuffield Ortholics Appeal, Nuffield Orthopaedic Appeal. *Miscellaneous:* Air Line Transport Pilots Licence; Flight Navigators Licence; Former office holder with BALPA (British Airline Pilots' Association). *Honours:* PC 1981; CH 1987. Liveryman, Guild of Air Pilots and Air Navigators. *Publications:* Author of: *Upwardly Mobile*, 1988; *Unfinished Business*, 1991. *Recreations:* Gardening. *Clubs:* Royal Air Force, Beefsteak, The Other Club. *Name, Style and Title:* Raised to the peerage as Baron Tebbit, of Chingford in the London Borough of Waltham Forest 1992. A Conservative. *Address:* The Rt Hon. the Lord Tebbit, CH, House of Lords, London, SW1A 0PW.

TEMPLEMAN (Life Baron, UK), Sydney William Templeman; cr. 1982; Kt 1972; PC 1978; MBE (Mil) 1946

Son of late Herbert William Templeman. Born March 3, 1920; educated Southall Grammar School; St John's College, Cambridge; Hon. DLitt, Reading 1980; Hon. Fellow, St John's College, Cambridge 1982; Hon. LLD: Birmingham 1986, Huddersfield Polytechnic CNAA 1990, Exeter 1991, West of England 1993, National Law School of India, University of Bangalore 1994. Married 1st, January 19, 1946, Margaret Rowles (died 1988) (2 sons); married 2nd, December 12, 1996, Mrs Sheila Edworthy. *Armed Forces:* Served War 1939–45; Commissioned 4/1st Gurkha Rifles 1941; NW Frontier 1942; Arakan 1943; Imphal 1944 (despatches, Hon. Major); Burma 1945. *Career:* Called to the Bar, Middle Temple and Lincoln's Inn 1947; Member, Bar Council 1961–65; Attorney-General of the Duchy of Lancaster 1970–72; A Judge of the High Court of Justice, Chancery Division 1972–78; President, Senate of the Inns of Court and the Bar 1974–76; Member, Royal Commission on Legal Services 1976–79; A Lord Justice of Appeal 1978–82; A Lord of Appeal in Ordinary 1982–94; Treasurer, Middle Temple 1987; Chairman, Ecclesiastical Committee 1992–. *Select Committees:* Member, Ecclesiastical Committee 1997–. *Honours:* MBE (Mil) 1946; Kt 1972; PC 1978. *Name, Style and Title:* Raised to the peerage as Baron Templeman, of White Lackington in the County of Somerset 1982. A Cross-Bencher. *Address:* The Rt Hon. the Lord Templeman, MBE, 'Mellowstone', 1 Rosebank Crescent, Exeter, Devon, EX4 6EJ *Tel:* 01392 275428.

TENBY (3rd Viscount, UK), William Lloyd-George; cr. 1957

Son of 1st Viscount, PC, TD. Born November 7, 1927. Succeeded his brother 1983; educated Eastbourne College; St Catharine's College, Cambridge (Late Exhibitioner). Married April 23, 1955, Ursula Diana Ethel, daughter of late Lieutenant-Colonel Henry Edward Medlicott, DSO (1 son 2 daughters). *Councils, Public Bodies:* Former JP, Hampshire, North East Hampshire Bench, retired 1997; Member, Hampshire Police Authority 1985–94. *Career:* Editorial Assistant, Herbert Jenkins Ltd 1951–54; Advertisement Department, Associated Newspapers 1954–57; Group Advertising Manager, United Dominions Trust Ltd 1957–74; P.R. Adviser to Chairman, Kleinwort Benson Ltd 1974–87; Consultant, Williams Lea Group 1985–93; Director, Ugland International plc 1993–95. *House of Lords:* An elected hereditary peer 1999–. *Select Committees:* Former Member: Finance and Building Sub-Committee, Committee on Procedure; Member, Select Committee on Selection. *Backbench Committees:* Member, Backbench Sub-Committees: on Smoking, on Broadcasting. *All-Party:* Member: All-Party Broadcasting Group All-Party Wildlife Protection Group 1999–; Founder, All-Party Magistrates' Group. *Trusts, etc:* Vice-Chairman Trustees, Byways Residential Home. *Miscellaneous:* President, Hampshire CPRE. *Special Interests:* Communications Industry, Magistracy, Railways, Environment. *Recreations:* Ornithology, music, reading. *Heir:* His son, Hon. Timothy Henry Gwilym Lloyd-George, born October 19, 1962. A Cross-Bencher. *Address:* The Viscount Tenby, The White House, Dippenhall Street, Crondall, Nr Farnham, Surrey, GU10 5PE *Tel:* 01252 850592 (Home) *Fax:* 01252 850913 (Home) *Tel:* 020 7219 5403 (Office).

THATCHER (Life Baroness, UK), Margaret Hilda Thatcher; cr. 1992; LG 1995; OM 1990; PC 1970; FRS 1983

Daughter of late Alfred Roberts. Born October 13, 1925; educated Kesteven and Grantham High School; Somerville College, Oxford (MA, BSc); Hon. Doctorates: Louisiana State University 1993, Mendeleyev University, Moscow 1993. Married, 1951, Denis Thatcher, MBE, TD (created Sir Denis Thatcher, 1st Bt 1991) (1 son 1 daughter twins). *Career:* Research Chemist 1947–51; Called to the Bar, Lincoln's Inn 1954. *House of Commons:* Contested (Conservative) Dartford in 1950, 1951 General Elections under her maiden name of Roberts; MP (Conservative) for Finchley 1959–92; Joint Parliamentary Secretary, Ministry of Pensions and National Insurance 1961–64; Shadow Minster of: Transport 1968–69, Education 1969–70; Secretary of State for Education and Science 1970–74; Leader of the Opposition 1975–79; Prime Minister, First Lord of the Treasury and Minister for the Civil Service 1979–90. *Spokesman (Commons):* Opposition Front Bench Spokesman on: Pensions and National Insurance 1964, Housing and Land 1965–66, The Treasury 1966–67; Chief Opposition Front Bench Spokesman on Power and Member of the Shadow Cabinet 1967; Opposition Treasury Spokesman 1974. *Chancellor:* Chancellor, Buckingham University 1992–98; Chancellor, College of William and Mary, Williamsburg, Virginia 1993–. *Party Groups (General):* Leader of Conservative and Unionist Party 1975–90. *Miscellaneous:* Hon. President, The Bruges Group 1991–. *Honours:* PC 1970; OM 1990; LG 1995; Hon. Bencher 1975; Elected Honorary Master of the Bench of Gray's Inn 1983; Presidential Medal of Freedom (USA) 1991; Order of Good Hope (South Africa) 1991; Order of the White Lion (First Class) (Czech Republic) 1999. FRS 1983. Freedom, London Borough of Barnet 1980; Hon. Freedom: Falkland Islands 1983, City of London 1989; Freeman, City of Westminster 1991. Hon. Freeman, Worshipful Company of Grocers 1980. *Recreations:* Music, reading. *Clubs:* Carlton. *Name, Style and Title:* Raised to the peerage as Baroness Thatcher, of Kesteven in the County of Lincolnshire 1992. A Conservative. *Address:* The Rt Hon. the Baroness Thatcher, LG, OM, FRS, House of Lords, London, SW1A 0PW.

Dod *on* Disk

The Vacher Dod Parliamentary Database – configured for PC or Network

For further details please telephone the Westminster Office

020 7828 7256

THOMAS OF GRESFORD (Life Baron, UK), (Donald) Martin Thomas; cr. 1996; OBE 1982; QC 1979

Son of late Hywel Thomas and of Olwen Thomas. Born March 13, 1937; educated Grove Park Grammar School, Wrexham; Peterhouse, Cambridge (MA, LLB). Married 1961, Nan Thomas (née Kerr) (3 sons 1 daughter). *Career:* Solicitor, Wrexham 1961–66; Lecturer in Law 1966–68; Called to the Bar, Gray's Inn 1967, Bencher 1989; Barrister, Wales and Chester Circuit 1968–; Deputy Circuit Judge 1974–76; Recorder of the Crown Court 1976–; Deputy High Court Judge 1985–. *Spokesman:* Liberal Democrat Spokesman on Welsh Affairs. *Party Groups (General):* Vice-Chairman, Welsh Liberal Party 1967–69, Chairman 1969–74; President: Wrexham Liberal Association 1975–, Welsh Liberal Party 1977, 1978, 1979, Welsh Liberal Democrats 1993, Vice-President 1991–93. *Other:* Chairman, Marcher Sound 1991–, Vice-Chairman 1983–91. *Miscellaneous:* Contested (Liberal): West Flintshire 1964, 1966, 1970, Wrexham February and October 1974, 1979, 1983, 1987; Member, Criminal Injury Compensation Board 1985–93. *Honours:* OBE 1982. *Recreations:* Rugby football, rowing, golf, music, fishing. *Sportsclubs:* Wrexham Rugby. *Clubs:* Reform, Western (Glasgow). *Name, Style and Title:* Raised to the peerage as Baron Thomas of Gresford, of Gresford in the County Borough of Wrexham 1996. A Liberal Democrat. *Address:* The Lord Thomas of Gresford, OBE, QC, Glasfryn, Gresford, Wrexham, LL12 8RG *E-Mail:* thomasm@parliament.uk.

THOMAS OF GWYDIR (Life Baron, UK), Peter John Mitchell Thomas; cr. 1987; PC 1964; QC 1965

Son of late David Thomas, Solicitor. Born July 31, 1920; educated Epworth College, Rhyl; Jesus College, Oxford (MA). Married December 20, 1947, Frances Elizabeth Tessa (died 1985), daughter of late Basil Dean, CBE, Theatrical Producer (2 sons 2 daughters). *Armed Forces:* War Service in RAF (POW Germany 1941–45). *Career:* Called to the Bar, Middle Temple 1947; Master of the Bench 1971, Emeritus 1991; Deputy Chairman, Cheshire Quarter Sessions 1966–70; Denbighshire Quarter Sessions 1968–70; Recorder of Crown Courts 1974–88; An Arbitrator, International Chamber of Commerce Courts of Arbitration, Paris 1974–88. *House of Commons:* MP (Conservative) for: Conway 1951–66, Hendon South 1970–87; PPS to Solicitor-General 1954–59; Parliamentary Secretary to Ministry of Labour 1959–61; Parliamentary Under-Secretary of State, Foreign Office 1961–63; Minister of State for Foreign Affairs 1963–64; Secretary of State for Wales and Member of the Cabinet June 1970–74. *Spokesman (Commons):* Opposition Frontbench Spokesman on Foreign Affairs and Law 1964–66. *Party Groups (General):* Chairman, Conservative Party 1970–72; President, National Union of Conservative and Unionist Association 1974–76; National President, Conservative Friends of Israel 1984–91. *Special Interests:* Foreign Affairs. *Honours:* PC 1964. *Clubs:* Carlton. *Name, Style and Title:* Raised to the peerage as Baron Thomas of Gwydir, of Llanrwst in the County of Gwynedd 1987. A Conservative. *Address:* The Rt Hon. the Lord Thomas of Gwydir, QC, 37 Chester Way, London, SE11 4UR *Tel:* 020 7735 6047; Millicent Cottage, Elstead, Surrey, GU8 6HD *Tel:* 01252 702052.

THOMAS OF MACCLESFIELD (Life Baron, UK), Terence James Thomas; cr. 1997; CBE 1997

Son of late William Emrys Thomas, and of Mildred Evelyn Thomas. Born October 19, 1937; educated Queen Elizabeth Grammar School, Carmarthen, Dyfed; School of Management, Bath University (Postgraduate Diploma); Hon. DLitt, University of Salford 1996; Hon. Dr Business Administration, Manchester Metropolitan University 1998; Hon. Degree Business Management, Manchester Federal School of Business and Management. Married 1963, Lynda, daughter of William John Stevens (3 sons). *Career:* National Provincial Bank (later National Westminster) 1962–71; Market Research Manager, later National Sales Manager, The Joint Credit Card Company 1971–73; Marketing Manager, The Co-operative Bank plc 1973–77, Assistant General Manager, later Joint General Manager 1977–83, General Manager, Customer Services 1984–87, Executive Director 1984–88, Managing Director 1988–; Visiting Professor, University of Stirling (Postgraduate MBA course for Banking) 1988–91; Various Company Directorships including: Unity Trust Bank plc 1983–95, Co-operative Commercial Ltd 1985–87, Co-operative City Investments

Ltd 1988–90, Vector Investments Ltd 1992–95 (Chairman), Stanley Leisure Organisation plc 1994–98, Venture Technic (Cheshire) Ltd (Chairman), FI Group Shareholders Trust (Chairman); Rathbone CI 1997–98; Capita Group 1997–98; Chairman, The North West Development Agency 1998–. *Select Committees:* Member, Select Committees on: European Affairs, Monetary Policy of the Bank of England 1998–. *International Bodies (General):* President, International Co-operative Banking Association (ICBA) 1988–95. *Other:* Chief Examiner, Chartered Institute of Bankers 1983–85; Trustee, Board of UNICEF 1998; President, Society for Co-operative Studies; Chairman: North West Partnership, East Manchester Partnership, Sustainability North West; Fellow and Member, General Council of the Institute of Bankers; Member: British Invisibles European Committee (Bank of England appointment), The Parliamentary Reneweable and Sustainable Energy Group (PRASEG), Court of Governors, UMIST 1996–; Patron, Northern Friends of ARMS (Multiple Sclerosis Therapy Centre); Appeal Chairman, City of Manchester and District Macmillan Nurse Appeal. *Awards Granted:* Mancunian of the Year 1998. *Trusts, etc:* Patron, Macclesfield Museums Trust. *Honours:* CBE 1997. FCIB; CIMgt; MCIM. *Clubs:* Reform. *Name, Style and Title:* Raised to the peerage as Baron Thomas of Macclesfield, of Prestbury in the County of Cheshire 1997. Labour. *Address:* The Lord Thomas of Macclesfield, CBE, House of Lords, London, SW1A 0PW.

THOMAS OF SWYNNERTON (Life Baron, UK), Hugh Swynnerton Thomas; cr. 1981

Son of late Hugh Whitelegge Thomas, and of Margery Swynnerton. Born October 21, 1931; educated Sherborne; Queens' College, Cambridge; The Sorbonne. Married May 5, 1961, Hon. Vanessa Jebb, daughter of 1st Baron Gladwyn, GCMG, GCVO, CB (2 sons 1 daughter). *Career:* Professor of History, University of Reading 1966–76; Chairman, Centre for Policy Studies 1979–90; King Juan Carlos I Professor of Spanish Civilisation, University of New York (NYU) 1995–96; University Professors' Programme, Boston University 1996–. *Honours:* Order of Isabel la Católica (Spain); Order of the Aztec Eagle (Mexico). *Publications: The Spanish Civil War,* 1961, new edition 1976; *The Suez Affair,* 1967; *Cuba or The Pursuit of Freedom,* 1971; *John Strachey,* 1973; *Goya and the Third of May,* 1973; *An Unfinished History of the World,* 1979; *Havannah!,* 1984; *Armed Truce,* 1986; *Ever Closer Union: Britain's Destiny in Europe,* 1991; *The Conquest of Mexico,* 1993; *The Slave Trade,* 1997; *The Future of Europe,* 1997. *Recreations:* Walking. *Name, Style and Title:* Raised to the peerage as Baron Thomas of Swynnerton, of Notting Hill in Greater London 1981. A Liberal Democrat. *Address:* The Lord Thomas of Swynnerton, 29 Ladbroke Grove, London, W11 3BB *Tel:* 020 7727-2288.

THOMAS OF WALLISWOOD (Life Baroness, UK), Susan Petronella Thomas; cr. 1994; OBE 1989; DL

Daughter of John Arrow, and of Mrs Ebba Fordham. Born December 20, 1935; educated Cranborne Chase; Lady Margaret Hall, Oxford University. Married 1958, David Churchill Thomas, CMG (1 son 2 daughters) (separated). *Councils, Public Bodies:* Councillor, Surrey County Council 1985–97; Former Vice-Chairman of County Council, Chairman 1996–97, Chairman of Highways and Transport Committee 1993–97; Former Surrey County Representative, Association of County Councils; Former Member, East Surrey Community Health Council; Non-executive Director, East Surrey Hospital and Community Healthcare Trust 1992–96; DL, Surrey 1996; Member, Surrey Probation Committee 1997–. *Career:* National Economic Development Office 1971–74; Chief Executive, British Clothing Industries, Council for Europe 1974–78. *Spokesman:* Liberal Democrat Spokesman on Transport 1994–. *Select Committees:* Member, Select Committee on House of Lords' Offices 1997–. *All-Party:* Member, All-Party: Sex Equality Group 1997, Rail Freight Group, Cycling Group. *International Bodies (General):* Member, IPU. *Party Groups (General):* Has served on many Liberal and Liberal Democrat policy committees; Former President, Women Liberal Democrats; Member, Liberal International 1999–. *Other:* School Governor 1985–. *Miscellaneous:* Contested (Liberal Alliance) Mole Valley in 1983, 1987 General Elections; Contested (Liberal Democrat) Surrey in 1994 European Elections. *Honours:* OBE 1989. *Recreations:* Gardening, reading, ballet, theatre, travel. *Name, Style and Title:* Raised to the peerage as Baroness Thomas of Walliswood, of Dorking in the County of Surrey 1994. A Liberal Democrat. *Address:* The Baroness Thomas of Walliswood, OBE, DL, House of Lords, London, SW1A 0PW.

THOMSON OF MONIFIETH (Life Baron, UK), George Morgan Thomson; cr. 1977; KT 1981; PC 1966

Son of late James Thomson, of Dundee. Born January 16, 1921; educated Grove Academy, Broughty Ferry; Hon. LLD, Dundee; Hon. D Litt, Herriot Watt. Married December 23, 1948, Grace, daughter of Cunningham Jenkins, of Glasgow (2 daughters). *Trades Union:* Member, NUJ. *Armed Forces:* RAF 1941–46. *Councils, Public Bodies:* DL, Kent 1992–98. *Career:* Journalist and Former Editor of "Forward"; Joint Chairman, Council for Education in the Commonwealth 1960–64; Chairman, David Davies Institute of International Affairs 1971–77; UK Commissioner for Regional Policy to EEC Brussels 1973–77; Chairman, British Council European Movement 1977–79; Chairman, Advertising Standards Authority 1977–80; First Crown Estate Commissioner 1977–80; Chairman, Independent Broadcasting Authority 1981–88; Deputy Chairman, Woolwich Building Society 1988–91; Member, Committee on Standards in Public Life 1994–97. *House of Commons:* Contested (Labour) Glasgow Hillhead Division 1950; MP (Labour) Dundee East 1952–72; Minister of State, Foreign Office 1964–66; Chancellor of the Duchy of Lancaster 1966–67; Secretary of State for Commonwealth Affairs 1967–68; Minister without Portfolio 1968-October 1969; Chancellor of the Duchy of Lancaster and Deputy Foreign Secretary 1969–70; Shadow Defence Minister 1970–72. *Spokesman (Commons):* Spokesman on Colonial Affairs 1957–64. *Chancellor:* Chancellor, Heriot-Watt University 1977–91. *Spokesman:* Liberal Democrat Party Spokesman on Broadcasting and Foreign Affairs in the House of Lords 1989–97. *Select Committees:* Chairman, Lords Select Committee on Broadcasting 1993–97. *All-Party:* Chairman, Scottish Peers Association 1996–98. *Party Groups (General):* Chairman, Labour Committee for Europe 1972–73. *Other:* Chairman: Franco-British Council 1977–80, Centre European Agricultural Studies 1978–82; European Television and Film Forum 1989–91. *Trusts, etc:* Trustee, Thomson Foundation 1978–; Trustee, Leeds Castle Foundation 1978–, Chairman 1994–; Pilgrim Trustee 1977–97; History of Advertising Trust 1985–. *Honours:* PC 1966; KT 1981. FRSE; Fellow of the Royal Television Society. Freeman: Monfieth 1967, Dundee 1973. *Recreations:* Swimming, cycling. *Name, Style and Title:* Raised to the peerage as Baron Thomson of Monifieth, of Monifieth in the District of the City of Dundee 1977. A Liberal Democrat. *Address:* The Rt Hon. the Lord Thomson of Monifieth, KT, Leeds Castle Foundation, Maidstone, Kent, ME17 1PL *Tel:* 01622 880656; House of Lords, London, SW1A 0PW *Tel:* House of Lords 020 7219 6718.

THORNTON (Life Baroness, UK), Dorothea Glenys Thornton; cr. 1998

Daughter of Peter and Jean Thornton, of Bradford, West Yorkshire. Born October 16, 1952; educated Thornton Secondary School, Bradford; LSE (BSc Economics 1976). Married February 1977, John Carr, of Holmfirth, West Yorkshire. *Trades Union:* Member, GMB. *Career:* Former General Secretary, Fabian Society; Former Public Affairs Adviser, CWS; Freelance Public Affairs Consultant. *Select Committees:* Member: Select Committee on European Communities Sub Committee C (Environment, Public Health and Consumer Protection) 1999–, Special Joint (both Houses) Select Committee on Local Government Legislation on Elected Mayors 1999. *All-Party:* Member, All-Party Homlessness and Housing Need Group. *Party Groups (General):* Chairman, The Greater London Labour Party 1986–91. *Special Interests:* Children, London, Media. *Recreations:* Canoeing, hill-walking, Star Trek. *Name, Style and Title:* Raised to the peerage as Baroness Thornton, of Manningham in the County of West Yorkshire 1998. Labour. *Address:* The Baroness Thornton, House of Lords, London, SW1A 0PW *E-Mail:* thorntong@parliament.uk.

TOMBS (Life Baron, UK), Francis Leonard Tombs; cr. 1990; Kt 1978

Son of late Joseph and Jane Tombs. Born May 17, 1924; educated Elmore Green School, Walsall; Birmingham College of Technology (BSc); Hon. LLD, Strathclyde 1976; Hon. DTech, Loughborough 1979; Hon. DSc: Aston 1979, Lodz (Poland) 1980, Cranfield 1985, Bradford 1986, City 1986; Hon. DSc(Eng), QUB 1986; Hon. DSc: Surrey 1988, Nottingham 1989; Hon. DEd, CNAA 1989; Hon. DSc: Warwick 1990, Cambridge 1990; DUniv, Strathclyde 1991. Married February 26, 1949, Marjorie, daughter of Albert Evans (3 daughters). *Career:* GEC 1939–45; Birmingham Corporation 1946–47; British Electricity Authority, Midlands, then Central Electricity Authority, Merseyside and North Wales 1948–57; General Manager, GEC, Erith 1958–67; Director and General Manager, James Howden and Co., Glasgow 1967–68; Successively Director of Engineering, Deputy Chairman and Chairman, South of Scotland Electricity Board 1969–77; Chairman, The Electricity Council 1977–80; Chairman: The Weir Group 1981–83, Turner and Newall 1982–89; Director: N M Rothschild & Sons Ltd 1981–94, Shell UK 1983–94; Chairman, Rolls-Royce plc 1985–92, Director 1982–92. *Chancellor:* Chancellor, Strathclyde University 1991–98. *Select Committees:* Member, House of Lords Select Committee on Science and Technology 1992–94, 1997–; Chairman, House of Lords Select Committee on Sustainable Development 1994–95; Chairman, Sub Committee II (Management of Nuclear Waste) 1998–99; Member, Select Committee on Science and Technology Sub-Committee II (Science and Society) 1999–. *Other:* Chairman, The Molecule Theatre of Science 1985–92, President 1992–94. *Trusts, etc:* Chairman, Brooklands Museum Trust 1993–. *Honours:* Kt 1978. FEng 1977; Hon. FIChemE 1985; Hon. FICE 1986; Hon. FIProdE 1986; Hon. FIMechE 1989; Hon. FIEE 1991; Hon. FRAeS 1995. Liveryman, Goldsmiths' Company 1981–, Prime Warden 1994–95. *Special Interests:* Science, Technology, Engineering. *Recreations:* Golf, music. *Name, Style and Title:* Raised to the peerage as Baron Tombs, of Brailes in the County of Warwickshire 1990. A Cross-Bencher. *Address:* The Lord Tombs, FEng, House of Lords, London, SW1A 0PW; Honington Lodge, Honington, Shipston-on-Stour, Warwickshire, CV36 5AA *Tel:* 01608 661437.

TOMLINSON (Life Baron, UK), John Edward Tomlinson; cr. 1998

Son of Frederick and Doris Tomlinson. Born August 1, 1939; educated Westminster City School; Co-operative College, Loughborough; Brunel University; Warwick University (MA). *Trades Union:* Member, TGWU. *Career:* Sometime Senior Lecturer in Industrial Relations and Management, Solihull College of Technology; Head of Research for AUEW 1968–70; MEP for Birmingham West 1984–99: Socialist Group Spokesman on: Budgetary Control Committee 1984–99; Member, Budgets Committee 1984–99; Member, Budgetary Control Committee 1984–99, Vice-Chairman 1997–99; Member, Delegation for South Asia and SAARC 1989–92, 1994–97, Substitute 1992–94; Substitute, Committee on Development and Cooperation 1994–97; Chairman, Temporary Committee Inquiry on Community Transit System 1996; Substitute, Committee on External Economic Relations 1997–99; Member, EU/Latvia Joint Parliamentary Delegation 1997–99; President, EP Intergroup on Sport. *House of Commons:* MP (Lab) for Meriden 1974–79; PPS to the Prime Minister 1975–76; Parliamentary Under-Secretary of State, Foreign and Commonwealth Office 1976–79; Parliamentary Secretary, Ministry of Overseas Development 1977–79. *Select Committees:* Member, Select Committee on European Communities 1998–. *Other:* Vice-President, The Hansard Society. *Trusts, etc:* Trustee, Industry and Parliament Trust. *Special Interests:* Finance, Europe, International Development, Foreign Policy. *Recreations:* Walking, reading, sport. *Clubs:* West Bromwich Labour. *Name, Style and Title:* Raised to the peerage as Baron Tomlinson, of Walsall in the County of West Midlands 1998. Labour. *Address:* The Lord Tomlinson, House of Lords, London, SW1A 0PW.

TOPE (Life Baron, UK), Graham Norman Tope; cr. 1994; CBE 1991

Son of late Leslie Tope. Born November 30, 1943; educated Whitgift School, South Croydon. Married July 22, 1972, Margaret, daughter of Frank East (2 sons). *Armed Forces:* London Scottish TA 1962–64. *Councils, Public Bodies:* London Borough of Sutton: Councillor 1974–, Leader of the Liberal (later Liberal Democrat) Group 1974–99, Leader of Opposition 1984–86, Leader of the Council 1986–99. *Career:* Former Company Secretary and Insurance Manager; Deputy General Secretary, Voluntary Action Camden 1975–90; Chairman, Community Investors Ltd 1995–98. *House of Commons:* MP (Liberal) Sutton and Cheam December 1972-February 1974; Contested (Liberal) Sutton and Cheam February and October 1974. *Spokesman (Commons):* Spokesman on The Environment and Northern Ireland 1973–74. *Whip:* Assistant Whip 1998–. *Spokesman:* Liberal Democrat Party Spokesman on Education 1994–. *Select Committees:* Member, House of Lords Select Committee on Relations between Central and Local Government 1995–96. *All-Party:* Member, All-Party London Group 1994–; Joint Vice-Chairman, All-Party Libraries Group 1998–. *International Bodies:* EU Committee of the Regions: Member 1994–, Vice-Chair, UK Delegation 1996–, Bureau Member 1996–; President (Leader), ELDR (Liberal) Group 1998–; Member, Council of Europe, Congress of Local and Regional Authorities in Europe 1996–. *Party Groups*

(General): Vice-Chairman, National League of Young Liberals 1971–73, President 1973–75; Member, Liberal Party National Council 1970–76; Executive Committee of London Liberal Party 1981–84; President, London Liberal Democrats 1991–. *Miscellaneous:* Member, London Boroughs Association Policy and Finance Committee 1986–95, Chair 1994–95; Member, Association of London Goverment Leaders' Committee 1995–; Deputy Leader of Opposition, Association of Metropolitan Authorities 1995–97; Member, London Fire and Civil Defence Authority 1995–97; Vice-President, Local Government Association 1997–; Vice-Chair, Association of London Government 1997–. *Honours:* CBE 1991. Freeman, City of London 1998. Member, Needle Makers Company. *Publications:* Joint Author of *Liberals and the Community,* 1974. *Special Interests:* Local Government, Education, Environment, Europe. *Name, Style and Title:* Raised to the peerage as Baron Tope, of Sutton in the London Borough of Sutton 1994. A Liberal Democrat. *Address:* The Lord Tope, CBE, 88 The Gallop, Sutton, Surrey, SM2 5SA *Tel:* 020 8770 7269 *Fax:* 020 8770 7269; House of Lords, London, SW1A 0PW *Tel:* House of Lords 020 8219 3098 *E-Mail:* Grahamtope.sutton@dial.pipex.com.

TORDOFF (Life Baron, UK), Geoffrey Johnson Tordoff; cr. 1981

Son of late Stanley Acomb Tordoff. Born October 11, 1928; educated Manchester Grammar School; Manchester University. Married October 22, 1953, Mary Patricia, daughter of late Thomas Swarbrick (2 sons 3 daughters). *Career:* Former: Marketing Executive, Shell Chemicals, Public Affairs Manager (Chemicals), Shell UK; Hon. President, British Youth Council 1986–92; Chairman, Middle East Committee, Refugee Council 1990–94; Member, Press Complaints Commission 1995–. *House of Lords:* Principal Deputy Chairman of Committees 1994–; A Deputy Speaker of the House of Lords. *Whip:* Deputy Whip 1983–84; Chief Whip 1984–88; Liberal Democrat Chief Whip 1988–94. *Spokesman:* Liberal Democrat Transport Spokesman 1988–94. *Select Committees:* Chairman, Select Committee on the European Communities 1994–; Member, Select Committee on House of Lords' Offices 1997–. *Party Groups (General):* Chairman: Liberal Party Assembly Committee 1974–76, Liberal Party 1976–79, Liberal Party Campaigns and Elections Committee 1980–82; President, Liberal Party 1983–84. *Miscellaneous:* Contested (Liberal): Northwich 1964, Knutsford 1966, 1970 General Elections. *Special Interests:* Foreign Affairs, Europe. *Clubs:* National Liberal. *Name, Style and Title:* Raised to the peerage as Baron Tordoff, of Knutsford in the County of Cheshire 1981. A Liberal Democrat. *Address:* The Lord Tordoff, House of Lords, London, SW1A 0PW *Tel:* House of Lords 020 7219 6613 *E-Mail:* tordoffg@parliament.uk.

TREFGARNE (2nd Baron, UK), David Garro Trefgarne; cr. 1947; PC 1989

Son of 1st Baron. Born March 31, 1941. Succeeded his father 1960; educated Haileybury; Princeton University. Married November 9, 1968, Hon. Rosalie Lane, daughter of Baron Lane of Horsell (*qv*) (2 sons 1 daughter). *Career:* Non-Exec Director, Siebe plc 1991–98; Chairman, Engineering and Marine Training Authority (EMTA) 1994–. *House of Lords:* Parliamentary Under-Secretary of State: Department of Trade 1980–81, Foreign and Commonwealth Office 1981–82, Department of Health and Social Security 1982–83, for the Armed Forces June 1983–85; Minister of State: for Defence Support 1985–86, for Defence Procurement 1986–89, Department of Trade and Industry (Minister for Trade) 1989–90; An elected hereditary peer 1999–. *Whip:* Opposition Whip House of Lords 1977–1979; A Lord in Waiting (Government Whip) 1979–80. *All-Party:* Vice-Chairman, All-Party Defence Study Group 1993–. *Other:* President: Mechanical and Metal Trades Confederation (METCOM) 1990–, Governor, Guildford School of Acting 1992–; Life Governor and Member of Council, Haileybury 1993–; Hon. President, British Association of Aviation Consultants 1993–; Vice-Chairman, Army Cadet Force 1993–. *Awards Granted:* Awarded Royal Aero Club Bronze Medal 1963. *Trusts, etc:* Member, Mary Rose Trust. *Honours:* PC 1989. *Special Interests:* Aviation. *Recreations:* Photography. *Clubs:* White's. *Heir:* His son, Hon. George Garro Trefgarne. Born January 4, 1970. A Conservative. *Address:* The Rt Hon. the Lord Trefgarne, House of Lords, London, SW1A 0PW.

TROTMAN (Life Baron, UK), Alexander James Trotman; cr. 1999; Kt 1996

Son of late Charles and Agnes Trotman. Born July 22, 1933; educated Boroughmuir School, Edinburgh; Michigan State University, USA (MBA); Hon. Doctorate, University of Edinburgh. Married 1963, Valerie Anne Edgar. *Armed Forces:* Flying Officer Navigator, Royal Air Force 1951–55. *Career:* Various positions with Ford of Britain 1955–67; Director, Car Product Planning, Ford Europe 1967–69; Positions in Car Product Planning and Sales Planning Departments, Ford US 1969–75; Chief Car Planning Manager, Ford Motor Co 1975–79; Vice-President, European Truck Operations 1979–83; President: Ford Asia Pacific 1983–84, Ford of Europe 1984–88; Executive Vice-President, North American Automotive Operations 1989–93; President, Ford Automotive Group 1993; Chairman and Chief Executive Officer, Ford Motor Company 1993–98; Director: IBM Corporation 1995–, New York Stock Exchange 1996–, ICI UK 1997–. *Trusts, etc:* Trustee, Shakespeare Globe Trust. *Honours:* Kt 1996. *Clubs:* Royal Air Force. *Name, Style and Title:* Raised to the peerage as Baron Trotman, of Osmotherley in the County of North Yorkshire 1999. *Address:* The Lord Trotman, House of Lords, London, SW1A 0PW.

TRUMPINGTON (Life Baroness, UK), Jean Alys Barker; cr. 1980; PC 1992

Daughter of late Major Arthur Edward Campbell-Harris, MC and of Doris Marie Robson. Born October 23, 1922; educated privately in England and France; Hon. Fellow, Lucy Cavendish College, Cambridge 1980. Married March 18, 1954, William Alan (died 1988), son of late T. L. Barker, of Edinburgh (1 son). *Armed Forces:* Landgirl to the Rt Hon. David Lloyd George, MP, at Churt 1939–41; Naval Intelligence at Bletchley Park 1941–45. *Councils, Public Bodies:* Cambridge City Councillor 1963–73; Hon. City Councillor (Cambridge) 1975; Mayor of Cambridge 1971–72, Deputy Mayor 1972–73; Cambridgeshire County Councillor 1973–75; JP, Cambridgeshire 1972–82; South Westminster. *Career:* European Central Inland Transport Organization (in London and Paris) 1946–49; Secretary to the Viscount Hinchingbrooke, MP 1949–52; Copywriter in Advertising Agency, New York City 1952–54; Member: Board of Visitors of HM Prison, Pentonville 1975–81, Mental Health Review Tribunal 1975–1981; General Commissioner of Taxes 1975–83; United Kingdom representative to the United Nations Status of Women Commission 1979–81. *House of Lords:* Parliamentary Under-Secretary of State for Health and Social Security 1985–87; Parliamentary Secretary, Ministry of Agriculture, Fisheries and Food 1987–89; Minister of State 1989–92. *Whip:* Baroness in Waiting (Government Whip) 1983–1985, 1992–97. *Spokesman:* A Former Government Spokesman for: The Foreign Commonwealth Office 1983–85, Home Office 1983–85, Office of Public Service 1996–97, Department of National Heritage. *International Bodies (General):* Vice-President, International League for the Protection of Horses 1990–99. *Party Groups (General):* Chairman, Cambridge City Conservative Association 1969–71. *Other:* Member, Airline Users Committee 1973–80, Deputy Chairman 1977, Chairman 1979–80; President, Association of Heads of Independent Schools 1980–90; Steward, Folkestone Racecourse 1980–92. *Trusts, etc:* Member, Council and Executive Committee of the Animal Health Trust 1981–87. *Miscellaneous:* A Extra Baroness in Waiting to HM The Queen 1998–. *Honours:* PC 1992. Hon. Fellow, Royal College of Pathologists; Hon. Associate, Royal College of Veterinary Surgeons 1994; Hon. Member, British Veterinary Association. *Recreations:* Antiques, bridge, cookery, golf, needlepoint, racing. *Clubs:* Grillions, Farmers'. *Name, Style and Title:* Raised to the peerage as Baroness Trumpington, of Sandwich in the County of Kent 1980. A Conservative. *Address:* The Rt Hon. the Baroness Trumpington, House of Lords, London, SW1A 0PW.

TUGENDHAT (Life Baron, UK), Christopher (Samuel) Tugendhat; cr. 1993; Kt 1990

Son of late Dr Georg Tugendhat and Mrs Mairé Tugendhat. Born February 23, 1937; educated Ampleforth College; Gonville and Caius College, Cambridge; Hon. LLD, Bath University 1998. Married 1967, Julia Dobson (2 sons). *Armed Forces:* National Service 1955–57; Second Lieutenant, Essex Regiment 1956–57. *Career:* Journalist with *The Financial Times* 1960–70; Director: Sunningdale Oils 1971–76, Phillips Petroleum International (UK) Ltd 1972–76, EEC Commission: Member 1977–85, A Vice-President 1981–85; Director: National Westminster Bank 1985–91, The BOC Group 1985–96; Chairman, Civil Aviation Authority 1986–91; Director, Commercial Union Assurance 1988–91; Deputy Chairman, National Westminster Bank 1990–91; Director: LWT (Holdings) plc 1991–94, Eurotunnel plc 1991–; Chairman: Abbey National plc 1991–, Blue Circle Industries plc 1996–; Non-executive Director, Rio Tinto plc 1997–. *House of Commons:* MP (Conservative): Cities of London and Westminster 1970–74, City of London and Westminster South 1974–76. *Spokesman (Commons):* Deputy Spokesman on: Employment 1975, Foreign Affairs 1975–76. *Select Committees (Commons):* Member, Select Committee on The Nationalised Industries. *Chancellor:* Chancellor, University of Bath 1998–. *Other:* Chairman, The Royal Institute for International Affairs (Chatham House) 1986–95; Governor, Council of Ditchley Foundation 1986–; Chairman: Construction Industry Trust for Youth 1997, European Policy Forum 1997; Member, National Portrait Gallery Advisory Committee. *Honours:* Kt 1990. Freeman, City of London. *Publications:* Author of: *Oil: the biggest business*, 1968; *The Multinationals*, 1971; *Making Sense of Europe*, 1986; *Options for British Foreign Policy in the 1990s*, 1988 (jointly). *Recreations:* Family, reading, conversation. *Clubs:* Buck's, Anglo-Belgian. *Name, Style and Title:* Raised to the peerage as Baron Tugendhat, of Widdington in the County of Essex 1993. A Conservative. *Address:* The Lord Tugendhat, 35 Westbourne Park Road, London, W2 5QD.

TURNER OF CAMDEN (Life Baroness, UK), Muriel Turner; cr. 1985

Daughter of Edward Price. Born September 18, 1927; Hon. LLD, Leicester University 1991. Married 1955, Wing-Commander Reginald Turner, MC, DFC (died April 15, 1995). *Trades Union:* Assistant General Secretary, Association of Scientific, Technical and Managerial Staffs 1970–87; Member, TUC General Council 1980–87. *House of Lords:* A Deputy Chairman of Committees 1997–. *Spokesman:* Opposition Spokesman on: Social Security 1987–96, Employment 1987–96. *Select Committees:* Former Member, European Select Committee (Consumer Affairs); Co-opted Member, Select Committee on European Communities Sub-Committee F (Social Affairs, Education and Home Affairs) 1997–; Member, Select Committee on House of Lords' Offices 1997–98. *Other:* Council Member, Save The Children Fund 1991–98. *Miscellaneous:* Member: Equal Opportunities Commission 1982–88, Occupational Pensions Board 1977–93; Chair, PIA Ombudsman Council 1994–97. *Special Interests:* Employment, Social Security, Pensions. *Recreations:* Reading, music. *Clubs:* RAF. *Name, Style and Title:* Raised to the peerage as Baroness Turner of Camden, of Camden in Greater London 1985. Labour. *Address:* The Baroness Turner of Camden, 87 Canfield Gardens, London, NW6 3EA *Tel:* 020 7624 3561.

U

UDDIN (Life Baroness, UK), Pola Manzila Uddin; cr. 1998

Born 1959; educated Plashet School for Girls, Newham; University of North London (Diploma in Social Work). Married 1976, Kemar Uddin (4 sons 1 daughter). *Councils, Public Bodies:* Councillor, London Borough of Tower Hamlets 1990–98, Deputy Leader of Council 1994–96; Vice-Chair: Policy and Resources Committee, Finance Committee; Member: Education Committee 1990–98, Social Services Committee to 1998. *Career:* Administrator 1976–79; Youth and Community Worker, YWCA 1980–82; Liaison Officer, Tower Hamlets Social Services 1982–84; Manager: Tower Hamlets Womens' Health Project 1984–88, Asian Family Counselling Services 1989–90; Policy Officer, Domestic Violence 1990–91; Newham Social Services: Social Worker

1993–96; Manager 1996–97; Management Consultant 1998–. *All-Party:* Member, All-Party: Health Group, Education and Employment Group, Foreign and Commonwealth Affairs Group. *Other:* Member: British Council of Churches/Board of Social Responsibility, Community Health Council 1982–86, Joint Health and Social Services Consultative Council 1985–88, Race Equality Council; Health Authority Board Member, EOP Implementation Committee; School Governor 1994–98. *Trusts, etc:* Trustee, St Katherine's and Shadwell Trust 1990–95. *Special Interests:* Education, Health, Children, Local Government, Equal Opportunities, Disability, Foreign and Commonwealth Affairs. *Recreations:* Family, community work. *Name, Style and Title:* Raised to the peerage as Baroness Uddin, of Bethnal Green in the London Borough of Tower Hamlets 1998. Labour. *Address:* The Baroness Uddin, House of Lords, London, SW1A 0PW.

V

VARLEY (Life Baron, UK), Eric Graham Varley; cr. 1990; PC 1974; DL

Son of late Frank Varley. Born August 11, 1932; educated Secondary School; Chesterfield Technical College; Ruskin College, Oxford; Sheffield University (extra mural studies). Married 1955, Marjorie, daughter of Alfred Turner (1 son). *Trades Union:* Branch Secretary, NUM 1955–64, Member, Area Executive Committee, Derbyshire 1956–64. *Councils, Public Bodies:* DL, Derbyshire 1989. *Career:* Craftsman in mining industry 1947–64; Chairman and Chief Executive, Coalite Group 1984–89; A Regional Director, Lloyds Bank plc 1987–91; Director: Cuthelco Ltd 1989–99, Laxgate Ltd 1991–92; Member, Thyssen (UK) Ltd Advisory Board 1991–98. *House of Commons:* MP (Labour) Chesterfield 1964–84; PPS to the Prime Minister 1968–69; Minister of State, Ministry of Technology 1969–70; Secretary of State for: Energy 1974–75, Industry 1975–79. *Whip (Commons):* Assistant Government Whip 1967–68. *Spokesman (Commons):* Principal Opposition Spokesman on Employment 1979–83. *Select Committees:* Former Member: House of Lords European Communities Select Committee, Sub-committee A. *Party Groups (General):* Chairman, Trade Union Group of Labour MPs 1971–74; Treasurer, Labour Party 1981–83. *Other:* Vice President, Ashgate Hospital Chesterfield. *Miscellaneous:* Visiting Fellow, Nuffield College 1981–83. *Honours:* PC, 1974. *Recreations:* Reading, gardening, music, sport. *Name, Style and Title:* Raised to the peerage as Baron Varley, of Chesterfield in the County of Derbyshire 1990. Labour. *Address:* The Rt Hon. the Lord Varley, DL, House of Lords, London, SW1A 0PW.

VINCENT OF COLESHILL (Life Baron, UK), Richard Frederick Vincent; cr. 1996; GBE 1990; KCB 1984; DSO 1972

Son of late Frederick Vincent and Frances Elizabeth (née Coleshill). Born August 23, 1931; educated Aldenham School; Royal Military College of Science; Hon. DSc, Cranfield 1985; Fellow, Imperial College of Science, Technology and Medicine 1996; Hon. Fellow, City and Guilds of London Institute. Married, 1955, Jean, daughter of late Kenneth Stewart (1 son 1 daughter and 1 son deceased). *Armed Forces:* Commissioned, Royal Artillery, National Service 1951, Germany 1951–55; Gunnery Staff 1959; Radar Research Establishment, Malvern 1960–61; BAOR 1962, Technical Staff Training 1963–64; Staff College 1965; Commonwealth Brigade, Malaysia 1966–68; Ministry of Defence 1968–70; Commanded 12th Light Air Defence Regiment, Germany, UK and Northern Ireland 1970–72; Instructor, Staff College 1972–73; Greenlands Staff College, Henley 1974; Military Director of Studies, Royal Military College of Science 1974–75; Commanded 19th Airportable Brigade 1975–77; Royal College of Defence Studies 1978; Deputy Military Secretary 1979–80; Commandant, Royal Military College of Science 1980–83; Colonel Commandant, REME 1981–87; Hon. Colonel 100 (Yeomanry) Field Regiment RA (TA) 1982–91; Master General of the Ordnance, Ministry of Defence 1983–87; Colonel Commandant, RA 1983– Hon. Colonel 12th Air Defence Regiment 1987–91; Vice-Chief, Defence Staff 1987–91, Chief 1991–92; Chairman, Military Committee, NATO 1993–96; Master Gunner, St James's Park 1996–. *Career:* Director: Vickers Defence Systems 1996–, Royal Artillery Museums Ltd; Chairman: Imperial College of Science,

Technology and Medicine 1996–, Hunting Defence Ltd 1996–, Hunting Engineering Ltd 1998–, Hunting – BRAE 1998. *Chancellor:* Chancellor, Cranfield University 1998–. *Other:* Member: Court, Cranfield Institute of Technology 1981–83, Advisory Council, Royal Military College of Science 1983–91; President: Army Ski-ing Association 1983–87, Combined Services Winter Sports Association 1983–90; Governor, Aldenham School 1987–; Kermit Roosevelt Lecturer 1988–; Governor, Ditchley Foundation 1992–; Vice-President, Defence Manufacturers Association 1996–; Chairman, Imperial College of Science, Technology and Medicine 1996–; Member: Royal United Service Institute for Defence Studies, Court of Greenwich University 1997–, Patron: Inspire, Aldenham 400 Appeal; Vice-President, Officers' Pension Society; President, Council of Military Education Committees. *Miscellaneous:* Visiting Fellow, Australian College of Defence and Strategic Studies 1995–; Member, Commission on Britain and Europe (Royal Institute of International Affairs) 1996–98; Adviser to Secretary of State on The Strategic Defence Review 1997–98. *Honours:* DSO 1972; KCB 1984; GBE 1990; Jordanian Order of Military Merit 1992; Commander, US Legion of Merit 1993. FRAeS 1990; FIMechE 1990; FIC 1996. Freeman, City of London 1992. Member, The Guild of Freemen of the City of London; Freeman, Worshipful Company of Wheelwrights 1997. *Publications:* Has contributed to military journals and publications. *Clubs:* Army and Navy, Royal Scots, Grillions. *Name, Style and Title:* Raised to the peerage as Baron Vincent of Coleshill, of Shrivenham in the County of Oxfordshire 1996. A Cross-Bencher. *Address:* Field Marshal The Lord Vincent of Coleshill, GBE, KCB, DSO, c/o The Midland Bank, The Commons, High Street, Shaftesbury, Dorset, SP7 8JX.

VINSON (Life Baron, UK), Nigel Vinson; cr. 1985; LVO 1979; DL

Son of late Ronald Vinson, farmer. Born January 27, 1931; educated Nautical College, Pangbourne. Married 1972, Yvonne, daughter of Dr Olaf Collin (3 daughters). *Armed Forces:* Lieutenant, Queen's Royal Regiment 1948–50. *Councils, Public Bodies:* DL, Northumberland 1990. *Career:* Founder, Plastic Coatings Ltd 1952; Director, Sugar Board 1968–75; Member: Crafts Advisory Committee 1971–77, Design Council 1973–80; Director, British Airports Authority 1973–; Co-Founder, Centre for Policy Studies 1974–80; Member: CBI Grand Council 1975–, President's Committee 1979–83; Deputy Chairman, CBI Smaller Firms Council 1979–84; Chairman, The 'Rural Development Commission 1980–90; Director, Barclays Bank UK 1982–87; Member, Industry Year Steering Committee, Royal Society of Arts, Chairman 1985; Deputy Chairman, Electra Investment Trust 1990–98. *Select Committees:* Former Member, Select Committee on Pollution; Member, Select Committee on Monetary Policy of the Bank of England 1998–. *Other:* Hon. Director, Queen's Silver Jubilee Appeal 1976–78; Member, Northumbrian National Parks and Countryside Committee 1977–87; President, Industrial Participation Association 1979–90; Member, Foundation of Science and Technology 1991–96. *Awards Granted:* Queen's Award to Industry 1971. *Trusts, etc:* Member, Regional Committee, National Trust 1977–84; Chairman, Trustees of Institute of Economic Affairs 1988–95; Trustee, St George's House, Windsor 1990–96. *Honours:* LVO 1979. CBIM; FRSA. *Publications:* Author of *Personal Pensions for All.* *Special Interests:* Small Businesses, De-Regulation, Tax, Pensions. *Recreations:* Objets d'art, farming, horses. *Clubs:* Boodle's. *Name, Style and Title:* Raised to the peerage as Baron Vinson, of Roddam Dene in the County of Northumberland 1985. A Conservative. *Address:* The Lord Vinson, LVO, DL, 34 Kynance Mews, London, SW7 4QR *Tel:* 01668 217230.

VIVIAN (6th Baron, UK), Nicholas Crespigny Laurence Vivian; cr. 1841; 6th Bt of Truro (UK) 1828

Son of 5th Baron. Born December 11, 1935. Succeeded his father 1991; educated Eton; Madrid University. Married 1st, 1960, Catherine Joyce, daughter of late James Kenneth Hope, CBE, DL, of West Park, Lanchester, Co. Durham (1 son 1 daughter) (marriage dissolved 1972), married 2nd, 1972, Carol, daughter of late Frederick Alan Martineau, MBE, of Valley End House, Chobham, Surrey (2 daughters). *Armed Forces:* Commissioned 3rd Carabiniers (Prince of Wales's Dragoon Guards) 1955; Royal Scots Dragoon Guards (Carabiniers and Greys) 1971; Commanded Independent Squadron, Royal Scots Dragoon Guards 1973; Principal Staff Officer to Commander British Contingent, UNFI-CYP 1975–76; Lieutenant Colonel, Commanding Officer, 16th/5th The Queen's Royal Lancers 1976–79; MoD Defence Intelligence Staff 1979–81; Colonel, General Staff Officer, Future Anti-Armour Study, MoD 1982–84; Chief of Staff and Deputy Commander, Land Forces,

Cyprus 1984–87; Brigadier; Commander, British Communication Zone (North West Europe, Netherlands, Belgium and North West France) 1987–90; Retired in rank of Brigadier 1990. *House of Lords:* An elected hereditary peer 1999–. *Select Committees:* Member, Joint Committee on Statutory Instruments 1997–. *All-Party:* Hon. Secretary, All-Party Defence Study Group. *International Bodies (General):* Member, RUSI. *Other:* Commissioner, Royal Hospital, Chelsea. *Trusts, etc:* Special Trustee, Westminster and Roehampton Hospitals. *Special Interests:* Defence, United Nations, Drug Abuse, Terrorism, Cyprus, Cornwall. *Clubs:* White's, Cavalry and Guards. *Heir:* His son, Hon. Charles Crespigny Hussey Vivian, born December 20, 1966. A Conservative. *Address:* The Lord Vivian, House of Lords, London, SW1A 0PW.

W

WADDINGTON (Life Baron, UK), David Charles Waddington; cr. 1990; GCVO 1994; PC 1987; QC 1971; DL

Son of late Charles Waddington, JP. Born August 2, 1929; educated Sedbergh; Hertford College, Oxford. Married December 20, 1958, Gillian Rosemary, daughter of late Alan Green, CBE (3 sons 2 daughters). *Armed Forces:* Second Lieutenant, 12th Royal Lancers 1951–53; Captain, Duke of Lancaster's Yeomanry 1953–60. *Councils, Public Bodies:* DL, Lancashire 1991–. *Career:* Called to Bar, Gray's Inn 1951; Bencher 1985; Recorder of the Crown Court 1972; Governor and Commander-in-Chief, Bermuda 1992–97. *House of Commons:* Contested (Conservative): Farnworth 1955, Nelson and Colne 1964, Heywood and Royton 1966; MP (Conservative) for: Nelson and Colne 1968–74, Clitheroe 1979–83, Ribble Valley 1983–90; Parliamentary Under-Secretary of State, Department of Employment 1981–83; Minister of State, Home Office 1983–87; Parliamentary Secretary to HM Treasury and Government Chief Whip 1987–89; Secretary of State for the Home Department 1989–90. *Whip (Commons):* A Lord Commissioner of HM Treasury (Government Whip) 1979–81. *House of Lords:* Lord Privy Seal and Leader of the House of Lords 1990–92. *Select Committees:* Member, Select Committee on Parliamentary Privilege (Joint Committee) 1997–. *Party Groups (General):* President, Oxford University Conservative Association 1950; Chairman, Clitheroe Constituency Young Conservatives 1953. *Honours:* PC 1987; GCVO 1994. *Special Interests:* Legal Affairs, Textile Industry, Lancashire. *Recreations:* Sailing. *Name, Style and Title:* Raised to the peerage as Baron Waddington, of Read in the County of Lancashire 1990. A Conservative. *Address:* The Rt Hon. the Lord Waddington, GCVO, DL, QC, House of Lords, London, SW1A 0PW; Stable House, Sabden, Nr Clitheroe, Lancashire, BB7 9HP *E-Mail:* waddingtond@parliament.uk.

WADE OF CHORLTON (Life Baron, UK), William Oulton Wade; cr. 1990; Kt 1982

Son of late Samuel Norman Wade, farmer, and late Joan Ferris Wade (née Wild). Born December 24, 1932; educated Birkenhead School; Queen's University, Belfast. Married May 9, 1959, Gillian Margaret, daughter of Desmond Leete, of Buxton, Derbyshire (1 son 1 daughter). *Councils, Public Bodies:* JP, Cheshire 1965; Councillor, Cheshire County Council 1973–77. *Career:* Farmer and Cheesemaster; President, North West Industrialists' Council; Chairman, Cheese Export Council 1982–84; Member, Food From Britain Export Council 1984–88; Chairman: William Wild and Son (Mollington) Ltd, Enterprise Business Solutions; Director: Murray Vernon Holdings Ltd, Murray Vernon Limited, Cartmel PR Limited, John Wilman Ltd; Chairman, NIMTECH; President, Campus Ventures Ltd. *Select Committees:* Member, European Committee D; Former Member: Science and Technology Committee Biotechnology Sub-Committee 1993, Committee on Relationship between Central and Local Government 1995–96. *International Bodies (General):* UK Representative to The International Business Advisory Council (IBAC) of UNIDO. *Party Groups (General):* Chairman, North West Area Conservative Association 1976–81; Member, National Union Executive Committee 1975–90; Joint Hon. Treasurer, Conservative Party 1982–90. *Other:* President: CHPA, Federation of Economic Development Authorities. *Trusts, etc:* Chairman: Cheshire Historic Churches Trust 1993–, Chester Heritage Trust 1994–, The Christie Hospital Against Cancer

Centenary Appeal. *Miscellaneous:* Chairman, Rural Economy Group. *Honours:* Kt 1982. Freeman, City of London 1980. Member, Worshipful Company of Farmers. *Special Interests:* Food Industry, Agriculture, Industry, Transport, Planning, Technology. *Recreations:* Shooting, reading, farming. *Clubs:* The City (Chester), Chester Grosvenor. *Name, Style and Title:* Raised to the peerage as Baron Wade of Chorlton, of Chester in the County of Cheshire 1990. A Conservative. *Address:* The Lord Wade of Chorlton, House of Lords, London, SW1A 0PW.

WAKEFIELD (11th Bishop of), Nigel Simeon McCulloch

Son of late Pilot Officer Kenneth McCulloch, RAFVR, and of Audrey McCulloch. Born January 17, 1942. Born Crosby, Liverpool; educated Liverpool College; Selwyn College, Cambridge (Kitchener Scholar, BA 1964, MA 1969); Cuddesdon College, Oxford. Married 1974, Celia Hume, daughter of Canon H. L. Townshend (2 daughters). *Career:* Ordained 1966; Curate of Ellesmere Port 1966–70; Chaplain of Christ's College, Cambridge 1970–73; Director of Theological Studies, Christ's College, Cambridge 1970–75; Diocesan Missioner, Norwich Diocese 1973–78; Rector of St Thomas' and St Edmund's, Salisbury 1978–86; Archdeacon of Sarum 1979–86; Prebendary of: Ogbourne, Salisbury Cathedral 1979–86, Wanstrow, Wells Cathedral 1986–92;
Bishop Suffragan of Taunton 1986–92; Canon Emeritus, Salisbury Cathedral 1989; Member, House of Bishops, General Synod of Church of England 1990–; Bishop of Wakefield 1992–; Chairman: Church of England Communications Unit 1993–99, Church of England Mission, Evangelism and Renewal Committee 1990–99; Took his seat in the House of Lords 1997; Lord High Almoner to HM The Queen 1997–. *All-Party:* Member, All-Party Drugs Misuse Group. *Other:* Council Member, Royal School of Church Music 1984–; Chaplain, St John Council: Somerset 1987–91, West and South Yorkshire 1991–; Chairman, Somerset County Scout Association 1988–92; President: Central Yorkshire Scouts 1992–, CALCB 1997–2000. *Trusts, etc:* Chairman, Sandford St Martin Trust 1999–. *Publications: A Gospel to Proclaim,* 1992; *Barriers to Belief,* 1995. *Special Interests:* Broadcasting and Communications. *Recreations:* Music, walking in the Lake District. *Clubs:* Athenaeum. *Address:* The Rt Rev. the Lord Bishop of Wakefield, Bishop's Lodge, Woodthorpe Lane, Wakefield, West Yorkshire, WF2 6JL.

WAKEHAM (Life Baron, UK), John Wakeham; cr. 1992; PC 1983; DL

Son of late Major Walter John Wakeham. Born June 22, 1932; educated Charterhouse; Hon. PhD, Anglia Polytechnic University 1992; Hon. DUniv, Brunel University 1998. Married 1st, September 9, 1965, Anne Roberta (died 1984), daughter of late H. E. Bailey (2 sons), married 2nd, July 19, 1985, Alison Ward, MBE, daughter of Venerable Edwin Ward, LVO, of Alresford, Hants (1 son). *Armed Forces:* National Service 1955–57, commissioned Royal Artillery. *Councils, Public Bodies:* JP, Inner London 1972; DL, Hampshire 1997. *Career:* Chartered Accountant; Non-Executive Director: British and West plc 19⊂ ─, Enron Corporation 1994–; Director, N. M. Rothschild & Sons 1995–; Non-Executive Chairman: Kalon 1995–, Vosper Thorneycroft 1995–;
Chairman, Press Complaints Commission 1995–; Chairman, Michael Page Group 1995–97, President 1997–; Chairman, British Horseracing Board 1996–98. *House of Commons:* Contested (Conservative): Coventry East 1966, Putney 1970 General Elections; MP (Conservative) for: Maldon 1974–83, South Colchester and Maldon 1983–92; Parliamentary Under-Secretary of State, Department of Industry 1981–82; Minister of State, HM Treasury 1982–83; Lord Privy Seal and Leader of the House of Commons 1987–88; Lord President of the Council and Leader of the House of Commons 1988–89; Secretary of State for Energy 1989–92; Given additional responsibility for co-ordinating the development of the presentation of Government policies 1990–92. *Whip (Commons):* Assistant Government Whip 1979–81; Lord Commissioner of HM Treasury January-September 1981; Parliamentary Secretary, HM Treasury and Government Chief Whip 1983–87. *Chancellor:* Chancellor, Brunel University 1997–. *House of Lords:* Lord Privy Seal and Leader of the House of Lords 1992–94. *Party Groups (General):* Chairman, Carlton Club 1992–98. *Other:* Member, Governing Body, Charterhouse 1986–; Governor, Sutton's Hospital, Charterhouse 1992–; Governor, St Swithun's School 1994–; President: GamCare 1997–, Brendoncare Foundation 1998–, Printers' Charitable Corporation 1998–; Chairman: Alexandra Rose Day 1998–, Cothill House 1998–. *Trusts, etc:* Trustee, HMS Warrior 1860 1997; Trustee and

Committee of Management, RNLI 1995–. *Miscellaneous:* Chairman, Royal Commission on the Reform of the House of Lords 1999. *Honours:* PC 1983. FCA. *Recreations:* Sailing, farming, racing, reading. *Clubs:* Buck's, Carlton, St Stephen's Constitutional, Garrick, Royal Yacht Squadron (Cowes). *Name, Style and Title:* Raised to the peerage as Baron Wakeham, of Maldon in the County of Essex 1992. A Conservative. *Address:* The Rt Hon. the Lord Wakeham, DL, House of Lords, London, SW1A 0PW *Tel:* House of Lords 020 7219 3162.

WALDEGRAVE OF NORTH HILL (Life Baron, UK), William Arthur Waldegrave; cr. 1999; PC 1990

Son of 12th Earl Waldegrave, KG, GCVO, TD, DL. Born August 15, 1946; educated Eton; Corpus Christi College, Oxford (Open Scholar, 1st Cl Lit Hum) (President of Union); Harvard University; Fellow, All Souls, Oxford 1971–86, 1999–. Married July 25, 1977, Caroline, daughter of Major and Mrs R. Burrows, of Tunbridge Wells, Kent (1 son 3 daughters). *Councils, Public Bodies:* JP, Inner London Juvenile Court 1975–79. *Career:* Member: Central Policy Review Staff, Cabinet Office 1971–73, Political Staff at 10 Downing Street 1973–74; Leader of Opposition's Office 1974–75; With GEC Ltd 1975–81; Director: Bristol and West plc (formerly Bristol and West Building Society) 1997–, Waldegrave Farms Ltd, Henry Sotherans Ltd; Director, Corporate Finance, Dresdner Kleinwort Benson 1998–. *House of Commons:* MP (Conservative) for Bristol West 1979–97; Parliamentary Under-Secretary of State at: Department of Education and Science 1981–83, Department of Environment 1983–85; Minister of State for: Department of the Environment 1985–86, Environment Countryside and Planning 1986–87, Housing and Planning 1987–88, Foreign and Commonwealth Office 1988–90; Secretary of State for Health 1990–92; Chancellor of the Duchy of Lancaster and Minister for Public Service and Science 1992–94; Minister of Agriculture, Fisheries and Food 1994–95; Chief Secretary to HM Treasury 1995–97. *Trusts, etc:* Trustee, Rhodes Trust 1992–. *Honours:* PC 1990. *Publications:* Author of *The Binding of Leviathan*, 1978. *Clubs:* Beefsteak, Pratt's, Clifton (Bristol). *Name, Style and Title:* Raised to the peerage as Baron Waldegrave of North Hill, of Chewton Mendip in the County of Somerset 1999. A Conservative. *Address:* The Rt Hon. the Lord Waldegrave of North Hill, 66 Palace Gardens Terrace, London, W8 4RR.

WALKER OF DONCASTER (Life Baron, UK), Harold Walker; cr. 1997; Kt 1992; PC 1979; DL

Son of late Harold Walker. Born July 12, 1927; educated Manchester College of Technology; NCLC. Married 1st, 1956, Barbara Hague (died 1981) (1 daughter), married 2nd, 1984, Mary Griffin. *Trades Union:* Former Chairman of stewards and convener, AEU. *Armed Forces:* Served Fleet Air Arm 1946–48. *Councils, Public Bodies:* DL, South Yorkshire 1997–. *Career:* Toolmaker; Industrial Administrator; Political and Trade Union Lecturer/Tutor. *House of Commons:* MP (Labour) for Doncaster 1964–83 and for Doncaster Central 1983–97; Parliamentary Under-Secretary of State, Department of Employment and Productivity 1968–70; Parliamentary Under-Secretary of State for Employment 1974–76; Minister of State for Employment 1976–79; Chairman, Ways and Means and Deputy Speaker 1983–92. *Whip (Commons):* Assistant Government Whip April 1967–68. *Spokesman (Commons):* Front Bench (Opposition) Spokesman on Employment 1970–74; Opposition Front Bench Spokesman on Employment 1979–83. *Select Committees (Commons):* Former Chairman: Chairmen's Panel, Court of Referees, Select Committee on Standing Orders. *All-Party Committees (Commons):* Chairman, All-Party: Gardens and Allotments Group, Gardening Group. *Select Committees:* Member, Joint Select Committee on Statutory Instruments 1998–. *Other:* President: St John's Hospice Appeal, Doncaster Multiple Sclerosis, Doncaster Mencap, Doncaster and District Punjab Association. *Trusts, etc:* President, Doncaster Cancer Detection Trust. *Honours:* PC 1979; Knighted 1992. Freeman, Doncaster 1998. *Special Interests:* Industrial Relations, Health and Safety at Work, Manpower Policy. *Name, Style and Title:* Raised to the peerage as Baron Walker of Doncaster, of Audenshaw in the County of Greater Manchester 1997. Labour. *Address:* The Rt Hon. the Lord Walker of Doncaster, DL, House of Lords, London, SW1A 0PW.

WALKER OF WORCESTER (Life Baron, UK), Peter Edward Walker; cr. 1992; PC 1970; MBE 1960

Son of late Sydney Walker. Born March 25, 1932; educated Latymer Upper School. Married February 22, 1969, Tessa, daughter of G. I. Pout, of Sunbury-on-Thames (3 sons 2 daughters). *Career:* Non-Executive Director: Smith New Court 1990–95, British Gas plc 1990–96, Tate & Lyle 1990–, Chairman: English Partnerships 1992–98, Cornhill Insurance plc 1992–; Non-Executive Director, Liffe 1995–; Chairman, Kleinwort Benson Group plc 1996–98; Vice-Chairman, Dresdner Kleinwort Benson 1998–. *House of Commons:* Contested (Conservative) Dartford in 1955, 1959 General Elections; MP (Conservative) for Worcester 1961–92; PPS to Rt Hon. Selwyn Lloyd, MP 1963–64; Minister of Housing and Local Government June-October 1970; Secretary of State for: The Environment 1970–72, Trade and Industry 1972–74; Minister of Agriculture, Fisheries and Food 1979–83; Secretary of State for: Energy 1983–87, Wales 1987–90. *Spokesman (Commons):* Opposition Front Bench Spokesman on: Finance and Economics 1964–66, Transport 1966–68, Local Government, Housing and Land 1968–70; Opposition Spokesman on: Trade, Industry and Consumer Affairs February-June 1974, Defence 1974–75. *Party Groups (General):* Member, National Executive Committee of Conservative Party 1956–62; National Chairman, Young Conservatives 1968–70. *Honours:* MBE 1960; PC 1970; Commander's Cross of the Order of Merit (Federal Republic of Germany) 1994; Chilean Order of Bernardo O'Higgins, Degree Gran Oficial 1995. *Publications:* Author of: *The Ascent of Britain,* 1977; *Trust the People,* 1987; *Staying Power,* 1991. *Clubs:* Carlton. *Name, Style and Title:* Raised to the peerage as Baron Walker of Worcester, of Abbots Morton in the County of Hereford and Worcester 1992. A Conservative. *Address:* The Rt Hon. the Lord Walker of Worcester, MBE, Abbots Morton Manor, Gooms Hill, Abbots Morton, Worcester, WR7 4LT.

WALLACE OF COSLANY (Life Baron, UK), George Douglas Wallace; cr. 1974

Son of late George Wallace. Born April 18, 1906; educated Cheltenham Central School. Married March 28, 1932, Vera, daughter of W. J. Randall, of Guildford, Surrey (1 son 1 daughter). *Trades Union:* Member, TGWU. *Armed Forces:* Sergeant, RAF 1941–45. *Councils, Public Bodies:* Councillor: Chislehurst, Sidcup UDC 1937–45, Kent County Council 1952–57. *House of Commons:* MP (Labour) for: Chislehurst 1945–50, Norwich North 1964–74; Contested (Labour): Chislehurst 1951, 1955, Norwich South 1959; PPS to: Lord President of Council 1964–66, Secretary of State for Commonwealth Affairs 1966–67, Minister of State, Housing and Local Government 1967–68. *Whip (Commons):* Assistant Government Whip 1947–50. *Select Committees (Commons):* Member, Panel of Chairman, House of Commons 1970–74. *International Bodies (Commons):* Member, UK delegation to IPU Conference, Stockholm 1949; Delegate to: CPA Conference, Ottawa 1966, IPU Conference, Delhi 1969. *Whip:* A Lord in Waiting (Government Whip) 1977–79; Opposition Whip 1979–84. *Spokesman:* Opposition Spokesman on Health, Social Security 1983–84. *Party Groups (General):* Joined Labour Party 1935. *Other:* President, Radio Society of Gt Britain 1977; Formerly President, London Society of Recreational Gardeners; President, League of Friends, Queen Mary's Hospital, Sidcup 1980–. *Miscellaneous:* A Commissioner, Commonwealth War Graves Commission 1970–86. *Recreations:* Amateur radio, gardening. *Sportsclubs:* President, Norwich City London Supporters. *Name, Style and Title:* Raised to the peerage as Baron Wallace of Coslany, of Coslany in the City of Norwich 1974. Labour. *Address:* The Lord Wallace of Coslany, 44 Shuttle Close, Sidcup, Kent, DA15 8EP *Tel:* 020 8300 3634; House of Lords, London, SW1A 0PW *Tel:* House of Lords 020 7219 5408.

WALLACE OF SALTAIRE (Life Baron, UK), William John Lawrence Wallace; cr. 1995

Son of late William Edward Wallace and late Mary Agnes Tricks. Born March 12, 1941; educated Westminster Abbey Choir School; St Edward's School, Oxford; King's College, Cambridge (BA History 1962); Cornell University (USA) (PhD Government 1968); Nuffield College, Oxford; Doctorate hc, Université Libre de Bruxelles. Married August 25, 1968, Helen Sarah, daughter of late Edward Rushworth (1 son 1 daughter). *Career:* Lecturer in Government, University of Manchester 1967–77; Director of Studies, Royal Institute of International Affairs 1978–90; Walter F. Hallstein Fellow, St Antony's College, Oxford 1990–95; Reader in International Relations, London School of Economics 1995–; Professor, International Relations LSE 1999–. *Spokesman:* Liberal Democrat Spokesman on: Defence 1997–, Foreign and Commonwealth Affairs 1998–. *Select Committees:* Member, Select Committee on European Communities 1997–; Chairman, Select Committee on European Communities Sub-Committee F (Social Affairs, Education and Home Affairs) 1997–; Member, Ecclesiastical Committee 1997–. *All-Party:* Co-Chairman, All-Party University Group 1999–. *Honours:* Chevalier, Ordre pour le Mérite (France) 1995. *Publications: The Foreign Policy Process in Britain,* 1977; *The Transformation of Europe,* 1990; *The Dynamics of European Integration,* 1990; *Regional Integration – The West European Experience,* 1994; *Policy-making in the European Union,* with Helen Wallace 1996. *Special Interests:* Foreign Affairs, Defence, Europe, Constitutional Affairs. *Recreations:* Swimming, walking, gardening. *Name, Style and Title:* Raised to the peerage as Baron Wallace of Saltaire, of Shipley in the County of West Yorkshire 1995. A Liberal Democrat. *Address:* The Lord Wallace of Saltaire, House of Lords, London, SW1A 0PW.

WALPOLE (10th Baron, GB), Robert (Robin) Horatio Walpole; cr 1723; 8th Baron Walpole of Wolterton (GB) 1756

Son of 9th Baron, TD. Born December 8, 1938. Succeeded his father 1989; educated Eton; King's College, Cambridge (MA, DipAgric); Hon. Fellow, St Mary's University College, Strawberry Hill 1997. Married 1st, 1962, Judith (later Mrs Judith Chaplin, OBE, MP – died 1993), daughter of late Theodore Schofield, of Stockingwood House, Harpenden, Herts (2 sons 2 daughters) (marriage dissolved 1979), married 2nd, 1980, Laurel Celia, daughter of S. T. Ball, of Swindon, Wilts (2 sons 1 daughter). *Councils, Public Bodies:* Councillor, Norfolk County Council 1970–81; Variously Chairman: Highways, Library and Recreation, Planning and Transportation, Norfolk Joint Museums Committees; JP, Norfolk 1972. *House of Lords:* An elected hereditary peer 1999–. *Select Committees:* Member: Agriculture Sub-Committee of European Communities Committee 1991–94, Environment Sub-Committee of European Communities Committee 1995–97, Select Committee on European Communities 1997–, Select Committee on European Communities Sub-Committee C (Environment, Public Health and Consumer Protection) 1997–. *All-Party:* Member, All-Party Conservation Group. *Other:* Chairman: Area Museums Service for South East England 1976–79, Norwich School of Art 1977–87; Chairman, Textile Conservation Centre 1981–88, President 1988; Member: CPRE, RSPB. *Miscellaneous:* Chairman, East Anglian Tourist Board 1982–88. *Special Interests:* Agriculture, Arts, Tourism, Conservation. *Heir:* His son, Hon. Jonathan Robert Hugh Walpole, born November 16, 1967. A Cross-Bencher. *Address:* The Lord Walpole, Mannington Hall, Norwich, Norfolk, NR11 7BB *Tel:* 01263 587763 *E-Mail:* walpolerh@parliament.uk.

WALTON OF DETCHANT (Life Baron, UK), John Nicholas Walton; cr. 1989; Kt. 1979; TD 1962

Son of late Herbert and Eleanor Walton. Born September 16, 1922; educated County Primary Schools in Co. Durham; Alderman Wraith Grammar School, Spennymoor, Co. Durham; Medical School, King's College, Newcastle upon Tyne (University of Durham) (MB, BS, MD, DSc, MA Oxon); Hon. DUniv, Aix Marseille; Hon. MD, Sheffield; Hon. DSc: Leeds, Leicester, Hull, Oxford Brookes; Hon. DCL, Newcastle; Laurea hc, Genoa; Hon. MD, Mahidol, Thailand. Married August 31, 1946, Mary Elizabeth, daughter of Joseph Bell Harrison (1 son 2 daughters). *Armed Forces:* Service in RAMC 1947–49; Colonel (late RAMC) and Officer Commanding 1 (N) General Hospital (TA) 1963–66. *Career:* Nuffield Foundation Fellow in Neurology, Massachusetts

General Hospital, Boston USA 1953–54; King's College Travelling Fellow in Medicine, National Hospital, London 1954–55; First Assistant in Neurology, King's College and Royal Infirmary, Newcastle 1956–58; Consultant Neurologist, Newcastle General Hospital 1958–83; Lecturer in Neurology, University of Newcastle upon Tyne 1966–68; Director, Muscular Dystrophy Group Research Laboratories, Newcastle General Hospital 1965–83; Professor of Neurology, Newcastle University 1968–83; Dean of Medicine, Newcastle University 1971–81; Warden, Green College, Oxford 1983–89. *Select Committees:* Member, House of Lords Select Committees on: Science and Technology 1992–96, 1997–, Medical Ethics 1993–94. *Other:* Chairman, Muscular Dystrophy Group of Great Britain and Northern Ireland 1971–95; Member: General Medical Council 1971–79, President 1982–89; Medical Research Council 1974–78; President: British Medical Association 1980–82, Royal Society of Medicine 1984–86, Association of British Neurologists 1987–88; First Vice-President, World Federation of Neurology 1987–89, President 1989–97. *Honours:* Kt 1979. FRCP; Hon. FRCPEd; Hon. FRCPC; Hon. FRCPsych; Hon. FRCPath; Hon. FRCPCH; FMedSci. Hon. Freeman, Newcastle upon Tyne 1980. *Publications:* Several medical titles including: *Essentials of Neurology*, 1961; *Disorders of Voluntary Muscle*, 1964; *The Spice of Life*, 1993 (autobiography); as well as numerous chapters in books and articles in scientific journals. *Special Interests:* Medicine, Health, Science, Education. *Recreations:* Golf, cricket, reading, music, opera. *Sportsclubs:* President, Bamburgh Castle Golf Club. *Clubs:* Athenaeum, United Oxford and Cambridge University, Royal Society of Medicine, MCC. *Name, Style and Title:* Raised to the peerage as Baron Walton of Detchant, of Detchant in the County of Northumberland 1989. A Cross-Bencher. *Address:* The Lord Walton of Detchant, TD, 13 Norham Gardens, Oxford, OX2 6PS *Tel:* Office: 01865 512492 *Fax:* 01865 512495.

WARNER (Life Baron, UK), Norman Reginald Warner; cr. 1998

Son of Albert and Laura Warner. Born September 8, 1940; educated Dulwich College; University of California, Berkeley (MPH) (Harkness Fellowship 1971–73). Married 1st, 1961, Anne Lesley Lawrence (1 son 1 daughter) (marriage dissolved 1981); married 2nd, 1990, Suzanne Elizabeth Reeve. *Councils, Public Bodies:* Chairman, City and East London FHSA 1991–94. *Career:* Joined Ministry of Health 1959; Assistant Private Secretary: to Minister of Health 1967–68, to Secretary of State for Social Services 1968–69; Executive Councils Division, Department of Health and Social Security 1969–71; NHS Reorganisation, DHSS 1973–74; Principal Private Secretary to Secretary of State for Social Services 1974–76; Supplementary Benefits Division 1976–78; Management Services, DHSS 1979–81; Regional Controller, Wales and South Western Region, DHSS 1981–83; Gwilym Gibbon Fellow, Nuffield College, Oxford 1983–84; Under-Secretary, Supplementary Benefits Division, DHSS 1984–85; Director of Social Services, Kent County Council 1985–91; Managing Director, Warner Consultancy and Training Services Ltd 1991–97; Senior Policy Adviser to the Home Secretary 1997–; Chairman, Youth Justice Board for England and Wales 1998–. *Other:* Member, Carers National Association 1991–94; Member, Royal Philanthropic Society 1991–, Chairman 1993–98; Chairman: Expert Panel for UK Harkness Fellowships 1994–97, Residential Forum, in Association with National Institute for Social Work 1994–97. *Trusts, etc:* Trustee: Leonard Cheshire Foundation 1994–96, MacIntyre Care 1994–97. *Miscellaneous:* Chairman, National Inquiry into Selection, Development and Management of Staff in Children's Homes 1991–92; Member, Local Government Commission 1995–96. *Publications:* Editor, *Commissioning Community Alternatives in European Social and Health Care*, 1993; several articles in specialised journals. *Recreations:* Reading, cinema, theatre, exercise, travel. *Name, Style and Title:* Raised to the peerage as Baron Warner, of Brockley in the London Borough of Lewisham 1998. Labour. *Address:* The Lord Warner, 8 College Gardens, Dulwich, London, SE21 7BE *Tel:* 020 8693 8083.

WARNOCK (Life Baroness, UK), Helen Mary Warnock; cr. 1985; DBE 1984

Daughter of late Archibald Edward Wilson. Born April 14, 1924; educated St Swithun's, Winchester; Lady Margaret Hall, Oxford (MA, BPhil); Hon. Degrees: Open University, Essex, Melbourne, Bath, Exeter, Manchester, Glasgow, York, Warwick, Liverpool, London, St Andrews, Leeds Metropolitan; Hon. Fellow: St Hugh's College, Lady Margaret Hall, Hertford College, Oxford; Life Fellow, Girton College, Cambridge. Married 1949, Sir Geoffrey James Warnock (died October 8, 1995), son of late Dr James Warnock, OBE (2 sons 3 daughters). *Career:* Fellow and Tutor in Philosophy, St Hugh's College, Oxford 1952–66, Headmistress, Oxford High School 1966–72; Chairman, Committee of Inquiry into Special Education 1974–78; Member, Royal Commission on Environmental Pollution 1979–84; Chairman, Committee of Inquiry on Human Fertility and Embryology 1982–84; Mistress, Girton College, Cambridge 1985–91; Gifford Lecturer, University of Glasgow 1991–92. *Select Committees:* Member, House of Lords Select Committees on: Medical Ethics 1993–94, Dangerous Dogs 1996. *All-Party:* Member, All-Party: Children Group, Higher Education Group. *Other:* President, British Dyslexia Association. *Awards Granted:* Albert Medalist, Royal Society of Arts 1998. *Trusts, etc:* Director, Girls' Public Dayschool Trust; Trustee, National Primary Trust. *Miscellaneous:* Research Fellow, St Hugh's College, Oxford 1972–84. *Honours:* DBE 1984; Hon. Bencher, Gray's Inn. Fellow, College of Teachers (formerly College of Preceptors); Hon. FRCM; Hon. Fellow, Royal Society of Physicians, Scotland. *Publications:* Author of books on ethics and education and philosophy of mind. *Special Interests:* Education, Broadcasting, Medicine, Environment. *Recreations:* Music, gardening. *Name, Style and Title:* Raised to the peerage as Baroness Warnock, of Weeke in the City of Winchester 1985. A Cross-Bencher. *Address:* The Baroness Warnock, DBE, 3 Church Street, Great Bedwyn, Marlborough, Wiltshire, SN8 3PE.

WARWICK OF UNDERCLIFFE (Life Baroness, UK), Diana Warwick; cr. 1999

Daughter of Jack and Olive Warwick. Born July 16, 1945; educated St Joseph's College, Bradford; Bedford College, University of London (BA Hons); Hon. DLitt: Bradford University 1993, Open University 1998. Married 1969, Sean Bowes Young, son of Terence Young and Dorothea Bennet. *Career:* Technical Assistant to General Secretary, NUT 1969–72; Assistant Secretary, Civil and Public Services Association 1972–83; General Secretary, Association of University Teachers 1983–92; Chief Executive: Westminster Foundation for Democracy 1992–95, Committee of Vice-Chancellors and Principals 1995–. *Other:* Chairman, Voluntary Service Overseas 1994–. *Trusts, etc:* Trustee: Royal Anniversary Trust 1991–93, St Catherine's Foundation, Windsor 1996–. *Miscellaneous:* Member: Board, British Council 1985–95, Employment Appeal Tribunal 1987–99, Executive and Council, Industrial Society 1987–, TUC General Council 1989–92, Council, Duke of Edinburgh's Seventh Commonwealth Study Conference 1991, Neill Committee on Standards in Public Life 1994–, OST Technology Foresight Steering Group 1997–, Commonwealth Institute 1988–95. FRSA 1984. *Recreations:* Theatre, reading, riding, looking at pictures. *Name, Style and Title:* Raised to the peerage as Baroness Warwick of Undercliffe, of Undercliffe in the County of West Yorkshire 1999. Labour. *Address:* The Baroness Warwick of Undercliffe, Committee of Vice-Chancellors and Principals, Woburn House, 20 Tavistock Square, London, WC1H 9HQ *Tel:* 020 7419 5402 *Fax:* 020 7380 0137 *E-Mail:* diana.warwick@cvcp.ac.uk.

WATSON OF INVERGOWRIE (Life Baron, UK), Michael Goodall Watson; cr. 1997

Son of late Clarke and Senga Watson. Born May 1, 1949; educated Invergowrie Primary School, Dundee; Dundee High School; Heriot-Watt University, Edinburgh (BA Hons Economics and Industrial Relations 1974); Hon. LLD, University of Abertay Dundee 1998. Married October 31, 1986, Lorraine Therese, daughter of late William McManus and of Mary McManus. *Trades Union:* Member, Manufacturing, Science and Finance Union (formerly ASTMS) 1975–. *Career:* Development Officer, WEA East Midlands District 1974–77; MSF: Full-time official 1977–89, Industrial Officer 1977–79, Regional Officer based in Glasgow 1979–89; Visiting Research Fellow, Department of Government, University of Strathclyde 1993–; Director, PS Communication Consultants Ltd, Edinburgh 1997–99. *House of Commons:* MP (Labour) for Glasgow

Central 1989–97. *Select Committees (Commons):* Member, Select Committees on: Parliamentary Commissioner for Administration 1990–95, Public Accounts 1995–97. *Backbench Committees (Commons):* Chairman, Parliamentary Labour Party Committee on Overseas Development Aid 1991–97. *Select Committees:* Member, Select Committee on European Communities Sub-Committee F (Social Policy) 1997–. *All-Party:* Member, All-Party Lords and Commons Population, Development and Reproductive Health Group. *Party Groups:* Member, Parliamentary Labour Party: Education and Employment Group, Foreign Affairs Group, Overseas Development Group. *Party Groups (General):* Member, Labour Party Scottish Executive Committee 1987–90. *Other:* Member: Board of Management, Volunteer Centre, Scotland 1994–; Scottish Youth Theatre 1998–. *Miscellaneous:* MSP for the Constituency of Glasgow Cathcart since May 6, 1999 (contested the seat as Mike Watson); Scottish Parliament Committees: Convener, Finance Committee 1999–; Member, Social Inclusion, Housing and Voluntary Sector Committee 1999–. *Publications: Rags to Riches: The Official History of Dundee United FC,* 1985; *The Tannadice Encyclopedia,* 1997. *Special Interests:* Scottish Parliament, Higher Education, Employment Law, Overseas Aid and Development, Foreign Affairs. *Recreations:* Supporting Dundee United FC, running, reading, especially political biographies. *Name, Style and Title:* Raised to the peerage as Baron Watson of Invergowrie, of Invergowrie in Perth and Kinross 1997. Labour. *Address:* The Lord Watson of Invergowrie, MSP, House of Lords, London, SW1A 0PW *E-Mail:* watsonm@parliament.uk; mike.watson.msp@scottish.parliament.uk.

WATSON OF RICHMOND (Life Baron, UK), Alan John Watson; cr. 1999; CBE 1985

Son of Rev. John William Watson and Edna Mary (née Peters). Born February 3, 1941; educated Diocesan College, Cape Town, South Africa; Kingswood School, Bath; Jesus College, Cambridge (Open Scholar in History 1959, State Scholar 1959) (MA Hons) (Vice-President, Cambridge Union). Married 1965, Karen Lederer (2 sons). *Career:* Research Assistant to Cambridge Professor of Modern History on post-war history of Unilever 1962–64; General Trainee, BBC 1965–66; Reporter, BBC TV, The Money Programme 1966–68; Chief Public Affairs Commentator, London Weekend Television 1969–70; Reporter, Panorama, BBC TV 1971–74; Presenter, The Money Programme 1974–75; Head of TV, Radio, Audio-Visual Division, EEC, and Editor, European Community Newsreel Service to Lomé Convention Countries 1975–79; Director, Charles Barker City Ltd 1980–85, Chief Executive 1980–83; Deputy Chairman, Sterling Public Relations 1985–86; Chairman: City and Corporate Counsel Ltd 1987–94, Threadneedle Publishing Group 1987–94, Corporate Vision Ltd 1989–, Corporate Television Networks 1992–; Director, Burson-Marsteller Worldwide 1992–; Chairman: Burson-Marsteller UK 1994–, Burson-Marsteller Europe 1996–. *International Bodies (General):* Chairman, British-German Association 1992–; Vice-Chairman, The European Movement 1995–; Chairman, English Speaking Union 2000–. *Party Groups (General):* Former President, Cambridge University Liberal Club. *Other:* Chairman of Governors, Westminster College, Oxford 1988–94; President, Heathrow Association for Control of Aircraft Noise 1992–95; Prince of Wales Business Leaders Forum 1996–. *Miscellaneous:* Member, Executive Board UNICEF 1985–92; Presenter: BBC 1 1990, Channel 4 1992; Visiting Fellow, Louvanium International Business Centre, Brussels 1990–95; Visiting Erasmus Professor in European Studies, Louvain University 1990;' Hon. Professor, German Studies, Birmingham University 1997–. *Honours:* CBE 1985; Order of Merit (Federal Republic of Germany) 1995. *Publications: Europe at risk,* 1972; *The Germans: who are they now?,* 1992; *Thatcher and Kohl: old rivalries renewed,* 1996. *Clubs:* Brooks's, Royal Automobile, Kennel. *Name, Style and Title:* Raised to the peerage as Baron Watson of Richmond, of Richmond in the London Borough of Richmond upon Thames 1999. A Liberal Democrat. *Address:* The Lord Watson of Richmond, CBE, Cholmondeley House, 3 Cholmondeley Walk, Richmond upon Thames, Surrey, TW9 1NS; Somerset Lodge, Nunney, Somerset, BA11 4NP *E-Mail:* alan_watson@uk.bm.com.

WAVERLEY (3rd Viscount, UK), John Desmond Forbes Anderson; cr. 1952

Son of 2nd Viscount. Born October 31, 1949. Succeeded his father 1990; educated Malvern. Married January 4, 1994, HE Dr Ursula Barrow (Former High Commissioner for Belize) (1 son). *Career:* Landscape Contractor (Europe/Middle East) 1975–85; Publishers' Agent (Latin America/Africa) 1985–93; Emerging Markets Support 1993–. *House of Lords:* An elected hereditary peer 1999–. *All-Party:* Vice-Chairman, All-Party Export Group 1998–; Member, Defence Study Group; Joint Vice-Chairman, All-Party Libya Country Group 1999–; Vice-Chairman, All-Party Central Asia Country Group. *International Bodies:* Member, Executive Committee, Commonwealth Parliamentary Association 1994–95; Member, Inter-Parliamentary Union; Parliamentary visits to: Japan, Falkland Islands, Bangladesh, Kashmir, Belize, Nigeria, Ghana, Burundi; Observer, 1994 San José X Ministerial Conference (EU/Central America); Aid Programme Evaluation, Nepal; Commonwealth Observer, Bangladesh General Elections 1996. *Other:* Member, Royal Institute of International Affairs. *Honours:* Order of San Carlos (Grand Cross) Colombia 1998. Companion, Institute of Export. *Special Interests:* Britain's Export Performance, Foreign Affairs, Commonwealth, Overseas Aid and Development, Conflict Resolution. *Recreations:* Golf, scuba diving, walking, travel. *Sportsclubs:* Rye Golf. *Heir:* His son, Hon. Forbes Alastair Rupert Anderson, born February 15, 1996. A Cross-Bencher. *Address:* The Viscount Waverley, House of Lords, London, SW1A 0PW *Tel:* 020 7219 3000 *E-Mail:* waverley@int-affairs.com.

WEATHERILL (Life Baron, UK), (Bruce) Bernard Weatherill; cr. 1992; PC 1980; DL

Son of late Bernard Weatherill and Gertrude Weatherill (née Creak). Born November 25, 1920; educated Malvern College; Hon. DCL: University of Kent, University of William and Mary USA, University of Denver, Colorado USA, Open University 1993. Married 1949, Lyn, daughter of late H. T. Eatwell (2 sons 1 daughter). *Armed Forces:* Commissioned 1940 in 4/7 Royal Dragoon Guards; Transferred to 19th King George V's Own Lancers (Indian Army) 1941–46; Served Burma and North-West Europe. *Councils, Public Bodies:* DL, Kent 1992. *Career:* Employed in family business of Bernard Weatherill Ltd, Tailors, of Savile Row, London, W1 1946–70, President of the Company 1992. *House of Commons:* MP (Conservative) for Croydon North East 1964–83; Chairman of Ways and Means and Deputy Speaker 1979–83; Elected Speaker of the House of Commons June 15, 1983 and chosen again June 17, 1987 until retirement in 1992. *Whip (Commons):* Opposition Whip 1967–70; A Lord Commissioner of HM Treasury (Government Whip) 1970–71; Vice-Chamberlain, HM Household 1971–72; Comptroller, HM Household 1972–73; Treasurer, HM Household and Deputy Chief Whip 1973–74; Opposition Deputy Chief Whip 1974–79. *House of Lords:* Alternate Convenor of the Cross-Bench Peers 1993–95, Convenor 1995–99. *Select Committees:* Member, Select Committees on: Offices, Finance and Staff, Administration and Works, Liaison Privileges, Procedure, Selection, House of Lords' Offices. *All-Party:* Patron, All-Party: Indo-British Parliamentary Group, Citizenship Group, Tibet Group; Member, All-Party: Anglo Pakistan Parliamentary Group, British Nepal Parliamentary Group. *International Bodies:* Vice-President: Commonwealth Parliamentary Association, Intra-Parliamentary Union. *Other:* Chairman, Commonwealth Speakers and Presiding Officers 1986–88; High Bailiff of Westminster Abbey and Searcher of the Sanctuary 1989–99; Chairman, Industry and Churches Forum; President: The Institute for Citizenship, Kent County Scout Association. *Trusts, etc:* Chairman, Industry and Parliamentary Trust 1993–; Trustee: The Prince's Trust, Prince's Youth Business Trust. *Honours:* PC 1980; KStJ 1992; Vice-Chancellor, Order of St John of Jerusalem; Hon. Bencher of Lincoln's Inn; Hilal-i-Pakistan 1993. Freeman: City of London 1949, Borough of Croydon 1983. Member: Gold and Silver Wyre Drawers, Merchant Taylors, Blacksmiths. *Publications: Acorns To Oaks*, (a policy for small businesses) 1967. *Recreations:* Tennis, Golf. *Sportsclubs:* President, Lucifer Golfing Society 1992; Tandridge Golf. *Clubs:* Cavalry and Guards, Reform. *Name, Style and Title:* Raised to the peerage as Baron Weatherill, of North East Croydon in the London Borough of Croydon 1992. A Cross-Bencher. *Address:* The Rt Hon. the Lord Weatherill, DL, Emmetts House, Ide Hill, Kent, TN14 6BA; House of Lords, London, SW1A 0PW *Tel:* House of Lords 020 7219 2224.

WEDDERBURN OF CHARLTON (Life Baron, UK), Kenneth William Wedderburn; cr. 1977; QC 1990; FBA 1980

Son of late Herbert J. Wedderburn. Born April 13, 1927; educated Aske's Hatcham Boys School; Whitgift School, Croydon; Queens' College, Cambridge (MA, LLB); Hon. Dottore Giur, University Pavia; Hon. Dottore Econ, University Siena; Hon. Doctor of Laws, University of Stockholm; Hon. Fellow: Clare College, Cambridge 1997–, London School of Economics 1999–. Married 1st, 1951, Nina, daughter of Dr M. Salaman (1 son 2 daughters) (marriage dissolved 1962), married 2nd, 1962, Mrs Dorothy Cole (marriage dissolved 1969), married 3rd, 1969, Frances, daughter of Basil Knight (1 son). *Trades Union:* Member, Association of University Teachers. *Armed Forces:* Served RAF 1949–51. *Career:* Fellow of Clare College, Cambridge and University Lecturer in Law 1952–64; Called to the Bar, Middle Temple 1953; Cassel Professor of Commercial Law, University of London (London School of Economics) 1964–92, Emeritus Professor 1992–; Visiting Professor, Harvard Law School 1969–70; General Editor, Modern Law Review 1971–88; QC 1990. *Spokesman:* Deputy Opposition Front Bench Spokesman on Employment 1980–92. *Select Committees:* Co-opted Member, Select Committee on European Communities Sub-Committee E (Law and Institutions) 1997–. *Party Groups (General):* Editorial Board, International Labour Law Reports 1975–. *Other:* Chairman, London and Provincial Theatre Councils 1973–93; Hon. President, Industrial Law Society 1997–. *Miscellaneous:* Chairman, TUC Independent Review Committee 1976–. FBA 1980. *Publications:* Author of: *Employment Rights in Britain and Europe*, 1991; *Labour Law and Freedom*, 1995; *The Worker and The Law*, 1986. *Special Interests:* Industrial Relations, Employment Law, Company Law, Education. *Recreations:* Charlton Athletic Football Club. *Name, Style and Title:* Raised to the peerage as Baron Wedderburn of Charlton, of Highgate in the County of Greater London 1977. Labour. *Address:* Professor The Lord Wedderburn of Charlton, QC, FBA, London School of Economics, Houghton Street, London, WC2A 2AE *Tel:* 020 7955 7265; Chambers: 1 Verulam Buildings, Gray's Inn, London, WC1R 5LQ *Tel:* 020 7831 0801; 29 Woodside Avenue, Highgate, London, N6 4SP *Tel:* 020 8444 8472.

WEIDENFELD (Life Baron, UK), (Arthur) George Weidenfeld; cr. 1976; Kt 1969

Son of late Max Weidenfeld. Born September 13, 1919; educated Piaristen Gymnasium, Vienna; Vienna University; Hon. PhD, Ben Gurion University of the Negev 1984; Hon. MA, Oxon 1992; Hon. Fellow: St Peter's College, Oxford, St Anne's College, Oxford; Hon. Senator (Ehrensenator), Bonn University; Magister, Diplomatic College, Vienna University. Married 1st, 1952, Jane, daughter of late Edward Sieff (1 daughter), married 2nd, 1956, Mrs Barbara Connolly (marriage dissolved 1961, she died January 1996), married 3rd, 1966, Mrs Sandra Meyer (marriage dissolved 1976), married 4th, July 14, 1992, Annabelle, daughter of late Commander Nicholas Whitestone, RN. *Career:* BBC Monitoring Service 1939–42; News Commentator, BBC Empire and North American Service 1942–46; Columnist, News Chronicle 1943–44; Formerly Political Adviser and Chief of Cabinet to President Weizmann of Israel; Chairman, Weidenfeld and Nicolson Ltd, Publishers; Director, Hollinger Group of Companies. *Spokesman:* SDP Spokesman on Foreign Affairs, the Arts, Broadcasting 1983–90. *Other:* Chairman, Board of Governors, Ben Gurion University of the Negev, Beer-Sheva, Israel; Governor: Weizmann Institute of Science, Tel Aviv University, Bezalel Academy of Art, Jerusalem, Jerusalem Foundation; Board Member, English National Opera 1988–98; Member, South Bank Board; Vice-President, Oxford University Development Programme; Board Member, Diplomatic Academy, Vienna 1997–. *Trusts, etc:* Trustee Emeritus, Aspen Foundation; Former Trustee, National Portrait Gallery. *Honours:* Kt 1969; Chevalier de l'Ordre National de la Legion d'Honneur; Golden Knight's Cross with Star of the Austrian Order of Merit; Knight Commander's Cross (Badge and Star) of the Order of Merit of the Federal Republic of Germany 1991. *Recreations:* Travel, opera. *Clubs:* Garrick, Athenaeum. *Name, Style and Title:* Raised to the peerage as Baron Weidenfeld, of Chelsea in the County of Greater London 1976. A Cross-Bencher. *Address:* The Lord Weidenfeld, Orion House, 5 Upper St Martin's Lane, London, WC2H 9EA *Tel:* 020 7240 3444.

WEINSTOCK (Life Baron, UK), Arnold Weinstock; cr. 1980; Kt 1970

Son of late Simon Weinstock. Born July 29, 1924; educated University of London (Degree in statistics); Hon. DSc: Salford 1975, Aston 1976, Bath 1978, Reading 1978; Hon. LLD, Leeds 1978; DTech, Loughborough 1981; Hon. Fellow: Peterhouse, Cambridge 1982, London School of Economics 1985; Hon. LLD, University of Wales 1985; Hon. DSc, Ulster 1987; Hon. DU, Anglia Polytechnic University 1994; Hon. LLD, Keele University 1997; Hon. DEconSci, University of London 1997. Married 1949, Netta, daughter of late Sir Michael Sobell (1 daughter and 1 son deceased). *Career:* Junior Administrative Officer at The Admiralty 1944–47; Joined Radio & Allied (Holdings) Ltd 1954; When it merged with the General Electric Co. Ltd in 1961, appointed director of GEC, MD January 1963–96, Chairman Emeritus 1996–; Director, Rolls-Royce (1971) Ltd 1971–73. *Trusts, etc:* Trustee, British Museum 1985–96. *Honours:* Kt 1970; Hon. Master of the Bench of Gray's Inn 1982; Officier, Legion d'Honneur (France) 1991; Commendatore of the Order of Merit (Italy) 1991. *Recreations:* Racing, Bloodstock, classical music. *Name, Style and Title:* Raised to the peerage as Baron Weinstock, of Bowden in the County of Wiltshire 1980. A Cross-Bencher. *Address:* The Lord Weinstock, 1 Bruton Street, London, W1X 8AQ *Tel:* 020 7493 8484.

WHADDON (Life Baron, UK), John Derek Page; cr. 1978

Son of late John Page. Born August 14, 1927; educated St Bedes College, Manchester; BSc Sociology London External. Married 1st, December 4, 1948, Catherine Audrey (died 1979), daughter of John and Rose Halls (1 son 1 daughter), married 2nd, 1981, Mrs Angela Rixon. *Career:* Sales Manager, Carnegies of Welwyn 1960–62; Director, Cambridge Chemical Co Ltd 1962–; Member, East Anglia Economic Planning Council until 1980; Director, Microautomatics Ltd 1981–87; Member, Lloyds 1981–94; Former Member, COSIRA Board; Director, Rindalbourne Ltd 1983–89; Chairman: Daltrade Ltd 1984–, Skorimpex-Rind Ltd 1985–, Britpol Ltd 1989–90, Crag Group Ltd 1996–. *House of Commons:* MP (Labour) for King's Lynn 1964–70. *Select Committees:* Former Member, House of Lords Select Committee on Science and Technology. *Other:* Patron, International Piano Festival, Warsaw. *Honours:* Golden Insignia of Order of Merit (Poland) 1989. *Special Interests:* Eastern Europe. *Recreations:* Private pilot. *Clubs:* Reform. *Name, Style and Title:* Raised to the peerage as Baron Whaddon, of Whaddon in the County of Cambridgeshire 1978. Labour. *Address:* The Lord Whaddon, The Old Vicarage, Whaddon, Royston, Hertfordshire *Tel:* 01223 207209.

WHARTON (Baroness, 11th in line, E), Myrtle Olive Felix (Ziki) Robertson; cr. 1544

Daughter of late David George Arbuthnot and Elizabeth Dorothy, Baroness Wharton (10th in line). Born February 20, 1934; educated Herschel School for Girls, Clarement, Cape, South Africa. Married November 17, 1958, Henry Macleod Robertson (died 1996), son of late Henry Robertson, of Elgin, Morayshire (3 sons of whom 2 are twins 1 daughter). *House of Lords:* An elected hereditary peer 1999–. *Select Committees:* Member, Select Committee on Broadcasting 1995–97. *All-Party:* Joint Hon. Secretary, All-Party Parliamentary Group for Animal Welfare; Secretary, All-Party FRAME Group 1998–. *Miscellaneous:* The barony was in abeyance from 1974–1990 when it was terminated in favour of the present peer. *Recreations:* Photography, opera, ski-ing. *Heir:* Her son, Hon. Myles Christopher David Robertson, born October 1, 1964. A Cross-Bencher. *Address:* The Baroness Wharton, House of Lords, London, SW1A 0PW.

Dod *on* Disk

The Vacher Dod Parliamentary Database – configured for PC or Network

For further details please telephone the Westminster Office

020 7828 7256

WHITAKER (Life Baroness, UK), Janet Alison Whitaker; cr. 1999

Daughter of Allan Harrison Stewart and Ella Stewart (née Saunders). Born 1936; educated Nottingham High School for Girls; Girton College, Cambridge (BA Hons). Married, December 18, 1964, Ben Whitaker, son of late Sir John Whitaker, 2nd Bt, CB, CBE, DL, JP (2 sons 1 daughter). *Trades Union:* Member, FDA. *Career:* André Deutsch (Publishers) 1961–66; Health and Safety Executive 1974–88; Department of Education and Employment 1988–96. *International Bodies:* Member, IPU *Other:* Chair, Working Men's College for Men and Women; Member: Employment Tribunals, Camden Racial Equality Council, SOS Sahel Population Concern, ACORD Gender Committee, Society of Labour Lawyers, Fabian Society, British Humanist Association. *Trusts, etc:* Trustee, Runnymede Trust. FRSA. *Special Interests:* Race Relations, International Development, Further Education. *Recreations:* Travel, walking, art, music, reading. *Clubs:* Reform. *Name, Style and Title:* Raised to the peerage as Baroness Whitaker, of Beeston in the County of Nottinghamshire 1999. Labour. *Address:* The Baroness Whitaker, House of Lords, London, SW1A 0PW.

WHITTY (Life Baron, UK), John Lawrence Whitty; cr. 1996

Son of late Frederick James and Kathleen May Whitty. Born June 15, 1943; educated Latymer Upper School; St John's College, Cambridge (BA Hons Economics). Married 1st, 1969, Tanya Margaret Gibson (2 sons) (marriage dissolved 1986); married 2nd, 1993, Angela Forrester. *Trades Union:* Member, GMB. *Career:* Hawker Siddeley Aviation 1960–62; Ministry of Aviation Technology 1965–70; Trades Union Congress 1970–73; General, Municipal, Boilermakers and Allied Trade Union 1973–85; The Labour Party: General Secretary 1985–94, European Co-ordinator 1994–. *House of Lords:* Parliamentary Under-Secretary of State, Department of the Environment, Transport and the Regions (Minister for Roads and Road Safety) 1998–. *Whip:* A Lord in Waiting (Government Whip) 1997–98. *Spokesman:* A Spokesman on European Affairs, International Development, Foreign and Commonwealth Affairs, Education and Employment 1997–98. *Party Groups (General):* Member, Fabian Society. *Other:* Member, Friends of the Earth. *Recreations:* Theatre, cinema, swimming. *Name, Style and Title:* Raised to the peerage as Baron Whitty, of Camberwell in the London Borough of Southwark 1996. Labour. *Address:* The Lord Whitty, 33 Gilbert House, Churchill Gardens, London, SW1V 3HN; 61 Bimport, Shaftesbury, Dorset, SP7 8AZ.

WIGODER (Life Baron, UK), Basil Thomas Wigoder; cr. 1974; QC 1966

Son of late Dr Philip Wigoder. Born February 12, 1921; educated Manchester Grammar School; Oriel College, Oxford (MA Hons) (President, Oxford Union 1946). Married August 30, 1948, Yoland, daughter of Ben Levinson (3 sons 1 daughter). *Armed Forces:* RA 1942–45. *Career:* Called to the Bar, Grays Inn 1946; General Council of the Bar 1970–74; A Recorder of the Crown Court 1972–84; Master of the Bench, Gray's Inn 1972; Chairman, Health Services Board 1977–80; Member, Council on Tribunals 1980; Chairman, BUPA 1981–92; Treasurer, Gray's Inn 1989. *Whip:* Liberal Chief Whip 1976–85. *Spokesman:* Liberal Party Spokesman on Home Affairs and Law 1983–88. *Select Committees:* Former Member: Consolidation Bills Joint Committee, Delegated Powers Scrutiny Committee, Member: Select Committee on European Communities Sub-Committee E (Law and Institutions) 1997–, Joint Committee on Parliamentary Privilege 1997–, Committee for Privileges, Sub-Committee on Lords' Interests. *Party Groups (General):* Chairman, Liberal Party Executive 1963–65. *Special Interests:* Home Office Affairs, Health Service. *Recreations:* Cricket. *Clubs:* National Liberal, MCC. *Name, Style and Title:* Raised to the peerage as Baron Wigoder, of Cheetham in the City of Manchester 1974. A Liberal Democrat. *Address:* The Lord Wigoder, QC, House of Lords, London, SW1A 0PW *Tel:* House of Lords 020 7219 3115.

WILBERFORCE (Life Baron, UK), Richard Orme Wilberforce; cr. 1964; Kt 1961; PC 1964; CMG 1956; OBE (Mil) 1944

Son of late Samuel Wilberforce. Born March 11, 1907; educated Winchester; New College, Oxford; Fellow, All Souls College, Oxford 1932; Hon. DCL, Oxford 1968; Hon. LLD: London 1972, Bristol. Married July 10, 1947, Yvette, daughter of late Roger Lenoan (1 son 1 daughter). *Armed Forces:* Served in the 1939–45 War in Norway, France and Germany, Hon. Brigadier; Under-Secretary, Control Office, Germany and Austria 1946–47. *Career:* Called to the Bar, Middle Temple 1932; QC 1954; Bencher 1961; A Judge of the High Court (Chancery division) 1961–64; A Lord of Appeal in Ordinary 1964–82. *Chancellor:* Chancellor, University of Hull 1978–94. *International Bodies (General):* Patron, International Law Association. *Other:* High Steward, University of Oxford 1967–90; Joint President, Anti-Slavery International; Vice-President, Royal College of Music. *Miscellaneous:* Hon. Member, Faculty of Advocates, Scotland. *Honours:* OBE (Mil) 1944; CMG 1956; Kt 1961; PC 1964. Hon. Companion, Royal Aeronautical Society. *Publications:* Author of *The Law of Restrictive Trade Practices.* *Clubs:* Athenaeum, Oxford and Cambridge University. *Name, Style and Title:* Raised to the peerage as Baron Wilberforce, of the City and County of Kingston-upon-Hull 1964. A Cross-Bencher. *Address:* The Rt Hon. the Lord Wilberforce, CMG, OBE, 8 Cambridge Place, London, W8 5PB.

WILCOX (Life Baroness, UK), Judith Ann Wilcox; cr. 1996

Daughter of John and Elsie Freeman. Born October 31, 1940; educated St Dunstan's Abbey, Devon; St Mary's Convent, Wantage; Plymouth University. Married 1st, 1961, Keith Davenport (1 son), (marriage dissolved 1986), married 2nd, 1986, Sir Malcom George Wilcox, CBE (died 1986). *Career:* Management of family business in Devon 1969–79; Founder/Financial Director, Capstan Fisheries Ltd, Devon 1979–84; Founder/Chairman, Channel Foods Ltd, Cornwall 1984–89; President Directeur-General, Pecheries de la Morinie, Boulogne-sur-Mer, France 1989–91; Chairman, National Consumer Council 1990–96; Chairman, Morinie et Cie, Boulogne-sur-Mere, France 1991–94; Board Member, Automobile Association 1991–; Member (non-executive), Inland Revenue Board 1992–95; Member, Prime Minister's Advisory Panel to Citizen's Charter Unit 1992–97; Commissioner, Local Government Commission 1992–95; Chairman, Citizen's Charter Complaints Task Force 1993–95; Board Member, Port of London Authority 1993–; Director: Cadbury Schweppes plc 1997–, Director, Carpetright plc 1997–. *Select Committees:* Member: Select Committee on European Communities Sub-Committee C (Environment, Public Health and Consumer Protection) 1997–, Ecclesiastical Committee 1997–; Select Committee on Science and Technology Sub-Committee II (Science and Society) 1999–. *All-Party:* Chair, All-Party Consumer Affairs and Trading Standards Group. *Other:* Member: Council of Institute of Directors 1991–, General Advisory Council of the BBC 1996, Lord Chancellor's Review of the Court of Appeal 1996–97, Tax Law Review Committee 1996–, Governing Body of Institute of Food Research 1996–; President: National Federation of Consumer Groups 1996–, Institute of Trading Standards Administration (ITSA) 1996–; Chairman, National Marine Aquarium at Plymouth 1998. FIMgt; FRSA. Freeman, City of London. Hon. Member, Fishmongers' Company 1998. *Special Interests:* Fishing Industry, Mariculture, Consumer Affairs, Environment. *Recreations:* Sailing, birdwatching, flyfishing, calligraphy. *Sportsclubs:* St Mawes Sailing. *Clubs:* Annabel's. *Name, Style and Title:* Raised to the peerage as Baroness Wilcox, of Plymouth in the County of Devon 1996. A Conservative. *Address:* The Baroness Wilcox, 17 Great College Street, London, SW1P 3RX *E-Mail:* wilcoxj@parliament.uk.

WILKINS (Life Baroness, UK), Rosalie Catherine Wilkins; cr. 1999

Daughter of late Eric Frederick and Marjorie Phyllis Elizabeth Wilkins. Born May 6, 1946; educated Dr Challoner's Grammar School, Amersham, Bucks; St Helen's School, Northwood, Middlesex; Manchester University (BA 1969). *Career:* PA to Director, Central Council for the Disabled 1971–74; Information Officer, MIND (National Association for Mental Health) 1974–78; Researcher/Presenter, The Link Programme (magazine programme for disabled people), ATV Network/Central Television 1975–88; Freelance Video and Documentary Producer 1988–96; Information Officer, National Centre for Independent Living 1997–99. *Awards Granted:* The Snowdon Award 1983. *Trusts, etc:* Trustee: Graeae Theatre Company, HAFAD (Hammersmith and Fulham Action for Disability). *Publications:* Contributing Author to *Able Lives – Women's Experience of Paralysis*, 1989. *Special Interests:* Disability. *Recreations:* Friends, gardening, theatre. *Name, Style and Title:* Raised to the peerage as Baroness Wilkins, of Chesham Bois in the County of Buckinghamshire 1999. Labour. *Address:* The Baroness Wilkins, House of Lords, London, SW1A 0PW *Tel:* 020 7381 1227 *Fax:* 020 7381 1227 *E-Mail:* roswilkins@compuserve.com.

WILLIAMS OF CROSBY (Life Baroness, UK), Shirley Vivien Teresa Brittain Williams; cr. 1993; PC 1974

Daughter of late Professor Sir George Catlin, and late Mrs Catlin (Vera Brittain). Born July 27, 1930; educated Schools in Great Britain and the United States; Somerville College, Oxford (Scholar, MA); Columbia University, New York (Fulbright Scholarship); Hon. Fellow: Somerville College, Oxford 1970, Newnham College, Cambridge 1977; Dr Pol Econ: Leuven University Belgium 1976, Radcliffe College, Harvard 1979; Hon. DLitt, Heriot-Watt 1980; Hon. LLD: Sheffield 1980, Southampton 1981, Bath 1981; Hon. DSc, Aston University 1981. Married 1st, 1955, Professor Sir Bernard Arthur Owen Williams, FBA, son of late Owen Williams, OBE (1 daughter) (marriage dissolved 1974), married 2nd, 1987, Professor Richard Elliott Neustadt. *Trades Union:* Member, NUGMW 1960–. *Career:* Journalist: *Daily Mirror* 1952–54, *Financial Times* 1954–58; General Secretary, Fabian Society 1960–64; Acting Director, Institute of Politics, Harvard University 1979–80; Professor of Elective Politics, John F. Kennedy School of Government, Harvard University 1988–; Lectureships: Pick Lecturer, University of Chicago, Godkin Lecturer, Harvard University, Janeway Lecturer, Princeton University, Regents Lecturer, University of California at Berkeley, Rede Lecturer, Darwin Lecturer, University of Cambridge, Dainton Lecturer, British Library, Gresham Lecturer, Mansion House. *House of Commons:* Contested: (Labour) Harwich 1954, 1955, Southampton Test 1959, (SDP) Crosby 1983, (SDP/Alliance) Cambridge 1987; MP: (Labour) Hitchin 1964–74, Hertford and Stevenage 1974–79, (SDP) Crosby 1981–83; PPS to Minister of Health 1964–66; Parliamentary Secretary, Ministry of Labour 1966–67; Minister of State: Department of Education and Science 1967–69, Home Office 1969–70; Secretary of State for: Prices and Consumer Protection 1974–76, Education and Science 1976–79; Paymaster General 1976–79. *Spokesman (Commons):* Opposition Spokesman on: Social Services 1970–71, Home Affairs 1971–73, Prices and Consumer Protection 1973–74. *House of Lords:* Deputy Leader, Liberal Democrat Party 1999–. *Spokesman:* A Spokesman on Foreign and Commonwealth Affairs 1998–. *Select Committees:* Member: Select Committee on European Communities 1997–99, Select Committee on European Communities Sub-Committee A (Economic and Financial Affairs, Trade and External Relations) 1997–99. *All-Party:* Joint Vice-Chairman, All-Party CAFOD Group 1999–. *Party Groups:* Deputy Leader, Liberal Democrat Peers in the House of Lords 1999–. *International Bodies (General):* International Advisory Committee Member, Council on Foreign Relations, USA; President, British-Russian Society and East-West Centre; Board Member, Moren School of Political Studies; Co-Chairman, Anglo-Dutch Society; Board Member, European Movement. *Party Groups (General):* Joined the Labour Party 1946; General Secretary, Fabian Society 1960–64, Chairman 1980–81; Member, Labour Party National Executive Committee 1970–81; Co-founder, Social Democratic Party 1981, President 1982–88. *Other:* Director, Turing Institute, Glasgow 1985–90; Board Member, Rand Corporation, Europe 1993–; Director, Ditchley Foundation 1994–. *Awards Granted:* Silver Medal, Royal Society of Arts. *Trusts, etc:* Trustee, 20th Century Foundation, New York. *Miscellaneous:* Visiting Fellow, Nuffield College, Oxford 1967–75; Member, Advisory Committee on Business Appointments 1999–. *Honours:* PC 1974; Grand Cross (second class),

Federal Republic of Germany. *Publications:* Author of: *Politics is for People,* 1981; *Jobs for the 1980s*; *Youth Without Work,* 1981; *Unemployment and Growth in the Western Economies,* 1984 (jointly); *A Job to Live,* 1985. *Recreations:* Music, hill-walking. *Name, Style and Title:* Raised to the peerage as Baroness Williams of Crosby, of Stevenage in the County of Hertfordshire 1993. A Liberal Democrat. *Address:* The Rt Hon. the Baroness Williams of Crosby, House of Lords, London, SW1A 0PW.

WILLIAMS OF ELVEL (Life Baron, UK), Charles Cuthbert Powell Williams; cr. 1985; CBE 1980

Son of late Dr N. P. Williams, DD, Lady Margaret Professor of Divinity at Oxford, and Mrs Muriel de Lérisson Williams, née Cazenove. Born February 9, 1933; educated Westminster; Christ Church, Oxford (MA); London School of Economics. Married March 1, 1975, Jane Gillian, DL, daughter of late Lieutenant-Colonel Gervase Portal (1 stepson). *Armed Forces:* National Service 1955–57, Subaltern KRRC (60th Rifles) HQ Battalion (Winchester) and Derna (Libya). *Career:* British Petroleum Co. Ltd 1958–64; Bank of London and Montreal 1964–66; Eurofinance SA Paris 1966–70; Baring Bros & Co. Ltd 1970–77, Managing Director 1971–77; Chairman, Price Commission 1977–79; Managing Director: Henry Ansbacher & Co. Ltd 1979–82, Henry Ansbacher Holdings 1982–85; Director, Mirror Group Newspapers plc 1985–92. *Spokesman:* Opposition Front Bench Spokesman on: Trade and Industry 1987–92, Defence 1990–97, the Environment 1992–97. *Select Committees:* Member, Ecclesiastical Committee 1997–. *Party Groups:* Deputy Leader of the Opposition in the House of Lords 1989–92. *Other:* Chairman, Academy of St Martin-in-the-Fields 1988; President, Campaign for the Protection of Rural Wales 1989–95, Immediate Past President and Vice-President 1995–; A Vice-President, Federation of Economic Development Authorities. *Trusts, etc:* A Busby Trustee, Westminster School 1989–99. *Honours:* CBE 1980. *Publications: The Last Great Frenchman: a life of General de Gaulle,* 1993; *Bradman: an Australian Hero,* 1996. *Special Interests:* Banking, Finance, Environment. *Clubs:* MCC, Reform. *Name, Style and Title:* Raised to the peerage as Baron Williams of Elvel, of Llansantffraed in Elvel in the County of Powys 1985. Labour. *Address:* The Lord Williams of Elvel, CBE, House of Lords, London, SW1A 0PW *Tel:* Home: 020 7581 1783.

WILLIAMS OF MOSTYN (Life Baron, UK), Gareth Wyn Williams; cr. 1992; PC 1999; QC 1978

Son of late Albert and Selina Williams. Born February 5, 1941; educated Rhyl Grammar School; Queens' College, Cambridge (Open Scholar History, LLM, MA). Married 1st, 1962, Pauline Clarke (1 son 2 daughters) (marriage dissolved), married 2nd, 1994, Veena Maya Russell (1 daughter). *Career:* Called to the Bar, Gray's Inn 1965; A Recorder of the Crown Court 1978–97; Deputy High Court Judge 1986–97; Member, Bar Council 1986–92; Leader of the Wales and Chester Circuit 1987–89; Bar Council: Vice-Chairman 1991–92, Chairman 1992–93; Fellow, University College of Wales, Aberystwyth 1993–; Hon. Professor, School of Sociology and Social Policy, University College of North Wales 1994; Visiting Professor, City University, London 1994–95; Fellow, University College of Wales, Bangor 1996. *Chancellor:* Pro-Chancellor, University of Wales 1994–. *House of Lords:* Parliamentary Under-Secretary of State, Home Office (Minister for Constitutional Issues) 1997–98; Minister of State, Home Office (Minister for Prisons and Probation) 1998–99; Deputy Leader of the House of Lords 1998–; Attorney-General 1999–. *Spokesman:* An Opposition Spokesman on: Legal Affairs 1992–97, Northern Ireland 1993–97, Wales 1995–96. *Other:* President: Commonwealth and Ethnic Bar Association 1993–97, Prisoners' Rights 1993–97, Welsh College of Music and Drama 1993–. *Trusts, etc:* Trustee: NSPCC 1993–97, Council of Justice 1993–97. *Honours:* PC 1999. Fellow, Institute of Advanced Legal Studies 1997–. *Special Interests:* Law, Foreign Affairs, Europe. *Name, Style and Title:* Raised to the peerage as Baron Williams of Mostyn, of Great Tew in the County of Oxfordshire 1992. Labour. *Address:* The Rt Hon. the Lord Williams of Mostyn, QC, House of Lords, London, SW1A 0PW.

WILLIAMSON OF HORTON (Life Baron, UK), David (Francis) Williamson; cr. 1999; GCMG 1998; CB 1984

Son of late Samuel and Marie Williamson. Born May 8, 1934; educated Tonbridge School; Exeter College, Oxford (MA); Hon. DEconSc, Limerick 1996; Hon. DCL, Kent 1998; Hon. DL, Robert Gordon University Aberdeen 1999. Married 1961, Patricia Margaret Smith (2 sons). *Armed Forces:* Second Lieutenant, Royal Signals 1956–58. *Career:* Joined Ministry of Agriculture, Fisheries and Food 1958; Private Secretary to Permanent Secretary and to successive Parliamentary Secretaries 1960–62; HM Diplomatic Service as First Secretary (Agriculture and Food) Geneva, for Kennedy Round Trade Negotiations 1965–67; Principal Private Secretary to successive Ministers of Agriculture, Fisheries and Food 1967–70; Head of Milk and Milk Products Division, Marketing Policy Division and Food Policy Division 1970–74; Under-Secretary, General Agricultural Policy Group 1974–76, EEC Group 1976–77; Deputy Director-General, Agriculture, European Commission 1977–83; Deputy Secretary, Cabinet Office 1983–87; Secretary-General, Commission of the European Communities 1987–97; Visiting Professor, University of Bath 1997–; Non-Executive Director, Whitbread plc 1998–. *Select Committees:* Member, Select Committee on Science and Technology Sub-Committee I (Non-Food Crops) 1999–. *Other:* Member, Wessex Regional Committee, National Trust. *Honours:* CB 1984; Knight Commander's Cross of the Order of Merit (Federal Republic of Germany) 1991; GCMG 1998; Commander Grand Cross of the Royal Order of the Polar Star (Sweden) 1998; Commander Légion d'Honneur (France) 1999. *Name, Style and Title:* Raised to the peerage as Baron Williamson of Horton, of Horton in the County of Somerset 1999. A Cross-Bencher. *Address:* The Lord Williamson of Horton, GCMG, CB, Thatchcroft, Broadway, Ilminster, Somerset, TA19 9QZ.

WILLOUGHBY DE BROKE (21st Baron, E), Leopold David Verney; cr. 1491; DL

Son of 20th Baron, MC, AFC. Born September 14, 1938. Succeeded his father 1986; educated Le Rosey, Switzerland; New College, Oxford. Married May 1, 1965, Petra, daughter of late Colonel Sir John Aird, 3rd Bt, MVO, MC (3 sons) (marriage dissolved 1989). *Councils, Public Bodies:* DL, Warwickshire 1999–. *Career:* Member, Council, Anglo-Hong Kong Trust 1989–; Chairman: St Martin's Magazines 1992–, SM Theatre ltd 1992–. *House of Lords:* An elected hereditary peer 1999–. *Select Committees:* Member: Select Committee on European Communities 1997–, Select Committee on European Communities Sub-Committee D (Agriculture, Fisheries and Food) 1997–. *All-Party:* Vice-President, All-Party Tibet Group. *Party Groups (General):* Vice-President, Conservatives Against a Federal Europe (CAFE) 1997–. *Other:* Patron, Warwickshire Association of Boys' Clubs 1990–; Governor, Royal Shakespeare Theatre 1992–; President, Heart of England Tourist Board 1996–. FRSA; FRGS. *Special Interests:* Hong Kong, Tibet, Europe. *Sportsclubs:* All England Lawn Tennis. *Clubs:* White's. *Heir:* His son, Hon. Rupert Greville Verney, born March 4, 1966. A Conservative. *Address:* The Lord Willoughby de Broke, DL, Ditchford Farm, Moreton in Marsh, Gloucestershire, GL56 9RD *Tel:* 01608 661990 *E-Mail:* willoughbyl@parliament.uk.

WILSON OF TILLYORN (Life Baron, UK), David (Clive) Wilson; cr. 1992; GCMG 1991

Son of late Rev. William Skinner Wilson and late Enid Wilson. Born February 14, 1935; educated Trinity College, Glenalmond; Keble College, Oxford (Scholar, MA, PhD (London) 1973); Hon. LLD, Aberdeen University 1990; Hon. DLitt, Sydney University 1991; Hon. LLD: University of Abertay, Dundee 1995, Chinese University of Hong Kong 1996. Married 1967, Natasha, daughter of late Bernard Gustav Alexander (2 sons). *Armed Forces:* National Service, The Black Watch 1953–55. *Career:* Entered Foreign Service 1958; Served Vientiane, Laos 1959–60; Language Student, Hong Kong 1960–62; First Secretary, British Embassy, Peking 1963–65; FCO 1965–68; Resigned 1968; Editor, China Quarterly 1968–74; Visiting Scholar, Columbia University, New York 1972; Rejoined Diplomatic Service 1974; Cabinet Office 1974–77; Political Adviser, Hong Kong 1977–81; Head of Southern European Department, FCO 1981–84; Assistant Under-Secretary of State, FCO 1984–87; Governor and Commander-in-Chief, Hong Kong 1987–92; Chairman: Scottish Hydro Electric plc 1993–98 (now Scottish and Southern Energy plc 1998–). *Chancellor:* Chancellor, University of Aberdeen 1997–. *Select Committees:* Chairman, Select Committee on Revised Red Deer

Act (Scotland) 1996. *All-Party:* Member, All-Party Hong Kong Country Group. *Other:* President, Bhutan Society of the UK; Member of Council, Glenalmond College; Member: Oxford University Expedition to Somaliland 1957, British Mount Kongur Expedition (North West China) 1981; President: Hong Kong Society, Hong Kong Association; Vice-President, Royal Scotish Geographical Society; Member, Royal Society for Asian Affairs. *Trusts, etc:* Member, Hopetown House Preservation Trust 1993–98; Trustee, Scotland's Churches Trust 1999–; Trustee, Museums of Scotland 1999–. *Miscellaneous:* Member, Board of British Council 1993–; Chairman, Scottish Committee of the British Council 1993–; Member of Council, CBI Scotland; Vice-Chairman, Scottish Peers Association 1998–. *Honours:* CMG 1985; KCMG 1987; KStJ 1987. FRGS. *Special Interests:* Hong Kong, East and South-East Asia, Scottish Affairs. *Recreations:* Mountaineering, skiing, reading. *Clubs:* Alpine, New (Edinburgh). *Name, Style and Title:* Raised to the peerage as Baron Wilson of Tillyorn, of Finzean in the District of Kincardine and Deeside and of Fanling in Hong Kong 1992. A Cross-Bencher. *Address:* The Lord Wilson of Tillyorn, GCMG, House of Lords, London, SW1A 0PW; Scottish and Southern Energy plc, 10 Dunkeld Road, Perth, PH15 5WA *Tel:* 01738 455200.

WINCHESTER (96th Bishop of), Michael Charles Scott-Joynt

Son of The Revd A. G. and Mrs D. B. M. Scott-Joynt. Born March 15, 1943; educated Bradfield College; King's College, Cambridge (MA); Cuddesdon Theological College. Married 1965, Louise White (2 sons 1 daughter). *Career:* Deacon 1967; Priest 1968; Curate, Cuddesdon 1967–70; Tutor, Cuddesdon College 1967–71, Chaplain 1971–72; Team Vicar, Newbury 1972–75; Priest-in-charge: Caversfield 1975–79, Bicester 1975–79, Bucknell 1976–79; Rural Dean of Bicester and Islip 1976–81; Rector, Bicester Area Team Ministry 1979–81; Canon Residentiary of St Albans 1982–87; Director, Ordinands and In-Service Training, Diocese of St Albans 1982–87; Suffragan Bishop of Stafford 1987–95; Bishop of Winchester 1995–; Prelate of the Most Noble Order of the Garter 1995–; Took his seat in the House of Lords 1996. *Special Interests:* Education, Local Government, Poverty, Welfare, Eastern Germany, Malaysia, Pensioners' Issues, Uganda, Rwanda. *Address:* The Rt Rev. the Lord Bishop of Winchester, Wolvesey, Winchester, Hampshire, SO23 9ND *Tel:* 01962 854050 *E-Mail:* michael.scott-joynt@dial.pipex.com.

WINDLESHAM (3rd Baron, UK), David James George Hennessy; cr. 1937; (Life) Baron Hennessy (UK) 1999; 3rd Bt of Winchester (UK) 1927; PC 1973; CVO 1981

Son of 2nd Baron. Born January 28, 1932. Succeeded his father 1962; educated Ampleforth; Trinity College, Oxford (MA); Brasenose College, Oxford (DLitt); Hon. Fellow, Trinity College, Oxford 1982. Married 1965, Prudence (died 1986), youngest daughter of Lieutenant-Colonel R. T. W. Glynn, MC (1 son 1 daughter). *Councils, Public Bodies:* Councillor, Westminster City Council 1958–62. *Career:* ATV Network: Managing Director 1974–81, Joint Managing Director 1974, Chairman 1981; Trustee, British Museum 1981–96, Chairman 1986–96; Chairman, The Parole Board 1982–88; Member, Museums and Galleries Commission 1984–86; Director, W. H. Smith Group plc 1986–95; Principal, Brasenose College, Oxford 1989–; Weinberg/Goldman, Sachs Visiting Professor, Princeton University 1997. *House of Lords:* Minister of State, Home Office 1970–72; Minister of State for Northern Ireland 1972–73; Lord Privy Seal and Leader of the House of Lords 1973–74; Leader of the Opposition 1974. *Select Committees:* Member, House of Lords Select Committee on Murder and Life Imprisonment 1988–89. *Party Groups (General):* Chairman, Bow Group 1959–60, 1962–63. *Other:* Vice-President, Royal Television Society 1977–82; Joint Deputy Chairman, Queen's Silver Jubilee Appeal 1977; President, Victim Support 1992–; Chairman, Oxford Society 1985–88. *Trusts, etc:* Deputy Chairman, Royal Jubilee Trust 1977–80; Chairman, Oxford Preservation Trust 1979–89; Trustee: The Royal Collection 1993–, Community Service Volunteers. *Miscellaneous:* Visiting Fellow, All Souls College, Oxford 1986. *Honours:* PC 1973; CVO 1981. *Publications: Communication and Political Power,* 1966; *Politics in Practice,* 1975; *Broadcasting in a Free Society,* 1980; *Responses to Crime,* Vol 1, 1987, Vol 2, 1993, Vol 3, 1996; *Politics, Punishment, and Populism,* 1998; *The Windlesham/Rampton Report on Death on the Rock,* 1989 (with Richard Rampton QC). *Clubs:* Brooks's. *Heir:* His son, Hon. James Rupert Hennessy, born November 9, 1968. *Name, Style and Title:* Created a life peer as Baron Hennessy, of Windlesham in the County of Surrey 1999. A Conservative. *Address:* The Rt Hon. the Lord Windlesham, CVO, House of Lords, London, SW1A 0PW.

WINSTON (Life Baron, UK), Robert Maurice Lipson Winston; cr. 1995

Son of late Laurence Winston, and of Ruth Winston-Fox, MBE. Born July 15, 1940; educated St Paul's School; London Hospital Medical College, London University (MB, BS 1964); Hon. Fellow, Queen Mary Westfield College. Married 1973, Lira Helen Feigenbaum (2 sons 1 daughter). *Career:* Wellcome Research Senior Lecturer, Institute of Obstetrics and Gynaecology 1974–78; Has held other posts in the United Kingdom, Belgium and USA; Consultant Obstetrician and Gynaecologist: Hammersmith Hospital 1978–; Presenter, *Your Life in their Hands*, BBC TV 1979–87; Dean, Institute of Obstetrics and Gynaecology, RPMS, London; Past Chairman, British Fertility Society; Professor of Fertility Studies, University of London at the Institute of Obstetrics and Gynaecology, Royal Postgraduate Medical School 1987–97; Imperial College, London; Presenter: *Making Babies*, BBC TV 1995, *The Human Body*, BBC TV 1998, *Secret Life of Twins*, BBC TV 1999. *Select Committees:* Member, Select Committee on Science and Technology 1996–, Chairman 1998–; Member, Select Committee on Science and Technology Sub-Committee II (Science and Society) 1999–. *All-Party:* Chairman, All-Party Research and Development in Fertility and Contraception Group 1998–. *Other:* Member: Council of Imperial Cancer Research Fund; Board of Lyric Theatre, Hammersmith. *Awards Granted:* Cedric Carter Medal, Clinical Genetics Society 1993; Victor Bonney Triennial Prize, Royal College of Surgeons of England 1993; Gold Medal, Royal Society for Promotion of Health 1998. *Miscellaneous:* Member, Parliamentary Office of Science and Technology (POST) 1998–. MRCS; LRCP; FRCOG 1983; FRSA; FScMed. *Publications: Reversibility of Sterilization*, 1978; (jointly) *Tubal Infertility*, 1981; *Infertility, a Sympathetic Approach*, 1987; *The IVF Revolution*, 1999; As well as over 250 papers in scientific journals on human and experimental reproduction. *Special Interests:* Health, Science and Technology, Education, Arts. *Recreations:* Theatre, broadcasting, music, wine. *Clubs:* Athenaeum. *Name, Style and Title:* Raised to the peerage as Baron Winston, of Hammersmith in the London Borough of Hammersmith and Fulham 1995. Labour. *Address:* Professor The Lord Winston, 11 Denman Drive, London, NW11 6RE *Tel:* 020 8455 7475 *E-Mail:* rwinston@globalnet.co.uk.

WOLFSON (Life Baron, UK), Leonard Gordon Wolfson; cr. 1985; 2nd Bt of St Marylebone (UK) 1962; Kt 1977

Son of late Sir Isaac Wolfson, 1st Bt, and late Lady Edith Wolfson. Born November 11, 1927. Succeeded his father to the baronetcy 1991; educated King's School, Worcester; Hon. Phd, Tel Aviv 1971 Hon. DCL, Oxon 1972; Hon. LLD, Strathclyde University 1972, Hon. DSC, Hull University 1977; Hon. Phd, Herbrew University 1978; Hon. LLD: Dundee 1979, Cambridge 1982, London 1982; Hon. Phd, Bar Ilan University 1983; Hon. DSC, Wales 1984; Hon. Fellow: London School of Hygiene and Tropical Medicine 1985, Queen Mary College, 1985; Hon. DSC, East Anglia 1986; Hon. Phd, Weitzmann Inst 1988; Hon. D Univ, Surrey 1990; Hon Fellow: University of Westminster 1991, Imperial College 1991; Hon. MD, Birmingham 1992; Dr hc, Edingburgh 1996; Hon. Member, Emmanuel College 1996, D Univ, Glasgow University 1997; Hon. Fellow: St Catherine's College, Oxford, Wolfson College, Oxford, Worcester College, Wolfson College, Cambridge, University College, London. Married 1st, 1949, Ruth, daughter of E. A. Sterling (4 daughters) (marriage dissolved 1991), married 2nd, September 1, 1991, Mrs Estelle Jackson, widow of Michael Jackson, FCA (1 step son, 1 step daughter). *Career:* Founder Trustee, Wolfson Foundation 1955–; Chairman: Wolfson Foundation 1972–, Burberry's Ltd 1978–96, Great Universal Stores 1981–96. *Other:* President, Jewish Welfare Board 1972–82. *Trusts, etc:* Trustee, Imperial War Museum 1988–94. Hon. FRCP 1977; Hon. FBA 1986; Hon. FRCS 1988; Hon. Member, Royal College of Surgeons, Edinburgh 1997; Hon. Fellow, Royal College of Engineering 1997. *Honours:* Kt 1977. *Recreations:* History, economics. *Heir:* Heir to baronetcy, none. *Name, Style and Title:* Raised to the peerage as Baron Wolfson, of Marylebone in the City of Westminster 1985. A Conservative. *Address:* The Lord Wolfson, 8 Queen Anne Street, London, W1M 9LD.

WOLFSON OF SUNNINGDALE (Life Baron, UK), David Wolfson; cr. 1991; Kt 1984

Son of late Charles and Hylda Wolfson. Born November 9, 1935; educated Clifton College; Trinity College, Cambridge (MA); Stanford University, California (MBA); Hon. Fellow, Hughes Hall, Cambridge 1989. Married 1st, 1962, Patricia Rawlings (created Baroness Rawlings, *qv*) (marriage dissolved 1967), married 2nd, 1967, Susan Davis (2 sons 1 daughter). *Career:* Director, Great Universal Stores 1973–78, 1993–, Chairman 1996–; Secretary to Shadow Cabinet 1978–79; Chief of Staff, Political Office, 10 Downing Street 1979–85; Chairman, Alexon Group plc 1982–86; Chairman, Next plc 1990–98. *Honours:* Kt 1984. Hon. FRCR; Hon. FRCOG. *Special Interests:* Health. *Recreations:* Golf, bridge. *Sportsclubs:* Sunningdale Golf, Woburn Golf, Trevose Golf.

Clubs: Portland. *Name, Style and Title:* Raised to the peerage as Baron Wolfson of Sunningdale, of Trevose in the County of Cornwall 1991. A Conservative. *Address:* The Lord Wolfson of Sunningdale, The Great Universal Stores plc, Leconfield House, London, W1Y 7FL *Tel:* 020 7495 0070 *Fax:* 020 7495 1567; 1 Portobello Studios, Haydens Place, London, W11 1LY *Tel:* 020 7792 2200 *Fax:* 020 7792 4400.

WOOLF (Life Baron, UK), Harry Kenneth Woolf; cr. 1992; Kt 1979; PC 1986

Son of late Alexander and Leah Woolf. Born May 2, 1933; educated Fettes College; University College, London (LLB); Fellow, University College, London 1981; Hon. LLD: Buckingham, Bristol, London, Manchester Metropolitan Universities; Hon. Fellow, Leeds Municipal University. Married 1961, Marguerite, daughter of late George and Victoria Sassoon (3 sons). *Armed Forces:* Commissioned (National Service) 15/19th Royal Hussars 1954; Seconded to Army Legal Services 1954; Captain 1955. *Career:* Called to Bar, Inner Temple 1954, Bencher 1976; Started Practice at Bar 1956; A Recorder of the Crown Court 1972–79; Junior Counsel, Inland Revenue 1973–74; First Treasury Junior Counsel (Common Law) 1974–79; A Judge of the High Court

of Justice, Queen's Bench Division 1979–86; Presiding Judge, South Eastern Circuit 1981–84; Member, Senate, Inns of Court and Bar 1981–85; Member, Board of Management, Institute of Advanced Legal Studies 1985–93; Chairman, Lord Chancellor's Advisory Committee on Legal Education 1986–90; A Lord Justice of Appeal 1986–92; Chairman, Board of Management, Institute of Advanced Legal Studies 1986–93; Held inquiry into prison disturbances 1990, part II with Judge Tumim, report 1991; A Lord of Appeal in Ordinary 1992–96; Held inquiry into Access to Justice 1994–96 (interim report 1995, final report and rules 1996); Master of the Rolls 1996–; Chairman, Advisory Committee on Public Records 1996; Visitor: University College, London 1996, Nuffield College, Oxford 1996. *Chancellor:* Pro Chancellor, London University 1994–. *Other:* President: Association of Law Teachers 1985–89, South West London Magistrates Association 1987–92, Central Council of Jewish Social Services 1989–; Governor, Oxford Centre of Hebrew Studies 1990–93 (Emeritus). *Trusts, etc:* Chairman: Butler Trust 1992–96, President 1996–, St Mary's Hospital Special Trustees 1993–97. *Honours:* Kt 1979; PC 1986. *Publications: Protection of the public: A New Challenge* (Hamlyn lecture) 1990; *Zamir and Woolf: The Declaratory Judgement* 2nd edition, 1993 (with another); *De Smith, Woolf and Jowell*, 1995 (with others, 5th edition). *Clubs:* Garrick, Royal Automobile. *Name, Style and Title:* Raised to the peerage as Baron Woolf, of Barnes in the London Borough of Richmond 1992. A Cross-Bencher. *Address:* The Rt Hon. the Lord Woolf, Royal Courts of Justice, Strand, WC2A 2LL.

WOOLMER OF LEEDS (Life Baron, UK), Kenneth John Woolmer; cr. 1999

Son of late Joseph Woolmer. Born April 25, 1940; educated Kettering Grammar School; Leeds University (BA Economics). Married September 23, 1961, Janice, daughter of Arthur Chambers, of Rothwell, Northamptonshire (3 sons). *Trades Union:* Member, AUT. *Councils, Public Bodies:* Councillor, Leeds County Borough Council 1970–74, Deputy Leader 1972–74; Councillor, Leeds Metropolitan District Council 1973–78; Councillor, West Yorkshire Metropolitan County Council 1973–80, Deputy Leader 1973–75, Leader 1975–77, Leader of the Opposition 1977–79; Chairman, Planning and Transportation Committee of Association of Metropolitan Authorities 1974–77. *Career:* Research Fellow, University of the West Indies 1961–62; Teacher, Friern Road Secondary Modern School, London 1963; Lecturer: Leeds University (Economics) 1963–66, University of Ahmadu Bello, Nigeria 1966–68, Leeds University 1968–79; Principal, Halton Gill

Associates 1979–96; University of Leeds, Leeds University Business School: Director of MBA Programmes 1991–97, Dean of External Relations 1997, Dean of Business School 1997–. *House of Commons:* MP (Labour) for Batley and Morley 1979–83; Contested Batley and Spen (Labour) 1983 and 1987. *Spokesman (Commons):* Front Bench Opposition Spokesman on: Trade, Aviation, Shipping, Film Industry 1981–82, Prices and Consumer Protection 1982. *Select Committees (Commons):* Member, Select Committee on The Treasury and the Civil Service 1979–81. *All-Party Committees (Commons):* Former Joint Secretary, All-Party Wool Textiles Industry Group. *Party Groups (Commons):* Chairman, PLP Finance and Economic Committee 1980–81, Vice-Chairman 1981–82. *Other:* Director, Leeds United AFC 1991–96. *Miscellaneous:* Former Parliamentary Adviser, Inland Revenue Staff Federation. *Recreations:* Football, cricket. *Sportsclubs:* Leeds United AFC supporter, Yorkshire CCC supporter. *Name, Style and Title:* Raised to the peerage as Baron Woolmer of Leeds, of Leeds in the County of West Yorkshire 1999. Labour. *Address:* The Lord Woolmer of Leeds, 8 Ancaster Crescent, Leeds, LS16 5HS *E-Mail:* kjw@lubs.leeds.ac.uk.

WRIGHT OF RICHMOND (Life Baron, UK), Patrick Richard Henry Wright; cr. 1994; GCMG 1989

Son of late Herbert Wright, of Wellington College, and of Rachel Wright, of Haslemere. Born June 28, 1931; educated Marlborough; Merton College, Oxford (MA); Hon. Fellow, Merton College, Oxford 1987. Married 1958, Virginia Anne Gaffney (2 sons 1 daughter). *Armed Forces:* Served Royal Artillery 1950–51. *Career:* Entered Diplomatic Service 1955; Middle East Centre for Arabic Studies 1956–57; Third Secretary, British Embassy, Beirut 1958–60; Private Secretary and later First Secretary, British Embassy, Washington 1960–65; Private Secretary to Permanent Under-Secretary, Foreign Office 1965–67; First Secretary and Head of Chancery, British Embassy, Cairo 1967–70; Deputy Political Resident, Bahrain 1971–72; Head of Middle East Department, FCO 1972–74; Private Secretary (Overseas Affairs) to Prime Minister 1974–77; British Ambassador to: Luxembourg 1977–79, Syria 1979–81; Deputy Under-Secretary of State, FCO 1982–84; British Ambassador to Saudi Arabia 1984–86; Permanent Under-Secretary of State and Head of the Diplomatic Service 1986–91; Director: Barclays Bank plc 1991–96, British Petroleum Co. (now BP Amoco) 1991–, De La Rue 1991–, Unilever 1991–99, BAA 1992–98; Member, Security Commission 1993–. *Other:* Member, Council of Royal Institute of International Affairs 1992–, Chairman 1995–99; Member of Council: Atlantic College 1993–, Royal College of Music 1991–; Governor: Ditchley Foundation 1986–, Wellington College 1991–; Registrar, OStJ 1991–95, Director of Overseas Relations 1995–97; Vice-President, Home-Start UK 1991–. *Honours:* CMG 1978; KCMG 1984; GCMG 1989; KStJ 1990. FRCM 1994. *Special Interests:* Foreign Affairs, Commonwealth. *Recreations:* Music, philately, walking. *Clubs:* United Oxford and Cambridge University. *Name, Style and Title:* Raised to the peerage as Baron Wright of Richmond, of Richmond upon Thames in the London Borough of Richmond upon Thames, 1994. A Cross-Bencher. *Address:* The Lord Wright of Richmond, GCMG, House of Lords, London, SW1A 0PW.

Y

YORK (96th Archbishop of), David Michael Hope; PC 1991; KCVO 1995

Son of late Jack and Florence Hope. Born April 14, 1940; educated Queen Elizabeth Grammar School, Wakefield; Nottingham University; St Stephen's House; Linacre College, Oxford (BA, DPhil); Hon. LLD CNAA; Hon. DD, Nottingham University. *Career:* Curate, St John, Tuebrook, Liverpool 1965–67, 1968–70; Chaplain, Church of the Resurrection, Bucharest 1967–68; Vicar, St Andrew, Orford, Warrington 1970–74; Principal, St Stephen's House, Oxford 1974–82; Vicar, All Saints, Margaret Street, London W1 1982–85; Diocesan Bishop of Wakefield 1985–91; Took his seat in the House of Lords 1990; Prelate of the Most Excellent Order of the British Empire 1991–95; Bishop of London 1991–95; Archbishop of York 1995–. *Honours:* PC 1991; KCVO 1995. *Publications:* Author of: *The Leonine Sacramentary, The Living Gospel, Friendship with God. Special Interests:* Eastern Europe, Inner Cities, Africa. *Recreations:* Music, fell walking, photography. *Clubs:* Athenaeum. *Address:* The Most Rev. and Rt Hon. the Lord Archbishop of York, KCVO, Bishopthorpe, York, North Yorkshire, YO23 2QE *Tel:* 01904 707021 *E-Mail:* office@bishopthorpe.u_net.com.

YOUNG (Life Baroness, UK), Janet Mary Young; cr. 1971; PC 1981; DL

Daughter of John Norman Leonard Baker. Born October 23, 1926; educated Dragon School Oxford; Headington School and in the USA; St Anne's College, Oxford (MA); Hon. Fellow, St. Anne's College, Oxford; Hon. DCL, Mt. Holyoke College, USA; Hon. DUniv, Greenwich. Married July 15, 1950, Geoffrey Tyndale Young (3 daughters). *Councils, Public Bodies:* Councillor, Oxford City Council 1957; Alderman and Leader of the Conservative Group on the Council 1967; DL, Oxfordshire 1989–; A Vice-President, Association of District Councils 1990–96. *Career:* Director, UK Provident Institution 1975; Member, British Railways Western Region Advisory Board 1977; Co-Chairman, Women's National Commission 1979–83; Director, National Westminster Bank 1987–96; Non-Executive Director, Marks & Spencer 1987–97; Chairman, Independent Schools Joint Council 1989–92, 1994–97. *Chancellor:* Chancellor, University of Greenwich 1993–98. *House of Lords:* Parliamentary Under-Secretary of State, Department of the Environment 1973–74; Minister of State, Department of Education and Science 1979–81; Chancellor of the Duchy of Lancaster and Leader of the House of Lords 1981–82; Minister in charge of: Civil Service Department 1981, Management and Personnel Office, November 1981–83; Lord Privy Seal and Leader of the House 1982–83; Minister of State, Foreign and Commonwealth Office 1983–87. *Whip:* Baroness in Waiting (Government Whip) 1972–73. *Spokesman:* Government Spokesman for Wales 1982. *Party Groups:* Chairman, Association of Conservative Peers 1995–. *Party Groups (General):* A Vice-Chairman, Conservative Party Organization 1975–83, Deputy Chairman 1977–79. *Other:* Vice-President, The West India Committee 1987–95, President 1995–; Member, Council of Royal Albert Hall, London 1988–, Vice-President 1996; Chairman, Governing Bodies of Girls Schools 1989–94, Vice-Chairman 1994–; Member, Council of Management, Ditchley Foundation 1990–; Member of Court, Cranfield University 1991–; Chairman, Council of Headington School 1992–; Patron, Family and Youth Concern 1996–. *Trusts, etc:* Trustee: Lucy Cavendish College, Cambridge 1992–97, Dorneywood Trust 1992–; Patron, Family Education Trust 1997–. Hon. Fellow, Institution of Civil Engineers. *Honours:* PC 1981. *Clubs:* University Women's. *Name, Style and Title:* Raised to the peerage as Baroness Young, of Farnworth in the County Palatine of Lancaster 1971. Recreation: Music. A Conservative. *Address:* The Rt Hon. the Baroness Young, DL, House of Lords, London, SW1A 0PW.

YOUNG OF DARTINGTON (Life Baron, UK), Michael Young; cr. 1978

Son of late Gibson Young, musician, and Edith Young, WEA tutor. Born August 9, 1915; educated Dartington Hall School; University of London; Hon. Degrees: Sheffield, Adelaide, Exeter, Queen Mary College, Open University, Keele University, Southampton University, University of East London; Hon. Fellow, Churchill College, Cambridge; Hon. Fellow, British Academy; Fellow, LSE. Married 1st, 1945, Joan Lawson (2 sons 1 daughter), married 2nd, 1960, Sasha Moorsom (died June 22, 1993) (1 son 1 daughter), married 3rd, November 5, 1995, Dorit Uhlemann (1 daughter). *Career:* Director, Political and Economic Planning 1941–45; Secretary, Labour Party Research Department 1945–51; Director, Institute of Community Studies 1953–; A Sociologist; Member, Central Advisory Council for Education 1963–66; Founder President, Consumers' Association 1965–; Member, National Economic Development Council 1975–78. *Other:* President, National Extension College 1970–; Chairman, Tawney Society 1982–84; President, College of Health 1983–. *Awards Granted:* Albert Medal, RSA. *Trusts, etc:* Trustee, Dartington Hall 1942–92. Hon. FBA. *Publications:* Author of: *The Rise of the Meritocracy*; *The Elmhirsts of Dartington – The Creation of an Utopian Community*; *The Metronomic Society -Natural Rhythms and Human Timetables*; *Life After Work*; Co-author of: *Family and Kinship in East London*; *A Good Death – Conversations with East Londoners*. *Name, Style and Title:* Raised to the peerage as Baron Young of Dartington, of Dartington in the County of Devon 1978. Labour. *Address:* The Lord Young of Dartington, 18 Victoria Park Square, London, E2 9PF.

YOUNG OF GRAFFHAM (Life Baron, UK), David Ivor Young; cr. 1984; PC 1984; DL

Son of late Joseph Young. Born February 27, 1932; educated Christ's College, Finchley; University College, London (LLB Hons). Married 1956, Lita Marianne Shaw (2 daughters). *Councils, Public Bodies:* DL, West Sussex 1999–. *Career:* Solicitor 1956; Executive, Great Universal Stores 1956–61; Chairman: Eldonwall Ltd 1961–75, Manufacturers Hanover Property Services Ltd 1974–84; Industrial Adviser/Special Adviser, Department of Industry 1979–82; Chairman, Manpower Services Commission 1982–84; Executive Chairman, Cable and Wireless plc 1990–95; Director, Salomon Inc 1990–94; Chairman, Young Associates Ltd 1996–; Currently Chairman of several companies, including: CDT Holdings plc, Inter Digital Networks Ltd, Pixology Ltd. *House of Lords:* Cabinet Minister without Portfolio 1984–85; Secretary of State for: Employment 1985–87, Trade and Industry 1987–89. *Party Groups (General):* Deputy Chairman, Conservative Party 1989–90. *Other:* President, Institute of Directors 1993–; Chairman of Council, University College, London 1995; Chairman: Chichester Festival Theatre Productions Company Ltd, West Sussex Economic Forum. *Honours:* PC 1984. *Publications:* Author of *The Enterprise Years*, 1990. *Recreations:* Fishing, photography. *Clubs:* Savile. *Name, Style and Title:* Raised to the peerage as Baron Young of Graffham, of Graffham in the County of West Sussex 1984. A Conservative. *Address:* The Rt Hon. the Lord Young of Graffham, DL, Young Associates Ltd, Harcourt House, 19 Cavendish Square, London, W1M 9AB *Tel:* 020 7447 8800 *E-Mail:* young@youngassoc.com.

YOUNG OF OLD SCONE (Life Baroness, UK), Barbara Scott Young; cr. 1997

Daughter of late George Young and of Mary Young. Born April 8, 1948; educated Perth Academy; Edinburgh University (MA Classics); Strathclyde University (DipSocSci, DipHSM 1971); DUniv, Stirling 1995; Hon. DSc; University of Hertfordshire 1997, Cranfield University 1998. *Career:* Sector Administrator, Glasgow Health Board 1973–78; Director of Planning and Development, St Thomas' Health District 1978–79; District General Administrator, NW District, Kensington and Chelsea and Westminster Area Health Authority 1979–82; District Administrator, Haringey Health Authority 1982–85; District General Manager: Paddington and North Kensington HA 1985–88, Parkside HA 1988–91; Chief Executive, Royal Society for the Protection of Birds 1991–98; Chairman, English Nature 1998–; Vice-Chairman, BBC 1998–; Non-Executive Director, Anglian Water. *Select Committees:* Member, Select Committee on European Communities Sub-Committee D (Agriculture, Fisheries and Food) 1998–. *Other:* Member: Committee, King's Fund Institute 1986–90, Delegacy, St Mary's Hospital Medical School 1991–94, World Council, Birdlife International 1994–98; Vice-President, Flora and Fauna International 1998–; Member Advisory Board, Forum for the Future 1999–. *Trusts, etc:* Trustee, National Council for Voluntary Organisations 1994–98. *Miscellaneous:* Member, BBC General Advisory Council 1985–88; President, Institute of Health Services Management 1987–88; Patron, Institute of Ecological and Environment Management 1993– Member: Committee of Secretary of State for the Environment's Going for Green Initiative 1994–96, UK Round Table on Sustainability 1995–, Commission on the Future of the Voluntary Sector 1995–97, Committee on the Public Understanding of Science 1996–97. *Recreations:* Cinema, gardening. *Name, Style and Title:* Raised to the peerage as Baroness Young of Old Scone, of Old Scone in Perth and Kinross 1997. Labour. *Address:* The Baroness Young of Old Scone, House of Lords, London, SW1A 0PW.

Dod *on* Disk
The Vacher Dod Parliamentary Database
that will run on your PC or Network
For further details please telephone the Westminster Office
020 7828 7256

YOUNGER OF LECKIE (4th Viscount, UK), George Kenneth Hotson Younger; cr. 1923; (Life) Baron Younger of Prestwick (UK) 1992; 4th Bt of Leckie (UK) 1911; KT 1995; PC 1979; KCVO 1993; TD 1964; DL

Son of 3rd Viscount, OBE, TD. Born September 22, 1931. Succeeded his father 1997; educated Winchester; New College, Oxford; Hon. LLD, Glasgow University 1992; Fellow, New College, Oxford 1992–; Hon. DLitt: Napier University, Edinburgh 1992; Hon. DU: Edinburgh 1992, Paisley 1994; Hon. LLD, Liverpool University 1995. Married 1954, Diana, daughter of late Captain G. S. Tuck, DSO, RN, of Chichester, West Sussex (3 sons 1 daughter). *Armed Forces:* Served Argyll and Sutherland Highlanders 1950–65. *Councils, Public Bodies:* DL, Stirlingshire 1968–. *Career:* Director: George Younger & Son Ltd 1958–68, Maclachlans Ltd 1968–70, Tennant Caledonian Breweries Ltd 1977–79, The Royal Bank of Scotland Group plc (Chairman) 1989, The Royal Bank of Scotland plc (Chairman) 1989, Murray Ventures plc (Chairman) 1989–98, Murray Income Trust plc (Chairman) 1989–99, Murray International Trust plc (Chairman) 1989, Murray Smaller Markets Trust plc (Now known as Murray Global Return) (Chairman) 1989, Siemens Plessey Electronic Systems Limited (Chairman) 1990–98; Chairman, Speed plc 1992–98; Banco Santander, SA (Now known as Banco Santander Central Hispano) 1991, PIK Holdings Limited (Chairman) 1991–98, Quality Scotland Foundation 1992, Quality Scotland Education Trust 1992, Scottish Partnership in Electronics for Effective Distribution Limited (Chairman) 1992–98, Scottish Council Development and Industry 1992, The New Atherton Investment Corporation Limited 1993–95, New Harrison Trust Limited 1993–95, Scottish Equitable Policyholders' Trust Limited 1993–98, Scottish Equitable Holdings Limited 1993–98, Scottish Equitable plc 1993–98; Murray Johnstone Holdings Limited 1993, Scottish Equitable Life Assurance Society 1994, Scottish European Educational Trust 1994, The Fleming Mercantile Investment Trust plc 1994, Alliance Logistics Limited 1994–99, Orangefield Investments Limited (Chairman) 1994, Royal Armouries' Board of Trustees (Chairman) 1994, European Children's Trust Limited (Now known as TECT Ltd) 1995. *House of Commons:* Contested (U) North Lanarkshire 1959 General Election; MP (Conservative) for Ayr 1964–92; Parliamentary Under-Secretary of State for Development, Scottish Office 1970–74; Minister of State for Defence, January-March 1974; Secretary of State for: Scotland 1979–86, Defence 1986–89. *Whip (Commons):* Scottish Conservative Whip 1965–67. *Select Committees (Commons):* Member, House of Commons Select Committees on: Scottish Affairs 1975–76, Parliamentary Procedure 1977–79. *Chancellor:* Chancellor, Napier University 1993–. *Party Groups (General):* Deputy Chairman, Conservative Party in Scotland 1967–70, Chairman 1974–75; President, National Union of Conservative and Unionist Associations 1988. *Other:* Former Governor, Royal Scottish Academy of Music; Director, The Romanian Orphanage Trust (Now known as The European Childrens' Trust Ltd) (Chairman) 1990–99; Chairman, Royal Anniversary Trust 1990–; President, Council of the Territorial Auxiliary and Volunteer Reserve Associations 1993–. *Miscellaneous:* Brigadier, The Queen's Bodyguard for Scotland (The Royal Company of Archers). *Honours:* TD 1964; PC 1979; KCVO 1993; KT 1995. *Special Interests:* Arts, Small Businesses. *Recreations:* Music, tennis, sailing, golf. *Clubs:* Caledonian, Highland Brigade. *Heir:* His son, Hon. James Edward George Younger, born November 11, 1955. *Name, Style and Title:* Created a life peer as Baron Younger of Prestwick, of Ayr in the District of Kyle and Carrick 1992. A Conservative. *Address:* The Rt Hon. Viscount Younger of Leckie, KT, KCVO, TD, DL, House of Lords, London, SW1A 0PW.

Whips and Spokesmen

GOVERNMENT WHIPS

The Rt Hon The Lord Carter — *Captain of the Honourable Corps of the Gentlemen-at-Arms (Chief Whip)*

The Lord McIntosh of Haringey — *Captain of The Queen's Bodyguard of the Yeoman of the Guard (Deputy Chief Whip)*

The Lord Bach — *Lord in Waiting*
The Lord Burlison, DL — *Lord in Waiting*

Baronesses in Waiting:
The Baroness Farrington of Ribbleton, The Baroness Ramsay of Cartvale, The Baroness Amos

GOVERNMENT SPOKESMEN

Lord Privy Seal, Leader of the House and Minister for Women:
Rt Hon the Baroness Jay of Paddington
Deputy Leader: Lord Williams of Mostyn
Agriculture: Baroness Hayman, Rt Hon the Lord Carter
Attorney-General: Lord Williams of Mostyn
Cabinet Office: Lord Falconer of Thoroton, QC, Lord Burlison
Culture, Media and Sport: Lord McIntosh of Haringey
Defence: Baroness Symons of Vernham Dean, Lord Burlison
Education and Employment: Baroness Blackstone, Lord Bach
Environment, Transport and the Regions: Rt Hon the Lord Macdonald of Tradeston, Lord Whitty, Baroness Farrington of Ribbleton *(Local Government)*
Foreign and Commonwealth Office: Baroness Scotland of Asthal, Baroness Ramsay of Cartvale
Health: Lord Hunt of Kings Heath, Lord Burlison
Home Office: Lord Bassam of Brighton, Lord Bach
International Development: Baroness Amos
Legal Affairs: Rt Hon the Lord Irvine of Lairg, Rt Hon the Lord Hardie
Lord Chancellor's Department: Rt Hon the Lord Irvine of Lairg, Lord Bach
Northern Ireland: Lord Dubs, Baroness Farrington of Ribbleton
Scotland Office: Baroness Ramsay of Cartvale
Social Security: Rt Hon the Baroness Hollis of Heigham, Baroness Amos
Trade and Industry: Lord Sainsbury of Turville, Lord McIntosh of Haringey
Treasury: Lord McIntosh of Haringey
The Wales Office: Baroness Farrington of Ribbleton
Women's Issues: Rt Hon. the Baroness Jay of Paddington, Baroness Amos

OPPOSITION WHIPS AND SPOKESMEN

Leader of the Opposition: Rt Hon the Lord Strathclyde
Deputy Leader of the Opposition: Rt Hon the Lord Mackay of Ardbrecknish
Chief Whip: Lord Henley
Deputy Chief Whip: Lord Burnham
Agriculture: Baroness Byford, Lord Luke *(Whip)*
Constitutional Affairs: Rt Hon the Lord Strathclyde, Rt Hon the Lord Mackay of Ardbrecknish *(Deputy Leader and Scotland)*, Rt Hon the Lord Mackay of Drumadoon *(Scotland)*, Lord Henley *(Wales)*, Earl of Northesk *(Whip)*
Culture, Media and Sport: Baroness Anelay of St Johns, Lord Luke *(Whip)*
Defence: Lord Burnham, Earl Attlee, Lord Northbrook *(Whip)*
Education and Employment: Rt Hon the Baroness Blatch *(Education)*, Viscount Astor *(Employment)*, Baroness Seccombe *(Whip)*
Environment, Transport and the Regions:
Lord Brabazon of Tara, Baroness Miller of Hendon *(London)*, Lord Dixon Smith *(Local Government)*, Earl Attlee *(Transport)*, Baroness Seccombe *(Whip)*
Foreign and Commonwealth Office: Lord Moynihan, Baroness Rawlings, Earl of Northesk *(Whip)*
Health: Earl Howe, Lord McColl of Dulwich, Lord Astor of Hever *(Whip)*
Home Office: Rt Hon the Lord Cope of Berkeley, Viscount Astor, Rt Hon the Lord Mackay of Drumadoon, Viscount Bridgeman *(Whip)*
International Development: Baroness Rawlings, Earl of Northesk *(Whip)*
Legal Affairs: Rt Hon the Lord Kingsland *(Shadow Lord Chancellor)*, Rt Hon the Lord Mackay of Drumadoon *(Shadow Lord Advocate)*, Baroness Buscombe, Viscount Bridgeman *(Whip)*

Northern Ireland: Lord Glentoran, Rt Hon the Lord Cope of Berkeley, Baroness Seccombe *(Whip)*

Scotland: Rt Hon the Lord Mackay of Ardbrecknish, Rt Hon the Lord Mackay of Drumadoon, Earl of Courtown *(Whip)*

Social Security: Rt Hon the Lord Higgins, Baroness Buscombe, Lord Astor of Hever *(Whip)*

Trade and Industry: Rt Hon the Lord Mackay of Ardbrecknish, Baroness Miller of Hendon, Baroness Buscombe, Lord Northbrook *(Whip)*

Treasury: Lord Saatchi, Rt Hon the Lord Kingsland, Earl of Northesk *(Whip)*

Wales: Rt Hon the Lord Roberts of Conwy, Earl of Courtown *(Whip)*

LIBERAL DEMOCRAT WHIPS AND SPOKESMEN

Leader: Rt Hon the Lord Rodgers of Quarry Bank

Deputy Leader: Rt Hon the Baroness Williams of Crosby

Chief Whip: Rt Hon the Lord Harris of Greenwich

Deputy Whip: Viscount of Falkland

Assistant Whips: Lord Tope, Lord Dholakia

Agriculture and Rural Affairs: Baroness Miller of Chilthorne Domer

Culture, Media and Sport: Viscount of Falkland, Rt Hon the Lord Thomson of Monifieth *(Media)*, Lord Addington *(Sport)*

Defence: Lord Wallace of Saltaire

Education and Employment: Lord Tope

Environment, Transport and the Regions: Baroness Hamwee

   Local Government and Planning: Baroness Hamwee

   Housing: Baroness Maddock, Lord Ezra

   Transport: Baroness Thomas of Walliswood Lord Methuen

Foreign and Commonwealth Affairs: Rt Hon the Baroness Williams of Crosby, Lord Wallace of Saltaire, Lord Avebury, Baroness Ludford

Health: Lord Clement-Jones, Lord Alderdice

Home Office: Lord McNally, Lord Thomas of Gresford, Lord Dholakia

International Development: (Vacant)

Northern Ireland: (Vacant)

Scotland: Lord Mackie of Benshie

Social Security: Earl Russell, Lord Goodhart Lord Addington *(Disability)*

Trade and Industry: Lord Razzall, Lord Ezra *(Energy)*, Lord Newby

Treasury: Lord Taverne, Lord Newby

Wales: Lord Thomas of Gresford, Lord Hooson, Lord Geraint

Chairman, General Election Campaign: Lord Razzall

Lord Lester of Herne Hill, Lord Thomas of Gresford and Lord Goodhart assist spokesmen on legal matters.

Peers' Special Interests

Abortion
Alton of Liverpool, L.
Brightman, L.

Adult Education
Mar, C.

Aerospace
Cope of Berkeley, L.

Africa
Chalker of Wallasey, B.
Lichfield, Bp.
York, Abp.

Ageing
Barker, B.

Agriculture
Brookeborough, V.
Callaghan of Cardiff, L.
Carlile of Berriew, L.
Carnegy of Lour, B.
Carter, L.
Cavendish of Furness, L.
Christopher, L.
Cope of Berkeley, L.
Courtown, E.
Deedes, L.
Dixon-Smith, L.
Geraint, L.
Home, E.
Hooson, L.
Howe, E.
Hughes of Woodside, L.
Inglewood, L.
Kimball, L.
Mackie of Benshie, L.
Mallalieu, B.
Mar, C.
Monro of Langholm, L.
Montrose, D.
Moyola, L.
Northbourne, L.
Northbrook, L.
Northesk, E.
O'Cathain, B.
Palmer, L.
Rotherwick, L.
Selborne, E.
Shrewsbury and Waterford, E.
Soulsby of Swaffham Prior, L.
Stodart of Leaston, L.
Wade of Chorlton, L.
Walpole, L.

Airport Policy
Morris of Manchester, L.
Smith of Leigh, L.

Alcohol and Drug Addiction
Falkland, V.

Alcoholism
Mancroft, L.

**Alternative Dispute
   Resolutions**
Ackner, L.

Alternative Medicine
Colwyn, L.

American Politics
Norton of Louth, L.

Amnesty International
Gilbert, L.

Anglo-American Relations
Blatch, B.

Anglo-Chinese Relations
Geddes, L.

Animal Welfare
Allenby of Megiddo, V.
Fookes, B.
Soulsby of Swaffham Prior, L.

Anti-Apartheid Work
Hughes of Woodside, L.

Anti-Pollution Matters
Mason of Barnsley, L.

Architecture
Lloyd-Webber, L.
Ryder of Warsaw, B.

Arms Control
Oxford, Bp.
Rea, L.

Army
Glentoran, L.

Art
Lloyd-Webber, L.
Luke, L.

Art and Design
Snowdon, E.

Arts
Alexander of Weedon, L.
Attenborough, L.
Blackstone, B.
Cameron of Lochbroom, L.
Carlile of Berriew, L.
Colwyn, L.
Crickhowell, L.
Davies of Oldham, L.
Donoughue, L.
Eatwell, L.
Fanshawe of Richmond, L.
Feldman, L.
Gibson, L.
Hamwee, B.
Healey, L.
Hoyle, L.
Inglewood, L.
James of Holland Park, B.
Jellicoe, E.
Jenkins of Putney, L.
McIntosh of Hudnall, B.
O'Cathain, B.
Oxford, Bp.
Quinton, L.
Renfrew of Kaimsthorn, L.
Renton of Mount Harry, L.
Rix, L.
Rogers of Riverside, L.
Sainsbury of Preston
   Candover, L.
Selkirk of Douglas, L.
Skidelsky, L.
Smith of Gilmorehill, B.
Sterling of Plaistow, L.
Stone of Blackheath, L.
Strange, B.
Walpole, L.
Winston, L.
Younger of Leckie, V.

Arts Sponsorship
Dean of Thornton-le-Fylde, B.

Australia
Parry, L.

Aviation
Brougham and Vaux, L.
Fanshawe of Richmond, L.
Glenarthur, L.

MacKenzie of Culkein, L.
Monro of Langholm, L.
Onslow of Woking, L.
Rotherwick, L.
Simon, V.
Trefgarne, L.

Banking
O'Cathain, B.
Williams of Elvel, L.

Blind People
Russell-Johnston, L.

Breast Cancer
Falkender, B.

**Britain's Export
Performance**
Waverley, V.

British Film Industry
Falkender, B.

British Politics
Norton of Louth, L.

British-Irish Relations
Hylton, L.

Broadcasting
Brigstocke, B.
Colwyn, L.
Griffiths of Fforestfach, L.
Holme of Cheltenham, L.
James of Holland Park, B.
Jay of Paddington, B.
Lipsey, L.
McNally, L.
Quirk, L.
Rawlings, B.
Taylor of Warwick, L.
Warnock, B.

**Broadcasting and
Communications**
Wakefield, Bp.

Building
Ryder of Warsaw, B.

Business
Hollick, L.

Business Ethics
Oxford, Bp.

Cane Sugar
Clark of Kempston, L.

Car Safety
Robertson of Port Ellen, L.

Central and Eastern Europe
Carlile of Berriew, L.

Charities
Rix, L.
Stewartby, L.

Charity
Arran, E.

Charity Law
Brightman, L.
Goudie, B.

Cheque-Book Journalism
Sharples, B.

Childcare
Hardie, L.
Knight of Collingtree, B.

Children
Blood, B.
David, B.
Goudie, B.
Harrison, L.
Murray of Epping Forest, L.
Nicholson of Winterbourne, B.
Strange, B.
Thornton, B.
Uddin, B.

China
Ashley of Stoke, L.
Marlesford, L.

Church Affairs
Luke, L.
Moore of Wolvercote, L.
Reverend Richardson of
   Calow, B.

Citizenship
Alton of Liverpool, L.

City
Alexander of Weedon, L.
Cuckney, L.
Northbrook, L.
Shawcross, L.

Civil Liberties
Barker, B.
Clinton-Davis, L.
Dubs, L.

Co-operative Movement
Morris of Manchester, L.

Coal Industry
Dormand of Easington, L.
Mason of Barnsley, L.

Commerce
Molloy, L.
Nicol, B.
O'Cathain, B.
Sainsbury of Preston
   Candover, L.

**Commercial and Intellectual
   Property Law**
Grabiner, L.

Commonwealth
Blaker, L.
Janner of Braunstone, L.
Molloy, L.
Moore of Wolvercote, L.
Russell-Johnston, L.
Stoddart of Swindon, L.
Taylor of Blackburn, L.
Waverley, V.
Wright of Richmond, L.

Communications Industry
Tenby, V.

Community Care
Brooke of Alverthorpe, L.
Carter, L.
Eames, L.

Community Relations
Howells of St Davids, B.

Company Law
Wedderburn of Charlton, L.

Complementary Medicine
Baldwin of Bewdley, E.

Conflict Resolution
Hylton, L.
Stone of Blackheath, L.
Waverley, V.

Conservation
Archer of Sandwell, L.
Gilbert, L.
Hardy of Wath, L.
Marlesford, L.
Nicol, B.
Northesk, E.
Onslow of Woking, L.
Renton of Mount Harry, L.
Roberts of Conwy, L.
Selborne, E.
Selkirk of Douglas, L.
Walpole, L.

Constitution
Carnegy of Lour, B.

Constitutional Affairs
Campbell of Alloway, L.
Dean of Harptree, L.
Gould of Potternewton, B.
Hogg of Cumbernauld, L.
Hollick, L.
Hooson, L.
Irvine of Lairg, L.
Molyneaux of Killead, L.
Norton of Louth, L.
Wallace of Saltaire, L.

Constitutional Reform
Currie of Marylebone, L.
Holme of Cheltenham, L.
Lester of Herne Hill, L.
Scarman, L.

Construction Industry
Feldman, L.
Howie of Troon, L.
Shrewsbury and Waterford, E.
Sterling of Plaistow, L.

Consumer Affairs
Campbell of Croy, L.
Graham of Edmonton, L.
Wilcox, B.

Consumer Protection
Janner of Braunstone, L.

Cornwall
Vivian, L.

Corporate Governance
Taverne, L.

**Council of Europe and
    Western European Union**
Knight of Collingtree, B.

Country Houses
Crathorne, L.

Countryside
Blackburn, Bp.
Carnegy of Lour, B.
Strange, B.

Cricket
Rix, L.

Crime and Criminal Justice
Bach, L.

Crime and Drugs
Taverne, L.

Criminal Justice
Harris of Greenwich, L.
Hilton of Eggardon, B.
James of Holland Park, B.
Stern, B.

Culture
Rawlings, B.

Current Affairs
Evans of Watford, L.

Cyprus
Stallard, L.
Vivian, L.

De-Regulation
Vinson, L.

Defence
Allenby of Megiddo, V.
Astor of Hever, L.
Attlee, E.
Blaker, L.
Bramall, L.
Brookeborough, V.
Campbell of Croy, L.
Carver, L.
Chalfont, L.
Craig of Radley, L.
Erroll, E.
Fanshawe of Richmond, L.
Fookes, B.
Gilbert, L.
Glenarthur, L.
Hardy of Wath, L.
Healey, L.
Hill-Norton, L.
Hooson, L.

Inge, L.
Judd, L.
Luke, L.
MacKenzie of Culkein, L.
Mason of Barnsley, L.
Monro of Langholm, L.
Moore of Wolvercote, L.
Murton of Lindisfarne, L.
Nicholson of Winterbourne,
    B.
Onslow of Woking, L.
Park of Monmouth, B.
Pym, L.
Robertson of Port Ellen, L.
Rogan, L.
Rotherwick, L.
Saltoun of Abernethy, Ly.
Selkirk of Douglas, L.
Selsdon, L.
Stewartby, L.
Strange, B.
Vivian, L.
Wallace of Saltaire, L.

Developing World
Falkland, V.

Development
Brett, L.
Desai, L.
Southwark, Bp.

Devolution
Hunt of Kings Heath, L.
Renton, L.

Devolution of Power
Geraint, L.

Disability
Ashley of Stoke, L.
Attenborough, L.
Carter, L.
Darcy de Knayth, B.
McColl of Dulwich, L.
Masham of Ilton, B.
Morris of Manchester, L.
Murray of Epping Forest, L.
Newton of Braintree, L.
Rix, L.
Simon, V.
Sterling of Plaistow, L.
Uddin, B.
Wilkins, B.

Disabled
Gould of Potternewton, B.
Jenkin of Roding, L.
O'Cathain, B.

Disadvantaged
Ashley of Stoke, L.

Disadvantaged and Excluded Children
Northbourne, L.

Disarmament
Jenkins of Putney, L.

Drafting of Legislation
Renton, L.

Drug Abuse
Masham of Ilton, B.
Vivian, L.

Drug Addiction
Mancroft, L.

Drug and Alcohol Rehabilitation
Cavendish of Furness, L.

East and South-East Asia
Wilson of Tillyorn, L.

East-West Relations
Russell-Johnston, L.

Eastern Europe
Harris of High Cross, L.
Whaddon, L.
York, L.

Eastern Germany
Winchester, Bp.

Ecological Economics
Beaumont of Whitley, L.

Economic Policy
Bruce of Donington, L.
Crickhowell, L.
Croham, L.
Cuckney, L.
Currie of Marylebone, L.
Davies of Oldham, L.
Desai, L.
Gilbert, L.
Griffiths of Fforestfach, L.

Harris of High Cross, L.
Hollick, L.
Jenkin of Roding, L.
Ludford, B.
Marsh, L.
O'Cathain, B.
Selsdon, L.
Sharp of Guildford, B.
Skidelsky, L.
Stoddart of Swindon, L.
Taverne, L.

Economics
Brett, L.
Christopher, L.
Eatwell, L.
Forsyth of Drumlean, L.
Howell of Guildford, L.
Lamont of Lerwick, L.
Roberts of Conwy, L.
Roll of Ipsden, L.
Sterling of Plaistow, L.

Economics and Monetary Union
Crawley, B.

Education
Addington, L.
Attenborough, L.
Baker of Dorking, L.
Baldwin of Bewdley, E.
Blackburn, Bp.
Blackstone, B.
Blake, L.
Blatch, B.
Bramall, L.
Briggs, L.
Brigstocke, B.
Brooke of Alverthorpe, L.
Buscombe, B.
Butterfield, L.
Butterworth, L.
Carlisle of Bucklow, L.
Carnegy of Lour, B.
Cavendish of Furness, L.
Chilver, L.
Cox, B.
Cumberlege, B.
Currie of Marylebone, L.
David, B.
Davies of Coity, L.
Davies of Oldham, L.
Desai, L.
Dormand of Easington, L.
Evans of Watford, L.

Griffiths of Fforestfach, L.
Hayman, B.
Hollis of Heigham, B.
Jellicoe, E.
Judd, L.
Kilpatrick of Kincraig, L.
King of West Bromwich, L.
Levy, L.
Lewis of Newnham, L.
Linklater of Butterstone, B.
Lockwood, B.
Lucas of Crudwell and Dingwall, L.
Macaulay of Bragar, L.
McFarlane of Llandaff, B.
Maddock, B.
Massey of Darwen, B.
Merlyn-Rees, L.
Nicholson of Winterbourne, B.
Northbourne, L.
Pearson of Rannoch, L.
Perry of Southwark, B.
Platt of Writtle, B.
Porter of Luddenham, L.
Quinton, L.
Quirk, L.
Renfrew of Kaimsthorn, L.
Roberts of Conwy, L.
St Albans, Bp.
Scarman, L.
Selborne, E.
Selkirk of Douglas, L.
Skidelsky, L.
Southwark, Bp.
Stallard, L.
Taylor of Blackburn, L.
Tope, L.
Uddin, B.
Walton of Detchant, L.
Warnock, B.
Wedderburn of Charlton, L.
Winchester, Bp.
Winston, L.

Electoral Affairs
Gould of Potternewton, B.

Electoral Reform
Blake, L.
Lipsey, L.

Employment
Brooke of Alverthorpe, L.
Davies of Oldham, L.
Durham, Bp.
Evans of Parkside, L.
Hoyle, L.
Turner of Camden, B.

Employment Law
Gladwin of Clee, L.
Janner of Braunstone, L.
Watson of Invergowrie, L.
Wedderburn of Charlton, L.

Energy
Cooke of Islandreagh, L.
Croham, L.
Evans of Parkside, L.
Gardner of Parkes, B.
Geddes, L.
Hardy of Wath, L.
Haslam, L.
Howell of Guildford, L.
Lindsay, E.
Lofthouse of Pontefract, L.
Lovell-Davis, L.
Naseby, L.
Nicol, B.
Skelmersdale, L.
Stoddart of Swindon, L.
Taylor of Blackburn, L.

Engineering
Attlee, E.
Tombs, L.

Environment
Addington, L.
Alton of Liverpool, L.
Baldwin of Bewdley, E.
Barber of Tewkesbury, L.
Beaumont of Whitley, L.
Bradshaw, L.
Bridgeman, V.
Campbell of Croy, L.
Cavendish of Furness, L.
Chilver, L.
Clinton-Davis, L.
Courtown, E.
Crickhowell, L.
David, B.
Dixon-Smith, L.
Erroll, E.
Flowers, L.
Forsyth of Drumlean, L.
Gibson, L.
Glentoran, L.
Graham of Edmonton, L.
Hanham, B.
Haslam, L.
Hereford, Bp.
Hilton of Eggardon, B.
Holme of Cheltenham, L.
Hunt of Kings Heath, L.

Hylton-Foster, B.
Inglewood, L.
Jellicoe, E.
Lewis of Newnham, L.
Lindsay, E.
London, Bp.
Maddock, B.
Mallalieu, B.
Mar, C.
Nicol, B.
Palmer, L.
Renton, L.
St John of Bletso, L.
Selkirk of Douglas, L.
Shrewsbury and Waterford, E.
Skelmersdale, L.
Soulsby of Swaffham Prior, L.
Strabolgi, L.
Tenby, V.
Tope, L.
Warnock, B.
Wilcox, B.
Williams of Elvel, L.

Equal Opportunities
Crawley, B.
Fookes, B.
Uddin, B.

Equality and Non-Discrimination
Lester of Herne Hill, L.

Ethics
Habgood, L.

Europe
Bowness, L.
Goudie, B.
Haskins, L.
Hooson, L.
Hylton, L.
Inglewood, L.
Ludford, B.
MacLehose of Beoch, L.
Montrose, D.
Pearson of Rannoch, L.
Skidelsky, L.
Tomlinson, L.
Tope, L.
Tordoff, L.
Wallace of Saltaire, L.
Williams of Mostyn, L.
Willoughby de Broke, L.

Europe (Anti-Federalist)
Shore of Stepney, L.

European Co-operation
Chalker of Wallasey, B.

European Legislation
Renton, L.

European Political Integration
Lester of Herne Hill, L.

European Union
Bruce of Donington, L.
Campbell of Alloway, L.
Carnegy of Lour, B.
Crawley, B.
Flather, B.
Gallacher, L.
Harris of High Cross, L.
Hooper, B.
Lovell-Davis, L.
Nicholson of Winterbourne, B.
Robertson of Port Ellen, L.
Russell-Johnston, L.
Stoddart of Swindon, L.
Taverne, L.

Exports
Falkender, B.
Naseby, L.
Oxfuird, V.

Family
Blood, B.
Northbourne, L.
Seccombe, B.

Far East
MacLehose of Beoch, L.
Marsh, L.

Farming
Barber of Tewkesbury, L.
Callaghan of Cardiff, L.
Nicholson of Winterbourne, B.

Film
Taylor of Warwick, L.

Film Industry
Dormand of Easington, L.
Falkland, V.

Finance
Boardman, L.
Bruce of Donington, L.
Clark of Kempston, L.

Croham, L.
Donoughue, L.
Haslam, L.
Higgins, L.
Howe, E.
Kimball, L.
Lucas of Crudwell and
   Dingwall, L.
Roll of Ipsden, L.
St John of Bletso, L.
Taylor of Gryfe, L.
Tomlinson, L.
Williams of Elvel, L.

Financial Institutions
Renton of Mount Harry, L.

Financial Markets
Stewartby, L.

Financial Regulation
Lipsey, L.

Financial Services
Christopher, L.
Jenkin of Roding, L.
Marsh, L.

Fishing
Hughes of Woodside, L.
Stodart of Leaston, L.
Wilcox, B.

Food and Nutrition
Naseby, L.
Rea, L.

Food Industry
Wade of Chorlton, L.

Football
Carter, L.

Foreign Affairs
Arran, E.
Blackstone, B.
Blake, L.
Blaker, L.
Bramall, L.
Campbell of Croy, L.
Cavendish of Furness, L.
Chalfont, L.
Clinton-Davis, L.
Fanshawe of Richmond, L.

Gilbert, L.
Glenarthur, L.
Hardy of Wath, L.
Healey, L.
Holme of Cheltenham, L.
Home, E.
Howell of Guildford, L.
Jellicoe, E.
Judd, L.
Lamont of Lerwick, L.
Lichfield, Bp.
McNally, L.
Molloy, L.
Moore of Wolvercote, L.
Moynihan, L.
Nicholson of Winterbourne, B.
Northbrook, L.
Park of Monmouth, B.
Prentice, L.
Pym, L.
Renfrew of Kaimsthorn, L.
Robertson of Port Ellen, L.
Russell-Johnston, L.
St John of Bletso, L.
Selkirk of Douglas, L.
Selsdon, L.
Shawcross, L.
Soulsby of Swaffham Prior, L.
Stern, B.
Stewartby, L.
Strange, B.
Thomas of Gwydir, L.
Tordoff, L.
Wallace of Saltaire, L.
Watson of Invergowrie, L.
Waverley, V.
Williams of Mostyn, L.
Wright of Richmond, L.

**Foreign and Commonwealth
   Affairs**
Uddin, B.

Foreign Policy
Tomlinson, L.

Forestry
Barber of Tewkesbury, L.
Cavendish of Furness, L.
McColl of Dulwich, L.
Nicol, B.
Taylor of Gryfe, L.

Former Soviet Union
Hylton, L.
Smith of Gilmorehill, B.

France
Astor of Hever, L.
Strabolgi, L.

Freedom of Information
Nicholson of Winterbourne, B.

Freemasonry
Burnham, L.

Further Education
Whitaker, B.

Future of Work
Sheppard of Liverpool, L.

Governance of the UK
Barker, B.

Health
Ashley of Stoke, L.
Barker, B.
Bridgeman, V.
Brigstocke, B.
Brookeborough, V.
Carter, L.
Colwyn, L.
Cox, B.
Dean of Harptree, L.
Ewing of Kirkford, L.
Falkender, B.
Gardner of Parkes, B.
Glenarthur, L.
Hanham, B.
Hayman, B.
Hollis of Heigham, B.
Hoyle, L.
Jay of Paddington, B.
Jenkin of Roding, L.
Kilpatrick of Kincraig, L.
Knight of Collingtree, B.
Lovell-Davis, L.
Ludford, B.
McColl of Dulwich, L.
McFarlane of Llandaff, B.
MacKenzie of Culkein, L.
Masham of Ilton, B.
Massey of Darwen, B.
Miller of Hendon, B.
Newton of Braintree, L.
Nicholson of Winterbourne, B.
Quirk, L.
Rea, L.
Roberts of Conwy, L.
Selkirk of Douglas, L.
Stallard, L.

Uddin, B.
Walton of Detchant, L.
Winston, L.
Wolfson of Sunningdale, L.

Health and Safety at Work
Walker of Doncaster, L.

Health Care
Forsyth of Drumlean, L.

Health Service
Carnegy of Lour, B.
Cumberlege, B.
Davies of Coity, L.
Dubs, L.
Hughes of Woodside, L.
McColl of Dulwich, L.
Mar, C.
Molloy, L.
Naseby, L.
Wigoder, L.

Hereditary Peers
Listowel, E.

Heritage
Gibson, L.
Hollis of Heigham, B.
Luke, L.
Monro of Langholm, L.
Montagu of Beaulieu, L.
Northesk, E.
Palmer, L.
Park of Monmouth, B.
Rawlings, B.
Selkirk of Douglas, L.

High Arctic
Brightman, L.

Higher Education
Flowers, L.
Grabiner, L.
Howie of Troon, L.
McColl of Dulwich, L.
Park of Monmouth, B.
Sharp of Guildford, B.
Soulsby of Swaffham Prior, L.
Watson of Invergowrie, L.

History
Baker of Dorking, L.

Home Affairs
Anelay of St Johns, B.

Carlile of Berriew, L.
David, B.
Hardy of Wath, L.
Irvine of Lairg, L.
Mackenzie of Framwellgate,
    L.
Mallalieu, B.
Shore of Stepney, L.

Home Office Affairs
Deedes, L.
Wigoder, L.

Homeless
Bristol, Bp.
Murray of Epping Forest, L.
Scarman, L.

Hong Kong
Ashley of Stoke, L.
Bramall, L.
Butterfield, L.
Geddes, L.
Marlesford, L.
Skidelsky, L.
Willoughby de Broke, L.
Wilson of Tillyorn, L.

Horse Racing
Carnarvon, E.
Lipsey, L.

Horticulture
Northbourne, L.
Skelmersdale, L.

Housing
Alton of Liverpool, L.
Bristol, Bp.
Clark of Kempston, L.
Dean of Thornton-le-Fylde, B.
Dixon, L.
Durham, Bp.
Fisher of Rednal, B.
Fookes, B.
Gardner of Parkes, B.
Goudie, B.
Hamwee, B.
Hylton, L.
Jenkin of Roding, L.
Lofthouse of Pontefract, L.
Maddock, B.
Merlyn-Rees, L.
Oxford, Bp.
Sanderson of Bowden, L.
Selkirk of Douglas, L.

Stallard, L.
Stoddart of Swindon, L.

Human Rights
Ahmed, L.
Alton of Liverpool, L.
Archer of Sandwell, L.
Brett, L.
Carlisle of Bucklow, L.
Cox, B.
Dubs, L.
Faulkner of Worcester, L.
Goodhart, L.
Hylton, L.
Janner of Braunstone, L.
Lester of Herne Hill, L.
Lofthouse of Pontefract, L.
Mason of Barnsley, L.
Nicholson of Winterbourne, B.
Rea, L.
Russell-Johnston, L.
St John of Bletso, L.
Scarman, L.
Stern, B.

Humanitarian Aid
Cox, B.

Immigration
Dubs, L.
Geddes, L.
Hoyle, L.

Import Substitution
Feldman, L.

India
Janner of Braunstone, L.

Industrial Issues
Sharp of Guildford, B.

Industrial Policy
Lamont of Lerwick, L.

Industrial Relations
Butterworth, L.
Campbell of Alloway, L.
Clarke of Hampstead, L.
Davies of Coity, L.
Evans of Parkside, L.
Evans of Watford, L.
Gladwin of Clee, L.
Haslam, L.
Hoyle, L.
Janner of Braunstone, L.

Lofthouse of Pontefract, L.
Prentice, L.
Robertson of Port Ellen, L.
Walker of Doncaster, L.
Wedderburn of Charlton, L.

Industrial Training
Lockwood, B.

Industry
Bruce of Donington, L.
Butterworth, L.
Cavendish of Furness, L.
Chilver, L.
Christopher, L.
Clark of Kempston, L.
Dean of Thornton-le-Fylde, B.
Feldman, L.
Geddes, L.
Gladwin of Clee, L.
Hanson, L.
Haslam, L.
Holme of Cheltenham, L.
Home, E.
Jenkin of Roding, L.
Knight of Collingtree, B.
Lockwood, B.
Marsh, L.
Molloy, L.
O'Cathain, B.
Oxfuird, V.
Sanderson of Bowden, L.
Stoddart of Swindon, L.
Taylor of Gryfe, L.
Wade of Chorlton, L.

Information Technology
Baker of Dorking, L.
Nicholson of Winterbourne, B.
Randall of St Budeaux, L.

Inner Cities
Alton of Liverpool, L.
Hooper, B.
Knights, L.
Lichfield, Bp.
Moynihan, L.
York, L.

Insurance
Clark of Kempston, L.

Intellectual Property
Nicholson of Winterbourne, B.

International Affairs
Hooson, L.
Islwyn, L.
Perry of Southwark, B.
Rawlings, B.
Sandwich, E.

**International Affairs
(Foreign and Defence)**
Owen, L.

International Development
Massey of Darwen, B.
Stern, B.
Tomlinson, L.
Whitaker, B.

International Finance
Howell of Guildford, L.

Iran
Nicholson of Winterbourne, B.

Iraq
Nicholson of Winterbourne, B.

Ireland
Dubs, L.

Islamic World
Nicholson of Winterbourne, B.

Jewish Causes
Janner of Braunstone, L.

Justice
Hanham, B.

Juvenile Justice
Elton, L.

**Kashmiri Right of Self
Determination**
Ahmed, L.

Kuwait
Nicholson of Winterbourne, B.

Labour Issues
Brett, L.

Lancashire
Waddington, L.

Land Reform
MacKenzie of Culkein, L.

Language and Culture
Geraint, L.

Latin America
Hooper, B.

Law
Ackner, L.
Alexander of Weedon, L.
Cameron of Lochbroom, L.
Carlisle of Bucklow, L.
Clinton-Davis, L.
Hooson, L.
Mallalieu, B.
Taylor of Warwick, L.
Williams of Mostyn, L.

Law and Order
Buscombe, B.
Knights, L.
Miller of Hendon, B.
Renton, L.

**Law and the Administration
of Justice**
Donaldson of Lymington, L.

Law Reform
Archer of Sandwell, L.
Grabiner, L.
Lester of Herne Hill, L.
Scarman, L.
Selkirk of Douglas, L.

Legal Affairs
Carlile of Berriew, L.
Inglewood, L.
Irvine of Lairg, L.
Mackenzie of Framwellgate,
 L.
St John of Bletso, L.
Waddington, L.

Legal Profession
Alexander of Weedon, L.

Legislatures
Norton of Louth, L.

Leisure Industries
McNally, L.

Licensed Trade
Evans of Parkside, L.

Light Rail Transport
Russell-Johnston, L.

Lighting
Robertson of Port Ellen, L.

Literature
James of Holland Park, B.

Local Government
Bach, L.
Bowness, L.
Bridgeman, V.
Cameron of Lochbroom, L.
Carnegy of Lour, B.
Cumberlege, B.
Dormand of Easington, L.
Fisher of Rednal, B.
Forsyth of Drumlean, L.
Graham of Edmonton, L.
Hamwee, B.
Hanham, B.
Hogg of Cumbernauld, L.
Hollis of Heigham, B.
Inglewood, L.
King of West Bromwich, L.
Knights, L.
Lofthouse of Pontefract, L.
Ludford, B.
Macaulay of Bragar, L.
Maddock, B.
Molyneaux of Killead, L.
Platt of Writtle, B.
Selkirk of Douglas, L.
Sewel, L.
Smith of Leigh, L.
Stodart of Leaston, L.
Stoddart of Swindon, L.
Taylor of Blackburn, L.
Tope, L.
Uddin, B.
Winchester, Bp.

Local Government Management
Blatch, B.

Local Issues
Cavendish of Furness, L.

London
Hamwee, B.
London, Bp.
Thornton, B.

Low Pay
Blood, B.

Machinery of Government
Goudie, B.
Lipsey, L.

Magistracy
Tenby, V.

Malaysia
Winchester, Bp.

Manpower Policy
Walker of Doncaster, L.

Manufacturing Industries
Cooke of Islandreagh, L.
Evans of Parkside, L.

Mariculture
Wilcox, B.

Marine Industry
Greenway, L.

Maritime Affairs
Cooke of Islandreagh, L.
Dixon, L.
Glentoran, L.
MacKenzie of Culkein, L.

Maritime Safety
Donaldson of Lymington, L..

Marketing
Naseby, L.

Media
Arran, E.
Cumberlege, B.
Dean of Thornton-le-Fylde, B.
Deedes, L.
Gibson, L.
Hamwee, B.
Hollis of Heigham, B.
Inglewood, L.
Jay of Paddington, B.
Jenkins of Putney, L.
Lester of Herne Hill, L.
Lovell-Davis, L.
Palmer, L.
Quinton, L.
Quirk, L.
Thornton, B.

Medical Drugs
Ashley of Stoke, L.

Medical Profession
Carlile of Berriew, L.

Medical Research Ethics
Carnegy of Lour, B.

Medicine
Butterfield, L.
Habgood, L.
McColl of Dulwich, L.
Walton of Detchant, L.
Warnock, B.

Mental Handicap
Forsyth of Drumlean, L.
Pearson of Rannoch, L.
Renton, L.

Mental Health
Alderdice, L.
Carlile of Berriew, L.
Fookes, B.
McCluskey, L.
Molyneaux of Killead, L.

Middle East
Hylton, L.
Janner of Braunstone, L.
Shore of Stepney, L.
Stone of Blackheath, L.

Middle Eastern History and Politics
Rochester, Bp.

Migration
Judd, L.

Military History
Luke, L.

Mineral Extraction
Shrewsbury and Waterford, E.

Monetary Union
Harrison, L.

Moral Issues
Oxford, Bp.

Motor Industry
Astor of Hever, L.
Brougham and Vaux, L.
Denton of Wakefield, B.
Islwyn, L.
Simon, V.

Motorcycle Industry
Falkland, V.

Museums and Galleries
Brigstocke, B.
Montagu of Beaulieu, L.
Renfrew of Kaimsthorn, L.

Music
Sterling of Plaistow, L.

**National Health Service
(Hospital Chaplaincy)**
St Albans, Bp.

National Heritage
Renfrew of Kaimsthorn, L.
Sandwich, E.
Strabolgi, L.

National Lottery
Naseby, L.

North American Matters
Parry, L.

North West
Taylor of Blackburn, L.

Northern Ireland
Alderdice, L.
Alton of Liverpool, L.
Archer of Sandwell, L.
Brookeborough, V.
Denton of Wakefield, B.
Eames, L.
Glentoran, L.
Hylton, L.
Mason of Barnsley, L.
Moyola, L.
Park of Monmouth, B.
Rogan, L.
Stallard, L.

Nuclear Disarmament
Jenkins of Putney, L.

Nursing
Cox, B.
MacKenzie of Culkein, L.

Oil
Howell of Guildford, L.

Oman
Butterfield, L.

**Overseas Aid and
Development**
Attlee, E.
Butterworth, L.
Chalker of Wallasey, B.
Clarke of Hampstead, L.
Deedes, L.
Durham, Bp.
Hughes of Woodside, L.
Jay of Paddington, B.
Lichfield, Bp.
Moynihan, L.
Oxford, Bp.
Sandwich, E.
Watson of Invergowrie, L.
Waverley, V.

Parliamentary Affairs
Norton of Louth, L.
Pym, L.

Parliamentary Procedure
Naseby, L.

Penal Affairs and Policy
Carlisle of Bucklow, L.
Christopher, L.
Fookes, B.
Glenarthur, L.
Howe, E.
Hylton, L.
Judd, L.
Linklater of Butterstone, B.
Masham of Ilton, B.

Penal Reform
Dubs, L.
Merlyn-Rees, L.

Pensioners' Issues
Winchester, Bp.

Pensions
Christopher, L.
Dean of Thornton-le-Fylde, B.
Newton of Braintree, L.
Taverne, L.
Turner of Camden, B.
Vinson, L.

Pet Quarantine
Sharples, B.

Planning
Bradshaw, L.
Gardner of Parkes, B.

Hamwee, B.
Jenkin of Roding, L.
Wade of Chorlton, L.

Police
Bradshaw, L.
Harris of Richmond, B.
Knights, L.
Mackenzie of Framwellgate,
  L.
Simon, V.

Policy Development
Filkin, L.

Policy Implementation
Ashton of Upholland, B.
Filkin, L.

Population and Development
Gould of Potternewton, B.

Post Office
Skelmersdale, L.

Poverty
Ashley of Stoke, L.
Barker, B.
Beaumont of Whitley, L.
Oxford, Bp.
Winchester, Bp.

Prison Reform
Addington, L.
McIntosh of Hudnall, B.

Prisoners' Wives
Sharples, B.

Prisons
Hylton, L.

Privatisation
Forsyth of Drumlean, L.
Renton of Mount Harry, L.

Privatised Utilities
Skelmersdale, L.

Professional Engineers
Howie of Troon, L.

Professional Self-Regulation
Kilpatrick of Kincraig, L.

Property
Courtown, E.
Shrewsbury and Waterford, E.

Psephology
Lipsey, L.

Psychoanalysis and Political Conflict Resolution
Alderdice, L.

Public Communication
Quirk, L.

Public Finance
Sewel, L.

Public Health
McIntosh of Hudnall, B.

Public Transport
Hogg of Cumbernauld, L.

Race Relations
Deedes, L.
Dubs, L.
Flather, B.
Gould of Potternewton, B.
Hilton of Eggardon, B.
Judd, L.
Sheppard of Liverpool, L.
Shore of Stepney, L.
Whitaker, B.

Railways
Taylor of Blackburn, L.
Tenby, V.

Recreation
Monro of Langholm, L.

Refugees
Alton of Liverpool, L.
Judd, L.
Moynihan, L.

Refugees/Displaced People
Nicholson of Winterbourne, B.

Regional Development
Goudie, B.
Morris of Manchester, L.

Regional Policy
Dormand of Easington, L.
Elliott of Morpeth, L.
Inglewood, L.

Regionalism
Smith of Leigh, L.

Research
Butterfield, L.

Restrictive Trade Practices and Monopolies
Campbell of Alloway, L.

Retail Industry
Denton of Wakefield, B.
Feldman, L.
McNally, L.
O'Cathain, B.

River Thames
Luke, L.

Road Programme
Islwyn, L.

Road Safety
Brougham and Vaux, L.
Simon, V.

Road Transport
Montagu of Beaulieu, L.

Rural Affairs
Carter, L.
Geraint, L.
Inglewood, L.
Mancroft, L.
Montrose, D.
Pym, L.

Russia
Harris of High Cross, L.
Smith of Gilmorehill, B.

Rwanda
Winchester, Bp.

Science
Habgood, L.
Porter of Luddenham, L.
Selborne, E.
Southwark, Bp.
Stone of Blackheath, L.
Tombs, L.
Walton of Detchant, L.

Science and Technology
Carver, L.
Flowers, L.

Haskel, L.
Morris of Manchester, L.
Sharp of Guildford, B.
Simon, V.
Taverne, L.
Winston, L.

Scotland
Erroll, E.
Glenarthur, L.
Goudie, B.
Monro of Langholm, L.
Robertson of Port Ellen, L.
Sewel, L.

Scottish Affairs
Carnegy of Lour, B.
Home, E.
Russell-Johnston, L.
Saltoun of Abernethy, Ly.
Sanderson of Bowden, L.
Selkirk of Douglas, L.
Wilson of Tillyorn, L.

Scottish Highlands
Pearson of Rannoch, L.

Scottish Law
Macaulay of Bragar, L.

Scottish Parliament
Watson of Invergowrie, L.

Sex Equality
Lockwood, B.

Shipping
Geddes, L.
Greenway, L.
Sterling of Plaistow, L.

Ships and Shipbuilding
Dixon, L.

Small Business
Harrison, L.

Small Businesses
Cope of Berkeley, L.
King of West Bromwich, L.
Miller of Hendon, B.
Roberts of Conwy, L.
Sanderson of Bowden, L.
Sharples, B.
Vinson, L.
Younger of Leckie, V.

Small Farmers
Listowel, E.

Social Issues
Eames, L.
Ludford, B.

Social Policy
Blackstone, B.
Briggs, L.
Griffiths of Fforestfach, L.
Harris of High Cross, L.

Social Security
Anelay of St Johns, B.
Carnegy of Lour, B.
Dean of Harptree, L.
Higgins, L.
Knight of Collingtree, B.
Mar, C.
Newton of Braintree, L.
Turner of Camden, B.

Social Services
Barker, B.
Bridgeman, V.
Dixon, L.
Ewing of Kirkford, L.
Newton of Braintree, L.
Stallard, L.

Social Welfare
Hylton-Foster, B.
Levy, L.

South Africa
St John of Bletso, L.

South East Asia
Geddes, L.
Naseby, L.

Southern Africa
Filkin, L.

Space
Tanlaw, L.

Speech Pathology
Quirk, L.

Sport
Arran, E.
Bach, L.
Donoughue, L.
Faulkner of Worcester, L.

Feldman, L.
Glentoran, L.
Higgins, L.
Islwyn, L.
Macaulay of Bragar, L.
Monro of Langholm, L.
Moynihan, L.

Steel
Islwyn, L.

Sufism
Rochester, Bp.

Sustainable Built Environment
Rogers of Riverside, L.

Tax
Newton of Braintree, L.
Stewartby, L.
Taverne, L.
Vinson, L.

Technology
Erroll, E.
Jenkin of Roding, L.
Southwark, Bp.
Tombs, L.
Wade of Chorlton, L.

Telecommunications
Dean of Thornton-le-Fylde, B.

Terrorism
Vivian, L.

Textile Industry
Sanderson of Bowden, L.
Waddington, L.

Theatre
Macaulay of Bragar, L.
Rix, L.

Third World
Archer of Sandwell, L.
Geraint, L.
Judd, L.
Rea, L.

Tibet
Willoughby de Broke, L.

Time
Tanlaw, L.

Tourism
Blaker, L.
Brookeborough, V.
Dormand of Easington, L.
Feldman, L.
Gladwin of Clee, L.
Harrison, L.
Luke, L.
McNally, L.
Montagu of Beaulieu, L.
Parry, L.
Roberts of Conwy, L.
Walpole, L.

Trade
Chalker of Wallasey, B.
Hoyle, L.

Trade and Industry
Boardman, L.
Buscombe, B.
Clark of Kempston, L.
Eatwell, L.
Haskel, L.
Lucas of Crudwell and
    Dingwall, L.
McNally, L.
Moynihan, L.
Rogan, L.
Selsdon, L.

Trade Union Law
Renton, L.

Trade Unions
Dixon, L.
Jenkins of Putney, L.

Training
Davies of Oldham, L.
Lockwood, B.
Roberts of Conwy, L.

Transition Economies
Skidelsky, L.

Transport
Attlee, E.
Blackburn, Bp.
Brabazon of Tara, L.
Bradshaw, L.
Brougham and Vaux, L.
Chalker of Wallasey, B.
Clinton-Davis, L.
Davies of Oldham, L.
Denton of Wakefield, B.

Dixon, L.
Dixon-Smith, L.
Evans of Parkside, L.
Falkland, V.
Faulkner of Worcester, L.
Gardner of Parkes, B.
Geddes, L.
Gilbert, L.
Hereford, Bp.
Higgins, L.
Hollick, L.
Hughes of Woodside, L.
Hunt of Kings Heath, L.
Laird, L.
Lindsay, E.
Roberts of Conwy, L.
Sanderson of Bowden, L.
Shrewsbury and Waterford, E.
Stoddart of Swindon, L.
Taylor of Gryfe, L.
Wade of Chorlton, L.

UFOs
Hill-Norton, L.

Uganda
Winchester, Bp.

Underdeveloped Countries
Attenborough, L.

Unemployment
Mar, C.
Sheppard of Liverpool, L.
Shore of Stepney, L.

United Nations
Carlile of Berriew, L.
Vivian, L.

Urban Policies
Crickhowell, L.
Jenkin of Roding, L.
Sheppard of Liverpool, L.

USA Affairs
Bach, L.

Visual and Performing Arts
Crathorne, L.

Visual Arts
Freyberg, L.

Vocational Education
Bristol, Bp.

Voluntary Sector
Chalker of Wallasey, B.
Evans of Watford, L.
Levy, L.
Rix, L.

Wales
Carlile of Berriew, L.
Geraint, L.
Hooson, L.
Parry, L.

Waste Management
Lindsay, E.

Welfare
Taverne, L.
Winchester, Bp.

Welsh Literature
Cledwyn of Penrhos, L.

Welsh Sport
Cledwyn of Penrhos, L.

West Africa
Filkin, L.

West Midlands
Shrewsbury and Waterford, E.

Wildlife
Hardy of Wath, L.

Women's Equality
Gould of Potternewton, B.

Women's Issues
Blood, B.
Dean of Thornton-le-Fylde, B.
Denton of Wakefield, B.
Miller of Hendon, B.
Seccombe, B.

Women's Opportunities in Engineering
Platt of Writtle, B.

Women's Rights
Crawley, B.

Working Class Issues
Blood, B.

World Government
Archer of Sandwell, L.

Young Under-privileged
Listowel, E.

Youth Affairs
Linklater of Butterstone, B.

Youth Work
Sheppard of Liverpool, L.

Summary of the House of Lords
(31 December 1999)

Archbishops	2	Bishops	24
Dukes	2	Hereditary Barons, Lords, Baronesses	
Marquesses	1	and Ladies	58
Earls and Countesses	27	Life Peers	537
Viscounts	16	*Total*	667

Number of Women Peers by Succession 5 (ie 1 Countess, 3 Baronesses and 1 Lady)
Number of Women Life Peers 100
Number of Hereditary Peers who have received Life Peerages 12

PARTY ALLEGIANCE IN THE HOUSE OF LORDS
(31 December 1999)

Conservative	233	Liberal Democrat	54
Cross-Bencher	162	Others*	34
Labour	180	Peers on Leave of Absence	4

*Includes Lords Spiritual and those peers who have not declared any party affiliation.

Women members

Women were first admitted into the House of Lords by the Life Peerage Act, 1958. At December 31, 1999, there were 100 women who had received life peerages. Women peers by succession (indicated with an asterisk) were not admitted into the Upper House until 1963. At December 31, 1999, there were were five, namely one Countess, three Baronesses and one Lady. The following list has been compiled in alphabetical order, showing the year of creation, for easy reference.

Amos, B.   1997
Anelay of St Johns, B.   1996
Ashton of Upholland, B.   1999
Barker, B.   1999
Blackstone, B.   1987
Blatch, B.   1987
Blood, B.   1999
Brigstocke, B.   1990
Brooke of Ystradfellte, B.   1964
Buscombe, B.   1998
Byford, B.   1996
Carnegy of Lour, B.   1982
Castle of Blackburn, B.   1990
Chalker of Wallasey, B.   1992
Cox, B.   1983
Crawley, B.   1998
Cumberlege, B.   1990
*Darcy de Knayth, B. (E)   1332
David, B.   1978
Dean of Thornton-le-Fylde, B.   1993
Delacourt-Smith of Alteryn, B.   1974
Denton of Wakefield, B.   1991
Dunn, B.   1990
Eccles of Moulton, B.   1990
Elles, B.   1972
Emerton, B.   1997
Falkender, B.   1974
Farrington of Ribbleton, B.   1994
Fisher of Rednal, B.   1974
Flather, B.   1990
Fookes, B.   1997
Gale, B.   1999
Gardner of Parkes, B.   1981
Goudie, B.   1998
Gould of Potternewton, B.   1993
Hamwee, B.   1991
Hanham, B.   1999
Harris of Richmond, B.   1999
Hayman, B.   1996
Hilton of Eggardon, B.   1991
Hogg, B.   1995
Hollis of Heigham, B.   1990
Hooper, B.   1985
Howells of St Davids, B.   1999
Hylton-Foster, B.   1965
James of Holland Park, B.   1991
Jay of Paddington, B.   1992
Jeger, B.   1979
Kennedy of The Shaws, B.   1997
Knight of Collingtree, B.   1997
Linklater of Butterstone, B.   1997
Lloyd of Highbury, B.   1996

Lockwood, B.   1978
Ludford, B.   1997
McFarlane of Llandaff, B.   1979
McIntosh of Hudnall, B.   1999
Maddock, B.   1997
Mallalieu, B.   1991
*Mar, C. (S)   1114/1404
Masham of Ilton, B.   1970
Massey of Darwen, B.   1999
Miller of Chilthorne Domer, B.   1998
Miller of Hendon, B.   1993
Nicholson of Winterbourne, B.   1997
Nicol, B.   1982
O'Cathain, B.   1991
O'Neill of Bengarve, B.   1999
Oppenheim-Barnes, B.   1989
Park of Monmouth, B.   1990
Perry of Southwark, B.   1991
Pike, B.   1974
Pitkeathley, B.   1997
Platt of Writtle, B.   1981
Prashar, B.   1999
Ramsay of Cartvale, B.   1996
Rawlings, B.   1994
Rendell of Babergh, B.   1997
Richardson of Calow, B.   1998
Ryder of Warsaw, B.   1979
*Saltoun of Abernethy, Ly. (S)   1445
Scotland of Asthal, B.   1997
Seccombe, B.   1991
Serota, B.   1967
Sharp of Guildford, B.   1998
Sharples, B.   1973
Smith of Gilmorehill, B.   1995
Stern, B.   1999
*Strange, B. (E)   1628
Symons of Vernham Dean, B.   1996
Thatcher, B.   1992
Thomas of Walliswood, B.   1994
Thornton, B.   1998
Trumpington, B.   1980
Turner of Camden, B.   1985
Uddin, B.   1998
Warnock, B.   1985
Warwick of Undercliffe, B.   1999
*Wharton, B. (E)   1544
Whitaker, B.   1999
Wilcox, B.   1996
Wilkins, B.   1999
Williams of Crosby, B.   1993
Young, B.   1971
Young of Old Scone, B.   1997

Select Committees

1a LORD CHANCELLOR
(*ex officio* Speaker)

The Lord Chancellor presides over the deliberations of the House, except when it is in Committee.

Lord Chancellor: Lord Irvine of Lairg.

1b DEPUTY SPEAKERS

Several Lords are appointed by the Crown by Commission under the Great Seal to act as Speaker of the House of Lords in the absence of the Lord Chancellor. Deputy Chairmen (see 2 below) may also act as Speaker. In the event of none of these Lords being present, the House may on Motion appoint its own Speaker.

Aberdare, *L.*
Allenby of Megiddo, *V.*
Ampthill, *L.*
Boston of Faversham, *L.*
Brougham and Vaux, *L.*
Burnham, *L.*
Carter, *L.*
Cocks of Hartcliffe, *L.*
Cox, *B.*
Dean of Harptree, *L.*
Elliott of Morpeth, *L.*
Elton, *L.*
Graham of Edmonton, *L.*
Henley, *L.*
Hooper, *B.*
Lockwood, *B.*
Lyell, *L.*
McColl of Dulwich, *L.*
McIntosh of Haringey, *L.*
Mar, *C.*
Murton of Lindisfarne, *L.*
Nicol, *B.*
Oxfuird, *V.*
Serota, *B.*
Simon, *V.*
Skelmersdale, *L.*
Strabolgi, *L.*
Tordoff, *L.*
Turner of Camden, *B.*

2 CHAIRMAN AND DEPUTY CHAIRMEN

At the beginning of every session, or whenever a vacancy occurs, Lords are appointed by the House to fill the offices of Chairman and Principal Deputy Chairman of Committees.

The Chairman takes the Chair in all Committees of the Whole House and is also chairman ex-officio of all committees of the House unless the House otherwise directs. In addition to his duties in the House, he exercises a general supervision and control over Provisional Order Confirmation Bills, Private Bills and Hybrid Instruments. He is also the first of the Deputy Speakers, appointed by Commission. The Principal Deputy Chairman of Committees, in addition to assisting the Chairman in his duties, is appointed to act as Chairman of the European Communities Committee. Other Deputy Chairmen may also take the Chair in Committees of the Whole House.

Chairman of Committees: Lord Boston of Faversham.
Principal Deputy Chairman of Committees: Lord Tordoff.
Panel of Deputy Chairmen:
Aberdare, *L.*
Allenby of Megiddo, *V.*
Ampthill, *L.*
Brougham and Vaux, *L.*
Burnham, *L.*
Carter, *L.*
Cocks of Hartcliffe, *L.*
Cox, *B.*
Dean of Harptree, *L.*
Elliott of Morpeth, *L.*
Elton, *L.*
Gardner of Parkes, *B.*
Graham of Edmonton, *L.*
Henley, *L.*
Hooper, *B.*
Lockwood, *B.*
Lofthouse of Pontefract, *L.*
Lyell, *L.*
McColl of Dulwich, *L.*
McIntosh of Haringey, *L.*
Mar, *C.*
Methuen, *L.*
Murton of Lindisfarne, *L.*
Nicol, *B.*
Oxfuird, *V.*
Serota, *B.*
Simon, *V.*
Skelmersdale, *L.*
Strabolgi, *L.*
Turner of Camden, *B.*

3 LORDS OF APPEAL

†*Lord of Appeal in Ordinary.*
Bingham of Cornhill, *L.*
†Browne-Wilkinson, *L.* (*Senior Lord of Appeal in Ordinary*)
Cameron of Lochbroom, *L.*
†Clyde, *L.*
Cooke of Thorndon, *L.*
Goff of Chieveley, *L.*
†Hobhouse of Woodborough, *L.*
†Hoffmann, *L.*
†Hope of Craighead, *L.*
†Hutton, *L.*
Irvine of Lairg, *L.* (*Lord Chancellor*)
Jauncey of Tullichettle, *L.*
Lloyd of Berwick, *L.*
McCluskey, *L.*
Mackay of Clashfern, *L.*
†Millett, *L.*
Mustill, *L.*
†Nicholls of Birkenhead, *L.*
†Phillips of Worth Matravers, *L.*
Rodger of Earlsferry, *L.*
†Saville of Newdigate, *L.*
†Slynn of Hadley, *L.*
†Steyn, *L.*
Woolf, *L.*

Note: Lords of Appeal who, having attained the age of 75, are no longer eligible to hear appeals, are excluded from this list.

4 SESSIONAL SELECT COMMITTEES

(other than those dealing with House administration)

CONSOLIDATION BILLS: JOINT COMMITTEE

The function of this Committee is to consider Consolidation Bills and report them with or without amendment to the House. These Bills fall into five categories:

(*a*) Consolidation Bills, whether public or private, which are limited to re-enacting existing law;
(*b*) Statute Law Revision Bills, which are limited to repeal of obsolete, spent, unnecessary or superseded enactments;
(*c*) Bills presented under the Consolidation of Enactments (Procedure) Act 1949, which include corrections and minor improvements to the existing law;
(*d*) Bills to consolidate any enactments with amendments to give effect to recommendations made by the Law Commissions;
(*e*) Bills prepared by the Law Commissions to promote the reform of the Statute Law by the repeal of enactments which are no longer of practical utility.

The committee consists of 24 members, 12 from each House, appointed on the recommendation of the Lord Chancellor and the Speaker respectively. The Committee appoints its own chairman.

Chairman: (Vacant).
Lords' Members: Lord Campbell of Alloway, Lord Clyde, Viscount Colville of Culross, Lord Hobhouse of Woodborough, Lord Janner of Braunstone, Baroness Mallalieu, Lord Razzall, Lord Strabolgi.
Clerk: Mr E. C. Ollard.

DELEGATED POWERS AND DEREGULATION COMMITTEE

The duty of this Committee is to report whether the provisions of any bill inappropriately delegate legislative power; to report on documents laid before Parliament under section 3(3) of the Deregulation and Contracting Out Act 1994 and on draft orders laid under section 1(4) of that Act; and to perform, in respect of such documents and orders, the functions performed in respect of other instruments by the Joint Committee on Statutory Instruments.

Chairman: Lord Alexander of Weedon.
Members: Lord Ampthill, Lord Dahrendorf, Lord Goodhart, Lord Hogg of Cumbernauld, Lord Mayhew of Twysden, Lord Merlyn-Rees, Lord Prys-Davies, Lord Waddington.
Clerk: Dr F. P. Tudor.
Counsel: Sir James Nursaw.

EUROPEAN UNION COMMITTEE

The duties of this Committee are to consider European Union documents and other matters relating to the European Union. The Committee has power to appoint Sub-Committees and to refer to them any of the matters within its terms of reference. The Committee may co-opt any Lord to serve on its Sub-Committees. The Chairman of the Committee is the Principal Deputy Chairman of Committees, and the Second Counsel to the Chairman of Committees acts as its legal adviser.

Chairman: Lord Tordoff.

Members: Viscount Bledisloe, Lord Borrie, Viscount Brookeborough, Lord Brooke of Alverthorpe, Baroness Crawley, Lord Geddes, Lord Goodhart, Lord Hope of Craighead, Lord Howell of Guildford, Lord Hussey of North Bradley, Lord Lamont of Lerwick, Baroness O'Cathain, Earl of Selborne, Lord Tomlinson, Lord Trefgarne, Lord Wallace of Saltaire, Lord Williams of Elvel, Lord Willoughby de Broke.

Clerk: Mr T. V. Mohan.

Legal Adviser: Dr C. S. Kerse.

Members of Sub-Committees with asterisks (*) after their names are co-opted members, i.e. they are not members of the main committee

SUB-COMMITTEES OF EUROPEAN COMMUNITIES COMMITTEE

SUB-COMMITTEE A:

ECONOMIC AND FINANCIAL AFFAIRS, TRADE AND EXTERNAL RELATIONS

Chairman: Lord Tomlinson.

Members: Lord Hussey of North Bradley, Lord Lamont of Lerwick, Lord Lea of Crondall*, Lord Randall of St Budeaux*, Lord Renton of Mount Harry*, Lord Sharman*, Baroness Sharp of Guildford*, Lord Shaw of Northstead*.

Clerk: Dr E. A. Hopkins.

SUB-COMMITTEE B:

ENERGY, INDUSTRY AND TRANSPORT

Chairman: Lord Brooke of Alverthorpe.

Members: Lord Bradshaw*, Viscount Brookeborough, Lord Cavendish of Furness*, Lord Chadlington*, Lord Faulkner of Worcester*, Baroness O'Cathain, Lord Paul*, Lord Sandberg*, Lord Skelmersdale*, Lord Woolmer of Leeds*.

Clerk: Mr R. Morgan.

SUB-COMMITTEE C:

COMMON FOREIGN AND SECURITY POLICY

Chairman: Lord Howell of Guildford.

Members: Lord Harrison*, Baroness Hilton of Eggardon*, Lord Inge*, Lord Jopling*, Lord Shore of Stepney*, Lord Trefgarne, Lord Watson of Richmond*, Lord Williams of Elvel, Lord Williamson of Horton*.

Clerk: Mr T. E. Radice.

SUB-COMMITTEE D:

ENVIRONMENT, AGRICULTURE, PUBLIC HEALTH AND CONSUMER PROTECTION

Chairman: Earl of Selborne.

Members: Lord Christopher*, Lord Judd*, Lord Lewis of Newnham*, Lord Mackie of Benshie*, Baroness Miller of Chilthorne Domer*, Lord Moran*, Baroness Thornton*, Baroness Wilcox*, Lord Willoughby de Broke, Baroness Young of Old Scone*.

Clerk: Mr D. J. Batt.

SUB-COMMITTEE E:

LAW AND INSTITUTIONS

Chairman: Lord Hope of Craighead.

Members: Viscount Bledisloe, Lord Borrie, Lord Fraser of Carmyllie*, Lord Goodhart, Baroness Goudie*, Lord Hunt of Wirral*, Lord Lester of Herne Hill*, Lord Norton of Louth*, Lord Plant of Highfield*, Lord Wedderburn of Charlton*, Lord Wigoder*.

Clerk: Mr T. E. Radice.

Legal Adviser: Dr C. S. Kerse.

SUB-COMMITTEE F:

SOCIAL AFFAIRS, EDUCATION AND HOME AFFAIRS

Chairman: Lord Wallace of Saltaire.

Members: Lord Bridges*, Lord Dholakia*, Lord Griffiths of Fforestfach*, Lord Harris of Richmond*, Baroness Knight of Collingtree*, Lord Pilkington of Oxenford*, Lord Rix*, Baroness Stern*, Baroness Turner of Camden*, Baroness Uddin*, Baroness Whitaker*.

Clerk: Dr C. Johnson.

HOUSE OF LORDS OFFICES

Chairman: Lord Boston of Faversham

Members: Earl of Caithness, Lord Carter, Lord Chalfont, Lord Colwyn, Lord Dholakia, Lord Dixon, Lord Elton, Lord Gilbert, Lord Harris of Greenwich, Lord Henley, Baroness Hilton of Eggardon, Lord Hunt of Wirral, Lord Irvine of Lairg, Baroness Jay of Paddington, Lord Laming, Lord Mackay of Ardbrecknish, Lord Marsh, Bishop of Oxford, Lord Renfrew of Kaimsthorn, Lord Rodgers of Quarry Bank, Baroness Seccombe, Baroness Serota, Lord Strathclyde, Baroness Thomas of Walliswood, Lord Tordoff, Lord Weatherill, Lord Williams of Mostyn, with the Clerk of the Parliaments and the Gentleman Usher of the Black Rod.

Clerk: Mr J. A. Vaughan.

SUB-COMMITTEES OF HOUSE OF LORDS' OFFICES COMMITTEE

ADMINISTRATION AND WORKS SUB-COMMITTEE:
Chairman: Lord Boston of Faversham.
Members: Viscount Allenby of Megiddo, Lord Carter, Lord Colwyn, Baroness David, Lord Harris of Greenwich, Lord Henley, Baroness Hilton of Eggardon, Lord Methuen, Baroness Rawlings, Lord Renfrew of Kaimsthorn, Lord Weatherill, with the Clerk of the Parliaments and the Gentleman Usher of the Black Rod.
Clerk: Miss M. Robertson.

ADVISORY PANEL ON WORKS OF ART:
Chairman: Baroness Hilton of Eggardon.
Members: Lord Crathorne, Viscount of Falkland, Lord Lloyd-Webber, Lord Morris of Castle Morris, Baroness Smith of Gilmorehill.
Clerk: Miss M. Robertson.

FINANCE AND STAFF SUB-COMMITTEE:
Chairman: Lord Boston of Faversham.
Members: Lord Astor of Hever, Lord Colwyn, Lord Cladwin of Clee, Lord Harris of Greenwich, Baroness Jay of Paddington, Lord Renfrew of Kaimsthorn, Lord Rodgers of Quarry Bank, Lord Sheppard of Didgemere, Lord Strathclyde, Lord Weatherill, Lord Williams of Elvel, with the Clerk of the Parliaments.
Clerk: Mr R. H. Walters.

LIBRARY AND COMPUTERS SUB-COMMITTEE:
Chairman: Lord Renfrew of Kaimsthorn.
Members: Lord Avebury, Lord Butterworth, Earl of Erroll, Lord Hoffman, Lord McIntosh of Haringey, Baroness Nicol, Earl of Northesk, Baroness Platt of Writtle, Baroness Rendell of Babergh, Lord St John of Bletso, with the Clerk of the Parliaments.
Clerk: Dr F. P. Tudor.

REFRESHMENT SUB-COMMITTEE:
Chairman: Lord Colwyn.
Members: Lord Burnham, Lord Carter, Baroness David, Lord Graham of Edmonton, Lord Harris of Greenwich, Lord Palmer, with the Clerk of the Parliaments.
Clerk: Mr R. H. Walters.

HYBRID INSTRUMENTS COMMITTEE

The function of the Committee is to consider Hybrid Instruments against which Petitions have been presented and to recommend to the House what action should be taken in each case.

Chairman: Lord Boston of Faversham.
Members: Lord Brougham and Vaux, Lord Burnham, Earl of Courtown, Viscount Craigavon, Lord King of West Bromwich, Baroness Wilkins.
Clerk: Dr F. P. Tudor.

LIAISON COMMITTEE

The duties of this Committee are to advise the House on the resources required for select committee work and to allocate resources between select committees; to review the select committee work of the House; to consider requests for *ad hoc* committees and report to the House with recommendations; to ensure effective coordination between the two Houses; and to consider the availability of Lords to serve on committees.

Chairman: Lord Boston of Faversham.
Members: Lord Clinton-Davis, Viscount Colville of Culross, Lord Craig of Radley, Baroness Jay of Paddington, Lord Kimball, Baroness Pitkeathley, Lord Rodgers of Quarry Bank, Lord Strathclyde, Lord Weatherill, Lord Wigoder, Baroness Young.
Clerk: Mr D. J. Batt.

PERSONAL BILLS COMMITTEE

The duties of the Committee are to examine Petitions for Personal Bills and the provisions of such Bills and consider whether the objects of the Bill are proper to be enacted by a Personal Bill; and if so, to see whether the provisions of the Bill are proper for carrying its purposes into effect, and to make any amendments, either of substance or drafting to the draft Bill for this purpose.

Chairman: Lord Boston of Faversham.
Members: Lord Astor of Hever, Lord Hogg of Cumbernauld, Lord Sandberg, Lord Templeman, Lord Wilberforce.
Clerk: Dr F. P. Tudor.

PRIVILEGES, COMMITTEE FOR

The House refers to this Committee questions regarding its privileges and claims of peerage and of precedence. In any claim of peerage, the Committee may not sit unless three Lords of Appeal are present. In certain circumstances claims to Irish Peerages are also referred to the Committee.

Chairman: Lord Boston of Faversham.

Members: Lord Allen of Abbeydale, Lord Carter, Lord Cledwyn of Penrhos, Lord Craig of Radley, Viscount Cranborne, Lord Glenamara, Lord Henley, Baroness Jay of Paddington, Lord Mackay of Clashfern, Lord Marsh, Lord Mayhew of Twysden, Lord Rodgers of Quarry Bank, Lord Strabolgi, Lord Strathclyde, Lord Weatherill, Lord Wigoder, together with any three Lords of Appeal.
Clerk: Mr B. P. Keith.
Clerk (Peerage Claims): Mr J. A. Vallance White.

SUB-COMMITTEE ON LORDS' INTERESTS
By resolutions of 7 November 1995, Lords are required to register consultancies, or similar arrangements, involving payment or other incentives or reward for providing Parliamentary advice or services, and financial interests in businesses involved in Parliamentary lobbying on behalf of clients; and are debarred for speaking, voting or lobbying in respect of such interests. They may also register other particulars relating to matters which they consider may affect the public perception of the way in which they discharge their Parliamentary duties.
Chairman: Lord Nolan.
Members: Earl Ferrers, Baroness Serota, Lord Wigoder, together with any two other Lords of Appeal.
Clerk to the Sub-Committee and Registrar of Lords' Interests: Mr J. A. Vallance White

PROCEDURE COMMITTEE

Chairman: Lord Boston of Faversham.
Members: Viscount Allenby of Megiddo, Baroness Anelay of St Johns, Viscount Bledisloe, Lord Burlison, Lord Burnham, Earl of Caithness, Lord Carter, Lord Clarke of Hampstead, Lord Craig of Radley, Lord Denham, Earl Ferrers, Baroness Gould of Potternewton, Baroness Hamwee, Lord Harris of Greenwich, Lord Henley, Lord Irvine of Lairg, Baroness Jay of Paddington, Lord Kimball, Baroness Lockwood, Lord Mackay of Ardbrecknish, Lord Mancroft, Lord Rodgers of Quarry Bank, Lord Shepherd, Viscount Simon, Lord Skelmersdale, Lord Strabolgi, Lord Strathclyde, Lord Tordoff, Lord Williams of Mostyn, with the Clerk of the Parliaments.
Clerk: Mr B. P. Keith.

SCIENCE AND TECHNOLOGY COMMITTEE

The duty of this Committee is to consider science and technology. The Committee reports on subjects of its own choosing within the fields of science and technology. Enquiries are conducted by two Sub-Committees, each comprising half the Committee's membership, and the Committee co-opts Lords to those Sub-Committees for the duration 'of specific enquiries. Specialist Advisers are also appointed to assist the Sub-Committees.

Chairman: Lord Winston.
Members: Lord Haskel, Baroness Hogg, Lord Howie of Troon, Lord Jenkin of Roding, Lord McColl of Dulwich, Lord Methuen, Lord Oxburgh, Lord Patel, Lord Perry of Walton, Baroness Platt of Writtle, Lord Quirk, Lord Rea, Lord Tombs, Lord Wade of Chorlton, Lord Walton of Detchant, Baroness Warwick of Undercliffe, Baroness Wilcox.
Clerk: Mr A. Makower.

SUB COMMITTEE I
Complementary and Alternative Medicine
Chairman: Lord Walton of Detchant.
Members: Lord Haskel, Lord Howie of Troon, Lord Perry of Walton, Baroness Platt of Writtle, Lord Quirk, Lord Soulsby of Swaffham Prior*, Lord Tombs, Lord Winston.
Clerk: Miss C. K. S. K. Mawson.

SUB COMMITTEE II
Science and Society
Chairman: Lord Jenkin of Roding.
Members: Lord Haskel, Lord Howie of Troon, Lord Oxburgh, Lord Perry of Walton, Baroness Platt of Writtle, Lord Porter of Luddenham*, Lord Quirk, Lord Tombs, Baroness Wilcox*, Lord Winston.
Clerk: Mr A. Makower.

SELECTION, COMMITTEE OF

The main function of the Committee is to select and propose to the House the names of the Lords to form each Select Committee of the House, and the Lords members of Joint Committees, except the Committee of Selection itself and any Committee otherwise provided for by statute or by order of the House (the Appellate and Appeal Committees and the Lords members of the Joint Committee on Consolidation Bills and the Ecclesiastical Committee). It may propose the name of a Lord to be the Chairman of such Committee. The Committee also selects and proposes to the House the panel of Lords to act as Deputy Chairmen of Committees for each session.

The Chairman of Committees has discretion to propose to the House, without reference to the Committee of Selection, the names of Lords to fill casual vacancies occurring in the membership of Select Committees.

In certain circumstances the Committee of Selection also has functions in relation to the appointment of Committees concerned with private legislation. If the Chairman of Committees is of the opinion that any such Committee should be appointed by the Committee of Selection or if two or more members of that Committee request a meeting for that purpose, the Committee is required to select and propose to the House the names of the Lords to form such a Committee. The Committees in question are the following:

(a) Select Committees on Private Bills;
(b) Select Committees on Opposed Personal Bills;
(c) Select Committees on Opposed Provisional Order Confirmation Bills;
(d) Joint Committees under the Private Legislation Procedure (Scotland) Act 1936 (Lords Members);
(e) Joint Committees under the Statutory Orders (Special Procedure) Act 1945 (Lords Members).

Chairman: Lord Boston of Faversham.
Members: Lord Burnham, Lord Carter, Lord Craig of Radley, Lord Harris of Greenwich, Lord Henley, Baroness Jay of Paddington, Lord McIntosh of Haringey, Lord Rodgers of Quarry Bank, Lord Strathclyde, Viscount Tenby.
Clerk: Mr J. A. Vaughan.

STANDING ORDERS (PRIVATE BILLS) COMMITTEE

The function of this Committee is to consider cases referred to them on a report from the Examiners of Petitions for Private Bills, who certify whether in the case of a particular Private Bill the Standing Orders have, or have not, been complied with and report the circumstances in cases where they have not. The Committee then consider whether, in such cases, the Standing Orders ought, or ought not, to be dispensed with and, if so, on what conditions.

The parties either appear in person or are represented by their parliamentary agents. Counsel are not heard.

Chairman: Lord Boston of Faversham.
Members: Baroness Ashton of Upholland, Lord Brett, Lord Brougham and Vaux, Viscount Bridgeman, Viscount of Falkland, Lord Gallacher, Earl of Liverpool, Earl of Sandwich.
Clerk: Dr F. P. Tudor.

STATUTORY INSTRUMENTS: JOINT COMMITTEE

This is a Joint Committee of seven members from each House.

All Statutory Instruments (except those made under Section 1 of the Deregulation and Contracting Out Act 1994), whether affirmative, negative or general, are subject to technical scrutiny by the Joint Committee on Statutory Instruments. This is a sessional Committee consisting of seven members of each House which is empowered to draw any such instrument to the special attention of both Houses on any ground which does not impinge on its merits or on the policy behind it. The orders of reference of the Joint Committee specify eight matters on which an instrument may be reported to both Houses the most important of which are:

(i)   that the instrument imposes a charge on the public revenues;
(ii) that the parent Act excludes challenge in the courts;
(iii) that the instrument has retrospective effect not authorised by its parent Act;
(iv) that there is doubt over the *vires* of the instrument;
(v)   that the meaning of the instrument is not clear.

Chairman: Mr D. Tredinnick, MP.
Lords' Members: Lord Greenway, Lord Hardy of Wath, Earl of Onslow, Lord Skelmersdale, Lord Thomas of Gresford, Lord Vivian, Lord Walker of Doncaster.
Clerk (Lords): Mr S. Burton.

5 HOUSE OF LORDS COLLECTION TRUST

The Trust is a registered charity whose aim (in brief) is to establish a collection of works of art, books etc. which will enhance public awareness and understanding of the British political system past and present, placing particular emphasis on the role of the House of Lords and its members.

Trustees

Baroness Jay of Paddington *(Chairman)*	The Clerk of the Parliaments
Lord Boston of Faversham	The Clerk of the Records

Secretary: Mr J. A. Vaughan.

6 LORDS' MEMBERS OF BRITISH–IRISH INTER-PARLIAMENTARY BODY

Lord Alderdice (associate member), Lord Blease, Lord Glentoran (associate member), Lord Holme of Cheltenham, Lord Lester of Herne Hill (associate member), Lord Lyell (associate member), Lord Merlyn-Rees, Baroness O'Cathain (associate member).

British Clerk to the Body: Mr F. A. Cranmer.

7 LORDS MEMBERS OF INTERNATIONAL ASSEMBLIES

a) Lords directly elected to the European Parliament.

	Party	Region
Lord Inglewood	Con	North West
Baroness Ludford	Lib Dem	London
Baroness Nicholson of Winterbourne	Lib Dem	South East

b) Lord nominated to serve as members of the United Kingdom delegation to the North Atlantic Assembly.

Representative
Lord Gladwin of Clee

Secretary: Mr J. D. W. Rhys.

c) Lords nominated to serve as members of the Parliamentary Assembly of the Council of Europe and the Assembly of Western European Union.

Representatives	Substitutes
Lord Kirkhill	Lord Lucas of Crudwell
Lord Russell-Johnston	
Lord Judd	Earl of Northesk

Secretary: Mr C. A. Shaw.

d) Lords nominated to serve as members of the Parliamentary Assembly of the Organisation for Security and Co-operation in Europe.

Representative	Substitute
Baroness Hilton of Eggardon	Lord Jopling

Secretary: Mr C. A. Shaw.

8 ECCLESIASTICAL COMMITTEE: JOINT COMMITTEE (LORDS' MEMBERS)

Lord Beaumont of Whitley, Lord Brightman, Lord Glenamara, Lord Hardy of Wath, Lord Pilkington of Oxenford, Lord Strabolgi, Lord Templeman, Lord Wallace of Saltaire, Baroness Wilcox, Lord Williams of Elvel.

Secretary: Mr E. C. Ollard.

Principal Officers and Officials

London, SW1A 0PW
020-7219 3000

Lord Chancellor: Rt Hon the Lord Irvine of Lairg

DEPARTMENT OF CHAIRMAN OF COMMITTEES

Chairman of Committees: Lord Boston of Faversham, QC
Principal Deputy Chairman of Committees: Lord Tordoff
Counsel to the Chairman of Committees: Sir James Nursaw, KCB, QC, Dr C S Kerse, D W Saunders, CB
Legal Assistant: Ms L. Gibson

DEPARTMENT OF CLERK OF THE PARLIAMENTS

Clerk of the Parliaments: J M Davies
Clerk Assistant and Clerk of Legislation: P D G Hayter, LVO
Reading Clerk and Principal Finance Officer: M G Pownall
Fourth Clerk at the Table (Judicial) and Clerk of the Judicial Office, and Registrar of Lords' Interests: J A Vallance White, CB
Clerk of the Journals: B P Keith
Clerk of Committees and Clerk of the Overseas Office: D R Beamish
Establishment Officer: R H Walters
Clerk of Private Bills: Dr F P Tudor
Clerk of Public Bills: E C Ollard
Clerks of Select Committees: A Makower, T V Mohan
Senior Clerks: Miss M B Robertson (seconded as Secretary to the Leader of the House and Chief Whip), S P Burton, T E Radice, D J Batt, R Morgan, Miss L J Mouland, Dr E A Hopkins, J A Vaughan
Clerks: Miss K Ball, A Mackersie, Miss C K S K Mawson, C Johnson, DPhil
Examiners of Petitions for Private Bills: Dr F P Tudor, W J Proctor
Taxing Officer (Private Bills): Dr F P Tudor
Judicial Taxing Officer: J A Vallance White, CB
Judicial Taxing Clerk: N I Cross
Clerk of the Records: S K Ellison
Assistant Clerks of the Records: D L Prior, Dr C Shenton
Assistant Archivist: Mrs K V Bligh
Records Manager: J Whiting
Librarian: D L Jones
Deputy Librarian: Dr P G Davis
Senior Library Clerk: Miss I L Victory

Library Clerks: S Kennedy, H Deadman, I S Cruse
Legal Library Executive: G R Dymond
Assistant Librarians: S J Owen, Miss P L Ward, Mr R L Anthony, Miss C C Auty, Ms A M Reilly, A Zelinger, Miss A Cowan
Senior Information Officer: Miss M L Morgan
Deputy Establishment Officer: G Embleton
Computer Executive: J W O'Meara, *Asst Computer Executive:* G Conway, *Computer Services Manager:* I T A McAllister
Computer Assistants: Mrs C Pepper, A K Morrison, Mrs L Midda
Internal Auditor: P M Thompson
Staff Adviser: D A W Dunn, ISO
Director of Works: H P Webber
Welfare Officer: Mrs A Mossop
Accountant: C Preece
Deputy Accountant: A D Underwood, ACMA
Catering Accountant: Mrs P Morris
Editor of the Official Report: Mrs M E E C Villiers
Deputy Editor: Mrs C J Boden, *Assistant Editors:* M L Hickes, Miss H J Sargent, Miss V A Sargent, Miss J D Collingwood, Miss J A Bradshaw
Chief Reporters: J C Donoghue, Ms C Shepherd
Reporters: Mrs P R Humphreys, Mrs G M Hoffmann, Mrs J K Dixon, Mrs M J Rogers, Miss G Callaby, Mrs S A Mitchell, Miss S E Burrell, M J Phoenix, Mrs A Mills, Mrs S Hussey, Mrs S Smith, L Bud, Mrs G J Reding
Assistant Reporters: Mrs B Y Franzmann, Miss E H Kumar
Shorthand Writer: Mrs P J Woolgar
Deputy Shorthand Writer: Miss A Archbold
Senior Executive Officer: G Bailey
Specialist Assistant Committee Office: Dr A E Heathfield
Higher Executive Officers: Miss C A Bolton, Mrs S A Collings, C Ross, Miss E A Murray, MBE, Miss S C Brown, Miss K P S Kavanagh, MAAT, Miss M P Pieroni, Ms S A Smith, M C Cooper
Personal Assistant to the Lords of Appeal: Mrs F P Rice
Executive Officers: C J Nicholls, LicIPD, S J Connor, G M Quin, Miss S K Hunt, S P Jones, R S Harrison, Miss A C Pickering, M Simpson, F Johnson, Mrs L J Fitt, Miss S E Fowler, S J Sperden, R K Kochhar, Miss J Sanders, Miss S J Myers, Ms A R Thomas, S A Gough

Senior Clerical Officers: J A Breslin, G B Newsome, Miss S E Condon, J G Frater, Miss A R Thomas, M J Troke, P C Goldstein, R Gee, J T Rhodes, Mrs K Crabtree-Taylor, N A Jackson, Mrs W J Chamberlain, Ms S M Utting, Ms A Townsend, Miss R Hyde, J P Rogers

Personal Secretaries: Miss P M L Hungerford, Miss J R Mitchley, Mrs R M Best, Miss A M Pinder, Lady Venetia Longstreth-Thompson, Miss A G V Piper, Miss R J Mannering, Miss E Minster, Miss E J Morgan, Mrs M M Byatt, Mrs J L Clark, Mrs A M Manning, Miss K B Sparrow, Mrs B D Wilkins, Miss V F Bath, Mrs H McMurdo, Miss N T Seaton, Ms P Jones, Mrs G Smith, Miss T M Perfect, MVO, Mrs Z Paul, Mrs S A Neale, Miss G Golding, Miss V Laslett, Miss M Sampson, Miss J Perodeau, C D McConnell, Mrs R Carter

DEPARTMENT OF GENTLEMAN USHER OF THE BLACK ROD

Gentleman Usher and Serjeant at Arms: General Sir Edward Jones, KCB, CBE

Yeoman Usher and Deputy Serjeant at Arms: Brigadier Hedley Duncan, MBE

Administration Officer: Brig A J McD Clark

Assistant Serjeant at Arms: Miss J Rowe

Personal Secretaries to the Gentleman Usher and Serjeant at Arms: Miss C J Bostock, Miss R M Wilkinson

Personal Secretary to the Yeoman Usher and Administration Officer: Miss J Fuller

Staff Superintendent: Major A M Charlesworth, BEM

Principal Attendant (Deputy Staff Superintendent): A R F Parsons

Personal Secretary to the Staff Superintendent: Mrs I Bowles

Principal Doorkeeper: R M Skelton

Second Principal Doorkeeper: V Crossfield

Senior Doorkeepers: W M Felkin, J E Blood, J B Kirtley, W C Quinn

Doorkeepers: A I Kendrick, H R Wright, G J Hyland, G J S Offer-Hoar, F L Biscoe, K C Phipps, A Dobson, R F Jones, W J Stocks, R G Waugh, D Evans, D M Stollery, D Foley, J Baldock, Ms S Devadason

Doorkeepers (Judicial): A J McConnon, M J Walsh

Clerk of the Crown in Chancery: Sir Hayden Phillips, KCB

Deputy Clerk of the Crown: M D Huebner, CB

REFRESHMENT DEPARTMENT

Superintendent: A D O Bibbiani

Banqueting Manager: R J Ellwood

Assistant Banqueting Manager: J K Harrison

Chef: M Thatcher

Assistant Managers: Miss C Sutton, O Stacchini, A Leaper

Dining Room Manager: B Lammoglia

Executive Officer: Miss S Myers

Senior Clerical Officers: Mrs L M P Jayaratne, Miss T McKenna, Miss A Connelly, Mrs C A Hunt, G S Hunt

Postmaster: L Ward

Transport Manager: J W Jones

Hereditary Peers' Election Results
27/28 October 1999

At the elections held on 27/28 October 1999 for 15 hereditary peers ready to serve as Deputy Speakers and other office holders, in accordance with the provisions of the House of Lords Bill and Standing Order 9(2)(ii), the candidates received the following number of votes:

Candidate	Votes	Place	Candidate	Votes	Place
C. Mar	570	1st	L. Colwyn	488	9th
L. Strabolgi	558	2nd	V. Oxfuird	482	10th
L. Elton	558	3rd	L. Reay	471	11th
L. Lyell	547	4th	L. Geddes	461	12th
L. Skelmersdale	544	5th	V. Simon	453	13th
L. Aberdare	530	6th	L. Methuen	421	14th
L. Brougham and Vaux	525	7th	L. Ampthill	418	15th
V. Falkland	519	8th			

3/4 November 1999

At the elections held on 3/4 November 1999 for 75 hereditary peers elected by the hereditary peers in their party or group, in accordance with the provisions of the House of Lords Bill and Standing Order 9(2)(i), the candidates received the following number of votes:

CONSERVATIVE PEERS

Candidate	Votes	Place	Candidate	Votes	Place
E. Ferrers	190	1st	V. Bridgeman	125	23rd
L. Strathclyde	174	2nd	L. Luke	124	24th
L. Trefgarne	173	3rd	E. Lindsay	116	25th
L. Denham	169	4th	L. Lucas of Crudwell		
L. Mancroft	168	5th	and Dingwall	115	26th
E. Howe	165	6th	L. Montagu of Beaulieu	113	27th
L. Brabazon of Tara	165	7th	E. Home	113	28th
E. Caithness	161	8th	L. Glentoran	104	29th
L. Henley	160	9th	E. Onslow	99	30th
L. Glenarthur	157	10th	L. Crathorne	97	31st
L. Astor of Hever	151	11th	L. Willoughby de Broke	96	32nd
V. Astor	146	12th	L. Inglewood	95	33rd
E. Courtown	143	13th	L. Northbrook	95	34th
E. Peel	142	14th	L. Swinfen	95	35th
L. Moynihan	137	15th	E. Shrewsbury	95	36th
E. Attlee	135	16th	L. Selsdon	94	37th
V. Goschen	132	17th	E. Liverpool	93	38th
D. Montrose	127	18th	E. Arran	90	39th
L. Burnham	127	19th	E. Dundee	90	40th
L. Vivian	126	20th	L. Mowbray and Stourton	88	41st
E. Northesk	126	21st	L. Rotherwick	88	42nd
E. Selborne	125	22nd			

CROSSBENCH PEERS

Candidate	Votes	Place	Candidate	Votes	Place
B. Darcy de Knathy	85	1st	L. Hylton	64	15th
L. Freyberg	82	2nd	E. Baldwin of Bewdley	63	16th
L. St John of Bletso	81	3rd	E. Carnarvon	58	17th
L. Northbourne	78	4th	E. Listowel	58	18th
E. Sandwich	78	5th	L. Moran	57	19th
V. Allenby of Megiddo	75	6th	B. Strange	53	20th
V. Tenby	74	7th	E. Erroll	52	21st
L. Palmer	72	8th	L. Walpole	52	22nd
V. Slim	72	9th	V. Craigavon	51	23rd
V. Bledisloe	70	10th	B. Wharton	48	24th
L. Monson	70	11th	V. Colville of Culross	47	25th
V. Brookeborough	68	12th	V. Waverley	47	26th
L. Bridges	68	13th	L. Greenway	47	27th
Lady Saltoun of Abernethy	64	14th	E. Rosslyn	45	28th

LABOUR PEERS

Candidate	Votes	Place	Candidate	Votes	Place
L. Milner of Leeds	8	1st	L. Rea	7	2nd

LIBERAL DEMOCRAT PEERS

Candidate	Votes	Place	Candidate	Votes	Place
E. Russell	17	1st	L. Addington	10	3rd
L. Avebury	13	2nd			

Hereditary Members

Those who have received life peerages have their titles listed in parenthesis. Peers of Ireland are marked*, with their British honours in parenthesis.
There are two hereditary office holders, The Duke of Norfolk (Earl Marshal), and The Marquess of Cholmondeley (Lord Great Chamberlain)

Aberdare, L.
Addington, L.
Aldington, L, (LP B. Low, 1999)
Allenby of Megiddo, V.
Ampthill, L.
Arran, E.* (B. Sudley)
Astor of Hever, L.
Astor, V.
Attlee, E.
Avebury, L.
Baldwin of Bewdley, E.
Belstead, L. (LP B. Ganzoni, 1999)
Bledisloe, V.
Brabazon of Tara, L.
Bridgeman, V.
Bridges, L.
Brookeborough, V.
Brougham and Vaux, L.
Burnham, L.
Caithness, E.

Carnarvon, E.
Carrington, L. (LP B. Carington of Upton, 1999)
Cholmondeley, M.
Colville of Culross, V.
Colwyn, L.
Courtown, E.* (B. Saltersford)
Craigavon, V.
Cranborne, V. (LP B. Gascoyne-Cecil, 1999)
Crathorne, L.
Crawford and Balcarres, E. (LP B. Balniel, 1974)
Darcy de Knayth, B.
Denham, L.
Dundee, E.
Elton, L.
Erroll, E.
Erroll of Hale, L. (LP B. Erroll of Kilmun, 1999)
Falkland, V.

Ferrers, E.
Freyberg, L.
Geddes, L.
Glenarthur, L.
Glentoran, L.
Goschen, V.
Greenway, L.
Henley, L.* (B. Northington)
Home, F.
Howe, E.
Hylton, L.
Inglewood, L.
Jellicoe, E. (LP B. Jellicoe of Southampton, 1999)
Lindsay, E.
Listowel, E.* (B. Hare)
Liverpool, E.
Longford, E.* (LP B. Pakenham of Cowley, 1999)
Lucas of Crudwell, L.
Luke, L.
Lyell, L.
Mancroft, L.
Mar, C.
Methuen, L.
Milner of Leeds, L.
Monson, L.
Montagu of Beaulieu, L.
Montrose, D.
Moran, L.
Mowbray and Stourton, L.
Moynihan, L.
Norfolk, D.
Northbourne, L.
Northbrook, L.
Northesk, E.

Onslow, E.
Oxfuird, V.
Palmer, L.
Peel, E.
Rea, L.
Reay, L.
Rosslyn, E.
Rotherwick, L.
Russell, E.
St John of Bletso, L.
Saltoun of Abernethy, Lady
Sandwich, E.
Selborne, E.
Selsdon, L.
Shepherd, L. (LP B. Shepherd of Spalding, 1999)
Shrewsbury and Waterford, E.
Simon, V.
Skelmersdale, L.
Slim, V.
Snowdon, E. (LP B. Armstrong-Jones, 1999)
Strabolgi, L.
Strange, B.
Strathclyde, L.
Swinfen, L.
Tenby, V.
Trefgarne, L.
Vivian, L.
Walpole, L.
Waverley, V.
Wharton, B.
Willoughby de Broke, L.
Windlesham, L. (LP B. Hennessy, 1999)
Younger of Leckie, V. (LP B. Younger of Prestwich, 1992)

HEREDITARY PEERS WHO HAVE RECEIVED LIFE PEERAGES

Aldington, L.   (Baron Low, 1999)
Belstead, L.   (Baron Ganzoni, 1999)
Carrington, L.   (Baron Carington of Upton, 1999)
Cranborne, V.   (Baron Gascoyne-Cecil, 1999)
Crawford and Balcarres, E.   (Baron Balniel, 1974)
Erroll of Hale, L.   (Baron Erroll of Kilmun, 1999)
Jellicoe, E.   (Baron Jellicoe of Southampton, 1999)
Longford, E.   (Baron Pakenham of Cowley, 1999)
Shepherd, L.   (Baron Shepherd of Spalding, 1999)
Snowdon, E.   (Baron Armstrong-Jones, 1999)
Windlesham, L.   (Baron Hennessy, 1999)
Younger of Leckie, V.   (Baron Younger of Prestwick, 1992)

PEERS WHO ARE MEMBERS OF THE SCOTTISH PARLIAMENT

The Rt Hon the Lord Selkirk of Douglas*	Con
The Rt Hon the Lord Steel of Aikwood*	Lib Dem
The Lord Watson of Invergowrie *(Glasgow Cathcart)*	Lab

*Lord Selkirk of Douglas and Lord Steel of Aikwood were elected as
  Additional Members for Lothian

PEER WHO IS A MEMBER OF THE NATIONAL ASSEMBLY FOR WALES

The Lord Elis-Thomas *(Meirionnydd Nant Conwy)*	Pl C

PEER WHO IS A MEMBER OF THE NORTHERN IRELAND ASSEMBLY

The Lord Alderdice *(Belfast East)*	Speaker

PEERS WHO ARE MEMBERS OF THE EUROPEAN PARLIAMENT

*The Lord Bethell *(London)*	Con
The Lord Inglewood *(North West)*	Con
The Baroness Ludford *(London)*	Lib Dem
The Baroness Nicholson of Winterbourne *(South East)*	Lib Dem
*The Earl of Stockton *(South West)*	Con

*No longer a Member of the House of Lords

Peerages created in 1999

Date of Creation

Earldom

Earl of Wessex and Viscount Severn (HRH Prince Edward Antony
  Richard Louis, CVO) — 19 June 1999

Life Baronies

Baron Armstrong-Jones (Antony Charles Robert, Earl of Snowdon, GCVO)	16 November 1999
Baroness Ashton of Upholland (Mrs Catherine Margaret Ashton)	2 August 1999
Baroness Barker (Miss Elizabeth Jean Barker)	31 July 1999
Baroness Blood (Miss May Blood, MBE)	31 July 1999
Baron Bradshaw (Professor William Peter Bradshaw)	22 July 1999
Baron Brett (William Henry Brett Esq)	20 July 1999
Baron Carington of Upton (Rt Hon Peter Alexander Rupert, Baron Carrington, KG, GCMG, CH, MC)	17 November 1999
Baron Carlile of Berriew (Alexander Charles Carlile Esq, QC)	27 July 1999
Baron Elder (Thomas Murray Elder Esq)	19 July 1999
Baron Erroll of Kilmun (Rt Hon Frederick James, Baron Erroll of Hale, TD)	16 November 1999
Baron Faulkner of Worcester (Richard Oliver Faulkner Esq)	14 July 1999
Baron Fellowes (Rt Hon. Sir Robert Fellowes, GCB, GCVO)	12 July 1999
Baron Filkin (David Geoffrey Nigel Filkin Esq, CBE)	29 July 1999
Baron Forsyth of Drumlean (Rt Hon. Sir Michael Forsyth, Kt)	14 July 1999
Baron Foster of Thames Bank (Sir Norman Robert Foster, Kt, OM)	19 July 1999
Baroness Gale (Mrs Anita Gale)	4 August 1999
Baron Ganzoni (Rt Hon John Julian, Baron Belstead, Baronet)	17 November 1999
Baron Gascoyne-Cecil (Rt Hon Robert Michael James, Baron Cecil and Viscount Cranborne)	17 November 1999
Baron Gavron (Robert Gavron Esq, CBE)	6 August 1999
Baron Goldsmith (Peter Henry Goldsmith Esq, QC)	29 July 1999
Baron Grabiner (Anthony Stephen Grabiner Esq, QC)	26 July 1999
Baroness Hanham (Mrs Joan Brownlow Hanham, CBE)	15 July 1999
Baroness Harris of Richmond (Mrs Angela Felicity Harris)	6 August 1999
Baron Harrison (Lyndon Henry Arthur Harrison Esq)	28 July 1999
Baron Hennessy (Rt Hon David James George, Baron Windlesham, CVO)	16 November 1999
Baroness Howells of St Davids (Mrs Rosalind Patricia-Anne Howells, OBE)	21 July 1999
Baron Imbert (Sir Peter Michael Imbert, QPM, JP)	10 February 1999
Baron Jellicoe of Southampton (Rt Hon George Patrick John Rushworth, Earl Jellicoe, KBE, DSO, MC)	17 November 1999
Baron King of West Bromwich (Tarsem King Esq)	22 July 1999
Baron Kirkham (Sir Graham Kirkham, Kt)	23 July 1999
Baron Laird (John Dunn Laird Esq)	16 July 1999
Baron Lea of Crondall (David Edward Lea Esq, OBE)	20 July 1999
Baron Lipsey (David Lawrence Lipsey Esq)	30 July 1999
Baron Low (Rt Hon Austin Richard William, Baron Aldington, KCMG, CBE, DSO, TD)	16 November 1999
Baroness McIntosh of Hudnall (Mrs Genista Mary McIntosh)	3 August 1999
Baron MacKenzie of Culkein (Hector Uisdean MacKenzie Esq)	4 August 1999
Baroness Massey of Darwen (Mrs Doreen Elizabeth Massey)	26 July 1999
Baroness O'Neill of Bengarve (Miss Onora Sylvia O'Neill, CBE)	25 February 1999
Baron Oxburgh (Sir Ernest Ronald Oxburgh, KBE)	27 July 1999
Baron Pakenham of Cowley (Rt Hon Francis Aungier, Baron Pakenham and Earl of Longford, KG)	16 November 1999
Baron Patel (Sir Narendra Babubhai Patel, Kt)	1 March 1999
Baron Phillips of Worth Matravers (Rt Hon Sir Nicholas Addison Phillips, Kt)	12 January 1999
Baroness Prashar (Miss Usha Kumari Prashar, CBE)	15 July 1999

Baron Rennard (Christopher John Rennard Esq, MBE)	21 July 1999
Baron Robertson of Port Ellen (The Rt Hon. George Islay MacNeill Robertson)	24 August 1999
Baron Rogan (Dennis Robert David Rogan Esq)	16 July 1999
Baron Sharman (Colin Morven Sharman Esq, OBE)	2 August 1999
Baron Shepherd of Spalding (Rt Hon Malcolm Newton, Baron Shepherd)	16 November 1999
Baron Smith of Leigh (Peter Richard Charles Smith Esq)	5 August 1999
Baroness Stern (Miss Vivien Helen Stern, CBE)	13 July 1999
Baron Stevenson of Coddenham (Sir Henry Dennistoun Stevenson, Kt, CBE)	13 July 1999
Baron Trotman (Sir Alexander James Trotman, Kt)	2 March 1999
Baron Waldegrave of North Hill (The Rt Hon. William Arthur Waldegrave)	28 July 1999
Baroness Warwick of Undercliffe (Miss Diana Mary Warwick)	10 July 1999
Baron Watson of Richmond (Professor Alan John Watson, CBE)	23 July 1999
Baroness Whitaker (Mrs Janet Alison Whitaker)	5 August 1999
Baroness Wilkins (Rosalie Catherine Wilkins)	30 July 1999
Baron Williamson of Horton (Sir David Francis Williamson, GCMG, CB)	5 February 1999
Baron Woolmer of Leeds (Kenneth John Woolmer Esq)	3 August 1999

Peers by succession who took their seats from 1 January to 11 November 1999

Arlington, B.	Cross-Bencher	Killanin, L.	Cross-Bencher
Cathcart, E.	Conservative	Lansdowne, M.	Conservative
Catto, L.	Cross-Bencher	Londesborough, L.	Cross-Bencher
Devon, E.	Cross-Bencher	Marks of Broughton, L.	Cross-Bencher
Eccles, V.	Conservative	Meath, E.	Cross-Bencher
Greenwood, V.	Cross-Bencher	Portman, V.	Cross-Bencher
Guilford, E.	Conservative	Rothermere, V.	Cross-Bencher
Hertford, M.	Conservative	Rutland, D.	Conservative
Hollenden, L.	Conservative	St Oswald, L.	Conservative
Hood, V.	Conservative	Seaford, L.	Conservative
Jersey, E.	Cross-Bencher	Winchilsea and	
Kemsley, V.	Conservative	Nottingham	Liberal Democrat

Peers of Ireland with British titles

A list of Lords usually addressed by their higher titles as Peers of Ireland, showing their titles as Peers of England, Great Britain and the United Kingdom.

Irish Peerage	UK Peerage	Irish Peerage	UK Peerage
E Arran	B Sudley	E Listowel	B Hare
E Courtown	B Saltersford	E Longford	B Pakenham
B Henley	B Northington		of Cowley (LP)

Bishops

ARCHBISHOPS (2) AND DIOCESAN BISHOPS (3) EX OFFICIO

Most Rev. George Leonard Carey	Canterbury
Most Rev. David Michael Hope	York
Rt Rev. Richard John Carew Chartres	London
Rt Rev. Anthony Michael Arnold Turnbull	Durham
Rt Rev. Michael Charles Scott-Joynt	Winchester

BISHOPS IN ORDER OF SENIORITY (21)

		Elected
Rt Rev. Eric Waldram Kemp	Chichester	1974
Rt Rev. Keith Norman Sutton	Lichfield	1984
Rt Rev. Barry Rogerson	Bristol	1985
Rt Rev. Robert Maynard Hardy	Lincoln	1987
Rt Rev. Richard Douglas Harries	Oxford	1987
Rt Rev. Mark Santer	Birmingham	1987
Rt Rev. Alan David Chesters	Blackburn	1989
Rt Rev. Ian Harland	Carlisle	1989
Rt Rev. John Keith Oliver	Hereford	1990
Rt Rev. Thomas Frederick Butler	Southwark	1991
Rt Rev. James Lawton Thompson	Bath and Wells	1991
Rt Rev. Nigel Simeon McCulloch	Wakefield	1992
Rt Rev. David John Smith	Bradford	1992
Rt Rev. Christopher John Mayfield	Manchester	1993
Rt Rev. David Staffurth Stancliffe	Salisbury	1993
Rt Rev. David Edward Bentley	Gloucester	1993
Rt Rev. Michael James Nazir-Ali	Rochester	1994
Rt Rev. John Warren Gladwin	Guildford	1994
Rt Rev. Kenneth William Stevenson	Portsmouth	1995
Rt Rev. Jonathan Sansbury Bailey	Derby	1995
Rt Rev. Christopher William Herbert	St Albans	1995

DIOCESAN BISHOPS WITHOUT SEATS

		Elected
Rt Rev. John Freeman Perry	Chelmsford	1996
Rt Rev. Ian Patrick Martyn Cundy	Peterborough	1996
Rt Rev. Peter Robert Forster	Chester	1996
Rt Rev. John Hubert Richard Lewis	St Edmundsbury and Ipswich	1997
Rt Rev. William Ind	Truro	1997
Rt Rev. Peter Selby	Worcester	1997
Rt Rev. John Martin Wharton	Newcastle	1997
Rt Rev. John Nicholls	Sheffield	1997
Rt Rev. Colin James Bennetts	Coventry	1997
Rt Rev. James Stuart Jones	Liverpool	1998
Rt Rev. Timothy John Stevens	Leicester	1999
Rt Rev. George Henry Cassidy	Southwell	1999
Rt Rev. Graham Richard James	Norwich	1999
Rt Rev. Michael Laurence Langrish	Exeter	1999

BISHOPS NOT ELIGIBLE TO HAVE A SEAT

		Appointed
Rt Rev. Noel Debroy Jones	Sodor and Man	1989
Rt Rev. John William Hind	Europe	1993

The Sees of Ely, Ripon and Leeds were vacant at the time of going to press

Peers' Obituaries 1999

Beloff (Life Baron, UK); d. 22 March; Extinct
*Belper (4th Baron, UK); d. 23 December; Succeeded by his son
Brandon of Oakbrook (Life Baron, UK); d. 24 March; Extinct
Bristol (7th Marquess, UK); d. 10 January; Succeeded by his half-brother
Caldecote (2nd Viscount, UK); d. 20 September; Succeeded by his son
Cathcart (6th Earl, UK); d. 15 June; Succeeded by his son
Cayzer (Life Baron, UK); d. 16 April; Extinct
Charteris of Amisfield (Life Baron, UK); d. 23 December; Extinct
*Chelmsford (3rd Viscount, UK); d. 15 December; Succeeded by his son
Dalhousie (16th Earl of, S); d. 15 July; Succeeded by his son
Dean of Beswick (Life Baron, UK); d. 26 February; Extinct
Denning (Life Baron, UK); d. 5 March; Extinct
Eccles (1st Viscount, UK); d. 24 February; Succeeded by his son
Gillmore of Thamesfield (Life Baron, UK); d. 20 March; Extinct
Grey of Naunton (Life Baron, UK); d. 17 October; Extinct
Guilford (9th Earl, GB); d. 26 March; Succeeded by his son
Hollenden (3rd Baron, UK); d. 12 April; Succeeded by his son
Hood (7th Viscount, GB); d. 2 October; Succeeded by his son
Howard de Walden (9th Baron, E); d. 9 July; Abeyant between four co-heiresses; and Seaford
    (5th Baron, UK); Succeeded by his cousin
*Howard of Penrith (2nd Baron, UK); d. 13 November; Succeeded by his son
Hughes (Life Baron, UK); d. 31 December; Extinct
Jakobovits (Life Baron, UK); d. 31 October; Extinct
Kemsley (2nd Viscount, UK); d. 28 February; Succeeded by his nephew
Killanin (3rd Baron, UK); d. 25 April; Succeeded by his son
Lambert (3rd Viscount, UK); d. 22 October; Extinct
Lansdowne (8th Marquess, GB); d. 25 August; Succeeded by his son
Lewin (Life Baron, UK); d. 23 January; Extinct
Lowry (Life Baron, UK); d. 15 January; Extinct
Macleod of Borve (Life Baroness, UK); d. 17 November; Extinct
Menuhin (Life Baron, UK); d. 12 March; Extinct
*Milford (3rd Baron, UK); d. 4 December; suc by his son.
Montague of Oxford (Life Baron, UK); d. 5 November; Extinct
Oram (Life Baron, UK); d. 5 September; Extinct
Orr-Ewing (Life Baron, UK); d. 19 August; Extinct
Phillips of Ellesmere (Life Baron, UK); d. 23 February; Extinct
Portman (9th Viscount, UK); d. 2 May; Succeeded by his son
Robens of Woldingham (Life Baron, UK); d. 27 June; Extinct
Robson of Kiddington (Life Baroness, UK); d. 9 February; Extinct
Rutland (10th Duke, E); d. 2 January; Succeeded by his son
St Oswald (5th Baron, UK); d. 18 March; Succeeded by his son
Sinha (5th Baron, UK); d. 19 January; Succeeded by his son
*Stuart of Findhorn (2nd Viscount, UK); d. 24 November; Succeeded by his son
White (Life Baroness, UK); d. 23 December; Extinct
Whitelaw (1st Viscount, UK); d. 1 July; Extinct
Wilton (7th Earl of, UK); d. 1 October; Succeeded by his kinsman 6th Baron Ebury
Winchilsea (16th Earl, E) and Nottingham (11th Earl, E); d. 26 June; Succeeded by his son
Wyfold (3rd Baron, UK); d. 8 April; Extinct

*Hereditary Peers who died after 11 November when the House of Lords Bill was passed

Peers' Obituaries 2000
Braine of Wheatley (Life Baron, UK); d. 5 January; Extinct
Henderson of Brompton (Life Baron, UK); d. 13 January; Extinct

Peers who are not Peers of Parliament

The following list includes all Peers of England, Scotland, Great Britain, Ireland and the United Kingdom who were excluded from the House of Lords in accordance with the House of Lords Act passed in November 1999. Peers of Ireland who do not hold British peerages, and who were never members of the House of Lords are also included in this list.

ABERCONWAY (3rd Baron, UK), Charles Melville McLaren; cr. 1911; 3rd Bt of Bodnant, Gwylgre and Hilders (UK) 1902

ABERCORN (5th Duke, I), James Hamilton; cr. 1868; Marquess of Hamilton; 6th Marquess of Abercorn (GB) 1790; 14th Earl of Abercorn (S) 1606; 9th Viscount Strabane (I) 1701; 7th Viscount Hamilton (GB) 1786; 15th Lord Paisley (S) 1587; 14th Lord Abercorn (S) 1603; 14th Lord Paisley, Hamilton, Mountcastell and Kilpatrick (S) 1606; 14th Baron Strabane (I) 1617; 15th Bt of Dunalong (I) 1660; KG 1999

ABERDEEN AND TEMAIR (6th Marquess of, UK), Alastair Ninian John Gordon; cr. 1916; 12th Earl of Aberdeen (S) 1682; 6th Earl of Haddo (UK) 1916; 12th Viscount Formartine, Lord Haddo, Methlic, Tarves and Kellie (all S) 1682; 9th Viscount Gordon (UK) 1814; 14th Bt of Haddo (NS) 1642

ABERGAVENNY (5th Marquess of, UK), John Henry Guy Nevill; cr. 1876; 9th Earl of Abergavenny (GB) 1784; 5th Earl of Lewes (UK) 1876; 9th Viscount Nevill (GB) 1784; 23rd Baron Abergavenny (E) 1450; KG 1974; OBE (Mil) 1945

ABINGER (8th Baron, UK), James Richard Scarlett; cr. 1835

ACTON (4th Baron, UK), Richard Gerald Lyon-Dalberg-Acton; cr. 1869; 11th Bt of Aldenham (E) 1644

ADDISON (4th Viscount, UK), William Matthew Wand Addison; cr. 1945; 4th Baron Addison (UK) 1937

AILESBURY (8th Marquess of, UK), Michael Sydney Cedric Brudenell-Bruce; cr. 1821; Earl of Cardigan (E) 1661; Earl of Ailesbury (GB) 1776; Earl Bruce and Viscount Savernake (UK) 1821; Baron Brudenell (E) 1627; Baron Bruce (GB) 1746; 14th Bt of Deene (E) 1611

AILSA (8th Marquess of, UK), Archibald Angus Charles Kennedy; cr. 1831; 19th Earl of Cassillis (S) 1509; 21st Lord Kennedy (S) 1457; 8th Baron Ailsa (UK) 1806

AIRLIE (13th Earl of, S), David George Coke Patrick Ogilvy; cr. 1639; 19th Lord Ogilvy of Airlie (S) 1491; Lord Ogilvy of Alyth and Lintrathen (S) 1639; KT 1985; GCVO 1984; PC 1984

ALANBROOKE (3rd Viscount, UK), Alan Victor Harold Brooke; cr. 1946; 3rd Baron Alanbrooke (UK) 1945

ALBEMARLE (10th Earl of, E), Rufus Arnold Alexis Keppel; cr. 1696; Viscount Bury and Baron Ashford

ALDENHAM (6th Baron, UK), Vicary Tyser Gibbs; cr. 1896; 4th Baron Hunsdon of Hunsdon (UK) 1923

ALEXANDER OF TUNIS (2nd Earl, UK), Shane William Desmond Alexander; cr. 1952; 2nd Viscount Alexander of Tunis (UK) 1946; 2nd Baron Rideau (UK) 1952

ALLENDALE (3rd Viscount, UK), Wentworth Hubert Charles Beaumont; cr. 1911; 4th Baron Allendale (UK) 1906; DL

ALVINGHAM (2nd Baron, UK), Robert Guy Eardley Yerburgh; cr. 1929; CBE (Mil) 1978; DL

AMHERST OF HACKNEY (4th Baron, UK), (William) Hugh Amherst Cecil; cr. 1892

AMWELL (3rd Baron, UK), Keith Norman Montague; cr. 1947

ANGLESEY (7th Marquess of, UK), George Charles Henry Victor Paget; cr. 1815; 8th Earl of Uxbridge (GB) 1784; 16th Baron Paget de Beaudesert (E) 1549; 10th Bt of Plas-Newydd (I) 1730

ANNALY (6th Baron, UK), Luke Richard White; cr. 1863

ANNANDALE AND HARTFELL (11th Earl of, S), Patrick Andrew Wentworth Hope Johnstone of Annandale and of that Ilk; cr. 1662 with precedence to 1643; Lord Johnstone

ANNESLEY (10th Earl, I), Patrick Annesley; cr. 1789; 11th Viscount Glerawly (I) 1766; 11th Baron Annesley (I) 1758.

ANTRIM (9th Earl of I), Alexander Randal Mark McDonnell; cr. 1785; Viscount Dunluce.

ARBUTHNOTT (16th Viscount of, S), John Campbell Arbuthnott; cr. 1641; Lord Inverbervie; KT 1996; CBE 1986; DSC 1945

ARGYLL (12th Duke of, S), Ian Campbell; cr. 1701; 5th Duke of Argyll (UK) 1892; Marquess of Kintyre and Lorne (S) 1701; Earl of Argyll (S) 1457; Earl of Campbell and Cowal (S) 1701; Viscount Lochow and Glenilla (S) 1701; Lord Campbell (S) 1445; Lord Lorne (S) 1470; Lord Inveraray, Mull, Morvern and Tiry (S) 1701; Baron Sundridge (GB) 1766; Baron Hamilton (GB) 1776; 14th Bt of Lundy (NS) 1627

ARLINGTON (Baroness, 11th in line, E), Jennifer Jane Forwood; cr. 1664

ASHBOURNE (4th Baron, UK), Edward Barry Greynville Gibson; cr. 1885

ASHBROOK (11th Viscount I), Michael Llowarch Warburton Flower; cr. 1751; 12th Baron of Castle Durrow (I) 1733; DL.

ASHBURTON (7th Baron, UK), John Francis Harcourt Baring; cr. 1835; KG 1994; KCVO 1990; Kt 1983; DL

ASHCOMBE (4th Baron, UK), Henry Edward Cubitt; cr. 1892

ASHTON OF HYDE (3rd Baron, UK), Thomas John Ashton; cr. 1911; TD

ASHTOWN (7th Baron, I), Nigel Clive Cosby Trench; cr. 1800; KCMG 1976.

ATHOLL (11th Duke of, S), John Murray; cr. 1703; Marquess of Tullibardine, Earl of Tullibardine, Earl of Strathtay and Strathardle, Viscount Glenalmond and Glenlyon; 12th Marquess of Atholl, Viscount Balquidder and Lord Murray, Balvenie and Gask (S) 1676; 16th Earl of Tullibardine (S) 1606; 13th Earl of Atholl (S) 1629; 16th Lord Murray of Tullibardine (S) 1604

AUCKLAND (10th Baron, I), Robert Ian Burnard Eden; cr. 1789; 10th Baron Auckland (GB) 1793

AYLESFORD (11th Earl of, GB), Charles Ian Finch-Knightley; cr. 1714; 11th Baron Guernsey (E) 1702

AYLMER (13th Baron I), Michael Anthony Aylmer; cr. 1718; 16th Bt of Balrath (I) 1662.

BADEN-POWELL (3rd Baron, UK), Robert Crause Baden-Powell; cr. 1929; 3rd Bt of Bentley (UK) 1922

BAGOT (9th Baron, GB), Heneage Charles Bagot; cr. 1780; 14th Bt of Blithfield (E) 1627

BAILLIEU (3rd Baron, UK), James William Latham Baillieu; cr. 1953

BALFOUR (4th Earl of, UK), Gerald Arthur James Balfour; cr. 1922; Viscount Traprain

BALFOUR OF BURLEIGH (de facto 8th Lord (S), 12th but for the attainder), Robert Bruce; cr. 1607

BALFOUR OF INCHRYE (2nd Baron, UK), Ian Balfour; cr. 1945

BANBURY OF SOUTHAM (3rd Baron, UK), Charles William Banbury; cr. 1924; 3rd Bt of Warneford Place (UK) 1903

BANGOR (8th Viscount, I), William Maxwell David Ward; cr. 1781; 8th Baron Bangor (I) 1770.

BARNARD (11th Baron, E), Harry John Neville Vane; cr. 1698; TD 1960

BASING (5th Baron, UK), Neil Lutley Sclater-Booth; cr. 1887

BATH (7th Marquess of, GB), Alexander George Thynn; cr. 1789; 9th Viscount Weymouth and Baron Thynne (E) 1682; 10th Bt of Caus Castle (E) 1641

BATHURST (8th Earl, GB), Henry Allen John Bathurst; cr. 1772; Baron Bathurst (GB) 1712; Baron Apsley (GB) 1771; DL

BEARSTED (5th Viscount, UK), Nicholas Alan Samuel; cr. 1925; 5th Baron Bearsted (UK) 1921; 5th Bt of The Mote and Portland Place (UK) 1903

BEATTY (3rd Earl, UK), David Beatty; cr. 1919; Viscount Borodale and Baron Beatty

BEAUFORT (11th Duke of, E), David Robert Somerset; cr. 1682; Marquess of Worcester (E) 1642; Earl of Worcester (E) 1513; Baron Herbert of Raglan, Chepstow and Gower (E) 1506

BEAVERBROOK (3rd Baron, UK), Maxwell William Humphrey Aitken; cr. 1917; 3rd Bt of New Brunswick (UK) 1916

BEDFORD (13th Duke of, E), John Robert Russell; cr. 1694; Marquess of Tavistock; Earl of Bedford (E) 1550; Baron Russell (E) 1540; Baron Russell of Thornhaugh (E) 1603; Baron Howland (E) 1695

BELHAVEN AND STENTON (13th Lord, S), Robert Anthony Carmichael Hamilton; cr. 1647

BELLEW (7th Baron, I), James Bryan Bellew; cr. 1848; 13th Bt of Barmeath (I) 1688.

BELMORE (8th Earl, I), John Armar Lowry-Corry; cr. 1797; 8th Viscount Belmore (I) 1789; 8th Baron Belmore (I) 1781.

BELPER (5th Baron, UK), Richard Henry Strutt; cr. 1856

BERKELEY (18th Baron, E), Anthony Fitzhardinge Gueterbock; cr. 1421; OBE 1989

BERNERS (Baroness, 16th in line, E), Pamela Vivien Kirkham; cr. 1455

BESSBOROUGH (11th Earl of, I), Arthur Mountifort Longfield Ponsonby; cr. 1739; Viscount Duncannon (I) 1722; Baron Bessborough (I) 1721; Baron Ponsonby (GB) 1749; Baron Duncannon of Bessborough (UK) 1834

BETHELL (4th Baron, UK), Nicholas William Bethell; cr. 1922; 4th Bt of Park House (UK) 1911

BICESTER (3rd Baron, UK), Angus Edward Vivian Smith; cr. 1938

BIDDULPH (5th Baron, UK), Anthony Nicholas Colin Maitland Biddulph; cr. 1903

BIRDWOOD (3rd Baron, UK), Mark William Ogilvie Birdwood; cr. 1938; 3rd Bt of Anzac and Totnes (UK) 1919

BIRKETT (2nd Baron, UK), Michael Birkett; cr. 1958

BLAKENHAM (2nd Viscount, UK), Michael John Hare; cr. 1963

BLYTH (4th Baron, UK), Anthony Audley Rupert Blyth; cr. 1907; 4th Bt of Blythwood (UK) 1895

BOLINGBROKE (7th Viscount, GB), cr. 1712; AND ST JOHN (8th Viscount, GB); cr. 1716; Kenneth Oliver Musgrave St John; Baron St John of Lydiard Tregoze (GB) 1712; Baron St John of Battersea (GB) 1716; 11th Bt of Lydiard Tregoze (E) 1611

BOLTON (7th Baron, GB), Richard William Algar Orde-Powlett; cr. 1797

BORTHWICK (24th Lord, S), John Hugh Borthwick of that Ilk; cr. 1452

BORWICK (4th Baron, UK), James Hugh Myles Borwick; cr. 1922; 4th Bt of Eden Lacy (UK) 1916; MC 1945

BOSTON (10th Baron, GB), Timothy George Frank Boteler Irby; cr. 1761; 11th Bt of Boston (E) 1704

BOYD OF MERTON (2nd Viscount, UK), Simon Donald Rupert Neville Lennox-Boyd; cr. 1960

BOYNE (11th Viscount, I), Gustavus Michael Stucley Hamilton-Russell; cr. 1717; 11th Baron Hamilton (I) 1715; 5th Baron Brancepeth (UK) 1866

BRABOURNE (7th Baron, UK), John Ulick Knatchbull; cr. 1880; 16th Bt of Mersham Hatch (E) 1641; CBE 1993

BRADBURY (3rd Baron, UK), John Bradbury; cr. 1925

BRADFORD (7th Earl of, UK), Richard Thomas Orlando Bridgeman; cr. 1815; Viscount Newport; 8th Baron Bradford (GB) 1794; 12th Bt of Great Lever (E) 1660

BRAIN (2nd Baron, UK), Christopher Langdon Brain; cr. 1962; 2nd Bt of Reading (UK) 1954

BRASSEY OF APETHORPE (3rd Baron, UK), David Henry Brassey; cr. 1938; 3rd Bt of Apethorpe (UK) 1922; OBE 1994; DL

BRAYBROOKE (10th Baron, GB), Robin Henry Charles Neville; cr. 1788

BRAYE (Baroness, 8th in line, E), Penelope Mary Aubrey-Fletcher; cr. 1529

BRENTFORD (4th Viscount, UK), Crispin William Joynson-Hicks; cr. 1929; 4th Bt of Holmbury (UK) 1919; 2nd Bt of Newick (UK) 1956

BRIDPORT (4th Viscount, UK), Alexander Nelson Hood; cr. 1868; 6th Baron Bridport (I) 1794; 7th Duke of Bronte (Sicily) 1799

BRISTOL (8th Marquess of, UK), Frederick William Augustus Hervey; cr. 1826; Earl Jermyn; 12th Earl of Bristol (GB) 1714; 12th Baron Hervey (E) 1703

BROADBRIDGE (3rd Baron, UK), Peter Hewett Broadbridge; cr. 1945; 3rd Bt of Wargrave Place (UK) 1937

BROCKET (3rd Baron, UK), Charles Ronald George Nall-Cain; cr. 1933; 3rd Bt of the Node (UK) 1921

BROOKE, Earldom of – see WARWICK (9th Earl)

BROUGHSHANE (3rd Baron, UK), (William) Kensington Davison; cr. 1945; DSO 1945; DFC

BROWNLOW (7th Baron, GB), Edward John Peregrine Cust; cr. 1776; 10th Bt of Stamford (E) 1677

BRUNTISFIELD (2nd Baron, UK), John Robert Warrender; cr. 1942; 9th Bt of Lochend (GB) 1715; OBE (Mil) 1962; MC 1942; TD 1967

BUCCLEUCH (9th Duke of, S), cr. 1663, AND QUEENSBERRY (11th Duke of, S) cr. 1684; Walter Francis John Montagu Douglas Scott; 12th Marquess of Dumfriesshire (S), 10th Earl of Doncaster (E) 1663; 12th Earl of Buccleuch (S) 1619; 9th Earl of Dalkeith (S) 1663; 11th Earl of Drumlanrig and Sanquhar (S) 1684; 11th Viscount of Nith, Torthorwold and Ross (S) 1684; 9th Baron Scott of Tyndale (E) 1663; 13th Lord Scott of Buccleuch (S) 1606; 12th Lord Scott of Whitchester and Eskdaill (S) 1619; 11th Lord Douglas of Kinmont, Middlebie and Dornoch (S) 1684; KT 1978

BUCHAN (17th Earl of, S), Malcolm Harry Erskine; cr. 1469; Lord Auchterhouse; 12th Lord Cardross (S) 1610; 8th Baron Erskine (UK) 1806

BUCKINGHAMSHIRE (10th Earl of, GB), George Miles Hobart-Hampden; cr. 1746; 10th Baron Hobart (GB) 1728; 14th Bt of Intwood (E) 1611

BUCKMASTER (3rd Viscount, UK), Martin Stanley Buckmaster; cr. 1933; 3rd Baron Buckmaster (UK) 1915; OBE 1979

BURDEN (3rd Baron, UK), Andrew Philip Burden; cr. 1950

BURGH (7th Baron, E), Alexander Peter Willoughby Leith; cr. 1529

BURTON (3rd Baron, UK), Michael Evan Victor Baillie; cr. 1897

BUTE (7th Marquess of, GB), John Colum Crichton-Stuart; cr. 1796; 12th Earl of Dumfries (S) 1633; 10th Earl of Bute (S) 1703; Earl of Windsor (GB) 1796; 7th Viscount of Air and Lord Crichton of Sanquhar and Cumnock (S) 1633; Viscount Kingarth (S) 1703; Viscount Mountjoy (GB) 1796; 20th Lord Crichton of Sanquhar (S) 1488; Lord Mountstuart, Cumrae and Inchmarnock (S) 1703; Baron Mount Stuart of Wortley (GB) 1761; 7th Baron Cardiff (GB) 1776; 12th Bt of Bute (NS) 1627

BYRON (13th Baron, E), Robert James Byron; cr. 1643

CADMAN (3rd Baron, UK), John Anthony Cadman; cr. 1937

CADOGAN (8th Earl, GB), Charles Gerald John Cadogan; cr. 1800; Viscount Chelsea; 10th Baron Cadogan (GB) 1718; 6th Baron Oakley (UK) 1831

CAIRNS (6th Earl, UK), Simon Dallas Cairns; cr. 1878; Viscount Garmoyle; Baron Cairns (UK) 1867; CBE 1992

CALDECOTE (3rd Viscount, UK), Piers James Hampden Inskip; cr. 1939

CALEDON (7th Earl of, I), Nicholas James Alexander; cr. 1800; 7th Viscount Caledon (I) 1797; 7th Baron Caledon (I) 1790.

CALVERLEY (3rd Baron, UK), Charles Rodney Muff; cr. 1945

CAMDEN (6th Marquess, UK), David George Edward Henry Pratt; cr. 1812; Earl of Brecknock; 7th Earl Camden and Viscount Bayham (GB) 1786; 7th Baron Camden (GB) 1765

CAMOYS (7th Baron, E), Ralph Thomas Campion Sherman Stonor; cr. 1383; PC 1997; GCVO 1998; DL

CAMROSE, Viscountcy of – see HARTWELL (Life Baron)

CARBERY (11th Baron, I), Peter Ralfe Harrington Evans-Freke; cr. 1715; 7th Bt of Castle Freke (I) 1768.

CAREW (7th Baron, I), Patrick Thomas Conolly-Carew; cr. 1834; 7th Baron Carew (UK) 1838

CARLISLE (13th Earl of, E), George William Beaumont Howard; cr. 1661; Viscount Howard of Morpeth and Baron Dacre of Gillesland (E) 1661; 13th Lord Ruthven of Freeland (S) 1651

CARNOCK (4th Baron, UK), David Henry Arthur Nicolson of that Ilk; cr. 1916; 16th Bt of Lasswade (NS) 1629; 14th Bt of Carnock (NS) 1637

CARRICK (10th Earl of, I), David James Theobald Somerset Butler; cr. 1748; 17th Viscount Ikerrin (I) 1629; 4th Baron Butler of Mount Juliet (UK) 1912

CASTLEMAINE (8th Baron, I), Roland Thomas John Handcock; cr. 1812; MBE (Mil) 1981.

CASTLE STEWART (8th Earl, I), Arthur Patrick Avondale Stuart; cr. 1800; 8th Viscount Castle Stuart (I) 1793; 16th Baron Castle Stuart (I) 1619; 15th Bt of Castle Stuart (NS) 1628.

CATHCART (7th Earl, UK), Charles Alan Andrew Cathcart; cr. 1814; 7th Viscount Cathcart and Baron Greenock (UK) 1807; 16th Lord Cathcart (S) 1447

CATTO (2nd Baron, UK), Stephen Gordon Catto; cr. 1936; 2nd Bt of Peterhead (UK) 1921

CAVAN (13th Earl of, I), Roger Cavan Lambart; cr. 1647; Viscount Kilcoursie; 14th Lord Lambart, Baron of Cavan (I) 1617.

CAWDOR (7th Earl, UK), Colin Robert Vaughan Campbell; cr. 1827; Viscount Emlyn; Baron Cawdor (GB) 1796; 25th Thane of Cawdor; DL

CAWLEY (3rd Baron, UK), Frederick Lee Cawley; cr. 1918; 3rd Bt of Prestwich (UK) 1906

CHANDOS (3rd Viscount, UK), Thomas Orlando Lyttelton; cr. 1954

CHARLEMONT (14th Viscount, I), John Day Caulfeild; cr. 1665; 18th Lord Caulfeild, Baron of Charlemont (I) 1620.

CHATFIELD (2nd Baron, UK), Ernle David Lewis Chatfield; cr. 1937

CHELMSFORD (4th Viscount, UK), Frederic Corin Piers Thesiger; cr. 1921; 6th Baron Chelmsford (UK) 1858

CHESHAM (6th Baron, UK), Nicholas Charles Cavendish; cr. 1858

CHETWODE (2nd Baron, UK), Philip Chetwode; cr. 1945; 8th Bt of Oakley (E) 1700

CHETWYND (10th Viscount, I), Adam Richard John Casson Chetwynd; cr. 1717; Baron Rathdowne.

CHICHESTER (9th Earl of, UK), John Nicholas Pelham; cr. 1801; Baron Pelham (GB) 1762; 14th Bt of Laughton (E) 1611

CHILSTON (4th Viscount, UK), Alastair George Akers-Douglas; cr. 1911; Baron Douglas of Baads

CHORLEY (2nd Baron, UK), Roger Richard Edward Chorley; cr. 1945

CHURCHILL (3rd Viscount, UK), Victor George Spencer; cr. 1902; 5th Baron Churchill (UK) 1815

CHURSTON (5th Baron, UK), John Francis Yarde-Buller; cr. 1858; 7th Bt of Lupton House (GB) 1790

CITRINE (3rd Baron, UK), Ronald Eric Citrine; cr. 1946

CLANCARTY (9th Earl of, I), Nicholas Power Richard Le Poer Trench; cr. 1803; 9th Viscount Dunlo (I), 1800; 8th Viscount Clancarty (UK) 1823; 9th Baron Kilconnel (I) 1797; 8th Baron Trench (UK) 1815; 8th Marquess of Heusden in the Netherlands 1818

CLANMORRIS (8th Baron, I), Simon John Ward Bingham; cr. 1800.

CLANWILLIAM (7th Earl of, I), John Herbert Meade; cr. 1776; Viscount Clanwilliam and Baron Gillford (I) 1766; Baron Clanwilliam (UK) 1828; 10th Bt of Ballintubber (I) 1703

CLARENDON (7th Earl of, GB), George Frederick Laurence Hyde Villiers; cr. 1776; 7th Baron Hyde (GB) 1756

CLIFFORD OF CHUDLEIGH (14th Baron, E), Thomas Hugh Clifford; cr. 1672; DL

CLINTON (22nd Baron, E), Gerard Nevile Mark Fane Trefusis; cr. 1299; DL

CLITHEROE (2nd Baron, UK), Ralph John Assheton; cr. 1955; 3rd Bt of Downham (UK) 1945; DL

CLWYD (3rd Baron, UK), John Anthony Roberts; cr. 1919; 3rd Bt of Bryngwenallt (UK) 1908

CLYDESMUIR (3rd Baron, UK), David Ronald Colville; cr. 1948

COBBOLD (2nd Baron, UK), David Antony Fromanteel Lytton Cobbold; cr. 1960; DL

COBHAM (11th Viscount, GB), John William Leonard Lyttelton; cr. 1718; Baron Cobham; Lord Lyttelton, Baron of Frankley (GB) 1794; Baron Westcote (I) 1776; 14th Bt of Frankley (E) 1618

COCHRANE OF CULTS (4th Baron, UK), (Ralph Henry) Vere Cochrane; cr. 1919; DL

COLERAINE (2nd Baron, UK), (James) Martin Bonar Law; cr. 1954

COLERIDGE (5th Baron, UK), William Duke Coleridge; cr. 1874

COLGRAIN (3rd Baron, UK), David Colin Campbell; cr. 1946

COLYTON (2nd Baron, UK), Alisdair John Munro Hopkinson; cr. 1956

COMBERMERE (5th Viscount, UK), Michael Wellington Stapleton-Cotton; cr. 1827; 5th Baron Combermere (UK) 1814; 10th Bt of Combermere (E) 1677

CONGLETON (8th Baron, UK), Christopher Patrick Parnell; cr. 1841; 11th Bt of Rathleague (I) 1766

CONYNGHAM (7th Marquess, I), Frederick William Henry Francis Conyngham; cr. 1816; Earl Conyngham (I) 1797; Earl of Mount Charles (I) 1816; Viscount Conyngham (I) 1789; Viscount Mount Charles (I) 1797; Viscount Slane (I) 1816; Baron Conyngham (I) 1781; 7th Baron Minster (UK) 1821

CORK AND ORRERY (14th Earl of, I), John William Boyle; cr. 1620 and 1660; 14th Viscount Dungarvan (I) 1620; 15th Viscount Boyle of Kinalmeaky and Baron of Bandon Bridge (I) 1627; 14th Baron Boyle of Yougal (I) 1616; 14th Baron Boyle of Broghill (I) 1621; 11th Baron Boyle of Marston (GB) 1711; DSC 1945; VRD 1952

CORNWALLIS (3rd Baron, UK), Fiennes Neil Wykeham Cornwallis; cr. 1927; OBE 1963; DL

COTTENHAM (8th Earl of, UK), Kenelm Charles Everard Digby Pepys; cr. 1850; Viscount Crowhurst; Baron Cottenham (UK) 1836; 11th Bt of Upper Brook Street (GB) 1784; 10th Bt of Wimpole Street (UK) 1801

COTTESLOE (5th Baron, UK), John Tapling Fremantle; cr. 1874; 5th Bt of Swanbourne (UK) 1821; Baron of the Austrian Empire 1816; DL

COVENTRY (11th Earl of, E), George William Coventry; cr. 1697; Viscount Deerhurst

COWDRAY (4th Viscount, UK), Michael Orlando Weetman Pearson; cr. 1917; 4th Baron Cowdray (UK) 1910; 4th Bt of Paddockhurst (UK) 1894; DL

COWLEY (7th Earl, UK), Garret Graham Wellesley; cr. 1857; Viscount Dangan; 8th Baron Cowley (UK) 1828

CRAIGMYLE (4th Baron, UK), Thomas Columba Shaw; cr. 1929

CRANBROOK (5th Earl of, UK), Gathorne Gathorne-Hardy; cr. 1892; Viscount Cranbrook (UK) 1878; Baron Medway (UK) 1892; DL

CRANWORTH (3rd Baron, UK), Philip Bertram Gurdon; cr. 1899

CRAVEN (9th Earl of, UK), Benjamin Robert Joseph Craven; cr. 1801; Viscount Uffington; 15th Baron Craven (E) 1666

CRAWSHAW (5th Baron, UK), David Gerald Brooks; cr. 1892; 5th Bt of Crawshaw Hall and Whatton House (UK) 1891

CROFT (3rd Baron, UK), Bernard William Henry Page Croft; cr. 1940; 3rd Bt of Knole (UK) 1924

CROFTON (7th Baron, I), Guy Patrick Gilbert Crofton; cr. 1797; 9th Bt of The Mote (I) 1758.

CROMARTIE (5th Earl of, UK), John Ruaridh Grant Mackenzie; cr. 1861; Viscount Tarbat; Baron Castlehaven and Baron McLeod

CROMER (4th Earl of, UK), Evelyn Rowland Esmond Baring; cr. 1901; Viscount Cromer (UK) 1899; Viscount Errington (UK) 1901; Baron Cromer (UK) 1892

CROMWELL (7th Baron, E), Godfrey John Bewicke-Copley; cr. 1375

CROOK (2nd Baron, UK), Douglas Edwin Crook; cr. 1947

CROSS (3rd Viscount, UK), Assheton Henry Cross; cr. 1886

CULLEN OF ASHBOURNE (2nd Baron, UK), Charles Borlase Marsham Cokayne; cr. 1920; MBE (Mil) 1945

CUNLIFFE (3rd Baron, UK), Roger Cunliffe; cr. 1914

DACRE (Baroness, 27th in line, E), Rachel Leila Douglas-Home; cr. 1321

DALHOUSIE (17th Earl of, S), James Hubert Ramsay; cr. 1633; 18th Lord Ramsay of Dalhousie (S) 1618; 17th Lord Ramsay of Keringtoun (S) 1633; 6th Baron Ramsay (UK) 1875

DARESBURY (4th Baron, UK), Peter Gilbert Greenall; cr. 1927; 5th Bt of Walton Hall (UK) 1876; DL

DARLING (2nd Baron, UK), Robert Charles Henry Darling; cr. 1924; DL

DARNLEY (11th Earl of, I), Adam Ivo Stuart Bligh; cr. 1725; 11th Viscount Darnley (I) 1723; 20th Baron Clifton of Leighton Bromswold (E) 1608; 11th Baron Clifton of Rathmore (I) 1721

DARTMOUTH (10th Earl of, GB), William Legge; cr. 1711; Viscount Lewisham; 11th Baron Dartmouth (E) 1682

DARWEN (3rd Baron, UK), Roger Michael Davies; cr. 1946

DAVENTRY (3rd Viscount, UK), Francis Humphrey Maurice FitzRoy Newdegate; cr. 1943

DAVIDSON (2nd Viscount, UK), John Andrew Davidson; cr. 1937

DAVIES (3rd Baron, UK), David Davies; cr. 1932; DL

DE CLIFFORD (27th Baron, E), John Edward Southwell Russell; cr. 1299

DE FREYNE (7th Baron, UK), Francis Arthur John French; cr. 1851

DE LA WARR (11th Earl, GB), William Herbrand Sackville; cr. 1761; Viscount Cantelupe; 17th Baron De La Warr (E) 1298/1572; 7th Baron Buckhurst (UK) 1864

DE L'ISLE (2nd Viscount, UK), Philip John Algernon Sidney; cr. 1956; 7th Baron De L'Isle and Dudley (UK) 1835; 10th Bt of Castle Goring (UK) 1806; 8th Bt of Penshurst Place (UK) 1818; MBE (Mil) 1977; DL

DE MAULEY (6th Baron, UK), Gerald John Ponsonby; cr. 1838

DE RAMSEY (4th Baron, UK), John Ailwyn Fellowes; cr. 1887; DL

DE ROS (28th Baron, E), Peter Trevor Maxwell; cr. 1264

DE SAUMAREZ (7th Baron, UK), Eric Douglas Saumarez; cr. 1831; 7th Bt of Guernsey (UK) 1801

DE VESCI (7th Viscount, I), Thomas Eustace Vesey; cr. 1776; 8th Baron Knapton (I) 1750; 9th Bt of Abbey Leix (I) 1698.

DE VILLIERS (3rd Baron, UK), Arthur Percy de Villiers; cr. 1910

DECIES (7th Baron, I), Marcus Hugh Tristam de la Poer Beresford; cr. 1812.

DELAMERE (5th Baron, UK), Hugh George Cholmondeley; cr. 1821

DENBIGH (12th Earl of, E), cr. 1622, AND DESMOND (11th Earl of, I), cr. 1622; Alexander Stephen Rudolf Feilding; 12th Viscount Feilding and Baron Feilding of Newnham Paddox (E) 1620; 11th Viscount Callan and Baron Feilding of Lecaghe (I) 1622; 11th Baron St Liz (E) 1663

DENMAN (5th Baron, UK), Charles Spencer Denman; cr. 1834; 2nd Bt of Staffield (UK) 1945; CBE 1976; MC 1942; TD 1945

DERAMORE (6th Baron, UK), Richard Arthur de Yarburgh-Bateson; cr. 1885; 7th Bt of Belvoir Park (UK) 1818

DERBY (19th Earl of, E), Edward Richard William Stanley; cr. 1485; 7th Baron Stanley of Bickerstaffe (UK) 1832; 4th Baron Stanley of Preston (UK) 1886; 13th Bt of Bickerstaffe (E) 1627; DL

DERWENT (5th Baron, UK), Robin Evelyn Leo Vanden-Bempde-Johnstone; cr. 1881; 7th Bt of Hackness Hall (GB) 1795; LVO 1957; DL

DEVON (18th Earl of, E), Hugh Rupert Courtenay; cr. 1553; 14th Bt of Powderham Castle (E) 1644; DL

DEVONPORT (3rd Viscount, UK), Terence Kearley; cr. 1917; 3rd Baron Devonport (UK) 1910; 3rd Bt of Wittington (UK) 1908

DEVONSHIRE (11th Duke of, E), Andrew Robert Buxton Cavendish; cr 1694; Marquess of Hartington; 14th Earl of Devonshire (E) 1618; 7th Earl of Burlington (UK) 1831; Baron Cavendish (E) 1605; Baron Cavendish (UK) 1831; KG 1996; PC 1964; MC 1944

DICKINSON (2nd Baron, UK), Richard Clavering Hyett Dickinson; cr. 1930

DIGBY (12th Baron, I), Edward Henry Kenelm Digby; cr. 1620; 6th Baron Digby (GB) 1765; KCVO 1999

DILHORNE (2nd Viscount, UK), John Mervyn Manningham-Buller; cr. 1964; 2nd Baron Dilhorne (UK) 1962; 5th Bt of Dilhorne Hall (UK) 1866

DILLON (22nd Viscount, I), Henry Benedict Charles Dillon; cr. 1622; 14th Count Dillon (France) 1711.

DINEVOR – see DYNEVOR (9th Baron)

DONEGALL (7th Marquess of, I), Dermot Richard Claud Chichester; cr. 1791; 11th Earl of Donegall (I) 1647; 7th Earl of Belfast (I) 1791; 12th Viscount and Baron Chichester (I) 1625; 7th Baron Fisherwick (GB) 1790; 5th Baron Templemore (UK) 1831; LVO 1986

DONERAILE (10th Viscount,I), Richard Allen St Leger; cr. 1785; 10th Baron Doneraile (I) 1776.

DONOUGHMORE (8th Earl of, I), Richard Michael John Hely-Hutchinson; cr. 1800; 8th Viscount Donoughmore (I) 1797; 8th Viscount Hutchinson (UK) 1821; 9th Baron Donoughmore (I) 1783

DORMER (17th Baron, E), Geoffrey Henry Dormer; cr. 1615; 17th Bt of Wyng (E) 1615

DOWDING (3rd Baron, UK), Piers Hugh Tremenheere Dowding; cr. 1943

DOWNE (11th Viscount, I), John Christian George Dawnay; cr. 1681; 4th Baron Dawnay (UK) 1897; DL

DOWNSHIRE (8th Marquess of, I), Arthur Robin Ian Hill; cr. 1789; Earl of Hillsborough (I) 1751 and (GB) 1772; Viscount Hillsborough (I) 1717; Viscount Kilwarlin (I) 1751; Viscount Fairford (GB) 1772; Baron Hill (I) 1717; Baron Harwich (GB) 1756

DROGHEDA (12th Earl of, I), Henry Dermot Ponsonby Moore; cr. 1661; Viscount Moore (I) 1621; Baron Moore (I) 1616; 3rd Baron Moore (UK) 1954

DUCIE (7th Earl of, UK), David Leslie Moreton; cr. 1837; 10th Baron Ducie (GB) 1763; Baron Moreton (UK) 1837

DUDLEY (4th Earl of, UK), William Humble David Ward; cr. 1860; Viscount Ednam; 14th Baron Ward (E) 1644

DUDLEY (Baroness, 14th in line, E), Barbara Amy Felicity Hamilton; cr. 1439

DUFFERIN AND CLANDEBOYE (11th Baron, I), John Francis Blackwood; cr. 1800; 12th Bt of Ballyleidy (I) 1763; 8th Bt (UK) 1814.

DULVERTON (3rd Baron, UK), (Gilbert) Michael Hamilton Wills; cr. 1929; 4th Bt of Manor Heath (UK) 1897

DUNALLEY (7th Baron, I), Henry Francis Cornelius Prittie; cr. 1800.

DUNBOYNE (28th Baron, by Summons; 18th Baron, by Patent, I), Patrick Theobald Tower Butler; cr. 1324 and 1541.

DUNDONALD (15th Earl of, S), Iain Alexander Douglas Blair Cochrane; cr. 1669; Lord Cochrane of Dundonald (S) 1647; Lord Cochrane of Paisley and Ochiltree (S) 1669

DUNLEATH (6th Baron, UK), Brian Henry Mulholland; cr. 1892; 3rd Bt of Ballyscullion Park (UK) 1945

DUNMORE (12th Earl of, S), Malcolm Kenneth Murray; cr. 1686; Viscount Fincastle and Lord Murray of Blair, Moulin and Tillimet

DUNRAVEN AND MOUNT-EARL (7th Earl of, I), Thady Windham Thomas Wyndham-Quin; cr. 1822; Viscount Adare; 7th Viscount Mount-Earl (I) 1816; 7th Baron Adare (I) 1800; 7th Bt of Adare (GB) 1781.

DUNROSSIL (2nd Viscount, UK), John William Morrison; cr. 1959; CMG 1981

DUNSANY (20th Baron of, I), Edward Carlos John Plunkett; cr. 1439; 24th Baron of Killeen (I) 1403.

DYNEVOR (9th Baron, GB), Richard Charles Uryan Rhys; cr. 1780

DYSART (Countess of, 11th in line, S), Rosamund Agnes Greaves; cr. 1643; Lady Huntingtower

EBURY, Barony of – see WILTON (8th Earl of)

ECCLES (2nd Viscount, UK), John Dawson Eccles; cr. 1964; 2nd Baron Eccles (UK) 1962; CBE 1985

EDINBURGH (1st Duke of, UK), H.R.H. The Prince Philip; cr 1947; Earl of Merioneth; Baron Greenwich of Greenwich; KG 1947; KT 1952; OM 1968; GBE 1953; AC; QSO; PC 1951

EFFINGHAM (7th Earl of, UK), David Mowbray Algernon Howard; cr. 1837; 17th Baron Howard of Effingham (E) 1554

EGLINTON (18th Earl of, S), cr. 1507 AND WINTON (6th Earl of, UK) cr. 1859; Archibald George Montgomerie; 20th Lord Montgomerie (S) 1449; 7th Baron Ardrossan (UK) 1806; 6th Baron Seton and Tranent (UK) 1859

EGMONT (11th Earl of, I), Frederick George Moore Perceval; cr. 1733; Viscount Perceval (I) 1722; Baron Perceval (I) 1715; Baron Lovel and Holland (GB) 1762; Baron Arden (I) 1770; Baron Arden (UK) 1802; 15th Bt of Burton (I) 1661

EGREMONT (2nd Baron, UK), John Max Henry Scawen Wyndham; cr. 1963; 7th Baron Leconfield (UK) 1859; DL

ELDON (5th Earl of, UK), John Joseph Nicholas Scott; cr. 1821; Viscount Encombe; Baron Eldon (GB) 1799

ELGIN (11th Earl of, S), cr. 1633, AND KINCARDINE (15th Earl of, S), cr 1647; Andrew Douglas Alexander Thomas Bruce; Lord Bruce of Torry (S) 1647; Lord Bruce of Kinloss (S) 1608; Baron Elgin (UK) 1849; KT 1981

ELIBANK (14th Lord, S), Alan D'Ardis Erskine-Murray; cr. 1643; 14th Bt of Elibank (NS) 1628

ELLENBOROUGH (8th Baron, UK), Richard Edward Cecil Law; cr. 1802

ELPHINSTONE (19th Lord, S), Alexander Mountstuart Elphinstone; cr. 1509; 5th Baron Elphinstone (UK) 1885

ELY (8th Marquess of, I), Charles John Tottenham; cr. 1801; 8th Earl of Ely (I) 1794; 8th Viscount Loftus (I) 1789; 8th Baron Loftus (I) 1785; 8th Baron Loftus (UK) 1801; 9th Bt of Tottenham Green (I) 1780

ENNISKILLEN (7th Earl of, I), Andrew John Galbraith Cole; cr. 1789; Viscount Enniskillen (I) 1776; Baron Mountflorence (I) 1760; Baron Grinstead (UK) 1815

ERNE (6th Earl of, I), Henry George Victor John Crichton; cr. 1789; Viscount Erne (I) 1781; Baron Erne (I) 1768; Baron Fermanagh (UK) 1876

ESHER (4th Viscount, UK), Lionel Gordon Baliol Brett; cr. 1897; 4th Baron Esher (UK) 1885; CBE 1970

ESSEX (10th Earl of, E), Robert Edward De Vere Capell; cr. 1661; Viscount Malden; Baron Capell (E) 1641

EXETER (8th Marquess of, UK), William Michael Anthony Cecil; cr. 1801; Earl of Exeter (E) 1605; Baron Burghley (E) 1571

EXMOUTH (10th Viscount, UK), Paul Edward Pellew; cr. 1816; 10th Baron Exmouth (UK) 1814; 10th Bt of Treverry (GB) 1796; Marquess de Olias (Spain) 1652

FAIRFAX OF CAMERON (14th Lord, S), Nicholas John Albert Fairfax; cr. 1627

FAIRHAVEN (3rd Baron, UK), Ailwyn Henry George Broughton; cr. 1961; DL

FALMOUTH (9th Viscount, GB), George Hugh Boscawen; cr. 1720; 26th Baron Le Despencer (E) 1264; 9th Baron Boscawen-Rose (GB) 1720

FARINGDON (3rd Baron, UK), Charles Michael Henderson; cr. 1916; 3rd Bt of Buscot Park (UK) 1902

FARNHAM (12th Baron, I), Barry Owen Somerset Maxwell; cr. 1756; 14th Bt of Calderwood (NS) 1627.

FERMOY (6th Baron, I), Patrick Maurice Burke Roche; cr. 1856.

FEVERSHAM (6th Baron, UK), Charles Antony Peter Duncombe; cr. 1826

FFRENCH (8th Baron, I), Robuck John Peter Charles Mario ffrench; cr. 1798; 8th Bt of Clogher (I) 1779.

FIFE (3rd Duke of, UK), James George Alexander Bannerman Carnegie; cr. 1900; Earl of Macduff; 12th Earl of Southesk (S) 1633; Lord Carnegie of Kinnaird (S) 1616; Lord Carnegie of Kinnaird and Leuchars (S) 1633; Baron Balinhard (UK) 1869; 9th Bt of Pittcarrow (NS) 1663

FISHER (3rd Baron, UK), John Vavasseur Fisher; cr. 1909; DSC 1944

FITZWALTER (21st Baron, E), Fitzwalter Brook Plumptre; cr. 1295

FOLEY (8th Baron, GB), Adrian Gerald Foley; cr. 1776

FORBES (22nd Lord, S), Nigel Ivan Forbes; cr. 1445; KBE 1960; DL

FORESTER (8th Baron, UK), George Cecil Brooke Weld-Forester; cr. 1821; DL

FORRES (4th Baron, UK), Alastair Stephen Grant Williamson; cr. 1922; 4th Bt of Glenogil (UK) 1909

FORTESCUE (8th Earl, GB), Charles Hugh Richard Fortescue; cr. 1789; Viscount Ebrington; 10th Baron Fortescue (GB) 1746

FORTEVIOT (4th Baron, UK), John James Evelyn Dewar; cr. 1917; 4th Bt of the City of Perth (UK) 1907

GAGE (8th Viscount, I), Henry Nicolas Gage; cr. 1720; Baron Gage; 7th Baron Gage (GB) 1790; 15th Bt of Firle (E) 1622; DL

GAINFORD (3rd Baron, UK), Joseph Edward Pease; cr. 1917

GAINSBOROUGH (5th Earl of, UK), Anthony Gerard Edward Noel; cr. 1841; Viscount Campden and Baron Noel; Baron Barham (UK) 1805; 7th Bt (GB) 1781

GALLOWAY (13th Earl of, S), Randolph Keith Reginald Stewart; cr. 1623; Lord Garlies (S) 1607; Baron Stewart of Garlies (GB) 1796; 12th Bt of Corsewell (S) 1627; 10th Bt of Burray (S) 1687

GALWAY (12th Viscount, I), George Rupert Monckton-Arundell; cr. 1727; Baron Killard.

GARVAGH (5th Baron, I), Alexander Leopold Ivor George Canning; cr. 1818.

GERARD (5th Baron, UK), Anthony Robert Hugo Gerard; cr. 1876; 17th Bt of Bryn (E) 1611

GIFFORD (6th Baron, UK), Anthony Maurice Gifford; cr. 1824; QC 1982

GISBOROUGH (3rd Baron, UK), Thomas Richard John Long Chaloner; cr. 1917

GLADWYN (2nd Baron, UK), Miles Alvery Gladwyn Jebb; cr. 1960

GLANUSK (5th Baron, UK), Christopher Russell Bailey; cr. 1899; 6th Bt of Glanusk Park (UK) 1852

GLASGOW (10th Earl of, S), Patrick Robin Archibald Boyle; cr. 1703; Viscount of Kelburn; 10th Lord Boyle (S) 1699/1703; 4th Baron Fairlie (UK) 1897; DL

GLENCONNER (3rd Baron, UK), Colin Christopher Paget Tennant; cr. 1911; 4th Bt of The Glen (UK) 1885

GLENDEVON (2nd Baron, UK), Julian John Somerset Hope; cr. 1964

GLENDYNE (3rd Baron, UK), Robert Nivison; cr. 1922; 3rd Bt of Branch Hill Lodge (UK) 1914

GLOUCESTER (2nd Duke of, UK), HRH Prince Richard Alexander Walter George; cr. 1928; Earl of Ulster and Baron Culloden; KG 1997; GCVO 1974

GORELL (4th Baron, UK), Timothy John Radcliffe Barnes; cr. 1909

GORMANSTON (17th Viscount, I), Jenico Nicholas Dudley Preston; cr. 1478; 20th Baron Gormanston (I) 1370; 5th Baron Gormanston (UK) 1868

GORT (9th Viscount, I), Foley Robert Standish Prendergast Vereker; cr. 1816; 9th Baron Kiltarton (I) 1810

GOSFORD (7th Earl of, I), Charles David Nicholas Alexander John Sparrow Acheson; cr. 1806; 8th Viscount Gosford (I) 1785; 8th Baron Gosford (I) 1776; 6th Baron Worlingham (UK) 1835; 5th Baron Acheson (UK) 1847; 13th Bt of Market Hill (NS) 1628

GOUGH (5th Viscount, UK), Shane Hugh Maryon Gough; cr. 1849; 5th Baron Gough (UK) 1846; 5th Bt of Synone and Drangan (UK) 1842

GOWRIE (2nd Earl of, UK), Alexander Patrick Greysteil Hore-Ruthven; cr. 1945; Viscount Ruthven of Canberra; 2nd Baron Gowrie (UK) 1935; 3rd Baron Ruthven of Gowrie (UK) 1919; PC 1984

GRAFTON (11th Duke of, E), Hugh Denis Charles FitzRoy; cr. 1675; 11th Earl of Euston, Viscount Ipswich and Baron Sudbury (E) 1672; KG 1976; DL

GRANARD (10th Earl of, I), Peter Arthur Edward Hastings Forbes; cr. 1684; 10th Viscount Granard and Baron Clanehugh (I) 1675; 5th Baron Granard (UK) 1806; 11th Bt of Castle Forbes (S) 1628

GRANTCHESTER (3rd Baron, UK), Christopher John Suenson-Taylor; cr. 1953

GRANTLEY (8th Baron, GB), Richard William Brinsley Norton; cr. 1782

GRANVILLE (6th Earl, UK), Granville George Fergus Leveson-Gower; cr. 1833; 6th Viscount Granville (UK) 1815; Baron Leveson (UK) 1833

GRAVES (9th Baron, I), Evelyn Paget Graves; cr. 1794.

GRAY (22nd Lord, S), Angus Diarmid Ian Campbell-Gray; cr. 1445

GREENHILL (3rd Baron, UK), Malcolm Greenhill; cr. 1950

GREENWOOD (3rd Viscount, UK), Michael George Hamar Greenwood; cr. 1937; 3rd Baron Greenwood (UK) 1929; 3rd Bt of Onslow Gardens (UK) 1915

GRENFELL (3rd Baron, UK), Julian Pascoe Francis St Leger Grenfell; cr. 1902

GRETTON (4th Baron, UK), John Lysander Gretton; cr. 1944

GREY (6th Earl, UK), Richard Fleming George Charles Grey; cr. 1806; Viscount Howick; Baron Grey of Howick (UK) 1801; 7th Bt of Howick (GB) 1746

GREY OF CODNOR (6th Baron, E), Richard Henry Cornwall-Legh; cr. 1397

GRIDLEY (3rd Baron, UK), Richard David Arnold Gridley; cr. 1955

GRIMSTON OF WESTBURY (2nd Baron, UK), Robert Walter Sigismund Grimston; cr. 1964; 2nd Bt of Westbury (UK) 1952

GRIMTHORPE (4th Baron, UK), Christopher John Beckett; cr. 1886; 8th Bt of Leeds (UK) 1813; OBE (Mil) 1958; DL

GUILFORD (10th Earl of, GB), Piers Edward Brownlow North; cr. 1752; 12th Baron Guilford (E) 1683

HACKING (3rd Baron, UK), Douglas David Hacking; cr. 1945; 3rd Bt of Altham (UK) 1938

HADDINGTON (13th Earl of, S), John George Baillie-Hamilton; cr. 1619; 13th Lord Binning (S) 1613; 13th Lord Byres and Binning (S) 1619

HADEN-GUEST (5th Baron, UK), Christopher Haden Haden-Guest; cr. 1950

HAIG (2nd Earl, UK), George Alexander Eugene Douglas Haig; cr. 1919; Viscount Dawick and Baron Haig of Bemersyde; 30th Laird of Bemersyde; OBE 1966; DL

HALIFAX (3rd Earl of, UK), Charles Edward Peter Neil Wood; cr. 1944; 5th Viscount Halifax (UK) 1866; 3rd Baron Irwin (UK) 1925; 7th Bt of Barnsley (GB) 1784

HALSBURY (4th Earl of, UK), Adam Edward Giffard; cr. 1898; Viscount Tiverton; Baron Halsbury (UK) 1885

HAMBLEDEN (4th Viscount, UK), William Herbert Smith; cr. 1891

HAMILTON (15th Duke of, S), cr. 1643, AND BRANDON (12th Duke of, GB), cr. 1711; Angus Alan Douglas Douglas-Hamilton; 12th Marquess of Douglas, Lord Abernethy and Jedburgh Forest (S) 1633; 15th Marquess of Clydesdale, Earl of Arran, Lanark and Cambridge, Lord Aven, Polmont, Machanshire and Innerdale (S) 1643; 22nd Earl of Angus (S) 1389; 12th Baron Dutton (GB) 1711

HAMILTON OF DALZELL (4th Baron, UK), James Leslie Hamilton; cr. 1886; DL

HAMPDEN (6th Viscount, UK), Anthony David Brand; cr. 1884; DL

HAMPTON (6th Baron, UK), Richard Humphrey Russell Pakington; cr. 1874; 6th Bt of Westwood Park (UK) 1846

HANKEY (3rd Baron, UK), Donald Robin Alers Hankey; cr. 1939

HANWORTH (3rd Viscount, UK), David Stephen Geoffrey Pollock; cr. 1936; 3rd Baron Hanworth (UK) 1926; 3rd Bt of Hanworth (UK) 1922

HARBERTON (10th Viscount, I), Thomas de Vautort Pomeroy; cr. 1791; 10th Baron Harberton (I) 1783.

HARDING OF PETHERTON (2nd Baron, UK), John Charles Harding; cr. 1958

HARDINGE (6th Viscount, UK), Charles Henry Nicholas Hardinge; cr. 1846; 8th Bt of Fermanagh (UK) 1801

HARDINGE OF PENSHURST (4th Baron, UK), Julian Alexander Hardinge; cr. 1910

HARDWICKE (10th Earl of, GB), Joseph Philip Sebastian Yorke; cr. 1754; Viscount Royston; 10th Baron Hardwicke (GB) 1733

HAREWOOD (7th Earl of, UK), George Henry Hubert Lascelles; cr. 1812; Viscount Lascelles; 7th Baron Harewood (GB) 1796; KBE 1986

HARLECH (6th Baron, UK), Francis David Ormsby-Gore; cr. 1876

HARMSWORTH (3rd Baron, UK), Thomas Harold Raymond Harmsworth; cr. 1939

HARRINGTON (11th Earl of, GB), William Henry Leicester Stanhope; cr. 1742; Viscount Petersham; 8th Viscount Stanhope of Mahon and Baron Stanhope of Elvaston (GB) 1717; 11th Baron Harrington (GB) 1730

HARRIS (8th Baron, UK), Anthony Harris; cr. 1815

HARROWBY (7th Earl of, UK), Dudley Danvers Granville Coutts Ryder; cr. 1809; Viscount Sandon; 8th Baron Harrowby (GB) 1776; TD 1953

HARVEY OF TASBURGH (2nd Baron, UK), Peter Charles Oliver Harvey; cr. 1954; 5th Bt of Crown Point (UK) 1868

HASTINGS (22nd Baron, E), Edward Delaval Henry Astley; cr. 1290; 12th Bt of Hill Morton (E) 1660

HATHERTON (8th Baron, UK), Edward Charles Littleton; cr. 1835

HAWARDEN (9th Viscount, I), Robert Connan Wyndham Leslie Maude; cr. 1793; 9th Baron de Montalt (I) 1785; 11th Bt of Dundrum (I)1705.

HAWKE (11th Baron, GB), Edward George Hawke; cr. 1776; TD 1993

HAYTER (3rd Baron, UK), George Charles Hayter Chubb; cr. 1927; 3rd Bt of Newlands (UK) 1900; KCVO 1977; CBE 1976

HAZLERIGG (2nd Baron, UK), Arthur Grey Hazlerigg; cr. 1945; 14th Bt of Noseley (E) 1622; MC 1945; TD 1948; DL

HEAD (2nd Viscount, UK), Richard Antony Head; cr. 1960

HEADFORT (6th Marquess of, I), Thomas Geoffrey Charles Michael Taylour; cr. 1800; 7th Earl of Bective (I) 1766; 7th Viscount Headfort (I) 1762; 7th Baron Headfort (I) 1760; 5th Baron Kenlis (UK) 1831; 9th Bt of Kells (I) 1704

HEMINGFORD (3rd Baron, UK), Dennis Nicholas Herbert; cr. 1943

HEMPHILL (5th Baron, UK), Peter Patrick Fitzroy Martyn Martyn-Hemphill; cr. 1906

HENNIKER (8th Baron, I), John Patrick Edward Chandos Henniker-Major; cr. 1800; 5th Baron Hartismere (UK) 1866; 9th Bt of Worlingworth Hall (GB) 1765; KCMG 1965; CVO 1960; MC 1945; DL

HEREFORD (18th Viscount, E), Robert Milo Leicester Devereux; cr. 1550; 15th Bt of Castle Bromwich (E) 1611

HERRIES OF TERREGLES (Lady, 14th in line, S), Anne Elizabeth Fitzalan-Howard; cr. 1490

HERSCHELL (3rd Baron, UK), Rognvald Richard Farrer Herschell; cr. 1886

HERTFORD (9th Marquess of, GB), Henry Jocelyn Seymour; cr. 1793; Earl of Yarmouth; 9th Earl of Hertford and Viscount Beauchamp (GB) 1750; 10th Baron Conway of Ragley (E) 1703; 10th Baron Conway of Killultagh (I) 1712

HESKETH (3rd Baron, UK), Thomas Alexander Fermor-Hesketh; cr. 1935; 10th Bt of Rufford (GB) 1761; PC 1991; KBE 1997

HEYTESBURY (6th Baron, UK), Francis William Holmes à Court; cr. 1828; 7th Bt of Heytesbury House (GB) 1795

HILL (8th Viscount, UK), Antony Rowland Clegg-Hill; cr. 1842; 8th Baron Hill (UK) 1816; 10th Bt of Hawkestone (GB) 1727

HINDLIP (6th Baron, UK), Charles Henry Allsopp; cr. 1886; 6th Bt of Hindlip Hall (UK) 1880

HIVES (3rd Baron, UK), Matthew Peter Hives; cr. 1950

HOLLENDEN (4th Baron, UK), Ian Hampden Hope-Morley; cr. 1912

HOLMPATRICK (4th Baron, UK), Hans James David Hamilton; cr. 1897

HOOD (8th Viscount, GB), Henry Lyttelton Alexander Hood; cr. 1796; 8th Baron Hood (I) 1782; 8th Baron Hood (GB) 1795; 8th Bt of Catherington (GB) 1778

HOTHAM (8th Baron, I), Henry Durand Hotham; cr. 1797; 18th Bt of Scarborough (E) 1622; DL.

HOTHFIELD (6th Baron, UK), Anthony Charles Sackville Tufton; cr. 1881; 7th Bt of Appleby Castle (UK) 1851

HOWARD OF PENRITH (3rd Baron, UK), Philip Esme Howard; cr. 1930

HOWICK OF GLENDALE (2nd Baron, UK), Charles Evelyn Baring; cr. 1960

HUNTINGDON (16th Earl of, E), William Edward Robin Hood Hastings-Bass; cr. 1529; LVO 1999

HUNTINGFIELD (7th Baron, I), Joshua Charles Vanneck; cr. 1796; 9th Bt of Putney (GB) 1751.

HUNTLY (13th Marquess of, S), Granville Charles Gomer Gordon; cr. 1599; 18th Earl of Huntly (S) 1445; Earl of Enzie (S) 1599; 9th Earl of Aboyne and Lord Gordon of Strathavon and Glenlivet (S) 1660; 5th Baron Meldrum (UK) 1815

IDDESLEIGH (4th Earl of, UK), Stafford Henry Northcote; cr. 1885; Viscount St Cyres; 11th Bt of Haine (E) 1641

ILCHESTER (9th Earl of, GB), Maurice Vivian de Touffreville Fox-Strangways; cr. 1756; 9th Lord Ilchester, Baron of Woodford Strangways (GB) 1741; 9th Lord Ilchester and Stavordale, Baron of Redlynch (GB) 1747

ILIFFE (3rd Baron, UK), Robert Peter Richard Iliffe; cr. 1933

INCHCAPE (4th Earl of, UK), Kenneth Peter Lyle Mackay; cr. 1929; Viscount Glenapp; 4th Viscount Inchcape (UK) 1924; 4th Baron Inchcape (UK) 1911

INCHIQUIN (18th Baron of, I), Conor Myles John O'Brien; cr. 1543; 10th Bt of Lemenagh (I) 1686.

INCHYRA (2nd Baron, UK), Robert Charles Reneke Hoyer Millar; cr. 1962

INGLEBY (2nd Viscount, UK), Martin Raymond Peake; cr. 1956

INVERFORTH (4th Baron, UK), Andrew Peter Weir; cr. 1919

IRONSIDE (2nd Baron, UK), Edmund Oslac Ironside; cr. 1941

IVEAGH (4th Earl of, UK), Arthur Edward Rory Guinness; cr. 1919; Viscount Elveden; 4th Viscount Iveagh (UK) 1905; 4th Baron Iveagh (UK) 1891; 4th Bt of Castle Knock (UK) 1885

JEFFREYS (3rd Baron, UK), Christopher Henry Mark Jeffreys; cr. 1952

JERSEY (10th Earl of, E), George Francis William Child Villiers; cr. 1697; 10th Viscount Villiers (E) 1691; 13th Viscount Grandison (I) 1620; 10th Baron Villiers of Hoo (E) 1691

JOICEY (5th Baron, UK), James Michael Joicey; cr. 1906; 5th Bt of Longhirst and Ulgham (UK) 1893

KEMSLEY (3rd Viscount, UK), Richard Gomer Berry; cr. 1945; 3rd Baron Kemsley (UK) 1936; 3rd Bt of Farnham Royal (UK) 1928

KENILWORTH (4th Baron, UK), John Randle Siddeley; cr. 1937

KENNET (2nd Baron, UK), Wayland Hilton Young; cr. 1935

KENSINGTON (8th Baron, I), Hugh Ivor Edwardes; cr. 1776; 5th Baron Kensington (UK) 1886

KENSWOOD (2nd Baron, UK), John Michael Howard Whitfield; cr. 1951

KENT (2nd Duke of, UK), HRH Prince Edward George Nicholas Paul Patrick; cr. 1934; Earl of St Andrews and Baron Downpatrick; KG 1985; GCMG 1967; GCVO 1960; FRS 1990

KENYON (6th Baron, GB), Lloyd Tyrell-Kenyon; cr. 1788; 6th Bt of Gredington (GB) 1784

KERSHAW (4th Baron, UK), Edward John Kershaw; cr. 1947

KEYES (2nd Baron, UK), Roger George Bowlby Keyes; cr. 1943; 2nd Bt of Zeebrugge and Dover (UK) 1919

KILBRACKEN (3rd Baron, UK), John Raymond Godley; cr. 1909; DSC 1945

KILLANIN (4th Baron, UK), (George) Redmond (Fitzpatrick) Morris; cr. 1900; 4th Bt of Spiddal (UK) 1885

KILLEARN (3rd Baron, UK), Victor Miles George Aldous Lampson; cr. 1943; 5th Bt of Rowfant (UK) 1866

KILMAINE (7th Baron, I), John David Henry Browne; cr. 1789; 13th Bt of The Neale (NS) 1636.

KILMOREY (6th Earl of, I), Richard Francis Needham; cr. 1822; Viscount Newry and Morne; 17th Viscount Kilmorey (I) 1625; PC 1994; Kt 1997 *(Does not use title)*.

KILMARNOCK (7th Baron, UK), Alastair Ivor Gilbert Boyd; cr. 1831

KIMBERLEY (4th Earl of, UK), John Wodehouse; cr. 1866; 6th Baron Wodehouse (GB) 1797; 11th Bt of Kimberley (E) 1611

KINDERSLEY (3rd Baron, UK), Robert Hugh Molesworth Kindersley; cr. 1941; DL

KINGSALE (35th Baron), John de Courcy; cr. 1223; Baron Courcy and Baron Ringrone.

KINGSTON (11th Earl of, I), Barclay Robert Edwin King-Tenison; cr. 1768; 11th Viscount Kingsborough (I) 1766; 7th Viscount Lorton (I) 1806; 11th Baron Kingston (I) 1764; 7th Baron Erris (I) 1800; 15th Bt of Boyle Abbey (I) 1682.

KINLOSS (Lady, 12th in line, S), Beatrice Mary Grenville Freeman-Grenville; cr. 1602

KINNOULL (15th Earl of, S), Arthur William George Patrick Hay; cr. 1633; Viscount Dupplin (S) 1627/1633/1697; Lord Hay of Kinfauns (S) 1627/1633; 8th Baron Hay of Pedwardine (GB) 1711

KINROSS (5th Baron, UK), Christopher Patrick Balfour; cr. 1902

KINTORE (13th Earl of, S), Michael Canning William John Keith; cr. 1677; 3rd Viscount Stonehaven (UK) 1938; 13th Lord Keith of Inverurie and Keith Hall (S) 1677; 3rd Baron Stonehaven (UK) 1925; 4th Bt of Urie (UK) 1897

KIRKWOOD (3rd Baron, UK), David Harvie Kirkwood; cr. 1951

KITCHENER OF KHARTOUM AND OF BROOME (3rd Earl, UK), Henry Herbert Kitchener; cr. 1914; Viscount Kitchener of Khartoum (UK) 1902; Viscount Broome and Baron Denton (UK) 1914; TD; DL

KNOLLYS (3rd Viscount, UK), David Francis Dudley Knollys; cr. 1911; Baron Knollys (UK) 1902

KNUTSFORD (6th Viscount, UK), Michael Holland-Hibbert; cr. 1895; 6th Baron Knutsford (UK) 1888; 7th Bt of Sandlebridge (UK) 1853; DL

LANGFORD (9th Baron, I), Geoffrey Alexander Rowley-Conwy; cr. 1800; OBE (Mil) 1943; DL.
LANSDOWNE (9th Marquess of, GB), Charles Maurice Petty-Fitzmaurice; cr. 1784; Earl of
    Wycombe and Viscount Calne and Calstone; 10th Earl of Kerry and Viscount ClanMaurice (I)
    1722; 10th Earl of Shelburne (I) 1753; 10th Viscount FitzMaurice and Baron Dunkeron (I) 1751;
    30th Baron of Kerry and Lixnaw (I) before 1253; 10th Baron Wycombe (GB) 1760; DL
LATHAM (2nd Baron, UK), Dominic Charles Latham; cr. 1942
LATYMER (8th Baron, E), Hugo Nevill Money-Coutts; cr. 1431
LAUDERDALE (17th Earl of, S), Patrick Francis Maitland; cr. 1624; 17th Viscount Lauderdale (S)
    1616; 17th Viscount Maitland (S) 1624; 18th Lord Maitland (S) 1590; 17th Lord Thirlestane and
    Boltoun (S) 1624; 13th Bt of Ravelrig (NS) 1680; Hereditary Bearer of National Flag of Scotland
    by Decrees of Lord Lyon King of Arms 1790 and 1952
LAWRENCE (5th Baron, UK), David John Downer Lawrence; cr. 1869; 5th Bt (UK) 1858
LAYTON (3rd Baron, UK), Geoffrey Michael Layton; cr. 1947
LEATHERS (3rd Viscount, UK), Christopher Graeme Leathers; cr. 1954; 3rd Baron Leathers (UK)
    1941
LECONFIELD, Barony of – see EGREMONT (2nd Baron)
LEICESTER (7th Earl of, UK), Edward Douglas Coke; cr. 1837; Viscount Coke
LEIGH (5th Baron, UK), John Piers Leigh; cr. 1839
LEIGHTON OF ST MELLONS (3rd Baron, UK), Robert William Henry Leighton Seager; cr. 1962;
    2nd Bt of St Mellons (UK) 1952
LEINSTER (8th Duke of, I), Gerald FitzGerald; cr. 1766; 8th Marquess of Kildare (I), 1761; 27th Earl
    of Kildare (I) 1316; 8th Earl of Offaly (I) 1761; 8th Viscount Leinster (GB) 1747; 32nd Baron
    of Offaly (I) 1193; 5th Baron Kildare (UK) 1870
LEVEN (14th Earl of, S), cr. 1641, AND MELVILLE (13th Earl of, S), cr. 1690; Alexander Robert
    Leslie Melville; 13th Viscount Kirkaldie (S) 1690; 16th Lord Melville of Monymaill (S) 1616;
    14th Lord Balgonie (S) 1641; 13th Lord Raith, Monymaill and Balwearie (S) 1690
LEVERHULME (3rd Viscount, UK), Philip William Bryce Lever; cr. 1922; 3rd Baron Leverhulme
    (UK) 1917; 3rd Bt of Thornton Manor (UK) 1911; KG 1988; TD
LICHFIELD (5th Earl of, UK), Thomas Patrick John Anson; cr. 1831; 6th Viscount Anson and Baron
    Soberton (UK) 1806; DL
LIFFORD (9th Viscount, I), Edward James Wingfield Hewitt; cr. 1781; 9th Baron Lifford (I) 1768.
LILFORD (7th Baron, GB), Vernon George Powys; cr. 1797
LIMERICK (6th Earl of, I), Patrick Edmund Pery; cr. 1803; 6th Viscount Limerick (I) 1800; 7th
    Baron Glentworth (I) 1790; 6th Baron Foxford (UK) 1815; KBE 1983; DL
LINCOLN (18th Earl of, E), Edward Horace Fiennes-Clinton; cr. 1572
LINDSAY OF BIRKER (3rd Baron, UK), James Francis Lindsay; cr. 1945
LINDSEY (14th Earl of, E), AND ABINGDON (9th Earl of, E), Richard Henry Rupert Bertie; cr.
    1626 and 1682; 13th Baron Norreys (E) 1572
LINLITHGOW (4th Marquess of, UK), Adrian John Charles Hope; cr. 1902; 10th Earl of Hopetoun,
    Viscount Aithrie and Lord Hope (S) 1703; 8th Baron Hopetoun (UK) 1809; 7th Baron Niddry
    (UK) 1814; 12th Bt of Kirkliston (NS) 1698
LISBURNE (8th Earl of, I), John David Malet Vaughan; cr. 1776; 11th Viscount Lisburne and Lord
    Vaughan, Baron of Fethard (I) 1695; DL.
LISLE (8th Baron, I), Patrick James Lysaght; cr. 1758.
LLOYD GEORGE OF DWYFOR (3rd Earl, UK), Owen Lloyd George; cr. 1945; Viscount Gwynedd;
    DL
LONDESBOROUGH (9th Baron, UK), Richard John Denison; cr. 1850
LONDONDERRY (9th Marquess of, I), Alexander Charles Robert Vane-Tempest-Stewart; cr. 1816;
    Earl of Londonderry (I) 1796; Earl Vane and Viscount Seaham (UK) 1823; Viscount Castlereagh
    (I) 1795; Baron Londonderry (I) 1789; Baron Stewart (UK) 1814
LONG (4th Viscount, UK), Richard Gerard Long; cr. 1921; CBE 1993
LONSDALE (7th Earl of, UK), James Hugh William Lowther; cr. 1807; 8th Viscount and Baron
    Lowther (GB) 1797; 8th Bt of Swillington (GB) 1764
LOTHIAN (12th Marquess of, S), Peter Francis Walter Kerr; cr. 1701; 13th Earl of Lothian (S) 1606;
    Earl of Ancram (S) 1633; Viscount of Briene (S) 1701; Lord Newbottle (S) 1591; Lord Jedburgh
    (S) 1622; Lord Kerr (S) 1633; Lord Ker (S) 1701; 7th Baron Ker (UK) 1821; KCVO 1983; DL

LOUDOUN (Countess of, 13th in line, S), Barbara Huddleston Abney-Hastings; cr. 1633; Lady Campbell of Loudoun (S), 1601; Lady Tarrinzean and Mauchline (S) 1633

LOUTH (16th Baron, I), Otway Michael James Oliver Plunkett; cr. 1541.

LOVAT (de facto 16th Lord (S), 18th but for the attainder), Simon Fraser; cr. between 1458 and 1464; 5th Baron Lovat (UK) 1837

LOVELACE (5th Earl of, UK), Peter Axel William Locke King; cr. 1838; Viscount Ockham; 12th Baron King of Ockham (GB) 1725

LUCAN (7th Earl of, I), Richard John Bingham; cr. 1795; Baron Lucan (I) 1776; 3rd Baron Bingham (UK) 1934; 13th Bt of Castlebar (NS) 1634

LUCAS OF CHILWORTH (2nd Baron, UK), Michael William George Lucas; cr. 1946

LYTTON (5th Earl of, UK), John Peter Michael Scawen Lytton; cr. 1880; Viscount Knebworth; 18th Baron Wentworth (E) 1529; 6th Baron Lytton (UK) 1866; 6th Bt of Knebworth (UK) 1838

LYVEDEN (6th Baron, UK), Ronald Cecil Vernon; cr. 1859

MacANDREW (3rd Baron, UK), Christopher Anthony Colin MacAndrew; cr. 1959

MACCLESFIELD (9th Earl of, GB), Richard Timothy George Mansfield Parker; cr. 1721; Viscount Parker; 9th Baron Parker (GB) 1716

MACDONALD (8th Baron, I), Godfrey James Macdonald of Macdonald; cr. 1776; DL.

MACDONALD OF GWAENYSGOR (2nd Baron, UK), Gordon Ramsay Macdonald; cr. 1949

McGOWAN (3rd Baron, UK), Harry Duncan Cory McGowan; cr. 1937

MACKINTOSH OF HALIFAX (3rd Viscount, UK), John Clive Mackintosh; cr. 1957; 3rd Baron Mackintosh of Halifax (UK) 1948; 3rd Bt of Halifax (UK) 1935

MACLAY (3rd Baron, UK), Joseph Paton Maclay; cr. 1922; 3rd Bt of Park Terrace (UK) 1914; DL

McNAIR (3rd Baron, UK), Duncan James McNair; cr. 1955

MACPHERSON OF DRUMOCHTER (2nd Baron, UK), James Gordon Macpherson; cr. 1951

MALMESBURY (6th Earl of, GB), William James Harris; cr. 1800; Viscount FitzHarris; Baron Malmesbury (GB) 1788; TD (2 clasps) 1944; DL

MALVERN (3rd Viscount, UK), Ashley Kevin Godfrey Huggins; cr. 1955

MANCHESTER (12th Duke of, GB), Angus Charles Drogo Montagu; cr. 1719; 15th Earl of Manchester (E) 1626; Viscount Mandeville and Baron Montagu (E) 1620

MANNERS (5th Baron, UK), John Robert Cecil Manners; cr. 1807; DL

MANSFIELD AND MANSFIELD (8th Earl of, GB), William David Mungo James Murray; cr. 1776 and 1792; 13th Viscount Stormont (S) 1621; 13th Lord Scone (S) 1605; 11th Lord Balvaird (S) 1641; DL

MANTON (3rd Baron, UK), Joseph Rupert Eric Robert Watson; cr. 1922; DL

MAR (14th Earl of, S); cr. 1565, AND KELLIE (16th Earl of, S); cr. 1619, James Thorne Erskine; 16th Viscount Fentoun (S) 1606; 19th Lord Erskine (S) 1429; 16th Lord Erskine of Dirleton (S) 1604; 16th Lord Dirleton (S) 1606; DL

MARCHAMLEY (4th Baron, UK), William Francis Whiteley; cr. 1908

MARCHWOOD (3rd Viscount, UK), David George Staveley Penny; cr. 1945; 3rd Baron Marchwood (UK) 1937; 3rd Bt of Singapore and Kingston-upon-Thames (UK) 1933

MARGADALE (2nd Baron, UK), James Ian Morrison; cr. 1964; TD 1963; DL

MARGESSON (2nd Viscount, UK), Francis Vere Hampden Margesson; cr. 1942

MARKS OF BROUGHTON (3rd Baron, UK), Simon Richard Marks; cr. 1961

MARLBOROUGH (11th Duke of, E), John George Vanderbilt Henry Spencer-Churchill; cr. 1702; Marquess of Blandford; 13th Earl of Sunderland (E) 1643; Earl of Marlborough (E) 1689; 15th Baron Spencer (E) 1603; Baron Churchill (E) 1685; Prince of the Holy Roman Empire (1704); Prince of Mindelheim in Suabia (1705); DL

MARTONMERE (2nd Baron, UK), John Stephen Robinson; cr. 1964

MASSEREENE (14th Viscount, I), cr. 1660, AND FERRARD (7th Viscount, I), cr. 1797; John David Clotworthy Whyte-Melville Foster Skeffington; Baron of Loughneagh (I) 1660; 7th Baron Oriel (I) 1790; 7th Baron Oriel (UK) 1821

MASSY (9th Baron, I), Hugh Hamon John Somerset Massy; cr. 1776.

MAY (3rd Baron, UK), Michael St. John May; cr. 1935; 3rd Bt of the Eyot (UK) 1931

MAYO (10th Earl of, I), Terence Patrick Bourke; cr. 1785; 10th Viscount Mayo (I) 1781; 10th Baron Naas (I) 1776.

MEATH (15th Earl of, I), John Anthony Brabazon; cr. 1627; 16th Baron Ardee (I) 1616; 6th Baron Chaworth (UK) 1831

MELCHETT (4th Baron, UK), Peter Robert Henry Mond; cr. 1928; 4th Bt of Hartford Hill (UK) 1910

MELVILLE (9th Viscount, UK), Robert David Ross Dundas; cr. 1802; Baron Duneira

MERRIVALE (3rd Baron, UK), Jack Henry Edmond Duke; cr. 1925

MERSEY (4th Viscount, UK), Richard Maurice Clive Bigham; cr. 1916; 13th Lord Nairne (S) 1681; 4th Baron Mersey (UK) 1910

MESTON (3rd Baron, UK), James Meston; cr. 1919; QC 1996

MEXBOROUGH (8th Earl of, I), John Christopher George Savile; cr. 1766; Viscount Pollington; 8th Baron Pollington (I) 1753.

MIDDLETON (12th Baron, GB), Digby Michael Godfrey John Willoughby; cr. 1711; 13th Bt of Wollaton (E) 1677; MC 1945; DL

MIDLETON (12th Viscount, I), Alan Henry Brodrick; cr. 1717; Baron Brodrick (I) 1715; Baron Brodrick (GB) 1796

MILFORD (4th Baron, UK), Guy Wogan Philipps; cr. 1939; 4th Bt of Llanstephan (UK) 1919

MILFORD HAVEN (4th Marquess of, UK), George Ivar Louis Mountbatten; cr. 1917; Earl of Medina and Viscount Alderney

MILLS (3rd Viscount, UK), Christopher Philip Roger Mills; cr. 1962; 3rd Baron Mills (UK) 1957; 3rd Bt of Alcester (UK) 1953

MILNE (2nd Baron, UK), George Douglass Milne; cr. 1933; TD

MILVERTON (2nd Baron, UK), Fraser Arthur Richard Richards; cr. 1947

MINTO (6th Earl of, UK), Gilbert Edward George Lariston Elliot-Murray-Kynynmound; cr. 1813; Viscount Melgund; 6th Baron Minto (GB) 1797; 9th Bt of Headshaw (NS) 1700; OBE 1986

MOLESWORTH (12th Viscount, I), Robert Bysse Kelham Molesworth; cr. 1716; Baron Philipstown.

MONCK (7th Viscount, I), Charles Stanley Monck; cr. 1801; 7th Baron Monck (I) 1797; 4th Baron Monck (UK) 1866

MONCKTON OF BRENCHLEY (2nd Viscount, UK), Gilbert Walter Riversdale Monckton; cr. 1957; CB (Mil) 1966; OBE (Mil) 1956; MC 1940; DL

MONCREIFF (5th Baron, UK), Harry Robert Wellwood Moncreiff; cr. 1874; 15th Bt of Moncreiff (NS) 1626; 5th Bt of Tulliebole (UK) 1871

MONK BRETTON (3rd Baron, UK), John Charles Dodson; cr. 1884; DL

MONKSWELL (5th Baron, UK), Gerard Collier; cr. 1885

MONTEAGLE OF BRANDON (6th Baron, UK), Gerald Spring Rice; cr. 1839

MONTGOMERY OF ALAMEIN (2nd Viscount, UK), David Bernard Montgomery; cr. 1946; CBE 1975

MORAY (20th Earl of, S), Douglas John Moray Stuart; cr. 1562; Lord Abernethy and Strathearn; Lord Doune (S) 1581; Lord St Colme (S) 1611; Baron Stuart of Castle Stuart (GB) 1796

MORLEY (6th Earl of, UK), John St Aubyn Parker; cr. 1815; Viscount Boringdon; 7th Baron Boringdon (GB) 1784; KCVO 1998

MORRIS (3rd Baron, UK), Michael David Morris; cr. 1918

MORRIS OF KENWOOD (2nd Baron, UK), Philip Geoffrey Morris; cr. 1950

MORTON (21st Earl of, S), John Charles Sholto Douglas; cr. 1458; Lord Aberdour

MOSTYN (5th Baron, UK), Roger Edward Lloyd Lloyd-Mostyn; cr. 1831; 6th Bt of Pengwern (GB) 1778; MC 1943

MOTTISTONE (4th Baron, UK), David Peter Seely; cr. 1933; CBE 1984

MOUNTBATTEN OF BURMA (Countess, 2nd in line, UK), Patricia Edwina Victoria Knatchbull; cr. 1947; Baroness Romsey; 2nd Viscountess Mountbatten of Burma (UK) 1946; CBE 1991; CD 1976; DL

MOUNT EDGCUMBE (8th Earl of, GB), Robert Charles Edgcumbe; cr. 1789; Viscount Mount Edgcumbe and Valletort (GB) 1781; Baron Edgcumbe (GB) 1742

MOUNTEVANS (3rd Baron, UK), Edward Patrick Broke Andvord Evans; cr. 1945

MOUNTGARRET (17th Viscount, I), Richard Henry Piers Butler; cr. 1550; Baron of Kells; 4th Baron Mountgarret (UK) 1911

MOYNE (3rd Baron, UK), Jonathan Bryan Guinness; cr. 1932

MUNSTER (7th Earl of, UK), Anthony Charles Fitz-Clarence; cr. 1831; Viscount Fitz-Clarence and Baron Tewkesbury

MUSKERRY (9th Baron, I), Robert Fitzmaurice Deane; cr. 1781; 14th Bt of Dromore (I) 1710.

NAPIER (14th Lord, S), cr. 1627, AND ETTRICK (5th Baron, UK), cr. 1872; Francis Nigel Napier, 11th Bt of Thirlestane (NS) 1666; KCVO 1992; DL

NAPIER OF MAGDALA (6th Baron, UK), Robert Alan Napier; cr. 1868

NATHAN (2nd Baron, UK), Roger Carol Michael Nathan; cr. 1940

NELSON (9th Earl, UK), Peter John Horatio Nelson; cr. 1805; Viscount Merton; Baron Nelson (UK) 1801

NELSON OF STAFFORD (3rd Baron, UK), Henry Roy George Nelson; cr. 1960; 3rd Bt of Hilcote Hall (UK) 1955

NETHERTHORPE (3rd Baron, UK), James Frederick Turner; cr. 1959

NEWALL (2nd Baron, UK), Francis Storer Eaton Newall; cr. 1946; DL

NEWBOROUGH (8th Baron, I), Robert Vaughan Wynn; cr. 1776; 10th Bt of Bodvean (GB) 1742.

NEWBURGH (12th Earl of, S), Prince Don Filippo Giambattista Francesco Aldo Maria Rospigliosi; cr. 1660; Viscount Kynnaird and Lord Levingston; 11th Prince Rospigliosi (Holy Roman Empire 1668)

NEWTON (5th Baron, UK), Richard Thomas Legh; cr. 1892

NOEL-BUXTON (3rd Baron, UK), Martin Connal Noel-Buxton; cr. 1930

NORBURY (6th Earl of, I), Noel Terence Graham-Toler; cr. 1827; Viscount Glandine; 7th Baron Norwood (I) 1797; 7th Baron Norbury (I) 1800.

NORMANBY (5th Marquess of, UK), Constantine Edmund Walter Phipps; cr. 1838; 6th Earl of Mulgrave and Viscount Normanby (UK) 1812; 8th Baron Mulgrave (I) 1767; 6th Baron Mulgrave (GB) 1794

NORMANTON (6th Earl of, I), Shaun James Christian Welbore Ellis Agar; cr. 1806; Viscount Somerton (I) 1800; 9th Baron Mendip (GB) 1794; Baron Somerton (I) 1795; 4th Baron Somerton (UK) 1873

NORRIE (2nd Baron, UK), George Willoughby Moke Norrie; cr. 1957

NORTHAMPTON (7th Marquess of, UK), Spencer Douglas David Compton; cr. 1812; 15th Earl of Northampton (E) 1618; Earl Compton and Baron Wilmington (UK) 1812; DL

NORTHUMBERLAND (12th Duke of, GB), Ralph George Algernon Percy; cr. 1766; Earl Percy; 13th Earl of Northumberland and Baron Warkworth (GB) 1749; 9th Earl of Beverley (GB) 1790; 13th Baron Percy (GB) 1722; 10th Baron Lovaine (GB) 1784; 15th Bt of Stanwick (E) 1660; DL

NORTON (8th Baron, UK), James Nigel Arden Adderley; cr. 1878

NORWICH (2nd Viscount, UK), John Julius Cooper; cr. 1952; CVO 1993

NUNBURNHOLME (5th Baron, UK), Charles Thomas Wilson; cr. 1906

OAKSEY, Barony of – see TREVETHIN (4th Baron)

OGMORE (2nd Baron, UK), Gwilym Rees Rees-Williams; cr. 1950

O'HAGAN (4th Baron, UK), Charles Towneley Strachey; cr. 1870

O'NEILL (4th Baron, UK), Raymond Arthur Clanaboy O'Neill; cr. 1868; TD 1970

ORANMORE AND BROWNE (4th Baron, I), Dominick Geoffrey Edward Browne; cr. 1836; 2nd Baron Mereworth (UK) 1926

ORKNEY (9th Earl of, S), Oliver Peter St John; cr. 1696; Viscount Kirkwall and Lord Dechmont

OXFORD AND ASQUITH (2nd Earl of, UK), Julian Edward George Asquith; cr. 1925; Viscount Asquith; KCMG 1964

PARMOOR (4th Baron, UK), (Frederick Alfred) Milo Cripps; cr. 1914

PEMBROKE (17th Earl of, E), cr. 1551; AND MONTGOMERY (14th Earl of, E), cr. 1605; Henry George Charles Alexander Herbert; Baron Herbert of Cardiff (E) 1551; Baron Herbert of Shurland (E) 1605; Baron Herbert of Lea (UK) 1861

PENDER (3rd Baron, UK), John Willoughby Denison-Pender; cr. 1937

PENRHYN (6th Baron, UK), Malcolm Frank Douglas-Pennant; cr. 1866; DSO 1945; MBE (Mil) 1943

PERTH (17th Earl of, S), John David Drummond; cr. 1605; 13th Viscount Strathallan (S) 1686; 20th Lord Drummond of Cargill (S) 1487; 17th Lord Maderty (S) 1609; Lord Drummond of Cromlix (S) 1686; PC 1957

PETRE (18th Baron, E), John Patrick Lionel Petre; cr. 1603; DL

PHILLIMORE (5th Baron, UK), Francis Stephen Phillimore; cr. 1918; 6th Bt of The Coppice (UK) 1881

PIERCY (3rd Baron, UK), James William Piercy; cr. 1945
PLUNKET (8th Baron, UK), Robin Rathmore Plunket; cr. 1827
PLYMOUTH (3rd Earl of, UK), Other Robert Ivor Windsor-Clive; cr. 1905; Viscount Windsor; 16th
    Baron Windsor (E) 1529; DL
POLTIMORE (7th Baron, UK), Mark Coplestone Bampfylde; cr. 1831; 12th Bt of Poltimore (E) 1641
POLWARTH (10th Lord, S), Henry Alexander Hepburne-Scott; cr. 1690; TD 1945; DL
PONSONBY OF SHULBREDE (4th Baron, UK), Frederick Matthew Thomas Ponsonby; cr. 1930
POOLE (2nd Baron, UK), David Charles Poole; cr. 1958
PORTARLINGTON (7th Earl of, I), George Lionel Yuill Seymour Dawson-Damer; cr. 1785; 8th
    Viscount Carlow (I) 1776; 8th Baron Dawson (I) 1770.
PORTLAND (12th Earl of, E), Timothy Charles Robert Bentinck; cr. 1689; Viscount Woodstock and
    Baron Cirencester; Count of the Holy Roman Empire, 1732
PORTMAN (10th Viscount, UK), Christopher Edward Berkeley Portman; cr. 1873; 10th Baron
    Portman (UK) 1837
PORTSMOUTH (10th Earl of, GB), Quentin Gerard Carew Wallop; cr. 1743; 10th Viscount
    Lymington (GB) 1720; 10th Baron Wallop (GB) 1720
POWERSCOURT (10th Viscount, I), Mervyn Niall Wingfield; cr. 1743; Baron Wingfield; 4th Baron
    Powerscourt (UK) 1885
POWIS (8th Earl of, UK), John George Herbert; cr. 1804; Viscount Clive; 9th Baron Clive (I) 1762;
    8th Baron Clive (GB) 1794; Baron Herbert of Chirbury (UK) 1804; Baron Powis (UK) 1804
QUEENSBERRY (12th Marquess of, S), David Harrington Angus Douglas; cr. 1682; Earl of
    Queensberry 1633; Viscount Drumlanrig and Lord Douglas of Hawick and Tibbers 1628; 11th
    Bt of Kelhead 1668 (all S)
RADNOR (8th Earl of, GB), Jacob Pleydell-Bouverie; cr. 1765; 9th Viscount Folkestone and Baron
    Longford (GB) 1747; 8th Baron Pleydell-Bouverie (GB) 1765; 11th Bt of St Catherine Cree
    (GB) 1714
RAGLAN (5th Baron, UK), FitzRoy John Somerset; cr. 1852; DL
RANFURLY (7th Earl of, I), Gerald Francoys Needham Knox; cr. 1831; Viscount Northland (I) 1791;
    Baron Welles (I) 1781; Baron Ranfurly (UK) 1826
RANKEILLOUR (4th Baron, UK), Peter St Thomas More Henry Hope; cr. 1932
RATHCAVAN (3rd Baron, UK), Hugh Detmar Torrens O'Neill; cr. 1953; 3rd Bt of Cleggan (UK)
    1929; DL
RATHCREEDAN (3rd Baron, UK), Christopher John Norton; cr. 1916
RATHDONNELL (5th Baron, I), Thomas Benjamin McClintock-Bunbury; cr. 1868.
RAVENSDALE (3rd Baron, UK), Nicholas Mosley; cr. 1911; 7th Bt of Ancoats (GB) 1781; MC 1944
RAVENSWORTH (8th Baron, UK), Arthur Waller Liddell; cr. 1821; 13th Bt of Ravensworth Castle
    (E) 1642
RAYLEIGH (6th Baron, UK), John Gerald Strutt; cr. 1821
READING (4th Marquess of, UK), Simon Charles Henry Rufus Isaacs; cr. 1926; Earl of Reading
    (UK) 1917; Viscount Reading (UK) 1916; Viscount Erleigh (UK) 1917; Baron Reading (UK)
    1914
REDESDALE (6th Baron, UK), Rupert Bertram Mitford; cr. 1902
REMNANT (3rd Baron, UK), James Wogan Remnant; cr. 1928; 3rd Bt of Wenhaston (UK) 1917;
    CVO 1979
RENDLESHAM (8th Baron, I), Charles Anthony Hugh Thellusson; cr. 1806.
RENNELL (3rd Baron, UK), John Adrian Tremayne Rodd; cr. 1933
RENWICK (2nd Baron, UK), Harry Andrew Renwick; cr. 1964; 3rd Bt of Coombe (UK) 1927
REVELSTOKE (5th Baron, UK), John Baring; cr. 1885
RICHMOND (10th Duke of, E), cr. 1675; LENNOX (10th Duke of, S), cr 1675 AND GORDON (5th
    Duke of, UK), cr. 1876, Charles Henry Gordon-Lennox; 10th Earl of March (E) 1675; 10th Earl
    of Darnley (S) 1675; 5th Earl of Kinrara (UK) 1876; 10th Baron Settrington (E) 1675; 10th Lord
    Torbolton (S) 1675; 10th Duc d'Aubigny (France) 1684
RIDLEY (4th Viscount, UK), Matthew White Ridley; cr. 1900; Baron Wensleydale; 8th Bt of
    Blagdon (GB) 1756; KG 1992; GCVO 1994; TD 1960
RITCHIE OF DUNDEE (5th Baron, UK), Harold Malcolm Ritchie; cr. 1905
RIVERDALE (3rd Baron, UK), Anthony Robert Balfour; cr. 1935; 3rd Bt of Sheffield (UK) 1929

ROBERTSON OF OAKRIDGE (2nd Baron, UK), William Ronald Robertson; cr. 1961; 3rd Bt of Welbourn (UK) 1919

ROBOROUGH (3rd Baron, UK), Henry Massey Lopes; cr. 1938; 6th Bt of Maristow House (UK) 1805

ROCHDALE (2nd Viscount, UK), St. John Durival Kemp; cr. 1960; 3rd Baron Rochdale (UK) 1913

ROCHESTER (2nd Baron, UK), Foster Charles Lowry Lamb; cr. 1931; DL

ROCKLEY (3rd Baron, UK), James Hugh Cecil; cr. 1934

RODEN (10th Earl of, I), Robert John Jocelyn; cr. 1771; 11th Viscount Jocelyn (I) 1755; 11th Baron Newport (I) 1743; 14th Bt of Hyde Hall (E) 1665.

RODNEY (10th Baron, GB), George Brydges Rodney; cr. 1782; 10th Bt of Alresford (GB) 1764

ROLLO (14th Lord, S), David Eric Howard Rollo; cr. 1651; 5th Baron Dunning (UK) 1869

ROMNEY (7th Earl of, UK), Michael Henry Marsham; cr. 1801; Viscount Marsham; 9th Baron Romney (GB) 1716; 13th Bt of Cuckston (E) 1663

ROOTES (3rd Baron, UK), Nicholas Geoffrey Rootes; cr. 1959

ROSEBERY (7th Earl of, S), Neil Archibald Primrose; cr. 1703; 3rd Earl of Midlothian (UK) 1911; 7th Viscount of Rosebery (S) 1700; Viscount Inverkeithing (S) 1703; Viscount Mentmore (UK) 1911; Lord Primrose and Dalmeny (S) 1700; Lord Dalmeny and Primrose (S) 1703; 4th Baron Rosebery (UK) 1828; Baron Epsom (UK) 1911; 11th Bt of Carrington (NS) 1651; DL

ROSSE (7th Earl of, I), William Brendan Parsons; cr. 1806; 7th Baron Oxmantown (I) 1792; 10th Bt of Birr Castle (I) 1677.

ROSSMORE (7th Baron, I), William Warner Westenra; cr. 1796; 6th Baron Rossmore (UK) 1838

ROTHERMERE (4th Viscount, UK), (Harold) Jonathan Esmond Vere Harmsworth; cr. 1919; 4th Baron Rothermere (UK) 1914; 4th Bt of Horsey (UK) 1910

ROTHES (21st Earl of, S), Ian Lionel Malcolm Leslie; cr. 1457; Lord Leslie and Ballinbreich (S) 1445

ROTHSCHILD (4th Baron, UK), (Nathaniel Charles) Jacob Rothschild; cr. 1885; 5th Bt of Grosvenor Place (UK) 1847; Baron of the Austrian Empire, 1822; GBE 1998

ROWALLAN (4th Baron, UK), John Polson Cameron Corbett; cr. 1911

ROXBURGHE (10th Duke of, S), Guy David Innes-Ker; cr. 1707; Marquis of Bowmont and Cessford; Earl of Roxburghe (S) 1616; Earl of Kelso (S) 1707; Earl Innes (UK) 1837; Viscount Broxmouth (S) 1707; Lord Roxburghe (S) 1600; Lord Ker of Cessford and Cavertoun (S) 1616; 11th Bt of Innes (NS) 1625

RUGBY (3rd Baron, UK), Robert Charles Maffey; cr. 1947

RUNCIMAN OF DOXFORD (3rd Viscount, UK), Walter Garrison Runciman; cr. 1937; 4th Baron Runciman (UK) 1933; 4th Bt of Jesmond (UK) 1906; CBE 1987; FBA 1974

RUSSELL OF LIVERPOOL (3rd Baron, UK), Simon Gordon Jared Russell; cr. 1919

RUTLAND (11th Duke of, E), David Charles Robert Manners; cr. 1703; Marquess of Granby; 19th Earl of Rutland (E) 1525; 11th Baron Manners of Haddon (E) 1679; 5th Baron Roos of Belvoir (UK) 1896

SACKVILLE (6th Baron, UK), Lionel Bertrand Sackville-West; cr. 1876

ST ALBANS (14th Duke of, E), Murray de Vere Beauclerk; cr. 1684; 14th Earl of Burford and Baron Heddington (E) 1676; 11th Baron Vere of Hanworth (GB) 1750

ST ALDWYN (3rd Earl, UK), Michael Henry Hicks Beach; cr. 1915; Viscount Quenington; 3rd Viscount St Aldwyn (UK) 1906; 11th Bt of Beverston Castle (E) 1619

ST DAVIDS (3rd Viscount, UK), Colwyn Jestyn John Philipps; cr. 1918; 16th Baron Strange of Knokin (E) 1299; 25th Baron Hungerford (E) 1425; 23rd Baron de Moleyns (E) 1444; 3rd Baron St Davids (UK) 1908; 15th Bt of Picton (E) 1621

ST GERMANS (10th Earl of, UK), Peregrine Nicholas Eliot; cr. 1815; 11th Baron Eliot (GB) 1784

ST HELENS (2nd Baron, UK), Richard Francis Hughes-Young; cr. 1964

ST LEVAN (4th Baron, UK), John Francis Arthur St Aubyn; cr. 1887; 5th Bt of St Michael's Mount (UK) 1866; DSC 1942

ST OSWALD (6th Baron, UK), Charles Rowland Andrew Winn; cr. 1885

ST VINCENT (7th Viscount, UK), Ronald George James Jervis; cr. 1801

SALISBURY (6th Marquess of, GB), Robert Edward Peter Gascoyne-Cecil; cr. 1789; Earl of Salisbury (E) 1605; Viscount Cranborne (E) 1604; Baron Cecil (E) 1603. DL

SAMUEL (3rd Viscount, UK), David Herbert Samuel; cr. 1937; OBE 1996

SANDFORD (2nd Baron, UK), John Cyril Edmondson; cr. 1945; DSC 1942

SANDHURST (5th Baron, UK), John Edward Terence Mansfield; cr. 1871; DFC 1944

SANDYS (7th Baron, UK), Richard Michael Oliver Hill; cr. 1802; DL

SAVILE (3rd Baron, UK), George Halifax Lumley-Savile; cr. 1888; DL

SAYE AND SELE (21st Baron, E), Nathaniel Thomas Allen Fiennes; cr. 1447 and 1603; DL

SCARBROUGH (12th Earl of, E), Richard Aldred Lumley; cr. 1690; 12th Viscount Lumley (E) 1689; 13th Viscount Lumley (I) 1628; 12th Baron Lumley (E) 1681

SCARSDALE (3rd Viscount, UK), Francis John Nathaniel Curzon; cr. 1911; 7th Baron Scarsdale (GB) 1761; 11th Bt of Kedleston (S) 1636; 11th Bt of Kedleston (E) 1641

SEAFIELD (13th Earl of, S), Ian Derek Francis Ogilvie-Grant; cr. 1701; Viscount Seafield (S) 1698; Viscount Reidhaven (S) 1701; Lord Ogilvy of Cullen (S) 1698; Lord Ogilvy of Deskford and Cullen (S) 1701

SEAFORD (6th Baron, UK), Colin Humphrey Felton Ellis; cr. 1826

SELBY (5th Viscount, UK), Edward Thomas William Gully; cr. 1905

SEMPILL (21st Lord, S), James William Stuart Whitemore Sempill; cr. 1489

SHAFTESBURY (10th Earl of, E), Anthony Ashley-Cooper; cr. 1672; Baron Cooper; Baron Ashley (E) 1661; 11th Bt of Rockbourne (E) 1622

SHANNON (9th Earl of, I), Richard Bentinck Boyle; cr. 1756; Viscount Boyle and Baron Castle Martyr; 8th Baron Carleton (GB) 1786

SHAUGHNESSY (3rd Baron, UK), William Graham Shaughnessy; cr. 1916; CD 1955

SHEFFIELD, Barony of – see STANLEY OF ALDERLEY (8th Baron)

SHERFIELD (2nd Baron, UK), Christopher James Makins; cr. 1964

SHUTTLEWORTH (5th Baron, UK), Charles Geoffrey Nicholas Kay-Shuttleworth; cr. 1902; 6th Bt of Gawthorpe Hall (UK) 1850

SIDMOUTH (7th Viscount, UK), John Tonge Anthony Pellew Addington; cr. 1805

SILSOE (2nd Baron, UK), David Malcolm Trustram Eve; cr. 1963; 2nd Bt of Silsoe (UK) 1943; QC 1972

SIMON OF WYTHENSHAWE (2nd Baron, UK), Roger Simon; cr. 1947

SINCLAIR (17th Lord, S), Charles Murray Kennedy St Clair; cr. 1449; CVO 1990

SINCLAIR OF CLEEVE (3rd Baron, UK), John Lawrence Robert Sinclair; cr. 1957

SINHA (6th Baron, UK), Arup Kumar Sinha; cr. 1919

SLIGO (11th Marquess of, I), Jeremy Ulick Browne; cr. 1800; 13th Earl of Altamont (I) 1771; 9th Earl of Clanricarde (I) 1800; 13th Viscount Westport (I) 1768; 13th Baron Mount Eagle (I) 1760; 11th Baron Monteagle (UK) 1806

SOMERLEYTON (3rd Baron, UK), Savile William Francis Crossley; cr. 1916; 4th Bt of Belle Vue and Somerleyton (UK) 1863; GCVO 1999; DL

SOMERS (9th Baron, GB), Philip Sebastian Somers Cocks; cr. 1784; 9th Bt of Dumbleton (GB) 1772

SOMERSET (19th Duke of, E), John Michael Edward Seymour; cr. 1546; Baron Seymour; 17th Bt of Berry Pomeroy (E) 1611; DL

SOULBURY (2nd Viscount, UK), James Herwald Ramsbotham; cr. 1954; 2nd Baron Soulbury (UK) 1941

SOUTHAMPTON (6th Baron, GB), Charles James FitzRoy; cr. 1780

SOUTHWELL (7th Viscount, I), Pyers Anthony Joseph Southwell; cr. 1776; 9th Baron Southwell (I) 1717; 10th Bt of Castle Mattress (I) 1662.

SPENCER (9th Earl, GB), Charles Edward Maurice Spencer; cr. 1765; Viscount Althorp; 9th Viscount and Baron Spencer (GB) 1761; 4th Viscount Althorp (UK) 1905

SPENS (3rd Baron, UK), Patrick Michael Rex Spens; cr. 1959

STAFFORD (15th Baron, E), Francis Melfort William Fitzherbert; cr. 1640; DL

STAIR (14th Earl of, S), John David James Dalrymple; cr. 1703; Viscount Dalrymple and Lord Newliston, Glenluce and Stranraer; 15th Viscount Stair and Lord Glenluce and Stranraer (S) 1690; 7th Baron Oxenfoord (UK) 1841; 15th Bt of Stair (S) 1664; 11th Bt of Killock (S) 1698

STAMP (4th Baron, UK), Trevor Charles Bosworth Stamp; cr. 1938

STANLEY OF ALDERLEY (8th Baron, UK), Thomas Henry Oliver Stanley; cr. 1839; 8th Baron Sheffield (I) 1783; 7th Baron Eddisbury (UK) 1848; 14th Bt of Alderley (E) 1660; DL

STOCKTON (2nd Earl of, UK), Alexander Daniel Alan Macmillan; cr. 1984; Viscount Macmillan of Ovenden

STRADBROKE (6th Earl of, UK), Robert Keith Rous; cr. 1821; Viscount Dunwich; Baron Rous (GB) 1796; 11th Bt of Henham (E) 1660

STRAFFORD (8th Earl of, UK), Thomas Edmund Byng; cr. 1847; Viscount Enfield; Baron Strafford (UK) 1835

STRANG (2nd Baron, UK), Colin Strang; cr. 1954

STRATHALMOND (3rd Baron, UK), William Roberton Fraser; cr. 1955

STRATHCARRON (2nd Baron, UK), David William Anthony Blyth Macpherson; cr. 1936; 2nd Bt of Drumalban (UK) 1933

STRATHCONA AND MOUNT ROYAL (4th Baron, UK), Donald Euan Palmer Howard; cr. 1900

STRATHEDEN (6th Baron, UK), cr. 1836, AND CAMPBELL (6th Baron, UK), cr. 1841; Donald Campbell

STRATHMORE AND KINGHORNE (18th Earl of, S), Michael Fergus Bowes Lyon; cr. 1606 and 1677; Earl of Strathmore and Kinghorne (UK) 1937; Viscount Lyon, Lord Glamis, Tannadyce, Sidlaw and Strathdichtie (S) 1677; Lord Glamis (S) 1445; Baron Bowes (UK) 1887; DL

STRATHSPEY (6th Baron, UK), James Patrick Trevor Grant of Grant; cr. 1884; 18th Bt of Grant (NS) 1625

STUART OF FINDHORN (3rd Viscount, UK), James Dominic Stuart; cr. 1959

SUDELEY (7th Baron, UK), Merlin Charles Sainthill Hanbury-Tracy; cr. 1838

SUFFIELD (11th Baron, GB), Anthony Philip Harbord-Hamond; cr. 1786; 12th Bt of Gunton (GB) 1746; MC 1950

SUFFOLK (21st Earl of, E), cr. 1603, AND BERKSHIRE (14th Earl of, E) cr. 1626; Michael John James George Robert Howard; 14th Viscount Andover and Baron Howard of Charlton (E) 1622

SUTHERLAND (6th Duke of, UK), John Sutherland Egerton; cr. 1833; Marquess of Stafford (GB) 1786; Earl Gower (GB) 1746; Earl of Ellesmere (UK) 1846; Viscount Trentham (GB) 1746; Viscount Brackley (UK) 1846; Baron Gower (E) 1703; 13th Bt of Stittenham (E) 1620; TD; DL

SUTHERLAND (Countess of, 24th in line, S), Elizabeth Millicent Sutherland; cr. 1235; Lady Strathnaver

SWANSEA (4th Baron, UK), John Hussey Hamilton Vivian; cr. 1893; 4th Bt of Singleton (UK) 1882; DL

SWAYTHLING (5th Baron, UK), Charles Edgar Samuel Montagu; cr. 1907; 5th Bt of South Stoneham House and Kensington Palace Gardens (UK) 1894

SWINTON (2nd Earl of, UK), David Yarburgh Cunliffe-Lister; cr. 1955; 2nd Viscount Swinton (UK) 1935; 2nd Baron Masham (UK) 1955; DL

SYSONBY (3rd Baron, UK), John Frederick Ponsonby; cr. 1935

TALBOT OF MALAHIDE (10th Baron, I), Reginald John Richard Arundell; cr. 1831; DL.

TANKERVILLE (10th Earl of, GB), Peter Grey Bennet; cr. 1714; 11th Baron Ossulston (E) 1682

TEDDER (3rd Baron, UK), Robin John Tedder; cr. 1946

TEMPLE OF STOWE (8th Earl, UK), Walter Grenville Algernon Temple-Gore-Langton; cr. 1822

TENNYSON (5th Baron, UK), Mark Aubrey Tennyson; cr. 1884; DSC 1943

TERRINGTON (5th Baron, UK), (Christopher) Montague Woodhouse; cr. 1918; DSO 1943; OBE (Mil) 1944

TEVIOT (2nd Baron, UK), Charles John Kerr; cr. 1940

TEYNHAM (20th Baron, E), John Christopher Ingham Roper-Curzon; cr. 1616

THOMSON OF FLEET (2nd Baron, UK), Kenneth Roy Thomson; cr. 1964

THURLOW (8th Baron, GB), Francis Edward Hovell-Thurlow-Cumming-Bruce; cr. 1792; KCMG 1961

THURSO (3rd Viscount, UK), John Archibald Sinclair; cr. 1952; 6th Bt of Ulbster (GB) 1786

TOLLEMACHE (5th Baron, UK), Timothy John Edward Tollemache; cr. 1876; DL

TORPHICHEN (15th Lord, S), James Andrew Douglas Sandilands; cr. 1564

TORRINGTON (11th Viscount, GB), Timothy Howard St George Byng; cr. 1721; Baron Byng; 11th Bt of Southill (GB) 1715

TOWNSHEND (7th Marquess, GB), George John Patrick Dominic Townshend; cr. 1787; 10th Viscount Townshend of Raynham (E) 1682; Baron Townshend of Lynn Regis (E) 1661; 12th Bt of Raynham (E) 1617

TRENCHARD (3rd Viscount, UK), Hugh Trenchard; cr. 1936; 3rd Baron Trenchard (UK) 1930; 3rd Bt of Wolfeton (UK) 1919

TREVETHIN (4th Baron, UK), cr. 1921, AND OAKSEY (2nd Baron, UK), cr. 1947; John Geoffrey Tristram Lawrence; (known as Lord Oaksey); OBE 1985

TREVOR (5th Baron, UK), Marke Charles Hill-Trevor; cr. 1880

TRIMLESTOWN (21st Baron, I), Raymond Charles Barnewall; cr. 1461.

TRYON (3rd Baron, UK), Anthony George Merrik Tryon; cr. 1940; DL

TWEEDDALE (13th Marquess of, S), Edward Douglas John Hay; cr. 1694; Earl of Tweeddale (S) 1646; Earl of Gifford and Viscount Walden (S) 1694; Lord Hay of Yester (S) 1488; Baron Tweeddale (UK) 1881

TWEEDSMUIR (3rd Baron, UK), William de l'Aigle Buchan; cr. 1935

ULLSWATER (2nd Viscount, UK), Nicholas James Christopher Lowther; cr. 1921; PC 1994

VALENTIA (15th Viscount, I), Richard John Dighton Annesley; cr. 1622; 15th Baron Mountnorris (I) 1628; 15th Bt of Mountnorris (I) 1620.

VAUX OF HARROWDEN (10th Baron, E), John Hugh Philip Gilbey; cr. 1523

VENTRY (8th Baron, I), Andrew Wesley Daubeny de Moleyns; cr. 1800; 8th Bt of Burnham 1797.

VERNON (10th Baron, GB), John Lawrance Venables-Vernon; cr. 1762

VERULAM (7th Earl of, UK), John Duncan Grimston; cr. 1815; Viscount Grimston; Viscount Grimston and Baron Dunboyne (I) 1719; Lord Forrester of Corstorphine (S) 1633; Baron Verulam (GB) 1790; 14th Bt of Little Waltham (E) 1629

VESTEY (3rd Baron, UK), Samuel George Armstrong Vestey; cr. 1922; 3rd Bt of Bessemer House (UK) 1913; DL

WAKEHURST (3rd Baron, UK), John Christopher Loder; cr. 1934

WALDEGRAVE (13th Earl, GB), James Sherbrooke Waldegrave; cr. 1729; Viscount Chewton; 14th Baron Waldegrave (E) 1685; 17th Bt of Hever Castle (E) 1643

WALES (Prince of), and Earl of Chester, HRH Prince Charles Philip Arthur George; cr. 1958. Duke of Cornwall and Rothesay, Earl of Carrick, Baron of Renfrew, Lord of the Isles and Great Steward of Scotland; cr. 1952; KG 1958; KT 1977; PC 1977; GCB 1975; AK; QSO

WALSINGHAM (9th Baron, GB), John de Grey; cr. 1780; MC 1952

WARDINGTON (2nd Baron, UK), Christopher Henry Beaumont Pease; cr. 1936

WARWICK (9th Earl of, GB), Guy David Greville; cr. 1759; 9th Earl Brooke (GB) 1746; 16th Baron Brooke (E) 1621

WATERFORD (8th Marquess of, I), John Hubert de la Poer Beresford; cr. 1789; 9th Earl of Tyrone (I) 1746; 9th Viscount Tyrone (I) 1720; 20th Baron Le Poer (I) 1375; 9th Baron Beresford (I) 1720; 8th Baron Tyrone (GB) 1786; 12th Bt of Coleraine (I) 1665

WATERPARK (7th Baron, I), Frederick Caryll Philip Cavendish; cr. 1792; 8th Bt of Doveridge (GB) 1755

WEDGWOOD (4th Baron, UK), Piers Anthony Weymouth Wedgwood; cr. 1942

WEIR (3rd Viscount, UK), William Kenneth James Weir; cr. 1938; 3rd Baron Weir (UK) 1918

WELLINGTON (8th Duke of, UK), Arthur Valerian Wellesley; cr. 1814; Marquess of Wellington (UK) 1812; Marquess of Douro (UK) 1814; Earl of Mornington (I) 1760; Earl of Wellington (UK) 1812; Viscount Wellesley (I) 1760; Viscount Wellington (UK) 1809; Baron Mornington (I) 1746; Baron Douro (UK) 1809; Prince of Waterloo (Netherlands) 1815; Duke of Vittoria and Marquess of Torres Vedras (Portugal) 1812; Count of Vimeiro (Portugal) 1811; Duke of Ciudad Rodrigo and a Grandee (1st Class) (Spain) 1812; KG 1990; LVO 1952; OBE (Mil) 1957; MC 1941; DL

WEMYSS (12th Earl of, S), Francis David Charteris; cr. 1633; AND 8th Earl of MARCH (S) 1697; Viscount Peebles (S) 1697; Lord Wemyss of Elcho (S) 1628; Lord Elcho and Methil (S) 1633; Lord Douglas of Neidpath, Lyne and Munard (S) 1697; 5th Baron Wemyss (UK) 1821; KT 1966

WESSEX (1st Earl of, UK), HRH Prince Edward Antony Richard Louis; cr. 1999; Viscount Severn; CVO 1989

WESTBURY (5th Baron, UK), David Alan Bethell; cr. 1861; CBE 1994; MC 1942; DL

WESTMEATH (13th Earl of, I), William Anthony Nugent; cr. 1621; 16th Baron Delvin (I) 1486.

WESTMINSTER (6th Duke of, UK), Gerald Cavendish Grosvenor; cr. 1874; Marquess of Westminster (UK) 1831; Earl Grosvenor and Viscount Belgrave (GB) 1784; Baron Grosvenor (GB) 1761; 15th Bt of Eaton (E) 1622; OBE (Mil) 1995; TD 1994; DL

WESTMORLAND (16th Earl of, E), Anthony David Francis Henry Fane; cr. 1624; Baron Burghersh

WESTWOOD (3rd Baron, UK), William Gavin Westwood; cr. 1944

WHARNCLIFFE (5th Earl of, UK), Richard Alan Montagu Stuart Wortley; cr. 1876; Viscount Carlton; 7th Baron Wharncliffe (UK) 1826

WIGRAM (2nd Baron, UK), George Neville Clive Wigram; cr. 1935; MC 1945; DL

WILLOUGHBY DE ERESBY (Baroness, 27th in line, E), Nancy Jane Marie Heathcote-Drummond-Willoughby; cr 1313; DL

WILSON (2nd Baron, UK), Patrick Maitland Wilson; cr. 1946

WILTON (8th Earl of, UK), Francis Egerton Grosvenor; cr. 1801; Viscount Grey de Wilton; 6th Baron Ebury (UK) 1857

WIMBORNE (4th Viscount, UK), Ivor Mervyn Vigors Guest; cr. 1918; 5th Baron Wimborne (UK) 1880; 4th Baron Ashby St Ledgers (UK) 1910; 6th Bt of Dowlais (UK) 1838

WINCHESTER (18th Marquess of, E), Nigel George Paulet; cr. 1551; Earl of Wiltshire (E) 1549; Baron St John of Basing (E) 1538

WINCHILSEA (17th Earl of, E), cr. 1628; AND NOTTINGHAM (12th Earl of, E), cr. 1681; Daniel James Hatfield Finch Hatton; 17th Viscount Maidstone (E) 1623; 12th Baron Finch (E) 1673; 18th Bt of Eastwell (E) 1611; 12th Bt of Raunston (E) 1660

WINTERTON (8th Earl, I), Donald David Turnour; cr. 1766; Viscount Turnour; 8th Baron Winterton (I) 1761.

WISE (2nd Baron, UK), John Clayton Wise; cr. 1951

WOLVERTON (7th Baron, UK), Christopher Richard Glyn; cr. 1869

WOOLTON (3rd Earl of, UK), Simon Frederick Marquis; cr. 1956; 3rd Viscount Woolton (UK) 1953; 3rd Viscount Walberton (UK) 1956; 3rd Baron Woolton (UK) 1939

WRAXALL (2nd Baron, UK), George Richard Lawley Gibbs; cr. 1928; DL

WRENBURY (3rd Baron, UK), John Burton Buckley; cr. 1915

WROTTESLEY (6th Baron, UK), Clifton Hugh Lancelot de Verdon Wrottesley; cr. 1838; 14th Bt of Wrottesley (E) 1642

WYNFORD (8th Baron, UK), Robert Samuel Best; cr. 1829; MBE (Mil) 1953; DL

YARBOROUGH (8th Earl of, UK), Charles John Pelham; cr. 1837; 9th Baron Yarborough (GB) 1794; Baron Worsley (UK) 1837

YORK (1st Duke of, UK), HRH Prince Andrew Albert Christian Edward; cr. 1986; Earl of Inverness and Baron Killyleagh; CVO 1979

ZETLAND (4th Marquess of, UK), Lawrence Mark Dundas; cr. 1892; 6th Earl of Zetland (UK) 1838; 4th Earl of Ronaldshay (UK) 1892; 7th Baron Dundas (GB) 1794; 8th Bt of Kerse (GB) 1762; DL

ZOUCHE OF HARYNGWORTH (18th Baron, E), James Assheton Frankland; cr. 1308; 12th Bt of Thirkleby (E) 1660

OBITUARY OF PEER OF IRELAND IN 1999

Dunsany (19th Baron of); d. February 6; suc. by his son.

OBITUARY OF NON-PARLIAMENTARY PEER IN 2000

Halsbury (3rd Earl, UK); d. January 14; suc. by his son

Former Peers who have disclaimed their Peerages under the Peerage Act 1963

(The year the peerage was disclaimed is in brackets)

Douglas-Hamilton, Lord J. (Selkirk, *E*.). (1994 but created a Life Baron 1997)

Grigg, J. E. P. (Altrincham, *B*.). (1963)

Hartwell, Lord (Camrose, *V*.). (1995)

Hogg, Q. M. (Hailsham, *V*. (1963) but created a Life Baron 1970)

Lambton, A. C. F. (Durham, *E*.). (1970)

Lewis, T. O. (Merthyr, *B*.). (1977)

Reith, C. J. (Reith, *B*.). (1972)

Sanderson, A. L. (Sanderson of Ayot, *B*.). (1971)

Silkin, A. (Silkin, *B*.). (1972)

Wedgwood Benn, A. N. (Stansgate, *V*.). (1963)

The Peerage

Those hereditary peers who were elected to the House of Lords are marked *. Hereditary office holders in the House of Lords are marked †. Peers of Ireland who are summoned by a Peerage of Great Britain or the United Kingdom have that title listed in parenthesis, eg Earl of Arran (Baron Sudley). Hereditary peers who have received life peerages are marked § and have their new titles listed after their names with the initials LP. Life peers are also indicated by the initials (LP).

PEERS OF THE BLOOD ROYAL
(1 Prince, 3 Dukes, 1 Earl)

HRH The Prince of Wales 1958
HRH The Duke of Gloucester 1928
HRH The Duke of Kent 1934
HRH The Duke of York 1986
HRH The Earl of Wessex 1999

ARCHBISHOPS (2)

Canterbury *translated* 1991
York *translated* 1983

DUKES (25)

†Norfolk 1483
Somerset 1546
Richmond, Lennox and Gordon 1675/1876
Grafton 1675
Beaufort 1682
Saint Albans 1684
Bedford 1694
Devonshire 1694
Marlborough 1702
Rutland 1703
Hamilton and Brandon 1643/1711
Buccleuch and Queensberry 1663/1684
Argyll 1701
Atholl 1703
*Montrose 1707
Roxburghe 1707
Manchester 1719
Northumberland 1766
Leinster 1766
Wellington 1814
Sutherland 1833
Abercorn 1868
Westminster 1874
Fife 1900
Edinburgh 1947

MARQUESSES (34)

Winchester 1551
Huntly 1599
Queensberry 1682
Tweeddale 1694
Lothian 1701
Lansdowne 1784
Townshend 1787
Salisbury 1789
Bath 1789
Waterford 1789
Downshire 1789
Donegall 1791
Hertford 1793
Bute 1796
Headfort 1800
Sligo 1800
Ely 1801
Exeter 1801
Northampton 1812
Camden 1812
Anglesey 1815
†Cholmondeley 1815
Conyngham 1816
Londonderry 1816
Ailesbury 1821
Bristol 1826
Ailsa 1831
Normanby 1838
Abergavenny 1876
Zetland 1892
Linlithgow 1902
Aberdeen and Temair 1916
Milford Haven 1917
Reading 1926

EARLS AND COUNTESSES (192)

*Shrewsbury and Waterford 1442/1446
Derby 1485
Huntingdon 1529
Pembroke and Montgomery 1551/1605
Devon 1553
Lincoln 1572
Suffolk and Berkshire 1603/1626

Denbigh and Desmond 1622
Westmorland 1624
Lindsey and Abingdon 1626/1682
Winchilsea and Nottingham 1628/1681
*Sandwich 1660
Carlisle 1661
Essex 1661
Shaftesbury 1672
Portland 1689
Scarbrough 1690
Albemarle 1696
Coventry 1697
Jersey 1697
*Mar 1114 (precedence of 1404)
Sutherland 1235
§Crawford and Balcarres 1398/1651 (LP Baron Balniel 1974)
*Erroll 1452
*Caithness 1455
Rothes 1457
Morton 1458
Buchan 1469
Eglinton and Winton 1507/1859
Mar and Kellie 1565/1619
Moray 1562
*Home 1604
Perth 1605
Strathmore and Kinghorne 1606/1677
Haddington 1619
Cork and Orrery 1620/1660
Westmeath 1621
Galloway 1623
Lauderdale 1624
Meath 1627
Kinnoull 1633
*Lindsay 1633
Loudoun 1633
Elgin and Kincardine 1633/1647
Wemyss and March 1633/1697
Dalhousie 1633
Airlie 1639

Leven and Melville 1641
Dysart 1643
*Northesk 1647
Cavan 1647
*Dundee 1660
Annandale and Hartfell 1662
Drogheda 1661
Dundonald 1669
Kintore 1677
Granard 1684
Dunmore 1686
Orkney 1696
Seafield 1701
Stair 1703
Rosebery 1703
Glasgow 1703
*Ferrers 1711
Dartmouth 1711
Tankerville 1714
Aylesford 1714
Macclesfield 1721
Darnley 1725
Waldegrave 1729
Egmont 1733
Bessborough 1739
Harrington 1742
Portsmouth 1743
Brooke and Warwick
  1746/1759
Buckinghamshire 1746
Carrick 1748
Guilford 1752
Hardwicke 1754
Ilchester 1756
Shannon 1756
De La Warr 1761
*Arran (Baron Sudley) 1762
*Courtown (Baron
  Saltersford) 1762
Radnor 1765
Spencer 1765
Mexborough 1766
Winterton 1766
Kingston 1768
Roden 1771
Bathurst 1772
Clarendon 1776
Mansfield 1776/1792
Lisburne 1776
Clanwilliam 1776
Antrim 1785
§Longford 1785 (LP Baron
  Pakenham of Cowley 1999)
Portarlington 1785
Mayo 1785
Mount Edgcumbe 1789

Fortescue 1789
Annesley 1789
Enniskillen 1789
Erne 1789
*Carnarvon 1793
Lucan 1795
Belmore 1797
Cadogan 1800
Malmesbury 1800
Castle Stewart 1800
Donoughmore 1800
Caledon 1800
*Rosslyn 1801
Craven 1801
*Onslow 1801
Romney 1801
Chichester 1801
Wilton 1801
Limerick 1803
Clancarty 1803
Powis 1804
Nelson 1805
Grey 1806
Gosford 1806
Rosse 1806
Normanton 1806
Lonsdale 1807
Harrowby 1809
Harewood 1812
Minto 1813
Cathcart 1814
Verulam 1815
St Germans 1815
Morley 1815
Bradford 1815
Eldon 1821
*Howe 1821
Stradbroke 1821
Temple of Stowe 1822
Kilmorey 1822
Dunraven and Mount-Earl
  1822
*Listowel (Baron Hare)
  1822
Norbury 1827
Cawdor 1827
Munster 1831
Lichfield 1831
Ranfurly 1831
Granville 1833
Effingham 1837
Ducie 1837
Yarborough 1837
Leicester 1837
Lovelace 1838
Gainsborough 1841

Strafford 1847
Cottenham 1850
Cowley 1857
Dudley 1860
*Russell 1861
Cromartie 1861
Kimberley 1866
Wharncliffe 1876
Cairns 1878
Lytton 1880
*Selborne 1882
Iddesleigh 1885
Cranbrook 1892
Halsbury 1898
Cromer 1901
Plymouth 1905
*Liverpool 1905
Kitchener of Khartoum 1914
St Aldwyn 1915
Beatty 1919
Haig 1919
Iveagh 1919
Balfour 1922
Oxford and Asquith 1925
§Jellicoe 1925 (LP Jellicoe
  of Southampton 1999)
Inchcape 1929
*Peel 1929
*Baldwin of Bewdley 1937
Halifax 1944
Gowrie 1945
Lloyd-George of Dwyfor
  1945
Mountbatten of Burma 1947
Alexander of Tunis 1952
Swinton 1955
*Attlee 1955
Woolton 1956
§Snowdon 1961 (LP Baron
  Armstrong-Jones 1999)
Stockton 1984

VISCOUNTS (116)
Hereford 1550
§Cranborne 1604 (LP Baron
  Gascoyne-Cecil 1999)
*Falkland 1620
Arbuthnott 1641
*Oxfuird 1651
Gormanston 1478
Mountgarret 1550
Valentia 1622
Dillon 1622
Massereene and Ferrard
  1660/1797
Charlemont 1665

Downe 1681
Bolingbroke and St John
    1712
Molesworth 1716
Chetwynd 1717
Boyne 1717
Midleton 1717
Cobham 1718
Falmouth 1720
Gage 1720
Torrington 1721
Galway 1727
Powerscourt 1743
Ashbrook 1751
Southwell 1776
De Vesci 1776
Lifford 1781
Bangor 1781
Doneraile 1785
Harberton 1791
Hawarden 1793
Hood 1796
Monck 1800
St Vincent 1801
Melville 1802
Sidmouth 1805
Gort 1816
Exmouth 1816
Combermere 1827
Hill 1842
Hardinge 1846
Gough 1849
Bridport 1868
Portman 1873
Hampden 1884
Cross 1886
Hambleden 1891
Knutsford 1895
Esher 1897
*Goschen 1900
Ridley 1900
*Colville of Culross 1902
Churchill 1902
Selby 1905
Knollys 1911
Allendale 1911
Chilston 1911
Scarsdale 1911
Mersey 1916
Cowdray 1916
Devonport 1917
*Astor 1917
Wimborne 1918
St Davids 1918
Rothermere 1919
*Allenby of Megiddo 1919

Chelmsford 1921
Long 1921
Ullswater 1921
Leverhulme 1922
§Younger of Leckie 1923
    (LP Baron Younger of
    Prestwick 1992)
Bearsted 1925
*Craigavon 1927
*Bridgeman 1929
Brentford 1929
Buckmaster 1932
Bledisloe 1935
Hanworth 1936
Trenchard 1936
Greenwood 1937
Samuel 1937
Runciman of Doxford 1937
Davidson 1937
Weir 1938
Caldecote 1939
*Simon 1940
Margesson 1942
Daventry 1943
Addison 1945
Kemsley 1945
Marchwood 1945
Alanbrooke 1946
Montgomery of Alamein
    1946
*Waverley 1952
Thurso 1952
*Brookeborough 1952
Norwich 1952
Leathers 1954
Soulbury 1954
Chandos 1954
Malvern 1955
De L'Isle 1956
Ingleby 1956
Monckton of Brenchley
    1957
*Tenby 1957
Mackintosh of Halifax
    1957
Dunrossil 1959
Stuart of Findhorn 1959
Rochdale 1960
*Slim 1960
Head 1960
Boyd of Merton 1960
Mills 1962
Blakenham 1963
Eccles 1964
Dilhorne 1964
BISHOPS (24)

For a full list, please see
    Bishops in the House of
    Lords on page 366.

BARONS, LORDS,
BARONESSES AND
LADIES (991)

De Ros 1264
*Mowbray and Stourton
    1283/1448
Hastings 1290
FitzWalter 1295
Clinton 1299
de Clifford 1299
Zouche of Haryngworth
    1308
Willoughby de Eresby 1313
*Strabolgi 1318
Dacre 1321
*Darcy de Knayth 1332
Cromwell 1375
Camoys 1383
Grey of Codnor 1397
Berkeley 1421
Latymer 1431
Dudley 1439
Saye and Sele 1447/1603
Berners 1455
*Willoughby de Broke 1491
Vaux of Harrowden 1523
Burgh 1529
Braye 1529
*Wharton 1544
*St John of Bletso 1558
Petre 1603
Dormer 1615
Teynham 1616
*Strange 1628
Stafford 1640
Byron 1643
*Lucas of Crudwell 1663
Arlington 1664
Clifford of Chudleigh 1672
Barnard 1698
Forbes 1445
*Saltoun of Abernethy 1445
Gray 1445
Sinclair 1449
Borthwick 1452
Lovat 1458
Sempill 1489
Herries of Terregles 1490
Elphinstone 1509
Torphichen 1564
Kinloss 1602
Balfour of Burleigh 1607

Napier and Ettrick
  1627/1872
Fairfax of Cameron   1627
*Reay   1628
Elibank   1643
Belhaven and Stenton   1647
Rollo   1651
Polwarth   1690
Middleton   1711
*Walpole   1723
*Monson   1728
Boston   1761
Vernon   1762
Digby 1765/1620
Hawke   1776
Brownlow   1776
Foley   1776
Kensington   1776
Dynevor   1780
Walsingham   1780
Bagot   1780
Southampton   1780
Grantley   1782
Rodney   1782
Somers   1784
Suffield   1786
Kenyon   1788
Braybrooke   1788
Thurlow   1792
Auckland   1793
Carrington   1796 (LP Baron
  Carington of Upton 1999)
Bolton   1797
Lilford   1797
Kingsale   1223/1397
Dunboyne   1324/1541
Dunsany   1439/1461
Trimlestown   1461
Louth   1541
Inchiquin   1543
Carbery   1715
Aylmer   1718
Farnham   1756
Lisle   1758
Macdonald   1776
Kensington   1776
Newborough   1776
Massy   1776
Muskerry   1781
Kilmaine   1789
Waterpark   1792
Graves   1794
Huntingfield   1796
Rossmore   1796
Hotham   1797
Crofton   1798

Ffrench   1798
*Henley (Baron Northington)
  1799
Langford   1800
Dufferin and Clandeboye
  1800
Henniker   1800
Ventry   1800
Dunalley   1800
Clanmorris   1800
Ashtown   1800
Ellenborough   1802
Sandys   1802
Rendlesham   1806
Manners   1807
Castlemaine   1812
Decies   1812
Harris   1815
Garvagh   1818
Ravensworth   1821
Delamere   1821
Forester   1821
Rayleigh   1821
Gifford   1824
Feversham   1826
Plunket   1827
Heytesbury   1828
*Skelmersdale   1828
Wynford   1829
Kilmarnock   1831
Talbot of Malahide   1831
Poltimore   1831
Mostyn   1831
De Saumarez   1831
Denman   1834
Carew   1834
Abinger   1835
Ashburton   1835
Hatherton   1835
Stratheden and Campbell
  1836/1841
Oranmore and Browne   1836
De Mauley   1838
Wrottesley   1838
Sudeley   1838
*Methuen   1838
Stanley of Alderley   1839
Leigh   1839
Monteagle of Brandon   1839
*Vivian   1841
Congleton   1841
Bellew   1848
Londesborough   1850
De Freyne   1851
Raglan   1852
Belper   1856

Fermoy   1856
Ebury   1857
Chesham   1858
Churston   1858
Leconfield and Egremont
  1859/1963
Lyveden   1859
*Brougham and Vaux   1860
Westbury   1861
Annaly   1863
*Northbrook   1866
*Hylton   1866
Penrhyn   1866
O'Neill   1868
Napier of Magdala   1868
Rathdonnell   1868
Lawrence   1869
Acton   1869
Wolverton   1869
O'Hagan   1870
Sandhurst   1871
*Aberdare   1873
Moncreiff   1874
Coleridge   1874
Cottesloe   1874
Hampton   1874
Harlech   1876
Tollemache   1876
Gerard   1876
Sackville   1876
Norton   1878
Trevor   1880
Brabourne   1880
Derwent   1881
Hothfield   1881
*Ampthill   1881
Tennyson   1884
Strathspey   1884
Monk Bretton   1884
*Northbourne   1884
Rothschild   1885
Revelstoke   1885
Monkswell   1885
Ashbourne   1885
Saint Oswald   1885
Deramore   1885
*Montagu of Beaulieu   1885
Herschell   1886
Hindlip   1886
Grimthorpe   1886
Hamilton of Dalzell   1886
Saint Levan   1887
Basing   1887
De Ramsey   1887
*Addington   1887
Savile   1888

Ashcombe 1892
Crawshaw 1892
Amherst of Hackney 1892
Newton 1892
Dunleath 1892
Swansea 1893
Aldenham 1896
HolmPatrick 1897
Burton 1897
Glanusk 1899
Cranworth 1899
*Avebury 1900
Killanin 1900
Strathcona and Mount Royal
  1900
Kinross 1902
Shuttleworth 1902
Grenfell 1902
Redesdale 1902
*Burnham 1903
Biddulph 1903
Ritchie of Dundee 1905
Hemphill 1906
Joicey 1906
Nunburnholme 1906
Swaythling 1907
Blyth 1907
Marchamley 1908
Gorell 1909
Fisher 1909
Kilbracken 1909
Hardinge of Penshurst 1910
de Villiers 1910
Glenconner 1911
Aberconway 1911
Rowallan 1911
Ashton of Hyde 1911
Ravensdale 1911
Hollenden 1912
Parmoor 1914
*Lyell 1914
Cunliffe 1914
Wrenbury 1915
Faringdon 1916
Shaughnessy 1916
Rathcreedan 1916
Somerleyton 1916
Carnock 1916
Beaverbrook 1917
Gainford 1917
Forteviot 1917
*Colwyn 1917
Gisborough 1917
Morris 1918
Cawley 1918
Terrington 1918

*Glenarthur 1918
Phillimore 1918
Inverforth 1919
Sinha 1919
Cochrane of Cults 1919
Clwyd 1919
Russell of Liverpool 1919
*Swinfen 1919
Meston 1919
Cullen of Ashbourne 1920
Trevethin and Oaksey
  1921/1947
Glendyne 1922
Manton 1922
Forres 1922
Vestey 1922
Borwick 1922
Maclay 1922
Bethell 1922
Darling 1924
Banbury of Southam 1924
Merrivale 1925
Bradbury 1925
*Greenway 1927
Hayter 1927
Cornwallis 1927
Daresbury 1927
Wraxall 1928
Melchett 1928
Remnant 1928
*Moynihan 1929
Craigmyle 1929
Dulverton 1929
*Luke 1929
Alvingham 1929
Baden-Powell 1929
Ponsonby of Shulbrede 1930
Dickinson 1930
Noel-Buxton 1930
Howard of Penrith 1930
Rochester 1931
*Selsdon 1932
Moyne 1932
Davies 1932
Rankeillour 1932
Brocket 1933
Milne 1933
Rennell 1933
Mottistone 1933
Iliffe 1933
*Palmer 1933
Rockley 1934
*Elton 1934
Wakehurst 1934
Hesketh 1935
Tweedsmuir 1935

Sysonby 1935
Wigram 1935
Riverdale 1935
May 1935
Kennet 1935
Strathcarron 1936
Catto 1936
Wardington 1936
§Windlesham 1937 (LP
  Baron Hennessy 1999)
*Mancroft 1937
McGowan 1937
*Denham 1937
*Rea 1937
Chatfield 1937
Cadman 1937
Kenilworth 1937
Pender 1937
Roborough 1937
Birdwood 1938
Brassey of Apethorpe 1938
§Belstead 1938 (LP Baron
  Ganzoni 1999)
Stamp 1938
Bicester 1938
Milford 1939
Hankey 1939
Harmsworth 1939
*Rotherwick 1939
*Glentoran 1939
Tryon 1940
Croft 1940
Teviot 1940
Nathan 1940
Kindersley 1941
Ironside 1941
Latham 1942
Wedgwood 1942
*Geddes 1942
Bruntisfield 1942
*Brabazon of Tara 1942
Keyes 1943
Hemingford 1943
*Moran 1943
Killearn 1943
Dowding 1943
Gretton 1944
Westwood 1944
Hazlerigg 1945
Hacking 1945
Balfour of Inchrye 1945
Chetwode 1945
Sandford 1945
Broadbridge 1945
Broughshane 1945
Mountevans 1945

Lindsay of Birker 1945
Piercy 1945
Chorley 1945
Calverley 1945
Tedder 1946
Colgrain 1946
Darwen 1946
Wilson 1946
Lucas of Chilworth 1946
§Shepherd 1946 (LP Baron
  Shepherd of Spalding 1999)
Citrine 1946
Newall 1946
Rugby 1947
Layton 1947
Simon of Wythenshawe
  1947
Kershaw 1947
*Trefgarne 1947
Crook 1947
Amwell 1947
Milverton 1947
Clydesmuir 1948
Macdonald of Gwaenysgor
  1949
Burden 1950
Haden-Guest 1950
Hives 1950
Greenhill 1950
Ogmore 1950
Morris of Kenwood 1950
Macpherson of Drumochter
  1951
Kenswood 1951
*Freyberg 1951
*Milner of Leeds 1951
Kirkwood 1951
Wise 1951
Jeffreys 1952
Rathcavan 1953
Baillieu 1953
Grantchester 1953
Strang 1954
Coleraine 1954
Harvey of Tasburgh 1954
Gridley 1955
Strathalmond 1955
*Strathclyde 1955
Clitheroe 1955
McNair 1955
Colyton 1956
*Astor of Hever 1956
Sinclair of Cleeve 1957
*Bridges 1957
Norrie 1957
Birkett 1957

Harding of Petherton 1958
Poole 1958
Shawcross (LP) 1959
Rootes 1959
Plowden (LP) 1959
Netherthorpe 1959
*Crathorne 1959
Spens 1959
MacAndrew 1959
Nelson of Stafford 1960
Howick of Glendale 1960
Gladwyn 1960
Cobbold 1960
Robertson of Oakridge 1961
Marks of Broughton 1961
Fairhaven 1961
Leighton of Saint Mellons
  1962
Brain 1962
§Aldington 1962 (LP Baron
  Low 1999)
Inchyra 1962
Silsoe 1963
Thomson of Fleet 1964
Martonmere 1964
Sherfield 1964
*Inglewood 1964
Glendevon 1964
Wilberforce (LP) 1964
Chalfont (LP) 1964
Brooke of Ystradfellte (LP)
  1964
Grimston of Westbury 1964
§Erroll of Hale 1964 (LP
  Baron Erroll of Kilmun
  1999)
Renwick 1964
St Helens 1964
Margadale 1964
Soper (LP) 1965
Annan (LP) 1965
Hylton-Foster (LP) 1965
Serota (LP) 1967
Beaumont of Whitley (LP)
  1967
Hartwell (LP) 1968
Taylor of Gryfe (LP) 1968
Stokes (LP) 1969
Masham of Ilton (LP) 1970
Hailsham of St Marylebone
  (LP) 1970
Diamond (LP) 1970
Simon of Glaisdale (LP)
  1971
Blake (LP) 1971
Tanlaw (LP) 1971

Young (LP) 1971
Moyola (LP) 1971
Elles (LP) 1972
Sharples (LP) 1973
Greenhill of Harrow (LP)
  1974
Harris of Greenwich (LP)
  1974
Mackie of Benshie (LP)
  1974
Pike (LP) 1974
Wigoder (LP) 1974
Lovell-Davies (LP) 1974
Fisher of Rednal (LP) 1974
Delacourt-Smith of Alteryn
  (LP) 1974
Falkender (LP) 1974
Barber (LP) 1974
Campbell of Croy (LP) 1974
Harmar-Nicholls (LP) 1974
Wallace of Coslany (LP)
  1974
Bruce of Donington (LP)
  1974
Greene of Harrow Weald (LP)
  1974
Gibson (LP) 1975
Gregson (LP) 1975
Ryder of Eaton Hastings (LP)
  1975
Kirkhill (LP) 1975
Brookes (LP) 1976
Carr of Hadley (LP) 1976
McCarthy (LP) 1976
Northfield (LP) 1976
Parry (LP) 1976
Bullock (LP) 1976
Weidenfeld (LP) 1976
Boston of Faversham (LP)
  1976
Allen of Abbeydale (LP)
  1976
Briggs (LP) 1976
Rayne (LP) 1976
McCluskey (LP) 1976
Keith of Kinkel (LP) 1976
Glenamara (LP) 1977
Thomson of Monifieth (LP)
  1977
Carver (LP) 1977
Chitnis (LP) 1977
Roll of Ipsden (LP) 1977
Wedderburn of Charlton (LP)
  1977
Scarman (LP) 1977
Croham (LP) 1978

Lockwood (LP)   1978
Young of Dartington (LP)
    1978
Cockfield (LP)   1978
Rawlinson of Ewell (LP)
    1978
Howie of Troon (LP)   1978
Whaddon (LP)   1978
David (LP)   1978
Sefton of Garston (LP)   1978
Taylor of Blackburn (LP)
    1978
Mishcon (LP)   1978
Buxton of Alsa (LP)   1978
Hutchinson of Lullington (LP)
    1978
Blease (LP)   1978
Ryder of Warsaw (LP)   1979
Richardson (LP)   1979
Hill-Norton (LP)   1979
Perry of Walton (LP)   1979
Scanlon (LP)   1979
Flowers (LP)   1979
Bellwin (LP)   1979
Mackay of Clashfern (LP)
    1979
Jeger (LP)   1979
Renton (LP)   1979
Cledwyn of Penrhos (LP)
    1979
Brooks of Tremorfa (LP)
    1979
Harris of High Cross (LP)
    1979
Murton of Lindisfarne (LP)
    1979
Hooson (LP)   1979
McFarlane of Llandaff (LP)
    1979
Holderness (LP)   1979
Dacre of Glanton (LP)   1979
Lane (LP)   1979
Gibson-Watt (LP)   1979
Coggan (LP)   1980
Trumpington (LP)   1980
Keith of Castleacre (LP)
    1980
Hunt of Tanworth (LP)   1980
Emslie (LP)   1980
Sieff of Brimpton (LP)   1980
Boardman (LP)   1980
Weinstock (LP)   1980
Bridge of Harwich (LP)
    1980
Molloy (LP)   1981
Tordoff (LP)   1981

Jenkins of Putney (LP)   1981
Elystan-Morgan (LP)   1981
Platt of Writtle (LP)   1981
Plummer of St Marylebone
    (LP)   1981
Stodart of Leaston (LP)   1981
Campbell of Alloway (LP)
    1981
Thomas of Swynnerton (LP)
    1981
Gardner of Parkes (LP)   1981
Marsh (LP)   1981
Constantine of Stanmore (LP)
    1981
Forte (LP)   1982
Brightman (LP)   1982
MacLehose of Beoch (LP)
    1982
Carnegy of Lour (LP)   1982
Templeman (LP)   1982
McIntosh of Haringey (LP)
    1983
Nicol (LP)   1983
Cox (LP)   1983
Ingrow (LP)   1983
Ezra (LP)   1983
Quinton (LP)   1983
Prys-Davies (LP)   1983
Bauer (LP)   1983
Richardson of Duntisbourne
    (LP)   1983
Gallacher (LP)   1983
Hanson (LP)   1983
Gray of Contin (LP)   1983
King of Wartnaby (LP)   1983
Stallard (LP)   1983
Graham of Edmonton (LP)
    1983
Stoddart of Swindon (LP)
    1983
Fanshawe of Richmond (LP)
    1983
Barnett (LP)   1983
Eden of Winton (LP)   1983
Peyton of Yeovil (LP)   1983
Carmichael of Kelvingrove
    (LP)   1983
Fitt (LP)   1983
Henderson of Brompton (LP)
    1984
McAlpine of West Green (LP)
    1984
Cameron of Lochbroom (LP)
    1984
Young of Graffham (LP)
    1984

Chapple (LP)   1985
Warnock (LP)   1985
Vinson (LP)   1985
Murray of Epping Forest (LP)
    1985
Kimball (LP)   1985
Butterworth (LP)   1985
Elliott of Morpeth (LP)   1985
Williams of Elvel (LP)   1985
Donoughue (LP)   1985
Griffiths (LP)   1985
Turner of Camden (LP)
    1985
Sanderson of Bowden (LP)
    1985
Hooper (LP)   1985
Wolfson (LP)   1985
Ackner (LP)   1986
Oliver of Aylmerton (LP)
    1986
Goff of Chieveley (LP)   1986
Moore of Wolvercote (LP)
    1986
Deedes (LP)   1986
Bramall (LP)   1987
Blackstone (LP)   1987
Carter (LP)   1987
Irvine of Lairg (LP)
    (Lord Chancellor)   1987
Peston (LP)   1987
Stevens of Ludgate (LP)
    1987
Johnston of Rockport (LP)
    1987
Plumb (LP)   1987
Blatch (LP)   1987
Chilver (LP)   1987
Knights (LP)   1987
Cocks of Hartcliffe (LP)
    1987
Thomas of Gwydir (LP)
    1987
Pym (LP)   1987
Dormand of Easington (LP)
    1987
Prior (LP)   1987
Crickhowell (LP)   1987
St John of Fawsley (LP)
    1987
Mason of Barnsley (LP)
    1987
Carlisle of Bucklow (LP)
    1987
Jenkin of Roding (LP)   1987
Callaghan of Cardiff (LP)
    1987

Rees (LP)   1987
Jenkins of Hillhead (LP)
   1987
Jauncey of Tullichettle (LP)
   1988
Donaldson of Lymington (LP)
   1988
Armstrong of Ilminster (LP)
   1988
Alexander of Weedon (LP)
   1988
Rees-Mogg (LP)   1988
Butterfield (LP)   1988
Mackenzie-Stuart (LP)   1988
Macaulay of Bragar (LP)
   1989
Sainsbury of Preston
   Candover (LP)   1989
Lewis of Newnham (LP)
   1989
Oppenheim-Barnes (LP)
   1989
Fraser of Carmyllie (LP)
   1989
Walton of Detchant (LP)
   1989
McColl of Dulwich (LP)
   1989
Park of Monmouth (LP)
   1990
Tombs (LP)   1990
Clinton-Davis (LP)   1990
Morris of Castle Morris (LP)
   1990
Eccles of Moulton (LP)
   1990
Richard (LP)   1990
Wade of Chorlton (LP)   1990
Cavendish of Furness (LP)
   1990
Cumberlege (LP)   1990
Brigstocke (LP)   1990
Soulsby of Swaffham Prior
   (LP)   1990
Holme of Cheltenham (LP)
   1990
Varley (LP)   1990
Hollis of Heigham (LP)
   1990
Flather (LP)   1990
Pearson of Rannoch (LP)
   1990
Castle of Blackburn (LP)
   1990
Porter of Luddenham   (LP)
   1990

Lane of Horsell (LP)   1990
Haslam (LP)   1990
Dunn (LP)   1990
Waddington (LP)   1990
Sterling of Plaistow (LP)
   1991
Runcie (LP)   1991
Palumbo (LP)   1991
Griffiths of Fforestfach (LP)
   1991
James of Holland Park (LP)
   1991
Laing of Dunphail (LP)
   1991
Seccombe (LP)   1991
Wolfson of Sunningdale (LP)
   1991
Desai (LP)   1991
Hamwee (LP)   1991
Marlesford (LP)   1991
Judd (LP)   1991
Denton of Wakefield (LP)
   1991
Hilton of Eggardon (LP)
   1991
Mallalieu (LP)   1991
Hollick (LP)   1991
O'Cathain (LP)   1991
Renfrew of Kaimsthorn (LP)
   1991
Mackay of Ardbrecknish (LP)
   1991
Skidelsky (LP)   1991
Perry of Southwark (LP)
   1991
Macfarlane of Bearsden (LP)
   1991
Craig of Radley (LP)   1991
Browne-Wilkinson (A Lord of
   Appeal)   1991
Mustill (A Lord of Appeal)
   1992
Rix (LP)   1992
Prentice (LP)   1992
Rodgers of Quarry Bank (LP)
   1992
Wilson of Tillyorn (LP)
   1992
Slynn of Hadley (A Lord of
   Appeal)   1992
Wakeham (LP)   1992
Chalker of Wallasey (LP)
   1992
Rodger of Earlsferry (LP)
   1992
Thatcher (LP)   1992

Parkinson (LP)   1992
Healey (LP)   1992
Owen (LP)   1992
Howe of Aberavon (LP)
   1992
Lawson of Blaby (LP)   1992
Merlyn-Rees (LP)   1992
Moore of Lower Marsh (LP)
   1992
Tebbit (LP)   1992
Walker of Worcester (LP)
   1992
Archer of Sandwell (LP)
   1992
Ashley of Stoke (LP)   1992
Eatwell (LP)   1992
Weatherill (LP)   1992
Ewing of Kirkford (LP)
   1992
Geraint (LP)   1992
Stewartby (LP)   1992
Clark of Kempston (LP)
   1992
Plant of Highfield (LP)   1992
Archer of Weston-Super-Mare
   (LP)   1992
Jay of Paddington (LP)   1992
Williams of Mostyn (LP)
   1992
Cooke of Islandreagh (LP)
   1992
Barber of Tewkesbury (LP)
   1992
Hayhoe (LP)   1992
Gilmour of Craigmillar (LP)
   1992
Elis-Thomas (LP)   1992
Woolf (LP)   1992
Williams of Crosby (LP)
   1993
Kingsdown (LP)   1993
Dahrendorf (LP)   1993
Attenborough (LP)   1993
Lloyd of Berwick (LP)   1993
Haskel (LP)   1993
Dean of Harptree (LP)   1993
Gould of Potternewton (LP)
   1993
Dixon-Smith (LP)   1993
Dean of Thornton-le-Fylde
   (LP)   1993
Lester of Herne Hill (LP)
   1993
Miller of Hendon (LP)   1993
Tugendhat (LP)   1993
Nolan (LP)   1994

Wright of Richmond (LP)
1994
Nickson (LP)   1994
Quirk (LP)   1994
Sheppard of Didgemere (LP)
1994
Hambro (LP)   1994
Dubs (LP)   1994
Gladwin of Clee (LP)   1994
Farrington of Ribbleton (LP)
1994
Shaw of Northstead (LP)
1994
Nicholls of Birkenhead (A
Lord of Appeal)   1994
Tope (LP)   1994
Rawlings (LP)   1994
Thomas of Walliswood (LP)
1994
Kingsland (LP)   1994
Blaker (LP)   1994
Steyn (A Lord of Appeal)
1995
Hogg (LP)   1995
McConnell (LP)   1995
Smith of Gilmorehill (LP)
1995
Hoffmann (A Lord of Appeal)
1995
Hope of Craighead (A Lord of
Appeal)   1995
Blyth of Rowington (LP)
1995
Cuckney (LP)   1995
Eames (LP)   1995
Habgood (LP)   1995
Mackay of Drumadoon (LP)
1995
Winston (LP)   1995
Wallace of Saltaire (LP)   1995
McNally (LP)   1995
Borrie (LP)   1995
Hayman (LP)   1996
Sewel (LP)   1996
Harris of Peckham (LP)
1996
Pilkington of Oxenford (LP)
1996
Feldman (LP)   1996
Wilcox (LP)   1996
Bowness (LP)   1996
Taverne (LP)   1996
Kilpatrick of Kincraig (LP)
1996
Cooke of Thorndon (LP)
1996

Bingham of Cornhill (Lord
Chief Justice)   1996
Lloyd of Highbury (LP)
1996
Vincent of Coleshill (LP)
1996
Hussey of North Bradley (LP)
1996
Thomas of Gresford (LP)
1996
Clyde (A Lord of Appeal)
1996
Currie of Marylebone (LP)
1996
Taylor of Warwick (LP)
1996
Saatchi (LP)   1996
Symons of Vernham Dean
(LP)   1996
Alderdice (LP)   1996
Paul (LP)   1996
Ramsay of Cartvale (LP)
1996
Anelay of St Johns (LP)
1996
Byford (LP)   1996
Chadlington (LP)   1996
Rogers of Riverside (LP)
1996
MacLaurin of Knebworth (LP)
1996
Whitty (LP)   1996
Hutton (A Lord of Appeal)
1997
Bagri (LP)   1997
Emerton (LP)   1997
Lloyd-Webber (LP)   1997
Hoyle (LP)   1997
Falconer of Thoroton (LP)
1997
Simon of Highbury (LP)
1997
Gilbert (LP)   1997
Hardie (LP)   1997
Biffen (LP)   1997
Jopling (LP)   1997
Shore of Stepney (LP)   1997
Howell of Guildford (LP)
1997
Steel of Aikwood (LP)   1997
Dixon (LP)   1997
Renton of Mount Harry (LP)
1997
Evans of Parkside (LP)   1997
Molyneaux of Killead (LP)
1997

Lofthouse of Pontefract (LP)
1997
Kelvedon (LP)   1997
Alton of Liverpool (LP)
1997
Mayhew of Twysden (LP)
1997
Hurd of Westwell (LP)   1997
Baker of Dorking (LP)   1997
Patten (LP)   1997
Cowdrey of Tonbridge (LP)
1997
Inge (LP)   1997
Russell-Johnston (LP)   1997
Levene of Portsoken (LP)
1997
Saville of Newdigate (A Lord
of Appeal) 1997
Levy (LP)   1997
Knight of Collingtree (LP)
1997
Amos (LP)   1997
Hogg of Cumbernauld (LP)
1997
Newby (LP)   1997
Randall of St Budeaux (LP)
1997
Renwick of Clifton (LP)
1997
Walker of Doncaster (LP)
1997
Hardy of Wath (LP)   1997
Hughes of Woodside (LP)
1997
Selkirk of Douglas (LP)   1997
Lang of Monkton (LP)   1997
Ludford (LP)   1997
Fookes (LP)   1997
Davies of Coity (LP)   1997
Roberts of Conwy (LP)   1997
Sandberg (LP)   1997
Blackwell (LP)   1997
Sainsbury of Turville (LP)
1997
Davies of Oldham (LP)   1997
Gordon of Strathblane (LP)
1997
Cope of Berkeley (LP)   1997
Pitkeathley (LP)   1997
Morris of Manchester (LP)
1997
Jacobs (LP)   1997
Hunt of Kings Heath (LP)
1997
Hunt of Wirral (LP)   1997
Orme (LP)   1997

Burlison (LP)   1997
Razzall (LP)   1997
Garel-Jones (LP)   1997
Goodhart (LP)   1997
Brooke of Alverthorpe (LP)
    1997
Rendell of Babergh (LP)
    1997
Dholakia (LP)   1997
Janner of Braunstone (LP)
    1997
Islwyn (LP)   1997
Puttnam (LP)   1997
Kennedy of The Shaws (LP)
    1997
Naseby (LP)   1997
Higgins (LP)   1997
Stone of Blackheath (LP)
    1997
Freeman (LP)   1997
Maddock (LP)   1997
Scotland of Asthal (LP)   1997
Onslow of Woking (LP)
    1997
Newton of Braintree (LP)
    1997
Linklater of Butterstone (LP)
    1997
Bassam of Brighton (LP)
    1997
Nicholson of Winterbourne
    (LP)   1997
Young of Old Scone (LP)
    1997
Smith of Clifton (LP)   1997
Thomas of Macclesfield (LP)
    1997
Simpson of Dunkeld (LP)
    1997
Monro of Langholm (LP)
    1997
Watson of Invergowrie (LP)
    1997
Ryder of Wensum (LP)   1997
Hattersley (LP)   1997
Neill of Bladen (LP)   1997
Butler of Brockwell (LP)
    1998
Dearing (LP)   1998
Sheppard of Liverpool (LP)
    1998
Hamlyn (LP)   1998
Mackenzie of Framwellgate
    (LP)   1998
Clement-Jones (LP)   1998
Alli (LP)   1998

Uddin (LP)   1998
Marshall of Knightsbridge
    (LP)   1998
Burns (LP)   1998
Goudie (LP)   1998
Tomlinson (LP)   1998
Buscombe (LP)   1998
Thornton (LP)   1998
Lamont of Lerwick (LP)
    1998
Crawley (LP)   1998
Phillips of Sudbury (LP)
    1998
Haskins (LP)   1998
Laming (LP)   1998
Bach (LP)   1998
Miller of Chilthorne Domer
    (LP)   1998
Evans of Watford (LP)   1998
Warner (LP)   1998
Clarke of Hampstead (LP)
    1998
Christopher (LP)   1998
Brookman (LP)   1998
Hanningfield (LP)   1998
Bell (LP)   1998
Norton of Louth (LP)   1998
Sharp of Guildford (LP)
    1998
Richardson of Calow (LP)
    1998
Ahmed (LP)   1998
Sawyer (LP)   1998
Bragg (LP)   1998
Harris of Haringey (LP)
    1998
Hobhouse of Woodborough (A
    Lord of Appeal)   1998
Millett (A Lord of Appeal)
    1998
Macdonald of Tradeston (LP)
    1998
Phillips of Worth Matravers
    (A Lord of Appeal)   1999
Williamson of Horton (LP)
    1999
Imbert (LP)   1999
O'Neill of Bengarve (LP)
    1999
Patel (LP)   1999
Trotman (LP)   1999
Warwick of Undercliffe (LP)
    1999
Fellowes (LP)   1999
Stevenson of Coddenham (LP)
    1999

Stern (LP)   1999
Forsyth of Drumlean (LP)
    1999
Faulkner of Worcester (LP)
    1999
Prashar (LP)   1999
Hanham (LP)   1999
Laird (LP)   1999
Rogan (LP)   1999
Foster of Thames Bank (LP)
    1999
Elder (LP)   1999
Lea of Crondall (LP)   1999
Brett (LP)   1999
Rennard (LP)   1999
Howells of St Davids (LP)
    1999
Bradshaw (LP)   1999
King of West Bromwich (LP)
    1999
Watson of Richmond (LP)
    1999
Kirkham (LP)   1999
Grabiner (LP)   1999
Massey of Darwen (LP)
    1999
Carlile of Berriew (LP)   1999
Oxburgh (LP)   1999
Harrison (LP)   1999
Waldegrave of North Hill (LP)
    1999
Goldsmith (LP)   1999
Filkin (LP)   1999
Lipsey (LP)   1999
Wilkins (LP)   1999
Blood (LP)   1999
Barker (LP)   1999
Sharman (LP)   1999
Ashton of Upholland (LP)
    1999
McIntosh of Hudnall (LP)
    1999
Woolmer of Leeds (LP)
    1999
Gale (LP)   1999
Mackenzie of Culkein (LP)
    1999
Smith of Leigh (LP)   1999
Whitaker (LP)   1999
Gavron (LP)   1999
Harris of Richmond (LP)
    1999
Robertson of Port Ellen (LP)
    1999

Surnames of Peers and Peeresses

WHERE THEY DIFFER FROM THEIR TITLE

Multiple Surnames are indexed under the First Surname

Abney-Hastings. Loudoun, *C.*

Acheson. Gosford, *E.*

Adderley. Norton, *L.*

Addington. Sidmouth, *V.*

Agar. Normanton, *E.*

Aitken. Beaverbrook, *L.*

Akers-Douglas. Chilston, *V.*

Alexander. Alexander of Tunis, *E.*, Alexander of Weedon, *L.* and Caledon, *E.*

Allen. Allen of Abbeydale, *L.* and Croham, *L.*

Allenby. Allenby of Megiddo, *V.*

Allsopp. Hindlip, *L.*

Alton. Alton of Liverpool, *L.*

Anderson. Waverley, *V.*

Anelay. Anelay of St Johns, *B.*

Annesley. Valentia, *V.*

Anson. Lichfield, *E.*

Archer. Archer of Sandwell, *L.* and Archer of Weston-Super-Mare, *L.*

Armstrong. Armstrong of Ilminster, *L.*

Armstrong-Jones. Snowdon, *E.*

Arthur. Glenarthur, *L.*

Arundell. Talbot of Malahide, *L.*

Ashley. Ashley of Stoke, *L.*

Ashley-Cooper. Shaftesbury, *E.*

Ashton. Ashton of Hyde, *L.* and Ashton of Upholland, *B.*

Asquith. Oxford and Asquith, *E.*

Assheton. Clitheroe, *L.*

Astley. Hastings, *L.*

Astor. Astor of Hever, *L.*

Aubrey-Fletcher. Braye, *B.*

Bailey. Glanusk, *L.*

Baillie. Burton, *L.*

Baillie-Hamilton. Haddington, *E.*

Baker. Baker of Dorking, *L.*

Baldwin. Baldwin of Bewdley, *E.*

Balfour. Balfour of Inchrye, *L.*, Kinross, *L.* and Riverdale, *L.*

Bampfylde. Poltimore, *L.*

Banbury. Banbury of Southam, *L.*

Barber. Barber of Tewkesbury, *L.*

Baring. Ashburton, *L.*, Cromer, *E.*, Northbrook, *L.*, Revelstoke, *L.* and Howick of Glendale, *L.*

Barker. Trumpington, *B.*

Barnewall. Trimlestown, *L.*

Barnes. Gorell, *L.*

Bassam. Bassam of Brighton, *L.*

Bathurst. Bledisloe, *V.*

Beauclerk. Saint Albans, *D.*

Beaumont. Allendale, *V.* and Beaumont of Whitley, *L.*

Beckett. Grimthorpe, *L.*

Bellow. Bellwin, *L.*

Bennet. Tankerville, *E.*

Bentinck. Portland, *E.*

Beresford. Waterford, *M.* and Decies, *L.*

Berry. Kemsley, *V.* and Hartwell, *L.*

Bertie. Lindsey and Abingdon, *E.*

Best. Wynford, *L.*

Bethell. Westbury, *L.*

Bewicke-Copley. Cromwell, *L.*

Bigham. Mersey, *V.*

Bingham. Lucan, *E.* and Clanmorris, *L.*

Blackwood. Dufferin and Clandeboye, *L.*

Bligh. Darnley, *E.*

Blyth. Blyth of Rowington, *L.*

Bootle-Wilbraham. Skelmersdale, *L.*

Boscawen. Falmouth, *V.*

Boston. Boston of Faversham, *L.*

Bourke. Mayo, *E.*

Bowes Lyon. Strathmore and Kinghorne, *E.*

Bowyer. Denham, *L.*

Boyd. Kilmarnock, *L.*

Boyle. Cork and Orrery, *E.* Glasgow, *E.* and Shannon, *E.*

Brabazon. Meath, *E.*

Brand. Hampden, *V.*

Brassey. Brassey of Apethorpe, *L.*

Brett. Esher, *V.*

Bridge. Bridge of Harwich, *L.*

Bridgeman. Bradford, *E.*

Brodrick. Midleton, *V.*

Brooke. Alanbrooke, *V.*, Brookeborough, *V.*, Brooke of Ystradfellte, *B* and Brooke of Alverthorpe, *L.*

Brooks. Crawshaw, *L.* and Brooks of Tremorfa, *L.*

Brougham. Brougham and Vaux, *L.*

Broughton. Fairhaven, *L.*

Browne. Oranmore and Browne, *L.*, Sligo, *M.* and Kilmaine, *L.*

Bruce. Aberdare, *L.*, Balfour of Burleigh, *L.*, Elgin and Kincardine, *E.* and Bruce of Donington, *L.*

Brudenell-Bruce. Ailesbury, *M.*

Buchan. Tweedsmuir, *L.*

Buckley. Wrenbury, *L.*

Butler. Butler of Brockwell, *L.*, Dunboyne, *L.*, Carrick, *E.* and Mountgarret, *V.*

Buxton. Buxton of Alsa, *L.*

Byng. Strafford, *E.* and Torrington, *V.*

Callaghan. Callaghan of Cardiff, *L.*

Cameron. Cameron of Lochbroom, *L.*

Campbell. Argyll, *D.*, Cawdor, *E.*, Stratheden and Campbell, *L.*, Colgrain, *L.*, Campbell of Croy, *L.* and Campbell of Alloway, *L.*

Campbell-Gray. Gray, *L.*

Canning. Garvagh, *L.*

Capell. Essex, *E.*

Carington. Carrington, *L.*

Carlile. Carlile of Berriew, *L.*

Carlisle. Carlisle of Bucklow, *L.*

Carmichael. Carmichael of Kelvingrove, *L.*

Carnegie. Fife, *D.* and Northesk, *E.*

Carr. Carr of Hadley, *L.*

Cary. Falkland, *V.*

Castle. Castle of Blackburn, *B.*

Caulfeild. Charlemont, *V.*

Cavendish. Chesham, *L.*, Devonshire, *D.*, Waterpark, *L.* and Cavendish of Furness, *L.*

Cayzer. Rotherwick, *L.*

Cecil. Amherst of Hackney, *L.*, Rockley, *L.* and Exeter, *M.*

Chalker. Chalker of Wallasey, *B.*

Chaloner. Gisborough, *L.*

Channon. Kelvedon, *L.*

Chapman. Northfield, *L.*

Charteris. Wemyss and March, *E.* and Charteris of Amisfield, *L.*

Chetwynd-Talbot. Shrewsbury and Waterford, *E.*

Chichester. Donegall, *M.*

Chichester-Clark. Moyola, *L.*

Child Villiers. Jersey, *E.*

Cholmondeley. Delamere, *L.*

Chubb. Hayter, *L.*

Clark. Clark of Kempston, *L.*

Clarke. Clarke of Hampstead, *L.*

Clegg-Hill. Hill, *V.*

Clifford. Clifford of Chudleigh, *L.*

Cochrane. Cochrane of Cults, *L.* and Dundonald, *E.*

Cocks. Somers, *L.* and Cocks of Hartcliffe, *L.*

Cokayne. Cullen of Ashbourne, *L.*

Coke. Leicester, *E.*

Cole. Enniskillen, *E.*

Collier. Monkswell, *L.*

Colville. Colville of Culross, *V.* and Clydesmuir, *L.*

Compton. Northampton, *M.*

Conolly-Carew. Carew, *L.*

Constantine. Constantine of Stanmore, *L.*

Cooke. Cooke of Islandreagh, *L.*

Cooper. Norwich, *V.*

Cope. Cope of Berkeley, *L.*

Corbett. Rowallan, *L.*

Cornwall-Legh. Grey of Codnor, *L.*

Courtenay. Devon, *E.*

Cowdrey. Cowdrey of Tonbridge, *L.*

Cox. Kings Norton, *L.*

Craig. Craigavon, *V.* and Craig of Radley, *L.*

Crichton. Erne, *E.*

Crichton-Stuart. Bute, *M.*

Cripps. Parmoor, *L.*

Crossley. Somerleyton, *L.*

Cubitt. Ashcombe, *L.*

Cunliffe-Lister. Swinton, *E.* and Masham of Ilton, *B.*

Curzon. Howe, *E.* and Scarsdale, *V.*

Cust. Brownlow, *L.*

Dalrymple. Stair, *E.*

Daubeny de Moleyns. Ventry, *L.*

Davies. Darwen, *L.*, Davies of Coity, *L.* and Davies of Oldham, *L.*

Davison. Broughshane, *L.*

Dawnay. Downe, *V.*

Dawson-Damer. Portarlington, *E.*

Dean. Dean of Harptree, *L.* and Dean of Thornton-le-Fylde, *B.*

Deane. Muskerry, *L.*

de Courcy. Kingsale, *L.*

de Grey. Walsingham, *L.*

Delacourt-Smith. Delacourt-Smith of Alteryn, *B.*

Denison. Londesborough, *L.*

Denison-Pender. Pender, *L.*

Denton. Denton of Wakefield, *B.*

Devereux. Hereford, *V.*

Dewar. Forteviot, *L.*

de Yarburgh-Bateson.

Deramore, *L.*

Dixon. Glentoran, *L.*

Dodson. Monk Bretton, *L.*

Donaldson. Donaldson of Lymington, *L.*

Dormand. Dormand of Easington, *L.*

Douglas. Morton, *E.* and Queensberry, *M.*

Douglas-Hamilton. Hamilton and Brandon, *D.* and Selkirk of Douglas, *L.*

Douglas-Home. Dacre, *B.* and Home, *E.*

Douglas-Pennant. Penrhyn, *L.*

Douglas-Scott-Montagu. Montagu of Beaulieu, *L.*

Drummond. Perth, *E.* and Strange, *B.*

Dugdale. Crathorne, *L.*

Duke. Merrivale, *L.*

Duncombe. Feversham, *L.*

Dundas. Melville, *V.* and Zetland, *M.*

Eady. Swinfen, *L.*

Eccles. Eccles of Moulton, *B.*

Eden. Auckland, *L.*, Henley, *L.* and Eden of Winton, *L.*

Edgcumbe. Mount Edgcumbe, *E.*

Edmondson. Sandford, *L.*

Edwardes. Kensington, *L.*

Edwards. Crickhowell, *L.*

Egerton. Sutherland, *D.*

Eliot. St Germans, *E.*

Elliot-Murray-Kynynmound. Minto, *E.*

Elliott. Elliott of Morpeth, *L.*

Ellis. Seaford, *L.*

Erroll. Erroll of Hale, *L.*

Erskine. Buchan, *E.* and Mar and Kellie, *E.*

Erskine-Murray. Elibank, *L.*

Evans. Mountevans, *L.*, Evans of Parkside, *L.* and Evans of Watford, *L.*

Evans-Freke. Carbery, *L.*

Eve. Silsoe, *L.*

Ewing. Ewing of Kirkford, *L.*

Fairfax. Fairfax of Cameron, *L.*

Falconer. Falconer of
Thoroton, *L.*

Fane. Westmorland, *E.*

Fane Trefusis. Clinton, *L.*

Farrington. Farrington of
Ribbleton, *L.*

Faulkner. Faulkner of
Worcester, *L.*

Feilding. Denbigh and
Desmond, *E.*

Fellowes. De Ramsey, *L.*

Fermor-Hesketh. Hesketh, *L.*

Fiennes. Saye and Sele, *L.*

Fiennes-Clinton. Lincoln, *E.*

Finch Hatton. Winchilsea
and Nottingham, *E.*

Finch-Knightley.
Aylesford, *E.*

Fisher. Fisher of Rednal, *B.*

Fitzalan-Howard. Norfolk,
D. and Herries of Terregles,
Ly.

Fitz-Clarence. Munster, *E.*

FitzGerald. Leinster, *D.*

Fitzherbert. Stafford, *L.*

FitzRoy. Grafton, *D.* and
Southampton, *L.*

FitzRoy Newdegate.
Daventry, *V.*

Fletcher-Vane. Inglewood, *L.*

Flower. Ashbrook, *V.*

Foljambe. Liverpool, *E.*

Forbes. Granard, *E.*

Forsyth. Forsyth of
Drumlean, *L.*

Forwood. Arlington, *B.*

Foster. Foster of Thames
Bank, *L.*

Fox-Strangways.
Ilchester, *E.*

Frankland. Zouche of
Haryngworth, *L.*

Fraser. Lovat, *L.*,
Strathalmond, *L.*, Fraser of
Carmyllie, *L.*, and Saltoun
of Abernethy, *Ly.*

Freeman-Grenville.
Kinloss, *Ly.*

Fremantle. Cottesloe, *L.*

French. De Freyne, *L.*

Galbraith. Strathclyde, *L.*

Ganzoni. Belstead, *L.*

Gardner. Gardner of Parkes,
B.

Gascoyne-Cecil. Salisbury,
M. and Cranborne, *V.*

Gathorne-Hardy.
Cranbrook, *E.*

Gibbs. Aldenham, *L.* and
Wraxall, *L.*

Gibson. Ashbourne, *L.*

Giffard. Halsbury, *E.*

Gilbey. Vaux of Harrowden,
L.

Gilmour. Gilmour of
Craigmillar, *L.*

Gladwin. Gladwin of Clee,
L.

Glyn. Wolverton, *L.*

Godley. Kilbracken, *L.*

Goff. Goff of Chieveley, *L.*

Gordon. Aberdeen and
Temair, *M.*, Huntly, *M.* and
Gordon of Strathblane, *L.*

Gordon-Lennox.
Richmond, Lennox and
Gordon, *D.*

Gore. Arran, *E.*

Gould. Gould of
Potternewton, *B.*

Graham. Montrose, *D.* and
Graham of Edmonton, *L.*

Graham-Toler. Norbury, *E.*

Grant. Strathspey, *L.*

Gray. Gray of Contin, *L.*

Greaves. Dysart, *C.*

Greenall. Daresbury, *L.*

Greene. Greene of Harrow
Weald, *L.*

Greenhill. Greenhill of
Harrow, *L.*

Greville. Warwick, *E.*

Griffiths. Griffiths of
Fforestfach, *L.*

Grimston. Verulam, *E.* and
Grimston of Westbury, *L.*

Grosvenor. Westminster, *D.*
and Wilton, *E.*

Guest. Wimborne, *V.*

Gueterbock. Berkeley, *L.*

Guinness. Iveagh, *E.* and
Moyne, *L.*

Gully. Selby, *V.*

Gummer. Chadlington, *L.*

Gurdon. Cranworth, *L.*

Gwynne Jones. Chalfont, *L.*

Hamilton. Abercorn, *D.*,
Belhaven and Stenton, *L.*,
Dudley, *B.*, Hamilton of
Dalzell, *L.* and Holm
Patrick, *L.*

Hamilton-Russell. Boyne, *V.*

Hamilton-Smith. Colwyn,
L.

Hanbury-Tracy. Sudeley,
L.

Handcock. Castlemaine, *L.*

Harbord-Hamond.
Suffield, *L.*

Harding. Harding of
Petherton, *L.*

Hardinge. Hardinge of
Penshurst, *L.*

Hardy. Hardy of Wath, *L.*

Hare. Listowel, *E.* and
Blakenham, *V.*

Harmsworth. Rothermere, *V.*

Harris. Malmesbury, *E.*,
Harris of Greenwich, *L.*,
Harris of High Cross, *L.*
Harris of Haringey, *L.* and
Harris of Richmond, *B.*

Harvey. Harvey of Tasburgh,
L.

Hastings-Bass. Huntingdon,
E.

Hay. Erroll, *E.*, Tweeddale,
M. and Kinnoull, *E.*

Heathcote-Drummond-
Willoughby.
Willoughby de Eresby, *B.*

Hely-Hutchinson.
Donoughmore, *E.*

Henderson. Faringdon, *L.*
and Henderson of
Brompton, *L.*

Hennessy. Windlesham, *L.*

Henniker-Major. Henniker,
L.

Hepburne-Scott. Polwarth,
L.

Herbert. Carnarvon, *E.*,
Hemingford, *L.*, Pembroke
and Montgomery, *E* and
Powis, *E.*

Hervey. Bristol, *M.*

Hewitt. Lifford, *V.*

Hicks Beach. St. Aldwyn,
E.

Hill. Downshire, *M.* and
Sandys, *L.*

Hill-Trevor. Trevor, *L.*

Hilton. Hilton of Eggardon,
B.

Hobart-Hampden.
Buckinghamshire, *E.*

Hobhouse. Hobhouse of
Woodborough, *L.*

Hogg. Hailsham of St.
Marylebone, *L.* and Hogg of
Cumbernauld, *L.*
Holland-Hibbert.
Knutsford, *V.*
Hollis. Hollis of Heigham,
B.
Holme. Holme of
Cheltenham, *L.*
Holmes à Court.
Heytesbury, *L.*
Hood. Bridport, *V.*
Hope. Linlithgow, *M.*, Hope
of Craighead, *L.*,
Rankeillour, *L.* and
Glendevon, *L.*
Hope Johnstone. Annandale
and Hartfell, *E.*
Hope-Morley. Hollenden, *L.*
Hopkinson. Colyton, *L.*
Hore-Ruthven. Gowrie, *E.*
Hovell-Thurlow-Cumming-
Bruce. Thurlow, *L.*
Howard. Carlisle, *E.*,
Effingham, *E.*, Suffolk and
Berkshire, *E.*, Strathcona
and Mount Royal, *L.* and
Howard of Penrith, *L.*
Howe. Howe of Aberavon,
L.
Howell. Howell of
Guildford, *L.*
Howells. Geraint, *L.* and
Howells of St Davids, *B.*
Howie. Howie of Troon, *L.*
Hubbard. Addington, *L.*
Huggins. Malvern, *V.*
Hughes. Cledwyn of
Penrhos, *L.*, Hughes of
Woodside, *L.* and Islwyn, *L.*
Hughes-Young. St. Helens,
L.
Hunt. Hunt of Tanworth, *L.*
Hurd. Hurd of Westwell, *L.*
Hutchinson. Hutchinson of
Lullington, *L.*
Ingrams. Darcy de Knayth,
B.
Innes-Ker. Roxburghe, *D.*
Inskip. Caldecote, *V.*
Irby. Boston, *L.*
Irvine. Irvine of Lairg, *L.*
Isaacs. Reading, *M.*
James. James of Holland
Park, *B.* and Northbourne,
L.

Janner. Janner of
Braunstone, *L.*
Jauncey. Jauncey of
Tullichettle, *L.*
Jay. Jay of Paddington, *B.*
Jebb. Gladwyn, *L.*
Jenkin. Jenkin of Roding, *L.*
Jenkins. Jenkins of Putney,
L. and Jenkins of Hillhead,
L.
Jervis. St. Vincent, *V.*
Jocelyn. Roden, *E.*
Johnston. Johnston of
Rockport, *L.*
Jolliffe. Hylton, *L.*
Joynson-Hicks. Brentford, *V.*
Kay-Shuttleworth.
Shuttleworth, *L.*
Kearley. Devonport, *V.*
Keith. Keith of Castleacre,
L., Kintore, *E.* and Keith of
Kinkel, *L.*
Kemp. Rochdale, *V.*
Kennedy. Ailsa, *M.* and
Kennedy of The Shaws, *B.*
Kenworthy. Strabolgi, *L.*
Keppel. Albemarle, *E.*
Kerr. Lothian, *M.* and
Teviot, *L.*
King. Lovelace, *E.*, King of
Wartnaby, *L.* and King of
West Bromwich, *L.*
King-Tenison. Kingston, *E.*
Kirkham. Berners, *B.*
Kitchener. Kitchener of
Khartoum, *E.*
Knatchbull. Brabourne, *L.*
and Mountbatten of Burma,
C.
Knight. Knight of
Collingtree, *B.*
Knox. Ranfurly, *E.*
Laing. Laing of Dunphail,
L.
Lamb. Rochester, *L.*
Lambart. Cavan, *E.*
Lamont. Lamont of Lerwick,
L.
Lampson. Killearn, *L.*
Lane. Lane of Horsell, *L.*
Lang. Lang of Monkton, *L.*
Lascelles. Harewood, *E.*
Law. Ellenborough, *L.* and
Coleraine, *L.*
Lawrence. Trevethin and
Oaksey, *L.*

Lawson. Burnham, *L.* and
Lawson of Blaby, *L.*
Lawson Johnston. Luke, *L.*
Lea. Lea of Crondall, *L.*
Legge. Dartmouth, *E.*
Legh. Newton, *L.*
Leigh-Pemberton.
Kingsdown, *L.*
Leith. Burgh, *L.*
Lennox-Boyd. Boyd of
Merton, *V.*
Le Poer Trench. Clancarty,
E.
Leslie. Rothes, *E.*
Leslie Melville. Leven and
Melville, *E.*
Lester. Lester of Herne Hill,
L.
Lever. Leverhulme, *V.*
Leveson-Gower. Granville,
E.
Lewis. Lewis of Newnham,
L.
Liddell. Ravensworth, *L.*
Lindesay-Bethune.
Lindsay, *E.*
Lindsay. Crawford and
Balcarres, *E.* and Lindsay of
Birker, *L.*
Linklater. Linklater of
Butterstone, *B.*
Littleton. Hatherton, *L.*
Lloyd. Lloyd of Berwick, *L,*
Lloyd of Highbury, *B.*
Lloyd George.
Lloyd-George of Dwyfor,
*E.*Lloyd-George. Tenby,
V.
Lloyd-Mostyn. Mostyn, *L.*
Lloyd Webber. Lloyd-
Webber, *L.*
Loder. Wakehurst, *L.*
Lofthouse. Lofthouse of
Pontefract, *L.*
Lopes. Roborough, *L.*
Low. Aldington, *L.*
Lowry-Corry. Belmore, *E.*
Lowther. Lonsdale, *E.* and
Ullswater, *V.*
Lubbock. Avebury, *L.*
Lucas. Lucas of Chilworth,
L.
Lumley. Scarbrough, *E.*
Lumley-Savile. Savile, *L.*
Lyon-Dalberg-Acton.
Acton, *L.*

Lysaght. Lisle, *L.*

Lyttelton. Cobham, *V.* and Chandos, *V.*

Lytton Cobbold. Cobbold, *L.*

McAlpine. McAlpine of West Green, *L.*

Macaulay. Macaulay of Bragar, *L.*

McClintock-Bunbury. Rathdonnell, *L.*

McColl. McColl of Dulwich, *L.*

Macdonald. Macdonald of Gwaenysgor, *L.* and Macdonald of Tradeston, *L.*

McDonnell. Antrim, *E.*

McDowell. Dean of Thornton-le-Fylde, *B.*

Macfarlane. Macfarlane of Bearsden, *L.*

McFarlane. McFarlane of Llandaff, *B.*

McIntosh. McIntosh of Haringey, *L.* and McIntosh of Hudnall, *B.*

Mackay. Inchcape, *E.*, Reay, *L.*, Tanlaw, *L.*, and Mackay of Clashfern, *L.* and Mackay of Drumadoon, *I.*

MacKay. MacKay of Ardbrecknish, *L.*

Mackenzie. Cromartie, *E.* and Mackenzie of Framwellgate, *L.*

MacKenzie. MacKenzie of Culkein, *L.*

Mackenzie Stuart. Mackenzie-Stuart, *L.*

Mackie. Mackie of Benshie, *L.*

Mackintosh. Mackintosh of Halifax, *V.*

McLaren. Aberconway, *L.*

MacLaurin. MacLaurin of Knebworth, *L.*

MacLehose. MacLehose of Beoch, *L.*

Macmillan. Stockton, *E.*

Macpherson. Strathcarron, *L.* and Macpherson of Drumochter, *L.*

Maffey. Rugby, *L.*

Maitland. Lauderdale, *E.*

Maitland Biddulph. Biddulph *L.*

Makgill. Oxfuird, *V.*

Makins. Sherfield, *L.*

Manners. Rutland, *D.*

Manningham-Buller. Dilhorne, *V.*

Mansfield. Sandhurst, *L.*

Marks. Marks of Broughton, *L.*

Marquis. Woolton, *E.*

Marshall. Marshall of Knightsbridge, *L.*

Marsham. Romney, *E.*

Martyn-Hemphill. Hemphill, *L.*

Mason. Mason of Barnsley, *L.*

Massey. Massey of Darwen, *B.*

Maude. Hawarden, *V.*

Maxwell. De Ros, *L.* and Farnham, *L.*

Mayhew. Mayhew of Twysden, *L.*

Meade. Clanwilliam, *E.*

Millar. Inchyra, *L.*

Miller. Miller of Hendon, *B.* and Miller of Chilthorne Domer, *B.*

Milner. Milner of Leeds, *L.*

Mitchell-Thomson. Selsdon, *L.*

Mitford. Redesdale, *L.*

Molyneaux. Molyneaux of Killead, *L.*

Monckton. Monckton of Brenchley, *V.*

Monckton-Arundell. Galway, *V.*

Mond. Melchett, *L.*

Money-Coutts. Latymer, *L.*

Monro. Monro of Langholm, *L.*

Montagu. Manchester, *D.* Sandwich, *E.* and Swaythling, *L.*

Montagu Douglas Scott. Buccleuch and Queensberry, *D.*

Montagu-Stuart-Wortley. Wharncliffe, *E.*

Montague. Amwell, *L.*

Montgomerie. Eglinton and Winton, *E.*

Montgomery. Montgomery of Alamein, *V.*

Moore. Drogheda, *E.*, Moore of Wolvercote, *L.* and Moore of Lower Marsh, *L.*

Moore-Brabazon. Brabazon of Tara, *L.*

Moreton. Ducie, *E.*

Morris. Killanin, *L.*, Morris of Kenwood, *L.*, Morris of Castle Morris, *L.*, Morris of Manchester, *L.* and Naseby, *L.*

Morrison. Dunrossil, *V.* and Margadale, *L.*

Mosley. Ravensdale, *L.*

Mountbatten. Edinburgh, *D.* and Milford Haven, *M.*

Muff. Calverley, *L.*

Mulholland. Dunleath, *L.*

Murray. Atholl, *D.*, Dunmore, *E.*, Mansfield, *E.* and Murray of Epping Forest, *L.*

Murton. Murton of Lindisfarne, *L.*

Nall-Cain. Brocket, *L.*

Napier. Napier and Ettrick, *L.* and Napier of Magdala, *L.*

Needham. Kilmorey, *E.*

Neill. Neill of Bladen, *L.*

Nelson. Nelson of Stafford, *L.*

Nevill. Abergavenny, *M.*

Neville. Braybrooke, *L.*

Newton. Newton of Braintree, *L.*

Nicholls. Nicholls of Birkenhead, *L.*

Nicholson. Nicholson of Winterbourne, *B.*

Nicolson. Carnock, *L.*

Nivison. Glendyne, *L.*

Noel. Gainsborough, *E.*

North. Guilford, *E.*

Northcote. Iddesleigh, *E.*

Norton. Grantley, *L.*, Rathcreedan, *L.* and Norton of Louth *L.*

Nugent. Westmeath, *E.*

O'Brien. Inchiquin, *E.*

Ogilvie-Grant. Seafield, *E.*

Ogilvy. Airlie, *E.*

Oliver. Oliver of Aylmerton, *L.*

O'Neill. Rathcavan, *L.* and O'Neill of Bengarve, *B.*

Onslow. Onslow of Woking, *L.*

Orde-Powlett. Bolton, *L.*

Ormsby-Gore. Harlech, *L.*

Page. Whaddon, *L.*

Paget. Anglesey, *M.*

Pakenham. Longford, *E.*

Pakington. Hampton, *L.*

Palmer. Selborne, *E.* and Lucas of Crudwell, *L.*

Park. Park of Monmouth, *B.*

Parker. Macclesfield, *E.* and Morley, *E.*

Parnell. Congleton, *L.*

Parsons. Rosse, *E.*

Paulet. Winchester, *M.*

Peake. Ingleby, *V.*

Pearson. Cowdray, *V.* and Pearson of Rannoch, *L.*

Pease. Gainford, *L.* and Wardington, *L.*

Pelham. Chichester, *E.* and Yarborough, *E.*

Pellew. Exmouth, *V.*

Penny. Marchwood, *V.*

Pepys. Cottenham, *E.*

Perceval. Egmont, *E.*

Percy. Northumberland, *D.*

Perry. Perry of Southwark, *B.* and Perry of Walton, *L.*

Pery. Limerick, *E.*

Petty-Fitzmaurice. Lansdowne, *M.*

Peyton. Peyton of Yeovil, *L.*

Philipps. St. Davids, *V.* and Milford, *L.*

Phillips. Phillips of Sudbury, *L.*

Phipps. Normanby, *M.*

Plant. Plant of Highfield, *L.*

Platt. Platt of Writtle, *B.*

Pleydell-Bouverie. Radnor, *E.*

Plummer. Plummer of St Marylebone, *L.*

Plumptre. FitzWalter, *L.*

Plunkett. Dunsany, *L.* and Louth, *L.*

Pollock. Hanworth, *V.*

Pomeroy. Harberton, *V.*

Ponsonby. Bessborough, *E.*, De Mauley, *L.* Ponsonby of Shulbrede, *L.* and Sysonby, *L.*

Porter. Porter of Luddenham, *L.*

Powys. Lilford, *L.*

Pratt. Camden, *M.*

Preston. Gormanston, *V.*

Primrose. Rosebery, *E.*

Prittie. Dunalley, *L.*

Prout. Kingsland, *L.*

Ramsay. Dalhousie, *E.* and Ramsay of Cartvale, *B.*

Ramsbotham. Soulbury, *V.*

Randall. Randall of St Budeaux, *L.*

Rawlinson. Rawlinson of Ewell, *L.*

Rees-Williams. Ogmore, *L.*

Rendell. Rendell of Babergh, *B.*

Renfrew. Renfrew of Kaimsthorn, *L.*

Renton. Renton of Mount Harry, *L.*

Renwick. Renwick of Clifton, *L.*

Rhys. Dynevor, *L.*

Richards. Milverton, *L.*

Richardson. Richardson of Duntisbourne, *L.* and Richardson of Calow, *B.*

Ritchie. Ritchie of Dundee, *L.*

Robens. Robens of Woldingham, *L.*

Roberts. Clwyd, *L.* and Roberts of Conwy, *L.*

Robertson. Robertson of Oakridge, *L.*, Robertson of Port Ellen, *L.* and Wharton, *B.*

Robinson. Martonmere, *L.*

Roche. Fermoy, *L.*

Rodd. Rennell, *L.*

Rodger. Rodger of Earlsferry, *L.*

Rodgers. Rodgers of Quarry Bank, *L.*

Rogers. Rogers of Riverside, *L.*

Roll. Roll of Ipsden, *L.*

Roper-Curzon. Teynham, *L.*

Rospigliosi. Newburgh, *E.*

Rous. Stradbroke, *E.*

Rowley-Conwy. Langford, *L.*

Royle. Fanshawe of Richmond, *L.*

Runciman. Runciman of Doxford, *V.*

Russell. Ampthill, *L.*, Bedford, *D.*, De Clifford, *L.* and Russell of Liverpool, *L.*

Ryder. Harrowby, *E.*, Ryder of Eaton Hastings, *L.*, Ryder of Warsaw, *B.* and Ryder of Wensum, *L.*

Sackville. De La Warr, *E.*

Sackville-West. Sackville, *L.*

Sainsbury. Sainsbury of Preston Candover, *L.* and Sainsbury of Turville, *L.*

St Aubyn. Saint Levan, *L.*

St Clair. Sinclair, *L.*

St Clair-Erskine. Rosslyn, *E.*

St John. Bolingbroke and St. John, *V.*, Orkney, *E.* and St. John of Bletso, *L.*

St John Stevas. St. John of Fawsley, *L.*

St Leger. Doneraile, *V.*

Samuel. Bearsted, *V.*

Sanderson. Sanderson of Bowden, *L.*

Sandilands. Torphichen, *L.*

Saumarez. De Saumarez, *L.*

Savile. Mexborough, *E.*

Scarlett. Abinger, *L.*

Schreiber. Marlesford, *L.*

Sclater-Booth. Basing, *L.*

Scotland. Scotland of Asthal, *B.*

Scott. Eldon, *E.*

Scrymgeour. Dundee, *E.*

Seager. Leighton of Saint Mellons, *L.*

Seely. Mottistone, *L.*

Sefton. Sefton of Garston, *L.*

Seymour. Somerset, *D.* and Hertford, *M.*

Sharp. Sharp of Guildford, *B.*

Shaw. Craigmyle, *L.* and Shaw of Northstead, *L.*

Sheppard. Sheppard of Didgemere, *L.* and Sheppard of Liverpool, *L.*

Shirley. Ferrers, *E.*

Shore. Shore of Stepney, *L.*

Short. Glenamara, *L.*

Siddeley. Kenilworth, *L.*

Sidney. De L'Isle, *V.*

Sieff. Sieff of Brimpton, *L.*

Simon. Simon of Wythenshawe, *L.*, Simon of Glaisdale, *L.* and Simon of Highbury, *L.*

Simpson. Simpson of Dunkeld, *L.*

Sinclair. Caithness, *E.*, Thurso, *V.* and Sinclair of Cleeve, *L.*

Skeffington. Massereene and Ferrard, *V.*

Slynn. Slynn of Hadley, *L.*

Smith. Hambleden, *V.*, Bicester, *L.* Kirkhill, *L.*, Smith of Gilmorehill, *B.*, Smith of Clifton, *L.* and Smith of Leigh, *L.*

Somerset. Beaufort, *D.* and Raglan, *L.*

Soulsby. Soulsby of Swaffham Prior, *L.*

Spencer. Churchill, *V.*

Spencer-Churchill. Marlborough, *D.*

Spring Rice. Monteagle of Brandon, *L.*

Stanhope. Harrington, *E.*

Stanley. Derby, *E.* and Stanley of Alderley, *L.*

Stapleton-Cotton. Combermere, *V.*

Steel. Steel of Aikwood, *L.*

Sterling. Sterling of Plaistow, *L.*

Stevens. Stevens of Ludgate, *L.*

Stevenson. Stevenson of Coddenham, *L.*

Stewart. Galloway, *E.* and Stewartby, *L.*

Stodart. Stodart of Leaston, *L.*

Stoddart. Stoddart of Swindon, *L.*

Stone. Stone of Blackheath, *L.*

Stonor. Camoys, *L.*

Stopford. Courtown, *E.*

Stourton. Mowbray and Stourton, *L.*

Strachey. O'Hagan, *L.*

Strutt. Belper, *L.* and Rayleigh, *L.*

Stuart. Castle Stewart, *E.* Moray, *E.* and Stuart of Findhorn, *V.*

Suenson-Taylor. Grantchester, *L.*

Taylor. Taylor of Blackburn, *L.*, Ingrow, *L.*, Taylor of Gryfe, *L.* and Taylor of Warwick, *L.*

Taylour. Headfort, *M.*

Temple-Gore-Langton. Temple of Stowe, *E.*

Tennant. Glenconner, *L.*

Thellusson. Rendlesham, *L.*

Thesiger. Chelmsford, *V.*

Thomas. Thomas of Macclesfield, *L.*, Thomas of Swynnerton, *L.*, Thomas of Gwydir, *L.* and Thomas of Walliswood, *B.*

Thomson. Thomson of Fleet, *L.* and Thomson of Monifieth, *L.*

Thynn. Bath, *M.*

Tottenham. Ely, *M.*

Trench. Ashtown, *L.*

Trevor-Roper. Dacre of Glanton, *L.*

Tufton. Hothfield, *L.*

Turner. Netherthorpe, *L.* and Turner of Camden, *B.*

Turnour. Winterton, *E.*

Tyrell-Kenyon. Kenyon, *L.*

Vanden-Bempde-Johnstone. Derwent, *L.*

Vane. Barnard, *L.*

Vane-Tempest-Stewart. Londonderry, *M.*

Vanneck. Huntingfield, *L.*

Vaughan. Lisburne, *E.*

Venables-Vernon. Vernon, *L.*

Vereker. Gort, *V.*

Verney. Willoughby de Broke, *L.*

Vernon. Lyveden, *L.*

Vesey. De Vesci, *V.*

Villiers. Clarendon, *E.*

Vivian. Swansea, *L.*

Wade. Wade of Chorlton, *L.*

Waldegrave. Waldegrave of North Hill, *L.*

Walker. Walker of Doncaster, *L.* and Walker of Worcester, *L.*

Wallace. Wallace of Coslany, *L.* and Wallace of Saltaire, *L.*

Wallop. Portsmouth, *E.*

Walton. Walton of Detchant, *L.*

Ward. Dudley, *E.* and Bangor, *V.*

Warrender. Bruntisfield, *L.*

Warwick. Warwick of Undercliffe, *B.*

Watson. Manton, *L.*, Watson of Invergowrie, *L.* and Watson of Richmond, *L.*

Wedderburn. Wedderburn of Charlton, *L.*

Weir. Inverforth, *L.*

Weld-Forester. Forester, *L.*

Wellesley. Cowley, *E.* and Wellington, *D.*

Westenra. Rossmore, *L.*

White. Annaly, *L.* and Hanningfield *L.*

Whiteley. Marchamley, *L.*

Whitfield. Kenswood, *L.*

Williams. Williams of Elvel, *L.* Williams of Mostyn, *L.* and Williams of Crosby, *B.*

Williamson. Forres, *L.*

Willoughby. Middleton, *L.*

Wills. Dulverton, *L.*

Wilson. Moran, *L.*, Nunburnholme, *L.* and Wilson of Tillyorn, *L.*

Windsor-Clive. Plymouth, *E.*

Wingfield. Powerscourt, *V.*

Winn. Saint Oswald, *L.*

Wodehouse. Kimberley, *E.*

Wolfson. Wolfson of Sunningdale, *L.*

Wood. Halifax, *E.* and Holderness, *L.*

Woodhouse. Terrington, *L.*

Woolmer. Woolmer of Leeds, *L.*

Wright. Wright of Richmond, *L.*

Wyndham. Egremont, *L.*

Wyndham-Quin. Dunraven and Mount-Earl, *E.*

Wynn. Newborough, *L.*

Yarde-Buller. Churston, *L.*

Yerburgh. Alvingham, *L.*

Yorke. Hardwicke, *E.*

Young. Kennet, *L.*, Young of Dartington, *L.*, Young of Graffham, *L.* and Young of Old Scone, *B.*

Younger. Younger of Leckie, *V.*

Addressing Letters to Persons of Title

Formal modes of address become less formal every year but there are occasions when a person may want to address someone with strict formality. The first form of address given is that which should always be used on the envelope, the second is the formal salutation and conclusion and the third is the less formal salutation and conclusion. Each is detailed respectively as (1), (2) and (3).

The following points should be noted:–
  1. The honorific prefix 'The Right Honourable' is not now generally used for Peers other than Privy Counsellors.
  2. The courtesy titles Honourable, Lady and Lord to which sons and daughters of Peers (depending on the rank of their father) are not prefixed by the definite article. These are the practices adopted by the Earl Marshal's Office and that of the Lord Chamberlain of the Household and consequently have been followed here.
  3. In the formal mode of address the conclusion '...... Obedient Servant' has been used. This is a matter of choice as it can be 'humble and obedient servant' or simply 'I am, Sir (my Lord or whatever) Yours faithfully'.
  4. In all appropriate cases the use of the masculine can be interpreted as including the feminine.

AMBASSADOR—(1) His Excellency Mr., Dr., etc. as appropriate, (Esquire is never used), Ambassador of the Italian Republic, (the name of the Country in full i.e. not The Italian Ambassador). (2) Your Excellency, conclude I am Your Excellency's Obedient Servant. (3) Dear Mr Ambassador, conclude Yours sincerely. A list of Ambassadors is given towards the end of the book. In conversation an Ambassador is addressed as 'Your Excellency', but once is sufficient, thereafter 'Sir' is normal.

AMBASSADOR'S WIFE—(1) As an ordinary married woman. She is not 'Your Excellency' nor 'Ambassadress'.

ARCHBISHOP—(1) The Most Rev. The Lord Archbishop of York. Or, The Most Rev. John Smith, Lord Archbishop of York. (2) Your Grace or My Lord Archbishop, conclude I am Your Grace's Obedient Servant. (3) Dear Archbishop, conclude Yours sincerely. Note: The Archbishops of Canterbury and York are Privy Counsellors and are therefore addressed as The Most Reverend and Right Honourable.

ARCHBISHOP'S WIFE—(1) As an ordinary married woman. She derives no precedence from her husband.

ARCHDEACON—(1) The Venerable John Smith, Archdeacon of Branchester. (2) Dear Sir or Reverend Sir, conclude Yours faithfully. (3) Dear Mr Archdeacon or Dear Archdeacon, conclude Yours sincerely.

BARON—(1) The Lord Barton. (2) My Lord, conclude I am, My Lord, Your Obedient Servant. (3) Dear Lord Barton, conclude Yours sincerely.

BARON'S DAUGHTER—(1) Hon. Mary Smith or, if married, Hon. Mrs Jones. (2) Dear Madam, conclude Yours faithfully. (3) Dear Miss Smith (or Mrs Jones if married), conclude Yours sincerely.

BARON'S SON—(1) Hon. James Smith. (2) Dear Sir, conclude Yours faithfully. (3) Dear Mr Smith, conclude Yours sincerely.

BARON'S SON'S WIFE—(1) Hon. Mrs John Smith. (2) Dear Madam, conclude Yours faithfully. (3) Dear Mrs Smith, conclude Yours sincerely.

BARON'S WIFE OR BARONESS IN HER OWN RIGHT—(1) The Lady Barton or, in the case of Baronesses in their own right, most prefer to be styled The Baroness Barton (see biographies of Members of the House of Lords). (2) Dear Madam, conclude Yours faithfully. (3) Dear Lady Barton or Dear Baroness Barton, conclude Yours sincerely.

BARONETS—(1) Sir John Smith, Bt. (the abbreviation Bart. is not much used today but is not incorrect). (2) Dear Sir, conclude Yours faithfully. (3) Dear Sir John, conclude Yours sincerely.

BARONET'S WIFE—(1) Lady Smith. (2) Dear Madam, conclude Yours faithfully. (3) Dear Lady Smith, conclude Yours sincerely.

BISHOP—(1) The Right Reverend The Lord Bishop of Buxton. Or, The Right Reverend John Smith, Lord Bishop of Buxton. (2) My Lord Bishop, conclude I am, My Lord, Your Obedient Servant. (3) Dear Lord Bishop, Dear Bishop or Dear Bishop of Buxton, conclude Yours sincerely. Note: Bishops suffragan are addressed by courtesy in the same way as diocesan bishops.

BISHOP'S WIFE—(1) As an Archbishop's wife.

COUNTESS—(1) The Countess of Poole. (2) Dear Madam, conclude Yours faithfully. (3) Dear Lady Poole, conclude Yours sincerely.

DAME—(1) Dame Mary Smith, followed by appropriate post-nominal letters (e.g. D.B.E.). (2) Dear Madam, conclude Yours faithfully. (3) Dear Dame Mary, conclude Yours sincerely.

DEAN—(1) The Very Reverend The Dean of Coventry, or The Very Reverend John Smith, Dean of Coventry. (2) Dear Sir or Reverend Sir, conclude Yours faithfully. (3) Dear Mr Dean, or Dear Dean, conclude Yours sincerely.

DUCHESS—(1) Her Grace The Duchess of Avon. (2) Your Grace, conclude I am, Your Grace's Obedient Servant. (3) Dear Duchess of Avon, conclude Yours sincerely.

DUKE—(1) His Grace The Duke of Avon. (2) Your Grace, or My Lord Duke, conclude I am, Your Grace's Obedient Servant. (3) Dear Duke of Avon, conclude Yours sincerely.

DUKE'S DAUGHTER—(1) Lady Mary Smith, or her husband's name if a commoner, (e.g. Lady Mary Jones). (2) Dear Madam, conclude Yours faithfully. (3) Dear Lady Mary, conclude Yours sincerely.

DUKE'S ELDEST SON—(1) The eldest sons of a Duke, Marquess and Earl, take a subsidiary title of their father's by courtesy and they, their wives and children are addressed in the same way as if such titles were substantive but the definite article is not used before the title. Thus, the Duke of Norfolk's eldest son is known as Earl of Arundel and Surrey, not The Earl etc. For titles used by eldest sons see biographies of Members of the House of Lords.

DUKE'S YOUNGER SON—(1) Lord William Smith. (2) Dear Sir, conclude Yours faithfully. (3) Dear Lord William, conclude Yours sincerely.

DUKE'S YOUNGER SON'S WIFE—(1) Lady William Smith. (2) Dear Madam, conclude Yours faithfully. (3) Dear Lady William, conclude Yours sincerely.

EARL—(1) The Earl of Hethe. (2) My Lord, conclude I am my Lord Your Obedient Servant. (3) Dear Lord Hethe, conclude Yours sincerely.

EARL'S DAUGHTER—As a Duke's Daughter.

EARL'S ELDEST SON—As a Duke's eldest son.

EARL'S YOUNGER SON—As a Baron's younger son.

EARL'S YOUNGER SON'S WIFE—As a Baron's younger son's wife.

GOVERNORS GENERAL, GOVERNORS AND LIEUTENANT GOVERNORS—As for Ambassadors but followed by description of office, such as Governor General and Commander-in-Chief of New Zealand. (3) Dear Governor General, Governor or Lieutenant-Governor, conclude Yours sincerely. The Lieutenant-Governors of Guernsey, Jersey and the Isle of Man enjoy this style. The Governor General of Canada has the style 'The Right Honourable' for life and a Lieutenant-Governor of a Canadian Province is 'His Honour' for life.

GOVERNOR GENERAL'S WIFE—She is accorded the style of 'Your Excellency' but the wife of a Governor or Lieutenant-Governor is addressed as an ordinary married woman.

HIGH COMMISSIONER—As an Ambassador, except for 'Ambassador' or 'Mr Ambassador' read 'High Commissioner'.

HIGH COMMISSIONER'S WIFE—As an Ambassador's wife.

JUDGE (LORD JUSTICE OF APPEAL)—(1) The Right Honourable Sir John Smith, as he is invariably a Privy Counsellor and a Knight, or the Right Honourable Lord Justice Smith. (2) My Lord, conclude I am My Lord, Your Obedient Servant. (3) Dear Sir John, conclude Yours sincerely.

JUDGE (JUSTICE OF THE HIGH COURT)—(1) The Honourable Sir John Smith, as he is invariably a Knight, or The Honourable Mr Justice Smith. (2) and (3) as for a Lord Justice of Appeal.

JUDGE (CIRCUIT JUDGE)—(1) His Honour Judge Smith. (2) Your Honour, conclude I have the honour to be Your Honour's Obedient Servant. (3) Dear Sir (or Judge Smith), conclude Yours sincerely.

JUDGE (WOMEN JUDGES)—(1) The Right Honourable Dame Ann Smith, D.B.E. (if a Lord of Appeal), The Honourable Dame Anne Smith, D.B.E. (if a High Court Judge). (2) and (3) as for a male Judge with suitable gender changes.

KNIGHT—(1) Sir John Smith, if a Knight Bachelor there is no post-nominal addition in this respect (Kt., K. Bach., or K.T. is quite wrong) but if a Knight or Knight Grand Cross or Grand Commander of an Order of Chivalry the appropriate post-nominal letters should be added. A Knight may be so addressed when his knighthood is announced, there is now no need to wait for the accolade to have been conferred. (2) Dear Sir, conclude Yours faithfully. (3) Dear Sir John, conclude Yours sincerely.

KNIGHT'S WIFE—(1) Lady Smith. (2) Dear Madam, conclude Yours faithfully. (3) Dear Lady Smith, conclude Yours sincerely.

LORD LIEUTENANT—(1) The normal form of address, followed by, for courtesy, H.M.'s Lord Lieutenant for the County of Newshire. (2) My Lord Lieutenant, conclude I have the honour to be my Lord Lieutenant, Your Obedient Servant. (3) Dear Lord (Sir John or Mr. as appropriate), conclude Yours sincerely.

LORD MAYOR—(1) The Right Worshipful the Lord Mayor of Graytown (even if a woman) but the Lord Mayors of London, York, Belfast and Cardiff have by tradition, or by grant of a privilege from the Crown, been accorded the additional style of Right Honourable. (2) My Lord Mayor, conclude I have the honour to be My Lord Mayor, Your Obedient Servant. (3) Dear Lord Mayor, conclude Yours sincerely.

LORD OF SESSION IN SCOTLAND—(1) The Honourable (or Right Honourable if a Privy

Counsellor), Lord Glentie. (2) My Lord, conclude I have the honour to be My Lord, Your Obedient Servant. (3) Dear Lord Glentie, conclude Yours sincerely. Note: The wife of a Lord of Session is styled as the wife of a Baron but her children have no courtesy titles. The Lord Justice General or Lord Justice Clerk is usually so addressed in correspondence, rather than by his juridical title.

MARCHIONESS—(1) The Most Honourable The Marchioness of Formby. (2) My Lady, conclude I have the honour to be my Lady, Your Obedient Servant. (3) Dear Lady Formby, conclude Yours sincerely.

MARQUESS—(1) The Most Honourable the Marquess of Formby. (2) My Lord (or my Lord Marquess), conclude I have the honour to be, my Lord, Your Obedient Servant. (3) Dear Lord Formby, conclude Yours sincerely. Note: Some Marquesses, mostly Scottish, spell the title 'Marquis', see biographies of Members of the House of Lords.

MARQUESS'S DAUGHTER—As a Duke's daughter.

MARQUESS'S ELDEST SON—As a Duke's eldest son.

MARQUESS'S YOUNGER SON—As a Duke's younger son.

MARQUESS'S YOUNGER SON'S WIFE—As a Duke's younger son's wife.

MAYOR—(1) The Right Worshipful the Mayor of Cromby, (if the Mayor of a City) or otherwise the Worshipful the Mayor of Drydale. A woman Mayor or Lord Mayor is so addressed, her consort being the Mayoress or Lady Mayoress. (2) Your Worship, conclude I have the honour to be Your Worship's Obedient Servant. (3) Dear Mr Mayor, conclude Yours sincerely.

MEMBER OF PARLIAMENT—(1) Address according to rank with the addition of the letters M.P. after the name. Privy Counsellors have the prefix 'The Right Honourable'. Letters to Ministers may start Dear Minister or, in the case of the Prime Minister Dear Prime Minister. Members of the Scottish Parliament should have the letters M.S.P. added after their name, e.g. Angus Fraser Esq., M.S.P. Members of the Welsh Assembly should have A.M. added, e.g. Hugh Jones Esq., A.M.

PREBENDARY—(1) The Reverend Prebendary John Smith. (2) Dear Sir, or Reverend Sir, conclude Yours faithfully. (3) Dear Prebendary, conclude Yours sincerely.

PRIME MINISTER—see Member of Parliament, also Privy Counsellor.

PRINCE—(1) H.R.H. The Prince Henry of Wales or, if a Duke, H.R.H. The Duke of Kent; the children of the Sovereign use the definite article before Prince (e.g. The Prince Edward). (2) Your Royal Highness or Sir, conclude I have the honour

to be Your Royal Highness's Obedient Servant. In conversation address as Your Royal Highness but once is sufficient, thereafter Sir is normal.

PRINCESS—(1) H.R.H. Princess Beatrice of York, or, if the wife of a Royal Duke, H.R.H. The Duchess of Kent; a daughter of the Sovereign uses the definite article before Princess (e.g. The Princess Margaret, Countess of Snowdon). (2) Your Royal Highness or Madam, conclude I have the honour to be Your Royal Highness's Obedient Servant. In conversation address as Your Royal Highness but once is sufficient, thereafter Ma'am (pronounced so as to rhyme with lamb) is normal.

PRINCE'S WIFE—As a Princess by birth (*q.v.*).

PRIVY COUNSELLOR—(1) The Right Honourable prefixes the name and style except in respect of Marquesses and Dukes when the letters P.C. are placed after the name. The letters follow those indicating membership of Orders of Chivalry. (2) Address according to rank. (See also Member of Parliament).

PRIVY COUNSELLOR'S WIFE—As an ordinary married woman. She derives no precedence from her husband.

QUEEN—(1) Her Majesty the Queen, although letters are usually addressed to The Private Secretary to Her Majesty the Queen. (2) Your Majesty or 'May it please your Majesty', conclude I have the honour to be Your Majesty's Obedient Subject. (3) Madam, conclude With my humble duty to Your Majesty. In conversation address as Your Majesty at first thereafter as Ma'am (see Princess).

SCOTTISH MEMBER OF PARLIAMENT—See Member of Parliament.

VISCOUNT—(1) The Viscount Totnes. (2) and (3) as for a Baron. Note: Viscounts in the Peerage of Scotland have the word 'of' in their titles (e.g. The Viscount of Falkland).

VISCOUNT'S WIFE—(1) The Viscountess Totnes (or of Totnes if appropriate). (2) and (3) as for a Baron (*q.v.*).

VISCOUNT'S DAUGHTER—As for a Baron's daughter (*q.v.*).

VISCOUNT'S SON—As for a Baron's son (*q.v.*).

VISCOUNT'S SON'S WIFE—As for a Baron's son's wife (*q.v.*).

WALES, MEMBER OF NATIONAL ASSEMBLY—See Member of Parliament.

WIDOWS—The widows of Peers and Baronets use either their christian name before their title (e.g. Jane, Lady Smith or Elizabeth, Countess of Humber) or else style themselves The Dowager Lady Smith or The Dowager Countess of Humber. If in doubt it is usually safest to use the christian name before the title as this is the preferred style. Widows or divorced persons who remarry take their style from that of their new husband.

HOUSE OF COMMONS

HER MAJESTY'S GOVERNMENT

The Cabinet

Formed May 1997, reshuffled July 1998, January, July and October 1999

Prime Minister, First Lord of the Treasury and Minister for the Civil Service	The Rt Hon Tony Blair, MP
Deputy Prime Minister and Secretary of State for the Environment, Transport and the Regions	The Rt Hon John Prescott, MP
Chancellor of the Exchequer	The Rt Hon Gordon Brown, MP
Secretary of State for Foreign and Commonwealth Affairs	The Rt Hon Robin Cook, MP
Lord Chancellor	The Rt Hon The Lord Irvine of Lairg
Secretary of State for the Home Department	The Rt Hon Jack Straw, MP
Secretary of State for Education and Employment	The Rt Hon David Blunkett, MP
President of the Council and Leader of the House of Commons	The Rt Hon Margaret Beckett, MP
Parliamentary Secretary, Treasury and Chief Whip	The Rt Hon Ann Taylor, MP
Secretary of State for Culture, Media and Sport	The Rt Hon Chris Smith, MP
Minister for the Cabinet Office and Chancellor of the Duchy of Lancaster	The Rt Hon Dr Marjorie Mowlam, MP
Secretary of State for International Development	The Rt Hon Clare Short, MP
Secretary of State for Social Security	The Rt Hon Alistair Darling, MP
Minister of Agriculture, Fisheries and Food	The Rt Hon Nick Brown, MP
*Leader of the House of Lords and Minister for Women**	The Rt Hon The Baroness Jay of Paddington
Secretary of State for Trade and Industry	The Rt Hon Stephen Byers, MP
Secretary of State for Health	The Rt Hon Alan Milburn, MP
Secretary of State for Scotland	The Rt Hon Dr John Reid, MP
Secretary of State for Wales	The Rt Hon Paul Murphy, MP
Secretary of State for Northern Ireland	The Rt Hon Peter Mandelson, MP
Secretary of State for Defence	The Rt Hon Geoffrey Hoon, MP
Chief Secretary to the Treasury	The Rt Hon Andrew Smith, MP

*The Minister is appointed as Lord Privy Seal

Departmental Ministers

MINISTRY OF AGRICULTURE, FISHERIES AND FOOD
Minister of Agriculture, Fisheries and Food   The Rt Hon Nick Brown, MP
Minister of State   The Rt Hon Joyce Quin, MP
Minister of State   The Baroness Hayman
Parliamentary Secretary   Elliot Morley Esq, MP

CABINET OFFICE
Minister for the Cabinet Office†   The Rt Hon Dr Marjorie Mowlam, MP
Minister of State   The Lord Falconer of Thoroton, QC
Minister of State   The Rt Hon Ian McCartney, MP
Parliamentary Secretary   Graham Stringer Esq, MP
Leader of the House of Lords and
    Minister for Women *   The Rt Hon The Baroness Jay of Paddington

DEPARTMENT FOR CULTURE, MEDIA AND SPORT
Secretary of State   The Rt Hon Chris Smith, MP
Parliamentary Under-Secretary of State   Janet Anderson, MP
Parliamentary Under-Secretary of State   Kate Hoey, MP
Parliamentary Under-Secretary of State   Alan Howarth Esq, CBE, MP

MINISTRY OF DEFENCE
Secretary of State   The Rt Hon Geoffrey Hoon, MP
Minister of State   John Spellar Esq, MP
Minister of State   The Baroness Symons of Vernham Dean
Parliamentary Under-Secretary of State   Peter Kilfoyle, Esq, MP

DEPARTMENT FOR EDUCATION AND EMPLOYMENT
Secretary of State   The Rt Hon David Blunkett, MP
Minister of State   The Rt Hon Tessa Jowell, MP
Minister of State   The Rt Hon Estelle Morris, MP
Minister of State   The Baroness Blackstone
Parliamentary Under-Secretary of State   Malcolm Wicks Esq, MP
Parliamentary Under-Secretary of State   Margaret Hodge, MBE, MP
Parliamentary Under-Secretary of State   Jacqui Smith, MP
Parliamentary Under-Secretary of State   Michael Wills Esq, MP

DEPARTMENT OF THE ENVIRONMENT, TRANSPORT AND THE REGIONS
Secretary of State   The Rt Hon John Prescott, MP
Minister of State (Transport)‡   The Rt Hon
    The Lord Macdonald of Tradeston, CBE
Minister of State   The Rt Hon Michael Meacher, MP
Minister of State   The Rt Hon Hilary Armstrong, MP
Minister of State   Nick Raynsford Esq, MP
Parliamentary Under-Secretary of State   Chris Mullin Esq, MP
Parliamentary Under-Secretary of State   Keith Hill Esq, MP
Parliamentary Under-Secretary of State   The Lord Whitty
Parliamentary Under-Secretary of State   Beverley Hughes, MP

*The Minister is appointed as Lord Privy Seal.
†The Minister is appointed as Chancellor of the Duchy of Lancaster.
‡Not a Member of the Cabinet but attends Cabinet Meetings.

FOREIGN AND COMMONWEALTH OFFICE

Secretary of State	The Rt Hon Robin Cook, MP
Minister of State	Peter Hain Esq, MP
Minister of State	John Battle Esq, MP
Minister of State	Keith Vaz Esq, MP
Parliamentary Under-Secretary of State	The Baroness Scotland of Asthal, QC

DEPARTMENT OF HEALTH

Secretary of State	The Rt Hon Alan Milburn, MP
Minister of State	John Denham Esq, MP
Minister of State	John Hutton Esq, MP
Parliamentary Under-Secretary of State	The Lord Hunt of Kings Heath, OBE
Parliamentary Under-Secretary of State	Yvette Cooper, MP
Parliamentary Under-Secretary of State	Gisela Stuart, MP

HOME OFFICE

Home Secretary	The Rt Hon Jack Straw, MP
Minister of State	The Rt Hon Paul Boateng, MP
Minister of State	Charles Clarke Esq, MP
Minister of State	Barbara Roche, MP
Parliamentary Under-Secretary of State	Mike O'Brien Esq, MP
Parliamentary Under-Secretary of State	The Lord Bassam of Brighton

DEPARTMENT FOR INTERNATIONAL DEVELOPMENT

Secretary of State	The Rt Hon Clare Short, MP
Parliamentary Under-Secretary of State	George Foulkes Esq, MP

LAW OFFICERS' DEPARTMENT

Attorney-General	The Rt Hon The Lord Williams of Mostyn, QC
Solicitor-General	Ross Cranston Esq, QC, MP

LORD CHANCELLOR'S DEPARTMENT

Lord Chancellor	The Rt Hon The Lord Irvine of Lairg, QC
Parliamentary Secretary	David Lock Esq, MP
Parliamentary Secretary	Jane Kennedy, MP

NORTHERN IRELAND OFFICE

Secretary of State	The Rt Hon Peter Mandelson, MP
Minister of State	The Rt Hon Adam Ingram, MP
Parliamentary Under-Secretary of State	George Howarth Esq, MP

PRIVY COUNCIL OFFICE

President of the Council and *Leader of the House of Commons*	The Rt Hon Margaret Beckett, MP
Parliamentary Secretary	Paddy Tipping Esq, MP

SCOTLAND OFFICE

Secretary of State	The Rt Hon Dr John Reid, MP
Minister of State	Brian Wilson Esq, MP
Advocate General for Scotland	Dr Lynda Clark, QC, MP

DEPARTMENT OF SOCIAL SECURITY

Secretary of State	The Rt Hon Alistair Darling, MP
Minister of State	The Rt Hon Jeff Rooker Esq, MP
Parliamentary Under-Secretary of State	The Rt Hon The Baroness Hollis of Heigham
Parliamentary Under-Secretary of State	Angela Eagle, MP
Parliamentary Under-Secretary of State	Hugh Bayley Esq, MP

DEPARTMENT OF TRADE AND INDUSTRY

Secretary of State	The Rt Hon Stephen Byers, MP
Minister of State	The Rt Hon Helen Liddell, MP
Minister of State	The Rt Hon Richard Caborn, MP
Minister of State	Patricia Hewitt, MP
Parliamentary Under-Secretary of State	Dr Kim Howells, MP
Parliamentary Under-Secretary of State	Alan Johnson Esq, MP
Parliamentary Under-Secretary of State (Minister for Science)*	The Lord Sainsbury of Turville

HM TREASURY

Prime Minister, First Lord of the Treasury and Minister for the Civil Service	The Rt Hon Tony Blair, MP
Chancellor of the Exchequer	The Rt Hon Gordon Brown, MP
Chief Secretary	The Rt Hon Andrew Smith, MP
Paymaster General	Dawn Primarolo, MP
Financial Secretary	Stephen Timms Esq, MP
Economic Secretary	Melanie Johnson, MP

WALES OFFICE

Secretary State for Wales	The Rt Hon Paul Murphy, MP
Parliamentary Under-Secretary of State	David Hanson Esq, MP

*Unpaid

Alphabetical List of Ministers

Ainsworth, Robert	Whip
Allen, Graham	Whip
Amos, The Baroness	Whip
Anderson, Janet	Parliamentary Under-Secretary of State, Department for Culture Media and Sport
Armstrong, Hilary	Minister of State, Department of the Environment, Transport and the Regions
Bach, The Lord	Whip
Bassam, The Lord	Parliamentary Under-Secretary of State, Home Office
Battle, John	Minister of State, Foreign and Commonwealth Office
Bayley, Hugh	Parliamentary Under-Secretary of State, Department of Social Security
Beckett, Margaret	President of the Council and Leader of the House of Commons
Betts, Clive	Whip
Blackstone, The Baroness	Minister of State, Department for Education and Employment
Blair, Tony	Prime Minister, First Lord of the Treasury and Minister for Civil Service
Blunkett, David	Secretary of State for Education and Employment
Boateng, Paul	Minister of State, Home Office and Deputy Home Secretary
Bradley, Keith	Deputy Chief Whip
Brown, Gordon	Chancellor of the Exchequer
Brown, Nick	Minister of Agriculture, Fisheries and Food
Byers, Stephen	Secretary of State for Trade and Industry
Burlison, The Lord	Whip
Caborn, Richard	Minister of State, Department of Trade and Industry
Carter, The Lord	Chief Whip
Clark, Lynda	Advocate General for Scotland
Clarke, Charles	Minister of State, Home Office
Clelland, David	Assistant Whip
Cook, Robin	Foreign Secretary
Cooper, Yvette	Parliamentary Under-Secretary of State, Department of Health
Cranston, Ross	Solicitor General
Darling, Alistair	Secretary of State for Social Security
Denham, John	Minister of State, Department of Health
Dowd, James	Whip
Eagle, Angela	Parliamentary Under-Secretary of State, Department of Social Security
Falconer of Thoroton, The Lord	Minister of State, Cabinet Office
Farrington of Ribbleton, The Baroness	Whip
Foulkes, George	Parliamentary Under-Secretary of State, Department for International Development
Hain, Peter	Minister of State, Foreign and Commonwealth Office
Hall, Michael	Assistant Whip
Hanson, David	Parliamentary Under-Secretary of State, Wales Office
Hayman, The Baroness	Minister of State, Ministry of Agriculture, Fisheries and Food
Hewitt, Patricia	Minister of State, Department of Trade and Industry
Hill, Keith	Parliamentary Under-Secretary of State, Department of the Environment, Transport and the Regions
Hodge, Margaret	Parliamentary Under-Secretary of State, Department for Education and Employment
Hoey, Kate	Minister for Sport (Parliamentary Under-Secretary of State, Department for Culture, Media and Sport)

Hollis, The Baroness	Parliamentary Under-Secretary of State, Department of Social Security
Hoon, Geoffrey	Secretary of State for Defence
Howarth, Alan	Parliamentary Under-Secretary of State, Department for Culture, Media and Sport
Howarth, George	Parliamentary Under-Secretary of State, Northern Ireland Office
Howells, Kim	Parliamentary Under-Secretary of State, Department of Trade and Industry
Hughes, Beverley	Parliamentary Under-Secretary of State, Department of the Environment, Transport and the Regions
Hughes, Kevin	Assistant Whip
Hunt of Kings Heath, The Lord	Parliamentary Under-Secretary of State, Department of Health
Hutton, John	Minister of State, Department of Health
Ingram, Adam	Minister of State, Northern Ireland Office
Irvine of Lairg, The Lord	Lord Chancellor
Jamieson, David	Whip
Jay of Paddington, The Baroness	Lord Privy Seal, Leader of the House of Lords and Minister for Women
Johnson, Alan	Parliamentary Under-Secretary of State, Department of Trade and Industry
Johnson, Melanie	Economic Secretary, HM Treasury
Jowell, Tessa	Minister of State, Department for Education and Employment
Kennedy, Jane	Parliamentary Secretary, Lord Chancellor's Department
Kilfoyle, Peter	Parliamentary Under-Secretary of State, Ministry of Defence
Liddell, Helen	Minister of State, Department of Trade and Industry
Lock, David	Parliamentary Secretary, Lord Chancellor's Department
McAvoy, Thomas	Whip
McCartney, Ian	Minister of State, Cabinet Office
Macdonald of Tradeston The Lord	Minister of Transport (Minister of State, Department of the Environment, Transport and the Regions)
McGuire, Anne	Assistant Whip
McIntosh of Haringey, The Lord	Deputy Chief Whip
McNulty, Tony	Assistant Whip
Mandelson, Peter	Secretary of State for Northern Ireland
Meacher, Michael	Minister of State, Department of the Environment, Transport and the Regions
Milburn, Alan	Secretary of State for Health
Morley, Elliot	Parliamentary Secretary, Ministry of Agriculture, Fisheries and Food
Morris, Estelle	Minister of State, Department for Education and Employment
Mowlam, Marjorie	Minister for the Cabinet Office and Chancellor of the Duchy of Lancaster
Murphy, Paul	Secretary of State for Wales
Mullin, Chris	Parliamentary Under-Secretary of State, Department of the Environment, Transport and the Regions
O'Brien, Mike	Parliamentary Under-Secretary of State, Home Office
Pope, Greg	Whip
Prescott, John	Deputy Prime Minister; Secretary of State for the Environment, Transport and the Regions
Primarolo, Dawn	Paymaster General, HM Treasury
Quin, Joyce	Minister of State, Ministry of Agriculture, Fisheries and Food
Ramsay of Cartvale, The Baroness	Whip

Raynsford, Nick	Parliamentary Under-Secretary of State, Department of Environment, Transport and the Regions
Reid, John	Secretary of State for Scotland
Roche, Barbara	Minister of State, Home Office
Rooker, Jeff	Minister of State, Department of Social Security
Sainsbury of Turville, The Lord	Minister for Science, (Parliamentary Under-Secretary of State, Department of Trade and Industry)
Scotland, The Baroness	Parliamentary Under-Secretary of State, Foreign and Commonwealth Office
Short, Clare	Secretary of State for International Development
Smith, Andrew	Chief Secretary, HM Treasury
Smith, Chris	Secretary of State for Culture, Media and Sport
Smith, Jacqui	Parliamentary Under-Secretary of State, Department for Education and Employment
Spellar, John	Minister of State, Ministry of Defence
Straw, Jack	Home Secretary
Stringer, Graham	Parliamentary Secretary, Cabinet Office
Stuart, Gisela	Parliamentary Under-Secretary of State, Department of Health
Sutcliffe, Gerry	Assistant Whip
Symons of Vernham Dean, The Baroness	Minister of State, Ministry of Defence
Taylor, Ann	Chief Whip
Timms, Stephen	Financial Secretary, HM Treasury
Tipping, Paddy	Parliamentary Secretary, Privy Council Office
Touhig, Don	Assistant Whip
Vaz, Keith	Minister of State, Foreign and Commonwealth Office
Whitty, The Lord	Parliamentary Under-Secretary of State, Department of the Environment, Transport and Regions
Wicks, Malcolm	Parliamentary Under-Secretary of State, Department for Education and Employment
Williams of Mostyn, The Lord	Attorney General
Wills, Michael	Parliamentary Under-Secretary of State, Department for Education and Employment
Wilson, Brian	Minister of State, Scotland Office

Ministerial Responsibilities

MINISTRY OF AGRICULTURE, FISHERIES AND FOOD

The Minister of Agriculture, Fisheries and Food **(The Rt Hon. Nick Brown MP)**
Has overall responsibility for all Departmental issues. He will normally represent the UK at EU Council of Agricultural Ministers.
Principal Private Secretary: Ms Sarah Hendry *Tel:* 020 7238 5339 *Fax:* 020 7238 5727 (Main Fax for Ministers) *Private Secretaries:* Fiona James, Adrian Dally *Tel:* 020 7238 5342/5343

The Minister of State and Deputy Minister of Agriculture, Fisheries and Food
(The Rt Hon. Joyce Quin MP)
Deputising for the Minister on EU agricultural policy issues; Responsibility for post-devolution agricultural policy and its implementation in England. Government policy on EU enlargement and CAP reform and euro changeover plan; external trade policy and export promotion; regional policy and organisation; food and drinks industry and marketing (including taking forward the food chain initiative with industry); competition issues; spokesperson in the Commons on food safety and Food Standards Agency issues.
Private Secretary: Miss Teresa Hart *Tel:* 020 7238 5404 *Fax:* 020 7238 5976

The Minster of State (Lords) **(The Baroness Hayman)**
Responsibility for food safety; food standards; meat hygiene; animal health (including BSE, Pet Travel Scheme and TB in cattle); pesticide safety; veterinary medicines, plant health; research and genetic modification.
Private Secretary: Vic Platten *Tel:* 020 7238 5379 *Fax:* 020 7238 5867

The Parliamentary Secretary (Commons) (Minister for Fisheries and the Countryside)
(Elliot Morley MP)
Responsibility for countryside matters; forestry; farm animal welfare; Departmental Green Minister. Normally represents the UK at meetings of the EU Council of Fisheries Ministers.
E-mail: parlsecc@sec.maff.gov.uk
Private Secretary: Mark Livesey *Tel:* 020 7238 5421 *Fax:* 020 7238 5996
Spokespersons in the House of Lords: The Baroness Hayman, The Lord Carter.

CABINET OFFICE

The Minister for the Cabinet Office **(The Rt Hon. Dr Mo Mowlam MP)**
Responsibility for oversight of the departmental work of Cabinet Office Ministers, including particular responsibilities for inter-departmental co-ordination on biotechnology, anti-drugs policy, regulation, rural affairs and equality and overall leadership of the Modernising Government programme. She will also be taking forward co-operation with the Treasury on ways of making the delivery of policies on the ground more efficient and effective.
E-mail: mmowlam@cabinet-office.x.gsi.gov.uk
Principal Private Secretary: Dr John Fuller *Tel:* 020 7270 0330 *Fax:* 020 7270 0196
Assistant Private Secretary: (Diary) N Massingham *Tel:* 020 7270 0296

The Minister of State **(The Lord Falconer of Thoroton QC)**
Responsibility for answering in the House of Lords for the full range of responsibilities of the Minister for the Cabinet Office; Working with the Secretary of State on taking forward work on the coherent formulation and implementation of policy across government; Preparation of the Government's Annual Report and on monitoring the overall performance of the Government; Specific regulatory issues as remitted to him, including transposition of EU directives into UK law; As sole shareholder, on behalf of the Government, of the New Millennium Experience Company, responsible for the Millennium Dome and the related national programme; With the Minister of State in the Home Office (Rt Hon Paul Boateng MP), responsible for the Active Community, a programme to promote and encourage the giving of time to community involvement.
E-mail: cfalconer@cabinet-office.x.gsi.gov.uk
Private Secretary: Mark Langdale *Tel:* 020 7270 0012/0013 *Fax:* 020 7270 1257

The Minister of State **(The Rt Hon. Ian McCartney MP)**
Responsibility for the parts of the modernising government agenda dealing with responsiveness and quality of public services and electronic government; Sponsor Minister for (CITU) project on lessons learned from big Government IT projects; Cabinet Office Agencies: GCDA, COI, including regional network; Creation of Office of Government Commerce; Sponsor Minister for (PIU) project on seizure and pursuit of criminal assets; Working with the Secretary of State as required in co-ordinating the anti-drugs policy; Co-ordinating the Government's arrangements for the 2002 Commonwealth Games.
E-mail: imccartney@cabinet-office.x.gsi.gov.uk
Private Secretary: Nicola Pitts *Tel:* 020 7270 0411 *Fax:* 020 7270 1171

Parliamentary Secretary **(Graham Stringer MP)**
Responsibility for Regulatory burdens, including the Bill to amend the Deregulation and Contracting Out Act, and enforcement; public appointments/NDPBs (creation of, and appointment to, quangos); issues relating to the Ombudsman (including review of 'joined-up' Ombudsmen); specific day-to-day civil service management issues such as pensions, TUPE; general oversight of the wider public sector workstream of modernising government; supporting Dr Mowlam and Ian McCartney in spreading the message to frontline deliverers; supporting the Secretary of State on networking with Junior Ministers and joint training events by Centre for Management and Policy Studies; departmental management, including Ministerial ownership of relevant PSA targets; departmental role on specific committees: Green Minister; Euro Minister.
E-mail: gstringer@cabinet-office.x.gsi.gov.uk
Private Secretary: Mark Holmes *Tel:* 020 7270 0652/0645 *Fax:* 020 7270 0655
Spokesmen in the House of Lords: The Lord Falconer of Thoroton, The Lord Burlison.

NB: The Women's Unit in the Cabinet Office reports to the Rt Hon Baroness Jay of Paddington in her capacity as Minister for Women

OFFICES OF THE CHANCELLOR OF THE DUCHY OF LANCASTER

The Chancellor of the Duchy of Lancaster **(The Rt Hon. Dr Mo Mowlam MP)**
Responsible to The Queen for the general administration of the Duchy of Lancaster, in which she is supported by the Duchy of Lancaster Office.
Principal Private Secretary: Dr John Fuller *Tel:* 020 7270 0330 *Fax:* 020 7270 0196
Private Secretary: Stephen Poole *Tel:* 020 7270 0225

See also Cabinet Office

DEPARTMENT FOR CULTURE, MEDIA AND SPORT

The Secretary of State for Culture, Media and Sport **(The Rt Hon. Chris Smith MP)**
Responsibility for Departmental strategy, expenditure and organisation; National Lottery policy; Public appointments; Chairman of the Millennium Commission; The Millennium.
E-mail: chris.smith@culture.gov.uk
Principal Private Secretary: Fergus Muir *Tel:* 020 7211 6243 *Fax:* 020 7211 6249
Private Secretary: Chris Carr *Tel:* 020 7211 6975

The Parliamentary Under-Secretary of State (Minister for Tourism, Film and Broadcasting)
(Janet Anderson MP)
Responsibility for Tourism; Broadcasting, Film and the Press; The creative industries (including the music industry); The Millennium; Regional and local authority policy issues; Women's Issues; Green Issues.
E-mail: janet.anderson@culture.gov.uk
Private Secretary: Dominic Tambling *Tel:* 020 7211 6303 *Fax:* 020 7211 6249
Assistant Private Secretary: Mark Mann *Tel:* 020 7211 6305

The Parliamentary Under-Secretary of State (Minister for Sport) **(Kate Hoey MP)**
Responsibility for sport; support for the Secretary of State on the National Lottery; Social policy, access and equal opportunities.
E-mail: kate.hoey@culture.gov.uk
Private Secretary: Simon Cooper *Tel:* 020 7211 6246 *Fax:* 020 7211 6249
Assistant Private Secretary: Philip Chamberlain *Tel:* 020 7211 6247

The Parliamentary Under-Secretary of State (Minister for the Arts) **(Alan Howarth CBE MP)**
Responsibility for European and international matters; The arts, the crafts, music and the Government Art Collection; Museums and galleries and libraries; The built heritage, the Royal estate, architecture and design; DCMS interest in information technology, training and education.
E-mail: alan.howarth@culture.gov.uk
Private Secretary: David Fitzgerald *Tel:* 020 7211 6421 *Fax:* 020 7211 6309
Spokesman in the House of Lords: The Lord McIntosh of Haringey.

MINISTRY OF DEFENCE

The Secretary of State for Defence **(The Rt Hon. Geoffrey Hoon MP)**
Has overall responsibility for the work of the Ministry.
Private Secretary: Julian Miller *Tel:* 020 7218 2111 *Fax:* 020 7218 7140

The Minister of State for the Armed Forces **(John Spellar MP)**
Responsibility for defence policy and planning, including: strategy including nuclear policy; size and shape of the Services (excluding equipment projects); Defence budget issues (including efficiency/asset use); arms control and disarmament; NATO, WEU; United Nations, OSCE, visiting forces. Operations, including: overseas commitments and garrisons; Northern Ireland; military aid to the civil authorities; UN peacekeeping; disaster relief; military assistance overseas; nuclear accident response; MoD Police operations. Service personnel policy, including: armed forces pay; equal opportunities, training and education, Defence medical services; reserves and cadets, veterans, Gulf veterans' illness; compensation policy. Operational sustainability; public presentation of defence.
Private Secretary: Daniel Applegate *Tel:* 020 7218 6385 *Fax:* 020 7218 6542

The Minister of State for Defence Procurement **(The Baroness Symons of Vernham Dean)**
Responsibility for procurement, including: forward equipment programme (including logistics strategy); project approval (including equipment capability upgrades); equipment collaboration; nuclear procurement (including safety and disposal); defence industrial questions; contracts policy. Science and technology strategy and research, including: Defence Evaluation Research Agency (DERA); civil use of defence research. Defence exports and disposals; intelligence and security policy; public-private partnerships*; all matters concerning Defence in the House of Lords.
*Decisions on specific projects and individual Agencies will be handled by the Minister with responsibility for the area concerned.
Private Secretary: David Hatcher *Tel:* 020 7218 6621 *Fax:* 020 7218 6625

The Parliamentary Under-Secretary of State **(Peter Kilfoyle MP)**
Responsibility for service personnel casework; civilian and MoD Police personnel policy and casework; market testing*. Defence estate and works, including: service housing; heritage and historic buildings. Regulatory issues, including: environmental matters; health and safety policy. Claims casework; public service matters, including: Service First, the new Charter programme; open Government; non-departmental public bodies; low flying; hydrographic and meteorological offices; service museums; visits by Peers and MPs/Armed Forces Parliamentary Scheme; Procurement matters in the House of Commons; Defence Diversification.
*Decisions on specific projects and individual Agencies will be handled by the Minister with responsibility for the area concerned.
Private Secretary: Andrew Dwyer *Tel:* 020 7218 2452 *Fax:* 020 7218 7610
Spokespersons in the House of Lords: The Baroness Symons of Vernham Dean, The Lord Burlison.

DEPARTMENT FOR EDUCATION AND EMPLOYMENT

The Secretary of State for Education and Employment **(The Rt Hon. David Blunkett MP)**
Has overall responsibility for the Department, its policies and strategy; finance and public expenditure; major appointments.
Principal Private Secretary: Mike Wardle *Tel:* 020 7925 5829 *Fax:* 020 7925 6995

The Minister of State (Minister for Employment, Welfare to Work and Equal Opportunities)
(The Rt Hon. Tessa Jowell MP)
Responsibility for employment policy; Employment Zones; Employment Service performance and programmes; New Deal (including an overview of the New Deal for Single Parents and the inter-relationship with childcare); Labour Market Statistics; EU and International employment policy; competitiveness; overview of equal opportunities; age discrimination. Also supports Mr Blunkett on economic issues; benefit reform and the Job Seekers Allowance.
Private Secretary: Alison Kerr *Tel:* 020 7925 6255 *Fax:* 020 7925 6996

The Minister of State (Minister for School Standards) **(The Rt Hon. Estelle Morris MP)**
Responsibility for school standards; Standards and Effectiveness Unit; specialist schools, technology colleges and related issues, including gifted children; independent schools; literacy and numeracy strategy; liaison with and responsibility for OFSTED; Education Action Zones; class sizes; education business links; overview of National Curriculum (including personal social and health education (PSHE) and citizenship democracy); overview of 5 to 16 – admissions and school organisation policy; local education authorities (including the new code, Fair Funding); school organisation and admissions casework (territorially split); schools recurrent funding; overview of early years; overview of special educational needs; implementation of the Social Exclusion Unit report on exclusion. Also supports Mr Blunkett on teachers' pay and conditions and Green Paper on teacher reform.
Private Secretary: Jane Whitfield *Tel:* 020 7925 5870 *Fax:* 020 7925 5151

The Minister of State (Minister for Education and Employment) (Lords) **(The Baroness Blackstone)**
Responsibility for lifelong learning; overview of: Higher Education, Further Education and Adult Education; overview of National Targets for Education and Training; 16-19 organisation – review of funding and organisation of sixth forms, sixth form colleges, Further Education and training; basic skills; overview of TEC Review; student support and the Student Loans Company; Modern Apprenticeships; Investors in People; University for Industry; overview of Individual Learning Accounts; public service reform; EU and International education policy; Social Exclusion*. Also works with Ms Morris on qualifications and examinations and Qualifications and Curriculum Authority; all DfEE business in the House of Lords.
*Baroness Blackstone is the lead Minister and works with other Ministers when proposals fall within their responsibilities.
Private Secretary: Elsa Wilkinson *Tel:* 020 7925 6242 *Fax:* 020 7925 5011

The Parliamentary Under-Secretary of State (Lifelong Learning) **(Malcolm Wicks MP)**
Supports Baroness Blackstone on: lifelong learning; Higher and Further Education, Adult Education and basic skills (business in the House of Commons); Training and Enterprise Councils – the review; Individual Learning Accounts; Modern Apprenticeships. Follow up to Learning Age Green Paper; co-ordination between TECs, further education and local authorities on post-16 education and training. Supports Mr Smith on: employability – skills and training; New Deal and economic issues. Development of the work of the Skills Task Force and its relevance for competitiveness; national training organisations; Investors in Young People (youth training and national traineeships); careers service; constitutional reform (including Regional Development Agencies); regeneration policy (co-ordination with DETR); youth policy and youth service. Works with Mr Clarke on overview of public private partnerships/PFI. Also supports Mr Blunkett on departmental efficiency and effectiveness (including budgetary issues).
Private Secretary: Steve Bartlett *Tel:* 020 7925 6341 *Fax:* 020 7925 6921

The Parliamentary Under-Secretary of State (Employment and Equal Opportunities)
(Margaret Hodge MBE MP)
Supports Mr Smith on: employment including the New Deal for Lone Parents; family friendly issues; equal opportunities issues. New Deal for disabled people; disability rights (and the Disability Rights Commission Bill); work permits; supports Ms Morris on early years education and childcare, and Mr Blunkett and Ms Jowell on the implementation of Sure Start; day care services. Also supports Mr Blunkett on volunteering policy and Millennium Volunteers.
Private Secretary: Graham Walker *Tel:* 020 7925 6951 *Fax:* 020 7925 6994

The Parliamentary Under-Secretary of State (School Standards) **(Jacqueline Smith MP)**
Supports Ms Morris on: school standards; school organisation and admissions casework (territorially split); special education needs. Grant-maintained schools; National Curriculum, assessment and performance information; out of school hours learning and New Opportunities Fund; teacher and headteacher supply, training and appraisal; teacher misconduct; teachers' pensions; General Teaching Council and liaison with Teacher Training Agency; The Funding Agency for Schools; Education Transfer Council; supports Baroness Blackstone on 14-19 issues; reducing bureaucracy; pupil welfare and school security; schools capital and public private partnerships; Section 11 and work with the Home Office; equality issues in education (including gender); information and communications technology (in schools and colleges, but also in the wider context of the National Grid for Learning and ICT training for teachers); the Millennium Dome; school transport and related cross-departmental issues; rural schools, including closures; green issues, rural issues and the environment; research.
Private Secretary: Karen Lumley *Tel:* 020 7925 6391 *Fax:* 020 7925 6688

The Parliamentary Under-Secretary of State **(Michael Wills MP)**
Responsibility for ICT in education and employment; National Grid for Learning; University for Industry and Learning Direct; broadcasting, including the development of world-class digital, satellite and home-based learning; overcoming exclusion in the information age, the gap between the haves and have nots; relationships with employers, including small and medium-sized enterprises; employability and competitiveness, Skills Task Force and skills development; constitutional reform; regional policy; Regional Development Agencies; departmental efficiency and effectiveness (including budgetary issues); completion of work on prevention of problems arising from the millennium bug; workforce development.
Private Secretary: Lucy Carter *Tel:* 020 7925 6823 *Diary Secretary:* Cathy Hare *Tel:* 020 7925 6821
Spokespersons in the House of Lords: The Baroness Blackstone, The Lord Bach.

DEPARTMENT OF THE ENVIRONMENT, TRANSPORT AND THE REGIONS

The Deputy Prime Minister and Secretary of State for the Environment, Transport and the Regions
(The Rt Hon. John Prescott MP)
Has responsibility for the overall direction of the Department and its agencies and has overall responsibility for the regions in England and London.
E-mail: john_prescott@detr.gsi.gov.uk
Private Secretary: Peter Unwin *Tel:* 020 7944 3011 *Fax:* 020 7944 4399

The Minister of State (Minister for Transport) **(The Rt Hon The Lord Macdonald of Tradeston CBE)**
Responsibility for Integrated Transport Strategy; Aviation; Railways; Shipping; Buses; Congestion and Workplace charging, National Roads; Local Transport Plans; London Transport; Environmental impacts of Transport; Road Safety.
E-mail: gus_macdonald@detr.gsi.gov.uk
Private Secretary: Seth Davis *Tel:* 020 7944 4483 *Fax:* 020 7944 4492

The Minister of State (Minister for the Environment) **(The Rt Hon. Michael Meacher MP)**
Responsibility for Sustainable Development Strategy; Environmental Protection; Countryside and Wildlife; Water; Health and Safety; Waste, National Waste Strategy; Climate Change; Energy Efficiency.
E-mail: michael_meacher@detr.gsi.gov.uk
Private Secretary: Colin Bird *Tel:* 020 7944 4494 *Fax:* 020 7944 4499

The Minister of State (Minister for Local Government and Regions)
(The Rt Hon. Hilary Armstrong MP)
Responsibility for Strategy for Regional and Local Government; Local Government; English Regions; Regeneration; Social Exclusion; Modernising Government.
E-mail: hilary_armstrong@detr.gsi.gov.uk
Private Secretary: Nick Carter *Tel:* 020 7944 4488 *Fax:* 020 7944 4489

The Minister of State (Minister for Housing, Planning and Construction) **(Nick Raynsford MP)**
Responsibility for Housing and Planning Strategy; Planning; Housing; Construction.
E-mail: nick_raynsford@detr.gsi.gov.uk
Private Secretary: Katy Willison *Tel:* 020 7944 4344 *Fax:* 020 7944 4539

The Parliamentary Under-Secretary of State **(Chris Mullin MP)**
Responsibility for Aviation; Housing – HMO Licensing, Gypsies, ROSA and RAPS, Research, Private Sector Renewal and HATs; Water; Coastal Policy; Waste – Implementation of Strategy at Local Level; Countryside and Wildlife; Trees, Zoos, CITEs, SSSIs, Access; Science and Technology Policy.
E-mail: chris_mullin@detr.gsi.gov.uk
Private Secretary: Jessica Matthew *Tel:* 020 7944 4324 *Fax:* 020 7944 4521

The Parliamentary Under-Secretary of State **(Keith Hill MP)**
Responsibility for Railways; Light Rail, Buses, Taxis, Cycling, Walking, Mobility; London; Local Transport Plans; Local Roads; Marine and Shipping; Maritime and Coastguard Agency; Freight Policy; Environmental protection issues at Local Level.
E-mail: keith_hill@detr.gsi.gov.uk
Private Secretary: Katherine Braddick *Tel:* 020 7944 4403 *Fax:* 020 7944 4521

The Parliamentary Under-Secretary of State **(The Lord Whitty)**
Responsibility for Climate Change, Energy Efficiency; Trunk Roads; Road Safety; Vehicle Safety and Environment; Highways Agency and DVO Agencies; British Waterways; Health and Safety; European Policy; Modernising Government.
E-mail: larry_whitty@detr.gsi.gov.uk
Private Secretary: Jenni Borg *Tel:* 020 7944 4536 *Fax:* 020 7944 4538

The Parliamentary Under-Secretary of State **(Beverley Hughes MP)**
Responsibility for Local Government; Planning; Regeneration; Regions; Construction; Tourism; Ordnance Survey; DETR Green Minister.
E-mail: beverley_hughes@detr.gsi.gov.uk
Private Secretary: Rory O'Donnell *Tel:* 020 7944 4334 *Fax:* 020 7944 4339
Spokespersons in the House of Lords: The Lord Macdonald of Tradeston, The Lord Whitty, The Baroness Farrington of Ribbleton (Local Government).

FOREIGN AND COMMONWEALTH OFFICE

The Secretary of State for Foreign and Commonwealth Affairs **(The Rt Hon. Robin Cook MP)**
Administration issues including honours, royal matters and the overall responsibility for the work of the department.
Private Secretary: Sherard Cowper-Coles *Tel:* 020 7270 2059 *Fax:* 020 7270 2144

The Minister of State **(Peter Hain MP)**
Africa Command: Africa Department (Equatorial), Africa Department (Southern), Commonwealth Co-ordination Department; (Part of) Asia Command: South Asian Department; Middle East and North Africa Command: Middle East Department, Near East and North Africa Department; Global Issues Command: Environmental Policy Department, United Nations Department, Human Rights Policy Department, Aviation and Maritime Department; (Part of) International Security Command: Non-Proliferation Department; Chief Economist and Economic Relations Department; (Part of) Public Services Command.
Private Secretary: Frank Baker *Tel:* 020 7270 2090 *Fax:* 020 7270 3731

The Minister of State **(John Battle MP)**
British Trade International; Invest in Britain Bureau (IBB); (Part of) Asia Command: South-East Asia Command, North-East Asia and Pacific Department, China and Hong Kong Department; (Part of) Americas Command: Latin America and Caribbean Department (Latin America only), Overseas Territories Department (Falklands and South Georgia only); Counter-Terrorism Policy Department; Drugs/International Crime Department; FCO Services Organisation: Technical Group, Estates Group, Support Group, Information Management Group, Consultancy Group, Resource Management Group, Conferences and Visits Group.
Private Secretary: Miss Pat Phillips *Tel:* 020 7270 2129 *Fax:* 020 7270 3539

The Minister of State for Europe **(Keith Vaz MP)**
European Union Command: European Union Department (Internal), European Union Department (External), European Union Department (Bilateral), Common Foreign and Security Policy Department, Devolved Administrations Department; Wider Europe Command: Central and North West European Department, Eastern Department, Southern European Department; Deputy Political Director Command, Eastern Adriatic Department; (Most of) International Security Command: Security Policy Department, OSCE/Council of Europe Department; Migration and Visa Department.
Private Secretary: Nick Hopton *Tel:* 020 7270 3367 *Fax:* 020 7270 2988

The Parliamentary Under-Secretary of State **(The Baroness Scotland of Asthal QC)**
(Most of) Americas Command: Latin America and Caribbean Department (Caribbean only), North America Department, Overseas Territories Department (not Falklands and South Georgia); (Most of) Public Services Command: Consular Division, Cultural Relations Department, Information Department; Records and Historical Services; Personnel Command; Resources Command: Financial Policy Department, Resource Planning Department, Internal Audit Department, Financial Compliance Unit, Purchasing Directorate; Central Administration: Change Management Unit, Estates Strategy Unit, Security Strategy Unit, IT Strategy Unit.
Private Secretary: Carl Newns *Tel:* 020 7270 2173 *Fax:* 020 7270 2148
Spokespersons in the House of Lords: The Baroness Scotland of Asthal, The Baroness Ramsay of Cartvale.

DEPARTMENT OF HEALTH

The Secretary of State for Health **(The Rt Hon. Alan Milburn MP)**
Overall responsibility for the work of the Department. Also has particular responsibility for: NHS finance – CSR preparation and follow-up; NHS resource allocation; NHS central budgets; performance monitoring; management costs and NHS efficiency; PFI and NHS capital; NHS Estates; strategic communications.
Principal Private Secretary: Janet Grauberg *Private Secretaries:* Heather Rogers, Mark Ferrero *Tel:* 020 7210 5798 *Fax:* 020 7210 5410

The Minister of State **(John Denham MP)**
Responsibility for NHS strategy and planning; NHS structure/organisation; service reconfiguration; commissioning; waiting times and lists; clinical quality including NICE and CHI; primary care; general medical services; GP walk-in centres; human resources in the NHS; NHS pay and conditions; NHS Pensions Agency; medical training and education; medical workforce planning; equal opportunities; race equality; regional NHS casework for London; appointments.
Private Secretary: Trish Fretten *Tel:* 020 7210 5103 *Fax:* 020 7210 5823
Assistant Private Secretaries: Giles Wilmore, James Adedeji

The Minister of State **(John Hutton MP)**
Responsibility for PSS resources; services for people with mental illness, special hospitals; homeless mentally ill; child and adolescent mental health services; Road Traffic (NHS Charges) Act; adult social services; services for elderly people (including NHS continuing care); long-term care; service for carers; NHS/PSS interface; Health Action Zones (HAZs); disabilities (including people with sensory and learning disabilities); children's services; adoption and fostering; child protection; Children Act 1989; children's residential care; children's secure units/juvenile offenders; voluntary sector (including Section 64 grant scheme); family issues; statistics; regional NHS casework for Northern and Yorkshire.
Private Secretary: Neil Paterson *Tel:* 020 7210 5564 *Fax:* 020 7210 5548
Assistant Private Secretaries: Bill Jobson, Anna McDevitt

The Parliamentary Under-Secretary of State (Lords) **(The Lord Hunt of Kings Heath)**
Responsibility for health services development; Pharmaceutical industry (including Pharmaceutical Price Regulation Schemes (PPRS)); pharmaceutical services (including Prescribing and Drugs Bill); Medicines (including licensing); renal services; NSF for diabetes; prison health care; community pharmacy; nursing strategy (including recruitment and retention); professions allied to medicine; transplants; blood; research and development; spreading good practice; medical devices; procurement and NHS Supplies; general dental services; general optical services; counter-fraud services; defence medical services; contingency planning (civil defence); departmental management (including agencies); Regional casework for Eastern and North West.
Private Secretary: Hester McLain *Tel:* 020 7210 5826 *Fax:* 020 7210 5066
Assistant Private Secretaries: Sue Cartwright, Lee McGill

The Parliamentary Under-Secretary of State (Minister for Public Health) **(Yvette Cooper MP)**
Responsibility for Saving Lives: Our Healthier Nation; public health in the NHS; cancer; coronary heart disease (including national service framework); ethnic health; health education and promotion; Health Development Agency; health inequalities; nutrition; substance misuse; communicable diseases (including AIDS); immunisation; women's health and related issues; maternity and child health; health visiting and school nursing; Sure Start; abortion; family planning; teenage pregnancy; ethical issues; Human Fertilisation and Embryology Authority (HFEA) and related issues; genetics and gene therapy; food hygiene and safety (including Food Standards Agency); spongiform encephalopathies; public health bodies; environment and health; air quality; radiation; regional NHS casework for Trent (TRRO) and North Western (NWRO). Office functions: management of PSS(PH)'s diary; management of ministerial invitations.
Private Secretary: Richard Carter *Tel:* 020 7210 5113 *Fax:* 020 7210 5534
Assistant Private Secretaries: Paul MacNaught, Iain Finlinson

The Parliamentary Under-Secretary of State for Health **(Gisela Stuart MP)**
Responsibility for NHS Direct; Millennium/winter planning; emergency services; Information Technology; confidentiality; regulatory impact; EU health council; World Health Organisation (WHO); Council of Europe; other international business; complaints; clinical negligence; CHCs; independent health care sector; policy on NHS appointments; SERO regional casework and appointments; SWRO regional casework and appointments.
Private Secretary: Steven Collins *Tel:* 020 7210 5325 *Fax:* 020 7210 5327
Assistant Private Secretary: Jon Orr *Tel:* 020 7210 5328
Spokesmen in the House of Lords: The Lord Hunt of Kings Heath, The Lord Burlison.

HOME OFFICE

The Secretary of State for the Home Department **(The Rt Hon. Jack Straw MP)**
Overall responsibility for the work of the Department; royal matters; security; Public Expenditure Survey; emergency and terrorism issues.
Principal Private Secretary: Ms Hilary Jackson *Tel:* 020 7273 4647 *Fax:* 020 7273 3965

The Minister of State and Deputy Home Secretary **(The Rt Hon. Paul Boateng MP)**
Responsibility for Prisons; Probation; Coroners; Family policy; Active Community; Mentally Disordered Offenders.
Private Secretary: Simon Hayes *Tel:* 020 7273 3458 *Fax:* 020 7273 4090

The Minister of State **(Charles Clarke MP)**
Responsibility for Criminal Policy; Crime Reduction; Police Policy; Organised and international crime, including IOCA Bill and Terrorism Bill.
Private Secretary: Jacquie Russell *Tel:* 020 7273 4606 *Fax:* 020 7273 2936

The Minister of State **(Barbara Roche MP)**
Responsibility for Immigration and Asylum; Nationality; Passport Agency; EU matters.
Private Secretary: Cathy Hume *Tel:* 020 7273 2742 *Fax:* 020 7273 2043

The Parliamentary Under-Secretary of State (Minister for Fire and Emergency Planning, Liquor, Drugs and Elections) **(Mike O'Brien MP)**
Responsibility for Constitutional issues; Freedom of Information; Fire and Emergency Planning; Race Relations; Byelaws; Animals; Liquor licensing; Gambling law; Data Protection; Action against Drugs.
Private Secretary: Lee Bailey *Tel:* 020 7273 2500 *Fax:* 020 7273 2565

The Parliamentary Under-Secretary of State **(The Lord Bassam of Brighton)**
Responsibility for prisons and probation, supporting Paul Boateng; The Metropolitan Police, supporting the Home Secretary; Policy on police discipline, police complaints and police training in support of Charles Clarke; Measures to combat football hooliganism; Judicial Co-operation and Extradition; alleged wrongful convictions; bribery and corruption; obscenity and video classification; Channel Islands and Isle of Man. Responsible for all Home Office business in the House of Lords.
Private Secretary: Paul Morrison *Tel:* 020 7273 2741 *Fax:* 020 7273 3094
Spokesmen in the House of Lords: The Lord Bassam of Brighton, The Lord Bach.

DEPARTMENT FOR INTERNATIONAL DEVELOPMENT

The Secretary of State for International Development **(The Rt Hon. Clare Short MP)**
Overall responsibility for the work of the Department; overseas development; certain overseas pensions.
Private Secretary: Chris Austin *Tel:* 020 7917 0419 *Fax:* 020 7917 0634

The Parliamentary Under-Secretary of State **(George Foulkes Esq MP)**
Assists the Secretary of State in her duties.
Private Secretary: Christine Atkinson *Tel:* 020 7917 0621 *Fax:* 020 7917 0634
Spokesperson in the House of Lords: The Baroness Amos.

LAW OFFICERS' DEPARTMENTS

The Attorney General **(The Rt Hon. the Lord Williams of Mostyn QC)**
Has overall responsibility for the work of the Departments under his superintendence (the Treasury Solicitor's Department, the Crown Prosecution Service, the Serious Fraud Office and the Legal Secretariat to the Law Officers); has a specific statutory duty to superintend the discharge of their duties by the Director of Public Prosecutions (who heads the Crown Prosecution Service) and the Director of the Serious Fraud Office; oversees the functions of the Director of Public Prosecutions for Northern Ireland; is the Government's principal legal adviser; deals with questions of law arising on Bills, and with issues of legal policy; is concerned with all major international and domestic litigation involving the Government; has specific responsibilities for the enforcement of the criminal law.
Private Secretary: Rupert Cazelet *Tel:* 020 7271 2405 *Fax:* 020 7271 2432

The Solicitor General **(Ross Cranston QC MP)**
Is responsible for such matters as the Attorney General delegates to him from time to time; presently takes the lead in the conduct of civil litigation and advice on civil law matters, including charity and family issues; proposed claims for public interest immunity; vexatious litigants; questions of European Community and international law.
Private Secretary: Rupert Cazelet *Tel:* 020 7271 2405 *Fax:* 020 7271 2432

LORD CHANCELLOR'S DEPARTMENT

The Lord High Chancellor **(The Rt Hon. the Lord Irvine of Lairg QC)**
The Lord Chancellor is responsible for promoting general reforms in the civil law, for the administration of the Supreme Court (Court of Appeal, High Court and Crown Court) and county courts in England and Wales. He also has ministerial responsibility for the locally administered Magistrates' Courts. He is responsible for advising the Crown on the appointment of judges and certain other officers and is himself responsible for the appointment of Masters and Registrars of the High Court and District Judges and magistrates. He is responsible for ensuring that letters patent and other formal documents are passed in the proper form under the Great Seal of the Realm, of which he is the custodian. The work in connection with this is carried out under his direction in the Office of the Clerk of the Crown in Chancery. He is also responsible for Legal Aid and has overall responsibility for the Public Record Office, HM Land Registry, the Public Trust Office and the Court Service, and the Northern Ireland Court Service.
Principal Private Secretary: Miss J Rowe *Tel:* 020 7219 3232 *Fax:* 020 7219 4711

The Parliamentary Secretary **(David Lock MP)**
Contributes to all major policy decisions and is jointly responsible for the development of the Community Legal Service as Lead Minister. He is responsible for Legal Aid and Legal Services (including the Legal Aid Board); Community Legal Service; Civil Justice; Civil Law Development (including the Law Commission); Northern Ireland Court Service; International Policy; Public Record Office; Legal Services Ombudsman; Statutory Publications Office. Oral parliamentary questions are shared between the two Parliamentary Secretaries.
Private Secretary: Diana Hulin *Tel:* 020 7210 0702 *Fax:* 020 7210 1472

The Parliamentary Secretary **(Jane Kennedy MP)**
Contributes to all major policy decisions and is jointly responsible for the development of the Community Legal Service. She is responsible for Criminal Policy; Magistrates' Courts; Court Service; Family Policy; Human Rights; Administrative Justice; Devolution Issues; Public Trust Office; Land Registry; Immigration and Asylum Policy; Official Solicitor's Department; Council on Tribunals. Oral parliamentary questions are shared between the two Parliamentary Secretaries.
Private Secretary: Robert Moore *Tel:* 020 7210 8562 *Fax:* 020 7210 8620
Spokesmen in the House of Lords: The Lord Irvine of Lairg, The Lord Bach.

LORD PRIVY SEAL

Leader of the House of Lords and Minister for Women (Lord Privy Seal)
(The Rt Hon. the Baroness Jay of Paddington)
The Leader of the House of Lords is responsible for the arrangement of Government business in the House and has a responsibility to the House itself to advise it on procedural matters and other difficulties as they arise; she is also Minister for Women and sits on a number of Cabinet Committees – chairing the Cabinet sub-committee on Women's Issues.
Principal Private Secretary: William Connon *Tel:* 020 7270 0501 (Cabinet Office) 020 7219 3201 (House of Lords) *Fax:* 020 7270 0491 (Cabinet Office) 020 7219 3051 (House of Lords)
Spokespersons in the House of Lords (Women's Issues): The Baroness Jay of Paddington, The Baroness Amos.

NORTHERN IRELAND OFFICE

The Secretary of State for Northern Ireland **(The Rt Hon. Peter Mandelson MP)**
Has responsibility for the work of the Northern Ireland Office matters not devolved to the Assembly. These include matters such as policing, security policy, prisons, criminal justice, international relations, taxation, national insurance, regulation of financial services and the regulation of telecommunications and broadcasting. The Secretary of State will represent Northern Ireland's interest in the United Kingdom Cabinet.
Private Secretary, Tel: 020 7210 6461 (London) 028 9052 8110/8107 (Belfast) *Fax:* 020 7210 0246 (London) 028 9052 8201 (Belfast)

The Minister of State and Deputy to the Secretary of State **(The Rt Hon. Adam Ingram MP)**
Private Secretary, Tel: 020 7210 6498 (London) 028 9052 8127 (Belfast)
Fax: 020 7210 6449 (London) 028 9052 8202 (Belfast)

The Parliamentary Under-Secretary of State **(George Howarth MP)**
Private Secretary, Tel: 020 7210 6488 (London) 028 9052 8128 (Belfast)
Fax: 020 7210 6449 (London) 028 9052 8202 (Belfast)

PRIVY COUNCIL OFFICE

The President of the Council and Leader of the House of Commons
(The Rt Hon. Margaret Beckett MP)
Responsible for the work of the Privy Council Office and, as Leader of the House of Commons, for the arrangement of Government business in the Commons and for planning and supervising the Government's legislative programme. She chairs the Ministerial Committees on the Queen's Speeches and Future Legislation, Legislation, Food Safety, and Health Strategy. Together with the Minister for the Cabinet Office, she acts as a spokesperson for the Government. She sits on a number of other Cabinet Committees and sub-committees.
Principal Private Secretary: Vanessa Scarborough *Tel:* 020 7210 1011 *Fax:* 020 7210 1075

Parliamentary Secretary **(Paddy Tipping MP)**
As Deputy Leader of the House of Commons, assists the President of the Council with her duties in supervising and arranging the Government's business in the Commons.
Private Secretary: Fiona Butcher *Tel:* 020 7210 1021 *Fax:* 020 7210 1073
Assistant Private Secretary: Frances Slee *Tel:* 020 7270 1022

SCOTLAND OFFICE

The Secretary of State for Scotland **(The Rt Hon. Dr John Reid MP)**

The main functions of the Secretary of State for Scotland are to represent Scottish interests within the UK Parliament in matters reserved to the UK Government, to ensure that the reserved policies of the UK Government are presented effectively in Scotland and to promote the devolution settlement for Scotland provided by the Scotland Act 1998.

E-mail: scottishsecretary@gov.uk

Private Secretary: Ms Jayne Colquhoun *Tel:* 020 7270 6740 (London) 0131-244 4011 (Edinburgh) *GTN:* 7188 44011 *Fax:* 020 7270 6815 (London) 0131-244 1512 (Edinburgh)

The Minister of State **(Brian Wilson MP)**

Private Secretary: David Ferguson *Tel:* 020 7270 6806 (London) 0131-244 9031 (Edinburgh) *Fax:* 020 7270 6703 (London) 0131-244 9028 (Edinburgh)

The Advocate General for Scotland **(Dr Lynda Clark QC MP)**

The Advocate General is a Law Officer and adviser to the UK Government on legal and constitutional matters in Scotland. Her office provides legal services to UK Departments in Scotland.

E-mail: claire.keggie@scotland.gov.uk

Private Secretary: Claire Keggie *Tel:* 020 7270 6720 *Fax:* 020 7270 6813

Spokesperson in the House of Lords: The Baroness Ramsay of Cartvale.

DEPARTMENT OF SOCIAL SECURITY

The Secretary of State for Social Security **(The Rt Hon. Alistair Darling MP)**

Has overall responsibility for all Social Security matters; public expenditure issues; handling of all major issues.

Principal Private Secretary: Rod Clark *Tel:* 020 7238 0654 *Fax:* 020 7238 0661

Private Secretaries: Alastair Levy *Tel:* 020 7238 0656 Beth Russell *Tel:* 020 7238 0655

The Minister of State for Social Security **(The Rt Hon. Jeff Rooker MP)**

Deputy to the Secretary of State across the board (including operations); management of legislation in the Commons; pensions review, state pensions, occupational and personal pensions, National Insurance contributions review; older people; long-term care policy development; fraud/methods of payment.

Private Secretary: David Higlett *Tel:* 020 7238 0671 *Fax:* 020 7238 0675

Assistant Private Secretaries: Robert Sanguinawzi *Tel:* 020 7238 0672

Denise Whitehead *Tel:* 020 7238 0674

The Parliamentary Under-Secretary of State **(The Rt Hon. the Baroness Hollis of Heigham)**

Responsibility for family policy; Child Benefit and One Parent Benefit; lone parents; child support; Child Support Agency; industrial injuries; compensation recovery; war pensions; War Pensions Agency; management of legislation in the Lords; Citizens Charter.

Private Secretary: Mary Curran *Tel:* 020 7238 0678 *Fax:* 020 7238 0682

Assistant Private Secretary: Nigel Carleton *Tel:* 020 7238 0681

The Parliamentary Under-Secretary of State **(Angela Eagle MP)**

Responsibility for Jobseeker's Allowance/Welfare to Work; Income Support; Family Credit; Housing Benefit; Council Tax Benefit; poverty/low income; social exclusion; Benefits Agency; active modern service; decision-making and appeals; Social Fund; Widows Benefit.

Private Secretary: Nicole Kett *Tel:* 020 7238 0690 *Fax:* 020 7238 0845

Assistant Private Secretaries: Deborah Topping *Tel:* 020 7238 0693

Chris Chapman *Tel:* 020 7238 0691

The Parliamentary Under-Secretary of State **(Hugh Bayley MP)**

Responsibility for Incapacity Benefit; Disability Living Allowance; Attendance Allowance; Motability; carers; Invalid Care Allowance; vaccine damage; deregulation; Statutory Sick and Maternity Pay; management of Department of Social Security headquarters; devolution issues; Independent Living Fund.

Private Secretary: Tricia Griffiths *Tel:* 020 7238 0684 *Fax:* 020 7238 0687

Assistant Private Secretaries: David Williams *Tel:* 020 7238 0685

Ms Chris McCoy *Tel:* 020 7238 0686

Spokespersons in the House of Lords: The Baroness Hollis of Heigham, Baroness Amos.

DEPARTMENT OF TRADE AND INDUSTRY

The Secretary of State for Trade and Industry **(The Rt Hon. Stephen Byers MP)**
Overall responsibility for the DTI, its agencies and Export Credits Guarantee Department. Cabinet Minister responsible for science.
E-mail: tlo.byers@tlo.dti.gov.uk
Principal Private Secretary: Antony Phillipson *Tel:* 020 7215 5621 *Fax:* 020 7215 5468

The Minister of State for Energy and Competitiveness in Europe **(The Rt Hon. Helen Liddell MP)**
Responsible for energy including sponsorship of the oil and gas industries, European Single Market, economic reform and enlargement, and business preparation for the Euro.
E-mail: tlo.liddell@tlo.dti.gov.uk
Senior Private Secretary: Richard Riley *Tel:* 020 7215 5109 *Fax:* 020 7215 5645

The Minister for Trade **(The Rt Hon. Richard Caborn MP)**
Responsible for Trade Policy, ECGD, British Trade International, inward investment and regional policy and export projects.
E-mail: tlo.caborn@tlo.dti.gov.uk
Private Secretary: Graeme Cornell *Tel:* 020 7215 5501

The Minister of State, Minister for Small Business and E-Commerce **(Patricia Hewitt MP)**
Responsible for small firms, e-commerce and the information society, industry (supported by Alan Johnson), environment, Radiocommunications Agency.
E-mail: tlo.hewitt@tlo.dti.gov.uk
Private Secretary: Gaynor Jeffrey *Tel:* 020 7215 5144
Assistant Private Secretary: Joanna Smith

The Parliamentary Under-Secretary of State (Minister for Competition and Consumer Affairs)
(Dr Kim Howells MP)
Responsible for competition, consumer affairs, company law, corporate governance, company investigations, Insolvency Service, Patent Office, Companies House, NWML, Export Licensing.
E-mail: tlo.howells@tlo.dti.gov.uk
Private Secretary: Dawn Parr *Tel:* 020 7215 5568 *Fax:* 020 7215 5560

The Parliamentary Under-Secretary of State (Minister for Competitiveness) **(Alan Johnson MP)**
Responsible for Industry (with Patricia Hewitt), Employment Relations and Post Office.
E-mail: tlo.johnson@tlo.dti.gov.uk
Private Secretary: Simon Lancaster *Tel:* 020 7215 6202

The Parliamentary Under-Secretary of State (Minister for Science) **(The Lord Sainsbury of Turville)**
Responsible for Science, Research Councils, innovation, design and space.
E-mail: sainsbury.tlo@tlo.dti.gov.uk
Private Secretary: Simon Evans *Tel:* 020 7215 5624 *Fax:* 020 7215 5410
Spokesmen in the House of Lords: The Lord Sainsbury of Turville, The Lord McIntosh of Haringey.

HM TREASURY

The Prime Minister **(The Rt Hon. Tony Blair MP)**
First Lord of the Treasury.

The Chancellor of the Exchequer **(The Rt Hon. Gordon Brown MP)**
As Second Lord is its Ministerial head and has overall responsibility for the work of the Treasury.
Principal Private Secretary: Tom Scholar *Tel:* 020 7270 5004 *Fax:* 020 7270 4580
Private Secretaries: James Papps, Nicholas Joicey

The Chief Secretary **(The Rt Hon. Andrew Smith MP)**
Responsibility for public expenditure planning and control; value for money in the public services, including Public Service Agreements; public/private partnerships and procurement policy; strategic oversight of banking, financial services and insurance; departmental investment strategies including Capital Modernisation Fund and Invest to Save budget; welfare reform; devolution; and resource accounting and budgeting.
Private Secretary: Deborah Nickerson *Tel:* 020 7270 4339 *Fax:* 020 7451 7600

The Paymaster General **(Dawn Primarolo MP)**
Responsibility for Inland Revenue, HM Customs and Excise and the Treasury and with overall responsibility for the Finance Bill. She leads on personal taxation, taxation; VAT; European and International tax issues.
Private Secretary: Sarah Knight *Tel:* 020 7270 4349 *Fax:* 020 7270 5179

The Financial Secretary **(Stephen Timms MP)**
Responsibility for growth and productivity; small firms and venture capital; science, research and development; competition and deregulation policy; export credit; HM Customs and Excise taxes, except VAT and road fuel duties; Parliamentary finance business (PAC, NAO). He provides support on the Finance Bill and Financial Services Bill.
Private Secretary: Chris Martin *Tel:* 020 7270 4340 *Fax:* 020 7270 5131

The Economic Secretary **(Melanie Johnson MP)**
Responsibility for National Savings, the UK Debt Management Office, National Investment and Loans Office, Office for National Statistics, Royal Mint and the Government Actuary's Department; banking, financial services and insurance; foreign exchange reserves and debt management policy. Environmental issues, including 'green' taxes, taxation of company cars and road fuel, Vehicle Excise Duty; financial services tax issues and charity taxation. She provides support to the Chancellor on EU and International issues.
Private Secretary: Jo-Anne Daniels *Tel:* 020 7270 4350 *Fax:* 020 7270 5419
Spokesman in the House of Lords: The Lord McIntosh of Haringey.

THE WALES OFFICE
(Office of the Secretary of State for Wales)

The Secretary of State for Wales **(The Rt Hon. Paul Murphy MP)**
The Office of the Secretary of State has responsibility for UK-wide policy. The Secretary of State is also responsible for Industry; Economic Development; Agriculture, Transport and Planning Issues.
Principal Private Secretary: Simon Morris *Tel:* 020 7270 0550
Assistant Private Secretary: Cherie Jones *Tel:* 020 7270 0538 *Fax:* 020 7270 0568

The Parliamentary Under-Secretary of State for Wales **(David Hanson MP)**
Responsibility for Education; Health; Local Government; Environment.
Private Secretary: Jo Salway *Tel:* 020 7270 0568
Head of Office of the Secretary of State for Wales: Alison Jackson
Tel: 020 7270 0558 *Fax:* 020 7270 0588
Spokesperson in the House of Lords: The Baroness Farrington of Ribbleton.

Ministerial Salaries

Figures include (where appropriate) Parliamentary salaries of £47,008 as Members of the House of Commons. These figures are effective from 1st April 1999. However, not all ministers or other office holders necessarily draw their full salary.

	Salary (£) Accepted	Entitled Salary (£)
Prime Minister	109,768	154,187
Lord Chancellor	160,011*	
Cabinet Minister (Commons)	94,157	111,315
Cabinet Minister (Lords)	70,608	83,560
Minister of State (Commons)	80,367	
Minister of State (Lords)	64,426	
Parliamentary Under-Secretary of State (Commons)	72,327	
Parliamentary Under-Secretary of State (Lords)	55,631	

*The Ministerial & Other Pensions and Salaries Act 1991, as amended by the Ministerial and Other Salaries Order 1996, determines that the Lord Chancellor should receive £2,500 a year more than the salary payable to the Lord Chief Justice.

Law Officers

Attorney-General	68,332
Solicitor-General	103,039
Advocate General for Scotland	103,039

Other Salaries

The Speaker	111,315	
Leader of the Opposition	105,957	
Opposition Chief Whip	80,367 (Commons)	51,161 (Lords)
MP	47,008	

Government Whips

HOUSE OF LORDS

The Rt Hon The Lord Carter	*Captain of the Honourable Corps of the Gentlemen-at-Arms (Chief Whip)*
The Lord McIntosh of Haringey	*Captain of The Queen's Bodyguard of the Yeoman of the Guard (Deputy Chief Whip)*
The Lord Burlison, DL	*Lord in Waiting*
The Lord Bach	*Lord in Waiting*

Baronesses in Waiting:
The Baroness Farrington of Ribbleton, The Baroness Ramsay of Cartvale, The Baroness Amos

HOUSE OF COMMONS

The Rt Hon Ann Taylor, MP	*Chief Whip and Parliamentary Secretary to the Treasury*
Keith Bradley Esq, MP	*Deputy Chief Whip and Treasurer of HM Household*
Thomas McAvoy Esq, MP	*Comptroller of HM Household*
Graham Allen Esq, MP	*Vice-Chamberlain of HM Household*
James Dowd Esq, MP	*Lord Commissioner of HM Treasury*
Robert Ainsworth Esq, MP	*Lord Commissioner of HM Treasury*
David Jamieson Esq, MP	*Lord Commissioner of HM Treasury*
Clive Betts Esq, MP	*Lord Commissioner of HM Treasury*
Greg Pope Esq, MP	*Lord Commissioner of HM Treasury*
David Clelland Esq, MP	*Assistant Whip*
Kevin Hughes Esq, MP	*Assistant Whip*
Michael Hall Esq, MP	*Assistant Whip*
Anne McGuire, MP	*Assistant Whip*
Gerry Sutcliffe Esq, MP	*Assistant Whip*
Tony McNulty Esq, MP	*Assistant Whip*
Don Touhig Esq, MP	*Assistant Whip*

Responsibilities

Keith Bradley, MP, *Deputy to the Chief Whip on all matters*

Thomas McAvoy, MP, *Pairing Whip*

Graham Allen, MP, *HM Treasury,* **East Midlands**

James Dowd, MP, *Culture, Media and Sport, Northern Ireland, London Bill,* **London**

Robert Ainsworth, MP, *Environment, Transport and the Regions,* **West Midlands**

David Jamieson, MP, *Health,* **South East and South West**

Clive Betts, MP, *Education and Employment, Committee Whip,* **Eastern**

Greg Pope, MP, *Trade and Industry,* **North West**

David Clelland, MP, *Defence, International Development,* **North East**

Kevin Hughes, MP, *Social Security,* **West Yorkshire**

Michael Hall, MP, *Home Affairs,* **North West**

Anne McGuire, MP, *Scotland, Agriculture,* **Scotland**

Gerry Sutcliffe, MP, *Cabinet Office,* **South Yorkshire**

Tony McNulty, MP, *Foreign Affairs,* **London**

Don Touhig, MP, *Wales,* **Wales**

Special Advisers

PRIME MINISTER
Rt Hon Tony Blair, MP

Policy Unit: David Miliband (Head of Unit),
Andrew Adonis, Robert Hill, Peter Hyman,
Roger Liddle, Liz Lloyd, Geoff Mulgan,
Geoffrey Norris, James Purnell, Ed Richards,
Derek Scott, Sharon White

AGRICULTURE, FISHERIES AND FOOD
Rt Hon Nick Brown, MP

Kieran Simpson
Jack Thurston

CABINET OFFICE
Minister for the Cabinet Office and
Chancellor of the Duchy of Lancaster
Rt Hon Dr Mo Mowlam, MP

Nigel Warner
Andrew Lappin
Clay Bendish (Adviser on Agencies)

CHIEF WHIP'S OFFICE
Rt Hon Ann Taylor, MP

Ian McKenzie
Sue Jackson

CULTURE, MEDIA AND SPORT
Rt Hon Chris Smith, MP

Andy Burnham
Ruth MacKenzie

DEFENCE
Rt Hon Geoffrey Hoon, MP

Alasdair McGowan
Andrew Hood

EDUCATION AND EMPLOYMENT
Rt Hon David Blunkett, MP

Tom Engel
Sophie Linden
Nick Pearce
Conor Ryan

ENVIRONMENT, TRANSPORT AND THE REGIONS
Rt Hon John Prescott, MP

Joe Irvin
Joan Hammell

Rt Hon Hilary Armstrong, MP
Chris Mullin, MP
Rt Hon Lord Macdonald of Tradeston

David Wilson
Paul Hackett
Adrian Long

FOREIGN AND COMMONWEALTH OFFICE
Rt Hon Robin Cook, MP

David Clark
David Mathieson

HEALTH
Rt Hon Alan Milburn, MP

Simon Stevens
Darren Murphy

HOME OFFICE
Rt Hon Jack Straw, MP

Ed Owen
Justin Russell

INTERNATIONAL DEVELOPMENT
Rt Hon Clare Short, MP

David Mepham
Dee Sullivan

LEADER OF THE HOUSE
Lords:
Rt Hon the Baroness Jay of Paddington

Clare Cozens
Jo Gibbons

Commons: Rt Hon Margaret Beckett, MP

Nicci Collins
Sheila Watson

LORD CHANCELLOR
Rt Hon Lord Irvine of Lairg, QC

Garry Hart

NORTHERN IRELAND OFFICE
Rt Hon Peter Mandelson, MP

To be confirmed

SCOTLAND OFFICE
Rt Hon Dr John Reid, MP

Richard Olszewski
Mike Elrick

SCOTTISH EXECUTIVE
First Minister's Office

Dave Whitton

SOCIAL SECURITY
Rt Hon Alistair Darling, MP

Andrew Maugham
Elsbeth Johnson

TRADE AND INDUSTRY
Rt Hon Stephen Byers, MP

Dan Corry
Jo Moore

HM TREASURY
Rt Hon Gordon Brown, MP

Ed Balls (Chief Economic Adviser)
Ian Austin
Sue Nye
Chris Wales

Rt Hon Andrew Smith, MP

Spencer Livermore
Edward Milliband

WALES OFFICE
Rt Hon Paul Murphy, MP

Hywel Francis

Parliamentary Private Secretaries

PRIME MINISTER
Rt Hon Tony Blair, MP

Bruce Grocott, MP

AGRICULTURE, FISHERIES AND FOOD
Rt Hon Nick Brown, MP
Rt Hon Joyce Quin, MP
The Baroness Hayman

Ruth Kelly, MP
Brian Jenkins, MP
Bob Blizzard, MP

CABINET OFFICE
Minister for the Cabinet Office and
Chancellor of the Duchy of Lancaster
Rt Hon Dr Mo Mowlam, MP
Rt Hon Ian McCartney, MP
The Lord Falconer of Thoroton, QC

Margaret Moran, MP
Frank Doran, MP
Christopher Leslie, MP

CULTURE, MEDIA AND SPORT
Rt Hon Chris Smith, MP

Fiona Mactaggart, MP

DEFENCE
Rt Hon Geoffrey Hoon, MP
John Spellar, MP
The Baroness Symons of Vernham Dean

Sylvia Heal, MP
Dave Watts, MP
Gillian Merron, MP

EDUCATION AND EMPLOYMENT
Rt Hon David Blunkett, MP

Jean Corston, MP
Alan Whitehead, MP

Rt Hon Tessa Jowel, MP (Employment)
Rt Hon Estelle Morris, MP (Education)

Jeff Ennis, MP
Rachel Squire, MP

ENVIRONMENT, TRANSPORT AND THE REGIONS
Rt Hon John Prescott, MP
   (Deputy Prime Minister)
Rt Hon The Lord Macdonald of Tradeston
   (Transport)
Rt Hon Michael Meacher, MP (Environment)
Rt Hon Hilary Armstrong, MP
Nick Raynsford, MP

John Heppell, MP

Phil Woolas, MP

Terry Rooney, MP
Sally Keeble, MP
Phil Hope, MP

FOREIGN AND COMMONWEALTH OFFICE
Rt Hon Robin Cook, MP
Keith Vaz, MP
Peter Hain, MP
John Battle, MP

Ken Purchase, MP
Dennis MacShane, MP
Caroline Flint, MP
Rosemary McKenna, MP

HEALTH
Rt Hon Alan Milburn, MP
John Denham, MP
John Hutton, MP

Jim Fitzpatrick, MP
Paul Goggins, MP
Maria Eagle, MP

HOME OFFICE
Rt Hon Jack Straw, MP
Rt Hon Paul Boateng, MP
Charles Clarke, MP
Barbara Roche, MP

Colin Pickthall, MP
Angela Smith, MP
Gareth R Thomas, MP
Tom Levitt, MP

INTERNATIONAL DEVELOPMENT
Rt Hon Clare Short, MP

Dennis Turner, MP

LAW OFFICERS
Attorney General: Rt Hon the Lord Williams
  of Mostyn, QC
Solicitor General: Ross Cranston, QC, MP

Michael Jabez Foster, MP

LEADER OF THE HOUSE
Lords: and Minister for Women
Rt Hon the Baroness Jay of Paddington
Commons: Rt Hon Margaret Beckett, MP

Eric Martlew, MP
Ivor Caplin, MP

LORD CHANCELLOR'S DEPARTMENT
Rt Hon the Lord Irvine of Lairg, QC

Bridget Prentice, MP
Paul Clark, MP

NORTHERN IRELAND OFFICE
Rt Hon Peter Mandelson, MP
Rt Hon Adam Ingram, MP

Helen Jackson, MP
Anthony Colman, MP

SCOTLAND OFFICE
Rt Hon Dr John Reid, MP
Brian Wilson, MP

Frank Roy, MP
Sandra Osborne, MP

SOCIAL SECURITY
Rt Hon Alistair Darling, MP
Rt Hon Jeff Rooker, MP

Ann Coffey, MP
Richard Burden, MP

TRADE AND INDUSTRY
Rt Hon Stephen Byers, MP
Rt Hon Helen Liddell, MP
Rt Hon Richard Caborn, MP
Patricia Hewitt, MP

Ivan Lewis, MP
Derek Twigg, MP
Ben Chapman, MP
Anne Campbell, MP

HM TREASURY
Rt Hon Gordon Brown, MP
Rt Hon Andrew Smith, MP
Dawn Primarolo, MP (Paymaster General)
Stephen Timms, MP

John Healey, MP
Joan Ryan, MP
Chris Pond, MP
Vernon Coaker, MP

WALES OFFICE
Rt Hon Paul Murphy, MP

Nick Ainger, MP

Ministerial Committees of the Cabinet

Economic Affairs

Chancellor of the Exchequer *(Chair)*
Deputy Prime Minister and Secretary of State for the Environment, Transport and the Regions
Secretary of State for the Home Department
Secretary of State for Education and Employment
President of the Council and Leader of the House of Commons
Parliamentary Secretary, Treasury and Chief Whip
Secretary of State for Culture, Media and Sport
Minister for the Cabinet Office and Chancellor of the Duchy of Lancaster
Secretary of State for Social Security
Minister of Agriculture, Fisheries and Food
Secretary of State for Trade and Industry
Secretary of State for Health
Secretary of State for Scotland
Secretary of State for Wales
Secretary of State for Northern Ireland
Chief Secretary, HM Treasury
Minister of Transport
Minister of State, Cabinet Office

Other Ministers are invited to attend for items in which they have a departmental interest. The Chief Scientific Adviser attends for issues relating to science and technology

Terms of Reference
To consider issues relating to the Government's economic policies

Energy Policy Sub-Committee

Chancellor of the Exchequer *(Chair)*
Deputy Prime Minister and Secretary of State for the Environment, Transport and the Regions
Secretary of State for Trade and Industry
Paymaster General, HM Treasury
Minister of State, Foreign and Commonwealth Office
Minister of State, Cabinet Office
Minister of State, Department of Trade and Industry
Minister of State, Scotland Office
Parliamentary Under-Secretary of State, Wales Office

Terms of Reference
To consider the principles and objectives which should underlie Great Britain's energy strategy; and make recommendations for an energy strategy to the Ministerial Committee on Economic Affairs

Productivity and Competitiveness Sub-Committee

Chancellor of the Exchequer *(Chair)*
Deputy Prime Minister and Secretary of State for the Environment, Transport and the Regions
Secretary of State for the Home Department
Secretary of State for Education and Employment
Secretary of State for Culture, Media and Sport
Minister for the Cabinet Office and Chancellor of the Duchy of Lancaster
Minister of Agriculture, Fisheries and Food
Secretary of State for Trade and Industry
Secretary of State for Scotland
Secretary of State for Wales
Secretary of State for Northern Ireland
Chief Secretary, HM Treasury

Minister of State, Foreign and Commonwealth Office
Miinister of State, Cabinet Office

Terms of Reference
To consider measures to improve the productivity and competitiveness of the United Kingdom economy

Welfare to Work Sub-Committee

Chancellor of the Exchequer *(Chair)*
Secretary of State for Education and Employment
Secretary of State for Social Security
Secretary of State for Scotland
Secretary of State for Wales
Secretary of State for Northern Ireland
Chief Secretary, HM Treasury
Minister of State, Department of the Environment, Transport and the Regions
Financial Secretary, Treasury
Minister of State, Home Office
Minister of State, Department for Education and Employment
Minister of State, Cabinet Office

The Secretary of State for Health also receives papers. Other Ministers are invited to attend for items in which they have a departmental interest

Terms of Reference
To develop policies to get people from welfare to work and to report as necessary to the Ministerial Committee on Economic Affairs

Public Services and Public Expenditure

Chancellor of the Exchequer *(Chair)*
Lord Chancellor
President of the Council and Leader of the House of Commons
Parliamentary Secretary, Treasury and Chief Whip
Minister for the Cabinet Office and Chancellor of the Duchy of Lancaster
Lord Privy Seal, Leader of the House of Lords and Minister for Women
Chief Secretary, Treasury
Minister of State, Cabinet Office

Other Ministers are invited to attend for matters in which they have a departmental interest

Terms of Reference
To monitor progress against public service agreements, to review public expenditure allocations and make recommendations to the Cabinet

The Environment

Deputy Prime Minister and Secretary of State for the Environment, Transport and the Regions
　　(Chair)
Chancellor of the Exchequer
Secretary of State for Foreign and Commonwealth Affairs
President of the Council and Leader of the House of Commons
Parliamentary Secretary, Treasury and Chief Whip
Secretary of State for Culture, Media and Sport
Minister for the Cabinet Office and Chancellor of the Duchy of Lancaster
Secretary of State for International Development
Minister of Agriculture, Fisheries and Food
Secretary of State for Trade and Industry
Secretary of State for Health
Secretary of State for Scotland

Secretary of State for Wales
Secretary of State for Northern Ireland
Chief Secretary, HM Treasury
Minister of Transport
Minister of State, Department of the Environment, Transport and the Regions

The Secretary of State for Social Security and the Secretary of State for Education and Employment also receive papers. They and other Ministers are invited to attend as necessary. The Chief Scientific Adviser attends for issues relating to science and technology

Terms of Reference
To consider environmental policies and to co-ordinate those on sustainable development

Local Government

Deputy Prime Minister and Secretary of State for the Environment, Transport and the Regions
    (Chair)
Chancellor of the Exchequer
Lord Chancellor
Secretary of State for the Home Department
Secretary of State for Education and Employment
President of the Council and Leader of the House of Commons
Parliamentary Secretary, Treasury and Chief Whip
Secretary of State for Culture, Media and Sport
Minister for the Cabinet Office and Chancellor of the Duchy of Lancaster
Secretary of State for Social Security
Secretary of State for Trade and Industry
Secretary of State for Health
Secretary of State for Wales
Chief Secretary, HM Treasury
Minister of Transport, Department of the Environment, Transport and the Regions
Minister of State, Department of the Environment, Transport and the Regions
Minister of State, Cabinet Office

Other Ministers are invited to attend for items in which they have a departmental interest

Terms of Reference
To consider issues affecting local government, including the annual allocation of resources

London Sub-Committee

Deputy Prime Minister and Secretary of State for the Environment, Transport and the Regions
    (Chair)
Minister of Transport, Department of the Environment, Transport and the Regions
Paymaster General, Treasury
Minister of State, Department for Education and Employment
Minister of State, Cabinet Office
Minister of State, Department of Health
Parliamentary Under-Secretary of State, Department of the Environment, Transport and the Regions
Parliamentary Under-Secretary of State, Home Office
Parliamentary Under-Secretary of State, Department for Culture, Media and Sport
Parliamentary Under-Secretary of State, Department of Social Security
Parliamentary Under-Secretary of State, Department of Trade and Industry

Terms of Reference
To co-ordinate the Government's policies on London, and report as necessary to the Ministerial Committee on Local Government and the Ministerial Committee on Devolution Policy

Biotechnology and Genetic Modification Group

Minister for the Cabinet Office *(Chair)*
Minister of State, Department of the Environment, Transport and the Regions
Minister of State, Foreign and Commonwealth Office
Minister of State, Cabinet Office and Chancellor of the Duchy of Lancaster
Minister of State, Ministry of Agriculture, Fisheries and Food
Minister of State, Department of Trade and Industry
Minister of State, Scotland Office
Economic Secretary, HM Treasury
Parliamentary Under-Secretary of State, Home Office
Parliamentary Under-Secretary of State, Department for International Development
Parliamentary Under-Secretary of State, Department of Trade and Industry
Parliamentary Under-Secretary, Department of Health
Parliamentary Under-Secretary of State, Wales Office
Parliamentary Under-Secretary of State, Northern Ireland Office
Minister of State, Scotland Office

The Chief Scientific Adviser also attends

Terms of Reference
To consider issues relating to biotechnology, in particular those arising from genetic modification

Better Government Group

Minister for the Cabinet Office and Chancellor of the Duchy of Lancaster *(Chair)*
Secretary of State for the Home Department
Secretary of State for Education and Employment
Secretary of State for Social Security
Secretary of State for Trade and Industry
Secretary of State for Health
Secretary of State for Wales
Chief Secretary, HM Treasury
Minister of State, Department of the Environment, Transport and the Regions
Minister of State, Foreign and Commonwealth Office
Minister of State, Department for Education and Employment
Minister of State, Cabinet Office
Minister of State, Cabinet Office
Minister of State, Scotland Office
Minister of State, Department of Health
Minister of State, Northern Ireland Office
Parliamentary Under-Secretary of State, Lord Chancellor's Department
Parliamentary Under-Secretary of State, Department for Culture, Media and Sport
Parliamentary Under-Secretary of State, Scotland Office

Terms of Reference
To develop the Government's programme for improving the quality, coherence and responsiveness of public services and to oversee its implementation

Home and Social Affairs

Deputy Prime Minister and Secretary of State for the Environment, Transport and the Regions
  (Chair)
Chancellor of the Exchequer
Lord Chancellor
Secretary of State for the Home Department
Secretary of State for Education and Employment
President of the Council and Leader of the House of Commons
Parliamentary Secretary, Treasury and Chief Whip
Secretary of State for Culture, Media and Sport

Minister for the Cabinet Office and Chancellor of the Duchy of Lancaster
Secretary of State for Social Security
Minister of Agriculture, Fisheries and Food
Leader of the House of Lords and Minister for Women (appointed as Lord Privy Seal)
Secretary of State for Trade and Industry
Secretary of State for Health
Secretary of State for Scotland
Secretary of State for Wales
Secretary of State for Northern Ireland
Chief Secretary, HM Treasury
Minister of Transport
Minister of State, Cabinet Office

The Attorney General, the Lord Advocate and the Captain of the Gentlemen-at-Arms also receive papers. They and others are invited to attend as necessary

Terms of Reference
To consider issues of home and social policy

Health Strategy Sub-Committee

President of the Council and Leader of the House of Commons *(Chair)*
Secretary of State for International Development
Secretary of State for Health
Minister of State, Department of the Environment, Transport and the Regions
Minister of State, Home Office
Minister of State, Ministry of Agriculture, Fisheries and Food
Parliamentary Under-Secretary of State, Department of the Environment, Transport and the Regions
Economic Secretary, HM Treasury
Parliamentary Under-Secretary of State, Department for Education and Employment
Parliamentary Under-Secretary of State, Department of Social Security
Parliamentary Under-Secretary of State, Department of Trade and Industry

The Chief Medical Officer is in attendance. The Secretary of State for Wales also receives papers and is invited to attend as necessary. Other Ministers are invited to attend for items in which they have a departmental interest

Terms of Reference
To oversee the development, implementation and monitoring of the Government's health strategy; and to report as necessary to the Ministerial Committee on Home and Social Affairs

Drug Misuse Sub-Committee

Minister for the Cabinet Office and Chancellor of the Duchy of Lancaster *(Chair)*
Secretary of State for International Development
Solicitor General
Financial Secretary, HM Treasury
Minister of State, Foreign and Commonwealth Office
Minister of State, Home Office
Minister of State, Cabinet Office
Minister of State, Department of Health
Minister of State, Scotland Office
Minister of State, Northern Ireland Office
Minister of State, Ministry of Defence
Parliamentary Under-Secretary of State, Department for Education and Employment
Parliamentary Under-Secretary of State, Department for Culture, Media and Sport
Parliamentary Under-Secretary of State, Wales Office

The Parliamentary Under-Secretary of State, Department of the Environment, Transport and the Regions also receives papers and may be invited to attend as appropriate

Terms of Reference
To co-ordinate the Government's national and international policies for tackling drugs misuse, and report as necessary to the Ministerial Committee on Home and Social Affairs

Women's Issues Sub-Committee

Lord Privy Seal, Leader of the House of Lords and Minister for Women *(Chair)*
Minister for the Cabinet Office and Chancellor of the Duchy of Lancaster
Secretary of State for International Development
Minister of State, Home Office
Minister of State, Department for Education and Employment
Minister of State, Scotland Office
Parliamentary Under-Secretary of State, Department of the Environment, Transport and the Regions
Economic Secretary, HM Treasury
Parliamentary Under-Secretary of State, Department of Social Security
Parliamentary Under-Secretary of State, Department of Trade and Industry
Parliamentary Under-Secretary of State, Department of Health
Parliamentary Under-Secretary of State, Wales Office
Parliamentary Under-Secretary of State, Northern Ireland Office

Terms of Reference

To review and develop the Government's policy and strategy on issues of special concern to women; to oversee their implementation; and to report as necessary to the Ministerial Committee on Home and Social Affairs

The Queen's Speeches and Future Legislation

President of the Council and Leader of the House of Commons *(Chair)*
Deputy Prime Minister and Secretary of State for the Environment, Transport and the Regions
Lord Chancellor
Parliamentary Secretary, Treasury and Chief Whip
Minister for the Cabinet Office and Chancellor of the Duchy of Lancaster
Lord Privy Seal, Leader of the House of Lords and Minister for Women
Chief Secretary, HM Treasury
Attorney General
Advocate General
Minister of State, Cabinet Office
Captain of the Gentlemen-at-Arms
The Parliamentary Secretary, Privy Council Office also attends

The Secretary of State for Foreign and Commonwealth Affairs is invited to attend for discussions of The Queen's Speeches

Terms of Reference

To prepare and submit to the Cabinet drafts of The Queen's Speeches to Parliament and proposals for the Government's legislative programme

Legislation

President of the Council and Leader of the House of Commons *(Chair)*
Lord Chancellor
Parliamentary Secretary, Treasury and Chief Whip
Lord Privy Seal, Leader of the House of Lords and Minister for Women
Secretary of State for Scotland
Secretary of State for Wales
Attorney General
Advocate General
Financial Secretary, HM Treasury
Minister of State, Foreign and Commonwealth Office
Minister of State, Home Office
Minister of State, Cabinet Office
Captain of the Gentlemen-at-Arms

The Parliamentary Secretary, Privy Council Office also attends. The Secretary of State for Northern Ireland also receives papers and is invited to attend as necessary

Terms of Reference
To examine all draft Bills; to consider the parliamentary handling of Government Bills, European Community documents and Private Members' business, and such other related matters as may be necessary; and to keep under review the Government's policy in relation to issues of Parliamentary procedures

Crime Reduction and Youth Justice Group

Secretary of State for the Home Department *(Chair)*
Lord Privy Seal, Leader of the House of Lords and Minister for Women
Chief Secretary, HM Treasury
Solicitor General
Minister of State, Home Office
Minister of State, Cabinet Office
Minister of State, Department of Health
Minister of State, Scotland Office
Parliamentary Under-Secretary of State, Department of the Environment, Transport and the Regions
Parliamentary Under-Secretary, Lord Chancellor's Department
Parliamentary Under-Secretary of State, Department for Education and Employment
Parliamentary Secretary, Cabinet Office
Parliamentary Under-Secretary of State, Department for Culture, Media and Sport
Parliamentary Under-Secretary of State, Wales Office

The Secretary of State for Northern Ireland also receives papers, and may attend or be represented as necessary

Terms of Reference
To oversee the Government's programme to reduce crime and the reform of youth justice and to make recommendations to the Ministerial Committee on Home and Social Affairs

Millennium Date Change Group

President of the Council and Leader of the House of Commons *(Chair)*
Secretary of State for Wales
Minister of State, Foreign and Commonwealth Office
Minister of State, Cabinet Office
Minister of State, Ministry of Agriculture, Fisheries and Food
Minister of State, Department of Trade and Industry
Minister of State, Scotland Office
Minister of State, Northern Ireland Office
Minister of State, Ministry of Defence
Parliamentary Under-Secretary of State, Department of the Environment, Transport and the Regions
Economic Secretary, HM Treasury
Parliamentary Under-Secretary of State, Home Office
Parliamentary Under-Secretary of State, Department for Education and Employment
Parliamentary Under-Secretary of State, Department for International Development
Parliamentary Under-Secretary of State, Department of Social Security
Parliamentary Under-Secretary of State, Department of Health
Captain of the Yeomen of the Guard

The Parliamentary Secretary, Privy Council Office also attends. Other Ministers are invited to attend for items in which they have a departmental interest. The Chairman of Action 2000 and the Prime Minister's Adviser on the Year 2000 problem are invited to attend

Terms of Reference
To drive action in the public and private sector, including the national infrastructure, to prevent damage from the failure of electronic systems related to the Year 2000 date change

Rural Affairs Group

Minister for the Cabinet Office and Chancellor of the Duchy of Lancaster *(Chair)*
Secretary of State for the Home Department
Secretary of State for Education and Employment
Secretary of State for Culture, Media and Sport
Minister of State, Ministry of Agriculture, Fisheries and Food
Secretary of State, Department of Trade and Industry
Secretary of State for Health
Chief Secretary, HM Treasury
Minister of State, Department of the Environment, Transport and the Regions

Other Ministers will be invited to attend as and when business requires

Terms of Reference
To co-ordinate the Government's policies affecting Rural Areas

Civil Contingencies

Secretary of State for the Home Department *(Chair)*

Representatives of government departments as appropriate

Terms of Reference
To co-ordinate, review and supervise plans for maintaining essential supplies and services in case of emergencies; and to report as necessary to the appropriate Ministerial Committee

Constitutional Reform Policy

Prime Minister *(Chair)*
Deputy Prime Minister and Secretary of State for the Environment, Transport and the Regions
Chancellor of the Exchequer
Secretary of State for Foreign and Commonwealth Affairs
Lord Chancellor
Secretary of State for the Home Department
President of the Council and Leader of the House of Commons
Parliamentary Secretary, Treasury and Chief Whip
Minister for the Cabinet Office and Chancellor of the Duchy of Lancaster
Lord Privy Seal, Leader of the House of Lords and Minister for Women
Secretary of State for Scotland
Secretary of State for Wales
Secretary of State for Northern Ireland

Other Ministers may be invited to attend as necessary

Terms of Reference
To consider strategic issues relating to the Government's constitutional reform policies

Incorporation of the European Convention of Human Rights Sub-Committee

Lord Chancellor *(Chair)*
Deputy Prime Minister and Secretary of State for the Environment, Transport and the Regions
Secretary of State for Foreign and Commonwealth Affairs
Secretary of State for the Home Department
Secretary of State for Education and Employment
President of the Council and Leader of the House of Commons
Parliamentary Secretary, Treasury and Chief Whip
Secretary of State for Culture, Media and Sport
Secretary of State for Social Security
Lord Privy Seal, Leader of the House of Lords and Minister for Women
Secretary of State for Health

Secretary of State for Scotland
Secretary of State for Wales
Secretary of State for Northern Ireland
Secretary of State for Defence
Chief Secretary, HM Treasury
Attorney General
Advocate General

Other Ministers are invited to attend for items in which they have a departmental interest. The Minister of State, Cabinet Office receives papers

Terms of Reference
To consider policy and other issues arising from the Government's decision to legislate for the incorporation of ECHR in UK law and to promote and oversee progress of the relevant legislation through Parliament and its subsequent implementation, and to report as necessary to the Ministerial Committee on Constitutional Reform Policy

Freedom of Information Sub-Committee

Lord Chancellor *(Chair)*
Chancellor of the Exchequer
Secretary of State for Foreign and Commonwealth Affairs
Secretary of State for the Home Department
Secretary of State for Education and Employment
President of the Council and Leader of the House of Commons
Parliamentary Secretary, Treasury and Chief Whip
Secretary of State for Culture, Media and Sport
Minister for the Cabinet Office and Chancellor of the Duchy of Lancaster
Secretary of State for International Development
Secretary of State for Social Security
Minister of Agriculture, Fisheries and Food
Lord Privy Seal, Leader of the House of Lords and Minister for Women
Secretary of State for Trade and Industry
Secretary of State for Health
Secretary of State for Scotland
Secretary of State for Wales
Secretary of State for Northern Ireland
Secretary of State for Defence
Attorney General
Advocate General
Minister of Transport
Minister of State, Cabinet Office

Other Ministers are invited to attend for items in which they have a departmental interest

Terms of Reference
To consider policy and other issues arising from the Government's decision to legislate on freedom of information; to promote and oversee progress of the relevant legislation through Parliament and its subsequent implementation; and to report as necessary to the Ministerial Committee on Constitutional Reform Policy

Reform of the House of Lords Sub-Committee

Lord Chancellor *(Chair)*
Secretary of State for the Home Department
President of the Council and Leader of the House of Commons
Parliamentary Secretary, Treasury and Chief Whip
Lord Privy Seal, Leader of the House of Lords and Minister for Women
Minister for the Cabinet Office and Chancellor of the Duchy of Lancaster
Attorney General
Captain of the Gentleman at Arms
Minister of State, Cabinet Office

Parliamentary Secretary, Privy Council Office also attends. Other Ministers are invited to attend as necessary

Terms of Reference

To consider policy and other issues arising from the Government's plans for reform of the House of Lords and to make recommendations to the Ministerial Committee on Constitutional Reform Policy

Devolution Policy Committee

Lord Chancellor *(Chair)*
Deputy Prime Minister and Secretary of State for the Environment, Transport and the Regions
Secretary of State for Foreign and Commonwealth Affairs
Secretary of State for the Home Department
Secretary of State for Education and Employment
President of the Council and Leader of the House of Commons
Parliamentary Secretary, Treasury and Chief Whip
Secretary of State for Culture, Media and Sport
Secretary of State for Social Security
Minister of Agriculture, Fisheries and Food
Lord Privy Seal, Leader of the House of Lords and Minister for Women
Secretary of State for Trade and Industry
Secretary of State for Health
Secretary of State for Scotland
Secretary of State for Wales
Secretary of State for Northern Ireland
Chief Secretary, HM Treasury
Captain of the Gentleman at Arms
Attorney General
Advocate General
Minister of State, Cabinet Office

Other Ministers are invited for items in which they have departmental interest

Terms of Reference

To consider policy and other issues arising from the Government's policies for devolution to Scotland, Wales and Northern Ireland and the regions of England and to promote and oversee progress of the relevant legislation through Parliament and its subsequent implementation

Liberal Democratic Party Joint Consultative Committee

The Committee will be chaired by the Prime Minister

Other Ministers are invited to attend for relevant items

Terms of Reference

To consider policy issues of joint interest to the Government and the Liberal Democrats

Defence and Overseas Policy

Prime Minister *(Chair)*
Deputy Prime Minister and Secretary of State for the Environment, Transport and the Regions
Chancellor of the Exchequer
Secretary of State for Foreign and Commonwealth Affairs
Secretary of State for Trade and Industry
Secretary of State for Defence

The Chief of the Defence Staff attends as required, as will the Chiefs of Staff when necessary. Others are invited to attend as necessary

Terms of Reference
To keep under review the Government's defence and overseas policy

Northern Ireland

Prime Minister *(Chair)*
Chancellor of the Exchequer
Secretary of State for Foreign and Commonwealth Affairs
Secretary of State for the Home Department
Secretary of State for Northern Ireland
Secretary of State for Defence

Terms of Reference
To oversee the Government's policy on Northern Ireland issues and relations with the Republic of Ireland on these matters

Intelligence Services

Prime Minister *(Chair)*
Deputy Prime Minister and Secretary of State for the Environment, Transport and the Regions
Chancellor of the Exchequer
Secretary of State for Foreign and Commonwealth Affairs
Secretary of State for the Home Department
Secretary of State for Defence

Terms of Reference
To keep under review policy on the security and intelligence services

Restructuring of the European Aerospace and Defence Industry Group

Secretary of State for Trade and Industry *(Chair)*
Secretary of State for Defence
Financial Secretary, HM Treasury
Minister of State, Foreign and Commonwealth Office
Parliamentary Under-Secretary of State, Department of Trade and Industry

Terms of Reference
To develop Government policy and co-ordinate related activity in promoting the restructuring of the European aerospace and defence industry

European Issues Sub-Committee

Secretary of State for Foreign and Commonwealth Affairs *(Chair)*
Deputy Prime Minister and Secretary of State for the Environment, Transport and the Regions
Chancellor of the Exchequer
Secretary of State for the Home Department
Secretary of State for Education and Employment
President of the Council and Leader of the House of Commons
Parliamentary Secretary, Treasury and Chief Whip
Minister for the Cabinet Office and Chancellor of the Duchy of Lancaster
Secretary of State for International Development

Minister of Agriculture, Fisheries and Food
Lord Privy Seal, Leader of the House of Lords and Minister for Women
Secretary of State for Trade and Industry
Secretary of State for Scotland
Secretary of State for Wales
Secretary of State for Northern Ireland
Secretary of State for Defence
Attorney General
Minister of State, Foreign and Commonwealth Office
Minister for Energy and Competitiveness in Europe, Department of Trade and Industry

Other Ministers are invited to attend as the nature of the business requires. The United Kingdom's Permanent Representative to the European Union is also in attendance

Terms of Reference
To consider questions relating to the United Kingdom's membership of the European Union and to report as necessary to the Ministerial Committee on Defence and Overseas Policy

European Trade Issues Sub-Committee

Secretary of State for Foreign and Commonwealth Affairs *(Chair)*
Chancellor of the Exchequer
Secretary of State for International Development
Minister of Agriculture, Fisheries and Food
Secretary of State for Trade and Industry

Other Ministers will be invited to attend as the nature of the business requires. The United Kingdom's Permanent Representative to the European Union is also in attendance

Terms of Reference
To consider questions relating to European Union trade policy issues and to report as necessary to the Ministerial Sub-Committee on European issues

Opposition Parliamentary Spokesmen

CONSERVATIVE PARTY

LEADER OF THE OPPOSITION
The Rt Hon William Hague, MP

AGRICULTURE, FISHERIES AND FOOD
Shadow Minister: **Tim Yeo, MP**
 Front Bench Spokesmen: James Paice, MP,
  Patrick Nicholls, MP
 Lords: The Baroness Byford, DBE

CABINET OFFICE
Shadow Minister for the Cabinet Office:
 Andrew Lansley, CBE, MP
 *Shadow Chancellor of the Duchy of
  Lancaster and Policy Renewal:*
 Ann Winterton, MP
 (responsible for policy on drugs misuse)
 Lords: The Rt Hon the Lord Mackay of
  Ardbrecknish, The Lord Henley

CULTURE, MEDIA AND SPORT
Shadow Secretary of State:
 Peter Ainsworth, MP
 Front Bench Spokesmen: Richard Spring, MP
 Lords: The Baroness Anelay of St Johns

DEFENCE
Shadow Secretary of State:
 Iain Duncan Smith, MP
 Front Bench Spokesmen:
  Richard Ottaway, MP, Robert Key, MP
 Lords: The Lord Burnham, The Earl Attlee

EDUCATION AND EMPLOYMENT
Shadow Secretary of State: **Theresa May, MP**
 *(also Shadow Cabinet Spokeswoman for
 Women's Issues)*
 Front Bench Spokesmen:
 People with Disabilities: Tim Boswell, MP,
  James Clappison, MP, John Bercow, MP
 Lords: The Rt Hon the Baroness Blatch, CBE
  (Education),
  The Viscount Astor *(Employment)*

ENVIRONMENT, TRANSPORT AND THE
REGIONS
Shadow Secretary of State:
 The Rt Hon John Redwood, MP
 Shadow Minister for Transport:
 The Hon Bernard Jenkin, MP
 Front Bench Spokesmen: Damian Green, MP,
  Nigel Waterson, MP
 Lords: The Lord Brabazon of Tara, The
  Baroness Miller of Hendon, MBE
  (London),
  The Lord Dixon Smith *(Local Government),*
  The Earl Attlee *(Transport)*

FOREIGN AND COMMONWEALTH
AFFAIRS
Shadow Foreign Secretary: **John Maples, MP**
 Front Bench Spokesmen:
  Archie Norman, MP, Cheryl Gillan, MP
 Lords: The Lord Moynihan,
  The Baroness Rawlings

HEALTH
Shadow Secretary of State: **Dr Liam Fox, MP**
 Front Bench Spokesmen:
  Philip Hammond, MP,
  Caroline Spelman, MP *(also Front Bench
  Spokesperson for Women's Issues reporting
  to Theresa May, MP)*
 Lords: The Earl Howe,
  The Lord McColl of Dulwich

HOME AFFAIRS
Shadow Home Secretary:
 The Rt Hon Ann Widdecombe, MP
 Front Bench Spokesmen:
  David Lidington, MP, John Greenway, MP
 Lords: The Rt Hon the Lord Cope of
  Berkeley, The Viscount Astor, The Rt Hon
  the Lord Mackay of Drumadoon, QC

INTERNATIONAL DEVELOPMENT
International Development:
Shadow Secretary of State: **Gary Streeter, MP**
 Lords: The Baroness Rawlings

LAW OFFICERS AND LORD
CHANCELLOR'S DEPARTMENT
Shadow Attorney General:
 Edward Garnier, QC, MP
 Shadow Lord Chancellor:
 The Rt Hon the Lord Kingsland, TD, QC
 Shadow Lord Advocate: **The Rt Hon the
  Lord Mackay of Drumadoon, QC**
 Front Bench Spokesman: Nick Hawkins, MP
 Lords: The Baroness Buscombe

NORTHERN IRELAND
Shadow Secretary of State:
 The Rt Hon Andrew Mackay, MP
 Front Bench Spokesman: Malcolm Moss, MP
 Lords: The Lord Glentoran,
  The Rt Hon the Lord Cope of Berkeley

SOCIAL SECURITY
Shadow Secretary of State: **David Willetts, MP**
 Front Bench Spokesmen:
  The Hon Michael Trend, CBE, MP,
  Eric Pickles, MP
 Lords: The Rt Hon the Lord Higgins, KBE,
  The Baroness Buscombe

SHADOW LEADER OF THE HOUSE OF COMMONS AND CONSTITUTIONAL AFFAIRS

The Rt Hon Sir George Young, Bt, MP

Deputy to the Shadow Leader of the House of Commons: Sir Patrick Cormack, MP

Spokesman for Scotland: Dominic Grieve, MP

Spokesman for Wales: Nigel Evans, MP, Robert Walter, MP

SHADOW LEADER OF THE HOUSE OF LORDS AND CONSTITUTIONAL AFFAIRS

The Rt Hon the Lord Strathclyde

Deputy Leader and Spokesman for Scotland: **The Rt Hon the Lord Mackay of Ardbrecknish**

Spokesman for Scotland: The Rt Hon the Lord Mackay of Drumadoon, QC

Spokesman for Wales: The Rt Hon the Lord Roberts of Conwy

TRADE AND INDUSTRY

Shadow Secretary of State: **Angela Browning, MP**

Front Bench Spokesmen: Alan Duncan, MP, Nick Gibb, MP

Lords: The Rt Hon the Lord Mackay of Ardbrecknish, The Baroness Miller of Hendon, MBE, The Baroness Buscombe

TREASURY

Shadow Chancellor: **The Rt Hon Francis Maude, MP**

Shadow Chief Secretary: The Rt Hon David Heathcoat-Amory, MP

Front Bench Spokesmen: Quentin Davies, MP, Oliver Letwin, MP, Howard Flight, MP

Lords: The Lord Saatchi, The Rt Hon the Lord Kingsland, TD, QC

WHIPS

House of Commons

Chief Whip: The Rt Hon James Arbuthnot, MP

Deputy Chief Whip: Patrick McLoughlin, MP

Pairing Whip; Northern Ireland: James Cran, MP

Foreign Office; Leader of the House: Oliver Heald, MP

Home Office; Private Members' Bills; Cabinet Office: Stephen Day, MP

Treasury; Health: Keith Simpson, MP

Environment, Transport and the Regions; Social Security: Jacqui Lait, MP

International Development; Trade and Industry; Wales: Eleanor Laing, MP

Education and Employment; Defence; Culture: Geoffrey Clifton-Brown, MP

Agriculture; Scotland: Peter Atkinson, MP

House of Lords

Chief Whip: The Lord Henley

Deputy Chief Whip: The Lord Burnham

Whips

The Earl of Courtown, The Lord Luke, The Baroness Seccombe, DBE, The Viscount Bridgeman, The Lord Astor of Hever, The Lord Northbrook, The Earl of Northesk

CONSERVATIVE CENTRAL OFFICE

Party Chairman: The Rt Hon Michael Ancram, QC, MP

Deputy Chairman and Chief Executive: The Hon David Prior, MP

Senior Vice-Chairman: Tim Collins, CBE, MP

Vice-Chairman, (Wales): Nigel Evans, MP

Vice-Chairman: John Hayes, MP

Parly Priv Secs to the Leader of the Conservative Party: John Whittingdale, OBE, MP *(Commons)*, The Baroness Hooper *(Lords)*

LIBERAL DEMOCRAT PARTY

Leader: **The Rt Hon Charles Kennedy, MP***

Deputy Leader: **The Rt Hon Alan Beith, MP***

Chief Whip and Shadow Leader of the House: Paul Tyler, MP*

Deputy Chief Whip: Andrew Stunell, MP

President: Baroness Maddock

Agriculture, Rural Affairs and Fisheries: **Colin Breed, MP***
David Heath, MP

Constitution, Culture and Sport: **The Rt Hon Robert Maclennan, MP***
Tourism: Ronnie Fearn, MP
Sport: Bob Russell, MP

Economy: **Matthew Taylor, MP***
Edward Davey, MP

Education and Employment: **Phil Willis, MP***
Employment and Childcare: Jackie Ballard, MP
Higher Education and Women: Dr Evan Harris, MP

Environment, Transport, the Regions and Social Justice: **Don Foster, MP***
Tom Brake, MP
Adrian Sanders, MP
Transport: **Michael Moore, MP***

Foreign Affairs and Defence: **The Rt Hon Menzies Campbell, QC, MP***
Mark Oaten, MP
Defence: Paul Keetch, MP
International Development: **Dr Jenny Tonge, MP***

Health: **Nick Harvey, MP***
  Public Health: Dr Peter Brand, MP
Home and Legal Affairs: **Simon Hughes, MP***
  Home Affairs: Richard Allan, MP
  Legal Affairs: John Burnett, MP
  Northern Ireland and Youth:
    Lembit Öpik, MP
Scotland: **Jim Wallace, QC, MP***
  Ray Michie, MP
  Sir Robert Smith, MP
Social Security: **Prof Steve Webb, MP***
  Andrew George, MP
  Pensions: Paul Burstow, MP
Trade and Industry: **Dr Vincent Cable, MP***
  Consumer Affairs and Broadcasting:
    Norman Baker, MP
  Small Business: Brian Cotter, MP
Wales: **Richard Livsey, MP***
Whips
  Chief Whip: Paul Tyler, MP
  Deputy Chief Whip: Andrew Stunell, MP
  Whips: Edward Davey, MP,
    Sir Robert Smith, MP, Adrian Sanders, MP,
    Bob Russell, MP
Party Chairman: Malcolm Bruce, MP
Church Commissioners: Simon Hughes, MP
*President of the Council and Leader of the
  House (House of Commons):* Paul Tyler, MP

**Members of the Shadow Cabinet*

ULSTER UNIONIST PARTY

Leader; Constitutional Affairs:
  The Rt Hon David Trimble, MP
*Deputy Leader; Foreign Affairs and
  International Development:*
  The Rt Hon John D Taylor, MP
*Chief Whip; Shadow Leader of the House;
  Health and Family Policy:*
  The Rev Martin Smyth, MP
Agriculture, Fisheries and Local Government:
  William Thompson, MP
Home Affairs and Defence: Ken Maginnis, MP

*Education and Employment; Community
  Relations; Culture, Media and Sport:*
  Roy Beggs, MP
Environment and Housing: Cecil Walker, MP
EU Issues: Jim Nicholson, MEP
Social Security; Transport:
  Clifford Forsythe, MP
Trade and Industry: Jeffrey Donaldson, MP
Treasury and the Civil Service:
  William Ross, MP

SCOTTISH NATIONAL PARTY

National Convenor; Constitution; Fishing:
  Alex Salmond, MP, MSP
*Parliamentary Leader; Europe and Foreign
  Affairs; Defence; Health; Highlands and
  Islands; Gaelic:* Margaret Ewing, MP, MSP
Education, Local Government; Housing:
  Andrew Welsh, MP, MSP
*Home Affairs; Environment and Land Reform;
  Arts and Broadcasting; Women's Issues:*
  Roseanna Cunningham, MP, MSP
*Chief Whip; Employment; Trade and Industry
  (tourism and small businesses); Energy;
  Forestry; Transport:*
  Alasdair Morgan, MP, MSP
Economy; Social Security; Agriculture:
  John Swinney, MP, MSP

PLAID CYMRU

*Leader of the Party; Constitutional Matters;
  Treasury and Economy; Trade and Industry;
  Social Security; Disability:*
  The Rt Hon Dafydd Wigley, MP
Whips
*Housing; Home Affairs; Local Government;
  Tourism; Northern Ireland; Organiser of
  House of Commons Business:*
  Elfyn Llwyd, MP
Health; Agriculture; Foreign Affairs; Defence:
  Ieuan Wyn Jones, MP

HANDBOOK

OF

HOUSE *of* COMMONS

PROCEDURE

2nd Edition 1999

This book is an essential reference work for anyone who needs to understand the procedures of the House of Commons.

Its author, a Clerk in the Commons with almost two decades' experience of working in the House, has completely revised his original guide to the procedures of the House. It describes the House, its organisation, rules and privileges; the business of the House and its committees; the role of the Speaker and chairmen; the timetables of Parliaments, sessions, weeks and days; question time; the rules of debate, procedures for bills, statutory instruments and European legislation; and the functions and procedures of the Select Committees of the House.

Also included is an extensive glossary of jargon of parliamentary procedure, and many figures and tables which summarise essential information and illustrate the text; and Standing Orders.

Vacher Dod Publishing Limited
PO Box 3700, Westminster, London SW1E 5NP
Tel: 020 7828 7256   Fax: 020 7828 7269
E-mail: politics@vacherdod.co.uk
Websites: www.vacherdod.co.uk   www.politicallinks.co.uk

MEMBERS' BIOGRAPHIES

A

ABBOTT, Diane *(Hackney North and Stoke Newington)* *Lab majority 15,627*

Daughter of late Reginald Abbott, welder, and late Mrs Julie Abbott, psychiatric nurse. Born September 27, 1953; educated Harrow County Girls' Grammar School; Newnham College, Cambridge (BA History 1976). Married 1991, David Thompson (1 son) (marriage dissolved 1993). *Trades Union:* Equality Officer, ACTT 1985–86. *Career:* Administration trainee, Home Office 1976–78; Race relations officer, National Council for Civil Liberties 1978–80; Journalist, Thames Television 1980–82, TV AM 1982–84, freelance 1984–85; Principal press officer, Lambeth Council 1986–87. *Councils, Public Bodies:* Westminster City Councillor 1982–86. *Select Committees (Current):* Member: Foreign Affairs 1997– *(Former):* Member: Treasury and Civil Service 1989–97, Entry Clearance Sub-Committee 1997–98. *Party Groups:* Member, Labour Party National Executive Committee 1994–. *Miscellaneous:* First black female MP. *Electoral Notes:* Member for Hackney North and Stoke Newington since June 1987. *Address:* Diane Abbott, MP, House of Commons, London, SW1A 0AA *Tel:* 020 7219 5062.

ADAMS, Gerry (Gerard) *(Belfast West)* *SF majority 7,909*

Son of Gerard Adams. Born October 6, 1948; educated St Mary's Christian Brothers' School, Belfast. Married 1971, Colette McArdle (1 son). *Career:* Bartender; Founder member of the civil rights movement. *Political Career:* Member, Northern Ireland Assembly 1981; Vice-President, Sinn Fein 1978–83, President 1983–; Member: Northern Ireland Forum 1996, New Northern Ireland Assembly for Belfast West 1998–. *International Bodies:* Member, PEN. *Publications: Before the Dawn, An Irish Voice, A Pathway to Peace, The Politics of Irish Freedom and Selected Writings, Falls Memories, Cage Eleven, The Street and Other Stories. Recreations:* Gaelic sports, Irish traditional music. *Electoral Notes:* Member for Belfast West 1983–92, and since May 1, 1997. *Address:* Gerry Adams Esq, MP, House of Commons, London, SW1A 0AA *Tel:* 020 7219 3000.

ADAMS, Mrs Irene *(Paisley North)* *Lab majority 12,814*

Born December 27, 1947; educated Stanley Green High School, Paisley. Married February 24, 1968, Allen Adams (MP for Paisley 1979–83 and for Paisley North 1983–90, died September 1990) (1 son 2 daughters). *Councils, Public Bodies:* Youngest woman ever to become a councillor in Britain, when elected to Paisley Town Council in 1970; Councillor: Renfrew District Council 1974–78, Strathclyde Regional Council 1979–84; JP. *Select Committees (Current):* Member: Scottish Affairs 1997–, Chairmen's Panel 1998– *(Former):* Member: Catering 1991–95. *Party Groups:* Member, Labour Party for over 25 years. *Recreations:* Reading, walking. *Electoral Notes:* Member for Paisley North since November 29, 1990 By-Election. *Address:* Mrs Irene Adams, JP, MP, House of Commons, London, SW1A 0AA *Tel:* 020 7219 3564.

Dod *on* Disk
The Vacher Dod Parliamentary Database – configured for PC or Network
For further details please telephone the Westminster Office
020 7828 7256

AINGER, Nick *(Carmarthen West and South Pembrokeshire)   Lab majority 9,621*

Son of Richard John Wilkinson and Marjorie Isabel Ainger (née Dye). Born October 24, 1949; educated Netherthorpe Grammar School, Staveley, Derbyshire. Married 1976, Sally Robinson (1 daughter). *Trades Union:* Branch secretary, TGWU. *Career:* Marine and Port Services Ltd., Pembroke Dock 1977–92. *Councils, Public Bodies:* Councillor, Dyfed County Council 1981–93; Previous member of committees: Public Protection, Cultural Services, Social Services, Education; Former Vice-Chairman, Dyfed County Council Labour Group. *Political Career:* PPS to Secretaries of State for Wales: Ron Davies, 1997–98, Alun Michael, 1998–99, Paul Murphy, 1999–. *Select Committees (Former):* Member: Broadcasting 1992–94, Welsh Affairs 1993–97. *Other:* Member: Amnesty International, RSPB. *Trust:* Member, Dyfed Wildlife Trust. *Countries of Interest:* Ireland. *Electoral Notes:* Member for Pembroke 1992–97, and for Carmarthen West and South Pembrokeshire since May 1, 1997. *Address:* Nick Ainger Esq, MP, House of Commons, London, SW1A 0AA *Tel:* 020 7219 4004 *Fax:* 020 7219 2690. *Constituency:* Ferry Lane Works, Ferry Lane, Pembroke Dock, Dyfed, SA71 4RE *Tel:* 01646 684404 *Fax:* 01646 682954.

AINSWORTH, Peter *(East Surrey)   Con majority 15,093*

Son of late Lieutenant-Commander Michael Lionel Yeoward Ainsworth and Patricia Mary (née Bedford). Born November 16, 1956; educated Ludgrove School; Bradfield College; Lincoln College, Oxford (MA Hons). Married 1981, Claire Burnett (1 son 2 daughters). *Career:* Research Assistant to Sir John Stewart-Clark MEP 1979–81; Investment Analyst, Laing & Cruickshank 1981–85; S G Warburg Securities 1985–: Investment Analyst 1985–87, Corporate Finance 1987–92, Director 1990–92. *Councils, Public Bodies:* Former Councillor, London Borough of Wandsworth; Chairman, Conservative Group on the Council 1990–92; Former Deputy Chairman, Policy and Finance Committee. *Political Career:* PPS: to Rt Hon. Jonathan Aitken, MP 1994–95, to Rt Hon. Virginia Bottomley, JP, MP 1995–96; Member, Shadow Cabinet 1998–; Shadow Secretary of State for Culture, Media and Sport 1998–. *Whip:* Assistant Government Whip 1996–97; Opposition Deputy Chief Whip 1997–98. *Select Committees (Former):* Member: Consolidation Bills Joint Committee 1993–96, Environment 1993–94, Public Service 1993–96, Selection 1997–98. *Party Groups:* Member, The Bow Group 1983–. *Other:* Secretary, Conservative and Unionist Agents' Superannuation Fund 1993–. *Awards: Country Life* Country MP of the Year 1994; *Green* Magazine Campaigning MP of the Year 1994. *Special Interests:* Economic Policy, Environment. *Recreations:* Family, music, gardening. *Electoral Notes:* Member for East Surrey since April 9, 1992. *Clubs:* MCC. *Address:* Peter Ainsworth Esq, MP, House of Commons, London, SW1A 0AA *Tel:* 020 7219 4047 *Fax:* 020 7219 2527. *Constituency:* 2 Hoskins Road, Oxted, Surrey, RH8 9HT *Tel:* 01883 715782 *Fax:* 01883 730576 *E-mail:* kyprianouc@parliament.uk.

AINSWORTH, Robert *(Coventry North East)   Lab majority 22,569*

Son of late Stanley and Pearl Ainsworth. Born June 19, 1952; educated Foxford Comprehensive School, Coventry. Married June 22, 1974, Gloria, daughter of Denis and Jean Sandall (2 daughters). *Trades Union:* Member, MSF: Shop steward 1974, Senior steward and secretary of joint shop stewards 1980–91, Union Branch President 1983–87. *Career:* Sheet metal worker; fitter with Jaguar Cars, Coventry 1971–91. *Councils, Public Bodies:* Councillor, Coventry City Council 1984–93, Deputy Leader 1988–91, Chairman, Finance Committee 1989–92. *Whip:* Opposition Whip 1995–97; A Lord Commissioner of HM Treasury (Government Whip) 1997–. *Party Groups:* Joined Labour Party 1975. *Sportsclubs:* Broad Street Rugby Football Old Boys'. *Special Interests:* Industry, Environment, Tax. *Countries of Interest:* France, India, Pakistan, USA. *Recreations:* Walking, chess, reading, cycling. *Electoral Notes:* Member for Coventry North East since April 9, 1992. *Clubs:* Bell Green Working Men's. *Address:* Robert Ainsworth Esq, MP, House of Commons, London, SW1A 0AA *Tel:* 020 7219 4047 *Tel (Constituency):* 024 7622 6707 *Fax (Constituency):* 024 7622 6707 *E-mail:* robert.ainsworth@hm-treasury.gov.uk.

ALEXANDER, Douglas Garven *(Paisley South)   Lab majority 2,731*

Son of Rev. Douglas N. Alexander and Dr. Joyce O. Alexander. Born October 26, 1967; educated Park Mains High School, Erskine, Renfrewshire; Lester B. Pearson College, Vancouver, Canada; Edinburgh University (MA 1990, LLB 1993, Diploma in Legal Practice 1994); University of Pennsylvania, USA. *Trades Union:* Member, TGWU. *Profession:* Solicitor. *Career:* Parliamentary Researcher for Gordon Brown 1990–91; Solicitor: Brodies W.S. 1994–96, Digby Brown 1996–97. *Party Groups:* General Election Campaign Co-ordinator 1999–. *Other:* Member, Muir Society; Rector's Assessor, University of Edinburgh 1993–96. Notary Public. *Publications:* Co-author *New Scotland, New Britain*, 1999. *Special Interests:* Constitutional Reform, Economic Policy, Employment Policy. *Recreations:* Running, angling. *Electoral Notes:* Contested Perth and Kinross by-election 1995 and Perth General Election 1997. Member for Paisley South since November 6, 1997 By-election. *Address:* Douglas Alexander Esq, MP, House of Commons, London, SW1A 0AA *Tel:* 020 7219 1345. *Constituency:* 19 Sir James Clark Building, Abbey Mill Business Centre, Paisley, PA1 1TJ *Tel:* 0141–561 0333 *Fax:* 0141–561 0334.

ALLAN, Richard *(Sheffield Hallam)   LD majority 8,271*

Son of John Allan, retired, and Elizabeth Allan, doctor's receptionist. Born February 11, 1966; educated Oundle School, Northants; Pembroke College, Cambridge (BA Hons Archaeology and Anthropology); Bristol Polytechnic (MSc Information Technology). Married May 25, 1991, Louise, daughter of Robin and Pat Netley (1 daughter). *Profession:* Information Technology Specialist. *Career:* Field Archaeologist in: Britain, France and The Netherlands 1984–85, Ecuador 1988–89; Computer Manager: Avon FHSA 1991–95, FHS 1995–97. *Councils, Public Bodies:* Councillor, Avon County Council 1993–95, Deputy Group Leader of Liberal Democrats; Councillor, Bath City Council 1994–95. *Spokesman:* A Spokesman for Home and Legal Affairs: Community Relations and Urban Affairs 1997–99, Immigration 1998–99, Home Affairs 1999–. *Select Committees (Current):* Member: Finance and Services 1998–; Chairman: Information 1998–; Member: Liaison 1998–. *(Former):* Member: Home Affairs 1997–98. *Trust:* Board Member, Sheffield City Trust 1999–. *Miscellaneous:* Member, World Development Movement; Board Member, Parliamentary Office of Science and Technology (POST) 1997–. *Special Interests:* Information Technology, Heritage, Home Affairs, Education. *Countries of Interest:* Latin America especially Ecuador, USA. *Recreations:* Visiting sites of natural beauty and historical interest, flying kites, walking. *Electoral Notes:* Member for Sheffield Hallam since May 1, 1997. *Address:* Richard Allan Esq, MP, House of Commons, London, SW1A 0AA *Tel:* 020 7219 1104 *Fax:* 020 7219 0971. *Constituency:* Belmayne House, 99 Clarkehouse Road, Sheffield, S10 2LN *Tel:* 0114–249 4774 *Fax:* 0114–249 4775 *E-mail:* allanr@parliament.uk.

ALLEN, Graham William *(Nottingham North)   Lab majority 18,801*

Son of Bill and Edna Allen. Born January 11, 1953; educated Robert Shaw Primary, Nottingham; Forest Fields Grammar School, Nottingham; City of London Polytechnic (BA Hons Politics and Economics); Leeds University (MA Political Sociology). Married Allyson (1 daughter). *Career:* Warehouseman 1974; Labour Party Research Officer 1979–83; Local Government Officer 1983–84; National Co-ordinator, Political Fund ballots 1984–86; GMBATU Research and Education Officer 1986–87. *Political Career:* Shadow Minister for: Social Security 1991–92, Constitutional Affairs 1992–94, Media and Broadcasting 1994–95, Transport 1995–96, Environment 1996–97. *Whip:* A Lord Commissioner of HM Treasury (Government Whip) 1997–98; Vice-Chamberlain of HM Household (Government Whip) 1998–. *Select Committees (Former):* Member: Public Accounts 1988–91. *Sportsclubs:* Secretary, Lords and Commons Cricket XI; Member, Dunkirk Cricket. *Publications:* Author, *Reinventing Democracy*, 1995. *Special Interests:* Economic Policy, Democratic Renewal. *Countries of Interest:* USA. *Recreations:* Cricket, walking, cooking, oil painting. *Electoral Notes:* Member for Nottingham North since June 1987. *Clubs:* Basford Hall Miners Welfare. *Address:* Graham Allen Esq, MP, House of Commons, London, SW1A 0AA *Tel:* 020 7219 3000 *Tel (Constituency):* 0115–979 2344.

AMESS, David Anthony Andrew *(Southend West)   Con majority 2,615*

Son of late James Amess and of Maud Amess. Born March 26, 1952; educated St Bonaventure's Grammar School; Bournemouth College of Technology (BSc Hons Economics). Married September 10, 1983, Julia, daughter of Graham and Faith Arnold (1 son 4 daughters). *Career:* Junior School Teacher 1970–71; Underwriter, Leslie Godwin Agency 1974–76; Accountancy Personnel 1976–79; Senior Consultant, Executemps Company Agency 1979–81, Chairman: Accountancy Solutions 1987–90, Accountancy Group 1990–96. *Councils, Public Bodies:* Redbridge Council: Councillor 1982–86, Vice-Chairman, Housing Committee 1982–85. *Political Career:* PPS: to Edwina Currie, to Lord Skelmersdale at DHSS 1987–88, to Rt Hon. Michael Portillo: at Department of Transport 1988–90, at Department of Environment 1990–92, at The Treasury 1992–94, at Department of Employment 1994–95, at Ministry of Defence 1995–97; Sponsored: Horses and Ponies Bill 1984–85, Members of Parliament (Minimum Age) Bill 1984–85, Horses, Ponies and Donkeys Bill 1987–88, Abortion (Right of Conscience) (Amendment) Bill 1988–89, British Nationality (Hon. Citizenship) Bill 1988–89, Adoption (Amendment) Bill 1989–90, Dogs Bill 1989–90, Pet Animals (Amendment) Bill 1990–91, Protection Against Cruel Tethering Act 1988, Human Fertilisation (Choice) Bill 1992–93, Voluntary Personal Security Cards Bill 1992–93, Football Matches (Violent and Disorderly Conduct) Bill 1992–93, Newly Qualified Drivers Bill 1993–94, Coercion in Family Planning (Prohibition) Bill 1994–95, Freezing of Human Embryos Bill 1995–96, Abortion (Amendment) Bill 1996–97, Reform of Quarantine Regulations Bill 1997–98, Voluntary Personal Security Cards Bill 1997–98. *Select Committees (Current):* Member: Health 1998– *(Former):* Member: Broadcasting 1994–97. *Party Groups:* Hon. Secretary, Conservative Friends of Israel 1998–. *Other:* Founder Member, Wallenberg Appeal Foundation; President, 1912 Club 1996–. Freeman, City of London. *Sportsclubs:* Kingswood Squash and Racketball. *Publications: The Basildon Experience,* 1995. *Special Interests:* Health, Education, Transport, Environment, Pro-Life Movement. *Countries of Interest:* USA, European Union, Middle East, Far East, Pacific Basin. *Recreations:* Socialising, reading, writing, sports, modern music, keeping animals, gardening. *Electoral Notes:* Contested Newham North West 1979. Member for Basildon 1983–97, and for Southend West since May 1, 1997. *Clubs:* Carlton, St Stephen's Constitutional. *Address:* David Amess Esq, MP, House of Commons, London, SW1A 0AA *Tel:* 020 7219 3452 *Fax:* 020 7219 2245. *Constituency:* Iveagh Hall, 67 Leigh Road, Leigh-on-Sea, Essex *Tel:* 01702 472391 *Fax:* 01702 480677 *E-mail:* amessd@parliament.uk.

ANCRAM, The Rt Hon. Earl of, Michael Andrew Foster Jude Kerr *(Devizes)   Con majority 9,782*

Son of 12th Marquess of Lothian, KCVO, DL. Born July 7, 1945; educated Ampleforth; Christ Church, Oxford (BA); Edinburgh University (LLB). Married June 7, 1975, Lady Jane Fitzalan-Howard, daughter of 16th Duke of Norfolk, KG, PC, GCVO, GBE, TD, and of late Lavinia, Duchess of Norfolk, LG, CBE (2 daughters). *Career:* Advocate, Scottish Bar 1970, QC 1996. *Councils, Public Bodies:* DL, Roxburgh, Ettrick and Lauderdale 1990–. *Political Career:* Parliamentary Under-Secretary of State, Scottish Office 1983–87; Northern Ireland Office: Parliamentary Under-Secretary of State 1993–94, Minister of State 1994–97; Member, Shadow Cabinet 1997–. *Spokesman:* Front Bench Spokesman on Constitutional Affairs, with overall responsibility for Scottish and Welsh issues 1997–98. *Select Committees (Former):* Member: Public Accounts 1992–93. *Party Groups:* Chairman, Conservative Party in Scotland 1980–83; Deputy Chairman, Conservative Party June-October 1998, Chairman October 1998–. *Other:* Member, Board of Scottish Homes 1988–90. *Miscellaneous:* Heir to the marquessate. *Honours:* PC 1996. *Recreations:* Skiing, photography, folksinging. *Electoral Notes:* Contested West Lothian 1970. Member for Berwickshire and East Lothian February-October 1974, and for Edinburgh South 1979–87; Member for Devizes since April 9, 1992. *Address:* The Rt Hon. Michael Ancram, QC, DL, MP (Earl of Ancram), House of Commons, London, SW1A 0AA *Tel:* 020 7219 4435 *Tel (Constituency):* 01672 563469.

ANDERSON, Donald *(Swansea East)   Lab majority 25,569*

Son of late David Robert Anderson, fitter and Eva Anderson (née Mathias). Born June 17, 1939; educated Swansea Grammar School; University College, Swansea (Modern History and Politics 1960); Inns of Court; Hon. Fellow, University College, Swansea 1985–; Visiting Parliamentary Fellow, St Antony's College, Oxford 1999–. Married September 28, 1963, Dr Dorothy Mary, eldest daughter of Rev. Frank Trotman (3 sons). *Trades Union:* RMT Sponsored. *Profession:* Barrister. *Career:* HM Diplomatic Service 1960–64; Lecturer, University College Swansea 1964–66; Barrister, South Eastern Circuit 1969–97. *Councils, Public Bodies:* Councillor, Royal Borough of Kensington and Chelsea 1970–75. *Political Career:* PPS: to Minister of Defence (Administration) 1969–70, to Attorney General 1974–79. *Spokesman:* Opposition Front Bench Spokesman on: Foreign and Commonwealth Affairs 1983–92, Defence, Disarmament and Arms Control 1993–94, Law Officers' Departments 1994–95. *Select Committees (Current):* Chairman: Foreign Affairs 1997–; Member: Liaison 1997– *(Former):* Member: Home Affairs 1994–95, Chairmen's Panel 1995–99, Entry Clearance Sub-Committee 1997–98. *Party Groups:* Vice-Chairman, Welsh Labour Group 1969–70, Chairman 1977–78. *International Bodies:* Member, Executive Committee, Commonwealth Parliamentary Association (CPA) UK Branch 1983–87–, Vice-Chairman 1987–88, Treasurer 1990–93, Special Representative 1989–90, Chairman 1997–; Vice-Chairman, IPU 1985–88, Treasurer 1988–90 and 1993–95; Member, UK Delegation to North Atlantic Assembly 1992–, Leader 1997–; Member, Organisation for Security and Co-operation in Europe 1997–, Leader 1997–98; Executive Committee Member, IPU British Group. *Other:* President, Gower Society 1976–78; Chairman, Parliamentary Campaign for the Homeless and Rootless (CHAR) 1984–90; Vice-President, Institute of Environmental Health Officers 1984–95; Senior Vice-President, Association of European Parliamentarians for Africa 1984–97; President, Swansea Male Choir; Vice-President, Morriston Orpheus Choir; Member: Morriston Big Band, Eastside Sportsmen's Association, HAFOD Brotherhood. *Miscellaneous:* Director, Campaign for a Political Europe 1966–67. Freeman, City of Swansea 2000. *Sportsclubs:* Bonymaen RFC. *Honours:* Commander's Cross, Order of Merit, Federal Republic of Germany 1986. *Special Interests:* Foreign Affairs, Housing Law, Transport, Wales, Environment. *Recreations:* Walking, Church work. *Electoral Notes:* Member for Monmouth 1966–70, and for Swansea East since October 1974. *Address:* Donald Anderson Esq, MP, House of Commons, London, SW1A 0AA *Tel:* 020 7219 3425 *E-mail:* trotmang@parliament.uk.

ANDERSON, Janet *(Rossendale and Darwen)   Lab majority 10,949*

Daughter of late Tom Anderson, Labour Party agent, and late Ethel Pearson. Born December 6, 1949; educated Kingsfield Comprehensive School, Bristol; Polytechnic of Central London (Diploma in Bi-lingual Business Studies); University of Nantes. Married 1972 (2 sons 1 daughter) (separated). *Career:* Secretary, *The Scotsman* and *The Sunday Times* 1971–74. *Political Career:* Personal Assistant: to The Rt Hon. Barbara Castle 1974–81, to Jack Straw MP 1981–87; PPS to Margaret Beckett MP, as Deputy Leader of the Labour Party 1992–93; Parliamentary Labour Party Representative, House of Commons Commission 1993–94; Parliamentary Under-Secretary of State, Department for Culture, Media and Sport (Minister for Tourism, Film and Broadcasting) 1998–. *Whip:* Opposition Whip 1995–96; Vice-Chamberlain of HM Household (Government Whip) 1997–98. *Spokesman:* Opposition Spokeswoman on Women 1996–97. *Select Committees (Former):* Member: Home Affairs 1994–95, Accommodation and Works 1997–98. *Party Groups:* Joined Labour Party 1970; Parliamentary Labour Party Campaign Organiser 1988–90; Vice-Chair, Labour Campaign for Electoral Reform; Steering Committee Member, Labour Women's Network; Secretary, Tribune Group 1993–96. *Other:* Northern Regional Organiser, Shopping Hours Reform Council 1991–92; Hon. Adviser, Emily's List UK; Member, Parliamentary Panel, Royal College of Nursing 1992–97; President, East Lancashire Environment Business Association. *Miscellaneous:* Vice-President, Association of District Councils. Fellow, Royal Society for the Arts. *Special Interests:* Footwear, Textile Industries, Quotas for Women, Health, Constitution/Constitutional Issues, Employment Rights and Protection, Home Affairs, Culture, Media and Sport. *Countries of Interest:* France, Cyprus, Italy. *Recreations:* Playing the piano, listening to opera. *Electoral Notes:* Contested Rossendale and Darwen 1987. Member for Rossendale and Darwen since April 9, 1992. *Clubs:* Rosemount Working Men's, Stacksteads.

Address: Janet Anderson, MP, House of Commons, London, SW1A 0AA *Tel:* 020 7219 6629 *Fax:* 020 7219 2148. *Constituency:* 23 Bolton Road, Darwen, Lancashire, BB3 1DF *Fax:* 01254 762077 *E-mail:* andersonj@parliament.uk; janet.anderson@culture.gov.uk.

ARBUTHNOT, The Rt Hon. James Norwich *(North East Hampshire)*   Con majority 14,398

Son of late Sir John Sinclair-Wemyss Arbuthnot, MP for Dover 1950–64 and Lady Arbuthnot. Born August 4, 1952, educated Wellesley House, Broadstairs; Eton; Trinity College, Cambridge (MA). Married September 6, 1984, Emma, daughter of Michael and Daphne Broadbent (1 son 3 daughters). *Career:* Called to the Bar 1975. *Councils, Public Bodies:* Councillor, Royal Borough of Kensington and Chelsea 1978–87. *Political Career:* PPS: to The Hon. Archie Hamilton MP, as Minister of State for the Armed Forces 1988–90, to Rt Hon. Peter Lilley, as Secretary of State for Trade and Industry 1990–92; Parliamentary Under-Secretary of State, Department of Social Security 1994–95; Minister of State for Procurement, Ministry of Defence 1995–97; Member, Shadow Cabinet 1997–. *Whip:* Assistant Government Whip 1992–94; Opposition Chief Whip in the House of Commons 1997–. *Party Groups:* Branch Chairman, Putney Conservative Association 1975–77; Joint Deputy Chairman, Chelsea Conservative Association 1980–82; President, Cynon Valley Conservative Association 1983–92. *Miscellaneous:* Heir presumptive to baronetcy. *Honours:* PC 1998. *Special Interests:* Tax, Defence, Foreign Affairs, Law. *Recreations:* Playing guitar, skiing. *Electoral Notes:* Contested Cynon Valley 1983 and By-election 1984. Member for Wanstead and Woodford 1987–97 and for North East Hampshire since May 1, 1997. *Clubs:* Buck's. *Address:* The Rt Hon. James Arbuthnot, MP, House of Commons, London, SW1A 0AA *Tel:* 020 7219 4649. *Constituency:* North East Hampshire Conservative Association, 14a Butts Road, Alton, Hampshire, GU34 1ND *Tel:* 01420 84122 *Fax:* 01420 84925.

ARMSTRONG, The Rt Hon. Hilary Jane *(North West Durham)*   Lab majority 24,754

Daughter of late Rt Hon. Ernest Armstrong, former MP for Durham North West, and of Mrs Hannah Armstrong. Born November 30, 1945; educated Monkwearmouth Comprehensive School, Sunderland; West Ham College of Technology; Birmingham University (BSc sociology; Diploma in social work). Married October 17, 1992, Dr Paul Corrigan. *Trades Union:* Chairman, ASTMS Northern Division Council 1981–88. *Career:* VSO teaching in Kenya 1967–69; Social Worker, Newcastle Social Services 1970–73; Community Worker, Southwick Neighbourhood Action Project 1973–75; Lecturer in Community and Youth Work, Sunderland Polytechnic 1975–86; Secretary/Researcher for Ernest Armstrong MP 1986–87. *Councils, Public Bodies:* Councillor, Durham County Council 1985–88. *Political Career:* PPS to Rt Hon. John Smith, MP, as Leader of the Opposition 1992–94; Minister of State, Department of the Environment, Transport and the Regions (Minister for Local Government and Housing) 1997–99, (Minister for Local Government and Regions) 1999–. *Spokesman:* Opposition Spokesperson on: Education 1988–92, Treasury and Economic Affairs 1994–95, The Environment and London 1995–97. *Select Committees (Former):* Member: Education 1998. *Party Groups:* Member, Labour Party National Executive Committee 1992–94, 1996–. *Other:* NCH Action for Children: Member NCH Board 1985–91, Vice-president 1991–97; Member, UNICEF National Committee 1995–97. *Miscellaneous:* Vice-Chair, The British Council 1994–97. *Honours:* PC 1999. *Special Interests:* Regional Development, World Development, Education, Environment. *Countries of Interest:* Central Africa, Kenya, South Africa, Tanzania, Uganda. *Recreations:* Theatre, reading. *Electoral Notes:* Member for North West Durham since June 1987. *Address:* The Rt Hon. Hilary Armstrong, MP, House of Commons, London, SW1A 0AA *Tel:* 020 7219 5076. *Constituency:* North House, 17 North Terrace, Crook, Co Durham, DL15 9AZ *Tel:* 01388 767065 *Fax:* 01388 767923 *E-mail:* hilary-armstrong@detr.gsi.gov.uk.

ASHDOWN, The Rt Hon. Paddy (Jeremy John Durham) *(Yeovil)*   *LD majority 11,403*

Son of late Lieutenant Colonel John W. R. D. Ashdown. Born February 27, 1941; educated Bedford School. Married February 10, 1961, Mary Jane Donne Courtenay (1 son 1 daughter). *Armed Forces:* Royal Marines Officer (Captain) 1959–72 with Commando Units in Far East, Middle East and Belfast; Commanded Unit of Special Boat Service in Far East. *Career:* Studied Chinese (Mandarin) at Hong Kong Language School 1967–70; 1st Class Interpreter, Chinese; First Secretary, UK Mission (Foreign Office) to UN in Geneva 1971–76; Westland Helicopters, Yeovil 1976–78; Morlands, Yeovil 1978–81; Youth Officer, Dorset County Council 1981–83. *Political Career:* Leader: Social and Liberal Democrats 1988–89, Liberal Democrats 1988–99. *Spokesman:* Liberal Spokesman on Trade and Industry 1985–87; Alliance Spokesman on Education and Science 1987; Liberal Spokesman on Education and Science 1987–88; Spokesman on Northern Ireland 1988–92. *Honours:* PC 1989. *Publications: Citizens' Britain: A Radical Agenda for the 1990s,* 1989; *Beyond Westminster: Finding Hope in Britain,* 1992. *Special Interests:* Youth Affairs, Foreign Affairs, Defence, Industry, New Technology. *Countries of Interest:* Bosnia, China, Hong Kong, Balkans. *Recreations:* Gardening, classical music, hill walking, wine making. *Electoral Notes:* Member for Yeovil since June 1983. *Clubs:* National Liberal. *Address:* The Rt Hon. Paddy Ashdown, MP, House of Commons, London, SW1A 0AA *Tel:* 020 7219 1430 *Fax:* 020 7219 3267. *Constituency:* Yeovil Liberal Club, 94 Middle Street, Yeovil, Somerset *Tel:* 01935 423284 *Fax:* 01935 433652 *E-mail:* paddyashdown@cix.compulink.co.uk.

ASHTON, Joseph William *(Bassetlaw)*   *Lab majority 17,460*

Son of late Arthur Ashton, steelsmelter. Born October 9, 1933; educated High Storrs Grammar School; Rotherham Technical College. Married December 24, 1957, Margaret, daughter of George Lee (1 daughter). *Trades Union:* Former AEU Shop Steward 1950s; Member, MSF. *Armed Forces:* National Service, RAF 1954–56 inc Suez Campaign. *Profession:* Engineering draughtsman and Journalist. *Career:* Engineering apprentice 1949–54; Journalist, weekly column for *Labour Weekly;* Columnist for: *Daily Star* 1979–87, *Sunday People* 1987–88, *Sheffield Star* 1970–75, 1979–80, *Plus Magazine* 1988–89; Director, Sheffield Wednesday FC 1990–99, Vice-President 1999–. *Councils, Public Bodies:* City Councillor and Chief Whip in Sheffield 1962–68. *Political Career:* PPS to Rt Hon. Anthony Wedgwood Benn 1974–76; Introduced Doctor Assisted Dying Bill (10 Minute Rule Bill) December 1987. *Whip:* Government Whip 1976–78. *Spokesman:* Opposition Front Bench Spokesman on Energy 1979–81. *Select Committees (Former):* Member: Home Affairs 1987–92, National Heritage 1992–97, Modernisation of the House of Commons 1997–98. *Party Groups:* Chairman, East Midlands Group of Labour MPs 1972–75. *Awards:* Columnist of the Year, Granada's *What the Papers Say* 1984. *Sportsclubs:* Director, Sheffield Wednesday Football Club 1990–99. *Publications: Grassroots,* a novel, later a radio play; *A Majority of One,* a stage play. *Special Interests:* Media, Trade Unions, National Lottery, Tourism, Labour Party, Elections. *Countries of Interest:* USA. *Recreations:* Football, films, travel, do-it-yourself. *Electoral Notes:* Member for Bassetlaw since October 1968 By-election. *Address:* Joseph Ashton Esq, MP, House of Commons, London, SW1A 0AA *Tel:* 020 7219 4453 *Fax:* 020 7219 0708. *Constituency:* 57 Church Walk, Worksop, Nottinghamshire *Tel:* 01909 482308.

ATHERTON, Candy *(Falmouth and Camborne)   Lab majority 2,688*

Daughter of late Denis Gordon Atherton, journalist, and Pamela Osborne, hairdresser/salon owner/ Former Mayoress of Falmouth. Born September 21, 1955; educated Convent of Sacred Hearts, Surrey; Midhurst Grammar School, Sussex; University of North London (BA Hons 2:1 Applied Social Studies). *Trades Union:* Member: UNISON, NUJ. *Profession:* Journalist. *Career:* Researcher for Jo Richardson MP and Judith Hart MP; Probation Officer; Launched Women's Magazine *Everywoman*; Press Officer, Labour Party; Journalist. *Councils, Public Bodies:* Councillor, London Borough of Islington 1986–92, Mayor 1989–90; Member, Islington Health Authority 1986–90. *Select Committees (Current):* Member: Education and Employment 1997–, Employment Sub-Committee 1997–. *Party Groups:* Joint Vice-Chair: South and West Group of Labour MPs 1997–99, South West Regional Group of Labour MPs 1999–. Freeman, City of London 1989. *Sportsclubs:* Falmouth Golf Club. *Publications: Housing in Camden, Hackney and Islington,* 1975. *Special Interests:* Environment, Disabled/Disability, Health. *Countries of Interest:* South Africa. *Recreations:* Gliding, gig racing, ornithology. *Electoral Notes:* Contested Chesham and Amersham 1992. Member for Falmouth and Camborne since May 1, 1997. *Clubs:* Falmouth Labour. *Address:* Candy Atherton, MP, House of Commons, London, SW1A 0AA *Tel:* 020 7219 4094 *Fax:* 020 7219 0982. *Constituency:* 4 Webber Hill, Falmouth, Cornwall, TR11 2BU *Tel:* 01326 314440 *Fax:* 01326 314415 *E-mail:* atherton@parliament.uk.

ATKINS, Charlotte *(Staffordshire Moorlands)   Lab majority 10,049*

Daughter of Ronald and Jessie Atkins. Born September 24, 1950; educated Colchester County High School, Essex; London School of Economics (BSc Economics); London University (MA, Area Studies). Married 1990, Gus Brain (1 daughter). *Trades Union:* Member: UNISON, NUJ. *Profession:* Parliamentary Officer. *Career:* Assistant Community Relations Officer, Luton CRC 1974–76; Research Officer/Head of Research, UCATT 1976–80; Research/Political Officer, AUEW(TASS) 1980–84; Press Officer/ Parliamentary Officer, COHSE/UNISON 1984–97. *Councils, Public Bodies:* Councillor, London Borough of Wandsworth 1982–86, Chief Whip and Deputy Leader of Labour Group. *Select Committees (Current):* Member: Education and Employment 1997–, Education Sub-Committee 1997–, Selection 1997–. *Party Groups:* Member: Labour Party 1966–, National Policy Forum to 1998, National Women's Committee to 1998. *Other:* Member, Liberty. *Publications:* Various articles in *Chartist* on parliamentary and equality issues; co-author with Chris Mullin *How to Select or Reselect Your MP. Special Interests:* Civil Liberties, Education, Employment, Health, Agriculture. *Recreations:* Family activities, theatre, keeping fit, cycling, conservation. *Electoral Notes:* Contested Eastbourne by-election 1990. Member for Staffordshire Moorlands since May 1, 1997. *Address:* Charlotte Atkins, MP, House of Commons, London, SW1A 0AA *Tel:* 020 7219 3591 *Tel (Constituency):* 01782 866666 *Fax (Constituency):* 01782 866666.

ATKINSON, David Anthony *(Bournemouth East)   Con majority 4,346*

Son of late Arthur Joseph Atkinson. Born March 24, 1940; educated St George's College, Weybridge; Southend College of Technology; College of Automobile and Aeronautical Engineering, Chelsea (Diplomas in Automobile Engineering and Motor Trade Management 1972). Married February 10, 1968, Susan Nicola Pilsworth (1 son 1 daughter). *Career:* Director: Chalkwell Motor Co Ltd 1963–72, David Graham Studios Ltd 1973–77. *Councils, Public Bodies:* Councillor: Southend County Borough Council 1969–72, Essex County Council 1973–78. *Political Career:* PPS to the Rt Hon. Paul Channon, MP: as Minister of State for the Civil Service 1979–81, as Minister for the Arts 1981–83, as Minister of State for Trade 1983–86, as Secretary of State for Trade and Industry 1986–87; Author of the Licencing (Occasional Permissions) Act 1983. *Select Committees (Former):* Member: Science and Technology 1997–98. *Party Groups:* Chairman, National Young Conservatives 1970–71. *International Bodies:* UK Representative on the Council of Europe and Western Europe Union 1979–86 and 1987–, Leader, Conservative delegation 1997–, Chairman, European

Democratic Group 1998–; Chairman, Council of Europe Committee for Non-Member Countries 1991–95. *Other:* National Chairman/President, Christian Solidarity International (UK). *Special Interests:* Human Rights, Small Businesses, Mental Health, Foreign Affairs, Arts, Heritage, Space Technology. *Countries of Interest:* Russia, former USSR. *Recreations:* Art and architecture, mountaineering. *Electoral Notes:* Contested Newham North West in February 1974 and Basildon in October 1974. Member for Bournemouth East since November 1977 By-election. *Address:* David Atkinson Esq, MP, House of Commons, London, SW1A 0AA *Tel:* 020 7219 3598 *Fax:* 020 7219 3847. *Constituency:* Bournemouth East Conservative Association, Haviland Road, Boscombe, Bournemouth, BH1 4JW *Tel:* 01202 397047 *E-mail:* atkinsond@parliament.uk.

ATKINSON, Peter *(Hexham)   Con majority 222*

Son of Major Douglas Atkinson, died on active service 1945, and of Amy Atkinson. Born January 19, 1943; educated Cheltenham College. Married April 7, 1976, Brione, daughter of late Commander A. T. Darley, of Bray, Co. Wicklow (2 daughters). *Profession:* Journalist. *Career:* Journalist 1961–82; Previously employed by *The Evening Standard* as a reporter and subsequently as News Editor; Director of Public Affairs, British Field Sports Society 1983–92. *Councils, Public Bodies:* Councillor, London Borough of Wandsworth 1978–82; Member, Wandsworth Health Authority 1982–89; Councillor, Suffolk County Council 1989–92. *Political Career:* PPS: to Rt Hon. Jeremy Hanley, MP, as Minister of State for the Armed Forces 1994, as Minister without Portfolio and Chairman of the Conservative Party 1994–95, to Rt Hon. Jeremy Hanley, MP and Sir Nicholas Bonsor, Bt., MP, as Ministers of State, Foreign and Commonwealth Office 1995–96, to Rt Hon. the Lord Parkinson, as Chairman of the Conservative Party 1997–99. *Whip:* An Opposition Whip (Agriculture; Scotland) 1999–. *Select Committees (Current):* Member: Court of Referees 1997–, Scottish Affairs 1997– *(Former):* Member: European Legislation 1992–97, Scottish Affairs 1992–97, Deregulation 1995–97, Chairmen's Panel 1997–99. *Sportsclubs:* Tynedale Rugby. *Special Interests:* Agriculture, Industry. *Countries of Interest:* Overseas Territories, Eastern Europe, USA. *Recreations:* Shooting, gardening, racing. *Electoral Notes:* Member for Hexham since April 9, 1992. *Clubs:* Albert Edward (Hexham), Northern Counties, Turf. *Address:* Peter Atkinson Esq, MP, House of Commons, London, SW1A 0AA *Tel:* 020 7219 3000 *Fax:* 020 7219 2775. *Constituency:* Hexham Conservative Association, Beaumont Street, Hexham, Northumberland *Tel:* 01434 603777.

AUSTIN, John Eric *(Erith and Thamesmead)   Lab majority 17,424*

Son of late Stanley Austin, electrician, and late Ellen Austin. Born August 21, 1944; educated Glyn Grammar School, Epsom; Goldsmiths' College, London (Certificate in Community and Youth Work 1972); Bristol University (Master's in Policy Studies 1990). Married October 6, 1965, Linda, daughter of Leonard and Hilda Walker (2 sons 1 daughter) (marriage dissolved 1988). *Trades Union:* Member, MSF; Chairman, MSF Parliamentary Group 1998–2000. *Career:* Medical laboratory technician 1961–63; Labour Party organiser/agent 1963–70; Social/community worker, London Borough of Bexley 1972–74; Director, Bexley Council for Racial Equality 1974–92. *Councils, Public Bodies:* Councillor, London Borough of Greenwich 1970–94: Chairman, Social Services Committee 1974–78, Deputy Leader 1981–82, Leader 1982–87, Mayor 1987–88, 1988–89. *Select Committees (Current):* Member: Health 1997–, Unopposed Bills (Panel) 1998– *(Former):* Member: Health 1994–97. *Party Groups:* Member, Labour Friends of Bosnia 1994–; Chair, Socialist Campaign Group of MPs 1994–97; Joint Vice-Chairman, London Regional Group of Labour MPs 1996–98, 1999 Treasurer, Labour First Past the Post Group 1997–. *International Bodies:* Co-Chair, Council for the Advancement of Arab British Understanding; Member, Executive Committee Inter-Parliamentary Union British Group 1996–; Vice-Chair, International Executive Parliamentary Association for Euro-Arab Co-operation 1997–; Member, Executive Committee, Commonwealth Parliamentary Association UK Branch 1999–. *Other:* Chairman, Greenwich MIND 1978–82. *Trust:* Trustee (unpaid): The Adolescent and Children's Trust, Greenwich MIND; Unpaid Director: London Marathon Charitable Trust, Grossness Engines Trust. *Miscellaneous:* Chairman, Greenwich Community Health Council 1976–80; National Chairman, Association of Community Health Councils for England and Wales 1980–82; Vice-Chairman: Association of London Authorities (ALA) 1983–87, London

Strategic Policy Unit 1985–87; Chairman: London Boroughs Emergency Planning Information Committee 1985–87, London Ecology Unit 1985–87; Member, Political Committee CWS (Retail South East) 1987–93; Environment spokesperson for ALA 1992–94. *Special Interests:* Health, Social Services, Mental Health, Equal Opportunity, Environment, Foreign Affairs. *Countries of Interest:* Eastern Europe, Ireland, Kurdistan, Middle East. *Recreations:* Gardening, cookery, running (including marathons). *Electoral Notes:* Member for Woolwich 1992–97, and for Erith and Thamesmead since May 1, 1997 (Contested the seat as John Austin-Walker). *Clubs:* St Patrick's Social (Plumstead), Northumberland Heath Working Men's (Erith), Woolwich Catholic. *Address:* John Austin Esq, MP, House of Commons, London, SW1A 0AA *Tel:* 020 7219 5195 *Fax:* 020 7219 2706 *E-mail:* austinj@parliament.uk *Website:* www.john-austin-mp.org.uk.

B

BAKER, Norman *(Lewes)   LD majority 1,300*

Born July 26, 1957; educated Royal Liberty School, Gidea Park; Royal Holloway College, University of London (BA Hons German). *Profession:* Teacher. *Career:* Regional Director, Our Price Records 1978–83; Teacher/Lecturer 1985–97; Lib Dem Environment Campaigner, House of Commons 1989–90. *Councils, Public Bodies:* Councillor: Lewis District Council 1987–99, Leader 1991-97, East Sussex County Council 1989–97. *Spokesman:* A Spokesman for Environment and Transport: Environment 1997–99, the Millennium Dome 1998–99, Transport 1998–99, Genetic Engineering and Animal Related Issues 1998–99, Genetic Modification and Animal Related Issues 1999; A Spokesman for Trade and Industry (Consumer Affairs, Broadcasting and Animal Welfare) 1999–. *Select Committees (Current):* Member: Environmental Audit 1997– *(Former):* Member: European Legislation 1997–98. *Other:* Member: Greenpeace, Amnesty International, Free Tibet, Liberty. *Publications:* Various environmental texts. *Special Interests:* Civil Liberties, Environment, Oppressed Minority Races. *Countries of Interest:* Tibet, Sweden. *Recreations:* Walking, music. *Electoral Notes:* Contested Lewes 1992, 1997. Member for Lewes since May 1, 1997. *Address:* Norman Baker Esq, MP, House of Commons, London, SW1A 0AA *Tel:* 020 7219 5138 *Fax:* 020 7219 0445. *Constituency:* 204 High Street, Lewes, East Sussex, BN7 2NS *Tel:* 01273 480281 *Fax:* 01273 480287 *E-mail:* bakern@parliament.uk.

BALDRY, Tony (Antony Brian) *(Banbury)   Con majority 4,737*

Son of Peter Baldry, consultant physician, and Oina Baldry (née Paterson). Born July 10, 1950; educated Leighton Park School, Reading; University of Sussex (BA, LLB). Married May 19, 1979, Catherine Weir (1 son 1 daughter) (marriage dissolved 1996). *Armed Forces:* Former TA Officer; Honorary Colonel RLC (TA). *Profession:* Barrister at Law. *Career:* Called to the Bar, Lincoln's Inn 1975; Publisher. *Political Career:* PA to Rt Hon. Margaret Thatcher 1974 General Election, served in her private office March-October 1975; PPS: to Rt Hon. Lynda Chalker, as Minister of State, FCO 1985–87, to Rt Hon. John Wakeham, as Lord Privy Seal 1987–88, as Leader of the House 1987–89, as Lord President of The Council 1988–89, as Secretary of State for Energy 1989–90; Parliamentary Under-Secretary of State at: Department of Energy January-November 1990, Department of Environment 1990–94, Foreign and Commonwealth Office 1994–95; Minister of State, Ministry of Agriculture, Fisheries and Food 1995–97. *Select Committees (Current):* Member: Trade and Industry 1997–. *Party Groups:* Chairman, Conservative Parliamentary Mainstream Group. *International Bodies:* Former Deputy Chairman, Conservative Group for Europe; Executive Committee Member, IPU British Group. *Other:* Former Vice-President, National Children's Homes. *Awards:* Robert Schumann Silver Medal 1978. Liveryman: Merchant Taylors Company, Stationers and Newspaper Makers Company. *Special Interests:* Employment Policy, Youth Affairs, Legal Affairs, Overseas Aid, European Union, Childcare. *Countries of Interest:* Asia, Africa, Caribbean, North America. *Recreations:* Walking, gardening, beagling. *Electoral Notes:* Contested Thurrock 1979 General Election. Member for Banbury since June 1983. *Clubs:* Carlton, Farmers. *Address:* Tony Baldry Esq, MP, House of Commons, London, SW1A 0AA *Tel:* 020 7219 4491 *Fax:* 020 7219 5826. *Constituency:* Dovecote House, Bloxham, OX15 4RT *Tel:* 01295 720368 (home) *Fax:* 01295 721302 (home) *Tel:* 01295 262341 (office) *Fax:* 01295 263140 (office) *E-mail:* dovecote.baldry@email.tory.org.uk; baldryt@parliament.uk.

BALLARD, Jackie (Jacqueline Margaret) *(Taunton)* *LD majority 2,443*

Daughter of late Alexander Mackenzie and Daisy Mackenzie. Born January 4, 1953; educated Monmouth School for Girls; London School of Economics (BSc Social Psychology); Yeovil College (FE Teachers' Certificate). Married October 11, 1975, Derek Ballard (marriage dissolved 1989) (1 daughter). *Career:* Social Worker, London Borough of Waltham Forest 1974–76; FE Lecturer, Psychology, Communication, Information Technology 1981–93; Council Support Officer, Association of Liberal Democratic Councillors 1993–97. *Councils, Public Bodies:* South Somerset District Council: Councillor 1987–91, Deputy Leader 1988–90, Leader 1990–91; Somerset County Council: Councillor 1993–97, Deputy Leader 1993–95. *Spokesman:* A Spokeswoman for: Local Government and Housing (Local Council Liaison) 1997–99, Women and Childcare 1997–99, Education and Employment (Employment and Childcare) 1999–. *Select Committees (Former):* Member: Catering 1997–99. *Party Groups:* Member: Liberal Democrat Federal Policy Committee 1990–95, Liberal Democrat Federal Executive 1997–. *Other:* Member: Friends of the Earth, National Trust, League Against Cruel Sports. *Miscellaneous:* Member, European Standing Committee A 1998–. *Sportsclubs:* Taunton School Sports Club. *Special Interests:* Environment, Youth Affairs, Civil Liberties, Local Government. *Recreations:* Swimming, working out in the gym, gardening, music. *Electoral Notes:* Member for Taunton since May 1, 1997. *Address:* Jackie Ballard, MP, House of Commons, London, SW1A 0AA *Tel:* 020 7219 6247 *Fax:* 020 7219 3962. *Constituency:* 10 Belvedere Road, Taunton, Devon, TA1 1BW *Tel:* 01823 337874 *Fax:* 01823 323075 *E-mail:* jackieballard@cix.compulink.co.uk.

BANKS, Tony *(West Ham)* *Lab majority 19,494*

Son of Albert Banks. Born April 8, 1943; educated State schools; University of York (BA); LSE. Married Sally Jones. *Trades Union:* Head of Research, AUEW 1969–75; Assistant General Secretary, Association of Broadcasting Staff 1976–83. *Councils, Public Bodies:* Councillor, GLC 1970–77, 1981–86, Chairman 1985–86. *Political Career:* Political Adviser to Minister for Overseas Development (Judith Hart MP) 1975; Parliamentary Under-Secretary of State, Department of National Heritage/Department for Culture, Media and Sport (Minister for Sport) 1997–99; Resigned from his ministerial post in the July 1999 Government reshuffle. Appointed Special Envoy for England's 2006 World Cup. *Spokesman:* Opposition Spokesman on Social Security 1990–91; Opposition Front Bench Spokesman on: Transport 1992–93, The Environment 1992–93. *Select Committees (Current):* Member: Procedure 1999– *(Former):* Member: Procedure 1989–97. *Party Groups:* Chairman, London Group Labour MPs 1987–91. *International Bodies:* Member, Council of Europe, WEU 1989–91; Representative, UK Delegation to Council of Europe and Western Europe Union. *Special Interests:* Economics, Local Government, Media, Arts, Animal Welfare. *Countries of Interest:* Europe, Lithuania, Nicaragua, Panama, USA. *Recreations:* Soccer, trade union history. *Electoral Notes:* Contested East Grinstead 1970, Newcastle North October 1974 and Watford 1979 General Elections. Member for Newham North West 1983–97, and for West Ham since May 1, 1997. *Address:* Tony Banks Esq, MP, House of Commons, London, SW1A 0AA *Tel:* 020 7219 3522. *Constituency:* 306 High Street, Stratford, London, E15 1AJ *Tel:* 020 8555 0036.

BARNES, Harry *(North East Derbyshire)* *Lab majority 18,321*

Son of the late Joseph Barnes and late Betsy Barnes. Born July 22, 1936; educated Easington Colliery Secondary Modern School; Ryhope Grammar School; Ruskin College, Oxford (Diploma in Economics and Political Science); Hull University (BA Hons). Married September 14, 1963, Elizabeth Ann, daughter of the late Richard and Evelyn Stephenson (1 son 1 daughter). *Armed Forces:* National Service 1954–56. *Career:* Railway clerk 1952–54, 1956–60; Adult student 1960–65; Lecturer: North Notts College of Further Education 1965–66, Sheffield University 1966–87; Member, National Administrative Council of Independent Labour Publications 1977–80, 1982–85; Director, Mature Matriculation Courses 1984–87 (Sheffield University). *Select Committees (Current):* Member: Northern Ireland Affairs 1997– *(Former):* Member: European Legislation 1989–97,

Members' Interests 1990–92. *Party Groups:* Vice-Chairman, East Midland Group of Labour MPs 1991–95; Campaign Officer, Central Regional Group, Labour MPs 1993–95; Hon. Treasurer: Central Region Group of Labour MPs 1997–99, East Midlands Regional Group of Labour MPs 1999–. *International Bodies:* Associate Member, British-Irish Parliamentary Body 1992–97, Full Member 1997–. *Miscellaneous:* Member, Standing Committees on: Poll Tax 1988, Employment and Football 1989, Student Loans 1990; Member, Standing Committee A on European Legislation 1990–97; Member, Standing Committees on: Northern Ireland Emergency Provisions 1991, Transport and Works 1992, Further and Higher Education 1992. *Special Interests:* Education, Industrial Relations, Local Government, European Union, Energy, Environment, Northern Ireland, Electoral Registration. *Countries of Interest:* Ireland, Malta, Africa. *Electoral Notes:* Member for North East Derbyshire since June 1987. *Address:* Harry Barnes Esq, MP, House of Commons, London, SW1A 0AA *Tel:* 020 7219 4521 *Fax:* 020 7219 2381 *Tel (Constituency):* 01246 412588.

BARRON, Kevin John *(Rother Valley)   Lab majority 23,485*

Son of Richard Barron, retired. Born October 26, 1946; educated Maltby Hall Secondary Modern; Ruskin College, Oxford. Married June 7, 1969, Carol McGrath (1 son 2 daughters). *Career:* National Coal Board 1962–83. *Political Career:* PPS to The Rt Hon. Neil Kinnock 1985–87. *Spokesman:* Opposition Spokesman on: Energy 1988–92, Employment 1993–95, Health 1995–97. *Select Committees (Former):* Member: Environment 1992–93. *Party Groups:* Member, area and local Labour Party; Chairman, Yorkshire Regional Group of Labour MPs 1987–. *Miscellaneous:* Member, General Medical Council 1999–. *Special Interests:* Energy, Environment, Home Affairs. *Countries of Interest:* Bulgaria. *Recreations:* Local history, family life, football, fly fishing. *Electoral Notes:* Member for Rother Valley since June 1983. *Address:* Kevin Barron Esq, MP, House of Commons, London, SW1A 0AA *Tel:* 020 7219 4432 *Tel (Constituency):* 01909 568611.

BATTLE, John *(Leeds West)   Lab majority 19,771*

Son of John Battle, electrical engineer, and late Audrey Battle. Born April 26, 1951; educated St Michael's College; Upholland College; Leeds University (BA Hons (1st Class)). Married April 12, 1977, Mary, daughter of Gerry and Elizabeth Meenan (1 son 2 daughters). *Career:* Research assistant 1979–83; National Coordinator, Church Action on Poverty 1983–87. *Councils, Public Bodies:* Councillor, Leeds City Council 1980–87. *Political Career:* Shadow Minister for Housing 1993–94, Science and Technology 1994–95, Energy 1995–97; Minister of State: Department of Trade and Industry 1997–99, Foreign and Commonwealth Office 1999–. *Whip:* Labour Whip 1990. *Spokesman:* Opposition Front Bench Spokesman on the Environment (Shadow Minister of Housing and Planning) 1992–94. *Select Committees (Former):* Member: Environment 1991–92. *Special Interests:* Poverty and Wealth at home and abroad, Housing, Economic Policy, International Development, Science, Engineering and Technology. *Countries of Interest:* South Korea, Latin America. *Recreations:* Folk music, poetry. *Electoral Notes:* Contested Leeds North West 1983. Member for Leeds West since June 1987. *Address:* John Battle Esq, MP, House of Commons, London, SW1A 0AA *Tel:* 020 7219 3000. *Constituency:* 2a Conference Place, Leeds, West Yorkshire, LS12 3DZ *Tel:* 0113-231 0258 *Fax:* 0113-279 5850 *E-mail:* johnbattlemp@dial.pipex.com.

BAYLEY, Hugh *(City of York)   Lab majority 20,523*

Son of Michael Bayley, architect, and Pauline Bayley. Born January 9, 1952; educated Haileybury; Universities of Bristol and York (BSc, BPhil). Married December 22, 1984, Fenella, daughter of Joseph Jeffers (1 son 1 daughter). *Trades Union:* NALGO 1975–82, District Officer 1975–77, National Officer 1977–82. *Career:* General Secretary, International Broadcasting Trust 1982–86; Lecturer in Social Policy, University of York 1986–87; Research Fellow in Health Economics, University of York 1987–92. *Councils, Public Bodies:* Councillor, Camden Borough Council 1980–86; York Health Authority 1988–90. *Political Career:* PPS to Rt Hon. Frank Dobson, MP, as Secretary of State for Health 1997–99; Parliamentary Under-Secretary of State, Department of Social Security 1999–. *Select Committees (Former):* Member: Health 1992–97. *Party Groups:* Joined Labour Party 1975. *International Bodies:* Member, Executive Committee: Inter-Parliamentary Union – UK Branch 1997–99, Commonwealth Parliamentary Association – UK Branch 1997–99; Member, UK Delegation to the North Atlantic Assembly 1997–99. *Publications: The Nation's Health*, 1995. *Special Interests:* Health, Economic Policy, Environment, International Development, Defence, Media, Electoral Reform. *Countries of Interest:* Africa. *Recreations:* Family life. *Electoral Notes:* Contested York 1987. Member for York 1992–97, and for City of York since May 1, 1997. *Address:* Hugh Bayley Esq, MP, House of Commons, London, SW1A 0AA *Tel:* 020 7219 5100 *Fax:* 020 7219 4293. *Constituency:* 59 Holgate Road, York, YO2 4AA *Tel:* 01904 623713 *Fax:* 01904 623260 *E-mail:* dellaganal@parliament.uk.

BEARD, Nigel *(Bexleyheath and Crayford)   Lab majority 3,415*

Son of late Albert Leonard Beard, and late Irene Bowes. Born October 10, 1936; educated Castleford Grammar School; University College, London (BSc Hons Physics). Married Jennifer Cotton (1 son 1 daughter). *Trades Union:* Member, GMB. *Profession:* Research and Development Manager. *Career:* Central Policy Staff, MoD 1961–73; Chief Planner, GLC 1973–74; Head, London Docklands Development Organisation 1974–79; Manager, Innovation and New Business Development, ICI 1979–93; Group Research and Development Manager, Zeneca 1993–. *Councils, Public Bodies:* Member, S.W. Thames Regional Health Authority for 10 years. *Select Committees (Current):* Member: Science and Technology 1997–, Unopposed Bills (Panel) 1998–. *Party Groups:* Member: Southern Region Executive of the Labour Party 1981–95, Labour Party National Constitutional Committee 1994–98, Fabian Society. *Other:* Board Member, Institute of Cancer Research for 10 years; Associate Board Member, Royal Marsden Hospital for 10 years; Comprehensive School Governor for 17 years, Chairman for 7 years. *Miscellaneous:* Member, Ecclesiastical Committee. FRSA. *Publications: Use of Linear Programming in Planning and Analysis. Special Interests:* Defence, Foreign Affairs, Economy (Industrial Renewal), Technology, Inner Cities. *Countries of Interest:* France. *Recreations:* Reading, walking, classical music, modern art. *Electoral Notes:* Contested Woking 1979, Portsmouth North 1983, Erith and Crayford 1992. Member for Bexleyheath and Crayford since May 1, 1997. *Clubs:* Athenaeum. *Address:* Nigel Beard Esq, MP, House of Commons, SW1A 0AA *Tel:* 020 7219 5061 *Fax:* 020 7219 2708. *Constituency:* 50 Peareswood Road, Sladegreen, Erith, Kent, DA8 2HP *Tel:* 01322 332261 *Fax:* 01322 332279 *E-mail:* nigel.beard@ee02.poptel.org.uk *Website:* www.mymp.org.uk/nigelbeard.

BECKETT, The Rt Hon. Margaret *(Derby South)   Lab majority 16,106*

Daughter of late Cyril Jackson, carpenter and Winifred Jackson, teacher. Born January 15, 1943; educated Notre Dame High School, Norwich; Manchester College of Science and Technology; John Dalton Polytechnic. Married July 7, 1979, Lionel Arthur, son of Arthur Beckett (2 step-sons). *Trades Union:* Member: T&GWU, NUJ, BECTU. *Profession:* Metallurgist. *Career:* Student apprentice in Metallurgy, AEI Manchester 1961–66; Experimental Officer, Department of Metallurgy, University of Manchester 1966–70; Research Assistant, Labour Party 1970–74; Principal Researcher, Granada Television 1979–83; Political Adviser, Ministry of Overseas Development 1974. *Political Career:* PPS to Rt Hon. Mrs Judith Hart MP 1974–75; Parliamentary Under-Secretary of State, Department of Education and Science 1976–79; Shadow

Minister, Social Security 1984–89; Shadow Chief Secretary to the Treasury 1989–92; Shadow Leader, House of Commons and Campaign Co-ordinator 1992–94; Deputy Leader, Labour Party 1992–94; Leader of Opposition May-July 1994; Shadow Secretary of State for Health 1994–95; Shadow President of the Board of Trade 1995–97; President of the Board of Trade and Secretary of State for Trade and Industry 1997–98; President of the Council and Leader of the House of Commons 1998–. *Whip:* Assistant Government Whip 1975–76. *Party Groups:* Member: Labour Party National Executive Committee 1980–81, 1985–86, 1988–98, Fabian Society, Tribune Group, Socialist Education Committee, Labour Women's Action Committee, Derby Co-Op Party, Socialist Environment and Resources Association. *Other:* Member: CND, Amnesty International, Anti-Apartheid Movement. *Honours:* PC 1993. *Publications: The Need For Consumer Protection,* 1972; *The National Enterprise Board*; *The Nationalisation of Shipbuilding, Ship Repair and Marine Engineering*; Relevant sections of Labour's Programme, 1972/73; *Renewing the NHS,* 1995; *Vision for Growth – A New Industrial Strategy for Britain,* 1996. *Special Interests:* Industry. *Recreations:* Cooking, reading, caravanning. *Electoral Notes:* Contested Lincoln February 1974. Member for Lincoln October 1974–79, and for Derby South since June 1983. *Address:* The Rt Hon. Margaret Beckett, MP, House of Commons, London, SW1A 0AA *Tel:* 020 7219 3000.

BEGG, Anne *(Aberdeen South)   Lab majority 3,365*

Daughter of David Begg, MBE, retired orthotist, and Margaret Catherine Begg, retired nurse. Born December 6, 1955; educated Damacre Primary School; Brechin High School; University of Aberdeen (MA); Aberdeen College of Education (Secondary Teaching Certificate). *Trades Union:* Member: Educational Institute of Scotland 1978–, EIS National Council 1990–95. *Profession:* Principal Teacher of English. *Career:* Teacher of English and History, Webster's High School, Kirriemuir 1978–88; Assistant Principal Teacher of English, Arbroath Academy 1988–91, Principal Teacher of English 1991–97. *Select Committees (Current):* Member: Scottish Affairs 1997–. *Party Groups:* Member, Labour Party 1983–; Held most positions at branch and constituency level; Member, Labour Party National Executive Committee 1998–99. *Other:* Patron: PHAB Scotland, Scottish Motor Neuron Society, Angus Special Playscheme. *Awards:* Disabled Scot of the Year 1988. *Miscellaneous:* Former Elected Member, General Teaching Council for Scotland. *Special Interests:* Education, Scottish Devolution, Health, Disabled/Disability, Arts, Broadcasting. *Recreations:* Reading, cinema, theatre, public speaking. *Electoral Notes:* Member for Aberdeen South since May 1, 1997. *Address:* Anne Begg, MP, House of Commons, London, SW1A 0AA *Tel:* 020 7219 2140 *Fax:* 020 7219 1264. *Constituency:* 166 Market Street, Aberdeen, AB11 5PP *Tel:* 01224 252704 *Fax:* 01224 252705 *E-mail:* begga@parliament.uk.

BEGGS, Roy *(East Antrim)   UUP majority 6,389*

Son of John Beggs. Born February 20, 1936; educated Ballyclare High School; Stranmillis Training College (DipEd). Married 1959, Wilma, daughter of Samuel Lorimer (2 sons 2 daughters). *Career:* Assistant Teacher, Science Department 1957–78; Vice-Principal, Larne High School 1978–83. *Councils, Public Bodies:* Councillor, Larne Borough Council 1973–; Mayor of Larne 1978–83. *Political Career:* Member, Northern Ireland Assembly 1982. *Spokesman:* Former Spokesman for Education, Employment and National Heritage; Spokesman for Education and Employment, Community Relations and Culture, Media and Sport 1997–. *Select Committees (Current):* Member: Northern Ireland Affairs 1997–. *Other:* Member, North Eastern Education and
Library Board 1973–, Vice-Chairman 1981–; President, Northern Ireland Association of Education and Library Boards 1984–. *Miscellaneous:* Member, House of Commons Public Accounts Commission 1983–. *Special Interests:* Education, Employment, National Heritage. *Recreations:* Fishing. *Electoral Notes:* Member for East Antrim since June 1983. *Address:* Roy Beggs Esq, MP, House of Commons, London, SW1A 0AA *Tel:* 020 7219 6305 *Fax:* 020 7219 3889.

BEITH, The Rt Hon. Alan James *(Berwick-upon-Tweed) LD majority 8,042*

Son of late James Beith, foreman packer, and Joan Beith. Born April 20, 1943; educated King's School, Macclesfield; Balliol College; Nuffield College, Oxford (BLitt, MA); Hon. DCL, University of Newcastle upon Tyne 1998. Married September 1, 1965, Barbara Jean Ward (died 1998) (1 son 1 daughter). *Trades Union:* Former Parliamentary Adviser, Association of University Teachers. *Profession:* Lecturer. *Career:* Lecturer, University of Newcastle upon Tyne 1966–73. *Councils, Public Bodies:* Councillor: Hexham RDC 1969–74, Tynedale DC 1974–75. *Whip:* Chief Whip, Liberal Party 1976–87. *Spokesman:* Liberal Spokesman on Foreign Affairs 1985–87; Alliance Spokesman on Foreign Affairs 1987; Liberal Treasury Spokesman 1987; SLD Treasury Spokesman 1988–89; Liberal Democrat: Treasury Spokesman 1989–94, Home Affairs Spokesman 1994–95, Spokesman for Police, Prison and Security Matters 1995–97, Spokesman for Home and Legal Affairs (Home Affairs) 1997–99. *Select Committees (Former):* Member: House of Commons Commission 1979–97, Treasury and Civil Service 1987–94. *Party Groups:* Deputy Leader: Liberal Party 1985–88, Liberal Democrat Parliamentary Party 1992–. *International Bodies:* Representative, Council of Europe Assembly 1976–84; Member, Western European Union Assembly 1976–84. *Trust:* Trustee, Historic Chapels Trust. *Miscellaneous:* Member, Intelligence and Security Committee 1994–. *Honours:* PC 1992. *Publications: Case for Liberal Party and Alliance*, 1983 (jointly); *Faith and Politics*, 1987. *Special Interests:* Parliamentary and Constitutional Affairs, Architectural and Artistic Heritage. *Countries of Interest:* Canada, Scandinavia, Zimbabwe. *Recreations:* Music, walking, boating. *Electoral Notes:* Contested Berwick-upon-Tweed 1970. Member for Berwick-upon-Tweed since 1973 By-election. *Clubs:* National Liberal. *Address:* The Rt Hon. Alan Beith, MP, House of Commons, London, SW1A 0AA *Tel:* 020 7219 3540 *Fax:* 020 7219 5890. *Constituency:* 5 Paikes Street, Alnwick, Northumberland, NE66 1HX *Tel:* 01665 602901 *Fax:* 01665 605700 *E-mail:* berwicklibdems@cix.compulink.co.uk; cheeseman@parliament.uk.

BELL, Martin, OBE *(Tatton) Ind majority 11,077*

Son of late Adrian Hanbury Bell. Born August 31, 1938; educated Taverham Hall Preparatory School; The Leys School, Cambridge; King's College, Cambridge (MA); DUniv, Derby 1996; Hon. MA, University of East Anglia 1997; Hon. LLD, Robert Gordon University 1998; Hon. MA, North London University 1998. Married 1st, 1971, Nelly Lucienne Gourdon (2 daughters); married 2nd, 1985, Rebecca Sobel; married 3rd, July 17, 1998, Fiona, daughter of Robert Goddard. *Armed Forces:* National Service, The Suffolk Regiment. *Career:* BBC TV News: Reporter 1965–77, Diplomatic Correspondent 1977–78, Chief Washington Correspondent 1978–89, Berlin Correspondent 1989–93, East European Correspondent 1993–94, Foreign Affairs Correspondent 1994–97 (resigned to fight the General Election). *Select Committees (Current):* Member: Standards and Privileges 1997–. *Other:* Vice-President, Hope and Homes for Children. *Awards:* Royal Television Society, Reporter of the Year 1977; TV Journalist of the Year 1992. *Miscellaneous:* Member, Ecclesiastical Committee. *Honours:* OBE 1992. *Publications: In Harm's Way*, 1995. *Special Interests:* Standards in Public Life, Foreign Affairs, Welfare of Armed Services Families. *Recreations:* Swimming. *Electoral Notes:* Member for Tatton since May 1, 1997. *Address:* Martin Bell Esq, OBE, MP, House of Commons, London, SW1A 0AA *Tel:* 020 7219 4010. *Constituency:* 9–11 Princess Street, Knutsford, Cheshire *Tel:* 01565 652882.

BELL, Stuart *(Middlesbrough)   Lab majority 25,018*

Son of late Ernest Bell, pitman. Born May 16, 1938; educated Hookergate Grammar School; Council of Legal Education, Gray's Inn. Married 1st, July 16, 1960, Margaret, daughter of Mary Bruce (1 son 1 daughter), married 2nd, June 6, 1980, Margaret, daughter of Mary Allan (1 son). *Trades Union:* Member, General Municipal Boilermakers and Allied Trades Union. *Career:* Barrister, called to the Bar, Gray's Inn 1970; Previously: colliery clerk, newspaper reporter, typist novelist; Conseil Juridique and International Lawyer Paris 1970–77. *Councils, Public Bodies:* Councillor, Newcastle City Council 1980–83, Member: Finance, Health and Environment, Arts and Education Committee, Association of Metropolitan Authorities, Education Committee, Council of Local Education Authorities, Newcastle Area Health Authority (teaching). *Political Career:* PPS to Deputy Leader of Opposition, Rt Hon. Roy Hattersley, 1983–84; Second Church Estates Commissioner 1997–. *Spokesman:* Opposition Front Bench Spokesman on: Northern Ireland 1984–87, Trade and Industry 1992–97. *Party Groups:* Member: Fabian Society, Society of Labour Lawyers. *International Bodies:* Founder member, British Irish Inter-Parliamentary Body 1990; Executive Member, British Group, Inter-Parliamentary Union 1992–95, Vice-Chairman 1992–95. *Publications: Paris 69; Days That Used to Be; When Salem Came to the Boro; The Children Act 1989 (annotated); Fabian Tract: How to Abolish the Lords; Legal Tract: United States Customs Valuation; Raising the Standard: The Case for First Past the Post; Where Jenkins Went Wrong: A Further Case for First Past the Post. Special Interests:* Economic Policy, European Union, Irish Affairs. *Countries of Interest:* Europe, USA, France. *Recreations:* Writing short stories, novels and feature articles. *Electoral Notes:* Contested Hexham 1979. Member for Middlesbrough since June 1983. *Clubs:* Beefsteak. *Address:* Stuart Bell Esq, MP, House of Commons, London, SW1A 0AA *Tel:* 020 7219 3000.

BENN, Hilary *(Leeds Central)   Lab majority 2,293*

Son of The Rt Hon Tony Benn, MP for Chesterfield (*qv*) and Caroline Middleton De Camp. Born November 26, 1953; educated Holland Park Comprehensive School; Sussex University (BA Hons Russian and East European Studies 1974). Married 1st, Rosalind (died); married 2nd, Sally Christina Clark (4 children). *Trades Union:* Member: MSF, GMB; Trustee, Unions 21. *Career:* Head of Policy and Communications, MSF; Special Adviser to David Blunkett, as Secretary of State for Education and Employment 1997–99. *Councils, Public Bodies:* London Borough of Ealing: Councillor 1979–99, Deputy Leader 1986–90, Chairman, Education Committee 1986–90. *Select Committees (Current):* Member: Environment, Transport and Regional Affairs 1999–, Environment Sub-Committee 1999–. *Other:* Chair of Governors, Southfield Primary School. *Miscellaneous:* Member, The Association of Metropolitan Authorities Education Committee 1986–90; Chair, Association of London Authorities Education Committee 1989–90. *Special Interests:* Education, Employment, Trade Unions, Environment, Urban Policy, Home Affairs. *Recreations:* Football, gardening, hillwalking. *Electoral Notes:* Contested Ealing North 1983 and 1987. Member for Leeds Central since June 10, 1999 By-election. *Address:* Hilary Benn Esq, MP, House of Commons, London, SW1A 0AA *Tel:* 020 7219 5770 *Fax:* 020 7219 2639. *Constituency:* South Point, South Accommodation Road, Leeds, West Yorkshire, LS10 1PP *Tel:* 0113–244 1097 *Fax:* 0113–234 1176 *E-mail:* bennh@parliament.uk.

BENN, The Rt Hon. Tony (Anthony Neil Wedgwood) *(Chesterfield)* *Lab majority 5,775*

Second son of late William Wedgwood Benn, Former Secretary of State and Labour MP for North Aberdeen and Gorton, and later created Viscount Stansgate. Born April 3, 1925; educated Westminster; New College, Oxford (MA); Five Hon. Doctorates from British and American Universities. Married June 17, 1949, Caroline Middleton, daughter of late James Milton De Camp (3 sons 1 daughter). *Trades Union:* Member: TGWU, NUJ; Hon. Member: NUM, GMBATU, SOGAT. *Armed Forces:* Pilot Officer, RAFVR 1945, Later Sub-Lieutenant (A) RNVR. *Profession:* Journalist and Author. *Career:* BBC Producer. *Political Career:* Postmaster General 1964–66; Minister of Technology July 1966–70; Minister of Power October 1969–70; Secretary of State for: Industry and Minister of Posts and Telecommunications 1974–75, Energy 1975–79. *Spokesman:* Spokesman on: RAF 1957–58, Transport 1959–60; Opposition Spokesman on Trade and Industry 1970. *Select Committees (Former):* Member: Privileges 1984–97. *Party Groups:* Member, Labour Party National Executive Committee 1959–94; Chairman, Labour Party 1971–72; President, Socialist Campaign Group of Labour MPs 1990–. *International Bodies:* Member, Inter-Parliamentary Union; President, EEC Energy Council of Ministers 1977. *Awards:* Channel 4 and House Award for Speechmaker of the Year 1999. *Miscellaneous:* Succeeded his father to the Viscountcy 1960, but disclaimed his peerage for life 1963. *Honours:* PC 1964. *Publications: Regeneration of Britain*, 1964; *Arguments for Socialism*, 1979; *Arguments for Democracy*, 1981; *Parliament, People and Power*, 1982; *The Sizewell Syndrome*, 1984; *Writing on the Wall*, editor 1984; *Out of the Wilderness, Diaries 1963–67*, 1987; *Fighting Back*, 1988; *Office without Power, Diaries 1968–72*, 1988; *Against the Tide, Diaries 1973–76*, 1989; *Conflicts of Interest, Diaries 1977–80*, 1990; *The End of an Era, Diaries 1980–90*, 1992; *Years of Hope, Diaries 1940–62*, 1994; *Common Sense*, 1993; *Speaking Up in Parliament*, (video) 1993; *Benn Diaries 1940–90*, 1995; *Westminster Behind Closed Doors*, (video) 1995; *Benn Diaries 1 & 2* – BBC Radio Collection; *Benn Diaries 1940–90* – on cassettes; *Writings on the Wall* – cassettes 1996; *New Labour in Focus*, (video) 1999 *Tony Benn Speaks*, (video) 1999. *Special Interests:* International Affairs, Industrial Policy, Labour History, Socialism, Constitution, Democracy, Technology. *Countries of Interest:* Europe, USA. *Electoral Notes:* Member for Bristol South-East 1950, 1951, 1955 and 1960. Re-elected May 1961; unseated by Election Court, July 1961; Member for Bristol South-East 1963–1983, and for Chesterfield since 1 March 1984 By-election. *Address:* The Rt Hon. Tony Benn, MP, House of Commons, London, SW1A 0AA *Tel:* 020 7219 6448. *Constituency:* Labour Club, 113 Saltergate, Chesterfield, S40 1NF *Tel:* 01246 2390779 *E-mail:* 106267.2444@compuserve.com.

BENNETT, Andrew F *(Denton and Reddish)* *Lab majority 20,311*

Born March 9, 1939; educated Birmingham University (BSocSc). Married 1961, Gillian (2 sons 1 daughter). *Trades Union:* Member, National Union of Teachers. *Career:* Geography Teacher. *Councils, Public Bodies:* Councillor, Oldham Borough Council 1964–74. *Spokesman:* Opposition Front Bench Spokesman on Education 1983–88. *Select Committees (Current):* Chairman (Environment): Environment, Transport and Regional Affairs 1997–; Chairman: Environment Sub-Committee 1997–; Member: Transport Sub-Committee 1997–, Liaison 1997–, Statutory Instruments (Joint Committee) 1997– *(Former):* Member: Social Security and Sittings of the House of Commons 1991–92, Environment 1992–97; Chairman: Joint and Select Committees on Statutory Instruments 1994–97; Member: Liaison 1994–97, Standing Orders Committee 1994–96; Chairman: Environment 1995–97; Chairman (Environment): Environment, Transport and Regional Affairs 1997–98. *Party Groups:* Joined Labour Party 1957. *Recreations:* Photography, walking, climbing. *Electoral Notes:* Contested Knutsford 1970. Member for Stockport North February 1974–83 and Denton and Reddish since 1983. *Address:* Andrew Bennett Esq, MP, House of Commons, London, SW1A 0AA *Tel:* 020 7219 4155. *Constituency:* Town Hall, Market Place, Denton, Greater Manchester, M34 2AP *Tel:* 0161-320 1504 *Fax:* 0161-320 1503 *E-mail:* bennett.andrew@pop3.poptel.org.uk *Website:* http://www.poptel.org.uk/andrew.bennett/indexhtml.

BENTON, Joseph *(Bootle)*   *Lab majority 28,421*

Son of late Thomas and Agnes Benton. Born September 28, 1933; educated St Monica's Primary and Secondary School; Bootle Technical College. Married March 30, 1959, Doris, daughter of Reuben and Lily Wynne (4 daughters). *Armed Forces:* Joined RAF 1955, National Service. *Career:* Apprentice fitter and turner 1949; Formerly with Pacific Steam Navigation Company as personnel manager; Girobank 1982–90. *Councils, Public Bodies:* Sefton Borough Council 1970–90· Councillor for Derby Ward, Leader, Labour Group 1985–90, Former education spokesman; JP, Bootle bench 1969. *Whip:* Opposition Whip 1994–97. *Select Committees (Current):* Member: Parliamentary Privilege (Joint Committee) 1997–, Chairman's Panel 1998– *(Former):* Member: Energy 1991–92, Speaker's Panel of Chairmen 1992–94, Education and Employment 1997–99, Education Sub-Committee 1997, Chairmen's Panel 1998. *Other:* Chairman of Governors, Hugh Baird College of Technology. *Miscellaneous:* Has working knowledge of Spanish. Member, Institute of Linguists; Affiliate Member, Institute of Personnel Management. *Special Interests:* Education, Housing, Local Government. *Recreations:* Reading, listening to classical music, squash, swimming. *Electoral Notes:* Member for Bootle since by-election November 8, 1990. *Address:* Joseph Benton Esq, JP, MP, House of Commons, London, SW1A 0AA *Tel:* 020 7219 6973. *Constituency:* 23A Oxford Road, Bootle, Liverpool, L20 9HJ *Tel:* 0151–933 8432 *Fax:* 0151–933 4746.

BERCOW, John Simon *(Buckingham)*   *Con majority 12,386*

Son of Mrs Brenda Bercow and of late Charles Bercow. Born January 19, 1963; educated Finchley Manorhill School; Essex University (BA government 1985). *Career:* Credit Analyst, Hambros Bank 1987–88; Public Affairs Consultant, Rowland Sallingbury Casey, Public Affairs Arm of Saatchi & Saatchi Group 1988–95; Board Director, Rowland Company 1994–95; Special Adviser: to Jonathan Aitken as Chief Secretary to the Treasury 1995, to Virginia Bottomley as Secretary of State for National Heritage 1995–96. *Councils, Public Bodies:* Lambeth Borough Council: Councillor, 1986–90, Deputy Leader, Conservative Opposition 1987–89. *Spokesman:* An Opposition Front Bench Spokesman for Education and Employment 1999–. *Select Committees (Former):* Member: Welsh Affairs 1997–98, Trade and Industry 1998–99. *Party Groups:* Chairman, University of Essex Conservative Association 1984–85; National Chairman, Federation of Conservative Students 1986–87; Vice-Chairman, Conservative Collegiate Forum 1987. *Miscellaneous:* Co-Director, Advanced Speaking and Campaigning Course; Executive Member, 1922 Committee 1998–99. *Publications: Turning Scotland Around,* 1987; *Faster Moves Forward for Scotland,* 1987. *Special Interests:* Education, Economic Policy, Small Businesses, Agriculture. *Countries of Interest:* Israel, USA, Far East. *Recreations:* Tennis, squash, golf, reading, swimming, music. *Electoral Notes:* Contested Motherwell South 1987 and Bristol South 1992. Member for Buckingham since May 1, 1997. *Address:* John Bercow Esq, MP, House of Commons, London, SW1A 0AA *Tel:* 020 7219 3462. *Constituency:* Buckingham Constituency Conservative Association, Buckingham Road, Winslow, Buckingham, MK18 3DY *Tel:* 01296 714240 *Fax:* 01296 714273.

BERESFORD, Sir (Alexander) Paul *(Mole Valley)*   *Con majority 10,221*

Born April 6, 1946; educated Waimea College, Richmond, Nelson, New Zealand; Otago University, Dunedin, New Zealand; BDS. Married Julie Haynes (3 sons 1 daughter). *Career:* Dental surgeon. *Councils, Public Bodies:* Councillor, Wandsworth Borough Council 1978–94, Leader 1983–92. *Political Career:* Parliamentary Under-Secretary of State, Department of the Environment 1994–97. *Select Committees (Current):* Member: Procedure 1997– *(Former):* Member: Education 1992–94. *Honours:* Knighted 1990. *Special Interests:* Inner Cities, Housing, Education. *Countries of Interest:* Fiji, New Zealand, Samoa, Australia. *Recreations:* DIY, reading. *Electoral Notes:* Member for Croydon Central 1992–97, and for Mole Valley since May 1, 1997. *Address:* Sir Paul Beresford, MP, House of Commons, London, SW1A 0AA *Tel:* 020 7219 3000. *Constituency:* Mole Valley Conservative Association, 86 South Street, Dorking, Surrey, RH4 2E2 *Tel:* 01306 883 312 *Fax:* 01306 885 194.

BERMINGHAM, Gerald Edward *(St Helens South)   Lab majority 23,739*

Son of late Dr Patrick Xavier Bermingham. Born August 20, 1940; educated Cotton College, North Staffordshire; Wellingborough Grammar School; Sheffield University (LLB Hons). Married (3 sons, 2 by 1st marriage). *Trades Union:* Vice-Chair, GMB Parliamentary Group; Various positions in APEX. *Profession:* Barrister. *Career:* Admitted Solicitor 1967; Barrister, Grays Inn, called to the Bar 1985. *Councils, Public Bodies:* Councillor, Sheffield City Council 1975–79, 1980–82. *Select Committees (Current):* Member: Catering 1999–. *Other:* Member: SERA, NCCL, Campaign for Criminal Justice. *Sportsclubs:* Vice-President, Sheffield Tigers RUFC. *Special Interests:* Home Affairs, Penal Reform, Energy Conservation, Investment. *Countries of Interest:* Europe, USA. *Recreations:* Music, theatre, sport. *Electoral Notes:* Contested South East Derbyshire 1979. Member for St Helens South since June 1983. *Address:* Gerald Bermingham Esq, MP, House of Commons, London, SW1A 0AA *Tel:* 020 7219 3502 *Fax:* 020 7219 2684 *Fax (Constituency):* 01744 811826.

BERRY, Dr Roger Leslie *(Kingswood)   Lab majority 14,253*

Son of Sydney and Mary Joyce Berry. Born July 4, 1948; educated Dalton County Junior School; Huddersfield New College; Bristol and Sussex Universities (BSc, DPhil). Alison Delyth. *Trades Union:* Member, MSF 1997–99: chair parliamentary group 1997–; Member, AUT 1997–99. *Profession:* Economist. *Career:* Temporary Lecturer in Economics, School of African and Asian Studies; Associate Fellow, Institute of Development Studies, University of Sussex 1973–74; Lecturer in Economics: University of Papua New Guinea 1974–78, Bristol University 1978–92. *Councils, Public Bodies:* Avon County Council: Councillor 1981–92, Chair, Finance and Administration Committee 1983–86, Deputy Leader 1985–86, Leader, Labour Group 1986–92. *Select Committees (Current):* Member: Trade and Industry 1997– *(Former):* Member: Deregulation 1994–95, Trade and Industry 1995–97. *Party Groups:* Joined Labour Party 1974; Chairman: South and West Group of Labour MPs 1997–99, South West Regional Group of Labour MPs 1999–. *Other:* Trustee: Disabled Law Centre, Snowdon Award Scheme; Patron: Artsline, Disabled Drivers' Association, Circomedia. *Awards:* Highland Park/Spectator Backbencher of the Year 1994. *Publications:* Numerous journal and newspaper articles and pamphlets. *Special Interests:* Economic Policy, Disabled/Disability, Third World, Local Government. *Countries of Interest:* India, USA, Ireland, Papua New Guinea. *Recreations:* Travel, food, cooking. *Electoral Notes:* Contested Weston-Super-Mare 1983 and Kingswood 1987 General Elections; Bristol 1984 European Parliamentary Election. Member for Kingswood since April 9, 1992. *Clubs:* Kingswood Labour. *Address:* Dr Roger Berry, MP, House of Commons, London, SW1A 0AA *Tel:* 020 7219 4106. *Constituency:* 2 Nelson Court, Nelson Road, Staple Hill, Bristol, BS16 5EY *Tel:* 0117–956 1837 *Fax:* 0117–970 3663 *E-mail:* berryr@parliament.uk.

BEST, Harold *(Leeds North West)   Lab majority 3,844*

Born December 18, 1937; educated Meanwood County School; Technical College. Married Mary Glyn (2 sons 2 daughters). *Trades Union:* Activist and full-time official. *Profession:* Electrical Technician. *Career:* Electrician; trade union official; electrical technician. *Councils, Public Bodies:* Councillor, West Yorkshire County Council 1981–86; Deputy Chair, West Yorkshire Police Authority. *Select Committees (Current):* Member: Joint Committee on Statutory Instruments 1999–. *Party Groups:* Member, Labour Party 1960–; Chair, North West Leeds Constituency Labour Party 1992–95. *Other:* Former National Executive Committee Member, National Council for Civil Liberties; Member: Amnesty International, Liberty National Executive Committee; Governor, two Leeds Schools; Chair, Headingley Network Community Group; Founder Member, Campaign Against Racial Discrimination, Leeds. *Miscellaneous:* Member, European Standing Committee A 1998. *Electoral Notes:* Member for Leeds North West since May 1, 1997. *Address:* Harold Best Esq, MP, House of Commons, London, SW1A 0AA *Tel:* 020 7219 6999 *Fax:* 020 7219 6979. *Constituency:* 7 Iveson Approach, Leeds, LS16 6LJ *Tel:* 0113–261 0002 *Fax:* 0113–261 0199.

BETTS, Clive James Charles *(Sheffield Attercliffe)   Lab majority 21,818*

Son of late Harold and Nellie Betts. Born January 13, 1950; educated King Edward VII School, Sheffield; Pembroke College, Cambridge (BA Hons Economics and Politics). *Trades Union:* Member, TGWU. *Career:* Economist, Trades Union Congress 1971–73; Local Government Economist: Derbyshire County Council 1973–74, South Yorkshire County Council 1974–86, Rotherham Borough Council 1986–91. *Councils, Public Bodies.* Sheffield City Council: Councillor 1976–92, Chairman: Housing Committee 1980–86, Finance Committee 1986–88, Deputy Leader 1986–87, Leader 1987–92. *Whip:* Opposition Whip 1996–97; Assistant Government Whip 1997–98; A Lord Commissioner of HM Treasury (Government Whip) 1998–. *Select Committees (Current):* Member: Selection 1997– *(Former):* Member: Treasury and Civil Service 1995–96, Treasury 1996–97. *Party Groups:* Joined Labour Party 1969; Member, Labour Leader's Campaign Team with responsibility for Environment and Local Government 1995–96; Member, Labour Housing Group. *Other:* Member, Anti-Apartheid Movement; Past Patron, National Association for Therapeutic Education; Patron: Mosborough Township Youth Project, British Deaf Sports Council; President, Mosborough Citizens' Advice Bureau; Past Vice-President, Energy from Waste Association. *Miscellaneous:* Vice-Chairman, Association of Metropolitan Authorities 1988–91; Chairman, AMA Housing Committee 1985–89; Vice-President, AMA; Chairman, South Yorkshire Pensions Authority 1989–92. *Special Interests:* Economic Policy, Local Government, Housing. *Countries of Interest:* Europe. *Recreations:* Supporting Sheffield Wednesday FC, playing squash, cricket, walking, real ale, scuba diving. *Electoral Notes:* Contested Sheffield Hallam October 1974 and Louth 1979 General Elections. Member for Sheffield Attercliffe since April 9, 1992. *Address:* Clive Betts Esq, MP, House of Commons, London, SW1A 0AA *Tel:* 020 7219 3588 *Fax:* 020 7219 2289. *Constituency:* 2nd Floor, Barkers Pool House, Burgess Street, Sheffield, S1 2HH *Tel:* 0114-273 4444 *Fax:* 0114-273 9666 *E-mail:* bettsc@parliament.uk.

BLACKMAN, Elizabeth *(Erewash)   Lab majority 9,135*

Born September 26, 1949; educated Carlisle County High School for Girls; Prince Henry's Grammar School, Otley; Clifton College, Nottingham (BEd Hons). Married Derek Blackman (1 son 1 daughter) (separated). *Trades Union:* Member, NASUWT. *Profession:* Teacher. *Career:* Head, Upper School, Bramcote Park Comprehensive, Nottingham. *Councils, Public Bodies:* Deputy Leader, Broxtowe Borough Council. *Select Committees (Current):* Member: Treasury 1997–, Treasury Sub-Committee 1998–. *Party Groups:* Member: Co-operative Party, Fabian Society. *Publications: Parliamentary Portions*, recipe book 1998. *Special Interests:* Education, Job Re-Training, Local Community, Economic Regeneration, Crime. *Recreations:* Family, music, reading. *Electoral Notes:* Member for Erewash since May 1, 1997. *Address:* Elizabeth Blackman, MP, House of Commons, London, SW1A 0AA *Tel:* 020 7219 2397 *Fax:* 020 7219 4837. *Constituency:* 23 Barratt Lane, Attenborough, Nottingham, NG9 6AG *Tel:* 0115–922 4380 *Fax:* 0115–943 1860.

BLAIR, The Rt Hon. Tony (Anthony Charles Lynton) *(Sedgefield)   Lab majority 25,143*

Son of Leo Charles Lynton Blair and late Hazel Elisabeth Blair. Born May 6, 1953; educated Durham Choristers School; Fettes College, Edinburgh; St John's College, Oxford (MA Law); Hon. DCL, Northumbria University 1995. Married 1980, Cherie Booth (2 sons 1 daughter). *Trades Union:* Sponsored until March 1996 by Transport and General Workers' Union. *Career:* Called to the Bar, Lincoln's Inn 1976; Barrister specialising in trade union and industrial law 1976–83. *Political Career:* Leader, Labour Party 1994–; Leader of the Opposition 1994–97; Prime Minister, First Lord of the Treasury and Minister for the Civil Service May 1997–. *Spokesman:* Opposition Front Bench Spokesman on: Treasury and Economic Affairs 1984–87, Trade and Industry 1987–88; Shadow Secretary of State for Energy 1988–89, Employment 1989–92, Shadow Home Secretary 1992–94. *Other:* Vice-President, Federation of Economic Development Authorities (FEDA). *Awards:* Charlemagne Prize 1999. *Miscellaneous:* Vice-President, Federation of Economic Development Authorities (FEDA). *Honours:* PC 1994. *Publications: New Britain: My Vision of a Young Country*, 1996.

Electoral Notes: Contested Beaconsfield By-election May 1982. Member for Sedgefield since June, 1983. *Address:* The Rt Hon. Tony Blair, MP, House of Commons, London, SW1A 0AA *Tel:* 020 7219 5676. *Constituency:* Myrobella, Farfield Terrace, Trindon Colliery, Co Durham *Tel:* 01429 882202 *Website:* http://www.number–10.gov.uk.

BLEARS, Hazel Anne *(Salford)* **Lab majority 17,069**

Daughter of Arthur and Dorothy Blears. Born May 14, 1956; educated Wardley Grammar School; Eccles VIth Form College; Trent Polytechnic; Chester College of Law (BA Hons, Law). Married October 21, 1989, Michael Halsall. *Trades Union:* Former Branch Secretary, TGWU; Member, TGWU. *Profession:* Solicitor. *Career:* Trainee Solicitor, Salford Council 1978–80; Private Practice Solicitor 1980–81; Solicitor: Rossendale Council 1981–83, Wigan Council 1983–85; Principal Solicitor, Manchester City Council 1985–. *Councils, Public Bodies:* Councillor, Salford Council 1984–92. *Political Career:* PPS to Rt Hon. Alan Milburn, MP: as Minister of State, Department of Health December 1997-December 1998, as Chief Secretary, HM Treasury January-October 1999. *Select Committees (Former):* Member: European Legislation 1997–98. *Party Groups:* Vice-Chair, North West Regional Group of Labour MPs 1997–98, Chair 1998–; Member: North West Executive 1997–, National Policy Forum 1997–; Leadership Campaign Team 1997–98; Labour Party Development Co-ordinator and Deputy to Ian McCartney. *Other:* Chair, Salford Community Health Council; Vice-Chair, Pendleton College Governors. *Trust:* Trustee: Working Class Movement Library, National Museum Labour History. *Special Interests:* Employment, Health, Engineering, Arts, Urban Regeneration. *Recreations:* Dance, motorcycling. *Electoral Notes:* Contested Tatton 1987, Bury South 1992. Member for Salford since May 1, 1997. *Address:* Hazel Anne Blears, MP, House of Commons, London, SW1A 0AA *Tel:* 020 7219 6595 *Fax:* 020 7219 0949. *Constituency:* Unit 4, Albion Place, The Crescent, Salford, Greater Manchester, M5 4NL *Tel:* 0161-925 0705 *Fax:* 0161-743 9173 *E-mail:* blearsh@parl.uk.

BLIZZARD, Bob (Robert John) *(Waveney)* **Lab majority 12,093**

Son of Arthur Blizzard, signwriter, and the late Joan Blizzard. Born May 31, 1950; educated Culford School, Bury St Edmunds; University of Birmingham (BA Hons). Married Lyn, daughter of Walter and Val Chance (1 son 1 daughter). *Trades Union:* Member, NUT. *Profession:* Teacher. *Career:* Teacher: Gravesend Secondary School 1973–75, Bexley Secondary School, Head of English 1976–86, Gorleston Secondary School, Head of English 1986–97. *Councils, Public Bodies:* Waveney District Council: Councillor 1987–, Leader 1991–; Vice-Chair, SCEALA 1995–. *Political Career:* PPS to the Baroness Hayman, as Minister of State, Ministry of Agriculture, Fisheries and Food 1999–. *Select Committees (Current):* Member: Environmental Audit 1997–. *Party Groups:* Joined Labour Party 1983. *Special Interests:* Employment, Health, Local Government, Education. *Countries of Interest:* Canada, USA, Europe, Asia. *Recreations:* Walking, skiing, listening to jazz. *Electoral Notes:* Member for Waveney since May 1, 1997. *Address:* Bob Blizzard Esq, MP, House of Commons, London, SW1A 0AA *Tel:* 020 7219 4088. *Constituency:* 27 Milton Road East, Lowestoft, Suffolk, NR32 1NT *Tel:* 01502 573452 *Fax:* 01502 561580 *E-mail:* bobblizzard@netmatters.co.uk.

BLUNKETT, The Rt Hon. David *(Sheffield Brightside)* **Lab majority 19,954**

Son of late Arthur and Doris Blunkett. Born June 6, 1947; educated Sheffield School for the Blind; Royal Normal College for the Blind; Shrewsbury Technical College; Sheffield Richmond College of Further Education (day release and evening courses); Sheffield University (BA political theory and institutions); Huddersfield College of Education (PGCE). Married July 18, 1970, Ruth Gwynneth Mitchell (3 sons) (marriage dissolved 1990). *Trades Union:* Shop steward 1967–69; Former member, NATFHE; Current member, UNISON. *Career:* Office work, East Midlands Gas Board 1967–69; industrial relations and politics, Barnsley College of Technology 1973-81. *Councils, Public Bodies:* Sheffield City Council 1970–1988, Chair, Social Services Committee 1976–80, Seconded as Leader 1980–87; South Yorkshire County Council 1973–77. *Political*

Career: Shadow Secretary of State for: Health 1992–94, Education 1994–95, Education and Employment 1995–97; Secretary of State for Education and Employment 1997–. *Spokesman:* Opposition Spokesman on Environment (Local Government) 1988–92;. *Party Groups:* Member, Labour Party National Executive Committee 1983–98; Vice-Chairman, Labour Party 1992–93, Chairman 1993–94. *Honours:* PC 1997. *Publications: Building from the Bottom,* 1983; *Democracy in Crisis – the Town Halls Respond,* 1987; *On a Clear Day* – (autobiography), 1995. *Special Interests:* Local Government, Education, Economic and Democratic Planning. *Recreations:* Walking, sailing, music, poetry. *Electoral Notes:* Contested Sheffield Hallam February 1974. Member for Sheffield Brightside since June 1987. *Address:* The Rt Hon. David Blunkett, MP, House of Commons, London, SW1A 0AA *Tel:* 020 7219 4043 *Fax:* 020 7219 5903. *Constituency:* Town Hall Chambers, 1 Barkers Pool, Sheffield, S1 2EN *Tel:* 0114–273 5987 *Fax:* 0114–278 0384.

BLUNT, Crispin *(Reigate)* Con majority 7,741

Son of Major-General Peter Blunt, CB, MBE, GM, and Mrs Adrienne Blunt. Born July 15, 1960; educated Wellington College; Royal Military Academy, Sandhurst; University College, University of Durham (BA); Cranfield Institute of Technology (MBA). Married September 15, 1990, Victoria, daughter of Kenneth Jenkins (1 son 1 daughter). *Armed Forces:* Army Officer 1979–90; Regimental duty 13th/18th Royal Hussars (QMO) in England, Germany and Cyprus. *Career:* District Agent, Forum of Private Business 1991–92; Political Consultant, Politics International 1993; Special Adviser to Malcolm Rifkind: as Secretary of State for Defence 1993–95, as Foreign Secretary 1995–97. *Select Committees (Current):* Member: Defence 1997–. *Sportsclubs:* Fantasians Cricket, Reigate Priory Cavaliers. *Special Interests:* Economic Policy, Defence, Foreign Affairs, Environment. *Recreations:* Cricket. *Electoral Notes:* Contested West Bromwich East 1992 General Election. Member for Reigate since May 1, 1997. *Clubs:* Redhill Constitutional, Royal Automobile. *Address:* Crispin Blunt Esq, MP, House of Commons, London, SW1A 0AA *Tel:* 020 7219 3454. *Constituency:* Reigate Conservative Association, 18 Warwick Road, Redhill, Surrey, RH1 1BU *Tel:* 01737 765411 *Fax:* 01737 765411 *E-mail:* crispin_blunt_mp@parliament.uk.

BOATENG, The Rt Hon. Paul *(Brent South)* Lab majority 19,691

Son of Kwaku Boateng, barrister, and Eleanor Boateng, teacher. Born June 14, 1951; educated Achimota; Accra Academy, Ghana; Apsley Grammar School; Bristol University (LLB Hons); College of Law. Married November 20, 1980, Janet Olivia, daughter of Leonard Carter and Sylvia Alleyne (2 sons 3 daughters). *Profession:* Barrister. *Career:* Solicitor 1975; Barrister-at-law. *Councils, Public Bodies:* Member of GLC for Walthamstow 1981–86, Chairman, Police Committee 1981–86, Vice-Chairman, Ethnic Minority Committee 1981–86. *Political Career:* Parliamentary Under-Secretary of State, Department of Health 1997–98; Home Office: Minister of State (Minister for Criminal Policy) 1998–99, Minister of State and Deputy Home Secretary 1999–. *Spokesman:* Opposition Front Bench Spokesman on: Treasury and Economic Affairs 1989–92, Lord Chancellor's Department 1992–97. *Party Groups:* Member: Labour Party NEC sub committee Human Rights 1979–83, Labour Party Joint Committee on Crime and Policing 1984–86. *Other:* Chairman: Afro-Caribbean Education Resource Project 1978–84, Westminster Community Relations Council 1979–81; Legal Adviser, Scrap Sus Campaign 1977–81; Vice-President, Waltham Forest Community Relations Council 1981–; Home Office Advisory Council on Race Relations 1981–86; World Council of Churches Commission on programme to combat racism 1984–91; Vice-Moderator 1984–91; Police Training Council 1981–85; Executive NCCL 1980–86; Chairman of Governors, Priory Park School 1978–84; Governor, Police Staff College Bramshill 1981–84; Board of English National Opera 1984–97. *Honours:* PC 1999. *Publications:* (contributor) *Reclaiming the Ground; Introduction to Sense and Sensibility: The Complete Jane Austen. Special Interests:* Home Affairs, Housing, Inner Cities, Overseas Aid and Development, Environment. *Countries of Interest:* Africa, Caribbean, USA, Southern Africa. *Recreations:* Family, swimming, opera. *Electoral Notes:* Contested Hertfordshire West 1983. Member for Brent South since June 1987. *Address:* The Rt Hon. Paul Boateng, MP, House of Commons, London, SW1A 0AA *Tel:* 020 7219 6816.

BODY, Sir Richard *(Boston and Skegness)   Con majority 647*

Son of Lieutenant-Colonel B. R. Body. Born May 18, 1927; educated Reading School. Married 1959, Marion Graham (1 son 1 daughter). *Trades Union:* Branch Secretary, AScW 1950–52; Delegate to Holborn Trades Council 1950–53. *Armed Forces:* RAFVR (India Command) 1945–48. *Profession:* Barrister. *Career:* Called to the Bar of the Middle Temple 1949; Farmer; Editor, *World Review* 1996–. *Other:* Former Chairman, Society for Individual Freedom. *Trust:* Chairman of Trustees, Centre for European Studies 1989. *Miscellaneous:* Joint Chairman, Council of the Get Britain Out Referendum Campaign, 1974. *Honours:* Knighted 1986. *Publications: The Architect and the Law*, 1954; (contributor) *Destiny or Delusion*, 1971; (edited jointly) *Freedom and Stability in the World Economy*, 1976; *Agriculture: the Triumph and the Shame*, 1982; *Farming in the Clouds*, 1984; *Red or Green for Farmers and the Rest of Us)*, 1987; *Europe of Many Circles*, 1990; *Our Food, Our Land*, 1991. *Special Interests:* Agriculture, Environment, European Union, Third World. *Countries of Interest:* Europe. *Electoral Notes:* Contested Rotherham 1950, Abertillery 1950 and Leek 1951. Member for Billericay 1955–59, for Holland with Boston 1966–97, and for Boston and Skegness since May 1, 1997. *Clubs:* Carlton, Reform, Athenaeum. *Address:* Sir Richard Body, MP, House of Commons, London, SW1A 0AA *Tel:* 020 7219 4100. *Constituency:* 5 Church Close, Boston, PE21 6NT *Tel:* 01205 355884.

BOOTHROYD, The Rt Hon. Betty *(West Bromwich West)   Speaker majority 15,423*

Daughter of late Archibald and Mary Boothroyd. Born October 8, 1929; educated Dewsbury College of Commerce and Art; Hon. LLD: Birmingham, Leeds Metropolitan, Leicester, South Bank, North London, Cambridge, Bradford, City, Oxford, Open University. *Career:* Former Personal/Political Assistant to Labour Ministers; Legislative Assistant, U.S. Congressman 1960–62. *Councils, Public Bodies:* Councillor, Hammersmith Borough Council 1965–68. *Political Career:* Second Deputy Chairman of Ways and Means and Deputy Speaker 1987–92; Speaker 1992–. *Whip:* Assistant Government Whip 1974–76. *Party Groups:* Member, Labour Party National Executive Committee 1981–87. *Other:* Chancellor, Open University October 1994–. *Awards: The Spectator* Parliamentarian of the Year Award 1992; Personality of the Year 1993; Communicator of the Year 1994. *Miscellaneous:* Chairman, House of Commons Commission 1992–. Freedom: Metropolitan Borough of Sandwell, Metropolitan Borough of Kirklees, City of London. *Honours:* PC 1992. *Electoral Notes:* Contested Leicester South East 1957 (by-election); Peterborough 1959; Nelson & Colne 1968 (by-election); Rossendale 1970; Member of European Parliament July 1975-March 1977. Member for West Bromwich 1973–74, and for West Bromwich West 1974–. *Clubs:* Reform, University Women's. *Address:* The Rt Hon. Betty Boothroyd, MP, House of Commons, London, SW1A 0AA *Tel:* 020 7219 5302.

BORROW, David Stanley *(South Ribble)   Lab majority 5,084*

Son of James Borrow, retired training officer, and Nancy Borrow, secretary. Born August 2, 1952; educated Mirfield Grammar School, Mirfield; Lanchester Polytechnic (BAHons Economics). Single. *Trades Union:* Member, UNISON; Former Branch Vice-Chair. *Career:* Clerk to Merseyside Valuation Tribunal 1983–97. *Councils, Public Bodies:* Councillor, Preston Borough Council 1987–98, Leader 1992–94, 1995–97. *Select Committees (Current):* Member: Agriculture 1999–. *Party Groups:* Member: Labour Party 1969–, Fabian Society, Co-operative Party. *Other:* President, Society of Clerks 1990–92 and 1996–97. *Miscellaneous:* Member: European Standing Committee A 1998, European Standing Committee C 1999–. TechIRRV. *Special Interests:* Regional Development, Local Government Finance, Aerospace. *Countries of Interest:* Southern Africa. *Electoral Notes:* Contested Wyre 1992. Member for South Ribble since May 1, 1997. *Clubs:* Lostock Hall Labour. *Address:* David Borrow Esq, MP, House of Commons, London, SW1A 0AA *Tel:* 020 7219 4126 *Fax:* 020 7219 4126. *Constituency:* Crescent House, 2–6 Sandy Lane, Leyland, Lancashire, PR5 1CB *Tel:* 01772 454727 *Fax:* 01772 422982 *E-mail:* david.borrow@labour.co.uk.

BOSWELL, Timothy Eric *(Daventry)   Con majority 7,378*

Son of late Eric Boswell and Mrs Joan Boswell. Born December 2, 1942; educated Marlborough College; New College, Oxford (MA, Diploma in Agricultural Economics). Married August 2, 1969, Helen Delahay, daughter of late Revd Arthur Rees (3 daughters). *Career:* Conservative Research Department 1966–73; Head, Economic Section 1970–73; Farmer 1974–87; Leicestershire, Northamptonshire and Rutland County Branch of NFU, County Chairman 1983; Part-time Special Adviser to Minister of Agriculture 1984–86. *Political Career:* PPS to Financial Secretary to HM Treasury 1989–90; Parliamentary Under-Secretary of State, Department for Education 1992–95; Parliamentary Secretary, Ministry of Agriculture, Fisheries and Food 1995–97. *Whip:* Assistant Government Whip 1990–92; Lord Commissioner of HM Treasury (Government Whip) April-December 1992. *Spokesman:* An Opposition Front Bench Spokesman for: the Treasury June-December 1997, Trade and Industry December 1997–99; Education and Employment (People with Disabilities) 1999–. *Party Groups:* Daventry Constituency Conservative Association Treasurer 1976–79, Chairman 1979–83. *Other:* Council of Perry Foundation 1967–90, President 1984–90. *Miscellaneous:* Member, Agricultural and Food Research Council 1988–90. *Special Interests:* Agriculture, Finance and Taxation, European Union. *Countries of Interest:* Europe. *Recreations:* Shooting. *Electoral Notes:* Contested Rugby February 1974. Member for Daventry since June 1987. *Clubs:* Farmers'. *Address:* Timothy Boswell Esq, MP, House of Commons, London, SW1A 0AA *Tel:* 020 7219 3520 *Fax:* 020 7219 4919. *Constituency:* Lloyds Bank Chambers, North Street, Daventry, Northamptonshire, NN11 5PN *Tel:* 01327 703192 *Fax:* 01327 310263.

BOTTOMLEY, Peter James *(Worthing West)   Con majority 7,713*

Son of Sir James Bottomley, KCMG, HM Diplomatic Service. Born July 20, 1944; educated Comprehensive School, Washington DC; Westminster; Trinity College, Cambridge (MA). Married 1967, Virginia, née Garnett, MP *(qv)* (1 son 2 daughters). *Trades Union:* Member, TGWU. *Profession:* Industrial Economist. *Career:* Industrial sales, industrial relations, industrial economics. *Political Career:* PPS: to Cranley Onslow, MP, at Foreign and Commonwealth Office 1982–83, to Norman Fowler, MP, at Department of Health and Social Security 1983–84; Parliamentary Under-Secretary of State: at Department of Employment 1984–86, at Department of Transport (Minister for Roads and Traffic) 1986–89, at Northern Ireland Office (Agriculture, Environment) 1989–90; PPS to Rt Hon. Peter Brooke MP, as Secretary of State for Northern Ireland September-November 1990. *Select Committees (Current):* Member: Standards and Privileges 1997–, Unopposed Bills (Panel) 1997– *(Former):* Member: Transport 1992–97. *Party Groups:* Former President, Conservative Trade Unionists. *International Bodies:* RIIA. *Other:* Chairman, Family Forum 1980–82; Hon. President, The Water Companies Association; Chairman, Church of England Children's Society 1982–84; Member, Council of NACRO. *Trust:* Trustee, Christian Aid 1978–84; Fellow, Industry and Parliament Trust. *Awards:* Gold Medal, Institute of the Motor Industry 1988. Court Member, Drapers' Company. *Sportsclubs:* Former Captain, House of Commons Football Club; Former Parliamentary swimming and occasional dinghy sailing champion. Former Fellow, Institute of Personnel Management; Fellow, Institute of Road Safety Officers. *Countries of Interest:* Southern Africa, El Salvador, USA. *Electoral Notes:* Contested Greenwich, Woolwich West February and October 1974. Member for Greenwich, Woolwich West By-election 1975–83, for Eltham 1983–97, and for Worthing West since May 1, 1997. *Address:* Peter Bottomley Esq, MP, House of Commons, London, SW1A 0AA *Tel:* 020 7219 6505. *Constituency:* Haverfield House, Union Place, Worthing, West Sussex, BN11 1LG *Tel:* 01903 235168.

Dod *on* Disk
The Vacher Dod Parliamentary Database – configured for PC or Network
For further details please telephone the Westminster Office
020 7828 7256

BOTTOMLEY, The Rt Hon. Virginia *(South West Surrey) Con majority 2,694*

Daughter of late W. John Garnett CBE. Born March 12, 1948; educated Putney High School; Essex University (BA sociology); London School of Economics (MSc social work and administration); Honorary LLD (University of Portsmouth). Married 1967, Peter Bottomley MP (*qv*), son of Sir James Bottomley, KCMG (1 son 2 daughters). *Career:* Researcher, Child Poverty Action Group 1971–73; Psychiatric social worker in South London, Social Policy Tutor 1973–74; Director, Mid Southern Water Company 1987–88. *Councils, Public Bodies:* Magistrate in Inner London Juvenile Courts 1975–84; Chairman, Lambeth Juvenile Court 1980–84. *Political Career:* PPS: to Chris Patten, MP, as Minister of State, Department of Education and Science 1985–86, as Minister of State (Minister for Overseas Development), FCO 1986–87, to Sir Geoffrey Howe QC, as Secretary of State for Foreign and Commonwealth Affairs 1987–88; Parliamentary Under-Secretary of State, Department of Environment 1988–89; Minister of State, Department of Health 1989–92; Secretary of State for: Health 1992–95, National Heritage 1995–97. *Select Committees (Former):* Member: Foreign Affairs 1997–99, Entry Clearance Sub-Committee 1997–98. *Other:* Governor, London School of Economics 1985–; Vice-President, Carers' National Association 1990–; Governor, Ditchley Foundation 1991–. *Trust:* Fellow, Industry and Parliament Trust. *Miscellaneous:* Member, Medical Research Council 1987–88; Chairman, Millennium Commission 1995–97; Government Co-Chairman, Women's National Commission 1991–92; Vice-Chairman, British Council Board 1997–. Freeman, City of London 1988. *Honours:* PC 1992. *Electoral Notes:* Contested Isle of Wight in 1983 General Election. Member for South West Surrey since May 3, 1984 By-election. *Address:* The Rt Hon. Virginia Bottomley, MP, House of Commons, London, SW1A 0AA *Tel:* 020 7219 6499 *Fax:* 020 7219 6279. *Constituency:* 2 Royal Parade, Tilford Road, Hindhead, Surrey, GU26 6TD *Tel:* 01428 604526 *Fax:* 01428 667498.

BRADLEY, Keith John Charles *(Manchester Withington) Lab majority 18,581*

Son of late John Bradley and Mrs Beatrice Harris. Born May 17, 1950; educated Bishop Vesey's Grammar School; Manchester Polytechnic; York University (BA Hons, MPhil, DipAcct). Married May 16, 1987, Rhona Ann Graham (2 sons 1 daughter). *Trades Union:* Member: MSF, UNISON. *Career:* Charles Impey and Co., Chartered Accountants 1969–73; Research Officer, Manchester City Council Housing Department 1978–81; Secretary, Stockport Community Health Council 1981–87. *Councils, Public Bodies:* Councillor, Manchester City Council 1983–88, Chairman, Environment and Consumer Services Committee 1984–88; Formerly City Council Director: Manchester Ship Canal Co, Manchester Airport plc. *Political Career:* Parliamentary Under-Secretary of State, Department of Social Security 1997–98. *Whip:* Treasurer of HM Household (Deputy Chief Whip) 1998–. *Spokesman:* Opposition Spokesman on: Social Security 1991–96, Transport 1996–97. *Select Committees (Current):* Member: Accommodation and Works 1998–, Finance and Services 1999–, Selection 1999– *(Former):* Member: Agriculture 1989–92. *Party Groups:* Member, Co-op Party. *Special Interests:* Local Government, Housing, Health, Pensions, Poverty. *Recreations:* All sports, theatre, cinema. *Electoral Notes:* Member for Manchester Withington since June 1987. *Address:* Keith Bradley Esq, MP, House of Commons, London, SW1A 0AA *Tel:* 020 7219 2279 *Fax:* 020 7219 5901. *Constituency:* Investment House, 425 Wilmslow Road, Withington, Manchester, M20 4AF *Tel:* 0161–446 2047 *Fax:* 0161–445 5543 *E-mail:* keith.bradley@hm-treasury.gov.uk.

BRADLEY, Peter Charles Stephen *(The Wrekin) Lab majority 3,025*

Son of Fred and Trudie Bradley. Born April 12, 1953; educated Abingdon; University of Sussex (BA Hons). Partner, Annie Hart (twin son and daughter). *Trades Union:* Member, MSF. *Profession:* Public Affairs Consultant. *Career:* Research Director, Centre for Contemporary Studies 1979–85; Director, Good Relations 1985–93; Managing Director, Millbank Consultants Ltd 1993–97. *Councils, Public Bodies:* Councillor, Westminster City Council 1986–96, Deputy Leader, Labour Group 1990–96. *Select Committees (Current):* Member: Public Administration 1997–. *Party Groups:* Member, Labour Party 1979–; Chair, Rural Group of Labour MPs. *Other:* Patron, Friends of Searchlight. *Miscellaneous:* Vice-President, UK Local Authority Forum of

World Heritage Sites. *Sportsclubs:* Warwickshire County Cricket Club. *Publications:* Various research and press articles. *Special Interests:* Economic Policy, Transport, Education, Health, Housing, Rural Affairs. *Recreations:* Playing cricket, watching football (especially Aston Villa) and rugby, walking. *Electoral Notes:* Member for The Wrekin since May 1, 1997. *Address:* Peter Bradley Esq, MP, House of Commons, London, SW1A 0AA *Tel:* 020 7219 4112 *Fax:* 020 7219 0536. *Constituency:* Wrekin Labour Party, 9A Queen Street, Wellington, Telford, Shropshire, TF1 1EH *Tel:* 01952 240010 *Fax:* 01952 240455 *E-mail:* taylorc@parliament.uk.

BRADSHAW, Benjamin Peter James *(Exeter)*   Lab majority 11,705

Son of late Canon Peter Bradshaw and late Daphne Bradshaw, teacher. Born August 30, 1960; educated Thorpe St Andrew School, Norwich; University of Sussex (BA Hons German); Freidburg University, Germany; Norfolk County Scholar. *Trades Union:* Member, NUJ. *Profession:* Journalist. *Career:* Award-winning BBC Reporter and Presenter; BBC Berlin correspondent during fall of Berlin Wall; Reporter for 'World At One' and 'World This Weekend' on BBC Radio 4. *Political Career:* Introduced Pesticides Act (Private Member's Bill) 1998. *Select Committees (Current):* Member: European Scrutiny 1998– *(Former):* Member: European Legislation 1998. *Party Groups:* Secretary, Labour Movement for Europe, Member: Labour Campaign for Electoral Reform, SERA, Christian Socialist Movement. *Awards:* Consumer Journalist of the Year 1989; Anglo-German Foundation Journalist of the Year 1990; Sony News Reporter Award 1993. *Publications:* Numerous for the BBC on domestic and foreign affairs. *Special Interests:* Foreign Affairs, Environment and Transport, Modernisation of Parliament. *Countries of Interest:* Europe – particularly Germany and Italy, USA. *Recreations:* Cycling, walking, cooking, music. *Electoral Notes:* Member for Exeter since May 1, 1997. *Clubs:* Whipton Labour, Exeter. *Address:* Benjamin Bradshaw Esq, MP, House of Commons, London, SW1A 0AA *Tel:* 020 7219 6597 *Fax:* 020 7219 0950. *Constituency:* Labour HQ, 26B Clifton Hill, Exeter, Devon, EX1 2DJ *Tel:* 01392 424464 *Fax:* 01392 425630 *E-mail:* bradshawb@parliament.uk.

BRADY, Graham Stuart *(Altrincham and Sale West)*   Con majority 1,505

Son of John Brady, accountant, and Maureen Brady (née Birch), medical secretary. Born May 20, 1967; educated Altrincham Grammar School; University of Durham (BA Hons Law). Married 1992, Victoria Lowther (1 son, 1 daughter). *Career:* Shandwick PLC 1989–90; Centre for Policy Studies 1990–92; Public Affairs Director, The Waterfront Partnership 1992–97. *Select Committees (Current):* Member: Education and Employment 1997–, Employment Sub-Committee 1997–. *Party Groups:* Chairman, Durham University Conservative Association 1987–88; National Union Executive Committee 1988; Chairman, Northern Area Conservative Collegiate Forum 1987–89; Vice-Chairman, East Berkshire Conservative Association 1993–95. *Other:* School Governor 1991–93; Vice-President, Greater Altrincham Chamber of Trade Commerce and Industry 1997–. *Miscellaneous:* Executive Member, 1922 Committee 1998–. *Publications: Towards an Employees' Charter – and Away From Collective Bargaining* (Centre for Policy Studies), 1991. *Special Interests:* European Union, Employment, Education, Foreign Affairs, Health. *Countries of Interest:* Commonwealth, Far East, British Overseas Territories. *Recreations:* Family, gardening, reading. *Electoral Notes:* Member for Altrincham and Sale West since May 1, 1997. *Address:* Graham Brady Esq, MP, House of Commons, London, SW1A 0AA *Tel:* 020 7219 4604. *Constituency:* Altrincham and Sale West Conservative Association, Thatcher House, Delahays Farm, Green Lane, Timperley, Cheshire, WA15 8QW *Tel:* 0161–904 8828 *Fax:* 0161–904 8868.

BRAKE, Tom (Thomas Anthony) *(Carshalton and Wallington)   LD majority 2,267*

Son of Michael and Judy Brake. Born May 6, 1962; educated Lycee International, St Germain-en-Laye, France; Imperial College, London (BSc Physics). Married August 23, 1998, Candida Goulden (1 daughter). *Profession:* IT Manager. *Career:* Principal Consultant (IT), Cap Gemini. *Councils, Public Bodies:* Councillor: London Borough of Hackney 1988–90, London Borough of Sutton 1994–98. *Spokesman:* A Spokesman for: Environment, Transport in London and Air Transport 1997–99, Environment, Transport, the Regions and Social Justice 1999–. *Select Committees (Current):* Member: Environment, Transport and Regional Affairs 1997–, Environment Sub-Committee 1997–, Transport Sub-Committee 1999–. *Other:* Member: Oxfam, Amnesty International, Greenpeace. *Special Interests:* Environment. *Countries of Interest:* France, Portugal, Russia. *Recreations:* Sport, film, eating. *Electoral Notes:* Contested Carshalton and Wallington 1992. Member for Carshalton and Wallington since May 1, 1997. *Address:* Tom Brake Esq, MP, House of Commons, London, SW1A 0AA *Tel:* 020 7219 6491 *Fax:* 020 7219 6491. *Constituency:* 6 Station Approach, Gordon Road, Carshalton, Surrey, SM5 3RF *Tel:* 020 8255 8155 *Fax:* 020 8395 4453 *E-mail:* cwlibs@cix.co.uk.

BRAND, Dr Peter *(Isle of Wight)   LD majority 6,406*

Son of late Louis H. Brand and late Ans (née Fredericks). Born May 16, 1947; educated Thornbury Grammar School; Birmingham University. Married 1972, Jane Vivienne, daughter of Dr Wilfrid Attlee and Mary Attlee (2 sons). *Trades Union:* Member, BMA: Former ARM Representative, Local Secretary, Local Chairman. *Profession:* General Practitioner. *Career:* Junior Hospital Posts, Kent and Dorset 1971–73; General Practice, Poole 1973–76, Isle of Wight 1976–. *Councils, Public Bodies:* County Councillor, Isle of Wight 1985–95; Councillor, Isle of Wight (Unitary Authority) 1995–97. *Spokesman:* A Spokesman for: Health (Public Health, Health Promotion, Family and Ethical Issues, Voluntary and Independent Sector, PFI) 1997–99, Health (Public Health) 1999–. *Select Committees (Current):* Member: Health 1997–. *International Bodies:* Member, Council of Europe. *Other:* Director of School for Children with Special Needs, The Mount School, Wadhurst 1971–75; Chairman, Islecare 1993–96; Governor: Medina House Special School 1985–97, Watergate Special School 1985–97; Member: Ventnor Railway Society, Amnesty, Charter 88; Patron: Medina Park Residents Association, IW Prosthetic Users Group, IW Gilten Market, Don Mills Variety Club, IW Group of Crohn's Disease and Ulcerative Colitis, ASCSA (Adult Survivors of Child Sexual Abuse). *Trust:* Member, National Trust. *Sportsclubs:* Brading Haven Yacht Club; Island Sailing Club; Royal Yachting Association; Royal Solent Yacht Club; Rear-Commodore, House of Commons Yacht Club. MRCS; LRCP; DORCOG; MRCGP. *Special Interests:* Health, Social Services, Isle of Wight. *Countries of Interest:* Europe. *Recreations:* Boating, maintenance of an ancient house, food and wine. *Electoral Notes:* Contested Isle of Wight 1992. Member for Isle of Wight since May 1, 1997. *Clubs:* National Liberal. *Address:* Dr Peter Brand, MP, House of Commons, London, SW1A 0AA *Tel:* 020 7219 4404 *Fax:* 020 7219 2165. *Constituency:* 30 Quay Street, Newport, Isle of Wight, PO30 5BA *Tel:* 01983 524427 *Fax:* 01983 525819 *E-mail:* island_mp@cix.co.uk *Website:* http://www.the_commons.com/peter_brand.

BRAZIER, Julian William Hendy, TD *(Canterbury)   Con majority 3,964*

Son of Lieutenant Colonel Peter Hendy Brazier, retired, and Patricia Audrey Helen Brazier (née Stubbs). Born July 24, 1953; educated Dragon School; Wellington College, Berks; Brasenose College, Oxford (Scholarship in Mathematics) (MA); London Business School. Married July 21, 1984, Katherine Elizabeth, daughter of Brigadier P. Blagden (3 sons). *Armed Forces:* Pre-university SSLC with Royal Engineers 1972; TA 1972–82, 1989–92. *Profession:* Management Consultant. *Career:* Charter Consolidated Ltd 1975–84, Economic Research, Corporate Finance and Secretary, Executive Committee of the Board; Management Consultant, H. B. Maynard International 1984–87. *Political Career:* PPS to Rt Hon. Gillian Shephard MP: as Minister of State, Treasury 1990–92; as Secretary of State for Employment 1992–93. *Select Committees (Current):*

Member: Defence 1997–. *Party Groups:* President, Conservative Family Campaign. *Awards:* Highland Park/*The Spectator* Backbencher of the Year (jointly) 1996. *Publications:* Co-author *Not Fit to Fight: The Cultural Subversion of the Armed Forces in Britain and America*, Social Affairs Unit 1999 Ten pamphlets on defence, social and economic issues (with Bow Group, Centre for Policy Studies and Conservative 2000). *Special Interests:* Defence, Economics, Law and Order, Family, Countryside. *Countries of Interest:* Middle East, South Africa, USA, Australia. *Recreations:* Cross-country running, science, philosophy. *Electoral Notes:* Contested Berwick-upon-Tweed 1983. Member for Canterbury since June 1987. *Address:* Julian Brazier Esq, TD, MP, House of Commons, London, SW1A 0AA *Tel:* 020 7219 3000. *Constituency:* c/o 9 Hawks Lane, Canterbury, Kent *Tel:* 01227 65332.

BREED, Colin Edward *(South East Cornwall)   LD majority 6,480*

Son of late Alfred and late Edith Violet Breed. Born May 4, 1947; educated Torquay Boys Grammar School. Married July 6, 1968, Janet, daughter of Ronald and Leonora Courtiour (1 son 1 daughter). *Profession:* Banker. *Career:* Manager, Midland Bank plc 1964–81; Managing Director, Dartington and Co plc 1981–91; Director, Gemini Abrasives Ltd 1991–96. *Councils, Public Bodies:* Councillor, Caradon District Council 1982–92; Mayor of Saltash 1989–90, 1995–96. *Spokesman:* A Spokesman for: Competition and Consumer Affairs 1997–99, Competition 1999; Principal Spokesman for Agriculture, Rural Affairs and Fisheries 1999–. *Select Committees (Current):* Member: European Scrutiny 1998– *(Former):* Member: European Legislation 1998.

International Bodies: Executive Committee Member, Council for Advancement of Arab-British Understanding. *Trust:* Chairman, Princes Trust Volunteers (Devon). *Miscellaneous:* Member, General Medical Council 1999–. *Sportsclubs:* St Mellion Golf and Country Club. ACIB. *Special Interests:* Cornwall. *Recreations:* Watching sport, golf. *Electoral Notes:* Member for South East Cornwall since May 1, 1997. *Clubs:* National Liberal. *Address:* Colin Breed Esq, MP, House of Commons, London, SW1A 0AA *Tel:* 020 7219 2588 *Fax:* 020 7219 5905. *Constituency:* Barras Street, Liskeard, Cornwall, PL14 6AD *Tel:* 01579 342150 *Fax:* 01579 347019.

BRINTON, Helen Rosemary *(Peterborough)   Lab majority 7,323*

Daughter of Phyllis May Dyche, ex infant headmistress, and George Henry Dyche, ex junior teacher. Born December 23, 1954; educated Spondon Park Grammar, Derby; Bristol University (BA Hons English Literature, MA Medieval Literature, PGCE). Divorced (1 son 1 daughter). *Trades Union:* Student Rep, NUT 1978–79; Member: NUT 1979–, TGWU 1989–; School Rep, NUT 1994–97. *Profession:* Teacher. *Career:* Assistant Teacher of English, Katharine Lady Berkeley Comprehensive 1979–82; 2nd Department, Harrogate College 1983–88; Year Head, Rochester Grammar For Girls 1993–97. *Select Committees (Current):* Member: Environmental Audit 1997–, Unopposed Bills (Panel) 1998–. *Party Groups:* Member: Fabian Society 1988–97, Co-op Party

1988–97; Has held many posts in Labour Party; Kent County Election Organiser 1993. *Other:* Volunteer: ASBAH, MIND-NCVO Parliamentary Secondment Scheme. *Miscellaneous:* Member, Standing Committees on: Crime and Disorder Bill 1997–98, Water Bill 1999, Finance Bill 1999, Financial Services and Markets Bill 1999. *Publications:* Articles and Letters in: *Co-op Members News, Tribune, Fabian News, New Statesman & Society, Progress, Labour Weekly*. *Special Interests:* Environment, Home Affairs, Health. *Recreations:* Reading, modern film. *Electoral Notes:* Member for Peterborough since May 1, 1997. *Address:* Mrs Helen Brinton, MP, House of Commons, London, SW1A 0AA *Tel:* 020 7219 4469. *Constituency:* Unity Hall, Northfield Road, Peterborough *Tel:* 01733 347979 *Fax:* 01733 897500.

BROOKE, The Rt. Hon. Peter Leonard, CH *(Cities of London and Westminster)   Con majority 4,881*

Son of Baroness Brooke of Ystradfellte, DBE *(qv)* and late Lord Brooke of Cumnor, PC, CH. Born March 3, 1934; educated Marlborough; Balliol College, Oxford (MA); Harvard Business School (MBA); Commonwealth Fund Fellow, Harvard; Senior Fellow, Royal College of Art 1987; Presentation Fellow, King's College, London 1989. Married 1st, Joan Margaret Smith (died 1985) (3 sons and 1 son deceased), married 2nd, January 25, 1991, Lindsay Allinson. *Armed Forces:* Royal Engineers. *Career:* Research Associate, IMEDE, Lausanne; Swiss Correspondent, *Financial Times* 1960–61; Spencer Stuart Management Consultants 1961–79, served in: New York 1969–71, Brussels 1971–72, Chairman 1974–79. *Political Career:* Parliamentary Under-Secretary of State, Department of Education and Science 1983–85; HM Treasury: Minister of State 1985–87, Paymaster General 1987–89; Secretary of State for: Northern Ireland 1989–92, National Heritage 1992–94. *Whip:* Government Whip 1979–83. *Select Committees (Current):* Chairman: Northern Ireland Affairs 1997–; Member: Liaison 1998–. *Party Groups:* Chairman, Conservative Party 1987–89. *Other:* Council, University of London 1995–; President, British Antique Dealers Association 1995–. *Trust:* Trustee, Wordsworth Trust 1975–; Trustee and former Chairman, Cusichaca Project 1978–; Chairman: COTAC 1994, Churches Conservation Trust 1995–; Trustee, Handel House Trust 1995–. Member, Drapers' Company. *Sportsclubs:* I Zingari, Lords' Taverners. *Honours:* PC 1988; CH 1992. *Recreations:* Churches, conservation, cricket. *Electoral Notes:* Member for City of London and Westminster South 1977–97, and for Cities of London and Westminster since May 1, 1997. *Clubs:* Beefsteak, Brooks's, City Livery, MCC, St George's (Hanover Sq). Conservative. *Address:* The Rt Hon. Peter Brooke, CH, MP, House of Commons, London, SW1A 0AA *Tel:* 020 7219 5041 *Fax:* 020 7219 0254. *Constituency:* 90 Ebury Street, SW1 *Tel:* 020 7730 8181 *Fax:* 020 7730 4520.

BROWN, The Rt Hon. (James) Gordon *(Dunfermline East)   Lab majority 18,751*

Son of late Rev. Dr John Brown. Born February 20, 1951; educated Kirkcaldy High School; Edinburgh University (MA 1972, PhD 1982). *Trades Union:* Member, TGWU. *Career:* Edinburgh University: Rector 1972–75, Temporary Lecturer 1975–76; Lecturer in Politics, Glasgow College of Technology 1976–80; Journalist, then Editor, Scottish Television Current Affairs Department 1980–83. *Political Career:* Shadow Chief Secretary to The Treasury 1987–89; Shadow Chancellor of the Exchequer 1992–97; Chancellor of the Exchequer 1997–. *Spokesman:* Opposition Front Bench Spokesman on Trade and Industry 1985–87; Shadow Spokesman for Trade and Industry 1989–92. *Party Groups:* Member, Scottish Executive Labour Party 1977–83; Chairman, Labour Party in Scotland 1983–84; Former Member, Labour Party National Executive Committee; Head, PLP General Election Campaign (Strategy) 1999–. *International Bodies:* Joint Hon Treasurer (ex-officio), Commonwealth Parliamentary Association (CPA) UK Branch 1997–99, Joint Hon Secretary 1999–. *Awards: The Spectator*/Highland Park Parliamentarian of the Year Award 1997. *Honours:* PC 1996. *Publications:* Co-editor *Values, Visions and Voices: An Anthology of Socialism*; Co-author *John Smith: Life and Soul of the Party; Maxton; Where There is Greed. Special Interests:* Economic and Employment Policy, Health, Social Security, Scotland. *Recreations:* Tennis, football, reading, writing. *Electoral Notes:* Member for Dunfermline East since June, 1983. *Address:* The Rt Hon. Gordon Brown, MP, House of Commons, London, SW1A 0AA *Tel:* 020 7270 3000. *Constituency:* 318–324 High Street, Cowdenbeath, Fife, KY4 9QS *Tel:* 01383 611702 *Fax:* 01383 611703.

BROWN, The Rt Hon. Nicholas H *(Newcastle upon Tyne East and Wallsend)   Lab majority 23,811*

Son of late R. C. Brown. Born June 13, 1950; educated Tunbridge Wells Technical High School; Manchester University (BA 1971). *Trades Union:* Legal Adviser for northern region of GMBATU 1978–83. *Career:* Proctor and Gamble advertising department. *Councils, Public Bodies:* Councillor, Newcastle upon Tyne City Council 1980–83. *Political Career:* Deputy to Margaret Beckett MP, as Shadow Leader of the Commons 1992–94; Minister of Agriculture, Fisheries and Food 1998–. *Whip:* Opposition Deputy Chief Whip 1995–97, Parliamentary Secretary, HM Treasury (Government Chief Whip) 1997–98. *Spokesman:* Opposition Front Bench Spokesman on: Legal Affairs 1985–92, Treasury and Economic Affairs 1988–94; Opposition Spokesman on Health 1994–95. *Select Committees (Former):* Member: Broadcasting 1994–95, Selection 1996–97. *Honours:* PC 1997. *Countries of Interest:* Australia, China, Japan, New Zealand, USA. *Electoral Notes:* Member for Newcastle upon Tyne East 1983–97, and for Newcastle upon Tyne East and Wallsend since May 1, 1997. *Address:* The Rt Hon. Nicholas Brown, MP, House of Commons, London, SW1A 0AA *Tel:* 020 7219 3000.

BROWN, Russell *(Dumfries)   Lab majority 9,643*

Son of late Howard Russell Brown and Muriel Brown. Born September 17, 1951; educated Annan Academy. Married March 3, 1973, Christine, daughter of John and Irene Calvert (2 daughters). *Trades Union:* Member, TGWU 1974–: Branch Secretary and Branch Chair. *Career:* ICI. *Councils, Public Bodies:* Councillor: Dumfries and Galloway Regional Council 1986–96, Annandale and Eskdale District Council 1988–96, Dumfries and Galloway Unitary Council 1995–97; Member, Dumfries and Galloway Tourist Board 1996–97. *Select Committees (Current):* Member: Deregulation 1999–, Scottish Affairs 1999– *(Former):* Member: European Legislation 1997–98, European Legislation 1997–98, European Scrutiny 1998–99. *Party Groups:* Member, Labour Party 1978. *Other:* Chair, Local Community Education Project 1991–97. *Special Interests:* Employment Legislation, Welfare State. *Countries of Interest:* European Union. *Recreations:* Sport. *Electoral Notes:* Member for Dumfries since May 1, 1997. *Address:* Russell Brown Esq, MP, House of Commons, London, SW1A 0AA *Tel:* 020 7219 4429 *Fax:* 020 7219 0922. *Constituency:* Loreburn Chambers, 11 Great King Street, Dumfries, DG1 1BA *Tel:* 01387 247902 *Fax:* 01387 247903.

BROWNE, Desmond Henry *(Kilmarnock and Loudoun)   Lab majority 7,256*

Son of late Peter Browne, process worker, and of Maureen Browne, catering manageress. Born March 22, 1952; educated Saint Michael's Academy, Kilwinning; University of Glasgow (LLB Hons). Married July 7, 1983, Maura, daughter of Joseph and Irene Taylor (2 sons). *Profession:* Advocate. *Career:* Qualified as Solicitor 1976; Called to Scottish Bar 1993. *Political Career:* PPS to Rt Hon. Donald Dewar, MP, as Secretary of State for Scotland 1998–99. *Select Committees (Current):* Member: Public Administration 1999– *(Former):* Member: Northern Ireland Affairs 1997–98. *Party Groups:* Secretary, Scottish Labour Party Working Party on Prison System 1988–. *Other:* Council Member, Law Society of Scotland 1988–91; Member, Scottish Council For Civil Liberties 1976–; Chairperson: Childrens Rights Group 1981–86, Scottish Child Law Centre 1988–. *Publications:* Briefing Paper for MPs on Criminal Justice (Scotland) Bill 1980; Report for Lord MacAulay's Working Party on the Prison System 1990. *Special Interests:* Legal Affairs, Human Rights, Disabled/Disability, Education, Northern Ireland, Constitutional Affairs, International Affairs. *Countries of Interest:* France, South Africa, Columbia. *Recreations:* Hill-walking, football, swimming, reading, computing. *Electoral Notes:* Contested Argyll and Bute 1992. Member for Kilmarnock and Loudoun since May 1, 1997. *Address:* Desmond Browne Esq, MP, House of Commons, London, SW1A 0AA *Tel:* 020 7219 4501 *Fax:* 020 7219 2423. *Constituency:* 24 Portland Road, Kilmarnock, KA1 2BS *Tel:* 01563 539439 *Fax:* 01563 572815 *E-mail:* browned@parliament.uk.

BROWNING, Mrs Angela *(Tiverton and Honiton)   Con majority 1,653*

Daughter of late Thomas Pearson and of Linda Pearson. Born December 4, 1946; educated Reading College of Technology; Bournemouth College of Technology. Married January 6, 1968, David Browning (2 sons). *Career:* Teacher of Home Economics, Adult Education 1968–74; Auxiliary Nurse 1976–77; Self-employed consultant, manufacturing industry 1977–85; Management consultant specialising in training, corporate communications and finance 1985–94; Director, Small Business Bureau 1985–94; Chairman, Women Into Business 1988–92; Member, Department of Employment Advisory Committee for Women's Employment 1989–92. *Political Career:* PPS to Minister of State, Department of Employment 1993–94; Parliamentary Secretary, Ministry of Agriculture, Fisheries and Food 1994–97; Member, Shadow Cabinet 1999–; Shadow Secretary of State for Trade and Industry 1999–. *Spokesman:* An Opposition Spokeswoman on Education and Employment (Education and Disability) 1997–98. *Select Committees (Former):* Member: Agriculture 1992–93. *Party Groups:* Has held various offices in Conservative Party in Devon. *Other:* Member, National Autistic Society, Special Councillor 1993–; National Vice-President, Alzheimers Disease Society 1997–. *Miscellaneous:* Co-Chairman, The Women's National Commission 1995–97; Vice-President, Institute of Sales and Marketing Management 1997–; President, Institute of Home Economics 1998–. Fellow, Institute of Sales and Marketing Management. *Special Interests:* Small Businesses, Education (Special Needs), Mental Health, Learning Disabilities. *Recreations:* Theatre, supporting family of keen oarsmen, member of Thomas Hardy Society. *Electoral Notes:* Contested Crewe and Nantwich in 1987 General Election. Member for Tiverton 1992–97, and for Tiverton and Honiton since May 1, 1997. *Address:* Mrs Angela Browning, MP, House of Commons, London, SW1A 0AA *Tel:* 020 7219 3000 *Tel (Constituency):* 01404 822103 *Website:* http://www.abrowning.demon.co.uk.

BRUCE, Ian *(South Dorset)   Con majority 77*

Son of late Henry Bruce, factory manager, and Mrs Ellen Flora Bruce (née Bingham), retired building society clerk. Born March 14, 1947; educated Chelmsford Technical High School; Bradford University; Mid-Essex Technical College. Married September 6, 1969, Hazel, daughter of late Edward Sidney and Kathleen Marjorie Roberts (1 son 3 daughters). *Career:* Marconi: Student Apprentice 1965–68, Work Study Engineer 1968–69; Pye Unicam, Method Study Engineer 1969–70; J. Sainsbury, Work Study Officer 1970–72; BEPI (part of Pye Group): Work Study Manager 1972–73, Production Manager 1970–74; Sinclair: Product Manager 1973–75, Works Manager 1975, Sales Manager 1975; Owner, Employment Agency and Consultancy Group 1975–. *Political Career:* PPS to Parliamentary Under-Secretaries of State, Department of Social Security 1993–94. *Select Committees (Current):* Member: Information 1997– *(Former):* Member: Employment 1990–92, Science and Technology 1995–97. *Party Groups:* President, Conservative Technology Forum 1997–. *International Bodies:* Vice-Chairman, European Infomatics Market Group 1994–. *Miscellaneous:* Member, Institute of Management Services; Vice-Chairman, EURIM. *Sportsclubs:* Weymouth Boardsailing Club, House of Commons Yacht Club. *Special Interests:* Employment, Energy, Defence, Information Technology, Tourism, Trade and Industry. *Countries of Interest:* Bahamas, Canada, Europe, Guatemala, Indonesia, USA, Zambia, Finland, Nepal, Cayman Islands, Former USSR and Eastern Bloc. *Recreations:* Badminton, camping, writing, sailing, gardening, scouting, squash, wind surfing. *Electoral Notes:* Contested Burnley in General Election 1983 and Yorkshire West in European Election 1984. Member for South Dorset since June 1987. *Address:* Ian Bruce Esq, MP, House of Commons, London, SW1A 0AA *Tel:* 020 7219 5086 *Fax:* 020 7219 6151 *Tel (Constituency):* 01305 833320 *Fax (Constituency):* 01305 833320 *E-mail:* brucei@parliament.uk.

Dod *on* Disk

The Vacher Dod Parliamentary Database – configured for PC or Network

For further details please telephone the Westminster Office

020 7828 7256

BRUCE, Malcolm *(Gordon)   LD majority 6,997*

Son of David Bruce, former agricultural merchant and hotelier, retired. Born November 17, 1944; educated Wrekin College; University of St Andrews; University of Strathclyde (Hons Graduate Economics and Political Science, MSc Marketing); CPE and Inns of Court School of Law. Married 1st, September 13, 1969, Jane Wilson (1 son 1 daughter) (marriage dissolved 1992); married 2nd, May 23, 1998, Rosemary Vetterlein (1 daughter). *Trades Union:* Member, NUJ. *Profession:* Barrister. *Career:* Trainee journalist, Liverpool Post 1966–67; Boots Section Buyer 1968–69; Research and Information Officer, NE Scotland Development Authority 1971–75; Director, Noroil Publishing House (UK) Ltd. 1975–81; Joint Editor/Publisher, Aberdeen Petroleum Publishing 1981–84. *Political Career:* Chairman, Liberal Democrat Parliamentary Party 1999–. *Spokesman:* Liberal Spokesman for Energy 1985–87; Scottish Liberal Spokesman for Education 1986–87; Alliance Spokesman for Employment 1987; Liberal Spokesman for Trade and Industry 1987–88; SLD Spokesman for Natural Resources (energy and conservation) 1988–89; Liberal Democrat Spokesman for: The Environment and Natural Resources 1989–90, Scottish Affairs 1990–92, Trade and Industry 1992–94, The Treasury 1994–99. *Select Committees (Current):* Member: Treasury 1997–99, Standards and Privileges 1999– *(Former):* Member: Scottish Affairs 1990–92, Trade and Industry 1992–94, Treasury and Civil Service 1994–97. *Party Groups:* Leader: Scottish Social and Liberal Democrats 1988–89, Liberal Democrats 1989–92. *Other:* Vice-President, National Deaf Children's Society, President, Grampian Branch. *Miscellaneous:* Elected Rector, Dundee University 1986–89; Vice-President, Federation of Economic Development Authorities (FEDA). *Special Interests:* Energy, Gas Industry, Oil Industry, Industrial Policy, Trade Policy, Deaf Children, Scottish Home Rule and Federalism. *Recreations:* Golf, cycling, walking, theatre and music. *Electoral Notes:* Contested Angus North and Mearns October 1974, Aberdeenshire West 1979. Member for Gordon since June 1983. *Address:* Malcolm Bruce Esq, MP, House of Commons, London, SW1A 0AA *Tel:* 020 7219 6233 *Fax:* 020 7219 2334. *Constituency:* 17b North Street, Inverurie, Aberdeenshire, AB51 4RJ *Tel:* 01467 623413 *Fax:* 01467 624994 *E-mail:* gordonlibdems@cix.co.uk.

BUCK, Karen *(Regent's Park and Kensington North)   Lab majority 14,657*

Born August 30, 1958; educated Chelmsford High School; LSE (BSc Econ, MSc Econ, MA Social Policy and Administration). Partner, Barrie Taylor (1 son). *Trades Union:* Former Member: ASTMS, NALGO; Member, TGWU. *Career:* Research and Development Worker, Outset (Charity Specialising in Employment for Disabled People) 1979–83; London Borough of Hackney: Specialist Officer Developing Services/Employment for Disabled People 1983–86, Public Health Officer 1986–87; Labour Party Policy Directorate (Health) 1987–92; Labour Party Campaign Strategy Co-ordinator 1992–99. *Councils, Public Bodies:* Councillor, Westminster City Council 1990–97; Member: Health Authority (late 1980s), Urban Regeneration Board. *Select Committees (Current):* Member: Social Security 1997–, Selection 1999–. *Party Groups:* Joined Labour Party 1978; Chair, Constituency Labour Party; Chair, London Regional Group of Labour MPs 1999–. *Miscellaneous:* Several radio interviews, notably on World At One coverage of Barratt Report on asbestos in Westminster Council Estates; Member, Queen's Park Single Regeneration Budget Board. *Special Interests:* Housing, Urban Regeneration, Health Care, Welfare, Children. *Recreations:* Music: rock, soul, jazz, opera. *Electoral Notes:* Member for Regent's Park and Kensington North since May 1, 1997. *Address:* Karen Buck, MP, House of Commons, London, SW1A 0AA *Tel:* 020 7219 3533 *Tel (Constituency):* 020 8968 7999 *Fax (Constituency):* 020 8960 0150.

BURDEN, Richard *(Birmingham Northfield)   Lab majority 11,443*

Son of Kenneth Rodney Burden, engineer, and of late Pauline Burden, secretary. Born September 1, 1954; educated Wallasey Technical Grammar School; Bramhall Comprehensive School; St John's College of Further Education, Manchester; York University (BA Hons Politics); Warwick University (MA Industrial Relations). Partner, Jane Slowey. *Trades Union:* Member, TGWU 1979–; Sponsored by TGWU 1989–96. *Career:* President, York University Students' Union 1976–77; NALGO: Branch Organiser, North Yorkshire 1979–81, West Midlands District Officer 1981–92. *Political Career:* PPS to Jeffrey Rooker, MP: as Minister of State and Deputy Minister, Ministry of Agriculture, Fisheries and Food (Minister for Food Safety) 1997–99, as Minister of State, Department of Social Security (Minister for Pensions) 1999–. *Party Groups:* Joined Labour Party 1980; Founder member, Bedale Labour Party 1980; Member, Labour Middle East Council, Vice-Chair 1994–95; Member, Co-operative Party; Chair, Labour Campaign for Electoral Reform 1996–98, Vice-Chair 1998–; Member, Fabian Society. *Other:* Member: CND, Greenpeace, SERA; Co-Chair, Parliamentary Advisory Council on Transport Safety (PACTS) 1995–98; Member, Northfield Community Development Association. *Miscellaneous:* Founded Joint Action for Water Services (Jaws) 1985 to oppose water privatisation, Secretary 1985–90. *Sportsclubs:* 750 Motor, Historic Sports Car Club. *Publications: Tap Dancing – Water, The Environment and Privatisation,* 1988. *Special Interests:* Motor Industry, Water Industry, Middle East, Poverty, Health, Employment Rights and Protection, Constitution, Electoral Reform. *Countries of Interest:* Europe, Middle East. *Recreations:* Cinema, motor racing. *Electoral Notes:* Contested Meriden in 1987 General Election. Member for Birmingham Northfield since April 9, 1992. *Clubs:* Kingshurst Labour, Austin Sports and Social. *Address:* Richard Burden Esq, MP, House of Commons, London, SW1A 0AA *Tel:* 020 7219 3000 *Fax:* 020 7219 2170 *Tel (Constituency):* 0121–475 9295 *Fax (Constituency):* 0121–476 2400 *E-mail:* burdenr@parliament.uk.

BURGON, Colin *(Elmet)   Lab majority 8,779*

Son of Thomas Burgon, tailoring worker, and Winifred Burgon, school secretary. Born April 22, 1948; educated St Charles School, Leeds; St Michael's College, Leeds; City of Leeds and Carnegie College. Divorced (1 daughter). *Career:* Former Teacher; Local Government Policy and Research Officer. *Select Committees (Current):* Member: Accommodation and Works 1999–, Procedure 1999– *(Former):* Member: Statutory Instruments (Joint Committee) 1997–99. *Party Groups:* Former Secretary, Elmet Constituency Labour Party; Former Chairman, Leeds Euro Constituency Labour Party. *Other:* Member: Amnesty International, Friends of the Earth. *Miscellaneous:* Member, CPRE. *Special Interests:* Youth Affairs, Planning Policy. *Countries of Interest:* USA, France, Italy, Spain. *Recreations:* Football (Leeds United), walking, the countryside, history (military and American Civil War). *Electoral Notes:* Contested Elmet 1987 and 1992 General Elections. Member for Elmet since May 1, 1997. *Address:* Colin Burgon Esq, MP, House of Commons, London, SW1A 0AA *Tel:* 020 7219 6487 *Tel (Constituency):* 0113–287 5198 *Fax (Constituency):* 0113–287 5958.

BURNETT, John Patrick Aubone *(Torridge and West Devon)   LD majority 1,957*

Son of late Lt-Col Aubone Burnett, OBE, and Joan Burnett (née Bolt). Born September 19, 1945; educated Ampleforth College, Yorks; Royal Marines Commando Training Centre; Britannia Royal Naval College, Dartmouth; College of Law, London. Married October 9, 1971, Elizabeth Sherwood, daughter of Sir Arthur and Lady de la Mare (2 sons 2 daughters). *Trades Union:* Member, NFU. *Armed Forces:* Royal Marines 1964–70: Troop Commander, 42 Commando in Borneo and Singapore, Troop Commander and Company Second-in-Command, 40 Commando in Far East and Middle East. *Profession:* Solicitor. *Spokesman:* A Spokesman for Home and Legal Affairs: (Legal Affairs) 1997–, (Legal Affairs and Attorney General, Solicitor General, Lord Chancellor) 1999. *Other:* Member: Law Society, Devon and Exeter Law Society, Law Society's Revenue (Tax) Law Committee 1984–96, Council of Devon Cattle Breeders' Association, Royal Marine Association, Royal British Legion. *Special Interests:* Economic Policy, Defence, Agriculture.

Recreations: Breeding Devon cattle, walking, sport. *Electoral Notes:* Contested Torridge and West Devon 1987 General Election. Member for Torridge and West Devon since May 1, 1997. *Address:* John Burnett Esq, MP, House of Commons, London, SW1A 0AA *Tel:* 020 7219 5132. *Constituency:* Liberal Democrats, 21–25 St James Street, Okehampton, Devon, EX20 1DH *Tel:* 01837 55881 *Fax:* 01837 55694.

BURNS, Simon *(Chelmsford West)   Con majority 6,691*

Son of late Major B. S. Burns MC and Mrs Anthony Nash. Born September 6, 1952; educated Christ the King School, Accra; Stamford School; Worcester College, Oxford (BA Hons History). Married September 22, 1982, Emma, daughter of late David Clifford and Susan Clifford (1 son 1 daughter) (separated). *Career:* Assistant to Rt Hon. Sally Oppenheim, MP for Gloucester 1975–81; Director and Co. Secretary, What to Buy for Business Ltd 1981–83; Conference organiser, Institute of Directors 1983–87. *Political Career:* PPS: to Timothy Eggar MP, as Minister of State: at Department of Employment 1989–90, at Department of Education and Science 1990–92, at Department of Trade and Industry 1992–93; to Rt Hon. Gillian Shephard, MP, as Minister of Agriculture, Fisheries and Food 1993–94; Parliamentary Under-Secretary of State, Department of Health 1996–97. *Whip:* Assistant Government Whip 1994–95; Lord Commissioner to HM Treasury (Government Whip) 1995–96. *Spokesman:* Opposition Front Bench Spokesman for: Social Security 1997-August 1998, Environment, Transport and the Regions (Planning, Housing and Construction) August 1998–99. *Select Committees (Current):* Member: Health 1999–. *Other:* President, Chelmsford Osteoporosis Society. *Miscellaneous:* Executive Member, 1922 Committee 1999–. *Special Interests:* Employment, Foreign Affairs. *Countries of Interest:* USA. *Recreations:* Photography, American politics, reading, antiques. *Electoral Notes:* Contested Alyn and Deeside 1983. Member for Chelmsford 1987–97, and for Chelmsford West since May 1, 1997. *Clubs:* Essex. *Address:* Simon Burns Esq, MP, House of Commons, London, SW1A 0AA *Tel:* 020 7219 4052.

BURSTOW, Paul Kenneth *(Sutton and Cheam)   LD majority 2,097*

Son of Brian Burstow, tailor, and Sheila Burstow. Born May 13, 1962; educated Glastonbury High School For Boys; Carshalton College of Further Education; South Bank Polytechnic (BA Hons Business Studies). Married Mary Kemm. *Profession:* Political Secretary. *Career:* Political Secretary, Association of Liberal Democrat Councillors 1996–97. *Councils, Public Bodies:* Councillor, London Borough of Sutton 1986–, Chair, Environment Services 1988–96, Deputy Leader 1994–99. *Spokesman:* A Spokesman for: Disabled People 1997–98, Local Government (Social Services and Community Care) 1997–99, Local Government (Team Leader) 1997–99, Older People 1999–. *Party Groups:* Former Member: SDP/Liberal Alliance, London Regional Liberal Democrat Executive; Member, Federal Policy Committee 1988–90. *Special Interests:* Environment, Disabled/Disability, Community Safety, Ageing. *Recreations:* Cooking, reading, cycling, walking, keeping fit. *Electoral Notes:* Contested Sutton and Cheam 1992. Member for Sutton and Cheam since May 1, 1997. *Clubs:* National Liberal. *Address:* Paul Burstow Esq, MP, House of Commons, London, SW1A 0AA *Tel:* 020 7219 1196. *Constituency:* 312–314 High Street, Sutton, Surrey, SM1 1PR *Tel:* 020 8288 6555 *Fax:* 020 8288 6550 *Website:* www.burstowmp.org.uk.

BUTLER, Christine *(Castle Point)   Lab majority 1,116*

Daughter of late Cecil and Gertrude Smith. Born December 14, 1943; educated Nelson Grammar School; Middlesex Polytechnic (BA Hons). Married 1964, Robert Butler, son of James and Theresa Butler (3 sons). *Trades Union:* Member, MSF. *Career:* Pharmaceutical Industry; NHS; Visual arts. *Councils, Public Bodies:* Former County Councillor; Former Chair, Essex Co-operative Development Agency. *Select Committees (Current):* Member: Environment, Transport and Regional Affairs 1997–, Environment Sub-Committee 1997–. *Party Groups:* Member: Co-operative Party, Fabian Society, SERA. *Other:* Former School Governor. *Special Interests:* Local Government, Environment, Employment, Education. *Recreations:* Walking, listening to music, art.

Electoral Notes: Member for Castle Point since May 1, 1997. *Address:* Christine Butler, MP, House of Commons, London, SW1A 0AA *Tel:* 020 7219 6955. *Constituency:* Labour Hall, Lionel Road, Canvey Island, Essex *Tel:* 01268 684722.

BUTTERFILL, John Valentine *(Bournemouth West)*   Con majority 5,710

Son of late George Thomas, Lloyd's broker, and late Elsie Amelia Butterfill (née Watts), Bank of England executive. Born February 14, 1941; educated Caterham School; College of Estate Management (London). Married October 2, 1965, Pamela Ross, daughter of late Frederick Ross Symons (1 son 3 daughters). *Profession:* Chartered Surveyor. *Career:* Valuer, Jones Lang Wootton 1962–64; Senior Executive, Hammerson Group 1964–69; Director, Audley Properties Ltd (Bovis Group) 1969–71; Managing Director, St Paul's Securities Group 1971–76; Senior Partner, Curchod & Co. Chartered Surveyors 1977–92; President, European Property Associates 1977–; Director: ISLEF Building and Construction Ltd 1985–91, Pavilion Services Group 1992–94. *Political Career:* PPS: to Rt Hon. Cecil Parkinson, MP: as Secretary of State for Energy 1988–89, as Secretary of State for Transport 1989–90, to Dr Brian Mawhinney MP, as Minister of State, Northern Ireland Office 1991–92. *Select Committees (Current):* Member: Chairmen's Panel 1997–, Court of Referees 1997–, Trade and Industry 1997–, Unopposed Bills (Panel) 1997– *(Former):* Member: Trade and Industry 1992–97. *Party Groups:* Chairman: Conservative Group for Europe 1989–92, Conservative Party Rules Committee 1997–; Member, Conservative Party Constitutional Committee 1998–; Vice-Chairman, Conservative Friends of Israel. *Other:* Member, Council of Management PDSA 1990–; Founder Chairman, Guildford/Freiburg Town Twinning Association. *Miscellaneous:* Joint Vice-Chairman, 1922 Committee 1997–. Fellow, Royal Institution of Chartered Surveyors 1974. *Special Interests:* Trade and Industry, Tourism, Foreign Affairs, Environment, Housing, Health. *Countries of Interest:* France, Germany, Scandinavia, Israel. *Recreations:* Skiing, tennis, riding, bridge, music. *Electoral Notes:* Contested London South Inner 1979 European Parliament election, Croydon North West by-election 1981. Member for Bournemouth West since June 1983. *Clubs:* Carlton. *Address:* John Butterfill Esq, MP, House of Commons, London, SW1A 0AA *Tel:* 020 7219 6383. *Constituency:* 135 Hankinson Road, Bournemouth, Dorset, BH9 1HR *Tel:* 01202 776607 *Fax:* 01202 521481.

BYERS, The Rt Hon. Stephen John *(North Tyneside)*   Lab majority 26,643

Son of late Robert Byers, chief technician, RAF. Born April 13, 1953; educated Chester City Grammar School; Chester College of Further Education; Liverpool Polytechnic (LLB). *Career:* Senior Lecturer in Law, Newcastle Polytechnic 1977–92. *Councils, Public Bodies:* North Tyneside Council: Councillor 1980–92, Chairman, Education Committee 1982–85, Deputy Leader of the Council 1985–92. *Political Career:* Minister of State, Department for Education and Employment (Minister for School Standards) 1997–98; Chief Secretary, HM Treasury July-December 1998; Secretary of State for Trade and Industry December 1998–. *Whip:* Opposition Whip 1994–95. *Spokesman:* Opposition Spokesman on Education and Employment 1995–97. *Select Committees (Former):* Member: Home Affairs 1993–94. *Party Groups:* Member, Labour Party 1974–. *Miscellaneous:* Member, Business and Technician Education Council 1985–89; Chairman, Association of Metropolitan Authorities Education Committee 1990–92; Leader, Council of Local Education Authorities 1990–92; Chairman, National Employers' Organisation for Teachers 1990–92. *Honours:* PC 1998. Fellow, Royal Society of Arts. *Special Interests:* Education, Treasury, Home Affairs, Trade and Industry, Local Government. *Recreations:* Cinema, travel, theatre, walking. *Electoral Notes:* Contested Hexham in 1983. Member for Wallsend 1992–97, and for North Tyneside since May 1, 1997. *Address:* The Rt Hon. Stephen Byers, MP, House of Commons, London, SW1A 0AA *Tel:* 020 7219 4085. *Constituency:* 7 Palmersville, Great Lime Road, Forest Hall, Newcastle upon Tyne, NE12 9HW *Tel:* 0191-268 9111 *Fax:* 0191-268 9777 *E-mail:* tlo.byers@tlo.dti.gov.uk.

C

CABLE, Dr (John) Vincent *(Twickenham)* *LD majority 4,281*

Son of late Leonard Cable and of Edith Cable. Born May 9, 1943; educated Nunthorpe Grammar School, York; Fitzwilliam College, Cambridge (President of Union) (BA Natural Science and Economics 1966); Glasgow University (PhD International Economics 1973); Visiting Fellow, Nuffield College, Oxford; Special Professor of Economics, University of Nottingham 1999; Research Fellow, International Economics Programme, Royal Institute of International Affairs. Married July 21, 1968, Dr Olympia, daughter of Mr and Mrs Rebelo (2 sons 1 daughter). *Profession:* Economist. *Career:* Finance Officer, Kenya Treasury 1966–68; Economics Lecturer, University of Glasgow 1968–74; Diplomatic Service 1974–76; Adviser to World Commission on Environment and Development (Brundtland Commission) 1975–77; Deputy Director, Overseas Development Institute 1976–83; Special Adviser to Rt Hon. John Smith, MP, as Secretary of State for Trade 1979; Special Adviser, Commonwealth Secretariat 1983–90; Group Planning, Shell 1990–95; Head, Economics Programme, Chatham House 1993–95; Chief Economist, Shell International 1995–97. *Councils, Public Bodies:* Councillor (Labour), Glasgow City Council 1971–74. *Spokesman:* A Spokesman for the Treasury (EMU and The City) 1997–99; Principal Spokesman for Trade and Industry 1999–. *Select Committees (Former):* Member: Treasury 1998–99, Treasury Sub-Committee 1998–99. *Other:* Member: HACAN (Aircraft Noise), Hospital Alert, Charter 88. *Miscellaneous:* Member, European Standing Committee B 1998–. *Publications:* Wide variety of books and pamphlets including: *Protectionism and Industrial Decline*, 1983, *Globalisation and Global Governance*, 1999; Journalism for the *Independent*. *Special Interests:* European Union, Trade and Industry, Economic Policy, Foreign Affairs, Energy, Environment. *Countries of Interest:* India, Russia, China, Nigeria, Kenya. *Recreations:* Ballroom and Latin dancing, classical music, cinema, walking. *Electoral Notes:* Contested Glasgow Hillhead (Labour) 1970, York (SDP/Alliance) 1983 and 1987, Twickenham (Liberal Democrat) 1992. Member for Twickenham since May 1, 1997. *Clubs:* Lensbury (Shell). *Address:* Dr Vincent Cable, MP, House of Commons, London, SW1A 0AA *Tel:* 020 7219 1106 *Fax:* 020 7219 1191. *Constituency:* 164c Heath Road, Twickenham, TW1 4BN *Tel:* 020 8892 0215 *Fax:* 020 8892 0218 *E-mail:* vincentcable@cix.co.uk.

CABORN, The Rt Hon. Richard George *(Sheffield Central)* *Lab majority 16,906*

Son of late George Caborn. Born October 6, 1943; educated Hurlfield Comprehensive School; Granville College; Sheffield Polytechnic. Married May 21, 1966, Margaret Hayes (1 son 1 daughter). *Trades Union:* Convenor of Shop Stewards. *Career:* Skilled engineer. *Political Career:* Minister of State: Department of the Environment, Transport and the Regions (Minister for the Regions, Regeneration and Planning) 1997–99, Department of Trade and Industry (Minister for Trade) 1999–. *Spokesman:* Opposition Spokesperson on: Trade and Industry 1988–90, with special responsibility for Regional Policy 1990–92, National Competitiveness and Regulation 1995–97. *Select Committees (Former):* Member: Liaison 1992–95; Chairman: Trade and Industry 1992–95. *Party Groups:* Chairman, Sheffield District Labour Party, served on Education Committee. *International Bodies:* Chairman, European Parliament British Labour Party Group 1979–84. *Miscellaneous:* Vice-President, Sheffield Trades Council 1968–79; Member, BBC Advisory Council 1975–78. *Honours:* PC 1999. *Special Interests:* European Union, Trade Unions, Steel Industry. *Countries of Interest:* South Africa. *Electoral Notes:* MEP for Sheffield District 1979–84. Member for Sheffield Central since June, 1983. *Address:* The Rt Hon. Richard Caborn, MP, House of Commons, London, SW1A 0AA *Tel:* 020 7219 4211 *Fax:* 020 7219 4866. *Constituency:* 2nd Floor, Barkers Pool House, Burgess Street, Sheffield, S1 2HF *Tel:* 0114–273 7947 *Fax:* 0114–273 7944 *E-mail:* tlo.caborn@tlo.dti.gov.uk.

CAMPBELL, Alan *(Tynemouth)   Lab majority 11,273*

Born July 8, 1957; educated Blackfyne Secondary School, Consett; University of Lancaster (BA Hons Politics); University of Leeds (PGCE); Newcastle Polytechnic (MA History). Married Jayne (1 son 1 daughter). *Trades Union:* Member, NAS/UWT. *Profession:* School Teacher. *Career:* Whitley Bay High School 1980–89; Hirst High School, Ashington, Northumberland: Teacher 1989–97, Head of Sixth Form, Head of Department. *Select Committees (Current):* Member: Public Accounts 1997–. *Party Groups:* Joined Labour Party 1987; Branch Secretary, Chairman, Agent; Tynemouth Constituency Labour Party: Secretary, Campaign Co-ordinator; Hon. Secretary and Hon. Treasurer, Northern Group of Labour MPs 1999–. *Miscellaneous:* Television Broadcasts: Newsnight, on Devolution 1995, North of Westminster, on Crime and Prisons 1996; Radio Broadcasts: North of Westminster, on Education 1996; Various radio phone-in and interview programmes. *Special Interests:* Education, Constitutional Reform. *Recreations:* Family. *Electoral Notes:* Member for Tynemouth since May 1, 1997. *Address:* Alan Campbell Esq, MP, House of Commons, London, SW1A 0AA *Tel:* 020 7219 6619. *Constituency:* 100 Howard Street, North Shields, Tyne and Wear, NE30 2NA *Tel:* 0191–257 1927 *Fax:* 0191–257 6537 *E-mail:* alan-campbellmp@office-mail.co.uk.

CAMPBELL, Mrs. Anne *(Cambridge)   Lab majority 14,137*

Daughter of late Frank Lucas, NHS clerical worker, and late Susan Lucas. Born April 6, 1940; educated Penistone Grammar School; Newnham College, Cambridge (MA); Honorary Doctorate. Married August 10, 1963, Dr Archie Campbell (1 son 2 daughters). *Trades Union:* Member, MSF. *Profession:* Statistician. *Career:* Assistant Maths teacher: Herts and Essex High School, Bishops Stortford 1962–64, Girls' Grammar School, Cambridge 1964–65; Various part-time teaching posts 1965–70; Lecturer, then senior lecturer in statistics, Cambridgeshire College of Arts and Technology 1970–83; Head, Statistics and Data Processing, National Institute of Agricultural Botany, Cambridge 1983–92. *Councils, Public Bodies:* Cambridgeshire County Councillor 1985–89. *Political Career:* PPS: to Ministers of State, Department of Trade and Industry: John Battle, MP 1997–99, to Patricia Hewitt, MP (Minister for Small Business and E-Commerce) 1999–. *Select Committees (Former):* Member: Science and Technology 1992–97. *Party Groups:* Joined Labour Party 1963; Chair: South and East Group of Labour MPs 1997–99, Eastern Regional Group of Labour MPs 1999. *Other:* Member, Greenpeace. *Miscellaneous:* Vice-Chair, Parliamentary Office of Science and Technology 1994–98. Fellow: Institute of Statisticians 1987, Royal Statistical Society 1987, Royal Society of Arts 1992. *Publications: Calculations for Commercial Students,* 1972. *Special Interests:* Education, Science Policy, Environment. *Recreations:* Gardening, tennis, mountain walking, skiing. *Electoral Notes:* Member for Cambridge since April 9, 1992. *Address:* Mrs Anne Campbell, MP, House of Commons, London, SW1A 0AA *Tel:* 020 7219 5089 *Fax:* 020 7219 2264. *Constituency:* Alex Wood Hall, Norfolk Street, Cambridge, CB1 2LD *Tel:* 01223 506500 *Fax:* 01223 311315 *E-mail:* anne.campbell.mp@dial.pipex.com.

CAMPBELL, The Rt Hon. (Walter) Menzies, CBE, QC *(North East Fife)   LD majority 10,356*

Son of late George and Elizabeth Campbell. Born May 22, 1941; educated Hillhead High School, Glasgow; Glasgow University (MA 1962, LLB 1965); Stanford University, California. Married June 13, 1970, Elspeth Mary, daughter of Major General R. E. Urquhart, CB, DSO. *Career:* Called to the Bar (Scotland) 1968; QC (Scotland) 1982; Amateur Athletics Association 220 yards champion 1964 and 1967; UK 100 Metres record holder 1967–74; UK Athletics Team Capt. 1965–66; Competed: 1964 (Tokyo) Olympics, 1966 Commonwealth Games (Jamaica); Chairman, Royal Lyceum Theatre Company, Edinburgh 1984–87. *Spokesman:* Liberal Spokesman for Arts, Broadcasting and Sport 1987–88; SLD Spokesman for Defence, Sport 1988–89; Liberal Democrat Spokesman for: Defence and Disarmament, Sport 1989–94, Foreign Affairs and Defence, Sport 1994–97, Foreign Affairs (Defence and Europe) 1997–99, Scotland (Legal Affairs, Lord Advocate) 1998–99; Principal Spokesman for Foreign Affairs and Defence 1999–. *Select Committees (Former):* Member: Trade and Industry 1990–92, Defence 1992–97, Defence 1997–99.

Party Groups: Chairman, Scottish Liberal Party 1975–77. *International Bodies:* Member: North Atlantic Assembly 1989–, UK Delegation, Parliamentary Assembly of OSCE 1992–97, 1999–. *Awards:* Highland Park/*The Spectator* Member to Watch 1996. *Miscellaneous:* Member, Board of the British Council 1998–. *Honours:* CBE 1987; PC 1999. *Special Interests:* Defence, Foreign Affairs, Legal Affairs, Sport, Arts. *Countries of Interest:* Middle East, North America. *Recreations:* All sports, theatre, music. *Electoral Notes:* Contested Greenock and Port Glasgow February and October 1974, East Fife 1979, North East Fife 1983. Member for North East Fife since June 1987. *Clubs:* Reform. *Address:* The Rt Hon. Menzies Campbell, CBE, QC, MP, House of Commons, London, SW1A 0AA *Tel:* 020 7219 4446 *Fax:* 020 7219 3878. *Constituency:* 16 Millbank, Cupar, Fife *Tel:* 01334 656361 *Fax:* 01334 654045 *E-mail:* nefifelibdem@cix.co.uk.

CAMPBELL, Ronnie *(Blyth Valley)*   Lab majority 17,736

Son of Ronnie and Edna Campbell. Born August 14, 1943; educated Ridley High School, Blyth. Married June 17, 1967, Deidre McHale (5 sons (2 twins) 1 daughter). *Trades Union:* NUM Lodge Secretary, Bates Colliery, Blyth 1982–86; NUM Sponsored MP. *Career:* Miner 1958–86. *Councils, Public Bodies:* Blyth Borough Council 1969–74; Blyth Valley Councillor 1974–88. *Select Committees (Current):* Member: Public Administration 1997– *(Former):* Member: Parliamentary Commissioner for Administration 1987–97. *Party Groups:* Labour Party member for over 28 years; Chair, Northern Regional Group of Labour MPs 1999–. *Recreations:* Furniture restoration, stamp collecting, antiques. *Electoral Notes:* Member for Blyth Valley since June 1987. *Address:* Ronnie Campbell Esq, MP, House of Commons, London, SW1A 0AA *Tel:* 020 7219 4216 *Fax:* 020 7219 4358. *Constituency:* 42 Renwick Road, Blyth, Northumberland, NE24 2LQ *Tel:* 01670 363050 *Fax:* 01670 363050 *E-mail:* ronnie@bvsocialistmp.netkonect.co.uk.

CAMPBELL-SAVOURS, Dale N *(Workington)*   Lab majority 19,656

Son of late John Lawrence. Born August 23, 1943; educated Keswick School; The Sorbonne, Paris. Married 1970, Gudrun Kristin Runolfsdottir (3 sons). *Trades Union:* Member: Transport & General Workers Union, UNISON Trade Union. *Career:* Former Company director. *Councils, Public Bodies:* Councillor, Ramsbottom Urban District Council 1972–74. *Spokesman:* Opposition Spokesman on Development and Co-operation 1991–92; Opposition Front Bench Spokesman on Food, Agriculture and Rural Affairs 1992–94. *Select Committees (Current):* Member: Standards and Privileges 1997– *(Former):* Member: Agriculture 1994–96, Standards and Privileges 1995–97. *Publications: The Case for the Supplementary Vote*, 1990; *The Case for The University of the Lakes*, 1995. *Special Interests:* Investigative Political and Social Work, Ending Privilege in Education and Health, Application of Industrial Democracy, Marketing. *Countries of Interest:* former Soviet Union, USA, Italy. *Recreations:* Angling, travelling. *Electoral Notes:* Contested Darwen in February and October 1974, Workington (By-election) 1976. Member for Workington since May 1979. *Address:* Dale Campbell-Savours Esq, MP, House of Commons, London, SW1A 0AA *Tel:* 020 7219 3513 *Tel (Constituency):* 017687 74747.

CANAVAN, Dennis Andrew *(Falkirk West)*   Lab majority 13,783

Son of late Agnes and late Thomas Canavan, electrician. Born August 8, 1942; educated St Bride's Primary School; St Columba's High School, Cowdenbeath; Edinburgh University (BSc(Hons), DipEd). *Trades Union:* Chair, Parliamentary Branch of Educational Institute of Scotland; Member, UNISON. *Career:* Principal Teacher of Mathematics, St Modan's High School, Stirling 1970–74; Assistant Head, Holy Rood High School, Edinburgh 1974. *Councils, Public Bodies:* District Councillor 1973–74; Labour Group Leader, Stirling District Council 1974. *Select Committees (Former):* Member: Foreign Affairs 1982–97, International Development 1997–99. *Miscellaneous:* Parliamentary Spokesperson for Scottish Committee on Mobility for the Disabled 1976–. *Special Interests:* Foreign Affairs, Health Service, Education, British-Irish Relations, Disarmament, Sport.

Countries of Interest: Ireland, Middle East, Southern Africa. *Recreations:* Hill-climbing, swimming, running, angling, football spectating (former Scottish Universities' football international). *Electoral Notes:* Member for Stirlingshire West October 1974–83, and for Falkirk West since June 1983. MSP for the Constituency of Falkirk West since May 6, 1999. *Clubs:* Camelon Labour, Bannockburn Miners' Welfare. *Address:* Dennis Canavan Esq, MP, MSP, House of Commons, London, SW1A 0AA *Tel:* 020 7219 4127 *Fax:* 020 7219 2513. *Constituency:* 37 Church Walk, Denny, Stirlingshire, FK6 6DF *Tel:* 01324 825922 *Fax:* 01324 823972 *E-mail:* dennis.canavan.msp@scottish.parliament.uk.

CANN, Jamie *(Ipswich)*   Lab majority 10,436

Son of Charles Cann, steel mill manager, and Brenda Cann, shopkeeper. Born June 28, 1946; educated Barton-on-Humber Grammar School. Married May 26, 1970, Rosemary, daughter of John Lovitt (2 sons). *Career:* Handford Hall Primary School, Ipswich: School teacher 1967–92, Deputy Head Teacher. *Councils, Public Bodies:* Ipswich Borough Council: Councillor 1973–92, Leader, Labour Group 1976–91, Leader of the Council 1979–91; Member, Ipswich Port Authority 1986–94. *Select Committees (Current):* Member: Defence 1997–. *Trust:* Fellow, Armed Forces Trust (Navy). *Special Interests:* British Constitution, Electoral Reform, Education, Tax, Social Issues, Defence, Environment. *Countries of Interest:* Former Soviet Union, Greece, Hong Kong, USA, Cyprus, Gibraltar. *Recreations:* Watching sport, squash, badminton, snooker, history, reading, walking. *Electoral Notes:* Member for Ipswich since April 9, 1992. *Address:* Jamie Cann Esq, MP, House of Commons, London, SW1A 0AA *Tel:* 020 7219 4171. *Constituency:* 33 Silent Street, Ipswich, Suffolk, IP1 1TF *Tel:* 01473 281559 *Fax:* 01473 217489.

CAPLIN, Ivor Keith *(Hove)*   Lab majority 3,959

Son of late Leonard Caplin, chartered accountant, and of Alma Caplin, market researcher. Born November 8, 1958; educated King Edward's School, Witley; Brighton College of Technology (National Certificate in Business Studies 1979). Married Maureen, daughter of Michael J. Whelan, retired, and of late Joan Ross (2 sons 1 daughter). *Trades Union:* Member, MSF. *Career:* Legal and General Assurance Society Ltd 1978–97, Former Quality Manager, Sales and Marketing. *Councils, Public Bodies:* Councillor, Hove 1991–97, Leader 1995–97; Councillor, Brighton and Hove Council 1996–98, former Deputy Leader. *Political Career:* PPS to Rt Hon. Margaret Beckett, MP, as President of the Council and Leader of the House of Commons 1998–. *Select Committees (Current):* Member: Modernisation of the House of Commons 1998–, Broadcasting 1999– *(Former):* Member: Broadcasting 1997–98. *Party Groups:* Chairman, Hove Constituency Labour Party 1986–92; Member: Co-operative Party, Labour Friends of Israel. *Other:* Member, League Against Cruel Sports. *Trust:* Trustee, Old Market Trust, Hove. *Sportsclubs:* Vice-President, Lewes Priory Cricket Club, Brighton and Hove Cricket Club. *Special Interests:* Finance, Heritage, Pensions, Sport, Arts, Local Government, Animal Welfare. *Recreations:* Football (Brighton and Hove Albion FC), music, cricket. *Electoral Notes:* Member for Hove since May 1, 1997. *Address:* Ivor Caplin Esq, MP, House of Commons, London, SW1A 0AA *Tel:* 020 7219 2146 *Fax:* 020 7219 0259. *Constituency:* Parliamentary Office, Town Hall, Norton Road, Hove, East Sussex, BN3 4AH *Tel:* 01273 292933 *Fax:* 01273 291054 *E-mail:* caplini@parliament.uk.

CASALE, Roger Mark *(Wimbledon)*   Lab majority 2,990

Son of Edward and Jean Casale. Born May 22, 1960; educated King's College, Wimbledon; Hurstpierpoint College, Sussex; Brasenose College, Oxford (BA Hons, Politics, Philosophy, Economics); Johns Hopkins, Bologna (MA International Affairs). Married August 30, 1997, Fernanda Miucci (1 daughter). *Trades Union:* Member, GMB. *Armed Forces:* Member, Oxford University Air Squadron. *Profession:* University Lecturer. *Career:* Former Head, Training Institute; Former Policy Adviser to office of John Prescott and Tony Blair; University Lecturer in European Studies, Greenwich. *Select Committees (Current):* Member: European Scrutiny 1998– *(Former):* Member: European Legislation 1997–98. *Party Groups:* Member: Fabian Society,

Labour Movement in Europe. *Trust:* Director, Future of Europe Trust Limited; Director/Hon President, Wimbledon Civic Trust Limited; Hon President, Wimbledon Hall Trust. *Special Interests:* Foreign Affairs, Treasury. *Countries of Interest:* Italy. *Recreations:* Spending time with family and friends. *Electoral Notes:* Member for Wimbledon since May 1, 1997. *Address:* Roger Casale Esq, MP, House of Commons, London, SW1A 0AA *Tel:* 020 7219 4565 *Fax:* 020 7219 0789. *Constituency:* Wimbledon Community Association, 28 St George's Road, Wimbledon, London, SW19 4DP *Tel:* 020 8540 1012 *Fax:* 020 8540 1018.

CASH, William *(Stone)*   Con majority 3,818

Son of Paul Cash, MC (killed in action, 1944). Born May 10, 1940; educated Stonyhurst College; Lincoln College, Oxford (MA). Married October 16, 1965, Bridget Mary, daughter of late James Rupert Lee (2 sons 1 daughter). *Career:* Solicitor, William Cash & Company. *Select Committees (Current):* Member: European Scrutiny 1998– *(Former):* Member: European Legislation 1985–97, European Legislation 1997–98. *Party Groups:* Chairman, Friends of Bruges Group in the House of Commons 1989–. *International Bodies:* Founder and Chairman, The European Foundation. *Other:* Vice-President, Conservative Small Business Bureau. *Miscellaneous:* Member, Standing Committees on: Financial Services 1985–86, Banking 1986–87. *Sportsclubs:* Secretary, Lords and Commons Cricket Club 1988–92. *Publications: Against a Federal Europe*, 1991; *Europe – The Crunch*, 1992. *Special Interests:* European Union, Trade and Industry, Media, Small Businesses, Heritage. *Countries of Interest:* East Africa, Europe. *Recreations:* Local history, cricket, jazz. *Electoral Notes:* Member for Stafford 1984–97, and for Stone since May 1, 1997. *Clubs:* Beefsteak, Carlton, Vincent's (Oxford). *Address:* William Cash Esq, MP, House of Commons, London, SW1A 0AA *Tel:* 020 7219 3431.

CATON, Martin Philip *(Gower)*   Lab majority 13,007

Son of William John Caton and Pauline Joan Caton, shopkeepers. Born June 15, 1951; educated Newport (Essex) Grammar School; Norfolk School of Agriculture; Aberystwyth College of Further Education (National Certificate in Agriculture, Higher National Certificate in Applied Biology). Married September 20, 1996, Bethan, daughter of late Hermus, and Menai Evans (2 step daughters). *Trades Union:* Member, GMB; Former Section Treasurer/Membership Secretary, IPCS. *Profession:* Political Researcher. *Councils, Public Bodies:* Councillor: Mumbles Community Council 1986–90, Swansea City Council 1988–95, City and County of Swansea 1995–97. *Select Committees (Current):* Member: Welsh Affairs 1997–. *Party Groups:* Member: Socialist Environmental Resources Association, Socialist Health Association. *Other:* Member, CND Cymru. *Special Interests:* Environment, Planning, Education, European Union. *Recreations:* Reading, walking, theatre, thinking about gardening. *Electoral Notes:* Member for Gower since May 1, 1997. *Address:* Martin Caton Esq, MP, House of Commons, London, SW1A 0AA *Tel:* 020 7219 5111 *Fax:* 020 7219 0905. *Constituency:* 26 Pontardulais Road, Gorseinon, Swansea, SA4 4FE *Tel:* 01792 892100 *Fax:* 01792 892375 *E-mail:* martin.caton@politics.demon.co.uk.

CAWSEY, Ian *(Brigg and Goole)*   Lab majority 6,389

Son of Arthur Henry Cawsey and Edith Morrison Cawsey. Born April 14, 1960; educated Wintringham School. Married July 19, 1987, Linda Mary, daughter of Henry Kirman and Joy Kirman (1 son 2 daughters). *Trades Union:* Member: ISTL, GMB. *Profession:* Information Technology Consultant. *Career:* Computer Operator 1977–78; Computer Programmer 1978–82; Systems Analyst 1982–85; IT Consultant 1985–87; Personal Assistant to Elliot Morley, MP 1987–97. *Councils, Public Bodies:* Former Councillor, Humberside County Council; Chairman, Humberside Police Authority 1993–; Leader, North Lincolnshire Council 1995–. *Select Committees (Current):* Member: Home Affairs 1999–. *Party Groups:* Member: Labour Party 1977–, Fabian Society. *Other:* Member, Scunthorpe Hospitals Broadcasting Organisation. *Miscellaneous:* Vice-President, Federation of Economic Development Authorities (FEDA). *Special Interests:* Police, Local Government.

Countries of Interest: Poland. *Recreations:* Football, playing in local 60s band 'The Moggies'. *Electoral Notes:* Member for Brigg and Goole since May 1, 1997. *Clubs:* Kinsley Labour, Ashby Mill Road. *Address:* Ian Cawsey Esq, MP, House of Commons, London, SW1A 0AA *Tel:* 020 7219 5237. *Constituency:* Brigg: 7 Market Place, Brigg, North Lincolnshire, DN20 8HA *Tel:* 01652 651327 *Fax:* 01652 657132, Goole: The Courtyard, Boothferry Road, Goole, East Riding of Yorkshire, DN14 6AE *Tel:* 01405 767744 *Fax:* 01405 767733 *E-mail:* ian-cawsey@msn.com.

CHAPMAN, Ben (James Keith) *(Wirral South)* Lab majority 7,004

Son of John Hartley and Elsie Vera Chapman. Born July 8, 1940; educated Appleby Grammar School, Appleby in Westmorland. Divorced (3 daughters); married 2nd, July 10, 1999, Maureen Ann. *Trades Union:* Former Member, FDA; Member: UNISON, MSF. *Armed Forces:* Pilot Officer, RAFVR 1959–61. *Profession:* Consultant (Retired Civil Servant). *Career:* Civil Servant: Ministry of Pensions and National Insurance 1958–62, Ministry of Aviation/BAA 1962–67, Rochdale Committee of Inquiry into Shipping 1967–70, Board of Trade 1970–74; First Secretary (Commercial) High Commission, Dar es Salaam, Tanzania 1974–78; First Secretary (Economic), High Commission, Accra, Ghana 1978–81; Assistant Secretary, Department of Trade and Industry 1981–87; Commercial Counsellor, Peking Embassy 1987–90; DTI North West: Director Merseyside and Deputy Regional Director 1991–93, Director Trade and Industry and Regional Director 1993–95; Director: On the Waterfront (Manchester) Ltd 1995–96, China Business Links Ltd 1995–97; Founder Consultant, Ben Chapman Associates 1995–97. *Political Career:* PPS to Richard Caborn, MP: as Minister of State, Department of the Environment, Transport and the Regions (Minister for the Regions, Regeneration and Planning) 1997–99, as Minister of State, Department of Trade and Industry (Minister for Trade) 1999–. *Other:* Director, Wirral Chamber of Commerce 1995–96; Council of Management, Lake District Summer Music Ltd 1996–97. *Trust:* Fellow, Industry and Parliament Trust elect. *Special Interests:* Economic Development, Regional Development, Trade and Industry, Foreign Affairs. *Countries of Interest:* China, Pacific Rim, Turkey. *Recreations:* Opera, theatre, music, reading, walking. *Electoral Notes:* Member for Wirral South since February 27, 1997 By-election. *Address:* Ben Chapman Esq, MP, House of Commons, London, SW1A 0AA *Tel:* 020 7219 1143 *Fax:* 020 7219 1179. *Constituency:* 32 Bebington Road, New Ferry, Merseyside, CH62 5BQ *Tel:* 0151–643 8797 *Fax:* 0151–643 8546 *E-mail:* chapmanb@parliament.uk.

CHAPMAN, Sir Sydney Brookes, RIBA, FRTPI *(Chipping Barnet)* Con majority 1,035

Son of late W. Dobson Chapman. Born October 17, 1935; educated Rugby School; Manchester University (DipArch 1958, DipTP 1961). Married 1976, Claire McNab (2 sons 1 daughter) (marriage dissolved). *Profession:* Chartered Architect and Surveyor, Chartered Town and Country Planner (non-practising). *Career:* Architect, Planner, Lecturer and occasional Journalist; Director (Information), British Property Federation 1976–79. *Political Career:* PPS: to Health and Social Security Ministers 1973–74; to Secretary of State for: Transport 1979–81, Social Services 1981–83. *Whip:* Assistant Government Whip 1988–90; Lord Commissioner of HM Treasury (Government Whip) 1990–92; Vice-Chamberlain of HM Household (Government Whip) 1992–95. *Select Committees (Current):* Chairman: Accommodation and Works 1997–; Member: Finance and Services 1997–, Liaison 1997– *(Former):* Member: Administration 1992–95, Accommodation and Works 1994–97, Public Service 1995–97. *Party Groups:* National Chairman, Young Conservatives 1964–66; Senior Vice-Chairman, North Western Area Conservatives and Unionist Associations 1966–70. *International Bodies:* Member, UK Delegation to Council of Europe and Western Europe Union. *Other:* Arboricultural Association: Vice-President 1973–83, President 1983–89; Instigator, National Tree Year 1973; Vice-President, RIBA 1974–75, Member of Council 1972–76; Vice-Chairman, United and Cecil Club since 1979; President, London Green Belt Council 1984–89; Formerly Vice-Chairman, Wildlife Link; Vice-President, Tree Council; Hon. Associate, British Veterinary Association; Former Vice-President, National Housing and Town Planning Council; Member, Sherlock Holmes Society of London. *Miscellaneous:* Formerly Member, Foreign Office Property Advisory Panel; Executive Member, 1922 Committee 1997–. *Honours:* HM The Queen's Silver Jubilee Medal 1977; Knighted 1995.

Fellowships, etc: RIBA; FRTPI; FRSA; Hon. MLI; Hon. FBEng; Hon. FFB; Hon. FISVA; Hon. FIAS. *Special Interests:* Environment, Architectural Heritage, Conservation, Construction Industry, Inner Cities, Arboriculture. *Countries of Interest:* Belize, Seychelles. *Electoral Notes:* Contested Stalybridge and Hyde 1964 General Election. Member for Birmingham Handsworth 1970–74, and for Chipping Barnet since May 1979. *Clubs:* United and Cecil. *Address:* Sir Sydney Chapman, MP, House of Commons, London, SW1A 0AA *Tel:* 020 7219 4542. *Constituency:* Chipping Barnet Conservative Association, 163 High Street, Barnet, Hertfordshire, EN5 5SU *Tel:* 020 8449 7345 *Fax:* 020 8449 7346.

CHAYTOR, David Michael *(Bury North)*   Lab majority 7,866

Born August 3, 1949; educated East Ward Primary School; Bury Grammar School; London University (BA Hons, MPhil); Leeds University (PGCE). Married (1 son 2 daughters). *Trades Union:* Member, TGWU. *Profession:* College Manager. *Career:* Senior Staff Tutor, Manchester College of Adult Education 1983–90; Head, Department of Continuing Education, Manchester College of Arts and Technology 1990–97. *Councils, Public Bodies:* Councillor, Calderdale Council 1982–97, Chair: Education Committee, Highways Committee, Economic Development Committee. *Select Committees (Current):* Member: Deregulation 1997–. *Miscellaneous:* Member, European Standing Committee A 1998–. *Special Interests:* Education, Transport, Environment, International Development. *Countries of Interest:* France, Albania, USA, Kazakhstan. *Recreations:* Walking, cycling, restoration of old buildings. *Electoral Notes:* Contested Calder Valley 1987, 1992. Member for Bury North since May 1, 1997. *Clubs:* Rochdale Labour. *Address:* David Chaytor Esq, MP, House of Commons, London, SW1A 0AA *Tel:* 020 7219 6625 *Fax:* 020 7219 0952. *Constituency:* Bury North Constituency Labour Party, 65A The Rock, Bury, Lancashire, BL9 0NB *Tel:* 0161–764 2023 *Fax:* 0161–763 3410.

CHIDGEY, David *(Eastleigh)*   LD majority 754

Son of Major Cyril Chidgey, and of Winifred Chidgey. Born July 9, 1942; educated Brune Park County High School, Gosport; Portsmouth Polytechnic (Dip CivilEng, CEng); Portsmouth Naval College. Married February 6, 1965, April Carolyn Idris-Jones (1 son 2 daughters). *Profession:* Consulting Engineer. *Career:* Consulting civil engineer; Senior Engineer, Hampshire County Council 1964–73; Coordinating Engineer, Brian Colquhoun and Partners 1973–78; Worked on projects in Guinea (West Africa) and South East Asia; Managing Director, Brian Colquhoun and Partners – Ireland 1981–87; Chief Consultant to Dublin Transport Authority; Associate Partner 1988–93; Associate Director, Thorburn Colquhoun 1994. *Councils, Public Bodies:* Winchester City Council: Councillor, Alresford 1987–91, Spokesman for: Health and Works 1987–90, Amenities 1987–89, Director, Direct Works Organisation 1990–91. *Spokesman:* Spokesman for: Employment 1994–95, Transport 1995–97, Trade and Industry 1997–99. *Select Committees (Current):* Member: Accommodation and Works 1998–, Foreign Affairs 1999–. *Party Groups:* Regional Chairman, Hampshire and Wight Liberal Democrats 1992–94. *Other:* Joint Founder and President, Association of Liberal Democrat Engineers and Applied Scientists; Member: Association of Liberal District Councillors, Council for the Protection of Rural England, President, NSPCC Eastleigh Branch. *Trust:* Member: National Trust, The Tramman Trust. Member, Worshipful Company of Carmen. *Sportsclubs:* Hampshire County Cricket. *Fellowships, etc:* FICE; FIHT; FIEI; MCIT; AConsEI. *Special Interests:* Manufacturing, Transport, Engineering Services. *Countries of Interest:* French speaking Africa, Pacific Rim, Middle East, Eastern Europe. *Recreations:* Reading, golf, tennis. *Electoral Notes:* Contested Hampshire Central European Parliamentary Constituency (SLD) 1988 By-Election and 1989 European Election; Contested Eastleigh (Lib Dem) 1992 General Election. Member for Eastleigh since June 9, 1994 By-Election. *Clubs:* National Liberal. *Address:* David Chidgey Esq, MP, House of Commons, London, SW1A 0AA *Tel:* 020 7219 4298 *Fax:* 020 7219 2810. *Constituency:* 113 Leigh Road, Eastleigh, Hampshire, SO50 9DS *Tel:* 023 8062 0007 *Fax:* 023 8061 8245.

CHISHOLM, Malcolm *(Edinburgh North and Leith)   Lab majority 10,978*

Son of George and Olive Chisholm. Born March 7, 1949; educated George Watson's College; Edinburgh University (MA Hons, DipEd). Married 1975, Janet Broomfield (2 sons 1 daughter). *Trades Union:* Member, Educational Institute of Scotland. *Career:* Teacher. *Political Career:* Parliamentary Under-Secretary of State, Scottish Office May-December 1997. *Whip:* Opposition Whip January-June 1996. *Spokesman:* Opposition Spokesman on Scotland 1996–97. *Party Groups:* Joined Labour Party 1980. *Special Interests:* Economic Policy, Health, Childcare, Housing. *Recreations:* Reading, cinema, theatre. *Electoral Notes:* Member for Edinburgh Leith 1992–97, and for Edinburgh North and Leith since May 1, 1997. MSP for Edinburgh North and Leith since May 6, 1999. *Address:* Malcolm Chisholm Esq, MP, MSP, House of Commons, London, SW1A 0AA *Tel:* 020 7219 4613. *Constituency:* 274 Leith Walk, Edinburgh *Tel:* 0131–555 3636 *Fax:* 0131–555 3737 *E-mail:* lamonta@parliament.uk.

CHOPE, Christopher, OBE *(Christchurch)   Con majority 2,165*

Son of late His Honour Judge Robert Chope and of Mrs Pamela Chope (née Durell). Born May 19, 1947; educated St Andrew's School, Eastbourne; Marlborough College; St Andrew's University (LLB 1970). Married April 20, 1987, Christine Mary Hutchinson (1 son 1 daughter). *Career:* Barrister, Inner Temple 1972; Consultant, Ernst and Young 1992–98. *Councils, Public Bodies:* Councillor, London Borough Wandsworth 1974–83, Chairman, Housing Committee 1978–79, Leader of the Council 1979–83. *Political Career:* PPS to Peter Brooke, as Minister of State, HM Treasury 1986; Parliamentary Under-Secretary of State: at Department of the Environment 1986–90, at Department of Transport (Minister for Roads and Traffic) 1990–92. *Spokesman:* An Opposition Front Bench Spokesman for: the Environment, Transport and the Regions 1997–98, Trade and Industry 1998–99. *Select Committees (Current):* Member: Trade and Industry 1999–. *Party Groups:* Member, Executive Committee, Society of Conservative Lawyers 1983–86; A Vice-Chairman, Conservative Party 1997–98. *Miscellaneous:* Member: Health and Safety Commission 1992–97, Local Government Commission for England 1994–95. *Honours:* OBE 1982. *Electoral Notes:* Member for Southampton Itchen 1983–92, and for Christchurch since May 1, 1997. *Address:* Christopher Chope Esq, OBE, MP, House of Commons, London, SW1A 0AA *Tel:* 020 7219 5808.

CHURCH, Judith *(Dagenham)   Lab majority 17,054*

Daughter of late Edmund Church, and of Helen Church. Born September 19, 1953; educated St Bernard's Convent School, Slough; Leeds University (Degree in Maths and Philosophy); Huddersfield Polytechnic (Postgraduate Certificate in Education (Technical Education)); Aston University (Postgraduate Diploma in Occupational Health and Safety); Thames Valley University (Postgraduate Diploma in Management Studies). (2 sons). *Trades Union:* First woman to be elected in union section of Labour Party National Executive Committee 1992. *Career:* Maths teacher in West Africa with Voluntary Service Overseas 1975–77; Process research, Mars UK 1979–80; Technical Officer, GAF UK 1978–79; HM Factory Inspector 1980–86; National Health and Safety Officer for MSF 1986–94. *Select Committees (Former):* Member: Deregulation 1995–97. *Party Groups:* Member, Labour Party 1980–; Former Chairman, Hornsey and Wood Green CLP; Joint Chairman, Labour Party Economic Policy Commission 1992–94; Member, Labour Party National Executive Committee 1992–94; Member, Fabian Society. *Special Interests:* Breast Cancer. *Recreations:* Reading, keeping fit. *Electoral Notes:* Contested Stevenage 1992 General Election; Member for Dagenham since June 9, 1994 By-Election. *Address:* Judith Church, MP, House of Commons, London, SW1A 0AA *Tel:* 020 7219 6000 *Fax:* 020 7219 0076 *Tel (Constituency):* 01279 757147 *Fax (Constituency):* 01279 757147 *E-mail:* dewdneyk@parliament.uk.

498   HOUSE OF COMMONS

CLAPHAM, Michael *(Barnsley West and Penistone)   Lab majority 17,267*

Son of late Thomas Clapham. Born May 15, 1943; educated Gawber Junior and Infant; Darton Secondary School; Barnsley Technical College; Leeds Polytechnic; Universities of Leeds and Bradford (BScHons, MPhil, Post Graduate Certificate of Education). Married December 4, 1965, Yvonne Hallsworth (1 son 1 daughter). *Trades Union:* NUM: Member, Claims Officer 1977–83, Head, Industrial Relations Department 1983–; Member, UCATT 1997–. *Career:* Miner 1958–70; Lecturer 1974–77, Deputy Head, Comp Dept, Yorkshire Area NUM 1977–83; Head, Industrial Relations NUM 1983–92. *Councils, Public Bodies:* Chairman, Barnsley Crime Prevention Partnership 1995–. *Political Career:* PPS to Alan Milburn, as Minister of State, Department of Health May-December 1997. *Select Committees (Former):* Member: Trade and Industry 1992–97. *Party Groups:* Member, Co-operative Party; Secretary, Higham Labour Party Branch 1981–83; Treasurer, Barnsley West and Penistone Constituency Labour Party 1983–92; Chairman, Dodworth Labour Party Branch 1984–86. *Special Interests:* Coal Industry, Energy, Employment, Health. *Countries of Interest:* Tibet, Nepal, South Africa. *Recreations:* Walking, gardening, reading. *Electoral Notes:* Member for Barnsley West and Penistone since April 9, 1992. *Address:* Michael Clapham Esq, MP, House of Commons, London, SW1A 0AA *Tel:* 020 7219 5015. *Constituency:* 18 Regent Street, Barnsley, South Yorkshire, S70 2HG *Tel:* 01226 731244 *Fax:* 01226 779429.

CLAPPISON, James *(Hertsmere)   Con majority 3,075*

Son of late Leonard Clappison, farmer, and of Dorothy Clappison. Born September 14, 1956; educated St Peter's School, York; The Queen's College, Oxford (Scholarship). Married July 6, 1984, Helen Margherita, daughter of Alan and Dorothy Carter (1 son 3 daughters). *Career:* Barrister 1981–. *Political Career:* PPS to Rt Hon. Baroness Blatch, CBE: as Minister of State, at the Department for Education 1992–94, Home Office 1994–95; Parliamentary Under-Secretary of State, Department of the Environment 1995–97. *Spokesman:* An Opposition Front Bench Spokesman for: Home Affairs (Crime, Immigration and Asylums) 1997–99, Education and Employment 1999–. *Select Committees (Former):* Member: Health 1992–94, Members' Interests 1994–95. *Special Interests:* Home Affairs, Economic Policy, Health, Education. *Countries of Interest:* Israel. *Recreations:* Bridge, walking. *Electoral Notes:* Contested Barnsley East 1987 General Election; Yorkshire South 1989 European Parliamentary Election; Bootle in two by-elections May and November 1990. Member for Hertsmere since April 9, 1992. *Clubs:* United Oxford and Cambridge University, Carlton. *Address:* James Clappison Esq, MP, House of Commons, London, SW1A 0AA *Tel:* 020 7219 5027. *Constituency:* 11 Stanhope Road, St Albans, Hertfordshire, AL1 5BH *Tel:* 01727 850661 *Fax:* 01727 868579 *E-mail:* clappisonj@parliament.uk.

CLARK, The Rt Hon. Dr David George *(South Shields)   Lab majority 22,153*

Son of George Clark. Born October 19, 1939; educated Windermere Grammar School; Manchester University (BA Economics 1963, MSc 1965) Sheffield University (PhD 1978). Married March 24, 1970, Christine, daughter of Ronald Kirkby (1 daughter). *Trades Union:* Member, UNISON. *Career:* Forester 1956–57; Laboratory worker in textile mill 1957–59; Student Teacher, Salford 1959–60; Lecturer in Public Administration, Salford University 1965–70; President, University of Manchester Union 1963–64. *Political Career:* Chancellor of the Duchy of Lancaster 1997–98. *Spokesman:* Front Bench Spokesman on: Agriculture, Fisheries and Food 1972–74, Defence 1980–81, The Environment 1981–87, Food, Agricultural and Rural Affairs 1987–92, Defence, disarmament and arms control 1992–97. *International Bodies:* Member, UK Delegation of the North Atlantic Assembly 1980–97, 1998–. *Trust:* Executive Member, National Trust 1980–94; Trustee: Vindolanda Trust 1983–, History of Parliament Trust 1986–. *Miscellaneous:* Chair, Atlantic Council of the UK. Borough of South Tyneside 1999. *Honours:* PC 1997. *Publications: Industrial Manager*, 1966; *Colne Valley: Radicalism to Socialism*, 1981; *Victor Grayson: Labour's Lost Leader*, 1985; *We do not want The Earth*, 1992. *Special Interests:* Open Spaces. *Countries of Interest:* New Zealand, Scandinavia.

Recreations: Gardening, fell-walking, reading, watching football. *Electoral Notes:* Contested Manchester Withington Division 1966; Member for Colne Valley 1970–74, and for South Shields since May 1979. *Address:* The Rt Hon. Dr David Clark, MP, House of Commons, London, SW1A 0AA *Tel:* 020 7219 4028. *Constituency:* Ede House, 143 Westoe Road, South Shields, Tyne and Wear, NE33 3PD *Tel:* 0191–456 0762 *Fax:* 0191–454 0364.

CLARK, Dr Lynda, QC *(Edinburgh Pentlands)   Lab majority 4,862*

Born February 26, 1949; educated Queens College, St Andrews University (LLB Hons 1970); Edinburgh University (PhD 1975). *Profession:* Queen's Counsel. *Career:* Part-time Tutor, Dundee University 1971–73; Lecturer in Jurisprudence, Dundee University 1973–76; Advocate, Scots Bar 1977–89; QC 1989; Called to the English Bar 1990. *Political Career:* Advocate General for Scotland 1999–. *Select Committees (Former):* Member: Public Administration 1997–99. *Other:* Former Member: Scottish Legal Aid Board, Edinburgh University Court. *Special Interests:* Constitutional Reform, Legal System, Health, Higher Education, Pensions. *Electoral Notes:* Contested North East Fife (Labour) 1992. Member for Edinburgh Pentlands since May 1, 1997.

Address: Dr Lynda Clark, QC, MP, House of Commons, London, SW1A 0AA *Tel:* 020 7219 4492. *Constituency:* The Reception Block, Princess Margaret Rose Hospital, 41/43 Frogston Road West, Edinburgh, EH10 7ED *Tel:* 0131–536 4834.

CLARK, Dr Michael *(Rayleigh)   Con majority 10,684*

Son of late Mervyn Clark. Born August 8, 1935; educated King Edward VI Grammar School, East Retford; King's College, London (BSc Hons Chemistry); University of Minnesota; St John's College, Cambridge (PhD); Fellow, King's College, London. Married July 26, 1958, Valerie Ethel Harbord (1 son 1 daughter). *Profession:* Industrial Chemist. *Career:* Won Fulbright Scholarship to USA 1956; Industrial chemist: ICI and Smiths Industries 1960–69; Management Consultant 1969–94. *Select Committees (Current):* Member: Chairmen's Panel 1997–; Chairman: Science and Technology 1997–; Member: Liaison 1998– *(Former):* Member: Energy 1983–92; Chairman: Energy 1989–92; Member: Liaison 1989–92, Trade and Industry 1992–94.

Party Groups: Cambridgeshire Conservative Association: Member 1969–83, Treasurer 1975–78, Vice-Chairman 1978–80, Chairman 1980–83; Member, Eastern Area Executive Council 1980–84. *International Bodies:* Executive Inter Parliamentary Union: Member 1987–95, Chairman 1990–93. *Other:* Melborn Village College: Governor 1974–82, Chairman of Governors 1977–80. *Awards:* Gold Medal, Coal Research Council 1992. *Miscellaneous:* Board of Parliamentary Office of Science and Technology 1988–, Chairman 1993–98; Executive Member, 1922 Committee 1997–. *Sportsclubs:* Rochford Hundred Golf. *Fellowships, etc:* Fellow: King's College, London 1987, Royal Society of Chemistry 1988; Companion, Institute of Energy 1991. *Publications: The History of Rochford Hall.* *Special Interests:* Energy, Manufacturing, Science and Technology, Animal Welfare. *Countries of Interest:* Russia, Venezuela, Turkey, Cyprus, Argentina. *Recreations:* Gardening, DIY, golf. *Electoral Notes:* Contested Ilkeston, Derbyshire 1979. Member for Rochford 1983–97, and for Rayleigh since May 1, 1997. *Clubs:* Rayleigh Conservative. *Address:* Dr Michael Clark, MP, House of Commons, London, SW1A 0AA *Tel:* 020 7219 4016 *Fax:* 020 7219 3548. *Constituency:* Conservative Office, 25 Bellingham Lane, Rayleigh, Essex, SS6 7ED *Tel:* 01268 742044 *Fax:* 01268 741833.

CLARK, Paul Gordon *(Gillingham)   Lab majority 1,980*

Son of Gordon Thomas Clark, retired journalist, and of Sheila Gladys Clark, Councillor, former Mayor of Gillingham. Born April 29, 1957; educated Gillingham Grammar School; Keele University (BA Hons Economics and Politics); University of Derby (DMS). Married Julie Hendrick (1 son 1 daughter). *Trades Union:* Member: TUC, AEU (Gillingham Branch). *Profession:* Centre Manager. *Career:* Centre Manager, Trades Union Congress, National Education Centre. *Councils, Public Bodies:* Councillor, Gillingham Borough Council 1982–90, Labour Group Leader 1988–90. *Political Career:* Joint PPS to Rt Hon. the Lord Irvine of Lairg, QC, as Lord Chancellor 1999–. *Party Groups:* Member, Labour Party 1975–. *Miscellaneous:* Member: European Standing Committee A 1998, European Standing Committee B 1998–. *Special Interests:* Education, Transport, Environment. *Countries of Interest:* Europe, including East Europe. *Recreations:* Historic buildings, reading. *Electoral Notes:* Contested Gillingham 1992 General Election. Member for Gillingham since May 1, 1997. *Clubs:* Anchorians Association. *Address:* Paul Clark Esq, MP, House of Commons, London, SW1A 0AA *Tel:* 020 7219 1232. *Constituency:* 6 Woodlands Road, Gillingham, Kent, ME7 2EG *Tel:* 01634 571655 *Fax:* 01634 571655.

CLARKE, Charles Rodway *(Norwich South)   Lab majority 14,239*

Son of late Sir Richard Clarke, KCB, and Lady Brenda Clarke. Born September 21, 1950; educated Highgate School, London; King's College, Cambridge (BA maths and economics). Married October 1984, Carol, daughter of Kenneth and Linda Pearson (2 sons). *Trades Union:* Sabbatical President, Cambridge Students' Union 1971–72; Member, National Union of Students' Executive, President 1975–77. *Career:* Part-time Adult Education Maths Lecturer, City Literary Institute 1981–83; Organiser, Community Challenge Conference, Gulbenkian Fund 1981–82; Researcher to Neil Kinnock, MP 1981–83; Chief of Staff to Neil Kinnock, MP 1983–92; Chief Executive, Quality Public Affairs 1992–97. *Councils, Public Bodies:* Councillor, London Borough of Hackney 1980–86, Chair, Housing Committee, Vice-Chair, Economic Development. *Political Career:* Parliamentary Under-Secretary of State (School Standards), Department for Education and Employment 1998–99; Minister of State, Home Office 1999–. *Select Committees (Former):* Member: Treasury 1997–98, Treasury Sub-Committee 1998. *Other:* Organiser, Hackney People In Partnership 1978–80. *Recreations:* Chess, reading, walking. *Electoral Notes:* Member for Norwich South since May 1, 1997. *Clubs:* Norwich Labour. *Address:* Charles Clarke Esq, MP, House of Commons, London, SW1A 0AA *Tel:* 020 7219 1194 *Fax:* 020 7219 0526. *Constituency:* Norwich Labour Party, 59 Bethel Street, Norwich, NR2 1NL *Tel:* 01603 661144 *Fax:* 01603 663502.

CLARKE, Eric Lionel *(Midlothian)   Lab majority 9,870*

Son of late Ernest Clarke, railway guard, and late Annie Clarke, laundress. Born April 9, 1933; educated St Cuthbert's; Holy Cross Academy; W. M. Ramsey Technical College, Edinburgh; Esk Valley College, Midlothian (Certificate for General Education – Mining Qualification Board). Married April 10, 1955, June, daughter of late Richard Hewat, boiler fireman (2 sons 1 daughter). *Trades Union:* General Secretary, Scottish Area NUM 1977–89; Sponsored by NUM. *Career:* Roslin Colliery 1949; Faceman, Lingerwood Colliery 1952; Trainer supervisor repairer, Bilstonglen Colliery 1967. *Councils, Public Bodies:* County and Regional Councillor 1962–78. *Whip:* Opposition Scottish and Defence Whip 1994–97. *Select Committees (Current):* Member: Finance and Services 1997–, Scottish Affairs 1997–, Liaison 1998– *(Former):* Member: Scottish Affairs 1992–94; Chairman: Broadcasting 1997–99. *Trust:* Member, Scottish Mining Museum Trust. *Honours:* Honorary Citizen, Morphu, Cyprus. *Special Interests:* Coal Industry, Scottish Affairs, Foreign Affairs. *Countries of Interest:* Cyprus, Middle East, Vietnam, Nepal. *Recreations:* Trout angling, carpentry, gardening, watching football. *Electoral Notes:* Member for Midlothian since April 9, 1992. *Clubs:* Mayfield Labour, Morris Workingmen's, Danderhall Miners' Welfare. *Address:* Eric Clarke Esq, MP, House of Commons, London, SW1A 0AA *Tel:* 020 7219 6373 *Fax:* 020 7219 2117. *Constituency:* PO Box 11, 34 Buccleuch Street, Dalkeith, Midlothian, EH22 1HL *Tel:* 0131–654 1585 *Fax:* 0131–654 1586.

CLARKE, The Rt Hon. Kenneth, QC *(Rushcliffe)* Con majority 5,055

Son of late Kenneth Clarke, watchmaker and jeweller, and Doris Clarke. Born July 2, 1940; educated Nottingham High School; Gonville and Caius College, Cambridge (BA, LLB) (President, Cambridge Union 1963); Hon. LLD: Nottingham University 1989, Huddersfield University 1992, Nottingham Trent University 1995; Honorary Fellow, Gonville and Caius College, Cambridge. Married November 7, 1964, Gillian Mary Edwards (1 son 1 daughter). *Profession:* Barrister-at-Law. *Career:* Called to the Bar 1963; Member, Midland Circuit, practising from Birmingham; QC 1980; Chairman, Alliance UniChem 1997–; Director, Foreign & Colonial Investment Trust 1997–; Deputy Chairman, British American Tobacco 1998–; Director, Independent News and Media (UK). *Political Career:* PPS to Solicitor General 1971–72; Parliamentary Secretary, Ministry of Transport 1979–80; Parliamentary Under-Secretary of State at Department of Transport 1980–82; Minister for Health 1982–85; Paymaster General and Employment Minister 1985–87; Chancellor, Duchy of Lancaster (Minister of Trade and Industry) 1987–88; Secretary of State for: Health 1988–90, Education and Science 1990–92, Home Department 1992–93, Chancellor of the Exchequer 1993–97; Contested Leadership of the Conservative Party June 1997. *Whip:* Assistant Government Whip 1972–74; Government Whip for Europe 1973–74; Lord Commissioner of the Treasury January-March 1974. *Spokesman:* Opposition Spokesman on: Social Services 1974–76, Industry 1976–79. *Party Groups:* Chairman: Cambridge University Conservative Association 1961, Federation Conservative Students 1963–65. Liveryman, The Clockmakers Company. *Electoral Notes:* Contested Mansfield Notts 1964 and 1966. Member for Rushcliffe since June 1970. *Clubs:* Garrick. *Address:* The Rt Hon. Kenneth Clarke, QC, MP, House of Commons, London, SW1A 0AA *Tel:* 020 7219 4528.

CLARKE, The Rt Hon. Thomas, CBE, JP *(Coatbridge and Chryston)* Lab majority 19,295

Son of late James Clarke. Born January 10, 1941; educated All Saints Primary School, Airdrie; Columba High School, Coatbridge; Scottish College of Commerce. *Trades Union:* Member, GMB. *Profession:* Film Executive. *Career:* Assistant Director, Scottish Council for Educational Technology (Scottish Film Council). *Councils, Public Bodies:* Councillor: Coatbridge Town Council 1964–74, Monklands District Council 1974–82; Provost of Monklands 1974–82; JP 1972; President, Convention of Scottish Local Authorities 1978–80. *Political Career:* Author and Sponsor Disabled Persons (Services, Representation and Consultation) Act 1986; Shadow Minister for UK Personal Social Services 1987–92; Shadow Secretary of State for Scotland 1992–93, for International Development 1994–95; Shadow Minister for Disabled People's Rights 1995–97; Minister of State (Film and Tourism), Department of National Heritage/for Culture, Media and Sport 1997–98. *Spokesman:* Principal Opposition Spokesman on Development and Co-operation 1993–94. *Trust:* Fellow, Industry and Parliament Trust. *Miscellaneous:* Director, Award-winning amateur film *Give Us A Goal.* *Sportsclubs:* Coatbridge Municipal Golf. *Honours:* CBE 1980; PC 1997. *Special Interests:* Film Industry, Foreign Affairs, Civil Service, Local Government. *Countries of Interest:* Central America, Philippines, Africa, Asia, Eastern Europe, USA. *Recreations:* Films, walking, reading, astrology. *Electoral Notes:* Member for Coatbridge and Airdrie by-election 1982–83, for Monklands West 1983–97, and for Coatbridge and Chryston since May 1, 1997. *Address:* The Rt Hon. Thomas Clarke, CBE, JP, MP, House of Commons, London, SW1A 0AA *Tel:* 020 7219 6997 *Fax:* 020 7219 6094 *Tel (Constituency):* 01236 600800 *Fax (Constituency):* 01236 600808.

CLARKE, Tony (Anthony Richard) *(Northampton South)   Lab majority 744*

Son of Walter Arthur Clarke, engineer, and Joan Ada Iris Clarke. Born September 6, 1963; educated Lings Upper School, Northampton; Institute of Training and Development; Institute of Safety and Health. Married Carole Chalmers (1 son 1 daughter). *Trades Union:* Member, GMB. *Profession:* Disability Training Officer. *Career:* Social Work Trainer, Northamptonshire County Council; Currently Disability Training Officer. *Councils, Public Bodies:* Councillor, Northampton Borough Council 1991–99; Chair, Environment Services. *Select Committees (Current):* Member: Consolidation of Bills (Joint Committee) 1997–. *Trust:* Vice-Chair, Northampton Town Football (Cobblers') Supporters Trust. *Miscellaneous:* Member, East Midlands Sports Council. *Sportsclubs:* Director, Northampton Town FC. *Special Interests:* Environment, Leisure, Constitution, Sport, Local Government. *Countries of Interest:* Europe. *Recreations:* Football. *Electoral Notes:* Member for Northampton South since May 1, 1997. *Address:* Tony Clarke Esq, MP, House of Commons, London, SW1A 0AA *Tel:* 020 7219 4465 *Fax:* 020 7219 0526. *Constituency:* 1 St Giles Terrace, Northampton, NN1 2BN *Tel:* 01604 250044 *Fax:* 01604 250055 *E-mail:* tonyclarkemp@lineone.com.

CLELLAND, David Gordon *(Tyne Bridge)   Lab majority 22,906*

Son of Archibald Clelland. Born June 27, 1943; educated Kelvin Grove Boys School; Gateshead Technical College; Hebburn Technical College. Married March 31, 1965, Maureen, daughter of William Potts (2 daughters) (separated). *Trades Union:* AEEU: Member, 35 years, Shop Steward, 14 years. *Career:* Electrical Fitter 1964–81; Local Government Association Secretary 1981–86. *Councils, Public Bodies:* Chairman, Gateshead Council Recreation Committee 1976–84; Secretary, Association of Councillors 1981–86; Vice-Chairman, Gateshead Health Authority 1982–84; Leader, Gateshead Council 1984–86. *Whip:* Opposition Whip 1995–97; Assistant Government Whip 1997–. *Party Groups:* Hon. Secretary and Hon. Treasurer, Northern Group of Labour MPs –1998, Vice-Chairman 1999. *Special Interests:* Local Government, Home Affairs, Transport, Environment, Employment, Energy. *Recreations:* Golf, music. *Electoral Notes:* Member for Tyne Bridge since December 5, 1985 By-election. *Address:* David Clelland Esq, MP, House of Commons, London, SW1A 0AA *Tel:* 020 7219 3669. *Constituency:* 19 Ravensworth Road, Dunston, Gateshead, Tyne and Wear, NE11 9AB *Tel:* 01914 200300 *Fax:* 01914 200301 *E-mail:* david.clelland@hm-treasury.gov.uk.

CLIFTON-BROWN, Geoffrey, ARICS *(Cotswold)   Con majority 11,965*

Son of Robert and Elizabeth Clifton-Brown. Born March 23, 1953; educated Eton; Royal Agricultural College, Cirencester. Married 1979, Alexandra Peto-Shepherd (1 son 1 daughter). *Profession:* Chartered Surveyor. *Career:* Graduate estate surveyor, Property Services Agency, Dorchester 1975; Investment surveyor, Jones Lang Wootton 1975–79; Managing Director, own farming business in Norfolk 1979–. *Political Career:* PPS to Rt Hon. Douglas Hogg, MP, as Minister of Agriculture, Fisheries and Food 1995–97. *Whip:* An Opposition Whip: (Agriculture; Education and Employment: Scotland) 1999, (Education and Employment; Defence; Culture, Media and Sport) 1999–. *Select Committees (Former):* Member: Environment 1992–97, Public Accounts 1997–99. *Party Groups:* Chairman, North Norfolk Constituency Association 1986–91. *Other:* Vice-Chairman: Charities Property Association 1993–, Small Business Bureau 1995–. *Miscellaneous:* Member: Eastern Area Executive and Agricultural Committees 1986–91. Liveryman, The Worshipful Company of Farmers. Freeman, City of London. ARICS. *Publications: Privatisation of the State Pension – Secure Funded Provision for all,* 1996. *Special Interests:* Economy and Taxation, Foreign Affairs, Environment, Agriculture. *Countries of Interest:* Brazil, France, Italy, Kashmir, Hong Kong. *Recreations:* Fishing, other rural pursuits. *Electoral Notes:* Member for Cirencester and Tewkesbury 1992–97, and for Cotswold since May 1, 1997. *Clubs:* Carlton, Farmers'. *Address:* Geoffrey Clifton-Brown Esq, ARICS, MP, House of Commons, London, SW1A 0AA *Tel:* 020 7219 5147 *Fax:* 020 7219 2550. *Constituency:* 7 Rodney Road, Cheltenham, Gloucestershire, GL50 1HX *Tel:* 01242 514551 *Fax:* 01242 514949 *E-mail:* gcb@gcbmp.demon.co.uk.

CLWYD, Ann *(Cynon Valley)   Lab majority 19,755*

Daughter of Gwilym Lewis and Elizabeth Lewis. Born March 21, 1937; educated Halkyn Primary School; Holywell Grammar School; The Queen's School; University College, Bangor. Married 1963, Owen Roberts. *Career:* Journalist; Broadcaster. *Political Career:* Shadow Minister of Education and Women's Rights 1987–88; Shadow Secretary of State for: Wales July–November 1992, National Heritage 1992–93; Assistant to Rt Hon. John Prescott, MP, as Deputy Leader of the Labour Party 1994–95. *Spokesman:* Opposition Spokesman on: Development and Co-operation 1989–92, Employment 1993–94, Foreign Affairs 1994–95. *Select Committees (Current):* Member: International Development 1997–. *Party Groups:* Member, Labour Party National Executive Committee 1983–84; Chairman, The Tribune Group 1986–87. *International Bodies:* Executive Committee Member, IPU British Group. *Other:* Member, Welsh Hospital Board 1970–74. *Miscellaneous:* Member, Arts Council 1975–79; Vice-Chairman, Welsh Arts Council 1975–79; Royal Commission on NHS 1976–79. *Countries of Interest:* Iraq, Turkey, Iran, Russia, South East Asia. *Electoral Notes:* Contested Denbigh 1970 and Gloucester October 1974 General Elections. MEP for Mid and West Wales 1979–84. Member for Cynon Valley since by-election May 3, 1984. *Address:* Ann Clwyd, MP, House of Commons, London, SW1A 0AA *Tel:* 020 7219 6609 *Tel (Constituency):* 01685 871394.

COAKER, Vernon Rodney *(Gedling)   Lab majority 3,802*

Son of Edwin Coaker. Born June 17, 1953; educated Drayton Manor Grammar School, London; Warwick University (BA Hons); Trent Polytechnic (PGCE). Married December 23, 1978, Jacqueline Heaton (1 son 1 daughter). *Trades Union:* Member, NUT. *Profession:* Deputy Head Teacher. *Career:* Teaching. *Councils, Public Bodies:* Councillor, Rushcliffe Borough Council 1983–97. *Political Career:* PPS to Stephen Timms, MP: as Minister of State, Department of Social Security 1999, as Financial Secretary, HM Treasury 1999–. *Select Committees (Former):* Member: Social Security 1998–99. *Other:* Member: League Against Cruel Sports, Friends of the Earth. *Miscellaneous:* Member, European Standing Committee B 1998. *Special Interests:* Environment, Education, Welfare Reform, Foreign Policy. *Countries of Interest:* France, Kosovo, Macedonia. *Recreations:* Sport, walking. *Electoral Notes:* Member for Gedling since May 1, 1997. *Address:* Vernon Coaker Esq, MP, House of Commons, London, SW1A 0AA *Tel:* 020 7219 6627. *Constituency:* 4 Arnot Hill Road, Arnold, Nottingham, NG5 6LJ *Tel:* 0115–920 4224 *Fax:* 0115–920 4500 *E-mail:* coakerv@parliament.uk.

COFFEY, Ann *(Stockport)   Lab majority 18,912*

Daughter of late John Brown, MBE, Flight-Lieutenant, RAF, and of Marie Brown, nurse. Born August 31, 1946; educated Nairn Academy; Bodmin and Bushey Grammar Schools; Polytechnic of South Bank, London (BSc sociology 1967); Walsall College of Education (Postgraduate Certificate in Education 1971); Manchester University (MSc psychiatric social work 1977). Married 1973, marriage dissolved 1989 (1 daughter). *Trades Union:* Member, USDAW. *Career:* Trainee Social Worker, Walsall Social Services 1971–72; Social Worker: Birmingham 1972–73, Gwynedd 1973–74, Wolverhampton 1974–75, Stockport 1977–82, Cheshire 1982–88; Team Leader, Fostering, Oldham Social Services 1988–92. *Councils, Public Bodies:* Stockport Metropolitan Borough Council: Councillor 1984–92, Leader of Labour Group 1988–92; Member, District Health Authority 1986–90. *Political Career:* Joint PPS to Rt Hon. Tony Blair, MP, as Prime Minister 1997–98; PPS to Rt Hon. Alistair Darling, MP, as Secretary of State for Social Security 1998–. *Whip:* Opposition Whip 1995–96. *Spokesman:* Opposition Spokeswoman on Health 1996–97. *Select Committees (Former):* Member: Trade and Industry 1993–95. *Special Interests:* Trade and Industry, Health, Personal Social Services, Voluntary Organisations. *Recreations:* Photography, drawing, cinema, swimming, reading. *Electoral Notes:* Contested Cheadle 1987 General Election. Member for Stockport since April 9, 1992. *Address:* Ann Coffey, MP, House of Commons, London, SW1A 0AA *Tel:* 020 7219 4546 *Fax:* 020 7219 0770 *Tel (Constituency):* 0161–491 0615 *Fax (Constituency):* 0161–491 0338 *E-mail:* coffeya@parliament.uk.

COHEN, Harry *(Leyton and Wanstead)*   *Lab majority 15,186*

Son of Emanuel and Anne Cohen. Born December 10, 1949; educated George Gascoigne Secondary Modern; East Ham Technical College (part-time); Birbeck College (MSc Politics and Administration). Married 1978, Ellen Hussain (1 step-son 1 step-daughter 1 foster-son). *Trades Union:* Member, UNISON. *Profession:* Accountant. *Career:* Accountant and Auditor, Local Government; Auditor, NALGO. *Councils, Public Bodies:* Waltham Forest Borough Council: Councillor 1972–83, Formerly Chairman, Planning Committee, Secretary, Labour Group; Member, Waltham Forest Area Health Authority. *Select Committees (Current):* Member: Defence 1997–. *International Bodies:* Member, UK Delegation to North Atlantic Assembly 1992–; Chairman, Sub-Committee for Economic Co-operation and Convergence with Central and Eastern Europe. *Miscellaneous:* Vice-President, The Royal College of Midwives. Member, CIPFA 1974. *Special Interests:* Defence, Women's Rights, Ecology, Conservation, Animal Rights. *Countries of Interest:* Middle East, Central Europe, Eastern Europe, India, Pakistan, Bangladesh, Tibet. *Electoral Notes:* Member for Leyton 1983–97, and for Leyton and Wanstead since May 1, 1997. *Address:* Harry Cohen Esq, MP, House of Commons, London, SW1A 0AA *Tel:* 020 7219 6376/4137 *Fax:* 020 7219 0438 *E-mail:* cohenh@parliament.uk.

COLEMAN, Iain *(Hammersmith and Fulham)*   *Lab majority 3,842*

Born January 18, 1958; educated Tonbridge School. Married Sally Powell (1 son). *Trades Union:* Member, MSF. *Profession:* Local Government Officer. *Career:* Senior Administrative Officer, London Borough of Islington. *Councils, Public Bodies:* Councillor, Hammersmith and Fulham 1986–97, Leader 1991–96, Mayor 1996–97. *Select Committees (Former):* Member: Deregulation 1997–99. *Party Groups:* Vice-Chair, London Regional Group of Labour MPs 1999–. *Miscellaneous:* Vice-Chair, Association of London Authorities 1993–95. *Sportsclubs:* Arsenal FC. *Special Interests:* Housing, Sport, Asylum and Immigration. *Countries of Interest:* Ireland, France. *Recreations:* Football, opera. *Electoral Notes:* Member for Hammersmith and Fulham since May 1, 1997. *Address:* Iain Coleman Esq, MP, House of Commons, SW1A 0AA *Tel:* 020 7381 5074 *Fax:* 020 7386 5415. *Constituency:* 28 Greyhound Road, London, W6 8NX *Tel:* 020 7381 5074 *Fax:* 020 7386 5415 *E-mail:* jacksona@parliament.uk.

COLLINS, Tim William George, CBE *(Westmorland and Lonsdale)*   *Con majority 4,521*

Son of late William Collins, and of Diana Collins. Born May 7, 1964; educated Chigwell School, Essex; London School of Economics (BSc Econ); King's College, London (MA). Married July 26, 1997, Clare Benson. *Career:* Conservative Research Department 1986–89; Special Adviser: to David Hunt and Michael Howard as Secretaries of State for the Environment 1989–90, to Michael Howard as Employment Secretary 1990–92; Press Secretary to the Prime Minister 1992; Director of Communications, Conservative Party 1992–95; Member, Prime Minister's Policy Unit, Downing Street 1995; Media Consultant to Conservative Party Chairman 1995–97; Senior Strategy Consultant, WCT Ltd 1995–97. *Political Career:* Senior Vice-Chairman, Conservative Party 1999–. *Whip:* An Opposition Whip (Social Security, Trade and Industry) 1998–99. *Select Committees (Current):* Member: Information 1998– *(Former):* Member: Agriculture 1997–98. *Party Groups:* Ex-officio Member, National Union Executive Committee 1992–95. *Honours:* CBE 1996. *Special Interests:* Defence, Media, Tourism, Constitution, Agriculture, European Union, Economic Policy, Employment, Northern Ireland. *Countries of Interest:* USA, Germany, Australia. *Recreations:* Literature, cinema, heritage. *Electoral Notes:* Member for Westmorland and Lonsdale since May 1, 1997. *Address:* Tim Collins Esq, CBE, MP, House of Commons, London, SW1A 0AA *Tel:* 020 7219 3378. *Constituency:* 112 Highgate, Kendal, Cumbria, LA9 4HE *Tel:* 01539 721010 *Fax:* 01539 733039 *E-mail:* listening@timcollins.co.uk *Website:* www.timcollins.co.uk.

COLMAN, Tony (Anthony John) *(Putney)* Lab majority 2,976

Son of late William and Beatrice Colman. Born July 24, 1943; educated Paston Grammar School, North Walsham, Norfolk; Magdalene College, Cambridge (MA Hons); Industrial Fellow, Kingston University. Married November 2, 1989, Juliet, daughter of Alec and June Owen (2 sons plus 1 stepson 1 stepdaughter and 3 sons 1 daughter from previous marriages). *Trades Union:* Member, GMB. *Career:* Unilever (United Africa Company) 1964–69; Associated Fisheries Ltd 1969–71; Burton Group 1969–90, Main Board Director 1981–90; Director, London First Centre Ltd 1994–. *Councils, Public Bodies:* Councillor, London Borough of Merton 1990–98, Leader of Council 1991–97. *Political Career:* PPS to Rt Hon. Adam Ingram, MP, as Minister of State, Northern Ireland Office (Minister for Security, Criminal Justice, Prisons, Economic Development and Victims of Violence) 1998–. *Select Committees (Former):* Member: Treasury 1997–98. *Party Groups:* Member: Labour Finance and Industry Group 1973–, Labour Party Enquiry into Education and Training in Europe 1991–93. *Other:* Chairman, Low Pay Unit 1990–98. *Trust:* Chairman, Wimbledon Theatre Trust 1991–97. *Miscellaneous:* Member, Prices Commission 1977–79; Vice-Chairman, Association of London Authorities 1991–95; Director, London Arts Board 1994–98; Chairman: UK Standing Committee Local Authority Pensions 1994–98, Public Private Partnership Program 1995–98; Director, CCLA 1995–98. Freeman, City of London 1997. FRSA 1983. *Special Interests:* Agenda 21, PFI, Pension Funds. *Recreations:* Swimming, theatre. *Electoral Notes:* Contested South West Hertfordshire 1979. Member for Putney since May 1, 1997. *Clubs:* Reform, Winchester (Putney). *Address:* Tony Colman Esq, MP, House of Commons, London, SW1A 0AA *Tel:* 020 7219 6639 *Fax:* 020 7219 1137. *Constituency:* 35 Felsham Road, London, SW15 1AY *Tel:* 020 8788 8961 *Fax:* 020 8785 2053.

COLVIN, Michael Keith Beale *(Romsey)* Con majority 8,585

Son of late Captain Ivan Beale Colvin, RN and Mrs Joy Colvin, OBE. Born September 27, 1932; educated Eton; Royal Military Academy, Sandhurst; Royal Agricultural College, Cirencester. Married 1956, Hon. Nichola, daughter of Lord Cayzer (1 son 2 daughters). *Trades Union:* Member, ASTMS 1975–85. *Armed Forces:* Temporary Captain, Grenadier Guards 1950–58; Served: Berlin and BAOR 1954–55, Malta 1956–57, Tripoli 1956–57, Suez Campaign 1956-57, Cyprus 1957–58. *Profession:* Farmer/Landowner. *Career:* J. Walter Thompson & Co. Ltd 1958–63; Landowner/Farmer 1963–; Member, Lloyd's. *Councils, Public Bodies:* Councillor, Andover Rural District Council 1964–73; First Deputy-Chairman, Test Valley District Council 1972–74. *Political Career:* PPS: to Ministers of State at the Foreign and Commonwealth Office 1983–85, to Minister for the Civil Service and the Arts 1985; Promoted: Computer Misuse Act 1990 (Private Member's Bill), Civil Aviation (Amendment) Bill 1996. *Select Committees (Current):* Member: Defence 1997– *(Former):* Member: Energy 1990–92, Defence 1992–97; Chairman: Defence 1995–97. *Party Groups:* Vice-Chairman, Winchester Conservative Association 1973–75; Part-time Conservative Research Department 1975–79; Chairman: West Country Conservative Members 1983–84, Conservatives Abroad 1992–97. *International Bodies:* Member, British-Irish Inter-Parliamentary Body 1993–97; Chairman, Committee B on International Affairs; Member, UK Delegation to Council of Europe and Western European Union; Member, Executive Committee, Commonwealth Parliamentary Association (CPA) UK Branch 1999–. *Other:* Member: NFU, CLA Council, British Horse Society, Kennel Club; Chairman, Council for Country Sports 1987–97; Vice-Chairman, British Field Sports Society 1986–94; Governor, Enham Village Centre; President: Andover Arts, Test Valley CPRE; Director: The Royal British Legion Training Company. *Trust:* Fellow, Industry and Parliament Trust. *Miscellaneous:* Executive Member, 1922 Committee 1997–. *Publications: Britain, the view from Westminster* (jointly). *Special Interests:* Defence, Foreign Affairs, Aerospace, Aviation, Civil Aviation, Training, Licensed Trade, Children's Play, Youth Affairs, Countryside, Agriculture, the Elderly. *Countries of Interest:* Canada, Gibraltar, Malta, South Africa, Sudan, USA, Kashmir, Bosnia-Herzegovina, Ireland, India. *Recreations:* Designing and painting, field sports. *Electoral Notes:* Member for Bristol North West 1979–83, for Romsey and Waterside 1983–97, and for Romsey since May 1, 1997. *Clubs:* Turf, Pratt's. *Address:* Michael Colvin Esq, MP, House of Commons, London, SW1A 0AA *Tel:* 020 7219 4208 *Fax:* 020 7219 5946. *Constituency:* 13 Market Place, Romsey, Hampshire, SO51 3AN *Tel:* 01794 512132 *Fax:* 01794 519226 *Website:* www.political.co.uk/michaelcolvin/index.html.

CONNARTY, Michael *(Falkirk East)   Lab majority 13,385*

Son of late Patrick Connarty, electrician, and Elizabeth (née Plunkett). Born September 3, 1947; educated St Patrick's High School, Coatbridge; Stirling University (BA Economics); Jordanhill College of Education (DCE); Glasgow University (DipEd). Married August 9, 1969, Margaret, Depute Director of Education, daughter of Patrick Doran, teacher and former coalminer, and Jessica Doran (1 son 1 daughter). *Trades Union:* Member: TGWU, EIS. *Career:* President, Student Association, Stirling University 1970 71; Teacher of children with special needs 1976–92; Chairman, Stirling Economic Development Co. 1987–90. *Councils, Public Bodies:* Stirling District Council: Councillor 1977–90, Council leader 1980–90; JP 1977–90. *Political Career:*
PPS to Rt Hon. Tom Clarke, as Minister of State, Department for Culture, Media and Sport (Film and Tourism) 1997–98. *Select Committees (Current):* Member: Information 1997–, European Scrutiny 1998– *(Former):* Member: European Directives Committee A (Agriculture, Environment, Health and Safety) 1993–97, Select Committee on Parliamentary Commissioner for Administration 1995–97. *Party Groups:* Member, Labour Party Scottish Exec Committee 1981–82, 1983–92; Chairman, LP Scottish Local Government Committee 1988–90; Member, LP Local Government Committee (UK) 1989–91; Vice-Chairman, COSLA Labour Group 1988–90; Chairman, Stirlingshire Co-operative Party 1990–92; Vice-Chair, Scottish Group of Labour MPs 1996–98, Chairman 1998–99. *International Bodies:* Life Member: International Parliamentary Union 1992–, Commonwealth Parliamentary Association 1992–. *Other:* Loch Lomond, Trossachs and Stirling Tourist Board: Financial Controller 1981–84, Member 1981–90; Member, Socialist Education Association 1978–; Central EIS President 1983–84; National Council EIS 1984–85; Rector, Stirling University 1983–84; Vice-Chairman, Scottish Medical Aid for Palestinians 1988–95. *Miscellaneous:* Board Member, Parliamentary Office of Science and Technology (POST) 1997–. *Special Interests:* Economy and Enterprise, Local Government, European Union, Industry, Skills and Training, Youth Affairs, Students, Crime, Drug Abuse. *Countries of Interest:* Middle East, Central America. *Recreations:* Family, music (jazz and classical), reading, walking. *Electoral Notes:* Contested Stirling 1983 and 1987. Member for Falkirk East since April 9, 1992. *Address:* Michael Connarty Esq, MP, House of Commons, London, SW1A 0AA *Tel:* 020 7219 5071 *Fax:* 020 7219 2541. *Constituency:* 47 Bo'Ness Road, Grangemouth, FK3 8AN *Tel:* 01324 474832 *Fax:* 01324 666811 *E-mail:* mc003@post.almac.co.uk; *Website:* www.mconnartymp.org.uk.

COOK, Francis *(Stockton North)   Lab majority 21,357*

Son of late James Cook. Born November 3, 1935; educated Corby School, Sunderland; De La Salle College, Manchester; Institute of Education, Leeds. Married March 30, 1959, Patricia, daughter of Thomas Lundrigan (1 son 3 daughters) (marriage dissolved). *Trades Union:* Member and Sponsored by MSF. *Career:* Previously: Schoolmaster, Gravedigger, Butlins Redcoat, Barman, Brewery hand, Gardener, Postman, Steel works transport manager; Construction, Planning, Field, Cost Engineer, Project Manager. *Political Career:* A Deputy Speaker, Westminster Hall 1999–. *Whip:* Opposition Whip 1987–92. *Select Committees (Current):* Member: Chairmen's Panel 1997– *(Former):* Member: Procedure 1989–92, Defence 1992–97. *International Bodies:* Member: North Atlantic Assembly, Vice-President 1999–; Organisation for Security and Co-operation in Europe Parliamentary Body. *Other:* Officer, Lucy Faithfull Foundation (for rehabilitation of paedophiles). *Trust:* Fellow, Industry and Parliament Trust. *Special Interests:* Engineering, Peace and Disarmament, Alternative Energy, Expatriate Workers, Pensioners' Rights, Education, Ecology, Race Relations, Landmine Victim Support, Landmine Eradication Measures, Child Protection and Safety, Shooters' Rights. *Countries of Interest:* North Korea, South Korea, Turkey, Laos. *Recreations:* Singing, climbing, fell-walking, swimming. *Electoral Notes:* Member for Stockton North since June 1983. *Address:* Francis Cook Esq, MP, House of Commons, London, SW1A 0AA *Tel:* 020 7219 4527 *Fax:* 020 7219 4303. *Constituency:* c/o The Health Centre, Queensway, Billingham, Teesside, TS23 2LA *Tel:* 01642 643288 *Fax:* 01642 643288 *E-mail:* cookf@parliament.uk.

COOK, The Rt Hon. Robin Finlayson *(Livingston)*   *Lab majority 11,747*

Son of late Peter Cook. Born February 28, 1946; educated Aberdeen Grammar School; University of Edinburgh. Married 1st, September 15, 1969, Margaret Whitmore, Medical Consultant (2 sons) (marriage dissolved 1998); married 2nd, April 9, 1998, Mrs Gaynor Regan, daughter of Alan Mansell Wellings. *Career:* Tutor-organiser, Workers' Educational Association 1970–74. *Councils, Public Bodies:* Edinburgh Town Council: Councillor 1971–74, Chairman, Edinburgh Housing Committee 1973–74. *Political Career:* Shadow Secretary of State for: Health and Social Security 1987–92, Trade and Industry 1992–94, Foreign and Commonwealth Affairs 1994–97; Chair, Parliamentary Labour Party 1997; Secretary of State for Foreign and Commonwealth Affairs 1997–.
Spokesman: Opposition Front Bench Spokesman on: Treasury and Economic Affairs 1980–83, European and Community Affairs 1983–84; Spokesman on the City 1986–87. *Party Groups:* Chairman, Scottish Association of Labour Student Organisations 1966–67; Secretary, Edinburgh City Labour Party 1970–72; Labour Party Campaign Co-ordinator 1984–86; Former Member, Labour Party National Executive Committee. *International Bodies:* Member, Executive Committee, Commonwealth Parliamentary Association (CPA) UK Branch 1999–. *Awards: The Spectator* Parliamentarian of the Year 1991, Debater of the Year 1996. *Honours:* PC 1996. *Special Interests:* Welfare, Environment, Defence. *Recreations:* Reading, eating and talking. *Electoral Notes:* Contested Edinburgh North 1970. Member for Edinburgh Central 1974–83, and for Livingston since June 1983. *Address:* The Rt Hon. Robin Cook, MP, House of Commons, London, SW1A 0AA *Tel:* 020 7219 1500.

COOPER, Yvette *(Pontefract and Castleford)*   *Lab majority 25,725*

Daughter of Tony and June Cooper. Born March 20, 1969; educated Eggars Comprehensive; Balliol College, Oxford (BA Hons, PPE 1st Class); Harvard University (Kennedy Scholar 1991); London School of Economics (MSc Economics). Married January 10, 1998, Ed Balls (1 daughter). *Trades Union:* Member, GMB. *Profession:* Journalist/Economist. *Career:* Economic Researcher for Rt Hon. John Smith, QC, MP 1990–92; Domestic Policy Specialist, Bill Clinton Presidential Campaign 1992; Policy Adviser to Labour Treasury Teams 1992–94; Economic Columnist/Leader Writer, *The Independent* 1995–97. *Political Career:* Parliamentary Under-Secretary of State, Department of Health (Minister for Public Health) 1999–. *Select Committees (Former):* Member: Education and Employment 1997–99, Employment Sub-Committee 1997–99. *Miscellaneous:* Member, Intelligence and Security Committee 1997–99. *Special Interests:* Unemployment, Coal Industry. *Countries of Interest:* USA. *Recreations:* Swimming, painting, watching soap operas. *Electoral Notes:* Member for Pontefract and Castleford since May 1, 1997. *Address:* Yvette Cooper, MP, House of Commons, London, SW1A 0AA *Tel:* 020 7219 5080 *Fax:* 020 7219 0912. *Constituency:* 2 Wesley Street, Castleford, West Yorkshire, WF10 1AE *Tel:* 01977 553388 *Fax:* 01977 553388.

CORBETT, Robin *(Birmingham Erdington)*   *Lab majority 12,657*

Son of late Thomas Corbett, foundry worker. Born December 22, 1933; educated Holly Lodge Grammar School, Smethwick, Staffordshire. Married May 1970, Val Hudson, daughter of Fred Jonas (1 son 2 daughters). *Trades Union:* Member, National Executive Council, National Union of Journalists 1964–69. *Armed Forces:* National Service RAF 1951–53. *Profession:* Journalist/Writer. *Career:* Journalist; Communications Consultant; Senior Labour Adviser, IPC Magazines; Editorial Staff Development Executive, ICP Magazines; Assistant Editor, *Farmers Weekly.* *Whip:* Former West Midlands Labour Whip. *Spokesman:* Opposition Front Bench Deputy Spokesman on Home Affairs 1987–92; Opposition Front Bench Spokesman on: National Heritage, Broadcasting and Press 1992–94, Disabled People's Rights 1994–95. *Select Committees (Current):* Chairman: Home Affairs 1997–99; Member: Liaison 1999– *(Former):* Member: Agriculture 1995–97; Chairman: Home Affairs 1997–99. *Party Groups:* Member, Parliamentary Labour Party Campaign Unit 1984–85. *Other:* Former Chairman, Farm Animal Welfare Co-ordinating Executive;

Member, Committee for the Reform of Animal Experiments; Former Council Member, Save the Children Fund; Director, Rehab UK. *Trust:* Fellow, Industry and Parliament Trust. *Publications: Can I Count on Your Support?* (for Save the Children Fund, with wife), 1986; *Tales from the Campaign Trail* (co-author, for Save the Children Fund). *Special Interests:* Home Affairs, Police, Civil Liberties, Motor Industry, Manufacturing, Disabled/Disability, Children's Rights, Alternative Energy, Environment, Agriculture, Animal Welfare, Press. *Countries of Interest:* Australia, Cyprus, India, New Zealand, South Africa. *Recreations:* Collecting bric-a-brac, walking. *Electoral Notes:* Member for Hemel Hempstead 1974–79, and for Birmingham Erdington since June 1983. *Clubs:* Castle Vale Residents', Forget Me-Not. *Address:* Robin Corbett Esq, MP, House of Commons, London, SW1A 0AA *Tel:* 020 7219 3420 *Fax:* 020 7219 2461. *Constituency:* 50a Reservoir Road, Erdington, Birmingham, B23 6DG *Tel:* 0121-373 1147 *Fax:* 0121-382 6347.

CORBYN, Jeremy *(Islington North)   Lab majority 19,955*

Son of David Benjamin and Naomi Loveday Jocelyn Corbyn. Born May 26, 1949; educated Adams Grammar School, Newport, Shropshire. (3 sons). *Trades Union:* Former full-time organiser, National Union of Public Employees; Also worked for Tailor and Garment workers and AUEW; NUPE sponsored MP. *Councils, Public Bodies:* Haringey Borough Council: Chairman: Community Development 1975–78, Public Works 1978–79, Planning 1980–81. *Select Committees (Former):* Member: Social Security 1991–97. *Special Interests:* People of Islington, Defence, Welfare State, Health Service, Campaigning for socialism in the community and against racism, Anti-imperialism and Internationalism, Safe Transport Systems in Cities, Environment, Irish Affairs, Liberation Islington Local Agenda 21. *Recreations:* Running, railways. *Electoral Notes:* Member for Islington North since June 1983. *Address:* Jeremy Corbyn Esq, MP, House of Commons, London, SW1A 0AA *Tel:* 020 7219 3545 *Tel (Constituency):* 020 7263 9450.

CORMACK, Sir Patrick Thomas *(South Staffordshire)   Con majority 7,821*

Son of late Thomas C. Cormack, local government officer. Born May 18, 1939; educated St James' Choir School; Havelock School, Grimsby; University of Hull (BA Hons 1961). Married August 18, 1967, Kathleen Mary McDonald (2 sons). *Profession:* Schoolmaster and Writer. *Career:* Industrial Consultant; Company Director; Second Master, St James' Choir School, Grimsby 1961–66; Training and Education Officer, Ross Group Ltd. 1966–67; Assistant Housemaster, Wrekin College, Shropshire 1967–69; Head of History, Brewood Grammar School, Staffordshire 1969–70; Associate Editor, *Time and Tide* 1977–79; Editor, *The House Magazine* 1983–; Visiting Lecturer, University of Texas 1984; Elected to Visiting Parliamentary Fellowship, St Anthony's College, Oxford 1994; Visiting Senior Lecturer, University of Hull 1994–; International President, *First* magazine 1994–. *Political Career:* PPS to the Joint Parliamentary Secretaries, Department of Health and Social Security 1970–73; Deputy to the Shadow Leader of the House of Commons 1997–. *Spokesman:* Spokesman on Constitutional Affairs 1997–. *Select Committees (Current):* Member: Accommodation and Works 1987–, Parliamentary Privilege (Joint Committee) 1997– *(Former):* Member: House of Commons Services 1979–92, Speaker's Panel of Chairmen 1983–97; Chairman: House of Commons Works of Art 1987–97; Member: Chairmen's Panel 1997–98, Modernisation of the House of Commons 1997–98. *International Bodies:* Vice-Chairman, De Burght Conference; Member, Council for Peace in the Balkans 1992–; Member, Executive Committee, Commonwealth Parliamentary Association (CPA) UK Branch 1997–99, Joint Vice-Chairman 1999–. *Other:* Member, Council of Historical Association 1963–66; Founder and Vice-Chairman, Heritage in Danger 1974–97; Member, Historic Buildings Council 1979–84; Chairman, Council for Independent Education from 1980–95; Member: Royal Commission on Historical Manuscripts 1981–, General Synod of the Church of England 1995–. *Trust:* Trustee, Historic Churches Preservation Trust 1973–; Member, Council of Winston Churchill Memorial Trust 1983–93; Trustee, Museum of Garden History; President, Staffordshire Historic Churches Trust. *Miscellaneous:* Member: Institute of Journalists 1979–89, Royal Commission on Historical Manuscripts 1981–, Lord Chancellor's Advisory Committee on Public Records 1982–87. Member, Worshipful Company of Glaziers. Freeman, City of London 1980. *Honours:* Hon. Citizen of Texas 1985; Knighted 1995; Commander of the Order of the Lion (Finland) 1998. Fellow, Society of Antiquaries 1978, Vice-President 1994–98. *Publications:*

Heritage in Danger, 1976; *Right Turn,* 1978; *Westminster: Palace and Parliament,* 1981; *Castles of Britain* 1982; *Wilberforce – The Nation's Conscience,* 1983; *English Cathedrals 1984. Special Interests:* Arts, Heritage, Defence and NATO, Parliamentary History, Education, Electoral Reform, Industrial Relations, Human Rights. *Countries of Interest:* Bosnia, former Soviet Union, Croatia, Finland, Netherlands, Lithuania, USA. *Recreations:* Walking, talking, fighting Philistines. *Electoral Notes:* Contested Bolsover 1964 and Grimsby 1966. Member for Cannock division 1970–74, for South-West Staffordshire 1974–83 and for South Staffordshire since June 1983. *Clubs:* Athenaeum. *Address:* Sir Patrick Cormack, FSA, MP, House of Commons, London, SW1A 0AA *Tel:* 020 7219 5514. *Constituency:* The Firs, Codsall, Staffordshire, WV8 1BX *Tel:* 01902 844985 *Fax:* 01902 844949.

CORSTON, Jean *(Bristol East)* *Lab majority 16,159*

Daughter of Laurie Parkin, trade union official, and late Eileen Parkin. Born May 5, 1942; educated Yeovil Girls' High School; London School of Economics (LLB 1989); Inns of Court School of Law 1989–90; Open University. Married 1st, September 23, 1961, Christopher Corston (1 son 1 daughter); married 2nd, January 4, 1985, Professor Peter Townsend. *Trades Union:* Member, TGWU. *Profession:* Barrister. *Career:* Barrister. *Political Career:* Joint PPS to Rt Hon. David Blunkett, MP, as Secretary of State for Education and Employment 1997–. *Select Committees (Former):* Member: Agriculture 1992–95, Home Affairs 1995–97. *Party Groups:* Joined Labour Party 1958; Organiser, Taunton Labour Party 1974–76; South West Region Labour Party: Assistant Regional Organiser 1976–81, Regional Organiser 1981–85; Assistant National Agent, The Labour Party, London 1985–86; Secretary, Labour Party Annual Conference Arrangements 1985–86; Deputy Chair, PLP 1997–98. *International Bodies:* Associate Member, British-Irish Inter-Parliamentary Body; Member, Executive Committee, Commonwealth Parliamentary Association (CPA) UK Branch 1999–. *Special Interests:* Employment Law, Legal Reform, Women's Rights, Disabled/Disability. *Countries of Interest:* India, Kenya, USA. *Recreations:* Gardening, reading, walking. *Electoral Notes:* Member for Bristol East since April 9, 1992. *Address:* Jean Corston, MP, House of Commons, London, SW1A 0AA *Tel:* 020 7219 4575 *Fax:* 020 7219 4878. *Constituency:* PO Box 1105, Bristol, BS99 2DP *Tel:* 0117–939 9901 *Fax:* 0117–939 9902.

COTTER, Brian Joseph *(Weston-Super-Mare)* *LD majority 1,274*

Son of late Michael Joseph and late Mary Cotter. Born August 24, 1938; educated Downside School; London Polytechnic, Business Studies. Married Eyleen Patricia, daughter of Mr and Mrs Len Wade (2 sons 1 daughter). *Profession:* Company Director. *Career:* Plasticable Ltd: Sales Manager, Managing Director. *Councils, Public Bodies:* Councillor, Woking Borough Council 1986–90. *Spokesman:* A Spokesman for Trade and Industry: (Small Business and Millennium Bug) 1997–99, (Small Business) 1999–. *Select Committees (Current):* Member: Deregulation 1997–. *Party Groups:* Member: Lib Dem Parliamentary Association, ASLDC, Green Liberal Democrat Association. *Special Interests:* Business, Tourism, Disabled/Disability, Youth Affairs. *Recreations:* Reading, walking, gardening, films. *Electoral Notes:* Contested Weston-Super-Mare 1992. Member for Weston-Super-Mare since May 1, 1997. *Clubs:* National Liberal. *Address:* Brian Cotter Esq, MP, House of Commons, London, SW1A 0AA *Tel:* 020 7219 5127 *Fax:* 020 7219 2277. *Constituency:* 8a Alexandra Parade, Weston-super-Mare, Somerset, BS23 1QT *Tel:* 01934 419200 *Fax:* 01934 419300 *E-mail:* briancottermp@liberty.compulink.co.uk.

Dod *on* Disk

The Vacher Dod Parliamentary Database – configured for PC or Network

For further details please telephone the Westminster Office

020 7828 7256

COUSINS, James MacKay *(Newcastle upon Tyne Central)   Lab majority 16,480*

Son of late Charles John Cousins, printing trade worker, and late Grace Ellen Cousins. Born February 23, 1944; educated New College, Oxford; London School of Economics. Married Anne Elizabeth (2 sons, 1 step-son, 1 step-daughter). *Career:* Industrial relations and research worker in industry 1967–72; Research worker, urban affairs and city labour markets 1972–82; Lecturer, Sunderland Polytechnic 1982–87. *Councils, Public Bodies:* Councillor, Wallsend Borough Council 1969–73; Tyne and Wear County Council: Councillor 1973–86, Deputy leader 1981–86. *Spokesman:* Opposition Front Bench Spokesman on: Trade and Industry 1992–94, Foreign and Commonwealth Affairs 1994–95. *Select Committees (Current):* Member: Treasury 1997–, Treasury Sub-Committee 1998– *(Former):* Member: Trade and Industry 1989–92, Public Service 1995–97. *Party Groups:* Chair, Northern Group of Labour MPs 1997–. *Special Interests:* Health, Science, Arms Control. *Countries of Interest:* Czechoslovakia, Ethiopia, Iran, Central Asian Republics. *Recreations:* Composting. *Electoral Notes:* Member for Newcastle upon Tyne Central since June 1987. *Address:* Jim Cousins Esq, MP, House of Commons, London, SW1A 0AA *Tel:* 020 7219 4204 *Fax:* 020 7219 6290. *Constituency:* 1st Floor, 21 Portland Terrace, Newcastle upon Tyne, NE2 1QQ *Tel:* 0191–281 9888 *Fax:* 0191–281 3383 *E-mail:* jcousins@globalnet.co.uk.

COX, Thomas Michael *(Tooting)   Lab majority 15,011*

Born January 19, 1930; educated State schools; London School of Economics. *Career:* Electrical Worker. *Councils, Public Bodies:* Former Alderman, Fulham Borough Council. *Whip:* Assistant Whip 1974–77; Lord Commissioner of the Treasury 1977–79. *International Bodies:* Member, UK Delegation of the Council of Europe and Western European Union; Representative, UK Delegation to Organisation for Security and Co-operation in Europe; Executive Committee Member, IPU British Group; Member, Executive Committee, Commonwealth Parliamentary Association (CPA) UK Branch 1999–. *Electoral Notes:* Contested Stroud 1966 General Election. Member for Wandsworth Central 1970–74, and for Tooting since 1974. *Address:* Thomas Cox Esq, MP, House of Commons, London, SW1A 0AA *Tel:* 020 7219 5034.

CRAN, James Douglas *(Beverley and Holderness)   Con majority 1,211*

Son of late James and Jane Macdonald-Cran. Born January 28, 1944; educated Ruthrieston School, Aberdeen (Dux Medallion Winner); King's College, University of Aberdeen (MA Hons). Married April 7, 1973, Penelope Barbara, daughter of Richard and Barbara Wilson (1 daughter). *Career:* Conservative Research Department 1970–71; Secretary and Chief Executive, National Association of Pension Funds 1971–79; CBI: Northern Director 1979–84, West Midlands Director 1984–87. *Councils, Public Bodies:* Councillor, London Borough of Sutton 1974–79, Chairman, Health and Housing Committee. *Political Career:* PPS to Rt Hon. Sir Patrick Mayhew, MP, as Secretary of State for Northern Ireland 1995–96. *Whip:* An Opposition Whip (Home Office, Northern Ireland: Northern and Yorkshire) 1997–98; Opposition Whip for Northern Ireland and Pairing Whip 1998–. *Select Committees (Current):* Member: Selection 1998– *(Former):* Member: Trade and Industry 1987–92, Northern Ireland Affairs 1994–95, Administration 1997–98, Selection 1998. *Other:* Member of Court: University of Birmingham 1984–87, University of Hull 1987–. *Trust:* Fellow, Armed Forces Parliamentary Scheme 1992; Council Member, Pensions Trustee Forum 1992–95; Fellow, Industry and Parliament Trust 1994. *Miscellaneous:* Treasurer, European Research Group 1994–97. *Honours:* OStJ. *Special Interests:* Trade and Industry, Pensions, Regional Policy, European Union, Irish Affairs, Economic Policy. *Countries of Interest:* Canada, Europe, Hong Kong, Taiwan, USA, Mexico, China. *Recreations:* Travelling, reading biographies and autobiographies, military history. *Electoral Notes:* Contested Glasgow Shettleston 1974 and Gordon 1983. Member for Beverley 1987–97, and for Beverley and Holderness since May 1, 1997. *Address:* James Cran Esq, MP, House of Commons, London, SW1A 0AA *Tel:* 020 7219 4445. *Constituency:* 9 Cross Street, Beverley, East Yorkshire *Tel:* 01482 881316.

CRANSTON, Ross Frederick, QC *(Dudley North)   Lab majority 9,457*

Son of F H and E E Cranston. Born July 23, 1948; educated University of Queensland; Harvard Law School; Oxford (DCL 1998). Divorced. *Trades Union:* Member: GMB, AUT. *Profession:* Lawyer and Academic. *Career:* Barrister, Gray's Inn 1976; Professor of Law (University of London, Queen Mary College, London School of Economics) 1986–97; Practising Barrister, Gray's Inn; Assistant Recorder 1991–97; Recorder 1997–98; QC 1998–. *Political Career:* Solicitor General 1998–. *Select Committees (Former):* Member: Home Affairs 1997–98, Home Affairs 1998. *International Bodies:* Consultant (1988–97) to: UNCTAD, Commonwealth Secretariat, World Bank, IMF. *Other:* President, Society of Public Teachers of Law 1992–93. *Trust:* Chair, Trustees of Public Concern at Work (The Whistleblowers Charity) 1996–97. *Miscellaneous:* Consultant to Woolf Inquiry into Access to Justice 1994–96. *Publications: Regulating Business,* 1979; *Consumers and the Law,* 2nd edition 1985; *Legal Foundations of the Welfare State,* 1985; *Legal Ethics and Professional Responsibility,* editor 1995; *Principles of Banking Law,* 1997. *Special Interests:* Home Affairs, Legal Affairs, Treasury. *Electoral Notes:* Contested Richmond, Yorkshire 1992. Member for Dudley North since May 1, 1997. *Address:* Ross Cranston Esq, QC, MP, House of Commons, London, SW1A 0AA *Tel:* 020 7219 4195 *Fax:* 020 7219 2726. *Constituency:* Holloway Chambers, 28 Priory Street, Dudley, West Midlands, DY1 1EZ *Tel:* 01384 233100 *Fax:* 01384 233 099.

CRAUSBY, David *(Bolton North East)   Lab majority 12,669*

Son of late Thomas Crausby, factory worker/club steward, and of Kathleen Crausby, cotton worker. Born June 17, 1946; educated Derby Grammar School, Bury; Bury Technical College. Married September 4, 1965, Enid, daughter of William and Anne Noon (2 sons). *Trades Union:* Shop Steward/Works Convenor, AEEU; Full-time Works Convenor 1978–97. *Profession:* Engineer. *Councils, Public Bodies:* Councillor, Bury Council 1979–92, Chair of Housing 1985–92. *Select Committees (Current):* Member: Administration 1997–, Social Security 1999–. *Miscellaneous:* Member, European Standing Committee C 1999–. *Special Interests:* Industrial Relations, Pensions, Housing. *Electoral Notes:* Contested Bury North 1987 and Bolton North East 1992. Member for Bolton North East since May 1, 1997. *Address:* David Crausby Esq, MP, House of Commons, London, SW1A 0AA *Tel:* 020 7219 4092 *Fax:* 020 7219 3713. *Constituency:* 60 St George's Road, Bolton, Greater Manchester *Tel:* 01204 523574 *Fax:* 01204 523574.

CRYER, (Constance) Ann *(Keighley)   Lab majority 7,132*

Daughter of late Allen and late Margaret Ann Place. Born December 14, 1939; educated St John's Church of England Primary School; Spring Bank Secondary Modern, Darwen; Bolton Technical College; Keighley Technical College (part-time). Married August 3, 1963, Bob Cryer, MP for Keighley and Bradford South (died 1994), son of John Arthur and Gladys Evelyn (1 son 1 daughter). *Trades Union:* Member, TGWU. *Career:* Clerk: ICI Ltd 1955–60, GPO 1960–64; Personal Assistant, Member of Parliament and Member of European Parliament 1974–94. *Councils, Public Bodies:* Member, Darwen Borough Council 1962–65; JP, Bradford Bench, appointed 1996. *Party Groups:* Member: Labour Party 1958–, Co-operative Party 1965–; Chair, PLP CND Group. *International Bodies:* Delegate, Parliamentary Assembly of the Council of Europe 1997–; Member, Legal Affairs on Human Rights Committee 1997–. *Other:* Former Governor: Shipley Church of England First School, Frizinghall First School; President, Keighley and Worth Valley Railway Preservation Society; Member: Friends of the Earth, CND, Brontë Society. *Trust:* Contributor to Canon Collins' Educational Trust for South Africa; Trustee, Keighley Bus Museum Trust. *Miscellaneous:* Member: Social Security Appeal Tribunal 1987–96, Keighley Business Forum. *Publications:* Compiled *Boldness Be My Friend – remembering Bob Cryer,* 1997. *Special Interests:* Early Years Education, Health, Benefits, Railways, Planning. *Countries of Interest:* South Africa, Pakistan, Afghanistan, Palestine. *Recreations:* Gardening, theatre, cinema, time with my six grandchildren, walking. *Electoral Notes:* Member for Keighley since May 1, 1997. *Address:* Mrs Ann Cryer, MP, House of Commons, London, SW1A 0AA *Tel:* 020 7219 6649. *Constituency:* Bob Cryer House, 35 Devonshire Street, Keighley, West Yorkshire *Tel:* 01535 210083 *Fax:* 01535 210085.

CRYER, John *(Hornchurch)   Lab majority 5,680*

Son of late Bob Cryer, Labour MP for Keighley 1974–83 and Bradford South 1987–94, and of Ann Cryer, MP for Keighley 1997– *(qv)*. Born April 11, 1964; educated Oakbank School, Keighley; Hatfield Polytechnic (BA Literature and History 1985); London College of Printing (Postgraduate Certificate in Print Journalism). Married Narinder Bains (2 sons 1 daughter). *Trades Union:* Member: TGWU 1986-, NUJ 1988-, UCATT 1997-. *Profession:* Journalist and Underwriter. *Career:* Journalist with: *Tribune* 1992–96, *Morning Star* 1989–92; Freelance Journalist with: *Labour Briefing* (editor), *Guardian*, *GMPU Journal, T&G Record*; Lloyd's of London Publications. *Select Committees (Current):* Member: Deregulation 1997–. *Party Groups:* Member, Labour Party, holding office in many positions 1979–; Member, Executive of Labour Euro Safeguards Committee; Press Officer, For Defend Clause Four Campaign 1995; Member, Co-operative Party. *Other:* Member: CND, Amnesty International, Transport on Water, Tibet Support Group, Keighley and Worth Valley Railway, RAF Hornchurch Association; Patron, St Frances Hospice. *Sportsclubs:* Member: House of Commons Cricket Club, House of Commons Rugby Club. *Publications:* Co-author, *Boldness be my Friend (Life of Bob Cryer, MP)*, 1996; Many articles mainly in political publications. *Special Interests:* Employment, Social Security, Education, Further and Higher Education, European Union, Health, Economic Policy, Industry, Coal Industry, Transport. *Countries of Interest:* Australia, India. *Recreations:* Swimming, reading, sport, old cars, cinema. *Electoral Notes:* Member for Hornchurch since May 1, 1997. *Address:* John Cryer Esq, MP, House of Commons, London, SW1A 0AA *Tel:* 020 7219 6988/1134 *Fax:* 020 7219 1183. *Constituency:* 11 Park Lane, Hornchurch, Essex *Tel:* 01708 742674 *Fax:* 01708 735576.

CUMMINGS, John Scott *(Easington)   Lab majority 30,012*

Son of late George and Mary Cummings, née Cain. Born July 6, 1943; educated Murton Council Infant, Junior, Senior Schools. *Trades Union:* Sponsored by NUM. *Career:* Murton Colliery 1958–87, Colliery Electrician and Secretary 1967–87. *Councils, Public Bodies:* Councillor, Easington Rural District Council 1970–73; Easington District Council: Councillor 1973–87, Chairman 1975–76, Leader 1979–87; Member: Northumbrian Water Authority 1977–83, Peterlee and Aycliffe Development Corporation 1980–87. *Whip:* Opposition Whip (Northern and Overseas Development) 1994–97. *Select Committees (Current):* Member: Environment, Transport and Regional Affairs 1997–, Environment Sub-Committee 1997–. *Party Groups:* Chairman, Northern Regional Group of Labour MPs 1999–. *International Bodies:* Member: Council of Europe 1992–, Western European Union 1992–. *Other:* Vice-Chairman, Coalfield Communities Campaign 1985–87. *Special Interests:* Energy, Environment, Coal Industry. *Countries of Interest:* Eastern Europe, Middle East. *Recreations:* Jack Russell terriers, walking, travel. *Electoral Notes:* Member for Easington since June 1987. *Address:* John Cummings Esq, MP, House of Commons, London, SW1A 0AA *Tel:* 020 7219 5122. *Constituency:* Seaton Holme, Easington Village, County Durham *Tel:* 01915 273773.

CUNLIFFE, Lawrence Francis *(Leigh)   Lab majority 24,496*

Born March 25, 1929; educated St. Edmund's Roman Catholic School, Worsley, Manchester; Ruskin College, Oxford (Economics, Industrial Relations). Married April 11, 1950, Winifred Haslem (3 sons 2 daughters) (marriage dissolved 1983). *Career:* Engineer, NCB 1949–79. *Councils, Public Bodies:* Councillor: Farnworth Borough Council 1960–74, Bolton Metropolitan District Council 1974–79; Magistrate 1967–79. *Whip:* Opposition Whip 1981–87. *International Bodies:* Deputy Leader, UK Delegation to Council of Europe and Western Europe Union. *Special Interests:* Energy, Industry, Aerospace, Aviation. *Recreations:* Cricket, football, swimming. *Electoral Notes:* Contested Rochdale October 1972 By-election and in February 1974. Member for Leigh since May, 1979. *Address:* Lawrence Cunliffe Esq, MP, House of Commons, London, SW1A 0AA *Tel:* 020 7219 4185.

CUNNINGHAM, The Rt Hon. Dr Jack (John A.) *(Copeland)   Lab majority 11,996*

Son of Andrew Cunningham. Born August 4, 1939; educated Jarrow Grammar School; Bede College, Durham University (BSc, PhD Chemistry). Married 1964, Maureen (1 son 2 daughters). *Trades Union:* Full-time Officer, GMWU 1969–70. *Career:* Research Fellow, Durham University 1966–68. *Councils, Public Bodies:* DL, Cumbria 1991. *Political Career:* PPS to the Rt Hon. James Callaghan, MP 1974–76; Parliamentary Under-Secretary for Energy 1976–79; Shadow Environment Secretary 1983–89; Shadow Leader, House of Commons and Campaigns Co-ordinator 1989–92; Shadow Secretary of State for: Foreign and Commonwealth Affairs 1992–94, Trade and Industry 1994–95, National Heritage 1995–97; Minister of Agriculture, Fisheries and Food 1997–98;

Minister for the Cabinet Office, and Chancellor of the Duchy of Lancaster 1998–99; Commissioner, Millennium Commission 1998–. *Spokesman:* Opposition Front Bench Spokesman on Industry 1979–83. *Select Committees (Former):* Member: Privileges 1989–95. *Trust:* Fellow, Industry and Parliament Trust. *Honours:* PC 1993. *Special Interests:* Regional Policy, Environment, Foreign Affairs. *Countries of Interest:* China, Japan, South Africa, Europe, USA. *Recreations:* Fell-walking, gardening, music, reading, fishing. *Electoral Notes:* Member for Whitehaven 1970–83, and for Copeland since June 1983. *Address:* The Rt Hon. Dr Jack Cunningham, DL, MP, House of Commons, London, SW1A 0AA *Tel:* 020 7219 3000 *Tel (Constituency):* 01946 62024.

CUNNINGHAM, James *(Coventry South)   Lab majority 10,953*

Son of Adam and Elizabeth Cunningham. Born February 4, 1941; educated Columbia High School, Coatbridge; Tillycoultry College, Ruskin Courses (Labour Movement, Industrial Law). Married March 1, 1985, Marion Douglas, daughter of Frank and Nancy Podmore (1 son 1 stepson 1 daughter 1 stepdaughter). *Trades Union:* Trade unionist for over 27 years; Shop steward 1968–88. *Profession:* Engineer. *Career:* Engineer. *Councils, Public Bodies:* Coventry City Council: Councillor 1972–92, Chairman, Consumer Services Committee 1975–77, Vice-Chairman, Finance Committee 1975–77, 1979–82, 1985–88, Vice-Chairman, Leisure Committee 1975–77, Chairman 1979–82, Vice-Chairman, Transportation and Highways Committee 1983–85, Chief Whip, Labour Group 1985–87, Deputy

Leader of the Council 1987–88, Leader of the Council 1988–92. *Select Committees (Current):* Member: Trade and Industry 1997–, Chairmen's Panel 1998– *(Former):* Member: Home Affairs 1993–97. *Party Groups:* Joined Labour Party 1966; Coventry South East CLP: Secretary 1976–77, Chairman 1977–79. *Special Interests:* Economic Policy, European Union, Industrial Relations, Health Service. *Countries of Interest:* USA, Eastern Europe, Russia. *Recreations:* Walking, reading, historical buildings. *Electoral Notes:* Member for Coventry South East 1992–97, and for Coventry South since May 1, 1997. *Address:* James Cunningham Esq, MP, House of Commons, London, SW1A 0AA *Tel:* 020 7219 6362 *Fax:* 020 7219 6362. *Constituency:* 2nd Floor, 107 New Union Street, Coventry, CV1 2NT *Tel:* 024 7655 3159 *Fax:* 024 7655 3159.

CUNNINGHAM, Roseanna *(Perth)   SNP majority 3,141*

Daughter of late Hugh Cunningham, and of Catherine Cunningham. Born July 27, 1951; educated University of Western Australia (Hons Degree in Politics); Edinburgh University (Degree in Law); Aberdeen University (Diploma in Legal Practice). *Trades Union:* Former convenor and shop steward for NALGO Member, NUJ. *Career:* SNP Research Department 1977–79; Solicitor: Dumbarton District Council 1983–86, Glasgow District Council 1986–89; Private practice as a solicitor 1989–; Called as Advocate 1990. *Spokesman:* SNP Spokeswoman for: Home Affairs 1995–, Environment and Land Reform, Arts and Broadcasting 1997–, Employment 1998, Women's Issues 1998–. *Party Groups:* Former SNP branch and constituency office holder; Member

SNP national executive. *Miscellaneous:* Former Member, European Standing Committee B. *Special Interests:* Constitution, Land. *Recreations:* Martial Art Aikido, reading – especially science fiction, cinema. *Electoral Notes:* Contested Perth and Kinross 1992 General Election. Member for Perth and Kinross May 25, 1995 By-election–1997, and for Perth since May 1, 1997. MSP for Perth since May 6, 1999. *Address:* Roseanna Cunningham, MP, MSP, House of Commons, London, SW1A 0AA *Tel:* 020 7219 3000. *Constituency:* 51 York Place, Perth, PH2 8EH *Tel:* 01738 444002 *Fax:* 01738 444602 *E-mail:* rcmp.perth@snp.org.uk; roseanna.cunningham.msp@scottish.parliament.uk.

CURRY, The Rt Hon. David Maurice *(Skipton and Ripon)*   Con majority 11,620

Son of Thomas Harold and late Florence Joan Curry (née Tyerman). Born June 13, 1944; educated Ripon Grammar School; Corpus Christi College, Oxford; Kennedy School of Government, Harvard University. Married July 24, 1971, Anne Helene Maude, daughter of late Yahn Roullet and Madame Madelaine Chambaud (1 son twin daughters). *Career:* Newspaper Reporter, *Newcastle Journal* 1966–70; *Financial Times*: World Trade Editor, International Companies Editor, Brussels Correspondent, Paris Correspondent 1970–79; Freelance Journalist. *Political Career:* Ministry of Agriculture, Fisheries and Food: Parliamentary Secretary 1989–92, Minister of State 1992–93; Minister of State, Department of the Environment for: Local Government and Planning 1993–94, Local Government, Housing and Urban Regeneration 1994–97; Shadow Minister of Agriculture, Fisheries and Food June-November 1997. *Spokesman:* Conservative Spokesman, Budget Committee 1984–89. *Select Committees (Current):* Member: Agriculture 1998–, Public Accounts 1999–. *International Bodies:* General rapporteur, EEC Budget for 1987. *Miscellaneous:* Director, British Association for Central and Eastern Europe; Vice-President, Local Government Association. *Honours:* PC 1996. *Publications: The Conservative Tradition in Europe*, 1988; *Lobbying Government*, 1999. *Special Interests:* Agriculture, Finance, Foreign Affairs, Trade. *Recreations:* Vegetable gardening, windsurfing. *Electoral Notes:* Contested Morpeth twice in 1974. MEP for Essex North East 1979–89. Member for Skipton and Ripon since June 1987. *Address:* The Rt Hon. David Curry, MP, House of Commons, London, SW1A 0AA *Tel:* 020 7219 5164. *Constituency:* 19 Otley Street, Skipton, North Yorks, BD23 1DY *Tel:* 01756 792092 *E-mail:* currydm@parliament.uk.

CURTIS-THOMAS, Claire *(Crosby)*   Lab majority 7,182

Daughter of Joyce Curtis-Thomas. Born April 30, 1958; educated Mynyddbach Comprehensive School For Girls, Swansea; University College, Cardiff (BSc Mechanical Engineering); Aston University (MBA Business Administration); Staffordshire University (PhD Technology); Senator, Engineering Council. Married Michael Lewis (1 son 2 daughters). *Trades Union:* Member, TGWU. *Profession:* University Dean. *Career:* Chartered Engineer; Head, Strategic Planning, Birmingham City Council; Shell Chemicals: Head, Environmental Affairs, Head, Distribution UK Ltd; Dean, Faculty of Business and Engineering, University of Wales College; Newport. *Councils, Public Bodies:* Councillor, Crewe and Nantwich Borough Council 1995–97. *Select Committees (Current):* Member: Science and Technology 1997–. *Party Groups:* Member: Co-operative Party, Fabian Society, Labour Women's Network; Membership Secretary, Rossett and Marford Labour Party; Secretary, Eddisbury Constituency Labour Party. *Other:* Member: Soroptimist International, Amnesty International, Women's Engineering Society, National Trust; Advisor, Control Division, Institution of Electrical Engineers. *Trust:* Member, two Education Trusts to promote science and engineering to the public (Founder and Chair of one, Founder and President of the other). *Miscellaneous:* Changed surname to Curtis-Thomas instead of Curtis-Tansley from May 1997. *Fellowships, etc:* CEng; FIMechE; Hon. FRICS. *Special Interests:* Economic Policy, Trade and Industry, Education, Foreign Affairs. *Countries of Interest:* USA, Pan-Pacific Nations, Malaysia, China. *Recreations:* Family. *Electoral Notes:* Member for Crosby since May 1, 1997 (Contested the seat as Claire Curtis-Tansley). *Address:* Claire Curtis-Thomas, MP, House of Commons, London, SW1A 0AA *Tel:* 020 7219 4193. *Constituency:* The Minster, 16 Beach Lawn, Waterloo, Liverpool, L22 8QA *Tel:* 0151–928 7250 *Fax:* 0151–928 9325.

Dod *on* Disk
The Vacher Dod Parliamentary Database
that will run on your PC or Network
For further details please telephone the Westminster Office
020 7828 7256

D

DAFIS, Cynog Glyndwr *(Ceredigion)* * *PC majority 6,961*

Son of late Rev. George and Annie Davies. Born April 1, 1938; educated Aberaeron Primary; County Secondary School; Neath Boys' Grammar School; University College of Wales, Aberystwyth. Married January 1, 1962, Llinos Iorwerth, daughter of Iorwerth and Eluned Jones (2 sons 1 daughter). *Career:* Teacher of English and Welsh, Pontardawe College of Further Education 1960–62; Head of English, Newcastle Emlyn Secondary Modern School, Dyfed 1962–80; Teacher of English, Aberaeron Comprehensive 1980–84; Head of English, Dyffryn Teifi Comprehensive School, Llandysul, Dyfed 1984–91; Research Officer, Department of Adult Continuing Education, University College, Swansea 1991–92. *Spokesman:* Spokesman for Environment and the Regions, Transport, Education and Employment, International Development, Energy, Culture, Media and Sport 1997–2000. *Select Committees (Former):* Member: Welsh Affairs 1995–97, Education and Employment 1997–98, Environmental Audit 1997–2000. *Miscellaneous:* Chair, GLOBE UK. *Special Interests:* Language and Culture, Environment, Wales, Education, Decentralisation of Government. *Countries of Interest:* Turkey. *Recreations:* Reading literature, listening to music, walking, jogging. *Electoral Notes:* Member for Ceredigion and Pembroke North 1992–97, and for Ceredigion 1997–2000 (*resigned January 2000). AM for the Region of Wales Mid and West since May 6, 1999.

DALYELL, Tam *(Linlithgow)* *Lab majority 10,838*

Son of late Gordon Dalyell, Indian Civil Servant and late Eleanor Dalyell. Born August 9, 1932; educated Edinburgh Academy, Harecroft; Eton College; King's College, Cambridge (MA 1956); Moray House, Edinburgh; Hon. DSc, Edinburgh University 1994; Hon. Doctorate, City University, London 1998. Married December 1963, Kathleen, only daughter of late Rt Hon. Lord Wheatley, Lord Justice Clerk of Scotland (1 son 1 daughter). *Trades Union:* Member: EIS, RMT. *Armed Forces:* National Service, Royal Scots Greys 1950–52. *Profession:* Teacher. *Career:* Deputy-Director of Studies, BI ship-school, Dunera, 1961-April 1962. *Political Career:* PPS to Rt Hon. Richard Crossman 1964–65, 1967–70. *Spokesman:* Opposition Front Bench Spokesman on Science 1980–82. *Party Groups:* Vice-Chairman, Parliamentary Labour Party 1974–76; Member, Labour Party National Executive Committee 1985–86. *International Bodies:* Member, Socialist Bureau of the Parliamentary and Budget Committee 1975; Vice-Chairman, Control Committee on Budgets of European Parliament 1976–79. *Publications: Case for Ship-Schools; Ship-School; Devolution: End of Britain*, 1977; *One Man's Falklands*, 1982; *A Science Policy for Britain*, 1983; *Thatcher's Torpedo*, 1983; *Misrule*, 1987; *Dick Crossman: a portrait*, 1989. *Special Interests:* Science Policy, Central Economic Issues, Wildlife and Countryside Legislation, Kidney Transplantation, Rainforest Issues. *Countries of Interest:* Brazil, Burma, Indonesia, Libya, Zaïre, Iran, Iraq, Peru. *Recreations:* Squash, tennis, hill-walking. *Electoral Notes:* Contested Roxburgh, Selkirk, Peebles for Labour 1959. Member for West Lothian 1962–83. MEP 1975–79. Member for Linlithgow since June 1983. *Clubs:* Congress Private Dining Club. *Address:* Tam Dalyell Esq, MP, House of Commons, London, SW1A 0AA *Tel:* 020 7219 3427.

DARLING, The Rt Hon. Alistair Maclean *(Edinburgh Central)* *Lab majority 11,070*

Born November 28, 1953; educated Loretto School; University of Aberdeen (LLB). Married November 12, 1986, Margaret McQueen Vaughan (1 son 1 daughter). *Profession:* Advocate. *Career:* Solicitor 1978–82; Advocate 1984–. *Councils, Public Bodies:* Lothian Regional Council: Councillor 1982–87, Chairman, Lothian Region Transport Committee 1986–87. *Political Career:* Sponsored Solicitors (Scotland) Act 1988 (Private Member's Bill); Chief Secretary to the Treasury 1997–98; Secretary of State for Social Security 1998–. *Spokesman:* Opposition Spokesman on Home Affairs 1988–92; Opposition Front Bench Spokesman on Treasury, Economic Affairs and the City 1992–96; Shadow Chief Secretary to the Treasury 1996–97. *Party Groups:* Member, Labour Party's Economic Commission 1994–97. *Honours:* PC 1997. *Special*

Interests: Transport, Education, Health, Economic Policy, Constitution. *Electoral Notes:* Member for Edinburgh Central since June 1987. *Address:* The Rt Hon. Alistair Darling, MP, House of Commons, London, SW1A 0AA *Tel:* 020 7219 4584. *Constituency:* 15A Stafford Street, Edinburgh, EH3 7BU *Tel:* 0131–476 2552 *Fax:* 0131–467 3574.

DARVILL, Keith Ernest *(Upminster)   Lab majority 2,770*

Son of late Ernest Arthur James, dockworker, and of late Ellen Darvill. Born May 28, 1948; educated Norlington Secondary Modern, Leyton; Central London Polytechnic; College of Law, Chester. Married Julia de Saran (2 sons 1 daughter). *Trades Union:* Member, TGWU. *Profession:* Solicitor. *Career:* Solicitor 1982–. *Select Committees (Current):* Member: Procedure 1997–. *Party Groups:* Member: Co-operative Society, Fabian Society, Society of Labour Lawyers. *Other:* Governor: Gaynes School (Upminster), Havering Sixth Form College. *Miscellaneous:* Member, European Standing Committee C 1999–. *Sportsclubs:* Cranston Park Lawn Tennis (Upminster). *Special Interests:* Environment, Education, Housing, Planning. *Recreations:* Sport, tennis, badminton, gardening. *Electoral Notes:* Member for Upminster since May 1, 1997. *Address:* Keith Darvill Esq, MP, House of Commons, London, SW1A 0AA *Tel:* 020 7219 5106 *Fax:* 020 7219 5106.

DAVEY, Edward Jonathon *(Kingston and Surbiton)   LD majority 56*

Son of late John George Davey, solicitor, and of late Nina Joan Davey (née Stanbrook), teacher. Born December 25, 1965; educated Nottingham High School; Jesus College, Oxford (College President) (BA 1st Class Hons); Birkbeck College, London (MSc Economics). *Profession:* Management Consultant. *Career:* Senior Economics Advisor to Liberal Democrat MPs 1989–93; Management Consultant, Omega Partners 1993; Director, Omega Partners Postal. *Whip:* London Whip. *Spokesman:* A Spokesman for: the Treasury (Public Spending and Taxation) 1997–99, Economy 1999–. *Select Committees (Current):* Member: Procedure 1997–, Treasury 1999–, Treasury Sub-Committee 1999–. *Party Groups:* Chair, Costing Group (costing all policies for manifesto) 1992 and 1997 General Elections; Member, Federal Policy Committee 1994–95; Liberal Democrat Policy Group (Economics, Tax and Benefits and Transport); Member, Association of Liberal Democrat Councillors. *Awards:* Awarded Honourable Testimonial by Royal Humane Society; Chief Constable London Transport Police Commendation. *Special Interests:* Tax, Macro Economics, European Monetary Union, Employment, Environment. *Countries of Interest:* Latin America. *Recreations:* Cinema, music, walking, squash, swimming. *Electoral Notes:* Member for Kingston and Surbiton since May 1, 1997. *Address:* Edward Davey Esq, MP, House of Commons, London, SW1A 0AA *Tel:* 020 7219 3512 *Fax:* 020 7219 0250. *Constituency:* Liberal Democrats, 23A Victoria Road, Surbiton, Surrey, KT6 4JZ *Tel:* 020 8288 0161 *Fax:* 020 8288 1090 *E-mail:* daveye@parliament.uk.

DAVEY, Mrs Valerie *(Bristol West)   Lab majority 1,493*

Born April 16, 1940; educated Birmingham University (MA); London University (PGCE). Married August 1966, Graham Davey (1 son 2 daughters). *Trades Union:* Member, NUT. *Profession:* Teacher. *Career:* Teacher, Wolverhampton; Teacher, Tanzania; Part-time Teacher, Further Education College. *Councils, Public Bodies:* Avon County Council: Councillor 1981–96, Leader, Labour Group 1992–96; Former Member, Avon Health Authority. *Select Committees (Current):* Member: Education and Employment 1997–, Education Sub-Committee 1997–. *Other:* Member: Bristol University Court (formerly Member of Council), Amnesty International, ACTSA, Muscular Disease Society. *Special Interests:* Education, Health, Local Government, Overseas Aid and Development. *Countries of Interest:* East Africa (especially Tanzania), Cyprus. *Recreations:* Walking, gardens, reading, making marmalade. *Electoral Notes:* Member for Bristol West since May 1, 1997. *Address:* Mrs Valerie Davey, MP, House of Commons, London, SW1A 0AA *Tel:* 020 7219 3576. *Constituency:* PO Box 1947, Bristol, BS99 2UG *Tel:* 0117–907 7464 *Fax:* 0117–907 7465 *E-mail:* valdavey@labourbriswest.demon.co.uk.

DAVIDSON, Ian Graham *(Glasgow Pollok)   Lab/Co-op majority 13,791*

Son of Graham Davidson and Elizabeth Crowe. Born September 8, 1950; educated Jedburgh Grammar School; Galashiels Academy; Edinburgh University (MA Hons); Jordanhill College. Married 1978, Morag Christine Anne Mackinnon (1 son 1 daughter). *Trades Union:* Chairman, MSF Parliamentary Group. *Career:* Sabbatical Chairman, National Organisation of Labour Students 1973–74; President, Students' Association, Jordanhill College 1975–76; Researcher for Janey Buchan, MEP 1978–85; Community Service Volunteers 1985–92. *Councils, Public Bodies:* Strathclyde Regional Council: Councillor 1978–92, Chairman, Education Committee 1986–92. *Select Committees (Current):* Member: Public Accounts 1997– *(Former):* Member: Selection 1997–99. *Party Groups:* Former Chair, Kelvingrove Constituency Labour Party; Executive: Glasgow Labour Party, Strathclyde Regional Labour Party; Member, Co-operative Party; Secretary: Tribune Group, Trade Union Group of Labour MPs; Former Chairman, Co-operative Parliamentary Group. *Other:* Chairman, COSLA Education Committee 1990–92. *Miscellaneous:* Chairman, COSLA Education Committee 1990–92. *Special Interests:* Local Government, Education, Commonwealth, Third World, Local Economic Development, Defence, Co-operative Movement. *Countries of Interest:* Africa, Europe, Scandinavia, The Commonwealth, USA, Belize, Japan, Germany, British Overseas Territories. *Recreations:* Sport, distance running, swimming, having a family. *Electoral Notes:* Member for Glasgow Govan 1992–97, and for Glasgow Pollok since May 1, 1997. *Address:* Ian Davidson Esq, MP, House of Commons, London, SW1A 0AA *Tel:* 020 7219 3610 *Fax:* 020 7219 2238. *Constituency:* 1829 Paisley Road West, Glasgow, G52 3SS *Tel:* 0141–883 8338 *Fax:* 0141–883 4116.

DAVIES, The Rt Hon. Denzil *(Llanelli)   Lab majority 16,039*

Son of G. Davies of Carmarthen. Born October 9, 1938; educated Carmarthen Grammar School; Pembroke College, Oxford University (First class Hons (Law)). Married 1963, Mary Ann Finlay (1 son 1 daughter) (marriage dissolved 1988). *Profession:* Barrister. *Career:* Lectured at Chicago and Leeds Universities; Called to Bar, Gray's Inn 1964. *Political Career:* Formerly PPS to Secretary of State for Wales; Minister of State, HM Treasury 1975–79. *Spokesman:* Opposition Front Bench Spokesman on: The Treasury and Economic Affairs 1979–80, Foreign and Commonwealth Affairs 1980–81, Defence and Disarmament 1981–1983; Deputy Spokesman on Defence and Disarmament 1983–84; Chief Opposition Spokesman 1984–88. *Select Committees (Former):* Member: Public Accounts 1992–97. *Honours:* PC 1978. *Special Interests:* Foreign Affairs, Treasury, Wales. *Electoral Notes:* Member for Llanelli since June 18, 1970. *Address:* The Rt Hon. Denzil Davies, MP, House of Commons, London, SW1A 0AA *Tel:* 020 7219 5197 *Tel (Constituency):* 01554 756374.

DAVIES, Geraint Richard *(Croydon Central)   Lab majority 3,897*

Son of David Thomas Morgan Davies, senior civil servant, and of Betty Ferrer Davies. Born May 3, 1960; educated Llanishen Comprehensive, Cardiff; Jesus College, Oxford (BA Philosophy, Politics and Economics 1982). Married September 7, 1991, Dr Vanessa Catherine Fry (2 daughters). *Trades Union:* Member, GMB. *Profession:* Company Director. *Career:* Group Product Manager, Unilever; Former Marketing Manager, Colgate Palmolive Ltd; Managing Partner, Pure Crete 1989. *Councils, Public Bodies:* Councillor, Croydon Council 1986–97: Chairman, Housing Committee, Leader of Council. *Select Committees (Current):* Member: Public Accounts 1997–. *Party Groups:* Chair, Labour Finance and Industry Group 1998–. *Miscellaneous:* Chairman, London Boroughs Association Housing Committee 1996. *Special Interests:* Treasury, Trade and Industry, Environment, Transport and the Regions. *Countries of Interest:* Wales, Crete. *Recreations:* Family. *Electoral Notes:* Contested Croydon South 1987 and Croydon Central 1992. Member for Croydon Central since May 1, 1997. *Clubs:* Ruskin House. *Address:* Geraint Davies Esq, MP, House of Commons, London, SW1A 0AA *Tel:* 020 7219 4599 *Fax:* 020 7219 5962.

DAVIES, Quentin *(Grantham and Stamford)   Con majority 2,692*

Son of Dr M. I. Davies, general practitioner, and Mrs Thelma Davies. Born May 29, 1944; educated Dragon School, Oxford; Leighton Park; Gonville and Caius College, Cambridge (BA); Harvard University, USA. Married April 9, 1983, Chantal, daughter of Lieutenant-Colonel and Mrs R. Tamplin (2 sons). *Career:* HM Diplomatic Service 1967–74: 3rd Secretary, FCO 1967–69, Second Secretary, Moscow 1969–72, First Secretary, FCO 1972–74; Manager then Assistant Director, Morgan Grenfell & Co. Ltd 1974–78; Director General and President, Morgan Grenfell France 1978–81; Director, Morgan Grenfell Co. Ltd. and certain group subsidiaries 1981–87, Consultant 1987–93; Consultant, National Westminster Securities plc 1993–; Director, Dewe Rogerson International 1987–94; Director, Société Generále d'Entreprises 1999–. *Political Career:* PPS to Rt Hon. Angela Rumbold MP, as Minister of State at: Department of Education and Science 1988–90, Home Office 1990–91; Shadow Minister for Pensions 1998–99; Shadow Paymaster General 1999–. *Spokesman:* An Opposition Front Bench Spokesman for: Social Security 1998–99, the Treasury 1999–. *Select Committees (Former):* Member: Treasury and Civil Service 1992–97, Standards and Privileges 1995–97, European Legislation 1997–98, Standards and Privileges 1997–98, Treasury 1997–98, European Scrutiny 1998. *International Bodies:* Executive Member, IPU (British Branch). *Miscellaneous:* Member of Executive Committee, Council for Economic Policy Research. Liveryman, Goldsmiths' Company. *Publications: Britain and Europe: A Conservative View*, 1996. *Special Interests:* Trade and Industry, Finance and Economics, Agriculture, Health, Welfare, Pensions. *Countries of Interest:* Other EU, USA, Russia. *Recreations:* Reading, riding, walking, skiing, travel. *Electoral Notes:* Contested Birmingham Ladywood 1977 (by-election). Member for Stamford and Spalding 1987–97, and for Grantham and Stamford since May 1, 1997. *Clubs:* Beefsteak, Brooks's, Travellers'. *Address:* Quentin Davies Esq, MP, House of Commons, London, SW1A 0AA *Tel:* 020 7219 5200 *Fax:* 020 7219 2963.

DAVIES, The Rt Hon. Ron (Ronald) *(Caerphilly)   Lab majority 25,839*

Son of late Ronald Davies, fitter. Born August 6, 1946; educated Bassaleg Grammar School; Portsmouth Polytechnic; University College of Wales, Cardiff. Married December 24, 1981, Christina Elizabeth Rees (1 daughter). *Career:* School-teacher 1968–70; Tutor-organiser, Workers' Educational Association 1970–74; Further education advisor, Mid-Glamorgan LEA 1974–83. *Councils, Public Bodies:* Councillor: Bedwas and Machen UDC and Rhymney Valley DC 1969–84. *Political Career:* Shadow Minister of Agriculture, Fisheries and Food July-November 1992; Shadow Secretary of State for Wales 1992–97; Secretary of State for Wales 1997–98. *Whip:* Opposition Whip 1985–87. *Spokesman:* Opposition Spokesman on: Agriculture and Rural Affairs 1987–92, Food 1989–92. *Other:* Member: Council of The Royal Society for the Protection of Birds 1993–, Highest Order Gorsedd of Bards, National Eisteddfod of Wales 1998. *Honours:* PC 1997. *Special Interests:* Regional Policy, Agriculture, Adult Education, Low Pay, Poverty, Environment, Conservation. *Recreations:* Sport (rugby and squash), walking, gardening, nature study. *Electoral Notes:* Member for Caerphilly since June 1983. AM for the Constituency of Caerphilly since May 6, 1999. *Address:* The Rt Hon. Ron Davies, MP, AM, House of Commons, London, SW1A 0AA *Tel:* 020 7219 3552. *Constituency:* Council Offices, Newport Road, Bedwas, Caerphilly, CF83 8YB *Tel:* 029 2085 2477 *Fax:* 029 2986 6022 *E-mail:* ron.davies@wales.gsi.gov.uk.

DAVIS, The Rt Hon. David Michael *(Haltemprice and Howden)   Con majority 7,514*

Son of late Ronald and Elizabeth Davis. Born December 23, 1948; educated Bec Grammar School; Warwick University (BSc molecular science, computing science 1971); London Business School (MSc Business Studies 1973); Harvard Business School (AMP 1985). Married July 28, 1973, Doreen Cook (1 son 2 daughters). *Career:* Joined Tate & Lyle 1974; Finance Director, Manbré & Garton 1976–80; Managing Director, Tate & Lyle Transport 1980–82; President, Redpath-Labatt joint venture 1982–84; Strategic Planning Director, Tate & Lyle 1984–87; Non-Executive Director, Tate & Lyle 1987–90. *Political Career:* PPS to Hon. Francis Maude, MP, as Financial Secretary to Treasury 1988–90; Parliamentary Secretary, Office of Public Service and Science 1993–94; Minister of State, Foreign and Commonwealth Office 1994–97. *Whip:* Assistant Government Whip 1990–93. *Select Committees (Current):* Chairman: Public Accounts 1997–; Member: Liaison 1998–. *Miscellaneous:* Member, Public Accounts Commission 1997–. *Honours:* PC 1997. *Publications: The BBC Viewer's Guide to Parliament, How to Turn Round a Company. Special Interests:* Health, Law and Order, Industry, Agriculture. *Recreations:* Mountaineering, flying light aircraft, writing. *Electoral Notes:* Member for Boothferry 1987–97, and for Haltemprice and Howden since May 1, 1997. *Address:* The Rt Hon. David Davis, MP, House of Commons, London, SW1A 0AA *Tel:* 020 7219 4183 *Tel (Constituency):* 01430 430365.

DAVIS, The Rt Hon. Terry *(Birmingham Hodge Hill)   Lab majority 14,200*

Son of late Gordon and Gladys Davis. Born January 5, 1938; educated King Edward VI Grammar School, Stourbridge; University College, London (LLB); University of Michigan, USA (MBA). Married 1963, Anne Cooper (1 son 1 daughter). *Trades Union:* Member, MSF. *Career:* Company Executive 1962–71; Manager in Motor Industry 1974–79. *Councils, Public Bodies:* Councillor, Yeovil Rural District Council 1967–68. *Whip:* Labour Whip for West Midlands 1979–80. *Spokesman:* Opposition Front Bench Spokesman on: The Health Service 1980–83, Treasury and Economic Affairs 1983–86, Trade and Industry 1986–87. *Select Committees (Former):* Member: Public Accounts 1987–94. *Party Groups:* Joined Labour Party 1965. *International Bodies:* Member, British Delegation to Council of Europe Assembly and Western European Union Assembly 1992–; Leader, Labour Delegation 1995–; Chairman: Economic Affairs and Development Committee, Council of Europe Assembly 1995–98, Rules Committee, Western European Union Assembly 1995–96; Leader, UK Delegation 1997–; Vice-President: Western European Union Assembly 1997–, Council of Europe Assembly 1998–; Executive Committee Member, IPU British Group. *Other:* Member, Socialist Health Association. *Miscellaneous:* Member, Advisory Council on Public Records 1989–94. *Honours:* PC 1999. *Countries of Interest:* Europe, USA. *Electoral Notes:* Contested Bromsgrove 1970 and October 1974. Member for Bromsgrove By-election 1971-February 74. Contested Birmingham Stechford By-election 1977. Member for Birmingham Stechford 1979–83, and for Birmingham Hodge Hill since June 1983. *Address:* The Rt Hon. Terry Davis Esq, MP, House of Commons, London, SW1A 0AA *Tel:* 020 7219 4509 *Fax:* 020 7219 6221 *Tel (Constituency):* 0121–747 9500 *Fax (Constituency):* 0121–747 9504.

DAWSON, (Thomas) Hilton *(Lancaster and Wyre)   Lab majority 1,295*

Son of late Harry Dawson, teacher, and Sally Dawson, teacher. Born September 30, 1953; educated Ashington Grammar School, Northumberland; Warwick University (BA Philosophy, Politics); Lancaster University (Diploma in Social Work). Married August 11, 1973, Susan, daughter of Ellis and Alice Williams (2 daughters). *Trades Union:* Member, UNISON. *Profession:* Social Work Manager. *Career:* Social Work Manager: Children's Homes, Fostering and Adoption, Day Care. *Councils, Public Bodies:* Councillor, Lancaster City Council 1987–97. *Select Committees (Current):* Member: Administration 1997–. *Party Groups:* Member, Labour Party 1978–. *Special Interests:* Community Politics, Children's Rights, Poverty, Jobs, Health, Development. *Electoral Notes:* Member for Lancaster and Wyre since May 1, 1997. *Address:* Hilton Dawson Esq, MP, House of Commons, London, SW1A 0AA *Tel:* 020 7219 4207 *Fax:* 020 7219 4207. *Constituency:* 15A Moor Lane, Lancaster, LA1 1GD *Tel:* 01524 380057 *Fax:* 01524 380057 *E-mail:* dawsonth@msn.com.

DAY, Stephen Richard *(Cheadle)   Con majority 3,189*

Son of late Francis Day, engineer and shop assistant and Mrs Annie Day. Born October 30, 1948; educated Otley Secondary Modern School; Park Lane College of Further Education; Leeds Polytechnic. Married 2nd, 1982, Frances, daughter of late James Booth and Mrs Edna Booth (1 son by former marriage). *Trades Union:* Parliamentary Consultant to NALGO Section of UNISON 1990–96. *Career:* William Sinclair and Sons: Sales Clerk 1965–70, Assistant Sales Manager 1970–77; Sales Representative: Larkfield Printing Co. 1977–80, A. H. Leach and Co. 1980–84; Sales Executive: PPL Chromacopy 1984–86, Chromagene 1986–87. *Councils, Public Bodies:* Councillor: Otley Town Council 1975–76, 1979–83, Leeds City Council 1975–80. *Political Career:* Sponsored Motor Vehicles (wearing of rear seat belts by children) Act 1988 (Private Member's Bill). *Whip:* An Opposition Whip: (Environment, Transport and the Regions, Agriculture: Greater London and North West) 1997–98, (Constitutional Affairs, Education and Employment) 1998–99, (Home Office, Culture, Media and Sport) 1999, (Health; Private Members' Bills; Defence) 1999, (Home Office; Private Members' Bills; Cabinet Office) 1999–. *Select Committees (Former):* Member: Social Security 1991–97, Catering 1997–98, Environment, Transport and Regional Affairs 1997 (May-Nov), Transport 1997–98. *Party Groups:* Vice-Chairman, Association of Conservative Clubs (ACC), Chairman 1999–. *International Bodies:* Vice-Chairman, Commonwealth Parliamentary Association (CPA) UK Branch 1996–97, Executive Committee Member 1999–. *Other:* Vice-President: Stockport Chamber of Commerce, Stockport Heart Foundation Hon. Member, Bromhall and Woodford Rotary Club. *Trust:* Patron, Humane Research Trust. Member, Institute of Export 1972–87. *Special Interests:* Transport, Israel, Constitution. *Countries of Interest:* Cyprus, Israel. *Recreations:* Music, films, Roman history. *Electoral Notes:* Contested Bradford West 1983. Member for Cheadle since June 1987. *Address:* Stephen Day Esq, MP, House of Commons, London, SW1A 0AA *Tel:* 020 7219 6200. *Constituency:* Conservative Offices, Mellor Road, Cheadle Hulme, Cheadle, Cheshire, SK8 5AT *Tel:* 0161–486 6875.

DEAN, Janet Elizabeth Ann *(Burton)   Lab majority 6,330*

Daughter of late Harry and late Mary Gibson. Born January 28, 1949; educated Winsford Verdin Grammar School. Married August 3, 1968, to Alan Dean (died) (2 daughters). *Career:* Bank Clerk 1965–69; Clerk 1969–70. *Councils, Public Bodies:* Member, Health Authority 1981–90; Staffordshire County Council: Councillor 1981–97, Vice-Chair, Highways 1985–93, Vice-Chair, Social Services 1993–96; Councillor: East Staffordshire Borough Council 1991–97, Uttoxeter Town Council 1995–97; Mayor, East Staffordshire Borough Council 1996–97. *Select Committees (Current):* Member: Catering 1997–, Home Affairs 1999–. *Party Groups:* Joined Labour Party 1971. *Other:* School Governor 1979–97; Member: Uttoxeter General Charities, Arthritis and Rheumatism Council (Uttoxeter Branch), Crime Prevention Panel. *Trust:* Chair, Burton Breweries Charitable Trust. *Miscellaneous:* Member, European Standing Committee A 1998–. *Special Interests:* Health, Social Services, Education, Transport, Housing, Home Affairs. *Recreations:* Dress-making, reading. *Electoral Notes:* Member for Burton since May 1, 1997. *Address:* Mrs Janet Dean, MP, House of Commons, London, SW1A 0AA *Tel:* 020 7219 6320 *Fax:* 020 7219 3010. *Constituency:* Suite 13, First Floor, Cross Street Business Centre, Cross Street, Burton upon Trent, DE14 1EF *Tel:* 01283 509166 *Fax:* 01283 569964.

DENHAM, John *(Southampton Itchen)   Lab majority 14,209*

Son of Edward and Beryl Denham. Born July 15, 1953; educated Woodroffe Comprehensive School, Lyme Regis; Southampton University (President, Student's Union 1976–77). Married October 6, 1979, Ruth Eleanore, daughter of Keith and Barbara Dixon (1 son 1 daughter) (separated). *Career:* Advice worker, Energy Advice Agency, Durham 1977–78; Transport campaigner, Friends of the Earth 1978–79; Head of Youth Affairs, British Youth Council 1979–83; Campaigner, War on Want 1984–88; Consultant to various voluntary organisations 1988–. *Councils, Public Bodies:* Hampshire County Council: Councillor 1981–89, Spokesperson on Education; Southampton City Council: Councillor 1989–92, Former Chairman, Housing Committee.

Political Career: Department of Social Security: Parliamentary Under-Secretary of State 1997–98, Minister of State 1998–99; Minister of State, Department of Health 1999–. *Spokesman:* Opposition Spokesman on Social Security 1995–97. *Select Committees (Former):* Member: Environment 1993–95. *Special Interests:* Development, Housing, Education, Pensions and Personal Financial Services. *Countries of Interest:* Latin America, Philippines. *Recreations:* Cricket, cooking, walking, family. *Electoral Notes:* Member for Southampton Itchen since April 9, 1992. *Address:* John Denham Esq, MP, House of Commons, London, SW1A 0AA *Tel:* 020 7219 4515. *Constituency:* 32 Henry Road, Southampton, SO1 3HA *Tel:* 023 8070 5656 *Fax:* 023 8077 0094.

DEWAR, The Rt Hon. Donald Campbell *(Glasgow Anniesland)   Lab majority 15,154*

Son of late Dr Alisdair Dewar. Born August 21, 1937; educated Glasgow Academy; Glasgow University (President of Union 1961–62). Married 1964, Alison McNair (1 son 1 daughter) (marriage dissolved 1973). *Political Career:* PPS to President of Board of Trade 1967; Shadow Cabinet 1984–97; Secretary of State for Scotland 1997–99; First Minister, Scottish Parliament 1999–. *Whip:* Opposition Chief Whip 1995–97. *Spokesman:* Principal Opposition Front Bench Spokesman on: Scottish Affairs 1981–92, Social Security 1992–95. *Party Groups:* Member, Labour Party 1957–. *Trust:* Fellow, Industry and Parliament Trust. *Honours:* PC 1996. *Electoral Notes:* Contested Aberdeen South 1964. Member for Aberdeen South 1966–70. Member for Glasgow Garscadden 1978–97, and for Glasgow Anniesland since May 1, 1997. MSP for the Constituency of Glasgow Anniesland since May 6, 1999. *Address:* The Rt Hon. Donald Dewar, MP, MSP, House of Commons, London, SW1A 0AA *Tel:* 020 7219 4265 *Fax:* 020 7219 4265 *Tel (Constituency):* 0141–552 2416.

DISMORE, Andrew *(Hendon)   Lab majority 6,155*

Son of late Ian Dismore, hotelier, and Brenda Dismore. Born September 2, 1954; educated Bridlington Grammar School; Warwick University (LLB); London School of Economics (LLM); Guildford College of Law. *Trades Union:* Member, GMB. *Profession:* Solicitor. *Career:* Formerly full-time, Education Department, GMWU; Solicitor: Robin Thomson and Partners 1978–95, Russell Jones and Walker 1995–. *Councils, Public Bodies:* Councillor, Westminster City Council 1982–97, Leader, Labour Group 1990–97. *Select Committees (Current):* Member: Social Security 1998– *(Former):* Member: Accommodation and Works 1997–99. *Party Groups:* Member, Labour Friends of Israel. *Other:* Member Executive Committee, Association of Personal Injury Lawyers. *Publications:* Various legal journals and articles. *Special Interests:* Health, Civil Justice, Rights of Victims of Accidents and Crime. *Countries of Interest:* Greece, Cyprus, Israel. *Recreations:* Art, opera, travel, gardening. *Electoral Notes:* Member for Hendon since May 1, 1997. *Address:* Andrew Dismore Esq, MP, House of Commons, London, SW1A 0AA *Tel:* 020 7219 4026. *Constituency:* Red Rose Shop, 63 Watling Avenue, Burnt Oak, Edgware, HA8 0LD *Tel:* 020 8952 5779 *Fax:* 020 8952 5771.

DOBBIN, Jim *(Heywood and Middleton)   Lab majority 17,542*

Son of William Dobbin, miner, and Catherine Dobbin (née McCabe), mill worker. Born May 26, 1941; educated St Columba's High, Cowdenbeath; St Andrew's High, Kirkcaldy; Napier College, Edinburgh. Married Pat (2 sons 2 daughters). *Trades Union:* Member, MSF. *Career:* Microbiologist (33 years' service, NHS). *Councils, Public Bodies:* Rochdale Metropolitan Borough Council: Former Councillor, Chairman of Housing, Leader of Labour Group, Deputy Leader, Leader of Council. *Select Committees (Current):* Member: European Scrutiny 1998– *(Former):* Member: European Legislation 1998, European Legislation 1998. *Party Groups:* Joined Labour Party 1975; Former Chairman, Rochdale District Labour Party: Former Executive Member, Rochdale Constituency Labour Party; Hon Treasurer, North West Regional Group of Labour MPs 1999–. *Other:* Chairman, Neighbourhood Services; Amnesty International. *Miscellaneous:* Member,

European Standing Committee A 1998–. *Special Interests:* Local Government, Health, Housing. *Recreations:* Walking, football. *Electoral Notes:* Contested Bury North 1992. Member for Heywood and Middleton since May 1, 1997. *Address:* Jim Dobbin Esq, MP, House of Commons, London, SW1A 0AA *Tel:* 020 7219 4530 *Fax:* 020 7219 2696. *Constituency:* 45 York Street, Heywood, Lancashire, OL10 4NN *Tel:* 01706 361135 *Fax:* 01706 361137.

DOBSON, The Rt Hon. Frank *(Holborn and St Pancras)   Lab majority 17,903*

Son of late James William Dobson, railwayman, and late Irene Dobson. Born March 15, 1940; educated Dunnington County Primary School; Archbishop Holgate's Grammar School, York; London School of Economics. Married February 18, 1967, Janet Mary, daughter of Henry and Edith Alker (1 daughter 2 sons). *Trades Union:* NUR sponsored MP. *Career:* Worked at HQ of: CEGB 1962–70, Electricity Council 1970–75; Assistant Secretary, Office of Local Ombudsman 1975–79. *Councils, Public Bodies:* Camden Borough Council: Councillor 1971–76, Leader of the Council 1973–75. *Political Career:* Shadow Health Minister 1983–87; Shadow Leader, House of Commons and Campaigns Co-ordinator 1987–89; Secretary of State for Health 1997–99. *Spokesman:* Opposition Front Bench Spokesman on Education 1982–83; Principal Opposition Front Bench Spokesman on: Energy 1989–92, Employment 1992–93, Transport and London 1993–94, Environment and London 1994–97. *Other:* Governor, London School of Economics and Political Science 1986–. *Honours:* PC 1997. *Electoral Notes:* Member for Holborn and St Pancras since May 1979. *Address:* The Rt Hon. Frank Dobson, MP, House of Commons, London, SW1A 0AA *Tel:* 020 7219 5040.

DONALDSON, Jeffrey Mark *(Lagan Valley)   UUP majority 16,925*

Son of James and Sarah Anne Donaldson. Born December 7, 1962; educated Kilkeel High School; Castlereagh College. Married June 26, 1987, Eleanor, daughter of late Gilbert and Kathleen Cousins (2 daughters). *Trades Union:* Former Member, AEEU. *Armed Forces:* Ulster Defence Regiment 1980–85. *Career:* Agent to Rt Hon. J. Enoch Powell, MP 1983–84; Personal Assistant to Sir James Molyneaux, MP 1984–85; Principal, Financial Services and Estate Agency Business 1986–96. *Political Career:* Member, Northern Ireland Assembly 1985–86; Member, Northern Ireland Forum 1996–98. *Spokesman:* Spokesman for Trade and Industry 1997–. *Select Committees (Current):* Member: Northern Ireland Affairs 1997–. *Party Groups:* Honorary Secretary, Ulster Unionist Council 1988–. *Other:* Member: Evangelical Alliance, CARE, Tear Fund. *Special Interests:* Northern Ireland, Christian Values, Trade and Industry, Constitution. *Countries of Interest:* USA, South Africa, Israel. *Recreations:* Hill-walking, reading, church. *Electoral Notes:* Member for Lagan Valley since May 1, 1997. *Address:* Jeffrey Donaldson Esq, MP, House of Commons, London, SW1A 0AA *Tel:* 020 7219 3407 *Fax:* 020 7219 0696. *Constituency:* 38 Railway Street, Lisburn, Co Antrim, BT28 2XP *Tel:* 028 9266 8001 *Fax:* 028 9267 1845 *E-mail:* mckeem@parliament.uk.

DONOHOE, Brian Harold *(Cunninghame South)   Lab majority 14,869*

Son of late George and Catherine Donohoe. Born September 10, 1948; educated Patna and Loudoun Montgomery primary schools; Irvine Royal Academy; Kilmarnock Technical College. Married July 16, 1973, Christine, daughter of Raymond Pawson (2 sons). *Trades Union:* NALGO District Officer 1981–; Convenor, Political and Education Committee TASS 1969–81; Secretary, Irvine Trades Council 1973–82. *Career:* Apprentice engineer, Ailsa Shipyard finishing apprenticeship in drawing office; Hunterston Nuclear Power Station 1977; ICI Organics Division, draughtsman 1977–81. *Councils, Public Bodies:* Chairman: Cunninghame Industrial Development Committee 1975–85, North Ayrshire and Arran Local Health Council 1977–79. *Select Committees (Current):* Member: Environment, Transport and Regional Affairs 1997–, Environment Sub-Committee 1997–, Transport Sub-Committee 1997– *(Former):* Member: Transport 1993–97. *Party Groups:* Treasurer, Cunninghame South Constituency Labour Party 1983–91; Chair, Scottish Group of Labour

MPs 1997–98. *Special Interests:* Health, Local Government, Transport. *Countries of Interest:* Singapore, Indonesia, Malaysia, USA. *Recreations:* Gardening. *Electoral Notes:* Member for Cunninghame South since April 9, 1992. *Address:* Brian Donohoe Esq, MP, House of Commons, London, SW1A 0AA *Tel:* 020 7219 6230 *Fax:* 020 7219 5388. *Constituency:* 17 Townhead, Irvine, Strathclyde *Tel:* 01294 276844 *Fax:* 01294 313463.

DORAN, Frank *(Aberdeen Central)* Lab majority 10,801

Son of Francis Anthony and Betty Hedges Doran. Born April 13, 1949; educated Ainslie Park Secondary School; Leith Academy; Dundee University (LLB Hons). Married February 4, 1967, Patricia Ann, daughter of Richard and Lilian Govan (2 sons) (separated). *Trades Union:* Member, GMB 1983–96. *Career:* Solicitor. *Political Career:* PPS to Rt Hon Ian McCartney, MP: as Minister of State, Department of Trade and Industry (Competitiveness) 1997–99, as Minister of State, Cabinet Office 1999–. *Spokesman:* Opposition Spokesman on Energy 1988–92. *Other:* Founder Member, Scottish Legal Action Group; Chairman, Dundee Association for Mental Health 1979–82. *Special Interests:* Energy, Childcare, Family, Mental Health. *Recreations:* Cinema, art, football, sport. *Electoral Notes:* Contested North-East Scotland, European Election 1984. Member for Aberdeen South 1987–92, and for Aberdeen Central since May 1, 1997. *Clubs:* Aberdeen Trades Council. *Address:* Frank Doran Esq, MP, House of Commons, London, SW1A 0AA *Tel:* 020 7219 3481.

DORRELL, The Rt Hon. Stephen James *(Charnwood)* Con majority 5,900

Son of late Philip Dorrell, Company Director. Born March 25, 1952; educated Uppingham School; Brasenose College, Oxford (BA). Married September 1980, Penelope Anne, daughter of James Taylor (3 sons). *Career:* Director, family industrial clothing firm 1975–87. *Political Career:* PPS to Secretary of State for Energy 1983–87; Parliamentary Under-Secretary of State, Department of Health 1990–92; Financial Secretary, HM Treasury 1992–94; Secretary of State for: National Heritage 1994–1995, Health 1995–97; Member, Shadow Cabinet 1997–98; Shadow Secretary of State for Education and Employment 1997–98. *Whip:* Assistant Government Whip 1987–88; Lord Commissioner of the Treasury (Government Whip) 1988–90. *Select Committees (Former):* Honorary Member: Public Accounts 1992–94. *Miscellaneous:* Chairman, Millennium Commission 1994–95. *Honours:* PC 1994. *Special Interests:* Economics, Foreign Affairs. *Recreations:* Reading, theatre. *Electoral Notes:* Contested Kingston-upon-Hull East in October 1974 General Election. Member for Loughborough 1979–97, and for Charnwood since May 1, 1997. *Address:* The Rt Hon. Stephen Dorrell, MP, House of Commons, London, SW1A 0AA *Tel:* 020 7219 4472 *Fax:* 020 7219 5838. *Constituency:* 19A The Nook, Anstey, Leicester, LE7 7AZ *Tel:* 0116–236 6898 *Fax:* 0116–236 6902.

DOWD, Jim *(Lewisham West)* Lab majority 14,317

Son of late James and Elfriede Dowd. Born March 5, 1951; educated Sedgehill Comprehensive School, London; London Nautical School. *Trades Union:* Member: POEU 1967–72, MSF (ASTMS) 1973–. *Career:* Apprentice telephone engineer, GPO (now BT) 1967–72; Station Manager, Heron Petrol Stations Ltd. 1972–73; Telecommunications Engineer, Plessey Company (now GPT) 1973–. *Councils, Public Bodies:* London Borough of Lewisham: Councillor 1974–94, Deputy Leader 1984–86, Chairman, Finance Committee, Deputy Mayor 1987, 1990, Mayor 1992; Formerly Member, Lewisham and North Southwark District Health Authority. *Whip:* Opposition Whip for London 1993–95; A Lord Commissioner of HM Treasury (Government Whip) 1997–. *Spokesman:* Opposition Spokesman on Northern Ireland 1995–97. *Party Groups:* Joined Labour Party 1970. *Other:* Member: Greenpeace, CND, International Fund for Animal Welfare, RSPB, WWFFN, Cats Protection League. *Trust:* Member, National Trust. *Special Interests:* Health Service, Transport, Economic Policy, Industrial Policy, Environment, Housing, Animal Welfare, Human Rights. *Recreations:*

Music, reading, theatre, Cornwall. *Electoral Notes:* Contested Beckenham in 1983 and Lewisham West in 1987 General Elections. Member for Lewisham West since April 9, 1992. *Address:* Jim Dowd Esq, MP, House of Commons, London, SW1A 0AA *Tel:* 020 7219 4617 *Fax:* 020 7219 2686. *Constituency:* 43 Sunderland Road, Forest Hill, London, SE23 2PS *Tel:* 020 8699 2001 *Fax:* 020 8291 5607 *E-mail:* james.dowd@hm-treasury.gov.uk.

DREW, David Elliott *(Stroud)   Lab/Co-op majority 2,910*

Son of Ronald Montague Drew, company accountant, and late Maisie Joan Drew, hospital administrator. Born April 13, 1952; educated Kingsfield School, Gloucestershire; Nottingham University (BA Economics 1974); Birmingham University (PGCE 1976); Bristol Polytechnic (MA historical studies); University of the West of England (MEd 1994). Married 1990, Anne Baker (2 sons 2 daughters). *Trades Union:* Member, NAS/UWT 1976–86, Former Branch Secretary; Member, NATFHE 1986–; Member, UNISON, then NUPE 1990–. *Career:* Teacher, various schools in Warwickshire, Hertfordshire and Gloucestershire 1976–86; Lecturer, Bristol University, University of the West of England 1986–97. *Councils, Public Bodies:* Councillor: Stevenage Borough Council 1981–82, Stroud District Council 1987–95, Stonehouse Town Council 1987–, Gloucestershire County Council 1993–97. *Select Committees (Current):* Member: Procedure 1997–, Modernisation of the House of Commons 1998–, Agriculture 1999–. *Party Groups:* Member: Labour Party 1969–; Stroud Constituency Labour Party, Secretary 1992–93; Gloucestershire County Labour Party, Treasurer 1987–93; Co-op Party 1980–; Christian Socialist Movement, Socialist Educational Association, Labour Party Rural Revival, Labour Campaign for Electoral Reform. *Other:* Member: Friends of the Earth, Greenpeace, ACTSA, Age Concern, Care and Repair, South Stroud Small Business Club, St Cyr's Parochial Church Council, Charter 88, NHS Support Federation; Governor, Maidenhill School. *Miscellaneous:* Spends 20–25 days per year with MoD on "work experience". *Sportsclubs:* Bristol Rugby Football Club, Forest Green FC. *Publications:* Various IT related materials. *Special Interests:* Housing, Poverty, Planning, Environment, Education, Agriculture, Rural Issues. *Countries of Interest:* South Africa. *Recreations:* Reading, watching rugby, football. *Electoral Notes:* Contested Stroud 1992. Member for Stroud since May 1, 1997. *Address:* David Drew Esq, MP, House of Commons, London, SW1A 0AA *Tel:* 020 7219 6479 *Fax:* 020 7219 0910. *Constituency:* 5A Lansdown, Stroud, Gloucestershire, G5 1BB *Tel:* 01453 764355 *Fax:* 01453 753756 *E-mail:* drewd@parliament.uk.

DROWN, Julia Kate *(South Swindon)   Lab majority 5,645*

Daughter of David Drown, picture restorer, and Audrey Drown (née Harris), nurse. Born August 23, 1962; educated Hampstead Comprehensive; University College, Oxford (BA Politics and Economics 1985). Partner, Bill Child (1 son 1 daughter deceased). *Trades Union:* Member: UNISON (formerly NALGO), TGWU. *Profession:* Public Sector Accountant. *Career:* NHS Accountancy Trainee, Oxfordshire 1985–88; Unit Accountant, Learning Disabilities, Oxfordshire 1989–90; Director, Finance, Contracts and Information, Radcliffe Infirmary 1990–96. *Councils, Public Bodies:* Councillor, Oxfordshire County Council 1989–96, Labour Spokesperson/Deputy Spokesperson on Social Services 1990–96, Vice-Chair, Labour Group 1994–95; Director/Chair, Oxfordshire Co-operative Development Agency 1994–95. *Select Committees (Former):* Member: Health 1997–99. *Party Groups:* Member: Labour Party 1984–, Co-operative Party 1992–, Labour Women's Network. *Other:* School Governor 1989–96; Member: World Development Movement, Amnesty International, Friends of the Earth, Greenpeace, Campaign to Close Campsfield. *Trust:* Trust Board Member, Radcliffe Infirmary NHS Trust 1993–96. Member, Chartered Institute of Public Finance and Accountancy (CIPFA) 1988. *Special Interests:* Health Service, Social Services, World Development, Co-operative Movement. *Recreations:* Family, music, walking. *Electoral Notes:* Member for South Swindon since May 1, 1997. *Address:* Julia Drown, MP, House of Commons, London, SW1A 0AA *Tel:* 020 7219 2392 *Fax:* 020 7219 0266. *Constituency:* 39 Victoria Road, Swindon, Wiltshire, SN1 3AT *Tel:* 01793 615444 *Fax:* 01793 644752.

DUNCAN, Alan *(Rutland and Melton)   Con majority 8,836*

Son of late Wing-Commander James Duncan, OBE, and Anne Duncan (née Carter). Born March 31, 1957; educated Beechwood Park School, St Albans; Merchant Taylors' School, Northwood; St John's College, Oxford (President, Oxford Union 1979); Harvard University (Kennedy Scholar). *Career:* Formerly graduate trainee, Shell International Petroleum; Oil trader and adviser to governments and companies on oil supply, shipping and refining 1989–. *Political Career:* PPS to Rt Hon. Dr. Brian Mawhinney, MP: as Minister of State, Department of Health 1993–94, as Chairman, Conservative Party 1995–97; A Vice-Chairman Conservative Party 1997–98; Parliamentary Political Secretary to Rt Hon. William Hague, MP, as Leader of the Conservative Party 1997–98.

Spokesman: An Opposition Front Bench Spokesman for: Health 1998–99, Trade and Industry 1999–. *Select Committees (Former):* Member: Social Security 1992–95. *Party Groups:* A Vice-Chairman, Conservative Party 1997–98. Freeman, City of London. *Publications:* Co-author: (CPC pamphlet) *Bearing the Standard: Themes for a Fourth Term,* 1991, *Who Benefits? Reinventing Social Security, An End to Illusions,* 1993, *Saturn's Children: How the State Devours Liberty, Prosperity and Virtue,* 1995; *Beware Blair,* 1997. *Special Interests:* International Trade and Finance, Social Security. *Recreations:* Shooting, Stalking, Fishing. *Electoral Notes:* Contested Barnsley West and Penistone in 1987 General Election. Member for Rutland and Melton since April 9, 1992. *Address:* Alan Duncan Esq, MP, House of Commons, London, SW1A 0AA *Tel:* 020 7219 5204 *Tel (Constituency):* 01664 566444 *Fax (Constituency):* 01664 566555.

DUNCAN SMITH, (George) Iain *(Chingford and Woodford Green)   Con majority 5,714*

Son of late Group Captain W. G. G. Duncan Smith, DSO, DFC, and of Mrs Pamela Duncan Smith (née Summers). Born April 9, 1954; educated HMS Conway (Cadet School); University of Perugia; RMA Sandhurst; Dunchurch College of Management. Married 1982, Hon. Elizabeth Wynne Fremantle, daughter of Commander 5th Baron Cottesloe (2 sons 2 daughters). *Armed Forces:* Commissioned, Scots Guards 1975; ADC to Major-General Sir John Acland, KCB, CBE, Commander of Commonwealth Monitoring Force in Zimbabwe 1979–81. *Career:* GEC Marconi 1981; Director: Bellwing Property 1988–89, Jane's Information Group 1989–92. *Political Career:* Member, Shadow Cabinet 1997–; Shadow Secretary of State for: Social Security

1997–99, Defence 1999–. *Select Committees (Former):* Member: Administration 1993–97, Health 1993–95, Standards and Privileges 1995–97. *Party Groups:* Vice-Chairman, Fulham Conservative Association 1991. Freeman, City of London 1993. *Publications:* Co-author *Who Benefits? Reinventing Social Security; Game, Set and Match?* (Maastricht); *Facing the Future* (Defence and Foreign and Commonwealth Affairs); *1994 and Beyond; A Response to Chancellor Kohl. Special Interests:* Finance, Small Businesses, Transport, Defence, Environment. *Countries of Interest:* India, Italy, Sri Lanka, USA. *Recreations:* Cricket, rugby, tennis, sport in general, painting, theatre, family. *Electoral Notes:* Contested Bradford West in 1987 General Election. Member for Chingford 1992–97, and for Chingford and Woodford Green since May 1, 1997. *Address:* Iain Duncan Smith Esq, MP, House of Commons, London, SW1A 0AA *Tel:* 020 7219 3574. *Constituency:* 20A Station Road, Chingford, London, E4 7BE *Tel:* 020 8524 4344.

DUNWOODY, The Hon. Mrs. Gwyneth Patricia *(Crewe and Nantwich)   Lab majority 15,798*

Daughter of late Morgan Phillips, sometime General Secretary of the Labour Party and late Baroness Phillips. Born December 12, 1930. Married May 28, 1954, Dr. John Elliott Orr Dunwoody, formerly Labour Member for Falmouth and Camborne (2 sons 1 daughter) (marriage dissolved 1975). *Career:* Director, Film Production Association of GB 1970–74. *Political Career:* Parliamentary Secretary to Board of Trade 1967–70. *Spokesman:* Opposition Front Bench Spokesman on: Foreign and Commonwealth Affairs 1979–80, The Health Service 1980–83, Parliamentary Campaigning and Information 1983–84; Opposition Spokesman on Transport 1984–85. *Select Committees (Current):* Member: Chairmen's Panel 1997–; Chairman (Transport): Environment,

Transport and Regional Affairs 1997–; Member: Environment Sub-Committee 1997–; Chairman: Transport Sub-Committee 1997–; Member: Liaison 1997–. *Party Groups:* Labour Friends of Israel: Former Chair, President 1993–95, Currently Life President. *International Bodies:* Vice-President, Socialist International Women; Vice-Chairman, European Parliament Social Affairs Committee. *Other:* Patron, BRAKE 1995–. *Special Interests:* Transport, Health Service, Arts. *Countries of Interest:* Botswana, Central Africa, East Africa, Middle East. *Recreations:* Reading, listening to music. *Electoral Notes:* Contested Exeter 1964. Member for Exeter 1966–70, and for Crewe February 1974–83. MEP 1975–79. Member for Crewe and Nantwich since June 1983 *Address:* The Hon. Mrs Gwyneth Dunwoody, MP, House of Commons, London, SW1A 0AA *Tel:* 020 7219 3490 *Fax:* 020 7219 6046. *Constituency:* 154 Nantwich Road, Crewe, CW2 6BG *Tel:* 01270 589132 *Fax:* 01270 589135.

E

EAGLE, Angela *(Wallasey)   Lab majority 19,074*

Daughter of André Eagle, printworker, and late Shirley Eagle, dressmaker and student. Born February 17, 1961; educated Formby High School; St John's College, Oxford (BA Hons Philosophy, Politics and Economics). *Trades Union:* Employed by COHSE 1984–: first as a researcher, then as National Press Officer, currently as Parliamentary Liaison Officer; Member: COHSE, NUJ. *Political Career:* Parliamentary Under-Secretary of State: Department of the Environment, Transport and the Regions (Minister for Green Issues and Regeneration) 1997–98, Department of Social Security 1998–. *Whip:* Opposition Whip 1996–97. *Select Committees (Former):* Member: Members' Interests 1992–97, Employment 1994–96, Public Accounts 1995–97. *Party Groups:* Member, Labour Party 1978–; Active at branch, women's section, general committee levels in Crosby Constituency 1978–80; Chairman: Oxford University Fabian Club 1980–83, National Conference of Labour Women 1991. *Other:* Member, British Film Institute. *Publications:* Columnist and regular contributor to *Tribune. Special Interests:* Economic Policy, Health Service, Politics of Sport. *Recreations:* Chess, cricket, cinema. *Electoral Notes:* Member for Wallasey since April 9, 1992. *Address:* Angela Eagle, MP, House of Commons, London, SW1A 0AA *Tel:* 020 7219 4074 *Tel (Constituency):* 0151–637 1979 *E-mail:* eaglea@parliament.uk *Website:* http://www2.poptel.org.uk/angela.eagle.mp.

EAGLE, Maria *(Liverpool Garston)   Lab majority 18,417*

Daughter of André Eagle, printworker, and late Shirley Eagle, dressmaker and student. Born February 17, 1961; educated St Peter's Church of England Primary School, Formby; Formby High School (Comprehensive); Pembroke College, Oxford (BA Hons Philosophy, Politics and Economics); College of Law, Lancaster Gate (Common Professional Exam, Law Society Finals). *Trades Union:* Member GMB. *Profession:* Solicitor. *Career:* Voluntary sector 1983–90; Articles of Clerkship, Brian Thompson & Partners, Liverpool 1990–92; Goldsmith Williams, Liverpool 1992–95; Senior Solicitor, Steven Irving & Co, Liverpool 1994–97. *Political Career:* PPS to John Hutton, MP, as Minister of State, Department of Health 1999–. *Select Committees (Former):* Member: Public Accounts 1997–99. *Party Groups:* Joined Labour Party 1978; Local activist; Campaigns organiser Crosby 1993–96; Campaigns organiser, Press officer, Merseyside West Euro Constituency Labour Party 1983–84; Constituency Labour Party secretary, Press officer, political education officer. *Miscellaneous:* Played cricket for Lancashire as a Junior; Played chess for England and Lancashire. *Publications: High Time or High Tide for Labour Women,* (jointly with Joni Lovenduski). *Special Interests:* Transport, Housing, Employment. *Countries of Interest:* Nicaragua, USA, Australia. *Recreations:* Cinema, chess, cricket. *Electoral Notes:* Contested Crosby 1992. Member for Liverpool Garston since May 1, 1997. *Address:* Maria Eagle, MP, House of Commons, London, SW1A 0AA *Tel:* 020 7219 5288 *Fax:* 020 7219 1157. *Constituency:* Unit House, Speke Boulevard, Liverpool, L24 9HZ *Tel:* 0151–448 1167 *Fax:* 0151–448 0976.

EDWARDS, Huw William Edmund *(Monmouth)   Lab majority 4,178*

Son of Rev Dr Ifor M. Edwards and Esme Edwards. Born April 12, 1953; educated Eastfields High School, Mitcham, Surrey; Manchester Polytechnic; York University (BA 1976, MA 1976, MPhil Social Policy 1984). Single. *Trades Union:* Member, NATFHE. *Profession:* University Lecturer. *Career:* Lecturer in Social Policy, Brighton Polytechnic/University 1988–97; Research Consultant, Low Pay Unit 1988–97; Tutor, Open University 1988–89, 1993–96. *Select Committees (Current):* Member: Welsh Affairs 1997– *(Former):* Member: Modernisation of the House of Commons 1997–98. *Party Groups:* Member, Fabian Society. *Other:* Member: Amnesty International (Monmouth), One World Action, Shelter (Cymru), Gwalia Male Choir (London), London Welsh Association. *Trust:* Member, Gwent Wildlife Trust. *Sportsclubs:* London Welsh AFC, Preston Park CC, Lords and Commons Cricket XI, Lords and Commons Rugby Football. *Publications: Low Pay in South Wales,* 1989; *Wales in the 1990s – Land of Low Pay,* 1995; Plus articles in new review of Low Pay Unit. *Special Interests:* Health, Housing, Education, Wales, Constitutional Reform, Low Pay and Social Inequality. *Countries of Interest:* Wales, Japan. *Recreations:* Playing football, cricket, squash, skiing, following rugby. *Electoral Notes:* Member for Monmouth 1991 Byelection–1992, and from May 1, 1997. *Clubs:* London Welsh Association. *Address:* Huw Edwards Esq, MP, House of Commons, London, SW1A 0AA *Tel:* 020 7219 3489 *Fax:* 020 7219 3949. *Constituency:* 2 Mill Street Close, Usk, Gwent *Tel:* 01291 672248 *Fax:* 01291 672248.

EFFORD, Clive *(Eltham)   Lab majority 10,182*

Son of Stanley Efford, retired civil servant. Born July 10, 1958; educated Walworth Comprehensive School. Married Gillian Vallius (3 daughters). *Trades Union:* Member, T&GWU. *Profession:* London Taxi Driver. *Career:* Worked in family-owned jewellery shop till 1987; Taxi Driver 1987–97. *Councils, Public Bodies:* Councillor, London Borough of Greenwich 1989–, Chair, Social Services, Chief Whip, Labour Group 1990–91. *Select Committees (Current):* Member: Procedure 1997–, Standing Orders 1999–. *Other:* Founder, Job Club 1980. *Special Interests:* Welfare State, Health, Transport, Education, Environment, Local Government. *Recreations:* Football (FA Coachers Club), Millwall. *Electoral Notes:* Contested Eltham 1992 General Election. Member for Eltham since May 1, 1997. *Address:* Clive Efford Esq, MP, House of Commons, London, SW1A 0AA *Tel:* 020 7219 4057. *Constituency:* Westmount Road, Eltham, London, SE9.

ELLMAN, Louise Joyce *(Liverpool Riverside)   Lab majority 21,799*

Daughter of late Harold and Anne Rosenberg. Born November 14, 1945; educated Manchester High School for Girls; Hull University (BA Hons); York University (MPhil). Married July 16, 1967, Geoffrey Ellman (1 son 1 daughter). *Trades Union:* Member, T&GWU. *Profession:* .Open University Tutor/Further Education Lecturer. *Councils, Public Bodies:* Councillor, Lancashire County Council 1970–97, Leader, County Labour Group 1977–97, Leader of Council 1981–97; Councillor, West Lancashire District Council 1974–87; Vice-Chairman, Lancashire Enterprise 1982–97; Founder Chairman, Northwest Regional Association 1991–92, Vice-Chairman 1996–97. *Select Committees (Current):* Member: Environment, Transport and Regional Affairs 1997–, Environment Sub-Committee 1997–. *Party Groups:* Member, Co-op Party. *Special Interests:* Public Services, Regional Economic Development, Devolution, Health, Europe, Environment, Transport, Local Government. *Electoral Notes:* Member for Liverpool Riverside since May 1, 1997. *Address:* Mrs Louise Ellman, MP, House of Commons, London, SW1A 0AA *Tel:* 020 7219 5210 *Fax:* 020 7219 2592. *Constituency:* First Floor, Threlfall Building, Trueman Street, Liverpool, L3 2EX *Tel:* 0151–236 2969 *Fax:* 0151–236 4301.

EMERY, The Rt Hon. Sir Peter *(East Devon)   Con majority 7,489*

Son of late F. G. Emery. Born February 27, 1926; educated Scotch Plains, New Jersey, USA; Oriel College, Oxford (MA). Married 1st, July 1954, Elizabeth, daughter of late Philip Nicholson (1 son 1 daughter); married 2nd, December 15, 1972, Elizabeth Monnington (1 son 1 daughter). *Trades Union:* Member, ASLEF 1952–57. *Armed Forces:* Served: RAF 1943–47, RAFVR 1942–72. *Profession:* Chairman of Companies. *Career:* Director, Institute of Purchasing and Supply 1961–72; Secretary General, European Federation of Purchasing 1962–72; Chairman, Consultative Council of Professional Management Organisations 1967–72; Director: Phillips Petroleum UK 1964–72, Property Growth Assurance 1969–72; Chairman: Shenley Trust Services Ltd 1972–94, The Winglaw Group 1984–. *Councils, Public Bodies:* Councillor, Hornsey Borough Council 1951–59; Chairman, Housing Committee 1953–57; Deputy Mayor 1957. *Political Career:* PPS: to Minister of State, Foreign Office 1960–63, to Secretary of State for War 1963, to Minister of Labour 1963–64; Parliamentary Under-Secretary of State for: Industry 1972, Industry and Consumer Affairs 1973–74, Energy 1974. *Spokesman:* Opposition Front Bench Spokesman on Trade, Treasury and Economic Affairs 1965–66. *Select Committees (Current):* Member: Science and Technology 1985–, Foreign Affairs 1997–, Modernisation of the House of Commons 1997– *(Former):* Member: Procedure 1976–97; Chairman: Procedure 1983–92; Member: Liaison 1992–97; Chairman: Procedure 1993–97. *Party Groups:* Joint Founder, Bow Group; Chairman, Conservative West Country Members. *International Bodies:* Delegate, Council of Europe and Western European Union 1964–66, 1970–72; North Atlantic Assembly: Member 1983–, Officer, Science Committee 1988–, Vice-President, Science and Technology Committee; OSCE Assembly: Member 1992–, Treasurer 1992–; Member, Advisory Board of the United States Center for Strategic and International Studies. *Other:* Member, Asthma Research Council 1968–89; Chairman, National Asthma Campaign 1989–. *Miscellaneous:* Secretary, 1922 Committee 1964–66, Treasurer 1997–. Freeman, City of: Reading, Pennsylvania, USA, Houston, Texas, USA. *Sportsclubs:* Captain, House of Commons Bridge Team 1984–; Member: Middlesex County Cricket Club, Camberley Heath Golf Club. *Honours:* Knighted 1982; PC 1993. FInstPS (now FCIPS). *Special Interests:* Trade and Industry, Purchasing and Supply, Commonwealth, Parliamentary Procedure, Foreign Affairs, Defence, Space. *Countries of Interest:* USA, Europe, Africa, Japan, The Commonwealth. *Recreations:* Skiing, tennis, golf, gardening, bridge, watching cricket. *Electoral Notes:* Contested Poplar 1951 and Lincoln 1955. Member for Reading 1959–66, for Honiton 1967–97, and for East Devon since May 1, 1997. *Clubs:* Carlton, Leander. *Address:* The Rt Hon. Sir Peter Emery, MP, House of Commons, London, SW1A 0AA *Tel:* 020 7219 4044 *Fax:* 020 7219 3021. *Constituency:* 45 Imperial Rd, Exmouth, Devon *Tel:* 01460 220309.

ENNIS, Jeffrey *(Barnsley East and Mexborough)   Lab majority 26,763*

Son of William, retired miner, and Jean Ennis. Born November 13, 1952; educated Hemsworth Grammar School; Redland College, Bristol (CertEd, BEd Hons). Married 1980, Margaret Angela, daughter of Martin and Margaret Knight (3 sons). *Trades Union:* Member, TU 1975–; Representative, NASUWT at Hillsborough Primary 1979–96; Member, TGWU 1997–. *Profession:* Teacher. *Career:* Raw Materials Inspector, Lyons Bakery 1975–76; Primary Teacher: Wolverhampton 1976–78, Hillsborough Primary School, Sheffield 1979–96. *Councils, Public Bodies:* Councillor, Brierley Ward, Barnsley Council 1980–96; Councillor, Barnsley Metropolitan Borough Council 1980–96, Deputy Leader 1988–95, Leader 1995–96; Chairman, South Yorkshire Fire and Civil Defence Authority 1995–96. *Political Career:* PPS to Rt Hon. Tessa Jowell, MP: as Minister for Public Health, Department of Health 1997–99, as Minister of State, Department for Education and Employment (Minister for Employment, Welfare to Work and Equal Opportunities) 1999–. *Other:* Chairman: Barnsley Economic Regeneration Forum, Barnsley City Challenge, Barnsley Partnership Ltd; Board Member, Dearne Valley Partnership; Board Director, Barnsley and Doncaster and Training and Enterprise Council; School Governor, Willowgarth High, Grimethorpe. *Special Interests:* Local Government, Environment, Education, Regeneration, Fire Service. *Countries of Interest:* Germany, Ukraine. *Recreations:* Family activities, hill walking, sport, music, swimming, caravanning. *Electoral Notes:* Member for Barnsley East from December 12, 1996 By-Election–1997, and for Barnsley East and Mexborough since May 1, 1997. *Address:* Jeffrey Ennis Esq, MP, House of Commons, London, SW1A 0AA *Tel:* 020 7219 5008 *Fax:* 020 7219 2728. *Constituency:* Dearne Town Hall, Bolton-on-Dearne, Rotherham, South Yorkshire, S63 9EJ *Tel:* 01226 775080 *Fax:* 01226 775080.

ETHERINGTON, William *(Sunderland North)   Lab majority 19,697*

Born July 17, 1941; educated Redby Infant and Junior School; Monkwearmouth Grammar School. Married April 3, 1963, Irene (2 daughters). *Trades Union:* Member: AEU 1957–, NUM 1963–, National Exec Committee of NUM; Trustee, Mineworkers' Pension Scheme 1985–87; Representative, North Regional TUC 1985–92; NUM delegate, TUC 1990–91; Vice-President, North East Area NUM 1988–92. *Career:* Apprentice fitter, Austin & Pickersgill Shipyard 1957–63; Fitter, Dawdon Colliery 1963–83; Full-time Official, NUM 1983–92. *Select Committees (Current):* Member: Court of Referees 1997– *(Former):* Member: Members' Interests 1994–95, Catering 1995–97, Parliamentary Commissioner for Administration 1996–97. *Party Groups:* Held various posts in the Labour Party including local ward treasurer; GMC delegate; CLP Executive Committee member. *International Bodies:* Member, UK Delegation to Council of Europe and Western Europe Union 1997–. *Special Interests:* Trades Union Legislation, Employment, Adult Education, Human Rights, Education, Equal Opportunity, Health Service, Homelessness, Disabled/Disability, Animal Welfare. *Recreations:* Fell walking, motorcycling, watching soccer, local, industrial and transport history, reading. *Electoral Notes:* Member for Sunderland North since April 9, 1992. *Clubs:* Kelloe Working Men's, Durham City Working Men's. *Address:* William Etherington Esq, MP, House of Commons, London, SW1A 0AA *Tel:* 020 7219 4603 *Fax:* 020 7219 4603. *Constituency:* 7 Bridge House, Bridge Street, Sunderland, SR1 1TE *Tel:* 0191–564 2489 *Fax:* 0191–564 2486.

EVANS, Nigel *(Ribble Valley)   Con majority 6,640*

Son of late Albert Evans, and of Betty Evans. Born November 10, 1957; educated Dynevor School; University College of Wales, Swansea (BA Hons Politics). *Career:* Took over running of family business of retail newsagent and convenience store 1979–90. *Councils, Public Bodies:* West Glamorgan County Council: Councillor 1985–91, Deputy Leader, Conservative Group 1990–91. *Political Career:* PPS: to Rt Hon. David Hunt, MBE, MP: as Secretary of State for Employment 1993–94, as Chancellor of the Duchy of Lancaster 1994–95, to Tony Baldry, MP, as Minister of State, Ministry of Agriculture, Fisheries and Food 1995–96, to Rt Hon. William Hague, MP, as Secretary of State for Wales 1996–97; A Vice-Chairman (Wales), Conservative Party 1999–. *Spokesman:* An Opposition Front Bench Spokesman for: Constitutional Affairs (Scotland and Wales) 1997–99, Constitutional Affairs (Wales) 1999–. *Select Committees (Former):* Member: Transport 1993, Public Service 1995–97. *Party Groups:* Chairman, Conservative Welsh Parliamentary Candidates Policy Group 1990; President, Conservative North West Parliamentary Candidates Group 1991; Secretary, North West Conservative MPs 1992–. *Miscellaneous:* Has worked on three US Presidential Elections in New York, Florida and California. *Special Interests:* Education, Small Businesses, US Elections, Local Government, Defence, Agriculture, International Politics, Europe, Telecommunications. *Countries of Interest:* Caribbean, Central America, Europe, USA, Asia, Far East. *Recreations:* Tennis, swimming, running. *Electoral Notes:* Contested Swansea West 1987 General Election, Pontypridd 1989 (by-election), Ribble Valley 1991 (by-election). Member for Ribble Valley since April 9, 1992. *Clubs:* Carlton, Stringfellows. *Address:* Nigel Evans Esq, MP, House of Commons, London, SW1A 0AA *Tel:* 020 7219 4165 *Fax:* 020 7219 2568. *Constituency:* 9 Railway View, Clitheroe, Lancashire *Tel:* 01200 425939 *E-mail:* nigelmp@hotmail.com *Website:* www.nigelmp.com.

EWING, Margaret Anne *(Moray)   SNP majority 5,566*

Daughter of late John McAdam, farmworker, and late Mrs Peggie McAdam. Born September 1, 1945; educated Biggar High School; Glasgow University (MA English and History); Strathclyde University (BA Economic History); Jordanhill College of Education. Married November 30, 1983, Fergus Stewart Ewing, son of Stewart Ewing and Winifred Ewing, former MP for Hamilton 1967–70 and Moray and Nairn 1974–79 and current MEP, Highlands and Islands. *Career:* Secondary School Teacher 1968–74; Principal Teacher, Remedial Education 1972–74; Freelance journalist 1979–81; Co-ordinator, West of Scotland Certificate in Social Service Scheme 1981–87. *Spokesman:* Spokeswoman for Europe and Foreign Affairs, Defence, Health, Highlands and Islands, Gaelic. *Select Committees (Current):* Member: European Scrutiny 1998– *(Former):* Member: European Legislation 1992–97, European Legislation 1997–98. *Party Groups:* Member, SNP 1965–; Member, NEC 1974–80, Vice-President 1981–83, Senior Vice-Convenor 1983–87; SNP Parliamentary Leader 1987–. *Special Interests:* Education, Social Services, European Union, Foreign Affairs. *Countries of Interest:* Baltic States, Europe. *Recreations:* Arts, gardening. *Electoral Notes:* Member for Dunbartonshire East (then as Mrs Margaret Bain) 1974–79. Contested Strathkelvin/Bearsden 1983. Member for Moray since June 1987. MSP for the Constituency of Moray since May 6, 1999. *Address:* Mrs Margaret Ewing, MP, MSP, House of Commons, London, SW1A 0AA *Tel:* 020 7219 5230 *Fax:* 020 7219 2797. *Constituency:* Mrs Marian Hoare, 7 Dunbar Street, Lossiemouth, Moray, IV31 6AG *Tel:* 01343 812222 *Fax:* 01343 813221 *E-mail:* margaret.ewing.msp@scottish.parliament.uk.

F

FABER, David James Christian *(Westbury)   Con majority 6,068*

Son of Julian Faber and Lady Caroline Faber, daughter of 1st Earl of Stockton, OM, PC, FRS. Born July 7, 1961; educated Summer Fields, Oxford; Eton; Balliol College, Oxford (BA/MA French and Spanish 1984). Married 1st, October 15, 1988, Sally Gilbert (1 son) (marriage dissolved 1996); married 2nd, November 20, 1998, Sophie, daughter of Martyn Hedley. *Career:* Conservative Research Assistant, House of Commons 1984–85; Conservative Central Office, including personal assistant to Jeffrey Archer when Deputy Chairman 1985–87; Founding director, Sterling Marketing Ltd., marketing consultants 1987–. *Political Career:* PPS: to Rt Hon. Baroness Chalker of Wallasey, as Minister for Overseas Development 1994–95, to Rt Hon. Stephen Dorrell, MP, as Secretary of State for Health 1995–97. *Spokesman:* An Opposition Spokesman on Foreign and Commonwealth Affairs 1997–98. *Select Committees (Current):* Member: Culture, Media and Sport 1998– *(Former):* Member: Social Security 1992–97. *Party Groups:* Ward Chairman, Cities of London and Westminster Conservative Association 1986–87. *Sportsclubs:* Royal St George's Golf, Sunningdale Golf. *Publications:* Co-author, *Bearing the Standard – Themes for a Fourth Term*, 1991. *Special Interests:* Education, Foreign Affairs, Drug Abuse, Alcohol Abuse and under-age drinking, Rural Affairs. *Recreations:* Cricket, golf, squash, watching Chelsea Football Club. *Electoral Notes:* Contested Stockton North 1987 General Election. Member for Westbury since April 9, 1992. *Clubs:* Vincent's (Oxford), MCC (Committee Member 1997–), Queen's. *Address:* David Faber Esq, MP, House of Commons, London, SW1A 0AA *Tel:* 020 7219 5215. *Constituency:* Lovemead House, Roundstone Street, Trowbridge, Wiltshire, BA14 8DG *Tel:* 01225 752141.

Dod *on* Disk
The Vacher Dod Parliamentary Database – configured for PC or Network
For further details please telephone the Westminster Office
020 7828 7256

FABRICANT, Michael *(Lichfield)* Con majority 238

Son of late Isaac Nathan Fabricant, and of Helena Fabricant (née Freed). Born June 12, 1950; educated State schools; Loughborough University (BSc Hons Economics and Law); Sussex University (MSc Systems and Econometrics); Oxford University; London University; University of Southern California, Los Angeles, USA (PhD Economics). *Profession:* Lawyer and Chartered Electronics Engineer. *Career:* Economist and founder director, leading broadcast and communications group, manufacturing and commissioning electronics equipment to radio stations in over 50 countries; Adviser, Home Office on broadcasting matters; Former radio broadcaster and journalist; Has been an adviser to foreign governments on the establishment and management of radio stations, including the Russian Federation; Has lived and worked extensively in Europe, Africa, the Far East, and former Soviet Union. *Political Career:* PPS to Michael Jack as Financial Secretary to the Treasury 1996–97. *Select Committees (Current):* Member: Catering 1999–, Home Affairs 1999– *(Former):* Member: European Legislation Scrutiny Committee B (Trade) 1992–97, National Heritage 1993–96, Culture, Media and Sport 1997–98, Culture, Media and Sport 1997–99. *Party Groups:* Former Chairman, Brighton Pavilion Conservative Association; Member, Conservative Way Forward. *International Bodies:* Member: Inter-Parliamentary Union, Commonwealth Parliamentary Association. *Other:* Member, Council of the Institution of Electrical Engineers 1996–. *Miscellaneous:* Presented Bills to strengthen economic and political ties between UK, United States, Canada, Australia and New Zealand; Promoted legislation to encourage the flying of the Union Jack. *Fellowships, etc:* CEng; FIEE. *Special Interests:* Trade and Industry, Foreign Affairs, Broadcasting. *Countries of Interest:* Russia, Israel, USA, Australia, Eastern Europe. *Recreations:* Reading, music, fell-walking, skiing and listening to the Omnibus Edition of The Archers. *Electoral Notes:* Contested South Shields 1987 General Election. Member for Mid-Staffordshire 1992–97, and for Lichfield since May 1, 1997. *Clubs:* Rottingdean (Sussex). *Address:* Michael Fabricant Esq, MP, House of Commons, London, SW1A 0AA *Tel:* 020 7219 5161 *Tel (Constituency):* 01543 419650.

FALLON, Michael *(Sevenoaks)* Con majority 10,461

Son of late Martin Fallon, OBE, FRICS, and Hazel Fallon. Born May 14, 1952; educated Epsom College, Surrey; St Andrews University (MA classics and ancient history 1974). Married September 27, 1986, Wendy Elisabeth, daughter of Peter and Elisabeth Payne (2 sons). *Profession:* Company Director. *Career:* European Educational Research Trust 1974–75; Conservative Research Department 1975–79 (seconded to Opposition Whips Office, House of Lords 1975–77, EEC Desk Officer 1977–79); Secretary, Lord Home's Committee on Future of the House of Lords 1977–78; Joint Managing Director, European Consultants Ltd 1979–81; Assistant to Baroness Elles 1979–83; Director, Quality Care Homes plc 1992–97; Chief Executive, Quality Care Developments Ltd 1996–97; Director of other companies. *Political Career:* PPS to Rt Hon. Cecil Parkinson, MP, as Secretary of State for Energy 1987–88; Parliamentary Under-Secretary of State, Department of Education and Science 1990–92. *Whip:* Assistant Government Whip 1988–90; Lord Commissioner of HM Treasury (Senior Government Whip) May-July 1990. *Spokesman:* A Front Bench Spokesman on: Trade and Industry June-December 1997, the Treasury (Tax, except VAT and Duties; Financial Services and City Issues; Competition and Deregulation) December 1997–98. *Select Committees (Current):* Member: Treasury 1999–, Treasury Sub-Committee 1999–. *Other:* Non-Executive Director, International Care and Relief. *Miscellaneous:* Member: Higher Education Funding Council 1992–97, Deregulation Task Force 1994–97, Advisory Council, Social Market Foundation 1994–. *Publications: Brighter Schools,* Social Market Foundation 1993. *Special Interests:* Constitution, Public Sector, Education. *Electoral Notes:* Contested Darlington By-election March 1983. Member for Darlington 1983–92, and for Sevenoaks since May 1, 1997. *Address:* Michael Fallon Esq, MP, House of Commons, London, SW1A 0AA *Tel:* 020 7219 6482. *Constituency:* 113 St John's Hill, Sevenoaks, TN13 3PF *Tel:* 01732 452261.

FEARN, Ronnie, OBE *(Southport)   LD majority 6,160*

Son of late James Fearn and late Martha Ellen Fearn. Born February 6, 1931; educated Norwood School; King George V Grammar School. Married June 11, 1955, Joyce Dugan, daughter of John and Alice Dugan (1 son 1 daughter). *Trades Union:* Member, Association of Liberal Democrat Trade Unionists. *Armed Forces:* Two years service in Royal Navy. *Profession:* Banker (Retired). *Career:* Banking, Royal Bank of Scotland 1947–87. *Councils, Public Bodies:* Former Councillor and Leader of Lib Dem Group: Southport Borough Council 1963–74, Merseyside Metropolitan County Council; Councillor, Sefton Metropolitan Borough Council 1974–. *Whip:* Deputy Whip 1988–90. *Spokesman:* A Liberal Democrat Spokesman for: Health, Tourism, Housing, Transport 1989–92, National Heritage, Constitution and Civil Service (Tourism) 1997, Culture, Media, Sport and Civil Service (Tourism) 1997–99, Constitution, Culture and Sport (Tourism) 1999–. *Select Committees (Current):* Member: Culture, Media and Sport 1997–. *International Bodies:* Member: IPU, CPA. *Other:* Voluntary Youth Leader in Southport for 21 years; President, Local Carers' Association; Local President, Sue Rider Association; Member: All Souls' Dramatic Association, Southport Offshore Lifeboat; Hon. Member, LIFE. *Miscellaneous:* Member, Sefton Sports Council. *Sportsclubs:* President, Southport and Waterloo Athletic Club. *Honours:* OBE 1985. Fellow, Chartered Institute of Bankers. *Special Interests:* Tourism, Health, Transport, Leisure, Local Government. *Recreations:* Amateur dramatics, badminton, athletics, community work. *Electoral Notes:* Member for Southport: (Liberal) 1987–88, (Liberal Democrat) 1988–92. Contested Southport 1992. Member for Southport since May 1, 1997. *Address:* Ronnie Fearn Esq, OBE, MP, House of Commons, London, SW1A 0AA *Tel:* 020 7219 5116 *Fax:* 020 7219 2331. *Constituency:* Liberal Democrat Headquarters, 35 Shakespeare Street, Southport, Merseyside, PR8 5AB *Tel:* 01704 533555 *Fax:* 01704 533535 *E-mail:* cixforliberaldemocrats-southportldp; fearnr@parliament.uk.

FIELD, The Rt Hon. Frank *(Birkenhead)   Lab majority 21,843*

Son of late Walter Field. Born July 16, 1942; educated St Clement Danes Grammar School; University of Hull. *Career:* Teacher in Further Education 1964–69; Director: Child Poverty Action Group 1969–79, Low Pay Unit 1974–80. *Councils, Public Bodies:* Councillor, Hounslow Borough Council 1964–68. *Political Career:* Minister of State, Department of Social Security (Welfare Reform) 1997–98. *Spokesman:* Opposition Front Bench Spokesman on Education 1980–81. *Select Committees (Former):* Chairman: Social Security 1990–97. *Honours:* PC 1997. *Publications:* Publications on low pay, poverty and social issues since 1971. *Special Interests:* Poverty and Income Redistribution, Ecclesiastical Matters. *Countries of Interest:* Poland. *Electoral Notes:* Contested Buckinghamshire South 1966. Member for Birkenhead since May 1979. *Address:* The Rt Hon. Frank Field, MP, House of Commons, London, SW1A 0AA *Tel:* 020 7219 6693 *Fax:* 020 7219 0332 *E-mail:* hendeyj@parliament.uk.

FISHER, Mark *(Stoke-on-Trent Central)   Lab majority 19,924*

Son of late Sir Nigel Fisher, MC, MP 1950–83 and late Lady Gloria Flower. Born October 29, 1944; educated Eton College; Trinity College, Cambridge (MA). Married December 16, 1971, Ingrid Hunt (2 sons 2 daughters) (marriage dissolved 1999). *Trades Union:* Member: NUT, MU. *Career:* Documentary film producer and scriptwriter 1966–75; Principal, The Tattenhall Centre of Education 1975–83. *Councils, Public Bodies:* Staffordshire County Council: Councillor 1981–85, Chairman, Libraries Committee 1981–83. *Political Career:* Parliamentary Under-Secretary of State: Department of National Heritage 1997, Department for Culture, Media and Sport 1997–98. *Whip:* Opposition Whip 1985–86. *Spokesman:* Spokesperson on Arts and Media 1987–92; Front Bench Spokesperson on: The Citizen's Charter 1992–93, National Heritage 1993–97. *Select Committees (Former):* Member: Treasury and Civil Service 1983–85. *Other:* Deputy Pro-Chancellor, Keele University 1989–97; Member, BBC General Advisory Council 1987–97; Member of Council, Policy Studies Institute 1989–97. *Trust:* Trustee: National Benevolent Fund for the Aged

1986–97, Education Extra 1992–97, Britten Peers Foundation 1998–. *Miscellaneous:* Museums and Galleries Commission 1999–. Hon. FRIBA 1992; Hon. Fellow, Royal College of Art 1993. *Publications: City Centres, City Cultures,* 1988; *Whose Cities?* (editor) 1991; *A New London,* 1992. *Special Interests:* Urban Policies, Freedom of Information, Human Rights, Overseas Aid and Development, Broadcasting, Press, Cultural Policy, Arts. *Countries of Interest:* Hong Kong, Kashmir, Pakistan, Central Asia. *Electoral Notes:* Contested Leek 1979 General Election. Member for Stoke-on-Trent Central since June 1983. *Address:* Mark Fisher Esq, MP, House of Commons, London, SW1A 0AA *Tel:* 020 7219 3000 *Fax:* 020 7219 4894. *Constituency:* 28 Hartshill Road, Stoke-on-Trent *Tel:* 01782 284009 *Fax:* 01782 283119 *E-mail:* fisherm@parliament.uk.

FITZPATRICK, Jim (James) *(Poplar and Canning Town)* Lab majority 18,915

Son of James and Jean Fitzpatrick. Born April 4, 1952; educated Holyrood Senior Secondary, Glasgow. Married July 12, 1980, Jane Lowe, daughter of Frederick Ronald Lowe and Gwyneth Lowe (1 son 1 daughter). *Trades Union:* Member, National Executive Council, Fire Brigades Union. *Career:* Trainee, Tytrak Ltd, Glasgow 1970–73; Driver, Mintex Ltd, London 1973–74; Firefighter, London Fire Brigade 1974–97. *Political Career:* PPS to Rt Hon. Alan Milburn, MP, as Secretary of State for Health 1999–. *Party Groups:* Barking Constituency Labour Party: Voluntary Agent 1986–91, Chairman 1989–90; Member, London Labour Executive 1988–; Chairman, Greater London Labour Party 1991–; Hon. Treasurer, London Regional Group of Labour MPs 1999–. *Other:* Parent Governor, Eastbury Comprehensive School; Member: War on Want, Amnesty International, Greenpeace, Labour Animal Welfare Society. *Awards:* Fire Brigade Long Service and Good Conduct Medal (20 years) 1994. *Sportsclubs:* West Ham United FC. *Special Interests:* Anti-Poverty, Regeneration, Anti-Racism. *Recreations:* Golf, cycling, reading, TV/film, football. *Electoral Notes:* Member for Poplar and Canning Town since May 1, 1997. *Address:* Jim Fitzpatrick Esq, MP, House of Commons, London, SW1A 0AA *Tel:* 020 7219 5085 *E-mail:* fitzpatrickj@parliament.uk.

FITZSIMONS, Lorna *(Rochdale)* Lab majority 4,545

Daughter of Derek Fitzsimons and Barbara Jean Fitzsimons (née Taylor). Born August 6, 1967; educated St James's Church of England, Wardle; Wardle High School, Rochdale; Rochdale College of Art and Design; Loughborough College of Art and Design (BA Hons Textile Design). *Trades Union:* National Union of Students: Part-time Executive Member 1989–90; Vice-President, Education 1990–92; President 1992–94; Member, MSF. *Profession:* Artist (Weaver)/Lobbyist. *Career:* Director: NUS Services 1990–94; Endsleigh Insurance 1992–94; Political Consultant (Associate Director), The Rowland Company 1994–. *Select Committees (Current):* Member: Procedure 1997–, Modernisation of the House of Commons 1999–. *Party Groups:* Member: Labour Campaign for Electoral Reform, Labour NEC Youth Committee 1990–94, LCC Executive 1994–97; Fabian Society, Labour Friends of Israel. *International Bodies:* Chair, The European Students Forum 1992–93; Parliamentary Vice-Chair, Council for Education in the Commonwealth. *Other:* Governor: Wardle High School 1982–83, Loughborough College of Art and Design 1988–89, Sheffield Hallam University 1995–96. *Trust:* Patron, Real Lancashire. *Awards:* Young Communicator of the Year Award, Institute of Public Relations 1996. *Miscellaneous:* Member, Further Education Funding Council Quality Committee 1993–94; Registered with The Sheffield Institute for Dyslexia. *Special Interests:* Education, Modernisation of Parliament, Health. *Countries of Interest:* USA, Italy, South Africa, Vietnam, Kashmir, Pakistan, Bangladesh. *Recreations:* Music, walking, cooking, cinema. *Electoral Notes:* Member for Rochdale since May 1, 1997. *Address:* Lorna Fitzsimons, MP, House of Commons, London, SW1A 0AA *Tel:* 020 7219 3433. *Constituency:* 81 Durham Street, Rochdale, Greater Manchester, OL11 1LR *Tel:* 01706 644911 *Fax:* 01706 759826 *E-mail:* lorna.fitzsimons@labour.co.uk.

FLIGHT, Howard Emerson *(Arundel and South Downs)   Con majority 14,035*

Son of late Bernard Thomas Flight and late Doris Mildred Emerson Flight. Born June 16, 1948; educated Brentwood School, Essex; Magdalene College, Cambridge (MA Economics); University of Michigan, USA (MBA). Married June 16, 1973, Christabel Diana Beatrice Norbury (1 son 3 daughters). *Profession:* Investment Management. *Career:* Investment Adviser, N M Rothschild 1971–73; Manager: Cayzer Ltd 1973–77, Wardley Ltd (HSBC) Hong Kong 1977–78; Hong Kong Bank, Merchant Banking Division, Bombay, India 1978–79; Director, Investment Division, Guinness Mahon 1979–86; Joint Managing Director, Guinness Flight Global Asset Management Ltd 1986–97; Chairman, Investec Guinness Flight Asset Management 1997–. *Political Career:* Shadow Economic Secretary to the Treasury 1999–. *Select Committees (Former):* Member: Environment, Transport and Regional Affairs 1997–98, Environment 1997–98, Social Security 1998–99. *Party Groups:* Chairman, Cambridge University Conservative Association 1968–69; Vice-Chairman, Federation of Conservative Students 1969. *International Bodies:* Power Exchange Scholar 1969–71. *Other:* President, Magdalene College Association, Cambridge. *Trust:* Trustee, Elgar Foundation. *Miscellaneous:* Member, Tax Consultative Committee to HM Treasury 1988–92. Member, Carpenters' Company. Freeman, City of London 1999. *Sportsclubs:* Marden (Skiing). *Fellowships, etc:* FRSA. *Publications: All You Need to Know About Exchange Rates* 1988. *Special Interests:* Tax, Economic Policy, Farming. *Countries of Interest:* India, South-East Asia, USA, China. *Recreations:* Skiing, classical music, antique collecting, gardening. *Electoral Notes:* Contested Southwark (Bermondsey) February and October 1974. Member for Arundel and South Downs since May 1, 1997. *Clubs:* Carlton. *Address:* Howard Flight Esq, MP, House of Commons, London, SW1A 0AA *Tel:* 020 7219 3461 *Fax:* 020 7219 2455. *Constituency:* The Old Town Hall, Steyning, West Sussex, BN44 3YE *Tel:* 01903 816886/879787 *Fax:* 01903 816880 *E-mail:* flighth@parliament.uk.

FLINT, Caroline Louise *(Don Valley)   Lab majority 14,659*

Daughter of late Wendy Flint (née Beasley), clerical/shop employee. Born September 20, 1961; educated Twickenham Girls School; Richmond Tertiary College; University of East Anglia (BA Hons American History/Literature and Film Studies). Marriage dissolved; partner, Phil Cole (1 son 1 daughter 1 stepson). *Trades Union:* Former Member: NALGO, TGWU, MSF; Member, GMB; Former Shop Steward: NALGO at GLC/LEA, GMB at Lambeth Council. *Career:* Management Trainee, GLC/ILEA 1984–85; Policy Officer, ILEA 1985–87; Head, Women's Unit, NUS 1988–89; Equal Opportunities Officer, Lambeth Council 1989–91; Welfare and Staff Development Officer, Lambeth Council 1991–93; Senior Researcher/Political Officer, GMB Trade Union 1994–97. *Political Career:* Joint PPS to the Ministers of State, Foreign and Commonwealth Office 1999–. *Select Committees (Former):* Member: Education and Employment 1997–99, Education Sub-Committee 1997–99. *Party Groups:* Member, Labour Party 1979–; National Women's Officer, Labour Students 1983–85; Executive Member, Labour Co-ordinating Committee 1984–85; Chair, Brentford and Isleworth Constituency Labour Party 1991–95; Branch Chair, Branch Secretary and GC Delegate; Facilitator, Labour National Policy Forums 1994–97; Associate Editor, *Renewal* 1995–; Member, Fabian Society; Member, Trade Union Group of Labour MPs. *International Bodies:* Member, Inter-Parliamentary Union 1997–. *Other:* Governor, Strand-on-the-Green Infant and Junior School 1991–97; Member, Working For Childcare 1989–99, Chair 1991–95. *Miscellaneous:* Member, GMB Group of MPs; Labour Party Adviser to the Police Federation of England and Wales 1999–. *Special Interests:* Employment, Education and Training, Childcare, Welfare to Work. *Recreations:* Cinema, tennis, being with my family and friends. *Electoral Notes:* Member for Don Valley since May 1, 1997. *Address:* Caroline Flint, MP, House of Commons, London, SW1A 0AA *Tel:* 020 7219 4407. *Constituency:* Room 10, 7 North Bridge Road, Doncaster, South Yorkshire, DN5 9AA *Tel:* 01302 366778 *Fax:* 01302 328833.

FLYNN, Paul *(Newport West)   Lab majority 14,537*

Son of late James and late Kathleen Flynn. Born February 9, 1935; educated St Illtyd's College, Cardiff; University College, Cardiff. Married 2nd, January 31, 1985, Samantha, daughter of Douglas and Elsie Cumpstone (1 step-son, 1 step-daughter and 1 son and 1 daughter (deceased) from previous marriage). *Career:* Chemist, steel industry 1962–83; Broadcaster, Gwent Community Radio 1983–84; Research officer for Llewellyn Smith, as Labour MEP for South Wales 1984–87. *Councils, Public Bodies:* Formerly Councillor: Newport Council, Gwent County. Council. *Spokesman:* Opposition Spokesman on: Health and Social Security 1988–89, Social Security 1989–90. *Select Committees (Former):* Member: Transport 1992–97, Welsh Affairs 1997–98. *Party Groups:* Vice-Chair, Welsh Group of Labour MPs 1997–. *International Bodies:* Member, UK Delegation to Council of Europe and Western European Union 1997–. *Awards:* Campaign for Freedom of Information Award 1991; Highland Park/*The Spectator* Backbencher of the Year (jointly) 1996. *Miscellaneous:* Board Member, Parliamentary Office of Science and Technology (POST) 1997–. *Publications: Commons Knowledge. How to be a Backbencher,* 1997; *Baglu Mlaen (Staggering Forward),* 1998; *Dragons Led by Poodles,* 1999. *Special Interests:* Health, Medicinal and Illegal Drugs, Social Security, Pensions, Animal Welfare, Devolution in Wales and Welsh Language, Parliamentary and Constitutional Reform. *Countries of Interest:* Baltic States, Eastern Europe, Hungary, Romania, Israel. *Recreations:* Local history, photography. *Electoral Notes:* Contested Denbigh October 1974. Member for Newport West since June 1987. *Address:* Paul Flynn Esq, MP, House of Commons, London, SW1A 0AA *Tel:* 020 7219 3478 *Fax:* 020 7219 2433 *Tel (Constituency):* 01633 262348 *E-mail:* info@paulflynnmp.co.uk; *Website:* www.paulflynnmp.co.uk.

FOLLETT, (Daphne) Barbara *(Stevenage)   Lab majority 11,582*

Daughter of late William Vernon Hubbard and Charlotte Hubbard. Born December 25, 1942; educated Sandford School, Addis Ababa, Ethiopia; Ellerslie Girls' High School, Cape Town; University of Cape Town; Open University; London School of Economics (BSc Econ). Married 1st, 1963, Richard Turner (2 daughters); married 2nd, Gerald Stonestreet; married 3rd, Les Broer (1 son); married 4th, Kenneth Martin Follett, son of Martin and Lavinia Follett (1 stepson 1 stepdaughter). *Trades Union:* Member, MSF. *Career:* Part-time Salesperson 1960–62: Ledger Clerk, Barclays Bank of South Africa 1962–63; EFL Teacher, Berlitz School of Languages 1964–66; Joint Manager, Fruit Farm 1966–70; Acting Regional Secretary, South African Institute of Race Relations 1970–71; Regional Manager, Kupugani 1971–74; National Health Education Director, Kupugani 1975–78; Lecturer and Assistant Course Organiser at the Centre for International Briefing 1980–84; Lecturer in Cross-cultural Communications 1985–87; Research Associate, Institute of Public Policy Research 1993–96, Visiting Fellow 1993–; Director, EMILY's List UK 1993–. *Select Committees (Current):* Member: International Development 1997–. *Party Groups:* Member: Fabian Society, SERA; Chair, Eastern Regional Group of Labour MPs 1999–. *Other:* Member: ACTSA, Charter 88, CPAG, FOE, Greenpeace, LCER, Liberty, OWA, Fawcett Society, NAWO; Head, South African Women's Movement for Peace 1976–78; Governor: Heath End Comprehensive 1981–84, Ashburnham School 1986–87, Bousefield School 1986–87, Nobel School Stevenage. RSA. *Special Interests:* Economic and Industrial Policy, Gender, Race Relations, Overseas Aid and Development, International Development, Trade and Industry, Housing, Film Industry. *Countries of Interest:* Africa, France. *Recreations:* Reading, Scrabble, photography, film, theatre and Star Trek. *Electoral Notes:* Contested Woking 1983, Epsom and Ewell 1987. Member for Stevenage since May 1, 1997. *Address:* Barbara Follett, MP, House of Commons, London, SW1A 0AA *Tel:* 020 7219 2649 *Fax:* 020 7219 1158. *Constituency:* The Old Rectory, Old Knebworth Lane, Stevenage, Hertfordshire, SG3 6PT *Tel:* 01438 817910 *Fax:* 01438 811410 *E-mail:* compuserve100064,3515; barbara@barbara-follett.org.uk *Website:* www.poptel.org.uk/barbara.follett.

FORSYTHE, Clifford *(South Antrim)   UUP majority 16,611*

Son of late Robert Forsythe. Born August 24, 1929; educated Glengormley Public Elementary School. *Career:* Professional footballer 1950–57; Plumbing and heating contractor 1957–83. *Councils, Public Bodies:* Newtownabbey Borough Council: Councillor 1981–85, Mayor 1983. *Political Career:* Elected to Northern Ireland Assembly 1982; Deputy Chairman, Northern Ireland Assembly January 1983. *Spokesman:* Party Spokesman for: Transport Communications and Local Government 1992–97, Social Security and Transport 1997–. *Select Committees (Current):* Member: Environment, Transport and Regional Affairs 1997–, Transport Sub-Committee 1997– *(Former):* Member: Social Security 1991–97. *Party Groups:* Chairman, South Antrim Official Unionist Association 1981–83. *Other:* Chairman, Glengormley Branch Chest, Heart and Stroke Association, Northern Ireland. *Trust:* Friend of Martin Trust; Fellow, Industry and Parliament Trust. *Special Interests:* Environment. *Recreations:* Soccer, running, drama, church choir. *Electoral Notes:* Member for South Antrim since June 1983. *Address:* Clifford Forsythe Esq, MP, House of Commons, London, SW1A 0AA *Tel:* 020 7219 4144.

FORTH, The Rt Hon. Eric *(Bromley and Chislehurst)   Con majority 11,118*

Son of late William Forth and Aileen Forth. Born September 9, 1944; educated Jordanhill College School, Glasgow; Glasgow University (MA (Hons) Politics and Economics). Married 1st, March 11, 1967, Linda, daughter of Peter St Clair (2 daughters) (marriage dissolved 1994), married 2nd, 1994, Mrs Carroll Goff (1 step-son). *Career:* Manager, Industry (Ford, Rank Xerox, etc). *Councils, Public Bodies:* Councillor, Brentwood Urban District Council 1968–72. *Political Career:* Joint Parliamentary Under-Secretary of State for Industry and Consumer Affairs, Department of Trade and Industry 1988–90; Joint Parliamentary Under-Secretary of State, Department of Employment 1990–92; Department for Education: Parliamentary Under-Secretary of State for Schools 1992–94, Minister of State 1994–95; Minister of State, Department for Education and Employment 1995–97. *Select Committees (Current):* Member: Procedure 1999–, Standards and Privileges 1999–. *Honours:* PC 1997. *Special Interests:* Economic Policy, European Union, USA. *Countries of Interest:* Canada, USA, Australia, New Zealand. *Recreations:* Cinema, political biographies. *Electoral Notes:* Contested Barking February and October 1974. MEP for Birmingham North 1979–84. Member for Mid Worcestershire 1983–97, and for Bromley and Chislehurst since May 1, 1997. *Clubs:* Bromley Conservative. *Address:* The Rt Hon. Eric Forth, MP, House of Commons, London, SW1A 0AA *Tel:* 020 7219 6344. *Constituency:* Bromley and Chislehurst Conservative Association, 5 White Horse Hill, Chislehurst, Kent, BR7 6DG *Tel:* 020 8295 2639 *E-mail:* forthe@parliament.uk.

FOSTER, The Rt Hon. Derek *(Bishop Auckland)   Lab majority 21,064*

Son of Joseph Foster, Shipyard worker. Born June 25, 1937; educated Bede Grammar School, Sunderland; Oxford University (BA Hons Philosophy, Politics and Economics). Married October 21, 1972, Florence Anne, daughter of Thomas Bulmer (3 sons 1 daughter). *Profession:* Education Administrator. *Career:* Ten years marketing in the private sector; Youth and Community 1970–73; Further Education Organiser 1973–74; Assistant Director of Education, Sunderland Borough Council 1974–79. *Councils, Public Bodies:* Councillor, Sunderland County Borough Council 1972–74; Tyne and Wear County Council: Councillor 1973–77, Chairman: Economic Development Committee 1974–76, North of England Development Council 1974–76. *Political Career:* PPS to Neil Kinnock as Leader of Opposition 1983–85; Member, Shadow Cabinet 1985–97; Shadow Chancellor of the Duchy of Lancaster 1995–97. *Whip:* Opposition Whip 1981–82; Opposition Chief Whip 1985–95. *Spokesman:* Opposition Front Bench Spokesman on Social Security 1982–83; Principal Opposition Spokesman for the Duchy of Lancaster 1995–97. *Select Committees (Current):* Chairman (Employment): Education and Employment 1997–; Member: Education Sub-Committee 1997–; Chairman: Employment Sub-Committee 1997–; Member: Liaison 1997–. *Party Groups:* Ex-Officio Member, Labour Party National Executive Committee 1985–95; Member: Fabian

Society, Christian Socialists Society. *Other:* Uniformed Member, Salvation Army; Former Vice-Chairman, Youthaid 1979–83. *Trust:* Fellow, Industry and Parliament Trust; Trustee, Auckland Castle. *Miscellaneous:* Vice-Chairman, Youth Affairs Lobby 1984–86; Hon. President, British Youth Council 1984–86; Vice-President, Christian Socialist Movement 1985–; Member: Ecclesiastical Committee 1997–, National Advisory Board of the Salvation Army, Advisory Committee for the Registration of Political Parties; Chairman: Pioneering Care Partnership 1997–, North Regional Information Society Initiative 1997–, National Prayer Breakfast 1998. *Sportsclubs:* Durham County Cricket. *Honours:* PC 1993. *Publications:* Articles in: *Guardian* newspaper, *Overview. Special Interests:* Youth Affairs, Education and Training, Regional Policy, Socialist Enterprise, Transport, Economics, Finance. *Countries of Interest:* USA, Japan. *Recreations:* Brass Bands, Male Voice Choirs, Cricket, Soccer. *Electoral Notes:* Member for Bishop Auckland since May 1979. *Address:* The Rt Hon. Derek Foster, MP, House of Commons, London, SW1A 0AA *Tel:* 020 7219 3582/6500 *Fax:* 020 7219 2711. *Constituency:* Hackworth House, Byerley Road, Shildon, Co Durham *Tel:* 01388 777175 *Fax:* 01388 777175.

FOSTER, Don *(Bath)*   LD majority 9,319

Son of late Rev. J. A. Foster and late I. E. Foster. Born March 31, 1947; educated Lancaster Royal Grammar School; Keele University (BSc Hons Physics and Psychology 1969, CEd 1969); Bath University (MEd 1981); Hon. Fellow, Bath College of High Education. Married December 31, 1968, Victoria Jane Dorcas, daughter of Major K. W. Pettegree, OBE (1 son 1 daughter). *Career:* Science teacher, Sevenoaks School, Kent 1969–75; Science Project Director, Resources for Learning Development Unit, Avon LEA 1975–80; Education lecturer, Bristol University 1980–89; Managing consultant, Pannell Kerr Forster 1989–92. *Councils, Public Bodies:* Avon County Council: Councillor, Cabot Ward, Bristol 1981–89, Chairman, Education Committee 1987–89.
Spokesman: Spokesman for: Education 1992–95, Education and Employment 1995–97; Spokesman for Education and Employment: Nursery Education and Schools 1997–99, Labour Market Statistics 1997–99; Principal Spokesman for Environment, Transport, the Regions and Social Justice 1999–. *Select Committees (Former):* Member: Education and Employment 1996–99, Education Sub-Committee 1997–99. *Party Groups:* President, Liberal Democrat Youth and Students 1993–95. *Other:* Vice-Chair, National Campaign for Nursery Education 1993–; President, British Association for Early Childhood Education 1998–. *Trust:* Trustee, Open School and Education Extra 1993–. *Miscellaneous:* Executive, Association of County Councils 1985–89; Joint Hon. President, British Youth Council 1992–99; Vice-Chair, British Association for Central and Eastern Europe 1994–97. *Fellowships, etc:* CPhys; MInstP. *Publications: Resource-based Learning in Science,* 1979; *Science With Gas,* 1981; Co-author: *Aspects of Science,* 1984, *Reading About Science,* 1984, *Nuffield Science,* 1986; Numerous educational and political articles and pamphlets. *Special Interests:* Education, Local Government. *Countries of Interest:* Africa, Israel, Central Europe. *Recreations:* Classical music, travel, sport. *Electoral Notes:* Contested (Liberal/Alliance) Bristol East 1987 General Election. Member for Bath since April 9, 1992. *Clubs:* National Liberal. *Address:* Don Foster Esq, MP, House of Commons, London, SW1A 0AA *Tel:* 020 7219 5001 *Fax:* 020 7219 2695. *Constituency:* 31 James Street West, Bath, BA1 2BT *Tel:* 01225 338973 *Fax:* 01225 463630 *E-mail:* fosterd@parliament.uk.

FOSTER, Michael Jabez *(Hastings and Rye)*   Lab majority 2,560

Son of Dorothy Foster. Born February 26, 1946; educated Hastings Secondary; Hastings Grammar School; Leicester University (LLM). Married September 13, 1969, Rosemary, daughter of Eric and Hilda Kemp (2 sons). *Trades Union:* Member and Legal Adviser to GMB. *Profession:* Solicitor. *Career:* Litigation Clerk 1963–72; Solicitor 1980–98. *Councils, Public Bodies:* Councillor: Hastings County Borough Council 1971–74, Hastings Borough Council 1973–79, 1983–87, East Sussex County Council 1973–77, 1981–97; Former Member: Sussex Police Authority, East Sussex Health Authority; DL, East Sussex. *Political Career:* PPS: to Attorneys General John Morris, QC, MP 1999 and Lord Williams of Mostyn, QC 1999–, and to Ross Cranston, QC, MP,
as Solicitor General 1999–. *Select Committees (Current):* Member: Standards and Privileges 1997– *(Former):* Member: Social Security 1998–99. *Party Groups:* Member: Society of Labour Lawyers, Christian Socialist Movement, Fabian Society. *Other:* Member, The Child Poverty Action Group.

Trust: Member, National Trust. *Miscellaneous:* Member: Methodist Church, European Standing Committee A 1998–, Law Society, The Chartered Institute of Arbitrators. *Sportsclubs:* Amherst Tennis Club. *Fellowships, etc:* ASCAb. *Special Interests:* Health and Poverty, Animal Welfare, Tax, Employment Law. *Countries of Interest:* United Kingdom. *Recreations:* Lawn Tennis, Table Tennis. *Electoral Notes:* Contested Hastings February and October 1974 and 1979. Member for Hastings and Rye since May 1, 1997. *Address:* Michael Jabez Foster Esq, DL, MP (Hastings and Rye), House of Commons, London, SW1A 0AA *Tel:* 020 7219 3613 *Fax:* 020 7219 1393. *Constituency:* Ellen Draper Centre, 84 Bohemia Road, St Leonards on Sea, East Sussex, TN37 6RN *Tel:* 01424 460070 *Fax:* 01424 460072 *E-mail:* mp@1066.net.

FOSTER, Michael John *(Worcester)   Lab majority 7,425*

Son of Brian William Foster, car worker, and Edna Foster, retired teacher. Born March 14, 1963; educated Great Wyrley High School, Staffordshire; Wolverhampton Polytechnic (BA Hons Economics, Post-graduate Certificate in Education). Married September 28, 1985, Shauna, daughter of Mr Edward and Mrs Dympna Ogle (1 son 2 daughters). *Trades Union:* Shop Steward, TGWU 1986–88; Current Member, GMB, NATFHE. *Profession:* Management Accountant, Lecturer. *Career:* Financial Planning and Control Department, Jaguar Cars Ltd: Financial Analyst 1984–5, Senior Analyst 1985–87, Manager 1989–91; Lecturer in Accountancy, Worcester College of Technology 1991–97. *Political Career:* Introduced Private Members' Bill to Ban Hunting With Dogs 1998. *Select Committees (Current):* Member: Education and Employment 1999–, Education Sub-Committee 1999–. *Party Groups:* Agent, Mid Worcester 1992; Secretary, Constituency Labour Party, Worcester 1992–95. *Other:* Patron: Maggs Day Centre for Homeless People, Worcester Barn Owls Society. *Sportsclubs:* Worcestershire County Cricket Club, House of Commons Soccer and Cricket Teams. Associate of Chartered Institute of Management Accountants (ACMA). *Special Interests:* Trade and Industry, Education and Training, Hunting With Dogs. *Recreations:* Sport. *Electoral Notes:* Member for Worcester since May 1, 1997. *Address:* Michael John Foster Esq, MP (Worcester), House of Commons, London, SW1A 0AA *Tel:* 020 7219 6379 *Fax:* 020 7219 6379. *Constituency:* 2a The Avenue, The Cross, Worcester *Tel:* 01905 26504 *E-mail:* fosterm@parliament.uk.

FOULKES, George *(Carrick, Cumnock and Doon Valley)   Lab/Co-op majority 21,062*

Son of late George Foulkes, engineer and Jessie Foulkes. Born January 21, 1942; educated Keith Grammar School, Banff; Haberdashers' Aske's School; Edinburgh University (BSc 1964). Married July 4, 1970, Elizabeth Anna, daughter of William and Florence Hope (2 sons 1 daughter). *Trades Union:* Member, GMB. *Profession:* Director of Voluntary Organisations. *Career:* President, Scottish Union of Students 1964–6; Director, ELEC 1966–68; Scottish Organiser, European Movement 1968–69; Director, Enterprise Youth 1969–73; Director, Age Concern Scotland 1973–79. *Councils, Public Bodies:* Councillor: Edinburgh Corporation 1970–75, Lothian Regional Council 1974–79; Chairman: Lothian Region Education Committee 1974–79, Education Committee of Convention of Scottish Local Authorities 1975–78; JP, Edinburgh 1975. *Political Career:* Parliamentary Under-Secretary of State, Department of International Development 1997–. *Spokesman:* Opposition Front Bench Spokesman on: Europe 1983–85, Foreign and Commonwealth Affairs 1985–92, Defence, Disarmament and Arms Control 1992–93, Overseas Development 1994–97. *Select Committees (Former):* Member: Foreign Affairs 1980–83. *Party Groups:* Chairman, Labour Campaign for a Scottish Parliament to 1997; Member, Co-operative Party. *International Bodies:* Delegate, Parliamentary Assemblies of the Council of Europe and Western European Union 1979–80; Vice-Chairman: UK-Netherlands Group of Inter-Parliamentary Union to 1997, UK-Canadian Group of Commonwealth Parliamentary Association to 1997; Treasurer, Anglo-Spanish Group of Inter-Parliamentary Union to 1997; Member: Executive UK Branch of Commonwealth Parliamentary Association 1989–97, Executive British Section of Inter-Parliamentary Union 1989–97. *Other:* Member, Board of St Cuthbert's Co-op Association 1975–79. *Trust:* Member, Commonwealth Parliamentary Association. *Awards:* Wilberforce Medal 1999. *Miscellaneous:* President, Edinburgh University SRC 1963–64; Rector's Assessor, University of Edinburgh 1968–71; Director, The Co-operative Press 1990–97; Chairman, The John Wheatley Centre 1990–97. *Publications:* Editor, *80 Years On*

(History of Edinburgh University SRC); Chapters in: *Scotland – A Claim of Right* (Editor: Owen Dudley Edwards), *Football and the Common People* (Editor: Alastair Campbell). *Special Interests:* International Development, Foreign Affairs, Devolution, Social Services, Tax Havens, Education, Aerospace, Aviation, Energy, Human Rights, Defence. *Countries of Interest:* Latin America, Canada, Netherlands, Eastern Europe. *Recreations:* Boating, season ticket holder and shareholder Heart of Midlothian FC. *Electoral Notes:* Contested Edinburgh West 1970 and Edinburgh Pentlands October 1974. Member for South Ayrshire 1979–83 and for Carrick, Cumnock and Doon Valley since June 1983. *Clubs:* Edinburgh University Staff. *Address:* George Foulkes Esq, MP, House of Commons, London, SW1A 0AA *Tel:* 020 7219 3474 *Fax:* 020 7219 6492. *Constituency:* South Wing, Skerrington Farm, Glaisnock Road, Netherthird, Cumnock, KA18 3BU *Tel:* 01290 422990.

FOWLER, The Rt Hon. Sir Norman *(Sutton Coldfield)* *Con majority 14,885*

Son of late N. F. Fowler and Katherine Fowler. Born February 2, 1938; educated King Edward VI School, Chelmsford; Trinity Hall, Cambridge (MA). Married May 29, 1979, Mrs Fiona Poole, daughter of Mr and Mrs John Donald (2 daughters). *Armed Forces:* National Service, Essex Regiment 1956–58. *Career: The Times:* Special Correspondent 1961–66, Home Affairs Correspondent 1966–70. *Political Career:* PPS to Secretary for Northern Ireland 1972–74; Minister of Transport 1979–81; Secretary of State for: Transport January-September 1981, Social Services 1981–87, Employment 1987–90; Chairman, Conservative Party 1992–94; Member, Shadow Cabinet 1997–99; Shadow Secretary of State for: the Environment, Transport and the Regions 1997–98, the Home Department 1998–99. *Spokesman:* Opposition Spokesman on Home Affairs 1974–75; Chief Opposition Spokesman on: Social Services 1975–76, Transport 1976–79. *Party Groups:* Chairman, Cambridge University Conservative Association 1960; Editorial Board, *Crossbow* 1962–70; Council Member, Bow Group 1967–69; Vice-Chairman, North Kensington Conservative Association 1967–68; Chairman: East Midlands Conservative Political Centre 1970–73, Conservative Party 1992–94. *Honours:* PC 1979; Knighted 1990. *Publications: After the Riots,* 1979; *Ministers Decide,* 1991. *Electoral Notes:* Member for Nottingham South 1970–74, and for Sutton Coldfield since February 1974. *Address:* The Rt Hon. Sir Norman Fowler, MP, House of Commons, London, SW1A 0AA *Tel:* 020 7219 3525 *Fax:* 020 7219 2412. *Constituency:* 36 High Street, Sutton Coldfield, B72 1UP *Tel:* 0121–354 2229 *Fax:* 0121–321 1762.

FOX, Dr Liam *(Woodspring)* *Con majority 7,734*

Son of William Fox, teacher, and Catherine Fox. Born September 22, 1961; educated St Bride's High School, East Kilbride; University of Glasgow (MB, ChB 1983, MROGP 1989). *Career:* General Practitioner; Divisional Surgeon, St John's Ambulance. *Political Career:* PPS to the Home Secretary 1993–94; Parliamentary Under-Secretary of State, Foreign and Commonwealth Office 1996–97; Member, Shadow Cabinet 1998–; Shadow Secretary of State for Health 1999–. *Whip:* Assistant Government Whip 1994–95; Lord Commissioner of HM Treasury (Government Whip) 1995–96. *Spokesman:* An Opposition Spokesman for Constitutional Affairs, Scotland and Wales 1997–98; Front Bench Spokesman for Constitutional Affairs, with overall responsibility for Scottish and Welsh issues 1998–99. *Select Committees (Former):* Member: Scottish Affairs 1992–93. *Party Groups:* Joined Conservative Party 1975; Chairman, West of Scotland Young Conservatives 1983; National Vice-Chairman, Scottish Young Conservatives 1983–84; Secretary, West Country Conservative Members' Committee 1992–93. *Other:* Member, Central Committee, Families for Defence 1987–89. *Awards:* World Debating Competition, Toronto (Individual speaking prize) 1982, Best Speaker's Trophy, University of Glasgow 1983. *Miscellaneous:* President, Glasgow University Club 1982–83; Guest of US State Department, involving study of drug abuse problems in USA, and Republican Party campaigning techniques 1985. *Publications: Making Unionism Positive,* 1988; *Review of Health Reforms* (House of Commons Magazine), 1989. *Special Interests:* Health, Defence, Economic Policy. *Recreations:* Tennis, swimming, cinema, theatre. *Electoral Notes:* Contested Roxburgh and Berwickshire in 1987 General Election. Member for Woodspring since April 9, 1992. *Address:* Dr Liam Fox, MP, House of Commons, London, SW1A 0AA *Tel:* 020 7219 4086 *Fax:* 020 7219 2617. *Constituency:* 71 High Street, Nailsea, North Somerset, BS48 1AW *Tel:* 01275 790090 *Fax:* 01275 790091.

FRASER, Christopher James *(Mid Dorset and Poole North)   Con majority 681*

Son of Mr and Mrs R. A. Fraser. Born October 25, 1962; educated Harrow College; Polytechnic of Central London (BA Hons). Married 1987, Lisa Margaret (1 son 1 daughter). *Profession:* Management Consultant. *Career:* Chairman, International Communications Group of Companies. *Councils, Public Bodies:* Councillor, Three Rivers District Council 1992–96. *Political Career:* Secretary to Rt Hon. the Lord Strathclyde, as Leader of the Opposition in the House of Lords 1999–. *Select Committees (Current):* Member: Culture, Media and Sport 1997 . *International Bodies:* Member: Inter-Parliamentary Union 1997–, Commonwealth Parliamentary Association 1997–. *Other:* Member, The Society of Dorset Men; LEA-appointed School Governor 1992–96; Director, Small Business Bureau; Patron, Firm Link, Business Forum, Dorset; Appeals Chairman, Pramacare Charity, Dorset; Member, County Committee, Holton Lee Charity, Dorset. *Miscellaneous:* Member, Institute of Directors. Freeman, City of London. *Special Interests:* Small Business and Enterprise, Arts, Media, Voluntary Organisations, Constitution, Foreign Affairs, Local Government, Rural Affairs, Tourism/Leisure Industry. *Countries of Interest:* SE Asia, Europe, USA, Canada, China, Australia. *Recreations:* Golf, sailing, skiing, riding. *Electoral Notes:* Member for Mid Dorset and Poole North since May 1, 1997. *Clubs:* Carlton, Athenaeum. *Address:* Christopher Fraser Esq, MP, House of Commons, London, SW1A 0AA *Tel:* 020 7219 6569 *Fax:* 020 7219 4499. *Constituency:* 38 Sandbanks Road, Poole, Dorset, BH14 8BX *Tel:* 01202 718080 *E-mail:* fraserc@parliament.uk.

FYFE, Maria *(Glasgow Maryhill)   Lab majority 14,264*

Daughter of late James and Margaret O'Neill (née Lacey). Born November 25, 1938; educated Notre Dame High School, Glasgow; Strathclyde University (Economic History). Married April 4, 1964, James (deceased), son of James and Elizabeth Fyfe (2 sons). *Career:* Secretary, Scottish Gas Board; Mature student 1970–75; Senior Lecturer, Trade Union Studies Unit, Central College of Commerce, Glasgow 1978–87. *Councils, Public Bodies:* Glasgow District Council: Councillor 1980–87, Vice-Convenor, Finance 1980–84, Convenor, Personnel 1984–87. *Spokesman:* Opposition Spokesperson on: Women 1988–91, Scottish Health and Social Services 1992–94, Scottish Education and Social Work 1994–95. *Party Groups:* Member, Labour Party Scottish Executive 1982–88; Chairperson, Local Government Committee 1985–87. *International Bodies:* Member: UK Delegation to Council of Europe and Western Europe Union, Chair, Labour Group 1997–; British-Irish Parliamentary Body. *Special Interests:* Local Government, Trade Unions, Employment Law, Women's Rights. *Countries of Interest:* Central America, Guyana, Nicaragua, Palestine, Ireland. *Recreations:* Reading, music, walking. *Electoral Notes:* Member for Glasgow Maryhill since June 1987. *Clubs:* Keir Hardie. *Address:* Mrs Maria Fyfe, MP, House of Commons, London, SW1A 0AA *Tel:* 020 7219 4430 *Fax:* 020 7219 4885. *Constituency:* c/o Maryhill Public Library, 1508 Maryhill Road, Glasgow, G20 9AB *Tel:* 0141–945 1495 *Fax:* 0141–945 1846.

G

GALBRAITH, Samuel Laird *(Strathkelvin and Bearsden)   Lab majority 16,292*

Son of late Sam and Cathie Galbraith. Born October 18, 1945; educated Greenock High School; University of Glasgow (BSc Hons 1968, MB ChB Hons 1971, MD 1977). Married 1987 (3 daughters). *Career:* Consultant Neurosurgeon. *Political Career:* Parliamentary Under-Secretary of State, Scottish Office (Minister for Health and the Arts) 1997–99; Minister for Children and Education, Culture, Arts and Sport, Scottish Parliament 1999–. *Spokesman:* Opposition Spokesperson on: Health 1988–92, Scotland 1988–92, Opposition Front Bench Spokesperson on Employment 1992–93. FRCS Glas. 1975. *Publications: An Introduction to Neurosurgery,* 1983. *Electoral Notes:* Member for Strathkelvin and Bearsden since June 1987. MSP for the Constituency of Strathkelvin and Bearsden since May 6, 1999. *Address:* Sam Galbraith Esq, MP, MSP, House of Commons, London, SW1A 0AA *Tel:* 020 7219 4079. *Constituency:* 110A Maxwell Avenue, Bearsden, Glasgow, G61 1HU *Tel:* 0141–942 9662 *Fax:* 0141–942 9658 *E-mail:* sam.galbraith.msp@scottish.parliament.uk.

GALE, Roger James *(North Thanet)   Con majority 2,766*

Son of Richard Byrne Gale, solicitor, and Phyllis Mary Gale (née Rowell). Born August 20, 1943; educated Hardye's School, Dorchester; Guildhall School of Music and Drama (LGSM&D). Married 1st, 1964, Wendy Bowman (marriage dissolved 1967), married 2nd, 1971, Susan Linda Sampson (marriage dissolved 1980) (1 daughter), married 3rd, 1980, Susan Gabrielle Marks (2 sons). *Trades Union:* Member: NUJ, Equity, BECTU. *Profession:* Television Producer/Director and Broadcaster. *Career:* Freelance broadcaster; Programme Director, Radio Scotland; Personal Assistant to General Manager, Universal Films 1963–72; Freelance reporter, BBC Radio London 1972–73; Producer: Radio 1 *Newsbeat,* BBC Radio 4 *Today* 1973–76; Director, BBC Children's Television 1976–79; Senior Producer, Children's Television, Thames TV; Editor, Teenage Unit; Producer special projects, Thames TV 1979–83. *Political Career:* PPS to Ministers of State for the Armed Forces: Rt Hon. Archibald Hamilton, MP 1992–93, Jeremy Hanley, MP 1993–94. *Select Committees (Current):* Member: Broadcasting 1997–, Chairmen's Panel 1997– *(Former):* Member: Home Affairs 1990–92. *Party Groups:* Vice-Chairman, Holborn & St Pancras Conservative Association 1971–72; Member, Greater London Young Conservative Committee 1972–82. *International Bodies:* Delegate, Council of Europe 1987–89; Joint Secretary, Esperanto Parliamentary Group Member, Delegation of Council of Europe, Western European Union 1987–89. *Other:* Fellow, Parliament and Armed Forces Fellowship; Inaugural Fellowship, Police and Parliamentary Fellowship 1995. *Trust:* Fellow, Industry and Parliament Trust. *Miscellaneous:* Hon. Associate, British Veterinary Association. Freeman, City of London. *Sportsclubs:* Kent County Cricket, Royal Temple Yacht. LGSM&D. *Special Interests:* Education, Animal Welfare, Media, Broadcasting, Tourism, Leisure Industry, Cable/Communications, Licensed Trade. *Countries of Interest:* Cyprus, Cuba, Tunisia. *Recreations:* Swimming, sailing. *Electoral Notes:* Contested Birmingham Northfield by-election 1982. Member for North Thanet since June 1983. *Clubs:* Farmer's. *Address:* Roger Gale Esq, MP, House of Commons, London, SW1A 0AA *Tel:* 020 7219 4087 *Fax:* 020 7219 6828. *Constituency:* The Old Forge, 15a Canterbury Road, Birchington, Kent, CT7 9AH *Tel:* 01843 848588 *Fax:* 01843 844856.

GALLOWAY, George *(Glasgow Kelvin)   Lab majority 9,665*

Son of George, engineer, and Sheila, née Reilly, factory worker. Born August 16, 1954; educated Charleston Primary; Harris Academy, Dundee. Married December 20, 1979, Elaine Fyffe (1 daughter) (marriage dissolved 1999). *Trades Union:* Member, TGWU 1974–99; Sponsored by TGWU 1987–96. *Career:* General labourer, Garden Works, Dundee 1972; Production worker, Michelin Tyres 1973; Labour Organiser 1977–83; General Secretary, War on Want 1983–87. *Select Committees (Current):* Member: Broadcasting 1997–. *Party Groups:* Labour Party organiser, Dundee East and West Constituencies 1977; Former Chairman, Scottish Labour Party. *Other:* General Secretary, War on Want 1983–87. *Awards:* Kashmir Centres Europe Kashmir Award for his work, efforts, support and services to the Kashmir cause 1998. *Honours:* Hilal-i-Quaid-Azam, the highest civil award in Pakistan for services to the restoration of democracy in Pakistan 1990, Hilal-i-Pakistan for services to the people of Kashmir 1996. *Publications: Downfall: The Ceausescus and the Romanian Revolution* (jointly) 1989. *Special Interests:* Foreign Affairs, Defence, Scotland. *Recreations:* Football, sport, films, music. *Electoral Notes:* Member for Glasgow Hillhead 1987–97, and for Glasgow Kelvin since May 1, 1997. *Clubs:* Groucho. *Address:* George Galloway Esq, MP, House of Commons, London, SW1A 0AA *Tel:* 020 7219 3000 *Fax:* 020 7219 2879. *Constituency:* 8a Parkgrove Terrace, Glasgow *Tel:* 0141–357 2073 *Fax:* 0141–357 2073 *E-mail:* george.galloway@btinternet.com.

GAPES, Mike (Michael John) *(Ilford South)   Lab/Co-op majority 14,200*

Son of Frank Gapes, retired postal worker, and Emily Gapes, retired office worker. Born September 4, 1952; educated Manford Primary School; Buckhurst Hill County High School; Fitzwilliam College, Cambridge (MA Hons Economics); Middlesex Polytechnic, Enfield (Diploma in Industrial Relations). Married September 4, 1992, Frances, daughter of Bruna and Roger Smith (3 daughters). *Trades Union:* Member, TGWU. *Career:* Voluntary Service Overseas (VSO) Teacher, Swaziland 1971–72; Secretary, Cambridge Students' Union 1973–74; National Organisation of Labour Students: Vice-Chair 1975–76, Chair 1976–77; National Student Organiser, The Labour Party 1977–80; Research Officer, Labour Party International Department 1980–88; Senior International Officer, The Labour Party 1988–92. *Political Career:* PPS to Rt Hon. Paul Murphy, MP, as Minister of State, Northern Ireland Office (Minister for Political Development) 1997–99. *Select Committees (Current):* Member: Defence 1999– *(Former):* Member: Foreign Affairs 1992–97. *Party Groups:* Member, The Co-operative Party; Deputy Chair, Parliamentary Labour Friends of Israel 1997–. *International Bodies:* Vice-President, Council of European National Youth Committees 1977–79; Council Member: Royal Institute of International Affairs 1996–99, Voluntary Service Overseas 1997–. *Other:* President, Redbridge United Chinese Association. *Sportsclubs:* Vice-President, Ilford Football Club; West Ham United Supporters' Association,. *Publications:* Contributor to several books and pamphlets; Author of Fabian Society pamphlet: *After the Cold War*, 1990. *Special Interests:* Defence, International Affairs, European Union, Economic Policy, Education. *Recreations:* My family and when I get time watching football at West Ham, blues and jazz music. *Electoral Notes:* Contested Ilford North in 1983 General Election. Member for Ilford South since April 9, 1992. *Address:* Mike Gapes Esq, MP, House of Commons, London, SW1A 0AA *Tel:* 020 7219 6485 *Fax:* 020 7219 0978. *Constituency:* 1 Coventry Road, Ilford, Essex, IG1 4QR *Tel:* 020 8554 3905 *E-mail:* gapesm@parliament.uk.

GARDINER, Barry Strachan *(Brent North)   Lab majority 4,019*

Son of late John Flannegan Gardiner, general manager, Kelvin Hall, and of late Sylvia Strachan, doctor. Born March 10, 1957; educated Glasgow High School; Haileybury College; St Andrews (MA Hons): Harvard (J. F. Kennedy Scholarship 1983); Cambridge (Research 1984–87). Married Caroline Smith (3 sons 1 daughter). *Trades Union:* Member: MSF, GMB. *Profession:* General Average Adjuster (Arbitrator, Maritime Casualties). *Career:* Occasional Lecturer, The Academy of National Economy, Moscow; Partner, Mediterranean Average Adjusting Co. *Councils, Public Bodies:* Cambridge City Council: Councillor 1988–94, Chair of Finance, Mayor 1992–93. *Select Committees (Current):* Member: Procedure 1997–, Broadcasting 1998–, Public Accounts 1999–. *Party Groups:* Member, Labour Finance and Industry Group; Chair, Labour Friends of India. *Other:* Member, Amnesty International. Member, Shipwrights' Company. Freeman, City of London. ACII. *Publications:* Various articles relating to shipping and maritime affairs; Articles on Political Philosophy in the *Philosophical Quarterly*. *Special Interests:* Economic Policy, Trade and Industry, Education, Foreign Affairs. *Countries of Interest:* India, Sri Lanka, Russia, Georgia. *Recreations:* Walking, music, reading philosophy, bird-watching. *Electoral Notes:* Member for Brent North since May 1, 1997. *Clubs:* Royal Overseas League. *Address:* Barry Gardiner Esq, MP, House of Commons, London, SW1A 0AA *Tel:* 020 7219 4046 *Fax:* 020 7219 2495.

GARNIER, Edward, QC *(Harborough)* Con majority 6,524

Son of late Colonel William d'Arcy Garnier, and Hon. Mrs Garnier. Born October 26, 1952; educated Wellington College; Jesus College, Oxford (BA 1974, MA 1976); College of Law, London; Visiting Parliamentary Fellow, St Anthony's College, Oxford 1996–97. Married April 17, 1982, Anna Caroline Mellows (2 sons 1 daughter). *Career:* Barrister; Called to the Bar, Middle Temple 1976; QC 1995. *Political Career:* PPS: to Ministers of State, Foreign and Commonwealth Office, Rt Hon. Alastair Goodlad, MP 1994–95, David Davis, MP 1994–95; to Attorney-General and Solicitor-General 1995–97, to Chancellor of the Duchy of Lancaster 1996–97; Shadow Minister, Lord Chancellor's Department 1997–99; Shadow Attorney General 1999–. *Select Committees (Former):* Member: Home Affairs 1992–95. *Party Groups:* Treasurer, Macleod Group of Conservative MPs 1995–97; Member, Society of Conservative Lawyers. *International Bodies:* Director, Great Britain–China Centre 1998–. *Miscellaneous:* Secretary, Foreign Affairs Forum 1988–92, Vice-Chairman 1992–. *Publications:* Co-author *Bearing the Standard: Themes for a Fourth Term*, 1991; *Facing the Future*, 1993; Contributor to *Halsbury's Laws of England*, 4th edition 1985. *Special Interests:* Agriculture, Defence, Foreign Affairs, Education. *Recreations:* Shooting, cricket, tennis, skiing, opera, biographical research. *Electoral Notes:* Contested Hemsworth 1987 General Election. Member for Harborough since April 9, 1992. *Clubs:* Pratt's, Vincent's (Oxford). *Address:* Edward Garnier Esq, QC, MP, House of Commons, London, SW1A 0AA *Tel:* 020 7219 6524. *Constituency:* 24 Nelson Street, Market Harborough, Leicestershire, LE16 9AY *Tel:* 01858 464146 *Fax:* 01858 410013 *E-mail:* garniere@parliament.uk.

GEORGE, Andrew Henry *(St Ives)* LD majority 7,170

Son of Reginald Hugh George, horticulturist, and Diana May (née Petherick), teacher and musician. Born December 2, 1958; educated Mullion County Primary School; Helston Grammar School; Sussex University (BA); University College, Oxford (MSc). Married July 4, 1987, Jill Elizabeth Marshall (1 son 1 daughter). *Career:* Charity Worker. *Spokesman:* A Spokesman for: Agriculture, Fisheries, Food and Rural Affairs (Fishing) 1997–99, Fishing 1999– Social Security (Disabilities) 1999–. *Select Committees (Former):* Member: Agriculture 1997–99. *Publications: Cornwall at the Crossroads*, 1989. *Special Interests:* Third World, Cornwall, Economic Development, Housing, Fishing, Agriculture, Social Exclusion, Devolution, Small Nations, Anti-Racism, Domestic Violence, Immigration, Environment, Minority Groups. *Countries of Interest:* All Small Nations. *Recreations:* Cricket, football, rugby, tennis, swimming, writing, walking, Cornish culture, cycling, gardening, drawing. *Electoral Notes:* Contested St Ives 1992. Member for St Ives since May 1, 1997. *Address:* Andrew George Esq, MP, House of Commons, London, SW1A 0AA *Tel:* 020 7219 4588 *Fax:* 020 7219 5572. *Constituency:* Knights Yard, Belgravia Street, Penzance, Cornwall TR18 2EL *Tel:* 01736 860020 *Fax:* 01736 332866 *E-mail:* mcguffiea@parliament.uk.

GEORGE, Bruce T *(Walsall South)* Lab majority 11,312

Son of late Edgar Lewis George and late Phyllis George. Born June 1, 1942; educated Mountain Ash Grammar School; University of Wales (BA); Warwick University (MA); Hon. Fellow, Warwick University. Married July 1992, Lisa Toelle. *Career:* Assistant Lecturer in Politics, Glamorgan College of Technology 1964–66; Lecturer in Politics, Manchester Polytechnic 1968–70; Senior Lecturer in Politics, Birmingham Polytechnic 1970–74; Visiting Lecturer, Essex University 1983; Former Tutor, Open University. *Select Committees (Current):* Chairman: Defence 1997–; Member: Liaison 1997–. *International Bodies:* Chairman, Mediterranean Special Group; Former Chairman, Political Committee, North Atlantic Assembly; Parliamentary Assembly of Organisation for Security and Co-operation in Europe: Chairman, General (First) Committee on Political Affairs and Security 1994–, Leader, UK Delegation 1997–, Vice-President 1999. *Other:* Member: RIIA, RUSI, International Institute of Strategic Studies, American Society for Industrial Security (UK); Patron: Institute of Security Management, Sister Dora Hospice Appeal Ltd, Hon. Adviser,

Royal British Legion 1997. *Trust:* Fellow, Industry and Parliament Trust. *Miscellaneous:* Councillor, Council for Arms Control. *Sportsclubs:* Founder, House of Commons Football Club. *Publications:* Numerous books and articles on defence and Foreign affairs; Editor, *Jane's NATO Handbook 1990–91*. *Special Interests:* Defence, International Affairs, Housing, Health, Social Services, Private Security. *Recreations:* Reading, supports Walsall Football Club. *Electoral Notes:* Contested Southport 1970. Member for Walsall South since February 1974. *Address:* Bruce George Esq, MP, House of Commons, London, SW1A 0AA *Tel:* 020 7219 4049/6610 *Fax:* 020 7219 3823. *Constituency:* 34 Bridge Street, Walsall, West Midlands, WS1 1HQ *Tel:* 01922 724960 *Fax:* 01922 621844.

GERRARD, Neil *(Walthamstow)   Lab majority 17,149*

Son of late Francis and Emma Gerrard, primary school teachers. Born July 3, 1942; educated Manchester Grammar School; Wadham College, Oxford; Chelsea College, London; Polytechnic of South Bank (BA, MEd, DPSE). Married 1968, Marian Fitzgerald (2 sons) (marriage dissolved 1983). *Trades Union:* Member: NATFHE, GMB. *Career:* Teacher, Queen Elizabeth's School, Barnet 1965–68; Lecturer, Hackney College –92. *Councils, Public Bodies:* London Borough of Waltham Forest: Councillor 1973–90, Leader, Labour Group 1983–90, Leader of Council 1986–90. *Political Career:* PPS to: Dawn Primarolo, MP, as Financial Secretary, HM Treasury May-December 1997. *Select Committees (Current):* Member: Information 1997–, Environmental Audit 1999– *(Former):* Member: Deregulation 1995–97, Environment 1995–97. *Party Groups:* Member, PLP Civil Liberties Group. *Other:* Board Member, Theatre Royal, Stratford, East London; Former Board Member, SHAC. *Special Interests:* Housing, Planning, Race Relations, Foreign Affairs, HIV/AIDS, Refugees/Asylum, Criminal Justice, Disabled/Disability. *Countries of Interest:* Middle East, Sri Lanka, Kashmir, India. *Recreations:* Theatre, cinema, reading, music, sport. *Electoral Notes:* Contested Chingford 1979 General Election. Member for Walthamstow since April 9, 1992. *Address:* Neil Gerrard Esq, MP, House of Commons, London, SW1A 0AA *Tel:* 020 7219 4529. *Constituency:* 23 Orford Road, Walthamstow, London, E17 9NL *Tel:* 020 8521 1223 *Fax:* 020 8521 1223 *E-mail:* gerrardn@parliament.uk.

GIBB, Nick (Nicolas) John *(Bognor Regis and Littlehampton)   Con majority 7,321*

Son of late John McLean Gibb, civil engineer, and Eileen Mavern Gibb, retired schoolteacher. Born September 3, 1960; educated Maidstone Boys' Grammar School; Roundhay School, Leeds; Thornes House School, Wakefield; University of Durham (BA Hons, Law). *Career:* Chartered accountant, specialising in taxation, KPMG, London 1984–97. *Spokesman:* An Opposition Front Bench Spokesman for: the Treasury (Tax, except VAT and Duties; Financial Services and City Issues; Competition and Deregulation) December 1998–99, Trade and Industry 1999–. *Select Committees (Former):* Member: Social Security 1997–98, Treasury 1998, Treasury Sub-Committee 1998. Member, Institute of Chartered Accountants in England and Wales; ACA.
Publications: Maintaining Momentum, Pamphlet on Tax Reform 1992; *Bucking the Market*, Pamphlet Opposing Membership of ERM 1990; *Duty to Repeal*, Pamphlet Calling for Abolition of Stamp Duty 1989; *Simplifying Taxes*, Pamphlet on Tax Reform 1987. *Special Interests:* Economics, Tax, Education, Social Security. *Countries of Interest:* USA, Israel. *Recreations:* Long-distance running, skiing. *Electoral Notes:* Contested Stoke-on-Trent Central 1992 and Rotherham By-election 1994. Member for Bognor Regis and Littlehampton since May 1, 1997. *Address:* Nick Gibb Esq, MP, House of Commons, SW1A 0AA *Tel:* 020 7219 6374 *Fax:* 020 7219 2634. *Constituency:* 4 The Precinct, West Meads, Bognor Regis, West Sussex, PO21 5SB *Tel:* 01243 826410 *Fax:* 01243 842076.

GIBSON, Dr Ian *(Norwich North)   Lab majority 9,470*

Son of late William and late Winifred Gibson. Born September 26, 1938; educated Dumfries Academy; Edinburgh University (BSc, PhD). Married March 1974 (2 daughters). *Trades Union:* National Executive Committee, ASTMS/MSF until 1996. *Profession:* Scientist. *Career:* Dean of Biology, University of East Anglia, Norwich. *Select Committees (Current):* Member: Science and Technology 1997–. *Party Groups:* Vice-Chairman, MSF Parliamentary Group. *Sportsclubs:* Football Supporters' Association. MIBiol; FIBiol. *Special Interests:* Science, Technology, Health, Environment. *Recreations:* Football. *Electoral Notes:* Contested Norwich North 1992. Member for Norwich North since May 1, 1997. *Address:* Dr Ian Gibson, MP, House of Commons, London, SW1A 0AA *Tel:* 020 7219 4419 *Fax:* 020 7219 2799. *Constituency:* Norwich Labour Centre, 59 Bethel Street, Norwich, NR1 1NL *Tel:* 01603 661144 *Fax:* 01603 663502.

GILL, Christopher *(Ludlow)   Con majority 5,909*

Born October 28, 1936; educated Shrewsbury School. Married July 2, 1960, Patricia Greenway (1 son 2 daughters). *Armed Forces:* RNVR 1952, RN 1955–57, Reserve Decoration 1971. *Career:* Chairman, family farming, meat processing and wholesaling business F. A. Gill Ltd. *Councils, Public Bodies:* Wolverhampton Borough Council: Councillor 1965–72, Chairman, Public Works Committee 1967–69; Chairman, Local Education Authority 1969–70. *Select Committees (Former):* Member: Agriculture 1989–95, Welsh Affairs 1995–97. *Party Groups:* Past President, Midlands West European Conservative Council. *Other:* Formerly Council member, Wolverhampton Chamber of Commerce. *Miscellaneous:* Executive Member, 1922 Committee 1997–; Member: Council of Europe 1997–99, Western European Union Assemblies 1997–99, European Standing Committee A 1998–. Liveryman, Worshipful Company of Butchers. Freeman, City of London. *Publications: In Their Own Words. Special Interests:* Agriculture, Fisheries, European Union. *Countries of Interest:* Europe. *Recreations:* Walking, golf, sailing, skiing, DIY. *Electoral Notes:* Member for Ludlow since June 1987. Conservative Whip withdrawn November 1994, restored April 1995. *Clubs:* Carlton. *Address:* Christopher Gill Esq, MP, House of Commons, London, SW1A 0AA *Tel:* 020 7219 5101 *Tel (Constituency):* 01746 861267 *Fax (Constituency):* 01746 861267.

GILLAN, Cheryl *(Chesham and Amersham)   Con majority 13,859*

Daughter of late Adam Mitchell Gillan, company director, and of Mona Gillan. Born April 21, 1952; educated Cheltenham Ladies' College; College of Law. Married December 7, 1985, John Coates Leeming, son of James Arthur Leeming. *Career:* International Management Group 1977–84; Director, British Film Year 1984–86; Senior Marketing Consultant, Ernst and Young 1986–91; Marketing Director, Kidsons Impey 1991–93. *Political Career:* PPS to Rt Hon. Viscount Cranborne, as Leader of the House of Lords and Lord Privy Seal 1994–95; Parliamentary Under-Secretary of State, Department of Education and Employment 1995–97. *Spokesman:* An Opposition Spokeswoman for: Trade and Industry 1997–98, Foreign and Commonwealth Affairs 1998–. *Select Committees (Former):* Member: Science and Technology 1992–95, Procedure 1994–95. *Party Groups:* Chairman, Bow Group 1987–88; Member, Highflyers' Conservative Group. *International Bodies:* Member, Executive Committee, Commonwealth Parliamentary Association (CPA) UK Branch 1998–. Member, Worshipful Company of Marketors. Freeman, City of London. FCIM. *Special Interests:* Industry, Space, International Affairs, Defence. *Countries of Interest:* Former Soviet Union, Europe, Hungary, Poland, USA, Japan, Pacific Rim. *Recreations:* Golf, music, gardening. *Electoral Notes:* Contested Greater Manchester Central in European Parliamentary Elections 1989. Member for Chesham and Amersham since April 9, 1992. *Clubs:* RAC. *Address:* Cheryl Gillan, MP, House of Commons, London, SW1A 0AA *Tel:* 020 7219 5146.

GILROY, Linda *(Plymouth Sutton)   Lab/Co-op majority 9,440*

Daughter of William and Gwendolen Jarvie. Born July 19, 1949; educated Maynards, Exeter; Stirling High School; Edinburgh University (MA Hons); Strathclyde University; Postgraduate Diploma, Secretarial Studies. Married March 10, 1986, Bernard Gilroy. *Trades Union:* Member, TGWU. *Profession:* MITSA Member, Institute of Trading Standards Administration. *Career:* Deputy Director, Age Concern, Scotland 1972–79; Regional Manager, Gas Consumers' Council 1979–96. *Select Committees (Former):* Member: European Legislation 1997 98, European Scrutiny 1998. *Trust:* Founder Member, Plymouth Energy Advice Centre and West Country Energy Action Trust. *Special Interests:* Pensioners' Rights, Trade and Industry, Energy, Utility Regulation. *Countries of Interest:* Turkey, Poland, New Zealand, Australia, America, Tanzania. *Recreations:* Theatre, swimming, walking. *Electoral Notes:* Contested South-East Cornwall 1992 General Election, Devon and East Plymouth 1994 European Election. Member for Plymouth Sutton since May 1, 1997. *Address:* Linda Gilroy, MP, House of Commons, London, SW1A 0AA *Tel:* 020 7219 3000.

GODMAN, Dr Norman Anthony *(Greenock and Inverclyde)   Lab majority 13,040*

Son of late Wilfrid Godman, fisherman and late Isabella Godman, fishergirl. Born April 19, 1938; educated Westbourne Street Boys' School, Hull; Hull University (BA Hons); Heriot-Watt University (PhD 1982). Married, Patricia. *Armed Forces:* National Service with the Royal Military Police. *Career:* Shipwright; Teacher, Scottish Further and Higher Education. *Spokesman:* Opposition Spokesman on: Fisheries 1988–89, Agriculture and Rural Affairs 1988–89. *Select Committees (Current):* Member: Foreign Affairs 1997– *(Former):* Member: European Legislation 1990–95. *Other:* Amnesty International; National Trust for Scotland; United Nations Association. *Trust:* Fellow, Industry and Parliament Trust. *Special Interests:* Foreign Affairs, Human Rights, Law Reform, Incomes Policies. *Recreations:* Hill-walking, reading, going to concerts, cinema and theatre, fishing, allotment. *Electoral Notes:* Contested Aberdeen South 1979. Member for Greenock and Port Glasgow 1983–97, and for Greenock and Inverclyde since May 1, 1997. *Address:* Dr Norman Godman, MP, House of Commons, London, SW1A 0AA *Tel:* 020 7219 4441.

GODSIFF, Roger *(Birmingham Sparkbrook and Small Heath)   Lab majority 19,526*

Son of late George Godsiff, chargehand/fitter, and of Gladys Godsiff. Born June 28, 1946; educated Catford Comprehensive School, London. Married 1977, Julia Brenda Morris (1 son 1 daughter). *Trades Union:* Member of and sponsored by GMB. *Career:* Banking 1965–70; Formerly Political Officer, APEX; Senior Research Officer, GMB. *Councils, Public Bodies:* London Borough of Lewisham: Councillor 1971–90, Labour Chief Whip 1974–77, Mayor 1977. *Party Groups:* Joined Labour Party 1966; Member, Co-operative Party. *International Bodies:* Member, Executive Committee, IPU 1999–. *Sportsclubs:* Member, Charlton Athletic Supporters Club. *Special Interests:* European Union, Foreign Affairs, Industrial Relations, Sport, Recreation, Immigration Policy. *Countries of Interest:* Indian Sub-Continent, America, Middle East, Asia. *Recreations:* Sport in general, particularly football, member of Charlton Athletic Supporters' Club. *Electoral Notes:* Contested (Labour) Birmingham Yardley in 1983 General Election. Member for Birmingham Small Heath 1992–97, and for Birmingham Sparkbrook and Small Heath since May 1, 1997. *Address:* Roger Godsiff Esq, MP, House of Commons, London, SW1A 0AA *Tel:* 020 7219 5191 *Fax:* 020 7219 2221 *Tel (Constituency):* 0121–772 2383 *Fax (Constituency):* 0121–772 2383.

GOGGINS, Paul Gerard *(Wythenshawe and Sale East)* *Lab majority 15,019*

Son of John Goggins and late Rita Goggins. Born June 16, 1953; educated St Bede's, Manchester; Ushaw College, Durham; Birmingham Polytechnic (Certificate in the Residential Care of Children and Young People); Manchester Polytechnic (Certificate of Qualification in Social Work). Married August 20, 1977, Wyn, daughter of Tom and Mary Bartley (2 sons 1 daughter). *Trades Union:* Shop Steward; Member, TGWU. *Profession:* Director, National Charity. *Career:* Child Care Worker, Liverpool Catholic Social Services 1974–75; Officer-in-Charge, Local Authority Children's Home, Wigan 1976–84; Project Director, NCH Action For Children, Salford 1984–89; National Director, Church Action On Poverty 1989–97. *Councils, Public Bodies:* Councillor, Salford City Council 1990–98. *Political Career:* PPS to John Denham, MP: as Minister of State, Department of Social Security 1998–99, as Minister of State, Department of Health 1999–. *Select Committees (Former):* Member: Social Security 1997–98. *Other:* Associate Member, CAFOD Board; Patron, Trafford Crossroads; Hon. President, Wythenshawe Mobile; Director, Campus Ventures Ltd. *Special Interests:* UK Poverty, Unemployment, Housing, Transport, Global Poverty, Democratic Renewal, Community Regeneration. *Recreations:* Watching Manchester City, walking, singing. *Electoral Notes:* Member for Wythenshawe and Sale East since May 1, 1997. *Address:* Paul Goggins Esq, MP, House of Commons, London, SW1A 0AA *Tel:* 020 7219 5865. *Constituency:* 2/10 Alderman Downward House, Civic Centre, Wythenshawe, Manchester, M22 5RF *Tel:* 0161–499 7900 *Fax:* 0161–499 7911 *E-mail:* gogginsp@parliament.uk.

GOLDING, Mrs Llin *(Newcastle-under-Lyme)* *Lab majority 17,206*

Daughter of late Rt Hon. Ness Edwards, MP. Born March 21, 1933; educated Caerphilly Girls Grammar School. Married 1st, 1957, Dr Roland Lewis (1 son 2 daughters), married 2nd, August 8, 1980, John Golding, MP for Newcastle-under-Lyme 1969–86 (died January 20, 1999). *Trades Union:* Former NUPE Branch Secretary. *Career:* Member, Society of Radiographers 1953–; Secretary and Assistant to her second husband, when he was an MP. *Councils, Public Bodies:* Former Member, North Staffs District Health Authority 1983–87. *Political Career:* Member of Opposition team on: Social Security 1992–93, Children and Families 1993–95, Food, Agriculture and Rural Affairs 1995–97. *Whip:* An Opposition Whip 1987–92. *Select Committees (Current):* Member: Culture, Media and Sport 1997–, Standing Orders 1998–. *(Former):* Member: Broadcasting the House of Commons 1990–92. *International Bodies:* Executive Committee Member, IPU British Group. *Other:* Secretary, Newcastle Staffs and District Trades Council 1976–86; Former Member, District Manpower Services Committee; Member: BBC Advisory Committee 1989–92, Commonwealth War Graves Commission 1992–; Trustee (unpaid): NSPCC 1988–, Second Chance 1988–, SAFE. *Special Interests:* Health Service, Trade Unions, Children. *Recreations:* Fishing. *Electoral Notes:* Member for Newcastle-under-Lyme since By-election July 17, 1986. *Address:* Mrs Llin Golding, MP, House of Commons, London, SW1A 0AA *Tel:* 020 7219 4209 *Fax:* 020 7219 2395. *Constituency:* 6 Lancaster Avenue, Newcastle-under-Lyme, Staffordshire, ST5 1DR *Tel:* 01782 636200 *Fax:* 01782 614336.

GORDON, Eileen *(Romford)* *Lab majority 649*

Daughter of late Charles Leatt and late Margaret Rose Leatt. Born October 22, 1946; educated Harold Hill Grammar School; Shoreditch Comprehensive; Westminster College of Education (Oxford) (Cert Ed). Married Tony Gordon (1 son 1 daughter). *Trades Union:* Member, TGWU. *Career:* Former Teacher; Caseworker/Assistant to Tony Banks MP 1990–97. *Select Committees (Current):* Member: Broadcasting 1997–, Health 1999–. *Party Groups:* Member: Labour Party 1964–, Co-operative Party; Greater London Party Regional Executive 1993–98. *Other:* Former Member, Community Health Council; Member: YMCA, League Against Cruel Sports; School Governor. *Miscellaneous:* Campaigned to save services at Oldchurch Hospital 1987–97; Member, European Standing Committee B 1998–. *Special Interests:* Education, Health, Housing, Equal Opportunities. *Recreations:* Cinema, family, keeping fit, socialising. *Electoral Notes:* Contested Romford 1992. Member for Romford since May 1, 1997. *Address:* Eileen Gordon, MP, House of Commons, London, SW1A 0AA *Tel:* 020 7219 4413 *Fax:* 020 7219 2779. *Constituency:* Saffron House, 273 South Street, Romford, Essex, RM1 2BE *Tel:* 01708 764020 *Fax:* 01708 732728.

GORMAN, Teresa *(Billericay)   Con majority 1,356*

Born September 30, 1931; educated Fulham County School; London University (BSc Hons, DipEd). Married. *Profession:* Teacher/Businesswoman. *Career:* Teacher; Entrepreneur; Writer. *Councils, Public Bodies:* Westminster City Council: Councillor 1982–86, Vice-Chairman: Housing, Social Services, General Purposes Committees, Whip. *Political Career:* Sponsored first ever Women into Politics exhibition and festival in House of Commons July 1993. *Select Committees (Current):* Member: Environment, Transport and Regional Affairs 1998–, Deregulation 1999–, Transport Sub-Committee 1999–. *Party Groups:* Conservative Women's National Committee 1983–88. *Trust:* Founder Chairman, Amarant Trust, a charity to raise awareness of HRT 1985–92.
Miscellaneous: Chairman, Alliance of Small Firms and Self Employed People 1973–87. *Fellowships, etc:* FLS. *Publications:* Papers for: Centre for Policy Studies, Institute of Economic Affairs, Adam Smith Institute; *The Amarant Book of HRT*, 1988; *Chickengate*, 1992; *The Bastards*, 1993; *Enterprise Culture*; *Worried to Death*; *Business Still Burdened*; *Not a Penny More*, 1994. *Special Interests:* Free Trade, Individual Freedom, Women's Issues, Environment. *Countries of Interest:* Botswana, Southern Africa, USA, Australia, SE Asia. *Recreations:* Natural history, travel. *Electoral Notes:* Contested (Independent) Lambeth, Streatham as Teresa Moore October 1974. Member for Billericay since June 1987. *Address:* Mrs Teresa Gorman, MP, House of Commons, London, SW1A 0AA *Tel:* 020 7219 6521 *Fax:* 020 7219 6856 *Tel (Constituency):* 01375 892683 *Fax (Constituency):* 01375 892683.

GORRIE, Donald Cameron Easterbrook, OBE *(Edinburgh West)   LD majority 7,253*

Son of late Robert MacLagan Gorrie, DSc, and late Sydney Grace Easterbrook Gorrie. Born April 2, 1933; educated Oundle School; Corpus Christi College, Oxford (MA Modern History). Married August 24, 1957, Astrid Margaret Salvesen, daughter of late Dr Cecil Salvesen and Elizabeth Reid Salvesen (2 sons). *Armed Forces:* Second Lieutenant, Royal Artillery 1951–53. *Profession:* Schoolmaster. *Career:* Schoolmaster, Gordonstoun School 1957–60; Director of Physical Education, Marlborough College 1960–66; Research at Edinburgh University (Scottish History), Adult Education Lecturer 1966–69; Director of Research, then Director of Administration, Scottish Liberal Party 1969–75; Started Small Business 1976–79; Full-Time Councillor 1980–97. *Councils, Public Bodies:* Councillor, Edinburgh Town Council 1971–75; Councillor/Group Leader: Lothian Regional Council 1974–96, Edinburgh District Council 1980–96, City of Edinburgh Council 1995–97. *Whip:* Liberal Democrat Whip 1997–99. *Spokesman:* Spokesman for Scotland: Education 1997–99, Housing 1997–99, Local Government 1997–99, Youth 1997–99, Sport 1997–99. *Other:* Former Convenor: Edinburgh City Youth Cafes, Diverse Attractions; Former Director/Committee Member: Edinburgh International Festival, Royal Lyceum Theatre, Queen's Hall, Edinburgh, Lothian Youth Clubs, Castle Rock Housing Association. *Awards:* Scottish Parliament Backbencher of the Year 1999. *Sportsclubs:* Honorary President: Corstorphine Amateur Athletic Club, Salvesen Boys' Club; Member: City of Edinburgh Athletic Club, Achilles Club. *Honours:* OBE 1984. *Special Interests:* Local Government, Education, Youth Affairs, Sport, Arts. *Recreations:* Reading, music, theatre, ruins, sight-seeing. *Electoral Notes:* Member for Edinburgh West since May 1, 1997. MSP for the Region of Central Scotland since May 6, 1999. *Clubs:* Scottish Liberal. *Address:* Donald Gorrie Esq, OBE, DL, JP, MP, MSP, House of Commons, London, SW1A 0AA *Tel:* 020 7219 4104. *Constituency:* West Edinburgh Liberal Democrats, 11 Drum Brae Avenue, Edinburgh, EH12 8TE *Tel:* 0131–339 0339 *Fax:* 0131–476 7101 *E-mail:* gorried@parliament.uk; donald.gorrie.msp@scottish.parliament.uk.

GRAHAM, Tommy *(West Renfrewshire)* *Lab majority 7,979*

Son of late William Graham, factory assembler, and Mrs Elizabeth Whitehead. Born December 5, 1943; educated Crookston Castle Secondary, Pollock; Stow College of Engineering, Glasgow, day release 1959–65. Married Joan Bagley (2 sons). *Trades Union:* AEUU; Sponsored by USDAW. *Career:* Machine and tool engineer; Served apprenticeship with Mathew Wylies; Rolls-Royce 1965–78; Office Manager, Robertson and Ross, Solicitors 1982–87. *Councils, Public Bodies:* Former Community Councillor, Linwood West; District Councillor, Renfrew District Council before reorganisation; Former Regional Councillor, Strathclyde. *Select Committees (Former):* Member: Catering 1997–98. *Other:* Chairman, Linwood Tenants Association. *Special Interests:* Social Security, Foreign Affairs, Elderly, Disabled/Disability, Unemployment, Urban Funding. *Recreations:* Walking, ornithology, family, reading, music, photography. *Electoral Notes:* Member for Renfrew West and Inverclyde 1987–97, and for West Renfrewshire since May 1, 1997. Labour Whip withdrawn September 1998, now sits as Scottish Labour. *Address:* Tommy Graham Esq, MP, House of Commons, London, SW1A 0AA *Tel:* 020 7219 4063. *Constituency:* 17 Murray Street, Paisley, Renfrewshire, PA3 1QW *Tel:* 0141-889 1736 *Fax:* 0141-848 9902.

GRANT, Bernie *(Tottenham)* *Lab majority 20,200*

Son of Eric and late Lily Grant, both teachers. Born February 17, 1944; educated St Stanislaus College, Georgetown, Guyana; Tottenham Technical College, London; Heriot Watt University (mining engineering); Hon LLD Pace University, New York 1993. 1st marriage dissolved (3 sons); married 2nd December 1998, Sharon. *Trades Union:* Area Officer, NUPE 1978–83. *Career:* Local Government Officer, London Borough of Newham 1984–87. *Councils, Public Bodies:* London Borough of Haringey: Councillor 1978–88, Leader 1985–87. *Select Committees (Current):* Member: International Development 1997–. *Party Groups:* Chairman, Campaign Group of Labour MPs 1990–93. *Other:* Chair, African Reparations Movement (UK); President, Caribbean Links Organisation; Race Equality in Europe Trust. *Miscellaneous:* Member, Anti-Apartheid Movement Executive 1988; Founder Member and Chairman, Parliamentary Black Caucus 1988–90; Chairman: Standing Conference on Racial Equality in Europe 1991–, National Committee on Reparations for Africa 1993–; Member, Group of Eminent Persons on Reparations for Africa (OAU) 1994–; Chair, The Global Trade Centre 1996–; Member, Home Secretary's Race Advisory Forum. *Special Interests:* Local Government, Third World, Equal Opportunity, Race Relations, Alternative Medicine. *Countries of Interest:* Africa, Caribbean. *Recreations:* Cooking, cricket, Internet. *Electoral Notes:* Member for Tottenham since June 1987. *Address:* Bernie Grant Esq, MP, House of Commons, London, SW1A 0AA *Tel:* 020 7219 4593 *Tel (Constituency):* 020 8880 9100 *Fax (Constituency):* 020 8880 9101 *E-mail:* grantb@parliament.uk.

GRAY, James Whiteside *(North Wiltshire)* *Con majority 3,475*

Son of late Very Revd John R. Gray and Dr Sheila Gray. Born November 7, 1954; educated Glasgow High School; Glasgow University (MA Hons); Christ Church, Oxford. Married July 11, 1980, Sarah Ann, daughter of Ronald and Valerie Beale (2 sons 1 daughter). *Armed Forces:* Honourable Artillery Company (TA) 1978–84. *Career:* Management Trainee, P & O 1977–78; Broker, Senior Broker then Department Manager, Anderson Hughes & Co Ltd (Shipbrokers) 1978–84; Member, The Baltic Exchange 1978–92, Hon. Member 1997–; Managing Director, GNI Freight Futures Ltd, Senior Manager, GNI Ltd (Futures Brokers) 1984–1992; Director: Baltic Futures Exchange 1989–91, Westminster Strategy 1995–96. *Political Career:* Special Adviser to Michael Howard and John Gummer as Secretaries of State for Environment 1991–93;. *Select Committees (Current):* Member: Environment, Transport and Regional Affairs 1997–, Environment Sub-Committee 1997–, Transport Sub-Committee 1997–. *Party Groups:* Deputy Chairman, Wandsworth Tooting Conservative Association 1994–96. *Other:* Governor, Hearnville Primary School, Balham 1989–92;

Governor, Chestnut Grove Secondary School, Balham 1993–96. *Miscellaneous:* Vice-President, HAC Saddle Club; Armed Forces Parliamentary Scheme (Army) 1998; Consultant, British Horse Industry Confederation 1995–. Member, Honourable Artillery Company. Freeman, City of London 1978–. *Sportsclubs:* Member, Royal Artillery Foxhounds. *Publications: Financial Risk Management in the Shipping Industry,* 1985; *Futures and Options for Shipping,* 1987 (Winner of Lloyds of London Book Prize); *Shipping Futures,* 1990. *Special Interests:* Housing, Local Government, Countryside, Agriculture, Defence, Scotland, Environment. *Countries of Interest:* America, China, Mongolia. *Recreations:* Riding Horses. *Electoral Notes:* Contested Ross, Cromarty and Skye 1992. Member for North Wiltshire since May 1, 1997. *Clubs:* Chippenham Constitutional, Wootton Bassett Conservative. *Address:* James Gray Esq, MP, House of Commons, London, SW1A 0AA *Tel:* 020 7219 6237 *Fax:* 020 7219 1169. *Constituency:* North Wilts Conservative Association, 8 St Mary Street, Chippenham, Wiltshire, SN15 3JJ *Tel:* 01249 652851 *Fax:* 01249 448582 *E-mail:* jamesgray.mp@parliament.uk.

GREEN, Damian Howard *(Ashford)*   Con majority 5,345

Son of Howard and late Audrey Green. Born January 17, 1956; educated Reading School; Balliol College, Oxford (MA Philosophy, Politics and Economics); President, Oxford Union 1997. Married 1988, Alicia, daughter of late Judge Jeffreys Collinson and Gwendolen Collinson-Stokes (2 daughters). *Profession:* Journalist. *Career:* BBC Radio Financial Journalist 1978–82; Channel 4 News, Business Producer 1982–84; *The Times* News Editor, Business News 1984–85; Channel 4 News, Business Editor 1985–87; *Business Daily* Programme Presenter and City Editor 1987–92; Special Adviser, Prime Minister's Policy Unit 1992–94; Public Affairs Consultant (Self-employed) 1995–97. *Spokesman:* An Opposition Front Bench Spokesman for: Education and Employment 1998–99,

Environment, Transport and the Regions 1999–. *Select Committees (Former):* Member: Culture, Media and Sport 1997–98, Procedure 1997–98. *Party Groups:* Vice-President, Tory Reform Group 1997–; Vice-Chairman, Conservative Parliamentary Mainstream Group 1997–. *Other:* Director, European Media Forum; Member, SPUC. *Trust:* Trustee, Community Development Foundations. *Sportsclubs:* Fowlers FC, MCC. *Publications: ITN Budget Fact Book,* 1984–85–86; *A Better BBC,* 1990; *The Cross-Media Revolution,* 1995; *Communities in the Countryside,* 1996; *Regulating the Media in the Digital Age,* 1997; *21st Century Conservatism,* 1998; *The Four Failures of the New Deal,* 1999. *Special Interests:* Economic Policy, Foreign Affairs, Media, Education, Employment, Rural Affairs. *Countries of Interest:* France. *Recreations:* Football, cricket, opera, cinema. *Electoral Notes:* Contested Brent East 1992. Member for Ashford since 1997. *Clubs:* Carlton. *Address:* Damian Green Esq, MP, House of Commons, London, SW1A 0AA *Tel:* 020 7219 3518. *Constituency:* c/o Hardy House, The Street, Bethenden, Ashford, Kent, TN26 3AG *Tel:* 01233 820454 *Fax:* 01233 820111 *E-mail:* greend@parliament.uk.

GREENWAY, John Robert *(Ryedale)*   Con majority 5,058

Son of Bill and Kathleen Greenway. Born February 15, 1946; educated Sir John Deane's Grammar School, Northwich; Hendon Police College; London College of Law. Married August 24, 1974, Sylvia Ann, daughter of James Francis Gant (2 sons 1 daughter). *Career:* Metropolitan Police Officer, stationed West End Central 1965–69; Insurance Co. representative 1970–72; Insurance broker and financial consultant 1973–; Financial journalist: *Post Magazine, Insurance Weekly. Councils, Public Bodies:* North Yorkshire County Council: Councillor 1985–87, Education and Schools Committees, Vice-Chairman, North Yorkshire Police Committee. *Political Career:* PPS to Baroness Trumpington, as Minister of State, Ministry of Agriculture, Fisheries and Food 1991–92. *Spokesman:* An

Opposition Spokesman for Home Affairs (Police, Criminal Policy, Constitution, Data Protection, Electoral Policy, Gambling and Licensing) 1997–. *Select Committees (Former):* Member: Home Affairs 1987–97. *Other:* Former Governor, York Theatre Royal. *Miscellaneous:* Member, Standing Committees 1997–98 to Consider: Data Protection Bill, Registration of Political Parties Bill, Special Immigration Appeals Commissioners Bill; Member, Executive, 1922 Committee 1997. *Sportsclubs:* President, York City FC. *Special Interests:* Law and Order, Personal Finance, Agriculture, Broadcasting, Sales Promotion and Marketing. *Recreations:* Opera, music, wine, travel. *Electoral Notes:* Member for Ryedale since June 1987. *Address:* John Greenway Esq, MP, House of Commons, London, SW1A 0AA *Tel:* 020 7219 6397 *Fax:* 020 7219 6059. *Constituency:* 109 Tower Street, Old Malton, North Yorkshire, YO17 0HD *Tel:* 01653 692023 *Fax:* 01653 696108 *E-mail:* greenwayj@parliament.uk.

GRIEVE, Dominic Charles Roberts *(Beaconsfield)*   Con majority 13,987

Son of late W. P. Grieve, QC, MP for Solihull 1964–83, and of late Evelyn Grieve (née Mijouain). Born May 24, 1956; educated Westminster School; Magdalen College, Oxford (MA Modern History); Central London Polytechnic (Diploma in Law). Married October 6, 1990, Caroline, daughter of Mr and Mrs Geoffrey Hutton (2 sons and 1 son deceased). *Armed Forces:* Territorial Army 1981–83. *Profession:* Barrister. *Councils, Public Bodies:* Councillor, London Borough of Hammersmith and Fulham 1982–86. *Spokesman:* An Opposition Front Bench Spokesman for Constitutional Affairs (Scotland) 1999–. *Select Committees (Current):* Member: Environmental Audit 1997–, Statutory Instruments (Joint Committee) 1997–. *Party Groups:* President, Oxford University Conservative Association 1997; Chairman, Research Committee, Society of Conservative Lawyers 1992–95. *Other:* Vice-Chairman/Director, Hammersmith and Fulham MIND 1986–89; Lay Visitor to Police Stations 1990–96; Member: Franco-British Society, Luxembourg Society. *Trust:* Member: National Trust, John Muir Trust. *Miscellaneous:* Member, London Diocesan Synod of Church of England 1994; Deputy Churchwarden. *Special Interests:* Law and Order, Environment, Defence, Foreign Affairs, European Union, Constitution. *Countries of Interest:* France, Luxembourg. *Recreations:* Mountaineering, skiing, fell-walking, travel, architecture and art. *Electoral Notes:* Contested Norwood 1987. Member for Beaconsfield since May 1, 1997. *Clubs:* Carlton. *Address:* Dominic Grieve Esq, MP, House of Commons, London, SW1A 0AA *Tel:* 020 7219 3000. *Constituency:* Disraeli House, 12 Aylesbury End, Beaconsfield, Buckinghamshire, HP9 1LW *Tel:* 01494 673745 *Fax:* 01494 670428.

GRIFFITHS, Jane *(Reading East)*   Lab majority 3,795

Daughter of late John Griffiths, advertising agent, and of Pat Griffiths, philosophy graduate. Born April 17, 1954; educated Cedars Grammar School, Leighton Buzzard; University of Durham (BA Hons Russian). Married 1999, Andrew Tattersall (1 son 1 daughter from previous marriage). *Trades Union:* Member, NUJ. *Profession:* Foreign News Editor, BBC World Service. *Career:* Linguist, GCHQ 1977–84; Asia Editor, BBC Monitoring 1984–97. *Councils, Public Bodies:* Councillor, Reading Borough Council 1989–99. *Select Committees (Former):* Member: Public Accounts 1997–99. *Party Groups:* Member, Labour Party 1983–; Branch Chair 1990–92. *Other:* Member, Transport 2000. *Trust:* Member, Ectopic Pregnancy Trust. *Miscellaneous:* Member, European Standing Committee B 1998–. *Sportsclubs:* Rivermead Fitness Factory. *Special Interests:* Transport, Arts, Leisure, Environment. *Countries of Interest:* Korea, Japan, Mongolia. *Recreations:* Cycling, cinema, theatre. *Electoral Notes:* Member for Reading East since May 1, 1997. *Address:* Jane Griffiths, MP, House of Commons, London, SW1A 0AA *Tel:* 020 7219 4122 *Fax:* 020 7219 2749. *Constituency:* St Giles House, 10 Church Street, Reading, Berkshire, RG1 2SD *Tel:* 0118–957 3756 *Fax:* 0118–958 0949 *E-mail:* griffithsj@parliament.uk.

GRIFFITHS, Nigel *(Edinburgh South)*   Lab majority 11,452

Son of late Lionel Griffiths and of Elizabeth Griffiths. Born May 20, 1955; educated Hawick High School; Edinburgh University (Hons 1977); Moray House College of Education (1978). Married 1979, Sally, daughter of Hugh and Sally McLaughlin. *Councils, Public Bodies:* City of Edinburgh District Council: Councillor 1980–87, Chairperson: Housing Committee, Decentralisation Committee 1986–87; Member: Edinburgh Festival Council 1984–87, Edinburgh Health Council 1982–87; Executive Member, Edinburgh Council of Social Service 1984–87. *Political Career:* Parliamentary Under-Secretary of State, Department of Trade and Industry (Competition and Consumer Affairs) 1997–98. *Whip:* Opposition Whip 1987–89. *Spokesman:* Opposition Spokesman on Trade and Industry Specialising in International Trade and Consumer Affairs 1989–97. *Select Committees (Current):* Member: Procedure 1999–, Public Accounts 1999–. *Party Groups:* Joined Labour Party 1970; President, EU Labour Club 1976–77. *Other:* Rights Adviser, Mental Handicap Pressure Group 1979–87; Member, Wester Hailes School Council 1981; Member: War on Want, SEAD, Amnesty International, Anti-apartheid, Friends of the Earth. *Trust:* Member, National Trust.

Miscellaneous: Secretary, Lothian Devolution Campaign 1978; Executive Member, Scottish Constitutional Convention 1988–90; Vice-President, Institute of Trading Standards Administration 1994–. *Publications: Guide to Council Housing in Edinburgh,* 1981; *Council Housing on the Point of Collapse,* 1982; *Welfare Rights Survey,* 1981; *Welfare Rights Guide,* 1982, 1983, 1984, 1985, 1986; *Rights Guide for Mentally Handicapped People,* 1988. *Special Interests:* Education, Housing, Health, Social Services, Disabled/Disability, Scotland, Arts, Economic Policy. *Recreations:* Travel, live entertainment, badminton, hill-walking and rock-climbing, architecture, reading, politics. *Electoral Notes:* Member for Edinburgh South since June, 1987. *Address:* Nigel Griffiths Esq, JP, MP, House of Commons, London, SW1A 0AA *Tel:* 020 7219 2424. *Constituency:* 93 Causewayside, Edinburgh, EH9 1QG *Tel:* 0131 662 4520 *E-mail.* ngriffithsmp@dial.pipex.com *Website:* http//ourworld.compuserve.com/homepages/ngriffiths/mp.

GRIFFITHS, Win (Winston James) *(Bridgend)   Lab majority 15,248*

Son of late Evan George Griffiths and late Rachel Elizabeth Griffiths. Born February 11, 1943; educated Brecon Boys' Grammar School; University College, Cardiff (BA Hons, DipEd). Married August 22, 1966, Elizabeth Ceri, daughter of John and Edith Gravell (1 son 1 daughter). *Trades Union:* Member, TGWU (ACTS). *Career:* Teacher: secondary school, Tanzania 1966–68, George Dixon Boys' Grammar School 1969–70, Barry Boys' Comprehensive School 1970–76; Head of History Department, Cowbridge Comprehensive School 1976–79. *Councils, Public Bodies:* Vale of Glamorgan Borough Council: Councillor (Chairman, Leisure Services Committee) 1973–76; Member, St Andrew's Major Community Council 1974–79. *Political Career:* Parliamentary Under-Secretary of State, Welsh Office 1997–98. *Spokesman:* Opposition Spokesman on: The Environment 1990–92, Education 1992–94, Welsh Affairs 1994–97. *International Bodies:* Vice-President, European Parliament 1984–87. *Other:* Member, Court of Governors, University College, Cardiff 1981–97. *Special Interests:* Education, European Union, Disabled/Disability, Overseas Aid and Development, Animal Welfare. *Countries of Interest:* European Union, Tanzania. *Recreations:* Reading, erstwhile runner, cultivating pot plants. *Electoral Notes:* MEP for South Wales 1979–89; Member for Bridgend since June 1987. *Address:* Win Griffiths Esq, MP, House of Commons, London, SW1A 0AA *Tel:* 020 7219 4461 *Fax:* 020 7219 6052. *Constituency:* 47 Nolton Street, Bridgend, CF31 3AA *Tel:* 01656 645432 *Fax:* 01656 767551.

GROCOTT, Bruce *(Telford)   Lab majority 11,290*

Son of Reginald Grocott and late Helen Grocott. Born November 1, 1940; educated Hemel Hempstead Grammar School; Leicester University; Manchester University (BA Politics, MA Economics). Married July 17, 1965, Sally, daughter of late James and Doris Ridgway (2 sons). *Trades Union:* Member: NUJ, BECTU. *Career:* Administration Officer, LCC 1963–64; Tutor in Politics, Manchester University 1964–65; Lecturer then Senior Lecturer in Politics, Birmingham Polytechnic 1965–72; Principal Lecturer, North Staffs Polytechnic 1972–74; Presenter then producer, Central Television 1979–87. *Councils, Public Bodies:* Councillor, Bromsgrove Urban District Council 1971–74. *Political Career:* PPS to John Silkin: as Minister for Planning and Local Government 1975–76, as Minister of Agriculture 1976–78; Deputy Shadow Leader of the House and Deputy Campaigns Co-ordinator 1987–92; PPS to Rt Hon. Tony Blair, MP: as Leader of the Labour Party 1994–, as Prime Minister 1997–. *Spokesman:* Opposition Front Bench Spokesman on Foreign and Commonwealth Affairs 1992–93. *Select Committees (Former):* Member: Broadcasting the House of Commons 1988–93, National Heritage 1993–94. *Special Interests:* Foreign Affairs, Media, Health Service, Machinery of Government. *Countries of Interest:* South Africa, The Commonwealth. *Recreations:* Football, steam railways, fiction writing, all sport. *Electoral Notes:* Contested South West Hertfordshire 1970, Lichfield and Tamworth February 1974. Member for Lichfield and Tamworth October 1974–79. Contested Lichfield and Tamworth 1979. Contested The Wrekin 1983. Member for The Wrekin 1987–97, and for Telford since May 1, 1997. *Clubs:* Trench Labour. *Address:* Bruce Grocott Esq, MP, House of Commons, London, SW1A 0AA *Tel:* 020 7219 5058 *Fax:* 020 7219 5136. *Constituency:* Suite 1, Matthew Webb House, High Street, Dawley, Telford, Shropshire, TF4 2EX *Tel:* 01952 507747 *Fax:* 01952 506064.

GROGAN, John *(Selby)   Lab majority 3,836*

Son of John Martin Grogan and late Maureen Grogan. Born February 24, 1961; educated St Michael's College, Leeds; St John's College, Oxford (Hons Degree Modern History and Economics). *Trades Union:* Member, GMB. *Career:* Self-employed Conference Organiser. *Select Committees (Current):* Member: Northern Ireland Affairs 1997–. *Party Groups:* Member, Fabian Society. *Special Interests:* Local Government, European Union, Economic Policy. *Recreations:* Football, running, cinema. *Electoral Notes:* Contested Selby 1987, 1992 General Elections, York European Parliament Election 1989. Member for Selby since May 1, 1997. *Address:* John Grogan Esq, MP, House of Commons, London, SW1A 0AA *Tel:* 020 7219 4403. *Constituency:* 58 Gunthorpe, Selby, North Yorkshire, YO8 4ET *Tel:* 01757 291152 *Fax:* 01757 291153.

GUMMER, The Rt Hon. John Selwyn *(Suffolk Coastal)   Con majority 3,254*

Son of late Canon Selwyn Gummer. Born November 26, 1939; educated King's School, Rochester; Selwyn College, Cambridge (BA Hons History 1961, MA 1971) (President of the Union 1962). Married 1977, Penelope Jane, daughter of John P. Gardner (2 sons 2 daughters). *Career:* Publisher; Journalist; Former Chairman, Siemssen Hunter Ltd; Chairman, Sancroft International. *Councils, Public Bodies:* Councillor, ILEA 1967–70. *Political Career:* PPS: to Minister of Agriculture, Fisheries and Food 1971–72, to Secretary of State for Social Services 1979–81; Parliamentary Under-Secretary of State, Department of Employment January-October 1983; Minister of State, Department of Employment 1983–84; Paymaster General 1984–85; Minister of State, Ministry of Agriculture, Fisheries and Food 1985–88; Minister for Local Government 1988–89; Minister of Agriculture, Fisheries and Food 1989–93; Secretary of State for the Environment 1993–97. *Whip:* Assistant Government Whip January 1981; Lord Commissioner of the Treasury 1981–83. *Party Groups:* Chairman, Cambridge University Conservative Association 1961; Conservative Party: Vice-Chairman 1972–74, Chairman 1983–85; Chairman, Conservative Group for Europe 1997–. *Other:* Member, General Synod of Church of England for St Edmundsbury and Ipswich Diocese 1978–92. *Honours:* PC 1985. *Publications: When the Coloured People Come*; *The Permissive Society*; Co-author *The Christian Calendar*, *Faith in Politics* 1987. *Electoral Notes:* Contested Greenwich 1964 and 1966 General Elections. Member for Lewisham West 1970–74, for Eye 1979–83, and for Suffolk Coastal since June 1983. *Address:* The Rt Hon. John Gummer, MP, House of Commons, London, SW1A 0AA *Tel:* 020 7219 4591 *Fax:* 020 7219 5906 *Tel (Constituency):* 01394 380001 *E-mail:* gummerj@parliament.uk.

GUNNELL, (William) John *(Morley and Rothwell)   Lab majority 14,750*

Son of late William and Norah Gunnell. Born October 1, 1933; educated King Edward's School, Birmingham; University of Leeds (BSc 1st Class Hons 1955). Married October 8, 1955, Jean Louise, daughter of late Frank Lacey (3 sons 1 daughter). *Trades Union:* Member, GMB 1955–. *Profession:* University Teacher. *Career:* Hospital porter, St Bartholomew's Hospital, London 1955–57; Leeds Modern School: Science teacher 1959–62, Head of Chemistry; Later Head of Science, United Nations International School, New York 1962–70; Lecturer, Centre for Studies in Science Education, University of Leeds 1970–88; Yorkshire Enterprise Ltd: Chairman 1982–90, 1995–6, Vice-Chairman 1990–95. *Councils, Public Bodies:* West Yorkshire Metropolitan County Council: Councillor 1977–86, Leader of the Council 1981–86; Yorkshire and Humberside Development Association: Chairman 1981–93, Hon. President 1993–; North of England Regional Consortium: Chairman 1982–92, Hon. President 1992–; Leeds City Council: Councillor 1986–92, Chairman, Social Services Committee 1990–92; Member: Leeds Healthcare 1990–92, Leeds Development Corporation 1988–92. *Select Committees (Current):* Member: Health 1997– *(Former):* Member: Broadcasting 1992–97, Public Service 1995–97. *Other:* Non-Executive Director, Opera North 1982–. *Trust:* Director, Leeds Theatre Trust (West Yorkshire Playhouse) 1986–93; Member: South Leeds Groundwork Trust, National Coal Mining Museum for England. *Miscellaneous:* Member, Audit Commission 1983–90. *Sportsclubs:* Warwickshire CC, Yorkshire CC. *Special Interests:* Industry, Venture

Capital, Investment, Regional Development, Health, Social Services. *Countries of Interest:* Middle East, Japan, Philippines, Belize. *Recreations:* Watching cricket and soccer, music, opera, photography. *Electoral Notes:* Contested Leeds North East February and October 1974. Member for Leeds South and Morley 1992–97, and for Morley and Rothwell since May 1, 1997. *Address:* John Gunnell Esq, MP, House of Commons, London, SW1A 0AA *Tel:* 020 7219 4549 *Fax:* 020 7219 2552. *Constituency:* Morley Town Hall, Leeds, LS27 9DY *Tel:* 0113–247 7138 *Fax:* 0113–247 7190 *E-mail:* gunnelljz@parliament.uk.

H

HAGUE, The Rt Hon. William *(Richmond (Yorkshire))*   Con majority 10,051

Son of Nigel and Stella Hague. Born March 26, 1961; educated Wath-on-Dearne Comprehensive School; Magdalen College, Oxford (President, Oxford Union 1981); INSEAD Business School, France. Married December 19, 1997, Ffion, daughter of Emyr and Myra Jenkins. *Career:* Shell UK 1982–83; McKinsey and Company 1983–88; Political Adviser: to Rt Hon. Sir Geoffrey Howe, QC, to Rt Hon. Leon Brittan, QC 1983. *Political Career:* PPS to Rt Hon. Norman Lamont MP, as Chancellor of the Exchequer 1990–93; Joint Parliamentary Under-Secretary of State, Department of Social Security 1993–94; Minister of State, Department of Social Security (Minister for Social Security and Disabled People) 1994–95; Secretary of State for Wales 1995–97; Leader of the Opposition 1997–. *Party Groups:* President, Oxford University Conservative Association 1981; Leader, Conservative Party June 1997–. *Awards: The Spectator*/Highland Park Parliamentarian of the Year Award 1998. *Honours:* PC 1995. *Special Interests:* Agriculture, Economic Policy. *Recreations:* Walking, swimming. *Electoral Notes:* Contested Wentworth 1987 General Election. Member for Richmond, Yorks. since February 23, 1989 By-election. *Clubs:* Beefsteak, Carlton, Buck's. *Address:* The Rt Hon. William Hague, MP, House of Commons, London, SW1A 0AA *Tel:* 020 7219 4553. *Constituency:* c/o 67 High Street, Northallerton, North Yorkshire, DL7 8EG *Tel:* 01609 779093 *Fax:* 01609 778172 *E-mail:* whague@conservative-party.org.uk.

HAIN, Peter *(Neath)*   Lab majority 26,741

Son of Walter and Adelaine Hain. Born February 16, 1950; educated London University (BSc Economics); Sussex University (MPhil). Married February 8, 1975, Patricia, daughter of Jack Western (2 sons) (separated). *Trades Union:* Head of Research, Union of Communication Workers 1976–91; Member, GMB. *Councils, Public Bodies:* Health Authority Member 1981–87. *Political Career:* Parliamentary Under-Secretary of State, Welsh Office 1997–99; Minister of State, Foreign and Commonwealth Office 1999–. *Whip:* Opposition Whip 1995–96. *Spokesman:* Opposition Spokesman on Employment 1996–97. *Party Groups:* Leader, Young Liberals 1971–73; Member: Co-op, Fabians. *Other:* Leader, Stop the Seventy Tour 1969–70; Anti-Nazi League 1977–79; Member: CND, Anti-Apartheid Movement; School Governor 1981–90; Tribune Newspaper Board of Directors. *Sportsclubs:* Resolven Rugby, Ynysygerwn Cricket. *Publications:* Author of thirteen books including *Ayes to the Left: A future for socialism,* 1995. *Special Interests:* Post Office, Telecommunications, Reform of Government, Economic Policy. *Countries of Interest:* Southern Africa. *Recreations:* Rugby, soccer, cricket, motor racing, rock and folk music. *Electoral Notes:* Contested Putney 1983 and 1987 General Elections. Member for Neath since by-election April 4, 1991. *Clubs:* Royal British Legion, Resolven. *Address:* Peter Hain Esq, MP, House of Commons, London, SW1A 0AA *Tel:* 020 7219 3925 *Fax:* 020 7219 3816. *Constituency:* 14 The Parade, Neath, SA11 1RA *Tel:* 01639 630152 *Fax:* 01639 641196.

HALL, Michael *(Weaver Vale)   Lab majority 13,448*

Son of late Thomas Hall, maintenance engineer, and of late Veronica Hall, mail order clerk. Born September 20, 1952; educated St Mary's Primary School, Ashton-under-Lyne; St Damian's Secondary Modern School; North Cheshire College (Teacher's Certificate); Padgate College of Higher Education (BEd (Hons) 1987); Bangor University (Diploma in Education). Married August 2, 1975, Lesley, daughter of Allen and Edna Gosling (1 son). *Career:* Scientific Assistant, chemical industry 1969–73; Padgate College of Higher Education 1973–77; Teacher of History and Physical Education, Bolton LEA 1977–85; Support Teacher, Halton Community Assessment Team 1985–92. *Councils, Public Bodies:* Warrington Borough Council: Councillor 1979–93; Chairman: Environmental Health Committee 1981–84, Finance Sub-Committee 1984–85, Policy and Resources Committee 1985–92; Council Leader 1985–92. *Political Career:* PPS to Rt Hon. Ann Taylor, MP, as Leader of the House and President of the Council 1997–98. *Whip:* Assistant Government Whip 1998–. *Select Committees (Former):* Member: Public Accounts Committee 1992–97, Modernisation of the House of Commons 1997–98. *Sportsclubs:* Lymm Lawn Tennis and Croquet. *Special Interests:* Poverty, Education, Local Government, Environment. *Recreations:* Tennis, walking, cooking, reading. *Electoral Notes:* Member for Warrington South 1992–97, and for Weaver Vale since May 1, 1997. *Address:* Michael Hall Esq, MP, House of Commons, London, SW1A 0AA *Tel:* 020 7219 3000. *Constituency:* Room 8, Castle Park, Frodsham, Cheshire, WA6 6UJ *Tel:* 01928 735000 *Fax:* 01928 735250 *E-mail:* michael.hall@geo2.poptel.org.uk; michael.hall@hm-treasury.gov.uk.

HALL, Patrick *(Bedford)   Lab majority 8,300*

Born October 20, 1951; educated Bedford Modern School; Birmingham University; Oxford Polytechnic. *Trades Union:* Member, NALGO. *Profession:* Local Government Planning Officer. *Career:* Local Government Planning Officer; Bedford Town Centre Co-ordinator. *Councils, Public Bodies:* Councillor, Bedfordshire County Council 1989–97; Member, North Bedfordshire Community Health Council. *Select Committees (Current):* Member: Consolidation of Bills (Joint Committee) 1997–, European Scrutiny 1999–. *Party Groups:* Hon. Secretary, Eastern Regional Group of Labour MPs 1999–. *Other:* Chairperson, Bedford Door to Door Dial-a-Ride 1989–; Governor, Beauchamp Middle School. Member, Chartered Institute of Public Finance and Accountancy. *Recreations:* Squash, gardens. *Electoral Notes:* Contested North Bedfordshire 1992 General Election. Member for Bedford since May 1, 1997. *Address:* Patrick Hall Esq, MP, House of Commons, London, SW1A 0AA *Tel:* 020 7219 3605. *Constituency:* 5 Mill Street, Bedford *Tel:* 01234 262699 *Fax:* 01234 272921.

HAMILTON, The Rt Hon. Sir Archibald Gavin *(Epsom and Ewell)   Con majority 11,525*

Son of late 3rd Baron Hamilton of Dalzell, GCVO, MC. Born December 30, 1941; educated Eton. Married December 14, 1968, Anne Napier (3 daughters). *Armed Forces:* Lieutenant, Coldstream Guards 1960–62. *Councils, Public Bodies:* Councillor, Royal Borough of Kensington and Chelsea 1968–71. *Political Career:* PPS To The Rt Hon. David Howell, MP: as Secretary of State for Energy 1979–81, as Secretary of State for Transport 1981–82; Parliamentary Under-Secretary of State for Defence Procurement 1986–87; PPS to Margaret Thatcher, as Prime Minister 1987–88; Minister of State for the Armed Forces, Ministry of Defence 1988–93. *Whip:* Assistant Government Whip 1982–84; Lord Commissioner to HM Treasury (Whip) 1984–86. *Select Committees (Former):* Member: Members' Interests 1995, Standards and Privileges 1995–97, Standards in Public Life 1995. *Other:* Governor, Westminster Foundation for Democracy 1993–. *Miscellaneous:* Member, Committee on Intelligence and Security 1994–97; Executive Member, 1922 Committee 1995–97, Chairman 1997–; Member, Conservative Ethics and Integrity Committee 1999–. *Honours:* PC 1991; Knighted 1994. *Special Interests:* Finance, Tax, Economic Policy, Trade and Industry, Defence. *Electoral Notes:* Parliamentary Candidate for Dagenham in February and October 1974 elections. Member for Epsom and Ewell since By-election April 27, 1978. *Address:* The Rt Hon. Sir Archibald Hamilton, MP, House of Commons, London, SW1A 0AA *Tel:* 020 7219 5109 *Fax:* 020 7219 2429. *Constituency:* 212 Barnet Wood Lane, Ashford, Surrey, KT21 2DB *Tel:* 013722 77066.

HAMILTON, Fabian *(Leeds North East)   Lab majority 6,959*

Son of late Mario Uziell-Hamilton, solicitor, and Adrianne Uziell-Hamilton (Her Honour Judge Uziell-Hamilton). Born April 12, 1955; educated Brentwood School, Brentwood, Essex; University of York (BA Hons). Married April 17, 1980, Rosemary, daughter of Shirley and Robert Ratcliffe (1 son 2 daughters). *Trades Union:* Member: SLADE 1978–82, NGA 1982–91, GPMU 1991–. *Profession:* Computer Systems Consultant. *Career:* Taxi Driver 1978–79; Graphic Designer 1979–94; Consultant and Dealer, Apple Macintosh Computer Systems 1994–97. *Councils, Public Bodies:* Councillor, Leeds City Council 1987–98, Chair: Race Equality Committee 1988–94, Economic Development Committee 1994–96, Education Committee 1996–97. *Select Committees (Current):* Member: Administration 1997–. *Party Groups:* Member: Co-op Party, Labour Friends of Israel. *Other:* School Governor; Member: Anti-Apartheid Movement, Poale Zion. *Trust:* Member, National Heart Research Fund. *Miscellaneous:* Member, European Standing Committee B 1998–. *Special Interests:* Education, Economic Development and Small Business, Anti-Racism, International Development, Alternative Fuels. *Countries of Interest:* Middle East, Europe, Southern Africa, Caribbean and Indian sub-continent, Cyprus. *Recreations:* Film, theatre, opera, music. *Electoral Notes:* Contested Leeds North East 1992. *Address:* Fabian Hamilton Esq, MP, House of Commons, London, SW1A 0AA *Tel:* 020 7219 3493 *Fax:* 020 7219 4945. *Constituency:* 6 Queenshill Approach, Leeds, LS17 6AY *Tel:* 0113–237 0022 *Fax:* 0113–237 0404 *E-mail:* fabian.mp@hamilton.go-serif.net.

HAMMOND, Philip *(Runnymede and Weybridge)   Con majority 9,875*

Son of Bernard Lawrence Hammond, AMICE, retired civil engineer and local government officer. Born December 4, 1955; educated Shenfield School, Brentwood, Essex; University College, Oxford (Open Scholarship) (MA philosophy, politics and economics). Married June 29, 1991, Susan Carolyn Williams-Walker (2 daughters 1 son). *Career:* Assistant to Chairman then Marketing Manager, Speywood Laboratories Ltd 1977–81; Director, Speywood Medical Ltd 1981–83; Established and ran medical equipment distribution agency 1983–94; Director, Castlemead Ltd 1984–; Director, various medical equipment manufacturing companies 1983–96; Partner, CMA Consultants 1993–95; Director, Castlemead Homes Ltd 1994–; Consultant to Government of Malawi 1995–97. *Spokesman:* An Opposition Spokesman for Health and Social Services 1998–. *Select Committees (Current):* Member: Unopposed Bills (Panel) 1997– *(Former):* Member: Environment, Transport and Regional Affairs 1998, Transport 1998. *Party Groups:* East Lewisham Conservative Association: Executive Council Member 1982–89, Chairman 1989–96; Member, Greater London Area Executive Council 1989–96; Vice-Chairman, Greenwich and Lewisham Conservative Action Group 1993–94. *Miscellaneous:* Member, European Standing Committee B 1997–1998. *Special Interests:* Economic Policy, International Trade, European Union, Defence, Social Security, Transport, Housing and Planning, Energy, Health. *Countries of Interest:* Latin America, Germany, Italy, Southern and Eastern Africa. *Recreations:* Travel, cinema, walking. *Electoral Notes:* Contested Newham North East By-Election 1994. Member for Runnymede and Weybridge since May 1, 1997. *Clubs:* Carlton. *Address:* Philip Hammond Esq, MP, House of Commons, London, SW1A 0AA *Tel:* 020 7219 4055 *Fax:* 020 7219 5851. *Constituency:* 74A Church Street, Weybridge, Surrey, KT13 8DL *Tel:* 01932 851239 *Fax:* 01932 854305 *E-mail:* hammondp@parliament.uk.

HANCOCK, Mike (Michael) Thomas, CBE *(Portsmouth South)   LD majority 4,327*

Son of Thomas William Hancock and Margaret Eva Hancock (née Cole). Born April 9, 1946. Married 1967, Jacqueline, daughter of Sidney and Gwen Elliott (1 son 1 daughter). *Trades Union:* Former Shop Steward and Convenor; Member, Engineering Union. *Career:* Director, BBC Daytime Club; District Officer for Hampshire, Isle of Wight and Channel Islands Mencap 1989–. *Councils, Public Bodies:* Councillor, Portsmouth City Council 1971, Fratton Ward 1973–, Leader, Liberal Democrat Group 1989–97, Chairman, Planning and Economic Development Committee 1991–; Councillor, Hampshire County Council 1973–, Leader of the Opposition 1977–81, 1989–93, Leader 1993–97. *Spokesman:* A Spokesman for Foreign Affairs, Defence and Europe (Defence) 1997–99. *Select Committees (Current):* Member: Defence 1999– *(Former):* Member: Public

Administration 1997–99. *Party Groups:* Member: Labour Party 1968–81, Social Democrat Party 1981–87, Liberal Democrat Party 1987–. *International Bodies:* Council of Europe, Western European Union, NATO. *Other:* Chairman, Southern Branch, NSPCC 1989–; Vice-Chairman, Portsmouth Docks 1992–. *Trust:* Trustee, Royal Marine Museum. *Honours:* CBE 1992. *Special Interests:* European Democracy, Defence, Sport. *Electoral Notes:* Contested Portsmouth South (SDP) 1983, (SDP/Alliance) 1987. Member (SDP) for Portsmouth South 1984–87. Contested (Liberal Democrat) Wight and Hampshire South, European Parliamentary Elections 1994. Member for Portsmouth South since May 1, 1997. *Address:* Mike Hancock Esq, CBE, MP, House of Commons, London, SW1A 0AA *Tel:* 020 7219 5180 *Fax:* 020 7219 2496. *Constituency:* 1A Albert Road, Southsea, Hampshire, PO5 2SE *Tel:* 023 9286 1055 *Fax:* 023 9283 0530 *E-mail:* portsmouthldp@cix.co.uk.

HANSON, David George *(Delyn)   Lab majority 12,693*

Son of Brian Hanson, retired fork lift driver and Glenda Hanson, retired wages clerk. Born July 5, 1957; educated Verdin Comprehensive School, Winsford, Cheshire; Hull University (BA Hons, Certificate of Education). Married September 6, 1986, Margaret, daughter of late Ronald Mitchell and of May Mitchell (1 son 2 daughters). *Profession:* Charity Director. *Career:* Vice-President, Hull University Students' Union 1978–79; Trainee, Co-operative Union 1980–81; Manager, Plymouth Co-operative 1981–82; Various posts with The Spastics Society 1982–89; Director, Re-Solv (The Society for the Prevention of Solvent Abuse) 1989–92. *Councils, Public Bodies:* Councillor: Vale Royal Borough Council 1983–91, Northwich Town Council 1987–91; Vale Royal Borough Council: Chairman, Economic Development Committee, Labour Leader 1989–91. *Political Career:* PPS to Rt Hon. Alastair Darling, MP, as Chief Secretary to the Treasury 1997–98; Parliamentary Under-Secretary of State, Wales Office 1999–. *Whip:* Assistant Government Whip 1998–99. *Select Committees (Former):* Member: Welsh Affairs 1992–95, Public Service 1995–97. *Party Groups:* Member, Leadership Campaign Team 1994–97. *Special Interests:* Foreign Affairs, Health, Heritage, Local Government, Solvent Abuse, Treasury. *Countries of Interest:* South Africa, Cyprus. *Recreations:* Football, cinema, family. *Electoral Notes:* Contested Eddisbury 1983 and Delyn 1987 General Elections, and Cheshire West 1984 European Parliamentary Election. Member for Delyn since April 9, 1992. *Address:* David Hanson Esq, MP, House of Commons, London, SW1A 0AA *Tel:* 020 7219 5064 *Fax:* 020 7219 2671. *Constituency:* 64 Chester Street, Flint, Flintshire, CH6 5DH *Tel:* 01352 763159 *Fax:* 01352 730140.

HARMAN, The Rt Hon. Harriet *(Camberwell and Peckham)   Lab majority 16,351*

Daughter of late John Bishop Harman, and of Anna Harman. Born July 30, 1950; educated St Paul's Girls' School; York University (BA Politics 1998). Married 1982, Jack Dromey (2 sons 1 daughter). *Career:* Legal Officer, National Council for Civil Liberties 1978–82. *Political Career:* Shadow Minister, Social Services 1984, 1985–87; Shadow Chief Secretary to the Treasury 1992–94; Shadow Secretary of State for: Employment 1994–95, Health 1995–96; Social Security 1996–97; Secretary of State for Social Security and Minister for Women 1997–98. *Spokesman:* Spokesperson on Health 1987–92. *Party Groups:* Member, Labour Party National Executive Committee 1993–. *Honours:* PC 1997. *Special Interests:* Women, Social Services, Provision for under 5s. *Electoral Notes:* Member for Peckham 1982–1997, and for Camberwell and Peckham since May 1, 1997. *Address:* The Rt Hon. Harriet Harman, MP, House of Commons, London, SW1A 0AA *Tel:* 020 7219 4218 *Fax:* 020 7219 4877 *E-mail:* harmanh@parliament.uk.

Dod *on* Disk
The Vacher Dod Parliamentary Database – configured for PC or Network
For further details please telephone the Westminster Office
020 7828 7256

HARRIS, Dr Evan *(Oxford West and Abingdon)* *LD majority 6,285*

Son of Prof Frank Harris, CBE, Dean of Medicine, Leicester University, and Mrs Brenda Harris, formerly scientific officer. Born October 21, 1965; educated Liverpool Blue Coat Secondary School; Wadham College, Oxford (BA Hons Physiology, Diploma in Med Sociology); Oxford University Medical School (BM, BCh); ESU Scholarship to Harvard High School 1984; Open Scholarship to Wadham College 1985. Divorced. *Trades Union:* Place of Work Representative, BMA 1992–94; BMA National Council 1994–97; Junior Doctors Committee Executive 1995–97. *Career:* NHS Hospital Doctor 1991–94; Public Health Registrar (Hon) 1994–97. *Spokesman:* A Spokesman for: Health (NHS Staff, Organisation and Planning) 1997–99, Education and Employment (Higher Education and Women) 1999–. *Select Committees (Current):* Member: Education and Employment 1999–, Education Sub-Committee 1999–. *Party Groups:* Member: SDP 1985, Oxford West and Abingdon SDP and LibDem Executive Committee 1986–97, Green Liberal Democrats; Hon. President, LibDems for Gay and Lesbian Rights. *Other:* Member: Oxford Asylum Welcome, OXAIDS, Liberty, Amnesty International, English Bridge Union, British Chess Federation. *Miscellaneous:* Member: Central Oxford Research Ethics Committee 1995–98, European Standing Committee C 1999–, BMA Ethics Committee, Oxford Diocesan Board of Social Responsibility. *Publications:* Various contributions and articles to medical journals. *Special Interests:* Health, Civil Liberties, Voting Systems, Asylum Issues, Science, Medical Ethics. *Countries of Interest:* Israel, South Africa, USA. *Recreations:* TV, Squash, Bridge. *Electoral Notes:* Member for Oxford West and Abingdon since May 1, 1997. *Clubs:* National Liberal. *Address:* Dr Evan Harris, MP, House of Commons, London, SW1A 0AA *Tel:* 020 7219 3614 *Fax:* 020 7219 2346. *Constituency:* The Old Jam Factory, 27 Park End Street, Oxford, OX1 1HU *Tel:* 01865 245584 *Fax:* 01865 245589 *E-mail:* harrise@parliament.uk.

HARVEY, Nick (Nicholas) *(North Devon)* *LD majority 6,181*

Son of Frederick Harvey, civil servant, and Christine Harvey, teacher. Born August 3, 1961; educated Queen's College, Taunton; Middlesex Polytechnic. *Career:* President, Middlesex Polytechnic Students' Union 1981–82; Communications and Marketing Executive: Profile PR Ltd 1984–86, Dewe Rogerson Ltd 1986–91; Communications Consultant 1989–. *Spokesman:* Liberal Democrat Spokesman for: Transport 1992–94, Trade and Industry 1994–97, Constitution (English Regions) 1997–99; Principal Spokesman for Health 1999–. *Select Committees (Former):* Member: Trade and Industry 1994–95. *Party Groups:* National Vice-Chairman, Union of Liberal Students 1981–82; Liberal Democrat Chair of Campaigns and Communications 1994–. *Special Interests:* Economics, European Union. *Recreations:* Travel, football, walking, music. *Electoral Notes:* Contested Enfield Southgate (Liberal/Alliance) 1987 General Election. Member for North Devon since April 9, 1992. *Clubs:* National Liberal. *Address:* Nick Harvey Esq, MP, House of Commons, London, SW1A 0AA *Tel:* 020 7219 5892 *E-mail:* harveyn@parliament.uk.

HASELHURST, The Rt Hon. Sir Alan Gordon Barraclough *(Saffron Walden)* *Con majority 10,573*

Son of late John Haselhurst. Born June 23, 1937; educated King Edward VI School, Birmingham; Cheltenham College; Oriel College, Oxford. Married April 16, 1977, Angela Margaret Bailey (2 sons 1 daughter). *Career:* Secretary, Treasurer, Librarian, Oxford Union Society 1959–60. *Political Career:* PPS to Secretary of State, Education and Science 1979–81; Chairman, Ways and Means and Deputy Speaker 1997–. *Select Committees (Current):* Chairman of Ways and Means: Chairmen's Panel 1997–, Court of Referees 1997–, Unopposed Bills (Panel) 1997–, Standing Orders 1998– *(Former):* Member: European Legislation 1982–97, Catering 1991–97, Transport 1992–97. *Party Groups:* President, Oxford University Conservative Association 1958; National Chairman, Young Conservative Movement 1966–68; Deputy Chairman, Conservative Group for Europe 1982–85. *International Bodies:* Chairman, Commonwealth Youth Exchange Council 1978–81. *Trust:* Chairman of Trustees, Community Projects Foundation 1986–97; Fellow, Industry and Parliament Trust. *Sportsclubs:* Essex County Cricket Club, Executive Committee Member 1996–. *Honours:* Knighted

1995; PC 1999. *Publications: Occasionaly Cricket. Special Interests:* Education, Aerospace, Aviation, Youth Affairs, European Union, Agriculture, Community Development. *Recreations:* Hi-fi, watching cricket, gardening. *Electoral Notes:* Member for Middleton and Prestwich 1970-February 1974, and for Saffron Walden from July 7, 1977 (By-election). *Clubs:* MCC. *Address:* The Rt Hon. Sir Alan Haselhurst, MP, House of Commons, London, SW1A 0AA *Tel:* 020 7219 5214 *Fax:* 020 7219 5600. *Constituency:* The Old Armoury, Saffron Walden, Essex, CB10 1JN *Tel:* 01799 506349 *Fax:* 01799 522349 *E-mail:* haselhursta@parliament.uk.

HAWKINS, Nicholas John *(Surrey Heath)*   Con majority 16,287

Son of Dr Arthur Ernest Hawkins and Mrs Patricia Jean Hawkins (née Papworth). Born March 27, 1957; educated Bedford Modern School; Lincoln College, Oxford (MA); Middle Temple, Inns of Court School of Law (Harmsworth Entrance Exhibition and Senior Scholar). Married July 21, 1979, Angela Margaret Turner (2 sons 1 daughter) (separated 1999). *Trades Union:* Member, NATSOPA 1976–77. *Armed Forces:* Royal Navy Cadet 1971–74; Senior Cadet, CCF RN Section, Coxswain, Chief Petty Officer. *Profession:* Barrister. *Career:* Barrister with chambers in Birmingham and Northampton 1979–86; Consultant 1986–87; Company Legal Adviser, Access (The Joint Credit Card Co. Ltd) 1987–89; Group Legal Adviser, Lloyds Abbey Life plc 1989–92. *Political Career:* PPS: to James Arbuthnot, MP and Hon. Nicholas Soames, MP, Ministers of State, Ministry of Defence 1995–96, to Rt Hon. Virginia Bottomley, MP as Secretary of State for National Heritage 1996–97; Political Aide, to Rt Hon. Gillian Shepherd MP, as Shadow Leader of the House and as Shadow Secretary of State, Department of the Environment Transport and the Regions 1997–99. *Whip:* Government Whip, Armed Forces Bill Committee 1996. *Spokesman:* Opposition Front Bench Spokesman for Lord Chancellor's Department 1999–. *Select Committees (Former):* Member: Transport 1992–95, Home Affairs 1998–99. *Party Groups:* Vice-Chairman, Rochford Constituency Conservative Association, Essex 1988–91; Bow Group 1990–92, Research Secretary 1990–91, Campaign Director 1991–92, Chairman 1992–93. *International Bodies:* Chairman, International Committee, Bar Association for Commerce, Finance and Industry 1989–92; Member, International Practice Committee, Bar Council 1989–91. *Other:* Area Chairman, Business Support Group, Marie Curie Cancer Care; Sponsor, Parliamentary Events, Association of Medical Research Charities; Founder Patron, Knight foundation for Cystic Fibrosis; NSPCC. *Awards:* Eastern Area CPC Public Speaking Competition 1990. *Miscellaneous:* Hon. Major, Armed Forces Parliamentary Scheme 1997–98; Government Whip on Armed Forces Bill Select Committee 1996. Co-Sponsor, Event for Coopers' Company 1999. *Sportsclubs:* Surrey CCC. *Publications:* Co-author *1992 – The Single Market in Insurance*, 1990; Author *Competitive Sport in Schools*, 1994; *Televising Sport – Responding to Debate*, 1996; *Bringing Order to the House*, 1997 Various articles on transport history. *Special Interests:* Defence, Home Affairs, Law and Order, Trade and Industry, Finance, Insurance, Financial Services, Environment, Transport, Education, Tourism, Sport, Small Businesses. *Countries of Interest:* France, Germany, Ireland, Austria, Italy, Baltic States, Scandinavia, Australia, West Indies, Israel, Gibraltar, Canada, USA. *Recreations:* Cricket, theatre, music, other sports including swimming, rugby union, soccer. *Electoral Notes:* Contested Huddersfield 1987. Member for Blackpool South 1992–97, and for Surrey Heath since May 1, 1997. *Address:* Nick Hawkins Esq, MP, House of Commons, London, SW1A 0AA *Tel:* 020 7219 6329 *Fax:* 020 7219 2693. *Constituency:* Curzon House, Church Road, Windlesham, Surrey, GU20 6BH *Tel:* 01276 472468 *Fax:* 01276 476110.

HAYES, John *(South Holland and The Deepings)   Con majority 7,991*

Son of Henry John Hayes and late Lily Hayes. Born June 23, 1958; educated Colfe's Grammar School, London; University of Nottingham (BA Hons Politics, PGCE History/English). Married July 1997, Susan Hopwell. *Profession:* Company Director. *Career:* IT company 1983–, executive director until 1997, non-executive director 1997–. *Councils, Public Bodies:* Councillor, Nottinghamshire County Council 1985–98, Conservative Spokesman on Education 1997–98, Former Chairman, County Conservative Group's Campaigns Committee. *Political Career:* A Vice-Chairman, Conservative Party 1999–. *Select Committees (Current):* Member: Education Sub-Committee 1999– *(Former):* Member: Agriculture 1997–99, Education and Employment 1998–99. *Party Groups:* Member, Conservative Party 1973–, Former Chairman: YC Branches, Nottingham University Conservative Association. *Other:* Member: British Field Sports Society, SPUC. *Trust:* Member, National Trust. *Publications:* Numerous articles and pamphlets. *Special Interests:* Education, Parties and Elections and Campaigning, Political Ideas and Philosophy, Local Government, Agriculture, Commerce, Industry, Welfare of Elderly and Disabled. *Countries of Interest:* England, Italy, USA, Spain. *Recreations:* The Arts, many sports, gardening, good food and wine. *Electoral Notes:* Contested Derby North East 1987, 1992. Member for South Holland and The Deepings since May 1, 1997. *Clubs:* Carlton, Spalding. *Address:* John Hayes Esq, MP, House of Commons, London, SW1A 0AA *Tel:* 020 7219 3453. *Constituency:* The Manor House, 11 Broad Street, Spalding, Lincolnshire, PE11 1TB *Tel:* 01775 713905 *Fax:* 01775 713905.

HEAL, Sylvia Lloyd *(Halesowen and Rowley Regis)   Lab majority 10,337*

Daughter of late John Lloyd Fox, steelworker, and Ruby Fox. Born July 20, 1942; educated Elfed Secondary Modern School, Buckley, North Wales; Coleg Harlech and Swansea University (BSc Econ, Politics and Social Administration). Married July 31, 1965, Keith, son of Cecil and Beatrice Heal (1son 1 daughter). *Trades Union:* Member, GMB. *Profession:* Social Worker. *Career:* Medical Records Clerk 1957–63; Social Worker: Department of Employment 1968–70, Rehabilitation Centre 1980–90; National Officer, Carers National Association 1992–97. *Councils, Public Bodies:* JP. *Political Career:* Shadow Minister of Health 1991–92; Deputy Shadow Minister for Women 1991–92; PPS to Secretaries of State for Defence: Rt Hon. the Lord Robertson of Port Ellen 1997–99, Rt Hon. Geoffrey Hoon, MP 1999–. *Select Committees (Former):* : Education and Science 1990–91. *Party Groups:* Member, Socialist Education Association. *Other:* Council Member, ASA 1992–97; Member: Action for South Africa (ACTSA), One World Action. *Special Interests:* Health Education, Equal Opportunities (Disability/Women). *Recreations:* Walking, gardening, listening to male voice choirs. *Electoral Notes:* Member for Mid Staffordshire 1990 By-election–1992. Member for Halesowen and Rowley Regis since May 1, 1997. *Clubs:* London-Welsh Association, Rowley and Blackheath Labour Club. *Address:* Mrs Sylvia Heal, MP, House of Commons, London, SW1A 0AA *Tel:* 020 7219 2317 *Fax:* 020 7219 0956. *Constituency:* Municipal Buildings, Barrs Road, Cradley Heath, West Midlands, B64 7JX *Tel:* 0121–569 4646 *Fax:* 0121–569 4647.

HEALD, Oliver *(North East Hertfordshire)   Con majority 3,088*

Son of J. A. Heald. Born December 15, 1954; educated Reading School; Pembroke College, Cambridge (MA). Married August 15, 1979, Christine Whittle (1 son 2 daughters). *Career:* Barrister, Middle Temple 1977–. *Political Career:* PPS: to Rt Hon. Sir Peter Lloyd, MP, as Minister of State, Home Office 1994, to Rt Hon. William Waldegrave, MP, as Minister of Agriculture, Fisheries and Food 1994–95; Parliamentary Under-Secretary of State, Department of Social Security 1995–97; Sponsored Private Member's Bill: Insurance Companies (Reserves) Act 1995. *Whip:* An Opposition Whip: (Chancellor of the Duchy of Lancaster, Constitutional, Private Members' Bills: East Midlands and West Midlands) 1997–98, (Treasury, Private Members' Bills) 1998–99, (Treasury, International Development) 1999, (Foreign Affairs; Leader of The House) 1999–. *Select Committees (Current):* Member: Administration 1998– *(Former):* Member: Employment 1992–94.

Party Groups: Chairman, North Hertfordshire Conservative Association 1984–86; Vice-President, Southwark and Bermondsey Conservative Association 1988–93, President 1993–98, Patron 1998–. *Special Interests:* Industrial Relations, Environment, Law and Order, Pensions. *Recreations:* Sport, family. *Electoral Notes:* Contested Southwark and Bermondsey in 1987 General Election. Member for North Hertfordshire 1992–97, and for North East Hertfordshire since May 1, 1997. *Address:* Oliver Heald Esq, MP, House of Commons, London, SW1A 0AA *Tel:* 020 7219 4505 *Tel (Constituency):* 01763 247640 *E-mail:* healdo@parliament.uk.

HEALEY, John *(Wentworth)*   Lab majority 23,959

Son of Aidan Healey, OBE, prison service, and Jean Healey, teacher. Born February 13, 1960; educated Lady Lumley's Comprehensive School, Pickering; St Peter's School, York; Christ's College, Cambridge (BA). Married October 25, 1993, Jackie, daughter of Leon and Jean Bate (1 son). *Trades Union:* Member: NUJ, GMB. *Profession:* Campaigns Director. *Career:* Journalist/Deputy Editor, *The House Magazine* 1983–84; Disability Campaigner for three national charities 1984–90; Tutor, Open University Business School 1989–92; Campaigns Manager, Issue Communications 1990–92; Head of Communications, MSF Union 1992–94; Campaigns and Communications Director, TUC 1994–97. *Political Career:* PPS to Rt Hon. Gordon Brown, MP, as Chancellor of the Exchequer 1999–. *Select Committees (Former):* Member: Education and Employment 1997–99, Employment Sub-Committee 1997–99. *Other:* Member: Child Poverty Action Group, Amnesty International Liberty World Development Movement. *Special Interests:* Employment, Trade Unions, Economic Regeneration, Industrial Relations, Disabled/Disability, Local Government Finance. *Recreations:* Family. *Electoral Notes:* Contested Ryedale 1992. Member for Wentworth since May 1, 1997. *Address:* John Healey Esq, MP, House of Commons, London, SW1A 0AA *Tel:* 020 7219 5170/2448 *Fax:* 020 7219 2451. *Constituency:* 79 High Street, Wath-upon-Deane, Rotherham, South Yorkshire, S63 7QB *Tel:* 01709 875665 *Fax:* 01709 874207 *E-mail:* healeyj@parliament.uk.

HEATH, David William St John, CBE *(Somerton and Frome)*   LD majority 130

Son of Eric and Pamela Heath. Born March 16, 1954; educated Millfield School, Street; St John's College, Oxford (MA physiological sciences); City University (ophthalmic optics). Married May 1987, Caroline Netherton (1 son 1 daughter). *Profession:* Qualified Optician. *Career:* Qualified Optician in Practice 1979–85; Parliamentary Consultant, Worldwide Fund for Nature 1990–91; Consultant to Various NGOs/Charities; Member, Audit Commission 1995–97. *Councils, Public Bodies:* Councillor, Somerset County Council 1985–97, Leader of Council 1985–89; Chairman, Avon and Somerset Police Authority 1993–96. *Spokesman:* A Spokesman for: Foreign Affairs, Defence and Europe (Europe) 1997–99, Agriculture, Rural Affairs and Fisheries 1999–. *Select Committees (Former):* Member: Foreign Affairs 1997–99, Foreign Affairs 1998–99, Entry Clearance Sub-Committee 1998. *Party Groups:* Member: Liberal Party National Executive 1988–89, Liberal Democrats Federal Executive 1990–92, 1993–95. *International Bodies:* Member: Council of Local Authorities and Regions of Europe 1993–97, Parliamentary Assembly of the Organisation for Security and Co-operation in Europe (OSCE) 1997–. *Other:* Member, Witham Friary Friendly Society. *Miscellaneous:* Vice-Chairman: Association of County Councils 1994–97, Committee of Local Police Authorities 1993–97; Member, Audit Commission 1994–97. *Honours:* CBE 1989. FRSA; FADO. *Special Interests:* Education, Local Government, Rural Affairs, Environment, Home Affairs. *Countries of Interest:* Europe, France. *Recreations:* Cricket, rugby football, until recently pig breeding. *Electoral Notes:* Contested Somerton and Frome 1992. Member for Somerton and Frome since May 1, 1997. *Clubs:* National Liberal. *Address:* David Heath Esq, CBE, MP, House of Commons, London, SW1A 0AA *Tel:* 020 7219 6245 *Fax:* 020 7219 5939. *Constituency:* 14 Catherine Hill, Frome, Somerset *Tel:* 01373 473618 *Fax:* 01373 455152 *E-mail:* davidheath@cix.co.uk.

HEATH, The Rt Hon. Sir Edward Richard George, KG, MBE *(Old Bexley and Sidcup)*
Con majority 3,569

Son of late William George Heath. Born July 9, 1916; educated Chatham House, Kent; Balliol College, Oxford (MA) (President, Oxford Union 1939); Various honorary degrees. *Armed Forces:* Served with Royal Artillery overseas 1940–46 (Mentioned in Despatches); Cmnd 2 Regt Honorable Artillery Company 1947–51; Master Gunner within the Tower of London 1951–54. *Political Career:* Minister of Labour 1959–60; Lord Privy Seal 1960–63; Secretary of State for Industry, Trade and Regional Development, and President of the Board of Trade 1963–64; Leader of the Opposition 1965–70, 1974–75; Prime Minister, First Lord of the Treasury and Minister for the Civil Service 1970–74; Responsible in 1971 for successfully completing the negotiations for Britain's entry into the EEC; Father of the House of Commons 1992–. *Whip:* Opposition Whip February 1951; Lord Commissioner of the Treasury November 1951; Joint Deputy Government Chief Whip May 1952; Deputy Government Chief Whip 1953–55; Parliamentary Secretary to the Treasury and Government Chief Whip 1955–59. *Party Groups:* President, Oxford University Conservative Association 1937; Chairman, Federation of University Conservative Association 1938; Leader, Conservative Party 1965-75. *International Bodies:* International Adviser, Praemium Imperiale (Japan). *Other:* Patron of many charities and voluntary organisations, nationally and within Old Bexley and Sidcup. *Awards:* Charlemagne Prize 1963; Channel 4 and House Award for Political Book of the Year 1999. *Honours:* MBE 1946; PC 1955; KG 1992. *Publications: One Nation: A Tory Approach to Social Problems*, 1950; *Old World New Horizons*, 1970; *Sailing: A Course in My Life*, 1975; *Music: A Joy for Life*, 1976, second edition 1997; *Travels: People and Places in My Life*, 1977; *Carols: The Joy of Christmas*, 1977; *The Course of My Life*, (autobiography) 1998. *Special Interests:* European Union, Economic Policy, Arts. *Countries of Interest:* All. *Recreations:* Sailing, music, travel. *Electoral Notes:* Member for Bexley 1950–74, for Bexley Sidcup 1974–83 and for Old Bexley and Sidcup since June 1983. *Clubs:* Royal Yacht Squadron (Cowes), Buck's, Pratt's, Carlton. *Address:* The Rt Hon. Sir Edward Heath, KG, MBE, MP, House of Commons, London, SW1A 0AA *Tel:* 020 7219 5559 *Fax:* 020 7219 5919 *Tel (Constituency):* 020 8300 3471 *Fax (Constituency):* 020 8300 9270.

HEATHCOAT-AMORY, The Rt Hon. David Philip *(Wells)* *Con majority 528*

Son of late Brigadier Roderick Heathcoat-Amory, MC. Born March 21, 1949; educated Eton College; Christ Church College, Oxford (MA Philosophy, Politics and Economics). Married February 4, 1978, Linda, daughter of Peter Adams (2 sons 1 daughter). *Career:* Qualified as Chartered Accountant 1974; Assistant Finance Director, British Technology Group 1980–83. *Political Career:* PPS: to Norman Lamont, MP, as Financial Secretary to the Treasury 1985–87, to Rt Hon. Douglas Hurd, MP, as Home Secretary 1987–88; Parliamentary Under-Secretary of State: at Department of Environment 1989–90, at Department of Energy 1990–92; Minister of State, Foreign and Commonwealth Office 1993–94; Paymaster General 1994–96; Member, Shadow Cabinet 1997–; Shadow Chief Secretary to the Treasury (Public Expenditure, Public Finances, Private Finance Initiative) 1997–. *Whip:* Assistant Government Whip 1988–89; Lord Commissioner of the Treasury and Government Whip July-October 1989; Treasurer of HM Household (Deputy Chief Whip) 1992–93. *Select Committees (Former):* Member: Broadcasting 1992–93, Finance and Services 1992–93. *Party Groups:* Treasurer, West Country Group of Conservative MPs 1983–85. *Honours:* PC 1996. FCA 1980. *Special Interests:* Industrial Policy, Agriculture, Forestry, Arms Control, Energy, European Union. *Recreations:* Fishing, shooting, music. *Electoral Notes:* Contested Brent South 1979. Member for Wells since June 1983. *Address:* The Rt Hon. David Heathcoat-Amory, MP, House of Commons, London, SW1A 0AA *Tel:* 020 7219 3543 *Tel (Constituency):* 01749 673146.

HENDERSON, Douglas *(Newcastle upon Tyne North)   Lab majority 19,332*

Son of John Henderson, railwayman, and Joy Henderson. Born June 9, 1949; educated Waid Academy, Fife; Central College, Glasgow; Strathclyde University, Glasgow. Married September 27, 1974, Janet, daughter of Robert Graham (1 son) (separated). *Trades Union:* Research Officer GMWU, Glasgow 1973; Scottish organiser GMB 1975–85, Organiser Newcastle 1985–87. *Career:* Apprentice, Rolls-Royce, Glasgow 1966–68; British Rail clerk, London 1969. *Political Career:* Minister of State (Europe), Foreign and Commonwealth Office 1997–98; Minister of State for the Armed Forces, Ministry of Defence 1998–99. *Spokesman:* Opposition Spokesman on: Trade and Industry 1988–92, The Environment (Local Government) 1992–94, Citizen's Charter 1994–95, Home Affairs 1995–97. *Sportsclubs:* Elswick Harriers, Cambuslang Harriers. *Special Interests:* Economic Policy, Industrial Policy, Employment Policy. *Countries of Interest:* former Soviet Union, USA. *Recreations:* Athletics, mountaineering, cross-country skiing. *Electoral Notes:* Member for Newcastle upon Tyne North since June 1987. *Clubs:* Lemington Labour, Newburn Memorial, Dinnington. *Address:* Douglas Henderson Esq, MP, House of Commons, London, SW1A 0AA *Tel:* 020 7219 5017 *Tel (Constituency):* 0191–286 2024.

HENDERSON, Ivan *(Harwich)   Lab majority 1,216*

Stepson of late Michael Bloice, son of Margaret Bloice. Born June 7, 1958; educated Sir Anthony Dean Comprehensive; Trade Union Courses – Political/Health and Safety. Married 1st (1 son 1 daughter), married 2nd, June 13, 1992, Jo'Anne Atkinson. *Trades Union:* Union Organiser, Docks; Member, NUR/RMT: Shop Steward 1984, Executive Officer 1991–94, Member, Political and Transport Committee, Former President, RMT Anglia District Council. *Profession:* Stevedore. *Career:* Former Dock Operative, Harwich International Port. *Councils, Public Bodies:* Councillor: Harwich Town Council 1986–97, Harwich District Council 1995–97. *Select Committees (Current):* Member: Joint Committee on Statutory Instruments 1999–. *Party Groups:* Member: Young Socialists, Labour Party prior to 1976; Executive Member, Harwich Constituency Labour Party; Member, Co-operative Party. *International Bodies:* Worked with International Transport Federation; European Works Council. *Other:* Member, PHAB (Harwich); President, Clacton and District Chamber of Trade & Commerce. *Miscellaneous:* Member: Trade's Council – Harwich Hospital Review Committee, European Standing Committee C 1999–. *Sportsclubs:* Harwich and Parkeston Football Club; Vice-President, Harwich and Dovercourt Cricket Club. *Special Interests:* Transport, Employment, Health. *Recreations:* Football, golf, sailing. *Electoral Notes:* Member for Harwich since May 1, 1997. *Address:* Ivan Henderson Esq, MP, House of Commons, London, SW1A 0AA *Tel:* 020 7219 3434. *Constituency:* 17 Hill Road, Dovercourt, Essex CO12 3PB *Tel:* 01255 552859 *Fax:* 01255 556771.

HEPBURN, Stephen *(Jarrow)   Lab majority 21,933*

Son of Peter and Margaret Hepburn. Born December 6, 1959; educated Springfield Comprehensive, Jarrow; Newcastle University (BA Hons). *Trades Union:* Member, UCATT. *Councils, Public Bodies:* Councillor, South Tyneside Council 1985–, Deputy Leader 1990–; Chair, Tyne & Wear Pensions 1989–. *Select Committees (Current):* Member: Administration 1997–, Defence 1999–. *Recreations:* Soccer, music, art. *Electoral Notes:* Member for Jarrow since May 1, 1997. *Address:* Stephen Hepburn Esq, MP, House of Commons, London, SW1A 0AA *Tel:* 020 7219 4134. *Constituency:* 35 Park Road, Jarrow, Tyne & Wear, NE32 5JL *Tel:* 0191–420 0648.

HEPPELL, John *(Nottingham East)   Lab majority 15,419*

Son of late Robert Heppell, miner, and late Helen Heppell. Born November 3, 1948; educated Rutherford Grammar School; South East Northumberland Technical College; Ashington Technical College. Married 1974, Eileen Golding (2 sons 1 daughter). *Trades Union:* Member, RMT (previously NUR). *Career:* Fitter: NCB 1964–70 and for number of firms in Nottingham area 1970–75; British Rail: Diesel fitter 1975–78, Workshop supervisor 1978–89. *Councils, Public Bodies:* Councillor, Nottinghamshire County Council 1981–93; Assistant Whip 1982; Vice-Chairman, Environment Committee 1983; Chairman: East Midlands Airport 1985, Resources Committee 1986, Deputy Leader, Nottinghamshire County Council 1989–92; Former Chairman, Equal Opportunities Committee; Former Chairman, Greater Nottingham LRT Board; Former Vice-Chairman, Policy Committee. *Political Career:* PPS to: The Rt Hon. the Lord Richard, as Lord Privy Seal and Leader of the House of Lords 1997–98; The Rt Hon. John Prescott, MP, as Deputy Prime Minister and Secretary of State for the Environment, Transport and the Regions 1998–. *Special Interests:* Equal Opportunity, Transport, Local Government. *Countries of Interest:* India, Pakistan, Cyprus. *Recreations:* Walking, reading. *Electoral Notes:* Member for Nottingham East since April 9, 1992. *Address:* John Heppell Esq, MP, House of Commons, London, SW1A 0AA *Tel:* 020 7219 4095 *Fax:* 020 7219 2969. *Constituency:* 1 Talbot Street, Nottingham, NG1 5GQ *Tel:* 0115–956 0450 *Fax:* 0115–956 0445.

HESELTINE, The Rt Hon. Michael Ray Dibdin, CH *(Henley)   Con majority 11,167*

Son of late Colonel R. D. Heseltine. Born March 21, 1933; educated Shrewsbury School; Pembroke College, Oxford (President of the Union); Hon. Fellow, Pembroke College 1986; Hon. LLD, Liverpool University 1990. Married 1962, Anne Williams (1 son 2 daughters). *Career:* Chairman: Haymarket Press (Magazine Publishers) 1964–70, Haymarket Publishing Group 1999–. *Political Career:* Parliamentary Secretary, Ministry of Transport June-October 1970; Parliamentary Under-Secretary of State, Department of the Environment October 1970–72; Minister for Aerospace and Shipping, DTI 1972–74; Secretary of State for: the Environment 1979–83, Defence 1983–86; Contested Leadership of the Conservative Party November 1990; Secretary of State for the Environment 1990–92; President of the Board of Trade and Secretary of State for Trade and Industry 1992–95; Deputy Prime Minister and First Secretary of State 1995–97. *Spokesman:* Opposition Spokesman for: Industry 1974–76, The Environment 1976–79. *Party Groups:* Chairman, Conservative Mainstream Group. *Miscellaneous:* Member, The Millennium Commission 1994–; Chairman, Anglo/Chinese Forum 1998–. *Honours:* CH 1997; PC 1979. *Publications: Where There's a Will* 1987; *The Challenge of Europe: Can Britain Win?* 1989. *Electoral Notes:* Contested Gower 1959 and Coventry North 1964. Member for Tavistock 1966–74 and for Henley from February 1974. *Clubs:* Carlton. *Address:* The Rt Hon. Michael Heseltine, CH, MP, House of Commons, London, SW1A 0AA *Tel:* 020 7219 5167.

HESFORD, Stephen *(Wirral West)*

Son of Bernard and Nellie Hesford. Born May 27, 1957; educated Urmston Grammar School; Bradford University; Central London Polytechnic (BSc Social Sciences, LLM). Married Elizabeth Anne Henshall (2 sons). *Trades Union:* Branch Equal Opportunities Officer, GMB. *Career:* Barrister for 17 years; Assistant to Joan Lestor, MP 1992–93. *Councils, Public Bodies:* Vice-Chair, North Manchester Community Health Council. *Select Committees (Current):* Member: Northern Ireland Affairs 1998–, Health 1999– *(Former):* Member: Deregulation 1997–98. *Party Groups:* Member, Fabian Society; NEC Member, Socialist Health Association. *Other:* Member: Greenpeace, Amnesty International, Child Poverty Action Group. *Miscellaneous:* Member, European Standing Committee C 1999–. *Sportsclubs:* Life Member, Lancashire Cricket Club. *Fellowships, etc:* Fellow: Royal Institue of Public Health and Hygiene, Society of Public Health. *Special Interests:* Economic Policy, Health, Social Services, Pensions, Education. *Countries of Interest:* France. *Recreations:* Sport, music, reading. *Electoral Notes:* Contested Suffolk South 1992. Member for Wirral West since May 1, 1997. *Address:* Stephen Hesford Esq, MP, House of Commons, London, SW1A 0AA *Tel:* 020 7219 6227 *Fax:* 020 7219 4953. *Constituency:* 140 Ford Road, Upton, Wirral, Merseyside *Tel:* 0151–522 0531 *Fax:* 0151–522 0558 *E-mail:* hesfords@parliament.uk.

HEWITT, Patricia Hope *(Leicester West)   Lab majority 12,864*

Daughter of Sir Lenox Hewitt, OBE and Lady Hope Hewitt. Born December 2, 1948; educated Canberra Girls' Grammar School; Newnham College, Cambridge (MA Cantab, MA Oxon). Married 1981, William Jack Birtles (1 son 1 daughter). *Trades Union:* Member, MSF. *Career:* Public Relations Officer, Age Concern 1971–73; National Council for Civil Liberties: Women's Rights Officer 1973–74, General Secretary 1974–83; To Neil Kinnock as Leader of the Opposition: Press Secretary 1983–87, Policy Co-ordinator 1987–89; Deputy Director, Institute for Public Policy Research 1989–94; Director of Research, Andersen Consulting 1994–97. *Political Career:* Economic Secretary, HM Treasury 1998–99; Minister of State, Department of Trade and Industry (Minister for Small Business and E-Commerce) 1999–. *Select Committees (Former):* Member: Social Security 1997–98, Social Security 1998. *Party Groups:* Member: Labour Women's Advisory Committee 1976–82, Labour Campaign for Social Justice, Fabian Society. *International Bodies:* Advisory Board, International Human Rights League. *Other:* Governor, Kentish Town Primary School 1993–96; Member: CPAG, Liberty. *Trust:* Trustee, Institute for Public Policy Research 1995–98. *Miscellaneous:* Member, Secretary of State's Advisory Committee on the Employment of Women 1976–83; Vice-Chair: Commission on Social Justice 1992–94, British Council Board 1997–98. Fellow, Royal Society for the Arts. *Publications:* Numerous, including books, pamphlets and articles for academic, specialist and popular journals. Also regular contributor on radio and television programmes. *Special Interests:* Social Security, Employment, Family, Information Technology. *Countries of Interest:* Australia, South Africa, India. *Recreations:* Gardening, music, theatre. *Electoral Notes:* Contested Leicester East 1983. Member for Leicester West since May 1, 1997. *Address:* Patricia Hewitt, MP, House of Commons, London, SW1A 0AA *Tel:* 020 7219 4022 *Fax:* 020 7219 2705. *Constituency:* Janner House, Woodgate, Leicester, LE3 5GH *Tel:* 0116–251 6160 *Fax:* 0116–251 0482 *E-mail:* hewittph@parliament.uk; tlo.hewitt@tlo.dti.gov.uk.

HILL, Keith *(Streatham)   Lab majority 18,423*

Son of Ernest Hill, printer, and Ida Hill, textile machine operative. Born July 28, 1943; educated City of Leicester Grammar School; Corpus Christi College, Oxford (MA); University College of Wales, Aberystwyth (DipEd (Wales)). Married May 19, 1972, Lesley Ann, daughter of Heinz Doktor. *Trades Union:* Political Liaison Officer, National Union of Rail, Maritime and Transport Workers (formerly NUR) 1976–92. *Career:* Research Assistant in Politics, University of Leicester 1966–68; Belgian Government Scholar, Brussels 1968–69; Lecturer in Politics, University of Strathclyde 1969–73; Research Officer, Labour Party International Department 1974–76. *Political Career:* Department of the Environment, Transport and the Regions: PPS to Hilary Armstrong, MP, as Minister of State (Minister for Local Government and Housing) 1997–98, Parliamentary Under-Secretary of State, 1999–. *Whip:* Assistant Government Whip 1998–99. *Select Committees (Former):* Member: Transport 1992–97. *Party Groups:* London Campaigner, Leadership Campaigns Team 1995; Hon. Secretary, London Group of Labour MPs 1997–98; Chair, Labour Movement in Europe 1997–98. *Publications: Belgium* in *European Political Parties* 1969; *Belgium: Political Change in A Segmented Society* in *Electoral Behaviour* 1974. *Special Interests:* Transport, European Union, Environment. *Countries of Interest:* Europe, Africa. *Recreations:* Walking, books, films, music. *Electoral Notes:* Contested Blaby 1979. Member for Streatham since April 9, 1992. *Address:* Keith Hill Esq, MP, House of Commons, London, SW1A 0AA *Tel:* 020 7219 6980 *Fax:* 020 7219 2565 *E-mail:* hillk@parliament.uk.

Dod *on* Disk

The Vacher Dod Parliamentary Database – configured for PC or Network

For further details please telephone the Westminster Office

020 7828 7256

HINCHLIFFE, David Martin *(Wakefield)   Lab majority 14,604*

Son of late Robert Hinchliffe, leading railman, and late Mrs Muriel Hinchliffe. Born October 14, 1948; educated Lawefield Lane Primary School; Cathedral Secondary School, Wakefield; Wakefield Technical College; Leeds Polytechnic (Certificate of Qualification in Social Work); Bradford University (MA). Married July 17, 1982, Julia North (1 son 1 daughter). *Career:* Trainee Social Worker, Leeds 1968–71; Social Worker, Leeds 1971–72, Senior Social Worker 1972–74, Principal 1974–79; Social Work Tutor, Kirklees MDC 1980–87. *Councils, Public Bodies:* Councillor: Wakefield City Council 1971–74, Wakefield Metropolitan District Council 1979–88. *Spokesman:* Opposition Front Bench Spokesman on Health (Shadow Minister for Personal Social Services and Community Care) 1992–95. *Select Committees (Current):* Chairman: Health 1997–; Member: Liaison 1997– *(Former):* Member: Health 1990–92. *Sportsclubs:* Vice-President, Wakefield Trinity RLFC. *Special Interests:* Health Service, Social Services. *Recreations:* Rugby League, researching family history. *Electoral Notes:* Member for Wakefield since June 1987. *Address:* David Hinchliffe Esq, MP, House of Commons, London, SW1A 0AA *Tel:* 020 7219 4447. *Constituency:* Wakefield NDC, Town Hall, Wakefield, WF1 2HQ *Tel:* 01924 305722 *Fax:* 01924 305706.

HODGE, Mrs Margaret Eve, MBE *(Barking)   Lab majority 15,896*

Daughter of Hans and Lisbeth Oppenheimer. Born September 8, 1944; educated Bromley High School; Oxford High School; London School of Economics (BSc Econ); Hon. Fellow, University of North London; Hon. DCL, City 1993. Married 1st, 1968, Andrew Watson (1 son 1 daughter) (marriage dissolved 1978), married 2nd, 1978, Henry Hodge, OBE (2 daughters). *Trades Union:* Member, TGWU. *Career:* Senior Consultant, Price Waterhouse 1992–94. *Councils, Public Bodies:* Councillor, London Borough of Islington 1973–94, Chair, Housing Committee 1975–79, Deputy Leader of Council 1981–82, Leader 1982–92. *Political Career:* Parliamentary Under-Secretary of State (Employment and Equal Opportunities), Department for Education and Employment 1998–. *Select Committees (Former):* Member: Deregulation 1996–97, Education and Employment 1996–98, Joint Chairman 1997–98; Chairman: Education Sub-Committee 1997–98; Member: Employment Sub-Committee 1997–98, Liaison 1997–98. *Party Groups:* Member, Labour Party Local Government Committee 1983–92; Chair, London Group of Labour MPs 1995–98; Vice-Chair, Fabians 1997–98. *Other:* Member, Home Office Advisory Committee on Race Relations 1988–92; Director: University College, Middlesex Hospitals; Governor, London School of Economics 1990–. *Miscellaneous:* Chair, Association of London Authorities 1984–92; Vice-Chair, AMA 1991–92. *Honours:* MBE 1978. *Publications: Quality, Equality and Democracy; Beyond the Town Hall;* Fabian pamphlet on London Government, *Not Just the Flower Show;* Contributed chapters to a number of books as well as articles in numerous journals and newspapers. *Special Interests:* Education, Local Government, Housing, Inner Cities, Democratic Reform, London Government. *Recreations:* Family, opera, piano, travel, cooking. *Electoral Notes:* Member for Barking since June 9, 1994 By-election. *Address:* Mrs Margaret Hodge, MBE, MP, House of Commons, London, SW1A 0AA *Tel:* 020 7219 6666 *Tel (Constituency):* 020 8594 1333 *Fax (Constituency):* 020 8594 1131 *E-mail:* haywoodmw@parliament.uk.

HOEY, Kate (Catharine Letitia) *(Vauxhall)   Lab majority 18,660*

Daughter of Thomas and Letitia Hoey. Born June 21, 1946; educated Lylehill Primary School; Belfast Royal Academy; Ulster College of Physical Education (Diploma in Physical Education); City of London College, London (BSc Economics). *Trades Union:* Member, GMB. *Career:* Senior Lecturer, Kingsway College 1976–85; Educational Adviser to Arsenal Football Club 1985–89. *Councils, Public Bodies:* Councillor: Hackney Borough Council 1978–82, Southwark Borough Council 1988–89. *Political Career:* PPS to Frank Field, MP, as Minister of State, Department of Social Security (Welfare Reform) 1997–98; Parliamentary Under-Secretary of State: Home Office (Metropolitan Police, European Union, Judicial Co-operation) 1998–99, Department for Culture, Media and Sport (Minister for Sport) 1999–. *Spokesman:* Member, Opposition team on Citizen's Charter and Women 1992–93. *Select Committees (Former):* Member: Broadcasting 1991–97, Social Security 1994–97. *Awards: The Spectator*/Highland Park Debater of the Year Award 1998. *Sportsclubs:* Member, Surrey County Cricket Club. *Publications:* Occasional articles on sport in the press. *Special Interests:* Environment, Sport, Foreign Affairs, Dog control, Housing. *Countries of Interest:* Angola, Bosnia. *Electoral Notes:* Contested Dulwich 1983 and 1987. Member for Vauxhall since June 15, 1989 By-election. *Address:* Kate Hoey, MP, House of Commons, London, SW1A 0AA *Tel:* 020 7219 5803 *Fax:* 020 7219 5989.

HOGG, The Rt Hon. Douglas Martin, QC *(Sleaford and North Hykeham)* Con majority 5,123

Son of Baron Hailsham of St Marylebone *(qv)*, former Lord Chancellor. Born February 5, 1945; educated Eton; Christ Church, Oxford (MA) (President, Oxford Union). Married 1968, Hon. Sarah Boyd-Carpenter (cr. Baroness Hogg, 1995) *(qv)* daughter of late Baron Boyd-Carpenter (1 son 1 daughter). *Profession:* Barrister. *Career:* Called to the Bar, Lincoln's Inn 1968 (Kennedy Law Scholar); QC 1990. *Political Career:* PPS to the Rt Hon. Leon Brittan, MP, Chief Secretary to the Treasury 1982–86; Parliamentary Under-Secretary, Home Office 1986–89; Minister of State at: Department of Trade and Industry (Minister for Industry and Enterprise) 1989–90, Foreign and Commonwealth Office 1990–95; Minister of Agriculture, Fisheries and Food 1995–97. *Whip:* Government Whip 1983–84. *Select Committees (Former):* Member: Home Affairs 1997–98. *Honours:* PC 1992. *Electoral Notes:* Member for Grantham 1979–97, and for Sleaford and North Hykeham since May 1, 1997. *Address:* The Rt Hon. Douglas Hogg QC, MP, House of Commons, London, SW1A 0AA *Tel:* 020 7219 3444/3484 *Fax:* 020 7219 4123. *Constituency:* Sleaford and North Hykeham Conservative Association, The Old Forge, Main Street, Leadenham, Lincolnshire, LN5 0PE *Tel:* 01400 272187 *Fax:* 01400 272189.

HOME ROBERTSON, John *(East Lothian)* Lab majority 14,221

Son of late Lieutenant-Colonel J. W. Home Robertson. Born December 5, 1948; educated Ampleforth; West of Scotland Agricultural College. Married 1977, Catherine Brewster (2 sons). *Career:* Farmer. *Councils, Public Bodies:* Councillor, Berwickshire District Council 1974–78; Member, Borders Health Board 1975–78. *Political Career:* PPS to Rt Hon. Dr Jack Cunningham, MP: as Minister of Agriculture, Fisheries and Food 1997–98, as Minister for the Cabinet Office and Chancellor of the Duchy of Lancaster 1998–99; Deputy Minister for Rural Affairs, Scottish Parliament, 1999-. *Whip:* Opposition Scottish Whip 1983–84. *Spokesman:* Opposition Front Bench Spokesman on: Agriculture 1984–87, Scottish Affairs 1987–88, Agricultural and Rural Affairs 1988–90. *Select Committees (Former):* Member: Defence 1990–97. *Party Groups:* Chairman, Scottish Group of Labour MPs 1982–83. *International Bodies:* British-Irish Parliamentary Body 1990–. *Other:* Member, Edinburgh District Aid to Bosnia. *Trust:* Member: The Paxton Trust, East Lothian Community Development Trust. *Miscellaneous:* Holds Heavy Goods Vehicle Driver's Licence; Member, Armed Forces Parliamentary Scheme 1996. *Special Interests:* Scottish Affairs, Defence, Rural Affairs. *Countries of Interest:* Ireland, Bosnia. *Electoral Notes:* Member for Berwick and East Lothian 1978–83, and for East Lothian since June 1983. MSP for the Constituency of East Lothian since May 6, 1999. *Address:* John Home Robertson Esq, MP, MSP, House of Commons, London, SW1A 0AA *Tel:* 020 7219 4135. *Constituency:* Town House, High Street, Dunbar, East Lothian, EH42 1ER *Tel:* 01368 861679.

HOOD, James *(Clydesdale)* *Lab majority 13,809*

Son of William Hood, retired miner, and Bridget Hood. Born May 16, 1948; educated Lesmahagow Higher Grade School, Coatbridge; Nottingham University. Married January 28, 1967, Marion Stewart, daughter of Ronald and late Rose McCleary (1 son 1 daughter). *Trades Union:* Member, NUM 1964–: Official 1973–87, Leader of Nottinghamshire striking miners in 1984–85 national miners strike; Member, AEEU 1996–. *Career:* Mining Engineer 1964–87. *Councils, Public Bodies:* Councillor, Newark and Sherwood District Council 1979–87 *Select Committees (Current):* Member: Chairmen's Panel 1997–, Defence 1997–, Liaison 1997–; Chairman: European Scrutiny 1998– *(Former):* Member: European Legislation 1987–97; Chairman: European Legislation 1992–98; Member: Liaison 1992–97. *Party Groups:* Member, Labour Party 1970–; Convenor, Scottish Parliamentary Group of Labour MPs; Member, Co-operative Party. *Trust:* Fellow, Industry and Parliament Trust; Armed Forces Parliamentary Scheme. *Special Interests:* Health Service, Home Affairs, Agriculture, Environment, Energy, Housing, Education, Alcohol Abuse and under-age drinking, European Union, Defence. *Recreations:* Gardening, reading, writing. *Electoral Notes:* Member for Clydesdale since June 1987. *Clubs:* Lesmahagow Miners. *Address:* James Hood Esq, MP, House of Commons, London, SW1A 0AA *Tel:* 020 7219 4585. *Constituency:* c/o Council Offices, South Vennel, Lanark, ML11 7JT *Tel:* 01555 673177 *Fax:* 01555 673188 *E-mail:* hoodj@parliament.uk.

HOON, The Rt Hon. Geoffrey William *(Ashfield)* *Lab majority 22,728*

Son of Ernest and June Hoon. Born December 6, 1953; educated Nottingham High School; Jesus College, Cambridge (MA). Married April 4, 1981, Elaine Anne, daughter of Roy and Betty Dumelow (1 son 2 daughters). *Career:* Lecturer in Law, University of Leeds 1976–81; Barrister 1978; Visiting Professor of Law, University of Louisville, USA 1980–81. *Political Career:* Lord Chancellor's Department: Parliamentary Secretary 1997–98, Minister of State 1998–99; Minister of State, Foreign and Commonwealth Office 1999; Secretary of State for Defence 1999–. *Whip:* Opposition Whip 1994–95. *Spokesman:* Opposition Spokesman on Trade and Industry 1995–97. *International Bodies:* Chairman, European Parliament Delegation for relations with: China 1986–89, United States 1989–93. *Honours:* PC 1999. *Special Interests:* Economic Policy, Trade and Industry, European Union. *Countries of Interest:* Europe, USA. *Recreations:* Sport, particularly cricket, football and running, cinema, music. *Electoral Notes:* MEP for Derbyshire 1984–94. Member for Ashfield since April 9, 1992. *Clubs:* Derby Labour, Long Eaton Labour. *Address:* The Rt Hon. Geoffrey Hoon, MP, House of Commons, London, SW1A 0AA *Tel:* 020 7219 3477. *Constituency:* 8 Station Street, Kirkby-in-Ashfield, Nottinghamshire, NG17 7AR *Tel:* 01623 720399 *Fax:* 01623 720399.

HOPE, Phil (Philip) Ian *(Corby)* *Lab majority 11,860*

Son of A. G. (Bob) Hope, former police commander, and Grace Hope. Born April 19, 1955; educated Wandsworth Comprehensive, London; St Luke's College, Exeter University (BEd (Hons) 1st Class). Married July 25, 1980, Allison, daughter of John and Margaret Butt (1 son 1 daughter). *Trades Union:* Former Member, NUT; Member, MSF 1979–. *Career:* Former Secondary School Teacher, Kettering School for Boys; Former Youth Policy Adviser, National Council for Voluntary Organisations; Former Head, Young Volunteer Resources Unit, National Youth Bureau; Management/Community Work Consultant, Framework 1985–97; Director, Framework in Print Publishing Co-operative. *Councils, Public Bodies:* Councillor, Kettering Borough Council 1983–87, Deputy Leader, Labour Group; Councillor, Northamptonshire County Council 1993–97, Chair, Equal Opportunities Sub-Committee, Chair, Labour Group. *Political Career:* PPS to Nick Raynsford, MP, as Minister of State, Department of the Environment, Transport and the Regions (Minister for Housing and Planning) 1999–. *Select Committees (Current):* Member: Selection 1999– *(Former):* Member: Public Accounts 1997–98. *Party Groups:* Member, Labour Party 1979–; Has held various posts in local constituency party; Former National Adviser on Youth Policy; Member, Co-operative Party 1982–; Delegate to National Conference; Member, Labour Party Leadership Campaign Team 1997–99.

International Bodies: Member, Commonwealth Parliamentary Association 1997–. *Other:* Member, Corby MIND; President: Corby Accommodation Project, Thrapston Volunteer Centre; Former Governor: Park Junior School, Montagu Secondary School; Member: The Wine Society Co-operative, The Midlands Co-operative Society. *Miscellaneous:* Member: National Advisory Group on Personal, Social and Health Education (DfEE), Development Awareness Working Group (DfID). *Sportsclubs:* Corby Tennis Centre. *Publications:* Author/Co-Author of many publications including: *Making the Best Use of Consultants,* 1993; *Education for Parenthood,* 1994; *Analysis and Action on Youth Health,* 1995; *Performance Appraisal,* 1995. *Special Interests:* Equal Opportunity, Youth Affairs. *Recreations:* Juggling, computing, gardening, tennis. *Electoral Notes:* Contested Kettering 1992. Member for Corby since May 1, 1997. *Address:* Phil Hope Esq, MP, House of Commons, London, SW1A 0AA *Tel:* 020 7219 4075 *Fax:* 020 7219 2673. *Constituency:* 2nd Floor, Chisholm House, Queen's Square, Corby, Northampton-shire, NN17 1PD *Tel:* 01536 443325 *Fax:* 01536 269462 *E-mail:* taylors@parliament.uk.

HOPKINS, Kelvin Peter *(Luton North)*   Lab majority 9,626

Son of late Professor Harold Horace Hopkins, FRS, physicist and mathemati-cian, and Joan Avery Frost, medical secretary. Born August 22, 1941; educated Queen Elizabeth's Grammar School, High Barnet; University of Nottingham (BA Hons Politics, Economics and Mathematics with Statistics); Hon. Fellow, University of Luton 1993. Married August 21, 1965, Patricia, daughter of late Alfred and Dorothy Langley (1 son 1 daughter). *Trades Union:* Member, GMB; Delegate, Luton Trades Union Council. *Profession:* Economist/Political Researcher. *Career:* TUC Economic Department 1969–70, 1973–77; Policy and Research Officer, NALGO/UNISON 1977–94. *Councils, Public Bodies:* Councillor, Luton Borough 1972–76. *Select Committees (Current):* Member: Broadcasting 1999–. *Party Groups:* Vice-Chair, Central Region Labour Party 1995–96. *Other:* Governor, Luton Sixth Form College; Chair of Governors, Luton College of Higher Education 1985–89; Member: Mary Seacole House, Luton, Wine Society, Hon. Vice-President, UK Carrom Federation. *Miscellaneous:* Member, European Standing Committee B 1998–. *Sportsclubs:* Luton Town Football Club, UK Carrom Federation. *Publications:* Various NALGO publications. *Special Interests:* Economic Policy, Employment, Transport, The Arts. *Countries of Interest:* France, Sweden. *Recreations:* Music, photogra-phy, sailing on the Norfolk Broads. *Electoral Notes:* Contested Luton North 1983 General Election. Member for Luton North since May 1, 1997. *Clubs:* Luton Socialist, Lansdowne (Luton). *Address:* Kelvin Hopkins Esq, MP, House of Commons, London, SW1A 0AA *Tel:* 020 7219 6670 *Fax:* 020 7219 0957. *Constituency:* 3 Union Street, Luton, Bedfordshire, LU1 3AN *Tel:* 01582 488208 *Fax:* 01582 480990.

HORAM, John Rhodes *(Orpington)*   Con majority 2,952

Son of Sydney and Catherine Horam. Born March 7, 1939; educated Silcoates School, Wakefield; St Catharine's College, Cambridge (MA Economics, Exhibition). Married 2nd, 1987, Judith Jackson (2 sons from previous mar-riage). *Career:* Market Research officer, Rowntree & Co. 1960–62; Leader and feature writer: *Financial Times* 1962–65, *The Economist* 1965–68; Managing Director: Commodities Research Unit Ltd 1968–70, 1983–87, CRU Holdings Ltd. 1988–92; Deputy Chairman, CRU International Ltd 1992–95. *Political Career:* Parliamentary Under-Secretary of State, Department of Transport 1976–79; Parliamentary Secretary, Office of Public Service July–November 1995; Parliamentary Under-Secretary of State, Department of Health 1995–97. *Spokesman:* Labour Spokesman on Economic Affairs 1979–81; SDP Spokesman 1981–83. *Select Committees (Current):* Chairman: Environmental Audit 1997–; Member: Liaison 1997– *(Former):* Member: Public Accounts Committee 1992–95. *Party Groups:* Joined Conservative Party February 1987. *Publications: Making Britain Competitive,* 1993. *Special Interests:* Economic Policy, Transport, Health, Tax, London. *Recreations:* Opera, ballet, gardening, walking. *Electoral Notes:* Contested (Labour) Folkstone and Hythe 1966. Member for Gateshead West 1970–83 (Labour 1970–81, SDP 1981–83). Contested Newcastle upon Tyne Central (SDP/Alliance) 1983 General Election. Member for Orpington since April 9, 1992. *Clubs:* Orpington Conservative. *Address:* John Horam Esq, MP, House of Commons, London, SW1A 0AA *Tel:* 020 7219 6328.

HOWARD, The Rt Hon. Michael, QC *(Folkestone and Hythe)   Con majority 6,332*

Son of late Bernard and Hilda Howard. Born July 7, 1941; educated Llanelli Grammar School; Peterhouse, Cambridge (MA, LLB) (President, Cambridge Union 1962). Married 1975, Sandra, daughter of Wing Commander Savile Paul (1 son 1 daughter and 1 step-son). *Career:* Called to the Bar, Inner Temple 1964; QC 1982; Junior Counsel to the Crown 1980–82. *Political Career:* PPS to the Solicitor-General 1984–85; Parliamentary Under-Secretary of State, Trade and Industry 1985–87; Minister for: Local Government 1987–88, Water and Planning 1988–89, Housing and Planning 1989–90; Secretary of State for: Employment 1990–92, The Environment 1992–93, The Home Department 1993–97; Contested Leadership of the Conservative Party June 1997; Member, Shadow Cabinet 1997–99; Shadow Secretary of State for Foreign and Commonwealth Affairs 1997–99. *Party Groups:* Chairman: Bow Group 1970, Coningsby Club 1972–73. *Honours:* PC 1990. *Special Interests:* Employment, Trade Union Law Reform. *Recreations:* Football and baseball. *Electoral Notes:* Contested Liverpool Edge Hill 1966 and 1970. Member for Folkestone and Hythe since June 1983. *Clubs:* Carlton. *Address:* The Rt Hon. Michael Howard, QC, MP, House of Commons, London, SW1A 0AA *Tel:* 020 7219 5493 *Fax:* 020 7219 5322. *Constituency:* Folkestone and Hythe Conservative Association, 4 Westcliff Gardens, Folkestone, Kent *Tel:* 01303 253524 *Fax:* 01303 251061 *E-mail:* howardm@parliament.uk.

HOWARTH, Alan, CBE *(Newport East)   Lab majority 13,523*

Son of late T. E. B. Howarth, MC, TD, and Margaret Howarth (née Teakle). Born June 11, 1944; educated Rugby School; King's College, Cambridge. Married September 23, 1967, Gillie Chance (2 sons 2 daughters) (marriage dissolved 1996). *Trades Union:* Member, GMB. *Career:* Senior Research Assistant to Field-Marshal Montgomery on *A History of Warfare* 1965–67; Assistant Master, Westminster School 1968–74. *Political Career:* PPS to Rt Hon. Sir Rhodes Boyson, MP 1985–87; Parliamentary Under-Secretary of State, Department for Education and Science 1989–92; Resigned from the Conservative Party and joined the Labour Party, October 1995; Parliamentary Under-Secretary of State: Department for Education and Employment (Employment and Equal Opportunities) 1997–98, Department for Culture, Media and Sport (Minister for the Arts) 1998–. *Whip:* Assistant Government Whip, 1987–88; Lord Commissioner of the Treasury (Government Whip) 1988–89. *Select Committees (Former):* Member: National Heritage 1992–93, Social Security 1996–97. *Party Groups:* Personal Assistant to Chairman of Conservative Party 1975–79; Director, Conservative Research Department 1979–81; Vice-Chairman, Conservative Party 1980–81. *Honours:* CBE 1982. *Publications:* Joint Author of *Changing Charity*, 1984; *Montgomery at Close Quarters*, 1986; *Save Our Schools*, 1986; *The Arts: The Next Move Forward*, 1987. *Special Interests:* Economic Policy, Employment, Education, Charities and the Voluntary Sector, Social Security, The Arts. *Recreations:* Books, arts, running. *Electoral Notes:* Member for Stratford-on-Avon (Conservative – June 1983 to Oct 1995, Labour – Oct 1995 to May 1997), and for Newport East since May 1, 1997. *Address:* Alan Howarth Esq, CBE, MP, House of Commons, London, SW1A 0AA *Tel:* 020 7219 3000. *Constituency:* Ringland Labour Club, Ringland, Newport, NP9 9PS *Tel:* 01633 277910/273111 *E-mail:* alan.howarth@culture.gov.uk.

HOWARTH, George *(Knowsley North and Sefton East)   Lab majority 26,147*

Born June 29, 1949; educated Schools in Huyton; Liverpool Polytechnic (Degree in Social Sciences). Married 1977, Julie Rodgers (2 sons 1 daughter). *Trades Union:* Joined AEU; Chief Executive, Wales TUC sponsored co-op. centre, Cardiff 1984–86. *Career:* Engineering apprentice; Teacher on Merseyside; Worked for CDS, Liverpool. *Councils, Public Bodies:* Former Councillor, Huyton Urban District Council; Councillor, Knowsley Borough Council 1975–86, Deputy Leader 1982–83. *Political Career:* Parliamentary Under-Secretary of State: Home Office (Minister for Fire and Emergency Planning, Liquor, Drugs and Elections) 1997–99, Northern Ireland Office 1999–. *Spokesman:* Opposition Spokesman on: the Environment 1989–92; Environmental Protection 1993–94; Home Affairs 1994–97. *Party Groups:* Former Chairman, Knowsley South Labour Party; Former Secretary, Knowsley Borough District Labour Party; Member, North West

Region Executive, Labour Party. *Special Interests:* Housing, Environment. *Recreations:* Coarse fishing, family, reading. *Electoral Notes:* Member Knowsley North November 13, 1986 By-election–1997, and for Knowsley North and Sefton East since May 1, 1997. *Address:* George Howarth Esq, MP, House of Commons, London, SW1A 0AA *Tel:* 020 7219 6902. *Constituency:* 149 Cherryfield Drive, Kirkby, Merseyside, L32 8SE *Tel:* 0151–546 9918 *Fax:* 0151–546 9918.

HOWARTH, Gerald *(Aldershot)* Con majority 6,621

Son of Mary and late James Howarth, retired company director. Born September 12, 1947; educated Haileybury and ISC Junior School, Windsor; Bloxham School, Banbury (Scholar); University of Southampton (BA Hons). Married 1973, Elizabeth, daughter of Muriel and the late Michael Squibb (2 sons 1 daughter). *Trades Union:* Member, National Union of Seamen 1966. *Armed Forces:* Commissioned RAFVR 1968. *Profession:* International Banker/Public Affairs Consultant. *Career:* Bank of America International Ltd 1971–77; European Arab Bank 1977–81: Manager and Personal Assistant to the Group Managing Director 1979, Manager, Loan Syndications 1980; Loan Syndication Manager responsible for arranging project and other loans in Africa, Middle East and South America, Standard Chartered Bank plc 1981–83; Joint Managing Director, Taskforce Communications 1993–95. *Councils, Public Bodies:* London Borough Council of Hounslow: Councillor 1982–82, Shadow Vice-Chairman, Environmental Planning Committee, Member, Finance and General Purposes Committee. *Political Career:* PPS to Michael Spicer, MP: as Parliamentary Under-Secretary of State, at Department of Energy 1987–90, as Minister of State, Department of the Environment (Minister for Housing and Construction) 1990; PPS: to Sir George Young, Bt, MP, as Minister of State, DoE 1990–91, to The Rt Hon. Margaret Thatcher, MP December 1991-April 1992. *Select Committees (Current):* Member: Home Affairs 1997–. *Party Groups:* Member, Greater London Area CPC Advisory Committee; Vice-Chairman, City Conservative Forum 1981–84; Founder Member, No Turning Back Group. *Other:* General Secretary, Society for Individual Freedom 1969–71; Director, Freedom Under Law. *Trust:* Fellow, Industry and Parliament Trust. *Miscellaneous:* Britannia Airways Parliamentary Pilot of the Year 1988. *Publications:* (Jointly) *No Turning Back*, 1985, and further publications by the Group. *Special Interests:* Aerospace, Aviation, Defence, Media, Education, Privatisation. *Countries of Interest:* Germany, Russia, South Africa, Chile, Pakistan. *Recreations:* Flying, squash, tennis, DIY, family. *Electoral Notes:* Member for Cannock and Burntwood 1983–92, and for Aldershot since May 1, 1997. *Clubs:* Aldershot Conservative. *Address:* Gerald Howarth Esq, MP, House of Commons, London, SW1A 0AA *Tel:* 020 7219 5650 *Fax:* 020 7219 1198. *Constituency:* Conservative Club, Victoria Road, Aldershot, Hampshire, GU11 1JX *Tel:* 01252 323637 *Fax:* 01252 323637.

HOWELLS, Dr Kim Scott *(Pontypridd)* Lab majority 23,129

Son of late Glanville Howells and of Glenys Howells. Born November 27, 1946; educated Mountain Ash Grammar School; Hornsey College of Art; Cambridge CAT (BA 1974); Warwick University (PhD 1979); Honorary Doctorate, Anglia Polytechnic University. Married September 22, 1983, Eirlys, daughter of William and Gwenda Davies (2 sons 1 daughter). *Trades Union:* Research Officer and Newspaper editor, NUM South Wales Area 1982–89. *Career:* Research officer, Coalfield History Project, University College, Swansea 1979–82; Freelance radio and television presenter and writer 1986–89. *Political Career:* Parliamentary Under-Secretary of State: Department for Education and Employment (Life-long Learning) 1997–98, Department of Trade and Industry 1998–99, (Minister for Consumers and Corporate Affairs) 1999–. *Spokesman:* Opposition Spokesman on: Development and Co-operation 1993–94, Foreign Affairs 1994, Home Affairs 1994–95, Trade and Industry 1995–97. *Select Committees (Former):* Member: Welsh Affairs 1989–90, Environment 1990–92, Public Accounts 1993–94. *Other:* President: Arthritis Care, Pontypridd, Taff Ely Drugs Support Group; Vice-President, Travol Pontypridd; Patron, Dragon Swimming Club for Disabled; Member, British Mountaineering Council. *Sportsclubs:* Llantwit Fadre Cricket, Hopkinstown Cricket, Pontypridd Rugby Football. *Special Interests:* Energy, Environment, Foreign Affairs, Transnational Broadcasting. *Countries of Interest:* Germany, Italy, Latin America, Switzerland, USA, South Africa, Austria, Romania. *Recreations:* Literature, films, jazz, mountain climbing, art. *Electoral Notes:* Member for Pontypridd from February 23, 1989 By-election. *Address:* Dr Kim Howells, MP, House of Commons, London, SW1A 0AA *Tel:* 020 7219 5813. *Constituency:* 16 Tyfica Road, Pontypridd, Mid Glamorgan, CF37 2DA *Tel:* 01443 402551 *Fax:* 01443 485628 *E-mail:* tlo.howells@tlo.dti.gov.uk.

HOYLE, Hon. Lindsay Harvey *(Chorley)   Lab majority 9,870*

Son of Baron Hoyle (*qv*) and late Pauline Hoyle. Born June 10, 1957; educated Anderton County Primary; Lords College, Bolton; Horwich FE; Bolton TIC (City & Guilds Construction). Married Catherine, daughter of John and Angela Swindley (2 daughters). *Trades Union:* Shop Steward; Member, MSF. *Career:* Company Director. *Councils, Public Bodies:* Councillor, Adlington Town Council; Councillor, Chorley Borough Council, Chairman, Economic Development, Deputy Leader and Mayor of Chorley. *Select Committees (Current):* Member: Catering 1997–, Trade and Industry 1998–. *Other:* Member: Royal Lancashire Agricultural Society, Adlington Cricket Club, Chorley Cricket Club; Former Chairman, Chorley Rugby League. *Trust:* Member, Cuerdon Valley Trust. *Miscellaneous:* Armed Forces Parliamentary Scheme (Royal Marines) 1998–. *Special Interests:* Trade and Industry, Sport, Defence. *Countries of Interest:* Gibraltar, Falkland Islands, British Overseas Territories. *Recreations:* Cricket. *Electoral Notes:* Member for Chorley since May 1, 1997. *Address:* Hon. Lindsay Hoyle, MP, House of Commons, London, SW1A 0AA *Tel:* 020 7219 1135 *Fax:* 020 7219 3831. *Constituency:* 35 Clifford Street, Chorley, Lancashire *Tel:* 01257 483887.

HUGHES, Beverley June *(Stretford and Urmston)   Lab majority 13,640*

Daughter of late Norman Hughes and Doris Hughes. Born March 30, 1950; educated Ellesmere Port Girls' Grammar School; Manchester University; Liverpool University (BSc Hons, MSc). Married March 31, 1973, Thomas, son of Thomas and Jean McDonald (1 son 2 daughters). *Profession:* University Lecturer. *Career:* Trainee Probation Officer, Merseyside 1971; Probation Officer, Merseyside 1972; Manchester University: Research Associate 1976; Lecturer 1981, Senior Lecturer and Head of Department 1993–97; Director: G-Mex Ltd, Modesole Ltd, Midas. *Councils, Public Bodies:* Trafford Metropolitan Borough Council: Councillor 1986, Labour Group Deputy Leader 1990, Labour Group Leader 1992, Council Leader 1995; Director: Trafford Park Development Corporation, Manchester Airport plc. *Political Career:* PPS to Hilary Armstrong, MP, as Minister of State, Department of the Environment, Transport and the Regions (Minister for Local Government and Housing) 1998–99; Parliamentary Under-Secretary of State, Department of the Environment, Transport and the Regions 1999–. *Select Committees (Former):* Member: Home Affairs 1997–98. *Other:* Chair, Age Concern, Trafford 1986–92. *Publications: Older People and Community Care: Critical Theory and Practice,* 1995; Numerous academic and professional publications. *Special Interests:* Economic Regeneration, Investment, Local Government, Health and Community Care, Family, Regional Development, Education, Criminal Justice, Child Protection and Safety. *Recreations:* Jazz, fell-walking. *Electoral Notes:* Member for Stretford and Urmston since May 1, 1997. *Address:* Beverley Hughes, MP, House of Commons, London, SW1A 0AA *Tel:* 020 7219 3802 *Fax:* 020 7219 2961 *Tel (Constituency):* 0161–749 9120 *Fax (Constituency):* 0161–749 9121 *E-mail:* beverley_hughes@detr.gsi.gov.uk.

HUGHES, Kevin Michael *(Doncaster North)   Lab majority 21,937*

Son of Leonard Hughes, retired coal miner, and Annie Hughes, retired school assistant. Born December 15, 1952; educated local schools; Sheffield University, Department of Extra Mural Studies (Industrial Relations, Trade Union History, Economics and Politics). Married August 26, 1972, Lynda, daughter of late Graham Saunders and of June Saunders (1 son 1 daughter). *Trades Union:* Branch delegate, Brodsworth NUM 1981–90; Member, Yorkshire NUM Executive Committee 1983–87. *Councils, Public Bodies:* Councillor, Doncaster Borough Council 1986–92, Chairman, Social Services Committee 1987–92. *Whip:* Opposition Whip 1996–97; Assistant Government Whip 1997–. *Select Committees (Former):* Member: European Legislation 1994–96. *Party Groups:* Secretary/Agent: Don Valley CLP 1980–83 Doncaster North 1983–89. *Other:* Hon. President, DIAL (Doncaster). *Trust:* Fellow, Industry and Parliament Trust 1995. *Special Interests:* Social Services, Childcare, Elderly. *Recreations:* Golf, walking, listening to opera. *Electoral Notes:* Member for Doncaster North since April 9, 1992. *Clubs:* Doncaster Trades and Labour, Skellow Grange Workingmen's. *Address:* Kevin Hughes Esq, MP, House of Commons, London, SW1A 0AA *Tel:* 020 7219 4107 *Fax:* 020 7219 2521 *Tel (Constituency):* 01302 873974 *Fax (Constituency):* 01302 876176 *E-mail:* kevin.hughes@hm-treasury.gov.uk.

HUGHES, Simon Henry Ward *(North Southwark and Bermondsey)   LD majority 3,387*

Son of late James Henry Hughes and of Sylvia Hughes (née Ward). Born May 17, 1951; educated Llandaff Cathedral School, Cardiff; Christ College, Brecon; Selwyn College Cambridge (BA, MA); Inns of Court School of Law; College of Europe, Bruges (Certificate in Higher European Studies). *Career:* Barrister Called to the Bar, Inner Temple 1974; In practice 1978–. *Councils, Public Bodies:* GLC candidate 1981; Southwark Borough Council candidate 1982. *Whip:* Liberal Democrat Deputy Whip 1989–99. *Spokesman:* Liberal Spokesman for the Environment 1983–88; Alliance Spokesman for Health January-June 1987; Spokesman for: Education, Science and Training 1989–92, Environment and Natural Resources 1992–94, Urban Affairs and Young People 1994–97, The Church of England 1988–97, Health and Social Welfare 1995–97, Health (Future of NHS) 1997–99; Principal Spokesman for Home and Legal Affairs 1999–. *Select Committees (Former):* Member: Ecclesiastical Committee 1987–97, Accommodation and Works 1992–97. *Party Groups:* President, National League of Young Liberals 1986–92, Vice-President, Liberal Democrat Youth and Students 1983–86, President 1992–; Vice-Chairman, Southwark and Bermondsey Liberal Association 1981–83; Former Chairman, Liberal Party's Home Affairs Panel; Member, Association of Liberal Lawyers. *International Bodies:* Trainee, EEC Brussels 1976; Trainee and member Secretariat, Directorate and Commission on Human Rights, Council of Europe, Strasbourg 1976–77. *Publications:* Co-author *Human Rights in Western Europe – The Next 30 Years*, 1981; *The Prosecutorial Process in England and Wales*, 1981; *Across the Divide – Liberal Values for Defence and Disarmament*, 1986; *Pathways to Power*, 1992. *Special Interests:* Human Rights, Civil Liberties, Youth Affairs, Social Issues, Housing, Environment. *Countries of Interest:* South Africa. *Recreations:* Music, theatre, history, sport (Millwall and Hereford FCs; Glamorgan CCC and Wales RFU), the countryside and open air. *Electoral Notes:* Member for Southwark and Bermondsey by-election February 1983–97, and for North Southwark and Bermondsey since May 1, 1997. *Clubs:* Redriff (Rotherhithe). *Address:* Simon Hughes Esq, MP, House of Commons, London, SW1A 0AA *Tel:* 020 7219 6256.

HUMBLE, Mrs Joan (Jovanka) *(Blackpool North and Fleetwood)   Lab majority 8,946*

Daughter of Jova Piplica and Darinka Piplica. Born March 3, 1951; educated Greenhead Grammar School, Keighley; Lancaster University (BA Hons). Married January 22, 1972, Paul Humble, son of Andrew and Emily Humble (2 daughters). *Trades Union:* Member, TGWU. *Career:* Civil servant, Department of Health and Social Security and Inland Revenue 1972–77. *Councils, Public Bodies:* Councillor, Lancashire County Council 1985–97, Chair, Lancashire Social Services 1990–97; JP, Preston Bench. *Select Committees (Current):* Member: Social Security 1998–. *Party Groups:* Member: Labour Party 1978–, Co-operative Party, Christian Socialist Movement; Hon. Secretary, North West Regional Group of Labour MPs 1999–. *Other:* School Governor for 15 years. *Miscellaneous:* Member, European Standing Committee A 1998. *Special Interests:* Social Services, Education, Economic Regeneration. *Recreations:* Reading, gardening, cooking. *Electoral Notes:* Member for Blackpool North and Fleetwood since May 1, 1997. *Address:* Mrs Joan Humble, MP, House of Commons, London, SW1A 0AA *Tel:* 020 7219 5025 *Fax:* 020 7219 2755. *Constituency:* 216 Lord Street, Fleetwood, Lancashire, FY7 6SW *Tel:* 01253 877346 *Fax:* 01253 777236.

HUME, John *(Foyle)   SDLP majority 13,664*

Son of Samuel Hume. Born January 18, 1937; educated Rosemount Primary School; St Columb's College, Derry; St Patrick's College, Maynooth (MA); Associate Fellow, Centre for International Affairs, Harvard 1976; Research Fellow in European Studies, Trinity College, Dublin 1976–77; Honorary Doctorate of Letters: University of Massachusetts 1985, Catholic University of America (Washington DC) 1986, St Joseph's University (Philadelphia) 1986, Tusculum College, Tennessee Presbyterian University of America 1988, Dublin City University 1994, Boston College 1995, Suffolk University 1995, University of Nice (France) 1995, University of Notre Dame (Indiana) 1996, University of St Andrew 1996, University College, Galway 1996, University of Santa Clara 1997, University of Missouri 1988. Married 1960, Patricia Hone (2 sons 3 daughters).

Trades Union: Member, SIPTU (Services, Industrial, Professional and Technical Union). *Profession:* Teacher. *Career:* Teacher; President, Credit Union League of Ireland 1964–68. *Political Career:* MP for Foyle, Northern Ireland Parliament 1969–72; Member (SDLP) for Londonderry: Northern Ireland Assembly 1973–75, Northern Ireland Constitutional Convention 1975–76, Northern Ireland Assembly 1982–86; Minister of Commerce Northern Ireland 1974; Member, New Ireland Forum 1983–84; Elected to the Northern Ireland Forum 1996–98; Elected to the New Northern Ireland Assembly 1998–. *Party Groups:* SDLP: Founder Member, Deputy Leader 1970–79, Leader 1979–. *International Bodies:* European Parliament: Member, Committee on Regional Policy 1989–; Member: United States Delegation 1994–97, Socialist Group Bureau. *Awards:* Irish 'People of the Year' Award 1984; American Federation of Teachers Human Rights Award 1986; St Thomas More Award, University of San Francisco 1991; Irishman of the Year awarded by 'Irish Abroad' 1992; International League for Human Rights Award for Peace and Human Rights 1994; Order of Thomas More, University of St Louis 1994; Pio Manzu Medal 1994; Communicators of the Year Award (RNID) 1995; European of the Year Award; President Roosevelt Award 1996; International Human Rights Award 1996; Global Citizens Award 1998; Sean McBride Peace Award 1998; The Nobel Peace Prize (jointly) 1998; Martin Luther King Award 1999. *Publications: Personal Views – Politics, Peace and Reconciliation in Ireland,* 1996. *Special Interests:* European Union, Third World, Poverty, Credit Unions, Northern Ireland. *Countries of Interest:* Belgium, Europe, France, USA. *Electoral Notes:* MEP for Northern Ireland since 1979. Member for Foyle since June 1983. *Address:* John Hume Esq, MP, House of Commons, London, SW1A 0AA *Tel:* 020 7219 3000. *Constituency:* 5 Bayview Terrace, Derry, BT48 7EE *Tel:* 028 7126 5340 *Fax:* 028 7136 3423.

HUNTER, Andrew Robert Frederick *(Basingstoke)   Con majority 2,397*

Son of late Squadron-Leader Roger Hunter, DFC and late Winifred Mary (née Nelson). Born January 8, 1943; educated St George's School, Harpenden; Durham University; Jesus College, Cambridge; Westcott House, Cambridge. Married March 24, 1972, Janet, daughter of late Samuel Bourne (1 son 1 daughter). *Armed Forces:* TAVR 1973–83. *Career:* In industry 1969; Assistant Master, Harrow School 1971–83. *Political Career:* PPS to Lord Elton, Minister of State, Department of Environment 1985–86; Sponsored Private Members' Bills: Control of Smoke Pollution Act 1989, Timeshare Act 1992, Noise and Statutory Nuisance (Amendment) Act 1993, Dogs (Fouling of Land) Act 1996 Road Traffic (Vehicle Testing Act) 1999. *Select Committees (Current):* Member: Northern Ireland Affairs 1994– *(Former):* Member: Environment 1986–92, Agriculture 1993–94. *Other:* Vice-President, National Prayer Book Society 1987–; Member: National Farmers' Union, British Field Sports Society; Honorary Member, Society of the Sealed Knot 1990–. *Miscellaneous:* Member, 1922 Executive Committee 1997–98. *Countries of Interest:* Ireland, Southern Africa. *Recreations:* Horse riding, watching cricket and rugby football. *Electoral Notes:* Contested Southampton Itchen, 1979. Member for Basingstoke since 1983. *Clubs:* St Stephen's Constitutional, Pratt's, Carlton. *Address:* Andrew Hunter Esq, MP, House of Commons, London, SW1A 0AA *Tel:* 020 7219 5216.

HURST, Alan *(Braintree)   Lab majority 1,451*

Son of late George Hurst. Born September 2, 1945; educated Westcliff High School; University of Liverpool (BA Hons History). Married 1976, Hilary Burch (2 sons 1 daughter). *Profession:* Solicitor. *Career:* Partner, Law Firm. *Councils, Public Bodies:* Councillor, Southend Borough Council 1968–96, Labour Group Leader 1990–95; Deputy Leader 1994–95, Councillor, Essex County Council 1993–98. *Select Committees (Current):* Member: Agriculture 1997–. *Other:* Member, Law Society; Former President, Southend Law Society. *Special Interests:* Employment, Housing, Conservation, Agriculture. *Recreations:* Bird watching, local history. *Electoral Notes:* Member for Braintree since May 1, 1997. *Address:* Alan Hurst Esq, MP, House of Commons, London, SW1A 0AA *Tel:* 020 7219 4068. *Constituency:* The Labour Hall, Collingwood Road, Witham, Essex, CM8 2EE *Tel:* 01376 520128 *Fax:* 01376 517709.

HUTTON, John *(Barrow and Furness)   Lab majority 14,497*

Son of late George Hutton, salesman and general labourer, and Rosemary Hutton, orthoptist. Born May 6, 1955; educated Westcliff High School, Southend; Magdalen College, Oxford (BA 1976, BCL 1978). Married April 28, 1978, Rosemary Caroline, daughter of Denis Little and late Jean Little (3 sons 1 daughter and 1 son deceased) (marriage dissolved 1993). *Career:* Research Associate, Templeton College, Oxford 1980–81; Senior Law Lecturer, Newcastle Polytechnic 1981–92. *Political Career:* PPS to Rt Hon. Margaret Beckett, MP: as President of the Board of Trade and Secretary of State for Trade and Industry 1997–98, as President of the Council and Leader of the House of Commons 1998; Department of Health: Parliamentary Under-Secretary of State 1998–99, Minister of State 1999–. *Select Committees (Former):* Member: Home Affairs 1994–97. *Special Interests:* Defence, Industry, Welfare State, Health. *Recreations:* Cricket, swimming. *Electoral Notes:* Contested Penrith and the Border in 1987 General Election; Cumbria and North Lancashire in 1989 European Parliamentary Election. Member for Barrow and Furness since April 9, 1992. *Clubs:* Cemetery Cottages Workingmen's (Barrow-in-Furness). *Address:* John Hutton Esq, MP, House of Commons, London, SW1A 0AA *Tel:* 020 7219 6228. *Constituency:* 22 Hartington Street, Barrow-in-Furness, Cumbria, LA14 5SL *Tel:* 01229 431204 *Fax:* 01229 432016 *E-mail:* huttonj@parliament.uk.

I

IDDON, Dr Brian *(Bolton South East)   Lab majority 21,311*

Son of late John Iddon and late Violet Iddon. Born July 5, 1940; educated Tarleton Church of England Primary School; Christ Church Boys' School, Southport; Southport Technical College; University of Hull (BSc Hons Chemistry, PhD in Organic Chemistry, DSc). Married May 15, 1965, Merrilyn-Ann Muncaster (2 daughters) (marriage dissolved 1989); married 2nd, September 16, 1995, Eileen Harrison (née Barker) (2 stepsons). *Trades Union:* Member, Association of University Teachers. *Profession:* Chartered Chemist. *Career:* Temporary Lecturer in Organic Chemistry, University of Durham 1964–65; Senior Demonstrator in Organic Chemistry, University of Durham 1965–66; Lecturer in Organic Chemistry, University of Salford 1966–78; Senior Lecturer in Organic Chemistry, University of Salford 1978–86; Reader in Organic Chemistry 1986–97. *Councils, Public Bodies:* Councillor, Bolton Metropolitan District Council 1977–98, Hon. Alderman 1998–, Vice-Chairman, Housing Committee 1980–82, Chairman, Housing Committee 1986–96. *Select Committees (Current):* Member: Environmental Audit 1997–. *Party Groups:* Member: North West Group of the Labour Party, Arts For Labour, Co-operative Party, Labour Middle East Council, Labour Friends of Remploy, Labour Housing Group, Labour PLP Keep The Link Group. *International Bodies:* Member: IPU, CPA. *Other:* Member, Amnesty International; Local Patron, Kids Club Network (Bolton-Bury Branch); National Patron, Society of Registration Officers; Patron, Bully Free Zone Programme. *Fellowships, etc:* FRSC; CChem. *Publications:* two books, research papers, research communications, major reviews, articles in magazines and a number of papers presented orally at conferences. *Special Interests:* Housing, Science, Engineering and Technology, Health, Education (FE in particular). *Countries of Interest:* Europe, Africa, India, Middle East. *Recreations:* Philately, gardening, cricket (spectator). *Electoral Notes:* Member for Bolton South East since May 1, 1997. *Clubs:* Former Member: Halliwell Labour, Tonge Ward Labour; Member, Bradford Ward Labour; Honorary Membership, Derby Ward Labour. *Address:* Dr Brian Iddon, MP, House of Commons, London, SW1A 0AA *Tel:* 020 7219 4064 *Fax:* 020 7219 2653. *Constituency:* 60 St Georges Road, Bolton, BL1 2DD *Tel:* 01204 371202 *Fax:* 01204 371374 *E-mail:* iddonb@parliament.uk.

ILLSLEY, Eric *(Barnsley Central)   Lab majority 24,501*

Son of John and Maud Illsley. Born April 9, 1955; educated Barnsley Holgate Grammar School; Leeds University (LLB Hons). Married September 16, 1978, Dawn, daughter of Robert and Freda Webb (2 daughters). *Career:* Yorkshire Area NUM: Compensation Officer 1978–81, Assistant Head of General Department 1981–84, Head of General Department and Chief Administration Officer 1984–87. *Whip:* Labour Whip 1991–94. *Spokesman:* Opposition Spokesman on: Health 1994–95, Local Government 1995, Northern Ireland 1995–97. *Select Committees (Current):* Member: Foreign Affairs 1997–, Procedure 1997– *(Former):* Member: Procedure 1991–97; Chairman: Entry Clearance Sub-Committee 1997–98. *Party Groups:* Former Treasurer, Yorkshire Group of Labour MPs; Secretary, Barnsley Constituency Labour Party 1981–83, Treasurer 1980–81; Secretary and Election Agent, Yorkshire South European Labour Party 1984–86; Member, Mining Group of MPs; Hon. Treasurer, Yorkshire Regional Group of Labour MP 1997–. *International Bodies:* Member, Executive Committee: IPU 1997–, Commonwealth Parliamentary Association (CPA) UK Branch 1997–. *Other:* Patron, Barnsley Alzheimer's Disease Society. *Special Interests:* Trade Unions, Mining, Energy, Social Security, Glass Industry. *Countries of Interest:* Australia, France. *Recreations:* Gymnasium. *Electoral Notes:* Member for Barnsley Central since June 1987. *Address:* Eric Illsley Esq, MP, House of Commons, London, SW1A 0AA *Tel:* 020 7219 3501 *Fax:* 020 7219 4863. *Constituency:* 18 Regent Street, Barnsley, S70 2HG *Tel:* 01226 730692 *Fax:* 01226 779429 *E-mail:* ericillsley104125,3557@compuserve.com.

INGRAM, The Rt Hon. Adam Paterson *(East Kilbride)   Lab majority 17,384*

Son of Bert Ingram, fitter, and Louisa Ingram. Born February 1, 1947; educated Cranhill Senior Secondary School. Married March 20, 1970, Maureen, daughter of Leo and late Flora McMahon. *Trades Union:* Full-time union official, NALGO 1977–87; Member of Parliament supported by TGWU. *Career:* Computer programmer/systems analyst 1967–77; Full-time Trade Union Official 1977–87. *Councils, Public Bodies:* District Councillor, East Kilbride 1980–87, Leader 1984–87; Member, COSLA Policy Committee 1984–87. *Political Career:* PPS to Rt Hon. Neil Kinnock MP, as Leader of the Opposition 1988–92; Minister of State, Northern Ireland Office (Minister for Security, Criminal Justice, Prisons) 1997– (with additional responsibility for Victims of Violence 1998–, Police 1999–). *Whip:* Opposition Whip for Scottish Affairs and Treasury Matters 1988–89. *Spokesman:* Opposition Spokesman on: Social Security 1993–95 Trade and Industry 1995–97. *Select Committees (Former):* Member: Trade and Industry 1992–93. *Party Groups:* Chairman, East Kilbride Constituency Labour Party 1981–85. *Honours:* PC 1999. *Special Interests:* Energy, Local Government, Aerospace. *Recreations:* Fishing, cooking, reading. *Electoral Notes:* Contested Strathkelvin and Bearsden 1983. Member for East Kilbride since June 1987. *Address:* The Rt Hon. Adam Ingram, MP, House of Commons, London, SW1A 0AA *Tel:* 020 7219 4093. *Constituency:* 17 Weaver Place, East Kilbride, Lanarkshire, G75 8SH *Tel:* 01355 235343 *Fax:* 01355 265252 *E-mail:* adam_ingram@compuserve.com.

J

JACK, The Rt Hon. (John) Michael *(Fylde)   Con majority 8,963*

Son of late Ralph Jack and Mrs Florence Edith Jack. Born September 17, 1946; educated Bradford Grammar School; Bradford Technical College; Leicester University (BA Hons Economics, MPhil Transport Economics). Married December 1976, Alison Jane, daughter of late Brian Musgrave and Mrs Barbara Musgrave (2 sons). *Career:* Proctor and Gamble 1971–75; Marks and Spencer 1975–80; PA to Lord Rayner; Director, L. O. Jeffs Ltd. *Councils, Public Bodies:* Member, Mersey Regional Health Authority 1984–87. *Political Career:* PA to Rt Hon. James Prior, MP 1979 General Election; PPS to Rt Hon. John Gummer, MP: as Minister for Local Government 1988–89, as Minister of Agriculture, Fisheries and Food 1989–90; Joint Parliamentary Under-Secretary of State for Social Security 1990–92; Minister of State at: Home Office 1992–93, Ministry of Agriculture,

Fisheries and Food 1993–95; Financial Secretary, HM Treasury 1995–97; Member, Shadow Cabinet 1997–98; Shadow Minister of Agriculture, Fisheries and Food November 1997-August 1998. *Spokesman:* Opposition Spokesman on Health June-November 1997. *Select Committees (Current):* Member: Agriculture 1999–. *Party Groups:* National Chairman, Young Conservatives 1976. *Other:* Member, Eastern Electricity Consultative Council 1979. *Miscellaneous:* Member: European Standing Committee C 1999–, Tax Law Rewrite Committee 1999–. Freeman, City of London. *Honours:* PC 1997. *Special Interests:* Health, Nuclear Industry, Horticulture, Sheltered Housing, Aerospace, Transport. *Countries of Interest:* China, USA, Italy. *Recreations:* Boule, motorsport, dinghy sailing, growing vegetables. *Electoral Notes:* Contested Newcastle Central February 1974. Member for Fylde since June 1987. *Address:* The Rt Hon. Michael Jack, MP, House of Commons, London, SW1A 0AA *Tel:* 020 7219 4454.

JACKSON, Glenda, CBE *(Hampstead and Highgate)   Lab majority 13,284*

Daughter of Harry and Joan Jackson. Born May 9, 1936; educated West Kirby County Grammar School for Girls; RADA. Married 1958, Roy Hodges (1 son) (marriage dissolved 1976). *Career:* Actress: Plays include: *The Idiot* 1962, *Love's Labour's Lost, Hamlet* 1965, *Three Sisters* 1967, *Hedda Gabler* 1975; Films include: *Women in Love, Mary, Queen of Scots, A Touch of Class*; Television includes *Elizabeth R* 1971; Member, Royal Shakespeare Company 1963–67, 1979–80. *Political Career:* Parliamentary Under-Secretary of State, Department of the Environment, Transport and the Regions 1997–99; Resigned in the July 1999 Government reshuffle. *Spokesman:* Opposition Spokeswoman on Transport 1996–97. *Other:* Member: Anti-Apartheid Movement, Amnesty International, Has campaigned for: Oxfam, Shelter, Friends of the Earth; President, The National Toy Libraries Association. *Awards:* Best film actress awards: Variety Clubs of Great Britain 1971, 1975, 1978, NY Film critics 1971, Oscar 1971, 1974. *Honours:* CBE 1978. *Special Interests:* Overseas Aid and Development, Housing, Environment. *Recreations:* Cooking, gardening, reading Jane Austen. *Electoral Notes:* Member for Hampstead and Highgate since April 9, 1992. *Address:* Glenda Jackson, CBE, MP, House of Commons, London, SW1A 0AA *Tel:* 020 7219 4008 *Fax:* 020 7219 2112.

JACKSON, Helen *(Sheffield Hillsborough)   Lab majority 16,451*

Daughter of late Stanley Price, MA, further education adviser, and late Katherine Price, health visitor. Born May 19, 1939; educated Berkhamsted School for Girls; St Hilda's College, Oxford (MA Modern History; Teaching Certificate); Post graduate teaching course at C. F. Mott College of Education 1971–72. Married 1960, Keith Jackson, son of Hugh Jackson, silver finisher (2 sons 1 daughter) (marriage dissolved 1998). *Career:* Assistant Librarian, The Queen's College, Oxford 1960–61; Assistant Teacher, City of Stoke-on-Trent 1961–62; Teacher: Lancashire Education Authority 1972–74, Sheffield Education Authority 1974–80. *Councils, Public Bodies:* Councillor: Huyton Urban District Council 1973–74, Sheffield City Council 1980–91; Chairman: Public Works Committee 1981–83, Employment and Economic Development Committee 1983–91, Sheffield Economic Regeneration Committee 1987–91; Board Member: Sheffield Partnerships Ltd, Sheffield Science Park, Sheffield Development Corporation; Founder Member and Chairman, Centre for Local Economic Strategies. *Political Career:* PPS to Secretaries of State of State for Northern Ireland: Rt Hon. Marjorie Mowlam, MP 1997–99, Rt Hon. Peter Mandelson, MP 1999–. *Select Committees (Current):* Member: Modernisation of the House of Commons 1997– *(Former):* Member: Environment 1992–97. *Party Groups:* Member: Labour Party National Policy Forum 1998–, Labour Party National Executive Committee 1999–. *International Bodies:* UK representative to AWEPA 1997–. *Other:* Child Care; Voluntary work as playgroup organiser; School governor; Occasional research work for Liverpool Council Social Services 1962–70. *Miscellaneous:* Occasional Tutor, WEA Yorkshire District; National Centre for Popular Music (Music Heritage Ltd). *Special Interests:* Environment, Women's Issues, Northern Ireland. *Countries of Interest:* Southern Africa. *Recreations:* Walking, music. *Electoral Notes:* Member for Sheffield Hillsborough since April 9, 1992. *Address:* Helen Jackson, MP, House of Commons, London, SW1A 0AA *Tel:* 020 7219 4587 *Fax:* 020 7219 2442. *Constituency:* Hillsborough Library, Middlewood Road, Sheffield, S6 4HD *Tel:* 0114–232 2439 *Fax:* 0114–285 5808.

JACKSON, Robert Victor *(Wantage)   Con majority 6,089*

Son of late Maurice Henry Jackson. Born September 24, 1946; educated Falcon College, Rhodesia; St Edmund Hall, Oxford; All Souls College, Oxford (MA) (President, Oxford Union 1967); Fellow, All Souls College, Oxford 1968–75. Married 1975, Caroline Frances Harvey (MEP for Wiltshire North and Bath 1994–) (1 son deceased). *Councils, Public Bodies:* Councillor, Oxford City Council 1969–71. *Political Career:* Political Adviser: to Secretary of State for Employment 1973–74, to Rt Hon. Sir Christopher Soames as EC Commissioner 1974–76; Chef de Cabinet to Basil De Ferranti, as President of EEC Economic and Social Committee 1976–78; Special Adviser to Lord Soames as Governor of Rhodesia 1980; Parliamentary Under-Secretary of State: at Department of Education and Science 1987–90, at Department of Employment 1990–92; Parliamentary Secretary, Office of Public Service and Science 1992–93. *Select Committees (Current):* Member: Science and Technology 1999–. *International Bodies:* EP Rapporteur on EEC Budget 1983. *Publications: The Round Table: The Commonwealth Journal of International Affairs,* 1970–74; *South Asian Crisis, Pakistan, Bangladesh,* 1974; *The European Parliament: a Guide for Direct Elections,* 1978; Editor: *International Affairs,* 1979–80. *Special Interests:* European Union, Agriculture, Science, Foreign Affairs. *Recreations:* Walking, gardening, singing. *Electoral Notes:* Contested Manchester Central October 1974. MEP for Upper Thames 1979–83. Member for Wantage since June 1983. *Address:* Robert Jackson Esq, MP, House of Commons, London, SW1A 0AA *Tel:* 020 7219 4557. *Constituency:* Orchard House, Portway, Wantage, Oxfordshire *Tel:* 01235 769090 *Fax:* 01235 224833.

JAMIESON, David Charles *(Plymouth Devonport)   Lab majority 19,067*

Son of late Frank Jamieson, engineer, and of Eileen Jamieson. Born May 18, 1947; educated Tudor Grange Grammar School, Solihull; St Peter's College, Birmingham; Open University (BA Social Science and Education Management). Married December 11, 1971, Patricia, daughter of Reginald and Lorna Hofton (2 sons 1 daughter). *Career:* Assistant teacher, mathematics, Riland-Bedford School, Sutton Coldfield 1970–76; Head of Mathematics, Crown Hills Community College, Leicester 1976–81; Senior Vice-Principal, The John Kitto Community College, Plymouth 1981–92. *Councils, Public Bodies:* Solihull Borough Council: Councillor 1970–74, Vice-Chairman, Housing Committee 1973–74. *Political Career:* Promoted as Private Member's Bill: Activity Centres (Young Persons' Safety) Act 1995. *Whip:* Assistant Government Whip 1997–98; A Lord Commissioner of HM Treasury (Government Whip) 1998–. *Select Committees (Current):* Member: Accommodation and Works 1998– *(Former):* Member: Education 1992–96, Education and Employment 1996–97. *Special Interests:* Education. *Recreations:* Music, classic cars, gardening. *Electoral Notes:* Contested Birmingham Hall Green February 1974 and Plymouth Drake 1987 General Elections. Member for Plymouth Devonport since April 9, 1992. *Address:* David Jamieson Esq, MP, House of Commons, London, SW1A 0AA *Tel:* 020 7219 6252 *Fax:* 020 7219 2388 *Tel (Constituency):* 01752 704677 *Fax (Constituency):* 01752 704677 *E-mail:* david_jamiesonmp@compuserve.com; david-jamieson@hm-treasury.gov.uk.

JENKIN, Hon. Bernard *(North Essex)   Con majority 5,476*

Son of Rt Hon. Baron Jenkin of Roding (*qv*). Born April 9, 1959; educated Highgate School; William Ellis School; Corpus Christi College, Cambridge (English Literature) (President, Cambridge Union Society 1982). Married 1988, Anne, daughter of late Hon. Charles Strutt (2 sons). *Career:* Previously employed by: Ford Motor Co Ltd and 3i plc; Manager, Legal and General Ventures Ltd 1989–92; Adviser, Legal and General Group plc 1992–95. *Councils, Public Bodies:* Chairman, Matching Parish Council 1985–87. *Political Career:* Political Adviser to Rt Hon. Leon Brittan, QC, MP 1986–88; PA to Hugh Rossi, MP, 1979 and 1983 General Elections; PPS to Michael Forsyth as Secretary of State for Scotland 1995–97; Member, Shadow Cabinet 1999–; Shadow Minister for Transport 1999–. *Spokesman:* Opposition Spokesman for: Constitutional Affairs, Scotland and Wales 1997–98, Environment, Transport and the Regions (Roads and Environment) 1998–99. *Select Committees (Former):* Member: Social Security 1993–97. *Other:* Governor, Central Foundation Girls' School ILEA 1985–89; Governor, London Goodenough Trust for Overseas Graduates 1992–.

Miscellaneous: Member, European Standing Committee B 1992–97. *Publications:* Co-author *Who Benefits: Reinventing Social Security,* 1993; *A Conservative Europe: 1994 and beyond,* 1994; *Fairer Business Rates,* 1996. *Special Interests:* Economic Policy, Trade, European Union, Defence, Foreign Affairs. *Countries of Interest:* USA, New Zealand, Singapore, Chile, France, Germany. *Recreations:* Sailing, music (especially opera), fishing, family, DIY. *Electoral Notes:* Contested Glasgow Central in 1987 General Election. Member for North Colchester 1992–97, and for North Essex since May 1, 1997. *Clubs:* Colchester Conservative. *Address:* Hon. Bernard Jenkin, MP, House of Commons, London, SW1A 0AA *Tel:* 020 7219 4029 *Fax:* 020 7219 5963. *Constituency:* North Essex Conservative Association, 1676 London Road, Stanway, Colchester, Essex, CO3 5PB *Tel:* 01206 717900 *Fax:* 01206 717909 *E-mail:* jenkinb@parliament.uk.

JENKINS, Brian *(Tamworth)   Lab majority 7,496*

Son of late Hiram and Gladys Jenkins. Born September 19, 1942; educated Kingsbury High School, Tamworth; Coventry College; Coleg Harlech; London School of Economics (BSc Econ); Wolverhampton Polytechnic (Post Graduate Certificate in Education). Married October 12, 1963, Joan, daughter of Charles and Marjorie Dix (1 son 1 daughter) (separated). *Career:* Instrument mechanic, CEGB 1961–68; Industrial engineer, Jaguar Cars 1968–73; Percy Lane 1973–75; Student 1975–81; College lecturer: Isle of Man College 1981–83, Tamworth College 1983–96. *Councils, Public Bodies:* Councillor, Tamworth Borough Council, Mayor 1993–94. *Political Career:* PPS: to Joyce Quin, MP, as Minister of State, Home Office (Minister for Prisons, Probation and Europe) 1997–98, to Rt Hon. Joyce Quin, MP, Derek Fatchett, MP and Tony Lloyd, MP, as Ministers of State, Foreign and Commonwealth Office 1998–99, to Rt Hon. Joyce Quin, MP, Geoff Hoon, MP and Tony Lloyd, MP, as Ministers of State, Foreign and Commonwealth Office 1999, to Rt Hon. Joyce Quin, MP, as Minister of State and Deputy Minister, Ministry of Agriculture, Fisheries and Food 1999–. *Select Committees (Current):* Member: Unopposed Bills (Panel) 1997–, Standing Orders 1998–. *Other:* School Governor. *Special Interests:* Trade and Industry, Training, Housing. *Countries of Interest:* Europe, North America. *Recreations:* Music, reading, watching sport. *Electoral Notes:* Contested South East Staffordshire in 1992 General Election. Member for South East Staffordshire By-election April 11, 1996–97, and for Tamworth since May 1, 1997. *Clubs:* Tamworth Royal British Legion. *Address:* Brian Jenkins Esq, MP, House of Commons, London, SW1A 0AA *Tel:* 020 7219 3000. *Constituency:* 11 Albert Road, Tamworth, Staffordshire, B79 7JN *Tel:* 01827 311957 *Fax:* 01827 311958.

JOHNSON, Alan Arthur *(Hull West and Hessle)   Lab majority 15,525*

Son of Stephen Arthur and late Lillian May Johnson. Born May 17, 1950; educated Sloane Grammar School, Chelsea. Married 1st, 1968, Judith Cox (1 son 2 daughters) (marriage dissolved); married 2nd, August 3, 1991, Laura Jane, daughter of John Patrick and Maureen Patient. *Trades Union:* Member, CWU. *Profession:* Trade Union Official. *Career:* Postman 1968; Local Officer, Slough UCW 1974–81; Union of Communication Workers: Branch Official 1976, Executive Council 1981–, National Officer 1987–93, General Secretary 1993–95; Member, General Council, TUC 1993–95; Executive Member, Postal, Telegraph and Telephone International 1993–97; Director, Unity Bank Trust plc 1993–97; Joint General Secretary, Communication Workers Union 1995–97. *Political Career:* PPS to Dawn Primarolo, MP: as Financial Secretary, HM Treasury 1997–99, as Paymaster General, HM Treasury 1999; Parliamentary Under-Secretary of State, Department of Trade and Industry (Minister for Competitiveness) 1999–. *Select Committees (Former):* Member: Trade and Industry 1997–98. *Party Groups:* Member: Eton and Slough Labour Party GMC 1976–87, Southern Regional Executive of Labour Party 1981–87, Member, Labour Party National Executive Committee 1995–97, Labour Campaign for Electoral Reform. *International Bodies:* Member, World Executive, Postal, Telegraph and Telephone International (PTTI) 1993–97. *Other:* Governor, Ruskin College. *Special Interests:* Education, Electoral Reform, Employment Law, Post Office. *Recreations:* Tennis, cooking, reading, Radio 4, music. *Electoral Notes:* Member for Hull West and Hessle since May 1, 1997. *Address:* Alan Johnson Esq, MP, House of Commons, London, SW1A 0AA *Tel:* 020 7219 5227 *Fax:* 020 7219 5856. *Constituency:* Unit 18, Lowgate Centre, 76–78 Lowgate, Hull, HU1 1HP *Tel:* 01482 219211 *Fax:* 01482 219691 *E-mail:* eked@parliament.uk; tlo.johnson@tlo.dti.gov.uk.

JOHNSON, Melanie Jane *(Welwyn Hatfield)* *Lab majority 5,595*

Daughter of David Johnson, retired civil engineer, and Angela Johnson, retired pharmacist. Born February 5, 1955; educated Clifton High School, Bristol; University College, London (BA Hons Philosophy and Ancient Greek); King's College, Cambridge (Postgraduate research). Partner, William Jordan (twin daughters 1 son). *Trades Union:* Member, UNISON. *Profession:* Lay Schools Inspector, OFSTED. *Career:* Member Relations Officer, Cambridge Co-op 1981–88; Retail Admin Manager, Cambridge Co-op 1988–90; Assistant General Manager, Quality Assurance, Cambridge FHSA 1990–92; Schools Inspector, OFSTED 1993–97. *Councils, Public Bodies:* Councillor, Cambridgeshire County Council 1981–97; JP 1994–. *Political Career:* HM Treasury: PPS to Barbara Roche, MP, as Financial Secretary 1999, Economic Secretary 1999–. *Select Committees (Former):* Member: Public Administration 1997–98, Home Affairs 1998–99. *Party Groups:* Labour Party Member since 1978; Vice-Chair, Eastern Regional Group of Labour MPs 1999. *Other:* School Governor. *Special Interests:* Business, Employment, Education, Health, Child Protection and Safety. *Recreations:* Family, gardening, a wide range of classical and rock music, films. *Electoral Notes:* Contested Cambridgeshire European Parliament Election 1994. Member for Welwyn Hatfield since May 1, 1997. *Address:* Melanie Johnson, MP, House of Commons, London, SW1A 0AA *Tel:* 020 7219 4119 *Fax:* 020 7219 0942. *Constituency:* 2 Queensway House, Hatfield, Herts, AL10 0LW *Tel:* 01707 262920 *Fax:* 01707 262834.

JOHNSON SMITH, The Rt Hon. Sir Geoffrey *(Wealden)* *Con majority 14,204*

Son of late J. Johnson Smith. Born April 16, 1924; educated Charterhouse; Lincoln College, Oxford (BA Hons). Married July 21, 1951, Jeanne Pomeroy (2 sons 1 daughter). *Armed Forces:* Army Service 1942–47, Captain, RA. *Career:* Information Officer, British Consulate-General, San Francisco 1950–52; Member, Production Staff, Talks Department, BBC TV 1953–54; Interviewer-Reporter, BBC TV 1954–59. *Councils, Public Bodies:* LCC Councillor, Putney 1955–58; DL, East Sussex 1986. *Political Career:* PPS: to Parliamentary Secretary, Board of Trade 1950–62; to Minister of Pensions July 1962–63; Under-Secretary of State for Defence (Army) 1971–72; Parliamentary Secretary, Civil Service Department 1972–74. *Whip:* Opposition Whip February-July 1965. *Select Committees (Former):* Chairman: House of Commons Members' Interests 1980–95; Member: Liaison 1992–96, Standards and Privileges 1994–96. *Party Groups:* Vice-Chairman, Conservative Party 1965–71. *International Bodies:* UK Delegate, North Atlantic Assembly 1980–; Chairman, Military Committee, North Atlantic Assembly 1985–89; Leader, UK Delegation 1987–, Elected Treasurer 1996–; Representative, UK Delegation to Organisation for Security and Co-operation in Europe. *Other:* Member, IBA General Advisory Council 1976–80; Patron, Wealden Mencap 1980–. *Trust:* Member: Thames Salmon Trust 1988–, Salmon and Trout Trust 1996–; Trustee, Handicapped Anglers Trust; President, London Youth Trust. *Miscellaneous:* Executive Member, 1922 Committee 1979–88, Joint Vice-Chairman 1988–. Freeman, City of London 1980. *Honours:* Knighted 1982; PC 1996. FRSA. *Special Interests:* Defence, Media, Agriculture, Health. *Countries of Interest:* USA. *Recreations:* Angling, visiting country houses and gardens. *Electoral Notes:* Member for Holborn and St Pancras South 1959–64; for East Grinstead 1965–83. Member for Wealden since June 1983. *Clubs:* Travellers'. *Address:* The Rt Hon. Sir Geoffrey Johnson Smith, DL, MP, House of Commons, London, SW1A 0AA *Tel:* 020 7219 4158 *Fax:* 020 7219 5333.

JONES, The Rt Hon. (Stephen) Barry *(Alyn and Deeside)* *Lab majority 16,403*

Son of late Stephen Jones, steelworker, and late Grace Jones. Born June 26, 1938; educated Hawarden Grammar School; Normal College, Bangor. Married Janet Davies (1 son). *Trades Union:* Regional Officer, National Union of Teachers. *Career:* Head of English Department, Deeside Secondary School, Flintshire. *Political Career:* Formerly PPS to Rt Hon. Denis Healey, MBE, MP; Parliamentary Under-Secretary of State for Wales 1974–79; Member, Shadow Cabinet 1983–92. *Spokesman:* Opposition Front Bench Spokesman on Employment 1980–83. *Select Committees (Current):* Member: Chairmen's Panel 1993–. *Party Groups:* Formerly Member, Executive of Labour Party, Wales. *International Bodies:* Member, Delegation of Council of Europe, Western European Union. *Other:* Governor: National Museum of Wales, National Library of Wales; Life Member, Liverpool Royal Philharmonic Society; Friend of: The Royal Academy, The Tate Gallery, National Trust, Museums and Galleries of Merseyside. *Miscellaneous:* Member, Prime Minister's Intelligence and Security Committee 1994–97, 1997–; Vice-President, Federation of Economic Development Authorities. *Honours:* PC 1999. *Special Interests:* Unemployment, Regional Policy, Education. *Countries of Interest:* Germany, France. *Electoral Notes:* Contested Northwich, Cheshire 1966, Member for East Flint 1970–83, and for Alyn and Deeside since June 1983. *Address:* The Rt Hon. Barry Jones, MP, House of Commons, London, SW1A 0AA *Tel:* 020 7219 3000. *Constituency:* 6 Cross Tree Close, Hawarden, Deeside, Clwyd, CH5 3PX *Tel:* 01244 543373.

JONES, Fiona *(Newark)* *Lab majority 3,016*

Born February 27, 1957; educated Mary Help of Christians Convent, Liverpool and North London; (Degree in Media and Communications). Married 1982, Chris Jones (2 sons). *Trades Union:* Member, NUJ. *Profession:* Journalist. *Councils, Public Bodies:* Councillor, West Lindsey 1990–94. *Select Committees (Current):* Member: Agriculture 1999–. *Party Groups:* Member, Labour Party. *Special Interests:* Employment, Crime, Health. *Electoral Notes:* Member for Newark since May 1, 1997. Disqualified over election expenses March 19, 1999; reinstated by the High Court, April 29, 1999. *Address:* Fiona Jones, MP, House of Commons, London, SW1A 0AA *Tel:* 020 7219 3445. *Constituency:* 1 Paxton's Court, Newark *Tel:* 01636 605530.

JONES, Helen Mary *(Warrington North)* *Lab majority 19,527*

Daughter of late Robert Edward Jones and of Mary Scanlan. Born December 24, 1954; educated St Werburgh's Primary School; Ursuline Convent, Chester; University College, London; Chester College; University of Liverpool; Manchester Metropolitan University (BA Hons, PGCE, MEd, CPE, LSF). Married July 23, 1988, Michael Vobe (1 son). *Trades Union:* MSF: Labour Party Liaison Officer, North West Coast Region, Former Member: National Women's Committee, National Appeals Panel. *Profession:* Solicitor. *Career:* Teacher of English; Development Officer, MIND; Justice and Peace Officer, Liverpool Archdiocese; Solicitor. *Councils, Public Bodies:* Councillor, Chester City Council 1984–91. *Select Committees (Current):* Member: Public Administration 1998–, Education and Employment 1999–, Education Sub-Committee 1999–, Standing Orders 1999–, Unopposed Bills (Panel) 1999– *(Former):* Member: Catering 1997–98. *Special Interests:* Education. *Recreations:* Gardening, reading, cooking. *Electoral Notes:* Contested Shropshire North 1983 General Election, Lancashire Central 1984 European Parliament Election, Ellesmere Port and Neston 1987 General Election. Member for Warrington North since May 1, 1997. *Address:* Helen Jones, MP, House of Commons, London, SW1A 0AA *Tel:* 020 7219 4048.

JONES, Ieuan Wyn *(Ynys Môn)   PC majority 2,481*

Son of late John Jones, minister of religion, and of Mair Elizabeth Jones, retired nurse. Born May 22, 1949; educated Pontardawe Grammar School, Glamorgan; Bala Comprehensive, Meirionnydd; Liverpool Polytechnic; London University (LLB Hons). Married August 17, 1974, Eirian Llwyd (2 sons 1 daughter). *Career:* Qualified as Solicitor 1973 Partner in Solicitors' firm 1974–87. *Political Career:* Sponsored Hearing Aid Council (Amendment) Act 1989 (Private Member's Bill). *Whip:* Plaid Cymru Whip 1991–95. *Spokesman:* Former Spokesman for Europe, Agriculture, Health, Housing, Home Affairs, Local Government, Tourism, Northern Ireland; Spokesman for Housing, Home Affairs, Local Government, Tourism, Northern Ireland, Health, Agriculture, Foreign Affairs, Defence 1997–. *Select Committees (Former):* Member: Welsh Affairs 1989–98, Agriculture 1992–97. *Party Groups:* Plaid Cymru: National Vice-Chairman 1975–79, National Chairman 1980–82, 1990–92. *Other:* President, North Wales Relate. *Trust:* Member, Industry and Parliament Trust. *Publications: Europe: The Challenge Facing Wales,* 1996; *Biography of Thomas Gee,* 1998. *Special Interests:* Agriculture, Transport, Elderly, Education and Industry Links, European Union. *Countries of Interest:* Scandinavia. *Recreations:* Sport, walking, reading. *Electoral Notes:* Contested West Denbigh October 1974 and 1979. Contested North Wales European Elections 1979. Contested Ynys Môn 1983. Member for Ynys Môn since June 1987. AM for the Constituency of Ynys Môn since May 6, 1999. *Address:* Ieuan Jones Esq, MP, AM, House of Commons, London, SW1A 0AA *Tel:* 020 7219 3439. *Constituency:* 45 Stryd-y-Bont, Llangefni, Ynys Môn, LL77 7PN *Tel:* 01248 723599 *Fax:* 01248 722868.

JONES, Jenny (Jennifer Grace) *(Wolverhampton South West)   Lab majority 5,118*

Born February 8, 1948; (BA Hons, MSocSci, Postgraduate qualifications CQSW, CITD). *Trades Union:* Member, MSF. *Career:* Social Worker; Business Adviser/Training manager. *Select Committees (Current):* Member: European Scrutiny 1998– *(Former):* Member: European Legislation 1997–98. *Party Groups:* Joined Labour Party 1979; Constituency Labour Party: Membership Secretary, Secretary, Vice/Chair, Chair. *International Bodies:* Member, UK Delegation to Council of Europe and Western European Union 1997–. *Miscellaneous:* BBC Newsnight, BSE Crisis 1996; Central TV, various local issues; Local Radio, regular broadcasts on local issues. *Special Interests:* Economic Development, Environment, Human Rights. *Recreations:* Swimming, gardening, keeping cats, craftwork. *Electoral Notes:* Member for Wolverhampton South West since May 1, 1997. *Address:* Jenny Jones, MP, House of Commons, London, SW1A 0AA *Tel:* 020 7219 4105 *Fax:* 020 7219 4105. *Constituency:* 57 Victoria Street, Wolverhampton, West Midlands, WV1 3NX *Tel:* 01902 714911 *Fax:* 01902 712580.

JONES, Jon Owen *(Cardiff Central)   Lab/Co-op majority 7,923*

Son of Gwynfor Owen Jones, retired optical salesman and former miner, and Dorothy Jones, retired teacher. Born April 19, 1954; educated Ysgol Gyfun Rhydfelin; University of East Anglia; University College, Cardiff (BSc Hons; PGCE). Married February 11, 1989, Allison Mary Clement (2 sons 1 daughter). *Trades Union:* President: Caerphilly NUT 1983, Mid Glamorgan NUT 1984. *Profession:* Teacher. *Career:* Teacher of biology and science in comprehensive schools 1977–92. *Councils, Public Bodies:* Cardiff City Council: Former Councillor, Vice-Chairman, Finance Committee 1987–91, Chairman, Economic Development Committee 1990–92. *Political Career:* Parliamentary Under-Secretary of State, Welsh Office 1998–99. *Whip:* Opposition Welsh/Agricultural Whip 1993–97; Transport Whip 1994–97; A Lord Commissioner of HM Treasury (Government Whip) 1997–98. *Select Committees (Current):* Member: Environmental Audit 1999– *(Former):* Member: Welsh Affairs 1992–93; Chairman: Information 1997–98; Member: Information 1998. *Party Groups:* Secretary, Cardiff Central Labour Party 1984–85; Member, Co-operative Party. *Miscellaneous:* Chairman, Campaign for Welsh Assembly 1988–91; Welsh speaking. *Special Interests:* Environment, Wales, Education. *Recreations:* Walking, cooking, natural history, watching rugby, family, golf. *Electoral Notes:* Contested Cardiff Central in 1987 General Election. Member for Cardiff Central since April 9, 1992. *Clubs:* Roath Labour. *Address:* Jon Owen Jones Esq, MP, House of Commons, London, SW1A 0AA *Tel:* 020 7219 4531/6352 *Fax:* 020 7219 2698 *Tel (Constituency):* 029 2048 5471 *Fax (Constituency):* 029 2048 5472 *E-mail:* jon@jonowen99.freeserve.co.uk.

JONES, Dr Lynne Mary *(Birmingham Selly Oak)   Lab majority 14,088*

Daughter of late Stanley Stockton and of Jean Stockton. Born April 26, 1951; educated Birmingham University (BSc, PhD). (2 sons). *Trades Union:* Member, MSF. *Career:* Research Fellow, Birmingham University 1972–86; Housing Association Manager 1987–92. *Councils, Public Bodies:* Birmingham City Councillor 1980–94, Chair, Housing Committee 1984–87. *Select Committees (Current):* Member: Science and Technology 1997– *(Former):* Member: Science and Technology 1992–97. *Other:* Member: Liberty, Greenpeace, CND. *Special Interests:* Economic Policy, Science, Criminal Justice, Housing. *Recreations:* Family. *Electoral Notes:* Member for Birmingham Selly Oak since April 9, 1992. *Address:* Dr Lynne Jones, MP, House of Commons, London, SW1A 0AA *Tel:* 020 7219 3000 *Fax:* 020 7219 3870 *Tel (Constituency):* 0121–486 2808 *Fax (Constituency):* 0121–486 2808 *E-mail:* jonesl@parliament.uk.

JONES, Martyn *(Clwyd South)   Lab majority 13,810*

Son of Vernon, engine driver, and Violet Jones. Born March 1, 1947; educated Grove Park Grammar School, Wrexham; Liverpool College of Commerce; Liverpool Polytechnic (CIBiol); Trent Polytechnic (MIBiol). Married January 5, 1974, Rhona, daughter of Roger Bellis (1 son 1 daughter) (marriage dissolved 1991). *Trades Union:* Member, TGWU 1974–; Vice-Chair, TGWU Parliamentary Group. *Profession:* Microbiologist. *Career:* Microbiologist, Wrexham Lager Beer Co. 1969-June 1987. *Councils, Public Bodies:* Councillor, Clwyd County Council 1981–89. *Whip:* Labour Whip 1988–92. *Spokesman:* Opposition Front Bench Spokesman on Food, Agricultural and Rural Affairs 1994–95. *Select Committees (Current):* Member: Liaison 1997–; Chairman: Welsh Affairs 1997– *(Former):* Member: Agriculture 1988–94, Speaker's Panel of Chairmen 1993–94, Agriculture 1996–97. *Party Groups:* Joined Labour Party 1977; Formerly Chairman, Clwyd County Party; Member: Christian Socialist Movement, Socialist Environment and Resources Association, Fabian Society. *Other:* Member, SERA. *Miscellaneous:* Council Member: Royal College of Veterinary Surgeons, National Rifle Association; Vice-President, Federation of Economic Development Authorities (FEDA). *Special Interests:* Science, Ecology, Agriculture. *Countries of Interest:* Spain, USA, Wales. *Recreations:* Backpacking, first aid, target shooting. *Electoral Notes:* Member for Clwyd South West 1987–97, and for Clwyd South since May 1, 1997. *Address:* Martyn Jones Esq, MP, House of Commons, London, SW1A 0AA *Tel:* 020 7219 3417 *Fax:* 020 7219 6090. *Constituency:* Foundry Buildings, Gutter Hill, Johnstown, Wrexham, LL14 1LU *Tel:* 01978 845938 *Fax:* 01978 843392.

JONES, Nigel *(Cheltenham)   LD majority 6,645*

Son of late A. J. Jones, and of Nora Jones. Born March 30, 1948; educated Prince Henry's Grammar School, Evesham. Married May 21, 1981, Katy, daughter of William and Freda Grinnell (1 son twin daughters). *Career:* Clerk; Computer operator, Westminster Bank 1965–67; Computer programmer, ICL Computers 1967–70; Systems analyst, Vehicle and General Insurance 1970–71; Systems programmer, Atkins Computing 1971; Systems Designer; Consultant; Project Manager, ICL Computers 1971–92. *Councils, Public Bodies:* Councillor, Gloucestershire County Council 1989–93. *Spokesman:* Liberal Democrat Spokesman for: England, Local Government and Housing 1992–93, Science and Technology 1993–, Consumer Affairs 1995–97, National Heritage, Constitution and Civil Service (Sport) 1997, Culture, Media, Sport, and Civil Service (Sport) 1997–99, Trade and Industry (Science and Technology) 1997–99, International Development 1999–. *Select Committees (Current):* Member: Science and Technology 1997–, International Development 1999–

(Former): Member: Broadcasting 1994–97, Standards and Privileges 1995–97. *International Bodies:* Member, Executive Committee: Inter-Parliamentary Union British Group 1997–, Commonwealth Parliamentary Association UK Branch 1999–, Governing Body British Association for Central and Eastern Europe. *Sportsclubs:* Gloucestershire County Cricket Club, Cheltenham Town FC Season Ticket Holder. *Special Interests:* Trade and Industry, Transport, Restructuring of Defence Industries, Information Technology, Sport, International Development. *Countries of Interest:* Middle East, Africa. *Recreations:* Watching Swindon Town and Cheltenham Town Football Club, playing cricket, gardening. *Electoral Notes:* Contested Cheltenham 1979. Member for Cheltenham since April 9, 1992. *Clubs:* National Liberal. *Address:* Nigel Jones Esq, MP, House of Commons, London, SW1A 0AA *Tel:* 020 7219 4415 *Fax:* 020 7219 2537. *Constituency:* 50 St George's Street, Cheltenham, Gloucestershire, GL50 4AF *Tel:* 01242 224889 *Fax:* 01242 256658 *E-mail:* nigeljonesmp@cix.co.uk.

JOWELL, The Rt Hon. Tessa *(Dulwich and West Norwood)   Lab majority 16,769*

Daughter of Dr. Kenneth Palmer, and of Rosemary Palmer, radiographer. Born September 17, 1947; educated St Margaret's School, Aberdeen; Aberdeen (MA), Edinburgh and London (Goldsmith's College) Universities; Visiting Fellow, Nuffield College, Oxford. Married 1st, 1970, Roger Jowell (marriage dissolved 1977), married 2nd, March 17, 1979, David Mills, son of Kenneth and Patricia Mills (1 son 1 daughter, 3 step-children). *Career:* Child Care Officer, London Borough of Lambeth 1969–71; Psychiatric Social Worker, Maudsley Hospital 1972–74; Assistant Director, MIND 1974–86; Director: Community Care Special Action Project, Birmingham 1987–90, Joseph Rowntree Foundation, Community Care Programme 1990–92; Senior Visiting Research Fellow: Policy Studies Institute 1987–90, King's Fund Institute 1990–92. *Councils, Public Bodies:* Councillor, London Borough of Camden 1971–86; Vice-Chairman, then Chairman, Social Services Committee of Association of Metropolitan Authorities 1978–86; Mental Health Act Commission 1985–90. *Political Career:* Minister of State: Department of Health (Minister for Public Health) 1997–99, Department for Education and Employment (Minister for Employment, Welfare to Work and Equal Opportunities) 1999–. *Whip:* Opposition Whip 1994–95. *Spokesman:* Frontbench Opposition Spokesperson on: Women 1995–96, Health 1994–95, 1996–97. *Select Committees (Former):* Member: Health 1992–94. *Other:* Governor, National Institute for Social Work 1985–97. *Miscellaneous:* Member: Central Council for Training and Education in Social Work 1983–89. *Honours:* PC 1998. *Special Interests:* Community Care, Human Rights, Constitutional Reform. *Electoral Notes:* Contested Ilford North 1978 By-election and 1979 General Election. Member for Dulwich 1992–97, and for Dulwich and West Norwood since May 1, 1997. *Address:* The Rt Hon. Tessa Jowell, MP, House of Commons, London, SW1A 0AA *Tel:* 020 7219 3409 *Fax:* 020 7219 2702 *E-mail:* jowellt@parliament.uk.

K

KAUFMAN, The Rt Hon. Gerald Bernard *(Manchester Gorton)   Lab majority 17,342*

Son of Louis Kaufman. Born June 21, 1930; educated Leeds Council Schools; Leeds Grammar School; The Queen's College, Oxford (MA). *Trades Union:* Member, GMB. *Profession:* Journalist. *Career:* Assistant General Secretary, Fabian Society 1954–55; Political Staff, *Daily Mirror* 1955–64; Political Correspondent, *New Statesman* 1964–65; Parliamentary Press Liaison Officer, Labour Party 1965–70. *Political Career:* Parliamentary Under-Secretary of State for the Environment 1974–75; Parliamentary Under-Secretary, Department of Industry 1975; Minister of State, Department of Industry 1975–79; Shadow Environment Secretary 1980–83; Shadow Home Secretary 1983–87; Shadow Foreign Secretary 1987–92. *Spokesman:* Opposition Front Bench Spokesman on the Environment 1979–80. *Select Committees (Current):* Chairman: Culture, Media and Sport 1997–; Member: Liaison 1997– *(Former):* Member: Liaison 1992–97; Chairman: National Heritage 1992–97. *Party Groups:* Member: Labour Party National Executive 1991–92, Fabian Society. *Other:* Member, Poale Zion. *Miscellaneous:* Member, Royal Commission on Lords Reform February 1999–. *Sportsclubs:* Member, East Levenshulme Cricket Club. *Honours:* PC 1978; Hilal-i-Pakistan 1999.

Publications: To Build the Promised Land; How to Be a Minister; Inside the Promised Land; My Life in the Silver Screen; How to Be a Minister (updated and revised edition); Co-author, *How to Live Under Labour;* Editor: *The Left; Renewal. Recreations:* Cinema, theatre, opera, concerts, travel. *Electoral Notes:* Contested Bromley 1955 and Gillingham 1959. Member for Ardwick 1970–1983, and for Manchester Gorton since 1983. *Address:* The Rt Hon. Gerald Kaufman, MP, House of Commons, London, SW1A 0AA *Tel:* 020 7219 5145 *Fax:* 020 7219 6825 *Tel (Constituency):* 0161–248 0073 *Fax (Constituency):* 0161–248 0073.

KEEBLE, Sally *(Northampton North)* **Lab majority 10,000**

Daughter of Sir Curtis Keeble, GCMG, and Lady Keeble. Born October 13, 1951; educated Cheltenham Ladies' College; St Hugh's College, Oxford (BA Hons Theology); University of South Africa (BA Hons Sociology); Honorary Fellow, South Bank University. Married June 9, 1990, Andrew Hilary Porter (1 son 1 daughter). *Trades Union:* Member: National Union of Journalists, GMB. *Profession:* Journalist. *Career:* Journalist: *Daily News,* Durban, South Africa 1973–79, *Birmingham Post* 1978–83; Press Officer, Labour Headquarters 1983–84; Assistant Director, External Relations, ILEA 1984–86; Head of Communications, GMB 1986–90; Public Affairs Consultant 1995–97. *Councils, Public Bodies:* Councillor, Southwark Council 1986–94, Leader 1990–93. *Political Career:* PPS to Rt Hon. Hilary Armstrong, MP, as Minister of State, Department of the Environment, Transport and the Regions (Minister for Local Government and Regions) 1999–. *Select Committees (Former):* Member: Agriculture 1997–99. *Other:* Chair, Northampton Rail Users' Group; Hon. Secretary, Friends of the Lakes. *Publications: Citizens Look At Congress Profiles,* 1971; *Flat Broke,* 1984; *Collectors Corner,* 1986; *Feminism, Infertility and New Reproductive Technologies,* 1994; *Conceiving Your Baby, How Medicine Can Help,* 1995. *Special Interests:* Economic Policy, Home Affairs, Education, Local Government, Financial Services. *Countries of Interest:* North Africa, South Africa, USA. *Recreations:* Antiques, walking, writing. *Electoral Notes:* Member for Northampton North since May 1, 1997. *Address:* Sally Keeble, MP, House of Commons, London, SW1A 0AA *Tel:* 020 7219 4039. *Constituency:* Unit 5, Barratt Building, Kingsthorpe Road, Northampton, NN2 6EZ *Tel:* 01604 27803 *Fax:* 01604 27805.

KEEN, Alan *(Feltham and Heston)* **Lab/Co-op majority 15,273**

Son of late Jack and Gladys Keen. Born November 25, 1937; educated St William Turner's School, Redcar, Cleveland. Married June 21, 1980, Ann Keen, MP for Brentford and Isleworth (*qv*), daughter of late John Fox, steel-worker, and of Ruby Fox (2 sons 1 daughter). *Trades Union:* Member, GMB. *Career:* Employed part-time Tactical Scout (assessing opposition tactics) 18 years by Middlesbrough FC; Miscellaneous positions in private industry and commerce, mainly in the fire protection industry; Systems Analyst; Accountant and Manager 1963–92. *Councils, Public Bodies:* Councillor, London Borough of Hounslow 1986–90. *Select Committees (Current):* Member: Culture, Media and Sport 1997– *(Former):* Member: Deregulation 1995–96, Education 1995–96. *Party Groups:* Co-operative Party MP; Secretary, Labour First Past the Post Group. *Sportsclubs:* Secretary, Lords and Commons Cricket. *Special Interests:* Commerce, Industry, Foreign Affairs, Development, Democracy, Defence, Sport, Culture. *Recreations:* Playing and listening to music, Association football, athletics. *Electoral Notes:* Member for Feltham and Heston since April 9, 1992. *Clubs:* Feltham Labour, Heston Catholic Social, Hanworth British Legion. *Address:* Alan Keen Esq, MP, House of Commons, London, SW1A 0AA *Tel:* 020 7219 2819 *Fax:* 020 7219 2233. *Constituency:* Labour Party, Manor Place, Feltham, Middlesex, TW14 9BT *Tel:* 020 8890 4489 *Fax:* 020 8893 2606.

KEEN, Mrs Ann *(Brentford and Isleworth)   Lab majority 14,424*

Daughter of late John Fox, and of Ruby Fox. Born November 26, 1948; educated Elfed Secondary Modern, Clwyd; University of Surrey (PGCEA). Married June 20, 1980, Alan Keen, MP (*qv*) (2 sons 1 daughter). *Trades Union:* Member, GMB. *Profession:* Community Nursing. *Career:* Registered Nurse; Former Head, Faculty of Advanced Nursing, Queen Charlotte's College, Hammersmith; General Secretary, Community and District Nursing Association. *Political Career:* PPS to Rt Hon. Frank Dobson, MP, as Secretary of State for Health 1999 *Select Committees (Former):* Member: Health 1997–99. *Party Groups:* Member, Labour Party for over 30 years. *Miscellaneous:* Hon. Professor of Nursing, Thames Valley University. *Sportsclubs:* Nurse/Physiotherapist, the House of Commons' Football Team. *Special Interests:* Health. *Countries of Interest:* South Africa, Cyprus. *Recreations:* Theatre, music, football, vegetarian cookery. *Electoral Notes:* Contested Brentford and Isleworth 1987 and 1992 General Elections. Member for Brentford and Isleworth since May 1, 1997. *Clubs:* Ewloe Social and Working Men's. *Address:* Mrs Ann Keen, MP, House of Commons, London, SW1A 0AA *Tel:* 020 7219 2819. *Constituency:* Brentford and Isleworth Labour Party, 367 Chiswick High Road, London, W4 4AG *Tel:* 020 8995 7289 *Fax:* 020 8742 1004.

KEETCH, Paul Stuart *(Hereford)   LD majority 6,648*

Son of late John Norton, engineer, and late Agnes (née Hughes). Born May 21, 1961; educated Hereford High School for Boys; Hereford Sixth Form College. Married December 21, 1991, Claire Elizabeth Baker, daughter of Gordon and Margaret Baker (1 son). *Career:* Self-employed Business Consultant; Non-executive Director, London Computer Company. *Councils, Public Bodies:* Councillor, Hereford City Council 1983–86. *Spokesman:* A Spokesman for: Health (Patients' and Community Health Council Issues, Dental, Ophthalmic and Pharmaceutical Services, Alternative Therapies) 1997, Education and Employment (Employment and Training) 1997–99, Foreign Affairs and Defence (Defence) 1999–. *Select Committees (Former):* Member: Education and Employment 1997–99, Education 1997–99, Employment Sub-Committee 1997–99, Catering 1998–99. *Party Groups:* Joined Liberal Party 1975. *Other:* Member: National Development Board, British Dyslexia Association 1993–. *Miscellaneous:* OSCE Observer, Albanian Elections 1996; Adviser, Lithuanian Local and National Elections 1995, 1996; Member, Council of The Electoral Reform Society. *Sportsclubs:* Herefordshire County Cricket Club. *Special Interests:* National Heritage, Defence, Foreign Affairs. *Countries of Interest:* Former Soviet Union, Eastern Bloc countries, Eastern Europe. *Recreations:* Cricket (watching), swimming, entertaining friends at home, country walks with my wife and son. *Electoral Notes:* Member for Hereford since May 1, 1997. *Clubs:* Hereford Liberal, Herefordshire Farmers', National Liberal. *Address:* Paul Keetch Esq, MP, House of Commons, London, SW1A 0AA *Tel:* 020 7219 5163 *Fax:* 020 7219 1184. *Constituency:* 39 Widemarsh Street, Hereford, HR4 9EA *Tel:* 01432 341483 *Fax:* 01432 341483 *E-mail:* keetch@cix.co.uk.

KELLY, Ruth Maria *(Bolton West)   Lab majority 7,072*

Daughter of Bernard James Kelly, pharmacist, and Gertrude Anne Kelly, teacher. Born May 9, 1968; educated Sutton High School; Westminster School; Queen's College, Oxford (BA Philosophy, Politics and Economics) (Exhibition); London School of Economics (MSc Economics). Married June 1, 1996, Derek John Gadd, son of late Frederick Gadd and of Joyce Gadd (1 son 1 daughter). *Trades Union:* Member, MSF. *Profession:* Journalist/Economist. *Career:* Economics Writer, *The Guardian* 1990–94; Deputy Head, Inflation Report Division, Bank of England 1994–97. *Political Career:* PPS to Nick Brown, MP, as Minister of Agriculture, Fisheries and Food 1998–. *Select Committees (Former):* Member: Treasury 1997–98, Treasury Sub-Committee 1998. *Party Groups:* Joined Labour Party 1990; Bethnal Green and Stepney/Bow Constituency Labour Party: Treasurer 1994–96, Ward Secretary. *Other:* Tower Hamlets Anti-Racist Committee. *Miscellaneous:* Member, Research Panel, Employment Policy Institute; Member, Council of Management, National Institute for Economic and Social Research; Member, Royal Economic Society Council.

Publications: Various Pamphlets on Finance and Taxation. *Special Interests:* Economic Policy, Europe, Social Policy, Welfare Reform, Employment Policy. *Countries of Interest:* France, Spain. *Recreations:* Walking, writing. *Electoral Notes:* Member for Bolton West since May 1, 1997. *Address:* Ruth Kelly, MP, House of Commons, London, SW1A 0AA *Tel:* 020 7219 3496. *Constituency:* Labour Party, 60 St George's Road, Bolton, Lancashire *Tel:* 01204 523920 *E-mail:* kellyr@parliament.uk.

KEMP, Fraser *(Houghton and Washington East)* Lab majority 26,555

Son of William and Mary Kemp. Born September 1, 1958; educated Washington Comprehensive. Married July 1, 1989, Patricia Mary, daughter of Patricia and Patrick Byrne (2 sons 1 daughter). *Trades Union:* Full-time Branch Secretary CPSA 1975–80; Member: GMB, AEEU. *Career:* Civil Servant 1975–81; Full-time Labour Party Organiser, Leicester 1981–84; Assistant Regional Organiser, East Midlands 1984–86; Regional Secretary, West Midlands 1986–94; National General Election Co-ordinator for the Labour Party 1994–96. *Select Committees (Former):* Member: Public Administration 1997–99, Selection 1997–99. *Party Groups:* Secretary: National Annual Labour Party Conference Arrangements Committee 1993–96, Labour's National General Election Planning Group 1994–96; Secretary, Labour's NEC Campaigns and Elections Committee 1995–96. *Other:* Vice-Chair, Herrington Burn YMCA; Honorary President, Northguard Roman Research and Living History Society; Member, Russell Foster Tyne & Wear Sports Foundation; Honorary Member, North East Chamber of Commerce; President, Washington MIND. *Trust:* Patron, The Friends of Houghton Parish Church Trust; Member, Beamish Development Trust (North of England Open Air Museum). *Sportsclubs:* Member, Houghton and Peterlee Athletics Club. *Special Interests:* Technology, Motor Industry. *Countries of Interest:* Australia. *Recreations:* Reading, cinema. *Electoral Notes:* Member for Houghton and Washington East since May 1, 1997. *Clubs:* Usworth and District Workmens and Institute (Washington); Hetton; Hetton-le-Hole CIU. *Address:* Fraser Kemp Esq, MP, House of Commons, London, SW1A 0AA *Tel:* 020 7219 5181 *Fax:* 020 7219 2536. *Constituency:* 5A Grangewood Close, Shiney Row, Houghton-le-Spring, Tyne and Wear, DH4 4SD *Tel:* 0191–385 7825 *Fax:* 0191–385 4785.

KENNEDY, The Rt Hon. Charles Peter *(Ross, Skye and Inverness West)* LD majority 4,019

Son of Ian Kennedy, crofter and Mary MacVarish MacEachen. Born November 25, 1959; educated Lochaber High School, Fort William; Glasgow University (MA Politics, Philosophy and English 1982); Indiana University (Fulbright Scholarship 1982–83). *Profession:* Journalist and broadcaster. *Career:* President, Glasgow University Union 1980–81; Winner, British Observer Mace Debating Tournament 1982; Journalist with BBC Highland, at Inverness 1982. *Political Career:* Leader, Liberal Democrat Party 1999–. *Spokesman:* Alliance Spokesman for Social Security 1987; SDP Spokesman for: Scotland and Social Security 1987–88, Trade and Industry 1988–89; Liberal Democrat Spokesman for: Health 1989–92, European Union Affairs 1992–97, Agriculture, Fisheries, Food and Rural Affairs 1997–99. *Select Committees (Former):* Member: Standards and Privileges 1997–99. *Party Groups:* Chairman, Glasgow University Social Democratic Club 1979–80; President, Liberal Democrat Party 1990–94; Deputy Convenor, Foreign Affairs, Defence and Overseas Development Committee 1994–. *Awards:* Member to Watch Award, The Spectator 1989. *Miscellaneous:* Associate Member, Scottish Crofters Union. *Honours:* PC 1999. *Special Interests:* Scotland, Social Policy, Broadcasting, European Union. *Recreations:* Reading, writing, music, swimming, golf, journalism, broadcasting. *Electoral Notes:* Member for Ross, Cromarty and Skye 1983–97, and for Ross, Skye and Inverness West since May 1, 1997. *Clubs:* National Liberal. *Address:* The Rt Hon. Charles Kennedy, MP, House of Commons, London, SW1A 0AA *Tel:* 020 7219 6226 *Fax:* 020 7219 4881. *Constituency:* 1a Montague Row, Inverness, IV3 5DX *Tel:* 01463 714377 *Fax:* 01463 714380 *E-mail:* charleskennedy@cix.co.uk.

KENNEDY, Mrs Jane *(Liverpool Wavertree)*   Lab majority 19,701

Daughter of Clifford Hodgson, engineer, and of Barbara Hodgson. Born May 4, 1958; educated Haughton School, Darlington; Queen Elizabeth Sixth Form College; Liverpool University. Married December 14, 1977, Malcolm Kennedy, son of Robert and Jesse Kennedy (2 sons) (marriage dissolved 1998). *Trades Union:* Branch Secretary, NUPE 1983–88, Area Organiser 1988–92. *Career:* Residential Child Care Officer, Liverpool City Council (LCC) 1979–83; Care Assistant, LCC Social Services 1983–88. *Political Career:* Parliamentary Secretary, Lord Chancellor's Department 1999–. *Whip:* Opposition Whip 1995–97; Assistant Government Whip 1997–98; A Lord Commissioner of HM Treasury (Government Whip) 1998–99. *Select Committees (Current):* Member: Administration 1997– *(Former):* Member: Social Security 1992–94. *Party Groups:* Member, Labour Party 1978–; Chair, Labour Friends of Israel 1997–. *Other:* Member, Governing Body: Liverpool Polytechnic 1986–88, Oldham Sixth Form College 1990–92; Member: Ramblers' Association, Youth Hostelling Association, Belgian Shepherd Dog Association. *Trust:* Fellow, Industry and Parliament Trust. *Special Interests:* Local Government, Public Services, Social Security, Foreign Affairs. *Countries of Interest:* Middle East and South East Asia. *Recreations:* Walking, training Belgian Shepherd dogs, horse-riding. *Electoral Notes:* Member for Liverpool Broadgreen 1992–97, and for Liverpool Wavertree since May 1, 1997. *Address:* Mrs Jane Kennedy, MP, House of Commons, London, SW1A 0AA *Tel:* 020 7219 4523 *Fax:* 020 7219 4880. *Constituency:* 1st Floor, Threlfall Building, Trueman Street, Liverpool, L3 2EX *Tel:* 0151–236 1117 *Fax:* 0151–236 0067.

KEY, Robert *(Salisbury)*   Con majority 6,276

Son of late Rt Rev. Maurice Key, former Bishop of Truro. Born April 22, 1945; educated Salisbury Cathedral School; Sherborne School; Clare College, Cambridge (MA, CertEd). Married 1968, Susan Priscilla Bright, daughter of Very Revd Thurstan Irvine, Dean of St Andrews, Scotland (1 son 2 daughters). *Trades Union:* Former Vice-Chairman, Wembley Branch ASTMS. *Profession:* Teacher. *Career:* Assistant Master: Loretto School, Edinburgh 1967–69, Harrow School (Economics Department) 1969–83. *Political Career:* Political Secretary to Rt Hon. Edward Heath, MBE, MP 1984–85; PPS: to Minister of State for Energy 1985–87, to Rt Hon. Christopher Patten, MP, as Minister for Overseas Development 1987–89, as Secretary of State for the Environment 1989–90; Parliamentary Under-Secretary of State: at Department of the Environment 1990–92, at Department of National Heritage 1992–93 at Department of Transport (Minister for Roads and Traffic) 1993–94. *Spokesman:* An Opposition Spokesman for Defence 1997–. *Select Committees (Former):* Member: Health 1994–95, Defence 1995–97. *Party Groups:* Treasurer, Conservative Candidates' Association 1976–79; Chairman, Harrow Central Conservative Association 1980–82; Vice-Chairman, London Central Euro-Constituency 1980–82; Member: Conservative Party National Advisory Committee on Education 1979–82, Executive Committee National Union of Conservative Party 1980–83. *International Bodies:* Member, Executive Council, Inter Parliamentary Union British Branch 1986–90; Chairman, Council for Education in the Commonwealth 1985–87; Substitute, UK Delegation to Council of Europe and Western Europe Union 1996–97. *Other:* Chairman, Governors of School at Great Ormond Street Children's Hospital 1976–79; Governor, Sir William Collins Comprehensive School 1976–79; Former Member of Council, Gap Activity Projects. *Trust:* Founding Chairman, the Alice Trust for Autistic Children 1977–80. *Miscellaneous:* Member: UK National Commission for UNESCO 1984–85, Medical Research Council 1989–90. Hon. Fellow, College of Preceptors 1989–. *Publications:* Author of *Reforming our Schools*, 1988. *Special Interests:* Education, Arts, Foreign Affairs, Defence, Agriculture. *Recreations:* Singing, cooking, countryside. *Electoral Notes:* Contested Camden, Holborn and St Pancras South 1979. Member for Salisbury since June 1983. *Address:* Robert Key Esq, MP, House of Commons, London, SW1A 0AA *Tel:* 020 7219 6501.

KHABRA, Piara Singh *(Ealing Southall) Lab majority 21,423*

Born November 20, 1924; educated Punjab University (BA Social Services, BEd Teaching); Whitelands College, Putney (Diploma in Teaching). Married Beulah Marian. *Trades Union:* Member, MSF. *Armed Forces:* Served Indian Armed Corps 1942–46. *Profession:* Teacher. *Career:* Clerical Work, British Oxygen; Teacher, ILEA; Community Worker. *Councils, Public Bodies:* Councillor, London Borough of Ealing 1978–82; JP 1977–. *Select Committees (Current):* Member: International Development 1997– *(Former):* Member: Members' Interests 1994–97. *Party Groups:* Joined Labour Party 1972. *Other:* Chairman, Indian Workers' Association, Southall, Middlesex. *Special Interests:* Employment, Education, Race Relations, European Union, International Development. *Countries of Interest:* India. *Recreations:* Reading, watching football. *Electoral Notes:* Member for Ealing Southall since April 9, 1992. *Address:* Piara S. Khabra Esq, JP, MP, House of Commons, London, SW1A 0AA *Tel:* 020 7219 5010 *Fax:* 020 7219 5699 *Tel (Constituency):* 020 8992 5614.

KIDNEY, David Neil *(Stafford) Lab majority 4,314*

Son of Neil Bernard Kidney, retired clerk, and late Doris Kidney. Born March 21, 1955; educated Longton High School; Sixth Form College, Stoke-on-Trent; Bristol University (LLB). Married September 9, 1979, Elaine (1 son 1 daughter). *Trades Union:* Member, MSF. *Career:* Solicitor: Hanley, Stoke-on-Trent 1977–79, Stafford 1979–97. *Councils, Public Bodies:* Councillor: Checkley Parish Council 1983–87, Stafford Borough Council 1987–97. *Select Committees (Current):* Member: Treasury 1998–, Treasury Sub-Committee 1998–. *Party Groups:* Member, Society of Labour Lawyers. *Other:* Member: Bethany Project for Homeless, ASIST (Citizen Advocacy), British Agencies for Adoption and Fostering, Law Society. *Special Interests:* Children, Housing. *Countries of Interest:* Britain. *Recreations:* Chess, bridge. *Electoral Notes:* Member for Stafford since May 1, 1997. *Address:* David Kidney Esq, MP, House of Commons, London, SW1A 0AA *Tel:* 020 7219 6472 *Fax:* 020 7219 0919. *Constituency:* Labour Rooms, Meyrick Road, Stafford, ST17 4DG *Tel:* 01785 224444/250356 *Fax:* 01785 250357 *E-mail:* kidneyd@parliament.uk.

KILFOYLE, Peter *(Liverpool Walton) Lab majority 27,038*

Son of late Edward and Ellen Kilfoyle. Born June 9, 1946; educated St Edward's College, Liverpool; University of Durham; Christ's College, Liverpool. Married July 27, 1968, Bernadette Slater (2 sons 3 daughters). *Career:* Labourer 1965–70, 1973–75; Student 1970–73; Teacher 1975–85. *Political Career:* Parliamentary Secretary: Office of Public Service 1997–98, Cabinet Office 1998–99; Parliamentary Under-Secretary of State, Ministry of Defence 1999–. *Whip:* Opposition Whip 1992–94. *Spokesman:* Opposition Spokesman on: Education 1994–96, Education and Employment 1996–97. *Party Groups:* Labour Party organiser 1986–91. *Special Interests:* Foreign Affairs, Commonwealth, Employment, Education. *Countries of Interest:* Australia, Latin America, The Commonwealth. *Recreations:* Reading, music, spectator sport. *Electoral Notes:* Member for Liverpool Walton since July 4, 1991 By-election. *Address:* Peter Kilfoyle Esq, MP, House of Commons, London, SW1A 0AA *Tel:* 020 7219 2591. *Constituency:* 4 Christopher Street, Liverpool, L4 4JX *Tel:* 0151–298 1148 *Fax:* 0151–298 1149.

Dod *on* Disk

The Vacher Dod Parliamentary Database – configured for PC or Network

For further details please telephone the Westminster Office

020 7828 7256

KING, Andy (Andrew) *(Rugby and Kenilworth)   Lab majority 495*

Son of late Charles King, labourer, and of late Mary King. Born September 14, 1948; educated St John the Baptist School, Uddingston; Coatbridge Technical College; Missionary Institute, London; Hatfield Polytechnic; Stevenage College; Nene College, Northants (CQSW, CMS). Married Semma (1 daughter). *Trades Union:* Member, UNISON. *Profession:* Social Worker. *Career:* Former: Labourer, Postal Officer, Apprentice Motor Vehicle Mechanic; Social Work Manager, Northamptonshire County Council 1989–. *Councils, Public Bodies:* Member, Warwickshire Police Authority 1989–97; Councillor, Warwickshire County Council 1989–98, Chair, Social Services Committee 1993–96; Councillor, Rugby Borough Council 1995–98. *Select Committees (Current):* Member: Deregulation 1999–, Social Security 1999–. *Party Groups:* Member, Co-operative Party; Treasurer, Rugby and Kenilworth Constituency Labour Party 1984–88. *Other:* Member, British Association of Social Workers. *Sportsclubs:* Rugby Golf Club; President, Rugby Town Junior FC. *Special Interests:* Health, Law and Order, Social Services, Home Affairs. *Countries of Interest:* Ethiopia, New Zealand, Brazil. *Recreations:* Golf, football, dominoes, theatre. *Electoral Notes:* Member for Rugby and Kenilworth since May 1, 1997. *Address:* Andy King Esq, MP, House of Commons, London, SW1A 0AA *Tel:* 020 7219 6229. *Constituency:* 12 Regent Place, Rugby, Warwickshire, CU21 2PN *Tel:* 01788 575504 *Fax:* 01788 575506 *E-mail:* kinga@parliament.uk.

KING, Oona *(Bethnal Green and Bow)   Lab majority 11,285*

Daughter of Preston King, professor of political science, and of Hazel King, teacher. Born October 22, 1967; educated Haverstock Comprehensive Secondary School; York University; Berkeley-University of California (Scholarship) (BA Hons Politics). Married July 15, 1994, Tiberio, son of Tullio and Esia Santomarco. *Trades Union:* Southern Region Equality Officer, GMB. *Profession:* Political Researcher/Trade Union Regional Organiser. *Career:* Researcher, Socialist Group, European Parliament 1990; Political Assistant to Glyn Ford MEP, as Leader, EPLP 1991; John Smith's Labour Party Leadership Campaign Team 1992; Freelance Speech-writer/Ghost Writer 1993–94; Political Assistant to Glenys Kinnock MEP 1994–95; Trade Union Organiser, GMB Southern Region 1995–97. *Select Committees (Current):* Member: International Development 1997–. *Party Groups:* Member, Fabian Society; Joint Vice-Chair, London Regional Group of Labour MPs 1997–; Committee Member, Labour Campaign for Electoral Reform. *Other:* Member: Oxfam, Campaign for Pension Fund Democracy, Amnesty International, Jewish Council for Racial Equality (J-Core), One World Action. *Trust:* Member, 1990 Trust, Toynbee Hall. *Special Interests:* Race Relations, Employment, Education, Health, Development, Women's Issues, Housing, Europe, Electoral Reform. *Countries of Interest:* Bangladesh, Nicaragua, USA, Italy, France, South Africa, Rwanda and Great Lakes Region (Africa). *Recreations:* Music, cinema. *Electoral Notes:* Member for Bethnal Green and Bow since May 1, 1997. *Address:* Oona King, MP, House of Commons, London, SW1A 0AA *Tel:* 020 7219 3000/5020 *Fax:* 020 7219 2798.

KING, The Rt Hon. Tom, CH *(Bridgwater)   Con majority 1,796*

Son of late J. H. King, JP, Company Director. Born June 13, 1933; educated Rugby; Emmanuel College, Cambridge (MA). Married January 20, 1960, Jane, daughter of late Robert Tilney, CBE, DSO, TD, DL (1 son 1 daughter). *Armed Forces:* Commissioned Somerset Light Infantry 1952 (NS); Seconded to KAR, served Tanganyika and Kenya, Acting Captain 1953. *Career:* Joined E. S. and A. Robinson Ltd, Bristol 1956, various positions up to Divisional General Manager 1964–69; Chairman, Sale, Tilney & Co. Ltd 1971–79. *Political Career:* PPS to Rt Hon. Christopher Chataway, MP: as Minister of Posts and Telecommunications 1970–72, as Minister for Industrial Development 1972–74; Minister for Local Government and Environmental Services 1979–83; Secretary of State for: Environment January-June 1983, Transport June-October 1983, Employment 1983–85, Northern Ireland 1985–89, Defence 1989–92. *Spokesman:* Opposition Front Bench Spokesman for Industry 1975–76; Shadow Spokesman for Energy 1976–79. *Select Committees*

(Former): Member: Standards in Public Life 1994–97. *Miscellaneous:* Chairman, Intelligence and Security Committee 1994–. *Honours:* PC 1979; CH 1992. *Countries of Interest:* Asia, Europe, USA. *Recreations:* Cricket, skiing. *Electoral Notes:* Member for Bridgwater since March 12, 1970 By-election. *Address:* The Rt Hon. Tom King, CH, MP, House of Commons, London, SW1A 0AA *Tel:* 020 7219 4566 *Fax:* 020 7219 0612 *Tel (Constituency):* 01278 423110 *Fax (Constituency):* 01278 431034 *E-mail:* tomkingmp@parliament.uk.

KINGHAM, Tess (Teresa Jane) *(Gloucester)   Lab majority 8,259*

Daughter of Roy Thomas Kingham, deeds clerk, and Patricia Ribbian Kingham (née Murphy). Born May 4, 1963; educated Dartford Girls Grammar School; Royal Holloway College, London University (BA Hons German with Italian); University of East Anglia (PGCE Modern Languages). Married October 26, 1991, Mark Luetchford (1 daughter, twin son and daughter). *Trades Union:* Member: TGWU. *Profession:* Communications Director. *Career:* Liaison Officer, Norfolk, British Trust for Conservation Volunteers 1984–85; National Appeals Director, War on Want 1985–90; Marketing and Communications Director, Blue Cross 1990–92; Editor, Youth Express 1992–94; Communications Manager, Oxfam 1994–96; Communications Director, War on Want 1996–97. *Select Committees (Current):* Member: International Development 1997–. *Party Groups:* Member: Oxford, Swindon and Gloucester Cooperative Society, Co-op Party, Labour Women's Network; Vice-Chair, Campaign Group of Labour MPs. *International Bodies:* Member, Inter-Parliamentary Union (IPU). *Other:* School Governor; Member: Campaign Vietnam Cinema; Vice-Chair, Gloucester Furniture Recycling Project; Member, Egypt Exploration Society; Nicaragua Solidarity Campaign; Western Sahara Campaign; Patron, Gloucester Family Support. *Miscellaneous:* President Mozambique Angola Committee. *Special Interests:* European Union, Foreign Affairs, Overseas Aid and Development. *Countries of Interest:* Central America (Nicaragua, El Salvador etc), Southern Africa (S Africa, Angola, Mozambique), Russia, Germany, Albania. *Recreations:* Modern music (not classical), art and dance, archaeology, Egyptology, walking, food, international travel, enjoying my family! (husband, children and dog). *Electoral Notes:* Contested Cotswolds 1994 European Parliament Elections. Member for Gloucester since May 1, 1997. *Clubs:* Royal Commonwealth Club. *Address:* Tess Kingham, MP, House of Commons, London, SW1A 0AA *Tel:* 020 7219 4611. *Constituency:* Gloucester Labour Party, Transport House, 1 Pullman Court, Gloucester GL1 3ND *Tel:* 01452 311870 *Fax:* 01452 311874 *E-mail:* hnewton@parliament.uk.

KIRKBRIDE, Julie *(Bromsgrove)   Con majority 4,895*

Daughter of late Henry Raymond Kirkbride and Barbara Kirkbride (née Bancroft). Born June 5, 1960; educated Highlands School, Halifax; Girton College, Cambridge (MA Economics and History); Graduate School of Journalism, University of California; Rotary Foundation Scholar 1982–83. Married 1997, The Rt Hon. Andrew Mackay, MP *(qv)*, son of late Robert and late Olive Mackay. *Profession:* Journalist. *Career:* Researcher, Yorkshire Television 1983–86; Producer, BBC News and Current Affairs 1986–89; ITN 1989–92; Political Correspondent, *Daily Telegraph* 1992–96; Social Affairs Editor, *Sunday Telegraph* 1996. *Select Committees (Current):* Member: Catering 1998–, Culture, Media and Sport 1999– *(Former):* Member: Social Security 1997–99. *Party Groups:* Vice-President, The Cambridge Union Society 1981. *International Bodies:* International Republican Institute Lecturer in Romania 1995; Member, Executive Committee, Commonwealth Parliamentary Association (CPA) UK Branch 1999–. *Special Interests:* Tax, European Union, Social Security, Law and Order, Health. *Recreations:* Walking, opera. *Electoral Notes:* Member for Bromsgrove since May 1, 1997. *Address:* Julie Kirkbride, MP, House of Commons, London, SW1A 0AA *Tel:* 020 7219 6417. *Constituency:* Conservative Association, 37 Worcester Road, Bromsgrove, Worcestershire *Tel:* 01527 872135.

KIRKWOOD, Archy *(Roxburgh and Berwickshire)   LD majority 7,906*

Son of David Kirkwood. Born April 22, 1946; educated Cranhill School; Heriot-Watt University (BSc (Pharmacy)). Married December 30, 1972, Rosemary, daughter of Edward Chester (1 son 1 daughter). *Career:* Solicitor; Notary Public. *Political Career:* Aide to Rt Hon. David Steel MP 1971–75 and 1977–78; Sponsored: Access to Personal Files Act 1987 (Private Member's Bill), Access to Medical Reports Act 1988 (Private Member's Bill). *Whip:* Liberal Democrat Deputy Chief Whip 1989–92, Chief Whip 1992–97. *Spokesman:* Liberal Spokesman on: Health and Social Services, Social Security 1985–87; Alliance Spokesman on Overseas Development 1987; Liberal Spokesman on Scotland 1987–88; Convenor and Spokesman on Welfare and Social Security 1989–94; Liberal Democrat Shadow Leader of the House 1994–97; Former Spokesman on Community Care; Spokesman on Social Security and Welfare 1997–. *Select Committees (Current):* Member: Court of Referees 1997–, Liaison 1997–; Chairman: Social Security 1997– *(Former):* Member: Finance and Services 1992–97, Liaison 1992–97, Selection 1992–97. *Party Groups:* Social and Liberal Democrat Convenor on Welfare, Health and Education 1988–89. *Trust:* Trustee: Joseph Rowntree Reform Trust 1985–, Chairman 1999–, Industry and Parliament Trust 1997–. *Awards:* Rowntree Political Fellow 1971. *Miscellaneous:* Member, House of Commons Commission 1997–. *Publications:* Author of *Long Term Care – a Framework for Reform* (with Julian Astle). *Special Interests:* Freedom of Information, Health, Social Security, Human Rights. *Recreations:* Music, photography. *Electoral Notes:* Member for Roxburgh and Berwickshire since June 1983. *Address:* Archy Kirkwood Esq, MP, House of Commons, London, SW1A 0AA *Tel:* 020 7219 4217 *Fax:* 020 7219 6437 *E-mail:* kirkwood@parliament.uk.

KUMAR, Ashok *(Middlesbrough South and East Cleveland)   Lab majority 10,607*

Son of Mr J. R. Saini and late Mrs S. Kumari. Born May 28, 1956; educated Rykenld School for Boys; Derby and District College of Art and Technology; University of Aston in Birmingham (BSc Chemical Engineering, MSc Process Analysis and Development, PhD Fluid Mechanics). *Trades Union:* Member: Association of University Teachers 1982–84, Steel and Industrial Managers' Union 1984–. *Profession:* Research Scientist. *Career:* Research Fellow, Imperial College, London 1982–85; Research Scientist, British Steel 1985–97. *Councils, Public Bodies:* Councillor, Middlesbrough Borough Council 1987–97. *Select Committees (Current):* Member: Science and Technology 1997–, Deregulation 1999–. *Party Groups:* Joined Labour Party 1972. *Other:* Member: Middlesbrough Law Centre 1985–95, Institute of Chemical Engineers, Institute of Energy. *Miscellaneous:* Board Member, Parliamentary Office of Science and Technology (POST) 1997–; Vice-President, Federation of Economic Development Authorities (FEDA). *Sportsclubs:* Marton Cricket Club. *Publications:* Articles in Scientific and Mathematical Journals. *Special Interests:* Trade and Industry, Education, Local Government. *Countries of Interest:* Japan, USA, India, Korea, Kazakhstan, Bahrain. *Recreations:* Listening to music, reading history and philosophy books, playing badminton and cricket. *Electoral Notes:* Member for Langbaurgh 1991 By-election – 1992, and for Middlesbrough South and East Cleveland since May 1, 1997. *Address:* Dr Ashok Kumar, MP, House of Commons, London, SW1A 0AA *Tel:* 020 7219 4460. *Constituency:* 6–8 Wilson Street, Guisborough, Cleveland, TS14 6NA *Tel:* 01287 610878 *Fax:* 01287 631894 *E-mail:* ashokkumarmp@parliament.uk.

L

LADYMAN, Dr Stephen John *(South Thanet)   Lab majority 2,878*

Son of Frank Ladyman, engineer, and of Winifred Ladyman. Born November 6, 1952; educated Birkenhead Institute; Liverpool Polytechnic (BSc Applied Biology); Strathclyde University (PhD for research into Isotopic Abundances in Soil Development). Married Janet Baker (1 daughter 2 stepsons 1 stepdaughter). *Trades Union:* Member, GMB. *Profession:* Computer Manager. *Career:* Computer Manager, Pfizer Central Research. *Councils, Public Bodies:* Councillor, Thanet District Council 1995–99, Chair, Labour Group 1995–97, Chairman, Finance Committee 1995–97. *Select Committees (Current):* Member: Environment, Transport and Regional Affairs 1999–. *Party Groups:* Former Chair, Thanet South Constituency Labour Party; Member, Fabian Society. *Miscellaneous:* Membe: European Standing Committee B 1998, European Standing Committee C 1999–. *Sportsclubs:* Manager, Under 15s Ramsgate Football Club. *Special Interests:* Environment, Economics, Industry, Science and Technology, Research. *Recreations:* Football, family, golf. *Electoral Notes:* Contested Wantage General Election 1987. Member for South Thanet since May 1, 1997. *Address:* Dr Stephen Ladyman, MP, House of Commons, London, SW1A 0AA *Tel:* 020 7219 6946. *Constituency:* Willson Hall, Willsons Road, Ramsgate, Kent, CT11 9LZ *Tel:* 01843 852696 *Fax:* 01843 852689 *E-mail:* ladymans@parliament.uk.

LAING, Eleanor *(Epping Forest)   Con majority 5,252*

Daughter of late Matthew Pritchard and Betty Pritchard (née McFarlane). Born February 1, 1958; educated St Columba's School, Kilmacolm, Renfrewshire; Edinburgh University (BA, LLB) (First Woman President of Union). Married June 25, 1983, Alan, son of Alan and Margaret Laing. *Profession:* Solicitor. *Career:* Practised Law in Edinburgh, City of London and Industry; Special Adviser to Rt Hon. John MacGregor, MP: as Secretary of State for Education 1989–90, as Leader of the House of Commons 1990–92, as Secretary of State for Transport 1992–94. *Whip:* An Opposition Whip: (Constitutional, Education and Employment) 1999, (Social Security; Trade and Industry) 1999, (International Development; Trade and Industry; Wales) 1999–. *Select Committees (Former):* Member: Education and Employment 1997–98, Employment Sub-Committee 1997–98, Environment, Transport and Regional Affairs 1998–99, Transport Sub-Committee 1998–99. *Special Interests:* Education, Transport, Economic Policy, Constitution, Devolution. *Countries of Interest:* Australia, Gibraltar, USA, New Zealand. *Recreations:* Theatre, music, golf. *Electoral Notes:* Contested Paisley North 1987. Member for Epping Forest since May 1, 1997. *Address:* Mrs Eleanor Laing, MP, House of Commons, London, SW1A 0AA *Tel:* 020 7219 4203 *Fax:* 020 7219 0980. *Constituency:* Thatcher House, 4 Meadow Road, Loughton, Essex, G10 4HX *Tel:* 020 8508 6608 *Fax:* 020 8508 8099.

LAIT, Mrs Jacqui *(Beckenham)   Con majority 1,227*

Daughter of late Graham Lait and of Margaret Lait. Born December 16, 1947; educated Paisley Grammar School; Strathclyde University. Married June 1, 1974, Peter Jones, son of late Anthony and Lilian Jones. *Career:* Public relations, Jute Industries Ltd 1968–70 Visnews Ltd 1970–74 Government Information Service 1974–79 Parliamentary Adviser, Chemical Industries Association 1980–84 Parliamentary Consultant – own business 1984–92. *Councils, Public Bodies:* Chairman, City and East London Family Health Services Authority 1987–91. *Political Career:* PPS: to Parliamentary Under-Secretaries of State, Department of Social Security 1994–95, to Rt Hon. William Hague, MP, as Secretary of State for Wales 1995–96,. *Whip:* Assistant Government Whip 1996–97; An Opposition Whip: (Cabinet Office; Duchy of Lancaster; Environment, Transport and the Regions) 1999, (Environment, Transport and the Regions; Social Security) 1999–. *Select Committees (Current):* Member: Deregulation 1997– *(Former):* Member: Health 1992–93, Scottish Affairs 1994–95, Catering 1998–99, Science and Technology 1998–99. *International Bodies:* Chairman, British Section, European Union of Women 1990–92. *Trust:* Trustee, National Missing

Persons Helpline. *Miscellaneous:* First woman in the Conservative Whips Office 1996–97; Executive Member, 1922 Committee 1998–99. *Special Interests:* Trade and Industry, European Union, Health. *Countries of Interest:* Australia, Europe, South Africa, USA. *Recreations:* Walking, swimming, theatre, food and wine. *Electoral Notes:* Contested Strathclyde West in Euro-Election 1984 and Tyne Bridge in Westminster By-election December 1985. Member for Hastings and Rye 1992–97, and for Beckenham since November 20, 1997 By-election. *Address:* Mrs Jacqui Lait, MP, House of Commons, London, SW1A 0AA *Tel:* 020 7219 4551 *Fax:* 020 7219 0141 *E-mail:* jacquilaitmp@parliament.uk.

LANSLEY, Andrew David, CBE *(South Cambridgeshire)*   Con majority 8,712

Son of Thomas Lansley, OBE, and Irene Lansley. Born December 11, 1956; educated Brentwood School; Exeter University (BA Politics 1979). Married November 30, 1985, Marilyn, general practitioner, daughter of Clive and Jennifer Biggs (3 daughters). *Career:* Department of Industry (Department of Trade and Industry 1984–87) 1979–87; Private Secretary to Secretary of State, at Department of Trade and Industry 1984–85; Principal Private Secretary, to Rt Hon Norman Tebbit, MP, as Chancellor of the Duchy of Lancaster 1985–87; Policy Director, British Chambers of Commerce 1987–89; Deputy Director-General, British Chambers of Commerce 1989–90; Director, Conservative Research Department 1990–95; Director, Public Policy Unit 1995–97.

Councils, Public Bodies: Vice-President, Local Government Association. *Political Career:* Member, Shadow Cabinet 1999–; Shadow Minister for the Cabinet Office 1999–. *Select Committees (Former):* Member: Health 1997–98. *Party Groups:* A Vice-Chairman, Conservative Party (with responsibility for Policy Renewal) 1998–. *Other:* Member, National Union Executive Committee 1990–95; Patron: Association for Spinal Injury Research Rehabilitation and Reintergration (ASPIRE), Stroke and Action for Dysphasic Adults (STRADA) Cambridgeshire Small Business Group, International Centre for Child Studies, Headway. *Honours:* CBE 1996. *Publications: A Private Route,* 1988; Co-author *Conservatives and the Constitution,* 1997. *Special Interests:* Trade and Industry, Economic Policy, Small Businesses, Health, Local Government, Police, Film Industry. *Countries of Interest:* USA, Japan, Egypt, Israel, France, Germany, South Africa. *Recreations:* Spending time with my children, films, biography, history, cricket. *Electoral Notes:* Member for South Cambridgeshire since May 1, 1997. *Address:* Andrew Lansley Esq, CBE, MP, House of Commons, London, SW1A 0AA *Tel:* 020 7219 6416 *Fax:* 020 7219 6835. *Constituency:* 153 St Neots Road, Harwick, Cambridge, CB3 7QJ *Tel:* 01954 212707 *Fax:* 01954 212707 *E-mail:* lansleya@parliament.uk.

LAWRENCE, Jackie *(Preseli Pembrokeshire)*   Lab majority 8,736

Daughter of the late Sidney and Rita Beale. Born August 9, 1948; educated Upperthorpe School, Darlington, County Durham; Upperthorpe College; Open University. Married David Lawrence, local government officer (2 sons 1 daughter). *Trades Union:* Member, TGWU. *Career:* Assistant to Nick Ainger, MP; TSB Bank plc. *Councils, Public Bodies:* Leader, Labour Group, Pembrokeshire County Council; Councillor, Dyfed County Council 1993–96; Member, Dyfed Powys Police Authority; Former Member, Pembrokeshire Coast National Park Committee. *Select Committees (Former):* Member: Welsh Affairs 1997–99. *Party Groups:* Member, Labour Party 24 years; Election Agent, Pembroke County Constituency 1992; Former Chairman, Pembroke Constituency Labour

Party; Former Secretary, Pembroke Constituency Labour Party; Hon. Treasurer, Welsh Regional Group of Labour MPs 1999, Hon. Secretary 1999–. *Other:* Member: RSPB, West Wales Naturalists Trust, Amnesty International, War on Want. *Recreations:* Walking. *Electoral Notes:* Member for Preseli Pembrokeshire since May 1, 1997. *Address:* Jackie Lawrence, MP, House of Commons, London, SW1A 0AA *Tel:* 020 7219 3510. *Constituency:* Fulke Street, Milford Haven, Pembrokeshire, SA73 2HH *Tel:* 01646 697969 *Fax:* 01646 698830 *E-mail:* lawrencej@parliament.uk.

LAXTON, Bob (Robert) *(Derby North) Lab majority 10,615*

Son of Alan and Elsie Laxton. Born September 7, 1944; educated Woodlands Secondary School; Derby College of Art and Technology. Divorced (1 son). *Trades Union:* Member, Communication Workers' Union. *Career:* TU Branch Officer, Communication Workers' Union; Telecommunications Engineer, BT plc 1961–. *Councils, Public Bodies:* Derby City Council: Councillor 1979–97, Council Leader 1986–88, 1994–97; Chair, East Midlands LGA to 1997. *Select Committees (Current):* Member: Trade and Industry 1997–. *Party Groups:* Joined Labour Party 1977; Ward Secretary. *Miscellaneous:* Labour Party Conference Debate, Local Government 1995; Various broadcasts on West Midlands BBC TV covering local government and Derby City Council issues. *Special Interests:* Local Government. *Countries of Interest:* Germany. *Recreations:* Hill walking. *Electoral Notes:* Member for Derby North since May 1, 1997. *Address:* Bob Laxton Esq, MP, House of Commons, London, SW1A 0AA *Tel:* 020 7219 4096 *Fax:* 020 7219 2329. *Constituency:* 1st Floor, Abbots Hill Chamber, Gower Street, Derby, DE1 1SD *Tel:* 01332 206699 *Fax:* 01332 206444.

LEIGH, Edward Julian Egerton *(Gainsborough) Con majority 6,826*

Son of late Sir Neville Leigh, KCVO, former Clerk to the Privy Council. Born July 20, 1950; educated Oratory School, Berkshire; French Lycee, London; Durham University (BA History 1972) (President of Union). Married July 25, 1984, Mary Goodman (3 sons 3 daughters). *Profession:* Barrister/Arbitrator. *Career:* Member: Conservative Research Department 1973–75, Private Office of Rt Hon. Margaret Thatcher, MP, as Leader of the Opposition 1976–77; Barrister, Inner Temple 1977. *Councils, Public Bodies:* Councillor: Richmond Borough Council 1974–78, GLC 1977–81. *Political Career:* PPS to the Rt Hon. John Patten, MP, Minister of State, Home Office 1990; Parliamentary Under-Secretary of State, Department of Trade and Industry 1990–93. *Select Committees (Current):* Member: Social Security 1997– *(Former):* Member: Social Security 1995–97, Agriculture 1996–97, Deregulation 1997. *Party Groups:* Former Chairman, Durham University Conservative Association. *Trust:* Fellow, Industry and Parliament Trust. *Miscellaneous:* Chairman, National Council for Civil Defence; Director, Coalition For Peace Through Security 1981–83. *Honours:* Knight of Honour and Devotion of the Sovereign Military Order of Malta. *Publications: Right Thinking,* 1982; *Onwards from Bruges,* 1989; *Choice and Responsibility – The Enabling State,* 1990. *Special Interests:* Defence, Foreign Affairs, Agriculture. *Recreations:* Walking, reading. *Electoral Notes:* Contested Teesside, Middlesbrough October 1974. Member for Gainsborough and Horncastle 1983–97, and for Gainsborough since May 1, 1997. *Address:* Edward Leigh Esq, MP, House of Commons, London, SW1A 0AA *Tel:* 020 7219 6480. *Constituency:* 23 Queen Street, Market Rasen, Lincolnshire *Tel:* 01673 844501.

LEPPER, David *(Brighton Pavilion) Lab/Co-op majority 13,181*

Son of late Harry Lepper, lorry driver, and Maggie Lepper. Born September 15, 1945; educated Gainsborough Secondary Modern, Richmond; Wimbledon Secondary School; University of Kent; University of Sussex; Polytechnic of Central London (BA Hons English and American Literature, Postgraduate CertEd, Postgraduate Diploma in Film, Postgraduate Certificate in Media Education); Fellow, University of Sussex. Married 1966, Jeane (1 son 1 daughter). *Trades Union:* Member, NUT 1969–. *Profession:* Teacher. *Career:* Secondary School Teacher 1969–96; Author of publications on the cinema. *Councils, Public Bodies:* Councillor, Brighton Council 1980–97, Council Leader 1986, Mayor 1993–94. *Select Committees (Current):* Member: Broadcasting 1997–. *Party Groups:* Member: Fabian Society, Socialist Education Association, Socialist Health Association, SERA, Labour Animal Welfare Society. *International Bodies:* Member: CPA 1997–, IPU. *Other:* Board Member, Alzheimers and Related Dementia Suffers Society, Brighton (ARDIS); Member: Alzheimers Disease Society, Brighton Cares, Brighton MENCAP; Patron, Brighton Age Concern. *Trust:* Trustee: Brighton Youth Orchestra, Lighthouse Media. *Miscellaneous:* Member, European Standing Committee B 1998–. Fellow, University of Sussex Society. *Publications:* Author of

John Wayne, 1986; Contributor to British Film Institute publications. *Special Interests:* Cultural Industries, Media, Multimedia, Community Regeneration, Consumer Issues, Animal Welfare, Leasehold Reform, Town Centre Issues, Cyprus. *Countries of Interest:* France, Italy, Japan, Cyprus. *Recreations:* Music, cinema, reading fiction and poetry, watching professional cycling. *Electoral Notes:* Contested Brighton Pavilion 1992. Member for Brighton Pavilion since May 1, 1997. *Clubs:* Brighton Trades and Labour. *Address:* David Lepper Esq, MP, House of Commons, London, SW1A 0AA *Tel:* 020 7219 4421 *Fax:* 020 7219 5814. *Constituency:* John Saunders House, 179 Preston Road, Brighton, East Sussex, BN1 6AG *Tel:* 01273 551532 *Fax:* 01273 550617.

LESLIE, Christopher *(Shipley)*   *Lab majority 2,996*

Born June 28, 1972; educated Bingley Grammar School; University of Leeds (BA Hons, MA Industrial and Labour Studies). *Trades Union:* Member: TGWU, GMB. *Career:* Political Research Assistant; Office Administrator. *Councils, Public Bodies:* Councillor, Bradford City Council 1994–98. *Political Career:* PPS to Lord Falconer of Thoroton, QC, as Minister of State, Cabinet Office 1998–. *Select Committees (Former):* Member: Public Accounts 1997–98. *Special Interests:* Industrial Policy, Economic Policy, Environment, Local Government. *Recreations:* Travel, tennis, cinema, opera, art. *Electoral Notes:* Member for Shipley since May 1, 1997. *Address:* Christopher Leslie Esq, MP, House of Commons, London, SW1A 0AA *Tel:* 020 7219 4424 *E-mail:* lesliec@currantbun.com.

LETWIN, Oliver *(West Dorset)*   *Con majority 1,840*

Son of Professor William Letwin and late Dr Shirley Robin Letwin. Born May 19, 1956; educated Eton College; Trinity College, Cambridge (BA, MA, PhD); London Business School. Married September 15, 1984, Isabel Grace, daughter of Professor and Mrs J. F. Davidson, FRS (1 son 1 daughter). *Profession:* Company Director. *Career:* Visiting Fellow (Procter Fellow), Princeton University, USA 1980–81; Research Fellow, Darwin College, Cambridge 1981–82; Special Adviser to Sir Keith Joseph as Secretary of State for Education 1982–83; Special Adviser, Prime Minister's Policy Unit 1983–86; N. M. Rothschild & Son, Merchant Bank 1986–: Manager 1986, Assistant Director 1987, Director 1991–. *Spokesman:* An Opposition Front Bench Spokesman for: Constitutional Affairs, Scotland and Wales 1998–99, the Treasury 1999–. *Select Committees (Former):* Member: Deregulation 1998–99. *Party Groups:* Member: Conservative Disability Group, Conservative Green Initiative. *Other:* Member, Tony Green Initiative; Patron, Joseph Weld Hospice. *Miscellaneous:* Member, European Standing Committee B 1998. Fellow, Royal Society of Arts. *Publications: Ethics, Emotion and the Unity of the Self*, 1985; *Aims of Schooling*, 1986; *Privatising the World*, 1989; *Aims of Sanity*, 1989; *Drift to Union*, 1989; *The Purpose of Politics*, 1999; Plus Articles and Reviews in learned and popular journals. *Special Interests:* Microeconomic Policy, Employment, Education. *Countries of Interest:* Eastern Europe, Africa. *Recreations:* Ski-ing, sailing, tennis, reading, writing books. *Electoral Notes:* Contested Hackney North 1987, Hampstead and Highgate 1992. Member for West Dorset since May 1, 1997. *Clubs:* St Stephen's Constitutional; Carlyle. *Address:* Oliver Letwin Esq, MP, House of Commons, London, SW1A 0AA *Tel:* 020 7219 4192 *Fax:* 020 7219 0805. *Constituency:* Chapel House, Dorchester Road, Maiden Newton, Dorset, DT2 0BG *Tel:* 01300 321188 *Fax:* 01300 321233.

LEVITT, Tom *(High Peak)   Lab majority 8,791*

Son of John and Joan Levitt. Born April 10, 1954; educated Westwood High School, Leek; Lancaster University (BSc Hons); Oxford University (PGCE). Married March, 1983, Teresa, daughter of Wacek and Halina Sledziewski (1 daughter). *Trades Union:* Member, NUT 1975–; School Representative, NUT 1977–79, 1984–90; Local Association President, NUT 1985; County Division President, NUT 1988; Member: NUPE 1988–94, GMB 1995–. *Profession:* Research Consultant (Sensory Impairment and Access Issues). *Career:* Teacher: Wiltshire County Council 1976–79, Gloucestershire County Council 1980–91; Supply Teacher, Staffordshire County Council 1991–95; Sensory Awareness Trainer 1993–97; Consultant, Access for People With Sensory Impairments 1993–97. *Councils, Public Bodies:* Councillor: Cirencester Town 1983–87, Stroud District 1990–92, Derbyshire County 1993–97, Vice-Chairman of Education 1994–95. *Political Career:* PPS to Barbara Roche, MP, as Minister of State, Home Office 1999–. *Select Committees (Current):* Member: Standards and Privileges 1997–. *Party Groups:* Member, SERA. *Other:* Member: Place (Educational Charity); Friends of Buxton Museum; British Deaf Association; League Against Cruel Sports; Friends of the Earth; Amnesty International; SEA. *Sportsclubs:* Tideswell Cricket Club. *Publications:* Local Government Management Board: *Sound Policies,* 1994, *Sound Practice,* 1995, *Clear Access,* 1996. *Special Interests:* Disabled/Disability, Education, Local Government, Quarrying. *Countries of Interest:* Western Europe, Poland. *Recreations:* Cricket, Walking, Theatre. *Electoral Notes:* Contested Stroud 1987, Cotswolds (European Election) 1989, High Peak 1992. Member for High Peak since May 1, 1997. *Address:* Tom Levitt Esq, MP, House of Commons, London, SW1A 0AA *Tel:* 020 7219 6599 *Fax:* 020 7219 0935 *Tel (Constituency):* 01298 71111 *Fax (Constituency):* 01298 71522 *E-mail:* tomlevittmp@parliament.uk; *Website:* www.cel.co.uk/labour.tom.

LEWIS, Ivan *(Bury South)   Lab majority 12,381*

Son of Joe and Gloria Lewis. Born March 4, 1967; educated William Hulme Grammar School; Stand College; Bury Further Education College. Married June 3, 1990, Juliette, daughter of Leslie and Joyce Fox (2 sons). *Trades Union:* Member, MSF. *Profession:* Charity Executive. *Career:* Coordinator, Contact Community Care Group 1986–89; Community Care Manager, Jewish Social Services 1989–92; Chief Executive, Manchester Jewish Federation 1992–97. *Councils, Public Bodies:* Councillor, Bury Metropolitan Borough Council 1990–98; Chairman, Social Services Committee 1991–95. *Political Career:* PPS to Rt Hon. Stephen Byers, MP, as Secretary of State for Trade and Industry 1999–. *Select Committees (Former):* Member: Deregulation 1997–99, Health 1999. *Party Groups:* Chair, Bury South Labour Party 1991–96; Vice-Chair, Labour Friends of Israel 1997–. *Other:* Chair: Bury MENCAP 1989–92, Sedgley Park County Primary School, Prestwich Regeneration Partnership; Member, Bury Carers Partnership Management Committee; Founder Member, Coordinator and Chair, Contact Community Care Group 1986–92; Honorary Consultant, Manchester Jewish Federation. *Trust:* Trustee, Holocaust Educational Trust. *Special Interests:* Health, Crime, Education. *Countries of Interest:* Israel, USA. *Recreations:* Keen supporter of Manchester City FC. *Electoral Notes:* Member for Bury South since May 1, 1997. *Address:* Ivan Lewis Esq, MP, House of Commons, London, SW1A 0AA *Tel:* 020 7219 6404 *Fax:* 020 7219 6866. *Constituency:* 513 Bury New Road, Prestwich, Manchester, M25 3JA *Tel:* 0161–773 5500 *Fax:* 0161–773 7959 *E-mail:* heneghonp@parliament.uk.

LEWIS, Dr Julian Murray *(New Forest East)   Con majority 5,215*

Son of Samuel Lewis and late Hilda Lewis. Born September 26, 1951; educated Dynevor Grammar School, Swansea; Balliol College, Oxford (MA); St Antony's College, Oxford (DPhil). *Armed Forces:* Seaman, HM Royal Naval Reserve 1979–82. *Profession:* Historian, Defence Consultant, Political Researcher. *Career:* Doctoral Research (Strategic Studies) 1975–77, 1978–81; Secretary, Campaign for Representative Democracy 1977–78; Research Director and Director, Coalition for Peace Through Security 1981–85; Director, Policy Research Associates 1985–; Deputy Director, Conservative Research Department 1990–96. *Select Committees (Current):* Member: Welsh Affairs 1998–. *Party Groups:* Treasurer, Oxford University Conservative Association 1971;

Secretary, Oxford Union 1972; Honorary Vice-President, Greater London and West London Young Conservatives, various dates. *Other:* Member: RNLI, Medical Charities. *Trust:* Trustee, British Military Powerboat Trust. *Miscellaneous:* Joint organiser of campaign against militant infiltration of the Labour Party 1977–78. *Publications: Changing Direction: British Military Planning for Post-War Strategic Defence, 1942–1947,* 1988; *Who's Left? An Index of Labour MPs and Left-Wing Causes, 1985–1992,* 1992; *Labour's CND Cover-Up,* 1992; *The Liberal Democrats: The Character of Their Politics,* 1993; *What's Liberal? Liberal Democrat Quotations and Facts,* 1996. *Special Interests:* Defence, Security, Foreign Affairs, Europe, Media, Education, Mental Health. *Countries of Interest:* Western Europe, Central and Eastern Europe, Russia. *Recreations:* History, fiction, films, music, photography. *Electoral Notes:* Contested Swansea West 1983. Member for New Forest East since May 1, 1997. *Clubs:* Athenaeum, Totton Conservative. *Address:* Dr Julian Lewis, MP, House of Commons, London, SW1A 0AA *Tel:* 023 8081 4817 (Parliamentary Office). *Constituency:* New Forest East Conservatives, 3 The Parade, Southampton Road, Cadnam, Hampshire, SO40 2NG *Tel:* 023 8081 4905 *Fax:* 023 8081 4906 *Website:* www.julianlewis.net.

LEWIS, Terry *(Worsley)   Lab majority 17,741*

Son of Andrew Lewis, dockworker. Born December 29, 1935; educated Our Lady of Mount Carmel School, Salford; Technical College. Married 1958, Audrey, daughter of William Clarke (1 son and 1 son deceased). *Trades Union:* Sponsored by TGWU. *Armed Forces:* RAMC 1954–56. *Career:* Personnel Officer 1961–76; Local Government 1976–84. *Councils, Public Bodies:* Deputy Leader, Bolton Borough Council 1980–83: Chairman, Education Committee 1981–83. *Select Committees (Current):* Member: Standards and Privileges 1997– *(Former):* Member: Environment 1991–92, Members' Interests 1992–97. *Special Interests:* Local Government. *Electoral Notes:* Member for Worsley since June 1983. *Address:* Terry Lewis Esq, MP, House of Commons, London, SW1A 0AA *Tel:* 020 7219 3479. *Constituency:* Emlyn Hall, Emlyn Street, Worsley, Greater Manchester, M28 3JZ *Tel:* 0161–703 8017 *Fax:* 0161–703 8346.

LIDDELL, The Rt Hon. Helen Lawrie *(Airdrie and Shotts)   Lab majority 15,412*

Daughter of Hugh and Bridget Reilly. Born December 6, 1950; educated St Patrick's High School, Coatbridge; Strathclyde University. Married 1972, Dr Alistair Liddell (1 son 1 daughter). *Trades Union:* Scottish TUC: Head of Economics Department 1971–75, Assistant Secretary 1975–76. *Career:* Economics Correspondent, BBC Scotland 1976–77; General Secretary, Labour Party in Scotland 1977–88; Director, Personnel and Public Affairs, Scottish Daily Record and Sunday Mail (1986) Ltd 1988–92; Chief Executive, Business Venture Programme 1993–94. *Political Career:* Economic Secretary, HM Treasury 1997–98; Minister of State: Scottish Office (Minister for Education) 1998–99, Department of the Environment, Transport and the Regions (Minister for Transport) 1999, Department of Trade and Industry (Minister for Energy and Competitiveness in Europe) 1999–. *Spokesman:* Opposition Spokeswoman on Scotland 1995–97. *Other:* Chair, Independent Review into the future of the Scottish Symphony; Vice-Chair, Rehab Scotland 1990–92; Orchestra and Orchestra of Scottish Opera 1993–94; Chair, UN5O: Scotland 1994. *Honours:* PC 1998. *Publications: Elite,* 1990. *Special Interests:* Media, Scottish Affairs, Economic Policy, Trade and Industry. *Countries of Interest:* USA, Europe, Russia. *Recreations:* Cooking, hill-walking, music, writing. *Electoral Notes:* Contested Fife East October 1974. Member for Monklands East from June 30, 1994 By-Election–1997, and for Airdrie and Shotts since May 1, 1997. *Address:* The Rt Hon. Helen Liddell, MP, House of Commons, London, SW1A 0AA *Tel:* 020 7219 6507 *Fax:* 020 7219 3390. *Constituency:* 115 Graham Street, Airdrie, Lanarkshire, ML6 6DE *Tel:* 01236 748777 *Fax:* 01236 748666 *E-mail:* tlo.liddell@tlo.dti.gov.uk.

LIDINGTON, David *(Aylesbury)* *Con majority 8,419*

Son of Roy and Rosa Lidington. Born June 30, 1956; educated Haberdashers' Aske's School, Elstree; Sidney Sussex College, Cambridge (MA History, PhD). Married August 5, 1989, Helen, daughter of late Lieutenant-Colonel and of Mrs T. F. Parry (4 sons). *Career:* British Petroleum 1983–86; Rio Tinto Zinc 1986–87; Special Adviser to Rt Hon. Douglas Hurd, CBE, MP, at Home Office 1987–89, at Foreign and Commonwealth Office 1989–90; Senior Consultant, The Public Policy Unit 1991–92. *Political Career:* PPS: to Rt Hon. Michael Howard, QC, MP, as Home Secretary 1994–97, to Rt Hon. William Hague, MP, as Leader of the Opposition 1997–99. *Spokesman:* An Opposition Front Bench Spokesman for Home Affairs 1999–. *Select Committees (Former):* Member: Education 1992–96. *Party Groups:* Joined Conservative Party 1975; Various offices in: Cambridge University (Chairman), Enfield North Conservative Association. *Special Interests:* Home Office, Foreign Office, Education. *Countries of Interest:* Europe, Hong Kong. *Recreations:* History, choral singing, reading. *Electoral Notes:* Contested Vauxhall in 1987 General Election. Member for Aylesbury since April 9, 1992. *Clubs:* Aylesbury Conservative. *Address:* David Lidington Esq, MP, House of Commons, London, SW1A 0AA *Tel:* 020 7219 3000 *Fax:* 020 7219 2564. *Constituency:* 100 Walton Street, Aylesbury, Buckinghamshire, HP21 7QP *Tel:* 01296 482102 *Fax:* 01296 398481 *E-mail:* richardsmall@aylesbury.tory.org.uk.

LILLEY, The Rt Hon. Peter Bruce *(Hitchin and Harpenden)* *Con majority 6,671*

Son of Arnold and Lillian (née Elliott) Lilley. Born August 23, 1943; educated Dulwich College; Clare College, Cambridge. Married May 24, 1979, Gail Ansell. *Career:* Director: Great Western Resources Ltd 1985–87, Greenwell Montague Stockbrokers 1986–87 (Head, oil investment department); Investment Advisor on North Sea oil and other energy industries 1972–84; Economic Advisor on underdeveloped countries 1966–72; Consultant Director, Conservative Research Department 1979–83. *Political Career:* PPS: to Lord Bellwin, as Minister of State for Local Government, Department of the Environment, to Hon. William Waldegrave 1984, MP, as Parliamentary Under-Secretary of State, Department of Environment 1984, to Rt Hon. Nigel Lawson, as Chancellor of the Exchequer 1984–87; Economic Secretary to the Treasury 1987–89; Financial Secretary to the Treasury 1989–90; Secretary of State for: Trade and Industry 1990–92, Social Security 1992–97; Contested Leadership of the Conservative Party June 1997; Member, Shadow Cabinet 1997–99; Shadow Chancellor of the Exchequer 1997–98; Deputy Leader of the Opposition (with overall responsibility for development of party policy) 1998–99. *Party Groups:* Chairman, Bow Group 1973–75. *Honours:* PC 1990. *Special Interests:* Economic Policy, European Union, Education, Race Relations. *Countries of Interest:* France. *Electoral Notes:* Contested Haringey, Tottenham October 1974. Member for St Albans 1983–97, and for Hitchin and Harpenden since May 1, 1997. *Clubs:* Carlton. *Address:* The Rt Hon. Peter Lilley, MP, House of Commons, London, SW1A 0AA *Tel:* 020 7219 4577 *Fax:* 020 7219 3840.

LINTON, Martin *(Battersea)* *Lab majority 5,360*

Son of Sydney Linton and late Karin Linton. Born August 11, 1944; educated Limpsfield Primary School, Surrey; Christ's Hospital, Sussex; Pembroke College, Oxford (MA Philosophy, Politics and Economics); Université de Lyon. Married 1975, Kathy (died 1995), daughter of Joseph and Jessie Stanley of Barrow-in-Furness (2 daughters). *Trades Union:* Former member, NUJ; Member, GMB. *Career:* Journalist on: *Daily Mail* 1966–71, *Financial Times* 1971, *Labour Weekly* 1971–79, *Daily Star* 1980–81, *The Guardian* 1981–97. *Councils, Public Bodies:* Councillor, London Borough of Wandsworth 1971–82, Chairman, Recreation Committee 1971–77. *Select Committees (Current):* Member: Home Affairs 1997–. *Party Groups:* Joined Labour Party 1968; Former Chairman, Constituency Labour Party. *International Bodies:* Treasurer, British Swedish Parliamentary Association. *Other:* President, Battersea Arts Centre. *Publications: Get Me Out Of Here*, 1980; *The Swedish Road to Socialism*, 1984; *Labour Can Still Win*, 1988; *The Guardian Guide to the House of Commons*, (editor) 1992; *What's wrong with first-past-the-post?*, 1993; *Money and Votes*, 1994;

Was It The Sun Wot Won It?, 1995; Editor, *Guardian Election Guide*, 1997; *Making Votes Count*, 1998. *Special Interests:* Housing, Education, Political Finance, Media Influence, Voting Systems. *Countries of Interest:* Sweden. *Recreations:* Playing music, watching football. *Electoral Notes:* Member for Battersea since May 1, 1997. *Address:* Martin Linton Esq, MP, House of Commons, London, SW1A 0AA *Tel:* 020 7219 4619 *Fax:* 020 7219 5728. *Constituency:* 177 Lavender Hill, London, SW11 5TE *Tel:* 020 7207 3060 *Fax:* 020 7207 3063 *E-mail:* lintonm@parliament.uk.

LIVINGSTONE, Ken *(Brent East)   Lab majority 15,882*

Son of late Robert Moffat Livingstone and late Ethel Ada Livingstone. Born June 17, 1945; educated Tulse Hill Comprehensive; Phillipa Fawcett College of Education (Teaching Certificate). Married 1973, Christine Pamela Chapman (marriage dissolved 1982). *Trades Union:* Member: MSF 1969–75, TGWU 1977–. *Career:* Cancer Research Worker 1962–70; Teacher Training College 1970–73. *Councils, Public Bodies:* Lambeth Council: Councillor 1971–78, Vice-Chairman, Housing Committee 1971–73; Camden Council: Councillor 1978–82, Chairman, Housing Committee 1978–80, Councillor, GLC 1973–86: Chairman, Ethnic Minorities Committee and Council Leader 1981–86. *Select Committees (Former):* Member: Northern Ireland Affairs 1997–99. *Party Groups:* Member, Labour Party National Executive Committee 1987–89, 1997–98. *Other:* Elected to Council, The Zoological Society of London 1994, Vice-President 1996–98. *Publications: If voting changed anything, they'd abolish it,* 1987; *Livingstone's Labour: A Programme for the Nineties,* 1989. *Special Interests:* Economic Policy, Democratising Britain, Northern Ireland. *Countries of Interest:* Former Soviet Union, Tibet, USA. *Recreations:* Films, science-fiction, walking, gardening. *Electoral Notes:* Contested Camden, Hampstead 1979. Member for Brent East since June 1987. *Address:* Ken Livingstone Esq, MP, House of Commons, London, SW1A 0AA *Tel:* 020 7219 6941 *Fax:* 020 7219 1202 *E-mail:* 105277.3653@compuserve.com *Website:* http://www.poptel.org.uk/ken-livingstone/.

LIVSEY, Richard Arthur Lloyd, CBE *(Brecon and Radnorshire)   LD majority 5,097*

Son of late Arthur Norman and Lilian Maisie Livsey. Born May 2, 1935; educated Talgarth County Primary School; Bedales; Seal Hayne Agricultural College (NDA); Reading University (MSc). Married April 3, 1964, Irene, daughter of Ronald and Margaret Earsman (2 sons 1 daughter). *Career:* Agricultural Development Officer, ICI 1961–67; Farm Manager, Blairdrummond Estate, Perthshire 1967–71; Senior Lecturer in Farm Management, Welsh Agricultural College, Llanbadarn Fawr, Aberystwyth 1971–85. *Spokesman:* Spokesman on: Agriculture 1985–87, Welsh Affairs 1987–92; Principal Spokesman for Wales 1997–. *Select Committees (Current):* Member: Welsh Affairs 1997–. *Party Groups:* Joined Liberal Party 1960; Leader, Welsh Liberal Democrats 1988–92, 1997–; Member, Constitution Reform Strategy Committee 1997–. *Honours:* CBE 1994. *Special Interests:* Agriculture. *Recreations:* Cricket, fishing, cycling. *Electoral Notes:* Contested (Liberal) Perth and East Perthshire 1970, Pembroke 1979, Brecon and Radnor 1983. Member for Brecon and Radnor from July 4, 1985 By-election to 1992 (Liberal 1985–88, Lib Dem 1988–92), and for Brecon and Radnorshire since May 1, 1997. *Address:* Richard Livsey Esq, CBE, MP, House of Commons, London, SW1A 0AA *Tel:* 020 7219 3000. *Constituency:* 99 The Street, Brecon, Powys, LD3 7LS *Tel:* 01874 625 739 *Fax:* 01874 625 635.

LLOYD, Anthony Joseph *(Manchester Central)* Lab majority 19,682

Son of late Sydney Lloyd, Lithographic printer. Born February 25, 1950; educated Stretford Grammar School; Nottingham University; Manchester Business School. Married September 21, 1974, Judith Ann, daughter of John Dynes and Eileen Tear (1 son 3 daughters). *Career:* University lecturer. *Councils, Public Bodies:* Councillor, Trafford District Council 1979–84. *Political Career:* Minister of State, Foreign and Commonwealth Office 1997–99. *Spokesman:* Opposition Spokesman on: Transport 1988–89, Employment 1988–92, 1993–94, Education (responsible for co-ordinating policies on education and training) 1992–94, The Environment and London 1994–95, Foreign and Commonwealth Affairs 1995–97. *Special Interests:* Civil Liberties, Disarmament, Immigration Policy, Race Relations, Industrial Policy, Human Rights, Overseas Aid and Development. *Countries of Interest:* CIS, Guatemala, Japan, Poland. *Recreations:* Family. *Electoral Notes:* Member for Stretford 1983–97, and for Manchester Central since May 1, 1997. *Address:* Anthony Lloyd Esq, MP, House of Commons, London, SW1A 0AA *Tel:* 020 7219 4442.

LLOYD, The Rt Hon. Sir Peter Robert Cable *(Fareham)* Con majority 10,358

Son of late David Lloyd, JP. Born November 12, 1937; educated Tonbridge School; Pembroke College, Cambridge. Married October 14, 1967, Hilary, daughter of Donald Creighton (1 son 1 daughter). *Career:* Until May 1979 was Marketing Manager, United Biscuits Ltd. *Political Career:* PPS: to Hon. Adam Butler, MP, as Minister of State for Northern Ireland 1981–82, to Rt Hon. Sir Keith Joseph, Bt, MP, as Secretary of State for Education and Science July 1983–84, Parliamentary Under Secretary of State: Department of Social Security 1988–89; Home Office: Parliamentary Under Secretary 1989–92, Minister of State 1992–94. *Whip:* Assistant Government Whip 1984–86; Lord Commissioner of the Treasury 1986–88. *Select Committees (Former):* Member: Public Service 1995–97, Treasury 1997–99; Chairman: Treasury Sub-Committee 1998–99; Member: Treasury Sub-Committee 1999. *Party Groups:* Chairman, Bow Group 1972–73; Editor, Crossbow 1974–76. *International Bodies:* Joint Chairman, Council for the Advancement of Arab British Understanding 1997–. *Other:* Chairman, New Bridge; Council Member, Howard League for Penal Reform. *Miscellaneous:* Member, House of Commons Commission 1997–. *Honours:* PC 1994; Knighted 1995. *Electoral Notes:* Contested Nottingham West February and October 1974 General Elections. Member for Fareham since May 1979. *Clubs:* Players Theatre. *Address:* The Rt Hon. Sir Peter Lloyd, MP, House of Commons, London, SW1A 0AA *Tel:* 020 7219 4442.

LLWYD, Elfyn *(Meirionnydd Nant Conwy)* PC majority 6,805

Son of late Huw Meirion Hughes, and of Hefina Hughes. Born September 26, 1951; educated Ysgol Dyffryn Conwy, Llanrwst Grammar School; University College, Aberystwyth; College of Law, Chester (LLB Hons Wales). Married July 27, 1974, Eleri Llwyd, daughter of Huw Lloyd Edwards, dramatist (1 son 1 daughter). *Profession:* Barrister. *Career:* Solicitor until 1997; President, Gwynedd Law Society 1990–91; Barrister 1997–. *Whip:* Plaid Cymru Parliamentary Whip 1995–. *Spokesman:* Former Spokesman for: Transport, Treasury and Economy, Trade and Industry, Social Security, Disability; Northern Ireland 1997–99, Spokesman for: Housing 1997–, Local Government 1997–, Tourism 1997–, Home Affairs 1999–. *Select Committees (Current):* Member: Welsh Affairs 1998– *(Former):* Member: Welsh Affairs 1992–95, 1996–97. *Party Groups:* Member, Plaid Cymru Policy Cabinet 1994–, Parliamentary Leader 1997–. *Other:* Council Member, NSPCC Wales; Member, Parliamentary Panel UNICEF; Hon Member, Gorsedd of Bards 1998. *Trust:* Chair, Dolgellan Hatchery Trust. *Sportsclubs:* President: Estimaner Angling Association, Betws-y-Coed Football Club, Llanuwchllyn Football Club, Bala Rugby Club; Vice-President, Dolgellau Old Grammarians' Rugby Club. *Special Interests:* Civil Liberties, Agriculture, Tourism, Home Affairs. *Countries of Interest:* Spain, Scotland, USA, Wales, Greece. *Recreations:* Pigeon breeding, choral singing, rugby, fishing, cycling. *Electoral Notes:* Member for Meirionnydd Nant Conwy since April 9, 1992. *Address:* Elfyn Llwyd Esq, MP, House of Commons, London, SW1A 0AA *Tel:* 020 7219 3555. *Constituency:* Bryn Meurig, Dolgellau, Gwynedd, LL40 1DS *Tel:* 01341 422661 *Fax:* 01341 423990.

LOCK, David Anthony *(Wyre Forest)   Lab majority 6,946*

Son of John, research engineer, and Jeanette Lock, nurse. Born May 2, 1960; educated Esher Grammar School; Woking Sixth Form College; Jesus College, Cambridge (MA); Central London Polytechnic (DipL); Gray's Inn (Wilson Scholar 1985) (Barrister); Wilson Scholar 1985. Married April 8, 1985, Bernadette Gregory (1 son 2 daughters). *Trades Union:* Member, MSF. *Profession:* Barrister. *Career:* Management Trainee, GEC; Barrister 1985–97. *Councils, Public Bodies:* Councillor, Wychavon District Council 1995–97, Chair: Amenities and Economic Development Committee, Wychavon Leisure Management Board. *Political Career:* PPS: Lord Chancellor's Department 1997–98, to Rt Hon. the Lord Irvine of Lairg, QC, as the Lord Chancellor 1998–99; Parliamentary Secretary 1999–. *Select Committees (Former):* Member: Deregulation 1997–98. *Party Groups:* Member, Society of Labour Lawyers. *Publications:* Various legal publications; Contributor to *Beyond 2002: Long-term Policies for Labour*, ed. Martin Linton, MP. *Special Interests:* Economics, Employment, Human Rights, Legal issues. *Countries of Interest:* Switzerland, USA, France. *Recreations:* Family, cycling, friends, squash, running. *Electoral Notes:* Member for Wyre Forest since May 1, 1997. *Address:* David Lock Esq, MP, House of Commons, London, SW1A 0AA *Tel:* 020 7219 4652 *Fax:* 020 7219 6193. *Constituency:* Lowland House, Green Street, Kidderminster, Worcestershire, DY10 1GJ *Tel:* 01562 827007 *Fax:* 01562 751007 *E-mail:* lock@parliament.uk.

LORD, Michael *(Central Suffolk and North Ipswich)   Con majority 3,538*

Son of late John Lord, Schoolmaster. Born October 17, 1938; educated William Hulme's Grammar School; Christ's College, Cambridge (MA) (Rugby Blue). Married 1965, Jennifer Margaret, daughter of late Thomas Childs (1 son 1 daughter). *Profession:* Arboricultural Consultant. *Career:* Farmer and taught agriculture 1962–66; Director, Power Line Maintenance Ltd 1966–68; Founded Lords Tree Services Ltd 1968; Aboricultural Consultant 1983. *Councils, Public Bodies:* North Bedfordshire Borough Council: Former Councillor, Chairman, Policy Commission 1974–77; Bedfordshire County Council: Former Councillor, Chairman, Further Education Committee 1981–83. *Political Career:* PPS to: Rt Hon. John MacGregor MP, as Minister of Agriculture, Fisheries and Food 1984–85, as Chief Secretary to the Treasury 1985–87; Second Deputy Chairman, Ways and Means 1997–. *Select Committees (Current):* Second Deputy Chairman of Ways and Means: Chairmen's Panel 1997–, Court of Referees 1997–, Standing Orders 1998– *(Former):* Member: Parliamentary Commissioner for Administration 1990–97. *International Bodies:* Parliamentary delegate, The Council of Europe and the Western European Union 1987–91; Member, Executive Committee, Inter Parliamentary Union (IPU) British Group 1995–97. *Other:* Vice-President, The Arboricultural Association, President 1989–95; Hon. Secretary, Parliamentary Golfing Society (Captain). *Miscellaneous:* Cambridge Rugby Blue. FArbA. *Special Interests:* Agriculture, Forestry, Environment. *Recreations:* Golf, sailing, gardening. *Electoral Notes:* Contested Manchester Gorton in 1979. Member for Central Suffolk 1983–97, and for Central Suffolk and North Ipswich since May 1, 1997. *Address:* Michael Lord Esq, MP, House of Commons, London, SW1A 0AA *Tel:* 020 7219 5055.

LOUGHTON, Timothy Paul *(East Worthing and Shoreham)   Con majority 5,098*

Son of Reverend Michael Loughton and Mrs Pamela Dorothy Loughton. Born May 30, 1962; educated The Priory School, Lewes, Sussex; University of Warwick (BA First Class Honours); Clare College, Cambridge. Married July 25, 1992, Elizabeth Juliet, daughter of John and Juliet MacLauchlan (1 son 2 daughters). *Trades Union:* Member: BIFU, CTU. *Profession:* Fund Manager. *Career:* Fund Manager, Fleming Private Asset Management, City of London 1984–, Director 1992–. *Select Committees (Current):* Member: Environmental Audit 1997–. *Party Groups:* Chairman, Lewes Young Conservatives 1978; Vice-Chairman: Sussex Young Conservatives 1979, Lewes Constituency Conservative Association 1979, South East Area Young Conservatives 1980; Secretary, Warwick University Conservative Association 1981–82; Member, Cambridge University Conservative Association 1983–84; Vice-Chairman, Battersea Conservative Association 1990–91;

Member, London Area Conservative Executive Committee 1993–; Life Vice-President, Sheffield Brightside Constituency Association 1993–; Deputy Chairman, Battersea Constituency Conservative Association 1994–; Executive Committee Member, Selsdon Group 1994–; Member, Carlton Club Political Committee 1994–; Member, Bow Group; Chairman, Conservative Disability Group. *International Bodies:* Member: CPA, IPU. *Other:* Chairman, Battersea Business Forum 1994–96; Member: Sussex Archaeological Society, Society of Sussex Downsmen, RNLI, RSPCA, British Museum Society, Centre for Policy Studies, Institute of Economic Affairs, Worldwide Fund for Nature, Tibet Action (UK), Court of Sussex University; Patron: League of Friends of Worthing Hospital, St Barnabas Hospice, Worthing, Patron, Worthing Hockey Club. *Trust:* Vice-Chairman, Shoreham Old Town Hall Trust. *Miscellaneous:* General Election PA to Tim Eggar, MP 1987; English Wine and Stock Exchange Lecturer; Member: Finance Bill Standing Committee 1997–98, Linking Agriculture and Farming (LEAF); Parliamentary Representative National Association Special Education Needs; Vice-President, Worthing United Nations Association; Member, European Standing Committee C 1999–. *Sportsclubs:* Captain, Fleming's Hockey Team. MSi(Dip). *Special Interests:* Finance, Foreign Affairs, Home Affairs, Drugs, Education (Special Needs), Environmental Taxation. *Countries of Interest:* Latin America, Middle East, India Sub-continent. *Recreations:* Skiing, tennis, hockey, wine, archaeology. *Electoral Notes:* Contested Sheffield Brightside 1992. Member for East Worthing and Shoreham since May 1, 1997. *Clubs:* Carlton. *Address:* Timothy Loughton Esq, MP, House of Commons, London, SW1A 0AA *Tel:* 020 7219 4471 *Fax:* 020 7219 0461. *Constituency:* Haverfield House, 4 Union Place, Worthing, West Sussex, BN11 1LG *Tel:* 01903 235168 *Fax:* 01903 219755 *E-mail:* loughtont@parliament.uk.

LOVE, Andrew *(Edmonton)* *Lab/Co-op majority 13,472*

Son of late James Love and Olive Love. Born March 21, 1949; educated Greenock High School; Strathclyde University (BSc Hons); Association of Chartered Institute of Secretaries. Married March 12, 1983, Ruth, daughter of late Jack and Esther Rosenthal. *Trades Union:* Member (former Branch Chairman), TGWU; Former National Executive Member, NACO. *Profession:* Chartered Secretary. *Career:* Parliamentary Officer, Co-operative Party. *Councils, Public Bodies:* Councillor, London Borough of Haringey 1980–86. *Select Committees (Current):* Member: Public Accounts 1997–, Deregulation 1999–. *Party Groups:* Joined Labour Party 1975; Chairman: Hornsey and Wood Green Labour Party 1987–89, Policy Committee, Greater London Labour Party 1990–94, Co-operative Parliamentary Group 1999–. *Other:* Former Member, NETRHA; Former Vice-Chairman, North London FE College; Member, St Pancras Housing Association; Vice-Patron, Helen Rollason Cancer Appeal 1999–. *Trust:* Trustee, ICOF. *Sportsclubs:* Muswell Hill Golf Club. ACIS. *Special Interests:* Housing, Regeneration, Health. *Countries of Interest:* France, Cyprus. *Recreations:* History, opera, cinema. *Electoral Notes:* Contested Edmonton 1992. Member for Edmonton since May 1, 1997. *Address:* Andrew Love Esq, MP, House of Commons, London, SW1A 0AA *Tel:* 020 7219 5497 *Fax:* 020 7219 6623. *Constituency:* 205 Fore Street, Edmonton, London, N18 *Tel:* 020 8807 6657/020 8803 0574 *Fax:* 020 8807 1673 *E-mail:* lovea@parliament.uk.

LUFF, Peter James *(Mid Worcestershire)* *Con majority 9,412*

Son of late Thomas Luff, master printer, and late Joyce Luff. Born February 18, 1955; educated Windsor Grammar School; Corpus Christi College, Cambridge (MA Economics). Married May 8, 1982, Julia, daughter of Lieutenant-Commander P. D. Jenks, RN (1 son 1 daughter). *Profession:* Public Relations Consultant. *Career:* Research Assistant to Rt Hon. Peter Walker, MBE, MP 1977–80; Head of private office to Rt Hon. Edward Heath, MBE, MP 1980–82; Company Secretary, family stationery business, Luff & Sons Ltd to 1987; Account Director, Director and Managing Director, Good Relations Public Affairs Ltd 1982–87; Assistant Managing Director, Good Relations Ltd 1990–92; Senior consultant, Lowe Bell Communications 1989–90. *Political Career:* PPS: to Rt Hon. Tim Eggar, MP, as Minister of State for Industry and Energy, Department of Trade and Industry 1993–96, to Rt Hon. Lord Mackay of Clashfern, as Lord Chancellor 1996–97, to Rt Hon. Ann Widdecombe MP, as Minister for Prisons 1996–97. *Select Committees (Current):* Chairman: Agriculture 1997–; Member: Liaison 1997– *(Former):* Member: Welsh Affairs 1992–97, Transport 1993,

Consolidation Etc Joint Bills Committee 1995–97, Public Service 1996–97. *Other:* Patron, Conservative Students 1995–98; Vice-President, Severn Valley Railway 1997–. *Miscellaneous:* Member, Joseph Rowntree Inquiry into Planning for Housing 1992–94; Member, Armed Forces Parliamentary Scheme (Royal Navy) 1996. *Sportsclubs:* Worcestershire County Cricket. Fellow, Institute of Public Relations. *Publications: Supporting Excellence – Funding Dance and Drama Students* (Bow Group), 1995. *Special Interests:* Railways, Trade and Industry, Rural Affairs, Performing Arts, International Development. *Countries of Interest:* Hong Kong, Falkland Islands, Israel, India, Mongolia. *Recreations:* Steam railways, theatre, photography. *Electoral Notes:* Contested Holborn and St Pancras in 1987 General Election. Member for Worcester 1992–97, and for Mid Worcestershire since May 1, 1997. *Clubs:* Royal Automobile. *Address:* Peter Luff Esq, MP, House of Commons, London, SW1A 0AA *Tel (Constituency):* 01905 763952 *Fax (Constituency):* 01905 763952 *E-mail:* luffpj@parliament.uk.

LYELL, The Rt Hon. Sir Nicholas Walter, QC *(North East Bedfordshire)   Con majority 5,883*

Son of late Hon. Mr. Justice Lyell (Sir Maurice Legat). Born December 6, 1938; educated Stowe School; Christ Church, Oxford; College of Law. Married September 2, 1967, Susanna Mary, daughter of Professor Charles Fletcher, CBE, MD (2 sons 2 daughters). *Armed Forces:* National Service, Royal Artillery (commissioned) 1957–59. *Profession:* Barrister. *Career:* Walter Runciman & Co. (Shipping) Newcastle upon Tyne 1962–64; Called to The Bar 1965; Private Practice at The Bar in Commercial and Employment Law 1965–86, 1997–; QC 1980; Bencher, Inner Temple 1986. *Political Career:* PPS to the Attorney General 1979–86; Parliamentary Under-Secretary of State DHSS 1986–87; Solicitor General 1987–92; Attorney General 1992–97; Shadow Attorney General 1997–99. *Select Committees (Former):* Member: Privileges 1994–96. *Party Groups:* Executive Chairman, Society of Conservative Lawyers 1985–86, 1997–. Member, Salters' Company. *Honours:* Knighted 1987; PC 1990. *Special Interests:* Home Affairs, Employment, Defence, Penal Affairs and Policy, Environment. *Recreations:* Gardening, shooting, drawing. *Electoral Notes:* Contested Lambeth Central October 1974 General Election. Member for Hemel Hempstead 1979–83, for Mid Bedfordshire 1983–97, and for North East Bedfordshire since May 1, 1997. *Clubs:* Brooks's, Pratt's, Beefsteak. *Address:* The Rt Hon. Sir Nicholas Lyell, QC, MP, House of Commons, London, SW1A 0AA *Tel:* 020 7219 6631. *Constituency:* Biggleswade Conservative Club, St Andrews Street, Biggleswade, Bedfordshire, SG18 1YB *Tel:* 01767 313385 *Fax:* 01767 316697.

M

McALLION, John *(Dundee East)   Lab majority 9,961*

Son of late Joseph and Norah McAllion. Born February 13, 1948; educated St Augustine's Secondary School, Glasgow; St Andrews University (MA, BEd). Married October 9, 1971, Dr Susan Jean, daughter of Alfred and Grace Godlonton (2 sons). *Career:* School teacher: St Saviour's High School, Dundee 1973–78; Balgowan School 1978–82; Research Assistant to Bob McTaggart, MP for Glasgow Central 1982–86. *Councils, Public Bodies:* Regional Councillor, Tayside 1984–87; Convenor, Tayside Regional Council 1986–87. *Spokesman:* Opposition Spokesman on Scotland 1994–96. *Select Committees (Former):* Member: Energy 1992, Scottish Affairs 1997–99. *Party Groups:* Member, Campaign Group 1997–. *Other:* Member, Shelter (Scotland) Advisory Board. *Special Interests:* Employment, Industry, Education, Housing. *Countries of Interest:* Cuba, Cyprus, Czechoslovakia, USA. *Recreations:* Football, reading, watching ice-hockey. *Electoral Notes:* Member for Dundee East since June 1987. MSP for the Constituency of Dundee East since May 6, 1999. *Address:* John McAllion Esq, MP, MSP, House of Commons, London, SW1A 0AA *Tel:* 020 7219 5048 *Fax:* 020 7219 5834. *Constituency:* 18B Marketgait, Dundee, DD1 1QR *Tel:* 01382 207000 *Fax:* 01382 221280.

McAVOY, Thomas McLaughlin *(Glasgow Rutherglen)* Lab/Co-op majority 15,007

Son of late Edward McAvoy, steelworker, and late Frances McLaughlin McAvoy. Born December 14, 1943; educated St Columbkilles Primary and Junior Secondary Schools. Married December 14, 1968, Eleanor, daughter of late William Kerr (4 sons). *Trades Union:* Former Shop Steward, AEU. *Councils, Public Bodies:* Chairman, Rutherglen Community Council 1980; Strathclyde Regional Councillor for Rutherglen and Toryglen 1982–87. *Whip:* Opposition Whip 1991–93, 1996–97; Comptroller of HM Household (Government Whip) 1997–. *Select Committees (Current):* Member: Finance and Services 1997– *(Former):* Member: Northern Ireland Affairs 1994–96. *Party Groups:* Member, Co-operative Party. *Other:* Chairman: Fernhill Tenants Association, Rutherglen Federation of Tenants Associations. *Special Interests:* Social Services. *Countries of Interest:* Ireland, USA. *Electoral Notes:* Member for Glasgow Rutherglen since June 1987. *Address:* Thomas McAvoy Esq, MP, House of Commons, London, SW1A 0AA *Tel:* 020 7219 3000 *E-mail:* thomas.mcavoy@hm-treasury.gov.uk.

McCABE, Stephen James *(Birmingham Hall Green)* Lab majority 8,420

Son of James and Margaret McCabe. Born August 4, 1955; educated Port Glasgow, Senior Secondary; Moray House College, Edinburgh (Diploma in Social Studies, Certificate Qualification Social Work); University of Bradford (MA). Married August 2, 1991, Lorraine Lea, daughter of Willis and Barbara Clendon (1 son 1 daughter). *Trades Union:* Member, MSF; Former Shop Steward, NALGO. *Profession:* Social Worker. *Career:* Social Work; Education Adviser. *Councils, Public Bodies:* Birmingham City Council: Councillor 1990–98, Chairman, Transportation Committee 1993–96. *Select Committees (Current):* Member: Northern Ireland Affairs 1998– *(Former):* Member: Deregulation 1997–99. *Other:* School Governor. *Miscellaneous:* Member of various local Management Committees. *Sportsclubs:* Local Cricket Club. *Special Interests:* Community Care, Transport, Economic Issues, Police. *Recreations:* Reading, football, hill walking. *Electoral Notes:* Member for Birmingham Hall Green since May 1, 1997. *Address:* Stephen McCabe Esq, MP, House of Commons, London, SW1A 0AA *Tel:* 020 7219 4842/3509 *Fax:* 020 7219 0367. *Constituency:* c/o The Labour Party, 14–16 Bristol Street, Birmingham *Tel:* 0121–622 6761 *Fax:* 0121–666 7322.

McCAFFERTY, Christine *(Calder Valley)* Lab majority 6,255

Daughter of late John and late Dorothy Livesley. Born October 14, 1945; educated Whalley Range Grammar School For Girls, Manchester; Footscray High School, Melbourne, Australia. Married 1st, Michael McCafferty (1 son), married 2nd, David Tarlo. *Trades Union:* Member: NALGO 1967–81, MSF 1994–. *Profession:* Women's Health Counsellor. *Career:* Welfare Worker (Disabled), CHS Manchester 1963–70; Education Welfare Officer, Manchester Education Committee 1970–72; Registrar of Marriages, Bury Registration District 1978–80; Project Worker, Calderdale Well Woman Centre 1989–96. *Councils, Public Bodies:* Councillor: Calderdale MBC, Calderdale District Council 1991–, Hebden Royd Town Council 1991–95; Member: West Yorkshire Police Authority 1994–, Police Complaints Committee 1994–. *Select Committees (Former):* Member: Procedure 1997–99. *Party Groups:* Member, Co-op Party 1990–. *Other:* Member: Calderdale Well Women Centre, Redwater Arts; Governor/Press Officer, Central St School 1988–92; Governor, Luddenden Dene School 1993–95; West Yorkshire Lay Prison Visitor 1994–. *Trust:* Trustee, Trades Club Building, Hebden Bridge 1992–; Director, Royd Regeneration Ltd 1996–. *Special Interests:* Health, Social Services. *Countries of Interest:* Gambia, India, Australia. *Recreations:* Swimming, reading, caravanning. *Electoral Notes:* Member for Calder Valley since May 1, 1997. *Address:* Christine McCafferty, MP, House of Commons, London, SW1A 0AA *Tel:* 020 7219 5026. *Constituency:* Labour Party, Trades Club, Holme Street, Hebden Bridge, West Yorkshire *Tel:* 01422 846791.

McCARTNEY, The Rt Hon. Ian *(Makerfield)   Lab majority 26,177*

Son of Hugh McCartney, Labour MP. Born April 25, 1951; educated State Schools. Married 1st (1 son deceased 2 daughters) (marriage dissolved), married 2nd, December 28, 1988, Mrs Ann Parkes, daughter of Thomas and Elizabeth Kevan. *Trades Union:* TGWU: Branch Secretary 1968, Shop steward 1970; Former Chairperson, TGWU Parliamentary Group. *Career:* Secretary to Roger Stott, CBE, MP *(qv)* until 1987. *Councils, Public Bodies:* Wigan Borough Councillor 1982–87. *Political Career:* Minister of State: Department of Trade and Industry 1997–99, Cabinet Office 1999–. *Spokesman:* Opposition Front Bench Spokesperson on: National Health Service 1992–94, Employment 1994–96, Education and Employment (Chief Employment Spokesperson) 1996–97. *Select Committees (Former):* Member: Social Security 1991–92. *Party Groups:* Labour Party full-time officer 1973; Member, Labour Party National Executive Committee 1996–; Member, PLP General Election Campaign (Country) 1999–; Vice-Chair, Labour Party National Policy Forum; Member, Labour Party Joint Policy Commission. *Other:* Chairman, Children's Wheelchair Fund; Vice-President, BARLA (British Amateur Rugby League Association). *Honours:* PC 1999. *Special Interests:* Local Government, Fire Service, Civil Defence, Health and Safety at Work, Health Service, Social Services, Employment. *Countries of Interest:* Australia. *Recreations:* Wigan Rugby League. *Electoral Notes:* Member for Makerfield since June 1987. *Clubs:* Platt Bridge Labour. *Address:* The Rt Hon. Ian McCartney, MP, House of Commons, London, SW1A 0AA *Tel:* 020 7219 4503. *Constituency:* 1st Floor, Gerrard Winstanley House, Crawford Street, Wigan, Greater Manchester, WN1 1NJ *Tel:* 01942 824029 *Fax:* 01942 828171 *E-mail:* mccartney@cabinet-office.gov.uk *Website:* http://www.cabinet-office.gov.uk.

McCARTNEY, Robert Law, QC *(North Down)   UKU majority 1,449*

Son of late William and Elizabeth McCartney. Born April 24, 1936; educated Grosvenor Grammar School, Belfast; Queen's University, Belfast. Married June 22, 1960, Maureen Ann, daughter of James and Sarah Bingham (1 son 3 daughters). *Profession:* Barrister. *Career:* Solicitor, Supreme Court of Justice, Northern Ireland 1962; Called to the Bar of Northern Ireland 1968; QC 1975. *Political Career:* Member, Northern Ireland Assembly representing North Down 1982–86; Northern Ireland Forum 1996–98; New Northern Ireland Assembly 1998–. *Party Groups:* Leader, United Kingdom Unionist Party. *Special Interests:* Northern Ireland's Constitutional future. *Recreations:* Reading political and military history, walking, all sport generally, particularly rugby football. *Electoral Notes:* Contested North Down in 1983 and 1987 General Elections. Member for North Down since June 15, 1995 By-Election. *Address:* Robert McCartney Esq, QC, MP, House of Commons, London, SW1A 0AA *Tel:* 020 7219 6590 *Fax:* 020 7219 0371. *Constituency:* 10 Hamilton Road, Bangor, Co Down, BT20 4LE *Tel:* 028 9127 2994 *Fax:* 028 9146 5037 *E-mail:* contactus@ukunionists.freeserve.co.uk *Website:* http://www.welcome.to/ukup.

McDONAGH, Siobhain *(Mitcham and Morden)   Lab majority 13,741*

Daughter of Cummin and Breda McDonagh, retired builder and nurse. Born February 20, 1960; educated Holy Cross Convent; University of Essex. *Career:* Clerical Officer, DHSS 1981–83; Housing Benefits Assistant 1983–84; Receptionist, Homeless Persons Unit, London Borough of Wandsworth 1984–86; Housing Adviser 1986–88; Development Co-ordinator, Battersea Church Housing Trust 1988–97. *Councils, Public Bodies:* Councillor, London Borough of Merton 1982–1997, Chair, Housing Committee 1990–95. *Select Committees (Former):* Member: Social Security 1997–98. *Party Groups:* Member, Labour Party 1976–. *Other:* Governor, Liberty Middle School and Tamworth Manor High School, Mitcham; Member: South Mitcham Community Centre, Colliers Wood Community Centre, Grenfell Housing Association, Merton MIND. *Miscellaneous:* Made first Conference Speech aged 23. *Special Interests:* Housing, Benefits, Private/Public Sector Partnership, Welfare Reform. *Recreations:* Shopping, clothes, music. *Electoral Notes:* Contested Mitcham and Morden 1987 and 1992. Member for Mitcham and Morden since May 1, 1997. *Address:* Siobhain McDonagh, MP, House of Commons, London, SW1A 0AA *Tel:* 020 7219 4678. *Constituency:* 1 Crown Road, Morden, Surrey, SM4 5DD *Tel:* 020 8542 4835 *Fax:* 020 8544 0377.

MacDONALD, Calum A *(Western Isles)   Lab majority 3,576*

Son of Malcolm MacDonald, crofter and weaver and Donella MacDonald. Born May 7, 1956; educated Bayble School; Nicholson Institute, Stornoway; Edinburgh University; University of California (PhD). *Career:* Former teaching fellow in political philosophy, University of California at Los Angeles. *Political Career:* PPS to Rt Hon. Donald Dewar, MP, as Secretary of State for Scotland May-December 1997; Parliamentary Under-Secretary of State, Scottish Office (Minister for Housing, Transport and European Affairs) December 1997–99. *Select Committees (Former):* Member: Agriculture 1987–92. *Countries of Interest:* CIS, Europe, USA. *Electoral Notes:* Member for Western Isles since June 1987. *Address:* Calum MacDonald Esq, MP, House of Commons, London, SW1A 0AA *Tel:* 020 7219 3000. *Constituency:* 4 South Beach Street, Stornoway, Isle of Lewis *Tel:* 01851 704684.

McDONNELL, John Martin *(Hayes and Harlington)   Lab majority 14,291*

Son of late Robert and Elsie McDonnell. Born September 8, 1951; educated Great Yarmouth Grammar School; Brunel University; Birkbeck, London University (BSc Government and Politics, MSc Politics and Sociology). Married 1995, Cynthia, daughter of Betsy Pinto and Richard Nunes (1 son 2 daughters). *Trades Union:* Former Shop Steward, UNISON. *Career:* Shopfloor Production Worker 1968–73; Assistant Head, Social Insurance Department, National Union of Mineworkers 1977–78; Researcher, TUC 1978–82; Head of Policy Unit, London Borough of Camden 1985–87; Chief Executive: Association of London Authorities 1987–95, Association of London Government 1995–. *Councils, Public Bodies:* GLC Councillor 1981–86: Chair Finance Committee, Deputy Leader. *Select Committees (Current):* Member: Deregulation 1999–, Unopposed Bills (Panel) 1999–. *Party Groups:* Member: Greater London Labour Party Regional Executive, National Policy Forum Labour Party, Labour Party Animal Welfare Society, Labour Party Committee on Ireland, Labour Party CND; Chair, Labour Party Irish Society. *International Bodies:* Chair, Britain and Ireland Human Rights Centre. *Other:* Member: Liberty, Action for South Africa, Hayes and Harlington Community Centre, League Against Cruel Sports. *Trust:* Member, London Wildlife Trust. *Miscellaneous:* Member, Friends of Ireland – Coalition in support of Belfast Agreement. *Sportsclubs:* Hillingdon Outdoor Activities Centre; Wayfarer Sailing Association; Vice-President, Hayes Football Club. *Publications:* Editor, *Labour Herald. Special Interests:* Economics, Local Government, Irish Affairs, Environment. *Countries of Interest:* Ireland, Kenya, Gambia, Tanzania. *Recreations:* Sailing, football, cycling, gardening, theatre, cinema. *Electoral Notes:* Member for Hayes and Harlington since May 1, 1997. *Clubs:* Member: Hayes Irish Society, Hayes and Harlington Workingmens, Hayes and Harlington History Society. *Address:* John McDonnell Esq, MP, House of Commons, London, SW1A 0AA *Tel:* 020 7219 6908 *Fax:* 020 7219 0927. *Constituency:* Hayes and Harlington Labour Party Shop, 65 Station Road, Hayes, Middlesex *Tel:* 020 8569 0010 *Fax:* 020 8569 0109 *E-mail:* mcdonnellj@parliament.uk.

McFALL, John *(Dumbarton)   Lab majority 10,883*

Son of late John and Jean McFall. Born October 4, 1944; educated St Patrick's Primary and Secondary School, Dumbarton; Paisley College of Technology; Strathclyde University (BSc Hons Chemistry, MBA); Open University (BA Education). Married October 11, 1969, Joan, daughter of Peter and Christina Ward (3 sons 1 daughter). *Career:* School teacher for 15 years; Assistant Head Teacher, Bellarmine Secondary School, Glasgow 1974–87. *Political Career:* Parliamentary Under-Secretary of State, Northern Ireland Office (Minister for Education, Training and Employment, Health and Community Relations) 1998–99, for Economy and Education 1999–. *Whip:* Opposition Whip 1989–91; A Lord Commissioner of HM Treasury (Government Whip) 1997–98. *Spokesman:* Opposition Front Bench Spokesman on Scottish Affairs (with responsibilities for Industry, Economic Affairs, Employment and Training, Home Affairs, Transport and Roads, Agriculture, Fisheries and Forestry) 1992–97. *Party Groups:* Member, Co-operative Party. *Special Interests:* Defence, Education, Economic Policy, Co-operative Development. *Countries of Interest:* Latin America, Middle East, Romania. *Recreations:* Jogging, golf, reading. *Electoral Notes:* Member for Dumbarton since June 1987. *Address:* John McFall Esq, MP, House of Commons, London, SW1A 0AA *Tel:* 020 7219 3521.

McGRADY, Edward K *(South Down)   SDLP majority 9,933*

Son of late Michael and Lilian McGrady. Born June 3, 1935; educated St Patrick's High School, Downpatrick. Married November 7, 1959, Patricia, daughter of late William and Margaret Swail (2 sons 1 daughter). *Profession:* Accountant. *Career:* Partner, M B McGrady & Co., Chartered Accountants. *Councils, Public Bodies:* Downpatrick Urban District Council: Councillor 1961–73, Chairman 1964–73; Down District Council: Councillor 1973–89, Chairman 1975. *Political Career:* Northern Ireland Assembly 1973; Minister for Co-ordination 1974; Northern Ireland Assembly 1982–86; Elected to the Northern Ireland Forum 1996–98; Elected to the Northern Ireland Assembly 1998–. *Whip:* Chief Whip, SDLP 1979–. *Spokesman:* Spokesman on: Housing, Local Government, Environment. *Select Committees (Current):* Member: Northern Ireland Affairs 1994–. *Party Groups:* Founder Member and First Chairman, SDLP 1970–72. Fellow, Institute Chartered Accountants. *Countries of Interest:* Ireland, USA. *Recreations:* Walking, gardening. *Electoral Notes:* Contested South Down in 1979 and 1983 General Elections and 1986 By-election. Member for South Down since June 1987. *Address:* Edward McGrady Esq, MP, House of Commons, London, SW1A 0AA *Tel:* 020 7219 4481. *Constituency:* 32 Saul Street, Downpatrick, County Down, BT30 6NQ *Tel:* 028 4461 2882 *Fax:* 028 4461 9574 *E-mail:* e.mcgrady@sdlp.ie.

MacGREGOR, The Rt Hon. John R. R., OBE *(South Norfolk)   Con majority 7,378*

Son of late Dr N. S. R. MacGregor. Born February 14, 1937; educated Merchiston Castle School, Edinburgh; St Andrews University (MA 1st Class Hons); King's College, London University (LLB); Fellow, King's College, London; Hon. LLD, Westminster University. Married September 22, 1962, Jean Mary Elizabeth, daughter of late L. W. E. Dungey (1 son 2 daughters). *Career:* Administrator, London University 1961–62; Editorial Staff, *New Society* 1962–63; Special Assistant to Rt Hon. Sir Alec Douglas-Home, MP 1963–64; Head of Private Office of Rt Hon. Edward Heath, MBE, MP 1965–68; Business executive in the City 1968–79; Formerly Director: Hill Samuel Registrars Ltd 1971–79, Hill Samuel & Co. Ltd 1973–79; Director: Associated British Foods 1994–, Slough Estates 1995–, Unigate 1996–; Deputy Chairman, Hill Samuel & Co. Ltd 1994–96; Director, Friends Provident 1998–. *Political Career:* Parliamentary Under-Secretary of State for Industry 1981–83; Minister of State, Ministry of Agriculture, Fisheries and Food 1983–85; Chief Secretary to the Treasury 1985–87; Minister of Agriculture, Fisheries and Food 1987–89; Secretary of State for Education and Science 1989–90; Lord President of the Council and Leader of the House of Commons 1990–92; Secretary of State for Transport 1992–94. *Whip:* Conservative Opposition Whip 1977–79; Lord Commissioner of the Treasury 1979–81. *Select Committees (Former):* Member: Privileges 1990–92, Standards and Privileges 1996–97. *Party Groups:* Formerly Chairman: Bow Group, Young Conservative External Relations Committee; First President, Conservative and Christian Democratic Youth Community. *Other:* Member, Council of King's College, London 1996–; Associate, Inner Magic Circle. *Miscellaneous:* Member, Council of Institute of Directors 1995–; Vice-President, Association of County Councils 1995–97; Member, Committee on Standards in Public Life 1997–; Deputy Chairman, Governing Bodies Association 1998–. *Honours:* OBE 1971; PC 1985. *Special Interests:* Economic and Financial Matters, Agriculture, Education, Industry, Housing, Countryside. *Countries of Interest:* Europe, USA, Australia and New Zealand, Japan. *Recreations:* Music, gardening, travel, conjuring. *Electoral Notes:* Member for South Norfolk since February 1974. *Address:* The Rt Hon. John MacGregor, OBE, MP, House of Commons, London, SW1A 0AA *Tel:* 020 7219 4439 *Fax:* 020 7219 0323. *Constituency:* Grasmere, Denmark Street, Diss, Norfolk, IP22 3LE *Tel:* 01379 642097 *Fax:* 01379 650765.

Dod *on* Disk

The Vacher Dod Parliamentary Database – configured for PC or Network

For further details please telephone the Westminster Office

020 7828 7256

McGUINNESS, Martin *(Mid Ulster)* *SF majority 1,883*

Born May 23, 1950; educated Christian Brothers' Technical College. *Career:* Chief negotiator of Sinn Fein. *Political Career:* Member, Northern Ireland Assembly 1982, 1998–; Minister for Education, Northern Ireland Assembly 1999–. *Electoral Notes:* Contested Foyle 1983, 1987 and 1992 General Elections. Member for Mid Ulster since May 1, 1997. *Address:* Martin McGuinness Esq, MP, House of Commons, London, SW1A 0AA *Tel:* 020 7219 3000. *Constituency:* 32 Burn Road, Cookstown, Co Tyrone *Tel:* 028 8676 5850 *Fax:* 028 8676 6734.

McGUIRE, Mrs Anne Catherine *(Stirling)* *Lab majority 6,411*

Daughter of late Albert Long, railway signalman, and late Agnes Long, shop worker. Born May 26, 1949; educated Our Lady of St Francis Secondary School, Glasgow; University of Glasgow (MA Hons Politics with History); Notre Dame College of Education (Diploma in Secondary Education). Married February 12, 1972, Len McGuire, son of Hugh and Ann McGuire (1 son 1 daughter). *Trades Union:* National Executive, GMB 1987–91. *Profession:* Teacher/Manager in Voluntary Sector. *Career:* Former Teacher; Development Worker/Senior Manager, Voluntary Sector; Depute Director, Scottish Council for Voluntary Organisations. *Councils, Public Bodies:* Councillor, Strathclyde Regional Council 1980–82. *Political Career:* PPS to Rt Hon. Donald Dewar, MP, as Secretary of State for Scotland December 1997–98. *Whip:* Assistant Government Whip 1998–. *Select Committees (Former):* Member: European Legislation 1997–98. *Party Groups:* Member: Labour Party for 31 years, Labour Party Scottish Executive 1984–; Chair, Labour Party Scotland 1992–93. *Trust:* Board Member, John Wheatly Centre. *Special Interests:* European Union, Rural Development, Urban Regeneration. *Countries of Interest:* USA, Germany. *Recreations:* Learning Gaelic, reading, walking. *Electoral Notes:* Member for Stirling since May 1, 1997. *Address:* Mrs Anne McGuire, MP, House of Commons, London, SW1A 0AA *Tel:* 020 7219 5014 *Fax:* 020 7219 2503. *Constituency:* 38 Forth Crescent, Stirling, FK8 1LG *Tel:* 01786 446515 *Fax:* 01786 446513 *E-mail:* mcguirea@parliament.uk.

McINTOSH, Anne Caroline Ballingall *(Vale of York)* *Con majority 9,721*

Daughter of Dr Alastair McIntosh, retired medical practitioner, and Mrs Grethe-Lise McIntosh. Born September 20, 1954; educated Harrogate College; Edinburgh University (LLB Hons 1977); Århus University, Denmark. Married September 19, 1992, John Harvey. *Profession:* Advocate. *Career:* Trainee, EEC Competition Directorate 1978; Legal Adviser, Didier and Associates, Brussels 1979–80; Apprentice, Scottish Bar, Edinburgh 1980–82; Admitted to Faculty of Advocates June 1982; Advocate, practising with Community Law Office, Brussels 1982–83; Adviser, European Democratic Group, principally on Transport, Youth Education, Culture, Tourism, Relations with Scandinavia, Austria and Yugoslavia 1983–89. *Select Committees (Current):* Member: Environment, Transport and Regional Affairs 1999–, Transport Sub-Committee 1999–. *International Bodies:* Member, European Parliament for: Essex North East 1989–94, Essex North and Suffolk South 1994–99; Assistant Whip, European Democratic Group 1989–92, Member, Committee on Transport and Tourism 1989–99, Substitute, Committee on Legal Affairs and Citizens' Rights 1989–99, Conservative Spokesman on Transport and Tourism 1992–99, Entered into Group of European People's Party 1992, Elected to Bureau of European People's Party 1994–97, Former Rapporteur on Air Transport, relations with third world countries and Trans-European Road Networks, EU Competition Policy, Air Transport Safety, Substitute, Committee on Women's Rights 1994–99, Member, Delegation to EU-Poland Joint Parliamentary Committee 1994–99; Co-Chairman, European Transport Safety Council; President, Anglia Enterprise in Europe. *Other:* President, Yorkshire (East) Enterprise in Yorkshire. *Trust:* Fellow, Industry and Parliament Trust 1995. *Miscellaneous:* Member, European Standing Committee C 1999–. *Special Interests:* Transport, Legal Affairs, Animal Welfare. *Countries of Interest:* Eastern Europe, Scandinavia. *Recreations:* Swimming, walking, cinema. *Electoral Notes:* Contested Workington,

Cumbria 1987. MEP for Essex North East 1989–94, and for Essex North and Suffolk South 1994–99. Member of Parliament for Vale of York since May 1, 1997. *Address:* Anne McIntosh, MP, House of Commons, London, SW1A 0AA *Tel:* 020 7219 0972 *Fax:* 020 7219 0972. *Constituency:* Vale of York Conservative Association, Thirsk Conservative Club, Westgate, Thirsk, North Yorkshire, YO7 1QS *Tel:* 01845 527240 *Fax:* 01845 527507.

McISAAC, Shona *(Cleethorpes)*   Lab majority 9,176

Daughter of Angus McIsaac, retired chief petty officer, and Isa (née Nicol), school dinner lady. Born April 3, 1960; educated SHAPE School, Belgium; Barne Barton Secondary Modern, Plymouth; Stoke Damerel High, Plymouth; Durham University (BSc Geography). Married April 2, 1994, Peter John Keith, son of William and Kathleen Keith. *Trades Union:* Member, NUJ. *Profession:* Sub-editor and food writer. *Career:* Senior Sub-editor, *Chat*; Deputy Chief-Sub-editor, *Bella*; Chief Sub-editor, *Woman*; Freelance Food Writer. *Councils, Public Bodies:* Councillor, London Borough of Wandsworth 1990–98. *Select Committees (Current):* Member: Standards and Privileges 1997–. *Party Groups:* Member, Labour Party 1983–. *Miscellaneous:* Member, Northern Ireland Grand Committee. *Publications:* Various work-related publications, mostly non-political. *Special Interests:* Finance, Tax, Benefits, Economic Policy. *Recreations:* Football, food, travel, cycling, archaeology of the UK, soap operas. *Electoral Notes:* Member for Cleethorpes since May 1, 1997. *Address:* Shona McIsaac, MP, House of Commons, London, SW1A 0AA *Tel:* 020 7219 5801 *Fax:* 020 7219 3047. *Constituency:* Immingham Resource Centre,, Margaret Street, Immingham, Lincolnshire, DN40 1LE *Tel:* 01469 574324 *Fax:* 01469 510841.

MACKAY, The Rt Hon. Andrew James *(Bracknell)*   Con majority 10,387

Son of late Robert and Olive Mackay. Born August 27, 1949; educated Solihull School. Married 1st, June 15, 1974, Diana Joy, daughter of late Leslie Kinchin (1 son 1 daughter) (marriage dissolved 1996); married 2nd, 1997, Julie Kirkbride, MP (*qv*), daughter of late Henry Raymond Kirkbride and Barbara Kirkbride (née Bancroft). *Career:* Consultant to various public companies. *Political Career:* PPS: to Secretary of State for Northern Ireland 1986–89, to Secretary of State for Defence 1989–92; Sponsored Licensing (Retail Sales) Act 1988 (Private Member's Bill); Member, Shadow Cabinet 1997–; Shadow Secretary of State for Northern Ireland 1997–. *Whip:* Assistant Government Whip 1992–93; Lord Commissioner of HM Treasury (Government Whip) 1993–95; Vice-Chamberlain of HM Household (Government Whip) 1995–96; Treasurer of HM Household (Deputy Chief Whip) 1996–97. *Select Committees (Former):* Member: Procedure 1994–95, Selection 1994–97. *Party Groups:* Chairman, Solihull Young Conservative 1971–74; Vice-Chairman, Solihull Conservative Association 1971–74; Member, Conservative Party National Executive 1979–82. *Miscellaneous:* Chairman, *Britain in Europe* Meriden Branch 1975 (Referendum). *Honours:* PC 1998. *Special Interests:* Foreign Affairs, Industry, Environment. *Recreations:* Golf, squash, tennis, good food, travel. *Electoral Notes:* Member for Birmingham Stechford 1977 by-election–1979. Member for Berkshire East 1983–97, and for Bracknell since May 1, 1997. *Address:* The Rt Hon. Andrew Mackay, MP, House of Commons, London, SW1A 0AA *Tel:* 020 7219 2989.

McKENNA, Mrs Rosemary, CBE *(Cumbernauld and Kilsyth)*   Lab majority 11,128

Daughter of late Cornelius Harvey, publican, and late Mary Susan Crossan. Born May 8, 1941; educated St Augustine's Comprehensive, Glasgow; Notre Dame College of Education (Diploma in Primary Education). Married September 28, 1963, James Stephen McKenna, son of Patrick and Catherine McKenna (3 sons 1 daughter). *Trades Union:* Member: Educational Institute of Scotland, GMB. *Profession:* Teacher. *Councils, Public Bodies:* Councillor, Cumbernauld and Kilsyth District Council 1984–96, Leader and Convenor of Policy and Resources 1984–88, Provost 1988–92, Leader 1992–94; Member: Cumbernauld Development Corporation 1985–97, Scottish Enterprise 1993–96, 1996–. *Political Career:* Joint PPS to Ministers of State, Foreign and

Commonwealth Office 1999–. *Select Committees (Former):* Member: Scottish Affairs 1997–98, Statutory Instruments (Joint Committee) 1997–99, Catering 1998–99, European Legislation 1998, European Scrutiny 1998–99. *Party Groups:* Member, Labour Party 1966–; Various positions at Branch and Constituency level; Chair, Constituency Party 1979–85; Member, Scottish Executive and National Local Government Committee 1994–98. *International Bodies:* Member, Committee of the Regions 1993–97; Chair, Ad-Hoc Committee on Equality Issues until 1997; Chair, Scotland Europa 1994–96; Chair, UK and European Standing Committees of Women Elected Members of the Council of European Municipalities and Regions 1995–98. *Other:* Chairman, SLIC (Scottish Libraries and Information Council) 1998–. *Trust:* Cumbernauld Theatre Trust 1984–95. *Miscellaneous:* Member, Convention of Scottish Local Authorities 1984–, Vice-President 1992–94, President 1994–96. *Honours:* CBE. *Special Interests:* Constitutional Reform, Democratic Renewal and Inclusive Politics. *Countries of Interest:* France, USA. *Recreations:* Reading. *Electoral Notes:* Member for Cumbernauld and Kilsyth since May 1, 1997. *Address:* Mrs Rosemary McKenna, CBE, MP, House of Commons, London, SW1A 0AA *Tel:* 020 7219 5804 *Fax:* 020 7219 2503. *Constituency:* Lennox House, Lennox Road, Cumbernauld Road, Strathclyde, G67 ILL *Tel:* 01236 457788 *Fax:* 01236 457313.

MACKINLAY, Andrew *(Thurrock)* *Lab majority 17,256*

Son of Daniel and Monica Mackinlay. Born April 24, 1949; educated Salesian College, Chertsey, Surrey; (DMA). Married October 21, 1972, Ruth, daughter of Joe and Selina Segar (2 sons 1 daughter). *Trades Union:* Former NALGO District Officer; Member, TGWU. *Profession:* Chartered Secretary. *Career:* Formerly local government officer with Surrey County Council 1965–75; NALGO Official 1975–92. *Councils, Public Bodies:* Councillor, London Borough of Kingston upon Thames 1971–78. *Whip:* Opposition Whip 1993–94. *Select Committees (Current):* Member: Foreign Affairs 1997–, Unopposed Bills (Panel) 1997– *(Former):* Member: Transport 1992–97. *Party Groups:* Joined Labour Party 1966; Vice-Chair, South and East Group of Labour MPs 1997–. *International Bodies:* Member, Parliamentary Delegation to OSCE; Member, Executive Committee, Commonwealth Parliamentary Association (CPA) UK Branch 1999–. *Miscellaneous:* Armed Forces Parliamentary Scheme (Royal Marines) 1997–98. *Sportsclubs:* Patron, Tilbury Football Club. Associate Member, Chartered Institute of Secretaries and Administrators. *Special Interests:* Constitution, Devolution, Electoral Reform, Police, Ports Industry, River Thames, Transport, Channel Islands, Isle of Man, Irish Affairs, Elderly, Environment. *Countries of Interest:* Poland, Belgium, France, Baltic States, Czech/Slovak Republics, Hungary, Falkland Islands, Gibraltar, USA. *Recreations:* Visiting and studying battlefields of World War 1 in France and Belgium, collecting Labour and Trade Union ephemera and memorabilia; non-league soccer. *Electoral Notes:* Contested Kingston-upon-Thames, Surbiton February and October 1974, Croydon Central 1983 and Peterborough 1987 General Elections; London South and Surrey East 1984 European Parliament Election. Member for Thurrock since April 9, 1992. *Clubs:* Chadwell Workingmens'. *Address:* Andrew Mackinlay Esq, MP, House of Commons, London, SW1A 0AA *Tel:* 020 7219 3000 *Tel (Constituency):* 01375 850359.

MACLEAN, The Rt Hon. David *(Penrith and The Border)* *Con majority 10,233*

Born May 16, 1953; educated Fortrose Academy; Aberdeen University. Married 1977. *Political Career:* Parliamentary Secretary, Ministry of Agriculture, Fisheries and Food 1989–92; Minister of State: at Department of the Environment 1992–93, at Home Office 1993–97. *Whip:* Assistant Government Whip 1987–89; Lord Commissioner of HM Treasury (Government Whip) 1988–89. *Honours:* PC 1995. *Electoral Notes:* Member for Penrith and The Border since July 1983 By-election. *Address:* The Rt Hon. David Maclean, MP, House of Commons, London, SW1A 0AA *Tel:* 020 7219 6494 *Tel (Constituency):* 01697 478519.

McLEISH, Henry *(Central Fife)   Lab majority 13,713*

Son of Harry McLeish, manual worker, local council, and late Mary McLeish. Born June 15, 1948; educated Buckhaven High School, Fife; Herriot Watt University, Edinburgh (BA Hons Urban Planning). Married 1st, March 16, 1968, Margaret Thomson Drysdale (died February 1995) (1 son 1 daughter); married 2nd, May 1, 1998, Julie Fulton. *Trades Union:* Member, UNISON. *Career:* Planning Officer, Glenrothes Development Corporation 1973–74; Research Officer, Edinburgh Social Work Department 1974–75, Planning and Employment Officer, Dunfermline District Council 1975–85; Employment Co-ordinator 1985–87; Part-time lecturer, Herriot Watt University 1973–87; Part-time Consultant on Employment Matters 1984–87. *Councils, Public Bodies:* Chairman, Planning Committee, Kirkcaldy District Council 1974–77; Chairman, Education Committee, Fife Regional Council 1978–82, Leader of Council 1982–87. *Political Career:* Minister of State, Scottish Office: (Minister for Health, Devolution and Transport) 1997–98, (Minister for Home Affairs, Devolution and Local Government) 1998–99; Minister for Enterprise and Lifelong Learning, Scottish Parliament 1999-. *Spokesman:* Opposition Spokesman on: Scotland 1988–89, 1992–94, Employment 1989–92, Transport 1994–95, Health 1995–96, Social Security 1996–97. *Trust:* Fellow, Industry and Parliament Trust 1993. *Special Interests:* Employment, Trade and Industry, Energy, Local Government, Health. *Countries of Interest:* China, CIS, France, Germany, USA. *Recreations:* Reading, sport, travel, history. *Electoral Notes:* Contested North East Fife 1979 General Election. Member for Central Fife since June 1987. MSP for the Constituency of Central Fife since May 6, 1999. *Address:* Henry McLeish Esq, MP, MSP, House of Commons, London, SW1A 0AA *Tel:* 020 7219 4561. *Constituency:* Unit 14A Hanover Court, North Street, Glenrothes, Fife, KY7 5SB *Tel:* 01592 755540 *Fax:* 01592 610325.

MACLENNAN, The Rt Hon. Robert Adam Ross *(Caithness, Sutherland and Easter Ross)* *LD majority 2,259*

Son of late Sir Hector Maclennan. Born June 26, 1936; educated Glasgow Academy; Balliol College, Oxford; Trinity College, Cambridge; Columbia University, New York. Married August 1968, Mrs Helen Noyes (1 son 1 daughter and 1 step-son). *Career:* Barrister. *Political Career:* PPS to: Rt Hon. George Thomson MP, as Minister without Portfolio 1967–69, as Chancellor of the Duchy of Lancaster 1969–70; Parliamentary Under-Secretary of State, Department of Prices and Consumer Protection 1974–79; Resigned the Labour Party and joined the Social Democrats 1981. *Spokesman:* Additional Opposition Spokesman for: Scottish Affairs 1970–71, Defence 1971–72; Opposition Front Bench Spokesman for Foreign and Commonwealth Affairs 1980–81; SDP Spokesman for: Agriculture, Fisheries and Food 1981–87, Home and Legal Affairs 1983–87, Northern Ireland 1983–87, Scotland (jointly) 1982–87; Alliance Spokesman for Agriculture and Fisheries and Food 1987; Former Liberal Democrat Spokesman for: Home Affairs and National Heritage 1988–94, National Heritage; Spokesman for: Constitutional Affairs (Arts and Broadcasting) 1994–97, Constitution 1997–99, Culture, Media and Sport and Civil Service, Arts and Broadcasting 1997–99; Principal Liberal Democrat Spokesman for Constitutional Affairs and Culture 1999-. *Select Committees (Former):* Member: Public Accounts 1979–99. *Party Groups:* Leader, SDP 1987–88; President, Liberal Democrat Party 1994–98. *Other:* Council Member: Foundation for Management Education, Cancer Research Council, Association of British Orchestras. *Honours:* PC 1997. *Special Interests:* Constitutional Reform, European Union, Energy, Rural Affairs, Arts. *Countries of Interest:* Norway, Sweden, Denmark, USA. *Recreations:* Theatre, music, visual arts. *Electoral Notes:* Member for Caithness and Sutherland, firstly as Labour, then as SDP and as a Liberal Democrat 1966–97, and for Caithness, Sutherland and Easter Ross since May 1, 1997. *Clubs:* Brooks's. *Address:* The Rt Hon. Robert Maclennan, MP, House of Commons, London, SW1A 0AA *Tel:* 020 7219 4133 *Tel (Constituency):* 01847 851203/01408 641310 *Fax (Constituency):* 01847 851289 *E-mail:* bobmaclennan@cix.compulink.co.uk.

McLOUGHLIN, Patrick Allan *(West Derbyshire) Con majority 4,885*

Son of Patrick Alphonsos McLoughlin. Born November 30, 1957; educated Cardinal Griffin Comprehensive School, Cannock; Staffordshire College of Agriculture. Married August 18, 1984, Lynne Patricia, daughter of Ralph and Margaret Newman (1 son 1 daughter). *Career:* Agricultural worker 1974–79; Various positions with National Coal Board 1979–86. *Councils, Public Bodies:* Councillor: Cannock Chase District Council 1980–87, Staffordshire County Council 1981–87. *Political Career:* PPS: to Angela Rumbold, CBE, MP, as Minister of State, Department of Education 1987–88, to Rt Hon. Lord Young of Graffham, as Secretary of State for Trade and Industry 1988–89; Parliamentary Under-Secretary of State, Department of Transport (Minister for Aviation and Shipping) 1989–92; Joint Parliamentary Under-Secretary of State, Department of Employment 1992–93; Parliamentary Under-Secretary of State for Trade and Technology, Department of Trade and Industry 1993–94. *Whip:* Assistant Government Whip 1995–96; A Lord Commissioner of HM Treasury (Government Whip) 1996–97; Opposition Pairing Whip 1997–98; Opposition Deputy Chief Whip 1998–. *Select Committees (Current):* Member: Selection 1997–, Finance and Services 1998– *(Former):* Member: Broadcasting 1994–95, National Heritage 1994–95. *Party Groups:* National Vice-Chairman, Young Conservatives 1982–84. *Electoral Notes:* Contested Wolverhampton South East 1983. Member for West Derbyshire since May 8, 1986 By-election. *Address:* Patrick McLoughlin Esq, MP, House of Commons, London, SW1A 0AA *Tel:* 020 7219 3000 *Tel (Constituency):* 01332 558125 *Fax (Constituency):* 01332 558125 *E-mail:* patrick.mcloughlin@talk21.com.

McNAMARA, (Joseph) Kevin *(Hull North) Lab majority 19,705*

Son of late Patrick McNamara. Born September 5, 1934; educated St Mary's College, Crosby; Hull University. Married August 4, 1960, Nora Jones (4 sons 1 daughter). *Trades Union:* Secretary, Parliamentary Group TGWU. *Career:* Lecturer in Law. *Spokesman:* Opposition Spokesman for Defence (Armed Forces) 1983–87; Principal Spokesperson on Northern Ireland 1987–94; Opposition Spokesperson on the Civil Service 1994–95. *Party Groups:* Secretary, National Association of Labour Student Organisations 1956–57. *International Bodies:* Formerly Member, British Delegation, Council of Europe; Member, UK Delegation, North Atlantic Assembly 1984–88; Substitute, UK Delegation to Council of Europe and Western Europe Union. *Special Interests:* Northern Ireland. *Countries of Interest:* Ireland. *Recreations:* Family, reading, walking. *Electoral Notes:* Contested Bridlington in 1964 General Election. Member for Kingston-upon-Hull North 1966–74, for Kingston-upon-Hull Central February 1974–83, and for Hull North since June 1983. *Address:* Kevin McNamara Esq, MP, House of Commons, London, SW1A 0AA *Tel:* 020 7219 5194.

McNULTY, Tony *(Harrow East) Lab majority 9,734*

Son of James Anthony McNulty, self-employed builder, and of Eileen McNulty. Born November 3, 1958; educated Salvatorian College; Stanmore Sixth Form College; Liverpool University (BA Hons Political Theory and Institutions); Virginia Polytechnic Institute and State University, USA (MA Political Science). *Trades Union:* Member: NUPE 1983–90, NATPHE 1983–97. *Profession:* Lecturer. *Career:* Lecturer, Business School, University of North London. *Councils, Public Bodies:* Councillor, London Borough of Harrow 1986–97, Deputy Leader, Labour Group 1990–95, Leader 1995–97. *Political Career:* PPS to Rt Hon. David Blunkett, MP, as Secretary of State for Education and Employment with responsibility for post–16 provision 1997–99. *Whip:* Assistant Government Whip 1999–. *Party Groups:* Member: Socialist Educational Association, Fabian Society; Co-founder, Labour Friends of India; Member, Labour Friends of Israel. *Publications:* Author of various academic papers. *Special Interests:* Education, Health, Local Government, Regeneration, London. *Countries of Interest:* Ireland, France, Germany. *Recreations:* Reading, theatre, rugby, cinema, football, gaelic games. *Electoral Notes:* Contested Harrow East 1992. Member for Harrow East since May 1, 1997. *Clubs:* Wealdstone CIU. *Address:* Tony McNulty Esq, MP, House of Commons, London, SW1A 0AA *Tel:* 020 7219 4108 *Fax:* 020 7219 2417. *Constituency:* 18 Byron Road, Wealdstone, Harrow, HA3 7ST *Tel:* 020 8427 2100 *Fax:* 020 8424 2319 *E-mail:* mcnultyt@parliament.uk.

MacSHANE, Dr Denis *(Rotherham)   Lab majority 21,469*

Born May 21, 1948; educated Merton College, Oxford (MA Modern History); London University (PhD International Economics). Married 1987, Nathalie Pham (1 son 4 daughters). *Trades Union:* President, National Union of Journalists 1978–79. *Career:* BBC Producer 1969–77; Policy Director, International Metal Workers' Federation 1980–92; Director, European Policy Institute 1992–94. *Political Career:* PPS: to Joyce Quin, MP, Derek Fatchett, MP and Tony Lloyd, MP, as Ministers of State, Foreign and Commonwealth Office 1997–99, to Geoff Hoon, MP, as Minister of State, Foreign and Commonwealth Office 1999; Joint PPS to Ministers of State, Foreign and Commonwealth Office 1999–. *Select Committees (Former):* Member:
Deregulation 1996–97. *Publications:* Author of several books on international politics. *Special Interests:* International Economics, European Union, Manufacturing. *Countries of Interest:* Europe, East and South East Asia. *Recreations:* Family, walking. *Electoral Notes:* Contested Solihull in October 1974 General Election. Member for Rotherham since May 5, 1994 By-Election. *Clubs:* East Dene Working Men's. *Address:* Dr Denis MacShane, MP, House of Commons, London, SW1A 0AA *Tel:* 020 7219 4060 *Fax:* 020 7219 6888 *Tel (Constituency):* 01709 837577 *Fax (Constituency):* 01709 835622.

MACTAGGART, Fiona *(Slough)   Lab majority 13,071*

Daughter of late Sir Ian Mactaggart and of late Rosemary Belhaven. Born September 12, 1953; educated London University: King's College (BA Hons, English), Goldsmiths' College (Postgraduate Teaching Certificate), Institute of Education (MA). *Trades Union:* Former Member: TGWU, NUJ, ASTMS; Member: NUT 1987–92, AUT 1992–1997, GMB 1997–. *Profession:* Teacher. *Career:* Vice-President, National Secretary, National Union of Students 1978–81; General Secretary, Joint Council for the Welfare of Immigrants 1982–86; Primary School Teacher 1987–92; Lecturer in Primary Education, Institute of Education 1992–97. *Councils, Public Bodies:* London Borough of Wandsworth: Councillor, Shaftesbury Ward 1986–90, Leader, Labour Group 1988–90. *Political Career:* PPS to Rt Hon. Chris Smith, MP, as Secretary of State for Culture, Media and Sport December 1997–. *Select Committees (Former):* Member: Public Administration 1997–98. *Party Groups:* Joined Labour Party 1980; Member, Fabian Society. *Other:* Chair, Liberty 1994–96, Editorial Board, Renewal. *Special Interests:* Human Rights, Civil Liberties, Home Affairs, Education. *Recreations:* Walking, talking, arts, watching Steve Bochco TV productions. *Electoral Notes:* Member for Slough since May 1, 1997. *Address:* Fiona Mactaggart, MP, House of Commons, London, SW1A 0AA *Tel:* 020 7219 3416 *Fax:* 020 7219 0989. *Constituency:* 29 Church Street, Slough, Berkshire, SL1 1PL *Tel:* 01753 518161 *Fax:* 01753 550293 *E-mail:* fionamac@netcomuk.co.uk.

McWALTER, Tony *(Hemel Hempstead)   Lab majority 3,636*

Son of late Joe McWalter, painter/decorator, and late Ann McWalter. Born March 20, 1945; educated St Benedict's, Ealing; University College of Wales, Aberystwyth (BSc); McMaster University, Canada (MA); University College, Oxford (BPhil, MLitt). Married March 30, 1991, Karen, daughter of Clive and Pam Omer (1 son 2 daughters). *Trades Union:* Member, TGWU. *Profession:* Philosophy Lecturer. *Career:* School Teacher, Cardinal Wiseman Secondary School 1963–64; Long-distance Lorry Driver, E. H. Paterson Ltd 1964–67; Teaching Fellow, McMaster University, Canada 1968–69; Lecturer: Thames Polytechnic 1972–74, Hatfield Polytechnic/University of Hertfordshire 1974–. *Councils, Public Bodies:* Councillor, North Hertfordshire District Council 1979–83. *Select Committees (Current):* Member: Northern Ireland Affairs 1997–. *Other:* Member: The Samaritans 1971–81, Greenpeace, Friends of the Earth, Compassion in World Farming, Amnesty International, World Development Movement, CND. *Publications:* Co-editor *Kant and His Influence*, 1990. *Special Interests:* Local Government, Green Issues, Political Philosophy, Science and Technology. *Countries of Interest:* Ireland, Canada, USA. *Recreations:* Club tennis, family pursuits, contract bridge, philosophy, theatre, the Arts. *Electoral Notes:* Contested Hertfordshire 1984, European Parliament Election,

St Albans 1987, Bedfordshire South, European Parliament 1989, North Luton 1992 General Elections. Member for Hemel Hempstead since May 1, 1997. *Address:* Tony McWalter Esq, MP, House of Commons, London, SW1A 0AA *Tel:* 020 7219 4547. *Constituency:* 5A Marlowes, Hemel Hempstead, Hertfordshire, AL1 1LA *Tel:* 01442 251251 *Fax:* 01442 241268 *E-mail:* tony.mcwalter@geo2.poptel.org.uk.

McWILLIAM, John David *(Blaydon)   Lab majority 16,605*

Son of late Alexander McWilliam, post office engineer. Born May 16, 1941; educated Leith Academy; Herriot-Watt College; Napier College of Science and Technology. Married 1st, February 2, 1965, Lesley Catling (2 daughters); married 2nd, March 31, 1994, Mary McLoughlin (marriage dissolved 1997). *Trades Union:* Former Branch Secretary and Regional Council Member, CWU. *Career:* Telecommunications Engineer. *Councils, Public Bodies:* Councillor, Edinburgh City Council 1970–75; City Treasurer, Edinburgh 1974–75; Member: Commission for Local Authority Accounts, Scotland 1974–78; Scottish Council for Technical Education 1994–98. *Political Career:* Deputy to the Shadow Leader of the House 1983–84; Assistant to Opposition Chief Whip 1984–87; Deputy Speaker (Westminster Hall) 1999–. *Whip:* Opposition Whip 1984–87. *Select Committees (Current):* Member: Chairmen's Panel 1997–; Chairman: Selection 1997– *(Former):* Member: Defence 1987–97, Speaker's Panel of Chairmen 1987–97, Defence 1997–99, Liaison 1997–99. *Miscellaneous:* Vice-Chairman, Pitcom 1987–. *Special Interests:* Defence, Technology, Education. *Countries of Interest:* Canada, Former Yugoslavia, New Zealand, USA. *Recreations:* Reading, angling, listening to music. *Electoral Notes:* Member for Blaydon since May 1979. *Address:* John McWilliam Esq, MP, House of Commons, London, SW1A 0AA *Tel:* 020 7219 4020 *Fax:* 020 7219 6536. *Constituency:* 15 Shibdon Road, Blaydon on Tyne, NE21 5AF *Tel:* 0191–414 2488 *Fax:* 0191–414 8036.

MADEL, Sir (William) David *(South West Bedfordshire)   Con majority 132*

Son of late William Madel. Born August 6, 1938; educated Uppingham School; Keble College, Oxford (MA 1965). Married October 16, 1971, Susan Catherine, daughter of late Lieutenant-Commander Hon. Peter and Mrs Carew (1 son 1 daughter). *Career:* Graduate Management Trainee 1963–64; Advertising Executive, Thomson Organisation 1964–70. *Political Career:* PPS to Minister of Defence 1973–74. *Whip:* An Opposition Whip (Education and Employment, Defence: Wessex) 1997–98; An Opposition Whip (Foreign and Commonwealth Office, International Development, Health) 1998–99. *Select Committees (Current):* Member: Chairmen's Panel 1999–, Foreign Affairs 1999– *(Former):* Member: European Legislation 1983–97, Administration 1992–95, Transport 1995–97, Chairmen's Panel 1997. *Trust:* Fellow, Industry and Parliament Trust. *Miscellaneous:* Member, Executive, 1922 Committee 1997. *Honours:* Knighted 1994. *Special Interests:* Education, Employment. *Electoral Notes:* Contested Erith and Crayford November 1965 By-election and March 1966. Member for South Bedfordshire 1970–83, and for South West Bedfordshire since June 1983. *Clubs:* Carlton. *Address:* Sir David Madel, MP, House of Commons, London, SW1A 0AA *Tel:* 020 7219 3000.

MAGINNIS, Ken *(Fermanagh and South Tyrone)   UUP majority 13,688*

Son of late Gilbert and Margaret Maginnis (née Wiggins). Born January 21, 1938; educated Royal School, Dungannon; Stranmillis Teacher Training College, Belfast. Married July 14, 1961, Joy, daughter of Jeannie and late Herbert Stewart (2 sons 2 daughters). *Armed Forces:* 8 Battalion, Ulster Defence Regiment (Substantive Major) 1970–81. *Career:* Teacher: Cookstown Secondary School 1959–60, Drumglass Primary School, Dungannon 1960–66; Principal, Pomeroy Primary School 1966–82. *Councils, Public Bodies:* Dungannon District Council: Councillor 1981–93, Member, Southern Health and Social Services Council 1989–93, Chairman, Finance and Personnel Committee. *Political Career:* Elected Northern Ireland Assembly October 1982; Elected to the Northern Ireland Forum 1996–98. *Spokesman:* Spokesman for Defence and Home Office 1997–. *Select Committees (Former):* Member: Northern Ireland Affairs 1994–97. *Party Groups:* Vice-President, Ulster Unionist Council. *Other:* Chairman, Moygashel Regeneration Group; Director,

Fermanagh Business Initiative (FBI). *Trust:* Chairman, Police Rehabilitation and Retraining Trust (RUC). *Special Interests:* Terrorism and Internal Security, Defence. *Countries of Interest:* Brazil, Northern Cyprus. *Electoral Notes:* Contested Fermanagh and South Tyrone By-election August 1981. Member for Fermanagh and South Tyrone since June 1983. Resigned December 1985 in protest against the Anglo-Irish Agreement. Re-elected at By-election January 23, 1986. *Address:* Ken Maginnis Esq, MP, House of Commons, London, SW1A 0AA *Tel:* 020 7219 5234. *Constituency:* 20 Brooke Street, Dungannon, BT71 7AN *Tel:* 028 8772 3265 *Fax:* 028 8772 5569.

MAHON, Alice *(Halifax)*   *Lab majority 11,212*

Daughter of late Thomas Edward Reginald Bottomley, bus driver, and late Edna Bottomley. Born September 28, 1937; educated Local Grammar School; Bradford University as a mature student (BA Hons). Married 1st (2 sons) (marriage dissolved), married 2nd, Tony Mahon. *Trades Union:* Activist with NUPE (now UNISON). *Career:* Worked in NHS; Nursing auxiliary for 10 years; Higher education 1980; Taught Trade Union studies at Bradford College. *Councils, Public Bodies:* Calderdale Borough Councillor 1982–87. *Political Career:* PPS to Rt Hon. Chris Smith, MP, as Secretary of State: for National Heritage 1997, for Culture, Media and Sport to December 1997. *Select Committees (Former):* Member: Health 1991–97. *International Bodies:* UK Delegate, North Atlantic Assembly 1992–. *Special Interests:* Health, Employment, Local Government, Trade Unions, Defence. *Countries of Interest:* Balkans, Russia. *Recreations:* Family. *Electoral Notes:* Member for Halifax since June 1987. *Address:* Mrs Alice Mahon, MP, House of Commons, London, SW1A 0AA *Tel:* 020 7219 4464 *Fax:* 020 7219 2450. *Constituency:* 2 West Parade, Halifax, West Yorkshire, HX1 2TA *Tel:* 01422 251800 *Fax:* 01422 251888.

MAJOR, The Rt Hon. John, CH *(Huntingdon)*   *Con majority 18,140*

Son of late Thomas Major and Gwendolyn Minny Coates. Born March 29, 1943; educated Rutlish School, Merton. Married October 1970, Norma Christina Elizabeth (Dame Norma Major, DBE), daughter of late Norman Johnson (1 son 1 daughter). *Career:* Executive, Standard Chartered Bank 1965–81; Director, Warden Housing Association 1974–82. *Councils, Public Bodies:* London Borough of Lambeth: Councillor 1968–71, Chairman, Housing Committee 1970. *Political Career:* PPS to Rt Hon. Timothy Raison, MP and Patrick Mayhew, QC, MP, as Ministers of State, Home Office 1981–83; Parliamentary Under-Secretary of State for Social Security 1985–86; Minister of State for Social Security and the Disabled 1986–87; Chief Secretary of HM Treasury 1987–89; Secretary of State for Foreign and Commonwealth Affairs July-October 1989; Chancellor of the Exchequer 1989–90; Prime Minister, First Lord of the Treasury and Minister of the Civil Service 1990–97; Leader of the Opposition May-June 1997. *Whip:* Appointed Government Whip 1983–85; Lord Commissioner of the Treasury 1984–85. *Party Groups:* Joined Conservative Party 1960; Brixton Conservative Association: Various offices 1960–69, Chairman 1970–71; Elected Leader, Conservative and Unionist Party November 1990, Re-elected 1995, Resigned 1997. *Other:* President, National Asthma Campaign. *Awards: The Spectator* Parliamentarian of the Year Award 1999. *Honours:* PC 1987; CH 1999. *Publications: John Major, The Autobiography,* 1999. *Special Interests:* Finance, Local Government, Agriculture, Race Relations, Social Policy, Housing. *Recreations:* Reading, watching opera, cricket, football and rugby. *Electoral Notes:* Contested Camden, St Pancras North February and October 1974 General Elections. Member for Huntingdonshire 1979–83, and for Huntingdon since June 1983. *Clubs:* Carlton, MCC. *Address:* The Rt Hon. John Major, CH, MP, House of Commons, London, SW1A 0AA *Tel:* 020 7219 5916.

Dod *on* Disk
The Vacher Dod Parliamentary Database – configured for PC or Network
For further details please telephone the Westminster Office
020 7828 7256

MALINS, Humfrey Jonathan, CBE *(Woking)   Con majority 5,678*

Son of Rev P. Malins and late Lilian Joan Malins. Born July 31, 1945; educated St John's School, Leatherhead; Brasenose College, Oxford (MA Jurisprudence 1967). Married July 21, 1979, Lynda Petman (1 son 1 daughter). *Profession:* Solicitor. *Career:* Deputy Metropolitan Stipendiary Magistrate 1992–97; Recorder of the Crown Court 1996–. *Councils, Public Bodies:* Mole Valley District Council: Member 1973–82, Chairman, Housing Committee 1980–81. *Political Career:* PPS: to Tim Renton as Minister of State, Home Office 1987–89, to Virginia Bottomley as Minister of State, Department of Health 1989–92. *Select Committees (Current):* Member: Home Affairs 1997–, Chairmen's Panel 1998–. *Party Groups:* Conservative Back Bench Legal Committee: Secretary 1983–86, Vice-Chairman 1986–87. *Trust:* Chairman, Trustees Immigration Advisory Service 1993–96. *Honours:* CBE 1997. *Special Interests:* Penal Affairs and Policy, Criminal Law Reform, European Union, Sport. *Recreations:* Rugby, golf, gardening, family. *Electoral Notes:* Contested Liverpool Toxteth Feb. and Oct. 1974, East Lewisham 1979. Member for Croydon North West 1983–92, and for Woking since May 1, 1997. *Clubs:* Vincents, Oxford, Walton Heath Golf, Richmond RFC. *Address:* Humfrey Malins Esq, CBE, MP, House of Commons, London, SW1A 0AA *Tel:* 020 7219 4169. *Constituency:* Woking Constituency Conservative Association, Churchill House, Chobham Road, Woking, Surrey, GU21 4AA *Tel:* 01483 773384 *Fax:* 01483 770060.

MALLABER, Judy *(Amber Valley)   Lab majority 11,613*

Daughter of late Kenneth Mallaber, librarian, and of late Margaret Joyce Mallaber, librarian. Born July 10, 1951; educated North London Collegiate School; St Anne's College, Oxford (BA Hons). *Trades Union:* Member, UNISON; Research Officer, NUPE 1975–85. *Career:* Research Officer, National Union of Public Employees 1975–85; Local Government Information Unit 1985–96, Director 1987–95. *Select Committees (Current):* Member: Education and Employment 1997–, Employment Sub-Committee 1997–. *Party Groups:* Labour Party posts include: Constituency Chair, Greater London Labour Party Regional Executive; Chair, Labour Research Department 1991–94. *Other:* Member: Action for Southern Africa, Liberty, Friends of the Earth, Amnesty. *Miscellaneous:* Advisory Council Member, Northern College for Adult Education, Barnsley. *Special Interests:* Economic Policy, Local Government, Education, Equal Opportunity, Employment. *Recreations:* Cinema, theatre, reading, family and friends. *Electoral Notes:* Member for Amber Valley since May 1, 1997. *Clubs:* Anvil, Ironville. *Address:* Judy Mallaber, MP, House of Commons, London, SW1A 0AA *Tel:* 020 7219 3428. *Constituency:* Prospect House, Nottingham Road, Ripley, Derbyshire, DE5 3AZ *Tel:* 01773 512792 *Fax:* 01773 742393.

MALLON, Seamus *(Newry and Armagh)   SDLP majority 4,889*

Son of late Francis and Jane Mallon. Born August 17, 1936; educated Abbey Grammar School, Newry; St Joseph's College of Education, Belfast. Married June 22, 1966, Gertrude Cush (1 daughter). *Career:* Headmaster, St James Primary School, Markethill 1960–73. *Councils, Public Bodies:* Elected Armagh District Council 1973–86. *Political Career:* Elected: Northern Ireland Assembly 1973–74, Northern Ireland Convention 1975–76; Member: Irish Senate 1982, New Ireland Forum 1983–84; Northern Ireland Forum 1996–98; Northern Ireland Assembly 1998–; Deputy First Minister, Northern Ireland Assembly 1998–. *Spokesman:* Spokesman on Justice 1978–. *Select Committees (Former):* Member: Agriculture 1987–92. *Party Groups:* Party Deputy Leader. *International Bodies:* Member, British-Irish Inter-Parliamentary Body. *Sportsclubs:* Member, House of Commons Golf Society. *Publications:* Author of *Adam's Children*; Regular contributor to *Tribune*. *Special Interests:* Justice, Social Services. *Countries of Interest:* Australia, USA. *Recreations:* Angling, horse racing. *Electoral Notes:* Contested Newry and Armagh, June 1983. Member for Newry and Armagh since by-election January 23, 1986. *Address:* Seamus Mallon Esq, MP, House of Commons, London, SW1A 0AA *Tel:* 020 7219 3000. *Constituency:* 2 Bridge Street, Newry, County Down, BT35 8AE *Tel:* 028 3026 7933 *Fax:* 028 3026 7828.

MANDELSON, The Rt Hon. Peter Benjamin *(Hartlepool)   Lab majority 17,508*

Son of late George Mandelson, and of Hon. Mary Joyce Morrison, daughter of late Baron Morrison of Lambeth. Born October 21, 1953; educated Hendon County Grammar School; St Catherine's College, Oxford (BA philosophy, politics and economics). *Trades Union:* Economic Department TUC 1977–78. *Career:* Producer LWT 1982–85; Director of Campaigns and Communications, Labour Party 1985–90; Industrial consultant, SRU Group 1990–92. *Councils, Public Bodies:* Councillor, London Borough of Lambeth 1979–82. *Political Career:* Minister without Portfolio, Cabinet Office 1997–98; Secretary of State for Trade and Industry July-December 1998, for Northern Ireland 1999–. *Whip:* Opposition Whip 1994–95. *Spokesman:* Opposition Spokesman on: The Duchy of Lancaster with responsibility for the Civil Service 1995–96, Election Planning 1996–97. *Party Groups:* Chair, PLP General Election Campaign (Planning) 1999–. *Miscellaneous:* Chairman, British Youth Council 1978–80; Vice-President, Federation of Economic Development Authorities (FEDA); Vice-Chairman, British Council 1999–. *Honours:* PC 1998. *Publications: Youth Employment: causes and cures,* 1977; *Broadcasting and Youth,* 1980; Co-author *The Blair Revolution – Can New Labour Deliver,* 1996. *Countries of Interest:* Europe, USA. *Recreations:* Walking and the countryside, swimming. *Electoral Notes:* Member for Hartlepool since April 9, 1992. *Address:* The Rt Hon. Peter Mandelson, MP, House of Commons, London, SW1A 0AA *Tel:* 020 7219 2632 *Tel (Constituency):* 01429 264956 *Fax (Constituency):* 01429 264956.

MAPLES, John *(Stratford-on-Avon)   Con majority 14,106*

Born April 21, 1943; educated Marlborough College; Cambridge University (MA); Harvard Business School. Married 1986, Jane Corbin (1 son 1 daughter). *Profession:* Barrister. *Career:* Barrister at Law 1965–. *Political Career:* PPS to Chief Secretary to the Treasury 1987–90; Economic Secretary, Treasury 1990–92; Member, Shadow Cabinet 1997–; Shadow Secretary of State for: Health 1997–98, Defence 1998–99, Foreign and Commonwealth Affairs 1999–. *Party Groups:* Deputy Chairman, Conservative Party 1994–95. *International Bodies:* Joint Vice-Chairman, British-American Parliamentary International Group 1999–. *Electoral Notes:* Member for Lewisham West 1983–92, and for Stratford-upon-Avon since May 1, 1997. *Address:* John Maples Esq, MP, House of Commons, London, SW1A 0AA *Tel:* 020 7219 5495 *Fax:* 020 7219 2829. *Constituency:* 3 Trinity Street, Stratford upon Avon *Tel:* 01789 292723 *Fax:* 01789 415866 *E-mail:* maplesj@parliament.uk.

MAREK, Dr John *(Wrexham)   Lab majority 11,762*

Son of late John Marek. Born December 24, 1940; educated Chatham House Grammar School; King's College, London (BSc Hons, PhD). Married 1964, Anne Pritchard. *Career:* Lecturer in Applied Mathematics, University College of Wales 1966–83. *Councils, Public Bodies:* Councillor, Ceredigion District Council 1979–83; Chairman, Finance Committee 1982–83. *Spokesman:* Opposition Front Bench Spokesman on: Health 1985–87, Treasury and Civil Service matters 1987–92. *Select Committees (Current):* Member: Catering 1997–. *Party Groups:* Secretary, Aberystwyth Labour Party 1971–79; Chairman, Dyfed County Labour Party 1978–80. *International Bodies:* Elected Member, International Astronomical Union 1983; Member, Executive Committee, Commonwealth Parliamentary Association (CPA) UK Branch 1987–; Member, Executive Committee, Commonwealth Parliamentary Association (CPA) 1997–. *Trust:* Fellow, Industry and Parliament Trust. *Special Interests:* Transport, Economic Policy. *Countries of Interest:* Gibraltar, Hong Kong, Korea, Mauritius, St Helena. *Electoral Notes:* Contested Ludlow October 1974. Member for Wrexham since June 1983. AM for the Constituency of Wrexham since May 6, 1999. *Address:* Dr John Marek, MP, AM, House of Commons, London, SW1A 0AA *Tel (Constituency):* 67 Regent Street, Wrexham, LL11 1PG *Tel:* 01978 364334 *Fax:* 01978 364334 *E-mail:* John.marek@wales.gsi.gov.uk.

MARSDEN, Gordon *(Blackpool South)   Lab majority 11,616*

Son of George Henry Marsden and Joyce Marsden. Born November 28, 1953; educated Stockport Grammar School; New College, Oxford (MA Hons History); London University; Harvard University; Gibbs Prize in History 1975; Kennedy Scholar, Harvard 1978–79. *Trades Union:* Member, GMB/APEX. *Profession:* Historian and Lecturer. *Career:* Open University Tutor/Associate Lecturer, Arts Faculty 1977–97; Public Relations Consultant 1980–85; Chief Public Affairs Adviser to English Heritage 1984–85; Editor, *History Today* 1985–97; Constituency posts in Hazel Grove, Oxford, London and Brighton. *Select Committees (Current):* Member: Education and Employment 1998–, Education Sub-Committee 1998– *(Former):* Member: Deregulation 1997–99.

Party Groups: Joined Labour Party 1971; Joined Fabian Society 1975; Former Chairman, Young Fabians; Vice-Chair Fabian Society, Chair, Research and and Public Committee 1998–. *Trust:* Member, National Trust; Trustee, Dartmouth Street Trust; Board, History Today Trust 1999–. *Miscellaneous:* Member, Association of British Editors; Editor, *New Socialist* 1989–90; Judge, Ford Conservation Awards UK 1990–97; Board Member, Institute of Historical Research 1996–; President, British Resorts Association 1998–. *Publications: Victorian Values* (ed.) 1990; Contributor to *The History Debate*, 1990; *Victorian Values*, 2nd edition 1998; *Low Cost Socialism*, 1997. *Special Interests:* Heritage, Education, International Affairs, Social Issues, Disabled/Disability. *Countries of Interest:* USA, Russia, Caribbean, Eastern Europe. *Recreations:* Theatre, early music and medieval culture, swimming, watching cricket, heritage sites, architecture. *Electoral Notes:* Contested Blackpool South 1992. Member for Blackpool South since May 1, 1997. *Address:* Gordon Marsden Esq, MP, House of Commons, London, SW1A 0AA *Tel:* 020 7219 4166 *Fax:* 020 7219 1262. *Constituency:* 132 Highfield Road, Blackpool, Lancashire, FY4 2JP *Tel:* 01253 344143.

MARSDEN, Paul William Barry *(Shrewsbury and Atcham)   Lab majority 1,670*

Son of late Tom Marsden and of Audrey Marsden. Born March 18, 1968; educated Helsby High School; Mid-Cheshire College of Further Education (National Diploma in Building Studies); Teesside Polytechnic; Open University (Professional Certificate in Management, Professional Diploma in Management). Married May 14, 1994, Shelly, daughter of Hugh and Dora Somerville (2 sons). *Trades Union:* Member, CWU. *Profession:* Quality Manager. *Career:* Quality Manager: Taylor Woodrow Group 1990–94, Natwest Bank 1994–96, Mitel Telecom 1996–97. *Select Committees (Current):* Member: Agriculture 1997–. *Party Groups:* Member, Labour Party; Personal Assistant to Parliamentary Candidate in Cheshire 1987; Key Organiser for Parliamentary Candidate in Halifax 1992; Campaign Manager/Social Secretary, Teesside Labour Party 1986–90; Branch Secretary/GC Delegate, Huddersfield CLP 1990–91; Member, National Executive Committee, Young Fabians 1990; Chairperson/Secretary, several local Labour Party Branches. *International Bodies:* Member, Commonwealth Parliamentary Association. *Other:* Member: English Heritage, Shropshire Chamber of Commerce, Training and Enterprise; Vice-President: Offa's Dyke Association, Heart of Wales Line Travellers Association. *Trust:* Member: National Trust, Shropshire Wildlife Trust. *Miscellaneous:* Member: Institute of Management, Health Bill Standing Committee 1999. MIMgt. *Special Interests:* Health, Agriculture, Rural Affairs, Environment, Education. *Countries of Interest:* USA, Europe. *Recreations:* Marathon running, reading, cinema, being with my family. *Electoral Notes:* Member for Shrewsbury and Atcham since May 1, 1997. *Address:* Paul Marsden Esq, MP, House of Commons, London, SW1A 0AA *Tel:* 020 7219 6913 *Fax:* 020 7219 0963. *Constituency:* The Labour Party, Morris Hall, Bellstone, Shrewsbury, Shropshire, SY1 1JB *Tel:* 01743 368604 *E-mail:* marsdenp@parliament.uk.

MARSHALL, David *(Glasgow Shettleston)   Lab majority 15,868*

Born May 7, 1941; educated Woodside Senior Secondary School, Glasgow; Larbert High School; Denny High School; Falkirk High School. Married, Christina (2 sons 1 daughter). *Trades Union:* Member, TGWU 1960–; Chairman, TGWU Group of 33 MPs 1987–88. *Career:* Former Transport Worker; Shop Steward. *Councils, Public Bodies:* Councillor, Glasgow Corporation 1972–75; Strathclyde Regional Council: Councillor 1974–79, Chairman, Manpower Committee; Former Chairman, Manpower Committee of Convention of Scottish Local Authorities; Former Member, Local Authorities Conditions of Service Advisory Board. *Political Career:* Put Private Member's Bill, The Solvent Abuse (Scotland) Act through Parliament, May 1983. *Select Committees (Current):* Member: Liaison 1997–; Chairman: Scottish Affairs 1997–; Member: Unopposed Bills (Panel) 1997– *(Former):* Member: Transport 1985–96, Liaison 1987–92; Chairman: Transport 1987–92; Member: Scottish Affairs 1994–97. *Party Groups:* Former Labour Party Organiser, Glasgow; Member, Labour Party 1962–; Hon. Secretary, Scottish Group of Labour MPs 1981–97; Hon. Secretary and Hon. Treasurer, Scottish Group of Labour MPs 1997–. *International Bodies:* Chairman, Inter-Parliamentary Union (IPU) British Group; Member, Executive Committee, Commonwealth Parliamentary Association (CPA) UK Branch 1997–99, Joint Vice-Chairman 1999–. *Other:* Co-Chairman, PACTS 1991–. *Special Interests:* Transport, Third World, Scottish Affairs, Drug Abuse, Solvent Abuse, Pensioners' Rights. *Recreations:* Gardening, music. *Electoral Notes:* Member for Glasgow Shettleston since May 1979. *Address:* David Marshall Esq, MP, House of Commons, London, SW1A 0AA *Tel:* 020 7219 3000.

MARSHALL, James *(Leicester South)   Lab majority 16,493*

Son of late Fred Marshall and Mrs Lilian Marshall. Born March 13, 1941; educated Sheffield City Grammar School; Leeds University (PhD 1968). Married 1st, June 9, 1962, Shirley Ellis (1 son 1 daughter) (marriage dissolved), married 2nd, July 15, 1986, Sue Carter. *Career:* Research scientist, Wool Industries Research Association 1963–67; Lecturer, Leicester Polytechnic 1968–74. *Councils, Public Bodies:* Leeds City Councillor 1965–68; Leicester City Council: Councillor 1971–76, Chairman, Finance Committee 1972–74, Leader 1974. *Whip:* Assistant Government Whip 1977–79. *Spokesman:* Opposition Spokesman on: Home Affairs 1982–83, Northern Ireland 1988–92. *Select Committees (Current):* Member: European Scrutiny 1998– *(Former):* Member: European Legislation 1997–98. *International Bodies:* Member, British Delegation to the Council of Europe and WEU. *Miscellaneous:* Labour Leader, Association of District Councils 1974. *Special Interests:* Housing, Education, Local Government. *Electoral Notes:* Contested the Harborough division of Leicestershire 1970 and Leicester South February 1974 General Elections. Member for Leicester South October 1974–83 and since June 1987. *Address:* James Marshall Esq, MP, House of Commons, London, SW1A 0AA *Tel:* 020 7219 5187. *Constituency:* 57 Regent Road, Leicester, CE1 6BF *Tel:* 0116–254 6900 *Fax:* 0116–255 3651.

MARSHALL-ANDREWS, Robert Graham, QC *(Medway)   Lab majority 5,354*

Son of late Robin and late Eileen Marshall. Born April 10, 1944; educated Mill Hill School; Bristol University (LLB). Married 1968, Gillian Diana, daughter of Capt and Diana Elliott (1 son 1 daughter). *Profession:* Barrister/QC, occasional novelist. *Career:* Called to the Bar, Gray's Inn 1967, QC 1987, Bencher 1996; A Recorder of the Crown Court 1982; Occasional novelist. *Select Committees (Current):* Member: Consolidation of Bills (Joint Committee) 1997–. *Party Groups:* Member, Society of Labour Lawyers. *Other:* Former Head Governor, Grey Court School. *Trust:* Trustee: George Adamson Wildlife Trust 1988–, Geffreye Museum 1990–. *Sportsclubs:* Vice-President, Old Millhillians Rugby. *Publications: Palace of Wisdom,* 1989/1990. *Special Interests:* Economic Policy, Environment. *Countries of Interest:* East Africa, USA. *Recreations:* Theatre, reading, watching rugby, writing, walking, travel. *Electoral Notes:* Contested Richmond 1974 and Medway 1992. Member for Medway since May 1, 1997. *Address:* Robert Marshall-Andrews Esq, QC, MP, House of Commons, London, SW1A 0AA *Tel:* 020 7219 5188/6920 *Fax:* 020 7219 2933. *Constituency:* Moat House, Castle Hill, Rochester, Kent, ME1 1QQ *Tel:* 01634 814687 *Fax:* 01634 831294.

MARTIN, Michael John *(Glasgow Springburn)   Lab majority 17,326*

Son of Michael Martin, merchant seaman and Mary McNeil, school cleaner. Born July 3, 1945; educated St Patrick's Boys' School, Glasgow. Married 1966, Mary McLay (1 son 1 daughter). *Trades Union:* Trade Union Organiser, NUPE; Member, AEEU (Craft Sector); Sponsored as MP by AEEU. *Career:* Time Served Metal Worker, Rolls-Royce Engineering; Full-time Trades Union Official. *Councils, Public Bodies:* Councillor: Glasgow Corporation 1973–75, Glasgow District Council 1975–79. *Political Career:* PPS to Rt Hon. Denis Healey, MP, as Deputy Leader of the Labour Party 1980–83; First Deputy Chairman, Ways and Means 1997–. *Select Committees (Current):* First Deputy Chairman of Ways and Means: Chairmen's Panel 1987–, Court of Referees 1997–, Unopposed Bills (Panel) 1997–, Standing Orders 1998– *(Former):* Chairman: Scottish Grand Committee 1987–97; Member: Speaker's Panel of Chairmen 1987–97; Chairman: Administration 1992–97, Liaison 1993–97. *Party Groups:* Joined Labour Party 1969. *Trust:* Fellow, Industry and Parliament Trust. *Special Interests:* Trade and Industry, Drug Abuse, Industrial Relations, Women's Rights, Care of the Elderly, Human Rights. *Countries of Interest:* Italy, Canada, USA. *Recreations:* Hillwalking, folk music, local history, playing the Highland Pipes and member of the College of Piping. *Electoral Notes:* Member for Glasgow Springburn since May 1979. *Address:* Michael Martin Esq, MP, House of Commons, London, SW1A 0AA *Tel:* 020 7219 1651.

MARTLEW, Eric Anthony *(Carlisle)   Lab majority 12,390*

Son of late George and Mary Jane Martlew. Born January 3, 1949; educated Harraby School, Carlisle; Carlisle College. Married December 19, 1970, Elsie Barbara, daughter of John and Ann Duggan. *Career:* Nestlé Co. 1966–87: Laboratory technician, Personnel Manager. *Councils, Public Bodies:* Councillor, Carlisle County Borough Council 1972–74; Cumbria County Council: Councillor 1973–88, Chairman 1983–85; Member, Cumbria Health Authority; East Cumbria Health Authority: Member 1975–88, Chairman 1977–79. *Political Career:* PPS: to Rt Hon. Dr David Clark, MP, as Chancellor of the Duchy of Lancaster 1997–98, to Rt Hon. Baroness Jay of Paddington, as Lord Privy Seal, Leader of the Lords and Minister for Women 1998–. *Whip:* Opposition Whip 1995–97. *Spokesman:* Opposition Front Bench Spokesman on Defence, Disarmament and Arms Control with special responsibilities for the RAF 1992–95. *Special Interests:* Transport, Health, Social Services, Agriculture, Defence. *Recreations:* Photography, fell-walking, horse-racing, watching rugby league. *Electoral Notes:* Member for Carlisle since June 1987. *Address:* Eric Martlew Esq, MP, House of Commons, London, SW1A 0AA *Tel:* 020 7219 4114 *Fax:* 020 7219 6898. *Constituency:* 3 Chatsworth Square, Carlisle, Cumbria, CA1 1HB *Tel:* 01228 511395 *Fax:* 01228 819798.

MATES, Michael John *(East Hampshire)   Con majority 11,590*

Son of Claude John Mates. Born June 9, 1934; educated Blundell's School; King's College, Cambridge. Married 1st, 1959, Mary Rosamund Paton (2 sons 2 daughters) (marriage dissolved 1980), married 2nd, May 26, 1982, Rosellen Bett (1 daughter) (marriage dissolved 1995). *Armed Forces:* Joined Army 1954; 2nd Lieutenant RUR 1955; Queen's Dragoon Guards, RAC 1961, Major 1967, Lieutenant-Colonel 1973, Resigned commission 1974. *Political Career:* Minister of State, Northern Ireland Office 1992–93. *Select Committees (Former):* Chairman: Defence 1987–92. *International Bodies:* UK Delegate, North Atlantic Assembly. *Miscellaneous:* Member, Committee on Intelligence and Security 1994–; Secretary, 1922 Committee 1987–88, Joint Secretary 1997–. Liveryman, Farriers' Company 1975, Master 1986–87. *Special Interests:* Defence, Northern Ireland, Home Affairs. *Recreations:* Music. *Electoral Notes:* Member for Petersfield October 1974–83, East Hampshire since June 1983. *Clubs:* MCC, Garrick. *Address:* Michael Mates Esq, MP, House of Commons, London, SW1A 0AA *Tel:* 020 7219 5166 *Fax:* 020 7219 4884. *Constituency:* 14A Butts Road, Alton, Hampshire *Tel:* 01420 84122.

MAUDE, The Rt Hon. Francis Anthony Aylmer *(Horsham)   Con majority 14,862*

Son of late Baron Maude of Stratford-upon-Avon, PC (Life Peer), author and journalist, and late Lady Maude. Born July 4, 1953; educated Abingdon School; Corpus Christi, Cambridge (MA Hons History) (Hulse Prize and Avory Studentship); College of Law (Forster Boulton Prize and Inner Temple Law Scholarship). Married 1984, Christina Jane, daughter of late Peter Hadfield (2 sons 3 daughters). *Profession:* Banker, Barrister. *Career:* Called to Bar, Inner Temple 1977; Practising Barrister 1977–85; Head of Global Privatisation, Saloman Bros International; Managing Director, Global Privatisation, Morgan Stanley & Co Ltd 1993–97; Chairman, Deregulation Task Force 1993–97; Non-executive Director: Asda Group plc 1993–, Benfield Reinsurance Ltd 1994–, Gartmore Shared Equity Trust 1997–. *Councils, Public Bodies:* Councillor, Westminster City Council 1978–84. *Political Career:* PPS to Hon. Peter Morrison, as Minister of State for Employment 1984; Minister for Corporate and Consumer Affairs, Department of Trade and Industry 1987–89; Minister of State, Foreign and Commonwealth Office 1989–90; Financial Secretary to the Treasury 1990–92; Member, Shadow Cabinet 1997–; Shadow Secretary of State: for National Heritage 1997, for Culture, Media and Sport 1997–98; Shadow Chancellor of the Exchequer 1998–. *Whip:* Government Whip 1985–87. *Select Committees (Former):* Member: Public Accounts 1990–92. *Other:* Chairman, Governors of Abingdon School. *Miscellaneous:* Member, Executive, 1922 Committee 1997. *Honours:* PC 1992. *Recreations:* Skiing, reading, opera. *Electoral Notes:* Member for North Warwickshire 1983–92, and for Horsham since May 1, 1997. *Address:* The Rt Hon. Francis Maude, MP, House of Commons, London, SW1A 0AA *Tel:* 020 7219 2494 *Fax:* 020 7219 0638. *Constituency:* Gough House, Madeira Avenue, Horsham, West Sussex, RH12 1AB *Tel:* 01403 242000 *Fax:* 01403 210600.

MAWHINNEY, The Rt Hon. Sir Brian Stanley *(North West Cambridgeshire)   Con majority 7,754*

Son of Frederick Stanley Arnot and Coralie Jean Mawhinney. Born July 26, 1940; educated Royal Belfast Academical Institution; Queen's University, Belfast (BSc); University of Michigan, USA (MSc); University of London (PhD). Married August 27, 1965, Betty Louise, daughter of Edwin Oja (2 sons 1 daughter). *Trades Union:* Life Member, AUT. *Career:* Assistant Professor of Radiation Research, University of Iowa, USA 1968–1970; Lecturer (subsequently Senior Lecturer), Royal Free Hospital School of Medicine 1970–84. *Political Career:* PPS: to Mr Barney Hayhoe, MP: as Minister of State at the Treasury 1982–84, to Rt Hon. Tom King, MP: as Secretary of State for Employment, as Secretary of State for Northern Ireland 1984–86; Northern Ireland Office: Parliamentary Under-Secretary of State 1986–90, Minister of State, 1990–92, Minister of State, Department of Health 1992–94; Secretary of State for Transport 1994–95; Minister without Portfolio 1995–97; Member, Shadow Cabinet 1997–98: Shadow Home Secretary 1997–98. *Party Groups:* National President, Conservative Trade Unionists 1987–90; Chairman, Conservative Party 1995–97. *Other:* Member: National Council, National Society for Cancer Relief 1981–85, General Synod 1985–90; President, Peterborough Association for the Blind. *Trust:* Fellow, Industry and Parliament Trust. *Miscellaneous:* Member, Medical Research Council 1979–83. *Sportsclubs:* Member, Etton Furze Golf Club. *Honours:* PC 1994; Kt 1997. *Publications:* Joint Author *Conflict and Christianity in Northern Ireland; In the Firing Line – Politics, Faith, Power and Forgiveness*, 1999. *Special Interests:* Health, Northern Ireland, Anglo-American Relations, Trade and Industry, Treasury. *Countries of Interest:* Middle East. *Recreations:* Sport, reading. *Electoral Notes:* Contested Teeside Stockton October 1974 General Election. Member for Peterborough 1979–97, and for North West Cambridgeshire since May 1, 1997. *Address:* The Rt Hon. Sir Brian Mawhinney, MP, House of Commons, London, SW1A 0AA *Tel:* 020 7219 6205. *Constituency:* 18 Peterborough Road, Wansford, Cambridgeshire, PE6 6JN *Tel:* 01780 783869 *Fax:* 01780 783770.

MAXTON, John Alston *(Glasgow Cathcart)   Lab majority 12,245*

Son of late John Maxton, Agricultural Economist, and late Jenny Maxton. Born May 5, 1936; educated Lord William's Grammar School, Thame; University College, Oxford (BA Modern History 1961, DipEd). Married July 9, 1970, Christine, daughter of Ken and Elspeth Waine (3 sons). *Trades Union:* Member: MSF, Educational Institute of Scotland. *Profession:* Teacher/Lecturer. *Career:* Lecturer in Social Studies, Hamilton College 1970–79. *Whip:* Scottish and Treasury Whip 1985. *Spokesman:* Opposition Front Bench Spokesman on Scotland 1985–92. *Select Committees (Current):* Member: Chairmen's Panel 1997–, Culture, Media and Sport 1997– *(Former):* Member: National Heritage 1992–97, Speaker's Panel of Chairmen 1994–97. *Party Groups:* Joined Labour Party 1970. *Other:* Member: Association of Lecturers in Colleges of Education, Socialist Educational Association, CND, Scottish Council for Civil Liberties. *Trust:* Member, Scottish Civil Liberties Trust; Council Member, National Trust for Scotland. *Special Interests:* Scotland, Devolution, Housing, Sport, The Arts. *Countries of Interest:* Spain. *Recreations:* Listening to Jazz, running, fitness, holiday golf on the Isle of Arran. *Electoral Notes:* Member for Glasgow Cathcart since May 1979. *Address:* John Maxton Esq, MP, House of Commons, London, SW1A 0AA *Tel:* 020 7219 4550. *Constituency:* Labour Club, Barlia Drive, Castlemilk, Glasgow.

MAY, Theresa Mary *(Maidenhead)   Con majority 11,981*

Daughter of late Rev Hubert Brasier and late Zaidee Brasier. Born October 1, 1956; educated Wheatley Park Comprehensive School; St Hugh's, Oxford University (MA Hons). Married September 6, 1980, Philip John May, son of John and Joy May. *Career:* Senior Adviser, International Affairs at Association for Payment Clearing Services. *Councils, Public Bodies:* Councillor, London Borough of Merton 1986–94. *Political Career:* Member, Shadow Cabinet 1999–; Shadow Secretary of State for Education and Employment 1999–. *Spokesman:* An Opposition Spokeswoman for Education and Employment (Schools, Disabled People and Women) 1998–99; Shadow Cabinet Spokeswoman for Women's Issues 1999–. *Select Committees (Former):* Member: Education and Employment 1997–98, Education Sub-Committee 1997–99. Fellow, Royal Geographical Society. *Special Interests:* Education, Disabled/Disability, Europe. *Electoral Notes:* Contested North-West Durham 1992, Barking 1994 (By-election). Member for Maidenhead since May 1, 1997. *Clubs:* Lady Associate, Carlton, Maidenhead Conservative. *Address:* Mrs Theresa May, MP, House of Commons, London, SW1A 0AA *Tel:* 020 7219 3471 *Fax:* 020 7219 1145. *Constituency:* Maidenhead Conservative Association, 2 Castle End Farm, Ruscombe, Berkshire, RG10 9XQ *Tel:* 0118 934 5433 *Fax:* 0118 934 5288 *E-mail:* mayt@parliament.uk.

MEACHER, The Rt Hon. Michael H *(Oldham West and Royton)   Lab majority 16,201*

Son of late George H. Meacher. Born November 4, 1939; educated Berkhamsted School, Hertfordshire; New College, Oxford. Married 1st, August 11, 1962, Molly Christine, daughter of W. F. Reid (2 sons 2 daughters) (marriage dissolved 1987), married 2nd, May 28, 1988, Mrs Lucianne Sawyer, daughter of W. H. Craven. *Trades Union:* Member, UNISON. *Career:* Secretary, Danilo Dolci Trust 1964; Sembal Research Fellow in Social Gerontology, University of Essex 1965–66; Lecturer in Social Administration: University of York 1966–69; London School of Economics 1970; Visiting Professor to Department of Sociology, University of Surrey 1980–86. *Political Career:* Parliamentary Under-Secretary of State: Department of Industry 1974–75, Department of Health and Social Security 1975–76, Department of Trade 1976–79; Member, Shadow Cabinet 1983–97; Minister of State, Department of the Environment, Transport and the Regions (Minister for the Environment) 1997–. *Spokesman:* Principal Opposition Front Bench Spokesman on: Health and Social Security 1983–87, Employment 1987–89, Social Security 1989–92, Overseas Development and Co-operation 1992–93, Citizen's Charter and Science 1993–94, Transport 1994–95, Education and Employment 1995–96, Environmental Protection 1996–97. *Select Committees (Current):* Ex-officio member: Environmental Audit 1997– *(Former):* Member: Environmental Audit 1998.

Party Groups: Candidate for Deputy Leadership, Labour Party 1983; Member, Labour Party National Executive Committee 1983–89. *Trust:* Fellow, Industry and Parliament Trust. *Honours:* PC 1997. *Publications: The Care of Old People,* Fabian Society 1969; *Taken For A Ride*; *Special Residential Homes for the Elderly Mentally Infirm*; *A Study of Separatism in Social Policy,* 1972; *Socialism with a Human Face – the Political Economy in the 1980s,* 1982; *Diffusing Power – The key to Socialist Revival,* 1992; Numerous articles and pamphlets on social and economic policy. *Special Interests:* Economics and Social Policy, Redistribution of Income and Wealth, Industrial Democracy, Civil Liberties, Housing. *Recreations:* Sport, music, reading. *Electoral Notes:* Contested Colchester 1966 and Oldham West 1968 By-election. Member for Oldham West 1970–97, and for Oldham West and Royton since May 1, 1997. *Address:* The Rt Hon. Michael Meacher, MP, House of Commons, London, SW1A 0AA *Tel:* 020 7219 4532/6461 *Fax:* 020 7219 5945. *Constituency:* 110 Union Street, Oldham, OL1 1DU *Tel:* 0161–626 5779 *Fax:* 0161–626 8572 *E-mail:* michael-meacher@detr.gsi.gov.uk.

MEALE, Alan *(Mansfield)   Lab majority 20,518*

Son of late Albert Henry Meale, and of Mrs Elizabeth Meale. Born July 31, 1949; educated St Joseph Roman Catholic School, Bishop Auckland; Durham University; Ruskin College, Oxford; Sheffield Hallam University. Married March 10, 1983, Diana, daughter of John and Eileen Gilhespy. *Trades Union:* National Employment Development Officer, NACRO 1977–80; Assistant to Ray Buckton, General Secretary of ASLEF 1979–84; Sponsored by MSF. *Career:* Author; Editor; Development Officer; Researcher for various MPs, B Castle, T Benn, D Skinner, A Booth; Parliamentary and political adviser to Michael Meacher, MP, as Principal Opposition Front Bench Spokesman on Health and Social Security 1984–87. *Councils, Public Bodies:* Deputy Leader, Local Authority. *Political Career:* PPS to Rt Hon. John Prescott, MP: as Deputy Leader of the Labour Party 1994–98, as Deputy Prime Minister and Secretary of State for the Environment, Transport and the Regions 1997–98; Parliamentary Under-Secretary of State, Department of the Environment, Transport and the Regions 1998–99. *Whip:* Opposition Whip 1992–94. *Select Committees (Current):* Member: Court of Referees 1999– *(Former):* : European Legislation 1988–90; Member: Home Affairs 1990–92, Court of Referees 1997–98. *Party Groups:* Member, Co-operative Party. *International Bodies:* Treasurer, CPA Cyprus Group (British Section); Executive Member: Commonwealth Parliamentary Association (CPA), Inter-Parliamentary Union (IPU). *Other:* Parliamentary Representative, SSAFA 1990–94; Member, War Pensions Board 1990–. *Trust:* Fellow and Postgraduate Fellow, Industry and Parliament Trust. *Miscellaneous:* Author; Vice-President, NAPP; Parliamentary Representative, SSAFA (Armed Forces Social Welfare Organisation) 1989–95 Member, War Pensions Board 1989–97;. Freeman, State of Louisiana, USA; Freeman, City of: Mansfield, Ohio, USA; Morphou, Cyprus. *Special Interests:* Home Affairs, Transport, Health, Social Security, Drug Abuse, Human Rights, Sport, Unemployment, Media, European Union, Music. *Countries of Interest:* Cyprus. *Recreations:* Reading, writing, arts, politics, sports, Mansfield Football Club. *Electoral Notes:* Member for Mansfield since June 1987. *Address:* Alan Meale Esq, MP, House of Commons, London, SW1A 0AA *Tel:* 020 7219 4159. *Constituency:* 5 Clumber Street, Mansfied, Nottinghamshire, NG18 1NT *Tel:* 01623 660531 *Fax:* 01623 420495 *E-mail:* alan.meale@geo2.poptel.org.uk.

MERRON, Gillian *(Lincoln)   Lab majority 11,130*

Born April 12, 1959; educated Wanstead High School; University of Lancaster (BSc Hons Management Sciences). *Trades Union:* Member, UNISON. *Career:* Business Development Adviser; Local Government Officer; Lay Representative and Official, National Union of Public Employees (now UNISON); Senior Officer for Lincolnshire, UNISON. *Political Career:* Sponsored, Football Sponsorship Levy Bill 1997; PPS: to Doug Henderson, MP, as Minister of State for the Armed Forces, Ministry of Defence 1998–99, to Baroness Symons of Vernham Dean, as Minister of State for Defence Procurement, Ministry of Defence 1999–. *Select Committees (Former):* Member: Trade and Industry 1997–98. *Party Groups:* Member, Labour Party 1982–; Constituency and Regional Labour Party Officer; Member, Co-operative Party; Vice-Chair, Central Region Group of Labour MPs 1997–99; Board Member, Westminster Foundation for Democracy; Chair, East Midlands Regional Group of Labour MPs 1999–. *Other:* Member: Amnesty International,

Cats Protection League, Action for Southern Africa (formerly Anti Apartheid), Greenpeace, National Campaign for Nursery Education. *Trust:* Fellow-Elect, Industry and Parliament Trust. *Miscellaneous:* Co-ordinated the Shadow Cabinet Central Region Campaign in General and European Elections; Campaigner on health, human rights and privatisation of public utilities; Member, Armed Forces Parliamentary Scheme (RAF) 1997–98; Member, Standing Committee on: National Minimum Wage Bill, Northern Ireland Arms Decommissioning, Local Authority Tendering, New Northern Ireland Assembly (Elections) Order 1998–. *Special Interests:* Economy, Employment, Low Pay, Business. *Recreations:* Football, walking, films. *Electoral Notes:* Member for Lincoln since May 1, 1997. *Address:* Gillian Merron, MP, House of Commons, London, SW1A 0AA *Tel:* 020 7219 4031 *Fax:* 020 7219 0489. *Constituency:* Grafton House, 32 Newland, Lincoln, LN1 1XJ *Tel:* 01522 888688 *Fax:* 01522 888686 *E-mail:* merrong@parliament.uk.

MICHAEL, The Rt Hon. Alun *(Cardiff South and Penarth)   Lab/Co-op majority 13,881*

Son of late Leslie Michael and of Elizabeth Michael. Born August 22, 1943; educated Colwyn Bay Grammar School; University of Keele (BA Hons). Married July 23, 1966, Mary, daughter of Mr and Mrs Ambrose Crawley (2 sons 3 daughters). *Trades Union:* Member, GMB; Former Member: TGWU, CYWU; Branch Secretary, National Union of Journalists 1967–70; General Secretary, Welsh Association of FE and Youth Service Officers 1973–75. *Profession:* Journalist, Youth and Community Worker. *Career:* Journalist, *South Wales Echo* 1966–72; Youth Worker, Cardiff City Council 1972–74; Youth and Community Worker, South Glamorgan CC 1974–87. *Councils, Public Bodies:* JP, Cardiff 1972–; Chairman, Cardiff Juvenile Bench 1986–87; Cardiff City Council: Councillor 1973–89, Past Chairman: Finance Committee, Planning Committee, Economic Development Committee 1987–89. *Political Career:* Minister of State, Home Office (Minister for Criminal Policy also responsible for Police and the Voluntary Sector) 1997–98; Secretary of State for Wales 1998–99; First Secretary, National Assembly for Wales 1999–. *Whip:* Opposition Whip 1987–88. *Spokesman:* Opposition Front Bench Spokesman on: Welsh Affairs 1988–92, Home Affairs 1992–97; The Voluntary Sector 1994–97. *Party Groups:* Former Chairman, Co-operative Group of MPs; Member, National Executive, Co-operative Party (representing Wales); Member, Christian Socialist Movement. *International Bodies:* Member: Commonwealth Parliamentary Association (CPA) (delegation to South Africa and Canada), Inter-Parliamentary Association (IPA). *Other:* National Vice-President, Youth Hostels Association; Member of Board, Crime Concern 1993–97. *Sportsclubs:* Penarth and Dinas Runners. *Honours:* PC 1998. *Publications:* Contributor, *Restoring Faith in Politics,* 1966, *Challenges to a Challenging Faith,* 1995; Editor, *Tough on Crime and Tough on the Causes of Crime,* 1997, *Building the Future Together,* 1997. *Special Interests:* Local Government, Housing, Youth Work, Juvenile Justice, Voluntary Sector, Community Development, Economic Development, Co-operative Development, Political Philosophy. *Countries of Interest:* Germany, South Africa, Israel, Canada, Somalia, USA, Japan. *Recreations:* Long-distance walking, running, reading, opera, music. *Electoral Notes:* Member for Cardiff South and Penarth since June 1987. AM for the Region of Wales Mid and West since May 6, 1999. *Clubs:* Penarth Labour, Grange Stars (Cardiff), Earlswood (Cardiff). *Address:* The Rt Hon. Alun Michael, JP, MP, AM, House of Commons, London, SW1A 0AA *Tel:* 020 7219 3000 *Tel (Constituency):* 029 2022 3533 *Fax (Constituency):* 029 2038 7465 *E-mail:* alun.michael@penarth.globalnet.co.uk.

MICHIE, Mrs Ray *(Argyll and Bute)   LD majority 6,081*

Daughter of late Lord and Lady Bannerman of Kildonan. Born February 4, 1934; educated Aberdeen High School for Girls; Lansdowne House, Edinburgh; Edinburgh College of Speech Therapy (MCST). Married May 11, 1957, Dr Iain Michie FRCP, son of Malcolm and Margaret Michie (3 daughters). *Trades Union:* Member: Scottish National Farmers Union, Scottish Crofters Union. *Career:* Area speech therapist, Argyll and Clyde Health Board 1977–87. *Spokesman:* Liberal Spokeswoman for Transport and Rural Development 1987–88; A Liberal Democrat Spokeswoman for: Women's Issues 1988–94, Scotland 1988–, (Scottish Team) for Agriculture, Community Care, Rural Affairs and National Heritage 1997–99. *Select Committees (Current):* Member: Chairmen's Panel 1997– *(Former):* Member: Scottish Affairs 1992–97. *Party Groups:* Vice-Chairman, Scottish Liberal Party 1976–78; Chair, Scottish Liberal Democrats

1992–93; Deputy Leader, Scottish Liberal Democrats 1997–99. *Other:* Vice-President, Royal College of Speech and Language Therapists; Hon. President, CFA (Clyde Fishermens Association); Member: An Comunn Gaidhealach, Scottish Constitutional Convention. *Miscellaneous:* Hon. Associate, National Council of Women of GB. *Special Interests:* Constitutional Reform, Home Rule for Scotland, Farming, Crofting, Gaelic language, Health Education, Fishing. *Countries of Interest:* Political Institutions in the EU. *Recreations:* Golf, swimming, gardening, watching rugby. *Electoral Notes:* Contested Argyll 1979, Argyll and Bute 1983. Member for Argyll and Bute since June 1987. *Clubs:* National Liberal. *Address:* Mrs Ray Michie, MP, House of Commons, London, SW1A 0AA *Tel:* 020 7219 4140. *Constituency:* 5 Stafford Street, Oban, Argyll, PA34 5NJ *Tel:* 01631 563551 *Fax:* 01631 565736.

MICHIE, William (Bill) *(Sheffield Heeley)   Lab majority 17,078*

Son of late Arthur Michie, engineer, and late Violet Michie. Born November 24, 1935; educated Abbeydale Secondary School, Sheffield; Sheffield Polytechnic (BA). Married May 1, 1987, Judith (2 sons, 1 step-son, 1 step-daughter). *Trades Union:* Chairman, AEEU Members Parliamentary Group. *Armed Forces:* National Service, RAF 1957–59. *Career:* Electrician 1952–61; Laboratory technician 1961–81. *Councils, Public Bodies:* Councillor: Sheffield City Council 1970–84, South Yorkshire County Council 1974–86; Sheffield City Council, Chairman: Planning 1974–81, Employment 1981–83. *Select Committees (Current):* Member: Parliamentary Privilege (Joint Committee) 1997– *(Former):* Member: Members' Interests 1992–96, Privileges 1994–96. *Party Groups:* Member, Co-operative Party. *Miscellaneous:* Chairman, AEEU Members Parliamentary Group. *Special Interests:* Industry, Local Government, Social Security. *Recreations:* Darts, soccer. *Electoral Notes:* Member for Sheffield Heeley since June 1983. *Clubs:* WMC Affiliated. *Address:* William Michie Esq, MP, House of Commons, London, SW1A 0AA *Tel:* 020 7219 4140. *Constituency:* Barkers Pool House, Burgess Street, Sheffield, S1 2HF *Tel:* 0114–270 1181 *Fax:* 0114–276 9874 *E-mail:* michieb@parliament.uk.

MILBURN, The Rt Hon. Alan *(Darlington)   Lab majority 16,025*

Son of Evelyn Metcalfe, former NHS secretary. Born January 27, 1958; educated John Marlay School, Newcastle; Stokesley Comprehensive School; Lancaster University (BA Hons History); Newcastle University. Partner, Ruth Briel (2 sons). *Trades Union:* Co-ordinator, Trade Union Studies Information Unit, Newcastle 1984–90; Co-ordinator, Sunderland Shipyards Campaign 1988–89; President, North East Region, MSF Union 1990–92. *Career:* Senior Business Development Officer, North Tyneside Council 1990–92. *Political Career:* Minister of State, Department of Health 1997–98; Chief Secretary, HM Treasury December 1998–99; Secretary of State for Health 1999–. *Spokesman:* Opposition Spokesman on: Health 1995–96, Treasury and Economic Affairs (Shadow Economic Secretary) 1996–97. *Select Committees (Former):* Member: Public Accounts 1994–95. *Party Groups:* Chairman, Newcastle Central Constituency Labour Party 1988–90; Member, Northern Region Labour Party Executive Committee 1990–92. *Honours:* PC 1998. *Publications: Jobs and Industry, the North Can Make It,* 1986; *Plan for the North,* 1987; *The Case for Regional Government,* 1989. *Special Interests:* Economic Policy, Industry, Regional Policy, Crime, Health. *Recreations:* Cricket, football, music, cinema. *Electoral Notes:* Member for Darlington since April 9, 1992. *Address:* The Rt Hon. Alan Milburn, MP, House of Commons, London, SW1A 0AA *Tel:* 020 7219 3000. *Constituency:* 123 Victoria Road, Darlington, County Durham, DL1 5JH *Tel:* 01325 380366.

Dod *on* Disk

The Vacher Dod Parliamentary Database – configured for PC or Network

For further details please telephone the Westminster Office

020 7828 7256

MILLER, Andrew *(Ellesmere Port and Neston)* *Lab majority 16,036*

Son of late Ernest and Daphne Miller. Born March 23, 1949; educated Hayling Island Secondary School; Highbury Technical College; London School of Economics (Diploma in Industrial Relations). Married Frances Ewan (2 sons 1 daughter). *Trades Union:* Regional official, MSF (formerly ASTMS) 1977–92. *Career:* Technician, Portsmouth Polytechnic, analyst in geology 1967–76; Mature student, LSE 1976–77. *Select Committees (Current):* Member: Information 1997– *(Former):* Member: Information 1992–97, Science and Technology 1992–97. *Party Groups:* Member: Labour Party 1968–, NW Regional Executive Committee 1984–92; President, Computing for Labour 1993–; Chair: Leadership Campaign Team 1997–98, North West Group of Labour MPs 1997–98; Member, Scientists for Labour 1997–. *Other:* Patron: Road Peace, Chester Childbirth Trust, Parents Against Drug Abuse. *Sportsclubs:* Vice-President: Alvanley Cricket Club, Chester and Ellesmere Port Athletics Club. *Special Interests:* Industry, Economic Policy. *Countries of Interest:* Europe, China, USA. *Recreations:* Walking, photography, tennis, cricket. *Electoral Notes:* Member for Ellesmere Port and Neston since April 9, 1992. *Address:* Andrew Miller Esq, MP, House of Commons, London, SW1A 0AA *Tel:* 020 7219 3580 *Fax:* 020 7219 3796. *Constituency:* Whitby Hall Lodge, Stanney Lane, Ellesmere Port, Cheshire, CH65 6QY *Tel:* 0151–357 3019 *Fax:* 0151–356 8226 *E-mail:* millera@parliament.uk.

MITCHELL, Austin Vernon *(Great Grimsby)* *Lab majority 16,244*

Son of Richard Vernon Mitchell, Dyer. Born September 19, 1934; educated Woodbottom Council School; Bingley Grammar School; Manchester University; Nuffield College, Oxford (BA, MA, DPhil). Married 1st, Patricia Dorothea Jackson (2 daughters) (marriage dissolved), married 2nd, Linda Mary McDougall (1 son 1 daughter). *Career:* Lecturer in History, Otago University, Dunedin, New Zealand 1959–63; Senior Lecturer in Politics, University of Canterbury, Christchurch, NZ 1963–67; Official Fellow, Nuffield College, Oxford 1967–69; Journalist: Yorkshire Television 1969–71, BBC 1972, Yorkshire Television 1973–77; Political commentator, Sky Television's Target programme 1989–98; Associate editor, *The House Magazine. Political Career:* PPS to John Fraser, MP, as Minister of State for Prices and Consumer Protection 1977–79. *Whip:* Former Opposition Whip. *Spokesman:* Front Bench Spokesman, Trade and Industry 1988–89. *Select Committees (Current):* Member: Agriculture 1997– *(Former):* : Treasury and Civil Service 1983–87. *Party Groups:* Member, Executive Council Fabian Society; Vice-Chairman: Labour Campaign for Electoral Reform, Labour Euro-Safeguards Campaign; Chairman, Labour Economic Policy Group. *International Bodies:* Member, Royal Institute of International Affairs; Joint Secretary, Esperanto Parliamentary Group. *Other:* Vice-Chairman, Hansard Society. *Trust:* Fellow, Industry and Parliament Trust. *Miscellaneous:* Member: Hairdressing Council, Advisory Council, National Fishing Heritage Centre, Public Accounts Commission 1997–; Vice-President, Federation of Economic Development Authorities (FEDA); President, Debating Group. *Publications: New Zealand Politics in Action 1962;* Government by Party, 1966; *Whigs in Opposition, 1815–30,* 1969; *Politics and People in New Zealand,* 1970; *Half Gallon Quarter Acre Pavlova – Paradise,* 1974; *Can Labour Win Again,* 1979; *Yes Maggie there is an Alternative; Westminster Man,* 1982; *The Case for Labour,* 1983; *Four Years in the Death of the Labour Party,* 1983; *Yorkshire Jokes; Teach Thissen Tyke; Britain, Beyond the Blue Horizon,* 1989; *Competitive Socialism,* 1989; *Election '45,* 1995; *Accounting for Change,* 1993; *Corporate Governance Matters,* 1996; *The Common Fisheries Policy, End or Mend?,* 1996; *Last Time: Labour's Lessons from the Sixties,* (with David Wienir) 1997; *Farewell My Lords,* 1999; *Parliament in Pictures,* 1999. *Special Interests:* Economics, Media, Fishing, Agriculture, Poverty, Accountancy, Legal Reform, European Union, Electoral Reform, Constitutional Reform. *Countries of Interest:* Canada, Iceland, New Zealand, France, Germany, China, Hong Kong, Nigeria. *Recreations:* Photography, contemplating exercise. *Electoral Notes:* Member for Grimsby 1977–83 and for Great Grimsby since June 1983. *Address:* Austin Mitchell Esq, MP, House of Commons, London, SW1A 0AA *Tel:* 020 7219 4559 *Fax:* 020 7219 4843. *Constituency:* 15 New Cartergate, Grimsby, NE Lincs, DN31 1RB *Tel:* 01472 342145 *Fax:* 01472 251484 *E-mail:* austin@austinmitchell.force9.co.uk.

MOFFATT, Laura Jean *(Crawley)* *Lab majority 11,707*

Daughter of Stanley and Barbara Field. Born April 9, 1954; educated Hazelwick School, Crawley; Crawley College of Technology. Married November 1, 1975, Colin Moffatt, son of Albert and Vera Moffatt (3 sons). *Trades Union:* Member, UNISON. *Profession:* Registered General Nurse. *Career:* State Registered Nurse, Crawley Hospital. *Councils, Public Bodies:* Crawley Borough Council: Councillor 1984–96, Mayor 1989–90, Chair, Environmental Services for 9 years. *Select Committees (Current):* Member: Defence 1997 . *Other:* Member, Lioness Club; Director, Furniaid (registered charity to provide furniture for needy); President, Relate. *Special Interests:* Health, Housing, Aerospace, Aviation, Defence, AIDS, Drug Abuse. *Recreations:* Family, friends, walking, pets, swimming. *Electoral Notes:* Member for Crawley since May 1, 1997. *Address:* Mrs Laura Moffatt, MP, House of Commons, London, SW1A 0AA *Tel:* 020 7219 3619 *Fax:* 020 7219 3619. *Constituency:* 6 The Broadway, Crawley, West Sussex, RH10 1DS *Tel:* 01293 526005 *Fax:* 01293 526005.

MOONIE, Dr Lewis *(Kirkcaldy)* *Lab/Co-op majority 10,710*

Son of late George Moonie, retired accountant, and of Eva Moonie. Born February 25, 1947; educated Grove Academy, Dundee; St Andrews University (MB, ChB 1970); Edinburgh University (DPM 1975, MRCPsych 1979, MSc 1981, MFCM 1984). Married December 28, 1971, Sheila Ann Burt, teacher (2 sons). *Career:* Junior Medical posts; One year as GP; Registrar training in psychiatry; Full-time research clinical pharmacologist and medical adviser in pharmaceutical industry in Netherlands, Switzerland and Edinburgh 1975–80; MSc course in Community Medicine 1980–81; Trainee Community Medicine, Fife Health Board 1980–84; Community Medicine specialists, Fife Health Board 1984–87. *Councils, Public Bodies:* Councillor, Fife Regional Council 1982–86. *Spokesman:* Opposition Front Bench Spokesman on: Technology, Trade and Industry 1991–92, Science and Technology 1992–94, Trade and Industry 1994–95, National Heritage 1995–97. *Select Committees (Current):* Chairman: Finance and Services 1997–; Member: Liaison 1997–, Treasury 1998–, Treasury Sub-Committee 1998– *(Former):* Member: Public Accounts Commission 1995–97. *Party Groups:* Member, Co-operative Party. *Miscellaneous:* Member, House of Commons Commission 1997–. *Special Interests:* Industry, Technology, Economic Policy. *Recreations:* A wide variety of sporting and recreational activities. *Electoral Notes:* Member for Kirkcaldy since June 1987. *Address:* Dr Lewis Moonie, MP, House of Commons, London, SW1A 0AA *Tel:* 020 7219 4097 *Tel (Constituency):* 01592 201873.

MOORE, Michael Kevin *(Tweeddale, Ettrick and Lauderdale)* *LD majority 1,489*

Son of Reverend W. Haisley Moore, Church of Scotland minister, and Jill Moore, physiotherapist. Born June 3, 1965; educated Strathallan School; Jedburgh Grammar School; University of Edinburgh (MA, Politics and Modern History). Single. *Profession:* Chartered Accountant. *Career:* Research Assistant to Archy Kirkwood, MP 1987–88; Coopers and Lybrand, Edinburgh 1988–: Trainee, Audit Practice 1988–91, Supervisor, Audit Practice 1991–93, Manager, Corporate Finance Practice 1993–97. *Spokesman:* A Spokesman for: Scotland (Industry, Employment, Health and Environment) 1997–99, Environment, Transport, the Regions and Social Justice (Transport) 1999–. *Select Committees (Former):* Member: Scottish Affairs 1997–99. *Party Groups:* Campaign Chairman, 1999 Scottish Elections. *Other:* Member, Amnesty International. *Miscellaneous:* Scottish Spokesman on Business and Employment 1995–; Liberal Democrat Party Conference, Debate on Economy 1995. Institute of Chartered Accountants of Scotland 1991. *Special Interests:* Business, Employment, Housing. *Recreations:* Rugby, hill-walking, music, films. *Electoral Notes:* Member for Tweeddale, Ettrick and Lauderdale since May 1, 1997. *Address:* Michael Moore Esq, MP, House of Commons, London, SW1A 0AA *Tel:* 020 7219 2236. *Constituency:* Tweeddale, Ettrick and Lauderdale Liberal Democrats, 46 High Street, Innerleithen, Borders, EH44 6HF *Tel:* 01896 831011 *Fax:* 01896 831011 *E-mail:* michaelmoore@cix.compulink.co.uk.

MORAN, Margaret *(Luton South)* Lab majority 11,319

Daughter of late Patrick (Jack) Moran, caretaker, of Mayo, and of Mary (née Murphy), home care worker, of West Cork. Born April 24, 1955; educated St Ursula's, South London; St Mary's, Strawberry Hill, Twickenham; Birmingham University (BSocSc 1978). *Trades Union:* Former National President, NALGO Housing Association Branch. *Career:* Director, Housing Association; Previously worked in Housing, Local Government, Social Services and Education. *Councils, Public Bodies:* Councillor, London Borough of Lewisham 1984–97, Leader 1993–95, Chair, Housing Committee (6 years). *Political Career:* PPS to Rt Hon. Gavin Strang, MP, as Minister of State (in Cabinet), Department of the Environment, Transport and the Regions (Minister for Transport) December 1997–98, to Rt Hon. Dr Mo Mowlam, as Minister for the Cabinet Office 1999–. *Select Committees (Current):* Member: Public Administration 1999– *(Former):* Member: Northern Ireland Affairs 1998. *Party Groups:* Member: Labour National Policy Forum, Labour Women's Network, Labour Housing Group. *Other:* School Governor: Denbigh Infants and Juniors, Luton, Cardinal Newman School, Luton; Luton Day Centre for the Homeless; Patron, Homes for Homeless People. *Miscellaneous:* Vice-Chair: Association of London Local Authorities, Association of Metropolitan Authorities; Chair, AMA Housing Committee. *Special Interests:* Economy and Employment, Welfare, Housing and Urban Regeneration, Childcare, E-Issues. *Countries of Interest:* Northern Ireland, Kashmir, Spain, Bangladesh, Ireland. *Recreations:* Visiting historic sites, rambling, cinema. *Electoral Notes:* Contested Carshalton and Wallington 1992. Member for Luton South since May 1, 1997. *Address:* Margaret Moran, MP, House of Commons, London, SW1A 0AA *Tel:* 020 7219 5049 *Fax:* 020 7219 5094. *Constituency:* 3 Union Street, Luton, Bedfordshire *Tel:* 01582 731882 *Fax:* 01582 731885 *E-mail:* moranm@parliament.uk *Website:* http://www.margaretmoran.org.

MORGAN, Alasdair Neil *(Galloway and Upper Nithsdale)* SNP majority 5,624

Son of late Alexander Morgan, insurance superintendent, and Emily Morgan. Born April 21, 1945; educated Breadalbane Academy, Aberfeldy; University of Glasgow (MA Mathematics and Political Economy); Open University (BA). Married August 28, 1969, Anne, daughter of Alexander and Jean Gilfillan (2 daughters). *Profession:* Computer Consultant. *Whip:* SNP Chief Whip 1999–. *Spokesman:* Spokesman for Employment, Trade and Industry (including Tourism and Small Businesses), Energy, Forestry, Transport 1997–99. *Select Committees (Current):* Member: Trade and Industry 1997–. *Party Groups:* SNP: National Treasurer 1983–90, Senior Vice-Convenor 1990–91, Election Director 1992, National Secretary 1992–97, Vice-President 1997–. *Special Interests:* European Union, Transport, Rural Affairs. *Recreations:* Hill-walking. *Electoral Notes:* Member for Galloway and Upper Nithsdale since May 1, 1997. MSP for Galloway and Upper Nithsdale since May 6, 1999. *Address:* Alasdair Morgan Esq, MP, MSP, House of Commons, London, SW1A 0AA *Tel:* 020 7219 3472 *Fax:* 020 7219 1235. *Constituency:* 106a High Street, Dalbeattie, Kirkcudbrightshire, DG5 4HB *Tel:* 01556 611956 *Fax:* 01556 613240 *E-mail:* morganal@parliament.uk.

MORGAN, Julie *(Cardiff North)* Lab majority 8,126

Daughter of late Jack Edwards and Grace Edwards. Born November 2, 1944; educated Dinas Powys Primary School; Howell's School, Llandaff, Cardiff; King's College, University of London (BA Hons); Manchester University; Cardiff University (Postgraduate Diploma in Social Administration, CQSW). Married April 22, 1967, Rhodri Morgan, MP *(qv)*, son of late T. J. Morgan and Huana Morgan (1 son 2 daughters). *Trades Union:* Member, TGWU. *Profession:* Social Worker. *Career:* Principal Officer and Development Officer, West Glamorgan County Council 1983–87; Senior Social Worker, Barry Social Services 1985–87; Assistant Director, Child Care, Barnados 1987–. *Councils, Public Bodies:* Councillor: South Glamorgan Council 1985–96, Cardiff Council 1996; Member, Probation Committee. *Select Committees (Current):* Member: Welsh Affairs 1997–. *Party Groups:* Hon. Treasurer, Welsh Regional Group of Labour MPs 1999–. *Other:* Chair of Governors, Albany Road School; Member: Welsh Refugee Council, Race Equality Council, Nicaragua

Solidarity Campaign; Permanent Waves, Women's Arts Association. *Special Interests:* Equal Opportunity, Social Services, Childcare. *Countries of Interest:* Nicaragua. *Recreations:* Swimming, walking. *Electoral Notes:* Contested Cardiff North 1992 General Election. Member for Cardiff North since May 1, 1997. *Address:* Mrs Julie Morgan, MP, House of Commons, London, SW1A 0AA *Tel:* 020 7219 6960. *Constituency:* Cardiff North Constituency Office, 17 Plasnewydd, Whitchurch, Cardiff *Tel:* 029 2052 2913 *Fax:* 029 2061 3662.

MORGAN, Rhodri *(Cardiff West)*   Lab majority 15,628

Son of late Thomas John Morgan, Vice-Principal of University College, Swansea, and Huana Morgan. Born September 29, 1939; educated Whitchurch Grammar School, Cardiff; St John's College, Oxford University (BA Hons Philosophy, Politics and Economics (Class II) 1961); Harvard University; Graduate School of Arts and Sciences (MA Government 1963). Married April 22, 1967, Julie Edwards (1 son 2 daughters). *Trades Union:* Member, TGWU. *Career:* Tutor, Organiser Workers' Educational Association 1963–65; Research Officer: Cardiff City Planning Department 1965–66; Welsh Office 1967–71; Economic Adviser, Department of Trade and Industry 1972–74; Industrial Development Officer, South Glamorgan County Council 1974–80; Head, European Commission Press and Information Office for Wales 1980–87. *Political Career:* Secretary for Economic Development, National Assembly for Wales 1999-. *Spokesman:* Opposition Front Bench Spokesman on Energy 1988–92; Opposition Front Bench Spokesman on Welsh Affairs 1992–97. *Select Committees (Former):* Member: Energy 1987–88, Members' Interests 1987–88, Liaison 1997–99; Chairman: Public Administration 1997–99. *Party Groups:* Chairman, Welsh Regional Group of Labour MPs 1999. *Other:* Founder Member, Wales Co-operative Centre 1985. *Sportsclubs:* Fairwater Rugby; Secretary, Lords and Commons Tennis Club. *Publications: Cardiff – Half and Half a Capital*, 1994. *Special Interests:* Industrial Policy, Regional Policy, Wild Life Conservation (especially bird and marine), Health. *Countries of Interest:* USA, France, Germany. *Recreations:* Running, wood-carving, watching rugby and athletics. *Electoral Notes:* Member for Cardiff West since June 1987. AM for Cardiff West since May 6, 1999. *Clubs:* Canton Labour, Grange, Riverside Labour. *Address:* Rhodri Morgan Esq, MP, AM, House of Commons, London, SW1A 0AA *Tel:* 020 7219 3498/2510 *Fax:* 020 7219 6838. *Constituency:* Transport House, 1 Cathedral Road, Cardiff, CF1 9SD *Tel:* 029 2022 3207/3370 *Fax:* 029 2023 0422.

MORLEY, Elliot *(Scunthorpe)*   Lab majority 14,173

Son of Anthony Morley and late Margaret Morley. Born July 6, 1952; educated St Margaret's High School, Liverpool; Hull College of Education (BEd); Hon. Fellow, Lincolnshire and Humberside University. Married September 1975, Patricia Hunt (1 son 1 daughter). *Trades Union:* Former President, Hull Teachers Association. *Career:* Teacher. *Councils, Public Bodies:* Hull City Council: Councillor 1979–86, Chairman, City Transport Committee 1981–85, Former Deputy Traffic Commissioner, NE Region; Member, NIJC of Municipal Bus Industries; Executive Member, Federation of Public Passenger Employers 1981–86. *Political Career:* Parliamentary Secretary, Ministry of Agriculture, Fisheries and Food (Minister for Fisheries and the Countryside) 1997-. *Spokesman:* Opposition Spokesman on Food, Agriculture and Rural Affairs with special responsibility for animal welfare 1989–97. *Select Committees (Former):* Member: Agriculture 1987–89. *Party Groups:* Parliamentary Convenor, Socialist Environmental Resources Association 1989–91. *Other:* Council Member, RSPB; Vice-President, Wildlife Link; President, South Humber and North Lincolnshire RSPCA; Vice-President, Steel Action. *Trust:* Former Council Member, British Trust for Ornithology; Trustee, Birds of the Humber Trust. *Miscellaneous:* Vice-President, Federation of Economic Development Authorities (FEDA). *Special Interests:* Education, Public Transport, Local Government, Green Issues, Countryside. *Countries of Interest:* Africa, Cyprus. *Recreations:* Ornithology, travel. *Electoral Notes:* Contested Beverley 1983. Member for Glanford and Scunthorpe 1987–97, and for Scunthorpe since May 1, 1997. *Address:* Elliot Morley Esq, MP, House of Commons, London, SW1A 0AA *Tel:* 020 7219 3569. *Constituency:* Kinsley Labour Club, Cole Street, Scunthorpe, Lincolnshire, DN15 6QS *Tel:* 01724 842000 *Fax:* 01724 281734 *E-mail:* elliot.morleymp@geo2.poptel.org.uk; parlsecc@sec.maff.gov.uk.

MORRIS, The Rt Hon. Estelle *(Birmingham Yardley) Lab majority 5,315*

Daughter of Rt Hon. Charles Morris, DL, and of Pauline Morris. Born June 17, 1952; educated Whalley Range High School; Coventry College of Education. *Career:* Teacher, Sidney Stringer School and Community College 1974–92. *Councils, Public Bodies:* Councillor, Warwick District Council 1979–91; Leader, Labour Group 1982–89. *Political Career:* Parliamentary Under-Secretary of State, Department for Education and Employment (School Standards) 1997–98, Minister of State (Minister for School Standards) 1998–. *Whip:* Opposition Whip 1994–95. *Spokesman:* Opposition Spokeswoman on Education and Employment 1995–97. *Honours:* PC 1999. *Special Interests:* Education and Training, Housing, Local Government. *Electoral Notes:* Member for Birmingham Yardley since April 9, 1992. *Address:* The Rt Hon. Estelle Morris, MP, House of Commons, London, SW1A 0AA *Tel:* 020 7219 6450 *Tel (Constituency):* 0121–789 7356 *Fax (Constituency):* 0121–789 9754 *E-mail:* estelle@morrisrthon.freeserve.co.uk.

MORRIS, The Rt Hon. Sir John, QC *(Aberavon) Lab majority 21,571*

Son of late D W Morris and M O A Lewis. Born November 5, 1931; educated Ardwyn School, Aberystwyth; University College of Wales, Aberystwyth; Gonville and Caius College, Cambridge (LLM); Hon. LLD, University of Wales; Hon. Fellow: University College, Aberystwyth, Trinity College, Carmarthen, University College, Swansea. Married 1959, Margaret, JP, daughter of late Edward Lewis, OBE, JP, of Llandysul (3 daughters). *Trades Union:* Member, GMB. *Armed Forces:* Commissioned Welch Regiment and served Royal Welsh Fusiliers. *Profession:* QC. *Career:* Called to the Bar, Gray's Inn 1954; QC 1973; Recorder of Crown Court 1982–97. *Political Career:* Parliamentary Secretary to the Ministry of Power 1964–1966; Joint Parliamentary Secretary Ministry of Transport 1966–1968; Minister of Defence for Equipment 1968–70; Secretary of State for Wales 1974–79; Opposition Attorney General 1979–81, 1983–97; Attorney General 1997–99. *Spokesman:* Former Principal Opposition Front Bench Spokesman on Legal Affairs. *Select Committees (Former):* Member: Privileges 1994–97. *International Bodies:* Member: UK Delegation Consultative Assemblies Council of Europe and WEU 1963–64, 1982–83, UK Delegates North Atlantic Assembly 1970. *Other:* Chairman, National Road Safety Advisory Council 1967–68. *Miscellaneous:* Chairman, Joint Review of British Railways 1966–67; Committee Member, Implementation of Nolan Report 1997. *Sportsclubs:* Vice-President, Aberavon RFC. *Honours:* PC 1970; Knighted 1999. *Electoral Notes:* Member for Aberavon since 1959. *Address:* The Rt Hon. Sir John Morris, QC, MP, House of Commons, London, SW1A 0AA *Tel:* 020 7219 3470 *Fax:* 020 7219 5999. *Constituency:* 22 Depot Road, Cwmaron, Port Talbot, West Glamorgan *Tel:* 01639 896807 *Fax:* 01639 891725.

MOSS, Malcolm Douglas *(North East Cambridgeshire) Con majority 5,101*

Son of late Norman Moss and Annie Moss, née Gay. Born March 6, 1943; educated Audenshaw Grammar School; St John's College, Cambridge (BA 1965, MA 1967); Larmor Award, St John's College. Married December 28, 1965, Vivien Lorraine (died February 1997), daughter of late Albert and Renee Peake (2 daughters). *Profession:* Teacher. *Career:* Blundell's School: Assistant Master 1966–68, Head of Department, Geography and Economics 1968–70; Barwick Associates Ltd: Insurance Consultant 1971–72, General Manager 1972–74; Mandrake Associates Ltd: Founder and Director 1974–94, Managing Director 1986–88; Chairman: Mandrake Group plc 1986–88, Mandrake Associates Ltd 1988–93. *Councils, Public Bodies:* Wisbech Town Councillor 1979–87; Fenland District Councillor 1983–87; Cambridgeshire County Councillor 1985–87. *Political Career:* PPS: to Rt Hon. Tristan Garel-Jones MP, as Minister of State, Foreign and Commonwealth Office 1991–93, to Rt Hon. Sir Patrick Mayhew, QC, MP, as Secretary of State for Northern Ireland 1993–94; Parliamentary Under-Secretary of State, Northern Ireland Office 1994–97. *Whip:* An Opposition Whip (Trade and Industry, Foreign Office and International Development: Western) June-November 1997. *Spokesman:* Opposition Spokesman for Northern Ireland November 1997–. *Select Committees (Former):* Member: Energy 1989–91. *Trust:* Trustee, Angles Theatre and Arts Centre, Wisbech. *Sportsclubs:*

Member, Lords and Commons: Ski Club, Tennis Club. *Special Interests:* Energy, Education, Housing, Small Businesses, Financial Services, Rural Development. *Countries of Interest:* France, Switzerland, USA. *Recreations:* Amateur dramatics, gardening, skiing, tennis. *Electoral Notes:* Member for North East Cambridgeshire since June 1987. *Address:* Malcolm Moss Esq, MP, House of Commons, London, SW1A 0AA *Tel:* 020 7219 6933 *Fax:* 020 7219 6840. *Constituency:* 111 High Street, March, Cambridgeshire, PE15 *Tel:* 01354 656541 *Fax:* 01354 660417.

MOUNTFORD, Kali *(Colne Valley)   Lab majority 4,840*

Born January 12, 1954; educated Crewe Grammar School for Girls; Crewe and Alsager College (DipHE, BA Hons). (1 son 1 daughter). *Trades Union:* Member, CPSA 1975–97: Shop Steward 1983–95, Branch Secretary 1985–90, Regional Secretary 1987–92, Department Employment Whitley Council Secretary 1988–95, Branch Chair 1990–92, Trades Council Executive 1990–95. *Councils, Public Bodies:* Councillor, Sheffield City Council 1992–96: Vice-Chair, Economic Development 1992–94, Chair, Personnel 1994–95, Deputy Chair, Finance 1995, Chair, Finance 1995–96. *Select Committees (Former):* Member: Social Security 1998–99. *Party Groups:* Member, Labour Party (Sheffield Brightside): General Management Committee 1985–95, Women's Officer 1989–91, Euro Constituency Vice-Chair 1989–91, Campaign Co-ordinator 1992, Recruitment Officer 1992–93. *Other:* Member: Sheffield Co-ordinating Committee Against Unemployment, National Centre for Popular Music 1994–95. *Miscellaneous:* Member, Sheffield Race Equality Council 1993–95. *Electoral Notes:* Member for Colne Valley since May 1, 1997. *Address:* Kali Mountford, MP, House of Commons, London, SW1A 0AA *Tel:* 020 7219 4507. *Constituency:* 1043 Manchester Road, Linthwaite, Huddersfield *Tel:* 01484 841470 *Fax:* 01484 841471.

MOWLAM, The Rt Hon. Dr Marjorie *(Redcar)   Lab majority 21,667*

Daughter of late Frank William Mowlam and late Bettina Mary Mowlam. Born September 18, 1949; educated Coundon Court Comprehensive School, Coventry; Durham University (BA); Iowa University, USA (MA, PhD); Honorary degrees Teeside, Durham and Coventry Universities. Married June 24, 1995, Peter Jon Norton. *Trades Union:* Member, TGWU. *Career:* Lecturer, Newcastle University 1979–83; Senior administrator, Northern College, Barnsley 1984–87. *Political Career:* Elected to Shadow Cabinet 1992–97; Shadow Secretary of State for Northern Ireland 1996–97; Secretary of State for Northern Ireland 1997–99; Minister for the Cabinet Office and Chancellor of the Duchy of Lancaster 1999–. *Spokesman:* Opposition Spokesperson on: Northern Ireland 1988–89, Trade and Industry specialising in City affairs 1989–92; Principal Opposition Spokesperson on: Citizen's Charter and Women's Affairs 1992–93, National Heritage 1993–94, Northern Ireland 1994–96. *Party Groups:* Member, Labour Party National Executive Committee 1995–. *Other:* Vice-President, The Big Issue Foundation. *Awards:* Channel 4 and House Award for Major Political Achievement 1999. Freeman: City of Sheffield, City of Coventry, Borough of Redcar and Cleveland. *Honours:* PC 1997. *Recreations:* Swimming, walking, travelling, jigsaws. *Electoral Notes:* Member for Redcar since June 1987. *Address:* The Rt Hon. Dr Marjorie Mowlam, MP, House of Commons, London, SW1A 0AA *Tel:* 020 7219 5066. *Constituency:* PO Box 77, Redcar, Cleveland, TS10 1YF *Tel:* 01642 490404 *Fax:* 01642 489260 *E-mail:* mmowlam@cabinet-office.x.gsi.gov.uk.

MUDIE, George *(Leeds East)   Lab majority 17,466*

Born February 6, 1945; educated Local state schools. Married (2 children). *Career:* Trade Union Official. *Councils, Public Bodies:* Former Leader, Leeds City Council. *Political Career:* Parliamentary Under-Secretary of State (Lifelong Learning), Department for Education and Employment 1998–99. *Whip:* Opposition Whip 1994–97; Pairing and Accommodation Whip 1995–97; Treasurer of HM Household (Deputy Chief Whip) 1997–98. *Select Committees (Former):* Member: Accommodation and Works 1992–98, Public Accounts 1994–95, Selection 1995–97, Finance and Services 1997–98, Selection 1997–98, Finance and Services 1998–99, Selection 1998–99. *Recreations:* Watching football. *Electoral Notes:* Member for Leeds East since April 9, 1992. *Clubs:* Harehills Labour. *Address:* George Mudie Esq, MP, House of Commons, London, SW1A 0AA *Tel:* 020 7219 5889.

MULLIN, Chris *(Sunderland South)   Lab majority 19,638*

Son of Leslie and Teresa Mullin. Born December 12, 1947; educated St Joseph's College, Ipswich; University of Hull (LLB Hons); Hon. LLD, City University, London. Married April 14, 1987, Nguyen Thi Ngoc, daughter of Nguyen Tang Minh (2 daughters). *Trades Union:* Member: NUJ, MSF. *Career:* Author; Journalist; travelled extensively in China, Vietnam and India; BBC World Service 1974–78; Worked for *Tribune* 1978–84, Editor 1982–84. *Political Career:* Parliamentary Under-Secretary of State, Department of the Environment, Transport and the Regions 1999–. *Select Committees (Former):* Member: Home Affairs 1992–97; Chairman: Home Affairs 1997–99; Member: Liaison 1997–99. *Awards:* Channel 4 and House Award for Questioner of the Year 1999. *Publications: How to Select or Reselect your MP*, 1981; *The Tibetans*, 1981; *A Very British Coup*, 1982; *Error of Judgement*, 1986; *The Last Man Out of Saigon*, 1986; *The Year of the Fire Monkey*, 1991. *Special Interests:* Home Affairs, Media Ownership, Justice. *Countries of Interest:* Cambodia, Tibet, Vietnam. *Recreations:* Walking, gardening. *Electoral Notes:* Contested Devon North 1970, Kingston Upon Thames February 1974. Member for Sunderland South since June 1987. *Address:* Chris Mullin Esq, MP, House of Commons, London, SW1A 0AA *Tel:* 020 7219 4343. *Constituency:* 3 The Esplanade, Sunderland, Tyne and Wear, SR2 7BQ *Tel:* Sunderland Office: 0191–567 2848 *Fax:* 0191–510 1063 *E-mail:* chris_mullin@detr.gsi.gov.uk.

MURPHY, Denis *(Wansbeck)   Lab majority 22,367*

Son of late John Murphy and of Josephine Murphy. Born November 2, 1948; educated St Cuthberts Grammar School, Newcastle-upon-Tyne; Northumberland College. Married September 1969, Nancy, daughter of Robert and Annie Moffat (1 son 1 daughter) (separated). *Trades Union:* Member, National Union of Mineworkers (Craft Section) 1965–; General Secretary, Northumberland Colliery Mechanics Association 1989–97. *Career:* Apprentice Electrician 1965–69; Underground Electrician, Ellington Colliery 1969–94. *Councils, Public Bodies:* Councillor, Wansbeck District Council 1990–97, former Chair of Planning, Leader of Council. *Select Committees (Current):* Member: Deregulation 1998–. *Party Groups:* Member, Labour Party 1974–. *Other:* Chair, Board of Governors, Northumberland Aged Mineworkers Homes Association. *Special Interests:* Economic Development, Planning Transport. *Recreations:* Cycling, walking. *Electoral Notes:* Member for Wansbeck since May 1, 1997. *Address:* Denis Murphy Esq, MP, House of Commons, London, SW1A 0AA *Tel:* 020 7219 6474. *Constituency:* 38 Belgrave Gardens, Ashington, Northumberland, NE63 9SW *Tel:* 01670 523100 *Fax:* 01670 813208.

MURPHY, Jim (James) *(Eastwood) Lab majority 3,236*

Son of Jim Murphy, pipe-fitter, and Anne Murphy, secretary. Born August 23, 1967; educated Bellarmine Secondary School, Glasgow; Milnerton High School, Cape Town; University of Strathclyde. Married Claire Cook (1 daughter). *Trades Union:* President: NUS (Scotland) 1992–94, NUS 1994–96; Member, GMB. *Career:* Director, Endsleigh Insurance 1994–96; Project Manager, Scottish Labour Party. *Select Committees (Current):* Member: Public Accounts 1999–. *Party Groups:* Vice-Chair, Labour Friends of Israel; Member, Co-operative Party. *Sportsclubs:* Bonnington Golf. Fellow, Royal Society of Arts. *Publications: The House of Lords – An Abuse of Power,* 1998. *Special Interests:* Economy, International Affairs, Defence, Consumer Issues, Sport. *Countries of Interest:* Southern Africa, Israel. *Recreations:* Football, travelling in Scotland, cinema, horse-racing, golf. *Electoral Notes:* Member for Eastwood since May 1, 1997. *Address:* Jim Murphy Esq, MP, House of Commons, London, SW1A 0AA *Tel:* 020 7219 4615 *Fax:* 020 7219 5657. *Constituency:* Millworks, 28 Field Road, Busby, Strathclyde, G76 8SE *Tel:* 0141–644 3330 *Fax:* 0141–644 4771.

MURPHY, The Rt Hon. Paul Peter *(Torfaen) Lab majority 24,536*

Son of late Ronald and late Marjorie Murphy. Born November 25, 1948; educated St Francis School, Abersychan; West Monmouth School, Pontypool; Oriel College, Oxford (MA). *Career:* Management trainee, CWS 1970–71; Lecturer in Government, Ebbw Vale College of Further Education 1971–87. *Councils, Public Bodies:* Torfaen Borough Council: Councillor 1973–87, Chairman, Finance Committee 1976–86. *Political Career:* Minister of State, Northern Ireland Office (Minister for Political Development) 1997–99; Secretary of State for Wales 1999–. *Spokesman:* Opposition Spokesman on: Welsh Affairs 1988–94, Northern Ireland 1994–95, Foreign Affairs 1995, Defence, Disarmament and Arms Control 1995–97. *Party Groups:* Secretary, Torfaen Constituency Labour Party 1971–87; Former Chair, Welsh Group of Labour MPs. *International Bodies:* Member, Royal Institute of International Affairs 1997–. *Other:* Former school and college governor. *Miscellaneous:* Former Treasurer, Anglo-Austrian Society. *Honours:* Knight of St Gregory (Papal Award); PC 1999. *Special Interests:* Local Government, Wales, Education, Housing, Foreign Affairs. *Recreations:* Classical music, cooking. *Electoral Notes:* Contested Wells 1979. Member for Torfaen since June 1987. *Address:* The Rt Hon. Paul Murphy, MP, House of Commons, London, SW1A 0AA *Tel:* 020 7219 3463 *Tel (Constituency):* 01495 750078 *Fax (Constituency):* 01495 752584.

N

NAYSMITH, Dr Doug (John Douglas) *(Bristol North West) Lab majority 11,382*

Son of late James Naysmith and late Ina Vass. Born April 1, 1941; educated Musselburgh Burgh School; George Heriots School, Edinburgh; Heriot Watt University; University of Edinburgh (BSc, PhD, MIBiol, CBiol). Married September 3, 1966, Caroline Hill (1 son 1 daughter) (separated). *Trades Union:* Past President and Secretary, Bristol AUT. *Profession:* Immunologist. *Career:* Research Assistant, Edinburgh University 1966–69; Post-doctoral Fellow, Yale University 1969–70; Research Immunologist, Beecham Research Laboratories 1970–72; Research Associate, Fellow, Lecturer in Immunology, Pathology Department, University of Bristol 1972–92; Administrator, Registrars Office, University of Bristol 1992–97. *Councils, Public Bodies:* Bristol City Council: Councillor 1981–98, Past Chair: Docks Committee, Health and Environmental Services Committee, Health Policy Committee, Past Labour Group Whip; Past member, Avon FPC; Past member, Bristol CHC. *Select Committees (Current):* Member: Deregulation 1998–, Social Security 1999–. *Party Groups:* Past Chair, Bristol District Labour Party; Past President, Socialist Health Association; National Vice-President, Socialist Health Association; Member, Co-operative Party. *International Bodies:* Former Treasurer, International Union of Immunology Societies; Former Secretary, European Federation of Immunology Societies; Former Delegate to Council of Europe and WEU. *Other:* Member: Citizens

Advice Bureau, CND, WDM. *Trust:* Member, Wildlife Trust; Trustee, Jenner Trust. FRSM; MIBiol. *Publications:* Various scientific papers and book chapters. *Special Interests:* Health, Co-operative Development, Local Government, International Development, Science, Higher Education. *Recreations:* Music, theatre, films, preserving paddle steamers. *Electoral Notes:* Member for Bristol North West since May 1, 1997. *Address:* Dr Doug Naysmith, MP, House of Commons, London, SW1A 0AA *Tel:* 020 7219 4187 *Fax:* 020 7219 2602. *Constituency:* Unit 7, Greenway Business Centre, Doncaster Road, Bristol, BS10 5PY *Tel:* 0117-950 2385 *Fax:* 0117-950 5302 *E-mail:* naysmithd@parliament.uk.

NICHOLLS, Patrick Charles Martyn *(Teignbridge)   Con majority 281*

Son of late Douglas Charles Martyn Nicholls, Solicitor. Born November 14, 1948; educated Redrice School, Andover; College of Law, Guildford. Married July 3, 1976, Bridget Elizabeth Fergus, daughter of E. A. Owens (1 son 2 daughters). *Career:* Qualified as solicitor 1974; Partner with firm of solicitors in Exeter 1976–; PA to Peter Emery, MP, in 1979 General Election; Steward, British Boxing Board of Control 1985–87. *Councils, Public Bodies:* Councillor, East Devon District Council 1980–84. *Political Career:* PPS: to David Mellor, QC, MP, as Parliamentary Under-Secretary of State, Home Office, and assisting Lord Elton at the Home Office 1984–86, to Rt Hon. John Selwyn Gummer, MP, as Minister of State, Ministry of Agriculture 1986–87; Parliamentary Under-Secretary of State: at Department of Employment 1987–90, at Department of Environment July-Oct 1990. *Spokesman:* Opposition Spokesman for: National Heritage 1997, Culture, Media and Sport June-November 1997, Health November 1997–98; An Opposition Spokesman for Agriculture, Fisheries and Food 1998–. *Select Committees (Former):* Member: Social Security 1990–93, Deregulation 1995–97. *Party Groups:* Secretary, West Country MPs' Group 1984–97; Vice-Chairman, Conservative Party 1993–94 Former Founder Member, Westminster Foundation for Democracy. *International Bodies:* Member, North Atlantic Assembly Delegation 1992–97. *Other:* Board Member, Westminster Foundation for Democracy 1992–93. *Miscellaneous:* Member, Standing Committees on: Police and Criminal Evidence Bill, Video Cassettes Bill. Freeman, City of London. *Special Interests:* Home Affairs, Defence, Construction Industry, Retail Industry. *Countries of Interest:* Indonesia, Malaysia, Venezuela, Bahrain. *Recreations:* Skiing, historical research, theatre, opera. *Electoral Notes:* Member for Teignbridge since June 1983. *Clubs:* Carlton. *Address:* Patrick Nicholls Esq, MP, House of Commons, London, SW1A 0AA *Tel:* 020 7219 4077 *Fax:* 020 7219 4957. *Constituency:* Unit D, Minerva Way, Brunel Road, Newton Abbot, Devon, TQ12 4JP *Tel:* 01392 204031 *Fax:* 01626 204033.

NORMAN, Archie John *(Tunbridge Wells)   Con majority 7,506*

Son of Dr Archie Norman, physician, and Aleida Elisabeth Norman. Born May 1, 1954; educated Charterhouse; Harvard Business School; Emmanuel College, Cambridge (Exhibitioner); University of Minnesota, Minneapolis (MBA, MA Economics); Hon. Degree, Leeds Metropolitan University. Married Vanessa Mary Peet (1 daughter). *Career:* Citibank NA 1975–77; Partner, McKinsey & Co Inc 1979–86; Group Finance Director, Kingfisher plc 1986–91; Non-Executive Director: British Rail, Railtrack plc, Geest plc 1989–91; Chief Executive, Asda Group plc 1991–96; Chairman, Asda Group plc 1996–. *Political Career:* A Vice-Chairman, Conservative Party (with responsibility for Organisation) 1997–98, Chief Executive and Deputy Chairman 1998–99. *Spokesman:* An Opposition Front Bench Spokesman for Europe 1999–. *Party Groups:* Chairman: Cambridge University Conservative Association 1975, East Region Federation of Conservative Students 1975; Council Member, Federation of Conservative Students 1975–76; Patron, North East Bow Group 1990–96; President, West Yorkshire (Conservative) Businessmen's Association 1990–96. *Miscellaneous:* DTI Deregulation Taskforce 1994–; ACISE Government Committee on Business and the Environment 1995–96; Member, Council of the Industrial Society; Fellow, Marketing Society. *Sportsclubs:* Vanderbuilt Tennis Club. *Special Interests:* Business, Transport, Agriculture. *Recreations:* Farming, music, opera, tennis, football. *Electoral Notes:* Member for Tunbridge Wells since May 1, 1997. *Address:* Archie Norman Esq, MP, House of Commons, London, SW1A 0AA *Tel:* 020 7219 3000. *Constituency:* 84 London Road, Tunbridge Wells, Kent, TN1 1EA *Tel:* 01892 522581 *Fax:* 01892 522582 *E-mail:* anorman@asda.u-net.com.

NORRIS, Dan *(Wansdyke)   Lab majority 4,799*

Son of David Norris and June Norris (née Allen). Born January 28, 1960; educated State Schools; University of Sussex (MSW); Hon. Fellow, School of Cultural and Community Studies, University of Sussex. *Trades Union:* Member, GMB. *Profession:* Researcher/Author. *Career:* Former Child Protection Officer. *Councils, Public Bodies:* Councillor: Bristol City Council 1989–92, 1995–97, Avon County Council 1994–96. *Party Groups:* Member: Co-op Party, Labour Leader's Campaign Team with responsibility for Health 1998–99, General Election Campaign Team with responsibility for campaigning against the Liberal Democrats 1999–. *Publications:* Various publications on prevention and reduction of violence. *Special Interests:* Freedom of Information, Child Protection and Safety, Animal Welfare. *Recreations:* Photography. *Electoral Notes:* Member for Wansdyke since May 1, 1997. *Clubs:* Radstock Working Men's. *Address:* Dan Norris Esq, MP, House of Commons, London, SW1A 0AA *Tel:* 020 7219 6395 *Tel (Constituency):* 0117–985 4856 *E-mail:* norrisd@parliament.uk.

O

OATEN, Mark *(Winchester)   LD majority 21,556*

Son of Ivor and Audrey Oaten. Born March 8, 1964; educated Queen's Comprehensive School, Watford; Hatfield Polytechnic (BA Hons, Diploma in International Public Relations). Married September 1992, Belinda, daughter of Bob Fordham (1 daughter). *Profession:* Company Director. *Career:* Managing Director, Westminster Communications Ltd; Director, Oasis Radio. *Councils, Public Bodies:* Councillor, Watford Borough Council 1986–94, Liberal Democrat Group Leader. *Political Career:* PPS to Rt Hon. Charles Kennedy, MP, as Leader of the Liberal Democrat Party 1999–. *Spokesman:* A Spokesman for: Social Security and Welfare (Disabled People) 1997–99, Foreign Affairs and Defence (Foreign Affairs) 1999–. *Select Committees (Current):* Member: Public Administration 1999–. *Miscellaneous:* Member, European Standing Committee C 1999–. *Recreations:* Gardening, swimming. *Electoral Notes:* Contested Watford 1992 General Election. Member for Winchester since May 1, 1997. (The two-vote victory was declared invalid and a by-election called for November 20). *Address:* Mark Oaten Esq, MP, House of Commons, London, SW1A 0AA *Tel:* 020 7219 5152. *Constituency:* 45 Southgate Street, Winchester, Hampshire, SO23 4EH *Tel:* 01962 868800.

O'BRIEN, Michael *(North Warwickshire)   Lab majority 14,767*

Son of Timothy O'Brien, railwayman, and Mary O'Brien (née Toomey). Born June 19, 1954; educated St George's School; Blessed Edward Oldcorne School; North Staffs Polytechnic (BA Hons History and Politics, PGCE). Married July 11, 1987, Alison Joy, daughter of Kenneth and Isobel Munro, of Brighton (2 daughters). *Trades Union:* Branch Secretary, NATFHE 1989–90. *Profession:* Solicitor and Lecturer in Law. *Career:* Trainee solicitor 1977–80; Teacher training 1980–81; Lecturer in Law, Colchester College of Further and Higher Education 1981–87; In practice as solicitor 1987–92. *Political Career:* Parliamentary Under-Secretary of State, Home Office: (Minister for Immigration and Nationality) 1997–99, (Minister for Fire and Emergency Planning, Liquor, Drugs and Elections) 1999–. *Spokesman:* Opposition Spokesman on Treasury and Economic Affairs 1995–96; Shadow Economic Secretary to the Treasury 1996–97. *Select Committees (Former):* Member: Home Affairs 1992–93, Treasury and Civil Service 1993–95. *Miscellaneous:* Parliamentary Adviser to the Police Federation of England and Wales 1993–96. *Special Interests:* Housing, Environment, West Midlands Industry, Police, Criminal Law, Coal Industry. *Countries of Interest:* CIS, Eastern Europe, USA. *Recreations:* Cinema and spending time with family. *Electoral Notes:* Contested Ruislip Northwood 1983 and North Warwickshire 1987. Member for North Warwickshire since April 9, 1992. *Clubs:* Bedworth Ex Servicemen's, Woodend Workingmen's. *Address:* Michael O'Brien Esq, MP, House of Commons, London, SW1A 0AA *Tel:* 020 7219 3000. *Constituency:* 2 Croft House, Croft Fields, Bedworth, Nuneaton, Warwickshire, CV12 8QT *Tel:* 024 7631 5084.

O'BRIEN, Stephen Rothwell *(Eddisbury)* Con majority 1,606

Son of David H O'Brien, MA, retired, and Pauline Ann O'Brien (née Rothwell). Born April 1, 1957; educated Handbridge School, Chester; Heronwater School; Abergele; Sedbergh School, Cumbria; Emmanuel College, Cambridge; College of Law, Chester (MA). Married August 30, 1986, Gemma, daughter of David and Clare Townshend (2 sons 1 daughter). *Profession:* Businessman. *Career:* Articles, Freshfields 1981–83, Senior Managing Solicitor 1983–88; Group Secretary and Director Corporate Affairs, Redland plc 1988–98; International Business Consultant 1998–. *Select Committees (Current):* Member: Education and Employment 1999–, Education Sub-Committee 1999–. *Party Groups:* Chairman, Chichester Conservative Association 1998–; Executive Committee Member, Westminster Candidates Association 1998–. *Other:* Non-Executive Director, Cambridge University Careers Service (SYNDIC) 1992–. *Miscellaneous:* Elected Member, CBI South East Regional Council 1995–98; Chairman, Public and Parliamentary Affairs Committee BMP (National Council of Building Materials Producers) 1995–99. FCIS. *Electoral Notes:* Member for Eddisbury since July 22, 1999. *Clubs:* Carlton, Institute of Director, Law Society. *Address:* Stephen O'Brien Esq, MP, House of Commons, London, SW1A 0AA. *Constituency:* Eddisbury Conservative Association, 4 Church Walk, High Street, Tarporley, Cheshire, CW6 0AJ *Tel:* 01829 733243 *Fax:* 01829 733243.

O'BRIEN, William *(Normanton)* Lab majority 15,893

Born January 25, 1929; educated State schools; Leeds University. Married Jean (3 daughters). *Trades Union:* Member, NUM 1945–. *Career:* Coalminer. *Councils, Public Bodies:* Councillor: Knottingly Urban District Council 1952–85, West Riding County Council 1964–74; Member, Yorkshire Water Authority 1973–83; Wakefield Council: Councillor 1973–83, Former Deputy Leader, Chairman, Finance and General Purposes Committee; JP, Wakefield Division. *Spokesman:* Opposition Front Bench Spokesman on: Environment (Local Government) 1988–92, Northern Ireland 1992–96. *Select Committees (Current):* Member: Environment, Transport and Regional Affairs 1997–, Transport Sub-Committee 1997–, Chairmen's Panel 1998–, Standing Orders 1998–. *International Bodies:* Executive Committee Member, IPU British Group. *Trust:* Fellow, Industry and Parliament Trust. *Miscellaneous:* Member, Public Accounts Commission 1997–. *Special Interests:* Local Government, Water Industry, Energy. *Recreations:* Reading, organising. *Electoral Notes:* Member for Normanton since June 1983. *Address:* William O'Brien Esq, MP, House of Commons, London, SW1A 0AA *Tel:* 020 7219 6464 *Fax:* 020 7219 0301.

O'HARA, Edward *(Knowsley South)* Lab majority 30,708

Son of late Robert O'Hara and of late Clara O'Hara, née Davies. Born October 1, 1937; educated Liverpool Collegiate School; Magdalen College, Oxford (MA). Married September 11, 1962, Lillian, daughter of late Thomas and Margaret Hopkins (2 sons 1 daughter). *Career:* Lecturer in Higher Education. *Councils, Public Bodies:* Councillor, Knowsley Borough Council 1975–90. *Select Committees (Current):* Member: Chairmen's Panel 1997– *(Former):* Member: Education 1992–96, Speaker's Panel of Chairmen 1993–97, Education and Employment 1996–97. *Party Groups:* Member: Socialist Education Association, Co-operative Party, Fabian Society. *International Bodies:* Merseyside delegate to Régions Européenes de Tradition Industrielle 1989–90, Permanent Committee, Assembly of European Regions 1989–90, Member, Labour Movement in Europe 1990–, Council of Europe 1997–. *Other:* Member: Merseyside Arts Association 1976–79, Board of Management, Royal Liverpool Philharmonic Society 1987–90, Board of Management, National Foundation for Educational Research 1987–90; Chairman of Governors, Cartbridge School 1976–; Governor, Knowsley Community College 1991–; Corresponding Fellow, Foundation for Hellenic Culture 1993–; Vice-President, *TS Iron Duke* (Huyton) 1994–; President, Knowsley South Juniors Football Club 1997–. *Trust:* Patron, Marilyn Houlton MND Trust 1991–; Trustee, Community Development Foundation 1992–, Chair 1997–; Vice-Chair, National Wild Flower Centre Development Trust 1996–.

Special Interests: Local Government, Regional Development, European Union, Education, Housing, Emergency Planning, Animal Welfare, Ageing Issues. *Countries of Interest:* CIS, Cyprus, Germany, Greece, Japan, USA. *Recreations:* Theatre, literature, music (classical, jazz, folk – especially Rembetiko), watching soccer, Greek language and culture. *Electoral Notes:* Member for Knowsley South since September 27, 1990 By-election. *Address:* Edward O'Hara Esq, MP, House of Commons, London, SW1A 0AA *Tel:* 020 7219 5232 *Fax:* 020 7219 4952 *Tel (Constituency):* 0151 449 3873 *Fax (Constituency):* 0151 449 3873.

OLNER, William John *(Nuneaton)   Lab majority 13,540*

Son of late C. William Olner, coalminer, and late Lillian Olner. Born May 9, 1942; educated Atherstone Secondary Modern School; North Warwickshire Technical College (City and Guilds Mechanical Engineering). Married March 10, 1962, Gillian, daughter of David Everitt, worsted fabric spinner. *Trades Union:* Member, AEU and branch secretary 1972–. *Career:* Engineer; Apprenticed with Armstrong Siddeley Motors; 35 years with Rolls Royce, Coventry as skilled machinist. *Councils, Public Bodies:* Nuneaton Borough Council: Councillor 1971–92, Chairman, Planning Committee 1974–76, Deputy Leader 1980–82, Leader 1982–87, Chairman, Policy and Resources Committee 1982–86, Mayor 1987–88, Chairman, Environmental Health Committee 1990–92. *Select Committees (Current):* Member: Environment, Transport and Regional Affairs 1997–, Environment Sub-Committee 1997–, Transport Sub-Committee 1997–, Chairmen's Panel 1998– *(Former):* Member: Environment 1995–97, Standing Orders 1998–99. *International Bodies:* Joint Vice-Chairman, Executive Committee, Commonwealth Parliamentary Association (CPA) UK Branch 1995–99, Member, 1999–. *Other:* Chairman, various school governing bodies. Freeman, City of Coventry. *Special Interests:* Engineering, Local Government. *Countries of Interest:* France, USA, China, Ghana, Australia. *Recreations:* Local Hospice Movement, walking, current affairs, television. *Electoral Notes:* Member for Nuneaton since April 9, 1992. *Address:* William Olner Esq, MP, House of Commons, London, SW1A 0AA *Tel:* 020 7219 4154. *Constituency:* 171 Queen's Road, Nuneaton, Warwickshire, CV11 5NB *Tel:* 024 7664 2222 *Fax:* 024 7664 2223.

O'NEILL, Martin John *(Ochil)   Lab majority 4,652*

Son of John O'Neill, fitter and turner. Born January 6, 1945; educated Wardie Primary School; Trinity Academy; Heriot Watt University (BA Economics); Moray House College of Education (all in Edinburgh). Married July 21, 1973, Elaine Marjorie Samuel (2 sons). *Career:* Insurance Clerk 1963–67; President, Scottish Union of Students 1970–71. *Councils, Public Bodies:* Candidate for Edinburgh Town Council 1973. *Spokesman:* Opposition Front Bench Spokesman on: Scotland 1980–84, Defence and Disarmament and Arms Control 1984–88; Principal Opposition Front Bench Spokesman on Defence 1988–92; Opposition Front Bench Spokesman on Trade and Industry (Energy) 1992–95. *Select Committees (Current):* Chairman: Trade and Industry 1995–; Member: Liaison 1997– *(Former):* Chairman: Trade and Industry 1995–97. *Party Groups:* Labour Party Member since 1963; Held most Party positions in Constituency and Local Government Organisations. *Special Interests:* Education, Defence, Trade and Industry. *Countries of Interest:* Argentina. *Recreations:* Cinema, jazz. *Electoral Notes:* Contested Edinburgh North October 1974 General Election. Member for Stirlingshire East and Clackmannan 1979–83, for Clackmannan 1983–97, and for Ochil since May 1, 1997. *Address:* Martin O'Neill Esq, MP, House of Commons, London, SW1A 0AA *Tel:* 020 7219 5059. *Constituency:* 19 Mar Street, Alloa, FK10 1HR *Tel:* 01259 721536 *Fax:* 01259 216716 *E-mail:* cartere@parliament.uk.

ÖPIK, Lembit *(Montgomeryshire)   LD majority 6,303*

Son of Dr Uno Öpik and Liivi Öpik. Born March 2, 1965; educated Royal Belfast Academical Institution; Bristol University (BA Hons Philosophy 1987) (President Union 1985-86). *Trades Union:* President, National Union of Students Executive 1987–88. *Profession:* Human Resources Training Manager. *Career:* Procter and Gamble Ltd: Brand Assistant/Assistant Brand Manager 1988–91, Corporate Training and Organisation Development Manager 1991–96, Global Human Resources Training Manager 1996–. *Councils, Public Bodies:* Councillor, Newcastle-upon-Tyne City Council 1992. *Spokesman:* A Spokesman for: Northern Ireland 1997–99, Welsh Affairs 1997–99, Young People 1997–99, Home and Legal Affairs (Northern Ireland and Youth) 1999–.

Select Committees (Current): Member: Agriculture 1999–. *Party Groups:* Member, Federal Executive Committee of Liberal Democrats 1991–; Welsh Vice-President, Liberal Democrat Federal Party 1999–. *Other:* President: Shropshire Astronomical Society, Clive Motorcycle Club. *Miscellaneous:* Member, Welsh Grand Committee 1997–. *Special Interests:* Public Transport, Education and Youth, Aerospace. *Countries of Interest:* Eastern Europe, China, Fiji. *Recreations:* Aviation, military history, astronomy, films. *Electoral Notes:* Contested Newcastle Central General Election 1992, Northumbria European Election 1994. Member for Montgomeryshire since May 1, 1997. *Address:* Lembit Öpik Esq, MP, House of Commons, London, SW1A 0AA *Tel:* 020 7219 1144 *Fax:* 020 7219 2210. *Constituency:* Montgomeryshire Liberal Democrats, 3 Park Street, Newtown, Powys, SY16 1EE *Tel:* 01686 625527 *Fax:* 01686 628891 *E-mail:* fionahall@cix.compulink.co.uk (political officer).

ORGAN, Diana Mary *(Forest of Dean)   Lab majority 6,343*

Daughter of Jack, company director, and Vera Pugh, voluntary organiser. Born February 21, 1952; educated Edgbaston Church of England College for Girls, Birmingham; St Hugh's College, Oxford (BA Hons Geography); Bath University School of Education (Postgraduate Certificate in Education); Bristol Polytechnic, Redland (Diploma in Special Education). Married August 9, 1975, Richard Thomas Organ, son of Terry and Edna Organ (2 daughters). *Trades Union:* Member: NUT, NUPE (now UNISON). *Profession:* Special Needs Teacher/Policy Researcher. *Career:* Assistant Teacher: Special School, Walsall 1974–75, Special Needs, Cardiff 1975–76, Special Needs, Plymouth 1976–77; Deputy Head Teacher, St Germans, Cornwall 1977–79; Head of Special Needs Unit, Somerset 1979–82; Supply Special School, Somerset 1982–88; Assistant English Teacher, Somerset 1988–92; Political Researcher, Oxfordshire County Council 1992–95. *Select Committees (Current):* Member: Culture, Media and Sport 1999– *(Former):* Member: Agriculture 1997–99, Statutory Instruments (Joint Committee) 1997–99. *Party Groups:* Joined Labour Party 1970–73; Rejoined 1982–; Secretary, Constituency Labour Party; Member: South-West Women's Committee, South-West Regional Executive, Labour REC 1990–92, 300 Group, Co-op Party. *Other:* Member, Amnesty International; School Governor; Secretary, 2 Playgroups. *Miscellaneous:* Political Board Member, TV South West; Labour Party Conference Debates: Nuclear Energy 1990, Defence 1992, Transport 1993, Education 1994, Rural issues 1995. *Special Interests:* Education, Transport, Rural Affairs. *Countries of Interest:* India, Tibet, China, Mongolia. *Recreations:* Swimming, sailing, tennis, gardening, cinema. *Electoral Notes:* Contested Somerset and Dorset West European Election 1989, Gloucestershire West 1992. Member for Forest of Dean since May 1, 1997. *Address:* Mrs Diana Organ, MP, House of Commons, London, SW1A 0AA *Tel:* 020 7219 5498 *Fax:* 020 7219 6860. *Constituency:* St Annals House, Bellevue Centre, Cinderford, Gloucestershire, GL14 1AB *Tel:* 01594 826835 *Fax:* 01594 827892.

Dod *on* Disk
The Vacher Dod Parliamentary Database
that will run on your PC or Network
For further details please telephone the Westminster Office
020 7828 7256

OSBORNE, Sandra *(Ayr)   Lab majority 6,543*

Daughter of Thomas Clark, labourer, and Isabella Clark, shop worker, meat factory worker, cleaner and laundry worker. Born February 23, 1956; educated Camphill Senior Secondary, Paisley; Anniesland College; Jordanhill College; Strathclyde University (Diploma in Community Education, Diploma in Equality and Discrimination, MSc Equality and Discrimination). Married February 20, 1982, Alastair Osborne (2 daughters). *Trades Union:* Member, APEX; Currently Branch Secretary, TGWU. *Profession:* Community Worker. *Councils, Public Bodies:* Councillor, Kyle and Carrick District Council 1990–95; South Ayrshire Council: Councillor 1994–, Convenor, Community Services (Housing and Social Work). *Political Career:* PPS to Brian Wilson, MP, as Minister of State for Scotland 1999–. *Select Committees (Current):* Member: Information 1997– *(Former):* Member: Scottish Affairs 1998–99. *Party Groups:* Labour Party Activist 1978–; Vice-Chair, Scottish Regional Group of Labour MPs 1998–99, Chair 1999–. *Other:* Member, Women's Aid. *Special Interests:* Women's Issues, Housing, Poverty. *Countries of Interest:* All countries. *Recreations:* Reading and television. *Electoral Notes:* Member for Ayr since May 1, 1997. *Address:* Mrs Sandra Osborne, MP, House of Commons, London, SW1A 0AA *Tel:* 020 7219 6402. *Constituency:* Room 1009, Aviation House, Glasgow Prestwick International Airport, Prestwick, Strathclyde, KA9 2PL *Tel:* 01292 286663 *Fax:* 01292 478540.

OTTAWAY, Richard Geoffrey James *(Croydon South)   Con majority 11,930*

Son of late Professor Christopher Ottaway and of Grace Ottaway. Born May 24, 1945; educated Backwell School, Somerset; Bristol University (LLB Hons). Married June 5, 1982, Nicola, daughter of John Kisch. *Armed Forces:* Officer in the Royal Navy 1961–70, Serving on: HMSs Beechampton, Nubian and Eagle 1967–70. *Profession:* Solicitor. *Career:* Admitted solicitor 1977, specialising in international, maritime and commercial law; Partner, William A. Crump & Son 1981–87; Director, Coastal States Petroleum (UK) Ltd 1988–95. *Political Career:* PPS: to Ministers of State, Foreign and Commonwealth Office 1985–87, to The Rt Hon. Michael Heseltine, MP: as President of the Board of Trade and Secretary of State for Trade and Industry 1992–95, as Deputy Prime Minister and First Secretary of State 1995; A Vice-Chairman, Conservative Party (with responsibility for Local Government) 1998–99. *Whip:* Assistant Government Whip 1995–96; Lord Commissioner of HM Treasury (Government Whip) 1996–97; An Opposition Whip (Environment, Transport and the Regions: Greater London) June-November 1997. *Spokesman:* An Opposition Front Bench Spokesman for: Environment, Transport and the Regions (Local Government and London) 1998–99, Defence 1999–. *Select Committees (Former):* Member: Procedure 1996–97. *Sportsclubs:* Royal Corinthian Yacht. *Publications:* Author of papers on international and maritime law, global pollution, debt and international fraud. *Special Interests:* Defence, Industry, Commerce, World Population. *Recreations:* Yacht racing, jazz, skiing. *Electoral Notes:* Member for Nottingham North 1983–87. Contested Nottingham North 1987 General Election. Member for Croydon South since April 9, 1992. *Address:* Richard Ottaway Esq, MP, House of Commons, London, SW1A 0AA *Tel:* 020 7219 6392 *Fax:* 020 7219 2256.

P

PAGE, Richard Lewis *(South West Hertfordshire)   Con majority 10,021*

Son of late Victor Charles Page. Born February 22, 1941; educated Hurstpierpoint College; Luton Technical College. Married October 3, 1964, Madeleine Ann Brown (1 son 1 daughter). *Councils, Public Bodies:* Councillor, Banstead Urban District Council 1968–71. *Political Career:* PPS to Leader of the House 1982–87; Parliamentary Under-Secretary of State, Department of Trade and Industry 1995–97. *Select Committees (Current):* Member: Public Accounts 1997– *(Former):* Member: Public Accounts 1987–95. *Party Groups:* Chairman, International Office CCO. *Other:* Governor, Rickmansworth Masonic School for Girls 1984–95; Hon. National Treasurer, Leukaemia Research Fund 1987–95; Member, Investment Committee LRF 1997–.

Liveryman, The Pattenmakers Company 1979–. Freeman, City of London. *Special Interests:* Small Businesses, Horses, Scientific Research and Development, Trade and Industry. *Countries of Interest:* Middle East, Eastern Europe. *Recreations:* Shooting. *Electoral Notes:* Contested Workington February and October 1974 General Elections. Member for Workington November 1976 (By-election)-May 1979. Member for South West Hertfordshire since December 1979. *Address:* Richard Page Esq, MP, House of Commons, London, SW1A 0AA *Tel:* 020 7219 5032. *Constituency:* SW Herts Conservative Association, 25 Church Street, Rickmansworth, Hertfordshire *Tel:* 01923 771781 *Fax:* 01923 779471.

PAICE, James Edward Thornton *(South East Cambridgeshire)* Con majority 9,349

Son of late Edward Paice and of Winifred Paice. Born April 24, 1949; educated Framlingham College; Writtle Agricultural College; Fellow, Writtle University College. Married January 6, 1973, Ava Patterson (2 sons). *Career:* Farm manager 1970–73; Farmer and contractor 1973–79; Training Manager, later General Manager, Framlingham Management and Training Services Ltd 1979–87, Non-Executive Director, 1987–89; Director, United Framlingham Farmers Ltd 1989–94. *Councils, Public Bodies:* Chairman, Suffolk Coastal District Council 1982–83. *Political Career:* PPS: to Baroness Trumpington, as Minister of State, Ministry of Agriculture, Fisheries and Food 1989–90, to Rt Hon. John Selwyn Gummer, MP: as Minister of Agriculture, Fisheries and Food 1990–93, as Secretary of State for the Environment 1993–94; Parliamentary Under-Secretary of State: at Department of Employment 1994–95, at Department for Education and Employment 1995–97. *Spokesman:* Opposition Spokesman for Agriculture, Fisheries and Food 1997–. *International Bodies:* Former UK delegate, EEC Council of Young Farmers. *Special Interests:* Small Businesses, Employment Promotion, Agriculture, Rural Affairs, Training, Waste Management. *Countries of Interest:* Europe, New Zealand. *Recreations:* Windsurfing, shooting. *Electoral Notes:* Contested Caernarvon 1979. Member for South East Cambridgeshire since June 1987. *Address:* James Paice Esq, MP, House of Commons, London, SW1A 0AA *Tel:* 020 7219 4101. *Constituency:* 153 St Neots Road, Hardwick, Cambridge, CB3 7QJ *Tel:* 01954 211450 *E-mail:* paicejet@parliament.uk.

PAISLEY, Rev. Ian Richard Kyle *(North Antrim)* DUP majority 10,574

Son of late Rev. J. Kyle Paisley. Born April 6, 1926; educated Ballymena Model School; Ballymena Technical High School; South Wales Bible College; Reformed Presbyterian Theological College, Belfast. Married 1956, Eileen Emily Cassells (2 twin sons 3 daughters). *Career:* Ordained 1946; Minister, Martyrs Memorial Free Presbyterian Church 1946–; Moderator, Free Presbyterian Church of Ulster 1951–; Founded *Protestant Telegraph* 1966. *Political Career:* Member, Northern Ireland Assembly 1973–74; Co-Chairman, World Congress of Fundamentalists 1978; Elected to second Northern Ireland Assembly 1982; MP (Protestant Unionist) for Bannside, Co. Antrim, Parliament of Northern Ireland (Stormont) 1970–72; Leader of Opposition 1972; Member: Northern Ireland Forum 1996–98, Northern Ireland Assembly 1998–. *Spokesman:* A Spokesman for Constitutional Affairs. *Party Groups:* Leader (co-founder), Democratic Unionist Party 1971–. *International Bodies:* Member: Rex Committee, Political Committee, European Parliament. *Other:* President, Whitefield College of the Bible, Laurencetown 1980. *Miscellaneous:* Member, Constitutional Convention 1975–76. *Publications:* Author of several publications. *Special Interests:* Foreign Affairs, Religious Affairs, Constitution. *Recreations:* History, Antiquarian book collecting. *Electoral Notes:* Member for North Antrim since June 1970; MEP for Northern Ireland 1979–. *Address:* The Rev. Ian Paisley, MP, House of Commons, London, SW1A 0AA *Tel:* 020 7219 3000.

Dod *on* Disk

The Vacher Dod Parliamentary Database – configured for PC or Network

For further details please telephone the Westminster Office

020 7828 7256

PALMER, Dr Nicholas *(Broxtowe)   Lab majority 5,575*

Son of late Reginald Palmer and of Irina Palmer. Born February 5, 1950; educated International Schools, Vienna and Copenhagen; Copenhagen University; Birkbeck College, London University (PhD Mathematics). *Trades Union:* Former Health and Safety Officer, MSF Brighton. *Profession:* Computing Manager. *Career:* Head of Internet Services, Novalis, Switzerland 1997–. *Select Committees (Current):* Member: Administration 1998–, European Scrutiny 1998–, Northern Ireland Affairs 1999–. *Party Groups:* National Executive Member, Labour Animal Welfare Society. *Other:* Member: Compassion in World Farming, World Development Movement, Cats Protection League, United Nations Association. *Miscellaneous:* Former Member, Danish and Swiss Social Democrats; Worked on Draft Swiss Social Democrat Economic Programme; Member, European Standing Committee B 1998–. *Publications: The Comprehensive Guide to Board Wargaming,* 1977; *The Best of Board Wargaming,* 1980; *Beyond the Arcade,* 1984; *Parliamentary Portions,* 1998. *Special Interests:* Training, Tax, Development, Animal Welfare. *Countries of Interest:* Scandinavia, Switzerland. *Recreations:* Postal games. *Electoral Notes:* Contested Chelsea 1983, East Sussex and South Kent European Election 1995. Member for Broxtowe since May 1, 1997. *Address:* Dr Nicholas Palmer, MP, House of Commons, London, SW1A 0AA *Tel:* 020 7219 2397 *Fax:* 020 7219 4837. *Constituency:* 23 Barratt Lane, Attenborough, Nottingham, NG9 6AD *Tel:* 0115 0943 0721 *Fax:* 0115–943 1860 *E-mail:* 76276.2147@compuserve.com.

PATERSON, Owen William *(North Shropshire)   Con majority 2,195*

Son of Alfred Dobell Paterson. Born June 24, 1956; educated Radley College; Corpus Christi College, Cambridge (MA History). Married January 26, 1980, Hon. Rose Ridley (2 sons 1 daughter). *Profession:* Tanner. *Career:* Managing Director, British Leather Co Ltd. *Select Committees (Current):* Member: Welsh Affairs 1997–, European Scrutiny 1999–. *Party Groups:* Member: 92 Group 1997–, Conservative Friends of Israel 1997–, Conservative Way Forward 1997–, Conservative 2000 1997–; Vice-President, Conservatives Against a Federal Europe 1998–, Member, No Turning Back Group 1998–. *International Bodies:* President, Cotance (European Tanners' Confederation) 1996–98, Vice-President 1998–; Member: World League For Freedom and Democracy 1997–, Inter-Parliamentary Union 1997–, Commonwealth Parliamentary Association 1997–; Member, Advisory Board, European Foundation 1998–. *Other:* Director, Orthopaedic Institute Ltd, Oswestry; President, Ellesmere Cadet Force; Member, Countryside Alliance. *Miscellaneous:* Member: Institute of Directors, European Standing Committee A 1998–, Welsh Grand Committee 1998–. Liveryman, Leathersellers' Company. *Sportsclubs:* Patron, Oswestry Cricket Club; Member, Shropshire Cricket Club. *Special Interests:* Trade, Industry, Agriculture, Foreign Affairs. *Countries of Interest:* Western and Eastern Europe, USA, China, India. *Recreations:* Travel, racing, hunting. *Electoral Notes:* Contested Wrexham 1992. Member for North Shropshire since May 1, 1997. *Address:* Owen Paterson Esq, MP, House of Commons, London, SW1A 0AA *Tel:* 020 7219 5185 *Fax:* 020 7219 3955. *Constituency:* 35 Willow Street, Oswestry, Shropshire, SY11 1AQ *Tel:* 01691 653596 *Fax:* 01691 671309.

PEARSON, Ian *(Dudley South)   Lab majority 13,027*

Born April 5, 1959; educated Brierley Hill Grammar School; Balliol College, Oxford (BA Hons Philosophy, Politics and Economics); Warwick University (MA Industrial Relations, PhD Industrial and Business Studies); Visiting Fellow, Warwick University. Married Annette Pearson (2 daughters 1 son). *Trades Union:* Member, TGWU. *Career:* Former Deputy Director, Urban Trust; Business and Economic Development Consultant; Joint Chief Executive, The West Midlands Enterprise Board;. *Councils, Public Bodies:* Councillor, Dudley Borough Council 1984–87. *Political Career:* PPS to Geoffrey Robinson, MP, as Paymaster General, HM Treasury 1997–98. *Select Committees (Current):* Member: Education and Employment 1999–, Employment Sub-Committee 1999– *(Former):* Member: Deregulation 1996–97, Treasury 1996–97. *Party Groups:* Joined Labour Party 1974; Former Local Government Policy Research Officer for the Labour Party. *Other:* Patron, Black Country Headway and Wardsley Kidney Patients Association.

Trust: Chairman, Redhouse Cone Trust. *Sportsclubs:* Stourbridge RFC, West Bromwich Albion FC. *Special Interests:* Economic and Industrial Policy, Regional Economic Development. *Countries of Interest:* Central and Eastern Europe, Latin and South America, Far East. *Recreations:* Playing rugby, literature, architecture. *Electoral Notes:* Member for Dudley West from December 15, 1994 By-election–1997, and for Dudley South since May 1, 1997. *Address:* Ian Pearson Esq, MP, House of Commons, London, SW1A 0AA *Tel:* 020 7219 6462 *Fax:* 020 7219 0390. *Constituency:* 139 High Street, Brierley Hill, West Midlands, DY5 3BU *Tel:* 01384 482123 *Fax:* 01384 482209 *E-mail:* pearsoni@parliament.uk.

PENDRY, Tom *(Stalybridge and Hyde)* *Lab majority 14,806*

Son of late Leonard E. Pendry. Born June 10, 1934; educated St Augustine's School, Ramsgate; Oxford University. Married February 19, 1966, Moira Ann Smith (1 son 1 daughter) (separated 1983). *Profession:* Electrical Engineer. *Career:* Steward, British Boxing Board of Control 1999–. *Councils, Public Bodies:* Councillor, Paddington Council 1962–65. *Political Career:* Resigned from Government February 1977; Under-Secretary of State Northern Ireland 1978–79. *Whip:* Opposition Whip 1971–74; Lord Commissioner of the Treasury 1974–77. *Spokesman:* Opposition Front Bench Spokesman on: Northern Ireland 1979–82, Regional Affairs and Devolution 1982–92, National Heritage (Sport and Tourism) 1992–97. *Party Groups:* Chairman, Derby Labour Party 1966. *International Bodies:* Member, Council of Europe and Western European Union 1973–75. *Trust:* Fellow, Industry and Parliament Trust; Chairman, The Football Trust; Member, Tameside Sports Trust. *Miscellaneous:* Middleweight Colonial champion, Hong Kong 1957; Boxed for Oxford University 1957–59; President, Stalybridge Public Band. Freeman, Borough of Tameside (Lord Mottram of Longendale). *Sportsclubs:* Lord's Taverners. *Special Interests:* Industrial Relations, Housing, Sport, Recreation, Finance, Social Security, Environment. *Recreations:* Watching all sport, meeting sportspersons. *Electoral Notes:* Member for Stalybridge and Hyde since 1970. *Clubs:* Wig and Pen, Vincent's. *Address:* Tom Pendry Esq, MP, House of Commons, London, SW1A 0AA *Tel:* 020 7219 5011. *Constituency:* Hyde Town Hall, Market Street, Hyde, Cheshire *Tel:* 0161–367 8077.

PERHAM, Linda *(Ilford North)* *Lab majority 3,224*

Daughter of George Sidney Conroy and Edith Conroy (née Overton). Born June 29, 1947; educated Mary Datchelor Girls' School, Camberwell, London, SE5; University of Leicester (BA Special Hons Classics 1969); Ealing Technical College (Postgraduate Diploma of the Library Association 1970). Married April 9 1972, Raymond Perham, son of Stanley and Joan Perham (2 daughters). *Trades Union:* Local Organiser, GLC Staff Association 1970–78; Chair, Joint Union Committee, City of London Polytechnic 1975–78; Member, UNISON (NALGO) 1985–. *Profession:* Librarian. *Career:* Library Assistant, London Borough of Southwark 1966; Information Officer, GLC Research Library 1970–72; City of London Polytechnic: Archives Librarian 1972–76, Staff Development Librarian 1976–78; Cataloguer, Fawcett Library 1981–92; Bibliographical Librarian, Epping Forest College 1992–97. *Councils, Public Bodies:* Member, Redbridge Community Health Council 1984–88; JP 1990–; London Borough of Redbridge: Former Councillor, Mayor 1994–95, Chair, Highways Committee 1995–96, Chair, Leisure Committee 1996–97. *Select Committees (Current):* Member: Accommodation and Works 1997–, Trade and Industry 1998–. *Party Groups:* Constituency Secretary, Ilford North Labour Party 1987–91; Member: Socialist Educational Association; Labour Friends of Israel. *Other:* Patron, Haven House Foundation (Children's Hospice Project). *Trust:* Post Natal Support Organiser, National Childbirth Trust 1979–85. ALA. *Publications: Directory of GLC Library Resources,* 1970, 2nd ed 1971; *Greater London Council Publications 1965–71,* 1972; *Libraries of London,* 1973; *How To Find Out In French,* 1977. *Special Interests:* Leisure, Environment, Education, Transport, Age Discrimination. *Countries of Interest:* Italy, Greece, Spain, Cyprus, USA, Israel, Saudi Arabia. *Recreations:* Art, cinema, theatre, organising quizzes. *Electoral Notes:* Prospective Parliamentary Candidate for Ilford North 1995. Member for Ilford North since May 1, 1997. *Address:* Linda Perham, MP, House of Commons, London, SW1A 0AA *Tel:* 020 7219 5853 *Fax:* 020 7219 1161. *Constituency:* Coventry House, 1 Coventry Road, Ilford, Essex, IG1 4GR *Tel:* 020 8554 3789 *Fax:* 020 8518 0594 *E-mail:* lindaperhammp@parliament.uk; *Website:* www.the-commons.com/linda-perham.

PICKLES, Eric *(Brentwood and Ongar)   Con majority 9,690*

Born April 20, 1952; educated Greenhead Grammar School; Leeds Polytechnic. Married September 1976, Irene. *Councils, Public Bodies:* Bradford Metropolitan District Council: Councillor 1979–91, Chairman: Social Services Committee 1982–84, Education Committee 1984–86, Leader of Conservative Group 1987–91; Member, Yorkshire Regional Health Authority 1982–90. *Spokesman:* An Opposition Spokesman for Social Security 1998–. *Select Committees (Former):* Member: Environment 1992–93, Transport 1995–97, Environment, Transport and Regional Affairs 1997–98, Transport Sub-Committee 1997–98. *Party Groups:* Member, Conservative Party National Union Executive Committee 1975–97; National Chairman, Young Conservatives 1980–81; Member, Conservative Party National Local Government Advisory Committee 1985–; Local Government Editor, Newsline 1990–; Deputy Leader, Conservative Group on Association of Metropolitan Authorities 1989–91; Vice-Chairman, Conservative Party 1993–97. *Other:* Chairman, National Local Government Advisory Committee 1992–. *Miscellaneous:* Member, One Nation Forum 1987–91. *Special Interests:* Housing, Health, Social Services, Local Government. *Countries of Interest:* Eastern Europe, India, Poland, USA. *Recreations:* Films, opera, serious walking. *Electoral Notes:* Member for Brentwood and Ongar since April 9, 1992. *Clubs:* Carlton. *Address:* Eric Pickles Esq, MP, House of Commons, London, SW1A 0AA *Tel:* 020 7219 4428. *Constituency:* 19 Crown Street, Brentwood, Essex *Tel:* 01277 210725 *Fax:* 01277 202221.

PICKTHALL, Colin *(West Lancashire)   Lab majority 17,119*

Son of Francis and Edith Pickthall. Born September 13, 1944; educated Ulverston Grammar School; University of Wales (BA); University of Lancaster (MA). Married 1973, Judith Ann, daughter of Dr R. A. Tranter 2 (daughters). *Trades Union:* Member, USDAW. *Profession:* Principal Lecturer in Higher Education. *Career:* Assistant Master, Ruffwood Comprehensive School, Kirkby, Liverpool 1967–70; Lecturer in English, Head of Modern European Cultural Studies, Edge Hill College, Ormskirk, Lancashire 1970–92. *Councils, Public Bodies:* County Councillor, Ormskirk, Lancashire County Council 1989–92. *Political Career:* PPS to: Alun Michael, MP, as Minister of State, Home Office (Minister for Criminal Policy) 1997–98, Rt Hon. Jack Straw, MP, as Home Secretary 1999–. *Select Committees (Former):* Member: Agriculture 1992–97. *Party Groups:* Hon. Secretary, North West Group of Labour MPs 1997–99. *Other:* President: West Lancashire Arthritis Care, West Lancashire Victim Support. *Sportsclubs:* Dalton-in-Furness Cricket. *Countries of Interest:* Canada, France. *Recreations:* Fell-walking, cricket, Shakespeare. *Electoral Notes:* Contested West Lancashire 1987; Member for West Lancashire since April 9, 1992. *Clubs:* Skelmersdale Labour. *Address:* Colin Pickthall Esq, MP, House of Commons, London, SW1A 0AA *Tel:* 020 7219 5011. *Constituency:* 127 Burscough Street, Ormskirk, Lancashire, L39 2EP *Tel:* 01695 570094 *Fax:* 01695 570094.

PIKE, Peter Leslie *(Burnley)   Lab majority 17,062*

Son of late Leslie Henry Pike. Born June 26, 1937; educated Hinchley Wood County Secondary School; Kingston Technical College (Evening Classes). Married December 8, 1962, Sheila Lillian, daughter of late Hubert J. Bull (2 daughters). *Trades Union:* Shop Steward, GMB 1976–83. *Armed Forces:* National Service, Royal Marines 1956–58. *Career:* Clerk: Midland Bank 1958–62, Twinings Tea 1962–63; Labour Party Organiser 1963–73; Final Inspector, Mullards (Simonstone) Ltd 1973–83. *Councils, Public Bodies:* Councillor, Merton and Morden Urban District Council 1962–63; Burnley Borough Council: Councillor 1976–84, Group Leader 1980–83. *Spokesman:* Opposition Front Bench Spokesperson on: Rural Affairs 1990–92, Environment (Housing) 1992–94. *Select Committees (Current):* Chair: Deregulation 1997–; Member: Liaison 1997–, Modernisation of the House of Commons 1997– *(Former):* Member: Deregulation 1995–97, Procedure 1995–97. *Party Groups:* Labour Party Member since 1957. *International Bodies:* Member, Executive Committee, Commonwealth Parliamentary Association (CPA) UK Branch 1999–.

Special Interests: Local Government, Energy, Employment, Trade and Industry, Pensions, Health Service, Environment. *Countries of Interest:* Bangladesh, Brazil, India, Pakistan, Romania, Southern Africa. *Recreations:* Burnley Football Club supporter, member of National Trust. *Electoral Notes:* Member for Burnley since June 1983. *Clubs:* Byerden House Socialist. *Address:* Peter Pike Esq, MP, House of Commons, London, SW1A 0AA *Tel:* 020 7219 3514 *Fax:* 020 7219 3872. *Constituency:* 2 Victoria Street, Burnley, Lancashire, BB11 1DD *Tel:* 01282 450840 *Fax:* 01282 839623 *E-mail:* peterpikemp@parliament.uk.

PLASKITT, James Andrew *(Warwick and Leamington)*   *Lab majority 3,398*

Son of late Ronald Edmund Plaskitt, and Phyllis Irene Plaskitt. Born June 23, 1954; educated Pilgrim School, Bedford; University College, Oxford (MA, MPhil). *Trades Union:* Member, MSF. *Profession:* Business Analyst. *Career:* University Lecturer; Business Analyst. *Councils, Public Bodies:* Councillor, Oxfordshire County Council 1985–97, Leader 1990–96. *Select Committees (Current):* Member: Consolidation of Bills (Joint Committee) 1997–, Treasury 1999–, Treasury Sub-Committee 1999– *(Former):* : Financial Services (Joint Committee) 1998–99. *Miscellaneous:* Member, Standing Committee on Finance Bill 1998. *Publications:* Contributor, *Beyond 2002 – A Programme for Labour's Second Term*, 1999. *Special Interests:* Constitution, European Union, Education, Local Government, Welfare Reform, Economic Policy. *Countries of Interest:* All EU, USA. *Electoral Notes:* Contested Witney 1992. Member for Warwick and Leamington since May 1, 1997. *Address:* James Plaskitt Esq, MP, House of Commons, London, SW1A 0AA *Tel:* 020 7219 6207 *Fax:* 020 7219 4993. *Constituency:* First Floor, 2A Leam Terrace, Leamington Spa, Warwickshire, CV31 1BB *Tel:* 01926 831151 *Fax:* 01926 831151 *E-mail:* plaskittj@parliament.uk.

POLLARD, Kerry Patrick *(St Albans)*   *Lab majority 4,459*

Son of late Patrick Joseph Pollard, and Iris Betty Pollard. Born April 27, 1944; educated St Josephs Primary, Heywood, Lancashire; Thornleigh Grammar School, Bolton. Married March 19, 1966, Maralyn, daughter of John and Ada Murphy (5 sons 2 daughters). *Trades Union:* Member: UNISON, MSF. *Profession:* Housing Association Director. *Career:* Process/Development Engineer, British Gas for 30 years. *Councils, Public Bodies:* Councillor: Hertfordshire County Council, St Albans District Council; JP. *Party Groups:* Member, Labour Party for 25 years; Vice-Chair, Eastern Regional Group of Labour MPs 1999–. *Other:* President, St Albans Community Forum. *Trust:* Director, Open Door Trust. *Special Interests:* Housing, Social Services. *Countries of Interest:* Ireland, Morocco, Bangladesh. *Recreations:* Relaxing with my family. *Electoral Notes:* Member for St Albans since May 1, 1997. *Address:* Kerry Pollard Esq, MP, House of Commons, London, SW1A 0AA *Tel:* 020 7219 4537. *Constituency:* 28 Alma Road, St Albans, Hertfordshire, AL1 3BW *Tel:* 01727 761031 *Fax:* 01727 761032 *E-mail:* kpollard@stalbansclp.u-net.com.

POND, Chris *(Gravesham)*   *Lab majority 5,779*

Son of late Charles Richard and late Doris Violet Pond. Born September 25, 1952; educated Minchenden School, Southgate; Sussex University (BA Hons Economics); Hon. Visiting Professor, Middlesex University. Married December, 1990, Carole Tongue, daughter of Archer Tongue and late Muriel Lambert (1 daughter); (divorced 1999). *Trades Union:* Member, TGWU. *Career:* Research Assistant (Economics) Birkbeck College, London 1974–75; Research Officer, Low Pay Unit 1975–79; Lecturer in Economics, Civil Service College 1979–80; Visiting Lecturer in Economics, University of Kent 1981–82; Visiting Professor/Research Fellow, University of Surrey 1984–86; Consultant, Open University 1987–88, 1991–92; 'Expert' DGV European Commission 1996. *Political Career:* PPS to Dawn Primarolo, MP, as Paymaster General, HM Treasury 1999–. *Select Committees (Former):* Member: Social Security 1997–99. *International Bodies:* European Commission. *Other:* Member, Editorial Board, Charity Magazine; Former Member, Management Committees of Unemployment Unit and Child Poverty Action Group; Chair, Low Pay Unit (unpaid) 1998–.

Sportsclubs: Former Member, London Road Runners' Club (eight marathons); Gravesend Road Runners and Athletics Club. Fellow, Royal Society of Arts 1994–95. *Publications: Inflation and Low Incomes,* 1975; *Trade Unions and Taxation,* 1976; *To Him Who Hath,* 1977; *The Poverty Trap: a study in statistical sources,* 1978; *Taxing Wealth Inequalities,* 1980; *Taxation & Social Policy,* 1981; *Low Pay: Labour's Response,* 1983; *The Changing Distribution of Income, Wealth & Poverty, in Restructuring Britain,* 1989; Plus numerous contributions to other publications, together with articles published in magazines and newspapers. *Special Interests:* Employment, Social Policy, Poverty. *Countries of Interest:* European Union. *Recreations:* Running, reading. *Electoral Notes:* Contested Welwyn-Hatfield 1987. Member for Gravesham since May 1, 1997. *Clubs:* Royal Academy. *Address:* Chris Pond Esq, MP, House of Commons, London, SW1A 0AA *Tel:* 020 7219 6493 *Fax:* 020 7219 0946. *Constituency:* 24 Overcliffe, Gravesend, Kent, DA11 0EH *Tel:* 01474 354725 *Fax:* 01474 351679 *E-mail:* cpond@parliament.uk.

POPE, Gregory *(Hyndburn)* *Lab majority 11,448*

Son of late Samuel Pope, ambulance officer, and of Sheila Pope. Born August 29, 1960; educated St Mary's College Roman Catholic Grammar School, Blackburn; Hull University (BA Hons Politics). Married August 2, 1985, Catherine Fallon (2 sons 1 daughter). *Career:* Vice-President, Hull University Students Union 1981–82; Co-ordinator, Blackburn Trade Union Centre for the unemployed 1983–85; Paperworker, Star newspaper, Blackburn 1985–87; Local government officer, Lancashire County Council 1987–92. *Councils, Public Bodies:* Councillor: Hyndburn Borough Council 1984–88, Blackburn Borough Council 1989–91. *Whip:* Opposition Whip 1995–97; Assistant Government Whip 1997–99; A Lord Commissioner of HM Treasury (Government Whip) 1999–. *Select Committees (Former):* Member: Education 1994–95. *Special Interests:* Education, Housing, Foreign Affairs. *Recreations:* Walking, chess, music. *Electoral Notes:* Contested Ribble Valley 1987 General Election. Member for Hyndburn since April 9, 1992. *Clubs:* Accrington Old Band (CIU). *Address:* Gregory Pope Esq, MP, House of Commons, London, SW1A 0AA *Tel:* 020 7219 5842 *Fax:* 020 7219 0685. *Constituency:* 149 Blackburn Road, Accrington, Lancs, BB5 0AA *Tel:* 01254 382283 *Fax:* 01254 392438 *E-mail:* popegj@parliament.uk.

PORTILLO, The Rt Hon. Michael Denzil Xavier *(Kensington and Chelsea)* *Con majority 6,706*

Son of late Luis Gabriel Portillo, and of Cora Blyth. Born May 26, 1953; educated Harrow County School for Boys; Peterhouse College, Cambridge (MA history 1975). Married February 12, 1982, Carolyn Claire Eadie. *Career:* Conservative Research Department 1976–79; Special adviser to David Howell, MP, as Secretary of State for Energy 1979–81; Oil industry consultant 1981–83; Special adviser to: Cecil Parkinson, MP, as Secretary of State for Trade and Industry 1983, Nigel Lawson, MP, as Chancellor of the Exchequer 1983–84. *Political Career:* PPS to Secretary of State for Transport 1986; Parliamentary Under-Secretary of State DHSS 1987–88; Minister of State: at Department of Transport 1988–90, at Department of Environment (Minister for Local Government and Inner Cities) 1990–92; Chief Secretary to HM Treasury 1992–94; Secretary of State for: Employment 1994–95, Defence 1995–97. *Whip:* Government Whip October 1986–87. *Honours:* PC 1992. *Electoral Notes:* Contested Birmingham Perry Barr June 1983. Member for Enfield Southgate 1984–97, for Kensington and Chelsea since November 25, 1999 by-election. *Address:* The Rt Hon. Michael Portillo, MP, House of Commons, London, SW1A 0AA *Tel:* 020 7219 3000.

Dod *on* Disk

The Vacher Dod Parliamentary Database
that will run on your PC or Network

For further details please telephone the Westminster Office

020 7828 7256

POUND, Stephen Pelham *(Ealing North)   Lab majority 9,160*

Son of Pelham Pound, journalist, and Dominica Pound, teacher. Born July 3, 1948; educated Hertford Grammar School; London School of Economics (Diploma in Industrial Relations, BSc Economics) (Sabbatical President of Union 1981–82). Married June 1976, Maggie, daughter of Lyndon Griffiths and Mary Griffiths (1 son 1 daughter). *Trades Union:* Branch Secretary, 640 Middlesex Branch, COHSE 1975–79; Branch Officer, T&GWU (ACTS) 1990–96. *Profession:* Housing Association Worker. *Career:* Seaman 1964–66; 'Bus Conductor 1966–68; Hospital Porter 1969–79; Student 1979–84; Housing Officer 1984–97. *Councils, Public Bodies:* Councillor, London Borough of Ealing 1982–98, Mayor 1995–96. *Select Committees (Current):* Member: Broadcasting 1997–, Northern Ireland 1999–. *Party Groups:* Member, Labour Party 1972–. *Other:* Director, Hanwell Community Centre. *Trust:* Trustee, Charity of Wm Hobbayne (Hanwell). *Sportsclubs:* Fulham FC Supporters Club. *Special Interests:* Housing, Transport. *Countries of Interest:* Ireland. *Recreations:* Watching football, playing cricket, snooker, jazz, gardening, collecting comics. *Electoral Notes:* Member for Ealing North since May 1, 1997. *Clubs:* St Joseph's Catholic Social, Hanwell. *Address:* Stephen Pound Esq, MP, House of Commons, London, SW1A 0AA *Tel:* 020 7219 1140 *Fax:* 020 7219 5982.

POWELL, Sir Raymond *(Ogmore)   Lab majority 24,447*

Son of late Albert Ernest Powell, miner. Born June 19, 1928; educated Pentre Grammar School; National Council of Labour Colleges; London School of Economics. Married January 28, 1950, Marion Grace Evans (1 son 1 daughter). *Trades Union:* Member, USDAW for over 50 years; Has held most Branch Positions; Sponsored by USDAW 1979–. *Career:* Fireman with British Rail 1946–51; Shop Assistant 1951–56; Own Business 1956–66; Administration Officer, PMSB 1969–74; Senior Administration Officer (Morgannwg Division), Welsh Water Authority 1974–79. *Councils, Public Bodies:* Councillor, Ogmore Borough Council 1973–79. *Whip:* Opposition Whip 1984–95, Pairing Whip 1987–95, Accommodation Whip 1987–95. *Select Committees (Current):* Member: Accommodation and Works 1997– *(Former):* Chairman: Accommodation and Works 1988–97; Member: Liaison 1993–95, Selection 1995. *Party Groups:* Secretary, Ogmore Constituency Labour Party; Agent to Walter Padley 1966–79; Chairman, Wales Labour Party 1977; Chairman, South Wales Euro Constituency Labour Party 1978–; Hon. Secretary: Welsh Parliamentary Party, Welsh Parliamentary Labour Party 1982–92; Member, Co-operative Party Fabian Group. *Other:* Chairman, Community Activities and Training in Ogmore Charity Organisation 1980–90; Member, Co-op Society, Bridgend. *Trust:* Fellow, Industry and Parliament Trust. *Miscellaneous:* Member, Keep Sunday Special Committee. *Sportsclubs:* Life President, Ogmore Constituency Labour Party Sports. *Honours:* Knighted 1996. *Special Interests:* Coal Industry, Steel Industry, CND, Childcare, Grandparents' Rights, Marketing, Keep Sunday Special, Sunday Trading, Sunday Drinking, Licensing Hours Pubs-Clubs, Parliamentary Buildings/Accommodation/Preservation. *Countries of Interest:* Cyprus (Greek), Bulgaria, America, Switzerland, Canada. *Recreations:* Gardening, sports. *Electoral Notes:* Member for Ogmore since May 1979. *Clubs:* Ogmore Labour Party. *Address:* Sir Raymond Powell, MP, House of Commons, London, SW1A 0AA *Tel:* 020 7219 4030. *Constituency:* 14 Blackmill Road, Bryncethin, Bridgend, Mid Glamorgan *Tel:* 01656 721300 *Fax:* 01656 729662.

PRENTICE, Bridget *(Lewisham East)   Lab majority 12,127*

Daughter of late James Corr, joiner, and of Bridget Corr, clerical worker. Born December 28, 1952; educated Our Lady and St Francis School, Glasgow; University of Glasgow (MA English Literature and Modern History); University of London (Postgraduate Certificate in Education); South Bank University (LLB). Married December 20, 1975, Gordon Prentice, MP for Pendle *(qv)*. *Career:* Rector's Assessor, Glasgow University 1972–73; London Oratory School: Teacher 1974–86, Head of Careers 1984–86; Head of Careers, John Archer School 1986–88. *Councils, Public Bodies:* London Borough of Hammersmith and Fulham: Councillor 1986–92, Chairman: Public Services Committee 1987–90, Labour Group 1986–89; JP 1985–. *Political Career:* PPS to Brian Wilson, MP, as Minister of State, Department of Trade and Industry (Minister for Trade) 1998–99;

Joint PPS to Rt Hon. the Lord Irvine of Lairg, QC, as Lord Chancellor 1999–. *Whip:* Opposition Whip 1995–97; Assistant Government Whip 1997–98. *Select Committees (Former):* Member: Parliamentary Commissioner for Administration 1992–96. *Party Groups:* Chairman, Fulham Constituency Labour Party 1982–85; Leadership Campaign Team Co-ordinator 1995–96. *Special Interests:* Education, Training, Constitutional Reform, Human Rights, Home Affairs. *Countries of Interest:* South Africa, USA. *Recreations:* Reading, music, crosswords, gardening, two cats, badminton (qualified coach), football. *Electoral Notes:* Contested Croydon Central 1987. Member for Lewisham East since April 9, 1992. *Address:* Bridget Prentice, MP, House of Commons, London, SW1A 0AA *Tel:* 020 7219 3000 *Fax:* 020 7219 5581. *Constituency:* 149 Lee High Road, London, SE13 5PF *Tel:* 020 8852 3995 *Fax:* 020 8852 2386 *E-mail:* prenticeb@parliament.uk.

PRENTICE, Gordon *(Pendle)   Lab majority 10,824*

Son of late William Prentice, and of Esther Prentice. Born January 28, 1951; educated George Heriot's School, Edinburgh; University of Glasgow (MA Politics and Economics). Married December 20, 1975, Bridget Corr, MP *(qv)*. *Trades Union:* Member, TGWU. *Career:* Labour Party Policy Directorate 1982–92; Labour Party Local Government Officer 1985–92. *Councils, Public Bodies:* London Borough of Hammersmith and Fulham: Councillor 1982–90, Deputy Leader, Labour Group 1982–84, Leader 1984–88. *Political Career:* PPS to Rt Hon. Gavin Strang, MP, as Minister of State (in Cabinet), Department of the Environment, Transport and the Regions (Minister for Transport) May-December 1997. *Select Committees (Current):* Member: Modernisation of the House of Commons 1999– *(Former):* Member: Statutory Instruments 1993–97, Deregulation 1995–97, Agriculture 1996–97. *International Bodies:* Executive Committee Member, Inter-Parliamentary Union (IPU) British Group. *Recreations:* Cooking, hillwalking. *Electoral Notes:* Member for Pendle since April 9, 1992. *Address:* Gordon Prentice Esq, MP, House of Commons, London, SW1A 0AA *Tel:* 020 7219 4011. *Constituency:* 33 Carr Road, Nelson, BB9 7JS *Tel:* 01282 695471 *Fax:* 01282 614097 *E-mail:* gordonprentice@compuserve.com.

PRESCOTT, The Rt Hon. John Leslie *(Hull East)   Lab majority 23,318*

Son of John Herbert Prescott, railway controller. Born May 31, 1938; educated Ellesmere Port Secondary Modern School; Ruskin College, Oxford; Hull University. Married November 11, 1961, Pauline Tilston (2 sons). *Trades Union:* TU Official, National Union of Seamen 1968–70. *Career:* Steward in the Merchant Navy 1955–63. *Political Career:* PPS to Secretary of State for Trade 1974–76; Member, Shadow Cabinet 1983–97; Deputy Prime Minister and Secretary of State for the Environment, Transport and the Regions 1997–. *Spokesman:* Opposition Front Bench Spokesman on: Transport 1979–81, Regional Affairs and Devolution 1981–83; Labour Party Spokesman on Transport 1983–84; Opposition Front Bench Spokesman on: Employment 1984–87, Energy 1987–88, Transport 1988–93, Employment 1993–94. *Party Groups:* Deputy Leader, Labour Party 1994–; Member, National Executive Committee of the Labour Party; Deputy Leader, Labour Party National Executive Committee 1997–. *International Bodies:* Member, Council of Europe 1972–75; Delegate, EEC Parliamentary 1975; Leader, Labour Party Delegation to European Parliament 1976–79. *Honours:* PC 1994. *Recreations:* Jazz, theatre, music, aqua diving. *Electoral Notes:* Contested Southport 1966. Member for Kingston-upon-Hull East June 18, 1970–83 and for Hull East 1983–. *Address:* The Rt Hon. John Prescott, MP, House of Commons, London, SW1A 0AA *Tel:* 020 7219 5030 *E-mail:* john-prescott@detr.gsi.gov.uk; *Website:* http://www.detr.gov.uk.

Dod *on* Disk

The Vacher Dod Parliamentary Database – configured for PC or Network

For further details please telephone the Westminster Office

020 7828 7256

PRIMAROLO, Dawn *(Bristol South)   Lab majority 19,328*

Born May 2, 1954; educated Thomas Bennett Comprehensive School, Crawley; Bristol Polytechnic; Bristol University (BA Social Science). Married 1st, October 7, 1972 (1 son) (marriage dissolved), married 2nd, November 29, 1990, Thomas Ian Ducat. *Career:* Secretary 1972–73; Secretary and Advice Worker, Law Centre East London; Secretary, Avon County Council 1975–78; Voluntary Work 1978–81; Mature Student 1981–87. *Councils, Public Bodies:* Councillor, Avon County Council 1985–87. *Political Career:* HM Treasury: Financial Secretary 1997–99, Paymaster General 1999–. *Spokesman:* Opposition Front Bench Spokesperson on: Health 1992–94, Treasury and Economic Affairs 1994–97. *Select Committees (Former):* Member: Members' Interests 1990–92, Public Accounts 1997–98. *Special Interests:* Education, Housing, Women's Rights, Social Security, Health, Economic Policy. *Electoral Notes:* Member for Bristol South since June 1987. *Address:* Dawn Primarolo, MP, House of Commons, London, SW1A 0AA *Fax:* 020 7219 2276. *Constituency:* PO Box 1002, Bristol, BS99 1WH *Tel:* 0117–909 0063 *Fax:* 0117–909 0064 *E-mail:* dawn.primarolo@hm-treasury.gov.uk.

PRIOR, Hon. David Gifford Leathes *(North Norfolk)   Con majority 1,293*

Son of The Rt Hon. Baron Prior (*qv*) and Lady Prior. Born December 3, 1954; educated Charterhouse; Cambridge (MA). Married February 14, 1987, Caroline Holmes (1 son 1 daughter). *Profession:* Barrister (did not practice). *Career:* Lehman Brothers and Lazard Freres, Investment Banks 1977–80; British Steel Corporation, last job Commercial Director 1980–87; Investor and Manager of various industrial businesses. *Political Career:* A Vice-Chairman, Conservative Party (with responsibility for Organisation) 1998, Deputy Chief Executive 1998–99; Deputy Chairman and Chief Executive, Conservative Party 1999–. *Select Committees (Former):* Member: Trade and Industry 1997–98. *Party Groups:* Chairman, Mid Norfolk Conservative Association 1995–96. *Special Interests:* City, Trade and Industry, Employment, Education, Agriculture. *Countries of Interest:* Asia, USA. *Recreations:* Gardening, sport. *Electoral Notes:* Member for North Norfolk since May 1, 1997. *Clubs:* RAC. *Address:* Hon. David Prior, MP, House of Commons, London, SW1A 0AA. *Constituency:* North Norfolk Conservative Association, 8 Louden Road, Norfolk, NR27 9EF *Tel:* 01263 510240 *Fax:* 01263 513473 *E-mail:* priordgl@parliament.uk.

PROSSER, Gwyn (Gwynfor Mathews) *(Dover)   Lab majority 11,739*

Son of late Glyn Prosser and of Doreen Prosser. Born April 27, 1943; educated Dunyant Secondary Modern; Swansea Technical School; Swansea College of Technology (National Diploma, Mechanical Engineering, First Class Certificate of Competency, Marine Engineering). Married April 6, 1972, Rhoda McLeod (1 son 2 daughters). *Trades Union:* Former Member, NUMAST NEC; Political Officer, MSF, South East Kent. *Profession:* Chartered Marine Engineer. *Career:* Merchant Navy Cadet Engineer 1960–64; Seagoing Fourth Engineer, BP 1964–67; Seagoing Second Engineer, Blue Funnel 1967–71; Chief Engineer, BR Shipping 1971–74; Test and Guarantee Engineer, Kincaid of Greenock 1974–77; Port Engineer, Aramco, Saudi Arabia 1977–78; Chief Engineer: Anscar 1978–79, Sealink Ferries at Dover 1979–92; Social Survey Interviewer, Civil Service 1993–96; Chartered Marine Engineer 1996–. *Councils, Public Bodies:* Councillor, Dover District Council 1987–; Kent County Council: Councillor 1989–, Co-Chairman, Economic Development and President, European Affairs 1993–. *Other:* Director, East Kent Women's Refuge; Member, Greenpeace. *Trust:* Trustee, Numerous Local Charities. *Miscellaneous:* Organising opposition, Channel Tunnel Bill. MIMarE; CEng. *Special Interests:* Transport, Shipping, Economic Development, Environment. *Countries of Interest:* Hungary. *Recreations:* Hill walking, swimming, awaiting revival of Welsh rugby. *Electoral Notes:* Member for Dover since May 1, 1997. *Address:* Gwyn Prosser Esq, MP, House of Commons, London, SW1A 0AA *Tel:* 020 7219 3524. *Constituency:* 26 Coombe Valley Road, Dover, Kent *Tel:* 01304 201199 *Fax:* 01304 207899.

PURCHASE, Kenneth *(Wolverhampton North East)   Lab/Co-op majority 12,987*

Son of late Albert Purchase, diecaster, and late Rebecca Purchase, cleaner. Born January 8, 1939; educated Springfield Secondary Modern School; Wolverhampton Polytechnic (BA Hons Social Science). Married August 20, 1960, Brenda, daughter of late Sam Sanders, steelworker (2 daughters). *Trades Union:* Member, TGWU (ACTSS). *Career:* Apprentice toolmaker, foundry industry 1956–60; Experimental component development, aerospace industry 1960–68; Toolroom machinist, motor industry 1968–76; Property division, Telford Development Corporation 1977 80; Housing Department, Walsall Metropolitan Borough Council 1981–82; Business Development Adviser, Black Country CDA Ltd 1982–92. *Councils, Public Bodies:* Councillor: Wolverhampton County Borough Council 1970–74; Wolverhampton Metropolitan Borough Council 1973–90; Member: Wolverhampton Health Authority 1978–82, 1985–87, 1988–90, Wolverhampton Community Health Council 1990–92. *Political Career:* PPS to Rt Hon. Robin Cook, MP, Foreign Secretary 1997–. *Select Committees (Former):* Member: Trade and Industry 1993–97. *Party Groups:* Sponsored by Co-operative Party. *Special Interests:* Trade and Industry, Health, Education. *Recreations:* Listening to jazz. *Electoral Notes:* Contested Wolverhampton North East 1987. Member for Wolverhampton North East since April 9, 1992. *Address:* Kenneth Purchase Esq, MP, House of Commons, London, SW1A 0AA *Tel:* 020 7219 3602 *Fax:* 020 7219 2110. *Constituency:* 492a Stafford Road, Wolverhampton, WV10 6AN *Tel:* 01902 397698 *Fax:* 01902 397538 *E-mail:* ken.purchase@cwmcon.net.

Q

QUIN, The Rt Hon. Joyce Gwendolen *(Gateshead East and Washington West)   Lab majority 24,950*

Daughter of late Basil Godfrey Quin, schoolmaster, and late Ida Quin, née Ritson, teacher. Born November 26, 1944; educated Whitley Bay Grammar School; Newcastle University (BA French 1967); LSE (MSc International Relations 1969); Hon. Fellow: Sunderland Polytechnic 1986, St Mary's College, University of Durham 1996. *Trades Union:* Member, TGWU. *Career:* Lecturer in French, University of Bath 1972–76; Tutor and lecturer in French and Politics, University of Durham 1976–79. *Political Career:* Minister of State: Home Office 1997–98, Foreign and Commonwealth Office 1998–99; Minister of State and Deputy Minister, Ministry of Agriculture, Fisheries and Food 1999–. *Spokesman:* Opposition Spokesperson on Trade and Industry 1989–92; Opposition Front Bench Spokesperson on: Employment 1992–93, Foreign and Commonwealth Affairs 1993–97. *Party Groups:* Research Officer, International Department, Labour Party HQ 1969–72. *Honours:* PC 1998. *Special Interests:* European Policy, Industrial Policy, Regional Policy. *Countries of Interest:* Australia, Europe, New Zealand, USA. *Recreations:* North-East local history, walking, music, reading, cycling, playing Northumbrian pipes. *Electoral Notes:* MEP for Tyne and Wear 1979–89. Member for Gateshead East 1987–97, and for Gateshead East and Washington West since May 1, 1997. *Address:* The Rt Hon. Joyce Quin, MP, House of Commons, London, SW1A 0AA *Tel:* 020 7219 4009. *Constituency:* Design Works, William Street, Felling, Gateshead, Tyne & Wear, NE10 0JP *Tel:* 01914 696006 *Fax:* 01914 696009.

QUINN, Lawrie *(Scarborough and Whitby)   Lab majority 5,124*

Son of late Jimmy and Sheila Quinn. Born December 25, 1956; educated Pennine Way Schools, Carlisle; Harraby School, Carlisle; Hatfield Polytechnic (BSc Civil Engineering). Married April 10, 1982, Ann. *Trades Union:* Chair/Secretary, TSSA. *Profession:* Chartered civil engineer. *Career:* Railway civil engineer and planning development engineer, Railtrack London NE. *Councils, Public Bodies:* Councillor, North Yorkshire County Council 1989–93, Member: Highways Committee, Policy and Resources Committee, Planning Committee. *Party Groups:* Member: Fabian Society, Labour Campaigning for Electoral Reform, SERA; Member, North and Yorks Labour Executive 1993–97; Chair, City of York CLP 1994–97. *Other:* Member:

Governing Board, York Sixth Form College 1989–93, Permanent Way Institution, Hon. Life Member, Civil Engineering Trainees, Transport 2000. *Miscellaneous:* Member, European Standing Committee A 1998–. *Fellowships, etc:* MICE; CEng. *Special Interests:* Transport, Devolution, Constitution, Health and Safety at Work, Tourism, Deep Sea Fishing Industry, Regional Assemblies. *Recreations:* Reading, history, cooking, theatre, avid internet user, long-distance supporter of Carlisle United, train travel around Europe. *Electoral Notes:* Member for Scarborough and Whitby since May 1, 1997. *Clubs:* York Speakers. *Address:* Lawrie Quinn Esq, MP, House of Commons, London, SW1A 0AA *Tel:* 020 7219 4170 *Fax:* 020 7219 2477. *Constituency:* 53 Westborough, Scarborough, North Yorkshire, YO11 1TU *Tel:* 01723 507000 *Fax:* 01723 507008 *E-mail:* quinnl@parliament.uk.

R

RADICE, The Rt Hon. Giles Heneage *(Durham North)* Lab majority 26,299

Born October 4, 1936; educated Winchester; Magdalen College, Oxford. Married March 4, 1971, Lisanne Koch. *Career:* Head of Research Department GMWU 1966–73. *Political Career:* PPS to Rt Hon. Mrs Shirley Williams, MP, as Secretary of State for Education and Science 1978–1979. *Spokesman:* Opposition Front Bench Spokesman on: Foreign Affairs 1981, Employment 1982–83, Education 1983–87. *Select Committees (Current):* Member: Liaison 1997–; Chairman: Treasury 1997–; Member: Treasury Sub-Committee 1998– *(Former):* Member: Treasury and Civil Service 1987–96, Public Service 1995–97, Liaison 1996–97; Chairman: Public Service 1996–97. *Miscellaneous:* Chairman, British Association for Central and Eastern Europe 1997–. *Honours:*
PC 1999. *Publications: Democratic Socialism,* 1965; *More Power to People,* 1968; Co-author *Will Thorne,* 1974; *The Industrial Democrats,* 1978; Co-author *Socialists in the Recession: a Survey of European Socialism,* 1986; *Labour's Path to Power: the New Revisionism,* 1989; *Offshore – Britain and the European Idea,* 1992; *The New Germans,* 1995; *What Needs to Change* Editor 1996. *Special Interests:* Economic and European Affairs, Labour Party policy revision. *Countries of Interest:* Eastern Europe, Europe, Poland, Germany, India. *Recreations:* Reading, tennis, gardening. *Electoral Notes:* Contested Chippenham 1964 and 1966. Member for Chester-le-Street by-election 1973–83 and for Durham North since June 1983. *Address:* The Rt Hon. Giles Radice, MP, House of Commons, London, SW1A 0AA *Tel:* 020 7219 4194. *Constituency:* Station Master's House, Station Lane, Chester-le-Street, Co Durham, DH3 3DU *Tel:* 0191–387 1107 *Fax:* 0191–387 1107.

RAMMELL, Bill (William Ernest) *(Harlow)* Lab majority 10,514

Son of William Ernest and Joan Elizabeth Rammell. Born October 10, 1959; educated Burnt Mill Comprehensive, Harlow; Cardiff University (BA Hons French/Politics). Married January 1, 1983, Beryl Jarhall (1 son 1 daughter). *Trades Union:* Member, MSF. *Career:* President, Cardiff University SU 1982–83; Management Trainee, British Rail 1983–84; Regional Officer, NUJ 1984–87; Head of Youth Services, Basildon Council 1987–89; General Manager, Kings College, London SU 1980–94; Senior University Business Manager, University of London 1994–. *Councils, Public Bodies:* Councillor, Harlow Council 1985–97; Former Member, Local Government Information Unit. *Select Committees (Current):* Member: European Scrutiny 1998–
(Former): Member: Education and Employment 1997–99, European Legislation 1997–98. *Party Groups:* Former Chair, CLP Chair, Labour Movement for Europe. *Other:* Member, Community Health Council; Chair, Community Safety Group. *Miscellaneous:* Member, European Standing Committee B 1998–. *Special Interests:* Education, Housing, Economic Policy, Europe, Media, Sport. *Countries of Interest:* France, Sweden, USA, Germany, Hungary, Netherlands. *Recreations:* Family, friends, sport, reading. *Electoral Notes:* Member for Harlow since May 1, 1997. *Address:* Bill Rammell Esq, MP, House of Commons, London, SW1A 0AA *Tel:* 020 7219 2828. *Constituency:* 1 Adams House, The High, Harlow, Essex, CM20 1BE *Tel:* 01279 439706.

RANDALL, (Alexander) John *(Uxbridge)* *Con majority 3,766*

Son of late Alec Albert Randall, company director, and of Joyce Margaret Randall (née Gore). Born August 5, 1955; educated Rutland House School, Hillingdon; Merchant Taylors School, Moor Park; School of Slavonic and East European Studies, University of London (BA Hons Serbo-Croat Language and Literature 1979). Married October 25, 1986, Katherine Frances, daughter of John and Frances Gray (2 sons 1 daughter). *Profession:* Company Director, Retail Department Store. *Career:* Randall's of Uxbridge: Sales Assistant, Buyer, Director 1980–, Managing Director 1988–; Tour Leader, Biroquest Holidays and Limosa Holidays as Specialist Ornithologist 1986–. *Select Committees (Current):* Member: Deregulation 1997–, Environment, Transport and Regional Affairs 1998–, Environment Sub-Committee 1998–. *Party Groups:* Hon. Treasurer, Uxbridge Conservative Association 1994, Chairman 1994–97. *Other:* Chairman: Uxbridge Retailers' Association to 1997, Cowley Residents' Association to 1997; Member: Uxbridge Town Centre Steering Committee to 1997, Royal Society for the Protection of Birds, British Ornithologists Union. *Sportsclubs:* Vice-President, Uxbridge Cricket Club. *Special Interests:* Environment, Trade and Industry, Foreign Affairs. *Recreations:* Local history, ornithology, theatre, opera, travel, music (plays piano), Uxbridge FC supporter. *Electoral Notes:* Member for Uxbridge since July 31, 1997 By-election. *Clubs:* Uxbridge Conservative. *Address:* John Randall Esq, MP, House of Commons, London, SW1A 0AA *Tel:* 020 7219 3400 *Fax:* 020 7219 2590. *Constituency:* 36 Harefield Road, Uxbridge, Middlesex, UB8 1PH *Tel:* 01895 239465 *Fax:* 01895 253105.

RAPSON, Syd (Sydney) Norman John, BEM *(Portsmouth North)* *Lab majority 4,323*

Son of late Sidney Rapson and of Doris Rapson (née Fisher), adopted by Lily and Sidney Rapson (grandparents). Born April 17, 1942; educated Southsea and Paulsgrove Secondary Modern; Portsmouth Dockyard College (City and Guilds); National Council of Labour Colleges. Married March 17, 1967, Phyllis Edna, daughter of Frank and Beatrice Williams (1 son 1 daughter). *Trades Union:* AEEU: Shop Steward 1965–97, Convenor 1979–97, National Delegate, District President. *Profession:* Aircraft Industrial Technician (MoD). *Career:* Ministry of Defence: apprentice aircraft fitter, MoD 1958–63; aircraft fitter 1963–96; industrial technician 1997. *Councils, Public Bodies:* Councillor, Portsmouth City Council 1971–99: Lord Mayor 1990–91, Deputy Leader 1994–95; Councillor, Hampshire County Council 1973–77; Hon Alderman, Portsmouth City Council 1999–. *Select Committees (Current):* Member: Accommodation and Works 1997–, Unopposed Bills (Panel) 1998–. *Party Groups:* Member, Co-operative Party; Joined Labour Party 1968; Chairman, Portsmouth South Constituency 1970–71; Member, Parliamentary Armed Forces Scheme (Royal Marines). *International Bodies:* Member: Britain Australia Society Portsmouth Branch, Portsmouth/Sydney Sister Link Committee, Vice-President, Portsmouth/Duisburg Friendship Committee, Portsmouth Haifa Friendship Committee, Council of Europe, Parliamentary Assembly, Council of Europe Science and Technology Committee, Western European Union, Western European Union Defence Committee. *Trust:* Former Non-executive Member, Portsmouth Healthcare NHS Trust. Freeman, City of London. *Sportsclubs:* Former President, Portsmouth Athletic Club. *Honours:* BEM 1984; Imperial Service Medal 1998. *Special Interests:* Leisure, Economic Development, Defence, Local Government. *Countries of Interest:* America, Germany, Australia. *Recreations:* Swimming, gardening. *Electoral Notes:* Contested Portsmouth South 1992. Member for Portsmouth North since May 1, 1997. *Address:* Syd Rapson Esq, BEM, MP, House of Commons, London, SW1A 0AA *Tel:* 020 7219 6351/6248 *Fax:* 020 7219 0915. *Constituency:* Portsmouth North Labour Party HQ, 1 Holbrook Road, Landport, Portsmouth, Hampshire, PO1 1JB *Tel:* 023 9235 0035 *Fax:* 023 9234 0451.

RAYNSFORD, Nick (Wyvill Richard Nicolls) *(Greenwich and Woolwich)* Lab majority 18,128

Son of late Wyvill and Patricia Raynsford. Born January 28, 1945; educated Repton School; Sidney Sussex College, Cambridge (MA Hons History); Chelsea School of Art (Diploma in Art and Design). Married 1968, Anne, daughter of late Marcus and Betty Jelley (3 daughters). *Career:* Director, SHAC, the London Housing Aid Centre 1976–86. *Councils, Public Bodies:* London Borough of Hammersmith and Fulham: Councillor 1971–75, Chairman, Leisure and Recreation Committee 1972–74. *Political Career:* Former PPS to Rt Hon. Roy Hattersley, MP; Department of the Environment, Transport and the Regions: Parliamentary Under-Secretary of State 1997–99, Minister of State, Department of the Environment, Transport and the Regions (Minister for Housing and Planning) 1999–. *Spokesman:* Opposition Spokesman on: Transport and London 1993–94, Housing, Construction and London 1994–97. *Select Committees (Former):* Member: Environment 1992–93. *Publications:* Author of: *A Guide to Housing Benefit*, 1982; Contributor to journals including *Building, Housing* and *New Statesman*. *Special Interests:* Housing, Social Policy, Transport, Environment. *Countries of Interest:* Europe. *Recreations:* Photography, walking, golf. *Electoral Notes:* Member for Fulham 1986–87 (by-election). Member for Greenwich 1992–97, and for Greenwich and Woolwich since May 1, 1997. *Address:* Nick Raynsford Esq, MP, House of Commons, London, SW1A 0AA *Tel:* 020 7219 2773 *Fax:* 020 7219 2619. *Constituency:* 32 Woolwich Road, London, SE10 0JU *Tel:* 020 7219 5895 *Fax:* 020 7219 2619 *E-mail:* seabeckaj@parliament.uk; nick-raynsford@detr.gsi.gov.uk.

REDWOOD, The Rt Hon. John *(Wokingham)* Con majority 9,365

Son of William and Amy Redwood (née Champion). Born June 15, 1951; educated Kent College, Canterbury; Magdalen College, Oxford (MA); St Antony's College, Oxford (DPhil). Married April 1974, Gail Felicity, daughter of Robert Chippington (1 son 1 daughter). *Career:* Fellow, All Souls College, Oxford 1972–87; Tutor and lecturer 1972–73; Investment analyst, Robert Fleming & Co. 1974–77; N. M. Rothschild: Bank Clerk 1977–78, Manager 1978–79, Assistant Director 1979–80, Director, Investment Division 1980–83, Overseas Corporate Finance Director and Head of International (non-UK) Privatisation 1986–87; Norcros plc: Non-Executive Director 1985–87, Chairman 1987–89. *Councils, Public Bodies:* Councillor, Oxfordshire County Council 1973–77. *Political Career:* Parliamentary Under-Secretary of State for Corporate Affairs, at Department of Trade and Industry 1989–90; Minister of State 1990–92; Minister of State, at Department of the Environment (Minister for Local Government) 1992–93; Secretary of State for Wales 1993–95; Contested Leadership of the Conservative Party 1995 and 1997; Member, Shadow Cabinet 1997–; Shadow Secretary of State for: Trade and Industry 1997–99, Environment, Transport and the Regions 1999–. *Other:* Governor, Oxford Polytechnic 1973–77; Governor of various schools in West Oxfordshire and Inner London 1973–82. *Miscellaneous:* Adviser, Treasury and Civil Service Select Committee 1981; Head, Prime Minister's policy unit 1983–85. *Sportsclubs:* Lords and Commons Cricket. *Honours:* PC 1993. *Publications: Reason, Ridicule and Religion*, 1976; *Public Enterprise in Crisis*, 1980; *Going for Broke*, 1984; *Popular Capitalism*, 1987; *The Global Marketplace*, 1993; *Our Currency, Our Country*, 1997; Several books and articles, especially on wider ownership and popular capitalism; *The Death of Britain*, 1999. *Special Interests:* British Business, Popular Capitalism. *Countries of Interest:* USA. *Recreations:* Village cricket, water sports. *Electoral Notes:* Contested Southwark Peckham 1982. Member for Wokingham since June 1987. *Address:* The Rt Hon. John Redwood, MP, House of Commons, London, SW1A 0AA *Tel:* 020 7219 3000. *Constituency:* 30 Rose Street, Wokingham, Berkshire *Tel:* 01734 629501 *E-mail:* redwoodj@parliament.uk.

REED, Andrew John *(Loughborough)   Lab majority 5,712*

Son of Mr James Donald Reed and Mrs Margaret Ann Reed. Born September 17, 1964; educated Riverside Junior, Birstall, Leicestershire; Stonehill High School, Birstall, Leicestershire; Longslade Community College, Birstall, Leicestershire; Leicester Polytechnic (BA Hons, Public Administration). Married August 29, 1992, Sarah Elizabeth, daughter of Mr Mike and Mrs Beryl Chester. *Trades Union:* NALGO 1988–; Unison 1990–, Steward, Convenor, Executive, Leicestershire County Council, Conference Delegate, Service Conditions Officer. *Career:* Parliamentary Assistant to Keith Vaz MP 1987–88; Urban Regeneration, Leicester City Council 1988–90; Economic Development Unit, Leicestershire County Council 1990–94; European Affairs Adviser, Leicestershire County Council 1994–97. *Councils, Public Bodies:* Councillor: Birstall Parish Council 1987–92, Charnwood Borough Council 1995–97, Chair, Economic Development; Vice-Chair, Loughborough Town Partnership; Board Member, Business Link Loughborough. *Party Groups:* Loughborough Constituency Labour Party: Chairman 1988–92, Regional Executive 1993–94; Member, East Midlands PLP; Vice-Chairman, East Midlands Regional Group of Labour MPs 1999–. *Other:* Director, Business Link, Loughborough. *Sportsclubs:* Leicester Rugby Football Club, Birstall Rugby Football Club (player), Sileby Tennis Club, Leicester PVC Volleyball Club. *Special Interests:* Economic Regeneration, Unemployment, Lifelong Learning, Education, Vocational Training, Sport, International Development, Co-operatives. *Countries of Interest:* South Africa, Germany. *Recreations:* Rugby, tennis, volleyball, any sport. *Electoral Notes:* Contested Loughborough 1992. Member for Loughborough since May 1, 1997. *Clubs:* Loughborough Labour. *Address:* Andrew Reed Esq, MP, House of Commons, London, SW1A 0AA *Tel:* 020 7219 3529 *Fax:* 020 7219 2405. *Constituency:* Unity House, Fennel Street, Loughborough, Leceistershire, LE11 1UQ *Tel:* 01509 261226 *Fax:* 01509 219398 *E-mail:* andrew.reed@geo2.poptel.org.uk.

REID, The Rt Hon. Dr John *(Hamilton North and Bellshill)   Lab majority 17,067*

Son of late Thomas Reid, postman, and of Mary Reid, factory worker. Born May 8, 1947; educated St Patrick's Senior Secondary School, Coatbridge; University of Stirling (Hons Degree History, PhD Economic History). Married 1969, Cathie McGowan (died 1998) (2 sons). *Trades Union:* Member, TGWU. *Career:* Scottish Research Officer, Labour Party 1979–83; Adviser to Rt Hon. Neil Kinnock MP, Leader of the Labour Party 1983–85; Scottish Organiser, Trade Unionists for Labour 1985–87. *Political Career:* Minister of State, Ministry of Defence (Minister for the Armed Forces) 1997–98; Minister of State, Department of the Environment, Transport and the Regions (Minister for Transport) 1998–99; Secretary of State for Scotland 1999–. *Spokesman:* Deputy Shadow Spokesman on Children 1989–90; Opposition Spokesman on Defence, Disarmament and Arms Control 1990–97; Shadow Deputy Secretary of State for Defence 1995–97. *Trust:* Fellow, Armed Services Parliamentary Scheme 1990–. *Honours:* PC 1998. *Special Interests:* Foreign Affairs, Defence, Transport, Economy. *Recreations:* Football, crosswords. *Electoral Notes:* Member for Motherwell North 1987–97, and for Hamilton North and Bellshill since May 1, 1997. *Address:* The Rt Hon. Dr John Reid, MP, House of Commons, London, SW1A 0AA *Tel:* 020 7219 4118. *Constituency:* Parliamentary Office, Montrose House, 154 Montrose Crescent, Hamilton, ML3 6LL *Tel:* 01698 454672 *Fax:* 01698 424732 *E-mail:* scottishsecretary@gov.uk; *Website:* http://www.scottishsecretary.gov.uk.

RENDEL, David Digby *(Newbury)   LD majority 8,517*

Son of late Alexander Rendel, CBE and of Elizabeth Rendel. Born April 15, 1949; educated Eton; Magdalen College; St Cross College, Oxford (Degree in Physics and Philosophy). Married September 7, 1974, Dr Susan Taylor, daughter of Dr William Taylor and Mrs June Taylor (3 sons). *Career:* Volunteer teacher in Cameroon and Uganda, Voluntary Service Overseas; Operational research analyst, Shell International 1974–76; Financial analyst, British Gas 1976–77; Various analytical and management posts (finance and computing), Esso Petroleum 1977–90. *Councils, Public Bodies:* Councillor: Newbury District Council 1987–95, St John's Ward 1987–91, Craven Ward 1991–95; Chairman: Finance and Property Sub-Committee 1991–92, Recreation and

Amenities Committee 1992–93. *Spokesman:* Spokesman for: Housing 1993–94, Local Government in England 1993–97, Local Government and Housing 1997, Social Security and Welfare 1997–99. *Select Committees (Current):* Member: Public Accounts 1999– *(Former):* Member: Accommodation and Works 1997–98. *Party Groups:* Member: Association of Liberal Democrat Councillors, Liberal Democrat Parliamentary Candidates Association, Green Liberal Democrats. *Miscellaneous:* Member, Oxford Boat Race crew 1974. *Recreations:* Family, sport, music, travel. *Electoral Notes:* Contested Hammersmith Fulham 1979 and Fulham 1983. Contested Newbury 1987 and 1992 General Elections. Member for Newbury since May 6, 1993 by-election. *Address:* David Rendel Esq, MP, House of Commons, London, SW1A 0AA *Tel:* 020 7219 3495 *Fax:* 020 7219 2941. *Constituency:* Kendrick House, Wharf Street, Newbury, Berkshire, RG14 5AP *Tel:* 01635 581048 *Fax:* 01635 581049.

ROBATHAN, Andrew Robert George *(Blaby)*   Con majority 6,474

Son of Douglas and Sheena Robathan (née Gimson). Born July 17, 1951; educated Merchant Taylors' School, Northwood; Oriel College, Oxford (MA); RMA, Sandhurst. Married December 20, 1991, Rachael Maunder (1 son 1 daughter). *Armed Forces:* Regular Army Officer, Coldstream Guards 1974–89; Rejoined Army for Gulf War January-April 1991. *Councils, Public Bodies:* Councillor, London Borough of Hammersmith and Fulham 1990–92. *Political Career:* PPS to Minister of State, Department of National Heritage 1995–97. *Select Committees (Current):* Member: International Development 1997– *(Former):* Member: Employment 1992–94. Freeman, Merchant Taylors Company. Freeman, City of London. *Special Interests:* Environment, Transport, Defence, Northern Ireland. *Countries of Interest:* Caucasus. *Recreations:* Mountain walking, skiing, wild life, shooting. *Electoral Notes:* Member for Blaby since April 9, 1992. *Address:* Andrew Robathan Esq, MP, House of Commons, London, SW1A 0AA *Tel:* 020 7219 3550. *Constituency:* Blaby Conservative Association, 35 Lutterworth Road, Blaby, Leicestershire, LE8 4DW *Tel:* 0116–277 9992 *Fax:* 0116–278 6664.

ROBERTSON, Laurence Anthony *(Tewkesbury)*   Con majority 9,234

Son of James Robertson, former colliery electrician, and Jean Robertson (née Larkin). Born March 29, 1958; educated St James' Church of England Secondary School; Farnworth Grammar School; Bolton Institute of Higher Education (Management Services Diploma). Married May 6, 1989, Susan, eldest daughter of James Lees, JP (2 step-daughters). *Career:* Warehouse Assistant 1976–77; Work Study Engineer 1977–83; Industrial Management Consultant 1983–89; Factory Owner 1987–88; Charity Fundraising, Public Relations and Special Events Consultant 1988–. *Select Committees (Current):* Member: Consolidation of Bills (Joint Committee) 1997–, Environmental Audit 1997–, European Scrutiny 1999–, Social Security 1999–. *Party Groups:* Former Member, Conservative 2000 Foundation; Member, Conservative Way Forward; Vice-Chairman, Association of Conservative Clubs (ACC). *Other:* Member, Freedom Association. *Miscellaneous:* Executive Member, 1922 Committee 1999–. *Publications: Europe: the Case Against Integration,* 1991; *The Right Way Ahead,* 1995. *Special Interests:* Constitution, European Policy, Education, Economic Policy, Law and Order. *Countries of Interest:* UK, USA, Switzerland, Mexico. *Recreations:* Sport (completed 6 marathons), reading, writing, countryside. *Electoral Notes:* Contested Makerfield 1987, Ashfield 1992. Member for Tewkesbury since May 1, 1997. *Address:* Laurence Robertson Esq, MP, House of Commons, London, SW1A 0AA *Tel:* 020 7219 3000 *Fax:* 020 7219 2325. *Constituency:* Tewkesbury Conservative Association, Lloyds Bank Chambers, Abbey Terrace, Winchcombe, Gloucestershire, GL54 5LL *Tel:* 01242 602388 *Fax:* 01242 604364.

ROBINSON, Geoffrey *(Coventry North West)   Lab majority 16,601*

Son of late Robert Norman Robinson and late Dorothy Jane Robinson. Born May 25, 1938; educated Emanuel School, London; Clare College, Cambridge; Yale University, USA. Married 1967, Marie Elena Giorgio (1 son 1 daughter). *Career:* Labour Party Research Assistant 1965–68; Senior Executive, Industrial Reorganisation Corporation 1968–70; Financial Controller, British Leyland 1970–72; Managing Director, Leyland Innocenti 1972–73; Chief Executive, Jaguar Cars Coventry 1974–75; Chief Executive (unpaid), Triumph Motorcycles (Meriden) Ltd 1978–80; Director, West Midlands Enterprise Board 1982–85; Chief Executive, TransTec plc 1986–97. *Political Career:* Paymaster General, HM Treasury 1997–98. *Spokesman:* Opposition Front Bench Spokesman on: Science 1982–83, Trade and Industry and Regional Affairs 1983–87. *Special Interests:* Regional Policy, Industry, Economic Policy, New Technology. *Countries of Interest:* France, Germany, Italy, USA. *Recreations:* Motorcars, gardens, architecture. *Electoral Notes:* Member for Coventry North West from 1976 By-election. *Address:* Geoffrey Robinson Esq, MP, House of Commons, London, SW1A 0AA *Tel:* 020 7219 4504 *Fax:* 0209 7219 4875. *Constituency:* Transport House, Short Street, Coventry, CV1 2LS *Tel:* 024 7625 7870 *Fax:* 024 7625 7813.

ROBINSON, Peter David *(Belfast East)   DUP majority 6,754*

Son of late David McCrea Robinson and of Sheila Robinson. Born December 29, 1948; educated Annadale Grammar School; Castlereagh College of Further Education. Married July 25, 1970, Iris Collins (2 sons 1 daughter). *Career:* Estate Agent. *Councils, Public Bodies:* Castlereagh Borough Council: Councillor 1977–, Alderman 1977, Deputy Mayor 1978, Mayor 1986. *Political Career:* Member, Northern Ireland Assembly 1982–86; Deputy Leader, Democratic Unionist Party: resigned 1987, re-elected 1988; Member, Northern Ireland Forum 1996–98; Elected to Northern Ireland Assembly 1998–; Minister for Regional Development, Northern Ireland Assembly 1999–. *Spokesman:* A Spokesman for Constitutional Affairs. *Select Committees (Current):* Member: Northern Ireland Affairs 1997– *(Former):* Member: Northern Ireland Affairs 1994–97. *Party Groups:* Foundation Member, Ulster Democratic Unionist Party, Party Executive Member 1973–; Secretary, Central Executive Committee 1974–79; General Secretary 1975. *Miscellaneous:* Member, NI Sports Council. *Publications: The North Answers Back; Capital Punishment for Capital Crime; Savagery and Suffering; Self-inflicted; Ulster the Prey; Ulster – The facts; Carson Man of Action; A War to be Won; It's Londonderry; Ulster in Peril; Give me Liberty; Hands off the UDR; Their cry was 'No Surrender'; IRA-Sinn Fein; The Union under Fire.* *Special Interests:* Housing, Shipbuilding, Community Care, Aerospace, Aviation, International Terrorism. *Recreations:* Golf, bowling, breeding Koi carp. *Electoral Notes:* Member for Belfast East since May 1979 (resigned seat December 1985 in protest against Anglo-Irish Agreement; re-elected January 1986). *Address:* Peter Robinson Esq, MP, House of Commons, London, SW1A 0AA *Tel:* 020 7219 3506 *Fax:* 020 7219 5854. *Constituency:* Strandtown Hall, 96 Belmont Avenue, Belfast, BT4 3DE *Tel:* 028 9047 3111 *Fax:* 028 9047 1797 *E-mail:* info@dup.org.uk.

ROCHE, Barbara *(Hornsey and Wood Green)   Lab majority 20,499*

Daughter of Barnet and Hannah Margolis. Born April 13, 1954; educated Comprehensive school; Lady Margaret Hall, Oxford University (BA Hons). Married August 1, 1977, Patrick Roche, son of Lawrence and Jocelyn Roche (1 daughter). *Career:* Barrister, called to the Bar 1977. *Political Career:* PPS to Rt Hon. Margaret Beckett, MP 1993–94; Parliamentary Under-Secretary of State, Department of Trade and Industry 1997–99; Financial Secretary, HM Treasury 1999; Minister of State, Home Office 1999–. *Whip:* Opposition Whip 1994–95. *Spokesman:* Opposition Spokeswoman on Trade and Industry 1995–97. *Select Committees (Former):* Member: Home Affairs 1992–94, Public Accounts 1999. *Special Interests:* Home Affairs, Legal Reform, Environment. *Countries of Interest:* Cyprus, Israel. *Recreations:* Theatre, family. *Electoral Notes:* Contested Surrey South West By-election in 1984 and Hornsey and Wood Green in 1987 General Election. Member for Hornsey and Wood Green since April 9, 1992. *Clubs:* Wood Green Labour. *Address:* Barbara Roche, MP, House of Commons, London, SW1A 0AA *Tel:* 020 7219 3411.

ROE, Marion Audrey *(Broxbourne)*   Con majority 6,653

Daughter of late William and Grace (née Bocking) Keyte. Born July 15, 1936; educated Bromley High School; Croydon High School; English School of Languages, Vevey, Switzerland. Married March 15, 1958, James Kenneth, son of Kenneth Alfred Roe (1 son 2 daughters). *Councils, Public Bodies:* Member, South East Thames Regional Health Authority 1980–83; Councillor, London Borough of Bromley 1975–78; GLC Councillor, Ilford North 1977–86; Leading Conservative Spokesman on GLC Police Committee 1982–83; Vice-Chairman, Historic Buildings Committee 1977–81; Whip for Planning and Communications Group; Vice-Chairman, General Management Committee; GLC Representative, General Services Committee of the Association of Metropolitan Authorities; UK Representative, Conference of Local and Regional Authorities of Europe. *Political Career:* Promoted: Prohibition of Female Circumcision Act 1985 (Private Member's Bill); PPS: to Parliamentary Under-Secretary of State for Transport 1985–86, to Minister of State for Transport 1986, to Rt Hon. John Moore, MP, as Secretary of State for Transport 1986–87; Parliamentary Under-Secretary of State, Department of Environment 1987–88. *Select Committees (Current):* Chairman: Administration 1997–; Member: Chairmen's Panel 1997–, Finance and Services 1997–, Liaison 1997– *(Former):* Member: Procedure 1990–92, Administration 1991–97, Sittings of the House 1991–92; Chairman: Health 1992–97; Member: Liaison 1992–97. *Party Groups:* Vice-President, Greater London Young Conservative Group 3 1977–80. *International Bodies:* Substitute Member, UK Delegation to Parliamentary Assemblies of Council of Europe and WEU 1989–92; Member, Executive Committee: Commonwealth Parliamentary Association (CPA) UK Branch 1997–, British Group of the Inter-Parliamentary Union (IPU) 1997–, A Vice-Chairman 1998–. *Other:* Patron, UN Development Fund for Women 1985–87; Vice-President, Women's Nationwide Cancer Control Campaign 1985–; Member: Greater London Area Local Government Advisory Committee 1978–82, BBC's General Advisory Council 1986–87. *Trust:* Fellow, Industry and Parliament Trust 1990; Managing Trustee, Parliamentary Contributory Pension Fund 1990–97. *Miscellaneous:* Member, Department of Employment's Advisory Committee on Women's Employment 1989–92; Executive Member, 1922 Committee 1992–94; Joint Secretary 1997–; Vice-President, Association of District Councils 1994–; Member, Armed Forces Parliamentary Scheme 1998. Freeman, Worshipful Company of Gardeners 1990, Liveryman 1993. Freeman, City of London 1981. FRSA 1990; Hon. Member, Institute of Horticulture 1993; Hon. Fellowship, Professional Business and Technical Management 1995. *Publications: The Labour Left in London – A Blueprint for a Socialist Britain,* 1985. *Special Interests:* Health, Social Security, Horticulture, Environment. *Countries of Interest:* Angola, Canada, Seychelles, South Africa, USA. *Recreations:* Ballet and opera. *Electoral Notes:* Contested Barking 1979. Member for Broxbourne since June 1983. *Address:* Mrs Marion Roe, MP, House of Commons, London, SW1A 0AA *Tel:* 020 7219 3528.

ROGERS, Allan Ralph *(Rhondda)*   Lab majority 24,931

Son of late John Henry Rogers, coalminer. Born October 24, 1932; educated Gelligaer Primary School; Bargoed Secondary School; University of Wales, Swansea (BSc Hons in Geology); Visiting professor, Glamorgan University. Married April 9, 1955, Ceridwen, daughter of Cynonfryn James (1 son 3 daughters). *Trades Union:* COHSE/UNISON sponsored. *Armed Forces:* Welsh Regiment/Royal Welsh Fusiliers 1951–53. *Profession:* Geologist. *Career:* Geologist: UK, Canada, USA, Australia, Africa; District Secretary, Workers' Educational Association for South Wales. *Councils, Public Bodies:* District Councillor 1965–71; County Councillor 1970–80. *Spokesman:* Opposition Spokesman on: Defence and Disarmament and Arms Control 1987–92, Foreign and Commonwealth Affairs 1992–94. *Select Committees (Former):* Member: Welsh Public Accounts. *International Bodies:* Vice-President, EP 1979–82, Secretary and Whip, British Labour Group 1979–84; Chairman, Inter-Parliamentary Union (IPU) British Group 1995–97, A Vice-Chairman 1998–; International President, Parliamentarians for Global Action. *Other:* Chairman, Polytechnic of Wales 1973–80. *Miscellaneous:* Member, Committee on Intelligence and Security 1994–; Vice-President, Federation of Economic Development Authorities (FEDA). *Sportsclubs:* Treorchy RFC. Fellow, Geological Society. *Special Interests:* European Union, Health, Education, Environment, Defence, Energy. *Countries of Interest:* Asia, Falkland Islands, Hong Kong, Japan, USA, Canada, Scandinavia. *Recreations:* All Sports. *Electoral Notes:* MEP for South East Wales 1979–84. Member for Rhondda since June 1983. *Clubs:* Treorchy Workmens, Penygraig Labour. *Address:* Allan Rogers Esq, MP, House of Commons, London, SW1A 0AA *Tel:* 020 7219 3560 *Tel (Constituency):* 01443 682925.

ROOKER, The Rt Hon. Jeffrey *(Birmingham Perry Barr)* *Lab majority 18,957*

Born June 5, 1941; educated Handsworth Technical College; Warwick University; Aston University. Married 1972, Angela. *Career:* Production Manager, Rola Celestion Ltd 1967–70; Lecturer, Lanchester Polytechnic, Coventry 1972–74. *Councils, Public Bodies:* Member, Birmingham Education Committee 1972–74. *Political Career:* PPS to the Government Law Officers 1977; Shadow Deputy Leader, House of Commons 1994–97; Minister of State and Deputy Minister, Ministry of Agriculture, Fisheries and Food (Minister for Food Safety) 1997–99; Minister of State, Department of Social Security 1999–. *Spokesman:* Opposition Front Bench Spokesman on: Social Services 1979–80, Social Security 1980–83, Treasury and Economic Affairs 1983–84, Environment 1984–88, Community Care and Social Services 1990–92, Education 1992–93. *Other:* Member of Council, Institution of Production Engineers 1975–80. *Honours:* PC 1999. *Electoral Notes:* Member for Birmingham Perry Barr since February 1974. *Address:* The Rt Hon. Jeffrey Rooker Esq, MP, House of Commons, London, SW1A 0AA *Tel:* 020 7219 4153.

ROONEY, Terence *(Bradford North)* *Lab majority 12,770*

Son of Eric and Frances Rooney. Born November 11, 1950; educated Buttershaw Comprehensive School; Bradford College. Married 1969, Susanne Chapman (1 son 2 daughters). *Career:* Commercial insurance broker; Welfare Rights Worker. *Councils, Public Bodies:* Bradford City Council (University Ward): Councillor 1983–91, Chairman, Labour Group 1988–91, Deputy Leader 1990–91. *Political Career:* PPS to Rt Hon. Michael Meacher, as Minister of State, Department of the Environment, Transport and the Regions (Minister for the Environment) 1997–. *Select Committees (Former):* Member: Broadcasting 1991–97. *Party Groups:* Campaign co-ordinator, Bradford West Labour Party in 1983 General Election Campaign; Hon. Secretary, Yorkshire Regional Group of Labour MPs 1997–. *Trust:* Trustee, Brierley Community Association. *Miscellaneous:* Member: Low Pay Unit, Unemployment Unit. *Special Interests:* Public Sector Housing, Poverty, Industrial Relations. *Countries of Interest:* Pakistan, India, Bangladesh. *Recreations:* Crosswords, football, tennis. *Electoral Notes:* Member for Bradford North since November 8, 1990 By-election. *Address:* Terence Rooney Esq, MP, House of Commons, London, SW1A 0AA *Tel:* 020 7219 6407. *Constituency:* 76 Kirkgate, Bradford, West Yorkshire, BD1 1SZ *Tel:* 01274 777821 *Fax:* 01274 777817.

ROSS, Ernie (Ernest) *(Dundee West)* *Lab majority 11,859*

Born July 27, 1942; educated St John's Junior Secondary School. Married (2 sons 1 daughter). *Trades Union:* Member, MSF. *Career:* Quality Control Engineer, Timex Ltd. *Select Committees (Current):* Member: Court of Referees 1997–, Standing Orders 1997– *(Former):* Member: Education and Employment 1996–97, Standards and Privileges 1996–97, Foreign Affairs 1997–99. *Party Groups:* Joined Labour Party 1957. *International Bodies:* UK Delegation to Organisation for Security and Co-operation in Europe. *Special Interests:* Social Services, Defence, Industry, Employment, Education. *Countries of Interest:* Bangladesh, Former Soviet Union, Cuba, Cyprus, Latin America, Middle East, South Africa, USA. *Recreations:* Football, cricket. *Electoral Notes:* Member for Dundee West since May 1979. *Address:* Ernie Ross Esq, MP, House of Commons, London, SW1A 0AA *Tel:* 020 7219 3480 *Fax:* 020 7219 2359. *Constituency:* 18B Marketgait, Dundee, DD1 1QR *Tel:* 01382 207000 *Fax:* 01382 221280 *E-mail:* rossm@parliament.uk.

Dod *on* Disk

The Vacher Dod Parliamentary Database – configured for PC or Network

For further details please telephone the Westminster Office

020 7828 7256

ROSS, William *(East Londonderry)   UUP majority 3,794*

Son of late Leslie Alexander Ross and late Mabel Ross. Born February 4, 1936; educated Dungiven Primary School; Northwest College of Agriculture. Married July 20, 1974, Christine, daughter of George Haslett (3 sons 1 daughter). *Career:* Farmer. *Whip:* Former UUP Whip. *Spokesman:* Spokesman for: Agriculture and Fisheries 1992–97, the Treasury and Civil Service 1997–. *Select Committees (Current):* Member: Administration 1997–, Deregulation 1997–, Statutory Instruments (Joint Committee) 1997– *(Former):* Member: Joint Committee on Statutory Instruments 1992–97, Deregulation 1995–97. *Party Groups:* Former Secretary: Mid-Londonderry Unionist Party (Northern Ireland Constituency), Londonderry Constituency Unionist Party.
Miscellaneous: Member, European Standing Committee B 1998–. *Special Interests:* Disabled/Disability, Housing, Local Government, Defence, Firearms Legislation, Marketing. *Countries of Interest:* Australia, Canada, New Zealand, South Africa. *Recreations:* Angling, shooting. *Electoral Notes:* Member for Londonderry February 1974–83. Member for East Londonderry since June 1983. *Clubs:* Northern Counties (Londonderry). *Address:* William Ross Esq, MP, House of Commons, London, SW1A 0AA *Tel:* 020 7219 3571. *Constituency:* Turmeel, Dungiven, County Londonderry, BT47 4SL *Fax:* 028 7174 2291.

ROWE, Andrew John Bernard *(Faversham and Mid Kent)   Con majority 4,173*

Son of late John Douglas Rowe. Born September 11, 1935; educated Eton College; Merton College, Oxford (MA Oxon). Married 1st, 1960, Alison Boyd (1 son) (marriage dissolved 1975); 2nd, November 1983, Sheila Leslie Finkle (2 step-daughters). *Armed Forces:* Sub-Lieutenant, RNVR 1954–56. *Career:* Assistant Master, Eton College 1959–62; Principal, Scottish Office 1962–67; Lecturer, Edinburgh University 1967–74; Consultant to Voluntary Service Unit 1973–74; Editor, *Small Business*; Consultant in Government Affairs 1979–83. *Political Career:* PPS: to Rt Hon. Richard Needham, MP, as Minister of State, Department of Trade and Industry 1992–95; to Rt Hon. the Earl Ferrers 1994–95. *Select Committees (Current):* Member: International Development 1997– *(Former):* Member: Health 1991–92, Public Accounts 1995–97. *Party Groups:* Director, Community Affairs, Conservative Central Office 1975–79; Member: Tory Reform Group, Mainstream Group, Positive European Group. *International Bodies:* Formerly Member, UK delegation to Council of Europe. *Other:* Member, NSPCC; President: Kent Engineering Society, North Downs Rail Concern. *Trust:* Trustee, Community Service Volunteers. *Miscellaneous:* Member, Swann Committee 1979–84; Formerly Chairman, Parliamentary Panel on Personal Social Services. *Publications: Democracy Renewed; Somewhere to Start;* and other pamphlets. *Special Interests:* Small Businesses, Employment, Conservation, Voluntary Organisations. *Countries of Interest:* China, Europe, Hong Kong, India, Nepal. *Recreations:* Photography, fishing, reading, theatre. *Electoral Notes:* Member for Mid Kent 1983–97, and for Faversham and Mid Kent since May 1, 1997. *Address:* Andrew Rowe Esq, MP, House of Commons, London, SW1A 0AA *Tel:* 020 7219 3536 *Fax:* 020 7219 3826.

ROWLANDS, Edward *(Merthyr Tydfil and Rhymney)   Lab majority 27,086*

Son of William Samuel Rowlands, Clerk of Works. Born January 23, 1940; educated Rhondda Grammar School; Wirral Grammar, Cheshire; King's College, London (BA (Hons) History 1962). Married 1968, Janice Williams (2 sons 1 daughter). *Career:* Research Student 1962; Research Assistant, History of Parliament Trust 1963–65; Lecturer: Modern History and Government, Welsh CAT 1965–, Law Department, LSC 1972–74. *Political Career:* Parliamentary Under-Secretary of State: Welsh Office October 1969–70, 1974–75, Foreign and Commonwealth Office 1975–76; Minister of State for Foreign and Commonwealth Affairs 1976–79. *Spokesman:* Opposition Front Bench Spokesman on: Foreign and Commonwealth Affairs 1979–1980, Energy December 1980–87. *Select Committees (Current):* Member: Foreign Affairs 1997– *(Former):* Member: Foreign Affairs 1987–97. *Other:* Judge, Booker McConnel Novel of the Year Competition 1984. *Trust:* Fellow, Industry and Parliament Trust; Chairman, History of Parliamentary Trust 1993–.

Publications: Robert Harley's Parliamentary Apprenticeship 1690–1695, (British Library Journal 1989); *Robert Harley and the Battle for Power in Radnorshire 1690–1693*, (Welsh History Review 1990). *Special Interests:* Energy, Overseas Aid, Disabled/Disability, Education, Publishing. *Countries of Interest:* Europe, Mozambique, Uganda. *Electoral Notes:* Member for Cardiff North 1966–70. Member for Merthyr Tydfil By-election 1972–83. Member for Merthyr Tydfil and Rhymney since June 1983. *Address:* Edward Rowlands Esq, MP, House of Commons, London, SW1A 0AA *Tel:* 020 7219 4480.

ROY, Frank *(Motherwell and Wishaw)   Lab majority 12,791*

Son of late James Roy, settler manager, and Esther McMahon, home-help. Born August 29, 1958; educated St Joseph's High School, Motherwell; Our Lady's High School, Motherwell; Motherwell College (HNC in Marketing); Glasgow Caledonian University (BA Consumer and Management Studies). Married September 17, 1977, to Ellen, daughter of Patrick and Ellen Foy (1 son 1 daughter). *Trades Union:* Member, GMB; Shop Steward, ISTC 1983–90. *Career:* Ravenscraig Steelworker 1977–91; Personal Assistant to Helen Liddell, MP 1994–97. *Political Career:* PPS: to Rt Hon. Helen Liddell, MP, as Minister of State, Scottish Office (Minister for Education) 1998–99, to Rt Hon. Dr John Reid, MP, as Secretary of State for Scotland 1999–. *Select Committees (Former):* Member: Social Security 1997–98. *Miscellaneous:* Parliamentary Election Agent to Dr Jeremy Bray 1987–92; Vice-President, Federation of Economic Development Authorities (FEDA). *Special Interests:* Employment Law, Social Welfare Issues. *Countries of Interest:* Europe, USA. *Recreations:* Football, reading, music. *Electoral Notes:* Member for Motherwell and Wishaw since May 1, 1997. *Address:* Frank Roy Esq, MP, House of Commons, London, SW1A 0AA *Tel:* 020 7219 6467. *Constituency:* Constituency Office, 265 Main Street, Wishaw, Lanarkshire, ML2 7NE *Tel:* 01698 303040 *Fax:* 01698 303060.

RUANE, Chris (Christopher) *(Vale of Clwyd)   Lab majority 8,955*

Son of late Michael Ruane, labourer, and Esther Ruane. Born July 18, 1958; educated Ysgol Mair RC, Rhyl Primary; Blessed Edward Jones Comprehensive, Rhyl; University College Wales, Aberystwyth (BSc Economics); Liverpool University (Post Graduate Certificate in Education); Glamorgan University (Diploma in Media Education); University College Wales, Bangor (Diploma in Teaching of Welsh as Second Language – Primary). Married February 14, 1994, Gill, daughter of Joe and Phil Roberts (2 daughters). *Trades Union:* National Union of Teachers: School Rep 1982–97, President, West Clwyd 1991, Vale of Clwyd 1997. *Profession:* Teacher. *Career:* Class Teacher, Primary School 1982–97; Deputy Head 1991–97. *Councils, Public Bodies:* Councillor, Rhyl Town Council 1988–99. *Select Committees (Current):* Member: Welsh Affairs 1999–. *Party Groups:* Has held numerous branch offices at all levels. *Other:* Member: Welfare Benefits Shop Management Committee, Steering Group forming Vale of Clwyd Credit Union; Founder Member: Rhyl Anti Apartheid 1987, Rhyl and District Amnesty International Group 1991, Rhyl Environmental Association 1988. *Special Interests:* Anti-Poverty, Human Rights, Education, Environment. *Recreations:* Cooking, walking, reading, humour. *Electoral Notes:* Contested Clwyd North West 1992 General Election. Member for Vale of Clwyd since May 1, 1997. *Address:* Chris Ruane Esq, MP, House of Commons, London, SW1A 0AA *Tel:* 020 7219 6378 *Fax:* 020 7219 6090. *Constituency:* 45–57 Kinmel Street, Rhyl, Clwyd, LL18 1AG *Tel:* 01745 334865 *Fax:* 01745 334827.

RUDDOCK, Joan *(Lewisham, Deptford)   Lab majority 18,878*

Daughter of late Kenneth Anthony and Mrs Eileen Anthony. Born December 28, 1943; educated Pontypool Grammar School for Girls; Imperial College, University of London (BSc); Hon. Fellow: Goldsmith's College, University of London; Laban Centre, London. Married July 3, 1963, Keith, son of Violet and late Charles Ruddock (separated 1990, died December 20, 1996). *Career:* Director: Research and Publications, Shelter, National Campaign for Homeless 1968–73; Oxford Housing Aid Centre 1973–77; Special Programmes Officer (MSC) for Unemployed Young People, Berks County Council 1977–79; Manager, Citizens Advice Bureau, Reading 1979–86. *Political Career:* Private Members' Bill on flytipping – Control of Pollution Act (amendment) 1989;

Parliamentary Under-Secretary of State for Women 1997–98; Promoted: Ten Minute Rule Bill 1999, Prophylactic Mastectomy Registry Presentation Bill 1999, Organic Food and Farming Targets Bill. *Spokesman:* Opposition Transport Spokesperson 1989–92; Opposition Front Bench Spokesperson on: Home Affairs 1992–94, Environmental Protection 1994–97. *International Bodies:* Member, British Delegation to Council of Europe and Western European Union 1988–89. *Other:* Chairperson, CND 1981–85. ARCS (1965). *Special Interests:* Foreign Affairs, Transport, Environment, Women. *Recreations:* Travel, music, gardening. *Electoral Notes:* Contested Newbury 1979. Member for Lewisham Deptford since June 1987. *Address:* Joan Ruddock, MP, House of Commons, London, SW1A 0AA *Tel:* 020 7219 6206 *Fax:* 020 7219 6045.

RUFFLEY, David *(Bury St Edmunds)   Con majority 368*

Son of Jack Laurie Ruffley LLB, Solicitor and Yvonne Grace (née Harris). Born April 18, 1962; educated Bolton Boys' School; Queens' College, Cambridge (Exhibitioner 1981, Foundation Scholar 1983, First Class Hons Historical Tripos Part I, BA Law 1985). *Profession:* Solicitor. *Career:* Clifford Chance Solicitors, London 1985–91; Special Adviser: to the Secretary of State for Education and Science 1991–92, to the Home Secretary 1992–93, to the Chancellor of the Exchequer 1993–96; Strategic Economic Consultant to the Conservative Party 1996–97; Vice-President, Small Business Bureau 1996–. *Select Committees (Current):* Member: Treasury 1998–, Treasury Sub-Committee 1999– *(Former):* Member: Public Administration 1997–99. *Party Groups:* Member, The Britain Club. *Other:* Adviser, Grant Maintained Schools Foundation 1993–; Governor: Marylebone Girls' School 1992–94, Pimlico School 1994–96, Bolton Boys' School 1997–99. *Miscellaneous:* Consultant: to Grant Maintained Schools Foundation 1991–, to 'Catch 'em Young' young offenders project 1992. *Sportsclubs:* Stowmarket FC, The Suffolk Golf and Country Club. *Special Interests:* Treasury, Home Affairs, Education. *Countries of Interest:* USA, China. *Recreations:* Football, cinema, golf, thinking. *Electoral Notes:* Member for Bury St Edmunds since May 1, 1997. *Clubs:* Athenaeum. *Address:* David Ruffley Esq, MP, House of Commons, London, SW1A 0AA *Tel:* 020 7219 2880 *Fax:* 020 7219 3998. *Constituency:* 3 Woolhall Street, Bury St Edmunds, Suffolk, IP33 1LA *Tel:* 01284 754072 *Fax:* 01284 476 3515 *E-mail:* davidruffleymp@parliament.uk.

RUSSELL, Bob (Robert Edward) *(Colchester)   LD majority 1,581*

Son of late Ewart Russell and late Muriel Russell (née Sawdy). Born March 31, 1946; educated Myland Primary, Colchester; St Helena Secondary Boys, Colchester; North-East Essex Technical College (NEETC) (Proficiency Certificate, National Council for the Training of Journalists). Married April 1, 1967, Audrey Blandon (twin sons 1 daughter, 1 daughter deceased). *Trades Union:* Branch Secretary, North-Essex, National Union of Journalists 1967–68. *Profession:* Journalist/Publicity Officer. *Career:* Trainee Reporter, *Essex County Standard* and *Colchester Gazette* 1963–66; News Editor, *Braintree and Witham Times* 1966–68; Editor, *Maldon and Burnham Standard* 1968–69; Sub-Editor: London *Evening News* 1969–72, London *Evening Standard* 1972–73; Press Officer, BT Eastern Region 1973–85; Publicity Information Officer, University of Essex 1986–97. *Councils, Public Bodies:* Councillor, Colchester Borough Council 1971, Mayor 1986–87, Council Leader 1987–91. *Whip:* North, Midlands and Wales Whip 1999–. *Spokesman:* A Spokesman for: Home and Legal Affairs (Immigration) 1997–99, Constitution, Culture and Sport (Sport) 1999–. *Select Committees (Current):* Member: Home Affairs 1998– *(Former):* Member: Home Affairs 1998. *Party Groups:* Member: Labour Party 1966, SDP May 1981, Liberal Democrats since formation. *Other:* Member: Oxfam, Colchester and East Essex Co-operative Society. *Awards:* Journalists Prize, NEETC 1965. *Sportsclubs:* Colchester United Football Club. *Special Interests:* Environment, Local Government, Sport, Transport, Animal Welfare. *Countries of Interest:* St Helena. *Recreations:* Local history, walking, camping, watching Colchester Utd FC. *Electoral Notes:* Member for Colchester since May 1, 1997. *Address:* Bob Russell Esq, MP, House of Commons, London, SW1A 0AA *Tel:* 020 7219 5150 *Fax:* 020 7219 2365. *Constituency:* Corporate House, Queen Street, Colchester, CO1 2PG *Tel:* 01206 710172 *Fax:* 01206 710184.

RUSSELL, Christine Margaret *(City of Chester)   Lab majority 10,553*

Daughter of late John Alfred William Carr, farmer, and Phyllis Carr. Born March 25, 1945; educated Spalding High School; London School of Librarianship; Polytechnic of North West London (Professional Librarianship Qualification, ALA). Married 30 July 1971, Dr James Russell, son of late Frederick and Mary Russell (marriage dissolved 1991) (1 son 1 daughter). *Trades Union:* Member, GMB. *Profession:* Chartered Librarian. *Career:* Librarian: London Borough of Camden 1967–70, University of Glasgow 1970–71, Dumbartonshire County Council 1971–73; Personal Assistant to: Lyndon Harrison, MEP 1989–91, Brian Simpson, MEP 1992–94; Coordinator of Advocacy Project, MIND 1994–97. *Councils, Public Bodies:* JP 1980–; Councillor, Chester City Council 1980–97, Chair, City Council Development Committee 1990–97. *Select Committees (Current):* Member: Environmental Audit 1999–. *Party Groups:* Joined Labour Party 1967; Agent, Chester Constituency Labour Party 1986–95, Chair/President 1989–92. *Other:* President, Chester Womens Hostel Association; Elected Member, Citizens Advice Bureau; Chair, Chester Film Society and Festival; Member, Magistrates Association. *Miscellaneous:* Among other broadcasts, On The Record: General Election 1992. ALA. *Special Interests:* Transport, Environment, Education, Urban Regeneration, Arts. *Countries of Interest:* South Africa, Romania, Portugal, South America, Eastern Europe. *Recreations:* Cinema, football, walking, art and architecture, travel. *Electoral Notes:* Member for City of Chester since May 1, 1997. *Address:* Mrs Christine Russell, MP, House of Commons, London, SW1A 0AA *Tel:* 020 7219 6398 *Fax:* 020 7219 0943. *Constituency:* York House, York Street, Chester, CH1 3LR *Tel:* 01244 400174 *Fax:* 01244 400487 *E-mail:* russellcm@parliament.uk.

RYAN, Joan *(Enfield North)   Lab majority 6,822*

Daughter of Michael Joseph and Dolores Marie Ryan (née Joyce). Born September 8, 1955; educated City of Liverpool College; Polytechnic of the South Bank (BA Hons, MSc). Married 2nd, Martin Hegarty (1 son 1 daughter). *Trades Union:* Member: NUT, MSF. *Profession:* Teacher. *Councils, Public Bodies:* Councillor, Barnet Council 1990–98, Deputy Leader 1994–98, Chair, Policy and Resources Committee 1994. *Political Career:* PPS to Rt Hon. Andrew Smith, MP: as Minister of State, Department for Education and Employment (Minister for Employment, Welfare to Work and Equal Opportunities) 1998–99, as Chief Secretary to the Treasury 1999–. *Party Groups:* Member, Labour Party 1984–; Chair: Finchley Constituency Labour Party 1992–96, London North European Constituency 1994–97; Hon. Secretary, London Regional Group of Labour MPs 1999–. *Other:* School Govenor, Lea Valley High School; Vice-President, Brimsdown Sports and Social Club; Director, Riders For Health. *Special Interests:* Jobs, Investment, Health Service, Local Government, Employment, Regeneration, Health. *Countries of Interest:* Cyprus, Ireland, Israel. *Recreations:* Swimming, reading, music, visiting historic buildings. *Electoral Notes:* Member for Enfield North since May 1; 1997. *Address:* Joan Ryan, MP, House of Commons, London, SW1A 0AA *Tel:* 020 7219 6502 *Fax:* 020 7219 2335. *Constituency:* Liberty House, 324 High Street, Ponders End, Enfield, EN3 4HF *Tel:* 020 8805 9470 *Fax:* 020 8373 0455 *E-mail:* joan-ryanmp@hotmail.com.

S

ST AUBYN, Nicholas Francis *(Guildford)   Con majority 4,791*

Son of Piers and late Mary St Aubyn. Born November 19, 1955; educated Eton College; Trinity College, Oxford (MA Hons PPE) (Open Exhibitioner). Married April 26, 1980, Jane Mary, daughter of William and Joan Brooks (2 sons, 3 daughters). *Profession:* Banking and Industry. *Career:* Investment Banking: Loan Officer for Morgan Guaranty 1979–81; Head of London Office, Morgan Futures 1981–84; Head of Morgan Guaranty's Sterling and Arbitrage Swaps Desk 1984–86; Vice-President: Kleinwort Benson Cross Finance 1986–87, American International Group's Financial Products Division 1987–89; Chairman: Gemini Ltd 1989–93, Fitzroy Joinery Ltd 1993–. *Councils, Public Bodies:* Councillor, Westminster City Council 1982–86.

Select Committees (Current): Member: Education and Employment 1997–, Education Sub-Committee 1997–, Unopposed Bills (Panel) 1997–, Employment Sub-Committee 1999–. *Party Groups:* Member, Bow Group. *Trust:* Member: National Trust; Council, Project Trust. *Special Interests:* Economic Policy, Education, Small Businesses, Planning, Housing. *Countries of Interest:* USA, South Africa. *Recreations:* Swimming, riding, shooting, walking, children. *Electoral Notes:* Contested Truro By-election 1987, General Elections 1987, 1992. Member for Guildford since May 1, 1997. *Clubs:* Guildford County, Brooks'. *Address:* Nicholas St Aubyn Esq, MP, House of Commons, London, SW1A 0AA *Tel:* 020 7219 3000. *Constituency:* Conservative Association, 63 Woodbridge Road, Guildford, Surrey, GU1 4RD *Tel:* 01483 575151 *Fax:* 01483 562855.

SALMOND, Alex (Alexander) Elliot Anderson *(Banff and Buchan)   SNP majority 12,845*

Son of Robert and Mary Salmond. Born December 31, 1954; educated Linlithgow Academy; St Andrew's University (MA (Hons) Economics and History). Married May 6, 1981, Moira French McGlashan. *Career:* Assistant Agriculture and Fisheries Economist, Department of Agriculture and Fisheries (Scotland) 1978–80; Assistant Economist, Royal Bank of Scotland 1980–82; Oil Economist 1982–87; Economist 1984–87. *Spokesman:* Parliamentary Spokesperson for: Constitution, Economy, Trade and Industry, Fishing 1992–97, Constitution and Fishing 1997–. *Party Groups:* SNP National Executive: Member 1981–, Vice-Chairman 1985–87, Deputy Leader 1987, Senior Vice-Convenor 1988–90, National Convenor 1990–. *Miscellaneous:* Hon. Vice-President, Scottish Centre for Economic and Social Research. *Special Interests:* Fishing, Agriculture, Energy, Third World, Scottish Economy. *Countries of Interest:* Europe. *Recreations:* Golf, reading, football. *Electoral Notes:* Member for Banff and Buchan since June 1987. MSP for the Constituency of Banff and Buchan since May 6, 1999. *Address:* Alex Salmond Esq, MP, MSP, House of Commons, London, SW1A 0AA *Tel:* 020 7219 4578. *Constituency:* 17 Maiden Street, Peterhead, Grampian, AB42 1EE *Tel:* 01779 470444 *Fax:* 01779 474460 *E-mail:* asmp.peterhead@snp.org.

SALTER, Martin John *(Reading West)   Lab majority 2,997*

Son of Raymond and Naomi Salter. Born April 19, 1954; educated Local Grammar School; University of Sussex. *Trades Union:* Member, TGWU; Former Shop Steward: TGWU, UCATT. *Career:* Former Co-ordinator, Reading Centre for the Unemployed; Former Regional Manager, Co-operative Home Services (a tenant-controlled Housing Association). *Councils, Public Bodies:* Councillor, Reading Borough Council 1984–96, Deputy Leader 1987–96. *Select Committees (Former):* Member: Northern Ireland Affairs 1997–99. *Party Groups:* Member, Co-operative Party; Organiser, Network of Labour Councils in South; Joint Vice-Chair, South and West Group of Labour MPs 1997–98; Chairman, South East Regional Group of Labour MPs 1998–. *Other:* Member: Greenpeace, Open Spaces Society, Amnesty International. *Trust:* Member, National Trust. *Miscellaneous:* Secretary, Punjab Human Rights Sub Group. *Sportsclubs:* Reading and District Angling Association and other Fishing Clubs. *Special Interests:* Environment, Local Government, Housing, Northern Ireland. *Countries of Interest:* India, Pakistan. *Recreations:* Angling, walking, football. *Electoral Notes:* Contested Reading East 1987. Member for Reading West since May 1, 1997. *Address:* Martin Salter Esq, MP, House of Commons, London, SW1A 0AA *Tel:* 020 7219 2416. *Constituency:* 413 Oxford Road, Reading, Berkshire, RG30 1HA *Tel:* 0118–954 6782 *Fax:* 0118–954 6784.

SANDERS, Adrian Mark *(Torbay)   LD majority 12*

Son of John Sanders, insurance official, and of Helen, nurse. Born April 25, 1959; educated Torquay Boys' Grammar School. Married Alison Nortcliffe. *Profession:* Grants Adviser to Charities. *Career:* Parliamentary Officer, Liberal Democrat Whips' Office 1989–90; Association of Liberal Democrat Councillors 1990–92; Policy Officer, National Council for Voluntary Organisations 1992–93; Worked for Paddy Ashdown, MP and Party Leader 1992–93, organised his tour of Britain 1993; Southern Association of Voluntary Action Groups for Europe 1993–97. *Councils, Public Bodies:* Councillor, Torbay Borough Council 1984–86. *Whip:* South and South West Regional Whip 1997–. *Spokesman:* A Spokesman for: Local Government and Housing (Housing) 1997–99, Environment, Transport, the Regions and Social Justice 1999–. *Select Committees (Current):* Member: Consolidation of Bills (Joint Committee) 1997–. *Party Groups:* Vice-President, National League of Young Liberals 1985; Political Secretary, Devon and Cornwall Regional Liberal Party 1983–84; Information Officer, Association of Liberal Councillors 1986–89. *International Bodies:* Member: CPA, IPU. *Other:* Member: Paignton Preservation Society, British Diabetic Association; Director (non-pecuniary), Southern Association of Voluntary Action Groups. *Countries of Interest:* USA. *Recreations:* Football. *Electoral Notes:* Contested Torbay General Election 1992, Devon and East Plymouth European Parliament Elections 1994. Member for Torbay since May 1, 1997. *Clubs:* Paignton Club. *Address:* Adrian Sanders Esq, MP, House of Commons, London, SW1A 0AA *Tel:* 020 7219 6304 *Fax:* 020 7219 3963. *Constituency:* 69 Belgrave Road, Torquay, Devon, TQ2 5HZ *Tel:* 01803 200036 *Fax:* 01803 200031.

SARWAR, Mohammed *(Glasgow Govan)   Lab majority 2,914*

Born August 18, 1952; educated University of Faisalabad, Pakistan (BA Political Science). Married Perveen Sarwar (3 sons, 1 daughter). *Trades Union:* Member, GMB. *Career:* Director, United Wholesale Ltd. *Councils, Public Bodies:* Councillor: Glasgow District Council 1992–95, Glasgow City Council 1995–. *Select Committees (Current):* Member: Scottish Affairs 1999–. *Party Groups:* Joined Labour Party 1984; Member: Scottish Labour Executive 1994–, Scottish Labour Gala Fund-raising Dinner Organising Committee; Constituency Labour Party: Former Branch Chairman, Membership Secretary, Trades Union Liaison Officer. *Miscellaneous:* Scottish Conference, Racism Debate 1994; BBC Scotland, Frontline Scotland 1995; BBC Newsnight 1995; Several appearances Reporting Scotland 1995–96. *Special Interests:* Housing, Employment, Economic Policy, Devolution, International Affairs. *Countries of Interest:* Pakistan, Middle East, Developing World. *Recreations:* Family and friends. *Electoral Notes:* Member for Glasgow Govan since May 1, 1997. *Address:* Mohammed Sarwar Esq, MP, House of Commons, London, SW1A 0AA *Tel:* 020 7219 3000. *Constituency:* 247 Paisley Road West, Glasgow *Tel:* 0141–427 5250.

SAVIDGE, Malcolm Kemp *(Aberdeen North)   Lab majority 10,010*

Son of late David Gordon Madgwick Savidge, FCA, and of Mrs Jean Kirkpatrick (née Kemp) Savidge. Born May 9, 1946; educated Wallington County Grammar School For Boys, Surrey; Aberdeen University (MA Hons); Aberdeen College of Education (Teaching Certificate); Hon. Fellow, Robert Gordon University, Aberdeen 1997. *Trades Union:* Educational Institute of Scotland: National Executive 1982–84, National Council 1980–86, 1989–90; Member, Transport and General Workers Union. *Profession:* Schoolteacher. *Career:* Production/Stock Control and Computer Assistant, Bryans' Electronics Ltd 1970–71; Teacher of Mathematics, Greenwood Dale Bilateral Secondary School, Nottingham 1971; Teacher of Mathematics and Religious/Social Education, Peterhead Academy 1972–73; Teacher of Maths, Kincorth Academy, Aberdeen 1973–97. *Councils, Public Bodies:* Aberdeen City Council: Councillor 1980–96, Vice-Chair, Labour Group 1980–88, Libraries Convenor 1984–87, 1988–94, Finance Convenor and Deputy Leader of the Council 1994–96; JP 1984–96. *Select Committees (Current):* Member: Environmental Audit 1997–. *Party Groups:* Member: Scottish Executive of the Labour Party 1993–94, Co-op Party.

International Bodies: Member, United Nations Association. *Other:* Governor: Aberdeen College of Education 1980–87, Robert Gordon Institute of Technology 1980–88; Member: Scientists For Global Responsibility, Amnesty International. *Special Interests:* International Affairs, Local Government, Education, Arms Conversion and Diversification. *Recreations:* Exploring life, spectator sport, crosswords and puzzles, reading, real ale, the Arts, heraldry. *Electoral Notes:* Contested Kincardine and Deeside 1991 by-election, 1992 General Election. Member for Aberdeen North since May 1, 1997. *Address:* Malcolm Savidge Esq, MP, House of Commons, London, SW1A 0AA *Tel:* 020 7219 3000. *Constituency:* Aberdeen Constituency Office, 166 Market Street, Aberdeen, AB11 5PP *Tel:* 01224 252708 *Fax:* 01224 252712 *E-mail:* mksavidge@aol.com/malcolm.savidge@geo2.poptel.org.uk.

SAWFORD, Philip Andrew *(Kettering)* *Lab majority 189*

Son of John William Sawford and Audrey Kathleen Sawford. Born June 26, 1950; educated Kettering Grammar School; Ruskin College, Oxford; Leicester University (BA Hons). Married May 1, 1971, Rosemary, daughter of John and Rene Stokes (2 sons). *Trades Union:* Member, GMB. *Profession:* Training Manager. *Career:* Apprentice Carpenter/Joiner, Moulton; British Steel Corporation, Corby 1977–80; Wellingborough Community Relations Council 1985–; Currently with Training Partnership, Wellingborough. *Councils, Public Bodies:* Councillor, Desborough Town Council 1977–97, Chair 1985; Councillor, Kettering Borough Council 1979–83, 1986–97, Leader 1991–97. *Select Committees (Current):* Member: Information 1997–. *Party Groups:* Member, Labour Party; Served as Branch Secretary, District Party Chair, Political Education Organiser, Constituency Vice-Chair, Annual Conference Delegate and various other capacities; Member, Co-operative Party. *Miscellaneous:* Member, Institute of Personnel and Development. MIPD. *Special Interests:* Education, Employment. *Countries of Interest:* France. *Recreations:* Playing guitar, music, reading. *Electoral Notes:* GMB supported candidate. Contested Wellingborough 1992. Member for Kettering since May 1, 1997. *Address:* Philip Sawford Esq, MP, House of Commons, London, SW1A 0AA *Tel:* 020 7219 6213 *Fax:* 020 7219 6174. *Constituency:* 1A Headlands, Kettering, Northamptonshire, NN15 7ER *Tel:* 01536 411900 *Fax:* 01536 410742 *E-mail:* sawfordp@parliament.uk.

SAYEED, Jonathan *(Mid Bedfordshire)* *Con majority 7,090*

Son of late M M Sayeed, chartered electrical engineer, and L S Sayeed. Born March 20, 1948; educated Britannia Royal Naval College, Dartmouth; Royal Naval Engineering College, Manadon, Plymouth. Married October 18, 1980, Nicola Anne Power (2 sons). *Armed Forces:* Royal Navy and Royal Naval Reserve 1964–74. *Career:* Founder Director, Wade Emerson & Co Ltd 1974–82; Chairman and Chief Executive, Calmady Insurance Services Ltd 1982–83; Chairman, Ranelagh Ltd 1992–96; Director (Non-Executive), Love Lane Investments Ltd (Holding Company) 1992–96; Chairman, Training Division Corporate Services Group plc 1996–97. *Political Career:* PPS to Paymaster General 1991–92. *Select Committees (Current):* Member: Broadcasting 1997–. *Party Groups:* President, Bristol East Conservative Association. *Recreations:* Golf, sailing, tennis, skiing, flying, classical music, books, architecture. *Electoral Notes:* Member for Bristol East 1983–92. Member for Mid Bedfordshire since May 1, 1997. *Clubs:* Carlton. *Address:* Jonathan Sayeed Esq, MP, House of Commons, London, SW1A 0AA *Tel:* 020 7219 2355 *Fax:* 020 7219 1294. *Constituency:* Mid-Bedfordshire Conservative Association, St Michaels Close, High Street, Shefford, Bedfordshire, SG17 5DD *Tel:* 01462 811992 *Fax:* 01462 811010.

SEDGEMORE, Brian *(Hackney South and Shoreditch)   Lab majority 14,980*

Son of late Charles John Sedgemore. Born March 17, 1937; educated State Schools; Oxford University (MA, Diploma in Public and Social Administration). Married December 19, 1966, Audrey, daughter of Juby Reece, QC (1 son) (marriage dissolved). *Trades Union:* Member, NUJ. *Armed Forces:* RAF 1956–58. *Profession:* Barrister. *Career:* Ministry of Housing and Local Government Principal 1962–66; Private Secretary to R. J. Mellish, MP (then a Junior Minister) 1964–66; Barrister 1966–74; Granada TV 1979–83. *Councils, Public Bodies:* Councillor, Wandsworth Council 1971–74, Chairman, Community Relations 1971–74. *Political Career:* PPS to Tony Benn, MP, as Secretary of State for Energy 1977–79. *Select Committees (Current):* Member: Treasury 1997–, Treasury Sub-Committee 1998– *(Former):* Member: Treasury and Civil Service 1987–96, Treasury 1996–97. *Party Groups:* Member: Fabian Society, Co-operative Party. *Other:* Member: World Development Movement, London Brook; Chair, East London Committee, Sanctuary Housing Association; Member, Defence of Literature and Arts. *Miscellaneous:* Member, Writers Guild of Great Britain. *Sportsclubs:* Vice-President, Esher RFC, Stockwood Park RFC. *Publications:* Contributor to *Tribune*; *The How and Why of Socialism*, 1977; *Mr Secretary of State* (fiction), 1979; *The Secret Constitution*, 1980; *Power Failure* (fiction), 1985; *Big Bang 2000*, 1986; *Pitless Pursuit* (fiction), 1994; *Insider's Guide to Parliament*, 1995. *Special Interests:* Economic Policy. *Countries of Interest:* Europe, USA. *Recreations:* Music, sleeping on the grass. *Electoral Notes:* Member for Luton West February 1974–79. Member for Hackney South and Shoreditch since June 1983. *Address:* Brian Sedgemore Esq, MP, House of Commons, London, SW1A 0AA *Tel:* 020 7219 3410 *Fax:* 020 7219 5969. *Constituency:* 17 Sutton Square, Urswick Road, Hackney, London, E9 6EQ *Tel:* 020 8533 1305 *Fax:* 020 7533 3392 *E-mail:* sedgemoreb@parliament.uk.

SHAW, Jonathan Rowland *(Chatham and Aylesford)   Lab majority 2,790*

Son of Alan James Shaw and Les Percival. Born June 3, 1966; educated Vinters Boys School, Maidstone; West Kent College of FE; Bromley College (Certificate in Social Services). Married Sue Gurmin (1 son 1 daughter). *Trades Union:* Member, UNISON. *Profession:* Social Worker. *Career:* Social Worker, Kent Council. *Councils, Public Bodies:* Councillor, Rochester 1993–98, Chairman, Community Development Committee 1995. *Select Committees (Current):* Member: Environmental Audit 1997–. *Party Groups:* Member, Fabian Society. *Special Interests:* Community Development, Economic Development, Housing, Welfare. *Recreations:* All music especially folk music, reading, walking, family. *Electoral Notes:* Member for Chatham and Aylesford since May 1, 1997. *Address:* Jonathan Shaw Esq, MP, House of Commons, London, SW1A 0AA *Tel:* 020 7219 6919 *Fax:* 020 7219 0938. *Constituency:* 5a New Road Avenue, Chatham, Kent, ME4 6BB *Tel:* 01634 811573 *Fax:* 01634 811006 *E-mail:* shawj@parliament.uk.

SHEERMAN, Barry John *(Huddersfield)   Lab/Co-op majority 15,848*

Son of late Albert William and Florence Sheerman. Born August 17, 1940; educated Hampton Grammar School; Kingston Technical College; London School of Economics (BSc Economics); London University (MSc). Married August 28, 1965, Pamela Elizabeth, daughter of late Charles William Brenchley, BEM (1 son 3 daughters). *Trades Union:* Member, AUT, MSF. *Career:* University Lecturer 1966–79. *Political Career:* Shadow Minister for: Education and Employment 1983–87, Home Affairs deputy to Roy Hattersley 1987–92, Disability 1992–94. *Spokesman:* Opposition Front Bench Spokesman on: Employment and Education 1983–88, Home Affairs 1988–92, Disabled People's Rights 1992–94. *Select Committees (Current):* Chairman (Education): Education and Employment 1999–; Chairman: Education Sub-Committee 1999–; Member: Liaison 1999–. *Party Groups:* Member, Co-operative Party; Chairman, Labour Forum for Criminal Justice. *International Bodies:* Chairman and Interparliamentary Director, Democracy International; Chairman, Interparle (Parliamentary Communication Across Europe). *Other:* Chairman: Parliamentary Advisory Council on Transport Safety, Urban Mines, Networking for Industry 1995–; Governor, LSE 1995–.

Trust: Chairman, National Educational Research and Development Trust; Fellow, Industry and Parliament Trust; Director and Trustee, National Childrens Centre. *Miscellaneous:* Chairman Cross-Party Advisory Group on Preparation for EMU 1998–; Vice-Chair, Joint Pre-Legislative Committee Investigating the Financial Services and Markets Bill 1998–. *Sportsclubs:* Member, Millbank Leisure. FRSA, FRGS. *Publications: Harold Laski: A Life on the Left*, (jointly) 1993. *Special Interests:* Trade, Industry, Finance, Further and Higher Education, Economy. *Countries of Interest:* European Union, South America, USA. *Recreations:* Walking, biography, films. *Electoral Notes:* Contested Taunton October 1974. Member for Huddersfield East 1979–83. Member for Huddersfield since June 1983. *Address:* Barry Sheerman Esq, MP, House of Commons, London, SW1A 0AA *Tel:* 020 7219 5037 *Fax:* 020 7219 2404. *Constituency:* Labour Party, 6 Cross Church Street, Huddersfield, West Yorkshire *Tel:* 01484 451382 *Fax:* 01484 451334 *E-mail:* barry.sheerman@virgin.net; sheerman.const@btconnect-com.

SHELDON, The Rt Hon. Robert Edward *(Ashton under Lyne) Lab majority 22,965*

Born September 13, 1923; educated Elementary; Grammar; Technical schools; London University (External graduate, Whitworth Scholar). Married 1st, 1945, Eileen Shamash (died 1969) (1 son 1 daughter), married 2nd, 1971, Mary Shield. *Career:* Qualified Engineer. *Political Career:* Minister of State: Department of Civil Service 1974, HM Treasury 1974–1975; Financial Secretary to HM Treasury 1975–79. *Spokesman:* Opposition Front Bench Spokesman on Civil Service, Treasury Matters and Machinery of Government 1970–74; Deputy Opposition Front Bench Spokesman on Treasury and Economic Affairs 1981–83. *Select Committees (Current):* Chairman: Liaison 1997–, Standards and Privileges 1997– *(Former):* Chairman: Public Accounts 1983–97. *Party Groups:* Chairman, Northwest Group Labour MPs 1970–74. *Miscellaneous:* Chairman, Public Accounts Commission 1997–. *Honours:* PC 1977. *Electoral Notes:* Contested Manchester Withington 1959 General Election. Member for Ashton under Lyne since October 15, 1964. *Address:* The Rt Hon. Robert Sheldon, MP, House of Commons, London, SW1A 0AA *Tel:* 020 7219 3618. *Constituency:* 27 Darley Avenue, Manchester, M20 2ZD *Tel:* 0161–799 6060 *Fax:* 0161–799 0001.

SHEPHARD, The Rt Hon. Gillian Patricia *(South West Norfolk) Con majority 2,464*

Daughter of Reginald and Bertha Watts. Born January 22, 1940; educated North Walsham Girls' High School; St Hilda's College, Oxford (MA); Hon. Fellow, St Hilda's College, Oxford 1991. Married December 27, 1975, Thomas, son of Frank and Lydia Shephard (2 stepsons). *Profession:* Educationalist. *Career:* Education Officer and Schools Inspector, Norfolk County Council 1963–75; Anglia TV 1975–77. *Councils, Public Bodies:* Norfolk County Council: Councillor 1977–89, Former Deputy Leader, Chairman: Social Services Committee 1978–83, West Norfolk Health Authority 1981–85, Education Committee 1983–85, Norwich Health Authority 1985–87. *Political Career:* PPS to Peter Lilley, MP 1988–89; Parliamentary Under-Secretary of State, Department of Social Security 1989–90; Minister of State, HM Treasury 1990–92; Secretary of State for Employment 1992–93; Minister of Agriculture, Fisheries and Food 1993–94; Secretary of State for: Education 1994–95; Education and Employment 1995–97; Shadow Leader of the House of Commons 1997–98; Shadow Chancellor of the Duchy of Lancaster 1997–98; Shadow Secretary of State for the Environment, Transport and the Regions 1998–99. *Select Committees (Former):* Member: Modernisation of the House of Commons 1997–98. *Party Groups:* Joint Deputy Chairman, Conservative Party 1991–92. *Miscellaneous:* Government Co-Chairman, Women's National Commission 1990; Member, House of Commons Commission 1997–. *Honours:* PC 1992. *Special Interests:* Health, Education, Penal Affairs and Policy, European Union. *Countries of Interest:* France, Latin America. *Recreations:* Music, gardening, France. *Electoral Notes:* Member for South West Norfolk since June 1987. *Address:* The Rt Hon. Gillian Shephard, MP, House of Commons, London, SW1A 0AA *Tel:* 020 7219 2898. *Constituency:* 17A Lynn Road, Downham Market, Norfolk, PE38 4NJ *Tel:* 01366 385072.

SHEPHERD, Richard Charles Scrimgeour *(Aldridge-Brownhills)   Con majority 2,526*

Son of late Alfred Shepherd and Davida Sophia (neé Wallace). Born December 6, 1942; educated The London School of Economics; John Hopkins School of Advanced International Studies (MSc Economics). *Profession:* Grocer. *Career:* Director, retail food business in London Underwriter, Lloyd's 1974–94. *Political Career:* Personal assistant to Edward Taylor, MP (Glasgow Cathcart) October 1974 General Election; Introduced four Private Member's Bills: The Crown Immunity Bill 1986, Protection of Official Information Bill 1988, The Referendum Bill 1992, Public Interest Disclosure Bill. *Select Committees (Current):* Member: Modernisation of the House of Commons 1997–, Public Administration 1997–. *Other:* Co-Chairman, Campaign for Freedom of Information. *Awards:* The Spectator's Award as: Backbencher of the Year 1987, Parliamentarian of the Year 1995; Campaign for Freedom of Information 1988. *Miscellaneous:* Member, South East Economic Planning Council 1970–74. *Electoral Notes:* Contested Nottingham East February 1974 General Election. Member for Aldridge-Brownhills since May 1979. *Clubs:* Carlton, Beefsteak, Chelsea Arts. *Address:* Richard Shepherd Esq, MP, House of Commons, London, SW1A 0AA *Tel:* 020 7219 3000 *Tel (Constituency):* 01922 451449 *Fax (Constituency):* 01922 451449.

SHIPLEY, Debra *(Stourbridge)   Lab majority 5,645*

Born June 22, 1957; educated Kidderminster High School; Kidderminster College; Oxford Polytechnic (BA Hons); London University (MA). *Trades Union:* Member, GMB. *Career:* Writer and Lecturer. *Political Career:* Initiated Private Member's Bill for Protection of Children Act 1999. *Select Committees (Former):* Member: Social Security 1999. *International Bodies:* Member; Western European Union Defence Committee 1998–99, Council of Europe 1998–99. *Other:* Board Member, Opportunities For Volunteering; Member, Amnesty; Patron, Headway Blackcountry. *Miscellaneous:* Member, Co-op. FRSA. *Publications:* Author of 17 books. *Special Interests:* Children, Elderly. *Countries of Interest:* Mongolia. *Recreations:* Walking, cooking/eating. *Electoral Notes:* Member for Stourbridge since May 1, 1997. *Address:* Debra Shipley, MP, House of Commons, London, SW1A 0AA *Tel:* 020 7219 3053 *Tel (Constituency):* 01384 374356 *Fax (Constituency):* 01384 370111.

SHORT, The Rt Hon. Clare *(Birmingham Ladywood)   Lab majority 23,082*

Daughter of late Frank and Joan Short. Born February 15, 1946; educated St Francis JI School, Handsworth; St Paul's Grammar, Birmingham; Keele and Leeds Universities (BA Hons Political Science). Married 1st, September 17, 1964, Andrew Moss (1 son) (marriage dissolved 1971); married 2nd, 1982, Alex Lyon, MP for York 1966–83 (died 1993). *Trades Union:* Member, Unison. *Career:* Civil Servant, Home Office 1970–75; Director: AFFOR – Community organisation concerned with race and urban deprivation in Handsworth 1976–77, Youth Aid 1979–83, Unemployment unit 1981–83. *Political Career:* Vice-Chair, Parliamentary Labour Party 1997–99; Secretary of State for International Development 1997–. *Spokesman:* Spokesperson on Employment 1985–88; Opposition Spokesperson on Social Security 1989–91; Opposition Front Bench Spokesperson on: Environmental Protection 1992–93, Women 1993–95; Principal Opposition Spokesperson on Transport 1995–96; Shadow Minister for Overseas Development 1996–97. *Party Groups:* Member, Labour Party National Executive Committee 1988–98. *International Bodies:* Former Chair, Human Rights Committee of Socialist International. *Honours:* PC 1997. *Special Interests:* Unemployment, Race Relations, Immigration Policy, Low Pay, Home Affairs, Northern Ireland, Women. *Recreations:* Swimming, family, friends. *Electoral Notes:* Member for Birmingham Ladywood since June 1983. *Address:* The Rt Hon. Clare Short, MP, House of Commons, London, SW1A 0AA *Tel:* 020 7219 4148 *Fax:* 020 7219 2586 *Tel (Constituency):* 020 7219 4264 (Constituency Secretary) *E-mail:* shortc@parliament.uk.

SIMPSON, Alan *(Nottingham South)   Lab majority 13,364*

Son of Reg and Marjorie Simpson. Born September 20, 1948; educated Bootle Grammar School; Nottingham Polytechnic (BSc Economics). Married (2 sons 1 daughter) (separated). *Trades Union:* Member, UNISON. *Career:* President, Students' Union, Nottingham Polytechnic 1969–70; Assistant General Secretary, Nottingham Council of Voluntary Service 1970–74; set up first pilot project for the national non-custodial treatment of offenders programme 1971–74; Community worker, Inner city anti-vandalism project 1974–78; Research Officer, Nottingham Racial Equality Council 1979–92. *Party Groups:* Secretary, Socialist Campaign of Labour MPs; Board Member, Tribune Newspaper. *Other:* Member: CND Oxfam. *Awards:* 1999 Green Ribbon Award, Environment Back Bencher of the Year. *Publications:* Author of books on: common security, community development, housing, employment, policing policies, Europe, racism. *Special Interests:* Environment, Economics, Disarmament. *Recreations:* Sport (lifelong supporter of Everton FC), vegetarian cooking, music (eclectic taste), reading. *Electoral Notes:* Contested Nottingham South in 1987. Member for Nottingham South since April 9, 1992. *Address:* Alan Simpson Esq, MP, House of Commons, London, SW1A 0AA *Tel:* 020 7219 3000. *Constituency:* 1 Talbot Street, Nottingham, NG1 5GQ *Tel:* 0115–956 0460 *Fax:* 0115–956 0445.

SIMPSON, Keith Robert *(Mid Norfolk)   Con majority 1,336*

Son of Harry Simpson and Jean Betty Simpson (née Day). Born March 29, 1949; educated Thorpe Grammar School, Norfolk; University of Hull; King's College, University of London (BA Hons). Married August 4, 1984, Pepita, daughter of Norman Hollingsworth (1 son). *Armed Forces:* University of London OTC 1970–72. *Profession:* Military Historian/Defence Consultant. *Career:* Senior Lecturer in War Studies, RMA Sandhurst 1973–86; Head of Foreign Affairs and Defence Section, Conservative Research Department 1987–88; Special Adviser to George Younger and Tom King as Secretaries of State for Defence 1988–90; Director, Cranfield Security Studies Institute, Cranfield University 1991–97. *Whip:* An Opposition Whip: (Home Office; Culture, Media and Sport: Wales) 1999, (Treasury; Health) 1999–. *Spokesman:* An Opposition Spokesman for Defence 1998–99. *Select Committees (Former):* Member: Catering 1998. *Party Groups:* National Vice-Chairman, Federation of Conservative Students 1971–72. *Other:* Member: International Institute for Strategic Studies, Royal United Services Institute for Defence Studies, British Field Sports Society, British Commission for Military History; Council Member, SSAFA 1997–. *Miscellaneous:* Member, European Standing Committee A 1998. *Publications: The Old Contemptibles*, 1981; Joint Editor *A Nations in Arms*, 1985; *History of the German Army*, 1985; Editor *The War the Infantry Knew 1914–1919*, 1986. *Special Interests:* Foreign Affairs, Defence, Education, Farming, Countryside. *Countries of Interest:* USA, Germany, France, Poland. *Recreations:* Walking dogs, reading, visiting restaurants, cinema, collecting and consuming malt whiskies, observing ambitious people. *Electoral Notes:* Contested Plymouth Devonport 1992. Member for Mid Norfolk since May 1, 1997. *Clubs:* Norfolk. *Address:* Keith Simpson Esq, MP, House of Commons, London, SW1A 0AA *Tel:* 020 7219 4059 *Fax:* 020 7219 0975. *Constituency:* Mid Norfolk Conservative Association, The Stable, Church Farm, Attlebridge, Norwich, Norfolk NR9 5ST *Tel:* 01603 261594 *Fax:* 01603 261794.

SINGH, Marsha *(Bradford West)   Lab majority 3,877*

Son of Harbans Singh and late Kartar Kaur. Born October 11, 1954; educated Belle Vue Boys Upper School; Loughborough University (BA Hons Languages, Politics and Economics of Modern Europe). Married 1971, Sital Kaur (1 son 1 daughter). *Trades Union:* Member, UNISON. *Profession:* Health Service Manager. *Career:* Senior Development Manager, Bradford Community Health 1990–97. *Select Committees (Current):* Member: Home Affairs 1997–. *Party Groups:* Chair: Bradford West Labour Party 1986–91, 1996–97, District Labour Party 1992. *Special Interests:* European Union, Health, Education. *Recreations:* Chess, Bridge, reading. *Electoral Notes:* Member for Bradford West since May 1, 1997. *Address:* Marsha Singh Esq, MP, House of Commons, London, SW1A 0AA *Tel:* 020 7219 4625 *Fax:* 020 7219 0965. *Constituency:* Bradford West Constituency Office, 2nd Floor, 76 Kirkgate, Bradford, West Yorkshire, BD1 1SZ *Tel:* 01274 402220 *E-mail:* singhmp@parliament.uk.

SKINNER, Dennis *(Bolsover)   Lab majority 27,149*

Son of Edward Skinner. Born February 11, 1932; educated Tupton Hall Grammar School; Ruskin College, Oxford. Married March 12, 1960, Mary, daughter of James Parker (1 son 2 daughters). *Trades Union:* President, Derbyshire Miners 1966–70. *Career:* Miner 1949–70. *Councils, Public Bodies:* Clay Cross UDC 1960–70; County Councillor, Derbyshire 1964–70; Former President, Derbyshire UDC Association. *Party Groups:* President, North East Derbyshire Constituency Labour Party 1968–71; Member, Labour Party National Executive Committee 1978–92, 1999–; Vice-Chairman, Labour Party 1987–88, Chairman 1988–89. *Miscellaneous:* Former Member, Scarsdale Valuation Panel. *Special Interests:* Inland Waterways, Energy, Economic Policy, Environment, Anti-Common Market, Third World. *Recreations:* Cycling, tennis, athletics (watching). *Electoral Notes:* Member for Bolsover since 1970. *Address:* Dennis Skinner Esq, MP, House of Commons, London, SW1A 0AA *Tel:* 020 7219 3000 *Fax:* 020 7219 0028. *Constituency:* 1 Elmhurst Close, South Normanton, Derbyshire *Tel:* 01773 581027.

SMITH, The Rt Hon. Andrew David *(Oxford East)   Lab majority 16,665*

Son of late David E. C. Smith and Mrs Georgina H. J. Smith. Born February 1, 1951; educated Reading Grammar School; St John's College, Oxford (BA, BPhil); Hon. Doctorate, Oxford Brookes University. Married March 26, 1976, Valerie, daughter of William and Annie Labert (1 son). *Trades Union:* Member, Union of Oxford Shop, Distributive and Allied Workers. *Career:* Member Relations Officer, Oxford and Swindon Co-op Society 1979–87. *Councils, Public Bodies:* Oxford City Councillor 1976–87; Chairman: Recreation and Amenities Committee 1980–83, Planning Committee 1985–87. *Political Career:* Minister of State, Department for Education and Employment (Minister for Employment, Welfare to Work and Equal Opportunities) 1997–99; Chief Secretary to the Treasury 1999–. *Spokesman:* Opposition Spokesman on Education 1988–92; Opposition Frontbench Spokesman on Treasury and Economic Affairs 1992–96; Shadow Chief Secretary to the Treasury 1994–96; Shadow Secretary of State for Transport 1996–97. *Select Committees (Former):* : Health and Social Services 1987–88. *Party Groups:* Member, Labour Party Economy Policy Commission. *Other:* Chairman of Governors, Oxford Polytechnic/Oxford Brookes University 1987–93. *Honours:* PC 1997. *Special Interests:* Car Industry, Education, Retail Industry, Transport, Employment. *Countries of Interest:* Europe. *Electoral Notes:* Contested Oxford East 1983. Member for Oxford East since June 1987. *Clubs:* Blackbird Leys Community Association. *Address:* The Rt Hon. Andrew Smith, MP, House of Commons, London, SW1A 0AA *Tel:* 020 7219 4512 *Fax:* 020 7219 2965 *Tel (Constituency):* 01865 772893 *Fax (Constituency):* 01865 715990.

SMITH, Angela Evans *(Basildon)   Lab/Co-op majority 13,280*

Daughter of Patrick Evans, factory worker, and Emily Evans (née Russell), supervisor of church pre-school. Born January 7, 1959; educated Chalvedon Comprehensive, Basildon; Leicester Polytechnic (BA Hons Public Administration). Married December 16, 1978, Nigel Smith. *Trades Union:* Member: TGWU, AEEU. *Career:* Trainee Accountant, London Borough of Newham 1982–83; League Against Cruel Sports, finally Head of Political and Public Relations 1983–95; Research Assistant to Alun Michael, MP 1995–97. *Councils, Public Bodies:* Essex County Council: Councillor 1989–97, Chief Whip 1993–96, Lead Spokesperson, Fire and Public Protection Committee 1993–96. *Political Career:* PPS to Paul Boateng, MP, as Minister of State, Home Office 1999–. *International Bodies:* Board Member, Cuba Initiative. *Other:* Voluntary Representative for Traidcraft; Patron: Basildon Home Start, Basildon Co-op Development Agency, Basildon Women's Refuge, Vange United Boys FC. *Special Interests:* Home Affairs, Animal Welfare, International Development, Employment Rights and Protection. *Electoral Notes:* Contested Southend West 1987. Member for Basildon since May 1, 1997. *Address:* Angela Smith, MP, House of Commons, London, SW1A 0AA *Tel:* 020 7219 6273 *Fax:* 020 7219 0926. *Constituency:* 16 Norwich Walk, Basildon, Essex, SS14 3QP *Tel:* 01375 645770 *Fax:* 01375 645771 *E-mail:* flackk@parliament.uk.

SMITH, The Rt Hon. Chris (Christopher) Robert *(Islington South and Finsbury)   Lab majority 14,563*

Son of Colin Smith, civil servant and Gladys Smith, teacher. Born July 24, 1951; educated George Watson's College, Edinburgh; Pembroke College, Cambridge (BA, PhD) (President, Cambridge Union 1972); Harvard University (Kennedy Scholar). *Trades Union:* Branch Secretary, ASTMS 1977–80, Branch Chairman 1980–83. *Career:* Worked for: The Housing Corporation 1976–77, Shaftesbury Society Housing Association 1977–80, Society for Co-operative Dwellings 1980–83. *Councils, Public Bodies:* Islington Borough Council: Councillor 1978–83, Chief Whip 1978–79, Chair of Housing 1981–83. *Political Career:* Shadow Treasury Minister 1987–92; Shadow Secretary of State for: Environmental Protection 1992–94, National Heritage 1994–95, Social Security 1995–96, Health 1996–97; Sponsored Environment and Safety Information Act 1988 (Private Member's Bill); Secretary of State: for National Heritage May-July 1997, for Culture, Media and Sport July 1997–. *Whip:* London Labour Whip 1986–87. *Select Committees (Former):* : Environment 1983–86. *Party Groups:* Secretary, Tribune Group 1984–88, Chairman 1988–89; Chairman, Labour Campaign for Criminal Justice 1985–88; Chairman, Board of *Tribune* newspaper 1990–93; Member, Executive of Fabian Society 1990–97, Vice-Chairman 1995–96, Chairman 1996–97; President, SERA 1992–; Chairman, Board of New Century Magazine 1993–96. *Other:* Member: Shelter Board 1986–92, Executive of National Council for Civil Liberties 1986–88; Board Member, Sadlers Wells Theatre 1986–92, Governor 1992–97; Vice-President, Wildlife Link 1986–90. *Trust:* Trustee, John Muir Trust 1991–97; Executive Committee, National Trust 1995–97. *Miscellaneous:* Co-opted Member, Council for National Parks 1980–89. *Honours:* PC 1997. *Publications:* Fabian Society: *National Parks*, 1977; Fabian Society: *New Questions for Socialism*, 1996; *Creative Britain*, 1998. *Special Interests:* Heritage, Housing, Local Government, Foreign Affairs, Environment, Civil Liberties, Criminal Justice, Economic Policy, Social Security, Health. *Countries of Interest:* Cyprus, Europe, Hong Kong, USA, Australia. *Recreations:* Mountaineering, literature, theatre, music. *Electoral Notes:* Contested Epsom and Ewell 1979. Member for Islington South and Finsbury since June 1983. *Address:* The Rt Hon. Chris Smith, MP, House of Commons, London, SW1A 0AA *Tel:* 020 7219 5119 *Fax:* 020 7219 5820. *Constituency:* 65 Barnsbury Street, London, N1 *Tel:* 020 7607 8373 *E-mail:* chris.smith@culture.gov.uk.

SMITH, Geraldine *(Morecambe and Lunesdale)   Lab majority 5,965*

Daughter of John and Ann Smith. Born August 29, 1961; educated Morecambe High School; Lancaster and Morecambe College (Diploma business studies). *Trades Union:* Member, Communication Workers Union 1980–, held various positions including Area Representative. *Career:* Postal Officer 1980–97. *Councils, Public Bodies:* Councillor, Lancaster City Council 1991–97. *Select Committees (Former):* Member: Deregulation 1997–99. *Party Groups:* Member, Labour Party 1979–, held various positions including Constituency Secretary. *International Bodies:* UK substitute delegate, Council of Europe 1999–. *Miscellaneous:* Member, European Standing Committee C 1999–. *Special Interests:* Economic Regeneration, Tourism, Public/Private Partnerships. *Countries of Interest:* Ireland, Eastern Europe. *Recreations:* Playing chess, walking and campaigning. *Electoral Notes:* Member for Morecambe and Lunesdale since May 1, 1997. *Address:* Geraldine Smith, MP, House of Commons, London, SW1A 0AA *Tel:* 020 7219 5816. *Constituency:* Morecambe and Lunesdale CLP, Labour Party Offices, 26–28 Victoria Street, Morecambe, Lancashire, LA4 4AJ *Tel:* 01524 411367/8 *Fax:* 01524 411369.

SMITH, Jacqui (Jacqueline) *(Redditch)   Lab majority 6,125*

Daughter of Michael L. Smith, headteacher, and Jill Smith, retired teacher. Born November 3, 1962; educated Dyson Perrins High School, Malvern, Worcs; Hertford College, Oxford University (BA Hons Philosophy, Politics and Economics); Worcester College of Higher Education (Post-graduate Certificate in Education). Married 1987, Richard Timney, son of Alan and Heather Timney (2 sons). *Trades Union:* Member: NUT, GMB. *Profession:* Teacher. *Career:* Teacher, Economics, Arrow Vale High School, Redditch 1986 88; Teacher, Worcester Sixth Form College 1988–90; Head of Economics, GNVQ Co-ordinator, Haybridge High School, Hagley 1990–97. *Councils, Public Bodies:* Councillor, Redditch Borough Council 1991–97. *Political Career:* Parliamentary Under-Secretary of State (School Standards), Department for Education and Employment 1999–. *Select Committees (Former):* Member: Treasury 1998–99, Treasury Sub-Committee 1998–99. *International Bodies:* Member, British East-West Centre. *Trust:* Member, Worcester Nature Conservation Trust. *Special Interests:* Industry, Education and Training, Economic Policy. *Recreations:* Family, football, theatre. *Electoral Notes:* Member for Redditch since May 1, 1997. *Address:* Jacqui Smith, MP, House of Commons, London, SW1A 0AA *Tel:* 020 7219 5845 *Fax:* 020 7219 4815 *Tel (Constituency):* 01527 585863 *Fax (Constituency):* 01527 585863 *E-mail:* smithjj@parliament.uk.

SMITH, John William Patrick *(Vale of Glamorgan)   Lab majority 10,532*

Son of John and Margaret Smith. Born March 17, 1951; educated Fairfield Primary School, Penarth; Penarth Grammar School; Gwent College of Higher Education; University College of Wales, Cardiff (BSc Economics). Married April 10, 1971, Kathleen, daughter of late Francis Mulvaney and Elizabeth Mulvaney (2 sons 1 daughter). *Trades Union:* Member: MSF 1970–, TASS, NATFHE, AUT, NUPE, UCATT. *Armed Forces:* RAF 1967–71. *Career:* Carpenter and Joiner, Vale Borough Council 1971–76; Mature Student 1976–81; University Tutor (UCC) 1981–85; Senior Lecturer in Business Studies 1985–89; Campaign Manager, Gwent Image Partnership, Chief Executive 1992–. *Councils, Public Bodies:* Councillor, Vale of Glamorgan Borough Council 1979–91, Opposition Finance and Housing Spokesperson 1979–87, Labour Group Secretary 1981–83, Labour Group Leader 1983–88. *Political Career:* PPS to Deputy Leader of Labour Party 1989–92; Contributed to: Trade Union Bill, Armed Forces Bill, Barry Old Harbour Bill, Seat Belt Regulation; PPS to Rt Hon. Dr John Reid, MP: as Minister of State, Ministry of Defence (Minister for the Armed Forces) 1997–98, Department of the Environment, Transport and the Regions (Minister of Transport) 1998–99. *Select Committees (Former):* Member: Welsh Affairs 1990–92. *Party Groups:* Chairman, Young Socialists 1967–94; Member: Vale of Glamorgan CLP 1972–, Welsh Executive 1985–89, 1996–; Chairman, Wales Labour Party 1988–89; Member, National Policy Forum 1996; Former Vice-Chairman, Welsh Parliamentary Labour Party; Vice-Chair, Welsh Regional Group of Labour MPs 1999, Chair 1999–. *International Bodies:* Member: Commonwealth Parliamentary Association (CPA), UK Delegation to North Atlantic Assembly. *Other:* Chairman, Anti-Apartheid Movement (ACTSA); Hon. Vice-President: Imperial Cancer Foundation, Rail Users Federation, Local Arthritis Care; President, Local Leisure and Community Centre; Team Manager, Valley and Vale Arts. *Miscellaneous:* Chairman, Parliamentary Advisory Council on Transport Safety 1989–92. *Special Interests:* Economic Development, Industrial Relations, Transport Safety, Defence. *Recreations:* Reading, walking, camping, boating. *Electoral Notes:* Contested Vale of Glamorgan 1987. Member for Vale of Glamorgan 1989–92 and since May 1, 1997. *Address:* John Smith Esq, MP, House of Commons, London, SW1A 0AA *Tel:* 020 7219 3589. *Constituency:* 29 Tynewydd Road, Barry *Tel:* 01446 743769 *Fax:* 01446 743769.

SMITH, Llewellyn Thomas *(Blaenau Gwent)* *Lab majority 28,035*

Son of late Ernest Smith, and of Cissie Smith. Born April 16, 1944; educated Greenfields Secondary Modern School; Colleg Harlech; Cardiff University (Bsc Hons, MSc). Married December 13, 1969, Pamela, daughter of Russell and Lilian Williams (2 sons 1 daughter). *Trades Union:* Member, TGWU. *Career:* Labourer, computer operator, tutor-organiser, Worker's Educational Association. *Other:* Member: CND, Socialist Education Association; Vice-President, Anti-Apartheid Wales. *Publications:* Co-author: *Bombing Ahead With Disarmament*, 1990, *The Politics of Poverty*, 1993. *Countries of Interest:* Cuba. *Electoral Notes:* MEP for South East Wales 1984–94. Member for Blaenau Gwent since April 9, 1992. *Address:* Llewellyn Smith Esq, MP, House of Commons, London, SW1A 0AA *Tel:* 020 7219 3000. *Constituency:* 23 Beaufort Street, Brynmawr, Gwent, NP3 4AQ *Tel:* 01495 313345.

SMITH, Sir Robert, Bt *(West Aberdeenshire and Kincardine)* *LD majority 2,662*

Son of late Sir (William) Gordon Smith, Bt, VRD, and of Diana Lady Smith. Born April 15, 1958; educated Merchant Taylors' School, Northwood; University of Aberdeen (BSc). Married August 13, 1993, Fiona Anne, daughter of Colonel Dennis Cormack, MD (2 daughters). *Profession:* Estate Manager. *Councils, Public Bodies:* Councillor, Aberdeenshire Council 1995–97; JP 1997. *Whip:* Liberal Democrat Whip 1999–. *Spokesman:* A Spokesman for: Police and Prisons, Environment and Transport 1999, Environment and Transport 1999, Scotland 1999–. *Select Committees (Current):* Member: Catering 1999–, Scottish Affairs 1999–. *Miscellaneous:* 3rd Bt (cr. 1945), succeeded his father 1983; General Council Assessor, University of Aberdeen 1994–98; Director, Grampian Transport Museum; Vice-Convenor, Grampian Joint Police Board 1995–97; Member, Electoral Reform Society. *Special Interests:* Electoral Reform. *Recreations:* Hill-walking, sailing. *Electoral Notes:* Contested (SDP/Liberal Alliance) Aberdeen North 1987. Member for West Aberdeenshire and Kincardine since May 1, 1997. *Clubs:* Royal Yacht Squadron, Royal Thames Yacht. *Address:* Sir Robert Smith, Bt, MP, House of Commons, London, SW1A 0AA *Tel:* 020 7219 3000 *Fax:* 020 7219 4930. *Constituency:* Crowmallie House, Pitcaple, Inverurie, AB51 5HR *Tel:* 01467 681595 *Fax:* 01467 681464 *E-mail:* bobsmith@cix.co.uk.

SMYTH, Rev. William Martin *(Belfast South)* *UUP majority 4,600*

Son of late James Smyth, JP. Born June 15, 1931; educated Methodist College, Belfast; Magee University College, Londonderry (BA general arts 1953); Presbyterian College, Belfast 1955; Trinity College, Dublin (BD 1961); San Francisco Theological Seminary. Married 1957, Kathleen Johnston (2 daughters and 1 daughter deceased). *Profession:* Minister of Religion. *Career:* Assistant Minister, Finaghy Presbyterian Church, Belfast 1953–57; Minister: Raffrey Church 1957–63, Alexandra Presbyterian Church 1963–82. *Political Career:* Member, Northern Ireland Constitutional Convention 1975; Assembly Member for Belfast South October 1982–86; Chairman, Northern Ireland Assembly: Health and Social Services Committee 1983–84, Finance and Personnel Committee 1984–86; Sponsored Disabled Persons (Northern Ireland) Act, 1989 (Private Member's Bill). *Whip:* Chief Whip 1996–. *Spokesman:* Party Spokesman for: Health and Social Services 1992–97, Health and Family Policy 1997–. *Select Committees (Former):* Member: Health 1990–97. *Party Groups:* Past Chairman, Ulster Unionist Executive Committee; Vice-President, Ulster Unionist Council 1974–. *International Bodies:* Member, Executive Committee: IPU (UK Branch) 1985–92, 1994–, Commonwealth Parliamentary Association (CPA) UK Branch 1989–. *Other:* Grand Master: Grand Orange Lodge of Ireland 1972–96, Grand Orange Council of the World 1973–82; Chairman, Belfast No. 1 School Management Committee 1972–80; President, Orange Council of the World 1985–88. *Trust:* Fellow, Industry and Parliament Trust. *Publications:* Editor *Faith For Today*, 1961; Pamphlets: *In Defence of Ulster; The Battle for Northern Ireland; A Federated People; Till Death Us Do Part; Why Presbyterian?*. *Special Interests:* World Protestantism, Health, Social Services, Education, Foreign Affairs, Human Rights, Transport. *Countries of Interest:* Brazil, Canada, Malawi, Morocco, New Zealand,

Taiwan, USA, India, Australia. *Recreations:* Reading and travel. *Electoral Notes:* Member for Belfast South since by-election March 1982. *Address:* The Rev. Martin Smyth, MP, House of Commons, London, SW1A 0AA *Tel:* 020 7219 4098 *Fax:* 020 7219 2347. *Constituency:* 117 Cregagh Road, Belfast, BT6 0LA *Tel:* 028 9045 7009 *Fax:* 028 9045 0837.

SNAPE, Peter *(West Bromwich East)   Lab majority 13,584*

Son of late Thomas Snape, Railway Chargeman. Born February 12, 1942; educated St. Joseph's School, Stockport. Married 1963, Winifred, daughter of Evelyn Grimshaw (2 daughters) (marriage dissolved 1980). *Armed Forces:* Regular Soldier, RE and RCT 1960–66. *Career:* Railwayman 1957–60, Goods Guard, BR 1966–70, Controller, BR 1970–74. *Councils, Public Bodies:* Bredbury and Romiley Urban District Council: Councillor 1971–74, Sometime Chairman, Finance Committee. *Whip:* Government Whip 1975–79. *Spokesman:* Opposition Front Bench Spokesman on: Defence 1979–82, Home Affairs 1982–83, Transport 1983–92. *Party Groups:* Chairman, West Midlands Regional Group of Labour MPs 1984–97, 1997–. *Special Interests:* Transport. *Countries of Interest:* Hungary, Iraq. *Electoral Notes:* Member for West Bromwich East since February 1974. *Address:* Peter Snape Esq, MP, House of Commons, London, SW1A 0AA *Tel:* 020 7219 5149. *Constituency:* Town Hall, High Street, West Bromwich, West Midlands, B70 8DK *Tel:* 0121-525 4408 *Fax:* 0121-525 4643.

SOAMES, Hon. Nicholas *(Mid Sussex)   Con majority 6,854*

Son of late Baron Soames, PC, GCMG, GCVO, CH, CBE, and of Lady Soames, DBE. Born February 12, 1948; educated Eton College. Married 1st, June 4, 1981, Catherine Weatherall (1 son) (marriage dissolved 1988), married 2nd, December 21, 1993, Serena, daughter of Sir John and Lady Smith. *Armed Forces:* 2nd Lieutenant, 11th Hussars 1967–70. *Career:* Equerry to HRH The Prince of Wales, KG 1970–72; Stockbroker 1972–74; PA to: Sir James Goldsmith 1974–76, US Senator Mark Hatfield 1976–78; Assistant Director, Sedgwick Group 1979–81. *Political Career:* PPS: to Rt Hon. John Gummer, MP, as Minister of State for Employment and Chairman of the Conservative Party 1984–86; to Rt Hon. Nicholas Ridley, MP as Secretary of State for the Environment 1987–89; Joint Parliamentary Secretary, Ministry of Agriculture, Fisheries and Food 1992–94; Minister of State for the Armed Forces, Ministry of Defence 1994–97. *Select Committees (Current):* Member: Public Administration 1999–. *Special Interests:* Defence, Foreign Affairs, Trade and Industry, Aerospace, Aviation. *Recreations:* Country pursuits. *Electoral Notes:* Contested Dumbartonshire Central 1979. Member for Crawley 1983–97, and for Mid Sussex since May 1, 1997. *Clubs:* White's, Turf. *Address:* Hon. Nicholas Soames, MP, House of Commons, London, SW1A 0AA *Tel:* 020 7219 4184.

SOLEY, Clive Stafford *(Ealing, Acton and Shepherd's Bush)   Lab majority 15,647*

Born May 7, 1939; educated Downshall Secondary Modern, Ilford; Newbattle Abbey Adult Education College; Strathclyde University (BA Hons Politics and Psychology); Southampton University (Diploma in Applied Social Studies). (1 son 1 daughter). *Career:* Probation Officer and Senior Probation Officer, Inner London Probation Service 1970–79. *Spokesman:* Opposition Spokesman on: Northern Ireland 1982–85, Home Affairs 1985–87, Housing and Local Government 1987–89, Housing and Planning 1989–92. *Select Committees (Current):* Member: Modernisation of the House of Commons 1997– *(Former):* Member: Northern Ireland Affairs 1994–97; Chairman: Northern Ireland Affairs 1995–97. *Party Groups:* Chairman: Labour Campaign for Criminal Justice 1983–97, Parliamentary Labour Party 1997–; Member, Labour Party National Executive Committee 1998–; Chair, London Selection Board for Labour candidate for Mayor 1999–. *International Bodies:* International Observer at: first National Elections in Mongolia 1990, Peruvian General Election 1995. *Other:* Chairman, Alcohol Education Centre to 1984. *Trust:* Fellow, Industry and Parliament Trust.

Miscellaneous: Member of several House of Commons Committees including: Prevention of Terrorism Bill 1983–84, Criminal Justice Bill 1987–99, Housing Bill 1987–88, Local Government and Housing Bill 1988–89, Planning and Compensation Bill 1990–91, Freedom and Responsibility of the Press 1992–93. *Special Interests:* Environment, Housing, Penal Affairs and Policy, Civil Liberties, Northern Ireland. *Countries of Interest:* China, South East Asia. *Recreations:* Walking, photography, scuba diving. *Electoral Notes:* Member for Hammersmith North 1979–83, for Hammersmith 1983–97, and for Ealing, Acton and Shepherds Bush since May 1, 1997. *Address:* Clive Soley Esq, MP, House of Commons, London, SW1A 0AA *Tel:* 020 7219 3000 *E-mail:* macleodn@parliament.uk.

SOUTHWORTH, Helen Mary *(Warrington South)*   Lab majority 10,807

Born November 13, 1956; educated Larkhill Convent School; University of Lancaster (BA Hons). Married Edmund Southworth (1 son). *Trades Union:* Member, MSF. *Career:* Director, Age Concern (St Helens); Non-executive Director, St Helens and Knowsley Health Authority; Representative on the Community Health Council for 8 years. *Councils, Public Bodies:* Councillor, St Helens Borough Council 1994–98, Chair, Leisure Committee 1994–96; Non-executive Member, St Helens and Knowsley Health Authority. *Select Committees (Current):* Member: Trade and Industry 1998– *(Former):* Member: Procedure 1997–99. *Other:* Governor, Age Concern; Director, Grosvenor Housing Association; Council Member, St Helen's College; Member, Sankey Canal Restoration Society. *Trust:* Trustee, History of Parliament Trust. *Publications:* Co-author, *National Standards for Day Care Provision. Special Interests:* Health, Housing, Democracy, Small Businesses. *Countries of Interest:* Denmark. *Recreations:* Family, gardening, painting, walking the dog. *Electoral Notes:* Contested Wirral South General Election 1992. Member for Warrington South since May 1, 1997. *Address:* Helen Southworth, MP, House of Commons, London, SW1A 0AA *Tel:* 020 7219 3568 *Fax:* 020 7219 2115 *Tel (Constituency):* 01925 240002.

SPELLAR, John Francis *(Warley)*   Lab majority 15,451

Son of late William David Spellar, and of Phyllis Kathleen Spellar. Born August 5, 1947; educated Bromley Parish Primary School; Dulwich College; St Edmund's Hall, Oxford (PPE). Married 1981, Anne Rosalind Wilmot (1 daughter). *Trades Union:* National Officer, Electrical, Electronic, Telecommunication and Plumbing Union 1969–97. *Political Career:* Ministry of Defence: Parliamentary Under-Secretary of State 1997–99, Minister of State for the Armed Forces 1999–. *Whip:* Opposition Whip 1992–94. *Spokesman:* Opposition Spokesman on: Northern Ireland 1994–95, Defence, Disarmament and Arms Control 1995–97. *Special Interests:* Energy, Industry (Electronics), Motor Industry, Construction Industry. *Countries of Interest:* Australia, Israel, USA. *Recreations:* Gardening. *Electoral Notes:* Contested Bromley 1970. Member for Birmingham Northfield from October 28, 1982 (By-election) to June 1983. Contested Birmingham Northfield 1987. Member for Warley West 1992–97, and for Warley since May 1, 1997. *Clubs:* Rowley Regis and Blackheath Labour. *Address:* John Spellar Esq, MP, House of Commons, London, SW1A 0AA *Tel:* 020 7219 5800 *E-mail:* spellarj@parliament.uk.

SPELMAN, Mrs Caroline Alice *(Meriden)*   Con majority 582

Daughter of Marshall Cormack and late Helen Margaret Cormack (née Greenfield). Born May 4, 1958; educated Herts and Essex Grammar School for Girls; Queen Mary College, London University (BA European studies 1980). Married April 25, 1987, Mark Spelman (2 sons 1 daughter). *Career:* Sugar Beet Commodity Secretary, National Farmers Union 1981–84; Deputy Director, International Confederation of European Beetgrowers, Paris 1984–89; Research Fellow, Centre for European Agricultural Studies 1989–93; Director, Spelman, Cormack and Associates, Food and Biotechnology Consultancy 1989–. *Whip:* An Opposition Whip (Agriculture; Environment, Transport and the Regions) 1998–99. *Spokesman:* An Opposition Front Bench Spokeswoman for Health and Women's Issues 1999–. *Select Committees (Former):* Member: Science and Technology 1997–98.

Trust: Trustee: Snowdon Awards Scheme for Disabled, Oxford Kilburn Club for Deprived Inner City Kids. *Miscellaneous:* Board Member, Parliamentary Office of Science and Technology (POST) 1997–. *Sportsclubs:* Member: Hampton in Arden Hockey Club, Lords and Commons Tennis Club, Lords and Commons Ski Club. *Publications: A Green and Pleasant Land,* Bow Group Paper. *Special Interests:* International Affairs, Trade and Industry, Environment, Agriculture. *Countries of Interest:* France, Germany, Brazil, South Africa. *Recreations:* Tennis, choral singing, ski-ing, sailing, hockey. *Electoral Notes:* Contested Bassetlaw 1992. Member for Meriden since May 1, 1997. *Address:* Mrs Caroline Spelman, MP, House of Commons, London, SW1A 0AA *Tel:* 020 7219 4189 *Fax:* 020 7219 0378. *Constituency:* 2 Manor Road, Solihull, West Midlands *Tel:* 0121–711 2955 *Fax:* 0121–711 2955 *E-mail:* spelmanc@parliament.uk.

SPICER, Sir (William) Michael (Hardy) *(West Worcestershire)* Con majority 3,846

Son of late Brigadier L. H. Spicer. Born January 22, 1943; educated Sacre Coeur, Vienna; Gaunts House Preparatory School; Wellington College; Emmanuel College, Cambridge (MA). Married April 7, 1967, Patricia Ann Hunter (1 son 2 daughters). *Career:* Director, Conservative Systems Research Centre 1968–70, Managing Director, Economic Models Limited 1970–80. *Political Career:* PPS to Ministers for Trade and Consumer Affairs 1979–81; Parliamentary Under-Secretary of State for Transport 1984–87; Aviation Minister 1985–87; Parliamentary Under-Secretary of State, Department of Energy 1987–90; Minister of State, Housing and Planning, Department of Environment January-November 1990. *Select Committees (Current):* Member: Treasury 1997–; Chairman: Treasury Sub-Committee 1999– *(Former):* Chairman: Treasury Sub-Committee 1999. *Party Groups:* Vice-Chairman, Conservative Party 1981–83; Deputy Chairman 1983–84. *Other:* Governor, Wellington College 1992–. *Miscellaneous:* Chairman: European Research Group; Member, Executive, 1922 Committee 1997–98. *Honours:* Knighted 1996. *Publications:* Author of: *A Treaty Too Far: A New Policy For Europe,* 1992; *The Challenge from the East: The Rebirth of the West,* 1996; Six novels. *Recreations:* Tennis, writing novels, painting. *Electoral Notes:* Contested Easington 1966 and 1970. Member for South Worcestershire 1974–97, and for West Worcestershire since May 1, 1997. *Clubs:* Pratts, Garrick. *Address:* Sir Michael Spicer, MP, House of Commons, London, SW1A 0AA *Tel:* 020 7219 3491.

SPRING, Richard *(West Suffolk)* Con majority 1,867

Son of late H. J. A. Spring and of late Marjorie Watson-Morris. Born September 24, 1946; educated Rondebosch, Cape; University of Cape Town; Magdalene College, Cambridge. Married December 13, 1979, Hon. Jane Henniker-Major, daughter of 8th Baron Henniker, KCMG, CVO, MC, DL (1 son 1 daughter) (marriage dissolved 1993). *Career:* Merrill Lynch Ltd 1971–86, Vice-President 1976–86; Deputy Managing Director, Hutton International Associates 1986–88; Executive Director, Shearson Lehman Hutton 1988–90; Managing Director, Xerox Furman Selz 1990–92. *Political Career:* PPS: to Rt Hon. Sir Patrick Mayhew, QC, MP, as Secretary of State for Northern Ireland 1994–95, to Tim Eggar, as Minister for Trade and Industry 1995–96, to Nicholas Soames, MP and James Arbuthnot, MP, as Ministers of State, Ministry of Defence 1996–97. *Spokesman:* Opposition Spokesman for Culture, Media and Sport November 1997–. *Select Committees (Former):* Member: Employment 1992–94, Health 1995–96, Northern Ireland Affairs 1995–97, Deregulation 1997. *Party Groups:* Has held various offices in Westminster Conservative Association 1976–87, including CPC Chairman 1990; Vice-Chairman, Conservative Industrial Fund 1993–96. *Other:* Deputy-Chairman, Small Business Bureau 1992–. *Countries of Interest:* Spain, South Africa, USA, Estonia. *Recreations:* Country pursuits, tennis, swimming. *Electoral Notes:* Contested Ashton-under-Lyne 1983 General Election. Member for Bury St Edmunds 1992–97, and for West Suffolk since May 1, 1997. *Clubs:* Boodle's. *Address:* Richard Spring Esq, MP, House of Commons, London, SW1A 0AA *Tel:* 020 7219 4062. *Constituency:* 4a Exeter Road, Newmarket, Suffolk, CB8 8LT *Tel:* 01638 669391 *Fax:* 01638 669410.

SQUIRE, Rachel *(Dunfermline West)   Lab majority 12,354*

Daughter of Louise Anne Squire. Born July 13, 1954; educated Godolphin and Latymer Girls' School; Durham University (BA Hons Anthropology); Birmingham University (Certificate of Qualification in Social Work). Married July 6, 1984, Allan Lee Mason. *Trades Union:* Trade Union Official 1981–92; Member, UNISON. *Career:* Social Worker, Birmingham City Council 1975–81; Area Officer, NUPE: Liverpool 1981–82, Ayrshire 1982–83, Renfrewshire 1983–85, All of Scotland Education Officer 1985–92. *Political Career:* PPS to Ministers of State, Department for Education and Employment: Stephen Byers, MP (School Standards) 1997–98, Estelle Morris, MP (Minister for School Standards) 1998–. *Select Committees (Former):* Member: Procedure 1992–97, European Legislation 1994–97, Modernisation of the House of Commons 1997–99. *Party Groups:* Head, Scottish Labour Party's Task Force on Community Care 1993–98; Member, Labour Movement in Europe; Chair, Scottish Policy Forum, Labour Party 1998–. *Other:* Member: Amnesty International, WEA, Council for British Archaeology, Council for Scotland Archaeology, Historic Scotland, Camping and Caravanning Club. *Trust:* Fellow, Industry and Parliament Trust (BAe); Member, National Trust (Scotland); Fellow (Navy), Armed Forces Parliamentary Scheme 1993–94. *Miscellaneous:* Labour Representative, Commission on Future of Scotland's Voluntary Sector. *Special Interests:* Defence, Health Service, Community Care, Foreign Affairs. *Countries of Interest:* Scandinavia, Europe, Former Eastern Bloc. *Recreations:* Archaeology, reading. *Electoral Notes:* Member for Dunfermline West since April 9, 1992. *Address:* Rachel Squire, MP, House of Commons, London, SW1A 0AA *Tel:* 020 7219 5144. *Constituency:* 10–14 Douglas Street, Dunfermline, KY12 7EB *Tel:* 01383 622889 *Fax:* 01383 623500.

STANLEY, The Rt Hon. Sir John P *(Tonbridge and Malling)   Con majority 10,230*

Son of late H. Stanley and late Mrs A. M. Stanley. Born January 19, 1942; educated Repton School; Lincoln College, Oxford. Married December 21, 1968, Susan Elizabeth, daughter of Leslie A. D. Giles (2 sons 1 daughter). *Career:* Conservative Research Department 1967–68; Research Associate, Institute for Strategic Studies 1968–69; Rio Tinto-Zinc Corp. Ltd 1969–79. *Political Career:* PPS to Rt Hon. Margaret Thatcher, MP as Leader of the Opposition 1976–79; Minister for Housing and Construction 1979–83; Minister for the Armed Forces 1983–87; Minister of State, Northern Ireland Office 1987–88. *Select Committees (Current):* Member: Foreign Affairs 1997– *(Former):* Member: Foreign Affairs 1992–97, Entry Clearance Sub-Committee 1997–98. *International Bodies:* Member, Executive Committee, Commonwealth Parliamentary Association (CPA) UK Branch 1999–. *Trust:* Trustee, ActionAid. *Honours:* PC 1984; Knighted 1988. *Recreations:* Music and the arts, sailing. *Electoral Notes:* Contested Newton 1970 General Election. Member for Tonbridge and Malling since February 1974. *Address:* The Rt Hon. Sir John Stanley, MP, House of Commons, London, SW1A 0AA *Tel:* 020 7219 3000.

STARKEY, Dr Phyllis Margaret *(Milton Keynes South West)   Lab majority 10,292*

Daughter of Dr John Williams, food chemist, and late Catherine Hooson Williams. Born January 4, 1947; educated Perse School for Girls, Cambridge; Lady Margaret Hall, Oxford (BA Hons); Clare Hall, Cambridge (PhD). Married September 6, 1969, Hugh Walton Starkey (2 daughters). *Trades Union:* Member: AUT 1974–93, MSF 1992–, PTC 1993–97. *Profession:* Research Scientist. *Career:* Research Scientist: Strangeways Laboratory, Cambridge 1974–81, Sir William Dunn School of Pathology, Oxford 1981–84; University Lecturer in Obstetrics, Oxford University and Fellow, Somerville College 1984–93; Science Policy Administrator, Biotechnology and Biological Sciences Research Council 1993–97; Parliamentary Fellow, St Antony's College, Oxford 1997–98. *Councils, Public Bodies:* Oxford City Council: Councillor 1983–97, Leader 1990–93, Chair of Transport 1985–88, Chair of Finance 1988–90, 1993–96. *Select Committees (Current):* Member: Foreign Affairs 1999– *(Former):* Member: Modernisation of the House of Commons 1997–99. *Party Groups:* Vice-Chair, South East Regional Group of Labour MPs 1998–. *Awards:* K M Stott Prize, Newnham College, Cambridge 1974. *Miscellaneous:* Chair, Local Government Information Unit 1992–97;

Representative of Labour Councillors on National Policy Forum 1995–97; Board Member, Parliamentary Office of Science and Technology (POST) 1997–. *Publications:* Seventy scientific papers 1977–96. *Special Interests:* Science, Health, Environmentally Sustainable Transport, Local Government and Devolution, Foreign Affairs, Middle East. *Countries of Interest:* Palestine, France, the Maghreb. *Recreations:* Gardening, cinema, walking, family. *Electoral Notes:* Member for Milton Keynes South West since May 1, 1997. *Address:* Dr Phyllis Starkey, MP, House of Commons, London, SW1A 0AA *Tel:* 020 7219 0456/6427 *Fax:* 020 7219 6865. *Constituency:* The Labour Hall, Newport Road, New Bradwell, Milton Keynes, MK13 0AA *Tel:* 01908 225522 *Fax:* 01908 312297 *E-mail:* starkey@miltonkeynes-sw.demon.co.uk.

STEEN, Anthony David *(Totnes)* Con majority 877

Son of late Stephen Steen. Born July 22, 1939; educated Westminster School; University of London. Married 1966, Carolyn, daughter of Colin Padfield (1 son 1 daughter). *Profession:* Barrister-at-Law. *Career:* Called to the Bar 1962; Barrister, Gray's Inn; Youth Leader and Social Worker; Founder, Task Force (Young helping the old) with Government grant 1964, First Director 1964–68; As Community Worker initiated Young Volunteer Force, Government Urban Development Foundation, First Director 1968–74; Lecturer in Law, Ghana High Commission and Council of Legal Education 1964–67; Ministry of Defence Court Martials Defence Counsel; Adviser to Federal and Provincial Canadian Governments on unemployment and youth problems 1970–71. *Political Career:* PPS to Secretary of State for National Heritage 1992–94. *Select Committees (Current):* Member: Deregulation 1997–, European Scrutiny 1998– *(Former):* Member: Environment 1989–92, House of Commons Catering 1991–95, European Legislation 1997–98, European Legislation 1998. *Party Groups:* Appointed by the Prime Minister to generate new activity amongst MPs in constituency work 1994; Conservative Central Office Co-ordinator for Critical Seats 1982–87; Joint National Chairman, Impact 80s Campaign 1980–82. *Other:* Founder of two national charities; Vice-President: International Centre for Child Studies, Association of District Councils, Malborough with South Huish Horticultural Society; Advisory Tutor to the School of Environment, Polytechnic of Central London 1982–83; Patron, Kidscape. *Trust:* Trustee of: Education Extra, Dartington Summer Arts Foundation. *Miscellaneous:* Member, Council for Christians and Jews. *Sportsclubs:* Lords and Commons Cycle, Lords and Commons Tennis. *Publications: New Life for Old Cities,* 1981; *Tested Ideas for Political Success,* 1983; *Public Land Utilisation Management Schemes (PLUMS),* 1988. *Special Interests:* Environment, Urban Regeneration, Community Care, Youth Affairs, Conservation, Heritage, Fishing, Agriculture, Deregulation. *Countries of Interest:* Middle East. *Recreations:* Piano playing, cycling, swimming, tennis, tree-hugging. *Electoral Notes:* Member for Liverpool Wavertree 1974–83, for South Hams 1983–97, and for Totnes since May 1, 1997. *Clubs:* Royal North Cape, Royal Automobile. *Address:* Anthony D. Steen Esq, MP, House of Commons, London, SW1A 0AA *Tel:* 020 7219 3000.

STEINBERG, Gerry (Gerald) *(City of Durham)* Lab majority 22,504

Son of late Harry and Mrs Esther Steinberg. Born April 20, 1945; educated Whinney Hill Secondary Modern School; Durham Johnston Grammar School; Sheffield College of Education; Newcastle Polytechnic (Certificate Ed. of Backward Children). Married August 25, 1969, Margaret, daughter of David and Ann Thornton (1 son 1 daughter). *Trades Union:* Member: TGWU, NUT. *Profession:* Teacher. *Career:* Teacher, Hexham Camp School 1966–69; Elemore Hall 1969–75, Deputy head 1975–79; Head teacher, Whitworth House School 1979–87. *Councils, Public Bodies:* Parish councillor, Pittington and Sherburn 1972–76; Durham City Councillor 1976–87. *Select Committees (Current):* Member: Catering 1998–, Public Accounts 1998– *(Former):* Member: Education 1987–96, Education and Employment 1997–98, Education Sub-Committee 1997–98. *Party Groups:* Secretary, Durham CLP and Agent to Dr Mark Hughes, MP 1973–83; Secretary, Durham City Labour Group 1981–87; Vice-Chair, Northern Group of Labour MPs 1997–98, Chair 1998–. *Special Interests:* Education, Local Government, Animal Welfare. *Recreations:* All sport, supporting Sunderland AFC. *Electoral Notes:* Member for City of Durham since June 1987. *Clubs:* Sherburn Village Workman's, Brandon Village Workman's, Crossgate Workman's, Neville's Cross Workman's, New Durham Workman's. *Address:* Gerald Steinberg Esq, MP, House of Commons, London, SW1A 0AA *Tel:* 020 7219 6909. *Constituency:* 32 Claypath, Durham, DH1 1RH *Tel:* 0191-386 0166 *Fax:* 0191-383 0047.

STEVENSON, George William *(Stoke-on-Trent South)   Lab majority 18,303*

Son of Harold and Elsie Stevenson. Born August 30, 1938; educated Queensberry Road Secondary Modern School. Married 1st, June 14, 1958, Doreen June (died March 20, 1989), daughter of late Joseph and Alice Parkes (2 sons 1 daughter), married 2nd, June 1, 1991, Pauline Margaret, daughter of late Sydney Barber and Mrs Ada Cuming. *Trades Union:* TGWU Shop steward 1968; Chairman, 5/24 Branch TGWU 1975–83. *Career:* Pottery industry 1953–57; Mining industry 1957–66. *Councils, Public Bodies:* Deputy Leader, Stoke-on-Trent City Council 1972–83, Chairman, Highways Committee; Deputy Leader, Staffordshire County Council 1981–85, Former Chairman, Social Services and Establishment Committees. *Select Committees (Current):* Member: Environment, Transport and Regional Affairs 1997–, Transport Sub-Committee 1997–, Chairmen's Panel 1998– *(Former):* Member: Agriculture 1992–96, European Legislation 1996–97, Chairmen's Panel 1998. *International Bodies:* Chairman: European Parliament Delegation for Relations with South Asia 1989, British Labour Group, European Parliament 1987–88. *Other:* Member: Amnesty International, ACTSA. *Miscellaneous:* Member: European Standing Committee B 1998, European Standing Committee A 1998–; Vice-President, Federation of Economic Development Authorities (FEDA). *Special Interests:* Transport, Energy, Agriculture, Human Rights, Education. *Countries of Interest:* India, Kashmir, Pakistan, Sri Lanka, Tibet, South Asia. *Recreations:* Walking, travel, reading. *Electoral Notes:* MEP for Staffordshire East 1984–94. Member for Stoke-on-Trent South since April 9, 1992. *Address:* George Stevenson Esq, MP, House of Commons, London, SW1A 0AA *Tel:* 020 7219 5012 *Fax:* 020 7219 2688. *Constituency:* 2A Stanton Road, Meir, Stoke-on-Trent, Staffs, ST3 6DD *Tel:* 01782 593393 *Fax:* 01782 593430 *E-mail:* stevensonp@parliament.uk.

STEWART, David *(Inverness East, Nairn and Lochaber)   Lab majority 2,339*

Son of John Stewart, retired postal executive, and Alice Stewart. Born May 5, 1956; educated Inverness High School; Paisley College; Stirling University; Open University Business School (BA Hons Social Science, CQSW, Professional Diploma Management). Married August 6, 1982, Linda (1 son 1 daughter). *Trades Union:* Member, UNISON. *Profession:* Social Work Manager. *Career:* Social Worker and Social Work Manager 1980–97. *Councils, Public Bodies:* Councillor: Nithsdale Council, Dumfries 1984–86, Inverness District Council 1988–96. *Select Committees (Former):* Member: Scottish Affairs 1997–99. *Party Groups:* Member, Scottish Executive Labour Party 1985–95. *International Bodies:* Member, Interparliamentary Union. *Other:* Governor, Eden Court Theatre 1992–96. *Sportsclubs:* Inverness Caledonian Thistle Football Club. *Special Interests:* Rural Affairs, Local Government, Health, International Development, Social Security. *Countries of Interest:* USA, Italy. *Recreations:* Football, films, fitness, American political biographies. *Electoral Notes:* Contested Inverness, Nairn and Lochaber General Elections 1987 and 1992. Member for Inverness East, Nairn and Lochaber since May 1, 1997. *Address:* David Stewart Esq, MP, House of Commons, London, SW1A 0AA *Tel:* 020 7219 3586. *Constituency:* Queensgate Business Centre, 1/3 Fraser Street, Inverness, IV1 1DY *Tel:* 01463 237441 *Fax:* 01463 237661.

STEWART, Ian *(Eccles)   Lab majority 21,916*

Son of John and Helen. Born August 28, 1950; educated David Livingstone Primary Memorial School, Blantyre; Calder St Secondary, Blantyre; Alfred Turner Secondary Modern, Irlam, nr Manchester; Stretford Technical College; Manchester Metropolitan University (currently registered for Master of Philosophy Degree, transferring to PhD); Visiting Fellow, Salford University. Married August 9, 1968, Merilyn, daughter of Arthur and Joyce Holding (2 sons 1 daughter). *Trades Union:* Member, Transport and General Workers 1966–. *Profession:* Union Officer. *Career:* Regional Full-time Officer, Transport and General Workers Union for 20 years. *Select Committees (Current):* Member: Deregulation 1997–, Information 1998–. *International Bodies:* Member: Society of International Industrial Relations, UK China Forum (Industry Group);

Executive Member, Great Britain–China Centre. *Other:* Member: International Society of Industrial Relations, UK Society of Industrial Tutors, Manchester Industrial Relations Society. *Miscellaneous:* Founder, European Foundation for Social Partnership and Continuing Training Initiatives. *Publications: Youth Unemployment and Government Training Strategies*, 1981. *Special Interests:* Employment, Education and Training, Economics, Trade and Industry, Investment, Regional Development, Information Technology, Democracy, International Affairs. *Countries of Interest:* EU, Central and Eastern Europe, China, USA, Commonwealth. *Recreations:* Tai-Chi, painting, research into philosophic religious and life systems, scientific and medical developments. *Electoral Notes:* Member for Eccles since May 1, 1997. *Address:* Ian Stewart Esq, MP, House of Commons, London, SW1A 0AA *Tel:* 020 7219 6175 *Fax:* 020 7219 0903. *Constituency:* Eccles Parliamentary Office, Eccles Town Hall, Church Street, Eccles, Greater Manchester, M30 0EL *Tel:* 0161–707 4688 *Fax:* 0161–789 8065 *E-mail:* ianstewartmp@parliament.uk.

STINCHCOMBE, Paul *(Wellingborough)*   *Lab majority 187*

Son of Lionel and Pauline Stinchcombe. Born April 25, 1962; educated High Wycombe Royal Grammar School; Trinity College, Cambridge (BA First Class Hons Law, MA); Harvard Law School, USA (LLM); Senior Scholar, Trinity College, Cambridge; Frank Knox Fellow, Harvard Law School. Married July 7, 1990, Suzanne, daughter of John and Diane Gardiner (2 sons 1 daughter). *Trades Union:* Member: GMB, MSF. *Profession:* Barrister. *Career:* Barrister, specialising in environmental law and judicial review. *Councils, Public Bodies:* Councillor, Camden Council, London 1990–94, Chair of Labour Group 1992–94; Member, Board of Management: Arlington House 1990–91, Central London Law Centre 1990–94. *Select Committees (Current):* Member: Home Affairs 1998– *(Former):* Member: Procedure 1997–99. *Party Groups:* Member: Christian Socialist Movement, Society of Labour Lawyers; Executive Committee Member, Labour Planning and Environment Group 1997–. *Other:* Member: Friends of the Earth, Liberty. *Publications: Law Reform For All*, 1996. *Special Interests:* Economics, Environment, Civil Liberties, Breast Cancer. *Countries of Interest:* Kenya, India, Philippines. *Recreations:* Football, cricket, golf. *Electoral Notes:* Member for Wellingborough since May 1, 1997. *Address:* Paul Stinchcombe Esq, MP, House of Commons, London, SW1A 0AA *Tel:* 020 7219 4066. *Constituency:* Queen Anne House, 29 High Street, Wellingborough, Northamptonshire, NN8 4JZ *Tel:* 01933 279022 *Fax:* 01933 279029.

STOATE, Dr Howard Geoffrey *(Dartford)*   *Lab majority 4,328*

Son of Alvan Stoate, retired engineer, and Maisie Stoate, retired teacher. Born April 14, 1954; educated Kingston Grammar School; Kings College, London University (MSc, DRCOG). Married September 22, 1979, Deborah, daughter of Desmond Dunkerley (2 sons). *Trades Union:* Member: MPU, MSF. *Profession:* General Practitioner. *Career:* Junior Hospital Doctor 1977–81; GP, Albion Surgery, Bexley Heath 1982–; GP Tutor, Queen Mary's Hospital, Sidcup 1989–; Chair, Bexley Ethics Research Committee 1995–97. *Councils, Public Bodies:* Councillor, Dartford Borough Council 1990–99, Chair, Finance and Corporate Business 1995–99. *Select Committees (Current):* Member: Health 1997–. *Party Groups:* Member, Labour Party 1970–; Vice-Chair, DCLP 1984–91; Chair, LP Branch 1985–97; Vice-Chair, Dartford Fabian Society. *Other:* Governor, Dartford Grammar School 1996–. *Miscellaneous:* Vice-Chair, Regional Graduate Education Board 1997–; Member, British Medical Association. *Sportsclubs:* Emsworth Sailing Club. MBBS. *Publications:* Many medical publications, particularly on health screening. *Special Interests:* Health, Education, Environment. *Countries of Interest:* Spain. *Recreations:* Running, sailing, reading, music. *Electoral Notes:* Member for Dartford since May 1, 1997. *Address:* Dr Howard Stoate, MP, House of Commons, London, SW1A 0AA *Tel:* 020 7219 4571 *Fax:* 020 7219 6820. *Constituency:* Civic Centre, Home Gardens, Dartford, Kent, DA1 1DR *Tel:* 01322 343234 *Fax:* 01322 343235 *E-mail:* stoateh@parliament.co.uk.

STRANG, The Rt Hon. Gavin Steel *(Edinburgh East and Musselburgh)*   *Lab majority 14,530*

Son of James S. Strang, tenant farmer. Born July 10, 1943; educated Morrison's Academy; Edinburgh University (BSc (Hons)); Churchill College, Cambridge University (DipAgriSci); Edinburgh University (PhD). Married August 1973, Bettina Morrison, daughter of James Smith (1 son, 2 stepsons). *Trades Union:* Member, TGWU. *Career:* Member, Tayside Economic Planning Consultative Group 1966–68; Scientist, Agricultural Research Council 1968–70. *Political Career:* Parliamentary Under-Secretary of State for Energy February-October 1974; Parliamentary Secretary to Ministry of Agriculture 1974–79; Minister of State (in Cabinet), Department of the Environment, Transport and the Regions (Minister for Transport) 1997–98. *Spokesman:* Opposition Front Bench Spokesman on: Agriculture 1979–82, Employment 1987–89, Food, Agriculture and Rural Affairs 1992–97. *Select Committees (Former):* Member: Agriculture, Science and Technology, Scottish Affairs. *Honours:* PC 1997. *Special Interests:* Agriculture, Transport, Fisheries. *Countries of Interest:* Europe. *Recreations:* Swimming, golf, watching football, walking in the countryside. *Electoral Notes:* Member for Edinburgh East 1970–97, and for Edinburgh East and Musselburgh since May 1, 1997. *Address:* The Rt Hon. Gavin Strang, MP, House of Commons, London, SW1A 0AA *Tel:* 020 7219 3000. *Constituency:* 54 Portobello High Street, Edinburgh, EH15 1DA *Tel:* 0131–669 6002.

STRAW, The Rt Hon. Jack (John Whitaker) *(Blackburn)*   *Lab majority 14,451*

Son of Walter Arthur Straw. Born August 3, 1946; educated Brentwood School; University of Leeds (LLB); Inns of Court School of Law; Visiting Fellow, Nuffield College, Oxford 1990–98; Hon. LLD, Leeds University 1999. Married November 10, 1978, Alice, daughter of late Derrick Perkins and Mrs Elsa Perkins, CBE (1 son 1 daughter). *Trades Union:* Member, GMB. *Profession:* Barrister. *Career:* President, National Union of Students 1969–71; Called to the Bar, Inner Temple 1972; Special Adviser: to Secretary of State for Social Services, Rt Hon. Mrs Barbara Castle, MP 1974–76, to Secretary of State for the Environment, Rt Hon. Peter Shore, MP 1976–77; staff of Granada Television *World in Action* 1977–79. *Councils, Public Bodies:* Councillor, Islington Borough Council 1971–78; ILEA: Member 1971–74, Deputy Leader 1973. *Political Career:* Shadow Education Secretary 1987–92; Shadow Environment Secretary 1992–94; Shadow Secretary of State for Home Affairs 1994–97; Secretary of State for the Home Department 1997–. *Spokesman:* Opposition Front Bench Spokesman on: Treasury and Economic Affairs 1980–83, Environment 1983–87. *Party Groups:* Member, Labour Party National Executive Committee 1994–95. *International Bodies:* Joint Vice-Chairman, British-American Parliamentary International Group 1999–. *Other:* Member of Council, University of Lancaster 1989–92; Governor: Blackburn College 1990–, Pimlico School 1994–, Chairman 1995–98. *Sportsclubs:* Vice-President, Blackburn Rovers FC 1998. *Honours:* PC 1997; Elected Master of Bench of the Inner Temple 1997. Fellow, Royal Statistical Society 1995–. *Publications: Policy and Ideology,* 1993. *Special Interests:* Education, Tax, Economic Policy, Local Government, Police, European Union. *Recreations:* Cooking, walking, music, watching Blackburn Rovers. *Electoral Notes:* Contested Tonbridge and Malling February 1974. Member for Blackburn since May 1979. *Address:* The Rt Hon. Jack Straw, MP, House of Commons, London, SW1A 0AA *Tel:* 020 7219 3000. *Constituency:* Richmond Chambers, Richmond Road, Blackburn *Tel:* 01254 52317 *Fax:* 01254 682213.

STREETER, Gary *(South West Devon)*   *Con majority 7,397*

Son of Kenneth and Shirley Streeter. Born October 2, 1955; educated Tiverton Grammar School; King's College, London (LLB 1st class hons). Married July 15, 1978, Janet Vanessa, daughter of Cyril and Joan Stevens (1 son 1 daughter). *Profession:* Solicitor. *Career:* Solicitor; Partner, Foot and Bowden, Plymouth 1984–98, specialist in company and employment law. *Councils, Public Bodies:* Plymouth City Council: Councillor 1986–92, Chairman, Housing Committee 1989–91. *Political Career:* PPS: to Sir Derek Spencer, QC, MP, as Solicitor General 1993–95, to Rt Hon. Sir Nicholas Lyell, QC, MP, as Attorney-General 1994–95; Assistant Government Whip 1995–96; Parliamentary Secretary, Lord Chancellor's Department 1996–97; Shadow Secretary of State for International Development 1998–. *Whip:* Assistant Government Whip 1995–96. *Spokesman:* An Opposition

Spokesman on: Foreign Affairs 1997–98, Europe 1997–98. *Select Committees (Former):* Member: Environment 1992–93. *Special Interests:* Law and Order, Family Moral and Social Issues, Developing World. *Recreations:* Watching cricket and rugby, family. *Electoral Notes:* Member for Plymouth Sutton 1992–97, and for South West Devon since May 1, 1997. *Address:* Gary Streeter Esq, MP, House of Commons, London, SW1A 0AA *Tel:* 020 7219 4070 *Fax:* 020 7219 2414 *Tel (Constituency):* 01752 335666 *Fax (Constituency):* 01752 338401 *E-mail:* garystreeter@compuserve.com.

STRINGER, Graham *(Manchester Blackley)* Lab majority 19,588

Son of late Albert Stringer, railway clerk, and Brenda Stringer, shop assistant. Born February 17, 1950; educated Moston Brook High School; Sheffield University (BSc chemistry 1971); Hon. RNCM. Married Kathryn. *Trades Union:* Branch Officer and Shop Steward, MSF. *Career:* Analytical Chemist; Chair of Board, Manchester Airport plc 1996–97. *Councils, Public Bodies:* Councillor, Manchester City Council 1979–98, Leader 1984–96. *Political Career:* Parliamentary Secretary, Cabinet Office 1999–. *Select Committees (Former):* Member: Environment, Transport and Regional Affairs 1997–99, Transport Sub-Committee 1997–99. *Sportsclubs:* Member: Manchester Tennis and Racquet Club, Cheetham Hill Cricket Club. *Electoral Notes:* Member for Manchester Blackley since May 1, 1997. *Address:* Graham Stringer Esq, MP, House of Commons, London, SW1A 0AA *Tel:* 020 7219 6055 *Tel (Constituency):* 0161–202 6600 *Fax (Constituency):* 0161–202 6626 *E-mail:* gstringer@cabinet-office.x.gsi.gov.uk.

STUART, Gisela Gschaider *(Birmingham Edgbaston)* Lab majority 4,842

Daughter of late Martin Gschaider and Liane Krompholz. Born November 26, 1955; educated Realschule Vilsbiburg; Manchester Polytechnic; London University (LLB). Married (2 sons). *Profession:* Law Lecturer. *Career:* Deputy Director, London Book Fair 1983; Translator; Lawyer and Lecturer, Worcester College of Technology and Birmingham University 1992–. *Political Career:* PPS to Rt Hon Paul Boateng, MP, as Minister of State, Home Office (Minister for Criminal Policy) 1998–99; Parliamentary Under-Secretary of State, Department of Health 1999–. *Select Committees (Former):* Member: Social Security 1997–98. *Other:* Chair of Governors, Primary School; Lay Visitor to Prisons; Member, Charter 88. *Special Interests:* Manufacturing, Pension Law. *Electoral Notes:* Member for Birmingham Edgbaston since May 1, 1997. *Address:* Gisela Stuart, MP, House of Commons, London, SW1A 0AA *Tel:* 020 7219 5051.

STUNELL, (Robert) Andrew, OBE *(Hazel Grove)* LD majority 11,814

Son of late Robert George Stunell and Trixie Stunell. Born November 24, 1942; educated Surbiton Grammar School; Manchester University; Liverpool Polytechnic (RIBA Part III). Married July 29, 1967, Gillian, daughter of late Jack and Margaret Chorley (3 sons 2 daughters). *Trades Union:* Member, NALGO: New Towns Whitley Council 1977–81. *Profession:* Political Secretary. *Career:* Architectural Assistant: CWS Manchester 1965–67, Runcorn New Town 1967–81; Freelance Architectural Assistant 1981–85; Various posts including Political Secretary, Association of Liberal Democrat Councillors (ALDC) 1985–87, Head of Service 1989–96. *Councils, Public Bodies:* Councillor: Chester City Council 1979–90, Cheshire County Council 1981–91, Stockport Metropolitan Borough Council 1994–. *Whip:* Deputy Chief Whip 1997–. *Spokesman:* Spokesman for: Environment and Transport 1997–98, Energy 1997–. *Select Committees (Current):* Member: Broadcasting 1997–, Modernisation of the House of Commons 1997–, Procedure 1997–, Unopposed Bills (Panel) 1997–, Standing Orders 1998–. *Party Groups:* Various Local and National Party Offices 1977–. *Other:* Member: United Nations Association 1959–, Romiley Methodist Church; President, Goyt Valley Rail Users Association. *Miscellaneous:* Vice-Chair, Association of County Councils 1985–90; Vice-President, Local Government Association 1997–. *Honours:* OBE 1995. *Publications: Life In The Balance,* 1986; *Budgeting For Real,* 1984, 2nd edition 1994, 3rd edition 1999; *Thriving In The Balance,* 1995; *Open Active & Effective,* 1995; *Local Democracy Guaranteed,* 1996;

Energy – Clean and Green to 2050, 1999. *Special Interests:* Local Democracy, Third World, Race Relations, Energy, Climate Change. *Countries of Interest:* All. *Recreations:* Theoretical astronomy, camping, table tennis. *Electoral Notes:* Contested City of Chester 1979, 1983, 1987, Hazel Grove 1992. Member for Hazel Grove since May 1, 1997. *Address:* Andrew Stunell Esq, OBE, MP, House of Commons, London, SW1A 0AA *Tel:* 020 7219 5223 *Fax:* 020 7219 2302. *Constituency:* Liberal Democrat HQ, 68A Compstall Road, Romiley, Stockport, Greater Manchester, SK6 4DE *Tel:* 0161–406 7070 *Fax:* 0161–494 2425.

SUTCLIFFE, Gerry *(Bradford South)* Lab majority 12,936

Son of Henry and Margaret Sutcliffe. Born May 13, 1953; educated Cardinal Hinsley Grammar School, Bradford. Married October 14, 1972, Maria, daughter of Eric and Mary Holgate (3 sons). *Trades Union:* Deputy Branch Secretary, SOGAT/GPMU 1980–94; Member: Yorkshire and Humberside Trade Union Friends of Labour, Regional TUC. *Career:* Salesperson 1969–72; Display advertising, *Bradford Telegraph and Argus* 1972–75; Field Printers, Bradford 1975–80. *Councils, Public Bodies:* Bradford City Council: Councillor 1982–94, Leader 1992–94. *Political Career:* PPS to Rt Hon. Harriet Harman, MP, as Secretary of State for Social Security and Minister for Women 1997–98; PPS to Rt Hon. Stephen Byers, MP: as Chief Secretary, HM Treasury July-December 1998, as Secretary of State for Trade and Industry 1999. *Whip:* Assistant Government Whip 1999–. *Select Committees (Former):* Member: Public Accounts 1996–98, Unopposed Bills (Panel) 1997–99. *Party Groups:* Member, Regional Labour Party Executive; Vice-Chairman, Yorkshire Regional Group of Labour MPs 1997–. *Other:* A School Governor; Director: Bradford TEC, Yorkshire Enterprise Ltd; Member: Friends of the Earth, Amnesty International. *Special Interests:* Employment, Local Government. *Countries of Interest:* Pakistan, Bangladesh, India, European Union. *Recreations:* Sport, music. *Electoral Notes:* Member for Bradford South since by-election June 9, 1994. *Address:* Gerry Sutcliffe Esq, MP, House of Commons, London, SW1A 0AA *Tel:* 020 7219 3247. *Constituency:* 3rd Floor, 76 Kirkgate, Bradford BD1 1SZ *Tel:* 01274 400007 *Fax:* 01274 400020 *E-mail:* sutcliffeg@parliament.uk.

SWAYNE, Desmond Angus *(New Forest West)* Con majority 11,332

Son of George Joseph Swayne and Elisabeth McAlister Swayne (née Gibson). Born August 20, 1956; educated Drumley House, Ayrshire; Bedford School; St Mary's College, University of St Andrews (Masters Degree, Theology). Married August 8, 1987, Moira Cecily Teek, daughter of Albert John Teek (1 son 2 daughters). *Armed Forces:* Major, Territorial Army;. *Career:* Schoolmaster, 'A' Level Economics: Charterhouse 1980–81, Wrekin College 1982–87; Manager, Risk Management Systems, Royal Bank of Scotland 1988–96. *Select Committees (Current):* Member: Scottish Affairs 1997–, Social Security 1999–. *Other:* Member, British Field Sports Society. *Sportsclubs:* Serpentine Swimming Club. *Electoral Notes:* Contested Pontypridd 1987, West Bromwich West 1992. Member for New Forest West since May 1, 1997. *Clubs:* Cavalry and Guards. *Address:* Desmond Swayne Esq, MP, House of Commons, London, SW1A 0AA *Tel:* 020 7219 3544. *Constituency:* New Forest West Conservative Association, 3 The Parade, Southampton Road, Cadnam, Hampshire, SO40 2NG *Tel:* 023 8081 4554 *Fax:* 023 8081 2019.

SWINNEY, John Ramsay *(North Tayside)* SNP majority 4,160

Son of Kenneth Swinney, garage manager, and Nancy Swinney. Born April 13, 1964; educated Forrester High School, Edinburgh; University of Edinburgh (MA Hons Politics). Married November 30, 1991, Lorna Ann, daughter of Francis and Margaret King (1 son 1 daughter) (separated 1998). *Career:* Managing Consultant, Development Options Ltd 1987–92; Strategic Planning Principal, Scottish Amicable 1992–97. *Spokesman:* Spokesman for Economy, Social Security and Agriculture 1997–. *Party Groups:* SNP: National Secretary 1986–92, Vice-Convenor Publicity 1992–97, Treasury Spokesperson 1995–99, Senior Vice-Convenor 1998–. *Miscellaneous:* Member: European Standing Committee A 1998, European Standing Committee C 1999. *Special Interests:* Economic Policy, Housing, Enterprise, Further and Higher Education. *Countries of Interest:* Eastern

Europe. *Recreations:* Hill-walking, reading, music. *Electoral Notes:* Member for North Tayside since May 1, 1997. MSP for the Constituency of North Tayside since May 6, 1999. *Address:* John Swinney Esq, MP, MSP, House of Commons, London, SW1A 0AA *Tel:* 020 7219 6581 *Fax:* 020 7219 3960. *Constituency:* 35 Perth Street, Blairgowrie, PH10 6DL *Tel:* 01250 876576 *Fax:* 01250 876991 *E-mail:* jsmp.blairg@snp.org.uk; john.swinney.msp@scottish.parliament.uk.

SYMS, Robert Andrew Raymond *(Poole)   Con majority 5,298*

Son of Raymond Syms, builder, and Mary Syms, teacher. Born August 15, 1956; educated Colston's School, Bristol. Married 1991 Nicola Guy (divorced 1999). *Career:* Managing Director, Family Building, Plant Hire and Property Group, based in Chippenham, Wiltshire. *Councils, Public Bodies:* Councillor: North Wiltshire District Council 1983–87, Wiltshire County Council 1985–97; Member, Wessex Regional Health Authority 1988–90. *Political Career:* PPS to Rt Hon. Michael Ancram, MP, as Chairman of the Conservative Party 1999–. *Spokesman:* Opposition Front Bench Spokesman for Environment, Transport and Regions 1999–; *Select Committees (Current):* Member: Health 1997– *(Former):* Member: Procedure 1998–99. *Party Groups:* North Wiltshire Conservative Association: Treasurer 1982–84, Deputy Chairman 1983–84, Chairman 1984–86. *Other:* Member, North Wiltshire Enterprise Agency 1986–90. *Trust:* Member, Calne Development Project Trust 1986–97. *Special Interests:* Economic Policy, Constitution, Local Government. *Countries of Interest:* USA, most of English speaking world. *Recreations:* Reading, music. *Electoral Notes:* Contested Walsall North 1992. Member for Poole since May 1, 1997. *Address:* Robert Syms Esq, MP, House of Commons, London, SW1A 0AA *Tel:* 020 7219 4601. *Constituency:* Poole Conservative Association, 38 Sandbanks Road, Poole, Dorset, BH14 8BX *Tel:* 01202 739922 *Fax:* 01202 739944.

T

TAPSELL, Sir Peter H B *(Louth and Horncastle)   Con majority 6,900*

Son of late Eustace Tapsell and late Jessie Tapsell (née Hannay). Born February 1, 1930; educated Tonbridge School; Merton College, Oxford (1st Class Hons Degree Modern History, MA); (Diploma in Economics); Honorary Fellow, Merton College, Oxford 1989. Married 1st, 1963, Hon. Cecilia Hawke, daughter of 9th Baron Hawke (1 son) (marriage dissolved 1971), married 2nd, 1974, Gabrielle, daughter of late Jean Mahieu. *Armed Forces:* Commissioned, The Royal Sussex Regiment 1948–50 (Middle East); Life Member, 6th Squadron RAF. *Profession:* Stockbroker. *Career:* Conservative Research Department 1954–57; Personal Assistant to Rt Hon. Sir Anthony Eden, KG, MC, MP during 1955 General Election campaign; Member, London Stock Exchange 1957–90; Adviser to Central Banks and international companies; Partner, James Capel and Co 1960–90. *Spokesman:* Opposition Front Bench Spokesman on: Foreign and Commonwealth Affairs 1976–77, Treasury and Economic Affairs 1977–78. *International Bodies:* Member, Trilateral Commission 1979–98. *Other:* Council Member, Institute of Fiscal Studies; Vice-President, Tennyson Society. *Trust:* Deputy-Chairman, Mitsubishi Trust Oxford Foundation. *Awards:* Spectator Backbencher of the Year 1993. *Honours:* Brunei Dato 1971; Knighted 1985. *Special Interests:* Foreign Affairs, Economics and Finance. *Recreations:* Overseas travel, walking, reading. *Electoral Notes:* Contested Wednesbury, By-election February 1957. Member for Nottingham West 1959–64, for Horncastle 1966–83, for Lindsey East 1983–97, and for Louth and Horncastle since May 1, 1997. *Clubs:* Athenaeum, Carlton, Hurlingham. *Address:* Sir Peter Tapsell, MP, House of Commons, London, SW1A 0AA *Tel:* 020 7219 4409 *Tel (Constituency):* 01507 603713 *Fax (Constituency):* 01507 602154.

TAYLOR, The Rt Hon. Ann *(Dewsbury)   Lab majority 8,323*

Daughter of late John Walker and Doreen Bowling. Born July 2, 1947; educated Bolton School; Bradford and Sheffield Universities; Hon. Fellow, Birkbeck College, University of London; Hon. D, University of Bradford. Married October 28, 1966, David Taylor (1 son 1 daughter). *Trades Union:* Member: Association of University Teachers GMB. *Career:* Part-time Tutor, Open University; Monitoring Officer, Housing Corporation 1985–87. *Councils, Public Bodies:* Holmfirth UDC 1972–74. *Political Career:* PPS: to Secretary of State for Education and Science 1975–76, to Secretary of State for Defence 1976–77; Shadow Secretary of State for Education 1992–94; Shadow Chancellor of the Duchy of Lancaster 1994–95; Shadow Leader of the House 1994–97; President of the Council and Leader of the House of Commons 1997–98. *Whip:* Government Whip 1977–79; Parliamentary Secretary, HM Treasury (Government Chief Whip) 1998–. *Spokesman:* Opposition Front Bench Spokesman on: Education 1979–81, Housing 1981–83, Home Office 1987–88, Environment 1988–92; Citizen's Charter 1994–95. *Select Committees (Current):* Member: Parliamentary Privilege (Joint Committee) 1997– *(Former):* Member: Standards and Privileges 1995–97; Chairman: Modernisation of the House of Commons 1997–98. *Miscellaneous:* Member: House of Commons Commission 1994–98, Public Accounts Commission 1997–98. *Honours:* PC 1997. *Publications: Choosing Our Future – Practical Politics of the Environment,* 1992. *Special Interests:* Education, Housing, Health, Home Office. *Electoral Notes:* Contested Bolton West February 1974. Member for Bolton West October 1974–83, contested Bolton North East 1983. Member for Dewsbury since June 1987. *Address:* The Rt Hon. Ann Taylor, MP, House of Commons, London, SW1A 0AA *Tel:* 020 7219 3000. *Constituency:* Dewsbury Business and Media Centre, Wellington Road, Dewsbury, West Yorkshire, WF12 1HF *Tel:* 01924 324999 *Fax:* 01924 324998.

TAYLOR, Dari (Daria Jean) *(Stockton South)   Lab majority 11,585*

Daughter of late Daniel Jones, MP for Burnley 1959–83, and late Phyllis Jones. Born December 13, 1944; educated Ynyshir Girls' School; Burnley Municipal College; Nottingham University (BA Hons); Durham University (MA). Married July 18, 1970, David E Taylor (1 daughter). *Trades Union:* Regional/Local Representative NATFHE; Member, General Municipal and Boilermakers (GMB); Trade Union Support and Information Unit. *Profession:* Lecturer. *Career:* Assistant Lecturer, Basford College of Further Education 1970; Lecturer, Westbridgeford College of Further Education; Lecturer (P.T.), North Tyneside College of Further Education 1986; General Municipal and Boilermakers: Research Support 1990, Regional Education Officer, Northern Region 1993. *Councils, Public Bodies:* Elected Member, Sunderland Metropolitan Council 1986–97. *Select Committees (Former):* Member: Defence 1997–99. *Party Groups:* Vice-Chairperson, Labour Women's Committee; Leadership Campaign Team. *Other:* Member, Domestic Violence Multi-Agency; Supporter: NSPCC, NSPCA, Children's Society. *Special Interests:* Economic Policy, Industry, Education, Housing. *Countries of Interest:* Europe, Africa, USA. *Recreations:* Choral singing, walking, travelling. *Electoral Notes:* Member for Stockton South since May 1, 1997. *Address:* Dari Taylor, MP, House of Commons, London, SW1A 0AA *Tel:* 020 7219 4608. *Constituency:* The Old Town Hall, Mandale Road, Thornaby on Tees, TS17 6AW *Tel:* 01642 604546 *Fax:* 01642 608395.

TAYLOR, David Leslie *(North West Leicestershire)   Lab majority 13,219*

Son of late Leslie Taylor, civil servant, and Eileen Mary Taylor, postal worker. Born August 22, 1946; educated Ashby-de-la-Zouch Boys Grammar School; Leicester Polytechnic; Lanchester Polytechnic (Chartered Public Finance Accountant); Open University (BA Maths and Computing);. Married September 13, 1969, Pamela, daughter of Sidney and Iris Caunt (4 daughters). *Trades Union:* Department Steward and Auditer, NALGO (now UNISON). *Profession:* Computer Manager/Accountant. *Career:* Accountant and Computer Manager, Leicestershire County Council 1977–. *Councils, Public Bodies:* Councillor, North West Leicestershire District Council 1981–87, 1992–95; Councillor, Heather Parish Council 1987– (Chairman); JP, Ashby-de-la-Zouch.

Select Committees (Current): Sub-Committee Staff: Environment Sub-Committee –. *Party Groups:* Joined Labour Party 1970; Member, Labour Campaign for Electoral Reform. *Other:* Member: CPRE, Greenpeace; Chair, North West Leicestershire Safer Communities Forum; Church Warden, St John The Baptist, Heather. *Miscellaneous:* Labour Party Conference, Environment Debate 1991; Appearances on regional TV news and BBC Radio Leicester news and phone-in programmes. *Sportsclubs:* President, Heather Sparkenhole Cricket Club. Member, Chartered Institute of Public Finance and Accountancy (Prize Winner in Accountancy Final Exams). *Special Interests:* Housing, Low Pay, Rural Affairs, Environment, Safer Communities (Crime), Security, CCTV. *Countries of Interest:* France. *Recreations:* Running, Cycling. *Electoral Notes:* Contested North West Leicestershire 1992. Member for North West Leicestershire since May 1, 1997. *Clubs:* Ibstock Working Mens; Coalville Labour. *Address:* David Taylor Esq, MP, House of Commons, London, SW1A 0AA *Tel:* 020 7219 4567. *Constituency:* Labour Office, 15 Hotel Street, Coalville, Leicestershire, LE67 3EQ *Tel:* 01530 814372 *Fax:* 01530 813833 *E-mail:* taylordl@parliament.uk.

TAYLOR, Ian Colin, MBE *(Esher and Walton)   Con majority 14,528*

Son of late Horace Stanley Taylor and late Beryl Harper. Born April 18, 1945; educated Whitley Abbey School, Coventry; University of Keele (BA Hons 1967); LSE (Research Scholar). Married 1974, Hon. Carole Alport, daughter of late Rt Hon. Lord Alport, TD, DL (2 sons). *Career:* Director, Mathercourt Securities Ltd 1980–91; Corporate Finance Consultant. *Political Career:* PPS to Rt Hon. William Waldegrave, MP, as: Minister of State, Foreign and Commonwealth Office 1988–90, as Secretary of State for Health 1990–92, as Chancellor of the Duchy of Lancaster, as Minister for Public Services and Science 1992–94; Parliamentary Under Secretary of State, Department of Trade and Industry (Minister for Science and Technology) 1994–97. *Spokesman:* Opposition Spokesman on Northern Ireland June-November 1997. *Select Committees (Current):* Member: Science and Technology 1998– *(Former):* Member: Foreign Affairs 1987–89. *Party Groups:* National Chairman, Federation of Conservative Students 1968–69; Chairman, European Union of Christian Democratic and Conservative Students 1969–70; Member, Conservative National Union Executive and other national committees 1966–75, 1990–95; National Chairman, Conservative Group for Europe 1985–88; Vice-Chairman, Association of Conservative Clubs 1988–92; Chairman, Conservative Foreign and Commonwealth Council 1990–95. *Other:* Chairman, Commonwealth Youth Exchange Council 1980–84, Vice-President 1984–; Patron, UK Centre for European Education 1991–94; Governor, Westminster Foundation for Democracy 1992–94; Member, Royal Society for International Affairs; Governor, Research into Ageing; Council Member, Anglo-German Foundation. *Trust:* Trustee, Painshill Park Trust 1998–. *Miscellaneous:* Member, Finance Bill Standing Committees 1987–94; Board Member, Parliamentary Office of Science and Technology (POST) 1997–; Council Member, Parliamentary Information Technology Committee; Director, EURIM (European Informatics Market) 1999–. Worshipful Company of Information Technologists 1998–. *Honours:* MBE 1974. Associate, Institute of Investment Management and Research 1972–. *Publications: Fair Shares for all the Workers,* 1988; *Releasing the Community Spirit – The Active Citizen,* 1990; *A Community of Employee Shareholders,* 1992; *The Positive Europe,* 1993; *Avoiding the Protectionist Trap,* 1995; *Net-Working,* 1996; *Conservative Tradition in Europe,* 1996; *Science, Government and Society,* 1998. *Countries of Interest:* Former Soviet Union, France, Germany, Middle East, Scandinavia, USA. *Recreations:* Country walks, shooting, cigars. *Electoral Notes:* Contested Coventry South East in 1974. Member for Esher 1987–97, and for Esher and Walton since May 1, 1997. *Clubs:* Carlton, Molesey Working Men's, Walton Conservative. *Address:* Ian Taylor Esq, MBE, MP, House of Commons, London, SW1A 0AA *Tel:* 020 7219 5221 *Fax:* 020 7219 5492. *Constituency:* 74A Church Street, Weybridge, Surrey, KT13 8DL *Tel:* 01932 843314 *Fax:* 01932 854246 *E-mail:* taylori@parliament.uk *Website:* http://www.political.co.uk/iantaylor.

Dod *on* Disk

The Vacher Dod Parliamentary Database – configured for PC or Network

For further details please telephone the Westminster Office

020 7828 7256

TAYLOR, The Rt Hon. John David *(Strangford)   UUP majority 5,852*

Son of late George David Taylor, architect, and late Georgina Taylor (née Baird). Born December 24, 1937; educated Royal School, Armagh; Queen's University, Belfast (BSc). Married December 30, 1970, Mary Frances, daughter of late Leslie Todd (1 son 5 daughters). *Career:* Company director; Chairman, Alpha Newspaper Group. *Councils, Public Bodies:* Leader, Ulster Unionists in Castlereagh Borough Council 1989–94. *Political Career:* MP (South Tyrone) Stormont 1965–73; Parliamentary Secretary, Ministry of Home Affairs, Northern Ireland 1969–70; Minister of State, Home Affairs 1970–72; Member: for Fermanagh and South Tyrone, Northern Ireland Assembly 1973–75, for North Down, Northern Ireland Constitutional Convention 1976–77, For North Down, Northern Ireland Assembly 1982–86; MEP (Northern Ireland) 1979–89; Northern Ireland Forum 1996–98; New Northern Ireland Assembly 1998–. *Spokesman:* Former Spokesman for Foreign and Commonwealth; Spokesman for: Trade and Industry 1992–97, Foreign and Commonwealth Affairs 1997–. *Select Committees (Former):* Member: Northern Ireland Affairs 1994–97. *Party Groups:* Chairman: Queen's University Conservative and Unionist Association 1959–60, Ulster Young Unionist Council 1961–62; Hon. Secretary, Ulster Unionist Party 1994–96, Deputy Leader 1995–. *International Bodies:* Member for Northern Ireland, European Parliament 1979–89; Member: Council of Europe, Western European Union. *Other:* Chairman, Gosford Housing Association; Member, Board of Charles Sheils Charity Homes. *Sportsclubs:* Ards Football Club. *Honours:* PC (Northern Ireland) 1970. *Fellowships, etc:* AMICEI; AMInstHE. *Publications: Ulster – The Economic Facts. Special Interests:* Irish Politics, European Union, Regional Policy, Agriculture. *Countries of Interest:* Asia, Cyprus, Gibraltar, Ireland, Turkey, Taiwan. *Recreations:* Antiques, Irish Art, Travelling, Horticulture. *Electoral Notes:* Member for Strangford since June 1983. *Clubs:* Farmers (London), County (Armagh). *Address:* The Rt Hon. John David Taylor, MP, House of Commons, London, SW1A 0AA *Tel:* 020 7219 4536 *Fax:* 020 7219 4536. *Constituency:* 6 William Street, Newtownards, BT23 4AE *Tel:* 028 9181 4123 *Fax:* 028 9181 4123.

TAYLOR, John Mark *(Solihull)   Con majority 11,397*

Son of late Wilfred and Eileen Martha Taylor. Born August 19, 1941; educated Bromsgrove School; College of Law. *Profession:* Solicitor. *Career:* Senior Partner, John Taylor & Co., Solicitors. *Councils, Public Bodies:* Councillor, Solihull County Borough Council 1971–74; West Midlands County Council: Councillor 1973–86, Leader of Opposition 1975–77, Leader of Council 1977–79; Member, West Midland Economic Planning Council 1977–79. *Political Career:* PPS to Rt Hon. Kenneth Clarke, QC, MP: as Chancellor of the Duchy of Lancaster, at the Department of Trade and Industry 1987–88; Parliamentary Secretary, Lord Chancellor's Department 1992–95; Parliamentary Under-Secretary of State, Department of Trade and Industry 1995–97. *Whip:* Assistant Government Whip 1988–89; Lord Commissioner of the Treasury and Government Whip 1989–90; Vice-Chamberlain of HM Household (Government Whip) 1990–92; An Opposition Whip: (Trade and Industry, Foreign Affairs, International Development: Western) 1997–98, (Defence, Legal Affairs, The Lord Chancellor's Department, The Duchy of Lancaster) 1997–99, (Foreign Office, Legal Affairs, The Lord Chancellor's Department) 1999. *Spokesman:* An Opposition Front Bench Spokesman on Northern Ireland 1999–. *Party Groups:* Member, Conservative Friends of Israel. *International Bodies:* European Parliament 1979–84: Group Budget Spokesman 1979–81, Group Deputy Chairman 1981–82, Council of Europe and WEU 1997–. *Other:* Chairman, Solihull Business Enterprise; President, Shirley Citizens' Advice Bureau; President, Oakenshaw Association; Founder Chairman, Solihull Institute for Medical Training and Research; Life Member, English Heritage; Shoreline (Life) Member, RNLI. *Trust:* Life Member, National Trust. *Miscellaneous:* Association of Metropolitan Authorities: Deputy Chairman 1978–79, Vice-President 1979–. *Sportsclubs:* Bromsgrove Martlets Cricket Club, Hampton-in-Arden Cricket Club, Olton Cricket Club, Olton Golf Club, Warwickshire County Cricket Club. *Special Interests:* Environment, European Union, Care of Ancient Monuments, Legal Affairs, Trade and Industry. *Countries of Interest:* USA. *Recreations:* Fellowship, cricket, golf, reading. *Electoral Notes:* Contested Dudley East, February and October 1974. MEP, Midlands East 1979–84. Member for Solihull since June 1983. *Clubs:* Carlton, MCC. *Address:* John M Taylor Esq, MP, House of Commons, London, SW1A 0AA *Tel:* 020 7219 4146 *Fax:* 020 7219 1243. *Constituency:* Northampton House, Poplar Road, Solihull, West Midlands, B91 3AW *Tel:* 0121–704 3071 *Fax:* 0121–705 6388.

TAYLOR, Matthew Owen John *(Truro and St Austell)   LD majority 12,501*

Son of Ken and Jill Taylor. Born January 3, 1963; educated Treliske School, Truro; University College School, London; Lady Margaret Hall, Oxford. *Career:* President, Oxford University Student Union 1985–86; Economic researcher to David Penhaligan, MP 1986. *Spokesman:* Liberal Spokesman for Energy 1987–88; Liberal Democrat Spokesman for: England (Local Government, Housing and Transport) 1988–89, Trade and Industry 1989–90, Education 1990–92, Citizen's Charter 1992–94; Principal Spokesman for: Environment 1994–97, the Environment and Transport 1997–99, Economy 1999–. *Select Committees (Former):* Member: Broadcasting 1992–94, Environment 1995–97, Environmental Audit 1997. *Party Groups:* Chairman, Liberal Democrat Campaigns and Communications 1989–95. *Electoral Notes:* Elected Member for Truro at By-election March 12, 1987–97, and for Truro and St Austell since May 1, 1997. *Address:* Matthew Taylor Esq, MP, House of Commons, London, SW1A 0AA *Tel:* 020 7219 6686.

TAYLOR, Sir Teddy (Edward Macmillan) *(Rochford and Southend East)   Con majority 4,225*

Son of late Edward Taylor. Born April 18, 1937; educated The High School of Glasgow; Glasgow University (MA Hons). Married December 12, 1970, Sheila Duncan (2 sons 1 daughter). *Career:* Commercial Editorial Staff, *Glasgow Herald* October 1958-April 1959; Industrial Relations Officer, Clyde Shipbuilders' Association 1959–1964. *Councils, Public Bodies:* Former Councillor, Glasgow Town Council representing Cathcart Ward. *Political Career:* Parliamentary Under-Secretary of State, Scottish Office 1970–71 (resigned over Government decision to join EC) and 1974. *Spokesman:* Shadow Spokesman on: Trade 1977, Scottish Affairs 1977–79. *Select Committees (Current):* Member: Treasury 1997–, Treasury Sub-Committee 1998–. *Honours:* Knighted 1991. *Special Interests:* Temperance Movement, Common Market, Home Affairs, Environment. *Countries of Interest:* Libya, Pakistan. *Recreations:* Golf, chess, history. *Electoral Notes:* Contested Glasgow Springburn 1959. Member for Glasgow Cathcart 1964–79, for Southend East from March 15, 1980 By-election–1997, and for Rochford and Southend East since May 1, 1997. *Address:* Sir Teddy Taylor, MP, House of Commons, London, SW1A 0AA *Tel:* 020 7219 3000.

TEMPLE-MORRIS, Peter *(Leominster)   Con majority 8,835**

Son of late His Hon. Sir Owen Temple-Morris, QC. Born February 12, 1938; educated Malvern; St. Catharine's College, Cambridge (MA). Married July 25, 1964, Tahere, daughter of His Excellency Senator Khozeime Alam, of Tehran (2 sons 2 daughters). *Trades Union:* Member, GMB. *Profession:* Former barrister; solicitor. *Career:* Barrister, Inner Temple 1962; Solicitor 1989–. *Political Career:* PPS to Minister of Transport, Rt Hon. Norman Fowler, MP 1979; *Select Committees (Former):* Member: Consolidation Bills (Joint Committee) 1991–92. *Party Groups:* Chairman: Cambridge University Conservative Association 1961, Bow Group Standing Committee on Home Affairs 1975–80, Society of Conservative Lawyers, Executive Committee 1995–97. *International Bodies:* Executive British Branch of Inter-Parliamentary Union: Member 1977–97, Chairman 1982–85, Delegate on their fact finding mission on Namibia 1977; Member, Parliamentary Delegation to United Nations 1980, 1984; Hon. Vice-President, United Nations Association 1987–; Founding Co-Chairman, British-Irish Parliamentary Body 1990–97, Member, 1997–; Vice-Chairman, GB-Russia and Eastern Europe Centre 1993–98; Member, Executive, Commonwealth Parliamentary Association 1994–98. *Other:* Member, Cambridge Afro-Asian Expedition 1961; Chairman, Afghanistan Support Committee 1981–82; Member, Academic Council, Wilton Park (FCO) 1990–97. *Trust:* Fellow, Industry and Parliament Trust; Trustee, Eveson Trust. *Awards:* Honorary Citizen: New Orleans, Havana, Cuba; Hon. Member, National Party of Australia, Queensland. *Miscellaneous:* Iran Society Council: Member 1968–80, President 1995–; Chevalier du Tastevin (Chat. de Vougeot); Chairman, Lords and Commons Solicitors Group 1992–. Liveryman, Barbers Companies. *Publications: Motoring Justice*, 1979, plus various articles on foreign affairs and Ireland. *Special Interests:* Foreign Affairs, Irish Affairs, European Union, Constitutional and Legal Affairs. *Countries of Interest:* Europe, Hong Kong, Iran,

Ireland, Middle East, Russia, USA, South Africa. *Recreations:* Wine and food, travel, family relaxation. *Electoral Notes:* Contested Newport 1964 and 1966. Contested Norwood Lambeth 1970. *Conservative Member for Leominster February 1974-October 1997, Independent Member October 1997-June 1998, Labour Member since October 1998. *Clubs:* Cardiff and County (Cardiff). *Address:* Peter Temple-Morris Esq, MP, House of Commons, London, SW1A 0AA *Tel:* 020 7219 4181 *Fax:* 020 7219 3801.

THOMAS, Gareth *(Clwyd West) Lab majority 1,848*

Son of late W. Thomas, toolmaker, and M. H. Thomas. Born September 25, 1954; educated Rock Ferry High School, Birkenhead; University College of Wales, Aberystwyth (LLB Hons); Council of Legal Education, London. Married December 5, 1987, Sioned Jones (1 son 1 daughter). *Trades Union:* Member, MSF. *Profession:* Barrister. *Career:* Insurance industry in UK and overseas; Formerly Loss Adjuster: Toplis and Harding Guardian Royal Exchange; Barrister 1986–: Oriel Chambers, Liverpool, Grays Inn. *Councils, Public Bodies:* Councillor, Flintshire County Council 1995–97. *Select Committees (Current):* Member: Welsh Affairs 1997–, Social Security 1999–. *Party Groups:* Member: Labour Party, Society of Labour Lawyers, SERA, Fabian Society, Campaign for Electoral Reform. *Other:* Member: Amnesty International, Oxfam, Local Credit Union, Country Landowners Association Legal and Parliamentary Committee; School Governor, Ysgol Maes Garmon. *Trust:* Member, National Trust. *Miscellaneous:* North Wales Campaign Co-ordinator for Labour Party in 1997 Welsh Referendum. ACII. *Special Interests:* Constitutional Reform, Pensions, Social Security, Criminal Justice, Police, Trade and Industry, Rural Development, Human Rights. *Countries of Interest:* West Indies, South America. *Recreations:* Rugby, walking, family, theatre. *Electoral Notes:* Member for Clwyd West since May 1, 1997. *Address:* Gareth Thomas Esq, MP (Clwyd West), House of Commons, London, SW1A 0AA *Tel:* 020 7219 3516 *Fax:* 020 7219 1263. *Constituency:* 23a Abergele Road, Colwyn Bay, LL29 7RS *Tel:* 01492 531154 *Fax:* 01492 535731.

THOMAS, Gareth Richard *(Harrow West) Lab majority 1,240*

Born July 15, 1967; educated Hatch End High School; Lowlands College; University College of Wales, Aberystwyth; King's College, London (BSc Hons Economics, MA); University of Greenwich (PGCE). *Trades Union:* Member, AEEU. *Profession:* Teacher. *Councils, Public Bodies:* Councillor, Harrow 1990–98, Labour Group Whip 1997–98. *Political Career:* PPS to Charles Clarke, MP, as Minister of State, Home Office 1999–. *Select Committees (Former):* Member: Environmental Audit 1997–99. *Party Groups:* Member: Co-operative Party, Fabian Society, SERA. *Miscellaneous:* Vice-Chair, Association of Local Government Social Services Committee. *Special Interests:* Health, Social Services, Environment, Renewable Energy. *Countries of Interest:* Europe. *Recreations:* Canoeing, running, theatre. *Electoral Notes:* Member for Harrow West since May 1, 1997. *Clubs:* United Services Club, Pinner. *Address:* Gareth R. Thomas Esq, MP (Harrow West), House of Commons, London, SW1A 0AA *Tel:* 020 7219 6436. *Constituency:* 132 Blenheim Road, West Harrow, Middlesex, HA2 7AA *Tel:* 020 8861 1300.

THOMPSON, William John *(West Tyrone) UUP majority 1,161*

Born October 26, 1939; educated Omagh Academy Grammar School. Married July 26, 1962, Violet Joyce Armstrong (1 son 2 daughters). *Profession:* Company Director. *Career:* Tyrone County Council 1957–66; Radio and TV Retailer, 1966–. *Councils, Public Bodies:* Councillor, Omagh District Council 1981–93. *Political Career:* Member: NI Assembly 1973–74, NI Convention 1975–76, NI Assembly 1982–84. *Spokesman:* Spokesman for Agriculture, Fisheries and Local Government 1997–. *Miscellaneous:* Member, European Standing Committee A 1998–. *Special Interests:* Political Biography. *Recreations:* Golf. *Electoral Notes:* Member for West Tyrone since May 1, 1997. *Address:* William Thompson Esq, MP, House of Commons, London, SW1A 0AA *Tel:* 020 7219 3553. *Constituency:* Donaghanie Post Office, 156 Donaghanie Road, Beragh, Co Tyrone, Northern Ireland, BT79 0XE *Tel:* 028 8224 5568 *Fax:* 028 8224 5742 *E-mail:* 100552.1524@compuserve.com.

TIMMS, Stephen *(East Ham)*   *Lab majority 19,358*

Son of late Ronald James Timms, engineer, and of Margaret Joyce Timms, retired school teacher. Born July 29, 1955; educated Farnborough Grammar School, Hampshire; Emmanuel College, Cambridge (MA Mathematics, MPhil Operational Research). Married July 26, 1986, Hui-Leng Lim. *Trades Union:* Member, MSF. *Career:* Computer and telecommunications industry; Logica Ltd 1978–86; Ovum Ltd 1986–94. *Councils, Public Bodies:* Little Ilford Ward, London Borough of Newham: Councillor 1984–97, Leader of the Council 1990–94, Formerly Chair, Economic Development Committee, Chair, Planning Committee 1987–90; Board Member, East London Partnership 1990–; Stratford Development Partnership 1992–94. *Political Career:* PPS to Rt Hon. Andrew Smith, MP, as Minister of State, Department for Education and Employment (Minister for Employment, Welfare to Work and Equal Opportunities) 1997–98; Joint PPS to Rt Hon. Marjorie Mowlam, as Secretary of State for Northern Ireland 1998; Parliamentary Under-Secretary of State, Department of Social Security 1998–99; Minister of State 1999; Financial Secretary, HM Treasury 1999–. *Select Committees (Current):* Member: Public Accounts 1999– *(Former):* Member: Treasury 1996–97. *Party Groups:* Joint Vice-Chair, Christian Socialist Movement. *Special Interests:* Urban Regeneration, Telecommunications, Economic Policy, Employment. *Electoral Notes:* Member for Newham North East from June 9, 1994 By-election–1997, and for East Ham since May 1, 1997. *Address:* Stephen Timms Esq, MP, House of Commons, London, SW1A 0AA *Tel:* 020 7219 3000 *Fax:* 020 7219 2949 *E-mail:* 100746.2456@compuserve.com.

TIPPING, Paddy *(Sherwood)*   *Lab majority 16,812*

Son of late Ernest Tipping, newsagent, and late Margaret Tipping, clerk. Born October 24, 1949; educated Hipperholme Grammar School; Nottingham University (BA 1972, MA 1978). Married January 8, 1970, Irene Margaret, daughter of Bert and Ida Quinn (2 daughters). *Trades Union:* Member, UNISON. *Career:* Social worker, Nottingham and Nottinghamshire 1972–79; Project Leader, Church of England Children's Society, Nottingham 1979–83. *Councils, Public Bodies:* Councillor, Nottinghamshire County Council 1981–93; Director: Nottinghamshire Co-operative Development Agency 1983–93, Nottingham Development Enterprise 1987–93. *Political Career:* PPS to Rt Hon. Jack Straw, MP, as Home Secretary 1997–99; Parliamentary Secretary, Privy Council Office 1999–. *Select Committees (Former):* Member: Parliamentary Commissioner for Administration 1996–97. *Party Groups:* Member, The Co-operative Party; Chair: Central Region Group of Labour MPs 1997–, East Midlands Group of Labour MPs until 1999. *Other:* Vice-President, The Ramblers' Association. *Trust:* Member: Industry and Parliament Trust, Armed Forces Parliamentary Trust. *Special Interests:* Local Government, Energy, Education, Police, Workers' Co-operatives. *Countries of Interest:* Former Soviet Union. *Recreations:* Family, gardening, running. *Electoral Notes:* Contested Rushcliffe in 1987 General Election. Member for Sherwood since April 9, 1992. *Clubs:* Clipstone Miners' Welfare. *Address:* Paddy Tipping Esq, MP, House of Commons, London, SW1A 0AA *Tel:* 020 7219 5044 *Fax:* 020 7219 3641. *Constituency:* Sherwood Parliamentary Office, 1st Floor, Council Offices, Watnall Road, Hucknall, Nottinghamshire, NG15 7LA *Tel:* 0115–964 0314 *Fax:* 0115–968 1639.

TODD, Mark Wainwright *(South Derbyshire)*   *Lab majority 13,967*

Son of Matthew and Viv Todd. Born December 29, 1954; educated Sherborne School; Emmanuel College, Cambridge. Married February 3, 1979, Sarah Margaret, daughter of late Peter and Margaret Dawson (1 son). *Trades Union:* ASTMS (now MSF), union chairman at employers. *Profession:* Publisher. *Career:* Longman Group, latterly Addison Wesley Longman 1977–96: Managing Director: Longman Industry and Public Service Management 1988–92, Longman Carter Mill 1990–92, Director: Information Technology 1992–94, Operations 1994–96. *Councils, Public Bodies:* Cambridge City Council 1980–92: Deputy Leader 1982–87, Leader of Council 1987–90. *Select Committees (Current):* Member: Agriculture 1997–.

Other: Member: Greenpeace, Royal Society of Arts and Manufacture. *Miscellaneous:* Director, Cambridge and District Co-operative Society 1986–89. FRSA. *Special Interests:* Business, Economics, Local Government, Environment, Agriculture. *Countries of Interest:* Europe, Third World. *Recreations:* Reading, cinema. *Electoral Notes:* Member for South Derbyshire since May 1, 1997. *Address:* Mark Todd Esq, MP, House of Commons, London, SW1A 0AA *Tel:* 020 7219 3549 *Fax:* 020 7219 2495. *Constituency:* 37 Market Street, Church Gresley, Swadlincote, Derbyshire, DE11 9PR *Tel:* 01283 551573 *Fax:* 01283 551573 *E-mail:* mark.todd@geo2.poptel.org.uk.

TONGE, Dr Jennifer Louise *(Richmond Park)* *LD majority 2,951*

Daughter of late Sidney Smith, school teacher, and late Violet Smith, school teacher. Born February 19, 1941; educated Dudley Girls' High School; University College, London; University College Hospital, London (MB, BS); College of Obstetrics and Gynaecology (MFFP). Married May 23, 1964, Keith Tonge (2 sons 1 daughter). *Trades Union:* SW Thames Representative, BMA Public and Community Health Committee. *Profession:* Medical Practitioner (Medical Gynaecology). *Career:* General Practice/Family Planning 1968–78; Senior Medical Officer, Women's Services (Ealing) 1980–85; Manager, Community Health Services (Ealing) 1992–96. *Councils, Public Bodies:* Councillor, London Borough of Richmond-on-Thames 1981–90, Chair, Social Services 1981–86. *Spokesman:* A Spokeswoman for: Foreign Affairs and Defence and Europe (International Development) 1997–99, Foreign Affairs and Defence (International Development) 1999–. *Select Committees (Former):* Member: International Development 1997–99. *Party Groups:* Chair, Richmond and Barnes Liberal Party 1978–80. *International Bodies:* Member, Parliamentary Assembly Organisation for Security and Co-operation in Europe. *Other:* Chair, Governors of Waldegrave School 1981–86; Member: RSPB, Amnesty International, Action For South Africa, Karuna Trust, Project Hope (UK). *Trust:* Trustee, Off the Record, Richmond. *Awards:* School – James Smellie Gold Medal. *Miscellaneous:* Member, Standing Committee on Asian Development Bank 1997–. MFFP; MFCH. *Special Interests:* Health, Environment, Social Services, International Development. *Countries of Interest:* India, Pakistan, Tibet, Indonesia. *Recreations:* Birdwatching. *Electoral Notes:* Contested Richmond and Barnes General Election 1992. Member for Richmond Park since May 1, 1997. *Address:* Dr Jennifer Tonge, MP, House of Commons, London, SW1A 0AA *Tel:* 020 7219 4596 *Fax:* 020 7219 4596. *Constituency:* Aaron House, 6 Bardolph Road, Richmond, Surrey, TW9 2LS *Tel:* 020 8332 7919 *Fax:* 020 8332 7919 *E-mail:* tonge@cix.compulink.co.uk.

TOUHIG, Don (James Donnelly) *(Islwyn)* *Lab/Co-op majority 23,931*

Son of late Michael and Catherine Touhig. Born December 5, 1947; educated St Francis School, Abersychan; Mid Gwent College. Married September 21, 1968, Jennifer Hughes (2 sons 2 daughters). *Trades Union:* Member, TGWU. *Profession:* Journalist. *Career:* Journalist 1968–76; Editor, Free Press of Monmouthshire 1976–90; General Manager and Editor in Chief, Free Press Group of Newspapers 1988–92; General Manager (Business Development), Bailey Group 1992–93, Bailey Print 1993–95. *Councils, Public Bodies:* County Councillor, Gwent 1973–; Former Chairman, Finance Committee. *Political Career:* Public Interest Disclosure (Private Member's Bill) 1995; PPS to Rt Hon. Gordon Brown, MP, as Chancellor of the Exchequer 1997–99. *Whip:* Assistant Government Whip 1999–. *Select Committees (Former):* Member: Welsh Affairs 1996–97. *Party Groups:* Hon. Secretary, Welsh Regional Group of Labour MPs 1995–99; Member, Labour Leadership Campaign Team (responsible for Devolution in Wales) 1996–97; Member, Co-Operative Party; Chair, Co-operative Parliamentary Group 1999. *Other:* Past President, South Wales Newspaper Society; Member: MENSA, MENCAP. Amnesty International, St David's Foundation, Credit Union; President: Home Start, Islwyn Drug and Alcohol Project, National Old Age Pensioners Association of Wales, Caerphilly County Borough Access Group. *Trust:* Member, Medical Council on Alcoholism. *Miscellaneous:* Member, European Standing Committee B 1995–96. *Honours:* Papal Knight of the Order of St Sylvester. *Special Interests:* Treasury, Employment, Health, Education, Local Government. *Recreations:* Reading, cooking for family and friends, music, walking. *Electoral Notes:* Contested Richmond and Barnes 1992 General Election. Member for Islwyn since February 16, 1995 By-election. *Address:* Don Touhig Esq, MP, House of Commons, London, SW1A 0AA *Tel:* 020 7219 6435 *Fax:* 020 7219 2070. *Constituency:* The Institute, Crumlin, Gwent *Tel:* 01495 244699 *Fax:* 01495 245109.

TOWNEND, John E *(Yorkshire East)   Con majority 3,337*

Son of late Charles Townend and Dorothy Townend. Born June 12, 1934; educated Hymers College, Hull; Plender Prize in CA Finals. Married May 4, 1963, Jennifer, daughter of G. Lawson (2 sons 2 daughters). *Armed Forces:* Served RAF 1957–59, Commissioned Pilot Officer. *Profession:* Chartered Accountant. *Career:* Articled clerk in chartered accountancy 1951–57 (in finals received Plender Prize for top paper); Joined family business as Company Secretary and Finance Director 1959, Managing Director 1961–79, now Chairman; Chairman, Yorkshire and Humberside Wine and Spirit Merchants' Association 1975–76; Underwriter, Lloyd's 1977. *Councils, Public Bodies:* Humberside County Council: Leader, Conservative Group 1973–77, Councillor 1973–79, Leader of the Council 1977–79, Chairman: Policy Committee 1977–79, Humber Bridge Board. *Political Career:* Former PPS to Sir Hugh Rossi, MP, as Minister of Pensions and Disabled. *Select Committees (Former):* Member: Treasury and Civil Service 1983–92. *Party Groups:* Member: Conservative National Advisory Committee on Local Government, Chairman, 92 Group, 1996–97, 1997–. *International Bodies:* Member, Council of Europe and Western European Union 1992–; Executive Committee Member, Inter-Parliamentary Union British Group. *Trust:* Fellow, Industry and Parliament Trust. *Miscellaneous:* Member, Policy Committee of the ACC 1977–79; Member, Executive 1922 Committee 1996–97, 1997–98; Vice-Chair, British Council. Liveryman: Woolmen's Company, Distillers Company. FCA. *Special Interests:* Treasury, Tax, Small Businesses, Employment, Europe. *Countries of Interest:* France, South Africa, USA, Southern Africa. *Recreations:* Swimming, tennis. *Electoral Notes:* Contested Kingston-upon-Hull North 1970. Member for Bridlington 1979–97, and for Yorkshire East since May 1, 1997. *Clubs:* Carlton. *Address:* John Townend Esq, MP, House of Commons, London, SW1A 0AA *Tel:* 020 7219 3000 *Fax:* 020 7219 2723. *Constituency:* Conservative Club, Tennyson Avenue, Bridlington, Humberside *Tel:* 01262 674072 *Fax:* 01262 401231.

TREDINNICK, David *(Bosworth)   Con majority 1,027*

Son of Stephen Victor Tredinnick and Evelyn Mabel, née Wates. Born January 19, 1950; educated Eton; Mons Officer Cadet School; Graduate School of Business; Cape Town University (MBA); St John's College, Oxford (MLitt). Married July 7, 1983, Rebecca, daughter of Mr and Mrs Roland Shott (1 son 1 daughter). *Armed Forces:* 2nd Lieutenant Grenadier Guards 1968–71. *Career:* Trainee, E. B. Savory Milln & Co. (Stockbrokers) 1972–73; Account Executive, Quadrant Int. 1974; Salesman, Kalle Infotech UK 1976; Sales Manager, Word Right Word Processing 1977–78; Consultant, Baird Communications NY 1978–79; Marketing Manager, QI Europe Ltd 1979–81; Manager, Malden Mitcham Properties 1981–87. *Political Career:* PPS to Rt Hon. Sir Wyn Roberts, MP, as Minister of State, Welsh Office 1991–94. *Select Committees (Current):* Member: Liaison 1997–; Chairman: Statutory Instruments (Joint Committee) 1997–. *International Bodies:* Chairman, British Atlantic Group of Young Politicians 1989–91. *Special Interests:* Foreign Affairs, Trade and Industry, Defence, Home Affairs, Police, Public Order, Employment, Environment. *Countries of Interest:* Eastern Europe. *Recreations:* Golf, skiing, tennis, windsurfing, sailing, shooting. *Electoral Notes:* Contested Cardiff South and Penarth 1983. Member for Bosworth since June 1987. *Address:* David Tredinnick Esq, MP, House of Commons, London, SW1A 0AA *Tel:* 020 7219 3000 *Tel (Constituency):* 01455 635741 *Fax (Constituency):* 01455 612023 *E-mail:* Tredinnickd@parliament.uk.

TREND, Hon. Michael St John, CBE *(Windsor)   Con majority 9,917*

Son of late Rt Hon. Baron Trend, GCB, CVO and Patricia Charlotte Shaw. Born April 19, 1952; educated Westminster School; Oriel College, Oxford (MA Oxon). Married 1987, Jill Kershaw (1 son 2 daughters). *Career:* Journalist; Editor; Broadcaster; Former Chief Leader Writer, *The Daily Telegraph.* *Political Career:* PPS; to Minister of State, Department of Environment 1993–94, to Rt Hon. Brian Mawhinney, MP: as Minister of State, Department of Health 1992–94, as Secretary of State for Transport 1994–95. *Spokesman:* An Opposition Front Bench Spokesman for: Foreign and Commonwealth Affairs 1998–99, Social Security 1999–. *Select Committees (Former):* Member: Health 1992–93. *Party Groups:* Deputy Chairman, Conservative

Party 1995–98. *Honours:* CBE 1997. *Special Interests:* Education, Health, Defence, Foreign Affairs. *Recreations:* Hill walking, cricket, playing the organ. *Electoral Notes:* Contested North East London 1989 European Parliament Elections. Member for Windsor and Maidenhead 1992–97, and for Windsor since May 1, 1997. *Address:* Hon. Michael Trend, CBE, MP, House of Commons, London, SW1A 0AA *Tel:* 020 7219 3000. *Constituency:* 87 St Leonards Road, Windsor, Berkshire, SL4 3BZ *Tel:* 01753 678693 *Fax:* 01753 832774.

TRICKETT, Jon *(Hemsworth)* Lab majority 23,992

Son of Laurence and Rose Trickett. Born July 2, 1950; educated Roundhay School, Leeds; Hull University (BA Politics); Leeds University (MA Political Sociology). Married October 31, 1993, Sarah, daughter of Thomas and Jean Balfour (1 son 2 daughters). *Trades Union:* Member, GMB Union. *Career:* Plumber/builder 1974–86. *Councils, Public Bodies:* Leeds City Council: Councillor 1984–96, Chair: Finance Committee 1985–88, Housing Committee 1988–89, Leader of the Council 1989–96. *Political Career:* PPS to Peter Mandelson, MP: as Minister without Portfolio 1997–98, as Secretary of State for Trade and Industry July–December 1998. *Select Committees (Current):* Member: Unopposed Bills (Panel) 1997–. *Sportsclubs:* Member: British Cycling Federation, West Riding Sailing Club; Hon Life Member, Cyclists' Touring Club. *Special Interests:* Economic Policy, Finance, Industry, Sport. *Countries of Interest:* Middle East, France, USA. *Recreations:* Cycle racing, windsurfing. *Electoral Notes:* Member for Hemsworth since February 1, 1996 By-election. *Clubs:* British Cycling Federation. *Address:* Jon Trickett Esq, MP, House of Commons, London, SW1A 0AA *Tel:* 020 7219 5074 *Fax:* 020 7219 2133. *Constituency:* 18 Market Street, Hemsworth, Dorset, WF9 5LB *Tel:* 01977 722290 *Fax:* 01977 722290.

TRIMBLE, The Rt Hon. (William) David *(Upper Bann)* UUP majority 9,252

Son of late William and Ivy Trimble. Born October 15, 1944; educated Bangor Grammar School; Queen's University, Belfast (LLB). Married 1978, Daphne Orr (2 sons 2 daughters). *Career:* Queen's University, Belfast: Lecturer in Law 1968–77, Senior Lecturer 1977–90. *Political Career:* Member, South Belfast, Northern Ireland Constitutional Convention 1975–76; Elected to the Northern Ireland Forum 1996–98; Elected to the Northern Ireland Assembly 1998–; First Minister, Northern Ireland Assembly 1998–. *Spokesman:* UUP Spokesman on Constitutional Affairs. *Party Groups:* Chairman, Lagan Valley Unionist Association 1985–90; Elected Leader, Ulster Unionist Party 1995–. *Awards:* Nobel Peace Prize (jointly) 1998. *Miscellaneous:* Chairman, Ulster Society 1985–90. *Honours:* PC 1998. *Recreations:* Music, reading. *Electoral Notes:* Member for Upper Bann since May 17, 1990 By-Election. *Address:* The Rt Hon. David Trimble, MP, House of Commons, London, SW1A 0AA *Tel:* 020 7219 3000. *Constituency:* 2 Queen Street, Lurgan, BT66 8BQ *Tel:* 028 3832 8088 *Fax:* 028 3832 2343.

TRUSWELL, Paul Anthony *(Pudsey)* Lab majority 6,207

Son of John Truswell, retired foundryman, and Olive Truswell, retired cleaner. Born November 17, 1955; educated Firth Park Comprehensive School; Leeds University (BA Hons). Married Suzanne, daughter of Desmond and Elizabeth Evans (2 sons). *Trades Union:* Member: UNISON, NUJ. *Profession:* Local Government Officer. *Career:* Journalist, Yorkshire Post Newspapers 1977–88; Local Government Officer, Wakefield MDC 1988–. *Councils, Public Bodies:* Councillor, Leeds City Council 1982–97; Member: Leeds Eastern Health Authority 1982–90, Leeds Community Health Council 1990–92, Leeds Family Health Services Authority 1992–96. *Select Committees (Former):* Member: Environmental Audit 1997–99. *Party Groups:* Member, Labour Party 1977–. *Special Interests:* Health, Social Services, Environment. *Electoral Notes:* Member for Pudsey since May 1, 1997. *Clubs:* Civil Service, Hawkshill Social (Guiseley). *Address:* Paul Truswell Esq, MP, House of Commons, London, SW1A 0AA *Tel:* 020 7219 3504 *Fax:* 020 7219 2252. *Constituency:* 10A Greenside, Pudsey, West Yorkshire, LS28 8PU *Tel:* 0113–229 3553 *Fax:* 0113–229 3800.

TURNER, Dennis *(Wolverhampton South East)   Lab/Co-op majority 15,182*

Son of late Thomas Herbert and Mary Elizabeth Turner. Born August 26, 1942; educated Stonefield Secondary School, Bilston; Bilston College of Further Education. Married June 19, 1976, Patricia, daughter of Joseph Henry and Mary Narroway (1 son 1 daughter). *Trades Union:* Former Chairman, Midlands Iron and Steel Trades Confederation Conference. *Career:* Director, Springvale Co-operative, sports, social and leisure centre. *Councils, Public Bodies:* Former Director, Black Country Co-operative Development Agency; Wolverhampton Borough Councillor 1966–86; West Midlands County Council: Councillor 1973–86, Former Chairman: Wolverhampton Social Services Committee, Higher Education Committee, Economic Development Committee, Housing Committee, Theatre Committee, Deputy Leader 6 years. *Political Career:* PPS to Rt Hon. Clare Short, MP, as Secretary of State for International Development 1997–. *Whip:* Opposition Whip 1992–97; Former Whip for Health and Education; Former Whip for Defence and West Midlands Region. *Select Committees (Current):* Chairman: Catering 1997–; Member: Court of Referees 1997–, Finance and Services 1997–, Liaison 1998– *(Former):* : Education 1988–94. *Party Groups:* Member, Co-operative Party; Vice-Chairman, West Midlands Regional Group of Labour MPs 1997–; Chairman, Parliamentary Labour Party Local Government Group 1997–. *International Bodies:* Member, Executive Committee: IPU (British Branch); Commonwealth Parliamentary Association (CPA) UK Branch 1999–, Vice-Chairman. *Other:* Vice-Chairman and Governor, Bilston Community College; President: Bilston Community Association, Wolverhampton Deaf Children's Society; Vice-President, Wolverhampton MENCAP. *Trust:* Trustee-Secretary, Bradley Old People's Trust. *Special Interests:* Education, Social Services, Housing. *Countries of Interest:* South Africa, The Commonwealth, British Overseas Territories. *Recreations:* Tasting traditional ales, all card games. *Electoral Notes:* Contested Halesowen and Stourbridge February and October 1974. Member for Wolverhampton South East since June 1987. *Clubs:* New Springvale Sports and Social (Bilston). *Address:* Dennis Turner Esq, MP, House of Commons, London, SW1A 0AA *Tel:* 020 7219 4210 *Fax:* 020 7219 4981. *Constituency:* Springvale House, Millfields Road, Bilston, West Midlands, WV14 0QS *Tel:* 01902 492364.

TURNER, Dr Des (Desmond Stanley) *(Brighton Kemptown)   Lab majority 3,534*

Son of late Stanley M. M. Turner and of Elsie Turner. Born July 17, 1939; educated Luton Grammar School; Imperial College, London; University College, London; Brighton Polytechnic (BSc, MSc, PhD, PGCE); R. D. Lawrence Memorial Fellow, British Diabetic Association 1970–72. Married 2nd, September 20, 1997 Lynne Rogers (1 daughter from previous marriage). *Trades Union:* Past Member: AUT, TGWU, NUT; Member, MSF. *Profession:* Scientist. *Career:* Medical Researcher; Teacher; Partner in Independent Brewery. *Councils, Public Bodies:* Councillor: East Sussex County Council 1985–96, Brighton Borough Council 1994–96, Brighton and Hove Unitary Council 1996–98. *Select Committees (Current):* Member: Science and Technology 1997–. *Other:* Member: Age Concern, West Sussex, Sussex Aids Centre and Helpline, Shelter. *Trust:* Member, Brighton Housing Trust. *Miscellaneous:* Parliamentary Observer: Albanian Elections 1997, Bosnian Elections 1998. *Sportsclubs:* Polytechnic Fencing Club. ARCS. *Publications:* Research papers and reviews. *Special Interests:* Health, Social Services, Employment, Housing and Science Policy. *Countries of Interest:* Europe. *Recreations:* Sailing, fencing. *Electoral Notes:* Contested Mid-Sussex 1979. Member for Brighton Kemptown since May 1, 1997. *Address:* Dr Des Turner, MP, House of Commons, London, SW1A 0AA *Tel:* 020 7219 4024 *Fax:* 020 7219 5814. *Constituency:* 179 Preston Road, Brighton, BN1 6AG *Tel:* 01273 330610 *Fax:* 01273 500966.

TURNER, Dr George *(North West Norfolk)   Lab majority 1,339*

Son of late George Turner and late Jane Turner. Born August 9, 1940; educated Laxton Grammar School, Oundle; Imperial College, London; Gonville and Caius, Cambridge (BSc Hons, PhD Physics). Married Lesley Duggan (2 daughters 1 stepson 1 stepdaughter). *Trades Union:* Member, AUT. *Profession:* University Lecturer. *Career:* Head, Electrical Engineering, University of East Anglia. *Councils, Public Bodies:* Councillor, Norfolk County Council 1977–97, Group Leader 1985–90, Chairman, Education 1992–97; Former Member, Norfolk Police Authority. *Select Committees (Current):* Member: Consolidation of Bills (Joint Committee) 1997–. *Other:* School Governor; Board Member, Kings Lyn Festival. *Special Interests:* Education, Trade and Industry. *Recreations:* Poetry, travelling, theatre, cinema, keeping fit, swimming. *Electoral Notes:* Contested North West Norfolk 1992 General Election. Member for North West Norfolk since May 1, 1997. *Address:* Dr George Turner, MP, House of Commons, London, SW1A 0AA *Tel:* 020 7219 4618. *Constituency:* 78 Chapel Street, Kings Lynn, Norfolk, PE30 1EF *Fax:* 01553 666112 *E-mail:* mp@nwnorfolk.demon.co.uk.

TURNER, Neil *(Wigan)   Lab majority 6,729*

Born September 16, 1945; educated Carlisle Grammar School. Married March 26, 1971, Susan (1 son). *Trades Union:* Member, MSF. *Profession:* Quantity Surveyor. *Career:* Quantity Surveyor, Fairclough Builders (later AMEC) 1967–94; Operations Manager, North Shropshire District Council 1995–97. *Councils, Public Bodies:* Councillor, Wigan County Borough Council 1972–74; Wigan Metropolitan Borough Council: Councillor 1975–, Vice-Chair, Highways and Works Committee 1978–80, Chair 1980–97, Chair, Best Value Review Panel 1998–. *Party Groups:* Member, Labour Party since age of 18; Former Member, Sale Young Socialists. *Miscellaneous:* Vice-Chair, Public Services Committee, Association of Metropolitan Authorities 1987–95, Chair 1995–97; Vice-Chair, Local Government Association Quality Panel 1997–98, Chair 1998–99. *Recreations:* Keen follower of Wigan Rugby League Club. *Electoral Notes:* Contested Oswestry 1970. Member for Wigan since September 23, 1999 By-election. *Address:* Neil Turner Esq, MP, House of Commons, London, SW1A 0AA *Tel:* 020 7219 3000. *Constituency:* Gerrard Winstanley House, Crawford Street, Wigan, Greater Manchester, WN1 1NG *Tel:* 01942 242047 *Fax:* 01942 828008.

TWIGG, Derek *(Halton)   Lab majority 23,650*

Son of Kenneth and Irene Twigg. Born July 9, 1959; educated Bankfield High School, Widnes; Halton College of Further Education. Married January 23, 1988, Mary, daughter of Thomas and Kathleen Cassidy (1 son 1 daughter). *Trades Union:* Trade Union Member for over 20 years; Branch Secretary, Branch Chairman 1978–84. *Career:* Civil Servant, Department for Education and Employment 1975–96; Political Consultant 1996–. *Councils, Public Bodies:* Councillor, Cheshire County Council 1981–85; Halton Borough Council: Councillor 1983–97, Chairman of Housing 1988–93, Chairman of Finance 1993–96, Education Spokesperson 1996–97. *Political Career:* PPS to Rt Hon. Helen Liddell, MP: as Minister of State, Department of the Environment, Transport and the Regions (Minister for Transport) 1999, as Minister of State, Department of Trade and Industry (Minister for Energy and Competitiveness in Europe) 1999–. *Select Committees (Former):* Member: Public Accounts 1998–99. *Party Groups:* Vice-Chairman, North West Regional Group of Labour MPs 1998–99, Chair 1999–. *Other:* Member, Halton Community Health Council. *Miscellaneous:* Member, European Standing Committee B 1997–98. *Special Interests:* Finance, Education, Health and Poverty, Housing. *Countries of Interest:* Greece. *Recreations:* Liverpool Football Club, various sporting activities, walking, reading history. *Electoral Notes:* Member for Halton since May 1, 1997. *Address:* Derek Twigg Esq, MP, House of Commons, London, SW1A 0AA *Tel:* 020 7219 3554 *Fax:* 020 7219 2115. *Constituency:* 76 Victoria Road, Widnes, Cheshire, WA8 7RA *Tel:* 0151–424 7030 *Fax:* 0151–495 3800.

TWIGG, Stephen *(Enfield Southgate)   Lab majority 1,433*

Son of Ian David Twigg and late Jean Barbara Twigg. Born December 25, 1966; educated Southgate Comprehensive; Balliol College, Oxford (BA Politics and Economics). *Trades Union:* Member, MSF. *Career:* Former President, National Union of Students; Former Parliamentary Officer: Amnesty International UK, NCVO; Former Research Assistant to Margaret Hodge, MP for Barking; Former Political Consultant, Rowland Sallingbury Casey; General Secretary, Fabian Society 1996–97. *Councils, Public Bodies:* Councillor, London Borough of Islington 1990–97, Chief Whip 1994–96, Deputy Leader 1996. *Select Committees (Current):* Member: Modernisation of the House of Commons 1998–, Education and Employment 1999–, Employment Sub-Committee 1999–. *Party Groups:* Member, Co-operative Party; Executive Member, Fabian Society; Chair, Labour Campaign for Electoral Reform; Chair, Labour Friends of Israel; Hon. Treasurer, London Group of Labour MPs 1997–. *Other:* Member: Amnesty International, Stonewall, League Against Cruel Sports; Director, Crime Concern; Governor: Merryhills Primary School, Southgate School; Patron: Body Positive, The Richmond and Kingston AIDS Project; Council Member, Electoral Reform Society. *Trust:* Member, Holocaust Educational Trust. *Sportsclubs:* Southgate Cricket. *Publications: The Cross We Bear: Electoral Reform in Local Government,* co-author with Andrew Adonis 1997. *Special Interests:* Education, Electoral Reform, Local Government, Foreign Affairs. *Countries of Interest:* Israel, Cyprus. *Electoral Notes:* Member for Enfield Southgate since May 1, 1997. *Clubs:* National Liberal. *Address:* Stephen Twigg Esq, MP, House of Commons, London, SW1A 0AA *Tel:* 020 7219 6554 *Fax:* 020 7219 0948 *E-mail:* twiggs@parliament.uk.

TYLER, Paul Archer, CBE *(North Cornwall)   LD majority 13,847*

Son of Oliver and Grace Tyler. Born October 29, 1941; educated Sherborne School; Exeter College, Oxford (MA). Married 1970, Nicola Mary Ingram (1 son 1 daughter). *Career:* Director, Public Affairs, Royal Institute of British Architects 1972–73; Board Member, Shelter: National Campaign for the Homeless 1975–76; Managing Director, Cornwall Courier Newspaper Group 1976–81; Public Affairs Division, Good Relations plc: Executive Director 1982–84, Chief Executive 1984–86, Chairman 1986–87; Senior Consultant, Public Affairs 1987–92; Director, Western Approaches Public Relations Ltd 1987–92. *Councils, Public Bodies:* Councillor, Devon County Council 1964–70; Member, Devon and Cornwall Police Authority 1965–70; Vice-Chairman, Dartmoor National Park Committee 1965–70. *Whip:* Chief Whip and Shadow Leader of the House 1997–. *Spokesman:* Spokesman for: Agriculture, Tourism, Transport and Rural Affairs 1992–95, Agriculture and Rural Affairs 1995–97, Food 1997–99. *Select Committees (Current):* Member: Finance and Services 1997–, Modernisation of the House of Commons 1997–, Selection 1997– *(Former):* Member: Procedure 1992–97, Procedure 1997–98. *Party Groups:* Chairman: Devon and Cornwall Region Liberal Party 1981–82, Liberal Party National Executive Committee 1983–86; Campaign Adviser to Rt Hon. David Steel, MP in 1983 and 1987 General Elections. *Other:* Vice-President: British Resorts Association, Youth Hostels Association, Action for Communities in Rural England. *Trust:* Vice-President, British Trust for Conservation Volunteers. *Miscellaneous:* Chairman, CPRE Working Party on the future of the village 1974–81; Vice-President, Federation of Economic Development Authorities (FEDA). *Honours:* CBE 1985. *Publications:* Author of: *A New Deal for Rural Britain,* 1978 (jointly); *Country Lives, Country Landscapes,* 1996. *Special Interests:* Tourism, Rural Affairs. *Recreations:* Sailing, gardening, walking. *Electoral Notes:* Contested (Liberal) Totnes 1966 and Bodmin 1970. Member for Bodmin February-October 1974. Contested Bodmin 1979 and Beaconsfield 1982 By-election. Contested (SLD) Cornwall and Plymouth in European Parliamentary Election 1989. Member (Liberal Democrat) for North Cornwall since April 9, 1992. *Clubs:* Launceston and District Liberal Democrat. *Address:* Paul Tyler Esq, CBE, MP, House of Commons, London, SW1A 0AA *Tel:* 020 7219 6208. *Constituency:* Church Stile, Launceston, Cornwall, PL15 8AT *Tel:* 01566 777123 *Fax:* 01566 772122 *E-mail:* paultylermp@cix.co.uk.

TYNAN, Bill *(Hamilton South)* **Lab majority 556**

Son of late James and Mary Tynan. Born August 18, 1940; educated Stow College (Mechanical Engineering). Married July 11, 1964, Elizabeth Mathieson (3 daughters). *Trades Union:* AEEU 1966–: Shop Steward, Convenor, local and national posts; Scottish Political Secretary; Treasurer, Scottish Trade Union Labour Liaison Committee. *Profession:* Toolmaker. *Career:* Press toolmaker; full-time union official: district secretary, regional office and political officer 1988–. *Select Committees (Current):* Member: Scottish Affairs 1999–. *Party Groups:* Member: Labour Party 1969–: Constituency and Scottish Labour Party posts; Labour's Scottish Policy Forum. *Special Interests:* Employment Law, Social Security, Equal Opportunities, Social Inclusion. *Recreations:* Golf, swimming, cycling, watching football, diy, gardening. *Electoral Notes:* Member for Hamilton South since September 23, 1999 By-election. *Address:* Bill Tynan, Esq, MP, House of Commons, London, SW1A 0AA *Tel:* 020 7219 6285 *Fax:* 020 7219 6285. *Constituency:* 154 Montrose Crescent, Hamilton, South Lanarkshire, ML3 6LL *Tel:* 01698 454925 *Fax:* 01698 454926 *E-mail:* commons@bill-tynan-mp.com.

TYRIE, Andrew *(Chichester)* **Con majority 9,734**

Son of the late Derek and Patricia Tyrie. Born January 15, 1957; educated Felstead School, Essex; Trinity College, Oxford (MA); College of Europe, Bruges; Wolfson College, Cambridge (MPhil). *Career:* Group Head Office, British Petroleum 1981–83; Adviser to Chancellors of the Exchequer: Nigel Lawson 1986–89, John Major 1989–90, Fellow, Nuffield College, Oxford 1990–91; Senior Economist, European Bank for Reconstruction and Development 1992–97. *Select Committees (Current):* Member: Consolidation of Bills (Joint Committee) 1997–, Public Administration 1997–. *International Bodies:* Member, Inter-Parliamentary Union. *Miscellaneous:* Member, Public Accounts Commission 1997–. *Publications:* Various works on economic and monetary union in Europe and other European issues; *The Prospects for Public Spending*, 1996; *Reforming the Lords: a Conservative Approach*, 1998; *Sense on EMU*, 1998. *Special Interests:* European Union, Economic Policy. *Recreations:* Golf. *Electoral Notes:* Contested Houghton and Washington 1992. Member for Chichester since May 1, 1997. *Clubs:* MCC, RAC, Goodwood Country. *Address:* Andrew Tyrie Esq, MP, House of Commons, London, SW1A 0AA *Tel:* 020 7219 6371 *Fax:* 020 7219 0625. *Constituency:* Chichester Conservative Association, 50 West Street, Chichester, West Sussex, PO19 1RP *Tel:* 01243 783519 *Fax:* 01243 536848.

V

VAZ, Keith *(Leicester East)* **Lab majority 18,422**

Son of Merlyn Verona Vaz, mother and teacher. Born November 26, 1956; educated St Joseph's Convent, Aden; Latymer Upper School, Hammersmith; Gonville and Caius College, Cambridge (BA 1979, MA 1987, MCFI 1988); College of Law, London. Married April 3, 1993, Maria Fernandes (1 son, 1 daughter). *Trades Union:* Member, UNISON 1985–. *Profession:* Barrister. *Career:* Articled clerk, Richmond Council 1980–82; Solicitor 1982; Senior solicitor, Islington LBC 1982–85; Solicitor: Highfields and Belgrave Law Centre 1985–86, North Leicester Advice Centre 1986–87. *Political Career:* PPS to: Rt Hon. John Morris, QC, MP, as Attorney General 1997–99, Solicitors General Lord Falconer of Thoroton 1997–98, Ross Cranston, MP 1998–99; Parliamentary Secretary, Lord Chancellor's Department 1999; Minister of State, Foreign and Commonwealth Office (Minister for Europe) 1999–. *Spokesman:* Opposition Front Bench Spokesman on: The Environment (Local Government) 1992–94, Planning and Regeneration 1994–97. *Select Committees (Former):* Member: Home Affairs 1987–92. *Party Groups:* Former Secretary, Parliamentary Labour Party Wool and Textiles Group; Chairman: Labour Party Race Action Group 1986–, Unison Group 1990–. *International Bodies:* Member, Executive Committee Inter-Parliamentary Union 1993–94. *Other:* President, Leicester and South Leicestershire RSPCA; Patron, Gingerbread; National Advisory Committee,

Crime Concern; Chair, City 2020 Urban Policy Commission 1993–. *Miscellaneous:* Member, Standing Committees on: Immigration Bill 1987–88, Legal Aid Bill 1988, Football Spectators Bill 1989, National Health Service and Community Care Bill 1989–90, Courts and Legal Services Bill 1990, Armed Forces Bill 1990–91, Promoter, Race Relations Remedies Act 1994; Board Member, The British Council 1999–. *Publications:* Co-author *Law Reform Now*, 1996. *Special Interests:* Education, Legal Services, Local Government, Race Relations, Urban Policies. *Countries of Interest:* India, Pakistan, Yemen, Bangladesh, Oman. *Electoral Notes:* Contested Richmond and Barnes 1983. Contested Surrey West Euro-election 1984. Member for Leicester East since June 1987. *Clubs:* Safari (Leicester). *Address:* Keith Vaz Esq, MP, House of Commons, London, SW1A 0AA *Tel·* 020 7219 4605 *Fax:* 020 7219 5743.

VIGGERS, Peter J *(Gosport)   Con majority 6,258*

Son of late John Sidney Viggers. Born March 13, 1938; educated Portsmouth Grammar School; Trinity Hall, Cambridge (MA Hons); College of Law. Married December 7, 1968, Dr Jennifer Mary, daughter of late Dr R. B. McMillan (2 sons 1 daughter). *Armed Forces:* National Service RAF Pilot 1956–58; Territorial Army Officer for five years. *Profession:* Solicitor and Company Chairman. *Career:* Solicitor 1967; Chairman and Director of Companies in banking, oil, hotels, textiles, pharmaceuticals, venture capital 1970–79; Elected Member, Council of Lloyd's of London 1992–95; Chairman: Tracer Petroleum Corporation 1996–98, Lloyd's Pension Fund 1996–; Director, Emerald Energy plc 1998–. *Political Career:* PPS: to Solicitor General, Rt Hon. Sir Ian Percival, QC, MP 1979–83, to Chief Secretary to the Treasury, Rt Hon. Peter Rees, QC, MP 1983–85; Parliamentary Under-Secretary of State (Industry Minister), Northern Ireland Office 1986–89. *Select Committees (Former):* Member: Defence 1992–97, Armed Forces Bill 1996. *Party Groups:* Chairman, Cambridge University Conservative Association 1960; Member, Bow Group. *International Bodies:* UK Delegate, North Atlantic Assembly 1981–86, 1992–. *Other:* RNLI: National Committee 1979–, Vice-President 1989–; Chairman, Governors of St Vincent College, Gosport 1993–97. *Trust:* Fellow, Industry and Parliament Trust. *Miscellaneous:* Executive Member, 1922 Committee 1997–; Member, European Standing Committee A 1998–. *Sportsclubs:* Member, House of Commons Yacht Club: Commodore 1982–83, Admiral 1997–99. *Special Interests:* Finance, Trade and Industry, Defence. *Countries of Interest:* China, Japan, South East Asia, USA. *Recreations:* Beagling, opera, travel. *Electoral Notes:* Member for Gosport since February 1974. *Address:* Peter Viggers Esq, MP, House of Commons, London, SW1A 0AA *Tel:* 020 7219 5081 *Fax:* 020 7219 3985.

VIS, Rudi (Rudolf) Jan *(Finchley and Golders Green)   Lab majority 3,189*

Son of late Laurens Vis, insurance broker, and late Helena Vis. Born April 4, 1941; educated High School, Alkmaar, The Netherlands; University of Maryland, USA (BSc Economics 1970); London School of Economics (MSc Economics 1972); Brunel University (PhD Economics 1976); Hon. Doctorate, Schiller International University. Married Joan Hanin (marriage dissolved) (1 son); partner, Jacqueline Suffling (twin sons). *Trades Union:* Member: NATFHE 1971–94, MSF 1994–. *Armed Forces:* Dutch Armed Services 1960–64. *Profession:* University Economics Lecturer. *Career:* Principal Lecturer, Economics, North East London Polytechnic/University of East London 1971–97. *Councils, Public Bodies:* Councillor, London Borough of Barnet 1986–98. *Party Groups:* Member: Labour Party 1971–, Co-op Party 1971–, SERA 1986–, Labour Movement in Europe 1997–, Labour Friends of Israel 1997–, Labour Friends of India 1997–, European Movement 1999–. *International Bodies:* Member: Council of Europe, Western European Union. *Other:* Member: CND 1971–, Friends of the Earth 1978–, Friends of Cyprus 1997–, UNA 1998–. *Trust:* Member: College Farm Finchley, Hendon Youth Club. *Miscellaneous:* Member, European Standing Committee A 1998–; Member, Finchley Society 1998–. *Special Interests:* Finance, European Union, Economics, Defence, Elderly. *Countries of Interest:* All. *Recreations:* Walking through London. *Electoral Notes:* Member for Finchley and Golders Green since May 1, 1997. *Address:* Rudi Vis Esq, MP, House of Commons, London, SW1A 0AA *Tel:* 020 7219 4562 *Fax:* 020 7219 0565. *Constituency:* 331 Ballards Lane, Finchley, London, N12 8LT *Tel:* 020 8343 9854 *Fax:* 020 8343 9854.

W

WALKER, A. Cecil, JP *(Belfast North)   UUP majority 13,024*

Son of late Alfred George Walker, police constable. Born December 17, 1924; educated Methodist College, Belfast. Married July 1953, Joan, daughter of William Verrant (2 sons). *Career:* Joined James P. Corry & Co. Ltd., Belfast as apprentice Timber Executive 1941; Joinery Sales Manager 1951–83. *Councils, Public Bodies:* Former Councillor, Belfast City Council; Former Member, Belfast Education and Library Board; JP 1966. *Spokesman:* Spokesman for: the Environment 1997–, Housing 1998–. *Sportsclubs:* Down Cruising, Magheramorne Sailing. *Special Interests:* Housing, Local Government, Fishing, Industry, Conservation, Timber, Irish Affairs, Elderly. *Countries of Interest:* Cyprus, South Africa, USA. *Recreations:* Sailing, angling, gardening. *Electoral Notes:* Contested Belfast North 1979. Member for Belfast North since June, 1983. *Address:* Cecil Walker Esq, JP, MP, House of Commons, London, SW1A 0AA *Tel:* 020 7219 6307 *Fax:* 020 7219 2347. *Constituency:* 20 Old Park Road, Belfast, BT14 6FR *Tel:* 028 9075 5996 *Fax:* 028 9084 4697.

WALLACE, James Robert *(Orkney and Shetland)   LD majority 6,968*

Son of John Fergus Thomson Wallace and Grace Wallace (née Maxwell). Born August 25, 1954; educated Annan Academy, Dumfriesshire; Downing College, Cambridge (MA); Edinburgh University (LLB). Married July 9, 1983, Rosemary Janet, daughter of William G. P. Fraser, OBE (2 daughters). *Profession:* Advocate. *Career:* Called to the Scottish Bar 1979; QC (Scot) 1997. *Councils, Public Bodies:* Member, Scottish Office Consultative Steering Group on the Scottish Parliament 1998. *Political Career:* Deputy First Minister and Minister for Justice, Scottish Parliament 1999-. *Whip:* Deputy Whip 1985–87; Chief Whip, Parliamentary Liberal Party 1987–88; First Chief Whip, Social and Liberal Democrats 1988; Liberal Democrat Chief Whip 1988–92. *Spokesman:* Liberal Parliamentary Spokesman for: Energy 1983–85, Fishing 1985–87, Defence 1985–88; Alliance Spokesman for Transport 1987; Liberal Democrat Spokesman for: Employment and Fishing 1988–92, Scotland and Fishing 1992–94, Scotland, Energy, Fisheries and Maritime Transport 1994–97; Principal Spokesman for Scotland 1997-. *Select Committees (Former):* Member: Selection 1987–92, Procedure 1988–92. *Party Groups:* Chairman, Edinburgh University Liberal Club 1976–77; Member, Scottish Liberal Party Executive 1976–85; Vice-Chairman (Policy), Scottish Liberal Party 1982–85; Hon. President, Scottish Young Liberals 1984–85; Elected Leader, Scottish Liberal Democrats 1992-. *Awards:* Joint recipient (with Donald Dewar and Alex Salmond) of Saltire Society's Andrew Fletcher Award for Services to Scotland 1998. *Special Interests:* Constitutional Reform, Scottish Home Rule and Federalism, Scottish Law, Rural Development, Energy Conservation, Fishing, Shipping, Amnesty International. *Recreations:* Golf, travel, novice horseriding. *Electoral Notes:* Contested European Parliament Election for South Scotland 1979. Contested Dumfries May 1979. Member for Orkney and Shetland since June 1983. MSP for the Constituency of Orkney since May 6, 1999. *Clubs:* Caledonian, Scottish Liberal. *Address:* James Wallace Esq, QC, MP, MSP, House of Commons, London, SW1A 0AA *Tel:* 020 7219 6254 *Fax:* 020 7219 1162. *Constituency:* 39 Junction Road, Kirkwall, Orkney; Albert Buildings, Lerwick, Shetland *Tel:* 01856 876541 (Orkney) *Fax:* 01856 876162 (Orkney) *E-mail:* jim.wallace@zetnet.co.uk; jimwallace@cix.compulink.co.uk.

WALLEY, Joan Lorraine *(Stoke-on-Trent North)   Lab majority 17,392*

Daughter of late Arthur and late Mary Emma Walley. Born January 23, 1949; educated Biddulph Grammar School; University of Hull; University College, Swansea. Married August 3, 1981, Jan, son of Adam and Marie Louise Ostrowski (2 sons). *Trades Union:* Member, UNISON. *Career:* Alcoholics Recovery Project 1970–73; Swansea City Council, Planning Department; Local Government Officer for three years; Wandsworth Council, Local Government Officer; NACRO Development Officer. *Councils, Public Bodies:* Lambeth Council: Formerly Councillor, Chair, Health and Consumer Services Committee. *Spokesman:* Opposition Spokesperson on: Environmental Protection and Development 1988–90, Transport 1990–95. *Select Committees (Current):*

Member: Environmental Audit 1997– *(Former):* Member: Trade and Industry 1995–97, Trade and Industry 1997–98. *Party Groups:* Member: SERA, SEA. *Other:* Vice-President, Institute Environmental Health Officers; President: West Midlands Home and Water Safety Council, City of Stoke on Trent Primary School Sports Association. *Miscellaneous:* Member, Armed Forces Parliamentary Scheme (RAF). *Special Interests:* Environment, Health. *Countries of Interest:* Eastern Europe. *Recreations:* Walking, swimming, music. *Electoral Notes:* Member for Stoke-on-Trent North since June 1987. *Clubs:* Newchapel Sports and Social Institute, Fegg Hayes Sports and Social. *Address:* Joan Walley, MP, House of Commons, London, SW1A 0AA *Tel:* 020 7219 3000 *Fax:* 020 7219 4397. *Constituency:* Unit 5, Burslem Enterprise Centre, Moorland Road, Burslem, Stoke-on-Trent, ST6 1JN *Tel:* 01782 577900 *Fax:* 01782 836462.

WALTER, Robert *(North Dorset)   Con majority 2,746*

Born May 30, 1948; educated Lord Weymouth School, Warminster; Aston University, Birmingham (BSc 1971). Widower (2 sons 1 daughter). *Profession:* Farmer and International Banker. *Career:* Farmer; Sheep Farm, South Devon; Director and Vice-President, Aubrey G. Langston and Co 1986–; Former Member, London Stock Exchange; Visiting Lecturer in East-West Trade, University of Westminster. *Spokesman:* An Opposition Front Bench Spokesman for Constitutional Affairs (Wales) 1999–. *Select Committees (Current):* Member: Unopposed Bills (Panel) 1997– *(Former):* Member: Health 1997–99, European Scrutiny 1999. *Party Groups:* Chairman: Aston University Conservative Association 1967–69, Westbury Constituency Young Conservative 1973–76, Conservative Foreign Affairs Forum 1986–88, Member: Carlton Club Political Committee 1991–, National Union Executive Committee 1992–95, Conservative Foreign and Commonwealth Council; Chairman, Conservative Group for Europe 1992–95, currently Vice-President. *International Bodies:* Former Chairman, European Democrat Forum. *Other:* Chairman, Governors of Tachbrook School 1980–; Founder Chairman, Wiltshire Europe Society; Member: National Farmers Union, National Sheep Association, Royal Agricultural Society of England. *Miscellaneous:* Member, European Standing Committee B 1998–. Liveryman, Worshipful Company of Needlemakers 1983. Freeman, City of London 1983. *Special Interests:* European Union, Environment, East-West Trade. *Electoral Notes:* Contested Bedwelty 1979. Member for North Dorset since May 1, 1997. *Address:* Robert Walter Esq, MP, House of Commons, London, SW1A 0AA *Tel:* 020 7219 6981 *Fax:* 020 7219 2608. *Constituency:* The Stables, White Cliff Gardens, Blandford Forum, Dorset, DT11 7BU *Tel:* 01258 452420 *Fax:* 01258 454231 *E-mail:* walterr@parliament.uk.

WARD, Claire Margaret *(Watford)   Lab majority 5,792*

Daughter of Frank and Catherine Ward. Born May 9, 1972; educated Loreto College, St Albans, Hertfordshire; University of Hertfordshire (LLB Hons); Brunel University (MA Britain and the European Union); College of Law, London. *Trades Union:* Member, TGWU 1987–; Winner: South East TUC Mike Perkins Memorial Award for Young Trade Unionists 1989, TGWU National Youth Award 1990; Delegate, TGWU Biennial Delegate Conference 1991. *Profession:* Solicitor. *Career:* Part-time Secretary, Graham Aitken & Associates 1985–88; Temporary Accounts Clerk, Hertsmere Borough Council 1988; Part-time Secretary/Receptionist, Clarendon House Business Centre 1989–92; Part-time Personal Assistant to Labour Group, Hertsmere Borough Council 1992–95 Trainee Solicitor 1995–98; Solicitor 1998–. *Councils, Public Bodies:* Councillor, Elstree and Boreham Wood Town Council 1994–97, Mayor 1996–97, Former Vice-Chair, Leisure and Entertainments Committee. *Select Committees (Current):* Member: Culture, Media and Sport 1997–. *Party Groups:* Member: Labour Party 1987–, Co-operative Party and CRS Ltd 1987–; Youth Representative, Labour Party National Executive Committee 1991–95; Chair: Boreham Wood Branch Labour Party 1991–97, Hertsmere Constituency Labour Party 1992–96; Member, Central Region Executive Committee 1993; Member: London Region CRS Political Committee 1993–, Co-operative Party Parliamentary Panel 1994–95; Member, Labour Party National Policy Commissions on: Democracy and Citizenship 1992–95, Social Policy 1992–95, Equalities 1992–95, Environment 1992–95; Member: Fabian Society, Society of Labour Lawyers. *Miscellaneous:* Youngest Woman MP. *Special Interests:*

Transport, Education, Employment, Home Affairs, Culture, Media, Sport. *Countries of Interest:* St Lucia. *Recreations:* Cinema, reading, restaurants, Watford Football Club. *Electoral Notes:* Member for Watford since May 1, 1997. *Clubs:* Reform. *Address:* Claire Ward, MP, House of Commons, London, SW1A 0AA *Tel:* 020 7219 4910 *Fax:* 020 7219 0468 *E-mail:* wardc@parliament.uk.

WARDLE, Charles Frederick *(Bexhill and Battle)*   Con majority 11,100

Son of late Frederick Maclean Wardle and Constance (née Roach). Born August 23, 1939; educated Tonbridge School; Lincoln College, Oxford; Harvard Business School. Married August 29, 1964, Lesley Ann, daughter of late Sidney and Doris Wells (1 daughter). *Career:* Assistant to the President, American Express Co., New York 1966–69; Merchant Banking, London 1969–72; Benjamin Priest Group: Director 1972–74, Managing Director 1974–77, Chairman 1977–84. *Political Career:* PPS: to Minister for Health 1984, to Secretary of State for Social Services 1984–87, to Rt Hon. Ian Lang, MP, as Secretary of State for Scotland 1991–92; Parliamentary Under-Secretary of State, Home Office 1992–94; Parliamentary Under-Secretary of State for Industry and Energy, Department of Trade and Industry 1994–95. *Party Groups:* Chairman, One Nation Forum 1989–90. *Miscellaneous:* Member: CBI Council 1980–84, CBI West Midlands Regional Council, Commercial and Economic Committee, Engineering and Employers' Federation 1980–83, Midlands Committee, Institute of Directors 1980–83. *Special Interests:* Industry, Employment, Economic Policy, Immigration, Police. *Recreations:* Books, sport, travel. *Electoral Notes:* Member for Bexhill and Battle since June 1983. *Address:* Charles Wardle Esq, MP, House of Commons, London, SW1A 0AA *Tel:* 020 7219 3426. *Constituency:* Bexhill and Battle Conservative Association, 6a Amherst Road, Bexhill-on-Sea, TN39 1QJ *Tel:* 01424 219117 *Fax:* 01424 218367 *E-mail:* charles@wardlecharles.tory.org.uk.

WAREING, Robert Nelson *(Liverpool West Derby)*   Lab majority 25,965

Son of late Robert and Florence Patricia Wareing. Born August 20, 1930; educated Ranworth Square Council School, Liverpool; Alsop High School, Liverpool; Bolton College of Education (Teacher's Certificate 1957); External student, London University (BSc economics 1956). Married August 16, 1962, Betty Coward (died 1989). *Trades Union:* Member, MSF. *Armed Forces:* RAF 1948–50. *Career:* Local Government Officer, Liverpool Corporation 1946–48, 1950–56; Lecturer: Brooklyn Technical College 1957–59, Wigan and District Mining and Technical College 1959–63, Liverpool College of Commerce 1963–64, Liverpool City Institute of Further Education 1964–72; Principal Lecturer/Deputy Head Adult Education, Central Liverpool College of FE 1972–83. *Councils, Public Bodies:* Merseyside County Council: Councillor 1981–86, Chairman, Economic Development Committee 1981–83, Chief Whip, Labour Group 1981–83. *Whip:* Assistant Opposition Whip 1987–92. *Select Committees (Former):* Member: Foreign Affairs 1992–97. *Party Groups:* President, Liverpool District Labour Party 1972–73, 1974–81. *Other:* Council Member, British-Russian Centre; Member, Hansard Society. *Miscellaneous:* Vice-President, AMA. *Special Interests:* Economic and Foreign Affairs, Regional Economic Policy, Disabled/Disability, NHS Tranquillisers Addiction, Motor Industry, Airports Policy. *Countries of Interest:* Russia, Yugoslavia, Germany, Latin America, Eastern Europe, Far East. *Recreations:* Watching soccer, concert-going, ballet, motoring, travel. *Electoral Notes:* Contested Berwick-upon-Tweed 1970 and Liverpool Edge Hill By-election and General Election of 1979. Member for Liverpool, West Derby since June 1983. *Clubs:* Dovecot Labour (Liverpool). *Address:* Robert Wareing Esq, MP, House of Commons, London, SW1A 0AA *Tel:* 020 7219 3482 *Fax:* 020 7219 6187. *Constituency:* c/o Walter Edwards, 78 Parkhurst Road, Liverpool L11 7DZ *Tel:* 0151-226 3562 *Fax:* 0151-230 0880.

WATERSON, Nigel Christopher *(Eastbourne)* **Con majority 1,994**

Son of late James Waterson and Katherine Mahon. Born October 12, 1950; educated Leeds Grammar School; The Queen's College, Oxford (MA Hons). Married 1st, 1979, Gisela Guettler (marriage dissolved), married 2nd, 1989, Bernadette Anne, daughter of late Denis O'Halloran (marriage dissolved 1998), married 3rd, 1999, Dr Barbara Judge. *Profession:* Solicitor. *Career:* Solicitor; Barrister; Founder and senior partner of law firm, Waterson Hicks; Research Assistant to Mrs Sally Oppenheim, MP 1972–73. *Councils, Public Bodies:* Councillor, London Borough of Hammersmith and Fulham 1974–78. *Political Career:* PPS to: Minister of State, Department of Health 1995–96, Michael Heseltine, MP as Deputy Prime Minister 1996–97. *Whip:* An Opposition Whip (Social Security, Health, Legal, Lord Chancellor: Eastern) 1997–98; An Opposition Whip (Home Office, Culture, Media and Sport) 1998–99. *Spokesman:* An Opposition Front Bench Spokesman for Local Government and Housing 1999–. *Select Committees (Former):* Member: Joint Committee on Statutory Instruments 1992–97, National Heritage 1995–96. *Party Groups:* President, Oxford University Conservative Association 1970; Chairman, Bow Group 1986–87; Chairman: Hammersmith Conservative Association 1987–90, Hammersmith and Fulham Joint Management Committee 1988–90; Member, CPC Advisory Committee 1986–90; Hon. Patron, Bow Group 1993–95. *International Bodies:* Member: IPU, CPA. *Other:* School governor 1986–88; Member, Management Committee of Stonham Housing Association Hostel for Ex-Offenders 1988–90; Vice-Chairman, Eastbourne Branch of BLESMA. *Sportsclubs:* Guards' Polo, Sussex County Cricket Club. *Special Interests:* Health, Foreign Affairs, Tourism, Shipping, Shipbuilding, Energy. *Recreations:* Sailing, polo, reading, music. *Electoral Notes:* Contested Islington South and Finsbury in 1979. Member for Eastbourne since April 9, 1992. *Clubs:* Carlton, Eastbourne Constitutional, Coningsby,. *Address:* Nigel Waterson Esq, MP, House of Commons, London, SW1A 0AA *Tel:* 020 7219 4576 *Fax:* 020 7219 2561. *Constituency:* Eastbourne Conservative Association, 7A Hyde Gardens, Eastbourne, East Sussex, BN21 4PN *Tel:* 01323 720776 *Fax:* 01323 410994 *E-mail:* nigelwatersonmp@parliament.uk.

WATTS, David Leonard *(St Helens North)* **Lab majority 23,417**

Born August 26, 1951; educated Seel Road Secondary Modern School. Married 1972, Avril (2 sons). *Trades Union:* Shop Steward, United Biscuits. *Profession:* Research Assistant. *Career:* Research Assistant to Angela Eagle, MP 1992–93 and John Evans, MP 1993–97. *Councils, Public Bodies:* Councillor, St Helens MBC 1979–97, Deputy Leader 1990–93, Leader 1993–97; Former Chair, Education and Economic Development Committee. *Political Career:* PPS to John Spellar, MP, as Minister of State for the Armed Forces, Ministry of Defence 1999–. *Select Committees (Current):* Member: Finance and Services 1997–. *Party Groups:* Vice-Chair, North West Regional Group of Labour MPs 1999–. *International Bodies:* UK President, Euro Group of Industrial Regions. *Miscellaneous:* Vice-Chairman, Association of Metropolitan Authorities. *Special Interests:* Regional Policy, Education, Training. *Recreations:* Watching football and rugby, reading. *Electoral Notes:* Member for St Helens North since May 1, 1997. *Address:* David Watts Esq, MP, House of Commons, London, SW1A 0AA *Tel:* 020 7219 6325. *Constituency:* Ann Ward House, 1 Milk Street, St Helens, Merseyside, WA10 1PX *Tel:* 01744 623416 *Fax:* 01744 623417.

WEBB, Prof Steve (Steven) *(Northavon)* **LD majority 2,137**

Son of Brian and Patricia Webb. Born July 18, 1965; educated Dartmouth High School, Birmingham; Hertford College, Oxford (BA PPE). Married July 10, 1993, Helen, daughter of Ron and Dorothy Edwards (1 daughter). *Profession:* Professor of Social Policy. *Career:* Researcher then Programme Director, Institute for Fiscal Studies 1986–95; Professor of Social Policy, University of Bath 1995–. *Spokesman:* A Spokesman for Social Security and Welfare (Pensions) 1997–99; Principal Spokesman for Social Security 1999–. *Party Groups:* Member: Liberal Democrat Tax and Benefits Working Group, Liberal Democrat Costings Group. *Other:* Member: Oxfam, Amnesty International, World Development Movement. *Miscellaneous:* Member, Commission on

Social Justice; Specialist Adviser to Social Security Select Committee. *Publications:* Include: *Beyond The Welfare State,* (with Sir Samuel Brittan) 1990; *For Richer, For Poorer,* (with Alissa Goodman) 1994; *Inequality in the UK,* (with Alissa Goodman and Paul Johnston) 1997. *Special Interests:* Social Issues, Welfare, Third World. *Recreations:* Football (West Bromwich Albion FC), cricket, music (play oboe, piano and organ), reading. *Electoral Notes:* Member for Northavon since May 1, 1997. *Address:* Prof Steve Webb Esq, MP, House of Commons, London, SW1A 0AA *Tel:* 020 7219 3000.

WELLS, Bowen *(Hertford and Stortford)   Con majority 6,885*

Son of late Reginald Laird Wells, chartered accountant, and Agnes Mary Wells (née Hunter). Born August 4, 1935; educated St Paul's School, Barnes; University of Exeter (BA Hons Political History and Government); Regent Street Polytechnic (Diploma in Business Management). Married October 25, 1975, Rennie, daughter of late Bernard Heyde (2 sons). *Armed Forces:* National Service, Royal Navy 1954–56; Promoted from Able Seaman to Sub-Lieutenant. *Career:* Schoolmaster 1956–57; Sales Trainee, British Aluminium Co. 1957–58; Exeter University, President of Guild of Students 1958–61; Senior Executive, in charge of subsidiary and associated Development Finance Companies of Commonwealth Development Corporation 1961–73; Director, Outward Bound School, Aberdovey 1979–92; Governor, Institute of Development Studies, Sussex University 1981–92. *Political Career:* PPS: to Minister of State for Employment June 1982–83, to Rt Hon. Roger Freeman, MP, as Minister for Public Transport, to Rt Hon. Earl of Caithness, as Minister for Aviation and Shipping 1992–94. *Whip:* Assistant Government Whip 1994–95; Lord Commissioner of HM Treasury (Government Whip) 1995–97. *Select Committees (Current):* Member: Chairmen's Panel 1997–; Chairman: International Development 1997–; Member: Liaison 1997– *(Former):* : European Legislation 1981–92; Member: Foreign Affairs 1990–92. *International Bodies:* Treasurer, International CPA and of UK Branch; Member, CPA Executive 1984–. *Other:* Chairman, Westminster for Europe 1975. *Trust:* Fellow and Trustee, Industry and Parliament Trust. *Miscellaneous:* Executive Member, 1922 Committee 1997–. *Publications: Managing Third World Debt; Growing out of Debt. Special Interests:* Foreign Affairs, Overseas Aid and Development, Trade and Industry, United Nations, Treasury. *Countries of Interest:* Africa, Caribbean, Central America, Europe, Hong Kong, West Indies. *Recreations:* Swimming, walking, sailing, gardening, cooking, music. *Electoral Notes:* Member for Hertford and Stevenage 1979–83 and for Hertford and Stortford since June 1983. *Address:* Bowen Wells Esq, MP, House of Commons, London, SW1A 0AA *Tel:* 020 7219 5154.

WELSH, Andrew Paton *(Angus)   SNP majority 10,189*

Son of late William and late Agnes (née Paton) Welsh. Born April 19, 1944; educated Govan High School; University of Glasgow (MA Hons Modern History and Politics, DipEd). Married 1971, Sheena Margaret, daughter of Douglas and Jean Cannon (1 daughter). *Trades Union:* Member: EIS, SHFEA. *Profession:* Teacher and Further Education Lecturer. *Career:* Teacher; Senior Lecturer in Business Studies and Public Administration. *Councils, Public Bodies:* Stirling District Councillor 1974; Provost, Angus District Council 1984–87. *Whip:* SNP Chief Whip 1977–79, 1987–99. *Spokesman:* SNP Parliamentary Spokesman for: Housing 1974–79, 1987–97, 1997–, Agriculture 1974–79, 1987–97, Self Employed and Small Businesses 1975–79, Local Government 1987–97, 1997–, Education 1997–. *Select Committees (Current):* Member: Chairmen's Panel 1997–, Scottish Affairs 1997– *(Former):* Member: Members' Interests 1990–92, Scottish Affairs 1992–97. *Trust:* Prayer Breakfast for Scotland. *Special Interests:* Local Government, Environment. *Countries of Interest:* China, France. *Recreations:* Music, football. *Electoral Notes:* Contested Dumbartonshire Central February 1974. Member for Angus South October 1974–79. Contested Angus East 1983. Member for Angus East 1987–97, and for Angus since May 1, 1997. MSP for the Constituency of Angus since May 6, 1999. *Address:* Andrew Welsh Esq, MP, MSP, House of Commons, London, SW1A 0AA *Tel:* 020 7219 6921 *Fax:* 020 7219 6716. *Constituency:* The Scottish Parliament Office, 31 Market Place, Arbroath, Angus, DD11 1HR *Tel:* 01241 439369 *Fax:* 01241 871561 *E-mail:* andrew.welsh.msp@scottish.parliament.uk.

WHITE, Brian Arthur Robert *(Milton Keynes North East)   Lab majority 240*

Son of William Edward White and Elinor White. Born May 5, 1957; educated Methodist College, Belfast. Married Leena Lindholm (2 stepsons). *Trades Union:* Member, MSF. *Profession:* Systems Analyst. *Career:* Civil Servant, HM Customs and Excise; IT Consultant; Systems Analyst, Abbey National. *Councils, Public Bodies:* Councillor, Milton Keynes Borough Council 1987–97, former Deputy Leader; Councillor, Buckinghamshire County Council 1994–97. *Select Committees (Current):* Member: Consolidation of Bills (Joint Committee) 1997–, Deregulation 1999–, Joint Committee on Statutory Instruments 1999–, Public Administration 1999–. *Other:* Member, Milton Keynes Energy Association. *Miscellaneous:* Agent, Milton Keynes South West General Election 1992; Local Government Association: Member, Policy and Strategy Committee, Chair, Planning Committee, Secretary, Labour Group. *Special Interests:* Environment, Transport, Economic Policy, European Union, International Trade, Information Technology, Animal Welfare. *Recreations:* Reading, ten-pin bowling. *Electoral Notes:* Member for Milton Keynes North East since May 1, 1997. *Address:* Brian White Esq, MP, House of Commons, London, SW1A 0AA *Tel:* 020 7219 3435 *Fax:* 020 7219 2887. *Constituency:* Labour Hall, Newport Road, New Bradwell, Milton Keynes, Buckinghamshire, MK13 0AA *Tel:* 01908 313933 *Fax:* 01908 313960 *E-mail:* whitebar@parliament.uk.

WHITEHEAD, Dr Alan Patrick Vincent *(Southampton Test)   Lab majority 13,684*

Born September 15, 1950; educated Isleworth Grammar School, Isleworth, Middlesex; Southampton University (BA Hons, PhD); Visiting Professor, Southampton Institute 1997–; Senior Research Fellow, Southampton University 1998–. Married December 1, 1979, Sophie Wronska (1 son 1 daughter). *Trades Union:* Member, UNISON (formerly NUPE). *Profession:* Professor of Public Policy. *Career:* Director, Outset 1979–83, Deputy 1976–79; Director, BIIT 1983–92; Professor of Public Policy, Southampton Institute 1992–97. *Councils, Public Bodies:* Councillor, Southampton City Council 1980–92, Leader of Council 1984–92. *Political Career:* Joint PPS to Rt Hon. David Blunkett, MP, as Secretary of State for Education and Employment 1999–. *Select Committees (Former):* Member: Environment, Transport and Regional Affairs 1997–99, Environment Sub-Committee 1997–99. *Party Groups:* Member, Labour Party National Policy Forum 1999–. *Other:* Governor, Cantell School, Southampton; Director/Board Member, Southampton Environment Centre. *Trust:* Director/Board Member, Mayflower Theatre Trust; Director, Southampton Environment Centre. *Miscellaneous:* Vice-President, Local Government Association 1998–. *Sportsclubs:* Season Ticket Holder, Southampton FC. *Publications:* Various chapters, articles and papers including: *TUPE – the EU's Revenge on the Iron Lady*, with M. Bennett 1994; *Spain, European Regions and City States*, 1995; *Rational Actors and Irrational Structures*, 1995; *Local Government Finance – Accountancy or Accountability?*, 1995; Joint editor, *Beyond 2002: Long-Term Policies for Labour. Special Interests:* Environment, Local and Regional Government, Further and Higher Education, Constitutional Affairs, Transport. *Countries of Interest:* Poland, France. *Recreations:* Football (playing and watching), writing, tennis. *Electoral Notes:* Contested Southampton Test 1983, 1987, 1992. Member for Southampton Test since May 1, 1997. *Address:* Dr Alan Whitehead, MP, House of Commons, London, SW1A 0AA *Tel:* 020 7219 6338 *Fax:* 020 7219 0918. *Constituency:* Southampton Labour Party, 20–22 Southampton Street, Southampton, SO15 1ED *Tel:* 023 8023 1942 *Fax:* 023 8023 1943 *E-mail:* whiteheada@parliament.uk *Website:* www.alan-whitehead.org.uk.

WHITNEY, Sir Raymond William, OBE *(Wycombe)   Con majority 2,370*

Son of late George William Whitney, hotel keeper. Born November 28, 1930; educated Wellingborough School; Royal Military Academy, Sandhurst; London University (BA Hons Oriental Studies); Hong Kong University. Married March 31, 1956, Sheila Margot Beswick, daughter of Walter Henry Prince (2 sons). *Armed Forces:* Commissioned, Northamptonshire Regt 1951; Service in Italy, Germany, Korea. *Career:* Seconded, Australian Government 1960–63; Diplomatic Service, Peking and Argentina 1964; Deputy High Commissioner, Bangladesh 1973–76; Head, Information Research Department, Overseas Information Department, Foreign and Commonwealth Office 1976–78. *Political Career:* PPS to Treasury Minister 1979–80; Parliamentary Under-Secretary of State: Foreign and Commonwealth Office 1983–84, Department of Social Security 1984–85, Department of Health 1985–86. *Party Groups:* Chairman, The Positive European Group 1993–. *Other:* Chairman, Mountbatten Community Trust. *Miscellaneous:* Executive Member, 1922 Committee 1997–; Member, European Standing Committee B 1998–. *Sportsclubs:* Windlesham Golf Club. *Honours:* OBE 1968; Knighted 1997. *Publications: National Health Crisis. A Modern Solution*; *Time to Return to Euro-Sanity*; *Europe: In or Out?* Co-author with Michael Welsh. *Special Interests:* European Union, Foreign Affairs, Defence, Economic Policy, Health. *Countries of Interest:* Bangladesh, China, Europe, Hong Kong, Latin America, Taiwan. *Recreations:* Golf, bridge, theatre. *Electoral Notes:* Member for Wycombe since April 1978 By-election. *Address:* Sir Raymond Whitney, OBE, House of Commons, London, SW1A 0AA *Tel:* 020 7219 5099 *Fax:* 020 7219 4614. *Constituency:* 150A West Wycombe Road, High Wycombe, Buckinghamshire, HP12 3AE *Tel:* 01494 521777 *Fax:* 01494 510042.

WHITTINGDALE, John Flasby Lawrance, OBE *(Maldon and Chelmsford East)*
Con majority 10,039

Son of late John Whittingdale, FRCS, and of Margaret Whittingdale. Born October 16, 1959; educated Sandroyd School, Wiltshire; Winchester College; University College, London (BSc Economics). Married 1990, Ancilla, daughter of late Dr Ian Murfitt (1 son 1 daughter). *Career:* Head, Political Section, Conservative Research Department 1982–84; Special Adviser to Secretary of State for Trade and Industry 1984–87; Manager, N. M. Rothschild & Sons 1987; Political Secretary to Rt Hon. Margaret Thatcher (MT) as Prime Minister 1988–90; Private Secretary to MT 1990–92. *Political Career:* PPS to Eric Forth, MP: as Minister of State for Education 1994–95, as Minister of State for Education and Employment 1994–96; private secretary to Rt Hon. William Hague, MP, as Leader of the Opposition 1999–. *Whip:* An Opposition Whip (Treasury, Culture, Media and Sport: South Eastern) 1997–98. *Spokesman:* A Front Bench Spokesman for the Treasury (Tax, VAT and Duties; EU Budget and other EU Issues) 1998–99. *Select Committees (Former):* Member: Health 1993–97, Information 1997–98. *Other:* Mensa. *Honours:* OBE 1990. *Publications: New Policies for the Media*, 1995. *Special Interests:* Home Affairs, Foreign Affairs, Health, Media. *Countries of Interest:* Israel, USA. *Recreations:* Cinema, music. *Electoral Notes:* Member for South Colchester and Maldon 1992–97, and for Maldon and Chelmsford East since May 1, 1997. *Clubs:* Essex. *Address:* John Whittingdale Esq, OBE, MP, House of Commons, London, SW1A 0AA *Tel:* 020 7219 3557 *Fax:* 020 7219 2522. *Constituency:* Maldon and East Chelmsford Conservative Association, 120B High Street, Maldon, Essex *Tel:* 01621 855663 *E-mail:* jwhittingdale.mp@email.tory.org.uk.

WICKS, Malcolm *(Croydon North)   Lab majority 18,398*

Son of Arthur Wicks and of late Daisy Wicks. Born July 1, 1947; educated Elizabeth College, Guernsey; North West London Polytechnic; London School of Economics (BSc Sociology). Married September 7, 1968, Margaret, daughter of George and Marjorie Baron (1 son 2 daughters). *Career:* Fellow, Department of Social Administration, University of York 1968–70; Research Worker, Centre for Environmental Studies 1970–72; Lecturer in Social Administration, Department of Government Studies, Brunel University 1970–74; Social Policy Analyst, Urban Deprivation Unit, Home Office 1974–77; Lecturer in Social Policy, Civil Service College 1977–78; Research Director and Secretary, Study Commission on the Family 1978–83; Director, Family Policy Studies Centre 1983–92; Co-Director, European Family and Social Policy Unit 1992–.

Political Career: Parliamentary Under-Secretary of State (Lifelong Learning), Department for Education and Employment 1999–. *Spokesman:* Opposition Spokesman on Social Security 1995–97. *Select Committees (Former):* Member: Social Security 1994–96, Social Security 1997–98; Chairman: Education Sub-Committee 1998–99; Member: Liaison 1998–99. *International Bodies:* Member, European Institute of Social Security. *Trust:* Trustee, National Energy Foundation. *Publications:* Author of several publications and articles on social policy and welfare including: *Old and Cold: hypothermia and social policy*, 1978; *Government and Urban Poverty*, 1983 (co-author); *A Future for All: do we need a welfare state?* 1987; *Family Change and Future Policy*, 1990 (co-author); *A New Agenda* (jointly) IPPR, 1993. *Special Interests:* Social Policy, Welfare State, Education. *Countries of Interest:* Australia, Europe, New Zealand. *Recreations:* Music, walking, gardening, very occasional white water rafting. *Electoral Notes:* Contested Croydon North West 1987. Member for Croydon North West 1992–97, and for Croydon North since May 1, 1997. *Clubs:* Ruskin House Labour (Croydon). *Address:* Malcolm Wicks Esq, MP, House of Commons, London, SW1A 0AA *Tel:* 020 7219 4554 *Fax:* 020 7219 2795. *Constituency:* 84 High Street, Thornton Heath, Surrey, CR7 8LF *Tel:* 020 8665 1214 *Fax:* 020 8683 0179.

WIDDECOMBE, The Rt Hon. Ann *(Maidstone and The Weald)   Con majority 9,603*

Daughter of late James Murray Widdecombe CB, OBE, retired Director General in Ministry of Defence, and of Rita Widdecombe. Born October 4, 1947; educated Royal Naval School, Singapore; La Sainte Union Convent, Bath; University of Birmingham (BA Hons Latin); Lady Margaret Hall, Oxford (BA Hons PPE, MA). *Career:* With Unilever in Marketing 1973–75; Senior Administrator, London University 1975–1987. *Councils, Public Bodies:* Councillor, Runnymede District Council 1976–78. *Political Career:* Introduced Abortion Amendment Bill 1988–89; PPS to Tristan Garel-Jones MP 1990; Joint Parliamentary Under-Secretary of State, Department of Social Security 1990–93; Department of Employment: Joint Parliamentary Under-Secretary of State 1993–94, Minister of State 1994–95; Minister of State, Home Office 1995–97; Member, Shadow Cabinet 1998–; Shadow Secretary of State for Health 1998–99; Shadow Home Secretary 1999–. *Select Committees (Former):* : Health and Social Security 1989–90; Member: Standards and Privileges 1997, Chairmen's Panel 1998. *Party Groups:* Vice-Chairman, National Association of Conservative Graduates 1974–76. *Other:* Founding Member and Vice-Chairman, Women and Families for Defence; National Patron, *Life*; Member, SPUC. *Awards:* Highland Park/*The Spectator* Minister of the Year 1996; Talk Radio, Straight Talker of the Year 1997. *Miscellaneous:* Member, Gas Consumers Council 1984–86. *Honours:* PC 1997. *Publications:* Various publications including *A Layman's Guide to Defence*, 1984; *Outspoken and Inspired*, 1999. *Special Interests:* Abortion, Health, Defence, Prisons. *Recreations:* Reading, researching Charles II's escape. *Electoral Notes:* Contested Burnley 1979. Contested Plymouth Devonport 1983. Member for Maidstone 1987–97, and for Maidstone and The Weald since May 1, 1997. *Address:* The Rt Hon. Ann Widdecombe, MP, House of Commons, London, SW1A 0AA *Tel:* 020 7219 5091. *Constituency:* Kloof Cottage, Sutton Valence, Maidstone, Kent *Tel:* 01622 843868 *Fax:* Home: 01622 844330, Office: 01622 752463.

WIGLEY, The Rt Hon. Dafydd *(Caernarfon)   PC majority 7,949*

Son of Elfyn Edward and Myfanwy Wigley. Born April 1, 1943; educated Caernarfon Grammar School; Rydal School, Colwyn Bay; Manchester University (BSc 1964); Married August 26, 1967, Elinor, daughter of late Emrys Bennett Owen (1 son 1 daughter, and 2 sons deceased). *Trades Union:* Former Member, ASTMS. *Profession:* Cost and Management Accountant. *Career:* Finance Staff, Ford Motor Co. 1964–67; Chief Cost Accountant and Financial Planning Manager, Mars Ltd. 1967–71; Financial Controller, Hoover Ltd., Merthyr Plant 1971–74; Chairman, Alpha-Dyffryn Ltd (Electronics) 1987–91. *Councils, Public Bodies:* Councillor, Merthyr Tydfil County Borough Council 1972–74. *Political Career:* Sponsor, 1981 Disabled Persons Act; Shadow First Secretary and Finance Secretary, National Assembly for Wales 1999–. *Whip:* Plaid Cymru Whip 1987–91. *Spokesman:* Spokesman for Constitutional Affairs 1997–. *Select Committees (Former):* Member: Public Accounts 1997–98. *Party Groups:* President, Plaid Cymru 1981–84, 1991–. *Other:* Vice-President, Wales Council for the Disabled; President, Spastic Society for Wales 1985–90; Member, Mencap Profound Mental Handicap Study Committee 1987–97; Vice-President, Mencap in Wales 1990–;

Member, National Committee for Electoral Reform; President, Epilepsy Wales 1998–. *Awards:* Awarded The Grimshaw Memorial Award by National Federation of the Blind 1981. *Miscellaneous:* Vice-President, Federation of Economic Development Authorities (FEDA). Freeman, Borough of Arfon (1995). *Sportsclubs:* Member, Caernarfon Town Football Club. *Honours:* PC 1997. *Publications:* Co-author *An Economic Plan for Wales*, 1970; Author: *Agenda i'r iaith*, 1988; Report *Tourism in Wales*, 1987; *O Ddifri*, 1992; *Dal Ati*, 1993; *A Democratic Wales in an United Europe*, 1994; *A Fair Choice for Wales*, 1996. *Special Interests:* Industry, Employment, Disabled/Disability, European Regional Issues, Minority Languages. *Countries of Interest:* Argentina, Ireland, USA, Slovenia. *Recreations:* Football, tennis, swimming, chess. *Electoral Notes:* Contested Merioneth 1970. Contested North Wales in 1994 European Election. Member for Caernarfon since Feb 1974. AM for the Constituency of Caernarfon since May 6, 1999. *Address:* The Rt Hon. Dafydd Wigley, MP, AM, House of Commons, London, SW1A 0AA *Tel:* 020 7219 4182 *Fax:* 020 7219 3705. *Constituency:* 8 Castle Street, Caernarfon, Gwynedd, LL55 1SE *Tel:* 01286 672076 *Fax:* 01286 672003 *E-mail:* wigleyd@parliament.uk.

WILKINSON, John Arbuthnot Du Cane *(Ruislip Northwood)* Con majority 7,794

Son of late Denys Wilkinson, schoolmaster, and late Gillian (née Nairn), university lecturer. Born September 23, 1940; educated Eton College (King's Scholar); RAF College, Cranwell; Churchill College, Cambridge (MA Hons History Tripos 1965); University of Aix/Marseilles (Diploma) 1961. Married 1st, July 5, 1969, Paula Adey (1 daughter) (marriage dissolved 1987), married 2nd, July 25, 1987, Cecilia Lyon (1 son). *Armed Forces:* Commissioned into RAF from Cranwell 1961; Qualified French Interpreter in RAF 1961; Flying Instructor: No. 8 FTS 1962; Trooper, 21 SAS Regiment (Artists') TA 1963–65; Qualified Flying Instructor, RAF College, Cranwell 1966–67; ADC to Commander, 2nd Allied Tactical Air Force, Germany 1967. *Career:* Head of University Department, Conservative Central Office 1967–68; Aviation Specialist, Conservative Research Department 1969; Senior Administration Officer (Anglo/French Jaguar Project), Preston Division BAC 1969–70; Correspondence Tutor, Open University 1970–71; Chief Flying Instructor, Skywork Ltd, Stansted 1974–75; Sales Manager, Brooklands Aviation 1975; Personal Assistant to Chairman, BAC 1976–77; Sales Manager, Executive Air Services 1978–79. *Political Career:* PPS: to Minister of State for Industry 1979–80, to Secretary of State for Defence 1981–82; Whip withdrawn over European Communities Finance Bill 1994–1995. *Select Committees (Former):* : Armed Forces Bill (Special Select Committee) 1990–91; Member: 1987 1990. *Party Groups:* Chairman, Anglo/Asian Conservative Society 1979–82. *International Bodies:* Delegate, Council of Europe and WEU 1979–90; Chairman: Aerospace Committee, WEU 1986–89, Space Sub-Committee, Council of Europe 1984–88. *Other:* Chairman: European Freedom Council 1982–90, Horn of Africa Council 1984–88. *Trust:* Fellow, Industry and Parliament Trust 1993. *Miscellaneous:* Commonwealth War Graves Commissioner 1997–; Member, European Standing Committee B 1998–; President, London Green Belt Council 1997–. *Honours:* Hilal-i-Quaid-i-Azam (HQA) Pakistan 1989; Cross of Land of Mary (Estonia) 1999. Companion, Royal Aeronautical Society. *Publications:* (jointly) *The Uncertain Ally*, 1982; *British Defence: A Blueprint for Reform*, 1987. *Special Interests:* International Affairs, Defence, Aerospace, Aviation, European Union, Industry. *Countries of Interest:* Latin America, Baltic States, Ukraine, Philippines and ASEAN States, Bosnia. *Recreations:* Cross country skiing, hill-walking. *Electoral Notes:* Member for Bradford West 1970-February 74. Contested Bradford West October 1974. Member for Ruislip Northwood since May 1979. *Address:* John Wilkinson Esq, MP, House of Commons, London, SW1A 0AA *Tel:* 020 7219 6317 *Tel (Constituency):* 01923 822876.

WILLETTS, David Lindsay *(Havant)   Con majority 3,729*

Son of John and Hilary Willetts. Born March 9, 1956; educated King Edward's School, Birmingham; Christ Church, Oxford (BA 1st class hons PPE). Married 1986, Hon. Sarah Butterfield, daughter of Lord Butterfield, OBE, FRCP (1 son 1 daughter). *Career:* HM Treasury 1978–84; Private Secretary to Financial Secretary 1981–82; Principal, Monetary Policy Division 1982–84; Prime Minister's Downing Street Policy Unit 1984–86; Director of Studies, Centre for Policy Studies 1987–92; Consultant Director, Conservative Research Department 1987–92; Director: Retirement Security Ltd 1988–94, Electra Corporate Ventures Ltd 1988–94. *Councils, Public Bodies:* Member: Lambeth and Lewisham Family Practitioners' Committee 1987–90, Parkside Health Authority 1988–90, Social Security Advisory Committee 1989–92. *Political Career:* PPS to Rt Hon. Sir Norman Fowler, MP, as Chairman of the Conservative Party 1993–94; Parliamentary Secretary, Office of Public Service 1995–96; Paymaster General, Office of Public Service July-December 1996; Shadow Secretary of State for: Education and Employment 1998–99, Social Security 1999–. *Whip:* Assistant Government Whip 1994–95; Lord Commissioner of HM Treasury (Government Whip) July-November 1995. *Spokesman:* An Opposition Spokesman on Education and Employment (Employment) 1997–98. *Select Committees (Former):* Member: Social Security 1992–93. *Party Groups:* Chairman, Conservative Research Department 1997. *Publications:* Author of: *Modern Conservatism*, 1992; *Civic Conservatism*, 1994; *Blair's Gurus*, 1996; *Why Vote Conservative*, 1997; *Welfare to Work*, 1998; *After the Landslide*, 1999. *Special Interests:* Economic Policy, Health, Social Security, Education. *Countries of Interest:* Japan, USA, Germany. *Recreations:* Swimming, reading. *Electoral Notes:* Member for Havant since April 9, 1992. *Clubs:* Athenaeum, Hurlingham. *Address:* David Willetts Esq, MP, House of Commons, London, SW1A 0AA *Tel:* 020 7219 4570 *Fax:* 020 7219 2567. *Constituency:* c/o Havant Conservative Association, Homewell House, 22 Homewell, Havant, Hampshire PO9 1EE *Tel:* 023 9247 5066.

WILLIAMS, The Rt Hon. Alan John *(Swansea West)   Lab majority 14,459*

Son of Emlyn Williams, coal miner. Born October 14, 1930; educated Cardiff High School; Cardiff College of Technology; University College, Oxford (BSc (Economics) (London), BA). Married June 1957, Patricia Rees (2 sons 1 daughter). *Trades Union:* Member, Association of Teachers at Technical Institutes, affiliated to the NUT since 1958; Member, Transport Salaried Staff Association (TSSA). *Career:* Lecturer in Economics, Welsh College of Advanced Technology. *Political Career:* PPS to Postmaster General 1966–67; Joint Parliamentary Secretary, Ministry of Technology 1969–70; Parliamentary Under-Secretary of State, Department of Economic Affairs 1967–69; Minister of State for: Prices and Consumer Protection 1974–76, Industry 1976–79; Shadow Secretary of State for Wales 1987–88; Deputy Shadow Leader of the House and Campaigns Co-ordinator 1983–89. *Spokesman:* Opposition Spokesman on: Industry 1970–71, Higher Education 1971–72, Consumer Affairs 1973–74; Opposition Front Bench Spokesman on: Wales 1979–80, Industry and Consumer Affairs 1979–87, The Civil Service 1980–83. *Select Committees (Current):* Member: Parliamentary Privilege (Joint Committee) 1997–, Public Accounts 1997–, Standards and Privileges 1997– *(Former):* Member: Public Accounts 1990–97, Privileges 1994–97. *Party Groups:* Joined Labour Party 1950; Member: Fabian Society, Co-operative Party; Chairman, Welsh Parliamentary Labour Group 1966–67. *International Bodies:* Visited Russia as Member of National Union of Students delegation 1954; Council of Europe and Western European 1966–67; Chairman, Welsh Branch of British-Russia Centre 1995–; Member, North Atlantic Alliance 1997–; Joint Hon. Treasurer, British-American Parliamentary International Group 1999–. *Miscellaneous:* Member: Lord Chancellor's Advisory Council on Committee Records 1995–, Public Accounts Commission 1997–. Freeman, City of Swansea. *Honours:* PC January 1977. *Special Interests:* Regional Policy, Industrial Policy, Job-Creating Strategies, Micro-Technology. *Recreations:* Golf. *Electoral Notes:* Contested Poole 1959. Member for Swansea West since October 15, 1964. *Clubs:* Clyne Golf. *Address:* The Rt Hon. Alan Williams, MP (Swansea West), House of Commons, London, SW1A 0AA *Tel:* 020 7219 3449 *Fax:* 020 7219 6943 *Fax (Constituency):* 01792 702048.

WILLIAMS, Dr Alan Wynne *(Carmarthen East and Dinefwr)   Lab majority 3,450*

Son of late Tom Williams and late Mary Williams. Born December 21, 1945; educated Carmarthen Grammar School; Jesus College, Oxford 1963–69 (BA Chemistry 1st class hons, DPhil). Married September 4, 1973, Marian Williams. *Career:* Lecturer in Environmental Science, Trinity College, Carmarthen 1971–87. *Select Committees (Former):* Member: Welsh Affairs 1987–91, Science and Technology 1992–97. *Party Groups:* Secretary, Carmarthen Constituency Labour Party 1981–84, Election Agent 1983. Oxfam. *Special Interests:* Agriculture, Environmental Protection, Trade and Industry, Economics. *Recreations:* Reading, television, watching sport. *Electoral Notes:* Member for Carmarthen 1987–97, and for Carmarthen East and Dinefwr since May 1, 1997. *Address:* Dr Alan Williams, MP (Carmarthen East and Dinefwr), House of Commons, London, SW1A 0AA *Tel:* 020 7219 3000. *Constituency:* 33 Wind Street, Ammanford, Carmarthenshire, SA18 3DN *Tel:* 01269 593809 *Fax:* 01269 597271.

WILLIAMS, Betty *(Conwy)   Lab majority 1,596*

Daughter of late Griffith Williams and of Elizabeth Williams. Born July 31, 1944; educated Ysgol Dyffryn Nantlle, Penygroes; Normal College, Bangor (BA Hons). Evan Glyn Williams (2 sons). *Trades Union:* Member, T&GWU. *Profession:* Freelance Media Researcher. *Career:* Secretarial; Freelance Journalist/Media Researcher. *Councils, Public Bodies:* Councillor: Parish/Community 1967–83, District Council 1970–91, County Council 1976–93; Mayor, Arfon Borough Council 1990–91; Former Member: Gwynedd Health Authority, Snowdonia National Park Committee (Northern). *Select Committees (Current):* Member: Welsh Affairs 1997–. *Other:* Chair, Governors of Special School in Caernarfon; Former Governor: Normal College, Bangor, Gwynedd Technical College; Former Chair, National Eisteddfod Local Finance Committee; Chair: Victims' Support, Arfon Carers' Committee; Christian Aid Organiser. *Awards:* HTV Student of the Year; National Eisteddfod Prize for video production about a Welsh heroine; John Evans Memorial Prize. *Miscellaneous:* Member, Gas Consumers' Council for Wales; Deacon, Seion C Talysarn. *Special Interests:* Social Services, Health, Health Education, Environmental Health, Consumer Issues, Education (Special Needs), Railways. *Recreations:* Eisteddfodau, opera, hymn singing festivals, sheep dog trials. *Electoral Notes:* Contested Caernarfon 1983, Conwy 1987 and 1992 General Elections. Member for Conwy since May 1, 1997. *Address:* Betty Williams, MP, House of Commons, London, SW1A 0AA *Tel:* 020 7219 5052 *Fax:* 020 7219 2759 *E-mail:* williamsbh@parliament.uk.

WILLIS, Phil (Philip George) *(Harrogate and Knaresborough)   LD majority 6,236*

Son of late George Willis, postman, and of late Norah, nurse. Born November 30, 1941; educated Burnley Grammar School; City of Leeds and Carnegie College; Birmingham University (CertEd 1963, BPhil 1978). Married Heather Sellars (1 son 1 daughter). *Trades Union:* Member, Secondary Heads Association. *Profession:* Teacher. *Career:* Head Teacher, Ormesby School, Cleveland 1978–82; Head Teacher, John Smeaton Community High School, Leeds 1983–97. *Councils, Public Bodies:* Councillor, Harrogate Borough Council 1988–, First Liberal Democrat Leader 1990–98; Councillor, North Yorkshire County Council 1993–97, Deputy Group Leader 1993–97. *Whip:* North, Midlands and Wales Whip 1997–99. *Spokesman:* Spokesman for Education and Employment (Further, Higher and Adult Education) 1997–99; Principal Spokesman for Education and Employment 1999–. *Select Committees (Current):* Member: Education and Employment 1999–, Education Sub-Committee 1999–. *Party Groups:* Member, Association of Liberal Democrat Councillors. *Other:* Member: Charter 88, Friends of the Earth, Amnesty International. *Sportsclubs:* Leeds United Football Club. *Special Interests:* Inclusive Education, Health, Local Government, Northern Ireland, Gibraltar. *Countries of Interest:* Ireland. *Recreations:* Theatre, music, dance (especially ballet), football (Leeds United). *Electoral Notes:* Member for Harrogate and Knaresborough since May 1, 1997. *Address:* Phil Willis Esq, MP, House of Commons, London, SW1A 0AA *Tel:* 020 7219 3846 *Fax:* 020 7219 0971. *Constituency:* Ashdown House, Station Parade, Harrogate, North Yorkshire, HG1 5BR *Tel:* 01423 528888 *Fax:* 01423 505700 *E-mail:* johnfox@cix.co.uk.

WILLS, Michael David *(North Swindon)   Lab majority 7,688*

Son of late Stephen Wills and Elizabeth Wills. Born May 20, 1952; educated Haberdashers Aske's, Elstree; Clare College, Cambridge (Double First Class BA Hons). Married January 19, 1984, Jill, daughter of David Freeman (3 sons 2 daughters). *Trades Union:* Member, TGWU. *Profession:* TV Producer. *Career:* Third Secretary later Second Secretary, HM Diplomatic Service 1976–80; Researcher, later Producer, London Weekend Television 1980–84; Director, Juniper Productions 1984–97. *Political Career:* Parliamentary Under-Secretary of State: Department of Trade and Industry (Minister for Small Firms, Trade and Industry) 1999, Department for Education and Employment 1999–. *Miscellaneous:* Chairman, Non-Ministerial Cross-Party Advisory Group on Preparation for the EMU 1998–. *Electoral Notes:* Member for North Swindon since May 1, 1997. *Address:* Michael Wills Esq, MP, House of Commons, London, SW1A 0AA *Tel:* 020 7219 3000. *Constituency:* People's Centre, Beech Avenue, Swindon, SN2 1JT *Tel:* 01793 481016 *Fax:* 01793 524483 *E-mail:* tlo.wills@tlo.dti.gov.uk.

WILSHIRE, David *(Spelthorne)   Con majority 3,473*

Born September 16, 1943; educated Kingswood School, Bath; Fitzwilliam College, Cambridge (MA Cantab). Married 1967, Margaret Weeks (1 son, and 1 daughter deceased). *Career:* Built up own group of small businesses; Worked for European MPs 1979–85; Partner, Western Political Research Services 1979–; Co-director, Political Management Programme, Brunel University 1985–90. *Councils, Public Bodies:* Formerly Parish, District and County Councillor; Leader, Wansdyke District Council (Avon) 1981–87. *Political Career:* PPS: to Rt Hon. Alan Clark, MP, as Minister for Defence Procurement 1991–92, to Rt Hon. Peter Lloyd MP, as Minister of State, Home Office 1992–94. *Select Committees (Current):* Member: Foreign Affairs 1997– *(Former):* Member: Northern Ireland Affairs 1994–97, Entry Clearance Sub-Committee 1997–98. *International Bodies:* Member, British-Irish Inter-Parliamentary Body 1990–; Substitute Member, Assembly of Council of Europe 1997–; Treasurer, IPU British Branch 1997–; Vice-Chairman, CPA UK Branch 1998–99. *Special Interests:* Foreign Affairs, Aviation, Local Government, Political Process, Northern Ireland. *Recreations:* Gardening, wine and cider-making. *Electoral Notes:* Member for Spelthorne since June 1987. *Address:* David Wilshire Esq, MP, House of Commons, London, SW1A 0AA *Tel:* 020 7219 3534. *Constituency:* 55 Cherry Orchard, Staines, Middx, TW8 2DQ *Tel:* 01784 450822.

WILSON, Brian *(Cunninghame North)   Lab majority 11,039*

Son of late John Forrest Wilson and Marion MacIntyre. Born December 13, 1948; educated Dunoon Grammar School; Dundee University; University College, Cardiff (MA Hons). Married December 11, 1981, Joni, daughter of Donald and Dolina Buchanan (2 sons 1 daughter). *Career:* Journalist; Founding Editor and Publisher, *West Highland Free Press* 1972–97; Contributor to: *The Guardian, Glasgow Herald. Political Career:* Minister of State: Scottish Office (Minister for Education and Industry) 1997–98, Department of Trade and Industry (Minister for Trade) 1998–99; Minister of State, Scotland Office 1999–. *Spokesman:* Opposition Spokesman on: Scotland 1988–92, Citizen's Charter and Women July–November 1992, Transport November 1992–94, Trade and Industry 1994–95, Transport 1995–96, Election Planning 1996–97. *Awards:* First winner, Nicholas Tomalin Memorial Award for outstanding journalism; *Spectator* Parliamentarian of the Year 'New Member' Award 1990. *Sportsclubs:* Kilbirnie Place Golf. FRSA (Scot). *Publications: Celtic: A Century with Honour,* 1988. *Electoral Notes:* Contested Ross and Cromarty October 1974, Inverness 1979 and Western Isles 1983. Member for Cunninghame North since June 1987. *Clubs:* Garnock Labour. *Address:* Brian Wilson Esq, MP, House of Commons, London, SW1A 0AA *Tel:* 020 7219 3000. *Constituency:* 37 Main Street, Kilbirnie, Ayrshire, KA25 7BX *Tel:* 01505 682847 *Fax:* 01505 684648.

WINNICK, David *(Walsall North)   Lab majority 12,588*

Son of late E. G. and Rose Winnick. Born June 26, 1933; educated Secondary school; London School of Economics. Married September 23, 1968, Bengisu Rona (marriage dissolved). *Trades Union:* Association of Professional, Executive, Clerical & Computer Staff (APEX): Member of Executive Council 1978–88, Vice-President 1983–88. *Councils, Public Bodies:* Councillor: Willesden Borough Council 1959–64, Brent Borough Council 1964–66. *Select Committees (Current):* Member: Home Affairs 1997– *(Former):* Member: Procedure 1989–97. *International Bodies:* British Co-Chair, British-Irish Inter-Parliamentary Body 1997–. *Other:* Chairman, United Kingdom Immigrants Advisory Service 1984–. *Electoral Notes:* Contested Harwich 1964. Member for Croydon South 1966–70. Contested Croydon Central October 1974 and Walsall North in 1976 By-election. Member for Walsall North since May 1979. *Address:* David Winnick Esq, MP, House of Commons, London, SW1A 0AA *Tel:* 020 7219 5003 *Fax:* 020 7219 0257 *Tel (Constituency):* 01922 495629.

WINTERTON, Ann *(Congleton)   Con majority 6,130*

Daughter of late Joseph Robert Hodgson and Ellen Jane Hodgson. Born March 6, 1941; educated Erdington Grammar School for Girls. Married 1960, Nicholas Winterton (MP for Macclesfield) *(qv)* (2 sons 1 daughter). *Political Career:* Member, Shadow Cabinet 1998–. *Spokesman:* An Opposition Frontbench Spokeswoman on National Drug Strategy 1998–. *Select Committees (Current):* Member: Unopposed Bills (Panel) 1997– *(Former):* Member: Agriculture 1987–97, Chairmen's Panel 1992–98, Chairmen's Panel 1998–99. *Party Groups:* Member, West Midlands Conservative Women's Advisory Committee 1969–71. *Other:* Vice-President: Townswomen's Guilds, East Cheshire and St Luke's Hospices; Patron: East Cheshire NSPCC, VISYON; President, Congleton Division of the St. John Ambulance. *Trust:* Fellow, Industry and Parliament Trust. *Miscellaneous:* Joint Master, South Staffordshire Hunt 1959–64. *Special Interests:* Textile Industries, Pharmaceutical and Chemical Industries, Agriculture, Transport, Think British Campaign. *Countries of Interest:* Austria, Namibia, South Africa, USA. *Recreations:* Cinema, theatre, music, tennis, riding, skiing. *Electoral Notes:* Member for Congleton since June, 1983. *Address:* Mrs Ann Winterton, MP, House of Commons, London, SW1A 0AA *Tel:* 020 7219 3585. *Constituency:* Riverside, Mountbatten Way, Congleton, Cheshire, CW12 1DY *Tel:* 01260 278866 *Fax:* 01260 278866.

WINTERTON, Nicholas *(Macclesfield)   Con majority 8,654*

Son of late Norman Harry Winterton. Born March 31, 1938; educated Bilton Grange Preparatory School; Rugby School. Married 1960, Ann (MP for Congleton) *(qv)*, daughter of J. R. Hodgson (2 sons 1 daughter). *Armed Forces:* Commissioned, 14th/20th Kings Hussars 1957–59. *Career:* Sales Executive Trainee, Shell-Mex B.P. Ltd. 1959–60; Sales & General Manager, Stevens & Hodgson Ltd 1960–71. *Councils, Public Bodies:* Warwickshire County Council: Councillor 1967–72, Chairman, County Youth Service Sub-Committee 1969–72, Deputy Chairman, Education Committee 1970–72. *Political Career:* A Deputy Speaker of the House of Commons 1999–. *Select Committees (Current):* Member: Chairmen's Panel 1997–, Modernisation of the House of Commons 1997–; Chairman: Procedure 1997–; Member: Liaison 1998–, Standing Orders 1998– *(Former):* Chairman: Health 1991–92; Member: Liaison 1997–98. *International Bodies:* Member of Council, League for Exchange of Commonwealth Teachers 1979–92; Member, Executive Committee, Commonwealth Parliamentary Association (CPA) UK Branch 1997–. *Other:* Patron, International Centre for Child Care Studies; Chairman, Zimbabwe Rhodesia Relief Fund; President: Macclesfield Riding for the Disabled Branch, Macclesfield Club for Physically Disabled, Macclesfield Branch of RNLI, Friends of Pallotti Day Care Centre, Rossendale Trust; Vice-President: Macclesfield Branch Multiple Sclerosis Society, Macclesfield and District Council for Voluntary Service, Macclesfield Division of St John Ambulance Brigade, East Cheshire Hospice. *Trust:* Fellow, Industry and Parliament Trust. *Miscellaneous:* Chairman, Executive Committee of Anglo/Austrian Society; Hon. Vice-President: National Association of Master Bakers, Confectioners and Caterers, The Royal College of Midwives; Executive Member, 1922 Committee 1997–; Vice-President, National Association of Local Councils. Immediate Past Upper Bailiff and Member of the Court of Assistants, Worshipful Company of Weavers. Freeman, City of London. *Sportsclubs:* Bollington Bowling Club; Bollington Cricket Club; Macclesfield Cricket Club; Macclesfield Hockey Club; New Century Bowman; Prince Albert Angling Society. *Special Interests:* Local Government, Health Service, Sport, Recreation, Paper Industries, Textile Industries, Foreign Affairs, Media, Pharmaceutical and Chemical Industries. *Countries of Interest:* South Africa, Indonesia, Taiwan, USA, Denmark, Sweden, Austria, Namibia. *Recreations:* Squash, tennis, swimming, jogging, skiing. *Electoral Notes:* Contested Newcastle-under-Lyme by-election October 1969 and General Election 1970. Member for Macclesfield since By-election Sept 30, 1971. *Clubs:* Cavalry and Guards, Lighthouse, Old Boys and Park Green Macclesfield. *Address:* Nicholas Winterton Esq, MP, House of Commons, London, SW1A 0AA *Tel:* 020 7219 3000. *Constituency:* Macclesfield Conservative and Unionist Association, West Bank Road, Macclesfield, Cheshire, SK10 3DU *Tel:* 01625 422848 *Fax:* 01625 617066.

WINTERTON, Rosie *(Doncaster Central)*   Lab majority 17,856

Daughter of Gordon Winterton, teacher, and late Valerie Winterton, teacher. Born August 10, 1958; educated Doncaster Grammar School; Hull University (BA Hons History). *Trades Union:* Former Branch Officer, TGWU; Member: NUJ, TGWU. *Career:* Constituency Personal Assistant to John Prescott 1980–86; Parliamentary Officer: Southwark Council 1986–88, Royal College of Nursing 1988–90; Managing Director, Connect Public Affairs 1990–94; Head of Office of Rt Hon. John Prescott, MP, Deputy Leader of the Labour Party. *Other:* Member, Amnesty International. *Special Interests:* Regional Policy, Employment, Transport, Housing, Home Affairs. *Recreations:* Sailing, reading. *Electoral Notes:* Member for Doncaster Central since May 1, 1997. *Clubs:* Doncaster Trades and Labour, Intake Social, Doncaster Catholic. *Address:* Rosie Winterton, MP, House of Commons, London, SW1A 0AA *Tel:* 020 7219 0925/6357 *Fax:* 020 7219 4581. *Constituency:* Guildhall Advice Centre, Old Guildhall Yard, Doncaster, South Yorkshire, DN1 1QW *Tel:* 01302 735241 *Fax:* 01302 735242 *E-mail:* wintertonr@parliament.uk.

WISE, Audrey *(Preston)*   Lab majority 18,680

Daughter of George and Elsie Crawford Brown. Born January 4, 1935. Married John Wise (1 son 1 daughter). *Trades Union:* President, USDAW 1991–97. *Career:* Shorthand typist. *Select Committees (Current):* Member: Health 1997–, Unopposed Bills (Panel) 1997– *(Former):* Member: Health 1991–97. *Other:* Member: War on Want, Labour Action for Peace, CND, Nicaragua Solidarity, The Soil Association, Socialist Environment and Resources Association. *Trust:* Member, National Trust. *Publications: Women and the Struggle for Workers' Control; Eye Witness in Revolutionary Portugal. Special Interests:* Women, Health, Nuclear Disarmament, Environment, Poverty and Low Pay, Children. *Countries of Interest:* Nicaragua, Vietnam. *Recreations:* Organic gardening. *Electoral Notes:* Member for Coventry South West February 1974–79. Contested Woolwich 1983. Member for Preston since June 1987. *Address:* Mrs Audrey Wise, MP, House of Commons, London, SW1A 0AA *Tel:* 020 7219 5220 *Fax:* 020 7219 5869 *Tel (Constituency):* 01772 556771 *Fax (Constituency):* 01772 556771.

WOOD, Mike *(Batley and Spen)*   Lab majority 6,141

Son of late Rowland L. Wood, foundry worker, and Laura M. Wood, retired cleaner. Born March 3, 1946; educated Nantwich and Acton Grammar School, Nantwich, Cheshire; Salisbury/Wells Theological College (Cert Theol); Leeds University (CQSW); Leeds Metropolitan University (BA). Married 1999 (1 son 1 daughter from previous marriage). *Trades Union:* Trade Unionist since 1962; Member: UNISON, GMB. *Profession:* Probation Officer. *Career:* Probation Officer, Social Worker, Community Worker 1965–97. *Councils, Public Bodies:* Kirklees Metropolitan District Council: Councillor 1980–88, Deputy Leader of Council 1986–87. *Select Committees (Former):* Member: Broadcasting 1997–98. *Party Groups:* Member, Labour Friends of India. *Other:* Former

Director, Housing Charity. *Publications: Probation Hostel Directory*, 1980. *Special Interests:* Poverty, Housing, Transport, Environmental Issues and World Development. *Countries of Interest:* France, Indian Sub-continent. *Recreations:* Sport, music, ornithology, walking. *Electoral Notes:* Contested Hexham 1987. Member for Batley and Spen since May 1, 1997. *Address:* Mike Wood Esq, MP, House of Commons, London, SW1A 0AA *Tel:* 020 7219 4125. *Constituency:* Tom Myer's House, 9 Cross Crown Street, Cleckheaton, West Yorkshire, BD19 3HW *Tel:* 01274 335233 *Fax:* 01274 335235 *E-mail:* mike.wood@geo2.pop.org.uk.

WOODWARD, Shaun Anthony *(Witney)   Con majority 7,028**

Son of Dennis George Woodward and Joan Lillian (née Nunn). Born October 26, 1958; educated Bristol Grammar School; Jesus College, Cambridge (MA English Literature); Visiting Professor, Queen Mary and Westfield College, London University; Visiting Fellow, John F. Kennedy School of Government, Harvard University. Married May 2, 1987, Camilla Davan Sainsbury, daughter of Rt Hon. Sir Timothy Sainsbury (1 son 3 daughters). *Profession:* Broadcaster. *Career:* BBC TV News and Current Affairs 1982–98; Director of Communications, Conservative Party 1991–92. *Spokesman:* An Opposition Front Bench Spokesman for Environment, Transport and the Regions 1999. *Select Committees (Current):* Member: Broadcasting 1997– *(Former):* Member: European Legislation 1997–98, European Legislation 1998, European Scrutiny 1998–99, Foreign Affairs 1999. *Trust:* Director: English National Opera, Marine Stewardship Council; Member, Foundation Board, RSC; Trustee, Childline. *Publications:* Co-author: *Tranquilisers,*1983, *Ben: The Story of Ben Hardwick*, 1984, *Drugwatch*, 1985. *Special Interests:* Finance, Environment, Education, Culture. *Countries of Interest:* USA. *Recreations:* Opera, tennis, reading, gardening, architecture. *Electoral Notes:* *Conservative Member for Witney May 1, 1997–December 1999, Labour Member since December 1999. *Address:* Shaun Woodward Esq, MP, House of Commons, London, SW1A 0AA *Tel:* 020 7219 2680 *Fax:* 020 7219 0979. *Constituency:* West Oxfordshire Conservative Association, 10 Bridge Street, Witney, Oxfordshire *Tel:* 01993 702302 *E-mail:* seelyr@parliament.uk.

WOOLAS, Philip James *(Oldham East and Saddleworth)   Lab majority 3,389*

Son of Dennis and Maureen Woolas. Born December 11, 1959; educated Nelson Grammar School; Walton Lane High School; Nelson and Colne College; University of Manchester (BA Hons Philosophy). Married June 25, 1988, Tracey, daughter of Phillip and Shirley Allen (1 son). *Trades Union:* Member, GMB. *Profession:* TV Producer. *Career:* President, National Union of Students 1984–86; BBC Newsnight Producer 1988–90; Channel 4 News Producer 1990; Head of Communication, GMB 1991–97. *Political Career:* PPS to Rt Hon. the Lord Macdonald of Tradeston, as Minister of State for Transport, Department of the Environment, Transport and the Regions (Minister for Transport) 1999–;. *Party Groups:* Chair, Tribune Newspaper 1997– Deputy Leader, Leadership Campaign Team 1997–99. *Awards:* RTS Award for Political Coverage 1990. *Sportsclubs:* Lancashire County Cricket Club, Manchester United Football Club. *Special Interests:* Employment, Economics, Media, Trade and Industry, Minimum Wage. *Countries of Interest:* Kashmir and Jammu. *Recreations:* Photography. *Electoral Notes:* Contested Littleborough and Saddleworth By-election 1995. Member for Oldham East and Saddleworth since May 1, 1997. *Clubs:* Groucho. *Address:* Philip Woolas Esq, MP, House of Commons, London, SW1A 0AA *Tel:* 020 7219 1149 *Fax:* 020 7219 0992. *Constituency:* Textile House, 110 Union Street, Oldham, Lancashire *Tel:* 0161–624 4248.

Dod *on* Disk
The Vacher Dod Parliamentary Database – configured for PC or Network
For further details please telephone the Westminster Office
020 7828 7256

WORTHINGTON, Tony (Anthony) *(Clydebank and Milngavie)   Lab majority 13,320*

Son of late Malcolm and Monica Worthington. Born October 11, 1941; educated City School, Lincoln; London School of Economics; York, Durham and Glasgow Universities. Married 1966, Angela, daughter of Cyril and May Oliver (1 son 1 daughter). *Career:* Lecturer: HM Borstal, Dover 1962–66, Monkwearmouth College of F.E., Sunderland 1967–71, Jordanhill College of Education 1971–87. *Councils, Public Bodies:* Clydebank North: Regional Councillor 1974–87, Chairman, Finance Committee 1986–87. *Political Career:* Parliamentary Under-Secretary of State, Northern Ireland Office 1997–98. *Spokesman:* Opposition Spokesman on: Education, Employment, Training and Social Work 1989–92, Development and Co-operation 1992–93; Opposition Spokesman on: Foreign and Commonwealth Affairs 1993–94, Northern Ireland 1995–97. *Select Committees (Current):* Member: International Development 1999– *(Former):* Member: Home Affairs 1987–88. *Special Interests:* International Development, Employment. *Countries of Interest:* Africa, Middle East, Eastern Europe. *Recreations:* Gardening. *Electoral Notes:* Member for Clydebank and Milngavie since June 1987. *Address:* Tony Worthington Esq, MP, House of Commons, London, SW1A 0AA *Tel:* 020 7219 3507 *Fax:* 020 7219 3507. *Constituency:* 24 Cleddans Crescent, Handgate, Clydebank, Dunbartonshire, G81 5NW *Tel:* 01389 873195 *Fax:* 01389 873195 *E-mail:* worthingtont@parliament.uk.

WRAY, James *(Glasgow Baillieston)   Lab majority 14,840*

Son of late Harold Wray and the late Elizabeth Wray. Born April 28, 1938; educated St Bonaventure's, Gorbals. Married (2 sons 2 daughters). *Trades Union:* Member of Committee, TGWU. *Councils, Public Bodies:* Strathclyde Regional Councillor, Gorbals for 1976–88; Councillor, Glasgow Corporation Mile-End Ward 1972–75. *Party Groups:* Parliamentary Agent for the late Frank McElhone, former Labour MP for Gorbals division of Glasgow 1969–74 and Queens Park division 1974–82; Former Parliamentary election agent for late Robert McTaggart, Labour MP for Glasgow Central. *International Bodies:* Substitute, UK Delegation to Council of Europe and Western Europe Union. *Other:* Leader: Anti-Dampness campaign, Anti-Eviction campaign, Anti-Fluoridation campaign, Gorbals rent strike. *Sportsclubs:* Hon. President, Scottish Pro-Amateur Ex-Boxers Association; President: Kelvin Amateur Boxing Club, Strathclyde Community Boxers Club. *Special Interests:* Social Services, Education, Foreign Affairs. *Recreations:* Boxing. *Electoral Notes:* Member for Glasgow Provan 1987–97, and for Glasgow Baillieston since May 1, 1997. *Address:* James Wray Esq, MP, House of Commons, London, SW1A 0AA *Tel:* 020 7219 4606.

WRIGHT, Anthony David *(Great Yarmouth)   Lab majority 8,668*

Son of late Arthur Wright and of Jean Wright. Born August 12, 1954; educated Secondary modern school. Married August 13, 1988, Barbara Fleming (1 son 1 daughter 1 stepdaughter). *Trades Union:* Member: AEEU, GMB. *Profession:* Engineer. *Career:* Engineering Apprentice; Engineer; Labour Party Organiser/Agent 1983–97. *Councils, Public Bodies:* Great Yarmouth Borough Council: Councillor 1980–82, 1986–98, Leader of Council 1996–97. *Miscellaneous:* Member, European Standing Committee C 1999–. *Special Interests:* Local Government, Trade and Industry. *Countries of Interest:* Cyprus. *Electoral Notes:* Member for Great Yarmouth since May 1, 1997. *Address:* Anthony David Wright Esq, MP (Great Yarmouth), House of Commons, London, SW1A 0AA *Tel:* 020 7219 4832 *Fax:* 020 7219 2304. *Constituency:* 21 Euston Road, Great Yarmouth, Norfolk, NR30 1DZ *Tel:* 01493 332291 *Fax:* 01493 332189 *E-mail:* wrighta@parliament.uk.

WRIGHT, Dr Anthony Wayland *(Cannock Chase)   Lab majority 14,478*

Son of Frank and Maud Wright. Born March 11, 1948; educated Desborough Primary School; Kettering Grammar School; London School of Economics (BSc Economics); Harvard University (Kennedy Scholar); Balliol College, Oxford (DPhil); Hon Professor, Birmingham University 1999–. Married July 21, 1973, Moira Elynwy, daughter of Edmor and Rhiannon Phillips (3 sons and 1 son deceased). *Career:* Lecturer in Politics, University College of North Wales, Bangor 1973–75; School of Continuing Studies, Birmingham University: Lecturer, Senior Lecturer, Reader in Politics 1975–92. *Councils, Public Bodies:* Chairman, South Birmingham Community Health Council 1983–85. *Political Career:* PPS to the Rt Hon. the Lord Irvine of Lairg, as Lord Chancellor 1997–98. *Select Committees (Current):* Member: Liaison 1999–; Chairman: Public Administration 1999– *(Former):* Member: Parliamentary Commissioner for Administration 1992–96, Public Service 1995–97. *Party Groups:* Executive Member, Fabian Society. *Other:* Parent Governor, St Laurence Church Schools, Northfield, Birmingham 1989–92; Co-Chair, Campaign for Freedom of Information –1999. *Publications:* Include: *G. D. H. Cole and Socialist Democracy*, 1979; *Local Radio and Local Democracy*, 1982; *British Socialism*, 1983; *Socialisms: Theories and Practices*, 1986; *R. H. Tawney*, 1987; *Matters of Death and Life: A Study of Bereavement Support in Hospitals*, 1988; *Consuming Public Services*, 1990 (editor); *Contemporary Political Ideologies*, 1993 (editor); *Subjects and Citizens*, 1993; *Socialisms: Old and New*, 1996; *The People's Party*, 1997; *Who Can I Complain To?*, 1997; *Why Vote Labour?*, 1997; Joint Editor, *The Political Quarterly*. *Special Interests:* Education, Health, Environment, Constitution. *Recreations:* Tennis, football, secondhand bookshops, walking, gardening. *Electoral Notes:* Contested Kidderminster 1979. Member for Cannock and Burntwood 1992–97, and for Cannock Chase since May 1, 1997. *Address:* Dr Anthony W Wright, MP (Cannock Chase), House of Commons, London, SW1A 0AA *Tel:* 020 7219 5029/5583 *Fax:* 020 7219 2665. *Constituency:* 6A Hallcourt Crescent, Cannock, Staffordshire, WS11 3AB *Tel:* 01543 467810 *Fax:* 01543 467811 *E-mail:* wrightt@parliament.uk.

WYATT, Derek *(Sittingbourne and Sheppey)   Lab majority 1,929*

Son of Reginald and Margaret Wyatt. Born December 4, 1949; educated Westcliff County High School; Colchester Royal Grammar School; St Luke's College, Exeter (Certificate of Education); Open University (BA Hons Art and Architecture); St Catherine's College, Oxford (Research). Married Joanna Willett (1 daughter 1 son). *Trades Union:* Member, NUJ. *Profession:* Software Specialist. *Career:* Former Head of Programmes, Wire TV; Former Director and a Publisher, William Heinemann; Former Director, Computer Channel, BSkyB. *Councils, Public Bodies:* Councillor, Archway Ward, London Borough of Haringey 1994–96, Chair, Alexandra Palace and Parks 1994–96. *Select Committees (Current):* Member: Culture, Media and Sport 1997–. *Party Groups:* Chair, Kent Labour MPs Group. *International Bodies:* Founder, World Internet Forum. *Other:* Member: RSPB, Charter 88, ANC, Amnesty International; Founded the Women's Sports Foundation 1986; Executive Member, European Media Forum. *Trust:* Major Stanley's, Oxford University 1993–; Fellow, Industry and Parliament Trust (Motorola) 1998–; Parliament Charitable Trust (Raleigh International) 1999–. *Awards:* Awarded The United Nations Commendation (Apartheid in Sport) 1987. *Sportsclubs:* Charlton Athletic FC, Penguin International RFC (Executive); Played Rugby for Oxford University, Barbarians and England. FRSA. *Publications:* 5 books to date including: *Wisecracks From The Movies*, 1987, *Rugby DisUnion*, 1995. *Special Interests:* Venture Capital, Sport, Internet Strategy, British Council, Foreign Affairs, Urban Parks, National Grid for Learning, Swiss Banking. *Countries of Interest:* Southern Africa, Middle East, China. *Recreations:* Reading, sport, writing, travel, jazz. *Electoral Notes:* Member for Sittingbourne and Sheppey since May 1, 1997. *Clubs:* RAC, Vincents (Oxford). *Address:* Derek Wyatt, MP, House of Commons, London, SW1A 0AA *Tel:* 020 7219 3000. *Constituency:* 29 Park Road, Sittingbourne, Kent *Tel:* 01795 477277 *E-mail:* wyattd@parliament.co.uk *Website:* http://www.derekwyattmp.co.uk.

Y

YEO, Timothy Stephen Kenneth *(South Suffolk)   Con majority 4,175*

Son of late Dr Kenneth John Yeo. Born March 20, 1945; educated Charterhouse; Emmanuel College, Cambridge (MA History); Exhibitioner 1963. Married March 30, 1970, Diane Helen, daughter of Brian Pickard, FRCS (1 son 1 daughter). *Career:* Assistant Treasurer, Bankers Trust Company 1970–73; Director: Worcester Engineering Co Ltd 1975–86, The Spastics Society 1980–83. *Political Career:* PPS to Rt Hon. Douglas Hurd, CBE, MP: as Home Secretary 1988–89, as Foreign and Commonwealth Secretary 1989–90; Joint Parliamentary Under-Secretary of State at: Department of the Environment 1990–92, Department of Health 1992–93; Minister of State for Environment and Countryside, Department of the Environment 1993–94; Shadow Minister of Agriculture, Fisheries and Food 1998–. *Spokesman:* An Opposition Spokesman on Environment, Transport and the Regions (Local Government, Regions, Planning and Housing) 1997–98. *Select Committees (Former):* Member: Employment 1994–96, Treasury 1996–97. *Party Groups:* A Vice-Chairman, Conservative Party (with responsibility for Local Government) 1998. *Other:* Chairman, Charities VAT Reform Group 1981–88; President, Charities Tax Reform Group 1988–90; Vice-President, International Voluntary Service 1984; Chairman, Tadworth Court Trust 1984–91. *Trust:* Trustee, Tanzania Development Trust 1980–97; Fellow, Industry and Parliament Trust. *Sportsclubs:* Captain, Parliamentary Golfing Society 1991–95. *Special Interests:* Health, Economic Policy, Unemployment, Charity Reform, Rural Affairs. *Recreations:* Golf, skiing. *Electoral Notes:* Contested Bedwelty February 1974. Member for South Suffolk since June 1983. *Clubs:* Royal St George's (Sandwich). *Address:* Timothy Yeo Esq, MP, House of Commons, London, SW1A 0AA *Tel:* 020 7219 6366 *Fax:* 020 7219 4857. *Constituency:* 7 Queen Street, Hadleigh, Suffolk, IP7 5DA *Tel:* 01473 823435.

YOUNG, The Rt Hon. Sir George, Bt *(North West Hampshire)   Con majority 11,551*

Son of Sir George Young, 5th Bt, CMG, and Elizabeth Young (née Knatchbull-Hugessen). Born July 16, 1941; educated Eton; Christ Church, Oxford (MA); University of Surrey (MPhil). Married July 11, 1964, Aurelia Nemon-Stuart (2 sons 2 daughters). *Career:* Economic Adviser, Post Office 1969–74. *Councils, Public Bodies:* Councillor, London Borough of Lambeth 1968–71; GLC Councillor for Ealing 1970–73; Chairman, Acton Housing Association 1972–79. *Political Career:* Parliamentary Under-Secretary of State at: Department of Health and Social Services 1979–81, Department of Environment 1981–86; Department of Environment: Minister for Housing and Planning 1990–93, Minister for Housing, Inner Cities and Construction 1993–94; Financial Secretary, HM Treasury 1994–95; Secretary of State for Transport 1995–97; Member, Shadow Cabinet 1997–; Shadow Secretary of State for Defence 1997–98; Shadow Leader of the House of Commons 1998–99; Shadow Chancellor of the Duchy of Lancaster 1998–99; Shadow Leader of the House of Commons and Constitutional Affairs 1999–. *Whip:* Opposition Whip 1976–79; Comptroller of HM Household (Government Whip) July–November 1990. *Select Committees (Current):* Member: Modernisation of the House of Commons 1998– *(Former):* Member: Public Accounts 1994–95. *Trust:* Trustee, Guinness Trust 1986–90. *Miscellaneous:* 6th Baronet, created 1813, succeeded his father 1960. *Honours:* PC 1993. *Publications:* Author of *Tourism – Blessing or Blight*, 1970. *Special Interests:* Housing, Disabled/Disability, Health Education. *Recreations:* Bicycling, opera, QPR supporter. *Electoral Notes:* Member for Ealing Acton 1974–97, and for North West Hampshire since May 1, 1997. *Address:* The Rt Hon. Sir George Young, Bt, MP, House of Commons, London, SW1A 0AA *Tel:* 020 7219 6665 *Fax:* 020 7219 2566. *Constituency:* 2 Church Close, Andover, Hampshire, SP10 1DP *Tel:* 01264 401401 *Fax:* 01264 391155 *E-mail:* sirgyoung@aol.com.

MPs' Special Interests

The political interests listed are supplied to Dod by MPs themselves.

*MP resigned January 2000

Abortion
Widdecombe, Ann *(Con)*

Accountancy
Mitchell, Austin *(Lab)*

Adult Education
Davies, Ron *(Lab)*
Etherington, William *(Lab)*

Aerospace
Borrow, David *(Lab)*
Colvin, Michael *(Con)*
Cunliffe, Lawrence *(Lab)*
Foulkes, George *(Lab/Co-op)*
Haselhurst, Sir Alan *(Con)*
Howarth, Gerald *(Con)*
Ingram, Adam *(Lab)*
Jack, Michael *(Con)*
Moffatt, Laura *(Lab)*
Öpik, Lembit *(Lib Dem)*
Robinson, Peter *(DUP)*
Soames, Nicholas *(Con)*
Wilkinson, John *(Con)*

Age Discrimination
Perham, Linda *(Lab)*

Ageing
Burstow, Paul *(Lib Dem)*

Ageing Issues
O'Hara, Edward *(Lab)*

Agenda 21
Colman, Tony *(Lab)*

Agriculture
Atkins, Charlotte *(Lab)*
Atkinson, Peter *(Con)*
Bercow, John *(Con)*
Body, Sir Richard *(Con)*
Boswell, Timothy *(Con)*
Burnett, John *(Lib Dem)*
Clifton-Brown, Geoffrey *(Con)*
Collins, Tim *(Con)*
Colvin, Michael *(Con)*
Corbett, Robin *(Lab)*
Curry, David *(Con)*
Davies, Quentin *(Con)*

Davies, Ron *(Lab)*
Davis, David *(Con)*
Drew, David *(Lab/Co-op)*
Evans, Nigel *(Con)*
Garnier, Edward *(Con)*
George, Andrew *(Lib Dem)*
Gill, Christopher *(Con)*
Gray, James *(Con)*
Greenway, John *(Con)*
Hague, William *(Con)*
Haselhurst, Sir Alan *(Con)*
Hayes, John *(Con)*
Heathcoat-Amory, David *(Con)*
Hood, Jimmy *(Lab)*
Hurst, Alan *(Lab)*
Jackson, Robert *(Con)*
Johnson Smith, Sir Geoffrey *(Con)*
Jones, Ieuan Wyn *(PC)*
Jones, Martyn *(Lab)*
Key, Robert *(Con)*
Leigh, Edward *(Con)*
Livsey, Richard *(Lib Dem)*
Llwyd, Elfyn *(PC)*
Lord, Michael *(Con)*
MacGregor, John *(Con)*
Major, John *(Con)*
Marsden, Paul *(Lab)*
Martlew, Eric *(Lab)*
Mitchell, Austin *(Lab)*
Norman, Archie *(Con)*
Paice, James *(Con)*
Paterson, Owen *(Con)*
Prior, David *(Con)*
Salmond, Alex *(SNP)*
Spelman, Caroline *(Con)*
Steen, Anthony *(Con)*
Stevenson, George *(Lab)*
Strang, Gavin *(Lab)*
Taylor, John D *(UUP)*
Todd, Mark *(Lab)*
Williams, Dr Alan *(Lab)*
Winterton, Ann *(Con)*

AIDS
Moffatt, Laura *(Lab)*

Airports Policy
Wareing, Robert *(Lab)*

Alcohol Abuse and Under-age Drinking
Faber, David *(Con)*
Hood, Jimmy *(Lab)*

Alternative Energy
Cook, Frank *(Lab)*
Corbett, Robin *(Lab)*

Alternative Fuels
Hamilton, Fabian *(Lab)*

Alternative Medicine
Grant, Bernie *(Lab)*

Amnesty International
Wallace, James *(Lib Dem)*

Anglo-American Relations
Mawhinney, Sir Brian *(Con)*

Animal Rights
Cohen, Harry *(Lab)*

Animal Welfare
Banks, Tony *(Lab)*
Caplin, Ivor *(Lab)*
Clark, Dr Michael *(Con)*
Corbett, Robin *(Lab)*
Dowd, Jim *(Lab)*
Etherington, William *(Lab)*
Flynn, Paul *(Lab)*
Foster, Michael Jabez *(Lab)*
Gale, Roger *(Con)*
Griffiths, Win *(Lab)*
Lepper, David *(Lab/Co-op)*
McIntosh, Anne *(Con)*
Norris, Dan *(Lab)*
O'Hara, Edward *(Lab)*
Palmer, Dr Nicholas *(Lab)*
Russell, Bob *(Lib Dem)*
Smith, Angela *(Lab/Co-op)*
Steinberg, Gerry *(Lab)*
White, Brian *(Lab)*

Anti-Common Market
Skinner, Dennis *(Lab)*

Anti-Imperialism and Internationalism
Corbyn, Jeremy *(Lab)*

Anti-Poverty
Fitzpatrick, Jim *(Lab)*
Ruane, Chris *(Lab)*

Anti-Racism
Fitzpatrick, Jim *(Lab)*
George, Andrew *(Lib Dem)*
Hamilton, Fabian *(Lab)*

Application of Industrial Democracy
Campbell-Savours, Dale *(Lab)*

Arboriculture
Chapman, Sydney *(Con)*

Architectural and Artistic Heritage
Beith, Alan *(Lib Dem)*

Architectural Heritage
Chapman, Sydney *(Con)*

Arms Control
Cousins, Jim *(Lab)*
Heathcoat-Amory, David *(Con)*

Arms Conversion and Diversification
Savidge, Malcolm *(Lab)*

Arts
Atkinson, David *(Con)*
Banks, Tony *(Lab)*
Begg, Anne *(Lab)*
Blears, Hazel *(Lab)*
Campbell, Menzies *(Lib Dem)*
Caplin, Ivor *(Lab)*
Cormack, Sir Patrick *(Con)*
Dunwoody, Gwyneth *(Lab)*
Fisher, Mark *(Lab)*
Fraser, Christopher *(Con)*
Gorrie, Donald *(Lib Dem)*
Griffiths, Jane *(Lab)*
Griffiths, Nigel *(Lab)*
Heath, Sir Edward *(Con)*
Key, Robert *(Con)*
Maclennan, Robert *(Lib Dem)*
Russell, Christine *(Lab)*

Asylum and Immigration
Coleman, Iain *(Lab)*

Asylum Issues
Harris, Evan *(Lib Dem)*

Aviation
Colvin, Michael *(Con)*
Cunliffe, Lawrence *(Lab)*
Foulkes, George *(Lab/Co-op)*
Haselhurst, Sir Alan *(Con)*
Howarth, Gerald *(Con)*
Moffatt, Laura *(Lab)*
Robinson, Peter *(DUP)*
Soames, Nicholas *(Con)*
Wilkinson, John *(Con)*
Wilshire, David *(Con)*

Benefits
Cryer, Ann *(Lab)*
McDonagh, Siobhain *(Lab)*
McIsaac, Shona *(Lab)*

Breast Cancer
Church, Judith *(Lab)*
Stinchcombe, Paul *(Lab)*

British Business
Redwood, John *(Con)*

British Constitution
Cann, Jamie *(Lab)*

British Council
Wyatt, Derek *(Lab)*

British-Irish Relations
Canavan, Dennis *(Lab)*

Broadcasting
Begg, Anne *(Lab)*
Fabricant, Michael *(Con)*
Fisher, Mark *(Lab)*
Gale, Roger *(Con)*
Greenway, John *(Con)*
Kennedy, Charles *(Lib Dem)*

Business
Cotter, Brian *(Lib Dem)*
Johnson, Melanie *(Lab)*
Merron, Gillian *(Lab)*
Moore, Michael *(Lib Dem)*
Norman, Archie *(Con)*
Todd, Mark *(Lab)*

Cable/Communications
Gale, Roger *(Con)*

Campaigning for Socialism in the Community and against Racism
Corbyn, Jeremy *(Lab)*

Car Industry
Smith, Andrew *(Lab)*

Care of Ancient Monuments
Taylor, John M *(Con)*

Care of the Elderly
Martin, Michael *(Lab)*
Öpik, Lembit *(Lib Dem)*

CCTV
Taylor, David *(Lab/Co-op)*

Central Economic Issues
Dalyell, Tam *(Lab)*

Channel Islands
Mackinlay, Andrew *(Lab)*

Charities and the Voluntary Sector
Howarth, Alan *(Lab)*

Charity Reform
Yeo, Tim *(Con)*

Child Protection and Safety
Cook, Frank *(Lab)*
Hughes, Beverley *(Lab)*
Johnson, Melanie *(Lab)*
Norris, Dan *(Lab)*

Childcare
Baldry, Tony *(Con)*
Chisholm, Malcolm *(Lab)*
Doran, Frank *(Lab)*
Flint, Caroline *(Lab)*
Hughes, Kevin *(Lab)*
Moran, Margaret *(Lab)*
Morgan, Julie *(Lab)*
Powell, Sir Raymond *(Lab)*

Children
Buck, Karen *(Lab)*
Golding, Llin *(Lab)*
Kidney, David *(Lab)*
Shipley, Debra *(Lab)*
Wise, Audrey *(Lab)*

Children's Play
Colvin, Michael *(Con)*

Children's Rights
Corbett, Robin *(Lab)*
Dawson, Hilton *(Lab)*

Christian Values
Donaldson, Jeffrey *(UUP)*

City
Prior, David *(Con)*

Civil Aviation
Colvin, Michael *(Con)*

Civil Defence
McCartney, Ian *(Lab)*

Civil Justice
Dismore, Andrew *(Lab)*

Civil Liberties
Atkins, Charlotte *(Lab)*
Baker, Norman *(Lib Dem)*
Ballard, Jackie *(Lib Dem)*
Corbett, Robin *(Lab)*
Harris, Evan *(Lib Dem)*
Hughes, Simon *(Lib Dem)*
Lloyd, Tony *(Lab)*
Llwyd, Elfyn *(PC)*
Mactaggart, Fiona *(Lab)*
Meacher, Michael *(Lab)*
Smith, Chris *(Lab)*
Soley, Clive *(Lab)*
Stinchcombe, Paul *(Lab)*

Civil Service
Clarke, Tom *(Lab)*

Climate Change
Stunell, Andrew *(Lib Dem)*

CND
Powell, Sir Raymond *(Lab)*

Co-operative Development
McFall, John *(Lab/Co-op)*
Michael, Alun *(Lab/Co-op)*
Naysmith, Dr Doug
 (Lab/Co-op)

Co-operative Movement
Davidson, Ian *(Lab/Co-op)*
Drown, Julia *(Lab)*

Co-operatives
Reed, Andrew *(Lab/Co-op)*

Coal Industry
Clapham, Michael *(Lab)*
Clarke, Eric *(Lab)*
Cooper, Yvette *(Lab)*
Cryer, John *(Lab)*
Cummings, John *(Lab)*
O'Brien, Mike *(Lab)*
Powell, Sir Raymond *(Lab)*

Commerce
Hayes, John *(Con)*
Keen, Alan *(Lab/Co-op)*
Ottaway, Richard *(Con)*

Common Market
Taylor, Sir Teddy *(Con)*

Commonwealth
Davidson, Ian *(Lab/Co-op)*
Emery, Peter *(Con)*
Kilfoyle, Peter *(Lab)*

Community Care
Jowell, Tessa *(Lab)*
McCabe, Stephen *(Lab)*
Robinson, Peter *(DUP)*
Squire, Rachel *(Lab)*
Steen, Anthony *(Con)*

Community Development
Haselhurst, Sir Alan *(Con)*
Michael, Alun *(Lab/Co-op)*
Shaw, Jonathan *(Lab)*

Community Politics
Dawson, Hilton *(Lab)*

Community Regeneration
Goggins, Paul *(Lab)*
Lepper, David *(Lab/Co-op)*

Community Safety
Burstow, Paul *(Lib Dem)*

Conservation
Chapman, Sydney *(Con)*
Cohen, Harry *(Lab)*
Davies, Ron *(Lab)*
Hurst, Alan *(Lab)*
Rowe, Andrew *(Con)*
Steen, Anthony *(Con)*
Walker, Cecil *(UUP)*

Constitution
Benn, Tony *(Lab)*
Burden, Richard *(Lab)*

Clarke, Tony *(Lab)*
Collins, Tim *(Con)*
Cunningham, Roseanna *(SNP)*
Darling, Alistair *(Lab)*
Day, Stephen *(Con)*
Donaldson, Jeffrey *(UUP)*
Fallon, Michael *(Con)*
Fraser, Christopher *(Con)*
Grieve, Dominic *(Con)*
Laing, Eleanor *(Con)*
Mackinlay, Andrew *(Lab)*
Paisley, The Rev. Ian *(DUP)*
Plaskitt, James *(Lab)*
Quinn, Lawrie *(Lab)*
Robertson, Laurence *(Con)*
Syms, Robert *(Con)*
Wright, Dr Tony *(Lab)*

Constitution/Constitutional
 Issues
Anderson, Janet *(Lab)*

Constitutional Affairs
Browne, Desmond *(Lab)*
Whitehead, Dr Alan *(Lab)*

Constitutional and Legal
 Affairs
Temple-Morris, Peter *(Lab)*

Constitutional Reform
Alexander, Douglas *(Lab)*
Campbell, Alan *(Lab)*
Clark, Dr Lynda *(Lab)*
Edwards, Huw *(Lab)*
Jowell, Tessa *(Lab)*
McKenna, Rosemary *(Lab)*
Maclennan, Robert *(Lib Dem)*
Michie, Ray *(Lib Dem)*
Mitchell, Austin *(Lab)*
Prentice, Bridget *(Lab)*
Thomas, Gareth *(Lab)*
Wallace, James *(Lib Dem)*

Construction Industry
Chapman, Sydney *(Con)*
Nicholls, Patrick *(Con)*
Spellar, John *(Lab)*

Consumer Issues
Lepper, David *(Lab/Co-op)*
Murphy, Jim *(Lab)*
Williams, Betty *(Lab)*

Cornwall
Breed, Colin *(Lib Dem)*
George, Andrew *(Lib Dem)*

Countryside
Brazier, Julian *(Con)*
Colvin, Michael *(Con)*
Gray, James *(Con)*
MacGregor, John *(Con)*
Morley, Elliot *(Lab)*
Simpson, Keith *(Con)*

Credit Unions
Hume, John *(SDLP)*

Crime
Blackman, Elizabeth *(Lab)*
Connarty, Michael *(Lab)*
Jones, Fiona *(Lab)*
Lewis, Ivan *(Lab)*
Milburn, Alan *(Lab)*

Criminal Justice
Gerrard, Neil *(Lab)*
Hughes, Beverley *(Lab)*
Jones, Dr Lynne *(Lab)*
Smith, Chris *(Lab)*
Thomas, Gareth *(Lab)*

Criminal Law
O'Brien, Mike *(Lab)*

Criminal Law Reform
Malins, Humfrey *(Con)*

Crofting
Michie, Ray *(Lib Dem)*

Cultural Industries
Lepper, David *(Lab/Co-op)*

Cultural Policy
Fisher, Mark *(Lab)*

Culture
Anderson, Janet *(Lab)*
Keen, Alan *(Lab/Co-op)*
Ward, Claire *(Lab)*
Woodward, Shaun *(Lab)*

Cyprus
Lepper, David *(Lab/Co-op)*

Deaf Children
Bruce, Malcolm *(Lib Dem)*

**Decentralisation of
  Government**
Dafis, Cynog *(PC)**

Deep Sea Fishing Industry
Quinn, Lawrie *(Lab)*

Defence
Arbuthnot, James *(Con)*
Ashdown, Paddy *(Lib Dem)*
Bayley, Hugh *(Lab)*
Beard, Nigel *(Lab)*
Blunt, Crispin *(Con)*
Brazier, Julian *(Con)*
Bruce, Ian *(Con)*
Burnett, John *(Lib Dem)*
Campbell, Menzies *(Lib Dem)*
Cann, Jamie *(Lab)*
Cohen, Harry *(Lab)*
Collins, Tim *(Con)*
Colvin, Michael *(Con)*
Cook, Robin *(Lab)*
Corbyn, Jeremy *(Lab)*
Davidson, Ian *(Lab/Co-op)*
Duncan Smith, Iain *(Con)*
Emery, Peter *(Con)*
Evans, Nigel *(Con)*
Foulkes, George *(Lab/Co-op)*
Fox, Dr Liam *(Con)*
Galloway, George *(Lab)*
Gapes, Mike *(Lab/Co-op)*
Garnier, Edward *(Con)*
George, Bruce *(Lab)*
Gillan, Cheryl *(Con)*
Gray, James *(Con)*
Grieve, Dominic *(Con)*
Hamilton, Sir Archie *(Con)*
Hammond, Philip *(Con)*
Hancock, Mike *(Lib Dem)*
Hawkins, Nick *(Con)*
Home Robertson, John *(Lab)*
Hood, Jimmy *(Lab)*
Howarth, Gerald *(Con)*
Hoyle, Lindsay *(Lab)*
Hutton, John *(Lab)*
Jenkin, Bernard *(Con)*
Johnson Smith, Sir Geoffrey
  (Con)
Keen, Alan *(Lab/Co-op)*
Keetch, Paul *(Lib Dem)*
Key, Robert *(Con)*
Leigh, Edward *(Con)*
Lewis, Dr Julian *(Con)*
Lyell, Sir Nicholas *(Con)*
McFall, John *(Lab/Co-op)*
McWilliam, John *(Lab)*
Maginnis, Ken *(UUP)*
Mahon, Alice *(Lab)*
Martlew, Eric *(Lab)*
Mates, Michael *(Con)*
Moffatt, Laura *(Lab)*
Murphy, Jim *(Lab)*
Nicholls, Patrick *(Con)*

O'Neill, Martin *(Lab)*
Ottaway, Richard *(Con)*
Rapson, Syd *(Lab)*
Reid, Dr John *(Lab)*
Robathan, Andrew *(Con)*
Rogers, Allan *(Lab)*
Ross, Ernie *(Lab)*
Ross, William *(UUP)*
Simpson, Keith *(Con)*
Smith, John *(Lab)*
Soames, Nicholas *(Con)*
Squire, Rachel *(Lab)*
Tredinnick, David *(Con)*
Trend, Michael *(Con)*
Viggers, Peter *(Con)*
Vis, Rudi *(Lab)*
Whitney, Sir Raymond *(Con)*
Widdecombe, Ann *(Con)*
Wilkinson, John *(Con)*

Defence and NATO
Cormack, Sir Patrick *(Con)*

Democracy
Benn, Tony *(Lab)*
Keen, Alan *(Lab/Co-op)*
Southworth, Helen *(Lab)*
Stewart, Ian *(Lab)*

Democratic Reform
Hodge, Margaret *(Lab)*

Democratic Renewal
Allen, Graham *(Lab)*
Goggins, Paul *(Lab)*

**Democratic Renewal and
  Inclusive Politics**
McKenna, Rosemary *(Lab)*

Democratising Britain
Livingstone, Ken *(Lab)*

Deregulation
Steen, Anthony *(Con)*

Developing World
Streeter, Gary *(Con)*

Development
Dawson, Hilton *(Lab)*
Denham, John *(Lab)*
Keen, Alan *(Lab/Co-op)*
King, Oona *(Lab)*
Palmer, Dr Nicholas *(Lab)*

Devolution
Ellman, Louise *(Lab/Co-op)*
Foulkes, George *(Lab/Co-op)*
George, Andrew *(Lib Dem)*
Laing, Eleanor *(Con)*
Mackinlay, Andrew *(Lab)*
Maxton, John *(Lab)*
Quinn, Lawrie *(Lab)*
Sarwar, Mohammed *(Lab)*

Devolution in Wales and Welsh Language
Flynn, Paul *(Lab)*

Disabled/Disability
Atherton, Candy *(Lab)*
Begg, Anne *(Lab)*
Berry, Dr Roger *(Lab)*
Browne, Desmond *(Lab)*
Burstow, Paul *(Lib Dem)*
Corbett, Robin *(Lab)*
Corston, Jean *(Lab)*
Cotter, Brian *(Lib Dem)*
Etherington, William *(Lab)*
Gerrard, Neil *(Lab)*
Graham, Tommy *(Scottish Labour)*
Griffiths, Nigel *(Lab)*
Griffiths, Win *(Lab)*
Healey, John *(Lab)*
Levitt, Tom *(Lab)*
Marsden, Gordon *(Lab)*
May, Theresa *(Con)*
Ross, William *(UUP)*
Rowlands, Edward *(Lab)*
Wareing, Robert *(Lab)*
Wigley, Dafydd *(PC)*
Young, Sir George *(Con)*

Disarmament
Canavan, Dennis *(Lab)*
Lloyd, Tony *(Lab)*
Simpson, Alan *(Lab)*

Dog Control
Hoey, Kate *(Lab)*

Domestic Violence
George, Andrew *(Lib Dem)*

Drug Abuse
Connarty, Michael *(Lab)*
Faber, David *(Con)*
Marshall, David *(Lab)*
Martin, Michael *(Lab)*
Meale, Alan *(Lab)*
Moffatt, Laura *(Lab)*

Drugs
Loughton, Tim *(Con)*

E-Issues
Moran, Margaret *(Lab)*

Early Years Education
Cryer, Ann *(Lab)*

East-West Trade
Walter, Robert *(Con)*

Ecclesiastical Matters
Field, Frank *(Lab)*

Ecology
Cohen, Harry *(Lab)*
Cook, Frank *(Lab)*
Jones, Martyn *(Lab)*

Economic and Democratic Planning
Blunkett, David *(Lab)*

Economic and Employment Policy
Brown, Gordon *(Lab)*

Economic and European Affairs
Radice, Giles *(Lab)*

Economic and Financial Matters
MacGregor, John *(Con)*

Economic and Foreign Affairs
Wareing, Robert *(Lab)*

Economic and Industrial Policy
Follett, Barbara *(Lab)*
Pearson, Ian *(Lab)*

Economic Development
Chapman, Ben *(Lab)*
George, Andrew *(Lib Dem)*
Jones, Jenny *(Lab)*
Michael, Alun *(Lab/Co-op)*
Murphy, Denis *(Lab)*
Prosser, Gwyn *(Lab)*
Rapson, Syd *(Lab)*
Shaw, Jonathan *(Lab)*
Smith, John *(Lab)*

Economic Development and Small Business
Hamilton, Fabian *(Lab)*

Economic Issues
McCabe, Stephen *(Lab)*

Economic Policy
Ainsworth, Peter *(Con)*
Alexander, Douglas *(Lab)*
Allen, Graham *(Lab)*
Battle, John *(Lab)*
Bayley, Hugh *(Lab)*
Bell, Stuart *(Lab)*
Bercow, John *(Con)*
Berry, Dr Roger *(Lab)*
Betts, Clive *(Lab)*
Blunt, Crispin *(Con)*
Bradley, Peter *(Lab)*
Burnett, John *(Lib Dem)*
Cable, Dr Vincent *(Lib Dem)*
Chisholm, Malcolm *(Lab)*
Clappison, James *(Con)*
Collins, Tim *(Con)*
Cran, James *(Con)*
Cryer, John *(Lab)*
Cunningham, James *(Lab)*
Curtis-Thomas, Claire *(Lab)*
Darling, Alistair *(Lab)*
Dowd, Jim *(Lab)*
Eagle, Angela *(Lab)*
Flight, Howard *(Con)*
Forth, Eric *(Con)*
Fox, Dr Liam *(Con)*
Gapes, Mike *(Lab/Co-op)*
Gardiner, Barry *(Lab)*
Green, Damian *(Con)*
Griffiths, Nigel *(Lab)*
Grogan, John *(Lab)*
Hague, William *(Con)*
Hain, Peter *(Lab)*
Hamilton, Sir Archie *(Con)*
Hammond, Philip *(Con)*
Heath, Sir Edward *(Con)*
Henderson, Doug *(Lab)*
Hesford, Stephen *(Lab)*
Hoon, Geoffrey *(Lab)*
Hopkins, Kelvin *(Lab)*
Horam, John *(Con)*
Howarth, Alan *(Lab)*
Jenkin, Bernard *(Con)*
Jones, Dr Lynne *(Lab)*
Keeble, Sally *(Lab)*
Kelly, Ruth *(Lab)*
Laing, Eleanor *(Con)*
Lansley, Andrew *(Con)*

Leslie, Christopher *(Lab)*
Liddell, Helen *(Lab)*
Lilley, Peter *(Con)*
Livingstone, Ken *(Lab)*
McFall, John *(Lab/Co-op)*
McIsaac, Shona *(Lab)*
Mallaber, Judy *(Lab)*
Marek, Dr John *(Lab)*
Marshall-Andrews, Robert *(Lab)*
Milburn, Alan *(Lab)*
Miller, Andrew *(Lab)*
Moonie, Lewis *(Lab/Co-op)*
Plaskitt, James *(Lab)*
Primarolo, Dawn *(Lab)*
Rammell, Bill *(Lab)*
Robertson, Laurence *(Con)*
Robinson, Geoffrey *(Lab)*
St Aubyn, Nicholas *(Con)*
Sarwar, Mohammed *(Lab)*
Sedgemore, Brian *(Lab)*
Skinner, Dennis *(Lab)*
Smith, Chris *(Lab)*
Smith, Jacqui *(Lab)*
Straw, Jack *(Lab)*
Swinney, John *(SNP)*
Syms, Robert *(Con)*
Taylor, Dari *(Lab)*
Timms, Stephen *(Lab)*
Trickett, Jon *(Lab)*
Tyrie, Andrew *(Con)*
Wardle, Charles *(Con)*
White, Brian *(Lab)*
Whitney, Sir Raymond *(Con)*
Willetts, David *(Con)*
Yeo, Tim *(Con)*

Economic Regeneration
Blackman, Elizabeth *(Lab)*
Healey, John *(Lab)*
Hughes, Beverley *(Lab)*
Humble, Joan *(Lab)*
Reed, Andrew *(Lab/Co-op)*
Smith, Geraldine *(Lab)*

Economics
Banks, Tony *(Lab)*
Brazier, Julian *(Con)*
Dorrell, Stephen *(Con)*
Foster, Derek *(Lab)*
Gibb, Nick *(Con)*
Harvey, Nick *(Lib Dem)*
Ladyman, Dr Stephen *(Lab)*
Lock, David *(Lab)*
McDonnell, John *(Lab)*

Mitchell, Austin *(Lab)*
Simpson, Alan *(Lab)*
Stewart, Ian *(Lab)*
Stinchcombe, Paul *(Lab)*
Todd, Mark *(Lab)*
Vis, Rudi *(Lab)*
Williams, Dr Alan *(Lab)*
Woolas, Philip *(Lab)*

Economics and Finance
Tapsell, Sir Peter *(Con)*

Economics and Social Policy
Meacher, Michael *(Lab)*

Economy
Merron, Gillian *(Lab)*
Murphy, Jim *(Lab)*
Reid, Dr John *(Lab)*
Sheerman, Barry *(Lab/Co-op)*

Economy (Industrial Renewal)
Beard, Nigel *(Lab)*

Economy and Employment
Moran, Margaret *(Lab)*

Economy and Enterprise
Connarty, Michael *(Lab)*

Economy and Taxation
Clifton-Brown, Geoffrey *(Con)*

Education
Allan, Richard *(Lib Dem)*
Amess, David *(Con)*
Armstrong, Hilary *(Lab)*
Atkins, Charlotte *(Lab)*
Barnes, Harry *(Lab)*
Begg, Anne *(Lab)*
Beggs, Roy *(UUP)*
Benn, Hilary *(Lab)*
Benton, Joe *(Lab)*
Bercow, John *(Con)*
Beresford, Sir Paul *(Con)*
Blackman, Elizabeth *(Lab)*
Blizzard, Bob *(Lab)*
Blunkett, David *(Lab)*
Bradley, Peter *(Lab)*
Brady, Graham *(Con)*
Browne, Desmond *(Lab)*
Butler, Christine *(Lab)*
Byers, Stephen *(Lab)*
Campbell, Alan *(Lab)*

Campbell, Anne *(Lab)*
Canavan, Dennis *(Lab)*
Cann, Jamie *(Lab)*
Caton, Martin *(Lab)*
Chaytor, David *(Lab)*
Clappison, James *(Con)*
Clark, Paul *(Lab)*
Coaker, Vernon *(Lab)*
Cook, Frank *(Lab)*
Cormack, Sir Patrick *(Con)*
Cryer, John *(Lab)*
Curtis-Thomas, Claire *(Lab)*
Dafis, Cynog *(PC)**
Darling, Alistair *(Lab)*
Darvill, Keith *(Lab)*
Davey, Valerie *(Lab)*
Davidson, Ian *(Lab/Co-op)*
Dean, Janet *(Lab)*
Denham, John *(Lab)*
Drew, David *(Lab/Co-op)*
Edwards, Huw *(Lab)*
Efford, Clive *(Lab)*
Ennis, Jeffrey *(Lab)*
Etherington, William *(Lab)*
Evans, Nigel *(Con)*
Ewing, Margaret *(SNP)*
Faber, David *(Con)*
Fallon, Michael *(Con)*
Fitzsimons, Lorna *(Lab)*
Foster, Don *(Lib Dem)*
Foulkes, George *(Lab/Co-op)*
Gale, Roger *(Con)*
Gapes, Mike *(Lab/Co-op)*
Gardiner, Barry *(Lab)*
Garnier, Edward *(Con)*
Gibb, Nick *(Con)*
Gordon, Eileen *(Lab)*
Gorrie, Donald *(Lib Dem)*
Green, Damian *(Con)*
Griffiths, Nigel *(Lab)*
Griffiths, Win *(Lab)*
Hall, Mike *(Lab)*
Hamilton, Fabian *(Lab)*
Haselhurst, Sir Alan *(Con)*
Hawkins, Nick *(Con)*
Hayes, John *(Con)*
Heath, David *(Lib Dem)*
Hesford, Stephen *(Lab)*
Hodge, Margaret *(Lab)*
Hood, Jimmy *(Lab)*
Howarth, Alan *(Lab)*
Howarth, Gerald *(Con)*
Hughes, Beverley *(Lab)*
Humble, Joan *(Lab)*
Jamieson, David *(Lab)*
Johnson, Alan *(Lab)*

Johnson, Melanie *(Lab)*
Jones, Barry *(Lab)*
Jones, Helen *(Lab)*
Owen Jones, Jon *(Lab/Co-op)*
Keeble, Sally *(Lab)*
Key, Robert *(Con)*
Khabra, Piara *(Lab)*
Kilfoyle, Peter *(Lab)*
King, Oona *(Lab)*
Kumar, Dr Ashok *(Lab)*
Laing, Eleanor *(Con)*
Letwin, Oliver *(Con)*
Levitt, Tom *(Lab)*
Lewis, Ivan *(Lab)*
Lewis, Dr Julian *(Con)*
Lidington, David *(Con)*
Lilley, Peter *(Con)*
Linton, Martin *(Lab)*
McAllion, John *(Lab)*
McFall, John *(Lab/Co-op)*
MacGregor, John *(Con)*
McNulty, Tony *(Lab)*
Mactaggart, Fiona *(Lab)*
McWilliam, John *(Lab)*
Madel, Sir David *(Con)*
Mallaber, Judy *(Lab)*
Marsden, Gordon *(Lab)*
Marsden, Paul *(Lab)*
Marshall, James *(Lab)*
May, Theresa *(Con)*
Morley, Elliot *(Lab)*
Moss, Malcolm *(Con)*
Murphy, Paul *(Lab)*
O'Hara, Edward *(Lab)*
O'Neill, Martin *(Lab)*
Organ, Diana *(Lab)*
Perham, Linda *(Lab)*
Plaskitt, James *(Lab)*
Pope, Greg *(Lab)*
Prentice, Bridget *(Lab)*
Primarolo, Dawn *(Lab)*
Prior, David *(Con)*
Purchase, Ken *(Lab/Co-op)*
Rammell, Bill *(Lab)*
Reed, Andrew *(Lab/Co-op)*
Robertson, Laurence *(Con)*
Rogers, Allan *(Lab)*
Ross, Ernie *(Lab)*
Rowlands, Edward *(Lab)*
Ruane, Chris *(Lab)*
Ruffley, David *(Con)*
Russell, Christine *(Lab)*
St Aubyn, Nicholas *(Con)*
Savidge, Malcolm *(Lab)*
Sawford, Philip *(Lab)*
Shephard, Gillian *(Con)*

Simpson, Keith *(Con)*
Singh, Marsha *(Lab)*
Smith, Andrew *(Lab)*
Smyth, Martin *(UUP)*
Steinberg, Gerry *(Lab)*
Stevenson, George *(Lab)*
Stoate, Dr Howard *(Lab)*
Straw, Jack *(Lab)*
Taylor, Ann *(Lab)*
Taylor, Dari *(Lab)*
Tipping, Paddy *(Lab)*
Touhig, Don *(Lab/Co-op)*
Trend, Michael *(Con)*
Turner, Dennis *(Lab/Co-op)*
Turner, Dr George *(Lab)*
Twigg, Derek *(Lab)*
Twigg, Stephen *(Lab)*
Vaz, Keith *(Lab)*
Ward, Claire *(Lab)*
Watts, David *(Lab)*
Wicks, Malcolm *(Lab)*
Willetts, David *(Con)*
Woodward, Shaun *(Lab)*
Wray, James *(Lab)*
Wright, Dr Tony *(Lab)*

Education (FE in particular)
Iddon, Dr Brian *(Lab)*

Education (Special Needs)
Browning, Angela *(Con)*
Loughton, Tim *(Con)*
Williams, Betty *(Lab)*

Education and Industry Links
Jones, Ieuan Wyn *(PC)*

Education and Training
Flint, Caroline *(Lab)*
Foster, Derek *(Lab)*
Foster, Michael John *(Lab)*
Morris, Estelle *(Lab)*
Smith, Jacqui *(Lab)*
Stewart, Ian *(Lab)*

Education and Youth
Öpik, Lembit *(Lib Dem)*

Elderly
Graham, Tommy *(Scottish Labour)*
Hughes, Kevin *(Lab)*
Jones, Ieuan Wyn *(PC)*
Mackinlay, Andrew *(Lab)*

Shipley, Debra *(Lab)*
Vis, Rudi *(Lab)*
Walker, Cecil *(UUP)*

Elections
Ashton, Joe *(Lab)*

Electoral Reform
Bayley, Hugh *(Lab)*
Burden, Richard *(Lab)*
Cann, Jamie *(Lab)*
Cormack, Sir Patrick *(Con)*
Johnson, Alan *(Lab)*
King, Oona *(Lab)*
Mackinlay, Andrew *(Lab)*
Mitchell, Austin *(Lab)*
Smith, Robert *(Lib Dem)*
Twigg, Stephen *(Lab)*

Electoral Registration
Barnes, Harry *(Lab)*

Emergency Planning
O'Hara, Edward *(Lab)*

Employment
Atkins, Charlotte *(Lab)*
Beggs, Roy *(UUP)*
Benn, Hilary *(Lab)*
Blears, Hazel *(Lab)*
Blizzard, Bob *(Lab)*
Brady, Graham *(Con)*
Bruce, Ian *(Con)*
Burns, Simon *(Con)*
Butler, Christine *(Lab)*
Clapham, Michael *(Lab)*
Clelland, David *(Lab)*
Collins, Tim *(Con)*
Cryer, John *(Lab)*
Davey, Edward *(Lib Dem)*
Eagle, Maria *(Lab)*
Etherington, William *(Lab)*
Flint, Caroline *(Lab)*
Green, Damian *(Con)*
Healey, John *(Lab)*
Henderson, Ivan *(Lab)*
Hewitt, Patricia *(Lab)*
Hopkins, Kelvin *(Lab)*
Howard, Michael *(Con)*
Howarth, Alan *(Lab)*
Hurst, Alan *(Lab)*
Johnson, Melanie *(Lab)*
Jones, Fiona *(Lab)*
Khabra, Piara *(Lab)*
Kilfoyle, Peter *(Lab)*
King, Oona *(Lab)*

Letwin, Oliver *(Con)*
Lock, David *(Lab)*
Lyell, Sir Nicholas *(Con)*
McAllion, John *(Lab)*
McCartney, Ian *(Lab)*
McLeish, Henry *(Lab)*
Madel, Sir David *(Con)*
Mahon, Alice *(Lab)*
Mallaber, Judy *(Lab)*
Merron, Gillian *(Lab)*
Moore, Michael *(Lib Dem)*
Pike, Peter *(Lab)*
Pond, Chris *(Lab)*
Prior, David *(Con)*
Ross, Ernie *(Lab)*
Rowe, Andrew *(Con)*
Ryan, Joan *(Lab)*
Sarwar, Mohammed *(Lab)*
Sawford, Philip *(Lab)*
Smith, Andrew *(Lab)*
Stewart, Ian *(Lab)*
Sutcliffe, Gerry *(Lab)*
Timms, Stephen *(Lab)*
Touhig, Don *(Lab/Co-op)*
Townend, John *(Con)*
Tredinnick, David *(Con)*
Turner, Dr Des *(Lab)*
Ward, Claire *(Lab)*
Wardle, Charles *(Con)*
Wigley, Dafydd *(PC)*
Winterton, Rosie *(Lab)*
Woolas, Philip *(Lab)*
Worthington, Tony *(Lab)*

Employment Law
Corston, Jean *(Lab)*
Foster, Michael Jabez *(Lab)*
Fyfe, Maria *(Lab)*
Johnson, Alan *(Lab)*
Roy, Frank *(Lab)*
Tynan, Bill *(Lab)*

Employment Legislation
Brown, Russell *(Lab)*

Employment Policy
Alexander, Douglas *(Lab)*
Baldry, Tony *(Con)*
Henderson, Doug *(Lab)*
Kelly, Ruth *(Lab)*

Employment Promotion
Paice, James *(Con)*

Employment Rights and Protection
Anderson, Janet *(Lab)*
Burden, Richard *(Lab)*
Smith, Angela *(Lab/Co-op)*

Ending Privilege in Education and Health
Campbell-Savours, Dale *(Lab)*

Energy
Barnes, Harry *(Lab)*
Barron, Kevin *(Lab)*
Bruce, Ian *(Con)*
Bruce, Malcolm *(Lib Dem)*
Cable, Dr Vincent *(Lib Dem)*
Clapham, Michael *(Lab)*
Clark, Dr Michael *(Con)*
Clelland, David *(Lab)*
Cummings, John *(Lab)*
Cunliffe, Lawrence *(Lab)*
Doran, Frank *(Lab)*
Foulkes, George *(Lab/Co-op)*
Gilroy, Linda *(Lab/Co-op)*
Hammond, Philip *(Con)*
Heathcoat-Amory, David *(Con)*
Hood, Jimmy *(Lab)*
Howells, Dr Kim *(Lab)*
Illsley, Eric *(Lab)*
Ingram, Adam *(Lab)*
McLeish, Henry *(Lab)*
Maclennan, Robert *(Lib Dem)*
Moss, Malcolm *(Con)*
O'Brien, William *(Lab)*
Pike, Peter *(Lab)*
Rogers, Allan *(Lab)*
Rowlands, Edward *(Lab)*
Salmond, Alex *(SNP)*
Skinner, Dennis *(Lab)*
Spellar, John *(Lab)*
Stevenson, George *(Lab)*
Stunell, Andrew *(Lib Dem)*
Tipping, Paddy *(Lab)*
Waterson, Nigel *(Con)*

Energy Conservation
Bermingham, Gerry *(Lab)*
Wallace, James *(Lib Dem)*

Engineering
Blears, Hazel *(Lab)*
Cook, Frank *(Lab)*
Olner, Bill *(Lab)*

Engineering and Technology
Battle, John *(Lab)*
Iddon, Dr Brian *(Lab)*

Engineering Services
Chidgey, David *(Lib Dem)*

Enterprise
Swinney, John *(SNP)*

Environment
Ainsworth, Peter *(Con)*
Ainsworth, Bob *(Lab)*
Amess, David *(Con)*
Anderson, Donald *(Lab)*
Armstrong, Hilary *(Lab)*
Atherton, Candy *(Lab)*
Austin, John *(Lab)*
Baker, Norman *(Lib Dem)*
Ballard, Jackie *(Lib Dem)*
Barnes, Harry *(Lab)*
Barron, Kevin *(Lab)*
Bayley, Hugh *(Lab)*
Benn, Hilary *(Lab)*
Blunt, Crispin *(Con)*
Boateng, Paul *(Lab)*
Body, Sir Richard *(Con)*
Brake, Tom *(Lib Dem)*
Brinton, Helen *(Lab)*
Burstow, Paul *(Lib Dem)*
Butler, Christine *(Lab)*
Butterfill, John *(Con)*
Cable, Dr Vincent *(Lib Dem)*
Campbell, Anne *(Lab)*
Cann, Jamie *(Lab)*
Caton, Martin *(Lab)*
Chapman, Sydney *(Con)*
Chaytor, David *(Lab)*
Clark, Paul *(Lab)*
Clarke, Tony *(Lab)*
Clelland, David *(Lab)*
Clifton-Brown, Geoffrey *(Con)*
Coaker, Vernon *(Lab)*
Cook, Robin *(Lab)*
Corbett, Robin *(Lab)*
Corbyn, Jeremy *(Lab)*
Cummings, John *(Lab)*
Cunningham, Dr Jack *(Lab)*
Dafis, Cynog *(PC)**
Darvill, Keith *(Lab)*
Davey, Edward *(Lib Dem)*
Davies, Geraint *(Lab)*
Davies, Ron *(Lab)*
Dowd, Jim *(Lab)*
Drew, David *(Lab/Co-op)*

Duncan Smith, Iain *(Con)*
Efford, Clive *(Lab)*
Ellman, Louise *(Lab/Co-op)*
Ennis, Jeffrey *(Lab)*
Forsythe, Clifford *(UUP)*
George, Andrew *(Lib Dem)*
Gibson, Dr Ian *(Lab)*
Gorman, Teresa *(Con)*
Gray, James *(Con)*
Grieve, Dominic *(Con)*
Griffiths, Jane *(Lab)*
Hall, Mike *(Lab)*
Hawkins, Nick *(Con)*
Heald, Oliver *(Con)*
Heath, David *(Lib Dem)*
Hill, Keith *(Lab)*
Hoey, Kate *(Lab)*
Hood, Jimmy *(Lab)*
Howarth, George *(Lab)*
Howells, Dr Kim *(Lab)*
Hughes, Simon *(Lib Dem)*
Jackson, Glenda *(Lab)*
Jackson, Helen *(Lab)*
Jones, Jenny *(Lab)*
Owen Jones, Jon *(Lab/Co-op)*
Ladyman, Dr Stephen *(Lab)*
Leslie, Christopher *(Lab)*
Lord, Michael *(Con)*
Lyell, Sir Nicholas *(Con)*
McDonnell, John *(Lab)*
Mackay, Andrew *(Con)*
Mackinlay, Andrew *(Lab)*
Marsden, Paul *(Lab)*
Marshall-Andrews, Robert
(Lab)
O'Brien, Mike *(Lab)*
Pendry, Tom *(Lab)*
Perham, Linda *(Lab)*
Pike, Peter *(Lab)*
Prosser, Gwyn *(Lab)*
Randall, John *(Con)*
Raynsford, Nick *(Lab)*
Robathan, Andrew *(Con)*
Roche, Barbara *(Lab)*
Roe, Marion *(Con)*
Rogers, Allan *(Lab)*
Ruane, Chris *(Lab)*
Ruddock, Joan *(Lab)*
Russell, Bob *(Lib Dem)*
Russell, Christine *(Lab)*
Salter, Martin *(Lab)*
Simpson, Alan *(Lab)*
Skinner, Dennis *(Lab)*
Smith, Chris *(Lab)*
Soley, Clive *(Lab)*
Spelman, Caroline *(Con)*

Steen, Anthony *(Con)*
Stinchcombe, Paul *(Lab)*
Stoate, Dr Howard *(Lab)*
Taylor, David *(Lab/Co-op)*
Taylor, John M *(Con)*
Taylor, Sir Teddy *(Con)*
Thomas, Gareth R *(Lab)*
Todd, Mark *(Lab)*
Tonge, Dr Jennifer *(Lib Dem)*
Tredinnick, David *(Con)*
Truswell, Paul *(Lab)*
Walley, Joan *(Lab)*
Walter, Robert *(Con)*
Welsh, Andrew *(SNP)*
White, Brian *(Lab)*
Whitehead, Dr Alan *(Lab)*
Wise, Audrey *(Lab)*
Woodward, Shaun *(Lab)*
Wright, Dr Tony *(Lab)*

Environment and Transport
Bradshaw, Ben *(Lab)*

Environmental Health
Williams, Betty *(Lab)*

**Environmental Issues and
    World Development**
Wood, Mike *(Lab)*

Environmental Protection
Williams, Dr Alan *(Lab)*

Environmental Taxation
Loughton, Tim *(Con)*

**Environmentally Sustainable
    Transport**
Starkey, Dr Phyllis *(Lab)*

Equal Opportunities
Gordon, Eileen *(Lab)*
Tynan, Bill *(Lab)*

**Equal Opportunities
    (Disability/Women)**
Heal, Sylvia *(Lab)*

Equal Opportunity
Austin, John *(Lab)*
Etherington, William *(Lab)*
Grant, Bernie *(Lab)*
Heppell, John *(Lab)*
Hope, Phil *(Lab/Co-op)*
Mallaber, Judy *(Lab)*
Morgan, Julie *(Lab)*

Europe
Ellman, Louise *(Lab/Co-op)*
Evans, Nigel *(Con)*
Kelly, Ruth *(Lab)*
King, Oona *(Lab)*
Lewis, Dr Julian *(Con)*
May, Theresa *(Con)*
Rammell, Bill *(Lab)*
Townend, John *(Con)*

European Democracy
Hancock, Mike *(Lib Dem)*

European Monetary Union
Davey, Edward *(Lib Dem)*

European Policy
Quin, Joyce *(Lab)*
Robertson, Laurence *(Con)*

European Regional Issues
Wigley, Dafydd *(PC)*

European Union
Baldry, Tony *(Con)*
Barnes, Harry *(Lab)*
Bell, Stuart *(Lab)*
Body, Sir Richard *(Con)*
Boswell, Timothy *(Con)*
Brady, Graham *(Con)*
Cable, Dr Vincent *(Lib Dem)*
Caborn, Richard *(Lab)*
Cash, William *(Con)*
Caton, Martin *(Lab)*
Collins, Tim *(Con)*
Connarty, Michael *(Lab)*
Cran, James *(Con)*
Cryer, John *(Lab)*
Cunningham, James *(Lab)*
Ewing, Margaret *(SNP)*
Forth, Eric *(Con)*
Gapes, Mike *(Lab/Co-op)*
Gill, Christopher *(Con)*
Godsiff, Roger *(Lab)*
Grieve, Dominic *(Con)*
Griffiths, Win *(Lab)*
Grogan, John *(Lab)*
Hammond, Philip *(Con)*
Harvey, Nick *(Lib Dem)*
Haselhurst, Sir Alan *(Con)*
Heath, Sir Edward *(Con)*
Heathcoat-Amory, David
    (Con)
Hill, Keith *(Lab)*
Hood, Jimmy *(Lab)*
Hoon, Geoffrey *(Lab)*

Hume, John *(SDLP)*
Jackson, Robert *(Con)*
Jenkin, Bernard *(Con)*
Jones, Ieuan Wyn *(PC)*
Kennedy, Charles *(Lib Dem)*
Khabra, Piara *(Lab)*
Kingham, Tess *(Lab)*
Kirkbride, Julie *(Con)*
Lait, Jacqui *(Con)*
Lilley, Peter *(Con)*
McGuire, Anne *(Lab)*
Maclennan, Robert *(Lib Dem)*
MacShane, Dr Denis *(Lab)*
Malins, Humfrey *(Con)*
Meale, Alan *(Lab)*
Mitchell, Austin *(Lab)*
Morgan, Alasdair *(SNP)*
O'Hara, Edward *(Lab)*
Plaskitt, James *(Lab)*
Rogers, Allan *(Lab)*
Shephard, Gillian *(Con)*
Singh, Marsha *(Lab)*
Straw, Jack *(Lab)*
Taylor, John D *(UUP)*
Taylor, John M *(Con)*
Temple-Morris, Peter *(Lab)*
Tyrie, Andrew *(Con)*
Vis, Rudi *(Lab)*
Walter, Robert *(Con)*
White, Brian *(Lab)*
Whitney, Sir Raymond *(Con)*
Wilkinson, John *(Con)*

Expatriate Workers
Cook, Frank *(Lab)*

Family
Brazier, Julian *(Con)*
Doran, Frank *(Lab)*
Hewitt, Patricia *(Lab)*
Hughes, Beverley *(Lab)*

Family Moral and Social Issues
Streeter, Gary *(Con)*

Farming
Flight, Howard *(Con)*
Michie, Ray *(Lib Dem)*
Simpson, Keith *(Con)*

Film Industry
Clarke, Tom *(Lab)*
Follett, Barbara *(Lab)*
Lansley, Andrew *(Con)*

Finance
Caplin, Ivor *(Lab)*
Curry, David *(Con)*
Duncan Smith, Iain *(Con)*
Foster, Derek *(Lab)*
Hamilton, Sir Archie *(Con)*
Hawkins, Nick *(Con)*
Loughton, Tim *(Con)*
McIsaac, Shona *(Lab)*
Major, John *(Con)*
Pendry, Tom *(Lab)*
Sheerman, Barry *(Lab/Co-op)*
Trickett, Jon *(Lab)*
Twigg, Derek *(Lab)*
Viggers, Peter *(Con)*
Vis, Rudi *(Lab)*
Woodward, Shaun *(Lab)*

Finance and Economics
Davies, Quentin *(Con)*

Finance and Taxation
Boswell, Timothy *(Con)*

Financial Services
Hawkins, Nick *(Con)*
Keeble, Sally *(Lab)*
Moss, Malcolm *(Con)*

Fire Service
Ennis, Jeffrey *(Lab)*
McCartney, Ian *(Lab)*

Firearms Legislation
Ross, William *(UUP)*

Fisheries
Gill, Christopher *(Con)*
Strang, Gavin *(Lab)*

Fishing
George, Andrew *(Lib Dem)*
Michie, Ray *(Lib Dem)*
Mitchell, Austin *(Lab)*
Salmond, Alex *(SNP)*
Steen, Anthony *(Con)*
Walker, Cecil *(UUP)*
Wallace, James *(Lib Dem)*

Footwear
Anderson, Janet *(Lab)*

Foreign Affairs
Anderson, Donald *(Lab)*
Arbuthnot, James *(Con)*
Ashdown, Paddy *(Lib Dem)*

Atkinson, David *(Con)*
Austin, John *(Lab)*
Beard, Nigel *(Lab)*
Bell, Martin *(Independent)*
Blunt, Crispin *(Con)*
Bradshaw, Ben *(Lab)*
Brady, Graham *(Con)*
Burns, Simon *(Con)*
Butterfill, John *(Con)*
Cable, Dr Vincent *(Lib Dem)*
Campbell, Menzies *(Lib Dem)*
Canavan, Dennis *(Lab)*
Casale, Roger *(Lab)*
Chapman, Ben *(Lab)*
Clarke, Eric *(Lab)*
Clarke, Tom *(Lab)*
Clifton-Brown, Geoffrey *(Con)*
Colvin, Michael *(Con)*
Cunningham, Dr Jack *(Lab)*
Curry, David *(Con)*
Curtis-Thomas, Claire *(Lab)*
Davies, Denzil *(Lab)*
Dorrell, Stephen *(Con)*
Emery, Peter *(Con)*
Ewing, Margaret *(SNP)*
Faber, David *(Con)*
Fabricant, Michael *(Con)*
Foulkes, George *(Lab/Co-op)*
Fraser, Christopher *(Con)*
Galloway, George *(Lab)*
Gardiner, Barry *(Lab)*
Garnier, Edward *(Con)*
Gerrard, Neil *(Lab)*
Godman, Dr Norman *(Lab)*
Godsiff, Roger *(Lab)*
Graham, Tommy *(Scottish Labour)*
Green, Damian *(Con)*
Grieve, Dominic *(Con)*
Grocott, Bruce *(Lab)*
Hanson, David *(Lab)*
Hoey, Kate *(Lab)*
Howells, Dr Kim *(Lab)*
Jackson, Robert *(Con)*
Jenkin, Bernard *(Con)*
Keen, Alan *(Lab/Co-op)*
Keetch, Paul *(Lib Dem)*
Kennedy, Jane *(Lab)*
Key, Robert *(Con)*
Kilfoyle, Peter *(Lab)*
Kingham, Tess *(Lab)*
Leigh, Edward *(Con)*
Lewis, Dr Julian *(Con)*
Loughton, Tim *(Con)*
Mackay, Andrew *(Con)*

Murphy, Paul *(Lab)*
Paisley, The Rev. Ian *(DUP)*
Paterson, Owen *(Con)*
Pope, Greg *(Lab)*
Randall, John *(Con)*
Reid, Dr John *(Lab)*
Ruddock, Joan *(Lab)*
Simpson, Keith *(Con)*
Smith, Chris *(Lab)*
Smyth, Martin *(UUP)*
Soames, Nicholas *(Con)*
Squire, Rachel *(Lab)*
Starkey, Dr Phyllis *(Lab)*
Tapsell, Sir Peter *(Con)*
Temple-Morris, Peter *(Lab)*
Tredinnick, David *(Con)*
Trend, Michael *(Con)*
Twigg, Stephen *(Lab)*
Waterson, Nigel *(Con)*
Wells, Bowen *(Con)*
Whitney, Sir Raymond *(Con)*
Whittingdale, John *(Con)*
Wilshire, David *(Con)*
Winterton, Nicholas *(Con)*
Wray, James *(Lab)*
Wyatt, Derek *(Lab)*

Foreign Office
Lidington, David *(Con)*

Foreign Policy
Coaker, Vernon *(Lab)*

Forestry
Heathcoat-Amory, David *(Con)*
Lord, Michael *(Con)*

Free Trade
Gorman, Teresa *(Con)*

Freedom of Information
Fisher, Mark *(Lab)*
Kirkwood, Archy *(Lib Dem)*
Norris, Dan *(Lab)*

Further and Higher Education
Cryer, John *(Lab)*
Sheerman, Barry *(Lab/Co-op)*
Swinney, John *(SNP)*
Whitehead, Dr Alan *(Lab)*

Gaelic language
Michie, Ray *(Lib Dem)*

Gas Industry
Bruce, Malcolm *(Lib Dem)*

Gender
Follett, Barbara *(Lab)*

Gibraltar
Willis, Phil *(Lib Dem)*

Glass Industry
Illsley, Eric *(Lab)*

Global Poverty
Goggins, Paul *(Lab)*

Grandparents' Rights
Powell, Sir Raymond *(Lab)*

Green Issues
McWalter, Tony *(Lab/Co-op)*
Morley, Elliot *(Lab)*

Health
Amess, David *(Con)*
Anderson, Janet *(Lab)*
Atherton, Candy *(Lab)*
Atkins, Charlotte *(Lab)*
Austin, John *(Lab)*
Bayley, Hugh *(Lab)*
Begg, Anne *(Lab)*
Blears, Hazel *(Lab)*
Blizzard, Bob *(Lab)*
Bradley, Keith *(Lab)*
Bradley, Peter *(Lab)*
Brady, Graham *(Con)*
Brand, Dr Peter *(Lib Dem)*
Brinton, Helen *(Lab)*
Brown, Gordon *(Lab)*
Burden, Richard *(Lab)*
Butterfill, John *(Con)*
Chisholm, Malcolm *(Lab)*
Clapham, Michael *(Lab)*
Clappison, James *(Con)*
Clark, Dr Lynda *(Lab)*
Coffey, Ann *(Lab)*
Cousins, Jim *(Lab)*
Cryer, Ann *(Lab)*
Cryer, John *(Lab)*
Darling, Alistair *(Lab)*
Davey, Valerie *(Lab)*
Davies, Quentin *(Con)*
Davis, David *(Con)*
Dawson, Hilton *(Lab)*
Dean, Janet *(Lab)*
Dismore, Andrew *(Lab)*
Dobbin, Jim *(Lab/Co-op)*

Donohoe, Brian *(Lab)*
Edwards, Huw *(Lab)*
Efford, Clive *(Lab)*
Ellman, Louise *(Lab/Co-op)*
Fearn, Ronnie *(Lib Dem)*
Fitzsimons, Lorna *(Lab)*
Flynn, Paul *(Lab)*
Fox, Dr Liam *(Con)*
George, Bruce *(Lab)*
Gibson, Dr Ian *(Lab)*
Gordon, Eileen *(Lab)*
Griffiths, Nigel *(Lab)*
Gunnell, John *(Lab)*
Hammond, Philip *(Con)*
Hanson, David *(Lab)*
Harris, Evan *(Lib Dem)*
Henderson, Ivan *(Lab)*
Hesford, Stephen *(Lab)*
Horam, John *(Con)*
Hutton, John *(Lab)*
Iddon, Dr Brian *(Lab)*
Jack, Michael *(Con)*
Johnson, Melanie *(Lab)*
Johnson Smith, Sir Geoffrey *(Con)*
Jones, Fiona *(Lab)*
Keen, Ann *(Lab)*
King, Andy *(Lab)*
King, Oona *(Lab)*
Kirkbride, Julie *(Con)*
Kirkwood, Archy *(Lib Dem)*
Lait, Jacqui *(Con)*
Lansley, Andrew *(Con)*
Lewis, Ivan *(Lab)*
Love, Andrew *(Lab/Co-op)*
McCafferty, Christine *(Lab)*
McLeish, Henry *(Lab)*
McNulty, Tony *(Lab)*
Mahon, Alice *(Lab)*
Marsden, Paul *(Lab)*
Martlew, Eric *(Lab)*
Mawhinney, Sir Brian *(Con)*
Meale, Alan *(Lab)*
Milburn, Alan *(Lab)*
Moffatt, Laura *(Lab)*
Morgan, Rhodri *(Lab)*
Naysmith, Dr Doug *(Lab/Co-op)*
Pickles, Eric *(Con)*
Primarolo, Dawn *(Lab)*
Purchase, Ken *(Lab/Co-op)*
Roe, Marion *(Con)*
Rogers, Allan *(Lab)*
Ryan, Joan *(Lab)*
Shephard, Gillian *(Con)*
Singh, Marsha *(Lab)*

Smith, Chris *(Lab)*
Smyth, Martin *(UUP)*
Southworth, Helen *(Lab)*
Starkey, Dr Phyllis *(Lab)*
Stewart, David *(Lab)*
Stoate, Dr Howard *(Lab)*
Taylor, Ann *(Lab)*
Thomas, Gareth R *(Lab)*
Tonge, Dr Jennifer *(Lib Dem)*
Touhig, Don *(Lab/Co-op)*
Trend, Michael *(Con)*
Truswell, Paul *(Lab)*
Turner, Dr Des *(Lab)*
Walley, Joan *(Lab)*
Waterson, Nigel *(Con)*
Whitney, Sir Raymond *(Con)*
Whittingdale, John *(Con)*
Widdecombe, Ann *(Con)*
Willetts, David *(Con)*
Williams, Betty *(Lab)*
Willis, Phil *(Lib Dem)*
Wise, Audrey *(Lab)*
Wright, Dr Tony *(Lab)*
Yeo, Tim *(Con)*

Health and Community Care
Hughes, Beverley *(Lab)*

Health and Poverty
Foster, Michael Jabez *(Lab)*
Twigg, Derek *(Lab)*

Health and Safety at Work
McCartney, Ian *(Lab)*
Quinn, Lawrie *(Lab)*

Health Care
Buck, Karen *(Lab)*

Health Education
Heal, Sylvia *(Lab)*
Michie, Ray *(Lib Dem)*
Williams, Betty *(Lab)*
Young, Sir George *(Con)*

Health Service
Canavan, Dennis *(Lab)*
Corbyn, Jeremy *(Lab)*
Cunningham, James *(Lab)*
Dowd, Jim *(Lab)*
Drown, Julia *(Lab)*
Dunwoody, Gwyneth *(Lab)*
Eagle, Angela *(Lab)*
Etherington, William *(Lab)*
Golding, Llin *(Lab)*

Grocott, Bruce *(Lab)*
Hinchliffe, David *(Lab)*
Hood, Jimmy *(Lab)*
McCartney, Ian *(Lab)*
Pike, Peter *(Lab)*
Ryan, Joan *(Lab)*
Squire, Rachel *(Lab)*
Winterton, Nicholas *(Con)*

Heritage
Allan, Richard *(Lib Dem)*
Atkinson, David *(Con)*
Caplin, Ivor *(Lab)*
Cash, William *(Con)*
Cormack, Sir Patrick *(Con)*
Hanson, David *(Lab)*
Marsden, Gordon *(Lab)*
Smith, Chris *(Lab)*
Steen, Anthony *(Con)*

Higher Education
Clark, Dr Lynda *(Lab)*
Naysmith, Dr Doug
  (Lab/Co-op)

HIV/AIDS
Gerrard, Neil *(Lab)*

Home Affairs
Allan, Richard *(Lib Dem)*
Anderson, Janet *(Lab)*
Barron, Kevin *(Lab)*
Benn, Hilary *(Lab)*
Bermingham, Gerry *(Lab)*
Boateng, Paul *(Lab)*
Brinton, Helen *(Lab)*
Byers, Stephen *(Lab)*
Clappison, James *(Con)*
Clelland, David *(Lab)*
Corbett, Robin *(Lab)*
Cranston, Ross *(Lab)*
Dean, Janet *(Lab)*
Hawkins, Nick *(Con)*
Heath, David *(Lib Dem)*
Hood, Jimmy *(Lab)*
Keeble, Sally *(Lab)*
King, Andy *(Lab)*
Llwyd, Elfyn *(PC)*
Loughton, Tim *(Con)*
Lyell, Sir Nicholas *(Con)*
Mactaggart, Fiona *(Lab)*
Mates, Michael *(Con)*
Meale, Alan *(Lab)*
Mullin, Chris *(Lab)*
Nicholls, Patrick *(Con)*
Prentice, Bridget *(Lab)*

Roche, Barbara *(Lab)*
Ruffley, David *(Con)*
Short, Clare *(Lab)*
Smith, Angela *(Lab/Co-op)*
Taylor, Sir Teddy *(Con)*
Tredinnick, David *(Con)*
Ward, Claire *(Lab)*
Whittingdale, John *(Con)*
Winterton, Rosie *(Lab)*

Home Office
Lidington, David *(Con)*
Taylor, Ann *(Lab)*

Home Rule for Scotland
Michie, Ray *(Lib Dem)*

Homelessness
Etherington, William *(Lab)*

Horses
Page, Richard *(Con)*

Horticulture
Jack, Michael *(Con)*
Roe, Marion *(Con)*

Housing
Battle, John *(Lab)*
Benton, Joe *(Lab)*
Beresford, Sir Paul *(Con)*
Betts, Clive *(Lab)*
Boateng, Paul *(Lab)*
Bradley, Keith *(Lab)*
Bradley, Peter *(Lab)*
Buck, Karen *(Lab)*
Butterfill, John *(Con)*
Chisholm, Malcolm *(Lab)*
Coleman, Iain *(Lab)*
Crausby, David *(Lab)*
Darvill, Keith *(Lab)*
Dean, Janet *(Lab)*
Denham, John *(Lab)*
Dobbin, Jim *(Lab/Co-op)*
Dowd, Jim *(Lab)*
Drew, David *(Lab/Co-op)*
Eagle, Maria *(Lab)*
Edwards, Huw *(Lab)*
Follett, Barbara *(Lab)*
George, Andrew *(Lib Dem)*
George, Bruce *(Lab)*
Gerrard, Neil *(Lab)*
Goggins, Paul *(Lab)*
Gordon, Eileen *(Lab)*
Gray, James *(Con)*
Griffiths, Nigel *(Lab)*
Hodge, Margaret *(Lab)*

Hoey, Kate *(Lab)*
Hood, Jimmy *(Lab)*
Howarth, George *(Lab)*
Hughes, Simon *(Lib Dem)*
Hurst, Alan *(Lab)*
Iddon, Dr Brian *(Lab)*
Jackson, Glenda *(Lab)*
Jenkins, Brian *(Lab)*
Jones, Dr Lynne *(Lab)*
Kidney, David *(Lab)*
King, Oona *(Lab)*
Linton, Martin *(Lab)*
Love, Andrew *(Lab/Co-op)*
McAllion, John *(Lab)*
McDonagh, Siobhain *(Lab)*
MacGregor, John *(Con)*
Major, John *(Con)*
Marshall, James *(Lab)*
Maxton, John *(Lab)*
Meacher, Michael *(Lab)*
Michael, Alun *(Lab/Co-op)*
Moffatt, Laura *(Lab)*
Moore, Michael *(Lib Dem)*
Morris, Estelle *(Lab)*
Moss, Malcolm *(Con)*
Murphy, Paul *(Lab)*
O'Brien, Mike *(Lab)*
O'Hara, Edward *(Lab)*
Osborne, Sandra *(Lab)*
Pendry, Tom *(Lab)*
Pickles, Eric *(Con)*
Pollard, Kerry *(Lab)*
Pope, Greg *(Lab)*
Pound, Stephen *(Lab)*
Primarolo, Dawn *(Lab)*
Rammell, Bill *(Lab)*
Raynsford, Nick *(Lab)*
Robinson, Peter *(DUP)*
Ross, William *(UUP)*
St Aubyn, Nicholas *(Con)*
Salter, Martin *(Lab)*
Sarwar, Mohammed *(Lab)*
Shaw, Jonathan *(Lab)*
Smith, Chris *(Lab)*
Soley, Clive *(Lab)*
Southworth, Helen *(Lab)*
Swinney, John *(SNP)*
Taylor, Ann *(Lab)*
Taylor, Dari *(Lab)*
Taylor, David *(Lab/Co-op)*
Turner, Dennis *(Lab/Co-op)*
Twigg, Derek *(Lab)*
Walker, Cecil *(UUP)*
Winterton, Rosie *(Lab)*
Wood, Mike *(Lab)*
Young, Sir George *(Con)*

Housing and Planning
Hammond, Philip *(Con)*

Housing and Science Policy
Turner, Dr Des *(Lab)*

Housing and Urban Regeneration
Moran, Margaret *(Lab)*

Housing Law
Anderson, Donald *(Lab)*

Human Rights
Atkinson, David *(Con)*
Browne, Desmond *(Lab)*
Cormack, Sir Patrick *(Con)*
Dowd, Jim *(Lab)*
Etherington, William *(Lab)*
Fisher, Mark *(Lab)*
Foulkes, George *(Lab/Co-op)*
Godman, Dr Norman *(Lab)*
Hughes, Simon *(Lib Dem)*
Jones, Jenny *(Lab)*
Jowell, Tessa *(Lab)*
Kirkwood, Archy *(Lib Dem)*
Lloyd, Tony *(Lab)*
Lock, David *(Lab)*
Mactaggart, Fiona *(Lab)*
Martin, Michael *(Lab)*
Meale, Alan *(Lab)*
Prentice, Bridget *(Lab)*
Ruane, Chris *(Lab)*
Smyth, Martin *(UUP)*
Stevenson, George *(Lab)*
Thomas, Gareth *(Lab)*

Hunting With Dogs
John Foster, Michael *(Lab)*

Immigration
George, Andrew *(Lib Dem)*
Wardle, Charles *(Con)*

Immigration Policy
Godsiff, Roger *(Lab)*
Lloyd, Tony *(Lab)*
Short, Clare *(Lab)*

Inclusive Education
Willis, Phil *(Lib Dem)*

Incomes Policies
Godman, Dr Norman *(Lab)*

Individual Freedom
Gorman, Teresa *(Con)*

Industrial Democracy
Meacher, Michael *(Lab)*

Industrial Policy
Benn, Tony *(Lab)*
Bruce, Malcolm *(Lib Dem)*
Dowd, Jim *(Lab)*
Heathcoat-Amory, David *(Con)*
Henderson, Doug *(Lab)*
Leslie, Christopher *(Lab)*
Lloyd, Tony *(Lab)*
Morgan, Rhodri *(Lab)*
Quin, Joyce *(Lab)*
Williams, Alan *(Lab)*

Industrial Relations
Barnes, Harry *(Lab)*
Cormack, Sir Patrick *(Con)*
Crausby, David *(Lab)*
Cunningham, James *(Lab)*
Godsiff, Roger *(Lab)*
Heald, Oliver *(Con)*
Healey, John *(Lab)*
Martin, Michael *(Lab)*
Pendry, Tom *(Lab)*
Rooney, Terence *(Lab)*
Smith, John *(Lab)*

Industry
Ainsworth, Bob *(Lab)*
Ashdown, Paddy *(Lib Dem)*
Atkinson, Peter *(Con)*
Beckett, Margaret *(Lab)*
Connarty, Michael *(Lab)*
Cryer, John *(Lab)*
Cunliffe, Lawrence *(Lab)*
Davis, David *(Con)*
Gillan, Cheryl *(Con)*
Gunnell, John *(Lab)*
Hayes, John *(Con)*
Hutton, John *(Lab)*
Keen, Alan *(Lab/Co-op)*
Ladyman, Dr Stephen *(Lab)*
McAllion, John *(Lab)*
MacGregor, John *(Con)*
Mackay, Andrew *(Con)*
Michie, Bill *(Lab)*
Milburn, Alan *(Lab)*
Miller, Andrew *(Lab)*
Moonie, Lewis *(Lab/Co-op)*
Ottaway, Richard *(Con)*
Paterson, Owen *(Con)*

Robinson, Geoffrey *(Lab)*
Ross, Ernie *(Lab)*
Sheerman, Barry *(Lab/Co-op)*
Smith, Jacqui *(Lab)*
Taylor, Dari *(Lab)*
Trickett, Jon *(Lab)*
Walker, Cecil *(UUP)*
Wardle, Charles *(Con)*
Wigley, Dafydd *(PC)*
Wilkinson, John *(Con)*

Industry (Electronics)
Spellar, John *(Lab)*

Information Technology
Allan, Richard *(Lib Dem)*
Bruce, Ian *(Con)*
Hewitt, Patricia *(Lab)*
Jones, Nigel *(Lib Dem)*
Stewart, Ian *(Lab)*
White, Brian *(Lab)*

Inland Waterways
Skinner, Dennis *(Lab)*

Inner Cities
Beard, Nigel *(Lab)*
Beresford, Sir Paul *(Con)*
Boateng, Paul *(Lab)*
Chapman, Sydney *(Con)*
Hodge, Margaret *(Lab)*

Insurance
Hawkins, Nick *(Con)*

International Affairs
Benn, Tony *(Lab)*
Browne, Desmond *(Lab)*
Gapes, Mike *(Lab/Co-op)*
George, Bruce *(Lab)*
Gillan, Cheryl *(Con)*
Marsden, Gordon *(Lab)*
Murphy, Jim *(Lab)*
Sarwar, Mohammed *(Lab)*
Savidge, Malcolm *(Lab)*
Spelman, Caroline *(Con)*
Stewart, Ian *(Lab)*
Wilkinson, John *(Con)*

International Development
Battle, John *(Lab)*
Bayley, Hugh *(Lab)*
Chaytor, David *(Lab)*
Follett, Barbara *(Lab)*
Foulkes, George *(Lab/Co-op)*
Hamilton, Fabian *(Lab)*

Jones, Nigel *(Lib Dem)*
Khabra, Piara *(Lab)*
Luff, Peter *(Con)*
Naysmith, Dr Doug
  (Lab/Co-op)
Reed, Andrew *(Lab/Co-op)*
Smith, Angela *(Lab/Co-op)*
Stewart, David *(Lab)*
Tonge, Dr Jennifer *(Lib Dem)*
Worthington, Tony *(Lab)*

International Economics
MacShane, Dr Denis *(Lab)*

International Politics
Evans, Nigel *(Con)*

International Terrorism
Robinson, Peter *(DUP)*

International Trade
Hammond, Philip *(Con)*
White, Brian *(Lab)*

**International Trade and
  Finance**
Duncan, Alan *(Con)*

Internet Strategy
Wyatt, Derek *(Lab)*

**Investigative Political and
  Social Work**
Campbell-Savours, Dale *(Lab)*

Investment
Bermingham, Gerry *(Lab)*
Gunnell, John *(Lab)*
Hughes, Beverley *(Lab)*
Ryan, Joan *(Lab)*
Stewart, Ian *(Lab)*

Irish Affairs
Bell, Stuart *(Lab)*
Corbyn, Jeremy *(Lab)*
Cran, James *(Con)*
McDonnell, John *(Lab)*
Mackinlay, Andrew *(Lab)*
Temple-Morris, Peter *(Lab)*
Walker, Cecil *(UUP)*

Irish Politics
Taylor, John D *(UUP)*

Isle of Man
Mackinlay, Andrew *(Lab)*

Isle of Wight
Brand, Dr Peter *(Lib Dem)*

Israel
Day, Stephen *(Con)*

Job Re-Training
Blackman, Elizabeth *(Lab)*

Job-Creating Strategies
Williams, Alan *(Lab)*

Jobs
Dawson, Hilton *(Lab)*
Ryan, Joan *(Lab)*

Justice
Mallon, Seamus *(SDLP)*
Mullin, Chris *(Lab)*

Juvenile Justice
Michael, Alun *(Lab/Co-op)*

Keep Sunday Special
Powell, Sir Raymond *(Lab)*

Kidney Transplantation
Dalyell, Tam *(Lab)*

Labour History
Benn, Tony *(Lab)*

Labour Party
Ashton, Joe *(Lab)*

**Labour Party Policy
  Revision**
Radice, Giles *(Lab)*

Land
Cunningham, Roseanna
  (SNP)

**Landmine Eradication
  Measures**
Cook, Frank *(Lab)*

**Landmine Victim
  Support**
Cook, Frank *(Lab)*

Language and Culture
Dafis, Cynog *(PC)**

Law
Arbuthnot, James *(Con)*

Law and Order
Brazier, Julian *(Con)*
Davis, David *(Con)*
Greenway, John *(Con)*
Grieve, Dominic *(Con)*
Hawkins, Nick *(Con)*
Heald, Oliver *(Con)*
King, Andy *(Lab)*
Kirkbride, Julie *(Con)*
Robertson, Laurence *(Con)*
Streeter, Gary *(Con)*

Law Reform
Godman, Dr Norman *(Lab)*

Learning Disabilities
Browning, Angela *(Con)*

Leasehold Reform
Lepper, David *(Lab/Co-op)*

Legal Affairs
Baldry, Tony *(Con)*
Browne, Desmond *(Lab)*
Campbell, Menzies *(Lib Dem)*
Cranston, Ross *(Lab)*
McIntosh, Anne *(Con)*
Taylor, John M *(Con)*

Legal Issues
Lock, David *(Lab)*

Legal Reform
Corston, Jean *(Lab)*
Mitchell, Austin *(Lab)*
Roche, Barbara *(Lab)*

Legal Services
Vaz, Keith *(Lab)*

Legal System
Clark, Dr Lynda *(Lab)*

Leisure
Clarke, Tony *(Lab)*
Fearn, Ronnie *(Lib Dem)*
Griffiths, Jane *(Lab)*
Perham, Linda *(Lab)*
Rapson, Syd *(Lab)*

Leisure Industry
Gale, Roger *(Con)*

Liberation Islington Local Agenda 21
Corbyn, Jeremy *(Lab)*

Licensed Trade
Colvin, Michael *(Con)*
Gale, Roger *(Con)*

Licensing Hours Pubs-Clubs
Powell, Sir Raymond *(Lab)*

Lifelong Learning
Reed, Andrew *(Lab/Co-op)*

Local and Regional Government
Whitehead, Dr Alan *(Lab)*

Local Community
Blackman, Elizabeth *(Lab)*

Local Democracy
Stunell, Andrew *(Lib Dem)*

Local Economic Development
Davidson, Ian *(Lab/Co-op)*

Local Government
Ballard, Jackie *(Lib Dem)*
Banks, Tony *(Lab)*
Barnes, Harry *(Lab)*
Benton, Joe *(Lab)*
Berry, Dr Roger *(Lab)*
Betts, Clive *(Lab)*
Blizzard, Bob *(Lab)*
Blunkett, David *(Lab)*
Bradley, Keith *(Lab)*
Butler, Christine *(Lab)*
Byers, Stephen *(Lab)*
Caplin, Ivor *(Lab)*
Cawsey, Ian *(Lab)*
Clarke, Tom *(Lab)*
Clarke, Tony *(Lab)*
Clelland, David *(Lab)*
Connarty, Michael *(Lab)*
Davey, Valerie *(Lab)*
Davidson, Ian *(Lab/Co-op)*
Dobbin, Jim *(Lab/Co-op)*
Donohoe, Brian *(Lab)*
Efford, Clive *(Lab)*
Ellman, Louise *(Lab/Co-op)*
Ennis, Jeffrey *(Lab)*
Evans, Nigel *(Con)*
Fearn, Ronnie *(Lib Dem)*
Foster, Don *(Lib Dem)*
Fraser, Christopher *(Con)*
Fyfe, Maria *(Lab)*
Gorrie, Donald *(Lib Dem)*
Grant, Bernie *(Lab)*

Gray, James *(Con)*
Grogan, John *(Lab)*
Hall, Mike *(Lab)*
Hanson, David *(Lab)*
Hayes, John *(Con)*
Heath, David *(Lib Dem)*
Heppell, John *(Lab)*
Hodge, Margaret *(Lab)*
Hughes, Beverley *(Lab)*
Ingram, Adam *(Lab)*
Keeble, Sally *(Lab)*
Kennedy, Jane *(Lab)*
Kumar, Dr Ashok *(Lab)*
Lansley, Andrew *(Con)*
Laxton, Bob *(Lab)*
Leslie, Christopher *(Lab)*
Levitt, Tom *(Lab)*
Lewis, Terry *(Lab)*
McCartney, Ian *(Lab)*
McDonnell, John *(Lab)*
McLeish, Henry *(Lab)*
McNulty, Tony *(Lab)*
McWalter, Tony *(Lab/Co-op)*
Mahon, Alice *(Lab)*
Major, John *(Con)*
Mallaber, Judy *(Lab)*
Marshall, James *(Lab)*
Michael, Alun *(Lab/Co-op)*
Michie, Bill *(Lab)*
Morley, Elliot *(Lab)*
Morris, Estelle *(Lab)*
Murphy, Paul *(Lab)*
Naysmith, Dr Doug *(Lab/Co-op)*
O'Brien, William *(Lab)*
O'Hara, Edward *(Lab)*
Olner, Bill *(Lab)*
Pickles, Eric *(Con)*
Pike, Peter *(Lab)*
Plaskitt, James *(Lab)*
Rapson, Syd *(Lab)*
Ross, William *(UUP)*
Russell, Bob *(Lib Dem)*
Ryan, Joan *(Lab)*
Salter, Martin *(Lab)*
Savidge, Malcolm *(Lab)*
Smith, Chris *(Lab)*
Steinberg, Gerry *(Lab)*
Stewart, David *(Lab)*
Straw, Jack *(Lab)*
Sutcliffe, Gerry *(Lab)*
Syms, Robert *(Con)*
Tipping, Paddy *(Lab)*
Todd, Mark *(Lab)*
Touhig, Don *(Lab/Co-op)*
Twigg, Stephen *(Lab)*

Vaz, Keith *(Lab)*
Walker, Cecil *(UUP)*
Welsh, Andrew *(SNP)*
Willis, Phil *(Lib Dem)*
Wilshire, David *(Con)*
Winterton, Nicholas *(Con)*
Wright, Anthony *(Lab)*

Local Government and Devolution
Starkey, Dr Phyllis *(Lab)*

Local Government Finance
Borrow, David *(Lab)*
Healey, John *(Lab)*

London
Horam, John *(Con)*
McNulty, Tony *(Lab)*

London Government
Hodge, Margaret *(Lab)*

Low Pay
Davies, Ron *(Lab)*
Merron, Gillian *(Lab)*
Short, Clare *(Lab)*
Taylor, David *(Lab/Co-op)*

Low Pay and Social Inequality
Edwards, Huw *(Lab)*

Machinery of Government
Grocott, Bruce *(Lab)*

Macro Economics
Davey, Edward *(Lib Dem)*

Manufacturing
Chidgey, David *(Lib Dem)*
Clark, Dr Michael *(Con)*
Corbett, Robin *(Lab)*
MacShane, Dr Denis *(Lab)*
Stuart, Gisela *(Lab)*

Marketing
Campbell-Savours, Dale *(Lab)*
Powell, Sir Raymond *(Lab)*
Ross, William *(UUP)*

Media
Ashton, Joe *(Lab)*
Banks, Tony *(Lab)*
Bayley, Hugh *(Lab)*
Cash, William *(Con)*

Collins, Tim *(Con)*
Fraser, Christopher *(Con)*
Gale, Roger *(Con)*
Green, Damian *(Con)*
Grocott, Bruce *(Lab)*
Howarth, Gerald *(Con)*
Johnson Smith, Sir Geoffrey *(Con)*
Lepper, David *(Lab/Co-op)*
Lewis, Dr Julian *(Con)*
Liddell, Helen *(Lab)*
Meale, Alan *(Lab)*
Mitchell, Austin *(Lab)*
Rammell, Bill *(Lab)*
Ward, Claire *(Lab)*
Whittingdale, John *(Con)*
Winterton, Nicholas *(Con)*
Woolas, Philip *(Lab)*

Media and Sport
Anderson, Janet *(Lab)*

Media Influence
Linton, Martin *(Lab)*

Media Ownership
Mullin, Chris *(Lab)*

Medical Ethics
Harris, Evan *(Lib Dem)*

Medicinal and Illegal Drugs
Flynn, Paul *(Lab)*

Mental Health
Atkinson, David *(Con)*
Austin, John *(Lab)*
Browning, Angela *(Con)*
Doran, Frank *(Lab)*
Lewis, Dr Julian *(Con)*

Micro-Technology
Williams, Alan *(Lab)*

Microeconomic Policy
Letwin, Oliver *(Con)*

Middle East
Burden, Richard *(Lab)*
Starkey, Dr Phyllis *(Lab)*

Minimum Wage
Woolas, Philip *(Lab)*

Mining
Illsley, Eric *(Lab)*

Minority Groups
George, Andrew *(Lib Dem)*

Minority Languages
Wigley, Dafydd *(PC)*

Modernisation of Parliament
Bradshaw, Ben *(Lab)*
Fitzsimons, Lorna *(Lab)*

Motor Industry
Burden, Richard *(Lab)*
Corbett, Robin *(Lab)*
Kemp, Fraser *(Lab)*
Spellar, John *(Lab)*
Wareing, Robert *(Lab)*

Multimedia
Lepper, David *(Lab/Co-op)*

Music
Meale, Alan *(Lab)*

National Grid for Learning
Wyatt, Derek *(Lab)*

National Heritage
Beggs, Roy *(UUP)*
Keetch, Paul *(Lib Dem)*

National Lottery
Ashton, Joe *(Lab)*

New Technology
Ashdown, Paddy *(Lib Dem)*
Robinson, Geoffrey *(Lab)*

NHS Tranquillisers Addiction
Wareing, Robert *(Lab)*

Northern Ireland
Barnes, Harry *(Lab)*
Browne, Desmond *(Lab)*
Collins, Tim *(Con)*
Donaldson, Jeffrey *(UUP)*
Hume, John *(SDLP)*
Jackson, Helen *(Lab)*
Livingstone, Ken *(Lab)*
McNamara, Kevin *(Lab)*
Mates, Michael *(Con)*
Mawhinney, Sir Brian *(Con)*
Robathan, Andrew *(Con)*
Salter, Martin *(Lab)*
Short, Clare *(Lab)*
Soley, Clive *(Lab)*

Willis, Phil *(Lib Dem)*
Wilshire, David *(Con)*

**Northern Ireland's
    Constitutional future**
McCartney, Robert *(UKU)*

Nuclear Disarmament
Wise, Audrey *(Lab)*

Nuclear Industry
Jack, Michael *(Con)*

Oil Industry
Bruce, Malcolm *(Lib Dem)*

Open Spaces
Clark, David *(Lab)*

**Oppressed Minority
    Races**
Baker, Norman *(Lib Dem)*

Overseas Aid
Baldry, Tony *(Con)*
Rowlands, Edward *(Lab)*

**Overseas Aid and
    Development**
Boateng, Paul *(Lab)*
Davey, Valerie *(Lab)*
Fisher, Mark *(Lab)*
Follett, Barbara *(Lab)*
Griffiths, Win *(Lab)*
Jackson, Glenda *(Lab)*
Kingham, Tess *(Lab)*
Lloyd, Tony *(Lab)*
Wells, Bowen *(Con)*

Paper Industries
Winterton, Nicholas *(Con)*

**Parliamentary and
    Constitutional Affairs**
Beith, Alan *(Lib Dem)*

**Parliamentary and
    Constitutional Reform**
Flynn, Paul *(Lab)*

**Parliamentary
    Buildings/Accommodation
    /Preservation**
Powell, Sir Raymond *(Lab)*

Parliamentary History
Cormack, Sir Patrick *(Con)*

Parliamentary Procedure
Emery, Peter *(Con)*

**Parties and Elections and
    Campaigning**
Hayes, John *(Con)*

Peace and Disarmament
Cook, Frank *(Lab)*

Penal Affairs and Policy
Lyell, Sir Nicholas *(Con)*
Malins, Humfrey *(Con)*
Shephard, Gillian *(Con)*
Soley, Clive *(Lab)*

Penal Reform
Bermingham, Gerry *(Lab)*

Pension Funds
Colman, Tony *(Lab)*

Pension Law
Stuart, Gisela *(Lab)*

Pensioners' Rights
Cook, Frank *(Lab)*
Gilroy, Linda *(Lab/Co-op)*
Marshall, David *(Lab)*

Pensions
Bradley, Keith *(Lab)*
Caplin, Ivor *(Lab)*
Clark, Dr Lynda *(Lab)*
Cran, James *(Con)*
Crausby, David *(Lab)*
Davies, Quentin *(Con)*
Flynn, Paul *(Lab)*
Heald, Oliver *(Con)*
Hesford, Stephen *(Lab)*
Pike, Peter *(Lab)*
Thomas, Gareth *(Lab)*

**Pensions and Personal
    Financial Services**
Denham, John *(Lab)*

People of Islington
Corbyn, Jeremy *(Lab)*

Performing Arts
Luff, Peter *(Con)*

Personal Finance
Greenway, John *(Con)*

Personal Social Services
Coffey, Ann *(Lab)*

Public Finance Initiative
Colman, Tony *(Lab)*

**Pharmaceutical and
    Chemical Industries**
Winterton, Ann *(Con)*
Winterton, Nicholas *(Con)*

Planning
Caton, Martin *(Lab)*
Cryer, Ann *(Lab)*
Darvill, Keith *(Lab)*
Drew, David *(Lab/Co-op)*
Gerrard, Neil *(Lab)*
St Aubyn, Nicholas *(Con)*

Planning Policy
Burgon, Colin *(Lab)*

Planning Transport
Murphy, Denis *(Lab)*

Police
Cawsey, Ian *(Lab)*
Corbett, Robin *(Lab)*
Lansley, Andrew *(Con)*
McCabe, Stephen *(Lab)*
Mackinlay, Andrew *(Lab)*
O'Brien, Mike *(Lab)*
Straw, Jack *(Lab)*
Thomas, Gareth *(Lab)*
Tipping, Paddy *(Lab)*
Tredinnick, David *(Con)*
Wardle, Charles *(Con)*

Political Biography
Thompson, William *(UUP)*

Political Finance
Linton, Martin *(Lab)*

**Political Ideas and
    Philosophy**
Hayes, John *(Con)*

Political Philosophy
McWalter, Tony *(Lab/Co-op)*
Michael, Alun *(Lab/Co-op)*

Political Process
Wilshire, David *(Con)*

Politics of Sport
Eagle, Angela *(Lab)*

Popular Capitalism
Redwood, John *(Con)*

Ports Industry
Mackinlay, Andrew *(Lab)*

Post Office
Hain, Peter *(Lab)*
Johnson, Alan *(Lab)*

Poverty
Bradley, Keith *(Lab)*
Burden, Richard *(Lab)*
Davies, Ron *(Lab)*
Dawson, Hilton *(Lab)*
Drew, David *(Lab/Co-op)*
Hall, Mike *(Lab)*
Hume, John *(SDLP)*
Mitchell, Austin *(Lab)*
Osborne, Sandra *(Lab)*
Pond, Chris *(Lab)*
Rooney, Terence *(Lab)*
Wood, Mike *(Lab)*

Poverty and Income Redistribution
Field, Frank *(Lab)*

Poverty and Low Pay, Children
Wise, Audrey *(Lab)*

Poverty and Wealth at Home and Abroad
Battle, John *(Lab)*

Press
Corbett, Robin *(Lab)*
Fisher, Mark *(Lab)*

Prisons
Widdecombe, Ann *(Con)*

Private Security
George, Bruce *(Lab)*

Private/Public Sector Partnership
McDonagh, Siobhain *(Lab)*

Privatisation
Howarth, Gerald *(Con)*

Pro-Life Movement
Amess, David *(Con)*

Provision for under 5s
Harman, Harriet *(Lab)*

Public Order
Tredinnick, David *(Con)*

Public Sector
Fallon, Michael *(Con)*

Public Sector Housing
Rooney, Terence *(Lab)*

Public Services
Ellman, Louise *(Lab/Co-op)*
Kennedy, Jane *(Lab)*

Public Transport
Morley, Elliot *(Lab)*
Öpik, Lembit *(Lib Dem)*

Public/Private Partnerships
Smith, Geraldine *(Lab)*

Publishing
Rowlands, Edward *(Lab)*

Purchasing and Supply
Emery, Peter *(Con)*

Quarrying
Levitt, Tom *(Lab)*

Quotas for Women
Anderson, Janet *(Lab)*

Race Relations
Cook, Frank *(Lab)*
Follett, Barbara *(Lab)*
Gerrard, Neil *(Lab)*
Grant, Bernie *(Lab)*
Khabra, Piara *(Lab)*
King, Oona *(Lab)*
Lilley, Peter *(Con)*
Lloyd, Tony *(Lab)*
Major, John *(Con)*
Short, Clare *(Lab)*
Stunell, Andrew *(Lib Dem)*
Vaz, Keith *(Lab)*

Railways
Cryer, Ann *(Lab)*
Luff, Peter *(Con)*
Williams, Betty *(Lab)*

Rainforest Issues
Dalyell, Tam *(Lab)*

Recreation
Godsiff, Roger *(Lab)*
Pendry, Tom *(Lab)*
Winterton, Nicholas *(Con)*

Redistribution of Income and Wealth
Meacher, Michael *(Lab)*

Reform of Government
Hain, Peter *(Lab)*

Refugees/Asylum
Gerrard, Neil *(Lab)*

Regeneration
Ennis, Jeffrey *(Lab)*
Fitzpatrick, Jim *(Lab)*
Love, Andrew *(Lab/Co-op)*
McNulty, Tony *(Lab)*
Ryan, Joan *(Lab)*

Regional Assemblies
Quinn, Lawrie *(Lab)*

Regional Development
Armstrong, Hilary *(Lab)*
Borrow, David *(Lab)*
Chapman, Ben *(Lab)*
Gunnell, John *(Lab)*
Hughes, Beverley *(Lab)*
O'Hara, Edward *(Lab)*
Stewart, Ian *(Lab)*

Regional Economic Development
Ellman, Louise *(Lab/Co-op)*
Pearson, Ian *(Lab)*

Regional Economic Policy
Wareing, Robert *(Lab)*

Regional Policy
Cran, James *(Con)*
Cunningham, Dr Jack *(Lab)*
Davies, Ron *(Lab)*
Foster, Derek *(Lab)*
Jones, Barry *(Lab)*
Milburn, Alan *(Lab)*
Morgan, Rhodri *(Lab)*
Quin, Joyce *(Lab)*
Robinson, Geoffrey *(Lab)*
Taylor, John D *(UUP)*
Watts, David *(Lab)*
Williams, Alan *(Lab)*
Winterton, Rosie *(Lab)*

Religious Affairs
Paisley, The Rev. Ian *(DUP)*

Renewable Energy
Thomas, Gareth R *(Lab)*

Research
Ladyman, Dr Stephen *(Lab)*

Restructuring of Defence Industries
Jones, Nigel *(Lib Dem)*

Retail Industry
Nicholls, Patrick *(Con)*
Smith, Andrew *(Lab)*

Rights of Victims of Accidents and Crime
Dismore, Andrew *(Lab)*

River Thames
Mackinlay, Andrew *(Lab)*

Rural Affairs
Bradley, Peter *(Lab)*
Faber, David *(Con)*
Fraser, Christopher *(Con)*
Green, Damian *(Con)*
Heath, David *(Lib Dem)*
Home Robertson, John *(Lab)*
Luff, Peter *(Con)*
Maclennan, Robert *(Lib Dem)*
Marsden, Paul *(Lab)*
Morgan, Alasdair *(SNP)*
Organ, Diana *(Lab)*
Paice, James *(Con)*
Stewart, David *(Lab)*
Taylor, David *(Lab/Co-op)*
Tyler, Paul *(Lib Dem)*
Yeo, Tim *(Con)*

Rural Development
McGuire, Anne *(Lab)*
Moss, Malcolm *(Con)*
Thomas, Gareth *(Lab)*
Wallace, James *(Lib Dem)*

Rural Issues
Drew, David *(Lab/Co-op)*

Safe Transport Systems in Cities
Corbyn, Jeremy *(Lab)*

Safer Communities (Crime)
Taylor, David *(Lab/Co-op)*

Sales Promotion and Marketing
Greenway, John *(Con)*

Science
Battle, John *(Lab)*
Cousins, Jim *(Lab)*
Gibson, Dr Ian *(Lab)*
Harris, Evan *(Lib Dem)*
Iddon, Dr Brian *(Lab)*
Jackson, Robert *(Con)*
Jones, Dr Lynne *(Lab)*
Jones, Martyn *(Lab)*
Naysmith, Dr Doug *(Lab/Co-op)*
Starkey, Dr Phyllis *(Lab)*

Science and Technology
Clark, Dr Michael *(Con)*
Ladyman, Dr Stephen *(Lab)*
McWalter, Tony *(Lab/Co-op)*

Science Policy
Campbell, Anne *(Lab)*
Dalyell, Tam *(Lab)*

Scientific Research and Development
Page, Richard *(Con)*

Scotland
Brown, Gordon *(Lab)*
Galloway, George *(Lab)*
Gray, James *(Con)*
Griffiths, Nigel *(Lab)*
Kennedy, Charles *(Lib Dem)*
Maxton, John *(Lab)*

Scottish Affairs
Clarke, Eric *(Lab)*
Home Robertson, John *(Lab)*
Liddell, Helen *(Lab)*
Marshall, David *(Lab)*

Scottish Devolution
Begg, Anne *(Lab)*

Scottish Economy
Salmond, Alex *(SNP)*

Scottish Home Rule and Federalism
Bruce, Malcolm *(Lib Dem)*
Wallace, James *(Lib Dem)*

Scottish Law
Wallace, James *(Lib Dem)*

Security
Lewis, Dr Julian *(Con)*
Taylor, David *(Lab/Co-op)*

Sheltered Housing
Jack, Michael *(Con)*

Shipbuilding
Robinson, Peter *(DUP)*
Waterson, Nigel *(Con)*

Shipping
Prosser, Gwyn *(Lab)*
Wallace, James *(Lib Dem)*
Waterson, Nigel *(Con)*

Shooters' Rights
Cook, Frank *(Lab)*

Skills and Training
Connarty, Michael *(Lab)*

Small Business and Enterprise
Fraser, Christopher *(Con)*

Small Businesses
Atkinson, David *(Con)*
Bercow, John *(Con)*
Browning, Angela *(Con)*
Cash, William *(Con)*
Duncan Smith, Iain *(Con)*
Evans, Nigel *(Con)*
Hawkins, Nick *(Con)*
Lansley, Andrew *(Con)*
Moss, Malcolm *(Con)*
Page, Richard *(Con)*
Paice, James *(Con)*
Rowe, Andrew *(Con)*
St Aubyn, Nicholas *(Con)*
Southworth, Helen *(Lab)*
Townend, John *(Con)*

Social Exclusion
George, Andrew *(Lib Dem)*

Social Inclusion
Tynan, Bill *(Lab)*

Social Issues
Cann, Jamie *(Lab)*
Hughes, Simon *(Lib Dem)*
Marsden, Gordon *(Lab)*
Webb, Prof Steve *(Lib Dem)*

Social Policy
Kelly, Ruth *(Lab)*
Kennedy, Charles *(Lib Dem)*
Major, John *(Con)*
Pond, Chris *(Lab)*
Raynsford, Nick *(Lab)*
Wicks, Malcolm *(Lab)*

Social Security
Brown, Gordon *(Lab)*
Cryer, John *(Lab)*
Duncan, Alan *(Con)*
Flynn, Paul *(Lab)*
Gibb, Nick *(Con)*
Graham, Tommy *(Scottish Labour)*
Hammond, Philip *(Con)*
Hewitt, Patricia *(Lab)*
Howarth, Alan *(Lab)*
Illsley, Eric *(Lab)*
Kennedy, Jane *(Lab)*
Kirkbride, Julie *(Con)*
Kirkwood, Archy *(Lib Dem)*
Meale, Alan *(Lab)*
Michie, Bill *(Lab)*
Pendry, Tom *(Lab)*
Primarolo, Dawn *(Lab)*
Roe, Marion *(Con)*
Smith, Chris *(Lab)*
Stewart, David *(Lab)*
Thomas, Gareth *(Lab)*
Tynan, Bill *(Lab)*
Willetts, David *(Con)*

Social Services
Austin, John *(Lab)*
Brand, Dr Peter *(Lib Dem)*
Dean, Janet *(Lab)*
Drown, Julia *(Lab)*
Ewing, Margaret *(SNP)*
Foulkes, George *(Lab/Co-op)*
George, Bruce *(Lab)*
Griffiths, Nigel *(Lab)*
Gunnell, John *(Lab)*
Harman, Harriet *(Lab)*
Hesford, Stephen *(Lab)*
Hinchliffe, David *(Lab)*
Hughes, Kevin *(Lab)*
Humble, Joan *(Lab)*
King, Andy *(Lab)*
McAvoy, Thomas *(Lab/Co-op)*
McCafferty, Christine *(Lab)*
McCartney, Ian *(Lab)*
Mallon, Seamus *(SDLP)*
Martlew, Eric *(Lab)*
Morgan, Julie *(Lab)*

Pickles, Eric *(Con)*
Pollard, Kerry *(Lab)*
Ross, Ernie *(Lab)*
Smyth, Martin *(UUP)*
Thomas, Gareth R *(Lab)*
Tonge, Dr Jennifer *(Lib Dem)*
Truswell, Paul *(Lab)*
Turner, Dennis *(Lab/Co-op)*
Turner, Dr Des *(Lab)*
Williams, Betty *(Lab)*
Wray, James *(Lab)*

Social Welfare Issues
Roy, Frank *(Lab)*

Socialism
Benn, Tony *(Lab)*

Socialist Enterprise
Foster, Derek *(Lab)*

Solvent Abuse
Hanson, David *(Lab)*
Marshall, David *(Lab)*

Space
Emery, Peter *(Con)*
Gillan, Cheryl *(Con)*

Space Technology
Atkinson, David *(Con)*

Sport
Campbell, Menzies *(Lib Dem)*
Canavan, Dennis *(Lab)*
Caplin, Ivor *(Lab)*
Clarke, Tony *(Lab)*
Coleman, Iain *(Lab)*
Godsiff, Roger *(Lab)*
Gorrie, Donald *(Lib Dem)*
Hancock, Mike *(Lib Dem)*
Hawkins, Nick *(Con)*
Hoey, Kate *(Lab)*
Hoyle, Lindsay *(Lab)*
Jones, Nigel *(Lib Dem)*
Keen, Alan *(Lab/Co-op)*
Malins, Humfrey *(Con)*
Maxton, John *(Lab)*
Meale, Alan *(Lab)*
Murphy, Jim *(Lab)*
Pendry, Tom *(Lab)*
Rammell, Bill *(Lab)*
Reed, Andrew *(Lab/Co-op)*
Russell, Bob *(Lib Dem)*
Trickett, Jon *(Lab)*
Ward, Claire *(Lab)*

Winterton, Nicholas *(Con)*
Wyatt, Derek *(Lab)*

Standards in Public Life
Bell, Martin *(Independent)*

Steel Industry
Caborn, Richard *(Lab)*
Powell, Sir Raymond *(Lab)*

Students
Connarty, Michael *(Lab)*

Sunday Drinking
Powell, Sir Raymond *(Lab)*

Sunday Trading
Powell, Sir Raymond *(Lab)*

Swiss Banking
Wyatt, Derek *(Lab)*

Tax
Ainsworth, Bob *(Lab)*
Arbuthnot, James *(Con)*
Cann, Jamie *(Lab)*
Davey, Edward *(Lib Dem)*
Flight, Howard *(Con)*
Foster, Michael Jabez *(Lab)*
Gibb, Nick *(Con)*
Hamilton, Sir Archie *(Con)*
Horam, John *(Con)*
Kirkbride, Julie *(Con)*
McIsaac, Shona *(Lab)*
Palmer, Dr Nicholas *(Lab)*
Straw, Jack *(Lab)*
Townend, John *(Con)*

Tax Havens
Foulkes, George *(Lab/Co-op)*

Technology
Beard, Nigel *(Lab)*
Benn, Tony *(Lab)*
Gibson, Dr Ian *(Lab)*
Kemp, Fraser *(Lab)*
McWilliam, John *(Lab)*
Moonie, Lewis *(Lab/Co-op)*

Telecommunications
Evans, Nigel *(Con)*
Hain, Peter *(Lab)*
Timms, Stephen *(Lab)*

Temperance Movement
Taylor, Sir Teddy *(Con)*

Terrorism and Internal Security
Maginnis, Ken *(UUP)*

Textile Industries
Anderson, Janet *(Lab)*
Winterton, Ann *(Con)*
Winterton, Nicholas *(Con)*

The Arts
Hopkins, Kelvin *(Lab)*
Howarth, Alan *(Lab)*
Maxton, John *(Lab)*

The Elderly
Colvin, Michael *(Con)*

Think British Campaign
Winterton, Ann *(Con)*

Third World
Berry, Dr Roger *(Lab)*
Body, Sir Richard *(Con)*
Davidson, Ian *(Lab/Co-op)*
George, Andrew *(Lib Dem)*
Grant, Bernie *(Lab)*
Hume, John *(SDLP)*
Marshall, David *(Lab)*
Salmond, Alex *(SNP)*
Skinner, Dennis *(Lab)*
Stunell, Andrew *(Lib Dem)*
Webb, Prof Steve *(Lib Dem)*

Timber
Walker, Cecil *(UUP)*

Tourism
Ashton, Joe *(Lab)*
Bruce, Ian *(Con)*
Butterfill, John *(Con)*
Collins, Tim *(Con)*
Cotter, Brian *(Lib Dem)*
Fearn, Ronnie *(Lib Dem)*
Gale, Roger *(Con)*
Hawkins, Nick *(Con)*
Llwyd, Elfyn *(PC)*
Quinn, Lawrie *(Lab)*
Smith, Geraldine *(Lab)*
Tyler, Paul *(Lib Dem)*
Waterson, Nigel *(Con)*

Tourism/Leisure Industry
Fraser, Christopher *(Con)*

Town Centre Issues
Lepper, David *(Lab/Co-op)*

Trade
Curry, David *(Con)*
Jenkin, Bernard *(Con)*
Paterson, Owen *(Con)*
Sheerman, Barry *(Lab/Co-op)*

Trade and Industry
Bruce, Ian *(Con)*
Butterfill, John *(Con)*
Byers, Stephen *(Lab)*
Cable, Dr Vincent *(Lib Dem)*
Cash, William *(Con)*
Chapman, Ben *(Lab)*
Coffey, Ann *(Lab)*
Cran, James *(Con)*
Curtis-Thomas, Claire *(Lab)*
Davies, Geraint *(Lab)*
Davies, Quentin *(Con)*
Donaldson, Jeffrey *(UUP)*
Emery, Peter *(Con)*
Fabricant, Michael *(Con)*
Follett, Barbara *(Lab)*
Foster, Michael John *(Lab)*
Gardiner, Barry *(Lab)*
Gilroy, Linda *(Lab/Co-op)*
Hamilton, Sir Archie *(Con)*
Hawkins, Nick *(Con)*
Hoon, Geoffrey *(Lab)*
Hoyle, Lindsay *(Lab)*
Jenkins, Brian *(Lab)*
Jones, Nigel *(Lib Dem)*
Kumar, Dr Ashok *(Lab)*
Lait, Jacqui *(Con)*
Lansley, Andrew *(Con)*
Liddell, Helen *(Lab)*
Luff, Peter *(Con)*
McLeish, Henry *(Lab)*
Martin, Michael *(Lab)*
Mawhinney, Sir Brian *(Con)*
O'Neill, Martin *(Lab)*
Page, Richard *(Con)*
Pike, Peter *(Lab)*
Prior, David *(Con)*
Purchase, Ken *(Lab/Co-op)*
Randall, John *(Con)*
Soames, Nicholas *(Con)*
Spelman, Caroline *(Con)*
Stewart, Ian *(Lab)*
Taylor, John M *(Con)*
Thomas, Gareth *(Lab)*
Tredinnick, David *(Con)*
Turner, Dr George *(Lab)*
Viggers, Peter *(Con)*
Wells, Bowen *(Con)*
Williams, Dr Alan *(Lab)*
Woolas, Philip *(Lab)*
Wright, Anthony *(Lab)*

Trade Policy
Bruce, Malcolm *(Lib Dem)*

Trade Union Law Reform
Howard, Michael *(Con)*

Trade Unions
Ashton, Joe *(Lab)*
Benn, Hilary *(Lab)*
Caborn, Richard *(Lab)*
Fyfe, Maria *(Lab)*
Golding, Llin *(Lab)*
Healey, John *(Lab)*
Illsley, Eric *(Lab)*
Mahon, Alice *(Lab)*

Trades Union Legislation
Etherington, William *(Lab)*

Training
Colvin, Michael *(Con)*
Jenkins, Brian *(Lab)*
Paice, James *(Con)*
Palmer, Dr Nicholas *(Lab)*
Prentice, Bridget *(Lab)*
Watts, David *(Lab)*

Transnational Broadcasting
Howells, Dr Kim *(Lab)*

Transport
Amess, David *(Con)*
Anderson, Donald *(Lab)*
Bradley, Peter *(Lab)*
Chaytor, David *(Lab)*
Clark, Paul *(Lab)*
Clelland, David *(Lab)*
Cryer, John *(Lab)*
Darling, Alistair *(Lab)*
Day, Stephen *(Con)*
Dean, Janet *(Lab)*
Donohoe, Brian *(Lab)*
Dowd, Jim *(Lab)*
Duncan Smith, Iain *(Con)*
Dunwoody, Gwyneth *(Lab)*
Eagle, Maria *(Lab)*
Efford, Clive *(Lab)*
Ellman, Louise *(Lab/Co-op)*
Fearn, Ronnie *(Lib Dem)*
Foster, Derek *(Lab)*
Goggins, Paul *(Lab)*
Griffiths, Jane *(Lab)*
Hammond, Philip *(Con)*
Hawkins, Nick *(Con)*
Henderson, Ivan *(Lab)*
Heppell, John *(Lab)*

Hill, Keith *(Lab)*
Hopkins, Kelvin *(Lab)*
Horam, John *(Con)*
Jack, Michael *(Con)*
Jones, Ieuan Wyn *(PC)*
Jones, Nigel *(Lib Dem)*
Laing, Eleanor *(Con)*
McCabe, Stephen *(Lab)*
McIntosh, Anne *(Con)*
Mackinlay, Andrew *(Lab)*
Marek, Dr John *(Lab)*
Marshall, David *(Lab)*
Martlew, Eric *(Lab)*
Meale, Alan *(Lab)*
Morgan, Alasdair *(SNP)*
Norman, Archie *(Con)*
Organ, Diana *(Lab)*
Perham, Linda *(Lab)*
Pound, Stephen *(Lab)*
Prosser, Gwyn *(Lab)*
Quinn, Lawrie *(Lab)*
Raynsford, Nick *(Lab)*
Reid, Dr John *(Lab)*
Robathan, Andrew *(Con)*
Ruddock, Joan *(Lab)*
Russell, Bob *(Lib Dem)*
Russell, Christine *(Lab)*
Smith, Andrew *(Lab)*
Smyth, Martin *(UUP)*
Snape, Peter *(Lab)*
Stevenson, George *(Lab)*
Strang, Gavin *(Lab)*
Ward, Claire *(Lab)*
White, Brian *(Lab)*
Whitehead, Dr Alan *(Lab)*
Winterton, Ann *(Con)*
Winterton, Rosie *(Lab)*
Wood, Mike *(Lab)*

Transport and the Regions
Davies, Geraint *(Lab)*

Transport Safety
Smith, John *(Lab)*

Transportation
Chidgey, David *(Lib Dem)*

Treasury
Byers, Stephen *(Lab)*
Casale, Roger *(Lab)*
Cranston, Ross *(Lab)*
Davies, Denzil *(Lab)*
Davies, Geraint *(Lab)*
Hanson, David *(Lab)*
Mawhinney, Sir Brian *(Con)*

Ruffley, David *(Con)*
Touhig, Don *(Lab/Co-op)*
Townend, John *(Con)*
Wells, Bowen *(Con)*

UK Poverty
Goggins, Paul *(Lab)*

Unemployment
Cooper, Yvette *(Lab)*
Goggins, Paul *(Lab)*
Graham, Tommy *(Scottish Labour)*
Jones, Barry *(Lab)*
Meale, Alan *(Lab)*
Reed, Andrew *(Lab/Co-op)*
Short, Clare *(Lab)*
Yeo, Tim *(Con)*

United Nations
Wells, Bowen *(Con)*

Urban Funding
Graham, Tommy *(Scottish Labour)*

Urban Parks
Wyatt, Derek *(Lab)*

Urban Policies
Fisher, Mark *(Lab)*
Vaz, Keith *(Lab)*

Urban Policy
Benn, Hilary *(Lab)*

Urban Regeneration
Blears, Hazel *(Lab)*
Buck, Karen *(Lab)*
McGuire, Anne *(Lab)*
Russell, Christine *(Lab)*
Steen, Anthony *(Con)*
Timms, Stephen *(Lab)*

US Elections
Evans, Nigel *(Con)*

USA
Forth, Eric *(Con)*

Utility Regulation
Gilroy, Linda *(Lab/Co-op)*

Venture Capital
Gunnell, John *(Lab)*
Wyatt, Derek *(Lab)*

Vocational Training
Reed, Andrew *(Lab/Co-op)*

Voluntary Organisations
Coffey, Ann *(Lab)*
Fraser, Christopher *(Con)*
Rowe, Andrew *(Con)*

Voluntary Sector
Michael, Alun *(Lab/Co-op)*

Voting Systems
Harris, Evan *(Lib Dem)*
Linton, Martin *(Lab)*

Wales
Anderson, Donald *(Lab)*
Dafis, Cynog *(PC)**
Davies, Denzil *(Lab)*
Edwards, Huw *(Lab)*
Owen Jones, Jon *(Lab/Co-op)*
Murphy, Paul *(Lab)*

Waste Management
Paice, James *(Con)*

Water Industry
Burden, Richard *(Lab)*
O'Brien, William *(Lab)*

Welfare
Buck, Karen *(Lab)*
Cook, Robin *(Lab)*
Davies, Quentin *(Con)*
Moran, Margaret *(Lab)*
Shaw, Jonathan *(Lab)*
Webb, Prof Steve *(Lib Dem)*

Welfare of Armed Services Families
Bell, Martin *(Independent)*

Welfare of Elderly and Disabled
Hayes, John *(Con)*

Welfare Reform
Coaker, Vernon *(Lab)*
Kelly, Ruth *(Lab)*
McDonagh, Siobhain *(Lab)*
Plaskitt, James *(Lab)*

Welfare State
Brown, Russell *(Lab)*
Corbyn, Jeremy *(Lab)*
Efford, Clive *(Lab)*
Hutton, John *(Lab)*
Wicks, Malcolm *(Lab)*

Welfare to Work
Flint, Caroline *(Lab)*

West Midlands Industry
O'Brien, Mike *(Lab)*

Wild Life Conservation (especially Bird and Marine)
Morgan, Rhodri *(Lab)*

Wildlife and Countryside Legislation
Dalyell, Tam *(Lab)*

Women
Harman, Harriet *(Lab)*
Ruddock, Joan *(Lab)*
Short, Clare *(Lab)*
Wise, Audrey *(Lab)*

Women's Issues
Gorman, Teresa *(Con)*

Jackson, Helen *(Lab)*
King, Oona *(Lab)*
Osborne, Sandra *(Lab)*

Women's Rights
Cohen, Harry *(Lab)*
Corston, Jean *(Lab)*
Fyfe, Maria *(Lab)*
Martin, Michael *(Lab)*
Primarolo, Dawn *(Lab)*

Workers' Co-operatives
Tipping, Paddy *(Lab)*

World Development
Armstrong, Hilary *(Lab)*
Drown, Julia *(Lab)*

World Population
Ottaway, Richard *(Con)*

World Protestantism
Smyth, Martin *(UUP)*

Youth Affairs
Ashdown, Paddy *(Lib Dem)*
Baldry, Tony *(Con)*
Ballard, Jackie *(Lib Dem)*
Burgon, Colin *(Lab)*
Colvin, Michael *(Con)*
Connarty, Michael *(Lab)*
Cotter, Brian *(Lib Dem)*
Foster, Derek *(Lab)*
Gorrie, Donald *(Lib Dem)*
Haselhurst, Sir Alan *(Con)*
Hope, Phil *(Lab/Co-op)*
Hughes, Simon *(Lib Dem)*
Steen, Anthony *(Con)*

Youth Work
Michael, Alun *(Lab/Co-op)*

Political Parties

LABOUR PARTY

Millbank Tower, Millbank,
London SW1P 4GT

020 7802 1000 Fax 020 7802 1234
E-mail: labour-party@geo2.poptel.org.uk
Website: www.labour.org.uk

Chair: Vernon Hince
Vice-Chair: Maggie Jones
Treasurer: Margaret Prosser
Leader: The Rt Hon Tony Blair, MP
Deputy Leader: The Rt Hon John Prescott, MP
General Secretary: Margaret McDonagh

**Parliamentary Labour Party's Office –
House of Commons**

Secretary: Alan Haworth (020 7219 4266)
Administrator: Rebecca Taylor (020 7219 4552)
Senior Committee Officer: Catherine Jackson
  (020 7219 5278)
Committee Officers: Liz Djilali (020 7219 5277),
  Fiona Twycross (020 7219 5953)
Press Officer: Don Brind (020 7219 2458)

CO-OPERATIVE PARTY

Victory House, 10–14 Leicester Square
London WC2H 7QH

020 7439 0123 Fax 020 7439 3434
E-mail: p.hunt@co-op-party.org.uk

Chair: Jim Lee
Vice-Chair: Peter Nurse
Chair of Parliamentary Group: Andy Love, MP
National Secretary: Peter Hunt

The Co-operative Party exists to put Co-
operators into Parliament. It is the political party
representing the Co-operative Movement.
Established in 1917. It is not affiliated to the
Labour Party at national level, but has a written
National Agreement. Our candidates stand as
Joint Candidates of both Parties and are badged
'Labour/Co-operative'. The Co-operative Party
published its own manifesto during the General
Election.

CONSERVATIVE AND UNIONIST PARTY

32 Smith Square
London SW1P 3HH

020 7222 9000 Fax 020 7222 1135
Website: www.tory.org.uk

Chairman:
  The Rt Hon Michael Ancram, QC, MP
Deputy Chairman and Chief Executive:
  Hon David Prior, MP
Senior Vice-Chairman: Tim Collins, CBE, MP
Vice-Chairman (Wales): Nigel Evans, MP

Vice-Chairman: John Hayes, MP
Senior Party Treasurer: Michael Ashcroft
Head of News and Media: Amanda Platell

LIBERAL DEMOCRAT PARTY

4 Cowley Street
London SW1P 3NB

020 7222 7999 Fax 020 7799 2170
E-mail: libdems@cix.co.uk
Website: www.libdems.org.uk

Leader: The Rt Hon Charles Kennedy, MP
President: Baroness Maddock
Vice-Presidents: Paul Farthing (England),
  Lembit Öpik, MP (Wales),
  Ian Yuill (Scotland)
Chief Executive: Ben Stoneham
Director of Campaigns: Chris Rennard, MBE
Director of Policy and Research:
  Dr Richard Grayson
*Director of Marketing, Fundraising and
  Members' Services:* David Loxton
Press Office:
Director of Media Communications:
  David Walter
Chief Broadcasting Officer: Jeremy Browne
Senior Press and Broadcasting Officer:
  Robert Blevin
Press and Broadcasting Officers: Lissa Bradley,
  Susannah Winter
Campaigns and Regional Media Officer:
  Ian Horner
Press Assistant: Gareth Thomas
E-mail: ldpressoffice@cix.co.uk
Conference and Events Organiser:
  Penny McCormack
Financial Controller: Irene Douglas
Head of International Office: Karla Hatrick

**Parliamentary Liberal Democrat's Office –
House of Commons**
Secretary: Ben Williams (020 7219 5654)
Parliamentary Assistant: David Oliver
  (020 7219 1415)
Fax: 020 7219 5894
E-mail: libdemcommons@cix.co.uk

ULSTER UNIONIST PARTY (UUP)

3 Glengall Street
Belfast BT12 5AE

028 9032 4601 Fax 028 9024 6738
E-mail: uup@uup.org
Website: www.uup.org

Patron: The Rt Hon the
  Lord Molyneaux of Killead, KBE

President: Josias Cunningham, DL
Leader: The Rt Hon David Trimble, MP
Chairman of the Executive Committee:
  Lord Rogan
Vice-Chairman of the Executive Committee:
  James Cooper
Vice-Presidents: Rev Martin Smyth, Ken
  Maginnis, MP, Jim Nicholson, MEP, Sir Reg
  Empey, OBE
Hon Secs: Jeffrey Donaldson, MP, Cllr Jim
  Rodgers, Mrs Arlene Foster, David Brewster
Hon Treasurer: Jack Allen, OBE
Asst Hon Treasurer: Mrs May Steele, JP
Whip: Rev Martin Smyth, MP
General Secretary: David Boyd

SCOTTISH NATIONAL PARTY

6 North Charlotte Street
Edinburgh EH2 4JH

0131-226 3661 Fax 0131-226 7373
E-mail:snp.hq@snp.org.uk
Website: www.snp.org.uk

President: Winnie Ewing, MSP
Parliamentary Leader:
  Alasdair Morgan, MP, MSP
Chief Whip: Alasdair Morgan, MP, MSP
National Convenor: Alex Salmond, MP, MSP
Senior Vice-Convenor: John Swinney, MP, MSP
National Secretary: Stewart Hosie
National Treasurer: Ian Blackford
Director of Organisation and Headquarters:
  Allison Hunter
Communications Manager: Kevin Pringle
Director of Administration: Irene White

PLAID CYMRU

Tŷ Gwynfor, 18 Park Grove, Cardiff CF1 3BN

029 2064 6000 Fax 029 2064 6001
E-mail: post@plaidcymru.org
Website: www.plaidcymru.org

President: The Rt Hon Dafydd Wigley, MP
Chair: Marc Phillips
Treasurer: Jeff Canning
Chief Executive: Karl Davies
Press Officer: Siôn Ffrancon

SOCIAL DEMOCRATIC AND LABOUR PARTY

121 Ormeau Road, Belfast BT7 1SH
028 9024 7700 Fax 028 9023 6699
E-mail: sdlp@indigo.ie
Website: www.indigo.ie/sdlp/

Leader: John Hume, MP, MEP, MLA
Deputy Leader: Seamus Mallon, MP, MLA
Chief Whip: Eddie McGrady, MP, MLA
Chairperson: Jim Lennon
Vice-Chairpersons: Mary McKeown,
  Sean McKee
Treasurer: Henry Doherty
Assistant Treasurer: Brian Heading
International Secretary: Denis Haughey, MLA
General Secretary: Gerry Cosgrove

MLA – Member of Legislative Assembly

DEMOCRATIC UNIONIST PARTY

91 Dundela Avenue
Belfast BT4 3BU
028 9047 1155 Fax 028 9047 1797
E-mail: info@dup.org.uk
Website: www.dup.org.uk

Leader: Dr Ian Paisley, MP, MEP
Deputy Leader: Ald Peter Robinson, MP
Chairman: Ald James McClure
Vice-Chairman: Cllr Samuel McConaghie
Party Secretary: Ald Nigel Dodds, LLB
Treasurer: Ald Gregory Campbell
Director of Communications:
  St Clair McAlister
Chief Executive: Allan Ewart

UK UNIONIST PARTY

10 Hamilton Road, Bangor
Co Down BT20 4LE
028 9127 2994 Fax 028 9146 5037
E-mail: contactus@ukunionists.freeserve.co.uk
Website: www.welcome.to/ukup

Leader: Robert McCartney, QC, MP
Chairman: Nelson Wharton
Treasurer: Flora Henderson
Secretary: Tom Sheridan

SINN FEIN

44 Parnell Square, Dublin 1
+353 1 8726932/8726100
Fax +353 1 8733441/8783595
E-mail: sinnfein@iol.ie
Website: www.sinnfein.ie

Press Officer: Miss Dawn Doyle
Assembly Nos:
028 9052 1470 Fax 028 9052 1474

Select Committees

AGRICULTURE

7 Millbank, London SW1P 3JA,
Telephone: 020 7219 6194

Remit: To examine the expenditure, administration and policy of the Ministry of Agriculture, Fisheries and Food and associated public bodies.

Members: (11) David Borrow; David Curry; David Drew; Alan Hurst; Michael Jack; Fiona Jones; Peter Luff (Chairman); Paul Marsden; Austin Mitchell; Lembit Öpik; Mark Todd; Ms Lynn Gardner (Clerk); Mr Richard Kelly (Specialist Assistant); Mr Mark Oxborough (Committee Assistant); Ms Anne Woolhouse (Secretary)

CONSOLIDATION OF BILLS (JOINT COMMITTEE)

Public Bill Offices, House of Lords/House of Commons, London SW1A 0AA
Telephone: 020 7219 3153/3256

Remit: Appointed under SO No 140 to consider consolidation bills, statute law revision bills and statute law repeal bills and Northern Ireland Orders in Council with like effect.

Members: (21) Earl Alexander of Tunis; Lord Campbell of Alloway; Lord Clyde; Viscount Colville of Culross; Viscount Dilhorne; Lord Hacking; Lord Hobhouse of Woodborough; Lord Janner of Braunstone; Baroness Mallalieu; Lord Meston; Lord Razzall; Lord Strabolgi; Tony Clarke; Patrick Hall; Robert Marshall-Andrews; James Plaskitt; Laurence Robertson; Adrian Sanders; George Turner; Andrew Tyrie; Brian White; Mr Fox (Clerk Commons); Mr Ollard (Clerk Lords)

CULTURE, MEDIA AND SPORT

7 Millbank, London SW1P 3JA
Telephone: 020 7219 6188

Remit: To examine the expenditure, administration and policy of the Department for Culture, Media and Sport and its associated public bodies. These include the Arts Council of England, the BBC, the British Tourist Authority, Channel 4, the Sports Council and the Office of the National Lottery (OFLOT).

Members: (11) Gerald Kaufman (Chairman); David Faber; Ronnie Fearn; Christopher Fraser; Llin Golding; Alan Keen; Julie Kirkbride; John Maxton; Diana Organ; Claire Ward; Derek Wyatt; Mr Colin Lee (Clerk); Mr Richard Cooke (Assistant Clerk); Mrs Nicole Mulloy (Committee Assistant); Mrs Amanda Waller (Secretary)

DEFENCE

Committee Office, House of Commons, London SW1A 0AA
Telephone: 020 7219 5745

Remit: To examine the expenditure, administration and policy of the Ministry of Defence and associated public bodies.

Members: (11) Bruce George (Chairman); Crispin Blunt; Julian Brazier; Jamie Cann; Harry Cohen; Michael Colvin; Mike Gapes; Mike Hancock; Stephen Hepburn; Jimmy Hood; Laura Moffatt; Mr Paul Evans (Clerk); Mr Simon Fiander (Audit Adviser); Carol Oxborough (Assistant Clerk); Ms Liz Partridge (Committee Assistant); Mrs Karen Watling (Secretary)

DEREGULATION
7 Millbank, London SW1P 3JA
Telephone: 020 7219 2833

Remit: Appointed under SO No 141 to examine documents containing proposals laid before the House and draft orders proposed under the Deregulation and Contracting Out Act 1994. The Committee makes recommendations on proposals either that a draft order should be laid, that the proposal be amended before an order is laid or that the order making power should not be used. The Committee reports to the House its recommendation as to whether a draft order should be approved.

Members: (18) Peter Pike (Chair); Russell Brown; David Chaytor; Brian Cotter; John Cryer; Teresa Gorman; Andy King; Ashok Kumar; Jacqui Lait; Andrew Love; John McDonnell; Denis Murphy; Doug Naysmith; John Randall; William Ross; Anthony Steen; Ian Stewart; Brian White; Mrs Susan Craig (Clerk); Mr John Vaux (Adviser); Kemi Alagbala (Adviser); Mr Brian Dye (Committee Assistant); Miss Susan Ramsay (Secretary)

EDUCATION AND EMPLOYMENT
7 Millbank, London SW1P 3JA
Telephone: 020 7219 6181

Remit: To examine the expenditure, administration and policy of the Department for Education and Employment, including the Employment Service and the TECs, and associated public bodies including the various funding agencies for education and the Office for Standards in Education. The Committee has the power to appoint two sub-committees.

Members: (16) Candy Atherton; Charlotte Atkins; Graham Brady; Valerie Davey; Derek Foster (Chairman (Employment); Michael Foster; Evan Harris; Helen Jones; Judy Mallaber; Gordon Marsden; Stephen O'Brien; Ian Pearson; Nicholas St Aubyn; Barry Sheerman (Chairman (Education); Stephen Twigg; Phil Willis; Mr Liam Laurence Smyth (Clerk); Mr Tom Healey (Assistant Clerk); Mr Eamon Lally (Specialist Assistant); Mr Robert Rees (Specialist Assistant); Mr Darren Hackett (Committee Assistant); Mr Richard Dawson (Committee Assistant); Ms Pam Morris (Secretary); Miss Claire Halls (Secretary)

EDUCATION AND EMPLOYMENT (EDUCATION SUB-COMMITTEE)
7 Millbank, London SW1P 3JA
Telephone: 020 7219 6181

Members: (12) Barry Sheerman (Chairman); Charlotte Atkins; Valerie Davey; Derek Foster; Michael John Foster; Evan Harris; John Hayes; Helen Jones; Gordon Marsden; Stephen O'Brien; Nicholas St Aubyn; Phil Willis; Mr Matthew Hamlyn (Clerk); Mr Robert Rees (Specialist Assistant); Mr Richard Dawson (Committee Assistant); Miss Claire Halls (Secretary)

EDUCATION AND EMPLOYMENT (EMPLOYMENT SUB-COMMITTEE)
7 Millbank, London SW1P 3JA,
Telephone: 020 7219 6181

Members: (7) Derek Foster (Chairman); Candy Atherton; Graham Brady; Judy Mallaber; Ian Pearson; Nick St Aubyn; Stephen Twigg; Mr Tom Healey (Clerk); Mr Eamon Lally (Specialist Assistant); Mr Darren Hackett (Committee Assistant); Ms Pam Morris (Secretary)

ENVIRONMENT, TRANSPORT AND REGIONAL AFFAIRS
7 Millbank, London SW1P 3JA
Telephone: 020 7219 4972

Remit: To examine the expenditure, administration and policy of the Department of the Environment, Transport and the Regions and associated public bodies including the Environment Protection Agency, the Health and Safety Executive and the Office of the Rail Regulator. The Environment, Transport and Regional Affairs Committee has the power to appoint two sub-committees.

Members: (17) Hilary Benn; Andrew F Bennett (Chairman (Environment)); Thomas Brake; Christine Butler; John Cummings; Brian Donohoe; Gwyneth Dunwoody (Chairman (Transport)); Louise Ellman; Clifford Forsythe; Teresa Gorman; James Gray; Stephen Ladyman; Anne McIntosh; William O'Brien; Bill Olner; John Randall; George Stevenson; Dr David Harrison (Clerk); Mr Gavin Devine (Clerk); Mr Huw Yardley (Clerk); Katie Smith (Specialist Assistant); Mr Kevin Lee (Specialist Assistant); Mr Dave Taylor (Specialist Assistant); Miss Frances Allingham (Committee Assistant); Miss Jackie Recardo (Committee Assistant);   Leslie Young (Secretary); Miss Susan Morrison (Secretary)

ENVIRONMENT, TRANSPORT AND REGIONAL AFFAIRS (ENVIRONMENT SUB-COMMITTEE)

7 Millbank, London SW1P 3JA
Telephone: 020 7219 1353

Members: (11) Andrew Bennett (Chairman); Hilary Benn; Thomas Brake; Christine Butler; John Cummings; Brian Donohoe; Gwyneth Dunwoody; Louise Ellman; James Gray; Bill Olner; John Randall; Dr David Harrison (Clerk); Mr Hugh Yardley (Clerk); Katie Smith (Specialist Assistant); Mr David Taylor (Specialist Assistant); Miss Jackie Recardo (Committee Assistant); Miss Susan Morrison (Secretary)

ENVIRONMENT, TRANSPORT AND REGIONAL AFFAIRS (TRANSPORT SUB-COMMITTEE)

7 Millbank, London SW1P 3JA
Telephone: 020 7219 6263

Members: (11) Gwyneth Dunwoody (Chairman); Andrew Bennett; Tom Brake; Brian Donohoe; Clifford Forsythe; Teresa Gorman; James Gray; Anne McIntosh; William O'Brien; Bill Olner; George Stevenson; Mr Gavin Devine (Clerk); Mr Kevin Lee (Specialist Assistant); Miss Frances Allingham (Committee Assistant); Miss Leslie Young (Secretary)

ENVIRONMENTAL AUDIT

7 Millbank, London SW1P 3JA,
Telephone: 020 7219 6150

Remit: Appointed under SO No 142A to consider to what extent the policies and programmes of government departments and non-departmental public bodies contribute to environmental protection and sustainable development; to audit their performance against such targets as may be set for them by ministers; and to report to the House.

Members: (15) John Horam (Chairman); Norman Baker; Bob Blizzard; Helen Brinton; Neil Gerrard; Dominic Grieve; Brian Iddon; Jon Owen Jones; Tim Loughton; Michael Meacher (Ex-officio member); Laurence Robertson; Christine Russell; Malcolm Savidge; Jonathan Shaw; Joan Walley; Mr Fergus Reid (Clerk); Mr Eric Lewis (Specialist Assistant); Ms Emma Downing (Specialist Assistant); Ms Tracy Herd (Committee Assistant); Jane Cooper (Secretary)

EUROPEAN SCRUTINY

7 Millbank, London SW1P 3JA
Telephone: 020 7219 5465

Remit: To examine European Community Documents and to report its opinion on the legal and political importance of each such document, and where it considers appropriate, to report also on the reasons for its opinion and on any matters of principle, policy or law which may be affected; to make recommendations for the further consideration of any such document in European Standing Committees and to consider any issues arising from such documents. These documents include: any proposal under the Community Treaties for legislation by the Council or the Council acting jointly with the European Parliament; any document published for submission to the European Council, the Council or the European Central Bank; any proposal to define a common position or for joint action under Title V of the Treaty on European Union or any proposal for a joint position, joint action or convention under Title VI of the Treaty on European Union, prepared for submission to the Council; any document published by one Union institution with a view to submission to another Union institution which does not relate exclusively to consideration of any proposal for legislation; and other document relating to European Union matters deposited in the House by a Minister of the Crown.

Members: (16) Jimmy Hood (Chairman); Ben Bradshaw; Colin Breed; Roger Casale; William Cash; Michael Connarty; Jim Dobbin; Margaret Ewing; Patrick Hall; Jenny Jones; James Marshall; Nick Palmer; Owen Paterson; Bill Rammell; Laurence Robertson; Anthony Steen; Mrs Elizabeth Flood (Clerk); Mrs Susan Craig (Clerk Adviser); Miss Josephine Eldred (Clerk Adviser); Mr David Griffiths (Clerk Adviser); Ms Rosemary Melling (Clerk Adviser); Mr Clive Wilson (Clerk Adviser); Ms Karen McLelland (Committee Assistant); Ms Keely Bishop (Secretary); Miss Susan Ramsey (Secretary); Miss Fiona Mearns (Secretary); Ms Alison Ross (Secretary); Ms Melanie Grant (Secretary)

FOREIGN AFFAIRS

Committee Office, House of Commons, London SW1A 0AA
Telephone: 020 7219 6394

Remit: To examine the expenditure, administration and policy of the Foreign and Commonwealth Office and associated public bodies, including the British Council and the BBC World Service.

Members: (12) Donald Anderson (Chairman); Diane Abbott; David Chidgey; Peter Emery; Norman Godman; Eric Illsley; Andrew Mackinlay; David Madel; Ted Rowlands; John Stanley; Phyllis Starkey; David Wilshire; Mr Paul Silk (Clerk); Ms Tabitha Brufal (Assistant Clerk); Mr Daniel Thornton (Committee Specialist); Mr James Davies (Committee Assistant); Ana Ferreira (Office Clerk); Mrs Sheryl Bertasius (Secretary)

HEALTH

7 Millbank, London SW1P 3JA,
Telephone: 020 7219 6182

Remit: To examine the expenditure, administration and policy of the Department of Health and associated public bodies, in particular the NHS in England and the responsibilities for personal social services and community care discharged by local authorities in England.

Members: (11) David Hinchliffe (Chairman); David Amess; John Austin; Peter Brand; Simon Burns; Eileen Gordon; John Gunnell; Stephen Hesford; Howard Stoate; Robert Syms; Audrey Wise; Mr John Benger (Clerk); Mr Tim Goldsmith (Second Clerk); Ms Suzanne O'Leary (Specialist Assistant); Mr Frank McShane (Committee Assistant); Ms Alex Richards (Secretary)

HOME AFFAIRS

7 Millbank, London SW1P 3JA
Telephone: 020 7219 3276

Remit: To examine the expenditure, administration and policy of the Home Office and associated public bodies; the policy administration and expenditure of the Lord Chancellor's Department (including the work of staff provided for the administrative work of courts and tribunals but excluding consideration of individual cases and appointments); and administration and expenditure of the Attorney General's Office, the Treasury Solicitor's Department, the Crown Prosecution Service and the Serious Fraud Office (but excluding individual cases and appointments and advice given within government by Law Officers).

Members: (11) Robin Corbett (Chairman); Ian Cawsey; Janet Dean; Michael Fabricant; Gerald Howarth; Martin Linton; Humfrey Malins; Bob Russell; Marsha Singh; Paul Stinchcombe; David Winnick; Mr Andrew Kennon (Clerk); Mr Martyn Atkins (Assistant Clerk); Mr Steve Barrett (Committee Assistant); Miss Elizabeth Booth (Secretary)

INTERNATIONAL DEVELOPMENT

7 Millbank, London SW1P 3JA
Telephone: 020 7219 1223

Remit: To examine the expenditure, administration and policy of the Department for International Development and associated public bodies.

Members: (11) Bowen Wells (Chairman); Ann Clwyd; Barbara Follett; Bernie Grant; Nigel Jones; Piara Khabra; Oona King; Tess Kingham; Andrew Robathan; Andrew Rowe; Tony Worthington; Mr Yusef Azad (Clerk); Miss Janet Hughes (Assistant Clerk); Mr William Benson (Specialist Assistant); Mr Ian Thomson (Committee Assistant); Sam Hill (Secretary)

LIAISON

Committee Office, House of Commons, London SW1A 0AA
Telephone: 020 7219 6432

Remit: Appointed under SO No 145 to consider general matters relating to the work of select committees; to give advice on the work of such committees to the House of Commons Commission; and to report to the House its choice of select committee reports for debate on appointed days, including "Estimates days". The Committee consists of the chairmen of all the other select committees of the House.

Members: (32) Robert Sheldon (Chairman); Richard Allan; Donald Anderson; Andrew Bennett; Peter Brooke; Sydney Chapman; Michael Clark; Eric Clarke; Robin Corbett; David Davis; Gwyneth Dunwoody; Derek Foster; Bruce George; David Hinchliffe; Jimmy Hood; John Horam; Martyn Jones; Gerald Kaufman; Archy Kirkwood; Peter Luff; David Marshall; Lewis Moonie; Martin O'Neill; Peter Pike; Giles Radice; Marion Roe; Barry Sheerman; David Tredinnick; Dennis Turner; Bowen Wells; Nicholas Winterton; Tony Wright; Mr Charles Winnifrith (Clerk); Ms Annie Power (Secretary)

MODERNISATION OF THE HOUSE OF COMMONS

Committee Office, House of Commons, London SW1A 0AA
Telephone: 020 7219 5978

Remit: Appointed for the current Parliament to consider how the practices and procedures of the House should be modernised and to make recommendations thereon.

Members: (15) Margaret Beckett (Chairman); Ivor Caplin; David Drew; Peter Emery; Lorna Fitzsimons; Helen Jackson; Peter Pike; Gordon Prentice; Richard Shepherd; Clive Soley; Andrew Stunell; Stephen Twigg; Paul Tyler; Nicholas Winterton; George Young; Mr Charles Winnifrith (Clerk); Mr Alan Sandall (Clerk); Carolyn Wilson (Committee Assistant); Ms Louise Sargent (Secretary)

NORTHERN IRELAND AFFAIRS

7 Millbank, London SW1P 3JA
Telephone: 020 7219 2172

Remit: To examine the expenditure, administration and policy of the Northern Ireland Office; the administration and expenditure of the Crown Solicitor's Office; and other matters within the responsibilities of the Secretary of State for Northern Ireland (but excluding the expenditure, administration and policy of the Office of the Director of Public Prosecutions, Northern Ireland and the drafting of legislation by the Office of the Legislative Counsel).

Members: (13) Peter Brooke (Chairman); Harry Barnes; Roy Beggs; Jeffrey Donaldson; John Grogan; Stephen Hesford; Andrew Hunter; Edward McGrady; Tony McWalter; Stephen McCabe; Nick Palmer; Stephen Pound; Peter Robinson; Dr Christopher Ward (Clerk); Mr Andrew Hubner (Committee Assistant); Ms Yvonne Platt (Secretary)

JOINT COMMITTEE ON PARLIAMENTARY PRIVILEGE

Journal Office, House of Commons, London SW1A 0AA
Telephone: 020 7219 3316

Remit: Appointed for the current Parliament to review parliamentary privilege and make recommendations thereon.

Members: (12) Lord Nicholls of Birkenhead (Chairman); Lord Archer of Sandwell; Lord Mayhew of Twysden; Lord Merlyn Rees; Lord Waddington; Lord Wigoder; Joe Benton; Patrick Cormack; Bill Michie; Ann Taylor; Paul Tyler; Alan Williams; Mr Jim Hastings (Clerk); Ms Louise Sargent (Secretary)

PROCEDURE

Journal Office, House of Commons, London SW1A 0AA
Telephone: 020 7219 3318

Remit: Appointed under SO No 147 to consider the practice and procedure of the House in the conduct of public business and to make recommendations.

Members: (14) Nicholas Winterton (Chairman); Tony Banks; Paul Beresford; Colin Burgon; Keith Darvill; Edward Davey; David Drew; Clive Efford; Lorna Fitzsimons; Eric Forth; Barry Gardiner; Nigel Griffiths; Eric Illsley; Andrew Stunell; Dr Robin James (Clerk); Shona McGlashan (Assistant Clerk); Ms Carolyn Wilson (Committee Assistant); Ms Louise Sargent (Secretary)

PUBLIC ACCOUNTS

7 Millbank, London SW1P 3JA
Telephone: 020 7219 5708

Remit: Appointed under SO No 149 to examine the appropriation accounts showing the sums granted by Parliament to meet the public expenditure and to examine any other such accounts laid before Parliament as the committee thinks fit; and, under the National Audit Act 1983, to inquire into the economy, efficiency and effectiveness of public expenditure by departments. The Public Accounts Committee works closely with the National Audit Office and uses that Office's reports as the basis of its inquiries.

Members: (15) David Davis (Chairman); Alan Campbell; David Curry; Ian Davidson; Geraint Davies; Barry Gardiner; Nigel Griffiths; Andrew Love; Jim Murphy; Richard Page; David Rendel; Gerry Steinberg; Stephen Timms; Charles Wardle; Alan Williams; Mr Ken Brown (Clerk); Miss Susan Monaghan (Committee Assistant); Miss Ronnie Jefferson (Secretary)

PUBLIC ADMINISTRATION

7 Millbank, London SW1P 3JA
Telephone: 020 7219 5730

Remit: Appointed under SO No 146 to examine the reports of the Parliamentary Commissioner for Administration, of the Health Service Commissioners for England, Scotland and Wales and of the Parliamentary Ombudsman for Northern Ireland; and to consider matters relating to the quality and standards of administration provided by civil service departments, and other matters relating to the civil service.

Members: (11) Tony Wright (Chairman); Peter Bradley; Desmond Browne; Ronnie Campbell; Helen Jones; Margaret Moran; Mark Oaten; Richard Shepherd; Nicholas Soames; Andrew Tyrie; Brian White; Ms Alda Barry (Clerk); Ms Clare Genis (Committee Assistant); Dr Devra Kay (Secretary)

SCIENCE AND TECHNOLOGY

7 Millbank, London SW1P 3JA
Telephone: 020 7219 2794

Remit: To examine the expenditure, administration and policy of the Office of Science and Technology, which is part of the Department of Trade and Industry.

Members: (12) Michael Clark (Chairman); Nigel Beard; Claire Curtis-Thomas; Peter Emery; Ian Gibson; Robert Jackson; Lynne Jones; Nigel Jones; Ashok Kumar; Ian Taylor; Desmond Turner; Alan Williams; Ms Jessica Mulley (Clerk); Mr Guy Rickett (Committee Specialist), Mrs Leonie Nugent (Committee Assistant); Ms Anna Browning (Secretary)

SCOTTISH AFFAIRS

Committee Office, House of Commons, London SW1A 0AA
Telephone: 020 7219 6295

Remit: To examine the expenditure, administration and policy of the Scottish Office and associated public bodies, including the NHS in Scotland and the Scottish development agencies; and administration and expenditure of the Lord Advocate's Departments, together with policy functions discharged by the Lord Advocate through the Scottish Courts Administration, but excluding consideration of individual cases and appointments, advice given within government by Scottish Law Officers, and the drafting of bills.

Members: (11) David Marshall (Chairman); Irene Adams; Peter Atkinson; Anne Begg; Russell Brown; Eric Clarke; Mohammed Sarwar; Robert Smith; Desmond Swayne; Bill Tynan; Andrew Welsh; Mr John Whatley (Clerk); Ms Jane Appleton (Committee Assistant); Ms Julie Storey (Secretary)

SELECTION

Committee Office, House of Commons, London SW1A 0AA
Telephone: 020 7219 3250

Remit: To nominate or propose Members to serve on Standing and Select Committees of the House of Commons.

Members: (9) John McWilliam (Chairman); Charlotte Atkins; Clive Betts; Keith Bradley; Karen Buck; James Cran; Philip Hope; Patrick McLoughlin; Paul Tyler; Ms Elizabeth Payne (Clerk)

SOCIAL SECURITY

7 Millbank, London SW1P 3JA
Telephone: 020 7219 5833

Remit: To examine the expenditure, administration and policy of the Department of Social Security, including the Benefits Agency, and associated public bodies.

Members: (11) Archy Kirkwood (Chairman); Karen Buck; David Crausby; Andrew Dismore; Joan Humble; Andy King; Edward Leigh; Doug Naysmith; Laurence Robertson; Desmond Swayne; Gareth Thomas; Mr Philip Moon (Clerk); Ms Janet Allbeson (Committee Specialist); Mrs Diane Nelson (Committee Assistant); Ms Mandy Sullivan (Secretary)

STANDARDS AND PRIVILEGES

Committee Office, House of Commons, London SW1A 0AA
Telephone: 020 7219 6615

Remit: Appointed under SO No 149 to consider specific matters relating to privileges referred to it by the House; to oversee the work of the Parliamentary Commissioner for Standards; to examine and review the arrangements for the compilation, maintenance and accessibility of the Register of Members' Interests; to consider specific complaints made in relation to the registering or declaring of interests referred to it by the Commissioner; to consider any matter relating to the conduct of Members; and to recommend any modification to any code of conduct relating to Members which the House has agreed as may from time to time appear to be necessary.

Members: (11) Robert Sheldon (Chairman); Martin Bell; Peter Bottomley; Malcolm Bruce; Dale Campbell-Savours; Eric Forth; Michael Foster; Tom Levitt; Terry Lewis; Shona McIsaac; Alan Williams; Mr Alan Sandall (Clerk); Mr Stephen Mark (Assistant Clerk); Miss Lisa Hasell (Secretary)

JOINT COMMITTEE ON STATUTORY INSTRUMENTS

Ways and Means Office, House of Commons, London SW1A 0AA
Telephone: 020 7219 3773

Remit: Appointed under SO No 151 to consider draft statutory instruments, statutory instruments and other instruments laid before each House of Parliament and upon which proceedings may be or might have been taken in either House of Parliament, in pursuance of an Act of Parliament. The Commons Members of the Committee meet as the Select Committee on Statutory Instruments from time to time to consider instruments subject to proceedings only in that House.

Members: (14) Lord Greenway; Lord Hardy; Lord Onslow; Lord Skelmersdale; Lord Thomas of Gresford; Lord Vivian; Lord Walker of Doncaster; David Tredinnick (Chairman); Andrew Bennett; Harold Best; Dominic Grieve; Ivan Henderson; William Ross; Brian White; Mr Mike Hennessy (Clerk); Mr Simon Burton (Clerk); Ms Michelle Owens (Secretary); Jane Lander (Secretary)

TRADE AND INDUSTRY

7 Millbank, London SW1P 3JA
Telephone: 020 7219 5777

Remit: To examine the expenditure, administration and policy of the Department of Trade and Industry (but excluding the Office of Science and Technology) and associated public bodies, including the regulatory authorities for the coal, gas, electricity and tele-communications industries.

Members: (11) Martin O'Neill (Chairman); Tony Baldry; Roger Berry; John Butterfill; Christopher Chope; James Cunningham; Lindsay Hoyle; Bob Laxton; Alasdair Morgan; Linda Perham; Helen Southworth; Mr David Natzler (Clerk); Charlotte Littleby (Assistant Clerk); Ms Julia Gleig (Committee Specialist); Mr Tony Catinella (Committee Assistant); Mrs Alison Game (Secretary)

TREASURY

7 Millbank, London SW1P 3JA
Telephone: 020 7219 5768

Remit: To examine the expenditure, administration and policy of the Treasury, the Board of Inland Revenue and the Board of Customs & Excise. The Committee also monitors the work of the Bank of England.

Members: (13) Giles Radice (Chairman); Elizabeth Blackman; Jim Cousins; Edward Davey; Michael Fallon; David Kidney; Lewis Moonie; James Plaskitt; David Ruffley; Brian Sedgemore; Michael Spicer; Teddy Taylor; Mr Simon Patrick (Clerk); Mr Mark Egan (Assistant Clerk); Ms Jane Fox (Committee Assistant); Mr Jonathan Lepper (Committee Specialist); Mr Timothy Jarrett (Committee Specialist); Ms Lisette Andrews (Secretary)

TREASURY (TREASURY SUB-COMMITTEE)

7 Millbank, London SW1P 3JA

Members: (12) Michael Spicer (Chairman); Elizabeth Blackman; Jim Cousins; Edward Davey; Michael Fallon; David Kidney; Lewis Moonie; James Plaskitt; Giles Radice; David Ruffley; Brian Sedgemore; Teddy Taylor; Mr Mark Egan (Clerk); Ms Jane Fox (Committee Assistant); Mr Jonathan Lepper (Committee Specialist); Mr Timothy Jarrett (Committee Specialist); Ms Lisette Andrews (Secretary)

WELSH AFFAIRS

7 Millbank, London SW1P 3JA
Telephone: 020 7219 6189

Remit: To examine the expenditure, administration and policy of the Welsh Office and associated public bodies, including the Welsh Development Agency and the NHS in Wales.

Members: (11) Martyn Jones (Chairman); Martin Caton; Huw Edwards; Julian Lewis; Richard Livsey; Elfyn Llwyd; Julie Morgan; Owen Paterson; Chris Ruane; Gareth Thomas; Betty Williams; Ms Philippa Helme (Clerk); Mr Paul Derrett (Committee Assistant); Ms Carys Thomas (Secretary)

Domestic Committees

ACCOMMODATION AND WORKS

Committee Office, House of Commons, London SW1A 0AA
Telephone: 020 7219 2471

Members: (9) Sydney Chapman (Chairman); Keith Bradley; Colin Burgon; David Chidgey; Patrick Cormack; David Jamieson; Linda Perham; Raymond Powell; Sydney Rapson; Ms Sarah Davies (Clerk); Miss Jo-Ann Crowder (Secretary)

ADMINISTRATION

Committee Office, House of Commons, London SW1A 0AA
Telephone: 020 7219 3299

Members: (9) Marion Roe (Chairman); David Crausby; Hilton Dawson; Fabian Hamilton; Oliver Heald; Stephen Hepburn; Jane Kennedy; Nicholas Palmer; William Ross; Mr Mike Clark (Clerk); Mrs Helen Agnew (Secretary); Mrs Karen Georgiou (Secretary)

BROADCASTING

Committee Office, House of Commons, London SW1A 0AA
Telephone: 020 7219 3275

Members: (10) Ivor Caplin; Roger Gale; George Galloway; Barry Gardiner; Eileen Gordon; Kelvin Hopkins; David Lepper; Stephen Pound; Jonathan Sayeed; Andrew Stunell; Mr Mike Clark (Clerk); Ms Lynda Young (Secretary)

CATERING

Committee Office, House of Commons, London SW1A 0AA
Telephone: 020 7219 3299

Members: (9) Dennis Turner (Chairman); Gerald Bermingham; Janet Dean; Michael Fabricant; Lindsay Hoyle; Julie Kirkbride; John Marek; Gerry Steinberg; Ms Sarah Davies (Clerk); Mrs Helen Agnew (Secretary); Mrs Karen Georgiou (Secretary)

FINANCE AND SERVICES

Committee Office, House of Commons, London SW1A 0AA
Telephone: 020 7219 3299

Members: (11) Lewis Moonie (Chairman); Richard Allan; Keith Bradley; Sydney Chapman; Eric Clarke; Thomas McAvoy; Patrick McLoughlin; Marion Roe; Dennis Turner; Paul Tyler; David Watts; Dr Malcolm Jack (Clerk); Mrs Karen Georgiou (Secretary); Mrs Helen Agnew (Secretary)

INFORMATION

Committee Office, House of Commons, London SW1A 0AA
Telephone: 020 7219 2471

Members: (9) Richard Allan (Chairman); Ian Bruce; Tim Collins; Michael Connarty; Neil Gerrard; Andrew Miller; Sandra Osborne; Philip Sawford; Ian Stewart; Mr Mike Clark (Clerk); Miss Jo-Ann Crowder (Secretary)

Internal Committees

CHAIRMEN'S PANEL

Public Bill Office, House of Commons, London SW1A 0AA
Telephone: 020 7219 3257

Members: (26) Alan Haselhurst (Chairman of Ways and Means); Michael Martin (First Deputy Chairman of Ways and Means); Michael Lord (Second Deputy Chairman of Ways and Means); Irene Adams; Joe Benton; John Butterfill; Michael Clark; Frank Cook; Jim Cunningham; Gwyneth Dunwoody; Roger Gale; Jimmy Hood; Barry Jones; John McWilliam; David Madel; Humfrey Malins; John Maxton; Ray Michie; Bill O'Brien; Edward O'Hara; Bill Olner; Marion Roe; George Stevenson; Bowen Wells; Andrew Welsh; Nicholas Winterton; Helen Irwin (Clerk)

COURT OF REFEREES

Public Bill Office, House of Commons, London SW1A 0AA
Telephone: 020 7219 3257

Members: (10) Alan Haselhurst (Chairman of Ways and Means); Michael Martin (First Deputy Chairman of Ways and Means); Michael Lord (Second Deputy Chairman of Ways and Means); Peter Atkinson; John Butterfill; William Etherington; Archy Kirkwood; Alan Meale; Ernest Ross; Dennis Turner; Helen Irwin (Clerk)

STANDING ORDERS

Ways & Means Office, House of Commons, London SW1A 0AA
Telephone: 020 7219 3771

Members: (11) Alan Haselhurst (Chairman of Ways and Means); Michael Martin (First Deputy Chairman of Ways and Means); Michael Lord (Second Deputy Chairman of Ways and Means); Clive Efford; Llin Golding; Brian Jenkins; Helen Jones; William O'Brien; Ernest Ross; Andrew Stunell; Nicholas Winterton; Mr Mike Hennessy (Clerk)

UNOPPOSED BILLS (PANEL)

Ways & Means Office, House of Commons, London SW1A 0AA
Telephone: 020 7219 3771

Members: (20) Alan Haselhurst (Chairman of Ways and Means); Michael Martin (First Deputy Chairman of Ways and Means); John Austin; Nigel Beard; Peter Bottomley; Helen Brinton; John Butterfill; Philip Hammond; Brian Jenkins; Helen Jones; Andrew Mackinlay; David Marshall; John McDonnell; Sydney Rapson; Nicholas St Aubyn; Andrew Stunell; Jon Trickett; Robert Walter; Ann Winterton; Audrey Wise; Mr Mike Hennessy (Clerk)

Principal Officers and Officials

The Speaker, The Rt Hon Betty Boothroyd, MP
Chairman of Ways and Means, The Rt Hon Sir Alan Haselhurst, MP
First Deputy Chairman, Michael Martin, MP
Second Deputy Chairman, Michael Lord, MP

OFFICES OF THE SPEAKER AND THE CHAIRMAN OF WAYS AND MEANS

Speaker's Secretary, N Bevan, CB
Speaker's Assistant Secretary, N P Wright
Trainbearer, P L Warwick
Diary Secretary, Mrs S Norvell
Office Manager, R P Edwards
Invitations Secretary, Mrs E Griffith-Okai
Secretary to N Bevan, Mrs H Parkhouse
Speaker's Chaplain, Rev Canon Robert Wright
Secretary to the Chairman of Ways and Means, M Hennessy
Parliamentary Commissioner for Standards, Ms Elizabeth Filkin
020 7219 0320 Fax: 020 7219 0490 E-mail: filkine@parliament.uk

DEPARTMENT OF THE CLERK OF THE HOUSE

Clerk of the House of Commons, W R McKay, CB
Clerk Assistant, G Cubie
Clerk of Committees, C B Winnifrith, CB
Clerk of Legislation, R B Sands
Principal Clerks, A J Hastings, CB *(Journals)*, R J Willoughby *(Registrar of Members' Interests, seconded to Speaker's Office)*, D G Millar *(Table Office)*, M R Jack, PhD *(Domestic Committees)*, R W G Wilson *(Overseas Office)*, W A Proctor *(Delegated Legislation)*, Ms H E Irwin *(Bills)*, Mrs J Sharpe *(Select Committees)*, F A Cranmer *(Select Committees)*, R J Rogers *(Select Committees)*
Deputy Principal Clerks, Ms A Barry, C R M Ward, PhD, D W N Doig, A Sandall, D L Natzler, E P Silk, L C Laurence Smyth, S J Patrick, A R Kennon, D J Gerhold, C J Poyser, D F Harrison, S J Priestley, A H Doherty, P A Evans, R I S Phillips, R G James, PhD, Ms P A Helme, D R Lloyd, B M Hutton, J S Benger, DPhil, Ms E C Samson, N P Walker, M D Hamlyn, Mrs E Flood, P C Seaward, DPhil, A Y A Azad
Senior Clerks, C G Lee, C D Stanton, C A Shaw, Ms L M Gardner, K J Brown, OBE, F J Reid, M Hennessy, G R Devine, P G Moon, M Clark, Mrs J N St J Mulley, T W P Healey, Mrs S A Davies, J D Whatley, K C Fox, J D W Rhys, Mrs S Craig, Miss E S Payne, Ms S McGlashan, Mrs C J Oxborough, Ms E J Eldred (acting), S T Fiander (acting), D H Griffiths (acting), Ms R Melling, CBE (acting), C Wilson (acting)
Assistant Clerks, H A Yardley, M P Atkins, M Egan, Ms J Hughes, Ms T H L Brufal, S Mark, P A Shelley, Ms C A Littleboy, R C A Cooke
Inward Visits Manager, Ms R J Challis
Senior Executive Officers, S D Barrett, Miss S J Fox (Vacancy)
Personnel and Establishments Officer, Mrs S D Pamphlett
Higher Executive Officers, L L Kaye, A P Hubner, Mrs P Fisher, F McShane, Miss F L Allingham, Mrs L M Nugent, M P Oxborough, Ms C M Genis, A Catinella, Ms A Fuki, Mrs D B Nelson, Mrs N Mulloy, J H Davies, Ms E C G Partridge, Miss J Appleton, P A Derrett, Miss K McClelland, Ms T Herd, R Dawson
Office Manager, S A Haher
Departmental Training and Support Officer, Ms S P Chubb
Committee Specialists, E C Lally, Ms S E O'Leary, Ms K R Smith, R Rees, K C Lee, Dr D Taylor, J R Lepper, Ms J Gleig, G Rickett, Ms J Allbeson, W Benson, D Thornton, K Alagbala, T Jarrett, E Lewis, R Kelly, Mrs E Downing
Editorial Supervisor of the Vote, B Tidball
Deputy, Miss L Lewis

Assistant Editorial Supervisers of the Vote, J Puricelli, K B Wood, P D Howlett, Mrs L R Shade, P A Jack, P Sullivan, D Mahoney, Mrs B Ward

Secretaries, Mrs G E C Sclater, MBE (Clerk of the House), Mrs D Gent, Miss A T Power, Mrs K J Georgiou, Ms L Young, Mrs H Agnew, Miss J Woodger, Miss K McClelland, Mrs B Hunter, Ms A M Allen, Ms S Marshall, Mrs K Watling, Miss J Allen, Miss M Owens, Mrs S Bertasius, Miss C Wilson (temp)

Examiners of Petitions for Private Bills, Ms H E Irwin, Dr F P Tudor

Taxing Officer, Ms H E Irwin

Superviser of Parliamentary Broadcasting, Ms B E Long, OBE

Director of Parliamentary Office of Science and Technology, Prof D Cope

Deputy Office Manager, R A Broomfield

Chief Office Clerks, J A Hole, I Blair, B Dye, Miss P Wainwright, R J Bartram, I Thomson, Ms J Recardo, Miss S Monaghan, Ms N Welfoot

Senior Office Clerks, S M Cruickshank, Miss R C Mead, D J Hackett, Miss A Ferreira, Miss K Phelan, Ms J Hunter, Miss D Fisher, Miss S Gorman, P J Lyon, A Mahoney

SPEAKER'S COUNSEL
Speaker's Counsel, J S Mason, CB
Speaker's Counsel (European Legislation), J E G Vaux
Speaker's Assistant Counsel, A Akbar, J R Mallinson

VOTE OFFICE
Deliverer, J F Collins
Deputy Deliverers, (Vacant) *(Distribution),* F W Hallett *(Production),* O B T Sweeney *(Parliamentary)*
Assistant Deliverer, C D Lister
IT Manager, G C Peek
Print Project Manager, Ms J Pitt
Bookshop Manager, Ms S Gowland
Higher Executive Officers, B G Underwood, Ms K M Barker
Computer Support Officer, R A Mulley
Superintending Clerks, Mrs S Fuzio, A J Ashton
Vote Office Assistants, G E Howard, C P Williams, P Hannet, J Harrington, M D Cook, J E Lawford, Mrs V Makhecha, P Smith, T J Green, Miss K Brown, Miss B Wilson
Assistant Computer Support Officers, T Dancey, R King
Senior Office Clerks, E J Weldin, I H Bright, J E Carroll, R Cao, N G Battley, Miss J Flint, Miss F Mohamed, A Mitchell, J Loades-Carter, Miss M Crainey
Docutech Operators, M D Loveday, S Campbell, M Stevens

OTHER PRINCIPAL OFFICERS
Clerk of the Crown in Chancery, Sir Hayden Phillips, KCB
Comptroller and Auditor General, Sir John Bourn, KCB
Parliamentary Commissioner for Administration, M S Buckley
Parliamentary Commissioner for Standards, Miss Elizabeth Filkin

DEPARTMENT OF THE SERJEANT AT ARMS
Serjeant at Arms, M J A Cummins
Deputy Serjeant at Arms, R M Morton
Assistant Serjeants at Arms, P A J Wright, J M Robertson, M C D Harvey

SECRETARIAT
Finance Manager, Ms S J Peterson
Finance and Purchasing Co-ordinator, C R Harris, BEM
Information Systems Manager, Ms J M M Carthew
Database Administrator, M F Goodman
IT Support Manager, J Taylor

Fire Safety Manager, R Bentley, MIFireE
Accommodation Implementation Manager, Mrs J Pay (acting)
Serjeant's Personal Assistant, Miss C Every

Clerk in Charge and Accommodation Co-ordinator, Miss S J Scott Thomson
Secretaries, Miss J Cheshire, Miss J McMillan, Miss A Goddard
Admission Order Office, Mrs S J Warren, A Evans
Principal Doorkeeper, T D Dann
Deputy Principal Doorkeepers, P E Overfield, H M Talbot
Senior Doorkeepers, R G Sterne, G J Dear, MBE, I Davis
Head Office Keeper, B Mulvihill (acting)
Senior Office Keepers, L Stockwell, N Kirby, Miss D Irving (acting)
Personnel and Training Assistant, A Vallins
Pass Office Manager, M Coombs

PARLIAMENTARY WORKS DIRECTORATE
Director of Works, H P Webber, CEng, FICE
Deputy Director of Works, L Brantingham, CEng, MICE, FCIArb
Project Sponsor, A Makepeace
Deputy Director, Contracts and Procurement, I Carr
Head of Secretariat, M C Trott
Manager, Building Project Branch, J Stone, FRICS
Principal Engineer, C Hillier, JP CEng, FIMechE, MIEE
Works Manager, L Benjamin, BEng(Hons) CEng, MCIBSE
Furnishing Manager, G Goode
Head of Administration, M Moone
Quantity Surveyor, J F Moore, ARICS
Project Managers, C Brown, ARICS, C Cowell, RIBA, J Eaton, CEng, MCIBSE, T Fox, CEng,
    MCIBSE, S Howard, T Jardine, TD, RIBA, T Nott, ARCIS
Deputy Works Manager, M McCann, CEng, BEng, MInstE, ACIBSE

PARLIAMENTARY COMMUNICATIONS DIRECTORATE
Director of Communications, C G Gilbert
PDVN Planning Officer, (Vacant)
Performance Assurance Manager, C Myers
Operations Manager, Mrs M Burns
Network Team Leader, M Luckins
Office Manager, Miss M Morrison
Telecommunications Manager, Dr G Williams
Deputy Telecommunications Manager, M Pollard

GENERAL SERVICES
Shorthand Writer to the House, Mrs P J Woolgar
Head of Security, Supt Gregory Roylance
Deputy Head of Security, Supt C P Facey
Postmaster, L Ward
Transport Manager, J Jones

DEPARTMENT OF THE LIBRARY
Librarian, Miss J B Tanfield
Directors, Miss P J Baines, BLitt *(Human Resources and Deputy Librarian)* , K G Cuninghame
    (Library Resources), Mrs J M Wainwright, FIInfSc *(Informations Systems)*, R C Clements
    (Parliamentary and Reference Services) , Richard Ware, DPhil *(Research Services)*

Heads of Section, C C Pond, PhD, Mrs C B Andrews, Mrs J M Lourie, C R Barclay, Mrs J M
    Fiddick, Mrs C M Gillie, R J Twigger, Mrs G L Allen, R J Cracknell, Cstat

Senior Clerks, Ms F Poole, T N Edmonds, Miss O M Gay, Miss E M McInnes, Ms D J Gore, PhD,
Miss M Baber, Ms A Walker, Mrs H V Holden, Mrs P L Carling, Mrs K Greener, Miss P J
Strickland, Miss V A Miller, M P Hillyard, Ms J Roll, Ms W T Wilson, S A Wise, E H Wood, P
Bowers, PhD, A C Seely, Mrs J K Hough, G Danby, PhD, Dr P M Richards, PhD, B C Morgan,
Ms K S Wright, Miss L A Conway, C Blair, PhD, C M Sear, M Oakes (period), A Presland
(period), Miss F M Whittle (acting)

Assistant Clerks, Miss L Bardgett, Dr A M Sleator, T Jarvis, Miss A Thorpe, Dr S McGinness, P
Bolton, T P Youngs (period)

Senior Executive Officers, P Skerratt, Ms D Gallagher (acting)

Senior Library Executives, K N H Parry, Miss C E Fretten, ALA, Ms I White, ALA, J A Prince,
Mrs D W Clark, ALA, Mrs B Brevitt, Miss C M Owens

Education Officer, Mrs C Weeds

Deputy Education Officer, Miss N Harland

Assistant Education Officer, Mrs C C O'Connor

Higher Executive Officers, Mrs F M Ward, E L V MacGregor, Ms B A Rowlands, ALA, J P Brevitt,
A J Fuller, D A Brown, P R Mann, Ms L Magee, Mrs B Onyskiw, P Ryan, Miss A Gual

Higher Library Executives, Mrs G C Brown, Mrs P E Cook, MBE, ALA, Ms H Armstrong, Mrs E
H Riley, ALA, T C Holmes, Ms J B Hall, ALA, R Freebury, ALA, A D Parker, ALA, Miss G M
Rose, Mrs J Priestley, Miss C M R Chambers, Miss A Hatton, Miss K Fitch, Mrs J Keddie, G G
Newell, Mrs G Griffin, Ms J Davies (acting), Ms E Armstrong (acting), G Howard (acting)

Library Executives, Mrs J M Smith, Miss C M Blair, ALA, Miss S Pepin, Mrs K E Burcher, Ms G
S Tyler, F Codd, Miss E Vaughan, Ms F Green, J Woodhouse, Ms L McGuire, Miss C Piper,
Miss B Jamnezhad, M Davies, Mrs A J Rushbrook, Mrs P Turley, J Rowe (temp), Miss S Brown
(temp)

Executive Officers, Mrs A J H Mara, Miss S Holland, M Greenhill, Mrs H Onyskiw, A Clark, Ms M
Moulton, Miss N M Sutherland, Mrs P M Burnett, Miss S K Priddy, Miss A H Penman, Ms S
Hayward, N Jolly, A T Adcock, J Wiltshire, Miss G Hughes, Miss C Bruce, Mrs H Weltman,
Miss A O'Rourke, Miss C Jenkins, S Howe, Miss J E Laker, Mrs C Randall, I Hook, Miss A
Bennell, N Johnston, D Lawson

Senior Office Clerks, Miss T Thomas, S Hammett, S Paston, Miss J Crawley, M Stewart, Miss E
Marah, J Garber, P M Alford, M Eagleton, M Michell, Ms R Maman, Ms J Page, Miss L Clay, E
Murphy, Ms J Ahrens, Miss L Campbell, Ms S Price, Miss S Haigh, N Walker, D Tewsley, Ms R
Winstone, Miss G Wallace, Miss J Watkins, Ms R Roche, Mrs V Fletcher, E Tetteh, T Godfrey,
Miss J Kitcher, T Robinson, P Carter, M O'Gorran, T Powell, Miss G Rou, A Lindsay, Miss J
Wilson (temp)

Office Assistants, Miss S A L Boyd-Moss, Ms B Woods, Miss J Baker, Mrs V Soanes, Miss L
Cogan, Miss K Barber

Office Clerk, R Borowski (temp)

Personal Secretaries Grade 2, Miss L M Palmer, Miss S Holt, Mrs J Page, Mrs L Mirams, Mrs
A Monk, Miss J M Laney

Personal Secretaries Grade 3, Mrs D Sullivan, Mrs L Reed, Mrs M E Walsh, Mrs L Baxter, Mrs J
Gouge, Mrs E Hasell, Miss A Vince, Mrs K Rose, Mrs S Jennings, Mrs H Mummery, Mrs J Cook

Senior Library Assistants, J O'Hagan, D Usher, S Haver, D Wright, J Brunger

Assistants, K Sargeant, B Blacksey, T Wheeler, J Coster, K Murray, C Richardson, R Ashburn

Head Library Cleaner, Mrs C Daley

Library Cleaners, Mrs S Wipperman, Mrs N Hannam, Mrs B Johnson

DEPARTMENT OF FINANCE AND ADMINISTRATION

Director of Finance and Administration, Andrew Walker
Director's Office:
Director's Assistant (DEO), Michael Page
Executive Personal Assistant, Angela Gladwin
Departmental Finance Officer, Nicky Price
Resources Manager, Stephen Furber
Resources Officer, Brian Palmer
Senior General Assistant, Elizabeth Mitchell

General Assistants, David Hankard, Nick Kenyon, Andrew Gibson
Head of Special Resource Team, Peter Barratt
Special Resource Team, Debbie McGuire, Janet Peach, Karen Baptiste, Louise Glennon
Training and Development/Communications Co-ordinator, Jane O'Mahoney

FEES OFFICE
Director of Operations and Head of the Fees Office, Archie Cameron
Personal Assistant, Paul Olden
Assistant Director of Operations, Gill Crowther
Bookstall Salesperson, Freda Bates
Payroll Team: Staff Payroll Manager, Tom White
Payroll Officers, David Yoxall, Kym Cook
Payroll Assistants, Roland Masterton, Gareth Bellinger, Carole Stanbury
Members and Members' Staff: Payroll Manager, Georgie Jessiman
Payroll Officers, Bhavna Parekh, Caroline Stockton, Perry French
Payroll Assistants, Ronald Bates, Emma Kearney, Susan Silvester, Nikki Carmen, Antonia
  Garroway
Payments Team: Chief Payments Manager, Merielle Morris
Administration Payments Team: Accounts Processing Manager, Guy Turner
Accounts Officer, Elaine Lavery
Processing Assistant, Gavin Murphy
Processing Assistant, Michael Mullen
Payments Assistants, Tim Mullen, Tim Balogun, Rizwan Quraishi
OCA & ACA Payments Team: Payments Manager, David Allen
OCA Payments Officer, Dan Gorman
Payment Assistant, Alan Brooks
ACA Payments Officer, Liz Johnson
Payments Assistants, James Hudson, Michelle Cummins
Secretarial Pensions Officer, Julia Nellis
Secretarial Pensions Assistants, Deirdre Euesden, Priya Ghadia
MPs' Travel Payments: Travel Payments Manager, Andy Martin
Rail and Air Warrants and Car Claims: Payments Officer, Paula Mills
Payments Assistants, Ann Williams, James Yankah-Ashun
Miscellaneous Payments and Extended Travel: Payments Office, Alan Rowlands
Payments Assistants, Jo Lush, Hannah van Schijndel, Michael De Tisi

PERSONNEL OFFICE
Head of Personnel, Neil Crawley
Senior Personnel Officer (SAA/Lib/RD), Jane Grieveson
Personnel Officers, Jason Travis, Sandra Deakins
Assistant Personnel Officers, Lucy Hallam, Heather Mann
Personnel Assistant, Pamela Lancaster
Senior Personnel Officer (Speakers' Office/Clerk/F&A/OR), Tara West
Personnel Officers, Maxine Seale, Denise Eltringham
Assistant Personnel Officers, Julie Diamond, Jenny Price
Senior Office Clerk, Charmaine McGusty

PENSIONS OFFICE
Pensions Office Manager, Lucy Watson
Senior Pensions Officers, Francene Graham, Dermot Woods
Database Administrator, Ryan Grenz (temp)
Pensions Officers, Jason Howard, Lyn Phillips

PERSONNEL POLICY DIRECTORATE (PPD): STAFF RESOURCE
Director, Brian Wilson, CBE
Personal Assistants, Tanya Harris, Michelle Garratty
Assistant Director (Members' Allowances and Pensions), Mike Fletcher
Personnel Policy and Planning Team: Assistant Director (Human Resources Policy), Heather Wood
Pay and Communications, Jane Leverton, Clare Jackson, Nigel Sequeira
Assistant Director (Occupational Health, Safety and Welfare Unit), Janice Tofts
Office Manager, Vanessa Traynor
Occupational Health Manager, Maggie Mainland
Welfare Officers, Anne Mossop, Anne Kidd
Health and Safety Adviser, Steve Wicks
Nursing Sister, Karen St Cyr
Editor, Staff News, Deryc Sands
Trade Union Side: Administrator, Josephine Newell
Occupational Health Physician, Dr Ira Madan

FINANCE POLICY DIRECTORATE (FPD): STAFF RESOURCE
Director of Finance, Michael Barram
Personal Assistant, Diane Ward
Finance Policy Team: Assistant Director (Management Accounts), Peter Lamb
Management Accountant, Kym Bigwood
Assistant Management Accountant, Patrick Dawson
Management Accounts Officers: Trudy Myers, Jenny Swann
Assistant Director (Resource Accounts), Norma Norman
Resource Accountant, Graham McAllister
Financial Accountant, Simon Little
Systems Administration Manager, Sarah Doyle
Fixed Assets Officer, David Johnson
MDIS Database Officer, Irene Brydon
Accounts Manager, Sarah Dearson
Control Officer, Teresa Ruewell
Bureau Services Officer, David Laryea
Procurement Adviser, Sue Cunningham
Information System Services: Assistant Director (ISS), Innis Montgomery
ISS Customer Services: IS Support Manager, Viv Browne
Webmaster, Robert Galbraith
Technical Support Officers, David Hodgson, John Gribbon
Help Desk Officer, Alex Lee
Assistant Support Officer, Laura Leeming
IT Technical Support Services: Operations Manager, Steve Judd
Project and Technical Support Officer, Paul Kane

DEPARTMENT OF THE OFFICIAL REPORT

Editor, I D Church
Deputy Editor (Personnel, Finance and Administration), Miss L Sutherland
Deputy Editor (House), W G Garland
Deputy Editor (Committees), Ms C Fogarty
Principal Assistant Editors, Miss H Hales, Miss V A Widgery, Ms K Stewart, P Hadlow, Ms J Dall,
    Miss C Hanly, M Watson, Mrs A M Browne (temp), Ms D A Jones (temp)
Assistant Editors, Miss V Grainger, S M Hutchinson
Committee Sub-Editors, D Crosswell, Mrs H Natzler, Mrs A P Street, Mrs E J Gregory, Miss K
    Myers, Ms J Warrington, Ms J Symons, Mrs J Davies, A Newton, Miss J Goodman, Miss J Levy,
    Ms V Wilson, Ms M Wright, J Prawer (temp), Miss V Hart (temp)
Reporters, Miss E M Morris, K Gall, F A Minichiello, Miss B Robins, Miss P Hill, M Lowes,
    Ms M Weinberg, S Nicholls, W Humphreys-Jones, P Kirby, Miss E Brazier, D Weir, R Wildman,
    Ms E Harrison, Miss L H Linchis (temp), R Gunby (temp)

Senior Transcribers, Miss J Beck, Miss F Stevenson, Miss P P A Simpson, Ms L Sinclair (temp)
Hansard Transcribers, Mrs A M Jerman, Mrs I Stringer, M Newman, P K Underhill, Miss B Jones,
   D W Hampton, J Vice, Miss K Trickey, Miss C M L Spencer, Ms A Dodd, Ms K Moss, Ms
   J Newell, B Tottle, R Hallas, Miss J Thompson, Ms S Michell, J Hoare, J Homer, B Geall, Ms F
   Reardon, Ms P Dadley, Ms J Wheway, J Staal, G Wigmore
Training Manager, P R Hadlow
Health and Safety Manager, Mrs M F Garland
Head of IT, R A Hill
IT Managers, Miss J L Brown, R Daniels, C J Bumstead, A Vyas
Junior Programming Analyst, P Oakley
Word Processing Assistants, Ms W Agnew, Ms D Cairns
Written Answers Supervisor, K Candy
Written Answers Operators, Ms S Dryden, Ms R Hanif, Mrs P A McGandy, Miss D Royle, Mrs G
   A Leslie, Mrs M T Valente, Miss L Rostron, Miss S Alexander
Principal Hansard Administrator, Miss R Washington
Senior Hansard Administrators, J Brake, S C O'Riordan, B Harrison
Hansard Administrators, B J Hudson, Miss C Hudson, A Jenner, M Woolfenden
Hansard Administrative Assistants, P Younger, Miss S Seal, Miss J Hoare
Personal Secretaries, Mrs B Donne *(Editor)*, Mrs C Rowlands *(Deputy Editor)*
Annunciator Superintendent, W A Holland
Annunciator Assistant Superintendent, A Wilkinson
Annunciator Operator, J R Griffin

REFRESHMENT DEPARTMENT

Director of Catering Services, Mrs Sue Harrison, MHCIMA
Personal Assistant to Director, Ms Belinda Woodiwiss
Executive Chef, David Dorricott
Head Chef, Laurence Colmer
Kitchen Co-ordinator, Miss Imogen Clist
Catering Manager (Terrace), Miss Suzanne Hovells, MHCIMA
Catering Manager (Bellamy's), Miss Della Herd, MHCIMA
Catering Manager (Millbank), Michael Simons
Food and Beverage Manager (acting), Matthew Johnson
Banqueting Co-ordinator, Miss Diane Elderfield
Assistant Banqueting Manager, Mrs Christina Gotthard
Financial Controller, Mrs Janet Rissen
Assistant Financial Controller, Miss Jackie Stone
Systems Manager, Jevern Partridge, MHCIMA
Purchasing Manager, Mrs Sara McKinnon-Snell, MHCIMA
Food and Beverage Controller, Stephen Fothergill
Cashier, Mrs Carol Prestidge
Personnel Manager, Andrew Wallace, MIPD
Personnel Officer, Mrs Jennie Horchover, Grad IPD

Parliamentary Commissioner for Standards

House of Commons, London SW1A 0AA
020 7219 0320   Fax 020 7219 0490
E-mail: filkine@parliament.uk
Parliamentary Commissioner for Standards, Ms Elizabeth Filkin
The Commissioner has responsibility for the operation of the Register of Members' Interests; advising
Members of Parliament and the Select Committee on Standards and Privileges on questions of
propriety; and receiving, and if she thinks fit, investigating complaints about the conduct of Members.

Office of the Commissioner for Public Appointments

Room 62/2 Horse Guards Road, London SW1P 3AL
020 7270 6472   Fax 020 7270 1981
E-mail: ocpa@gtnet.gov.uk
Website: www.open.gov.uk/ocpa
Commissioner, Dame Rennie Fritchie, DBE
The Commissioner for Public Appointments is independent of government. Her role is to monitor, regulate and provide advice on ministerial appointments to the boards of executive and advisory non-departmental public bodies, NHS bodies, public corporations and nationalised industries. In addition, the three regulatory posts for gas, electricity, water and telecommunications also fall within her remit. She has the right to investigate complaints.

Parliamentary Office of Science and Technology

7 Millbank, London SW1P 3JA
020 7219 2848   Fax 020 7219 2849
E-mail: coped@parliament.uk
Website: www.parliament.uk/post/home.htm
Chairman, Dr Ian Gibson, MP
Vice-Chairman, Lord Flowers
Director, Prof David Cope
POST Board Members, (Lords) Baroness Nicol, Lord Flowers, Prof The Lord Winston, *(Commons)* Mr Richard Allan, MP, Dr Michael Clark, MP, Mrs Anne Campbell, MP, Mr Michael Connarty, MP, Mr Paul Flynn, MP, Dr Ashok Kumar, MP, Dr Phyllis Starkey, MP, Ms Caroline Spelman, MP, Mr Ian Taylor, MP
POST is an independent office within Parliament, and is administratively part of the House of Commons. It is an office run by its Board and analyses issues of interest to Parliament on matters of science and technology and also provides assistance to Select Committees in both Houses.

Parliamentary Press Gallery

DESK NUMBERS: 020 7219

Press Gallery Chairman	Michael Brunson 3387
Vice-Chairman	Jon Craig 4751
Hon. Secretary	John Deans 6140/6561
Hon. Treasurer	Rodney Foster 7973-6160
Gallery Secretary	Stella Thomas 4395
Gallery Superintendents	5371
Lobby Journalists' Chairman	Colin Brown 2037
Lobby Journalists' Vice Chairman	John Hipwood 3381
Press Bar	4284
Press Dining Room	6406/4393/4240

The Parliamentary Lobby Journalists are those journalists authorised to work in Parliament by the inclusion of their names on a list kept by the Serjeant at Arms for the Speaker. There are about 120 British and Irish journalists on this List who are allowed access to the Members' Lobby of the House of Commons. A further 50 or so foreign correspondents are also on this Lobby List and have access to the Lobby.

*Members of the Lobby

DAILY NEWSPAPERS

The Daily Telegraph
*George Jones 5719
*Robert Shrimsley 3687
*Jon Hibbs 3688
Virginia Utley 3685 (admin)
*Andrew Sparrow 3689
*Polly Newton 6890
*Rachel Sylvester
Marie Woolf

The Financial Times
*Robert Peston 4380
*Andrew Parker 3680
*David Wighton 6892
*Rosemary Bennett 6142
*Cathy Newman

The Independent
*Andy Grice 4665
*Don Macintyre 5285
*Colin Brown 2037
*Fran Abrams 4392
Sarah Schaefer 4392
Tom Sutcliffe
*Paul Waugh 4392

The Guardian
*Michael White 6143
*David Hencke 6769
Simon Hoggart 6738
*Ewen McAskill 3681
Hugo Young 0026
*Lucy Ward 6831
Jonathan Freedland 0026
*Nick Watt 6831

The Times
*Peter Riddell 4751
Matthew Parris 5284
Jill Sherman 6543
*Phil Webster 5241
*James Landale 5284
*Roland Watson 5284
*Tom Baldwin 6543
*Melisa Kite

The Express
*Anthony Bevins 3389
*Alison Little 3387/3389
*Sarah Womack 6743/6149
*Patrick O'Flynn 6764
Alice Miles

Daily Mail
*David Hughes 3679
*John Deans 6140
*Paul Eastham 3683
*Gaby Hinsliff 0616
Gill Watmough (admin) 6894
*Graeme Wilson 6561

The Mirror
*Peter MacMahon 4379
*Nigel Morris 6733
*James Hardy 4377
*Oona Blackman 4379
Paul Routledge 4377

The Daily Star
*Henry Macrory 6743

The Sun
*Trevor Kavanagh 6144
*George Pascoe-Watson 3337
*Bill Coles 0141
*Paul Gilfeather 4683
Chris Davis 7782-4087

Morning Star
*Mike Ambrose 4681

SUNDAY NEWSPAPERS

The Sunday Times
*Michael Jones 5397
*Michael Prescott 5397
*Eben Black

The Sunday Telegraph
*Joe Murphy 0615
Matthew D'Ancona
*David Cracknell 6116

The Observer
*Patrick Wintour 3380
*Andrew Rawnsley 7713-4286
*Andy McSmith 6687

The Express on Sunday
*Jon Craig 5596
*Mark Fox 5596
*Peter Oborne 5596
Richard Whitely 6149
Jonathan Oliver

Sunday Mirror
*Chris Buckland 6733
*Chris MacLaughlan

The Independent on Sunday
*Jon Carr-Brown 6580
Alan Watkins 5285
*Jo Dillon

The Mail on Sunday
*Simon Walters
*Vince Moss 4386

The People
*Nigel Nelson 4377

News of the World
*Ian Kirby 6768

Scotland on Sunday
*Francis Elliott 6763

Sunday Mercury
*Peter Hooley 4700

Sunday Post

Sunday Business
*Steve Bevan
*Sebastian Hamilton 3673

Newcastle Sunday Sun
*Ian Hernon 5396

Wales on Sunday
*Julia Langdon

Birmingham Sunday Mercury
*Richard Williamson

Sunday Herald
*Iain Watson

OTHERS

Evening Standard
*Charles Reiss 5718
*Patrick Hennessy 0052
*David Shaw 4680
*Ben Leapman 4281
*Peter Kelliner

The Scotsman
*Joy Copley 4370
*Severin Carrell 6740
*Jenny Percival 4682

Glasgow Herald
*Ben Brogan 6722
Jim McKillop 7405-2121
Roy Rogers 7405-2121
*Catherine McLeod 6147
*Mike Settle 0156

Glasgow Evening Times
*Ian Hernon 5396

Aberdeen Press and Journal
*David Perry 4390

Dundee Courier
*Gordon Campbell, OBE 3338
*Steve Bargeton 01382-23131

Daily Record
3336
*Dave King
*David Thompson

Aberdeen Evening Express
Middlesbrough Evening Gazette
*Bill Doult 4388

Edinburgh Evening News
Bolton Evening News
Lancashire Evening Telegraph
4391
*Bill Jacobs
Ian Swanson

Cambridgeshire Evening News
Worcester Evening News
Yorkshire Evening News
3385
*Nick Cecil

Stoke Evening Sentinel
Plymouth Evening News
Torquay Herald Express
Gloucestershire Echo
Gloucestershire Citizen
*Bob Podmore 3682

Nottingham Post
Leicester Mercury
Lincolnshire Echo
*Kristiina Cooper 0875

Hull Daily Mail
Grimsby Telegraph
South Wales Evening Post
Derby Evening Telegraph
Scunthorpe Telegraph
Kirsty Buchanon 4691

Derby Telegraph
*Bob Podmore 3682

Manchester Evening News
*Ian Craig 6672
*Ian Wylie 6672

Birmingham Post
*Chris Gray 3765
John Lewis 4700

East Anglian Daily Times
*Graham Dines 4700

Coventry Evening Telegraph
*Paul Dale 4700

Portsmouth and Sunderland News
*Brian Brady 6539

Eastern Daily Press
*Chris Fisher 3384
*Ian Collins 3384/3339

Liverpool Daily Post
*David Rose 3383

Journal, The Newcastle
*Paul Linford 4389

Yorkshire Post
*Sarah Neville 3674/222 1137

Northern Echo
*Brendan Carlin

Western Daily Press
*Matthew George 3673

Western Morning News
*Andrew Porter

Western Mail
South Wales News
*Mike Speed 4382
Leslie Able

Birmingham Mail
*Shaun Connolly 4277

Bristol Evening Post
Oldham Chronicle
Carlisle News and Star
North West Evening Mail
Rob Merrick 5287

Liverpool Echo
*Keith Gladdis 6723

Shropshire Express
*

Southern Daily Echo
South Wales Argus
Bournemouth Daily Echo
Dorset Evening Echo
*Greg Hurst 3386

Wolverhampton Express & Star
Shropshire Star
*John Hipwood 3381
*Scott Watson 3381

Yorkshire Evening Post
Sheffield Star
Lancashire Evening Post
*Hugh Lawrence 6766

Belfast Telegraph
*Des McCartan 6725

South Wales Echo
*6146

Irish Independent
*Bernard Purcell 4700

Irish Press
*Aiden Hennigan 4700

Irish Times
*Frank Millar 4700

Belfast Newsletter
*Mervyn Pauley 4700
*Donna Carton

MAGAZINES

Spectator
*Bruce Anderson 3689

New Statesman/Society
*Steve Richards 6564

Tribune
*Hugh Macpherson 4700

The Economist
*Peter Barnes 7830-7047
*Peter David

Punch
Jerry Hayes

Marketing News
David Oakley 4700

The House Magazine
Daisy Sampson 7233-1388

AFX News
*Frank Prenesti 4700

Bridge News
*Christopherson Davison
*David Robinson 0618
Stephen Ball

Dow-Jones
*Lucy Farmdon 4700

Gallery News
*Robert Gibson 2908

AGENCIES

Reuters
*5389
*Michael Peacock 5380
*John Morrison 5380
Edna Fernandez

Bloomberg News
*David Healy 2035
Andrew Atkinson

Central Press
*Matthew George 3385
*Nick Cecil 3385

Press Association (PA News)
Trevor Mason 4299/4288
*Martin Hickman
*Jon Smith
Chris Mead 4299/4282
Roger Smith 4299/4282
*Chris Moncrieff 4299
*Gavin Cordon
Jackie Storer 4282
*Michael Clarke 4282
David Roberts
Benjamin Davies
Martin Evans
*Bob Roberts
Dominic Hayes
*Amanda Brown
Chris Hamilton

Robinson's Parliamentary News Agency
*Mike Peters 4283
*Julian Robinson 4283
*Reg Robinson 4283

Newspoint Agency
4279
4279
*Simon Page 6148
*Mike Steele 4278
*Malcolm MacMillan 4279
*David Bearfield 4279

BROADCASTING

Independent Radio News
7799-2360
*Desmond Fahy
*Peter Murphy
*Peter Russell
*Kevin Murphy

IRN Scotland
*Gordon Campbell 3338

Israel Radio
*Jerry Lewis 0452

London Weekend TV (LWT)
4700
Dollan Cannell
Charles Harrison
*David Mapstone

Channel One TV
Stephen Punter 4700

HTV – Wales
*Max Perkins 4278

HTV – West
Bob Constantine 3673
*Jo Kiernan

London News Radio
*Max Cotton 4700

Tyne Tees TV
*Gerry Foley 6739

RTE – Irish Broadcasting
*Brian O'Connell 4700

Ulster TV
*Ken Reid 5381

Welsh Fourth Channel
*Vaughan Roderick 4700
*Beth Kilfoil 4700

Yorkshire TV
*Geoff Druett 6720
Richard Whiteley 6720

West Country TV
*John Ray 7976-0831
*Deborah Geraghty
Angus Walker

Scottish TV
Bernard Ponsonby 6724
*Fiona Ross 6724
*Michael Crow 6724

Granada TV
*Mark Lyons 6891
*Benedict Fitzgerald 6891
Rob McLoughlin

London News Network
*Clare Rewcastle 4700

Southern Radio
*Brian Shallcross 6729

Meridian
*Richard Brock
*Alan Clark 6729

Grampian TV
*Michael Crow 6148

Central TV
*Peter Hayes 3765
*Simon Mares 4681
Simon Garrett
Vivienne Read

Anglia TV
*Graham Donaldson 4700
*Sean Walsh 6671

Border TV
*Simon Page 6148

Sky TV
*Richard Bestic 7976-7120
*Adam Boulton 7976-7120
*Judith Dawson 7976-7120
*Peter Spencer 7976-7120
*Paul Bromley 7976-7120

GM-TV
*Sara Holden 3678
*Sue Jameson
Rae Stewart

Carlton TV
*Paul Larsmon 4700
*Joanne Scard 4700

Channel 5 News
*Andrew Bell 4700
*Vincent Dowd

BBC
National Correspondents
020 7973 6057/6044/6010
*Robin Oakley (Political Editor – 7973 6010)
*John Sergeant (Chief Political
Correspondent – 7973 6010)
Reeta Chakrabarti
Guto Harri
Laura Trevelyan
*Max Cotton (News 24)
*Mark Mardell (7973 6072)
Polly Billington   *Carolyn Quinn
*Nick Jones   *Charlotte
Udwin
*John Kampfner   *Carole Walker
*John Pienaar
*Paul Rowley
    (Political
    Correspondent)

Regional Correspondents
020 7973 6170
*Robin Chrystal (North West)
John Turnbull (North)
Zahid Warley (West Midlands)
Nick Thatcher (East Midlands)
Steve Kingston (East Anglia)
Shaun Ley (South East)
*Bruce Parker
*Paul Cannon
Mark Sanders (South)
Tim Finch (South West)
Viv Robbins (West)
Jane Dodge (Northern Ireland)

*Luke Waltone
Other BBC Correspondents
David Cornock (Wales) 7973 6240
Mike Fairbairn (Parliamentary) 7973 6058
Tim Franks (World) 7973 6249
David Porter (Scotland) 7973 6245

ITN
3334/4387
*Michael Brunson
*Graham Forrester
Stephen Mawhinney
Anne Lingley
*Harry Smith
*Lauren Taylor
*Jo Andrews

Channel 4
3334/4387
*Elinor Goodman
*Gary Gibbon
*Jonathan Hawker 7430-4932
Malcolm Boughen 7430 4935
Chris Banatvala 7430-4935
7430 4909
Andrew Brown
Oliver King
Celia Ellacott
Adam Vandermark

Parliamentary Agents

Parliamentary Agents provide general information on Parliament to both individuals and firms, fully reporting on progress of Bills. There are two types of Agent, those registered to propose and oppose bills on behalf of their clients and those who only oppose Bills.

The Register of authorised Parliamentary Agents is kept in the Private Bills Office of the House of Commons. Generally associated with the legal profession, Agents carry out their duties under the rules, originally laid down by the Speaker in 1837, of both the Houses of Parliament.

One or more of the Partners of the firms listed below are authorised to practise as Parliamentary Agents.

DYSON BELL MARTIN
1 Dean Farrar Street, Westminster
London SW1H 0DY
020 7222 9458
Fax: 020 7222 0650
E-mail: dysonbell@bircham.co.uk
Partners: I H McCulloch, P H Thompson,
    E N W Brown, R J V Owen, D N Mundy

LEWIN GREGORY & CO
1 The Sanctuary, Westminster
London SW1P 3JT
020 7222 5381
Fax: 020 7222 4646
E-mail: enquiries@1thesanctuary.com
Partners: J Durkin, P Cronin, P Lane,
    M Peto, G Fountain, P Sergeant

REES & FRERES
1 The Sanctuary, Westminster
London SW1P 3JT
020 7222 5381
Fax: 020 7222 4646
E-mail: enquiries@1thesanctuary.com
Partners: J Durkin, P Cronin, P Lane,
    M Peto, G Fountain, P Sergeant,
    J Taplin, K Wallace, P Robinson,
    A Davies, P Beesley, Z Reisman,
    M Fletcher, N Richens

SHARPE PRITCHARD
Elizabeth House, Fulwood Place
London WC1V 6HG
020 7222 3551
Fax: 020 7222 1451
E-mail: parliamentary@sharpepritchard.co.uk
Partners: H M V Pritchard, W A Lewis

VIZARD OLDHAM
42 Bedford Row
London WC1R 4JL
020 7663 2222
Fax: 020 7663 2226
E-mail: ron.perry@vizold.co.uk
Partner: R E Perry

WINCKWORTH SHERWOOD
35 Great Peter Street, Westminster
London SW1P 3LR
DX 2312 Victoria
020 7593 5000
Fax: 020 7593 5199
E-mail: cmvine@winckworths.co.uk
Parliamentary Agents (Partners): Mrs A M H
Gorlov, C M Vine, P M C F Irving, H S Wiggs

GENERAL ELECTION 1997

POLLING RESULTS

Parties with seats in the House of Commons:
Lab – Labour
Lab/Co-op – Labour Co-operative
Con – Conservative
Lib Dem – Liberal Democrat
Pl C – Plaid Cymru
SNP – Scottish National Party

UUP – Ulster Unionist Party
DUP – Democratic Unionist Party
SDLP – Social Democratic and Labour Party
SF – Sinn Fein
UKU – United Kingdom Unionist

21st Cent – 21st Century Independent Foresters; *Albion* – Albion Party; *Alliance* Alliance; *ANP* – All Night Party; *Alt LD* – Alternative Liberal Democrat; *Embryo* – Anti Abortion Euthanasia Embryo Experiments; *ACA* – Anti Child Abuse; *ACA* – Anti-Corruption Candidate; *AS* – Anti-sleaze; *AS Lab* – Anti-sleaze Labour; *B Ind* – Beaconsfield Ind: Unity Through Electoral Reform; *Bert* – Berties Party; *BHMBCM* – Black Haired Medium Build Caucasian Male; *BDP* – British Democratic Party; *BFAIR* – British Freedom And Individual Rights; *Home Rule* – British Home Rule; *BIPF* – British Isles People First Party; *BNP* – British National Party; *Fair* – Building A Fair Society; *Care* – Care in the Community; *Rights* – Charter For Basic Rights; *Ch D* – Christian Democrat; *Ch Nat* – Christian Nationalist; *Ch P* – Christian Party; *Ch U* – Christian Unity; *CSSPP* – Common Sense Sick of Politicians Party; *Comm Lge* – Communist League; *Comm Brit* – Communist Party of Britain; *CRP* – Community Representative Party; *CASC* – Conservatives Against The Single Currency; *Cvty* – Conservatory; *Constit* – Constitutionalist; *CFSS* – Country Field and Shooting Sports; *Dem* – Democratic Party; *D Nat* – Democratic Nationalist; *EDP* – English Democratic Party; *Ind Hum* – English Independent Humanist Party; *EUP* – European Unity Party; *FDP* – Fancy Dress Party; *Fellowship* – Fellowship Party For Peace and Justice; *Dynamic* – First Dynamic Party; *NIFT* – Former Captain NI Football Team; *FP* – Freedom Party; *FEP* – Full Employment Party; *Glow* – Glow Bowling Party; *Green* – Green; *Green Ref* – Green Party for Euro Referendum; *GRLNSP* – Green Referendum Lawless Naturally Street Party; *Stan* – Happiness Stan's Freedom To Party; *Party Heart* – Heart 106.2 Alien Party; *Hemp* – Hemp Coalition; *HR* – Human Rights '97; *Hum* – Humanist Party; *Ind* – Independent; *Ind AFE* – Independent Against a Federal Europe; *IAC* – Independent Anti Corruption in Government/TGWU; *Anti-maJ Independent* – Anti-majority Democracy; *Ind BB* – Independent Back To Basics; *Ind C* – Independent Conservative; *Ind CRP* – Independent Conservative Referendum Party; *Consult* – Independent Democracy Means Consulting The People; *Ind Dem* – Independent Democrat; *Ind ECR* – Independent English Conservative and Referendum; *Ind F* – Independent Forester; *Ind Green* – Independent Green: Your Children's Future; *Ind Lab* – Independent Labour; *Ind No* – Independent No To Europe; *Ind OAP* – Independent OAP; *Ind Dean* – Independent Royal Forest of Dean; *Barts* – Independent Save Barts Candidate; *Beaut* – Independently Beautiful Party; *IZB* – Islam Zinda Baad Platform; *Ind Isl* – Island Independent; *Juice* – Juice Party; *JP* – Justice Party; *Ind JRP* – Justice and Renewal Independent Party; *KBF* – Keep Britain Free and Independent Party; *Lab Change* – Labour Time For Change Candidate; *LCP* – Legalise Cannabis Party; *Lib* – Liberal; *Loc C* – Local Conservative; *LGR* – Local Government Reform; *Loc Ind* – Local Independent; *Logic* – Logic Party Truth Only Allowed; *Byro* – Lord Byro versus The Scallywag Tories; *LC* – Loyal Conservative; *Mal* – Mal Voice of the People Party; *Meb Ker* – Mebyon Kernow; *Miss M* – Miss Moneypenny's Glamorous One Party; *Loony* – Monster Raving Loony Party; *MRAC* – Multi-racial Anti-Corruption Alliance; *Musician* – Musician; *Nat Dem* – National Democrat; *NF* – National Front; *NLP* – Natural Law Party; *N Lab* – New Labour; *New Way* – New Millenium New Way Hemp Candidate; *Bypass* – Newbury Bypass Stop Construction Now; *NPC* – Non-party Conservative; *None* – None Of The Above Parties; *NIP* – Northern Ireland Party; *NI Women* – Northern Ireland Women's Coalition; *O Lab* – Old Labour; *Pacifist* – Pacifist for Peace, Justice, Co-operation, Environment; *PEC* – Pro European Conservative Party; *PF* – Pathfinders; *Slough* – People in Slough Shunning Useless Politicians; *Choice* – People's Choice; *PLP* – People's Labour Party; *PP* – People's Party; *Plymouth* – Plymouth First Group; *Shields* – Pro Interests of South Shields People; *ProLife* – ProLife Alliance; *PUP* – Progressive Unionist Party; *PAYR* – Protecting All Your Rights Locally Effectively; *R Alt* – Radical Alternative; *Rain Isl* – Rainbow Connection Your Island Candidate; *Dream* – Rainbow Dream Ticket Party; *Rain Ref* – Rainbow Referendum; *R Lab* – Real Labour Party; *Ref* – Referendum Party; *Ren Dem* – Renaissance Democrat; *Rep GB* – Republican Party of Great Britain; *RA* – Residents Association; *Rizz* – Rizz Party; *Ronnie* – Ronnie The Rhino Party; *Route 66* – Route 66 Party Posse Party; *SCU* – Scottish Conservative Unofficial;

SLI – Scottish Labour Independent; *SLU* – Scottish Labour Unofficial; *SSA* – Scottish Socialist Alliance; *Scrapit* – Scrapit Stop Avon Ring Road Now; *SIP* – Sheffield Independent Party; *Soc Dem* – Social Democrat; *Socialist* – Socialist; *SEP* – Socialist Equality Party; *Soc Lab* – Socialist Labour Party; *Soc* – Socialist Party; *Beanus* – Space Age Superhero from Plant Beanus; *Spts All* – Sportsman's Alliance: Anything but Mellor; *SFDC* – Stratford First Democratic Conservative; *SG* – Sub-genius Party; *Teddy* – Teddy Bear Alliance Party; *FP* – The Fourth Party; *Mongolian* – The Mongolian Barbeque Great Place to Party; *NLPC* – The New Labour Party Candidate; *PPP* – The People's Party Party; *Speaker* – The Speaker; *Third* – Third Way; *Top* – Top Choice Liberal Democrat; *UKIP* – UK Independence Party; *UKPP* – UK Pensioners Party; *UKU* – United Kingdom Unionist; *UA* – Universal Alliance; *Value* – Value Party; *Wessex Reg* – Wessex Regionalist; *WCCC* – West Cheshire College in Crisis Party; *Whig* – Whig Party; *WP* Workers' Party; *WRP* – Workers Revolutionary Party.

ABERAVON

		%
*Morris, J. (Lab)	25,650	71.3
McConville, R. (LD)	4,079	11.3
Harper, P. (Con)	2,835	7.9
Cockwell, P. (PC)	2,088	5.8
David, P. (Ref)	970	2.7
Beany, C. (Beanus)	341	0.9
Lab majority 21,571		59.98%
Electorate 50,025		
Total Vote 35,963	Poll 71.9%	

*Member of last parliament
Lab Hold (2.7% Swing from LD to Lab)

ABERDEEN CENTRAL

		%
Doran, F. (Lab)	17,745	49.8
Wisely, J. (Con)	6,944	19.5
Topping, B. (SNP)	5,767	16.2
Brown, J. (LD)	4,714	13.2
Farquharson, J. (Ref)	446	1.3
Lab majority 10,801		30.33%
Electorate 54,257		
Total Vote 35,616	Poll 65.6%	

Lab Gain (8% Swing from Con to Lab)

ABERDEEN NORTH

		%
Savidge, M. (Lab)	18,389	47.9
Adam, B. (SNP)	8,379	21.8
Gifford, J. (Con)	5,763	15.0
Rumbles, M. (LD)	5,421	14.1
McKenzie, A. (Ref)	463	1.2
Lab majority 10,010		26.06%
Electorate 54,302		
Total Vote 38,415	Poll 70.7%	

Lab Hold (6.7% Swing from SNP to Lab)

ABERDEEN SOUTH

		%
Begg, A. (Lab)	15,541	35.3
Stephen, N. (LD)	12,176	27.6
*Robertson, R. (Con)	11,621	26.4
Towers, J. (SNP)	4,299	9.8
Wharton, R. (Ref)	425	1.0
Lab majority 3,365		7.64%
Electorate 60,490		
Total Vote 44,062	Poll 72.8%	

*Member of last parliament
Lab Gain (11.2% Swing from Con to Lab)

AIRDRIE AND SHOTTS

		%
*Liddell, H. (Lab)	25,460	61.8
Robertson, K. (SNP)	10,048	24.4
Brook, N. (Con)	3,660	8.9
Wolseley, R. (LD)	1,719	4.2
Semple, C. (Ref)	294	0.7
Lab majority 15,412		37.43%
Electorate 57,673		
Total Vote 41,181	Poll 71.4%	

*Member of last parliament
Lab Hold (3.5% Swing from Lab to SNP)

ALDERSHOT

		%
Howarth, G. (Con)	23,119	42.7
Collett, A. (LD)	16,498	30.5
Bridgeman, T. (Lab)	13,057	24.1
Howe, J. (UKIP)	794	1.5
Pendragon, A. (Ind)	361	0.7
Stevens, D. (BNP)	322	0.6
Con majority 6,621		12.23%
Electorate 76,189		
Total Vote 54,151	Poll 71.1%	

Con Hold (9.7% Swing from Con to LD)

ALDRIDGE-BROWNHILLS

		%
*Shepherd, R. (Con)	21,856	47.1
Toth, J. (Lab)	19,330	41.7
Downie, C. (LD)	5,184	11.2
Con majority 2,526		5.45%
Electorate 62,441		
Total Vote 46,370	Poll 74.3%	

*Member of last parliament
Con Hold (7.8% Swing from Con to Lab)

ALTRINCHAM AND SALE WEST

		%
Brady, G. (Con)	22,348	43.2
Baugh, J. (Lab)	20,843	40.3
Ramsbottom, M. (LD)	6,535	12.6
Landes, A. (Ref)	1,348	2.6
Stephens, J. (Pro-Life)	313	0.6
Mrozinski, R. (UKIP)	270	0.5
Renwick, J. (NLP)	125	0.2
Con majority 1,505		2.91%
Electorate 70,625		
Total Vote 51,782	Poll 73.3%	

Con Hold (12.6% Swing from Con to Lab)

ALYN AND DEESIDE

		%
*Jones, B. (Lab)	25,955	61.9
Roberts, T. (Con)	9,552	22.8
Burnham, E. (LD)	4,076	9.7
Jones, M. (Ref)	1,627	3.9
Hills, S. (PC)	738	1.8
Lab majority 16,403		39.11%
Electorate 58,091		
Total Vote 41,948	Poll 72.2%	

*Member of last parliament
Lab Hold (12.5% Swing from Con to Lab)

AMBER VALLEY

		%
Mallaber, J. (Lab)	29,943	54.7
*Oppenheim, P. (Con)	18,330	33.5
Shelley, R. (LD)	4,219	7.7
McGibbon, I. (Ref)	2,283	4.2
Lab majority 11,613		21.20%
Electorate 72,005		
Total Vote 54,775	Poll 76%	

*Member of last parliament
Lab Gain (11.7% Swing from Con to Lab)

ANGUS

		%
*Welsh, A. (SNP)	20,792	48.3
Leslie, S. (Con)	10,603	24.6
Taylor, C. (Lab)	6,733	15.6
Speirs, R. (LD)	4,065	9.4
Taylor, B. (Ref)	883	2.0
SNP majority 10,189		23.65%
Electorate 59,708		
Total Vote 43,076	Poll 72.1%	

*Member of last parliament
SNP Hold (11.3% Swing from Con to SNP)

ARGYLL AND BUTE

		%
*Michie, R. (LD)	14,359	40.2
MacCormick, N. (SNP)	8,278	23.2
Leishman, R. (Con)	6,774	19.0
Syed, A. (Lab)	5,596	15.7
Stewart, M. (Ref)	713	2.0
LD majority 6,081		17.02%
Electorate 49,451		
Total Vote 35,720	Poll 72%	

*Member of last parliament
LD Hold (3% Swing from SNP to LD)

ARUNDEL AND SOUTH DOWNS

		%
Flight, H. (Con)	27,251	53.1
Goss, J. (LD)	13,216	25.7
Black, R. (Lab)	9,376	18.3
Herbert, J. (UKIP)	1,494	2.9
Con majority 14,035		27.34%
Electorate 67,641		
Total Vote 51,337		Poll 75.9%

Con Hold (5.2% Swing from Con to LD)

ASHFIELD

		%
*Hoon, G. (Lab)	32,979	65.2
Simmonds, M. (Con)	10,251	20.3
Smith, W. (LD)	4,882	9.6
Betts, M. (Ref)	1,896	3.7
Belshaw, S. (BNP)	595	1.2
Lab majority 22,728		44.91%
Electorate 72,269		
Total Vote 50,603		Poll 70%

Member of last parliament
Lab Hold (11.3% Swing from Con to Lab)

ASHFORD

		%
Green, D. (Con)	22,899	41.4
Ennals, J. (Lab)	17,544	31.7
Williams, J. (LD)	10,901	19.7
Cruden, C. (Ref)	3,201	5.8
Boden, R. (Green)	660	1.2
Tyrell, S. (NLP)	89	0.2
Con majority 5,355		9.66%
Electorate 74,149		
Total Vote 55,294		Poll 74.6%

Con Hold (12.5% Swing from Con to Lab)

ASHTON UNDER LYNE

		%
*Sheldon, R. (Lab)	31,919	67.5
Mayson, R. (Con)	8,954	18.9
Pickstone, T. (LD)	4,603	9.7
Clapham, L. (Ref)	1,346	2.8
Cymbal, P. (Loony)	458	1.0
Lab majority 22,965		48.57%
Electorate 72,206		
Total Vote 47,280		Poll 65.4%

Member of last parliament
Lab Hold (10.2% Swing from Con to Lab)

AYLESBURY

		%
*Lidington, D. (Con)	25,426	44.2
Bowles, S. (LD)	17,007	29.5
Langridge, R. (Lab)	12,759	22.2
John, M. (Ref)	2,196	3.8
Sheaff, L. (NLP)	166	0.3
Con majority 8,419		14.63%
Electorate 79,047		
Total Vote 57,554		Poll 72.8%

Member of last parliament
Con Hold (7.5% Swing from Con to LD)

AYR

		%
Osborne, S. (Lab)	21,679	48.4
*Gallie, P. (Con)	15,136	33.8
Blackford, I. (SNP)	5,625	12.6
Hamblen, C. (LD)	2,116	4.7
Enos, J. (Ref)	200	0.4
Lab majority 6,543		14.62%
Electorate 55,829		
Total Vote 44,756		Poll 80.2%

Member of last parliament
Lab Gain (5.2% Swing from Con to Lab)

BANBURY

		%
*Baldry, T. (Con)	25,076	42.9
Peperell, H. (Lab)	20,339	34.8
Bearder, C. (LD)	9,761	16.7
Ager, J. (Ref)	2,245	3.8
Cotton, B. (Green)	530	0.9
King, L. (UKIP)	364	0.6
Pearson, I. (NLP)	131	0.2
Con majority 4,737		8.10%
Electorate 77,456		
Total Vote 58,446		Poll 75.1%

Member of last parliament
Con Hold (9.9% Swing from Con to Lab)

BANFF AND BUCHAN

		%
*Salmond, A. (SNP)	22,409	55.8
Bell-Frain, W. (Con)	9,564	23.8
Harris, M. (Lab)	4,747	11.8
Fletcher, N. (LD)	2,398	6.0
Buchan, A. (Ref)	1,060	2.6
SNP majority 12,845		31.97%
Electorate 58,493		
Total Vote 40,178		Poll 68.7%

Member of last parliament
SNP Hold (7.9% Swing from Con to SNP)

BARKING

		%
*Hodge, M. (Lab)	21,698	65.8
Langford, K. (Con)	5,802	17.6
Marsh, M. (LD)	3,128	9.5
Taylor, C. (Ref)	1,283	3.9
Tolman, M. (BNP)	894	2.7
Mearns, D. (Pro-Life)	159	0.5
Lab majority 15,896		48.22%
Electorate 53,682		
Total Vote 32,964		Poll 61.4%

Member of last parliament
Lab Hold (14.9% Swing from Con to Lab)

BARNSLEY CENTRAL

		%
*Illsley, E. (Lab)	28,090	77.0
Gutteridge, S. (Con)	3,589	9.8
Finlay, D. (LD)	3,481	9.5
Walsh, J. (Ref)	1,325	3.6
Lab majority 24,501		67.15%
Electorate 61,133		
Total Vote 36,485		Poll 59.7%

Member of last parliament
Lab Hold (7.5% Swing from Con to Lab)

BARNSLEY EAST AND MEXBOROUGH

		%
*Ennis, J. (Lab)	31,699	73.1
Ellison, J. (Con)	4,936	11.4
Willis, D. (LD)	4,489	10.4
Capstick, K. (SLP)	1,213	2.8
Miles, A. (Ref)	797	1.8
Hyland, J. (SEP)	201	0.5
Lab majority 26,763		61.76%
Electorate 67,840		
Total Vote 43,335		Poll 63.9%

Member of last parliament
Lab Hold (3.1% Swing from Con to Lab)

BARNSLEY WEST AND PENISTONE

		%
*Clapham, M. (Lab)	25,017	59.3
Watkins, P. (Con)	7,750	18.4
Knight, W. (LD)	7,613	18.0
Miles, J. (Ref)	1,828	4.3
Lab majority 17,267		40.91%
Electorate 64,894		
Total Vote 42,208		Poll 65%

Member of last parliament
Lab Hold (5.3% Swing from Con to Lab)

BARROW AND FURNESS

		%
*Hutton, J. (Lab)	27,630	57.3
Hunt, R. (Con)	13,133	27.2
Metcalfe, A. (LD)	4,264	8.8
Hamezeian, A. (PLP)	1,995	4.1
Mitchell, D. (Ref)	1,208	2.5
Lab majority 14,497		30.06%
Electorate 66,960		
Total Vote 48,230		Poll 72%

Member of last parliament
Lab Hold (11.8% Swing from Con to Lab)

BASILDON

		%
Smith, A. (Lab/Co-op)	29,646	55.8
Baron, J. (Con)	16,366	30.8
Granshaw, L. (LD)	4,608	8.7
Robinson, C. (Ref)	2,462	4.6
Lab/Co-op majority 13,280		25.02%
Electorate 73,989		
Total Vote 53,082		Poll 71.6%

Lab/Co-op Gain (14.7% Swing from Con to Lab)

BASINGSTOKE

		%
*Hunter, A. (Con)	24,751	43.3
Lickley, N. (Lab)	22,354	39.1
Rimmer, M. (LD)	9,714	17.0
Selim, E. (Ind)	310	0.5
Con majority 2,397		4.20%
Electorate 77,035		
Total Vote 57,129		Poll 73.8%

Member of last parliament
Con Hold (12.1% Swing from Con to Lab)

BASSETLAW

		%
*Ashton, J. (Lab)	29,298	61.0
Cleasby, M. (Con)	11,838	24.8
Kerrigan, M. (LD)	4,950	10.3
Graham, R. (Ref)	1,838	3.9
Lab majority 17,460		36.43%
Electorate 68,101		
Total Vote 47,924		Poll 70.5%

Member of last parliament
Lab Hold (8.9% Swing from Con to Lab)

BATH

		%
*Foster, D. (LD)	26,169	48.5
McNair, A. (Con)	16,850	31.2
Bush, T. (Lab)	8,828	16.4
Cook, A. (Ref)	1,192	2.2
Scrase, R. (Green)	580	1.1
Sandell, P. (UKIP)	315	0.6
Pullen, N. (NLP)	55	0.1
LD majority 9,319		17.26%
Electorate 70,815		
Total Vote 53,989		Poll 75.5%

Member of last parliament
LD Hold (6.9% Swing from Con to LD)

BATLEY AND SPEN

		%
Wood, M. (Lab)	23,213	49.4
*Peacock, E. (Con)	17,072	36.4
Pinnock, K. (LD)	4,133	8.8
Wood, E. (Ref)	1,691	3.6
Smith, R. (BNP)	472	1.0
Lord, C. (Green)	384	0.8
Lab majority	6,141	13.08%
Electorate	64,209	
Total Vote	46,965	Poll 73.1%

*Member of last parliament
Lab Gain (7.4% Swing from Con to Lab)

BATTERSEA

		%
Linton, M. (Lab)	24,047	50.7
*Bowis, J. (Con)	18,687	39.4
Keaveney, P. (LD)	3,482	7.3
Slater, M. (Ref)	804	1.7
Banks, A. (UKIP)	250	0.5
Marshall, J. (Dream)	127	0.3
Lab majority	5,360	11.31%
Electorate	66,928	
Total Vote	47,397	Poll 69%

*Member of last parliament
Lab Gain (10.2% Swing from Con to Lab)

BEACONSFIELD

		%
Grieve, D. (Con)	24,709	49.2
Mapp, P. (LD)	10,722	21.4
Hudson, A. (Lab)	10,063	20.0
Lloyd, H. (Ref)	2,197	4.4
Story, C. (IndCon)	1,434	2.9
Cooke, C. (UKIP)	451	0.9
Duval, G. (Pro-Life)	286	0.6
Dyball, T. (NLP)	193	0.4
Matthews, R. (Ind)	146	0.3
Con majority	13,987	27.86%
Electorate	68,959	
Total Vote	50,201	Poll 70.8%

Con Hold (8.2% Swing from Con to LD)

BECKENHAM

		%
*Merchant, P. (Con)	23,084	42.5
Hughes, R. (Lab)	18,131	33.4
Vetterlein, R. (LD)	9,858	18.1
Mead, L. (Ref)	1,663	3.1
Rimmer, P. (Lib)	720	1.3
Pratt, C. (UKIP)	506	0.9
McAuley, J. (NF)	388	0.7
Con majority	4,953	9.11%
Electorate	72,807	
Total Vote	54,350	Poll 74%

*Member of last parliament
Con Hold (15% Swing from Con to Lab)

BEDFORD

		%
Hall, P. (Lab)	24,774	50.6
Blackman, R. (Con)	16,474	33.7
Noyce, C. (LD)	6,044	12.3
Conquest, P. (Ref)	1,503	3.1
Saunders, N. (NLP)	149	0.3
Lab majority	8,300	16.96%
Electorate	66,560	
Total Vote	48,944	Poll 73.5%

Lab Gain (13% Swing from Con to Lab)

BELFAST EAST

		%
*Robinson, P. (DUP)	16,640	42.6
Empey, R. (UUP)	9,886	25.3
Hendron, J. (APNI)	9,288	23.8
Dines, S. (Con)	928	2.4
Corr, D. (SF)	810	2.1
Lewsley, P. (SDLP)	629	1.6
Dougan, D. (Ind)	541	1.4
Bell, J. (Workers)	237	0.6
Collins, D. (NLP)	70	0.2
DUP majority	6,754	17.31%
Electorate	61,744	
Total Vote	39,029	Poll 63.2%

*Member of last parliament
DUP Hold (0% Swing from to)

BELFAST NORTH

		%
*Walker, C. (UUP)	21,478	51.8
Maginness, A. (SDLP)	8,454	20.4
Kelly, G. (SF)	8,375	20.2
Campbell, T. (APNI)	2,221	5.4
Emerson, P. (Green)	539	1.3
Treanor, P. (Workers)	297	0.7
Gribben, A. (NLP)	88	0.2
UUP majority	13,024	31.42%
Electorate	64,577	
Total Vote	41,452	Poll 64.2%

*Member of last parliament
UUP Hold (1.2% Swing from UUP to SDLP)

BELFAST SOUTH

		%
*Smyth, M. (UUP)	14,201	36.0
McDonald, A. (SDLP)	9,601	24.3
Ervine, D. (PUP)	5,687	14.4
McBride, S. (APNI)	5,112	12.9
Hayes, S. (SF)	2,019	5.1
Campbell, A. (Women)	1,204	3.0
Boal, M. (Con)	962	2.4
Cusack, N. (Lab)	292	0.7
Lynn, P. (Workers)	286	0.7
Anderson, J. (NLP)	120	0.3
UUP majority	4,600	11.65%
Electorate	63,439	
Total Vote	39,484	Poll 62.2%

*Member of last parliament
UUP Hold (13.4% Swing from UUP to SDLP)

BELFAST WEST

		%
Adams, G. (SF)	25,662	55.9
*Hendron, J. (SDLP)	17,753	38.7
Parkinson, F. (UUP)	1,556	3.4
Lowry, J. (Workers)	721	1.6
Kennedy, L. (HR)	102	0.2
Daly, M. (NLP)	91	0.2
SF majority	7,909	17.24%
Electorate	61,785	
Total Vote	45,885	Poll 74.3%

*Member of last parliament
SF Gain (9.7% Swing from SDLP to SF)

BERWICK-UPON-TWEED

		%
*Beith, A. (LD)	19,007	45.5
Brannen, P. (Lab)	10,965	26.2
Herbert, N. (Con)	10,056	24.1
Lambton, N. (Ref)	1,423	3.4

Dodds, I. (UKIP)	352	0.8
LD majority	8,042	19.24%
Electorate	56,428	
Total Vote	41,803	Poll 74%

*Member of last parliament
LD Hold (1.1% Swing from LD to Lab)

BETHNAL GREEN AND BOW %

King, O. (Lab)	20,697	46.3
Choudhury, K. (Con)	9,412	21.1
Islam, S. (LD)	5,361	12.0
King, D. (BNP)	3,350	7.5
Milsom, T. (Lib)	2,963	6.6
Osman, S. (Real Labour)	1,117	2.5
Petter, S. (Green)	812	1.8
Abdullah, M. (Ref)	557	1.2
Hamid, A. (SLP)	413	0.9
Lab majority	11,285	25.26%
Electorate	73,008	
Total Vote	44,682	Poll 61.2%

Lab Hold (5.9% Swing from Lab to Con)

BEVERLEY AND HOLDERNESS

		%
*Cran, J. (Con)	21,629	41.2
O'Neill, N. (Lab)	20,418	38.9
Melling, J. (LD)	9,689	18.4
Barley, D. (UKIP)	695	1.3
Withers, S. (NLP)	111	0.2
Con majority	1,211	2.30%
Electorate	71,916	
Total Vote	52,542	Poll 72.9%

*Member of last parliament
Con Hold (16.1% Swing from Con to Lab)

BEXHILL AND BATTLE %

*Wardle, C. (Con)	23,570	48.1
Field, K. (LD)	12,470	25.5
Beckwith, R. (Lab)	8,866	18.1
Thompson, V. (Ref)	3,302	6.7
Pankhurst, J. (UKIP)	786	1.6
Con majority	11,100	22.66%
Electorate	65,584	
Total Vote	48,994	Poll 74.3%

*Member of last parliament
Con Hold (4.4% Swing from Con to LD)

BEXLEYHEATH AND CRAYFORD

		%
Beard, N. (Lab)	21,942	45.5
*Evennett, D. (Con)	18,527	38.4
Montford, F. (LD)	5,391	11.2
Thomas, B. (Ref)	1,551	3.2
Smith, P. (BNP)	429	0.9
Jenner, W. (UKIP)	383	0.8
Lab majority	3,415	7.08%
Electorate	63,334	
Total Vote	48,223	Poll 76.1%

*Member of last parliament
Lab Gain (15% Swing from Con to Lab)

BILLERICAY

		%
*Gorman, T. (Con)	22,033	39.8
Richards, L. (Lab)	20,677	37.3
Williams, G. (LD)	8,763	15.8
Hughes, B. (LoyalCon)	3,377	6.1

Buchanan, J.
(Pro-Life) 570 1.0

Con majority	1,356	2.45%
Electorate	76,550	
Total Vote	55,420	Poll 72.1%

*Member of last parliament
Con Hold (17.6% Swing from Con to Lab)

BIRKENHEAD %

*Field, F. (Lab)	27,825	70.8
Crosby, A. (Con)	5,982	15.2
Wood, R. (LD)	3,548	9.0
Cullen, M. (SLP)	1,168	3.0
Evans, R. (Ref)	800	2.0
Lab majority	21,843	55.56%
Electorate	59,782	
Total Vote	39,323	Poll 65.8%

*Member of last parliament
Lab Hold (8.5% Swing from Con to Lab)

BIRMINGHAM EDGBASTON %

Stuart, G. (Lab)	23,554	48.6
Marshall, A. (Con)	18,712	38.6
Gallagher, J. (LD)	4,691	9.7
Oakton, J. (Ref)	1,065	2.2
Campbell, D. (BDP)	443	0.9
Lab majority	4,842	9.99%
Electorate	70,204	
Total Vote	48,465	Poll 69%

Lab Gain (10% Swing from Con to Lab)

BIRMINGHAM ERDINGTON %

*Corbett, R. (Lab)	23,764	58.8
Tomkins, A. (Con)	11,107	27.5
Garrett, I. (LD)	4,112	10.2
Cable, G. (Ref)	1,424	3.5
Lab majority	12,657	31.32%
Electorate	66,380	
Total Vote	40,407	Poll 60.9%

*Member of last parliament
Lab Hold (7.3% Swing from Con to Lab)

BIRMINGHAM HALL GREEN %

McCabe, S. (Lab)	22,372	53.5
*Hargreaves, A. (Con)	13,952	33.4
Dow, C. (LD)	4,034	9.6
Bennett, P. (Ref)	1,461	3.5
Lab majority	8,420	20.13%
Electorate	58,767	
Total Vote	41,819	Poll 71.2%

*Member of last parliament
Lab Gain (14% Swing from Con to Lab)

BIRMINGHAM HODGE HILL %

*Davis, T. (Lab)	22,398	65.6
Grant, E. (Con)	8,198	24.0
Thomas, H. (LD)	2,891	8.5
Johnson, P. (UKIP)	660	1.9
Lab majority	14,200	41.58%
Electorate	56,086	
Total Vote	34,147	Poll 60.9%

*Member of last parliament
Lab Hold (12.1% Swing from Con to Lab)

BIRMINGHAM LADYWOOD %

*Short, C. (Lab)	28,134	74.1
Vara, S. (Con)	5,052	13.3
Marwa, S. (LD)	3,020	8.0
Gurney, R. (Ref)	1,086	2.9
Carmichael, A. (Nat Dem)	685	1.8
Lab majority	23,082	60.78%
Electorate	70,813	
Total Vote	37,977	Poll 54.2%

*Member of last parliament
Lab Hold (4.9% Swing from Con to Lab)

BIRMINGHAM NORTHFIELD %

*Burden, R. (Lab)	22,316	57.4
Blumenthal, A. (Con)	10,873	28.0
Ashall, M. (LD)	4,078	10.5
Gent, D. (Ref)	1,243	3.2
Axon, K. (BNP)	337	0.9
Lab majority	11,443	29.46%
Electorate	56,842	
Total Vote	38,847	Poll 68.3%

*Member of last parliament
Lab Hold (13% Swing from Con to Lab)

BIRMINGHAM PERRY BARR %

*Rooker, J. (Lab)	28,921	63.0
Dunnett, A. (Con)	9,964	21.7
Hassall, R. (LD)	4,523	9.9
Mahmood, S. (Ref)	843	1.8
Baxter, W. (Lib)	718	1.6
Windridge, L. (BNP)	544	1.2
Panesar, A. (4th Party)	374	0.8
Lab majority	18,957	41.31%
Electorate	71,031	
Total Vote	45,887	Poll 64.6%

*Member of last parliament
Lab Hold (13.4% Swing from Con to Lab)

BIRMINGHAM SELLY OAK %

*Jones, L. (Lab)	28,121	55.6
Green, G. (Con)	14,033	27.8
Osborne, D. (LD)	6,121	12.1
Marshall, L. (Ref)	1,520	3.0
Gardner, G. (Pro-Life)	417	0.8
Sherriff-Knowles, P. (Loony)	253	0.5
Meads, H. (NLP)	85	0.2
Lab majority	14,088	27.87%
Electorate	72,049	
Total Vote	50,550	Poll 70.2%

*Member of last parliament
Lab Hold (12.1% Swing from Con to Lab)

BIRMINGHAM SPARKBROOK AND SMALL HEATH %

*Godsiff, R. (Lab)	26,841	64.3
Hardeman, K. (Con)	7,315	17.5
Harmer, R. (LD)	3,889	9.3
Clawley, A. (Green)	959	2.3
Dooley, R. (Ref)	737	1.8
Patel, P. (4th Party)	538	1.3
Syed, R. (Rights)	513	1.2

Bi, S. (Ind)	490	1.2
Wren, C. (SLP)	483	1.2
Lab majority	19,526	46.75%
Electorate	73,130	
Total Vote	41,765	Poll 57.1%

*Member of last parliament
Lab Hold (4.6% Swing from Con to Lab)

BIRMINGHAM YARDLEY %

*Morris, E. (Lab)	17,778	47.0
Hemming, J. (LD)	12,463	33.0
Jobson, A. (Con)	6,736	17.8
Livingston, D. (Ref)	646	1.7
Ware, A. (UKIP)	164	0.4
Lab majority	5,315	14.07%
Electorate	53,058	
Total Vote	37,787	Poll 71.2%

*Member of last parliament
Lab Hold (4.7% Swing from LD to Lab)

BISHOP AUCKLAND %

*Foster, D. (Lab)	30,359	65.9
Fergus, J. (Con)	9,295	20.2
Ashworth, L. (LD)	4,293	9.3
Blacker, D. (Ref)	2,104	4.6
Lab majority	21,064	45.74%
Electorate	66,754	
Total Vote	46,051	Poll 69%

*Member of last parliament
Lab Hold (15.5% Swing from Con to Lab)

BLABY %

*Robathan, A. (Con)	24,564	45.8
Willmott, R. (Lab)	18,090	33.8
Welsh, G. (LD)	8,001	14.9
Harrison, R. (Ref)	2,018	3.8
Peacock, J. (BNP)	523	1.0
Stokes, T. (Ind)	397	0.7
Con majority	6,474	12.08%
Electorate	70,471	
Total Vote	53,593	Poll 75.9%

*Member of last parliament
Con Hold (11.5% Swing from Con to Lab)

BLACKBURN %

*Straw, J. (Lab)	26,141	55.0
Sidhu, S. (Con)	11,690	24.6
Fenn, S. (LD)	4,990	10.5
Bradshaw, D. (Ref)	1,892	4.0
Wingfield, T. (Nat Dem)	671	1.4
Drummond, H. (SLP)	637	1.3
Field, R. (Green)	608	1.3
Carmichael-Grimshaw, M. (KBFIP)	506	1.1
Batchelor, W. (Common Sense)	362	0.8
Lab majority	14,451	30.43%
Electorate	73,058	
Total Vote	47,497	Poll 65%

*Member of last parliament
Lab Hold (9.7% Swing from Con to Lab)

BLACKPOOL NORTH AND
FLEETWOOD   %
Humble, J. (Lab)   28,051   52.2
*Elletson, H. (Con)   19,105   35.5
Hill, B. (LD)   4,600   8.6
Stacey, K. (Ref)   1,704   3.2
Ellis, J. (BNP)   288   0.5
Lab majority   8,946   16.64%
Electorate   74,989
Total Vote   53,748   Poll 71.6%
*Member of last parliament
Lab Gain (14.4% Swing from Con to Lab)

BLACKPOOL SOUTH   %
Marsden, G. (Lab)   29,282   57.0
Booth, R. (Con)   17,666   34.4
Holt, D. (LD)   4,392   8.6
Lab majority   11,616   22.63%
Electorate   75,720
Total Vote   51,340   Poll 67.7%
Lab Gain (11.6% Swing from Con to Lab)

BLAENAU GWENT   %
*Smith, L. (Lab)   31,493   79.5
Layton, G. (LD)   3,458   8.7
Williams, M.
   (Con)   2,607   6.6
Criddle, J. (PC)   2,072   5.2
Lab majority   28,035   70.74%
Electorate   54,800
Total Vote   39,630   Poll 72.3%
*Member of last parliament
Lab Hold (0.9% Swing from Lab to LD)

BLAYDON   %
*McWilliam, J.
   (Lab)   27,535   60.0
Maughan, P. (LD)   10,930   23.8
Watson, M. (Con)   6,048   13.2
Rook, R. (IndLab)   1,412   3.1
Lab majority   16,605   36.16%
Electorate   64,699
Total Vote   45,925   Poll 71%
*Member of last parliament
Lab Hold (2.1% Swing from LD to Lab)

BLYTH VALLEY   %
*Campbell, R. (Lab)   27,276   64.2
Lamb, A. (LD)   9,540   22.5
Musgrave, B. (Con)   5,666   13.3
Lab majority   17,736   41.75%
Electorate   61,761
Total Vote   42,482   Poll 68.7%
*Member of last parliament
Lab Hold (12.7% Swing from LD to Lab)

BOGNOR REGIS AND
LITTLEHAMPTON   %
Gibb, N. (Con)   20,537   44.2
Nash, R. (Lab)   13,216   28.5
Walsh, J. (LD)   11,153   24.0
Stride, G. (UKIP)   1,537   3.3
Con majority   7,321   15.76%
Electorate   66,480
Total Vote   46,443   Poll 69.6%
Con Hold (13.8% Swing from Con to Lab)

BOLSOVER   %
*Skinner, D. (Lab)   35,073   74.0
Harwood, R. (Con)   7,924   16.7
Cox, I. (LD)   4,417   9.3
Lab majority   27,149   57.26%
Electorate   66,476
Total Vote   47,414   Poll 71.3%
*Member of last parliament
Lab Hold (9% Swing from Con to Lab)

BOLTON NORTH EAST   %
Crausby, D. (Lab)   27,621   56.1
Wilson, R. (Con)   14,952   30.4
Critchley, E. (LD)   4,862   9.9
Staniforth, D. (Ref)   1,096   2.2
Kelly, W. (SLP)   676   1.4
Lab majority   12,669   25.75%
Electorate   67,930
Total Vote   49,207   Poll 72.4%
Lab Win (10.2% Swing from Con to Lab)

BOLTON SOUTH EAST   %
Iddon, B. (Lab)   29,856   68.9
Carter, P. (Con)   8,545   19.7
Harasiwka, F. (LD)   3,805   8.8
Pickering, W. (Ref)   973   2.2
Walch, L. (NLP)   170   0.4
Lab majority   21,311   49.16%
Electorate   66,459
Total Vote   43,349   Poll 65.2%
Lab Hold (11.8% Swing from Con to Lab)

BOLTON WEST   %
Kelly, R. (Lab)   24,342   49.5
*Sackville, T. (Con)   17,270   35.1
Ronson, B. (LD)   5,309   10.8
Kelly, D. (SLP)   1,374   2.8
Frankl-Slater, G. (Ref)   865   1.8
Lab majority   7,072   14.39%
Electorate   63,535
Total Vote   49,160   Poll 77.4%
*Member of last parliament
Lab Gain (11.3% Swing from Con to Lab)

BOOTLE   %
*Benton, J. (Lab)   31,668   82.9
Matthews, R. (Con)   3,247   8.5
Reid, K. (LD)   2,191   5.7
Elliot, J. (Ref)   571   1.5
Glover, P. (SLP)   420   1.1
Cohen, S. (NLP)   126   0.3
Lab majority   28,421   74.36%
Electorate   57,284
Total Vote   38,223   Poll 66.7%
*Member of last parliament
Lab Hold (6% Swing from Con to Lab)

BOSTON AND SKEGNESS   %
*Body, Sir R. (Con)   19,750   42.4
McCauley, P. (Lab)   19,103   41.0
Dodsworth, J. (LD)   7,721   16.6
Con majority   647   1.39%
Electorate   67,623
Total Vote   46,574   Poll 68.9%
*Member of last parliament
Con Hold (10.6% Swing from Con to Lab)

BOSWORTH   %
*Tredinnick, D.
   (Con)   21,189   40.6
Furlong, A. (Lab)   20,162   38.7
Ellis, J. (LD)   9,281   17.8
Halborg, S. (Ref)   1,521   2.9
Con majority   1,027   1.97%
Electorate   68,113
Total Vote   52,153   Poll 76.6%
*Member of last parliament
Con Hold (11.7% Swing from Con to Lab)

BOURNEMOUTH EAST   %
*Atkinson, D. (Con)   17,997   41.4
Eyre, D. (LD)   13,651   31.4
Stevens, J. (Lab)   9,181   21.1
Musgrave-Scott, A.
   (Ref)   1,808   4.2
Bennet, K. (UKIP)   791   1.8
Con majority   4,346   10.01%
Electorate   61,862
Total Vote   43,428   Poll 70.2%
*Member of last parliament
Con Hold (7.2% Swing from Con to LD)

BOURNEMOUTH WEST   %
*Butterfill, J. (Con)   17,115   41.7
Dover, J. (LD)   11,405   27.8
Gritt, D. (Lab)   10,093   24.6
Mills, R. (Ref)   1,910   4.7
Tooley, L. (UKIP)   281   0.7
Morse, J. (BNP)   165   0.4
Springham, A. (NLP)   103   0.3
Con majority   5,710   13.90%
Electorate   62,028
Total Vote   41,072   Poll 66.2%
*Member of last parliament
Con Hold (5.6% Swing from Con to LD)

BRACKNELL   %
*Mackay, A. (Con)   27,983   47.4
Snelgrove, A. (Lab)   17,596   29.8
Hilliar, A. (LD)   9,122   15.4
Tompkins, J.
   (New Labour)   1,909   3.2
Cairns, W. (Ref)   1,636   2.8
Boxall, L. (UKIP)   569   1.0
Roberts, D.
   (Pro-Life)   276   0.5
Con majority   10,387   17.58%
Electorate   79,292
Total Vote   59,091   Poll 74.5%
*Member of last parliament
Con Hold (11.3% Swing from Con to Lab)

BRADFORD NORTH   %
*Rooney, T. (Lab)   23,493   56.1
Skinner, R. (Con)   10,723   25.6
Browne, T. (LD)   6,083   14.5
Wheatley, H. (Ref)   1,227   2.9
Beckett, W.
   (Loony)   369   0.9
Lab majority   12,770   30.48%
Electorate   66,228
Total Vote   41,895   Poll 63.1%
*Member of last parliament
Lab Hold (7.4% Swing from Con to Lab)

BRADFORD SOUTH %
*Sutcliffe, G. (Lab)   25,558   56.7
Hawkesworth, A.
(Con)   12,622   28.0
Wilson-Fletcher, A.
(LD)   5,093   11.3
Kershaw, M. (Ref)   1,785   4.0
Lab majority 12,936   28.71%
Electorate   68,391
Total Vote   45,058 Poll 65.8%
*Member of last parliament
Lab Hold (9.7% Swing from Con to Lab)

BRADFORD WEST %
Singh, M. (Lab)   18,932   41.5
Riaz, M. (Con)   15,055   33.0
Wright, H. (LD)   6,737   14.8
Khan, A. (SLP)   1,551   3.4
Royston, C. (Ref)   1,348   3.0
Robinson, J. (Green)   861   1.9
Osborn, G. (BNP)   839   1.8
Shah, S. (Soc)   245   0.5
Lab majority 3,877   8.51%
Electorate   71,961
Total Vote   45,568 Poll 62.9%
Lab Hold (5.5% Swing from Lab to Con)

BRAINTREE %
Hurst, A. (Lab)   23,729   42.7
*Newton, T. (Con)   22,278   40.1
Ellis, T. (LD)   6,418   11.5
Westcott, N. (Ref)   2,165   3.9
Abbott, J. (Green)   712   1.3
Nolan, M. (New Way)   274   0.5
Lab majority 1,451   2.61%
Electorate   72,772
Total Vote   55,576 Poll 76.1%
*Member of last parliament
Lab Gain (12.9% Swing from Con to Lab)

BRECON AND RADNORSHIRE %
Livsey, R. (LD)   17,516   40.8
*Evans, J. (Con)   12,419   29.0
Mann, C. (Lab)   11,424   26.6
Phillips, L. (Ref)   900   2.1
Cornelius, S. (PC)   622   1.5
LD majority   5,097   11.89%
Electorate   52,142
Total Vote   42,881 Poll 82.2%
*Member of last parliament
LD Gain (6.1% Swing from Con to LD)

BRENT EAST %
*Livingstone, K. (Lab) 23,748 67.3
Francois, M. (Con)   7,866   22.3
Hunter, I. (LD)   2,751   7.8
Keable, S. (SLP)   466   1.3
Shanks, A. (Pro-Life)   218   0.6
Warrilow, C. (Dream)   120   0.3
Jenkin, D. (NLP)   103   0.3
Lab majority 15,882   45.03%
Electorate   53,548
Total Vote   35,272 Poll 65.9%
*Member of last parliament
Lab Hold (14.4% Swing from Con to Lab)

BRENT NORTH %
Gardiner, B. (Lab)   19,343   50.7
*Boyson, R. (Con)   15,324   40.1
Lorber, P. (LD)   3,104   8.1
Davids, T. (NLP)   204   0.5
Clark, G. (Dream)   199   0.5
Lab majority 4,019   10.53%
Electorate   54,149
Total Vote   38,174 Poll 70.5%
*Member of last parliament
Lab Gain (18.8% Swing from Con to Lab)

BRENT SOUTH %
*Boateng, P. (Lab)   25,180   73.0
Jackson, S. (Con)   5,489   15.9
Brazil, J. (LD)   2,670   7.7
Phythian, J. (Ref)   497   1.4
Edler, D. (Green)   389   1.1
Howard, C.
(Dream)   175   0.5
Mahaldar, A. (NLP)   98   0.3
Lab majority 19,691   57.08%
Electorate   53,505
Total Vote   34,498 Poll 64.5%
*Member of last parliament
Lab Hold (15.3% Swing from Con to Lab)

BRENTFORD AND ISLEWORTH %
Keen, A. (Lab)   32,249   57.4
*Deva, N. (Con)   17,825   31.8
Hartwell, G. (LD)   4,613   8.2
Bradley, J. (Green)   687   1.2
Simmerson, B.
(UKIP)   614   1.1
Ahmed, M. (NLP)   147   0.3
Lab majority 14,424   25.70%
Electorate   79,058
Total Vote   56,135 Poll 69.5%
*Member of last parliament
Lab Gain (14.3% Swing from Con to Lab)

BRENTWOOD AND ONGAR %
*Pickles, E. (Con)   23,031   45.4
Bottomley, E. (LD)   13,341   26.3
Young, M. (Lab)   11,231   22.1
Kilmartin, A. (Ref)   2,658   5.2
Mills, D. (UKIP)   465   0.9
Con majority 9,690   19.10%
Electorate   66,005
Total Vote   50,726 Poll 76.9%
*Member of last parliament
Con Hold (4% Swing from Con to LD)

BRIDGEND %
*Griffiths, W. (Lab) 25,115   58.1
Davies, D. (Con)   9,867   22.8
McKinlay, A. (LD)   4,968   11.5
Greaves, T. (Ref)   1,662   3.8
Watkins, D. (PC)   1,649   3.8
Lab majority 15,248   35.25%
Electorate   59,721
Total Vote   43,261 Poll 72.3%
*Member of last parliament
Lab Hold (9.8% Swing from Con to Lab)

BRIDGWATER %
*King, T. (Con)   20,174   36.9
Hoban, M. (LD)   18,378   33.6
Lavers, R. (Lab)   13,519   24.8
Evens, F. (Ref)   2,551   4.7
Con majority 1,796   3.29%
Electorate   73,038
Total Vote   54,622 Poll 74.6%
*Member of last parliament
Con Hold (6.9% Swing from Con to LD)

BRIGG AND GOOLE %
Cawsey, I. (Lab)   23,493   50.2
Stewart, D. (Con)   17,104   36.5
Hardy, M. (LD)   4,692   10.0
Rigby, D. (Ref)   1,513   3.2
Lab majority 6,389   13.65%
Electorate   63,648
Total Vote   46,802 Poll 73.5%
Lab Gain (13.9% Swing from Con to Lab)

BRIGHTON KEMPTOWN %
Turner, D. (Lab)   21,479   46.6
*Bowden, Sir A.
(Con)   17,945   39.2
Gray, C. (LD)   4,478   9.8
Inman, D. (Ref)   1,526   3.3
Williams, H. (SLP)   316   0.7
Bowler, J. (NLP)   172   0.4
Newman, L. (Loony)   123   0.3
Darlow, R. (Dream)   93   0.2
Lab majority 3,534   7.66%
Electorate   65,147
Total Vote   46,132 Poll 70.4%
*Member of last parliament
Lab Gain (13.6% Swing from Con to Lab)

BRIGHTON PAVILION %
Lepper, D.
(Lab/Co-op)   26,737   54.6
*Spencer, Sir D. (Con) 13,556 27.9
Blanshard, K. (LD)   4,644   9.5
Stocken, P. (Ref)   1,304   2.6
West, P. (Green)   1,249   2.5
Huggett, R. (IndCon)   1,098   2.2
Stevens, F. (UKIP)   179   0.4
Dobbs, B. (Sub-Genius) 125   0.3
Card, A. (Dream)   59   0.1
Lab/Co-op
majority   13,181   26.9%
Electorate   66,431
Total Vote   48,951 Poll 73.7%
*Member of last parliament
Lab/Co-op Gain (16% Swing from Con to Lab)

BRISTOL EAST %
*Corston, J. (Lab)   27,418   56.9
Vaizey, E. (Con)   11,259   23.4
Tyzack, P. (LD)   7,121   14.8
Philp, G. (Ref)   1,479   3.1
Williams, P. (SLP)   766   1.6
McLaggan, J. (NLP)   158   0.3
Lab majority 16,159   33.52%
Electorate   68,990
Total Vote   48,201 Poll 69.7%
*Member of last parliament
Lab Hold (11.9% Swing from Con to Lab)

BRISTOL NORTH WEST   %
Naysmith, D.
(Lab/Co-op)   27,575   49.9
*Stern, M. (Con)   16,193   29.3
Parry, I. (LD)   7,263   13.1
Horton, C. (IndLab)   1,718   3.1
Quintanilla, J. (Ref)   1,609   2.9
Shorter, G. (SLP)   482   0.9
Parnell, S. (BNP)   265   0.5
Leighton, T. (NLP)   140   0.3
Lab/Co-op
majority   11,382   20.60%
Electorate   75,009
Total Vote   55,245   Poll 73.3%
*Member of last parliament
Lab Hold (7.1% Swing from Con to Lab)

BRISTOL SOUTH   %
*Primarolo, D. (Lab)   29,890   59.9
Roe, M. (Con)   10,562   21.2
Williams, S. (LD)   6,691   13.4
Guy, D. (Ref)   1,486   3.0
Boxall, J. (Green)   722   1.4
Marshall, I. (Soc)   355   0.7
Taylor, L.
(Go Bowling)   153   0.3
Lab majority   19,328   38.77%
Electorate   72,393
Total Vote   49,859   Poll 68.7%
*Member of last parliament
Lab Hold (12.3% Swing from Con to Lab)

BRISTOL WEST   %
Davey, V. (Lab)   22,068   35.2
*Waldegrave, W. (Con)   20,575   32.8
Boney, C. (LD)   17,551   28.0
Beauchamp, R. (Ref)   1,304   2.1
Quinnell, J. (Green)   852   1.4
Nurse, R. (SLP)   244   0.4
Brierley, J. (NLP)   47   0.1
Lab majority   1,493   2.38%
Electorate   84,870
Total Vote   62,641   Poll 72.7%
*Member of last parliament
Lab Gain (12.1% Swing from Con to Lab)

**BROMLEY AND
CHISLEHURST**   %
*Forth, E. (Con)   24,428   46.3
Yeldham, R. (Lab)   13,310   25.2
Booth, P. (LD)   12,530   23.8
Bryant, R. (UKIP)   1,176   2.2
Speed, F. (Green)   640   1.2
Stoneman, M. (NF)   369   0.7
Aitman, G. (Lib)   285   0.5
Con majority   11,118   21.08%
Electorate   71,104
Total Vote   52,738   Poll 73.6%
*Member of last parliament
Con Hold (11.8% Swing from Con to Lab)

BROMSGROVE   %
Kirkbride, J. (Con)   24,620   47.2
McDonald, P. (Lab)   19,725   37.8
Davy, J. (LD)   6,200   11.9
Winsor, D. (Ref)   1,411   2.7
Wetton, B. (UKIP)   251   0.5

Con majority   4,895   9.38%
Electorate   67,744
Total Vote   52,207   Poll 77.1%
Con Hold (7% Swing from Con to Lab)

BROXBOURNE   %
*Roe, M. (Con)   22,952   48.9
Coleman, B. (Lab)   16,299   34.7
Davies, J. (LD)   5,310   11.3
Millward, D. (Ref)   1,633   3.5
Bruce, D. (BNP)   610   1.3
Cheetham, B.
(Third Way)   172   0.4
Con majority   6,653   14.16%
Electorate   66,720
Total Vote   46,976   Poll 70.4%
*Member of last parliament
Con Hold (13.4% Swing from Con to Lab)

BROXTOWE   %
Palmer, N. (Lab)   27,343   47.0
*Lester, J. (Con)   21,768   37.4
Miller, T. (LD)   6,934   11.9
Tucker, R. (Ref)   2,092   3.6
Lab majority   5,575   9.59%
Electorate   74,144
Total Vote   58,137   Poll 78.4%
*Member of last parliament
Lab Gain (12.9% Swing from Con to Lab)

BUCKINGHAM   %
Bercow, J. (Con)   24,594   49.8
Lehmann, R. (Lab)   12,208   24.7
Stuart, N. (LD)   12,175   24.6
Clements, G. (NLP)   421   0.9
Con majority   12,386   25.07%
Electorate   62,945
Total Vote   49,398   Poll 78.5%
Con Hold (10.6% Swing from Con to Lab)

BURNLEY   %
*Pike, P. (Lab)   26,210   57.9
Wiggin, W. (Con)   9,148   20.2
Birtwistle, G. (LD)   7,877   17.4
Oakley, R. (Ref)   2,010   4.4
Lab majority   17,062   37.71%
Electorate   67,582
Total Vote   45,245   Poll 66.9%
*Member of last parliament
Lab Hold (7.7% Swing from Con to Lab)

BURTON   %
Dean, J. (Lab)   27,810   51.0
*Lawrence, I. (Con)   21,480   39.4
Fletcher, D. (LD)   4,617   8.5
Sharp, K. (Nat Dem)   604   1.1
Lab majority   6,330   11.61%
Electorate   72,601
Total Vote   54,511   Poll 75.1%
*Member of last parliament
Lab Gain (9.3% Swing from Con to Lab)

BURY NORTH   %
Chaytor, D. (Lab)   28,523   51.8
*Burt, A. (Con)   20,657   37.5
Kenyon, N. (LD)   4,536   8.2
Hallewell, R. (Ref)   1,337   2.4

Lab majority   7,866   14.29%
Electorate   70,515
Total Vote   55,053   Poll 78.1%
*Member of last parliament
Lab Gain (11.2% Swing from Con to Lab)

BURY SOUTH   %
Lewis, I. (Lab)   28,658   56.9
*Sumberg, D. (Con)   16,277   32.3
D'Albert, V. (LD)   4,227   8.4
Slater, B. (Ref)   1,216   2.4
Lab majority   12,381   24.6%
Electorate   66,568
Total Vote   50,378   Poll 75.7%
*Member of last parliament
Lab Gain (13.2% Swing from Con to Lab)

BURY ST EDMUNDS   %
Ruffley, D. (Con)   21,290   38.3
Ereira, M. (Lab)   20,922   37.7
Cooper, D. (LD)   10,102   18.2
McWhirter, I. (Ref)   2,939   5.3
Lillis, J. (NLP)   272   0.5
Con majority   368   0.66%
Electorate   74,017
Total Vote   55,525   Poll 75%
Con Hold (9.6% Swing from Con to Lab)

CAERNARFON   %
*Wigley, D. (PC)   17,616   51.0
Williams, E. (Lab)   10,167   29.5
Williams, E. (Con)   4,230   12.3
MacQueen, J. (LD)   1,686   4.9
Collins, C. (Ref)   811   2.4
PC majority   7,449   21.5%
Electorate   46,815
Total Vote   34,510   Poll 73.7%
*Member of last parliament
PC Hold (10.6% Swing from PC to Lab)

CAERPHILLY   %
*Davies, R. (Lab)   30,697   67.8
Harris, H. (Con)   4,858   10.7
Whittle, L. (PC)   4,383   9.7
Ferguson, A. (LD)   3,724   8.2
Morgan, M. (Ref)   1,337   3.0
Williams, C. (Pro-Life)   270   0.6
Lab majority   25,839   57.08%
Electorate   64,621
Total Vote   45,269   Poll 70%
*Member of last parliament
Lab Hold (5.8% Swing from Con to Lab)

**CAITHNESS, SUTHERLAND
AND EASTER ROSS**   %
*Maclennan, R. (LD)   10,381   35.6
Hendry, J. (Lab)   8,122   27.8
Harper, E. (SNP)   6,710   23.0
Miers, T. (Con)   3,148   10.8
Ryder, C. (Ref)   369   1.3
Martin, J. (Green)   230   0.8
Carr, M. (UKIP)   212   0.7
LD majority   2,259   7.74%
Electorate   41,566
Total Vote   29,172   Poll 70%
*Member of last parliament
LD Hold (10.5% Swing from LD to Lab)

CALDER VALLEY

		%
McCafferty, C. (Lab)	26,050	46.1
*Thompson, Sir D.		
(Con)	19,795	35.1
Pearson, S. (LD)	8,322	14.7
Mellor, A. (Ref)	1,380	2.4
Smith, V. (Green)	488	0.9
Jackson, C. (BNP)	431	0.8
Lab majority	6,255	11.08%
Electorate	74,901	
Total Vote	56,466	Poll 75.4%

*Member of last parliament
Lab Gain (9.5% Swing from Con to Lab)

CAMBERWELL AND PECKHAM

		%
*Harman, H. (Lab)	19,734	69.5
Humphreys, M. (Con)	3,383	11.9
Williams, N. (LD)	3,198	11.3
China, N. (Ref)	692	2.4
Ruddock, A. (SLP)	685	2.4
Williams, G. (Lib)	443	1.6
Barker, J. (Soc)	233	0.8
Eames, C. (WRP)	106	0.4
Lab majority	16,351	57.42%
Electorate	50,214	
Total Vote	28,474	Poll 55.6%

*Member of last parliament
Lab Hold (10.7% Swing from Con to Lab)

CAMBRIDGE

		%
*Campbell, A. (Lab)	27,436	53.4
Platt, D. (Con)	13,299	25.9
Heathcock, G. (LD)	8,287	16.1
Burrows, W. (Ref)	1,262	2.5
Wright, M. (Green)	654	1.3
Johnstone, A. (Pro-Life)	191	0.4
Athow, R.		
(Workers Rev)	107	0.2
Gladwin, M. (NLP)	103	0.2
Lab majority	14,137	27.54%
Electorate	71,669	
Total Vote	51,339	Poll 69.2%

*Member of last parliament
Lab Hold (13.2% Swing from Con to Lab)

CANNOCK CHASE

		%
*Wright, T. (Lab)	28,705	54.8
Backhouse, J. (Con)	14,227	27.2
Kirby, R. (LD)	4,537	8.7
Froggatt, P. (Ref)	1,663	3.2
Hurley, W.		
(New Labour)	1,615	3.1
Conroy, M. (SLP)	1,120	2.1
Hartshorne, M.		
(Loony)	499	1.0
Lab majority	14,478	27.65%
Electorate	72,362	
Total Vote	52,366	Poll 72.4%

*Member of last parliament
Lab Hold (8.4% Swing from Con to Lab)

CANTERBURY

		%
*Brazier, J. (Con)	20,913	38.6
Hall, C. (Lab)	16,949	31.3
Vye, M. (LD)	12,854	23.8
Osborne, J. (Ref)	2,460	4.5
Meaden, G. (Green)	588	1.1
Moore, J. (UKIP)	281	0.5
Pringle, A. (NLP)	64	0.1
Con majority	3,964	7.33%
Electorate	74,548	
Total Vote	54,109	Poll 72.6%

*Member of last parliament
Con Hold (13.8% Swing from Con to Lab)

CARDIFF CENTRAL

		%
*Jones, J. (Lab/Co-op)	18,464	43.7
Randerson, J. (LD)	10,541	24.9
Melding, D. (Con)	8,470	20.0
Burns, T. (SLP)	2,230	5.3
Vernon, W. (PC)	1,504	3.6
Lloyd, N. (Ref)	760	1.8
James, C. (Loony)	204	0.5
Hobbs, A. (NLP)	80	0.2
Lab/Co-op majority	7,923	18.75%
Electorate	60,354	
Total Vote	42,253	Poll 68.9%

*Member of last parliament
Lab/Co-op Hold (0.9% Swing from Lab to LD)

CARDIFF NORTH

		%
Morgan, J. (Lab)	24,460	50.4
*Jones, G. (Con)	16,334	33.7
Rowland, R. (LD)	5,294	10.9
Palfrey, C. (PC)	1,201	2.5
Litchfield, E. (Ref)	1,199	2.5
Lab majority	8,126	16.76%
Electorate	60,430	
Total Vote	48,488	Poll 79.7%

*Member of last parliament
Lab Gain (11.5% Swing from Con to Lab)

CARDIFF SOUTH AND PENARTH

		%
*Michael, A.		
(Lab/Co-op)	22,647	53.4
Roberts, C. (Con)	8,786	20.7
Wakefield, S. (LD)	3,964	9.3
Foreman, J.		
(New Labour)	3,942	9.3
Haswell, D. (PC)	1,356	3.2
Morgan, P. (Ref)	1,211	2.9
Shepherd, M. (Soc)	344	0.8
Caves, B. (NLP)	170	0.4
Lab/Co-op majority	13,861	32.74%
Electorate	61,838	
Total Vote	42,420	Poll 68.6%

*Member of last parliament
Lab/Co-op Hold (5.4% Swing from Con to Lab)

CARDIFF WEST

		%
*Morgan, R. (Lab)	24,297	60.3
Hoare, S. (Con)	8,669	21.5
Gasson, J. (LD)	4,366	10.8
Carr, G. (PC)	1,949	4.8
Johns, T. (Ref)	996	2.5
Lab majority	15,628	38.80%
Electorate	58,198	
Total Vote	40,277	Poll 68.9%

*Member of last parliament
Lab Hold (9.2% Swing from Con to Lab)

CARLISLE

		%
*Martlew, E. (Lab)	25,031	57.4
Lawrence, R. (Con)	12,641	29.0
Mayho, C. (LD)	4,576	10.5
Fraser, A. (Ref)	1,233	2.8
Stevens, W. (NLP)	126	0.3
Lab majority	12,390	28.41%
Electorate	59,917	
Total Vote	43,607	Poll 72.7%

*Member of last parliament
Lab Hold (12.2% Swing from Con to Lab)

CARMARTHEN EAST AND DINEFWR

		%
*Williams, A. (Lab)	17,907	42.9
Thomas, R. (PC)	14,457	34.6
Hayward, E. (Con)	5,022	12.0
Hughes, J. (LD)	3,150	7.5
Humphries-Evans, I. (Ref)	1,196	2.9
Lab majority	3,450	8.27%
Electorate	53,079	
Total Vote	41,732	Poll 78.6%

*Member of last parliament
Lab Hold (2.1% Swing from Lab to PC)

CARMARTHEN WEST AND PEMBROKESHIRE SOUTH

		%
*Ainger, N. (Lab)	20,956	49.1
Williams, O. (Con)	11,335	26.6
Llewellyn, D. (PC)	5,402	12.7
Evans, K. (LD)	3,516	8.2
Poirrier, J. (Ref)	1,432	3.4
Lab majority	9,621	22.56%
Electorate	55,724	
Total Vote	42,641	Poll 76.4%

*Member of last parliament
Lab Hold (9.8% Swing from Con to Lab)

CARRICK, CUMNOCK AND DOON VALLEY

		%
*Foulkes, G.		
(Lab/Co-op)	29,398	59.8
Marshall, A. (Con)	8,336	17.0
Hutchison, C. (SNP)	8,190	16.7
Young, D. (LD)	2,613	5.3
Higgins, J. (Ref)	634	1.3
Lab/Co-op majority	21,062	42.83%
Electorate	65,593	
Total Vote	49,171	Poll 75%

*Member of last parliament
Lab/Co-op Hold (7.2% Swing from Con to Lab)

CARSHALTON AND WALLINGTON

		%
Brake, T. (LD)	18,490	38.2
*Forman, N. (Con)	16,223	33.5
Theobald, A. (Lab)	11,565	23.9
Storey, J. (Ref)	1,289	2.7
Hickson, P. (Green)	377	0.8
Ritchie, G. (BNP)	261	0.5
Povey, L. (UKIP)	218	0.5
LD majority	2,267	4.68%
Electorate	66,038	
Total Vote	48,423	Poll 73.3%

*Member of last parliament
LD Gain (11.8% Swing from Con to LD)

CASTLE POINT

		%
Butler, C. (Lab)	20,605	42.4
*Spink, R. (Con)	19,462	40.1
Baker, M. (LD)	4,477	9.2
Maulkin, H. (Ref)	2,700	5.6
Kendall, L. (Consult)	1,301	2.7
Lab majority	1,143	2.30%
Electorate	67,146	
Total Vote	48,545	Poll 72.3%

*Member of last parliament
Lab Gain (16.9% Swing from Con to Lab)

CENTRAL FIFE

		%
*McLeish, H. (Lab)	23,912	58.7
Marwick, T. (SNP)	10,199	25.0
Rees-Mogg, J. (Con)	3,669	9.0
Laird, R. (LD)	2,610	6.4
Scrymgeour-Wedderburn, J. (Ref)	375	0.9
Lab majority	13,713	33.64%
Electorate	58,315	
Total Vote	40,765	Poll 69.8%

*Member of last parliament
Lab Hold (3.9% Swing from SNP to Lab)

CENTRAL SUFFOLK AND NORTH IPSWICH

		%
*Lord, M. (Con)	22,493	42.6
Jones, C. (Lab)	18,955	35.9
Goldspink, M. (LD)	10,886	20.6
Bennell, S. (Ind)	489	0.9
Con majority	3,538	6.70%
Electorate	70,222	
Total Vote	52,823	Poll 75.2%

*Member of last parliament
Con Hold (14.2% Swing from Con to Lab)

CEREDIGION

		%
*Dafis, C. (PC)	16,728	41.6
Harris, R. (Lab)	9,767	24.3
Davies, D. (LD)	6,616	16.5
Aubel, F. (Con)	5,983	14.9
Leaney, C. (Ref)	1,092	2.7
PC majority	6,961	17.32%
Electorate	54,378	
Total Vote	40,186	Poll 73.7%

*Member of last parliament
PC Hold (2.5% Swing from Lab to PC)

CHARNWOOD

		%
*Dorrell, S. (Con)	26,110	46.5
Knaggs, D. (Lab)	20,210	36.0
Wilson, R. (LD)	7,224	12.9
Meechan, H. (Ref)	2,104	3.7
Palmer, M. (BNP)	525	0.9
Con majority	5,900	10.50%
Electorate	72,692	
Total Vote	56,173	Poll 77.2%

*Member of last parliament
Con Hold (14.2% Swing from Con to Lab)

CHATHAM AND AYLESFORD

		%
Shaw, J. (Lab)	21,191	43.1
Knox-Johnston, R. (Con)	18,401	37.4
Murray, R. (LD)	7,389	15.0

Riddle, K. (Ref)	1,538	3.1
Harding, A. (UKIP)	493	1.0
Martel, T. (NLP)	149	0.3
Lab majority	2,790	5.68%
Electorate	69,172	
Total Vote	49,161	Poll 70.8%

Lab Gain (15.1% Swing from Con to Lab)

CHEADLE

		%
*Day, S. (Con)	22,944	43.7
Calton, P. (LD)	19,755	37.7
Diggett, P. (Lab)	8,253	15.7
Brook, A. (Ref)	1,511	2.9
Con majority	3,189	6.08%
Electorate	67,627	
Total Vote	52,463	Poll 77.3%

*Member of last parliament
Con Hold (11% Swing from Con to LD)

CHELMSFORD WEST

		%
*Burns, S. (Con)	23,781	40.6
Bracken, M. (LD)	17,090	29.2
Chad, R. (Lab)	15,436	26.4
Smith, T. (Ref)	1,536	2.6
Rumens, G. (Green)	411	0.7
Levin, M. (UKIP)	323	0.6
Con majority	6,691	11.42%
Electorate	76,086	
Total Vote	58,577	Poll 76.9%

*Member of last parliament
Con Hold (7.2% Swing from Con to LD)

CHELTENHAM

		%
*Jones, N. (LD)	24,877	49.5
Todman, W. (Con)	18,232	36.2
Leach, B. (Lab)	5,100	10.1
Powell, A. (Ref)	1,065	2.1
Hanks, K. (Loony)	375	0.7
Cook, G. (UKIP)	302	0.6
Harriss, A. (Pro-Life)	245	0.5
Brighouse, S. (NLP)	107	0.2
LD majority	6,645	13.21%
Electorate	67,950	
Total Vote	50,303	Poll 74%

*Member of last parliament
LD Hold (4.9% Swing from Con to LD)

CHESHAM AND AMERSHAM

		%
*Gillan, C. (Con)	26,298	50.4
Brand, M. (LD)	12,439	23.8
Farrelly, C. (Lab)	10,240	19.6
Andrews, P. (Ref)	2,528	4.8
Shilson, C. (UKIP)	618	1.2
Godfrey, H. (NLP)	74	0.1
Con majority	13,859	26.55%
Electorate	69,244	
Total Vote	52,197	Poll 73.7%

*Member of last parliament
Con Hold (6.2% Swing from Con to LD)

CHESTERFIELD

		%
*Benn, T. (Lab)	26,105	50.8
Rogers, T. (LD)	20,330	39.6
Potter, J. (Con)	4,752	9.2

Scarth, N. (Ind OAP)	202	0.4
Lab majority	5,775	11.24%
Electorate	72,472	
Total Vote	51,389	Poll 70.9%

*Member of last parliament
Lab Hold (0.1% Swing from Lab to LD)

CHICHESTER

		%
Tyrie, A. (Con)	25,895	46.4
Gardiner, P. (LD)	16,161	29.0
Smith, C. (Lab)	9,605	17.2
Denny, D. (Ref)	3,318	5.9
Rix, J. (UKIP)	800	1.4
Con majority	9,734	17.45%
Electorate	74,489	
Total Vote	55,779	Poll 74.6%

Con Hold (7.6% Swing from Con to LD)

CHINGFORD AND WOODFORD GREEN

		%
*Duncan Smith, I. (Con)	21,109	47.5
Hutchinson, T. (Lab)	15,395	34.6
Seeff, G. (LD)	6,885	15.5
Gould, A. (BNP)	1,059	2.4
Con majority	5,714	12.86%
Electorate	62,904	
Total Vote	44,448	Poll 70.7%

*Member of last parliament
Con Hold (13.8% Swing from Con to Lab)

CHIPPING BARNET

		%
*Chapman, S. (Con)	21,317	43.0
Cooke, G. (Lab)	20,282	40.9
Hooker, S. (LD)	6,121	12.3
Ribekow, V. (Ref)	1,190	2.4
Miskin, B. (Loony)	253	0.5
Scallan, B. (Pro-Life)	243	0.5
Derksen, D. (NLP)	159	0.3
Con majority	1,035	2.09%
Electorate	69,049	
Total Vote	49,565	Poll 70.9%

*Member of last parliament
Con Hold (14.1% Swing from Con to Lab)

CHORLEY

		%
Hoyle, L. (Lab)	30,607	53.0
*Dover, D. (Con)	20,737	35.9
Jones, S. (LD)	4,900	8.5
Heaton, A. (Ref)	1,319	2.3
Leadbetter, P. (NLP)	143	0.2
Lab majority	9,870	17.10%
Electorate	74,387	
Total Vote	57,706	Poll 77.6%

*Member of last parliament
Lab Gain (10.6% Swing from Con to Lab)

CHRISTCHURCH

		%
Chope, C. (Con)	26,095	46.4
*Maddock, D. (LD)	23,930	42.6
Mannan, C. (Lab)	3,884	6.9
Spencer, R. (Ref)	1,684	3.0
Dickinson, R. (UKIP)	606	1.1
Con majority	2,165	3.85%
Electorate	71,488	
Total Vote	56,199	Poll 78.6%

*Member of last parliament
Con ReGain (18.3% Swing from Con to LD)

CITIES OF LONDON AND WESTMINSTER

		%
*Brooke, P. (Con)	18,981	47.3
Green, K. (Lab)	14,100	35.1
Dumigan, M. (LD)	4,933	12.3
Walters, A. (Ref)	1,161	2.9
Wharton, P. (Barts)	266	0.7
Merton, C. (UKIP)	215	0.5
Johnson, R. (NLP)	176	0.4
Walsh, N. (Loony)	138	0.3
Webster, G. (Hemp)	112	0.3
Sadowitz, J. (Dream)	73	0.2
Con majority	4,881	12.16%
Electorate	69,047	
Total Vote	40,155	Poll 58.2%

*Member of last parliament
Con Hold (11.5% Swing from Con to Lab)

CITY OF CHESTER

		%
Russell, C. (Lab)	29,806	53.0
*Brandreth, G. (Con)	19,253	34.2
Simpson, D. (LD)	5,353	9.5
Mullan, R. (Ref)	1,487	2.6
Sanderson, I. (Loony)	204	0.4
Johnson, W. (WCCC)	154	0.3
Lab majority	10,553	18.76%
Electorate	71,730	
Total Vote	56,257	Poll 78.1%

*Member of last parliament
Lab Gain (11.4% Swing from Con to Lab)

CITY OF DURHAM

		%
*Steinberg, G. (Lab)	31,102	63.3
Chalk, R. (Con)	8,598	17.5
Martin, N. (LD)	7,499	15.3
Robson, M. (Ref)	1,723	3.5
Kember, P. (NLP)	213	0.4
Lab majority	22,504	45.80%
Electorate	69,340	
Total Vote	49,135	Poll 70.9%

*Member of last parliament
Lab Hold (8.1% Swing from Con to Lab)

CITY OF YORK

		%
*Bayley, H. (Lab)	34,956	59.9
Mallett, S. (Con)	14,433	24.7
Waller, A. (LD)	6,537	11.2
Sheppard, J. (Ref)	1,083	1.9
Hill, M. (Green)	880	1.5
Wegener, E. (UKIP)	319	0.5
Lightfoot, A. (Chr Nat)	137	0.2
Lab majority	20,523	35.18%
Electorate	79,383	
Total Vote	58,345	Poll 73.2%

*Member of last parliament
Lab Hold (12.6% Swing from Con to Lab)

CLEETHORPES

		%
McIsaac, S. (Lab)	26,058	51.6
*Brown, M. (Con)	16,882	33.4
Melton, K. (LD)	5,746	11.4
Berry, J. (Ref)	1,787	3.5
Lab majority	9,176	18.18%
Electorate	68,763	
Total Vote	50,473	Poll 73.4%

*Member of last parliament
Lab Gain (15.1% Swing from Con to Lab)

CLWYD SOUTH

		%
*Jones, M. (Lab)	22,901	58.1
Johnson, B. (Con)	9,091	23.1
Chadwick, A. (LD)	3,684	9.4
Williams, G. (PC)	2,500	6.3
Lewis, A. (Ref)	1,207	3.1
Lab majority	13,810	35.07%
Electorate	53,495	
Total Vote	39,383	Poll 73.6%

*Member of last parliament
Lab Hold (7.8% Swing from Con to Lab)

CLWYD WEST

		%
Thomas, G. (Lab)	14,918	37.1
*Richards, R. (Con)	13,070	32.5
Williams, E. (PC)	5,421	13.5
Williams, W. (LD)	5,151	12.8
Bennett-Collins, H. (Ref)	1,114	2.8
Neal, D. (Conserv)	583	1.4
Lab majority	1,848	4.59%
Electorate	53,467	
Total Vote	40,257	Poll 75.2%

*Member of last parliament
Lab Gain (11.1% Swing from Con to Lab)

CLYDEBANK AND MILNGAVIE

		%
*Worthington, A. (Lab)	21,583	55.2
Yuill, J. (SNP)	8,263	21.1
Morgan, N. (Con)	4,885	12.5
Moody, K. (LD)	4,086	10.5
Sanderson, J. (Ref)	269	0.7
Lab majority	13,320	34.08%
Electorate	52,092	
Total Vote	39,086	Poll 75%

*Member of last parliament
Lab Hold (1.1% Swing from SNP to Lab)

CLYDESDALE

		%
*Hood, J. (Lab)	23,859	52.5
Doig, A. (SNP)	10,050	22.1
Izatt, M. (Con)	7,396	16.3
Grieve, S. (LD)	3,796	8.4
Smith, K. (BNP)	311	0.7
Lab majority	13,809	30.41%
Electorate	63,428	
Total Vote	45,412	Poll 71.6%

*Member of last parliament
Lab Hold (4.4% Swing from SNP to Lab)

COATBRIDGE AND CHRYSTON

		%
*Clarke, T. (Lab)	25,694	68.3
Nugent, B. (SNP)	6,402	17.0
Wauchope, P. (Con)	3,216	8.6
Daly, M. (LD)	2,048	5.4
Bowsley, B. (Ref)	249	0.7
Lab majority	19,292	51.30%
Electorate	52,024	
Total Vote	37,609	Poll 72.3%

*Member of last parliament
Lab Hold (3.1% Swing from SNP to Lab)

COLCHESTER

		%
Russell, R. (LD)	17,886	34.4
Shakespeare, S. (Con)	16,305	31.4
Green, R. (Lab)	15,891	30.5
Hazell, J. (Ref)	1,776	3.4
Basker, L. (NLP)	148	0.3
LD majority	1,581	3.04%
Electorate	74,743	
Total Vote	52,006	Poll 69.6%

LD Gain (6.2% Swing from Con to LD)

COLNE VALLEY

		%
Mountford, K. (Lab)	23,285	41.3
*Riddick, G. (Con)	18,445	32.7
Priestley, N. (LD)	12,755	22.6
Brooke, A. (SLP)	759	1.3
Cooper, A. (Green)	493	0.9
Nunn, J. (UKIP)	478	0.8
Staniforth, M. (Loony)	196	0.3
Lab majority	4,840	8.58%
Electorate	73,338	
Total Vote	56,411	Poll 76.8%

*Member of last parliament
Lab Gain (10.4% Swing from Con to Lab)

CONGLETON

		%
*Winterton, A. (Con)	22,012	41.2
Walmsley, J. (LD)	15,882	29.7
Scholey, F. (Lab)	14,713	27.5
Lockett, J. (UKIP)	811	1.5
Con majority	6,130	11.48%
Electorate	68,873	
Total Vote	53,418	Poll 77.4%

*Member of last parliament
Con Hold (2.7% Swing from Con to LD)

CONWY

		%
Williams, B. (Lab)	14,561	35.0
Roberts, D. (LD)	12,965	31.2
Jones, D. (Con)	10,085	24.3
Davies, R. (PC)	2,844	6.8
Barham, A. (Ref)	760	1.8
Bradley, R. (Alt LD)	250	0.6
Hughes, D. (NLP)	95	0.2
Lab majority	1,596	3.84%
Electorate	55,092	
Total Vote	41,560	Poll 75.3%

Lab Gain (9.4% Swing from Con to Lab)

COPELAND

		%
*Cunningham, J. (Lab)	24,077	58.2
Cumpsty, A. (Con)	12,081	29.2
Putnam, R. (LD)	3,814	9.2
Johnston, C. (Ref)	1,036	2.5
Hanratty, G. (Pro-Life)	389	0.9
Lab majority	11,996	29.0%
Electorate	54,263	
Total Vote	41,397	Poll 76.3%

*Member of last parliament
Lab Hold (11.8% Swing from Con to Lab)

CORBY

		%
Hope, P. (Lab/Co-op)	29,888	55.4
*Powell, W. (Con)	18,028	33.4
Hankinson, I. (LD)	4,045	7.5
Riley-Smith, S. (Ref)	1,356	2.5
Gillman, I. (UKIP)	507	0.9
Bence, J. (NLP)	133	0.2
Lab/Co-op majority	11,860	21.98%
Electorate	69,252	
Total Vote	53,957	Poll 77.7%

*Member of last parliament
Lab Gain (11.3% Swing from Con to Lab)

COTSWOLD %
*Clifton-Brown, G.
(Con)	23,698	46.4
Gayler, D. (LD)	11,733	23.0
Elwell, D. (Lab)	11,608	22.7
Lowe, R. (Ref)	3,393	6.6
Michael, V. (Green)	560	1.1
Brighouse, H. (NLP)	129	0.3
Con majority	11,965	23.41%
Electorate	67,333	
Total Vote	51,121	Poll 75.9%

*Member of last parliament
Con Hold (1.2% Swing from LD to Con)

COVENTRY NORTH EAST %
*Ainsworth, B.
(Lab)	31,856	66.2
Burnett, M. (Con)	9,287	19.3
Sewards, G. (LD)	3,866	8.0
Brown, N. (Lib)	1,181	2.5
Hurrell, R. (Ref)	1,125	2.3
Khamis, H. (SLP)	597	1.2
Sidwell, C. (Dream)	173	0.4
Lab majority	22,569	46.94%
Electorate	74,274	
Total Vote	48,085	Poll 64.4%

*Member of last parliament
Lab Hold (12.7% Swing from Con to Lab)

COVENTRY NORTH WEST %
*Robinson, G. (Lab)
*Robinson, G. (Lab)	30,901	56.9
Bartlett, P. (Con)	14,300	26.3
Penlington, N. (LD)	5,690	10.5
Butler, D. (Ref)	1,269	2.3
Spencer, D. (SLP)	940	1.7
Wheway, R. (Lib)	687	1.3
Mills, P. (Pro-Life)	359	0.7
Francis, L. (Dream)	176	0.3
Lab majority	16,601	30.56%
Electorate	76,439	
Total Vote	54,322	Poll 70.7%

*Member of last parliament
Lab Hold (8.1% Swing from Con to Lab)

COVENTRY SOUTH %
*Cunningham, J.
(Lab)	25,511	50.9
Ivey, P. (Con)	14,558	29.0
Macdonald, G. (LD)	4,617	9.2
Nellist, D. (Soc)	3,262	6.5
Garratt, P. (Ref)	943	1.9
Jenking, R. (Lib)	725	1.4
Astbury, J. (BNP)	328	0.7
Bradshaw, A. (Dream)	180	0.4
Lab majority	10,953	21.85%
Electorate	71,826	
Total Vote	50,124	Poll 68.7%

*Member of last parliament
Lab Gain (13.5% Swing from Con to Lab)

CRAWLEY %
Moffatt, L. (Lab)	27,750	55.0
Crabb, J. (Con)	16,043	31.8
De Souza, H. (LD)	4,141	8.2
Walters, R. (Ref)	1,931	3.8
Saunders, E. (UKIP)	322	0.6
Khan, A. (Justice)	230	0.5

Lab majority	11,707	23.22%
Electorate	69,040	
Total Vote	50,417	Poll 72.5%

Lab Gain (13.4% Swing from Con to Lab)

CREWE AND NANTWICH %
*Dunwoody, G. (Lab) 29,460 58.2
*Dunwoody, G. (Lab)	29,460	58.2
Loveridge, M. (Con)	13,662	27.0
Cannon, D. (LD)	5,940	11.7
Astbury, P. (Ref)	1,543	3.0
Lab majority	15,798	31.22%
Electorate	68,694	
Total Vote	50,605	Poll 73.5%

*Member of last parliament
Lab Hold (11.3% Swing from Con to Lab)

CROSBY %
Curtis-Tansley, C.
(Lab)	22,549	51.1
*Thornton, M. (Con)	15,367	34.8
McVey, P. (LD)	5,080	11.5
Gauld, J. (Ref)	813	1.8
Marks, J. (Lib)	233	0.5
Hite, W. (NLP)	99	0.2
Lab majority	7,182	16.27%
Electorate	57,190	
Total Vote	44,141	Poll 77.2%

*Member of last parliament
Lab Gain (18.2% Swing from Con to Lab)

CROYDON CENTRAL %
Davies, G. (Lab)	25,432	45.6
*Congdon, D. (Con)	21,535	38.6
Schlich, G. (LD)	6,061	10.9
Cook, C. (Ref)	1,886	3.4
Barnsley, M. (Green)	595	1.1
Woollcott, J. (UKIP)	290	0.5
Lab majority	3,897	6.98%
Electorate	80,152	
Total Vote	55,799	Poll 69.6%

*Member of last parliament
Lab Gain (15.5% Swing from Con to Lab)

CROYDON NORTH %
*Wicks, M. (Lab)	32,672	62.2
Martin, I. (Con)	14,274	27.2
Morris, M. (LD)	4,066	7.7
Billis, R. (Ref)	1,155	2.2
Feisenberger, J.		
(UKIP)	396	0.8
Lab majority	18,398	35.00%
Electorate	77,063	
Total Vote	52,563	Poll 68.2%

*Member of last parliament
Lab Gain (17.6% Swing from Con to Lab)

CROYDON SOUTH %
*Ottaway, R. (Con)	25,649	47.3
Burling, C. (Lab)	13,719	25.3
Gauge, S. (LD)	11,441	21.1
Barber, T. (Ref)	2,631	4.9
Ferguson, P. (BNP)	354	0.7
Harker, A. (UKIP)	309	0.6
Samuel, M.		
(People's Choice)	96	0.2
Con majority	11,930	22.01%
Electorate	73,787	
Total Vote	54,199	Poll 73.5%

*Member of last parliament
Con Hold (11.7% Swing from Con to Lab)

**CUMBERNAULD AND
KILSYTH** %
McKenna, R. (Lab)	21,141	58.7
Barrie, C. (SNP)	10,013	27.8
Sewell, I. (Con)	2,441	6.8
Biggam, J. (LD)	1,368	3.8
Kara, J. (Pro-Life)	609	1.7
McEwan, K. (ScotSoc)	345	1.0
Cook, P. (Ref)	107	0.3
Lab majority	11,128	30.89%
Electorate	40,032	
Total Vote	36,024	Poll 75%

Lab Hold (2.9% Swing from SNP to Lab)

CUNNINGHAME NORTH %
*Wilson, B. (Lab)	20,686	50.3
Mitchell, M. (Con)	9,647	23.5
Nicoll, K. (SNP)	7,584	18.4
Freel, K. (LD)	2,271	5.5
McDaid, L. (SLP)	501	1.2
Winton, I. (Ref)	440	1.1
Lab majority	11,039	26.84%
Electorate	54,526	
Total Vote	41,129	Poll 74.1%

*Member of last parliament
Lab Hold (10% Swing from Con to Lab)

CUNNINGHAME SOUTH %
*Donohoe, B. (Lab)	22,233	62.7
Burgess, M. (SNP)	7,364	20.8
Paterson, P. (Con)	3,571	10.1
Watson, E. (LD)	1,604	4.5
Edwin, K. (SLP)	494	1.4
Martlew, A. (Ref)	178	0.5
Lab majority	14,869	41.95%
Electorate	49,543	
Total Vote	35,444	Poll 71.5%

*Member of last parliament
Lab Hold (6.6% Swing from SNP to Lab)

CYNON VALLEY %
*Clwyd, A. (Lab)	23,307	69.7
Davies, A. (PC)	3,552	10.6
Price, H. (LD)	3,459	10.3
Smith, A. (Con)	2,262	6.8
John, G. (Ref)	844	2.5
Lab majority	19,755	59.10%
Electorate	48,286	
Total Vote	33,424	Poll 69.2%

*Member of last parliament
Lab Hold (0.5% Swing from PC to Lab)

DAGENHAM %
*Church, J. (Lab)	23,759	65.7
Fairrie, J. (Con)	6,705	18.5
Dobrashian, T. (LD)	2,704	7.5
Kraft, S. (Ref)	1,411	3.9
Binding, W. (BNP)	900	2.5
Dawson, R. (Ind)	349	1.0
Hipperson, M.		
(Nat Dem)	183	0.5
Goble, K. (Pro-Life)	152	0.4
Lab majority	17,054	47.16%
Electorate	58,573	
Total Vote	36,163	Poll 61.7%

*Member of last parliament
Lab Hold (16.2% Swing from Con to Lab)

DARLINGTON

		%
*Milburn, A. (Lab)	29,658	61.6
Scrope, P. (Con)	13,633	28.3
Boxell, L. (LD)	3,483	7.2
Blakey, M. (Ref)	1,399	2.9
Lab majority 16,025		33.27%
Electorate 65,140		
Total Vote 48,173	Poll 74%	

*Member of last parliament
Lab Hold (14.1% Swing from Con to Lab)

DARTFORD

		%
Stoate, H. (Lab)	25,278	48.6
*Dunn, B. (Con)	20,950	40.3
Webb, D. (LD)	4,872	9.4
McHale, P. (BNP)	424	0.8
Homden, P. (Fancy)	287	0.6
Pollitt, J. (ChriDem)	228	0.4
Lab majority 4,328		8.32%
Electorate 69,726		
Total Vote 52,039	Poll 74.6%	

*Member of last parliament
Lab Gain (11.5% Swing from Con to Lab)

DAVENTRY

		%
*Boswell, T. (Con)	28,615	46.3
Ritchie, K. (Lab)	21,237	34.4
Gordon, J. (LD)	9,233	15.0
Russocki, B. (Ref)	2,018	3.3
Mahoney, B. (UKIP)	443	0.7
France, R. (NLP)	204	0.3
Con majority 7,378		11.95%
Electorate 80,151		
Total Vote 61,750	Poll 76.8%	

*Member of last parliament
Con Hold (11% Swing from Con to Lab)

DELYN

		%
*Hanson, D. (Lab)	23,300	58.4
Lumley, K. (Con)	10,607	26.0
Lloyd, D. (LD)	4,160	10.2
Drake, A. (PC)	1,558	3.8
Soutter, E. (Ref)	1,117	2.7
Lab majority 12,693		31.20%
Electorate 53,693		
Total Vote 40,742	Poll 75.9%	

*Member of last parliament
Lab Hold (12% Swing from Con to Lab)

DENTON AND REDDISH

		%
*Bennett, A. (Lab)	30,137	65.4
Nutt, B. (Con)	9,826	21.3
Donaldson, I. (LD)	6,121	13.3
Lab majority 20,311		44.07%
Electorate 68,866		
Total Vote 46,084	Poll 66.8%	

*Member of last parliament
Lab Hold (12.5% Swing from Con to Lab)

DERBY NORTH

		%
Laxton, R. (Lab)	29,844	53.2
*Knight, G. (Con)	19,229	34.3
Charlesworth, R. (LD)	5,059	9.0
Reynolds, P. (Ref)	1,816	3.2
Waters, J. (Pro-Life)	195	0.3
Lab majority 10,615		18.91%
Electorate 76,116		
Total Vote 56,143	Poll 73.5%	

*Member of last parliament
Lab Gain (13.2% Swing from Con to Lab)

DERBY SOUTH

		%
*Beckett, M. (Lab)	29,154	56.3
Arain, J. (Con)	13,048	25.2
Beckett, J. (LD)	7,438	14.4
Browne, J. (Ref)	1,862	3.6
Evans, R. (Nat Dem)	317	0.6
Lab majority 16,106		31.08%
Electorate 76,386		
Total Vote 51,819	Poll 67.6%	

*Member of last parliament
Lab Hold (11.8% Swing from Con to Lab)

DEVIZES

		%
*Ancram, M. (Con)	25,710	42.8
Vickers, A. (LD)	15,928	26.5
Jeffrey, F. (Lab)	14,551	24.2
Goldsmith, J. (Ref)	3,021	5.0
Oram, S. (UKIP)	622	1.0
Haysom, S. (NLP)	204	0.3
Con majority 9,782		16.29%
Electorate 80,383		
Total Vote 60,036	Poll 74.4%	

*Member of last parliament
Con Hold (2.1% Swing from Con to LD)

DEWSBURY

		%
*Taylor, A. (Lab)	21,286	49.4
McCormick, P.		
(Con)	12,963	30.1
Hill, K. (LD)	4,422	10.3
Taylor, F. (BNP)	2,232	5.2
Goff, W. (Ref)	1,019	2.4
Daniel, D. (IndLab)	770	1.8
McCourtie, I. (Green)	383	0.9
Lab majority 8,323		19.32%
Electorate 61,523		
Total Vote 43,075	Poll 70%	

*Member of last parliament
Lab Hold (6% Swing from Con to Lab)

DON VALLEY

		%
Flint, C. (Lab)	25,376	58.3
Gledhill, C. (Con)	10,717	24.6
Johnston, P. (LD)	4,238	9.7
Davies, P. (Ref)	1,379	3.2
Ball, N. (SLP)	1,024	2.4
Platt, S. (Green)	493	1.1
Johnson, C. (Pro-Life)	330	0.8
Lab majority 14,659		33.65%
Electorate 65,643		
Total Vote 43,557	Poll 66.3%	

Lab Hold (9.9% Swing from Con to Lab)

DONCASTER CENTRAL

		%
Winterton, R. (Lab)	26,961	62.1
Turtle, D. (Con)	9,105	21.0
Tarry, S. (LD)	4,091	9.4
Cliff, M. (Ref)	1,273	2.9
Kenny, M. (SLP)	854	2.0
Redden, J.		
(Pro-Life)	694	1.6
Davies, P. (UKIP)	462	1.1
Lab majority 17,856		41.10%
Electorate 67,965		
Total Vote 43,440	Poll 63.8%	

Lab Hold (10.1% Swing from Con to Lab)

DONCASTER NORTH

		%
*Hughes, K. (Lab)	27,843	69.8
Kennerley, P. (Con)	5,906	14.8
Cook, M. (LD)	3,369	8.4
Thornton, R. (Ref)	1,589	4.0
Swan, N.		
(Anti-Sleaze Lab)	1,181	3.0
Lab majority 21,937		55.00%
Electorate 63,019		
Total Vote 39,888	Poll 63.3%	

*Member of last parliament
Lab Hold (6.4% Swing from Con to Lab)

DOVER

		%
Prosser, G. (Lab)	29,535	54.5
*Shaw, D. (Con)	17,796	32.8
Corney, M. (LD)	4,302	7.9
Anderson, S. (Ref)	2,124	3.9
Hyde, C. (UKIP)	443	0.8
Lab majority 11,739		21.66%
Electorate 68,669		
Total Vote 54,200	Poll 78.6%	

*Member of last parliament
Lab Gain (11.6% Swing from Con to Lab)

DUDLEY NORTH

		%
Cranston, R. (Lab)	24,471	51.2
MacNamara, C.		
(Con)	15,014	31.4
Lewis, G. (LD)	3,939	8.2
Atherton, M. (SLP)	2,155	4.5
Bavester, S. (Ref)	1,201	2.5
Cartwright, G. (NF)	559	1.2
Darby, S. (Nat Dem)	469	1.0
Lab majority 9,457		19.78%
Electorate 68,835		
Total Vote 47,808	Poll 69.3%	

Lab Hold (9% Swing from Con to Lab)

DUDLEY SOUTH

		%
*Pearson, I. (Lab)	27,124	56.6
Simpson, G. (Con)	14,097	29.4
Burt, R. (LD)	5,214	10.9
Birch, C. (Ref)	1,467	3.1
Lab majority 13,027		27.20%
Electorate 66,731		
Total Vote 47,902	Poll 71.7%	

*Member of last parliament
Lab Hold (11% Swing from Con to Lab)

DULWICH AND WEST NORWOOD

		%
*Jowell, T. (Lab)	27,807	61.0
Gough, R. (Con)	11,038	24.2
Kramer, S. (LD)	4,916	10.8
Coles, B. (Ref)	897	2.0
Goldie, A. (Lib)	587	1.3
Goodman, D.		
(Dream)	173	0.4
Pike, E. (UKIP)	159	0.3
Captain Rizz (Rizz)	38	0.1
Lab majority 16,769		36.79%
Electorate 69,655		
Total Vote 45,615	Poll 65.5%	

*Member of last parliament
Lab Hold (16.6% Swing from Con to Lab)

DUMBARTON

		%
*McFall, J. (Lab/Co-op)	20,470	49.6
Mackechnie, B. (SNP)	9,587	23.2
Ramsay, P. (Con)	7,283	17.6
Reid, A. (LD)	3,144	7.6
Robertson, L. (ScotSoc)	283	0.7
Dempster, G. (Ref)	255	0.6
Lancaster, R. (UKIP)	242	0.6
Lab/Co-op majority	10,883	26.37%
Electorate	56,229	
Total Vote	41,264	Poll 73.4%

*Member of last parliament
Lab Hold (0.6% Swing from SNP to Lab)

DUMFRIES

		%
Brown, R. (Lab)	23,528	47.5
Stevenson, S. (Con)	13,885	28.0
Higgins, R. (SNP)	5,977	12.1
Wallace, N. (LD)	5,487	11.1
Parker, D. (Ref)	533	1.1
Hunter, E. (NLP)	117	0.2
Lab majority	9,643	19.47%
Electorate	62,759	
Total Vote	49,527	Poll 78.9%

Lab Gain (16.5% Swing from Con to Lab)

DUNDEE EAST

		%
*McAllion, J. (Lab)	20,718	51.1
Robison, S. (SNP)	10,757	26.5
Mackie, B. (Con)	6,397	15.8
Saluja, G. (LD)	1,677	4.1
Galloway, T. (Ref)	601	1.5
Duke, H. (ScotSoc)	232	0.6
MacKenzie, E. (NLP)	146	0.4
Lab majority	9,961	24.58%
Electorate	58,388	
Total Vote	40,528	Poll 69.4%

*Member of last parliament
Lab Hold (6.2% Swing from SNP to Lab)

DUNDEE WEST

		%
*Ross, E. (Lab)	20,875	53.8
Dorward, J. (SNP)	9,016	23.2
Powrie, N. (Con)	5,105	13.2
Dick, E. (LD)	2,972	7.7
Ward, M. (ScotSoc)	428	1.1
MacMillan, J. (Ref)	411	1.1
Lab majority	11,859	30.56%
Electorate	57,346	
Total Vote	38,807	Poll 67.7%

*Member of last parliament
Lab Hold (3.7% Swing from SNP to Lab)

DUNFERMLINE EAST

		%
*Brown, G. (Lab)	24,441	66.8
Ramage, J. (SNP)	5,690	15.6
Mitchell QC, I. (Con)	3,656	10.0
Tolson, J. (LD)	2,164	5.9
Dunsmore, T. (Ref)	632	1.7
Lab majority	18,751	51.26%
Electorate	52,072	
Total Vote	36,583	Poll 70.3%

*Member of last parliament
Lab Hold (1.6% Swing from SNP to Lab)

DUNFERMLINE WEST

		%
*Squire, R. (Lab)	19,338	53.1
Lloyd, J. (SNP)	6,984	19.2
Harris, E. (LD)	4,963	13.6
Newton, K. (Con)	4,606	12.6
Bain, J. (Ref)	543	1.5
Lab majority	12,354	33.91%
Electorate	52,467	
Total Vote	36,434	Poll 69.4%

*Member of last parliament
Lab Hold (6.1% Swing from SNP to Lab)

DURHAM NORTH

		%
*Radice, G. (Lab)	33,142	70.3
Hardy, M. (Con)	6,843	14.5
Moore, B. (LD)	5,225	11.1
Parkin, I. (Ref)	1,958	4.2
Lab majority	26,299	55.76%
Electorate	67,891	
Total Vote	47,168	Poll 69.4%

*Member of last parliament
Lab Hold (10.4% Swing from Con to Lab)

EALING NORTH

		%
Pound, S. (Lab)	29,904	53.7
*Greenway, H. (Con)	20,744	37.2
Gupta, A. (LD)	3,887	6.8
Slysz, G. (UKIP)	689	1.2
Seibe, A. (Green)	502	0.9
Lab majority	9,160	16.44%
Electorate	78,144	
Total Vote	55,726	Poll 72.3%

*Member of last parliament
Lab Gain (16.0% Swing from Con to Lab)

EALING SOUTHALL

		%
*Khabra, P. (Lab)	32,791	60.0
Penrose, J. (Con)	11,368	20.8
Thomson, N. (LD)	5,687	10.4
Brar, H. (SLP)	2,107	3.9
Goodwin, N. (Green)	934	1.7
Cherry, D. (Ref)	854	1.6
Klepacka, K. (Pro-Life)	473	0.9
Mead, R. (UKIP)	428	0.8
Lab majority	21,423	39.21%
Electorate	81,704	
Total Vote	54,642	Poll 65.7%

*Member of last parliament
Lab Hold (15.1% Swing from Con to Lab)

EALING, ACTON AND SHEPHERD'S BUSH

		%
*Soley, C. (Lab)	28,052	58.4
Yerolemou, B. (Con)	12,405	25.8
Mitchell, A. (LD)	5,163	10.7
Winn, C. (Ref)	637	1.3
Gilbert, J. (SLP)	635	1.3
Gomm, J. (UKIP)	385	0.8
Danon, P. (Pro-Life)	265	0.6
Beasley, C. (Glow)	209	0.4
Edwards, W. (Christian)	163	0.3
Turner, K. (NLP)	150	0.3
Lab majority	15,647	32.55%
Electorate	72,078	
Total Vote	48,064	Poll 64%

*Member of last parliament
Lab Hold (12.8% Swing from Con to Lab)

EASINGTON

		%
*Cummings, J. (Lab)	33,600	80.2
Hollands, J. (Con)	3,588	8.6
Heppell, J. (LD)	3,025	7.2
Pulfrey, R. (Ref)	1,179	2.8
Colborn, S. (Socialist)	503	1.2
Lab majority	30,012	71.64%
Electorate	62,518	
Total Vote	41,895	Poll 67%

*Member of last parliament
Lab Hold (7.8% Swing from Con to Lab)

EAST ANTRIM

		%
*Beggs, R. (UUP)	13,318	38.8
Neeson, S. (APNI)	6,929	20.2
McKee, J. (DUP)	6,682	19.5
Dick, T. (Con)	2,334	6.8
Donaldson, B. (PUP)	1,757	5.1
O'Connor, D. (SDLP)	1,576	4.6
Mason, R. (Ind)	1,145	3.3
McAuley, C. (SF)	543	1.6
McCann, M. (NLP)	69	0.2
UUP majority	6,389	18.60%
Electorate	58,963	
Total Vote	34,353	Poll 58.3%

*Member of last parliament
UUP Hold (0.1% Swing from APNI to UUP)

EAST DEVON

		%
*Emery, Sir P. (Con)	22,797	43.4
Trethewey, R. (LD)	15,308	29.1
Siantonas, A. (Lab)	9,292	17.7
Dixon, W. (Ref)	3,200	6.1
Halliwell, G. (Lib)	1,363	2.6
Giffard, C. (UKIP)	459	0.9
Needs, G. (Nat Dem)	131	0.2
Con majority	7,489	14.25%
Electorate	69,094	
Total Vote	52,550	Poll 75.9%

*Member of last parliament
Con Hold (5.6% Swing from Con to LD)

EAST HAM

		%
*Timms, S. (Lab)	25,779	64.6
Bray, A. (Con)	6,421	16.1
Khan, I. (SLP)	2,697	6.8
Sole, M. (LD)	2,599	6.5
Smith, C. (BNP)	1,258	3.2
McCann, J. (Ref)	845	2.1
Hardy, G. (Nat Dem)	290	0.7
Lab majority	19,358	48.53%
Electorate	65,591	
Total Vote	39,889	Poll 60.3%

*Member of last parliament
Lab Hold (13.3% Swing from Con to Lab)

EAST HAMPSHIRE

		%
*Mates, M. (Con)	27,927	48.0
Booker, R. (LD)	16,337	28.1
Hoyle, R. (Lab)	9,945	17.1
Hayter, J. (Ref)	2,757	4.7
Foster, I. (Green)	649	1.1
Coles, S. (UKIP)	513	0.9
Con majority	11,590	19.94%
Electorate	76,604	
Total Vote	58,128	Poll 75.8%

*Member of last parliament
Con Hold (6.6% Swing from Con to LD)

EAST KILBRIDE

		%
*Ingram, A. (Lab)	27,584	56.5
Gebbie, G. (SNP)	10,200	20.9
Herbertson, C. (Con)	5,863	12.0
Philbrick, K. (LD)	3,527	7.2
Deighan, J. (Pro-Life)	1,170	2.4
Gray, J. (Ref)	306	0.6
Gilmour, E. (NLP)	146	0.3
Lab majority 17,384		35.63%
Electorate 65,229		
Total Vote 48,796 Poll 74.8%		

*Member of last parliament
Lab Hold (5.9% Swing from SNP to Lab)

EAST LONDONDERRY

		%
*Ross, W. (UUP)	13,558	35.6
Campbell, G. (DUP)	9,764	25.6
Docherty, A. (SDLP)	8,273	21.7
O'Kane, M. (SF)	3,463	9.1
Boyle, Y. (APNI)	2,427	6.4
Holmes, J. (Con)	436	1.1
Gallen, C. (NLP)	100	0.3
Anderson, I. (Nat Dem)	81	0.2
UUP majority 3,794		9.96%
Electorate 58,831		
Total Vote 38,102 Poll 64.8%		

*Member of last parliament
UUP Hold (0% Swing from to)

EAST LOTHIAN

		%
*Home Robertson, J.		
(Lab)	22,881	52.7
Fraser, M. (Con)	8,660	19.9
McCarthy, D. (SNP)	6,825	15.7
MacAskill, A. (LD)	4,575	10.5
Nash, N. (Ref)	491	1.1
Lab majority 14,221		32.74%
Electorate 57,441		
Total Vote 43,432 Poll 75.6%		

*Member of last parliament
Lab Hold (8.7% Swing from Con to Lab)

EAST SURREY

		%
*Ainsworth, P. (Con)	27,389	50.1
Ford, B. (LD)	12,296	22.5
Ross, D. (Lab)	11,573	21.2
Sydney, M. (Ref)	2,656	4.9
Stone, A. (UKIP)	569	1.0
Bartrum, S. (NLP)	173	0.3
Con majority 15,093		27.61%
Electorate 72,852		
Total Vote 54,656 Poll 74.6%		

*Member of last parliament
Con Hold (3.3% Swing from Con to LD)

EAST WORTHING AND SHOREHAM

		%
Loughton, T. (Con)	20,864	40.5
King, M. (LD)	15,766	30.6
Williams, M. (Lab)	12,335	23.9
McCulloch, J. (Ref)	1,683	3.3
Jarvis, R. (UKIP)	921	1.8
Con majority 5,098		9.89%
Electorate 70,771		
Total Vote 51,569 Poll 72.9%		

Con Hold (3.9% Swing from Con to LD)

EASTBOURNE

		%
*Waterson, N. (Con)	22,183	42.1
Berry, C. (LD)	20,189	38.3
Lines, D. (Lab)	6,576	12.5
Lowe, T. (Ref)	2,724	5.2
Williamson, M. (Lib)	741	1.4
Dawkins, J. (UKIP)	254	0.5
Con majority 1,994		3.79%
Electorate 72,347		
Total Vote 52,667 Poll 72.8%		

*Member of last parliament
Con Hold (4% Swing from Con to LD)

EASTLEIGH

		%
*Chidgey, D. (LD)	19,453	35.1
Reid, S. (Con)	18,699	33.7
Lloyd, A. (Lab)	14,883	26.8
Eldridge, V. (Ref)	2,013	3.6
Robinson, P.		
(UKIP)	446	0.8
LD majority 754		1.36%
Electorate 72,155		
Total Vote 55,494 Poll 76.6%		

*Member of last parliament
LD Win (11.3% Swing from Con to LD)

EASTWOOD

		%
Murphy, J. (Lab)	20,766	39.7
Cullen, P. (Con)	17,530	33.5
Yates, D. (SNP)	6,826	13.1
Mason, C. (LD)	6,110	11.7
Miller, D. (Ref)	497	1.0
Tayan, M. (Pro-Life)	393	0.8
McPherson, D.		
(UKIP)	130	0.2
Lab majority 3,236		6.19%
Electorate 66,697		
Total Vote 52,252 Poll 78.2%		

Lab Gain (14.3% Swing from Con to Lab)

ECCLES

		%
Stewart, I. (Lab)	30,468	66.7
Barker, G. (Con)	8,552	18.7
Boyd, R. (LD)	4,905	10.7
de Roeck, J. (Ref)	1,765	3.9
Lab majority 21,916		47.97%
Electorate 69,645		
Total Vote 45,690 Poll 65.6%		

Lab Hold (10.7% Swing from Con to Lab)

EDDISBURY

		%
*Goodlad, A. (Con)	21,027	42.5
Hanson, M. (Lab)	19,842	40.1
Reaper, D. (LD)	6,540	13.2
Napier, N. (Ref)	2,041	4.1
Con majority 1,185		2.40%
Electorate 65,256		
Total Vote 49,450 Poll 75.6%		

*Member of last parliament
Con Hold (9.6% Swing from Con to Lab)

EDINBURGH CENTRAL

		%
*Darling, A. (Lab)	20,125	47.1
Scott-Hayward, M.		
(Con)	9,055	21.2
Hyslop, F. (SNP)	6,750	15.8

Utting, K. (LD)	5,605	13.1
Hendry, L. (Green)	607	1.4
Skinner, A. (Ref)	495	1.2
Benson, M. (Ind Dem)	98	0.2
Lab majority 11,070		25.90%
Electorate 63,695		
Total Vote 42,735 Poll 67.1%		

*Member of last parliament
Lab Hold (8.4% Swing from Con to Lab)

EDINBURGH EAST AND MUSSELBURGH

		%
*Strang, G. (Lab)	22,564	53.6
White, D. (SNP)	8,034	19.1
Ward, K. (Con)	6,483	15.4
MacKellar, C. (LD)	4,511	10.7
Sibbet, J. (Ref)	526	1.2
Lab majority 14,530		34.50%
Electorate 59,648		
Total Vote 42,118 Poll 70.6%		

*Member of last parliament
Lab Hold (3.9% Swing from SNP to Lab)

EDINBURGH NORTH AND LEITH

		%
*Chisholm, M. (Lab)	19,209	46.9
Dana, A. (SNP)	8,231	20.1
Stewart, E. (Con)	7,312	17.9
Campbell, H. (LD)	5,335	13.0
Graham, S. (Ref)	441	1.1
Brown, G. (ScotSoc)	320	0.8
Douglas-Reid, P.		
(NLP)	97	0.2
Lab majority 10,978		26.81%
Electorate 61,617		
Total Vote 40,945 Poll 66.5%		

*Member of last parliament
Lab Hold (6.1% Swing from SNP to Lab)

EDINBURGH PENTLANDS

		%
Clark, L. (Lab)	19,675	43.0
*Rifkind, M. (Con)	14,813	32.4
Gibb, S. (SNP)	5,952	13.0
Dawe, J. (LD)	4,575	10.0
McDonald, M. (Ref)	422	0.9
Harper, R. (Green)	224	0.5
McConnachie, A.		
(UKIP)	81	0.2
Lab majority 4,862		10.63%
Electorate 59,635		
Total Vote 45,742 Poll 76.7%		

*Member of last parliament
Lab Gain (9.8% Swing from Con to Lab)

EDINBURGH SOUTH

		%
*Griffiths, N. (Lab)	20,993	46.8
Smith, E. (Con)	9,541	21.3
Pringle, M. (LD)	7,911	17.6
Hargreaves, J. (SNP)	5,791	12.9
McLean, I. (Ref)	504	1.1
Dunn, B. (NLP)	98	0.2
Lab majority 11,452		25.54%
Electorate 62,467		
Total Vote 44,838 Poll 71.8%		

*Member of last parliament
Lab Hold (8.1% Swing from Con to Lab)

EDINBURGH WEST

		%
Gorrie, D. (LD)	20,578	43.2
*Douglas-Hamilton, J. (Con)	13,325	28.0
Hinds, L. (Lab)	8,948	18.8
Sutherland, G. (SNP)	4,210	8.8
Elphick, S. (Ref)	277	0.6
Coombes, P. (Lib)	263	0.6
Jack, A. (AntiSleaze)	30	0.1
LD majority	7,253	15.23%
Electorate	61,133	
Total Vote	47,631	Poll 77.9%

*Member of last parliament
LD Gain (11.8% Swing from Con to LD)

EDMONTON

		%
Love, A. (Lab/Co-op)	27,029	60.3
*Twinn, I. (Con)	13,557	30.2
Wiseman, A. (LD)	2,847	6.3
Wright, J. (Ref)	708	1.6
Cowd, B. (BNP)	437	1.0
Weald, P. (UKIP)	260	0.6
Lab/Co-op majority	13,472	30.05%
Electorate	63,718	
Total Vote	44,838	Poll 70.4%

*Member of last parliament
Lab/Co-op Gain (15.6% Swing from Con to Lab)

ELLESMERE PORT AND NESTON

		%
*Miller, A. (Lab)	31,310	59.6
Turnbull, L. (Con)	15,275	29.1
Pemberton, J. (LD)	4,673	8.9
Rodden, C. (Ref)	1,305	2.5
Lab majority	16,036	30.51%
Electorate	67,573	
Total Vote	52,563	Poll 77.6%

*Member of last parliament
Lab Hold (12.4% Swing from Con to Lab)

ELMET

		%
Burgon, C. (Lab)	28,348	52.4
*Batiste, S. (Con)	19,569	36.2
Jennings, B. (LD)	4,691	8.7
Zawadski, C. (Ref)	1,487	2.7
Lab majority	8,779	16.23%
Electorate	70,423	
Total Vote	54,095	Poll 76.7%

*Member of last parliament
Lab Gain (10.9% Swing from Con to Lab)

ELTHAM

		%
Efford, C. (Lab)	23,710	54.6
Blackwood, C. (Con)	13,528	31.2
Taylor, A. (LD)	3,701	8.5
Clark, M. (Ref)	1,414	3.3
Middleton, H. (Lib)	584	1.3
Hitches, W. (BNP)	491	1.1
Lab majority	10,182	23.45%
Electorate	57,358	
Total Vote	43,428	Poll 75.2%

Lab Gain (13.6% Swing from Con to Lab)

ENFIELD NORTH

		%
Ryan, J. (Lab)	24,148	50.7
Field, M. (Con)	17,326	36.4
Hopkins, M. (LD)	4,264	8.9
Ellingham, R. (Ref)	857	1.8
Griffin, J. (BNP)	590	1.2
O'Ware, J. (UKIP)	484	1.0
Lab majority	6,822	14.31%
Electorate	67,748	
Total Vote	47,669	Poll 70.4%

Lab Gain (16.1% Swing from Con to Lab)

ENFIELD SOUTHGATE

		%
Twigg, S. (Lab)	20,570	44.2
*Portillo, M. (Con)	19,137	41.1
Browne, J. (LD)	4,966	10.7
Luard, N. (Ref)	1,342	2.9
Storkey, A. (Christ Dem)	289	0.6
Malakouna, A. (Mal Voice)	229	0.5
Lab majority	1,433	3.08%
Electorate	65,796	
Total Vote	46,533	Poll 70.7%

*Member of last parliament
Lab Gain (17.4% Swing from Con to Lab)

EPPING FOREST

		%
Laing, E. (Con)	24,117	45.5
Murray, S. (Lab)	18,865	35.6
Robinson, S. (LD)	7,074	13.3
Berry, J. (Ref)	2,208	4.2
Henderson, P. (BNP)	743	1.4
Con majority	5,252	9.91%
Electorate	72,795	
Total Vote	53,007	Poll 72.8%

Con Hold (13.6% Swing from Con to Lab)

EPSOM AND EWELL

		%
*Hamilton, A. (Con)	24,717	45.6
Woodford, P. (Lab)	13,192	24.3
Vincent, J. (LD)	12,380	22.8
MacDonald, C. (Ref)	2,355	4.3
Green, H. (UKIP)	544	1.0
Charlton, H. (Green)	527	1.0
Weeks, K. (Pro-Life)	466	0.9
Con majority	11,525	21.27%
Electorate	73,322	
Total Vote	54,181	Poll 74%

*Member of last parliament
Con Hold (12.4% Swing from Con to Lab)

EREWASH

		%
Blackman, E. (Lab)	31,196	51.7
*Knight, A. (Con)	22,061	36.6
Garnett, M. (LD)	5,181	8.6
Stagg, S. (Ref)	1,404	2.3
Simmons, M. (SLP)	496	0.8
Lab majority	9,135	15.14%
Electorate	77,402	
Total Vote	60,338	Poll 77.8%

*Member of last parliament
Lab Gain (12.1% Swing from Con to Lab)

ERITH AND THAMESMEAD

		%
*Austin-Walker, J. (Lab)	25,812	62.1
Zahawi, N. (Con)	8,388	20.2
Grigg, A. (LD)	5,001	12.0
Flunder, J. (Ref)	1,394	3.4
Dooley, V. (BNP)	718	1.7
Jackson, M. (UKIP)	274	0.7
Lab majority	17,424	41.90%
Electorate	62,887	
Total Vote	41,587	Poll 66%

*Member of last parliament
Lab Hold (15.3% Swing from Con to Lab)

ESHER AND WALTON

		%
*Taylor, I. (Con)	26,747	49.8
Reay, J. (Lab)	12,219	22.8
Miles, G. (LD)	10,937	20.4
Cruickshank, A. (Ref)	2,904	5.4
Collignon, B. (UKIP)	558	1.0
Kay, S. (Dream)	302	0.6
Con majority	14,528	27.07%
Electorate	72,382	
Total Vote	53,667	Poll 74.3%

*Member of last parliament
Con Hold (8.1% Swing from Con to Lab)

EXETER

		%
Bradshaw, B. (Lab)	29,398	47.5
Rogers, A. (Con)	17,693	28.6
Brewer, D. (LD)	11,148	18.0
Morrish, D. (Lib)	2,062	3.3
Edwards, P. (Green)	643	1.0
Haynes, C. (UKIP)	638	1.0
Meakin, J. (Pensioners)	282	0.5
Lab majority	11,705	18.92%
Electorate	79,154	
Total Vote	61,864	Poll 77.6%

Lab Gain (11.9% Swing from Con to Lab)

FALKIRK EAST

		%
*Connarty, M. (Lab)	23,344	56.1
Brown, K. (SNP)	9,959	23.9
Nicol, M. (Con)	5,813	14.0
Spillane, R. (LD)	2,153	5.2
Mowbray, S. (Ref)	325	0.8
Lab majority	13,385	32.18%
Electorate	56,792	
Total Vote	41,594	Poll 73.2%

*Member of last parliament
Lab Hold (8.2% Swing from SNP to Lab)

FALKIRK WEST

		%
*Canavan, D. (Lab)	22,772	60.01
Alexander, D. (SNP)	8,989	23.4
Buchanan, C. (Con)	4,639	12.1
Houston, D. (LD)	1,970	5.1
Lab majority	13,783	35.92%
Electorate	52,850	
Total Vote	38,370	Poll 72.6%

*Member of last parliament
Lab Hold (4% Swing from SNP to Lab)

FALMOUTH AND CAMBORNE

		%
Atherton, C. (Lab)	18,151	33.8
*Coe, S. (Con)	15,463	28.8
Jones, T. (LD)	13,512	25.2
de Savary, P. (Ref)	3,534	6.6
Geach, J. (Ind Lab)	1,691	3.2
Holmes, P. (Lib)	527	1.0
Smith, R. (UKIP)	355	0.7
Lewarne, R. (MK)	238	0.4
Glitter, G. (Loony)	161	0.3
Lab majority	2,688	5.01%
Electorate	71,383	
Total Vote	53,632	Poll 75.1%

*Member of last parliament
Lab Gain (6.4% Swing from Con to Lab)

FAREHAM

		%
*Lloyd, Sir P. (Con)	24,436	46.8
Prior, M. (Lab)	14,078	27.0
Hill, G. (LD)	10,234	19.6
Markham, W. (Ref)	2,914	5.6
O'Brian, W. (Ind)	515	1.0
Con majority	10,358	19.85%
Electorate	68,787	
Total Vote	52,177	Poll 75.9%

*Member of last parliament
Con Hold (13% Swing from Con to Lab)

FAVERSHAM AND MID KENT

		%
*Rowe, A. (Con)	22,016	44.4
Stewart, A. (Lab)	17,843	36.0
Parmenter, B. (LD)	6,138	12.4
Birley, R. (Ref)	2,073	4.2
Davidson, N. (Loony)	511	1.0
Cunningham, M. (UKIP)	431	0.9
Currer, D. (Green)	380	0.8
Morgan, C. (Street)	115	0.2
Pollard, N. (NLP)	99	0.2
Con majority	4,173	8.41%
Electorate	67,490	
Total Vote	49,606	Poll 73.3%

*Member of last parliament
Con Hold (13.9% Swing from Con to Lab)

FELTHAM AND HESTON   %

*Keen, A. (Lab/Co-op)	27,836	60.0
Ground, R. (Con)	12,563	26.7
Penning, C. (LD)	4,264	9.2
Stubbs, R. (Ref)	1,099	2.4
Church, R. (BNP)	682	1.5
Fawcett, D. (NLP)	177	0.4
Lab/Co-op majority	15,273	32.76%
Electorate	71,093	
Total Vote	46,621	Poll 65.6%

*Member of last parliament
Lab/Co-op Hold (15.4% Swing from Con to Lab)

FERMANAGH AND SOUTH TYRONE   %

*Maginnis, K. (UUP)	24,862	51.5
McHugh, G. (SF)	11,174	23.1
Gallagher, T. (SDLP)	11,060	22.9

Farry, S. (APNI)	977	2.0
Gillan, S. (NLP)	217	0.4
UUP majority	13,688	28.35%
Electorate	64,600	
Total Vote	48,290	Poll 74.8%

*Member of last parliament
UUP Hold (2.4% Swing from UUP to SF)

FINCHLEY AND GOLDERS GREEN   %

Vis, R. (Lab)	23,180	46.1
*Marshall, J. (Con)	19,991	39.7
Davies, J. (LD)	5,670	11.3
Shaw, G. (Ref)	684	1.4
Gunstock, A. (Green)	576	1.1
Barraclough, D. (UKIP)	205	0.4
Lab majority	3,189	6.34%
Electorate	72,225	
Total Vote	50,306	Poll 68.2%

*Member of last parliament
Lab Gain (15.1% Swing from Con to Lab)

FOLKESTONE AND HYTHE   %

*Howard, M. (Con)	20,313	39.0
Laws, D. (LD)	13,981	26.9
Doherty, P. (Lab)	12,939	24.9
Aspinall, J. (Ref)	4,188	8.0
Baker, J. (UKIP)	378	0.7
Segal, E. (Soc)	182	0.3
Saint, R. (Field Sport)	69	0.1
Con majority	6,332	12.17%
Electorate	71,153	
Total Vote	52,050	Poll 72.7%

*Member of last parliament
Con Hold (2.4% Swing from Con to LD)

FOREST OF DEAN   %

Organ, D. (Lab)	24,203	48.2
*Marland, P. (Con)	17,860	35.6
Lynch, A. (LD)	6,165	12.3
Hopkins, J. (Ref)	1,624	3.2
Morgan, G. (Ind)	218	0.4
Palmer, C. (21stCent)	80	0.2
Porter, S. (IndForest)	34	0.1
Lab majority	6,343	12.64%
Electorate	63,465	
Total Vote	50,184	Poll 79.1%

*Member of last parliament
Lab Gain (5.6% Swing from Con to Lab)

FOYLE   %

*Hume, J. (SDLP)	25,109	52.5
McLaughlin, M. (SF)	11,445	23.9
Hay, W. (DUP)	10,290	21.5
Bell, E. (APNI)	817	1.7
Brennan, D. (NLP)	154	0.3
SDLP majority	13,664	28.58%
Electorate	67,620	
Total Vote	47,815	Poll 70.7%

*Member of last parliament
SDLP Hold (4% Swing from SDLP to SF)

FYLDE   %

*Jack, M. (Con)	25,443	48.9
Garrett, J. (Lab)	16,480	31.7
Greene, W. (LD)	7,609	14.6

Britton, D. (Ref)	2,372	4.6
Kerwin, T. (NLP)	163	0.3
Con majority	8,963	17.21%
Electorate	71,385	
Total Vote	52,067	Poll 72.8%

*Member of last parliament
Con Hold (12.2% Swing from Con to Lab)

GAINSBOROUGH   %

*Leigh, E. (Con)	20,593	43.1
Taylor, P. (Lab)	13,767	28.8
Taylor, N. (LD)	13,436	28.1
Con majority	6,826	14.28%
Electorate	63,106	
Total Vote	47,796	Poll 74.6%

*Member of last parliament
Con Hold (9.1% Swing from Con to Lab)

GALLOWAY AND UPPER NITHSDALE   %

Morgan, A. (SNP)	18,449	43.9
*Lang, I. (Con)	12,825	30.5
Clark, K. (Lab)	6,861	16.3
McKerchar, J. (LD)	2,700	6.4
Wood, R. (Ind)	566	1.3
Kennedy, A. (Ref)	428	1.0
Smith, J. (UKIP)	189	0.4
SNP majority	5,624	13.38%
Electorate	52,751	
Total Vote	42,018	Poll 79.7%

*Member of last parliament
SNP Gain (9.5% Swing from Con to SNP)

GATESHEAD EAST AND WASHINGTON WEST   %

*Quin, J. (Lab)	31,047	72.1
Burns, J. (Con)	6,097	14.2
Ord, A. (LD)	4,622	10.7
Daley, M. (Ref)	1,315	3.1
Lab majority	24,950	57.91%
Electorate	64,114	
Total Vote	43,081	Poll 67.2%

*Member of last parliament
Lab Hold (13.8% Swing from Con to Lab)

GEDLING   %

Coaker, V. (Lab)	24,390	46.8
*Mitchell, A. (Con)	20,588	39.5
Poynter, R. (LD)	5,180	9.9
Connor, J. (Ref)	2,006	3.8
Lab majority	3,802	7.29%
Electorate	68,820	
Total Vote	52,164	Poll 75.6%

*Member of last parliament
Lab Gain (13% Swing from Con to Lab)

GILLINGHAM   %

Clark, P. (Lab)	20,187	39.8
*Couchman, J. (Con)	18,207	35.9
Sayer, R. (LD)	9,649	19.0
Cann, G. (Ref)	1,492	2.9
MacKinlay, C. (UKIP)	590	1.2
Robinson, D. (Loony)	305	0.6
Jury, C. (BNP)	195	0.4
Duguay, G. (NLP)	58	0.1
Lab majority	1,980	3.91%
Electorate	70,389	
Total Vote	50,683	Poll 72%

*Member of last parliament
Lab Gain (16% Swing from Con to Lab)

GLASGOW ANNIESLAND %
*Dewar, D. (Lab)	20,951	61.8	
Wilson, W. (SNP)	5,797	17.1	
Brocklehurst, R.			
(Con)	3,881	11.5	
McGinty, C. (LD)	2,453	7.2	
Majid, A. (Pro-Life)	374	1.1	
Bonnar, B. (ScotSoc)	229	0.7	
Milligan, A. (UKIP)	86	0.3	
McKay, G. (Ref)	84	0.2	
Pringle, T. (NLP)	24	0.1	
Lab majority	15,154	44.73%	
Electorate	52,955		
Total Vote	33,879	Poll 63.8%	

*Member of last parliament
Lab Hold (4.3% Swing from SNP to Lab)

GLASGOW BAILLIESTON %
*Wray, J. (Lab)	20,925	65.7
Thomson, P. (SNP)	6,085	19.1
Kelly, M. (Con)	2,468	7.7
Rainger, S. (LD)	1,217	3.8
McVicar, J. (ScotSoc)	970	3.0
McClafferty, J. (Ref)	188	0.6
Lab majority	14,840	46.59%
Electorate	51,152	
Total Vote	31,853	Poll 62.2%

*Member of last parliament
Lab Hold (3% Swing from SNP to Lab)

GLASGOW CATHCART %
*Maxton, J. (Lab)	19,158	57.4
Whitehead, M. (SNP)	6,193	18.5
Muir, A. (Con)	4,248	12.7
Dick, G. (LD)	2,302	6.9
Indyk, Z. (Pro-Life)	687	2.1
Stevenson, R.		
(ScotSoc)	458	1.4
Haldane, S. (Ref)	344	1.0
Lab majority	12,965	38.83%
Electorate	49,312	
Total Vote	33,390	Poll 67.7%

*Member of last parliament
Lab Hold (4.3% Swing from SNP to Lab)

GLASGOW GOVAN %
Sarwar, M. (Lab)	14,216	44.1
Sturgeon, N. (SNP)	11,302	35.1
Thomas, W. (Con)	2,839	8.8
Stewart, R. (LD)	1,918	5.9
McCombes, A.		
(ScotSoc)	755	2.3
Paton, P. (Ind)	325	1.0
Badar, I. (IndLab)	319	1.0
Abbassi, Z. (IndCon)	221	0.7
MacDonald, K. (Ref)	201	0.6
White, J. (BNP)	149	0.5
Lab majority	2,914	9.04%
Electorate	49,836	
Total Vote	32,245	Poll 64.7%

Lab Hold (3.2% Swing from Lab to SNP)

GLASGOW KELVIN %
*Galloway, G. (Lab)	16,643	51.0
White, S. (SNP)	6,978	21.4
Buchanan, E. (LD)	4,629	14.2
McPhie, D. (Con)	3,539	10.8

Green, A. (Scot Soc)	386	1.2
Grigor, R. (Ref)	282	0.9
Vanni, V. (SPGB)	102	0.3
Stidolph, G. (NLP)	95	0.3
Lab majority	9,665	29.60%
Electorate	57,438	
Total Vote	32,654	Poll 56.1%

*Member of last parliament
Lab Hold (1% Swing from SNP to Lab)

GLASGOW MARYHILL %
*Fyfe, M. (Lab)	19,301	64.9
Wailes, J. (SNP)	5,037	16.9
Attwooll, E. (LD)	2,119	7.1
Baldwin, S. (Con)	1,747	5.9
Blair, L. (NLP)	651	2.2
Baker, M. (Scot Soc)	409	1.4
Hanif, J. (Pro-Life)	344	1.2
Paterson, R. (Ref)	77	0.3
Johnstone, S. (SEP)	36	0.1
Lab majority	14,264	47.99%
Electorate	52,523	
Total Vote	29,721	Poll 56.4%

*Member of last parliament
Lab Hold (2.4% Swing from SNP to Lab)

GLASGOW POLLOK %
*Davidson, I.		
(Lab/Co-op)	19,653	59.9
Logan, D. (SNP)	5,862	17.9
Sheridan, T.		
(Scot Soc)	3,639	11.1
Hamilton, E. (Con)	1,979	6.0
Jago, D. (LD)	1,137	3.5
Gott, M. (Pro-Life)	380	1.2
Haldane, D. (Ref)	152	0.5
Lab/Co-op		
majority	13,791	42.04%
Electorate	49,284	
Total Vote	32,802	Poll 66.5%

*Member of last parliament
Lab/Co-op Hold (8.6% Swing from SNP to Lab)

GLASGOW RUTHERGLEN %
*McAvoy, T.		
(Lab/Co-op)	20,430	57.5
Gray, I. (SNP)	5,423	15.3
Brown, R. (LD)	5,167	14.5
Campbell-Bannerman,		
D. (Con)	3,288	9.3
Easton, G. (IndLab)	812	2.3
Kane, R. (ScotSoc)	251	0.7
Kerr, J. (Ref)	150	0.4
Lab/Co-op		
majority	15,007	42.25%
Electorate	50,646	
Total Vote	35,521	Poll 70.1%

*Member of last parliament
Lab/Co-op Hold (2.2% Swing from SNP to Lab)

GLASGOW SHETTLESTON %
*Marshall, D. (Lab)	19,616	73.2
Hanif, H. (SNP)	3,748	14.0
Simpson, C. (Con)	1,484	5.5
Hiles, K. (LD)	1,061	4.0

McVicar, C. (Scot Soc)	482	1.8
Currie, R. (BNP)	191	0.7
Montguire, T. (Ref)	151	0.6
Graham, J. (WRP)	80	0.3
Lab majority	15,868	59.18%
Electorate	47,990	
Total Vote	26,813	Poll 54.6%

*Member of last parliament
Lab Hold (4.9% Swing from SNP to Lab)

GLASGOW SPRINGBURN %
*Martin, M. (Lab)	22,534	71.4
Brady, J. (SNP)	5,208	16.5
Holdsworth, M. (Con)	1,893	6.0
Alexander, J. (LD)	1,349	4.3
Lawson, J. (Scot Soc)	407	1.3
Keating, A. (Ref)	186	0.6
Lab majority	17,326	54.87%
Electorate	53,473	
Total Vote	31,577	Poll 58.9%

*Member of last parliament
Lab Hold (4.9% Swing from SNP to Lab)

GLOUCESTER %
Kingham, T. (Lab)	28,943	50.0
*French, D. (Con)	20,684	35.7
Munisamy, P. (LD)	6,069	10.5
Reid, A. (Ref)	1,482	2.6
Harris, A. (UKIP)	455	0.8
Hamilton, M. (NLP)	281	0.5
Lab majority	8,259	14.26%
Electorate	78,682	
Total Vote	57,914	Poll 73.6%

*Member of last parliament
Lab Gain (11.5% Swing from Con to Lab)

GORDON %
*Bruce, M. (LD)	17,999	42.6
Porter, J. (Con)	11,002	26.0
Lochhead, R. (SNP)	8,435	20.0
Kirkhill, L. (Lab)	4,350	10.3
Pidcock, F. (Ref)	459	1.1
LD majority	6,997	16.56%
Electorate	58,767	
Total Vote	42,245	Poll 71.9%

*Member of last parliament
LD Win (18.7% Swing from Con to LD)

GOSPORT %
*Viggers, P. (Con)	21,085	43.6
Gray, I. (Lab)	14,827	30.7
Hogg, S. (LD)	9,479	19.6
Blowers, A. (Ref)	2,538	5.2
Ettie, P. (Ind)	426	0.9
Con majority	6,258	12.94%
Electorate	68,830	
Total Vote	48,355	Poll 70.3%

*Member of last parliament
Con Hold (15.8% Swing from Con to Lab)

GOWER %
Caton, M. (Lab)	23,313	53.8
Cairns, A. (Con)	10,306	23.8
Evans, H. (LD)	5,624	13.0
Williams, D. (PC)	2,226	5.1
Lewis, R. (Ref)	1,745	4.0
Popham, A. (Freedom)	122	0.3

Lab majority 13,007   30.01%
Electorate   57,691
Total Vote   43,336 Poll 74.9%
Lab Hold (7.5% Swing from Con to Lab)

GRANTHAM AND STAMFORD

		%
*Davies, Q. (Con)	22,672	42.8
Denning, P. (Lab)	19,980	37.7
Sellick, J. (LD)	6,612	12.5
Swain, M. (Ref)	2,721	5.1
Charlesworth, M. (UKIP)	556	1.0
Clark, R. (Pro-Life)	314	0.6
Harper, I. (NLP)	115	0.2
Con majority	2,692	5.08%
Electorate	72,310	
Total Vote	52,970	Poll 73.3%

*Member of last parliament
Con Hold (13.3% Swing from Con to Lab)

GRAVESHAM

		%
Pond, C. (Lab)	26,460	49.7
*Arnold, J. (Con)	20,681	38.8
Canet, J. (LD)	4,128	7.8
Curtis, P. (Ref)	1,441	2.7
Leyshon, A. (Ind)	414	0.8
Palmer, D. (NLP)	129	0.2
Lab majority	5,779	10.85%
Electorate	69,234	
Total Vote	53,253	Poll 76.7%

*Member of last parliament
Lab Gain (10% Swing from Con to Lab)

GREAT GRIMSBY

		%
*Mitchell, A. (Lab)	25,765	59.8
Godson, D. (Con)	9,521	22.1
De Freitas, A. (LD)	7,810	18.1
Lab majority	16,244	37.69%
Electorate	65,043	
Total Vote	43,096	Poll 66.1%

*Member of last parliament
Lab Hold (11.5% Swing from Con to Lab)

GREAT YARMOUTH

		%
*Wright, T. (Lab)	26,084	53.4
Carttiss, M. (Con)	17,416	35.6
Wood, D. (LD)	5,381	11.0
Lab majority	8,668	17.73%
Electorate	68,625	
Total Vote	48,881	Poll 71.1%

*Member of last parliament
Lab Gain (13.9% Swing from Con to Lab)

GREENOCK AND INVERCLYDE

		%
*Godman, N. (Lab)	19,480	56.2
Goodall, B. (SNP)	6,440	18.6
Ackland, R. (LD)	4,791	13.8
Swire, H. (Con)	3,976	11.5
Lab majority	13,040	37.59%
Electorate	48,818	
Total Vote	34,687	Poll 71.1%

*Member of last parliament
Lab Hold (3.5% Swing from SNP to Lab)

GREENWICH AND WOOLWICH

		%
*Raynsford, N. (Lab)	25,630	63.4
Mitchell, M. (Con)	7,502	18.6
Luxton, C. (LD)	5,049	12.5
Ellison, D. (Ref)	1,670	4.1
Mallone, R. (Fellowship)	428	1.1
Martin-Eagle, D. (Constit)	124	0.3
Lab majority	18,128	44.87%
Electorate	61,352	
Total Vote	40,403	Poll 64.9%

*Member of last parliament
Lab Hold (9.3% Swing from Con to Lab)

GUILDFORD

		%
St Aubyn, N. (Con)	24,230	42.5
Sharp, M. (LD)	19,439	34.1
Burns, J. (Lab)	9,945	17.5
Gore, J. (Ref)	2,650	4.7
McWhirter, R. (UKIP)	400	0.7
Morris, J. (Pacifist)	294	0.5
Con majority	4,791	8.41%
Electorate	75,541	
Total Vote	56,958	Poll 75.4%

Con Hold (7.1% Swing from Con to LD)

HACKNEY NORTH AND STOKE NEWINGTON

		%
*Abbott, D. (Lab)	21,110	65.2
Lavender, M. (Con)	5,483	16.9
Taylor, D. (LD)	3,306	10.2
Chong, Y. (Green)	1,395	4.3
Maxwell, B. (Ref)	544	1.7
Tolson, D. (None)	368	1.1
Lovebucket, L. (Rainbow Ref)	176	0.5
Lab majority	15,627	48.26%
Electorate	62,045	
Total Vote	32,382	Poll 51.2%

*Member of last parliament
Lab Hold (8.7% Swing from Con to Lab)

HACKNEY SOUTH AND SHOREDITCH

		%
*Sedgemore, B. (Lab)	20,048	59.4
Pantling, M. (LD)	5,068	15.0
O'Leary, C. (Con)	4,494	13.3
Betts, T. (New Labour)	2,436	7.2
Franklin, R. (Ref)	613	1.8
Callow, G. (BNP)	531	1.6
Goldman, M. (Comm)	298	0.9
Goldberg, M. (NLP)	145	0.4
Rogers, W. (WRP)	139	0.4
Lab majority	14,980	44.36%
Electorate	61,728	
Total Vote	33,772	Poll 54%

*Member of last parliament
Lab Hold (3% Swing from LD to Lab)

HALESOWEN AND ROWLEY REGIS

		%
Heal, S. (Lab)	26,366	54.1
Kennedy, J. (Con)	16,029	32.9
Todd, E. (LD)	4,169	8.5
White, P. (Ref)	1,244	2.6

Needs, K. (Nat Dem)	592	1.2
Weller, T. (Green)	361	0.7
Lab majority	10,337	21.20%
Electorate	66,245	
Total Vote	48,761	Poll 73.6%

Lab Gain (10.7% Swing from Con to Lab)

HALIFAX

		%
*Mahon, A. (Lab)	27,465	54.3
Light, R. (Con)	16,253	32.1
Waller, E. (LD)	6,059	12.0
Whitaker, C. (UKIP)	779	1.5
Lab majority	11,212	22.18%
Electorate	71,701	
Total Vote	50,556	Poll 70.5%

*Member of last parliament
Lab Hold (10.7% Swing from Con to Lab)

HALTEMPRICE AND HOWDEN

		%
*Davis, D. (Con)	21,809	44.0
Wallis, D. (LD)	14,295	28.8
McManus, G. (Lab)	11,701	23.6
Pearson, T. (Ref)	1,370	2.8
Bloom, G. (UKIP)	301	0.6
Strevens, B. (NLP)	74	0.1
Con majority	7,514	15.16%
Electorate	65,602	
Total Vote	49,550	Poll 75.4%

*Member of last parliament
Con Hold (9.5% Swing from Con to LD)

HALTON

		%
Twigg, J. (Lab)	31,497	70.9
Balmer, P. (Con)	7,847	17.7
Jones, J. (LD)	3,263	7.3
Atkins, R. (Ref)	1,036	2.3
Proffitt, D. (Lib)	600	1.4
Alley, J. (Republican)	196	0.4
Lab majority	23,650	53.22%
Electorate	64,987	
Total Vote	44,439	Poll 68.4%

Lab Hold (11.9% Swing from Con to Lab)

HAMILTON NORTH AND BELLSHILL

		%
*Reid, J. (Lab)	24,322	64.0
Matheson, M. (SNP)	7,255	19.1
McIntosh, G. (Con)	3,944	10.4
Legg, K. (LD)	1,924	5.1
Conn, R. (Ref)	554	1.5
Lab majority	17,067	44.91%
Electorate	53,607	
Total Vote	37,999	Poll 70.9%

*Member of last parliament
Lab Hold (3.2% Swing from SNP to Lab)

HAMILTON SOUTH

		%
*Robertson, G. (Lab)	21,709	65.6
Black, I. (SNP)	5,831	17.6
Kilgour, R. (Con)	2,858	8.6
Pitts, R. (LD)	1,693	5.1
Gunn, C. (Pro-Life)	684	2.1
Brown, S. (Ref)	316	1.0
Lab majority	15,878	47.98%
Electorate	46,562	
Total Vote	33,091	Poll 71.1%

*Member of last parliament
Lab Hold (5.7% Swing from SNP to Lab)

HAMMERSMITH AND FULHAM %
Coleman, I. (Lab) 25,262 46.8
*Carrington, M.
(Con) 21,420 39.6
Sugden, A. (LD) 4,728 8.8
Bremner, M. (Ref) 1,023 1.9
Johnson-Smith, W.
(New Labour) 695 1.3
Streeter, E. (Green) 562 1.0
Roberts, G. (UKIP) 183 0.3
Phillips, A. (NLP) 79 0.1
Elston, A. (Care) 74 0.1
Lab majority 3,842 7.11%
Electorate 78,637
Total Vote 54,026 Poll 68.7%
*Member of last parliament
Lab Gain (10.1% Swing from Con to Lab)

HAMPSTEAD AND HIGHGATE %
*Jackson, G. (Lab) 25,275 57.4
Gibson, E. (Con) 11,991 27.2
Fox, B. (LD) 5,481 12.4
Siddique, M. (Ref) 667 1.5
Leslie, J. (NLP) 147 0.3
Carroll, R. (Dream) 141 0.3
Prince, P. (UKIP) 123 0.3
Harris, R. (Humanist) 105 0.2
Rizz, C. (Rizz) 101 0.2
Lab majority 13,284 30.24%
Electorate 64,889
Total Vote 44,031 Poll 67.9%
*Member of last parliament
Lab Hold (12.4% Swing from Con to Lab)

HARBOROUGH %
*Garnier, E. (Con) 22,170 41.8
Cox, M. (LD) 15,646 29.5
Holden, N. (Lab) 13,332 25.2
Wright, N. (Ref) 1,859 3.5
Con majority 6,524 12.31%
Electorate 70,424
Total Vote 53,007 Poll 75.3%
*Member of last parliament
Con Hold (3% Swing from Con to LD)

HARLOW %
Rammell, B. (Lab) 25,861 54.1
*Hayes, J. (Con) 15,347 32.1
Spenceley, L. (LD) 4,523 9.5
Wells, M. (Ref) 1,422 3.0
Batten, G. (UKIP) 340 0.7
Bowles, J. (BNP) 319 0.7
Lab majority 10,514 21.99%
Electorate 64,072
Total Vote 47,812 Poll 74.4%
*Member of last parliament
Lab Gain (12.6% Swing from Con to Lab)

HARROGATE AND KNARESBOROUGH %
Willis, P. (LD) 24,558 51.5
*Lamont, N. (Con) 18,322 38.5
Boyce, B. (Lab) 4,151 8.7
Blackburn, J.
(IndCon) 614 1.3

LD majority 6,236 13.09%
Electorate 65,155
Total Vote 47,645 Poll 72.9%
*Member of last parliament
LD Gain (15.7% Swing from Con to LD)

HARROW EAST %
McNulty, T. (Lab) 29,923 52.5
*Dykes, H. (Con) 20,189 35.4
Sharma, B. (LD) 4,697 8.2
Casey, B. (Ref) 1,537 2.7
Scholefield, A. (UKIP) 464 0.8
Planton, A. (NLP) 171 0.3
Lab majority 9,734 17.09%
Electorate 79,846
Total Vote 56,981 Poll 71.4%
*Member of last parliament
Lab Gain (18.1% Swing from Con to Lab)

HARROW WEST %
Thomas, G. (Lab) 21,811 41.5
*Hughes, R. (Con) 20,571 39.2
Nandhra, P. (LD) 8,127 15.5
Crossman, H. (Ref) 1,997 3.8
Lab majority 1,240 2.36%
Electorate 72,005
Total Vote 52,506 Poll 72.2%
*Member of last parliament
Lab Gain (17.5% Swing from Con to Lab)

HARTLEPOOL %
*Mandelson, P. (Lab) 26,997 60.7
Horsley, M. (Con) 9,489 21.3
Clark, R. (LD) 6,248 14.1
Henderson, M. (Ref) 1,718 3.9
Lab majority 17,508 39.39%
Electorate 67,712
Total Vote 44,452 Poll 65.6%
*Member of last parliament
Lab Hold (11.2% Swing from Con to Lab)

HARWICH %
Henderson, I. (Lab) 20,740 38.8
*Sproat, I. (Con) 19,524 36.5
Elvin, A. (LD) 7,037 13.1
Titford, J. (Ref) 4,923 9.2
Knight, R.
(Community) 1,290 2.4
Lab majority 1,216 2.27%
Electorate 75,775
Total Vote 53,514 Poll 70.5%
*Member of last parliament
Lab Gain (14.6% Swing from Con to Lab)

HASTINGS AND RYE %
Foster, M. (Lab) 16,867 34.4
*Lait, J. (Con) 14,307 29.2
Palmer, M. (LD) 13,717 28.0
McGovern, C. (Ref) 2,511 5.1
Amstad, J. (Lib) 1,046 2.1
Andrews, W. (UKIP) 472 1.0
Tiverton, D. (Loony) 149 0.3
Lab majority 2,560 5.22%
Electorate 70,388
Total Vote 49,069 Poll 69.7%
*Member of last parliament
Lab Gain (18.5% Swing from Con to Lab)

HAVANT %
*Willetts, D. (Con) 19,204 39.7
Armstrong, L.
(Lab) 15,475 32.0
Kooner, M. (LD) 10,806 22.4
Green, A. (Ref) 2,395 5.0
Atwal, M.
(People-1st) 442 0.9
Con majority 3,729 7.72%
Electorate 68,420
Total Vote 48,322 Poll 70.4%
*Member of last parliament
Con Hold (12.7% Swing from Con to Lab)

HAYES AND HARLINGTON %
McDonnell, J. (Lab) 25,458 62.0
Retter, A. (Con) 11,167 27.2
Little, A. (LD) 3,049 7.4
Page, F. (Ref) 778 1.9
Hutchins, G. (NF) 504 1.2
Farrow, D.
(AllNight) 135 0.3
Lab majority 14,291 34.78%
Electorate 56,829
Total Vote 41,091 Poll 72.3%
Lab Gain (17.4% Swing from Con to Lab)

HAZEL GROVE %
Stunell, A. (LD) 26,883 54.5
Murphy, B. (Con) 15,069 30.5
Lewis, J. (Lab) 5,882 11.9
Stanyer, J. (Ref) 1,055 2.1
Black, G. (UKIP) 268 0.5
Firkin-Flood, D.
(Humanist) 183 0.4
LD majority 11,814 23.94%
Electorate 63,694
Total Vote 49,340 Poll 77.3%
LD Gain (12.8% Swing from Con to LD)

HEMEL HEMPSTEAD %
McWalter, T.
(Lab/Co-op) 25,175 45.7
*Jones, R. (Con) 21,539 39.1
Lindsley, P. (LD) 6,789 12.3
Such, P. (Ref) 1,327 2.4
Harding, D.
(NLP) 262 0.5
Lab/Co-op majority 3,636 6.60%
Electorate 71,468
Total Vote 55,092 Poll 76.7%
*Member of last parliament
Lab/Co-op Gain (12% Swing from Con to Lab)

HEMSWORTH %
*Trickett, J. (Lab) 32,088 70.6
Hazell, N. (Con) 8,096 17.8
Kirby, J. (LD) 4,033 8.9
Irvine, D. (Ref) 1,260 2.8
Lab majority 23,992 52.76%
Electorate 66,964
Total Vote 45,477 Poll 67.9%
*Member of last parliament
Lab Hold (7.4% Swing from Con to Lab)

HENDON

		%
Dismore, A. (Lab)	24,683	49.3
*Gorst, Sir J. (Con)	18,528	37.0
Casey, W. (LD)	5,427	10.8
Rabbow, S. (Ref)	978	2.0
Wright, B. (UKIP)	267	0.5
Taylor, S. (WRP)	153	0.3
Lab majority	6,155	12.30%
Electorate	76,195	
Total Vote	50,036	Poll 64.6%

*Member of last parliament
Lab Gain (16.2% Swing from Con to Lab)

HENLEY

		%
*Heseltine, M. (Con)	23,908	46.4
Horton, T. (LD)	12,741	24.7
Enright, D. (Lab)	11,700	22.7
Sainsbury, S. (Ref)	2,299	4.5
Miles, S. (Green)	514	1.0
Barlow, N. (NLP)	221	0.4
Hibbert, T. (Whig)	160	0.3
Con majority	11,167	21.67%
Electorate	66,424	
Total Vote	51,543	Poll 77.6%

*Member of last parliament
Con Hold (7.2% Swing from Con to LD)

HEREFORD

		%
Keetch, P. (LD)	25,198	47.9
*Shepherd, C. (Con)	18,550	35.3
Chappell, A. (Lab)	6,596	12.6
Easton, C. (Ref)	2,209	4.2
LD majority	6,648	12.65%
Electorate	69,864	
Total Vote	52,553	Poll 75.2%

*Member of last parliament
LD Gain (9.2% Swing from Con to LD)

HERTFORD AND STORTFORD

		%
*Wells, B. (Con)	24,027	44.0
Speller, S. (Lab)	17,142	31.4
Wood, M. (LD)	9,679	17.7
Page Croft, H. (Ref)	2,105	3.9
Smalley, B. (UKIP)	1,233	2.3
Franey, M. (Pro-Life)	259	0.5
Molloy, D. (Logic)	126	0.2
Con majority	6,885	12.62%
Electorate	71,759	
Total Vote	54,571	Poll 75.6%

*Member of last parliament
Con Hold (13.5% Swing from Con to Lab)

HERTSMERE

		%
*Clappison, J. (Con)	22,305	44.3
Kelly, B. (Lab)	19,230	38.2
Gray, A. (LD)	6,466	12.8
Marlow, J. (Ref)	1,703	3.4
Saunders, R. (UKIP)	453	0.9
Kahn, N. (NLP)	191	0.4
Con majority	3,075	6.11%
Electorate	68,011	
Total Vote	50,348	Poll 73.4%

*Member of last parliament
Con Hold (15% Swing from Con to Lab)

HEXHAM

		%
*Atkinson, P. (Con)	17,701	38.8
McMinn, I. (Lab)	17,479	38.3
Carr, P. (LD)	7,959	17.4
Waddell, R. (Ref)	1,362	3.0
Lott, D. (UKIP)	1,170	2.6
Con majority	222	0.49%
Electorate	58,914	
Total Vote	45,671	Poll 77.5%

*Member of last parliament
Con Hold (13.9% Swing from Con to Lab)

HEYWOOD AND MIDDLETON

		%
Dobbin, J. (Lab/Co-op)	29,179	57.7
Grigg, E. (Con)	11,637	23.0
Clayton, D. (LD)	7,908	15.6
West, C. (Ref)	1,076	2.1
Burke, P. (Lib)	750	1.5
Lab/Co-op majority	17,542	34.70%
Electorate	73,898	
Total Vote	50,550	Poll 68.3%

Lab Hold (9.9% Swing from Con to Lab)

HIGH PEAK

		%
Levitt, T. (Lab)	29,052	50.8
*Hendry, C. (Con)	20,261	35.5
Barber, S. (LD)	6,420	11.2
Hanson-Orr, C. (Ref)	1,420	2.5
Lab majority	8,791	15.38%
Electorate	72,315	
Total Vote	57,153	Poll 78.9%

*Member of last parliament
Lab Gain (11.7% Swing from Con to Lab)

HITCHIN AND HARPENDEN

		%
*Lilley, P. (Con)	24,038	45.9
Sanderson, R. (Lab)	17,367	33.1
White, C. (LD)	10,515	20.1
Cooke, D. (NLP)	290	0.6
Horton, J. (Soc)	217	0.4
Con majority	6,671	12.72%
Electorate	67,219	
Total Vote	52,427	Poll 78%

*Member of last parliament
Con Hold (15.4% Swing from Con to Lab)

HOLBORN AND ST PANCRAS

		%
*Dobson, F. (Lab)	24,707	65.0
Smith, J. (Con)	6,804	17.9
McGuinness, J. (LD)	4,750	12.5
Carr, J. (Ref)	790	2.1
Bedding, T. (NLP)	191	0.5
Smith, S. (Justice)	173	0.5
Conway, B. (WRP)	171	0.4
Rosenthal, M. (Dream)	157	0.4
Rice-Evans, P. (EU Party)	140	0.4
Quintavalle, B. (Pro-Life)	114	0.3
Lab majority	17,903	47.12%
Electorate	63,037	
Total Vote	37,997	Poll 57.2%

*Member of last parliament
Lab Hold (10.5% Swing from Con to Lab)

HORNCHURCH

		%
Cryer, J. (Lab)	22,066	50.2
*Squire, R. (Con)	16,386	37.3
Martins, R. (LD)	3,446	7.8
Khilkoff-Boulding, R. (Ref)	1,595	3.6
Trueman, J. (Third Way)	259	0.6
Sowerby, J. (Pro-Life)	189	0.4
Lab majority	5,680	12.93%
Electorate	60,775	
Total Vote	43,941	Poll 72.2%

*Member of last parliament
Lab Gain (16% Swing from Con to Lab)

HORNSEY AND WOOD GREEN

		%
*Roche, B. (Lab)	31,792	61.7
Hart, H. (Con)	11,293	21.9
Featherstone, L. (LD)	5,794	11.3
Jago, H. (Green)	1,214	2.4
Miller, R. (Ref)	808	1.6
Sikorski, P. (SLP)	586	1.1
Lab majority	20,499	39.81%
Electorate	74,537	
Total Vote	51,487	Poll 66.9%

*Member of last parliament
Lab Hold (15.3% Swing from Con to Lab)

HORSHAM

		%
Maude, F. (Con)	29,015	50.8
Millson, M. (LD)	14,153	24.8
Walsh, M. (Lab)	10,691	18.7
Grant, R. (Ref)	2,281	4.0
Miller, H. (UKIP)	819	1.4
Corbould, M. (FullEmp)	206	0.4
Con majority	14,862	26.00%
Electorate	75,432	
Total Vote	57,165	Poll 75.8%

Con Hold (6.8% Swing from Con to LD)

HOUGHTON AND WASHINGTON EAST

		%
Kemp, F. (Lab)	31,946	76.4
Booth, P. (Con)	5,391	12.9
Miller, K. (LD)	3,209	7.7
Joseph, C. (Ref)	1,277	3.1
Lab majority	26,555	63.49%
Electorate	67,343	
Total Vote	41,823	Poll 62.1%

Lab Hold (9.1% Swing from Con to Lab)

HOVE

		%
Caplin, I. (Lab)	21,458	44.6
Guy, R. (Con)	17,499	36.4
Pearce, T. (LD)	4,645	9.7
Field, S. (Ref)	1,931	4.0
Furness, J. (IndCon)	1,735	3.6
Mulligan, P. (Green)	644	1.3
Vause, J. (UKIP)	209	0.4
Lab majority	3,959	8.23%
Electorate	69,016	
Total Vote	48,121	Poll 69.7%

Lab Gain (16.4% Swing from Con to Lab)

HUDDERSFIELD

		%
*Sheerman, B.		
(Lab/Co-op)	25,171	56.5
Forrow, B. (Con)	9,323	20.9
Beever, G. (LD)	7,642	17.2
McNulty, P. (Ref)	1,480	3.3
Phillips, J. (Green)	938	2.1
Lab/Co-op		
majority	15,848	35.57%
Electorate	65,824	
Total Vote	44,554	Poll 67.5%

*Member of last parliament
Lab/Co-op Hold (10.4% Swing from Con to Lab)

HULL EAST

		%
*Prescott, J. (Lab)	28,870	71.3
West, A. (Con)	5,552	13.7
Wastling, J. (LD)	3,965	9.8
Rogers, G. (Ref)	1,788	4.4
Nolan, M.		
(Pro-Life)	190	0.5
Whitley, D. (NLP)	121	0.3
Lab majority	23,318	57.60%
Electorate	68,733	
Total Vote	40,486	Poll 58.9%

*Member of last parliament
Lab Hold (9.2% Swing from Con to Lab)

HULL NORTH

		%
*McNamara, K.		
(Lab)	25,542	65.8
Lee, D. (Con)	5,837	15.0
Nolan, D. (LD)	5,667	14.6
Scott, A. (Ref)	1,533	4.0
Brotheridge, T. (NLP)	215	0.6
Lab majority	19,705	50.79%
Electorate	68,106	
Total Vote	38,794	Poll 57%

*Member of last parliament
Lab Hold (9.2% Swing from Con to Lab)

HULL WEST AND HESSLE

		%
Johnson, A. (Lab)	22,520	58.7
Tress, R. (LD)	6,995	18.2
Moore, C. (Con)	6,933	18.1
Bate, R. (Ref)	1,596	4.2
Franklin, B. (NLP)	310	0.8
Lab majority	15,525	40.48%
Electorate	65,840	
Total Vote	38,354	Poll 58.2%

Lab Hold (3.1% Swing from LD to Lab)

HUNTINGDON

		%
*Major, J. (Con)	31,501	55.3
Reece, J. (Lab)	13,361	23.5
Owen, M. (LD)	8,390	14.7
Bellamy, D. (Ref)	3,114	5.5
Coyne, C. (UKIP)	331	0.6
Hufford, V.		
(ChriDem)	177	0.3
Robertson, D. (Ind)	89	0.2
Con majority	18,140	31.85%
Electorate	76,094	
Total Vote	56,963	Poll 74.9%

*Member of last parliament
Con Hold (6.8% Swing from Con to Lab)

HYNDBURN

		%
*Pope, G. (Lab)	26,831	55.6
Britcliffe, P. (Con)	15,383	31.9
Jones, L. (LD)	4,141	8.6
Congdon, P. (Ref)	1,627	3.4
Brown, J.		
(Anti-Corruption)	290	0.6
Lab majority	11,448	23.72%
Electorate	66,806	
Total Vote	48,272	Poll 72.3%

*Member of last parliament
Lab Hold (10% Swing from Con to Lab)

ILFORD NORTH

		%
Perham, L. (Lab)	23,135	47.4
*Bendall, V. (Con)	19,911	40.8
Dean, A. (LD)	5,049	10.3
Wilson, P. (BNP)	750	1.5
Lab majority	3,224	6.60%
Electorate	68,218	
Total Vote	48,845	Poll 71.6%

*Member of last parliament
Lab Gain (17.3% Swing from Con to Lab)

ILFORD SOUTH

		%
*Gapes, M.		
(Lab/Co-op)	29,273	58.5
Thorne, N. (Con)	15,073	30.1
Khan, A. (LD)	3,152	6.3
Hodges, D. (Ref)	1,073	2.1
Ramsay, B. (SLP)	868	1.7
Owens, A. (BNP)	580	1.2
Lab/Co-op		
majority	14,200	28.39%
Electorate	72,104	
Total Vote	50,019	Poll 69.4%

*Member of last parliament
Lab/Co-op Win (16.6% Swing from Con to Lab)

INVERNESS EAST, NAIRN AND LOCHABER

		%
Stewart, D. (Lab)	16,187	33.9
Ewing, F. (SNP)	13,848	29.0
Gallagher, S. (LD)	8,364	17.5
Scanlon, M. (Con)	8,355	17.5
Wall, W. (Ref)	436	0.9
Falconer, M. (Green)	354	0.7
Hart, D. (Christian)	224	0.5
Lab majority	2,339	4.90%
Electorate	65,701	
Total Vote	47,768	Poll 72.5%

Lab Gain (9.9% Swing from LD to Lab)

IPSWICH

		%
*Cann, J. (Lab)	25,484	52.7
Castle, S. (Con)	15,048	31.1
Roberts, N. (LD)	5,881	12.2
Agnew, T. (Ref)	1,637	3.4
Vinyard, W. (UKIP)	208	0.4
Caplan, E. (NLP)	107	0.2
Lab majority	10,436	21.59%
Electorate	68,064	
Total Vote	48,365	Poll 71.1%

*Member of last parliament
Lab Hold (10.5% Swing from Con to Lab)

ISLE OF WIGHT

		%
Brand, P. (LD)	31,274	42.7
Turner, A. (Con)	24,868	34.0
Gardiner, D. (Lab)	9,646	13.2
Bristow, T. (Ref)	4,734	6.5
Turner, M. (UKIP)	1,072	1.5
Rees, H. (Ind)	848	1.2
Scivier, P. (Green)	544	0.7
Daly, C. (NLP)	87	0.1
Eveleigh, J. (Rainbow)	86	0.1
LD majority	6,406	8.76%
Electorate	101,680	
Total Vote		Poll 71.7%

LD Gain (5.5% Swing from Con to LD)

ISLINGTON NORTH

		%
*Corbyn, J. (Lab)	24,834	69.3
Kempton, J. (LD)	4,879	13.6
Fawthrop, S. (Con)	4,631	12.9
Ashby, C. (Green)	1,516	4.2
Lab majority	19,955	55.65%
Electorate	57,385	
Total Vote	35,860	Poll 61.4%

*Member of last parliament
Lab Hold (6.7% Swing from LD to Lab)

ISLINGTON SOUTH AND FINSBURY

		%
*Smith, C. (Lab)	22,079	62.5
Ludford, S. (LD)	7,516	21.3
Berens, D. (Con)	4,587	13.0
Bryett, J. (Ref)	741	2.1
Laws, A. (ACA)	171	0.5
Creese, M. (NLP)	121	0.3
Basarik, E. (Ind)	101	0.3
Lab majority	14,563	41.24%
Electorate	55,468	
Total Vote	35,316	Poll 60.1%

*Member of last parliament
Lab Hold (6.6% Swing from LD to Lab)

ISLWYN

		%
*Touhig, D.		
(Lab/Co-op)	26,995	74.2
Worker, C. (LD)	3,064	8.4
Walters, D. (Con)	2,864	7.9
Jones, D. (PC)	2,272	6.2
Monaghian, S. (Ref)	1,209	3.3
Lab/Co-op		
majority	23,931	65.74%
Electorate	50,540	
Total Vote	36,404	Poll 71.9%

*Member of last parliament
Lab/Co-op Hold (1.5% Swing from Lab to LD)

JARROW

		%
Hepburn, S. (Lab)	28,497	64.9
Allatt, M. (Con)	6,564	14.9
Stone, T. (LD)	4,865	11.1
Le Blond, A. (IndLab)	2,538	5.8
Mailer, P. (Ref)	1,034	2.4
Bisset, J. (Socialist)	444	1.0
Lab majority	21,933	49.91%
Electorate	63,828	
Total Vote	43,942	Poll 68.8%

Lab Hold (5.4% Swing from Con to Lab)

KEIGHLEY

		%
Cryer, A. (Lab)	26,039	50.6
*Waller, G. (Con)	18,907	36.7
Doyle, M. (LD)	5,064	9.8
Carpenter, C. (Ref)	1,470	2.9
Lab majority	7,132	13.85%
Electorate	67,231	
Total Vote	51,480	Poll 76.3%

*Member of last parliament

Lab Gain (10.2% Swing from Con to Lab)

KENSINGTON AND CHELSEA

		%
Clark, A. (Con)	19,887	53.6
Atkinson, J. (Lab)	10,368	28.0
Woodthorpe Browne, R. (LD)	5,668	15.3
Ellis-Jones, A. (UKIP)	540	1.5
Bear, E. (Teddy)	218	0.6
Oliver, G. (Pensioners)	176	0.5
Hamza, S. (NLP)	122	0.3
Sullivan, P. (Dream)	65	0.2
Parliament, P. (Heart)	44	0.1
Con majority	9,519	25.67%
Electorate	67,786	
Total Vote	37,088	Poll 49.6%

Con Hold (12.9% Swing from Con to Lab)

KETTERING

		%
Sawford, P. (Lab)	24,650	43.3
*Freeman, R. (Con)	24,461	42.9
Aron, R. (LD)	6,098	10.7
Smith, A. (Ref)	1,551	2.7
Le Carpentier, R. (NLP)	197	0.3
Lab majority	189	0.33%
Electorate	75,153	
Total Vote	56,957	Poll 75.5%

*Member of last parliament

Lab Gain (10.6% Swing from Con to Lab)

KILMARNOCK AND LOUDOUN

		%
Browne, D. (Lab)	23,621	49.8
Neil, A. (SNP)	16,365	34.5
Taylor, D. (Con)	5,125	10.8
Stewart, J. (LD)	1,891	4.0
Sneddon, W. (Ref)	284	0.6
Gilmour, W. (NLP)	123	0.3
Lab majority	7,256	15.31%
Electorate	61,376	
Total Vote	47,409	Poll 77.2%

Lab Hold (0.6% Swing from SNP to Lab)

KINGSTON AND SURBITON %

Davey, E. (LD)	20,411	36.7
*Tracey, R. (Con)	20,355	36.6
Griffin, S. (Lab)	12,811	23.0
Tchiprout, G. (Ref)	1,470	2.6
Burns, A. (UKIP)	418	0.8
Port, C. (Dream)	100	0.2
Leighton, M. (NLP)	100	0.2
LD majority	56	0.10%
Electorate	73,879	
Total Vote	55,665	Poll 75.3%

*Member of last parliament

LD Gain (13.6% Swing from Con to LD)

KINGSWOOD

		%
*Berry, R. (Lab)	32,181	53.7
Howard, J. (Con)	17,928	29.9
Pinkerton, J. (LD)	7,672	12.8
Reather, A. (Ref)	1,463	2.4
Hart, P. (BNP)	290	0.5
Harding, A. (NLP)	238	0.4
Nicolson, A. (Scrappit)	115	0.2
Lab majority	14,253	23.80%
Electorate	77,026	
Total Vote	59,887	Poll 77.7%

*Member of last parliament

Lab Win (14.5% Swing from Con to Lab)

KIRKCALDY

		%
*Moonie, L. (Lab/Co-op)	18,730	53.6
Hosie, S. (SNP)	8,020	22.9
Black, C. (Con)	4,779	13.7
Mainland, J. (LD)	3,031	8.7
Baxter, V. (Ref)	413	1.2
Lab/Co-op majority	10,710	30.62%
Electorate	52,186	
Total Vote	34,973	Poll 66.9%

*Member of last parliament

Lab/Co-op Hold (3.8% Swing from SNP to Lab)

KNOWSLEY NORTH AND SEFTON EAST %

*Howarth, G. (Lab)	34,747	69.9
Doran, C. (Con)	8,600	17.3
Bamber, D. (LD)	5,499	11.1
Jones, C. (SLP)	857	1.7
Lab majority	26,147	52.61%
Electorate	70,918	
Total Vote	49,703	Poll 70.1%

*Member of last parliament

Lab Hold (12.5% Swing from Con to Lab)

KNOWSLEY SOUTH

		%
*O'Hara, E. (Lab)	36,695	77.1
Robertson, G. (Con)	5,987	12.6
Mainey, C. (LD)	3,954	8.3
Wright, A. (Ref)	954	2.0
Lab majority	30,708	64.53%
Electorate	70,532	
Total Vote	47,590	Poll 67.5%

*Member of last parliament

Lab Hold (7.8% Swing from Con to Lab)

LAGAN VALLEY

		%
Donaldson, J. (UUP)	24,560	55.4
Close, S. (APNI)	7,635	17.2
Poots, E. (DUP)	6,005	13.6
Kelly, D. (SDLP)	3,436	7.8
Sexton, S. (Con)	1,212	2.7
Ramsey, S. (SF)	1,110	2.5
McCarthy, F. (Workers)	203	0.5
Finlay, H. (NLP)	149	0.3
UUP majority	16,925	38.20%
Electorate	71,225	
Total Vote	44,310	Poll 62.2%

UUP Hold (8.5% Swing from UUP to APNI)

LANCASTER AND WYRE %

Dawson, T. (Lab)	25,173	42.8
*Mans, K. (Con)	23,878	40.6
Humberstone, J. (LD)	6,802	11.6
Ivell, V. (Ref)	1,516	2.6
Barry, J. (Green)	795	1.4
Whittaker, J. (UKIP)	698	1.2
Lab majority	1,295	2.20%
Electorate	78,168	
Total Vote	58,862	Poll 74.9%

*Member of last parliament

Lab Gain (10.6% Swing from Con to Lab)

LEEDS CENTRAL

		%
*Fatchett, D. (Lab)	25,766	69.6
Wild, W. (Con)	5,077	13.7
Freeman, D. (LD)	4,164	11.3
Myers, P. (Ref)	1,042	2.8
Rix, M. (SLP)	656	1.8
Hill, C. (Soc)	304	0.8
Lab majority	20,689	55.90%
Electorate	67,664	
Total Vote	37,009	Poll 54.2%

*Member of last parliament

Lab Hold (7.3% Swing from Con to Lab)

LEEDS EAST

		%
*Mudie, G. (Lab)	24,151	67.5
Emsley, J. (Con)	6,685	18.7
Kirk, M. (LD)	3,689	10.3
Parrish, L. (Ref)	1,267	3.5
Lab majority	17,466	48.80%
Electorate	56,963	
Total Vote	35,792	Poll 62.8%

*Member of last parliament

Lab Hold (9.7% Swing from Con to Lab)

LEEDS NORTH EAST %

Hamilton, F. (Lab)	22,368	49.2
*Kirkhope, T. (Con)	15,409	33.9
Winlow, B. (LD)	6,318	13.9
Rose, I. (Ref)	946	2.1
Egan, J. (SLP)	468	1.0
Lab majority	6,959	15.29%
Electorate	63,185	
Total Vote	45,509	Poll 71.8%

*Member of last parliament

Lab Gain (11.9% Swing from Con to Lab)

LEEDS NORTH WEST %

Best, H. (Lab)	19,694	39.9
*Hampson, K. (Con)	15,850	32.1
Pearce, B. (LD)	11,689	23.7
Emmett, S. (Ref)	1,325	2.7
Lamb, R. (SLP)	335	0.7
Toone, R. (ProLife)	251	0.5
Duffy, D. (Ronnie)	232	0.5
Lab majority	3,844	7.79%
Electorate	69,972	
Total Vote	49,376	Poll 69.7%

*Member of last parliament

Lab Gain (11.8% Swing from Con to Lab)

LEEDS WEST

		%
*Battle, J. (Lab)	26,819	66.7
Whelan, J. (Con)	7,048	17.5
Amor, N. (LD)	3,622	9.0
Finley, B. (Ref)	1,210	3.0
Blackburn, D.		
(Green)	896	2.2
Nowosielski, N. (Lib)	625	1.6
Lab majority 19,771		49.16%
Electorate	63,965	
Total Vote	40,220	Poll 62.7%

*Member of last parliament
Lab Hold (10.1% Swing from Con to Lab)

LEICESTER EAST

		%
*Vaz, K. (Lab)	29,083	65.5
Milton, S. (Con)	10,661	24.0
Matabudul, J. (LD)	3,105	7.0
Iwaniw, P. (Ref)	1,015	2.3
Singh Sidhu, S.		
(SLP)	436	1.0
Slack, N. (Glow)	102	0.2
Lab majority 18,422		41.49%
Electorate	64,012	
Total Vote	44,402	Poll 69.1%

*Member of last parliament
Lab Hold (9.4% Swing from Con to Lab)

LEICESTER SOUTH

		%
*Marshall, J. (Lab)	27,914	58.0
Heaton-Harris, C.		
(Con)	11,421	23.7
Coles, B. (LD)	6,654	13.8
Hancock, J. (Ref)	1,184	2.5
Dooher, J. (SLP)	634	1.3
Sills, K. (Nat Dem)	307	0.6
Lab majority 16,493		34.28%
Electorate	71,750	
Total Vote	48,114	Poll 66.3%

*Member of last parliament
Lab Hold (8.3% Swing from Con to Lab)

LEICESTER WEST

		%
Hewitt, P. (Lab)	22,580	55.2
Thomas, R. (Con)	9,716	23.7
Jones, M. (LD)	5,795	14.2
Shooter, W. (Ref)	970	2.4
Forse, G. (Green)	586	1.4
Roberts, D. (SLP)	452	1.1
Nicholls, J. (Soc)	327	0.8
Belshaw, A. (BNP)	302	0.7
Potter, C. (Nat Dem)	186	0.5
Lab majority 12,864		31.44%
Electorate	64,570	
Total Vote	40,914	Poll 63.1%

Lab Hold (11.6% Swing from Con to Lab)

LEIGH

		%
*Cunliffe, L. (Lab)	31,652	68.9
Young, E. (Con)	7,156	15.6
Hough, P. (LD)	5,163	11.2
Constable, R. (Ref)	1,949	4.2
Lab majority 24,496		53.34%
Electorate	69,908	
Total Vote	45,920	Poll 65.7%

*Member of last parliament
Lab Hold (10.7% Swing from Con to Lab)

LEOMINSTER

		%
*Temple-Morris, P.		
(Con)	22,888	45.3
James, T. (LD)	14,053	27.8
Westwood, R. (Lab)	8,831	17.5
Parkin, A. (Ref)	2,815	5.6
Norman, F. (Green)	1,086	2.1
Chamings, R. (UKIP)	588	1.2
Haycock, J. (BNP)	292	0.6
Con majority 8,835		17.48%
Electorate	65,993	
Total Vote	50,553	Poll 76.6%

*Member of last parliament
Con Hold (5.5% Swing from Con to LD)

LEWES

		%
Baker, N. (LD)	21,250	43.2
*Rathbone, T. (Con)	19,950	40.6
Patton, M. (Lab)	5,232	10.6
Butler, L. (Ref)	2,481	5.0
Harvey, J. (UKIP)	256	0.5
LD majority 1,300		2.64%
Electorate	64,340	
Total Vote	49,169	Poll 76.4%

*Member of last parliament
LD Gain (7.4% Swing from Con to LD)

LEWISHAM DEPTFORD

		%
*Ruddock, J. (Lab)	23,827	70.8
Kimm, I. (Con)	4,949	14.7
Appiah, K. (LD)	3,004	8.9
Mulrenan, J. (SLP)	996	3.0
Shepherd, S. (Ref)	868	2.6
Lab majority 18,878		56.11%
Electorate	58,141	
Total Vote	33,644	Poll 57.9%

*Member of last parliament
Lab Hold (11.6% Swing from Con to Lab)

LEWISHAM EAST

		%
*Prentice, B. (Lab)	21,821	58.3
Hollobone, P.		
(Con)	9,694	25.9
Buxton, D. (LD)	4,178	11.2
Drury, S. (Ref)	910	2.4
Croucher, R. (NF)	431	1.2
White, P. (Lib)	277	0.7
Rizz, C. (Dream)	97	0.3
Lab majority 12,127		32.50%
Electorate	56,333	
Total Vote	37,408	Poll 66.4%

*Member of last parliament
Lab Hold (14.9% Swing from Con to Lab)

LEWISHAM WEST

		%
*Dowd, J. (Lab)	23,273	62.0
Whelan, C. (Con)	8,956	23.8
McGrath, K. (LD)	3,672	9.8
Leese, A. (Ref)	1,098	2.9
Long, N. (SLP)	398	1.1
Oram, E. (Lib)	167	0.4
Lab majority 14,317		38.11%
Electorate	58,659	
Total Vote	37,564	Poll 64%

*Member of last parliament
Lab Hold (17% Swing from Con to Lab)

LEYTON AND WANSTEAD

		%
*Cohen, H. (Lab)	23,922	60.8
Vaudry, R. (Con)	8,736	22.2
Anglin, C. (LD)	5,920	15.1
Duffy, S. (Pro-Life)	488	1.2
Mian, A. (Ind)	256	0.7
Lab majority 15,186		38.62%
Electorate	62,176	
Total Vote	39,322	Poll 63.2%

*Member of last parliament
Lab Hold (11.8% Swing from Con to Lab)

LICHFIELD

		%
*Fabricant, M. (Con)	20,853	42.9
Woodward, S. (Lab)	20,615	42.4
Bennion, R. (LD)	5,473	11.3
Seward, G. (Ref)	1,652	3.4
Con majority 238		0.49%
Electorate	62,720	
Total Vote	48,593	Poll 77.5%

*Member of last parliament
Con Hold (10% Swing from Con to Lab)

LINCOLN

		%
Merron, G. (Lab)	25,563	54.9
Brown, A. (Con)	14,433	31.0
Gabriel, L. (LD)	5,048	10.8
Ivory, J. (Ref)	1,329	2.9
Myers, A. (NLP)	175	0.4
Lab majority 11,130		23.91%
Electorate	65,485	
Total Vote	46,548	Poll 70.9%

Lab Win (11% Swing from Con to Lab)

LINLITHGOW

		%
*Dalyell, T. (Lab)	21,469	54.1
MacAskill, K. (SNP)	10,631	26.8
Kerr, T. (Con)	4,964	12.5
Duncan, A. (LD)	2,331	5.9
Plomer, K. (Ref)	259	0.7
Lab majority 10,838		27.33%
Electorate	53,706	
Total Vote	39,654	Poll 73.8%

*Member of last parliament
Lab Hold (4.1% Swing from SNP to Lab)

LIVERPOOL GARSTON

		%
Eagle, M. (Lab)	26,667	61.3
Clucas, F. (LD)	8,250	19.0
Gordon-Johnson, N.		
(Con)	6,819	15.7
Dunne, F. (Ref)	833	1.9
Copeland, G. (Lib)	666	1.5
Parsons, J. (NLP)	127	0.3
Nolan, S. (SEP)	120	0.3
Lab majority 18,417		42.36%
Electorate	66,755	
Total Vote	43,482	Poll 65.1%

Lab Hold (6.4% Swing from LD to Lab)

LIVERPOOL RIVERSIDE

		%
Ellman, L. (Lab/Co-op)	26,858	70.4
Fraenkel, B. (LD)	5,059	13.3
Sparrow, D. (Con)	3,635	9.5
Wilson, C. (Soc)	776	2.0
Green, D. (Lib)	594	1.6

Skelly, G. (Ref)	586	1.5
Nielsen, H. (ProLife)	277	0.7
Braid, D. (MRAC)	179	0.5
Gay, G. (NLP)	171	0.4
Lab/Co-op majority	21,799	57.16%
Electorate	73,429	
Total Vote	38,135	Poll 51.6%

Lab Hold (3.6% Swing from LD to Lab)

LIVERPOOL WALTON %

*Kilfoyle, P. (Lab)	31,516	78.4
Roberts, R. (LD)	4,478	11.1
Kotecha, M. (Con)	2,551	6.3
Grundy, C. (Ref)	620	1.5
Mahmood, L. (Soc)	444	1.1
Williams, H. (Lib)	352	0.9
Mearns, V. (Pro-Life)	246	0.6
Lab majority	27,038	67.33%
Electorate	67,527	
Total Vote	40,207	Poll 59.5%

Member of last parliament
Lab Hold (3.4% Swing from LD to Lab)

LIVERPOOL WAVERTREE %

*Kennedy, J. (Lab)	29,592	64.4
Kemp, R. (LD)	9,891	21.5
Malthouse, C. (Con)	4,944	10.8
Worthington, P. (Ref)	576	1.3
McCullough, K. (Lib)	391	0.9
Kingsley, R. (Pro-Life)	346	0.8
Corkhill, C. (WRP)	178	0.4
Lab majority	19,701	42.90%
Electorate	73,063	
Total Vote	45,918	Poll 62.8%

Member of last parliament
Lab Hold (18.2% Swing from LD to Lab)

LIVERPOOL WEST DERBY %

*Wareing, R. (Lab)	30,002	71.2
Radford, S. (Lib)	4,037	9.6
Hines, A. (LD)	3,805	9.0
Morgan, N. (Con)	3,656	8.7
Forest, P. (Ref)	657	1.6
Lab majority	25,965	61.59%
Electorate	68,682	
Total Vote	42,157	Poll 61.3%

Member of last parliament
Lab Hold (0% Swing from to)

LIVINGSTON %

*Cook, R. (Lab)	23,510	54.9
Johnston, P. (SNP)	11,763	27.5
Craigie Halkett, H. (Con)	4,028	9.4
Hawthorn, E. (LD)	2,876	6.7
Campbell, H. (Ref)	444	1.0
Culbert, M. (SPGB)	213	0.5
Lab majority	11,747	27.42%
Electorate	60,296	
Total Vote	42,834	Poll 70.9%

Member of last parliament
Lab Hold (3.8% Swing from SNP to Lab)

LLANELLI %

*Davies, D. (Lab)	23,851	57.9
Phillips, M. (PC)	7,812	19.0
Hayes, A. (Con)	5,003	12.1
Burree, N. (LD)	3,788	9.2
Willock, J. (SLP)	757	1.8
Lab majority	16,039	38.92%
Electorate	58,323	
Total Vote	41,211	Poll 70.7%

Member of last parliament
Lab Hold (0.1% Swing from PC to Lab)

LOUGHBOROUGH %

Reed, A. (Lab/Co-op)	25,448	48.6
Andrew, K. (Con)	19,736	37.7
Brass, D. (LD)	6,190	11.8
Gupta, R. (Ref)	991	1.9
Lab/Co-op majority	5,712	10.91%
Electorate	68,945	
Total Vote	52,365	Poll 75.5%

Lab Gain (8.9% Swing from Con to Lab)

LOUTH AND HORNCASTLE %

*Tapsell, Sir P. (Con)	21,699	43.4
Hough, J. (Lab)	14,799	29.6
Martin, F. (LD)	12,207	24.4
Robinson, R. (Green)	1,248	2.5
Con majority	6,900	13.81%
Electorate	68,824	
Total Vote	49,953	Poll 72.4%

Member of last parliament
Con Hold (12.6% Swing from Con to Lab)

LUDLOW %

*Gill, C. (Con)	19,633	42.4
Huffer, I. (LD)	13,724	29.7
O'Kane, N. (Lab)	11,745	25.4
Andrewes, T. (Green)	798	1.7
Freeman-Keel, E. (UKIP)	385	0.8
Con majority	5,909	12.77%
Electorate	61,267	
Total Vote	46,285	Poll 75.5%

Member of last parliament
Con Hold (6.6% Swing from Con to LD)

LUTON NORTH %

Hopkins, K. (Lab)	25,860	54.6
Senior, D. (Con)	16,234	34.3
Newbound, K. (LD)	4,299	9.1
Brown, C. (UKIP)	689	1.5
Custance, A. (NLP)	250	0.5
Lab majority	9,626	20.34%
Electorate	64,618	
Total Vote	47,332	Poll 73.2%

Lab Gain (17.2% Swing from Con to Lab)

LUTON SOUTH %

Moran, M. (Lab)	26,428	54.8
*Bright, Sir G. (Con)	15,109	31.4
Fitchett, K. (LD)	4,610	9.6
Jacobs, C. (Ref)	1,205	2.5
Lawman, C. (UKIP)	390	0.8
Scheimann, M. (Green)	356	0.7
Perrin, C. (NLP)	86	0.2
Lab majority	11,319	23.49%

Electorate	68,395	
Total Vote	48,184	Poll 70.4%

Member of last parliament
Lab Gain (12.3% Swing from Con to Lab)

MACCLESFIELD %

*Winterton, N. (Con)	26,888	49.6
Jackson, J. (Lab)	18,234	33.6
Flynn, M. (LD)	9,075	16.7
Con majority	8,654	15.97%
Electorate	72,049	
Total Vote	54,197	Poll 74.9%

Member of last parliament
Con Hold (8.6% Swing from Con to Lab)

MAIDENHEAD %

May, T. (Con)	25,344	49.8
Ketteringham, A. (LD)	13,363	26.3
Robson, D. (Lab)	9,205	18.1
Taverner, C. (Ref)	1,638	3.2
Munkley, D. (Lib)	896	1.8
Spiers, N. (UKIP)	277	0.5
Ardley, K. (Glow)	166	0.3
Con majority	11,981	23.54%
Electorate	67,302	
Total Vote	50,889	Poll 75.6%

Con Hold (4.1% Swing from Con to LD)

MAIDSTONE AND THE WEALD %

*Widdecombe, A. (Con)	23,657	44.1
Morgan, J. (Lab)	14,054	26.2
Nelson, J. (LD)	11,986	22.4
Hopkins, S. (Ref)	1,998	3.7
Cleator, M. (SLP)	979	1.8
Kemp, P. (Green)	480	0.9
Owen, R. (UKIP)	339	0.6
Oldbury, J. (NLP)	115	0.2
Con majority	9,603	17.91%
Electorate	72,466	
Total Vote	53,608	Poll 73.7%

Member of last parliament
Con Hold (12.9% Swing from Con to Lab)

MAKERFIELD %

*McCartney, I. (Lab)	33,119	73.6
Winstanley, M. (Con)	6,942	15.4
Hubbard, B. (LD)	3,743	8.3
Seed, A. (Ref)	1,210	2.7
Lab majority	26,177	58.15%
Electorate	67,358	
Total Vote	45,014	Poll 66.8%

Member of last parliament
Lab Hold (9.6% Swing from Con to Lab)

MALDON AND CHELMSFORD EAST %

*Whittingdale, J. (Con)	24,524	48.7
Freeman, K. (Lab)	14,485	28.7
Pooley, G. (LD)	9,758	19.4
Overy-Owen, L. (UKIP)	935	1.9
Burgess, E. (Green)	685	1.4
Con majority	10,039	19.92%
Electorate	66,184	
Total Vote	50,387	Poll 76%

Member of last parliament
Con Hold (15.6% Swing from Con to Lab)

MANCHESTER BLACKLEY %
Stringer, G. (Lab)   25,042   70.0
Barclay, S. (Con)   5,454   15.3
Wheale, S. (LD)   3,937   11.0
Stanyer, P. (Ref)   1,323   3.7
Lab majority   19,588   54.78%
Electorate   62,227
Total Vote   35,756   Poll 57.3%
Lab Hold (9.3% Swing from Con to Lab)

MANCHESTER CENTRAL %
*Lloyd, T. (Lab)   23,803   71.0
Firth, A. (LD)   4,121   12.3
McIlwaine, S. (Con)   3,964   11.8
Rafferty, F. (SLP)   810   2.4
Maxwell, B. (Ref)   742   2.2
Rigby, T. (Comm)   97   0.3
Lab majority   19,682   58.69%
Electorate   63,815
Total Vote   33,537   Poll 52%
*Member of last parliament
Lab Hold (0.3% Swing from LD to Lab)

MANCHESTER GORTON %
*Kaufman, G. (Lab)   23,704   65.3
Pearcey, J. (LD)   6,362   17.5
Senior, G. (Con)   4,249   11.7
Hartley, K. (Ref)   812   2.2
Fitz-Gibbon, S. (Green)   683   1.9
Wongsam, T. (SLP)   501   1.4
Lab majority   17,342   47.76%
Electorate   64,349
Total Vote   36,311   Poll 55.8%
*Member of last parliament
Lab Hold (0.3% Swing from Lab to LD)

MANCHESTER WITHINGTON %
*Bradley, K. (Lab)   27,103   61.6
Smith, J. (Con)   8,522   19.4
Zalzala, Y. (LD)   6,000   13.6
Sheppard, M. (Ref)   1,079   2.5
Caldwell, S. (Pro-Life)   614   1.4
White, J. (Soc)   376   0.9
Kingston, S. (Dream)   181   0.4
Gaskell, M. (NLP)   152   0.3
Lab majority   18,581   42.20%
Electorate   66,116
Total Vote   44,027   Poll 66%
*Member of last parliament
Lab Hold (10.4% Swing from Con to Lab)

MANSFIELD %
*Meale, A. (Lab)   30,556   64.4
Frost, T. (Con)   10,038   21.2
Smith, P. (LD)   5,244   11.1
Bogusz, J. (Ref)   1,588   3.3
Lab majority   20,518   43.26%
Electorate   67,057
Total Vote   47,426   Poll 70.6%
*Member of last parliament
Lab Hold (11% Swing from Con to Lab)

MEDWAY %
Marshall-Andrews,
R. (Lab)   21,858   48.9
*Fenner, Dame P.
(Con)   16,504   36.9

Roberts, R. (LD)   4,555   10.2
Main, J. (Ref)   1,420   3.2
Radlett, S. (UKIP)   405   0.9
Lab majority   5,354   11.97%
Electorate   61,736
Total Vote   44,742   Poll 72.2%
*Member of last parliament
Lab Gain (14.9% Swing from Con to Lab)

MEIRIONNYDD NANT CONWY %
*Llwyd, E. (PC)   12,465   50.7
Rees, H. (Lab)   5,660   23.0
Quin, J. (Con)   3,922   16.0
Feeley, R. (LD)   1,719   7.0
Hodge, P. (Ref)   809   3.3
PC majority   6,805   27.69%
Electorate   32,345
Total Vote   24,575   Poll 76%
*Member of last parliament
PC Hold (1.3% Swing from Lab to PC)

MERIDEN %
Spelman, C. (Con)   22,997   42.0
Seymour-Smith, B.
(Lab)   22,415   41.0
Dupont, A. (LD)   7,098   13.0
Gilbert, P. (Ref)   2,208   4.0
Con majority   582   1.06%
Electorate   76,287
Total Vote   54,718   Poll 71.6%
Con Hold (11.6% Swing from Con to Lab)

MERTHYR TYDFIL AND RHYMNEY %
*Rowlands, T. (Lab)   30,012   76.7
Anstey, D. (LD)   2,926   7.5
Morgan, J. (Con)   2,508   6.4
Cox, A. (PC)   2,344   6.0
Cowdell, A. (IndLab)   691   1.8
Hutchings, R. (Ref)   660   1.7
Lab majority   27,086   69.20%
Electorate   56,507
Total Vote   39,141   Poll 69.2%
*Member of last parliament
Lab Hold (4.5% Swing from LD to Lab)

MID BEDFORDSHIRE %
Sayeed, J. (Con)   24,176   46.0
Mallett, N. (Lab)   17,086   32.5
Hill, T. (LD)   8,823   16.8
Marler, S. (Ref)   2,257   4.3
Lorys, M. (NLP)   174   0.3
Con majority   7,090   13.50%
Electorate   66,979
Total Vote   52,516   Poll 78.3%
Con Hold (14.6% Swing from Con to Lab)

MID DORSET AND POOLE NORTH %
Fraser, C. (Con)   20,632   40.7
Leaman, A. (LD)   19,951   39.3
Collis, D. (Lab)   8,014   15.8
Nabarro, D. (Ref)   2,136   4.2
Con majority   681   1.34%
Electorate   67,049
Total Vote   50,733   Poll 75.7%
Con Hold (5.4% Swing from Con to LD)

MID NORFOLK %
Simpson, K. (Con)   22,739   39.6
Zeichner, D. (Lab)   21,403   37.3
Frary, S. (LD)   8,617   15.0
Holder, N. (Ref)   3,229   5.6
Park, T. (Green)   1,254   2.2
Parker, B. (NLP)   215   0.4
Con majority   1,336   2.33%
Electorate   75,311
Total Vote   57,457   Poll 76.1%
Con Hold (13.1% Swing from Con to Lab)

MID SUSSEX %
*Soames, N. (Con)   23,231   43.5
Collins, M. (LD)   16,377   30.6
Hamilton, M. (Lab)   9,969   18.6
Large, T. (Ref)   3,146   5.9
Barnett, J. (UKIP)   606   1.1
Tudway, E.
(Ind JRP)   134   0.3
Con majority   6,854   12.82%
Electorate   68,784
Total Vote   53,463   Poll 77.7%
*Member of last parliament
Con Hold (8.9% Swing from Con to LD)

MID ULSTER %
McGuiness, M. (SF)   20,294   40.1
*McCrea, W. (DUP)   18,411   36.3
Haughey, D.
(SDLP)   11,205   22.1
Bogues, E. (APNI)   460   0.9
Donnelly, M.
(Workers)   238   0.5
Murray, M. (NLP)   61   0.1
SF majority   1,883   3.72%
Electorate   58,836
Total Vote   50,669   Poll 86.1%
*Member of last parliament
SF Gain (10.3% Swing from DUP to SF)

MID WORCESTERSHIRE %
*Luff, P. (Con)   24,092   47.4
Smith, D. (Lab)   14,680   28.9
Barwick, D. (LD)   9,458   18.6
Watson, T. (Ref)   1,780   3.5
Ingles, D. (UKIP)   646   1.3
Dyer, A. (NLP)   163   0.3
Con majority   9,412   18.52%
Electorate   68,381
Total Vote   50,819   Poll 74.3%
*Member of last parliament
Con Hold (9.4% Swing from Con to Lab)

MIDDLESBROUGH %
*Bell, S. (Lab)   32,925   71.4
Benham, L. (Con)   7,907   17.2
Charlesworth, A.
(LD)   3,934   8.5
Edwards, R. (Ref)   1,331   2.9
Lab majority   25,018   54.27%
Electorate   70,931
Total Vote   46,097   Poll 64.8%
*Member of last parliament
Lab Hold (11.5% Swing from Con to Lab)

MIDDLESBROUGH SOUTH AND EAST CLEVELAND %

Kumar, A. (Lab)	29,319	54.7
*Bates, M. (Con)	18,712	34.9
Garrett, H. (LD)	4,004	7.5
Batchelor, R. (Ref)	1,552	2.9
Lab majority	10,607	19.79%
Electorate	70,481	
Total Vote	53,587	Poll 75.9%

*Member of last parliament
Lab Gain (11.1% Swing from Con to Lab)

MIDLOTHIAN %

*Clarke, E. (Lab)	18,861	53.5
Millar, L. (SNP)	8,991	25.5
Harper, A. (Con)	3,842	10.9
Pinnock, R. (LD)	3,235	9.2
Docking, K. (Ref)	320	0.9
Lab majority	9,870	28.00%
Electorate	47,552	
Total Vote	35,249	Poll 74%

*Member of last parliament
Lab Hold (1.5% Swing from SNP to Lab)

MILTON KEYNES NORTH EAST %

White, B. (Lab)	20,201	39.4
*Butler, P. (Con)	19,961	39.0
Mabbutt, G. (LD)	8,907	17.4
Phillips, M. (Ref)	1,492	2.9
Francis, A. (Green)	576	1.1
Simson, M. (NLP)	99	0.2
Lab majority	240	0.47%
Electorate	70,395	
Total Vote	51,236	Poll 72.8%

*Member of last parliament
Lab Gain (14.2% Swing from Con to Lab)

MILTON KEYNES SOUTH WEST %

Starkey, P. (Lab)	27,298	53.8
*Legg, B. (Con)	17,006	33.6
Jones, P. (LD)	6,065	12.0
Kelly, H. (NLP)	389	0.8
Lab majority	10,292	20.28%
Electorate	71,070	
Total Vote	50,758	Poll 71.4%

*Member of last parliament
Lab Gain (14.6% Swing from Con to Lab)

MITCHAM AND MORDEN %

McDonagh, S. (Lab)	27,984	58.4
*Rumbold, Dame A. (Con)	14,243	29.7
Harris, N. (LD)	3,632	7.6
Isaacs, P. (Ref)	810	1.7
Miller, L. (BNP)	521	1.1
Walsh, T. (Green)	415	0.9
Vaikuntha Vasan, K. (Ind)	144	0.3
Barrett, J. (UKIP)	117	0.2
Dixon, N. (Anti-Corr)	80	0.2
Lab majority	13,741	28.66%
Electorate	65,385	
Total Vote	47,946	Poll 72.4%

*Member of last parliament
Lab Gain (16% Swing from Con to Lab)

MOLE VALLEY %

*Beresford, Sir P. (Con)	26,178	48.0
Cooksey, S. (LD)	15,957	29.3
Payne, C. (Lab)	8,057	14.8
Taber, N. (Ref)	2,424	4.4
Burley, R. (Ind Con Ref)	1,276	2.3
Cameron, I. (UKIP)	435	0.8
Thomas, J. (NLP)	197	0.4
Con majority	10,221	18.75%
Electorate	69,140	
Total Vote	54,524	Poll 78.9%

*Member of last parliament
Con Hold (7% Swing from Con to LD)

MONMOUTH %

Edwards, H. (Lab)	23,404	47.7
*Evans, R. (Con)	19,226	39.2
Williams, M. (LD)	4,689	9.6
Warry, N. (Ref)	1,190	2.4
Cotton, A. (PC)	516	1.1
Lab majority	4,178	8.52%
Electorate	60,703	
Total Vote	49,025	Poll 80.8%

*Member of last parliament
Lab Gain (7.4% Swing from Con to Lab)

MONTGOMERYSHIRE %

Opik, L. (LD)	14,647	45.9
Davies, G. (Con)	8,344	26.1
Davies, A. (Lab)	6,109	19.1
Jones, H. (PC)	1,608	5.0
Bufton, J. (Ref)	879	2.8
Walker, S. (Green)	338	1.1
LD majority	6,303	19.74%
Electorate	42,618	
Total Vote	31,925	Poll 74.9%

LD Hold (2% Swing from Con to LD)

MORAY %

*Ewing, M. (SNP)	16,529	41.6
Findlay, A. (Con)	10,963	27.6
Macdonald, L. (Lab)	7,886	19.8
Storr, D. (LD)	3,548	8.9
Meiklejohn, P. (Ref)	840	2.1
SNP majority	5,566	14.00%
Electorate	58,302	
Total Vote	39,766	Poll 68%

*Member of last parliament
SNP Hold (3.5% Swing from Con to SNP)

MORECAMBE AND LUNESDALE %

Smith, G. (Lab)	24,061	48.9
*Lennox-Boyd, Sir M. (Con)	18,096	36.7
Greenwell, J. (LD)	5,614	11.4
Ogilvie, I. (Ref)	1,313	2.7
Walne, D. (NLP)	165	0.3
Lab majority	5,965	12.11%
Electorate	68,013	
Total Vote	49,249	Poll 72.3%

*Member of last parliament
Lab Gain (16% Swing from Con to Lab)

MORLEY AND ROTHWELL %

*Gunnell, J. (Lab)	26,836	58.5
Barraclough, A. (Con)	12,086	26.3
Galdas, M. (LD)	5,087	11.1
Mitchell Innes, D. (Ref)	1,359	3.0
Wood, R. (BNP)	381	0.8
Sammon, P. (Pro-Life)	148	0.3
Lab majority	14,750	32.14%
Electorate	68,385	
Total Vote	45,897	Poll 67.1%

*Member of last parliament
Lab Hold (9.8% Swing from Con to Lab)

MOTHERWELL AND WISHAW %

Roy, F. (Lab)	21,020	57.4
McGuigan, J. (SNP)	8,229	22.5
Dickson, S. (Con)	4,024	11.0
Mackie, A. (LD)	2,331	6.4
Herriot, C. (SLP)	797	2.2
Russell, T. (Ref)	218	0.6
Lab majority	12,791	34.93%
Electorate	52,252	
Total Vote	36,619	Poll 70.1%

Lab Hold (0.1% Swing from Lab to SNP)

NEATH %

*Hain, P. (Lab)	30,324	73.5
Evans, D. (Con)	3,583	8.7
Jones, T. (PC)	3,344	8.1
Little, F. (LD)	2,597	6.3
Morris, P. (Ref)	975	2.4
Marks, H. (Cannabis)	420	1.0
Lab majority	26,741	64.84%
Electorate	55,425	
Total Vote	41,243	Poll 74.3%

*Member of last parliament
Lab Hold (6% Swing from Con to Lab)

NEW FOREST EAST %

Lewis, J. (Con)	21,053	42.9
Dawson, G. (LD)	15,838	32.3
Goodfellow, A. (Lab)	12,161	24.8
Con majority	5,215	10.63%
Electorate	65,717	
Total Vote	49,052	Poll 74.4%

Con Hold (4.5% Swing from Con to LD)

NEW FOREST WEST %

Swayne, D. (Con)	25,149	50.6
Hale, R. (LD)	13,817	27.8
Griffiths, D. (Lab)	7,092	14.3
Elliott, M. (Ref)	2,150	4.3
Holmes, M. (UKIP)	1,542	3.1
Con majority	11,332	22.78%
Electorate	66,522	
Total Vote	49,750	Poll 74.5%

Con Hold (3.7% Swing from Con to LD)

NEWARK %

Jones, F. (Lab)	23,496	45.2
*Alexander, R. (Con)	20,480	39.4
Harris, P. (LD)	5,960	11.5
Creedy, G. (Ref)	2,035	3.9
Lab majority	3,016	5.80%
Electorate	69,763	
Total Vote	51,971	Poll 74.4%

*Member of last parliament
Lab Gain (10.2% Swing from Con to Lab)

NEWBURY

		%
*Rendel, D. (LD)	29,887	52.9
Benyon, R. (Con)	21,370	37.8
Hannon, P. (Lab)	3,107	5.5
Snook, T. (Ref)	992	1.8
Stark, R. (Green)	644	1.1
Tubb, R. (UKIP)	302	0.5
Howse, K. (SLP)	174	0.3
LD majority	8,517	15.1%
Electorate	73,680	
Total Vote	56,476	Poll 76.7%

*Member of last parliament
LD Hold (17% Swing from Con to LD)

NEWCASTLE UPON TYNE CENTRAL

		%
*Cousins, J. (Lab)	27,272	59.2
Newmark, B. (Con)	10,792	23.4
Berry, R. (LD)	6,911	15.0
Coxon, C. (Ref)	1,113	2.4
Lab majority	16,480	35.76%
Electorate	69,781	
Total Vote	46,088	Poll 65.3%

*Member of last parliament
Lab Hold (9.8% Swing from Con to Lab)

NEWCASTLE UPON TYNE EAST AND WALLSEND

		%
*Brown, N. (Lab)	29,607	71.2
Middleton, J. (Con)	5,796	13.9
Morgan, G. (LD)	4,415	10.6
Cossins, R. (Ref)	966	2.3
Carpenter, B. (SLP)	642	1.5
Levy, M. (Comm)	163	0.4
Lab majority	23,811	57.25%
Electorate	63,272	
Total Vote	41,589	Poll 65.5%

*Member of last parliament
Lab Hold (11.3% Swing from Con to Lab)

NEWCASTLE UPON TYNE NORTH

		%
*Henderson, D. (Lab)	28,125	62.2
White, G. (Con)	8,793	19.4
Allen, P. (LD)	6,578	14.5
Chipchase, D. (Ref)	1,733	3.8
Lab majority	19,332	42.74%
Electorate	65,357	
Total Vote	45,229	Poll 69.1%

*Member of last parliament
Lab Hold (12.6% Swing from Con to Lab)

NEWCASTLE-UNDER-LYME

		%
*Golding, L. (Lab)	27,743	56.5
Hayes, M. (Con)	10,537	21.4
Studd, R. (LD)	6,858	14.0
Suttle, K. (Ref)	1,510	3.1
Mountford, S. (Lib)	1,399	2.8
Bell, B. (SLP)	1,082	2.2
Lab majority	17,206	35.02%
Electorate	66,686	
Total Vote	49,129	Poll 73.7%

*Member of last parliament
Lab Hold (8.3% Swing from Con to Lab)

NEWPORT EAST

		%
*Howarth, A. (Lab)	21,481	57.7
Evans, D. (Con)	7,958	21.4
Cameron, A. (LD)	3,880	10.4
Scargill, A. (SLP)	1,951	5.2
Davis, G. (Ref)	1,267	3.4
Holland, C. (PC)	721	1.9
Lab majority	13,523	36.30%
Electorate	50,997	
Total Vote	37,258	Poll 73.1%

*Member of last parliament
Lab Hold (6.3% Swing from Con to Lab)

NEWPORT WEST

		%
*Flynn, P. (Lab)	24,331	60.5
Clarke, P. (Con)	9,794	24.4
Wilson, S. (LD)	3,907	9.7
Thompsett, C. (Ref)	1,199	3.0
Jackson, H. (PC)	648	1.6
Moelwyn Hughes, H. (UKIP)	323	0.8
Lab majority	14,537	36.16%
Electorate	53,914	
Total Vote	40,202	Poll 74.6%

*Member of last parliament
Lab Hold (9.5% Swing from Con to Lab)

NEWRY AND ARMAGH

		%
*Mallon, S. (SDLP)	22,904	43.0
Kennedy, D. (UUP)	18,015	33.8
McNamee, P. (SF)	11,218	21.1
Whitcroft, P. (APNI)	1,015	1.9
Evans, D. (NLP)	123	0.2
SDLP majority	4,889	9.18%
Electorate	70,652	
Total Vote	53,275	Poll 75.4%

*Member of last parliament
SDLP Hold (1.9% Swing from SDLP to UUP)

NORMANTON

		%
*O'Brien, B. (Lab)	26,046	60.6
Bulmer, F. (Con)	10,153	23.6
Ridgway, D. (LD)	5,347	12.4
Shuttleworth, K. (Ref)	1,458	3.4
Lab majority	15,893	36.96%
Electorate	62,980	
Total Vote	43,004	Poll 68.3%

*Member of last parliament
Lab Hold (10.7% Swing from Con to Lab)

NORTH ANTRIM

		%
*Paisley, I. (DUP)	21,495	46.5
Leslie, J. (UUP)	10,921	23.6
Farren, S. (SDLP)	7,333	15.9
McCarry, J. (SF)	2,896	6.3
Alderdice, D. (APNI)	2,845	6.2
Hinds, B. (Women)	580	1.3
Wright, J. (NLP)	116	0.3
DUP majority	10,574	22.89%
Electorate	72,411	
Total Vote	46,186	Poll 63.8%

*Member of last parliament
DUP Hold (5% Swing from DUP to UUP)

NORTH CORNWALL

		%
*Tyler, P. (LD)	31,100	53.2
Linacre, N. (Con)	17,253	29.5
Lindo, A. (Lab)	5,523	9.4
Odam, F. (Ref)	3,636	6.2
Bolitho, J. (MK)	645	1.1
Winfield, R. (Lib)	186	0.3
Cresswell, N. (NLP)	152	0.3
LD majority	13,847	23.78%
Electorate	80,076	
Total Vote	58,495	Poll 72.9%

*Member of last parliament
LD Hold (10.3% Swing from Con to LD)

NORTH DEVON

		%
*Harvey, N. (LD)	27,824	50.8
Ashworth, R. (Con)	21,643	39.5
Brenton, E. (Lab)	5,347	9.8
LD majority	6,181	11.3%
Electorate	70,350	
Total Vote	54,814	Poll 77.9%

*Member of last parliament
LD Hold (5% Swing from Con to LD)

NORTH DORSET

		%
Walter, R. (Con)	23,294	44.3
Yates, P. (LD)	20,548	39.1
Fitzmaurice, J. (Lab)	5,380	10.2
Evans, M. (Ref)	2,564	4.9
Wheeler, D. (UKIP)	801	1.5
Con majority	2,746	5.22%
Electorate	68,923	
Total Vote	52,587	Poll 76.3%

Con Hold (6.9% Swing from Con to LD)

NORTH DOWN

		%
*McCartney, R. (UKU)	12,817	35.1
McFarland, A. (UUP)	11,368	31.1
Napier, O. (APNI)	7,554	20.7
Fee, A. (Con)	1,810	5.0
Farrell, M. (SDLP)	1,602	4.4
Morrice, J. (Women)	1,240	3.4
Mullins, T. (NLP)	108	0.3
Mooney, R. (NI Party)	67	0.2
UKU majority	1,449	3.96%
Electorate	63,010	
Total Vote	36,566	Poll 58%

*Member of last parliament
UKU Hold (0% Swing from to)

NORTH EAST BEDFORDSHIRE

		%
*Lyell, Sir N. (Con)	22,311	44.3
Lehal, J. (Lab)	16,428	32.6
Bristow, P. (LD)	7,179	14.2
Taylor, J. (Ref)	2,490	4.9
Foley, F. (IndCon)	1,842	3.7
Bence, B. (NLP)	138	0.3
Con majority	5,883	11.68%
Electorate	64,743	
Total Vote	50,388	Poll 77.6%

*Member of last parliament
Con Hold (13.8% Swing from Con to Lab)

NORTH EAST CAMBRIDGESHIRE %
*Moss, M. (Con)   23,855   43.0
Bucknor, V. (Lab)   18,754   33.8
Nash, A. (LD)   9,070   16.4
Bacon, M. (Ref)   2,636   4.8
Bennett, C. (SLP)   851   1.5
Leighton, L. (NLP)   259   0.5
Con majority   5,101   9.20%
Electorate   76,056
Total Vote   55,425   Poll 72.8%
*Member of last parliament
Con Hold (15.4% Swing from Con to Lab)

NORTH EAST DERBYSHIRE %
*Barnes, H. (Lab)   31,425   60.5
Elliott, S. (Con)   13,104   25.2
Hardy, S. (LD)   7,450   14.3
Lab majority 18,321   35.25%
Electorate   72,653
Total Vote   51,979   Poll 72.6%
*Member of last parliament
Lab Hold (12.3% Swing from Con to Lab)

NORTH EAST FIFE %
*Campbell, M. (LD)   21,432   51.2
Bruce, A. (Con)   11,076   26.5
Welsh, C. (SNP)   4,545   10.9
Milne, C. (Lab)   4,301   10.3
Stewart, W. (Ref)   485   1.2
LD majority   10,356   24.75%
Electorate   58,794
Total Vote   41,839   Poll 70.6%
*Member of last parliament
LD Hold (8.4% Swing from Con to LD)

NORTH EAST HAMPSHIRE %
*Arbuthnot, J. (Con)   26,017   50.9
Mann, I. (LD)   11,619   22.7
Dare, P. (Lab)   8,203   16.0
Rees, D. (Ref)   2,420   4.7
Jessavala, K. (Ind)   2,400   4.7
Berry, C. (UKIP)   452   0.9
Con majority 14,398   28.17%
Electorate   69,111
Total Vote   51,111   Poll 73.6%
*Member of last parliament
Con Hold (5.4% Swing from Con to LD)

NORTH EAST HERTFORDSHIRE %
*Heald, O. (Con)   21,712   41.8
Gibbons, I. (Lab)   18,624   35.8
Jarvis, S. (LD)   9,493   18.3
Grose, J. (Ref)   2,166   4.2
Con majority   3,088   5.94%
Electorate   67,161
Total Vote   51,995   Poll 77.4%
*Member of last parliament
Con Hold (12.2% Swing from Con to Lab)

NORTH ESSEX %
*Jenkin, B. (Con)   22,480   43.9
Young, T. (Lab)   17,004   33.2
Phillips, A. (LD)   10,028   19.6
Lord, R. (UKIP)   1,202   2.3

Ransome, S. (Green)   495   1.0
Con majority   5,476   10.69%
Electorate   68,008
Total Vote   51,209   Poll 75.3%
*Member of last parliament
Con Hold (14% Swing from Con to Lab)

NORTH NORFOLK %
Prior, D. (Con)   21,456   36.5
Lamb, N. (LD)   20,163   34.4
Cullingham, M. (Lab)   14,736   25.1
Allen, J. (Ref)   2,458   4.2
Con majority   1,293   2.20%
Electorate   77,113
Total Vote   58,813   Poll 76.2%
Con Hold (9.5% Swing from Con to LD)

NORTH SHROPSHIRE %
Paterson, O. (Con)   20,730   40.2
Lucas, I. (Lab)   18,535   36.0
Stevens, J. (LD)   10,489   20.4
Allen, D. (Ref)   1,764   3.4
Con majority   2,195   4.26%
Electorate   70,852
Total Vote   51,518   Poll 72.7%
Con Hold (10.2% Swing from Con to Lab)

NORTH SOUTHWARK AND BERMONDSEY %
*Hughes, S. (LD)   19,831   48.6
Fraser, J. (Lab)   16,444   40.3
Shapps, G. (Con)   2,835   6.9
Davidson, M. (BNP)   713   1.7
Newton, B. (Ref)   545   1.3
Grant, I. (Comm)   175   0.4
Munday, J. (Lib)   157   0.4
Yngvisson, I. (Nat Dem)   95   0.2
LD majority   3,387   8.30%
Electorate   65,598
Total Vote   40,795   Poll 60.9%
*Member of last parliament
LD Hold (4.3% Swing from LD to Lab)

NORTH TAYSIDE %
Swinney, J. (SNP)   20,447   44.8
*Walker, B. (Con)   16,287   35.7
McFatridge, I. (Lab)   5,141   11.3
Regent, P. (LD)   3,716   8.2
SNP majority   4,160   9.12%
Electorate   61,398
Total Vote   45,591   Poll 74.3%
*Member of last parliament
SNP Gain (8.4% Swing from Con to SNP)

NORTH THANET %
*Gale, R. (Con)   21,586   44.1
Johnson, I. (Lab)   18,820   38.4
Kendrick, P. (LD)   5,576   11.4
Chambers, M. (Ref)   2,535   5.2
Haines, J. (UKIP)   438   0.9
Con majority   2,766   5.65%
Electorate   71,112
Total Vote   48,955   Poll 68.8%
*Member of last parliament
Con Hold (14% Swing from Con to Lab)

NORTH TYNESIDE %
*Byers, S. (Lab)   32,810   72.7
McIntyre, M. (Con)   6,167   13.7
Mulvenna, T. (LD)   4,762   10.6
Rollings, M. (Ref)   1,382   3.1
Lab majority 26,643   59.05%
Electorate   66,449
Total Vote   45,121   Poll 67.8%
*Member of last parliament
Lab Hold (12.1% Swing from Con to Lab)

NORTH WARWICKSHIRE %
*O'Brien, M. (Lab)   31,669   58.4
Hammond, S. (Con)   16,902   31.2
Powell, W. (LD)   4,040   7.4
Mole, R. (Ref)   917   1.7
Cooke, C. (UKIP)   533   1.0
Moorcroft, I. (Bert)   178   0.3
Lab majority 14,767   27.23%
Electorate   72,602
Total Vote   54,239   Poll 74.6%
*Member of last parliament
Lab Hold (12.4% Swing from Con to Lab)

NORTH WEST CAMBRIDGESHIRE %
*Mawhinney, B. (Con)   23,488   48.1
Steptoe, L. (Lab)   15,734   32.2
McCoy, B. (LD)   7,388   15.1
Watt, A. (Ref)   1,939   4.0
Wyatt, W. (UKIP)   269   0.6
Con majority   7,754   15.88%
Electorate   65,791
Total Vote   48,818   Poll 74.2%
*Member of last parliament
Con Hold (10.3% Swing from Con to Lab)

NORTH WEST DURHAM %
*Armstrong, H. (Lab)   31,855   68.8
St John Howe, L. (Con)   7,101   15.3
Gillings, A. (LD)   4,991   10.8
Atkinson, R. (Ref)   2,372   5.1
Lab majority 24,754   53.44%
Electorate   67,156
Total Vote   46,319   Poll 69%
*Member of last parliament
Lab Hold (11.4% Swing from Con to Lab)

NORTH WEST HAMPSHIRE %
*Young, Sir G. (Con)   24,730   45.2
Fleming, C. (LD)   13,179   24.1
Mumford, M. (Lab)   12,900   23.6
Callaghan, P. (Ref)   1,533   2.8
Rolt, T. (UKIP)   1,383   2.5
Baxter, B. (Green)   486   0.9
Anscomb, H. (No Bypass)   231   0.4
Dodd, J. (Ind)   225   0.4
Con majority 11,551   21.13%
Electorate   73,222
Total Vote   54,667   Poll 74.4%
*Member of last parliament
Con Hold (4.5% Swing from Con to LD)

NORTH WEST LEICESTERSHIRE %

Taylor, D.		
(Lab/Co-op)	29,332	56.4
Goodwill, R. (Con)	16,113	31.0
Heptinstall, S. (LD)	4,492	8.6
Abney-Hastings, M. (Ref)	2,088	4.0
Lab/Co-op majority	13,219	25.41%
Electorate	65,069	
Total Vote	52,025	Poll 79.8%

Lab Gain (13.5% Swing from Con to Lab)

NORTH WEST NORFOLK %

Turner, G. (Lab)	25,250	43.8
*Bellingham, H. (Con)	23,911	41.5
Knowles, E. (LD)	5,513	9.6
Percival, R. (Ref)	2,923	5.1
Lab majority	1,339	2.32%
Electorate	77,083	
Total Vote	57,597	Poll 74.6%

*Member of last parliament
Lab Gain (10.4% Swing from Con to Lab)

NORTH WILTSHIRE %

Gray, J. (Con)	25,390	43.8
Cordon, S. (LD)	21,915	37.8
Knowles, N. (Lab)	8,261	14.2
Purves, M. (Ref)	1,774	3.1
Wood, A. (UKIP)	410	0.7
Forsyth, J. (NLP)	263	0.5
Con majority	3,475	5.99%
Electorate	77,237	
Total Vote	58,013	Poll 74.6%

Con Hold (9.3% Swing from Con to LD)

NORTHAMPTON NORTH %

Keeble, S. (Lab)	27,247	52.7
*Marlow, T. (Con)	17,247	33.4
Dunbar, L. (LD)	6,579	12.7
Torbica, D. (UKIP)	464	0.9
Spivack, B. (NLP)	161	0.3
Lab majority	10,000	19.34%
Electorate	73,664	
Total Vote	51,698	Poll 69.9%

*Member of last parliament
Lab Gain (13.3% Swing from Con to Lab)

NORTHAMPTON SOUTH %

Clarke, T. (Lab)	24,214	42.4
*Morris, M. (Con)	23,470	41.1
Worgan, A. (LD)	6,316	11.1
Petrie, C. (Ref)	1,405	2.5
Clark, D. (UKIP)	1,159	2.0
Woollcombe, G. (NLP)	541	0.9
Lab majority	744	1.30%
Electorate	79,384	
Total Vote	57,105	Poll 71.7%

*Member of last parliament
Lab Gain (13.4% Swing from Con to Lab)

NORTHAVON %

Webb, S. (LD)	26,500	42.4
*Cope, Sir J. (Con)	24,363	39.0
Stone, R. (Lab)	9,767	15.6
Parfitt, J. (Ref)	1,900	3.0
LD majority	2,137	3.42%
Electorate	78,943	
Total Vote	62,530	Poll 79.1%

*Member of last parliament
LD Gain (10.4% Swing from Con to LD)

NORWICH NORTH %

Gibson, I. (Lab)	27,346	49.7
Kinghorn, R. (Con)	17,876	32.5
Young, P. (LD)	6,951	12.6
Bailey-Smith, T. (Ref)	1,777	3.2
Marks, H. (Cannabis)	512	0.9
Hood, J. (SLP)	495	0.9
Mills, D. (NLP)	100	0.2
Lab majority	9,470	17.20%
Electorate	72,521	
Total Vote	55,057	Poll 75.7%

Lab Gain (10.6% Swing from Con to Lab)

NORWICH SOUTH %

Clarke, C. (Lab)	26,267	51.7
Khanbhai, B. (Con)	12,028	23.7
Aalders-Dunthorne, A. (LD)	9,457	18.6
Holdsworth, D. (Ref)	1,464	2.9
Marks, H. (LCP)	765	1.5
Holmes, A. (Green)	736	1.4
Parsons, B. (NLP)	84	0.2
Lab majority	14,239	28.03%
Electorate	70,009	
Total Vote	50,801	Poll 72.6%

Lab Hold (10.1% Swing from Con to Lab)

NOTTINGHAM EAST %

*Heppell, J. (Lab)	24,755	62.3
Raca, A. (Con)	9,336	23.5
Mulloy, K. (LD)	4,008	10.1
Brown, B. (Ref)	1,645	4.1
Lab majority	15,419	38.80%
Electorate	65,581	
Total Vote	39,744	Poll 60.2%

*Member of last parliament
Lab Hold (11.3% Swing from Con to Lab)

NOTTINGHAM NORTH %

*Allen, G. (Lab)	27,203	65.7
Shaw, G. (Con)	8,402	20.3
Oliver, R. (LD)	3,301	8.0
Neal, J. (Ref)	1,858	4.5
Belfield, A. (Soc)	637	1.5
Lab majority	18,801	45.41%
Electorate	65,698	
Total Vote	41,401	Poll 62.9%

*Member of last parliament
Lab Hold (12.4% Swing from Con to Lab)

NOTTINGHAM SOUTH %

*Simpson, A. (Lab)	26,825	55.3
Kirsch, B. (Con)	13,461	27.7
Long, G. (LD)	6,265	12.9
Thompson, K. (Ref)	1,523	3.1
Edwards, S. (Nat Dem)	446	0.9
Lab majority	13,364	27.54%
Electorate	72,418	
Total Vote	48,520	Poll 66.6%

*Member of last parliament
Lab Hold (10.8% Swing from Con to Lab)

NUNEATON %

*Olner, B. (Lab)	30,080	56.2
Blunt, R. (Con)	16,540	30.9
Cockings, R. (LD)	4,732	8.8
English, R. (Ref)	1,533	2.9
Bray, D. (LocInd)	390	0.7
Everitt, P. (UKIP)	238	0.4
Lab majority	13,540	25.30%
Electorate	72,032	
Total Vote	53,513	Poll 74.2%

*Member of last parliament
Lab Hold (11.3% Swing from Con to Lab)

OCHIL %

*O'Neill, M. (Lab)	19,707	45.0
Reid, G. (SNP)	15,055	34.4
Hogarth, A. (Con)	6,383	14.6
Watters, A. (LD)	2,262	5.2
White, D. (Ref)	210	0.5
Macdonald, I. (Dem Nat)	104	0.2
Sullivan, M. (NLP)	65	0.1
Lab majority	4,652	10.62%
Electorate	56,572	
Total Vote	43,786	Poll 76.9%

*Member of last parliament
Lab Hold (3.2% Swing from Lab to SNP)

OGMORE %

*Powell, R. (Lab)	28,163	74.0
Unwin, D. (Con)	3,716	9.8
Williams, K. (LD)	3,510	9.2
Rogers, J. (PC)	2,679	7.0
Lab majority	24,447	64.22%
Electorate	52,078	
Total Vote	38,068	Poll 73.1%

*Member of last parliament
Lab Hold (3.8% Swing from Con to Lab)

OLD BEXLEY AND SIDCUP %

*Heath, Sir E. (Con)	21,608	42.0
Justham, R. (Lab)	18,039	35.1
King, I. (LD)	8,284	16.1
Reading, B. (Ref)	2,457	4.8
Bullen, C. (UKIP)	489	1.0
Tyndall, V. (BNP)	415	0.8
Stephens, R. (NLP)	99	0.2
Con majority	3,569	6.94%
Electorate	68,044	
Total Vote	51,391	Poll 75.5%

*Member of last parliament
Con Hold (14.1% Swing from Con to Lab)

OLDHAM EAST AND SADDLEWORTH %

Woolas, P. (Lab)	22,546	41.7
*Davies, C. (LD)	19,157	35.4
Hudson, J. (Con)	10,666	19.7
Findley, D. (Ref)	1,116	2.1
Smith, J. (SLP)	470	0.9
Dalling, I. (NLP)	146	0.3
Lab majority	3,389	6.26%
Electorate	73,189	
Total Vote	54,101	Poll 73.9%

*Member of last parliament
Lab Gain (13.6% Swing from Con to Lab)

OLDHAM WEST AND ROYTON

		%
*Meacher, M. (Lab)	26,894	58.8
Lord, J. (Con)	10,693	23.4
Cohen, H. (LD)	5,434	11.9
Choudhury, G. (SLP)	1,311	2.9
Etherden, P. (Ref)	1,157	2.5
Dalling, S. (NLP)	249	0.5
Lab majority	16,201	35.42%
Electorate	69,203	
Total Vote	45,738	Poll 66.1%

*Member of last parliament
Lab Hold (12.2% Swing from Con to Lab)

ORKNEY AND SHETLAND

		%
*Wallace, J. (LD)	10,743	52.0
Paton, J. (Lab)	3,775	18.3
Ross, W. (SNP)	2,624	12.7
Anderson, H. (Con)	2,527	12.2
Adamson, F. (Ref)	820	4.0
Wharton, C. (Artist)	116	0.6
Robertson, A. (Ind)	60	0.3
LD majority	6,968	33.72%
Electorate	32,291	
Total Vote	20,665	Poll 63.9%

*Member of last parliament
LD Hold (3.6% Swing from Lab to LD)

ORPINGTON

		%
*Horam, J. (Con)	24,417	40.6
Maines, C. (LD)	21,465	35.7
Polydorou, S. (Lab)	10,753	17.9
Clark, D. (Ref)	2,316	3.8
Carver, J. (UKIP)	526	0.9
Almond, R. (Lib)	494	0.8
Wilton, N. (Pro-Life)	191	0.3
Con majority	2,952	4.91%
Electorate	78,749	
Total Vote	60,162	Poll 76.4%

*Member of last parliament
Con Hold (11% Swing from Con to LD)

OXFORD EAST

		%
*Smith, A. (Lab)	27,205	56.8
Djanogly, J. (Con)	10,540	22.0
Kershaw, G. (LD)	7,038	14.7
Young, M. (Ref)	1,391	2.9
Simmons, C. (Green)	975	2.0
Harper-Jones, D. (Pro-Life)	318	0.7
Gardner, P. (UKIP)	234	0.5
Thompson, J. (NLP)	108	0.2
Mylvaganam, P. (Anti-Maj)	68	0.1
Lab majority	16,665	34.81%
Electorate	69,339	
Total Vote	47,877	Poll 69%

*Member of last parliament
Lab Hold (9.1% Swing from Con to Lab)

OXFORD WEST AND ABINGDON

		%
Harris, E. (LD)	26,268	42.9
Harris, L. (Con)	19,983	32.7
Brown, S. (Lab)	12,361	20.2
Eustace, G. (Ref)	1,258	2.1
Woodin, M. (Green)	691	1.1

Buckton, R. (UKIP)	258	0.4
Hodge, L. (Pro-Life)	238	0.4
Wilson, A. (NLP)	91	0.1
Rose, J. (Local Govt)	48	0.1
LD majority	6,285	10.27%
Electorate	79,324	
Total Vote	61,196	Poll 77.1%

LD Gain (10.3% Swing from Con to LD)

PAISLEY NORTH

		%
*Adams, I. (Lab)	20,295	59.5
Mackay, I. (SNP)	7,481	21.9
Brookes, K. (Con)	3,267	9.6
Jelfs, A. (LD)	2,365	6.9
Graham, R. (Pro-Life)	531	1.6
Mathew, E. (Ref)	196	0.6
Lab majority	12,814	37.54%
Electorate	49,725	
Total Vote	34,135	Poll 68.5%

*Member of last parliament
Lab Hold (4.6% Swing from SNP to Lab)

PAISLEY SOUTH

		%
*McMaster, G. (Lab/Co-op)	21,482	57.5
Martin, B. (SNP)	8,732	23.4
McCartin, E. (LD)	3,500	9.4
Reid, R. (Con)	3,237	8.7
Lardner, J. (Ref)	254	0.7
Clerkin, S. (ScotSoc)	146	0.4
Lab/Co-op majority	12,750	34.14%
Electorate	54,040	
Total Vote	37,351	Poll 69.5%

*Member of last parliament
Lab Hold (3.9% Swing from SNP to Lab)

PENDLE

		%
*Prentice, G. (Lab)	25,059	53.3
Midgley, J. (Con)	14,235	30.3
Greaves, T. (LD)	5,460	11.6
Hockney, D. (Ref)	2,281	4.8
Lab majority	10,824	23.01%
Electorate	63,049	
Total Vote	47,035	Poll 74.5%

*Member of last parliament
Lab Hold (9.5% Swing from Con to Lab)

PENRITH AND THE BORDER

		%
*Maclean, D. (Con)	23,300	47.6
Walker, K. (LD)	13,067	26.7
Meling, M. (Lab)	10,576	21.6
Pope, C. (Ref)	2,018	4.1
Con majority	10,233	20.90%
Electorate	66,496	
Total Vote	48,961	Poll 73.6%

*Member of last parliament
Con Hold (4.4% Swing from Con to LD)

PERTH

		%
*Cunningham, R. (SNP)	16,209	36.4
Godfrey, J. (Con)	13,068	29.3
Alexander, D. (Lab)	11,036	24.8
Brodie, C. (LD)	3,583	8.0

MacAuley, R. (Ref)	366	0.8
Henderson, M. (UKIP)	289	0.6
SNP majority	3,141	7.05%
Electorate	60,313	
Total Vote	44,551	Poll 73.9%

*Member of last parliament
SNP Gain (6.6% Swing from Con to SNP)

PETERBOROUGH

		%
Brinton, H. (Lab)	24,365	50.3
Foster, J. (Con)	17,042	35.2
Howarth, D. (LD)	5,170	10.7
Slater, P. (Ref)	924	1.9
Brettell, C. (NLP)	334	0.7
Linskey, J. (UKIP)	317	0.7
Goldspink, S. (Pro-Life)	275	0.6
Lab majority	7,323	15.12%
Electorate	65,926	
Total Vote	48,427	Poll 72.8%

Lab Gain (13.4% Swing from Con to Lab)

PLYMOUTH DEVONPORT

		%
*Jamieson, D. (Lab)	31,629	60.9
Johnson, A. (Con)	12,562	24.1
Copus, R. (LD)	5,570	10.7
Norsworthy, C. (Ref)	1,486	2.9
Farrand, C. (UKIP)	478	0.9
Ebbs, S. (Nat Dem)	238	0.5
Lab majority	19,067	36.69%
Electorate	74,483	
Total Vote	51,963	Poll 69.8%

*Member of last parliament
Lab Hold (12.7% Swing from Con to Lab)

PLYMOUTH SUTTON

		%
Gilroy, L. (Lab/Co-op)	23,881	50.1
Crisp, A. (Con)	14,441	30.3
Melia, S. (LD)	6,613	13.9
Hanbury, T. (Ref)	1,654	3.5
Bullock, R. (UKIP)	499	1.0
Kelway, K. (Plymouth)	396	0.8
Lyons, F. (NLP)	168	0.4
Lab/Co-op majority	9,440	19.81%
Electorate	70,666	
Total Vote	47,652	Poll 67%

Lab/Co-op Gain (10.9% Swing from Con to Lab)

PONTEFRACT AND CASTLEFORD

		%
Cooper, Y. (Lab)	31,339	75.7
Flook, A. (Con)	5,614	13.6
Paxton, W. (LD)	3,042	7.3
Wood, R. (Ref)	1,401	3.4
Lab majority	25,725	62.14%
Electorate	62,350	
Total Vote	41,396	Poll 66.4%

Lab Hold (6.6% Swing from Con to Lab)

PONTYPRIDD   %
*Howells, K. (Lab)   29,290   .63.9
Howells, N. (LD)   6,161   13.5
Cowen, J. (Con)   5,910   12.9
Llewelyn, O. (PC)   2,977   6.5
Wood, J. (Ref)   874   1.9
Skelly, P. (SLP)   380   0.8
Griffiths, R. (Comm)   178   0.4
Moore, A. (NLP)   85   0.2
Lab majority   23,129   50.44%
Electorate   64,185
Total Vote   45,855   Poll 71.4%
*Member of last parliament
Lab Hold (0.9% Swing from Lab to LD)

POOLE   %
Syms, R. (Con)   19,726   42.1
Tetlow, A. (LD)   14,428   30.9
White, H. (Lab)   10,100   21.6
Riddington, J. (Ref)   1,932   4.1
Tyler, P. (UKIP)   487   1.0
Rosta, J. (NLP)   137   0.3
Con majority   5,298   11.32%
Electorate   66,078
Total Vote   46,810   Poll 70.8%
Con Hold (7.2% Swing from Con to LD)

POPLAR AND CANNING
TOWN   %
Fitzpatrick, J. (Lab)   24,807   63.2
Steinberg, B. (Con)   5,892   15.0
Ludlow, J. (LD)   4,072   10.4
Tyndall, J. (BNP)   2,849   7.3
Hare, I. (Ref)   1,091   2.8
Joseph, J. (SLP)   557   1.4
Lab majority   18,915   48.17%
Electorate   67,172
Total Vote   39,268   Poll 58.5%
Lab Hold (11.3% Swing from Con to Lab)

PORTSMOUTH NORTH   %
Rapson, S. (Lab)   21,339   47.1
*Griffiths, P. (Con)   17,016   37.6
Sollitt, S. (LD)   4,788   10.6
Evelegh, S. (Ref)   1,757   3.9
Coe, P. (UKIP)   298   0.7
Bex, C. (Wessex Reg)   72   0.2
Lab majority   4,323   9.55%
Electorate   64,539
Total Vote   45,270   Poll 70.1%
*Member of last parliament
Lab Gain (13.5% Swing from Con to Lab)

PORTSMOUTH SOUTH   %
Hancock, M. (LD)   20,421   39.5
*Martin, D. (Con)   16,094   31.1
Burnett, A. (Lab)   13,086   25.3
Trim, C. (Ref)   1,629   3.2
Thompson, J. (Lib)   184   0.4
Evans, J. (UKIP)   141   0.3
Treend, W. (NLP)   140   0.3
LD majority   4,327   8.37%
Electorate   80,514
Total Vote   51,695   Poll 63.8%
*Member of last parliament
LD Gain (4.4% Swing from Con to LD)

PRESELI
PEMBROKESHIRE   %
Lawrence, J. (Lab)   20,477   48.3
Buckland, R. (Con)   11,741   27.7
Clarke, J. (LD)   5,527   13.0
Jones, A. (PC)   2,683   6.3
Berry, D. (Ref)   1,574   3.7
Cato, M. (Green)   401   0.9
Lab majority   8,736   20.60%
Electorate   54,088
Total Vote   42,403   Poll 78.2%
Lab Gain (11% Swing from Con to Lab)

PRESTON   %
*Wise, A. (Lab)   29,220   60.8
Gray, P. (Con)   10,540   21.9
Chadwick, W. (LD)   7,045   14.7
Porter, J. (Ref)   924   1.9
Ashforth, J. (NLP)   345   0.7
Lab majority   18,680   38.86%
Electorate   72,933
Total Vote   48,074   Poll 65.7%
*Member of last parliament
Lab Hold (9% Swing from Con to Lab)

PUDSEY   %
Truswell, P. (Lab)   25,370   48.1
Bone, P. (Con)   19,163   36.3
Brown, J. (LD)   7,375   14.0
Crabtree, D. (Ref)   823   1.6
Lab majority   6,207   11.77%
Electorate   70,922
Total Vote   52,731   Poll 74.3%
Lab Gain (13.2% Swing from Con to Lab)

PUTNEY   %
Colman, A. (Lab)   20,084   45.7
*Mellor, D. (Con)   17,108   38.9
Pyne, R. (LD)   4,739   10.8
Goldsmith, J. (Ref)   1,518   3.5
Jamieson, W. (UKIP)   233   0.5
Beige, L. (Stan)   101   0.2
Yardley, M. (Spts All)   90   0.2
Small, J. (NLP)   66   0.2
Poole, A. (Beaut)   49   0.1
Van Braam, D.
(Ren Dem)   7   0.0
Lab majority   2,976   6.76%
Electorate   60,176
Total Vote   43,995   Poll 71.4%
*Member of last parliament
Lab Gain (11.2% Swing from Con to Lab)

RAYLEIGH   %
*Clark, M. (Con)   25,516   49.7
Ellis, R. (Lab)   14,832   28.9
Cumberland, S. (LD)   10,137   19.8
Farmer, A. (Lib)   829   1.6
Con majority   10,684   20.82%
Electorate   68,737
Total Vote   51,314   Poll 74.7%
*Member of last parliament
Con Hold (12.7% Swing from Con to Lab)

READING EAST   %
Griffiths, J. (Lab)   21,461   42.7
*Watts, J. (Con)   17,666   35.2

Samuel, R. (LD)   9,307   18.5
Harmer, P. (Ref)   1,042   2.1
Buckley, J. (NLP)   254   0.5
Thornton, A. (UKIP)   252   0.5
Packer, B. (BNP)   238   0.5
Lab majority   3,795   7.56%
Electorate   71,586
Total Vote   50,220   Poll 70.2%
*Member of last parliament
Lab Gain (13.9% Swing from Con to Lab)

READING WEST   %
Salter, M. (Lab)   21,841   45.1
Bennett, N. (Con)   18,844   38.9
Tomlin, D. (LD)   6,153   12.7
Brown, S. (Ref)   976   2.0
Dell, I. (BNP)   320   0.7
Black, D. (UKIP)   255   0.5
Lab majority   2,997   6.19%
Electorate   69,073
Total Vote   48,389   Poll 70.1%
Lab Gain (15% Swing from Con to Lab)

REDCAR   %
*Mowlam, M. (Lab)   32,975   67.3
Isaacs, A. (Con)   11,308   23.1
Benbow, J. (LD)   4,679   9.6
Lab majority   21,667   44.25%
Electorate   68,965
Total Vote   48,962   Poll 71.0%
*Member of last parliament
Lab Hold (12.3% Swing from Con to Lab)

REDDITCH   %
Smith, J. (Lab)   22,280   49.8
McIntyre, A. (Con)   16,155   36.1
Hall, M. (LD)   4,935   11.0
Cox, R. (Ref)   1,151   2.6
Davis, P. (NLP)   227   0.5
Lab majority   6,125   13.69%
Electorate   60,841
Total Vote   44,748   Poll 73.5%
Lab Gain (10.2% Swing from Con to Lab)

REGENT'S PARK AND
KENSINGTON NORTH   %
Buck, K. (Lab)   28,367   59.9
McGuinness, P. (Con)   13,710   29.0
Gasson, E. (LD)   4,041   8.5
Dangoor, S. (Ref)   867   1.8
Hinde, J. (NLP)   192   0.4
Sadowitz, D. (Dream)   167   0.4
Lab majority   14,657   30.96%
Electorate   73,752
Total Vote   47,344   Poll 64.2%
Lab Hold (11.8% Swing from Con to Lab)

REIGATE   %
Blunt, C. (Con)   21,123   43.8
Howard, A. (Lab)   13,382   27.8
Samuel, P. (LD)   9,615   20.0
*Gardiner, G. (Ref)   3,352   7.0
Higgs, R. (Loc Ind)   412   0.9
Smith, S. (UKIP)   290   0.6
Con majority   7,741   16.07%
Electorate   64,750
Total Vote   48,174   Poll 73.8%
*Member of last parliament
Con Re-gain (12% Swing from Con to Lab)

RHONDDA %
*Rogers, A. (Lab)   30,381   74.5
Wood, L. (PC)   5,450   13.4
Berman, R. (LD)   2,307   5.7
Whiting, S. (Con)   1,551   3.8
Gardener, S. (Ref)   658   1.6
Jakeway, K. (Green)   460   1.1

Lab majority 24,931   61.09%
Electorate   57,105
Total Vote   40,807 Poll 71.5%
*Member of last parliament
Lab Hold (0.8% Swing from Lab to PC)

RIBBLE VALLEY %
*Evans, N. (Con)   26,702   46.7
Carr, J. (LD)   20,062   35.1
Johnstone, M. (Lab)   9,013   15.8
Parkinson, J. (Ref)   1,297   2.3
Holmes, N. (NLP)   147   0.3

Con majority 6,640   11.60%
Electorate   72,664
Total Vote   57,221 Poll 78.5%
*Member of last parliament
Con Hold (1.4% Swing from Con to LD)

RICHMOND (YORKS) %
*Hague, W. (Con)   23,326   48.9
Merritt, S. (Lab)   13,275   27.8
Harvey, J. (LD)   8,773   18.4
Bentley, A. (Ref)   2,367   5.0

Con majority 10,051   21.05%
Electorate   65,058
Total Vote   47,741 Poll 73.4%
*Member of last parliament
Con Hold (13.9% Swing from Con to Lab)

RICHMOND PARK %
Tonge, J. (LD)   25,393   44.7
*Hanley, J. (Con)   22,442   39.5
Jenkins, S. (Lab)   7,172   12.6
Pugh, J. (Ref)   1,467   2.6
Beaupre, D. (Loony)   204   0.4
D'Arcy, B. (NLP)   102   0.2
Davies, P. (Dream)   73   0.1

LD majority 2,951   5.19%
Electorate   71,572
Total Vote   56,853 Poll 77.3%
*Member of last parliament
LD Gain (9.7% Swing from Con to LD)

ROCHDALE %
Fitzsimons, L. (Lab) 23,758   49.4
*Lynne, L. (LD)   19,213   40.0
Turnberg, M. (Con)   4,237   8.8
Bergin, G. (BNP)   653   1.4
Salim, M. (Islam)   221   0.5

Lab majority 4,545   9.45%
Electorate   68,529
Total Vote   48,082 Poll 70%
*Member of last parliament
Lab Gain (4.8% Swing from LD to Lab)

ROCHFORD AND SOUTHEND EAST %
*Taylor, T. (Con)   22,683   48.7
Smith, N. (Lab)   18,458   39.7
Smith, P. (LD)   4,387   9.4

Lynch, B. (Lib)   1,007   2.2
Con majority 4,225   9.08%
Electorate   72,848
Total Vote   46,535 Poll 63.6%
*Member of last parliament
Con Hold (11.2% Swing from Con to Lab)

ROMFORD %
Gordon, E. (Lab)   18,187   43.2
*Neubert, Sir M.
    (Con)   17,538   41.6
Meyer, N. (LD)   3,341   7.9
Ward, S. (Ref)   1,431   3.4
Hurlstone, T. (Lib)   1,100   2.6
Carey, M. (BNP)   522   1.2

Lab majority   649   1.54%
Electorate   59,611
Total Vote   42,119 Poll 70.5%
*Member of last parliament
Lab Gain (15.6% Swing from Con to Lab)

ROMSEY %
*Colvin, M. (Con)   23,834   46.0
Cooper, M. (LD)   15,249   29.4
Ford, J. (Lab)   9,623   18.6
Sked, A. (UKIP)   1,824   3.5
Wigley, M. (Ref)   1,291   2.5

Con majority 8,585   16.57%
Electorate   67,306
Total Vote   51,821 Poll 76.4%
*Member of last parliament
Con Hold (11.8% Swing from Con to LD)

ROSS, SKYE AND INVERNESS WEST %
*Kennedy, C. (LD)   15,472   38.7
Munro, D. (Lab)   11,453   28.7
Paterson, M. (SNP)   7,821   19.6
MacLeod, M. (Con)   4,368   10.9
Durance, A. (Ref)   535   1.3
Hopkins, A. (Green)   306   0.8

LD majority 4,019   10.06%
Electorate   55,639
Total Vote   39,955 Poll 71.6%
*Member of last parliament
LD Hold (4.9% Swing from LD to Lab)

ROSSENDALE AND DARWEN %
*Anderson, J. (Lab) 27,470   53.6
Buzzard, P. (Con)   16,521   32.3
Dunning, B. (LD)   5,435   10.6
Newstead, R. (Ref)   1,108   2.2
Wearden, A. (BNP)   674   1.3

Lab majority 10,949   21.38%
Electorate   69,749
Total Vote   51,208 Poll 73.4%
*Member of last parliament
Lab Hold (10.6% Swing from Con to Lab)

ROTHER VALLEY %
*Barron, K. (Lab)   31,184   67.6
Stanbury, S. (Con)   7,699   16.7
Burgess, S. (LD)   5,342   11.6
Cook, S. (Ref)   1,932   4.2

Lab majority 23,485   50.88%

Electorate   68,622
Total Vote   46,157 Poll 67.2%
*Member of last parliament
Lab Hold (8.6% Swing from Con to Lab)

ROTHERHAM %
*MacShane, D. (Lab) 26,852   71.3
Gordon, S. (Con)   5,383   14.3
Wildgoose, D. (LD)   3,919   10.4
Hollebone, R. (Ref)   1,132   3.0
Neal, F. (Pro-Life)   364   1.0

Lab majority 21,469   57.02%
Electorate   59,895
Total Vote   37,650 Poll 62.8%
*Member of last parliament
Lab Hold (8.4% Swing from Con to Lab)

ROXBURGH AND BERWICKSHIRE %
*Kirkwood, A. (LD)   16,243   46.5
Younger, D. (Con)   8,337   23.9
Eadie, H. (Lab)   5,226   15.0
Balfour, M. (SNP)   3,959   11.3
Curtis, J. (Ref)   922   2.6
Neilson, P. (UKIP)   202   0.6
Lucas, D. (NLP)   42   0.1

LD majority 7,906   22.63%
Electorate   47,259
Total Vote   34,931 Poll 73.8%
*Member of last parliament
LD Hold (5.2% Swing from Con to LD)

RUGBY AND KENILWORTH %
King, A. (Lab)   26,356   43.1
*Pawsey, J. (Con)   25,861   42.3
Roodhouse, J. (LD)   8,737   14.3
Twite, M. (NLP)   251   0.4

Lab majority   495   0.81%
Electorate   79,384
Total Vote   61,205 Poll 77.1%
*Member of last parliament
Lab Gain (10.6% Swing from Con to Lab)

RUISLIP NORTHWOOD %
*Wilkinson, J. (Con) 22,526   50.2
Barker, P. (Lab)   14,732   32.9
Edwards, C. (LD)   7,279   16.2
Griffin, C. (NLP)   296   0.7

Con majority 7,794   17.38%
Electorate   60,393
Total Vote   44,833 Poll 74.2%
*Member of last parliament
Con Hold (12.8% Swing from Con to Lab)

RUNNYMEDE AND WEYBRIDGE %
Hammond, P. (Con)   25,051   48.6
Peacock, I. (Lab)   15,176   29.4
Taylor, G. (LD)   8,397   16.3
Rolt, P. (Ref)   2,150   4.2
Slater, S. (UKIP)   625   1.2
Sleeman, J. (NLP)   162   0.3

Con majority 9,875   19.15%
Electorate   72,177
Total Vote   51,561 Poll 71.5%
Con Hold (13.1% Swing from Con to Lab)

RUSHCLIFFE %
*Clarke, K. (Con)   27,558   44.4
Pettitt, J. (Lab)   22,503   36.2
Boote, S. (LD)   8,851   14.3
Chadd, S. (Ref)   2,682   4.3
Moore, J. (UKIP)   403   0.6
Miszewska, A. (NLP)   115   0.2
Con majority   5,055   8.14%
Electorate   78,735
Total Vote   62,112   Poll 78.9%
*Member of last parliament
Con Hold (11.5% Swing from Con to Lab)

RUTLAND AND MELTON %
*Duncan, A. (Con)   24,107   45.8
Meads, J. (Lab)   15,271   29.0
Lee, K. (LD)   10,112   19.2
King, R. (Ref)   2,317   4.4
Abbott, J. (UKIP)   823   1.6
Con majority   8,836   16.79%
Electorate   70,150
Total Vote   52,630   Poll 74.9%
*Member of last parliament
Con Hold (14.5% Swing from Con to Lab)

RYEDALE %
*Greenway, J. (Con)   21,351   43.8
Orrell, J. (LD)   16,293   33.4
Hiles, A. (Lab)   8,762   18.0
Mackfall, J. (Ref)   1,460   3.0
Feaster, S. (UKIP)   917   1.9
Con majority   5,058   10.37%
Electorate   65,215
Total Vote   48,783   Poll 74.7%
*Member of last parliament
Con Hold (7.5% Swing from Con to LD)

SAFFRON WALDEN %
*Haselhurst, Sir A.
  (Con)   25,871   45.3
Caton, M. (LD)   15,298   26.8
Fincken, M. (Lab)   12,275   21.5
Glover, R. (Ref)   2,308   4.0
Evans, I. (UKIP)   658   1.2
Tyler, R. (Ind)   486   0.9
Edwards, C. (NLP)   154   0.3
Con majority 10,573   18.53%
Electorate   74,097
Total Vote   57,050   Poll 76.6%
*Member of last parliament
Con Hold (4.7% Swing from Con to LD)

SALFORD %
Blears, H. (Lab)   22,848   69.0
Bishop, E. (Con)   5,779   17.4
Owen, N. (LD)   3,407   10.3
Cumpsty, R. (Ref)   926   2.8
Herman, S. (NLP)   162   0.5
Lab majority 17,069   51.53%
Electorate   58,610
Total Vote   33,122   Poll 56.3%
Lab Hold (9.5% Swing from Con to Lab)

SALISBURY %
*Key, R. (Con)   25,012   42.9
Emmerson-Peirce,
  Y. (LD)   18,736   32.2

Rogers, R. (Lab)   10,242   17.6
Farage, N. (UKIP)   3,332   5.7
Soutar, H. (Green)   623   1.1
Holmes, W. (Ind)   184   0.3
Haysom, S. (NLP)   110   0.2
Con majority   6,276   10.78%
Electorate   78,973
Total Vote   58,239   Poll 73.7%
*Member of last parliament
Con Hold (2% Swing from Con to LD)

**SCARBOROUGH AND
WHITBY** %
Quinn, L. (Lab)   24,791   45.6
*Sykes, J. (Con)   19,667   36.2
Allinson, M. (LD)   7,672   14.1
Murray, S. (Ref)   2,191   4.0
Lab majority   5,124   9.43%
Electorate   75,862
Total Vote   54,321   Poll 71.6%
*Member of last parliament
Lab Gain (14.7% Swing from Con to Lab)

SCUNTHORPE %
*Morley, E. (Lab)   25,107   60.4
Fisher, M. (Con)   10,934   26.3
Smith, G. (LD)   3,497   8.4
Smith, P. (Ref)   1,637   3.9
Hopper, B. (SLP)   399   1.0
Lab majority 14,173   34.09%
Electorate   60,393
Total Vote   41,574   Poll 68.8%
*Member of last parliament
Lab Hold (7.9% Swing from Con to Lab)

SEDGEFIELD %
*Blair, T. (Lab)   33,526   71.2
Pitman, E. (Con)   8,383   17.8
Beadle, R. (LD)   3,050   6.5
Hall, M. (Ref)   1,683   3.6
Gibson, B. (SLP)   474   1.0
Lab majority 25,143   53.36%
Electorate   64,923
Total Vote   47,116   Poll 72.6%
*Member of last parliament
Lab Hold (9.6% Swing from Con to Lab)

SELBY %
Grogan, J. (Lab)   25,838   45.9
Hind, K. (Con)   22,002   39.1
Batty, T. (LD)   6,778   12.0
Walker, D. (Ref)   1,162   2.1
Spence, P. (UKIP)   536   1.0
Lab majority   3,836   6.81%
Electorate   75,141
Total Vote   56,316   Poll 74.9%
Lab Gain (11.1% Swing from Con to Lab)

SEVENOAKS %
Fallon, M. (Con)   22,776   45.4
Hayes, J. (Lab)   12,315   24.6
Walshe, R. (LD)   12,086   24.1
Large, N. (Ref)   2,138   4.3
Lawrence, M. (Green)   443   0.9
Ellis, M. (Path)   244   0.5
Hankey, A. (NLP)   147   0.3

Con majority 10,461   20.86%
Electorate   66,474
Total Vote   50,149   Poll 75.4%
Con Hold (10.3% Swing from Con to Lab)

SHEFFIELD ATTERCLIFFE %
*Betts, C. (Lab)   28,937   65.3
Doyle, B. (Con)   7,119   16.1
Smith, A. (LD)   6,973   15.7
Brown, J. (Ref)   1,289   2.9
Lab majority 21,818   49.23%
Electorate   68,548
Total Vote   44,318   Poll 64.7%
*Member of last parliament
Lab Hold (9% Swing from Con to Lab)

SHEFFIELD BRIGHTSIDE %
*Blunkett, D. (Lab)   24,901   73.5
Butler, F. (LD)   4,947   14.6
Buckwell, C. (Con)   2,850   8.4
Farnsworth, B. (Ref)   624   1.8
Davidson, P. (SLP)   482   1.4
Scott, R. (NLP)   61   0.2
Lab majority 19,954   58.92%
Electorate   58,930
Total Vote   33,865   Poll 57.5%
*Member of last parliament
Lab Hold (0.5% Swing from LD to Lab)

SHEFFIELD CENTRAL %
*Caborn, R. (Lab)   23,179   63.6
Qadar, A. (LD)   6,273   17.2
Hess, M. (Con)   4,341   11.9
D'Agorne, A. (Green)   954   2.6
Brownlow, A. (Ref)   863   2.4
Douglas, K. (Soc)   466   1.3
Aitken, M. (Pro-Life)   280   0.8
Driver, M. (WRP)   63   0.2
Lab majority 16,906   46.42%
Electorate   68,667
Total Vote   36,419   Poll 53%
*Member of last parliament
Lab Hold (2.8% Swing from LD to Lab)

SHEFFIELD HALLAM %
Allan, R. (LD)   23,345   51.3
*Patnick, I. (Con)   15,074   33.1
Conquest, S. (Lab)   6,147   13.5
Davidson, I. (Ref)   788   1.7
Booler, P. (SIP)   125   0.3
LD majority   8,271   18.19%
Electorate   62,834
Total Vote   45,479   Poll 72.4%
*Member of last parliament
LD Gain (18.5% Swing from Con to LD)

SHEFFIELD HEELEY %
*Michie, B. (Lab)   26,274   60.7
Davison, R. (LD)   9,196   21.3
Harthman, J. (Con)   6,767   15.6
Mawson, D. (Ref)   1,029   2.4
Lab majority 17,078   39.47%
Electorate   66,599
Total Vote   43,266   Poll 65%
*Member of last parliament
Lab Hold (1.1% Swing from LD to Lab)

SHEFFIELD HILLSBOROUGH %
*Jackson, H. (Lab)   30,150   56.9
Dunworth, A. (LD)   13,699   25.8
Nuttall, D. (Con)   7,707   14.5
Rusling, J. (Ref)   1,468   2.8

Lab majority 16,451   31.03%
Electorate   74,642
Total Vote   53,024   Poll 71%
*Member of last parliament
Lab Hold (9.6% Swing from LD to Lab)

SHERWOOD %
*Tipping, P. (Lab)   33,071   58.5
Spencer, R. (Con)   16,259   28.8
Moult, B. (LD)   4,889   8.6
Slack, L. (Ref)   1,882   3.3
Ballard, P. (BNP)   432   0.8

Lab majority 16,812   29.74%
Electorate   74,788
Total Vote   56,533   Poll 75.5%
*Member of last parliament
Lab Hold (12.5% Swing from Con to Lab)

SHIPLEY %
Leslie, C. (Lab)   22,962   43.4
*Fox, Sir M. (Con)   19,966   37.8
Cole, J. (LD)   7,984   15.1
Ellams, S. (Ref)   1,960   3.7

Lab majority   2,996   5.67%
Electorate   69,281
Total Vote   52,872   Poll 76.1%
*Member of last parliament
Lab Gain (13.8% Swing from Con to Lab)

SHREWSBURY AND ATCHAM %
Marsden, P. (Lab)   20,484   37.0
*Conway, D. (Con)   18,814   34.0
Woolland, A. (LD)   13,838   25.0
Barker, D. (Ref)   1,346   2.4
Rowlands, D. (UKIP)   477   0.9
Dignan, A. (Farming)   257   0.5
Williams, A. (People's)   128   0.2

Lab majority   1,670   3.02%
Electorate   73,542
Total Vote   55,344   Poll 75.3%
*Member of last parliament
Lab Gain (11.4% Swing from Con to Lab)

SITTINGBOURNE AND SHEPPEY %
Wyatt, D. (Lab)   18,723   40.6
*Moate, Sir R. (Con)   16,794   36.4
Truelove, R. (LD)   8,447   18.3
Moull, P. (Ref)   1,082   2.3
Driver, C. (Loony)   644   1.4
Risi, N. (UKIP)   472   1.0

Lab majority   1,929   4.18%
Electorate   63,850
Total Vote   46,162   Poll 72.3%
*Member of last parliament
Lab Gain (14.5% Swing from Con to Lab)

SKIPTON AND RIPON %
*Curry, D. (Con)   25,294   46.5
Mould, T. (LD)   13,674   25.2
Marchant, R. (Lab)   12,171   22.4

Holdsworth, N. (Ref)   3,212   5.9

Con majority 11,620   21.38%
Electorate   72,042
Total Vote   54,351   Poll 75.4%
*Member of last parliament
Con Hold (4.6% Swing from Con to LD)

SLEAFORD AND NORTH HYKEHAM %
*Hogg, D. (Con)   23,358   43.9
Harriss, S. (Lab)   18,235   34.3
Marriott, J. (LD)   8,063   15.2
Clery, P. (Ref)   2,942   5.5
Overton, R. (Ind)   578   1.1

Con majority   5,123   9.63%
Electorate   71,486
Total Vote   53,176   Poll 74.2%
*Member of last parliament
Con Hold (13.4% Swing from Con to Lab)

SLOUGH %
Mactaggart, F. (Lab)   27,029   56.6
Buscombe, P. (Con)   13,958   29.2
Bushill, C. (LD)   3,509   7.4
Bradshaw, A. (Lib)   1,835   3.8
Sharkey, T. (Ref)   1,124   2.4
Whitmore, P. (Slough)   277   0.6

Lab majority 13,071   27.64%
Electorate   70,283
Total Vote   47,732   Poll 67.9%
Lab Win (13.7% Swing from Con to Lab)

SOLIHULL %
*Taylor, J. (Con)   26,299   44.6
Southcombe, M. (LD)   14,902   25.3
Harris, R. (Lab)   14,334   24.3
Nattrass, M. (Ref)   2,748   4.7
Caffery, J. (Pro-Life)   623   1.1

Con majority 11,397   19.35%
Electorate   78,898
Total Vote   58,906   Poll 74.4%
*Member of last parliament
Con Hold (10.3% Swing from Con to LD)

SOMERTON AND FROME %
Heath, D. (LD)   22,684   39.5
*Robinson, M. (Con)   22,554   39.3
Ashford, R. (Lab)   9,385   16.3
Rodwell, R. (Ref)   2,449   4.3
Gadd, R. (UKIP)   331   0.6

LD majority   130   0.23%
Electorate   73,988
Total Vote   57,403   Poll 77.4%
*Member of last parliament
LD Gain (3.7% Swing from Con to LD)

SOUTH ANTRIM %
*Forsythe, C. (UUP)   23,108   57.5
McClelland, D.
   (SDLP)   6,497   16.2
Ford, D. (APNI)   4,668   11.6
Smyth, H. (PUP)   3,490   8.7
Cushnahan, H. (SF)   2,229   5.5
Briggs, B. (NLP)   203   0.5

UUP majority 16,611   41.33%
Electorate   69,414
Total Vote   40,195   Poll 57.9%
*Member of last parliament
UUP Hold (8.2% Swing from UUP to SDLP)

SOUTH CAMBRIDGESHIRE %
Lansley, A. (Con)   22,572   42.0
Quinlan, J. (LD)   13,860   25.8
Gray, T. (Lab)   13,485   25.1
Page, R. (Ref)   3,300   6.1
Norman, D. (UKIP)   298   0.6
Chalmers, F. (NLP)   168   0.3

Con majority   8,712   16.23%
Electorate   69,850
Total Vote   53,683   Poll 76.1%
Con Hold (8.7% Swing from Con to LD)

SOUTH DERBYSHIRE %
Todd, M. (Lab)   32,709   54.5
*Currie, E. (Con)   18,742   31.3
Renold, R. (LD)   5,408   9.0
North, R. (Ref)   2,491   4.2
Crompton, I.
   (UKIP)   617   1.0

Lab majority 13,967   23.29%
Electorate   76,672
Total Vote   59,967   Poll 78.2%
*Member of last parliament
Lab Gain (13.2% Swing from Con to Lab)

SOUTH DORSET %
*Bruce, I. (Con)   17,755   36.1
Knight, J. (Lab)   17,678   35.9
Plummer, M. (LD)   9,936   20.2
McAndrew, P. (Ref)   2,791   5.7
Shakesby, M.
   (UKIP)   861   1.8
Napper, G. (NLP)   161   0.3

Con majority   77   0.16%
Electorate   66,318
Total Vote   49,182   Poll 74%
*Member of last parliament
Con Hold (15% Swing from Con to Lab)

SOUTH DOWN %
*McGrady, E.
   (SDLP)   26,181   52.9
Nesbitt, D. (UUP)   16,248   32.8
Murphy, M. (SF)   5,127   10.4
Crozier, J. (APNI)   1,711   3.5
McKeon, R. (NLP)   219   0.4

SDLP majority 9,933   20.07%
Electorate   69,855
Total Vote   49,486   Poll 70.8%
*Member of last parliament
SDLP Hold (0.3% Swing from SDLP to UUP)

SOUTH EAST CAMBRIDGESHIRE %
*Paice, J. (Con)   24,397   42.9
Collinson, R. (Lab)   15,048   26.5
Brinton, S. (LD)   14,246   25.1
Howlett, J. (Ref)   2,838   5.0
Lam, K. (Fair)   167   0.3
While, P. (NLP)   111   0.2

Con majority   9,349   16.46%
Electorate   75,666
Total Vote   56,807   Poll 74.8%
*Member of last parliament
Con Hold (10.8% Swing from Con to Lab)

SOUTH EAST CORNWALL %
Breed, C. (LD)	27,044	47.1
Lightfoot, W. (Con)	20,564	35.8
Kirk, D. (Lab)	7,358	12.8
Wonnacott, J. (UKIP)	1,428	2.5
Dunbar, P. (MK)	573	1.0
Weights, B. (Lib)	268	0.5
Hartley, M. (NLP)	197	0.3
LD majority	6,480	11.28%
Electorate	75,825	
Total Vote	57,432	Poll 75.5%

LD Gain (12.1% Swing from Con to LD)

SOUTH HOLLAND AND THE DEEPINGS %
Hayes, J. (Con)	24,691	49.3
Lewis, J. (Lab)	16,700	33.3
Millen, P. (LD)	7,836	15.6
Erwood, G. (Non-party)	902	1.8
Con majority	7,991	15.94%
Electorate	69,642	
Total Vote	50,129	Poll 71.8%

Con Hold (8.5% Swing from Con to Lab)

SOUTH NORFOLK %
*MacGregor, J. (Con)	24,935	40.2
Hacker, B. (LD)	17,557	28.3
Ross, J. (Lab)	16,188	26.1
Bateson, P. (Ref)	2,533	4.1
Ross-Wagenknecht, S. (Green)	484	0.8
Boddy, A. (UKIP)	400	0.6
Con majority	7,378	11.88%
Electorate	79,239	
Total Vote	62,097	Poll 78.4%

Member of last parliament
Con Hold (6.8% Swing from Con to LD)

SOUTH RIBBLE %
Borrow, D. (Lab)	25,856	46.8
*Atkins, R. (Con)	20,772	37.6
Farron, T. (LD)	5,879	10.6
Adams, M. (Ref)	1,475	2.7
Ashton, N. (Lib)	1,127	2.0
Leadbetter, J. (NLP)	122	0.2
Lab majority	5,084	9.20%
Electorate	71,670	
Total Vote	55,231	Poll 77.1%

Member of last parliament
Lab Gain (12.1% Swing from Con to Lab)

SOUTH SHIELDS %
*Clark, D. (Lab)	27,834	71.4
Hoban, M. (Con)	5,681	14.6
Ord, D. (LD)	3,429	8.8
Lorraine, A. (Ref)	1,660	4.3
Wilburn, I. (Shields)	374	1.0
Lab majority	22,153	56.83%
Electorate	62,261	
Total Vote	38,978	Poll 62.6%

Member of last parliament
Lab Hold (11.2% Swing from Con to Lab)

SOUTH STAFFORDSHIRE %
*Cormack, P. (Con)	25,568	50.0
LeMaistre, J. (Lab)	17,747	34.7
Calder, J. (LD)	5,797	11.3

Carnell, P. (Ref)	2,002	3.9
Con majority	7,821	15.30%
Electorate	68,896	
Total Vote	51,114	Poll 74.2%

Member of last parliament
Con Hold (9% Swing from Con to Lab)

SOUTH SUFFOLK %
*Yeo, T. (Con)	19,402	37.3
Bishop, P. (Lab)	15,227	29.3
Pollard, A. (LD)	14,395	27.7
de Chair, S. (Ref)	2,740	5.3
Holland, A. (NLP)	211	0.4
Con majority	4,175	8.03%
Electorate	67,323	
Total Vote	51,975	Poll 77.2%

Member of last parliament
Con Hold (10.7% Swing from Con to Lab)

SOUTH SWINDON %
Drown, J. (Lab)	23,943	46.8
*Coombs, S. (Con)	18,298	35.8
Pajak, S. (LD)	7,371	14.4
McIntosh, D. (Ref)	1,273	2.5
Charman, R. (Route 66)	181	0.4
Buscombe, K. (NLP)	96	0.2
Lab majority	5,645	11.03%
Electorate	70,207	
Total Vote	51,162	Poll 72.9%

Member of last parliament
Lab Gain (14.6% Swing from Con to Lab)

SOUTH THANET %
Ladyman, S. (Lab)	20,777	46.2
*Aitken, J. (Con)	17,899	39.8
Hewitt-Silk, B. (LD)	5,263	11.7
Crook, C. (UKIP)	631	1.4
Wheatley, D. (Green)	418	0.9
Lab majority	2,878	6.40%
Electorate	62,792	
Total Vote	44,988	Poll 71.6%

Member of last parliament
Lab Gain (15% Swing from Con to Lab)

SOUTH WEST BEDFORDSHIRE %
*Madel, Sir D. (Con)	21,534	40.7
Date, A. (Lab)	21,402	40.5
Owen, S. (LD)	7,559	14.3
Hill, R. (Ref)	1,761	3.3
Wise, T. (UKIP)	446	0.8
Le Carpentier, A. (NLP)	162	0.3
Con majority	132	0.25%
Electorate	69,781	
Total Vote	52,864	Poll 75.2%

Member of last parliament
Con Hold (15.1% Swing from Con to Lab)

SOUTH WEST DEVON %
*Streeter, G. (Con)	22,659	42.9
Mavin, C. (Lab)	15,262	28.9
Baldry, K. (LD)	12,542	23.8
Sadler, R. (Ref)	1,668	3.2
King, H. (UKIP)	491	0.9
Hyde, J. (NLP)	159	0.3

Con majority	7,397	14.0%
Electorate	69,293	
Total Vote	52,781	Poll 76.2%

Member of last parliament
Con Hold (13.9% Swing from Con to Lab)

SOUTH WEST HERTFORDSHIRE %
*Page, R. (Con)	25,462	46.0
Wilson, M. (Lab)	15,441	27.9
Shaw, A. (LD)	12,381	22.3
Millward, T. (Ref)	1,853	3.3
Adamson, C. (NLP)	274	0.5
Con majority	10,021	18.08%
Electorate	71,671	
Total Vote	55,411	Poll 76.8%

Member of last parliament
Con Hold (11.8% Swing from Con to Lab)

SOUTH WEST NORFOLK %
*Shephard, G. (Con)	24,694	42.0
Heffernan, A. (Lab)	22,230	37.8
Buckton, D. (LD)	8,178	13.9
Hoare, R. (Ref)	3,694	6.3
Con majority	2,464	4.19%
Electorate	80,236	
Total Vote	58,796	Poll 73.2%

Member of last parliament
Con Hold (11.8% Swing from Con to Lab)

SOUTH WEST SURREY %
*Bottomley, V. (Con)	25,165	44.6
Sherlock, N. (LD)	22,471	39.8
Leicester, M. (Lab)	5,333	9.4
Clementson, J. (Ref)	2,830	5.0
Kirby, P. (UKIP)	401	0.7
Quintavalle, J. (Pro-Life)	258	0.5
Con majority	2,694	4.77%
Electorate	72,350	
Total Vote	56,458	Poll 78%

Member of last parliament
Con Hold (10.1% Swing from Con to LD)

SOUTHAMPTON ITCHEN %
*Denham, J. (Lab)	29,498	54.8
Fleet, P. (Con)	15,289	28.4
Harrison, D. (LD)	6,289	11.7
Clegg, J. (Ref)	1,660	3.1
Rose, K. (SLP)	628	1.2
Hoar, C. (UKIP)	172	0.3
Marsh, G. (Soc)	113	0.2
Barry, R. (NLP)	110	0.2
McDermott, F. (Pro-Life)	99	0.2
Lab majority	14,209	26.38%
Electorate	76,869	
Total Vote	53,858	Poll 70.6%

Member of last parliament
Lab Hold (12.3% Swing from Con to Lab)

SOUTHAMPTON TEST %
Whitehead, A. (Lab)	28,396	54.1
*Hill, Sir J. (Con)	14,712	28.1
Dowden, A. (LD)	7,171	13.7
Day, P. (Ref)	1,397	2.7
Marks, H. (Cannabis)	388	0.7

McCabe, A. (UKIP)	219	0.4
Taylor, P. (Glow)	81	0.2
Sinel, J. (NLP)	77	0.1
Lab majority 13,684		26.09%
Electorate 72,983		
Total Vote 52,441		Poll 71.2%

*Member of last parliament
Lab Win (10.5% Swing from Con to Lab)

SOUTHEND WEST %
*Amess, D. (Con)	18,029	38.8
Stimson, N. (LD)	15,414	33.1
Harley, A. (Lab)	10,600	22.8
Webster, C. (Ref)	1,734	3.7
Lee, B. (UKIP)	636	1.4
Warburton, P. (NLP)	101	0.2
Con majority 2,615		5.62%
Electorate 66,493		
Total Vote 46,514		Poll 69.8%

*Member of last parliament
Con Hold (9.1% Swing from Con to LD)

SOUTHPORT %
Fearn, R. (LD)	24,346	48.1
*Banks, M. (Con)	18,186	35.9
Norman, S. (Lab)	6,129	12.1
Buckle, F. (Ref)	1,368	2.7
Ashton, S. (Lib)	386	0.8
Lines, E. (NLP)	93	0.2
Middleton, M. (Nat Dem)	92	0.2
LD majority 6,160		12.17%
Electorate 70,194		
Total Vote 50,600		Poll 72.1%

*Member of last parliament
LD Gain (8.9% Swing from Con to LD)

SPELTHORNE %
*Wilshire, D. (Con)	23,306	44.9
Dibble, K. (Lab)	19,833	38.2
Glynn, E. (LD)	6,821	13.1
Coleman, B. (Ref)	1,495	2.9
Fowler, J. (UKIP)	462	0.9
Con majority 3,473		6.69%
Electorate 70,562		
Total Vote 51,917		Poll 73.6%

*Member of last parliament
Con Hold (14.5% Swing from Con to Lab)

ST ALBANS %
Pollard, K. (Lab)	21,338	42.0
Rutley, D. (Con)	16,879	33.2
Rowlands, A. (LD)	10,692	21.0
Warrilow, J. (Ref)	1,619	3.2
Craigen, S. (Dream)	166	0.3
Docker, I. (NLP)	111	0.2
Lab majority 4,459		8.78%
Electorate 65,560		
Total Vote 50,805		Poll 77.5%

Lab Gain (14.7% Swing from Con to Lab)

ST HELENS NORTH %
Watts, D. (Lab)	31,953	64.9
Walker, P. (Con)	8,536	17.3
Beirne, J. (LD)	6,270	12.7
Johnson, D. (Ref)	1,276	2.6

Waugh, R. (SLP)	833	1.7
Rudin, R. (UKIP)	363	0.7
Lab majority 23,417		47.57%
Electorate 71,380		
Total Vote 49,231		Poll 69%

Lab Hold (9.1% Swing from Con to Lab)

ST HELENS SOUTH %
*Bermingham, G.
(Lab)	30,367	68.6
Russell, M. (Con)	6,628	15.0
Spencer, B. (LD)	5,919	13.4
Holdaway, W. (Ref)	1,165	2.6
Jump, H. (NLP)	179	0.4
Lab majority 23,739		53.64%
Electorate 66,526		
Total Vote 44,258		Poll 66.5%

*Member of last parliament
Lab Hold (8.5% Swing from Con to Lab)

ST IVES %
George, A. (LD)	23,966	44.5
Rogers, W. (Con)	16,796	31.2
Fegan, C. (Lab)	8,184	15.2
Faulkner, M. (Ref)	3,714	6.9
Garnier, P. (UKIP)	567	1.1
Stephens, G. (Lib)	425	0.8
Lippiatt, K. (Radical)	178	0.3
Hitchins, W. (Male)	71	0.1
LD majority 7,170		13.30%
Electorate 71,680		
Total Vote 53,901		Poll 75%

LD Gain (8.1% Swing from Con to LD)

STAFFORD %
Kidney, D. (Lab)	24,606	47.5
Cameron, D. (Con)	20,292	39.2
Hornby, P. (LD)	5,480	10.6
Culley, S. (Ref)	1,146	2.2
May, A. (Loony)	248	0.5
Lab majority 4,314		8.33%
Electorate 67,555		
Total Vote 51,772		Poll 76.6%

Lab Gain (10.7% Swing from Con to Lab)

STAFFORDSHIRE MOORLANDS %
Atkins, C. (Lab)	26,686	52.2
Ashworth, A. (Con)	16,637	32.5
Jebb, C. (LD)	6,191	12.1
Stanworth, D. (Ref)	1,603	3.1
Lab majority 10,049		19.66%
Electorate 66,095		
Total Vote 51,117		Poll 77.3%

Lab Win (8.7% Swing from Con to Lab)

STALYBRIDGE AND HYDE %
*Pendry, T. (Lab)	25,363	58.9
de Bois, N. (Con)	10,557	24.5
Cross, M. (LD)	5,169	12.0
Clapham, R. (Ref)	1,992	4.6
Lab majority 14,806		34.37%
Electorate 65,468		
Total Vote 43,081		Poll 65.7%

*Member of last parliament
Lab Hold (9.3% Swing from Con to Lab)

STEVENAGE %
Follett, B. (Lab)	28,440	55.3
*Wood, T. (Con)	16,858	32.8
Wilcock, A. (LD)	4,588	8.9
Coburn, J. (Ref)	1,194	2.3
Bundy, D. (Pro-Life)	196	0.4
Calcraft, A. (NLP)	110	0.2
Lab majority 11,582		22.54%
Electorate 66,889		
Total Vote 51,386		Poll 76.8%

*Member of last parliament
Lab Gain (13.9% Swing from Con to Lab)

STIRLING %
McGuire, A. (Lab)	20,382	47.4
*Forsyth, M. (Con)	13,971	32.5
Dow, E. (SNP)	5,752	13.4
Tough, A. (LD)	2,675	6.2
McMurdo, W. (UKIP)	154	0.4
Olsen, E. (Value)	24	0.1
Lab majority 6,411		14.92%
Electorate 52,491		
Total Vote 42,958		Poll 81.8%

*Member of last parliament
Lab Gain (7.7% Swing from Con to Lab)

STOCKPORT %
*Coffey, A. (Lab)	29,338	62.9
Fitzsimmons, S. (Con)	10,426	22.3
Roberts, S. (LD)	4,951	10.6
Morley-Scott, W. (Ref)	1,280	2.7
Southern, G. (SLP)	255	0.5
Newitt, C. (Loony)	213	0.5
Dronsfield, C. (Ind)	206	0.4
Lab majority 18,912		40.52%
Electorate 65,232		
Total Vote 46,669		Poll 71.3%

*Member of last parliament
Lab Hold (15.2% Swing from Con to Lab)

STOCKTON NORTH %
*Cook, F. (Lab)	29,726	66.8
Johnston, B. (Con)	8,369	18.8
Fletcher, S. (LD)	4,816	10.8
McConnell, K. (Ref)	1,563	3.5
Lab majority 21,357		48.02%
Electorate 64,380		
Total Vote 44,474		Poll 69%

*Member of last parliament
Lab Hold (13.5% Swing from Con to Lab)

STOCKTON SOUTH %
Taylor, D. (Lab)	28,790	55.2
*Devlin, T. (Con)	17,205	33.0
Monck, L. (LD)	4,721	9.1
Horner, J. (Ref)	1,400	2.7
Lab majority 11,585		22.66%
Electorate 68,470		
Total Vote 52,116		Poll 76.1%

*Member of last parliament
Lab Gain (15.8% Swing from Con to Lab)

STOKE-ON-TRENT CENTRAL

		%
*Fisher, M. (Lab)	26,662	66.2
Jones, D. (Con)	6,738	16.7
Fordham, E. (LD)	4,809	11.9
Stanyer, P. (Ref)	1,071	2.7
Coleman, M. (BNP)	606	1.5
Oborski, F. (Lib)	359	0.9
Lab majority	19,924	49.51%
Electorate	64,113	
Total Vote	40,245	Poll 62.5%

*Member of last parliament
Lab Hold (9.7% Swing from Con to Lab)

STOKE-ON-TRENT NORTH %

*Walley, J. (Lab)	25,190	65.1
Day, C. (Con)	7,798	20.2
Jebb, H. (LD)	4,141	10.7
Tobin, J. (Ref)	1,537	4.0
Lab majority	17,392	44.98%
Electorate	59,030	
Total Vote	38,666	Poll 65.4%

*Member of last parliament
Lab Hold (11.9% Swing from Con to Lab)

STOKE-ON-TRENT SOUTH

*Stevenson, G. (Lab)	28,645	62.0
Scott, S. (Con)	10,342	22.4
Barnett, P. (LD)	4,710	10.2
Adams, R. (Ref)	1,103	2.4
Micklem, A. (Lib)	580	1.3
Batkin, S. (BNP)	568	1.2
Lawrence, B. (Nat Dem)	288	0.6
Lab majority	18,303	39.59%
Electorate	69,968	
Total Vote	46,236	Poll 66%

*Member of last parliament
Lab Hold (13.3% Swing from Con to Lab)

STONE %

*Cash, W. (Con)	24,859	46.8
Wakefield, J. (Lab)	21,041	39.6
Stamp, B. (LD)	6,392	12.0
Winfield, A. (Lib)	545	1.0
Grice, D. (NLP)	237	0.4
Con majority	3,818	7.19%
Electorate	68,242	
Total Vote	53,074	Poll 77.8%

*Member of last parliament
Con Hold (10% Swing from Con to Lab)

STOURBRIDGE %

Shipley, D. (Lab)	23,452	47.2
*Hawksley, W. (Con)	17,807	35.8
Bramall, C. (LD)	7,123	14.3
Quick, P. (Ref)	1,319	2.7
Lab majority	5,645	11.36%
Electorate	64,966	
Total Vote	49,701	Poll 76.4%

*Member of last parliament
Lab Gain (11% Swing from Con to Lab)

STRANGFORD %

*Taylor, J. (UUP)	18,431	44.3
Robinson, I. (DUP)	12,579	30.2
McCarthy, K. (APNI)	5,467	13.1

O'Reilly, P. (SDLP)	2,775	6.7
Chalk, G. (Con)	1,743	4.2
O Fachtna, G. (SF)	503	1.2
Mullins, S. (NLP)	121	0.3
UUP majority	5,852	14.06%
Electorate	69,980	
Total Vote	41,619	Poll 59.5%

*Member of last parliament
UUP Hold (7.6% Swing from UUP to DUP)

STRATFORD-ON-AVON %

Maples, J. (Con)	29,967	48.3
Juned, S. (LD)	15,861	25.5
Stacey, S. (Lab)	12,754	20.5
Hilton, A. (Ref)	2,064	3.3
Spilsbury, J. (UKIP)	556	0.9
Brewster, J. (NLP)	307	0.5
Marcus, S. (SFDC)	306	0.5
Miller, S. (ProLife)	284	0.5
Con majority	14,106	22.72%
Electorate	81,434	
Total Vote	62,099	Poll 76.3%

*Member of last parliament
Con Re-gain (5.2% Swing from Con to LD)

STRATHKELVIN AND BEARSDEN %

*Galbraith, S. (Lab)	26,278	52.9
McCormick, G. (SNP)	9,986	20.1
Sharpe, D. (Con)	8,111	16.3
Morrison, J. (LD)	4,843	9.7
Wilson, D. (Ref)	339	0.7
Fisher, C. (NLP)	155	0.3
Lab majority	16,292	32.8%
Electorate	62,974	
Total Vote	49,712	Poll 78.9%

*Member of last parliament
Lab Hold (9.6% Swing from Con to Lab)

STREATHAM %

*Hill, K. (Lab)	28,181	62.8
Noad, E. (Con)	9,758	21.7
O'Brien, R. (LD)	6,082	13.6
Wall, J. (Ref)	864	1.9
Lab majority	18,423	41.04%
Electorate	74,509	
Total Vote	44,885	Poll 59%

*Member of last parliament
Lab Hold (15% Swing from Con to Lab)

STRETFORD AND URMSTON %

Hughes, B. (Lab)	28,480	58.5
Gregory, J. (Con)	14,840	30.5
Bridges, J. (LD)	3,978	8.2
Dore, C. (Ref)	1,397	2.9
Lab majority	13,640	28.01%
Electorate	69,913	
Total Vote	48,695	Poll 69.7%

*Member of last parliament
Lab Hold (9.9% Swing from Con to Lab)

STROUD %

Drew, D. (Lab/Co-op)	26,170	42.7
*Knapman, R. (Con)	23,260	37.9
Hodgkinson, P. (LD)	9,502	15.5
Marjoram, J. (Green)	2,415	3.9

Lab/Co-op majority	2,910	4.74%
Electorate	77,494	
Total Vote	61,347	Poll 78.8%

*Member of last parliament
Lab/Co-op Gain (10.8% Swing from Con to Lab)

SUFFOLK COASTAL %

*Gummer, J. (Con)	21,696	38.6
Campbell, M. (Lab)	18,442	32.8
Jones, A. (LD)	12,036	21.4
Caulfield, S. (Ref)	3,416	6.1
Slade, T. (Green)	514	0.9
Kaplan, F. (NLP)	152	0.3
Con majority	3,254	5.78%
Electorate	74,219	
Total Vote	56,256	Poll 75.8%

*Member of last parliament
Con Hold (11.7% Swing from Con to Lab)

SUNDERLAND NORTH %

*Etherington, W. (Lab)	26,067	68.2
Selous, A. (Con)	6,370	16.7
Pryke, G. (LD)	3,973	10.4
Nicholson, M. (Ref)	1,394	3.6
Newby, K. (Loony)	409	1.1
Lab majority	19,697	51.55%
Electorate	64,711	
Total Vote	38,213	Poll 59.1%

*Member of last parliament
Lab Hold (9.9% Swing from Con to Lab)

SUNDERLAND SOUTH %

*Mullin, C. (Lab)	27,174	68.1
Schofield, T. (Con)	7,536	18.9
Lennox, J. (LD)	4,606	11.5
Wilkinson, A. (UKIP)	609	1.5
Lab majority	19,638	49.19%
Electorate	67,937	
Total Vote	39,925	Poll 58.8%

*Member of last parliament
Lab Hold (10.5% Swing from Con to Lab)

SURREY HEATH %

*Hawkins, N. (Con)	28,231	51.6
Newman, D. (LD)	11,944	21.8
Jones, S. (Lab)	11,511	21.0
Gale, J. (Ref)	2,385	4.4
Squire, R. (UKIP)	653	1.2
Con majority	16,287	29.76%
Electorate	73,813	
Total Vote	54,724	Poll 74.1%

*Member of last parliament
Con Hold (5.4% Swing from Con to LD)

SUTTON AND CHEAM %

Burstow, P. (LD)	19,919	42.3
*Maitland, O. (Con)	17,822	37.8
Allison, M. (Lab)	7,280	15.5
Atkinson, P. (Ref)	1,784	3.8
McKie, S. (UKIP)	191	0.4
Wright, D. (NLP)	96	0.2
LD majority	2,097	4.45%
Electorate	62,785	
Total Vote	47,092	Poll 75.1%

*Member of last parliament
LD Gain (12.9% Swing from Con to LD)

SUTTON COLDFIELD %
*Fowler, N. (Con)   27,373   52.2
York, A. (Lab)   12,488   23.8
Whorwood, J. (LD)   10,139   19.3
Hope, D. (Ref)   2,401   4.6
Con majority 14,885   28.41%
Electorate   71,864
Total Vote   52,401   Poll 72.9%
*Member of last parliament
Con Hold (10.9% Swing from Con to Lab)

SWANSEA EAST %
*Anderson, D. (Lab)   29,151   75.4
Dibble, C. (Con)   3,582   9.3
Jones, E. (LD)   3,440   8.9
Pooley, M. (PC)   1,308   3.4
Maggs, C. (Ref)   904   2.3
Job, R. (Soc)   289   0.7
Lab majority 25,569   66.11%
Electorate   57,373
Total Vote   38,674   Poll 67.2%
*Member of last parliament
Lab Hold (6.8% Swing from Con to Lab)

SWANSEA WEST %
*Williams, A. (Lab)   22,748   56.2
Baker, A. (Con)   8,289   20.5
Newbury, J. (LD)   5,872   14.5
Lloyd, D. (PC)   2,675   6.6
Proctor, D. (SLP)   885   2.2
Lab majority 14,459   35.73%
Electorate   58,703
Total Vote   40,469   Poll 68.2%
*Member of last parliament
Lab Hold (7.1% Swing from Con to Lab)

SWINDON NORTH %
Wills, M. (Lab)   24,029   49.8
Opperman, G. (Con)   16,341   33.9
Evemy, M. (LD)   6,237   12.9
Goldsmith, G. (Ref)   1,533   3.2
Fisken, A. (NLP)   130   0.3
Lab majority 7,688   15.93%
Electorate   65,535
Total Vote   48,270   Poll 73.6%
Lab Hold (7.1% Swing from Con to Lab)

TAMWORTH %
*Jenkins, B. (Lab)   25,808   51.8
Lightbown, A. (Con)   18,312   36.7
Pinkett, J. (LD)   4,025   8.1
Livesey, D. (Ref)   1,163   2.3
Lamb, C. (UKIP)   369   0.7
Twelvetrees, C. (Lib)   177   0.4
Lab majority 7,496   15.04%
Electorate   67,205
Total Vote   49,854   Poll 74.2%
*Member of last parliament
Lab Win (12.6% Swing from Con to Lab)

TATTON %
Bell, M. (Ind)   29,354   60.2
*Hamilton, N. (Con)   18,277   37.5
Hill, S. (Ind)   295   0.6
Kinsey, S. (Ind)   187   0.4
Penhaul, B. (Miss M)   128   0.3

Muir, J. (Albion)   126   0.3
Kennedy, M. (NLP)   123   0.3
Bishop, D. (Byro)   116   0.2
Nicholas, R. (Ind)   113   0.2
Price, J. (Juice)   73   0.1
Ind majority 11,077   22.70%
Electorate   63,822
Total Vote   48,792   Poll 76.5%
*Member of last parliament
Ind Gain

TAUNTON %
Ballard, J. (LD)   26,064   42.7
*Nicholson, D.
(Con)   23,621   38.7
Lisgo, E. (Lab)   8,248   13.5
Ahern, B. (Ref)   2,760   4.5
Andrews, L. (BNP)   318   0.5
LD majority   2,443   4.00%
Electorate   79,783
Total Vote   61,011   Poll 76.5%
*Member of last parliament
LD Gain (4.6% Swing from Con to LD)

TEIGNBRIDGE %
*Nicholls, P. (Con)   24,679   39.2
Younger-Ross, R.
(LD)   24,398   38.8
Dann, S. (Lab)   11,311   18.0
Stokes, S. (UKIP)   1,601   2.5
Banwell, N. (Green)   817   1.3
Golding, L. (Dream)   139   0.2
Con majority   281   0.45%
Electorate   81,667
Total Vote   62,945   Poll 76.9%
*Member of last parliament
Con Hold (7.3% Swing from Con to LD)

TELFORD %
*Grocott, B. (Lab)   21,456   57.8
Gentry, B. (Con)   10,166   27.4
Green, N. (LD)   4,371   11.8
Morris, C. (Ref)   1,119   3.0
Lab majority 11,290   30.42%
Electorate   56,558
Total Vote   37,112   Poll 65.6%
*Member of last parliament
Lab Hold (5.5% Swing from Con to Lab)

TEWKESBURY %
Robertson, L. (Con)   23,859   45.8
Sewell, J. (LD)   14,625   28.0
Tustin, K. (Lab)   13,665   26.2
Con majority 9,234   17.71%
Electorate   68,208
Total Vote   52,149   Poll 76.5%
Con Hold (0.5% Swing from Con to LD)

THE WREKIN %
Bradley, P. (Lab)   21,243   46.9
Bruinvels, P. (Con)   18,218   40.2
Jenkins, I. (LD)   5,807   12.8
Lab majority 3,025   6.68%
Electorate   59,126
Total Vote   45,268   Poll 76.5%
Lab Gain (11.3% Swing from Con to Lab)

THURROCK %
*MacKinlay, A. (Lab)   29,896   63.3
Rosindell, A. (Con)   12,640   26.8
White, J. (LD)   3,843   8.1
Compobassi, P. (UKIP)   833   1.8
Lab majority 17,256   36.55%
Electorate   71,600
Total Vote   47,212   Poll 65.8%
*Member of last parliament
Lab Hold (17.2% Swing from Con to Lab)

TIVERTON AND HONITON %
*Browning, A. (Con)   24,438   41.3
Barnard, J. (LD)   22,785   38.5
King, J. (Lab)   7,598   12.8
Lowings, S. (Ref)   2,952   5.0
Roach, J. (Lib)   635   1.1
McIvor, E. (Green)   485   0.8
Charles, D. (Nat Dem)   236   0.4
Con majority   1,653   2.80%
Electorate   75,744
Total Vote   59,129   Poll 77.9%
*Member of last parliament
Con Hold (8.4% Swing from Con to LD)

TONBRIDGE AND MALLING%
*Stanley, J. (Con)   23,640   48.0
Withstandley, B.
(Lab)   13,410   27.2
Brown, K. (LD)   9,467   19.2
Scrivener, J. (Ref)   2,005   4.1
Bullen, B. (UKIP)   502   1.0
Valente, G. (NLP)   205   0.4
Con majority 10,230   20.78%
Electorate   64,798
Total Vote   49,229   Poll 75.6%
*Member of last parliament
Con Hold (11.5% Swing from Con to Lab)

TOOTING %
*Cox, T. (Lab)   27,516   59.7
Hutchings, J. (Con)   12,505   27.1
James, S. (LD)   4,320   9.4
Husband, A. (Ref)   829   1.8
Rattray, J. (Green)   527   1.1
Boddington, P. (BFAIR)   161   0.3
Koene, J. (Rights)   94   0.2
Bailey-Bond, P. (Dream)   83   0.2
Miller, P. (NLP)   70   0.2
Lab majority 15,011   32.56%
Electorate   66,653
Total Vote   46,105   Poll 67.9%
*Member of last parliament
Lab Hold (12.3% Swing from Con to Lab)

TORBAY %
Sanders, A. (LD)   21,094   39.6
*Allason, R. (Con)   21,082   39.5
Morey, M. (Lab)   7,923   14.9
Booth, G. (UKIP)   1,962   3.7
Cowling, B. (Lib)   1,161   2.2
Wild, P. (Dream)   100   0.2
LD majority   12   0.02%
Electorate   72,258
Total Vote   53,322   Poll 73.8%
*Member of last parliament
LD Gain (5.1% Swing from Con to LD)

TORFAEN %
*Murphy, P. (Lab) 29,863 69.1
Parish, N. (Con) 5,327 12.3
Gray, J. (LD) 5,249 12.1
Holler, D. (Ref) 1,245 2.9
Gough, R. (PC) 1,042 2.4
Coghill, R. (Green) 519 1.2

Lab majority 24,536 56.74%
Electorate 60,343
Total Vote 43,245 Poll 71.6%
*Member of last parliament
Lab Hold (6.4% Swing from Con to Lab)

**TORRIDGE AND WEST
DEVON** %
Burnett, J. (LD) 24,744 41.8
Liddell-Grainger, I.
(Con) 22,787 38.5
Brenton, D. (Lab) 7,319 12.4
Lea, R. (Ref) 1,946 3.3
Jackson, M. (UKIP) 1,841 3.1
Pithouse, M. (Lib) 508 0.9

LD majority 1,957 3.31%
Electorate 75,919
Total Vote 59,145 Poll 77.7%
LD Gain (4.4% Swing from Con to LD)

TOTNES %
*Steen, A. (Con) 19,637 36.5
Chave, R. (LD) 18,760 34.9
Ellery, V. (Lab) 8,796 16.4
Cook, P. (Ref) 2,552 4.7
Venmore, C.
(Loc C) 2,369 4.4
Thomas, H. (UKIP) 999 1.9
Pratt, A. (Green) 548 1.0
Golding, J. (Dream) 108 0.2

Con majority 877 1.63%
Electorate 70,473
Total Vote 53,769 Poll 76%
*Member of last parliament
Con Hold (6.8% Swing from Con to LD)

TOTTENHAM %
*Grant, B. (Lab) 26,121 69.3
Scantlebury, A.
(Con) 5,921 15.7
Hughes, N. (LD) 4,064 10.8
Budge, P. (Green) 1,059 2.8
Tay, L. (Pro-Life) 210 0.6
Anglin, C. (WRP) 181 0.5
Kent, T. (SEP) 148 0.4

Lab majority 20,200 53.58%
Electorate 66,173
Total Vote 37,704 Poll 55%
*Member of last parliament
Lab Hold (13.4% Swing from Con to Lab)

TRURO AND ST AUSTELL %
*Taylor, M. (LD) 27,502 48.5
Badcock, N. (Con) 15,001 26.4
Dooley, M. (Lab) 8,697 15.3
Hearn, C. (Ref) 3,682 6.5
Haithwaite, A. (UKIP) 576 1.0
Robinson, D. (Green) 482 0.8
Hicks, D. (MK) 450 0.8
Yelland, L. (PP) 240 0.4

Boland, P. (NLP) 117 0.2

LD majority 12,501 22.03%
Electorate 76,824
Total Vote 56,747 Poll 73.9%
*Member of last parliament
LD Hold (4.9% Swing from Con to LD)

TUNBRIDGE WELLS %
*Norman, A. (Con) 21,853 45.2
Clayton, A. (LD) 14,347 29.7
Warner, P. (Lab) 9,879 20.4
Macpherson, T. (Ref) 1,858 3.8
Anderson-Smart, M.
(UKIP) 264 0.5
Levy, P. (NLP) 153 0.3

Con majority 7,506 15.52%
Electorate 65,259
Total Vote 48,354 Poll 74.1%
*Member of last parliament
Con Hold (5% Swing from Con to LD)

**TWEEDDALE, ETTRICK AND
LAUDERDALE** %
Moore, M. (LD) 12,178 31.2
Geddes, K. (Lab) 10,689 27.4
Jack, A. (Con) 8,623 22.1
Goldie, I. (SNP) 6,671 17.1
Mowbray, C. (Ref) 406 1.0
Hein, J. (Lib) 387 1.0
Paterson, D. (NLP) 47 0.1

LD majority 1,489 3.8%
Electorate 50,891
Total Vote 39,001 Poll 76.6%
LD Hold (7.4% Swing from LD to Lab)

TWICKENHAM %
Cable, V. (LD) 26,237 45.1
*Jessel, T. (Con) 21,956 37.8
Tutchell, E. (Lab) 9,065 15.6
Harrison, M.
(IndECR) 589 1.0
Haggar, T. (Dream) 155 0.3
Hardy, A. (NLP) 142 0.2

LD majority 4,281 7.36%
Electorate 73,281
Total Vote 58,144 Poll 78.1%
*Member of last parliament
LD Gain (8.8% Swing from Con to LD)

TYNE BRIDGE %
*Clelland, D. (Lab) 26,767 76.8
Lee, A. (Con) 3,861 11.1
Wallace, M. (LD) 2,785 8.0
Oswald, G. (Ref) 919 2.6
Brunskill, E. (Soc) 518 1.5

Lab majority 22,906 65.73%
Electorate 61,058
Total Vote 34,850 Poll 57.1%
*Member of last parliament
Lab Hold (10.5% Swing from Con to Lab)

TYNEMOUTH %
Campbell, A. (Lab) 28,318 55.4
Callanan, M. (Con) 17,045 33.3
Duffield, A. (LD) 4,509 8.8
Rook, C. (Ref) 819 1.6

Rogers, F. (UKIP) 462 0.9

Lab majority 11,273 22.04%
Electorate 66,341
Total Vote 51,153 Poll 77%
Lab Gain (14.2% Swing from Con to Lab)

UPMINSTER %
Darvill, K. (Lab) 19,085 46.2
*Bonsor, N. (Con) 16,315 39.5
Peskett, P. (LD) 3,919 9.5
Murray, T. (Ref) 2,000 4.8

Lab majority 2,770 6.70%
Electorate 57,149
Total Vote 41,319 Poll 72.1%
*Member of last parliament
Lab Gain (15.4% Swing from Con to Lab)

UPPER BANN %
*Trimble, D. (UUP) 20,836 43.6
Rodgers, B. (SDLP) 11,584 24.2
O'Hagan, B. (SF) 5,773 12.1
Carrick, M. (DUP) 5,482 11.5
Ramsey, W. (APNI) 3,017 6.3
French, T. (Workers) 554 1.2
Price, B. (Con) 433 0.9
Lyons, J. (NLP) 108 0.2

UUP majority 9,252 19.36%
Electorate 70,398
Total Vote 47,787 Poll 67.9%
*Member of last parliament
UUP Hold (8.1% Swing from UUP to
SDLP)

UXBRIDGE %
*Shersby, M. (Con) 18,095 43.6
Williams, D. (Lab) 17,371 41.8
Malyan, A. (LD) 4,528 10.9
Aird, G. (Ref) 1,153 2.8
Leonard, J. (Soc) 398 1.0

Con majority 724 1.74%
Electorate 57,497
Total Vote 41,545 Poll 72.3%
*Member of last parliament
Con Hold (12.8% Swing from Con to Lab)

VALE OF CLWYD %
Ruane, C. (Lab) 20,617 52.7
Edwards, D. (Con) 11,662 29.8
Munford, D. (LD) 3,425 8.8
Kensler, G. (PC) 2,301 5.9
Vickers, S. (Ref) 834 2.1
Cooke, S. (UKIP) 293 0.7

Lab majority 8,955 22.88%
Electorate 52,418
Total Vote 39,132 Poll 74.6%
Lab Gain (13.9% Swing from Con to Lab)

VALE OF GLAMORGAN %
Smith, J. (Lab) 29,054 53.9
*Sweeney, W. (Con) 18,522 34.4
Campbell, S. (LD) 4,945 9.2
Corp, M. (PC) 1,393 2.6

Lab majority 10,532 19.53%
Electorate 67,213
Total Vote 53,914 Poll 80%
*Member of last parliament
Lab Gain (9.8% Swing from Con to Lab)

VALE OF YORK %
McIntosh, A. (Con)   23,815   44.7
Carter, M. (Lab)   14,094   26.5
Hall, C. (LD)   12,656   23.8
Fairclough, C. (Ref)   2,503   4.7
Pelton, T. (SDP)   197   0.4
Con majority   9,721   18.25%
Electorate   70,077
Total Vote   53,265   Poll 76%
Con Hold (15.6% Swing from Con to Lab)

VAUXHALL %
*Hoey, K. (Lab)   24,920   63.8
Kerr, A. (LD)   6,260   16.0
Bacon, R. (Con)   5,942   15.2
Driver, I. (SLP)   983   2.5
Collins, W. (Green)   864   2.2
Headicar, R. (Socialist)   97   0.2
Lab majority   18,660   47.77%
Electorate   70,402
Total Vote   39,066   Poll 53.5%
*Member of last parliament
Lab Hold (3.1% Swing from LD to Lab)

WAKEFIELD %
*Hinchliffe, D. (Lab)   28,977   57.4
Peacock, J. (Con)   14,373   28.5
Dale, D. (LD)   5,656   11.2
Shires, S. (Ref)   1,480   2.9
Lab majority   14,604   28.93%
Electorate   73,210
Total Vote   50,486   Poll 69%
*Member of last parliament
Lab Hold (10.6% Swing from Con to Lab)

WALLASEY %
*Eagle, A. (Lab)   30,264   64.6
Wilcock, M. (Con)   11,190   23.9
Reisdorf, P. (LD)   3,899   8.3
Hayes, R. (Ref)   1,490   3.2
Lab majority   19,074   40.72%
Electorate   67,714
Total Vote   46,843   Poll 73.5%
*Member of last parliament
Lab Hold (16.8% Swing from Con to Lab)

WALSALL NORTH %
*Winnick, D. (Lab)   24,517   56.6
Bird, M. (Con)   11,929   27.5
O'Brien, T. (LD)   4,050   9.4
Bennett, D. (Ref)   1,430   3.3
Pitt, M. (Ind)   911   2.1
Humphries, A. (NF)   465   1.1
Lab majority   12,588   29.07%
Electorate   67,587
Total Vote   43,302   Poll 64.1%
*Member of last parliament
Lab Hold (10.9% Swing from Con to Lab)

WALSALL SOUTH %
*George, B. (Lab)   25,024   57.9
Leek, L. (Con)   13,712   31.7
Harris, H. (LD)   2,698   6.2
Dent, T. (Ref)   1,662   3.8
Meads, L. (NLP)   149   0.3
Lab majority   11,312   26.16%

Electorate   64,221
Total Vote   43,245   Poll 67.3%
*Member of last parliament
Lab Hold (9.9% Swing from Con to Lab)

WALTHAMSTOW %
*Gerrard, N. (Lab)   25,287   63.1
Andrew, J. (Con)   8,138   20.3
Jackson, J. (LD)   5,491   13.7
Hargreaves, G. (Ref)   1,139   2.8
Lab majority   17,149   42.81%
Electorate   63,818
Total Vote   40,055   Poll 62.8%
*Member of last parliament
Lab Hold (17.9% Swing from Con to Lab)

WANSBECK %
Murphy, D. (Lab)   29,569   65.5
Thompson, A. (LD)   7,202   15.9
Green, P. (Con)   6,299   13.9
Gompertz, P. (Ref)   1,146   2.5
Best, N. (Green)   956   2.1
Lab majority   22,367   49.5%
Electorate   62,998
Total Vote   45,172   Poll 71.7%
Lab Hold (2.5% Swing from LD to Lab)

WANSDYKE %
Norris, D. (Lab)   24,117   44.1
Prisk, M. (Con)   19,318   35.3
Manning, J. (LD)   9,205   16.8
Clinton, K. (Ref)   1,327   2.4
Hunt, T. (UKIP)   438   0.8
House, P. (Loony)   225   0.4
Lincoln, S. (NLP)   92   0.2
Lab majority   4,799   8.77%
Electorate   69,032
Total Vote   54,722   Poll 79.1%
Lab Gain (14.4% Swing from Con to Lab)

WANTAGE %
*Jackson, R. (Con)   22,311   39.8
Wilson, C. (Lab)   16,222   28.9
Riley, J. (LD)   14,862   26.5
Rising, S. (Ref)   1,549   2.8
Kennet, M. (Green)   640   1.1
Tolstoy, N. (UKIP)   465   0.8
Con majority   6,089   10.86%
Electorate   71,657
Total Vote   56,049   Poll 78.2%
*Member of last parliament
Con Hold (11.9% Swing from Con to Lab)

WARLEY %
*Spellar, J. (Lab)   24,813   63.8
Pincher, C. (Con)   9,362   24.1
Pursehouse, J. (LD)   3,777   9.7
Gamre, K. (Ref)   941   2.4
Lab majority   15,451   39.73%
Electorate   59,758
Total Vote   38,893   Poll 64.9%
*Member of last parliament
Lab Hold (10.5% Swing from Con to Lab)

WARRINGTON NORTH %
Jones, H. (Lab)   31,827   62.1
Lacey, R. (Con)   12,300   24.0

Greenhalgh, I. (LD)   5,308   10.4
Smith, A. (Ref)   1,816   3.5
Lab majority   19,527   38.10%
Electorate   72,694
Total Vote   51,251   Poll 70.5%
Lab Hold (9.9% Swing from Con to Lab)

WARRINGTON SOUTH %
Southworth, H. (Lab)   28,721   52.1
Grayling, C. (Con)   17,914   32.5
Walker, P. (LD)   7,199   13.1
Kelley, G. (Ref)   1,082   2.0
Ross, S. (NLP)   166   0.3
Lab majority   10,807   19.62%
Electorate   72,262
Total Vote   55,082   Poll 76.2%
Lab Win (12.3% Swing from Con to Lab)

WARWICK AND
LEAMINGTON %
Plaskitt, J. (Lab)   26,747   44.5
*Smith, D. (Con)   23,349   38.9
Hicks, N. (LD)   7,133   11.9
Davis, V. (Ref)   1,484   2.5
Baptie, P. (Green)   764   1.3
Warwick, G. (UKIP)   306   0.5
Gibbs, M. (EDP)   183   0.3
McCarthy, R. (NLP)   125   0.2
Lab majority   3,398   5.65%
Electorate   79,374
Total Vote   60,091   Poll 75.2%
*Member of last parliament
Lab Gain (12% Swing from Con to Lab)

WATFORD %
Ward, C. (Lab)   25,019   45.3
Gordon, R. (Con)   19,227   34.8
Canning, A. (LD)   9,272   16.8
Roe, P. (Ref)   1,484   2.7
Davis, L. (NLP)   234   0.4
Lab majority   5,792   10.49%
Electorate   74,015
Total Vote   55,236   Poll 74.6%
Lab Gain (12.3% Swing from Con to Lab)

WAVENEY %
Blizzard, R. (Lab)   31,486   56.0
*Porter, D. (Con)   19,393   34.5
Thomas, C. (LD)   5,054   9.0
Clark, N. (Ind)   318   0.6
Lab majority   12,093   21.50%
Electorate   75,266
Total Vote   56,251   Poll 74.6%
*Member of last parliament
Lab Gain (14.4% Swing from Con to Lab)

WEALDEN %
*Johnson Smith,
  G. (Con)   29,417   49.8
Skinner, M. (LD)   15,213   25.7
Levine, N. (Lab)   10,185   17.2
Taplin, B. (Ref)   3,527   6.0
English, M. (UKIP)   569   1.0
Cragg, P. (NLP)   188   0.3
Con majority   14,204   24.03%
Electorate   79,519
Total Vote   59,099   Poll 74.3%
*Member of last parliament
Con Hold (5.3% Swing from Con to LD)

WEAVER VALE   %
*Hall, M. (Lab)   27,244   56.4
Byrne, J. (Con)   13,796   28.6
Griffiths, T. (LD)   5,949   12.3
Cockfield, R. (Ref)   1,312   2.7
Lab majority 13,448   27.84%
Electorate   66,011
Total Vote   48,301   Poll 73%
*Member of last parliament
Lab Hold (7.4% Swing from Con to Lab)

WELLINGBOROUGH   %
Stinchcombe, P.
  (Lab)   24,854   44.2
*Fry, P. (Con)   24,667   43.8
Smith, P. (LD)   5,279   9.4
Ellwood, A. (UKIP)   1,192   2.1
Lorys, A. (NLP)   297   0.5
Lab majority   187   0.33%
Electorate   74,955
Total Vote   56,289   Poll 74.8%
*Member of last parliament
Lab Gain (9.9% Swing from Con to Lab)

WELLS   %
*Heathcoat-Amory,
  D. (Con)   22,208   39.4
Gold, P. (LD)   21,680   38.5
Eavis, M. (Lab)   10,204   18.1
Phelps, P. (Ref)   2,196   3.9
Royse, L. (NLP)   92   0.2
Con majority   528   0.94%
Electorate   72,178
Total Vote   56,380   Poll 77.8%
*Member of last parliament
Con Hold (5.3% Swing from Con to LD)

WELWYN HATFIELD   %
Johnson, M. (Lab)   24,936   47.1
*Evans, D. (Con)   19,341   36.5
Schwartz, R. (LD)   7,161   13.5
Cox, V. (WelHat)   1,263   2.4
Harrold, H. (Pro-Life)   267   0.5
Lab majority   5,595   10.56%
Electorate   67,395
Total Vote   52,968   Poll 78.6%
*Member of last parliament
Lab Gain (11% Swing from Con to Lab)

WENTWORTH   %
Healey, J. (Lab)   30,225   72.3
Hamer, K. (Con)   6,266   15.0
Charters, J. (LD)   3,867   9.3
Battley, A. (Ref)   1,423   3.4
Lab majority 23,959   57.34%
Electorate   63,951
Total Vote   41,781   Poll 65.3%
Lab Hold (5.3% Swing from Con to Lab)

**WEST ABERDEENSHIRE AND
  KINCARDINE**   %
Smith, Sir R. (LD)   17,742   41.1
*Kynoch, G. (Con)   15,080   34.9
Mowatt, J. (SNP)   5,639   13.0
Khan, Q. (Lab)   3,923   9.1
Ball, S. (Ref)   805   1.9

LD majority   2,662   6.16%
Electorate   59,123
Total Vote   43,189   Poll 73%
*Member of last parliament
LD Gain (8.3% Swing from Con to LD)

WEST BROMWICH EAST   %
*Snape, P. (Lab)   23,710   57.2
Matsell, B. (Con)   10,126   24.4
Smith, M. (LD)   6,179   14.9
Mulley, G. (Ref)   1,472   3.5
Lab majority 13,584   32.74%
Electorate   63,401
Total Vote   41,487   Poll 65.4%
*Member of last parliament
Lab Hold (11.4% Swing from Con to Lab)

WEST BROMWICH WEST   %
*Boothroyd, B.
  (Speaker)   23,969   65.3
Silvester, R. (Ind Lab)   8,546   23.3
Edwards, S.
  (Nat Dem)   4,181   11.4
Speaker
  majority   15,423   42.03%
Electorate   67,496
Total Vote   36,696   Poll 54.3%
*Member of last parliament
Speaker Hold (0% Swing from to)

WEST DERBYSHIRE   %
*McLoughlin, P. (Con) 23,945   42.1
Clamp, S. (Lab)   19,060   33.5
Seeley, C. (LD)   9,940   17.5
Gouriet, J. (Ref)   2,499   4.4
Meynell, G. (IndGreen)   593   1.0
Price, H. (UKIP)   484   0.9
Delves, N. (Loony)   281   0.5
Kyslun, M. (Ind)   81   0.1
Con majority   4,885   8.59%
Electorate   72,716
Total Vote   56,883   Poll 78.1%
*Member of last parliament
Con Hold (11.6% Swing from Con to Lab)

WEST DORSET   %
Letwin, O. (Con)   22,036   41.1
Legg, R. (LD)   20,196   37.7
Bygraves, R. (Lab)   9,491   17.7
Jenkins, P. (UKIP)   1,590   3.0
Griffiths, M. (NLP)   239   0.4
Con majority   1,840   3.44%
Electorate   70,369
Total Vote   53,552   Poll 76%
Con Hold (5.6% Swing from Con to LD)

WEST HAM   %
*Banks, T. (Lab)   24,531   72.9
MacGregor, M. (Con)   5,037   15.0
McDonough, S. (LD)   2,479   7.4
Francis, K. (BNP)   1,198   3.6
Jug, T. (Loony)   300   0.9
Rainbow, J. (Dream)   116   0.3
Lab majority 19,494   57.91%
Electorate   57,058
Total Vote   33,661   Poll 58.4%
*Member of last parliament
Lab Hold (15% Swing from Con to Lab)

WEST LANCASHIRE   %
*Pickthall, C. (Lab)   33,022   60.3
Varley, C. (Con)   15,903   29.1
Wood, A. (LD)   3,938   7.2
Carter, M. (Ref)   1,025   1.9
Collins, J. (NLP)   449   0.8
Hill, D. (Home Rule)   392   0.7
Lab majority 17,119   31.28%
Electorate   73,175
Total Vote   54,729   Poll 74.8%
*Member of last parliament
Lab Hold (12.1% Swing from Con to Lab)

WEST RENFREWSHIRE   %
*Graham, T. (Lab)   18,525   46.6
Campbell, C. (SNP)   10,546   26.5
Cormack, C. (Con)   7,387   18.6
MacPherson, B.
  (LD)   3,045   7.7
Lindsay, S. (Ref)   283   0.7
Lab majority   7,979   20.05%
Electorate   52,348
Total Vote   39,786   Poll 75.9%
*Member of last parliament
Lab Hold (1.1% Swing from Lab to SNP)

WEST SUFFOLK   %
*Spring, R. (Con)   20,081   40.9
Jeffreys, M. (Lab)   18,214   37.1
Graves, A. (LD)   6,892   14.0
Carver, J. (Ref)   3,724   7.6
Shearer, A. (NLP)   171   0.3
Con majority   1,867   3.80%
Electorate   68,638
Total Vote   49,082   Poll 71.5%
*Member of last parliament
Con Hold (13% Swing from Con to Lab)

WEST TYRONE   %
Thompson, W. (UUP) 16,003   34.6
Byrne, J. (SDLP)   14,842   32.1
Doherty, P. (SF)   14,280   30.9
Gormley, A. (APNI)   829   1.8
Owens, T. (Workers)   230   0.5
Johnstone, R. (NLP)   91   0.2
UUP majority   1,161   2.51%
Electorate   58,168
Total Vote   46,275   Poll 79.6%
UUP Gain (0% Swing from to)

WEST WORCESTERSHIRE   %
*Spicer, M. (Con)   22,223   45.0
Hadley, M. (LD)   18,377   37.2
Stone, N. (Lab)   7,738   15.7
Cameron, S. (Green)   1,006   2.0
Con majority   3,846   7.79%
Electorate   64,712
Total Vote   49,344   Poll 76.3%
*Member of last parliament
Con Hold (8.8% Swing from Con to Lab)

WESTBURY   %
*Faber, D. (Con)   23,037   40.6
Miller, J. (LD)   16,969   29.9
Small, K. (Lab)   11,969   21.1
Hawkins, G. (Lib)   1,956   3.4

Hawkings-Byass, N.
(Ref) 1,909 3.4
Westbury, R. (UKIP) 771 1.4
Haysom, C. (NLP) 140 0.2
Con majority 6,068 10.69%
Electorate 74,301
Total Vote 56,751 Poll 76.2%
*Member of last parliament
Con Hold (3.8% Swing from Con to LD)

WESTERN ISLES %
*MacDonald, C. (Lab) 8,955 55.6
Gillies, A. (SNP) 5,379 33.4
McGrigor, J. (Con) 1,071 6.6
Mitchison, N. (LD) 495 3.1
Lionel, R. (Ref) 206 1.3
Lab majority 3,576 22.20%
Electorate 22,983
Total Vote 16,106 Poll 70.1%
*Member of last parliament
Lab Hold (5.8% Swing from SNP to Lab)

WESTMORLAND AND LONSDALE %
Collins, T. (Con) 21,463 42.3
Collins, S. (LD) 16,942 33.4
Harding, J. (Lab) 10,452 20.6
Smith, M. (Ref) 1,924 3.8
Con majority 4,521 8.90%
Electorate 68,389
Total Vote 50,781 Poll 74.3%
Con Hold (10.3% Swing from Con to LD)

WESTON-SUPER-MARE %
Cotter, B. (LD) 21,407 40.1
Daly, M. (Con) 20,133 37.7
Kraft, D. (Lab) 9,557 17.9
Sewell, T. (Ref) 2,280 4.3
LD majority 1,274 2.39%
Electorate 72,445
Total Vote 53,377 Poll 73.7%
LD Gain (6% Swing from Con to LD)

WIGAN %
*Stott, R. (Lab) 30,043 68.6
Loveday, M. (Con) 7,400 16.9
Beswick, T. (LD) 4,390 10.0
Bradborne, A. (Ref) 1,450 3.3
Maile, C. (Green) 442 1.0
Aycliffe, W. (NLP) 94 0.2
Lab majority 22,643 51.67%
Electorate 64,689
Total Vote 43,819 Poll 67.7%
*Member of last parliament
Lab Hold (8.2% Swing from Con to Lab)

WIMBLEDON %
Casale, R. (Lab) 20,674 42.8
*Goodson-Wickes,
C. (Con) 17,684 36.6
Willott, A. (LD) 8,014 16.6
Abid, H. (Ref) 993 2.1
Thacker, R. (Green) 474 1.0
Davies, S. (Pro-Life) 346 0.7
Kirby, M. (Mongolian) 112 0.2
Stacey, G. (Dream) 47 0.1

Lab majority 2,990 6.18%
Electorate 64,070
Total Vote 48,344 Poll 73.3%
*Member of last parliament
Lab Gain (17.9% Swing from Con to Lab)

WINCHESTER %
Oaten, M. (LD) 26,100 42.0
*Malone, G. (Con) 26,098 42.0
Davies, P. (Lab) 6,528 10.6
Strand, P. (Ref) 1,598 2.6
Huggett, R. (Top) 640 1.0
Rumsey, D. (UKIP) 476 0.8
Stockton, P. (Loony) 307 0.5
Browne, J.
(Ind AFE) 307 0.5
LD majority 2 0.00%
Electorate 78,884
Total Vote 62,054 Poll
*Member of last parliament
LD Hold (0.0% Swing from Con to LD)

WINDSOR %
*Trend, M. (Con) 24,476 48.2
Fox, C. (LD) 14,559 28.7
Williams, A. (Lab) 9,287 18.3
McDermott, J. (Ref) 1,676 3.3
Bradshaw, P. (Lib) 388 0.8
Bigg, E. (UKIP) 302 0.6
Parr, R. (Dynamic) 93 0.2
Con majority 9,917 19.53%
Electorate 69,132
Total Vote 50,781 Poll 73.5%
*Member of last parliament
Con Hold (3.8% Swing from Con to LD)

WIRRAL SOUTH %
*Chapman, B. (Lab) 24,499 50.9
Byrom, L. (Con) 17,495 36.4
Gilchrist, P. (LD) 5,018 10.4
Wilcox, D. (Ref) 768 1.6
Nielsen, J.
(Pro-Life) 264 0.5
Mead, G. (NLP) 51 0.1
Lab majority 7,004 14.56%
Electorate 59,372
Total Vote 48,095 Poll 81%
*Member of last parliament
Lab Hold (15.4% Swing from Con to Lab)

WIRRAL WEST %
Hesford, S. (Lab) 21,035 44.9
*Hunt, D. (Con) 18,297 39.0
Thornton, J. (LD) 5,945 12.7
Wharton, D. (Ref) 1,613 3.4
Lab majority 2,738 5.84%
Electorate 60,908
Total Vote 46,890 Poll 77%
*Member of last parliament
Lab Gain (13.8% Swing from Con to Lab)

WITNEY %
Woodward, S. (Con) 24,282 43.1
Hollingsworth, A.
(Lab) 17,254 30.6
Lawrence, A. (LD) 11,202 19.9
Brown, G. (Ref) 2,262 4.0

Montgomery, M.
(UKIP) 765 1.4
Chaple-Perrie, S. (Green) 636 1.1
Con majority 7,028 12.46%
Electorate 73,520
Total Vote 56,401 Poll 76.7%
Con Hold (13.6% Swing from Con to Lab)

WOKING %
Malins, H. (Con) 19,553 38.4
Goldenberg, P. (LD) 13,875 27.3
Hanson, K. (Lab) 10,695 21.0
Bell, H. (IndCon) 3,933 7.7
Skeate, C. (Ref) 2,209 4.3
Harvey, M. (UKIP) 512 1.0
Sleeman, D. (NLP) 137 0.3
Con majority 5,678 11.15%
Electorate 70,053
Total Vote 50,914 Poll 72.7%
Con Hold (10.4% Swing from Con to LD)

WOKINGHAM %
*Redwood, J. (Con) 25,086 50.1
Longton, R. (LD) 15,721 31.4
Colling, P. (Lab) 8,424 16.8
Owen, P. (Loony) 877 1.8
Con majority 9,365 18.69%
Electorate 66,161
Total Vote 50,108 Poll 75%
*Member of last parliament
Con Hold (8.7% Swing from Con to LD)

WOLVERHAMPTON NORTH EAST %
*Purchase, K.
(Lab/Co-op) 24,534 59.3
Harvey, D. (Con) 11,547 27.9
Niblett, B. (LD) 2,214 5.3
Hallmark, C. (Lib) 1,560 3.8
Muchall, A. (Ref) 1,192 2.9
Wingfield, M.
(Nat Dem) 356 0.9
Lab/Co-op
majority 12,987 31.37%
Electorate 61,642
Total Vote 41,403 Poll 67%
*Member of last parliament
Lab/Co-op Hold (11.9% Swing from Con to Lab)

WOLVERHAMPTON SOUTH EAST %
*Turner, D.
(Lab/Co-op) 22,202 63.7
Hanbury, W. (Con) 7,020 20.2
Whitehouse, R. (LD) 3,292 9.5
Stevenson-Platt, T.
(Ref) 980 2.8
Worth, N. (SLP) 689 2.0
Bullman, K. (Lib) 647 1.9
Lab/Co-op
majority 15,182 43.59%
Electorate 54,291
Total Vote 34,830 Poll 64.1%
*Member of last parliament
Lab/Co-op Hold (9.3% Swing from Con to Lab)

WOLVERHAMPTON
SOUTH WEST   %
Jones, J. (Lab)   24,657 50.4
*Budgen, N. (Con)   19,539 39.9
Green, M. (LD)   4,012   8.2
Hyde, M. (Lib)   713   1.5

Lab majority   5,118   10.46%
Electorate   67,482
Total Vote   48,921 Poll 72%
*Member of last parliament
Lab Gain (9.9% Swing from Con to Lab)

WOODSPRING   %
*Fox, L. (Con)   24,425 44.4
Kirsen, N. (LD)   16,691 30.4
Sander, D. (Lab)   11,377 20.7
Hughes, R. (Ref)   1,641   3.0
Lawson, R. (Green)   667   1.2
Glover, A. (Ind)   101   0.2
Mears, M. (NLP)   52   0.1

Con majority   7,734   14.00%
Electorate   69,964
Total Vote   54,954 Poll 78.5%
*Member of last parliament
Con Hold (3.8% Swing from Con to LD)

WORCESTER   %
Foster, M. (Lab)   25,848 50.1
Bourne, N. (Con)   18,423 35.7
Chandler, P. (LD)   6,462 12.5
Wood, P. (UKIP)   886   1.7

Lab majority   7,425   14.38%
Electorate   69,234
Total Vote   51,619 Poll 74.6%
Lab Gain (10% Swing from Con to Lab)

WORKINGTON   %
*Campbell-Savours,
  D. (Lab)   31,717 64.2
Blunden, R. (Con)   12,061 24.4
Roberts, P. (LD)   3,967   8.0
Donnan, G. (Ref)   1,412   2.9
Austin, C. (UniAll)   217   0.4

Lab majority 19,656   39.81%
Electorate   65,766
Total Vote   49,374 Poll 75.1%
*Member of last parliament
Lab Hold (11% Swing from Con to Lab)

WORSLEY   %
*Lewis, T. (Lab)   29,083 62.2
Garrido, D. (Con)   11,342 24.2
Bleakley, R. (LD)   6,356 13.6

Lab majority 17,741   37.92%
Electorate   68,978
Total Vote   46,781 Poll 67.8%
*Member of last parliament
Lab Hold (8.1% Swing from Con to Lab)

WORTHING WEST   %
*Bottomley, P. (Con)   23,733 46.1
Hare, C. (LD)   16,020 31.1
Adams, J. (Lab)   8,347 16.2
John, N. (Ref)   2,313   4.5
Cross, T. (UKIP)   1,029   2.0

Con majority   7,713   14.99%
Electorate   71,329
Total Vote   51,442 Poll 71.8%
*Member of last parliament
Con Hold (9.6% Swing from Con to LD)

WREXHAM   %
*Marek, J. (Lab)   20,450 56.1
Andrew, S. (Con)   8,688 23.9
Thomas, A. (LD)   4,833 13.3
Cronk, J. (Ref)   1,195   3.3
Plant, J. (PC)   1,170   3.2
Low, N. (NLP)   86   0.2

Lab majority 11,762   32.29%
Electorate   50,741
Total Vote   36,422 Poll 71.8%
*Member of last parliament
Lab Hold (7.4% Swing from Con to Lab)

WYCOMBE   %
*Whitney, R. (Con)   20,890 39.9
Bryant, C. (Lab)   18,520 35.4
Bensilum, P. (LD)   9,678 18.5
Fulford, A. (Ref)   2,394   4.6
Laker, J. (Green)   716   1.4
Heath, M. (NLP)   121   0.2

Con majority   2,370   4.53%
Electorate   73,589
Total Vote   52,319 Poll 71.1%
*Member of last parliament
Con Hold (13.6% Swing from Con to Lab)

WYRE FOREST   %
Lock, D. (Lab)   26,843 48.8
*Coombs, A. (Con)   19,897 36.1
Cropp, D. (LD)   4,377   8.0
Till, W. (Ref)   1,956   3.6
Harvey, C. (Lib)   1,670   3.0
Millington, A. (UKIP)   312   0.6

Lab majority   6,946   12.62%
Electorate   73,063
Total Vote   55,055 Poll 75.4%
*Member of last parliament
Lab Gain (14.4% Swing from Con to Lab)

WYTHENSHAWE AND
SALE EAST   %
Goggins, P. (Lab)   26,448 58.1
Fleming, P. (Con)   11,429 25.1
Tucker, V. (LD)   5,639 12.4
Stanyer, B. (Ref)   1,060   2.3
Flannery, J. (SLP)   957   2.1

Lab majority 15,019   32.98%
Electorate   71,986
Total Vote   45,533 Poll 63.2%
Lab Hold (9.2% Swing from Con to Lab)

YEOVIL   %
*Ashdown, P. (LD)   26,349 48.7
Cambrook, N.
  (Con)   14,946 27.7
Conway, P. (Lab)   8,053 14.9
Beveridge, J. (Ref)   3,574   6.6
Taylor, D. (Green)   728   1.3
Archer, J.
  (Musician)   306   0.6
Hudson, C. (Dream)   97   0.2

LD majority   11,403   21.10%
Electorate   74,165
Total Vote   54,053 Poll 72.7%
*Member of last parliament
LD Hold (3.2% Swing from Con to LD)

YNYS MON   %
*Jones, I. (PC)   15,756 39.5
Edwards, O. (Lab)   13,275 33.2
Owen, G. (Con)   8,569 21.5
Burnham, D. (LD)   1,537   3.8
Gray Morris, R.
  (Ref)   793   2.0

PC majority   2,481   6.21%
Electorate   52,952
Total Vote   39,930 Poll 75.4%
*Member of last parliament
PC Hold (3.7% Swing from PC to Lab)

YORKSHIRE EAST   %
*Townend, J. (Con)   20,904 42.7
Male, I. (Lab)   17,567 35.9
Leadley, D. (LD)   9,070 18.5
Allerston, R.
  (SDP)   1,049   2.1
Cooper, M.
  (Nat Dem)   381   0.8

Con majority   3,337   6.81%
Electorate   69,409
Total Vote   48,971 Poll 70.5%
*Member of last parliament
Con Hold (8.7% Swing from Con to Lab)

State of the Parties

	1997 General Election	1992 General Election
Labour Party	418*	270
Conservative Party	165	336
Liberal Democrats	46	20
Ulster Unionist Party	10	9
Scottish Nationalist Party	6	3
Plaid Cymru	4	4
Social Democratic and and Labour Party	3	4
Democratic Unionist Party	2	3
Sinn Fein	2	0
Independent	1	0
UK Unionist	1	0
UPUP	0	1
The Speaker	1	1
Total	**659**	**651**

*Includes 26 Labour/Co-operative MPs

Votes Cast by party

England, Scotland and Wales (GB)

Lab	13,551,381
Con	9,590,565
Lib Dem	5,243,322
SNP	620,434
PC	161,030
Ref	810,778
UKIP	106,019
NLP	30,165
Green	65,997
SocLab	52,516
Liberal	45,166
Ind Con	12,153
Ind Lab	18,497
BNP	35,393
New Lab	10,597
ScotSoc	9,740
SocP	9,486
Comm	911
Loony	7,906
Nat Front	2,716
Rainbow	3,745
MK	1,906
Others	421,292

Northern Ireland:

UUP	258,349
DUP	107,348
SDLP	190,814
Sinn Fein	126,921
APNI	62,972
PUP	10,928
Others	44,358

GB Vote Share

Lab	45%
Con	31%
Lib Dem	17%
Others	7%

Northern Ireland Vote Share

UUP	32.7%
SDLP	24.1%
SF	16.1%
DUP	13.6%
APNI	8.0%
Con	1.2%
Others	4.4%

Women Members

ABBOTT Diane
ADAMS Irene
ANDERSON Janet
ARMSTRONG Hilary
ATHERTON Candy
ATKINS Charlotte
BALLARD Jackie
BECKETT Margaret
BEGG Anne
BLACKMAN Elizabeth
BLEARS Hazel
BOOTHROYD Betty
BOTTOMLEY Virginia
BRINTON Helen
BROWNING Angela
BUCK Karen
BUTLER Christine
CAMPBELL Anne
CHURCH Judith
CLARK Lynda
CLWYD Ann
COFFEY Ann
COOPER Yvette
CORSTON Jean
CRYER Ann
CUNNINGHAM Roseanna
CURTIS-THOMAS Claire
DAVEY Valerie
DEAN Janet
DROWN Julia
DUNWOODY Gwyneth
EAGLE Angela
EAGLE Maria
ELLMAN Louise
EWING Margaret
FITZSIMONS Lorna
FLINT Caroline
FOLLETT Barbara
FYFE Maria
GILLAN Cheryl
GILROY Linda
GOLDING Llin
GORDON Eileen
GORMAN Teresa
GRIFFITHS Jane
HARMAN Harriet
HEAL Sylvia
HEWITT Patricia
HODGE Margaret
HOEY Kate
HUGHES Beverley
HUMBLE Joan
JACKSON Glenda
JACKSON Helen

JOHNSON Melanie
JONES Fiona
JONES Helen
JONES Jenny
JONES Lynne
JOWELL Tessa
KEEBLE Sally
KEEN Ann
KELLY Ruth
KENNEDY Jane
KING Oona
KINGHAM Tess
KIRKBRIDE Julie
LAING Eleanor
LAIT Jacqui
LAWRENCE Jackie
LIDDELL Helen
McCAFFERTY Christine
McDonagh Siobhain
McGUIRE Anne
McINTOSH Anne
McISAAC Shona
McKENNA Rosemary
MACTAGGART Fiona
MAHON Alice
MALLABER Judy
MAY Theresa
MERRON Gillian
MICHIE Ray
MOFFATT Laura
MORAN Margaret
MORGAN Julie
MORRIS Estelle
MOUNTFORD Kali
MOWLAM Marjorie
ORGAN Diana
OSBORNE Sandra
PERHAM Linda
PRENTICE Bridget
PRIMAROLO Dawn
QUIN Joyce
ROCHE Barbara
ROE Marion
RUDDOCK Joan
RUSSELL Christine
RYAN Joan
SHEPHARD Gillian
SHIPLEY Debra
SHORT Clare
SMITH Angela
SMITH Geraldine
SMITH Jacqui
SOUTHWORTH Helen
SPELMAN Caroline

SQUIRE Rachel
STARKEY Phyllis
STUART Gisela
TAYLOR Ann
TAYLOR Dari
TONGE Jennifer
WALLEY Joan

WARD Claire
WIDDECOMBE Ann
WILLIAMS Betty
WINTERTON Ann
WINTERTON Rosie
WISE Audrey

The 300 Group

PO Box 166, Horsham RH13 7YS Tel: 01403 733797 Fax: 01403 734432

The 300 Group is an all party campaign for more women in Parliament, Local Government and all areas of public life. Its members are women and men from all walks of life across the country. It encourages and trains women to seek and hold public office and to participate in public decision making processes at all levels.

Chair: Ann Swain
Finance Director: Sara Phillp
Directors: Rhian Chilcott, Fiona Bell, Dionysia Bovijn, Jane Evans, Carolyn Hilder

Constituencies

ENGLAND – 529 Members

LABOUR (330 Members)
(*Labour/Co-operative)

Amber Valley	Judy Mallaber
Ashfield	Geoffrey Hoon
Ashton under Lyne	Robert Sheldon
Barking	Margaret Hodge
Barnsley Central	Eric Illsley
Barnsley East and Mexborough	Jeffrey Ennis
Barnsley West and Penistone	Michael Clapham
Barrow and Furness	John Hutton
Basildon	Angela Smith*
Bassetlaw	Joe Ashton
Batley and Spen	Mike Wood
Battersea	Martin Linton
Bedford	Patrick Hall
Bethnal Green and Bow	Oona King
Bexleyheath and Crayford	Nigel Beard
Birkenhead	Frank Field
Birmingham Edgbaston	Gisela Stuart
Birmingham Erdington	Robin Corbett
Birmingham Hall Green	Stephen McCabe
Birmingham Hodge Hill	Terry Davis
Birmingham Ladywood	Clare Short
Birmingham Northfield	Richard Burden
Birmingham Perry Barr	Jeffrey Rooker
Birmingham Selly Oak	Lynne Jones
Birmingham Sparkbrook and Small Heath	Roger Godsiff
Birmingham Yardley	Estelle Morris
Bishop Auckland	Derek Foster
Blackburn	Jack Straw
Blackpool North and Fleetwood	Joan Humble
Blackpool South	Gordon Marsden
Blaydon	John McWilliam
Blyth Valley	Ronnie Campbell
Bolsover	Dennis Skinner
Bolton North East	David Crausby
Bolton South East	Brian Iddon
Bolton West	Ruth Kelly
Bootle	Joe Benton
Bradford North	Terence Rooney
Bradford South	Gerry Sutcliffe
Bradford West	Marsha Singh
Braintree	Alan Hurst
Brent East	Ken Livingstone
Brent North	Barry Gardiner
Brent South	Paul Boateng
Brentford and Isleworth	Ann Keen
Brigg and Goole	Ian Cawsey
Brighton Kemptown	Des Turner
Brighton Pavilion	David Lepper*
Bristol East	Jean Corston
Bristol North West	Doug Naysmith*
Bristol South	Dawn Primarolo
Bristol West	Valerie Davey
Broxtowe	Nicholas Palmer
Burnley	Peter Pike
Burton	Janet Dean
Bury North	David Chaytor
Bury South	Ivan Lewis
Calder Valley	Christine McCafferty
Camberwell and Peckham	Harriet Harman
Cambridge	Anne Campbell
Cannock Chase	Tony Wright
Carlisle	Eric Martlew
Castle Point	Christine Butler
Chatham and Aylesford	Jonathan Shaw
Chesterfield	Tony Benn
Chorley	Lindsay Hoyle
City of Chester	Christine Russell
City of Durham	Gerry Steinberg
City of York	Hugh Bayley
Cleethorpes	Shona McIsaac
Colne Valley	Kali Mountford
Copeland	Jack Cunningham
Corby	Phil Hope*
Coventry North East	Bob Ainsworth
Coventry North West	Geoffrey Robinson
Coventry South	James Cunningham
Crawley	Laura Moffatt
Crewe and Nantwich	Gwyneth Dunwoody
Crosby	Claire Curtis-Thomas
Croydon Central	Geraint Davies
Croydon North	Malcolm Wicks
Dagenham	Judith Church
Darlington	Alan Milburn
Dartford	Howard Stoate
Denton and Reddish	Andrew Bennett
Derby North	Bob Laxton
Derby South	Margaret Beckett
Dewsbury	Ann Taylor
Don Valley	Caroline Flint
Doncaster Central	Rosie Winterton
Doncaster North	Kevin Hughes
Dover	Gwyn Prosser
Dudley North	Ross Cranston

Dudley South	Ian Pearson	Hemsworth	Jon Trickett
Dulwich and West		Hendon	Andrew Dismore
Norwood	Tessa Jowell	Heywood and Middleton	Jim Dobbin*
Durham North	Giles Radice	High Peak	Tom Levitt
Ealing North	Stephen Pound	Holborn and St Pancras	Frank Dobson
Ealing Southall	Piara Khabra	Hornchurch	John Cryer
Ealing, Acton and		Hornsey and Wood Green	Barbara Roche
Shepherd's Bush	Clive Soley	Houghton and	
Easington	John Cummings	Washington East	Fraser Kemp
East Ham	Stephen Timms	Hove	Ivor Caplin
Eccles	Ian Stewart	Huddersfield	Barry Sheerman*
Edmonton	Andrew Love*	Hull East	John Prescott
Ellesmere Port and		Hull North	Kevin McNamara
Neston	Andrew Miller	Hull West and Hessle	Alan Johnson
Elmet	Colin Burgon	Hyndburn	Greg Pope
Eltham	Clive Efford	Ilford North	Linda Perham
Enfield North	Joan Ryan	Ilford South	Mike Gapes*
Enfield Southgate	Stephen Twigg	Ipswich	Jamie Cann
Erewash	Elizabeth	Islington North	Jeremy Corbyn
	Blackman	Islington South and	
Erith and Thamesmead	John Austin	Finsbury	Chris Smith
Exeter	Ben Bradshaw	Jarrow	Stephen Hepburn
Falmouth and Camborne	Candy Atherton	Keighley	Ann Cryer
Feltham and Heston	Alan Keen*	Kettering	Philip Sawford
Finchley and Golders		Kingswood	Roger Berry
Green	Rudi Vis	Knowsley North and	
Forest of Dean	Diana Organ	Sefton East	George Howarth
Gateshead East and		Knowsley South	Edward O'Hara
Washington West	Joyce Quin	Lancaster and Wyre	Hilton Dawson
Gedling	Vernon Coaker	Leeds Central	Hilary Benn
Gillingham	Paul Clark	Leeds East	George Mudie
Gloucester	Tess Kingham	Leeds North East	Fabian Hamilton
Gravesham	Chris Pond	Leeds North West	Harold Best
Great Grimsby	Austin Mitchell	Leeds West	John Battle
Great Yarmouth	Anthony Wright	Leicester East	Keith Vaz
Greenwich and Woolwich	Nick Raynsford	Leicester South	James Marshall
Hackney North and		Leicester West	Patricia Hewitt
Stoke Newington	Diane Abbott	Leigh	Lawrence
Hackney South and			Cunliffe
Shoreditch	Brian Sedgemore	Leominster	Peter Temple-
Halesowen and Rowley			Morris
Regis	Sylvia Heal	Lewisham East	Bridget Prentice
Halifax	Alice Mahon	Lewisham West	Jim Dowd
Halton	Derek Twigg	Lewisham, Deptford	Joan Ruddock
Hammersmith and		Leyton and Wanstead	Harry Cohen
Fulham	Iain Coleman	Lincoln	Gillian Merron
Hampstead and Highgate	Glenda Jackson	Liverpool Garston	Maria Eagle
Harlow	Bill Rammell	Liverpool Riverside	Louise Ellman*
Harrow East	Tony McNulty	Liverpool Walton	Peter Kilfoyle
Harrow West	Gareth R Thomas	Liverpool Wavertree	Jane Kennedy
Hartlepool	Peter Mandelson	Liverpool West Derby	Robert Wareing
Harwich	Ivan Henderson	Loughborough	Andrew Reed*
Hastings and Rye	Michael Jabez	Luton North	Kelvin Hopkins
	Foster	Luton South	Margaret Moran
Hayes and Harlington	John McDonnell	Makerfield	Ian McCartney
Hemel Hempstead	Tony McWalter*	Manchester Blackley	Graham Stringer

Manchester Central	Tony Lloyd	Portsmouth North	Syd Rapson
Manchester Gorton	Gerald Kaufman	Preston	Audrey Wise
Manchester Withington	Keith Bradley	Pudsey	Paul Truswell
Mansfield	Alan Meale	Putney	Tony Colman
Medway	Robert Marshall-Andrews	Reading East	Jane Griffiths
		Reading West	Martin Salter
Middlesbrough	Stuart Bell	Redcar	Marjorie Mowlam
Middlesbrough South and East Cleveland	Ashok Kumar	Redditch	Jacqui Smith
		Regent's Park and Kensington North	Karen Buck
Milton Keynes North East	Brian White	Rochdale	Lorna Fitzsimons
Milton Keynes South West	Phyllis Starkey	Romford	Eileen Gordon
		Rossendale and Darwen	Janet Anderson
Mitcham and Morden	Siobhain McDonagh	Rother Valley	Kevin Barron
		Rotherham	Denis MacShane
Morecambe and Lunesdale	Geraldine Smith	Rugby and Kenilworth	Andy King
		Salford	Hazel Blears
Morley and Rothwell	John Gunnell	Scarborough and Whitby	Lawrie Quinn
Newark	Fiona Jones	Scunthorpe	Elliot Morley
Newcastle upon Tyne Central	Jim Cousins	Sedgefield	Tony Blair
		Selby	John Grogan
Newcastle upon Tyne East and Wallsend	Nick Brown	Sheffield Attercliffe	Clive Betts
		Sheffield Brightside	David Blunkett
Newcastle upon Tyne North	Doug Henderson	Sheffield Central	Richard Caborn
		Sheffield Heeley	Bill Michie
Newcastle-under-Lyme	Llin Golding	Sheffield Hillsborough	Helen Jackson
Normanton	William O'Brien	Sherwood	Paddy Tipping
North East Derbyshire	Harry Barnes	Shipley	Christopher Leslie
North Swindon	Michael Wills	Shrewsbury and Atcham	Paul Marsden
North Tyneside	Stephen Byers	Sittingbourne and Sheppey	Derek Wyatt
North Warwickshire	Mike O'Brien		
North West Durham	Hilary Armstrong	Slough	Fiona Mactaggart
North West Leicestershire	David Taylor*	South Derbyshire	Mark Todd
		South Ribble	David Borrow
North West Norfolk	George Turner	South Shields	David Clark
Northampton North	Sally Keeble	South Swindon	Julia Drown
Northampton South	Tony Clarke	South Thanet	Stephen Ladyman
Norwich North	Ian Gibson	Southampton Itchen	John Denham
Norwich South	Charles Clarke	Southampton Test	Alan Whitehead
Nottingham East	John Heppell	St Albans	Kerry Pollard
Nottingham North	Graham Allen	St Helens North	David Watts
Nottingham South	Alan Simpson	St Helens South	Gerry Bermingham
Nuneaton	Bill Olner		
Oldham East and Saddleworth	Philip Woolas	Stafford	David Kidney
		Staffordshire Moorlands	Charlotte Atkins
Oldham West and Royton	Michael Meacher	Stalybridge and Hyde	Tom Pendry
		Stevenage	Barbara Follett
Oxford East	Andrew Smith	Stockport	Ann Coffey
Pendle	Gordon Prentice	Stockton North	Frank Cook
Peterborough	Helen Brinton	Stockton South	Dari Taylor
Plymouth Devonport	David Jamieson	Stoke-on-Trent Central	Mark Fisher
Plymouth Sutton	Linda Gilroy*	Stoke-on-Trent North	Joan Walley
Pontefract and Castleford	Yvette Cooper	Stoke-on-Trent South	George Stevenson
		Stourbridge	Debra Shipley
Poplar and Canning Town	Jim Fitzpatrick	Streatham	Keith Hill
		Stretford and Urmston	Beverley Hughes

Stroud	David Drew*
Sunderland North	William Etherington
Sunderland South	Chris Mullin
Tamworth	Brian Jenkins
Telford	Bruce Grocott
The Wrekin	Peter Bradley
Thurrock	Andrew Mackinlay
Tooting	Tom Cox
Tottenham	Bernie Grant
Tyne Bridge	David Clelland
Tynemouth	Alan Campbell
Upminster	Keith Darvill
Vauxhall	Kate Hoey
Wakefield	David Hinchliffe
Wallasey	Angela Eagle
Walsall North	David Winnick
Walsall South	Bruce George
Walthamstow	Neil Gerrard
Wansbeck	Denis Murphy
Wansdyke	Dan Norris
Warley	John Spellar
Warrington North	Helen Jones
Warrington South	Helen Southworth
Warwick and Leamington	James Plaskitt
Watford	Claire Ward
Waveney	Bob Blizzard
Weaver Vale	Mike Hall
Wellingborough	Paul Stinchcombe
Welwyn Hatfield	Melanie Johnson
Wentworth	John Healey
West Bromwich East	Peter Snape
West Ham	Tony Banks
West Lancashire	Colin Pickthall
Wigan	Neil Turner
Wimbledon	Roger Casale
Wirral South	Ben Chapman
Wirral West	Stephen Hesford
Witney	Shaun Woodward
Wolverhampton North East	Ken Purchase*
Wolverhampton South East	Dennis Turner*
Wolverhampton South West	Jenny Jones
Worcester	Michael John Foster
Workington	Dale Campbell-Savours
Worsley	Terry Lewis
Wyre Forest	David Lock
Wythenshawe and Sale East	Paul Goggins

CONSERVATIVE (163 Members)

Aldershot	Gerald Howarth
Aldridge-Brownhills	Richard Shepherd
Altrincham and Sale West	Graham Brady
Arundel and South Downs	Howard Flight
Ashford	Damian Green
Aylesbury	David Lidington
Banbury	Tony Baldry
Basingstoke	Andrew Hunter
Beaconsfield	Dominic Grieve
Beckenham	Jacqui Lait
Beverley and Holderness	James Cran
Bexhill and Battle	Charles Wardle
Billericay	Teresa Gorman
Blaby	Andrew Robathan
Bognor Regis and Littlehampton	Nick Gibb
Boston and Skegness	Sir Richard Body
Bosworth	David Tredinnick
Bournemouth East	David Atkinson
Bournemouth West	John Butterfill
Bracknell	Andrew Mackay
Brentwood and Ongar	Eric Pickles
Bridgwater	Tom King
Bromley and Chislehurst	Eric Forth
Bromsgrove	Julie Kirkbride
Broxbourne	Marion Roe
Buckingham	John Bercow
Bury St Edmunds	David Ruffley
Canterbury	Julian Brazier
Central Suffolk and North Ipswich	Michael Lord
Charnwood	Stephen Dorrell
Cheadle	Stephen Day
Chelmsford West	Simon Burns
Chesham and Amersham	Cheryl Gillan
Chichester	Andrew Tyrie
Chingford and Woodford Green	Iain Duncan Smith
Chipping Barnet	Sydney Chapman
Christchurch	Christopher Chope
Cities of London and Westminster	Peter Brooke
Congleton	Ann Winterton
Cotswold	Geoffrey Clifton-Brown
Croydon South	Richard Ottaway
Daventry	Timothy Boswell
Devizes	Michael Ancram
East Devon	Peter Emery
East Hampshire	Michael Mates
East Surrey	Peter Ainsworth
East Worthing and Shoreham	Tim Loughton
Eastbourne	Nigel Waterson
Eddisbury	Stephen O'Brien

Epping Forest	Eleanor Laing
Epsom and Ewell	Sir Archie Hamilton
Esher and Walton	Ian Taylor
Fareham	Sir Peter Lloyd
Faversham and Mid Kent	Andrew Rowe
Folkestone and Hythe	Michael Howard
Fylde	Michael Jack
Gainsborough	Edward Leigh
Gosport	Peter Viggers
Grantham and Stamford	Quentin Davies
Guildford	Nicholas St Aubyn
Haltemprice and Howden	David Davis
Harborough	Edward Garnier
Havant	David Willetts
Henley	Michael Heseltine
Hertford and Stortford	Bowen Wells
Hertsmere	James Clappison
Hexham	Peter Atkinson
Hitchin and Harpenden	Peter Lilley
Horsham	Francis Maude
Huntingdon	John Major
Kensington and Chelsea	Michael Portillo
Lichfield	Michael Fabricant
Louth and Horncastle	Sir Peter Tapsell
Ludlow	Christopher Gill
Macclesfield	Nicholas Winterton
Maidenhead	Theresa May
Maidstone and The Weald	Ann Widdecombe
Maldon and Chelmsford East	John Whittingdale
Meriden	Caroline Spelman
Mid Bedfordshire	Jonathan Sayeed
Mid Dorset and Poole North	Christopher Fraser
Mid Norfolk	Keith Simpson
Mid Sussex	Nicholas Soames
Mid Worcestershire	Peter Luff
Mole Valley	Sir Paul Beresford
New Forest East	Julian Lewis
New Forest West	Desmond Swayne
North Dorset	Robert Walter
North East Bedfordshire	Sir Nicholas Lyell
North East Cambridgeshire	Malcolm Moss
North East Hampshire	James Arbuthnot
North East Hertfordshire	Oliver Heald
North Essex	Bernard Jenkin
North Norfolk	David Prior
North Shropshire	Owen Paterson
North Thanet	Roger Gale
North West Cambridgeshire	Sir Brian Mawhinney
North West Hampshire	Sir George Young
North Wiltshire	James Gray
Old Bexley and Sidcup	Sir Edward Heath
Orpington	John Horam
Penrith and The Border	David Maclean
Poole	Robert Syms
Rayleigh	Michael Clark
Reigate	Crispin Blunt
Ribble Valley	Nigel Evans
Richmond (Yorkshire)	William Hague
Rochford and Southend East	Sir Teddy Taylor
Romsey	Michael Colvin
Ruislip Northwood	John Wilkinson
Runnymede and Weybridge	Philip Hammond
Rushcliffe	Kenneth Clarke
Rutland and Melton	Alan Duncan
Ryedale	John Greenway
Saffron Walden	Sir Alan Haselhurst
Salisbury	Robert Key
Sevenoaks	Michael Fallon
Skipton and Ripon	David Curry
Sleaford and North Hykeham	Douglas Hogg
Solihull	John M Taylor
South Cambridgeshire	Andrew Lansley
South Dorset	Ian Bruce
South East Cambridgeshire	James Paice
South Holland and The Deepings	John Hayes
South Norfolk	John MacGregor
South Staffordshire	Sir Patrick Cormack
South Suffolk	Tim Yeo
South West Bedfordshire	Sir David Madel
South West Devon	Gary Streeter
South West Hertfordshire	Richard Page
South West Norfolk	Gillian Shephard
South West Surrey	Virginia Bottomley
Southend West	David Amess
Spelthorne	David Wilshire
Stone	William Cash
Stratford-on-Avon	John Maples
Suffolk Coastal	John Gummer
Surrey Heath	Nick Hawkins
Sutton Coldfield	Sir Norman Fowler
Teignbridge	Patrick Nicholls
Tewkesbury	Laurence Robertson
Tiverton and Honiton	Angela Browning
Tonbridge and Malling	Sir John Stanley

Totnes	Anthony Steen	Sutton and Cheam	Paul Burstow
Tunbridge Wells	Archie Norman	Taunton	Jackie Ballard
Uxbridge	John Randall	Torbay	Adrian Sanders
Vale of York	Anne McIntosh	Torridge and West Devon	John Burnett
Wantage	Robert Jackson	Truro and St Austell	Matthew Taylor
Wealden	Sir Geoffrey Johnson Smith	Twickenham	Vincent Cable
		Weston-Super-Mare	Brian Cotter
Wells	David Heathcoat-Amory	Winchester	Mark Oaten
		Yeovil	Paddy Ashdown
West Derbyshire	Patrick McLoughlin		

INDEPENDENT (1 Member)

Tatton	Martin Bell

		THE SPEAKER	
West Dorset	Oliver Letwin		
West Suffolk	Richard Spring	West Bromwich West	Betty Boothroyd
West Worcestershire	Sir Michael Spicer		
Westbury	David Faber		
Westmorland and Lonsdale	Tim Collins		
Windsor	Michael Trend	**SCOTLAND** – 72 Members	
Woking	Humfrey Malins		
Wokingham	John Redwood	LABOUR (55 Members)	
Woodspring	Liam Fox	(*Labour/Co-operative)	
Worthing West	Peter Bottomley	Aberdeen Central	Frank Doran
Wycombe	Sir Raymond Whitney	Aberdeen North	Malcolm Savidge
		Aberdeen South	Anne Begg
Yorkshire East	John Townend	Airdrie and Shotts	Helen Liddell
		Ayr	Sandra Osborne

		Carrick, Cumnock and Doon Valley	George Foulkes*
LIBERAL DEMOCRAT (34 Members)		Central Fife	Henry McLeish
Bath	Don Foster	Clydebank and Milngavie	Tony Worthington
Berwick-upon-Tweed	Alan Beith	Clydesdale	Jimmy Hood
Carshalton and Wallington	Tom Brake	Coatbridge and Chryston	Tom Clarke
Cheltenham	Nigel Jones	Cumbernauld and Kilsyth	Rosemary McKenna
Colchester	Bob Russell		
Eastleigh	David Chidgey	Cunninghame North	Brian Wilson
Harrogate and Knaresborough	Phil Willis	Cunninghame South	Brian Donohoe
		Dumbarton	John McFall*
Hazel Grove	Andrew Stunell	Dumfries	Russell Brown
Hereford	Paul Keetch	Dundee East	John McAllion
Isle of Wight	Peter Brand	Dundee West	Ernie Ross
Kingston and Surbiton	Edward Davey	Dunfermline East	Gordon Brown
Lewes	Norman Baker	Dunfermline West	Rachel Squire
Newbury	David Rendel	East Kilbride	Adam Ingram
North Cornwall	Paul Tyler	East Lothian	John Home Robertson
North Devon	Nick Harvey		
North Southwark and Bermondsey	Simon Hughes	Eastwood	Jim Murphy
		Edinburgh Central	Alistair Darling
Northavon	Steve Webb	Edinburgh East and Musselburgh	Gavin Strang
Oxford West and Abingdon	Evan Harris		
Portsmouth South	Mike Hancock	Edinburgh North and Leith	Malcolm Chisholm
Richmond Park	Jennifer Tonge		
Sheffield Hallam	Richard Allan	Edinburgh Pentlands	Lynda Clark
Somerton and Frome	David Heath	Edinburgh South	Nigel Griffiths
South East Cornwall	Colin Breed	Falkirk East	Michael Connarty
Southport	Ronnie Fearn		
St Ives	Andrew George		

Falkirk West	Dennis Canavan
Glasgow Anniesland	Donald Dewar
Glasgow Baillieston	James Wray
Glasgow Cathcart	John Maxton
Glasgow Govan	Mohammed Sarwar
Glasgow Kelvin	George Galloway
Glasgow Maryhill	Maria Fyfe
Glasgow Pollok	Ian Davidson*
Glasgow Rutherglen	Thomas McAvoy*
Glasgow Shettleston	David Marshall
Glasgow Springburn	Michael Martin
Greenock and Inverclyde	Norman Godman
Hamilton North and Bellshill	John Reid
Hamilton South	Bill Tynan
Inverness East, Nairn and Lochaber	David Stewart
Kilmarnock and Loudoun	Desmond Browne
Kirkcaldy	Lewis Moonie*
Linlithgow	Tam Dalyell
Livingston	Robin Cook
Midlothian	Eric Clarke
Motherwell and Wishaw	Frank Roy
Ochil	Martin O'Neill
Paisley North	Irene Adams
Paisley South	Douglas Alexander
Stirling	Anne McGuire
Strathkelvin and Bearsden	Sam Galbraith
Western Isles	Calum MacDonald

LIBERAL DEMOCRAT (10 Members)

Argyll and Bute	Ray Michie
Caithness, Sutherland and Easter Ross	Robert Maclennan
Edinburgh West	Donald Gorrie
Gordon	Malcolm Bruce
North East Fife	Menzies Campbell
Orkney and Shetland	James Wallace
Ross, Skye and Inverness West	Charles Kennedy
Roxburgh and Berwickshire	Archy Kirkwood
Tweeddale, Ettrick and Lauderdale	Michael Moore
West Aberdeenshire and Kincardine	Robert Smith

SCOTTISH NATIONAL PARTY (6 Members)

Angus	Andrew Welsh
Banff and Buchan	Alex Salmond
Galloway and Upper Nithsdale	Alasdair Morgan
Moray	Margaret Ewing
North Tayside	John Swinney
Perth	Roseanna Cunningham

SCOTTISH LABOUR PARTY (1 Member)

West Renfrewshire	Tommy Graham

WALES – 40 Members

LABOUR (34 Members)

Aberavon	Sir John Morris
Alyn and Deeside	Barry Jones
Blaenau Gwent	Llewellyn Smith
Bridgend	Win Griffiths
Caerphilly	Ron Davies
Cardiff Central	Jon Owen Jones*
Cardiff North	Julie Morgan
Cardiff South and Penarth	Alun Michael*
Cardiff West	Rhodri Morgan
Carmarthen East and Dinefwr	Alan Williams
Carmarthen West and South Pembrokeshire	Nick Ainger
Clwyd South	Martyn Jones
Clwyd West	Gareth Thomas
Conwy	Betty Williams
Cynon Valley	Ann Clwyd
Delyn	David Hanson
Gower	Martin Caton
Islwyn	Don Touhig*
Llanelli	Denzil Davies
Merthyr Tydfil and Rhymney	Edward Rowlands
Monmouth	Huw Edwards
Neath	Peter Hain
Newport East	Alan Howarth
Newport West	Paul Flynn
Ogmore	Sir Raymond Powell
Pontypridd	Kim Howells
Preseli Pembrokeshire	Jackie Lawrence
Rhondda	Allan Rogers
Swansea East	Donald Anderson
Swansea West	Alan Williams
Torfaen	Paul Murphy
Vale of Clwyd	Chris Ruane
Vale of Glamorgan	John Smith
Wrexham	John Marek

PLAID CYMRU (4 Members)

Caernarfon	Dafydd Wigley
Ceredigion	Cynog Dafis*
Meirionnydd Nant Conwy	Elfyn Llwyd
Ynys Môn	Ieuan Wyn Jones

*resigned January 2000

LIBERAL DEMOCRAT (2 Members)

Brecon and Radnorshire	Richard Livsey
Montgomeryshire	Lembit Öpik

NORTHERN IRELAND – 18 Members

ULSTER UNIONIST PARTY (10 Members)

Belfast North	Cecil Walker
Belfast South	Martin Smyth
East Antrim	Roy Beggs
East Londonderry	William Ross
Fermanagh and South Tyrone	Ken Maginnis
Lagan Valley	Jeffrey Donaldson
South Antrim	Clifford Forsythe
Strangford	John D Taylor
Upper Bann	David Trimble
West Tyrone	William Thompson

SOCIAL DEMOCRATIC AND LABOUR PARTY (3 Members)

Foyle	John Hume
Newry and Armagh	Seamus Mallon
South Down	Edward McGrady

DEMOCRATIC UNIONIST PARTY (2 Members)

Belfast East	Peter Robinson
North Antrim	Ian Paisley

SINN FEIN (2 Members)

Belfast West	Gerry Adams
Mid Ulster	Martin McGuinness

UK UNIONIST PARTY (1 Members)

North Down	Robert McCartney

Geographical Whereabouts

Aberavon	South Wales
Airdrie and Shotts	North Lanarkshire
Aldershot	Hampshire
Aldridge-Brownhills	West Midlands
Altrincham and Sale West	Greater Manchester
Alyn and Deeside	Flintshire
Amber Valley	Derbyshire
Angus	East Scotland
Antrim, East	Northern Ireland
Antrim, North	Northern Ireland
Antrim, South	Northern Ireland
Argyll and Bute	West Scotland
Arundel and South Downs	West Sussex
Ashfield	Nottinghamshire
Ashford	Kent
Ashton under Lyne	Greater Manchester
Aylesbury	Buckinghamshire
Ayr	South Ayrshire
Banbury	Oxfordshire
Banff and Buchan	Aberdeenshire
Barking	East London
Barnsley Central	South Yorkshire
Barnsley East and Mexborough	South Yorkshire
Barnsley West and Penistone	South Yorkshire
Barrow and Furness	Cumbria
Basildon	Essex
Basingstoke	Hampshire
Bassetlaw	Nottinghamshire
Bath	Somerset
Batley and Spen	West Yorkshire
Battersea	South London
Beaconsfield	Buckinghamshire
Beckenham	Kent
Berwick-upon-Tweed	Northumberland
Bethnal Green and Bow	East London
Beverley and Holderness	East Yorkshire
Bexhill and Battle	East Sussex
Bexleyheath and Crayford	South London
Billericay	Essex
Birkenhead	Merseyside
Bishop Auckland	County Durham
Blaby	Leicestershire
Blackburn	Lancashire
Blaenau Gwent	South Wales
Blaydon	Tyne and Wear
Blyth Valley	Northumberland
Bognor Regis and Littlehampton	West Sussex
Bolsover	Derbyshire
Bolton North East	Greater Manchester
Bolton South East	Greater Manchester
Bolton West	Greater Manchester
Bootle	Merseyside
Boston and Skegness	Lincolnshire
Bosworth	Leicestershire
Bracknell	Berkshire
Braintree	Essex
Brecon and Radnorshire	Powys
Brent East	North London
Brent North	North London
Brent South	North London
Brentford and Isleworth	West London
Brentwood and Ongar	Essex
Bridgend	South Wales
Bridgwater	Somerset
Brigg and Goole	Lincolnshire
Bromley and Chislehurst	Kent
Bromsgrove	Worcestershire
Broxbourne	Hertfordshire
Broxtowe	Nottinghamshire
Burnley	Lancashire
Burton	Staffordshire
Bury North	Greater Manchester
Bury South	Greater Manchester
Bury St Edmunds	Suffolk
Caernarfon	Gwynedd
Caerphilly	South Wales
Caithness, Sutherland and Easter Ross	Highland
Calder Valley	West Yorkshire
Camberwell and Peckham	South London
Cannock Chase	Staffordshire
Carmarthen East and Dinefwr	Carmarthenshire
Carmarthen West and South Pembrokeshire	South West Wales
Carrick, Cumnock and Doon Valley	Ayrshire
Carshalton and Wallington	South London
Castle Point	Essex
Ceredigion	West Wales
Charnwood	Leicestershire

Chatham and Aylesford	Kent
Cheadle	Greater Manchester
Chelmsford West	Essex
Cheltenham	Gloucestershire
Chesham and Amersham	Buckinghamshire
Chesterfield	Derbyshire
Chichester	West Sussex
Chingford and Woodford Green	Essex
Chipping Barnet	North London
Chorley	Lancashire
Christchurch	Dorset
Cleethorpes	Lincolnshire
Clwyd South	North Wales
Clwyd West	North Wales
Clydebank and Milngavie	Dunbartonshire
Clydesdale	South Lanarkshire
Coatbridge and Chryston	Central Scotland
Colchester	Essex
Colne Valley	West Yorkshire
Congleton	Cheshire
Conwy	North Wales
Copeland	Cumbria
Corby	Northamptonshire
Cotswold	Gloucestershire
Crawley	West Sussex
Crewe and Nantwich	Cheshire
Crosby	Merseyside
Cumbernauld and Kilsyth	North Lanarkshire
Cunninghame North	North Ayrshire
Cunninghame South	North Ayrshire
Cynon Valley	South Wales
Dagenham	Essex
Darlington	County Durham
Dartford	Kent
Daventry	Northamptonshire
Delyn	Flintshire
Denton and Reddish	Greater Manchester
Devizes	Wiltshire
Dewsbury	West Yorkshire
Don Valley	South Yorkshire
Down, North	Northern Ireland
Down, South	Northern Ireland
Dudley North	West Midlands
Dudley South	West Midlands
Dulwich and West Norwood	South London
Dunfermline East	Fife
Dunfermline West	Fife
Ealing North	West London
Ealing Southall	West London
Ealing, Acton and Shepherd's Bush	West London
Easington	County Durham
East Ham	East London
East Kilbride	South Lanarkshire
East Lothian	South East Scotland
Eastbourne	East Sussex
Eastleigh	Hampshire
Eastwood	East Renfrewshire
Eccles	Greater Manchester
Eddisbury	Cheshire
Edmonton	North London
Ellesmere Port and Neston	Cheshire
Elmet	West Yorkshire
Eltham	South London
Enfield North	North London
Enfield Southgate	North London
Epping Forest	Essex
Epsom and Ewell	Surrey
Erewash	Derbyshire
Erith and Thamesmead	South London
Esher and Walton	Surrey
Exeter	Devon
Falkirk East	Central Scotland
Falkirk West	Central Scotland
Falmouth and Camborne	Cornwall
Fareham	Hampshire
Feltham and Heston	West London
Fermanagh and South Tyrone	Northern Ireland
Finchley and Golders Green	North London
Folkestone and Hythe	Kent
Forest of Dean	Gloucestershire
Foyle	Northern Ireland
Fylde	Lancashire
Gainsborough	Lincolnshire
Galloway and Upper Nithsdale	Dumfries and Galloway
Gateshead East and Washington West	Tyne and Wear
Gedling	Nottinghamshire
Gillingham	Kent
Gordon	North Eastern Scotland
Gosport	Hampshire
Gower	South Wales
Grantham and Stamford	Lincolnshire
Gravesham	Kent
Great Grimsby	Lincolnshire
Great Yarmouth	Norfolk

Greenock and Inverclyde	West Scotland
Greenwich and Woolwich	South East London
Guildford	Surrey
Hackney North and Stoke Newington	North London
Hackney South and Shoreditch	North London
Halesowen and Rowley Regis	West Midlands
Halifax	West Yorkshire
Haltemprice and Howden	East Yorkshire
Halton	Cheshire
Hamilton North and Bellshill	Lanarkshire
Hamilton South	South Lanarkshire
Hammersmith and Fulham	West London
Hampstead and Highgate	North London
Harborough	Leicestershire
Harlow	Essex
Harrogate and Knaresborough	North Yorkshire
Harrow East	Middlesex
Harrow West	Middlesex
Hartlepool	County Durham
Harwich	Essex
Hastings and Rye	East Sussex
Havant	Hampshire
Hayes and Harlington	Middlesex
Hazel Grove	Greater Manchester
Hemel Hempstead	Hertfordshire
Hemsworth	West Yorkshire
Hendon	North London
Henley	Oxfordshire
Hertsmere	Hertfordshire
Hexham	Northumberland
Heywood and Middleton	Greater Manchester
High Peak	Derbyshire
Hitchin and Harpenden	Hertfordshire
Holborn and St Pancras	Central London
Hornchurch	Essex
Hornsey and Wood Green	North London
Horsham	West Sussex
Houghton and Washington East	Tyne and Wear
Hove	East Sussex
Huddersfield	West Yorkshire
Huntingdon	Cambridgeshire
Hyndburn	Lancashire
Ilford North	Essex
Ilford South	Essex
Inverness East, Nairn and Lochaber	Highland
Ipswich	Suffolk
Islington North	North London
Islington South and Finsbury	Central London
Islwyn	South Wales
Jarrow	Tyne and Wear
Keighley	West Yorkshire
Kettering	Northamptonshire
Kilmarnock and Loudoun	East Ayrshire
Kingston and Surbiton	South West London
Kingswood	Gloucestershire
Kirkcaldy	Fife
Knowsley North and Sefton East	Merseyside
Knowsley South	Merseyside
Lagan Valley	Northern Ireland
Leigh	Greater Manchester
Leominster	Herefordshire
Lewes	East Sussex
Lewisham Deptford	South East London
Lewisham East	South East London
Lewisham West	South East London
Leyton and Wanstead	East London
Lichfield	Staffordshire
Linlithgow	West Lothian
Livingston	West Lothian
Llanelli	Carmarthenshire
Londonderry, East	Northern Ireland
Loughborough	Leicestershire
Louth and Horncastle	Lincolnshire
Ludlow	Shropshire
Luton North	Bedforshire
Luton South	Bedforshire
Macclesfield	Cheshire
Maidenhead	Berkshire
Maidstone and The Weald	Kent
Makerfield	Greater Manchester
Maldon and Chelmsford East	Essex
Mansfield	Nottinghamshire
Medway	Kent
Meirionnydd Nant Conwy	North Wales
Meriden	West Midlands

Merthyr Tydfil and Rhymney	South Wales
Middlesbrough	North Yorkshire
Middlesbrough South and East Cleveland	North Yorkshire
Midlothian	South East Scotland
Milton Keynes North East	Buckinghamshire
Milton Keynes South West	Buckinghamshire
Mitcham and Morden	South West London
Mole Valley	Surrey
Monmouth	South East Wales
Montgomeryshire	Powys
Moray	North Eastern Scotland
Morecambe and Lunesdale	Lancashire
Morley and Rothwell	West Yorkshire
Motherwell and Wishaw	North Lanarkshire
Neath	South Wales
New Forest East	Hampshire
New Forest West	Hampshire
Newark	Nottinghamshire
Newbury	Berkshire
Newcastle-under-Lyme	Staffordshire
Newport East	South Wales
Newport West	South Wales
Newry and Armagh	Northern Ireland
Normanton	West Yorkshire
Northavon	Gloucestershire
Nuneaton	Warwickshire
Ochil	Eastern Central Scotland
Ogmore	South Wales
Old Bexley and Sidcup	South London
Oldham East and Saddleworth	Greater Manchester
Oldham West and Royton	Greater Manchester
Orpington	Kent
Paisley North	Renfrewshire
Paisley South	Renfrewshire
Pendle	Lancashire
Penrith and The Border	Cumbria
Perth	Central Scotland
Peterborough	Cambridgeshire
Pontefract and Castleford	West Yorkshire
Pontypridd	South Wales
Poole	Dorset
Poplar and Canning Town	East London
Preston	Lancashire
Pudsey	West Yorkshire
Putney	South West London
Rayleigh	Essex
Redcar	North Yorkshire
Redditch	Worcestershire
Regent's Park and Kensington North	North London
Reigate	Surrey
Rhondda	South Wales
Ribble Valley	Lancashire
Ribble, South	Lancashire
Richmond Park	South West London
Rochdale	Greater Manchester
Rochford and Southend East	Essex
Romford	Essex
Romsey	Hampshire
Ross, Skye and Inverness West	Highland
Rossendale and Darwen	Lancashire
Rother Valley	South Yorkshire
Rotherham	South Yorkshire
Roxburgh and Berwickshire	Scottish Borders
Rugby and Kenilworth	Warwickshire
Ruislip Northwood	Middlesex
Runnymede and Weybridge	Surrey
Rushcliffe	Nottinghamshire
Ryedale	North Yorkshire
Saffron Walden	Essex
Salford	Greater Manchester
Salisbury	Wiltshire
Scarborough and Whitby	North Yorkshire
Scunthorpe	East Riding of Yorkshire
Sedgefield	County Durham
Selby	North Yorkshire
Sevenoaks	Kent
Sherwood	Nottinghamshire
Shipley	West Yorkshire
Shrewsbury and Atcham	Shropshire
Sittingbourne and Sheppey	Kent
Skipton and Ripon	North Yorkshire
Sleaford and North Hykeham	Lincolnshire
Slough	Berkshire
Solihull	West Midlands
Somerton and Frome	Somerset
South Holland and The Deepings	Lincolnshire
South Shields	Tyne and Wear

Southend West	Essex	**Tyneside, North**	Tyne and Wear
Southport	Merseyside	**Tyrone, West**	Northern Ireland
Southwark and		**Upminster**	Essex
Bermondsey, North	South London	**Upper Bann**	Northern Ireland
Spelthorne	Surrey	**Uxbridge**	Middlesex
St Albans	Hertfordshire	**Vale of Clwyd**	North Wales
St Helens North	Merseyside	**Vale of Glamorgan**	South Wales
St Helens South	Merseyside	**Vauxhall**	South London
St Ives	Cornwall	**Wakefield**	West Yorkshire
Stalybridge and Hyde	Greater Manchester	**Wallasey**	Merseyside
Stevenage	Hertfordshire	**Walsall North**	West Midlands
Stirling	Central Scotland	**Walsall South**	West Midlands
Stockport	Greater Manchester	**Walthamstow**	East London
Stockton North	County Durham	**Wansbeck**	Northumberland
Stockton South	County Durham	**Wansdyke**	Somerset
Stone	Staffordshire	**Wantage**	Oxfordshire
Stourbridge	West Midlands	**Warley**	West Midlands
Strangford	Northern Ireland	**Warrington North**	Cheshire
Stratford-on-Avon	Warwickshire	**Warrington South**	Cheshire
Strathkelvin and		**Watford**	Hertfordshire
Bearsden	East Dunbartonshire	**Waveney**	Suffolk
Streatham	South London	**Wealden**	East Sussex
Stretford and		**Weaver Vale**	Cheshire
Urmston	Greater Manchester	**Wellingborough**	Northamptonshire
Stroud	Gloucestershire	**Wells**	Somerset
Sunderland North	Tyne and Wear	**Welwyn Hatfield**	Hertfordshire
Sunderland South	Tyne and Wear	**Wentworth**	South Yorkshire
Surrey Heath	Surrey	**West Bromwich East**	West Midlands
Sutton and Cheam	Surrey	**West Bromwich West**	West Midlands
Sutton Coldfield	West Midlands	**West Ham**	East London
Swindon, North	Wiltshire	**Westbury**	Wiltshire
Swindon, South	Wiltshire	**Westmorland and**	
Tamworth	Staffordshire	**Lonsdale**	Cumbria
Tatton	Cheshire	**Weston-Super-Mare**	Somerset
Taunton	Somerset	**Wigan**	Greater Manchester
Tayside, North	Central East Scotland	**Wimbledon**	South West London
Teignbridge	Devon	**Winchester**	Hampshire
Telford	Shropshire	**Windsor**	Berkshire
Tewkesbury	Gloucestershire	**Wirral South**	Merseyside
Thanet, North	Kent	**Wirral West**	Merseyside
Thanet, South	Kent	**Witney**	Oxfordshire
Thurrock	Essex	**Woking**	Surrey
Tiverton and Honiton	Devon	**Wokingham**	Berkshire
Tonbridge and		**Woodspring**	Somerset
Malling	Kent	**Workington**	Cumbria
Tooting	South London	**Worsley**	Greater Manchester
Torbay	Devon	**Worthing East and**	
Torfaen	South Wales	**Shoreham**	West Sussex
Totnes	Devon	**Worthing West**	West Sussex
Tottenham	North London	**Wrekin, The**	Shropshire
Truro and St Austell	Cornwall	**Wycombe**	Buckinghamshire
Tunbridge Wells	Kent	**Wyre Forest**	Worcestershire
Tweeddale, Ettrick		**Wythenshawe and**	
and Lauderdale	South East Scotland	**Sale East**	Greater Manchester
Twickenham	South West London	**Yeovil**	Somerset
Tyne Bridge	Tyne and Wear	**Ynys Môn**	Anglesey
Tynemouth	Tyne and Wear		

State of the Parties as at 31 December 1999

Labour	418
Conservative	161
Liberal Democrats	46
Ulster Unionists	10
Scottish National Party	6
Plaid Cymru	4
Social Democratic and Labour	3
Democratic Unionists	2
Sinn Fein	2
Independent	1
Scottish Labour	1*
UK Unionist Party	1
The Speaker	1
Deputy Speakers	3†
Total	659

*Tommy Graham, MP *(West Renfrewshire)* had the Labour Whip withdrawn and now sits as Scottish Labour.
†The three Deputy Speakers are Rt Hon Sir Alan Haselhurst MP (Con), Michael Lord MP (Con) and Michael Martin, MP (Lab). Government majority 179.

Deceased and Resigned MPs since the 1997 General Election

Previous MP	Constituency	New MP	Date elected
Sir **Michael Shersby** (Con) Died 8 May 1997	Uxbridge	**John Randall** (Con)	31 July 1997 by-election
Gordon McMaster (Lab/Co-op) Died 28 July 1997	Paisley South	**Douglas Alexander** (Lab)	6 November 1997 by-election
Piers Merchant (Con) Resigned 21 October 1997	Beckenham	**Jacqui Lait** (Con)	20 November 1997 by-election
The Rt Hon **Derek Fatchett** (Lab) Died 9 May 1999	Leeds Central	**Hilary Benn** (Lab)	10 June 1999 by-election
The Rt Hon Sir **Alastair Goodlad** (Con) Resigned 28 June 1999	Eddisbury	**Stephen O'Brien** (Con)	22 July 1999 by-election
Roger Stott (Lab) Died 8 August 1999	Wigan	**Neil Turner** (Lab)	23 September 1999 by-election
The Rt Hon **George Robertson** (Lab) created life peer 24 August 1999	Hamilton South	**Bill Tynan** (Lab)	23 September 1999 by-election
The Rt Hon **Alan Clark** (Con) Died 5 September 1999	Kensington and Chelsea	The Rt Hon **Michael Portillo** (Con)	25 November 1999 by-election

By-Election results

UXBRIDGE

Sir Michael Shersby died on 8 May 1997 and a by-election was held on 31 July 1997.

		%
Randall, J. (Con)	16,288	51.1
Slaughter, A. (Lab)	12,522	39.3
Kerr, K. (LD)	1,792	5.6
Sutch, D. (Looney)	396	1.2
Leonard, J. (Soc)	259	0.8
Taylor, F. (BNP)	205	0.6
Anderson, I. (Nat Dem)	157	0.5
McCauley, J. (Nat Front)	110	0.3
Middleton, H. (Orig Lib)	69	0.2
Feisenberger, J. (UKIP)	39	0.1
Carroll, R. (Rainbow)	30	0.1

Con Majority   3,766   11.8%
Electorate 57,733
Total Vote 31,867   Poll 55.2
Con Hold

PAISLEY SOUTH

Gordon McMaster died on 28 July 1997 and a by-election was held on 6 November 1997.

		%
Alexander, D. (Lab)	10,346	44.1
Blackford, I. (SNP)	7,615	32.5
McCartin, E. (LD)	2,582	11.0
Laidlaw, S. (Con)	1,643	7.0
Deighan, J. (Pro-Life)	578	2.5
Curran, F. (Scot Soc)	306	1.3
McLauchlan, C. (Scot Ind Lab)	155	0.7
Herriot, C. (SLP)	153	0.7
Blair, K. (NLP)	57	0.2

Lab Majority   2,731   11.65%
Electorate 54,573
Total Vote 23,435   Poll 42.94%
Lab Hold

BECKENHAM

Piers Merchant resigned on 21 October 1997 and a by-election was held on 20 November 1997.

		%
Lait, J. (Con)	13,162	41.2
Hughes, B. (Lab)	11,935	37.4
Vetterlein, R. (LD)	5,864	18.4
Rimmer, P. (Lib)	330	1.0
Mcauley, J. (NF)	267	0.8
Mead, L. (New Brit/Ref.)	237	0.7
Campion, T. (SFP)	69	0.2
Small, J. (NLP)	44	0.1

Con Majority   1,227   3.84%
Electorate 74,019
Total Vote 31,908   Poll 43.57%
Con Hold

WINCHESTER

General Election result of 1 May 1997 was overturned by the High Court and a by-election was held on 20 November 1997.

		%
Oaten, M. (LD)	37,006	68.0
Malone, G. (Con)	15,450	28.5
Davies, P. (Lab)	944	1.7
Page, R. (Ref/UKI/ALL)	521	0.9
Sutch, D. (Looney)	316	0.6
Huggett, R. (Lit Dem MHTW)	59	0.1
Barry, R. (NLP)	48	0.1
Everest, R. (Euro Con)	40	0.1

LD Majority   21,556   39.63%
Electorate 79,121
Total Vote 54,384   Poll 68.7%
LD Hold

LEEDS CENTRAL

Rt Hon Derek Fatchett died on 9 May 1999 and a by-election was held on 10 June 1999.

		%
Benn, H. (Lab)	6,361	48.2
Wild, P. (LD)	4,068	30.8
Wild, W. E. (Con)	1,618	12.3
Blackburn, D. (Green)	478	3.6
Northgreaves, R. (UKIP)	353	2.7
Hill, C. (Left Alliance)	258	2.0
Fitzgerald, J.(Equal Parenting)	51	0.4

Lab Majority   2,293   17.38%
Electorate 67,569
Total Vote 13,187   Poll 19.5%
Lab Hold

EDDISBURY

Rt Hon Sir Alistair Goodlad resigned on 28 June 1999 and a by-election was held on 22 July 1999.

		%
O'Brien, S. (Con)	15,465	44.8
Hanson, M. (Lab)	13,859	40.2
Roberts, P. (LD)	4,757	13.8
Hope, A. (Looney)	238	0.7
Everest, R. (Ind Europe Cons)	98	0.3
Grice, D. (NLP)	80	0.2

Con Majority   1,606   2.23%
Electorate 60,026
Total Vote 34,497   Poll 57.5%
Con Hold

WIGAN

Roger Stott died on 8 August 1999 and a by-election was held on 23 September 1999.

		%
Turner, N. (Lab)	9,641	59.6
Peet, T (Con)	2,912	18.0
Rule, J. (LD)	2,148	13.3
Whittaker, J. (UKIP)	834	5.2
Kelly, W. (Soc Lab)	240	1.5
Maile, C. (Green)	190	1.2
Ebbs, S. (NDR)	100	0.6
Davis, P. (NLP)	64	0.4
Braid, D. (Reverend)	58	0.4

Lab Majority   6,729   41.57%
Electorate 64,755
Total Vote 16,187   Poll 25.0%
Lab Hold

HAMILTON SOUTH

Rt Hon George Robertson elevated to the House of Lords 24 August 1999 and a by-election was held on 23 September 1999.

		%
Tynan, B. (Lab)	7,172	36.8
Ewing, A (SNP)	6,616	34.0
Blackall, S. (SSP)	1,847	9.5
Ferguson, C. (Con)	1,406	7.2
Mungall, S. (Accies)	1,075	5.5
MacLaren, M. (Green)	634	3.3
Burns, M. (ProLife)	257	1.3
Dewar, T. (Soc Lab)	238	1.2
Reid, J. (SUP)	113	0.6
McConnachie, A. (UKIP)	61	0.3
Stidolph, G (NLP)	18	0.1
Drummon Moray, J. (Status Quo)	17	0.1

Lab Majority   556   2.85%
Electorate 47,081
Total Vote 19,485   Poll 41.4%
Lab Hold

KENSINGTON AND CHELSEA

Rt Hon Alan Clark died on 5 September 1999 and a by-election was held on 25 November 1999.

		%
Portillo, M. (Con)	11,004	56.4
Atkinson, J. (Lab)	4,298	22.0
Browne, R. (LD)	1,831	9.4
Stevens, J. (PEC)	740	3.8
Hockney, N. (UKIP)	450	2.3
Charlton, H. (Green)	446	2.3
Burford, C. (Dem)	182	0.9
Paisley, C. (LCA)	141	0.7
Irwin, M. (LWL)	97	0.5
Oliver, G, (UKPP)	75	0.4
Scott-Fawcett, S. (Ref)	57	0.3
Hodges, L. (D&SP)	48	0.3
Valente, G. (NLP)	35	0.2
Lovebucket, L. (PNDT)	26	0.1
Davies, J. (IESCC)	24	0.1
May, P. (EP)	24	0.1
Hope, A. (Looney)	20	0.1
Samuelson, T. (STCFOC)	15	0.1

Con Majority   6,706   34.37%
Electorate 65,752
Total Vote 19,513   Poll 29.7%
Con Hold

VACHER'S PARLIAMENTARY COMPANION

Published continuously since 1832 and updated quarterly

Opening with comprehensive details of the Government, the new look quarterly *Vacher's* pocket book continues with the Cabinet Office, Ministerial Responsibilities, Permanent Secretaries and Opposition Spokesmen, up-to-date lists of MPs, Constituency results and By-elections, Select Committees and Political Parties' Organisations followed by the House of Lords. New sections on the Scottish Parliament, the National Assembly for Wales and the Northern Ireland Assembly are treated with the same thoroughness of detail. Then follow sections on Senior Civil Servants, Government Departments and UK MEPs – all designed for speed and handiness.

Vacher Dod Publishing Limited
PO Box 3700, Westminster, London SW1E 5NP
Tel: 020 7828 7256   Fax: 020 7828 7269
E-mail: politics@vacherdod.co.uk
Websites: www.vacherdod.co.uk   www.politicallinks.co.uk

GOVERNMENT AND PUBLIC OFFICES

GOVERNMENT DEPARTMENTS

Agriculture, Fisheries and Food, Ministry of

Nobel House, 17 Smith Square,
London SW1P 3JR (LNH)
020 7238 3000 *Fax:* 020 7238 6591
MAFF Helpline (Public Enquiries)
0645 335577
E-mail: helpline@inf.maff.gov.uk
Website: www.maff.gov.uk/maffhome.htm

OTHER HEADQUARTER ADDRESSES

Ergon House, c/o 17 Smith Square,
London SW1P 3JR (LER)
020 7238 3000 *Fax:* 020 7238 6591

Eastbury House, 30-34 Albert Embankment,
London SE1 7TL (LEA)
020 7238 6000 *Fax:* 020 7238 6616

Foss House, 1-2 Peasholme Green, Kings Pool,
York YO1 7PX (YKF)
01904 641000

Government Buildings, Epsom Road,
Guildford, Surrey GU1 2LD (GUI)
01483 568121 *Fax:* 01483 37396

1a Page Street, London SW1P 4PQ (LPS)
020 7904 6000

St Christopher House, 80-112 Southwark Street,
London SE1 0TE (LCH)

55 Whitehall, London SW1A 2EY (L55W)
020 7238 6000 *Fax:* 020 7270 8721

Whitehall Place, London SW1A 2HH (LWP)
020 7238 6000 *Fax:* 020 7270 8721

Government Buildings (Toby Jug Site),
Hook Rise South, Tolworth, Surbiton,
Surrey KT6 7NF (TOL)
020 8330 4411 *Fax:* 020 8337 3640

White House Lane, Huntingdon Road,
Cambridge CB3 0LE (CWL)
01223 277151 *Fax:* 01223 342386

19-29 Woburn Place, London WC1H 0LU
(LWO)
020 7273 3000

The Ministry of Agriculture, Fisheries and Food is responsible for Government policies on agriculture, horticulture and fisheries in England and for policies relating to safety and quality of food in the United Kingdom, including composition, labelling, additives, contaminants and new production processes. In association with the other Agriculture Departments in the UK and the Intervention Board Executive Agency it is responsible for negotiations in the European Community on the Common Agricultural and Common Fisheries Policies and for Single European Market questions which relate to its agricultural, fisheries and food responsibilities. The Ministry exercises responsibilities for the protection and the enhancement of the countryside and the marine environment, for flood and coastal defence and for other rural issues. It is the licensing authority for veterinary medicines and the registration authority for pesticides. It administers policies relating to control of animal, plant and fish diseases. It provides scientific, technical and professional services and advice to farmers, growers and ancillary industries, and it commissions research to assist in the formulation and assessment of policy and to underpin applied research and development work done by industry.

Minister:
   The Rt Hon Nick Brown, MP
Prin Priv Sec: Ms Sarah Hendry
Priv Secretaries: Fiona James, Adrian Dally
Parly Priv Sec: Ruth Kelly, MP
Special Advisers: Kieran Simpson,
   Jack Thurston
Minister of State and Deputy Minister:
   The Rt Hon Joyce Quin, MP
Priv Sec: Miss Teresa Hart
Parly Priv Sec: Brian Jenkins, MP
Minister of State (Lords):
   The Baroness Hayman
Priv Sec: Vic Platten
Parly Priv Sec: Bob Blizzard, MP
Parliamentary Secretary (Commons):
   Elliot Morley, MP
Priv Sec: Mark Livesey

Spokespersons in the House of Lords: The Baroness Hayman, The Lord Carter

Permanent Secretary: (Vacant)
Priv Sec: Lloyd Burdett
Parliamentary Branch (for all MAFF
Ministers) 020 7238 5456
Parliamentary Clerk: Mark Stickings
*Head of Agricultural Crops and Commodities
   Directorate:* Ms Kate Timms, CB *(SCS)*
*Head of Food Safety and Environment
   Directorate:* Richard Carden, CB *(SCS)*
Based at LNH

Chief Scientist:
  David Shannon, PhD, BAgr, DMS *(SCS)*
  (LCH)
Legal Adviser and Solicitor:
  Miss Kathyrn Morton *(SCS)* (L55W)

AGRICULTURAL CROPS AND COMMODITIES DIRECTORATE
European Union and International Policy Group
Head of European Union and International
  Policy Group: Andy Lebrecht *(SCS)*
Heads of Division (SCS): John Robbs,
  Tom Eddy

AGRICULTURAL GROUP
Head of Agricultural Group:
  David Hunter *(SCS)*
Heads of Division (SCS): Henry Brown,
  Richard Cowan, Peter Nash, Andrew Kuyk
G6, Alan Taylor
Based at LWP
George Noble *(SCS)* (LEA)

FOOD INDUSTRY COMPETITIVENESS AND CONSUMERS
Head of Food Industry Competitiveness and
  Consumers: Neil Thornton *(SCS)*
Heads of Division (SCS): David Orchard,
  Miss Jane Rabagliati, Ms Judy Allfrey,
David Dawson
G6, Mrs Ann Waters
Based at LWP
Mrs Alison Blackburn *(SCS)* (LNH)

REGIONAL SERVICES AND DEFENCE GROUP
Head of Regional Services and Defence Group:
  Mrs Jane Brown *(SCS)* (LWP)
Head of Division: Mrs Janet Purnell *(SCS)*
  (LWP)
Head of Unit: G7, David Putley (LNH)
Heads of Division: Andrew Perrins *(SCS)*
  (YKF), David Boreham (CWL), Dr Jim Park
  (LEA)

REGIONAL SERVICE CENTRE DIRECTORS
ANGLIA REGION
Bedfordshire, Cambridgeshire, Essex,
Hertfordshire, Norfolk and Suffolk
Block B, Government Buildings
Brooklands Avenue, Cambridge CB2 2DR
01223 462727 *Fax:* 01223 455652
Martin Edwards

NORTHERN REGION
Cumbria, Lancashire, Northumberland
and Tyne and Wear
Eden Bridge House, Lowther Street
Carlisle, Cumbria CA3 8DX
01228 523400 *Fax:* 01228 640205
Ian Pearson

EAST MIDLANDS REGION
Derbyshire, Leicestershire, Lincolnshire,
Northamptonshire and Nottinghamshire
Block 7, Government Buildings,
Chalfont Drive, Nottingham NG8 3SN
0115-929 1191 *Fax:* 0115-929 4886
Graham Norbury

SOUTH EAST REGION
Berkshire, Buckinghamshire, Hampshire,
Isle of Wight, Kent, Greater London,
Oxfordshire, Surrey and Sussex (East
and West)
Block A, Government Buildings
Coley Park, Reading, Berks RG1 6DT
0118-958 1222 *Fax:* 0118-939 2399
Mrs Virginia Silvester

SOUTH WEST REGION
Cornwall, Devon and Isles of Scilly
Clyst House, Winslade Park,
Clyst St Mary, Exeter, Devon EX5 1DY
01392 447400 *Fax:* 01392 266000
Mike Highman

NORTH EAST REGION
Cleveland, Durham, Humberside and Yorkshire
(North, South and West)
Government Buildings, Crosby Road
Northallerton, North Yorkshire DL6 1AD
01609 773751 *Fax:* 01609 780179
Peter Watson

SOUTH MERCIA REGION
Hereford and Worcester,
Gloucestershire, Warwickshire and
West Midlands
Block C, Government Buildings
Whittington Road, Worcester WR5 2LQ
01905 763355 *Fax:* 01905 763180
Brinley Davies

NORTH MERCIA REGION
Cheshire, Merseyside, Greater Manchester,
Shropshire and Staffordshire
Electra Way, Crew Business Park,
Crewe CW1 6GJ
01270 754000 *Fax:* 01270 669494
Frank Whitehouse

WESSEX REGION
Avon, Dorset, Somerset and Wiltshire
Block 3, Government Buildings
Burghill Road, Westbury-on-Trym
Bristol BS10 6NJ
0117-959 1000 *Fax:* 0117-950 5392
Mrs Angela Ould

FOOD SAFETY AND ENVIRONMENT DIRECTORATE

FOOD SAFETY AND STANDARDS GROUP
Head of Food Safety and Standards Group:
  Geoffrey Podger *(SCS)* (LNH)
Heads of Division (SCS): Dr Jonathan Bell,
  Dr Richard Burt, Miss Jill Wordley,
  Grant Meekings, Dr Mike Segal,
  Dr Richard Harding, Chris Lawson,
  Peter Hewson, Richard McIvor
Based at LER

CHIEF VETERINARY OFFICER'S GROUP

Chief Veterinary Officer: Jim Scudamore *(SCS)*
Assistant Chief Veterinary Officer:
  Richard Cawthorne *(SCS)*
Heads of Division (SCS): Robin Bell,
  David Pritchard, Debby Reynolds,
  Danny Matthews
Director of Veterinary Field Service:
  Martin Atkinson
Head of Division: Fred Landeg
Asst Directors Veterinary Field Service (SCS):
  John Cross, BVM&S, DVSM, MRCVS
  (Bristol), Richard Drummond, BVM&S,
  MSc, FRCVS (Harrogate), Gareth Jones,
  BVetMed, DipAH, MRCVS (Reading),
  Derick McIntosh, BVM&S, MRCVS
  (Edinburgh), Tony Edwards, BVetMed, MSc,
  MRCVS (Cardiff)
Based at LPS

ANIMAL HEALTH GROUP
Head of Animal Health: Brian Dickinson *(SCS)*
Heads of Division: Valerie Smith,
  Dr Mandy Bailey, Roy Hathaway, Chris Ryder
G6, Robert Gurd
Based at LPS

ENVIRONMENT GROUP

Head of Environment Group:
  Dudley Coates *(SCS)*
Heads of Division (SCS): John Osmond,
  Ms Lindsey Cornish, David Jones
Based at LNH

ECONOMICS AND STATISTICS GROUP

Head of Economics and Statistics:
  David Thompson *(SCS)*
Heads of Division: Peter Muriel, Nigel Atkinson
G6, Howard Fearn
Based at LWP
  Stuart Platt *(SCS)*
Chief Statistician (Census and Surveys):
  Peter Helm
Based at YKF

FISHERIES

Fisheries Secretary: Stephen Wentworth *(SCS)*
Heads of Division: Peter Boyling,
  Miss Sue Brown, Ivor Lewellyn
G6, Barry Edwards
Chief Inspector, Sea Fisheries Inspectorate:
  George Ellson
Based at LNH

LEGAL DEPARTMENT

Legal Adviser and Solicitor:
  Miss Kathryn Morton *(SCS)*
Prin Asst Solicitors (SCS):
  Ms Catherine Crisham, David Pearson
Heads of Division (SCS): Charles Allen,
  Ian Corbett, Dr Gisela Davis, Peter Davis,
  Nigel Lambert, Ms Susan Spence
Chief Investigation Officer:
  G7, Miss Jan Panting
Based at L55W
  Colin Gregory *(SCS)*
  Anne Werbicki
Based at LWP

CHIEF SCIENTIST GROUP

Chief Scientist:
  David Shannon, PhD, BAgr, DMS *(SCS)*
Heads of Division (SCS):
  Dr John Sherlock, BSc, PhD, FRSC, CChem,
  FIFST, Dr Ken MacOwan, BVM&S, PhD,
  MRCVS, Dr Tony Burne
Based at LPS

ESTABLISHMENTS GROUP

Director of Establishments:
  Roger Saunderson *(SCS)* (LNH)
Heads of Division: Tony Nickson *(SCS)* (LEA),
  Mrs Teresa Newell (LNH)
Director of IT: Tony Matthews *(SCS)* (LCH)
Heads of Division: G6, David Brown,
  Peter Barber, Sean Soper
Based at GUI

FINANCE

Prin Finance Officer: Paul Elliott *(SCS)* (LWP)
Heads of Division (SCS): David Rabey (LWO),
   Brian Harding (LWP)
Head of Unit: Vivien Bodnar (LWP)
*Director of Audit Consultancy and Management
   Services:* David Fisher, FCCA (LWO)
Head of Resource Management Division:
   G6, Mrs Julie Flint (YKF)

CHANGE MANAGEMENT UNIT
Head of Unit: David Rossington *(SCS)*
Head of IIP Unit: G6, Gavin Ross
Based at LWP

AGENCY OWNERSHIP UNIT
Head of Unit: G6, Dr Mike Tas (LWP)

DIRECTOR OF COMMUNICATIONS
Director of Communications:
   Robert Lowson *(SCS)* (LNH)

Executive Agencies: Central Science
Laboratory (CSL); Centre for Environment,
Fisheries and Aquaculture Science (CEFAS);
Farming and Rural Conservation Agency
(FRCA); Meat Hygiene Service (MHS);
Pesticides Safety Directorate (PSD); Veterinary
Laboratories Agency (VLA); Veterinary
Medicines Directorate (VMD)

Cabinet Office

10 Downing Street, London SW1A 2AA
Tel: Direct Line from 020 7930 4433
Website: www.number—10.gov.uk

To help the Prime Minister and Ministers collectively to reach well informed and timely decisions on policy and its presentation, and to drive
forward its implementation, together with their
agenda for modernising Government, for
improving the quality, coherence and repson-
siveness of public services, and for promoting a
strong and well managed Civil Service.

The Prime Minister:
   The Rt Hon Tony Blair, MP

Details of the Prime Minister's staff may be
found under Prime Minister's Office in this
Section.

70 Whitehall, London SW1A 2AS
020 7270 0400 *Fax:* 020 7270 0196
Website: www.cabinet-office.gov.uk
The Minister for the Cabinet Office:
   The Rt Hon Dr Mo Mowlam, MP
Prin Priv Sec: Dr John Fuller

Parly Priv Sec: Margaret Moran, MP
Special Advisers: Nigel Warner, Andrew Lappin,
   Clay Bendish (Adviser on Agencies)

Minister of State:
   The Lord Falconer of Thoroton, QC
Priv Sec: Mark Langdale
Parly Priv Sec: Christopher Leslie, MP
Minister of State:
   The Rt Hon Ian McCartney, MP
E-mail: imccartney@cabinet-office.x.gsi.gov.uk
Priv Sec: Nicola Pitts
Parly Priv Sec: Frank Doran, MP
Parliamentary Secretary: Graham Stringer, MP
E-mail: gstringer@cabinet-office.x.gsi.gov.uk
Priv Sec: Mark Holmes
Asst Priv Sec: Neil Massingham
Parly Clerk: Selvin Brown

Spokesmen in the House of Lords: The Lord
Falconer of Thoroton, The Lord Burlison

*Sec of the Cabinet and Head of the
   Home Civil Service:*
   Sir Richard Wilson, KCB *(SCS)*
Prin Priv Sec: Sebastian Wood
Priv Sec: Richard Abel
Asst Priv Secs: Ashley Ibbett, Lynne Sheasgreen,
   Karen Chong

Permanent Secretary: Brian Bender, CB, *(SCS)*
Priv Sec: Patrick White (020 7270 0003)

SECRETARIATS
70 Whitehall, London SW1A 2AS
020 7270 3000
Economic and Domestic Secretariat (SCS):
   W Rickett, J Gallagher, P Britton, A Kennon
Defence and Overseas Affairs Secretariat (SCS):
   Hon M A Pakenham, CMG, T McKane
Joint Intelligence Organisation (SCS): J Alpass,
   R Gozney
European Secretariat (SCS): D Bostock,
   M Donnelly, M Roberts
Constitution Secretariat (SCS):
   Sir Quentin Thomas, D Brew,
   Miss J Simpson, Miss R Jeffreys

CENTRAL SECRETARIAT
020 7270 1829 *Fax:* 020 7270 1860
E-mail: open.co.wh@gtnet.gov.uk
Director: David Wilkinson, CB *(SCS)*

PUBLIC SERVICE DELIVERY
Government Offices, Horse Guards Road,
London SW1P 3AL

REGULATORY IMPACT UNIT
Government Offices, Horse Guards Road,
London SW1P 3AL
E-mail: plewis@cabinet-office.x.gsi.gov.uk
Director: (Vacant) *(SCS)*
Fax: 020 7270 1983

CENTRAL IT UNIT
53 Parliament Street, London SW1
020 7238 2015 GTN 238 2015
Fax: 020 7238 2006 GTN 238 2006
E-mail: citu@citu.gov.uk
Website: www@citu.gov.uk
Director: David Cooke *(SCS)*

GOVERNMENT DIRECT TEAM
Mark Gladwyn *(SCS)*, Ian White *(SCS)*,
Jeremy Crump, P Waller, Mrs A Steward

YEAR 2000 TEAM
Mandy Mayer

MODERNISING PUBLIC SERVICES GROUP
Government Offices, Horse Guards Road,
London SW1P 3AL
Fax: 020 7270 3000
E-mail: servicefirst@gtnet.gov.uk
E-mail: efficiency.unit@gtnet
Director: Jonathan Rees *(SCS)*

MODERNISING GOVERNMENT
Government Offices, Horse Guards Road,
London SW1P 3AL
E-mail: moderngov@cabinet-office.gov.uk
Director: Andrew Wells *(SCS)*

CIVIL SERVICE MANAGEMENT MATTERS

CIVIL SERVICE CORPORATE MANAGEMENT
COMMAND
Government Offices, Horse Guards Road,
London SW1P 3AL
E-mail: cseg@gtnet.gov.uk
Head of Unit: B Fox, CB *(SCS)*

RECRUITMENT AND DEVELOPMENT OF PEOPLE
GROUP
Government Offices, Horse Guards Road,
London SW1P 3AL
Fax: 020 7270 6058
Director: John Barker *(SCS)*

PERFORMANCE MANAGEMENT GROUP
Government Offices, Horse Guards Road,
London SW1P 3AL
Director: Sally Hinkley, CBE

CENTRE FOR MANAGEMENT AND POLICY STUDIES
Government Offices, Horse Guards Road,
London SW1P 3AL
Director-General: Prof Ronald Amann
Corporate Development and Training Director:
  Robert Green
Business Director: Peter Tebby

GOVERNMENT INFORMATION AND
COMMUNICATIONS SERVICE
Head of Communications: M Grannatt *(SCS)*

INFORMATION DIVISION/PRESS OFFICE
70 Whitehall, London SW1A 2AS
020 7270 0516
E-mail: bsutlieff@cabinet-office.gov.uk
Director of Information: Barry Sutlieff

UK ANTI-DRUGS CO-ORDINATION UNIT
Government Offices, Horse Guards Road,
London SW1P 3AL
020 7270 5776
Head of Unit: (Vacant)
UK Anti-Drugs Co-ordinator:
  Keith Hellawell *(SCS)*
Deputy Anti-Drugs Co-ordinator:
  Michael Trace *(SCS)*

CORPORATE RESOURCES AND SERVICES GROUP
Queen Anne's Chambers, 28 Broadway
London SW1H 9JS
Director: Nicky Oppenheimer *(SCS)*

Executive Agencies: The Buying Agency
(TBA); Central Computer and Telecommuni-
cations Agency (CCTA); Central Office of
Information (COI); Civil Service College (CSC);
Government Car and Despatch Agency
(GCDA); Property Advisers to the Civil Estate
(PACE)

Crown Office

25 Chambers Street, Edinburgh
EH1 1LA, Scotland
0131-226 2626 *Fax:* 0131-226 6910
E-mail: co.isunit@dial.pipex.com

The Law Officers for Scotland are the Lord
Advocate and the Solicitor General for Scotland.
The Lord Advocate's Department is responsible
for drafting Scottish legislation, for providing
legal advice to other departments on Scottish
questions and for assistance to the Law Officers
for Scotland in certain of their legal duties.

Lord Advocate:
  The Rt Hon the Lord Hardie, QC

Solicitor General for Scotland:
Colin Boyd, Esq, QC
Private Secretary to Lord Advocate and Solicitor General for Scotland: J A Gibbons
Assistant Private Secretary to Lord Advocate and Solicitor General for Scotland:
Mrs C McDivitt
Crown Agent: A C Normand *(SCS)*
Deputy Crown Agent: F R Crowe *(SCS)*
Asst Solicitors: Miss E C Munro, T H Dysart, Mrs E F Angiolini, Mrs J E Cameron, A N Brown
Head of Practice and Quality Review: G Napier
Senior Deputes: B M Logan, C B McClory
Legal Assistant to the Crown Agent:
Miss M A M McLaughlin
Principal Deputes: Miss S C Barrie, J Brisbane, L A Brown, Miss C E S Bryden, Mrs S M Burns, Miss G Y Climie, W C Craig, Mrs A M Di Rollo, Ms C M D Duncan, J A Dunn, Miss C R Frame, Miss L Glancy, D S A Green, A S D Laing, A Miller, Miss M R Paterson, S Pattison, Miss A B Swarbrick, Miss M B Watson, A K Youngson
Depute Fiscals: Miss G E Wallace, Miss S T Swan, Mrs E A Knox, J T Logue, Miss L R Anderson, D B Harvie, S Latif, Miss A Galbraith
Senior Legal Assistants: Miss A Ogg, Miss P M Collins, Ms A V Forbes

Culture, Media and Sport, Department for

2–4 Cockspur Street, London SW1Y 5DH
020 7211 6200 *Fax:* 020 7211 6032
E-mail: enquiries@culture.gov.uk
Website: www.culture.gov.uk

The Department for Culture, Media and Sport is responsible for Government policies on arts and libraries, broadcasting and press issues; sports issues including the safety of sports grounds; tourism and heritage issues; film policy; the export licensing of antiques; the National Lottery; volunteering and charities; museums and galleries.

Secretary of State: The Rt Hon Chris Smith, MP
Principal Priv Sec: Fergus Muir
Priv Sec: Chris Carr
Asst Priv Sec: Suzi Daley
Diary Sec: Raymond Toth
Parly Priv Sec: Fiona Mactaggart, MP

Special Advisers:
020 7211 6101 *Fax:* 020 7211 6249
Andy Burnham
E-mail: andy.burnham@culture.gov.uk
Ruth MacKenzie
E-mail: ruth.mackenzie@culture.gov.uk
Parliamentary Under-Sec of State (Minister for Tourism, Film and Broadcasting):
Ms Janet Anderson, MP
Private Secretary: Dominic Tambling
Assistant Private Secretary: Mark Mann
Diary Secretary: Oswin Taylor
Parliamentary Under-Sec of State (Minister for Sport): Kate Hoey, MP
Private Secretary: Simon Cooper
Assistant Private Secretary: Philip Chamberlain
Diary Sec: Nicholas Hercules
Parliamentary Under-Sec of State (Minister for the Arts): Alan Howarth, CBE, MP
Priv Sec: David Fitzgerald
Asst Priv Sec: Steven Harding
Diary Secretary: Emily Adams

Spokesman in the House of Lords: The Lord McIntosh of Haringey

Permanent Secretary: Robin Young *(SCS)*
E-mail: robin.young@culture.gov.uk
Priv Sec: Keith Gibbins
Diary Sec: Barbara McOgg

Corporate Services Group
Head of Group: Andrew Ramsay *(SCS)*
Director of Finance: Andy Mclellan *(SCS)*
Head of Personnel and Central Services Division: Ruth Siemaszko *(SCS)*
Head of National Lottery Division:
Andy McLellan *(SCS)*
Head of Accounts: John Kempsell *(SCS)*
Head of Internal Audit: David Rix
Head of Statistics: Paul Allin
Head of Economics: Dr Stephen Creigh-Tyte
Head of Central Appointments Unit:
Rosemary Griggs

Creative Industries, Media and Broadcasting Group
Head of Group: Nicholas Kroll *(SCS)*
Head of Media Division: Janet Evans *(SCS)*
Head of Broadcasting Policy Division:
Melanie Leech *(SCS)*
Head of Creative Industries Unit: Allan Ferries

Museums, Galleries, Libraries and Heritage Group
Head of Group: Alexandra Stewart *(SCS)*
Head of Buildings, Monuments and Sites Division: Nigel Pittman *(SCS)*

Head of Museums and Galleries Division:
Hugh Corner *(SCS)*
Head of Libraries, Information and Archives Division: Neville Mackay *(SCS)*
Head of Government Art Collection:
Penny Johnson *(SCS)*

Strategy and Communications Group
Director of Strategy and Communications:
Paul Bolt *(SCS)*
Head of Strategy: Zoe McNeill-Ritchie
(Secretary to the Management Board)
Head of News: Iain Hepplewhite
Head of Publicity and Communications:
Graham Newsom

Education, Training, Arts and Sports Group
Head of Group: Phillippa Drew
Head of Sports and Recreation Division:
Harry Reeves *(SCS)*
Head of Arts Division: William Nye *(SCS)*
Head of Education and Training Unit:
Tony Dyer

Regions, Tourism, Millennium and International Group
Head of Group: Brian Leonard *(SCS)*
Head of Local, Regional and International Division: Paul Douglas *(SCS)*
Head of Tourism Division:
Simon Broadley *(SCS)*
Head of Millennium Unit: Clare Pillman

Legal Adviser
Isabel Letwin
DCMS Legal Advisers, 28 Broadway,
London SW1
020 7210 3278 *Fax:* 020 7210 3448

Parliamentary Branch
Parly Clerk: Trevor English 020 7211 6288
Ministerial Support Unit
Rob Goodyear 020 7211 6253

Executive Agency: Royal Parks

Defence, Ministry of
FOR SECURITY REASONS, CERTAIN
DEPARTMENTS NOT PUBLISHED
Main Building, Whitehall,
London SW1A 2HB
Switchboard 020 7218 9000
Parliamentary Section 020 7218 6169
E-mail: public@ministers.mod.uk
for all Ministers
Website: www.mod.uk

The Ministry of Defence is concerned with the control, administration, equipment and support of the Armed Forces of the Crown. The research,

development, production and purchase of weapons systems and equipment for the Armed Forces is the concern of the Defence Procurement Agency of the Ministry of Defence.

Secretary of State:
The Rt Hon Geoffrey Hoon, MP
Priv Sec: Julian Miller
Parly Priv Sec: Sylvia Heal, MP
Parly Clerk: Patricia Parkin
Special Adviser: Alasdair McGowan
Minister of State for the Armed Forces:
John Spellar, MP
Priv Sec: Daniel Applegate
Parly Priv Sec: David Watts, MP
Minister of State for Defence Procurement:
The Baroness Symons of Vernham Dean
Priv Sec: David Hatcher
Parly Priv Sec: Gillian Merron, MP
Parliamentary Under-Sec of State:
Peter Kilfoyle, MP
Priv Sec: Andrew Dwyer

Spokespersons in the House of Lords: The Baroness Symons of Vernham Dean, The Lord Burlison

Chief of the Defence Staff:
General Sir Charles Guthrie, GCB, LVO, OBE, ADC Gen
Permanent Under-Secretary:
Kevin Tebbit, CMG *(SCS)*
Priv Sec: Guy Lester 020 7218 2839
Second Permanent Under-Secretary:
Roger Jackling, CBE *(SCS)*

DEFENCE INFORMATION DIVISION
As part of the Defence Information Division the **Public Enquiry Office** acts as a first point of contact for the public. The telephone number for all enquiries relating to MoD business is as follows:

Public Enquiry Office
020 7218 6645

For specific public relations queries a full contact list of Defence Information Staff is shown below:

Director-General of Corporate Communications: John Pitt-Brooke *(SCS)*
(020 7218 0546)
Director of Corporate Services:
A Boardman *(SCS)* (020 7218 6181)
Director of News: Oona Muirhead *(SCS)*
(020 7218 2717)
Head of Communication Planning: Nick Gurr
Director Corporate Communications (Navy):
Cdre Hugh Edleston, RN (020 7218 7906)

Director Corporate Communications (Army):
Brig Sebastian Roberts, OBE (020 7218 2500)
Director Corporate Communications (RAF):
Air Cdre David Walker (020 7218 3559)
Director News/Chief Press Officer:
D Gregg (020 7218 7950)

CENTRAL STAFFS
Vice-Chief of the Defence Staff:
Adm Sir Peter Abbott, KCB
*Deputy Chief of the Defence Staff (Equipment
Capability):* Vice-Adm Jeremy Blackham,
KCB, BA
Capability Manager (Strategic Deployment):
Rear Adm R G J Ward
Directorate of Science (Sea): C D Fallows *(SCS)*
Capability Manager (Manoeuvre):
Maj Gen P J Russell-Jones, OBE
Capability Manager (Strike): Air Vice-Marshal
S M Nicholl, CBE, AFC, BA, FRAeS (RAF)
Deputy Chief of the Defence Staff (Personnel):
Air Marshal Malcolm Pledger, RAF
Assistant Chief of Defence Staff (Programmes):
Maj Gen J P Kiszely, MC
*Assistant Under-Secretary of State (Service
Personnel):* Barry Miller *(SCS)*
*Defence Housing Executive
Chief Executive:* John Wilson *(SCS)*
Surgeon Generals Department (SGD): Surg
General, Air Marshal J A Baird, CBE, QHP
Defence Medical Training Organisation:
Maj Gen C G Callow, OBE, QHP
Principal Finance Officer: C V Balmer *(SCS)*
Director-General (Resources and Plans):
T Woolley *(SCS)*
Director-General (Equipment):
N K J Witney *(SCS)*
Director-General (Financial Management):
D G Jones *(SCS)*
Assistant Under-Secretary of State: C T Sandars
(SCS)
Defence Bills Agency: I S Elrick
Defence Services Secretary: Rear Adm R Lees
Directorate of Reserve Forces and Cadets:
Brig E R Holmes
*Deputy Chief of the Defence Staff
(Commitments):* Lt Gen J R Day, OBE
*Assistant Chief of the Defence Staff
(Operations):* Rear Adm S Moore
*Assistant Under Secretary of State (Home and
Overseas):* Simon Webb *(SCS)*
Gulf Veterans' Illnesses Unit:
Christopher Baker *(SCS)*
Chief of the Defence Staff (Logistics):
Gen Sir S Cowen, KCB, CBE
Policy Director: R P Hatfield *(SCS)*

*Assistant Under-Secretary of State (Service
Personnel):* D J Bowen *(SCS)*
NATO European Policy Group: Brig Jim Dutton
Assistant Chief of the Defence Staff (Policy):
Maj Gen C F Drewry, CBE
Director of Defence Policy: Patrick Turner *(SCS)*
*Deputy Under Secretary of State (Civilian
Management):* J J M Legge *(SCS)*
*Assistant Under Secretary of State (Civilian
Management):* B A E Taylor *(SCS)*
MoD Police, Chief Constable:
W E E Boreham, OBE *(SCS)*
*Assistant Under Secretary (Security and
Support):* A G Rucker *(SCS)*
Legal Adviser: M J Hemming *(SCS)*
Capability Manager (Information Superiority):
A Sleigh *(SCS)*
Defence Estate Organisation: I Andrews *(SCS)*
*Joint Service Command and Staff College
(Bracknell):* Maj Gen T J Granville-Chapman,
CBE

CHIEFS OF STAFF
Chief of Naval Staff and First Sea Lord: Adm Sir
Michael Boyce, KCB, CBE
Assistant Chief of the Naval Staff:
Rear Adm J Band
Chief of the General Staff:
Gen Sir Roger Wheeler, GCB, CBE,
ADC Gen
Assistant Chief of the General Stafff:
Maj Gen K O'Donohue, CBE
Director-General Development and Doctrine:
Maj Gen A D Pigott, CBE
Chief of the Air Staff: Air Chief Marshal Sir
Richard Johns, KCB, CBE, LVO
Assistant Chief of the Air Staff:
Air Vice-Marshal G E Stirrup
British-American Community Relations: Air
Marshal Sir John Kemball (RTD), KCB, CBE
Chief Executive, National Air Traffic Services:
D J McLauchlan *(SCS)*
Directorate of Airspace Policy:
Air Vice-Marshal J R D Arscott

DEFENCE INTELLIGENCE STAFF
Chief of Defence Intelligence:
Vice-Admiral Alan West, DSC
*Director Intelligence Programmes and
Resources:* P I Bailey *(SCS)*
*Director Defence Intelligence Secretariat and
Communications Information Sytems:*
R C Hack *(SCS)*
*Deputy Chief of Defence Intelligence
Defence Intelligence Analysis Staff:*
J N L Morrison *(SCS)*

Director Regional Assessments:
Brig N J Cottam, OBE
Director Intelligence Global Issue:
J M Cunningham *(SCS)*
Director Intelligence Scientific and Technical:
P H West *(SCS)*
Director General Intelligence and Geographic
Resources: Air Vice-Marshal
J C French, CBE, RAF

DEFENCE SCIENTIFIC STAFF
Chief Scientific Adviser: Prof Sir D Davies,
KBE *(SCS) (from January 2000 Prof Sir Keith*
O'Nions, FRS)
Chief Scientist: G H B Jordan *(SCS)*

SECOND SEA LORD/COMMANDER-IN-CHIEF
NAVAL HOME COMMAND
Second Sea Lord/Commander-in-Chief Naval
Home Command:
Adm Sir John Brigstocke, KCB, ADC
Director-General Naval Personnel Strategy and
Plans: Rear Adm P A Dunt
Flag Officer Training and Recruiting:
Rear Adm J Chadwick
Medical Director-General (Naval):
Surg Rear Adm I L Jenkins

NAVAL SUPPORT COMMAND
Chief of Fleet Support:
Vice-Adm Sir John Dunt, KCB
Director-General Fleet Support (Operations and
Plans): Rear Adm M G Wood
Assistant Under Secretary of State (Fleet
Support): D J Gould *(SCS)*
Director-General Aircraft (Navy):
Rear Adm J A Burch
Flag Officer Scotland, Northern England and
Northern Ireland and Naval Base Commander
Clyde: Rear Adm A M Gregory, OBE, RN

CINCFLEET (INCLUDING CGRM)
Commander in Chief Fleet – Cincfleet:
Adm Nigel Essenhigh, KCB
Deputy Commander Fleet and Chief of Staff:
Vice-Adm F Malbon
Chief of Staff Operations and Flag Officer
Submarines: Rear Adm R P Stevens, OBE
Flag Officer Surface Flotilla:
Rear Adm P M Franklyn, CB, MVO
Commander UK Task Group:
Rear Adm I A Forbes, CBE
Flag Officer Naval Aviation:
Rear Adm I R Henderson, CBE
Commandant-General Royal Marines:
Maj Gen R H Fulton

Flag Officer, Sea Training:
Rear Adm R J Lippiet, MBE
Commodore Royal Fleet Auxiliary:
Commodore P J Lannin, RFA

QUARTERMASTER GENERAL'S DEPARTMENT
Quartermaster General: Lt Gen Sir S C Grant
Chief of Staff HQ/QMG:
Maj Gen C L Elliot, KCB
Assitant Under-Secretary (QMG):
N H R Evans *(SCS)*
Director-General Logistics Support (Army):
Maj-Gen A W Lyons, CBE
Director-General Equipment Support (Army):
Maj-Gen P V R Besgrove, CBE

ADJUTANT GENERAL'S DEPARTMENT
Headquarters Adjutant General
(Personnel and Training Command)
Adjutant General:
Gen Sir Alex Harley, KBE, CB, ADC Gen
Chief of Staff to the Adjutant General:
Maj Gen A P N Currie
Director-General Army Training and
Recruiting: Maj Gen A Palmer, CBE
Directorate General Army Medical Services:
Maj Gen W R Short, QHP
Director-General Development and Doctrine:
Maj-Gen A D Pigott, CBE
Directorate of Army Legal Services:
Maj Gen G Risius
Military Secretary: Maj Gen A S H Irwin, CBE
HQ Advisory: Brig P J Bryant
Headquarters Army Personnel Centre:
Maj Gen D L Burden
Directorate of Individual Training Policy (Army)
Organisation: Brig J P Weller
Royal Military Academy Sandhurst:
Maj Gen A G Denaro, CBE
Royal Military College of Science:
Maj Gen J C B Sutherell, CBE, ADC

CINCLAND
Commander-in-Chief Land Command:
General Sir Michael Walker,
KCB, CM, CBE, ADC Gen
Deputy Commander-in-Chief Land Command:
Maj Gen J F Deverell, KCB, OBE
Chief of Staff Headquarters Land Command:
Maj Gen P Trousdell
Deputy Chief of Staff Headquarters Land
Command: Maj Gen Chambers

STRIKE COMMAND
Air Officer Commanding-in-Chief (Strike
Command): Air Chief Marshal Sir John
Allison, KCB, CBE

Chief of Staff/Deputy Commander-in-Chief (Strike Command): Air Marshal T I Jenner
Air Staff (Strike Command):
   Air Vice-Marshal P O Sturley
Air Officer Logistcs and CIS (Strike Command):
   Air Vice-Marshal P J Scott
Air Officer Administration (Strike Command):
   Air Vice-Marshal A G Burton
Command Secretariat (Strike Command):
   C J Wright *(SCS)*
Air Officer Commanding 1 Group:
   Air Vice-Marshal J H Thompson
Air Officer Commanding 11/18 Group:
   Air Vice-Marshal B K Burridge
Air Officer Commanding 38 Group:
   Air Vice-Marshal P O Sturley

HEADQUARTERS LOGISTIC COMMAND (RAF)
Air Officer Commanding in Chief/Air Member for Logistics: Air Marshal M D Pledger, OBE, AFC, BSc, FRAeS, RAF
Chief of Staff/Air Officer Commanding Directly Administered Units: Air Vice-Marshal G Skinner, MBE, MSc, BSc, CEng, FILog, FMechI, FIMgt, MFRAeS
Command Secretary: Paul Hatt *(SCS)*
Air Officer Communications Information Systems/Air Officer Commanding Signals Units: Air Vice-Marshal P Liddell, BSc, CEng, FIEE, FRAeS, RAF
Directorate General of Support Management (RAF): Air Vice-Marshal P Henderson, MBE, MSc, BA, CEng, FRAeS, RAF

PERSONNEL AND TRAINING COMMAND (RAF)
Air Member for Personnel/Air Office Commanding in Chief: Air Marshal Sir Anthony Bagnall, KCB, OBE, FRAeS
Chief of Staff/Air Member for Personnel:
   Air Vice-Marshal R Wright
Air Officer Commanding and Commandant RAF College Cranwell:
   Air Vice-Marshal C R Fowler
Directorate General Medical Services (RAF):
   Air Vice-Marshal C J Sharples, QHP, MS, FFOM, MRCS, LRCP, DArmed, MRAeS, RAF
Clinical Director:
   Air Cdre D J Rainford, MBE, MB, BS, FRCP, MRCS
Directorate of RAF Legal Services:
   Air Vice-Marshal J Weeden, LLB, RAF
Command Secretary: L D Kyle *(SCS)*

Executive Agencies: Armed Forces Personnel Administration Agency (AFPAA); Army Base Repair Organisation (ABRO); Army Personnel Centre (APC); Army Technical Support Agency (ATSA); Army Training and Recruiting Agency (ATRA); British Forces Post Office (BFPO); Defence Analytical Services Agency (DASA); Defence Aviation Repair Agency (DARA); Defence Bills Agency (DBA), Defence Clothing and Textiles Agency (DCTA); Defence Communication Services Agency (DCSA); Defence Dental Agency (DDA); Defence Estates (DE); Defence Evaluation and Research Agency (DERA); Defence Housing Executive (DHE); Defence Intelligence and Security Centre (DISC); Defence Medical Training Organisation (DMTO); Defence Procurement Agency (DPA); Defence Secondary Care Agency (DSCA); Defence Storage and Distribution Agency (DSDA); Defence Transport and Movements Agency (DTMA); Defence Vetting Agency (DVA); Disposal Sales Agency (DSA); Duke of York's Royal Military School (DYRMS); Joint Air Reconnaissance Intelligence Centre (JARIC); Logistic Information Systems Agency (LISA); Medical Supplies Agency (MSA); Meteorological Office; Military Survey Defence Agency (MSDA); Ministry of Defence Police Agency (MDP); Naval Bases and Supply Agency (NBSA); Naval Manning Agency (NMA); Naval Recruiting and Training Agency (NRTA); Pay and Personnel Agency (PPA), Queen Victoria School (QVS); RAF Logistics Support Services (LSS); RAF Personnel Management Agency (RAFPMA); RAF Signals Engineering Establishment (RAFSEE); RAF Training Group Defence Agency (RAF TGDA); Service Children's Education (SCE); Ships Support Agency (SSA); UK Hydrographic Office (UKHO)

Education and Employment, Department for

Sanctuary Buildings, Great Smith Street, London SW1P 3BT

Caxton House, Tothill Street, London SW1H 9NA

Moorfoot, Sheffield S1 4PQ

East Lane, Runcorn WA7 2DN

Mowden Hall, Staindrop Road, Darlington DL3 9BG

Press Office: 020 7925 5106

Information Office: 020 7925 5189
Main switchboard: 0870 0012345
Website: www.dfee.gov.uk
E-mail: dfee.ministers@dfee.gov.uk for all
ministers

The Department for Education and Employment
(DfEE) is working with others, in Government
and beyond, towards two overarching goals:
- an inclusive society, where everyone has an
equal chance to achieve their full potential; and
- a globally competitive economy, with successful firms and a fair and efficient labour market.
Objectives
The Department makes its distinctive contribution by concentrating on three central objectives:
1. Ensuring that all young people reach 16 with
the skills, attitudes and personal qualities that
will give them a secure foundation for lifelong
learning, work and citizenship in a rapidly
changing world.
- in particular by substantially improving literacy and numeracy skills in primary schools,
pupil achievement in secondary schools and
support for the family through early education
and the availability of affordable, good quality
childcare in every neighbourhood.
2. Developing in everyone a commitment to lifelong learning, so as to enhance their lives,
improve their employability in a changing labour
market and create the skills that our economy
and employers need.
- in particular by making learning attractive and
accessible, improving the relevance and quality of provision, and persuading employers to
invest in those they employ.
3. Helping people wihout a job into work.
- in particular by helping young people, the
long-term unemployed and others at a disadvantage in the labour market, including lone
parents, to move into sustainable jobs, within a
fair and diverse employment market.

Secretary of State:
The Rt Hon David Blunkett, MP
Principal Priv Sec: Mike Wardle
Parly Priv Secs: Jean Corston, MP,
Alan Whitehead, MP
Special Advisers: Tom Engel, Sophie Linden,
Nick Pearce, Conor Ryan
*Minister of State (Minister for Employment,
Welfare to Work and Equal Opportunities):*
The Rt Hon Tessa Jowell, MP
Priv Sec: Alison Kerr
Parly Priv Sec: Jeff Ennis, MP

*Minister of State (Minister for School
Standards):*
The Rt Hon Ms Estelle Morris, MP
Priv Sec: Jane Whitfield
Parly Priv Sec: Rachel Squire, MP
*Minister of State (Minister for Education and
Employment (Lords):*
The Baroness Blackstone
Priv Sec: Elsa Wilkinson
*Parliamentary Under-Sec of State (Employment
and Equal Opportunities):*
Mrs Margaret Hodge, MBE, MP
Priv Sec: Graham Walker
*Parliamentary Under-Sec of State (Lifelong
Learning):* Malcolm Wicks, MP
Priv Sec: Steve Bartlett
*Parliamentary Under-Sec of State (School
Standards):* Ms Jacqueline Smith, MP
Priv Sec: Karen Lumley
Parliamentary Under-Sec of State:
Michael Wills, MP
Priv Sec: Lucy Carter

Spokespersons in the House of Lords: The
Baroness Blackstone, The Lord Bach

Permanent Secretary:
Sir Michael Bichard, KCB *(SCS)*
Priv Sec: Margaret Doherty (020 7925 6234)
Parliamentary Clerk: Tim O'Sullivan

PERSONNEL AND SUPPORT SERVICES
DIRECTORATE
Director: Hilary Douglas *(SCS)*

AIMS AND OBJECTIVES
The Directorate's aim is to help build an out-
ward-looking, open minded and innovative
Department that values people, partnerships,
standards and outcomes, through developing
policies and providing services that respond to
customer's needs and are high quality and value
for money.
*Divisional Manager, Training and Development
Division:* Jim Gordon
*Divisional Manager, Information Systems
Division:* Ray Hinchcliffe
*Divisional Manager, Corporate Change and
Senior Staff:* Graham Archer
Divisional Manager, Personnel Division:
Mike Ship
Divisional Manager, Facilities Management:
Les Webb
*Divisional Manager, Procurement and
Contracting:* Paul Neill
Divisional Manager, Equal Opportunities Unit:
Bernadette Hillon

FINANCE AND ANALYTICAL SERVICES DIRECTORATE
Director-General: Peter Shaw *(SCS)*

AIMS AND OBJECTIVES
To assist Ministers and Permanent Secretary to secure and allocate the financial resources needed to deliver the Department for Education and Employment's overall aim and objectives; to monitor, account for and evaluate the use of resources so as to optimise value for money and ensure adherence to sound control systems and the requirements of Government Accounting.
Director Analytical Services:
  Denis Allnutt *(SCS)*
Divisional Manager, Analytical Services – Equal Opportunities and Research Programme:
  Richard Bartholomew
Divisional Manager, Analytical Services – Employability and Adult Learning:
  Bob Butcher
Divisional Manager, Analytical Services – Qualifications, Pupil Assessment and IT Support: Malcolm Britton
Divisional Manager, Analytical Services – Youth and Further Education: John Elliott
Divisional Manager, Analytical Services – Higher Education Evaluation Strategy and International: Simon Field
Divisional Manager, Analytical Services – Schools, Teachers and Resources:
  Audrey Brown
Divisional Manager, Efficiency: Rob Wye
Divisional Manager, Financial Accounting:
  Peter Connor
Divisional Manager, Programmes: Carol Hunter
Divisional Manager, Planning and Expenditure:
  Susanna Todd
Divisional Manager, Capital Investment:
  Stephen Burt
Divisional Manager, Internal Audit:
  Neville Thirtle

SCHOOLS DIRECTORATE
Director-General: David Normington, CB *(SCS)*

Ensuring that all young people reach 16 with the skills, attitudes and personal qualities that will give them a secure foundation fo lifelong learning, work and citizenship in a changing world.
Director School Organisation and Funding Group: Helen Williams *(SCS)*
Divisional Manager, School and LEA Funding:
  Andrew Wye
Divisional Manager, Schools Admissions Organisation and Governance:
  Caroline Macready

Divisional Manager, Organisation of School Places: Alan Cranston
Divisional Manager, LEA Support:
  Elizabeth Wylie
Divisional Manager, Schools Capital and Buildings: Ken Beeton
Architects and Building: Mukund Patel
Director Teachers Group: Peter Makeham *(SCS)*
Divisional Manager, Teacher Development and Leadership Division: Christina Bienkowska
Divisional Manager, Teachers' Pay and Policy:
  Anne Jackson
Divisional Manager, Teachers Standards and Pensions: Penny Jones
Divisional Manager, Teacher Supply and Training: Graham Holley
Director, Pupils Support and Inclusion Group:
  Rob Smith *(SCS)*
Divisional Manager, Special Educational Needs:
  Chris Wells
Divisional Managers, School Plus: Mrs Anne-Marie Lawlor, Ms Susan Johnson
Divisional Manager, Pupil Support and Independent Schools: Michael D Phipps
Divisional Manager, School Inclusion:
  Paul Cohen
Divisional Manager, Sure Start Unit:
  Naomi Eisenstat
Early Years: Alan Cranston
Head of Standards and Effectiveness Unit:
  Prof Michael Barber
Divisional Manager, Standards Division:
  Sandy Adamson
Divisional Manager, LEA Effectiveness:
  Sheila Scales
School Effectiveness: Stephen Crowne
Director, Curriculum Communications and Technology: Imogen Wilde
Divisional Manager, Curriculum and Assessment: Ian Berry
Divisional Manager, Schools Communications:
  Stuart Edwards
Divisional Manager, Education and Training Technology: Ralph Taberner
Divisional Manager, Parents' Performance:
  Nick Baxter

FURTHER AND HIGHER EDUCATION AND YOUTH TRAINING DIRECTORATE
Director-General: Roger Dawe *(SCS)*

AIMS AND OBJECTIVES
To ensure that all young people (14–19) develop the skills, behaviour and attitudes critical to success in adult and working life; and maximise the number gaining rigorous qualifications that fully meet their needs and those of the labour market.

To develop the further and higher education sectors and the system of vocational and academic qualifications for school children, young people and adults, so that they make the most effective and efficient contribution to the aim for young people and to the Government's objectives for the education and training of adults.

WORKING RELATIONS
The Directorate works in partnership with a wide range of bodies, including the Further and Higher Education Funding Councils, the School Curriculum and Assessment Authority, the National Council for Vocational Qualifications (to merge in 1997-98 to form the Qualifications and Curriculum Authority), the Higher Education Quality Council, the Student Loans Company, the Further Education Development Agency, the TEC National Council, Local Authorities and the Careers Service.

Director, Review of Student Support, Higher Education: Tony Clark *(SCS)*
Director of Higher Education:
Nick Sanders *(SCS)*
Divisional Manager, Higher Education, Quality and Employability: Trevor Fellowes
Divisional Manager, Student Support 1:
Neil Flint
Divisional Manager, Student Support 2:
Beverley Evans
Divisional Manager, Higher Education and Organisation Funding: Michael Hipkins
Director, Qualifications: Rob Hull *(SCS)*
Divisional Manager, Schools and College Qualifications: Celia Johnson
Divisional Manager, Qualifications for work:
John West
Review of Support for Learning Project: Michael Stone
Director Further Education and Youth Training:
David Forrester
Divisional Manager, Careers and Information Division: Steve Geary
Divisional Manager, Funding and Organisation:
Stephen Hillier
Divisional Manager, Connexions Unit:
Claire Tyler
Divisional Manager, Partnership Skills and Young People: Alan Davies

EMPLOYMENT, LIFELONG LEARNING AND INTERNATIONAL DIRECTORATE
Director-General: Nick Stuart *(SCS)*

AIMS AND OBJECTIVES
To support economic growth and personal development by promoting lifelong learning and an efficient, flexible, fair and competitive labour market. ELLID has a particular focus on adults and disadvantaged groups in the labour market helping them to acquire skills and to get and keep jobs. The Directorate also has policy responsibility for employment, including the New Deal for Young People and the wider Welfare to Work agenda; establishing a framework and targets for the Employment Service, key elements of the Lifelong Learning Strategy including the University for Industry and Individual Learning Accounts; equal opportunities in employment, education and training, and sex equality and disability issues more generally and the effective use of technology in education and training.

WORKING RELATIONS
The Directorate is the main link for the Department to:
the Employment Service;
the Commission for Racial Equality;
Investors in People UK;
the Basic Skills Agency;
the National Council for the Employment of Disabled People;
the Equal Opportunities Commission;
the new National Disabilities Council;
the Management Charter Initiative;
the National Council for Education Technology.

New Deal for Young People.
Fax: 020 7925 5091
Enquiry Point: 020 7925 6943
Director Skills and Lifelong Learning:
Derek Grover, CB *(SCS)*
Divisional Manager, Individual Learning:
Tim Down
Divisional Manager, Work Place Learning:
Linda Ammon
Divisional Manager, Skills Unit: John Temple
Divisional Manager, University for Industry:
Jeanette Pugh
Director, Employment Policy:
Michael J Richardson *(SCS)*
Divisional Manager, Economy and Labour Market: Bill Wells
Divisional Manager, Sructural Unemployment Policy: Mark Neale
Divisional Manager, Welfare to Work:
Chris Barnham
Divisional Manager, Adult Disadvantage:
Eric Galvin
Divisional Manager, New Deal Task Force Secretariat: Liz Tillett
Divisional Manager, Work Bank Project:
Neil Atkinson

Director, Equal Opportunities, Technology and Overseas Labour: Bob Niven *(SCS)*
Divisional Manager, Overseas Labour: Martyn Craske
Divisional Manager, Disability Policy: Deirdre Fordham
Divisional Manager, Child Care Unit: Shirley Trundle
Divisional Manager, Sex and Race Equality: Jenny Eastabrook
Divisional Manager, Family Friendly Employment Project: Philip Chorley
Director, International: Clive Tucker *(SCS)*
Divisional Manager, International Relations: Barnaby Shaw
Divisional Manager, European Union: Win Harris
Divisional Manager, European Social Fund: Elaine Trewartha

OPERATIONS DIRECTORATE
Director: John Hedger, CB *(SCS)*

AIMS AND OBJECTIVES
The aim of the Directorate is to influence and promote the cost effective implementation and influence the development of the Department's for: providing and improving the advice and training available to young people, and those out of work; promoting equality of opportunity and tackling social exclusion; raising standards of training across different sectors of employment; and supporting economic growth and regeneration.

WORKING RELATIONS
The Directorate's main links are with Government Offices for the Regions, with national bodies representing TECs and providers of training and careers advice; and with the sector organisations (including National Training Organisations) responsible for developing relevant occupational standards.

Divisional Manager, National Training Organisations: John Fuller
Divisional Manager, Resources and Contract Management: Peter Holme
Divisional Manager, Regional Development and Government Offices: Gordon McKenzie
Divisional Manager, Quality and Financial Assurance Division: Suzanne Orr
Divisional Manager, Millennium Volunteers Unit: Anne Weinstock
Director, Learning to Succeed Directorate: Peter Lauener

STRATEGY AND COMMUNICATIONS DIRECTORATE
To ensure that strategic thinking and excellent communications are at the heart of the Department's policies development and delivery.
Director: Peter Wanless *(SCS)*
Communications Division: Caroline Bicknell
Divisional Manager, Speeches and General Briefing: Gary McKenzie
Divisional Manager, Strategy: Richard Harrison
Divisional Manager, Media Relations: Julia Simpson
Divisional Manager, Media Relations: Trevor Cook
Divisional Manager, Publicity: John Ross
Divisional Manager, Welfare to Work Campaign: Helena Ratalowska

Executive Agency: Employment Service

Environment, Transport and the Regions, Department of the

The Department of the Environment, Transport and the Regions is mainly based in 3 Central London locations:

Eland House
Bressenden Place, London SW1E 5DU
020 7944 3000

Ashdown House
123 Victoria Street, London SW1E 6DE
020 7944 3000

Great Minster House
76 Marsham Street, London SW1P 4DR
020 7944 3000
Website: www.detr.gov.uk

The aim of DETR is to improve the quality of life by promoting sustainable development at home and abroad, fostering economic prosperity and supporting local democracy.

To protect and improve the environment, and to integrate the environment with other policies across government and in international fora.

To offer everyone the opportunity of a decent home and so promote social cohesion, well-being and self-dependence.

To promote efficient and integrated transport services across different modes and reduce road trafic growth, in order better to meet the mobility needs of the travelling public and industry.

To deliver regulatory and other transport services to the public and industry and to collect taxes efficiently and fairly.

To enhance opportunity in rural areas, improve enjoyment of the countryside and conserve and manage wildlife resources.

To create a fair and efficient land use planning system that respects regional differences and promotes development which is of high quality and sustainable.

To promote a system of elected government in England which responds to the needs of local communities.

To enhance economic development and social cohesion throughout England through effective regional action and integrated local regeneration programmes.

To ensure an efficient market in the construction industry, with innovative and successful UK firms that meet the needs of clients and society and are competitive at home and abroad.

To improve health and safety by reducing risks from work activity, travel and the environment.

Deputy Prime Minister and Secretary of State:
The Rt Hon John Prescott, MP
Priv Sec: Peter Unwin
Parly Priv Sec: John Heppell, MP
Special Advisers: Joe Irvin, Joan Hammell
Priv Sec: Rosemary Jeboo
Minister of State (Minister for Transport):
The Rt Hon The Lord Macdonald of
Tradeston, CBE
Priv Sec: Seth Davies
Parly Priv Sec: Phil Woolas, MP
Special Adviser: Adrian Long
Minister of State (Minister for the Environment):
The Rt Hon Michael Meacher, MP
Priv Sec: Colin Bird
Parly Priv Sec: Terry Rooney, MP
Minister of State (Minister for Local
Government and Regions):
The Rt Hon Ms Hilary Armstrong, MP
Priv Sec: Nick Carter
Parly Priv Sec: Sally Keeble, MP
Special Adviser: David Wilson
Minister of State (Minister for Housing,
Planning and Construction):
Nick Raynsford, MP
Priv Sec: Katy Willison
Parly Priv Sec: Phil Hope, MP
Parliamentary Under-Secretary of State:
Chris Mullin, MP
Priv Sec: Jessica Matthew
Special Adviser: Paul Hackett
Parliamentary Under-Secretary of State:
Keith Hill, MP
Priv Sec: Katherine Braddick

Parliamentary Under-Secretary of State:
The Lord Whitty
Priv Sec: Jenni Borg
Parliamentary Under-Secretary of State:
Ms Beverley Hughes, MP
Priv Sec: Rory O'Donnell
Parly Clerk: Paul Davies

Spokespersons in the House of Lords: The Lord Macdonald of Tradeston, The Lord Whitty, The Baroness Farrington of Ribbleton (Local Government)

Permanent Secretary:
Sir Richard Mottram, KCB *(SCS)*
Priv Sec: Sandy Bishop (020 7944 4388)

Parliamentary Branch:
(Ministers) 020 7944 3019
Ministerial Correspondence Section:
020 7944 3085

DIRECTORATE OF COMMUNICATION
Acting Director: Derek Plews *(SCS)*
Deputy Director (Publicity): Charles Skinner
Deputy Director (Press): (Vacant)

ENVIRONMENTAL PROTECTION GROUP
Director-General: Dinah Nichols, CB *(SCS)*

ENERGY, ENVIRONMENT AND WASTE
DIRECTORATE
Director: Philip Ward *(SCS)*
Leslie Packer, David Vincent, Henry Cleary,
Bob Ryder, Lisette Simcock, Duncan Prior

ENVIRONMENT: RISKS AND ATMOSPHERE
Director: Henry Derwent *(SCS)*
Martin Williams, Peter Hinchcliffe,
Steve Brown, Pete Betts, Martin Hurst

ENVIRONMENT PROTECTION STRATEGY
DIRECTORATE
Director: Andrew Burchell *(SCS)*
Robin Wilson, Hilary Hillier, Brian Glicksman,
John Adams, Sheila McCabe

WATER AND LAND DIRECTORATE
Director: Alan Davis *(SCS)*
Michael Rouse, Alan Simcock, Stuart Hoggan,
Bob Dinwiddy

FINANCE GROUP
Director and Principal Finance Officer:
John Ballard *(SCS)*
Ian McBrayne, Alan Beard, Rodney Anderson,
Campbell Arnott

HOUSING, CONSTRUCTION,
REGENERATION AND COUNTRYSIDE
GROUP
Director-General: Mavis McDonald, CB *(SCS)*

HOUSING
Director: Michael Gahagan *(SCS)*
Michael Faulkner, Philip Cox, Judith Littlewood,
   Hilary Chipping, Bruce Delman,
   Andrew Allberry, Richard Horsman,
   George Clark, Rachel Sharpe

CONSTRUCTION DIRECTORATE
Director: John Hobson *(SCS)*
Paul Everall, Richard Wood,
   John Stambollouian, Nigel Dorling,
   Bob Davies

LONDON ROUGH SLEEPERS' UNIT
Director: Louise Casey *(SCS)*
Joan Bailey

WILDLIFE AND COUNTRYSIDE DIRECTORATE
Director: Sophia Lambert *(SCS)*
Diana Kahn, Susan Carter, Roger Pritchard,
   Robert Hepworth, Chris Braun

REGENERATION DIRECTORATE
Director: Paul Evans *(SCS)*
John Roberts, Linda Derrick, Helen Ghosh

LEGAL GROUP
Director-General: David Hogg, CB *(SCS)*

COUNTRYSIDE, PLANNING AND TRANSPORT
Director: Sandra Unerman *(SCS)*
Nigel Lefton, Gloria Hedley-Dent,
   Richard Lines, Neil Thomas, Alan Jones,
   Colin Ingram, Judith-Anne MacKenzie,
   Hussein Kaya, David Ingham

COMMERCIAL, ENVIRONMENT, HOUSING AND
LOCAL GOVERNMENT
Director: Christopher Muttukumaru *(SCS)*
John Comber, Pamela Conlon,
   Donatella Phillips, Ken Baublys,
   Dudley Aries, David Jordan

ENVIRONMENT (INTERNATIONAL AND EC)
Director: Patrick Szell *(SCS)*
Alistair McGlone

LEGISLATIVE UNIT
Director: Allan Roberts *(SCS)*

LOCAL AND REGIONAL GOVERNMENT
GROUP
Director-General: Philip Wood, CB *(SCS)*

LOCAL GOVERNMENT DIRECTORATE
Director: Andrew Whetnall *(SCS)*
Paul Rowsell, Richard Footitt, Tony Redpath,
   Terry Crossley

LOCAL GOVERNMENT FINANCE POLICY
DIRECTORATE
Director: Mark Lambirth *(SCS)*
Richard Gibson, Ian Scotter, Pauline Penneck,
   Pam Williams, Stephen Claughton

GOVERNMENT OFFICES AND REGIONAL POLICY
DIRECTORATE
Director: Lindsay Bell *(SCS)*
Mike Ross, Jan Scoones, Andrew Murray

PLANNING, ROADS AND LOCAL
TRANSPORT
Director-General: Chris Brearley *(SCS)*

MOBILITY UNIT
Divisional Manager: Ann Frye

PLANNING DIRECTORATE
Director: Jeff Jacobs *(SCS)*
Lester Hicks, Mike Ash, Jeff Channing,
   John Zetter, Alan Oliver, Martin Leigh-Pollitt,
   Christopher Bowden

ROADS AND TRAFFIC DIRECTORATE
Director: Diane Phillips, CB *(SCS)*
Neil McDonald, Mike Talbot, Tom Worsley,
   Roger Donachie

INTEGRATED AND LOCAL TRANSPORT
Director: Richard Bird *(SCS)*
Edward Neve, Mike Walsh, Peter McCarthy,
   Andrew Whybrow, Peter Capell

ROAD SAFETY AND ENVIRONMENT
Director: John Plowman *(SCS)*
Roger Peal, Iain Todd, Malcolm Fendick,
   Richard Jones, Tim Carter, Martin Brasher

RAILWAYS, AVIATION LOGISTICS AND
MARITIME
Director-General: David Rowlands, CB *(SCS)*

RAILWAYS
Director: Bob Linnard *(SCS)*
Peter Thomas, Stuart Connolly, Alison Munro,
   Mark Coulshed

LOGISTICS AND MARITIME TRANSPORT
Director: Brian Wadsworth *(SCS)*
Rear Adm John Lang, Mike Hughes,
Angela Moss, David Liston-Jones,
Stephen Reeves, Frank Wall, David Cooke,
David Rowe

AVIATION
Director: Roy Griffins *(SCS)*
Tony Baker, Mike Smethers, Michael Fawcett,
Elizabeth Duthie, Michael Mann,
David McMillan
Ken Smart, CBE, Douglas Evans

LONDON UNDERGROUND TASK FORCE GROUP
Director: Mike Fuhr *(SCS)*
Richard Bennett

TRANSPORT SECURITY
Director: David Lord
William Gillan

STRATEGY AND CORPORATE SERVICES
GROUP
Director-General: Richard Dudding *(SCS)*
Ian Heawood, Ian Harris, Peter Walton,
Gareth Jones, Richard Long

PERSONNEL AND CHANGE MANAGEMENT
Director: Hazel Parker-Brown *(SCS)*
Mike Bailey, Bernard Meakins, Ken Arnold,
Liz Godfrey

CENTRAL STRATEGY (AND CHIEF SCIENTIST)
Director: David Fisk, CBE *(SCS)*
Bronwyn Hill, John Stevens, Murray Devine,
Alan Apling, Graham Pendlebury

CHIEF ECONOMIST
Director: Chris Riley *(SCS)*
Elizabeth Cleary, Maureen Holkam

Executive Agencies: Driver and Vehicle Licensing Agency (DVLA); Driving Standards Agency (DSA); Highways Agency; Maritime and Coastguard Agency (MCA); Ordnance Survey (OS); Planning Inspectorate (PINS); Queen Elizabeth II Conference Centre; Vehicle Certification Agency (VCA); Vehicle Inspectorate

Export Credits Guarantee Department

PO Box 2200
2 Exchange Tower,
Harbour Exchange Square,
London E14 9GS
020 7512 7000 *Fax:* 020 7512 7649
Telex: 290350 ECGD HQ G
Website: www.ecgd.gov.uk

ECGD is the UK's official export credit insurer and reports directly to the Secretary of State for Trade and Industry. Deriving its statutory powers from the Export and Investment Guarantees Act (EIGA) 1991, its main role is to assist the export of UK capital and project-related goods by providing exporters with insurance against the commercial and political risks of not being paid by their buyers. ECGD also guarantees the repayment of bank loans to overseas borrowers which finance the purchase of UK goods and services and insures UK investors against the political risks of not receiving earnings from their overseas investments. ECGD reinsurance is available for private sector insurers who cover the export of UK goods sold on credit terms of less than two years.

MINISTERS
Secretary of State for Trade and Industry:
    The Rt Hon Stephen Byers, MP
Minister for Trade: Richard Caborn, MP
Chief Executive: Mr Vivian Brown *(SCS)*

UNDERWRITING GROUP
Group Director: J R Weiss *(SCS)*
Directors: S R Dodgson, R Gotts, C J Leeds,
    M D Pentecost, G G Welsh

ASSET MANAGEMENT GROUP
Group Director: V P Lunn-Rockliffe *(SCS)*
Directors: R F Lethbridge Mrs M E Maddox,
    J S Snowdon, Ms L Woods

RESOURCE MANAGEMENT GROUP
*Group Director and Principal Establishment and
    Finance Officer:* T M Jaffray *(SCS)*
Directors: P J Callaghan, G Cassell,
    J C W Croall, R J Healey, Ms R A Kaufman,
    P J Radford, E J Walsby

LEGAL BRANCH
ECGD General Counsel: N Ridley *(SCS)*

EXPORT GUARANTEES ADVISORY COUNCIL
Chairman: D H A Harrison

Members: Ms E P Airey, Dr A K Banerji,
R F T Binyon, A E Brown, R F T Binyon,
S J Doughty, Mrs L Knox, G W Lynch, OBE,
P J Mason, R H Maudslay, D G McLachlan,
Sir David Wright

Foreign and Commonwealth Office

Whitehall, London SW1A 2AH
020 7270 1500
Consular/Travel Advice: 020 7238 4503/4
Media Section Information:
E-mail: newmedia@info.mail.fco.gov.uk
Website: www.fco.gov.uk

Telegraphic address: Prodrome, London
Telex: 297711 (a/b PRDRME G)

The Foreign and Commonwealth Office provides mainly through diplomatic missions, the means of communication between Her Majesty's Government and other governments and international organisations for the discussion and negotiation of all matters falling within the field of international relations. It is responsible for alerting the Government to the implications of developments overseas; for protecting British interests overseas; for protecting British citizens abroad; for explaining British policies to, and cultivating friendly relations with, Governments overseas and for the discharge of British responsibilities to the overseas territories.

Secretary of State (Foreign Secretary):
   The Rt Hon Robin Cook, MP
Priv Sec: Sherard Cowper-Coles
Parliamentary Private Secretary: Ken
   Purchase, MP
Special Advisers: David Clark, Andrew Hood,
   David Mathieson
Minister of State: Peter Hain, MP
Priv Sec: Frank Baker
Minister of State: John Battle, MP
Priv Sec: Miss Pat Phillips
Minister of State for Europe: Keith Vaz, MP
Priv Sec: Nick Hopton
*Parliamentary Private Secretaries to the
   Ministers:* Denis MacShane, MP,
   Rosemary McKenna, MP, Caroline Flint, MP
Parliamentary Under-Sec of State:
   The Baroness Scotland of Asthal, QC
Priv Sec: Carl Newns

Spokespersons in the House of Lords:
The Baroness Scotland of Asthal, The Baroness
Ramsay of Cartvale

*Permanent Under-Secretary and Head of HM
   Diplomatic Service:*
   Sir John Kerr, KCMG *(SCS)*
Priv Sec: David Frost
Chief Executive British Trade International:
   Sir David Wright, KCMG, LVO
Priv Sec: Ann Sherriff
Deputy Under-Secs of State (SCS): Christopher
   Hum, CMG (and Chief Clerk),
   Colin Budd, CMG (Director for EU and
   Economic Affairs), John Shepherd, CMG,
   David Manning, CMG, Emyr Jones Parry,
   CMG (and Political Director)
Michael Wood *(SCS)* (and Legal Adviser)
Directors (SCS): Ann Grant (Africa and the
   Commonwealth), Peter Westmacott, CMG
   (the Americas), Stephen Wright, CMG,
   (Wider Europe), Nigel Sheinwald (European
   Union), R E Dibble (General Services), Tony
   Brenton (Global Issues), Peter Ricketts, CMG
   (International Security), Derek
   Plumbly, CMG (Middle East and North
   Africa), David Hall (Overseas Trade), Denise
   Holt (Personnel), Charles Crawford, CMG
   (Deputy Political Director), David Reddaway
   (Public Services), Peter Collecott (Resources),
   Robert Cooper (Asia Pacific)

HEADS OF DEPARTMENTS
African (Equatorial): James Bevan
African (Southern): Neil Chrimes
Aviation and Maritime: Norman Ling
Diplomatic Service Families Association:
   Howard John
Central North and West European:
   John Ramsden
Change Management Unit: Sheena Matthews
China and Hong Kong: David Warren
Commonwealth Co-ordination: Colin Bright
Common Foreign and Security Policy:
   Colin Roberts
Conference and Visits: Ntil Hook
Consular Division: Duncan Taylor
Counter Terrorism Policy Department:
   Keith Bloomfield
Cultural Relations: Ann Lewis
Devolved Administration Dept: June Milligan
DS Whitley Council (TUS): Philippa Hadley
Drugs and International Crime: Michael Ryder
Eastern Adriatic Dept: Stephen Wordsworth
Eastern: Ann Pringle
Economic Relations: Creon Butler
Environment, Science and Energy: John Ashton
Estates Command: Boyd McCleary
European Unit (Bilateral): Jeremy Cresswell
European Union (External): Simon Featherstone

European Union (Internal): Mark Lyall Grant
Financial Compliance Dept: Mike Purves
Financial Policy: Mike Brown
Government Hospitality Fund: Col T J Earl
Human Rights Policy: Carolyne Browne
Information: Peter Dun
Information Systems Division: Nigel Stickells
Internal Audit: Roger Elias
Invest in Britain Bureau: Andrew Fraser
Joint Export Promotion Directorate:
    Peter Beckingham
Latin America and Caribbean: Henry Hogger
Legal Adviser:
    Sir F D Berman, KCMG, QC *(SCS)*
Library and Records: John Thompson
Management Consultancy Services: Vivien Life
Middle East: Edward Chaplin
Migration and Visa: Richard White
National Audit Office: John Pearce
Near East and North Africa:
    Christopher Prentice
News: Kim Darroch
Non-Proliferation: Paul Hare
North America: Philip Priestley, CBE
North East Asia and Pacific: Peter Carter
Overseas Territories: John White
*Organisation for Security and Co-operation in
    Europe:* Alan Huckle
Parliamentary Relations: Mark Hutton
Prosper: Colin J Edgerton, OBE
Personnel Management: Peter Jones
Personnel Services: Richard Fell
Personnel Policy Unit: Scott Wightman
Policy Planning Staff: Richard Clarke
Protocol: Kathryn Colvin
Purchasing Directorate: Michael Gower
Research Analyst: Stuart Jack
Resource Planning: Martin Williamson
Security: Tom Duggin
Security Policy: Adam Thomson
Services, Planning and Resources Dept:
    Ms Joan Link
South Asian: Stephen Evans
South-East Asian: Robert Gordon
Southern European: Jeremy Hill
Support Services: Michael Carr
United Nations: Rosalind Marsden
Whitehall Liaison Department: Lyn Parker

Executive Agency: Wilton Park

Government Offices for the Regions

The Government Offices for the Regions were established in April 1994. There are 9 Government Offices, which combine the former regional offices of the Departments of the Environment, Transport and the Regions, (previously Department of Environment and Transport), Trade and Industry and Education and Employment (previously the Employment Department). The offices deliver Government programmes, such as Technology Development and Training and Enterprise. They are also responsible for planning and transport issues. Each Government Office is headed by a Regional Director who is accountable to the Secretary of States of all the Government Departments.

CENTRAL UNIT
1st Floor, Eland House
Bressenden Place, London SW1E 5DU
020 7890 5157 *Fax:* 020 7890 5019

Director: Lindsay Bell *(SCS)*
Head of Unit: Jan Scoones
Secretariat: Ceri King (Organisation and
    planning of Management Board and Regional
    Directors' meetings, purchasing, branding,
    directories, Open Government, Citizen's
    Charter, records management, libraries,
    security and accommodation issues relating to
    nine Government Offices)
Finance: Nita Murphy (Finance and Planning,
    Resource Accounting System – including in-
    year financial monitoring and reporting)
Personnel: Jane Bishop (General personnel
    issues in Government Offices)
Pay: Paul Arkell (Government Offices pay and
    grading issues)
IT: Andy Bentley (IT support to the Government
    Offices)

EAST OF ENGLAND
Building A, Westbrook Centre
Milton Road, Cambridge CB4 1YG
01223 346700

Victory House, Vision Park, Histon
Cambridge CB4 4ZR
01223 202000

Heron House, 49–53 Goldington Road
Bedford MK40 3LL
01234 796332

Regional Director (Westbrook Centre):
Alan Riddell *(SCS)*
E-mail: ariddell.goe@go.regions.gov.uk
Director Strategy and Resources (Westbrook Centre): Chris Beesley
E-mail: cbeesley.goe@go-regions.gov.uk
Director Economic Development (Westbrook Centre): Martin Oldham
E-mail: moldham.goe@go-regions.gov.uk
Director Skills and Enterprise (Victory House): John Street
E-mail: jstreet.goe@go-regions.gov.uk
Deputy Director Skills and Enterprise (Victory House): Steve Halls
E-mail: shalls.goe@go-regions.gov.uk
Director Planning and Transport (Heron House): Caroline Bowdler
E-mail: cbowdler.goe@go-regions.gov.uk
Director Housing, Environment and Regeneration (Heron House): Chris Dunabin
E-mail: cdunabin.goe@go-regions.gov.uk

EAST MIDLANDS
The Belgrave Centre, Stanley Place,
Talbot Street, Nottingham NG1 5GG
0115-971 9971 *Fax:* 0115-971 2404
E-mail: enquiries.goem@go-regions.gov.uk
Website: www.go_em.gov.uk

Regional Director: Dennis Morrison *(SCS)*
Director Environment and Community Development: Dr Stephen Kennett
Director, Corporate Affairs: Ken Lussey
Deputy Director Environment and Community Development: Robert Smith
Director Competitiveness and European Policy: Roger Poole
Acting Director Skills and Enterprise: Pauline Bailey
Acting Deputy Director Skills and Enterprise: Peter Ward

LONDON
Riverwalk House, 157–161 Millbank
London SW1P 4RR
020 7217 3456 *Fax:* 020 7217 3450
E-mail:
enquiries-london.gol@go-regions.gov.uk
Website: www.open.gov.uk/glondon

Director: Genie Turton, CB *(SCS)*
Director Transport and Corporate: Stuart Lord *(SCS)*
Division Head Corporate: Corinne Lyons
Division Head London Readiness 2000/Millennium Access: Zyg Kowalczyk

Division Head Transport Division: Andrew Morrison
Division Head Transport Task Force: Andrew Weeden
Director Skills, Education and Regeneration: John Owen *(SCS)*
Division Head London East and European Programmes: Marie Winckler
Division Head London South: Peter Fiddeman
Division Head Planning: Joyce Bridges
Director London Development Unit: John Sienkiewicz
Director Enterprise and North West: Ken Timmins *(SCS)*
Business Development: Nick Robinson
Director Skills and Education: Andrew Sargent *(SCS)*
Division Head Operations and Business Management: Richard Wragg
Director New London Governance: Richard Allan *(SCS)*
Division Head Greater London Authority Division: Liz Meek, CBE
Division Head Greater London Authority Implementation: Andrew Melville
Division Head Transport for London Project Division: Ian Jordan
Division Head Transport for London Bill Division: Peter Sanders
Division Head London Transport: Beth-Ann Bostock
Home Office Liaison: Bertie Mann

NORTH EAST
Wellbar House, Gallowgate,
Newcastle upon Tyne NE1 4TD
0191-201 3300 *Fax:* 0191-202 3744

Regional Director: Dr Bob Dobbie, CB *(SCS)*
Director Education, Skills, Enterprise and Regeneration: Miss Denise Caudle
Deputy Director Education, Skills, Enterprise and Regeneration: Michael Gilbey
Director Europe, Industry, Trade and Technology: Tony Dell
Director Planning Environment and Transport: Jim Darlington
Director Strategy and Resources: Mrs Diana Pearce

NORTH WEST
Sunley Tower, Piccadilly Plaza
Manchester M1 4BE
0161-952 4000 *Fax:* 0161-952 4099
Website: www.go-nw.gov.uk

Cunard Building, Pier Head
Liverpool L3 1QB
0151-224 6300 *Fax:* 0151-224 6470

Regional Director:
Marianne Neville-Rolfe *(SCS)*
Director, Corporate Services: David Hopewell
Director, Environment and Transport:
Peter Styche
Director, Planning: Eira Hughes
Director, Business and Europe:
Dr David Higham
Director, Europe: Ian Jamieson
Director, Europe (Merseyside): Sylvia Yates
Director, Skills and Enterprise: David Duff
Director, Operations: Mike Hill
Director, New Business: Nigel Burke

SOUTH WEST
Bristol: The Pithay, Bristol BS1 2PB
0117-900 1700 *Fax:* 0117-900 1900
E-mail: goswbris@online.rednet.co.uk
Websitel: www.gosw.gov.uk/gosw

Plymouth: Mast House, Shepherds Wharf
24 Sutton Road, Plymouth PL4 0HJ
01752 635000 *Fax:* 01752 227647
E-mail: goswdc@eurobell.co.uk

Regional Director: Jane Henderson *(SCS)*
Director Environment and Regeneration:
Bryony Houlden
Director Competitiveness and Skills:
Thoss Shearer
Director Devon and Cornwall (Plymouth):
Richard Bayly
Director Corporate Services: Celia Carrington

SOUTH EAST
Bridge House, 1 Walnut Tree Close
Guildford, Surrey GU1 4GA
01483 882255 *Fax:* 01483 882259
E-mail: [firstinitialandsurname].gose@
go-regions.co.uk

Regional Director: David Saunders
Area Director, Hants/IoW: Lucy Robinson
Area Director, Berks/Oxon/Bucks: Nick Wilson
Area Director, Surrey/E Sussex/W Sussex:
David Andrews
Area Director, Kent: Andrew Campbell
Director, Regional Strategy Team:
Charlotte Dixon
Director, Finance and Corporate Management:
Nick Patel

WEST MIDLANDS
77 Paradise Circus Queensway
Birmingham B1 2DT
0121-212 5050 *Fax:* 0121-212 1010
Website: www.go-wm.gov.uk
GTN: 76177 5050

Regional Director: David Ritchie *(SCS)*
(E-mail: jwilkes.gowm@go-regions.gov.uk)
Director of Business and Learning Division:
David Way
(E-mail: dway.gowm@go-regions.gov.uk)
Director of Local Government Division:
Philippa Holland
(E-mail: pholland.gowm@go-regions.gov.uk)
*Director of Policy Co-ordination and Europe
Division and Acting Director of Resource
Management Division:* Chris Marsh
(E-mail: cmarsh.gowm@go-regions.gov.uk)

YORKSHIRE AND THE HUMBER
PO Box 213, City House,
New Station Street, Leeds LS1 4US
0113-280 0600 *Fax:* 0113-233 8301

Regional Director: Felicity Everiss *(SCS)*
(E-mail: feveriss.goyh@go-regions.gov.uk)
Director Strategy and Europe:
Greg Dyche *(SCS)*
(E-mail: gdyche.goyh@go-regions.gov.uk)
Director Planning and Transport: John Jarvis
(E-mail: jjarvis.goyh@go-regions.gov.uk)
Director Business Enterprise and Skills:
Simon Perryman *(SCS)*
(E-mail: sperryman.goyh@go-regions.gov.uk)
Operations Director: Nick Best
(E-mail: nbest.goyh@go-regions.gov.uk)
Director Regeneration: Margaret Jackson
(E-mail: mjackson.goyh@go-regions.gov.uk)
Director Personnel and Resources:
Martin Doxey
(E-mail: mdoxey.goyh@go-regions.gov.uk)

Health, Department of

Richmond House, 79 Whitehall
London SW1A 2NS
020 7210 3000 *Fax:* 020 7210 5523
Website: www.doh.gov.uk

Skipton House, 80 London Road
London SE1 6LH
020 7972 2000

Wellington House,
133–155 Waterloo Road,
London SE1 8UG
020 7972 2000

Quarry House, Quarry Hill,
Leeds LS2 7UE
0113-254 5000

Hannibal House, Elephant and Castle,
London SE1 6TE
020 7972 2000
(non MDA Staff)

Hannibal House, Elephant and Castle,
London SE1 6TQ
020 7972 8000
(MDA Staff)

Market Towers, 1 Nine Elms Lane,
London SW8 5NQ
020 7273 3000

Eileen House
80–94 Newington Causeway,
London SE1 6EF
020 7972 2000

Eastern Regional Office
6–12 Capital Drive, Linford Wood,
Milton Keynes MK14 6QP
01908 844400

London Regional Office
40 Eastbourne Terrace,
London W2 3QR
020 7725 5300

North West Regional Office
930–932 Birchwood Boulevard,
Millennium Park, Birchwood,
Warrington WA3 7QN
0192-570 4000

Northern and Yorkshire Regional Office
John Snow House,
Durham University Science Park,
Durham DH1 3YG
0191-301 1300

South East Regional Office
40 Eastbourne Terrace,
London W2 3QR
020 7725 2500

South and West Regional Office
Westward House, Lime Kiln Close,
Stoke Gifford, Bristol BS12 6SR
0117-984 1750

Trent Regional Office
Fullwood House, Old Fullwood Road,
Sheffield S10 3TH
0114-263 0300

West Midlands Regional Office
Bartholomew House, 142 Hagley Road,
Edgbaston, Birmingham B16 9PA
0121-224 4600

40 Berkely Square, Clifton, Bristol BS8 1HU
0117-941 6501

2nd Floor, John Rothschild House, Castle Quay,
Castle Boulevard, Nottingham NG7 1FW
0115-959 7500

Ladywood House, 45/46 Stephenson Street,
Birmingham B2 4DH
0121-606 4360

Tyne Bridge Tower, Church Street, Gateshead,
Tyne and Wear NE28 2DU
0191-490 3400

West Point, 501 Chester Road, Old Trafford,
Manchester M16 9HU
0161-876 2400

St Thomas's Hospital, Lambeth Palace Road,
London SE1 7EH
020 7928 9292

The Department of Health's overall aim is to improve the health and well-being of the people of England, through the resources available, by:
– supporting activity at national level to protect, promote and improve the nation's health.
– securing the provision of comprehensive, high quality care for all those who need it, regardless of their ability to pay or where they live.
– securing responsive social care and child protection for those who lack the support they need.

Richmond House
Secretary of State and Chairman of the NHS Policy Board:
   The Rt Hon Alan Milburn, MP
Prin Priv Secretary: Janet Grauberg
Priv Secs: Heather Rogers, Mark Ferrero
Parly Priv Sec: Jim Fitzpatrick, MP
Special Advisers: Darren Murphy,
   Simon Stevens (020 7210 5942)
Minister of State: John Denham, MP
Priv Sec: Trish Fretten
Asst Priv Secs: Giles Wilmore, James Adedeji
Parly Priv Sec: Paul Goggins, MP
Minister of State: John Hutton, MP
Priv Sec: Neil Paterson
Asst Priv Secs: Bill Jobson, Anna McDevitt
Parly Priv Sec: Maria Eagle, MP
Parliamentary Under-Secretary of State (Lords):
   The Lord Hunt of Kings Heath, OBE
Priv Sec: Hester McLain

Asst Priv Secs: Sue Cartwright, Lee McGill
*Parliamentary Under-Secretary of State
(Minister for Public Health):*
Yvette Cooper, MP
Priv Sec: Richard Carter
Asst Priv Secs: Paul MacNaught,
Iain Finlinson
*Parliamentary Under-Secretary of State for
Health:* Gisela Stuart, MP
Priv Sec: Steven Collins
Asst Priv Sec: Jon Orr
Parliamentary Clerk: Jeremy Mear
Private Office Manager: Simon Stephenson

Spokesmen in the House of Lords: The Lord
Hunt of Kings Heath, The Lord Burlison

Permanent Secretary: Chris Kelly *(SCS)*
Priv Sec: Sammy Foster
Asst Priv Sec: Ruth Wetterstad
Chief Medical Officer:
Prof Liam Donaldson, QHP *(SCS)*
Priv Sec: Rachel Dickson
Asst Priv Sec: Anne Handicott
Deputy Chief Medical Officers:
Dr Pat Troop *(SCS)*, Dr Sheila Adam *(SCS)*
National Cancer Director:
Prof Michael Richards, MA, MD, FRCP
(Based at St Thomas's Hospital)
Chief Executive, NHS Management Executive:
Sir Alan Langlands *(SCS)*
Priv Sec: Kirsty Jarvie
Personal Sec: Gill MacKenzie

Ministerial Correspondence Section:
020 7210 5615

REGIONAL CHAIRMAN'S MEETING
Chairman: The Rt Hon Alan Milburn, MP
Board Members: John Hutton, MP, The Lord
Hunt of Kings Heath OBE, Yvette Cooper,
MP, Chris Kelly, Sir Alan Langlands, Zahida
Manzoor, John Denham, MP, Ian Mills, Ms
Janet Trotter, OBE, Mrs Rosie Varley,
Sir William Wells, Clive Wilkinson,
Prof Joan Higgins, Dr Peter Barrett
Secretariat: Chris Walker

NATIONAL HEALTH SERVICE EXECUTIVE
NATIONAL HEALTH SERVICE EXECUTIVE BOARD
Chairman: Sir Alan Langlands *(SCS)*
NHS Executive Headquarters Directors (SCS):
Dr Sheila Adam, Prof M Green,
Ron Kerr, CBE, Alasdair Liddell, CBE,
Sarah Mullally, Colin Reeves, CBE,
Hugh Taylor

NHS Executive Regional Directors (SCS):
Nigel Crisp, Stephen Day, Peter Garland,
Peter Houghton *(acting)*, Tony Laurance,
Neil McKay, Barbara Stocking, CBE,
Robert Tinston
Secretariat: Giles Wilmore

COMMUNICATIONS DIRECTORATE
Richmond House, Skipton House and
Quarry House
Liaison with the press, radio and television,
advertising and other paid publicity; corporate
communications for the NHS Executive; Direct
marketing and print services and Public Enquiry
office
Director of Communications:
Helen McCallum *(SCS)*
Head of Planning Unit: Gavin Larner
Chief Press Officer: Laurence Knight
Head of Administration: Carol Hulkes
Deputy Director of Publicity: Wyn Roberts
Deputy Director of Media Relations: Sian Jarvis
Acting Deputy Director NHS Comms:
Peter Addison-Child

CORPORATE MANAGEMENT
DIRECTORATE
Richmond House
Group Head: Alice Perkins *(SCS)*
Personal Asst: Helena Edwards

ORGANISATIONAL DEVELOPMENT
BRANCH
Richmond House
The purpose of the OD Branch is to drive, sup-
port and evaluate the organisational change
agenda within DoH, and to develop the
Department's capacity to deliver Ministers'
objectives

PERSONNEL SERVICES
Director of Personnel: Flora Goldhill *(SCS)*
Skipton House

PS (F) FIELD SERVICES
Skipton House
Personnel services for the wider department,
NHS Executive, Security Service Centre, Senior
Civil Service Unit. Honours, support and advice
to staff and line management and strategic
advice to top management in the NHS Executive
HQ on human resources
Branch Head: Stephen Redmond

PS (CS) CORPORATE SERVICES
Pay policy for DH; Pay operations; terms and conditions of service; development and audit of corporate personnel policies; industrial relations; health and safety
Branch Head: Craig Muir

PS (STAFF DEVELOPMENT UNIT)
Eileen House
Implementing and embedding core values (new understanding), developing policies on training and development and equity assurance, co-ordinating investors in people (IIP) re-assessment
Head of Unit: Ian Forsyth

RESOURCE MANAGEMENT AND FINANCE
Richmond House
Division Head: D Clark *(SCS)*

RMF1 PROGRAMME SUPPORT:
Personal Social Services public expenditure; PSS Finance liaison; Public Health group finance liaison; Demand led finance liaison; Arms Length bodies
Branch Head: Jonathan Stopes-Roe

RMF2 BUSINESS DEVELOPMENT:
Departmental running costs finance liaison; Corporate Governance business development claims; Accounts system development; Estimates; Accounts and cashiers
Branch Head: Peter Kendall

RMF-IA (INTERNAL AUDIT BRANCH)
Provision of Internal Audit services to the Department of Health and Departmental Next Step Agencies, financial appraisal of Non-Departmental Public Bodies and Voluntary Organisations
Branch Head: B Burleigh

INTERNATIONAL AND INDUSTRY DIVISION
Richmond House
Health and Social Services Aspects of International Relations. Co-ordination of DH involvement in EC, WHO and Council of Europe; Health Co-operation agreements; International Nursing Matters; Promotion of Export of Health Care Products. Pharmaceutical Price Regulation Scheme; Sponsorship of the Health Care Industry including liaison with other Government Departments, Trade Associations and Individual Companies; EC Pharmaceutical Pricing

Head of IID: J H Barnes *(SCS)*

INFORMATION SERVICES DIVISION
Skipton House
Director: Dr A A Holt

ISD1
Provision and management of building and offices for London HQ buildings; management of departmental estate; IT security; IT project support; ISD personnel
Branch Head: M J Rainsford

ISD2
Applications development and support – project management, scoping studies and requirements analysis, commissioned project work, end-user development, mainframe systems support; applications support, pay and personnel systems support
Branch Head: C Horsey

ISD3-ICL
OIS Network voice and video conferencing support, vendor services, procurement, service support
Head of Branch: Paul Charman

ISD4
Corporate information management and web development, knowledge management, departmental internet/extranet strategy, libraries and information services, departmental records, internet policy, corporate data administration, external contact data
Branch Head: Mrs L Wishart

ISD5
IT Strategy and Standards, OIS development and exploitation user support services, service management, IT procurement management
Skipton House
Head of Branch: R Long

ISD6 RMF2D
Resource Accounts and Finance Systems
Eileen House
Branch Head: P Cobb

ISD8
Financial Management Unit
Skipton House
Head of Branch: Mrs J A Dainty

POLICY MANAGEMENT UNIT (PMU)
Richmond House
Supports the Departmental Board (DB) in its oversight of management and policy issues affecting the whole Department. A key feature of this role is to provide intelligence to DB on ongoing and future cross-sectoral policy and management issues; and commission out-work as appropriate to them. The Unit also co-ordinates DH input to major pan-Governmental initiatives (e.g. Better Regulation, Freedom of Information) and has responsibility for Communications within DH
Acting Head of Unit: Richard Walsh *(SCS)*

SOCIAL CARE GROUP (SCG)
Wellington House
Head of Social Care Policy:
David Walden, *(SCS)*
Chief Inspector: Ms Denise Platt, CBE *(SCS)*

SC1
(BUSINESS SUPPORT)
IT Systems development; Management and Financial Information Systems, staff development and training; publications; Equal Opportunities Monitoring Group; Personnel system support; Group Business Planning, Valuing Diversity
Section Head: Robin Wilson

SC2
(GENERAL SOCIAL CARE POLICY AND PERSONAL SOCIAL SERVICES TRAINING)
DH interests in local government structure and other general local government issues. Policy on regulation and inspection in the PSS and nursing homes. Group interests in general PSS finance and other general PSS issues. Management of Section 64 Grants general scheme, and Opportunities for Volunteering Schemes, Policy on voluntary sector in PSS, PSS training and complaints. Sponsorship of CCETSW. Relations with NISW, including DH core grant funding. Social Services Bill 1999/2000. Management of Training Support Programme. Joint Reviews. Access to Social Service Records
Head of Branch: S Mitchell

SC3
(CHILDREN'S SERVICES)
DH lead role in children's services. Children's Services Plans. Children Act 1989 general issues; all child protection issues; adoption; day care; Family Support. UN Convention on the Rights of the Child and related matters. Family policy. Domestic violence
Head of Branch: Tom Jeffrey

SC4
(CHILDREN'S RESIDENTIAL CARE, SECURE ACCOMMODATION AND JUVENILE JUSTICE)
All DH issues in these fields. Family placement including fostering. Policy on inspection of independent boarding schools. Children's employment. DH responsibilities for the Glenthorne Youth Treatment Centre
Head of Branch: Ann Stephenson

SC5
(GENERAL COMMUNITY CARE, ELDERLY SOCIAL CARE)
DH lead on community care and responsibility for continued development of 'Caring for People' policies, including carer's issues. Community Care and adult services research and information including monitoring. DH lead role and all social care issues for elderly people. Housing aspects of Community Care
Head of Branch: Giles Denham

HSD-SC (JU) (HSD-SC JOINT UNIT)
To ensure NHS and social services work collaborating across the interface to achieve the policy objectives set up by Ministers in the NHS White Paper, Social Services White Paper and other departmental initiatives to meet the best interests of patients and clients
Team Leader: Mark Davies

SC6
(DISABILITIES AND MENTAL ILLNESS ISSUES)
DH lead role and all social care issues for learning disabilities, physical disability and sensory impairment; Social care issues in mental health, drugs and alcohol, AIDS and HIV. Social Care Group interests in homelessness, ethnic minorities and inner cities
Head of Branch: Mrs A Gross
Social Care Regions:
  Northern: P Brearley
  Central: J Cypher
  Southern: Ms F McCabe
  London: Ms J Cleary
Inspection Division:
Head of Inspection Division: Ms Averil Nottage
  North West: B Riddell
  North East: J Fraser
  West: Richard Balfe

South: Hoare
East: Alan Jones
Inspection Resource Group: J Owen
Joint Review Group:
Project Director: Dr A Webster

JOINT FOOD SAFETY AND STANDARDS GROUP (A DH/MAFF GROUP)
Skipton House
Head of JFSSG: G Podger
Personal Sec (MAFF): Ms S Springall

FSAD 1
FOOD STANDARDS AGENCY DIVISION 1
MAFF and DH teams dealing with policy on charging, review of public analysts, LA enforcement; communicable diseases, and External Relations and Consumer Branch. Responsible for briefing, speeches, the Food Safety Information Bulletin, support to the Consumer Panel, and food safety enquiries from the general public

Head: Miss Jill Wordley

FSAD 2
Lead for JFSSG on implementation of the Agency, including infrastructure, support and accountability arrangements; personnel issues, structure and funding; Joint DH/MAFF Risk Communications Unit

Branch Head: Pat Stewart

FSAD 3
Aspects of FSA Implementation Programme, including external communications accountability; concordats and corporate governance issues. Risk communication, development of JFSSG/FSA Press and Media Relations Unit

Branch Head: Ms Pat Stewart

FSP (DH)
Microbiology of food; food hygiene (including UK and EC legislation); liaison with local authorities on food issues; Advisory Committee on Microbiological Safety of Food (ACMSF); management of food poisoning outbreaks and hazards; safety of chemicals in food; novel foods and processes; medical and scientific aspects of nutrition

Branch Head: Dr Roger Skinner

PUBLIC HEALTH DIVISION
Wellington House

Division Head: Edmund Waterhous *(SCS)*

PH – DCMO
Policy on Communicable Diseases for the Corporate Management of the Public Health Group

Deputy Chief Medical Officer: Dr Pat Troop

PH – TPU TEENAGE PREGNANCY UNIT
Responsible for implementing the Social Exclusion Unit's report on Teenage Parenthood

Head of Unit: Miss C Hamlyn

PH1 – HEALTH STRATEGY BRANCH
Our Healthier Nation, Strategy Implementation Team, Public Health Standards and Health Development Agency Team, Health Impact Assessment, Health Monitoring and Surveillance, Ethnic Minority Health

Acting Branch Head: Nick Dean

PH2 – HEALTHY PEOPLE AND COMMUNITIES BRANCH
Coronary Heart Disease/Stroke and Accidents Team, Health Settings Team, Community Development Team, Access to Retail Services Team

Head of Branch: Miss Amy Edwards

PH3 – SUBSTANCE MISUSE BRANCH
Alcohol Misuse Team, Tackling Smoking Team, Services for Drug Misuses Team, Prevention of Drug Misuse Team

Acting Head of Branch: Chris Kenny

PH4 – SEXUAL HEALTH – GENETICS BRANCH
Genetics Policy Unit, Human Genetics Commission Unit, Embryology and Assisted Conception Team, Bio Ethics Team, Sexual Health Policy Team, sexual health education

Branch Head: Marcia Fry

PH5 – ENVIRONMENTAL HEALTH BRANCH
Sustainable Development Team, Radiation Team, Air Pollution Team, Environmental Chemicals Team

Branch Head: Janet Walden

PH6 – COMMUNICABLE DISEASE BRANCH
CJD/BSE – New and Emerging Infections Team, environmental transmission, Microbiological Risk Assessment and Biotechnology Unit; Immunisation, Blood–Bone Infections Team, communicable disease and policy standards, Antimicrobial Resistance and Hospital Acquired Infection Team

Branch Head: Dr Elisabeth Smales

PH7 – Corporate Management Branch
Organisational development, business support, management of non-departmental public bodies, complementary medicine, welfare foods and BSE inquiry/CJD litigation, Emergency Planning Co-ordination Unit

Branch Head: Andy Smith

Support Services for Medical Functions (MED SUPP)
CMO's Office, Richmond House

Dr Pat Troop
DCMO's Office, Richmond House
Jim Connelly
Editorial Unit, Eileen House
Ed Davis

HM Inspector of Anatomy
Wellington House
Dr Jeremy Metters

PLANNING DIRECTORATE
Richmond House and Quarry House
Planning, analytical services, primary care, pharmacy, drugs and prescribing, information and IT

Director of Planning:
    Alisdair Liddell, CBE *(SCS)*
Head of Planning: Les Bradley
Chief Economic Adviser: Clive Smee, CB
Director of Statistics: Dr John Fox *(SCS)*
Head of Communications: Helen McCallum
Head of Primary Care: Andy McKeon *(SCS)*
Head of General Medical Services: M Farrar
Chief Dental Officer: Robin Wild
Head of Pharmacy and Prescribing:
    Kevin Guinness
*Acting Heads of White Paper Implementation
    Team:* Tim Sands – HAZ Issues,
    Paul Atkinson – Non-HAZ Aspects
Head of Dental and Optical Services:
    Helen Robinson
Acting Chief Pharmaceutical Officer:
    Jeanette Howe
Head of Information Policy Unit: Dr Peter Drury

ECONOMICS AND OPERATIONAL RESEARCH DIVISION
Skipton House and Quarry House
Chief Economic Adviser: C H Smee, CB *(SCS)*
Economic support to the NHS Executive
(EOR1 – Quarry House)
Senior Economic Adviser: Nick York (EOR1)
Economic support to the wider Department and NHS Executive HQ in London
(EOR3 – Skipton House)

Senior Economic Adviser: Dr S Harding (EOR3)
Operational Research/ Management Science support to the NHS Executive in Leeds
(EOR2 – Quarry House)
Head of Operational Research:
    Dr G H D Royston (EOR2)
Operational Research/Management Science support in London
(EOR4 – Skipton House)
Head of Operational Research: A P G Hare

STATISTICS DIVISION
Skipton House
Director of Statistics: Dr John Fox *(SCS)*
Deputy Director: Greg Phillpotts

SD1
Remuneration, work-force and activity statistics of general dental, pharmaceutical and ophthalmic services, prescription analysis, weekly returns
Chief Statistician: Jim Stokoe

SD2
Statistics on Mental Health, Drugs Misuse, Community and cross sector services, women's health, smoking, drinking, hospital episodes, demographics, public health information co-ordination
Chief Statistician: Richard Willmer

SD3
Local authority personal social services (PSS) statistics and information strategy, and analytical support to social care group and finance division, DH survey programme including health surveys and National Survey of NHS patients. Policy on statistical publications, co-ordination of office for national statistics (ONS) publications. General statistical advice
Acting Chief Statistician: Antonia Roberts

STATS (W)
Quarry House
Workforce and remuneration statistics for the hospital and community services and the general medical service
Chief Statistician: Gill Eastabrook

NURSING SERVICES
Richmond House and Quarry House
All aspects of nursing, midwifery and health visiting
Chief Nursing Officer and Director of Nursing:
    Sarah Mullally

Richmond House
Assistant Chief Nursing Officer (NUR-PS):
  Mrs G Stephens, BSc(Econ), RGN, RHV

Quarry House
*Assistant Chief Nursing Officer – Clinical
  Practice:* Liz Fradd
*Assistant Chief Nursing Officer – Corporate
  Management:* D Moore

Richmond House
QUAL – NHS Quality Management
Branch Head: Dr Felicity Harvey

RESEARCH AND DEVELOPMENT DIVISION
Richmond House and Skipton House
Department of Health R&D programme; NHS
R&D Strategy and Programme: Research Policy;
Scientific Aspects of R&D
Acting Director of Research and Development:
  Prof Sir John Pattison
Deputy Director of Research and Development:
  Dr C Henshall

RD1
Richmond House*
**Private Office, R&D Strategy Policy and Co-
ordination, Business Management Unit**
Ms A Kauder

RD2
Skipton House
**Research Management, Policy Research
Programme**
Mrs J Griffin

RD3
NHS Research and Development Directorate
Quarry House
Branch Head: Marc Taylor

RD4
Health Care, Science and Technology
Skipton House*
Chief Scientific Officer: Dr P Greenaway

Branches highlighted by * report to the
Permanent Secretary, the remainder to the NHS
Management Executive

HEALTH AND PERSONAL SOCIAL SERVICES
MATTERS (OTHER THAN NATIONAL HEALTH
SERVICE SUPERANNUATION)
Director of Legal Services: Mrs G S Kerrigan
Asst Directors: Gillian Aitken, David Dunleavy,
  Sue Edwards, Anita James, P Milledge,
  Ron Powell, Rachel Sandby-Thomas,
  Miss M Trefgarne, Mrs S A Walker

OPERATIONS DIRECTORATE
Director of Operations: Ron Kerr, CBE
Implementation; working with headquarters'
staff and regional directors to ensure that key
changes are properly implemented. Management
of specific issues including the transfer of
responsibilities from the High Security
Psychiatric Services Commissioning Board to
regional commissioning team, changes in the
NHS Procurement Support for the Chief
Executive across the whole range of his general
management duties. Close cross-government
regional working.

HUMAN RESOURCES DIVISION
Quarry House
Pay and conditions of service of directly
employed staff of Health Authorities and family
practitioner committees, excluding dentists. Staff
groups as specified. General NHS personnel
matters. Non-medical manpower and training.
NHS superannuation policy, Human Resources
Strategy.

Director of Human Resources:
  Hugh Taylor *(SCS)*

HRD NHS PAY
Branch Head: Ms A Simkins

HRD EMPLOYMENT ISSUES
Branch Head: R Heron

HRD EQUAL OPPORTUNITIES UNIT
Branch Head: Ms E Al-Khalifa

HRD NHS DEVELOPMENT UNIT
Branch Head: Ms H Fields

HRD EDUCATION AND REGULATION
Branch Head: Miss G Newton

HRD WORKFORCE PLANNING
Acting Branch Head: Mrs G Redhead

HRD MEDICAL EDUCATION UNIT
Acting Branch Head: Dr G Cairncross

HRD APPOINTMENTS UNIT
Branch Head: Dr Roger J Moore

HEALTH SERVICES DIRECTORATE

Director of Health Services:
  Dr Sheila Adam *(SCS)*
Deputy Director: (Vacant)

HSD CORPORATE MANAGEMENT COMMISSIONING

HEALTH SERVICES DIRECTORATE – 1
Emergency services, adult intensive care and hospital policy, blood and pathology, imaging

Branch Head: David Hewlett

HEALTH SERVICES DIRECTORATE – 2
Cancer services, cardiac/renal/general medicine, transplantation, NSCAG Secretariat

Branch Head: Jane McKessack
Head of Business Management and Development: Linda Percival

HEALTH SERVICES DIRECTORATE – 3
Women's and Children's Health Services

Branch Head: Kathryn Tyson

HEALTH SERVICES DIRECTORATE – 4
Policy and services for people with mental health problems, Mental Health Review Tribunal Service

Acting Branch Head: Ms Elaine Edgar

MENTAL HEALTH ACT COMMISSION

Chief Executive Officer: William Bingley

NHS PUBLIC HEALTH DEVELOPMENT UNIT – PHDU

Head: Dr Gina Radford

HEALTH SERVICES DIRECTORATE – 7
Physical and Sensory Disabilities; Clinical and professional advice related to therapy and other professions allied to medicine and psychogeriatric medicine

Branch Head: (Vacant)

FINANCE AND PERFORMANCE DIVISION
Quarry House and Richmond House

Director of Finance and Performance:
Colin Reeves, CBE *(SCS)*

FINANCE AND PERFORMANCE DIVISION A
Public expenditure on health and personal social services

Deputy Director of Finance:
Bill McCarthy *(SCS)*

FINANCE AND PERFORMANCE DIVISION B
Health Authority and Trust financial allocations, plans and monitoring, NHS Trust financial management, private finance initiative and NHS financial development

Deputy Director of Finance:
Christine Daws *(SCS)*

DIRECTORATE OF COUNTER FRAUD SERVICES
Matters relating to the uncovering and prevention of fraud in the health service

Director: Jon Gee

REGIONAL OFFICES

EASTERN REGIONAL OFFICE
Chairman: Rosie Varley
Regional Director: Peter Houghton *(SCS)*

LONDON REGIONAL OFFICE
Chairman: Ian Mills
Regional Director: Nigel Crisp *(SCS)*

NORTH WEST REGIONAL OFFICE
Chairman: Prof Joan Higgins
Regional Director: Robert Tinston *(SCS)*

NORTHERN AND YORKSHIRE REGIONAL OFFICE
Chair: Zahida Manzoor
Acting Regional Director: Peter Garland *(SCS)*

SOUTH EAST REGIONAL OFFICE
Chairman: Sir William Wells
Regional Director: Barbara Stocking, CBE *(SCS)*

SOUTH AND WEST REGIONAL OFFICE
Chair: Janet Trotter, OBE
Regional Director: Tony Laurence *(SCS)*

TRENT REGIONAL OFFICE
Chairman: Dr Peter Barrett
Regional Director: Neil McKay *(SCS)*

WEST MIDLANDS REGIONAL OFFICE
Chairman: Clive Wilkinson
Regional Director: Stephen Day *(SCS)*

AGENCIES

MEDICAL DEVICES AGENCY
Chief Executive: Alan Kent

MEDICINES CONTROL AGENCY
Chief Executive: Dr K H Jones, CB *(SCS)*

NHS ESTATES
Chief Executive: Kate Priestley *(SCS)*

NHS PENSIONS AGENCY
Chief Executive: A F Cowan

SOLICITOR'S OFFICE
Solicitor: Marilynne Morgan, CB
New Court

Executive Agencies: Medical Devices Agency (MDA); Medicines Control Agency (MCA); NHS Estates; NHS Pensions

Home Office

50 Queen Anne's Gate,
London SW1H 9AT
020 7273 4000 *Fax:* 020 7273 3965
Gen *Fax:* 020 7273 2190
E-mail: gen.ho@gtnet.gov.uk
Website: www.homeoffice.gov.uk/

Statement of Purpose
To build a safe, just and tolerant society in which the rights and responsibilities of individuals, families and communities are properly balanced, and the protection and security of the public are maintained.
Aims
- Reduction in crime, particularly youth crime, and in the fear of crime; and the maintenance of public safety and good order.
- Delivery of justice through effective and efficient investigation, prosecution, trial and sentencing, and through support for victims.
- Prevention of terrorism, reduction in other organised and international crime, and protection against threats to national security.
- Effective execution of the sentences of the courts so as to reduce re-offending and protect the public.
- Helping to build, under a modernised constitution, a fair and prosperous society, in which everyone has a stake, and in which rights and responsibilities of individuals, families and communities are properly balanced.
- Regulation of entry to and settlement in the UK in the interests of social stability and economic growth and facilitation of travel by UK citizens.
- Reduction in the incidence of fire and related death, injury and damage, and ensuring the safety of the public through civil protection.
In pursing its aims the Home Office seeks to:
- Provide high quality services to the public and to Parliament including the provision of accurate, timely information about those services and about citizens' rights and obligations in relation to them;
- Secure best value for money and take account of the needs of the environment;
- Deal honestly, fairly, sensitively and openly with people; and
- Encourage all services for which it is responsible to share its commitment to those aims and principles and to help them in their work.

Secretary of State (Home Secretary):
   The Rt Hon Jack Straw, MP
Prin Priv Sec: Ms Hilary Jackson
   Priv Secs: S Harrison, Ms M Goldstein,
   Ms A Pearce
Parly Priv Sec: Colin Pickthall, MP
Special Advisers to the Secretary of State:
   Justin Russell (020 7273 2713), Ed Owen
   (020 7273 2852 *Fax:* 020 7273 2745)
Minister of State and Deputy Home Secretary:
   The Rt Hon Paul Boateng, MP
   Priv Sec: Simon Hayes
Parly Priv Sec: Angela Smith, MP
Minister of State: Charles Clarke, MP
   Priv Sec: Jacquie Russell
Parly Priv Sec: Gareth R Thomas, MP
Minister of State: Mrs Babara Roche, MP
   Priv Sec: Cathy Hume
Parly Priv Sec: Tom Levitt, MP
Parliamentary Under-Sec of State:
   Mike O'Brien, MP
   Priv Sec: Lee Bailey
   Parly Clerk: Ms Diane Caddle
Parliamentary Under-Sec of State:
   The Lord Bassam of Brighton, MP
   Priv Sec: Paul Morrison
Lord in Waiting: The Lord Hoyle

Spokesmen in the House of Lords: The Lord Bassam of Brighton, The Lord Bach

Permanent Under-Secretary:
   Sir David Omand, KCB *(SCS)*
   Priv Sec:
      Miss Alison Rutherford
      (*Fax:* 020 7273 2972)
   Asst Priv Sec: C A Jones
   Asst Priv Sec: David Rasmussen
J Lyon *(SCS) (Director, Police Policy Directorate)*
   Personal Asst: Pat Bromley
Ms Lynda Lockyer *(SCS) (Director, Corporate Resources Directorate)*
   Personal Asst: Ms B Neville
J Halliday, CB *(SCS) (Director, Criminal Policy Group)*
   Personal Asst: Miss C Goodwin

Mrs S Street *(SCS) (Director, Criminal Policy Group)*

W Fittall *(SCS) (Director, Criminal Policy Group)*

R Fulton *(SCS) (Director, Planning and Finance Directorate)*
Personal Asst: Miss J Dwyer

B Butler *(SCS) (Director, Communications Directorate)*
Personal Asst: Miss G Ford, MBE

P Wiles *(SCS) (Director, Research, Development and Statistics)*
Personal Asst: Mrs M Washer

Dr D Pepper *(SCS) (Director, Corporate Development Directorate)*
Personal Asst: Miss C Dartnall

Miss C E C Sinclair *(SCS) (Director, Constitutional and Community Policy Directorate)*
Personal Asst: Mrs T Nelson

Director: C Everett *(Director, Fire and Emergency Planning Directorate)*
Personal Asst: Miss C Thomas

Martin Narey *(SCS) (Director-General, HM Prison Service)*
Personal Asst: Sue Bryant

Stephen Boys-Smith *(SCS) (Director-General, Immigration and Nationality Directorate)*
Personal Asst: Mrs V Scott

F J Warne, CB *(SCS) (Director, Organised and International Crime Directorate)*
Personal Asst: Mrs D M Cramer

Advisers –
Legal Adviser: Miss J Wheldon, CB *(SCS)*
Personal Asst: Ms Lesley Beck

Chief Medical Officer (at Department of Health and Social Security):
Prof Liam Donaldson, QHP

DIRECTORATES

COMMUNICATION DIRECTORATE
50 Queen Anne's Gate, London SW1H 9AT
020 7273 4000
Director, Communications (Head of News):
B Butler *(SCS)*
Head of Publicity and Corporate Services:
Miss A Nash

CONSTITUTIONAL AND COMMUNITY POLICY DIRECTORATE
50 Queen Anne's Gate, London SW1H 9AT
020 7273 4000
(SCS): Mrs P G Catto, R G Evans,
Ms S Marshall, L Hughes, M de Pulford,
E Grant, N Varney

Gaming Board for Great Britain SCS:
T J Kavanagh* *(Secretary to the Board)*
*Based at Berkshire House,
168/173 High Holborn, London WC1V 7AA

ANIMALS (SCIENTIFIC PROCEDURE)
INSPECTORATE
Chief Inspector: Dr J Richmond

CORPORATE DEVELOPMENT DIRECTORATE
50 Queen Anne's Gate, London SW1H 9AT
020 7273 4000
(SCS): T Edwards, Ms S Rae
T Williams, C Welsh, C Burrows, D Rigby

CORPORATE RESOURCES DIRECTORATE
Grenadier House, 99/105 Horseferry Road,
London SW1P 2DD
020 7273 4000
(SCS): Ms L Lockyer
Mrs E Moody, T Cobley, R Creedon,
J G Jones, Ms D Loudon, Ms F Spencer,
S Wharton

CRIMINAL POLICY GROUP
50 Queen Anne's Gate,
London SW1H 9AT
020 7273 4000
Director, Criminal Justice Policy:
J Halliday *(SCS)*
Director, Sentencing and Correctional Policy:
Mrs S Street *(SCS)*
Director, Crime Reduction and Community Programmes: W Fittall *(SCS)*
(SCS): M D Boyle, J I Chisholm, V Hogg,
G H Marriage, OBE, C Stewart, J Powls,
A Norbury, C Byrne, N Warner,
Howard Webber*, J Thompson, Ms S Atkins,
Ms G Fletcher-Cooke, Ms K Bramwell,
P Pugh
(G6): A D Macfarlane, Ms L Rogerson,
V Clayton, J Nicholson, Ms J Furniss,
S Trimmins, Ms V George, Mrs A Johnstone,
S Thornton
*Based at Morley House,
26/30 Holborn Viaduct, London EC1A 2JQ

HM INSPECTORATE OF PROBATION
Chief Insp: Sir Graham Smith, CBE
Asst Chief Insp (G6): G W Childs

FIRE AND EMERGENCY PLANNING
DIRECTORATE
Horseferry House, Dean Ryle Street,
London SW1P 2AW
020 7273 4000
(SCS): C Everett, Dr D M Peace, P Davies,
G E Guy, Ms V Harris

Marketing Group Manager: R Smith*
(G6): T Lewis, P Jones

*Based at The Hawkhills, Easingwold,
York YO6 3EG

HM FIRE SERVICE INSPECTORATE
Chief Insp: G Meldrum, CBE, QFSM, DUniv,
FIFireE, CIMgt

IMMIGRATION AND NATIONALITY DIRECTORATE
Lunar House, 40 Wellesley Road,
Croydon, Surrey CR9 2BY
020 8760 plus ext
Director-General: S Boys-Smith *(SCS)*
Deputy Director-General – Operations:
Miss K Collins* *(SCS)*
Deputy Dir-Gen – Policy: M J Eland* *(SCS)*
Deputy Dir-Gen – Projects: Dr C Mace
Directors (SCS): J Acton*, Miss V M Dews,
Mrs L Pallett*, R M Whalley*, R G Yates,
B Eagle, Mrs M Bishop
Director (Enforcement): Ian Boon*
Director (Ports): P Higgins*
Grade 6: T Mercer, C Harbin*, D Roberts*
*Located at Apollo House
36 Wellesley Road, Croydon CR9 3RR
†Located at 50 Queen Anne's Gate
London SW1H 9AT
‡Located at India Buildings
3rd Floor, Water Street, Liverpool L2 0QN

EU AND INTERNATIONAL UNIT
50 Queen Anne's Gate, London SW1H 9AT
020 7273 4000
(SCS): P Edwards

LEGAL ADVISER'S BRANCH
50 Queen Anne's Gate, London SW1H 9AT
020 7273 4000
Deputy Leg Advs: Mrs S A Evans *(SCS)*,
T Middleton *(SCS)*

ORGANISED AND INTERNATIONAL CRIME
DIRECTORATE
50 Queen Anne's Gate, London SW1H 9AT
020 7273 4000
(SCS): J Warne, G Stadlen, P Storr, B Paterson

PRISONS OMBUDSMEN
Ashley House, 2 Monck Street,
London SW1P 2BQ
Ombudsmen (SCS): Stephen Shaw
See **Ombudsmen and Consumer Protection**

BOARD OF VISITORS SECRETARIAT
Horseferry House, Dean Ryle Street
London SW1P 2AW
Director: D Sandiford

PLANNING AND FINANCE DIRECTORATE
50 Queen Anne's Gate, London SW1H 9AT
020 7273 4000
(SCS): R Fulton, R Scotland, C Harnett,
A Mortimore
(G6): R B Woodland

POLICE POLICY DIRECTORATE
50 Queen Anne's Gate, London SW1H 9AT
020 7273 4000
(SCS): B Coleman†, P Honour, J Duke-Evans,
A Cory**, R Kornicki, Miss D Loudon
(G6): R A Ginman*, S Wells**
**Located at Horseferry House

HM INSPECTORATE OF CONSTABULARY
50 Queen Anne's Gate,
London SW1H 9AT
020 7273 4000
HM Chief Inspector:
David O'Dowd, CBE, QPM

RESEARCH, DEVELOPMENT AND STATISTICS
DIRECTORATE
50 Queen Anne's Gate,
London SW1H 9AT
020 7273 4000
(SCS): C G Lewis, A D Moxon, P Ward*,
Prof K Pease
(G6): G Barclay, Ms M Colledge, Mrs P
Dowdeswell, Mrs C L Lehman, Mrs
P Mayhew, OBE, P Collier, B Webb,
R Walmsley, Dr J Youell, R Price
*Located at Abell House, John Islip Street,
London SW1P 4LH

STRATEGY UNIT (SU)
50 Queen Anne's Gate,
London SW1H 9AT
020 7273 4000
(SCS): R Weatherill

HM INSPECTORATE OF PRISONS
50 Queen Anne's Gate,
London SW1H 9AT
020 7273 4000
HM Chief Inspector of Prisons:
Sir David Ramsbotham
HM Deputy Chief Inspector of Prisons: C Allen

Executive Agencies: Fire Service College;
Forensic Science Service; HM Prison Service;
UK Passport Agency

International Development, Department for

94 Victoria Street, London SW1E 5JL
020 7917 7000 *Fax:* 020 7917 0016
GTN: 3535 7000

Abercrombie House, Eaglesham Road,
East Kilbride, Glasgow G75 8EA
01355 844000 *GTN:* 7243 1000
E-mail: dfid.gov.uk
Website: www.dfid.gov.uk

The Department for International Development, reporting to the Secretary of State for International Development, is the government department responsible for managing Britain's bilateral and multilateral development programmes in poorer countries and for ensuring that Government policies which affect developing countries, including the environment, trade, investment and agricultural policies, take account of developing country issues.

DfID's aim is the elimination of poverty in developing countries. As set out in the November 1997 White Paper on International Development, "Eliminating World Poverty: A Challenge for the 21st Century", the Government is committed to the internationally agreed targets to halve the proportion of people living in abject poverty by 2015, together with the associated targets, including universal access to primary education and basic health care by the same date.

DfID works in partnership with developing countries which are committed to the international targets, and is putting in place new ways of working with the UK private and voluntary sectors, and the research community. DfID works closely with other donors and development agencies to strengthen the commitment to the elimination of poverty, and uses its influence to help mobilise the political will to achieve the international development targets.

Secretary of State: The Rt Hon Clare Short, MP
Priv Sec: Chris Austin
Parly Priv Sec: Dennis Turner, MP
Special Advisers: David Mepham,
  Ms Dee Sullivan
Parliamentary Under-Sec of State:
  George Foulkes, MP
Priv Sec: Christine Atkinson
Asst Priv Sec: Phillipa Hoffman
Parliamentary Unit, Head of Unit and
  Asst Priv Sec: Ian Ruff
Parliamentary Assistant: Craig French

Spokesperson in the House of Lords:
The Baroness Amos
Permanent Secretary:
  Sir John Vereker, KCB *(SCS)*
Priv Sec: Arvind Mungur (020 7917 0514)

Director-General Programmes:
  Barrie Ireton *(SCS)*
Director-General Resources:
  Richard Manning, CB *(SCS)*

CHAD
Disaster preparedness and relief; monitoring reports from all sources and research on possible disaster situations. Liaison with Ministry of Defence, Department of Health, voluntary societies and international organisations; UN High Commissioner for Refugees; UN Relief and Works Agency; Voluntary organisations working for refugees overseas.
Head of Department: Dr Mukesh Kapila

AFRICA DIVISION
Acting Director: Barbara Kelly *(SCS)*

AFRICA POLICY AND ECONOMICS DEPARTMENT
Head of Unit: Peter Landymore

AFRICA, GREATER HORN AND CO-ORDINATION DEPARTMENT
Angola, Burundi, the Comoros, Congo, Djibouti, Eritrea, Ethiopia, Madagascar, Mauritius, Rwanda, Sao Tome & Principe, Seychelles, Somalia, Sudan, Zaïre. Liaison with British Development Divisions in Central, Eastern and Southern Africa.
Acting Head of Department: Bob Smith *(SCS)*

WEST AND NORTH AFRICA DEPARTMENT
Algeria, Benin, Burkina Faso, Cameroon, Cape Verde, Central African Republic, Chad, Egypt, Equatorial Guinea, Gabon, the Gambia, Ghana, Guinea, Guinea Bissau, Ivory Coast, Liberia, Mali, Mauritania, Morocco, Niger, Nigeria, the Sahel, Senegal, Sierra Leone, Togo, Tunisia.
Head of Department: Brian Thompson *(SCS)*

DfID EASTERN AFRICA (NAIROBI)
Kenya, Tanzania, Uganda.
Head of Division: Mark Lowcock *(SCS)*

DfID CENTRAL AFRICA (HARARE)
Malawi, Mozambique, Zambia, Zimbabwe.
Head of Division: Jim Drummond *(SCS)*

DfID SOUTHERN AFRICA (PRETORIA)
Botswana, Lesotho, Namibia, South Africa, Swaziland.
The division organises regional programmes for Southern Africa and supports regional initiatives undertaken by the Southern African Development Community (SADC) and other similar organisations.
Head of Division: Stephen Chard *(SCS)*

ASIA AND PACIFIC DIVISION
Director: Sue Unsworth *(SCS)*
Asia Regional and Economic Policy Unit
Head of Unit: Paul Ackroyd
DfID Nepal (Katmandu)
Head of Department: Sue Wardell
DfID Pacific (Suva)
Head of Department: Jackie Creighton

EASTERN ASIA AND PACIFIC
DEPARTMENT
Brunei, China, Fiji, Hong Kong, Kiribati, Korea, Mongolia, Papua New Guinea, Solomon Islands, Tonga, Tuvalu, Vanuatu, Western Samoa, University of South Pacific and Aid and Trade projects in South East Asia.
Head of Department: Sarah Smith *(SCS)*

DEPARTMENT FOR INTERNATIONAL
DEVELOPMENT IN INDIA (DFID INDIA)
India, Bhutan.
Head of Department:
    Robert Graham-Harrison *(SCS)*

WESTERN ASIA DEPARTMENT
Iraq, Jordan, Pakistan, Yemen, Occupied Territories; regional programmes.
Head of Department: Margaret Vowles *(SCS)*

DfID SOUTH EAST ASIA (BANGKOK)
Cambodia, Indonesia, Maldives, Nepal Philippines, Sri Lanka.
Head of Division: Adam Wood *(SCS)*

DfID BANGLADESH (DHAKA)
Bangladesh.
Head of Department: Kevin L Sparkhall *(SCS)*

INTERNATIONAL DIVISION
Director: Tony Faint *(SCS)*

EUROPEAN UNION DEPARTMENT
EU aid and development policies; European Development Fund and operations of the European Investment Bank in developing countries; Asia/Latin America Programme; EU Technical Assistance to Eastern and Central Europe (PHARE) and the former Soviet Union (TACIS); Mediterranean Programme; EC Humanitarian Aid and EC Sector Programmes.
Head of Department: Anthony Smith *(SCS)*

UNITED NATIONS AND
COMMONWEALTH DEPARTMENT
The UN development system including aspects of ECOSOC and the General Assembly; DfID interests in UN Reform; UN Development Group (UNDP); UNICEF and World Food Programme; UNESCO (United Nations Educational, Scientific and Cultural Organisation, UNIDO, FAO, IFAD, UN Regional Economic Commissions. Food aid and food security; Commonwealth Fund for Technical Co-operation; Commonwealth Youth Programme, Commonwealth Foundation.
Head of Department: Michael Mosselnars *(SCS)*

INTERNATIONAL FINANCIAL
INSTITUTIONS DEPARTMENT
World Bank Group; IBRD/IMF Development Committee: Asian Development Bank/Fund; African Development Bank/Fund; Caribbean Development Bank; Inter-American Development Bank; debt, IMF and export credits.
Head of Department: Margaret Cund *(SCS)*

CONFLICT AND HUMANITARIAN
AFFAIRS DEPARTMENT
Conflict prevention and post-conflict peace-building including human rights; General humanitarian policy; Disaster preparedness, response and mitigation; Refugees and migration; Military–Civilian Co-operation. Relations with United Nations humanitarian system (including UN Secretariat, OCHA, OHCHR, UNHCR) IOM and International Red Cross; Country responsibilities for Afghanistan and North Korea.
Head of Department and Senior Humanitarian Adviser: Dr Mukesh Kapila

INTERNATIONAL ECONOMICS
DEPARTMENT
Economic advice to all International Division Departments including multilateral budgets, financial forecasting, economic policies, project cycle management in MDIs, reporting, effectiveness and economic aspects of disaster preparedness and relief. Quarterly in-depth reports on international economic issues. Specific focus on debt issues, multilateral impact, private sector, migration and financial flows.
Head of Department: Eric Hawthorn

EASTERN EUROPEAN AND WESTERN HEMISPHERE DIVISION
Head of Division: John Kerby *(SCS)*

CENTRAL AND SOUTH EASTERN EUROPE DEPARTMENT
Head of Department: Simon Ray

EASTERN EUROPE AND CENTRAL ASIA DEPARTMENT
Head of Department: Matthew Wyatt

EASTERN EUROPE AND WESTERN HEMISPHERE ECONOMICS DEPARTMENT
Head of Department: Catriona Laing

UK REPRESENTATIVE AT THE EUROPEAN BANK FOR RECONSTRUCTION AND DEVELOPMENT
Head of Unit: Michael McCulloch

LATIN AMERICA, CARIBBEAN AND ATLANTIC DEPARTMENT
Argentina, Bolivia, Brazil, Chile. Colombia, Costa Rica, Cuba, Dominican Republic, Ecuador, El Salvador, Guatemala, Haiti, Honduras, Latin America general, Mexico, Nicaragua, Panama, Paraguay, Peru, Uruguay. Antigua. Bahamas, Barbados, Belize, Dominica, Grenada, Guyana, Jamaica, St Kitts and Nevis, St Lucia, St Vincent, Suriname, Trinidad and Tobago. Anguilla, British Virgin Islands, Cayman Islands, Montserrat, Turks and Caicos Islands, University of West Indies, Caribbean Group for Co-operation in Economic Development (CGCED), EDF aid to the Caribbean. Falkland Islands, Gibraltar, St Helena, Tristan da Cunha.
Head of Department: Alex Archbold

DFID CARIBBEAN
Independent Caribbean countries, Associated States and Dependencies.
Head of Division: Desmond Curran *(SCS)*

EDUCATION DEPARTMENT
Education aid policy and research; functional programmes of assistance to formal and non-formal education.
Chief Education Adviser: Myra Harrison

INFRASTRUCTURE AND URBAN DEVELOPMENT DEPARTMENT
Policy and knowledge generation; synthesis and dissemination in the broad engineering sector including transport, water and sanitation, power and energy, telecommunications, geosciences and mining, physical planning and architecture.
Chief Engineering Adviser: John Hodges

HEALTH AND POPULATION DEPARTMENT
World Health Organisation (WHO); Medical and Nutrition Research projects; population policy and family planning.
Chief Health and Population Adviser:
Dr Julian Lobb-Levyt *(SCS)*

RURAL LIVELIHOODS AND ENVIRONMENT DIVISION
Director, Production Capacity & Environment and Chief Natural Resources Adviser:
Andrew Bennett *(SCS)*

ENVIRONMENT POLICY DEPARTMENT
Sectoral policy on agricultural and rural development and co-operatives and institutions; co-ordination of environmental advice; support for international agricultural research renewable natural resources research: general co-ordinating responsibility for DfID-funded contract research; Stirling University – Institute of Aquaculture, International Institute for Environment and Development, Co-ordination of Environmental Advice; relations with Natural Resources Institute, Silsoe Research Institute (Overseas Division), Tsetse Research Laboratory, Langford, Centre for Tropical Veterinary Medicine and Oxford Forestry Institute; science and technology for development (Commonwealth and European Community aspects).
Head of Department: Adrian Davis *(SCS)*

RURAL LIVELIHOOD DEPARTMENT
Head of Department: Michael Scott *(SCS)*

ECONOMICS, STATISTICS AND ENTERPRISE DEVELOPMENT DIVISION
Chief Economist: Alan Coverdale *(SCS)*

ASIA, REGIONAL ECONOMICS AND POLICY DEPARTMENT
Head of Department: Paul Ackroyd *(SCS)*

AFRICA ECONOMICS DEPARTMENT
Head of Department: Peter Landymore *(SCS)*

ECONOMICS POLICY AND RESEARCH DEPARTMENT
Head of Department: Peter Grant *(SCS)*

INTERNATIONAL ECONOMIC POLICY DEPARTMENT
Head of Department: John Roberts *(SCS)*

ENTERPRISE DEVELOPMENT GROUP
Chief Enterprise Development Adviser:
David Wright

GOVERNANCE DEPARTMENT
Chief Governance Adviser: Roger Wilson *(SCS)*

STATISTICS DEPARTMENT
Compilation and publication of statistics on British Aid. Technical assistance to statistical offices in developing countries and countries in transition.
Chief Statistician: Tony Williams *(SCS)*
Principal Finance Officer:
  Graham Stegmann *(SCS)*

AID POLICY DEPARTMENT
Size, distribution and composition of the aid programme; overview of DfID policies; aid aspects of the work of the Organisation of European Co-operation and Development (OECD); development policies of other donor countries and OPEC aid institutions; bilateral aid systems; Crown Agents for Overseas Governments and Administrations.
Head of Department: David Sands Smith *(SCS)*

FINANCE DEPARTMENT
Head of Department: Colin Raynor

ACCOUNTS DEPARTMENT
Head of Department: Mike Smithson

ASIA REGIONAL ECONOMICS AND POLICY DEPARTMENT
Head of Department: Paul Ackroyd

BUSINESS PARTNERSHIPS DEPARTMENT
Head of Department: Rosemary Stevenson

SOCIAL DEVELOPMENT DEPARTMENT
Chief Social Development Adviser:
  Dr Ros Eyben *(SCS)*

MEDICAL AND WELFARE DEPARTMENT
Head of Department: Elaine Kennedy

INTERNAL AUDIT UNIT
Head of Department: Roger Elias *(SCS)*

EVALUATION DEPARTMENT
Ex-post evaluation of aid activities.
Head of Department: Christopher Raleigh *(SCS)*

PERSONNEL DEPARTMENT
Personnel, accommodation and office services.
Principal Establishment Officer:
  Martin Dinham *(SCS)*

PROCUREMENT APPOINTMENTS AND NGO DEPARTMENT
General policy on manpower and terms of service of all staff overseas; recruitment policy.
Head of Department: Robin Russell *(SCS)*

OVERSEAS PENSIONS DEPARTMENT
Overseas service pensions including pensions supplements.
Head of Department: Richard Plumb *(SCS)*

INFORMATION SYSTEMS AND SERVICES DEPARTMENT
Head of Department: David Gillett *(SCS)*

INFORMATION DEPARTMENT/LIBRARY
Press and public relations: publicity; development education in the UK.
Head of Department: Richard Calvert *(SCS)*

LIBRARY
Material on aid and developing countries.

Enquiries: 01355 843599/843246
GTN: 7243 359913246

Law Officers' Departments
Attorney General's Chambers,
9 Buckingham Gate, London SW1E 6JP
020 7271 2400 *Fax:* 020 7271 2432
E-mail: islo@gtnet.gov.uk

Overall responsibility for the work of the Departments (the Treasury Solicitor's Department, the Crown Prosecution Service, the Serious Fraud Office and the Legal Secretariat to the Law Officers). He has a specific statutory duty to superintend the discharge of their duties by the Director of Public Prosecutions (who is head of the Crown Prosecution Service) and the Director of the Serious Fraud Office.

The Director of Public Prosecution for Northern Ireland is also responsible to the Attorney General for the due performance of his functions.

He is the Government's principal legal adviser; he deals with questions of law arising on Bills, and with issues of legal policy; he is concerned with all major international and domestic litigation involving the Government; and he has specific responsibilities for the enforcement of the criminal law.

Attorney General:
  The Rt Hon the Lord Williams of Mostyn, QC
Solicitor General: Ross Cranston, QC, MP
Legal Secretary to the Law Officers:
  David Seymour

Deputy Legal Sec: Stephen Parkinson
Parly Priv Sec: Michael Jabez Foster, MP
Priv Sec to the Law Officers:
   Rupert Cazelet (020 7271 2405)
Assistant Priv Sec, Parly Clerk:
   Jeff Thompson (020 7271 2406)
Diary Sec: Jacque Kugler (020 7271 2407)

Executive Agency: Treasury Solicitor's Department

Lord Chancellor's Department

House of Lords, London SW1A OPW
020 7219 3232 *Fax:* 020 7219 4711

The Lord Chancellor is responsible for promoting general reforms in the civil law, for the procedure of the civil courts and for the administration of the Supreme Court (Court of Appeal, High Court and Crown Court) and county courts in England and Wales. He also has ministerial responsibility for the locally administered Magistrates' Courts. He is responsible for advising the Crown on the appointment of judges and certain other officers and is himself responsible for the appointment of Masters and Registrars of the High Court and District Judges and magistrates. He is responsible for ensuring that letters patent and other formal documents are passed in the proper form under the Great Seal of the Realm, of which he is the custodian. The work in connection with this is carried out under his direction in the Office of the Clerk of the Crown in Chancery. He is also responsible for Legal Aid and has overall responsibility for the Public Record Office, HM Land Registry, the Public Trust Office and the Court Service, and the Northern Ireland Court Service.

Lord Chancellor:
   The Rt Hon the Lord Irvine of Lairg
Principal Priv Sec: Miss J Rowe *(SCS)*
Parly Priv Secs: Bridget Prentice, MP,
   Paul Clark, MP
Parly Clerk: Alexander Clark
Special Adviser: Garry Hart

Spokesmen in the House of Lords:
The Lord Irvine of Lairg, The Lord Bach

Selborne House, 54/60 Victoria Street
London SW1E 6QW
020 7210 8562 *Fax:* 020 7210 8620
Parliamentary Secretary:
David Lock, MP
Priv Sec: Diana Hulin

Parliamentary Secretary:
Jane Kennedy, MP
Priv Sec: Robert Moore
Permanent Secretary:
   Sir Hayden Phillips, KCB *(SCS)*
Priv Sec: Mark Camley

CROWN OFFICE
House of Lords
Clerk of the Crown in Chancery:
   Sir Hayden Phillips, KCB *(SCS)*
Deputy Clerk of the Crown in Chancery:
   Michael Huebner, CB *(SCS)*
Clerk of the Chamber: C I P Denyer

POLICY GROUP
Selborne House, 54/60 Victoria Street,
London SW1E 6QW
020 7210 8851
Director-General:
   Miss J M MacNaughton *(SCS)*
Heads of Divisions (SCS):
Director, Civil Justice and Legal Services:
   Alan Cogbill *(SCS)*
Director, Magistrates' Courts and Criminal
   Policy: Mark Ormerod
Civil Justice Division: David Gladwell
Legal Aid Division: Peter Harris
Civil Law Development Division: Ray Sams
Legal Services Development Division:
   Derek Hill
Community Legal Services Division:
   Colin Myerscough
Public and Private Rights Directorate:
   Ms Amanda Finlay
Family Policy Division: William Arnold
Administrative Justice Division: Alistair Shaw
Magistrates' Courts IT Division: Peter White

Magistrates' Courts Division: Ms Sally Field
Policy Group Secretariat: Mrs Kerry Allen
Social Policy Unit: Mrs Jackie Brown
Human Rights Act Implementation Team:
   Ian Rees

JUDICIAL GROUP
Selborne House, 54/60 Victoria Street,
London SW1E 6QW
020 7210 8928
Director: M D Huebner, CB *(SCS)*
D E Staff, J W Tanner, Mrs M Pigott,
   Miss J Killick, P L Jacob, S Humphreys

LEGAL ADVISER'S GROUP
3rd Floor, Southside, 105 Victoria Street,
London SW1E 6QT
020 7210 0711

Paul Jenkins *(SCS)*
M Collon, A Wallace, P Fish

CORPORATE SERVICES GROUP
Selborne House, 54/60 Victoria Street,
London SW1E 6QW
020 7210 8503 *Fax:* 020 7210 8752

Mrs E Grimsey *(SCS)*
S Smith, Ms S Webber, Mrs J Anderson,
  K T Cregeen, A Rummins, K W Garrett,
  A Maultby

COMMUNICATIONS GROUP
Selbourne House, 54-60 Victoria Street,
London SW1E 6QW
Press enquiries:
020 7210 8512 *Fax:* 020 7210 8633

Director of Communications:
  Allan Percival, LVO *(SCS)*
Chief Press Officer: Mike Wicksteed

MAGISTRATES COURT SERVICES INSPECTORATE
C J A Chivers

ECCLESIASTICAL PATRONAGE
No. 10 Downing Street, London SW1
020 7930 4433

Secretary for Ecclesiastical Patronage:
  J H Holroyd, CB
Asst Sec for Ecclesiastical Patronage:
  N C Wheeler

Executive Agencies: Court Service; HM Land
Registry; Public Record Office (PRO); Public
Trust Office (PTO)

NORTHERN IRELAND COURT SERVICE
Windsor House, Bedford Street,
Belfast BT2 7LT
028 9032 8594 *Fax:* 028 9032 9110

Director
Maintenance of Court's Charter, customer services and communications

OPERATIONS
Administrative support for Supreme Court of
Judicature, Northern Ireland (comprising Court
of Appeal, High Court and Crown Court), coun-
ty courts, magistrates' courts, the Enforcement
of Judgments Office, coroners' courts and
Offices of the Social Security and Child Support
Commissioners
Deputy Director

POLICY AND LEGISLATION
Formulation and implementation of policy initiatives, including those for legal aid; preparation
and drafting of primary and secondary legislation; secretarial support to Court Rules
Committees, Advisory Committees and Judicial
Studies Board for Northern Ireland; provision of
legal services and strategic control and monitoring of legal aid expenditure and administration
Deputy Director

CORPORATE SERVICES
Personnel and Training, Resource Management,
Procurement, Judicial Appointments, Internal
Audit
Deputy Director

Northern Ireland Office
11 Millbank, Whitehall, London SW1 4PN
020 7210 3000 *Fax:* 020 7210 0249

Castle Buildings, Belfast BT4 3SG
028 9052 0700 *Fax:* 028 9052 8195
E-mail: press.nio@nics.gov.uk
Website: www.nio.gov.uk

The Northern Ireland Office is the United
Kingdom government department in which the
Secretary of State for Northern Ireland, assisted
by one Minister of State and a Parliamentary
Under-Secretary of State, has overall responsi-
bility for the government of Northern Ireland.

The Secretary of State is directly responsible
for political and constitutional matters, security
policy, broad economic questions and other
major policy issues, while responsibility for such
matters as agriculture, economic development,
education, environment, finance and personnel,
and health and social services has been devolved
to the Northern Ireland Assembly.

For the purposes of local government, NI is
divided into 26 districts, each with its own council, elected on the basis of PR and universal adult
suffrage. These district councils are responsible
for local environmental services, including street
cleaning, refuse disposal, consumer protection,
environmental health and the provision of leisure
facilities.

The Parliamentary Commissioner for
Administration investigates complaints of maladministration against government departments
and personnel matters in the Northern Ireland
Civil Service.

Secretary of State:
  The Rt Hon Peter Mandelson, MP
Parly Priv Sec: Helen Jackson, MP

Minister of State: The Rt Hon Adam Ingram, MP
Parly Priv Sec: Anthony Colman, MP
Parliamentary Under-Sec of State:
  George Howarth, MP

Spokesperson in the House of Lords: The
Baroness Farrington of Ribbleton

Permanent Under-Secretary:
  Joe Pilling, CB *(SCS)*
*Head of NI Civil Service (2nd Permanent Under-
Secretary):* John Semple, CB *(SCS)*

Parliamentary Branch for all Ministers
020 7210 6551

NORTHERN IRELAND CIVIL SERVICE
Central Secretariat
Parliament Buildings, Belfast BT4 8SG
028 9052 0700
Head of NICS: John Semple, CB *(SCS)*

Executive Agencies: Business Development
Service (BDS); Compensation Agency;
Construction Service; Driver and Vehicle
Licensing (NI) (DVLNI); Driver and Vehicle
Testing Agency (DVTA); Environment and
Heritage Service (EHS); Forensic Science
Agency of NI (FSANI); Forest Service:
Government Purchasing Agency (GPA); Health
Estates; Industrial Research and Technology
Unit (IRTU); Land Registers of NI; NI Child
Support Agency; NI Prison Service (NIPS); NI
Statistics and Research Agency (NISRA);
Ordnance Survey of NI (OSNI); Planning
Service; Public Record Office of NI (PRONI);
Rate Collection Agency (RCA); Rivers Agency;
Roads Service; Social Security Agency (SSA);
Training and Employment Agency (TEA);
Valuation and Lands Agency (VLA); Water
Service

Prime Minister's Office

10 Downing Street, London SW1A 2AA
Telephone: Direct line from 020 7270 3000
Press Office 020 7270 3000
Website: www.number—10.gov.uk

*Prime Minister and First Lord of the Treasury
  and Minister for the Civil Service:*
  The Rt Hon Tony Blair, MP
Chief of Staff: Jonathan Powell
Deputy Chief of Staff: Pat McFadden
Prin Priv Secretary to the Prime Minister:
  Jeremy Heywood *(SCS)*
Private Secretary Foreign Affairs:
  John Sawers, CMG *(SCS)*
Parly Priv Sec: Bruce Grocott, MP

Private Secretaries to Prime Minister:
  Owen Barder *(SCS)* (Economic Affairs), Clare
  Sumner (Parliamentary Affairs), David
  North *(SCS)* (Home Affairs), Philip Barton,
  OBE (Assistant on Overseas Affairs),
  Michael Tatham (Assistant Overseas Affairs)
Personal Asst to Prime Minister:
  Miss Kate Garvey (Diary)
Secretary for Appointments: William Chapman
Special Assistant for Presentation and Planning:
  Anji Hunter
Policy Unit Special Advisers: David Miliband
  (Head of Unit), Andrew Adonis, Robert Hill,
  Peter Hyman, Roger Liddle, Liz Lloyd, Geof
  Mulgan, Geoffrey Norris, James Purnell, Ed
  Richards, Derek Scott, Sharon White
Chief Press Sec: Alastair Campbell
Dep Press Sec: Godric Smith
Head of Strategic Communications Unit:
  Alun Evans *(SCS)*
Executive Secretary: Ms Pat Dixon
Political Sec: Sally Morgan
Political Office: John Cruddas,
  Michael Stephenson, Faz Hakim,
  Caroline Adams, Gill Christopher-Chambers,
  Angela Goodchild
Parliamentary Clerk: Clive Barbour

Privy Council Office

Regency Building, 2 Carlton Gardens,
London SW1Y 5AA
020 7210 1033 *Fax:* 020 7210 1071
E-mail: spowell@cabinet-office.gov.uk

The Office is responsible for the arrangements
leading to the making of all Royal Proclamations
and Orders in Council; for certain formalities
connected with Ministerial changes; for considering applications for the grant (or amendment)
of Royal Charters; for the scrutiny and approval
of Bye-laws and Statutes of Chartered Bodies;
and for the appointment of High Sheriffs and
many Crown and Privy Council appointments to
Governing Bodies.

The President of the Council and Leader of the
House of Commons is responsible for the work
of the Privy Council Office; supervising the
Government's legislative programme and
upholding the rights and privileges of the House.
She Chairs the Select Committee on
Modernisation of the House of Commons and
the Ministerial Committees on the Queen's
Speeches and Future Legislation, and on
Legislation. Together with the Minister for the
Cabinet Office, she also acts as a spokesperson
for Government.

The Leader of the House of Lords is responsible for the arrangement of Government business in the House and has a responsibility to the House itself to advise it on procedural matters and other difficulties as they arise; she is also Minister for Women and sits on a number of Cabinet Committees – chairing the Cabinet sub-committee on Women's Issues.

A list of privy counsellors appears at the end of this section.

PRIVY COUNCIL OFFICE

Clerk of the Council: Alex Galloway *(SCS)*
Deputy Clerk: Graham Donald
Senior Clerk: Miss Muriel McCullagh

JUDICIAL COMMITTEE OF THE PRIVY COUNCIL
Downing Street, London SW1A 2AJ
020 7270 0483 *Fax:* 020 7270 0460
Registrar of the Privy Council:
J A C Watherston
Chief Clerk: F G Hart
Second Clerk: K W May

OFFICE OF PRESIDENT OF THE COUNCIL
Privy Council Office, Regency Building,
2 Carlton Gardens, London SW1Y 5AA
020 7210 1025/020 7219 4040
President of the Council and Leader of the House of Commons:
    The Rt Hon Margaret Beckett, MP
Prin Priv Sec: Vanessa Scarborough
Parly Priv Sec: Ivor Caplin, MP
Priv Sec – Policy: Matthew Hill
Priv Sec – Parly Affairs: Jonathan Capstick
Diary Sec: Sheron McDougall
Special Advisers: Sheila Watson, Nicci Collins
Priv Sec to Special Advisers: (020 7210 1082)
Parliamentary Secretary: Paddy Tipping, MP
Priv Sec: Fiona Butcher
Asst Priv Sec: Frances Slee (020 7210 1022)

OFFICE OF LORD PRIVY SEAL
70 Whitehall, London SW1A 2AT
020 7270 0501 *GTN:* 270 0501

House of Lords, London SW1A 0PW
020 7219 3201 *GTN:* 219 3200
Leader of the House of Lords and Minister for Women (Lord Privy Seal):
    The Rt Hon the Baroness Jay of Paddington
Parly Priv Sec: Eric Martlew, MP
Prin Priv Sec: William Connon
Priv Sec: Russell Hamblin-Boone
Asst Priv Sec: Sharon Wallace

Diary Sec: Sandra Simpson
Support Officer: Anthony Glover
Priv Sec (House of Lords): Mary Robertson
Special Advisers: Clare Cozens, Jo Gibbons
    (020 7270 1294 *Fax:* 020 7270 0491)
Admin Officer: Tracey Goddard

Spokespersons in the House of Lords (Women's Issues): The Baroness Jay of Paddington, The Baroness Amos

Scotland Office

Dover House, Whitehall,
London SW1A 2AU
020 7270 3000 *Fax:* 020 7270 6812
E-mail: scottishsecretary@gov.uk
Website: www.scotland.gov.uk

Parliamentary Branch for all Ministers:
020 7270 6727

The Secretary of State for Scotland represents Scottish interests in the UK Government in matters reserved to the UK Parliament. He is also responsible for ensuring that the reserved policies of the UK Government are presented effectively in Scotland.

The reserved functions include: The constitution, foreign affairs, defence, the civil service, financial and economic matters, national security, immigration and nationality, misuse of drugs, trade and industry, energy (eg electricity, coal, oil and gas, nuclear energy), many aspects of transport (eg railways), social security, employment, abortion, genetics, surrogacy, medicines, broadcasting and equal opportunities.

Secretary of State:
    The Rt Hon Dr John Reid, MP
Priv Sec: Ms Jayne Colquhoun
Asst Priv Sec: Mrs M Thomson
Parly Priv Sec: Frank Roy, MP
Special Advisers:
    Richard Olszewski (020 7270 6779),
    Mike Elrick (020 7270 6757)
Minister of State: Brian Wilson, MP
Priv Sec: David Ferguson
Parly Priv Sec: Sandra Osborne, MP
Advocate General for Scotland:
    Dr Lynda Clark, QC, MP
Priv Sec: Claire Keggie (020 7270 6720)
Legal Secretary to the Advocate General:
    George Duke (020 7270 6810)
Parliamentary Clerk: Michael Chalmers
    (020 7270 6727)

Spokesperson in the House of Lords: The Baroness Ramsay of Cartvale

Scotland Office Management Group
Head of Department: Ian Gordon *(SCS)*
(020 7270 6769)
Head of Division: Eric Ferguson
(020 7270 6800)
Head of Division: Stuart Macdonald
(0131-244 2093)
Principal Finance and Administration Officer:
Norman Kernohan (Edinburgh)
(0131-244 2498)

Social Security, Department of

Richmond House, 79 Whitehall
London SW1A 2NS
020 7238 0800
E-mail: ministers@ms41.dss.gov.uk
Website: www.dss.gov.uk

Adelphi
1–11 John Adam Street
London WC2N 6HT
020 7962 8000

Benefits Agency, Quarry House,
Quarry Hill, Leeds LS2 7UH
0113-232 4000

Central Office DSS
Newcastle upon Tyne NE98 1YX
0191-2135000

New Court, 48 Carey Street
London WC2A 2LS
020 7962 8000

North Fylde Central Offices,
Norcross, Blackpool, Lancs FY5 3TA
01253 856123

Parliamentary Branch for all Ministers
020 7238 0715

The Department is responsible for the social security system in England, Wales and Scotland. The system includes cash benefits for sick and disabled people, Job Seekers Allowance, Retirement Pensions, War Pensions, Family Credit, Child Benefit, and Child Support, The Social Fund, Income Support, Housing Benefit, Community Charge Benefit and the collection and assessment of National Insurance contributions.

Secretary of State:
The Rt Hon Alistair Darling, MP
Prin Priv Sec: Rod Clark
Parly Priv Sec: Ann Coffey, MP
Priv Secs: Beth Russell, Alastair Levy

Diary Sec: Juliet Rogers
Special Advisers: Andrew Maugham,
Elsbeth Johnson
Minister of State for Social Security:
The Rt Hon Jeff Rooker, MP
Priv Sec: David Higlett
Parly Priv Sec: Richard Burden, MP
Asst Priv Secs: Robert Sanguinazzi,
Denise Whitehead
Parliamentary Under-Sec of State:
The Rt Hon the Baroness Hollis of Heigham
Priv Sec: Mary Curran
Asst Priv Sec: Rawlston Wrightman
Parliamentary Under-Sec of State:
Ms Angela Eagle, MP
Priv Sec: Nicole Kett
Asst Priv Secs: Deborah Topping,
Chris Chapman
Parliamentary Under-Sec of State:
Hugh Bayley, MP
Priv Sec: Tricia Griffiths
Asst Priv Secs: Ms Chris McCoy,
David Williams
Parliamentary Clerk: Tim Elms

Spokespersons in the House of Lords: The Baroness Hollis of Heigham, The Baroness Amos

Permanent Secretary: Mrs Rachel Lomax
(*E-mail:* rlomax@rch001.dss.gov.uk)
Priv Sec: Colin Jackson
Director of Corporate Management:
Jonathan Tross *(SCS)*
(*E-mail:* jtross@rch001.dss.gov.uk)
Director of Social Security Policy:
Paul Gray *(SCS)*
(*E-mail:* pgray@ms41.dss.gov.uk)

BENEFITS AGENCY PRINTING AND STATIONERY SERVICE
Norcross, Blackpool
Unit Manager: A Dowlman
01253 332217 *Fax:* 01253 333254

ANALYTICAL SERVICES DIVISION (ASD)
The Adelphi
Director: D Stanton *(SCS)*
020 7962 8611 *Fax:* 020 7962 8795
E-mail: David@asdlondon.dss-asd.gov.uk

ASD1
Collection of statistics relating to Social Security Benefits
DSS Longbenton, Newcastle
Chief Statistician: N Dyson

ASD2
Advice on Operational Issues
Adelphi
Deputy Chief Scientific Officer: D Barnbrook

ASD3
Incapacity, Low Income and Take-up Statistics,
Income Related Benefits
Adelphi
Senior Economic Adviser: G Harris

ASD4
Social Security Statistics, Housing Benefit and
Family Credit, PES Forecasting and Monitoring
Adelphi
Chief Statistician: Ms S Rice

ASD5
Social Research Branch
Adelphi
Chief Research Office: Ms S Duncan

ASD6
Pensions, Disability and Carer Benefits and the
Labour Market Data Base
Adelphi
Senior Economic Adviser: J Ball

ASD7
Labour Market, Incentives and Income-related
Benefits
Senior Economic Adviser: Richard D'Souza

HQ PERSONNEL AND SUPPORT SERVICES
DIVISION
Richmond House
Director of Personnel and Support Services:
  Michael Cayley *(SCS)*

Adelphi
Heads of HQ Personnel: Rita Spicer,
  Nicola Bastin

PLANNING AND FINANCE (SOCIAL SECURITY)
Richmond House
Under-Sec: Stephen Hickey *(SCS)*

COMMUNICATIONS DIRECTORATE
Richmond House
*Director of Information and Press Secretary to
Secretary of State:* Simon Macdowall *(SCS)*

OFFICE OF CHIEF MEDICAL ADVISER
MEDICAL POLICY AND RESEARCH
Adelphi
020 7962 8000
Chief Medical Adviser: Dr Mansel Aylward
Head of Profession. Medical Advice and input to
disability, sickness and carer benefits; industrial
injuries disablement benefit and Industrial
Injuries Advisory Council; War Pensions;
Disability Living Allowance Advisory Board;
Rehabilitation and Back to Work incentives for
disabled people; Welfare Reform Unit; Vaccine
Damage Payments. Senior accountable official
for professional standards and medical quality.
Medical advice and support to medical services'
outsourcing and contract management. Liaison
with external medical profession and Royal
Medical Colleges. Medical Services to Central
Ajudication Services. International relationships.

MEDICAL POLICY MANAGERS
State Incapacity Benefits. Decision Making and
Appeals. Sickness, Disability and Carer Benefits
Review. Welfare Reform Rehabilitation and
Back to Work incentives.
Medical Policy Manager: Dr Philip Sawney
  (Adelphi)

Disability and Carer Benefits: Disability Living
Allowance, Attendance Allowance, Disability
Living Allowance Advisory Board. NHS
Pensions Agency.
Medical Policy Manager: Dr Peter Dewis
  (Adelphi)

DMA (Implementation). European Union of
Medical Advisers in Social Security (UEMASS).
Medical Policy Manager: Dr Paul Stidolph
  (Adelphi)

Contractorisation of Medical Services (IMPACT
Project). Contract Monitoring. Medical Quality
Assurance. Vaccine Damage Payments.
Disability Handbook. Accreditation Issues.
Faculty of Occupational Medicine. Professional
Development.
Medical Policy Manager: Dr Moira Henderson
  (Adelphi)

War Pensions Policy. Validation of medical qual-
ity.
Medical Policy Manager: Dr Anne Braidwood
  (Norcross)

BENEFIT AGENCY MEDICAL SERVICES
Albert Edward House, Preston
01772 898352 *Fax:* 01772 898392
All operational matters relating to the provision
of a medical service to support the delivery of
Incapacity Benefit, Industrial Injuries Scheme,
Disability Living Allowance, Attendance
Allowance, Disability Working Allowance,
Vaccine Damage Payments Scheme. Design and
implementation of work processes, delivery of
service level agreements to a national standard,
agreeing and assuring quality standards to a
national level. Nationwide recruitment and training of doctors including professional and career
development, reward and remuneration systems.

SOLICITOR'S OFFICE
New Court
Solicitor: Marilynne Morgan, CB *(SCS)*
E-mail: mmorgan@nct001.dss.gov.uk
Advice and services on Social Security policy,
War Pensions, and Occupational and Personal
Pensions, Child Support, EC and International
Matters. Legal services to Central Adjudication
Services

SOLA
Director of Legal Services: J Catlin *(SCS)*
Asst Directors of Legal Services:
  J H Swainson, CBE, Mrs G Massiah,
  Mrs F A Logan, S M Cooper, P Milledge,
  C Cooper, H Connell

CIVIL AND CRIMINAL PROCEEDINGS, INDUSTRIAL
RELATIONS AND ESTABLISHMENT MATTERS
SOLB
Solicitor: Ms M A Morgan, CB *(SCS)*
Asst Directors of Legal Services: R G S Aitken,
  Ms S Edwards, S Cooper

POLICY GROUP
Policy Director: Paul Gray *(SCS)*
Head of Policy Group. Overall responsibility for
leadership and management of the policy func-
tion of DSS
Private Secretary: Ina Perry

Ursula Brennan *(SCS)*
Policy Director with special responsibility for
disability, sickness and carer benefits; the War
Pensions and the Contributory Benefits Project.
Oversight of the Medical Policy Branch. Policy
Group lead on people management.

Stephen Hewitt *(SCS)*
Policy Director with special responsibility for
benefits for the economically active; welfare to
work; dependency; and relations with the Child
Support Agency. Policy Group lead on resource
accounting, piloting, project management and
information technology. Oversight of policy
management teams dealing with family support,
child support, job seekers and incentives, international and European relations. ITSA and welfare to work.

Margaret Peirson, CB *(SCS)*
Policy Director with special responsibility for
pensions; policy group lead on deregulation,
audit, the elderly and the self-employed.
Oversight of policy management teams dealing
with pensions (private and state).

Don Brereton *(SCS)*
Policy Director with special responsibility for
income support, housing benefit, council tax
benefit and the social fund; policy group lead on
devolution, social exclusion, training, MPs' correspondence, and relations with the Benefits
Agency and the Social Security Advisory
Committee. Oversight for policy management
teams dealing with income support policy, housing benefit, social fund and homelessness, Social
Security Advisory Committee, central correspondence unit.

Alan Woods *(SCS)*
Policy Director for welfare reform; policy group
lead on active modern service, private provision
and objectives for expenditure. Oversight for
policy management teams dealing with welfare
reform.

Robert Devereux
Policy Director with special responsibility for
fraud strategy

Policy Managers
Child Support (CS)
Policy on child support and liable relatives
Policy Manager: Mike Street

JOB SEEKERS AND PROJECTS LIAISON
Job seekers allowance; job seekers allowance for
16/17 year olds; work incentives; tax-benefits
interaction; earnings top-up
Policy Manager: Angela Lingwood

INCOME SUPPORT POLICY (ISP)

Income Support for elderly and disabled people and lone parents; 16/17 year olds – income support, learning credits and general briefing; persons from abroad; residential and community care issues; structure of income related benefits; income support mortgage interest; uprating; poverty/low income/adequacy – policy, briefing and statistics, EC anti-poverty programme/social exclusion, inner cities; Ministerial sub-committee on London

Policy Manager: Janice Shersby

HOUSING BENEFIT POLICY (HBP)

Policy on housing benefit and council tax benefit; housing benefit and council tax benefit subsidy; students; residual questions on Community Charge Benefit

Policy Manager: Hilary Reynolds

HOUSING BENEFIT MANAGEMENT (HBM)

Housing benefit and council tax benefit administration; monitoring of local authorities; housing benefit and council tax benefit administration subsidy

Policy Manager: Ruth Thompson

WAR AND INDUSTRIAL INJURIES (WII)

War Pensions scheme, War widows; Industrial Injuries

Policy Manager: Pauline Barrett

DISABILITY AND CARER BENEFITS (DCB)

Disability Living Allowance, Attendance Allowance, the Independent Living Funds; Invalid Care Allowance and care benefits issues; Vaccine Damage Payments; Funding of the voluntary sector and Motability

Policy Manager: Charles Ramsden

INCAPACITY BENEFITS AND DISABILITY REFORM (IBDR)

Incapacity Benefit; Disability Working Allowance; Severe Disablement Allowance; Rehabilitation and Back to Work incentives for sick and disabled people; Maternity Benefits and Statutory Sick Pay

Policy Manager: Lesley Richards

FAMILY SUPPORT (FS)

Child Benefit, one-parent benefit and guardian's allowance; family credit; lone parent issues; Cabinet sub-committee on women's issues/ Ministerial group on domestic violence/ family law and policy co-ordination group; interactions between tax and benefit system

Policy Manager: Garvin Bowen

SOCIAL FUND AND RESETTLEMENT (SFR)

Social Fund, Homelessness and the residual functions of the Resettlement Agency

Policy Manager: Ian Williams

OCCUPATIONAL AND PERSONAL PENSIONS (OPP)

Contracting-out of State Earnings-Related Pensions Schemes for salary-related occupational schemes; equal treatment in occupational pensions

Personal and occupational money-purchase pensions; portability and flexibility in non-state pensions

Policy Manager: John Hughes

STATE PENSIONS (SP)

State pensions, Widow's Benefit, incomes of the elderly

Policy Manager: Phillip Morgan

PENSIONS REVIEW TEAM (PRT)

Departmental Maxwell issues; strengthening and supporting occupational pensions, including 'default' options; raising awareness of, and improving availability of information on pensions

Policy Manager: John Hughes

INTERNATIONAL AND EUROPEAN UNION RELATIONS (IER)

Advice on EU and international matters; representation of DSS interests including negotiations; information on other countries' systems, provision of information on UK social security to other countries; policy on migrant workers

Policy Manager: Peter Cleasby

FRAUD STRATEGY PROJECTS

The role of the Fraud Strategy Directorate is to focus on the delivery of the Government's four anti-fraud aims contained in the Green Paper *Beating Fraud is Everyone's Business: securing the future*. These aims are: changing public culture to be less tolerant of fraud; building security into departmental systems from beginning to end; creating an environment in which work against fraud can flourish; and developing a highly skilled anti-fraud profession

Policy Manager: Norman Cockett

DEVOLUTION OF CONSTITUTIONAL REFORM

Policy Manager: Jill Moore

WELFARE REFORM UNIT (WRU)

Policy Director: Alan Woods *(SCS)*

PENSION PROVISION GROUP (PPG)
Policy Manager: Guy Fiegehen

INCAPACITY BENEFITS AND DISABILITY REFORM
Policy Manager: Lesley Richards

WELFARE TO WORK
Policy Manager: Jeremy Groombridge

Executive Agencies: Benefits Agency (BA); Child Support Agency (CSA); Information Technology Services Agency (ITSA); War Pensions Agency

Trade and Industry, Department of

1 Victoria Street, London SW1H 0ET
020 7215 5000 *Fax:* 020 7222 0613
Minicom: 020 7215 6740
Website: www.dti.gov.uk

Business in Europe Enquiries: 020 7215 4080
Fax: 020 7215 8884

Parliamentary Branch for all Ministers:
020 7215 6630

The Headquarters of the Department of Trade and Industry are based in London. Outside London, the DTI is one of the three Departments represented in the Government Offices for the Regions.

The DTI is headed by the Secretary of State for Trade and Industry, who is supported by three Ministers of State and three Parliamentary Under-Secretaries of State. The DTI aims to help business to compete successfully at home, in the rest of Europe and throughout the world. It has a wide range of responsibilities, including industrial sponsorship, trade policy, inward investment, export promotion, energy policy, science and technology, consumer and investor protection, corporate government, industrial relations, company law, support for small and medium-sized industries, e-commerce and the information society. It is also responsible for a number of Executive Agencies: Companies House, the Patent Office, the Insolvency Service, the Employment Tribunals Service, the Radiocommunications Agency and the National Weights and Measures Laboratory.

DTI incorporates the Office of Science and Technology, whose aim is to develop and coordinate, transdepartmentally, Government policy on science, engineering and technology (SET), so as to strengthen the UK's SET capability and maximise its contribution to national economic performance and quality of life. The Head of OST is also the Chief Scientific Adviser to the Government, with direct access to the Prime Minister.

Fuller information on DTI policies, functions and services are available on the DTI worldwide website on the Internet: www.dti.gov.uk

Secretary of State:
The Rt Hon Stephen Byers, MP
Prin Priv Sec: Antony Phillipson
Parly Priv Sec: Ivan Lewis, MP
Special Advisers: Dan Corry, Ms Jo Moore
Private Secs: Edward Barker,
Christopher Woolard
Asst Priv Secs: Nick Wellington, David Snell
Minister of State for Energy and Competitiveness in Europe:
The Rt Hon Helen Liddell, MP
Senior Priv Sec: Richard Riley
Parly Priv Sec: Derek Twigg, MP
Minister for Trade:
The Rt Hon Richard Caborn, MP
Priv Sec: Graeme Cornell
Parly Priv Sec: Ben Chapman, MP
Minister of State (Minister for Small Business and E-Commerce): Patricia Hewitt, MP
Priv Sec: Gaynor Jeffrey
Assist Priv Sec: Joana Smith
Parly Priv Sec: Anne Campbell, MP
Parliamentary Under-Sec of State (Minister for Competition and Consumer Affairs):
Dr Kim Howells, MP
Priv Sec: Dawn Parr
Parliamentary Under-Sec of State (Minister for Competitiveness): Alan Johnson, MP
Priv Sec: Simon Lancaster
Parliamentary Under-Sec of State (Minister for Science and Innovation):
The Lord Sainsbury of Turville
Priv Sec: Simon Evans

Spokesmen in the House of Lords: The Lord Sainsbury of Turville, The Lord McIntosh of Haringey

British Trade International Board Chairman:
Sir Martin Laing, CBE
Priv Sec: Sarah Borron
Chief Executive, British Trade International:
Sir David Wright, KCMG, LVO *(SCS)*
Permanent Secretary:
Sir Michael Scholar, KCB *(SCS)*
Priv Sec: Julie Davis
(SCS): A Hutton, CB, Dr Catherine Bell,
A Macdonald, CB, A Walker, D Nissen (The Solicitor), J Spencer, CB, D Durie, CMG,
John Taylor, OBE

Parliamentary Clerk: Tim Williams
Chief Scientific Adviser to the Government and Head of Office of Science and Technology:
Sir Robert May, FRS *(SCS)*
Priv Sec: Dr Robert Clay
Director-General, Research Councils:
Dr John Taylor, OBE *(SCS)*
Senior Personal Sec: Wendy Carless

TRADE POLICY GROUP
151 Buckingham Palace Road,
London SW1W 9SS

Director-General: Tony Hutton, CB *(SCS)*
Director Trade Policy: John Hunt *(SCS)*
Director New Issues and Developing Countries:
Charles Bridge *(SCS)*
Director Trade Facilitation and Import Policy:
Alec Berry *(SCS)*
Director International Economics:
Christopher Moir *(SCS)*
Director Europe: John Alty *(SCS)*
Director Export Control and Non-proliferation:
Dr Roger Heathcote *(SCS)*
Director Export Control Organisation:
Susan Haird
Director Non-proliferation: John Neve

EXPORT PROMOTION GROUP
Kingsgate House, 66–74 Victoria Street,
London SW1E 6SW
020 7215 5000

Chief Executive:
Sir David Wright, KCMG, LVO *(SCS)*
Director Markets and Sectors:
Mark Gibson *(SCS)*
Director Export Promotion (Middle East, Near East and North Africa): Suresh Khanna *(SCS)*
Director Export Promotion (Asia Pacific):
Mike Cohen *(SCS)*
Director Export Promotion (Business in Europe): Keith Levinson *(SCS)*
Director Export Promotion (Former Soviet Union, Central and Eastern Europe):
Keith Levinson *(SCS)*
Director Export Promotion (The Americas):
Michael Mowlam *(SCS)*
Director Trade Promotions (Sub Saharan Africa and South Asia): Vincent Fear *(SCS)*
Director Sectors, Services, Outward Investment:
Robin Lamb *(SCS)*
Deputy Director-General and Director:
David Hall *(SCS)*
Policy, Resources and Personnel Directorate, British Trade International PRPD2:
Director: Clive Stitt

Head PRPD1: Ian Fletcher
Director Export Services: Alan Reynolds *(SCS)*
Director Infrastructure and Energy Projects:
John Rhodes *(SCS)*

INDUSTRY GROUP
151 Buckingham Palace Road
London SW1W 9SS
020 7215 5000

Director-General: Alastair Macdonald *(SCS)*
Director Space and Director-General British National Space Centre: Dr Colin Hicks *(SCS)*
Director Innovation, Research and Technology Policy: Peter Bunn
Deputy Director-General Space Technology, Chairman BNSC and Space Technology Advisory Board: Dr David Leadbeater
Director Space Applications and Transportation: Miss Paula Freedman
Director Chemicals and Biotechnology:
Derek Davis *(SCS)*
Director Chemicals: Geraldine Alliston
Director Biotechnology:
Dr Monica Darnbrough *(SCS)*
Director Engineering Industries:
Mike O'Shea *(SCS)*
Director, Aerospace and Defence Industries Policy: John Neilson
Director, Aerospace and Defence Industries Technology and Equipment:
Shelley Ian Charik
Technical Director, Aerospace and Defence Industries: Malcolm Ralph
Director Mechanical and Electrical Engineering Industries: Hugh Brown
Director Automotive Components and Technology: Iain Cameron
Director Motor Vehicles: John Dennis
Director Metals, Minerals and Shipbuilding:
Erica Zimmer
Director Innovation Policy and Standards:
Robert Foster *(SCS)*
Assistant Director Innovation Policy:
Gillian Hunter
Director Technology Economics Statistics and Evaluation: John Barber
Director Standards and Technical Regulations:
David Reed
Director National Measurement System:
John Hobday
Director Innovation Unit: (Vacant) *(SCS)*
Director Environment: Alistair Keddie *(SCS)*
Director Consumer Goods, Business and Postal Services: Derek Davis *(SCS)*
Director Posts, Director Post Office Reform:
Judy Britton

Director Consumer Goods/Materials, Consumer and Business Services: Brian Hopson
Head of Communications and Information Industries: Bill Macintyre *(SCS)*
Director UK Communications Policy:
David Lumley
Director Emu and Enlargement:
Tim Abraham, CMG
Director Technology Policy and Innovation:
Christopher Holmes
Director Content and Applications:
Chris Matthews
Director Electronic Communications Bill:
Stephen Pride
Director Industrial Sponsorship Support Unit:
Martin Berry *(SCS)*
Director Industry Economics and Statistics:
Nicholas Owen *(SCS)*

ENERGY GROUP
1 Victoria Street, London SW1H 0ET
020 7215 5000

Director-General: Anna Walker *(SCS)*
Deputy Director-General: Neil Hirst
Energy Policy Technology, Analysis and Coal Director Coal: Mike Atkinson *(SCS)*
Director Energy Utilities Technologies: Jonathan Green *(SCS)*
Director Energy Technologies:
Godfrey Bevan *(SCS)*
Chief Engineering Inspector:
Peter Fenwick *(SCS)*
Director Energy Policy and Analysis Unit: Nigel Peace *(SCS)*
Director, BNFL Public Private Partnership Team: Dr Stephen Sklaroff *(SCS)*
Director Economics: Adrian Gault
Energy Head, Energy Statistics: Dissemination and Analysis: Chris Bryant
Director Nuclear Industries: Helen Leiser *(SCS)*
Director UKAEA, Nuclear Decommissioning and Fusion: Melvyn Draper
Director, Reform of Energy Regulation:
Keith Long
Director Euratom, Nuclear Safety, Security and Emergency Planning: Dr Elaine Drage
Director Oil and Gas: Geoff Dart *(SCS)*
Director International Economics, Oil, Taxation, Downstream Oil and Gas Markets and Policy:
Geoffrey Riggs
Director Hydrocarbons Exploration and Licensing: John Brooks, CBE
Director Oil and Gas Development and Production: Simon Toole

REGIONAL AND SME GROUP
1 Victoria Street, London SW1H 0ET
020 7215 5558

Director-General: David Durie, CMG *(SCS)*
Deputy Director/Director Business Links:
Peter Waller *(SCS)*
Director Regional Policy: David Smith *(SCS)*
Director Regional European Funds:
Keith Masson *(SCS)*
Director Regional Assistance:
Andrew Steele *(SCS)*
Director Resources: John Thompson *(SCS)*
Director Management Best Practice:
Dr Kenneth Poulter *(SCS)*
Director, SME Policy: Callum Johnston
Director SME Technology:
Richard Allpress *(SCS)*
Director Business Link Development and Operations: Haf Merrifield
Director Business Link Finance: Peter Bentley
Director Business Link Services:
Mrs Pat Jackson
Director, People and Services: Tim Evans
Chief Executive of Invest in Britain Bureau:
Andrew Fraser

CORPORATE AND CONSUMER AFFAIRS GROUP
1 Victoria Street, London SW1H 0ET
020 7215 5000

Director-General: Dr Catherine Bell *(SCS)*
Director Employment Relations:
Paul Salvidge *(SCS)*
Director, Consumer Affairs: Stephen Naddrill
Director Consumer Safety Strategy and Safety:
Peter Mason
Director Consumer Policy: Janice Munday
Director (UK) Competition and Regulation Economics: David Mines
Director EC and International Competition Policy: Mark Hutton
Director Competition and Regulation Economics: David Mines
Director Enterprise Unit: Mark Higson
Director Employee Involvement, EU and Partnership and Working Time:
Dr Elizabeth Baker
Director Special Employment Rights:
Robert Niblett
Director National Minimum Wage: Nicola Carter
Director Employment Market Analysis and Research: Mark Beatson
Director, Employment Rights and Tribunals:
Nicola Carter
Director, Fairness at Work: Jonathan Startup

Director Company Law and Investigations:
Richard Rogers *(SCS)*
Director Company Law Reform: Robert Burns
Director Financial Reporting Policy:
John Grewe
Director of Investigations and Inspector of
Companies: Grahame Harp
Director, Competition Policy and Utilities
Review Team: Ms Rolande Anderson *(SCS)*

LEGAL SERVICES GROUP
10 Victoria Street, London SW1H 0NN
020 7215 5000

The Solicitor and Director-General:
David Nissen, CB *(SCS)*
Director Legal Services A: John Stanley *(SCS)*
Legal Director A1: Gillian Richmond
Legal Director A2: John Roberts
Legal Director A3: Nuala O'Flynn
Legal Director A4: Stephen Hyett
Legal Adviser A5: Kate Lee
Director Legal Services B: Philip Bovey *(SCS)*
Legal Director B1: Richard Baker
Legal Director B2: Richard Perkins
Legal Director B3: Charles Raikes
Legal Director B4: Bryan Welch
Legal Director B5: Serena Hardy
Legal Adviser B6: Nisha Arora
Director Legal Services C:
Alex Brett-Holt *(SCS)*
Legal Director C1: Mark Bucknill
Legal Director C2: Alan Woods
Legal Director C3: Clive Osborne
Legal Director C4: Tony Susman
Director Legal Services D: Tessa Dunstan *(SCS)*
Legal Director D1: Scott Milligan
Legal Director D2: Lal Nawbatt
Director Legal Resources Management and
Business Law Unit: Karl Warren *(SCS)*

RESOURCES AND SERVICES GROUP
1 Victoria Street, London SW1H 0ET
020 7215 5000

Director-General: Jonathan Spencer *(SCS)*
Director Staff Personnel Operations:
Rob Wright *(SCS)*
Director Senior Staff Management:
Katharine Elliott *(SCS)*
Director, Staff Policy and Pay:
Barbara Habberjam *(SCS)*
Director Information Management and Process
Engineering: Dick Wheeler *(SCS)*
Director Estates and Facilities Management:
Michael Coolican *(SCS)*
Director Internal Audit: Roger Louth *(SCS)*

Director Finance and Resource Management:
Jonathan Phillips *(SCS)*
Director Finance: Edmund Hosker
Director Resource Management: Hugh Savill
Director Resource Accounting: Keith Hills
Director Knowledge Management Unit:
Tim Soane

OFFICE OF SCIENCE AND TECHNOLOGY
Albany House, 94–98 Petty France
London SW1H 9ST
020 7271 2000

Chief Scientific Adviser and Head of Office of
Science and Technology:
Sir Robert May, FRS *(SCS)*
Director Transdepartmental Science and
Technology: Jo Durning *(SCS)*
Director International Science and Technology:
Dr Miles Parker
Director LINK: Alan Wootton
Director Foresight: Stephen Spivey
Director Science in Government: Mrs Pat Sellers
Director-General Research Councils:
Dr John Taylor, OBE *(SCS)*
Director Science and Engineering Base:
Dr Martin Earwicker *(SCS)*
Director Research Councils: Miss Fiona Price
Director Projects: Richard King
Director Finance and Central Issues:
Keith Root

CENTRAL FUNCTIONS AND THE MINISTERIAL
ORGANISATION
1 Victoria Street, London SW1H 0ET
020 7215 5000

Chief Economic Adviser: David Coates *(SCS)*
Chief Adviser on Statistics: Ms Janet Dougharty
Director, Competitiveness, Central Directorate:
David Evans
Director, Competitiveness Unit: Sarah Chambers
Director, Enterprise Unit: Mark Hyson
Director, Future Unit: John Reynolds
Principal Private Secretary: Antony Phillipson

COMMUNICATIONS
Director Publicity and Internal
Communications: Peter Burke *(SCS)*
Director of News: Matt Tee
Deputy Director News: Colin Seabrook
Director Publicity: Peter Burke *(SCS)*

Executive Agencies: Companies House;
Employment Tribunals Service (ETS);
Insolvency Service; National Weights and
Measures Laboratory (NWML); Patent Office;
Radiocommunications Agency (RA)

HM Treasury

Treasury Chambers, Parliament Street,
London SW1P 3AG
020 7270 5000 *Fax:* 020 7270 5653
E-mail: firstname.surname@hm-treasury.gov.uk
Website: www.hmt.gov.uk

Parliamentary Branch (for all Ministers)
020 7270 5005/07/5183
Ministerial Correspondence (for all Ministers)
020 7270 5163

The offices of the Prime Minister and First Lord of the Treasury, and of the Government Whips (some of whom are formally members of the Treasury Board) are not part of the Departmental Treasury headed by the Chancellor of the Exchequer.

Prime Minister and First Lord of the Treasury:
   The Rt Hon Tony Blair, MP
Chancellor of the Exchequer:
   The Rt Hon Gordon Brown, MP
Prin Priv Sec: Tom Scholar
Priv Secretaries: James Papps, Nicholas Joicey
Asst Priv Sec: Pam Keenan
Parly Priv Sec: John Healey, MP
Parly Clerk: David S Martin
Senior Economic Adviser: Ed Balls
   (020 7270 4941)
Special Advisers: Ian Austin, Sue Nye,
   Chris Wales
Chief Sec to the Treasury:
   The Rt Hon Andrew Smith, MP
Priv Sec: Deborah Nickerson
Parly Priv Sec: Joan Ryan, MP
Special Advisers: Spencer Livermore
   (020 7270 5027), Edward Milliband
Paymaster General: Ms Dawn Primarolo, MP
Priv Sec: Sarah Knight
Parly Priv Sec: Chris Pond, MP
Financial Secretary: Stephen Timms, MP
Priv Sec: Chris Martin
Parly Priv Sec: Vernon Coaker, MP
Economic Secretary: Ms Melanie Johnson, MP
Priv Sec: Jo-Anne Daniels
Parliamentary Secretary to the Treasury:
   The Rt Hon Ann Taylor, MP
Prin Priv Sec: M Maclean
Lords Commissioners: Robert Ainsworth, MP,
   Graham Allen, MP, Clive Betts, MP, Keith
   Bradley, MP, James Dowd, MP, David
   Jamieson, MP, Thomas McAvoy, MP, Greg
   Pope, MP
Assistant Whips: David Clelland, MP, Michael
   Hall, MP, Kevin Hughes, MP, Anne McGuire,
   MP, Tony McNulty, MP, Gerry Sutcliffe, MP,
   Don Touhig, MP

Spokesman in the House of Lords: The Lord
McIntosh of Haringey

DIRECTORATE MANAGEMENT
Permanent Secretary:
   Sir Andrew Turnbull, KCB, CVO *(SCS)*

MACROECONOMIC POLICY AND PROSPECTS
Director: Gus O'Donnell, CB *(SCS)*
Deputy Directors: Jonathan Taylor** *(SCS)*,
   Joe Grice *(SCS)*

INTERNATIONAL FINANCE
Director:
   Sir Nigel Wicks, KCB, CVO, CBE *(SCS)*
Deputy Directors: Paul McIntyre** *(SCS)*,
   Jon Cunliffe *(SCS)*

BUDGET AND PUBLIC FINANCES
Director: Robert Culpin *(SCS)*
Deputy Director: Colin Mowl *(SCS)*
Nick Macpherson

PUBLIC SERVICES
Director: John Gieve, CB *(SCS)*
Deputy Directors: Norman Glass, CB*,
   Gill Noble, CB, Peter Sedgwick,
   Adam Sharples *(SCS)*

FINANCIAL MANAGEMENT, REPORTING AND AUDIT
Director: Andrew Likierman** *(SCS)*
Deputy Director: Jamie Mortimer* *(SCS)*

FINANCE REGULATION AND INDUSTRY
Director: Sir Steve Robson, CB *(SCS)*
Deputy Directors: Brian Rigby,
   Harry Bush *(SCS)*, Robin Fellgett *(SCS)*

PERSONNEL ACCOMMODATION AND INFORMATION
SERVICES
Director: Margaret O'Mara *(SCS)*
Non-Executive Director: Margaret Exley
*combined deputy director and head of standing
   team
**head of cross-directorate standing team
Heads of Directorate Standing Teams: Sam
   Beckett, Malcolm Bradbury,
   John Breckenridge, Rob Brightwell,
   Alastair Bridges, Simon Brooks, Mike Burt,
   Harry Bush, Chris Butler, Ian Carruthers,
   Anita Charlesworth, John Colling, Ian Cooper,
   Peter Curwen, Melanie Dawes, David Deaton,
   Paula Diggle, John Dodds, Tim Dowse,
   Ros Dunn, Elwyn Evans, Colin Farthing,
   Robin Fellgett, Chris Ford, Donald Franklin,
   Alex Gibbs, John Gieve, Norman Glass,
   Dilwyn Griffiths, Joseph Halligan,
   Jim Hibberd, Andrew Hudson,
   Nicholas Holgate, Anne-Marie Jones,
   Peter Kane, Bernadette Kelly, Chris M Kelly,

Sue Killen, Andrew Kilpatrick,
John Kingman, Ruth Kosmin, David Lawton,
Sue Lewis, David Loweth, Stephen Matthews,
Jeremy Moore, Jamie Mortimer,
Graham Parker, Mark Parkinson,
Dave Ramsden, Mike Richardson,
Brian Rigby, Allen Ritchie, David Roe,
Kevin Ross, Philip Rutnam, Peter Schofield,
Adam Sharples, Michael Swan, Ian Taylor,
Rick Todd, Helen Tuffs, Ian Walker,
Mike Williams, Tim Wilson, Phil Wynn Owen
Treasury Representative Abroad:
Stephen Pickford

Executive Agencies: HM Customs and Excise;
Inland Revenue; National Savings (NS); Office
for National Statistics (ONS); Royal Mint; UK
Debt Management Office (DMO); Valuation
Office

Treasury Solicitor and HM Procurator General

Queen Anne's Chambers
28 Broadway, London SW1H 9JS
020 7210 3000 *Fax:* 020 7222 6006

Provides litigation and advisory services to
Government departments and other publicly
funded bodies in England and Wales. Also
administers estates of people who die intestate
with no known kin.

HM Procurator-General and Treasury Solicitor:
Sir Anthony Hammond, KCB *(SCS)*
Deputy Treasury Solicitor: A Inglese *(SCS)*
M A Blythe, CB *(SCS)*
R N Ricks, M Thomas *(SCS)*,
  D Brummell *(SCS)*, D Macrae *(SCS)*
Mrs L Addison, R Aitken, Mrs D Babar,
  J R J Braggins, J Burnet, M C L Carpenter,
  F D W Clarke, Mrs V Collett, J E Collins,
  Mrs D Collins, S T Harker, M J Hemming,
  C House, Miss R Jeffreys, J Jones,
  P Kilgarreff, A D Lawton, A Leithead,
  Mrs I G Letwin, B McKay, P R Messer,
  Miss F Nash, Ms L Nicoll, Mrs J B C Oliver,
  D Palmer, A Perrett, R J Phillips, A Ridout,
  A J Sandal, E B Solomons, Miss J V Stokes

Wales Office

OFFICE OF THE SECRETARY OF STATE
FOR WALES
Gwydyr House, Whitehall,
London SW1A 2ER
020 7270 3000 *GTN:* 1208
E-mail: 020 7270 0568
Website: www.ossw.wales.gov.uk

The National Assembly for Wales
Cardiff Bay, Cardiff CF99 1NA
029 2082 5111
Website: www.wales.gov.uk

New Crown Building, Cathays Park,
Cardiff CF1 3NQ
029 2082 5111 *GTN:* 1208
Telex: 498228
Fax enquiries should be made through
the switchboard

Parliamentary Branch for all Ministers:
020 7270 0554

The Welsh Office was established in 1965, following the creation of the Office of the Secretary
of State for Wales in October 1964. In 1997, the
Welsh electorate voted for the establishment of a
directly-elected Assembly which on 1 July 1999
took over the responsibilities of the Welsh
Office, for the implementation of Government
policies in Wales including health, the environment, transport and agriculture, as well as many
other functions. The Secretary of State continues
to represent Wales in the Cabinet. The Welsh
Office was renamed The Wales Office in
October 1999.

Secretary of State:
  The Rt Hon Paul Murphy, MP
  Prin Priv Sec: Simon Morris
  Asst Priv Sec: Ms Cherie Jones
Special Adviser: Hywel Francis
Parly Private Sec: Nick Ainger, MP
Parliamentary Under-Secretary of State: David
  Hanson, MP
Priv Sec: Stephen George
*Head of Office of the Secretary of State for
  Wales:* Alison Jackson
Parly Clerk: Michael Williams

Spokesperson in the House of Lords:
The Baroness Farrington of Ribbleton

INFORMATION DIVISION
Director of News: Pat Wilson

FINANCE
Head of Finance Services: John Williams
POLICY GROUP 1
Head of Group: Anne Morrice
Responsibility for: Industry and Training;
Agriculture; Transport, Planning and
Environment
POLICY GROUP 2
Head of Group: Sarah Canning
Responsibility for: Education; Health; Local
Government Finance, Housing and Social
Services

NON-MINISTERIAL DEPARTMENTS

Building Societies Commission

25 The North Colonnade, Canary Wharf,
London E14 5HS
020 7676 1000
First Commissioner and Chairman:
G E Fitchew, CMG *(SCS)*
Deputy Chairman: Ms C Sergeant
Commissioners: Sir James Birrell, N Fox-
Bassett, J M Palmer, S Mundy,
F G Sunderland, F E Worsley
Secretary: G Johnson
Legal Adviser: Ms P Henderson
*For Information on Registry of Friendly
Societies and Friendly Societies Commission –
see separate entries*

Charity Commission

Harmsworth House, 13-15 Bouverie Street,
London EC4Y 8DP
0870-333 0123 *Fax:* 020 7674 2300
The Commission is responsible for the registration and supervision of registered charities in
England and Wales. Under the Charities Act
1993 it maintains a Register of Charities.
Registered charities with a turnover of over
£10,000 a year are monitored on the basis of the
annual report and accounts they are required to
submit. The Commission provides advice and
has powers to investigate misconduct and mis-
management and take remedial action.

Chief Commissioner: John Stoker *(SCS)*
Commissioner: Michael Carpenter *(SCS)*
Commissioners (part-time): John Bonds,
Julia Unwin
Executive Director: Lynne Berry
Director of Resources: Bill Richardson
Director of Policy: Richard Carter
Regional Operations Manager: Christina Parry

2nd Floor, 20 Kings Parade,
Queens Dock, Liverpool L3 4DQ
0870 333 0123 *Fax:* 0151-703 1555

Commissioner (part-time): Jean Warburton
Regional Operations Manager: Neil Peterson

Woodfield House, Tangier, Taunton
Somerset TA1 4BL
0870 333 0123 *Fax:* 01823 345003

Regional Operations Manager:
Ms Ceinwen Thorne

Crown Estate

16 Carlton House Terrace,
London SW1Y 5AH
020 7210 4377 *Fax:* 020 7930 8187
Website: www.crownestate.co.uk
The Crown Estate is an estate in land. Its origins
go back at least to the reign of King Edward the
Confessor. It includes a wide variety of land and
landed property deriving from a number of different sources.
Up to the reign of King George III the reigning Sovereign received the rents and profits of
the Crown Estate. Since 1760 the surplus rents
and profits (after deducting management expenses) have been, at the beginning of each reign,
surrendered by the Sovereign to Parliament as
part of the arrangements for the Civil List. The
estate itself remains part of the hereditary pos-
sessions of the Sovereign in right of the Crown.
It is not a government department but neither is
it part of the private estate of the reigning
monarch.
The Crown Estate is administered by a Board
of Commissioners appointed by the Sovereign.
Today the Crown Estate includes valuable urban
property, mostly in London; Windsor Great
Parks and Forest; agricultural estates in various
parts of England and Scotland; and foreshore and
seabed around the coast of the United Kingdom.

First Commissioner and Chairman (part-time):
Sir Denys Henderson, Kt, MA, LLB, FRSA
Second Commissioner and Chief Executive:
Sir Christopher Howes, KCVO, CB, BSc,
MPhil, FRICS, HonFRIBA
Commissioners (part-time): J H M Norris, CBE,
DL, FRAgS, HonFCIWEM,
The Lord De Ramsey, DL, FRAgS,
D E G Griffiths, CBE, FCMA,
I Grant, CBE, FRAgS, Mrs Honor Chapman,
CBE, FRICS, MRTPI, BSc, MPhil,
R R Spinney, FRICS
Director of Finance and Administration:
R Bright, MA(Cantab)
Director of Urban Estates: N Borrett, FRICS
Legal Adviser: D Harris, MA(Oxon)
Head of Corporate Policy and Personnel:
M J Gravestock

HM Customs and Excise

New King's Beam House,
22 Upper Ground, London SE1 9PJ
020 7620 1313 *Fax:* 020 7865 5048
Website:
www.open.gov.uk/customs/c&ehome.htm

HM Customs and Excise is one of the two main tax collecting Departments in the United Kingdom. It collects and administers taxes and duties imposed in the annual Finance Acts and by other legislation. This amounts to over 40% of the total central government revenue from taxation and consists mainly of indirect taxes on consumer expenditure (indirect taxation), including Value Added Tax (VAT), excise duties on hydrocarbon oils, tobacco products, alcoholic drinks, betting and gaming and Insurance Premium Tax and Air Passenger Duty. The Department is also responsible for the collection and administration of the landfill tax. It also collects customs duties and agricultural levies on behalf of the EU.

Customs' other main responsibility is the enforcement of import prohibitions and restrictions on drugs, firearms, indecent material and endangered species. The Department is also responsible for the compilation of trade statistics and undertakes a variety of non-revenue functions on behalf of other government departments and public bodies.

Ministers: Chancellor of the Exchequer:
 The Rt Hon Gordon Brown, MP
Paymaster General: Ms Dawn Primarolo, MP

THE BOARD
Chairman: Dame Valerie Strachan, DCB *(SCS)*
 (Richard Broadbent from 1 February 2000)
Priv Sec: Paul Gerrard
Asst Priv Sec: Julie Mellon
Deputy Chairman: T Walker, CB *(SCS)*
 (020 7865 5013)
Priv Sec: Shahida Rai
Personal Sec: Angela Pinto
Commissioners (SCS):
 Richard Allen (020 7865 5933),
 Mike Norgrove (020 7865 5978),
 Martin Brown (020 7865 5016),
 David Howard (020 7865 5019),
 Terry Byrne (020 7865 5025),
 Ray McAfee (020 7865 5445),
 Tony Rawsthorne (020 7865 5405)
Solicitor: David Pickup *(SCS)* (020 7865 5123)
Deputy Solicitor: Gordon Fotherby *(SCS)*
 (020 7865 5123)

Director, Corporate Services:
 Alan Paynter *(SCS)* (01702 367036)
Board Secretariat: John Bone
Corporate Development Group: Gary Jones
Director of Communications: Peter Rose
Director, Personnel and Finance:
 Richard Allen *(SCS)*
Directorate Support Unit: Jim Williamson
Financial Management Division: Mike Hanson
Estates and Security: Diana Barrett
Personnel Management: Mike Rickwood
Internal Audit Division: Carol Piper
Director, VAT Policy: Martin Brown *(SCS)*
Strategy and International: Lance Railton
Supply: Ian Stewart
Commercial: Stewart Kingaby
Social: Chris Talbot
Collection: Liz Allen
Director, Customs Policy:
 Tony Rawsthorne *(SCS)*
Strategy and International Group:
 William Parker
Criminal and Enforcement Policy: Donald Toor
Trade Policy Group: Athol Cowley
International Assistance: Peter Bachelor
European Union: Kathy Barnes
Director, Excise and Central Policy:
 David Howard *(SCS)*
Excise and Policy Group: Sarah Harlen
Excise and Policy Group: Heather Massie
Economics and Statistics Division:
 Derek Hodgson
Budget and Central Unit: Robin MacLachlan
Director, Fraud and Intelligence:
 Terry Byrne *(SCS)*
Fraud and Intelligence Policy Unit: Mike Wells
National Investigation Service: Paul Evans
National Intelligence Division: Mike Blythe
Operations Anti-Smuggling: Graham Hooker
Director, Operational Policy:
 Mike Norgrove *(SCS)*
Compliance Projects (Non-IS): David Chilver
Taxes and Duties Management: Andre Howard
IS Compliance Projects: Maurice Kingdon
Director, Outfield: Ray McAfee *(SCS)*
Solicitor: David Pickup *(SCS)*
Deputy Solicitor: Gordon Fotherby *(SCS)*
Corporate Legal Services: Ian Napper
Head of Prosecutions Group: David North
Prosecutions International Criminal:
 Annabelle Bolt
Prosecutions Special Casework: Derek Pratt
VAT and Excise Advisory: Michael Michael
Customs International Advisory:
 David McIntyre
LEGIS: Angelos Agathanglelou

VAT and Excise Tribunals: John Flood
Senior Legal Specialist Indirect Taxes:
　Sara Linton
Senior Legal Specialist Indirect Taxes:
　John Tester
Director, Corporate Services:
　Alan Paynter *(SCS)*
Accounting Services Divisions: Doug Robinson
Central Services Division: Robin Tough
Corporate Services Southend: Fiona Porter
Departmental Purchasing Unit: Dave Mooney
Management Consultancy Services:
　Peter Cox-Bisham
Training Services Division: Malcolm Smith
Tariff and Statistical Office: Mike McDowall
VAT Operations: Matt Corcoran
Single Currency Programme Team:
　John Moscrop
Corporate IS Division: Dave Gostling
Information Technology Division:
　Steve Cracknell
Infrastructure PFI: Tim Doran
Strategy/Closer Working: John Spencer
Customer Services: Eunice Simpkins
IT Development: Nigel Green

Executive Agencies: 24 HM Customs and Excise Executive Units

Estyn: Her Majesty's Inspectorate for Education and Training in Wales

Phase 1, Government Buildings,
Ty Glas Road, Llanishen, Cardiff CF14 2FQ
029 2032 5000 *Fax:* 029 2075 8182
or *Secure Fax* 029 2076 5201

Estyn's aim is to raise standards and quality in education and training in Wales through independent inspection and advice.
Estyn's objectives are to:
– set up and maintain system of inspection of schools and funded nursery provision;
– to provide well-informed and sound advice on education and training to the National Assembly for Wales and to make public good practice based on inspection evidence;
– to provide well-informed and sound assessments of further education provision;
– to undertake the planning and recruitment for the inspection of government-funded training and the work of the careers companies.

HM Chief Inspector: Miss S Lewis
Head of Administration: Mrs Shan Howells

Forestry Commission

231 Corstorphine Road,
Edinburgh EH12 7AT
0131-334 0303 *Fax:* 0131-334 3047
E-mail: enquiries@forestry.gov.uk
Website: www.forestry.gov.uk

The Forestry Commission is the government department responsible for forestry policy in Great Britain. It reports directly to forestry ministers to whom it is responsible for advice on forestry policy and for the implementation of that policy. The Minister of Agriculture, Fisheries and Food has responsibility for forestry in England, Scottish Ministers have responsibility for forestry in Scotland, and the National Assembly for Wales has responsibility for forestry in Wales. For matters affecting forestry in Britain as a whole, all three Ministers have equal responsibility, but the Minister of Agriculture, Fisheries and Food takes the lead.

Chairman: Sir Peter Hutchison, Bt, CBE
Director-General and Deputy Chairman:
　D J Bills
Chief Executive Forest Enterprise:
　Dr R McIntosh
Secretary to the Commissioners: W F G Strang
Commissioners (Non-Executive):
　T A Bruce Jones, J W Edmonds,
　Dr V Edwards, H G Fetherstonhaugh,
　John James, OBE, G Wardell

SECRETARIAT
Head of Secretariat: F Strang
　Policy Support: P Edwards
　Communications: C Morton

CORPORATE SERVICES
Head of Corporate Services: D Macniven *(SCS)*
　Personnel: W J Anderson
　Finance and Corporate Planning:
　　E K Arthurs
　Internal Audit: Mrs L Holmes
　Business Services: A T Mitchell
Head of Policy Practice: P Hill-Tout
Head of Country Services: R C Herbert
Chief Conservators:
　England (Cambridge): T J D Rollinson
　Scotland (Edinburgh): D B Henderson-Howat
　Wales (Aberystwyth): S E Hewitt

Executive Agencies: Forest Enterprise; Forest Research

Friendly Societies Commission

25 The North Colonnade, Canary Wharf,
London E14 5HS
020 7676 1000
Chairman: M Roberts
Commissioners: F da Rocha, Mrs S Brown,
   J A Geddes, B Richardson, Miss P Triggs
Secretary: Ms J Erskine
Legal Adviser: J Wylde

*For information on Building Societies
Commission and Registry of Friendly Societies –
see separate entries*

Inland Revenue

Somerset House, Strand,
London WC2R 1LB
020 7438 6622 *Fax:* 020 7438 6494
Website: www.open.gov.uk/inrev/
The Board of Inland Revenue administers and
collects income tax, corporation tax, capital
gains tax, stamp duty, inheritance tax, petroleum
revenue tax and National Insurance
Contributions, and advises the Chancellor of the
Exchequer on tax policy. The Head Office is in
London.

The Department is organised into a series of
accountable management units under Next
Steps. The day to day operations, collecting tax
and National Insurance Contributions and providing internal support services are carried out
by Executive Offices. The Department's
Valuation Office is an Executive Agency responsible for providing valuation services for rating,
council tax, Inland Revenue and other public
sector purposes.

Ministers: Chancellor of the Exchequer
Paymaster General: Ms Dawn Primarolo, MP
Chairman: Nick Montagu, CB *(SCS)*
Priv Sec to Chairman: Miss C Lunney
Asst Priv Sec to Chairman: Mrs E Neads
Deputy Chairmen: S C T Matheson, CB *(SCS)*,
   G H Bush, CB *(SCS)*
Director General: T Flesher *(SCS)*
Chief Executive VOA: M A Johns *(SCS)*
Head Office, Directors (SCS): J Gant,
   G Makhlouf, D Hartnett, S Jones, B A Mace,
   E J Gribbon, Ms J Williams, J E Yard,
   R R Martin, N C Munro, D A Smith
Director Analytical Services Division:
   R Ward *(SCS)*
Sen Economic Adviser: W M McNie *(SCS)*

NICO – National Insurance Contribution Office:
Director: George Bertram (Executive Office)

Executive Agencies: Valuation Office; 25
Inland Revenue Executive Units

National Investment and Loans Office

1 King Charles Street, London SW1A 2AP
020 7270 3861 *Fax:* 020 7270 6075
The National Investment and Loans Office was
formed on April 1, 1980, to provide common
office services to the National Debt Office and
the Public Works Loan Board. Since 1
November 1996 it has also incorporated the
Office of HM Paymaster General.

The National Debt Office was established in
1786 with the purpose of reducing, or eliminating, the National Debt. Only rudimentary elements of that function remain and its current role
is mainly the investment of a series of
Government funds (National Insurance Fund,
National Savings and the National Lottery).

The Public Works Loan Board is an independent and unpaid statutory body which originated
in 1793 and became established on a permanent
basis in 1817. Since 1946 it has consisted of 12
unpaid Commissioners appointed by the Crown
to hold office for 4 years. Their functions,
derived chiefly from the Public Works Loan Act
1875 and the National Loan Act 1968, are to
consider loan applications from local authorities
and other prescribed bodies and, where loans are
made, to collect the repayments.

The Office of HM Paymaster General has continuously existed in its present form since 1836;
the Paymaster General has responsibilities
assigned from time to time by the Prime Minister
and is currently a Treasury Minister. The
Assistant Paymaster General is responsible for
the banking and financial information services
provided to the Government and public sector
bodies by the Office of HM Paymaster General.

Director: Ian Peattie

NATIONAL DEBT OFFICE
020 7270 3868 *Fax:* 020 7270 3863
Comptroller General: Ian Peattie
Establishment Officer and Head of Finance:
   Alex Lawrie

PUBLIC WORKS LOAN BOARD
020 7270 3874 *Fax:* 020 7270 3860
Chairman: A D Loehnis, CMG
Deputy Chairman: Miss V J Di Palma, OBE

Other Commissioners: J Andrews, R Burton,
T W Fellowes, Mrs R V Hale, Dame Sheila
Masters, DBE, D W Midgley, L M Nippers,
J A Parkes, CBE, B M Tanner, CBE,
Mrs R Terry
Secretary: Ian Peattie
Head of Lending: David Hockey

OFFICE OF HM PAYMASTER GENERAL
020 7270 6074 *Fax:* 020 7270 6075
Paymaster General: Ms Dawn Primarolo, MP
Assistant Paymaster General: Ian Peattie
Head of Banking: Lee Palmer

Banking Operations
National Investment and Loans Office
Sutherland House, Russell Way, Crawley,
West Sussex RH10 1UH
01293 604410 *Fax:* 01293 551780
Banking Manager: Peter Harris

Office for Standards in Education (OFSTED)

Alexandra House, 33 Kingsway
London WC2B 6SE
020 7421 6800 *Fax:* 020 7421 6707
Website: www.ofsted.gov.uk

OFSTED was set up under the Education
(Schools) Act 1992 to establish and maintain the
system of independent inspections of schools.
OFSTED monitors standards in England's
schools and regulates the work of the independent registered inspectors. All schools are now
inspected during a six-year period. OFSTED
also arranges the inspection of funded education
for 4-year olds. It is developing a similar system
relating to 3-year olds. OFSTED HMI inspect
initial teacher training, local education authorities, independent schools and LEA-funded youth
and adult education.

The government has recently announced that
OFSTED is to take over the inspection and regulation of child care provision.

OFSTED is a non-ministerial government
department, separate from the Department for
Education and Employment. HMCI advises the
Secretary of State for Education, other government departments and education services on a
range of educational matters.

HM Chief Inspector: Chris Woodhead
Directors of Inspection: M J Tomlinson, CBE,
D Taylor
Director of Policy, Planning and Resources:
Miss J M Phillips, CBE

Head of Research, Analysis and International:
Mrs C Agambar
Head of School Improvement:
Miss E L Passmore, OBE
Head of Secondary: M Raleigh
Head of Primary: K Lloyd
Head of Nursery: D Bradley
Head of SEN: C Marshall
Head of Post Compulsory: D West
Head of Contracts: C Bramley
Head of Teacher Education: C Gould
Head of Personnel Management: C Payne
Head of IT: M Worthy
*Head of Communications, Media and Public
Relations:* J Lawson
Head of Accommodation: K Francis
Head of Inspection Quality: P Matthews
Head of Curriculum Advice and Inspection:
B McCafferty
Head of LEA Reviews: D Singleton
Head of Finance: P Jolly
Heads of Corporate Services: R Knight,
J Parsons

Office for the Regulation of Electricity and Gas

Brookmount Buildings, 42 Fountain Street,
Belfast BT1 5EE
028 9031 1575 *Fax:* 028 9031 1740
E-mail: ofreg@nics.gov.uk
Website: ofreg.nics.gov.uk/

OFREG is the joint regulatory authority for the
electricity and natural gas industries in Northern
Ireland. It is responsible for promoting competition in the generation and supply of electricity;
promoting the development of the natural gas
industry, and regulating certain electricity and
gas prices. OFREG also assists electricity customers with complaints against Northern Ireland
Electricity plc, protects customers' interests generally, and promotes the efficient use of electric-
ty and gas.

Director-General of Electricity Supply NI:
Director-General of Gas NI: Douglas McIldoon
*Deputy Director-General of
Electricity Supply NI:*
Deputy Director-General of Gas NI:
Charles Coulthard

Office of Fair Trading

Field House, 15–25 Bream's Buildings,
London EC4A 1PR
020 7211 8000 *Fax:* 020 7211 8800
E-mail: enquiries@oftuk.demon.co.uk
Website: www.oft.gov.uk

The Office of Fair Trading is a small Non-Ministerial Government Department, headed by an independent Director-General. The Office:
– has responsibility to keep all commercial activities under review, to identify behaviour that adversely affects the consumer or damages competition;
– has the power to take regulatory enforcement action to protect the interests of consumers, for example, revocation or refusal of consumer credit licences and prevention of unfair standard terms in consumer contracts;
– has the power among other things, to make references to the Competition Commission and following its introduction on 1 March 2000 to impose penalties on companies found to be in breach of prohibitions under the Competition Act 1998;
– has the statutory duty to publish advice and information for consumers and assists the European Commission in the enforcement of the competition rules of the European Union.

Director-General: John Bridgeman

CONSUMER AFFAIRS DIVISION
Director of Consumer Affairs:
  Miss Caroline Banks *(SCS)*
Director Consumer Affairs Policy and Regulation: David Wray *(SCS)*
Director Consumer Affairs Policy and Research:
  Dr Martin Graham *(SCS)*
Director Consumer Credit and Regulation:
  Ray Watson *(SCS)*

COMPETITION POLICY DIVISION
Director of Competition Policy:
  Mrs Margaret Bloom *(SCS)*
Director, Competition Policy Co-ordination:
  Edward Whitehorn *(SCS)*
Chief Economist: Peter Bamford *(SCS)*
Director, Mergers: Andrew White *(SCS)*
Director, Cartels Investigations:
  Adrian Walker-Smith
Director, Industries: Steven Wood *(SCS)*
Director, Consumer Goods Industries:
  Donald Mason
Director, Media, Sport and Information Industries: Alan Williams
Director, Basic Industries, Energy and Vehicles:
  Ms Gisela Davis

LEGAL DIVISION
Legal Director: Miss Pat Edwards *(SCS)*
Legal Director Consumer Affairs:
  Arif Khan *(SCS)*
Legal Director Competition Policy:
  Simon Brindley *(SCS)*

INFORMATION BRANCH
Director of Information: Dermod Hill

RESOURCES AND SERVICES BRANCH
Director of Resources and Services:
  Mrs Rosemary Heyhoe *(SCS)*

Office of Gas and Electricity Markets

Stockley House, 130 Wilton Road,
London SW1V 1LQ
020 7828 0898 *Fax:* 020 7932 1600

The Office of Gas and Electricity Markets is the regulatory body for gas and electricity. It follows the merger which started in 1999 of the Office of Gas Supply (OFGAS) and the Office of Electricity Regulation (OFFER).

The office is responsible for regulating the gas and electricity markets and protecting customers' interests. It also encourages competition in both markets which since May 1999 have seen all domestic customers free to choose which company supplies their gas and electricity.

Director-General of the Office of Gas and Electricity Markets: Callum McCarthy
Deputy Director-General, Electricity and Gas Transportation Regulation: Richard Morse
Deputy Director-General, Supply Chain:
  Dr Eileen Marshall, CBE *(SCS)*
Deputy Director-General, Customers:
  Tony Boorman
Acting Chief Operating Officer:
  Gill Whittington
Director of Public Affairs: Sarah Harrison
Legal Adviser: William Sprigge

Office of Telecommunications (OFTEL)

50 Ludgate Hill, London EC4M 7JJ
020 7634 8700 *Fax:* 020 7634 8943
E-mail: press.office.oftel@gtnet.gov.uk
Website: www.oftel.gov.uk

The Office of Telecommunications (OFTEL) is the independent regulator of the UK telecommunications industry. Its goal is to deliver the best deal for UK telecommunications customers in terms of quality, choice and value for money.

Director-General: David Edmonds
Director of Operations: Ms Anne Lambert *(SCS)*
Director of Regulatory Policy: Mrs Ann Taylor
Director of Compliance: Mrs Jane Whittles
Director of Technology: Peter Walker
Director of Strategy and Forecasting: Alan Bell
Director of Business Support: David Smith
Director of Communications: Duncan Stroud

Office of the International Rail Regulator

1 Waterhouse Square, 138–142 Holborn,
London EC1N 2TQ
020 7282 2000 *Fax:* 020 7282 2040
E-mail: orr@dial.pipex.com
Website: www.rail-reg.gov.uk
International Rail Regulator: Tom Winsor
Head of Information: Ian Cooke

Office of the Rail Regulator

1 Waterhouse Square, 138–142 Holborn,
London EC1N 2TQ
020 7282 2000 *Fax:* 020 7282 2040
E-mail: orr@dial.pipex.com
Website: www.rail-reg.gov.uk
The Office of the Rail Regulator is the independent regulatory body set up under the Railways Act 1993, headed by the Rail Regulator, who is independent of ministerial control. His functions include licensing of operators and protecting the interests of rail users.

Rail Regulator: Tom Winsor
Director of Communications, Strategy and Planning: Keith Webb
Director, Railway Network Group: Michael Beswick
Director, Operator Regulation: Melanie Leech
Chief Economist: Paul Plummer
Chief Legal Adviser: Michael Brocklehurst
Head of Information: Ian Cooke

Office of Water Services (OFWAT)

Centre City Tower, 7 Hill Street,
Birmingham B5 4UA
0121-625 1300 *Fax:* 0121-625 1400
E-mail: enquiries@ofwat.gtnet.gov.uk
Website: www.open.gov.uk/ofwat/
The Director of Water Services is responsible for regulating the water and sewerage industry in England and Wales. His primary duty is to ensure that the 26 appointed companies properly carry out their functions and can finance them.

From this stem the Director's further duties to protect customers, facilitate competition and promote economy and efficiency.

The Director established ten independent Customer Service Committees (CSCs). They are concerned solely with the interests of water customers and do not share the wider duties of the Director. They have their own legal duties which include identifying the main concerns of water customers and making representations to the companies; investigating complaints and advising the Director.

The Ofwat National Customer Council, whose membership brings together the ten regional CSC chairmen, represents customers' interests at a national level. Its current chairman is Sheila Reiter, Chairman of Wessex CSC.

Director General: I C R Byatt
Assistant Director and Chief Engineer: Dr W Emery
Assistant Director and Head of Consumer Affairs: M Saunders
Assistant Director and Head of Operations: R Dunshea
Legal Adviser: A Merry
Head of External Relations: Ms J Havard
Corporate Finance Adviser and Head of Financial Affairs: D Rees
Parliamentary Affairs Officer: I Olsen
Secretary to Ofwat National Customer Council: R Wardle

Registry of Friendly Societies

Victory House, 30–34 Kingsway,
London WC2B 6ES
020 7663 5025 *Fax:* 020 7663 5059
The Registry of Friendly Societies now comprises the Central Office of the Registry of Friendly Societies (together with the Assistant Registrar of Friendly Societies for Scotland). The Chief Registrar is the Head of the Department.

The Central Office of the Registry of Friendly Societies provides a public registry for mutual organisations registered under the Building Societies Act 1986, Friendly Societies Acts 1974 and 1992 and the Industrial and Provident Societies Act 1965. The Chief Registrar is responsible for the supervision of credit unions, and advises the Government on issues affecting them.

The Registry of Friendly Societies will be subsumed into the Financial Services Authority at a date to be fixed following the enactment of the Financial Services and Markets Bill.

Chief Registrar: G E Fitchew, CMG *(SCS)*
Assistant Registrars: A J Perrett, Ms S Eden, E Engstrom, N Fawcett, S Mundy
Assistant Registrar: J L J Craig
   (Registry of Friendly Societies (Scotland), 58 Frederick Street, Edinburgh EH2 1NB)
Establishment and Finance Officer: R E Merrick

Shadow Strategic Rail Authority

26 Old Queen Street, London SW1H 9HP
020 7960 1500 *Fax:* 020 7960 1517
Website: www.sra.gov.uk

The Strategic Rail Authority is currently operating in Shadow form as the SSRA, pending the passage of legislation through Parliament.

The SSRA monitors and manages the passenger train franchises operating on the national railway network in Great Britain, and seeks to strategically direct the growth of passenger and freight rail transport.

Chairman: Sir Alastair Morton

Goldings House, 2 Hay's Lane,
London SE1 2HB
020 7940 4200 *Fax:* 020 7940 4210
Chief Executive and Director of Passenger Rail Franchising: Mike Grant
PA to Mike Grant: Margaret Ritchie
Executive Director, Strategic Development: Chris Stokes
Executive Director, Franchise Management: Nick Newton
Executive Director, Finance and Administration: David Revolta
The Solicitor: Terence Jenner
Freight Director: Julia Clarke
Chief Economist: Bob Stannard
Head of Secretariat: James McArthur Watson
Head of Public Affairs: Paul McKie

EXECUTIVE AGENCIES

Armed Forces Personnel Administration Agency

Building 182, RAF Innsworth,
Gloucester GL3 1HW
01452 712612 ext 7347 Fax: 01452 510887

Provides, on a tri-Service basis, the data and systems for the payment of military personnel (including pensions), and supports the Armed Forces personnel management function.

Chief Executive: T S Lord
Director Personnel and Finance: C J Boyle
Director Centurion: Captain D W Pond, RN
Director Worthy Down: Brigadier M L Ward
Director Innsworth:
   Air Commodore P R Thomas, MBE
Director Business Development:
   Captain T A Spires, RN
EDS Account Director: D J Whitfield

Department: Defence
Launched: 1/4/97

Army Base Repair Organisation

Monxton Road, Andover,
Hampshire SP11 8HT
01264 383295 *Fax:* 01264 383144

Provides an equipment repair and refurbishment service for the Army.

Chief Executive: Jim Drew, CBE, BSc(Eng),
   CEng, FIEE, FIMgt
Deputy Chief Executive:
   Dr Les Salmon, BSc, PhD, MInstP CPhys
Commercial Director: Alan Lewis
Director Workshops: Graham Benjamin,
   BSc(Eng), MSc, CEng, MIEE
Non-Executive Director:
   John Barnes, MA, MS, FCA, CIMgmt
Non-Executive Director: Dr Mike Goodfellow,
   PhD, FIEE, CEng, FInstP FIMgt

Department: Defence
Launched: 1/4/93

Army Personnel Centre

Kentigern House, 65 Brown Street,
Glasgow G2 8EX
0141-224 2070 *Fax:* 0141-224 3555

The Agency's task is to man the Army, manage the careers of Army personnel (including both officers and soldiers) and to provide Army pay, personnel and pensions administration.

Military Secretary/Chief Executive:
   Major General Alister Irwin, CB
Deputy Military Secretary:
   Brigadier Mark Elcomb, OBE
Director Personnel Administration:
   Brigadier Malcolm Duncan
APC Secretary: Dr Alec Stevenson

Department: Defence
Launched: 2/12/96

Army Technical Support Agency

Monxton Road, Andover,
Hampshire SP11 8HT
01264 383004 *Fax:* 01264 383294
E-Mail: all.atsa@gtnet.gov.uk
Website: www.army.mod.uk/army/atsa/atsa.htm

Primarily involved with providing technical and engineering advice and services to Armed Forces users and managers of military equipment.

Chief Executive: Brigadier Tony Ball
Director Engineering: Colonel Mike Capper
Director Aircraft Branch: Lt Col David Eke
Director Technical Services: John Denyer
Director Andover North Site Redevelopment:
   Mike Stockbridge
Director of Administration: Colin Knapman
Director Business Development: (Vacant)

Department: Defence
Launched: 16/10/95

Army Training and Recruiting Agency

Trenchard Lines, Upavon, Pewsey,
Wiltshire SN9 6BE
01980 615024 *Fax:* 01980 615300

Provides manpower trained in the individual skills required to sustain the Army's military effectiveness.

Chief Executive:
  Major General Anthony Palmer, CBE
Deputy Chief Executive: Charles Gordon
Head of Policy, Strategy and Communications:
  Colonel David Santa-Olalla, DSO, MC
Head of Operations and Plans:
  Colonel Tom Richardson
Head of Resources, Programmes and Finance:
  John Thornton
Agency Secretary: David Simpson
Head of Personnel: Ms Wendy Barnes
Head of Commerce and Estates:
  John Marchbank
Head of Management Information Systems:
  Colonel Tim Wilton, MBE

Department: Defence
Launched: 1/4/97
Re-launched as an enlarged agency: 1/7/97

Benefits Agency

Quarry House, Quarry Hill
Leeds LS2 7UA
0113-232 4000 *Fax:* 0113-232 4476
For details of Agency local offices
0113-232 4605 *Fax:* 0113-232 4476
E-Mail: baadmin@baadmin.demon.co.uk
Website: www.dss.gov.uk/ba

The Benefits Agency is responsible for administering claims and payments of social security benefits.

Chief Executive: Peter Mathison *(SCS)*
Personal Assistant: Margaret Moor
Strategy and Planning Director:
  Steve Heminsley *(SCS)*
Finance Director: John Codling *(SCS)*
Personnel and Communications Director:
  Mark Fisher *(SCS)*
Projects Director: Norman Haighton *(SCS)*
Operations Support Director:
  Alexis Cleveland *(SCS)*
Director of Field Operations (North):
  Charlie Mackinnon *(SCS)*
Director of Field Operations (South):
  Tony Edge *(SCS)*
Branches within Directorates:
Strategy and Planning Directorate
  Benefit Management Branch: Terry Moran
  Business Development Branch:
    Ms Florence Lea
  BA Security: Hilary Reynolds
Finance Directorate
  BA Resources: Peter Ward
  Banking and Accountancy Branch:
    Rob Langford

Benefits Agency Audit: Brian Eason
  Financial Services Branch: Jeff Taylor
Personnel and Communications Directorate
  Communications and Customer Liaison
    Branch: Steve O'Neill
  Personnel and Development Branch:
    John Parker
Projects Directorates
  IMPACT: Ms Jane Brady
  CAPS: Vincent Gaskill
Operations Support Directorate
  Commercial Services Branch: Alan Dowlman

Department: Social Security
Launched: 2/4/91
Review completed: March 1995 (agency
  status confirmed)

British Forces Post Office

Inglis Barracks, Mill Hill, London NW7 1PX
020 8818 6315 *Fax:* 020 8818 6309
E-Mail: bfpo@compuserve.com

The mission of the BFPO is to provide the highest quality of postal and courier services to its customers whilst maintaining best value for money and sufficient military capability to meet Government's defence requirements in peace and war.

Chief Executive: Brigadier B J Cash
Deputy Chief Executive/Head Policy and
  Strategy: Colonel R W Bugler
Head Postal and Courier Services:
  Colonel D J Kent
Head Finance and Corporate Affairs: (Vacant)
Contact: Ms A D Davidson – Public Relations
  020 8818 6343 *Fax:* 020 8818 6291

Department: Defence
Launched: 1/7/92 as DPCSA
Re-launched: 1/7/99 as BFPO

Business Development Service

Craigantlet Buildings, Stoney Road,
Belfast BT4 3SX
028 9052 0444 *Fax:* 028 9052 7447
E-Mail: bds@nics.gov.uk
Website: www.nics.gov.uk/bds/

Provides business support services to Northern Ireland departments, their executive agencies and the wider public sector.

Chief Executive: Ken Millar

Department: Northern Ireland – Finance and
  Personnel
Launched: 1/10/96

Buying Agency

Royal Liver Building, Pier Head,
Liverpool L3 1PE
0151-227 4262 *Fax:* 0151-227 3315
Procurement Advice
0151-224 2242/3
E-Mail: marketing@tba.gov.uk
Website: www.open.gov.uk/tba/tbahome.htm

TBA provides a high quality, professional procurement service to government, public sector organisations and their private sector contractors.

TBA's procurement teams offer access to over 500,000 competitively priced goods and services across a broad range of negotiated contracts in major product areas.

Chief Executive: Stephen Sage
Finance Director: Alan Philips
Human Resource Director: Keith Pope
Commercial Director: Dr Clare Poulter
Operations Director: Kevin Cahill

Department: Cabinet Office
Launched: 31/10/91
Trading Fund Status

Cadw: Welsh Historic Monuments

Crown Buildings,
Cathays Park, Cardiff CF10 3NQ
029 2050 0200 *Fax:* 029 2082 6375

Maintains and preserves the built heritage of Wales and presents those monuments in the care of the National Assembly for Wales to the public.

Chief Executive: Thomas Cassidy
Director of Policy and Administration: (Vacant)
Chief Architect: J D Hogg
Chief Inspector: J R Avent
Head of Presentation: A J Hood
Head of Corporate Services: J Jenkins

Responsible Assembly Members: First
Secretary and Peter Law, AM
Launched 2/4/91
Review completed: July 1995 (agency status
confirmed)

Central Computer and Telecommunications Agency

Rosebery Court, St Andrew's Business Park, Norwich NR7 0HS
01603 704567 *Fax:* 01603 704817
E-Mail: info@ccta.gov.uk
Website: www.ccta.gov.uk/cctahome.htm

Provides information technology expertise to public sector organisations.

Chief Executive: Bob Assirati *(SCS)*

Responsible Minister: Minister for the
Cabinet Office
Launched: 1/4/96

Central Office of Information

Hercules Road, London SE1 7DU
020 7928 2345 *Fax:* 020 7928 5037

The Central Office of Information (COI) is an Executive Agency which provides consultancy, procurement and project management services to central government for publicity and provides specialist services in certain areas.

Chief Executive: Ms Carol Fisher
Group Directors,
  Establishment and Finance: Keith Williamson
  Marketing Communications: Peter Buchanan
  Publications: Michael Reid
  Films, Radio Events: Ms Sally Whetton
  Client Services: Ian Hamilton
Regional Network Director: Rob Haslam
Network Office Directors,
  East: Philip Powell
  North East: Ms Lynn Taylor
  North West: Ms Eileen Jones
  Yorkshire and Humberside: Ms Wendy Miller
  Midlands West: Brent Garner
  Midlands East: Peter Smith
  South East: Ms Virginia Burdon
  South West: Peter Whitbread

Responsible Minister: Minister for the
Cabinet Office
Launched: 5/4/90
Review completed: March 1998 (agency
status confirmed)
Trading Fund Status

Central Science Laboratory

Sand Hutton, York YO41 1LZ
01904 462000 *Fax:* 01904 462111
E-Mail: science@csl.gov.uk
Website: www.csl.gov.uk

Provides a wide range of scientific services including:
– plant health
– the authenticity, chemical and microbiological safety and nutritional value of the food supply
– pesticide safety, including monitoring of residues in food
– veterinary drug residues
– the control of pests and diseases of growing and stored foodstuffs
– wildlife management, and
– the impact of food production on the environment and the consumer.

The work is carried out primarily for MAFF, but also for other government departments and public and private sector organisations both nationally and internationally on a commercial basis.

Chief Executive: Prof Peter Stanley *(SCS)*
Research Director (Agriculture and Environment): Prof Tony Hardy
Research Director (Food): Prof John Gilbert
Business Support Director: Brian Simmons
Commercial Director: Dr Robert Bolton
Science Group Heads:
  Plant Health: Prof Stephen Hill
  Conservation and Environment Protection: Dr Stephen Hunter
  Pest Management: Prof Nick Price
  International Centre for Safe Commodity Storage: Dr Ken Wildey
  Alternative Crops and Biotechnology: Melvyn Askew
  Pesticides: Dr Michael Wilson
  Food Safety and Quality: Dr Rob Massey
  Microbiology: Dr Lynton Cox
Facilities and Procurement: Jim Hill
Communications, Human Resources and Quality: Mrs Heather Hamilton

Department: Agriculture, Fisheries and Food
Launched: 1/4/92
Re-launched as an enlarged CSL Agency following the merger with the MAFF Food Science Laboratories: 1/4/94
Review completed: December 1996 (agency status confirmed)

Centre for Environment, Fisheries and Aquaculture Science

Lowestoft Laboratory, Pakefield Road
Lowestoft, Suffolk NR33 0HT
01502 562244 *Fax:* 01502 513865
E-Mail: marketing@cefas.co.uk
Website: www.cefas.co.uk

Provides scientific research, assessment and advice in fisheries management, environmental protection, and fish health, hygiene and aquaculture, in order to enhance the protection of the public, the conservation of the aquatic environment and the rational management of natural resources.

Chief Executive: Dr Peter Greig-Smith *(SCS)*
Deputy to the Chief Executive: Dr J W Horwood

Department: Agriculture, Fisheries and Food
Launched: 1/4/97

Child Support Agency

Room 158A, Longbenton,
Newcastle upon Tyne NE98 1YX
E-Mail:
csa-chief-execs-office@new100.dss.gov.uk
Website: www.gov.dss.uk/csa

Operates the system under the guidelines of the Child Support Act, 1991 for assessing, collecting and, where necessary, enforcing Child Support maintenance.

Chief Executive: Faith Boardman *(SCS)*
  0191-225 9738
Deputy Chief Executive: Mike Isaac
  0191-225 7699
Director of Operations: John Lutton
  0191-225 9292
Resources Director: Mick Davison
  0191-225 7508
HR Director: Chris Peters
  0191-225 9513

Department: Social Security
Launched: 5/4/93

Civil Service College

Sunningdale Park, Ascot,
Berkshire SL5 0QE
01344 634000 *Fax:* 01344 842491

London: 11 Belgrave Road SW1V 1RB
020 7834 6644
E-Mail: [name]@cscolleg.attmail.com
Website:
www.open.gov.uk/college/cschome.htm

Provides a wide range of training and development opportunities for civil servants and others plus international consultancy services.

Director and Chief Executive: Ewart Wooldridge
Director of Finance: M Timmis
Business Group Directors: M Barnes,
  R Behrens, G Llewellyn, Dr A Wyatt

**Responsible Minister: Minister for the
  Cabinet Office
Launched: 6/6/89
Review completed: June 1995 (agency status
  confirmed); additional review completed:
  April 1996**

Companies House

Crown Way, Cardiff CF14 3UZ
029 2038 8588 *Fax:* 029 2038 0900
Website: www.companieshouse.gov.uk

Registers companies and collects statutory documents and returns and makes information available to the public.

*Chief Executive and Registrar of Companies for
  England and Wales:* John Holden *(SCS)*
Director of Operations: Tim Lonsdale
Director of Development: Ms Jeanne Spinks
Director of Finance: Jack Mansfield
Director of Policy and Planning: Ms Liz Carter
Director of Personnel: John David
Marketing and Sales Manager: Mark Pacey

LONDON INFORMATION CENTRE
Companies House
21 Bloomsbury Street, London WC1B 3XD
029 2038 8588 *Fax:* 029 2038 0900

COMPANIES HOUSE
37 Castle Terrace, Edinburgh EH1 2EB
0131-535 5800 *Fax:* 0131-535 5820

Registrar for Scotland: J Henderson

**Department: Trade and Industry
Launched: 3/10/88
Trading Fund Status**

Compensation Agency

Royston House, 34 Upper Queen Street
Belfast BT1 6FD
028 9024 9944 *Fax:* 028 9024 6956
E-Mail: comp-agency@nics.gov.uk
Website: www.nics.gov.uk/ca

Administers the criminal injuries and criminal damage compensation schemes and pays compensation under the emergency provisions legislation.

Chief Executive: Denis A Stanley
Head of Operations Frank W Brannigan

**Department: Northern Ireland Office
Launched: 1/4/92
Review completed: October 1995 (agency
  status confirmed)**

Construction Service

Churchill House, Victoria Square
Belfast BT1 4QW
028 9025 0283 *Fax:* 028 9025 0333
E-Mail: info.cs.doe@nics.gov.uk
Website: www.doeni.gov.uk/const.htm

Provides a professional design, maintenance and advisory service to government departments, agencies and other public bodies covering a wide range of construction industry disciplines.

Acting Chief Executive: Billy Walker

**Department: Northern Ireland –
  Environment
Launched: 1/4/96**

Court Service

Southside, 105 Victoria Street,
London SW1E 6QT
020 7210 1672 *Fax:* 020 7210 1797
E-Mail: cust.ser.cs@gtnet.gov.uk
Website: www.courtservice.gov.uk
Chief Executive: Ian Magee *(SCS)*

**Department: Lord Chancellor's
Launched: 3/4/95**
For full details of the Court Service see Judiciary

HM Customs and Excise

The Board of HM Customs and Excise – see also Non-Ministerial Government Departments

New King's Beam House
22 Upper Ground, London SE1 9PJ
020 7620 1313 *Fax:* 020 7865 5048
Website:
www.open.gov.uk/customs/c&ehomc.htm
Chairman: Richard Broadbent

24 EXECUTIVE UNITS

ACCOUNTING SERVICES DIVISION
D J Robinson
Accountant & Comptroller General, 9SE
Alexander House
Southend-on-Sea, Essex SS99 1AU
01702 367176 *Fax:* 01702 367055

ANGLIA COLLECTION
Collector: M Hill
HM Customs and Excise, Haven House
17 Lower Brook Street, Ipswich IP4 1DN
01473 235922 *Fax:* 01473 235922

CENTRAL ENGLAND COLLECTION
Collector: D Garlick
HM Customs and Excise, Two Broadway,
Broad Street, Fiveways, Birmingham B15 1BG
0121-697 4234 *Fax:* 0121-697 4002

EASTERN ENGLAND COLLECTION
Collector: A Durrant
HM Customs and Excise
Bowman House, 100/102 Talbot Street
Nottingham NG1 5NF
0115-971 2277 *Fax:* 0115-941 8164

INTERNAL AUDIT DIVISION
Chief Internal Auditor: C Piper
HM Customs and Excise
Baryta House, Victoria Avenue,
Southend, Essex SS2 6AZ
01702 366234 *Fax:* 01702 367472

IT DIVISION
Head: S Cracknell
HM Customs and Excise
Alexander House, 21 Victoria Avenue
Southend-on-Sea, Essex SS99 1AA
01702 348944 *Fax:* 01702 366089

LONDON AIRPORTS COLLECTION
Collector: M Peach
HM Customs and Excise, Custom House
Nettleton Road, North Side,
Heathrow Airport London, Hounslow
Middlesex TW6 2LA
020 8910 3646 *Fax:* 020 8910 3616

LONDON CENTRAL COLLECTION
Collector: J Maclean
HM Customs and Excise, Thomas Paine
House (3rd Floor), Angel Square,
Torrens Street, London EC1V 1TA
020 7865 3090 *Fax:* 020 7865 3102

MANAGEMENT CONSULTANCY SERVICES
Head: Peter Cox-Bisham
HM Customs and Excise
7th Floor, Dorset House, Stamford Street
London SE1 9PS
020 7865 5884 *Fax:* 020 7865 5898

NATIONAL INTELLIGENCE DIVISION
Head of Intelligence: M Blythe
Dorset House, Stamford Street
London SE1 9PY
020 7202 4430 *Fax:* 020 7202 4428

NATIONAL INVESTIGATION SERVICE
Chief Investigation Officer: P Evans
HM Customs and Excise
Custom House, Lower Thames Street
London EC3R 6EE
020 7283 5353 *Fax:* 020 7696 7799

NORTH WEST COLLECTION
Collector: A P Allen
HM Customs and Excise, 1st Floor
Queen's Dock, Liverpool L74 4AG
0151-703 1303 *Fax:* 0151-703 1336

NORTHERN ENGLAND COLLECTION
Collector: H Peden
HM Customs and Excise
Peter Bennett House, Redvers Close
West Park Ring Road, Leeds LS16 6RQ
0113-230 3024 *Fax:* 0113-288 3322

NORTHERN IRELAND COLLECTION
Collector: T W Logan
HM Customs and Excise, Custom House,
Custom House Square, Belfast BT1 3ET
028 9056 2600 *Fax:* 028 9056 2976

SCOTLAND COLLECTION
Collector: I Mackay
HM Customs and Excise, 44 York Place
Edinburgh EH1 3JW
0131-469 7275 *Fax:* 0131-469 7340

SOLICITOR'S OFFICE
Solicitor: D F W Pickup
HM Customs and Excise
New King's Beam House
22 Upper Ground, London SE1 9PJ
020 7620 1313 *Fax:* 020 7865 5022

SOUTH EAST COLLECTION
Collector: Jerry Tullberg
HM Customs and Excise
Priory Court, St Johns Road
Dover, Kent CT17 9SH
01304 224392 *Fax:* 01304 224420

SOUTH LONDON AND THAMES COLLECTION
Collector: J Hendry
HM Customs and Excise
Dorset House, Stamford Street
London SE1 9PS
020 7202 4152 *Fax:* 020 7202 4216

SOUTHERN ENGLAND COLLECTION
Collector: H Burnard
HM Customs and Excise, Custom House
Orchard Place, Southampton SO14 3NF
023 8082 7001 *Fax:* 023 8082 7909

TARIFF AND STATISTICAL OFFICE
Controller: Dr M McDowall
HM Customs and Excise
Portcullis House, 27 Victoria Avenue
Southend-on-Sea, Essex SS2 6AL
01702 348944 *Fax:* 01702 367163

THAMES VALLEY COLLECTION
Collector: J C Barnard, CBE
HM Customs and Excise, Eaton Court
104-112 Oxford Road, Reading RG1 7FU
01734 583921 *Fax:* 01734 505618

TRAINING SERVICES DIVISION
Departmental Training Officer: M Smith
HM Customs and Excise, Carby House
73 Victoria Avenue, Southend-on-Sea
Essex SS2 6EB
01702 348944 *Fax:* 01702 365042

VAT OPERATIONS LIVERPOOL
Collector: M Corcoran
Room 3/1 NW, Queen's Dock
Liverpool L74 4AA
0151-703 8000 *Fax:* 0151-703 8212

WALES, THE WEST AND THE BORDERS
COLLECTION
Collector: R Flavill
HM Customs and Excise
Portcullis House, 21 Cowbridge Road East
Cardiff CF1 9SS
029 2023 8531 *Fax:* 029 2039 5096

Launched: 1/4/91
Review completed: 23/1/96

Defence Analytical Services Agency

MoD, Northumberland House,
Northumberland Avenue,
London WC2N 5BP
020 7218 0729 *Fax:* 020 7218 5203
E-Mail: postmast@dasa.mod.uk

Provides services including compilation of manpower, financial and logistical statistics, a manpower planning and forecasting service to the Armed Services. It also provides project-based consultancy services to Ministers and senior officials.

Chief Executive: Colin Youngson
Director (Manpower and Finance):
   Fred Johnson
Director (Information Services and Logistics):
   Glen Watson
Head of Business Services: Ms Sue Johnston

Department: Defence
Launched: 1/7/92

Defence Aviation Repair Agency

DARA Head Office, St Athan, Barry,
Vale of Glamorgan CF62 4WA
01446 798727 *Fax:* 01446 798187

The DARA's primary role is to provide the MoD's strategic in-house deep repair, maintenance, modification and overhaul facility for aircraft and aerosystems of the UK Armed Forces.

DARA also provides aircraft storage services, marine gas turbine engine repair and overhaul, and complementary support services for the logistics supply chain and UK Armed Forces operations.

In accordance with Government policies, these services may also be provided to external military and civilian customers.

Chief Executive: Stephen Hill, OBE *(SCS)*
Deputy Chief Executive: Air Commodore P Dye
Finance Director: D Roberts
Commercial Director: R Jones
Information Systems Director:
   Captain (RN) P Bishop
Human Resources Director: B Galton
Contracts Director: J Kershaw
Corporate Development Director: A Hamilton

Department: Defence
Launched: 1/4/99

Defence Bills Agency

Ministry of Defence, Mersey House,
Drury Lane, Liverpool L2 7PX
Fax: 0151-242 2470
E-Mail: cao.dba@gtnet.gov.uk
Website: www.defencebills.gov.uk

Provides bill payment, debt collection and associated management information services for MoD.

Chief Executive: Iain Elrick 0151-242 2234

Department: Defence
Launched: 1/1/96

Defence Clothing and Textiles Agency

Skimmingdish Lane, Caversfield,
Oxfordshire OX6 9TS
01869 875501 *Fax:* 01869 875509
E-Mail: dcta@dial.pipex.com

Supplies uniforms, clothing, textiles, common user items and engineer stores required by the Armed Forces.

Chief Executive: Brigadier Michael Roycroft
Product Director: Group Captain Dave Bernard
Deputy Product Director/Science Adviser:
   Dr Claire Millard
Director Business Management: John Deas
Director Science and Technology Division:
   Prof Colin Lewis
Director Quality and Product Support Division:
   Alan Beattie
Finance Director: Bob Dixson
Contracts Director: Neil Manners

Department: Defence
Launched: 22/11/94

Defence Communication Services Agency

HQ DCSA, Basil Hill Site,
Corsham, Wiltshire SN13 9NR
01225 814785 *Fax:* 01225 814966
E-Mail: hqdcsa@dial.pipex.com

The Defence Communication Services Agency manages the provision of world-wide communications and information transfer services for the Ministry of Defence and Armed Forces. The DCSA brings together into one organisation a number of separate units previously in the three Services and the MoD Centre with a range of functional responsibilities including satellite communications, radio and messaging as well as telephone, fax, data, e-mail, and e-commerce.

The creation of the DCSA has provided the opportunity for significant improvements in the range and level of services provided to Defence customers and other government departments.

Chief Executive: Major General A J Raper, CBE
Deputy Chief Executive/Director Operations:
   Commodore P J Tyrrell, OBE, RN
Director Resources: Norman Swanney
Director Networks: Brigadier H H Ham, CBE

Department: Defence
Launched: 1/4/98

Defence Dental Agency

Ministry of Defence, Headquarters DDA
RAF Halton, Aylesbury
Buckinghamshire HP22 5PG
01296 623535 ext 6103
Fax: 01296 626535 ext 6251
E-Mail: dda@hqdda.demon.co.uk

Provides dental treatment to service personnel, entitled dependants and other entitled civilians.

Chief Executive:
   Air Vice-Marshal I G McIntyre
Director of Plans and Resources (Director Naval Dental Services):
   Surgeon Commodore (D) J Hargraves
Director Clinical Services (Director Army Dental Services): Brigadier J A Gamon
Director of Dental Services (RAF):
   Air Commodore R M Butler
Head of Finance and Secretariat:
   T L O'Regan

Department: Defence
Launched: 1/3/96

Defence Estates

DE Head Office, Blakemore Drive,
Sutton Coldfield, West Midlands B75 7RL
0121-311 3850 *Fax:* 0121-311 2100
E-Mail: de_hq@dial.pipex.com

Mission – "to deliver estate solutions to defence needs".

Vision – "to be recognised as being at the forefront of excellence in estate management".

Chief Executive: Ian Andrews, CBE, TD *(SCS)*
Functional Directors all based at DE Head Office Sutton Coldfield (except where shown)
   Operations Director: Alan Threadgold
   Finance Director: Stephen Dolan, FMCA
   Commercial Director: Ted Pearson, MAPM
   Personnel Director: Stephen Harmer
      (Waterbeach 01223 255051)

Estates Director: Allan Baillie, FRICS
Projects Director: Howard Lawrence, DEng, MSc, MICE, MIHT
Quality Director: Clive Cain, ARIBA
Service Liaison Director:
    Group Captain David Evans, OBE, RAF
Agency Secretary: Richard Howard
Information Services Director: Glyn Owens
Regional and Functional Business Unit Managers
South East and Germany – Aldershot:
    Stephen Rice, BSc, FRICS (01252 348933)
East – Waterbeach: Barry Sygrove, FRICS
    (01223 255411)
Scotland and Northern Ireland – Rosyth:
    Phil Gibb, CEng, MICE, MIHT
    (01383 648022)
Training Estate – Wilton:
    Gwyn Powell, ARICS (01722 436591)
South West – Portsmouth:
    Paul Champney, BSc, CEng, MIMechE
    (023 9272 2721)
Central and Rest of the World – Sutton Coldfield: Chris Burrows, FRICS, MCIPS
    (0121-311 2255)
US Forces – Waterbeach:
    John Regan, MBA, BSc, CEng, MICE
    (01223 255031)

Department: Defence
Launched as Defence Estate Organisation:
    18/3/97
Re-launched as Defence Estates: 29/3/99

Defence Evaluation and Research Agency

DERA, Ively Road, Farnborough,
Hampshire GU14 0LX
General Enquiries
01252 393300 *Fax:* 01252 393399
E-Mail: centralenquiries@dera.gov.uk
Website: www.dera.gov.uk

Provides non-nuclear research for the MoD, government departments and other customers.

Chief Executive: Sir John Chisholm
Finance: S Park
Technical: Dr A L Mears
Corporate Affairs: Mrs E Peace
MD DERAtec: J Mabberley
MD Programmes: Dr M Goodfellow
MD Facilities: C R Stonehouse
MD Science: Dr G Coley
Director, Corporate Development: D Steeds
Director, Personnel: E W L Hedley
Senior Military Officer: Commodore R Pelly

Department: Defence
Launched: 1/4/95
Trading Fund Status

Defence Housing Executive

St Christopher House, Southwark Street,
London SE1 0TD
020 7921 1035 *Fax:* 020 7921 1564

Provides a housing service to Service families across mainland UK, including allocation, maintenance and construction.

Chief Executive: John Wilson
Director Housing: Wendy Jarvis
Director Services Liaison:
    Brigadier Christopher Price, CBE
Director Finance and Secretariat:
    Ashley Adams

Department: Defence
Launched: 1/4/99

Defence Intelligence and Security Centre

Chicksands, Shefford,
Bedfordshire SG17 5PR
01462 752228 *Fax:* 01462 752291
E-Mail: ync30@dial.pipex.com

Defence Intelligence and Security Centre trains authorised personnel in the intelligence, security and information support disciplines while maintaining an operational capability.

Chief Executive: Brigadier Chris Holtom
Chief of Staff/Deputy Chief Executive:
    Group Captain Martin Hallam

Department: Defence
Launched: 1/10/96

Defence Medical Training Organisation

Building 87, Fort Blockhouse, Gosport,
Hampshire PO12 2AB
023 9276 5223 *Fax:* 023 9276 5501
E-Mail: ygb91@dial.pipex.com

Trains specialist defence medical personnel and provides medical services training for other service personnel to meet the operational requirements of all three services.

Chief Executive: Brigadier J R Brown

Department: Defence
Launched: 1/4/97

Defence Procurement Agency

Abbey Wood, Bristol BS34 8JH
0117-913 2724 *Fax:* 0117-913 2923
Website: www.mod.uk/dpa

The DPA procures new equipment for the Armed Forces in response to approved requirements and provides other procurement related services to its customers in and beyond the Ministry of Defence.

Chief of Defence Procurement and Chief Executive:
   Sir Robert Walmsley, KCB, FREng *(SCS)*
Deputy Chief Executive:
   John F Howe, CB, OBE *(SCS)*
Deputy Chief of Defence Procurement (Operations): Air Marshal P C Norriss, CB, AFC, MA, FRAeS

EXECUTIVE DIRECTORS
Executive Director 1: Ian Fauset *(SCS)*
Executive Director 2: Maj Gen David Jenkins
Executive Director 3: Geoff Beaven *(SCS)*
Executive Director 4: Rear Adm Peter Spencer
Executive Director 5: Stan Porter *(SCS)*
Executive Director 6: Nick Evans *(SCS)*
Integration and Aerospace Adviser to the Board:
   Air Vice-Marshal Tony Nicholson
Engineering Adviser to the Board:
   Maj Gen Liam Curran

Department: Defence
Launched: 1/4/99

Defence Secondary Care Agency

St Christopher House, Southwark Street, London SE1 0TD
020 7305 6190 *Fax:* 020 7305 6043

Provides deployable, trained Service medical staff to supply medical care and support to the Armed Forces in exercises and military operations and works very closely with the NHS.

Chief Executive: Major General C G Callow
Director of Personnel and Services:
   Air Commodore Warwick Pike
Director of Corporate Development:
   Mrs Maggie Somekh
Director of Finance and Management Information: Miss Kathy Makin

Department: Defence
Launched: 30/4/96

Defence Storage and Distribution Agency

Ploughley Road, Lower Arncott, Bicester, Oxfordshire OX6 0LD
01869 256818 *Fax:* 01869 256516
E-Mail: dsda@gtnet.gov.uk

The role of the Agency is to store, maintain and distribute stock to consumers of the Royal Navy, Army units both Regular and Territorial, the RAF, the Procurement Executive, other government departments, MoD administrative and training units and other authorities including NATO allies, Commonwealth and Foreign Governments, defence contractors and other agencies.

Chief Executive: Brigadier P D Foxton
Deputy Chief Executive: Paul Clasper
Director Plans:
   Group Captain Don Cannon, RAF
Director Human Resources/Personnel:
   Stewart Murray
Director Storage: Colonel O'Hare
Director Finance: J J Kelly
Director Distribution: Colonel N Lloyd
Director Commercial: Colonel S L Bennett
Non-Executive Director: R B Blaxland

Department: Defence
Launched: 1/4/99

Defence Transport and Movements Agency

Headquarters Quartermaster General, Monxton Road, Andover, Hampshire SP11 8HT
01264 383766 *Fax:* 01264 382881

The Defence Transport and Movements Agency mission is to provide Defence and other authorised users with agreed transport and movements services to meet their world-wide requirements in peace, crisis and war.

DTMA services include planning, acquiring and allocating Land, Sea and Air movements capability, to meet the operational and routine requirements of the Ministry of Defence and other authorised customers, by the most efficient and cost effective means available.

It is a tri-Service Defence Agency having the Director-General Logistic Support (Army) as its Owner on behalf of the Secretary of State for Defence. DTMA has been formed as a result of recommendations contained in the Strategic Defence Review. It subsumes the Defence

Transport and Movements Executive, the Joint Transport and Movements Staff and elements of the Air Movements Executive.

Chief Executive: Air Commodore Tim Leaning
Private Secretary: Mrs Linda Stringer
   (01264 382537)

Department: Defence
Launched: 1/4/99

Defence Vetting Agency

Metropole Building, Northumberland Avenue, London WC2N 5BP
020 7218 2892 *Fax:* 020 7218 1352

The Defence Vetting Agency grants and maintains security clearances for Armed Forces Personnel, MoD Staff, Defence Industry employees and undertakes investigation work for other government departments.

Chief Executive: Michael Wilson
Head of Secretariat: Clive Hodgson
Personnel Manager: Jim Simmonds
Management Accountant: Rosemary Hampson

Department: Defence
Launched: 1/4/97

Disposal Sales Agency

6 Hercules Road, London SE1 7DJ
020 7261 8836 *Fax:* 020 7261 8696
Website: www.deso.mod.uk

The mission of the DSA is to secure the best return to the taxpayer from the sale of surplus publicly owned equipment and stockholdings, whilst minimising the cost of disposal. The Agency was established to manage the disposals of MoD surpluses, but it now offers its Disposals Service across the public sector as a whole.

Chief Executive: A J S Taylor, CBE
Agency Administrator: Joan Lyons
   020 7261 8836

Department: Defence
Launched: 1/10/94

Driver and Vehicle Licensing Agency

Longview Road, Morriston
Swansea SA6 7JL
01792 782341 *Fax:* 01792 782793
E-Mail: dvla@gtnet.gov.uk
Website: www.open.gov.uk/dvla/dvla.htm

Its principal responsibilities are:
(a) the registration and licensing of drivers in Great Britain;
(b) the registration and licensing of vehicles, together with the collection and enforcement of vehicle excise duty in the UK;
(c) the Agency also offers for sale attractive registration marks through the Sale of Marks Scheme.

It provides a wide range of services for the Department of Environment, Transport and the Regions, other government departments, the police, the public and other external operations. In providing these services it is required to assist law enforcement agencies, help to promote road safety and to provide efficient services to the motor industry.

Chief Executive: Dr S J Ford, CBE *(SCS)*
Director of Operations: R Verge
Director of External and Corporate Services:
   T J Horton
Director of Development: R Ley
Director of Finance: P Houston
Director of Personnel: Mrs A Beynon

Department: Environment, Transport and
   the Regions
Launched: 2/4/90
Review completed: April 1995 (agency status
   confirmed)

Driver and Vehicle Licensing Northern Ireland

County Hall, Castlerock Road, Coleraine, County Londonderry BT51 3HS
028 7034 1249 *Fax:* 028 7034 1424
E-Mail: dvlni@nics.gov.uk
Website: www.dvlni@nics.gov.uk

Issues driving licences to appropriately qualified drivers, and as an agent of the Secretary of State for Transport, registers and licenses vehicles in Northern Ireland and collects and enforces vehicle excise duty.

Chief Executive: Brendan Magee
Deputy Chief Executive: Trevor Evans
Director of Vehicle Licensing: Mrs Aileen Gault
Director of Driver Licensing and Corporate
   Affairs: George Dillon
Director of Finance and Personnel:
   Ms Lucia O'Connor

Department: Northern Ireland –
   Environment
Launched: 2/8/93

Driver and Vehicle Testing Agency

Balmoral Road, Belfast BT12 6QL
028 9068 1831 *Fax:* 028 9066 5520
E-Mail: dvta@nics.gov.uk
Website: www.doeni.gov.uk/dvta

Promotes and improves road safety in Northern Ireland by testing drivers and vehicles as required by legislation.

Chief Executive: J B Watson
Director of Operations: A Peoples
Acting Director of Personnel and Quality:
  Ms P Carey
Director of Corporate Services: G McKenna
Director of Test Administration: S Duncan
Director of Finance: C Berry
Deputy Chief Driving Examiner: B Morrison
Deputy Chief Vehicle Examiners:
  T Hassin, G McDermott

**Department: Northern Ireland –
  Environment**
Launched: 1/4/92
Trading Fund Status: 1/4/96
**Awarded Charter Mark: December 1996;
  Renewed 1999**
**Attained Investor in People (IiP):
  February 1999**

Driving Standards Agency

Stanley House, 56 Talbot Street,
Nottingham NG1 5GU
0115-901 2500 *Fax:* 0115-901 2510
E-Mail: excomms.dsa@prima.net

Driver testing for cars, motorcycles, lorries and buses and supervision of car and lorry driving instructors and approved training bodies for motorcyclists in Great Britain.

Acting Chief Executive and Finance Director:
  Ms Laraine M Manley
Operations Director: Paul Hedley
Director of Personnel: Alan Evans
Chief Driving Examiner: Robin G Cummins
Registrar of Approved Driving Instructors:
  Mike Ambrose
IT Director: Gordon Court
Head of Policy: Paul Butler

**Department: Environment, Transport and
  the Regions**
Launched: 2/4/90
**Review completed: April 1995 (agency status
  confirmed)**
Trading Fund Status

Duke of York's Royal Military School

Dover, Kent CT15 5EQ
01304 245024 *Fax:* 01304 245019
E-Mail: duke@easynet.co.uk

Provides boarding school education for the children, aged between 11 and 18 years, of serving and retired Service personnel.

Headmaster and Chief Executive:
  J A Cummings, BA, MA
Bursar and Clerk to HM Commissioners:
  Lt Col (retd) R Say, FCMA, ACIS, Mimgt
Deputy Headmasters: P A James, A K Bisby

Department: Defence
Launched: 1/4/92

Employment Service

Level 6, Caxton House,
Tothill Street, London SW1H 9NA
020 7273 3000 *Fax:* 020 7273 6143

Steel City House, West Street,
Sheffield S1 2GQ
0870 001 0171 *Fax:* 0114-259 5003
E-Mail: erb.es@gtnet.gov.uk
Website: www.employmentservice.co.uk

The Employment Service aims to provide a competitive, efficient and flexible labour market by helping into work unemployed people, while ensuring they understand and fulfil the conditions for receipt of the Jobseeker's Allowance.

Chief Executive: Leigh Lewis *(SCS)*
ES Board:
  Director, Jobcentre Services:
    Clare Dodgson *(SCS)*
  Director, Human Resources: K White *(SCS)*
  Director, Welfare to Work Delivery:
    R Foster *(SCS)*
  Director, Finance and Commercial Policy:
    (Vacant)
Non-Executive Members:
  Lucy De Groot, Chief Executive Bristol City
    Council
  Richard Dykes, Managing Director of Royal
    Mail
Divisions:
  Strategy and Communications Division,
    Head: M Williams
  Commercial Policy, Head: R Wormald
  Corporate Governance, Head: Ms I Morrison
  Employer and Marketing Services, Head:
    S Norton
  Estates and National Contracts, Head:
    J Davies

Finance, *Head:* Ms S Newton
Information Systems Division, Head: R Harris
Jobcentre Performance, Head: P Hughes
Jobseeker Disability Services, Head: P Keen
Jobseeker Mainstream Services, Head:
  M Nicholas
Joint Planning and Operations Division,
  Head: J Myers
Product Development, Head: H Tollyfield
Occupational Psychology, Head:
  Ms M Dalgleish
Personnel, Head: Gill Adey
Training and Development: Jon Ashe
Timebound Projects:
  Customer Service Strategy, Head:
    Ms K Chaplain
  HR Partnership, Head: M Rennard
  One Project, Head: L Brown
  Year 2000 Programme, Head: G Macnair
Regional Directors:
  East Mids and Eastern: M Groves
  London and South East: S Holt, OBE
  Northern: Vincent Robinson
  North West: Ms M John
  South West: K Pascoe
  West Midlands: Ms R Thew
  Yorkshire and The Humber: R Lasko
  Office for Scotland: A R Brown
  Office for Wales: Ms S Keyse

Department: Education and Employment
Launched: 2/4/90
Review completed: October 1996 (agency
status confirmed)

Employment Tribunals Service

19-29 Woburn Place, London WC1H 0LU
020 7273 8510 *Fax:* 020 7273 8670

Provides administrative support to the employment tribunals and to the Employment Appeal Tribunal (EAT).

Chief Executive: Ian Jones *(SCS)*
Director of Operations, Employment Tribunals:
  Martin Wilson
Registrar EAT: Veronica Selio
Director of Resources and Strategic Planning:
  Steve Loach
Director of Personnel: Gerard Oates
Director of Information Technology: Jeremy Ilic
Director of Estates: Alastair Scott

Department: Trade and Industry
Launched: 1/4/97

Environment and Heritage Service

Headquarters, Corporate Affairs
and Natural Heritage,
Commonwealth House, 35 Castle Street,
Belfast BT1 1GU
028 9025 1477 *Fax:* 028 9054 6660
E-Mail: ehs@nics.gov.uk
Website: www.nics.gov.uk/ehs

Environmental Protection
Calvert House, 23 Castle Place,
Belfast BT1 1FY
028 9025 4754 *Fax:* 028 9025 4865
E-Mail: ehs@nics.gov.uk
Website: www.nics.gov.uk/ehs

Built Heritage
5–33 Hill Street, Belfast BT1 2LA
028 9023 5000 *Fax:* 028 9054 3111
E-Mail: ehs@nics.gov.uk
Website: www.nics.gov.uk/ehs

Protects and conserves the natural and built environment and promotes its appreciation for the benefit of present and future generations.

Acting Chief Executive: Jim Lamont
  028 9054 6569
Director of Natural Heritage: Dr John Faulkner
  028 9054 6571
Director of Environmental Protection:
  Jim Lamont 028 9054 6614
Director of Built Heritage:
  Nick Brannon 028 9054 3024
Acting Director of Corporate Affairs:
  Liam Gibson 028 9054 6620

Department: Northern Ireland –
Environment
Launched: 1/4/96

Farming and Rural Conservation Agency

Nobel House, 17 Smith Square
London SW1P 3JR
020 7238 5432 *Fax:* 020 7238 5588
E-Mail: frca.genenq@frca.maff.gov.uk
Website: www.maff.gov.uk/aboutmaf/
agency/frca/frca.htm

It assists government in the design, development and implementation of policies on the integration of farming and conservation, environmental protection, rural land use and the rural economy. This includes agri-environment schemes such as Environmentally Sensitive Areas, Countryside

Stewardship and Access Schemes, Land Use and Tenure, Milk Hygiene Inspections and Wildlife Management.

Chief Executive: Sarah Nason
(020 7238 5960 *Fax:* 020 7238 5372)
Policy Director: John Archer
(020 7238 5775 *Fax:* 020 7238 5372)
Resources Director: Terry Bird
(020 7238 6597 *Fax:* 020 7238 5588)
Director, Eastern Region: Clive Whitworth
(01223 455907 *Fax:* 01223 455829)
Director, Northern Region: Mike Silverwood
(0113-230 3900 *Fax:* 0113-230 3963)
Director, Western Region: David Sisson
(0117-959 1000 *Fax:* 0117-959 0463)
Director, Wales: Jeff Robinson
(029 2058 6101 *Fax:* 029 2058 6763)

Department: Agriculture, Fisheries and Food and the National Assembly for Wales
Launched: 1/4/97

Fire Service College

Moreton-in-Marsh,
Gloucestershire GL56 0RH
01608 650831 *Fax:* 01608 651788
E-Mail: enquiries@fireservicecollege.uk.co

Provides a wide range of specialist fire related and management and finance training for fire officers. It also provides training for commerce and industry, and for students from overseas fire brigades.

Chief Executive and Commandant:
T L Glossop, OStJ, QFSM, BSc, FIMgt, AIFireE
E-Mail: tglossop@fireservicecollege.uk.co
Director, Sales and Marketing: Mrs Julie Tew

Department: Home Office
Launched: 1/4/92
Trading Fund Status

Fisheries Research Services

Marine Laboratory, PO Box 101
Victoria Road, Aberdeen AB11 9DB
01224 876544 *Fax:* 01224 295511
E-Mail: heaths@marlab.ac.uk
Website: www.marlab.ac.uk

Provides expert scientific and technical advice and information on marine and freshwater fisheries, on aquaculture, and on the protection of the aquatic environment and its wildlife.

Director: Prof A D Hawkins

Deputy Director: Dr J M Davies
Environment Programme: Dr C Moffat
Fisheries Management: Dr R M Cook
Aquaculture and Animal Health: Dr R M Stagg
Freshwater Fisheries Laboratory:
Dr R G J Shelton

Department: Scottish Executive – Rural Affairs Department
Launched: 1/4/97

Forensic Science Agency of Northern Ireland

151 Belfast Road, Carrickfergus,
Co Antrim BT38 8PL
028 9036 1888 *Fax:* 028 9036 1900
E-Mail: fsani@nics.gov.uk
Website: www.fsani.org.uk

The provision of effective scientific advice and support to enhance the delivery of justice through:
– scientific support for police in the investigation of crime;
– scientific advice for the legal profession and objective expert testimony to the Courts;
– training in the effective and efficient application of forensic science;
– analytical support for pathologists.
In the pursuit of its Vision and Mission, the Agency operates principally in support of the Royal Ulster Constabulary.

Chief Executive: Dr Richard W Adams

Department: Northern Ireland Office
Launched: 1/9/95

Forensic Science Service

Priory House, Gooch Street North,
Birmingham B5 6QQ
0121-607 6800 *Fax:* 0121-622 5889
Website: www.fss.org.uk

The purpose of the FSS is to serve the administration of justice principally by providing scientific support in the investigation of crime and expert evidence to the courts. It aims to do so with efficiency, effectiveness and economy.

Chief Executive: Dr J Thompson* *(SCS)*
Director of Quality and Head of Profession:
M Loveland
Chief Scientist: Dr R K Bramley
Service Delivery Director (Operations and DNA): Dr D Werrett
Director of Finance: R J Anthony*

Director of Research and Service Development:
  T Howitt
UK Sales and Marketing Director:
  Ms S Thompson
Human Resources Director: K Gilliver

CORPORATE OFFICE
109 Lambeth Road, London SE1 7LP
020 7230 6700 *Fax:* 020 7230 6253
*All correspondence for Chief Executive and
Director of Finance to Corporate Office

REGIONAL OPERATIONAL
LABORATORIES

BIRMINGHAM
Priory House, Gooch Street North,
Birmingham B65 6QQ
0121-607 6800 *Fax:* 0121-622 5889

CHEPSTOW
Usk Road, Chepstow, Gwent NP6 6YE
01291 637100 *Fax:* 01291 629482

CHORLEY
Washington Hall, Euxton, Chorley,
Lancashire PR7 6HJ
01257 265666 *Fax:* 01257 274752

HUNTINGDON
Hinchingbrooke Park, Huntingdon,
Cambridgeshire PE18 8NU
01480 450071 *Fax:* 01480 450079

LONDON
Metropolitan Laboratory, 109 Lambeth Road,
London SE1 7LP
020 7230 6700 *Fax:* 020 7230 6253

WETHERBY
Sandbeck Way, Audby Lane, Wetherby, West
Yorkshire LS22 7DN
01937 548100 *Fax:* 01937 587683

WOODLEY LOCAL OFFICE
Suite C, Loddon Vale House,
Hurricane Way, Woodley,
Reading RG5 4UX
01189 440391 *Fax:* 01189 440408

Department: Home Office
Launched: 1/4/91

Forest Enterprise

231 Corstorphine Road
Edinburgh EH12 7AT
0131-334 0303 *Fax:* 0131-334 3047
E-Mail: carol.finlayson@forestry.gov.uk
Website: www.forestry.gov.uk
Manages the national forest to produce the envi-

ronmental, financial, social and other outputs
sought by Ministers and the Forestry
Commissioners.

Chief Executive: Dr R McIntosh
Heads of Divisions:
  Forest Planning: Mrs W Harper
  Forest Enterprise Personnel: I Miller
  Forest Operations: I Forshaw
  Estate Management: P C Ranken
  Corporate Services: K Gliddon
  Environment and Communications:
    A Stevenson
Territorial Directors:
Forest Enterprise England (Bristol):
  G R Hatfield
Forest Enterprise Wales (Aberystwyth):
  R A Farmer
Forest Enterprise Scotland (North) (Inverness):
  H Insley
Forest Enterprise Scotland (South) (Dumfries):
  M Lofthouse

Department: Forestry Commission
Launched: 1/4/96

Forest Research

Northern Research Station, Roslin,
Nr Edinburgh, Midlothian EH25 9SY
0131-445 2176 *Fax:* 0131-445 5124
E-Mail: nrs@forestry.gov.uk
Website: www.forestry.gov.uk
Provides research, development, surveys and
technical services to the forest industry and provides authoritative advice in support of development and implementation of the Government's
forest policies.

Chief Executive: Jim Dewar
Chief Research Officer:
  Dr Peter Freer-Smith

Alice Holt Lodge, Wrecclesham,
Farnham, Surrey GU10 4LH
01420 22255 *Fax:* 01420 23653

Department: Forestry Commission
Launched: 1/4/97

Forest Service

Dundonald House, Upper Newtownards Road,
Belfast BT4 3SB
028 9052 4949 *Fax:* 028 9052 4570
E-Mail: forest.customer@dani.gov.uk
Website: www.dani.gov.uk/forestry/

Sustainable management of Northern Ireland forests and the development of afforestation to provide a range of economic, social and environmental benefits.

Chief Executive
Malcolm Beatty, BSc(For), MSc, MICFor
Head of Operations: Ken Ellis
Forest Services Officer:
Pat Hunter Blair, BSc(For), MICFor
Forest Management Officer:
Stan Milner, BSc, MICFor
Administration and Finance Officer:
Brian O'Hara

**Department: Northern Ireland – Agriculture
and Rural Development**
Launched: 1/4/98

Government Car and Despatch Agency

46 Ponton Road, London SW8 5AX
020 7217 3821 *Fax:* 020 7217 3875
E-Mail: gcda@compuserve.com

Provides secure transport and mail services to central government and comprises: the Government Car Service (GCS), meeting personal transport needs by supplying allocated chauffeur, short term chauffeur hire and taxi services; InterDespatch Service (IDS), which supplies secure mail and distribution services to all main government departments and the public sector through national and local networks.

Chief Executive: Nick Matheson
Operations Director: Jerry Doyle
Finance and IT Director: Chris Powell
Personnel Director: Alan Westover

Department: Cabinet Office
Launched: 1/4/97

Government Purchasing Agency

Rosepark House, Upper Newtownards Road,
Belfast BT4 3NR
028 9052 6560 *Fax:* 028 9052 6440
Website: www.gpa-ni.gov.uk

Establishes on behalf of customers effective contracts for the procurement of goods and services and provides advice and support to enable them to achieve value for money improvements in procurement.

Chief Executive: David Court

**Department: Northern Ireland – Finance and
Personnel**
Launched: 1/4/96

Health Estates

Stoney Road, Dundonald,
Belfast BT16 1US
028 9052 0025 *Fax:* 028 9052 3900
E-Mail: health.estates@dhssni.gov.uk
Website:
www.dhssni.gov.uk/hpss/health-estates

Provides policy, advice, guidance and support on estate matters at strategic and operational levels to the various bodies charged with responsibility for the Health and Social Services estate in Northern Ireland.

Chief Executive: R H Browne

**Department: Northern Ireland – Health,
Social Services and Public Safety**
Launched: 2/10/95

Highways Agency

St Christopher House, Southwark Street
London SE1 0TE
Information Line: 0345 504030
Enquiries: 0645 556575
Website: www.highways.gov.uk

It is responsible for contributing to sustainable development by maintaining, operating and improving the trunk road network in support of the government's integrated transport and land use planning policies.

Acting Chief Executive: Peter Nutt *(SCS)*
Director, Network and Customer Services:
Richard Thorndike

Director, Project Services: David York
Director, Quality Services: John Kerman
Director, Finance Services: Jon Seddon
Director, Human Resource Services:
  Hazel Parker-Brown
**Department: Environment, Transport and
the Regions**
Launched 1/4/94

Historic Scotland

Longmore House, Salisbury Place,
Edinburgh EH9 1SH
0131-668 8600 Fax: 0131-668 8699
Website: www.historic—scotland.gov.uk

Protects and promotes public understanding and
enjoyment of Scotland's ancient monuments and
archaeological sites and landscapes, historic
buildings, parks, gardens and designed landscapes.

Director and Chief Executive:
  Graeme N Munro, MA (SCS)
Directors: F J Lawrie, B Naylor, B O'Neil,
  L Wilson, I Maxwell
Chief Inspector of Historic Buildings:
  R Emerson, BA, FSA, FSA(Scot), IHBC
Chief Inspector of Ancient Monuments:
  D J Breeze, BA, PhD, FSA, FSAScot, FRSE,
  MIFA
Department: Scottish Executive
Launched: 1/4/91
**Review completed: November 1994 (agency
status confirmed)**

Industrial Research and Technology Unit

17 Antrim Road, Lisburn, BT28 3AL
028 9262 3000 Fax: 028 9267 6054
E-Mail: info.irtu@nics.gov.uk
Website: www.nics.gov.uk/irtu

Responsible for spearheading the drive for competitiveness in NI companies through innovation, R&D, use of technology and technology
transfer. The Agency administers a range of
R&D support programmes and provides scientific, technological and environmental services to
government and industry.

Chief Executive: Greg McConnell

**Department: Northern Ireland – Economic
Development**
Launched: 3/4/95

Information Technology Services Agency

PP 36, Peel Park, Phase 2A,
Blackpool Industrial Estate, Brunel Way,
Blackpool FY4 5ES
01253 689821 Fax: 01253 689841
Website: www.dss.gov.uk/itsa

The Agency works closely with the centre of the
department to set out their vision of an active
modern service; set the IS/IT strategic direction
for the DSS; secure the cost effective delivery of
the systems necessary to support the day-to-day
social security operations; increase the opportunities to improve business operations by max-
imising the effectiveness of the use of IS/IT; and,
work with external suppliers in the development
and provision of IT services.

Chief Executive: George McCorkell (SCS)
01253 688850 Fax: 01253 689743
Deputy Chief Executive: Pete Sharkey
01253 335678 Fax: 01253 334254
E-Mail: psharkey@eus002.dss.gov.uk
Control IS/IT Supply Director: Chris Nicholls
01253 688902 Fax: 01253 689840
IT Provider Director: Dave Imrie
0191-213 9661 Fax: 0191-213 9220
Corporate Services Director: John Thomas
01253 334417 Fax: 01253 335762
Business Unit Delivery Director:
  Christine Goodfellow
0191-225 2540 Fax: 0191-225 2793
ACCORD Security and Paris Director:
  John Delamore
01253 334073 Fax: 01253 334597
Director for HR, Business Improvement and
  Communications: Bill Gormley
01253 688992 Fax: 01253 688306
IS/IT Technical Strategy and Regulation:
  George Brown
01253 688888 Fax: 01253 688769
IS/IT Commercial Strategy and Regulation:
  Brian Barnes
0191-225 4296 Fax: 0191-225 3110

Department: Social Security
Launched: 2/4/90

Inland Revenue

The Board of Inland Revenue – see also Non-Ministerial Government Departments

25 EXECUTIVE OFFICES

INLAND REVENUE EAST
Director: S Banyard *(SCS)*
Churchgate, New Road
Peterborough PE1 1TD
01733 754321 *Fax:* 01733 755001

INLAND REVENUE LARGE BUSINESS OFFICE
Director: Mrs M E Williams *(SCS)*
6th Floor, North West Wing, Bush House,
London WC2B 4BB
020 7438 7977 *Fax:* 020 7438 6633

INLAND REVENUE LONDON
Director: R Massingale
New Court, Carey Street,
London WC2A 2JE
020 7324 1290 *Fax:* 020 7324 1542

INLAND REVENUE NORTH
Director: R Cooke *(SCS)*
Ground Floor, Regent House, 10 Commercial
Street, Darlington, Co Durham DL3 6TN
01325 349900 *Fax:* 01325 349904

INLAND REVENUE NORTH WEST
Director: G W Lunn *(SCS)*
The Triad, Stanley Road, Bootle,
Merseyside L75 2DD
0151-300 3000 *Fax:* 0151-300 3750

INLAND REVENUE NORTHERN IRELAND
Director: D Hinstridge
Dorchester House, 52–58 Great Victoria Street
Belfast BT2 7QE
028 9050 5050 *Fax:* 028 9050 5058

INLAND REVENUE SCOTLAND
Director: I S Gerrie *(SCS)*
Clarenden House, 114–116 George Street
Edinburgh EH2 4LH
0131-473 4100 *Fax:* 0131-473 9118

INLAND REVENUE SOUTH EAST
Director: A C Sleeman *(SCS)*
4th Floor, Dukes Court, Duke Street, Woking,
Surrey GU21 5XR
01483 264402 *Fax:* 01483 264410

INLAND REVENUE SOUTH WEST
Director: R S Hurcombe
Longbrook House, New North Road,
Exeter EX4 4UA
01392 663210 *Fax:* 01392 216803

INLAND REVENUE SOUTH YORKSHIRE
Director: Ms M Hay
Concept House, 5 Young Street
Sheffield S1 4LF
0114-296 9696 *Fax:* 0114-296 9797

INLAND REVENUE WALES & MIDLANDS
Director: M W Kirk *(SCS)*
1st Floor, Phase II Building, Ty Glas
Llanishen, Cardiff CF14 5TS
029 2032 6601 *Fax:* 029 2075 5730

ACCOUNTS OFFICE (CUMBERNAULD)
Director: A Geddes, OBE
Inland Revenue, St Mungo's Road
Cumbernauld, Glasgow G70 5TR
01236 783600 *Fax:* 01236 725959

ACCOUNTS OFFICE (SHIPLEY)
Director: R J Warner
Inland Revenue, Victoria Street, Shipley, West
Yorkshire BD98 8AA
01274 530750 *Fax:* 01274 580385

CAPITAL TAXES OFFICE
Director: E McKeegan
Inland Revenue, Ferrers House
PO Box 38, Castle Meadow Road
Nottingham NG2 1BB
0115-974 3043 *Fax:* 0115-974 3041

ENFORCEMENT OFFICE
Director: Mrs C A Mellor
Inland Revenue, Durrington Bridge House
Barrington Road, Worthing
West Sussex BN12 4SE
01903 700222 *Fax:* 01903 701401

FINANCIAL ACCOUNTING OFFICE
Acting Director: R F Jones
Inland Revenue, South Block
Barrington Road, Worthing
West Sussex BN12 4XH
01903 700222 *Fax:* 01903 509107

FINANCIAL INTERMEDIARIES AND CLAIMS
OFFICE
Director: J Johnston
Inland Revenue, St Johns House
Merton Road, Bootle, Merseyside L69 9BB
0151-472 6010 *Fax:* 0151-944 1254

INTERNAL AUDIT OFFICE
Director: N R Buckley
Inland Revenue, Fifth Floor
North West Wing, Bush House
Aldwych, London WC2B 4PP
020 7438 7280 *Fax:* 020 7438 7197

NATIONAL INSURANCE CONTRIBUTIONS OFFICE
Director: G Bertram, CB *(SCS)*
Room C1830, Benton Park Road, Longbenton,
Newcastle upon Tyne, NE98 1ZZ
0191-225 7665 *Fax:* 0191-225 4198

OIL TAXATION OFFICE
Director: R C Mountain
Inland Revenue, Melbourne House
Aldwych, London WC2B 4LL
020 7438 6908 *Fax:* 020 7438 6910

PENSION SCHEMES OFFICE
Director: A G Nield
Inland Revenue, Yorke House
PO Box 62, Castle Meadow Road
Nottingham NG2 1BG
0115-974 1599 *Fax:* 0115-974 1651

SOLICITOR'S OFFICE
Solicitor: Philip Ridd *(SCS)*
Inland Revenue, East Wing
Somerset House, Strand
London WC2R 1LB
020 7438 7259 *Fax:* 020 7438 6246

SPECIAL COMPLIANCE OFFICE
Director: J Middleton
Inland Revenue, Angel Court
199 Borough High Street, London SE1 1HZ
020 7234 3701 *Fax:* 020 7234 3730

STAMP OFFICE
Director: Ms L Martin
Inland Revenue, Ground Floor
Ferrers House, PO Box 38,
Castle Meadow Road,
Nottingham NG2 1BB
0115-974 2604 *Fax:* 0115-974 2507

TRAINING OFFICE
Director: A W Kuczys
Inland Revenue, Lawress Hall
Riseholme Park, Lincoln LN2 2BJ
01522 561761 *Fax:* 01522 561750

Launched: 1/4/92
Review completed: 8/1/96

Insolvency Service

PO Box 203, 21 Bloomsbury Street
London WC1B 3QW
020 7637 1110 *Fax:* 020 7636 4709
Website: www.insolvency.gov.uk

Administers and investigates the affairs of bankrupts and companies in compulsory liquidation, deals with the disqualification of directors in all corporate failures, regulates insolvency practitioners and their professional bodies, provides banking and investment services for bankruptcy and liquidation estates, and advises ministers on insolvency policy issues.

The Insolvency Service also has responsibility in Scotland for disqualifications, insolvency practitioner regulation and certain aspects of corporate insolvency policy.

Inspector General and Agency Chief Executive:
    Peter Joyce *(SCS)*
Deputy Inspectors General:
    Desmond Flynn *(SCS)*, Les Cramp *(SCS)*
Director of Corporate Resources: (Vacant)
Director of Enforcement: Patrick Chillery
Director of Policy/Technical: Eamon Murphy
Director of Finance and Planning: Lesley Beech

Department: Trade & Industry
Launched: 21/3/90

Intervention Board

PO Box 69, Reading RG1 3YD
0118-958 3626 *Fax:* 0118-953 1370
Website: www.ib-uk.gov.uk

The Board is responsible for the implementation of EU regulations covering the market support arrangements of the Common Agriculture Policy.

Chairman: I Kent
Chief Executive: G Trevelyan
Secretary: Mrs A Couch
Operations Directorate: H MacKinnon
Corporate Services Division: Mrs A Parker
Finance Division: G Trantham
Legal Division: P Kent
Operations Newcastle: J P Bradbury
Operations Reading: J A Sutton
Information Systems: D Mitcham
Procurement and Supply: D Younger

Department: Members of the Board are
appointed by and are responsible to the
four Agriculture Ministers.
Launched: 2/4/90
Review completed: June 1995 (agency status
confirmed)

Joint Air Reconnaissance Intelligence Centre

Royal Air Force, Brampton, Huntingdon
Cambridgeshire PE18 8QL
01480 52151 ext 7508
Fax: 01480 52151 ext 7476

JARIC's mission is to exploit and analyse imagery from all available sources and produce intelligence products and services to meet MoD and operational command requirements.

Chief Executive: Group Captain Steve Lloyd
Head of Business Support: Mike Bowen
Head of Operations:
Wing Commander Ian Denholm
Head of Technical Support:
Wing Commander Steve Gale

Department: Defence
Launched: 19/4/96

Land Registers of Northern Ireland

Lincoln Building, 27–45 Great Victoria Street, Belfast BT2 7SL
028 9025 1515 *Fax:* 028 9025 1550

Supports the conveyancing and property markets in Northern Ireland by: guaranteeing the validity of title to registered land; protecting the priority of conveyancing transactions for unregistered properties; supplying accurate, reliable and cost effective information about the ownership and other rights affecting land; and providing a forum for the resolution of disputes regarding registered land.

Chief Executive: Arthur Moir

Department: Northern Ireland – Finance and Personnel
Launched: 1/4/96

HM Land Registry

Lincoln's Inn Fields, London WC2A 3PH
020 7917 8888 *Fax:* 020 7955 0110
E-Mail: hmlr@dial.pipex.com
Website: www.landreg.gov.uk

Maintains and develops a unified and reliable system of land registration in England and Wales.

Chief Land Registrar and Chief Executive:
P Collis *(SCS)*
Management Board:
Solicitor to HM Land Registry:
C J West *(SCS)*
Director of Corporate Services:
E G Beardsall *(SCS)*
Land Registrar: J Timothy *(SCS)*
Director of Operations: A W Howarth *(SCS)*
Director of Information Technology: P J Smith *(SCS)*
Director of Finance: Miss H Jackson *(SCS)*
Controller Management Services: P R Laker

Land Registrar: M L Wood *(SCS)*
Head of Policy and Strategy Group:
A S Pemberton

Department: The Land Registry is a separate Government Department reporting directly to the Lord Chancellor
Launched: 2/7/90
Review completed: January 1996 (agency status confirmed)
Trading Fund Status: 1/4/93

Logistic Information Systems Agency

HQ QMG, Monxton Road, Andover, Hampshire SP11 8HT
01264 382745 *Fax:* 01264 382820
E-Mail: hq.lisa@gtnet.gov.uk

LISA has four main functions: Maintenance of QMG's IS strategy; Information systems consultancy; Development of logistic information systems; Operation of logistic area information systems.

Chief Executive: Brigadier P Flanagan
Director IS Strategy and Policy: A Withey
Director Finance: A Fisher
Director Applications: Colonel N Knudsen
Director Infrastructure: R Neath
Personnel Director: L C Milne
Director Central Support Services: A C Targett

Department: Defence
Launched: 21/11/94

Maritime and Coastguard Agency

Bay 3/29, Spring Place
105 Commercial Road
Southampton SO15 1EG
023 8032 9100 *Fax:* 023 8032 9298
E-Mail: infoline@swan.mcagency.org.uk
Website: www.mcagency.org.uk

The Agency was created by the merger of the Coastguard Agency (TCA) and the Marine Safety Agency (MSA) and is responsible for carrying out the functions of both organisations.

The primary aim of the Agency is to develop, promote and enforce high standards of marine safety; to minimise loss of life amongst seafarers and coastal users; to respond to maritime emergencies 24hrs a day; and to minimise the risk of pollution of the marine environment from ships and where pollution occurs, minimise the impact on UK interests.

The Agency is managed by a four-member Board comprising:

Chief Executive: M Storey
Maritime Operations Director: J Astbury
Maritime Standards and Pollution Prevention Director: A Cubbin
Corporate Services Director: D Lawrence

Department: Environment, Transport and the Regions
Launched: 1/4/98

Meat Hygiene Service

Foss House, Kings Pool
1–2 Peasholme Green, York YO1 7PX
01904 455501 *Fax:* 01904 455502

Protects public health and animal welfare through veterinary supervision and meat inspection in licensed fresh meat establishments.

Chief Executive: Johnston McNeill, MBA, MA, BA, DipM, DipPM *(SCS)*
Director of Operations:
  Peter Soul, BVetMed, MSc, MRCVS
  01904 455520 *Fax:* 01904 455502
Director of Finance:
  Alex Kerr, BSc, FCMA
  01904 455510 *Fax:* 01904 455516
Director of Human Resources:
  Monica Redmond, MBA, BA(Hons)
  01904 455503 *Fax:* 01904 455211
Director of Information Technology:
  Graham Perry, BSc
  01904 455530 *Fax:* 01904 455502

Department: Agriculture, Fisheries and Food
Launched: 1/4/95

Medical Devices Agency

Hannibal House, Elephant and Castle
London SE1 6TQ
020 7972 8000 *Fax:* 020 7972 8108
E-Mail: mail@medical-devices.gov.uk
Website: www.medical-devices.gov.uk

Protects the public health and safeguards the interests of patients and users by ensuring that medical devices and equipment meet appropriate standards of safety, quality and performance and that they comply with relevant Directives of the EU.

Chief Executive: Alan Kent
European and Regulatory Affairs: Steve Owen
Device Technology and Safety:
  Dr Eamonn Hoxey
Device Evaluations and Publications:
  Tom Crawley

Clinical: Dr Susanne Ludgate,
  Miss Carol Williams
Corporate Finance: Keith Cornelius
Corporate Services: Tom Crawley

Department: Health
Launched: 27/9/94

Medical Supplies Agency

Drummond Barracks, Ludgershall
Andover, Hampshire SP11 9RU
01980 608622 *Fax:* 01980 608676

Provides medical, dental and veterinary material, blood and blood products, trained personnel and technical and logistic support to the armed forces.

Chief Executive: Brian Nimick
Director of Customer and Technical Services:
  Graham North
Director of Operational Support:
  Lt Col Brian Eadon, RAMC
Director of Management Services:
  Jeremy Baines

Department: Defence
Launched: 1/3/96

Medicines Control Agency

Market Towers, 1 Nine Elms Lane
London SW8 5NQ
020 7273 3000 *Fax:* 020 7273 0353
Central Enquiry Point 020 7273 0000
Website:
www.open.gov.uk/mca/mcahome.htm

Safeguards public health by controlling medicines through a system of licensing, monitoring, inspection, and enforcement of standards which ensure that medicines marketed in the UK meet rigorous standards of safety, quality and efficacy.

Chief Executive: Dr Keith Jones, CB
Licensing Division: Dr David Jefferys
Post Licensing Division: Dr June Raine
Inspection and Enforcement: Dr Gordon Munro
Executive Support: Roy Alder
Finance, IT and Corporate Planning:
  Dr Jim Stockwell

Department: Health
Launched: 11/7/91
Review completed: July 1997 (agency status confirmed)
Trading Fund Status

Meteorological Office

London Road, Bracknell
Berkshire RG12 2SZ
01344 854455 (enquiries)
Fax: 01344 854412
E-Mail: dchardy@email.meto.gov.uk
Website: www.met-office.gov.uk

The Met Office is the State Meteorological Service, with responsibility for provision of meteorological services to the Armed Forces and civil aviation, shipping, emergency services, media, commerce, industry and the public, and for undertaking research related to meteorology and climate.

Chief Executive: Peter Ewins *(SCS)*
Chief Scientist: Dr Paul Mason, FRS *(SCS)*
Company Secretary: Miss Ann Tourle *(SCS)*
Finance Director: Philip Mabe *(SCS)*
Business Director: Roger Hunt *(SCS)*
Forecasting Director: Colin Flood *(SCS)*
Managing Director, Commercial Division:
  Stephen Lawrenson *(SCS)*
Technical Director: Dr Jim Caughey *(SCS)*
Director Numerical Weather Prediction:
  Dr David Carson *(SCS)*
Director Climate Research:
  Prof Alan Thorpe *(SCS)*
Director Information Technology:
  John Ponting *(SCS)*

Department: Defence
Launched: 2/4/90
Review completed: May 1996 (agency status confirmed)
Trading Fund Status: 1/4/96

Military Survey Defence Agency

Elmwood Avenue, Feltham
Middlesex TW13 7AH
020 8818 2232 *Fax:* 020 8818 2148

To ensure the provision of geographic support to defence operations, planning and training.

Chief Executive:
  Brigadier Philip Wildman, OBE
Director of Geographic Resources:
  Paul Hancock
Director of Geographic Commitments:
  Colonel Iain Whittington
Director of Geographic Production:
  Tony Painter
Director of Geographic Systems: Bob Russell

Director of Geographic Information:
  Stuart Haynes
Director of Geographic Field Support:
  Colonel Chris Dorman
Director of Finance: Mike Thatcher

Department: Defence
Launched: 2/4/91

Ministry of Defence Police Agency

Wethersfield, Braintree
Essex CM7 4AZ
01371 854000 *Fax:* 01371 854060

The primary role of the Ministry of Defence Police is the prevention, detection and investigation of crime within the MoD and Crown Estate and other locations policed under repayment arrangements.

In addition to its policing role, MDP also provides a security and guarding service, armed when required, at a number of key defence and other installations.

The Chief Constable is also responsible for the professional management and training of the Ministry of Defence Guard Service.

Chief Constable/Chief Executive: Walter
  Boreham, OBE, OStJ, D Univ(Middx) *(SCS)*
Deputy Chief Constable:
  Anthony Comben, BSc *(SCS)*
Agency Secretary and Director of Finance and
  Administration: Paul Crowther *(SCS)*
Assistant Chief Constable (Personnel and
  Training): Barry Smith
Assistant Chief Constable (Territorial
  Operations): Richard Miles
Assistant Chief Constable (Support): David Ray

Department: Defence
Launched: 1/4/96

National Archives of Scotland (formerly Scottish Record Office)

HM General Register House,
Edinburgh EH1 3YY
0131-535 1314 *Fax:* 0131-535 1360
E-Mail: enquiries@nas.gov.uk

Responsible for preserving the public records of Scotland and other records which have been transmitted to it, and for making them available for public inspection. Also promotes the growth and maintenance of proper archive provision.

Keeper: Patrick Cadell
Deputy Keeper: Peter Anderson

Responsible Minister: First Minister, Scottish Parliament
Launched: 1/4/93

National Savings

Charles House, 375 Kensington High Street, London W14 8SD
020 7605 9300
E-Mail: hq.ns.london@gtnet.gov.uk
Website: www.nationalsavings.co.uk

To add value by helping to reduce the costs to the taxpayer of Government borrowing and by supporting Government savings policies.
Objectives:
– To market Government debt to retail investors so as to help to minimise the combined cost and risk of the total national debt and to contribute to the Government's funding needs
– To promote Government savings policies among personal investors

In meeting these objectives the Agency will operate cost effectively and in a competitive and commercial manner that does not distort the savings market; and in a manner that benefits both Government and personal savers – now and in future.

Chief Executive: Peter Bareau
Director of Sourcing: Ms Jeannie Bevan
Director of Funding: Michael Corcoran
Director of Commerce: Christopher Moxey
Director of Finance: Richard Douglas
Director of Personnel: Scott Speedie

Department: National Savings reports directly to the Chancellor of the Exchequer
Launched: 1/7/96

National Weights and Measures Laboratory

Stanton Avenue, Teddington, Middlesex TW11 0JZ
020 8943 7272 *Fax:* 020 8943 7270
E-Mail: info@nwml.dti.gov.uk
Website: www.nwml.gov.uk

Administers weights and measures legislation; regulation and certification of equipment in use for trade; EC Directives on measuring instruments; equipment testing, calibration and training services.

Chief Executive: Dr Seton Bennett

Directors of Units,
  Legal Metrology Policy: Peter Badger
  Measuring Instruments Certification:
    Michael Koch
  Metrology and Training: Chris Rosenberg
  International: Martin Birdseye
  Business Support: Iain MacGregor

Department: Trade & Industry
Launched: 18/4/89
Review completed: July 1995 (agency status confirmed)

Naval Bases and Supply Agency

Ministry of Defence, Ensleigh, Bath BA1 5AB
01225 467854 *Fax:* 01225 468307

To provide cost-effective engineering, supply naval personnel and other support services to the Fleet and other customers in war, crises and peace.

Chief Executive: Rear Admiral Brian Perowne
Deputy Chief Executive and Director Personnel and Corporate Services: Malcolm Westgate
Naval Base Commander, Clyde:
  Rear Admiral Mike Gregory, OBE
Naval Base Commander, Devonport:
  Cdre (RN) Jonathon Reeve
Naval Base Commander, Portsmouth:
  Cdre (RN) Steve Graham, OBE
Director, Commercial: Stewart Yeo
Director, Physical Supply Chain: Mike Skeet
Director Finance and Plans: Keith Earley
Director, Base Support:
  Captain (RN) Neil Latham
Non-Executive Board Member: Alan Howell

Department: Defence
Launched: 11/12/96

Naval Manning Agency

Victory Building, HM Naval Base
Portsmouth, Hampshire PO1 3LS
023 9272 7400 *Fax:* 023 9272 7413

Ensures that sufficient naval manpower is available in trained strength and effectively deployed at all times.

Chief Executive: Rear Admiral J M de Halpert
Board of Directors:
  Naval Assistant to the Naval Secretary:
    Commodore B Burns, CBE, RN

Director Naval Manning:
  Commodore R J N Hibbert, CBE, RN
Commodore Naval Officer Appointments:
  Commodore S M Williams, RN
Commodore Naval Drafting:
  Commodore J B A Musters, RN
Head of Naval Manning Secretariat: D Aldis
Executive Secretary:
  Commander C E W King, RN
*Chief Staff Officer Personnel (Royal
  Marines):* Colonel N E Pounds, RM
Non-Executive Director: B E Toye

Department: Defence
Launched: 1/7/96

Naval Recruiting and Training Agency

Room 041, Victory Building
HM Naval Base, Portsmouth,
Hampshire PO1 3LS
023 9272 7600 *Fax:* 023 9272 7613

Primarily involved in providing and maintaining a pool of suitably trained manpower for deployment in the Naval Service.

Chief Executive:
  Rear Admiral John Chadwick, CEng, FIEE
Personnel Director and Deputy Chief Executive:
  Commodore S R J Goodall, RN
Director Naval Recruiting: Commodore
  A L Chilton, LVO, OBE, ADC, RN
Director of Naval Reserves:
  Captain J A Rimington, RN
Projects Director: Captain M J Potter, RN
Training Director:
  Captain C P R Montgomery, RN
Commercial Director: P Clark
Finance Director: P Hurst

Department: Defence
Launched: 1/4/95

NHS Estates

Department of Health, 1 Trevelyan Square,
Boar Lane, Leeds LS1 6AE
0113-254 7000 *Fax:* 0113-254 7299
E-Mail: nhs.estates@doh.gov.uk
Website: www.nhsestates.gov.uk

Property advisers and consultants for the management and development of the National Health Service estate. Aim to encourage effective, efficient and economical management of property and to promote excellence of design, with value for money, in new buildings.

Chief Executive: Kate Priestley *(SCS)*
Executive Director of Trading: David Lawrence
Executive Finance Director: Tim Straughan
*Executive Director of Policy and Performance
  Management:* Peter Wearmouth
Chief Engineer: John Parkin

Department: Health
Launched: 1/4/91
**Review completed: October 1995 (agency
  status confirmed)**

NHS Pensions Agency

Hesketh House, 200–220 Broadway
Fleetwood, Lancashire FY7 8LG
01253 774774 *Fax:* 01253 774860
E-Mail: acowan@nhspa.gov.uk
Website: www.nhspa.gov.uk

Administers the NHS Occupational Pension Scheme. It also provides information and advice on NHS pension matters.

Chief Executive: Alec Cowan
Resource and Development Director:
  Nigel Holden
Information Systems (IS) Director:
  Bill McCallum

Department: Health
Launched: 20/11/92

Northern Ireland Child Support Agency

Great Northern Tower
17 Great Victoria Street, Belfast BT2 7AD
028 9089 6666 *Fax:* 028 9089 6850
E-Mail: csa@nics.gov.uk
Website: www.dhssni.gov.uk/child_support/

We are responsible for implementing the Child Support (Northern Ireland) Orders 1991 and 1995 within Northern Ireland and the 1991 and 1995 Child Support Acts for our business in Eastern England

Chief Executive: Gerry Keenan

**Department: Northern Ireland – Health,
  Social Services, Public Safety**
Launched: 5/4/93

Northern Ireland Prison Service

Dundonald House, Upper Newtownards Road, Belfast BT4 3SU
028 9052 0700 *Fax:* 028 9052 5160
Press Office: 028 9052 5354/5139
Fax: 028 9052 5100
E-Mail: nips@nics.gov.uk

Protects the community by holding in secure and humane confinement persons who have been given into custody by the courts, and reduces the risk of re-offending by encouraging them to take full advantage of the opportunities offered during their confinement.

Director-General: Robin Halward *(SCS)*

Department: Northern Ireland Office
Launched: 3/4/95

Northern Ireland Statistics and Research Agency

McAuley House, 2–14 Castle Street, Belfast BT1 1SA
028 9034 8100 *Fax:* 028 9034 8106
E-Mail: edgar.jardine@dfpni.gov.uk
Website: www.nisra.gov.uk

Provides Government in Northern Ireland with a statistical and research service to support decision making; informs debate in Parliament and the wider community about social and economic issues; and registers key life events.

Chief Executive: Edgar Jardine
Registrar General: Dr Norman Caven
Head of Corporate Affairs: Dr Gerry Mulligan

Department: Northern Ireland – Finance and Personnel
Launched: 1/4/96

Office for National Statistics

Headquarters
1 Drummond Gate, London SW1V 2QQ
020 7533 5888 *Fax:* 020 7533 6261
E-Mail: info@ons.gov.uk
Website: www.ons.gov.uk

Government Buildings, Cardiff Road
Newport, Gwent NP9 1XG
01633 815696 *Fax:* 01633 812343

Segensworth Road, Titchfield, Fareham
Hampshire PO15 5RR
01329 842511

Smedley Hydro, Trafalgar Road
Birkdale, Southport, Lancashire PR8 2HH
01704 569824

East Lane, Runcorn, Cheshire WA7 2DN
01928 715151

Somerford Road, Christchurch
Dorset BH23 3QA
01202 486154

ONS provides government at all levels with a statistical service to support the formulation and monitoring of economic and social policies, informs Parliament and the citizen about the state of the nation and provides a window on the work and performance of government, allowing the impact of government policies and actions to be assessed. ONS provides business with a statistical service which promotes the efficient functioning of industry and commerce, as well as providing a statistical service which meets EU and international requirements.

Chief Executive: Dr Tim Holt *(SCS)*
Private Secretary: Graham Horry
Assistant Private Secretary: Landes Land
Directors: Julian Calder *(SCS)*,
    Alan Goldsmith *(SCS)* (Principal Finance
    Officer), John Kidgell *(SCS)*,
    John Pullinger *(SCS)*
Principal Establishment Officer: Eryl Williams
Head of Information: Ian Scott
Parliamentary Clerks: Rosalyn Crich,
    John Bailey

Department: HM Treasury
Launched: 1/4/96

Ordnance Survey

Romsey Road, Southampton,
Hampshire SO16 4GU
023 8079 2000 *Fax:* 023 8079 2452
E-Mail: custinfo@ordsvy.gov.uk
Website: www.ordsvy.gov.uk

Carries out official topographic surveying and mapping of Great Britain. From its databases, Ordnance Survey provides a wide range of maps and computer data products for Government, business, administrative, educational and leisure use.

Director-General: Dr G Robinson, CBE *(SCS)*
Director of Strategic Operations: A Black
Director of Business Strategy and Finance:
    D Willey
Director of Data Collection: I Logan
Director of Staff Development: B Nanson
Director of Sales and Marketing: M H Mayes

Director of Solutions Group: Dr N Land
Director of Product Development: S Erskine
Assistant to Director-General: A King
Senior Press Officer: P Round

Department: Ordnance Survey is a separate Government Department and Trading Fund, reporting directly to the Secretary of State for the Environment, Transport and the Regions
Launched: 1/5/90
Review completed: April 1995 (agency status confirmed)
Trading Fund Status: 1/4/99

Ordnance Survey of Northern Ireland

Colby House, Stranmillis Court
Belfast BT9 5BJ
028 9025 5755 *Fax:* 028 9025 5700
E-Mail: osni@nics.gov.uk
Website: www.nics.gov.uk/doe/ordnance/ordnance.htm

Ordnance Survey of Northern Ireland is the official survey and cartographic organisation for Northern Ireland.

Chief Executive: Michael Cory, BSc, MPhil, FSCS, ARICS, FIS

Department: Northern Ireland – Environment
Launched: 1/4/92

Patent Office

Concept House, Cardiff Road,
Newport, Gwent NP10 8QQ
01633 814000 *Fax:* 01633 814444
E-Mail: enquiries@patent.gov.uk
Website: www.patent.gov.uk

Grants patents and trade marks, registers designs, and formulates policy on intellectual property.

Chief Executive: Alison Brimelow
Director Patents and Designs: R J Marchant
Director Trade Marks: P Lawrence
Director Intellectual Property Policy: G Jenkins
Director Copyright: A Murphy
Secretary: Claire Clancy
Financial Controller: J Thompson

Department: Trade & Industry
Launched: 1/3/90
Review completed: August 1994 (agency status confirmed)
Trading Fund Status

Pay and Personnel Agency

Ministry of Defence, Warminster Road,
Bath BA1 5AA
01225 828105 *Fax:* 01225 828728

Provides a central payroll service to MoD and other departments.

Chief Executive: Mike Rowe
Director Business Operations: Ray Pollard
Director Information Systems: David Wealthall
Director Corporate Services: Val Hudspeth

Department: Defence
Launched: 1/2/96

Pesticides Safety Directorate

Mallard House, Kings Pool
3 Peasholme Green, York YO1 7PX
01904 640500 *Fax:* 01904 455733
E-Mail: psd.information@psd.maff.gov.uk
Website: www.maff.gov.uk/aboutmaff/agency/psd/psdhome.htm

Protects the health of human beings, creatures and plants, safeguards the environment and secures safe, efficient and humane methods of pest control, by controlling the sale, supply and use of pesticides.

Chief Executive: G Bruce *(SCS)*
Director (Policy): J A Bainton
Director of Finance: Ms K Dyson
Director (Approvals): Dr A D Martin
Deputy Director (Approvals): R P Davis

Department: Agriculture, Fisheries and Food
Launched: 1/4/93

Planning Inspectorate

Tollgate House, Houlton Street
Bristol BS2 9DJ
Cathays Park, Cardiff CF1 3NQ
01225 825007 *Fax:* 01225 825150
E-Mail: enquiries.pins@gtnet.gov.uk
Website: www.open.gov.uk/pi/pihome.htm

Appeals and other casework under Planning, Housing, Environment, Highways, Transport and Works Legislation. Also provision of Inspectors to hold local inquiries into objections to local authority plans, and administration of the Lord Chancellor's Panel of Independent Inspectors.

Chief Planning Inspector (Chief Executive):
C Shepley, BA, DipTP, PPRTPI *(SCS)*
0117-987 8963 *Fax:* 0117-987 8408

Deputy Chief Planning Inspector: D Hanchet
0117-987 8961 *Fax:* 0117-987 8408
Directors:
Highways, Rights of Way: B Dodd
Rights of Way: 0117-987 8895
Highways: 0117-987 8905/8907
Enforcement Casework: R Davies
0117-987 8916/8917 *Fax:* 0117-987 8782
All Welsh Office Appeals and Casework: R
Davies
(based at Cardiff Office) 01225 825 3861
Structure and Local Plans: R Wilson
0117-987 8529
*Head of Planning Appeals Administration,
Appeals Procedure and Casework:*
G Saunders 0117-987 8727
Director of Finance and Management Services:
M Headicar 0117-987 8391
Group Managers:
Inspector Training: A Gray
0117-987 8954
Housing and Planning: T Cookson
0117-987 8444
Planning Casework; Environmental Protection:
M Culshaw 0117-987 8919
Planning Casework: C Richardson
0117-987 8706
Architect Adviser: C Cockrane
0117-987 6264
**Departments: Environment, Transport and
the Regions and the National Assembly for
Wales**
Launched: 1/4/92
**Review completed: March 1998 (agency
status confirmed)**

Planning Service

Clarence Court, 10-18 Adelaide Street
Belfast BT2 8GB
028 9054 0651 *Fax:* 028 9054 0662
E-Mail: planning.service.hq@nics.gov.uk
Website: www.doeni.gov.uk/planning/index.htm
Implements the Government's policies and strat-
egy for town and country planning in Northern
Ireland.

Chief Executive: H McKay
Director of Corporate Services: Mrs C Smith
Acting Director of Professional Services:
J Cleland
Professional Services Manager: Miss H Heslip

**Department: Northern Ireland –
Environment**
Launched: 1/4/96

HM Prison Service

Cleland House, Page Street,
London SW1P 4LN
020 7217 6000 (enquiries)
Fax: 020 7217 6403

Provides prison services in England and Wales,
both directly and through contractors.

Prison Service Strategy Board:
   Chairman: The Rt Hon Paul Boateng, MP
      (Minister for Prisons and Probation)
   Director-General Martin Narey *(SCS)*
   Deputy Director-General:
      Phil Wheatley *(SCS)*
   Director of Security: Elaine Bailey *(SCS)*
   Director of Health Care:
      Dr Mike Longfield *(SCS)*
   Director of Regimes: Ken Sutton *(SCS)*
   Director of Finance: Julian Le Vay *(SCS)*
   Director of Personnel: Gareth Hadley *(SCS)*
   Director of High Security Prisons:
      Brodie Clark *(SCS)*
   Director of Corporate Affairs:
      Clare Pelham *(SCS)*
Non-Executive Directors:
   Sir Duncan Nichol, CBE,
   Rosemary Thomson, CBE, Patrick Carter
Secretary and Head of Secretariat:
   Clare Checksfield

AREA MANAGERS

CENTRAL AREA
Enquiries: 020 7217 6588
Area Manager: John Dring *(SCS)*

EAST MIDLAND AREA
Enquiries: 020 7217 6711
Area Manager: Mitch Egan (temp) *(SCS)*

KENT AREA
Enquiries: 020 7217 6479
Area Manager: Tom Murtagh *(SCS)*

LONDON NORTH AND EAST ANGLIA AREA
Enquiries: 020 7217 6528
Area Manager: Ivor Ward *(SCS)*

LONDON SOUTH AREA
Enquiries: 020 7217 2893
Area Manager: Peter Atherton *(SCS)*

MERCIA AREA
Enquiries: 020 7217 6589
Area Manager: Dai Curtis *(SCS)*

MERSEY AND MANCHESTER AREA
Enquiries: 020 7217 6593
Area Manager: Tony Fitzpatrick *(SCS)*

NORTH EAST AREA
Enquiries: 020 7217 6597
Area Manager: Ray Mitchell *(SCS)*

NORTH WEST AREA
Enquiries: 020 7217 6288
Area Manager: Ian Lockwood *(SCS)*

SOUTH COAST AREA
Enquiries: 020 7217 2812
Area Manager: Adrian Smith *(SCS)*

WALES AND THE WEST AREA
Enquiries: 020 7217 6925
Area Manager: John May*(SCS)*

YORKSHIRE AREA
Enquiries: 020 7217 6288
Area Manager: Peter Earnshaw *(SCS)*

DIRECTORATE OF HIGH SECURITY PRISONS
Enquiries: 020 7217 2888
Director and Area Manager: Brodie Clark *(SCS)*

Department: Home Office
Launched: 1/4/93

Property Advisers to the Civil Estate

Trevelyan House, Great Peter Street
London SW1P 2BY
General Enquiries: 020 7271 2833
Fax: 020 7271 2715
E-Mail: enquiries@property.gov.uk
Website: www.property.gov.uk

PACE is responsible for promoting co-operation between Departments to enable them to obtain best value for money in the management of their property assets. It identifies and promotes opportunities to co-ordinate Departments' market activity and to rationalise their estates. Its Central Advice Unit promotes best practice by providing general property guidance to Departments. Also, where commissioned by Departments, PACE will provide property related intelligent client services on a repayment basis.

Chief Executive:
John Locke, FRICS, HonFIHEEM *(SCS)*
020 7271 2610 *Fax:* 020 7271 2612
E-Mail: jclsc@property.gov.uk
Co-ordination Director: John Hathaway
020 7271 2760 *Fax:* 020 7271 2733
E-Mail: jhsc@property.gov.uk
Central Advice Unit Director: Arnold Butler
020 7271 2705 *Fax:* 020 7271 2715
E-Mail: ajbsc@property.gov.uk

Intelligent Client Service Director:
Jay Jayasundara
020 7271 2823 *Fax:* 020 7271 2733
E-Mail: jaysc@property.gov.uk
Corporate Services Director: Barry Redfern
020 7271 2619 *Fax:* 020 7271 2644
E-Mail: brsc@property.gov.uk

Department: Cabinet Office
Launched: 1/4/96

Public Record Office

Ruskin Avenue, Kew, Richmond
Surrey TW9 4DU
020 8876 3444 *Fax:* 020 8878 8905
E-Mail: enquiry@pro.gov.uk
Website: www.pro.gov.uk

The Public Record Office houses the national archives of England and Wales and the UK, that is, records created by the actions of central government and the courts of law. Its responsibilities include ensuring the selection of records which should be permanently preserved, their preservation and their use by the public.

Keeper of Public Records and Chief Executive:
Mrs Sarah Tyacke, CB *(SCS)*
Director of Public Services:
Dr Elizabeth Hallam-Smith
Director of Government, Information and Corporate Services: Dr D Simpson

Department: The Public Record Office is a separate Government Department reporting directly to the Lord Chancellor
Launched: 1/4/92

Public Record Office of Northern Ireland

66 Balmoral Avenue, Belfast BT9 6NY
028 9025 1318 *Fax:* 028 9025 5999
E-Mail: proni@doeni.gov.uk
Website: http://proni.nics.gov.uk/index.htm

Identifies and preserves Northern Ireland's archival heritage and ensures public access to that heritage which fully meets Open Government standards.

Acting Chief Executive: Dr Gerry Slater

Department: Northern Ireland – Culture, Arts and Leisure
Launched: 3/4/95

Public Trust Office

MENTAL HEALTH AND TRUST DIVISIONS
Stewart House, 24 Kingsway
London WC2B 6JX
020 7664 7000 *Fax:* 020 7664 7705
E-Mail: enquiries@publictrust.gov.uk
Website: www.publictrust.gov.uk

COURT FUNDS OFFICE
22 Kingsway, London WC2B 6LE
020 7936 6000

Looks after the private assets and financial affairs of members of the public who are suffering from mental disorder, those involved with trusts where the Public Trustee is executor of trust, those involved in civil actions in the courts and those interested in some institutional funds.

Chief Executive, Public Trustee and Accountant General: Ms Julia Lomas *(SCS)*
Deputy Public Trustee: Ms Jill Martin

Department: Lord Chancellor's
Launched: 1/7/94

Queen Elizabeth II Conference Centre

Broad Sanctuary, London SW1P 3EE
020 7222 5000 *Fax:* 020 7798 4200
E-Mail: gillp@qeiicc.co.uk
Website: www.qeiicc.co.uk

Provides superior conference and banqueting facilities for government and commercial use on a national and international scale.

Chief Executive: Marcus Buck
Commercial Director: Gill Price

Department: Environment, Transport and the Regions
Launched: 6/7/86
Trading Fund Status

Queen Victoria School

Dunblane, Perthshire FK15 0JY
01786 822288 *Fax:* 0131-310 2926

An MoD-funded boarding school for the children of Scottish Sailors, Soldiers and Airmen, educating pupils from the age of 11 to 18 years.

Headmaster and Chief Executive:
Brian Raine, BA, PGCE
Deputy Head: Colin Philson, BA, PGCE
Assistant Head: Alice Hainey, MA, TCert
Bursar: Ian McGregor
Estate Manager: Lt Col J Sharp, MBE

Department: Defence
Launched: 1/4/92

Radiocommunications Agency

Wyndham House, 189 Marsh Wall,
London E14 9SX
020 7211 0211 *Fax:* 020 7211 0507
E-Mail: library.ra@gtnet.gov.uk
Website: www.radio.gov.uk

It is responsible for the management of the civil radio spectrum in the UK. It also represents UK radio interests internationally.

Chief Executive: David Hendon *(SCS)*
Spectrum Policy Director: Mike Goddard
Spectrum Services Director: Ms Hazel Canter
Customer Services Director: Barry Maxwell
Corporate Services and Facilities Director:
Chris de Grouchy

Department: Trade and Industry
Launched: 2/4/90
Review completed: August 1996 (agency status confirmed)

RAF Logistics Support Services

RAF Wyton, Huntingdon,
Cambridgeshire PE17 2EA
01480 446961 *Fax:* 01480 446747
Website: www.lss-raf.com

To provide specialist logistics support services to enhance UK defence capability.

Chief Executive: Air Commodore Ian Sloss

Department: Defence
Launched: 10/12/96

RAF Personnel Management Agency

RAF Innsworth, Gloucester GL3 1EZ
01452 712612 Ext 7849
Fax: 01452 712612 Ext 7309

RAFPMA provides personnel to meet the RAF's world-wide manpower commitments in times of crisis, war and peace and manages individuals' careers making best use of their skills and potential whilst maintaining an adequate nucleus of trained personnel to meet the manning needs of the Service.

Air Secretary and Chief Executive:
Air Vice-Marshal I M Stewart, AFC
Director of Personnel Management Agency (Officers and Airmen Aircrew):
Air Commodore A E Neal, AFC

Director of Personnel Management Agency
(Airmen and Reserve Forces):
Air Commodore C Davison, MBE
Director of Personnel Management Agency
(Policy): Air Commodore J A Collier, CBE
Personnel Management Agency Air Secretary 1:
Air Commodore (Retired) R D Arnott, CBE
Personnel Management Agency (Casework):
Group Captain D G Barton
Personnel Management Agency (Agency
Secretary): A Cowpe

Department: Defence
Launched: 2/2/97

RAF Signals Engineering Establishment

RAF Henlow, Bedfordshire SG16 6DN
01462 851515 Ext 7087
Fax: 01462 814517
E-Mail: name@rafsee.demon.co.uk

The Agency's mission is to provide timely communications, information systems and electronic support to the Armed Forces of the UK for military operations world-wide. In support of this mission, the Agency carries out design, installation and integration of airborne and ground-based communications and electronic systems.

Chief Executive: Air Commodore C M
Davison, BSc, CEng, MIEE, MIMgt, RAF
Group Captain Policy and Services Division:
Group Captain H G Britten-Austin, MSc, BSc,
CEng, FIEE
Director Projects Division:
A Palmer, BA, CEng, FIEE
Officer Commanding Support Unit:
Wing Commander G E P Pattenden, LLB,
ACIS
Financial Controller: Mrs B S Hudson
Non-Executive Director:
Dr G G Flower, PhD, BSc, CEng, FIEE
Wing Commander Plans:
Wing Commander J S Parker, MBE, MBA,
BSc, CEng, MRAeS
Head Business Development:
Wing Commander N Little, BSc, CEng, MIEE

Department: Defence
Launched: 22/11/94

RAF Training Group Defence Agency

Royal Air Force Innsworth, Gloucester,
Gloucestershire GL3 1EZ
01452 712612 Ext 5312 *Fax:* 01452 510825
E-Mail: ca@tgda.gov.uk
Website: www.tgda.gov.uk

The recruitment and selection of all Royal Air Force personnel and for the policy and delivery of Royal Air Force non-operational training. The aim of the Agency is to underpin the military effectiveness of the Royal Air Force by the timely provision of trained military and civilian personnel.

Chief Executive:
Air Vice-Marshal I S Corbitt, RAF
Director of Training: Air Commodore A P
Waldron, CBE, AFC, RAF
Director of Corporate Development:
Air Commodore G E Willis, BSc, FRAeS,
RAF

Department: Defence
Launched: 1/4/94
Re-launched as an enlarged agency: 1/4/97

Rate Collection Agency

Oxford House, 49–55 Chichester Street,
Belfast BT1 4HH
028 9025 2252 *Fax:* 028 9025 2113
E-Mail: rca@doeni.gov.uk
Website: www.nics.gov.uk/rca

Collects rates and administers the Housing Benefit Scheme for owner-occupiers.

Chief Executive: Arthur Scott
Director of Operations: Anne McKenna
Director of Finance: Fred Hempton
Director of Personnel: Janet Lunn
Director of Information Systems:
Margaret Taylor

Department: Northern Ireland –
Environment
Launched: 1/4/91
Review completed: February 1996 (agency
status confirmed)

Registers of Scotland

Meadowbank House, 153 London Road,
Edinburgh EH8 7AU
0131-659 6111 Ext 3293
Fax: 0131-459 1221
E-Mail: keeper@ros.gov.uk
Website: www.ros.gov.uk
Maintains registers of land etc. in Scotland.

Chief Executive: Alan W Ramage
Deputy Keeper: A G Rennie, LLB
Managing Director: Frank Manson
Head of Legal Services: Ian Davis, LLB

Responsible Minister: First Minister, Scottish Parliament
Launched: 6/4/90
Review completed: March 1999 (agency status confirmed)
Trading Fund Status

Rivers Agency

Hydebank, 4 Hospital Road,
Belfast BT8 8JP
028 9025 3355 *Fax:* 028 9025 3455
E-Mail: enquiry.rivers@dani.gov.uk
Maintains watercourses, flood and sea defences in Northern Ireland.

Chief Executive (Acting): John Hagan

Department: Northern Ireland – Agriculture and Rural Development
Launched: 1/10/96

Roads Service

Clarence Court, 10–18 Adelaide Street
Belfast BT2 8GB
028 9054 0540 *Fax:* 028 9054 0024
E-Mail: roads@doeni.gov.uk
Website: www.doeni.gov.uk/doeroads
The aim of Roads Service is to ensure that Northern Ireland has a safe and effective road based transportation network, in support of the Department's strategic aims and policies.

Chief Executive: Colin James
Director of Corporate Services: Jim Carlisle
Director of Finance: (Vacant)
Director of Network and Customer Services: Grahame Fraser
Director of Engineering: Victor Crawford

Department: Northern Ireland – Department of the Environment
Launched: 1/4/96

Royal Mint

Llantrisant, Pontyclun, CF72 8YT
01443 222111 *Fax:* 01443 623190
7 Grosvenor Gardens, London SW1W 0BH
020 7592 8601 *Fax:* 020 7592 8634
E-Mail: ewilliams@rmint.demon.co.uk
Website: www.royalmint.com
The manufacture and distribution of UK and overseas coins (circulating and commemorative); medals and seals.

Chief Executive: R de L Holmes
Director of Finance: G J Davies
Director of Sales: K R Cottrell
Director of Human Resources: A E Pearce
Director of Collector Coin: A W Wallace
Director of Engineering Services: G J Payne

Department: HM Treasury
Launched: 1/4/90
Review completed: July 1999 (agency status confirmed)
Trading Fund Status

Royal Parks

The Old Police House, Hyde Park,
London W2 2UH
020 7298 2000 *Fax:* 020 7298 2005
Website: www.open.gov.uk/rp/rphome.htm
Manages and polices the Royal Parks in London – St James's Park, Green Park, Hyde Park, Kensington Gardens, Regent's Park, Primrose Hill, Greenwich Park, Richmond Park and Bushy Park. It also manages and polices a number of other areas.

Chief Executive: David Welch, CBE
Chief Officer, Royal Parks Constabulary: Walter Ross
Head of Policy: Viviane Robertson
Head of Finance and IT: Sandra Smith
Head of Commerce and Inner Parks: Jennifer Adams
Head of Estates and Outer Parks: Mike Fitt

Department: Culture, Media and Sport
Launched: 1/4/93

Scottish Agricultural Science Agency

82 Craigs Road, East Craigs,
Edinburgh EH12 8NJ
0131-244 8876 *Fax:* 0131-244 8940
E-Mail: library@sasa.gov.uk
Website: www.sasa.gov.uk

Provides Government, primarily the Scottish Executive, with expert scientific information and advice on agricultural and horticultural crops and aspects of the environment. Also performs statutory and regulatory work consistent with national and European legislation on topics such as plant health, variety registration, crop improvement and protection of crops, food and the environment.

Director: Dr Robert Hay
Deputy Director: S R Cooper
Head of Administration: Mrs Shelagh Quinn

Department: Scottish Executive – Rural Affairs Department
Launched: 1/4/92

Scottish Court Service

Hayweight House, 23 Lauriston Street
Edinburgh EH3 9DQ
0131-229 9200 *Fax:* 0131-221 6895
E-Mail: enquiries@scotcourts.gov.uk

Responsible for the provision and maintenance of Court Houses, and for ensuring the supply of trained staff and of administrative and organisational services, to support the judiciary, in the Supreme and Sheriff Courts in Scotland.

Chief Executive: John Ewing
Deputy Chief Executive and Area Director West:
  Ian Scott
Head of Operations and Policy Unit:
  Eric Cumming
Head of Resources and Efficiency Unit:
  Mrs Nicola Bennett
Head of Personnel and Development Unit:
  Alan Swift
Head of Property and Services Unit:
  Ron Gardiner

Department: Scottish Executive – Justice Department
Launched: 3/4/95

Scottish Fisheries Protection Agency

Pentland House, 47 Robb's Loan
Edinburgh EH14 1TY
0131-244 6059 *Fax:* 0131-244 6086
E-Mail: sfpa.agency@.so003.scotoff.gov.uk
Website: www.scotland.gov.uk

Enforces UK, EU and international fisheries law and regulations in Scottish waters and ports.

Chief Executive: P E Du Vivier
Director of Corporate Strategy and Resources:
  J B Roddin
Director, Operations: R J Walker
Marine Superintendent: Captain W A Brown

Department: Scottish Executive – Rural Affairs
Launched: 12/4/91
Review completed: June 1996 (agency status confirmed)

Scottish Prison Service

Headquarters, Calton House
5 Redheughs Rigg, Edinburgh EH12 9HW
0131-244 8745 *Fax:* 0131-244 8774
Website: www.sps.gov.uk

Provides prison services in Scotland.

Chief Executive: T Cameron *(SCS)*
Director of Custody: J Durno
Area Director (North and East): P Withers
Area Director (South and West): M Duffy
Director of Strategy and Corporate Affairs:
  Ms J Hutchison
Director of Human Resources: P Russell
Director of Finance and Information Systems:
  W Pretswell
Deputy Director of Custody: D Croft
*Deputy Director of Regime Services and
  Supplies:* J McNeill
*Deputy Director of Estates and Building
  Division:* B Paterson

Department: Scottish Executive – Justice Department
Launched: 1/4/93

Scottish Public Pensions Agency

St Margaret's House, 151 London Road
Edinburgh EH8 7TG
0131-244 3288 *Fax:* 0131-244 3334

Responsible for the pension arrangements of some 330,000 people, mainly employees of the NHS and teaching service, including pensioners and former employees with preserved rights.

Chief Executive: Ralph Garden
Director of Policy: G Mowat
Director of Operations: A M Small
Director of Resources and Customer Services:
  M McDermott

Department: Scottish Executive
Launched: 1/4/93

Service Children's Education

BFPO 40
00 49 2161 908 + Ext 2372
Fax: 00 49 2161 908 + Ext 2396
E-Mail: tutor1@bfgnet.com
Website: www.childrens-education.org

Provides an education service for the dependent children of service personnel and UK based civilian support staff residing overseas, and advice and support to service parents in the UK on the provision of schooling.

Chief Executive Officer:
  David Wadsworth, MA, MPhil, HonDEd
Assistant Chief Executive (Operations):
  Paul S Niedzwiedzki, BA
Assistant Chief Executive (Corporate Affairs):
  Doug F Weidner
Assistant Chief Executive (Quality Assurance):
  Ian G Forrest, BSc

Department: Defence
Launched: 1/4/96

Ships Support Agency

B Block, Foxhill, Bath BA5 5AB
01225 883935 *Fax:* 01225 884313

Defines and directs the materiel support of the Royal Navy's ships and submarines.

Director-General Equipment Support
  (Maritime) and Chief Executive:
  J D Coles *(SCS)*
Director Resources: A McClelland
Director Engineering: A Jenkins
Director Operations Platform: M Frowde

Director Support Chain: P Montague
Director Technical: R Cummings
Director Business Development: A Rossi
Director Commercial: J Hall
Frigates IPT/TL: A Fisher
Submarine Support IPT/TL:
  Cdre T C Chittenden
Strategic Systemsx IPT/TL: Cdre M J Holmes

Department: Defence
Launched: 11/12/96

Social Security Agency

Churchill House, Victoria Square,
Belfast BT1 4SS
028 9056 9127 *Fax:* 028 9056 9178
E-Mail: ssa@nics.gov.uk
Website: http://ssa.nics.gov.uk

Delivers a wide range of social security benefits and services. It also provides processing services for the Benefits Agency in Great Britain.

Department: Northern Ireland – Health,
  Social Services and Public Safety
Launched: 1/7/91
Review completed: February 1997 (agency
  status confirmed)

Student Awards Agency for Scotland

Gyleview House, 3 Redheughs Rigg
Edinburgh EH12 9HH
0131-476 8212 *Fax:* 0131-244 5887
Website: www.student-support-saas.gov.uk

Administers student awards and other related services for Scottish domiciled students in full-time higher education.

Chief Executive: K MacRae
Director of Operations: D Stephen

Department: Scottish Executive – Education
  and Lifelong Learning Department
Launched: 5/4/94

Training and Employment Agency

Adelaide House, 39-49 Adelaide Street,
Belfast BT2 8FD
028 9025 7777 *Fax:* 028 9025 7778
E-Mail: derekblack.tea@nics.gov.uk
Website: www.tea-ni.org/

Administration of employment and training services in Northern Ireland.

Department: Northern Ireland – Economic Development
Launched: 2/4/90
Review completed: February 1996 (agency status confirmed)

Treasury Solicitor

Queen Anne's Chambers, 28 Broadway,
London SW1H 9JS
020 7210 3079 *Fax:* 020 7210 3004
E-Mail: tsol.tsd.qac@gtnet.gov.uk

Provides litigation and advisory services to government departments and other publicly funded bodies in England and Wales. Also administers estates of people who die intestate with no known kin.

Chief Executive:
Anthony Hammond, CB, QC *(SCS)*

Responsible Minister: The Attorney General
Launched: 1/4/96

For full details of Treasury Solicitor's Department – see Government Departments

UK Passport Agency

Clive House, Petty France,
London SW1H 9HD
020 7271 8500 *Fax:* 020 7271 8824
Website:
www.open.gov.uk/ukpass/ukpass.htm

The United Kingdom Passport Agency is chiefly concerned with issuing and servicing UK passports to British nationals who are resident in the UK.

Chief Executive: Bernard Herdan
Deputy Chief Executive and Director of Operations: Kevin Sheehan

Department: Home Office
Launched: 2/4/91
Review completed: November 1994 (agency status confirmed)

United Kingdom Debt Management Office

Cheapside House, 138 Cheapside,
London EC2V 6BB
020 7862 6500 *Fax:* 020 7862 6509
E-Mail: [firstname.surname]@dmo.gov.uk
Website: www.dmo.gov.uk

Aim is to carry out the Government's debt management policy of minimising its financing costs over the long term, taking account of risk, and to manage the aggregate cash needs of the Exchequer in the most cost-effective way. Debt management responsibilities include issuing gilts, monitoring the secondary gilt market and intervening if necessary to help it function properly, and advising on new instruments and reforms to make the market more efficient for the benefit of both issuer and purchaser of gilts. Will in due course take on responsibility for management of the Exchequer's daily cash flow.

Chief Executive: Mike Williams *(SCS)*
  020 7862 6533
Policy and Analysis: Paul Mills
  020 7862 6521
Markets: Jo Whelan
  020 7862 6531
Business Services: Dave Curtis
  020 7862 6515

Department: HM Treasury
Launched: 1/4/98

United Kingdom Hydrographic Office

Admiralty Way, Taunton
Somerset TA1 2DN
01823 337900 *Fax:* 01823 284077
E-Mail: [name]@hydro.gov.uk
Website: www.ukho.gov.uk

Produces charts and navigational publications for the Royal Navy and other customers at home and abroad.

Hydrographer/Chief Executive:
  Rear Admiral John P Clarke, CB, LVO, MBE
Director of Production: V Jenkins
Director of Finance: W Burgess
Director Defence Requirements:
  Captain D Conley, RN
Director of Marketing: I Harkness
Director Planning: N Beadle
Director of Human Resources: K Wilson
Director New Business Processes: S Parnell
Technical Adviser: Dr C Drinkwater

Department: Defence
Launched: 6/4/90
Review completed: January 1996 (agency status confirmed)
Trading Fund Status

Valuation and Lands Agency

Queen's Court,
56–66 Upper Queen Street,
Belfast BT1 6FD
028 9025 0700 *Fax:* 028 9054 3800
E-Mail: bobby.stranaghan@dfpni.gov.uk
Website: http://vla.nics.gov.uk

The Valuation and Lands Agency's three main business areas are:
- The maintenance of the Valuation List for rating purposes in Northern Ireland and, periodically, the preparation of a new Valuation List.
- The provision of a valuation, estate management and property data service to the public sector.
- The Central Advisory Unit established within VLA promotes a more proactive approach to estate management.

Chief Executive and Commissioner of Valuation:
  N D Woods
Assistant Commissioner: D C Rainey
Assistant Commissioner: B R McClure

Department: Northern Ireland – Finance & Personnel
Launched: 1/4/93

Valuation Office

New Court, Carey Street,
London WC2A 2JE
020 7506 1700 *Fax:* 020 7506 1998
E-Mail: custserv.voa@gtnet.gov.uk
Website: www.voa.gov.uk

Provides land and buildings valuation service to government departments, other public bodies and a number of local authorities throughout Great Britain.

Ministers: Chancellor of the Exchequer, Paymaster General
Chief Executive: M A Johns *(SCS)*
Deputy Chief Executive:
  J H Ebdon, BSc(EM), FRICS *(SCS)*
Director of Professional and Customer Services:
  A B Prior, FRICS, IRRV
Director of Business Resources:
  Mrs A Wheatcroft
Director Finance, Planning and Strategy:
  D K Park, MA, FRICS

Director of Financial Operations:
  D A Cruden
Director of Business Development:
  R A Dales, FRICS
Director of Corporate Communications:
  Mrs A J McKenna
Director of Modernisation:
  B G Jones, FRICS, IRRV
Chief Valuer, Scotland: A Ainslie
Chief Valuer, Wales: Peter Clement

Department: Inland Revenue
Launched: 30/9/91
Review completed: July 1995 (agency status confirmed)

Vehicle Certification Agency

1 The Eastgate Office Centre
Eastgate Road, Bristol BS5 6XX
0117-951 5151 *Fax:* 0117-952 4103
E-Mail: general.vca.eoc@gtnet.gov.uk
Website: www.vca.gov.uk

Tests and certificates vehicles and their components to UK and international standards.

Chief Executive: Derek Harvey
Deputy Chief Executive: Peter Nicholl

Department: Environment, Transport and the Regions
Launched: 2/4/90
Review completed: September 1994 (agency status confirmed)

Vehicle Inspectorate

Berkeley House, Croydon Street
Bristol BS5 0DA
0117-954 3200 *Fax:* 0117-954 3212
E-Mail: enquiries@via.gov.uk
Website: www.via.gov.uk

It contributes to the maintenance and improvement of road safety and environmental protection by the enforcement of relevant legislation. It does this by checking vehicles and drivers at roadside and other enforcement checks and through the annual testing of all vehicles including Heavy Goods Vehicles, Light Goods Vehicles, Public Service Vehicles, cars and motorcycles.

Chief Executive: Maurice Newey
Product Strategy and Policy Director:
  Hugh Edwards
Business Performance Director: Bob Tatchell
Process Director: Jeff Belt
People Director: Judith Smith

Department: Environment, Transport and the Regions
Launched: 1/8/88
Review completed: August 1996 (agency status confirmed)
Trading Fund Status

Veterinary Laboratories Agency

Woodham Lane, New Haw, Addlestone,
Surrey KT15 3NB
01932 341111 *Fax:* 01932 347046
E-Mail: enquiries@vla.maff.gov.uk
Website:
www.maff.gov.uk/aboutmaf/agency/vla

It provides specialist veterinary advice to MAFF based on sound investigation and surveillance, laboratory testing, research and development. It also offers this service to other government departments and the private sector.

Chief Executive: Dr Tony Little *(SCS)*
Research Director: Dr John Morris
Director of Laboratory Services and
 Surveillance: Dr Steve Edwards

Department: Agriculture, Fisheries and Food
Launched: 1/10/95

Veterinary Medicines Directorate

Woodham Lane, New Haw, Addlestone,
Surrey KT15 3LS
01932 336911 *Fax:* 01932 336618
E-Mail: postbk@vmd.maff.gov.uk
Website: www.open.gov.uk/vmd/vmdhome.htm

Assesses applications for veterinary medicines, issues authorisations and monitors suspected adverse reactions and the presence of residues of veterinary medicines in meat and animal products. Advises Ministers on policy for veterinary medicines.

Director and Chief Executive: Dr J M Rutter
Director of Licensing: S P Dean
Director of Policy: R Anderson
VMD Secretary and Head of Business Unit:
 J F FitzGerald

Department: Agriculture, Fisheries and Food
Launched: 2/4/90
Review completed: April 1994 (agency status confirmed)

War Pensions Agency

Norcross, Blackpool, Lancashire FY5 3WP
01253 858858 *Fax:* 01253 330561
E-Mail: warpension@gtnet.gov.uk
Website: www.dss.gov.uk/wpa/index.htm

Responsible for the assessment and payment of war pensions, the War Pensions Welfare Offices and the Ilford Park Polish Home in Devon.

Chief Executive: Gordon Hextall
Director of Operations, Welfare, IT and Policy:
 Alan Burnham
Director of Finance and Personnel:
 Stuart Munslow
Medical Director: Dr Paul Kitchen
Head of Operations and Welfare Service:
 Peter Hulme
Head of IT and Product Development:
 Lynn Holden
DMA Programme Manager: Tony Burke
Head of Finance and Business Assurance:
 Vic McGeown

Department: Social Security
Launched: 1/4/94

Water Service

Northland House, 3–5 Frederick Street
Belfast BT1 2NR
028 9024 4711 *Fax:* 028 9035 4888
E-Mail: water.service@nics.gov.uk
Website: www.waterni.gov.uk

Provides water and sewerage services, in a cost effective manner, to meet the requirements of existing and future customers and, thereby, to contribute to the health and well-being of the community and the protection of the environment.

Chief Executive: Robert C Martin
Director of Corporate Services: J Crowther
Director of Operations: J Kelly
Director of Development: J McMillen
Director of Finance: D Carson
Technical Director: H Thompson

Department: Northern Ireland –
 Environment
Launched: 1/4/96

Wilton Park

Wiston House, Steyning,
Sussex BN44 3DZ
01903 815020 *Fax:* 01903 815931
E-mail: wilton@pavilion.co.uk

Arranges and runs conferences on international affairs for politicians, officials, academics and others from around the world. Also hosts conferences for public and private sector customers.

Chief Executive and Director, Wilton Park Conferences: Colin Jennings

Manager, Wiston House Conference Centre:
Roger Barr
Deputy Director: Dr Richard Latter
Associate Directors: Nicholas Hopkinson,
Chris Langdon, Virginia Crowe, Robin Hart

Department: Foreign and Commonwealth Office
Launched: 1/9/91
Review completed: March 1997 (agency status confirmed)

OMBUDSMEN AND COMPLAINT-HANDLING BODIES

Ombudsmen deal with complaints about the public or private sector bodies within their jurisdiction. Ombudsman services are free. The majority of Ombudsman schemes are set up by statute. Others are voluntary, non-statutory schemes set up on the initiative of the service sectors concerned. In most schemes there are individual Ombudsmen.

All the schemes listed below, other than the European Ombudsman, are recognised or associate members of the British and Irish Ombudsman Association. To be recognised they have to meet four key criteria: independence from the organisations the Ombudsman has the power to investigate; effectiveness; fairness; and public accountability.

Further information about Ombudsmen is available on the Association's Website: www.intervid.co.uk/bioa or from the Secretary, British and Irish Ombudsman Association, 70 Gray's Inn Road, London WC1X 8NB, Tel: 020 7242 5713, Fax: 020 7405 5052, E-mail: gordon.adams@obo.org.uk. For information about an individual scheme contact the appropriate scheme direct.

Adjudicator's Office

Haymarket House, 28 Haymarket, London SW1Y 4SP
020 7930 2292 *Fax:* 020 7930 2298
E-mail: adjudicators@gtnet.gov.uk
Website: www.open.gov.uk/adjoff/aodemo1.htm

The Adjudicator investigates complaints from people and businesses about the way the Inland Revenue (including the Valuation Office Agency) and Customs and Excise, have handled their affairs, and recommends how complaints should be settled.

The Adjudicator: Dame Barbara Mills, DBE, QC
Head of Office: Charlie Gordon

Assembly Ombudsman and Commissioner for Complaints – Northern Ireland

Progressive House, 33 Wellington Place, Belfast BT1 6HN
028 9023 3821 *Fax:* 028 9023 4912
Free call Information Service: 0800 343424
E-mail: ombudsman@nics.gov.uk
Website: www.ni-ombudsman.org.uk

Included are matters relating to the Code of Practice on Access to Government Information duties in relation to Health Services and matters in the Public Service. The Ombudsman investigates complaints from those who think they have been unfairly treated by a government department or other public body.

Ombudsman: Gerry Burns, MBE
Deputy Ombudsman: J MacQuarrie

Banking Ombudsman, Office of the

70 Gray's Inn Road, London WC1X 8NB
020 7404 9944 *Fax:* 020 7405 5052
E-mail: banking.ombudsman@obo.org.uk
Website: www.obo.org.uk

The Ombudsman, responsible to an independent Council, seeks to resolve disputes between banks and customers. The scheme covers most banks (including all the High Street banks) with personal account business in the UK. Awards up to £100,000. Individuals, clubs, associations, sole traders, partnerships and small limited businesses (with turnover less than £1m) are covered.

This scheme will be merged in mid-2000 with other similar ombudsman schemes to form a single Financial Services Ombudsman Scheme – *see separate entry.*

Chairman of the Council: Sir David Calcutt, QC
Banking Ombudsman: David Thomas
Deputy Ombudsmen: Chris Eadie,
    Michael Reddy
Assistant Ombudsman: Ms Jane Hingston
Administration Manager: Ian Pattison

Broadcasting Standards Commission

7 The Sanctuary, London SW1P 3JS
020 7233 0544 *Fax:* 020 7233 0397
E-mail: bsc@bsc.org.uk
Website: www.bsc.org.uk

The Broadcasting Standards Commission is the

statutory body for standards and fairness in broadcasting. It is the only organisation within the regulatory framework of UK broadcasting to cover all television and radio. This includes BBC and commercial broadcasters as well as text, cable, satellite and digital services.

The Commission has three main tasks:
- produce codes of practice relating to standards and fairness
- consider and adjudicate on complaints
- monitor, research and report on standards and fairness in broadcasting

Chairman: Lord Holme of Cheltenham, CBE
Deputy Chairmen: Jane Leighton, Lady Warner
Commissioners: Ms Danielle Barr,
David Boulton, Dame Fiona Caldicott, DBE,
Uday Dholakia, Strachan Heppell, CB,
The Rev Rose Hudson-Wilkin,
Jeremy Mitchell, Ms Sally O'Sullivan,
Ms Sioned Wyn Thomas, Michael Unger

Building Societies Ombudsman, Office of the

Millbank Tower, Millbank,
London SW1P 4XS
020 7931 0044 *Fax:* 020 7931 8485
E-mail: bldgsocombudsman@easynet.co.uk
DX: 120555, Victoria 6

The Ombudsman investigates and decides complaints against building societies. Complainants should first go through the internal complaints procedure of the building society/connected undertaking. If satisfaction is not obtained, the complaint should go in writing to the Ombudsman.

Ombudsman: Ms Josephine Thompson
Registrar to the Council: Ms Barbara Cheney

Complaints Adjudicator for Companies House

PO Box 2, Fakenham, Norfolk NR21 0RS

Customers who are not content with a decision by Companies House may be referred to The Adjudicator who will act as an impartial referee.

Adjudicator: Bill Thomas

Complaints Commissioner to the General Council of the Bar

2/3 Cursitor Street, London EC4A 1NE
020 7440 4000 *Fax:* 020 7440 4001
E-mail: laycommissioner@barcouncil.org.uk
Website: www.barcouncil.org.uk

The Complaints Commissioner, who is independent of the Bar Council, investigates all complaints against barristers. Complaints disclosing possible evidence of misconduct or inadequate professional service are remanded for the Professional Conduct and Complaints Committee.

Complaints Commissioner:
Michael Scott, CB, CBE, DSO

Estate Agents, Ombudsman for

Beckett House, 4 Bridge Street
Salisbury, Wiltshire SP1 2LX
01722 333306 *Fax:* 01722 332296
E-mail: post@oea.co.uk
Website: www.oea.co.uk

Deals with disputes between actual and potential buyers and sellers of residential property in the UK and Member Agencies.

Ombudsman: Stephen Carr-Smith

European Ombudsman

1 avenue du Président Robert Schuman,
BP 403, 67001 Strasbourg Cedex, France
00 33 (0) 3 88 17 24 22
Fax: 00 33 (0) 3 88 17 90 62
E-mail: euro-ombudsman@europarl.eu.int
Website: www.euro-ombudsman.eu.int

The European Ombudsman is empowered to receive complaints from any citizen of the European Union concerning instances of maladministration in the activities of the EU institutions or bodies.

Ombudsman: Jacob Söderman

Financial Services Ombudsman Scheme

11th Floor, 25 The North Colonnade,
Canary Wharf, London E14 5HS
020 7676 0822 *Fax:* 020 7676 9713
E-mail: walter.merricks@fsa.gov.uk

From mid-2000, the FSOS will bring all the current eight financial services ombudsman schemes under one roof. These are: The Banking Ombudsman, The Building Societies Ombudsman, The Investment Ombudsman, The Insurance Ombudsman, The PIA Ombudsman Bureau, The Personal Insurance Arbitration Service, The SFA Complaints Bureau and Arbitration Service and the FSA Independent Investigator.

Chief Ombudsman: Walter Merricks

Funeral Ombudsman Scheme

Fifth Floor, 26-28 Bedford Row,
London WC1R 4HE
020 7430 1112 *Fax:* 020 7430 1012
E-mail: fos@dircon.co.uk

The Funeral Ombudsman Scheme provides free, impartial and independent investigation into complaints against member funeral directors and crematoria. Compensation is awarded where appropriate. The Scheme covers a substantial proportion of the UK funeral profession.

Chairman of the Council: John Hosker
Ombudsman: Prof Geoffrey Woodroffe
Scheme Manager: Regina Weston

Health Service Commissioner Ombudsman for England

Millbank Tower, Millbank,
London SW1P 4QP
0845 015 4033 *Fax:* 020 7217 4940
Website: www.ombudsman.org.uk

The Health Service Ombudsman investigates complaints about NHS authorities including NHS trusts, and family health service providers in England.

Commissioner: M S Buckley
Deputy: Miss H Scott
Directors: Miss H Bainbridge, N J Jordan, D R G Pinchin, R Tyrrell

Health Service Commissioner Ombudsman for Scotland

28 Thistle Street, Edinburgh EH2 1EN
0131-225 7465 *Fax:* 0131-226 4447

The Health Service Ombudsman investigates complaints about NHS authorities, including NHS trusts, and family health service providers in Scotland.

Commissioner: M S Buckley
Deputy Commissioner: Miss H Scott

Health Service Commissioner Ombudsman for Wales

5th Floor, Capital Tower,
Greyfriars Road, Cardiff CF10 3AG
0845 601 0987 *Fax:* 029 2022 6909

The Health Service Ombudsman investigates complaints about NHS authorities, including NHS trusts, and family health service providers in Wales.

Commissioner: M S Buckley
Deputy Commissioner: Miss H Scott
Investigations Manager (Wales): S Drummond

Housing Association Ombudsman for Scotland

2 Belford Road, Edinburgh EH4 3BL
0131-220 0599 *Fax:* 0131-220 0577

The Housing Association Ombudsman for Scotland examines complaints from tenants and customers of housing associations and co-operatives registered with Scottish Homes and certain other landlords, who claim to have suffered personal injustice as a result of bad, inefficient or improper administration.

Ombudsman: John Richards

Independent Case Examiner for the Child Support Agency

PO Box 155, Chester CH99 9SA
0151-801 8800 *Fax:* 0151-801 8801
Minicom: 0151-801 8888
Local call rate number: 0845 606 0777
E-mail: ice@ukgov.demon.co.uk
Website: www.ind-case-exam.org.uk

PO Box 1245, Belfast BT2 7DF

The Independent Case Examiner deals with complaints about maladministration against the

Child Support Agency, where the client has received a response from or on behalf of the Chief Executive within the last six months. She cannot consider complaints which the Parliamentary Commissioner for Administration has investigated or is investigating, nor complaints about legislation.

Independent Case Examiner: Mrs Anne Parker
Office Manager: Phil Latus

Independent Complaints Reviewer to HM Land Registry

Newspaper House (First Floor),
8-16 Great New Street, London EC4A 3EU
020 7583 1172 *Fax:* 020 7583 1173
DX461 London Chancery Lane
E-mail: icr2hmlr@icrev.demon.co.uk
Website:
www.icrev.demon.co.uk/icrbook.htm

The ICR investigates complaints of maladministration, complaints including complaints about the Registry's failure to meet standards of service, quality, speed and performance. Following review, the ICR can make recommendations aimed at putting matters right for individual complainants and at improving Land Registry services in the future.

The ICR issues an annual report which is available on our website or from our office.

Independent Complaints Reviewer:
  Mrs Jodi Berg
Assistant to ICR: Andrew Robertson

Independent Housing Ombudsman Scheme

Norman House, 105–109 Strand,
London WC2R 0AA
020 7836 3630 *Fax:* 020 7836 3900
Lo-call Tel: 0345 125973
E-mail: ombudsman@ihos.org.uk

IHO deals with complaints against social landlords registered with the Housing Corporation, and other landlords who have volunteered to join the scheme.

Chair: Ms Pam Brown
Ombudsman: Roger Jefferies
General Manager and Company Secretary:
  Lawrence Greenberg

Insurance Ombudsman Bureau

City Gate One, 135 Park Street,
London SE1 9EA
020 7902 8100 *Fax:* 020 7902 8197
E-mail: complaint@theiob.org.uk
Website: www.theiob.org.uk

The Insurance Ombudsman Bureau investigates and resolves disputes between policyholders and general insurance companies which are members of the scheme.

Enquiries 0845 600 6666
Advice Centre Helpline 020 7902 8144

Chairman of the Council: Maurice Healy
Ombudsman: Laurie Slade
Deputy Ombudsman: Peter Hart
Communications Manager: Graham Cox
Head of Information Services: Reidy Flynn

Investment Ombudsman, Office of the

6 Frederick's Place, London EC2R 8BT
020 7796 3065

The Office of the Investment Ombudsman is an independent organisation which considers and resolves disputes between investors and companies regulated in the conduct of investment business by IMRO.

Investment Ombudsman: Peter Dean, CBE
Executive Director: Ronald Bennett

Lay Observer for Northern Ireland

Lancashire House, 1st Floor,
5 Linenhall Street, Belfast BT2 8AA
028 9054 2900 *Fax:* 028 9054 2909

The Lay Observer is an independent non-legal person appointed to monitor the nature of complaints against solicitors made to the Law Society and to report on the manner in which the Law Society handles them.

Lay Observer: Professor Vincent Mageean, OBE

Legal Services Ombudsman, Office of the

22 Oxford Court, Oxford Street,
Manchester M2 3WQ
0161-236 9532 *Fax:* 0161-236 2651
E-mail: enquiries.olso@gtnet.gov.uk

Appointed under the Courts and Legal Services Act 1990 to oversee the handling of complaints against solicitors, barristers, licensed conveyancers and legal executives by professional bodies.

Ombudsman: Ms Ann Abraham

Local Administration In England, Commission for

21 Queen Anne's Gate, London SW1H 9BU
020 7915 3210 *Fax:* 020 7233 0396

The Local Government Ombudsmen investigate complaints from members of the public alleging injustice caused by maladministration by local authorities with a view to securing, where appropriate, satisfactory redress for the complainant and better administration by the authorities.

Chairman of the Commission and Ombudsman for London, Kent and East Sussex:
E B C Osmotherly, CB
Secretary to the Commission: N Karney
Ombudsman for East Anglia, Essex, Surrey, West Sussex, the South West, the West, the South and most of Central England (excluding Birmingham): J R White
No 2 The Oaks, Westwood Way, Westwood Business Park, Coventry CV4 8JB
024 7669 5999 *Fax:* 024 7669 5902

Ombudsman for Birmingham, Cheshire, Derbyshire, Nottinghamshire, Lincolnshire and the North of England: Mrs P A Thomas
Beverley House, 17 Shipton Road,
York YO30 5FZ
01904 663200 *Fax:* 01904 663269

Website: www.open.gov.uk/lgo

Local Administration in Scotland, Commissioner for

23 Walker Street, Edinburgh EH3 7HX
0131-225 5300 *Fax:* 0131-225 9495

Handles complaints of administrative shortcoming against local authorities in Scotland and housing complaints against Scottish Homes.

Commissioner (Ombudsman):
Frederick C Marks, OBE
Deputy Commissioner and Secretary:
Ms Janice H Renton, LLB

Local Administration in Wales, Commission for

Derwen House, Court Road, Bridgend,
Mid Glamorgan CF31 1BN
01656 661325 *Fax:* 01656 658317
E-mail: lgombudsmanwales@btinternet.com
Website: www.ombudsman-wales.org

Investigation of complaints of maladministration made against local government bodies in Wales where such maladministration is alleged to have caused personal injustice to the complainant. Reports on investigations are sent to the complainant, the authority which is the subject of the complaint, and the press.

Local Commissioner (Ombudsman):
E R Moseley
Secretary to the Commission: D Bowen
Parliamentary Commissioner (ex officio):
M S Buckley

Office for the Supervision of Solicitors

Victoria Court, 8 Dormer Place,
Leamington Spa, Warwickshire CV32 5AE
01926 820082 *Fax:* 01926 431435
Website: www.lawsociety.org.uk

The Office for the Supervision of Solicitors was established by the Law Society in September 1996 to handle complaints about the conduct and standard of service of solicitors in England and Wales. The independence of the Office's decision making is guaranteed by the Law Society's Council. The majority of its work is carried out through conciliation. The Office prosecutes serious misconduct cases in the independent Solicitors Disciplinary Tribunal. It also investigates breaches of the Solicitors A/Cs Rules, intervenes to wind up practices, administers the Compensation Fund and houses the department which issues Remuneration Certificates.

Director: (Vacant)

Office of the Subsidence Adviser

The Belgrave Centre, Talbot Street,
Nottingham NG1 5GG
0115-971 2776 *Fax:* 0115-971 2779
E-mail: osanotts@cix.co.uk

The Office of the Subsidence Adviser is an independent statutory body which provides free information and advice to people whose property is affected by coal mining subsidence damage. OSA also has the power to investigate complaints of maladministration against The Coal Authority and private mine operators who have responsibility for administering coal mining subsidence damage claims.

The Subsidence Adviser:
    Malcolm Webb, FRICS, ACIArb

Parliamentary Commissioner for Administration, Office of the

Millbank Tower, Millbank,
London SW1P 4QP
020 7217 4212 *Fax:* 020 7217 4067
Website:
www.ombudsman.org.uk/pca-hsc.htm

The Parliamentary Ombudsman investigates complaints (which must be referred on behalf of individuals by MPs) about injustice resulting from maladministration of government departments and certain non-departmental public bodies, including complaints against their own grievance procedures and complaints that they have refused access to information to which the public are entitled under the 1994 Code of Practice on Access to Government Information.

Parliamentary Commissioner: M S Buckley
Deputy: J E Avery
Directors: Mrs S Maunsell, A Watson, N Cleary,
    G R Monk, D Reynolds

Pensions Ombudsman

6th Floor, 11 Belgrave Road,
London SW1V 1RB
020 7834 9144 *Fax:* 020 7821 0065

Primarily complaints investigated relate to alleged maladministration of occupational pension schemes. Personal pension complaints would normally be dealt with only if outside the jurisdiction of The Personal Investment Authority (PIA).

Pensions Ombudsman: Dr Julian Farrand

Personal Investment Authority Ombudsman Bureau

Hertsmere House, Hertsmere Road,
London E14 4AB
020 7216 0016 *Fax:* 020 7712 8742

Principal Ombudsman: Tony Holland
Ombudsmen: Richard Prior, Philip Roberts
General Manager: Christopher J Hamer
Press and Information Officer: Iris Baker

Police Complaints Authority

10 Great George Street,
London SW1P 3AE
020 7273 6450 *Fax:* 020 7273 6401

The Police Complaints Authority was established in 1985 as an independent body with powers to supervise the investigation of the more serious complaints by members of the public against police officers and over the disciplinary outcome of such investigations.

Chairman: Peter Moorhouse
Deputy Chairman: Ms Molly Meacher
Members: Ian Bynoe, Ms Jo Dobry,
    James Elliott, Mrs Linda Allan,
    Ms Lorna Whyte, Ms Mehmuda Mian,
    Mrs Caroline Mitchell, Alan Potts,
    Tony Williams

Police Complaints for Northern Ireland, Independent Commission for

Chamber of Commerce House,
22 Great Victoria Street, Belfast BT2 7LP
028 9024 4821 *Fax:* 028 9024 8563

The Independent Commission for Police Complaints for Northern Ireland was established in 1988 with powers to supervise the investigation of serious complaints by members of the public against members of the Royal Ulster Constabulary; to review disciplinary action on all complaints; and to monitor the informal resolution procedure.

Chairman: Paul A Donnelly
Chief Executive: Brian McClelland

Prisons Ombudsman

Ashley House, 2 Monck Street
London SW1P 2BQ
020 7276 2876 *Fax:* 020 7276 2860

The Prisons Ombudsman considers complaints submitted by individual prisoners who have failed to obtain satisfaction from the Prison Service requests and complaints system.

Prisons Ombudsman: Stephen Shaw

Scottish Legal Services Ombudsman

Mulberry House, 16 Picardy Place,
Edinburgh EH1 3JT
0131-556 5574 *Fax:* 0131-556 1519
E-mail: complaints@scot-legal-ombud.org.uk
Website: www.scot-legal-ombud.org.uk

The Scottish Legal Services Ombudsman is appointed by the First Minister to examine complaints about how the Law Society of Scotland, the Faculty of Advocates and the Scottish Conveyancing and Executry Services Board have handled complaints against practitioners who are members of those bodies.

Ombudsman: Garry S Watson

Scottish Parliamentary Commissioner for Administration

28 Thistle Street, Edinburgh EH2 1EN
0845 601 0456 *Fax:* 0131-226 4447

The Scottish Parliamentary Commissioner investigates complaints made to him via members of the Scottish Parliament about injustice resulting from maladministration by the Scottish Executive, the Parliamentary corporation and a range of bodies involved in devolved Scottish affairs. He can also look at complaints that individuals have been refused information to which they are entitled under the Code of Practice on Access to Scottish Executive Information.

Ombudsman: M S Buckley
Investigations Manager: G Keil

Waterways Ombudsman

PO Box 406, Haywards Heath,
West Sussex RH17 5GF
Tel/Fax: 01273 832624

The independent Waterways Ombudsman investigates and resolves complaints of maladministration against British Waterways, where the complainant has completed the internal complaints procedure. Exclusions from the Ombudsman's jurisdiction include complaints concerning personnel matters and things that have been, or are being, considered by a court, or otherwise involve legal interpretation.

Ombudsman: Stephen Edell

Welsh Administration Ombudsman

5th Floor, Capital Tower, Greyfriars Road,
Cardiff CF10 3AG
0845 601 0987 *Fax:* 029 2022 6909

The Welsh Administration Ombudsman investigates complaints about injustice resulting from maladministration by the National Assembly for Wales or certain public bodies involved in devolved Welsh affairs. He can also look at complaints that individuals have been refused information to which they are entitled under the Code of Practice on Public Access to Information adopted by the National Assembly.

Ombudsman: M S Buckley
Investigations Manager: S Drummond

PRIVY COUNSELLORS

HRH The Duke of Edinburgh
HRH The Prince of Wales
Lord Aberdare
Lord Ackner
Earl of Airlie
Lord Aldington (sits as Lord Low)
Sir William Aldous
Ezekiel Alebua
Michael James Hugh Alison
Lord Ampthill
Michael Ancram
Hon John Douglas Anthony
James Norwich Arbuthnot
Lord Archer of Sandwell
Hilary Jane Armstrong
Sir John Lewis Arnold
Hon Owen Seymour Arthur
Jeremy John Durham (Paddy) Ashdown
Lord Ashley of Stoke
Robert James Atkins
Sir Robin Ernest Auld
Lord Baker of Dorking
Sir Alfred John Balcombe
Lord Barber
Lord Barnett
Margaret Mary Beckett
Alan James Beith
Sir Alexander Roy Asplan Beldam
Lord Belstead (sits as Lord Ganzoni)
Anthony Neil Wedgwood Benn
Sir Frederic Mackarness Bennett
Lord Biffen
Lord Bingham of Cornhill
Hon William Francis Birch
*Sir Gordon Ellis Bisson
Anthony Charles Lynton Blair
Lord Blaker
Hon Peter Blanchard (appt)
Baroness Blatch
David Blunkett
Paul Yaw Boateng
James Brendan Bolger
Albert Edward Booth
Betty Boothroyd
Robert Thomas Boscawen
Virginia Hilda Brunette Maxwell Bottomley
Sir Michael Hardie Boys
Sir Rhodes Boyson
Sir Nicholas Alexander Brathwaite
Lord Bridge of Harwich
Lord Brightman
Sir Leon Brittan
Sir Henry Brooke

Peter Leonard Brooke
James Gordon Brown
Nicholas Brown
Sir Simon Denis Brown
Sir Stephen Brown
Lord Browne-Wilkinson
Sir Adam Courtauld Butler
Dame Ann Elizabeth Oldfield
   Butler-Sloss
Sir Richard Joseph Buxton
Stephen Byers
Richard George Caborn
Earl of Caithness
Lord Callaghan of Cardiff
Lord Cameron of Lochbroom
Lord Camoys
Walter Menzies Campbell
Sir William Campbell
Lord Campbell of Croy
Archbishop of Canterbury
Lord Carlisle of Bucklow
Lord Carr of Hadley
Lord Carrington
   (sits as Lord Carington of Upton)
Sir Robert Douglas Carswell
Lord Carter
*Hon Sir Maurice Eugene Casey
Baroness Castle of Blackburn
Sir John Murray Chadwick
Lord Chalfont
Baroness Chalker of Wallasey
Hon Sir Julius Chan
Sir Christopher John Chataway
David George Clark
Helen Elizabeth Clark
Lord Clark of Kempston
Sir Anthony Clarke
Kenneth Harry Clarke
Thomas Clarke
Lord Cledwyn of Penrhos
Lord Clinton-Davis
Lord Clyde
Lord Cockfield
Lord Cocks of Hartcliffe
Lord Coggan
Fraser McDonald Colman
Sir John George Melvin Compton
John Dennis Concannon
Robin Finlayson Cook
Lord Cooke of Thorndon
Sir Frank Cooper
Lord Cope of Berkeley
Sir Frederick Vernon Corfield

Sir Zelman Cowen
Sir Percy Cradock
Viscount Cranborne
  (sits as Lord Gascoyne-Cecil)
Earl of Crawford & Balcarres
  (sits as Lord Balniel)
The Hon Wyatt Creech
Lord Crickhowell
Sir David Powell Croom-Johnson
William Douglas Cullen
Sir James Roualeyn Hovell-Thurlow-
  Cumming-Bruce
John Anderson Cunningham
David Maurice Curry
Alistair Maclean Darling
David John Denzil Davies
Ronald Davies
David Michael Davis
Terence Davis
*Hon Sir Ronald Keith Davison
Lord Dean of Harptree
Baroness Dean of Thornton-le-Fylde
Lord Deedes
Lord Denham
Duke of Devonshire
Donald Campbell Dewar
Lord Diamond
Sir George Brian Hugh Dillon
Lord Dixon
Frank Dobson
Lord Donaldson of Lymington
Stephen James Dorrell
*Sir William Randolph Douglas
Sir Edward Dillon Lott Du Cann
Sir Arthur Antony Duff
Sir Robin Horace Walford Dunn
Paul Clayton East
Lord Eden of Winton
Timothy John Crommelin Eggar
*Sir Johann Thomas Eichelbaum
The Hon Dame Sian Elias
Sir Peter Frank Hannibal Emery
Lord Emslie
Lord Erroll of Hale
  (sits as Lord Erroll of Kilmun)
Manuel Esquivel
Sir Anthony Howell Meurig Evans
Sir Edward Walter Eveleigh
Sir Donald Henry Farquharson
Lord Fellowes
Earl Ferrers
Frank Field
*Sir Vincent Floissac
Michael Mackintosh Foot
Lord Forsyth of Drumlean
Eric Forth

Derek Foster
Sir Peter Norman Fowler
Sir John Marcus Fox
Sir Michael John Fox
Hon John Malcolm Fraser
Lord Fraser of Carmyllie
John Freeman
Lord Freeman
Reginald Freeson
Lord Garel-Jones
*Hon Thomas Munro Gault
Edward Alan John George
*Philip Telford Georges
*Hon Sir Harry Talbot Gibbs
Sir Peter Leslie Gibson
Sir Ralph Brian Gibson
Lord Gibson-Watt
Lord Gilbert
Lord Gilmour of Craigmillar
Lord Glenamara
Sir Iain Derek Laing Glidewell
Lord Goff of Chieveley
Alastair Robertson Goodlad
Hon Sir John Grey Gorton
Earl of Gowrie
Lord Graham of Edmonton
Hon Douglas Arthur Montrose Graham (appt)
Lord Gray of Contin
Lord Griffiths
John Selwyn Gummer
Lord Habgood
William Hague
Lord Hailsham of St Marylebone
Dame Brenda Hale
Sir Archibald Hamilton
Jeremy James Hanley
Lord Hardie
Harriet Harman
Lord Harris of Greenwich
Walter Harrison
Sir Alan Gordon Barraclough Haselhurst
Lord Hattersley
Lord Hayhoe
Lord Healey
Sir Edward Richard George Heath
David Philip Heathcote-Amory
Sir Denis Robert Maurice Henry
Hon John Steele Henry
Michael Ray Dibdin Heseltine
Sir William Frederick Payne Heseltine
Lord Hesketh
Lord Higgins
Sir David Cozens-Hardy Hirst
Lord Hobhouse of Woodborough
Lord Hoffmann
Douglas Martin Hogg

Lord Holderness
Baroness Hollis of Heigham
Geoffrey Hoon
Lord Hope of Craighead
Sir Peter Maudslay Hordern
Michael Howard
Lord Howe of Aberavon
Lord Howell of Guildford
Lord Hunt of Wirral
Jonathan Lucas Hunt
Lord Hurd of Westwall
Sir Michael Hutchison
Lord Hutton
Hubert Ingraham
Adam Paterson Ingram
Lord Irvine of Lairg
John Michael Jack
Sir Robin Janvrin
Lord Jauncey of Tullichettle
Baroness Jay of Paddington
Earl Jellicoe
    (sits as Lord Jellicoe of Southampton)
Lord Jenkin of Roding
Lord Jenkins of Hillhead
Aubrey Jones
Stephen Barry Jones
Lord Jopling
Tessa Jowell
Sir Igor Judge
Hon Anerood Jugnauth
Gerald Bernard Kaufman
Lord Keith of Kinkel
Hon Sir Kenneth James Keith (appt)
Sir John William Basil Kelly
Lord Kelvedon
Hon Sir Peter Kenilorea
Charles Kennedy
Sir Paul Joseph Morrow Kennedy
Sir Michael Robert Emanuel Kerr
Thomas Jeremy King
Lord Kingsdown
Lord Kingsland
Neil Gordon Kinnock
Gregory Knight
Lord Lamont of Lerwick
Lord Lane
Lord Lang of Monkton
David Russell Lange
Hon Kamuta Latasi
Hon Toaripi Lauti
Sir John Laws
Lord Lawson of Blaby
Sir Frederick Horace Lawton
Sir Andrew Peter Leggatt
Graham Douglas Leonard (Bishop)
Helen Lawrie Liddell

Peter Bruce Lilley
Lord Lloyd of Berwick
Sir Peter Robert Cable Lloyd
Bishop of London
Earl of Longford
    (sits as Lord Pakenham of Cowley)
Hon Allan Louisy
Sir Richard Napier Luce
Sir Nicholas Walter Lyell
Jesse Dickson Mabon
Sir John Clarke MacDermott
Lord Macdonald of Tradeston
John Roddick Russell MacGregor
Hon Duncan MacIntyre
Lord Mackay of Ardbrecknish
Lord Mackay of Clashfern
Lord Mackay of Drumadoon
Andrew James Mackay
David John Maclean
Robert Adam Ross Maclennan
John Major
Sir Jonathan Mance
Peter Benjamin Mandelson
Sir Charles Barrie Knight Mantell
Hon Ratu Sir Kamisese Mara
Lord Marsh
Lord Mason of Barnsley
Francis Anthony Aylmer Maude
Sir Brian Stanley Mawhinney
Sir Anthony Tristram Kenneth May
Lord Mayhew of Twysden
*Hon Sir Thaddeus Pearcey McCarthy
Ian McCartney
Sir William Paschal McCollum
Sir Anthony James Denys McCowan
*Hon Ian Lloyd McKay
Hon Donald Charles McKinnon
*Sir Duncan Wallace McMullin
Michael Hugh Meacher
Sir Robert Edgar Megarry
David John Mellor
Lord Merlyn-Rees
Alun Michael
Alan Milburn
Bruce Millan
Lord Millett
Hon James Fitzallen Mitchell
Lord Molyneaux of Killead
Lord Monro of Langholm
Lord Moore of Lower Marsh
Lord Moore of Wolvercote
Michael Kenneth Moore
Lord Morris of Manchester
Charles Richard Morris
Estelle Morris
John Morris

Sir Robert Andrew Morritt
Marjorie Mowlam
Roland Dunstan Moyle
Sir John Frank Mummery
Paul Peter Murphy
Sir Donald Bruce Murray
Lord Murray of Epping Forest
Lord Murray
Lord Murton of Lindisfarne
Lord Mustill
Sir Patrick Dalmahoy Nairne
Rabbie Lainagau Namaliu
Lord Naseby
Richard Francis Needham
Sir Brian Thomas Neill
Lord Newton of Braintree
Lord Nicholls of Birkenhead
Sir James Michael Anthony Nicholson
Lord Nolan
Sir John William Frederic Nott
Sir Martin Charles Nourse
Gordon James Oakes
Sir Patrick McCarthy O'Connor
Turlough O'Donnell
Francis Duncan O'Flynn
Sir Angus James Bruce Ogilvy
Lord Oliver of Aylmerton
Lord Onslow of Woking
Baroness Oppenheim-Barnes
Lord Orme
Sir Philip Howard Otton
Lord Owen
Hon Bikenibeu Paeniu
Sir Arthur Michael Palliser
Sir Geoffrey Winston Russell Palmer
Sir Roger Jocelyn Parker
Lord Parkinson
Christopher Francis Patten
Lord Patten
Percival Patterson
Sir Geoffrey Edwin Pattie
Earl of Perth
Hon Winston Raymond Peters
Lord Peyton of Yeovil
Lord Phillips of Worth Matravers
Sir Malcolm Thomas Pill
Hon Sir Lynden Oscar Pindling
Michael Denzil Xavier Portillo
Sir Mark Howard Potter
Lord Prentice
John Leslie Prescott
Hon George Cadle Price
Lord Prior
Sir Tomasi Puapua
Sir Francis Brooks Purchas
Lord Pym

Joyce Gwendolen Quin
Giles Heneage Radice
Sir Timothy Hugh Francis Raison
James Edward Ramsden
Lord Rawlinson of Ewell
John Alan Redwood
Lord Rees
John Reid
Lord Renton
Lord Renton of Mount Harry
Lord Richard
*Hon Sir Ivor Lloyd Morgan Richardson
Lord Richardson of Duntisbourne
Sir Malcolm Leslie Rifkind
Lord Roberts of Conwy
Lord Robertson of Port Ellen
Sir John Ormond Roch
Lord Rodger of Earlsferry
Lord Rodgers of Quarry Bank
Jeffrey William Rooker
Sir Christopher Dudley Roger Rose
Lord Ross
Dame Angela Claire Rosemary Rumbold
Lord Runcie
Sir Thomas Patrick Russell
Lord Ryder of Wensum
Hon Timothy Alan Davan Sainsbury
Lloyd Erskine Sandiford
Lord Saville of Newdigate
Lord Scarman
Sir Konrad Hermann Theodor
   Schiemann
Sir Nicholas Paul Scott
Sir Richard Rashleigh Folliott Scott
Hon Edward Phillip George Seaga
Sir Stephen Sedley
Lord Selkirk of Douglas
Lord Shawcross
Hon Hugh Lawson Shearer
Robert Edward Sheldon
Gillian Patricia Shephard
Lord Shepherd
   (sits as Lord Shepherd of Spalding)
Lord Shore of Stepney
Hon Jennifer Mary Shipley
Clare Short
Hon Kennedy Alphonse Simmonds
Lord Simon of Glaisdale
Hon Ian McCahon Sinclair
Sir Christopher John Slade
Lord Slynn of Hadley
Andrew David Smith
Christopher Robert Smith
Sir Geoffrey Johnson Smith
Hon Sir Michael Thomas Somare
*Hon Sir Edward Jonathan Somers

Lord St John of Fawsley
Sir John Paul Stanley
Sir Christopher Stephen Thomas Jonathan
    Thayer Staughton
Lord Steel of Aikwood
Sir Ninian Martin Stephen
Lord Stewartby
Lord Steyn
Lord Stodart of Leaston
Gavin Steel Strang
Lord Strathclyde
John (Jack) Whitaker Straw
Sir Murray Stuart-Smith
Hon Sir Brian Edward Talboys
Ann Taylor
Lord Tebbit
Lord Templeman
Baroness Thatcher
Lord Thomas of Gwydir
Hon Edmund Walter Thomas
Sir Swinton Barclay Thomas
Lord Thomson of Monifieth
John Jeremy Thorpe
Sir Mathew Alexander Thorpe
Hon Andrew Patrick Charles Tipping
Robert James Tizard
Lord Trefgarne
William David Trimble
Baroness Trumpington
Sir Simon Tuckey
Viscount Ullswater
Hon Simon Upton

Lord Varley
Lord Waddington
Sir John Douglas Waite
Lord Wakeham
Lord Waldegrave of North Hill
Lord Walker of Doncaster
Lord Walker of Worcester
Sir Robert Walker
Sir Mark Waller
Sir Alan Hylton Ward
Sir Tasker Watkins
Lord Weatherill
Sir John Daniel Wheeler
Ann Noreen Widdecombe
Dafydd Wigley
Lord Wilberforce
Alan John Williams
Baroness Williams of Crosby
Lord Williams of Mostyn
Lord Windlesham (sits as Lord Hennessy)
Hon Paias Wingti
Hon Reginald Grieve Withers
*Hon Sir Arthur Owen Woodhouse
Lord Woolf
Norman Russell Wylie
Archbishop of York
Baroness Young
Lord Young of Graffham
Sir George Samuel Knatchbull Young
Viscount Younger of Leckie
    (sits as Lord Younger of Prestwick)
*Edward Zacca

* Judges from the Commonwealth, members of the Judicial Committee – see Privy Council Office.

Privy Counsellors of Northern Ireland

By virtue of the Northern Ireland Constitution Act 1973 no further appointments will be made to the Privy Council of Northern Ireland, but existing members will retain their existing style and dignity.

R J Bailie
D W Bleakley
W Craig
J Dobson
Rt Hon Lord Justice Kelly
H V Kirk
W J Long

Lord McConnell
W B McIvor
Lord Moyola
Sir Ivan Neill
Sir Robert Porter
J D Taylor
H W West

Two important new books from Vacher Dod

THE SCOTTISH PARLIAMENT

and

THE NATIONAL ASSEMBLY FOR WALES
CYNULLIAD CENEDLAETHOL CYMRU

Members' Biographies and Photographs,
Historical Background, 1999 Election Results,
Structure and Functions, Contact Directories

Vacher Dod Publishing Limited
PO Box 3700, Westminster, London SW1E 5NP
Tel: 020 7828 7256   Fax: 020 7828 7269
E-mail: politics@vacherdod.co.uk
Websites: www.vacherdod.co.uk   www.politicallinks.co.uk

NEW PARLIAMENT AND
NATIONAL ASSEMBLIES

SCOTTISH PARLIAMENT

George IV Bridge, Edinburgh EH99 1SP
0131-348 5000 *General Enquiries:* 0845 278 1999
Public Information: E-mail: sp.info@scottish.parliament.uk
Presiding Officer: E-mail: presiding.officer@scottish.parliament.uk
Websites:
www.scottish.parliament.uk/contact.html
www.sp.media@scottish.parliament.uk (Media enquiries)
www.education.service@scottish.parliament.uk
www.chamber.office@scottish.parliament.uk (Debating chamber)
www.committee.office@scottish.parliament.uk
www.petitions@scottish.parliament.uk
www.presiding.officer@scottish.parliament.uk
www.webmaster@scottish.parliament.uk

Election 6 May 1999
1 July 1999 Official Opening by HM The Queen

Future elections are to be held every four years.

ELECTORAL SYSTEM

The election was conducted using a method combining the traditional first past the post system and a form of proportional representation called the Additional Member System. Each voter cast two votes. One vote was for one of 73 constituency members, based on the Westminster parliament constituencies. The second went towards the election of 56 regional members, seven for each of the eight regions used in the European Parliament elections. These seats ensure that each party's representation in the Parliament reflects its overall share of the vote.

ELECTION RESULT

	Constituency MSPs	Regional MSPs	Total MSPs
Scottish Labour Party	53	3	56
(includes Scottish Labour/Co-operative Party)			
Scottish National Party	7	28	35
Scottish Conservative and Unionist Party	0	18	18
Scottish Liberal Democrats	12	5	17
Scottish Green Party	0	1	1
Scottish Socialist Party	0	1	1
MSP for Falkirk West	1	0	1
Turnout 58%	**73**	**56**	**129**

POWERS AND RESPONSIBILITIES

The Parliament has administrative and legislative powers relating to Scotland in the following areas:

agriculture
economic development
education
environment
health

law and order
local government
social work
transport

It can vary the basic rate of income tax in Scotland by 3p in the £.

Westminster retains responsibility for:

defence
employment
international relations

national finance and economics
social security

The interests of Scotland in the United Kingdom Government are represented by the Secretary of State for Scotland and the Westminster Parliament allocates a budget to the Scottish Parliament.

OPERATION/PROCEDURES

The First Minister is elected by Members and appoints Ministers from among Members to be responsible for specific areas of policy. The First Minister, Ministers and the Law Officers, the Lord Advocate and the Solicitor General for Scotland (who do not have to be Members), make up the Scottish Executive. The Cabinet consists of all these except the Solicitor General.

The Parliament appoints a Presiding Officer and deputy from among its members, to oversee debates, advise on procedure in a similar role to the Speaker of the House of Commons.

Committees made up of members of the Parliament consider in detail various policy areas.

Parliament will sit for 30 to 33 weeks a year, fitting in with school holidays, and will work normal business hours.

Members (MSPs)

Lab	Labour Party
SNP	Scottish National Party
Con	Conservative
Lib Dem	Liberal Democrats
Green	Green Party
SSP	Scottish Socialist Party
MSPFW	MSP for Falkirk West

	Party	Constituency/Region*	Majority
ADAM Brian	SNP	North East Scotland*	
AITKEN Bill	Con	Glasgow*	
ALEXANDER Wendy	Lab	Paisley North	4,616
BAILLIE Jackie	Lab	Dumbarton	4,758
BARRIE Scott	Lab	Dunfermline West	5,021
BOYACK Sarah	Lab	Edinburgh Central	4,626
BRANKIN Rhona	Lab/Co-op	Midlothian	5,525
BROWN Robert	Lib Dem	Glasgow*	
CAMPBELL Colin	SNP	West of Scotland*	
†CANAVAN Dennis	MSPFW	Falkirk West	12,192
†CHISHOLM Malcolm	Lab	Edinburgh North and Leith	7,736
CRAIGIE Cathie	Lab	Cumbernauld and Kilsyth	4,259
CRAWFORD Bruce	SNP	Mid Scotland and Fife*	
†CUNNINGHAM Roseanna	SNP	Perth	2,027
CURRAN Margaret	Lab	Glasgow Baillieston	3,072
DAVIDSON David	Con	North East Scotland*	
DEACON Susan	Lab	Edinburgh East and Musselburgh	6,714
†DEWAR Rt Hon Donald	Lab	Glasgow Anniesland	10,993
‡DOUGLAS-HAMILTON Rt Hon Lord James	Con	Lothian*	
EADIE Helen	Lab/Co-op	Dunfermline East	8,699
ELDER Dorothy-Grace	SNP	Glasgow*	
EWING Fergus	SNP	Inverness East, Nairn and Lochaber	441
†EWING Margaret	SNP	Moray	4,129
EWING Winifred	SNP	Highlands and Islands*	
FABIANI Linda	SNP	Central Scotland*	
FERGUSON Patricia	Lab	Glasgow Maryhill	4,326
FERGUSSON Alex	Con	South of Scotland*	
FINNIE Ross	Lib Dem	West of Scotland*	
†GALBRAITH Sam	Lab	Strathkelvin and Bearsden	12,121
GALLIE Phil	Con	South of Scotland*	
GIBSON Kenneth	SNP	Glasgow*	
GILLON Karen	Lab	Clydesdale	3,880

GODMAN Trish	Lab	West Renfrewshire	2,893
GOLDIE Annabel	Con	West of Scotland*	
†GORRIE Donald	Lib Dem	Central Scotland*	
GRAHAME Christine	SNP	South of Scotland*	
GRANT Rhoda	Lab	Highlands and Islands*	
GRAY Iain	Lab	Edinburgh Pentlands	2,885
HAMILTON Duncan	SNP	Highlands and Islands*	
HARDING Keith	Con	Mid Scotland and Fife*	
HARPER Robin	Green	Lothian*	
HENRY Hugh	Lab	Paisley South	4,495
†HOME ROBERTSON John	Lab	East Lothian	10,946
HUGHES Janis	Lab	Glasgow Rutherglen	7,287
HYSLOP Fiona	SNP	Lothian*	
INGRAM Adam	SNP	South of Scotland*	
JACKSON Gordon	Lab	Glasgow Govan	1,756
JACKSON Sylvia	Lab	Stirling	3,981
JAMIESON Cathy	Lab/Co-op	Carrick, Cumnock and Doon Valley	8,803
JAMIESON Margaret	Lab	Kilmarnock and Loudoun	2,760
JENKINS Ian	Lib Dem	Tweeddale, Ettrick and Lauderdale	4,478
JOHNSTON Nick	Con	Mid Scotland and Fife*	
JOHNSTONE Alex	Con	North East Scotland*	
KERR Andy	Lab	East Kilbride	6,499
LAMONT Johann	Lab/Co-op	Glasgow Pollok	4,642
LIVINGSTONE Marilyn	Lab/Co-op	Kirkcaldy	4,475
LOCHHEAD Richard	SNP	North East Scotland*	
LYON George	Lib Dem	Argyll and Bute	2,057
†McALLION John	Lab	Dundee East	2,854
MacASKILL Kenny	SNP	Lothian*	
McAVEETY Frank	Lab/Co-op	Glasgow Shettleston	5,467
McCABE Tom	Lab	Hamilton South	7,176
McCONNELL Jack	Lab	Motherwell and Wishaw	5,046
MACDONALD Lewis	Lab	Aberdeen Central	2,696
MacDONALD Margo	SNP	Lothian*	
McGRIGOR Jamie	Con	Highlands and Islands*	
McGUGAN Irene	SNP	North East Scotland*	
MACINTOSH Kenneth	Lab	Eastwood	2,125
McINTOSH Lyndsay	Con	Central Scotland*	
MacKAY Angus	Lab	Edinburgh South	5,424
MacLEAN Kate	Lab	Dundee West	121
†McLEISH Henry	Lab	Central Fife	8,675
McLEOD Fiona	SNP	West of Scotland*	
McLETCHIE David	Con	Lothian*	
McMAHON Michael	Lab	Hamilton North and Bellshill	5,606
MACMILLAN Maureen	Lab	Highlands and Islands*	
McNEIL Duncan	Lab	Greenock and Inverclyde	4,313
McNEILL Pauline	Lab	Glasgow Kelvin	4,408
McNULTY Des	Lab	Clydebank and Milngavie	4,710
MARTIN Paul	Lab	Glasgow Springburn	7,893
MARWICK Tricia	SNP	Mid Scotland and Fife*	
MATHESON Michael	SNP	Central Scotland*	
MONTEITH Brian	Con	Mid Scotland and Fife*	
†MORGAN Alasdair	SNP	Galloway and Upper Nithsdale	3,201
MORRISON Alasdair	Lab	Western Isles (Eilean Siar)	2,093
MULDOON Bristow	Lab	Livingston	3,904
MULLIGAN Mary	Lab	Linlithgow	2,928
MUNDELL David	Con	South of Scotland*	

MUNRO John Farquhar	Lib Dem	Ross, Skye and Inverness West	1,539
MURRAY Elaine	Lab	Dumfries	3,654
NEIL Alex	SNP	Central Scotland*	
OLDFATHER Irene	Lab	Cunninghame South	6,541
PATERSON Gil	SNP	Central Scotland*	
PEACOCK Peter	Lab	Highlands and Islands*	
PEATTIE Cathy	Lab	Falkirk East	4,139
QUINAN Lloyd	SNP	West of Scotland*	
RADCLIFFE Nora	Lib Dem	Gordon	4,195
RAFFAN Keith	Lib Dem	Mid Scotland and Fife*	
REID George	SNP	Mid Scotland and Fife*	
ROBISON Shona	SNP	North East Scotland*	
ROBSON Euan	Lib Dem	Roxburgh and Berwickshire	3,585
RUMBLES Mike	Lib Dem	West Aberdeenshire and Kincardine	2,289
RUSSELL Michael	SNP	South of Scotland*	
†SALMOND Alex	SNP	Banff and Buchan	11,292
SCANLON Mary	Con	Highlands and Islands*	
SCOTT Tavish	Lib Dem	Shetland	3,194
SHERIDAN Tommy	SSP	Glasgow*	
SIMPSON Richard	Lab	Ochil	1,303
SMITH Elaine	Lab	Coatbridge and Chryston	10,404
SMITH Iain	Lib Dem	North East Fife	5,064
SMITH Margaret	Lib Dem	Edinburgh West	4,583
‡STEEL Rt Hon Sir David	Lib Dem	Lothian*	
STEPHEN Nicol	Lib Dem	Aberdeen South	1,760
STONE Jamie	Lib Dem	Caithness, Sutherland and Easter Ross	4,391
STURGEON Nicola	SNP	Glasgow*	
†SWINNEY John	SNP	North Tayside	4,192
THOMSON Elaine	Lab	Aberdeen North	398
TOSH Murray	Con	South of Scotland*	
ULLRICH Kay	SNP	West of Scotland*	
WALLACE Ben	Con	North East Scotland*	
†WALLACE Jim	Lib Dem	Orkney	4,619
‡WATSON Mike	Lab	Glasgow Cathcart	5,374
†WELSH Andrew	SNP	Angus	8,901
WHITE Sandra	SNP	Glasgow*	
WHITEFIELD Karen	Lab	Airdrie and Shotts	8,985
WILSON Allan	Lab	Cunninghame North	4,796
WILSON Andrew	SNP	Central Scotland*	
YOUNG John	Con	West of Scotland*	

† *Also a Member of the House of Commons*
‡ *Also a Member of the House of Lords*

Ian Welsh, MSP for Ayr, resigned December 1999

Regions* and Constituencies

Central Scotland*
Airdrie and Shotts
Coatbridge and Chryston
Cumbernauld and Kilsyth
East Kilbride
Falkirk East
Falkirk West
Hamilton North and Bellshill
Hamilton South
Kilmarnock and Loudoun
Motherwell and Wishaw

Glasgow*
Glasgow Anniesland
Glasgow Baillieston
Glasgow Cathcart
Glasgow Govan
Glasgow Kelvin
Glasgow Maryhill
Glasgow Pollok
Glasgow Rutherglen
Glasgow Shettleston
Glasgow Springburn

Highlands and Islands*
Argyll and Bute
Caithness, Sutherland and Easter Ross
Inverness East, Nairn and Lochaber
Moray
Orkney
Ross, Skye and Inverness West
Shetland
Western Isles (Eilean Siar)

Lothians*
Edinburgh Central
Edinburgh East and Musselburgh
Edinburgh North and Leith
Edinburgh Pentlands
Edinburgh South
Edinburgh West
Linlithgow
Livingston
Midlothian

Mid Scotland and Fife*
Central Fife
Dunfermline East
Dunfermline West
Kirkcaldy
North East Fife
North Tayside
Ochil
Perth
Stirling

North East Scotland*
Aberdeen Central
Aberdeen North
Aberdeen South
Angus
Banff and Buchan
Dundee East
Dundee West
Gordon
West Aberdeenshire and Kincardine

South of Scotland*
Ayr
Carrick, Cumnock and Doon Valley
Clydesdale
Cunninghame South
Dumfries
East Lothian
Galloway and Upper Nithsdale
Roxburgh and Berwickshire
Tweeddale, Ettrick and Lauderdale

West of Scotland*
Clydebank and Milngavie
Cunninghame North
Dumbarton
Eastwood
Greenock and Inverclyde
Paisley North
Paisley South
Strathkelvin and Bearsden
West Renfrewshire

Scottish Government

THE CABINET (Labour/Liberal Democrat Partnership)

The First Minister: The Rt Hon Donald Dewar, MSP
Deputy First Minister and Minister for Justice: Jim Wallace, QC, MSP
  Deputy Minister for Justice: Angus MacKay, MSP
Minister for Finance: Jack McConnell, MSP
Minister for Health and Community Care: Susan Deacon, MSP
  Deputy (Community Care): Iain Gray, MSP
Minister for Communities: Wendy Alexander, MSP
  Deputy (Local Government): Frank McAveety, MSP
  Deputy (Social Inclusion, Equality and the Voluntary Sector): Jackie Baillie, MSP
Minister for Transport and the Environment (including Land Reform and Water): Sarah Boyack, MSP
Minister for Enterprise and Lifelong Learning: Henry McLeish, MSP
  Deputy Minister for Enterprise and Lifelong Learning: Nicol Stephen, MSP
  Deputy (Highlands and Islands and Gaelic): Alasdair Morrison, MSP
Minister for Rural Affairs: Ross Finnie, MSP
  Deputy Minister for Rural Affairs: John Home Robertson, MSP
Minister for Children and Education, Culture, Arts and Sport: Sam Galbraith, MSP
  Deputy (Culture and Sport): Rhona Brankin, MSP
  Deputy (Children and Education): Peter Peacock, MSP
Minister for Parliament (Chief Whip): Tom McCabe, MSP
  Deputy Minister for Parliament (Deputy Chief Whip): Iain Smith, MSP

Law Officers
Lord Advocate: The Rt Hon the Lord Hardie, QC
  Deputy (Solicitor General for Scotland): Colin Boyd, Esq, QC *(not a member of the Cabinet)*

Source: Scottish Parliament Information Centre

PRINCIPAL OFFICERS AND OFFICIALS

OFFICE OF THE PRESIDING OFFICER

Presiding Officer: The Rt Hon Sir David Steel, KBE, MSP
Private Secretary: Huw Williams

SCOTTISH PARLIAMENTARY CORPORATE BODY
(responsible for administration)

Robert Brown, MSP   Andrew Welsh, MSP
Des McNulty, MSP   John Young, MSP
Secretary to the SPCB: Huw Williams

PARLIAMENTARY BUREAU
(responsible for all-party business programme and forward planning)

The Rt Hon Sir David Steel, MSP   Tom McCabe, MSP (Lab)
  (Presiding Officer)   Michael Russell, MSP (SNP)
The Rt Hon Lord James   Iain Smith, MSP (Lib Dem)
  Douglas-Hamilton, MSP (Con)

PRINCIPAL OFFICERS

Clerk/Chief Executive: Paul Grice
Legal Adviser: Ann Nelson
Director of Clerking: Carol McCracken
Director of Corporate Services: Stewart Gilfillan
Director of Communications: Lesley Beddie
Holyrood Project Director: Barbara Doig

Audit Adviser: Dave Ferguson
Head of Chamber Office: Bill Thomson
Head of Committee Office: Elizabeth Watson
Head of Information Systems: Bethan Hubbard
Head of Scottish Parliament Information Centre: Janet Seaton
Editor of the Official Report: Henrietta Hales
Head of Corporate IT Services: Cathy Watkins
Head of Security: Bill Anderson
Head of Finance: Robin Andrews
Head of Procurement: Lynn Garvie
Head of Personnel: Ian Macnicol
Head of Broadcasting: Alan Smart
Head of Facilities Management: Charlie Fisher

Ministerial Responsibilities

THE FIRST MINISTER

First Minister (The Rt Hon **Donald Dewar** MSP)
Head of Scottish Executive. With the Deputy First Minister is responsible for the development, implementation and presentation of Scottish Executive policies.
Principal Special Adviser: John Raffety *Tel:* 0131-244 5223 *Fax:* 0131-244 2756
Official Spokesman: David Whitton *Tel:* 0131-244 5202 *Fax:* 0131-244 5201
Strategic Communications: Philip Chalmers *Tel:* 0131-244 5055 *Fax:* 0131-244 2240
Principal Private Secretary: Jonathan Pryce *Tel:* 0131-244 5218
Deputy Private Secretary: A Nichol *Tel:* 0131-244 5214
Assistant Private Secretary: Karen Jackson *Tel:* 0131-244 5215
Diary Secretary: Billy McLaren *Tel:* 0131-244 5216
Personal Secretary: Sandra Buckle *Tel:* 0131-244 5213 *Fax:* 0131-244 2756
Based at St Andrew's House (SAH)

JUSTICE

Deputy First Minister and Minister for Justice (**Jim Wallace** QC MSP)
With the First Minister, responsible for the development, implementation and presentation of Scottish Executive policies. Responsible for Home Affairs, including civil law and criminal justice, criminal justice social work services, police, fire, prisons and courts, law reform, land reform policy and freedom of information.
Private Secretary: Michael Kellett *Tel:* 0131-244 4576 (SH) 0131-244 5228 (SAH)
Assistant Private Secretary: Fiona Armstrong *Tel:* 0131-244 4575 (SH) 0131-244 5227 (SAH)
Based at St Andrew's House (SAH)

Deputy Minister for Justice (**Angus Mackay** MSP)
Deputy to the Minister for Justice, with particular responsibility for land reform and co-ordination of Executive policy in relation to drugs.
Private Secretary: Helen Buckley *Tel:* 0131-244 4579 *Fax:* 0131-244 2121
Based at Saughton House (SH)

CHILDREN AND EDUCATION

Minister for Children and Education (**Sam Galbraith** MSP)
Responsible for pre-school and school education, children and young people, culture and the arts, the built heritage, architecture, sport and lottery funding.
Private Secretary: Gabby Pieraccini *Tel:* 0131-244 7716 *Fax:* 0131-244 7715

Deputy Minister for Children and Education (**Peter Peacock** MSP)
Deputy to the Minister for Children and Education with responsibility for pre-school and school education, children and young people.
Private Secretary: Steven Szymoszowski *Tel:* 0131-244 1469

Deputy Minister for Culture and Sport (**Rhona Brankin** MSP)
Deputy to the Minister for Children and Education with responsibility for culture and the arts, the built heritage, architecture, sport and lottery funding.
Private Secretary: Fiona McLauchlan *Tel:* 0131-244 7717 *Fax:* 0131-244 7715
Based at Victoria Quay (VQ)

ENTERPRISE AND LIFELONG LEARNING

Minister for Enterprise and Lifelong Learning (**Henry McLeish** MSP)
Responsible for the Economy, Business and Industry including Scottish Enterprise, Highlands and Islands Enterprise, tourism, trade and inward investment, further and higher education, the science base, lifelong learning, training and the delivery of the new deal.
Private Secretary: Karen McAvenue *Tel:* 0141-242 5475 0131-244 1472 (VQ)

Deputy Minister for Enterprise and Lifelong Learning (**Nicol Stephen** MSP)
Deputy to the Minister for Enterprise and Lifelong Learning, with particular responsibility for training further and higher education and the delivery of the new deal.
Private Secretary: Liz Shea *Tel:* 0141-242 5587

Deputy Minister for Enterprise in the Highlands and Islands and Gaelic (**Alasdair Morrison** MSP)
Deputy to the Minister for Enterprise and Lifelong Learning with responsibility for Highlands and Islands Enterprise, the University of the Highlands and Islands and Tourism, and Gaelic.
Private Secretary: Juliet Grimes *Tel:* 0141-242 5777
Diary Secretary: Gary Crombie *Tel:* 0141-242 5778
Based at Meridian Court (MC)

FINANCE

Minister for Finance (**Jack McConnell** MSP)
Responsible for the Scottish Budget, including local government finance, and European structural funds, resource allocation and accounting and for Modernising Government. Assists the First Minister and Deputy First Minister on the development and co-ordination of Executive policy.
Private Secretary: Deborra Smith *Tel:* 0131-348 5590 *Fax:* 0131-348 5562/3
Temporarily based at Parliament Headquarters (PHQ)

HEALTH AND COMMUNITY CARE

Minister for Health and Community Care (**Susan Deacon** MSP)
Responsible for health policy, the National Health Service in Scotland, community care, and food safety.
Private Secretary: Rachel Sunderland *Tel:* 0131-244 4017
Personal Secretary: Joanne Ramsay *Tel:* 0131-244 2135 *Fax:* 0131-244 3563

Deputy Minister for Community Care (**Iain Gray** MSP)
Deputy to the Minister for Health and Community Care with particular responsibility for community care.
Private Secretary: David Thomson *Tel:* 0131-244 2186
Based at St Andrew's House (SAH)

LAW OFFICERS

The Lord Advocate (The Rt Hon the **Lord Hardie** QC)
Legal advice to the Scottish Executive; prosecution in the Scottish criminal courts; tribunals.
Private Secretary: Jeff Gibbons *Tel:* 0131-226 2525
Assistant Private Secretary: Carol McDivitt *Tel:* 0131-226 2500
Diary Secretary: Alison Shields *Tel:* 0131-226 2521 *Fax:* 0131-226 6910

Solicitor-General for Scotland (**Colin Boyd** QC)
Assists the Lord Advocate, with particular responsibility for prosecutions.
Private Secretary: Jeff Gibbons *Tel:* 0131-226 2525
Based at the Crown Office (CO)

PARLIAMENT

Minister for Parliament (**Tom McCabe** MSP)
Responsible for Parliamentary Affairs and the management of Executive business in the Parliament. Labour Business Manager.
Private Secretary: Ian Campbell *Tel:* 0131-348 5593
Assistant Private Secretary: Audrey Snedden *Tel:* 0131-348 5592 *Fax:* 0131-348 5562

Deputy Minister for Parliament (**Iain Smith** MSP)
Deputy to the Minister for Parliament, with particular responsibility for the Parliamentary handling of the legislative programme. Liberal Democrat Business Manager.
Private Secretary: Callum Stanners *Tel:* 0131-348 5572
Temporarily based at Parliament Headquarters (PHQ)

RURAL AFFAIRS

Minister for Rural Affairs (**Ross Finnie** MSP)
Responsible for policy in relation to rural development including agriculture, fisheries and forestry.
Private Secretary: Jacqueline Conlan *Tel:* 0131-244 4456 *Fax:* 0131-244 4458

Deputy Minister for Rural Affairs (**John Home Robertson** MSP)
Deputy to the Minister for Rural Affairs with particular responsibility for fisheries, forestry and research. Assists the Minister for Rural Affairs on policy in relation to rural development.
Private Secretary: Mike Watson *Tel:* 0131-244 4425 *Fax:* 0131-244 4458
Based at Pentland House (PH)

COMMUNITIES

Minister for Communities (**Wendy Alexander** MSP)
Responsible for social inclusion, local government and housing. Lead responsibility for Executive policy on equality issues and the voluntary sector.
Private Secretary: Linda Sinclair *Tel:* 0131-244 7818
Diary Secretary: Sarah Hobkirk *Tel:* 0131-244 7327

Deputy Minister for Local Government (**Frank McAveety** MSP)
Deputy to the Minister for Communities with particular responsibility for local government.
Private Secretary: Gary Cox *Tel:* 0131-244 0228
Diary Secretary: Helen Doyle *Tel:* 0131-244 0362 *Fax:* 0131-244 7403

Deputy Minister for Communities (**Jackie Baillie** MSP)
Deputy to the Minister for Communities with particular responsibility for social inclusion; for co-ordination of Executive policy on equality and the voluntary sector.
Private Secretary: Scott Rogerson *Tel:* 0131-244 5539
Diary Secretaries: Tracy Rae, Jacqueline D'Arcy *Tel:* 0131-244 5538 *Fax:* 0131-244 7404
Based at Victoria Quay (VQ)

TRANSPORT AND THE ENVIRONMENT

Minister for Transport and the Environment (**Sarah Boyack** MSP)
Responsible for transport including the development for integrated transport policies for rural areas, the environment, natural heritage, sustainable development, strategic environmental assessments and the land-use planning system.
Private Secretary: Neil MacLennan *Tel:* 0131-244 0627 *Fax:* 0131-244 7405
Based at Victoria Quay (VQ)

LOCATION GUIDE

SAH   St Andrew's House, Regent Road, Edinburgh EH1 3DG.
       Tel: 0131-556 8400

PHQ   Parliament Headquarters, George IV Bridge,
       Edinburgh EH99 1SP
       Tel: 0131-348 5000

MC   Meridian Court, 5 Cadogan Street, Glasgow G2 6AT.
       Tel: 0141-248 2855 and 0131-556 8400

PH   Pentland House, 47 Robbs Loan, Edinburgh EH14 1TY.
       Tel: 0131-556 8400

VQ   Victoria Quay, Edinburgh EH6 6QQ.
       Tel: 0131-556 8400

SH   Saughton House, Broomhouse Drive, Edinburgh EH11 3XD.
       Tel: 0131-556 8400

CO   Crown Office, 25 Chambers Street, Edinburgh EH1 1LA.
       Tel: 0131-226 2626 Fax: 0131-226 6910
       E-mail: co.isunit@dial.pipex.com

Committees

The following committees have been established.

Audit
Education, Culture and Sport
Enterprise and Lifelong Learning
Equal Opportunities
European
Finance
Health and Community Care
Justice and Home Affairs

Local Government
Procedures
Public Petitions
Rural Affairs
Social Inclusion, Housing and Voluntary Sector
Standards
Subordinate Legislation
Transport and Environment

THE SCOTTISH PARLIAMENT

Biographies of MSPs available now on

Dod *on* Disk

Tel: 020 7828 7256

The Scottish Executive (Civil Service)

The Scottish Executive is the Government in Scotland for all devolved matters. It is accountable to the Scottish Parliament. The Executive consists of the First Minister plus a team of 12 Scottish Ministers including Law Officers. The statutory powers and duties exercised by UK Ministers in Scotland in relation to devolved matters have been transferred to the Scottish Ministers.

The Scottish Executive consists of six main departments:

Development Department; Education Department; Enterprise and Lifelong Learning Department; Justice Department*; Health Department; Rural Affairs Department – together with Executive Secretariat, Corporate Services and Finance.

Includes Scottish Courts Administration

Senior Management

OFFICE OF THE PERMANENT SECRETARY – ST ANDREW'S HOUSE

Permanent Secretary: Muir Russell
Private Secretary: Sarah Morrel
 Tel: 0131-244 4026 and 0131-270 6796 (DH)
Assistant Private Secretary: Neil Cuthbert
 Tel: 0131-244 2348 *Fax:* 0131-244 2756

Departments

DEVELOPMENT DEPARTMENT – VICTORIA QUAY

Head: Kenneth MacKenzie, CB
Private Secretary: John Peerless
 Tel: 0131-244 0760
Assistant Private Secretary: Alison Knox
 Tel: 0131-244 0763 *Fax:* 0131-244 0785
Heads of Groups:
Housing and Area Regeneration Group:
 David Belfall
Local Government Group: David Middleton
Director, Construction and Building Control Group: John Gibbons, CBE
Transport and Planning Group: John Martin
National Roads Directorate:
Chief Road Engineer, Trunk Roads Design and Construction Division: John Howison
Chief Planner, Planning and Development Control Group: Alastair Mackenzie, CBE
Director, Road Network Management and Maintenance Division: Neil Mackenzie

EDUCATION DEPARTMENT – VICTORIA QUAY

Head: John Elvidge
Private Secretary: Johann MacDougall
 Tel: 0131-244 1484
Assistant Private Secretary: Jock Steward
 Tel: 0131-244 1479 *Fax:* 0131-244 1475
Head of Primary and Secondary Education Group: Mike Ewart

Heads of Divisions:
School Standards and Improvement:
 Bob Irvine
Curriculum, International and Information Technology: Eleanor Emberson
Children and Young People's Group:
 Gillian Stewart
Early Education and Childcare:
 Roma Menlowe
Children and Families: Jane Morgan
Young People and Looked After Children:
 Gerald McHugh
Sports Policy Unit: John Gilmour
Arts and Cultural Heritage: Jim Lonie
Chief Inspector, Social Work Service Inspectorate: Angus Skinner
 (based at James Craig Walk)
HM Senior Inspector of Schools:
 D A Oslser
Chief Statistician, Education Statistics:
 Rob Wishart
Chief Architect: Dr J G Gibbons

ENTERPRISE AND LIFELONG LEARNING DEPARTMENT – MERIDIAN COURT

Head: Eddie Frizzell
Private Secretary: Alison Latimer
 Tel: 0131-242 5704
Assistant Private Secretary: Janet Smith
 Tel: 0131-242 5703 *Fax:* 0131-242 5477
Head of Lifelong Learning Group:
 Ed Weeple
Head of New Deal and Childcare Group:
 M B Foulis
Head of Economics and Industrial Affairs:
 Geoffrey Robson
Industrial Adviser: Douglas Blair
Chief Scientific Adviser: Prof David Tedford
Director, Scottish Trade International:
 David Taylor
Director, Locate in Scotland: David Macdonald

JUSTICE DEPARTMENT –
SAUGHTON HOUSE

Head: Hamish Hamill, CB
Private Secretary: Jackie Knox
  Tel: 0131-244 2791
Assistant Private Secretary: Linda Craik
  Tel: 0131-244 2122 *Fax:* 0131-244 2121
Head of Police, Fire and Emergencies Group:
  Colin Baxter
Head of Civil and Criminal Law Group:
  Niall Campbell
HM Chief Inspector of Prisons:
  Clive Fairweather, OBE
HM Chief Inspector of Fire Services:
  Dennis Davis, OBE
HM Chief Inspector of Constabulary:
  William Taylor, QPM
Chief Research Officer, Central Research Unit:
  Dr Peter Leveln
Head of Social Work Services Group:
  Gillian Stewart

HEALTH DEPARTMENT
NHS SCOTLAND –
ST ANDREW'S HOUSE

Head of Department and Chief Executive:
  Geoff Scaife, CB
Private Secretary: Gill Wylie
  Tel: 0131-244 2410
Assistant Private Secretary:
  Miss Beverely Currie *Tel:* 0131-244 2440
  Fax: 0131-244 2162
Public Health Policy Unit
Chief Medical Officer:
  Prof Sir David Carter
Private Secretary: Laura Crooks
  Tel: 0131-244 2317 *Fax:* 0131-244 2835
Deputy Chief Medical Officer:
  Dr Andrew Fraser
Senior Management:
Director of Purchasing: Dr Kevin Woods
Director of Trusts: Paul Wilson
Director of Primary Care: Agnes Robson
Director of Finance: John Aldridge
Deputy Director of Finance: David Palmer
Director of Human Resources: Gerry Marr
Medical Adviser: Dr David Ewing
Director and Chief Nursing Officer:
  Anne Jarvie
Chief Scientist: Prof Graeme Catto
Chief Dental Officer: Ray Watkins
Chief Pharmacist: Bill Scott
Public Health Policy Unit, Head
  of Administrative Group:
  Nicola Munro

RURAL AFFAIRS DEPARTMENT –
PENTLAND HOUSE

Head: John Graham
Private Secretary: David Brown
  Tel: 0131-244 6022
Assistant Private Secretary: Lorraine Irving
  Tel: 0131-244 6308 *Fax:* 0131-244 6116
*Head of Division, Research, Education and
  Advisory Services:* Andrew Rushworth
Food and Agricultural Group:
Head of Group: David Crawley
Head of Division A: Jim Wildgoose
Head of Division D: Ian Anderson
Head of Fisheries Group: Dr Paul Brady
Head of Environment Group: Stephen Hampson

Scottish Executive Secretariat

St Andrew's House
Edinburgh EH1 3DG
Enquiries: 0131-556 8400

EXECUTIVE SECRETARIAT

Head of Executive: Robert Gordon
  Tel: 0131-244 7937
Personal Assistant: Jane McEwan
  Tel: 0131-244 5598
Personal Secretary: Liz Fanning
  Tel: 0131-244 7938

CABINET

Head of Secretariat: Ian Walford
  Tel: 0131-244 5532
Personal Secretary: Tracy Ramsay
  Tel: 0131-244 5533

CONSTITUTIONAL POLICY AND
PARLIAMENTARY DIVISION

Head of Division: Ken Thomson
  Tel: 0131-244 0357
Personal Secretary: Linda Landles
  Tel: 0131-244 7661
Parliamentary Liaison Branch: David Spence
  Tel: 0131-244 1433
Constitutional Policy Branch: George Burgess
  Tel: 0131-244 7432

EXTERNAL RELATIONS

Head of Division: Owen Kelly
  Tel: 0131-244 7944
Personal Secretary: Lisa Nugent
  Tel: 0131-244 7362
European Affairs: David Wallace
  Tel: 0131-244 0735
UK, Ireland and International:
  Donald Henderson *Tel:* 31-244 0375

EQUALITY AND VOLUNTARY ISSUES GROUP

Head: Valerie Macniven *Tel:* 0131-244 2631

EU OFFICE (BRUSSELS)

Scotland House, Rond-Point, Schuman 6, Brussels 1040, Belgium.
Tel: +32 2 282 8330
Head: George Calder

OFFICE OF THE CHIEF ECONOMIC ADVISER

Chief Economic Adviser: Dr Andrew Goudie
Tel: 0131-244 3430
Personal Secretary: Linda Boag
Tel: 0131-244 2788

OFFICE OF THE SCOTTISH PARLIAMENTARY COUNSEL – VICTORIA QUAY

First Scottish Parliamentary Counsel:
John McCluskie, QC *Tel:* 0131-244 1673
Personal Secretary: Anne Williams
Tel: 0131-244 1672
Counsel: Gregor Clark, Colin Wilson
Deputes: John Harkness, Madelaine Mackenzie

OFFICE OF THE SOLICITOR TO THE SCOTTISH EXECUTIVE – VICTORIA QUAY

Tel: 0131-244 0549
Solicitor: Richard Henderson
Tel: 0131-244 0531
Deputy Solicitor: Jim Maclean
Tel: 0131-244 0494
Personal Secretary: Sheena Cooper
Tel: 0131-244 0495

OFFICE OF THE LEGAL SECRETARY TO THE LORD ADVOCATE

Crown Office, 25 Chamber Street, Edinburgh EH1 1LA.
Tel: 0131-247 2665
Legal Secretary: Patrick Layden

INFORMATION DIRECTORATE

Provision of advice to Ministers and Scottish Executive Departments on public presentation and policy.
Headquarters: St Andrew's House

Director: Roger Williams
Chief Press Officers:
Susan Stewart (Communities, Finance, Justice and Education)
Tel: 0131-244 2972
Andrew Baird (Environment and Transport, Rural Affairs, Health, Enterprise and Lifelong Learning) *Tel:* 0131-244 2661
Anne Shevas (First Minister's Press Desk)
Tel: 0131-244 2718
Strategic Communications Branch
Judy Waterman *Tel:* 0131-244 2398
Chief Publicity Officer: Sandy Sutherland
Tel: 0131-244 2676

CORPORATE SERVICES

16 Waterloo Place, Edinburgh EH1 3DN
Principal Establishment Officer and Head of Corporate Services: Colin MacDonald, CB
Private Secretary: Lesley Simpson
Tel: 0131-244 3939
Private Secretary (PEO): Caroline Banks
Tel: 0131-244 4593
Assistant Private Secretary: Steven Feeney
Tel: 0131-244 3921 *Fax:* 0131-244 3095

PRINCIPAL FINANCE OFFICER AND HEAD OF FINANCE

Principal Finance Officer and Head of Finance: Dr Peter Collings
Senior Personal Secretary:
Sylvia Cunningham, MBE
Tel: 0131-244 7285 *Fax:* 0131-244 7287
Heads of Division:
Mark Batho, John Henderson, Alasdair McLeod, David Reid, Bill Tait
Head of Accountancy Services Unit: Ian Smith

SCOTTISH EXECUTIVE AGENCIES

Fisheries Research Service (FRS); Historic Scotland; Intervention Board (IB); Scottish Agricultural Science Agency (SASA); Scottish Court Service; Scottish Fisheries Protection Agency (SFPA); Scottish Prison Service (SPS); Scottish Public Pensions Agency (SPPA); Student Awards Agency for Scotland (SAAS). Registers of Scotland and National Archives of Scotland (NAS) both report directly to the First Minister.

Source: Scottish Executive Secretariat

Political Party Headquarters and Shadow Cabinet Spokespeople

SCOTTISH LABOUR PARTY

Delta House, 4th Floor, 50 West Nile Street,
Glasgow G1 2NA
0141-572 6900 Fax 0141-572 2566
E-mail: general@scottish-labour.org
Website: www.labour.org.uk
Acting Assistant General Secretary:
   Lesley Quinn
Press and Broadcasting Officer:
   Angus Macleod

SCOTTISH NATIONAL PARTY

6 North Charlotte Street, Edinburgh EH2 4JH
0131-226 3661 Fax 0131-226 7373
E-mail: snp.hq@snp.org.uk
Website: www.snp.org.uk
National Convener: Alex Salmond, MSP
Senior Vice-Convenor: John Swinney, MSP
Manager of Communications: Kevin Pringle
Parliamentary Group Convenor:
   Margaret Ewing, MSP
Parliamentary Group Secretary:
   Shona Robison, MSP

SHADOW CABINET

*First Minister, Constitution and External
   Affairs:* Alex Salmond, MSP
*Deputy Leader and Enterprise and Lifelong
   Learning:* John Swinney, MSP
Justice, Equality and Land Reform:
   Roseanna Cunningham, MSP
Children and Education: Nicola Sturgeon, MSP
Finance: Andrew Wilson, MSP
Health and Community Care: Kay Ullrich, MSP
Rural Affairs: Alasdair Morgan, MSP
Housing and Social Justice: Fiona Hyslop,
   MSP
Local Government: Kenneth Gibson, MSP
Transport and the Environment:
   Kenny MacAskill, MSP
*Business Manager and Culture, Broadcasting
   and Gaelic:* Michael Russell, MSP
Chief Whip: Bruce Crawford, MSP
Reserved Matters:
Defence: Colin Campbell, MSP
Social Security: Alex Neil, MSP
Europe: Ian Hudghton, MEP

The above team of 15 represents the members of
the SNP's Shadow Cabinet, encompassing
devolved and non-devolved functions.

Junior Ministers
*Deputy Tourism, Small Business and Highlands
   and Islands:* Fergus Ewing, MSP
Deputy Justice and Equality:
   Michael Matheson, MSP
Deputy Children and Sport:
   Fiona McLeod, MSP
*Deputy Health, Public Health and Community
   Care:* Duncan Hamilton, MSP
Deputy Fisheries and Water Industry:
   Richard Lochhead, MSP
*Deputy Social Inclusion, Trade Unions and the
   Voluntary Sector:* Lloyd Quinan, MSP
Deputy Transport and Environment:
   Linda Fabiani, MSP
Deputy Local Government: Cllr Peter Johnson
Deputy Business Manager:
   Tricia Marwick, MSP
Deputy Whips: Brian Adam, MSP,
   Sandra White, MSP

SCOTTISH CONSERVATIVE AND UNIONIST PARTY

Suite 1/1, 14 Links Place, Leith,
Edinburgh EH6 7EZ
0131-555 2900 Fax 0131-555 2869
Press and Research: 0131-554 8872
E-mail: scuco@scottish.tory.org.uk
Chairman: Raymond Robertson
Leader: David McLetchie, MSP

SHADOW CABINET

Leader: David McLetchie, MSP
*Deputy Leader, Economy, Industry and
   Finance:* Annabel Goldie, MSP
Chief Whip and Business Manager:
   Rt Hon Lord James Douglas-Hamilton, MSP
Home Affairs: Phil Gallie, MSP
Education, Arts, Culture and Sport:
   Brian Monteith, MSP
Transport and Environment: Murray Tosh, MSP
Rural Affairs: Alex Johnstone, MSP
Health and Social Work: Mary Scanlon, MSP
Local Government and Housing:
   Keith Harding, MSP
Deputies:
   Economy, Industry and Finance:
      David Davidson, MSP,
      Nick Johnstone, MSP
   Homes Affairs: Lyndsay McIntosh, MSP
   Education: David Mundell, MSP

Transport and Environment:
John Young, MSP
Rural Affairs (Fisheries):
Jamie McGrigor, MSP,
Alex Fergusson, MSP
Health and Social Work: Ben Wallace, MSP
Local Government and Housing, Deputy
Business Manager: Bill Aitken, MSP

SCOTTISH LIBERAL DEMOCRATS

4 Clifton Terrace, Edinburgh EH12 5DR
0131-337 2314 Fax 0131-337 3566
and 0131-346 1653
E-mail: scotlibdem@cix.co.uk
Website: www.scotlibdems.org.uk
Chief Executive: Willie Rennie
Party Administrator: Mrs Rae Grant

PARLIAMENTARY SPOKESPEOPLE

Leader: Jim Wallace, MSP
Health, Community Care and Housing:
Robert Brown, MSP
Local Government; Procedures:
Donald Gorrie, MSP
Culture, Arts and Sport: Ian Jenkins, MSP
Enterprise and Life-Long Learning:
George Lyon, MSP
Highlands and Islands and Gaelic:
John Farquhar Munro, MSP
Equal Opportunities: Nora Radcliffe, MSP
Finance; Social Inclusion, Voluntary Sector and
Drugs: Keith Raffan, MSP
Justice: Euan Robson, MSP
Rural Affairs; Convenor of Standards
Committee: Mike Rumbles, MSP
Transport, the Environment and Europe:
Tavish Scott, MSP
Convenor of Health and Community Care
Committee: Margaret Smith, MSP
Children and School Education:
Jamie Stone, MSP

SCOTTISH GREEN PARTY

14 Albany Street (3F4), Edinburgh EH1 3QB
0131-478 7896 Fax 0131-478 7896
E-mail: info@scottishgreens.org.uk
Website: www.scottishgreens.org.uk
Council Convenor: Dr Nina Baker
Executive Convenor: Caroline Hoffman

PRINCIPAL SPOKESPEOPLE
Robin Harper MSP, Dr Eleanor Scott

Scottish Parliament Office
Robin Harper, MSP
0131-348 5927 Fax 0131-348 5972
E-mail:
robin.harper.msp@scottish.parliament.uk
Policy Support Officer: Dr Steve Burgess
Administrative Support Officer: Alison Johnstone
Lothians Office
14 Albany Street (3F2), Edinburgh EH1 3QB
0131-478 7895 Fax: 0131-478 7891

SCOTTISH SOCIALIST PARTY

73 Robertson Street, Glasgow G2 8QD
0141-221 7714 Fax 0141-221 7715
E-mail: ssv@mail.ndirect.co.uk
Website: www.scotsocialistparty.org
West of Scotland Organiser: Richie Venton
Convenor: Tommy Sheridan, MSP
Scottish Parliament Office: 0131-348 5632
Fax 0131-348 5948
E-mail:
thomas.sheridan.msp@scottish.parliament.uk
Glasgow City Council: 0141-287 3934
Fax 0141-287 3933

MSP FOR FALKIRK WEST

Dennis Canavan MSP
Constituency Office, 37 Church Walk, Denny,
Stirlingshire FK6 6DF
01324 825922 Fax 01324 823972

NATIONAL ASSEMBLY FOR WALES

CYNULLIAD CENEDLAETHOL CYMRU

Cardiff Bay
Cardiff CF99 1NA
029 2089 5111 Cardiff Bay
029 2082 5111 Cathays Park
E-mail: assembly.info@wales.gsi.gov.uk
Website: www.wales.gov.uk
(To move to new Assembly building at Pier Head, Cardiff in 2001)

Election 6 May 1999
26 May 1999 Official Opening by HM The Queen

Future elections are to be held every four years.

ELECTORAL SYSTEM

The election was conducted using a method combining the traditional first past the post system and a form of proportional representation called the Additional Member System. Each voter cast two votes. One vote was for one of 40 constituency members, based on the Westminster parliament constituencies. The second went towards the election of 20 regional members, four for each of the five regions used in the European Parliament elections. These seats ensure that each party's representation in the Assembly reflects its overall share of the vote.

The Assembly operates a three-day week conducted during normal business hours.

ELECTION RESULT

	First past post	Top up	Total seats
Labour	27	1	28
Plaid Cymru	9	8	17
Conservative	1	8	9
Liberal Democrat	3	3	6
Turnout 46%			**60 seats**

POWERS AND RESPONSIBILITIES

The Assembly decides on its priorities and allocates funds in the following policy areas as they apply to Wales:

agriculture
ancient monuments and historic buildings
culture
economic development
education and training
environment
health
highways
housing

industry
local government
social services
sport and leisure
tourism
town and country planning
transport and roads
Welsh language

The Assembly does not have powers to enact legislation.

The following areas remain the responsibility of Westminster:

broadcasting policy
competition policy
defence
fiscal and common markets policy
fire service
foreign affairs
justice system

labour market policy
macro-economic policy
National Lottery
police service
prisons
social security benefits
taxation

The Secretary of State for Wales represents the interests of Wales in the Cabinet of the UK Government.

COMPOSITION

The Assembly has 60 members elected by universal sufferage.

The members elect the First Secretary, who appoints Assembly Secretaries to be responsible for particular policy areas. The Secretaries and the First Secretary make up the Cabinet, which is responsible to the Assembly.

Members (AMs)

Lab	Labour Party
PC	Plaid Cymru
Con	Conservative
Lib Dem	Liberal Democrats
Lab/Co-op	Labour/Co-operative

	Party	Constituency/Region*	Majority
BARRETT Lorraine	Lab/Co-op	Cardiff South and Penarth	6,803
BATES Michael	Lib Dem	Montgomeryshire	5,504
BLACK Peter	Lib Dem	South Wales West*	
BOURNE Nicholas	Con	Mid and West Wales*	
BUTLER Rosemary	Lab	Newport West	4,710
CAIRNS Alun	Con	South Wales West*	
CHAPMAN Christine	Lab/Co-op	Cynon Valley	677
DAFIS Cynog	PC	Mid and West Wales*	
DAVIDSON Jane	Lab	Pontypridd	1,575
DAVIES Andrew	Lab	Swansea West	1,926
DAVIES David	Con	Monmouth	2,712
DAVIES Geraint	PC	Rhondda	2,285
DAVIES Glyn	Con	Mid and West Wales*	
DAVIES Janet	PC	South Wales West*	
DAVIES Jocelyn	PC	South Wales East*	
†DAVIES Rt Hon Ron	Lab	Caerphilly	2,861
EDWARDS Dr Richard	Lab	Preseli Pembrokeshire	2,738
‡ELIS-THOMAS Dafydd	PC	Meirionnydd Nant Conwy	8,742
ESSEX Sue	Lab	Cardiff North	2,304
FELD Val	Lab	Swansea East	3,781
GERMAN Michael	Lib Dem	South Wales East*	
GIBBONS Brian	Lab	Aberavon	6,743
GRAHAM William	Con	South Wales East*	
GREGORY Janice	Lab	Ogmore	4,565
GRIFFITHS John	Lab/Co-op	Newport East	5,111
GWYTHER Christine	Lab	Carmarthen West and South Pembrokeshire	1,492
HALFORD Alison	Lab	Delyn	5,417
HANCOCK Brian	PC	Islwyn	604
HART Edwina	Lab	Gower	3,160
HUMPHREYS Christine	Lib Dem	North Wales*	
HUTT Jane	Lab	Vale of Glamorgan	926
JARMAN Pauline	PC	South Wales Central*	
JONES Ann	Lab	Vale of Clwyd	3,341
JONES Carwyn	Lab	Bridgend	4,258
JONES Elin	PC	Ceredigion	10,249
JONES Gareth	PC	Conwy	114
JONES Helen Mary	PC	Llanelli	688
†JONES Ieuan Wyn	PC	Ynys Môn	9,288
LAW Peter	Lab/Co-op	Blaenau Gwent	10,568
LEWIS Huw	Lab/Co-op	Merthyr Tydfil and Rhymney	4,214
LLOYD Dr David	PC	South Wales West*	

†MAREK John	Lab	Wrexham	6,472
MELDING David	Con	South Wales Central*	
†MICHAEL Rt Hon Alun	Lab	Mid and West Wales*	
MIDDLEHURST Tom	Lab	Alyn and Deeside	6,359
MORGAN Jonathan	Con	South Wales Central*	
†MORGAN Rhodri	Lab	Cardiff West	10,859
NEAGLE Lynne	Lab	Torfaen	5,285
PUGH Alun	Lab	Clwyd West	760
RANDERSON Jennifer	Lib Dem	Cardiff Central	3,168
RICHARDS Rod	Con	North Wales*	
ROGERS Peter	Con	North Wales*	
RYDER Janet	PC	North Wales*	
SINCLAIR Karen	Lab	Clwyd South	3,685
THOMAS Gwenda	Lab	Neath	2,618
THOMAS Owen John	PC	South Wales Central*	
THOMAS Rhodri	PC	Carmarthen East and Dinefwr	6,980
†WIGLEY Rt Hon Dafydd	PC	Caernarfon	12,273
WILLIAMS Kirsty	Lib Dem	Brecon and Radnorshire	5,852
WILLIAMS Dr Philip	PC	South Wales East*	

† *Also a Member of the House of Commons*
‡ *Also a Member of the House of Lords*

Regions* and Constituencies

Mid and West Wales*
Brecon and Radnorshire
Carmarthen East and Dinefwr
Carmarthen West and South Pembrokeshire
Ceredigion
Llanelli
Meirionydd Nant Conwy
Montgomeryshire
Presli Pembrokeshire

North Wales*
Alyn and Deeside
Caernarfon
Clwyd South
Clwyd West
Conwy
Delyn
Vale of Clwyd
Wrexham
Ynys Môn

South Wales Central*
Cardiff Central
Cardiff North
Cardiff South and Penarth
Cardiff West
Cynon Valley
Pontypridd
Rhondda
Vale of Glamorgan

South Wales East*
Blaenau Gwent
Caerphilly
Islwyn
Merthyr Tydfil and Rhymney
Monmouth
Newport East
Newport West
Torfaen

South Wales West*
Aberavon
Bridgend
Gower
Neath
Ogmore
Swansea East
Swansea West

National Assembly for Wales
Cynulliad Cenedlaethol Cymru

THE RT HON ALUN MICHAEL, AM
First Secretary

Presiding Officer: Lord Dafydd Elis-Thomas, AM
Private Secretary: Mark Maguire *(Official)*
Deputy Presiding Officer: Jane Davidson, AM

THE CABINET

First Secretary: The Rt Hon Alun Michael, AM
Agriculture and the Rural Economy: Christine Gwyther, AM
Finance Secretary: Edwina Hart, AM
Health and Social Services: Jane Hutt, AM
Environment (Local Government and Planning): Peter Law, AM
Economic Development: Rhodri Morgan, AM
Education: Children and Young People (up to 16): Rosemary Butler, AM
Education and Training (Post 16): Tom Middlehurst, AM
Business Secretary: Andrew Davies, AM

PRINCIPAL OFFICERS AND OFFICIALS

Permanent Secretary: Jon D Shortridge
Clerk to the Assembly: John W Lloyd, CBE
Deputy Clerk and Head of Office of Presiding Officer: Barbara J M Wilson
Counsel General: Winston Roddick, QC
Principal Establishment Officer: Bryan Mitchell
Principal Finance Officer: David T Richards

Assembly Secretaries' Responsibilities

The First Secretary (The Rt Hon **Alun Michael** AM)
The First Secretary is accountable and responsible for the exercise of functions by the Assembly Cabinet, and for the policy development and co-ordination of cross-cutting issues. The First Secretary's primary cross-cutting responsibilities are Co-ordination of overall resources (Finance, Personnel and Property); Social Inclusion; Voluntary Sector Partnership, Community Action and Volunteering; Partnership with Business; European Dimensions of Assembly Policy; Image and promotion of Wales; Youth issues; Welsh culture and language; Crime reduction.
Special Advisers: Gareth Williams, Julie Crowley, Andrew Bould, Delyth Evans
Principal Private Secretary: Anna Coleman *Tel:* 029 2082 5129
E-mail: anna.coleman@wales.gsi.gov.uk
Private Secretaries: Rose Stewart *Tel:* 029 2082 5480 *E-mail:* rose.stewart@wales.gsi.gov.uk
Prys Davies *Tel:* 029 2082 6642 *E-mail:* prys.davies@wales.gsi.gov.uk
Diary Secretary: Bev Summers *Tel:* 029 2082 6031 *E-mail:* bev.summers@wales.gsi.gov.uk

Agriculture and Rural Development Secretary (**Christine Gwyther** AM)
Responsible for food promotion, development of the rural economy, National parks.
Private Secretary: Andrew Cousins *Tel:* 029 2089 8769 029 2082 6540
E-mail: andy.cousins@wales.gsi.gov.uk
Diary Secretary: Daphne Allen *Tel:* 029 2082 5639 *E-mail:* christine.gwyther@wales.gsi.gov.uk

Finance Secretary (**Edwina Hart** AM)
Responsible for local government finance, best value and performance review.
Private Secretary: Jo-Ann Bainton *Tel:* 029 2089 8774 029 2082 6333
E-mail: jo-ann.bainton@wales.gsi.gov.uk
Diary Secretary: Mandy Lewis *Tel:* 029 2082 6326 *E-mail:* edwina.hart@wales.gsi.gov.uk

Health and Social Services Secretary (**Jane Hutt** AM)
Responsible for child protection, health inequalities, community care and public health.
Private Secretary: Shaun Chainey *Tel:* 029 2089 8771 029 2082 6955
E-mail: shaun.chainey@wales.gsi.gov.uk
Diary Secretary: Daphne Allen *Tel:* 029 2082 5639 *E-mail:* jane.hutt@wales.gsi.gov.uk

Environment and Local Government Secretary (**Peter Law** AM)
Responsible for housing, town and country planning, transport, general local government issues, waste, water and flood defences.
Private Secretary: Susanne Powell *Tel:* 029 2089 8768 029 2082 6557
E-mail: susanne.powell@wales.gsi.gov.uk
Diary Secretary: Terry Harper *Tel:* 029 2082 3492 *E-mail:* peter.law@wales.gsi.gov.uk

Economic Development Secretary (**Rhodri Morgan** AM)
Responsible for European economic issues; tourism; business support and inward investment.
Private Secretary: Sarah Austin *Tel:* 029 2089 8773 029 2082 6652
E-mail: sarah.austin@wales.gsi.gov.uk
Diary Secretary: Terry Harper *Tel:* 029 2082 3492 *E-mail:* rhodri.morgan@wales.sgi.gov.uk

Secretary for Education and Children (**Rosemary Butler** AM)
Responsible for pre-16 education, together with early-learning, child care and children's issues.
Private Secretary: Sian Mitchell *Tel:* 029 2089 8767 029 2082 6334
E-mail: sian.mitchell@wales.gsi.gov.uk
Diary Secretary: Heather Harris *Tel:* 029 2082 6694 *E-mail:* rosemary.butler@wales.gsi.gov.uk

Secretary for Education and Training (**Tom Middlehurst** AM)
Responsible for post-16 education in sixth forms, further education colleges and workplace training, higher education, Welsh language, arts, culture and sport.
Private Secretary: Megan Jones *Tel:* 029 2089 8770 029 2082 6335
E-mail: megan.jones@wales.gsi.gov.uk
Diary Secretary: Heather Harris *Tel:* 029 2082 6694 *E-mail:* tom.middlehurst@wales.gsi.gov.uk

Business Secretary (**Andrew Davies** AM)
The Assembly Business Secretary has responsibility for the planning and management of the Assembly's business and the organisation of the majority group. The post combines the Westminster roles of Leader of the House and Government Chief Whip. Each week the Assembly meets in plenary, the Business Secretary proposes a statement about the organisation of its business for the next three weeks. The Business Secretary decides on the management of the Assembly's business after weekly discussions with the Business Committee, which comprises one member from each political group in the Assembly.
Private Secretary: Marion Stapleton *Tel:* 029 2089 8772 029 2082 5444
E-mail: marion.stapleton@wales.gsi.gov.uk
Assistant Private Secretary: Amanda Berry *Tel:* 029 2089 8135
E-mail: amanda.berry@wales.gsi.gov.uk
Diary Secretary: Nicola Britton *Tel:* 029 2089 8132 029 2082 6651
E-mail: andrew.davies@wales.gsi.gov.uk

Executive Agencies

CADW: Welsh Historic Monuments
Farming and Rural Conservation Agency

Intervention Board
Planning Inspectorate

Committees

Subject Committees

Members are elected onto various subject committees in proportion to their party's representation in the Assembly.

Agriculture and Rural Development
Economic Development
Health and Social Services
Local Government and Environment
Post-16 Education, Schools and Early Learning
Pre-16 Education, Schools and Early Learning

Standing Committees
Audit
Equal Opportunities
European Affairs
Legislation
Standards of Conduct

Regional Committees
Mid Wales
North Wales
South East Wales
South West Wales

Political Parties and Shadow Assembly Spokespeople

WALES LABOUR PARTY
PLAID LAFUR CYMRU

Transport House, 1 Cathedral Road,
Cardiff CF11 9HA
029 2087 7700 Fax 029 2022 1153
E-mail: lp-wales@new.labour.org.uk
Website: www.waleslabourparty.org.uk
General-Secretary: Jessica Morden
Director of Communications: Huw Evans
Press Officer: Jackie Aplin

PLAID CYMRU
PARTY OF WALES

Ty Gwynfor, 18 Park Grove, Cardiff CF1 3BN
029 2064 6000 Fax 020 2064 6001
E-mail: post@plaidcymru.org
Website: www.plaidcymru.org
Assembly Office: 029 2089 8250
Chief Executive: Karl Davies
Press Officer: Emyr Williams 029 2089 8401

ASSEMBLY SPOKESPEOPLE

*Shadow First Secretary and Shadow Finance
Assembly Secretary:*
Rt Hon Dafydd Wigley, AM
Business Manager: Ieuan Wyn Jones, AM
Social Inclusion and Equal Opportunity:
Helen Mary Jones, AM
Policy Co-ordinator: Cynog Dafis, AM
Economic Development: Phil Williams, AM
Education (up to 16): Gareth Jones, AM
Education and Training (Post 16):
Elin Jones, AM
Agriculture and the Rural Economy:
Rhodri Glyn Thomas, AM
Environment, Local Government and Planning:
Janet Ryder, AM
Health and Social Services: Dr Dai Lloyd, AM

WELSH CONSERVATIVE PARTY
PLAID GEIDWADOL CYMRU

4 Penlline Road, Whitchurch,
Cardiff CF14 2XS
029 2061 6031 Fax 029 2061 0544
E-mail: cco@wales.tory.org.uk
Assembly: 029 2082 5111
Chairman: Henri Lloyd Davies
Leader: Nick Bourne, AM
Director of the Party, Leigh Jeffes

ASSEMBLY SPOKESPEOPLE

Leader: Nick Bourne, AM
Economic Development: Alun Cairns, AM
*Chief Whip; Environment, Transport and
Planning; Policy Presentation:*
David Davies, AM
Finance: Glyn Davies, AM
Business Secretary: William Graham, AM
Health and Social Services: David Melding,
AM
Education: Jonathan Morgan, AM
Agriculture and the Rural Economy:
Peter Rogers, AM
Chief of Staff: Susan Inkin

LIBERAL DEMOCRATS WALES
DEMOCRATIAID RHYDDFRYDOL CYMRU

Bay View House, 102 Bute Street,
Cardiff CF10 5AD
029 2031 3400 Fax 029 2031 3401
E-mail: ldwales@cix.co.uk
Website: www.libdemwales.org.uk
Chief Executive: Chris Lines
Administrative Officer: Helen Northmore-
Thomas

ASSEMBLY SPOKESPEOPLE

Leader and Economic Development:
Michael German, AM
Education (under 16) (Whip):
Jenny Randerson, AM
Education (16+): Christine Humphreys, AM
Health and Social Services:
Kirsty Williams, AM
Rural Development: Mike Bates, AM
Local Government, Environment and Housing:
Peter Black, AM

NORTHERN IRELAND ASSEMBLY

Parliament Buildings
Stormont
Belfast BT4 3XX
028 9052 1333 Fax 028 9052 1961
E-mail: info.office@ni.assembly.gov.uk
Website: www.niassembly.gov.uk

Background

From 1921, Northern Ireland was governed by a devolved parliament under the terms of the Government of Ireland Act 1920 which provided for separate parliaments in the north and south of Ireland. In 1972, the Government at Westminster prorogued the Northern Ireland Parliament and introduced a system of 'Direct Rule'. Various political initiatives attempted to restore some form of devolved government at different times during the following 25 years. Eventually, following the Westminster election of May 1997, a series of talks, under the chairmanship of American Senator George Mitchell, led to the publication on 10 April 1998 of what has become known as the 'Good Friday' or Belfast Agreement.

The Good Friday Agreement

The governments of the United Kingdom and Ireland, together with a number of the political parties in Northern Ireland, agreed to support a three stranded approach to resolving the historical differences which had provided the context for political instability in Northern Ireland. The three strands provided for arrangements within Northern Ireland; within Ireland north and south; and within the British Isles as a whole. The Agreement was endorsed by referenda in both parts of Ireland in May 1998.

The Assembly

Under Strand One of the Agreement, a new democratic institution was created within Northern Ireland. Elections to this body of 108 members were held in June 1998 and the new Northern Ireland Assembly held its first meeting at Castle Buildings, Stormont on 1 July 1998.

The Assembly is responsible for all 'transferred matters', ie for all public services not 'reserved' or 'excepted' in the Northern Ireland Act 1998, including areas such as taxation, foreign affairs, defence etc. The powers were devolved to the Northern Ireland Assembly on 2 December 1999.

The Assembly has agreed to the structure of the administration after devolution. Ten Departments will be formed out of the existing six. Each Department will also be 'shadowed' by a Departmental Committee which will scrutinise the policy of the Department and play a role in the initiation and development of legislation. The new Assembly has also developed its own Standing Orders.

The Assembly met on 29 November during which time ten Ministers were nominated, as well as the Chairpersons, Deputy Chairpersons and members for the ten Departmental Committees.

New Institutions

On 2 December 1999, the day power was devolved to the Assembly, the following became fully functioning institutions:
North/South Ministerial Council
and its six implementation bodies:
Waterways Ireland
Food Safety Promotion Board
Trade and Business Development Board
Special European Union Programmes Body
Foyle, Carlingford and Irish Lights Commission
North/South Language Body
The British-Irish Council
British-Irish Inter-governmental Conference

State of the Parties at December 1999

UUP	Ulster Unionist Party	28 seats
SDLP	Social Democratic and Labour Party	24 seats
DUP	Democratic Unionist Party	20 seats
SF	Sinn Fein	18 seats
A	Alliance	*6 seats
NIUP†	Northern Ireland Unionist Party	§3 seats
UUAP‡	United Unionist Assembly Party	3 seats
PUP	Progressive Unionist Party	2 seats
NIWC	Women's Coalition	2 seats
UKUP	UK Unionist Party	1 seat
Ind Un	Independent Unionists	1 seat
		108 seats

18 Constituencies
  6 Members per constituency
108 Members

*Includes the Presiding Officer
†Elected as UK Unionist candidates. Formed Northern Ireland Unionist Party 15 January 1999
‡Independents formed United Unionist Assembly Party 21 September 1998
§One member left the NIUP 1 December 1999

Members (MLAs)

	Party	*Constituency*
*ADAMS Gerry	SF	Belfast West
ADAMSON Ian	UUP	Belfast East
AGNEW Fraser	UUAP	Belfast North
‡ALDERDICE Lord	Speaker	Belfast East
ARMITAGE Pauline	UUP	East Londonderry
ARMSTRONG Billy	UUP	Mid Ulster
ATTWOOD Alex	SDLP	Belfast West
BEGGS Jnr Roy	UUP	East Antrim
BELL Billy	UUP	Lagan Valley
BELL Eileen	A	North Down
BENSON Thomas	UUP	Strangford
BERRY Paul	DUP	Newry and Armagh
BIRNIE Esmond	UUP	Belfast South
BOYD Norman	NIUP	South Antrim
BRADLEY P J	SDLP	South Down
BYRNE Joe	SDLP	West Tyrone
CAMPBELL Gregory	DUP	East Londonderry
CARRICK Mervyn	DUP	Upper Bann
CARSON Joan	UUP	Fermanagh and South Tyrone
CLOSE Seamus	A	Lagan Valley
CLYDE Wilson	DUP	South Antrim
COBAIN Fred	UUP	Belfast North
COULTER Rev Robert	UUP	North Antrim
DALLAT John	SDLP	East Londonderry
DAVIS Ivan	UUP	Lagan Valley
DE BRÚN Bairbre	SF	Belfast West
DODDS Nigel	DUP	Belfast North
DOHERTY Pat	SF	West Tyrone
DOHERTY Arthur	SDLP	East Londonderry
DOUGLAS Boyd	UUAP	East Londonderry
DURKAN Mark	SDLP	Foyle

EMPEY Sir Reg	UUP	Belfast East
ERVINE David	PUP	Belfast East
FARREN Sean	SDLP	North Antrim
FEE John	SDLP	Newry and Armagh
FORD David	A	South Antrim
FOSTER Sam	UUP	Fermanagh and South Tyrone
GALLAGHER Tommy	SDLP	Fermanagh and South Tyrone
GIBSON Oliver	DUP	West Tyrone
GILDERNEW Michelle	SF	Fermanagh and South Tyrone
GORMAN Sir John	UUP	North Down
HANNA Carmel	SDLP	Belfast South
HAUGHEY Denis	SDLP	Mid Ulster
HAY William	DUP	Foyle
HENDRON Joe	SDLP	Belfast West
HILDITCH David	DUP	East Antrim
*HUME John†	SDLP	Foyle
HUSSEY Derek	UUP	West Tyrone
HUTCHINSON Roger	Ind Un	East Antrim
HUTCHINSON Billy	PUP	Belfast North
KANE Gardiner	DUP	North Antrim
KELLY John	SF	Mid Ulster
KELLY Gerry	SF	Belfast North
KENNEDY Danny	UUP	Newry and Armagh
LESLIE James	UUP	North Antrim
LEWSLEY Patricia	SDLP	Lagan Valley
McCARTHY Kieran	A	Strangford
*McCARTNEY Robert	UKUP	North Down
McCLARTY David	UUP	East Londonderry
McCLELLAND Donovan	SDLP	South Antrim
McCREA Rev William	DUP	Mid Ulster
McDONNELL Alasdair	SDLP	Belfast South
McELDUFF Barry	SF	West Tyrone
McFARLAND Alan	UUP	North Down
McGIMPSEY Michael	UUP	Belfast South
*McGRADY Eddie	SDLP	South Down
*McGUINNESS Martin	SF	Mid Ulster
McHUGH Gerry	SF	Fermanagh and South Tyrone
McLAUGHLIN Mitchel	SF	Foyle
McMENAMIN Eugene	SDLP	West Tyrone
McNAMEE Pat	SF	Newry and Armagh
McWILLIAMS Prof Monica	NIWC	Belfast South
MAGINNESS Alban	SDLP	Belfast North
*MALLON Seamus	SDLP	Newry and Armagh
MASKEY Alex	SF	Belfast West
MOLLOY Francie	SF	Mid Ulster
MORRICE Jane	NIWC	North Down
MORROW Maurice	DUP	Fermanagh and South Tyrone
MURPHY Connor	SF	Newry and Armagh
MURPHY Mick	SF	South Down
NEESON Sean	A	East Antrim
NELIS Mary	SF	Foyle
NESBITT Dermot	UUP	South Down
O'CONNOR Danny	SDLP	East Antrim
O'HAGAN Dara	SF	Upper Bann
O'NEILL Eamon	SDLP	South Down
*PAISLEY Rev Ian†	DUP	North Antrim
PAISLEY Ian Jnr	DUP	North Antrim

POOTS Edwin	DUP	Lagan Valley
RAMSEY Sue	SF	Belfast West
ROBINSON Mark	DUP	Belfast South
ROBINSON Ken	UUP	East Antrim
ROBINSON Iris	DUP	Strangford
*ROBINSON Peter David	DUP	Belfast East
ROCHE Patrick	NIUP	Lagan Valley
RODGERS Brid	SDLP	Upper Bann
SAVAGE George	UUP	Upper Bann
SHANNON Jim	DUP	Strangford
SHIPLEY-DALTON Duncan	UUP	South Antrim
*TAYLOR The Rt Hon John D	UUP	Strangford
TIERNEY John	SDLP	Foyle
*TRIMBLE The Rt Hon David	UUP	Upper Bann
WATSON Denis	UUAP	Upper Bann
WEIR Peter	UUP	North Down
WELLS Jim	DUP	South Down
WILSON Sammy	DUP	Belfast East
WILSON Cedric	NIUP	Strangford
WILSON Jim	UUP	South Antrim

* *Also a Member of the House of Commons*
† *Also a Member of the European Parliament*
‡ *Also a Member of the House of Lords*

MLA   Member of Legislative Assembly

Northern Ireland Assembly

First Minister: The Rt Hon David Trimble MLA (UUP)
Deputy First Minister: Seamus Mallon (SDLP)
Speaker: The Lord Alerdice MLA

PRINCIPAL OFFICERS AND OFFICIALS

The Speaker: The Lord Alderdice MLA, FRCPI, FRCPsych

OFFICE OF THE SPEAKER

Speaker's Private Secretary: Georgina Campbell
Speaker's Special Adviser: Niall Johnston
Speaker's Counsel: Nicolas Hanna, QC

PRINCIPAL OFFICERS

Clerk to the Assembly: Vacant
Deputy Clerk: Vacant
Head of Administration: Gerry Cosgrove
Clerk Assistant: Murray Barnes
Editor of Debates: Alex Elder
Keeper of the House: Peter Waddell
Director of Research and Information: Allan Black
Director of Finance and Personnel: Dennis Millar
Clerk of Bills: Alan Patterson
Clerk of Business: Joe Reynolds
Clerk of Committees: John Torney

Northern Ireland Executive Committee

First Minister: The Rt Hon David Trimble MLA
Deputy First Minister: Seamus Mallon MLA
Minister of Agriculture and Rural Development: Brid Rogers MLA
Minister of Culture, Arts and Leisure: Michael McGimpsey MLA
Minister of Education: Martin McGuinness MLA
Minister of Enterprise, Trade and Investment: Sir Reg Empey MLA
Minister of the Environment: Sam Foster MLA
Minister of Finance and Personnel: Mark Durkan MLA
Minister of Health, Social Services and Public Safety: Bairbre de Brun MLA
Minister of Higher and Further Education, Training and Employment: Dr Sean Farren MLA
Minister for Regional Development: Peter Robinson MLA
Minister for Social Development: Nigel Dodds MLA

Powers

The Secretary of State will retain responsibility for excepted and reserved matters as defined in the Northern Ireland Act 1998. However, it is open to the Secretary of State to lay appropriate legislation at any time following devolution if it appears to him that any reserved matter should become a transferred matter or that any transferred matter should become a reserved matter. This transfer has to have the cross-community support of the Assembly before any legislation can be laid.

Ministerial Responsibilities

OFFICE OF THE FIRST MINISTER AND DEPUTY FIRST MINISTER

Parliament Buildings, Stormont, Belfast BT4 3XX
First Minister (**The Rt Hon David Trimble** MLA)
Areas of responsibility: Economic Policy Unit; Equality Unit; liaison with NSMC including Secretariat; liaison with BIC; Civic Forum (administrative and other arrangements, including Secretariat support); liaison with Secretary of State (excepted or reserved); European affairs/international matters/Washington Bureau; liaison with IFI; information services; community relations; Executive Committee Secretariat; Legislative Progress Unit; Office of the Legislative Counsel; public appointments policy; visits; honours; freedom of information; victims; Nolan standards; Public Service Office; machinery of government; emergency planning; women's issues; Policy Innovation Unit; cross-departmental co-ordination; Assembly Ombudsmen (liaison and appointment issues).
Principal Private Secretary: David Lavery *Tel:* 028 9052 1013 *Fax:* 028 9052 1963
Private Secretary: Maura Quinn

Deputy First Minister (**Seamus Mallon** MLA)
Areas of responsibility: Economic Policy Unit; Equality Unit; liaison with NSMC including Secretariat; liaison with BIC; Civic Forum (administrative and other arrangements, including Secretariat support); liaison with Secretary of State (excepted or reserved); European affairs/international matters/Washington Bureau; liaison with IFI; information services; community relations; Executive Committee Secretariat; Legislative Progress Unit; Office of the Legislative Counsel; public appointments policy; visits; honours; freedom of information; victims; Nolan standards; Public Service Office; machinery of government; emergency planning; women's issues; Policy Innovation Unit; cross-departmental co-ordination; Assembly Ombudsmen (liaison and appointment issues).
Principal Private Secretary: Peter May *Tel:* 028 9052 1126 *Fax:* 028 9052 1687
Private Secretary: Billy Gamble

AGRICULTURE AND RURAL DEVELOPMENT

Dundonald House, Upper Newtownards Road, Belfast BT4 3SB
Tel: 028 9052 0100
Minister of Agriculture and Rural Development (**Brid Rogers** MLA)
Areas of responsibility: Food, farming and envronment policy; agri-food development; science; veterinary matters; science service; rural development; forestry; sea fisheries, rivers.
Private Secretary: Tommy Breslin *Tel:* 028 9052 4140 *Fax:* 028 9052 4170

CULTURE, ARTS AND LEISURE

Interpoint Building, 3rd Floor, 20-24 York Street, Belfast BT15 1AQ
Tel: 028 9025 8825
Minister of Culture, Arts and Leisure (**Michael McGimpsey** MLA)
Areas of responsibility: Arts and culture; sport and leisure; libraries; museums; Armagh Planetarium; Ulster Historical Foundation; inland waterways; inland fisheries; Ordnance Survey; Public Record Office; language policy; lottery matters; millennium events and events companies; visitors' amenities.
Private Secretary: Mrs Arlene McCreight *Tel:* 028 9025 8807 *Fax:* 028 9025 8906

EDUCATION

Rathgael House, Balloo Road, Bangor BT19 7PR
Tel: 028 9127 9279
Minister of Education (**Martin McGuinness** MLA)
Areas of responsibility: Schools' funding and administration; special education; school effectiveness; school planning and provision; Schools' Inspectorate; pre-school education; Youth Service; teachers (numbers and remuneration); Education and Library Board appointments.
Private Secretary: Mrs Jacqui Loughrey *Tel:* 028 9127 9303 *Fax:* 028 9127 9271

ENTERPRISE, TRADE AND INVESTMENT

Netherleigh House, Massey Avenue, Belfast BT4 2JP
Tel: 029 9052 9900
Minister of Enterprise, Trade and Investment (**Sir Reg Empey** MLA)
Areas of responsibility: Economic development policy; industry (IDB, LBDU); research and development (IRTU); tourism; Health and Safety Executive; Employment Medical Advisory Service; company regulation; consumer affairs; energy policy; Minerals and Petroleum Unit (including Geological Survey); NICO; company training grant schemes (Company Development Programme and Explorers).
Private Secretary: Miss Marian Magill *Tel:* 028 9052 9211 *Fax:* 028 9052 9545

ENVIRONMENT

Clarence Court, 10-18 Adelaide Street, Belfast BT2 8GB
Tel: 028 9054 0540
Minister of the Environment (**Sam Foster** MLA)
Areas of responsibility: Planning control; environment and heritage; protection of the countryside; waste management; pollution control; wildlife protection; local government; sustainable development; mineral resources (planning aspects); Driver and Vehicle Testing Agency; road safety; Driver and Vehicle Licensing Agency; transport licensing and enforcement.
Private Secretary: David Steele *Tel:* 028 9054 1166 *Fax:* 028 9054 0092

FINANCE AND PERSONNEL

Rathgael House, Balloo Road, Bangor BT19 7PR
Tel: 028 9127 9279
Minister of Finance and Personnel (**Mark Durkan** MLA)
Areas of responsibility: Finance; personnel, IT and common services; accommodation; legal services; NI Statistics and Research Agency; Land Registry of NI; Rates Collection Agency; Valuation and Lands Agency; Construction Service; Northern Ireland Construction Industry Advisory Council; Government Purchasing Agency; Office of Law Reform.
Private Secretary: Stephen Orr (temp) *Tel:* 028 9185 8170 *Fax:* 028 9185 8282

HEALTH, SOCIAL SERVICES AND PUBLIC SAFETY

Castle Buildings, Stormont Estate, Belfast BT4 3SJ
Tel: 028 9052 0500
Minister of Health, Social Services and Public Safety (**Bairbre de Brun** MLA)
Areas of responsibility: Health; social services; public health and safety; health promotion; Fire Authority.
Private Secretary: Craig Allen *Tel:* 028 9052 0642 *Fax:* 028 9052 0557

HIGHER AND FURTHER EDUCATION, TRAINING AND EMPLOYMENT

Adelaide House, Adelaide Street, Belfast BT2 8FD
Tel: 028 9025 7777
Minister of Higher and Further Education, Training and Employment (**Dr Sean Farren** MLA)
Areas of responsibility: Higher education; further education; vocational training; employment services; employment law and labour relations; teacher training and teacher education; student support and postgraduate awards; training grants.
Private Secretary: Mrs Bernie Rooney *Tel:* 028 9025 7921 028 9025 7919

REGIONAL DEVELOPMENT

Clarence Court, 10-18 Adelaide Street, Belfast BT2 8GB
Tel: 028 9054 0540
Minister for Regional Development (**Peter Robinson** MLA)
Areas of responsibility: Transport planning; public transport; roads; rail; ports and airports; city visioning; water; strategic planning.
Private Secretary: Ms Sheila McClelland *Tel:* 028 9054 1182 *Fax:* 028 9054 0028

SOCIAL DEVELOPMENT

Churchill House, Victoria Square, Belfast BT2 4BA
Tel: 028 9056 9100
Minister for Social Development (**Nigel Dodds** MLA)
Areas of responsibility: Housing policy; Northern Ireland Housing Executive; voluntary activity; urban renewal; community sector; Laganside Corporation; Rent Assessment Panel; Housing Benefit Review Boards; Social Security Agency; Child Support Agency; Lands Division; Independent Tribunal Service; Office of Social Fund Commissioner; social legislation.
Private Secretary: Mark O'Donnell *Tel:* 028 9056 9216 *Fax:* 028 9056 9244

Departmental Committees

Ten Departmental Committees have been established to advise and assist each Northern Ireland Minister in the formulation of policy with respect to matters within his/her responsibilities and to undertake a scrutiny, policy development and consultation role. They are:

Agriculture and Rural Development
Culture, Arts and Leisure
Education
Enterprise, Trade and Investment
Environment
Finance and Personnel

Health, Social Services and Public Safety
Higher and Further Education, Training and
   Development
Regional Development
Social Development

Political Party Headquarters

ULSTER UNIONIST PARTY
Parliament Buildings, Stormont, Belfast
BT4 3XX
028 9052 1327 Fax 028 9052 1395
E-mail: uup@uup.org
Website: www.uup.org
Chief Whip, Jim Wilson, MLA
028 9052 1544
Press Officer: Alex Benjamin
028 9052 1328

SOCIAL DEMOCRATIC AND LABOUR PARTY
121 Ormeau Road, Belfast BT7 1SH
028 9024 7700 Fax 028 9023 6699
E-mail: sdlp@indigo.ie
Website: www.indigo.le/sdlp/
General Secretary, Gerry Cosgrove
Assembly Nos:
Room 272
028 9052 1319/1649 Fax 028 9052 1329

DEMOCRATIC UNIONIST PARTY
Room 207, Parliament Buildings, Stormont,
Belfast BT4 3XX
028 9052 1322/1323 Fax 028 9052 1289
E-mail: info@dup.org.uk
Website: www.dup.org.uk
Director of Communications, St Clair McAlister
Chief Executive, Allan Ewart

SINN FEIN
44 Parnell Square, Dublin 1
+353 1 8726932/8726100
Fax +353 1 8733441/8783595
E-mail: sinnfein@iol.ie
Website: www.sinnfein.ie
Press Officer, Miss Dawn Doyle
Assembly Nos:
028 9052 1470 Fax 028 9052 1474

ALLIANCE
88 University Street, Belfast BT7 1HE
028 9032 4274 Fax 028 9033 3147
E-mail: alliance@allianceparty.org
Website: www.allianceparty.org
General Secretary, Richard Good
Assembly:
Assistant to Chief Whip, Pam Tilson
Assistant to Assembly Party, Elizabeth Hanna
028 9052 1314 Fax 028 9052 1313
E-mail: alliance@unite.net

NORTHERN IRELAND UNIONIST PARTY
Parliament Buildings, Stormont, Belfast
BT4 3XX
Party Leader, Cedric Wilson, MLA
028 9052 1294 Fax 028 9052 1293
Website: www.niup.org
Party Whip, Norman Boyd, MLA
028 9052 1733 Fax 028 9052 1754
E-mail: norman.j.boyd.niup@ni-
  assembly.gov.uk
Patrick Roche, MLA
028 9052 1994 Fax 028 9052 1848
E-mail: pj.roche@ni-assembly.gov.uk
NIUP Party Office:
028 9052 1533/1901 Fax 028 9052 1845
Assembly Nos:
028 9052 1294 Fax 028 9052 1293

UNITED UNIONIST ASSEMBLY PARTY
Party Leader, Denis Watson, MLA
Assembly Nos:
028 9052 1466 Fax 028 9052 1461

PROGRESSIVE UNIONIST PARTY
182 Shankill Road, Belfast BT13 2BH
028 9032 6233 Fax 028 9032 9602
David Ervine, MLA
Billy Hutchinson, MLA
Assembly Nos:
028 9052 1469 Fax 028 9052 1468

NORTHERN IRELAND WOMEN'S COALITION
50 University Street, Belfast BT7 1HB
028 9023 3100 Fax 028 9024 0021
E-mail: niwc@iol.ie
Prof Monica Williams, MLA
Jane Morrice, MLA
Assembly Nos:
028 9052 1463 Fax 028 9052 1461

UK UNIONIST PARTY
10 Hamilton Road, Bangor,
Co Down BT20 4LE
028 9127 2994 Fax 028 9146 5037
Press Officer, David Vance
Assembly Nos:
028 9052 1484 Fax 028 9052 1483
E-mail: contactus@ukunionists.freeserve.co.uk
Website: www.welcome.to/ukup

The Parliamentarian

Journal of the Parliaments of the Commonwealth

provides an authoritative insight into the political, parliamentary and constitutional development of the Commonwealth written by the Parliamentarians and senior officials directly involved in setting policy. Factual reports and expert assessments of important advances in the evolution of political policy and systems of government present a broad picture of the state of democracy in approximately 140 Commonwealth Parliaments and Legislatures. Recent editions have covered:

Summary Report of the 45th Commonwealth Parliamentary Conference

Summary Report of the 19th Small Countries Conference

The Peace Process in Northern Ireland

Democracy in Trinidad and Tobago

Political Peace in Zanzibar

Redefining Political Parties in Canada

Information Technology in the Chamber

Electoral Reform in Cyprus and Mauritius

Constitutional Reform in Sri Lanka

The Banana Trade and the Caribbean

Aboriginal Parliament in Australia

Parliamentarians and UNESCO

Parliament and Politics in Singapore

Published quarterly by:

The Headquarters Secretariat
Commonwealth Parliamentary Association
Suite 700, Westminster House, 7 Millbank
London SW1P 3JA, United Kingdom
Phone: 020 7799 1460   Fax: 020 7222 6073
E-mail: comparlhq.org.uk

Price:

Per Copy: £8 (U.K.), £9 (world, surface mail). £10 (air mail)
Per Year: £28 (U.K.), £30 (world, surface mail), £36 (air mail)

THE JUDICIARY

SUPREME COURT OF JUDICATURE

LORD HIGH CHANCELLOR OF
GREAT BRITAIN
Rt Hon The Lord Irvine of Lairg

HOUSE OF LORDS
LORDS OF APPEAL IN ORDINARY
(In order of seniority)
Rt Hon The Lord Browne-Wilkinson *(Senior Lord of Appeal in Ordinary)*, Rt Hon The Lord Slynn of Hadley, Rt Hon The Lord Nicholls of Birkenhead, Rt Hon The Lord Steyn, Rt Hon The Lord Hoffmann, Rt Hon The Lord Hope of Craighead, Rt Hon The Lord Clyde, Rt Hon The Lord Hutton, Rt Hon The Lord Saville of Newdigate, Rt Hon The Lord Hobhouse of Woodborough, Rt Hon The Lord Millett, Rt Hon The Lord Phillips of Worth Matravers
Clerk of the Parliaments and Registrar,
    J M Davies
Fourth Clerk at the Table (Judicial),
    J A Vallance White, CB
Website: www.publications.parliament.uk/pa/ld/ldjudinf.htm

RETIRED LORDS OF APPEAL IN
ORDINARY who are eligible to hear appeals
(In order of seniority)
Rt Hon The Lord Goff of Chieveley, Rt Hon The Lord Jauncey of Tullichettle, Rt Hon The Lord Mustill, Rt Hon The Lord Lloyd of Berwick, Rt Hon The Lord Nolan

OTHER LORDS OF APPEAL who are eligible to hear appeals
(In order of seniority)
Rt Hon The Lord Mackay of Clashfern, Rt Hon The Lord McCluskey, Rt Hon The Lord Cameron of Lochbroom, Rt Hon The Lord Mackenzie-Stuart, Rt Hon The Lord Rodger of Earlsferry *(Lord Justice General and Lord President of the Court of Session in Scotland)*, Rt Hon The Lord Woolf *(Master of the Rolls)*, Rt Hon The Lord Cooke of Thorndon, Rt Hon The Lord Bingham of Cornhill *(Lord Chief Justice of England)*

RETIRED LORDS OF APPEAL IN
ORDINARY who, having attained the age of 75, are no longer eligible to hear appeals (Judicial Pensions and Retirement Act 1993)
(In order of their place in the Roll of the Lords Spiritual and Temporal)

Rt Hon The Lord Wilberforce, Rt Hon The Lord Simon of Glaisdale, Rt Hon The Lord Keith of Kinkel, Rt Hon The Lord Scarman, OBE, Rt Hon The Lord Lane of Horsell, Rt Hon The Lord Bridge of Harwich, Rt Hon The Lord Brightman, Rt Hon The Lord Templeman, MBE, Rt Hon The Lord Griffiths, MC, Rt Hon The Lord Ackner, Rt Hon The Lord Oliver of Aylmerton

OTHER LORDS OF APPEAL who, having attained the age of 75, are no longer eligible to hear appeals
(In order of their place in the Roll of the Lords Spiritual and Temporal)
Rt Hon The Lord Hailsham of Saint Marylebone, Rt Hon The Lord Emslie, Rt Hon The Lord Donaldson of Lymington

COURT OF APPEAL
Rt Hon The Lord Woolf *(Master of the Rolls)*
Rt Hon Sir Martin Charles Nourse
Rt Hon Sir Murray Stuart-Smith
Rt Hon Sir Alexander Roy Asplan Beldam
Rt Hon Sir Paul Joseph Morrow Kennedy
Rt Hon Sir David Cozens-Hardy Hirst
Rt Hon Sir Simon Denis Brown
Rt Hon Sir Anthony Howell Meurig Evans, RD
Rt Hon Sir Christopher Dudley Roger Rose
Rt Hon Sir John Ormond Roch
Rt Hon Sir Peter Leslie Gibson
Rt Hon Sir Denis Robert Maurice Henry
Rt Hon Sir Swinton Barclay Thomas
Rt Hon Sir Robert Andrew Morritt, CVO
Rt Hon Sir Philip Howard Otton
Rt Hon Sir Robin Ernest Auld
Rt Hon Sir Malcolm Thomas Pill
Rt Hon Sir William Aldous
Rt Hon Sir Alan Hylton Ward
Rt Hon Sir Konrad Hermann Theodor Schiemann
Rt Hon Sir Mathew Alexander Thorpe
Rt Hon Sir Mark Howard Potter
Rt Hon Sir Henry Brooke
Rt Hon Sir Igor Judge (senior presiding Judge)
Rt Hon Sir George Mark Waller
Rt Hon Sir John Frank Mummery
Rt Hon Sir Charles Mantell
Rt Hon Sir John Chadwick, ED
Rt Hon Sir Robert Walker
Rt Hon Sir Richard Joseph Buxton
Rt Hon Sir Anthony Tristram May
Rt Hon Sir Simon Tuckey

Rt Hon Sir Anthony Clarke
Rt Hon Sir John Grant McKenzie Laws
Rt Hon Sir Stephen John Sedley
Rt Hon Sir Jonathan Hugh Mance
Dame Brenda Marjorie Hale, DBE

HIGH COURT OF JUSTICE
CHANCERY DIVISION

Rt Hon The Lord Irvine of Lairg
  (Lord High Chancellor)
Rt Hon Sir Richard Rashleigh Folliott Scott
  (Vice-Chancellor)
Hon Sir Donald Keith Rattee
Hon Sir Francis Mursell Ferris, TD
Hon Sir Jonathan Frederic Parker
Hon Sir John Edmund Frederic Lindsay
Hon Dame Mary Howarth Arden, DBE
Hon Sir Edward Christopher Evans-Lombe
Hon Sir Robert Raphael Hayim (Robin) Jacob
Hon Sir William Anthony Blackburne
Hon Sir Gavin Anthony Lightman
Hon Sir Robert John Anderson Carnwath, CVO
Hon Sir Colin Percy Farquharson Rimer
Hon Sir Hugh Ian Lang Laddie
Hon Sir Timothy Andrew Wigram Lloyd
Hon Sir David Edmund Neuberger
Hon Sir Edward Wilson Park
Hon Sir Nicholas Richard Pumfrey
Hon Sir Michael Christopher Campbell Hart
Hon Sir Andrew Wilson Park

QUEEN'S BENCH DIVISION

Rt Hon The Lord Bingham of Cornhill
  (Lord Chief Justice of England) (President)
Hon Sir Oliver Bury Popplewell
Hon Sir Richard Howard Tucker
Hon Sir Patrick Neville Garland
Hon Sir Michael John Turner
Hon Sir John Downes Alliott
Hon Sir Harry Henry Ognall
Hon Sir John Arthur Dalziel Owen
Hon Sir Francis Humphrey Potts
Hon Sir Richard George Rougier
Hon Sir Ian Alexander Kennedy
Hon Sir Stuart Neil McKinnon
Hon Sir Thomas Scott Gillespie Baker
Hon Sir Edwin Frank Jowitt
Hon Sir Douglas Dunlop Brown
Hon Sir Michael Morland
Hon Sir Roger John Buckley
Hon Sir Anthony Brian Hidden
Hon Sir John Michael Wright
Hon Sir John Christopher Calthorpe Blofeld
Hon Sir Peter John Cresswell
Hon Dame Ann Marian Ebsworth, DBE
Hon Sir David Nicholas Ramsey Latham
Hon Sir Christopher John Holland

Hon Sir John William Kay
Hon Sir Richard Herbert Curtis
Hon Dame Janet Hilary Smith, DBE
Hon Sir Anthony David Colman
Hon Sir John Anthony Dyson
Hon Sir John Thayne Forbes
Hon Sir Michael Alexander Geddes Sachs
Hon Sir Stephen George Mitchell
Hon Sir Rodger Bell
Hon Sir Michael Guy Vicat Harrison
Hon Sir Bernard Anthony Rix
Hon Dame Anne Heather Steel, DBE
Hon Sir William Marcus Gage
Hon Sir Jonathan Hugh Mance
Hon Sir Andrew Centlivres Longmore
Hon Sir Thomas Richard Atkin Morison
Hon Sir David Wolfe Keene
Hon Sir Andrew David Collins
Hon Sir Maurice Ralph Kay
Hon Sir Frank Brian Smedley
Hon Sir Anthony Hooper
Hon Sir Alexander Neil Logie Butterfield
Hon Sir George Michael Newman
Hon Sir David Anthony Poole
Hon Sir Martin James Moore-Bick
Hon Sir Gordon Julian Hugh Langley
Hon Sir Roger John Laugharne Thomas
Hon Sir Robert Franklyn Nelson
Hon Sir Roger Grenfell Toulson
Hon Sir Michael John Astill
Hon Sir Alan George Moses
Hon Sir Timothy Edward Walker
Hon Sir David Eady
Hon Sir Jeremy Mirth Sullivan
Hon Sir Stephen Price Richards
Hon Sir David Herbert Penry-Davey
Hon Sir David William Steel
Hon Sir Rodney Conrad Klevan
Hon Sir Charles Gray
Hon Sir Nicolas Dusán Bratza
Hon Sir Michael John Burton
Hon Sir Rupert Matthew Jackson
Hon Dame Heather Carol Hallett, DBE
Hon Sir Patrick Elias
Hon Sir Richard Pearson Aikens

FAMILY DIVISION

Rt Hon Dame Elizabeth Butler-Sloss
Hon Sir Edward Stephen Cazalet, DL
Hon Sir Robert Lionel Johnson
Hon Dame Joyanne Winifred Bracewell, DBE
Hon Sir Michael Bryan Connell
Hon Sir Jan Peter Singer
Hon Sir Nicholas Alan Roy Wilson
Hon Sir Nicholas Peter Rathbone Wall
Hon Sir Andrew Tristram Hammett Kirkwood
Hon Sir Hugh Peter Derwyn Bennett

Hon Sir Edward James Holman
Dame Mary Claire Hogg, DBE
Hon Sir Christopher John Sumner
Hon Sir Anthony Philip Gilson Hughes
Hon Sir Arthur William Hessin Charles
Hon Sir David Roderick Lessiter Bodey
Dame Jill Margaret Black

CENTRAL OFFICE OF THE SUPREME COURT

Royal Courts of Justice
London WC2A 2LL
020 7936 6000
Senior Master of the Queen's Bench Division and Queen's Remembrancer, R L Turner
Masters of the Queen's Bench Division, D L Prebble, G H Hodgson, J Trench, M I Tennant, P M Miller, N O G Murray, I H Foster, G H Rose, P G A Eyre, J Ungley, L Leslie

SUPREME COURT TAXING OFFICE

Cliffords Inn, Fetter Lane
London EC4A 1DQ
020 7936 6000
Chief Taxing Master, P T Hurst
Masters, C C Wright, M Ellis, T Seager Berry, P R Rogers, D N Pollard, J O'Hare, C D N Campbell

CHANCERY CHAMBERS

Royal Courts of Justice
London WC2A 2LL
020 7936 6000
Chief Master, J I Winegarten
Masters, J A Moncaster, R Bowman, Master Bragge

ADMIRALTY AND COMMERCIAL REGISTRY

Royal Courts of Justice
London WC2A 2LL
020 7936 6000
Registrar, P M Miller

COURT OF PROTECTION
Stewart House, 24 Kingsway
London WC2B 6JX
020 7664 7300
Master, D Lush

OFFICIAL SOLICITOR'S DEPARTMENT

81 Chancery Lane, London WC2A 1DD
020 7911 7127
Official Solicitor, L Oates
Deputy Official Solicitor, H J Baker, LLB

BANKRUPTCY COURT AND COMPANIES COURT

Thomas More Building
Royal Courts of Justice
Strand, London WC2A 2ZZ
020 7936 6448
Telex 296933 DX 44450 STRAND
Chief Registrar, Mr Registrar Buckley
Registrars, W S James, J A Simmonds, P J S Rawson, Mr Baister

PRINCIPAL REGISTRY OF THE FAMILY DIVISION

1st Avenue House, 42-49 High Holborn
London WC1V 6NP
Sen District Judge, G B N A Angel
District Judges, R B Rowe, B P F Kenworthy-Browne, Mrs K T Moorhouse, M J Segal, R Conn, Miss I M Plumstead, G J Maple, Miss H C Bradley, K J White, N A Grove, M C Berry, P A Waller, C E Million, P Cushing, S M Bowman, A O S Bassett-Cross, R S Harper, G Brasse

COURT OF ARCHES

16 Beaumont Street, Oxford OX1 2LZ
01865 241974 Fax 01865 726274
Judge, The Right Worshipful Sir John Arthur Dalziel Owen
Registrar and Record Keeper, Dr Frank E Robson

CONSISTORY COURT OF LONDON

Registry Chambers, The Old Deanery
Dean's Court, London EC4V 5AA
020 7593 5110 Fax 020 7248 3221
Chancellor, Sheila Cameron, QC
Registrar, P C E Morris
Deputy Registrar, M C Thatcher

CONSISTORY COURT OF SOUTHWARK

Registry Chambers, The Old Deanery
Dean's Court, London EC4V 5AA
020 7593 5110 Fax 020 7248 3221
Chancellor, Charles George, QC
Registrar, P C E Morris

FACULTY OFFICE

1 The Sanctuary, London SW1P 3JT
020 7222 5381 Fax 020 7222 7502
E-mail: registrar@facultyoffice.org.uk
Website: www.facultyoffice.org.uk
Office for Marriage Licences (Special and Common), Appointment of Notaries Public, etc
Master, The Right Worshipful Sir John Arthur Dalziel Owen
Registrar, P F B Beesley, LLB
Chief Clerk and Sealer, S J Borton
Asst Clerk, S E Turner, LLB

VICAR-GENERAL'S OFFICE

16 Beaumont Street, Oxford OX1 2LZ
01865 241974 Fax 01865 726274
Vicar-General, Miss Sheila M Cameron, QC
Registrar, Dr Frank E Robson

JUDGE ADVOCATE GENERAL OF THE FORCES, OFFICE OF THE

(Lord Chancellor's Establishment)
(Joint Service for the Army and
Royal Air Force)
22 Kingsway, London WC2B 6LE
020 7218 8079 Fax 020 7218 8090
Judge Advocate General,
    His Honour Judge J W Rant, CB, QC
Vice-Judge Advocate General,
    Edmwnd G Moelwyn-Hughes
Assistant Judge Advocates General,
    Judge Advocate M A Hunter, Judge
    Advocate J P Camp, Judge Advocate
    S E Woollam, R C C Seymour, Judge
    Advocate I H Pearson, Judge Advocate
    R G Chapple, Judge Advocate J F T Bayliss
Registrar, D Murray
Seven Assistant Judge Advocates General
comprise the judicial staff, three of whom are
stationed in the German Federal Republic.

THE COURT SERVICE

Southside, 105 Victoria Street
London SW1E 6QT
020 7210 1672 Fax 020 7219 1797
E-mail: cust.ser.cs@gtnet.gov.uk
Website: www.courtservice.gov.uk
The Court Service provides administrative
support to the Supreme Court of England and
Wales (comprising the Court of Appeal, the
High Court of Justice – including the probate
service – and the Crown Court), county courts
and a number of tribunals. While the outcome
of cases coming before these courts and
tribunals is determined by a judge or judicial
officer, much of the work necessary to enable
these decisions to be made and given effect is
carried out by the staff of the Court Service.
The Court Service does not provide support for
the magistrates' courts, which are supported by
a separate locally administered service.
Chief Executive, Ian Magee *(SCS)*
Change Director, Kevin Pogson
Director of Operational Policy,
    Miss Bernadette Kenny
Director of Finance, (Vacant)
*Director of Purchasing and Contract
    Management,* (Vacant)

Head of Information Services Division,
    Ms Annette Vernon
Head of Personnel and Training,
    Ms Helen Dudley
Director of Civil and Family Business, John
    Silis
Director of Criminal Operations, (Vacant)
Director of Tribunals, Paul Stockton
Director of Supreme Court Group, Ian Hyams
NB: See Executive Agencies

SUPREME COURT GROUP

ROYAL COURTS OF JUSTICE
Strand, London WC2A 2LL
020 7936 6000
Director, I Hyams

CIRCUIT ADMINISTRATORS

Midland and Oxford Circuit
P Handcock
The Courts
33 Bull Street, Birmingham B4 6DU
0121-681 3000 Fax 0121-681 3210
North Eastern Circuit
P J Farmer
17th Floor West Riding House
Albion Street, Leeds LS1 5AA
0113-251 1200 Fax 0113-234 0948
Northern Circuit
R A Vincent
15 Quay Street
Manchester M60 9PD
0161-833 1005 Fax 0161-832 8596
South Eastern Circuit
R J Clark
New Cavendish House
18 Maltravers Street, London WC2R 3EU
020 7936 6000 Fax 020 7936 7230
South Eastern (Provincial Administrator)
J Powell
1st Floor, Steeple House,
Church Lane, Chelmsford CM1 1NH
01245 257425 Fax 01245 493216
Wales and Chester Circuit
P Risk
2nd Floor, Churchill House
Churchill Way, Cardiff CF1 4HH
029 2041 5500 Fax 029 2034 5786
Western Circuit
D Ryan
Bridge House
Clifton Down, Bristol BS8 4BN
0117-974 3763 Fax 0117-974 4133

SUPREME COURTS, SCOTLAND
(COURT OF SESSION)

INNER HOUSE

First Division, The Rt Hon the Lord Rodger of Earlsferry (Lord President), The Hon Lord Sutherland, The Hon Lord Prosser, The Hon Lord Caplan

Second Division, The Rt Hon Lord Cullen (Lord Justice Clerk), The Rt Hon the Lord McCluskey, The Hon Lord Kirkwood, The Hon Lord Coulsfield

OUTER HOUSE

The Hon Lord Milligan, The Rt Hon the Lord Cameron of Lochbroom, The Hon Lord Marnoch, The Hon Lord MacLean, The Hon Lord Penrose, The Hon Lord Osborne, The Hon Lord Abernethy, The Hon Lord Johnston, The Hon Lord Gill (seconded to the Scottish Law Commission), The Hon Lord Hamilton, The Hon Lord Dawson, The Hon Lord Macfadyen, The Hon Lady Cosgrove, The Hon Lord Nimmo Smith, The Hon Lord Philip, The Hon Lord Kingarth, The Hon Lord Bonomy, The Hon Lord Eassie, The Hon Lord Reed

Principal Clerk of Session, J L Anderson, Parliament House, Edinburgh EH1 1RQ

HIGH COURT OF JUSTICIARY

Lord Justice-General, The Rt Hon the Lord Rodger of Earlsferry

Lord Justice-Clerk, The Rt Hon Lord Cullen

The remaining judges of the Court of Session are also Lords Commissioners of Justiciary

Principal Clerk of Justiciary, J L Anderson, Parliament House, Edinburgh EH1 1RQ

0131-225 2595 Fax: 0131-240 6755 Website: www.scotcourts.gov.uk

SUPREME COURT, NORTHERN IRELAND

Royal Courts of Justice, Chichester Street,
Belfast BT1 3JF   028 9023 5111
Principal Secretary to the Lord Chief Justice,
    G W Johnston (gjohnston@nicts.dnet.co.uk)
Senior Personal Secretary to the Lord Chief
    Justice, kwray@nicts.dnet.co.uk

DEPARTMENTS OF THE SUPREME COURT

Central Office
Master (Queen's Bench and Appeals),
    J W Wilson, QC
Master (High Court), Mrs D M Kennedy
Chancery Office
Master, R A Ellison
Bankruptcy and Companies Office:
    Master, C W G Redpath
Probate and Matrimonial Office:
    Master, Miss M J McReynolds
Office of Care and Protection: *Master,* F B Hall

Official Solicitor's Office: *Official Solicitor,*
    Miss B M Donnelly
Taxing Office, Bedford House, Bedford Street,
    Belfast BT2 7DS. 028 9024 5081
Master, J C Napier

SUPREME COURT OF JUDICATURE OF NORTHERN IRELAND

The Lord Chief Justice of Northern Ireland,
    The Rt Hon Sir Robert Carswell
The Rt Hon Lord Justice Nicholson, The Rt
    Hon Lord Justice McCollum, The Rt Hon
    Lord Justice Campbell, The Hon Mr Justice
    Sheil, The Hon Mr Justice Kerr, The Hon Mr
    Justice Pringle, The Hon Mr Justice Higgins,
    The Hon Mr Justice Girvan, The Hon Mr
    Justice Coghlin, The Hon Mr Justice Gillen,
    The Hon Mr Justice McLaughlin

NATIONAL AND INTERNATIONAL ORGANISATIONS

NATIONAL ORGANISATIONS

Advertising Standards Authority

2 Torrington Place, London WC1E 7HW
020 7580 5555 Fax: 020 7631 3051
Website: www.asa.org.uk

Supervises the British Codes of Advertising and Sales Promotion to ensure all advertisements and promotions in print and the cinema are legal, decent, honest and truthful. Investigates complaints, conducts extensive research and provides free and confidential pre-publication advice to advertisers, agencies and the media. Funded by a levy on advertising space, the ASA is independent of both government and the advertising industry.

Chairman:
The Rt Hon the Lord Rodgers of Quarry Bank
Director-General: Mrs Matti Alderson
Deputy Director-General: Tony Butler

Advisory Committee on Protection of the Sea

11 Dartmouth Street, London SW1H 9BN
020 7799 3033 Fax: 020 7799 2933
E-mail: acopsorg@netcomuk.co.uk
Website: www.acops.org

The Advisory Committee on Protection of the Sea, ACOPS, was founded in 1952 by James (now Lord) Callaghan. It is a non-governmental organisation and a registered charity, which aims to promote the control of marine pollution worldwide. This ACOPS seeks to achieve through scientific research and seeking appropriate legal solutions.

ACOPS also fulfils an educational role by providing a forum for the exchange of information and views on the great variety of sources of marine pollution. It has consultative status at the International Maritime Organisation, the International Oil Pollution Compensation Fund, the London Dumping Convention and UNEP and produces a unique compendium on the subject of sea pollution in the form of a Yearbook.

President: The Rt Hon the
Lord Callaghan of Cardiff, KG
Chairman: The Rt Hon the Lord Clinton-Davis
Vice-Chairman: Trygve Meyer
Honorary Treasurer: Paul Phillips
Executive Director: Dr Viktor Sebek
Director of Programmes: Dr Ljubomir Jeftic

Vice-Presidents: Prof Nizar Tawfiq (Saudi Arabia), Cheikh Cissokho (Senegal), Senor Manuel Rodriguez (Colombia), Hon John Fraser, PC, QC (Canada), Adm Igor Kasatonov (Russian Fed), Jan Henry Olsen (Norway), Sir Hugh Rossi, KT (UK), Thierry Chambolle (France), Rui Manuel Godinho (Portugal), Senator Heherson Alvarez (Philippines), Congressman Curt Weldon (United States), Prof Dr HRH Princess Chulabhorn Mahidol (Thailand), Jeremie Bonnelame (Seychelles), Peter Mokaba (South Africa), Mr Yang Zhenhuai (People's Republic of China)

Advisory Committee on Statute Law

Lord Chancellor's Department
Statutory Publications Office,
Selborne House, 54-60 Victoria Street,
London SW1E 6QW
020 7210 2615 Fax: 020 7210 2678

The Advisory Committee provides the Lord Chancellor with advice on all matters relating to the publication of the statute book including the availability of up-to-date texts in both printed and electronic form.

The Lord Chancellor: The Rt Hon the Lord
Irvine of Lairg *(Chairman)*
Permanent Secretary to the Lord Chancellor:
Sir Hayden Phillips, KCB *(Deputy Chairman)*
Clerk of the Parliaments: J M Davies
Clerk of the House of Commons:
W R McKay, CB
Chairman of the Law Commission:
The Hon Mr Justice Carnwath
Chairman of the Scottish Law Commission:
The Hon Lord Gill
First Parliamentary Counsel:
E G Caldwell, CB *(SCS)*
First Scottish Parliamentary Counsel:
J C McCluskie, CB, QC *(SCS)*
Treasury Solicitor:
A H Hammond, CB, QC *(SCS)*
Solicitor to the Scottish Office:
Richard Henderson *(SCS)*
Counsel General, Welsh Office:
Winston Roddick, QC *(SCS)*
Head of Corporate Services Group in LCD:
Ms Jenny Rowe

The Legal Adviser, LCD: Paul Jenkins *(SCS)*
Head of the Statutory Publications Office:
K Garrett
Consultant Legal Editor, Statutory Publications Office: C E Carey
Controller of HMSO and Queen's Printer:
Mrs Carol Tullo
First Legislative Counsel, Northern Ireland, is also a member
Secretary (acting): Claire Malthouse

Advisory Committee on Telecommunications for Disabled and Elderly People

50 Ludgate Hill, London EC4M 7JJ
020 7634 8773 Fax: 020 7634 8924
E-mail: diel@acts.org.uk
Website: www.acts.org.uk

An independent body set up under the Telecommunications Act 1984 to advise the Director-General of OFTEL on the additional needs of telecommunications users who happen to be disabled or elderly. The committee takes up policy issues but does not handle individual complaints, which should be referred to OFTEL on 0845 714 5000.

Chairman: Mrs Jean Gaffin, OBE
Secretaries: Terry Walker, David Edwards

Advisory, Conciliation and Arbitration Service (ACAS)

Brandon House, 180 Borough High Street, London SE1 1LW
020 7210 3613
Website: www.acas.org.uk

The Advisory, Conciliation and Arbitration Service (ACAS) was established on a statutory basis under the Employment Protection Act 1975. The current statutory provisions covering the Service are included in the Trade Union and Labour Relations Act 1992 as amended by the Trade Union Reform and Employment Rights Act 1993. It has the general duty of promoting the improvement of industrial relations. In addition to its full-time Chairman, the Council of ACAS currently comprises eleven part-time members, four appointed after consultation with employers' organisations, four appointed after consultation with the unions and three are independent members.

Chairman: John Hougham, CBE

Council Members: W Brown, J Cridland, Ms J Williams, W Knox, B Warman, J Edmonds, W Morris, B Barber, A Pointon, Ms J Gaymer, Ms C Wells, OBE
Chief Conciliator: D Evans
Directors: D Evans, F Noonan, J Thompson, A Wareing
Head of Information: D H Mattes

Air Transport Users Council

CAA House, 45-59 Kingsway, London WC2B 6TE
020 7240 6061 Fax: 020 7240 7071
Website: www.auc.org.uk

The AUC is an independent, non-statutory organisation which seeks to further the interests of all users of air transport. It publishes Annual Reports and Flight Plan, a guide to planning and using air travel. Both are available free from the AUC's office.

Chairman: Ian Hamer
Director-General: Philip Martin

Ancient Monuments Board for Scotland

Longmore House, Salisbury Place, Edinburgh EH9 1SH
0131-668 8764 Fax: 0131-668 8765

The Ancient Monuments Board for Scotland advises the Scottish Ministers on the exercise of their functions, under the Ancient Monuments and Archaeological Areas Act 1979, of providing protection for monuments of national importance. Protection may be provided by including a monument in a statutory list of protected monuments, by acquisition or by guardianship in which the Scottish Ministers assume responsibility for maintenance.

Chairman: Prof Michael Lynch, MA, PhD, FRSE, FSA Scot, FRHistS
Secretary: R A J Dalziel

Ancient Monuments Board for Wales

c/o Cadw: Welsh Historic Monuments
Crown Buildings, Cathays Park, Cardiff CF1 3NQ
029 2082 6430 Fax: 029 2082 6375

The Ancient Monuments Board for Wales is an advisory board created by the Ancient Monuments Consolidation Act of 1913 (now repealed) and confirmed by the Ancient

Monuments and Archaeological Areas Act of 1979. The function of the Board is to advise the National Assembly for Wales on matters concerned with the preservation of Ancient Monuments, including which monuments should be taken into its care and how those monuments should be preserved and displayed to the public.

Chairman: Prof Rees Davies, CBE, FBA, MA, DPhil, FRHistS
Secretary: Mrs Jean M Booker

Architects Registration Board

8 Weymouth Street, London W1N 3FB
020 7580 5861 Fax: 020 7436 5269

The Architects Registration Board was established by statute in 1997. As an independent body, its aim is to protect consumers and safeguard the reputation of architects by:
- maintaining an accurate register of all those entitled to use the term 'architect'
- maintaining and improving standards for education and practice
- taking action if we think somebody should not be on the register
- operating an efficient and effective complaints handling and information service.

Chair: Dr Barbara Kelly, CBE, DL
Acting Registrar: Jane Rees

Arts and Business

Nutmeg House, 60 Gainsford Street
Butler's Wharf, London SE1 2NY
020 7378 8143 Fax: 020 7407 7527
E-mail: head.office@aandb.org.uk
Website: www.AandB.org.uk

Arts and Business exists to promote and encourage partnerships between the private sector and the arts, to their mutual benefit and to that of the community at large.

Arts and Business provides a wide range of services to its 350 business members as well as to 700 arts organisations and museums through the Development Forum.

To enable individual business people to share their skills with the arts, Arts and Business manages the Placement Scheme and the NatWest Board Bank.

On behalf of the Department for Culture, Media and Sport and the Department of Education for Northern Ireland, Arts and Business manages the Pairing Scheme, an incentive programme for new and established sponsors of the arts.

The scheme is funded by the Arts Council of England. Increasingly, Arts and Business is working with forward looking businesses to determine the future of partnerships between business and the arts through its Creative Forum. With the support of its Patron, HRH The Prince of Wales, it is exploring and developing new ways for business, the arts and society to interact.

Arts and Business runs its programmes from London and a network of offices nationwide. It is the world's foremost agency in the field of business partnership with the arts.

Patron: HRH The Prince of Wales
Chairman: Robin Wight
Chief Executive: Colin Tweedy

Arts Council of England

14 Great Peter Street, London SW1P 3NQ
020 7333 0100 Fax: 020 7973 6590
Minicom: 020 7973 6564
E-mail: enquiries@artscouncil.org.uk
Website: www.artscouncil.org.uk

The Arts Council of England was formed in April 1994 as the successor to the Arts Council of Great Britain (founded in 1946). It operates under a Royal Charter, is independent of Government and registered as a charity. Its chartered objectives are to develop and improve the knowledge, understanding and practice of the arts, to increase the accessibility of the arts to the public and to advise government departments, local authorities and other bodies on the arts. An annual grant from the Government enables the Council to carry out its work in co-operation with ten regional Arts Boards which it funds.

The Arts Council of England is also responsible for distributing the arts share of the proceeds of the National Lottery to arts, crafts and film projects in England.

Chairman: Mr Gerry Robinson
Chief Executive: Peter Hewitt
Executive Director of Arts and Policy:
  Kim Evans
Executive Director of Finance and Operations:
  Graham Long
Executive Director of Communications:
  Wendy Andrews
Executive Director of Research and Policy:
  Pauline Tambling
Director of Finance and Resources:
  Nigel Copeland
Director of Dance: Hilary Carty
Director of Drama: Anna Stapleton

Director of Education and Training: (Vacant)
Director of Music: Hilary Boulding
Director of Literature: Gary McKeone
Director of Touring: Kate Devey
Director of Visual Arts:
   Marjorie Allthorpe-Guyton

Arts Council of Northern Ireland

MacNeice House, 77 Malone Road, Belfast, BT9 6AQ
028 9038 5200 Fax: 028 9066 1715
E-mail: publicaffairs@artscouncil-ni.org
Website: www.artscouncil-ni.org/

The Arts Council of Northern Ireland is the prime distributor of public support for the arts. It was established in 1962 as a successor to the Committee for the Encouragement of Music and the Arts (CEMA) which had operated since 1942. It is now a statutory body. In addition to providing funding for the arts, its principal functions are to develop and improve the knowledge, appreciation and practice of arts; to increase public access to and participation in the arts; and to advise the Department for Education and other government departments, district councils and other bodies, on matters relating to the arts.

Chairman: Prof Brian Walker
Vice-Chair: Ms Marnie O'Neill
Chief Executive: Brian Ferran

Arts Council of Wales

Museum Place, Cardiff CF10 3NX
029 2037 6500 Fax: 029 2022 1447
E-mail: information@ccc-acw.org.uk
Website: www.ccc-acw.org.uk
and offices at Colwyn Bay and Carmarthen

The new Arts Council of Wales is an independent body, incorporated by Royal Charter, with the following objects:
(a) to develop and improve the knowledge, understanding and practice of the arts;
(b) to increase the accessibility of the arts to the public
(c) to advise and co-operate with departments of the Government, local authorities, the Arts Councils of England, Scotland and Northern Ireland and other bodies on any matters concerned, whether directly or indirectly with the foregoing objects, and
(d) to carry out the objects through the medium of both the Welsh and English languages.
The Council receives annual grants from the

National Assembly for Wales, the Crafts Council and Local Authorities in Wales and is the distributing body for National Lottery funds for the Arts in Wales.

Chief Executive: Joanna Weston

Association for Payment Clearing Services

Mercury House, Triton Court, 14 Finsbury Square, London EC2A 1LQ
020 7711 6200 Fax: 020 7711 6276
Website: www.apacs.org.uk

Chairman: Ian Harley
Chief Executive: Christopher Pearson
Head of Public Affairs: Richard Tyson-Davies

Association of Community Health Councils for England and Wales

Earlsmead House, 30 Drayton Park, London N5 1PB
020 7609 8405 Fax: 020 7700 1152
E-mail: mailbox@achew.org.uk
Website: www.achcew. org.uk

Community Health Councils (CHCs) are local statutory bodies, whose job is to keep under review the operation of the NHS in their Districts and to recommend improvements. ACHCEW advises and helps CHCs in their work and represents at national level the consumer interest in the NHS.

Chair: Ms Joyce Struthers
Director: Ms Donna Covey

Association of Local Authorities of Northern Ireland

123 York Street, Belfast BT15 1AB
028 9024 9286 Fax: 028 9023 3328

The Association represents the interests of district councils in Northern Ireland. It considers, and takes action on, matters related to the functions and duties of the councils.

President: Cllr W J Dillon
Secretary and Treasurer:
   Raymond McKay, BSc (Econ) LLB, FHSM

Association of London Government

36 Old Queen Street, London SW1H 9JP
020 7222 7799 Fax: 020 7799 2339
E-mail: ikeating@alg.gov.uk

The ALG represents all 33 London local authorities and its role is to serve as the voice of London local government and to co-ordinate the activities of its member authorities, give them a corporate identity in talks with government and other bodies, and provide a forum in which they can discuss common problems.

Joint Presidents:
  The Rt Hon the Lord Jenkin of Roding,
  The Rt Hon the Lord Graham of Edmonton
Chair: Lord Harris of Haringey
Deputy Chair: Cllr Len Duvall
Chief Executive: Martin Pilgrim
Deputy Chief Executive: Madeleine Williams
Head of Communications: Sue Rhodes
Head of Community Services: Hilary McCollum
Head of Environment, Europe and
  Regeneration: Derek Whyte
Head of Local Government Finance:
  Stephen Fitzgerald
Parliamentary Officer: Ian Keating

Association of Town Centre Management

1 Queen Anne's Gate, Westminster,
London SW1H 9BT
020 7222 0120 Fax: 020 7222 4440
E-mail: atcm@btinternet.com

Formed in 1991, created by representatives from both the public and private sectors to:

– Encourage co-operation among those with a common vision for their town centre
– Research–Advocate the role of Town Centres
– Act as a national forum for the identification and exchange of good practice
– Consider national and local government practice and seek priority for the funding of town centres
– Liaise with other relevant organisations having similar aims
– Act as Secretariat to the All-Party Parliamentary Group on Town Centre Management Issues

The Association organises conferences and training courses, has published a best practice guide, offering help with skills training, action and business plan preparation advice, and conducts relevant research responding to government consultations

Chairman: Alan K Tallentire

Audit Commission

1 Vincent Square, London SW1P 2PN
020 7828 1212 Fax: 020 7976 6187
Website: www.audit-commission.gov.uk

The Audit Commission for Local Authorities and the National Health Service in England and Wales is an independent body, established under the provisions of the 1982 Local Government Finance Act. Its objectives are to appoint auditors to local authorities and health authorities and to help authorities to bring about improvements in efficiency, through the "value for money" studies which the Commission carries out.

Under the 1999 Local Government Act, the Commission is also responsible for carrying out inspections of certain local government services. It also carries out inspections of social service department with the Social Services Inspectorate and assists OFSTED with local education authority inspections.

The auditors appointed may be the District Audit Service or private firms of accountants.

The Commission members include senior people from industry, local government, the accounting profession and the health service.

Chairman: Dame Helena Shovelton, DBE
Deputy Chairman: Jeremy Orme
Commission Members: Richard Arthur,
  Julie Baddeley, Dr Judy Curson, John Foster,
  Adrienne Fresko, Rosalynde Lowe,
  Prof Sue Richards, Hilary Rowland,
  Peter Soulsby, Mrs Iris Tarry, CBE,
  Sir Ron Watson, CBE, Sir David Williams,
  Brian Wolfe
Controller of Audit: Andrew Foster

Bank of England

Threadneedle Street, London EC2R 8AH
020 7601 4444
E-mail: enquiries@bankofengland.co.uk
Website: www.bankofengland.co.uk

The Bank was established in 1694 by Act of Parliament and Royal Charter as a commercial bank with private shareholders. In 1946 it was brought into public ownership and a new Royal Charter was granted. As the central bank of the United Kingdom, the Bank's overriding objective is to maintain a stable and efficient monetary and financial framework for the effective functioning of the economy. The Bank's monetary policy objective is to deliver price stability as defined by the Government's inflation target. Legislation, approved by Parliament in 1998, gave the responsibility for setting short-term interest rates, previously held by the Chancellor of the Exchequer, to the Bank. Under the new legislation, the Bank's responsibilities for supervising banks passed to a new single regulator, the Financial Services Authority, which is responsible for all financial services regulation. The Bank retains its responsibilities for maintaining the stability of the financial system as a whole. Among its priorities are the security and efficiency of payment and settlement systems and ensuring that the City maintains its position as a leading international financial centre. The Bank acts as a banker, with the Government and other banks as its customers, and is the Registrar of Government stocks. It is also responsible for the Note Issue. The Bank is governed by a Court of Directors, all of whom are appointed by the Crown.

Governor:
The Rt Hon Edward Alan John George
Deputy Governors: David Clementi,
Mervyn King
Secretary: Peter Rodgers

Biotechnology and Biological Sciences Research Council

Polaris House, North Star Avenue,
Swindon SN2 1UH
01793 413200 *Fax:* 01793 413201
Website: www.bbsrc.ac.uk

The Biotechnology and Biological Sciences Research Council was formed on 1 April 1994 by an incorporation of the research programmes of the former Agricultural and Food Research Council, and the Biotechnology Directorate and Biological Sciences Committee of the former Science and Engineering Research Council.

The Council is funded principally through the Science Budget of the Office of Science and Technology and receives funds from the Ministry of Agriculture, Fisheries and Food (MAFF) in respect of commissioned research and also from other Government Departments. The BBSRC supports research within departments in universities throughout the United Kingdom. Institutes sponsored by the Council also undertake research commissions from commercial organisations.

The mission of the Council is:
– to promote and support high-quality basic, strategic and applied research and related postgraduate training relating to the understanding and exploitation of biological systems;
– to advance knowledge and technology, and provide trained scientists and engineers, which meet the needs of users and beneficiaries (including the agriculture, bioprocessing, chemical, food, healthcare, pharmaceutical and other biotechnological related industries), thereby contributing to the economic competitiveness of the United Kingdom and the quality of life;
– to provide advice, disseminate knowledge, and promote public understanding in the fields of biotechnology and the biological sciences.
Research Activities: Basic, strategic and applied research in biological sciences and related areas in chemistry, physics, engineering and mathematics.

Chairman: Dr Peter Doyle, CBE, FRSE
Deputy Chairman and Chief Executive to the Council: Prof Raymond Baker, FRS
Members: Prof B Atkinson, FREng, M M Baker, M Calvert, Prof Sir Brian Follett, FRS, Prof J M Goodfellow, J Graham, Prof K Gull, Prof C F Higgins, FRSE, Dr J Padfield, Prof L Partridge, FRS, FRSE, Prof P R Schroeder, FBIM, Dr D W F Shannon, Dr M A Stanley, W G Walker, CBE
Group Directors: R J Price (Human and Corporate Resources Group), S H Visscher (Finance Group), Prof D C S White (Science and Technology Group), Dr D Yarrow (Business Innovation and International Group)
Public Affairs: Dr M A Winstanley

Boundary Commission for England

Room RG/11, Drummond Gate,
London SW1V 2QQ
020 7533 5177 Fax: 020 7533 5176
E-mail: bcomm.england@ons.gov.uk
Website: www.ons.gov.uk

The Commission is required by the Parliamentary Constituencies Act 1986, as amended, to review the representation of England in the House of Commons and, every 8 to 12 years, submit to the Home Secretary a report showing the constituencies it recommends to give effect to the Rules for Redistribution of Seats which include a need to create constituencies with equal electorates whilst taking account of local government boundaries, local ties and geography.

Chairman: The Rt Hon Betty Boothroyd, MP, The Speaker of the House of Commons
Deputy Chairman: The Hon Mr Justice Harrison
Joint Secretaries: R W Farrance, M Rawlings

Boundary Commission for Scotland

3 Drumsheugh Gardens, Edinburgh EH3 7QJ
0131-538 7200
The Commission is required by the Parliamentary Constituencies Act 1986, as amended, to review the representation of Scotland in the House of Commons and to report to the Secretary of State for Scotland within 8 to 12 years of the date of its last report. The Commission recommends, in accordance with the Rules for Redistribution of Seats, constituencies which are as near the average electorate as possible, while having regard to other factors such as local government boundaries, local ties and special geographical considerations. Under the Scotland Act 1998, the Commission is also required to review the regions for elections to the Scottish Parliament.

Chairman: The Rt Hon Betty Boothroyd, MP, The Speaker of the House of Commons
Dep Chairman: The Hon Lady Cosgrove
Secretary: Bob Smith

Boundary Commission for Wales

1 Drummond Gate, London SW1V 2QQ
020 7533 5170/5171 Fax: 020 7533 5176
E-mail: bcomm.wales@ons.gov.uk
Website: www.ons.gov.uk
The Commission is required by the Parliamentary Constituencies Act 1986, as amended, to review the representation of Wales in the House of Commons and, every 8 to 12 years, submit to the Home Secretary a report showing the constituencies it recommends to give effect to the Rules for Redistribution of Seats which include a need to create constituencies with equal electorates whilst taking account of local government boundaries, local ties and geography.

Chairman: The Rt Hon Betty Boothroyd, MP, The Speaker of the House of Commons
Deputy Chairman:
The Hon Mr Justice Maurice Kay
Joint Secretaries: R W Farrance, M Rawlings

British Board of Agrément

PO Box 195, Bucknalls Lane, Garston,
Watford, Hertfordshire WD2 7NG
01923 665300 Fax: 01923 665301
E-mail: mail@bba.star.co.uk
Website: www.bbacerts.co.uk
The British Board of Agrément (BBA) is an organisation whose Governing Board includes representation on behalf of the Secretary of State for the Environment, Transport and the Regions. Originally set up by Government in 1966 as The Agrément Board, the BBA's principal function is the testing and assessment of innovative building products, for which no British Standard has yet been agreed, and the issuing of Agrément Certificates to those which meet the required criteria.

These Certificates include details on the performance of the products concerned as well as statements on their compliance, or contribution to compliance, with Building Regulations throughout the United Kingdom. They are used by architects and other building professionals as an important source of independent product information and a guide to fitness for specific purposes.

The BBA has been designated by Government to issue European Technical Approvals – the system of approval for new products which will apply throughout the Single European Market – and to represent the UK in the co-ordinating European Organisation for Technical Approvals.

Chairman: A J Jackson, CBE
Chief Executive: Dr P C Hewlett
Governing Board: R F Gainsford, B J Griffiths, D J Harper, Dr D J Johns, CBE, D Smith
Observer: P F Everall
Solicitor: J P Rodier

British Broadcasting Corporation

Broadcasting House, London W1A 0AA
020 7580 4468
E-mail: info@bbc.co.uk
The BBC is a body corporate set up by Royal Charter and operating under Licence to provide a public service of broadcasting at home and over-

seas. Its domestic services are financed by an annual licence fee (payable by people who have television sets) and its world service by an annual Grant-in Aid from the Foreign Office. It began life as the British Broadcasting Company in 1922 and became a corporation under a Royal Charter in 1927. Its current Charter and Licence Agreement took effect on 1 May 1996 and expires in December 2006.

At home, the BBC provides national services on two colour television channels and five radio networks, as well as regional broadcasting and local radio. A 24-hour television news service, News 24, is broadcast free to air on selected cable channels, BBC-1 overnight and on Digital Satellite and Digital Terrestrial. BBC Choice is a free to air digital channel offering complementary programming to BBC-1 and BBC-2 and is available on all digital platforms. BBC Parliament which carries live unedited coverage from Westminster is available on selected cable channels and Digital Satellite. BBC Knowledge, the new education channel is also available on all digital platforms. BBC Online is available at www.bbc.co.uk.

BBC World Service broadcasts in English and 42 other languages and has a global audience of 143 million.

The BBC aims to provide a balanced output of information, education and entertainment. Unlike newspapers, it expresses no editorial opinion on public issues or matters of controversy, and it applies a policy of strict impartiality in its coverage of these matters.

BBC BOARD OF GOVERNORS
Chairman: Sir Christopher Bland
Vice-Chairman:
   The Baroness Young of Old Scone
National Governor for Scotland:
   Sir Robert Smith
National Governor for Northern Ireland:
   Prof Fabian Monds, CBE
National Governor for Wales:
   Roger Spencer Jones, OBE
Other Governors: Richard Eyre, CBE, Dame Pauline Neville-Jones, DCMG, Sir David Scholey, CBE, Ranjit Sondhi, Adrian White, CBE, Tony Young, Heather Rabbatts

BBC EXECUTIVE COMMITTEE
Director-General: Sir John Birt *(until 31 March 2000, Greg Dyke from 1 April 2000)*
Chief Executive, BBC Broadcast: Will Wyatt
Chief Executive, BBC Production:
   Matthew Bannister
Chief Executive, BBC News: Tony Hall

Chief Executive, BBC Resources:
   Margaret Salmon
Director of Personnel: (Vacant)
Director of Finance: John Smith
Director of Policy and Planning:
   Patricia Hodgson, CBE
Director of Corporate Affairs: Colin Browne
Chief Executive, World Service: Mark Byford
Chief Executive, BBC Worldwide Ltd:
   Rupert Gavin

BOARD OF MANAGEMENT
The Board of Management is made up of members of the Executive Committee, together with:
Director of Television: Alan Yentob
Director of Radio: Jenny Abramsky
Director, National and Regional Broadcasting:
   Mark Thompson
Director of Education: Michael Stevenson
Director of Technology: Philip Langsdale
Director of New Services and Deputy Director of Television: David Doherty
Director, Online: Nigel Chapman
Managing Director of UK Regions and Deputy Chief Executive Worldwide: Peter Teague
Director of Programmes and Deputy Chief Executive: Lorraine Heggessey

British Chambers of Commerce

Manning House, 22 Carlisle Place, London SW1P 1JA
020 7565 2000 Fax: 020 7565 2049
E-mail: info@britishchambers.org.uk
Website: www.britishchambers.org.uk

The British Chambers of Commerce (BCC) is the largest business representative body in the UK. Its membership comprises a national network of quality assured Approved Chambers of Commerce which collectively represent over 120,000 businesses of all sizes and in all sectors of the economy.

Approved Chambers of Commerce are the UK's largest provider of business services in the private sector, offering support in areas central to the needs of business such as exports and international trade, business training, information and independent representation. Approved Chambers also provide a range of exclusive commercial benefits to business members on essential services including telecom, fleet, energy and healthcare.

Approved Chambers articulate the views and interests of business to government, and play a central role in the progress and promotion of economic development at the local and regional level.

The BCC's policy on issues ranging from Skills, Transport and the Economy to the Environment, Europe and Business Support is reached only after thorough and detailed consultation with Approved Chambers of Commerce and their business members.

President: John Entwistle
Director-General: Chris Humphries, CBE
Deputy Director-General: Dr Ian Peters
Principal Economic Adviser: Ian Fletcher
Principal Policy Adviser: Mark Sharman
Head of Communications: Andrew Parkinson

British Council

10 Spring Gardens, London SW1A 2BN
020 7930 8466 Fax: 020 7839 6347

The British Council promotes a wider knowledge of the United Kingdom as a forward-looking and dynamic democracy and advances the use of the English language.

Drawing on the country's intellectual capital and immense creativity the British Council reinforces the UK's positive role in the international community through cultural, scientific, technological and educational co-operation.

The Council works with partners in the UK and overseas to build long-term relations with people and institutions in other countries.

Board Members:
Chair: Baroness Kennedy of the Shaws, QC
Deputy Chairman: Sir Tim Lankester, KCB
Vice-Chairmen:
   The Rt Hon Virginia Bottomley, MP,
   Oona King, MP
Ms Lesley Abdela, MBE, Michael Bichard,
   Sir Christopher Bland, Prof Robert Boucher,
   The Rt Hon Menzies Campbell, CBE, QC, M
   P, Prof David Crystal, OBE,
   Dr John Hemming, CMG, Ms Ffion Jenkins,
   Sir John Kerr, KCMG, Gerard Lemos,
   Ms Penelope Lively, Ms Heather Rabbatts,
   Joan Smyth,
   Lord Stevenson of Coddenham, CBE,
   Prof Eric Sunderland, John Vereker, CB,
   The Lord Wilson of Tillyorn, GCMG
Director-General: David Green
Secretary: Sarah Ewans
Parliamentary Officers: Brionie Huish,
   Christopher Graffius, Jane Ladbury

British Dental Association

64 Wimpole Street, London W1M 8AL
020 7935 0875 Fax: 020 7487 3024
E-mail:
press.parliamentary@bda-dentistry.org.uk
Website: www.bda-dentistry.org.uk
Head of Press and Parliamentary Department:
   Kate Cinamon

British Educational Communications and Technology Agency

Milburn Hill Road, Science Park,
Coventry CV4 7JJ
024 7641 6994 Fax: 024 7641 1418
E-mail: becta@becta.org.uk
Website: www.becta.org.uk

Becta is the government agency for information and communications technology in education. It supports and develops the use of technology to raise educational standards. Responsible for the National Grid for Learning, Becta also encourages schools and colleges to become effective and critical purchasers and users of ICT by supporting and disseminating good practice and quality in educational technology.

Chairman: H Du Quesnay, CBE
Chief Executive: O Lynch
Directors: F Daly, J Brown, N McLean, J Wedge

British Film Institute

21 Stephen Street, London W1P 2LN
020 7255 1444 Fax: 020 7436 7950
Website: www.bfi.org.uk

The British Film Institute offers opportunities to experience, enjoy and discover more about the world of film and moving images. It publishes film books and educational resources, runs the BFI National Library, supports cinemas and film festivals UK-wide, cares for the UK's film heritage and promotes access to these collections in a variety of ways.

Chairman: Joan Bakewell, CBE
Acting Director: Jon Teckman

British Library

96 Euston Road, London NW1 2DB
020 7412 7000 Fax: 020 7412 7168

The British Library is the national library for the United Kingdom and the world's leading reference library for the arts and sciences. It was established on 1 July 1973 under the British Library Act 1972 although its oldest collections stem from the foundation of the British Museum in 1753. Its purpose is to provide comprehensive reference, lending, document supply, bibliographic, publishing, computer searches and other services based on its vast collections of books, manuscripts (both western and oriental), maps, sound recordings, music scores, periodicals, patents, and other material. Since July 1999, the Library has been fully open at its new centre in St Pancras, and is now based on two geographical centres – London for reference material and Boston Spa for document supply, bibliographic work, legal deposit of books and administration.

The British Library's three new exhibition galleries, public events, tours and bookshop are now available at St Pancras.

Chairman: Dr John M Ashworth
Chief Executive: Dr Brian A Lang
Board Members:
    Prof Michael Anderson, FBA, FRSE,
    Henry Boyd-Carpenter, CVO,
    Sir Matthew Farrer, GCVO, C G R Leach,
    B Naylor, Dr Jessica Rawson, CBE, FBA,
    J Ritblat, FSA,
    Viscount Runciman of Doxford, CBE, FBA,
    P Scherer
Deputy Chief Executive: D Russon
Director-General: D Bradbury
Secretary to the Board: (Vacant)
Assistant Secretary: A Stephens
Head of Corporate Communication:
    Greg Hayman
Press and Public Relations: Kenneth Shirreffs

British Medical Association

BMA House, Tavistock Square,
London WC1H 9JP
020 7387 4499
Website: www.bma.org.uk
Chairman of Council: Dr Ian Bogle
Secretary: Dr Mac Armstrong, BSc, FRCPEd, FRCP(Glas), FRCGP
Treasurer: Dr W James Appleyard, MA(Oxon), BM, Bch, FRCP, Glasgow
Head of Public Affairs:
    Nigel Duncan (020 7383 6113)
Head of Parliamentary Unit: Ms Sue Marks
    (020 7383 6590 Fax: 020 7383 6830)

British Museum

Great Russell Street, Bloomsbury,
London WC1B 3DG
020 7636 1555 Fax: 020 7323 8616
E-mail: info@british-museum.ac.uk
Website: www.british-museum.ac.uk

The British Museum was founded by an Act of Parliament of 1753 which appointed Trustees to take charge of the library, natural history collections, antiquities and works of art of Sir Hans Sloane. The natural history collections were removed to South Kensington between 1880 and 1883 and were finally constituted as a separate museum in 1963 by the British Museum Act of that year. The library departments became part of a separate institution, the British Library, in 1973.

At the present time the British Museum comprises the national collections of antiquities, ethnography, prints, drawings, coins and medals. Its purpose is to advance learning for both scholars and the general public by its permanent and special exhibitions, by the provision of material and facilities for research and by other special services.

Chairman of the Board of Trustees:
    Graham Greene, CBE, MA
Director: Dr Robert G W Anderson, MA, DPhil, FSA, FRSC
Managing Director: Ms Suzanna Taverne
Secretary: (Ian) Tony Doubleday, LLB

British Nuclear Industry Forum

22 Buckingham Gate, London SW1E 6LB
020 7828 0116 Fax: 020 7931 0646
E-mail: info@bnif.co.uk
Website: www.bnif.co.uk

BNIF is the trade association and information body for the British civil nuclear industry. It represents over 60 companies including the operators of the nuclear power stations, those engaged in decommissioning, waste management and all aspects of the nuclear fuel cycle, nuclear equipment suppliers, engineering and construction firms and the nuclear research facilities.

Chairman: Ray Hall, CBE, FEng
Director of Communications and Public Affairs:
    Keith Parker
Director of Trade and Industry: John Haddon

British Ports Association

Africa House, Kingsway,
London WC2B 6AH
020 7242 1200 Fax: 020 7405 1069
E-mail: ports@compuserve.com
Director: David Whitehead
Secretary: Betty Redmond

British Railways Board

Whittles House, 14 Pentonville Road
London N1 9HF
020 7904 5000 Fax: 020 7904 5040
E-mail: ji79@dial.pipex.com

The Board (whose members are appointed by the Secretary of State for Environment, Transport and the Regions) is a Public Authority established under the terms of the Transport Act 1962.

Since April 1994, ownership of track, stations and infrastructure has been vested in a new company – Railtrack. Train operations and other activities of the British Railways Board have been restructured into smaller companies transferred to the private sector.

The Board has various duties as a residuary body, for certain property matters and the BT Police. It also has an advisory role in regard to strategic transport planning. Since April 1999 the Board and the Office of Passenger Rail Franchising have been working together within the Shadow Strategic Rail Authority.

Board Members
Chairman (part-time): Sir Alastair Morton
Vice-Chairman: J J Jerram, CBE
Part-time Members: L Adams, OBE, D A Begg,
   Lord Bradshaw, D Jefferies, CBE,
   P H Kent, CBE, D Quarmby
The Secretary: P C Trewin

Department: Environment, Transport and the Regions

British Retail Consortium

5 Grafton Street, London W1X 3LB
020 7647 1500 Fax: 020 7647 1599

The British Retail Consortium represents the interests of the retail industry to the UK Government and Parliament, to the European Union and to the public via the media.

The BRC represents over 90% of the retail industry, from multiple retailers to corner shops, from food and drink to clothing and DIY, and from the High Street to out-of-town and mail order. The BRC seeks to inform and influence policy makers and opinion formers at all levels and maintains links with a wide range of organisations with related interests to ensure that the industry's views are professionally represented at all times.

The British Retail Consortium is based in central London and maintains a Brussels office. It is affiliated to EuroCommerce – the retail, wholesale and international trade representation to the European Communities.

Director-General: Ann Robinson
Director of External Affairs: Ann Grain
Parliamentary Officer: Leigh Tomkins

British Safety Council

70 Chancellors Road, London W6 9RS
020 8741 1231 Fax: 020 8741 4555
E-mail: mail@britsafe.org
Website: www.britishsafetycouncil.org

The British Safety Council came into existence following a debate in the House of Commons on 7 June 1957. It is the largest independent specialist occupational health and safety body in Europe, with 12,700 corporate members from all fields of industry and commerce, representing 4.5 million employees. It campaigns vigorously on a range of health, safety and environmental issues. The Council runs 30,000 delegate days of training a year in accident and ill-health prevention techniques and is an approved assessment centre for the Vocational Qualification in Occupational Health and Safety Practice. It provides a comprehensive range of training, risk management, auditing, advisory and assessment programmes and publications, including the journal *Safety Management* (23,717 copies monthly). It is anxious to provide an authoritative source of information to Members of Parliament.

Director-General: Sir Neville Purvis, KCB

British Standards Institution

389 Chiswick High Road, London W4 4AL
020 8996 9000 Fax: 020 8996 7400
Website: www.bsi.org.uk

An independent body established by Royal Charter, BSI prepares and promulgates nationally agreed standards and codes of practice. It provides a range of certification for products including the Kitemark, indicating the adherence to agreed standards. The Customer Services department provides assistance and advice on British and overseas technical certification and licencing requirements. BSI is the United Kingdom member of the International Organization for Standardization and the European standards-making bodies. Through these fora BSI works to gain advantage for UK industry, technology and systems and to ensure that unfair barriers to trade are removed.

Chairman: Vivian Thomas, CBE
Chief Executive: Keith Tozzi
Company Secretary: Stanley K Williams
Head of Corporate Affairs: Brian Bannister

British Urban Regeneration Association

33 Great Sutton Street,
London EC1V 0DX
020 7253 5054 Fax: 020 7490 8735
Freephone: 0800 0181260
E-mail: info@bura.org.uk

Founder President:
  The Rt Hon the Lord Jenkin of Roding
President: Sir Jeremy Beecham
Chair: Bernadette Marjoram
Directors: Ralph Luck, Lesley Chalmers,
  Jacqueline Sadek, David Scougall,
  Graham Farrant, Sir Hugh Sykes,
  June Barnes, Malcolm Iley, Imtiaz Farookhi,
  Greg Clark
Chief Executive: David Fitzpatrick
Treasurer: John Francis, FCA
Company Secretary: Gerald Cary-Elwes
Development Director: Paul Way
Director of Operations: Elspeth Burrage

British Waterways Board

Willow Grange, Church Road, Watford,
Hertfordshire WD1 3QA
01923 226422 *Fax:* 01923 226081
Website: www.britishwaterways.co.uk

The British Waterways Board was established under the Transport Act 1962. Its duties are to provide services and facilities on inland waterways and at harbours owned by the Board. Under the Transport Act 1968, the waterways were divided into three types, commercial, cruising waterways, and the remainder. The Board has the specific duty to maintain commercial waterways for use by freight-carrying vessels and cruising waterways for use by cruising craft. Of some 2,000 miles of waterway owned by the Board in the UK, 388 miles are classified as commercial and 1,169 as cruising. The remainder are to be dealt with in the most economical manner possible, consistent with the requirements of public health and amenity and safety.

Chairman: Dr G P Greener
Vice-Chairman: D H R Yorke, CBE
Board Members: Sir Neil Cossons, OBE,
  C Christie, CBE, Mrs C Dobson,
  Mrs C J Elvy, Dr P F King, Ms J A Lewis-
  Jones, Sir Peter Soulsby
Chief Executive: D J Fletcher
Corporate Services Director: R J Duffy

**Department: Environment, Transport and
  the Regions**

British Youth Council

65–69 White Lion Street, London N1 9PP
020 7278 0582 Fax: 020 7278 0583
E-mail: mail@byc.org.uk
Website: www.byc.org.uk

The British Youth Council was formed in 1948, and is the representative voice for young people aged 16–25 in the UK, with an affiliated membership of over four million in its 130 member organisations. The Council's primary aim is to advance the interests and views of young people, and to work towards their effective participation and involvement in society as a whole.

Chairperson: David Jones
Vice-Chair, Finance: Roz Mascarenhas
Vice-Chair: Phil Pinder
Chief Executive: Samantha Peters

Building Societies Association

3 Savile Row, London W1X 1AF
020 7437 0655 Fax: 020 7734 6416/6317
Website: www.bsa.org.uk

The Building Societies Association represents the UK's building societies. There are 70 mutual societies with assets in excess of £150 billion and around 25% of the mortgage market.

The BSA is the principal source of information on building societies, providing briefing material and statistics on matters relating to their activities. It also provides analysis on financial markets generally. The BSA publishes a range of publications on societies' business and the services they provide.

Chairman: David Smith, OBE
Deputy Chairman: David Anderson
Director-General: Adrian Coles
Head of Financial Policy: Christopher French
Head of Personnel, Finance and Administration:
  Jane Jones
Head of Legal Services: Christopher Lawrenson
External Affairs Manager: Pam O'Keeffe

Cardiff Bay Development Corporation

Baltic House, Mount Stuart Square
Cardiff CF1 6DH
029 2058 5858 Fax: 029 2025 5651

The Cardiff Bay Development Corporation was established under the provisions of the Local Government Planning and Land Act 1980 in April 1987, with the overall objective of establishing Cardiff as a superlative maritime city which will stand comparison with any such city in the world, thereby enhancing the image and economic well-being of Cardiff and Wales as a whole.

To achieve this objective the Corporation may acquire, hold, manage, reclaim and dispose of land, carry out building and other operations, ensure the provision of services and carry on any other activities as necessary.

Board Members:
Chairman: Sir Geoffrey Inkin, OBE
Deputy Chairman:
   The Rt Hon the Lord Brooks of Tremorfa
   J A Beveridge, Sir Alan Cox, CBE,
   Cllr Marion Drake, Cllr Russell Goodway
   (Leader, Cardiff City Council),
   Sir John Gray, KBE, CMG,
   Cllr Gordon Houlston, Ms Menna Richards,
   J Sainsbury, Professor H R Silverman,
   Cllr John Smith, BSc, DL,
   Cllr Anthony J Williams
Executive:
Chief Executive: Michael Boyce
Director of Finance and Administration:
   Glyn Stone
Commercial Director: Duncan Syme
Director of Engineering Operations:
   David Crompton, OBE

(Will cease operating in March 2000)

Central Arbitration Committee

Brandon House, 180 Borough High Street
London SE1 1LW
020 7210 3737/3738

The Central Arbitration Committee (CAC), established under the Trade Union and Labour Relations (Consolidation) Act 1992 but with its origin in the Industrial Court (set up in 1919), is a permanent, independent arbitration body working nationally in the field of industrial relations. It adjudicates on disclosure of information complaints made under the 1992 Act and claims for trade union recognition made under the Employment Relations Act 1999.

Chairman: (Vacant)
Secretary: C Johnston

Central Bureau for International Education and Training

10 Spring Gardens, London SW1A 2BN
020 7389 4004 Fax: 020 7389 4426
E-mail: cblon.information@britishcouncil.org
Website: www.britishcouncil.org/cbeve/

Offices at: 3 Bruntsfield Crescent,
Edinburgh EH10 4HD
0131-447 8024 *Fax:* 0131-452 8569

1 Chlorine Gardens, Belfast BT9 5DJ
028 9066 4418 Fax: 028 9066 1275

The Central Bureau for International Education and Training is the UK national office for information and professional advice on educational exchange, the administration of exchange programmes and support for developing an international dimension in education and training. The Bureau offers international opportunities for mobility, linking and exchange, partnerships and vocational and in-service training.

The Bureau's services enhance the quality of learning provision, especially in the areas of foreign languages, communications and other key skills. They add value to primary and secondary education and training provision, and promote and support training and curriculum development, thereby raising standards of achievement and extending the professional development of educators.

The Central Bureau forms part of the British Council. It is funded by the UK Education Departments and is the UK National Agency for many parts of the EU's education and training programmes: SOCRATES and LEONARDO. The British Council is registered in England as a charity and is the UK's international network for education, culture and development services.

Chairman: Keith Anderson
Director: Peter Upton
Deputy Directors: Bill Musk, Graham Davey,
   Elspeth Cardy, Judith Hemery

Central Rail Users' Consultative Committee

Clements House, 14–18 Gresham Street, London EC2V 7NL
020 7505 9090 Fax: 020 7505 9004

The Central Rail Users' Consultative Committee, established under the 1993 Railways Act, is the statutory consumer organisation representing the interests of rail users nationally. It monitors and investigates the policies and performance of train and station operators and has the legal right to make recommendations for changes. The Committee can refer matters to the Regulator with a view to him exercising his powers. The Regulator can commission work from the CRUCC.

Members of the CRUCC include the Chairman of the eight Rail Users' Consultative Committees (RUCCs) which deal with matters affecting rail users locally, and of the London Regional Passengers' Committee, and up to six other members.

The Central Committee co-ordinates the work of the RUCCs and collates information fed in by them on key issues.

The chairman of the CRUCC and of each RUCC is appointed by the Secretary of State for the Environment, Transport and the Regions in consultation with the Rail Regulator. Appointments of other members are made by the Regulator in consultation with the Secretary of State.

The Office of the Rail Regulator resources both the CRUCC and RUCCs.

Chairman: David Bertram, BA, FIM
National Director: Anthony Smith
Deputy Director: Jon Carter
External Relations and Policy Manager:
   Philip Wilks

Certification Office for Trade Unions and Employers' Associations

Brandon House, 180 Borough High Street, London SE1 1LW
020 7210 3734/5 Fax: 020 7210 3612

The Certification Officer is responsible for maintaining a list of trade unions and employers' associations; for receiving and scrutinising annual returns from trade unions and employers' associations; for dealing with complaints concerning trade union elections and certain other ballots; for ensuring observance of statutory requirements governing mergers between trade unions and between employers' associations; for overseeing the political funds and the finances of trade unions and employers' associations; and for certifying the independence of trade unions.

Certification Officer: E G Whybrew
Asst Certification Officer: G S Osborne
Legal Adviser: Ms C Croft
Asst Certification Officer for Scotland:
   J L J Craig*, WS
*At 58 Frederick Street, Edinburgh EH2 1LN

Church Commissioners for England

1 Millbank, Westminster, London SW1P 3JZ
020 7898 1000
E-mail: corporate.affairs@c-of-e.org.uk

The Church Commissioners were established in 1948, by the amalgamation of Queen Anne's Bounty and the Ecclesiastical Commissioners. They are responsible for the management of the greater part of the Church of England's historic assets, most of the income from which goes towards the pay, housing and pension of the clergy. Their investment portfolio includes stocks and shares and property. Their property portfolio comprises over 131,000 acres of agricultural land, a number of residential estates in central London, and commercial property in this country. They also carry out administrative duties in connection with pastoral reorganisation and the future of redundant churches.

Chairman: The Archbishop of Canterbury
First Church Estates Commissioner:
   John Sclater
Second (Parliamentary) Church Estates
   Commissioner: Stuart Bell, MP
Third Church Estates Commissioner:
   The Viscountess Brentford, OBE, FCA
Secretary: H H Hughes
Deputy Secretary: C W Daws, FCA
Official Solicitor: N Johnson
Chief Surveyor: A C Brown, ARICS
Pastoral and Redundant Churches Secretary:
   M D Elengorn
Investments Manager: A S Hardy
Management Accountant: B J Hardy
Computer Manager: J W Ferguson
Senior Architect: J A Taylor
Corporate Affairs Officer: Catherine Skinner
Bishoprics Secretary: E Peacock

Churches Together in Britain and Ireland

Inter-Church House, 35–41 Lower Marsh,
London SE1 7RL
020 7620 4444 Fax: 020 7928 0010
Website: www.ctbi.org.uk

Churches Together in Britain and Ireland was renamed in 1999; it was previously the Council of Churches for Britain and Ireland. CTBI coordinates the work of its 32 member Churches and liaises with ecumenical bodies in Britain and Ireland as well as ecumenical organisations at European and world levels. Its work includes Church life, Church and Society, Mission, International Affairs and Racial Justice. It provides a forum for joint decision-making and enables the Churches to take action together.

General Secretary: Dr David Goodbourn
Communications Officer: Mary Houston

Citizens Advice Bureaux, National Association of

Myddelton House,
115–123 Pentonville Road, London N1 9LZ
020 7833 2181 Fax: 020 7833 4371
Website: www.nacab.org.uk

Patron: HRH The Princess Royal
Chair: Sir Graham Hart, KCB
Chief Executive: David Harker

Citizens Advice Bureaux, Northern Ireland Association of

11 Upper Crescent, Belfast BT7 1NT
028 9023 1120 Fax: 028 9023 6522
E-mail: niacab@btinternet.com

Chairman: John Hunter
Chief Executive: Derek Alcorn

Citizens Advice Scotland

26 George Square, Edinburgh EH8 9LD
0131-667 0156 *Fax:* 0131-668 4359
E-mail: info@cas.org.uk
Website: www.cas.org.uk

Chairman: Bob Brodie
Chief Executive: Kaliani Lyle

Civil Aviation Authority

CAA House, 45–59 Kingsway,
London WC2B 6TE
020 7832 5712 Fax: 020 7379 4784
Website: www.caa.co.uk

The Civil Aviation Authority (CAA) plays a leading role in the development of the aviation industry through the safety and economic regulation of British aviation and by providing air traffic services in UK airspace. Through its skills and expertise, the CAA is recognised as a world leader in its field.

Its specific responsibilities include:
- Air safety – airworthiness of aircraft and operational aspects including licensing flight crew, aircraft engineers, air traffic controllers and aerodromes; certificating UK airlines and aircraft and maintaining air traffic services standards
- Economic regulation – through licensing of routes, approval of airfares for journeys outside the EU, regulation of certain airport charges, and licensing of air travel organisers
- Air traffic services – providing air traffic control services and radio and navigational aids through a subsidiary company, National Air Traffic Services Limited (NATS).

In addition, the CAA advises the Government on aviation issues, represents consumer interests, conducts economic and scientific research, produces statistical data and provides specialist services.

Board Members
Chairman: Sir Malcolm Field
Group Director Safety Regulation:
    Richard Profit
Group Director Economic Regulation:
    Doug Andrew
Chairman (National Air Traffic Services):
    Sir Roy McNulty
Chief Executive National Air Traffic Services:
    William K Semple
Members: Bryan Austin, Anthony Herron, David Lusher, Rod Lynch, Colin Senior, Roy Swainson
Secretary and Legal Adviser: Rupert Britton
Director Corporate Communications:
    Adrian Moorey
Parliamentary Liaison Officer: Anne Noonan

Department: Environment, Transport and the Regions

Coal Authority

200 Lichfield Lane, Berry Hill,
Mansfield, Nottinghamshire NG18 4RG
01623 427162
Fax: 01623 622072 (General)

The Coal Authority was established under the Coal Industry Act 1994.

It has four principle functions: licensing coal mining operations; handling subsidence damage claims; dealing with historic liabilities; and providing coal mining information.

Chairman: J C Harris, DL
Chief Executive and Authority Member:
  K J Fergusson
Authority Members: E R Hassall, CBE, T W Slee
Director of Operations and Authority Member:
  A Schofield
Director of Finance/Admin and Authority
  Member: M V Edwards
Solicitor and Secretary:
  Mrs S A Brook Shanahan

College of Arms

Queen Victoria Street, London EC4V 4BT
020 7248 2762 Fax: 020 7248 6448

The College of Arms is the official repository of the arms and pedigrees of English and Commonwealth families. The thirteen royal heralds or officers of arms were incorporated and given the site of their present building in 1555. The Three Kings of Arms are empowered by the Crown to grant arms to worthy individuals and corporations on receipt of a Warrant from the Earl Marshal, who has jurisdiction over, but is not part of the College. All the officers undertake heraldic and genealogical research professionally for clients. The College is open from 10 am to 4 pm Monday to Friday and an officer is always in attendance during those hours.

Earl Marshal: The Duke of Norfolk, KG,
  GCVO, CB, CBE, MC
Garter King of Arms:
  Peter Gwynn-Jones, CVO, MA, FSA
Clarenceux King of Arms and Registrar:
  D H B Chesshyre, LVO, MA, FSA
Earl Marshal's Secretary: Patric Dickinson, MA

Commission for Architecture and the Built Environment

7 St James's Square, London SW1Y 4JU
020 7839 6537 Fax: 020 7839 8475
E-mail: enquiries@cabe.org.uk
Website: www.cabe.org.uk

Established on 1 September 1999 to promote high quality design and architecture in the public and private sectors and to raise the quality of the built environment generally. CABE will continue the design review work previously undertaken by the Royal Fine Art Commission.

Chairman: Stuart Lipton, HonRIBA
Commissioners: Miss Sophie Andreae, MA, Paul Finch, HonRIBA, Sunand Prasad, MA, AADipl, PhD, RIBA, Ian Ritchie, DipArch, RA, RIBA, FRSA, Sir Nicholas Serota, Les Sparks, OBE. Further Commissioners will be announced in early 2000
Chief Executive: Francis Golding

Commission for Racial Equality

Head Office, Elliot House,
10-12 Allington Street, London SW1E 5EH
020 7828 7022 Fax: 020 7630 7605
E-mail: media@cre.gov.uk
Website: www.cre.gov.uk

The Commission for Racial Equality was set up by the Race Relations Act 1976 with the duties of: a) working towards the elimination of discrimination; b) promoting equality of opportunity and good relations between persons of different racial groups generally; and c) keeping under review the working of the Act, and, when required by the Secretary of State or when it otherwise thinks it necessary, to draw up and submit to the Secretary of State proposals for amending it.

The CRE provides extensive guidance and information on all matters to do with racial equality and the promotion of equality of opportunity. At its head office there are Media Information and Parliamentary units.

Commissioners
Chairman: (Vacant)
Chief Executive: Susie Parsons
Deputy Chairs: Hugh Harris,
  Dr Moussa Jogee, JP
  Mohammed Amran, Dr Raj Chandran,
  Michael Hastings, Shahid Malik,
  Ms Julie Mellor, Patrick Passley,

Ms Sushila Patel, Bob Purkiss,
Ms Cherry Short, Dr Jaslien Singh,
Ray Singh, Ms Gita Sootarsingh
Director of Policy and Communications:
Phil Barnett (020 7932 5342)
Parliamentary/Public Affairs Officer:
Richard Jarman (020 7932 5454)

Commissioners of Irish Lights

16 Lower Pembroke Street, Dublin 2
00 353 1 662 4525 *Fax:* 00 353 1 6618094
Telex: 93311 CIL EI
E-mail: post@cil.ie
Website: www.cil.ie

The Commissioners of Irish Lights are the General Lighthouse Authority for the coast of Ireland and maintain aids to navigation for shipping in general. Aids to navigation maintained by Local Authorities, Harbour Boards etc., are subject to the approval of the Commissioners.

Commmissioners: Richie Ryan, M A O'Neill,
M W S Maclaran, BA,
J Gore-Grimes, BA, LLB,
Commodore L S Moloney,
The Lord Glentoran, CBE, DL, T C Johnson,
L D McGonagle, BA, LLB, W B Lyster, FCA,
Ms S M Tyrrell, F J Boland, together with The Lord Mayor of Dublin and three Aldermen
Chief Executive:
T M Boyd, CEng, BA, BAI, DIC, MICE

Commissioners of Northern Lighthouses

84 George Street, Edinburgh EH2 3DA
0131-473 3100 *Fax:* 0131-220 2093
E-mail: enquiries@nlb.org.uk
Website: www.nlb.org.uk

The Commissioners of Northern Lighthouses are the General Lighthouse Authority for Scotland and the Isle of Man. The present Board owes its origin to an Act of Parliament passed in 1786 which authorised the erection of four lighthouses. At the present time the Commissioners operate under the Merchant Shipping Act 1995 and are 19 in number.

The Commissioners control 84 major automatic lighthouses, 116 minor lights and many lighted and unlighted buoys. They have a fleet of two motor vessels.

Commissioners: The Lord Advocate, the Solicitor General for Scotland; the Lord Provosts of Edinburgh, Glasgow and Aberdeen; the Provost of Inverness; Convener of the Council for Argyll and Bute; the Sheriffs-Principal of North Strathclyde; Tayside, Central and Fife; Grampian, Highlands and Islands; South Strathclyde, Dumfries and Galloway; Lothians and Borders; Glasgow and Strathkelvin; Admiral Sir Michael Livesay, KCB, P MacKay, K MacLeod, Captain D M Cowell, Lord Maclay, Captain G Sutherland
Chief Executive:
Captain J B Taylor, FIMgt *(Royal Navy)*
Director of Engineering:
W Paterson, BSc(Eng), CEng, FIEE, MRAeS
Director of Operations: P J Christmas, FIMgt
Director of Finance:
D M Gorman, ACMA, MIIA

Committee of Vice-Chancellors and Principals of the Universities of the UK

Woburn House, 20 Tavistock Square, London WC1H 9HQ
020 7419 4111 Fax: 020 7383 5766
E-mail: info@cvcp.ac.uk
Website: www.cvcp.ac.uk

The CVCP consists of the executive heads of all UK universities. CVCP aims to promote public understanding of the roles and achievements of UK universities and to improve the funding, regulatory and marketing environment within which UK universities pursue their diverse missions.

UK President: Prof Howard Newby
Chairman, English and Northern Ireland Council: Prof Roderick Floud
Chairman, Scottish Council (COSHEP): Dr Ian Graham-Bryce
Chairman, Welsh Council (HHEW): Prof John Williams
Chief Executive: Baroness Warwick
Members: Heads of all UK universities
Parliamentary Office: Lucy Burns (Government Relations Manager), Christopher Walden (Parliamentary Officer), Lynn Collie (EU Affairs Officer)

Committee on Standards in Public Life

Horse Guards Road, London SW1P 3AL
020 7270 5875 Fax: 020 7270 5874
Website: www.public-standards.gov.uk

The Prime Minister announced the setting up of the Committee under the Chairmanship of Lord Nolan on 25 October 1994. Its terms of reference are: "to examine current concerns about standards of conduct of all holders of public office, including arrangements relating to financial and commercial activities, and to make recommendations as to any changes in present arrangements which might be required to ensure the highest standards of propriety in public life." The Committee's work covers Ministers, civil servants and advisers, MPs, MEPs, members and senior staff of Quangos, NHS bodies and local authorities, and Ministerial office holders. It does not investigate individual cases.

Lord Neill of Bladen, QC succeeded Lord Nolan as Chairman on 10 November 1997.

The Committee's terms of reference were extended on 12 November 1997 "to review issues in relation to the funding of political parties, and to make recommendations as to any changes in present arrangements".

The report on party funding, the Committee's fifth report, was published on 12 October 1998. It made 100 recommendations for a fundamentally new framework of control of the funding arrangements for political parties in the UK.

The Committee's first report, covering MPs, Ministers and Civil Servants, and executive NDPSs, was published in May 1995. During 1999 the Committee is conducting a review of the effect of its first report.

The second report, published in May 1996, covered local public spending bodies; further and higher education; housing associations; grant-maintained schools; training and enterprise councils and local enterprise companies. The Committee reported on aspects of conduct in local government in July 1997.

In November 1997, the Committee published its fourth report, a review of standards of conduct in executive NDPBs, NHS Trusts and local public spending bodies; and in June 1998 published a legal research study – personal liability of public appointees.

Further background on the Committee, its reports and programme of work available from the Committee or via the Internet.

Chairman: Lord Neill of Bladen, QC

Members: Sir Clifford Boulton, GCB,
Sir Anthony Cleaver, The Lord Goodhart, QC
Frances Heaton, Prof Alice Brown,
The Rt Hon John MacGregor, OBE, MP,
The Rt Hon The Lord Shore of Stepney,
Sir William Utting, CB,
Baroness Warwick of Undercliffe
Secretary to the Committee:
Sarah Tyerman *(SCS)*
(020 7270 5875)
Press Secretary: Philip Aylett *(SCS)*
(020 7270 6345)
Assistant Secretary: Christine Salmon
(020 7270 5869)

Commonwealth Development Corporation

One Bessborough Gardens, London SW1V 2JQ
020 7828 4488 Fax: 020 7828 6505
E-mail: depcr@cdc.co.uk
Website: www.cdc.co.uk

The Corporation was established in 1948 to assist overseas countries in the development of their economies. A new public/private partnership for CDC was announced in 1997 for which legislation was passed in 1999. CDC may operate with ministerial approval in any developing country whether or not a member of the Commonwealth. At the end of 1998 CDC had investments of £1.5bn in 55 countries. CDC provides risk capital in the form of equity and loan investments and in some cases management, to encourage the development of sustainable businesses in the private sector.

Chairman: The Earl Cairns, CBE
Deputy Chairman: Jayne Almond
Members: Carolyn Hayman, Pen Kent,
Prof Jonathan Kydd, Roger Murray,
Prof D W Pearce, Russell Seal
Chief Executive: Dr Alan Gillespie

Commonwealth War Graves Commission

2 Marlow Road, Maidenhead,
Berkshire SL6 7DX
01628 634221 *Fax:* 01628 771208
Telex: 847526 COMGRA G
E-mail:
general.enq@cwgc.org (general enquiries)
casualty.enq@cwgc.org
(casualty and cemetery enquiries)
Website: www.cwgc.org

The Commonwealth War Graves Commission was established by Royal Charter in 1917. It is responsible for the commemoration of some 1.75 million members of the forces of the Commonwealth who fell in the two world wars. Over one million graves are maintained in 23,000 burial grounds throughout the world. More than three-quarters of a million men and women who have no known grave or who were cremated are commemorated by name on memorials built and maintained by the Commission. Its funds are derived from the six governments participating in its work – United Kingdom, Canada, Australia, India, New Zealand and South Africa.

President: HRH The Duke of Kent, KG, GCMG, GCVO, ADC
Chairman: The Secretary of State for Defence in the United Kingdom
Vice-Chairman:
   Admiral Sir John Kerr, GCB, DL
Commissioners: The High Commissioners in London for Canada, New Zealand, South Africa, Australia and India; Professor Robert J O'Neill, AO; Mrs Llin Golding, MP; John Wilkinson, MP; Sir John Gray, KBE, CMG; Paul D Orchard-Lisle, CBE, TD, DL; Air Chief Marshal Sir Michael Stear, KCB, CBE; General Sir John Wilsey, GCB, CBE, DL, Dame Sue Tinson, DBE
Director-General: David Kennedy, CMG
Deputy Director-General: Roger J Dalley
Legal Adviser and Solicitor: Graham C Reddie
Director of Personnel: David R Parker
Director of Works: Alan Coombe
Director of Finance: Ronald D Wilson, ACMA
Director of Horticulture:
   Derek C Parker, Dip Hort (Kew), M.I.Hort.
Director of Information and Secretariat:
   Liam J Hanna
Personal Secretary to the Director-General:
   Mrs Rubena M Truran

Communications for Business

(The Business Advisory Committee on Telecommunications)
50 Ludgate Hill, London EC4M 7JJ
020 7634 5301 Fax: 020 7634 8924
Text: 020 7634 8769
E-mail: cfb@acts.org.uk
Website: www.acts.org.uk

An independent body set up under the Telecommunications Act 1984 to advise the Director-General of OFTEL on the particular problems and needs of smaller businesses. The committee takes up policy issues but does not handle individual complaints, which should be referred to OFTEL on 0845 714 5000.

Chairman: (Vacant)
Secretaries: Terry Walker, David Edwards

Competition Commission
(formerly Monopolies and Mergers Commission)

New Court, 48 Carey Street, London WC2A 2JT
020 7271 0100 Fax: 020 7271 0367
Public Enquiries: 020 7271 0243
Press Office: 020 7271 0242
E-mail: info@competition-commission.org.uk
Website:
www.competition-commission.org.uk

The Commission is an independent statutory body which investigates monopolies, mergers and other matters referred to it under provisions of the Fair Trading Act 1973, the Competition Act 1980, the Telecommunications Act 1984, the Airports Act 1986, the Gas Act 1986, the Water Industry Act 1991, the Electricity Act 1989, the Broadcasting Act 1990, the Railways Act 1993, the Gas (Northern Ireland) Order 1996, the Electricity (Northern Ireland) Order 1992, the Airports (Northern Ireland) Order 1994, the EC Competition Law (Articles 88 and 89) Enforcement Regulations 1996 and the Competition Act 1998. Under the provisions of the Competition Act 1998 (which are expected to be brought into force during 2000), independent tribunals of the Competition Commission will hear appeals against certain decisions of the Director-General of Fair Trading.

Chairman: Dr Derek J Morris
President of the Appeal Tribunals:
   Christopher Bellamy, QC
Deputy Chairmen: G Corbett, CBE,
   Mrs D P B Kingsmill
Members: Hugh Aldous, Prof Jack Beatson, QC, Robert Bertram, Mrs Sarah Brown, Prof Martin Cave, Anthony Clothier, Roy Croft, CB, Christopher Darke, Prof Paul Geroski, David Hammond, Miss Judith Hanratty, Charles Henderson, CB, David Jenkins, MBE, Roger Lyons, Peter Mackay, CB, Mrs Kate Mortimer, Roger Munson, Prof David Newbery, FBA, Dr Gill Owen, Richard Prosser, Arthur Pryor, CB, Richard Rawlinson, Prof Judith Rees, Timothy Richmond, MBE, Jonathan Rickford, Dame Helena Shovelton, DBE,

Graham Stacy, CBE, David Stark,
Prof Anthony Steele
Secretary: Miss P Boys
Team Managers: J A Banfield, G M Field,
D Fisher, A Mantle, Miss P M Smith,
A Williams
Chief Legal Adviser: Ms J Richardson
Legal Advisers: P Coopman, C Dhanowa,
Chief Accounting Adviser: A T Head
Chief Economist: G P Sumner
Chief Industrial Adviser: Dr C Rix
Personnel Manager: J A Dyble

Confederation of British Industry

Centre Point, 103 New Oxford Street
London WC1A 1DU
020 7395 8089 Fax: 020 7497 2596
E-mail: paul.morris@cbi.org.uk
      emmaline.owens@cbi.org.uk
Website: www.cbi.org.uk

The Confederation of British Industry, CBI, is an independent non party-political body financed entirely by industry and commerce. It exists primarily to ensure that Governments of all political complexions understand the intentions, needs and problems of British business. It is the acknowledged spokesman for business and is consulted as such by Governments.

President: Sir Clive Thompson
Deputy President: Sir Iain Vallance
Director-General: Digby Jones
Deputy Director-General: Peter Agar
Director of Communications: Audrey Nelson
Head of Paliamentary Affairs: Paul Morris

Construction Industry Training Board

Bircham Newton, Kings Lynn,
Norfolk PE31 6RH
01485 577577
Website: www.citb.org.uk

The CITB's mission is to promote and facilitate the training of sufficient people in the skills needed for a world-class construction industry. It is an employer led organisation but also with representatives from government, education and the trade unions. The DfEE has appointed it as a National Training Organisation and as an Industry Training Board it raises a statutory training levy from in-scope employers over a certain size. The main services that it provides are: the latest research into construction training

issues; work towards a fully qualified workforce; training advice and support (including grants) for employers; the recruitment of motivated new entrants into the industry; and four national construction training centres.

@half:
Chairman: Hugh W Try, CBE, PPCIOB,
HonFIStructE, FRSA
Deputy Chairman:
Peter Rainbird, CBE, FRICS, FCIOB
Chief Executive: Peter W M Lobban
Employer Members of the Board:
Howard Baggaley, David J Barrass,
Stewart Bonnette, Maurice Denyer, MBE,
Michael J Fitchett, Dermot Gleeson,
Malcolm Harris, Ian M McAlpine, OBE, MA,
Dermot F McGinley, John E D Milne,
Geoffrey Snow, Brian G Tierney, MBE, FASI,
Stewart A Tilley, LLB, FRICS, FCIArb, FInst
CES, Stephen Watson, FIOR
Employee Members of the Board:
Robert Blackman, George B Brumwell,
George P Henderson, OBE
Client Member of the Board:
David M Adamson, MA DipHM, FICE, CEng
Education Members of the Board:
Prof Brian E Lee, BSc, PhD, CEng, FICE, FH
KIE, Gordon Robbins, BA(Hons), MIMgt
Government Members of the Board:
Mitch J Brown, BSc, MSc, MCIOB, MIMgt,
James D Kirkwood, Robert Lowenstein

Consumers in Europe Group

20 Grosvenor Gardens,
London SW1W 0DH
020 7881 3021 Fax: 020 7730 8540
E-mail: ceg@ceg.co.uk
Website: www.ceg.co.uk

CEG is an independent voluntary umbrella organisation concerned with the effects of EU policies and proposals on UK consumers.

Chairman: Susan Knox
Secretary: Stephen Crampton

Convention of Scottish Local Authorities

Rosebery House, 9 Haymarket Terrace
Edinburgh EH12 5XZ
0131-474 9200 *Fax:* 0131-474 9292
E-mail: carol@cosla.gov.uk
Website: www.cosla.gov.uk

The Convention of Scottish Local Authorities (COSLA) is the association promoting and protecting the interests of local authorities in Scotland by providing a forum for discussion of matters of common concern. It ascertains the views of member councils and communicates these to central government, public bodies and general public.

President: Cllr Norman Murray
Vice-Presidents: Cllr Pat Watters,
Cllr Hugh Halcro-Johnston
Chief Executive: Oonagh Aitken

Corporation of London

Guildhall, London EC2P 2EJ
020 7606 3030 Fax: 020 7332 1119

Lord Mayor's Official Residence
Mansion House, London, EC4N 8BH

The Corporation of London consists of the Lord Mayor, 25 Aldermen and 130 Common Councilmen. The Lord Mayor is nominated by the Liverymen of the 100 Livery Companies, and elected by the Court of Aldermen for the term of one year, on the 29 September each year.

The Sheriffs are elected by the Livery at Midsummer, and take office at Michaelmas for one year.

The Rt Hon The Lord Mayor of the City of
London: Alderman Clive Martin
The Recorder: Judge Michael Hyam
Sheriffs: Robert Finch, Pauline Halliday

PRINCIPAL OFFICIALS
Town Clerk: Tom Simmons, BA
Chamberlain: Peter Derrick
City Secretary: (Vacant)
Common Serjeant: Judge Neil Denison, QC
Judges who sit regularly at the Central Criminal
Court: Brian Capstick, QC, Michael Coombe, Henry Pownall, QC, Richard Hawkins, QC, Geoffrey Grigson, Ann Goddard, QC, Gerald Gordon, Giles Forrester, Ian Davies, TD, Peter Beaumont, QC, Graham Boal, QC
Commissioner of the City Police: Perry Nove
Comptroller and City Solicitor:
Andrew James Colvin, LLM
Remembrancer: Adrian F. P. Barnes, CVO, MA
Secondary and Under Sheriff and High Bailiff of
Southwark: Group Captain John Hurn Constable, BA, FCIS, FInst, AM, FIMet
Coroner for the City of London:
Dr Douglas Robert Chambers, MA, MAPhil, BS, LLB, FInst. Biol., Barrister
High Steward of Southwark: (Vacant)

City Surveyor:
Edward Theodore Hartill, BSc, FRICS, FRSA
City Planning Officer: Peter Wynne Rees, BSc, BArch, BTP, RIBA, FRTPI, FRSA
Director of Technical Services:
William George Row, OBE, FRICS
Director of Public Relations: Tony Halmos

Corporation of London Records Office

PO Box 270, Guildhall,
London EC2P 2EJ
020 7332 1251 Fax: 020 7710 8682
E-mail: clro@corpoflondon.gov.uk
Website:
www.cityoflondon.gov.uk/archives/clro

The Records Office holds the official archives of the Corporation of the City of London. The accumulation of archives, on account of its antiquity, continuity and wide range, is perhaps the most complete and valuable series of municipal records in the country and contains much material that is of national, as well as of civic interest. A reading room is open to members of the public, Monday to Friday inclusive, 9.30 a.m. to 4.45 p.m.

Keeper of the City Records: The Town Clerk
City Archivist: J R Sewell, MA, FSA
Deputy City Archivist: Mrs J M Bankes, MA

Corporation of Trinity House

Trinity House, Tower Hill,
London EC3N 4DH
020 7481 6900 Fax: 020 7480 7662
Website: www.trinityhouse.co.uk
Telex: 987526 *Answer Back:* NAVAID G

Trinity House is the General Lighthouse Authority for England, Wales and the Channel Islands, a Maritime charitable organisation and a Deep Sea Pilotage Authority.

Master: HRH The Duke of Edinburgh, KG, KT
Deputy Master and Executive Chairman: Rear Admiral Patrick Barton Rowe, CBE, LVO
Members of the Board: Capt Duncan Glass, Sir Brian Piers Shaw, Capt Peter King, Cdr Miles Rivett-Carnac, Capt Colin Stewart, Capt John Burton-Hall, RD, Capt Ian Gibb, FNI, FRIN, FRSA, FRGS, Commodore Peter Melson, CBE, Richard Dobb (Secretary)
Media and Communication Officer:
Howard Cooper

Council for Science and Technology

Albany House, 94–98 Petty France,
London SW1H 9ST
020 7271 2052 Fax: 020 7271 2028
Website: www.cst.gov.uk

Chairman: The Rt Hon Stephen Byers, MP,
Secretary of State for Trade and Industry
Deputy Chairman: Sir Robert May, FRS,
(Chief Scientific Adviser)
Members:
Prof S Kumar Bhattacharyya, CBE, FREng,
Prof Sir Alec Broers, FRS, FREng,
Dr Chris Evans, OBE, DSc,
Prof Julia Higgins, CBE, FRS,
Prof Sir Aaron Klug, OM, FRS,
Dr Rob Margetts, CBE, FREng,
Sir Robin Nicholson, FRS, FREng,
Dame Bridget Ogilvie, ScD,
Prof Sir Keith O'Nions, FRS,
Mr David Potter, CBE,
Miss Emma Rothschild,
Prof Sir Stewart Sutherland, FBA,
Sir Richard Sykes, DSc, FRS,
Mr J Martin Taylor
Secretary: Steve Elton

Council for the Central Laboratory of the Research Councils

The Council for the Central Laboratory of the Research Councils (CCLRC) promotes and supports scientific research by providing large-scale facilities and associated expertise, at its laboratories in Cheshire, Hampshire and Oxfordshire. Some 12,000 researchers from the UK and abroad use its facilities in X-ray, neutron, muon and laser research, in space science and particle physics, and in supporting disciplines such as engineering, electronics and information technology.

Chairman and Chief Executive:
Dr A R C Westwood
Director Research and Development:
Dr T G Walker

RUTHERFORD APPLETON LABORATORY
Chilton, Didcot, Oxon OX11 0QX
01235 821900

DARESBURY LABORATORY
Daresbury, Warrington,
Cheshire WA4 4AD
01925 603000

Website: www.cclrc.ac.uk

Council for the Protection of Rural England

Warwick House,
25 Buckingham Palace Road
London SW1W 0PP
020 7976 6433 Fax: 020 7976 6373
E-mail: info@cpre.org.uk
Website: www.greenchannel.com/cpre

The Council for the Protection of Rural England is a registered charity (Reg. No. 233179) working for a living and beautiful countryside. CPRE is the only independent environmental group working for the whole countryside. It has a strong impact wherever decisions shaping the countryside are made – from town hall, Parliament and Whitehall to Brussels – using the expertise of its Westminster office and local branches.

CPRE's principal weapons are careful research, constructive ideas, reasoned argument and a knowledge of how to get things done. Its business is effective lobbying and real influence.

CPRE's growing membership currently stands at 46,000. The members are organised into county branches (and district committees in rural areas) covering the whole countryside.

CPRE is acknowledged as an authoritative source of guidance and advice on rural conservation issues by MPs, peers, the news media and other organisations.

President: Prunella Scales
Chairman: Sir David Ford
Director: Kate Parminter
Deputy Director: David Conder

Council of Mortgage Lenders

3 Savile Row, London W1X 1AF
020 7437 0075 Fax: 020 7434 3791
E-mail: info@cml.org.uk
Website: www.cml.org.uk

The Council of Mortgage Lenders is a central trade body representing mortgage lending institutions, providing research, technical and statistical services and data related to the housing finance industry.

The CML was established in 1989 in response to the deregulation of financial markets. It has 122 members, including building societies, banks, centralised mortgage lenders and other institutions which undertake mortgage lending. Since its formation the CML has worked on matters such as legislation affecting the mortgage market, prevention of mortgage fraud and the provision of statistics and business information

Chairman: George Wise
Deputy Chairmen: Gren Folwell,
Philip Williamson
Director-General: Michael Coogan
Deputy Director-General: Peter Williams

Council on Tribunals

7th Floor, 22 Kingsway, London WC2B 6LE
020 7936 7045 Fax: 020 7936 7044

The Council operates under the Tribunals and Inquiries Act 1992 and consists of sixteen members, including the Chairman and, by virtue of his office, the Parliamentary Commissioner for Administration. One of its members is appointed to represent the interests of persons in Wales.

Its main function is to advise on and keep under review the constitution and working of administrative tribunals, as well as to consider and report on administrative procedures involving statutory inquiries. The 1992 Act lists in a schedule the seventy or so tribunal systems which fall within its supervisory jurisidiction, and also those tribunals in Scotland which are separately supervised by its Scottish Committee.

The Council is consulted by and advises government departments on a wide range of subjects relating to adjudicative procedures. It has to be consulted on all procedural rules for tribunals under its supervision, and on procedural rules made by the Lord Chancellor in connection with statutory inquiries, both when first-made and when amended. It has no powers to investigate or adjudicate on complaints from members of the public about the conduct or decisions of tribunals in particular cases.

The Council is required to make an Annual Report to the Lord Chancellor and the Lord Advocate which is normally published and printed in December as a House of Commons Paper. It may also make Special reports on matters which it considers to be particularly important.

Chairman:
Rt Hon the Lord Newton of Braintree, OBE
Members: R John Elliot, DKS
(Chairman of the Scottish Committee)
Mrs C Berkeley, JP, S M D Brown, JP,
S R Davie, CB, J H Eames, Mrs A Galbraith,
Mrs S R Howdle, Ian J Irvine, CA,
Sam Jones, CBE, DL, Prof T M Partington,
I D Penman, CB, D G Readings, E P Roberts,
P A A Waring, *Michael S Buckley
Secretary: Mrs P Fairbairn

COUNCIL ON TRIBUNALS (SCOTTISH COMMITTEE)
44 Palmerston Place, Edinburgh EH12 5BJ
0131-220 1236 *Fax:* 0131-225 4271
Chairman: R John Elliot, DKS
Members: Mrs P Y Berry JP, Mrs B Bruce,
Ian J Irvine, CA, Mrs A Middleton,
I D Penman, CB, Mrs H B Sheerin, OBE,
*Michael S Buckley
Secretary: Mrs E M MacRae

*ex officio (as Parliamentary Commissioner for Administration)

Countryside Agency

Head Office: John Dower House,
Crescent Place, Cheltenham,
Gloucestershire GL50 3RA
01242 521381 *Fax:* 01242 584270
Press and Parliamentary Unit: Dacre House,
19 Dacre Street, London SW1H 0DH
020 7340 2906/2908 *Fax:* 020 7340 2910
Website: www.countryside.gov.uk

The Countryside Agency is responsible for advising government and taking action on issues relating to the social, economic and environmental well-being of the English countryside.

Chairman: Ewen Cameron
Deputy Chairman: Pam Warhurst
Board Members: Kate Ashbrook,
Janet Bradbury, Bishop Alan Chesters,
Martin Doughty, Dr Victoria Edwards,
Professor Philip Lowe, Catherine Mack,
Miles Middleton, Frances Rowe,
David Woodhall
Chief Executive: Richard Wakeford
Directors: Margaret Clark, OBE,
David Coleman, Jon Tomlinson

Countryside Council for Wales

Cyngor Cefn Gwlad Cymru
Plas Penrhos, Ffordd Penrhos
Bangor, Gwynedd LL57 2LQ
01248 385500 *Fax:* 01248 355782
Website: www.ccw.gov.uk

The Countryside Council for Wales is the statutory adviser to government on sustaining natural beauty, wildlife and the opportunity for outdoor enjoyment throughout Wales and its inshore waters. With English Nature and Scottish Natural Heritage, CCW delivers its statutory responsibilities for Great Britain as a whole, and internationally, through the Joint Nature Conservation Committee.

Chairman: E M W Griffith, CBE, DL
Chief Executive: Paul Loveluck, CBE
Senior Director: Dr M E Smith
Director of Conservation: Dr D Parker
Director of Countryside Policy: Dr J Taylor

NORTH WEST AREA
Bryn Menai, Holyhead Road,
Bangor LL57 2EF
01248 373100

NORTH EAST AREA
Victoria House, Grosvenor Street,
Mold CH7 1EJ
01352 754000

EAST AREA
3rd Floor, The Gwalia, Ithon Road,
Llandrindod Wells, Powys LD1 6AA
01597 824661

WEST AREA
Plas Gogerddan, Aberystwyth,
Ceredigion SY23 3EE
01970 828551

SOUTH AREA
Unit 4, Castleton Court, Fortran Road,
St Mellons, Cardiff CF3 0LT
01222 772400

Covent Garden Market Authority

Covent House, New Covent Garden Market,
London SW8 5NX
020 7720 2211 Fax: 020 7622 5307
E-mail: info@cgma.gov.uk
Website: www.cgma.gov.uk

The Covent Garden Market Authority is a statutory corporation, established by Act of Parliament in 1961 and is responsible to the Minister of Agriculture, Fisheries and Food.

The function and responsibility of the Authority is to operate an efficient wholesale market at Nine Elms. The members of the Authority are appointed by the Minister of Agriculture.

Chairman: L A Mills, CBE
Members of the Authority: Mrs P H Challens,
    A J Cole, R Gidoomal, CBE,
    Mrs C J Nicholson, G K Noon, MBE,
    D Williams
General Manager: Dr P M Liggins
Secretary: C R Farey
Information Officer: Mrs H Evans

Crafts Council

44a Pentonville Road, Islington,
London N1 9BY
020 7278 7700 Fax: 020 7837 6891

The Crafts Council is the national body for promoting the crafts. It is an independent organisation funded by the Arts Council of England. The Council was formed as the Crafts Advisory Committee in 1971, and in 1982 it received a Royal Charter as the Crafts Council. Members serve at the invitation of the Secretary of State for Culture, Media and Sport.

Chairman: Sir Nicholas Goodison
Director: Janet Barnes

Criminal Cases Review Commission

Alpha Tower, Suffolk Street Queensway,
Birmingham B1 1TT
0121-633 1800 *Fax:* 0121-633 1804
E-mail: info@ccrc.gov.uk
Website: www.ccrc.gov.uk

The Criminal Cases Review Commission is an independent public body which was established on 1 January 1997 to investigate suspected miscarriages of justice in England, Wales and Northern Ireland.

The Commission considers cases which present a new argument or evidence and have already been turned down by the judicial appeal system; or can claim exceptional circumstances. Each case is examined afresh to decide whether it would have a real possibility of succeeding at a further hearing in an appeal court. If so, it is referred to the appropriate court of appeal.

Chairman: Sir Frederick Crawford, DL
Chief Executive: Glenys Stacey
Members: Barry Capon, Laurence Elks,
    Tony Foster, Jill Gort, Fiona King, John Knox,
    David Kyle, John Leckey,
    Prof Leonard Leigh, Dr James MacKeith,
    Karamjit Singh, Baden Skitt, Edward Weiss

Criminal Injuries Compensation Board/ Authority

Tay House, 300 Bath Street,
Glasgow G2 4LN
0141-331 2726 *Fax:* 0141-331 2287

and Morley House, 26–30 Holborn Viaduct
London EC1A 2JQ
020 7842 6800 Fax: 020 7436 0804

All applications for compensation for personal injury arising from crimes of violence in England, Scotland and Wales are dealt with at the above locations. (Separate arrangements apply in Northern Ireland.) Applications received up to 31 March 1996 are assessed on the basis of common law damages under the 1990 Compensation Scheme by the Criminal Injuries Compensation Board (CICB), which also hears appeals. Applications received on or after 1 April 1996 are assessed under a Tariff-based Scheme, made under the Criminal Injuries Compensation Act 1995, by the Criminal Injuries Compensation Authority (CICA). There is a separate avenue of appeal to the Criminal Injuries Compensation Appeals Panel (CICAP).

The Board was founded in 1964 by the Home Secretary and the Secretary of State for Scotland under the prerogative powers of the Crown. The Authority and the Panel are established by the Tariff-based scheme made on the 12 December 1995 under the Criminal Injuries Compensation Act 1995.

Chairman of the CICB:
The Rt Hon Lord Carlisle of Bucklow, QC
Chief Executive of CICA: Howard Webber
Head of Legal Services: Mrs Anne Johnstone
Operations Manager: E M McKeown
Chairman of the CICAP: Michael Lewer, QC
Secretary to the Panel: Miss V Jenson

Crown Agents for Oversea Governments and Administrations Limited

St Nicholas House, St Nicholas Road,
Sutton, Surrey SM1 1EL
020 8643 3311 Fax: 020 8643 8232
E-mail: crownagents@attmail.com

The Crown Agents for Oversea Governments and Administrations Limited is a private limited company which provides on commercial terms services which assist in the process of develop-ment. It is owned by The Crown Agents Foundation, which dervies its income from dividends paid by Crown Agents and applies that income in pursuit of its developmental objectives. The British government is a special member of the Foundation.

The company delivers specialist and multidisciplinary services in institutional development, procurement, finance and international trade. Projects are often in joint venture or partnership with other companies or organisations, frequently in the private sector and, increasingly, with local firms in client countries.

Crown Agents work for 130 countries, as well as for multilateral and bilateral donors. It is involved in projects with an estimated annual value of $6 billion. It is independent of any commercial interest in Britian or elsewhere.

Executive Chairman and Managing Director:
P F Berry, CMG
Non-Executives: J D Andrewes, F I Sumner,
R S W H Wiggs, Mrs J E Borden, OBE
Chief Operating Officer: K G White
Director Procurement: A M Slater
Director Corporate Marketing and
Development: D F Cook
Company Secretary: Mrs H A Kent
Director, Institutional Development Group:
D Phillips
Managing Director, Crown Agents Financial
Services Ltd: A H Oxford
Finance Director: J P Pigott

Crown Prosecution Service

Headquarters, 50 Ludgate Hill,
London EC4M 7EX
020 7796 8000 Fax: 020 7796 8650
E-mail: enquiries@cps.gov.uk
Website: www.cps.gov.uk

The Crown Prosecution Service is responsible for the independent review and conduct of criminal proceedings instituted by police forces in England and Wales (with the exception of cases conducted by the Serious Fraud Office and certain minor offences).

The Director of Public Prosecutions is the Head of the Service and discharges his statutory functions under the superintendence of the Attorney General.

The Service comprises a Headquarters and 42 Areas – one Area corresponding to each police force in England and Wales outside London, and one for London. Each of the Areas is headed by a Chief Crown Prosecutor, supported by an Area Business Manager.

Director of Public Prosecutions:
David Calvert-Smith, QC
Chief Executive: Mark Addison
Chief Inspector: Stephen Wooler
Director, Business Information Systems:
Lonny Carey
Director, Casework: Chris Newell
Director, Finance: John Graham
Director, Human Resources: Indi Seehra
Director, Policy: Garry Patten
Head of Communications: Lyn Salisbury
Head of Management Audit Services:
Rosemary Read

Data Protection Registrar, Office of the

Wycliffe House, Water Lane,
Wilmslow, Cheshire SK9 5AF
Switchboard: 01625 545700
Enquiries: 01625 545745 *Fax:* 01625 524510
E-mail: data@wycliffe.demon.co.uk
Website: www.dataprotection.gov.uk

The Office of the Data Protection Registrar was created by the Data Protection Act 1984.

The Registrar has a number of specific duties under the Act, and she is given discretion in the manner in which she fulfils them. Much of her work, and that of her staff, involves informal advice and consultation with Data Users, Computer Bureaux and Data Subjects, and the various bodies which represent them.

It is the Registrar's duty to compile and maintain the Register of Data Users and Computer Bureaux and provide facilities for members of the public to examine the Register; promote observance of the Data Protection Principles; consider complaints made by Data Subjects; disseminate information to the public about the Act and her functions under the Act; encourage where appropriate the production of codes of practice, by trade associations and other bodies, to guide Data Users in complying with the Data Protection Principles; co-operate with other parties to the Council of Europe Convention and act as United Kingdom authority for the purposes of Article 13 of the Convention; report annually to Parliament on the performance of her functions under the Act.

Registrar: Mrs E I France
Deputy Registrar: F G B Aldhouse
Director of Operations: Dr J N Woulds
Asst Registrars: J Bamford, P Jones, D Smith

As a result of the new Data Protection Law the Registrar's title will change to the Data Protection Commissioner on 1st March 2000

Deer Commission for Scotland

Knowsley, 82 Fairfield Road,
Inverness IV3 5LH
01463 231751 *Fax:* 01463 712931
E-mail: deercom@aol.com

The Deer Commission for Scotland has the general functions of furthering the conservation and control of all wild deer in Scotland and of keeping under review all matters relating to all deer. It has the statutory duty, with powers, to prevent damage to agriculture and forestry by deer. A field staff of skilled stalkers, with transport and equipment, is available for direct action, where necessary, anywhere in Scotland. The Commission also has balancing duties to take account of deer populations and their impact on the natural heritage, the needs of agriculture and forestry and the interests of owners and occupiers of land and to carry out research into matters of scientific importance relating to deer.

Chairman: Andrew Raven
Director: Nick Reiter
Technical Director:
Richard W Youngson, BSc (Forestry)

Design Council

34 Bow Street, London WC2E 7DL
020 7420 5200 Fax: 020 7420 5300
Website: www.design-council.org.uk

The Design Council's purpose is to inspire the best use of design by the UK, in the world context, to improve prosperity and well-being. To do this we work at local, national and international levels; gathering knowledge on how design works to inform and enable people in business, education and government.

Locally, we are providing support for business advisory services, particularly the Design Counsellors in Business Links. 'Design in Business Week' will continue our annual programme of national events and conferences dedicated to showing design's value to business. Our annual 'Design in Education Week' held in March also involves thousands of people in events throughout the UK.

Nationally, we are working in partnership with research, business and education organisations to generate new knowledge about the effective use of design, and to develop practical tools to allow this information to be used. We are also working with the media, politicians and the civil service to promote the benefits of effective design.

Internationally, we are working to position the UK as a world leader in innovation and design through initiatives such as Millennium Products which aims to identify, encourage and promote forward-thinking and innovative products and services created in the UK for the 21st Century.

Chief Executive: Andrew Summers
Chairman: John Sorrell, CBE

Duchy of Cornwall

10 Buckingham Gate, London SW1E 6LA
020 7834 7346 Fax: 020 7931 9541

The Duchy of Cornwall, instituted by Edward III in 1337, provides the revenue for the heir to the Throne in his capacity as Duke of Cornwall. The Duchy is a private estate regulated by Acts of Parliament and comprises agricultural, commercial and residential property, mostly located in south-west of England.

Lord Warden of the Stannaries:
  The Earl Peel, DL
Receiver General: The Earl Cairns, CBE
Attorney General: Nicholas E Underhill, QC
Secretary and Keeper of the Records:
  W R A Ross
Deputy Secretary: K J S Knott, LVO
Solicitor: James Furber

Duchy of Lancaster

Lancaster Place, Strand, London WC2E 7ED
020 7836 8277

The estates and jurisdiction known as the Duchy and County Palatine of Lancaster have been attached to the Crown since 1399, when John of Gaunt's son came to the throne as Henry IV. As the Lancaster inheritance it goes back to 1265. Edward III raised Lancashire into a County Palatine in 1351.

Chancellor:
  The Rt Hon Dr Marjorie Mowlam, MP
Receiver-General: Sir Michael Peat, KCVO
Attorney-General: Richard McCombe, QC
Vice-Chancellor of the County Palatine:
  The Hon Mr Justice Blackburne
Clerk of the Council:
  Michael Ridley, CVO, MA, FRICS
Secretary for Appointments:
  Col Nicolas Davies, DL

Chancellor of the Duchy of Lancaster, Office of

Cabinet Office, 70 Whitehall
London SW1A 2AS
020 7270 0400 Fax: 020 7270 0196
E-mail:
mmowlam@cabinet-office.x.gsi.gov.uk
The Rt Hon Dr Marjorie Mowlam, MP
Prin Priv Sec: Dr John Fuller
Priv Sec: Ms Brigid Feeny
Asst Priv Sec (Diary): Ms Tracey Temple
Parly Priv Sec: Margaret Moran, MP
Special Advisers: Tim Walker, Ms Anna Healy

Chancellor of the Duchy of Lancaster:
(see also Cabinet Office)

Ecclesiastical Committee

House of Lords, London SW1A 0PW
020 7219 3152 Fax: 020 7219 5933
(Constituted under the Church of England Assembly (Powers) Act, 1919)
Lords Members: Lord Beaumont of Whitley, Viscount Brentford, The Rt Hon the Lord Brightman, The Rt Hon the Lord Glenamara, CH, Lord Hardy of Wath, Lord Pilkington of Oxenford, Lord Robertson of Oakridge, Lord Strabolgi, The Rt Hon the Lord Templeman, MBE, Lord Teviot, Lord Wallace of Saltaire, Lord Westbury, CBE, MC, Baroness Wilcox, Lord Williams of Elvel, CBE
Commons Members: Nigel Beard, MP, Martin Bell, OBE, MP, Stuart Bell, MP, Peter Bottomley, MP, Ben Bradshaw, MP, Sir Sydney Chapman, RIBA, FRTPI, MP, Sir Patrick Cormack, MP, David Drew, MP, Gwyneth Dunwoody, MP, The Rt Hon Frank Field, MP, The Rt Hon Derek Foster, MP, The Rt Hon John Gummer, MP, Simon Hughes, MP, Gordon Marsden, MP, Peter Pike, MP
Secretary: E C Ollard
  House of Lords, SW1A 0PW
Legal Adviser: Sir James Nursaw, KCB, House of Lords, SW1A 0PW

Economic and Social Research Council

Polaris House, North Star Avenue,
Swindon SN2 1UJ
01793 413000 *Fax:* 01793 413001
E-mail: exrel@esrc.ac.uk
Website: www.esrc.ac.uk

The Economic and Social Research Council is the UK's leading research agency for the social sciences. It is an independent organisation, established by Royal Charter in 1965, and funded mainly by the government.

The ESRC's mission is:
to promote and support, by any means, high quality basic, strategic and applied research and related post-graduate training in the social sciences;

to advance knowledge and provide trained social scientists which meet the needs of users and beneficiaries, thereby contributing to the economic competitiveness of the UK, the effectiveness of public services and policy, and the quality of life;

to provide advice on, and disseminate knowledge and promote public understanding of, the social sciences.

Chairman: Dr Bruce Smith, CBE
Chief Executive: Dr Gordon Marshall
Director of Research: Chris Caswill
Director of Resources: Glyn Davies
Director of External Relations: Tim Whitaker

Electoral Reform Society

6 Chancel Street, Blackfriars,
London SE1 0UU
020 7928 1622 Fax: 020 7401 7789
E-mail: ers@reform.demon.co.uk
Website: www.electoral-reform.org.uk

The Society promotes the modernisation of our democracy through improvements in voting systems for all levels of government. Together with an associated charity, the McDougall Trust, it provides information services on electoral issues. Electoral Reform Ballot Services (ERBS: 020 8365 8909) conducts and advises on ballots and market research.

Electoral Reform International Services (ERIS: 020 7620 3794) provides electoral assistance in Africa, Asia and eastern Europe.

President: Prof The Earl Russell, FBA
Chair: Keith Best
Vice-Chair: Dr Peter Jackson
Treasurer: Dr Crispin Allard

Chief Executive and Company Secretary:
  Dr Ken Ritchie
Managing Director, ERBS: Owen Thomas
Programme Director, ERIS: Simon Osborn

Electricity Arbitration Association

5 Meadow Road, Great Gransden,
Sandy, Bedfordshire SG19 3BD
Tel/Fax: 01767 677043

The EAA gives back-up in the speedy and effective resolution of disputes relating to the UK electricity industry.

President: Sir Derek Oulton, GCB, QC, PhD
Secretary: Donald H J Lester, FCIS, ACIArb

Electricity Association Limited, Electricity Association Services Limited

30 Millbank, London, SW1P 4RD
020 7963 5700 Fax: 020 7963 5959
Website: www.electricity.org.uk

The Electricity Association is the trade body which represents the UK electricity industry on a national and international level. Members comprise all the major electricity generation, transmission, distribution and supply companies in the UK.

As the industry's voice, the EA's main role is to promote the policies determined by its members through established contacts in government, parliament, the media, regulatory bodies, and other organisations with an interest in the industry.

Electricity Association Services Limited is the principal subsidiary through which Electricity Association Limited operates.

ELECTRICITY ASSOCIATION LIMITED (EAL)

President and Director:
  M A Hughes, MSc, CEng, MIEE
Chief Executive and Director:
  P E G Daubeney, MA(Oxon)
Company Secretary:
  B R Venables, BA, FCIS, MBIM

ELECTRICITY ASSOCIATION SERVICES LIMITED (EASL)

Chief Executive: P E G Daubeney, MA(Oxon)
Company Secretary:
  B R Venables, BA, FCIS, MBIM

Divisional Heads
Commercial Services:
B R Venables, BA, FCIS, MBIM
Policy and Communication:
Dr D F Porter, BSc, PhD
Engineering and Safety:
Dr J E J Cottrill, BSc, MSc, PhD, CEng, MIEE
Finance: J L M Grint, MA, ACA
Legal Services: J W Cotterell, BA

Electricity Consumers' Committees and the National Electricity Consumers' Council

FORMERLY THE ECC CHAIRMEN'S GROUP (ECCCG)
11 Belgrave Road, London SW1V 1RB
020 7828 7790 Fax: 020 7233 6449

The NECC is the independent national voice for electricity consumers. It is a non-statutory group set up by Chairmen in 1993 to provide a forum to raise national issues for electricity consumers. NECC is officially recognised by the Regulator, Government, the industry and the media.

The Electricity Consumers' Committees (ECCs) are statutory bodies set up under the Electricity Act 1989 to promote and protect the interests of all domestic and business consumers. There are 14 regional ECCs, one for each public electricity supply region. Each ECC reviews all matters affecting electricity consumers' interests for their region. Some areas covered by the ECC include: investigation of individual consumer complaints – monitoring all complaints to identify trends – advising the regional electricity suppliers on the setting of their Codes of Practice.

Committee Chairmen,
Yorkshire and NECC:
    Rodney Brooke, CBE, DL
Eastern: Malcolm Roberts
East Midlands: Ms Irene Bloor, OBE
London: Andrew Horsler *(Acting Chairman)*
Merseyside and North Wales:
    David Owen, CBE, QPM
Midlands: Ray O'Brien
North Eastern: Ms Elizabeth Derrington
North of Scotland: Hugh Duncan
North Western: Prof Lorraine Baric
South Eastern: Ms Pauline Ashley
Southern: Ken Prior
South of Scotland: Graeme Millar
South Wales: Ms Janet Candler
South Western: Peter Weston

Employment Tribunals

(ENGLAND AND WALES)
The President's Office
Albion Tower, 11 Albion Street,
Leeds LS1 5ES
0113-388 3040 *Fax:* 0113-244 2871

Established under the Industrial Training Act 1964 the Tribunals are independent judicial bodies established to try certain matters of dispute in the employment field.

President: His Hon. Judge John Prophet

Secretary's Office
7th Floor, 19–29 Woburn Place
London WC1H 0LU
020 7273 8653 Fax: 020 7273 8673
Secretary: M B Wilson

(SCOTLAND)
President and Secretary's Office
The Eagle Building, 3rd Floor,
215 Bothwell Street, Glasgow G2 7TS
0141-204 0730 *Fax:* 0141-204 0732
President: D Littlejohn, CBE
Secretary: D J Easton

FOR FULL DETAILS OF EMPLOYMENT TRIBUNALS SERVICE SEE EXECUTIVE AGENCIES

Engineering and Marine Training Authority

Vector House, 41 Clarendon Road, Watford,
Hertfordshire WD1 1HS
01923 238441 *Fax:* 01923 256086
Website: www.emta.org.uk

The Engineering and Marine Training Authority (EMTA) is the National Training Organisation (NTO) for engineering. As such it has three main tasks: to identify the skill needs of its sector; to develop and maintain standards for key occupations in its sector in conjunction with employers; to represent to Government the interests of its sector on training issues.

EMTA wholly owns an awarding body – EMTA Awards Ltd. – recognised by the Qualifications and Curriculum Authority (QCA) and by the Scottish Qualifications Authority (SQA) for the award of National Vocational Qualifications and Scottish Vocational Qualifications.

EMTA also operates an Engineering Careers Information Service (ECIS) for young people on behalf of the industry.

EMTA is the successor organisation to the Engineering Training Authority (EnTra) and the

Marine and Engineering Training Association (M&ETA) and came into being on 1 October 1996. It is governed by a Council, most of whose members are engineering employers elected to ensure a broad representation of the industry.

Chairman: Rt Hon the Lord Trefgarne
Deputy Chairmen: D'A T N Payne, R G Davies
Chief Executive: Dr M D Sanderson
Secretary: P W Whiteman
Council Members: J Allen, A A Brewster,
    R Cartwright, M P Chapman, R Etches,
    Mrs M Gildea, I Grant, P J F Horton,
    Cllr G Lane, A Lowth, S Pallas, T Pye,
    M W Regan, A Robson, A Shipton,
    N Stockbridge, P N P Watts, I R Young
For Information: Nicolas Heslop

Engineering and Physical Sciences Research Council

Polaris House, North Star Avenue,
Swindon SN2 1ET
01793 444000 *Fax:* 01793 444010
Website: www.epsrc.ac.uk

The Engineering and Physical Sciences Research Council (EPSRC) has a mission to promote and support high quality basic, strategic and applied research and postgraduate training in engineering and the physical sciences.
– to advance knowledge and technology, and provide trained engineers and scientists, to meet the needs of users and beneficiaries thereby contributing to the economic competitiveness of the United Kingdom and the quality of life of its citizens.
– to provide advice, disseminate knowledge and promote public understanding in the field of engineering and the physical sciences.
    EPSRC spends £391 million (1998–99) from the Science Budget overseen by the Office of Science and Technology.

Chairman: Professor Tony Ledwith
Chief Executive: Prof Richard Brook
Director, Science and Engineering:
    Dr David Clark
Director, Finance and Administration:
    Stuart Ward
Director, Planning and Communications:
    Dr David Leech

Engineering Construction Industry Training Board

Blue Court, Church Lane, Kings Langley,
Hertfordshire, WD4 8JP
01923 260000 *Fax:* 01923 270969
E-mail: ecitb@ecitb.org.uk
Website: www.ecitb.org.uk

The Engineering Construction Industry Training Board (ECITB) is a Statutory Body appointed by the Secretary of State for Education and Employment to give a lead to companies in the engineering construction industry on the need to invest in the training of people they employ, and to set standards, create a framework and stimulate appropriate action to support the industry's training efforts.

The Board comprises employer, trade union and education members, representatives of the major clients in the industry and representatives from the Scottish Education Department and the Department for Education and Employment. It works closely with a wide range of bodies in the education, training and employment fields.

The ECITB has many activities including the setting of training standards, producing recommendations, issuing certificates of training including N/SVQ certificates and developing new training methods and projects. It is itself a trainer on a collective basis on behalf of its industry of both apprentices and adults undergoing their initial training. It is also a significant provider of management and supervisory training programmes on behalf of its industry. It has an information database which is updated each year and which is used as a basis for research and the disseminating of employment information and training trends. The Board actively encourages its industry to train for its needs more effectively. It does this through a network of field and manpower development advisors who provide advisory and certification services to employers in the industry.

Chairman: J Rowland
Board Members: R Angus, M Ashbrook,
    I M Bell, S Bush, P Corby, M Hockey, J Lee,
    R McCaffer, P Miller, D Mowforth, A Probert,
    H Rees, B Rider, K Turnbull, D Walker,
    B Williams
Director and Chief Executive: D Edwards
Secretary: P Johnston

Engineering Council

10 Maltravers Street, London WC2R 3ER
020 7240 7891 Fax: 020 7240 7517
E-mail: publicaffairs@engc.org.uk
Website: www.engc.org.uk

The Engineering Council is the co-ordinating and regulating body for the engineering profession.

The Senate of the Engineering Council is the central representative body. Its 54 members are made up of 24 elected by the engineering Institutions, 24 directly elected by the registered engineers and six nominated by the Privy Council.

The Senate operates through two executive boards, each composed of members of the Senate – The Board for the Engineering Profession, which promotes the profession, and The Board for Engineers' Regulation, which maintains the register of 260,000 Chartered Engineers, Incorporated Engineers and Engineering Technicians.

Chairman: Dr Robert Hawley, CBE, BSc, PhD, DSc, FRSE, FEng, FIMechE, CPhys, FInstP
Director-General:
Malcolm Shirley, BSc, CEng, FIMarE, MInstD
Director of Personnel, Finance, Administration and Senate Secretary: Chris Hall, FCA
Director, Engineers' Regulation:
Andrew Ramsay, MA, CEng, MIEE
Director, Engineering Profession:
Rob Jones, CEng, FRAeS
Director, Marketing and Public Affairs:
Brian O'Neill

Engineering Employers' Federation

Broadway House, Tothill Street
London SW1H 9NQ
020 7222 7777 Fax: 020 7222 2782
Website: www.eef.org.uk

President: Bruce Ralph
Director-General: Martin Temple
Director of Marketing and External Affairs:
Jeremy Miller
Director of Policy and Association Affairs:
David Giachardi
Media Relations Manager: Mark Swift
Political Officer: John Letizia
Chief Economist: (Vacant)

English Heritage

HISTORIC BUILDINGS AND MONUMENTS
COMMISSION FOR ENGLAND
23 Savile Row, London W1X 1AB
020 7973 3000 Fax: 020 7973 3001

English Heritage, Historic Buildings and Monuments Commission for England came into existence on April 1, 1984.

The Commission was set up by the Government under the National Heritage Act 1983 to create an independent body devoted to the conservation and presentation of England's inheritance of ancient monuments and historic buildings. To protect and promote England's built heritage, English Heritage identify important buildings and monuments and if necessary, recommend that they be protected by the government, either by listing or scheduling. They also provide expert advice and give grants to many of England's 450,000 listed buildings, 15,400 ancient monuments and 9,000 conservation areas, as well as manage and open to the public over 400 historic sites and buildings on behalf of the nation.

Chairman: Sir Jocelyn Stevens, CVO,
Hon DLitt (Lough), Hon DLitt (Buckingham),
Hon FCSD
Members: Ms Amanda Arrowsmith,
Mrs Bridget Cherry, FSA, Hon FRIBA,
Cllr Philip Davis, Andrew Fane, MA, FCA,
The Rt Hon the Lord Faringdon,
Prof Eric Fernie, BA, CBE, FSA, FRSE,
Lady Gass, DL,
HRH The Duke of Gloucester, KG, GCVO,
ARIBA, KStJ, FSA,
Mrs Candida Lycett Green,
Loyd Grossman, MA, Miss Kirsty McLeod,
Prof Richard Morris, FSA, MIFA,
Miss Sue Underwood

NATIONAL MONUMENTS RECORD CENTRE
Kemble Drive, Swindon SN2 2GZ
01793 414600 *Fax:* 01793 414606

English Nature

Northminster House,
Peterborough PE1 1UA
01733 455000 *Fax:* 01733 568834
and 01733 455375 (Private Office only)
E-mail: enquiries@english-nature.org.uk
Website: www.english-nature.org.uk

Established by Act of Parliament in 1991. Responsible for advising Government on nature conservation in England.

Promotes, directly and through others, the conservation of England's wildlife and natural features within the wider setting of the United Kingdom and its international responsibilities. Selects, establishes and manages National Nature Reserves and identifies and notifies Sites of Special Scientific Interest. Provides advice and information about nature conservation and supports and conducts research relevant to these functions. Through the Joint Nature Conservation Committee works with sister organisations in Scotland and Wales on UK and international nature conservation issues.

Chairman: The Baroness Young of Old Scone
Members: Miss M Appleby, D T Burke, CBE, Dr S Gubbay, Mrs A Kelaart, Miss J Kelly, Dr D R Langslow, Prof G L Lucas, OBE, Dr M Moser, Prof D Norman, S Tromans, Prof R C L Wilson, MBE, G N Woolley
Chief Executive: D Arnold-Forster, OBE
Directors: Dr A E Brown, Sue Collins, Dr Keith L Duff, Caroline Wood

English Partnerships

16–18 Old Queen Street, London SW1H 9HP
020 7976 7070 Fax: *020 7976 7740*
Website: www.englishpartnerships.co.uk

English Partnerships works with central and local Government, the Regional Development Agencies (RDAs), the private sector and other partners to bring about sustainable economic regeneration and development in the English regions.

It was created by combining the roles of the Commission for the New Towns (CNT) and the national functions of the Urban Regeneration Agency (URA) (formerly known as English Partnerships). The regions of the URA were transferred to the RDAs on 1 April 1999, with the exception of London, which will remain part of English Partnerships until the creation of the London RDA.

English Partnerships will retain the statutory bases of both the CNT and the URA. It therefore has all of the powers that these two organisations possessed in the past. By operating as a single organisation it will seek to use these powers in new, more creative ways.

Chairman: Sir Alan Cockshaw, BSc, HonDEng, HonDSc, FEng, FICE, FIHT
Non Executive Board Members:
   Sir Idris Pearce, CBE, TD, DL, FRICS,
   Michael Mallinson, CBE, FRICS,
   Andrew Fraser,
   Sir Brian Jenkins, GBE, MA, FCA,
   Bill Jordan, CBE, Derek Mapp,
   Lord Stevenson of Coddenham, CBE,
   Lord Thomas of Macclesfield, CBE
Executive Management Board:
Chief Executive: Paula Hay-Plumb
Corporate Strategy and Communications Director: Trevor Beattie
Commercial Director: Jim Gill
Finance and Administration Director (CNT): Dennis Hone
Finance and Administration Director (EP): John Walker
Development Director: David Shelton

Environment Agency

Head Office, Rio House
Waterside Drive, Aztec West
Almondsbury, Bristol BS32 4UD
01454 624400 *Fax:* 01454 624409
Websites: www.environment-agency.gov.uk
www.environment-agency.wales.gov.uk

The Environment Agency, which came into being on 1 April 1996, was created by the 1995 Environment Act. It brings together, the Waste Regulation Authorities, Her Majesty's Inspectorate of Pollution, the National Rivers Authority and some technical units from the Department of the Environment. It is responsible, in England and Wales, for pollution prevention and control, and for the management and use of water resources, including flood defences, fisheries and navigation. It has a head office in London and Bristol and 8 regional offices which are mainly concerned with operational activities.

The Board
Chairman: Sir John Harman
Deputy Chairman: (Vacant)
Members: Ed Gallagher *(Chief Executive),*
   Cllr Colin Beardwood, Alan Dalton,
   Andrew Dare, CBE, Nigel Haigh, OBE,
   Chris Hampson, CBE, Prof Richard Macrory,
   Gerald Manning, Prof Jacqueline McGlade,
   Dr Anne Powell, Prof Donald Ritchie,
   Tony Rodgers, Gareth Wardell
The Executive:
Chief Executive: E Gallagher
Director of Finance: N Reader
Director of Personnel: G Duncan
Director of Environmental Protection: P Leinster
Director of Water Management: G Mance
Director of Operations: A Robertson
Director of Corporate Affairs: M Wilson
Director of Legal Services: R Navarro
Chief Scientist: J Pentreath

Environmental Pollution, Royal Commission on

Steel House, 11 Tothill Street,
London SW1H 9RE
020 7273 6635

This standing commission was established in February 1970 to advise on matters, both national and international, concerning the pollution of the environment; on the adequacy of research in this field; and the future possibilities of danger to the environment.

Chairman: Sir Tom Blundell
Commissioners: Sir Geoffrey Allen, FRS,
    The Revd Prof Michael Banner,
    Prof G S Boulton, FRS, FRSE,
    Prof R Clift, OBE, J Flemming,
    Sir Martin Holdgate,
    Prof Brian Hoskins, CBE, FRS,
    Prof R Macrory, FRSA, Prof M G Marmot,
    Prof J G Morris, CBE, FRS,
    Dr Susan Owens, OBE, John Roberts,
    Dr P A Rowlatt
Secretary: D R Lewis

Equal Opportunities Commission

Overseas House, Quay Street
Manchester M3 3HN
Tel and Minicom: 0161-833 9244
Fax: 0161-835 1657
E-mail: info@eoc.org.uk
Website: www.eoc.org.uk

The Equal Opportunities Commission was created in 1975 to ensure effective enforcement of the Sex Discrimination Act 1975 and the Equal Pay Act 1970. The EOC's mission is to work for a society free from sex discrimination in which everyone has equal opportunities in all aspects of their lives. The EOC has offices in Glasgow and Cardiff.

Chair: Julie Mellor
Deputy Chairs: Elizabeth Hodder,
    Georgina James
Commissioners: Mary Berg, Kay Carberry,
    Richard Grayson, Richard Penn, Teresa Rees,
    Janet Rubin, Michael Schofield, Peter Smith,
    Joan Stringer, Jenny Watson, Tess Woodcraft
Chief Executive: Lynne Berry

Federation of Economic Development Authorities

36 Sheep Street, Shipston-on-Stour,
Warwickshire CV36 4AE
01608 664661 *Fax:* 01608 664662

Founded in 1943, FEDA is the oldest National Local Authority Organisation. FEDA considers all aspects of economic development and tourism affecting Local Authorities and acts to further relations between Local Authorities, Industry and Government. An annual seminar, half-yearly Regional Meetings, incorporating Study Tours, are organised and FEDA Journals are issued.

President: Lord Wade of Chorlton
Vice-Presidents: Lord Northfield of Telford,
    Lord Williams of Elvel, CBE,
    Lord Berkeley, OBE,
    Rt Hon the Lord Molyneaux of Killead, KBE,
    Rt Hon Tony Blair, MP, Malcolm Bruce, MP,
    Ian Cawsey, MP, Rt Hon Barry Jones, MP,
    Martyn Jones, MP, Ashok Kumar, MP,
    Rt Hon Peter Mandelson, MP,
    Austin Mitchell, MP, Elliot Morley, MP,
    Allan Rogers, MP, Frank Roy, MP,
    George Stevenson, MP, Paul Tyler, CBE, MP,
    Rt Hon Dafydd Wigley, MP,
    Stephen Hughes, MEP,
    James Nicholson, MEP, Mel Read, MEP
Chair: Cllr Harold Scrimshaw, OBE
Administrator: Maureen Proud

Federation of Small Businesses

Press and Parliamentary Office
2 Catherine Place, Westminster
London SW1E 6HF
020 7233 7900 Fax: 020 7233 7899
E-mail: london@fsb.org.uk
Website: www.fsb.org.uk

The Federation of Small Businesses (FSB) is a non-party political organisation financed entirely by subscriptions from the members who are mainly self employed and small businesses. Its aims are to ensure that Government, opposition parties and civil servants are aware of the problems and needs of Britain's small business sectors. It is the recognised spokesman for small businesses. It is consulted on a daily basis by Government.

Chairman: Ian Handford
Policy Committee Chairman: Brendan Burns
Parliamentary Adviser: Stephen Alambritis,
    BA(Govt), MA(Law), MSc(Econ)

Financial Services Authority

25 The North Colonnade, Canary Wharf,
London E14 5HS
020 7676 1000 Fax: 020 7676 1099
Website: www.fsa.gov.uk

The FSA, formerly the Securities and Investments Board, became the designated agency under the Financial Services Act 1986 in 1987 to regulate the activities of investment businesses in the UK. Its major aims are to achieve a high level of investor protection and to promote integrity in financial markets. On 1 June 1998, with the passage of the Bank of England Act 1998, the FSA assumed responsibility for banking supervision.

The FSA will eventually be a single regulator for all financial firms and markets, bringing together the functions previously handled by a number of regulatory bodies. This will happen when the Financial Services and Markets Bill takes effect. The Bill sets out statutory objectives for the FSA, including maintaining confidence in the UK financial system and promoting public understanding of it, protecting consumers and reducing financial crime.

Executive Chairman: Howard Davies
Managing Director, Head of Financial
Supervision: Michael Foot
Managing Director, Head of Authorisation,
Enforcement and Consumer Relations:
Phillip Thorpe
Other non-Executive Board Members:
Moira Black, Stewart Boyd, David Clementi, Deirdre Hutton, Gillian Nott, Keith Oates, Christopher Rodrigues, Shamit Saggar, Robert Smith, Stephen Thieke, Keith Whitson

Food from Britain

123 Buckingham Palace Road
London SW1W 9SA
020 7233 5111 Fax: 020 7233 9515
E-mail: uk@foodfrombritain.com

Food from Britain is a government and industry funded organisation with the role of increasing food and drink exports and assisting the development of smaller speciality food companies in the UK. Through a network of overseas offices, FFB helps exporters in identifying opportunities, negotiating with trade buyers and organising consumer promotions.

Chairman: Geoffrey R John, CBE
Chief Executive: Patrick Davis
Council: Stanley Bernard, Don Curry, CBE,
Ben Gill, CBE, Christine Gray, Prof Michael Haines, Liam McKibbon, Kirit Pathak, CBE, Jan Polley, Meurig Raymond, Prof Susan Shaw, Gordon Summerfield, David Thomas, Neil Thornton, Tom Vyner, CBE, Lionel Walford, James N Walker, CBE, Robert Watson

Football Licensing Authority

27 Harcourt House, 19 Cavendish Square,
London W1M 9AD
020 7491 7191 Fax: 020 7491 1882
E-mail: fla@flaweb.org.uk
Website: www.flaweb.org.uk/fla

The Football Licensing Authority was set up under the Football Spectators Act 1989. It is responsible for:
- operating a licensing scheme for grounds at which designated football matches are played;
- advising the Government on the introduction of all-seated accommodation at Premier League and First Division grounds and the national stadia;
- ensuring that any terracing which is retained at Football League Second and Third Division grounds meets the necessary safety standards; and
- keeping under review the discharge by local authorities of their functions under the Safety of Sports Grounds Act 1975.

Chairman: C R Sherling
Members: T J Gee, Dr J M Fisher, MB, BS, FRCGP, C Lewis, CPsychol, AFBPsS, M J Sheldon, OStJ, QFSM, DMS, GIFireE, Prof M Talbot, PhD, OBE, Prof S Thorburn, OBE, DSc, FEng, FIStructE, FICE
Chief Executive: J R K de Quidt

Forum of Private Business

Ruskin Chambers, Drury Lane
Knutsford, Cheshire WA16 6HA
01565 634467/8/9 *Fax:* 01565 650059
Brussels Office (UEAPME) 0032 22 3075 99
E-mail: fpbltd@fpb.co.uk
Website: www.fpb.co.uk

Permanent Brussels Representative:
Garry Parker
Chief Executive: Stan Mendham, OBE
Head of Policy: Nicholas Goulding
Parliamentary Officer: Alison Beer
Research Officer: James Redman
Press Officer: Dave Harrop

Further and Higher Education Funding Councils - Wales

Linden Court, The Orchards, Ty Glas Avenue,
Llanishen, Cardiff CF14 5DZ
029 2076 1861 Fax: 029 2076 3163
Website: www.wfc.ac.uk

The Further Education Funding Council for Wales and the Higher Education Funding Council for Wales are served by a common Executive. Each Council is an independent body with its own Chairman and members. Professor John Andrews is the Chief Executive of both Councils. The Welsh Funding Councils are statutory public bodies established under the Further and Higher Education Act 1992. The Further Education Funding Council is responsible for funding further education colleges, and certain other institutions and associations concerned with the provision of further education in Wales. The Higher Education Funding Council is concerned with the funding of colleges and institutes of higher education and universities, and also has power to fund higher education in further education colleges. The Councils assumed (funding) responsibility on 1 April 1993.

FURTHER EDUCATION FUNDING COUNCIL
FOR WALES (FEFCW)
Chairman: Kenneth Young, CBE
Chief Executive: Prof J Andrews
Members: S Dunster, OBE, H Evans,
    Mrs R Lawrence, Prof R Norris,
    Mrs J Pierce, MBE, I Price, Dr S Reynolds,
    G Roberts, Mrs A Warman

HIGHER EDUCATION FUNDING COUNCIL
FOR WALES (HEFCW)
Chairman: Sir Philip Jones, CB
Chief Executive: Prof J Andrews
Members: Prof B Clarkson, Dr E Edwards,
    Dr K Gray, CBE, A Morris,
    Dr B F Roberts, CBE, H Thomas,
    Prof R Williams

Further Education Funding Council

Cheylesmore House, Quinton Road,
Coventry CV1 2WT
024 7686 3000 Fax: 024 7686 3100
Website: www.fefc.ac.uk

The Further Education Funding Council (FEFC) was set up under the Further and Higher Education Act (1992). Its purpose is to secure further education provision in England which meets the needs and demands of individuals, employers and the requirements of government. It allocates funds mainly to the further education and sixth form colleges which make up the English further education sector, but also to universities and other institutions which provide further education courses. The Council assesses the quality of further education and reports publicly on each college every four years. As a non-departmental public body the Council is responsible to Parliament for the use of the public funds allocated to it. Members of the Council are appointed by the Secretary of State for Education. The Council has nine regional committees and nine regional offices.

Chairman: Lord Davies of Oldham
Chief Executive: Prof David Melville
Chief Inspector and Director of Audit:
    Jim Donaldson
Director of Education and Institutions:
    Kate Anderson
Director of Finance and Corporate Services:
    David Russell
Director of Funding and Strategy: Geoff Hall

Gaming Board for Great Britain

Berkshire House, 168–173 High Holborn,
London WC1V 7AA
020 7306 6200 Fax: 020 7306 6267
E-mail: enqs@gbgb.org.uk

The Gaming Board was established under the Gaming Act 1968 and is the regulatory body for casinos, bingo clubs, gaming machines and the larger society and all local authority lotteries in Great Britain. The Board's responsibilities may be summarised as:

1. to ensure that those involved in organising gaming and lotteries are fit and proper to do so and to keep gaming free from criminal infiltration;
2. to ensure gaming and lotteries are run fairly and in accordance with the law;
3. to advise the Secretary of State on developments in gaming and lotteries so that the law can respond to change.

In pursuit of these aims the Board:
(a) keeps the extent, character and location of gaming and lotteries in general and in licensed premises in particular under review;
(b) initiates proposals for changes in the law and regulations on gaming and lotteries and advises Ministers on proposals from interest groups;

(c) determines applications made for certificates of consent in respect of casino and bingo licences, for certificates to sell, supply and/or maintain gaming machines, for certificates of approval required by gaming employees, for the registration of societies and local authority lottery schemes and for the certification of external lottery managers.

(d) supervises the conduct of holders of certificates, licences and registrations and takes action against those no longer considered fit and proper;

(e) makes representations to licensing authorities concerning the grant, revocation or renewal of gaming licences;

(f) maintains close contact with the gaming industry's trade associations with a view to informing itself about developments in the industry and encouraging the issue of appropriate codes of conduct and other co-operation in pursuit of the Board's aims.

Chairman: P H Dean, CBE
Members: D Elliott, CBE, QPM,
R C Lockwood, D M C E, Steen, MA, FCA,
Mrs M Stevens
Secretary: T Kavanagh

Gas Consumers Council

6th Floor, Abford House, 15 Wilton Road,
London SW1V 1LT
020 7931 0977 Fax: *020 7630 9934*

The Council of 10 members includes six who represent the interests of gas consumers by regions and four appointed for their special knowledge and experience.

Chairman: Ms Jenny Kirkpatrick
Director: Phil Hamer

General Aviation Safety Council

Rochester Airport, Chatham, Kent ME5 9SD
Tel/Fax: 01634 816620

GASCO was established in 1965 with the aim of fostering the development of general aviation in the UK along safe lines by encouraging competence among pilots and operators. The GASCO consists of representatives of most leading UK general aviation organisations and of those with an interest in promoting the Council's aims such as the AAIB, CAA, MoD, Royal Meterological Society and Lloyd's Aviation. The Council also publishes a quarterly *Flight Safety Bulletin* which is distributed free of charge to UK regis-

tered owners of aircraft, flying instructors, and many flying and gliding clubs and groups.

Chief Executive: John Campbell
Publication: Flight Safety Bulletin
Members: AAME, AOA, AOPA, BAeA, BAUA, BBAC, BGA, BHAB, BHPA, BMAA, BMFA, BPA, CAA, FFA, GAMTA, GAPAN, GATCO, HAA, HC of GB, LFA, Lloyd's Aviation Ltd, MAF, Met Office, MoD, PFA, PPL I/R Network, RAeS, RIN, UKFSC

General Consumer Council for Northern Ireland

Elizabeth House, 116 Holywood Road,
Belfast BT4 1NY
028 9067 2488 Fax: *028 9065 7701*
E-mail: info@gccni.org.uk
Website: www.gccni.org.uk

As Northern Ireland's leading consumer body, GCCNI's aim is to promote and safeguard the interests of consumers and to campaign for the best possible standards of service and protection. Set up by statute in 1985, the Council is funded by the Department of Economic Development. The Council consists of a Chairman, deputy and 12 other appointed members.

Since 1985, its job has been to give consumers a voice – and to make sure that voice is heard by those who make decisions which affect consumers.

It has further specific responsibilities relating to: transport (both within and to and from Northern Ireland); gas; and coal.

Chairman: Mrs Joan Whiteside, OBE
Deputy Chairman: Mrs Felicity Huston
Director: Mrs Maeve Bell

General Council of the Bar

3 Bedford Row, London WC1R 4DB
020 7242 0082 Fax: *020 7831 9217*
Press Office: 020 7222 2525
E-mail: chiefexec@barcouncil.org.uk
Website: www.barcouncil.org.uk

There are 9,500 barristers in independent practice in England and Wales, representing a specialist core of approximately 12 per cent of all lawyers.

Membership of the Bar is open to all who have qualified as barristers, whether now in private practice or employed. The professional conduct of barristers is governed by the General Council of the Bar [otherwise referred to as the Bar Council] which is responsible for discipline and for dealing with complaints against members of the profession.

A new complaints system was established in 1997, headed by a Lay Complaints Commissioner. Under the system the Bar Council will be able to require barristers to reduce fees or pay compensation to lay clients in respect of inadequate professional service.

The Bar Council is also responsible for the development of the profession and looks after its interests, for example, in negotiating with the Government over publicly funded work.

The Council and its officers – the Chairman, Vice-Chairman and Treasurer provide a voice for the Bar on matters both of immediate concern to the profession and to the public in general.

The General Council is maintained by subscriptions which vary in amount according to the status of individual barristers and their years of practice.

Chairman: Daniel Brennan, QC
Chief Executive: Niall Morison

General Dental Council

37 Wimpole Street, London W1M 8DQ
020 7887 3800 Fax: 020 7224 3294
Website: www.gdc-uk.org

The GDC is the regulatory body of the dental profession.

It protects the public by means of its statutory responsibilities for dental education, registration, professional conduct and health.

It supports dentists and dental auxiliaries in the practice of dentistry and encourages their continuing professional development.

President: Prof Nairn Wilson
Chief Executive and Registrar:
   Mrs Ros Hepplewhite

General Medical Council

178 Great Portland Street, London W1N 6JE
020 7580 7642 Fax: 020 7915 3641
Website: www.gmc-uk.org

The General Medical Council licenses doctors to practise medicine in the UK. Its purpose is summed up in the phrase: *Protecting patients, guiding doctors.*

The GMC has four main functions:
– keeping up-to-date registers of qualified doctors;
– fostering good medical practice;
– promoting high standards of medical education;

– dealing firmly and fairly with doctors whose fitness to practise is in doubt.

There are approximately 190,000 registered doctors.

The GMC has 104 members. 54 are doctors elected by doctors, 25 are lay (non-medical) people who represent the public. The other 25 are doctors appointed by the universities with medical schools and by the medical royal colleges.

For further information about GMC please contact the External Relations Office on 020 7915 3720.

President: Sir Donald Irvine, CBE
Registrar and Chief Executive: Finlay Scott

General Optical Council

41 Harley Street, London W1N 2DJ
020 7580 3898 Fax: 020 7436 3525
E-mail: goc@optical.org
Website: www.optical.org

The Opticians Act, 1958, established the profession as a new statutory profession generally similar to the older healing professions. The Council's duties are to register opticians, enrol bodies corporate, maintain and publish registers and lists, approve training institutions and qualifications, and promote proper professional conduct.

Chairman: Mrs R Varley
Registrar: R D Wilshin, FIMgt, FRSA

General Register Office for Scotland

New Register House, Edinburgh EH1 3YT
Ladywell House, Edinburgh EH12 7TF
0131-334 0380 *Fax:* 0131-314 4344
E-mail: reception@gro-scotland.gov.uk
Website: www.open.gov.uk/gros/groshome.htm

The General Register Office for Scotland has central responsibility in Scotland for the registration of births, deaths and marriages; the administration of the law on marriage; the taking of censuses of population; the production and supply of a wide range of population and vital statistics; and the maintenance of the National Health Service Central Register.

Registrar General: J N Randall
Deputy Registrar General: B V Philp
Census and Population Statistics: D A Orr

General Synod of the Church of England

Church House, Great Smith Street,
London SW1P 3NZ
020 7898 1000 Fax: 020 7898 1369

The General Synod was constituted in 1970, under the Synodical Government Measure 1969, in succession to the former Church Assembly. There are in total some 560 members of the General Synod, divided into three Houses – Bishops, Clergy and Laity. The function of the General Synod is to consider and make provision for all matters concerning the Church of England, and to consider and express opinion on any other matters of religious or public interest. Under the Church of England Assembly (Powers) Act 1919 the General Synod has the power – delegated by Parliament – to frame Statute Law on any matter concerning the Church of England. The Synod also has the power (inherited from the Convocations of Canterbury and York) to make Canons and other ecclesiastical regulations provided that they are not contrary to the Royal Prerogative or the customs, laws or statutes of the Realm.

Secretary General: P J C Mawer
Legal Adviser: B J T Hanson, CBE, LLM
Clerk to General Synod: D M Williams
Financial Secretary: M G S Farrell

THE CONVOCATION OF CANTERBURY
Church House, Great Smith Street,
London SW1P 3NZ
020 7898 1000 Fax: 020 7898 1369
President: The Archbishop
Prolocutor of the Lower House:
    Canon H Wilcox
Registrar: B J T Hanson, CBE

THE CONVOCATION OF YORK
Church House, Great Smith Street,
London SW1P 3NZ
020 7898 1000 Fax: 020 7898 1369
President: The Archbishop
Prolocutor of the Lower House: Canon J Stanley
Joint Registrars: L P M Lennox,
    B J T Hanson, CBE

Government Actuary's Department

New King's Beam House, 22 Upper Ground,
London SE1 9RJ
020 7211 2600 Fax: 020 7211 2640
E-mail: enquiries@gad.gov.uk
Website: www.gad.gov.uk/

The Government Actuary's Department provides a consultancy service to departments, and to the public sector, both in the United Kingdom and overseas. It advises on a wide range of actuarial issues including social security, occupational and personal pensions, population projection and the financial supervision of insurance companies and friendly societies.

Government Actuary: C D Daykin, CB
Directing Actuaries: D G Ballantine,
    T W Hewitson, A G Young
Chief Actuaries: A I Johnston, Mrs B J Hall,
    E I Battersby, J C Rathbone, D Lewis,
    Miss C Cresswell, A J M Chamberlain,
    G T Russell

Government Art Collection

c/o Department for Culture, Media and Sport,
2-4 Cockspur Street, London SW1Y 5DH
020 7211 6200 Fax: 020 7211 6032
E-mail: enquiries@culture.gov.uk

Works of art from the Government Art Collection (GAC) are displayed in major government buildings in the UK and throughout the world. The objectives of the GAC are to help promote the image of Britain and reflect its culture, history and creativity in the visual arts. The GAC contains a core collection of about 11,500 British works of art dating from the 16th century to the present, acquired by purchase, gift and commission, and acts in an administrative or advisory capacity for many more. The Collection is a division of the Department for Culture, Media and Sport. Its purchasing policy is guided by an Advisory Committee comprising three independent members (including the Chairman) and four *ex officio* members (the Directors of the National, Tate and National Portrait Galleries and the Government Art Collection).

Chairman: John Tusa
Members: Neil MacGregor, Nicholas Serota,
    Charles Saumarez-Smith, Richard Dorment,
    Mary Rose Beaumont, Penny Johnson,
    (Director of the Government Art Collection)

Hansard Society for Parliamentary Government

St Philips Building North, Sheffield Street,
London WC2A 2EX
020 7955 7459 Fax: 020 7955 7492
E-mail: hansard-society@lse.ac.uk
Website: www.hansard-society.org.uk

The Hansard Society promotes effective parliamentary democracy. Supported by Madam Speaker, Party leaders, MPs and Peers, the Society's activities range from mock elections in schools to research, on-line debates, study days and publications. In 1999 the Society launched two important new programmes on Parliamentary Reform and Parliament and the Electronic Media which will be continuing throughout the year 2000.

President: The Rt Hon Betty Boothroyd, MP
Vice-Presidents: The Rt Hon Tony Blair, MP,
    The Rt Hon William Hague, MP,
    The Rt Hon Charles Kennedy, MP
Chairman: Dr David Butler, CBE
Vice-Chairmen: Austin Mitchell, MP,
    The Rt Hon Gillian Shephard, MP, The
    Lord Holme of Cheltenham, CBE,
    Lord Tomlinson
Hon Treasurer: Wilf Weeks
Director: Shelagh Diplock, OBE

Health and Safety Commission

Rose Court, 2 Southwark Bridge
London SE1 9HS
Enquiries: 020 7717 6000
Fax: 020 7717 6717
GTN: 3053

The Commission is responsible to the appropriate Minister for the administration of the Health and Safety at Work etc. Act 1974; it also reviews health and safety legislation and submits proposals for new or revised regulations.

The Health and Safety Commission appointed, with effect from 1 January 1975, the three Members of the Health and Safety Executive, a body corporate, which, together with its officers and servants, is responsible for implementing the provisions of the HSW Act 1974 and which reports to the Commission.

Chairman: Bill Callaghan
Members of the Commission: George Brumwell,
    Margaret Burns, A Chowdry, Joyce Edmond-
    Smith, Anne Gibson, S Hamid,

Michael McKiernan, Rex Symons,
    Owen Tudor
Commission Secretary: Rosemary Banner

HEALTH AND SAFETY EXECUTIVE (HSE)
Secretariat
Rose Court, 2 Southwark Bridge
London SE1 9HS
Enquiries: 020 7717 6000

HSE MANAGEMENT BOARD
Director-General: Ms J H Bacon, CB *(SCS)*
Deputy Director-General:
    D C T Eves, CB *(SCS)*
Director, Safety Policy: C Norris
Director, Resources and Planning: R Hillier
Director, Field Operations Division:
    Dr A Ellis *(SCS)*
Director, Directorate of Science and Technology:
    (Vacant)
Director, Health Directorate:
    Dr P J Graham *(SCS)*

HEALTH AND SAFETY EXECUTIVE (HSE)
Public Enquiries, Information Centre,
Broad Lane, Sheffield S3 7HQ
0541 545500 Fax: 0114-289 2333
E-mail: public.enquiries@hse.gov.uk
Website:
www.open.gov.uk/hse/feedback.htm

SOLICITOR'S OFFICE
Rose Court, 2 Southwark Bridge
London SE1 9HS
020 7717 6000
Solicitor to Commission and Executive:
    B J Ecclestone
Assistant Solicitor: R P Humm

SENIOR MANAGEMENT SUPPORT UNIT
Head of Unit: C D Byrne

SAFETY POLICY DIVISION
Rose Court, 2 Southwark Bridge
London SE1 9HS
020 7717 6000
Director: C Norris *(SCS)*

Division A:
Safety Policy for the Channel Tunnel;
Construction; Explosives, Marine Matters;
Railways and Transport of Dangerous Goods by
Road
Head of Division: J Grubb

Division B:
General and Technical Safety Policy
Head of Division: J Willis

Division C: Extractive Industries
Head of Division: A Sharp

Division D: Flammables and Gas Policy
Head of Division: A J Williams

Division E: Hazardous Installations
Head of Division: N Starling

RESOURCES AND PLANNING DIVISION
Rose Court, 2 Southwark Bridge
London SE1 9HS
020 7717 6000
Director: R Hillier *(SCS)*

Planning Efficiency and Finance Division
Head of Division: B Ledsome

Business Services Division
Head of Division: J S R Pugh

Personnel Division
Director of Personnel: D Ashton

Directorate of Information and Advisory
Services
Director of DIAS: P H Rimmer

Press Office
Rose Court, 2 Southwark Bridge
London SE1 9HS
Enquiries: 020 7717 6000
Chief Press Officer: (Vacant)

HEALTH DIRECTORATE
Rose Court, 2 Southwark Bridge
London SE1 9HS
Enquiries: 020 7717 6000
Director, Health Directorate: Dr P J Graham

HEALTH STRATEGY, MANAGEMENT AND
RESEARCH: AND MUSCULOSKELETAL AND
PSYCHOSOCIAL POLICY DIVISION
Head of Division: Mrs E Gyngell

Physical and Biological Agents Division
Head of Division: M Clare

Chemical Division
Head of Division: Dr J Cruikshank

Health Sciences Division
Head of Division: Dr P Oldershaw

CHEMICALS & HAZARDOUS INSTALLATIONS
DIVISION
St Annes House, Stanley Precinct, Bootle,
Merseyside L20 3QZ
Enquiries: 0151-951 4000
Head of Division: Dr P Davies

HM INSPECTORATE OF MINES
Daniel House, Trinity Road,
Bootle L20 7HA
Enquiries: 0151-951 4000
HM Chief Inspector of Mines: B Langdon, CBE
Deputy Chief Inspector: D Mitchell

NUCLEAR SAFETY DIRECTORATE
Rose Court, 2 Southwark Bridge
London SE1 9HS
Enquiries: 020 7717 6000
Director, Nuclear Safety Directorate, HM Chief
　Inspector of Nuclear Installations:
　L Williams *(SCS)*

Division 1 – British Energy
Head of Division: J Cowley
Division 2 – BNFL
Head of Division: J Furness
Division 3 – General Sites
Head of Division: Dr R Pape

HEALTH AND SAFETY LABORATORY
Broad Lane, Sheffield S3 7HQ
Enquiries: 0114 289 2000
Chief Executive, Health and Safety Laboratory:
　Dr D Buchanan
Director, Operations: Dr A Jones
Head of Finance: J A Verney
Head of Planning and Administration:
　Dr C Jackson
Science Group 1, Fire and Explosion:
　Dr K Moody
Science Group 2, Engineering Control:
　Dr C Nicholson
Science Group 3, Human Factors:
　Dr N West
Science Group 4, Biomedical Sciences:
　Dr H Wilson
Science Group 5, Environmental Measurement:
　Dr S Gentry
Science Group 6, Technical Services:
　Dr G Ince

ELECTRICAL EQUIPMENT CERTIFICATION
SERVICE (EECS)
Harpur Hill, Buxton,
Derbyshire SK17 9JN
Enquiries: 0114 289 2000
Director: I M Cleare

DIRECTORATE OF SCIENCE AND TECHNOLOGY
Rose Court, 2 Southwark Bridge
London SE1 9HS
020 7717 6000
Director: (Vacant)

OFFSHORE SAFETY DIVISION
Rose Court, 2 Southwark Bridge
London SE1 9HS
020 7717 6000
Head of Division: Dr A Sefton

FIELD OPERATIONS DIRECTORATE
Daniel House, Trinity Road
Bootle, Merseyside L20 7HE
Enquiries: 0151-951 4000
Director: Dr A E Ellis
HM Chief Inspector of Construction:
  S Caldwell
HM Chief Agricultural Inspector: D J Mattey
Regional Directors
  Midlands D J Mattey
  Yorkshire and North East C Willby
  London and South East S Caldwell
  Scotland Mrs L Williams
  North West J Taylor
  Wales and South West T Rose
  Home Counties K Myers

REGIONAL ORGANISATION
WALES AND WEST REGIONAL OFFICE
Government Buildings, Phase 1, Ty Glas,
Llanishen, Cardiff CF14 5SH
029 2026 3000 Fax: 029 2026 3120

HOME COUNTIES REGIONAL OFFICE
14 Cardiff Road, Luton LU1 1PP
01582 444200 *Fax:* 01582 444320

LONDON AND SOUTH EAST REGIONAL OFFICE
St Dunstans House, 201/211 Borough High
Street, Southwark, London SE1 1GZ
020 7556 2100 Fax: 020 7556 2200

MIDLANDS REGIONAL OFFICE
McClaren Building, 35 Dale End
Birmingham B4 7NP
0121-607 6200 *Fax:* 0121-607 6349

YORKS AND NORTH EAST REGIONAL OFFICE
Woodside House, 261 Low Lane
Horsforth, Leeds LS18 5TW
0113 283 4200 *Fax:* 0113 258 8029

NORTH WEST REGIONAL OFFICE
Quay House, Quay Street, Manchester M3 3JB
0161-952 8200 *Fax:* 0161-952 8222

SCOTLAND OFFICE
Belford House, 59 Belford Road
Edinburgh EH4 3UE
0131-247 2000 *Fax:* 0131-247 2121

RAILWAY INSPECTORATE
Rose Court, 2 Southwark Bridge
London SE1 9HS
Enquiries: 020 7717 6000
HM Chief Inspecting Officer of Railways:
  V Coleman
Deputy Chief Inspecting Officer: A Cooksey

Health Development Agency

Trevelyan House, 30 Great Peter Street,
London SW1P 2HW
020 7222 5300 Fax: 020 7413 8900
Chair: Ms Yve Buckland
Chief Executive: Richard Parish
Non-Executive Directors: Tahera Aanchawan
  (Independent Consultant),
  Prof Michael Adler, Colin Browne
  (BBC Director of Corporate Affairs),
  Ken Crossland *(Managing Partner at Price*
  Waterhouse Coopers), Dr John Noakes, OBE,
  Michael Peters *(Director of Education at York*
  City Council), Jude Williams *(Director of*
  Community Relations and Health Promotion
  at the East London and City Health Authority)
NOTE: HEALTH DEVELOPMENT AGENCY IS THE
SUCCESSOR TO HEALTH EDUCATION AUTHORITY
FROM 1 JANUARY 2000

Heathrow Airport Consultative Committee

First Floor, Heathrow Point East,
234 Bath Road, Hayes, Middlesex UB3 5AP
020 8745 7589 Fax: 020 8745 0580

The Heathrow Airport Consultative Committee
(HACC) was formed in 1948. It is a statutory
advisory body established by Heathrow Airport
Limited to provide a forum for users of the airport and community representatives to discuss
any matter connected with the airport. The
Committee has 40 members drawn from environmental groups, local business and aviation
industry groups.

Chairman: Sam Jones, CBE
Secretary: Mrs Sue Heeps

Heritage Lottery Fund

7 Holbein Place, London SW1W 8NR
020 7591 6000 Fax: 020 7591 6001
E-mail: nhmf@nhmf.demon.co.uk
Website: www.hlf.org.uk

Using money raised by the National Lottery, the
aim of the Heritage Lottery Fund is to improve
quality of life by safeguarding and enhancing the
heritage of buildings, objects and the environment, whether man-made or natural, which have
been important in the formation of the character
and identity of the United Kingdom; assisting
people to appreciate and enjoy their heritage, and
allowing them to hand it on in good heart to
future generations.

Chairman: Dr Eric Anderson
Trustees: Prof Chris Baines, Robert Boas,
Sir Richard Carew Pole, Sir Angus Grossart,
Sir Ernest Hall, Caryl Hubbard, John Keegan,
Patricia Lankester, Prof Palmer Newbould,
Susan Palmer, Catherine Porteous,
Prof Tom Pritchard, Mary Ann Sieghart,
Dame Sue Tinson

EXPERT PANELS
HISTORIC BUILDINGS AND LAND
Chairman: Les Sparks
Members: Alan Barber, Peter Inskip,
David Lambert, Michael Morrison,
Adrian Phillips, Anna Ritchie,
Matthew Saunders, Jane Sharman,
David Streeter, Prof David Walker,
Sir Jack Zunz

MUSEUMS, LIBRARIES AND ARCHIVES
Chairman: Richard Foster
Members: Dr Celina Fox, Dr J Patrick Greene,
Karen Hull, Sally MacDonald,
Dr Charles Saumaurez-Smith,
Dr Michael Smethurst, Terence Suthers,
David Vaisey, Giles Waterfield

REVIEW AND COMPLAINTS COMMITTEE
Chairman: Michael Gale, QC
Members: Brian McGeough, Sally Sampson,
Mike Taylor

MANAGEMENT GROUP
Director: Anthea Case
Director of Resources and Planning:
Steve Willis
Director of Operations: Stephen Johnson
Director of Heritage Policy: Simon Olding
*Secretary to Trustees and Head of Corporate
Policy:* Melanie Rickman
Head of Communications: Louise Lane
Deputy Director of Operations: Judith Cligman
*Deputy Director of Operations and Head of
National Heritage Memorial Fund:*
Robert Dufton
Deputy Director of Operations:
Claire Arokiasamy

Higher Education Funding Council for England

*Northavon House, Coldharbour Lane,
Bristol BS16 1QD*
0117 931 7317 *Fax:* 0117 931 7203

The Higher Education Funding Council for
England was established on 6 May 1992 under
the Further and Higher Education Act 1992 to
administer funds made available by the Secretary
of State for Education for the provision of teaching and research in higher education institutions
in England.

Chairman: Sir Michael Checkland
Chief Executive: Prof Sir Brian Fender, CMG
Members: Anthony Booth, CBE,
Stephen Bundred, Prof Marilyn Butler,
Prof Ron Cooke, Dr David Fussey,
Ms Caroline Neville, Dr David Potter, CBE,
Prof Sir Gareth Roberts,
Ms Barbara Stephens,
Prof Sir Stewart Sutherland,
Dr John Taylor, OBE, Dr Keith Taylor,
Miss Dorma Urwin
Assessor: Roger Dawe, CB, OBE
Observers: Peter Holmes (DENI),
Prof John Sizer, CBE (SHEFC),
Prof John Andrews (HEFCW),
Mike Mercer (TTA)

Highlands and Islands Enterprise

*Bridge House, 20 Bridge Street,
Inverness IV1 1QR*
01463 234171 *Fax:* 01463 244469
E-mail: hie.general@hient.co.uk
Website: www.hie.co.uk

Highlands and Islands Enterprise (HIE) is a non-
departmental public body charged with the economic and social development of the northern
half of Scotland, from the Clyde estuary to
Shetland, the Western Isles to Morayshire, working to the Scottish Parliament's Enterprise and
Lifelong Learning Department.

HIE's stated strategic aims are: strengthening
communities; developing skills; and growing
businesses. It is active in sectors such as manufacturing and production, tourism, food and
drink, and knowledge, information and telecommunications.

HIE comprises a central, strategic body in
Inverness at the core of a wider network (known
as the Highland and Islands Enterprise network)
consisting of 10 private sector-led Local
Enterprise Companies, contracted by HIE to
deliver a range of development and training
functions in their own local areas. The Network
provides financial assistance by way of grant,
loan or equity; builds factories, workshops and
offices; promotes the area's products, facilities
and location as a base for inward investment and
offers a wide range of business advisory services. In addition, it delivers and develops a wide
range of training schemes at all levels and pro-

vides learning and training programme support. It also exercises powers of environmental renewal and land reclamation and spends £1m a year on social development projects. Its annual budget is *c.* £75m.

Chairman: Jim Hunter
Chief Executive: Iain Robertson

Historic Royal Palaces

Hampton Court Palace, Surrey KT8 9AU
020 8781 9750 Fax: 020 8781 9754
Website: www.hrp.org.uk

The Historic Royal Palaces was a Government Executive Agency established in October 1989. As from 1 April 1998, it became a Royal Charter Body with charitable status. The Chief Executive is responsible for the day-to-day management of five Historic Royal Palaces: HM Tower of London; Hampton Court Palace; Kensington Palace State Apartments and Royal Ceremonial Dress Collection; The Banqueting House, Whitehall; Kew Palace and Queen Charlotte's Cottage in Kew Gardens, Richmond, Surrey. The objectives of the Historic Royal Palaces are: to improve the interpretation, presentation and visitor services at the Palaces in order to provide a high standard of service to the public which is consistent with best practice and achievement in the public and private sector; and, to maintain the Palaces and their associated gardens to a standard consistent with their architectural, historical and royal status in a manner which ensures value for money.

Chief Executive: A Coppin
Director of Finance: Ms A McLeish
Surveyor of the Fabric: R Davidson
Curator: Dr E Impey
Human Resources Director: M Bridger
Governor, HM Tower of London:
  Maj-Gen G Field, CB, OBE
Palaces Director, Hampton Court Palace;
  Kensington Palace; Banqueting House,
  Whitehall; Kew Palace: D McGuiness

As from 1 April 1998 HRP became a Royal Charter Body with charitable status

Home-Grown Cereals Authority

Caledonia House, 223 Pentonville Road,
London N1 9HY
020 7520 3926 Fax: 020 7520 3954
E-mail: pr@hgca.com

Established by the Cereals Marketing Act 1965, the Authority is empowered to carry out a number of functions under the Act for the purpose of improving the production and marketing of home-grown cereals and oilseeds. Specifically, HGCA provides a market information service to the industry, sponsors research and development on cereals and oilseeds by means of grants in aid to research establishments, promotes the export of UK grain and greater consumption of cereal-based products in Britain and abroad. The Chairman and Directors of the Board of the Authority are appointed by the Agriculture Ministers of the UK.

Chairman: Antony Pike
Chief Executive: Dr Paul Biscoe

Horserace Betting Levy Board

52 Grosvenor Gardens,
London SW1W 0AU
020 7333 0043 Fax: 020 7333 0041
E-mail: hblb@hblb.org.uk

The Horserace Betting Levy Board is a statutory body, established in 1961 following the legalisation of off-course betting offices, which collects a levy from bookmakers and the Horserace Totalisator Board, and applies it for the improvement of breeds of horses, veterinary science and education, and the improvement of horseracing. It currently has an annual budget of about £55 million.

The Board owns the Horseracing Forensic Laboratory at Newmarket which provides a drug-screening service for both the Jockey Club and commercial clients. The Board is also responsible for the National Stud at Newmarket.

Chairman: R Hughes
Deputy Chairman: Sir John Robb
Members: W Bartlett, A Crichton-Miller,
  K Elliott, P I Jones, A D G Oldrey, P Savill
Chief Executive: R L Brack
Scientific Liaison Executive:
  Ms E K Archer, BSc
Head of Legal Affairs: Ms L Evers
Project Development Executive: G Ayres
Head of Finance: R Haincock
Racing Executive: D Bradshaw

Horserace Totalisator Board

Tote House, 74 Upper Richmond Road,
London SW15 2SU
020 8874 6411 Fax: 020 8875 1882
E-mail: rhartnett@tote.co.uk

Established by the Betting, Gaming and Lotteries Act 1963 as successor in title to the Racecourse Betting Control Board established by the Racecourse Betting Act 1928.

Its function is to operate totalisators, on approved racecourses in Great Britain, and it also provides off-course cash and credit offices which offer bets at tote odds and starting price.

Chairman: P I Jones
Members: Ms F Driscoll, G Grimstone,
  W J Heaton, D L Lipsey, R W Miller,
  T J Phillips, P Savill, C H Sporborg

Housing Corporation

149 Tottenham Court Road, London W1P 0BN
020 7393 2000 Fax: 020 7393 2111
E-mail: enquiries@housingcorp.gov.uk
Website: www.housingcorp.gov.uk

Established by Parliament in 1964, the Housing Corporation has since had its functions broadened by the Housing Act 1996. It now registers, supervises and funds non-profit making Registered Social Landlords (RSLs) throughout England. Some 2,200 organisations are currently registered with the Corporation. The Corporation also supports RSLs in the rehabilitation of older houses and in new building to help people with special needs, including the elderly, the disabled, and single homeless people, and backs initiatives to provide homes for sale to people on lower incomes, through schemes for shared equity and leasehold for the elderly.

Chairman: The Rt Hon The Baroness Dean of
  Thornton-le-Fylde
Deputy Chairman: Eric Armitage, OBE
Chief Executive: Anthony Mayer
Board Members: John Foster, OBE,
  Dr Peter Williams, Derek Waddington, OBE,
  George Cracknell, Julia Unwin,
  Ken Griffin, OBE, Sylvia Denman, CBE,
  Sheila Button, Yvonne Hutchinson,
  Andrew Winckler, Ivan Monckton

Human Fertilisation and Embryology Authority

Paxton House, 30 Artillery Lane,
London E1 7LS
020 7377 5077 Fax: 020 7377 1871
Website: www.hfea.gov.uk

The principal statutory function of the HFEA is to regulate certain practices involved in the treatment of infertility and research on human embryos. Specifically, it is required to operate a licensing system for embryo research and for infertility treatment which involve the use of donated eggs or sperm or which involve the creation or use of embryos outside the body. The storage of sperm, eggs and embryos is also a licensable activity.

The HFEA has a number of other responsibilities, including publishing a Code of Practice giving guidance to centres on how they should carry out licensed activities. The HFEA also keeps a confidential register of information about donors, patients and treatments and their outcomes. It publishes an annual Patients' Guide to DI and IVF clinics, listing the success rates of all licensed clinics.

Chairman: Mrs Ruth Deech
Deputy Chairman: Mrs Jane Denton
Chief Executive: Mrs Suzanne McCarthy

Independent Review Service for the Social Fund

4th Floor, Centre City Podium,
5 Hill Street, Birmingham B5 4UB
0121-606 2100 *Fax:* 0121-606 2180

The Social Fund Commissioner is appointed by the Secretary of State for Social Security. The Commissioner appoints Social Fund Inspectors who provide an independent review of decisions made by Social Fund Officers in the Benefits Agency of the Department of Social Security.

Social Fund Commissioner: John Scampion
Office Manager: Pauline Adey

Independent Schools Council

Grosvenor Gardens House,
35–37 Grosvenor Gardens,
London SW1W 0BS
020 7798 1590 Fax: 020 7798 1591
E-mail: abc@isis.org.uk

The Council comprises the eight independent schools' associations which together have some

1,300 member schools, and the Independent Schools' Information Service (ISIS) which is the press and media arm of the Council.

Chairman: Ian Beer, CBE
General Secretary: Dr Alistair B Cooke, OBE
Administrator: Mrs Vivian Harris

Independent Television Commission

33 Foley Street, London W1P 7LB
020 7255 3000 Fax: 020 7306 7800
E-mail: publicaffairs@itc.org.uk

The Independent Television Commission (ITC) is the public body responsible for licensing and regulating all commercially-funded television in the UK, whether delivered terrestrially (i.e. ITV, Channel 4 and Channel 5) or by cable or satellite, public teletext, digital television services and certain other text and data services.

The ITC has a duty under the Broadcasting Acts 1990 and 1996 to ensure that a wide range of television programme services is available throughout the UK and that, taken as a whole, they are of high quality and appeal to a variety of tastes and interests, and that there is a fair and effective competition in the provision of such services.

The ITC regulates these services through licence conditions and through its various codes on programmes content, advertising, sponsorship and technical standards. The ITC has the statutory powers to impose penalties on licensees if they do not comply with their licence conditions. It monitors compliance through its headquarters and regional staff and with the assistance of eleven regional Viewer Consultative Councils.

Chairman: Sir Robin Biggam
Deputy Chairman: Lord Holme of Cheltenham
Members: Miss J Goffe, Prof Derec Llwyd Morgan, Dr M Moloney, Dr J Beynon, Dr Michael Shea, Sir Michael Checkland, Alastair Balls
Chief Executive: Peter Rogers
Director of Economic Regulation: Sheila Cassells
Director of Programmes and Cable Division: Sarah Thane
Director of Regions and Public Affairs: (Vacant)
Director of Engineering: Gary Tonge
Director of Advertising and Sponsorship: Stephen Locke
Secretary to the Commission: Michael Redley

Regional Officers: Brian Marjoribanks (Scotland), Janet Wootton (Midlands), Denis Wolinski (Northern Ireland), Jean Young (South and South East England), Stella Mair Thomas (Wales and West of England), Michael Fay (North of England)
Regional Executives: Nicholas Bull (South-West England), Peter Monteith (East of England), Louise Bennett (North-West England), Alan Stewart (Scotland), Robert Conlon (North-East England)
Regional Assistants: Joyce Young (South and South East), Hywel Wiliam (Wales and West of England)

Independent Tribunal Service/The Appeals Service

The Presidents Office, 4th Floor,
Whittington House, 19-30 Alfred Place,
London WC1E 7LW
020 7814 6500 Fax: 020 7814 6540

President: His Hon Judge Michael Harris
Chief Executive: Neil Ward
Regional Chairmen: Mrs T Parker (Scotland), R Martin (Midlands), R G Smithson (South East), N Warren (North West), C B Stephens (Wales and South Western), J W Tinnion (North East)
Acting National Chairman: D Turrell

Industrial Society

Customer Centre, 49 Calthorp Road
Edgbaston, Birmingham B15 1TH
0870 400 1000 Fax: 0870 400 1099
Website: www.indsoc.co.uk

The Industrial Society was founded in 1918 and campaigns to improve working life through training, consultancy, advisory services, publishing and advocacy. The Society is incorporated under Royal charter and is a fully independent and non-profit organisation. It has over 10,500 member organisations.

Chairman: Sir Christopher Wates
Chief Executive: Will Hutton
Director: Yvonne Bennion
Company Secretary: Lesley Thornley
Director of Communications: Patrick Burns

Industry and Parliament Trust

1 Buckingham Place, London SW1E 6HR
020 7976 5311 Fax: 020 7828 7778
E-mail: admin@ipt.org.uk
Website: www.ipt.org.uk

The Trust, an independent educational charity, was established in 1977 to make a positive contribution towards improving understanding between the world of industry including finance and commerce and Members and Officers of both Houses of Parliament and MEPs – of all parties. Its activities include the arrangement of Fellowship study courses for parliamentarians, seminars and conferences. It also provides study courses and seminars about Parliament and the EU for personnel of its member companies. These are elected to help the Trust to provide a complete picture of British Business in relation to size sector and geographical spread.

The Trust is non-partisan, non-profit making and is not a parliamentary lobby.

Eleven other parallel organisations modelled on the Trust have been established overseas. In 1997 they and the Trust established the International Association of Business and Parliament electing the Trust to administer the Association for its first two years.

Presidents: The Rt Hon the Lord Irvine of Lairg, QC (The Lord Chancellor), The Rt Hon Betty Boothroyd, MP (Speaker of the House of Commons)
Trustees: The Rt Hon the Lord Weatherill DL (Chairman), The Rt Hon Richard Caborn MP (Minister for Trade), George Cubie (Clerk Assistant of the House of Commons), Michael Davies (Clerk of the Parliaments), The Rt Hon the Baroness Dean of Thornton-le-Fylde, Judge David Edward CMG, QC, The Baroness Hooper, Sir Ken Jackson (General Secretary, AEEU), Ieuan Wyn Jones MP, Archy Kirkwood, MP, Ken Minton, CBE (Chairman, SGB Group plc), Bill Olner, MP, The Lord Tomlinson, Bowen Wells MP
Chairman of the Council: Barry Stickings (Managing Director, BASF plc)
Director: Fredrick R Hyde-Chambers
General Secretary (Operations) and Finance Director: Peter Sharp
General Secretary (Trust Administration) and Small Business Fellowship Officer: Susan Chaytor
Office Manager: Eunice Anthony

Fellowships Development Manager: Andrew Clark
Fellowships and European Officer: Yvonne D'Inverno
Fellowships and Political Service Officer: Ian Stokes
Fellowships and International Officer: Sharon Garfinkel

Inland Waterways Amenity Advisory Council

City Road Lock, 38 Graham Street, London N1 8JX
020 7253 1745 Fax: 020 7490 7656
E-mail: iwaac@btinternet.com

IWAAC was established by the Transport Act 1968 to advise the Secretary of State for the Environment and British Waterways on the classification and use of the Board's inland waterways for amenity and recreational purposes. The Council's Chairman and Members are appointed for their knowledge in the relevant fields and include representatives with knowledge of boating, tourism, heritage and recreation etc. The Council may investigate matters it considers relevant and within its terms of reference. Reports to the Secretary of State and British Waterways on its findings and publishes reports and papers concerned with current issues and their effect on the waterways.

Chairman: The Viscountess Knollys, DL
Manager: Anthony McCann
Members: Prof Anthony Collier, David Morgan, Mike Palmer, Audrey Smith, OBE, R Bell, D Court, OBE, Dr J W Eaton, A Hirst, OBE, Prof I Mercer, J R Hume, OBE, J Barron, P Chambers, H Green, S Stacey, L Tatham

Institute of Directors

116 Pall Mall, London SW1Y 5ED
020 7839 1233 Fax: 020 7839 2337
E-mail: policy-unit@iod.co.uk

The Institute of Directors was founded in the United Kingdom in 1903 and granted a Royal Charter in 1906.

It is an international organisation with a membership composed of individual directors and business leaders in every continent.

It is committed to free market economics and to high standards of corporate governance.

Its constituent organisations share the following aims:
– to encourage and help members to develop their professional competence;

- to bring the experience of members to bear on the conduct of public affairs for the common good.
- to provide facilities and services for members; The Institute actively represents the interests of members to both the UK government and the EC institutions.

The Institute's membership is confined to company directors and persons of equivalent status. There are 47,000 UK members – total membership 63,000. From its Pall Mall premises the Institute provides advisory and training services and banquetting, meeting and other business facilities for its members. It distributes a number of publications, including the monthly *Director* magazine,

Director-General: George Cox
Head of Policy Unit: Ruth Lea
Taxation Executive and Deputy Head of Policy Unit: Richard Baron
Chief Economist: Graeme Leach
Business Research Executive: Geraint Day
Business Policy Executive: Richard Wilson

Institute of Logistics and Transport

Registered Office:
80 Portland Place, London W1N 4DP
020 7467 9400 Fax: 020 7467 9440

Administration and Membership Enquiries:
Supply-Chain Centre,
Earlstrees Court, Earlstrees Road,
Corby, Northants NN17 4AX
01536 740100 Fax: 01536 740101
E-mail: membership@iolt.org.uk
Website: www.iolt.org.uk

Formed in June 1999 from the merger of The Chartered Institute of Transport in the UK (CIT-UK) and the Institute of Logistics (IoL), The Institute of Logistics and Transport (ILT) is the leading professional body for those concerned with the movement of people or goods. It aims to promote understanding of and provide training in the concepts and practice of logistics and transport. It has a UK membership of around 23,000 and is the UK Territorial Organisation of The Chartered Institute of Transport (CIT) which has 33,000 members in 60 countries.

President: John Welsby
Chairman: Richard Hunt
Chief Executive: Graham Ewar
Director of Marketing: Nicholas Pope
Director of Publications and Public Relations:
Gerald Fisher

Director of Education:
Mrs Dorothea de Carvalho
Director of Supply-Chain Management:
Mrs Christine Rowat
Director of Logistics and Transport Policies:
Reg Harman

Institute of Management

3rd Floor, 2 Savoy Court, Strand,
London WC2R 0EZ
020 7497 0580 Fax: 020 7497 0463
Website: www.inst-mgt.org.uk

The Institute of Management was inaugurated on 1 November 1992 following the merger of BIM and IIM. It exists to foster and encourage the highest standards of professional excellence at every level of management. To this end, IM's aim is to provide to all its members – individual or corporate – the information, consultation, training and advice vital to the effective day-to-day fulfilment of the managerial role. The Institute has more than 86,000 individual and 600 corporate members.

IM's Public Affairs Department seeks to protect and further the interests of good management at every level. The Department's reports, briefings and submissions influence and inform government and opinion formers, both in the United Kingdom and throughout Europe.

President: Sir Anthony Cleaver
Director-General: Mary Chapman
Director of Public and Professional Affairs:
Christine Hayhurst
Policy Adviser: Mark Hastings
Media Relations Manager: Karen Dale

Investors Compensation Scheme

Cottons Centre, Cottons Lane,
London SE1 2QB
020 7367 6000 Fax: 020 7367 6001
Website: www.fsa.gov.uk

The Investors Compensation Scheme was established under the Financial Services Act (1986), as part of the investor protection framework. The Scheme is the final safety net for investors. It can pay compensation of up to £48,000 each to clients of UK authorised investment firms which are unable to return money or investments owed to investors.

Chairman: Sir John Wickerson
Chief Executive: Ms Myra Kinghorn, FCA

Board Members: Sir John Caines, KCB *(Deputy Chairman),* Allan Daffern, FCII, Nicholas Durlacher, CBE, David Enock, FCIS, Ms Philippa Foster Back, Kit Jebens, CBE, Dr Oonagh McDonald, CBE, Luke March, Ms Helena Wiesner

Joint Nature Conservation Committee

Monkstone House, City Road,
Peterborough PE1 1JY
01733 562626 *Fax:* 01733 555948

The Joint Nature Conservation Committee is a forum through which the three country nature conservation agencies, the Countryside Council for Wales, English Nature and Scottish Natural Heritage, deliver their special statutory responsibilities for Great Britain as a whole and internationally. These special responsibilities, known as the special functions, contribute to sustaining and enriching biological diversity, enhancing geological features and sustaining natural systems. The special functions are:
- to devise and maintain common standards and protocols for nature conservation;
- to promote, through common standards, the free interchange of data between the country agencies and with external partners;
- to advise on nature conservation issues affecting Great Britain as a whole;
- to pursue wider international goals for nature conservation (encouraging sustainable development, biological diversity and earth science conservation), including the provision of relevant advice to the Government;
- to commission new research and collate existing knowledge in support of these activities, and to disseminate the results.

Chairman: Sir Angus Stirling
Members: E Cameron, Prof M J Crawley, Dr J S Faulkner, E M W Griffith, CBE, DL, R J Hanna, Prof O W Heal, Prof D Ingram, Dr J Markland, CBE, Prof J I Sprent, OBE, Prof L Warren, Prof R C L Wilson, MBE, Baroness Young of Old Scone
Managing Director: D Steer
Projects Director: Dr M A Vincent

Judicial Studies Board

9th Floor, Millbank Tower,
Millbank, London SW1P 4QU
020 7217 4708 Fax: 020 7217 4779
E-mail: jsboard@compuserve.com
Website: www.jsboard.co.uk

The Judicial Studies Board, established in 1979, is an independent advisory non-departmental public body, financed by the Lord Chancellor's Department, which provides training for all full-time and part-time members of the judiciary and advises on the training of magistrates and chairmen and members of tribunals.

Chairman: The Rt Hon Lord Justice Waller
Director of Studies: His Honour Judge Pearl
Secretary to the Board: Edward Adams

Lands Tribunal for Scotland

1 Grosvenor Crescent,
Edinburgh EH12 5ER
0131-225 7996 *Fax:* 0131-226 4812

The Lands Tribunal for Scotland is an independent judicial body constituted in 1971 by Order of the Secretary of State for Scotland under the Lands Tribunal Act 1949. Jurisdiction has been extended by numerous Acts of Parliament to include determining questions relating to the valuation of land, compensation for the compulsory acquisition of land, appeals against the Keeper of the Registers of Scotland, discharge or variation of restrictive land obligations and disputes in relation to the purchase of council houses by tenants and the transfer of council house landlords.

President: The Hon Lord McGhie
Members: J Devine, FRICS, R A Edwards, CBE, WS, Sheriff A C Henry, A MacLeary, FRICS,
Clerk: N M Tainsh

Law Commission

Conquest House, 37/38 John Street,
Theobalds Road, London WC1N 2BQ
020 7453 1220 Fax: 020 7453 1297
Website: www.open.gov.uk/lawcomm/home-page.htm

The Law Commission, established by the Law Commissions Act 1965, is a permanent body constituted to promote the reform of the law with a view to its systematic development, simplification and modernisation. The Commission reports to the Lord Chancellor and its programme includes projects in the fields of common law, contract and tort, criminal law, family law, property law (including landlord and tenant law) and public law. The Commission also has a separate programme covering the consolidation of statutes and the repeal of obsolete and unnecessary enactments.

Chairman: The Hon Mr Justice Carnwath
Commissioners: Miss D Faber, C Harpum,
  S Silber, QC
Secretary: Michael Sayers
Parliamentary Draftsmen: G Lyne, D Ramsey,
  J Sellers, Ms E White, Ms C Wynter

Law Society

Head Office, 113 Chancery Lane,
London WC2A 1PL
020 7320 5858 Fax: 020 7242 1309
Website: www.lawsociety.org.uk

Regional Offices:
Preston, Bristol, Cambridge, Cardiff, Wakefield,
Greater London and Brussels

The Law Society, founded in 1825 by Royal Charter, is both the governing body and the professional association for solicitors in England and Wales. Although membership of the Society is voluntary, the great majority of solicitors are members. The Society is funded by the fees charged for practising certificates and by subscriptions from members. The Society publishes a weekly journal. *The Law Society's Gazette,* which is sent to all members and a monthly *Guardian Gazette,* sent to all practising lawyers. The Society is governed by a Council of 75 solicitors most of whom are elected by members in geographical constituencies.

President: R Sayer
Vice-President: Ms Kamlesh Bahl, CBE
Deputy Vice-President: Mike Napier
Secretary-General: Jane Betts
Director of Communications: Barbara Cahalane
Head of Parliamentary Unit: John Ludlow

Law Society of Scotland

26 Drumsheugh Gardens,
Edinburgh EH3 7YR
0131-226 7411 *Fax:* 0131-225 2934
Website: www.lawscot.org.uk

The Law Society of Scotland is the regulatory body for Solicitors in Scotland. It is established under the Solicitors (Scotland) Act 1980. It is funded by subscription from all Scottish Solicitors. The Society is responsible for deter-

mining the education and training required of solicitors, the regulation and control of solicitors and the investigation of complaints regarding the conduct and services of solicitors. The Society is active in further legal education, law reform, and the promotion of solicitors services.

President: Michael Scanlan

Legal Aid Board

Head Office, 85 Gray's Inn Road,
London WC1X 8AA
020 7813 1000 Fax: 020 7813 8637

The Legal Aid Board is a non departmental public body, set up under the Legal Aid Act 1988. The Legal Aid Board administers legal aid on behalf of the Lord Chancellor and advises on developing and improving the legal aid system. The Board took over the responsibility for this function, previously administered by the Law Society, on 1 April 1989. The Board's overall remit from the Lord Chancellor is to ensure that "Legal advice, assistance, mediation and representation are made available to those in England and Wales who need it — in ways which are effective and give the best possible value for money". The Board administers legal advice and assistance including assistance by way of representation and legal aid for civil proceedings. It also assesses claims for payment of magistrates' court work and deals with some aspects of criminal legal aid. The Board, its Head Office and central departments are based in London. Applications for civil legal aid certificates and amendments/authorities and extensions of authority for advice and assistance as well as the payment of the various types of bills are dealt with through offices across England and Wales. Each office is run by a Regional Director and has an area committee made up of practising solicitors and barristers.

The Board is involved in a wide range of initiatives in the context of the Lord Chancellor's reform plans to transform the legal aid system. The initiatives are designed to improve access to legal services, while controlling spending and targeting the available resources to people who need them most.

Regional Legal Services Committees (RLSCs) have been established by the Legal Aid Board to help achieve these claims. RLSCs advise the Legal Aid Board and the Government on needs and priorities and how best to ensure that legal services provision is related to the needs of local people. Information about RLSCs can be obtained from Legal Aid Head Office.

The Legal Services Commission, a new body to be established in April 2000, will take on the responsibilities of the Legal Aid Board. In addition it will create and develop a Community Legal Service to ensure that legal needs throughout England and Wales are met through quality-driven and cost effective mechanisms. It will also establish a new Criminal Defence Service to provide defence services through a mix of contracts with private lawyers and salaried defenders.

Chairman: Sir Tim Chessells
Members: Michael Barnes, CBE,
  Mrs D Charnock, Ms J Dunkley, Philip Ely,
  Brian Harvey *(Director of Resources and Supplier Development),* Mrs S Hewitt,
  Peter Hollingworth, Steve Orchard, CBE
  (Chief Executive), Jim Shearer
Secretary: Mrs A-M Roberts

Local Authorities Co-ordinating Body on Food and Trading Standards

10 Albert Embankment, London SE1 7SP
020 7840 7200 Fax: 020 7735 9977
E-mail: lynne.skelton@lacots.org.uk
Website: www.lacots.org.uk

LACOTS is a national co-ordinating body set up by the local authority Associations to co-ordinate the enforcement of food safety and trading standards laws and regulations.

Its functions are to co-ordinate enforcement work; promote uniform interpretation of laws; be a centre of information and assist Government, trade associations and consumer organisations with the development of fair trading policies. It liaises closely with enforcement practitioners in Europe and elsewhere.

Executive Director: Nick Cull

Local Government Association

Local Government House, Smith Square,
London SW1P 3HZ
020 7664 3000 Fax: 020 7664 3030
E-mail: info@lga.gov.uk
Website: www.lga.gov.uk

The Local Government Association (LGA) was formed by the merger of the Association of County Councils, the Association of District Councils and the Association of Metropolitan Authorities on the 1 April 1997. The LGA has just under 500 members, including 238 shire district councils, 36 metropolitan district councils, 34 county councils, 46 new unitary authorities, 33 London authorities, and 22 Welsh authorities. In addition, the LGA represents police authorities, fire authorities and passenger transport authorities. The LGA provides the national voice for local communities in England and Wales; its members represent over 50 million people, employ more than 2 million staff and spend over £65 billion on local services.

Local authorities have a unique role in leading communities and working with the private and voluntary sectors to solve national problems at local levels. Now, at a time when the need for community leadership is greater than ever, the LGA is assisting local authorities to:

- raise standards in schools;
- work for better local government;
- prevent social exclusion;
- regenerate local communities;
- focus on improving child care and early years services;
- work to produce healthy communities;
- develop integrated transport services.@half:

Chief Executive: Brian Briscoe
Director of Policy and Research:
  Janet Rutherford
Director of Local Government Finance:
  Neil Kinghan
Director of Management and Member Services:
  Joan Jones
Director of Communications and Public Affairs:
  Phil Swann
Head of Education: Neil Fletcher
Head of Environment and Public Protection:
  Mike Ashley
Head of Strategy: Matthew Warburton
Head of Social Services and Housing:
  John Ransford
LGA Leading Members:
President: The Lord Hunt of Tanworth, GCB
Chair: Sir Jeremy Beecham (Labour, Newcastle)
Vice-Chair: Harry Jones, CBE (Labour, Newport)
Deputy Chairs: Ian Swithenbank (Labour, Northumberland), David Williams, CBE (Liberal Democrat, Richmond), Lord Hanningfield (Conservative, Essex), Ron Gee (Independent, Epsom and Ewell)

NB: The Welsh Local Government Association (WLGA) is part of the LGA. See separate entry.

Local Government Boundary Commission for Scotland

3 Drumsheugh Gardens,
Edinburgh EH3 7QJ
0131-538 7510
E-mail: lgbcs@cableinet.co.uk

The Commission reviews local government administrative areas and electoral arrangements under the provisions of the Local Government (Scotland) Act 1973 as amended by the Local Government etc (Scotland) Act 1994.

Chairman: The Hon Lord Osborne
Deputy Chairman: Brian Wilson, OBE
Members: Dr Elspeth Graham, Prof Hugh Begg,
  Dr Iseabel Glen
Secretary: R Smith

Local Government Boundary Commission for Wales

Caradog House, 1–6 St Andrew's Place,
Cardiff CF10 3BE
029 2039 5031 Fax: 029 2039 5250
E-mail: lgbc@lgbc-wales.gov.uk
Website: www.lgbc-wales.gov.uk

The Local Government Boundary Commission for Wales is an advisory body set up under terms of Section 53 of the Local Government Act 1972. Its main task is to review local government areas and electoral arrangements in Wales, with a view to considering whether or not to make proposals to the National Assembly for Wales for effecting changes which appear to the Commission to be desirable in the interests of effective and convenient local government.

Chairman: Prof E Sunderland, OBE, DL, MA,
  PhD, LLD, FIBiol
Deputy Chairman: E F L FitzHugh, OBE, DL
Member: Mrs S G Smith, LLB
Secretary: Roger Knight, BA, MSC, MRTPI

Local Government Commission for England

Dolphyn Court, 10/11 Great Turnstile,
London WC1V 7JU
020 7430 8400 Fax: 020 7404 6142
E-mail: press@lgce.gov.uk
Website: www.lgce.gov.uk

Established in 1992 under the Local Government Act 1992, the Commission's functions are to review and make recommendations to the Government on the boundaries of wards within individual local authority areas and to their electoral arrangements (such as the number of councillors for each area) so as to ensure electoral equality. The Commission comprises a Chairman and several Commissioners drawn from various backgrounds. They include academics, business people and former local government officers. All are appointed by the Secretary of State for the Environment, Transport and the Regions but are independent from Government and political parties. The Commissioners are supported by a Chief Executive and a small full time staff. The Commission can also undertake structural reviews on the direction of the Secretary of State but does not do so currently.

Chairman: Prof Malcolm Grant
Chief Executive: Barbara Stephens

London Chamber of Commerce and Industry

33 Queen Street, London EC4R 1AP
020 7248 4444 Fax: 020 7489 0391
E-mail: press@londonchamber.co.uk
Website: www.londonchamber.co.uk

The London Chamber of Commerce is the capital's largest business organisation with over 3,500 member companies.

It runs two European Information Centres, a Regional Supply Office and one of the country's biggest programmes of overseas trade missions and exhibitions.

It also handles 30,000 requests for business information each year and runs the busiest export documentation centre in the UK. It also organises nearly 200 events annually, enabling businesses to network with each other or improve their business skills.

President: Colin Parsons
Chief Executive: Simon Sperryn
Director of Campaigns: Andrew Hawkins
Press Officer: Vincent Burke

London Regional Passengers' Committee

Clements House, 14–18 Gresham Street,
London EC2V 7PR
020 7505 9000 Fax: 020 7505 9003

The independent statutory body set up to represent the interests of the users of London Transport Buses, the Underground and facilities at Victoria Coach Station, the Docklands Light Railway, Eurostar, Heathrow Express Railway and other rail services in and around London.

Chairman: Sir Alan Greengross
Director: Rufus Barnes

London Transport

55 Broadway, London SW1H 0BD
020 7222 5600 Fax: *020 7222 5719*
Website: www.londontransport.co.uk
LT is the authority responsible for the Underground, and for regulating bus services. Its network of services extends over an area of about 610 square miles within a radius of approximately 15 miles of Charing Cross. LT is responsible to the Secretary of State for the Environment, Transport and the Regions.

Chairman (non Executive): Sir Malcolm Bates
Chief Executive: Denis Tunnicliffe, CBE
Managing Director, London Transport Buses:
   Clive Hodson, CBE
Managing Director, London Underground:
   Derek Smith
LT Director of Finance: John Hughes
Secretary: Frances Low
Public Affairs Manager: Claire Filby

Lord Chamberlain

Buckingham Palace, London SW1A 1AA
020 7930 4832
The Lord Chamberlain is head of the Royal Household.

Lord Chamberlain:
   The Rt Hon the Lord Camoys, GCVO

Lord Great Chamberlain's Office

Palace of Westminster, London SW1A 0PW
020 7219 3100
The Lord Great Chamberlain has particular responsibility for the internal administrative arrangements within the House of Lords for the State Openings. The Lord Great Chamberlain is responsible for the Royal Apartments of the Palace of Westminster, i.e. The Queen's Robing Room, the Royal Gallery and, in conjunction with the Lord Chancellor and the Speaker, Westminster Hall.

Lord Great Chamberlain: The Most Hon
   the Marquess of Cholmondeley

Secretary to the Lord Great Chamberlain:
   General Sir Edward Jones, KCB, CBE
Clerk to the Lord Great Chamberlain:
   Miss C J Bostock
Staff Superintendent:
   Major A M Charlesworth, BEM

Low Pay Commission

5th Floor, 151 Buckingham Palace Road,
London SW1W 9SS
020 7215 3646 Fax: *020 7215 1560*
Website: www.lowpay.gov.uk
The Low Pay Commission is a statutory body, established in July 1997, to advise Government on the National Minimum Wage.

Chairman of Commission: Prof George Bain
Commissioners: Stephanie Monk,
   Rita Donaghy, OBE, Prof David Metcalf,
   Prof Willy Brown, Bill Callaghan,
   John Cridland, Paul Gates,
   Lawrie Dewar, MBE
Secretary to the Commission: Claire Durkin

Meat and Livestock Commission

PO Box 44, Winterhill House, Snowdon Drive,
Winterhill, Milton Keynes MK6 1AX
01908 677577 Telex: 82227
Fax: 01908 609221
Website: www.meatmatters.com

The Meat and Livestock Commission established as a result of the Agriculture Act 1967 came into operation on 1 October 1967. It is an independent body, charged with the general duty of promoting greater efficiency in the livestock industry and the livestock products industry. The fifteen members of the Commission are appointed by Ministers and have no financial or commercial interests likely to prejudice the proper discharge of their functions as members.

In carrying out its functions the Commission has regard to the interests of consumers as well as to the interests of the various sections of the livestock and livestock products industry. The Commission is concerned with cattle, pigs and sheep but is excluded from concern with the production of milk or milk products or fleece wool and with the production of dairy cattle.

Chairman: D T Y Curry, CBE
Deputy Chairman: P Kirk

Members: J Baker, MBE, Mrs H Browning,
J Bundy, R Campbell, R Green, OBE,
Ms D McCrea, Prof R Moody, R Roberts,
J Ross, CBE, R F Sadler, J Taylor,
D Walker, MBE, TD, J Whitehead
Director-General: G Howells
Marketing Director: R Lowe
Technical Director: M Attenborough
Corporate Strategy Director: R J Bansback
Commercial Service Director: K J Roberts

Medical Research Council

20 Park Crescent, London W1N 4AL
020 7636 5422 Fax: 020 7436 6179
Website: www.mrc.ac.uk
The MRC is a public body reporting to the
Office of Science and Technology. It nevertheless remains independent in its choice of which
research to support. Its principal objectives are to
promote the balanced development of medical
and related biological research and to advance
knowledge that will lead to the maintaining and
improvement of human health. The Council
employs its own research staff in over 40
research establishments which include the
National Institute for Medical Research, the
Laboratory of Molecular Biology and the
Clinical Sciences Centre. It also provides grants
to enable scientists who are not members of its
own staff to undertake research programmes and
projects, thus complementing the research
resources of universities and teaching hospitals,
using a multidisciplinary approach where appropriate. Research training is supported by means
of fellowships and studentships. Extensive
details about the MRC's research and structure
can be found on its website at www.mrc.ac.uk.
Useful publications include the quarterly magazine MRC News (updates on research activities)
and the Strategic Plan (for the MRC's approach
to funding research).

Chairman: Sir Anthony Cleaver
Chief Executive:
Prof G K Radda, CBE, DPhil, FRS
Executive Director: N H Winterton, MA

CORPORATE AFFAIRS GROUP
Director: J M Lee, BA

RESEARCH MANAGEMENT GROUP
Director of Research Management:
D R Dunstan, PhD

FINANCE GROUP
Director: D L Smith, PhD

HUMAN RESOURCES GROUP
Director: G M Breen, LLB

COMMERCIAL OPERATIONS
Director of Industrial Collaboration and
Licensing: D A A Owen, PhD

NATIONAL INSTITUTE FOR MEDICAL RESEARCH
Director: Sir John James Skehel, PhD, FRS

MRC LABORATORY OF MOLECULAR BIOLOGY
Director: Dr R Henderson, PhD, FRS

MRC CLINICAL SCIENCES CENTRE
Director: Prof C Higgins, FRSE

Mental Welfare Commission for Scotland

K Floor, Argyle House,
3 Lady Lawson Street
Edinburgh EH3 9SH
0131-222 6111 *Fax:* 0131-222 6112
The Commission was established under the
Mental Health (Scotland) Act 1960 and its duties
were considerably extended by the Mental
Health (Scotland) Act 1984. The statutory duties
are to generally exercise protective functions in
respect of persons who may, by reason of mental
disorder, be incapable of adequately protecting
themselves or their interests, and, where those
persons are liable to be detained in hospital, or
subject to guardianship under the provisions of
the Act.

Chairman:
Sir William Reid, KCB, MA, LLD, FRCPEd
Director: Dr James A T Dyer, MB, ChB(Hons),
FRCPsych
Vice-Chairman: Mrs Norma Bennie, DipCot
Social Work Commissioner:
Prof Juliet Cheetham, MA, OBE
Medical Commissioners:
Dr Adrian Lodge, BSc, MB, CHB, FRCPsych,
Dr Madeleine Osborn, MB, CHB,
MRCPsych, FRCPsych
Secretary: David M Hogg
Medical Officers:
Dr E Calder, BSc, MB, ChB, MRCPsych,
Dr H Cash, MB, ChB, DRCOG, MRCPsych,
Dr Christopher Fleming, MB, ChB, DCH,
DPM, MRCPsych, FRCPEd,
Dr Carolyn Greenwood, MB, ChB,
MRCPsych,
Dr F Sinclaire, MB, ChB, MRCPsych
Nursing Officer: Jamie Malcolm, RMN, RGN
Social Work Officer: George Kappler, MSW

Social Worker:
  Ms Marion Shawcross, BA(Hons), DipAss
Complaints Officer: Mrs Yvonne Osman
Part-time Commissioners: Mrs Norma Bennie,
  DipCot, Colin Campbell, QC, Mrs Faith
  Cotter, MB, LLB, William Gent, OBE,
  RNMH, Dr Pramod Jauhar, MB, BS, DPM,
  MRCPsych, Dr Shainool Jiwa, BA, MA, PhD,
  Tom Keenan, CQSW, Dr Elizabeth McCall-
  Smith, MB, ChB, MRCGP, DRCOG, Donald
  J MacDonald, MA, RGN, RMN,
  Rev Dr Joe Morrow, JP, Malcolm Murray, CA,
  Dr Linda Pollock, RGN, DNC, DCN, RMN,
  BSc, PhD, MBA,
  Archie Robb, CQSW, DipSW, ACIS,
  Mrs Margaret Ross, LLB(Hons),
  Dr E Margaret Thomas, MB, ChB, CRCOG,
  DCH, MRCGP, Dr Margaret Whoriskey,
  BA(Hons), MPhil, CPsychol, PhD

Millennium Commission

Portland House, Stag Place,
London SW1E 5EZ
020 7880 2001 Fax: 020 7880 2000

The Millennium Commission (created by the
National Lottery etc Act 1993) is one of the five
distributors of money raised for good causes by
the National Lottery. The Commission assists
communities in marking the close of the second
millennium and in celebrating the start of the
third by giving grants to projects throughout the
UK which enjoy public support and which will
be lasting monuments to the achievements and
aspirations of the nation.

The Commission supports three main types of
project: capital projects (application rounds now
closed), an Exhibition and Festival during the
year 2000, and Awards schemes for individuals.

Chairman: Rt Hon Chris Smith, MP
Commissioners:
  Rt Hon Michael Heseltine, CH, MP,
  Rt Hon Dr Marjorie Mowlam, MP
  The Earl of Dalkeith, KBE, DL,
  The Lord Glentoran, CBE, DL, Sir John Hall,
  Simon Jenkins, Dr Heather Couper, FRAS

Museums and Galleries Commission

16 Queen Anne's Gate,
London SW1H 9AA
020 7233 4200 Fax: 020 7233 3686
Website: www.museums.gov.uk

The MGC advises the United Kingdom
Government, including the Department of
Education for Northern Ireland, the Scottish
Education Department and the National
Assembly for Wales, on museum affairs. There
are 15 Commissioners, appointed by the Prime
Minister.

The MGC'S executive functions include the
services of the National Museums Security
Adviser, allocation of grants to the 7 Area
Museum Councils (AMCs) in England (and the
monitoring of the 10 AMCs generally); funding
and monitoring of the work of the mda; and
administers various grant schemes. Since 1986
the MGC has helped fund the Tyne and Wear
Museums Service and supports certain research
and publication projects of a national character
which benefit museums. The MGC also advises
on disability and environmental standards in
museums.

In 1993 the MGC completed the first phase of
a programme to set up a national Registration
scheme for museums. The MGC administers the
arrangements for government indemnities and
acceptance of works of art in lieu of Inheritance
Tax and it has responsibility for the two Purchase
Grant Funds for local museums managed on its
behalf by the V & A and Science Museums.

In 1996, as a result of the Government's
review of museum policy, the MGC was asked to
fulfil a number of additional functions. These
include: a review of the Area Museum Councils;
the implementation of a Designation Scheme
identifying those museums with outstanding collections; advising the Department for Culture,
Media and Sport on possible recognition of
smaller museums with important collections;
develop the Registration Scheme; publish guidance on the legal status of collections, advise
Government how to encourage greater collaboration between local authority and independent
museums; work with the BTA and British
Council regarding presentation of Britain's heritage and culture overseas; and develop support
for UK museum initiatives abroad.

Chairman: James Joll
Vice-Chairman: Prof Patrick Bateson ScD, FRS
Members: Sir J Baer, The Baroness Brigstocke,
  Prof Ronald Buchanan, OBE,
  Viscountess Cobham, Mark Fisher, MP,
  R Foster, Loyd Grossman,
  Adm Sir John Kerr, GCB, DL,
  Alan Warhurst, CBE, Catherine Wilson, OBE,
  Robert Hiscox, Mrs Rosemary Butler, AM,
  Dr Ian McKenzie Smith, OBE
Director: Timothy Mason

National Association of Local Councils

109 Great Russell Street,
London WC1B 3LD
020 7637 1865 Fax: 020 7436 7451
The Association, founded in 1947, is the representative body for town, parish and community councils in England and Wales. Its role is to promote the interests and privileges of member councils; to advise and assist them to perform their duties; to develop the social, cultural, economic and recreational life of the areas they serve; and to promote good local government at community level.

Chairman: Tony Hayward, OBE
Vice Chairman: Mrs Irene Chatfield
Chief Executive: John Findlay
Solicitor and Deputy Chief Executive:
  Rosemary Lansdowne, BA(Hons)
Senior Solicitor: Tola Amodu, LLB, MA Cantab
Financial Officer/Accountant: Stephen Walker
Policy Officer: Sarah Thomas, BA
Legal Executive: Ian Mark

National Audit Office

157–197 Buckingham Palace Road,
Victoria, London SW1W 9SP
020 7798 7000 Press 020 7798 7400
Fax: 020 7828 3774
E-mail: nao@gtnet.gov.uk
Website: www.open.gov.uk/nao/home.htm

22 Melville Street, Edinburgh EH3 7NS
0131-244 2736 *Fax:* 0131-244 2721
E-mail: edin.nao@gtnet.gov.uk

Audit House, 23–24 Park Place,
Cardiff CF1 3BA
029 2037 8661 Fax: 029 2038 8415
E-mail: cardiff.nao@gtnet.gov.uk
The National Audit Office (NAO) came into existence under the National Audit Act 1983 to replace and continue the work of the former Exchequer and Audit Department. The act reinforced the Office's total financial and operational independence from the government and brought its head, the Comptroller and Auditor-General, into a closer relationship with Parliament as an officer of the House of Commons.

The NAO provides independent information, advice and assurance to Parliament and about all aspects of the financial operations of government departments and many other bodies receiving public funds. It does this by examining and cer-

tifying the accounts of these organisations and by regularly publishing reports to Parliament of the results of its value for money investigations of economy, efficiency and effectiveness with which public resources have been used. The NAO is also the auditor by agreement of the accounts of certain international and other organisations. In addition, the Office authorises the issue of public funds to government departments.

Comptroller and Auditor-General:
  Sir John Bourn, KCB
Private Secretary: Mark Davies
Deputy Comptroller and Auditor-General:
  R N Le Marechal
Assistant Auditors-General: T Burr, J Colman,
  L H Hughes, CB, J Marshall, C Mawhood,
  M C Pfleger, M Sinclair
Directors: Mrs C Allen, Miss J Angus,
  J Ashcroft, T Banfield, Mrs G Body,
  A Burchell, P Cannon, J Cavanagh, D Clarke,
  M Daynes, S Doughty, R J Eales, A Fiander,
  R Frith, N Gale, F Grogan, Mrs A Hands,
  K Hawkeswell, Jeff Jones, Joe Jones,
  Ms W Kenway-Smith, Mrs P Leahy,
  R Maggs, G Miller, J McEwen, R Parker,
  J M Pearce, Ms M Radford, J Rickleton,
  M Reeves, A Roberts, J Robertson, B Skeen,
  N Sloan, Mrs P Smith, I Summers, R Swan,
  J Thorpe, Miss J Wheeler, M Whitehouse,
  D Woodward, P Woodward
Press Officer: H Everton

National Biological Standards Board

(NATIONAL INSTITUTE FOR BIOLOGICAL STANDARDS AND CONTROL) (NIBSC)

Blanche Lane, South Mimms,
Potters Bar, Hertfordshire EN6 3QG
01707 654753 *Fax:* 01707 646730
E-mail: enquiries@nibsc.ac.uk
Website: www.nibsc.ac.uk
The National Biological Standards Board, under the Biological Standards Act 1975, is responsible on behalf of the Health Ministers of the United Kingdom for the provision of biological standards, reference preparations and reagents, and for functions related to the control of biological substances used in human medicine. The Board executes its functions through management of the National Institute for Biological Standards and Control, which provides the scientific facilities and expertise for discharging the Board's responsibilities.

Chairman: N J B Evans, CB, MA
Director: G C Schild, CBE, DSC, FIBiol,
    FRCPath, HonMRCP
Secretary: R A Stewart, BSc, PhD

National Centre for Volunteering

Regent's Wharf, 8 All Saints Street,
London N1 9RL
020 7520 8900 Fax: 020 7520 8910
E-mail: volunteering@thecentre.org.uk
Website: www.volunteering.org.uk
Chair: John Shaw
Chief Executive: Christopher Spence
Head of Policy: Judith Hanna

National Consumer Council

20 Grosvenor Gardens,
London SW1W 0DH
020 7730 3469 Fax: 020 7730 0191
E-mail: info@ncc.org.uk
Website: www.ncc.org.uk
Funded by government to give a vigorous, independent voice to consumers in the UK. The Council's research and campaigns on behalf of consumers are largely targeted at decision makers in central and local government, business, public utilities and professions. The NCC has a particular responsibility to represent disadvantaged consumers.

Chairman: David Hatch, CBE, JP
Vice-Chairman: Deirdre Hutton, CBE
Director: Anna Bradley

National Crime Squad

PO Box 2500, London SW1V 2WF
020 7238 2500
The National Crime Squad was formed on 1 April 1998 by statute. Working in partnership with other law enforcement and intelligence agencies the National Crime Squad's mission is to provide leadership and expertise to combat serious and organised crime nationally and internationally. The squad is made up of 1450 police officers, the majority seconded from forces, assisted by 300 support staff.

Director-General: Roy Penrose, OBE, QPM
Deputy Director-General:
    Bob Packham, QPM, BSc
Director of Support Services:
    Trevor Nash, MA, DMS, FIMgt

Assistant Chief Constables:
    D Milburn, MA(Oxon) (East Area),
    D A Wakenshaw, BSc (North Area),
    R C Aldridge, LLB(Hons), MPhil(Cantab)
    (West Area)

National Federation of Consumer Groups

527 Leeds Road, Scholes, Leeds LS15 4DA
Tel/Fax: 0113-264 8341
The National Federation of Consumer Groups brings together local voluntary Consumer Groups to investigate and campaign on consumer topics. It supports and promotes these local groups and provides them with an avenue to government departments and to manufacturers and retailers.

Honorary Secretary: Mrs Stella Walsh

National Galleries of Scotland

National Gallery, The Mound,
Edinburgh EH2 2EL
0131-624 6200
Under the National Galleries of Scotland Act 1906, a Board of Trustees was established for the purpose of managing the National Galleries of Scotland and for such other purposes connected with the promotion of the Fine Arts in Scotland as might be prescribed by the First Minister for Scotland. The Board consists of eleven members appointed by the First Minister for Scotland. Each member holds office for five years from the date of his appointment and is eligible for reappointment on the expiry of that period.

Chairman of the Board of Trustees: Lady Airlie
Director:
    T Clifford, BA, AMA, FRSA, FSA(Scot)
Head of Press and Information:
    Anne-Marie Wagener
Head of Education: Michael Cassin, BA

National Gallery

Trafalgar Square, London WC2N 5DN
020 7747 2885 *(Information)*
Fax: 020 7747 2423 (Information)
E-mail: information@ng-london.org.uk
Website: www.nationalgallery.org.uk
The National Gallery was instituted in 1824 when the government bought the collection of paintings belonging to John Julius Angerstein. Subsequent gifts and acquisitions have formed a

comprehensive collection of over 2,300 Western European paintings dating from *c.* 1260 to 1900. The Sainsbury Wing opened in 1991 and holds the Early Renaissance Collection as well as temporary exhibition galleries, the Micro Gallery computer information room and other facilities.

The Gallery holds a constantly changing programme of exhibitions. Major loan exhibitions are held in the Sainsbury Wing and others usually highlight certain aspects of the Collection. The Education Department organizes daily lectures as well as a variety of events for children and adult study programmes.

Chairman of Trustees: Philip Hughes
Director: Neil MacGregor
Senior Curator: David Jaffé
Keeper: Dr Nicholas Penny
Curators: Dr Dillian Gordon, Dr Susan Foister, Dr Humphrey Wine, Dr Gabriele Finaldi, Christopher Riopelle, Xavier Bray, Lorne Campbell, Carol Plazzotta, Axel Rüger, Sarah Herring
Head of Exhibitions and Display:
  Michael Wilson
Head of Education: Kathleen Adler
Director of Administration: John MacAuslan
Head of Building: Peter Fotheringham
Head of Press and PR: Jean Liddiard
Chief Conservator: Martin Wyld
Head of Scientific: Dr Ashok Roy
Managing Director, NGCo: Geoffrey Matthews
Head of Design: Herb Gillman
Head of Development: Colin McKenzie
Head of Finance: Andrew Robson
Head of Framing: John England
Head of Security: Jon Campbell
Head of Library: Elspeth Hector
Head of Personnel: Margaret Pegler
Head of Photographic: Sara Hattrick
Registrar: Rosalie Cass
Head of Information: Miranda Carroll
Head of Multimedia: Julian Blom
Front of House Manager: Martin Wyatt

National House-Building Council

Buildmark House, Chiltern Avenue
Amersham, Buckinghamshire HP6 5AP
01494 434477 *Fax:* 01494 735201
E-mail: dhknight@nhbc.co.uk

NHBC is the standard setting and independent regulatory body for the UK house-building industry and has 18,000 house builders on its register and over 1.7 million homes under its warranty and insurance cover. It has enjoyed 60 years at the heart of the house-building industry and is a highly respected authority on housing construction and home buyer protection.

NHBC sets the standards for home building, monitors homes built to those standards and then provides 10 year cover on around 90 per cent of new homes built each year in the UK. Independent actuaries have confirmed that housing defects are now less than half what they otherwise would have been without NHBC's insistence on raising standards.

Independent of government, the Governing Council of NHBC represents all those interested in improving the standard of new home construction.

Public Affairs Manager:
  Derek Hamilton-Knight

National Library of Scotland

George IV Bridge,
Edinburgh EH1 1EW
0131-226 4531 *Fax:* 0131-622 4803
E-mail: enquiries@nls.uk
Website: www.nls.uk

The Library, which was founded as the Advocates' Library in the early 1680s, became the National Library of Scotland by Act of Parliament in 1925. It is one of the Copyright Libraries, entitled to claim works published in the United Kingdom and Ireland, and it also buys modern foreign literature extensively. The Library's collections of printed books, manuscripts and maps, augmented by purchase and gift, are very large, and it has an unrivalled Scottish collection. The Reading Rooms are for research and reference which cannot conveniently be pursued elsewhere, but the Library also lends foreign and out-of-print British books for use within other libraries, and is the administrative centre for interlibrary lending in Scotland.

Chairman of the Board of Trustees:
  The Rt Hon the Earl of Crawford and Balcarres, KT
Librarian and Secretary to the Trustees:
  I D McGowan, BA
Secretary of the Library: M C Graham, MA

National Library of Wales

Penglais, Aberystwyth, Ceredigion,
Wales SY23 3BU
01970 632800 *Fax:* 01970 615709
E-mail: holi@llgc.org.uk
Website: www.llgc.org.uk

Founded by Royal Charter, 1907, and maintained by annual grant from the National Assembly for Wales. It is one of the six libraries entitled to most privileges under the Copyright Act. It contains about 4,000,000 printed books, 30,000 manuscripts, 3,500,000 deeds and documents, numerous maps, prints and drawings, and audio-visual material. The National Library specializes in manuscripts and books relating to Wales and the Celtic peoples and is the repository for pre-1858 Welsh probate records. It is approved by the Master of the Rolls as a repository for manorial records and tithe documents and by the Lord Chancellor for certain legal records. The Readers' room is open on weekdays 9.30 a.m. to 6 p.m. (Saturdays 5 p.m.); closed on Sundays, Bank Holidays and 1st week of October. Admission by Reader's Ticket to Reading Rooms. Open admission to Exhibitions.

Librarian:
    A M W Green, MA, DipLib, ALA
Director of Administration and Technical
    Services:
    M W Mainwaring, MA, Solicitor MIMgt
Keeper of Printed Books: W R M Griffiths, MA,
    MLitt, PhD, DipLib, ALA
Keeper of Manuscripts and Records:
    Gwyn Jenkins, MA
Keeper of Pictures and Maps:
    D Huw Owen, BA, PhD, DAA

National Lottery Charities Board

St Vincent House, 16 Suffolk Street,
London SW1Y 4NL
020 7747 5300 Fax: 020 7747 5214
Enquiry Line: 020 7747 5299
Application Line: 0845 7919191
Minicom/Textphone: 020 7747 5347
E-mail: enquiries@nlcb.org.uk
Website: www.nlcb.org.uk

The National Lottery Charities Board is an independent grant making body set up by Parliament to distribute a portion of the twenty-eight pence from each Lottery ticket that goes to "good causes". The Board's main aim is to give grants to help meet the needs of those at greatest disadvantage in society and to improve the quality of life in the community. There are seventeen Board Members, including the Chair. Decisions on grants are made by the Board Members in five grant making Committees: England, Wales, Scotland, Northern Ireland and the UK as a whole.

For an application pack telephone 0845 791 9191.

Chair: Lady Diana Brittan
Chief Executive: Timothy Hornsby

National Lottery Commission

2 Monck Street, London SW1P 2BQ
020 7227 2000 Fax: 020 7227 2005

The National Lottery Commission, a non departmental public body set up under the National Lottery Act 1998, is responsible for the granting, varying and enforcing of Licences to run the National Lottery. The Commission's duties are to ensure that the National Lottery is run with all due propriety, that players are protected, and subject to these, to maximise the money raised for the Good Causes.

The National Lottery Commission took over the statutory duties of regulating the National Lottery, previously carried out by the Director-General of the Office of the National Lottery (OFLOT), on 1 April 1999. It is headed by five Commissioners, supported by a full time Chief Executive.

Commissioners: Hilary Blume, Brian Pomeroy
    (Chair), Dame Helena Shovelton,
    Harriet Spicer, Robin Squire
Chief Executive: Mark Harris
Director of Licensing: Kingsley Jones

National Museums and Galleries of Wales

Cathays Park, Cardiff CF10 3NP
029 2039 7951 Fax: 029 2037 3219
Website: www.nmgw.ac.uk

Incorporated by Royal Charter in 1907, the Museum's main institutions are the National Museum & Gallery Cardiff, Museum of Welsh Life St Fagans, Cardiff, Roman Legionary Museum Caerleon and the Welsh Slate Museum Llanberis, Gwynedd. There are in addition three smaller specialist national museums and galleries in Wales.

The National Museum & Gallery Cardiff houses the Welsh national collections of archaeology, art, botany, geology and zoology. The Museum has recently been extensively refurbished and developed to establish it as a national centre of excellence for the visual arts in Wales, while preserving its multi-disciplinary nature.

The Museum of Welsh Life's collections illustrate the life and culture of the Welsh nation from the 16th century onwards. Situated in a 100 acre parkland, it is one of Europe's foremost open air museums.

The Roman Legionary Museum Caerleon illustrates the history of Isca, one of the three principal military bases in Roman Britain.

The Welsh Slate Museum Llanberis, interprets the economic, social and cultural history of the quarrying communities of Wales.

The three other smaller museums are: Turner House Gallery Penarth, near Cardiff; Museum of the Welsh Woollen Industry Dre-fach Felindre, Dyfed, and the Segontium Roman Museum Caernarfon, Gwynedd.

President: M C T Prichard, CBE, DL
Vice-President: A Thomas
Treasurer: G Wyn Howells
Director: A Southall
Deputy Director and Assistant Director (Collections and Education): E Wiliam
Assistant Director (Public Affairs): C Thomas
Assistant Director (Exhibitions and Interpretation): I Fell
Assistant Director (Social and Industrial History) and Keeper, Museum of Welsh Life St Fagans: J Williams-Davies
Assistant Director (Arts and Sciences) and Keeper, National Museum & Gallery Cardiff: M Tooby

National Museums and Galleries on Merseyside

Liverpool Museum, William Brown Street, Liverpool L3 8EN
0151-207 0001 *Fax:* 0151-478 4321
E-mail: @nmgmdir1.demon.co.uk
Website: www.nmgm.org.uk

The Board of Trustees of the National Museums & Galleries on Merseyside administers the first National Museum to be established in an English provincial city. The Trustees are custodians of collections of national and international importance in art, history and science. It is substantially grant-aided by the Secretary of State for Culture, Media and Sport and is an exempt charity. The principal institutions administered by the Board are Liverpool Museum, the Walker Art Gallery, Merseyside Maritime Museum, HM Customs & Excise National Museum, Museum of Liverpool Life, the Lady Lever Art Gallery, the Conservation Centre, Sudley House and the Oratory. Fourth Triennial Report was published in November 1998.

Chairman of the Board of Trustees:
  D C McDonnell, FCA
Director: Dr R A Foster, DL, MA, FSA, FMA
Secretary to the Trustees: M A Harrison, FCIS
Keeper of Art Galleries: J Treuherz, MA, AMA
Keeper of Conservation:
  A Durham, MA (Cantab)
Keeper of Liverpool Museum:
  Loraine Knowles, BA, FMA
Keeper of Maritime Museum:
  M K Stammers, BA, FMA
Head of Central Services:
  A J F Archard, CIPFA
Head of Education: Caroline Rowley
General Manager (NMGM Enterprises Ltd):
  James Forrester

National Museums of Scotland

Chambers Street, Edinburgh EH1 1JF
0131-225 7534 *Fax:* 0131-220 4819
E-mail: rmos@nms.ac.uk
Website: www.nms.ac.uk
Website Feedback: feedback@nms.ac.uk

The National Museums of Scotland was established in 1985, with a Board of Trustees who have responsibility for many of Scotland's museum collections of national and international importance. The collections include decorative art, working life, science and technology, military history and geology and zoology. The trustees of NMS have a responsibility to add to, care for and preserve the collections, to ensure that research is undertaken on them, and to ensure that public access is provided to them through exhibition and education and other appropriate activities. NMS currently has six display sites open to the public, the Royal Museum and Museum of Scotland, both in Edinburgh, the Scottish Agricultural Museum at Ingliston in Midlothian, the Piping Centre in Glasgow, the Museum of Flight at East Fortune (East Lothian) and Shambellie House Museum of Costume at New Abbey (Dumfriesshire), together with a storage and conservation centre in Leith. The Scottish National War Museum re-opened to the public in March 2000 after a major renovation.

In addition to services at its permanent sites NMS has an active outreach policy based on partnerships with many museums and other organisations throughout Scotland and internationally. Outreach includes loans, fieldwork, touring exhibitions and increasingly the use of new technology to extend access to schools and other users.

Chairman:
Sir Robert Smith, CA, FCIBS, FSA(Scot)
Director:
Mark Jones, MA, FMA, FSA, FSA(Scot),
Hon Prof (Edinburgh)
Head of Public Affairs:
Miss Mary Bryden, MA, DipEd

National Portrait Gallery

St Martin's Place, London WC2H 0HE
020 7306 0055 Fax: 020 7306 0056
Website: www.npg.org.uk

The National Portrait Gallery was founded in 1856 with the aim of collecting the likenesses of famous British men and women. The display shows images of famous British faces from the Tudors to the present day, including paintings, sculpture, etchings, photographs and miniatures.

The Gallery holds special exhibitions throughout the year, along with a programme of musical and dramatic events and lectures for the general public.

Director: Charles Saumarez Smith, PhD
Senior Curator: Robin Gibson, BA
Curators: Catharine Macleod, MA (16th & 17th century), Jacob Simon, MA (18th century), Peter Funnell, DPhil (19th century), Honor Clerk, BA (20th century), Terence Pepper, LLB (Curator of Photographs)
Head of Documentation:
Robin Francis, BSc, MA, ALA
Head of Public Relations and Development:
Pim Baxter, MA
Head of Exhibitions and Collections Management: Kathleen Soriano, BA
Head of Education: John Cooper, MA
Head of Administration and Finance:
John Wykeham, PhD
Head of Retail and Publications:
Robert Carr-Archer

National Radiological Protection Board

Chilton, Didcot, Oxfordshire OX11 0RQ
01235 831600 *Fax:* 01235 833891
E-mail: nrpb@nrpb.org.uk
Website: www.nrpb.org.uk

The National Radiological Protection Board is an independent government body set up under the Radiological Protection Act 1970. The Board is the national point of authoritative reference for radiological protection.

Its functions are to advance the acquisition of knowledge about the protection of mankind from radiation hazards, by means of research and otherwise, and to provide information and advice to persons (including government departments) with responsibilities in the UK in relation to the protection from radiation hazards either of the community as a whole or particular sections of it. In 1974 the Board's functions were extended to include all electromagnetic radiations.

The Board advises the government on the acceptability to the UK of standards recommended or proposed by international bodies, and on their application. It is also responsible for specifying Emergency Reference Levels, for use following an accident at a nuclear installation.

Chairman:
Sir Walter Bodmer, PhD, FRCPath, FRS
Director: Prof R H Clarke
Board Members: Prof A D Baddeley, CBE, FRS, Mrs P M Castle, Prof K E Davies, CBE, Prof W Gelletly, OBE, Prof J M Harrington, CBE, Prof W R Lees, Prof R M MacKie, CBE, Prof J McEwen, Mr J C White, FCA
Secretary: Mr D B Talbot, FCCA
Deputy Director: Dr J W Stather
Divisional Heads: Dr J W Stather, Miss F A Fry

National Trust

36 Queen Anne's Gate,
London SW1H 9AS
020 7222 9251 Fax: 020 7222 5097
E-mail: lddpxb@smtp.ntrust.org.uk

The National Trust is a charity, founded in 1895 for the preservation of places of historic interest or natural beauty in England, Wales and Northern Ireland and their protection for the benefit of the nation. It is the largest conservation charity in the world with a membership of over 2.5 million.

The main objectives of the National Trust's work are preservation through ownership and conservation management of its wide variety of properties which include 244,000 hectares owned of open countryside, 565 miles of coastline, 280 historic buildings open to the public, nature reserves, gardens, archaeological sites, farms and villages.

The National Trust's constitution is laid down in the National Trust Acts 1907-71. Under the Acts the Trust is governed by a Council of 52, half of whom are elected by the membership whilst the other half are appointed from organisations relevant to the Trust's work.

President:
HM Queen Elizabeth The Queen Mother
Vice President: HRH The Prince of Wales
Chairman: Charles Nunneley
Director-General: Martin Drury
Deputy Director-General: Julian Prideaux
Director of Marketing and Communications:
Michael Taylor
Policy Liaison Officer: Patrick Begg

National Trust for Scotland

28 Charlotte Square, Edinburgh EH2 4ET
0131-243 9300 *Fax:* 0131-243 9301
E-mail: information@nts.org.uk
Website: www.nts.org.uk

The National Trust for Scotland was formed in 1931 to promote the permanent preservation of Scotland's heritage of architectural, historic and scenic treasures and to encourage public enjoyment of them. In its care are more than 100 properties covering some 185,000 acres and including castles and great houses, historic sites, gardens, islands, vernacular architecture, mountains, waterfalls, coastline and the birthplaces of some famous Scots. They attract almost two million visitors each year. NTS is a charity dependent on donations, legacies and the subscriptions of its 230,000 members.

Chairman: Prof J McC M Cunningham, CBE
(from May 2000 Prof Roger Wheater, OBE)
Director: Trevor A Croft

Natural Environment Research Council

Headquarters:
Polaris House, North Star Avenue,
Swindon SN2 1EU
01793 411500 *Fax:* 01793 411501
Website: www.nerc.ac.uk

The Natural Environment Research Council (NERC) was established by Royal Charter in 1965 under the Science and Technology Act with responsibility to encourage, plan and execute research in the physical and biological sciences that relate to man's natural environment and its resources.

The sciences supported by the Council include geology, geophysics and geochemistry; physical oceanography and marine ecology; hydrology and atmospheric sciences. Council also makes awards for postgraduate training, research grants and fellowships.

The Council employs directly about 3,000 people. Its budget this year is about £200m, of which about 80% is given as a grant from the Office of Science and Technology. The remaining income is mainly earned from research commissioned by industry, government departments, local authorities and overseas governments.

Chairman: James Smith, CBE, FEng, FRSE
Chief Executive: Prof John Lawton, CBE, FRS

CENTRAL ADMINISTRATION
NERC, Polaris House, North Star Avenue,
Swindon SN2 1EU
01793 411500 *Fax:* 01793 411501

RESEARCH INSTITUTES

BRITISH ANTARCTIC SURVEY
High Cross, Madingley Road,
Cambridge CB3 0ET
01223 221400
Website: www.nerc-bas.ac.uk
Director: Prof Chris Rapley

BRITISH GEOLOGICAL SURVEY
Kingsley Dunham Centre, Keyworth,
Nottingham NG12 5GG
0115-936 3100
Website: www.nerc-bgs.ac.uk
Director: Dr David Falvey

CENTRE FOR ECOLOGY AND HYDROLOGY
Website: www.mwnta.nmw.ac.uk/ceh
Director: Prof T M Roberts

Incorporating the following institutes:

INSTITUTE OF TERRESTRIAL ECOLOGY
Monks Wood, Abbots Ripton,
Huntingdon PE17 2LS
01487 773381

INSTITUTE OF FRESHWATER ECOLOGY
The Ferry House, Far Sawrey,
Ambleside, Cumbria LA22 0LP
015394 42468
Director: Prof A D Pickering

INSTITUTE OF HYDROLOGY
Maclean Building, Crowmarsh Gifford,
Wallingford, Oxon OX10 8BB
01491 838800
Director: Prof J Wallace

INSTITUTE OF VIROLOGY AND ENVIRONMENTAL
MICROBIOLOGY
Mansfield Road, Oxford OX1 3SR
01865 281630
Director: Prof P A Nuttall

CENTRE FOR COASTAL AND MARINE SCIENCE
Website: www.nerc.ac.uk/ccms
Director: Prof Jacqueline McGlade (based at
Plymouth Marine Laboratory)

Incorporating the following institutes:

PLYMOUTH MARINE LABORATORY
Prospect Place, Plymouth PL1 3DH
01752 633100
Director: Prof R F C Mantoura

PROUDMAN OCEANOGRAPHIC LABORATORY
Bidston, Birkenhead L43 7RA
0151-653 8633
Director: Dr Ed Hill

DUNSTAFFNAGE MARINE LABORATORY
PO Box 3, Oban, Argyll PA34 4AD
01631 562244
Director: Dr G Shimmield

SOUTHAMPTON OCEANOGRAPHY CENTRE
(A joint venture between NERC and the
University of Southampton)
Express Dock, Southampton SO14 3ZH
023 8059 6666
Website: www.soc.soton.ac.uk

Also based at Southampton Oceanography
Centre:

RESEARCH VESSEL SERVICES
Superintendent: Dr C W Fay

SEA MAMMAL RESEARCH UNIT
University of St Andrews,
Gatty Marine Laboratory,
St Andrews, Fife KY16 8LB
01334 462630
Director: Dr P Hammond

CENTRE FOR POPULATION BIOLOGY
Imperial College, Silwood Park
Ascot, Berkshire SL5 7PY
01344 294346
Director: Prof C Godfray

ENVIRONMENTAL SYSTEMS SCIENCE CENTRE
Harry Pitt Building,
Reading University, Whiteknights,
PO Box 238, Reading RG6 2AL
0118-931 8741
Director: Prof R Gurney

ATMOSPHERIC CHEMISTRY MODELLING SUPPORT
UNIT
University Chemical Laboratory
University of Cambridge
Lensfield Road, Cambridge CB2 1EP
01223 336473 *Fax:* 01223 336473
Director: Dr J A Pyle

CENTRE FOR GLOBAL ATMOSPHERIC MODELLING
Department of Meteorology
University of Reading
Earley Gate, Whiteknights,
Reading RG6 2BB
0118-931 8315 *Fax:* 0118-931 8316
Director: Prof A O'Neill

Natural History Museum

Cromwell Road, South Kensington,
London SW7 5BD
020 7942 5000
Website: www.nhm.ac.uk

The Natural History Museum began life as a
department of the British Museum in
Bloomsbury when the private collection of Sir
Hans Sloane, a wealthy physician, was sold to
the nation in 1753. The natural history collections grew so extensively during the 19th
century that they were moved in 1881 to a new
purpose built Museum in South Kensington. In
1963 the British Museum Act made The Natural
History Museum completely independent with
its own trustees.

Today the Museum is a complex and active
institution with a mission to maintain and
develop the national collections and use them to
promote the discovery, understanding, responsible use and enjoyment of the natural world.

As one of the UK's most popular museums it
attracted 1.859 million visitors in 1998/99 and is
world renowned for its exhibitions and educational resources. Adding to its popular galleries,
such as Dinosaurs and Ecology, in July 1998 the
Museum completed a massive earth science
exhibition complex entitled Earth Galleries. This
project, with the support of the Heritage Lottery
Fund, transformed the former Geological
Museum, and represented the biggest exhibition
development on site since 1881.

The Museum also plays an internationally significant role in the science of systematics – the naming, describing and classifying of organisms, fossils, rocks and minerals, and the study of their inter-relationships. The Museum's collections of more than 68 million specimens in the earth and life sciences lie at the heart of much of this work.

With more than 300 scientists working in conjunction with scientific institutions in more than 60 countries across the globe, the Museum uses its expertise to respond to the scientific needs of society both nationally and internationally. It does so through a range of activities, from providing identification services, consultancy on habitat impact assessment and environmental monitoring, to contributing to tackling world health problems and issues. Museum scientists publish hundreds of academic research papers every year and contribute to many other publications, including books produced by the Museum's own publishing unit.

The Walter Rothschild Zoological Museum at Tring has formed part of the Museum since 1938.

The Museum was the first UK museum to launch a website in 1994. The site is a content-rich resource, www.nhm.ac.uk.

Chairman of the Board of Trustees:
  Lord Oxburgh, KBE, FRS
Members: Ms Jana Bennett,
  Prof Michael Hassell, FRS,
  Prof Christopher Leaver, FRS, FRSE,
  Miss Judith Mayhew,
  Dr Anne McLaren, DBE, FRS, FRCOG,
  Sir Keith O'Nions, FRS, Lord Palumbo,
  Prof Linda Partridge, FRS, FRSE,
  Oliver Stocken, Sir Richard Sykes, FRS,
  Sir Crispin Tickell, GCMG, KCVO
Director: Dr N R Chalmers
Director of Science: Prof P Henderson
Heads of Department: David Thorpe (*Audit and Review*), Dr Richard Bateman (*Botany*), Ms Sharon Ament (*Development and Marketing*), Dr R Vane-Wright (*Entomology*), G Pellow (*Estates*), Dr G Clarke (*Exhibitions and Education*), Neil Greenwood (*Finance*), Dr R G Lester (*Library and Information Services*), Prof A Fleet (*Mineralogy*), Prof S Donovan (*Palaeontology*), Jane Rowe (*Human Resources*), (Vacant) (*Visitor Services*), Prof P Rainbow (*Zoology*)
Policy and Planning Co-ordinator:
  Paul Kirkman
Sub Department of Ornithology, Director Zoological Museum, Tring: Teresa Wild
  020 7942 6171

NHS Supplies Authority

Premier House, 60 Caversham Road, Reading, Berkshire RG1 7EB
0118-980 8600 *Fax:* 0118-980 8650

NHS Supplies' role is to enable the NHS to obtain the maximum possible benefit from the money it spends on the goods and services it requires for the delivery of health care, constantly seeking value for money, reliability, responsiveness and innovation.

Working within the NHS and with its suppliers, NHS Supplies aims to be the NHS' own centre of expertise, knowledge and excellence in matters of supply.

Chairman: David Hall, CBE, TD
Chief Executive: Terry Hunt, CBE
Director of Finance and IT: Richard Chantler
Director of Strategy: Roxanne Sutton
Director of Human Resources: Chris Uden
Managing Director, Purchasing: Eric Jackson
Managing Director, Wholesaling: Ian Bradshaw

Northern Ireland Advisory Committee on Telecommunications

22 Great Victoria Street, Belfast BT2 7QA
028 9024 4113 Fax: 028 9024 7024
E-mail: niact@acts.org.uk
Website: www.acts.org.uk

NIACT is an independent consumer body and aims to represent the opinions and needs of everyone in Northern Ireland who uses telecoms. It is responsible for handling complaints on telecoms issues from consumers in Northern Ireland.

Chairman: Courtenay Thompson, DL, BA, BBS
Secretary: John Stringer

Northern Ireland Audit Office

106 University Street, Belfast BT7 1EU
028 9025 1000 Fax: 028 9025 1051
E-mail: auditoffice@nics.gov.uk
Website: www.niauditoffice.gov.uk

The Northern Ireland Audit Office was created by the Audit (Northern Ireland) Order 1987 and replaced the former Exchequer and Audit Department on 1 April 1987. The head of the Office is the Comptroller and Auditor General for Northern Ireland who has responsibility for controlling receipts into and issues from the NI

Consolidated Fund and for the audit of the accounts of government departments and many public sector bodies in Northern Ireland. In addition he has statutory power to carry out examinations of the economy, efficiency and effectiveness in the use of resources by government departments and various other bodies in receipt of public funds. He reports direct to Parliament on the results of such audits and examinations.

Comptroller and Auditor General: J M Dowdall
Secretary: B H Poulter

Occupational Pensions Regulatory Authority

Invicta House, Trafalgar Place
Brighton BN1 4DW
01273 627600 *Fax:* 01273 627688
E-mail: helpdesk@opra.gov.uk
Website: www.opra.gov.uk

The Occupational Pensions Regulatory Authority (OPRA) was set up under the Pensions Act 1995 to regulate the operation of occupational pensions in the UK. OPRA enforces a wide range of duties placed on people who run occupational pensions schemes. The aim is to ensure that the interests of members of occupational pension schemes are properly protected.

Chairman: John Hayes, CBE
Chief Executive: Caroline Instance
Board Members: Ron Amy, OBE,
    John Bowman, Hugh Brown, Mike Jones,
    Harriet Maunsell, OBE, Joanne Segars,
    Sue Ward, Anne Wood

Office of Manpower Economics

Oxford House, 76 Oxford Street,
London W1N 9FD
020 7467 7244 Fax: 020 7467 7248
E-mail: ome.dti@dial.pipex.com

The Office of Manpower Economics, established in 1971, is an independent non-statutory organisation responsible for servicing independent review bodies which advise on the pay of various public sector groups. These are the:
– Review Body on Senior Salaries (SSRB);
– Armed Forces' Pay Review Body (AFPRB);
– Review Body on Doctors' and Dentists' Remuneration (DDRB);
– Review Body for Nursing Staff, Midwives, Health Visitors and Professions Allied to Medicine (NAPRB);

– School Teachers' Review Body (STRB).
The Office also provides services for the Pharmacists Review Panel and the Police Negotiating Board. It is also responsible for servicing ad hoc bodies of inquiry and for undertaking research into pay and associated matters as requested by Government.

Director: M J Horsman
Deputy Director: Graeme Charles

Oil and Pipelines Agency

35–38 Portman Square, London W1H OEU
020 7935 2585 Fax: 020 7935 3510

The Oil and Pipelines Agency is an executive non-departmental public body constituted under the Oil and Pipelines Act 1985. Its role is to manage, in a safe, efficient and effective manner, the Government Pipeline and Storage System on behalf of the Secretary of State for Defence.

Chairman (Part-time): Dr John D Hastie
Members (Part-time): John C Morgan,
    Paul W D Hatt
Secretary: John R Merrett

Department: Defence

Parliamentary Counsel Office

36 Whitehall, London SW1A 2AY
020 7210 6637 Fax: 020 7210 6632/0950

Parliamentary Counsel draft all Government Bills except commonform ones and those relating exclusively to Scotland. They also advise on all aspects of Parliamentary procedure in connection with such Bills and draft Government amendments to them as well as any motions (including financial resolutions) necessary to secure their introduction into, and passage through, Parliament.

First Parly Counsel: E G Caldwell, CB *(SCS)*
Parly Counsel: E G Bowman, CB *(SCS)*,
    G B Sellers, CB *(SCS)*,
    E R Sutherland, CB *(SCS)*,
    P F A Knowles, CB *(SCS)*,
    S C Laws, CB *(SCS)*, R S Parker, CB *(SCS)*,
    Miss C E Johnston *(SCS)*, P J Davies *(SCS)*,
    *J M Sellers *(SCS)*
Dep Parly Counsel: A J Hogarth *(SCS)*,
    †Dr H J Caldwell *(SCS)*, *D J Ramsay *(SCS)*,
    D J Cook *(SCS)*, D Greenberg *(SCS)*
Principal Asst Parly Counsel: R J Dormer *(SCS)*

Senr Assistants (SCS): Mrs E A F Gardiner,
†Miss C I H Dillon, Miss J M Piesse, Miss
B A Waplington, Mrs A M Bertlin, E J Stell,
†Mrs H Rogers, Miss L R Baines, D J Sewell,
D M Sprackling
Assts: Miss C N O'Riordan, *Miss E C White,
*Ms C D Wynter, *G J Lyne,
Mrs J C de Mounteney, Miss J Crawford,
N W Rendell, M J Hudson, F T Coleman,
D P Hall, Miss B Walsh,
Ms C M McLoughlin, A C Scott
*Law Commission
†Counsel at Inland Revenue

Parole Board for England and Wales

Abell House, John Islip Street
London SW1 4LH
020 7217 5800 Fax: 020 7217 5677

The Board was constituted under Section 59 of
The Criminal Justice Act 1967 and continued
under Section 32 of the Criminal Justice Act
1991. Its duty is to advise the Secretary of State
for the Home Department with respect to any
matter referred to it by him, which is connected
with the early release or recall of prisoners. Its
functions include giving directions concerning
the release on licence of prisoners serving discretionary life sentences and of certain prisoners
serving long term determinate sentences; and
making recommendations to the Secretary of
State concerning the early release on licence of
other prisoners, the conditions of parole and the
licences and the variation and cancellation of
such conditions, and the recall of long term and
life prisoners while on licence.

Chairman: Baroness Prashar, CBE
Vice-Chairman: The Hon Mr Justice Tucker
Members: K Appiah, Mrs A B C Barker, JP,
A Barrow, Dr C Berry, TD, FRCPsych,
Dr I Bronks, FRCPsych, D Brown,
Miss P Buller, Mrs I Butcher,
His Hon Judge Capstick, QC,
His Hon Judge Coltart,
His Hon Judge Connor, A Corless, CBE,
His Hon Judge J A Cotton, Mrs J Coward,
Dr S Davenport, MRCPsych, DPM, MB,
HBS, H Dillon, MBE, R Doven, JP,
Mrs R Draycott, OBE, JP, J Entwistle, DL,
Mrs D J Fawcett, JP, His Hon Judge Griffiths,
Dr E Gordon, MB, ChB, FRCPsych,
P Grattan, His Hon Judge Harris, QC,
Mrs D Hayle, JP, M Hennessey, Mrs L Hilton,
Her Hon Judge Hindley, QC, Mrs V Horman,

Miss S Hubbard,
Dr C C Hunter, MB, BS(Lond),
MRCS, LRCP, FRCPsych, M Hursey, JP,
Ms B M Kane,
Dr I Keitch, MB, ChB, MRCPsych,
Dr Z Khan, OBE, JP, Ms A King, Dr D Kohen,
Dr D D Kothari, BSc, MB,BS, MRCPsych,
His Hon Judge Lawrence,
Mrs W Lloyd, RMN, RGN, Mrs B Lorge,
Prof R D Mackay,
Dr H McClelland, MB, FRCP, FRCPsych,
His Hon Judge McNaught, Dr J MacKenzie,
His Hon Judge Maddison, Mrs L March, JP,
P Martin, R Mathers,
His Hon Judge K Matthewman, QC,
Dr D Mawson, FRCPsych, Mrs H Morgan,
Prof R Morgan, S Murphy,
Miss E Norton, OBE, Dr R B L Osborn,
P Palmer, G Park, CBE, E Parry, OBE,
Mrs S M Peach, OBE, JP, A Pembrooke,
His Hon Judge Petre, M Pirani,
Mrs J Pitchers, MBE, JP, M A Price-
Jones, LLB, His Hon Judge Pugsley,
Mrs P Rance, A Reeve, JP, Mrs S Reiter, JP,
Sir Samuel Roberts, Bt, R P Robson,
Ms A E Roy, T Russell, J Sadlik, JP,
Prof A Sanders, Mrs R Sargent, JP,
D Scott, BSc(Hons),
His Hon Mr Justice Scott Baker, Dr A Sheikh,
Dr G Shetty, MB, BS, MRCPsych,
D A G Smith, OBE, JP,
Dr D E M Speed, MB, ChB, MRCPsych
(Affiliate), J Staples, R S Statham,
His Hon Judge Stephens, QC, N Stone,
His Hon Judge Stroyan, QC,
Mrs Janet Summers, JP, D Swaysland,
Dr D Tamlyn, Mrs D Tolan,
Mrs W A Towers, JP, P J Trusler,
Mrs J Turnbull, JP, LLB, Mrs S Turquet, JP,
His Hon Judge Viljoen, Ms M Weatheritt,
Ms T West, C Wheeler, A Whiffin,
R Whitfield, P Wilshaw, Dr S Wood,
His Hon Judge Young
Chief Executive: Jon Casey

Parole Board for Scotland

Saughton House, Broomhouse Drive,
Edinburgh EH11 3XD
0131-244 8755 *Fax:* 0131-244 6974
Text: 0131-244 8755

The Board was set up in 1968. It advises and
directs Scottish Ministers on the release of prisoners under licence, on the conditions of such
licences, the revocation of such licences and
allied matters.

Chairman: Dr Jim J McManus
Vice-Chairmen: (Vacant)
Members: Dr John Baird, Mrs Megan Casserly,
   Mrs Linda Costelloe Baker,
   Dr John P Donnelly, Mrs Johan Findlay,
   Dr Judith Greenwood, OBE, Mrs Irene Guild,
   Hamish S Hyslop, Sheriff Brian A Lockhart,
   Hon Lord Maclean,
   Sheriff Principal J Maguire, James Milne,
   John Muirhead, Ms Morag Owens,
   The Rt Hon Lord Ross,
   Prof Lorraine Waterhouse, Dr Peter Young
Secretary: Hugh Boyle

Particle Physics and Astronomy Research Council

Polaris House, North Star Avenue,
Swindon SN2 1SZ
01793 442000 *Fax:* 01793 442002
E-mail: pr_pus@pparc.ac.uk

The Particle Physics and Astronomy Research
Council (PPARC) is the UK's strategic science
investment agency. It funds research, education
and public understanding in four areas of science
– particle physics, astronomy, cosmology and
space science.

PPARC is government funded and provides
research grants and studentships to scientists in
British universities, gives researchers access to
world-class facilities and funds the UK member-
ship of international bodies such as the European
Laboratory for Particle Physics, CERN, and the
European Space Agency. It also contributes
money for the UK telescopes overseas on La
Palma, Hawaii, Australia and in Chile, the UK
Astronomy Technology Centre at the Royal
Observatory, Edinburgh and the MERLIN/VLBI
National Facility.

PPARC's Public Understanding of Science
and Technology Awards Scheme provides funding to both small local projects and national initiatives aimed at improving public understanding
of its areas of science.

Chairman (part-time):
   Dr Robert Hawley, CBE, FRSE, FREng
Chief Executive: Prof Ian Halliday
Director for Science: Dr Ian Corbett
Head of Astronomy: Dr Paul Murdin
Head of Particle Physics: Dr Dave Morrell
Members: Tony Brenton (Foreign and
   Commonwealth Office), Prof Len Culhane,
   FRS (Mullard Space Science Laboratory),
   Prof Roger Davies (University of Durham),
   Prof Brian Eyre, CBE, FEng (University of

Oxford), Robert Foster (Department of Trade
and Industry), Prof James Hough, BSc, PhD
(University of Hertfordshire), Dr Sue Ion,
CEng, FIM, FEng (British Nuclear Fuels plc),
Prof John Pendry, FRS (Imperial College,
London), Prof Ian Ritchie, Prof Chris
Sachrajda, FRS (University of Southampton),
Prof David Saxon, FRSE (Glasgow
University)

UK ASTRONOMY TECHNOLOGY CENTRE
Blackford Hill, Edinburgh EH9 3HJ
0131-668 8100
Director: Dr Adrian Russell

THE ISAAC NEWTON GROUP OF TELESCOPES
Royal Greenwich Observatory
Apartado de Coreos, 321
Santa Cruz De La Palma, Tenerife 38780
Canary Islands
00 34 922 411048
Head: Dr Rene Rutten

JOINT ASTRONOMY CENTRE
660 N A'ohoku Place, University Park,
Hilo, Hawaii, 96720
00 1 808 961 3756
Head: Prof Ian Robson

Patients' Association

PO Box 935, Harrow, Middlesex HA1 3YJ
020 8423 9111 Fax: 020 8423 9119
Helpline: 020 8423 8999
E-mail: user@patients-association.com
Website: www.patients-association.com

The Patients' Association promotes patients'
interests nationally to government, professional
bodies and the media; gives advice to individuals
on patients' rights, complaints procedures and
sources of help. Publishes advice leaflets, a quarterly newsletter and produces a Health Address
Book of self-help groups.

General Manager: M Stone

Policy Studies Institute

100 Park Village East,
London NW1 3SR
020 7468 0468 Fax: 020 7388 0914
E-mail: postmaster@psi.org.uk
Website: www.psi.org.uk

The Policy Studies Institute (PSI), one of the
leading independent social and economic
research centres in the UK, contributing bench-
mark studies to the policy process since 1932.

PSI is a registered charity, run on a non-profit
basis, and is not associated with any political

party, pressure group or commercial interest. In January 1998 it became a wholly owned subsidiary of The University of Westminster.

PSI's mission is to inform policy by establishing the facts.

Director: Prof Jim Skea

Political Honours Scrutiny Committee

Ashley House, 2 Monck Street,
London SW1P 2BQ
020 7276 2770 Fax: 020 7276 2766
E-mail: amerifield@cabinet-office.x.gsi.gov.uk
Examines all recommendations for Honours made in respect of political services and reports to the Prime Minister.

Chairman: The Rt Hon The Lord Thomson of Monifieth, KT, DL
Members:
The Rt Hon The Baroness Dean of Thornton-le-Fylde, The Rt Hon The Lord Hurd of Westwell, CH, CBE
Secretary: A J Merifield, CB

Port of London Authority

Devon House, 58–60 St Katharine's Way,
London E1 9LB
020 7265 2656 Fax: 020 7265 2699
The PLA is a public trust constituted under the Port of London Act 1968 and Harbour Revision Orders of 1975 and 1992.

The PLA has statutory responsibilities for the conservancy and regulation of navigation of the 150 kms of the tidal River Thames and owns much of the river bed and foreshore to the high-water mark. It provides navigational services for ships using the Port including the maintenance of shipping channels and moorings, and navigational lights up-river of Sea Reach No 1 Buoy. The PLA is also the pilotage authority for the tidal Thames.

Other responsibilities include registration of craft, and licensing of watermen and lightermen and of river works extending into, over, or under the Thames below mean high water level. The PLA is actively engaged in the promotion of the Port of London.

Chairman: Sir Brian Shaw
Vice-Chairman: Juan Kelly, CBE

Board Members: S Cuthbert *(Chief Executive):*
C Jonas, CBE, P M Castle, R D Clegg,
The Baroness Wilcox, G P Ellis *(Executive),*
Capt J Burton-Hall, RD
Chief Harbour Master:
Rear Adm Bruce Richardson, CB
Secretary: G E Ennals

Post Office

148 Old Street, London EC1V 9HQ
020 7490 2888
Website: www.postoffice.co.uk
The Post Office is a Public Corporation established under the terms of the Post Office Act 1969. The Post Office Group comprises Royal Mail, which has responsibility for letter services; Parcelforce Worldwide, which operates parcel services; and Post Office Counters Ltd.

Under proposed legislation, The Post Office would become a plc, with the Government being the sole shareholder.

Chairman: Dr Neville Bain
Chief Executive: John Roberts, CBE
Group Managing Director Strategy and
Personnel: Jerry Cope
Group Managing Director Finance:
Richard Close
Secretary of The Post Office: Jonathan Evans
Group Corporate Affairs Director:
Alan Williams
Non Executive Members: Mike Kinski,
John Lloyd, Miles Templeman,
Rosemary Thorne

Department: Trade & Industry

Post Office Users' Council for Northern Ireland

22 Great Victoria Street, Belfast BT2 7PU
028 9024 4113 Fax: 028 9024 7024
The Post Office Users' Council for Northern Ireland is an independent statutory body established under the Post Office Act 1969. The Council represents the interests of users in Northern Ireland and is directly represented on the Post Office Users' National Council.

Chairman: Gerard Trainor, LLB, LLM, FCIArb
Secretary: John Stringer

Post Office Users' Council for Scotland

2 Greenside Lane, Edinburgh EH1 3AH
0131-244 5576 *Fax:* 0131-244 5696
E-mail: help@poucs.org
Website: www.poucs.org

The Post Office Users' Council for Scotland was established under the Post Office Act 1969 to represent the interests of users of Post Office monopoly services, and to ensure that customers have a voice in matters affecting them, such as the standard or quality of services provided.

Chairman: Dr T N A Begg
Secretary: R L L King

Post Office Users' Council for Wales

First Floor, Caradog House, St Andrews Place, Cardiff CF10 3BE
029 2037 4028
E-mail: enquiries@poucw.org.uk
Website: www.poucw.org.uk

A statutory consumer council monitoring the Post Office monopoly services for customers in Wales.

Chairman:
Eifion Pritchard, QPM, BA(Hons), FIMgt
Secretary: Gordon Mackenzie

Post Office Users' National Council

6 Hercules Road, London SE1 7DN
020 7928 9458 Fax: 020 7928 9076
E-mail: enquiry@pounc.org.uk

An independent statutory body funded by the Department of Trade and Industry, with members appointed by the Secretary of State, to represent users of Post Office services. POUNC takes up complaints, makes representations and examines proposals for tariff and service changes put forward by The Post Office.

Chairman: J P Hackney, FCA
Secretary: J Dodds

Press Complaints Commission

1 Salisbury Square, London EC4Y 8JB
020 7353 1248 Fax: 020 7353 8355
Help-line: 020 7353 3732
Scottish Helpline: 0131-220 6652
E-mail: pcc@pcc.org.uk
Website: www.pcc.org.uk

The Press Complaints Commission, a self-regulating body, was established by the newspaper and magazine industry in 1991 replacing the Press Council on the recommendation of the Committee on Privacy and Related Matters. It investigates complaints from the public about the contents and conduct of newspapers and magazines, enforcing a Code of Practice agreed by the press.

Chairman: The Rt Hon the Lord Wakeham, FCA
Director: Guy Black
Commission Members: Arzina Bhanji,
Sir Brian Cubborn, Paul Dacre, Phil Hall,
Alison Hastings, Dr Arthur Hearnden, OBE,
Dominic Lawson, John McGurk,
Prof Robert Pinker,
Viscountess Runciman, DBE,
Baroness Smith of Gilmorehill,
Malcolm Starbrook, Lord Tordoff,
Russell Twisk, The Rt Rev John Waine

Public Health Laboratory Service Board

61 Colindale Avenue, London NW9 5DF
020 8200 1295 Fax: 020 8200 8130
E-mail: (initial)(surname)@phls.nhs.uk
Website: www.phls.co.uk

The Public Health Laboratory Service is established under the National Health Service Act for England and Wales. It protects the population from infection through detection, diagnosis, surveillance, prevention and control of infections and communicable diseases. It achieves its aims through its network of microbiology laboratories, epidemiology and field investigation services, research and development, and education and training programmes. This requires collaboration with NHS and local authorities, universities and other institutions, central Government and world-wide initiatives on the sources and control of infections.

There is a network of laboratories based in NHS Trusts in England and Wales and organised into nine groups. At the heart of the network is the PHLS Headquarters at Colindale in North

London together with the Communicable Disease Surveillance Centre and the Central Public Health Laboratory. The network of grouped laboratories and Centres enables the PHLS to keep track of what infections are appearing where, to advise on remedial or preventative action and to provide clinical diagnostic services.

Director: Dr Diana Walford, BSc, MSc, MD, FRCP, FRCPath, FFPHM
Deputy Director:
Prof Brian I Duerden, BSc, MD, FRCPath
Deputy Director and Board Secretary:
K M Saunders, IPFA, MIMgt

Qualifications and Curriculum Authority

29 Bolton Street, London W1Y 7PD
020 7509 5555 Fax: 020 7509 6666
E-mail: info@qca.org.uk
Website: www.qca.org.uk/

The Qualifications and Curriculum Authority (QCA) is a public body responsible for promoting quality and coherence in education and training.

QCA's remit ranges from early years education to higher level vocational qualifications. It is responsible for ensuring that the curriculum and qualifications available to children, young people and adults are of a high quality, coherent and flexible.

As a body committed to enhancing quality in education, QCA aims to help raise national standards of achievement. This includes promoting greater access to, and participation in, education and training, enhancing lifelong learning opportunities, creating ways of giving credible national recognition for all learners and encouraging greater achievement.

Chairman: Sir William Stubbs
Deputy Chairman: Sir Dominic Cadbury
Chief Executive: Dr Nicholas Tate
Press Office Contact: Sue Stevens

Qualifications, Curriculum and Assessment Authority for Wales

Castle Buildings, Womanby Street,
Cardiff CF11 9SX
029 2037 5400 Fax: 029 2034 3612
E-mail: info@accac.org.uk
Website: www.accac.org.uk

The Qualifications, Curriculum and Assessment Authority for Wales (ACCAC) came into being on 1 October 1997 through the amalgamation of Curriculum and Assessment Authority for Wales (ACAC) and the Wales office of the National Council for Vocational Qualifications (NCVQ).

ACCAC is responsible in Wales for keeping under review all aspects of the curriculum and of statutory assessment arrangements for maintained schools, for external and vocational qualifications; for commissioning classroom materials to support the teaching of Welsh, other subjects through the medium of Welsh and Wales-specific aspects of the curriculum; and for advising the National Assembly for Wales as required.

Chairman: Brian Connolly
Deputy Chairman: Owen Rees, CB
Chief Executive: John V Williams

Quality Assurance Agency for Higher Education

Southgate House, Southgate Street,
Gloucester GL1 1UB
01452 557000 *Fax:* 01452 557070
E-mail: comms@qaa.ac.uk

The QAA was established in 1997 to provide a unified quality assurance service for higher education institutions throughout the UK. It succeeded to the functions of the former Higher Education Quality Council and to those of the Quality Assessment Divisions of the Higher Education Funding Councils for England and Wales.

The mission of the Agency is to promote public confidence that quality of provision and standards of awards in higher education are being safeguarded and enhanced. The Agency conducts programmes of review of performance of universities and colleges resulting in published reports on the quality and standards of academic programmes and the overall academic management of institutions.

The Agency advises government on the grant of degree awarding powers and university title, promulgates codes of practice and works with higher education institutions to promote and support continuous improvement in the quality and standards of provision; and to develop and manage the framework of higher education qualifications.

Chairman: Christopher Kenyon
Chief Executive: John Randall
Director of Programme Review: Peter Milton

Director of Institutional Review: Peter Williams
Director of Development: Julie Swan
Director of Administration and Company Secretary: Stuart Bushell

Radio Authority

Holbrook House, 14 Great Queen Street, London WC2B 5DG
020 7430 2724 Fax: *020 7405 7062*
Website: www.radioauthority.org.uk

The Radio Authority officially began its regulatory and licensing role on 1 January 1991, when the Broadcasting Act 1990 came into force. It plans frequencies, awards licences with a view to broadening listener-choice, enforces ownership rules and regulates radio programming and advertising. It also plays an active role in the discussion and formulation of policies which affect the independent radio industry and its listeners.

Chairman: Sir Peter Gibbings
Deputy Chairman: Michael Moriarty, CB
Members: Helen Tennant, Feargal Sharkey,
    Sheila Hewitt, David Witherow, Sara Nathan
Chief Executive: Tony Stoller
Deputy Chief Executive and Head of Development: David Vick
Head of Programming and Advertising: Martin Campbell
Head of Engineering: Mark Thomas
Head of Finance: Neil Romain
Secretary to the Authority and Head of Legal Services: Eve Salomon

Rail Users' Consultative Committee for Wales

St David's House, Wood Street, Cardiff CF1 1ES
029 2022 7247 Fax: *029 2022 3992*

A statutory body dealing with issues affecting rail users in Wales. It has the legal right to make recommendations for improvements.

Chairman: Charles A Hogg, MBE
Secretary: Clive G Williams

Regional Development Agencies

Regional Development Agencies in the 8 English regions outside London began work on 1 April 1999. They are the lead bodies at the regional level for co-ordinating inward investment, raising people's skills, improving the competitiveness of business and social and physical regeneration. The regional activities of English Partnerships transferred to the appropriate RDA on that date together with the Government Offices for the Regions' work on the Single Regeneration Budget and some of the responsibilities of the Rural Development Commission (RDC). The remainder of the RDC merged with the Countryside Commission to form the Countryside Agency. The activities of the Commission for the New Towns have merged with the national activities of English Partnerships.

EAST MIDLANDS
East Midlands Development Agency, Apex Court, City Link, Nottingham NG2 4LA
0115-988 8300
Website: www.emda.org.uk
Chairman: Derek Mapp
Chief Executive: Martin Briggs

EASTERN REGION
East of England Development Agency, Compass House, Chivers Way, Histon, Cambridge CB4 9ZR
01223 713900 Fax: 01223 713940
Website: www.eeda.org.uk
Chairman: Vincent Watts
Chief Executive: Bill Samuel

NORTH EAST
One North East, Great North House, Sandyford Road, Newcastle upon Tyne NE1 8ND
0191-261 2000 Fax: 0191-201 2021
Website: www.onenortheast.co.uk
Chairman: Dr John Bridge
Chief Executive: Michael Collier

NORTH WEST
North West Development Agency, New Town House, Buttermarket Street, Warrington WA1 2LF
01925 644734 Fax: 01925 644671
Website: www.nwda.co.uk
Chairman: Lord Thomas of Macclesfield, CBE
Chief Executive: Mike Shields

SOUTH EAST
South East of England Development Agency (SEEDA), SEEDA Headquarters, Cross Lanes, Guildford GU1 1YA
01483 484226 Fax: 01483 484247
Website: www.seeda.co.uk
Chairman: Allan Willett
Chief Executive: Anthony Dunnett

SOUTH WEST
South West of England Regional Development Agency,
Sterling House, Dix's Field, Exeter EX1 1QA
01392 214747 *Fax:* 01392 214848
Website: www.southwestengland.co.uk
Chairman: Sir Michael Lickiss
Chief Executive: Jill Barrow

WEST MIDLANDS
Advantage West Midlands,
2 Priestley Wharf, Holt Street,
Aston Science Park, Birmingham B7 4BZ
0121-380 3500 *Fax:* 0121-380 3501
Website: www.advantage-westmidlands.co.uk
Chairman: Alex Stephenson
Chief Executive: Anthony Cassidy

YORKSHIRE AND THE HUMBER
Yorkshire Forward,
Westgate House, 100 Wellington Street,
Leeds LS1 4LT
0113-243 9222 *Fax:* 0113-243 1088
Website: www.yorkshire-forward.com
Chairman: Graham Hall
Chief Executive: Martin Havenhand

Registrar of Political Parties

Companies House, Crown Way,
Cardiff CF14 3UZ
029 2038 0380 Fax: 029 2038 0149
E-mail: rppuser@companieshouse.gov.uk
Website: www.party-register.gov.uk

The function is to create, maintain and provide access to a register of political parties as required by the Registration of Political Parties Act, 1998. The Registrar is accountable to the Home Office.

Registrar: John Holden *(SCS)*

Royal Botanic Garden Edinburgh

20A Inverleith Row, Edinburgh EH3 5LR
Enquiries: 0131-552 7171

The Garden, founded in 1670, and an integral part of the Scottish Office from 1969, was established on April 1, 1986 as a corporate body, under the control of trustees in terms of the National Heritage (Scotland) Act 1985.

In addition to the main activities at Inverleith, Edinburgh there are three specialist gardens at Younger Botanic Garden Benmore near Dunoon, Logan Botanic Garden near Stranraer and Dawyck Botanic Garden near Peebles. The main functions of the Garden are: scientific research on the classification, biology, ecology and conservation of plants; the maintenance of a living collection of over 17,000 species for research and the conservation of endangered species which is also displayed for the enjoyment and education of the public; the curation of the herbarium collection of preserved plants; the provision of education including post-graduate and under-graduate training, public education, work with schools and the training of horticultural students.

Chairman of the Board of Trustees:
    Dr Paul A Nicholson
Regius Keeper: Prof Stephen Blackmore
Acting Director and General Manager:
    Dr Colin Will
Head of Science: Dr Richard Bateman
Head of Horticulture: John Main
Development and Communications Director:
    David Wood
Development Manager: Elaine Carmichael

Royal Botanic Gardens, Kew

Richmond, Surrey TW9 3AB
020 8332 5000 Fax: 020 8332 5197
E-mail: info@rbgkew.org.uk

The Royal Botanic Gardens, Kew, which also includes the estate of Wakehurst Place at Ardingly in West Sussex, was transferred from the Ministry of Agriculture, Fisheries and Food on April 1, 1984 to a Board of Trustees under the provisions of the National Heritage Act 1983.

Kew is an international centre for the study, classification and identification of plants and fungi, and plays a world role in conservation and the utilisation of plants for the benefit of mankind. In addition many of the properties and collections are open for the enjoyment and interest of visitors.

Chairman of the Board of Trustees:
    The Viscount Blakenham
Director: Prof Peter Crane, FRS
Deputy Director and Director of Operations:
    John J Lavin

Royal Commission for the Exhibition of 1851

Sherfield Building, Imperial College,
London SW7 2AZ
020 7594 8790 Fax: 020 7594 8794
E-mail: royalcom1851@ic.ac.uk
Website: www.royalcommission1851.org.uk

Incorporated by Supplemental Charter as a permanent Commission after winding up the affairs of the Great Exhibition of 1851. Under the terms of its Charter the Commission is enjoined to "increase the means of industrial education, and extend the influence of science and art upon productive industry" by means of funds deriving from the surplus left over from the Great Exhibition.

Approximately £1m pa is dispensed as educational and other grants.

President of the Royal Commission: HRH the
    Duke of Edinburgh, KG, KT, OM, GBE, AC,
    QSO
Chairman, Board of Management:
    Sir Denis Rooke, OM, CBE, FRS, FREng
Secretary to Commissioners:
    J P W Middleton, CB

Royal Commission on Historical Manuscripts

Quality House, Quality Court,
Chancery Lane, London WC2A 1HP
020 7242 1198 Fax: 020 7831 3550
E-mail: nra@hmc.gov.uk
Website: www.hmc.gov.uk

The Commission, set up in 1869, is the United Kingdom's central investigatory and advisory body on the care and use of historical manuscripts other than the Public Records. It collects and disseminates information about the sources of British history, and maintains the National Register of Archives which contains over 42,000 lists of manuscripts and may be consulted in the search room. The Commission offers independent advice to ministers and central government departments on national policies affecting archives; to grant-awarding bodies on applications for support towards the purchase, conservation and cataloguing of manuscripts; to local government, the universities and other custodians and to private and corporate owners of historical manuscripts on aspects of their storage and use. Its publications have included over 250 texts, calendars and guides to sources for British history, as well as an *Annual Review*, periodic

Reports to the Crown, and a directory of *Record repositories in Great Britain.*

Chairman of the Commissioners:
    The Rt Hon the Lord Bingham of Cornhill
Secretary: C J Kitching, PhD, FSA

Royal Commission on the Ancient and Historical Monuments of Scotland

John Sinclair House, 16 Bernard Terrace,
Edinburgh, EH8 9NX
0131-662 1456 *Fax:* 0131-662 1477/1499
Website: www.rcahms.gov.uk

RCAHMS was appointed in 1908 to make an inventory of the Ancient and Historical Monuments of Scotland and to specify those that seem most worthy of preservation. It also has a responsibility to record monuments threatened with destruction, including a statutory duty to record historic buildings for which Listed Building Consent for demolition has been granted. The National Monuments Record of Scotland, curated by the RCAHMS, contains an extensive collection of pictorial and documentary material relating to Scottish ancient monuments and historic buildings and is open daily for public reference. RCAHMS is also responsible for the supply of archaeological information to the Ordnance Survey for mapping purposes.

Publications include surveys of ancient and historical monuments, lists of archaeological sites and monuments, catalogues of aerial photographs.

Chairman:
    Sir William Fraser, GCB, MA, LLD, FRSE
Secretary: R J Mercer, MA, FSA, FRSE, MIFA

Royal Commission on the Ancient and Historical Monuments of Wales

Crown Building, Plas Crug, Aberystwyth,
Dyfed SY23 1NJ
01970 621200 *Fax:* 01970 621246
E-mail: admin.rcahmw@rcahmw.org.uk
Website: www.rcahmw.org.uk

The Royal Commission was established in 1908 to make an inventory of the ancient and historical monuments of Wales and Monmouthshire. It is currently empowered by a Royal Warrant of 1992 to survey, record, publish and maintain a database of ancient and historical and maritime sites and structures, and landscapes in Wales. It is responsible for the National Monuments Record of Wales which is open daily for public reference, for the supply of archaeological information to the Ordnance Survey for mapping purposes, for the co-ordination of archaeological aerial photography in Wales, and for the sponsorship of the regional Sites and Monuments Records.

Chairman:
Prof R A Griffiths, PhD, DLitt, FRHistS
Commissioners: D Gruffydd Jones, BA, FRSA,
Mrs A Nicol, MA, BLitt, FRHistS,
Prof P Sims-Williams, PhD, FBA,
Prof G J Wainwright, MBE, PhD, FSA,
E Wiliam, PhD, FSA
Secretary: P R White, BA, FSA

Royal Fine Art Commission for Scotland

Bakehouse Close, 146 Canongate,
Edinburgh EH8 8DD
0131-556 6699 *Fax:* 0131-556 6633
E-mail: rfacscot@gtnet.gov.uk

The Commission, established in 1927, advises government on the visual impact and quality of design of construction projects. Major buildings of different types, bridges, roads, squares and other open spaces may all constitute examples of the Commission's cases. The sizes of the projects vary from a group of power stations in its landscape setting to a detail such as a street lamp in a particularly sensitive, historic place.

The Commission reports its views to Ministers and local authorities and may recommend that planning applications be called in by the Scottish Ministers for their determination. It may visit sites, invite the production of papers, and call people before it to give explanations. It publicises its work in various ways including exhibitions and publishes Annual Reports to HM the Queen through Parliament. It is important to note that although the government finances it the Commission remains totally independent and gives its opinions impartially.

Chairman: The Rt Hon the Lord Cameron of
Lochbroom, MA, LLB, FRSE, Hon FRIAS
Secretary: Charles Prosser, DFA, DAEd, FRSA,
Hon. FRIAS

Royal Warrant Holders Association

No 1 Buckingham Place, London SW1E 6HR
020 7828 2268 Fax: 020 7828 1668
E-mail: warrants@rwha.co.uk

The Royal Warrant Holders Association which was founded in 1840 and granted a Royal Charter in 1907, has three main functions:

(a) In accordance with its Royal Charter of Incorporation and the authority delegated to it by the Lord Chamberlain, to take such legal action as may be necessary for the protection of the Royal Arms under the Trade Marks Act, 1938.

(b) To promote the interests of Royal Warrant Holding firms generally.

(c) To act as an authorised channel of communication between Royal Warrant Holding firms and the Royal Household on all matters relating to the Royal Warrant of Appointment.

President: Roger Mitchell
Vice-President: Michael Skinner
Secretary: Colonel Christopher Pickup, OBE
Assistant Secretary: Mrs Philippa Dutton

Sainsbury Centre for Mental Health

134–138 Borough High Street, London SE1 1LB
020 7403 8790 Fax: 020 7403 9482
Website: www.sainsburycentre.org.uk

The Sainsbury Centre for Mental Health is the leading policy and practice development centre for mental health services in the UK.

The Sainsbury Centre aims to improve the quality of life for people with severe mental health problems by enabling the development of excellent mental health services which are valued by users, carers and professionals. The centre seeks to achieve this by influencing policy and practice through a co-ordinated programme of research and evaluation, communications and development.

Director: Matt Muijen

Science Museum

Exhibition Road, South Kensington,
London SW7 2DD
020 7942 4000 Fax: 020 7942 4447
Website: www.nmsi.co.uk

As the largest museum of its kind in the world, the Science Museum houses over 200,000 different exhibits, covering almost every imaginable sector of science, technology, industry and medicine.

The Museum dates back to Prince Albert's Great Exhibition of 1851 and its aim is to promote the public's understanding of historical and contemporary science. It has over 45 different galleries, spread over seven floors, holding exhibits that are among the finest in the world, recording the emergence of modern scientific and industrial man. Many of the Museum's exhibits are interactive, allowing visitors to explore and discover science and technology for themselves.

The Science Museum receives more visits from educational groups than any other place in the UK, and is widely recognised as a centre for scholarship and expertise. Patrons of its Corporate Partnership scheme include BT, Glaxo Wellcome and SmithKline Beecham, while Benefactors include McLaren International and BG plc.

The Science Museum in London has two sister museums: the National Museum of Photography, Film & Television in Bradford, and the National Railway Museum in York. In total these three Museums receive over 2.53 million visitors each year, with the Science Museum in London accounting for approximately 1.53 million.

Chairman of the Trustees: Sir Peter Williams, CBE, MA, PhD, FEng
Trustees: HRH The Duke of Kent, KG, GCMG, GCVO, ADC, Dr Mary Archer, MA(Oxon), MA(Cantab), PhD(Lond) HonDSc, CCHEM, FRSC, Prof Ann Dowling, FREng, FIMechE, FRAeS, Greg Dyke, Prof Susan Greenfield, MA, DPhil, Dsc, Dr Anne Grocock, MA, Mrs Anita Higham, OBE, BA, LèsL, MEd, Mrs Joanna Kennedy, OBE, MA, HonDSc, FEng, FICE, Dr Nathan Myhrvold, Dr Bridget M Ogilvie, DBE, FIBiol, Lord Puttnam, CBE, LLD, DLitt, Sir Michael Quinlan, GCB, David E Rayner, CBE, Prof Michael Richards, MA, MD, FRCP, Martin G Smith, Sir Christopher Wates, FCA
Director: Sir Neil Cossons, OBE
Assistant Directors: Prof J R Durant (*Assistant Director, Wellcome Wing Project Director and Head of Science Communication Division*), C M Pemberton (*Assistant Director and Head of Public Affairs*), D Swade (*Assistant Director and Head of Collections Division*), A Scott (*Head of the National Railway Museum, York*), A Nevill (*Head of the National Museum of Photography, Film & Television, Bradford*)

Scottish Advisory Committee on Telecommunications

2 Greenside Lane, Edinburgh EH1 3AH
0131-244 5576 *Fax:* 0131-244 5696
E-mail: sacot@csi.com
Website: www.acts.org.uk

The Scottish Advisory Committee on Telecommunications (SACOT) was established by the Telecommunications Act 1984 to advise the Director-General of the Office of Telecommunications (OFTEL) on any matter in respect of which the Director-General has a legitimate interest. Companies operating telecommunications systems are also required by their licences to consider its representations.

Members of the committee are appointed by the Secretary of State for Trade and Industry, and are independent of OFTEL. They are selected to represent the varying interests of consumers and other users of public telecommunications services (including cellular mobile services) in Scotland.

Chairman: Jeremy Mitchell
Secretary: R L L King

Scottish Arts Council

12 Manor Place, Edinburgh EH3 7DD
0131-226 6051 *Fax:* 0131-225 9833
E-mail: administrator@scottisharts.org.uk

The Scottish Arts Council is one of the principle channels for Government funding of the arts in Scotland. Formerly part of the Arts Council of Great Britain, SAC is now an autonomous organisation, responsible to and financed by the Scottish Executive. SAC also distributes funds from the National Lottery to the arts in Scotland. The Council gives around 1300 grant a year to artists and arts organisations. As well as funding the arts, SAC has an important role to play in encouraging support for the arts from others – local authorities, economic development agencies, private sponsors and charitable trusts.

Director: Ms Tessa Jackson
Director of Finance and Administration: Graham Berry
Director of Planning and Development: Barclay Price
Visual Arts Director: Susan Daniel-McElroy
Crafts Director: Dr Helen Bennet
National Lottery Director: David Bonnar
Combined Arts Director: Jim Tough
Drama and Dance Director: David Taylor
Literature Director: Jenny Brown
Music Director: Nod Knowles

Scottish Consumer Council

Royal Exchange House, 100 Queen Street,
Glasgow G1 3DN
0141-226 5261 *Fax:* 0141-221 0731
Minicom: 0141-226 8459
E-mail: scc@scotconsumer.org.uk
Website: www.scotconsumer.org.uk

SCC promotes and represents the interests of Scottish consumers in general and in particular the disadvantaged. SCC researches areas of consumer concern and the resulting published reports are then used to influence and persuade the relevant bodies, such as central and local government, nationalised and independent industries and public, professional and private sector services.

Chairman: Ms Deirdre Hutton, CBE
Director: Martyn Evans

Scottish Council for Educational Technology

74 Victoria Crescent Road,
Glasgow G12 9JN
0141-337 5000 *Fax:* 0141-337 5050
E-mail: enquiries@scet.com
Website: www.scet.com

SCET is a Non-Departmental Public Body which provides direction to the Scottish Executive in the use of new technologies in Scottish education, including policy shaping and advice on ICT within schools and for lifelong learning.

SCET is involved in software and internet development, mulitmedia production, consultancy, training and providing information and support on all aspects of learning through technology.

Chairman: Tom Wilson
Chief Executive: Richard Pietrasik

Scottish Design

120 Bothwell Street, Glasgow, G2 7JP
0141-221 6121

A product development organisation, Scottish Design offers services for businesses in all aspects of the design and product development process. It is a unique organisation of multi-disciplinary specialists in best practice design and product development methods.

As part of the overall economic development strategy for Scotland, Scottish Design operates in partnership with the Scottish Enterprise Network, industrial and educational organisations and the Scottish 'design' industry to stimulate successful product development across all business sectors.

Public Relations: Ms Nuala Walsh

Scottish Enterprise

120 Bothwell Street, Glasgow G2 7JP
0141-248 2700 *Fax:* 0141-221 3217
Telex: 777600 SEGLW G

Scottish Enterprise – helping create jobs and prosperity for Scotland.

The Scottish Enterprise Network is made up of Scottish Enterprise and 13 local enterprise companies. Scottish Enterprise provides a framework for the operation of the network and carries out Scotland-wide projects and programmes. Through Locate in Scotland it helps attract jobs to Scotland and through Scottish Trade International helps Scottish companies compete in world export markets.

The local enterprise companies deliver a wide range of economic development services to meet local needs, including company development, business start-up programmes and training programmes such as Skillseekers and Training for Work.

Scottish Enterprise is a statutory body charged with enhancing Scotland's economy and environment and improving the skills levels of its people.

Chairman: Sir Ian Wood
Deputy Chairman: Cameron McLatchie, CBE
Board Members:
  Sir Iain Vallance, Janet Lowe, Eric Hagman,
  Campbell Christie, CBE,
  Crawford W Beveridge, CBE, *(Chief*
  Executive), Jim Sillars
Senior Management Team:
  Crawford Beveridge, Charlie Woods,
  Ray Macfarlane, Alistair Proctor, Alan Sim

Scottish Environment Protection Agency

Erskine Court, The Castle Business Park,
Stirling FK9 4TR
01786 457700 *Fax:* 01786 446885

The Scottish Environment Protection Agency (SEPA) is a non-departmental public body which is responsible for the protection of the environment and is accountable to the Scottish Parliament. The control of pollution to air, land

and water falls under SEPA's responsibilities, as does the control of radioactive waste. SEPA has 22 offices covering the whole of Scotland, comprising a Head Office, 3 Regional Headquarters and locally based offices within each region, providing locally based operational services.

Chairman: Ken Collins
Deputy Chairman: Deirdre Hutton
Chief Executive: Alasdair Paton
Board Members: Prof Brian Clark,
  Cllr Susan Clark, Prof Stanley Dagg,
  Fred Edwards, Bill Furness,
  Cllr Bill Howatson, David Hughes-Hallet,
  Nick Kuenssberg, Cllr Corrie McChord
Executive Team:
  West Region Director: John Beveridge
  East Region Director: Willie Halcrow
  North Region Director: Prof David Mackay
  Director of Environmental Strategy:
    Tricia Henton
  Director of Finance: John Ford

Scottish Further Education Funding Council

*Donaldson House, 97 Haymarket Terrace,
Edinburgh EH12 5HD*
0131-313 6500 *Fax:* 0131-313 6501
E-mail: info@sfc.ac.uk

The Scottish Further Education Funding Council was established in shadow form in January 1999 under the Further and Higher Education (Scotland) Act 1992 to secure the adequate and efficient provision of further education in Scotland on behalf of the Secretary of State. Since July 1999 the Council has been responsible for allocating funds, monitoring the financial health of the further education sector, and advising the First Minister on further education matters.

Chairman: Robert Beattie, MBE
Chief Executive: Prof John Sizer, CBE
Members: David Batty, Bill Gold, MBE,
  John Gray, Mrs Joyce Johnston,
  Prof Tom McCool, CBE, Brian Minto,
  Ms Esther Roberton, Fred Shedden,
  Prof Michael Thorne, Alan Tripp
Secretary: Ms Julia Amour

Scottish Higher Education Funding Council

*Donaldson House, 97 Haymarket Terrace,
Edinburgh EH12 5HD*
0131-313 6500 *Fax:* 0131-313 6501
E-mail: info@sfc.ac.uk
Website: www.shefc.ac.uk/shefc/welcome.htm

The Scottish Higher Education Funding Council was established in June 1992 under the Further and Higher Education (Scotland) Act to provide financial support for teaching, research and associated activities in Scottish higher education institutions: there are currently 18 such institutions. The Council is also responsible for advising the First Minister on higher education matters and has a statutory responsibility to secure that provision is made for the assessment of the quality of provision funded by the Council.

Chairman: Dr Chris Masters
Chief Executive: Prof John Sizer, CBE
Members: Ms Rowena Arshad, Prof Colin Bell,
  Prof Alice Brown, Prof Geoffrey Boulton,
  Prof Vicki Bruce, OBE,
  Prof Graeme R D Catto, Prof Georgina Follett,
  John Gray, Ms Ann Kettle, James McColl,
  Prof Tom McCool, CBE, Dr Valerie Maehle
Secretary: Laurence Howells
Observers: Representatives from DENI,
  HEFCW and HEFCE

Scottish Homes

*Thistle House, 91 Haymarket Terrace,
Edinburgh EH12 5HE*
0131-313 0044 *Fax:* 0131-313 4527
Website: www.scot-homes.gov.uk

Scottish Homes is the National Housing Agency for Scotland. The organisation works in partnership with housing associations and co-operatives, private developers, local authorities, financial institutions, the voluntary sector, and local communities to tackle Scotland's housing problems. It aims to help provide good quality affordable hosing and contribute to the regeneration of local communities. The agency believes the value of housing investment goes beyond bricks and mortar to impact on the local economy, health, education and crime levels, and therefore sees its work as a vital contribution to the delivery of the Government's social inclusion agenda. The agency has an annual development budget of around £200 million and is transferring its remaining 14,000 rented houses to other landlords because of the benefits to tenants. Since it was established in 1989, it has invested £2 billion in helping to provide over 60,000 new and improved houses for sale or rent throughout Scotland, attracting a further £1 billion of private funding in the process.

Chairman and Chief Executive: John Ward, CBE
Board Members: Ms Rani Dhir,
 Mrs Pat Greenhill, OBE, William McKelvey,
 Mrs Christine May,
 Canon Lewis Shand Smith,
 Prof John Small, CBE, John Spencely
Director of Communications: Bill Hoy

Scottish Law Commission

140 Causewayside,
Edinburgh EH9 1PR
0131-668 2131 *Fax:* 0131-662 4900
E-mail: info@scotlawcom.gov.uk

The Scottish Law Commission was established in 1965 under the Law Commissions Act 1965, to keep under review, and to promote the reform of, the Law of Scotland.

Chairman (part-time): The Hon Lord Gill
Commissioners (full-time): Dr E M Clive, CBE,
 Prof K G C Reid, N R Whitty
Commissioner (part-time): P S Hodge, QC
Secretary: N Raven
Parliamentary Draftsmen:
 G M Clark (0131-244 1671)
 Miss M Mackenzie (0131-244 1667)

Office of Scottish Parliamentary Counsel,
Victoria Quay, Edinburgh EH6 6QQ

Scottish Museums Council

County House, 20–22 Torphichen Street
Edinburgh EH3 8JB
0131-229 7465 *Fax:* 0131-229 2728
E-mail: inform@scottishmuseums.org.uk
Website: www.scottishmuseums.org.uk

The Scottish Museums Council is the national agency for central government support to non-national museums in Scotland. It is one of ten Area Museum Councils in the United Kingdom. The Council was founded in 1964 and is an independent company with charitable status, funded principally by the Secretary of State for Scotland.

The Council's purpose is to improve the quality of museum and gallery provision in Scotland. It provides a wide range of advice, services, and financial assistance to its membership, which includes private sector museum trusts, local authorities, Universities and regimental museums. It represents the interests of this membership at national level.

Policies are determined by the Council's membership, who elect the Chairman and Board of Directors. The Council has a small permanent staff of about 25 based at its Edinburgh headquarters. They are active in providing advisory and consultancy services in the fields of management and development planning, conservation, fundraising and marketing, information and training. Conservation staff provide practical conservation. The Council also supports a number of special research projects on aspects of Scottish museums and their collections.

Chair: Prof Malcolm McLeod
Director: Jane Ryder, MA, WS

Scottish Natural Heritage

12 Hope Terrace, Edinburgh EH9 2AS
0131-447 4784 *Fax:* 0131-446 2277
Website: www.snh.org.uk

Scottish Natural Heritage was set up under the Natural Heritage (Scotland) Act 1991. It has duties relating to landscape and nature conservation, promoting enjoyment and understanding of the environment and encouraging sustainable use of natural resources.

It is responsible for landscape and nature conservation designations including National Nature Reserves and National Scenic Areas; advising government, local authorities and others on natural heritage issues; supporting, commissioning and undertaking relevant research; and making available grants within its sphere of interest.

Chairman: Dr John Markland, CBE
Members: Simon Fraser,
 Prof David Ingram, OBE,
 Barbara Kelly, CBE, David L Laird,
 Alice Lambert, Ivor Lewis,
 Dr Patricia Macdonald, Peter MacKay, CB,
 Prof Jeremy Rowan Robinson, Michael Scott,
 Prof Roger Wheater, OBE
Chief Executive: Prof Roger Crofts, CBE
Chief Scientist: Prof Michael B Usher
Director of Strategy and Operations (North):
 Dr Jeff Watson
Director of Strategy and Operations (East):
 Dr Ian Jardine
Director of Strategy and Operations (West):
 John Thomson
Director of Corporate Services:
 Ian Edgeler
Head of National Strategy: Jane Clark
Head of Advisory Services: Dr Colin Galbraith
Secretary: Iain Rennick

Scottish Retail Consortium

Federation House, 222–224 Queensferry Road,
Edinburgh EH4 2BN
0131 332 6619 *Fax:* 0131 332 6597

The Scottish Retial Consortium co-ordinates the views and represents the interests of indigenous Scottish retailers and UK based retailers with concerns in Scotland, as well as feeding the policy on Scottish issues into its parent association, the British Retail Consortium, which represents over 90% of the UK's retail sector.

Director: Patrick Browne
Press and Parliamentary Officer: Scott Wright

Sea Fish Industry Authority

18 Logie Mill, Logie Green Road,
Edinburgh EH7 4HG
0131-558 3331 *Fax:* 0131-558 1442
E-mail: seafish@seafish.co.uk
Website: www.seafish.co.uk

The Authority provides a wide range of services to help all sectors of the UK fish industry look after its customers better.

It develops and tests more conservation-friendly methods of fishing; sets training standards and organises training opportunities; provides economic information and advice; promotes consumption and carries out research into fish and shellfish cultivation techniques.

Chairman: Eric Davey
Deputy Chairman: Derek Reid
Chief Executive: Alasdair Fairbairn

Serious Fraud Office

Elm House, 10-16 Elm Street
London WC1X 0BJ
020 7239 7272 Fax: 020 7837 1689
Britdoc: DX135896 London (Grays Inn) 3
Website: www.sfo.gov.uk

The Serious Fraud Office was created by the Criminal Justice Act 1987 following recommendations by the Fraud Trials Committee chaired by Lord Roskill. It is a government department, headed by the Director, who discharges her statutory functions under the superintendence of the Attorney General.

The SFO has been given powers to investigate and prosecute serious or complex fraud in England, Wales and Northern Ireland. It is staffed by lawyers, accountants and others with relevant expertise. It works closely with the police, other investigative authorities and other government departments.

Director of the Serious Fraud Office:
  Mrs Rosalind Wright
Assistant Directors: F Coford, G Dickinson,
  P Henry, J Kellock, P Kiernan, S Low,
  D Morrison, R Wardle
Principal Establishment and Finance Officer:
  P Rayner
Case Controllers: A Dodsworth, A Farries,
  Mrs H Garlick, R Gillanders, Miss J Glass,
  Miss L Griffiths, Mrs L Harris, P Lewis,
  P Lund, G Mills, S Myers, M Pinfold,
  P Roberts, D Smith, Miss E Venton, C Walker,
  Miss C Whitaker

Simpler Trade Procedures Board

151 Buckingham Palace Road,
London SW1W 9SS
020 7215 0825 Fax: 020 7215 0824
E-mail: info@sitpro.org.uk

SITPRO is the UK's trade facilitation agency sponsored by the DTI. It seeks to reduce the cost and complexity of international trade by removing the barriers, simplifying international trade procedures and rationalising the documentation and informations flows associated with them.

SITPRO's objective is to: 1) help and encourage UK traders to improve their competitive position by using the most effective trading practices and information systems; 2) improve the efficiency of the trading process.

Chief Executive: M Doran
Contact: G Cragge

Social Security Advisory Committee

New Court, Carey Street,
London WC2A 2LS
020 7412 1507 Fax: 020 7412 1570
E-mail: ssac@ms42.dss.gov.uk
Website: www.ssac.org.uk

The Committee is the statutory UK advisory body on most social security matters. The Committee's remit does not include industrial injuries, war pensions or occupational pensions, all of which are dealt with by other advisory bodies. Nor does the remit extend to subjects which may interrelate with social security benefits but which are not the responsibility of the Department of Social Security. Examples of this are: social services; employment, training and education policies; health care; taxation. The Committee takes an interest in the impact of these policy areas on social security but has no statutory advisory responsibility for them. In the case of National Insurance contributions and Tax Credits, an informal agreement with Inland Revenue has been made to that the Committee is able to comment on proposals for changes, particularly when they are likely to impact upon social secuity matters.

Chairman: Sir Thomas Boyd-Carpenter, KBE
Members: N Barlow, Mrs S Denman, CBE,
A W Dilnot, Mrs E Elias, JP, R Exell,
N Hardwick, Dr Pui-Ling Li,
Prof E McLaughlin, Prof A Ogus,
Prof O Stevenson, CBE, Dr A V Stokes, OBE,
R G Wendt, CBE, DL
Sec (Prin): Ms Gill Saunders
Asst Sec (HEO): R J Elbert
Asst Sec (HEO): Mrs C Watkins

Social Security and Child Support Commissioners, Office of the

5th Floor, Newspaper House,
8–16 Great New Street, London EC4A 3BN
020 7353 5145
23 Melville Street, Edinburgh EH3 7PW
0131-225 2201

The Social Security Commissioners are independent adjudicating authorities appointed by the Crown to rule upon applications for leave to appeal and to decide appeals under the Social Security Acts. The Commissioners' Offices are located in London and Edinburgh.

Chief Social Security and Child Support
Commissioner:
His Hon Judge Kenneth Machin, QC
Social Security and Child Support
Commissioners: M Heald, QC,
Mrs R F M Heggs, D J May, QC (Edinburgh),
R A Sanders, W M Walker, QC (Edinburgh),
M Rowland, J Mesher, J Henty, P Howell,
R Angus, S J Pacey, P Powell, N Levenson,
D Williams, E Jacobs, A Lloyd-Davies,
Miss C Fellner
Sec: L Pereira (London),
Mrs M Watts (Edinburgh)
Nominated Officers (Legal): Mrs J C Fowler,
G C Hall, A James, I K Murray (Edinburgh),
Mrs J Payne, Ms M M Teo, Miss J Walker,
R Baker, D Stanhill, K McIntyre, M Revell

Solicitors' Disciplinary Tribunal

113 Chancery Lane, London WC2A 1PL
020 7242 0219 Fax: 020 7320 5967
DocExch.LDE395

The Solicitors' Disciplinary Tribunal is a statutory body having a quasi judicial function created by the Solicitors Act 1974. There are currently 20 solicitor members and 9 lay members. The members are appointed by the Master of the Rolls. The Tribunal members sit in divisions of three made up of two solicitor members and one lay member. The Tribunal hears applications relating to professional misconduct alleged against individually named solicitors, former solicitors and registered foreign lawyers as well as applications for restoration to the Roll by struck off solicitors. It also has jurisdiction pursuant to Section 43 of the Solicitors Act 1974 in respect of solicitor's clerks and to deal with applications for revocation of orders made pursuant to Section 43. Appeal from the Tribunal lies to the Divisional Court in most cases and in cases of refusal to restore to the Roll direct to the Master of the Rolls.

President: G Barrie Marsh
Members: Richard Bamford, Adrian Gaynor-Smith, Anthony G Gibson, Anthony H Isaacs,
K I B Yeaman, John R C Clitheroe,
David W Faull, David J Leverton,
John C Potter, Mrs Elodie Stanley,
J Colin Chesterton, Jeremy N Barnecutt,
Alan Ground, Andrew Spooner,
Andrew Holmes, William Hartley,
Laurence Gilford, Theresa Cullen
Lay Members: Lady Bonham-Carter,
Kenneth Griffin, OBE, D E Marlow,
Dame Simone Prendergast, DBE, JP, DL,
M C Baughan, Mrs Caroline Pickering,
Lady Maxwell-Hyslop, Gerald Fisher,
David Gilbertson, Anjali Arya
Clerk to the Tribunal: Mrs S C Elson (Solicitor)

Special Commissioners of Income Tax

15-19 Bedford Avenue, London, WC1B 3AS
020 7631 4242 Fax: 020 7436 4151

The Special Commissioners (as they are usually called) are an independent appeal tribunal. They hear and determine appeals by taxpayers against tax assessments etc. made on them by the Inland Revenue under the Taxes Acts.

Presiding Special Commissioner:
    His Hon S J L Oliver, QC
Clerk to the Special Commissioners: R P Lester

Sport England

16 Upper Woburn Place, London WC1H 0QP
020 7273 1500 Fax: 020 7383 5740
E-mail: info@english.sports.gov.uk
Website: www.english.sports.gov.uk

Sport England is an independent body established by Royal Charter in January 1997. Together with UK Sport it has replaced the Sports Council which had a GB remit. It receives an annual grant from central government which it uses to promote the development of sport. Currently it focuses on more people being involved in sport, more places to play sport, and more medals through higher performance in sport. Sport England also has a responsibility for distributing grants from the Sport England Lottery Fund. Sport England has ten regional offices and operates five national sports centres.

Chairman: Trevor Brooking, CBE
Vice-Chairman: Des Wilson
Chief Executive: Derek Casey

Sports Council for Northern Ireland

House of Sport, Upper Malone Road,
Belfast BT9 5LA
028 9038 1222 Fax: 028 9068 2757

The Sports Council for Northern Ireland was established on 31 December 1973 under the provisions of Article 3 of the Recreation and Youth Service (Northern Ireland) Order 1973. Its objects are the furtherance of sport and physical recreation and its functions are provided by Article 3 of the Recreation and Youth Service (Northern Ireland) Order 1986.

Chairman: D F Allen, FInstD, OBE
Chief Executive:
    E G McCartan, MBA, DMS, BEd, DASE

Sports Council for Wales

Welsh Institute of Sport
Sophia Gardens, Cardiff CF11 9SW
029 2030 0500 Fax: 029 2030 0600
E-mail: scw@scw.co.uk
Website: www.sports-council-wales.co.uk

The Sports Council for Wales is the national organisation responsible for developing and promoting sport and recreation. It is the main adviser to the Welsh Assembly on all sporting matters. The Council's main aims are to:
– encourage and help more people take part in sport
– help sportspeople improve their performances and reach high standards
– promote the best use of Wales's man-made and natural sports facilities
– supply advice and information to help people understand the issues and technical matters facing sport.

The Council is also responsible for distributing funds from the National Lottery to sport in Wales through the SPORTLOT Fund and managing Sportsmatch, the Government's business sponsorship incentive scheme for sport.

Chairman: G Davies
Chief Executive: Dr H G Jones
Information Officer: J R Hinton

Sportscotland

Caledonia House, South Gyle
Edinburgh EH12 9DQ
0131-317 7200 *Fax:* 0131-317 7202
Website: sportscotland.org.uk

Sportscotland's mission is to lead the development of sport and physical recreation in Scotland, with the aim of increasing participation and improving standards of performance. To achieve its aim, Sportscotland focuses its resources on two priorities: investing in quality sporting opportunities for young people which will increase participation in sport, and investing in a comprehensive, integrated excellence programme for Scotland's aspiring and top performers which will improve standards of performance. Sportscotland also distributes more than £20 million annually to develop the infrastructure of Scottish sport through the Sportscotland Lottery Fund.

Chairman: Alastair Dempster
Chief Executive: Allan Alstead, CBE, DL

Statute Law Society

c/o Institute of Advanced Legal Studies,
17 Russell Square, London WC1B 5DR
020 7637 1731 Fax: 020 7637 5216

The Statute Law Society is an association of statute users which aims to secure improvements in the system of expressing, producing and publishing laws so that they are made more intelligible and to further education in legislative processes.

Its methods include encouraging research, promoting publications and meetings, making representations and liaison with appropriate bodies and individuals.

The Society is associated with the Statute Law Review, published by Oxford University Press.

President:
Rt Hon the Lord Renton, KBE, QC, TD
Chairman: Rt Hon the Lord Slynn of Hadley
Secretary: Juliet Fussell
Hon Treasurer: Hilary Farley

Student Loans Company Limited

100 Bothwell Street, Glasgow G2 7JD
0141-306 2000 *Fax:* 0141-306 2006
Website: www.slc.co.uk

Student loans, which were introduced in 1990, are part of the financial support package available to students. Loans are governed by regulations which are revised by the Government from time to time.

Chairman: Sir Anthony Battishill, CBE
Chief Executive and Director:
Colin Ward, BA, CA
Directors: John Morrison, Erik Ostman,
Peter Gregory, Anne Weatherston
Non-Executive Directors:
Prof Sir Eric Ash, CBE, FEng, FRS,
Brian Booth, Paul Grace, Maurice Paterson

Tate Gallery

Millbank, London SW1P 4RG
020 7887 8000 Fax: 020 7887 8007

The Tate Gallery opened in 1897 as a result of the generosity of Sir Henry Tate (who also contributed the nucleus of the original collection). The building has been extended considerably over the years and now contains over 70 galleries, including the Clore Gallery, for the Turner collection. Tate Liverpool was opened by HRH The Prince of Wales at the Albert Dock, Liverpool on 28 May 1988.

The Tate Gallery has begun an exciting new phase of development. In spring 2000 the Tate Gallery will create two new galleries in London. Tate Britain, at the original Millbank site, will open to the public on 24 March 2000, and Tate Modern, in the transformed Bankside Power Station in Southwark, will open from 12 May 2000.

The Tate Gallery houses the national collections of British art and of international 20th-century art. There are three major loan exhibitions each year. Displays from the Permanent Collection change annually to explore the wealth and variety of the Tate Gallery's collection within a chronological sequence leading from the 16th century to the present day. Free lectures, films and guided tours are offered nearly every day throughout the year.

The Friends of the Tate Gallery, formed in 1958, raise funds for the purchase of works of art for the Tate collections. Two special groups, the Patrons of New Art and the Patrons of British Art, were formed in 1982.

The Tate Gallery Foundation and the International Council, both formed in 1986, support the work of the Gallery. They are raising funds on a large scale for the further development of the Tate Gallery and help to stimulate gifts and bequests to the Gallery.

Tate St Ives on Porthmeor Beach, St Ives, Cornwall was opened by HRH The Prince of Wales on 23 June 1993. Tate St Ives is managed in conjunction with the Barbara Hepworth Museum in St Ives which the Tate Gallery has maintained since 1980.

Chairman: David Verey
Director: Sir Nicholas Serota, MA
Director, Tate Britain: Stephen Deuchar
Director, Tate Modern: Lars Nittve
Director of National Programmes: Sandy Nairne
Director of Finance and Administration:
Alex Beard
Head of Communications: Damien Whitmore
Development Director: Andrea Nixon
Director of Buildings and Gallery Services:
Peter Wilson
Director of Collection Services: Jim France
Head of Library and Archive: Beth Houghton
Head of Collections: Jeremy Lewison
Head of Education, Tate Britain:
Richard Humphreys
Head of Education, Tate Modern: Toby Jackson
Head of Exhibitions and Display, Tate Modern:
Iwona Blazwick

Head of Exhibitions and Display, Tate Britain:
  Sheena Wagstaff
Tate St Ives Curator: Michael Tooby
Tate Liverpool Curator: Lewis Biggs
Publications Manager: Celia Clear
Restaurant Director: Duncan Carew
Head of Membership: Rachel Oglethorpe

TEC National Council
(TRAINING AND ENTERPRISE COUNCILS)
Westminster Tower
3 Albert Embankment, London SE1 7SX
020 7735 0010 Fax: 020 7735 0090
E-mail: info@tec.co.uk
Chairman: Neville Chamberlain
Chief Executive: Mrs Jacqui Henderson

Trades Union Congress
Congress House, Great Russell Street,
London WC1B 3LS
020 7636 4030 Fax: 020 7636 0632

The Trades Union Congress is a voluntary association of independent unions. It consists of 77 unions representing 6.7 million workers. Its governing body is the annual Congress consisting of 811 delegates. Between Congresses, a General Council of 48 members meets seven times a year. The main job of the TUC is to campaign for trade union aims and values. It prepares common policies on matters of importance to people at work and has representatives on a number of public bodies. It maintains close links with trade union movements overseas and runs a substantial education service for union officers on issues such as employment law. There is also an extensive regional network.

President: Rita Donaghy
General Secretary: John Monks
Deputy-General Secretary: Brendan Barber
Head, Economic and Social Affairs Dept:
  (Vacant)
Head, Organisation and Services Dept:
  Frances O'Grady
Head, Equality and Rights Dept: Kay Carberry
Head, Europe and International Dept:
  Tom Jenkins
Head, Management Services Dept: Mike Jones
Head, Campaigns and Communications Dept:
  Nigel Stanley
Parliamentary Officer: Isobel Larkin

Traffic Director for London
College House, Great Peter Street,
London SW1P 3LN
020 7222 4545 Fax: 020 7976 8640
E-mail: messages@tdfl.gov.uk
Website: www.tdfl.gov.uk

The Traffic Director for London is an Executive non-departmental public body created by power of the Road Traffic Act 1991. Its role is to co-ordinate the introduction, monitoring and maintenance of the Priority (Red) Route Network in London and is funded by grant-in-aid from the Department of Environment, Transport and the Regions (DETR). The Traffic Director is a Corporation Sole and an Accounting Officer independent from the DETR but reporting to the Secretary of State and to Parliament.

Traffic Director for London: Derek Turner,
  BEng, CEng, FICE, FCIT, FIHT, MIMgt
Senior Assistant Director (Finance & Admin):
  Robert Chapman, FCCA, CPFA
Senior Assistant Director (Technical):
  Mark Allan, MEng, CEng, MICE
Media and Public Relations: Heather Bolton
FROM JULY 2000 THE TRAFFIC DIRECTOR'S WORK
WILL TRANSFER TO TRANSPORT FOR LONDON

United Kingdom Atomic Energy Authority
Marshall Building, 521 Downs Way,
Harwell, Didcot, Oxfordshire OX11 0RA
01235 820220
Website: www.ukaea.org.uk

The United Kingdom Atomic Energy Authority (UKAEA) was created by an Act of Parliament in 1954 to take over responsibility for the research and development of the civil nuclear power programme. The Authority increasingly evolved its operations selling it products and services to the nuclear and non-nuclear sectors while also continuing with the development of nuclear R&D. In March 1994 the Authority was re-organised into two main divisions, the commercial division, trading under the name AEA Technology, and UKAEA Government Division.

AEA Technology plc was vested as a legally separate organisation on 31 March 1996 and has now been privatised as a science and engineering services business. From March 31 1996 UKAEA Government Division formally became UKAEA. It has responsibility for the safe management and decommissioning of its nuclear plant and facilities, optimising the income from its site and active facilities, the management of the UK's contribution to the international fusion programme.

Chairman: Sir Kenneth Eaton, GBE, KCB
E-mail: kenneth.eaton@ukaea.org.uk
Chief Executive: Dr John McKeown
E-mail: john.mckeown@ukaea.org.uk
Department: Trade & Industry

United Kingdom Sports Council

Walkden House, 3-10 Melton Street,
London NW1 2EB
020 7380 8000 Fax: 020 7380 8005
Website: www.uksport.gov.uk

Chairman: Sir Rodney Walker
Members: Don Allen, OBE, Gareth Davies,
    Craig Reedie, CBE,
    Dr Sarah Springman, OBE, Dr Mary Nevill,
    Judy Simpson, Trevor Brooking, CBE,
    Tanni Grey, MBE, Zahara Hyde Peters,
    Diana King, Adrian Metcalfe,
    Prof Myra Nimmo, Gavin Stewart,
    Alastair Dempster

ASSESSOR
Department for Culture, Media and Sport:
    Harry Reeves

OFFICERS
Chief Executive: Richard Callicott
Director of Corporate Services: Neil Shearer
Director of International Relations and Major
    Events: John Scott
Director of Performance Services: Liz Nicholl
Director of Ethics and Anti-Doping:
    Michele Verroken
Director of UK Sport Institute Project:
    Roger Moreland
Head of Strategic Planning: Jerry Bingham

Unrelated Live Transplant Regulatory Authority

c/o Room 311, Wellington House,
133–155 Waterloo Road, London SE1 8UG
020 7972 4812 Fax: 020 7972 4852
Website: www.doh.gov.uk/ultra.htm

The Unrelated Live Transplant Regulatory Authority is a statutory body established by the Human Organ Transplant (Unrelated Persons) Regulations 1989. From April 1, 1990 it has been an offence to carry out a transplant between living persons who are not genetically related

within the degrees specified in the Act, unless the Authority is satisfied as to certain matters specified in the Regulations. The Authority comprises a Chairman and ten members appointed by the Secretary of State. The Authority's secretariat is provided by officials working in the Department of Health.

Chairman: Prof Roderick MacSween
Members: Mrs Judy Callman,
    Dr James Douglas, Dr Heather Draper,
    Miss Patricia Franklin, Dr Susan Fuggle,
    Anthony J Hooker, Prof Stuart Macpherson,
    Prof Sir Netar Mallick, Prof Andrew Rees,
    Mrs Stephanie J Sullivan
Administrative Secretary: E Scarlett
Medical Secretary: Dr P Doyle

VAT and Duties Tribunals

Headquarters
15–19 Bedford Avenue,
London WC1B 3AS
020 7631 4242

The Tribunals exist to hear appeals against decisions of the Commissioners of Customs and Excise

President: His Honour S J L Oliver, QC
Registrar: R Lester

LONDON TRIBUNAL CENTRE
15–19 Bedford Avenue
London WC1B 3AS
020 7631 4242 Fax: 020 7436 4150/1

EDINBURGH TRIBUNAL CENTRE
44 Palmerston Place
Edinburgh EH12 5BJ
0131-226 3551 *Fax:* 0131-220 6817

MANCHESTER TRIBUNAL CENTRE
First Floor, Warwickgate House
Warwick Road, Old Trafford
Manchester M16 0GP
0161-872 6471 *Fax:* 0161-876 4479

Victoria and Albert Museum

South Kensington, London, SW7 2RL
020 7992 2000
Website: www.vam.ac.uk

The Victoria and Albert Museum is The National Museum of Art and Design and covers all branches of fine and applied art. It descends direct from the Museum of Manufactures (later called Museum of Ornamental Art), opened in Marlborough House in 1852. The Museum was moved in 1857 to become part of the collective South Kensington Museum. It was renamed the Victoria and Albert Museum in 1899. The Victoria and Albert Museum is administered by a Board of Trustees established under the National Heritage Act 1983.

Chair of the Board of Trustees: Ms Paula Ridley
Trustees: Miss Nina Campbell,
   The Viscountess Cobham, Lady Copisarow,
   Rodney Fitch, CBE, Prof Christopher
   Frayling, MA, PhD, Sir Terence Heiser, GCB,
   Mrs Anne Heseltine, Alton Irby III, Jonathan
   Scott, CBE, FSA *(Deputy Chairman),*
   Anthony Snow, Prof John Steer, MA, DLitt,
   Alan Wheatley, FCA, Prof Christopher
   White, CVO, FBA
Secretary to the Board of Trustees: P A Wilson
Director: Dr A C N Borg, CBE, FSA
Assistant Director, (Administration): J W Close
Assistant Director (Collections): T J Stevens
Heads of Department:
Buildings and Estate: R Whitehouse
Ceramics and Glass: Dr O J Watson
Conservation: Dr J Ashley-Smith
Education: D Anderson, OBE
Far Eastern: Miss R Kerr
Finance and Central Services: Miss R M Sykes
Furniture and Woodwork: C Wilk
Indian and South-East Asian: Dr D A Swallow
Major Projects and Collections Management:
   Mrs G F Miles
Metalwork, Silver and Jewellery: (Vacant)
National Art Library: J van der Wateren
Personnel: Mrs G Henchley
Prints, Drawings and Paintings:
   Miss S B Lambert
Public Services: R Cole-Hamilton
Research: P Greenhalgh
Safety and Security: R Bland
Sculpture: Dr P E D Williamson
Textiles and Dress: Mrs V D Mendes
V&A Enterprises Ltd: M Cass
Branch Museums:
Bethnal Green Museum of Childhood:
   Dr S Laurence *(Acting Head)*
Theatre Museum: Miss M Benton
Wellington Museum: Miss A Robinson

Water Industry Commissioner for Scotland

Ochil House, Springkerse Business Park,
Stirling FK7 7XE
01786 430200 (Textphone available)
Fax: 01786 462018
E-mail: enquiries@watercommissioner.co.uk

The Water Industry Commissioner for Scotland has responsibility for promoting the interests of all Scottish water consumers and ensuring that they receive the best value for money. His functions include the advising of Ministers on the fixing of water and sewerage charges over a period of years. He is advised by three Water Industry Consultative Committees.

Water Industry Commissioner: Alan Sutherland

Welsh Advisory Committee on Telecommunications

First Floor, Caradog House, St Andrews Place,
Cardiff CF10 3BE
029 2023 9174 or
0845 145000 (within Wales)
Fax: 029 2066 8536
E-mail: wact@acts.org.uk
Website: www.acts.org.uk

The Welsh Advisory Committee on Telecommunications is an independent body set up under the Telecommunications Act 1984 to advise the Director-General of Telecommunications (OFTEL) and to promote the interests of all telecommunications users in Wales.

Chairman: Prof Mike Tedd
Secretary: Gordon Mackenzie

Welsh Consumer Council

5th Floor, Longcross Court
47 Newport Road, Cardiff CF24 0WL
029 2025 5454 Fax: 029 2025 5464
E-mail: info@wales.consumer.org.uk
Website: www.wales.consumer.org.uk

The Welsh Consumer Council was established in 1975 as a result of a government White Paper. It aims to be the authoritative voice of consumers in Wales by working with consumers and others to present their interests and needs to industry, commerce and government. The Council also works with other organisations in the public, private and voluntary sector developing projects on consumer related issues.

Chair: Mrs Barbara Hicks
Director: Dr Nich Pearson

Welsh Development Agency

Principality House, The Friary,
Cardiff CF10 3FE
0345 775577 Fax: 01443 845589
Welshline: 0345 775566
International: +44 1443 845500
E-mail: enquiries@wda.co.uk
Website: www.wda.co.uk

The original Welsh Development Agency was created in 1976 with a brief to engineer the long term economic regeneration of Wales. Under the Welsh Development Agency Act of 1975, which established the Agency and which governs its activities, the WDA has three main roles: to further the economic development of Wales and to provide, maintain and safeguard quality employment; to promote industrial efficiency and the international competitiveness of Welsh business; and to improve the environment.

On 1st October 1998 the WDA merged with the Development Board for Rural Wales and the Land Authority to form a unified organisation to promote economic development in Wales. The new organisation retained the name "Welsh Development Agency". The move was part of the Government of Wales Act for which Royal Assent was given in July 1998.

The enlarged Agency currently employs around 460 people and will have a budget of £225 million for 1999-2000. In addition to the head office in Cardiff, the WDA has divisional offices in South West, South East, North and Mid Wales. It is also represented in North America, Europe, the Far East and Australia. In addition to its own activities the WDA works closely with a wide range of other bodies throughout Wales creating a powerful partnership of interests committed to the economic development of the Principality.

Chairman: David Rowe-Beddoe
Deputy Chairman: Graham Hawker
Chief Executive: Brian Willott
Principal Finance Officer: Richard Beaumont
Legal Director and Agency Secretary:
    Roy Thomas
Managing Director, International Division:
    Geoff Sheppard
Managing Director, South West Wales Division:
    Gareth Hall
Managing Director, North Wales Division:
    Chris Farrow
Managing Director, South East Wales Division:
    Karen Thomas
Managing Director, Mid Wales Division:
    Sian Lloyd-Jones

Director of Business and Product Development:
    Alan Morgan
Board Members: Sir John Allen,
    Mrs Susan Balsom, Cllr Noel Crowley,
    Trefor Jones, Dewi Lewis, Robin Lewis,
    Dr Ruth Williams, George Wright,
    Sir Brian Smith

From 1st October 1998, the Development Board for Rural Wales and the Land Authority for Wales merged with the WDA

Welsh Local Government Association

10-11 Raleigh Walk, Atlantic Wharf,
Cardiff CF10 5LN
029 2046 8600 Fax: 029 2046 8601
E-mail: gen.office@wlga.org

The WLGA was established in April 1996 as the collective voice of the local authorities in Wales. It aims to represent and promote the interests of Welsh local government and of Wales in general. A constituent part of the Local Government Association for England and Wales it enjoys autonomy in its dealing with the Welsh Office and other Welsh institutions and in representing the interests of Wales within the European Community.

Political Structure: The Council of the Association, comprising 70 representatives of the member authorities, meets twice a year. A Co-ordinating Committee, comprising political leaders of the authorities meets monthly to determine policy and provide general political direction over the Association's affairs. Apart from these two bodies, the Association has no standing committees but, rather, establishes advisory groups, comprising both elected members and officers of the member authorities, on a "task and finish" basis to consider specific policy issues.

Secretary: Colin Jones
Head of Corporate Affairs: Paul Griffiths
Head of Economic and Environmental Affairs:
    Victoria Winckler
Head of Education, Training and Cultural
    Affairs: Peter Tyndall
Head of Finance: Steve Dunster, OBE
Head of Social Affairs: Lynda Bransbury

Whitehall and Industry Group

22 Queen Anne's Gate, London SW1H 9AA
020 7222 1166 Fax: 020 7222 1167
E-mail: info@wig.co.uk
Website: www.wig.co.uk

The Whitehall & Industry Group, established in 1984, is an independent, not-for-profit organisation which works to improve communication and understanding between government and the private sector through exchange of people, ideas, information and best practice.

It works in close co-operation with all major government departments and agencies, with local government and with companies, encouraging and organising a wide variety of interchange activity. This ranges from information, awareness raising and networking events, attachments and secondments (both short and longer term) to workshops and leadership development programmes.

Chief Executive: Will Wesson

Women's National Commission

Cabinet Office, 4th Floor, Horse Guards Road, London SW1P 3AL
020 7238 0386 Fax: 020 7238 0387

The WNC acts as a focal point for women's organisations, putting their views and concerns to government departments and ministers on all issues that concern women.

Chair: Baroness Crawley
Director: Janet Veitch

Youth Justice Board for England and Wales

Sixth Floor, 50 Queen Anne's Gate, London SW1H 9AT
020 7273 2240 Fax: 020 7273 2256
E-mail: yjb@gtnet.gov.uk
Website: www.youth-justice-board.gov.uk

The Youth Justice Board, which was established on 30 September 1998, aims to prevent or reduce offending by children and young people. Objectives include tackling delays in youth justice and promoting programmes that prevent or reduce offending by children and young people.

Chairman: Lord Warner of Brockley
Board Members: Rob Allen, Jonathan Black, Cedric Fullwood, CBE, Ms Joyce Moseley, Dr Theodore Mutale, Ms Janet Paraskeva, JP, Charles Pollard, Mrs Annabella Scott, JP, Martin Stephenson, Ms Lorna Whyte, Charles Wilson
Chief Executive: Mark Perfect
   020 7273 3217/2821
Secretary to the Board: Andrew Brown
   020 7273 4142
Adviser on Development Fund: Louise Bennett
   020 7273 3822
Adviser on Secure Accommodation (Regimes) and Assessments: Ruth Allan
   020 7273 3694
Adviser on Secure Accommodation (Purchasing): Robert Newman
   020 7273 4178
Adviser on Local Area Teams and Justice Plans: Adrian Bell
   020 7273 4184
Director of Communications: Rachel Pitkeathley
   020 7273 4586

INTERNATIONAL ORGANISATIONS

British-American Parliamentary Group

Houses of Parliament, London SW1A 0AA
020 7219 6209

Formed during the Second World War to promote closer relations and mutual understanding between Members of both Houses of Parliament of the UK and Members of both Houses of the Congress of the United States of America, by providing opportunities for discussion on problems common to the United States and to the UK and for exchange of visits and information.

Presidents: The Lord Chancellor, The Speaker of the House of Commons
Vice-Presidents: The Rt Hon the Lord Callaghan of Cardiff, KG, The Rt Hon the Lord Carrington, KG, GCMG, CH, MC, The Rt Hon Robin Cook, MP, The Rt Hon William Hague, MP, The Rt Hon Sir Edward Heath, KG, MBE, MP, The Rt Hon the Lord Howe of Aberavon, CH, QC, The Rt Hon the Lord Hurd of Westwell, CH, CBE, The Rt Hon the Lord Mackay of Clashfern, KT, FRSE, The Rt Hon John Major, CH, MP, The Rt Hon the Lord Owen of Plymouth, CH, The Rt Hon the Lord Pym, MC, The Rt Hon the Baroness Thatcher, LG, OM, FRS, The Rt Hon the Lord Weatherill, DL
Chairman: The Prime Minister
Joint Vice-Chairmen:
The Rt Hon Jack Straw, MP,
John Maples, MP
Joint Hon Treasurers:
The Rt Hon Alan Williams, MP,
The Rt Hon Sir Geoffrey Johnson-Smith, MP
Honorary Secretary:
The Rt Hon the Lord Jopling, DL
Assistant Secretary: Lady Moate

British-Irish Inter-Parliamentary Body

All correspondence regarding the Administration of the Body to:
Miss Amanda Hay,
Administrator, British Secretariat,
British-Irish Inter-Parliamentary Body,
7 Millbank, London SW1P 3JA
020 7219 6800 Fax: 020 7219 0455
E-mail: haya@parliament.uk

All correspondence regarding the Business of the Body to:
Frank A Cranmer, British Clerk to the Body,
Committee Office, House of Commons,
London SW1A 0AA
020 7219 1365 Fax: 020 7219 2731

The Body was founded on the initiative of the British and Irish Groups of the Inter-Parliamentary Union with the support of both Governments. It held its Inaugural Plenary Session in London in February 1990 and meets in Plenary Session twice a year, alternately in the UK and in Ireland. It has a full and formally appointed membership of 25 British and 25 Irish members of both Houses from each Parliament, and further Associate members. The Body is run by a Steering Committee, jointly chaired by David Winnick, MP and Michael O'Kennedy, TD, and divides into four Standing Committees who meet regularly to consider matters referred to them by Plenary Sessions or which they may wish to bring forward at these Sessions.

Co-Chairmen: David Winnick, MP,
Michael O'Kennedy, TD

Cab International

Wallingford, Oxfordshire OX10 8DE
01491 832111 *Fax:* 01491 833508
E-mail: cabi@cabi.org
Telex: 847964 (COMAGG G)
Website: www.cabi.org/

An international, intergovernmental, not-for-profit organisation dedicated to improving human welfare through the dissemination, application and generation of scientific knowledge in support of sustainable development worldwide, with emphasis on agriculture, forestry, human health and the management of natural resources, and with particular attention to the needs of developing countries.

Executive Council: Dr John C Radcliffe, OAM (Chairman) (Australia), Dr Keith T H Farrer, OBE (alternate), Frank Davis (The Bahamas), A F M Yeahyea Choudhury (Bangladesh), HE Dr Ursula Barrow (Belize), J M Moreti (Botswana), Dr Morni bin Othman (Brunei Darussalam), Dr Caroline Martin (Canada), Rolando Ortega (Chile), Prof Fan Mingyi (China), Dra Amparo Araújo (Colombia), K Kallinicos (Cyprus), Sung Kangwai (Fiji), HE Mr John Bojang (The Gambia), Simon

A Nyamikeh (Ghana), HE Mr Laleshwar K N Singh (Vice-Chairman) (Guyana), Mrs Vera Balint (Hungary), M S Grover (India), Suprapto Martosetomo (Indonesia), Mrs Angella V Brown (Jamaica), Joseph Ngetich (Kenya), B L Namul (Malawi), Husni Zai Yaacob (Malaysia), S Chuckowree (Mauritius), HE Dr Kyaw Win (Myanmar), Y D Gukas (Nigeria), HE Mian Riaz Samee (Pakistan), Kikereng Wargem (Papua New Guinea), Mrs M Z Collinson (Philippines), E M Sankoh (Sierra Leone), Robert Sislo (Solomon Islands), Siphiwe Mkhize (South Africa), Mrs Chitranganee Wagiswara (Sri Lanka), Simba Mbenna (Tanzania), Miss Reita G Toussaint (Trinidad & Tobago), D Nyakairu (Uganda), R Carlisle (UK Overseas Territories), Dr D W F Shannon (United Kingdom), Ngo Tien Long (Vietnam), Miss Udi Soko (Zambia), Mrs P T Musaka (Zimbabwe)

Director-General: Jim Gilmore

Commonwealth Foundation

Marlborough House, Pall Mall
London SW1Y 5HY
020 7930 3783 Fax: 020 7839 8157
E-mail: geninfo@commonwealth.int
Website: www.commonwealthfoundation.com

The Commonwealth Foundation is an inter-governmental organisation with a mandate from Commonwealth Heads of Government to promote people to people interaction and collaboration within the non-governmental sector of the Commonwealth. The Foundation supports non-governmental organisations, Commonwealth professional associations and Commonwealth arts and culture.

Director: Dr Humayan Khan

Commonwealth Parliamentary Association

Formed in 1911, the CPA exists to promote understanding among Parliamentarians who, irrespective of race, religion, gender or culture, are united in the Commonwealth by community of interest, respect for the rule of law and pursuit of the positive ideals of parliamentary democracy. CPA Branches exist in nearly all of the Legislatures of the Commonwealth.

Patron: HM Queen Elizabeth, Head of the Commonwealth

Vice-Patron: Rt Hon Tony Blair, MP, Prime Minister, United Kingdom
President: Rt Hon Betty Boothroyd, MP, Speaker of the House of Commons, United Kingdom
Vice-President: Sen the Hon Margaret Reid, President of the Senate, Australia
Chairman of the Executive Committee: Hon Pius Msekwa, MP, Speaker of the House of Representatives, Tanzania
Vice-Chairman of the Executive Committee: Bob Spellar, MP, Canada
Treasurer: Bowen Wells, MP, United Kingdom
Regional Representatives: Africa: HM Chief Fon Doh Gwanyin III, MP, Cameroon; Hon Simon Mwila, MP, Deputy Speaker of the National Assembly, Zambia; Hon Francis Ayume, MP, Speaker of the Parliament, Uganda; Sen the Hon S Lejaha, President of the Senate, Lesotho. *Asia:* Hon Chaudhary Parvez Elahi, MPA, Speaker of the Provincial Assembly, Punjab, Pakistan; Shri P A Sangma, MP, Lok Sabha, India; Hon K B Ratnayake, MP, Speaker of the Parliament, Sri Lanka; Hon Y Ramakrishnudu, MLA, Speaker of the Legislative Assembly, Andhra Pradesh; Hon Sardar Charnjit Singh Atwal, MLA, Speaker of the Legislative Assembly, Punjab; Md Abdul Hamid, MP, Deputy Speaker of the Parliament, Bangladesh. *Australia:* Member to be appointed by the Parliament of Australia; Hon George Strickland, MLA, Speaker of the Legislative Assembly, Western Australia; Hon David Buffett, MLA, Deputy Speaker of the Legislative Assembly, Norfolk Island. *British Islands and Mediterranean:* Dr John Marek, MP, United Kingdom; Demetris Eliades, MP, Cyprus; Hon Mario Galea, MP, Malta. *Canada:* Bob Speller, MP, Canada; Hon Sam Gargon, MLA, Speaker of the Legislative Assembly, Northwest Territories; Member to be determined. *The Caribbean, the Americas and the Atlantic:* Hon Matthew Vernon Roberts, MP, Speaker of the House of Assembly, St Lucia; Dr the Hon Howard Fergus, CBE, MLC, Speaker of the Legislative Council, Montserrat; Hon Hector McClean, MP, Speaker of the House of Representatives, Trinidad and Tobago. *Pacific:* Hon Tewareka Tentoa, MP, Vice-President and Minister of Home Affairs and Rural Development, Kiribati; Hon O'Love Jacobsen, MP, Niue; Member to be determined, Solomon Islands. *South-East Asia:* Hon Ruhanie bin Haji Ahmad, MP,

Chairman of Malaysian Backbenchers Club, Malaysia; Hon Dato' Hasan Arifin, MLA, Deputy Chief Minister, Pahang; Dr Yaacob Ibrahim, MP, Parliamentary Secretary in the Ministry of Communications and Information Technology, Singapore.

CPA Secretariat
Secretary-General: Arthur Donahoe, QC
Director of Planning and Development:
  Raja Gomez
Director of Information Services:
  Andrew Imlach
Director of Finance and Administration:
  Mahbub Alam

Suite 700, Westminster House,
7 Millbank, London SW1P 3JA
020 7799 1460 Fax: 020 7222 6073
E-mail: hq.sec@comparlhq.org.uk

Commonwealth Parliamentary Association – United Kingdom Branch

Westminster Hall, Houses of Parliament,
London SW1A 0AA
020 7219 5373 Fax: 020 7233 1202
E-mail: cpa@parliament.uk
Presidents: The Lord Chancellor, The Speaker of the House of Commons
Chairman of the CPA United Kingdom Branch: The Rt Hon Tony Blair, MP (ex-officio)
Vice Presidents: The Rt Hon William Hague, MP, The Rt Hon the Lord Callaghan of Cardiff, KG, The Rt Hon the Lord Carlisle of Bucklow, QC, DL, The Rt Hon the Lord Carrington, KG, GCMG, CH, MC, DL, The Rt Hon the Lord Hailsham of Saint Marylebone, KG, CH, FRS, The Rt Hon Sir Edward Heath, KG, MBE, MP, The Rt Hon the Lord Howe of Aberavon, CH, QC, The Rt Hon the Lord Hurd of Westwell, CH, CBE, The Rt Hon the Earl of Longford, KG, The Rt Hon the Lord Mackay of Clashfern, KT, FRSE, The Rt Hon John Major, CH, MP, The Rt Hon the Lord Owen, CH, The Rt Hon the Lord Pym, MC, The Rt Hon the Baroness Thatcher, LG, OM, FRS, The Rt Hon the Lord Weatherill, DL
Chairman of the Executive Committee:
  Donald Anderson, MP
Joint Vice-Chairmen of the Executive Committee:
  Sir Patrick Cormack, FSA, MP,
  David Marshall, MP

Joint Hon Treasurers:
  The Rt Hon Gordon Brown, MP (ex-officio), Bowen Wells, MP
Executive Committee: John Austin, MP, Michael Colvin, MP, The Rt Hon Robin Cook, MP (ex-officio), Mrs Jean Corston, MP, Tom Cox, MP, Stephen Day, MP, The Lord Evans of Parkside, Mrs Cheryl Gillan, MP, Eric Illsley, MP, Nigel Jones, MP, Miss Julie Kirkbride, MP, Professor Lord McColl of Dulwich, CBE, Andrew Mackinley, MP, Dr John Marek, MP, The Rt Hon the Lord Merlyn-Rees, The Rt Hon the Lord Morris of Manchester, AO, QSO, Bill Olner, MP, James Paice, MP, Peter Pike, MP, Mrs Marion Roe, MP, Rev Martin Smyth, MP, The Rt Hon Sir John Stanley, MP, Dennis Turner, MP, Nicholas Winterton, MP
Secretary: Andrew Pearson
Deputy Secretary: Christopher Jones
Assistant Secretary: Paul Jackson
Administrator: Helen Haywood

Commonwealth Secretariat

Marlborough House, Pall Mall
London SW1Y 5HX
020 7839 3411 Fax: 020 7930 0827
Telex: 27678
Website: thecommonwealth.org

The Commonwealth Secretariat is the principal organisation of the Commonwealth. Together with its sister organisations, the Commonwealth Foundation and the Commonwealth of Learning (in Canada), the Secretariat is the Commonwealth's own civil service, effectively carrying out the priorities of its 54 member governments.

Among other things, the Secretariate promotes:
– Good governance and democracy;
– Sustainable economic and social development;
– The rule of law, human rights and gender equality.

The Commonwealth Secretariat is located at Marlborough House in London, close to the diplomatic missions of many Commonwealth countries. It was established by Head of Government in 1965.

Commonwealth Secretary-General:
  Chief Emeka Anyaoku, CON
Deputy Secretary-General (Economic and Social Affairs):
  Dame Veronica Sutherland, DBE, CMG
Deputy Secretary-General (Development Co-operation): Nick Hare

Deputy Secretary-General (Political):
K Srinivasan
Director and Head of the Secretary-General's Private Office: Stuart G Mole, OBE

STRATEGIC PLANNING AND EVALUATION UNIT
Director: Dr Siripurapu K Rao

POLITICAL AFFAIRS DIVISION
Director: Jon Sheppard

LEGAL AND CONSTITUTIONAL AFFAIRS DIVISION
Director: Richard C Nzerem

INFORMATION AND PUBLIC AFFAIRS DIVISION
Director: Kaye Whiteman

ADMINISTRATION DIVISION
Director: Dr Gelase Mutahaba

ECONOMIC AFFAIRS DIVISION
Director: Rumman A Faruqi

HUMAN RESOURCE DEVELOPMENT DIVISION
Director: Prof Stephen Matlin

GENDER AND YOUTH AFFAIRS DIVISION
Director: Ms Nancy Spence

SCIENCE AND TECHNOLOGY DIVISION
Director: Dr Ken Lum

ECONOMIC AND LEGAL ADVISORY SERVICES DIVISION
Director and Head: Mohammad Abdul Malik

EXPORT AND INDUSTRIAL DEVELOPMENT DIVISION
Director: Richard N Gold

MANAGEMENT AND TRAINING SERVICES DIVISION
Special Adviser (Commercialisation) and Acting Director: Michael Gillibrand

GENERAL TECHNICAL ASSISTANCE SERVICES DIVISION
Director: Ms Tendai R W Bare

Esperanto Parliamentary Group

Esperanto Centre
43 St Giles Close, Maldon, Essex CM9 6HU
07957 417526
E-mail:
esperantolobby@esperanto.demon.co.uk
Website: www.esperanto.org/uk

The Esperanto Parliamentary Group was formed in 1973 and exists to support the teaching and use of Esperanto as a solution to language difficulties encountered universally both in the commercial and social fields.

Chairman:
Rt Hon Lord Archer of Sandwell, QC
Joint Secretaries: Roger Gale, MP,
Dr Evan Harris, MP, Austin Mitchell, MP
Organising Secretary: Brian Barker

Inter-Parliamentary Union British Group

All communications regarding Subscriptions, Meetings, Hospitality arrangements and Administrative matters, should be addressed to: The Secretary, Inter-Parliamentary Union, Palace of Westminster, London SW1A 0AA 020 7219 3011/2/3 Fax: 020 7222 1213
E-mail: bgipu@parliament.uk

Founded in 1889 to promote personal contact between the members of all Parliaments, the IPU now includes 138 national groups committed to the development of representative institutions and the advancement of international peace and co-operation. At the Annual General Meeting held on 23 November 1999 the undermentioned were elected as officers and members of the Executive Committee of the British Group, IPU, for the year 1999-2000.

At the Annual General Meeting held on 23 November 1999 the undermentioned were elected as officers and members of the Executive Committee of the British Group, IPU, for the year 1999-2000.
Hon Presidents: The Rt Hon the Lord Irvine of Lairg, The Rt Hon Betty Boothroyd, MP
President: The Rt Hon Tony Blair, MP
Vice-Presidents: The Rt Hon Paddy Ashdown, MP, The Rt Hon the Lord Callaghan of Cardiff, KG, The Rt Hon the Lord Carrington, KG, GCMG, CH, MC, DL, The Rt Hon Robin Cook, MP, The Rt Hon William Hague, MP, The Rt Hon Sir Edward Heath, KG, MBE, MP, The Rt Hon Lord Howe of Aberavon, CH, QC, The Rt Hon the Lord Hurd of Westwell, CH, CBE, The Rt Hon John Major, CH, MP, The Rt Hon the Lord Owen, CH, The Rt Hon the Lord Steel of Aikwood, KBE, DL, The Rt Hon the Baroness Thatcher, LG, OM, FRS, The Rt Hon the Lord Weatherill, DL
Chairman: David Marshall, MP
Vice-Chairmen: Marion Roe, MP,
Allan Rogers, MP
Treasurer: David Wilshire, MP
Executive Committee:
Government: Donald Anderson, MP, John Austin, MP, Ann Clwyd, MP, Tom Cox, MP, Terry Davis, MP, Lord Desai, Llin Golding,

MP, Eric Illsley, MP, Tony Lloyd, MP, William O'Brien, MP, Gordon Prentice, MP, Baroness Smith of Gilmorehill, Dennis Turner, MP
Opposition: Tony Baldry, MP, Quentin Davies, MP, The Rt Hon the Lord Jopling, John Townend, MP
Minority Parties: The Lord Mackie of Benshie, CBE, DSO, DFC, LLD, Nigel Jones, MP, Rev Martin Smyth, MP, Baroness Strange
Secretary: David Ramsay

Inter-Parliamentary Union

Founded in 1889, the IPU is the world organisation of parliaments of Sovereign States. It is the focal point for world-wide parliamentary dialogue and works for peace and co-operation among peoples and for the firm establishment of representative institutions. In October 1999, the IPU had 138 member-parliaments, operating through National IPU Groups. Through its twice-annual inter-parliamentary conferences and other meetings, the IPU discusses the main issues before the international community and for which proposals and solutions can be advanced by parliamentary co-operation and diplomacy: democracy and human rights, including equality between men and women, sustainable development in all its dimensions, international security. The IPU supports the efforts of the United Nations, whose objectives it shares, and works in close co-operation with it. The IPU has concluded co-operation agreements with the UN and several of its specialised agencies.

Acting President of the Inter-Parliamentary Council (IPU governing body), and Chairman of the Executive Committee:
Mrs N Heptulla, MP, India
Executive Committee: Mr I Fjuk, MP, Estonia; Mrs Barbara Imiolczyk, MP, Poland; Mrs F Kefi, MP, Tunisia; Senator Eduardo Menem, Argentina; Mr Diego Novelli, MP, Italy; Mr Fernando Solana, MP, Mexico; Mr Mélégué Traoré, MP, Burkina Faso; Mr Fawzi Tuaimeh, MP, Jordan; Mrs Tatiana Yariguina, MP, Russian Federation; Mr Chung-Soo Park, MP, Republic of Korea, Mr M P Tjitendero, MP, Namibia, Mr G Versnick, MP, Belgium

IPU SECRETARIAT
Secretary General: Anders Johnsson
Official Publication, Inter-Parliamentary Bulletin (twice annual).
Place du Petit-Saconnex, BP 438, CH-1211 Geneva 19, Switzerland
00 41 22 919 41 50 *Fax:* (41 22) 733 31 41
E-mail: postbox@mail.ipu.org
Website: www.ipu.org

International Association of Business and Parliament

1 Buckingham Place, London SW1E 6HR
020 7976 5311 Fax: 020 7828 7778
E-mail: admin@ipt.org.uk
Website: www.iabp.org

The aim of the Association is to improve dialogue between those organisations which manage schemes for legislators, business people and public administrators and to educate and inform each other about their respective functions.

To enhance and facilitate improved interaction between member organisations and their participating business personnel with administrators and parliamentarians.

President: The Rt Hon the Lord Weatherill, DL
Secretary-General: Fredrick R Hyde-Chambers
International Co-ordination Manager: Sharon Garfinkel
Board: Dr William de Ridder, Director, Stichting Maatschappij en Onderneming (Society and Enterprise Foundation) [The Netherlands], Lucila Gomez-Baeza, Director, Industry and Parliament Scheme, and Deputy Secretary General, Circulo de Empresarios [Spain], Fredrick R Hyde-Chambers, Director, The Industry and Parliament Trust (Administrating Member) [UK], Jukka Koivisto, Executive Director, Politiika – Elinkeinoelama-Seura (Economic Information Bureau) [Finland], Goran Lagerholm, Director of Sallskapet & Naringlsiv (Society of Politics and Business) [Sweden], Stephen Lakis, President, The State Legislative Leaders Foundation [USA], Lindsay McCallum, Director, The New Zealand Business and Parliament Trust [New Zealand], Will Wesson, Chief Executive, The Whitehall and Industry Group [UK], Enterprise et Progres [France], (Director to be nominated) Vlaams Economisch Verbond, VEV [Belgium]

International Criminal Police Organization

50 quai Achille Lignon, BP 6041
69411 Lyon, France
00 334 7 244 70 00 *Fax:* 00 334 7 244 71 63
Website: www.interpol-pr.com

Secretary-General:
Raymond Kendall, QPM (UK)

UK OFFICE:
NCIS-Interpol, PO Box 8000,
London SE11 5EN
020 7238 8115 Fax: 020 7238 8112

British Representative:
J M Abbott, QPM, BA(Hons)

International Oil Pollution Compensation Funds

4 Albert Embankment, London SE1 7SR
020 7582 2606 Fax: 020 7735 0326
E-mail: info@iopcfund.org

Director: M Jacobsson
Legal Counsel: S Osanai
Head, Claims Department: J Nichols
Head, Finance and Administration Department:
R Pillai
Claims Officers: Miss S T Gregory, J Maura
Head, External Relations and Conference
Department: Ms H Warson
Finance Officer:
Mrs P Binkhorst-van Romunde

North Atlantic Treaty Organization

Autoroute Bruxelles Zaventem, Evere,
B-1110 Brussels, Belgium
00 32 2 707 41 11 *Fax:* 00 32 2 707 41 17
E-mail: natodoc@hq.nato.int
Telex: 23867
Website: www.nato.int

Secretary-General: The Rt Hon the Lord
Robertson of Port Ellen (UK)
UK Representative:
HE Sir John Goulden, KCMG

NORTH ATLANTIC COUNCIL
Chairman: The Rt Hon the Lord Robertson of
Port Ellen (UK) Secretary-General of NATO
Deputy Chairman: HE Mr Sergio Balanzino
(Italy), Deputy Secretary-General of NATO

PERMANENT REPRESENTATIVES ON THE
NORTH ATLANTIC COUNCIL
Belgium: Baron Thierry de Gruben

Canada: S E M David Wright
Czech Republic: Karel Kovanda
Denmark: Gunnar Riberholdt
France: Philippe Guelluy
Germany: Joachim Bitterlich
Greece: George Savvaides
Hungary: Andras Simonyi
Iceland: Gunnar Pálsson
Italy: Amadeo de Franchis
Luxembourg: Jean-Jacques Kasel
Netherlands: Nicolaas Hendrik Biegman
Norway: Hans Jacob Biørn Lian
Poland: Andrzej Towpik
Portugal: Fernando Andresen-Guimarães
Spain: Javier Conde de Saro
Turkey: Onur Öymen
United Kingdom: Sir John Goulden, KCMG
United States: Alexander R Vershbow

Organisation for Economic Co-operation and Development

2 rue André-Pascal, F-75775 Paris Cedex 16,
France
00 33 1 45 24 82 00
Fax: 00 33 1 45 24 85 00
E-mail: webmaster@oecd.org
Website: http://www.oecd.org

OECD came into existence on 30 September
1961 when it succeeded OEEC (Organisation for
European Economic Co-operation). The aims of
the Organisation are to promote economic and
social welfare throughout the OECD area by
assisting its member governments in the formulation of policies designed to this end and by co-
ordinating these policies; and to stimulate and
harmonise its members' efforts in favour of
developing countries.

Member Countries:
Australia, Austria, Belgium, Canada, Czech
Republic, Denmark, Finland, France,
Germany, Greece, Hungary, Iceland, Ireland,
Italy, Japan, Korea, Luxembourg, Mexico,
Netherlands, New Zealand, Norway, Poland,
Portugal, Spain, Sweden, Switzerland, Turkey,
United Kingdom, United States.
Secretary-General: Donald J Johnston
Deputy Secretaries-General: Thorvald Moe,
Herwig Schlögl, Seiichi Kondo, Mrs Sally
Shelton-Colby
UK Representative: HE Mr Chris Crabbie
19 rue de Franqueville, F-75116 Paris 16, France
00 33 1 45 24 98 28 Fax: 00 33 1 45 24 98 37

Overseas Development Institute

Portland House, Stag Place
London SW1E 5DP
020 7393 1600 Fax: 020 7393 1699
E-mail: odi@odi.org.uk
Website: www.oneworld.org/odi/

The Overseas Development Institute is an independent non-governmental centre for development research and a forum for discussion of the problems facing developing countries. Its research programme has four main components: Rural Policy and Environment, Forestry Policy and Environment, Humanitarian Policy, and International Economic Development. There are also networks linking research to practitioners in Agricultural Research and Extension, Rural Development Forestry, and Relief and Rehabilitation.

The Institute also has an information programme of publications, meetings, conferences and library services. ODI works closely with the All Party Parliamentary Group for Overseas Development (APGOOD) providing research and advice to both Houses of Parliament. The Institute regularly advises government, the EU and international organisations such as the World Bank and the United Nations. ODI also briefs journalists and maintains a close relationship with other development NGOs.

As a registered charity, ODI is dependent on outside funds and is supported by grants and donations from public and private sources.

Chairman of Council: The Earl Cairns, CBE
Director: Simon Maxwell
Secretary to Council: Allen Brown

Royal Institute of International Affairs

Chatham House, 10 St James's Square
London SW1Y 4LE
020 7957 5700 Fax: 020 7957 5710
E-mail: contact@riia.org
Website: www.riia.org

Patron: Her Majesty The Queen
Presidents: The Rt Hon the Lord Callaghan of Cardiff, KG, The Rt Hon the Lord Carrington, KG, GCMG, CH, MC, The Rt Hon the Lord Jenkins of Hillhead, OM
Chairman: Lord Marshall of Knightsbridge
Director: Dr Chris Gamble

United Nations

THE GENERAL ASSEMBLY
THE SECURITY COUNCIL
THE ECONOMIC & SOCIAL COUNCIL
THE TRUSTEESHIP COUNCIL
THE SECRETARIAT
United Nations,
New York, NY 10017, USA
00 1 212 963 1234 *Fax:* 00 1 212 963 4879
Telex: 232 422
Websites: www.un.org
unsystem.org (the official Website locator for UN Programmes, specialised agencies, autonomous bodies, inter-agency co-ordination mechanisms and other groups dealing with UN issues)

Secretary-General: Kofi Annan
Deputy Secretary-General: Ms Louise Fréchette
Chef de Cabinet, Executive Office of the Secretary-General: Iqbal S Riza
Under Secretary-General, Office of Internal Oversight Services: Karl Theodor Paschke
Under Secretary-General for Legal Affairs and Legal Counsel: Hans Corell
Under Secretary-General, Department of Political Affairs:
  Sir Kieran Prendergast, KCVO, CMG
Under Secretary-General, Department of Peacekeeping Operations: Bernard Miyet
Under Secretary-General, Department of Economic and Social Affairs: Nitin Desai
Under Secretary-General, Department of General Assembly Affairs and Conference Services: Yongjian Jin
Under Secretary-General, Department of Administration and Management:
  Joseph E Connor
Under-Secretary-General, Disarmament Affairs:
  Jayartha Dhanapala
Under Secretary-General, Department of Public Information: Kensaku Hogen
Under Secretary-General, Office of the Special Representative of the Secretary-General for Children and Armed Conflict: Olara Otunnu
Under Secretary-General, Office for the Co-ordination of Humanitarian Affairs (OCHA):
  Veira de Mello

INTERNATIONAL COURT OF JUSTICE
The Peace Palace, 2517 KJ, The Hague,
The Netherlands
00 31 70 302 23 23 *Fax:* 00 31 70 364 99 28
Website: www.icj-cij.org
Telex: 32323
President: Stephen M Schwebel

INTERNATIONAL TRADE CENTRE
(UNCTAD/WTO)
Postal address: Palais des Nations
CH-1211 Geneva 10, Switzerland
00 41 22 907 1234
Fax: 00 41 22 907 0057/0043
and 54-56 rue de Montbrillant, CH-1202
Geneva, Switzerland
00 41 22 730 0111 *Fax:* 00 41 22 733 44 39
Secretary General: J Denis Belisle

UNITED NATIONS OFFICE AT GENEVA (UNOG)
UN Office, Palais des Nations
CH-1211 Geneva 10, Switzerland
00 41 22 907 1234 *Fax:* 00 41 22 917 0123
Telex: 28 9696 UNO CH
Director-General: Vladimir Petrovsky
High Commissioner for Human Rights:
   Mary Robinson
00 41 22 917 34 56 Fax: 00 41 22 917 02 13
E-mail: wabadmin.hchr@unog.ch

UNITED NATIONS OFFICE AT VIENNA
Vienna International Centre, PO Box 500, A-
1400 Vienna, Austria
Info phone: 00 43 1 21 13 10
Fax: 00 43 1 23 72 71
Telex: 135612
Director-General: Pino Arlacchi
UK Representative: HE Dr John Freeman

UNITED NATIONS INFORMATION CENTRE (UK)
Millbank Tower (21st Floor),
21–24 Millbank, London SW1P 4QH
020 7630 1981 Fax: 020 7976 6478
E-mail: info@uniclondon.org
Website: unitednations.org.uk
Director: Ahmad Fawzi
Deputy Representative: Tina Jorgensen

UK MISSION TO THE UNITED NATIONS IN
NEW YORK
One Dag Hammarskjold Plaza, 28th Floor, 885
Second Avenue, New York, NY 10017, USA
Postal address: PO Box 5238,
New York NY 10150-5238, USA
00 1 212 745 9200 *Fax:* 00 1 212 745 9316
E-mail: gbrun@undp.org
Permanent Representative:
   HE Sir Jeremy Greenstock, KCMG
Deputy Permanent Representative:
   HE Mr S Eldon, CMG, OBE

UK MISSION TO THE OFFICE OF THE UNITED
NATIONS AND OTHER INTERNATIONAL
ORGANISATIONS AT GENEVA
37–39 rue de Vermont,
CH-1211 Geneva 20, Switzerland
00 41 22 918 23 00 *Fax:* 00 41 22 918 23 33
E-mail:
UKMis (Humanitarian/Human Rights):
human.uk@ties.itu.int
UKMis (Economic/WTO):
trade.uk@ties.itu.int
UKMis (Specialised Agencies):
specag.uk@ties.itu.int
UKDis: disarm.uk@ties.itu.int
Commercial Section:
commercial.uk@ties.itu.int
Joint Management Unit:
mission.uk@ties.itu.int
Permanent Representative:
   HE Mr Simon Fuller, CMG
Deputy Permanent Representative: P R Jenkins

UK MISSION TO THE INTERNATIONAL ATOMIC
ENERGY AGENCY, THE UNITED NATIONS
INDUSTRIAL DEVELOPMENT ORGANIZATION AND
THE UNITED NATIONS OFFICE AT VIENNA
Jaurèsgasse 12, A-1030 Vienna, Austria
00 43 1 71 61 30 *Fax:* 00 43 1 71 61 34 900
Permanent Representative:
   HE Dr John Freeman
Deputy Permanent Representative:
   M R Etherton

UN FUNDS PROGRAMMES

UNITED NATIONS INSTITUTE FOR
DISARMAMENT RESEARCH (UNIDIR)
Palais des Nations, CH-1211 Geneva 10
Switzerland
00 41 22 917 3186 *Fax:* 00 41 22 917 0176
E-mail: Internet,unidir.unidir@itu.ch

Director: Patricia Lewis
UK Representative: HE Mr S I Soutar
37–39 rue de Vermont
CH-1211 Geneva 20, Switzerland
00 41 22 734 3800 *Fax:* 00 41 22 734 5254

UNITED NATIONS INTERNATIONAL DRUG
CONTROL PROGRAMME (UNDCP)
Vienna International Centre,
Wagramerstrasse 5, PO Box 500,
A-1400, Vienna, Austria
00 43 1 21345 4116 *Fax:* 00 43 1 21345 5931
Telex: 135612 UNO A
Executive Director: Pino Arlacchi

UNITED NATIONS CHILDREN'S FUND
(UNICEF)
3 UN Plaza, New York, NY 10017, USA
00 1 212 326 7000 *Fax:* 00 1 212 888 7465
Telex: 239521
Executive Director: Carol Bellamy
*UK Committee: 55 Lincoln's Inn Fields
London WC2A 3NB*
020 7405 5592 Fax: 020 7405 2332
UK Director: David Bull

UNICEF GREETING CARD OPERATION
*Unit 1, Rignalls Lane, Galleywood
Chelmsford, Essex CM2 8TU*
01245 476315

UNITED NATIONS DEVELOPMENT
PROGRAMME (UNDP)
1 UN Plaza, New York, NY 10017, USA
00 1 212 906 5000 *Fax:* 00 1 212 906 5001
Telex: 125980
Administrator: Mark Malloch Brown

UNITED NATIONS HIGH COMMISSIONER FOR
REFUGEES (UNHCR)
*PO Box 2500, 94 rue de Montbrillant,
CH-1211 Geneva 2, Dépot
Switzerland*
00 41 22 739 81 11 *Fax:* 00 41 22 739 7377
High Commissioner: Sadako Ogata
*UK Office: 21st Floor, Millbank Tower,
21–24 Millbank, London SW1P 4QP*
020 7828 9191 Fax: 020 7630 5349
Representative in the UK: Hope Hanlan
Deputy Representative in the UK:
    Peter van der Vaart

UNITED NATIONS RELIEF AND WORKS AGENCY
FOR PALESTINE REFUGEES IN THE NEAR EAST
(UNRWA)
*PO Box 371, Gamal Abdul Nasser Street, Gaza
City, Israel*
00 972 7 677 7700 *Fax:* 00 972 7 677 7555
Commissioner-General: Peter Hansen

UNITED NATIONS CENTRE FOR HUMAN
SETTLEMENTS
PO Box 30030, Nairobi, Kenya
00 254 2 621234
Fax: 00 254 2 624266/624267
Telex: 22996 UNHAB KE
Assistant Secretary-General: Klaus Töpfer
UK Permanent Representative:
    HE Mr J R James, CMG
*British High Commission, Upper Hill Road,
PO Box 30465, Nairobi, Kenya*

UNITED NATIONS CONFERENCE ON TRADE &
DEVELOPMENT (UNCTAD)
*Palais des Nations, CH-1211 Geneva 10,
Switzerland*
00 41 22 907 12 34 *Fax:* 00 41 22 907 00 57
Telex: 289696
Secretary-General: Rubens Ricupero

UNITED NATIONS ENVIRONMENT
PROGRAMME (UNEP)
*PO Box 30552, United National Avenue, Gigiri,
Nairobi, Kenya*
00 254 2 621234 *Fax:* 00 254 2 622624
Telex: 22068, 22173
Executive Director: Klaus Töpfer
UK Permanent Representative:
    HE Mr J R James, CMG
*British High Commission, Upper Hill Road,
PO Box 30465, Nairobi, Kenya*

UNITED NATIONS POPULATION FUND
(UNFPA)
*220 East 42nd Street, New York
NY10017-5880, USA*
00 1 212 297 5000 *Fax:* 00 1 212 370 0201
Telex: 7607883 UNFPA
Executive Director: Nafis Sádik

UNITED NATIONS RESEARCH INSTITUTE FOR
SOCIAL DEVELOPMENT (UNRISD)
*Palais des Nations, CH-1211 Geneva 10,
Switzerland, or Pavillons du Petit-Saconnex 16,
avenue Jean Trembley, Geneva, Switzerland*
00 41 22 798 3400 *Fax:* 00 41 22 740 07 91
Telex: 412 962 UNO CH
Director: Thandika Mkandawire

INTERNATIONAL RESEARCH AND TRAINING
INSTITUTE FOR THE ADVANCEMENT OF WOMEN
(INSTRAW)
*Calle César Nicolás Penson 702-A,
Santo Domingo, Dominican Republic*
00 500 809 685 2111
Fax: 00 500 809 685 2117
Telex: (326) 4280 WRA SD
Director: Ms Yakin Erturk

UNITED NATIONS INSTITUTE FOR TRAINING &
RESEARCH (UNITAR)
*Palais des Nations, CH-1211, Geneva 10,
Switzerland, or Pavillons du Petit-Saconnex 16,
avenue Jean Trembley, Geneva, Switzerland*
00 41 22 798 58 50 *Fax:* 00 41 22 733 1383
Telex: 41 29 62
Acting Executive Director: Marcel Boisard

UNITED NATIONS INTER-REGIONAL CRIME &
JUSTICE RESEARCH INSTITUTE (UNICRI)
Via Giulia 52, 00186 Rome, Italy
00 39 6 6877437 *Fax:* 00 39 6 6892638
Telex: 610181 FAU I UNICRI
Director: Alberto Bradanini

UNITED NATIONS UNIVERSITY (UNU)
*53–70 Gingumae 5-Chome, Shibuya-Ku, Tokyo
150-8925, Japan*
00 81 3 3499 2811 *Fax:* 00 81 3 3499 2828
Telex: J25442 UNATUNIV
Rector: Hans Van Ginkel

WORLD FOOD PROGRAMME (WFP)
*Via Cesare Giulio Viola, 68/70, 00148 Rome,
Italy*
00 39 6 65131 *Fax:* 00 39 6 59 0632/0637
Telex: 626675 WFP I
Executive Director: Ms Catherine A Bertini
UK Permanent Representative: A Beattie
Viale Aventino 36/1, 00153 Rome, Italy
00 39 06 578 1535 *Fax:* 00 39 06 572 85010
Paris Office
c/o Unesco, Room M1-32, 1 rue Miollis,
F-75732 Paris Cedex 15, France
00 331 4568 3005/10 *Fax:* 00 331 4065 9186

UN SPECIALISED AGENCIES

FOOD AND AGRICULTURE ORGANIZATION OF THE
UNITED NATIONS (FAO)
*Viale delle Terme di Caracalla, 00100 Rome,
Italy*
00 39 6 57051 *Fax:* 00 39 6 5705 3152
Website: www.fao.org
Telex: 610181 FAOI

Director-General: Jacques Diouf
UK Permanent Representative: A Beattie
Viale Aventino 36/1, 00153 Rome, Italy
00 39 06 578 1535 *Fax:* 00 39 06 572 85010

GENERAL AGREEMENT ON TARIFFS AND TRADE
(GATT)
*See World Trade Organization (the WTO is the
successor to GATT)*

INTERNATIONAL ATOMIC ENERGY AGENCY
(IAEA)
*Vienna International Centre,
Wagramerstrasse 5, PO Box 100,
A-1400 Vienna, Austria*
00 43 1 2600 0 *Fax:* 00 43 1 2600 7
Website: www.iaea.org
Telex: 1-12645 ATOM A
Director-General: Mohamed M El Barquei
UK Representative: HE Dr John Freeman

INTERNATIONAL CIVIL AVIATION ORGANIZATION
(ICAO)
*999 University Street, PO Box 400,
H3C 5H7 Montreal, Quebec H3A 2R2, Canada*
00 1 514 954 8219 *Fax:* 00 1 514 954 6077
Telex: 05 24513
President of the Council: Dr Assad Kotaite
Secretary-General: Mr R C Costa Pereira
UK Representative: D S Evans
Suite 1415
00 1 514 954 8302 *Fax:* 00 1 514 954 8001

INTERNATIONAL FUND FOR AGRICULTURAL
DEVELOPMENT (IFAD)
Via del Serafico 107, 00142 Rome, Italy
00 39 6 54 591 *Fax:* 00 39 6 504 3463
Telex: 620330 IFAD-I
President: Fawzi Hamad Al-Sultan
UK Permanent Representative: A Beattie
Viale Aventino 36/1, 00153 Rome, Italy
00 39 06 578 1535 *Fax:* 00 39 06 572 85010

INTERNATIONAL LABOUR ORGANIZATION (ILO)
*4 route des Morillons, CH-1211 Geneva 22,
Switzerland*
00 41 22 799 61 11 *Fax:* 00 41 22 798 86 85
Website: www.ilo.org
Telex: 415647 ILO CH
Director-General: Juan Somavia
*London Branch Office: Millbank Tower, 21–24
Millbank, London SW1P 4QP*
020 7828 6401 Fax: 020 7233 5925
Director: Peter Brannen

INTERNATIONAL MARITIME ORGANIZATION
(IMO)
4 Albert Embankment, London SE1 7SR
020 7735 7611 Fax: 020 7587 3210
Website: www.imo.org
Telex: 23588 IMOLDN G
Secretary-General: William A O'Neil

INTERNATIONAL MONETARY FUND (IMF)
*700 19th Street NW,
Washington DC 20431, USA*
00 1 202 623 7000 *Fax:* 00 1 202 623 4661
Telex: RCA 248331 IMF UR
*Chairman of the Executive Board and Managing
Director:* Michel Camdessus
UK Executive Directors: S Pickford,
M Wickstead, S Collins
Room 11–120
00 1 202 623 4562 *Fax:* 00 1 202 623 4965

INTERNATIONAL TELECOMMUNICATION UNION
(ITU)
Place des Nations, CH-1211 Geneva 20,
Switzerland
00 41 22 730 51 11 *Fax:* 00 41 22 733 72 56
Telex: 421000 UIT CH
Secretary-General: Pekka J Tarjanne

UNITED NATIONS EDUCATIONAL, SCIENTIFIC
AND CULTURAL ORGANIZATION (UNESCO)
7 Place de Fontenoy, F-75352 Paris, 07 SP,
France
00 33 1 45 68 10 00
Fax: 00 33 1 45 67 16 90
Telex: 270 602 PARIS
Director-General: Federico Mayor

UNITED NATIONS INDUSTRIAL DEVELOPMENT
ORGANIZATION (UNIDO)
Vienna International Centre
PO Box 300, A-1400 Vienna, Austria
00 43 1 260 260 *Fax:* 00 43 1 269 2669
Telex: 135612
Director-General: Carlos Magariños
UK Representative: Dr John Freeman

UNIVERSAL POSTAL UNION (UPU)
Weltpoststrasse 4, CH-3000 Berne 15,
Switzerland
00 41 31 350 31 11
Fax: 00 41 31 350 31 10
Telex: 912761 UPU CH
Director-General: Thomas E Leavey

WORLD BANK/INTERNATIONAL FINANCE
CORPORATION (IFC) – A GROUP OF THREE
ORGANISATIONS:
INTERNATIONAL BANK FOR RECONSTRUCTION
AND DEVELOPMENT (IBRD), INTERNATIONAL
DEVELOPMENT ASSOCIATION (IDA) AND
MULTILATERAL INVESTMENT GUARANTEE AGENCY
1818 H Street NW, Washington DC 20433, USA
00 1 202 477 1234
Fax: 00 202 477 6391
Telex: RCA 248423, ITT 440098, WUI 64145
President of the World Bank: James Wolfensohn
UK Executive Directors to the IBRD:
H P Evans, D L Stanton
c/o International Monetary Fund,
Room 11–120, 700 19th Street NW,
Washington DC 20431, USA
00 1 202 623 7000 *Fax:* 00 1 202 623 4661
London Office:
World Bank Group, New Zealand House,
Haymarket, London SW1Y 4TE
020 7930 8511 Fax: 020 7930 8515
Director: Andrew Rogersson

WORLD HEALTH ORGANIZATION (WHO)
20 avenue Appia, CH-1211 Geneva 27,
Switzerland
00 41 22 791 21 11
Fax: 00 41 22 791 07 46
Telex: 41 54 16
Director-General:
Dr Gro Harlem Brundtland

WORLD INTELLECTUAL PROPERTY ORGANIZATION
(WIPO)
34 chemin des Colombettes
CH-1211 Geneva 20, Switzerland
00 41 22 730 91 11
Fax: 00 41 22 338 81 11
Telex: 412 912 OMPI CH
Director-General: Kamil Idris

WORLD METEOROLOGICAL ORGANIZATION
(WMO)
41 avenue Giuseppe Motta, Geneva,
Switzerland
Mailing address: Case Postale No. 2300, CH-
1211 Geneva 2, Switzerland
00 41 22 730 81 11
Fax: 00 41 22 734 23 26
Telex: 414199 OMM CH
Secretary-General: G O P Obasi

WORLD TOURISM ORGANIZATION (WTO)
Capitán Haya 42, 28020 Madrid, Spain
00 34 91 567 6100
Fax: 00 34 91 571 37 33
Telex: 42188 OMT E
Secretary-General: Francesco Frangialle
(The UK is not a member)

UN REGIONAL ECONOMIC COMMISSIONS

ECONOMIC COMMISSION FOR AFRICA (ECA)
Africa Hall, PO Box 3001
Addis Ababa, Ethiopia
00 251 1 51 72 00 *Fax:* 00 251 1 51 44 16
Telex: 21029

Executive Director: Kingsley Y Amoako

ECONOMIC COMMISSION FOR EUROPE (ECE)
Palais des Nations, 8-14 Avenue de la Paix,
CH-1211 Geneva 10, Switzerland
00 41 22 917 2670/2673
Fax: 00 41 22 917 0036
Website: www.unece.org
Executive Secretary: Yves Berthelot

ECONOMIC COMMISSION FOR LATIN AMERICA AND THE CARIBBEAN (ECLAC)
Avenida Vitacura 3030, PO Box 179-D, Santiago, Chile
00 56 2 210 2000
Fax: 00 56 2 2080252/2081946
Telex: 441054 UN SGO CZ
Executive Secretary: José Antonio Ocampo

ECONOMIC AND SOCIAL COMMISSION FOR ASIA AND THE PACIFIC (ESCAP)
United Nations Building, Rajdamnern Avenue, Bangkok 10200, Thailand
00 66 2 288 1234 *Fax:* 00 66 2 288 1000
Telex: 82392/82315 escap th
Executive Secretary: Dr Adrianius Mooy

ECONOMIC AND SOCIAL COMMISSION FOR WESTERN ASIA (ESCWA)
PO Box 11-8575, Beirut, Lebanon
00 9611 981 301 *Fax:* 00 9611 981 510
Executive Secretary: Hazem El-Beblawi

World Trade Organization

Centre William Rappard
154 rue de Lausanne, CH-1211 Geneva 21
Switzerland
00 41 22 739 51 11
Fax: 00 41 22 731 42 06
Telex: 41 2 324 OMC/WTO CH

Director-General: Mike Moore
Information and Media Relations Division
  Director: Keith Rockwell
00 41 22 739 50 07
Fax: 00 41 22 739 54 58
E-mail: enquiries@wto.org
Website: www.wto.org
NB: WTO is the successor to GATT

HISTORICAL INFORMATION

Parliaments of the 20th Century

Assembled	Dissolved	Length	Ministries	Took Office
		yrs. m. d.		
VICTORIA				
Dec. 3, 1900	Jan. 8, 1906	5 1 5	{ Salisbury (C)	Dec. 6, 1900
			{ Balfour (C)	July 12, 1902
EDWARD VII				
Feb. 13, 1906	Jan. 10, 1910	3 10 28	{ C. Bannerman (L)	Dec. 5, 1905
			{ Asquith (L)	April 5, 1908
Feb. 15, 1910	Nov. 28, 1910	9 13	Asquith (L)	Feb. 15, 1910
GEORGE V				
Jan. 31, 1911	Nov. 25, 1918	7 9 25	{ Asquith (L)	May 25, 1915
Feb. 4, 1919	Oct. 25, 1922	3 8 21	{ Lloyd George (L)	Dec. 6, 1916
			{ Coalition	
Nov. 20, 1922	Nov. 16, 1923	11 27	A. Bonar Law (C)	Oct. 23, 1922
Jan. 8, 1924	Oct. 9, 1924	9 1	J. R. MacDonald (Lab.)	Jan. 22, 1924
Dec. 2, 1924	May 10, 1929	4 5 8	S. Baldwin (C)	Nov. 4, 1924
June 25, 1929	Oct. 7, 1931	2 3 12	J. R. MacDonald (Lab.)	June 5, 1929
			{ J. R. MacDonald	Aug. 24, 1931
Nov. 3, 1931	Oct. 25, 1935	3 11 22	{ (Nat. Govt.)	
			{ S. Baldwin	
Nov. 26, 1935			S. Baldwin	June 7, 1935
			(Nat. Govt.)	
EDWARD VIII			N. Chamberlain	May 28, 1937
			(Nat. Govt.)	
GEORGE VI	June 15, 1945	9 6 20	W. Churchill	May 10, 1940
			(Nat. Govt.)	
Aug. 1, 1945	Feb. 3, 1950	4 6 2	C. R. Attlee (Lab.)	July 26, 1945
Mar. 1, 1950	Oct. 5, 1951	1 7 4	C. R. Attlee (Lab.)	Feb. 25, 1950
Oct. 31, 1951	May 6, 1955	3 6 6	{ W. Churchill (C)	Oct. 26, 1951
			{ A. Eden (C)	
ELIZABETH II			A. Eden (C)	Apr. 6, 1955
June 7, 1955	Sept. 18, 1959	4 3 11	{ H. Macmillan (C)	Jan. 10, 1957
			{ H. Macmillan (C)	Oct. 9, 1959
Oct. 20, 1959	Sept. 25, 1964	4 11 5	A. Douglas-Home (C)	Oct. 9, 1963
Oct. 27, 1964	Mar. 10, 1966	1 4 11	{ H. Wilson (Lab.)	Oct. 16, 1964
Apr. 18, 1966	May 29, 1970	4 1 11	{ H. Wilson (Lab.)	Apr. 1, 1966
June 29, 1970	Feb. 8, 1974	3 7 10	E. R. G. Heath (C)	June 19, 1970
Mar. 6, 1974	Sept. 20, 1974	6 14	H. Wilson (Lab.)	Mar. 4, 1974
			(Minority Govt.)	
Oct. 22, 1974	April 7, 1979	4 5 15	{ H. Wilson (Lab.)	Oct. 11, 1974
			{ J. Callaghan (Lab.)	Apr. 5, 1976
May 9, 1979	May 13, 1983	4 0 4	Mrs M. Thatcher (C)	May 3, 1979
June 15, 1983	May 18, 1987	3 11 3	Mrs M. Thatcher (C)	June 9, 1983
June 17, 1987	Mar. 16, 1992	4 8 28	{ Mrs M. Thatcher (C)	June 11, 1987
			{ J. Major (C)	Nov. 28, 1990
April 27, 1992	April 8, 1997	4 11 19	J. Major (C)	April 10, 1992
May 7, 1997			T. Blair (Lab.)	May 1, 1997

Size of the House of Commons since 1801

With the Union of Great Britain and Ireland in 1801 the number of members of Parliament of the United Kingdom was fixed at 658. This number was adhered to by the Reform Act, 1832. In 1885 the total was increased to 670, and by the Act of 1918 to 707. With the creation of the Irish Free State in 1922, the Irish representation was reduced to 13 members from Ulster, making the membership of the House of Commons 615. In 1945, owing to the division of large Constituencies, the number was increased by 25 to 640. Under the Act of 1948 the number was decreased to 625. Under the Orders passed in 1954 and 1955 the number was increased to 630. As the result of redistribution and boundary changes, the total number of MPs elected at the 1979 General Election was 635. The House of Commons (Redistribution of Seats) Act 1979 and the Boundary Commission reports of 1983 resulted in an increase of 15 seats after the 1983 Election. The size of the House of Commons up until the 1992 General Election was 650 members. At the 1992 Election, 651 Members were elected, an extra seat having been created for Milton Keynes. Reports from the Boundary Commission caused an increase to 659 at the 1997 Election.

General Election Majorities since the Reform Act

(NB *In certain cases, such as the election of 1910, the Government party had a working arrangement with other parties, which ensured them a majority in the House*)

1832	Lib.	300	1923	Con.	No majority
1835	Lib.	108	1924	Con.	223
1837	Lib.	40	1929	Lab.	No majority
1841	Con.	78	1931	Nat. Govt.	493
1847	Lib.	2	1935	Nat. Govt.	249
1852	Con.	8	1945	Lab.	146
1857	Lib.	92	1950	Lab.	5
1859	Lib.	40	1951	Con.	17
1865	Lib.	62	1955	Con.	58
1868	Lib.	106	1959	Con.	100
1874	Con.	52	1964	Lab.	4
1880	Lib.	176	1966	Lab.	96
1885	Lib.	No majority	1970	Con.	30
1886	Unionist	120	1974	(Feb.) Lab.	No majority
1892	Lib.	No majority	1974	(Oct.) Lab.	3
1895	Unionist	152	(3 over all parties, 42 over Cons.)		
1900	Unionist	135	1979	Con.	43
1906	Lib.	130	1983	Con.	144
1910	(Jan.) Lib.	No majority	1987	Con.	101
1910	(Dec.) Lib.	No majority	1992	Con.	21
1918	Coalition	249	1997	Lab.	177
1922	Con.	75			

Long Parliaments

The longest lived Parliaments in English history have been the Elizabethan Parliament of 1572–83, the Long Parliament of 1640–53, and the Cavalier Parliament of 1661–79. The First World War Parliament met on 31 January 1911, and was dissolved on 25 November 1918. That of the Second met 26 November 1935, and was dissolved 15 June 1945.

Prime Ministers since 1721

1721–42	Sir Robert Walpole (Whig)
1742–43	Spencer Compton (Whig)
1743–54	Henry Pelham (Whig)
1754–56	Duke of Newcastle (Whig)
1756–57	Duke of Devonshire (Whig)
1757–62	Duke of Newcastle (Whig)
1762–63	Earl of Bute (Tory)
1763–65	George Grenville (Whig)
1765–66	Marquess of Rockingham (Whig)
1766–67	William Pitt (the Elder) (Whig)
1767–70	Duke of Grafton (Whig)
1770–82	Lord North (Tory)
1782	Marquess of Rockingham (Whig)
1782–83	Earl of Shelburne (Whig)
1783	Duke of Portland (Coalition)
1783–1801	William Pitt (the Younger) (Tory)
1801–04	Henry Addington (Tory)
1804–06	William Pitt (the Younger) (Tory)
1806–07	Lord Grenville (Whig)
1807–09	Duke of Portland (Tory)
1809–12	Spencer Perceval (Tory)
1812–27	Earl of Liverpool (Tory)
1827	George Canning (Tory)
1827–28	Viscount Goderich (Tory)
1828–30	Duke of Wellington (Tory)
1830–34	Earl Grey (Whig)
1834	Viscount Melbourne (Whig)
1834–35	Sir Robert Peel (Tory)
1835–41	Viscount Melbourne (Whig)
1841–46	Sir Robert Peel (Tory)
1846–52	Lord John Russell (Whig)
1852	Earl of Derby (Con)
1852–55	Earl of Aberdeen (Coalition)
1855–58	Viscount Palmerston (Lib)
1858–59	Earl of Derby (Con)
1859–65	Viscount Palmerston (Lib)
1865–66	Earl Russell (Lib)
1866–68	Earl of Derby (Con)
1868	Benjamin Disraeli (Con)
1868–74	William Gladstone (Lib)
1874–80	Benjamin Disraeli (Con)
1880–85	William Gladstone (Lib)
1885–86	Marquess of Salisbury (Con)
1886	William Gladstone (Lib)
1886–92	Marquess of Salisbury (Con)
1892–94	William Gladstone (Lib)
1894–95	Earl of Rosebery (Lib)
1895–1902	Marquess of Salisbury (Con)
1902–05	Arthur Balfour (Con)
1905–08	Sir Henry Campbell-Bannerman (Lib)
1908–16	Herbert Asquith (Lib)
1916–22	David Lloyd George (Coalition)
1922–23	Andrew Bonar Law (Con)
1923–24	Stanley Baldwin (Con)
1924	Ramsay MacDonald (Lab)
1924–29	Stanley Baldwin (Con)
1929–35	Ramsay MacDonald (Lab)
1935–37	Stanley Baldwin (Nat Govt)
1937–40	Neville Chamberlain (Nat Govt)
1940–45	Winston Churchill (Coalition)
1945–51	Clement Attlee (Lab)
1951–55	Winston Churchill (Con)
1955–57	Sir Anthony Eden (Con)
1957–63	Harold Macmillan (Con)
1963–64	Sir Alec Douglas-Home (Con)
1964–70	Harold Wilson (Lab)
1970–74	Edward Heath (Con)
1974–76	Harold Wilson (Lab)
1976–79	James Callaghan (Lab)
1979–90	Margaret Thatcher (Con)
1990–97	John Major (Con)
1997–	Tony Blair (Lab)

Presiding Officers and Speakers of the House of Commons

1258   Peter de Montfort
1327   William Trussell
1332 (March) Henry Beaumont
1332 (Sept) Sir Geoffrey Le Scrope
1340   William Trussell
1343   William Trussell
1347–48 William de Thorpe
1351–52 William de Shareshull
1376   Sir Peter de la Mare
1377 (Jan.–Mar.) Sir Thomas Hungerford (the
          first to be designated Speaker)
1377 (Oct.–Nov.) Sir Peter de la Mare
1378 (Oct.–Nov.) Sir James Pickering
1380   Sir John Guildesborough
1381–82 Sir Richard Waldegrave
1383–90 Sir James Pickering (during these
          years the records are defective and
          this Speaker's service might not
          have been unbroken)
1394–98 Sir John Bussy
1399 (Oct.) Sir John Cheyne or Cheney
1399 (Oct.–Nov.) John Dorewood
1401 (Jan.–Mar.) Sir Arnold Savage
1402 (Oct.–Nov.) Sir Henry Redford
1404 (Jan.–Apr.) Sir Arnold Savage
1404 (Oct.–Nov.) Sir William Sturmy or
          Esturmy
1406   Sir John Tiptoft
1407–11 Thomas Chaucer
1412   Speaker unknown
1413 (May–June) William Stourton
1413 (June) John Dorewood
1414 (May) Sir Walter Hungerford
1414   Thomas Chaucer
1415 (Nov.) Richard Redman or Redmayne
1416 (Mar.–May) Sir Walter Beauchamp
1416–19 Roger Flower
1420   Roger Hunt
1421   Thomas Chaucer
1421   Richard Baynard
1422 (Nov.–Dec.) Roger Flower
1423–24 Sir John Russell
1425 (May–July) Sir Thomas Walton or
          Wauton
1426 (Feb.–June) Sir Richard Vernon
1427–28 Sir John Tyrrell
1429–30 William Alington
1431 (Jan.–Mar.) Sir John Tyrrell
1432 (May–July) Sir John Russell
1433 (July–Dec.) Roger Hunt
1435 (Oct.–Dec.) John Bowes
1437 (Jan.–Mar.) Sir John Tyrrell
1437 (Mar.) William Burley or Boreley
1439–42 William Tresham

1445 (Feb.–Apr.) William Burley
1447 (Feb.–Mar.) William Tresham
1449 (Feb.–July) Sir John Say
1449 (Nov. 8th) Sir John Popham
1449–50 William Tresham
1450–51 Sir William Oldhall
1453–54 Thomas Thorpe
1454 (Feb.–Apr.) Sir Thomas Charlton
1455–56 Sir John Wenlock
1459 (Nov.–Dec.) Sir Thomas Tresham
1460 (Oct.) John Green
1461–62 Sir James Strangeways
1463–68 Sir John Say
1469–71 No particulars known
1472–78 William Alington
1483 (Jan.–Feb.) John Wood or Wode
1484 (Jan.–Feb.) William Catesby
1485–86 Sir Thomas Lovell
1487   Sir John Mordaunt
1489–90 Sir Thomas Fitzwilliam
1491–92 Sir Richard Empson
1495   Sir Robert Drury
1496 (Oct.) Sir Reginald Bray (not a Speaker
          in the true sense of the word as he
          presided over a Great Council
          rather than a Parliament)
1497   Sir Thomas Englefield of Inglefield
1504   Edmond Dudley
1510 (Jan.–Feb.) Sir Thomas Englefield
1512–13 Sir Robert Sheffield
1515 (Feb.–Dec.) Sir Thomas Nevill
1523 (Apr.–Aug.) Sir Thomas More
1529–33 Sir Thomas Audley
1533–36 Sir Humphrey Wingfield
1536 (June–July) Sir Richard Rich
1539–40 Sir Nicholas Hare
1542–44 Sir Thomas Moyle
1545–52 Sir John Baker
1553 (March) Sir James Dyer
1553 (Oct.–Dec.) Sir John Pollard
1554 (Apr.–May) Sir Robert Brooke
1554–55 Sir Clement Heigham
1555 (Oct.–Dec.) Sir John Pollard
1558 (Jan.–Nov.) Sir William Cordell
1559 (Jan.–May) Sir Thomas Gargrave
1563 (Jan.–Apr.) Thomas Williams
1566–67 Richard Onslow
1571 (Apr.–May) Sir Christopher Wray
1572–76 Sir Robert Bell
1581–83 Sir John Popham
1584–87 Sir John Puckering
1589 (Feb.–Mar.) Thomas Snagge
1593 (Feb.–Apr.) Sir Edward Coke
1597–98 Sir Christopher Yelverton

1601 (Oct.–Dec.) Sir John Croke
1604–11 Sir Edward Phelips
1614 (Apr.–June) Sir Randolph Crewe
1621–22 Sir Thomas Richardson
1624–25 Sir Thomas Crewe
1626 (Feb.–June) Sir Heneage Finch
1628–29 Sir John Finch
1640 (Apr.–May) Sir John Glanville
1640–47 William Lenthall
1647 (July–Aug.) Henry Pelham
1647–53 William Lenthall
1653 (July–Dec.) Rev. Francis Rous
1654–55 William Lenthall
1656–58 Sir Thomas Widdrington
1657 Bulstrode Whitelocke (appointed *pro tem.* during absence of Widdrington through indisposition)
1659 (Jan.–Mar.) Chaloner Chute
1659 (March) Sir Lislebone Long
1659 (Mar.–Apr.) Thomas Bampfylde
1659–60 William Lenthall
1660 (Jan.) William Say (appointed *pro tem.* during Lenthall's absence)
1660 (Apr.–Dec.) Sir Harbottle Grimston
1661–71 Sir Edward Turnour
1673 (Feb.) Sir Job Charlton
1673–78 Sir Edward Seymour
1678 (Apr.–May) Sir Robert Sawyer
1678–79 Sir Edward Seymour
1679 (Mar.–July) Sir William Gregory
1680–81 Sir William Williams
1685–87 Sir John Trevor
1689 (Jan.–Feb.) Henry Powle
1690–95 Sir John Trevor

1695–98 Paul Foley
1698–1700 Sir Thomas Littleton
1701–05 Robert Harley
1705–08 John Smith
1708–10 Sir Richard Onslow
1710–13 William Bromley
1714–15 Sir Thomas Hanmer
1715–27 Sir Spencer Compton
1728–61 Arthur Onslow
1761–70 Sir John Cust
1770–80 Sir Fletcher Norton
1780–89 Charles Cornwall
1789 (Jan.–June) William Wyndham Grenville
1789–1801 Henry Addington
1801–02 Sir J. Milford
1802–17 C. Abbot
1817–34 C. Manners-Sutton
1835–39 J. Abercromby
1839–57 C. Shawe-Lefevre
1857–72 J. E. Denison
1872–84 H. B. W. Brand
1884–95 A. W. Peel
1895–1905 W. C. Gully
1905–21 J. W. Lowther
1921–28 J. H. Whitley
1928–43 E. A. FitzRoy
1943–51 D. Clifton Brown
1951–59 W. S. Morrison
1959–65 Sir Harry Hylton-Foster
1965–71 Dr Horace King
1971–76 Selwyn Lloyd
1976–83 George Thomas
1983–92 Bernard Weatherill
1992– Betty Boothroyd

Lord Chancellors

1255 Henry Wingham
1260 Nicholas of Ely
1261 Walter of Merton
1263 Nicholas of Ely
1264 Thomas Cantilupe
1265 Walter Giffard
1267 Godfrey Giffard
1268 John Chishull
1269 Richard Middleton
1272 Walter Merton
1274 Robert Burnell
1292 John Langton
1302 William Greenfield
1305 William Hamilton
1307 Ralph Baldock
1307 John de Langton
1310 Walter Reynolds
1314 John Sandall

1318 John Hotham
1320 John Salmon
1323 Robert Baldock
1327 John Hotham
1327 Henry Burghersh
1330 John Stratford
1334 Richard Bury
1335 John Stratford
1337 Robert Stratford
1338 Richard Bintworth
1340 John Stratford
1340 Robert Stratford
1340 Sir Robert Bourchier
1341 Sir Robert Parving
1343 Robert Sadington
1345 John Offord
1349 John Thoresby
1356 William Edington

1363 Simon Langham
1367 William Wykeham
1371 Sir Robert Thorp
1372 Sir John Knyvet
1377 Adam Houghton
1378 Lord Scrope of Bolton
1380 Simon Sudbury
1381 William Courtenay
1381 Lord Scrope of Bolton
1382 Robert Braybrooke
1383 Sir Michael de la Pole
1386 Thomas Arundel
1389 William Wykeham
1391 Thomas Arundel
1396 Edmund Stafford
1399 Thomas Arundel
1399 John Scarle
1401 Edmund Stafford

1403 Cardinal Beaufort
1405 Thomas Langley
1407 Thomas Arundel
1410 Sir Thomas Beaufort
1412 Thomas Arundel
1413 Cardinal Beaufort
1417 Thomas Langley
1422 Thomas Langley
1424 Cardinal Beaufort
1426 Cardinal Kempe
1432 John Stafford
1450 Cardinal Kempe
1454 Richard Neville, Earl of
       Salisbury
1455 Cardinal Bourchier
1456 William Waynflete
1460 George Neville
1461 George Neville
1467 Robert Stillington
1470 George Nevill
1473 Lawrence Booth
1475 Thomas Rotherham
1483 John Russell
1485 John Alcock
1487 Cardinal Morton
1500 Henry Deane
1504 Archbishop Warham
1509 Archbishop Warham
1515 Cardinal Wolsey
1529 Sir Thomas More
1533 Lord Audley
1544 Earl of Southampton
1547 William Paulet
1547 Lord Rich
1552 Thomas Goodrich,
       Bishop of Ely
1553 Bishop Gardiner
1556 Archbishop Heath
1558 Sir Nicholas Bacon
1579 Sir Thomas Bromley
1587 Sir Christopher Hatton
1592 Sir John Puckering
1596 Lord Ellesmere
1603 Lord Ellesmere
1618 Lord Bacon
1621 Lord Keeper Williams
1625 Lord Keeper Williams
1625 Lord Keeper Coventry
1640 Lord Keeper Finch
1641 Lord Keeper Littleton
1643 Earl of Kent*
1645 Lord Keeper Lane

1646 Earl of Salisbury*
1646 Earl of Manchester*
1648 Earl of Kent*
1649 Sir Thomas Whitelock*
1653 Sir E Herbert*
1654 Sir Thomas Whitelock*
1655 Colonel Fiennes*
1659 Speaker Lenthall*
1659 Thomas Tirrell*
1660 Sir Thomas
       Widdington*
       and Earl of Manchester*
1660 Lord Clarendon
1667 Sir Orlando Bridgeman
1672 Lord Shaftesbury
1673 Lord Nottingham
1682 Lord Keeper Guildford
1685 Lord Jeffreys
1689 Lord Maynard and
       Others
1690 Lord Maynard and
       Others
1690 Lord Trevor and Others
1693 Lord Somers
1700 Lord Keeper Wright
1702 Lord Keeper Wright
1705 Lord Cowper
1710 Lord Harcourt
1714 Lord Harcourt
1714 Lord Cowper
1718 Lord Macclesfield
1725 Lord King
1727 Lord King
1733 Lord Talbot of Hensol
1737 Lord Hardwicke
1757 Lord Keeper Henley
1760 Lord Northington
1766 Lord Camden
1770 Charles Yorke
1771 Lord Bathurst
1778 Lord Thurlow
1783 Lord Thurlow
1793 Lord Loughborough
1801 Lord Eldon
1806 Lord Erskine
1807 Lord Eldon
1820 Lord Eldon
1827 Lord Lyndhurst
1830 Lord Brougham
1834 Lord Lyndhurst
1836 Lord Cottenham
1841 Lord Lyndhurst

1846 Lord Cottenham
1850 Lord Truro
1852 Lord St Leonards
1852 Lord Cranworth
1858 Lord Chelmsford
1859 Lord Campbell
1861 Lord Westbury
1865 Lord Cranworth
1866 Lord Chelmsford
1868 Lord Cairns
1868 Lord Hatherley
1871 Lord Selborne
1874 Lord Cairns
1880 Lord Selborne
1885 Lord Halsbury
1886 Lord Herschell
1886 Lord Halsbury
1892 Lord Herschell
1895 Lord Halsbury
1905 Lord Loreburn
1912 Lord Haldane
1915 Lord Buckmaster
1916 Lord Finlay
1919 Lord Birkenhead
1922 Viscount Cave
1924 Viscount Haldane
1924 Viscount Cave
1928 Lord Hailsham
1929 Lord Sankey
1935 Viscount Hailsham
1938 Lord Maugham
1939 Viscount Caldecote
1940 Viscount Simon
1945 Lord Jowitt
1951 Lord Simonds
1954 Viscount Kilmuir
1962 Lord Dilhorne
1964 Lord Gardiner
1970 Lord Hailsham of St
       Marylebone
1974 Lord Elwyn-Jones
1979 Lord Hailsham of St
       Marylebone
1987 Lord Havers
1987 Lord Mackay of
       Clashfern
1997–Lord Irvine of Lairg

* Commissioners 1643–1660
sometimes in conjunction with
others.

UK GOVERNMENT REPRESENTATIVES/ OVERSEAS REPRESENTATIVES IN UK

HM Lord-Lieutenants

ENGLAND

Bedfordshire	Samuel Charles Whitbread, Esq
Berkshire	Philip Lavallin Wroughton, Esq
Bristol	James Napier Tidmarsh, Esq, MBE
Buckinghamshire	Sir Nigel Mobbs
Cambridgeshire	James Gee Pascoe Crowden, Esq
Cheshire	William Arthur Bromley-Davenport, Esq
Cornwall	Lady Mary Holborow
Cumbria	James Cropper, Esq
Derbyshire	John Knollys Bather, Esq
Devon	Eric Dancer, Esq, CBE
Dorset	Captain Michael Fulford-Dobson, CVO, RN
Durham	Sir Paul Nicholson
East Riding of Yorkshire	Richard Marriott, Esq, TD
East Sussex	(Vacant)
Essex	The Lord Braybrooke
Gloucestershire	Henry William George Elwes, Esq
Greater London	The Lord Imbert, QPM
Greater Manchester	Colonel John Bradford Timmins, OBE, TD
Hampshire	Mrs Mary Fagan
Herefordshire	Sir Thomas Dunne, KCVO
Hertfordshire	Simon Alexander Bowes Lyon, Esq
Isle of Wight	Christopher Donald Jack Bland, Esq
Kent	The Rt Hon the Lord Kingsdown, KG
Lancashire	The Lord Shuttleworth
Leicestershire	Timothy Gerald Martin Brooks, Esq
Lincolnshire	Mrs Bridget Cracroft-Eley
Merseyside	Alan William Waterworth, Esq
Norfolk	Sir Timothy Colman, KG
Northamptonshire	Lady Juliet Margaret Townsend, LVO
Northumberland	The Viscount Ridley, KG, GCVO, TD
North Yorkshire	The Lord Crathorne
	The Lord Gisborough, TD *(HM Lieutenant)*
Nottinghamshire	Sir Andrew George Buchanan, Bt
Oxfordshire	Hugo Brunner, Esq
Rutland	Air Chief Marshal Sir Thomas Kennedy, GCB, AFC
Shropshire	Algernon Heber-Percy, Esq
Somerset	Lady Gass
South Yorkshire	The Earl of Scarbrough
Staffordshire	James Appleton Hawley, Esq, TD
Suffolk	The Rt Hon the Lord Belstead
Surrey	Mrs Sarah Goad
Tyne and Wear	Colonel Sir Ralph Carr-Ellison, KCVO, TD
Warwickshire	Martin Dunne, Esq
West Midlands	Robert Richard Taylor, Esq, OBE
West Sussex	Hugh Wyatt, Esq
West Yorkshire	John Lyles, Esq, CBE
Wiltshire	Lieutenant-General Sir Maurice Johnston, KCB, OBE
Worcestershire	Sir Thomas Dunne, KCVO

WALES

Clwyd	Sir Erskine William Gladstone, Bt, KG
Dyfed	Sir David Courtenay Mansel Lewis, KCVO
Gwent	Sir Richard Hanbury Tenison, KCVO
Gwynedd	Richard Ellis Meuric Rees, Esq, CBE
Mid Glamorgan	Murray Adams McLaggan, Esq
Powys	Hon Mrs Shän Legge-Bourke, LVO
South Glamorgan	Captain Norman Lloyd-Edwards, RD, RNR (retired)
West Glamorgan	Robert Cameron Hastie, Esq, CBE, RD

SCOTLAND

The Lord Provosts for the time being of the four City Districts (Aberdeen, Dundee, Edinburgh and Glasgow) are Lord-Lieutenants of those districts ex-officio

Aberdeen City	Lord Provost *ex officio* Margaret Smith
Aberdeenshire (Grampian Region)	Angus Farquharson, Esq, OBE
Angus (Tayside Region)	The Rt Hon the Earl of Airlie, KT, GCVO
Argyll and Bute (Strathclyde Region)	His Grace the Duke of Argyll
Ayrshire and Arran (Strathclyde Region)	Major Richard Henderson, TD
Banffshire (Grampian Region)	James Alexander Strachan McPherson, Esq, CBE
Berwickshire (Borders Region)	Major-General Sir John Swinton, KCVO, OBE
Caithness (Highland Region)	Major Graham Dunnett, TD
Clackmannan (Central Region)	Lieutenant-Colonel Robert Christie Stewart, CBE, TD
Dumfries (Dumfries and Galloway Region)	Captain Ronald Charles Cunningham-Jardine
Dunbartonshire (Strathclyde Region)	Brigadier Donald David Graeme Hardie, TD
Dundee	Lord Provost *ex officio* Mrs Helen Wright
East Lothian (Lothian Region)	Major Sir Hew Hamilton-Dalrymple, Bt, KCVO
Edinburgh	Lord Provost *ex officio* Eric Milligan, Esq
Fife	Mrs Margaret Dean
Glasgow	Lord Provost *ex officio* Alex Mosson, Esq
Inverness (Highland Region)	The Rt Hon the Lord Gray of Contin
Kincardineshire (Grampian Region)	The Viscount of Arbuthnott, KT, CBE, DSC
Lanarkshire (Strathclyde Region)	Hutchison Burt Sneddon, Esq, CBE
Midlothian (Lothian Region)	Captain George Wardlaw Burnet, LVO
Moray (Grampian Region)	Air Vice-Marshal George Arthur Chesworth, CB, OBE, DFC
Nairn (Highland Region)	Ewen Brodie, Esq
Orkney	George Robert Marwick, Esq
Perth and Kinross (Tayside Region)	Sir David Montgomery, Bt
Renfrewshire (Strathclyde Region)	Cameron Holdsworth Parker, Esq, OBE
Ross and Cromarty (Highland Region)	Captain Roderick William Kenneth Stirling of Fairburn, TD
Roxburgh, Ettrick and Lauderdale (Borders Region)	Dr June Paterson-Brown, CBE
Shetland	John Hamilton Scott, Esq
Stewartry of Kirkcudbright (Dumfries and Galloway Region)	Lieutenant-General Sir Norman Arthur, KCB
Stirling and Falkirk (Central Region)	Colonel James Stirling of Garden, CBE, TD
Sutherland (Highland Region)	Major-General David Houston, CBE
Tweeddale (Borders Region)	Captain David Younger
Western Isles	The Viscount Dunrossil, CMG
West Lothian (Lothian Region)	The Earl of Morton
Wigtown (Dumfries and Galloway Region)	Major Edward Orr Ewing

NORTHERN IRELAND

Antrim	The Lord O'Neill, TD
Armagh	The Earl of Caledon
Belfast	Colonel J. Elliott Wilson, OBE
Down	William Joseph Hall, Esq
Fermanagh	The Earl of Erne
Londonderry	Colonel Sir Michael McCorkell, KCVO, OBE, TD
Londonderry City	James Thompson Eaton, Esq, CBE, TD
Tyrone	His Grace the Duke of Abercorn, KG

Association of Lord-Lieutenants

Chairman	The Rt Hon the Lord Kingsdown, KG
Secretary	Andrew Makower, Esq
	(House of Lords, London SW1P 3JY)

Isle of Man

Lieutenant-Governor,
  HE Sir Timothy Daunt, KCMG
The President of Tynwald,
  Hon Sir Charles Kerruish, OBE, CP
Speaker of the House of Keys,
  Hon Noel Q Cringle, SHK
Chief Minister,
  Hon Donald James Gelling, FInstMM, MHK
Population: 71,714
Area: 221 square miles
Capital: Douglas

The Isle of Man, situated in the centre of the British Isles, is an internally self-governing dependent territory of the Crown which is not part of the UK.

The Tynwald Parliament makes its own laws and oversees all internal administration, fiscal and social policies. External issues, such as foreign representation and defence, are administered on the Island's behalf by the UK Government and the Island makes an annual payment for these services. As a British Crown dependency, the ultimate responsibility for the Island's good government is vested in the Crown but by long standing convention, the UK Government does not legislate for the Island except with the specific consent of the Island's Government.

HM the Queen as Lord of Mann is Head of State. Her personal representative on the Island is His Excellency the Lieutenant Governor, who is appointed by the Crown for a five-year term.

Clerk to Tynwald,
  Prof T St John Bates, MA, LLM
Legislative Buildings, Douglas,
Isle of Man IM1 3PW
01624 685500 Fax 01624 685504
Tynwald (www.tynwald.isle-of-man.org.im)
Government offices: 01624 685685
Isle of Man Government (www.gov.im)

Jersey

Lieutenant-Governor,
  HE General Sir Michael Wilkes, KCB, CBE
The Bailiff (President of the States Assembly and the Royal Court),
  Sir Philip Bailhache
Population: 85,150
Area: 45 square miles
Capital: St Helier

Constitutionally, Jersey is a dependency of the Crown, owing allegiance to the Sovereign, but without incorporation into the UK. Effectively it is self-governing in internal matters, but the UK Government is responsible for defence, overseas representation and international affairs generally.

The Assembly of the States of Jersey is the Island's legislature and oversees all domestic administration and fiscal, social and other policies. Laws passed by the States are subject to the sanction of Her Majesty in Council.

The Lieutenant-Governor is Her Majesty's personal representative in the Bailiwick and is appointed by the Sovereign by Royal Warrant usually for a term of five years. He is the official channel of communication between the Crown (through the Secretary of State for the Home Department) and the Insular Authorities. He attends meetings of the States Assembly but takes no part in debates.

The Crown Officers are the Bailiff, the Deputy Bailiff, the Attorney General and the Solicitor General. All are appointed by the Sovereign by Letters Patent. The Attorney General and the Solicitor General, as the Law Officers, are the legal advisers of the Crown and of the States. They have the right to attend the States Assembly and to speak but not to vote. Points of law raised in debate are referred to them for explanation, clarification and advice.

The Bailiff's Chambers,
Royal Court House, St Helier,
Jersey, JE1 1DD, Channel Islands
01534 502100 Fax 01534 502199

G H C Coppock, MA (Cantab),
Greffier (Clerk) of the States,
Morier House, Halkett Place, St Helier,
Jersey, JE1 1DD, Channel Islands
01534 502013 Fax 01534 502098
E-mail: stgreffe@itl.net

Guernsey

Lieutenant-Governor,
  Vice-Admiral Sir John Coward, KCB, DSO
The Bailiff, de V G Carey
Population: 60,000 approx
Area: 24 square miles
Capital: St Peter Port

Guernsey is not a sovereign state but a dependent territory of the Crown and under international law Her Majesty's Government is responsible for the Island's international relations.

The offices held under the Crown in Guernsey are those of Lieutenant-Governor, Bailiff, Deputy Bailiff, Procureur, Comptroller, Greffier, Receiver-General, Sheriff and Sergeant. Their appointments are made by HM the Queen on the advice of the Secretary of State for the Home Department, the member of the Privy Council with responsibility for the Islands.

The Lieutenant-Governor is Her Majesty's personal representative in the Bailiwick and is appointed by the Sovereign by Royal Warrant under the Sign Manual. He normally holds office for five years. He is the official channel of communication between the Crown and the Insular Authorities. The Lieutenant-Governor is commander-in-chief in the Bailiwick. Alderney, Sark, Herm, Jethou, Brechou and Lihou are included in the Bailiwick.

The Bailiff's Chambers,
The Royal Court House,
Guernsey, GY1 2PB, Channel Islands
01481 726161

The Commonwealth

Of the 54 member countries of the Commonwealth, Queen Elizabeth II is Head of State of 16 (including the United Kingdom), 33 are republics, and 5 are monarchies with other sovereigns. The Queen remains symbolically Head of the Commonwealth.

Governors-General of the Queen's Realms

In the overseas realms of which she is Queen, Her Majesty is represented by a Governor-General:

Antigua and Barbuda	HE Sir James Carlisle, KCMG *Prime Minister:* The Hon Lester B Bird
Australia	HE Sir William Deane *Prime Minister:* The Hon John Howard, MP
Bahamas	HE Sir Orville Turnquest, KCMG *Prime Minister:* The Rt Hon Hubert A Ingraham
Barbados	HE Sir Clifford Husbands, GCMG *Prime Minister:* The Rt Hon Owen Arthur
Belize	HE Sir Colville Norbert Young, Sr, KCMG *Prime Minister:* The Hon Said Musa
Canada	HE The Hon Mrs Adrienne Clarkson *Prime Minister:* The Rt Hon Jean Chretien
Grenada	HE Sir Charles Daniel Williams, GCMG, QC *Prime Minister:* The Hon Dr Keith Mitchell
Jamaica	HE Sir Howard Felix Cooke, GCMG, CD *Prime Minister:* The Rt Hon P J Patterson, QC
New Zealand	HE The Rt Hon Sir Michael Hardie Boys, GCMG *Prime Minister:* The Rt Hon Mrs Jenny Shipley
Papua New Guinea	HE Sir Sailas Atopare, GCMG *Prime Minister:* The Hon Sir Mekere Morauta
Solomon Islands	HE Rev John Ini Lapli, GCMG *Prime Minister:* The Hon Bartholomew Ulufa'alu
*St Christopher and Nevis	HE Sir Cuthbert M Sebastian, GCMG, OBE *Prime Minister:* The Hon Dr Denzil Douglas
*St Lucia	HE Dame Calliopa Pearlette Louisy, GCMG *Prime Minister:* Dr The Hon Kenny D Anthony
*St Vincent and The Grenadines	HE Sir Charles James Antrobus, GCMG, OBE *Prime Minister:* The Rt Hon Sir James Fitz Allen Mitchell, KCMG
Tuvalu	HE The Rt Hon Sir Tomasi Puapua, KBE *Prime Minister:* The Hon Ionatana Ionatana

*Eastern Caribbean States

Republics and other Commonwealth Monarchies
Heads of State and Heads of Government

Bangladesh	*President and Head of State:* HE Mr Shahabuddin Ahmed *Prime Minister and Head of Government:* The Hon Sheikh Hasina
Botswana	*President and Head of Government:* HE Mr Festus G Mogae
Brunei	*Sultan and Head of Government:* HM Paduka Seri Baginda Sultan Haji Hassanal Bolkiah Mu'izzaddin Waddaulah; Sultan and Yang Di-Pertuan Negara Brunei Darussalam
Cameroon	*President and Head of Government:* HE Mr Paul Biya
Cyprus	*President and Head of Government:* HE Mr Glafkos Clerides
Dominica	*President and Head of State:* HE Mr Vernon Shaw *Prime Minister and Head of Government:* The Hon Edison James
Fiji Islands	*President:* HE Ratu Sir Kamisese Mara, GCMG, KBE

The Gambia	*President and Head of Government:* HE Mr Yahya A J J Jammeh
Ghana	*President and Head of Government:* HE Flt Lt (rtd) Jerry J Rawlings
Guyana	*President and Head of Government:* HE Mr Bharrat Jagdeo
India	*President and Head of State:* HE Mr K R Narayanan
	Prime Minister and Head of Government: The Hon Atal Behari Vajpayee
Kenya	*President and Head of Government:* HE Mr Daniel arap Moi, CGH
Kiribati	*President and Head of Government:* HE Mr Teburoro Tito
Lesotho	*Head of State:* HM King Letsie III
	Prime Minister and Head of Government: The Hon Bethuel Pakalitha Mosisili
Malawi	*President and Head of Government:* HE Mr Bakili Muluzi
Malaysia	*Head of State:* HM Sultan Salahuddin Abdul Aziz Shah *(King of Malaysia)*
	Prime Minister and Head of Government: The Hon Datuk Seri Dr Mahathir Mohamad
Maldives	*President and Head of Government:* HE Mr Maumoon Abdul Gayoom, GCMG
Malta	*President and Head of State:* HE Professor Guido de Marco
	Prime Minister and Head of Government: The Hon Dr Edward Fenech Adami
Mauritius	*President and Head of State:* HE Mr Cassam Uteem, GCSK
	Prime Minister and Head of Government: The Hon Dr Navinchandra Ramgoolam
Mozambique	*President and Head of State:* HE Mr Joaquim A Chissano
Namibia	*President and Head of Government:* HE Dr Sam Nujoma
Nauru	*President and Head of Government:* HE Mr René Harris
Nigeria	*President and Head of State:* HE General (Rtd) Olusegun Obasanjo
*Pakistan	*President and Head of State:* HE Mr Rafiq Tarar
	Chief Executive: General Pervaiz Musharraf
Samoa	*Head of State:* HH Malietoa Tanumafili II, GCMG, CBE
	Prime Minister and Head of Government: The Hon Tuilaepa Sailele Malielegaoi
Seychelles	*President and Head of Government:* HE Mr France Albert René
Sierra Leone	*President:* HE Alhaji Dr Ahmed Tejan Kabbah
Singapore	*President and Head of State:* HE Mr Ong Teng Cheong
	Prime Minister and Head of Government: The Hon Goh Chok Tong
South Africa	*President and Head of Government:* HE Mr Thabo Mbeki
Sri Lanka	*President and Head of Government:* HE Mrs Chandrika Bandaranaike Kumaratunga
Swaziland	*Head of State:* HM King Mswati III
	Prime Minister and Head of Government: The Hon Dr Barnabas Dlamini
Tanzania	*President and Head of Government:* HE Mr Benjamin William Mkapa
Tonga	*Head of State:* HM King Taufa'ahau Tupou IV, GCMG
	Prime Minister and Head of Government: The Hon Baron Vaea of Houma
Trinidad and Tobago	*President and Head of State:* HE Mr A N R Robinson
	Prime Minister and Head of Government: The Hon Basdeo Panday
Uganda	*President and Head of Government:* HE Mr Yoweri Museveni
Vanuatu	*President and Head of State:* HE Fr John Bani
	Prime Minister and Head of Government: The Hon Donald Kalpokas
Western Samoa	– See Samoa
Zambia	*President and Head of Government:* HE Mr Frederick Chiluba
Zimbabwe	*President and Head of Government:* HE Mr Robert Mugabe, MP

*Membership of the Commonwealth suspended, October 1999

British Overseas Territories
Governors and Commanders-in-Chief

Anguilla	HE Mr Peter Johnstone *(Governor)*
Bermuda	HE Mr Thorold Masefield, CMG *(Governor and Commander-in-Chief)*
British Antarctic Territory	Mr C J B White *(Commissioner)* (Resident in London)
British Indian Ocean Territory	Mr C J B White *(Commissioner)* (Resident in London)
British Virgin Islands	HE Mr Frank Savage, CMG, LVO, OBE *(Governor)*
Cayman Islands	HE Mr Peter Smith, CBE *(Governor)*
Falkland Islands	HE Mr Donald Lamont *(Governor)*
Gibraltar	HE The Rt Hon Sir Richard Luce, DL *(Governor and Commander-in-Chief)*
Montserrat	HE Mr Anthony Abbott, OBE *(Governor)*
Pitcairn,	HE Mr Martin Williams, CVO, OBE *(Governor)* (Non-resident)
Henderson, Ducie and Oeno Islands	see New Zealand – British Embassies and High Commissions Overseas section
St Helena and Dependencies	HE Mr D Hollamby *(Governor and Commander-in-Chief)*
South Georgia and South Sandwich Islands	HE Mr Donald Lamont *(Commissioner)* (Resident in Stanley)
Turks and Caicos Islands	HE Mr Mervyn Jones *(Governor)*

ANGUILLA

Governor   HE Mr Peter Johnstone
Deputy Governor   Roger Cousins, OBE
Chief Minister   Hon. Hubert B. Hughes
Area   35 square miles
Population   Approx. 10,000 (1998)

Constitution   Ministerial system. The Governor is responsible for defence, external affairs, internal security, the public service and offshore finance. House of Assembly (7 elected members plus 2 nominated and 2 ex-officio members (the Deputy Govenor and the Attorney General). Executive Council (chaired by the Governor with participation of the Chief Minister, 3 ministers and 2 ex-officio members) advises the Governor on the exercise of executive powers other than those for which the Governor is responsible.

Electoral System   Universal adult suffrage for those aged 18 or over. Elections take place at intervals of not more than five years. The last election was held on the 16th March 1994. The next election is scheduled for March 2000.

Acting Director of Information and Broadcasting   Wycliffe Richardson
Information Officer   Kenneth Hodge

BERMUDA

Governor   HE Mr Thorold Masefield, CMG
Premier   The Hon. Jennifer Smith, MP
Area   20 square miles
Population   60,000 (1990)

Constitution   Internal self-government. Governor's Council (Governor, Premier, 2 or 3 other cabinet ministers nominated by Premier) deals with the Governor's reserve powers on defence, external affairs, internal security and the police. House of Assembly (40 elected members). Senate (11 nominated members – 3 by the Governor at his discretion, 5 on the advice of the Premier and 3 on the advice of the Leader of the Opposition). Cabinet headed by the Premier, who is appointed by the Governor and who is the leader of the majority party in the House of Assembly. The Governor also appoints the leader of the largest minority party as Leader of the Opposition.

Party Strength in House of Assembly 1998 election: Progressive Labour Party 26; United Bermuda Party 14.

Electoral System Elections at intervals of not more than five years; universal adult suffrage for those aged 18 and over; 20 double-member constituencies.

BRITISH ANTARCTIC TERRITORY

Commissioner Mr C. J. B. White (resides in London)
Administrator Dr M. G. Richardson (resides in London)
Area approximately 660,000 square miles
Population None except for scientists manning the British Antarctic Survey scientific stations

BRITISH INDIAN OCEAN TERRITORY

Commissioner Mr C. J. B. White (resides in London)
Administrator Ms L. M. Savill (resides in London)
Area 21 square miles
Population 2,000 United States and British Military personnel, and 1,500 Civilian personnel

BRITISH VIRGIN ISLANDS

Governor HE Mr F. J. Savage, CMG, LVO, OBE
Chief Minister Hon. Ralph T. O'Neal, OBE
Area 59 square miles
Population 19,107 (1997)

Constitution Ministerial system. The Governor has responsibility for defence, internal security, external affairs and the public service. Executive Council (Governor as Chairman, 1 ex-officio member, Chief Minister and 3 other ministers). Legislative Council (13 elected, 1 ex-officio member, presided over by Speaker).

Party Strength in Legislative Council 1999 election: Virgin Islands Party, 7; National Democratic Party, 5; Concerned Citizens Movement, 1.

Electoral System Elections every four years unless Legislative Council dissolved earlier; universal adult suffrage with 18 years as the voting age; single-member constituencies.

CAYMAN ISLANDS

Governor HE Mr Peter Smith, CBE
Area 100 square miles
Population 35,000 (1996)

Constitution The Governor is responsible for defence, external affairs, the police and internal security. Legislative Assembly (Speaker, 15 elected, 3 official members and 5 Ministers elected by and from the 15 elected members of the Legislative Assembly).

Electoral System Elections at intervals of not more than four years (the last took place in 1996); universal adult suffrage with the voting age at 18; six constituencies, two electing 4 members each, one electing 3 members, one electing 2 members and two electing 1 member each. No organised political parties.

Cayman Islands Government Representative in the United Kingdom, Mr T. Russell, CMG, CBE. *6 Arlington Street, London, SW1A 1RE.*   (020 7491 7772).

FALKLAND ISLANDS

Governor HE Mr Donald Lamont
Area 4,700 square miles
Population 2,221 (1996)

Constitution Amended in 1997, it provides for a Governor exercising executive powers, assisted by an Executive Council (2 ex-officio, and 3 members of the Legislative Council) and a Legislative Council (2 ex-officio and 8 elected members). The 3 elected Legislative Councillors who also sit on the Executive Council are elected by their colleagues on the Legislative Council. Defence and security (apart from the police) are the responsibility of the Commander British Forces. The constitution contains a chapter on the protection of human rights and the right of peoples to self-determination.

Electoral System Elections held at intervals of not more than 4 years: universal adult suffrage for those aged 18 and over. Two constituencies, of which Stanley elects five members to Council and Camp elects three members. The last election was held in 1997.

The Falkland Islands Government Office, Falkland House, 14 Broadway, London, SW1H 0BH. (020 7222 2542) *Fax:* 020 7222 2375 *E-Mail:* rep@figo.u-net.com.

GIBRALTAR

Governor and Commander-in-Chief HE The Rt Hon. Sir Richard Luce, DL
Chief Minister The Hon. Peter Caruana
Area 2.25 square miles
Population 31,265 (1990)

Constitution Ministerial system with a large measure of internal self-government. The Governor retains responsibility for defence, external affairs, internal security and certain other matters. House of Assembly (Speaker, 15 elected, 2 ex-officio members). Council of Ministers (Chief Minister, 4 to 8 other ministers). Gibraltar Council (Deputy Governor and 3 other ex-officio members, Chief Minister and 4 other ministers, presided over by the Governor). The Governor normally acts in accordance with the advice of the Gibraltar Council in exercising his functions relating to matters not dealt with by ministers.

Party Strength in House of Assembly 1996 election: Gibraltar Social Democrats, 8; Gibraltar Socialist Labour Party, 7.

Electoral System Elections take place at intervals of not more than four years; universal suffrage for those over 18; a block voting system in which each elector may vote for up to eight candidates.

Government of Gibraltar, London Bureau, 179 Strand, London, WC2R 1EH (020 7836 0777).

Representative Albert A. Poggio, MBE.

MONTSERRAT

Governor HE Mr Anthony Abbott, OBE
Chief Minister Hon. David Brandt
Speaker Hon. Dr Howard Fergus, CBE
Area 39 square miles
Population 4,000 (1998)

Constitution The Governor is responsible for external affairs, defence, internal security, international financial services and the public service. Ministerial system. Legislative Council (2 ex-officio, 2 nominated and 7 elected members presided over by the Speaker). Executive Council (2 ex-officio members, the Chief Minister and 3 other ministers, presided over by the Governor).

Party Strength in Legislative Council 1996 election: National Progressive Party 1; Progressive Peoples Alliance 2; Movement for National Reconstruction 2; Independent 2.

Electoral System Elections are held at intervals of not more than five years; universal adult suffrage, the voting age being 18 years; single-member constituencies.

PITCAIRN, HENDERSON, DUCIE AND OENO

Governor HE Mr M. J. Williams, CVO, OBE (resident in Wellington, New Zealand)
Deputy Governor Mr C. D. Shute (resident in Wellington, New Zealand)
Island Magistrate and President of Council Mr J. Warren
Area 19.5 square miles* (Pitcairn I. 1.75 square miles)
Population 50 (1998)

Constitution Island Council (10 members: 1 ex-officio; 6 elected, including the Island Magistrate who presides; and 3 nominated, 1 by the elected members and 2 by the Governor).

*The territory also includes the uninhabited islands of Ducie, Henderson and Oeno.

ST HELENA

Governor HE Mr David Hollamby
Area 47 square miles
Population 5,157 (1998)

Constitution Legislative Council (Speaker, 3 ex-officio and 12 elected members). Executive Council (the Chief Secretary, the Financial Secretary and the Attorney General as ex-officio members and the chairmen of the five council committees). These committees, of which the chairmen and the majority of the members are also members of the Legislative Council, are appointed by the Governor and have executive powers and the oversight of the government departments.

Electoral System Elections held at intervals of not more than four years (the last in 1997) and on the basis of universal adult suffrage for those aged 18 and over. There are 8 electoral areas; 4 return one Councillor and 4 return two each.

Information Officer Mr J. Drummond.

ST HELENA DEPENDENCIES

ASCENSION

Governor HE Mr David Hollamby (resident St Helena)
Administrator Mr G. C. Fairhurst
Area 34 square miles
Population 719 (1998) non indigenous, mostly employees of Ascension Island Services, Cable and Wireless plc, the BBC and US Base

Constitution The Administrator acts on behalf of the Governor of St Helena. (The St Helena Legislative and Executive Councils have no jurisdiction on the island.) An Advisory Forum, composed of representatives of the organisations using the island, assists the Administrator.

TRISTAN DA CUNHA

Governor HE Mr David Hollamby (resident St Helena)
Administrator Mr B. P. Baldwin
Area 38 square miles
Population 288 (1998)

Constitution The Administrator acts on behalf of the Governor of St Helena. (The St Helena Legislative and Executive Councils have no jurisdiction over the island.) The Administrator is advised by an Island Council comprising 3 appointed members and 8 elected members: 1 elected member is required to be a woman.

Electoral System Elections are held at intervals of not more than three years (the last in 1997). Universal adult suffrage for those aged 18 and over.

The Tristan da Cunha group also includes Inaccessible Island, The Nightingale Islands and Gough Island.

SOUTH GEORGIA AND THE SOUTH SANDWICH ISLANDS

Commissioner   HE Mr Donald Lamont (resident in Stanley, Falkland Islands)
Area   South Georgia 1,450 square miles; South Sandwich Islands approximately 130 square miles
Population   Very small transient population including scientists manning a British Antarctic Survey Station

TURKS AND CAICOS ISLANDS

Governor   HE Mr Mervyn Jones
Chief Secretary   Mrs Cynthia Astwood, MBE
Chief Minister   Hon. Derek Taylor, MLC
Area   193 square miles
Population   19,000 (1995 estimate)

Constitution   The Governor exercises powers in respect of defence, external affairs, offshore finance, internal security and the public service. Ministerial system of Government. Legislative Council: 13 elected members from single-member constituencies; 3 appointed members; 2 ex-officio members and a Speaker. Executive Council (the Chief Minister, and 5 Ministers (who must be elected members of legislative council), and 2 ex-officio members) presided over by the Governor.

Party Strength in the Legislative Council   1999 election: People's Democratic Movement, 9; Progressive National Party, 4.

Electoral System   Elections held at intervals of not more than four years; universal adult suffrage for all 'belongers' of the territory aged 18 or over.

British Embassies and High Commissions

Source: HM Diplomatic Service Overseas List – updated November 1999

AFGHANISTAN
(Post currently vacant)

ALBANIA
British Embassy
Rruga, Skenderberg 12, Tirana
+ 900 355 42 34973 Fax + 900 355 42 47697
Ambassador: HE Dr Peter January

ALGERIA
British Embassy
Résidence Cassiopée, Bâtiment B, 7 Chemin
des Glycines (B P 08, Alger-Gare 16000)
+ 213 2 23 00 92 Fax + 213 2 23 00 67
Telex: 66266 (a/b 66266 VISA DZ)
Ambassador: HE Mr William Sinton

ANDORRA – see Spain

ANGOLA
British Embassy
Rua Diogo Cað, 4 (Caixa Postal 1244), Luanda
+ 244 2 334582 Fax + 244 2 333331
Ambassador: HE Miss Caroline Elmes
Commercial: Mr C Gedge
(Non-resident: Sao Tome)

ANTIGUA & BARBUDA
British High Commission
PO Box 483, Price Waterhouse Centre,
11 Old Parham Road, St John's
+ 001268 462 0008/463 0010
Fax + 001268 462 2806
High Commissioner: HE Mr Gordon M Baker
(Resides in Barbados)
Resident High Commissioner:
HE Miss M J Maxwell

ARGENTINA
British Embassy
Dr Luis Agote 2141, 1425 Buenos Aires
+ 54 11 4803 7070/1 Fax + 54 11 4803 1731
Ambassador: HE Mr William Marsden, CMG
Commercial: Mr G M Wise – Second Secretary

ARMENIA
British Embassy
28 Charents Street, Yerevan
+ 3742 151841 Fax + 3742 151064
Ambassador: HE Mr Timothy Jones

AUSTRALIA
British High Commission
Commonwealth Avenue, Yarralumla, Canberra,
ACT 2600
+ (02) 6270 6666
Fax Chancery + (02) 6270 6653
High Commissioner:
HE The Rt Hon. Sir Alastair Goodlad, KCMG

AUSTRIA
British Embassy
Jaurèsgasse 12, 1030 Vienna
+ 43 1 716130 Fax + 43 1 71613 2999
Ambassador:
HE Sir Anthony Figgis, KCVO, CMG

AZERBAIJAN
British Embassy
2 Izmir Street, Baku 370065
+ 99412 9248 13 Fax + 99412 922739
Ambassador: HE Mr Roger Thomas

BAHAMAS
British High Commission
Ansbacher House (3rd Floor), East Street,
PO Box N7516, Nassau
+ (001) 242 325 7471/2/3
Fax + (001) 242 323-3871
High Commissioner: HE Mr P Heigl
Commercial: Ms E J Huggins –
Commercial/Information Officer

BAHRAIN
British Embassy
21 Government Avenue, Manama 306,
PO Box 114, Bahrain
+ 973 534404 Fax + 973 531273
Telegrams: PRODROME, BAHREIN
Ambassador and Consul-General:
HE Mr P Ford
Commercial: Mr K J Shaughnessy –
Second Secretary

BANGLADESH
British High Commission
United Nations Road, Baridhara Dhaka
+ 880 2 882705 Fax + 880 2 883 437
High Commissioner:
HE Mr Mr David Carter, CVO

BARBADOS
British High Commission
Lower Collymore Rock (PO Box 676),
Bridgetown
+ 001 246 430 7800
Fax + 001 246 430 7851
High Commissioner: HE Mr Gordon M Baker
(Non-resident: St Lucia, Grenada, St Kitts &
Nevis, Commonwealth of Dominica, St Vincent
& the Grenadines, Antigua & Barbuda)

BELARUS
British Embassy
37 Karl Marx Street, 220030 Minsk
+ 375 172 292303 Fax + 375 172 292306
Ambassador: HE Mr Iain Kelly

BELGIUM
British Embassy
Rue d'Arlon 85, 1040 Brussels
+ 32 2 287 6211 Fax + 32 2 287 6355
Ambassador: HE Mr David H Colvin, CMG
Commercial: Mr D J Currie – First Secretary
Fax + 32 2 287 6240

BELIZE
British High Commission
PO Box 91 Belmopan, or BFPO 12
+ 501 8 22146/7 Fax + 501 8 22761
Telex 284 (a/b 284 UKREP BZE)
High Commissioner: HE Mr Timothy David

BENIN – see Nigeria

BOLIVIA
British Embassy
Avenida Arce 2732 (Casilla 694), La Paz
+ 591 2 433424 Fax: + 591 2 431073
Ambassador: HE Mr Graham Minter
Commercial: Mr E Suarez –
Commercial Officer

BOSNIA AND HERZEGOVINA
8 Tina Ujevica, Sarajevo
+ (00 387 71) 444429
Fax + (00 387 71) 666131
Ambassador: HE Mr Graham Hand
Commercial: Mr C J Poole, MBE –
First Secretary

BOTSWANA
British High Commission
Private Bag 0023, Gaborone
+ 267 3 52841/2/3 Fax + 267 356105
High Commissioner: HE Mr J Wilde

BRAZIL
British Embassy
Setor de Embaixadas Sul, Quadra 801,
Conjunto K, CEP 70.408-900 or
Avenida das Naçoes, Caixa Postal 07-0586,
70359 Brasilia-DF
+ 55 61 225-2710 Fax + 55 61 225 1777
Ambassador: HE Mr Roger Bone, CMG

BRUNEI
British High Commission
2/01, 2nd Floor, Block D,
Kompleks Bangunan Yayasan,
Sultan Haji Hassanal Bolkiah, Jalan Pretty,
PO Box 2197, Bandar Seri Begawan 1921
+ 673 2 222231/223121 Fax + 673 2 226002
High Commissioner: HE Mr Stuart Laing
Commercial: Mr M Y Moon –
Second Secretary

BULGARIA
British Embassy
38 Boulevard Vassil Levski, Sofia
+ 359 2980 1220 Fax: + 359 2980 1229
Ambassador: HE Mr Richard Stagg
Commercial: Mr M J Carbine – First Secretary

BURKINA FASO – see Cote d'Ivoire

BURMA
British Embassy
80 Strand Road (Box No 638), Rangoon
+ 95 1 295300/295309 Fax + 95 1 295306
Ambassador: HE Dr John Jenkins, LVO

BURUNDI – see Rwanda

CAMBODIA
British Embassy
29 Street 75, Phnom Penh
+ 855 23 427124 Fax + 855 23 427125
Ambassador: HE Mr George Edgar

CAMEROON
British High Commission
Avenue Winston Churchill, BP 547, Yaoundé
+ 237 22 05 45/07 96 Fax + 237 22 01 48
High Commissioner: HE Mr Peter Boon
(Non-resident: Chad, Central African Republic,
Equatorial Guinea, Gabon)
Commercial: Mr P D Brown – First Secretary,
Consul and Deputy Head of Mission

CANADA
British High Commission
80 Elgin Street, Ottawa K1P 5K7
+ 1 613 237-1530 Fax + 1 613 237 7980
Telegraphic address: UKREP OTTAWA
High Commissioner:
HE Sir Anthony Goodenough, KCMG
Commercial: Ms E Miller – Third Secretary

CAPE VERDE – see Senegal

CENTRAL AFRICAN REPUBLIC –
see Cameroon

CHAD – see Cameroon

CHILE
British Embassy
Av El Bosque 0125, Casilla 72-D or Casilla
16552, Santiago 9
+ 56 2 2313737 Fax + 56 2 2319771
Ambassador: HE Miss M Glynne D Evans, CMG
Commercial: Mr T A Torlot – First Secretary

CHINA
British Embassy
11 Guang Hua Lu, Jian Guo Men Wai,
Peking 100 600
+ 86 10 6532 1961 Fax + 86 10 6532 1937
Ambassador:
HE Sir Anthony Galsworthy, KCMG
Commercial: Mr C M J Segar – Counsellor

Hong Kong
British Consulate General,
No 1 Supreme Court Road, Central,
Hong Kong (PO Box 528)
+ (852) 2901 3000 Fax + (852) 2901 3066
Consul-General: Sir Andrew Burns, KCMG
*British Senior Representative to the Sino-British
Joint Liaison:* Mr A Paul, CMG

COLOMBIA
British Embassy
Edificio Ing Barings, Carrera 9 No 76-49 Piso
9, Bogotá
+ (57) (1) 317 6690/6310/6321
Fax + (57) (1) 317 6298
Ambassador: HE Mr Jeremy Thorp

COMOROS – see Madagascar

CONGO, DEMOCRATIC REPUBLIC OF
British Embassy
Avenue le Mera, Kinshasa
+ 243 88 34775/33130/33453
Fax Satellite + 871 144 7753
Ambassador: HE Mr D Scrafton, CMG
(Non-resident: Congo, Peoples Republic)

CONGO, PEOPLES REPUBLIC OF
Ambassador: HE Mr D Scrafton, CMG
(resident in Democratic Republic of Congo)

COSTA RICA
British Embassy
Apartado 815, Edificio Centro Colon,
(11th Floor), San José 1007
+ 506 258 20 25 Fax + 506 233 99 38
Ambassador and Consul-General:
HE Mr P J Spiceley, MBE

COTE D'IVOIRE
British Embassy
3rd Floor, Immeuble "Les Harmonies",
Angle Boulevard Carde et Avenue, Dr Jamot,
Plateau, Abidjan
Postal address: 01 BP 2581, Abidjan 01
+ 225 22 68 50 Fax + 225 22 32 21
Ambassador and Consul-General:
HE Mr Haydon Warren-Gash
(Non-resident: Burkina Faso, Niger and
Liberia)
Commercial: Mr F G Geere – First Secretary,
Consul and Deputy Head of Mission

CROATIA
British Embassy
Vlaska, 121, 3rd Floor, PO Box 454,
10000 Zagreb
+ 385 1 455 5310 Fax + 385 1 455 1685
Ambassador: HE Mr Colin Munro
Commercial: Mr Peter Ivey – First Secretary

CUBA
British Embassy
Calle 34 No. 702/4 entre 7ma Avenida 17,
Miramar, Havana
+ 53 7 24-1771/2 Fax + 53 7 24-8104
Ambassador: HE Mr David Ridgway, OBE
Commercial: Mr N D Sutcliffe –
First Secretary

CYPRUS
British High Commission
Alexander Pallis Street (PO Box 1978), Nicosia
or BFPO 567
+ 357 2 861100 Fax + 357 2 861125
High Commissioner:
HE Mr Edward Clay, CMG
Commercial: Mr W E J Preston –
First Secretary

CZECH REPUBLIC
British Embassy
Thunovská 14, 11800 Prague 1
+ 420 2 5732 0355 Fax 420 2 5732 1023
Ambassador: HE Mr David Broucher
Commercial: Palac Myslbek,
Na Prikope 21, 117 19 Prague 1
+ 420 2 2424-0021/2/3
Fax + 420 2 2224-3625
Mr M L Connor – First Secretary

DENMARK
British Embassy
Kastelsvej 36/38/40, DK-2100 Copenhagen Ø
+ 45 35 44 52 00 Fax + 45 35 44 52 93
Ambassador: HE Mr Philip Astley, CVO
Commercial: Mr F J Martin – First Secretary
Fax + 45 35 44 52 46

DJIBOUTI – see Ethiopia

DOMINICA – see Barbados

DOMINICAN REPUBLIC
British Embassy
Edificio Corominas Pepin, Ave 27 de Fabrero
No 233, Santo Domingo
+ 001 809 472 7111/7905
Ambassador: HE Mr David Ward
(Non-resident: Haiti)

ECUADOR
British Embassy
Calle González Suárez, 111 (Casilla 314), Quito
+ 593 2 560669 Fax + 593 2 560730
Ambassador: HE Mr I Gerken, LVO

EGYPT
British Embassy
Ahmed Ragheb Street, Garden City, Cairo
+ 20 2 354-0850/0852 Fax +20 2 354-0859
Ambassador: HE Mr Graham Boyce, CMG
Commercial: Mr D G Reader – First Secretary

EL SALVADOR
British Embassy
Edifio Inter-Inversiones, Paseo General Escalón
4828, PO Box 1591, San Salvador
+ 503 263 6527 Fax + 503 263 6516
Ambassador and Consul-General:
HE Mr Patrick Morgan

EQUATORIAL GUINEA – see Cameroon

ERITREA – see Ethiopia

ESTONIA
British Embassy
Wismari 6, Tallinn 10136
+ 372 6774 700 Fax + 372 6774 724
Ambassador: HE Mr Tim Craddock

ETHIOPIA
British Embassy
Fikre Mariam Abatechan Street, Addis Ababa
+ 251 161 2354 Fax 251 161 0588
Postal address: PO Box 858
Telex: 1299 (a/b PROAD ET)
Ambassador: HE Mr G G Wetherell
(Non-resident: Eritrea and Djibouti)

FIJI ISLANDS
British High Commission
Victoria House, 47 Gladstone Road, Suva
(PO Box 1355)
+ 679 311033 Fax + 679 301406
High Commissioner: HE Mr Michael Dibben
(Non-resident: Nauru, Tuvalu and Kiribati)
HE Mr Vernon M Scarborough – Deputy Head
of Mission and Consul, and non-resident
Ambassador to Micronesia, Marshall Islands,
Palau and Deputy High Commissioner to
Kiribati, Nauru and Tuvalu

FINLAND
British Embassy
Itainen Puistotie 17, 00140 Helsinki
+ 358 9 2286 5100 Fax + 358 9 2286 5284
Ambassador: HE Mr Gavin Hewitt, CMG
Commercial: Mr H B Formstone, OBE –
First Secretary

FRANCE
British Embassy
35 rue du Faubourg St Honoré, 75383 Paris
Cedex 08
+ 331 44 51 31 00 Fax + 331 47 05 77 02
Ambassador:
HE Sir Michael Jay, KCMG
Commercial: Mr R J Codrington – Counsellor
(Trade, Promotion and Investment)

GABON – see Cameroon

GAMBIA, THE
British High Commission
48 Atlantic Road, Fajara (PO Box 507), Banjul
+ 220 4 95133 Fax + 220 4 96134
High Commissioner: HE Mr M Tony Millson

GEORGIA
British Embassy
Metechi Palace Hotel, 380003 Tbilisi
+ 995 32 955 497 Fax + 995 32 001 065
Ambassador: HE Mr Richard Jenkins, OBE

GERMANY
British Embassy
Berlin: Unter den Linden 32/34, 10117 Berlin
+ 49 030 201 84-0 Fax + 49 030 201 84-158
Ambassador: HE Sir Paul Lever, KCMG
Minister: Mr A Ford, CMG
Commercial: Mr D S Schroeder –
First Secretary

GHANA
British High Commission
Osu Link, off Gamel Abdul Nasser Avenue
(PO Box 296), Accra
+ 00 233 21 221665
Fax + 00 233 21 66 46 52
High Commissioner:
HE Mr Ian W Mackley, CMG
(Non-resident: Togo)
Commercial: Mr M A Ives – First Secretary

GREECE
British Embassy
1 Ploutarchou Street, 106 75 Athens
+ 30 1 727 2600 Fax + 30 1 727 2734
Ambassador: HE Mr David Madden, CMG
Commercial: Mr G G Thomas – First Secretary

GRENADA
British High Commission
14 Church Street, St Georges
+ (1) (473) 440 3222 Fax + (1) (473) 440 4939
High Commissioner: HE Mr Gordon M Baker
(Resides in Barbados)
Resident Acting High Commissioner:
Mr D R Miller

GUATEMALA
British Embassy
Avenida La Reforma 16-00, Zona 10,
Edificio Torre Internacional, Nivel 11,
Guatemala City
+ 502 367 5425/29 Fax + 502 367 5430
Ambassador: HE Mr Andrew Caie

GUINEA – see Senegal

GUINEA-BISSAU – see Senegal

GUYANA
British High Commission
44 Main Street (PO Box 10849), Georgetown
+ 592 2 65881 Fax + 592 2 53555

High Commissioner:
HE Mr Edward Glover, MVO
(Non-resident: Suriname)

HAITI – see Dominican Republic

HOLY SEE
British Embassy
91 Via dei Condotti, I-00187 Rome
+ 39 6 699 23561 Fax + 39 6 6994 0684
Ambassador: HE Mr Mark Pellew, LVO

HONDURAS
British Embassy
Edificio Palmira, 3er Piso, Colonia Palmira,
PO Box 290, Tegucigalpa
+ 504 232 0612 Fax + 504 232 5480
Ambassador and Consul-General:
HE Mr David Osborne

HUNGARY
British Embassy
Harmincad Utca 6, Budapest 1051
+ 36 1 266-2888 Fax + 36 1 266 0907
Ambassador: HE Mr Nigel Thorpe, CVO
Commercial: Mr S C Martin – First Secretary

ICELAND
British Embassy
Laufasvegur 31, 101 Reykjavik
(Postal address: PO Box 460, 121 Reykjavik)
+ 354 550 5100/2 Fax + 354 550 5104
Ambassador and Consul-General:
HE Mr James R McCulloch
Commercial: Mr Orn Valdimarsson –
Commercial Officer

INDIA
British High Commission
 Chanakyapuri, New Delhi 11000-21
+ 91 11 687 2161 Fax + 91 11 6872882
High Commissioner:
HE Sir Robertson Young, KCMG
Commercial: Mr G C Gillham – Counsellor
(Economic and Commercial)
Bombay: Deputy High Commissioner's Office,
Maker Chambers IV, 222 Jamnalal Bajaj Road,
(PO Box 11714) Nariman Point,
Bombay 400 021
+ 91 22 283 0517/283 2330
Fax + 91 22 202 7940
Deputy High Commissioner:
Mr M C Bates, OBE
Commercial: Mr P O D McCoy –
First Secretary

INDONESIA
British Embassy
Jalan M. H. Thamrin 75, Jakarta 10310
+ 62 21 315 6264 Fax: + 62 21 314 6263
Ambassador:
HE Mr Duncan Christopher, CMG
Commercial: Mr A Godson – Counsellor
(Commercial/Development)

IRAN
British Embassy
143 Ferdowsi Avenue, Tehran 11344,
(PO Box No 11365-4474)
+ 98 21 675011 Fax + 98 21 6708021
Ambassador: HE Mr N W Browne, CMG
Commercial: Mr A F Bedford – First Secretary

IRAQ – No representation

IRELAND, REPUBLIC OF
British Embassy
29 Merrion Road, Ballsbridge, Dublin 4
+ 00 353 1 205 3700 Fax + 00 353 1 205 3885
Ambassador: HE Mr Ivor Roberts, CMG
Commercial: Mr R N J Baker – First Secretary

ISRAEL
British Embassy
192 Hayarkon Street, Tel Aviv 63405
+ 972 3-5249171 Fax + 972 3 524 3313
Ambassador: HE Mr F Cornish, CMG, LVO
Commercial: Mr W W Magor – First Secretary

ITALY
British Embassy
Via XX Settembre 80a, 00187 Rome
+ 39 06 482 5441/5551 Fax + 39 06 487 3324
Ambassador:
HE Sir Thomas Richardson, KCMG
(Non-resident: San Marino)
Commercial: Mr M A Hatfull – Counsellor

IVORY COAST – see Cote D'Ivoire

JAMAICA
British High Commission
PO Box 575, Trafalgar Road, Kingston 10
+ 001 876 92 69050 Fax + 001 876 92 97869
High Commissioner: HE Mr Antony Smith

JAPAN
British Embassy
No 1 Ichiban-cho, Chiyoda-ku,
Tokyo 102-8381
+ 81 3 5211 1100 Fax: + 81 3 5275-3164

Ambassador:
HE Mr Stephen Gommersall, CMG
Commercial: Mr P Bateman – Counsellor
Fax + 81 3 3265 5580

JERUSALEM
British Consulate-General
19 Nashashibi Street, Sheikh Jarrah Quarter
PO Box 19690, East Jerusalem 97200
+ 972 25 828281 Fax + 972 25 322368
Consul General: Mr R A Kealy, CMG

JORDAN
British Embassy
(PO Box 87) Abdoun, Amman
+ 00 9626 5923100 Fax + 00 9626 5923759
Telex: 22209 (a/b 22209 PRODRM JO)
Ambassador: HE Mr Edward Chaplin
Commercial: Mr B Wilson – Second Secretary

KAZAKHSTAN
British Embassy
Ul Furmanova 173, Almaty
+ 73272 506191/192/229 Fax + 73272 506260
Ambassador: HE Mr Richard Lewington
(Non-resident: Kyrgyzstan)

KENYA
British High Commission
Upper Hill Road, Nairobi, PO Box 30465
+ 254 2 714699 Fax + 254 2 719082
High Commissioner: HE Mr J R James, CMG
Commercial: PO Box 30133, Nairobi
Mr J Chandler – First Secretary

KIRIBATI – see Fiji Islands

KOREA
British Embassy
4, Chung-Dong, Chung-Ku, Seoul 100-120
+ 82 2 735-7341/3 Fax + 82 2 725 1738
Ambassador: HE Sir Stephen Brown, KCVO
Commercial: Mr D R Marsh, CVO –
Counsellor (Economic/Commercial) and
Deputy Head of Mission
Fax + 82 2 736 6241

KUWAIT
British Embassy
Arabian Gulf Street
Postal address: PO Box 2 Safat, 13001 Safat
+ 965 240 3334 Fax + 965 242 6799
Ambassador: HE Mr Richard Muir, CMG
Commercial: PO Box 300, Safat, 13001 Safat
Fax + 965 240 7395
Mr M Hurley, MBE – First Secretary

KYRGHYZSTAN – see Kazakhstan

LAOS
British Embassy
PO Box 6626, Vientiane, Laos, PDR
+ 856 21 413606 Fax + 856 21 413607
Ambassador:
HE Mr B Smith (Resides in Thailand)

LATVIA
British Embassy
5 Alunana Iela Street, Riga LV 1010
+ 371 7 338126 Fax + 371 7 338132
Ambassador: HE Mr Stephen Nash, CMG

LEBANON
British Embassy
East Beirut: 8th Street, Rabieh
+ 961 4 417007/405070 Fax + 961 4 402032
Ambassador: HE Mr David R MacLennan

LESOTHO
British High Commission
PO Box Ms 521, Maseru 100
+ 266 313961 Fax + 266 310120
High Commissioner:
HE Ms Kaye Oliver, OBE

LIBERIA – see Cote d'Ivoire

LIBYA
British Embassy
Sharia Uahran 1, PO Box 4206, Tripoli
+ 00 218 21 333 1191/2/3
Ambassador: HE Mr Richard Dalton, CMG

LIECHTENSTEIN – see Switzerland

LITHUANIA
British Embassy
2 Antakalnio, 2055 Vilnius
+ 370 2 22 20 70 Fax + 370 2 72 75 79
Ambassador: HE Mr C Robbins

LUXEMBOURG
British Embassy
14 Boulevard Roosevelt, L-2450
Luxembourg
+ 352 22 98 64/65/66 Fax + 352 22 98 67
Ambassador and Consul-General:
HE Mr William Ehrman
Commercial: Mr S Smith – Counsellor
(Resides at Brussels)

MACEDONIA
British Embassy
Veljko Vlakovic 26 (4th Floor), 9100 Skopje
+ 389 91 116 772 Fax + 389 91 117 005
Ambassador: HE Mr W M L Dickinson

MADAGASCAR
British Embassy
First Floor, Immeuble "Ny Havana", Cite de 67
Ha, BP 167, Antananarivo
+ 00 2612 22 277 49/273 70/337 65
Fax + 00 2612 022 266 90
Ambassador: HE Mr Charles Mochan
(Non-resident: Comoros)
Commercial: Mr M Rakotolehibe –
Commercial Officer

MALAWI
British High Commission
PO Box 30042, Lilongwe 3
+ 265 782 400 Fax + 265 782 657
High Commissioner: HE Mr G Finlayson

MALAYSIA
British High Commission
185 Jalan Ampang, 50450 Kuala Lumpur, or
PO Box 11030, 50732 Kuala Lumpur
+ 60 3 2482122 Fax + 60 3 2447766
High Commissioner: HE Mr Graham Fry
Commercial: Mr H Parkinson, CVO, OBE –
Counsellor
Fax + 60 3 2480880

MALDIVES – see Sri Lanka

MALI – see Senegal

MALTA
British High Commission
PO Box 506, 7 St Anne Street, Floriana
+ 356 233134 Fax + 356 242001
High Commissioner:
HE Mr Howard Pearce, CVO
Commercial: Mr P Tissot – Deputy High
Commissioner and First Secretary
(Commercial/Economic)

MARSHALL ISLANDS – see Fiji Islands
Ambassador:
HE Mr Vernon M Scarborough (Non-resident)

MAURITANIA – see Morocco

MAURITIUS
British High Commission
Les Cascades Building, Edith Cavell Street,
Port Louis, PO Box 1063
+ 230 211 1361 Fax + 230 211 1369
High Commissioner: HE Mr James Daly, CVO
Commercial: Mr J S Taylor – Deputy High
Commissioner and First Secretary
(Commercial)
+ 230 208 9850 Fax + 230 212 1369

MEXICO
British Embassy
Rio Lerma 71, Col Cuauhtémoc,
06500 Mexico City
+ 525 207 2089 Fax + 525 207 7672
Ambassador: HE Mr A C Thorpe, CMG
Commercial: Mr A C Stephens – First Secretary

MICRONESIA – see Fiji Islands
Ambassador: HE Mr Vernon M Scarborough
(Non-resident)

MOLDOVA – see Russian Federation

MONACO
British Consulate-General
33 Boulevard Princesse Charlotte BP 265,
MC98005 Monaco CEDEX
+ 377 93 50 99 66
Fax + 377 93 50 14 47
Consul-General: Mr I Davies
(Resides Marseilles)

MONGOLIA
British Embassy
30 Enkh Taivny Gudamzh (PO Box 703),
Ulaanbaatar 13
+ 976 1 458133 Fax + 976 1 458036
Ambassador and Consul-General:
HE Miss Kay Coombs

MOROCCO
British Embassy
17 Boulevard de la Tour Hassan (BP 45), Rabat
+ 212 7 72 96 96 Fax + 212 7 70 45 31
Ambassador: HE Mr Anthony Layden
(Non-resident: Mauritania)

MOZAMBIQUE
British High Commission
Av Vladimir I Lenine 310, Caixa Postal 55,
Maputo
+ 2581 420111 Fax + 2581 421666
High Commissioner: HE Mr Bernard J Everett
Commercial: Mr D G Harries, OBE –
Third Secretary (Commercial/Development)

MYANMAR – see Burma

NAMIBIA
British High Commission
116 Robert Mugabe Avenue, Windhoek 9000
+ 264 61 223022 Fax + 264 61 228895
High Commissioner: HE Mr R H G Davies

NAURU – see Fiji Islands

NEPAL
British Embassy
Lainchaur Kathmandu (PO Box 106)
+ 977 1 410583/414588 Fax + 977 1 411789
Ambassador: HE Mr Ronald Nash, LVO
Commercial: Mr M L Alcock – First Secretary
(Development/Commercial)

NETHERLANDS
British Embassy
Lange Voorhout 10, 2514 ED, The Hague
+ 31 70 427 0427 Fax + 31 70 427 0345
Ambassador:
HE Dame Rosemary Spencer, DCMG
Commercial: Miss C Bradley – Counsellor and
Consul-General
Fax + 31 70 427 0346

NEW ZEALAND
British High Commission
44 Hill Street, Wellington 1
+ 64 4 472 6049 Fax + 64 4 473 4982
High Commissioner:
HE Mr Martin Williams, CVO, OBE
(Non-resident: Samoa)
(Also Governor of Pitcairn, Henderson, Ducie
& Oeno Islands)
Commercial: Mr M A Capes – First Secretary

NICARAGUA
British Embassy
Plaza Churchill, Reparto "Los Robles",
Managua, Apartado A-169, Managua
+ 505 2 780014/780887 Fax + 505 2 784085
Ambassador and Consul-General:
HE Mr R Osborne

NIGER – see Cote d'Ivoire

NIGERIA
British High Commission
Shehu Shangari Way (North), Maitama, Abuja
+ 234 9 5232010/5232011
Fax + 234 9 5233552
High Commissioner:
HE Sir Graham Burton, KCMG, LVO
(Non-resident: Benin)
Commercial: Mr D S Adamson –
Second Secretary

NORWAY
British Embassy
Thomas Heftyesgate 8, 0244 Oslo
+ 47 23 13 27 00 Fax + 47 23 13 27 41
Ambassador: HE Mr Richard Dales, CMG
Commercial: Dr C M Sweeney – First Secretary
Fax 47 23 13 27 05

OMAN
British Embassy
PO Box 300, Muscat, Postal Code 113
+ 968 693077 Fax + 968 693087
Ambassador: HE Sir Ivan Callan, KCVO, CMG
Commercial:
Mr R Mackenzie – First Secretary
Fax + 968 693088

PAKISTAN
British High Commission
Diplomatic Enclave, Ramna 5, PO Box 1122,
Islamabad
+ 92 51 822131 Fax + 92 51 823439
High Commissioner:
HE Sir David Dain, KCVO, CMG
Commercial: Ms A Thornton – First Secretary

PALAU – see Fiji Islands
Ambassador: HE Mr Vernon M Scarborough
(Non-resident)

PANAMA
British Embassy
Torre Swiss Bank, Calle 53 (Apartado 889)
Zona 1, Panama City
+ 507 269-0866 Fax + 507 223-0730
Ambassador and Consul-General:
HE Mr Glyn Davies

PAPUA NEW GUINEA
British High Commission
PO Box 212, Waigani NCD 131
+ 675 3251643/45 Fax + 675 3253547
High Commissioner:
HE Mr Charles Drace-Francis, CMG

PARAGUAY
British Embassy
Avenida Boggiani 5848, C/R 16 Boqueron,
Asunción
+ 595 21 612611 Fax + 595 21 605007
Ambassador and Consul-General:
HE Mr Andrew George
Commercial: Mr H Silvero –
Commercial Officer

PERU
British Embassy
Edificio El Pacifico Washington (Piso 12),
Plaza Washington, Avenida Arequipa
(PO Box No 854), Lima 100
+ 51 14 33 4738 Fax + 51 14 33 4735
Ambassador: HE Mr Roger Hart, CMG
Commercial: Mr S J Collier, MVO –
First Secretary

PHILIPPINES
British Embassy
Floors 15–17 LV Locsin Building, 6752 Ayala
Avenue, Cor Makati Avenue, 1226 Makati,
(PO Box 2927 MCPO), Manila
+ 63 2 816 7116 Fax + 63 2 819 7206
Telex: 63282 (a/b 63282 PRODME PN)
Ambassador: HE Mr Alan Collins, CMG
Commercial: Mr E J McAvoy – First Secretary
Fax + 63 2815 815 6233

POLAND
British Embassy
Aleje Roz No 1, 00-556 Warsaw
+ 00 48 22 6281001
Fax + 00 48 22 621 7161
Ambassador:
HE Mr J Macgregor, CVO
Commercial: Warsaw Corporate Centre,
2nd Floor, Emilii Platter 28 00 688
+ 00 48 22 625 3030 Fax + 00 48 22 625 3472
Mr S D Pattison –
Director of Trade Promotion/Consul-General

PORTUGAL
British Embassy
Rua de São Bernardo 33, 1200 Lisbon
+ 351 1 392 40 00 Fax + 351 1 392 41 83
Ambassador:
HE Sir John Holmes, KCMG
Commercial: Mr P A Sinkinson –
First Secretary

QATAR
British Embassy
PO Box 3, Doha
+ 974 421991 Fax + 974 438692
Ambassador:
HE Mr David Wright, OBE
Commercial: 8th Floor, Toyota Tower
+ 974 353543 Fax + 974 356131
Mr P Cole – First Secretary and
Deputy Head of Mission

ROMANIA
British Embassy
24 Strada Jules Michelet, 70154 Bucharest
+ 40 1 312 0303 Fax + 40 1 312 0229
Ambassador:
HE Mr Richard Ralph, CMG, CVO
Commercial: Mr R J Cork – First Secretary
Fax + 40 1 312 9742

RUSSIAN FEDERATION
British Embassy
Sofiskaya Naberezhnaya 14, Moscow 109072
+ 007 503 956 7200 Fax + 007 503 956 7420
Ambassador: HE Sir Roderic Lyne, KBE, CMG
(Non-resident: Moldova)
Commercial: Mr J Dauris – First Secretary
Fax + 007 503 956 7480

RWANDA
British Embassy
Parcelle No 1131, Boulevard de l'Umuganda,
Kacyira-Sud, BP 576, Kigali
+ 250 84098 Fax + 250 82044
Ambassador: HE Mr Graeme Loten
(Non-resident: Burundi)

ST CHRISTOPHER AND NEVIS
British High Commission
PO Box 483, Price Waterhouse Centre,
11 Old Parham Road, St John's, Antigua
+ (1) (268) 462 0008/9
Fax + (1) (268) 462 2806
High Commissioner: HE Mr Gordon M Baker
(Resident in Barbados)
Resident Acting High Commissioner:
Miss M J Maxwell

ST LUCIA
British High Commission
NIS Waterfront Building,
2nd Floor (PO Box 227), Castries
+ 001 758 45 22484 Fax + 001 758 45 31543
High Commissioner: HE Mr Gordon M Baker
(Resident in Barbados)
Resident Acting High Commissioner:
Mr P J Hughes

ST VINCENT AND THE GRENADINES
British High Commission
Granby Street (PO Box 132), Kingstown
+ (1) (784) 457 1701/2
Fax + (1) (784) 456 2750
High Commissioner: HE Mr Gordon M Baker
(Resident in Barbados)
Resident Acting High Commissioner:
Mr B Robertson

SAMOA – see New Zealand

SAN MARINO – see Italy

SÃO TOMÉ & PRINCIPÉ – see Angola

SAUDI ARABIA
British Embassy
PO Box 94351, Riyadh 11693
+ 966 1 488 0077 Fax + 966 1 488 2373/0623
Telex: 406488 (a/b 406488 BRITEM SJ)
Ambassador:
HE Sir Andrew Green, KCMG
Commercial: Mr R J Northern, MBE –
Counsellor

SENEGAL
British Embassy
20 Rue du Docteur Guillet (Boîte Postale
6025), Dakar
+ 221 823 7392, 823 9971 Fax + 221 823 2766
Ambassador: HE Mr David R Snoxell
(Non-resident: Cape Verde, Guinea-Bissau,
Mali, Guinea)

SEYCHELLES
British High Commission
Oliaji Trade Centre, PO Box 161, Victoria,
Mahé
+ 248 225225/356/396 Fax + 248 225127
High Commissioner: HE Mr John Yapp

SIERRA LEONE
British High Commission
Spur Road, Freetown
+ 232 22 233961 Fax + 232 22 228169
High Commissioner:
HE Mr P A Penfold, CMG, OBE

SINGAPORE
British High Commission
Tanglin Road, Singapore 247919
+ 65 4739333 Fax + 65 474 1958
High Commissioner:
HE Mr Alan Hunt, CMG
Commercial:
+ 65 474 0461 Fax + 65 475 2320
Mr A J Gooch – Counsellor and
Deputy High Commissioner

SLOVAK REPUBLIC
British Embassy
Panska 16, 811 01 Bratislava
+ 421 7 531 9632 Fax + 421 7 531 0002
Ambassador: HE Mr D Lyscom
Commercial: Fax + 421 7 531 0003

SLOVENIA
British Embassy
4th Floor, Trg Republike 3, 61000 Ljubljana
+ 386 61 125 7191 Fax: + 386 61 125 0174
Ambassador: HE Mr David A Lloyd, OBE

SOLOMON ISLANDS
British High Commission
Telekom House, Mendana Avenue, Honiara
Postal address: PO Box 676
+ 677 21705/706 Fax + 677 21549
High Commissioner: HE Mr Alan Waters

SOMALIA – No representation

SOUTH AFRICA
British High Commission
91 Parliament Street, Cape Town 8001
+ 27 21 461-7220 Fax + 27 21 4610017
and at 255 Hill Street,
Arcadia 0083, Pretoria
+ 27 12 4831200 Fax + 27 12 4831302
High Commissioner:
HE Dame Maeve Fort, DCMG

SPAIN
British Embassy
Calle de Fernando el Santo 16, 28010 Madrid
+ (34) (91) 700 82 00
Fax + (34) (91) 700 83 09
Ambassador: HE Mr Peter Torry
(Non-resident: Andorra)
Commercial: Mr M H Connor – Counsellor

SRI LANKA
British High Commission
190 Galle Road, Kollupitiya (PO Box 1433),
Colombo 3
+ 94 1 437336/43 Fax + 94 1 430308
High Commissioner:
HE Miss Linda Duffield
(Non-resident: Maldives)
Commercial: Mr A Madeley – First Secretary

SUDAN
British Embassy
off Sharia Al Baladia, Khartoum East
(PO Box No 801)
+ 249 11 777105/780828 Fax + 249 11 776457
Telex: 22189 (a/b PRDRM SD)
Ambassador: HE Mr Alan F Goulty, CMG

SURINAME – see Guyana

SWAZILAND
British High Commission
Callers: Allister Miller Street, Mbabane
Postal address: Private Bag, Mbabane
+ 268 404 2581 Fax + 268 404 2585
High Commissioner:
HE Mr Neil Hook, MVO

SWEDEN
British Embassy
Skarpögatan 6–8, Box 27819, 115 93
Stockholm
+ 46 8 671 9000 Fax + 46 8 662 9989
Ambassador: HE Mr John Grant
Commercial: Mr P J Mathers, LVO –
Counsellor

SWITZERLAND
British Embassy
Thunstrasse 50, 3005 Berne
+ 41 31 359 77 00 Fax + 41 31 359 77 01
Ambassador:
HE Mr Christopher Hulse, CMG, OBE
(Non-resident: Liechtenstein)
Commercial: Miss A J Pring – First Secretary

SYRIA
British Embassy
Kotob Building, 11 Mohammad Kurd Ali
Street, Malki, PO Box 37, Damascus
+ 963 11 371 2561 Fax + 963 11 373 1600
Telex: BRITEM 411049
Ambassador: HE Mr Basil S T Eastwood, CMG

TAJIKESTAN – see Uzbekistan

TANZANIA
British High Commission
Social Security House, Samora Avenue
(PO Box 9200)
+ 255 51 117659/64,112953
Fax + 225 51 112952
High Commissioner: HE Mr Bruce Dinwiddy
Commercial: Mr K E Green – Second Secretary

THAILAND
British Embassy
Wireless Road, Bangkok 10330
+ 66 2 253-0191 Fax + 66 2 254 9578
Ambassador:
HE Mr B Smith (Non-resident: Laos)
Commercial: Mr M J Greenstreet – Counsellor
Fax + 66 2 255 8619

TOGO – see Ghana

TONGA
British High Commission
PO Box 56, Nuku'alofa
+ 676 24285/24395 Fax 676 24285/24395
*High Commissioner and Consul for American
Samoa:* HE Mr Brian Connelly

TRINIDAD AND TOBAGO
British High Commission
19 St Clair Avenue, St Clair, Port of Spain
+ 001 868 622 2748/9895
Fax + 001 868 622 4555
High Commissioner:
HE Mr Peter Harborne
Commercial: Mr B Nicholas –
Second Secretary

TUNISIA
British Embassy
5 Place de la Victoire, Tunis
+ 216 1 341 444 Fax + 216 1 354 877
Ambassador and Consul-General:
HE Mr Ivor Rawlinson, OBE
Commercial: Mrs J M Quinn –
Second Secretary

TURKEY
British Embassy
Sehit Ersan Caddesi 46/A, Cankaya, Ankara
+ 90 312 468 6230 Fax + 90 312 468 6249
Ambassador: HE Sir David Logan, KCMG
Commercial: Ms J MacPherson –
First Secretary
Fax + 90 312 468 3214

TURKMENISTAN
British Embassy
3rd Floor, Office Building, Ak Altin Plaza
Hotel, Ashgabat
+ 00 993 12 510661 Fax + 00 993 12 510861
Ambassador: HE Mr Fraser Wilson, MBE

TUVALU – see Fiji Islands

UGANDA
British High Commission
10/12 Parliament Avenue, PO Box 7070,
Kampala
+ 256 41 257054 Fax + 256 41 257304
High Commissioner:
HE Mr Michael E Cook, CMG
Commercial: Miss H C Rawlins –
Second Secretary

UKRAINE
British Embassy
252025 Kiev Desyatinna 9
+ 380 44 462 0011 Fax + 380 44 462 0013
Ambassador: HE Mr Roland Smith, CMG
Commercial: Mr R C C Cook – First Secretary

UNITED ARAB EMIRATES
British Embassy
PO Box 248, Abu Dhabi
+ 971 2 326600/321364 Fax + 971 2 318138
Ambassador: HE Mr Patrick Nixon, CMG, OBE
Commercial: Mr D A Bell –
Commercial Secretary
  Dubai:
  PO Box 65, Dubai
  + 971 4 521070 Fax + 971 4 525750
  Consul-General and Counsellor:
  Mr N H S Armour
  Commercial: Mr H Dunnachie, MBE –
  First Secretary/Deputy Head of Post
  + 971 4 521893/524993
  Fax + 971 4 527095

UNITED STATES OF AMERICA
British Embassy
3100 Massachusetts Avenue NW,
Washington DC 20008
+ 1 202 588 6500 Fax + 1 202 588 7870
Ambassador:
HE Sir Christopher Meyer, KCMG
Trade: Fax + 1 202 588 7901
Mr N J Westcott – Counsellor
(Trade and Transport)

URUGUAY
British Embassy
Calle Marco Bruto 1073, 11300 Montevideo,
PO Box 16024
+ 598 2 6223630/650 Fax + 598 2 6227815
Ambassador: HE Mr Andrew Murray

UZBEKISTAN
British Embassy
Ul-Gogolya 67, Tashkent 700000
+ 99871 1206822 Fax + 99871 1206549
Ambassador: HE Mr Christopher Ingham
(Non-resident: Tajikistan)

VANUATU
British High Commission
KPMG House, Rue Pasteur, Port Vila, Vanuatu,
PO Box 567
+ 678 23100 Fax + 678 27153
High Commissioner:
HE Mr Malcolm G Hilson

VATICAN CITY – see Holy See

VENEZUELA
British Embassy
Edificio Torre Las Mercedes (Piso 3),
Avenida La Estancia, Chuao, Caracas 1061
(Postal address: Embajada Britanica,
Apartado 1246 Caracas 1010-A)
+ 58 2 993 41 11 Fax + 58 2 993 99 89
Ambassador:
HE Mr Richard D Wilkinson, CVO
Commercial: Mr A F N Goodworth –
First Secretary
Fax + 58 2 933 03 39

VIETNAM
British Embassy
Central Building, 31 Hai Ba Trung, Hanoi
+ 84 4 8252510 Fax + 84 4 8265762
Ambassador: HE Mr David W Fall
Commercial: Mr J Wales – Second Secretary

YEMEN
British Embassy
129 Haddah Road, Sana'a
Postal address: PO Box 1287
+ 967 1 264081 Fax + 967 1 263059
Ambassador and Consul-General:
HE Mr Victor Henderson, CMG

**YUGOSLAVIA, FEDERAL REPUBLIC OF
(Serbia & Montenegro)**
British Embassy
Generala Zdanova, 46, 11000 Belgrade
+ 381 11 645055/034/043/087
Fax + 381 11 659651
(Embassy Closed)

ZAIRE – see Democratic Republic of Congo

ZAMBIA
British High Commission
Independence Avenue (PO Box 50050),
15101, Lusaka
+ 260 1 251133 Fax + 260 1 253798
High Commissioner: HE Mr Thomas Young
Commercial: Miss I M Mulvaney –
Third Secretary
Fax + 260 1 251923

ZIMBABWE
British High Commission
Corner House, Samora Machel Avenue/
Leopold Takawaira Street (PO Box 4490),
Harare
+ 263 4 772990 Fax + 263 4 774617
High Commissioner: HE Mr Peter Longworth
Commercial: Mr D Seddon – First Secretary

British High Commissioners

Baker, G.	Barbados, Antigua and Barbuda, Dominica, Grenada, St Christopher and Nevis, St Lucia, St Vincent and the Grenadines	Fry, G.	Malaysia
		Glover, E.	Guyana, Suriname
		Goodenough, Sir A.	Canada
		Goodlad, Sir A.	Australia
		Harborne, P.	Trinidad and Tobago
		Heigl, P.	Bahamas
Boon, P.	Cameroon	Hemans, S. N.	Kenya
Burton, Sir G.	Nigeria, Benin	Hilson, M. G.	Vanuatu
Carter, D.	Bangladesh	Hook, N.	Swaziland
Clay, E.	Cyprus	Hunt, A.	Singapore
Connelly, B.	Tonga	Laing, S.	Brunei
Cook, M. E.	Uganda	Longworth, P.	Zimbabwe
Dain, D. J. M.	Pakistan	Mackley, I.	Ghana, Togo
Daly, J.	Mauritius	Millson, T.	Gambia
David, T.	Belize	Oliver, K.	Lesotho
Davies, R. H.	Namibia	Pearce, H.	Malta
Dibben, M.	Fiji, Kiribati, Nauru, Tuvalu	Penfold, P.	Sierra Leone
		Smith, A.	Jamaica
Dinwiddy, B.	Tanzania	Waters, A.	Solomon Islands
Drace-Francis, C.	Papua New Guinea	Wilde, J.	Botswana
Duffield, L.	Sri Lanka, Maldives	Williams, M.	New Zealand, Samoa
Everett, B. J.	Mozambique	Yapp, J.	Seychelles
Finlayson, G.	Malawi	Young, Sir R.	India
Fort, Dame M.	South Africa	Young, T.	Zambia

British Ambassadors

Astley, P.	Denmark	Fall, D.	Vietnam
Bone, R.	Brazil	Figgis, Sir A.	Austria
Boon, P.	Chad, Central African Republic, Equatorial Guinea, Gabon	Ford, P.	Bahrain
		Galsworthy, Sir A.	China
		George, A.	Paraguay
Boyce, G.	Egypt	Gerken, I.	Ecuador
Broucher, D. S.	Czech Republic	Gomersall, S.	Japan
Brown, Sir S.	Korea	Goulty, A. F.	Sudan
Browne, N.	Iran	Grant, J.	Sweden
Caie, A.	Guatemala	Green, A. F.	Saudi Arabia
Callan, Sir I.	Oman	Hand, G.	Bosnia and Herzegovina
Chaplin, E.	Jordan		
Christopher, D. R. C.	Indonesia	Hart, R.	Peru
Collins, A.	Philippines	Henderson, V.	Yemen
Colvin, D.	Belgium	Hewitt, G.	Finland
Coombs, K.	Mongolia	Holmes, Sir J.	Portugal
Cornish, F.	Israel	Hulse, C.	Switzerland, Liechtenstein
Craddock, T.	Estonia		
Dales, R.	Norway	Ingham, C.	Uzbekistan, Tajikistan
Dalton, R.	Libya	Jackson, R. M.	Costa Rica
Davies, G.	Panama	James, J.	Iran
Dickinson, W.	Macedonia	January, P.	Albania
Eastwood, B.	Syria	Jay, M. A.	France
Edgar, G.	Cambodia	Jenkins, J.	Burma
Ehrman, W.	Luxembourg	Jenkins, R.	Georgia
Elmes, Miss C.	Angola, Sao Tome and Principe	Jones, T.	Armenia
		Kelly, I.	Belarus
Evans, Miss G.	Chile	Layden, A.	Morocco, Mauritania

Lever, Sir P.	Germany
Lewington, J.	Kazakhstan, Kyrgyzstan
Lloyd, D.	Slovenia
Logan, Sir D.	Turkey
Loten, G.	Rwanda, Burundi
Lyne, Sir R.	Russian Federation, Moldova
Lyscom, D.	Slovak Republic
Macgregor, J.	Poland
Maclean, P. A.	Cuba
MacLennan, D. R.	Lebanon
MacRae, Sir C. D. S.	Afghanistan
Madden, D.	Greece
Marsden, W.	Argentina
Meyer, Sir C.	USA
Minter, G.	Bolivia
Mochan, C.	Madagascar, Comoros
Morgan, P.	El Salvador
Muir, R.	Kuwait
Munro, C.	Croatia
Murray, A.	Uruguay
Nash, R.	Nepal
Nash, S.	Latvia
Nixon, P.	United Arab Emirates
Osborne, D.	Honduras
Osbourne, R.	Nicaragua
Pellew, M.	Holy See
Ralph, R.	Romania
Rawlinson, I.	Tunisia
Richardson, Sir T.	Italy, San Marino
Ridgway, D.	Cuba
Robbins, C.	Lithuania
Roberts, I.	Irish Republic
Scarborough, V.	Marshall Islands, Micronesia, Palau
Scrafton, D.	Congo DR, Congo PR
Short, R.	Bulgaria
Sinton, W. B.	Algeria
Smith, B.	Thailand, Laos
Smith, R. B.	Ukraine
Snoxell, D.	Senegal, Guinea, Guinea Bissau, Cape Verde, Mali
Spencer, Dame R.	Netherlands
Spiceley, P.	Costa Rica
Stagg, R.	Bulgaria
Thomas, A. R.	Haiti
Thomas, D. R.	Azerbaijan
Thorp, J.	Colombia
Thorpe, A. C.	Mexico
Thorpe, N.	Hungary
Torry, P.	Spain, Andorra
Ward, D.	Dominican Republic
Warren-Gash, H.	Cote d'Ivoire, Burkina, Niger, Liberia
Wetherell, G. C.	Ethiopia, Eritrea, Djibouti
Whitehead, I.	Guyana
Wilkinson, R.	Venezuela
Williams, P. K.	Vietnam
Wilson, F.	Turkmenistan
Wright, D.	Qatar

London Embassies and High Commissions

Source: London Diplomatic List – updated November 1999

AFGHANISTAN
Embassy of the Islamic State of Afghanistan
31 Prince's Gate, London SW7 1QQ
020 7589 8891 Fax 020 7581 3452
Telex: 916641
Mr Ahmad Wali Masud *(Chargé d'Affaires)*

ALBANIA
Embassy of the Republic of Albania
4th Floor, 38 Grosvenor Gardens,
London SW1W 0EB
020 7730 5709 Fax 020 7730 5747
Ambassador: HE Mr Agim Besim Fagu

ALGERIA
Embassy of Algeria
54 Holland Park, London W11 3RS
020 7221 7800 Fax 020 7221 0448
Ambassador: HE Mr Ahmed Benyamina

ANGOLA
Embassy of the Republic of Angola
98 Park Lane, London W1Y 3TA
020 7495 1752 Fax 020 7495 1635
Telex: 8813258 EMBAUK G
Ambassador:
HE Senhor Antonio DaCosta Fernandes

ANTIGUA AND BARBUDA
High Commission for Antigua and Barbuda
15 Thayer Street, London W1M 5LD
020 7486 7073 Fax 020 7486 9970
Telex: 814503AK ANTEGA G
High Commissioner:
HE Mr Ronald Sanders, CMG

ARGENTINA
Embassy of the Argentine Republic
65 Brook Street, London W1Y 1YE
020 7318 1300 Fax 020 7318 1301
Ambassador: HE Señor Rogelio Pfirter
Commercial: 4th Floor, 65 Brook Street,
London W1Y 1YE
020 7318 1330 Fax 020 7318 1331
Senor Gustavo A Martino – Counsellor
(Economic and Commercial)

ARMENIA
Embassy of the Republic of Armenia
25A Cheniston Gardens, London W8 6TG
020 7938 5435 Fax 020 7938 2595
Ambassador: HE Dr Armen Sarkissian

AUSTRALIA
Australian High Commission
Australia House, Strand,
London WC2B 4LA
020 7379 4334 Fax 020 7240 5333
High Commissioner: HE Mr Philip Flood, AO
Commercial: Mr Mark Jenkins – Minister
(Commercial)

AUSTRIA
Austrian Embassy
18 Belgrave Mews West,
London SW1X 8HU
020 7235 3731 Fax 020 7344 0292
Ambassador: (Vacant)
Mrs Brigitte Oppinger-Walchshofer
(Chargé d'Affaires)
Commercial: Dr Rudolf J Engel – Counsellor
and Trade Commissioner

AZERBAIJAN
Embassy of the Azerbaijan Republic
4 Kensington Court, London W8 5DL
020 7938 5482/3412 Fax 020 7937 1783
Ambassador: HE Mr Mahmud Mamed-Kuliyev

BAHAMAS
High Commission for the Commonwealth of
the Bahamas
10 Chesterfield Street, London W1X 8AH
020 7408 4488 Fax 020 7499 9937
High Commissioner:
HE Mr Basil O'Brien, CMG

BAHRAIN
Embassy of the State of Bahrain
98 Gloucester Road, London SW7 4AU
020 7370 5132/3 Fax 020 7370-7773
Telex: 917829
Ambassador:
HE Shaikh Abdul Aziz Mubarak Al Khalifa

BANGLADESH
High Commission for the People's Republic of
Bangladesh
28 Queen's Gate, London SW7 5JA
020 7584 0081 Fax 020 7225 2130
Telex: 918016
High Commissioner: HE Mr A H Mahmood Ali

BARBADOS
Barbados High Commission
1 Great Russell Street, London WC1B 3JY
020 7631 4975 Fax 020 7323 6872
High Commissioner:
HE Mr Peter Patrick Simmons

BELARUS
Embassy of the Republic of Belarus
6 Kensington Court, London W8 5DL
020 7937 3288 Fax 020 7361 0005
Ambassador: HE Mr Uladzimir Shchasny

BELGIUM
Belgian Embassy
103–105 Eaton Square, London SW1W 9AB
020 7470 3700 Fax 020 7259 6213
Telex: 22823 BELAM G
Ambassador: HE Mr Lode Willems

BELIZE
Belize High Commission
22 Harcourt House, 19 Cavendish Square,
London W1M 9AD
020 7499 9728 Fax 020 7491 4139
Telex: 94082284 BHCOM
High Commissioner: HE Mr Assad Shoman

BENIN
No London Embassy
Embassy of the Republic of Benin
87 Avenue Victor Hugo, 75116 Paris, France
+ 45-009882 Fax + 42-223244
Ambassador:
HE Mons André-Guy Ologoudou
(Resident in Paris)
Honorary Consulate:
Dolphin House, 16 The Broadway,
Stanmore, Middlesex HA7 4DW
020 8954 8800

BOLIVIA
Bolivian Embassy
106 Eaton Square, London SW1W 9AD
020 7235 4248/2557 Fax 020 7235 1286
Telex: 918885 COMBOL G
Ambassador:
HE Senor Jaime Quiroga-Matos

BOSNIA AND HERZEGOVINA
Embassy of the Republic of Bosnia and
Herzegovina
4th Floor, Morley House,
320 Regent Street, London W1R 5AB
020 7255 3758 Fax 020 7255 3760
Ambassador: HE Mr Osman Topcagic

BOTSWANA
Botswana High Commission
6 Stratford Place, London W1N 9AE
020 7499 0031 Fax 020 7495 8595
High Commissioner:
HE Mr Roy Blackbeard

BRAZIL
Brazilian Embassy
32 Green Street, Mayfair, London W1Y 4AT
020 7499 0877 Fax 020 7493 5105
Telex: 261157 BRASLO G
Ambassador:
HE Senhor Sergio Silva do Amaral, KBE
Commercial: Senhor João de Mendonça Lima
Neto – Counsellor

BRUNEI
Brunei Darussalam High Commission
19–20 Belgrave Square, London SW1X 8PG
020 7581 0521 Fax 020 7235 9717
Telex: 888 369
High Commissioner: (Vacant)

BULGARIA
Embassy of the Republic of Bulgaria
186–188 Queen's Gate, London SW7 5HL
020 7584 9400/9433 Fax 020 7584 4948
Ambassador: HE Mr Valentin Dobrev
Commercial: Mr Christo Charenkov –
Counsellor (Commercial/Economic)
020 7581 3144 Fax 020 7589 4875

BURKINA
No London Embassy
Embassy of the Republic of Burkina
16 Place Guy d'Arezzo 16, 1060 Brussels,
Belgium
+ 345 99 12 Fax + 345 06 12
Ambassador: (Vacant)
Monsieur Raymond Balima
(Chargé d'Affaires)
(Resident in Brussels)
Honorary Consulate:
5 Cinnamon Row, Plantation Wharf,
London SW11 3TW 020 7738 1800

BURMA
19A Charles Street, Berkeley Square,
London W1X 8ER
020 7499 8841 Fax 020 7629 4169
Telex: 267609 MYANMA G
Ambassador: HE Dr Kyaw Win

BURUNDI
No London Embassy
Embassy of the Republic of Burundi
26 Armitage Road, London NW11 8RD
020 8381 4092 Fax 020 8458 8596
Ambassador: HE Mr Jonathas Niyungeko
(Resident in Brussels)

CAMEROON
High Commission of the Republic of Cameroon
84 Holland Park, London W11 3SB
020 7727 0771 Fax 020 7792 9353
Telex: 921880
High Commissioner:
HE Mr Samuel Libock Mbei

CANADA
Canadian High Commission
Macdonald House, 1 Grosvenor Square,
London W1X 0AB
020 7258 6600 Fax 020 7258 6333
High Commissioner:
HE The Hon Roy MacLaren, PC
Commercial: Mr Tom MacDonald – Minister

CAPE VERDE
No London Embassy
Embassy of the Republic of Cape Verde
Burgemeester Patijnlaan 1930, 2585 CB,
The Hague, Netherlands
+ 355-36-51
Ambassador: HE Mr Julio Vasco de Sousa Lobo
(Resident in The Hague)

CENTRAL AFRICAN REPUBLIC
No London Embassy
Embassy of the Central African Republic
30 rue des Perchamp, 75016 Paris, France
+ 42 24 42 56
Ambassador: (Vacant) (Resident in Paris)

CHAD
No London Embassy
Embassy of the Republic of Chad
Boulevard Lambermont 52, 1030 Brussels,
Belgium
+ 215 19 75
Mons Idriss Adjide *(Chargé d'Affaires)*
(Resident in Brussels)

CHILE
Embassy of Chile
12 Devonshire Street, London W1N 2DS
020 7580 6392 Fax 020 7436 5204
Ambassador: HE Senor Pablo Cabrera
Commercial: Señor Marcial Ubilla – Counsellor

CHINA
Embassy of the People's Republic of China
49–51 Portland Place, London W1N 4JL
020 7636 9375/5726
Ambassador: HE Mr Ma Zhengang
Commercial: 13 Leinster Gardens,
London W2 6DP 020 7723 8923

COLOMBIA
Colombian Embassy
Flat 3A, 3 Hans Crescent, London SW1X 0LN
020 7589 9177/5037 Fax 020 7581 1829
Ambassador:
HE Señor Humberto de la Calle-Lombana

CONGO, DEMOCRATIC REPUBLIC OF
Embassy of the Democratic Republic of Congo
26 Chesham Place, London SW1X 8HH
020 7235 6137 Fax 020 7235 9048
Telex: 25651
Mr Henri N'Swana *(Chargé d'Affaires)*

CONGO, REPUBLIC OF
No London Embassy
Embassy of the Republic of Congo
37 bis Rue Paul Valery, 75116 Paris, France
+ 4500 60 57
Ambassador: HE Mons Henri Lopes
(Resident in Paris)
Honorary Consulate:
4 Wendle Court, 131–137 Wandsworth Road,
London SW8 2LH 020 7622 0419

COSTA RICA
Costa Rican Embassy
Flat 1, 14 Lancaster Gate, London W2 3LH
020 7706 8844 Fax 020 7706 8655
Ambassador: HE Señor Rodolfo Gutiérrez

COTE D'IVOIRE
Embassy of the Republic of Côte d'Ivoire
2 Upper Belgrave Street, London SW1X 8BJ
020 7235 6991 Fax 020 7259 5320
Telex: 23906 IVORY G
Ambassador: HE Mons Kouadio Adjoumani
Commercial: 2 Upper Belgrave Street,
London SW1X 8BJ 020 7235 6991
Mons Kouame Clement Goli – Attaché

CROATIA
Embassy of the Republic of Croatia
21 Conway Street, London W1P 5HL
020 7387 2022 Fax 020 7387 0310
Ambassador: HE Mr Andrija Kojakovic

CUBA
Embassy of the Republic of Cuba
167 High Holborn, London WC1 6PA
020 7240 2488 Fax 020 7836 2602
Ambassador:
HE Señor Rodney A Lopez Clemente
Commercial: Ms Elena Blanco Diaz –
Counsellor

CYPRUS
Cyprus High Commission
93 Park Street, London W1Y 4ET
020 7499 8272 Fax 020 7491 0691
High Commissioner:
HE Mr Michalis Attalides
Commercial: 3rd Floor, 29 Princes Street,
London W1R 7RG 020 7629 6288
Mr Andreas Georgiades – Counsellor

CZECH REPUBLIC
Embassy of the Czech Republic
26–30 Kensington Palace Gardens,
London W8 4QY
020 7243 1115 Fax 020 7727 9654
Ambassador: HE Mr Pavel Seifter

DENMARK
Royal Danish Embassy
55 Sloane Street, London SW1X 9SR
020 7333 0200 Fax 020 7333 0270
Ambassador: HE Mr Ole Lønsmann Poulsen
Commercial: Mr Gunner Richard Tetler –
Counsellor

DJIBOUTI
No London Embassy
Embassy of the Republic of Djibouti
26 Rue Emile Mènier, 75116 Paris, France
+ 47 27 49 22
Ambassador: HE Mr Djama Omar Idleh
(Resident in Paris)

DOMINICA
Office of the High Commissioner for the
Commonwealth of Dominica
1 Collingham Gardens, South Kensington,
London SW5 0HW
020 7370 5194/5 Fax 020 7373 8743
Telex: 8813931 DACOM G
High Commissioner: HE Mr George E Williams

DOMINICAN REPUBLIC
Embassy of the Dominican Republic
139 Inverness Terrace, Bayswater,
London W2 6JF
020 7727 6285 Fax 020 7727 3693
Ambassador: HE Dr Pedro L Padilla Tonos

EASTERN CARIBBEAN STATES
see St Christopher and Nevis; St Lucia;
St Vincent and the Grenadines

ECUADOR
Embassy of Ecuador
Flat 3B, 3 Hans Crescent, Knightsbridge,
London SW1X 0LS
020 7584 2648/8084 Fax 020 7823 9701
Telex: 8811087
Ambassador
HE Senor Oswaldo Ramirez-Landazuri

EGYPT
Embassy of the Arab Republic of Egypt
12 Curzon Street, London W1Y 7FJ
020 7499 2401 Fax 020 7355 3568
Telex: 23650 BOSTAN G
Ambassador: HE Mr Adel El Gazzar
Commercial: 23 South Street,
London W1Y 6EL
020 7499 3002 Fax 020 7493 8110
Dr Ismail M Roushdy – Minister
Plenipotentiary (Commercial)

EL SALVADOR
Embassy of El Salvador
Tennyson House, 159 Great Portland Street,
London W1N 5FD
020 7436 8282 Fax 020 7436 8181
Ambassador:
HE Senor Mauricio Castro-Aragôn

EQUATORIAL GUINEA
No London Embassy
Embassy of the Republic of Equatorial Guinea
6 Rue Alfred de Vigny, 75008 Paris, France
+ 47 66 44 33/95 70
Ambassador: HE Mr Lino-Sima Ekua Avomo
(Resident in Paris)

ERITREA
No London Embassy
Embassy of the State of Eritrea
15–17 Avenue de Wolvendael, 1180 Brussels,
Belgium
+ 02/374.44.34 Fax + 02/372.07.30
Ambassador: HE Mr Andrebrhan Weldegiorgis
(Resident in Brussels)
Consulate:
96 White Lion Street, London N1 9PF
020 7713 0096

ESTONIA
Embassy of the Republic of Estonia
16 Hyde Park Gate, Kensington,
London SW7 5DG
020 7589 7690/3428 Fax 020 7589 3430
Ambassador: HE Mr Raul Mälk

ETHIOPIA
Embassy of the Federal Democratic Republic of
Ethiopia
17 Prince's Gate, London SW7 1PZ
020 7589 7212/5 Fax 020 7584 7054
Ambassador: HE Dr Beyone Negewo
Commercial: Mr Osman Imam Beshir –
Counsellor

FIJI ISLANDS
High Commission of the Fiji Islands
34 Hyde Park Gate, London SW7 5DN
020 7584 3661 Fax 020 7584 2838
High Commissioner: HE Mr Filimone Jitoko
Commercial: Mr Sung Kangwai –
Counsellor 020 7584 3661

FINLAND
The Embassy of Finland
38 Chesham Place, London SW1X 8HW
020 7838 6200 Fax 020 7235 3680
Ambassador: HE Mr Pertti Salolainen
Commercial: 3rd Floor, 30–35 Pall Mall,
London SW1 020 7747 3000
Mr Marcus Moberg – Counsellor

FRANCE
French Embassy
58 Knightsbridge, London SW1X 7JT
020 7201 1000 Fax 020 7201 1004
Telex: 261 95 FRALON
Ambassador: HE Monsieur Daniel Bernard
Commercial: Mons Philippe O'Quin –
Minister-Counsellor

GABON
Embassy of the Republic of Gabon
27 Elvaston Place, London SW7 5NL
020 7823 9986 Fax 020 7584 0047
Telex: 919418 AMBGAB G
Ambassador:
HE Madame Honorine Dossou-Naki
(Resident in Paris)

GAMBIA
The Gambia High Commission
57 Kensington Court, Kensington,
London W8 5DG
020 7937 6316/7/8 Fax 020 7937 9095
High Commissioner: HE Mr John P Bojang

GEORGIA
Embassy of the Republic of Georgia
3 Hornton Place, Kensington, London W8 4LZ
020 7937 8233 Fax 020 7938 4108
Ambassador: HE Mr Teimuraz Mamatsashvili

GERMANY
Embassy of the Federal Republic of Germany
23 Belgrave Square, 1 Chesham Place,
London SW1X 8PZ
020 7824 1300 Fax 020 7824 1435
Telex: 21650 AALDN E
Ambassador:
HE Herr Dr Hans-Friedrich von Ploetz

GHANA
Office of the High Commissioner for Ghana
13 Belgrave Square, London SW1X 8PN
020 7235 4142 Fax 020 7245 9552
High Commissioner: HE Mr James Emmanuel
Kwegyir Aggrey-Orleans

GREECE
Embassy of Greece
1A Holland Park, London W11 3TP
020 7229 3850 Fax 020 7229 7221
Telex: 266751 GREEMB G
Ambassador: (Vacant)
Mr Constantine Bitsios *(Chargé d'Affaires)*
Commercial: 020 7727 8860
Fax 020 7727 9934

GRENADA
High Commission for Grenada
1 Collingham Gardens, Earl's Court,
London SW5 0HW
020 7373 7809 Fax 020 7370 7040
High Commissioner: HE Miss Ruth Rouse

GUATEMALA
Embassy of Guatemala
13 Fawcett Street, London SW10 9HN
020 7351 3042 Fax 020 7376 5708
Telex: 926556 GUATEM
Ambassador:
HE Mr Fernando Andrade Díaz-Durán

GUINEA
No London Embassy
Embassy of the Republic of Guinea
51 rue de la Faisanderie, 75016 Paris, France
+ 47 04 81 48
Ambassador HE Mons Ibrahim Sylla
(Resident in Paris)
Honorary Consulate:
20 Upper Grosvenor Street, London W1X 9PB
020 7333 0044

GUINEA-BISSAU
No London Embassy
Embassy of the Republic of Guinea-Bissau
94 rue St Lazare, Paris 9, France
+ 45 26 18 51
Senhora Maria Filomena Embala Araujo Vieira
(Chargé d'Affaires) (Resident in Paris)
Honorary Consulate:
Flat 5, 8 Palace Gate, London W8 5NF
020 7589 5253

GUYANA
High Commission for Guyana
3 Palace Court, Bayswater Road,
London W2 4LP
020 7229 7684-8 Fax 020 7727 9809
High Commissioner:
HE Mr Laleshwar K N Singh

HAITI
Embassy closed 30 March 1987

HOLY SEE
Apostolic Nunciature
54 Parkside, London SW19 5NF
020 8946 1410/7971 Fax 020 8947 2494
Apostolic Nuncio:
HE Archbishop Pablo Puente

HONDURAS
Embassy of Honduras
115 Gloucester Place, London W1H 3PJ
020 7486 4880 Fax 020 7486 4550
Telex: 296368
Ambassador:
HE Senor Hernan Antonio Bermudez

HUNGARY
Embassy of the Republic of Hungary
35 Eaton Place, London SW1X 8BY
020 7235 5218 Fax 020 7823 1348
Ambassador: HE Mr Gabor Szentivanyi
Commercial: 46 Eaton Place, London SW1
020 7235 8767
Dr Jenö Hámori – Counsellor (Commercial)

ICELAND
Embassy of Iceland
1 Eaton Terrace, London SW1W 8EY
020 7590 1100 Fax 020 7730 1683
Telex: 918226 ICEMBY G
Ambassador: HE Mr Thorsteinn Pálsson

INDIA
Office of the High Commissioner for India
India House, Aldwych, London WC2B 4NA
020 7836 8484 Fax 020 7836 4331
Telex: 267166 HCILDNG 263581 INDSUPG
24104 INDSUPG
High Commissioner: (Vacant)
Mr H S Puri *(Acting High Commissioner)*

INDONESIA
Embassy of the Republic of Indonesia
38 Grosvenor Square, London W1X 9AD
020 7499 7661 Fax 020 7491 4993
Ambassador:
HE Mr Nana Sutresna Sastradidjaja
Commercial: 61 Welbeck Street,
London W1M 7HB
020 7935 1616 Fax 020 7935 0034
Mr Andreas Anugerah – Attaché

IRAN
Embassy of the Islamic Republic of Iran
16 Prince's Gate, London SW7 1PT
020 7225 3000 Fax 020 7589 4440
Ambassador: HE Mr Gholamreza Ansari

IRAQ
Diplomatic Relations broken
February 1991
Iraqi Interests Section: Embassy of the
Hashemite Kingdom of Jordan,
21 Queen's Gate, London SW7 5JG
020 7584 7141 Fax 020 7584 7716
Minister/Head: (Vacant)

IRELAND
Irish Embassy
17 Grosvenor Place, London SW1X 7HR
020 7235 2171 Fax 020 7245 6961
Telex: 916104
Ambassador: HE Mr Edward Barrington
Commercial: Ms Orla Maher
(Commercial Attaché)

ISRAEL
Embassy of Israel
2 Palace Green, Kensington, London W8 4QB
020 7957 9500 Fax 020 7957 9555
Ambassador: HE Mr Dror Zeigerman
Commercial: Mrs Ronit Kan – Counsellor

ITALY
Italian Embassy
14 Three Kings Yard, Davies Street,
London W1Y 2EH
020 7312 2200 Fax 020 7312 2230
Telex: 05123520 ITADIPG
Ambassador: HE Signor Luigi Amaduzzi

IVORY COAST – see Côte D'Ivoire

JAMAICA
Jamaican High Commission
1–2 Prince Consort Road, London SW7 2BZ
020 7823 9911 Fax 020 7589 5154
Telex: 263304
High Commissioner:
HE Hon David Muirhead, QC

JAPAN
Embassy of Japan
101–104 Piccadilly, London W1V 9FN
020 7465 6500 Fax 020 7491 9348
Ambassador: HE Mr Sadayuki Hayashi
Commercial: Mr Masayoshi Amano – Minister

JORDAN
Embassy of the Hashemite Kingdom of Jordan
6 Upper Phillimore Gardens, Kensington,
London W8 7HB
020 7937 3685 Fax 020 7937 8795
Ambassador: HE Mr Timoor Ghazi Daghistani

KAZAKHSTAN
Embassy of the Republic of Kazakhstan
33 Thurloe Square, London SW7 2DS
020 7581 4646 Fax 020 7584 8481
Ambassador: (Vacant)
Mr Konstantin Zhigalov *(Chargé d'Affaires)*

KENYA
Kenya High Commission
45 Portland Place, London W1N 4AS
020 7636 2371/5 Fax 020 7323 6717
Telex: 262551
High Commissioner: (Vacant)
Mr L N Ngaithe *(Acting High Commissioner)*
Commercial: Mr D Mbugua – Attaché

KIRIBATI
Kiribati High Commission
c/o Office of the President, PO Box 68,
Bairiki, Tarawa, Kiribati
Acting High Commissioner:
Mr Peter T Timeon
(Resident in Tarawa, Kiribati)

KOREA
Embassy of the Republic of Korea
60 Buckingham Gate, London, SW1E 6AJ
020 7227 5500 Fax 020 7227 5503
Ambassador: HE Mr Choi Sung-hong
Commercial: Mr Kim Chil-doo – Counsellor

KUWAIT
Embassy of the State of Kuwait
2 Albert Gate, Knightsbridge,
London SW1X 7JU
020 7590 3400 Fax 020 7823 1712
Ambassador:
HE Mr Khaled A A S Al Duwaisan, GCVO

KYRGYZ REPUBLIC
Embassy of the Kyrgyz Republic
Ascot House, 119 Crawford Street,
London W1H 1AF
020 7935 1462 Fax 020 7935 7449
Ambassador: HE Mrs Roza Otunbayeva

LAOS
No London Embassy
Embassy of the Lao People's
Democratic Republic
74 Avenue Raymond-Poincaré,
75116 Paris, France
+ 45 53 02 98 Telex: 61-07-11
Ambassador: HE Mr Khamphan Simmalavong
(Resident in Paris)

LATVIA
Embassy of the Republic of Latvia
45 Nottingham Place, London W1M 3FE
020 7312 0040 Fax 020 7312 0042
Ambassador: HE Mr Normans Penke

LEBANON
Lebanese Embassy
21 Kensington Palace Gardens,
London W8 4QM
020 7229 7265 Fax 020 7243 1699
Telex: 262048 ALIBAN G
Ambassador: HE Mr Jihad Mortada

LESOTHO
High Commission for the Kingdom of Lesotho
7 Chesham Place, Belgravia,
London SW1 8HN
020 7235 5686 Fax 020 7235 5023
Telex: 262995
High Commissioner: HE Mr Benjamin Masilo

LIBERIA
Embassy of the Republic of Liberia
2 Pembridge Place, London W2 4XB
020 7221 1036
Ambassador: HR Mr William V S Bull

LIBYA
Libyan People's Bureau
119 Harley Street, London W1
020 7486 8387
Mr Isa Baruni Edaeki *(Chargé d'Affaires)*

LITHUANIA
Embassy of the Republic of Lithuania
84 Gloucester Place, London W1H 3HN
020 7486 6401 Fax 020 7486 6403
Ambassador: HE Mr Justas Vincas Paleckis

LUXEMBOURG
Embassy of Luxembourg
27 Wilton Crescent, London SW1X 8SD
020 7235 6961 Fax 020 7235 9734
Ambassador: HE Mons Joseph Weyland

MACEDONIA
Embassy of the Republic of Macedonia
Suite 10, 4th Floor, Harcourt House,
19–19A Cavendish Square, London W1M 9AD
020 7499 5152 Fax 020 7499 2864
Ambassador: HE Mr Stevo Crvenkovski

MADAGASCAR
No London Embassy
Embassy of the Republic of Madagascar
4 Avenue Raphael, 75016 Paris, France
+ 45 04 62 11
Ambassador: HE Mr Malala Zo Raolison
(Resident in Paris)
Honorary Consulate:
16 Lanark Mansions, Pennard Road,
London W12 8DT 020 8746 0133

MALAWI
High Commission for the Republic of Malawi
33 Grosvenor Street, London W1X 0DE
020 7491 4172/7 Fax 020 7491 9916
High Commissioner: HE Mr Bright Mcbin Msaka

MALAYSIA
Malaysian High Commission
45 Belgrave Square, London SW1X 8QT
020 7235 8033 Fax 020 7235 5161
Telex: 262550
High Commissioner:
HE Dato Mohamad Amir bin Jaafar
Commercial Counsellor: Mr Zulkepli Mohd Perai

MALDIVES
High Commission of the Republic of Maldives
22 Nottingham Place, London W1M 3FB
020 7224 2135 Fax 020 7224 2157
Mr Adam Hassan *(Acting High Commissioner)*

MALI
No London Embassy
Embassy of the Republic of Mali
Avenue Moliere 487, 1050 Brussels, Belgium
+ 345 74 32
Ambassador: (Vacant)
Mons Moussa Kouyate *(Chargé d'Affaires)*
(Resident in Brussels)

MALTA
Malta High Commission
Malta House, 36–38 Piccadilly,
London W1P 0PQ
020 7292 4800 Fax 020 7734 1831
Telex: 261102
High Commissioner:
HE Dr George Bonello Dupuis

MAURITANIA
Embassy of the Islamic Republic of
Mauritania
5 Rue de Montevideo, Paris XVIe, France
+ 45 04 88 54
Ambassador: HE Mons Dah Ould Adbi
(Resident in Paris)
Honorary Consulate:
140 Bow Common Lane, London E3 4BH
020 8980 4382

MAURITIUS
Mauritius High Commission
32/33 Elvaston Place, London SW7 5NW
020 7581 0294 Fax 020 7823 8437
High Commissioner:
HE Sir Satcam Boolell, QC
Commercial: Mr Devesh Dukhira –
Second Secretary
020 7225 3331 Fax 020 7225 1580

MEXICO
Embassy of Mexico
42 Hertford Street, Mayfair,
London W1Y 7TF
020 7499 8586 Fax 020 7495 4035
Ambassador: HE Señor Santiago Oñate
Commercial: 5th Floor Rear,
3 St James's Square, London SW1W 4JU
020 7839 6586 Fax 020 7839 4425

MOLDOVA
No London Embassy
Embassy of the Republic of Moldova
Avenue Emile Max 175, 1040 Brussels,
Belgium
+ 732 9659/9300 Fax + 732 9660
Ambassador: HE Mr Ion Capatina
(Resident in Brussels)

MONGOLIA
Embassy of Mongolia
7 Kensington Court, London W8 5DL
020 7937 0150
Ambassador: HE Mr Tsedenjavyn Suhbaatar

MOROCCO
Embassy of the Kingdom of Morocco
49 Queen's Gate Gardens, London SW7 5NE
020 7581 5001/4 Fax 020 7225 3862
Telex: 28389
Ambassador: HE Mr Mohammed Belmahi

MOZAMBIQUE
High Commission of the Republic of
Mozambique
21 Fitzroy Square, London W1P 5HJ
020 7383 3800 Fax 020 7383 3801
High Commissioner: HE Dr Eduardo J B Koloma

MYANMAR – see Burma

NAMIBIA
High Commission of the Republic of Namibia
6 Chandos Street, London W1M 0LQ
020 7636 6244 Fax 020 7637 5694
High Commissioner: HE Mrs Monica Nashandi

NAURU
No London High Commission
Honorary Consulate:
Romshed Courtyard, Under River,
Nr Sevenoaks, Kent TN15 0SD
01732 746016

NEPAL
Royal Nepalese Embassy
12A Kensington Palace Gardens,
London W8 4QU
020 7229 1594 Fax 020 7792 9861
Ambassador: HE Dr Singha B Basnyat

NETHERLANDS
Royal Netherlands Embassy
38 Hyde Park Gate, London SW7 5DP
020 7590 3200 Fax 020 7225 0947
Ambassador:
HE Baron William Bentinck van Schoonheten

NEW ZEALAND
New Zealand High Commission
New Zealand House, Haymarket,
London SW1Y 4TQ
020 7930 8422 Fax 020 7839 4580
High Commissioner:
HE The Rt Hon Paul East, QC
Commercial: Mr J N Waugh – Minister

NICARAGUA
The Embassy of Nicaragua
Suite 12, Vicarage House,
58–60 Kensington Church Street,
London W8 4DP
020 7938 2373 Fax: 020 7937 0952
Ambassador:
HE Senora Nora Campos de Lankes

NIGER
No London Embassy
Embassy of the Republic of Niger
154 Rue de Longchamp, 75116 Paris, France
+ 45 04 80 60
Ambassador: HE Madame Mariama Hima
(Resident in Paris)

NIGERIA
High Commission for the Federal Republic of
Nigeria
Nigeria House, 9 Northumberland Avenue,
London WC2N 5BX
020 7839 1244 Fax 020 7839 8746
Telex: 23665/916814/8952931
High Commissioner: HE Prince Bola A. Ajibola

NORWAY
Royal Norwegian Embassy
25 Belgrave Square, London SW1X 8QD
020 7591 5500 Fax 020 7245 6993
Ambassador: (Vacant)
Mr Rolf Baltzersen *(Chargé d'Affaires)*
Commercial: Charles House, 5th Floor,
5–11 Lower Regent Street, London SW1
020 7973 0188 Fax 020 7973 0189
Mr Sverre Johan Lindtvedt –
Counsellor (Trade)

OMAN
Embassy of the Sultanate of Oman
167 Queen's Gate, London SW7 5HE
020 7225 0001 Fax 020 7589 2505
Ambassador: HE Mr Hussain Ali Abdullatif

PAKISTAN
High Commission for the Islamic Republic of Pakistan
35–36 Lowndes Square, London SW1X 9JN
020 7664 9200 Fax 020 7664 9299
High Commissioner:
HE Mr Akhar S. Ahmad

PANAMA
Embassy of the Republic of Panama
48 Park Street,
London W1Y 3PD
020 7493 4646 Fax 020 7493 4333
Ambassador: (Vacant)
Mr Alberto Watson Fabrega *(Chargé d'Affaires)*
Commercial: Flat 2, 48 Park Street, London W1Y 3PD
Mr Salim Kheireddine – Counsellor

PAPUA NEW GUINEA
Papua New Guinea High Commission
3rd Floor, 14 Waterloo Place,
London SW1R 4AR
020 7930 0922/7 Fax 020 7930 0828
Telex: 25827 Kundu G
High Commissioner: HE Sir Kina Bona, KBE

PARAGUAY
Embassy of Paraguay
Braemar Lodge, Cornwall Gardens,
London SW7 4AQ
020 7937 1253 Fax 020 7937 5687
Ambassador: HE Senor Raul dos Santos

PERU
Embassy of Peru
52 Sloane Street, London SW1X 9SP
020 7235 1917/2545 Fax 020 7235 4463
Ambassador: (Vacant)
Senor Pedro Rey-Daly *(Chargé d'Affaires)*

PHILIPPINES
Embassy of the Philippines
9A Palace Green, London W8 4QE
020 7937 1600 Fax 020 7937 2925
Ambassador: HE Hon. César B Bautista
Commercial: 1a Cumberland House,
Kensington Court Road, London W8
020 7937 1898
Mr Vicente Casim – Commercial Attaché

POLAND
Embassy of the Republic of Poland
47 Portland Place, London W1N 3AG
020 7580 4324/9 Fax 020 7323 4018
Telex: 265691

Ambassador: HE Dr Stanislaw Komorowski
Commercial: 15 Devonshire Street,
London W1N 2AR 020 7580 5481
Mr Piotr Kozerski – Commercial
Counsellor/Minister Plenipotentiary

PORTUGAL
Portuguese Embassy
11 Belgrave Square, London SW1X 8PP
020 7235 5331/4 Fax 020 7245 1287
Telex: 28484
Ambassador: HE Senhor José Gregório Faria
Commercial: Senhor Antonio Silva –
Counsellor

QATAR
Embassy of the State of Qatar
1 South Audley Street, London W1Y 5DQ
020 7493 2200 Fax 020 7493 2661
Telex: 284 69
Ambassador: HE Mr Ali M Jaidah
Commercial: 020 7581 8611

ROMANIA
Embassy of Romania
4 Palace Green, London W8 4QD
020 7937 9666 Fax 020 7937 8069
Telex: 22232
Ambassador: HE Mr Radu Onofrei

RUSSIA
Embassy of the Russian Federation
13 Kensington Palace Gardens,
London W8 4QX
020 7229 3628/2666/6412 Fax 020 7727 8625
Ambassador: HE Mr Yuri Fokine

RWANDA
Embassy of the Republic of Rwanda
Uganda House, 58–59 Trafalgar Square,
London WC2N 5DX
020 7930 2570 Fax 020 7930 2572
Ambassador: HE Dr Zac Nsenga

ST CHRISTOPHER AND NEVIS
High Commission for St Christopher and Nevis
10 Kensington Court, London W8 5DL
020 7937 9522 Fax 020 7937 5514
High Commissioner: HE Mr Aubrey E Hart

ST LUCIA
High Commission for St Lucia
10 Kensington Court, London W8 5DL
020 7937 9522 Fax 020 7937 5514
High Commissioner:
HE Mr Emmanuel Cotter, MBE

ST VINCENT AND THE GRENADINES
High Commission for St Vincent and the
Grenadines
10 Kensington Court, London W8 5DL
020 7565 2874
High Commissioner: HE Mr Carlyle Dougan, QC

SAMOA
No London Embassy
Embassy of the Independent State of Samoa
Avenue Franklin D Roosevelt 123,
1050 Brussels, Belgium
+ 02 660 84 54 Fax + 02 675 03 36
High Commissioner:
HE Mr Tau'ili'ili U'ili Meredith
(Resident in Brussels)

SÃO TOMÉ AND PRINCIPÉ
Embassy of the Democratic Republic of São
Tomé and Principé:
Square Montgomery, 175 Avenue de Tervuren,
1150 Brussels, Belgium
+ 734 89 66 Fax + 734 88 15
Mons Antonio de Lima Viegas
(Chargé d'Affaires) (Resident in Brussels)

SAUDI ARABIA
Royal Embassy of Saudi Arabia
30 Charles Street, Mayfair, London W1X 7PM
020 7917 3000
Ambassador: HE Dr Ghazi A Algosaibi
Commercial: Mr Mohammed Abdullah
Al-Sheddi – Attaché

SENEGAL
Embassy of the Republic of Senegal
39 Marloes Road, London W8 6LA
020 7937 7237 Fax 020 7938 2546
Ambassador: HE Mr Gabriel Alexandre Sar

SEYCHELLES
High Commission for Seychelles
Box 4PE, 2nd Floor, Eros House, 111 Baker
Street, London W1M 1FE
020 7224 1660 Fax 020 7487 5756
High Commissioner: HE Mr Bertrand Rassool

SIERRA LEONE
Sierra Leone High Commission
33 Portland Place, London W1N 3AG
020 7636 6483/6 Fax 020 7927 8130
High Commissioner: HE Professor Cyril Foray

SINGAPORE
High Commission for the Republic of Singapore
9 Wilton Crescent, London SW1X 8RW
020 7235 8315 Fax 020 7245 6583
Telex: 262564

High Commissioner:
HE Professor Pang Eng Fong
Commercial: 5 Chesham Street,
London SW1X 8ND
020 7235 4558 Fax 020 7235 4557
Mr Kheng Hian Philip Ho – First Secretary

SLOVAK REPUBLIC
Embassy of the Slovak Republic
25 Kensington Palace Gardens,
London W8 4QY
020 7243 0803 Fax 020 7727 5824
Ambassador: HE Mr Igor Slobodnik
Commercial: Mr Jozef Chovan – First Secretary

SLOVENIA
Embassy of the Republic of Slovenia
Suite 1, Cavendish Court,
11–15 Wigmore Street, London W1H 9LA
020 7495 7775 Fax 020 7495 7776
Ambassador: HE Mr Marjan Setinc
Commercial: Mr Ciril Košak – Counsellor

SOLOMON ISLANDS
Embassy of the Solomon Islands
Boulevard Saint Michel, (First Floor),
Box 23, 1040 Brussels, Belgium
+ 2732 7085 Fax + 2732 6885
High Commissioner: Mr Robert Sisilo
(Resident in Brussels)

SOMALIA
Embassy closed 2 January 1992

SOUTH AFRICA
High Commission of the Republic of South
Africa
South Africa House, Trafalgar Square,
London WC2N 5DP 020 7451 7299
Fax 020 7451 7284 Telex: 8952626
High Commissioner:
HE Ms Cheryl Ann Carolus

SPAIN
Spanish Embassy
39 Chesham Place, London SW1X 8SB
020 7235 5555/6/7 Fax 020 7235 9905
Telex: 21110/261333
Ambassador:
HE The Marques de Tamarón
Commercial: 66 Chiltern Street,
London W1M 1PR
020 7486 0101 Fax 020 7487 5586
Señor Don Juan Sebastián de Erice, Head of
Commercial Office

SRI LANKA

High Commission for the Democratic Socialist
Republic of Sri Lanka
13 Hyde Park Gardens, London W2 2LU
020 7262 1841/7 Fax 020 7262 7970
High Commissioner: HE Dr Lal Jayawardena
Commercial: Mr T G Ariyaratne – Minister

SUDAN

The Embassy of the Republic of the Sudan
3 Cleveland Row, St James's,
London SW1A 1DD
020 7839 8080 Fax 020 7839 7560
Ambassador: (Vacant)
Mr Abdel Mahmoud Nour El Daiem Al
Koronky *(Chargé d'Affaires)*

SURINAME

No London Embassy
Embassy of the Republic of Suriname
2 Alexander Gogelweg, The Hague 2517JH,
The Netherlands
+ 3 650 844
Ambassador:
HE Mr Evert Guillaume Azimullah
(Resident in The Hague)

SWAZILAND

Kingdom of Swaziland High Commission
20 Buckingham Gate, London SW1E 6LB
020 7630 6611 Fax 020 7630 6564
Telex: 28853
High Commissioner:
HE Rev Percy Sipho Mngomezulu

SWEDEN

Embassy of Sweden
11 Montagu Place, London W1H 2AL
020 7917 6400 Fax 020 7724 4174
Telex: 28249
Ambassador: HE Mr Mats Bergquist, CMG
Commercial/Trade: 73 Welbeck Street, London
W1M 8AN 020 7935 9601
Mr Jonas Brogardh – Commercial Counsellor
and Trade Commissioner

SWITZERLAND

Embassy of Switzerland
16/18 Montagu Place, London W1H 2BQ
020 7616 6000 Fax 020 7724 7001
Telex 28212
Ambassador: (Vacant)
Commercial: Herr Jürg Schneeberger –
Counsellor (Commercial)

SYRIA

Embassy of the Syrian Arab Republic
8 Belgrave Square, London SW1X 8PH
020 7245 9012 Fax 020 7235 4621
Ambassador: (Vacant)
Dr Sami Glaiel *(Chargé d'Affaires)*

TAJIKISTAN

No London Embassy
Honorary Consulate:
33 Ovington Square, London SW3 1LJ
020 7584 5111

TANZANIA

High Commission for the United Republic of
Tanzania
43 Hertford Street, London W1Y 8DB
020 7499 8951/4 Fax 020 7491 9321
Telex: 262504 TANLDN G
High Commissioner:
HE Dr Abdul-Kader A Shareef
Commercial: Mr Simon U R Mlay –
Minister-Counsellor

THAILAND

Royal Thai Embassy
29–30 Queen's Gate, London SW7 5JP
020 7589 2944 Fax 020 7823 9695
Telex: 27661
Ambassador:
HE Mr Vidhya Rayananonda, KCVO
Commercial: 11 Hertford Street,
London W1Y 7DX
020 7493 5749 Fax 020 7493 7416
Mr Suraphol Jaovisidha – Minister/Counsellor

TOGO

No London Embassy
Embassy of the Republic of Togo
8 rue Alfred-Roll, 75017 Paris, France
+ 42 80 12 13

TONGA

Tonga High Commission
36 Molyneux Street, London W1H 6AB
020 7724 5828
High Commissioner:
HE Mrs Akosita Fineanganofo

TRINIDAD AND TOBAGO
Office of the High Commissioner for the
Republic of Trinidad and Tobago:
42 Belgrave Square, London SW1X 8NT
020 7245 9351 Fax 020 7823 1065
High Commissioner:
HE Mrs Sheelagh de Osuna
Commercial: Miss Candyce Kelshall –
Commercial Attaché

TUNISIA
Tunisian Embassy
29 Prince's Gate, London SW7 1QG
020 7584 8117 Fax 020 7225 2884
Telex: 23736
Ambassador: HE Mr Khemaies Jhinaoui

TURKEY
Turkish Embassy
43 Belgrave Square, London SW1X 8PA
020 7393 0202
Ambassador: HE Mr Ozdem Sanberk
Commercial: Mr Münir Aksoy –
Counsellor 020 7235 4233/4991

TURKMENISTAN
Embassy of Turkmenistan, 2nd Floor South,
St George's House, 14-17 Wells Street,
London W1P 3FP
020 7255 1071 Fax 020 7323 9184
Ambassador: HE Mr Chary Babaev

TUVALU
No London High Commission
Honorary Consulate:
Tuvalu House, 230 Worple Road,
London SW20 8RH 020 8879 0985

UGANDA
Uganda High Commission
Uganda House, 58/59 Trafalgar Square,
London WC2N 5DX
020 7839 5783 Fax 020 7839 8925
Telex: 915141
High Commissioner:
HE Prof George Kirya
(Doyen of the Diplomatic Corps)

UKRAINE
Embassy of Ukraine
60 Holland Park, London W11 3SJ
020 7727 6312 Fax 020 7792 1708
Ambassador:
HE Mr Volodimir Vassylenko

UNITED ARAB EMIRATES
Embassy of the United Arab Emirates
30 Princes Gate, London SW7 1PT
020 7581 1281 Fax 020 7581 9616
Telex: 918459
Ambassador: HE Mr Easa Sakh Al Gurg, CBE
Commercial: 48 Princes Gate, London SW7
020 7589 3434

UNITED STATES OF AMERICA
American Embassy
24 Grosvenor Square, London W1A 1AE
020 7499 9000
Ambassador: HE Mr Philip Lader
Commercial: Mr Charles A Ford –
Minister-Counsellor

URUGUAY
Embassy of the Oriental Republic of Uruguay
2nd Floor, 140 Brompton Road,
London SW3 1HY
020 7584 8192 Fax 020 7581 9585
Telex: 264180 URUBRI G
Ambassador:
HE Dr Agustin Espinosa-Lloveras

UZBEKISTAN
Embassy of the Republic of Uzbekistan
41 Holland Park, London W11 2RP
020 7221 7679 Fax 020 7229 7029
Ambassador: (Vacant)

VANUATU
No London High Commission
c/o Department for Foreign Affairs,
Port Vila, Vanuatu
High Commissioner: (Vacant)
(Residence in Vanuatu)

VENEZUELA
Venezuelan Embassy
1 Cromwell Road, London SW7
020 7584 4206/7 Fax 020 7589 8887
Ambassador: Señor Roy Chaderton-Matos
Commercial: Senorita Elba Rodriguez-Pulgar –
Counsellor (Economic and Commercial)

VIETNAM
Embassy of the Socialist Republic of Vietnam
12–14 Victoria Road, London W8 5RD
020 7937 1912 Fax 020 7937 6108
Telex: 887361
Ambassador: HE Mr Vuong Thua Phong
Commercial: Mr Dinh Van Hoi – Counsellor

WESTERN SAMOA – see Samoa

YEMEN
Embassy of the Republic of Yemen
57 Cromwell Road, London SW7 2ED
020 7584 6607 Fax 020 7589 3350
Ambassador:
HE Dr Hussain Abdullah Al-Amri
Commercial: Mr Othman Salem Obeid –
Assistant Attaché

YUGOSLAVIA
Diplomatic relations broken March 25, 1999. A
Yugoslav Interests Section has been established
in the Cyprus High Commission

ZAÏRE – See Democratic Republic of Congo

ZAMBIA
High Commission for the Republic of Zambia
2 Palace Gate, Kensington, London W8 5NG
020 7589 6655 Fax 020 7581 1353
Telex: 263544
High Commissioner:
HE Professor Moses Musonda

ZIMBABWE
High Commission for the Republic of
Zimbabwe
Zimbabwe House, 429 Strand,
London WC2R 0SA 020 7836 7755
High Commissioner:
HE Mr Simbarashe S Mumbengegwi

EUROPE

EUROPEAN UNION

In 1957 France, Germany and Italy joined Belgium, the Netherlands and Luxembourg in setting up the European Economic Community (EEC) and the European Atomic Energy Agency (EAEC) through the Treaties of Rome. The United Kingdom joined, together with Ireland and Denmark in 1973. The Community continued to expand in membership and the policy areas within its competence. In 1981 Greece became the tenth member state followed by Spain and Portugal in 1986. In 1990 the unification of Germany automatically brought the former East German territory within the Community. In 1995 the European Community became the European Union, and was further enlarged with the accession of Austria, Finland and Sweden. In March 1998, accession discussions were launched with Cyprus, Poland, Hungary, the Czech Republic, Slovenia and Estonia. In October 1999 the European Commission proposed that accession talks should be opened in 2000 with Bulgaria, Latvia, Lithuania, Malta, Romania and the Slovak Republic. At the same time the Commission proposed that Turkey should now be regarded as a candidate country. These proposals were to be discussed at the European Council meeting in Helsinki in December 1999.

The European Union is managed by five institutions:

Council of the European Union

rue de la Loi, 170, 1048 Brussels, Belgium
Tel: 00 322 285 6511 *Fax:* 00 322 285 7397/7381 *Website:* http://www.ue.eu.int

The 15-member Council of the European Union is the only institution which directly represents the member governments. For major decisions the Foreign Ministers are usually present – at other times the appropriate Ministers according to the subject before the Council. The Presidency rotates every six months. From 1 January 2000 the Presidency will succeed, in the following order: Portugal, France, Sweden, Belgium.

European Commission

rue de la Loi, 200, 1049 Brussels, Belgium
Tel: 00 322 299 1111
E-mail: [forename.surname]@cec.eu.int *Website:* http://www.europa.eu.int/comm/index—en.htm

The Commission's principal functions are to propose legislation, to manage established Community policies, and to be the guardian of the Treaties setting up the Union.

REPRESENTATION IN THE UNITED KINGDOM

The Representation in the United Kingdom, through its four offices, reports directly to the Commission on political, economic and social developments throughout the UK; in partnership with others, it explains the likely impact of policies programmes, and proposals for future action, and stimulates debate on the future of the EU.

The European Commission's Representation is directly responsible to the Commission's headquarters in Brussels. Its Representation offices are independent of the governments of the countries in which they are based.

LONDON OFFICE
8 Storey's Gate, London SW1P 3AT
Tel: 020 7973 1992 *Fax:* 020 7973 1900 *Website:* http://www.cec.org.uk
Head of the Representation: Geoffrey Martin

REGIONAL OFFICES
Windsor House, 9/15 Bedford Street, Belfast BT2 7EG
Tel: 028 9024 0708 *Fax:* 028 9024 8241
Head of the Representation: Jim Dougal
4 Cathedral Road, Cardiff CF1 9SG
Tel: 029 2037 1631 *Fax:* 029 2039 5489
Head of the Representation: Catherine Eva
9 Alva Street, Edinburgh, EH2 4PH
Tel: 0131-225 2508 *Fax:* 0131-226 4105
Head of the Representation: Elizabeth Holt

European Parliament

The European Parliament exercises democratic control over the running of the European Union. Its 626 members (MEPs) are elected every five years. The most recent elections took place in June 1999. Each member state returns a specific number of MEPs, elected by its national electorate. Most of the members sit in one of seven transnational party groups. The Parliament meets and debates in public, with plenary sessions taking place in Strasbourg for on average one week in each month except for August. In addition there are mini sessions in Brussels to facilitate contacts with the Commission and the Council. The major working unit of the European Parliament is the specialised committee where much of the legislative scrutiny takes place. The current Parliament has 17 permanent committees. As well as legislative powers, the Parliament also has powers relating to the Budget, to the conclusion of international agreements and general supervisory powers.

UK INFORMATION OFFICE
2 Queen Anne's Gate, London SW1H 9AA
Tel: 020 7227 4300 *Fax:* 020 7227 4302 *Library Fax:* 020 7227 4301
Website: http://www.europarl.eu.int/uk
Head of Office: Chris Piening
Press Officer: Edward McVeigh
Librarian: Avis Furness

REGIONAL OFFICE IN SCOTLAND
9 Alva Street, Edinburgh EH2 4PH
Tel: 0131-225 2058 *Fax:* 0131-226 4105
Head: Dermot Scott

UK MEMBERS

Conservative	36
Labour	29
Liberal Democrat	10
UK Independence Party	3
Green Party	2
Scottish National Party	2
Plaid Cymru	2
Democratic Unionist Party (DUP)	1
Social Democratic & Labour (SDLP)	1
Ulster Unionist Party (UUP)	1
Total	**87**

England	71
Scotland	8
Wales	5
Northern Ireland	3
Total	**87**

Con **ATKINS, Rt Hon Sir Robert** – *North West*
Lib Dem **ATTWOOLL, Elspeth** – *Scotland*
Lab **BALFE, Richard** – *London*
Con **BEAZLEY, Christopher** – *Eastern*
Con **BETHELL, The Lord**† – *London*
Lab **BOWE, David** – *Yorkshire & Humber*
Con **BOWIS, John** – *London*
Con **BRADBOURN, Philip** – *West Midlands*
Con **BUSHILL-MATTHEWS, Philip** – *West Midlands*
Con **CALLANAN, Martin** – *North East*
Lab **CASHMAN, Michael** – *West Midlands*
Con **CHICHESTER, Giles** – *South West*
Lib Dem **CLEGG, Nick** – *East Midlands*

Lab **CORBETT, Richard** – *Yorkshire & Humber*
Con **CORRIE, John** – *West Midlands*
Lib Dem **DAVIES, Chris** – *North West*
Con **DEVA, Nirj** – *South East*
Con **DOVER, Den** – *North West*
Lib Dem **DUFF, Andrew** – *Eastern*
Con **ELLES, James** – *South East*
Pl C **EVANS, Jill** – *Wales*
Con **EVANS, Jonathan** – *Wales*
Lab **EVANS, Robert** – *London*
UKIP **FARAGE, Nigel** – *South East*
Lab **FORD, Glyn** – *South West*
Con **FOSTER, Jacqueline** – *North West*
Lab **GILL, Neena** – *West Midlands*
Con **GOODWILL, Robert** – *Yorkshire & Humber*

Con **HANNAN, Daniel** – *South East*
Con **HARBOUR, Malcolm** – *West Midlands*
Con **HEATON-HARRIS, Chris** – *East Midlands*
Con **HELMER, Roger** – *East Midlands*
UKIP **HOLMES, Michael** – *South West*
Lab **HOWITT, Richard** – *Eastern*
SNP **HUDGHTON, Ian** – *Scotland*
Lab **HUGHES, Stephen** – *North East*
Lib Dem **HUHNE, Chris** – *South East*
SDLP **HUME, John*** – *Northern Ireland*
Con **INGLEWOOD, The Lord†** – *North West*
Con **JACKSON, Dr Caroline** – *South West*
Con **KHANBHAI, Bashir** – *Eastern*
Lab **KINNOCK, Glenys** – *Wales*
Con **KIRKHOPE, Timothy** – *Yorkshire & Humber*
Green **LAMBERT, Jean** – *London*
Green **LUCAS, Dr Caroline** – *South East*
Lib Dem **LUDFORD, The Baroness†** – *London*
Lib Dem **LYNNE, Liz** – *West Midlands*
Lab **McAVAN, Linda** – *Yorkshire & Humber*
Lab **McCARTHY, Arlene** – *North West*
SNP **MacCORMICK, Neil** – *Scotland*
Con **McMILLAN-SCOTT, Edward** – *Yorkshire & Humber*
Lab **McNALLY, Eryl** – *Eastern*
Lab **MARTIN, David** – *Scotland*
Lab **MILLER, Bill** – *Scotland*
Lab **MORAES, Claude** – *London*
Lab **MORGAN, Eluned** – *Wales*

Lab **MURPHY, Simon** – *West Midlands*
Con **NEWTON DUNN, Bill** – *East Midlands*
UUP **NICHOLSON, James** – *Northern Ireland*
Lib Dem **NICHOLSON OF WINTER-BOURNE, The Baroness†** – *South East*
Lab **O'TOOLE, Mo** – *North East*
DUP **PAISLEY, The Rev Ian*** – *Northern Ireland*
Con **PARISH, Neil** – *South West*
Con **PERRY, Roy** – *South East*
Con **PROVAN, James** – *South East*
Con **PURVIS, John** – *Scotland*
Lab **READ, Mel** – *East Midlands*
Lab **SIMPSON, Brian** – *North West*
Lab **SKINNER, Peter** – *South East*
Con **STEVENSON, Struan** – *Scotland*
Con **STOCKTON, Earl of†** – *South West*
Con **STURDY, Robert** – *Eastern*
Con **SUMBERG, David** – *North West*
Con **TANNOCK, Dr Charles** – *London*
Lab **TAYLOR, Catherine** – *Scotland*
UKIP **TITFORD, Jeffrey** – *Eastern*
Lab **TITLEY, Gary** – *North West*
Con **VAN ORDEN, Geoffrey** – *Eastern*
Con **VILLIERS, Theresa** – *London*
Lib Dem **WALLIS, Diana** – *Yorkshire & Humber*
Lib Dem **WATSON, Graham** – *South West*
Lab **WATTS, Mark** – *South East*
Lab **WHITEHEAD, Phillip** – *East Midlands*
Pl C **WYN, Eurig** – *Wales*
Lab **WYNN, Terry** – *North West*

* MP
† Also a Member of the House of Lords

At the time of going to press there are two Labour Party vacancies following the resignations of Pauline Green (London) in December 1999 and Alan Donnelly (North East) in January 2000.

Court of Justice of the European Communities

2025 Luxembourg
Tel: 00 352 43031 *Fax:* 00 352 4303 2500 (Press and Information)
Fax: 00 352 4303 2600 (Registry) *Website:* http://www.curia.eu.int

The Court of Justice of the European Communities and the Court of First Instance rule on questions of Union law, and whether actions by the Commission, the Council of Ministers, member governments and other bodies are compatible with the Treaties.

European Court of Auditors

12 rue Alcide de Gasperi, 1615 Luxembourg
Tel: 00 352 43981 *Fax:* 00352 439342 *E-mail:* euraud@eca.eu.int *Website:* http://www.eca.eu.int

The European Court of Auditors examines all revenue and expenditure accounts of the Union. There are 15 members, one per member state.

Committee of the Regions

rue Belliard, 79, 1040 Brussels, Belgium
Tel: 00 322 282 2211 *Fax:* 00 322 282 2085
E-mail: [forename.surname]@cdr.be *Website:*http://www.cor.eu.int

A consultative assembly of representatives of regional and local authorities such as mayors, county councillors and regional presidents. It began working in 1994. There are 24 members and 24 alternate members from the UK.

Economic and Social Committee

2 rue Ravenstein, 1000 Brussels, Belgium
Tel: 00 322 546 9011 *Fax:* 00 322 513 4893
E-mail: info@ces.be *Website:* http://www.esc.eu.int

An advisory body of the EU established by the Rome Treaties. It is consulted by the Commission and the Council and may deliver opinions on its own initiative. It has 222 members from the 15 member states, including 24 from the UK.

European Central Bank

Postfach 160319, 60066 Frankfurt-am-Main, Germany
Tel: 00 49 69 13 440 *Fax:* 00 49 69 13 44 6000 *Website:* http://www.ecb.int

European Investment Bank

100 Boulevard Konrad Adenauer, 2950 Luxembourg
Tel: 00352 43791 *Fax:* 00 352 437704 *Videoconferencing:* 00 352 439367
E-mail: info@eib.bei.org *Website: http://www.eib.org*

LONDON OFFICE
68 Pall Mall, London SW1Y 5ES *Tel:* 020 7343 1200

The EU's financing institution, providing long-term loans for capital investment.

OTHER EUROPEAN ORGANISATIONS

Council of Europe

Palais de l'Europe, 67075 Strasbourg Cedex, France
Tel: 00 33 3 88 41 20 00 *Fax:* 00 33 3 88 41 27 81/82/83 *Website:* http://www.coe.fr

Member Countries
Albania, Andorra, Austria, Belgium, Bulgaria, Croatia, Cyprus, Czech Republic, Denmark, Estonia, Finland, France, Germany, Georgia, Greece, Hungary, Iceland, Ireland, Italy, Latvia, Liechtenstein, Lithuania, Luxembourg, Malta, Moldova, Netherlands, Norway, Poland, Portugal, Romania, Russia, San Marino, Slovakia, Slovenia, Spain, Sweden, Switzerland, the former Yugoslav Republic of Macedonia, Turkey, Ukraine, United Kingdom
Special guest status in the Parliamentary Assembly:
Bosnia-Herzegovina, Armenia, Azerbaijan

The Council of Europe was founded by ten nations on 5 May 1949, as the first European political institution with the first international parliament. Today, with 41 member states, it is the European organisation with the widest representation and is currently providing a framework for welcoming the new democracies of Central and Eastern Europe. The Council was set up 'to achieve a greater unity between its members for the purpose of safeguarding and realising the ideals and principles which are their common heritage and facilitating their economic and social progress'. It is to achieve this aim 'by discussion of questions of common concern and by agreements and common action in economic, social, cultural, scientific, legal and administrative matters and in the maintenance and further realisation of human rights and fundamental freedoms' (Article 1 of the Statute). Only the military aspects of defence are outside its competence.

The two organs of the Council of Europe are the Committee of Ministers, comprising the Foreign Ministers of the 41 member states, and the Parliamentary Assembly, consisting of 291 representatives appointed by the national parliaments as well as delegations 'with special guest status' from Central and Eastern Europe. Both organs are served by the Secretariat. The headquarters of the Council are at the Palais de l'Europe, Strasbourg.

United Kingdom Delegation of the Parliamentary Assembly

Full members: Terry Davis MP *(Leader of the Delegation)*, David Atkinson MP, Sir Sydney Chapman MP, Tom Cox MP *(Labour Whip)*, Lawrence Cunliffe MP *(Labour Deputy Leader)*, Bill Etherington MP, Paul Flynn MP, Maria Fyfe MP *(Labour Chairwoman)*, Lord Kirkhill, Baroness Knight of Colingtree DBE, Kevin McNamara MP, Jim Marshall MP, Edward O'Hara MP, Lord Ponsonby of Shulbrede, Lord Russell-Johnston *(President of the Assembly)*, Rt Hon John D Taylor MP, John Townend MP, Jimmy Wray MP
Substitute Members: Dr Peter Brand MP, Lord Clinton-Davis, Michael Colvin MP, Ann Cryer MP, Christopher Gill MP, Michael Hancock CBE MP, Jenny Jones MP, Lord Judd, Lord Lucas of Crudwell, Christine McCafferty MP, Lord Northesk, Gwynfor Prosser MP, Sir Sydney Rapson MP, Geraldine Smith MP, David Taylor MP, Dr Rudi Vis MP, David Wilshire MP, Dr Anthony Wright MP
Secretary to the Delegation: Chris Shaw
Overseas Office, European Section, House of Commons, London SW1A 0AA
Tel: 020 7219 3293 *Fax:* 020 7219 6832

European Bank for Reconstruction and Development

One Exchange Square, London EC2A 2JN
Tel: 020 7338 6000 *Fax:* 020 7338 6100 *Website:* http://www.ebrd.com
Project enquiries: *Tel:* 020 7338 6282 Fax: 020 7338 6102
EBRD publications: *Tel:* 020 7338 7533 *Fax:* 020 7338 6102
General enquiries: Tel: 020 7338 7931/7236

The EBRD was established in 1991 to foster the transition towards open market-orientated economies and to promote private and entrepreneurial initiative in Central and Eastern European countries. It has 60 members (58 countries and two institutions, the European Community and the European Investment Bank).

European Free Trade Association

Secretariat Headquarters: 9-11 rue de Varembé, 1211 Geneva 20, Switzerland
Tel: 00 41 22 74 91 111 *Fax:* 00 41 22 733 92 91 *Website: http://www.efta.int*

Secretariat in Brussels: 74 rue de Trèves, 1040 Brussels, Belgium
Tel: 00 32 2 286 1711 *Fax:* 00 32 2 286 1750 *E-mail:* efta-mailbox@secrbru.efta.be

EFTA Court: 1 rue du Fort Thüngen, 1499 Luxembourg
Tel: 00 352 42 108-1 *Fax:* 00 352 43 43 89

Member countries: Iceland, Liechtenstein, Norway, Switzerland

EFTA was established in 1960 by the Stockholm Convention with the goal of removing import duties, quotas and other obstacles to trade in Western Europe and of upholding liberal, non-discriminatory practices in world trade. Its founder members were Austria, Denmark, Norway, Portugal, Sweden, Switzerland and the United Kingdom. Iceland joined EFTA in 1970, Finland became an associate member in 1961 and a full member in 1986. Liechtenstein became a member in 1991.

Of the original members, six have left to join the EU: the United Kingdom and Denmark in 1972, Portugal in 1986, and on 1 January 1995 Austria, Finland and Sweden joined the EU.

Western European Union

Member countries: Belgium, France, Germany, Greece, Italy, Luxembourg, Netherlands, Portugal, Spain, United Kingdom
Observers: Austria, Denmark, Finland, Ireland, Sweden
Associate members: Czech Republic, Hungary, Iceland, Norway, Poland, Turkey
Associate partners: Bulgaria, Estonia, Latvia, Lithuania, Romania, Slovak Republic, Slovenia
Presidency: Portugal 1 January–30 June 2000 France 1 July–31 December 2000
4 rue de la Régence, 1000 Brussels, Belgium
Tel: 00 32 2 500 44 11 *Fax:* 00 32 2 511 32 70
Press and Information *Tel:* 00 32 2 500 44 55 *Fax:* 00 32 2 511 35 19 *Website:* http://www.weu.int

Western European Union originated as the Brussels Treaty Organisation. This was established under the Treaty of Brussels, signed in 1948 by Belgium, France, Luxembourg, the Netherlands and UK, to provide collective self-defence and economic, cultural and social collaboration amongst its signatories. With the collapse of the European Defence Community and the decision of NATO to incorporate the Federal Republic of Germany into the Western security system, the Organisation was modified to become WEU in 1954 with the admission of West Germany and Italy.

Owing to the overlap with NATO and the Council of Europe, the Union became largely defunct. From the late 1970s onwards efforts were made to add a security dimension to the EC's European Political Co-operation. Opposition to these efforts from Denmark, Greece and Ireland led the remaining EC countries, all WEU members, to decide to reactivate the Union in 1984. Members committed themselves to harmonizing their views on defence and security and developing a European security identity, while bearing in mind the importance of transatlantic relations. Portugal and Spain joined WEU in 1990, and Greece became a full member in 1995.

After much debate about the future of WEU, the EC Maastricht Treaty designated WEU as the future defence component of the EU and is the beginning of a process of strengthening the European pillar in NATO. WEU foreign ministers agreed in the Petersberg Declaration 1992 to assign forces to WEU. On 20 November 1992 WEU's role was enhanced when WEU ministers signed a declaration with remaining European NATO members to give them associate membership. Ireland and Denmark, Austria, Finland and Sweden are observer members. In May 1994 WEU reached agreements with nine eastern European states, Estonia, Latvia, Lithuania, Poland, Czech Republic, Slovak Republic, Hungary, Romania and Bulgaria, under which they all became associate partners. In June 1996 Slovenia became the tenth Associate Partner of WEU. In March 1999, following their accession to membership of NATO, the Czech Republic, Hungary and Poland became associate members of WEU.

Principal Clubs

All England Lawn Tennis and Croquet, *Church Road, Wimbledon, SW19 5AE* 020 8944 1066.

Alpine, *55 Charlotte Road, EC2A 3QF* 020 7613 0755.

Anglo-Belgian, *60 Knightsbridge, SW1X 7LF* 020 7235 2121.

Army and Navy, *36/39 Pall Mall, SW1Y 5JN* 020 7930 9721.

Arts, *40 Dover Street, W1X 3RB* 020 7499 4204.

Athenaeum, *107 Pall Mall, SW1Y 5ER* 020 7930 4843.

Authors, *40 Dover Street, W1X 3RB* 020 7499 4204.

Beefsteak, *9 Irving Street, WC2H 7AT* 020 7930 5722.

Boodle's, *28 St. James's Street, SW1A 1HJ* 020 7930 7166.

Brooks's, *St. James's Street, SW1A 1LN* 020 7493 4411.

Buck's, *18 Clifford Street, W1X 1RG* 020 7734 6896.

Caledonian, *9 Halkin Street, SW1X 7DR* 020 7235 5162.

Canning, *4 St. James's Square, SW1Y 4JU* 020 7499 5163.

Cardiff and County, *Westgate Street, Cardiff, CF1 1DA* 029 2022 0846

Carlton, *69 St. James's Street, SW1A 1PJ* 020 7493 1164.

Cavalry and Guards, *127 Piccadilly, W1V 0PX* 020 7499 1261.

City Livery, *20 Aldermanbury, EC2V 7HP* 020 7814 0200.

City of London, *19 Old Broad Street, EC2N 1DS* 020 7588 7991/4.

Civil Service, *13/15 Great Scotland Yard, SW1A 2HJ* 020 7930 4881.

East India, Devonshire, Sports and Public Schools, *16 St. James's Square, SW1Y 4LH* 020 7930 1000.

English Speaking Union, *Dartmouth House, 37 Charles Street, W1X 8AB* 020 7493 3328.

Farmers', *3 Whitehall Court, SW1A 2EL* 020 7930 3557.

Flyfishers', *69 Brook Street, London, W1Y 2ER* 020 7629 5958.

Garrick, *15 Garrick Street, WC2E 9AY* 020 7379 6478.

Hawks', *18 Portugal Place, Cambridge, CB5 8AF* 01223 314666.

Hurlingham, *Ranelagh Gardens, Fulham, SW6 3PR* 020 7736 8411.

Institute of Directors, *116 Pall Mall, SW1Y 5ED* 020 7839 1233.

Kildare Street and University, *17 St Stephen's Green, Dublin 2* +353 1 676 2975

Lansdowne, *9 Fitzmaurice Place, Berkeley Square, W1X 6JD* 020 7629 7200.

Leander, *Henley-on-Thames, Oxon, RG9 2LP* 01491-575782

MCC, *Lord's Cricket Ground, NW8 8QN* 020 7289 1611.

National Liberal, *Whitehall Place, SW1A 2HE* 020 7930 9871.

Naval, *38 Hill Street, W1X 8DP* 020 7493 7672.

Naval and Military, *4 St. James's Square, SW1Y 4JU* 020 7499 5163.

New, *86 Princes Street, Edinburgh, EH2 2BB* 0131-226 4881.

New Cavendish, *44 Great Cumberland Place, W1H 8BS* 020 7723 0391.

Norfolk, *17 Upper King Street, Norwich, NR3 1RB* 01603-660478.

Northern Counties, *Hood Street, Newcastle-upon-Tyne, NE1 6LH* 0191-232 2744

Oriental, *Stratford House, 11 Stratford Place, W1N 0ES* 020 7629 5126.

Portland, *69 Brook Street, W1Y 2ER* 020 7499 1523.

Pratt's, *14 Park Place, St James's Street, SW1A 1LP* 020 7493 0397.

Puffin's, *c/o Woodbury Hall, Everton, Sandy, Bedfordshire, SG19 2HR* 01767-650251

Queen's, *Palliser Road, W. Kensington, W14 9EQ* 020 7385 3421.

Reform, *104 Pall Mall, SW1Y 5EW* 020 7930 9374.

Roehampton, *Roehampton Lane, SW15 5LR* 020 8480 4200.

Royal Air Force, *128 Piccadilly, W1V 0PY* 020 7499 3456.

Royal Automobile, *89 Pall Mall, SW1Y 5HS* 020 7930 2345.

Royal Commonwealth Society, *18 Northumberland Avenue, WC2N 5BJ* 020 7930 6733

Royal Ocean Racing, *20 St James's Place, SW1A 1NN* 020 7493 2248

Royal Over-Seas League, *Over-Seas House, Park Place, St. James's Street SW1A 1LR* 020 7408 0214

Royal Scottish Automobile, *11 Blythswood Square, Glasgow, G2 4AG* 0141-221 3850

Royal Thames Yacht, *60 Knightsbridge,*
SW1X 7LF　020 7235 2121.

Royal Yacht Squadron, *The Castle, Cowes, Isle*
of Wight, PO31 7QT　01983-292743.

St. James's, *6th Floor, Peter House, St. Peter's*
Square, Manchester, M1 5AN
0161-236 2235.

St. Stephen's Constitutional, *34 Queen Anne's*
Gate, London, SW1H 9AB　020 7222 1382.

Savage, *1 Whitehall Place, SW1A 2HD*
020 7930 8118.

Savile, *69 Brook Street, W1Y 2ER*
020 7629 5462

Ski Club of Great Britain, *The White House,*
57-63 Church Road, Wimbledon SW19 5SB
020 8410 2000

Thames Rowing, *Putney Embankment,*
SW15 1LB　020 8788 0676

Travellers', *106 Pall Mall, SW1Y 5EP*
020 7930 8688.

Turf, *5 Carlton House Terrace, SW1Y 5AQ*
020 7930 8555.

United Oxford and Cambridge University,
71 Pall Mall, SW1Y 5HD
020 7930 5151.

University Women's, *2 Audley Square, South*
Audley Street, W1Y 6DB
020 7499 6478.

Victoria, *1 North Court, Great Peter Street,*
SW1P 3LL　020 7222 7070.

Vincent's, *1A King Edward Street, Oxford,*
OX1 4HS　01865-722984.

Western, *32 Royal Exchange Square, Glasgow,*
G1 3AB　0141-221 2016.

White's, *37 St. James's Street, SW1A 1JG*
020 7493 6671/5.

Wig and Pen, *229–230 Strand, WC2R 1BA*
020 7583 7255

Glossary of Parliamentary Terms and Proceedings

ACT OF PARLIAMENT—When a Bill (*qv*) has completed its parliamentary progress, it is submitted for Royal Assent (*qv*). Once this is given, the Bill becomes an Act of Parliament and is part of the statute law. Acts of Parliament are known as "primary legislation" in contrast to secondary or delegated legislation (*qv*).

ADJOURNMENT—When a sitting ends, the House is adjourned. Debate on an individual piece of business may also be adjourned, and the parliamentary recesses are properly called "periodic adjournments". The motion to adjourn can be divided upon, and in most circumstances is debatable. However, adjournment debates are not normally concerned with the mechanics or timing of adjournment. There are four main types of adjournment debate. The daily adjournment debate normally lasts 30 minutes and allows a backbencher chosen by ballot to raise a subject of his or her choice and to receive a reply from a Minister. A second type of adjournment debate are the backbencher-initiated debates at a Tuesday or Wednesday morning sitting in Westminster Hall (*qv*). Normally there are one 1½-hour and three ½-hour debates on Tuesday mornings and two 1½-hour debates and three ½-hour debates on Wednesday mornings. Subjects are chosen in a similar way to those of the daily adjournment debate. On three Wednesdays each session, the Liaison Committee chooses select committee reports to be debated in the two longer slots. A third type of adjournment motion is government-initiated: frequently a full day or half day of debate takes place "on the adjournment" in order to discuss a matter without there being a substantive Motion for Resolution before the House. Finally, under Standing Order No. 24, Members may apply in speeches lasting no more than three minutes for an emergency adjournment debate on "a specific and important matter that should have urgent consideration". The Speaker has discretion whether to grant these applications. If granted, the debate either takes place at 7 pm on the same day or at the beginning of business on the following day, and lasts three hours. Very few, if any such emergency debates are granted in the average Session.

In the House of Lords, at the end of Business a member of the Government Front Bench moves "That the House do now adjourn". The Lord Chancellor or his deputy puts the Question but does not collect the voices, as this Question is not normally debated. In the House of Lords Unstarred Questions, which may give rise to debate, are often taken as last business and perform a similar function to that of the daily adjournment debates in the House of Commons. When the House intends to sit late, it often adjourns "during pleasure" for a short specified interval at dinner time. Again, such a motion is not normally debated. Debate on an individual piece of business may also be adjourned.

AGENDA—*See* ORDER OF BUSINESS PAPER.

ALL-PARTY GROUP—An unofficial group consisting exclusively of MPs and Peers which acts as a focus of cross-party discussion of a particular topic—for example, cycling, penal affairs or science. The term "registered group" is used for groups which admit outsiders as members as well as MPs and Peers.

AMENDMENTS—Amendments may generally be proposed to Bills and Motions being discussed in the Chamber or in Committee. A Question proposed from the Chair may be amended by omitting certain words in order to insert other words, or by leaving out certain words, or by inserting or adding other words. Prior notice of Amendments need not be given, though it is usual to do so. Any Member may move an Amendment, not just the one who tabled it. In the Commons, the Chair normally has the power to select Amendments and to group them so as to encourage rational debate.

APPROPRIATION ACT—The annual Appropriation Act "appropriates" to individual purposes the sums of money voted by Parliament for government expenditure during the year. It does not merely give statutory authority for the total amount of money voted for supply, but sets out in detail the precise wording of each estimate presented with the sum voted by the House to be granted for that specific service. The Appropriation Act completes the regular financial business of the year. (*See also* CONSOLIDATED FUND and SUPPLY.)

BALLOT—A ballot is held to decide the precedence at second reading of the first 20 private Members' Bills to be presented in the session (see PRIVATE MEMBERS' TIME). The ballot is held in a Committee Room.

The Speaker holds ballots to determine the subjects to be raised at backbencher-initiated adjournment debates, including Wednesday morning debates in Westminster Hall.

In the Lords, a ballot is used to select two backbench motions for the short (2½ hour) debates which are held on one Wednesday a month till the Spring Bank Holiday recess and each Wednesday and Thursday for a topical question to be taken at question time on those days.

BILL OF AIDS AND SUPPLIES—By ancient convention, these Bills may not be amended by the House of Lords or initiated in that House. In modern times, two types of Bill of Aids and Supplies can be distinguished: Consolidated Fund and Appropriation Bills (*qv*) and Bills imposing taxation, the principal of which are the annual Finance Bills (*qv*).

BILLS, HYBRID—Hybrid Bills are public bills (*qv*) which contain some clauses of a private bill (*qv*) nature. Select Committees in both Houses are constituted to hear any petitions from those directly affected by the Bill. Otherwise they proceed as public bills.

BILLS, PERSONAL—*see* BILLS, PRIVATE.

BILLS, PRIVATE—Private bills are bills for the particular benefit of any person or body of persons. Most are local in character and allow local authorities or organisations or groups of individuals or others to undertake works of public utility at their own risk and, in a degree, to their own advantage. Private bills may also deal with the affairs of an individual, such as naturalisation, marriage or the settling of estates. These are called personal bills and originate in the House of Lords.

BILLS, PRIVATE MEMBERS'—Private Members' Bills are public bills which are introduced by private members—or backbenchers—of either House. They may not raise taxes or have as their first objective the expenditure of public money, but otherwise may deal with any matter appropriate for any public bill. They are subject to considerable time restraints in the Commons. (*See* PRIVATE MEMBERS' TIME.)

BILLS, PUBLIC—A bill is a draft statute or Act of Parliament. It passes through a number of stages in each House before it is ready to receive the Royal Assent (*qv*) and become law. The Commons procedure is here described, followed by an indication of differences in practice in the Lords. Bills (other than Bills of aids and supplies) may be introduced in either House, though the Government usually introduce Bills of major political content in the Commons. It is possible for Bills to be passed without the concurrence of the Lords (*see* PARLIAMENT ACTS).

Introduction

There are three methods of introducing Bills and so giving them a "first reading". Bills may be introduced by "Order of the House". This is uncommon except for major financial bills and "ten minute rule" bills (*qv*). Secondly, Bills may be brought from the Lords when their passage there is complete. Once the Member who proposes to take charge of a Lords Bill makes application at the Table, the Bill is "taken up" and receives a first reading. Finally, Bills may be presented by any Member if he or she gives notice at least the previous sitting day. Short, formal proceedings in the Chamber are involved with the first and third of these methods. When a Bill has been introduced, it is printed, and a day is fixed for second reading. Government bills are normally put down for second reading "to-morrow", when they will be deferred from day to day until time is found to debate them. Private Members normally nominate one of the days set aside for their bills as the day for second reading.

Second Reading

The second reading, which is the next stage, is not taken until the bill has been published and a copy made available to every Member. Conventionally, two weekends intervene in the case of Government Bills. The question is proposed "That the bill be now read a second time" and a debate, lasting usually up to six hours, takes place on the Bill's general principle. Any Member may seek to table a so-called "reasoned amendment", setting out the reasons he or she believes the bill should not be given a second reading. Another, but now uncommon, means of registering opposition to a bill is by tabling an amendment to the effect that the bill be read "this day six (or three) months". A procedure exists in the Commons to allow debate on the second reading of uncontroversial Bills to take place in a Standing Committee known as a Second Reading Committee. Bills whose main purpose is to give effect to proposals contained in a report from the Law Commission or the Scottish Law Commission and tax simplification bills are normally automatically so referred. Bills relating exclusively to Scotland or Wales may also be debated in the Scottish or Welsh Grand Committees (*see* COMMITTEES, STANDING).

Committee

After second reading, bills are considered in Committee. (*See* COMMITTEE OF THE WHOLE HOUSE, COMMITTEE, STANDING etc.) This provides an opportunity for the details of the bill to be considered. Committees have power to make any amendments they think fit relevant to the subject matter of the Bill. The Bill is considered clause by clause, and sometimes largely remodelled. Under the Commons Standing Orders, Bills are committed automatically to a standing committee, unless the House decides, on motion being made immediately after second reading (or, with notice, subsequently), to commit the bill to a committee of the whole House or to a select committee or to a special standing committee. Bills of a constitutional character are almost always committed to a committee of the whole House after second reading. A Bill may be committed to a standing committee in respect of some of its clauses, and to a committee of the whole House in respect of other clauses. The Finance Bill is frequently so divided, the major tax proposals remaining on the floor of the House.

Debate may take place on any amendment after it has been moved, the Chairman of the Committee having complete discretion in the selection of amendments. When the amendments to a clause have been disposed of, the Chairman proposes the question "That the clause (as amended) stand part of the bill," and a debate on the clause as a whole may then take place. The Chairman may at this point, if he or she thinks that the principle of the clause has already been adequately discussed in the course of debate on the amendments, put this question forthwith, no further debate on the clause being allowed.

Report

When the Committee stage is concluded, a bill is reported to the House. The "Report stage" (or "consideration stage") then takes place on the floor of the House (except for bills which were considered in Committee of the whole House and were unamended: these pass straight to third reading).

At the report stage, amendments to meet points raised in committee and reserved for consideration are proposed, and other changes may be made. New clauses, of which notice must be given, are taken first. For Bills committed to Standing Committees, this is the opportunity for Members who did not serve on the Committee to propose changes, though no distinction is made between those who served on the Committee and those who did not so far as the tabling of proposed changes is concerned. The bill is not considered clause by clause, but is dealt with as a whole, amendments being moved by reference solely to the particular line and page. Unlike at Committee stage, Members may normally only speak once to each amendment.

Third Reading

The final debate on a Bill occurs at third reading. This is an opportunity to express dissatisfaction or satisfaction with the Bill in its final form. Once third reading has been agreed to, the Bill has been passed, and will be taken up to the House of Lords by the Clerk with a Message requesting that House's concurrence.

Possible reforms

The Select Committee on Modernisation of the House of Commons has proposed a number of experimental reforms. These are being adopted gradually. These include the programming of legislation to ensure that all parts of a bill are scrutinised; pre-legislative scrutiny of bills by select committees; greater use of select and special standing committees for the committee stage of bills; the taking of report stage and Lords amendments in standing committee, and the possibility that bills could be carried over from one session to another.

House of Lords procedures

In the Lords, bills pass through the same stages as in the Commons. A bill arriving from the Commons is almost invariably given a first reading forthwith out of courtesy. Lords bills may be introduced by any Lord without notice. Government bills are not normally opposed at second reading, though reasoned amendments may be tabled. After second reading a bill is usually committed to a committee of the whole House. Some less controversial bills may be considered by a Grand Committee of the whole House off the floor. Under this relatively new (1995) procedure, all Lords may attend and participate but no divisions may take place. Occasionally, a bill may be committed to a select committee of some kind – a Public Bill Committee (the Lords equivalent of a Commons Standing Committee), rarely used; a Special Public Bill Committee (*qv*), usual in the case of Law Commission Bills; or a select committee (to consider the merits of the bill). Where a bill is committed to a select committee the bill is normally re-committed to a committee of the whole House before Report stage, but otherwise bills taken through Committee stage off the floor normally proceed directly to Report on the floor of the House. There is no selection of amendments in the Lords and all the amendments that have been tabled are discussed; and there is no guillotine. Amendments may, subject to certain restrictions, be tabled at third reading. A further opportunity for general debate takes place on the motion "that the bill do now pass", after any Third Reading amendments have been considered. No two stages of a bill may be taken on one day and certain minimum intervals between stages are also observed.

When the Lords agree with the Commons on the principle of the measure, but differ on matters of detail, they return the bill with amendments to which the Commons agree, with or without amendments, or disagree. If no amendments are made in the Lords, or amendments made to which the Commons agree, the bill then only awaits the Royal Assent. Disagreement between the two Houses is usually resolved by one House not insisting on its amendments or an alternative proposal being found acceptable. If no agreement can be reached the bill is lost. The same proceedings are adopted *mutatis mutandis* when the bill originates in the Upper House.

A bill having passed both Houses remains with the Lords. The assent of the Crown is the final proceeding which converts a bill into an Act of Parliament, which is printed by the Stationery Office. A copy on vellum is preserved for posterity in the House of Lords Record Office.

BLACK ROD—The Gentleman Usher of the Black Rod is an officer of the House of Lords. His duties correspond to those of the Serjeant-at-Arms in the House of Commons, and he executes the orders for the commitment of persons guilty of breaches of privilege and contempt. He or his deputy, the Yeoman Usher, is present when the House sits, and acts as the messenger of the Sovereign whenever the attendance of the Commons is required. He is the Agent of the Administration and Works Sub-Committee on whose behalf he is responsible for accommodation, services and security in the House of Lords area of the Palace of Westminster. He also acts as the Secretary to the Lord Great Chamberlain and as such is responsible for certain ceremonial duties. He assists at the introduction of peers and at other ceremonies. Black Rod also holds the office of Serjeant-at-Arms. In this capacity he attends upon the Lord Chancellor or the person who is acting as Speaker of the House for the time being.

BROADCASTING—Regular sound broadcasting of both Houses and their Committees has existed since 1978; the House of Lords has been televised since 1984, and the House of Commons since 1989. Overall control of television rests with the two Houses and is exercised by the Supervisor of Broadcasting who reports to the Select Committee on Broadcasting in the House of Commons and the Administration and Works Sub-Committee in the House of Lords.

BUDGET—Every year the Chancellor of the Exchequer makes a general statement to the House of Commons known as the Budget Statement. He reviews the income and expenditure of the last year, estimates those of the ensuing year and discusses the country's financial prospects. He also describes the government's proposals for the repeal, modification or imposition of taxes. The Chancellor's proposals are embodied in "the Budget Resolutions". These are discussed over several days in the Commons, and, when agreed, form the basis of the Finance Bill which will give them legislative effect. This bill is subject to normal procedures, except that its various stages must be taken on different days and it is exempted business (*qv*).

Budget resolutions varying or amending existing taxes (but not any imposing new taxes) may have immediate effect under the Provisional Collection of Taxes Act 1968. These resolutions are given a provisional validity for 10 sitting days by a resolution passed immediately the Chancellor sits down. Confirmatory resolutions are passed at the end of the general budget debate. The Finance Bill must be read a second time within 30 days of the passing of the provisional resolutions, and receive Royal Assent by 5th August, or within 4 months in the case of bills not introduced in March or April.

From 1998, the Budget has been delivered in the Spring, as it was before 1993. A Pre-Budget Statement is made in November.

BUSINESS, ARRANGEMENT OF—Government business has precedence at every sitting in the Commons, except for (a) certain days set aside for Private Members' business (*see* PRIVATE MEMBERS' TIMES) and (b) 20 Opposition Days a year (*see* OPPOSITION DAY). There are also three Estimates Days, where the Estimate for debate is recommended by the Liaison Committee (*qv*), and the Chairman of Ways and Means may set down private business for consideration at 7 pm on any day. The agenda is thus set on most days by the government's business managers (*see* USUAL CHANNELS).

The House meets on Mondays to Wednesdays at 2.30 pm. The first item is unopposed private business. Then comes question time. This ends at 3.30, unless extended by a private notice question.

Ministerial statements (*qv*) follow. At this stage, backbenchers may propose emergency adjournment debates (*see* ADJOURNMENT). The Speaker then calls the name of any MP who has given notice of business coming under the heading of "At the commencement of public business". This includes notice of presentation of bills, government motions relating to the business or sittings of the House, and motions for leave to bring in a bill under the Ten Minute Rule (*qv*). The main business of the day is thus usually reached at any time between 3.30 and 5.30 pm or even later. This usually lasts until 10 pm ("the hour of interruption"), unless it is exempted business (*qv*) when it may last longer, or unless it has been agreed by arrangement that the business will end earlier, or it is business which is time-limited (e.g. consideration of a statutory instrument) or simply too few MPs wish to discuss the business in hand. After 10 pm, only exempted business may be taken. The final business of each day is the half-hour adjournment debate, initiated by a backbencher chosen by ballot. Occasionally business lasts until midnight or later, though late sittings have become rarer since 1995.

On Thursdays, the same pattern is advanced by three hours: the House meets at 11.30 am and the hour of interruption is 7 pm.

On Fridays, the House meets at 9.30 am, and the hour of interruption is 2.30 pm. No questions are taken (except private notice questions) and statements interrupt business at 11 am Applications for emergency adjournment debates cannot be made. The House does not sit on ten so-called "constituency Fridays" each session. The House does not normally sit on Saturdays; sittings on that day, and the even rarer Sunday sittings are appointed, and the times fixed, by resolution or by the Speaker. The House also sits in Westminster Hall (*qv*).

The House of Lords normally meets on Mondays, Tuesdays and Wednesdays at 2.30 pm and on Thursdays at 3 pm. The House meets on Fridays at 11 am in the latter part of the session. When there are judgments in appeal cases, the House of Lords usually meets at 2 pm on Thursdays. No hour is fixed for the adjournment of the House, the question being put by the Lord Speaker at the conclusion of business and agreed to by the House.

While in theory Government business does not take precedence in the Lords, in practice business is arranged by the Government Whips' Office in consultation with the usual channels (*qv*) and, where necessary, individual members of the House.

Business is taken in the order in which it is tabled, subject to the conditions that "starred" questions for oral answer are entered first; private business precedes public business (except when it is opposed when it may be taken later); Business of the House motions and Chairman of Committees business come before public business; public bills, measures, affirmative instruments and reports from Select Committees have precedence over other motions except on Wednesday when motions (usually for lengthy debates) have precedence; and "unstarred" questions for debate before answer usually come last.

On the day the Queen opens Parliament, both Houses meet a little before 11.30 am when the speech from the Throne is delivered in the House of Lords. The sittings in both Houses are then suspended until the afternoon at 2.30 pm in the Commons and 3.30 pm in the Lords.

BY-ELECTION—A by-election is caused when a vacancy occurs because of the death, bankruptcy, mental illness or disqualification of an MP. Technically an MP cannot resign, but he or she can apply for a nominal office of profit under the Crown, acceptance of which acts as a disqualification. The two offices traditionally used for this purpose are that of steward or bailiff of Her Majesty's Three Chiltern Hundreds of Stoke, Desborough and Burnham, and that of Steward of the Manor of Northstead. No duties are involved and no pay received. An application to hold one of these offices is always granted.

When a seat is vacant, the Chief Whip of the party to which the former Member belonged is generally responsible for "moving a writ" in the Chamber to set in motion the procedure to cause the by-election. This is a debatable Motion but, since it deals with a matter of privilege, may be moved without notice by any Member. During a recess, two Members may apply to the Speaker for a by-election to take place if a vacancy exists because of death, bankruptcy or accession to the peerage.

By convention, almost all vacancies are filled within three to four months, but there is no formal limit to the period during which a constituency may be unrepresented. (*See also* WRITS *and* DISQUALIFICATION.)

CHAIR—The Chair in the Chamber is occupied by the Speaker or Deputy Speakers, who have the titles of Chairman of Ways and Means (*qv*) and First and Second Deputy Chairmen of Ways and Means. The Speaker does not occupy the Chair when the House is in Committee. Not fewer than 10

MPs are also appointed by the Speaker to the Chairmen's Panel at the beginning of each session. These MPs take the Chair in Standing Committee and, occasionally, in the Chamber when the House is in Committee. Four of these Chairmen sit in Westminster Hall as Deputy Speakers in addition to the Chairman of Ways and Means and his Deputies. The Chairmen's Panel (of which the Chairman of Ways and Means and his two deputies are *ex officio* members) has power to report its resolutions on matters of procedure relating to Standing Committees. Each Select Committee chooses its own Chairman. A Liaison Committee, which considers general matters relating to the work of Select Committees, is made up mostly of the Chairmen of Select Committees.

In the Lords, the Lord Chancellor, as Speaker (*qv*), and the Deputy Speakers sit on the Woolsack (*qv*). When the House is in Committee the Speaker leaves the Woolsack and the Chairman of Committees (*qv*) or one of the Deputy Chairmen presides from the Chair at the Table of the House, facing the Clerks.

CHAIRMAN OF COMMITTEES (Lords)—The Chairman of Committees is Chairman of every Select Committee in the Lords unless another chairman is appointed. He is also Principal Deputy Speaker and takes the Chair of Committees of the Whole House. He is elected by the House at the beginning of every Session. Like the Chairman of Ways and Means in the Commons, the Chairman of Committees is entrusted with important duties relating to the examination and supervision of private legislation. In the absence of the Lord Chancellor he may recall the House if the public interest so requires.

The Principal Deputy Chairman of Committees is also appointed by the House and acts as Chairman of the European Communities Committee.

A number of Lords are appointed each session to be Deputy Chairmen of Committees.

The Chairman of Committees and the Principal Deputy Chairman are assisted in their work by three Counsel.

CHAIRMAN OF WAYS AND MEANS—The Chairman of Ways and Means, who is a Member, is appointed by the House on motion made by the Leader of the House of Commons at the beginning of each Parliament. He and his two deputies do not vote, except to give a casting vote. As well as his functions in the Chair (*qv*), he has a responsibility for the conduct of private business in the House, for example examining private bills with the assistance of the Speaker's Counsel to ensure that they comply with the rules of the House.

CHILTERN HUNDREDS—*See* BY-ELECTIONS.

CLAUSE—The individual articles of bills are referred to as clauses. When a bill becomes an Act, the clauses are called sections.

CLERK OF THE HOUSE OF COMMONS—The senior official of the House is its Clerk. He and his deputies (the senior of whom is called the Clerk Assistant) sit at the Table of the House immediately in front of the Speaker. The Clerk gives advice both inside the Chamber and outside on parliamentary procedure, and is responsible for recording the proceedings of the House. The Clerks in his department are advisers on particular areas of procedure to MPs and act as secretaries of Select Committees. The Clerk of the House is appointed by the Crown by letters patent, and the Clerk Assistant by Royal Warrant. The Clerk of the House is Accounting Officer and Corporate Officer for the House of Commons Vote.

CLERK OF THE PARLIAMENTS—As Clerk of the House of Lords the Clerk of the Parliaments signs all Orders of the House and all other official communications. He calls the Business of the House and advises generally on points of order and procedure. He is responsible for the due record and publication of the proceedings and journals of the House. In these duties he is assisted by the Clerk Assistant and the Reading Clerk, who sit with him at the Table of the House. He endorses the bills communicated between the two Houses and is responsible for the conveyance of messages between them. He is responsible for the accuracy of the text of Acts of Parliament and Measures, and is also the custodian of the records of both Houses preserved in the House of Lords Records Office. He is Registrar of the Court in respect of the judicial business of the House of Lords, Accounting Officer for the House of Lords Vote and Corporate Officer. The Clerk of the Parliaments is head of the Parliament Office. He is appointed by the Crown under letters patent. The Clerk Assistant and the Reading Clerk are appointed by the Lord Chancellor. The other Clerks and all staff of the House of Lords are appointed by the Clerk of the Parliaments.

CLOSURE—A Member who wishes to bring a debate to a close—for example, because he or she believes that their opponents want to protract discussion and so delay the House's business—may try to "move the closure" by moving a Motion "That the question be now put." Unless the motion appears to the Chair to be an abuse of the rules of the House or an infringement of the rights of the minority, it is put to the vote at once, and if it is carried, the original question is then put without further debate. A closure motion is not carried unless at least one hundred Members vote in its support. The chairman of a standing committee also has power to accept a motion for the closure, and a number of Members equivalent to the quorum of the Committee is required in support of the motion.

A more drastic form of closure is occasionally applied in order to expedite the passage of controversial Government bills which may be subject to prolonged debate. These motions, known as allocation of time, or "guillotine" motions, subject the bill through all its remaining stages to a strict time schedule. Such motions may be made at any stage during a Bill's progress. The question on a "guillotine" motion is put after three hours' debate.

Following the recommendations of the Select Committee on the Modernisation of the House of Commons, a number of bills have been subject to a programming order, moved after second reading. Such orders typically provide for the committee route the bill will take; the day by which the bill will be reported from committee, and the amount of time proposed for report stage and third reading. Programming orders are agreed under the same standing order (No. 83) which deals with guillotine motions. But, unlike guillotines, programmes represent compromises agreed between the political parties.

The Chairman of Ways and Means and not more than eight other Members nominated by the Speaker in respect of each bill form the Business Committee whose duty it is, when an allocation of time order (including a programming order) has been made in respect of a bill, to arrange for the detailed application of the order in respect of the committee stage and report stage. These recommendations must then be reported to the House; and if agreed to (no debate being allowed), they have the effect of an order of the House. When there is a timetable in respect of a bill in standing committee, a sub-committee of that committee is appointed to make recommendations on its application.

In the Lords the closure is a most exceptional procedure and the "guillotine" does not exist.

COMMAND PAPER—A document formally presented to Parliament on the initiative of the Government is known as a Command Paper because it is said to be presented "at Her Majesty's Command". (*See* GREEN PAPER; WHITE PAPER.)

COMMITTEES, JOINT—Joint Committees are Select Committees of both Houses meeting jointly. A joint committee to examine the *vires* of, and other technical matters related to, Statutory Instruments and one to examine Consolidation Bills (*qv*) are appointed by Standing Order in the Commons and each session in the Lords.

Other Joint Committees may be appointed *ad hoc*. The Ecclesiastical Committee, appointed by the Lord Chancellor and the Speaker each Parliament for the consideration of Church of England Measures (*qv*), consists of members of both Houses, but is not regarded as a Joint Committee.

COMMITTEES, SELECT—Select Committees are so called because their membership is selected from the House. They are appointed to inquire into, and to report to the House on, specified matters, or to consider Bills.

In the Commons, a Committee on Public Accounts has existed by Standing Order for many years, and other Standing Orders provide for a Committee on Standards and Privileges, and Select Committees on Public Administration, on Environmental Audit, on European Scrutiny and on Procedure. The Statutory Instruments Committee has certain technical responsibilities with regard to statutory instruments (*qv*), and a Deregulation Committee was first appointed in 1994/95 to examine deregulatory orders proposed to be made under the Deregulation and Contracting Out Act 1994. There are also four Domestic Committees and a Finance and Services Committee. Sixteen Select Committees, with a broad brief to examine the expenditure, administration and policy of particular government departments and their related public bodies, are provided for under Standing Order No. 152. All principal Departments are covered by these Committees. Further Select Committees may be appointed at any time *ad hoc*; in recent years there has been, for example, a Committee on Standards in Public Life, and there is at present a Select Committee on Modernisation of the House of Commons. The Liaison Committee and the Committee of Selection (*qv*) are themselves Select Committees.

Each Select Committee has a quorum, laid down in the order of reference under which it was appointed. Select Committees may not exceed 15 Members without leave of the House (there is no such restriction in the Lords), and they are usually given power to send for persons, papers and records. They may discharge an investigative function, and they are often aided in this by the appointment of specialist advisers in addition to their full-time Clerk. Witnesses may be examined (on oath, if necessary: false evidence in such circumstances carries the penalties attaching to perjury), and Reports are prepared by the Committee and made to the House. These Reports may be very substantial documents, and their preparation may have involved taking evidence from a large number of distinguished witnesses. Reports are not automatically debated, though they may be – on estimates days, in debates in Westminster Hall or, indeed, in government or opposition-initiated debates in the House. Other reports, while not specifically debated, are "tagged" on the Order Paper as relevant to debates.

In the Lords, Select Committees on the European Communities and on Science and Technology broadly correspond to the policy committees in the Commons, though their activities are not linked to any specific Department of State. Other Select Committees on policy matters or on the merits of bills may be appointed *ad hoc*. Select Committees are also appointed sessionally on Consolidation Bills, House of Lords' Offices, Privileges, Procedure, Delegated Powers Scrutiny (including deregulation) and Statutory Instruments. Select Committees are appointed by the House on recommendation of the Committee of Selection. Select Committees are also appointed in both Houses to consider private bills (*qv*).

COMMITTEE OF SELECTION—This Committee appoints members to Standing Committees, opposed Private Bill Committees and other private legislation Committees. It also nominates members to the departmental Select Committees and domestic committees. In these cases, its nominations must be endorsed by the House.

In the Lords, most Select Committees are appointed by the House on recommendation of the Committee of Selection of that House. The exceptions are the Joint Committee on Consolidation Bills (appointed by the Lord Chancellor) and Select Committees on private legislation (proposed by the Chairman of Committees unless he is of the opinion that the membership be proposed by the Committee of Selection).

COMMITTEE OF THE WHOLE HOUSE—This consists of all Members of the House, meeting in the Chamber and presided over by a Chairman instead of by the Speaker. Committees are appointed to consider certain—usually major—bills in detail, clause by clause. The Speaker leaves the Chair without putting any question whenever the order is read for the House to go into committee. The Mace is placed under the Table, and the Chairman of Ways and Means, or in his absence one of the Deputy Chairmen, takes the chair at the Table. In the House of Lords the Chairman of Committees, or one of the Deputy Chairmen, takes the chair. The Committee stage of most public bills in the Lords is taken in a Committee of the whole House. Some less controversial bills may, under a relatively new (1995) procedure, be considered by a Grand Committee off the floor.

COMMITTEES, SPECIAL STANDING—After its second reading, any MP may make a motion that a bill should be referred to one of these Committees for its Committee stage. Their principal feature is that, in the 28 days after the bill's committal, they have power to send for persons, papers and records and may hold three three-hour hearings to hear oral evidence (these sittings follow a first, private sitting). After these investigative sittings, the bill is considered clause by clause as in a normal Standing Committee (*qv*). A similar procedure was initiated in the House of Lords in 1992, principally for the consideration of Law Commission bills, but has rarely been used.

COMMITTEES, STANDING—

Legislative Standing Committees

Unless otherwise ordered, all Bills are committed to Standing Committee for their committee stage. Committees are essentially *ad hoc* bodies: they have no continuing existence after the bill they are considering has been dealt with. As many Standing Committees as necessary may be appointed, and government bills have precedence in all Standing Committees except one, where Private Members' Bills have precedence. The procedure of a Standing Committee in considering a bill is generally similar to that of a Committee of the whole House. The Chairman has power to control proceedings, select amendments and accept the closure. The first meeting to consider a Bill takes place on a day and time specified by the Chairman.

Second reading committees are also appointed from time to time (*see* BILLS, PUBLIC) and there is a rarely-used provision for bills considered by such committees to have their report stage taken in a standing committee also. The Modernisation Committee favours more frequent use of standing committees for report stage, and the use of such committees to consider Lords amendments.

Regional Standing Committees

All public bills relating exclusively to Scotland and committed to a standing committee are considered by a Scottish Standing Committee, but, since the establishment of the Scottish Parliament, such bills are now unlikely. The Scottish Grand Committee consists of all members representing Scottish constituencies. Its role was extended substantially in the 1994–95 session but has largely been superseded since the Scottish Parliament came into existence. However, the Grand Committee can meet in Scotland; can, in effect, replace the Chamber for the second reading and report stages of some Scottish bills; can consider Scottish statutory instruments and holds general debates, some initiated by the government and some by opposition parties. There are also provisions for periodic question times; opportunities to hear statements from Scottish Office ministers, other ministers of the Crown and Scottish law officers (whether or not they are MPs); half hour adjournment debates, and a novel procedure for short debates with short speeches on topical matters.

The Welsh Grand Committee consists of all Members sitting for constituencies in Wales, together with not more than five other Members nominated by the Committee of Selection. It considers bills or specified matters relating to Wales referred to it on a motion made by a Minister, and there is provision for question times; short debates; ministerial statements and adjournment debates. When the Committee meets in Wales, Members may speak in Welsh – simultaneous translations are provided. Again, the Welsh Grand Committees's role has largely been superseded since the establishment of the National Assembly for Wales.

The Northern Ireland Grand Committee consists of all Members sitting for constituencies in Northern Ireland together with not more than 25 members nominated by the Committee of Selection. It can consider similar matters to the Welsh Grand Committee.

The Standing Committee on Regional Affairs consists of all Members sitting for constituencies in England, together with not more than five other Members nominated by the Committee of Selection, and considers specified matters relating to regional affairs in England.

The future of the regional Standing Committees representing Scotland, Wales and Northern Ireland remains under debate, following legislative devolution to those countries. There have also been suggestions that an English Grand Committee should be established or the Regional Affairs Committee revived.

Delegated Legislation

One or more Standing Committees on Delegated Legislation consider Statutory Instruments or draft Statutory Instruments referred to them: this is automatic, unless the House decides otherwise, in the case of statutory instruments requiring affirmative resolution. The Committee has 1½ hours to consider the instrument (2½ hours for a Northern Ireland instrument) and has no power to amend the instrument. Members other than those nominated may attend and speak, but not vote. After consideration by a Standing Committee, any decision by the House on the instrument is taken without debate. Church of England Measures (*qv*) may also be considered by the Committees.

European Standing Committees

There are three European Standing Committees concerned with matters within the responsibility of (A) the Departments of: Agriculture, Fisheries and Food; Environment, Transport and the Regions; Forestry Commission; and analogous responsibilities of Scotland, Wales and Northern Ireland Offices (B); HM Treasury (including HM Customs and Excise; Social Security; Foreign and Commonwealth Office; International Development; Home Office; Lord Chancellor's Department, together with any matters not otherwise allocated (C); Trade and Industry; Education and Employment; Culture, Media and Sport; Health, respectively. Members are nominated for the whole session, but others may attend and speak, but not vote. The Committees consider documents recommended by the European Scrutiny Committee for further consideration. These documents are normally referred automatically to the Committees. The Committees meet once to consider a document. They may hear a statement from a Minister on the Document, and the Minister may then reply to questions. This process may take no longer than one hour. After this, a Motion may be moved in the Committee, and Amendments proposed. Proceedings are interrupted after 2½ hours. The Committee reports to the House any Resolution to which it has come. When the Committee has reported to the House, any motion relating to the document is taken without debate.

General

Except for the Scottish and Welsh Grand Committees, the Northern Ireland Committee, the European Standing Committees, the Standing Committee on Regional Affairs and the Report Stage

Committee, all Standing Committees have between 16 and 50 members. These are nominated by the Committee of Selection, having regard to individual Members' qualifications and the need to represent the political parties in proportion to their numbers in the House. With the exception of European Standing Committees (which are nominated for a whole session), the Committees are not "standing" in the sense generally understood by the word, and their membership alters depending on the Bill or other matter which they are considering. The quorum of a Standing Committee is 17, or one-third of its membership, whichever is less (three in the case of the European Standing Committees). Standing Committees may meet on any day, including a day when the House is not sitting. The only restriction is that they cannot meet on sitting days on Mondays to Wednesday, between 1 pm and 3.30 pm or Thursdays between 11.25 am and 12.30 pm. Except for the Grand Committees, all meetings must take place within the precincts.

COMPTROLLER AND AUDITOR GENERAL—*See* National Audit Office.

CONDUCT OF MEMBERS—Certain disciplinary powers are available to the Chair in the Commons to deal with Members who misconduct themselves. The Chair may direct Members who persist in irrelevance or tedious repetition to discontinue their speeches. A Member whose conduct is grossly disorderly can, under Standing Order No. 43, be ordered to leave the Chamber. If this Standing Order proves inadequate, the Speaker or Chairman may "name" a Member. When a Member is named, the Leader of the House or the senior Minister present moves a Motion that the Member be suspended from the service of the House. For the first offence in one session, the period of suspension is until the fifth sitting day, for the second offence until the twentieth day and for the third offence suspension is indefinite. If a Member has to be removed by force after he or she is named, the suspension automatically lasts for the remainder of the session. If grave disorder arises in the Chamber, the Speaker can adjourn the House or suspend the sitting.

A Code of Conduct and a Guide to the Rules relating to the Conduct of Members were agreed by the House in July 1996. The Committee on Standards and Privileges is authorised to make minor amendments to the Guide to the Rules. The Parliamentary Commissioner for Standards (*qv*) has responsibilities in this area.

In the House of Lords, the preservation of order and the maintenance of the rules of debate are the responsibility of the House itself, i.e. of all Lords present, any of whom may call attention to any breach of order or custom. Lords usually bring to the notice of the House any transgression of a rule or convention either by saying "Order, Order" or by indicating briefly the nature of the transgression. If two Lords rise simultaneously and one does not promptly give way, Lords indicate their preference by naming the Lord they wish to hear. The Leader of the House expresses the attitude of the House in drawing attention to a transgression or abuse of the rules of procedure. The Leader has, however, no special disciplinary powers and can only appeal to Members to exercise restraint.

CONSOLIDATED FUND—The Consolidated Fund is the fund formed of the proceeds of taxation and other sums received by the Exchequer.

Consolidated Fund Bills are introduced normally three times a year to give statutory confirmation to the granting of money to the Government by Parliament. The details of the areas of expenditure for which the money is granted are set out in the Estimates (*qv*). The final Consolidated Fund Bill of the financial year becomes, when enacted, the Appropriation Act (*qv*). Consolidated Fund Bills are not debated in the Commons (though a vote could be held on their second and third readings—there is no Committee stage) and they are invariably passed without debate or vote by the Lords. (*see* SUPPLY).

CONSOLIDATION BILL—A bill which merely brings together several existing Acts into one, with the object of simplifying the statutes. An expedited procedure exists for the consideration of these bills. They always begin in the Lords where they are committed to a Joint Select Committee of both Houses. This Committee also considers consolidating legislation which applies to Northern Ireland alone and is in the form of a Statutory Instrument because of the provisions of the Northern Ireland Acts. Under the Consolidation of Enactments (Procedure) Act 1949, the bills may contain corrections and minor improvements. If the bills contain more substantial improvements recommended by one of the Law Commissions, those improvements are open to debate and amendment in the usual way.

CONSTITUENCY—There are at present 659 constituencies, each represented by one MP. Every 10 to 15 years constituency boundaries are altered on the recommendation of the Boundary Commissions, which are responsible for ensuring that constituency size throughout each country of the United Kingdom is as equal as possible. Nevertheless, the population of different constituencies ranges widely. A large part of MPs' work is concerned with issues brought to them by their constituents, and the majority hold constituency "surgeries" on Fridays or Saturdays when they make themselves readily available to constituents. A "constituency week" is a week when a backbencher is excused from attending the House and is expected to work in his or her constituency.

CONTINGENCIES FUND—A fund which allows the Treasury to meet urgent and unforeseen expenditure in advance of the parliamentary authority which must ultimately be obtained.

CROWN—*See* QUEEN

DEBATE, RULES OF—In the Commons, Members who wish to speak rise and address themselves to the Chair. They may not speak from below the bar. The Speaker calls the Member who "catches her eye": normally she alternates between the two sides of the House. Priority is given to "maiden" speakers (i.e. those who have not spoken before in the Chamber). Normally, except in Committee, Members may speak only once on any individual question. No Member may speak after the question has been put by the Chair.

Members may not read their speeches, but may refer to notes. At the Speaker's discretion, a limit on speeches may be imposed in most circumstances.

There are certain rules restricting what MPs may say. They must not refer to other Members by name but by constituency or office. Insulting or offensive language is not permitted. Members may not refer to the alleged views of members of the royal family. Matters before the courts which are covered by the House's *sub judice* rule may not be raised. Speeches must be relevant, and Members who rise to speak must direct their speech to the question before the House, or to a motion or amendment which they wish to move or to a question of order. Members present in the Chamber must also follow certain rules. They must not heckle or disrupt other speakers. They must not cross the floor of the House between the Chair and the MP who is speaking, and they must bow to the Chair when entering or leaving the Chamber.

In the House of Lords the rules of debate differ in some respects from those observed in the Commons. In debate a Lord addresses the rest of the Lords in general. No Lord may speak twice except in committee, or in explanation or reply, or if he is Chairman of Committees or Chairman of a Select Committee whose report is under consideration. The Lord who sits on the Woolsack or in the Chair when in committee has no duties to perform except to put the question. For debates on Second Readings, motions and occasionally on Affirmative Instruments and private legislation, the order of speaking is determined by lists prepared by the Leader of the House in consultation with the usual channels and the mover of the motion. In other proceedings, if several Lords rise together, the House decides who shall be heard first. The occupant of the Woolsack does not possess the power to direct a Lord to resume his or her seat, although in exceptional circumstances a motion may be moved that a noble Lord be no longer heard. Lords speak in their place, standing and "uncovered". Reading of speeches is discouraged and speeches are expected to be relevant to the question before the House. Lords must refrain from "asperity of speech". Matters which are *sub judice* may not be raised except in cases of national importance, where there is no danger of prejudice to proceedings, and only by leave of the Leader of the House.

DEBATES—Strictly speaking any formal discussion of any motion (*qv*) in either House of Parliament may be termed a debate. But the term is popularly more commonly applied to discussions not related to legislative or financial business.

There is no specific time set aside in the Commons for debates, but debates arise on adjournment motions (*see* ADJOURNMENT) and on specific motions brought before the House by the Government or by the opposition parties on Opposition Days (*qv*). Most Sessions include—among many others—debates on the armed forces, foreign affairs, the government's expenditure plans, and any important Select Committee reports relating to the House's procedures or privileges.

In the Lords, most debates take place on Wednesdays when motions have precedence over bills and other business. Each session's Wednesdays are allocated to the political parties and the Cross-bench Peers by agreement through the usual channels. These debates may be time-limited by order of the House to 2, 2½, 3, 3½, 4 or 5 hours. One Wednesday a month up to the Spring Bank Holiday is given over to two 2½ hour debates on motions by backbench peers, drawn by ballot (*qv*). These Wednesday debates are usually conducted on motions for papers (*qv*) and no division takes place. Occasionally debate may take the form of a divisible motion for resolution, requiring the House to express a collective opinion.

Time is also made available on other days to debate reports of Select Committees, usually on a motion to take note moved by the Chairman of the Committee in question. Emergency debates on a government motion to take note of a particular circumstance are occasionally used when circumstances so require.

The adjournment is not normally debated in the Lords but debatable unstarred questions may be tabled at the end of business or, by agreement, in an adjournment of other business for dinner.

DELEGATED LEGISLATION—Delegated legislation (or 'subordinate legislation') is so called because the power to make law has been delegated by Parliament in specific circumstances to other persons and bodies. For example, Statutory Instruments and other orders having the force of law may be made by Ministers and other persons on authority delegated to them by Acts of Parliament. Some parliamentary control is often retained by means of the requirement for a resolution to bring or continue an instrument in force (the "affirmative procedure") or by motions praying Her Majesty that an instrument be annulled ("prayers"—the "negative procedure"). Most orders and regulations are subject to the provisions of the Statutory Instruments Act 1946, and the usual time permitted for a prayer is forty days from the date of laying before the House (not counting periods when both Houses stand adjourned for more than four days or periods when Parliament is prorogued or dissolved). A Joint Select Committee of both Houses considers Statutory Instruments in relation to their form and legal propriety except for those Instruments (mainly financial) that are laid before the Commons only, which are considered by a Select Committee of that House. In the Lords, no motion to approve an affirmative instrument may be moved until the report from the Joint Committee has been made. There is no comparable provision in the Commons. In the Commons, Statutory Instruments subject to negative or affirmative procedures (as well as Statutory Instruments which are not subject to any parliamentary procedure) may be referred to a Standing Committee for debate on their merits. Normally affirmative instruments are automatically so referred. Statutory Instruments debated on the floor of the House are limited to 1½ hours debate. In the Lords, the Delegated Powers Scrutiny Committee reports on whether the provisions of any Bill inappropriately delegate legislative power or whether they subject the exercise of legislative power to an inappropriate degree of parliamentary scrutiny.

Under the Government of Wales Act 1998, the Welsh Assembly has taken over the majority of powers previously held by the Secretary of State for Wales to make delegated legislation and may have other areas of legislative competence delegated to it. Subordinate legislation made by the Welsh Assembly will not normally be subject to any parliamentary control.

Orders made under Chapter I of the Deregulation and Contracting Out Act 1994 (deregulation orders) amend primary legislation. They are (unusually) available in draft for a 60-day period before the normal 40 days for affirmative instruments. During this time, they are considered by the Commons Deregulation Committee and by the Lords Delegated Powers Scrutiny Committee who report whether the order should be made in the form of the draft, or amended. The eventual order is then considered again by these Committees rather than the Joint Committee on Statutory Instruments. Deregulation orders must then be approved by both Houses; in the Commons, they may be debated for 90 minutes or, if the Government seeks to overturn a recommendation from the Deregulation Committee that the order should not be made, for three hours. (*See also* EUROPEAN COMMUNITY DOCUMENTS.)

DEPARTMENTAL REPORTS—These are presented to Parliament each February by each Government Department. The documents follow certain common reporting principles, and outline the work of the Departments and their financial performance. They are frequently used as the basis of inquiries by departmental Select Committees.

DEREGULATION ORDERS—*see* DELEGATED LEGISLATION.

DILATORY MOTION—In order to bring about the adjournment of business to another day, a Member may move the adjournment of the House or of the debate (in Committee, that the Chairman do report progress or do leave the Chair). If of the opinion that this motion is an abuse of the rules of the House, the Chair may put the question on the dilatory motion forthwith, or may refuse to put the question to the House or Committee at all.

DISQUALIFICATION—The following are disqualified for membership of the House of Lords: (i) *Aliens.* By the Act of Settlement 1701 "no person born out of the Kingdoms of England, Scotland or Ireland, or the Dominions thereunto belonging . . . (except such as are born of English parents)" may be a member of either House. By virtue of the British Nationality Act 1981, this provision does not apply to Commonwealth citizens or citizens of the Republic of Ireland.

"Commonwealth citizen" means a British citizen, a British Overseas Territories citizen, a British Overseas citizen, a British subject under that Act or a citizen of an independent Commonwealth country.

(ii) *Those under the age of twenty-one.*

(iii) Bankrupts.   Under the Insolvency Act 1986, a Lord adjudged bankrupt, or in Scotland whose estate is sequestered, is disqualified for sitting and voting in the House of Lords or in any committee of the House; and a Writ is not issued to any Lord for the time being so disqualified. The court certifies the bankruptcy or sequestration to the Speaker of the House of Lords and a record thereof is entered in the Journals. Disqualification ceases in accordance with the provisions of s.427 of the 1986 Act.

(iv) *Peers convicted of treason.*   The Forfeiture Act 1870 provides that anyone convicted of treason shall be disqualified for sitting or voting as a member of the House of Lords until he has either suffered his term of imprisonment or received a pardon.

The following are the principal categories of individuals who are disqualified from membership of the House of Commons: aliens; persons under 21; the mentally ill; members of the House of Lords; those adjudged bankrupt (under section 427 of the Insolvency Act 1986); those convicted of treason (under similar provisions as apply in the House of Lords); those detained (in the United Kingdom or Republic of Ireland) for more than a year for any offence, or those unlawfully at large; those guilty of certain corrupt electoral practices; clergy of the Church of England and Church of Ireland; Ministers of the Church of Scotland; Roman Catholic priests; civil servants; members of the armed forces; police officers (except officers of private police forces); members of legislatures outside the Commonwealth; judges; holders of a number of public offices specified in the regularly amended Schedule to the House of Commons Disqualification Act 1975, and (in the case of serving Members who voluntarily wish to resign) those who accept the Chiltern Hundreds or the Manor of Northstead (see also BY-ELECTIONS).

DISSOLUTION—A Parliament ends with dissolution which is followed in turn by a General Election. Dissolution normally takes place by royal proclamation after the Queen has been advised by the Prime Minister of the latter's wish to call an election. Under the Parliament Act 1911, a Parliament would automatically be dissolved five years after the date on which it had first met.

DIVISIONS—At the end of a debate, the Chair "puts the question". This is done by asking the House to decide with the words: "as many as are of that opinion say 'Aye' , the contrary 'No'." The Chair then says either "I think the Ayes have it" or "I think the Noes have it". If this statement is challenged, an order is given to "clear the lobby" and a division takes place. The tellers' doors to the "No" and "Aye" lobbies on either side of the Chamber are locked, and division bells are rung throughout the precincts. After the lapse of not more than two minutes the question is again put, and if the statement from the Chair is again challenged, the Speaker, or Chairman, directs the "Ayes" to go into the right lobby and the "Noes" into the left lobby, and names tellers for each side. As the Members pass through the lobbies, the Division Clerks mark their names on lists, and they are counted by the tellers. After the lapse of at least eight minutes from the order to clear the lobby, the doors leading into both lobbies are ordered to be locked, and remain locked until the figures are declared. When the result has been reported by the tellers to the Speaker, or Chairman, she or he declares the number to the House. Members may vote in a division although they did not hear the question put. A Member is not obliged to vote. There is no formal way in which an abstention can be recorded. Procedures exist to allow the Chair to prevent divisions being claimed unnecessarily.

Voting is very similar in the Lords. When a motion has been moved a question is usually proposed "that the motion be agreed to" and the forms of voices are "Contents" and "Not-Contents". Three minutes elapse before the question is put a second time and eight minutes before the doors are locked.

EARLY DAY MOTION—In the Commons, the majority of Motions tabled by backbenchers are put down "for an early day". This is because the MP tabling the Motion realises that there is very unlikely to be any actual day when the Motion will be debated. In any case, he or she may not wish this to happen. A number of early day motions (known as EDM) are nevertheless tabled in each sitting day. By this means, MPs are able to express their views on particular issues with the protection of parliamentary privilege. They can also gauge the popularity of their views in the House by the number of signatures of other MPs which the Motion attracts.

ELECTORAL SYSTEM—The British parliamentary electoral system is known as the relative majority or "first past the post" method. The country is divided into constituencies (*qv*), each represented by one MP. Electors choose just one candidate. No order of priority is expressed between candidates. The candidate with the greatest number of votes is the winner. Elections take place at least every five years. An earlier general election may take place if the Prime Minister advises the Queen to dissolve Parliament.

EMERGENCY DEBATE—Some emergency debates are granted by the Speaker (these are adjournment motions under Standing Order No. 24—*see* ADJOURNMENT). Other emergency debates may occur in both Houses when government business managers re-arrange the parliamentary timetable at short notice because of a widespread desire that a particular debate should take place.

ERSKINE MAY—Thomas Erskine May (1815–1886) was the Clerk of the House of Commons from 1871 to 1886. His *Treatise on the Law, Privilege, Proceedings and Usage of Parliament* was first published in 1844 and has since passed through twenty-two editions. The Treatise is now commonly known as *Erskine May* and is considered the authoritative work of reference on Parliament.

ESTIMATES—Estimates are presented to Parliament at least four times a year—the main estimates in March, and supplementary estimates in Spring, Summer and Winter. These estimates set out the estimated totals of the part of public expenditure (known as "Supply expenditure") which can only be incurred with parliamentary authority. For further information, *see* SUPPLY.

EUROPEAN UNION DOCUMENTS—European Union Documents are defined under Standing Order No. 143 as (i) any proposal under the Community Treaties for legislation by the Council or the Council acting jointly with the European Parliament; (ii) any document which is published for submission to the European Council, the Council or the European Central Bank; (iii) any proposal for a common strategy, a joint action or a common position under Title V of the Treaty on European Union which is prepared for submission to the Council or to the European Council; (iv) any proposal for a common position, framework decision, decision or a convention under Title VI of the Treaty on European Union which is prepared for submission to the Council; (v) Any document (not falling within (ii), (iii) or (iv) above) which is published by one Union institution for or with a view to submission to another Union institution and which does not relate exclusively to consideration of any proposal for legislation; (vi) any other document relating to European Union matters deposited in the House by a Minister of the Crown. In the Commons, these documents are examined by the Select Committee on European Legislation, which reports its opinion on the legal and political importance of each, recommends which documents should be considered by a European Standing Committee (*see* COMMITTEES, STANDING) and considers any other issue arising from a document or group of documents. The House has resolved that in normal circumstances, no Minister should give agreement in the Council of Ministers to a proposal for EU legislation (or certain decisions under Title IV or Title VI) which has not completed the scrutiny process in the House. If special factors lead the Minister to conclude that agreement should be given before the scrutiny process is complete, he or she must explain his or her reasons to the Select Committee and (if appropriate) the House. A similar practice applies in the House of Lords. (*See* COMMITTEES.)

In the House of Lords, European Union proposals are scrutinised by the Select Committee on the European Union. This Committee has at present six Sub-Committees covering the different areas of EU activity. The Committee frequently makes detailed reports to the House on those proposals which raise important matters of policy and principle, taking evidence from a wide variety of witnesses and interested parties: these reports may be debated. The Government has undertaken not to agree to the adoption of proposals under scrutiny, or awaiting debate, subject to the same exceptions as apply in the House of Commons.

EXEMPTED BUSINESS—Under Standing Order No. 9, business in the Commons is interrupted at 10 pm (or 7 pm on a Thursday or 2.30 pm on a Friday). Except for the half-hour adjournment debate (*qv*), only "exempted business" can then be discussed. However, certain types of business are automatically exempted for an unlimited period (e.g. bills such as the Finance Bill which are brought in upon Ways and Means Resolutions) or for a specific period (e.g. "prayers" [*qv*]). In addition, the House is sometimes asked to agree a Motion which exempts particular business for that day's sitting from interruption at 10 pm. Standing Order No. 15 deals with exempted business. Since 1995, the classes of exempted business have been reduced as part of a series of measures designed to secure earlier rising of the House.

FATHER OF THE HOUSE—The MP who has sat longest in the House of Commons without a break (irrespective of whether he or she has sat for the same constituency) is known as the Father of the House. At present he is The Rt Hon. Sir Edward Heath, KG, MBE, Prime Minister from 1970-1974, who was first elected in 1950.

FINANCE BILL—*See* BUDGET

GREEN PAPER—*See* WHITE PAPER

GUILLOTINE—*See* CLOSURE

HANSARD—There have been official verbatim records of debate since 1909. The name Hansard has been associated with Parliamentary reporting since 1812, when T. C. Hansard took over Cobbett's Parliamentary Debates. The business was sold in 1889, but the popular title Hansard survived and was replaced on the cover of the official report of debates in 1943. Lords and Commons debates appear in two separate series of publications; the reports are prepared by members of the staff of the two respective Houses, and are published daily by the Stationery Office. Hansard contains the texts of answers to written questions, including letters written to Members by Chief Executives of Executive Agencies in response to parliamentary questions. Hansard is also available in electronic form through the internet. Verbatim records of Standing Committee debates are also produced.

"HENRY VIII" ORDERS—These are pieces of delegated legislation which amend primary legislation (for example, remedial orders under the Human Rights Act 1998). These are so named because of King Henry VIII's Statute of Proclamations which allowed the King to rule by decree.

HOURS OF SITTING—*See* BUSINESS, ARRANGEMENT OF.

HOUSE OF COMMONS, CHAMBER—The House originally met in the Painted Chamber of the Palace of Westminster, or in the Chapter House or in the Refectory of Westminster Abbey, and then, from about 1550, in St Stephen's Chapel, the chapel of the Royal Palace of Westminster, until 1834, when that building was largely destroyed by fire. St Stephen's Hall now occupies the site of the original debating Chamber; but the basement storey of St Stephen's Chapel still exists and contains the crypt chapel. When the Palace was rebuilt after the fire of 1834, the Commons debating chamber was placed in the Northern part of the building, the Speaker's chair facing due South, towards the Central Lobby and the House of Lords, whose chamber was built on the south side of the Lobby. This Commons Chamber was destroyed by enemy action on 10th May 1941, and on 28th October 1943, a Select Committee was appointed to consider and report on plans for the rebuilding of the House "and upon such alterations as may be considered desirable while preserving all its essential features." This Committee's report was agreed to by the House in January 1945, and the construction of the new chamber was begun in March 1947, with Sir Giles Gilbert Scott as architect. It was first occupied on 26th October, 1950. It was deliberately decided that the Chamber should remain intimate, and it is of the same size as the one which was destroyed. This means that there are only 427 seats for 659 MPs. However, the rebuilding provided an opportunity to increase considerably the accommodation in the galleries for press and public. Special galleries are also reserved for peers and for Commonwealth and diplomatic representatives. The galleries at the north end of the chamber above and behind the Speaker's chair are used by the media and Hansard; opposite them are the special galleries and those provided for members of the public. The side galleries are reserved for Members, who may in certain circumstances speak from them. Under the press gallery, on the Speaker's right, is a row of seats reserved for civil servants who attend to give such advice as may be required by ministers during the sittings of the House. During the period between the destruction of the old chamber in 1941 and the opening of the new in 1950, the House occupied the House of Lords debating chamber, while the Lords used the King's Robing Room. Emergency accommodation in Church House was used at various times by both Houses during the Second World War.

HOUSE OF COMMONS COMMISSION—The House of Commons Commission is a statutory body which consists of the Speaker (Chairman), the Leader of the House, a Member appointed by the Leader of the Opposition and three other non-ministerial MPs appointed by the House. It is responsible (with a few exceptions) for the appointment, pay and conditions of the House's staff, and also has the task of preparing estimates of the expenses of the House.

HOUSE OF LORDS, CHAMBER—The present Chamber of the House of Lords was first used in 1847, after the fire of 1834 had destroyed the greater part of the Palace of Westminster.

The Lords had at some time previously met in the White Chamber, the White Hall and the Painted Chamber. The new Parliament Chamber, designed by Sir Charles Barry, assisted by Augustus W. N. Pugin, has been used continuously by the Lords since 1847, except between 1941 and 1951, when the Lords gave it up to the Commons (whose own Chamber had been destroyed by enemy action) and met in the Robing Room, and on certain occasions in Church House.

The Chamber is 85 feet long, 45 feet wide, and 47 feet high. At its southern end, facing the Strangers' Gallery, is the Throne, designed by Pugin. The Canopy above the Throne represents the

Cloth of Estate, to which Lords bow on entering. When the House is sitting, Bishops who are not members of the House, Privy Counsellors and certain other distinguished persons may sit on the steps of the Throne. For the State Opening of Parliament the brass rail around the Throne is removed and the Queen reads the Gracious Speech from the Throne. The members of the House of Commons then stand behind the Bar of the House—a barrier, situated below the Strangers' Gallery, which marks the boundary of the House.

In front of the Throne is the Woolsack, which is stuffed with wool from England, Wales, Scotland, Northern Ireland and the countries of the Commonwealth. The Lord Chancellor or his deputy sits, as Speaker of the House of Lords, on the Woolsack, on which is placed the Mace, the emblem of Her Majesty's authority.

In front of the Lord Chancellor's Woolsack are two other woolsacks and the Table of the House. Two Despatch Boxes are placed on the Table, at which Front Bench speakers stand when addressing the House. Seated at the Table, facing the Throne, are the Clerks, whose responsibilities include the calling and recording of the business of the House. (*See* CLERK OF THE PARLIAMENTS.)

Behind the Clerks, just in front of the Bar of the House, are the Cross Benches. On these sit those Lords (apart from Bishops) who are not associated with either the Government or Opposition parties. Below the Bar, to the left facing the floor of the House, are the shorthand writers, preparing copy for Hansard (the Official Report). The Benches on the right of the Throne are for supporters of the Government, and those on the left for supporters of the Opposition. Liberal Democrats normally occupy the benches on the left nearest the Woolsack, and the two front benches opposite are reserved for the Bishops, the front of these being the only bench with elbow-rests.

The Government side of the House, where the Leader of the House and Ministers of the Crown sit, is known as the "Spiritual Side" and the Opposition side as the "Temporal Side".

Accommodation is provided in the side galleries for spouses, ambassadors and other distinguished persons. The Press Gallery and the Strangers' Gallery are above the Bar.

HOUSE OF LORDS, FUNCTIONS, POWERS AND MEMBERSHIP—The House of Lords is a chamber of the legislature (*see* PARLIAMENT). Generally speaking, no bill may receive Royal Assent unless it has been passed by the Lords. However, under the Parliament Acts 1911 and 1949 (*qv*) certain bills known as Money Bills (*qv*) may be presented for Royal Assent without the agreement of the Lords; and any other public bill rejected by the Lords in one session may, after reintroduction and further rejection, be presented for Royal Assent in the following session without the agreement of the Lords. By convention, the Lords may not amend bills of aids and supplies (*qv*) nor do they reject outright any bill passed by the Commons which fulfils a manifesto commitment on the part of the Government (*see* SALISBURY CONVENTION).

The House of Lords is a forum of general debate and of scrutiny of the executive and it is also the ultimate Court of Appeal in the United Kingdom (*see* LAW LORDS).

The following are members of the House of Lords: the Archbishops of Canterbury and York, the Bishops of London, Durham and Winchester and the 21 most senior diocesan bishops of the Church of England; Lords created under the Appellate Jurisdiction Act 1876 (as amended); Life Peers created under the Life Peerages Act 1958; and 92 Hereditary Peers who have been excepted from the provisions of the House of Lords Act 1992 (90 by election and two—the Earl Marshal and Lord Great Chamberlain—*ex officio*).

A Peer not in the House of Lords is eligible to sit in the House of Commons. (*See also* BUSINESS, ARRANGEMENT OF *and* DISQUALIFICATION.)

INTERESTS, FINANCIAL—An MP may not vote on any question in which he or she has a direct pecuniary interest, nor take part in Select Committee inquiries where such an interest arises. The interest must be immediate and personal, not general or remote. No Member may enter into a contractual relationship with an outside body which limits his or her freedom of action, and no Member may, in consideration of a material benefit he or she, or his or her immediate family, receive, act as an advocate for an outside body or individual by means of any speech, question, motion, bill or amendment. Relevant pecuniary interests must be declared by Members in debate or other proceedings, including when tabling questions, motions or amendments, or adding signatures to motions or amendments already tabled. When such an interest is declared, the relevant entry is marked with a "[R]" in the House's published papers. Members must also register certain interests (these are published in the Register of Members' Interests), and must deposit copies of any agreements into which they enter for provision of services in their capacity as Members of Parliament, with certain details of the fees payable, with the Parliamentary Commissioner for Standards (*qv*). The work of the Commissioner, and certain other matters relating to the conduct of Members, is overseen by the Committee on Standards and Privileges. This was first established in 1995 as part of the response to the first report of the Committee on Standards in Public Life.

On the basis of recommendations made by the sub-committee of the Procedure Committee on Declaration and Registration of Interests in July 1995, the rules in the Lords are that Lords should always act on their personal honour and never accept any financial inducement as an incentive or reward for exercising Parliamentary influence. Lords who accept payment or other incentive or reward for providing Parliamentary advice or services (i.e. as consultants), or who have any financial interest in a business involved in parliamentary lobbying on behalf of clients should not speak, vote, lobby or otherwise take advantage of their position as Members of the House on behalf of their clients. This restriction does not apply to matters relating to Lords' outside employment or directorships where the interest does not arise from membership of the House. Lords who have a direct financial or other interest in a subject on which they speak should declare it. A public register is maintained by the House and all Lords in receipt of a writ of summons to Parliament and not on leave of absence are expected to declare any parliamentary consultancies, financial interests in businesses involved in lobbying and other particulars which relate to matters which may affect the public perception of the way in which they discharge their parliamentary duties. The register is published annually.

JOURNALS—The authorised record of the daily proceedings of the two Houses (as distinct from the verbatim report of debates) which have been preserved from 1510 in the case of the Lords and from 1547 in the case of the Commons.

LANGUAGE, UNPARLIAMENTARY—Various expressions or words have been ruled to be unparliamentary over the years. However, there is no comprehensive list. As Erskine May says, "good temper and moderation are the characteristics of parliamentary language". Unparliamentary language can often depend on the circumstances in which it is spoken. When a phrase or word is ruled unparliamentary, the MP who spoke the phrase or word must withdraw it. If he or she does not, the disciplinary sanctions of the Chair are liable to be enforced. (*See* CONDUCT OF MEMBERS.)

LAW LORDS (LORDS OF APPEAL)—The House of Lords is the ultimate court of appeal in the United Kingdom (save in Scottish criminal cases). The Lords of Appeal consist of the Lord Chancellor and a maximum of 12 Lords of Appeal in Ordinary, three constituting a quorum, and Lords who hold or have held high judicial office. Appeals are normally heard by five Lords of Appeal sitting as an Appellate Committee, but judgments are delivered at judicial sittings of the House. The Lords of Appeal in Ordinary—if not already peers—are raised to the peerage usually as life barons under the Appellate Jurisdiction Act 1876 as amended.

LEADER OF THE HOUSE—In each House, the member of the Government (usually holding one of the "sinecure" offices, such as Lord President of the Council) who is responsible for planning and supervising the Government's legislative programme is known as the Leader of the House. It is the Leader's duty to uphold the rights and privileges of the House as a whole, and in this capacity to move motions relating to the procedure of the House.

LIAISON COMMITTEE—In the Commons, this Committee, which is made up largely of Select Committee Chairmen, considers general matters relating to the work of Select Committees. It also reports its recommendations on the allocation of time for consideration by the House of the Estimates. In the Lords, a Liaison Committee chaired by the Leader of the House allocates resources between Select Committees and advises the House on other matters relating to Committee work.

LIBRARIES—Both Houses have extensive libraries. Both also provide research assistance to Members. This is especially comprehensive in the Commons.

LOBBY GROUPS—Lobby groups can broadly be defined as any group organised to influence opinion among MPs, Peers and others either in favour of or in opposition to some cause. Firms of professional lobbyists, sometimes known as parliamentary consultants, also exist.

LOBBY, PRESS—The press lobby consists of those journalists (about 150 in number) who are authorised to work in Parliament by the Serjeant at Arms. Lobby journalists have access to the Members' Lobby in the House of Commons and certain other areas of the Palace. They attend briefings given by Ministers and civil servants, sometimes on an "off-the-record" basis. They, as well as other reporters, have access to the press gallery in the Chamber above the Speaker's Chair.

LORD CHANCELLOR—The Lord High Chancellor or Lord Keeper of the Great Seal is also Speaker of the House of Lords. It is his duty ordinarily to attend as Speaker, to sit on the Woolsack and to preside over the deliberations of the House, except when it is in Committee. He puts the Question on all Motions which are submitted to the House, but he has no power either to maintain order or to act in any way as the representative or mouthpiece of the House, unless the House confers the necessary authority upon him. He is responsible for the recall of the House during a period of adjournment. When royal commissions are issued for opening the Session, for giving the royal assent to bills, or for proroguing Parliament, the Lord Chancellor is usually the senior of the Commissioners, and reads the commission upon each occasion. He also reads the Speech from the Throne when Parliament is opened by Commission, or when the Sovereign is present but incapacitated. More usually, when the Sovereign opens the Session in person the Lord Chancellor stands on the right of the throne and hands to the Monarch the speech in which the Government policies and programme for the Session are announced.

The Lord Chancellor is a member of the Government and like other Peers he may take part in debate and vote. (*See also*: SPEAKER OF THE HOUSE OF LORDS.)

LORDS OF PARLIAMENT—*See* HOUSE OF LORDS, FUNCTIONS, POWERS AND MEMBERSHIP.

LORDS SPIRITUAL—The Archbishops of Canterbury and York, the Bishops of London, Durham and Winchester and twenty-one other diocesan Bishops of the Church of England according to their seniority of appointment to diocesan sees are members of the House of Lords and are collectively known as the Lords Spiritual. On his retirement, a Bishop ceases to be a member of the House of Lords but he is entitled to sit on the steps of the Throne and use the facilities of the House. A Bishop reads prayers (*qv*) before each sitting.

MEASURE—Any legislation concerning the Church of England may be contained in a Measure. After it has been approved by the Church's General Synod, a Measure is submitted to Parliament and considered by the Ecclesiastical Committee, a Committee of Members of both Houses. The Measure must then be approved by Resolution of both Houses and receive the Royal Assent before it becomes part of church law.

Neither the Ecclesiastical Committee nor either House has power to amend a Measure, but either House can reject it by disagreeing to the Resolution.

MEETING, HOURS OF—*See* BUSINESS, ARRANGEMENT OF.

MEMBERS' PAY, RESOURCES AND STAFF—For the year ending 31 March 2000 MPs are paid £47,008, and they are also entitled to an office costs allowance of up to £50,264 to meet general office expenses and secretarial and research assistance. MPs are responsible for engaging and paying their own personal staff. Other allowances are payable in respect of travel to and from the constituency, other travel on parliamentary business and for accommodation for non-London MPs. MPs are provided with office accommodation (which sometimes has to be shared, though there has been an extensive programme of providing extra accommodation in outbuildings in recent years), and—for their parliamentary business—free telephone calls and postage within the United Kingdom and free stationery. Salaries are uprated in line with those of the senior civil service, and allowances in line with the movements in the retail price index.

Members of the House of Lords do not receive a salary but they receive expenses and allowances of various kinds. The most important of these are free travel to and from Westminster, an overnight and day subsistence allowance and a modest secretarial and office expenses allowance. All allowances must relate to attendance at the House. The total allowances claimable, excluding travel expenses, are £152.50 a day.

MONEY BILL—The Parliament Act 1911 defines a money bill as a public bill which, in the opinion of the Speaker, contains only provisions dealing with any of the following subjects—the imposition, repeal, remission, alteration, or regulation of taxation; the imposition for the payment of debt or other financial purposes of charges on the Consolidated Fund, or on money provided by Parliament, or the variation or repeal of any such charges; supply; the appropriation, receipt, custody, issue or audit of accounts of public money; the raising, or guarantee, or the repayment of any loan. The expressions, "taxation", "public money" and "loan", do not include any raised by local authorities or bodies for local purposes. For the restrictions on the power of the House of Lords in respect of Money Bills, *see* PARLIAMENT ACTS. Paradoxically, most Finance Bills are not Money Bills because they contain wider provisions than those strictly defined in the 1911 Act. However they are Bills of aids and supplies (*qv*).

MONEY RESOLUTION—The creation of a charge on public funds by a Bill is normally authorised by a "money resolution" which is normally taken forthwith after the Bill's second reading. If amendments passed later in a Bill's passage require, further money resolutions can be moved subsequently.

MOTIONS—With the exception of occasions like question time and ministerial statements, most proceedings or debates in Parliament are based on Motions: for example, "That the Bill be read a Second Time", "That the Amendment be made" or "That this House has no confidence in Her Majesty's Government". The Motion is proposed or "made" by a Member, is "put" from the Chair, normally debated and then decided by the House, on a division if necessary. A substantive motion generally requires notice and can only be made by the Member in whose name it stands on the Order Paper, except a motion standing in the name of a Member of the Government, which can be moved by any other Minister. (Certain formal motions mainly relating to the transaction of business do not require notice.) A motion can only be withdrawn by the unanimous leave of the House. Seconders are not required, except, by custom, for the address in reply to the Queen's Speech and on ceremonial occasions. Amendments may be proposed to most Motions (*see* AMENDMENTS).

NAMING A MEMBER—*See* CONDUCT OF MEMBERS.

NATIONAL AUDIT OFFICE—The National Audit Office (NAO) was created by the National Audit Act 1983. Its head is the Comptroller and Auditor General, who is an officer of the House of Commons. The NAO examine the accounts of government departments and certain public bodies and the Comptroller reports on these to the House of Commons. He also has the statutory power to examine the economy, efficiency and effectiveness in the use of resources by government departments and various other bodies in receipt of public funds and to report to the House on these matters. The Comptroller is also responsible for controlling the issue of money sanctioned by Parliament.

NEW PARLIAMENT—Before it begins its work, a new Parliament has certain ceremonial and domestic tasks to perform. Both Houses meet in their respective Chambers before the Commons are summoned to the Lords. The Lord Chancellor there reads the Royal Commission and requires the Commons to elect a Speaker. The Commons return to their Chamber, and, under the Chairmanship of the Father of the House (*qv*), elect a Speaker. The next day the Commons return to the Lords, and present the Speaker-elect for royal approbation. In a formal exchange of speeches, the Lord Chancellor on behalf of the Crown promises that the Commons will receive "all their ancient and undoubted rights". The Commons again return to their Chamber, and MPs take the oath, the Speaker doing so first. In the Lords, Peers may take the oath on both these days.

Several days later, the State opening of Parliament takes place, with the Queen's Speech setting out the business for the Session. Real political work in the respective Chambers then begins.

NORTHSTEAD, MANOR OF—*See* BY-ELECTION.

OATH—No Member of either House may sit or vote without making the oath or affirmation of allegiance to the Sovereign and her successors in the hearing of the House. The oath or affirmation must be repeated after each election. Members returned after by-elections normally take the oath or affirm after ministerial statements have been concluded in the Chamber. Peers sitting first in a new Parliament take the oath immediately after Prayers. In the Commons, Members who do not take the oath have only limited access to the facilities of the Palace.

OFFICIAL REPORT OF DEBATES—*See* HANSARD.

OMBUDSMAN—*See* PARLIAMENTARY COMMISSIONER FOR ADMINISTRATION

OPPOSITION DAY—There are 20 of these each session. On 17 of the days, the Leader of the Opposition decides the topic for debate, and on three days the choice rests with the Leader of the second largest opposition party.

ORDER—*See* RESOLUTION.

ORDER IN THE HOUSE—*See* CONDUCT OF MEMBERS.

ORDER OF BUSINESS—In the Commons, the daily Order of Business paper contains notice of the oral Questions, Motions, Orders of the Day (*qv*) and other business to be considered on that day. It also gives notice of Committee meetings. The Order of Business forms part of the daily Vote. As well as the Order of Business, there is a paper called "Future Business", which is divided into three sections: (a) listing business for the week ahead; (b) listing business for which no day has been fixed; and (c) listing business for other named future days. The Government largely has control over the make-up of each day's "effective" Order of Business and such of its own business as it does not want considered that day is consigned to section (b). A Summary Agenda is also published daily, and there has been an attempt since October 1997 to make Vote papers more informative and easier to understand.

ORDERS OF THE DAY—These are the stages of bills and other matters already ordered to be taken into consideration, and so forming part of the appointed business of each day's sitting. An order of the day becomes "dropped" if no action is taken upon it when it is called, or if, when the moment of interruption is reached, no day is named for its resumption. Each day's agenda is called "Orders of the Day and Notices of Motions".

OUTLAWRIES BILL—To show their independence of the Crown, both Houses consider for form's sake a bill of their own choice at the very beginning of each session before considering the Queen's Speech. In the Commons, this is the Outlawries Bill, in the Lords the Select Vestries Bill.

PAIRING—Pairing is an unofficial system under which two MPs, one from each of the two major parties, agree to be absent from the Chamber from particular votes or for agreed periods of time. In this way the government's majority is not affected by absences.

PAPERS, MOVING FOR—In the House of Lords a common method of initiating a general debate is for a peer to call attention to a matter "and to move for papers". Since this is a debating device, the motion is generally withdrawn at the conclusion of the debate.

PARLIAMENT—Formally, the Legislature of Parliament consists of the two Houses, the Commons and the Lords, convened by royal authority and acting jointly with the Crown. The Crown, Lords Temporal and Spiritual and Commons are sometimes referred to as the "three branches of the Legislature". The power of Parliament has, in the British constitution, traditionally been regarded as transcendent and subject to no limitation whatever, other than those accepted by Parliament in connection with membership of the European Union. An Act of Parliament can apply to any citizen, and can even bind the Sovereign.

PARLIAMENT ACTS 1911 AND 1949—The Parliament Acts 1911 and 1949 allow legislation to be passed without the concurrence of the House of Lords. Under the Acts, if a money bill, having been passed by the House of Commons, and sent up to the House of Lords at least one month before the end of the session, is not passed by the Lords without amendment within one month after it has been sent up, the bill shall, unless the House of Commons direct to the contrary, be presented to the Sovereign and become an Act when the Royal Assent is given, even though the House of Lords have not consented to the bill. If any public bill (other than a money bill) is passed by the House of Commons in two successive sessions—whether of the same Parliament or not—and having been sent up to the House of Lords at least one month before the end of the session, is rejected by the Lords in each of these sessions, that bill shall, on its rejection for the second time by the Lords, unless the House of Commons direct to the contrary, be presented to the Sovereign and become an Act when the Royal Assent is given, even though the Lords have not consented to the bill. This provision can not take effect unless one year has elapsed between the date of the second reading in the first of those sessions in the House of Commons and the date on which it is passed by the Commons in the second session. In 1991 the War Crimes Act received Royal Assent under these provisions after the bill had been rejected by the Lords at second reading in two successive sessions. In December 1998 the European Parliamentary Elections Bill, which had been the subject of disagreement between the two Houses in the previous session, was rejected at second reading by the Lords and received Royal Assent in like manner. These are the only occasions since 1949 that the Parliament Acts have been invoked in this way. A Bill to extend the life of a Parliament (i.e. to postpone elections) is not subject to these provisions.

PARLIAMENTARY COMMISSIONER FOR ADMINISTRATION (or Ombudsman)—is responsible for investigating complaints referred to him by Members of the House of Commons from members of the public, who claim to have suffered injustice through maladministration by government departments and certain non-departmental public bodies. He also investigates complaints received directly from the public about the National Health Service or about the non-disclosure of official information.

PARLIAMENTARY COMMISSIONER FOR STANDARDS—The Parliamentary Commissioner for Standards was appointed in November 1995 to guide and monitor those issues relating to the interests and activities of Members of Parliament discussed in the First Report of the Committee on Standards in Public Life. Functions include maintaining and monitoring the operation of the Register of Members' Interests; and receiving and investigating complaints about the conduct of Members and reporting findings to the Committee on Standards and Privileges.

PARLIAMENTARY COUNSEL—Parliamentary Counsel are lawyers employed by the Government to draft Bills which the Government intends to present to Parliament.

PARLIAMENTARY PRIVATE SECRETARY—Parliamentary Private Secretaries (who are commonly referred to as PPSs) are backbench MPs from the government party who are chosen by individual Cabinet Ministers and Ministers of State to assist them in their parliamentary duties. They are not paid a salary and are not Ministers, though they are not supposed to vote against government policy.

PETITION, PUBLIC—Advice on the rules which govern the admissibility of public petitions is available from the Clerk of Public Petitions at the House of Commons. Petitions must set out the reasons why the Petitioner(s) is/are petitioning the House; they must conclude with a specific request that the House should do something which it is within its powers to do; the top copy of the petition must be hand-written, and there are other restrictions on the form of petitions. Petitions are presented by Members. This is done before the half-hour adjournment debate on Mondays to Thursdays or after Prayers on Fridays. No debate is allowed except on the very rare petitions "complaining of some present personal grievance, for which there may be an urgent necessity for providing an immediate remedy." Normally MPs must restrict themselves to a brief statement on the source of the petition, the number of signatures and subject matter. Petitions may also be presented without any activity in the Chamber, simply by placing them in the bag kept for the purpose behind the Speaker's chair. However a petition is presented, it is printed and circulated with the Vote. A copy is sent for comment to the appropriate government department. In turn, the government comments (if any) are also printed and circulated with the Vote.

Public Petitions may also be presented in the Lords but they are now rare. They are presented by a Member of the House who confines himself to reading out the prayer and stating the number of petitioners who have signed. A petition is not printed unless a Lord puts down a motion to debate it on a particular day.

POINT OF ORDER—MPs may draw attention to procedural problems by rising "on a point of order", if necessary interrupting a speech in progress, and addressing the Chair from whom they seek a ruling. Points of order may not normally be raised during question time, and on most sitting days some minutes are given over to "points of order" at the end of ministerial statements and before the main business of the day.

PRAYER—*See* DELEGATED LEGISLATION.

PRAYERS—Each House begins each day's sitting with Prayers, which in the Lords are read by a Lord spiritual or a Peer who is a clergyman of the Church of England, and in the House of Commons by the Speaker's Chaplain.

PREVIOUS QUESTION, MOVING THE—Moving the previous question is a procedural device which allows the House to move on to its next business without coming to any decision on the matter before it at the time. The device is very rarely used.

PRIVATE MEMBERS' TIME—A "Private Member" is also called a "backbencher". He or she is an MP who is neither a Minister nor a shadow minister. The general rule of the Commons is that Government business has precedence at every sitting. However, under Standing Orders, 13 Fridays each Session are set aside for Private Members' Bills. Precedence between bills is initially determined by ballot. On and after the eighth Friday on which Private Members' Bills have precedence, priority is given to those bills which have made most progress—except that bills whose report stage has been adjourned fall below consideration of reports not already entered upon. Time constraints are so severe that it is difficult for a controversial bill to make progress unless government time is given to it. This has not happened for some years. Further opportunities for Private Members to initiate matters arise on the daily half-hour adjournment debate; in the Wednesday morning adjournment debates in Westminster Hall; on emergency adjournment motions under S.O. No. 24; on the procedure under the Ten Minute Rule; and in the regular questioning of Ministers. Backbenchers are also, of course, called to speak on government bills and government and opposition motions. In the Lords, Peers have an unrestricted right to introduce Private Members' Bills, and time is normally found to consider them on the floor of House. While only a few of these bills reach Royal Assent (because of the limitations on Private Members' time in the Commons) they nevertheless provide a useful method of floating legislative proposals. One Wednesday a month is given over to debating backbench motions (*see* BALLOT) and members may also table questions (*qv*), including debatable "unstarred" questions, to ministers.

PRIVILEGE—Each House has a number of privileges or special rights and immunities beyond those normally held by non-parliamentary bodies. Parliamentary privilege is extensive, but its limits are not always clear. For this reason, both Houses appoint Committees to help ascertain these limits in individual cases. However, parliamentary privilege may not be extended into new areas without specific statutory authority. The most important areas covered by the Houses' privilege are: (1) the right to regulate their own internal affairs and procedure free from interference by the courts (2) the right to institute enquiries and to require the attendance of witnesses and the production of documents (3) the right to punish persons guilty of breaches of privilege and contempt and (4) the right to publish papers without being subject to any action for defamation. The only substantial privilege of individual Members of Parliament is freedom of speech, though they are also exempt from jury service and from obeying subpoenas. Questions of privilege take precedence over any other business in the Chamber. However, in the Commons, when the facts are known in advance, it is necessary to seek the Speaker's permission before raising a matter of privilege in the Chamber. The most usual allegation of breach of privilege is that an MP or other person has committed a contempt of the House by actions that obstruct its working or tend to bring it into disrepute. If the Speaker is satisfied that a *prima facie* breach of privilege has occurred, he or she will announce so in the Chamber, and on the following day the MP who has raised the issue is able to move a motion to refer the matter to the Committee on Standards and Privileges. This is decided upon by the whole House, if necessary by a vote. The Committee on Standards and Privileges enquires into the affair and produces a report which in due course is debated by the House.

In the House of Lords questions of privilege are normally taken after question time. Matters of privilege may be referred to the Committee for Privileges. The Committee for Privileges formerly determined claims of peerage and will, in future, determine any claim of eligibility to stand in a by-election for a seat as an "excepted" Hereditary Peer.

A Joint Committee of both Houses has recently conducted an extensive review of parliamentary privilege.

PROGRAMMING—*See* CLOSURE.

PROROGATION—*See* SESSIONAL ORGANISATION.

PROVISIONAL ORDER—*See* BILLS, PROVISIONAL ORDER

QUEEN—The Queen is one Estate of Parliament. Bills only become Acts when they receive the Royal Assent (*qv*) and the form of Statutory Instrument known as an Order in Council can be made only by the Queen in Council. The Queen's recommendation is required to sanction any proposal for a charge on public funds, and her consent is necessary for any Bill affecting the Royal prerogative, hereditary revenues, personal property or interests of the Crown. The Queen is also responsible for dissolving or proroguing Parliament. Peerages are also created in the Queen's name. The only occasion on which she normally attends Parliament is to open it on the day of State Opening at the beginning of a new Session when she delivers the Queen's Speech in the House of Lords to the assembled Lords, Commons, judges and diplomatic corps. The speech sets out the Government's programme for the coming Session.

As well as having these parliamentary functions, foreign relations are conducted in the Queen's name; she is responsible for declaring war or concluding peace; she directs the armed forces, and she is the source of justice and of mercy and of all honours and many offices. However, functions which Sovereigns once exercised in person are now largely exercised by Ministers on her behalf or by her on the advice of Ministers. These Ministers must be members of one House of Parliament. The choice of the Prime Minister remains the Sovereign's, but she must take account of the acceptability of her choice to a majority of the House of Commons.

MPs are restricted in the references which they may make to the Queen and her family in debate or in motions. Since King Charles I entered the Commons Chamber in 1642 to arrest five Members, no Sovereign has attended Commons debates, even as a spectator. No such restriction applies in the Lords.

QUESTION—When a Motion is made in debate, the Speaker is said to "put a question" to the House. Once a question is before the House, it must be disposed of one way or another before the House can move on to next Business.

QUESTION, PRIVATE NOTICE—A private notice question (PNQ) is one which deals with a matter of particular urgency on which an MP wishes to secure an oral answer without any delay. He or she applies to the Speaker before noon (10 am on a Thursday or Friday) for the PNQ to be allowed, and the Speaker has absolute discretion whether or not to do so. The Speaker's decision is made known at 1 pm (soon after 10 am on Thursday or Friday) and a Minister attends to answer the question (and any supplementaries) that day at 3.30 pm (12.30 pm on a Thursday and 11 am on a Friday).

In the Lords, it is the Leader of the House who decides in the first instance whether a PNQ is of sufficient urgency to justify an immediate reply. Notice of such a question must be given by noon on the day it is proposed to ask it. Private Notice Questions are rare, and are taken immediately after starred questions (*qv*). Answers to Commons PNQs are often repeated as statements in the Lords.

QUESTIONS, PARLIAMENTARY—In the Commons, questions to Ministers for oral answer are taken on Mondays, Tuesdays and Wednesdays from about 2.35 to 3.30 pm (on Thursdays from 11.35 am to 12.30 pm). Ministers answer in accordance with a rota, drawn up in advance. The Prime Minister at present answers for half an hour on Wednesdays. Notice of questions for oral answer must be given in the Table Office by a Member in person at least three days before they are due to be answered. The maximum notice period is normally 10 sitting days. Because of the growth in the numbers of oral questions in recent years, it is effectively only those oral questions which are handed in with the maximum period of notice, which is usually between 10 am and 5 pm 10 sitting days in advance of the day on which they are due to be asked, which have any chance of receiving an oral answer.

Questions handed in between these hours are "shuffled" by computer and the order of oral questions is then determined, all having an equal chance of coming high in that order. Not all questions are published: between 40 and 50 are printed, depending on the length of time the minister concerned is due to answer questions. 20 questions to the Prime Minister are printed. Oral Questions handed in after 5 pm on the first tabling day are only accepted if these numbers have not been received. A Member is not entitled to have on the order paper more than two oral questions at the same sitting with one only to any particular Minister, but may, at the Speaker's discretion, put supplementary questions to elucidate answers given by Ministers.

There is no limit to the number of written questions which an MP may table. A Member may also designate a specific day on which he or she requires an answer—a minimum notice period is necessary. The MP asking the question receives written notification of the reply, and this is also published in Hansard.

There are various rules restricting the contents of both oral and written questions. The most fundamental of these is that they must relate only to areas for which Ministers have responsibility. For example, they must not deal with matters devolved to the Scottish Parliament or National Assembly for Wales. Advice on the rules for parliamentary questions in the Commons may be obtained from the Clerks in the Table Office.

Questions in the Lords are always addressed to Her Majesty's Government rather than to a particular minister. Every day at the beginning of business up to four "starred" questions (marked with a star on the Order Paper) may be asked. No Lord may have more than one starred question on the Order Paper at any one time. The fourth question each Wednesday and Thursday is a "topical" question tabled not before the previous Tuesday or Wednesday respectively and drawn by lot before the sitting of the House on the day on which it is to be taken. Peers may also table questions for written answer. At the end of business, by arrangement with the Whips Office, a Peer may also ask one "unstarred" question on which debate is permitted. These debates are akin to adjournment debates in the Commons. "Unstarred" questions may occasionally also be taken in the dinner adjournment of business on major bills. (*See also* QUESTIONS, PRIVATE NOTICE.)

QUORUM—There is no requirement in the Commons that a certain number of MPs be present for business to be transacted. However, if a division is called and fewer than 40 MPs (including the tellers and the occupant of the Chair) take part, the business under consideration stands over, and the next business is taken. It is possible to move "That the House sit in private" once in any sitting. This motion (on which the Question must be put forthwith) allows Members to ascertain whether 40 MPs are present. The quorum of a Standing Committee of the House of Commons is one third of the membership, or 17, whichever is the less, and debate cannot continue in the absence of a quorum. The quorum of a Select Committee is appointed by a Standing Order, or by the House, in each case.

The quorum of the House of Lords is three. But if, on a division upon any stage of a bill or on a motion to approve delegated legislation, fewer than 30 vote, the question is not decided and further debate is adjourned. The quorum of a Select Committee (unless otherwise ordered in the motion appointing the Committee) is also three.

RECALL OF PARLIAMENT—*See* SESSIONAL ORGANISATION

RECESS—*See* SESSIONAL ORGANISATION

RESIGNATION—*See* BY-ELECTION

RESOLUTION—The decisions of the House take the form of "Resolutions" or of "Orders". It is not always clear why the one or the other is used in the House's records. However, a typical example of a Resolution would be one in which the House's collective opinion on some matter were expressed, whereas an Order might set out some rule governing the House's future conduct.

ROYAL ASSENT—The action by which the Crown agrees to a Bill is known as Royal Assent. The moment the Royal Assent has been given, the Bill becomes an Act, and has the force and effect of law from the beginning of that day, unless some date for the commencement of its operation has been provided in the Act itself. Although the Royal Assent may be given by the Sovereign in person, robed, crowned and seated on the throne in the House of Lords, or by Royal Commissioners appointed for the purpose, the normal method is for the Lord Chancellor and the Speaker to interrupt proceedings in their respective Chambers at a convenient time, and to read out the titles of the Bills to which the Queen has given her assent and of which they have received documentary notice. Royal Assent is given by Royal Commissioners nowadays only at the end of the Session, just before prorogation. This allows the traditional ceremony to continue. The commissioners sit on the steps of the throne, and the Commons come to the bar of the Chamber. The titles of the bills are read out, and the Clerk of the Parliaments signifies the Queen's pleasure in Norman French. For a bill of supply, the phrase used is "La reine remercie ses bons sujets, accepte leur benevolence et ainsi le veult". For private and public bills, he says simply "La reine le veult". For personal bills, "Soit fait comme il est desiré." If Royal Assent were to be refused, the phrase would be "La reine s'avisera"—but this has not happened since 1707.

SALISBURY CONVENTION—This is the convention that the Lords do not reject at second reading any government legislation which carries out a manifesto commitment and which has been passed by the House of Commons. This was an understanding reached between the Conservative opposition in the Lords (led by the then Marquis of Salisbury) and the Labour government in 1945.

SECONDARY LEGISLATION—Secondary legislation is another term for delegated legislation (*qv*). It is contrasted with primary legislation, which is contained in Acts of Parliament (*qv*).

SELECT VESTRIES BILL—*See* OUTLAWRIES BILL.

SERJEANT AT ARMS—Each House has a Serjeant at Arms, appointed by the Crown. In the Lords, the Serjeant is also the Gentleman Usher of the Black Rod (*qv*). In the Commons, the Serjeant is responsible for some ceremonial duties, for housekeeping in the precincts and for security arrangements. Any warrant, for example for the attendance of a witness, would also be served by him.

SESSIONAL ORGANISATION—The sittings of both Houses are broken up in three ways: adjournment, prorogation and dissolution.

Each House may adjourn independently of the other. In the Lords, the House adjourns each day to a named day and hour. In the Commons, under Standing Orders, the House adjourns from day to day and from Fridays (or Thursdays, when Friday is a non-sitting day) to Mondays. However, both Houses also take "periodic adjournments" (sometimes, improperly, called recesses—see below). These need not be of the same length in both Houses. Roughly speaking, they last from two to three weeks at Christmas, a week each at Easter and the Spring holiday and 10 to 12 weeks in August, September and the first half of October. A "half term" adjournment in February is also likely from 2000. Both Houses have procedures allowing them to be recalled during an adjournment. The normal method is for the Lord Chancellor (or in his absence, the Lord Chairman) and the Speaker respectively to call the House together on a day earlier than that to which it has been adjourned. The initiative for requesting a recall of Parliament rests with the Government, who inform the Speaker and Lord Chancellor of their belief that the public interest requires a recall. Parliament must also meet within five days if the reserve forces are mobilised, or if a state of emergency is proclaimed under the Emergency Powers Act 1920.

Prorogation is generally an annual event which marks the end of a session of Parliament. In recent non-election years, a session has usually lasted from early or mid November to late October or early November, and the period of prorogation (which is properly called a recess) has been between 4 and 12 days. Both Houses are prorogued at the same time, and all unfinished business (except appeals to the House of Lords and private bills specifically exempted) is ended by prorogation. This means that the legislative programme of the government must be tailored to what can realistically be achieved in one year. It is also a major constraint on private members' bills. However, in session 1998-99, for the first time, a public bill was suspended at the end of the session, to be started again in session 1999-2000 at the stage which it had reached in the previous session. This may become more common in future. References to parliamentary events are frequently made by reference to the session in which they occurred. The beginning and end of each session is marked with ceremony: at the beginning, in the State Opening of the Session, the Queen delivers the Speech from the throne outlining the government's programme for the session ahead, and at the end another speech is made by the Lord Chancellor outlining the session's achievements before he announces the prorogation. On this occasion the Lord Chancellor, together with four other Lords Commissioners, sit on the steps of the throne in their parliamentary robes and the Commons are summoned to attend by Black Rod as they were at the beginning of the session.

A session can also be brought to a close by dissolution. Dissolution has the effect of bringing the whole Parliament to a close as well, and a general election will follow. In normal circumstances, there are four or five sessions in each parliament, though there may be only one as in 1974 when two general elections followed each other in the same year. The most recent Parliament was the 1992-97 Parliament, which was divided into the 1992-93, 1993-94, 1994-95, 1995-96 and 1996-97 Sessions. The "normal length" sessions were 1993-94, 1994-95 and 1995-96, with 1992-93 being long and 1996-97 short because of the timing of the dissolutions in 1992 and 1997.

See also ADJOURNMENT, DISSOLUTION.

SPEAKER (HOUSE OF COMMONS)—The Speaker is presiding officer of the House of Commons. The Mace is her symbol of office. Like her predecessors, the current Speaker is an MP herself, but ceased to belong to a political party on her election to the Chair.

The term "Speaker" derives from the Speaker's function as spokesman for the House of Commons. Most of the Speaker's modern functions are connected directly or indirectly with the control of proceedings. Because the Speaker commands the respect of the House, he or she is able to maintain order in the Chamber through personal authority. The Speaker's powers are also enhanced by Standing Orders. Rulings on matters of order may not be challenged except by the tabling of a Motion and these rulings establish precedent for future conduct. The Speaker has a number of specific functions under statute, and is *ex officio* Chairman of the House of Commons Commission (*qv*). The Speaker also has certain responsibilities for accommodation and services for MPs. Modern Speakers have always acted with impartiality, and have been willing to advise MPs of all parties who consult them privately.

A Speaker is elected by fellow MPs at the beginning of each new Parliament or when an incumbent has decided to resign. He or she holds office until the dissolution of the Parliament in which he or she was elected, and he or she is usually re-elected in the new Parliament. As a candidate at the General Election, he or she stands as the Speaker seeking re-election, and not with a party affiliation. More than one candidate can be proposed as Speaker. If this happens, the claims of each nominee are discussed in a debate and decided upon, if necessary, by a division. There can be a division if only one candidate is nominated. More usually, one agreed candidate is put forward and his or her election is proposed and seconded by senior backbenchers from the two sides of the House. When elected, the Speaker makes a speech of thanks, and then is congratulated by the Prime Minister, other party leaders and others.

The Speaker is paid a Cabinet Minister's salary. He or she is a Privy Counsellor, ranking next after the Lord President of the Council, and occupies a residence in the Palace of Westminster. At the end of their terms of office, Speakers are usually made Peers.

SPEAKER (HOUSE OF LORDS)—The Lord Chancellor is *ex officio* Speaker of the House of Lords. Deputy Speakers are appointed to act as Speaker during the absence of the Lord Chancellor. Lords appointed by the House as Deputy Chairmen may also act as Deputy Speakers. When the Lord Chancellor, the Deputy Speaker and Deputy Chairmen are absent, the House appoints any Lord to act temporarily as Speaker. The Speaker of the House of Lords, unlike the Speaker of the Commons, has no power or authority in matters of order. He puts the question from the Woolsack; he may speak in debate and vote in divisions, but has no casting vote. (*See also* LORD CHANCELLOR.)

STANDING ORDERS—The first Roll of Standing Orders was prepared in the Lords in 1621. Since then both Houses have passed Standing Orders which regulate their proceedings. These orders do not, however, provide a complete code of procedure, the greater part of which in the House of Commons is based upon custom, precedent and rulings from the Chair. There are also many resolutions governing the procedure of the House made in past Parliaments and continually observed without formally being termed Standing Orders: the seventeenth century rule against smoking in the Chamber is an interesting example. The Standing Orders are permanent and have effect until repealed. They can, however, be suspended for a particular purpose, though it is necessary for notice to be given and a motion moved for this to occur. It is also possible to make Standing Orders for the duration of one Parliament only. Copies of Standing Orders of both Houses may be obtained from the Parliamentary Bookshop.

STATEMENTS—When the Government wishes to announce a new policy initiative or give its views on some important matter, a minister will often make a statement to either House of Parliament. Most statements are made in the Commons and repeated, if requested by the Opposition, in the Lords. In both Houses statements are normally taken after question time. A statement will not be repeated in the other House until after it has been delivered in the House in which it originates. After delivery, there follows a period of comment and questions from the Opposition spokesmen and backbenchers.

STATUTORY INSTRUMENTS—*See* DELEGATED LEGISLATION.

STRANGERS—The term "stranger" is used to describe those who are not Members or officials of either House. Historically, strangers were excluded from Commons debates, but the public is now admitted to all debates in the Chamber, to Standing Committees and to most non-deliberative meetings of Select Committees. It remains possible for strangers to be excluded. The motion "that the House sit in private" may be moved without notice, but the Speaker is empowered by Standing Order to order the withdrawal of strangers.

SUBORDINATE LEGISLATION—*see* DELEGATED LEGISLATION.

SUPPLY—Supply expenditure is that part of public spending which can only be incurred with specific parliamentary authority. In the Queen's Speech at the beginning of each Session are included the words "Members of the House of Commons, Estimates for the Public Service will be laid before you". These Estimates are laid usually four times a year. The expenditure which they list is eventually authorised by Consolidated Fund or Appropriation Acts.

Before the financial year begins, a Vote on Account is presented, and after the year has ended any Excess Votes are also presented. The Main Estimates are usually presented in March and they and the Summer Supplementary Estimates (presented in July) must be agreed by 5th August. In November or December and in February, the Winter and Spring Supplementary Estimates are presented. These must be voted, respectively, by 6th February and 18th March.

Appropriation Accounts are proposed at the end of the financial year. As well as the formal voting of the Estimates, three days each session are allotted for the consideration of specific Estimates. Estimates for debate are proposed by the Liaison Committee (*qv*) whose recommendation must be endorsed by the House. The House, if it agrees with the Committee's recommendations, debates government Motions that Supply be voted to cover the estimate, to which Amendments, if selected by the Speaker or the Deputy Speaker, may be moved. All questions necessary to dispose of proceedings are deferred until ten o'clock. Amendments cannot be proposed, whether by a Minister or any other Member, to increase the amount in the estimate. If an increase is necessary, the original estimate must be withdrawn and a revised estimate presented. The three days allotted for consideration of the estimates may coincide with the days on which specific blocks of Supply expenditure have to be voted, but need not necessarily do so.

TAX SIMPLIFICATION BILLS—Special expedited procedures apply to bills intended to simplify tax law. The procedures include committal to a Joint Committee.

TEN MINUTE RULE—Ten Minute Rule Bills are so described because their introduction is proposed by backbenchers at the beginning of public business on Tuesdays and Wednesdays usually from the seventh week of a session (but not on Budget day) by means of a single speech limited to ten minutes. If the Bill is opposed, one ten-minute speech is also permitted against it, and the House may divide on the question of whether the MP proposing the introduction of the Bill should have leave to do so. Not more than one ten-minute rule motion may be made on any one sitting day, and there are restrictions on the notice which may be given. Ten Minute Rule Motions are popular because of the opportunity which they give backbenchers to canvass legislative ideas. However, even when leave is given for the Bill to be introduced, it will still face the considerable hurdles which private members' bills must surmount in the Commons. The Ten Minute rule procedure can also be used by Ministers to introduce bills or by any member to nominate a Select Committee. These uses are extremely rare.

TIMETABLING—In the Commons, some bills may be subject to timetabling or programming or guillotine motions (*see* CLOSURE). Individual pieces of business may also be subject to time limits because of the Standing Orders or a special Business of the House order. However, an informal timetable for the business of each House is determined by the Government's business managers (*see* WHIPS) and agreed in the "usual channels". This informal timetable is always liable to last-minute change or even disruption as the House responds to events outside. Much legislation is now subject either to formal programming motions fixing its timetable, or to informal arrangements between the usual channels, or to a combination of both. *See also* GUILLOTINE.

USUAL CHANNELS—*see* WHIPS.

VOTES AND PROCEEDINGS—The daily—and rather laconic—minutes of the Commons proceedings are known as the Votes and Proceedings. This document is published each sitting day and, together with the Order of Business and other material for the business of the House and its Committees, constitutes the "Vote".

WAYS AND MEANS—Ways and Means is the term used for the provision of revenue to meet national expenditure and to influence the national economy. All taxes, duties, revenue, imposts and loans are first considered as Ways and Means Resolutions. For example, the Budget proposals are set out in Ways and Means Resolutions on which the Finance Bill is said to be founded. The Lords may reject, but cannot modify those parts of a bill which are founded on Ways and Means Resolutions.

WESTMINSTER HALL—For an experimental period starting in November 1999 the House has sat in Westminster Hall. This is a parallel but subordinate Chamber in the former Grand Committee Room off Westminster Hall. The intention is to provide more opportunity to discuss less controversial issues which are often squeezed out from the floor of the House. Procedure largely follows the procedure of the House. The times of meetings are on Tuesdays from 10 am to 1 pm; on Wednesdays from 9.30 am to 2 pm, and on Thursdays from 2.30 pm to 5.30 pm (plus time for suspensions for divisions in the House). All Members may take part. Private Members' business (adjournment debates) is taken on Tuesdays and Wednesdays. Business on Thursdays is appointed by Chairman of Ways and Means following consultations through the usual channels and is announced in the Business Statement. This includes debates on Reports of Select Committees. The Chairman of Ways and Means and the two Deputy Chairman and four Additional Deputy Speakers appointed by the House for the purpose sit as Deputy Speaker. The quorum is three. No votes are taken at sittings in Westminster Hall, but if the opinion of the Chair as to the decision of a question (on collecting voices) is challenged, the Deputy Speaker so reports to the House (where the Question is put immediately). On business other than adjournment debates, if six Members signify objection to further proceedings, that business cannot be proceeded with. Standing orders dealing with selection of amendments, dilatory motions, irrelevance or repetition and short speeches apply to sittings in Westminster Hall. Papers for the sitting are published in the Vote Bundle and notices appear in the Order of Business/Future Business paper.

WHIPS—In both Houses Members are appointed by the parties to organize attendance at debates and in divisions. The Government Whips receive salaries (the Government Chief Whip in the Commons is the Parliamentary Secretary to the Treasury and other senior Whips hold office in the Treasury and the Royal Household) and so do certain Opposition Whips. The announcement of business circulated weekly among members of a party is referred to as the Whip. It indicates, by underlining, the importance that is attached to attendance at particular business. A "three line" Whip is the most urgent summons.

In both Houses the Whips Offices of all the parties are collectively known as the "usual channels". The Government Whips' Office in each House is responsible for arranging the business, in consultation where appropriate through the "usual channels" with the Whips of other parties.

The Government Chief Whips and the Leaders of the two Houses are sometimes referred to as the "business managers".

WHITE PAPER—Government papers presented to Parliament and which are statements of policy are known generally as White Papers. "Green Papers" are documents published for consultative purposes before the final formulation of policy. House of Commons Committee Reports are printed with blue covers, House of Lords reports with red covers. In recent times there has been a great variety in the covers of the other documents presented to Parliament. (*See also* COMMAND PAPER.)

WITNESSES—Either House may summon witnesses to give evidence to it. Evidence is given on oath and refusal to attend is a breach of privilege. Most witnesses in modern times give expert evidence to Select Committees, attend voluntarily by invitation of the Committee and do not give sworn evidence. However, they can be required to attend and are bound to answer all questions which the Committees may pose. Witnesses' expenses are met, and it is a contempt (and possibly a criminal offence under the Witnesses (Public Inquiries) Protection Act 1892) for those outside the House to take action against a witness because of evidence he or she may have given.

WOOLSACK—*see* HOUSE OF LORDS (CHAMBER)

WRIT OF SUMMONS—Writs of Summons are issued by direction of the Lord Chancellor from the Office of the Clerk of the Crown in Chancery. New Writs are issued before the meeting of each Parliament to all Lords spiritual and temporal who are members of the House of Lords. Writs in a slightly different form are also issued to any newly created Life Peers or to any Hereditary Peer who during the course of a Parliament becomes eligible to sit by filling a vacancy caused by the death of one of the Hereditary Peers "excepted" from the provisions of the House of Lords Act 1999.

WRITS—The writs for the election of a new Parliament are issued by the Lord Chancellor upon a warrant from the Sovereign in Council and, for a by-election during a Parliament, by order of the House or upon the Speaker's warrant. A motion for a writ to fill a vacancy caused by death, or by acceptance of a disqualifying office or government contract, or by accession to the peerage, or by bankruptcy or by mental illness, etc., is usually moved in the House of Commons by the Chief Whip of the Party to which the Member whose seat is vacated belonged. Power exists for vacancies caused by death, by acceptance of office and by accession to the peerage, to be filled when the House is in recess. On receipt of a notice signed by two Members certifying the cause of the vacancy and applying for a new writ to be issued, the Speaker inserts a notice in the London Gazette and, six days after such notice appears, issues a warrant to the Clerk of the Crown for the preparation of a new writ to fill the vacancy. Similar power exists to fill a vacancy caused by bankruptcy, but writs cannot be issued during a recess on acceptance of the Chiltern Hundreds or similar offices or on account of mental illness.

Electoral Dates

The Representation of the People Act 1983 sets out the timetable for parliamentary elections. In the case of a General Election, the last day for the delivery of nomination papers is the sixth day after the date of the proclamation summoning the new Parliament, and the poll is held in every constituency on the eleventh day after the last day for delivery of nomination papers. In the case of a by-election, the last day for the delivery of nomination papers is fixed by the Returning Officer and must be not earlier than the third day after the date of publication of the notice of election nor later than the seventh day after that on which the writ is received. Polling takes place on the day fixed by the Returning Officer, which is not earlier than the ninth nor later than the eleventh day after the last day for delivery of nomination papers. In calculating these dates, a Sunday, a Saturday, Christmas Eve, Christmas Day, Maundy Thursday, Good Friday, a bank holiday and a day appointed for public thanksgiving or mourning are disregarded.

Thus the whole process from the last sitting of the old Parliament to the State Opening of the new took just over seven weeks in 1992 and almost six weeks in 1997. The 1997 timetable ran as follows:

Friday 21 March: Parliament met for the last time and was prorogued.

Tuesday 8 April: Parliament dissolved.

Thursday 1 May: General Election.

Wednesday 7 May: Parliament meets pursuant to the Proclamation of 8 April to swear members and, in the Commons, to elect a Speaker.

Wednesday 14 May: State Opening of Parliament.

Breakdown of Seats by Country

England: 529 seats; Scotland: 72 seats; Wales: 40 seats; Northern Ireland: 18 seats.

Parliamentary Franchise

A person resident in the United Kingdom on the annual qualifying date (10 October) (15 September in Northern Ireland) is entitled to be entered on the register of electors if he or she is (a) a British or other Commonwealth citizen or a citizen of the Republic of Ireland, and
(b) is at least 18 years of age (or will become 18 during the currency of the register) and is not otherwise disqualified. Under the Representation of the People Act 1985, certain British citizens resident abroad may also vote in parliamentary elections.

Parliamentary Candidates

A candidate must be at least 21 years old.

Each candidate must deposit £500 with the Returning Officer at the time of nomination. This sum is returned when he has taken the oath, if elected, or if he is not elected but has polled 5% of the number of votes polled, otherwise the deposit is forefeited.

The maximum expenditure which may be incurred by a candidate is £4965 plus, in a county constituency, 5.6p and, in a borough constituency, 4.2p for every entry in the Register of Electors to be used at the election (as first published). These figures are approximately quadrupled in the case of a by-election.

The Returning Officer's expenses are paid by the Treasury.

Number of Voters

In 1999 there was a total of 44,388,885 names on the parliamentary electoral register of the United Kingdom. This is broken down as follows: England 36,947,525; Scotland 4,011,450; Wales 2,227,571; and Northern Ireland 1,202,339.

Bibliography

Adonis, A. *Parliament Today*, Manchester University Press, 2nd edition, 1993.

Bagehot, W. *The English Constitution*, Introduction by R. H. S. Crossman. London, Fontana, 1963.

Biffen, John. *Inside the House of Commons*, Grafton, 1989.

Bradshaw, K. A., and Pring, D. A. M. *Parliament and Congress*. Quartet Books, Revised Edition, 1981.

Butler, D. and Kavanagh, D. *The British General Election of 1997*. London, Macmillan, 1997.

Cook, Sir Robert. *The Palace of Westminster*. Burton Skira, 1987.

Crewe, Ivor and Fox A. *British Parliamentary Constituencies: A Statistical Compendium*. London, Faber, 1984.

de Smith, S. A. *Constitutional and Administrative Law*, 8th edn. Penguin, 1998.

Drewry, G. (ed.) *The New Select Committees*. Oxford, 2nd Ed., 1989.

Englefield, D. J. T. *Westminster and Whitehall*. Longman, 1985.

Englefield, D. J. T. (Ed.) *Workings of Westminster*. Dartmouth, 1991.

Evans, Paul. *Handbook of House of Commons Procedure*, 2nd edition, Vacher Dod Publishing, 1999.

Fell, Sir Bryan and Mackenzie, K. R. *The Houses of Parliament: A guide to the Palace of Westminster*, 15th edn. Editor: D. L. Natzler. London, HMSO, 1994.

Franklin, Mark and Norton, Philip (eds.). *Parliamentary Questions*, Oxford, 1993.

Garrett, John, *Westminster—Does Parliament Work?* Gollancz, 1992.

Giddings, Philip and Drewry, Gavin (eds.), *Westminster and Europe*. Macmillan 1995.

Griffith, J. A. G. *Parliamentary Scrutiny of Government Bills*. London, Allen & Unwin, 1974.

Griffith J. A. G. and Ryle M. T., *Parliament*, Sweet and Maxwell, 1989.

Jones, Christopher. *The Great Palace: the Story of Parliament*. London, BBC Books, 1983.

Judge, D. (ed.). *The Politics of Parliamentary Reform*. Heinemann, 1983.

Liaison Select Committee. *The Select Committee System* (HC Paper 92 (1982–83)), HMSO.

McDonald, Oonagh, *Parliament at Work*, Methuen, 1989.

May, Sir T. Erskine. *Parliamentary Practice*, 22nd edn. London, Butterworth, 1997.

Miers, D. and Page, A., *Legislation*, Sweet and Maxwell, 2nd edition 1990.

Norton, Philip. *The Commons in Perspective*, Martin Robertson, 1981.

Norton, Philip, *Legislatures*, Oxford, 1990.

Norton, Philip (ed.), *National Parliaments and the European Union*, Frank Cass, 1996.

Norton, Philip (ed.). *Parliament in the 1980's*. Basil Blackwell, 1985.

Radice, L., Vallance, E. and Willis, V. *Member of Parliament*. London, Macmillan, 1987.

Riddell, P. *Parliament Under Pressure*. London, Gollancz, 1997.

Rush, Michael (ed), *Parliament and Pressure Groups*, Oxford, 1990.

Rush, Michael, *Parliamentary Government in Britain*. Pitman, 1981.

Ryle, M. and Richards, P. *The Commons Under Scrutiny*, Routledge, 1988.

Ryle, M and Griffith, J. *Parliament*, Sweet and Maxwell, 1989.

Shell, Donald. *The House of Lords*, Harvester Wheatsheaf, 2nd edition, 1992.

Shell, Donald and Beamish, David (eds.). *The House of Lords at Work*, Oxford, 1993.

Silk, Paul and Walters, Rhodri. *How Parliament Works*, 4th edn. Longman, 1998.

Walkland, S. A. *The Legislative Process in Great Britain*. London, Allen & Unwin, 1968, and *The House of Commons in the Twentieth Century*. Oxford University Press, 1979.

Parliamentary Papers (including Hansard and the Votes and Proceedings) are available from the Parliamentary Bookshop, or from the Stationery Office. Various fact sheets are also available from the Public Information Offices of both Houses (see Index).

Abbreviations

AA	Automobile Association	AIF	Australian Imperial Forces
AAA	Amateur Athletic Association	AIM	Alternative Investment Market
ABRO	Army Base Repair Organisation	ALG	Association of London Government
ABSDA	Army Base Storage and Distribution Agency	AM	Assembly Member
AC	Companion of the Order of Australia	AMA	Association of Metropolitan Authorities
ACA	Associate, Institute of Chartered Accountants	AMS	Additional Member System
		AMS	Army Medical Services
ACAS	Advisory, Conciliation and Arbitration Service	AMS	Assistant Military Secretary
		ANAF	Arab Non-Arab Friendship
ACC	Anglican Consultative Council	ANZAC	Australia and New Zealand All-Party Committee
ACC	Association of County Councils		
ACCA	Association of Chartered Certified Accountants	AOC	Association of Colleges
		APACS	Association for Payment Clearing Services
ACCAC	Qualifications, Curriculum and Assessment Authority for Wales	APC	Army Personnel Centre
		APEX	Association of Professional, Executive, Clerical and Computer Staff
ACE	Action for Community Employment		
ACF	Army Cadet Force		
ACF	Association of Charitable Foundations	APGOOD	All-Party Parliamentary Group on Overseas Development
ACHCEW	Association of Community Health Councils for England and Wales	ARA	Associate, Royal Academy
		ARCM	Associate, Royal College of Music
ACOPS	Advisory Committee on Protection of the Sea	ARCS	Associate, Royal College of Science
		ARICS	Professional Associate, Royal Institution of Chartered Surveyors
ACP	African/Caribbean/Pacific		
ACPO	Association of Chief Police Officers	ASA	Advertising Standards Authority
ACRE	Action with Communities in Rural England	ASEAN	Association of South East Asian Nations
ACTT	Association of Cinematograph, Television and Allied Technicians	ASLEF	Associated Society of Locomotive Engineers and Firemen
ADC	Aide-de-camp	ASLIB	Association of Special Libraries and Information Bureaux (now Association for Information Management)
AE	Air Efficiency Award		
AEC	Agriculture Executive Council		
AEC	Atomic Energy Commission		
AEEU	Amalgamated Engineering and Electrical Union	ASTMS	Association of Scientific, Technical and Management Staffs (now part of MSF, qv)
AEF	Amalgamated Union of Engineering and Foundry Workers		
		ATII	Associate Member, Incorporated Institute of Taxation
AEP	Association of Electricity Producers		
AERE	Atomic Energy Research Establishment (Harwell)	ATRA	Army Training and Recruiting Agency
AEU	Amalgamated Engineering Union	ATSA	Army Technical Support Agency
AFC	Air Force Cross	AUA	Association of University Administrators
AFFOR	All Faiths for One Race		
AFHQ	Allied Force Headquarters	AUC	Air Transport Users Council
AFPAA	Armed Forces Personnel Administration Agency	AUEW	Amalgamated Union of Engineering Workers
AFPRB	Armed Forces' Pay Review Body	BA	Bachelor of Arts
AGI	Association for Geographic Information	BA	Benefits Agency
		BAA	British Airports Authority
Agric	Agricultural	BAFTA	British Academy of Film and Television Arts
Agric	Agriculture		
ai	ad interim	BBA	British Board of Agre{a}ment
AIB	Associate, Institute of Bankers		

BBC	British Broadcasting Corporation	CABE	Commission for Architecture and the Built Environment
BBSRC	Biotechnology and Biological Sciences Research Council	CAC	Central Arbitration Committee
BCC	British Chambers of Commerce	CAFOD	Catholic Aid Fund for Overseas Development
BCCI	Bank of Credit and Commerce International	Cantab	Cantabrigiensis (of Cambridge)
BChir	Bachelor of Surgery	CAO	Chief Adjudication Officer
BCL	Bachelor of Civil Law	Capt	Captain
BCom	Bachelor of Commerce	CAS	Central Adjudication Services
BD	Bachelor of Divinity	CB	Companion of the Order of the Bath
BDA	British Dental Association	CBC	County Borough Council
BDS	Business Development Service	CBE	Commander of the Order of the British Empire
BECTa	British Educational Communications and Technology agency	CBI	Confederation of British Industry
BECTU	Broadcasting, Entertainment, Cinematograph and Theatre Union	CBIM	Companion, British Institute of Management
		CC	City Council
BEd	Bachelor of Education	CC	County Council
BEF	British Equestrian Federation	CC	Cricket Club
BEF	British Expeditionary Force	CCBI	Council of Churches for Britain and Ireland
BEM	British Empire Medal		
BFI	British Film Institute	CCF	Combined Cadet Force
BFPO	British Forces Post Office	CCLRC	Council for the Central Laboratory of the Research Councils
BIC	British-Irish Council		
BIGC	British-Irish Governmental Conference	CCSO	Chief Child Support Officer
		CCTA	Central Computer and Telecommunications Agency
BIS	Bank for International Settlements		
BLESMA	British Limbless Ex-Servicemen's Association	CCW	Countryside Council for Wales
		CD	Canadian Forces Decoration
BLitt	Bachelor of Literature	CDA	Co-operative Development Agency
BMA	British Medical Association	CDC	Commonwealth Development Corporation
BMus	Bachelor of Music		
BNAF	British North Africa Force	CDipAF	Certified Diploma in Accounting and Finance
BNIF	British Nuclear Industry Forum		
BOAC	British Overseas Airways Corporation	CDS	Chief of the Defence Staff
		CEE	Communaute{a} Economique Europe{a}enne
BPA	British Ports Association		
BR	British Rail	CEFAS	Centre for Environment, Fisheries and Aquaculture Science
BRB	British Railways Board		
BRC	British Retail Consortium	CEG	Consumers in Europe Group
BRCS	British Red Cross Society	CEGB	Central Electricity Generating Board
BRE	Building Research Establishment	CEng	Chartered Engineer
BSc	Bachelor of Science	CertEd	Certificate of Education
BSI	British Standards Institution	CFF	National Funding Formula
Bt	Baronet	CH	Companion of Honour
BT	British Telecommunication Plc	ChB	Bachelor of Surgery
BTA	British Tourist Authority	CHC	Community Health Council
BUPA	British United Provident Association	CHD	Coronary Heart Disease
BURA	British Urban Regeneration Association	Chev	Chevalier
		ChM	Master of Surgery
BWI	British West Indies	CI	Imperial Order of the Crown of India
BYC	British Youth Council		
C	Conservative	CICA	Criminal Injuries Compensation Authority
C-in-C	Commander-in-Chief		
CA	Contributions Agency	CICAP	Criminal Injuries Compensation Appeals Panel
CAA	Civil Aviation Authority		

CICB	Criminal Injuries Compensation Board		CSI	Committee on the Intelligence Services
CIE	Companion of the Order of the Indian Empire		CSI	Companion of the Order of the Star of India
CIMA	Chartered Institute of Management Accountants		CSL	Central Science Laboratory
			CST	Council for Science and Technology
CIPFA	Chartered Institute of Public Finance and Accountancy		CStJ	Commander, Most Venerable Order of the Hospital of St. John of Jerusalem
CIS	Institute of Chartered Secretaries and Administrators		CTBI	Churches Together in Britain and Ireland
CIT	Chartered Institute of Transport		CVCP	Committee of Vice-Chancellors and Principals of the Universities of the UK
CITB	Construction Industry Training Board			
CITES	Convention on International Trade in Endangered Species		CVO	Commander of the Royal Victorian Order
CITU	Central IT Unit			
CIU	Club and Institute Union		CVS	Council for Voluntary Service
CLA	Country Landowners' Association		CWP	Community Work Programme
CLP	Constituency Labour Party		CWS	Co-operative Wholesale Society
CMG	Companion of the Order of St Michael and St George		CWU	Communication Workers Union
			DANI	Department of Agriculture for Northern Ireland
CML	Council of Mortgage Lenders			
CNAA	Council for National Academic Awards		DARA	Defence Aviation Repair Agency
			DASA	Defence Analytical Services Agency
CND	Campaign for Nuclear Disarmament			
CNT	Commission for the New Towns		DBA	Defence Bills Agency
COHSE	Confederation of Health Service Employees (see Unison)		DBE	Dame Commander of the Order of the British Empire
COI	Central Office of Information		DC	District Council
Con	Conservative		DCA	Defence Codification Agency
COPUS	Committee on the Public Understanding of Science		DCB	Dame Commander of the Order of the Bath
COSHEP	Committee of Scottish Higher Education Principals		DCL	Doctor of Civil Law
			DCM	Distinguished Conduct Medal
COSLA	Convention of Scottish Local Authorities		DCMG	Dame Commander of the Order of St Michael and St George
CPA	Commonwealth Parliamentary Association		DCMS	Department for Culture, Media and Sport
CPAS	Church Pastoral Aid Society		DCSA	Defence Communication Services Agency
CPC	Conservative Political Centre			
CPRE	Council for the Protection of Rural England		DCTA	Defence Clothing and Textiles Agency
CPS	Crown Prosecution Service		DCVO	Dame Commander of the Royal Victorian Order
cr	Created			
CRE	Commission for Racial Equality		DD	Doctor of Divinity
CRP	Constitutional Reform Policy		DDA	Defence Dental Agency
CRP(EC)	Incorporation of the European Convention of Human Rights		DDRB	Review Body on Doctors' and Dentists' Remuneration
CRP(FOI)	Freedom of Information		DE	Defence Estates
CRP(HL)	House of Lords Reform		DENI	Department of Education for Northern Ireland
CRUCC	Central Rail Users' Consultative Committee			
			DERA	Defence Evaluation and Research Agency
CSA	Child Support Agency			
CSC	Civil Service College		DETR	Department of the Environment, Transport and the Regions
CSCE	Conference on Security and Co-operation in Europe			
			DFC	Distinguished Flying Cross

DfEE	Department for Education and Employment
DFID	Department for International Development
DFM	Distinguished Flying Medal
DHE	Defence Housing Executive
DHSS	Department of Health and Social Security
DI	Donor Insemination
DipAgriSci	Diploma in Agricultural Science
DipEd	Diploma in Education
DipObst	Diploma in Obstetrics
DISC	Defence Intelligence and Security Centre
DL	Deputy Lieutenant
DLI	Durham Light Infantry
DMO	UK Debt Management Office
DMS	Diploma in Management Studies
DMTO	Defence Medical Training Organisation
DoH	Department of Health
DOP	Defence and Overseas Policy
DOP(E)	European Issues
DOP(E)(T)	European Trade Issues
DP	Devolution Policy
DPA	Defence Procurement Agency
DPCSA	Defence Postal and Courier Services
DPH	Diploma in Public Health
DPhil	Doctor of Philosophy
Dr	Doctor
DSA	Disposal Sales Agency
DSA	Driving Standards Agency
DSC	Distinguished Service Cross
DSc	Doctor of Science
DSCA	Defence Secondary Care Agency
DSDA	Defence Storage and Distribution Agency
DSO	Distinguished Service Order
DSS	Department of Social Security
DStJ	Dame of Grace/Dame of Justice, Most Venerable Order of the Hospital of St. John of Jerusalem
DSTJ	Dame of Grace/or Dame of Justice, Order of the Hospital of St John of Jerusalem
DTI	Department of Trade and Industry
DTMA	Defence Transport and Movements Agency
DU	Doctor of the University
DUP	Democratic Unionist Party
DVA	Defence Vetting Agency
DVLA	Driver and Vehicle Licensing Agency
DVLNI	Driver and Vehicle Licensing Northern Ireland
DVTA	Driver & Vehicle Testing Agency

DYRMS	Duke of York's Royal Military School
E	England
EA	Economic Affairs
EA(N)	Energy Policy
EA(PC)	Productivity and Competitiveness
EA(WW)	Welfare to Work
EA	Environment Agency
EA	Executive Agency
EAA	Electricity Arbitration Association
EAL	Electricity Association Limited
EASL	Electricity Association Services Limited
EAT	Employment Appeal Tribunal
EC	European Community
ECA	Economic Commission for Africa (UN)
ECCCG	Electricity Consumers' Committees Chairmen's Group
ECCs	Electricity Consumers' Committees
ECE	Economic Commission for Europe (UN)
ECHR	European Convention of Human Rights
ECITB	Engineering Construction Industry Training Board
ECLAC	Economic Commission for Latin America and the Caribbean (UN)
Econ	Economics
EDC	Economic Development Committee
EDG	European Democratic Group
EEC	European Economic Community
EEF	Engineering Employers' Federation
EETPU	Electrical, Electronic Telecommunications and Plumbing Union
EHS	Environment and Heritage Service
ELLID	Employment, Lifelong Learning and International Directorate
EMTA	Engineering and Marine Training Authority
EMU	European Monetary Union
ENV	The Environment
EOC	Equal Opportunities Commission
EP	English Partnerships
EP	European Parliament
EPSRC	Engineering and Physical Sciences Research Council
ERD	Emergency Reserve Decoration (Army)
ES	Employment Service
ESCAP	Economic and Social Commission for Asia and the Pacific (UN)
ESCWA	Economic and Social Commission for Western Asia (UN)

ESRC	Economic and Social Research Council
ETS	Employment Tribunals Service
EU	European Union
FANY	First Aid Nursing Yeomanry
FAO	Food and Agriculture Organization of the UN
FAS	Funding Agency for Schools
FBA	Fellow, British Academy
FBIM	Fellow, British Institute of Management
FC	Football Club
FCCA	Fellow, Chartered Association of Certified Accountants
FCIM	Fellow, Chartered Institute of Marketing
FCIT	Fellow, Chartered Institute of Transport
FCO	Foreign and Commonwealth Office
FDA	Association of First Division Civil Servants
FEDA	Federation of Economic Development Authorities
FEFC	Further Education Funding Council
FEFCW	Further Education Funding Council for Wales
FFB	Food from Britain
FHCIMA	Fellow, Hotel, Catering and Institutional Management Association
FICE	Fellow, Institution of Civil Engineers
FICO	Financial Intermediaries and Claims Office
FIEE	Fellow, Institution of Electrical Engineers
FILA	Fellow, Institute of Landscape Architects
FIMechE	Fellow, Institution of Mechanical Engineers
FIMgt	Fellow, Institute of Management
FIMI	Fellow, Institute of the Motor Industry
FIMT	Fellow, Institute of the Motor Trade
FInstM	Fellow, Institute of Marketing
FInstPS	Fellow, Institute of Purchasing and Supply
FIQA	Fellow, Institute of Quality Assurance
FIRTE	Fellow, Institute of Road Transport Engineers
FKC	Fellow, King's College, London
FOI	Freedom of Information
FOS	Funeral Ombudsman Scheme
FPC	Family Practitioner Committee
FRAM	Fellow, Royal Academy of Music

FRAME	Fund for the Replacement of Animals in Medical Experiments
FRCA	Farming and Rural Conservation Agency
FRCOG	Fellow, Royal College of Obstetricians and Gynaecologists
FRCP	Fellow, Royal College of Physicians, London
FRCS	Fellow, Royal College of Surgeons of England
FRCVS	Fellow, Royal College of Veterinary Surgeons
FREng	Fellow, Royal Academy (formerly Fellowship) of Engineering
FRES	Federation of Recruitment and Employment Services
FRGS	Fellow, Royal Geographical Society
FRIBA	Fellow, Royal Institute of British Architects
FRPS	Fellow, Royal Photographic Society
FRS	Fellow, The Royal Society
FRS	Fisheries Research Services
FRSA	Fellow, Royal Society of Arts
FRSE	Fellow, The Royal Society of Edinburgh
FSA	Fellow, Society of Antiquaries
FSA	Financial Services Authority
FSAA	Fellow, Society of Incorporated Accountants and Auditors
FSANI	Forensic Science Agency of Northern Ireland
FSB	Federation of Small Businesses
FSOS	Financial Services Ombudsman Scheme
FSS	Forensic Science Service
GAC	Government Art Collection
GATT	General Agreement on Tariffs and Trade
GB	Great Britain
GBE	Knight or Dame Grand Cross of the Order of the British Empire
GC	George Cross
GCB	Knight or Dame Grand Cross of the Order of the Bath
GCCNI	General Consumer Council for Northern Ireland
GCDA	Government Car and Despatch Agency
GCIE	Knight Grand Commander, Order of the Indian Empire
GCMG	Knight or Dame Grand Cross of the Order of St Michael and St George
GCS	Government Car Service
GCSI	Knight Grand Commander, Order of the Star of India

GCVO	Knight or Dame Grand Cross of the Royal Victorian Order	Hon	Honourable
GDC	General Dental Council	HQ	Headquarters
GEST	Grant for Education, Support and Training	HRH	His (or Her) Royal Highness
		HRP	Historic Royal Palaces
GL	Local Government	HS	Health and Safety
GL(L)	London	HS	Home and Social Affairs
GLA	Greater London Assembly	HS(D)	Drug Misuse
GLA	Greater London Authority	HS(H)	Health Strategy
GLC	Greater London Council	HS(W)	Women's Issues
GM	Genetic Modification	HSC	Health and Safety Commission
GMB	General Municipal Boilermakers Union	HSE	Health and Safety Executive
		HSH	His (or Her) Serene Highness
GMBATU	General, Municipal, Boilermakers and Allied Trades Union (see GMB)	HSW	Health and Safety at Work
		I	Ireland
		IA	Indian Army
		IAEA	International Atomic Energy Agency (UN)
GMC	General Medical Council		
GMW	General Municipal Boilermakers and Allied Trades Union	IAS	Immigration Advisory Service
		IB	Intervention Board
GMWU	General Municipal Workers' Union	IBA	Independent Broadcasting Authority
GOC	General Officer Commanding	IBA	International Bar Association
GOC	General Optical Council	IBRD	International Bank for Reconstruction and Development (World Bank)
GOL	Government Office for London		
GP	General Practitioner		
GPA	Government Purchasing Agency	ICAO	International Civil Aviation Organization (UN)
GPDST	Girls' Public Day School Trust		
GPMU	Graphical, Paper, Media Union	ICE	Independent Case Examiner for the Child Support Agency
GPO	General Post Office		
GSO	General Staff Officer	ICFTU	International Confederation of Free Trade Unions
GSO1	General Staff Officer 1		
GTN	Government Telephone Network	ICPC	Independent Commission for Police Complaints for Northern Ireland
HAC	Honourable Artillery Company		
HACC	Heathrow Airport Consultative Committee	ICR	Independent Complaints Reviewer to HM Land Registry
HAT	Housing Action Trusts	ICRC	Inner Cities Religious Council
HAZ	Health Action Zones	ICRC	International Committee of the Red Cross
HBLB	Horserace Betting Levy Board		
HE	His (Her) Excellency	ICS	Indian Civil Service
HEA	Health Education Authority	ICS	Investors Compensation Scheme
HEFCE	Higher Education Funding Council for England	ICT	Information and Communications Technology
HEFCW	Higher Education Funding Council for Wales	IDA	International Development Association (World Bank)
HFEA	Human Fertilisation and Embryology Authority	IDB	Industrial Development Board
		IDC	Imperial Defence College
HGCA	Home-Grown Cereals Authority	IDS	InterDespatch Service
HHEW	Heads of Higher Education Institutions in Wales	IFAD	International Fund for Agricultural Development (UN)
HIE	Highlands and Islands Enterprise	IFC	International Finance Corporation (UN)
HLI	Highland Light Infantry		
HM	His (or Her) Majesty (Majesty's)	IFI	International Fund for Ireland
HMCI	Her Majesty's Chief Inspector	IFRC	International Federation of Red Cross and Red Crescent Societies
HMS	His (or Her) Majesty's Ship		
HMT	Her Majesty's Treasury	IFS	Institute for Fiscal Studies
HO	Home Office	IHO	Independent Housing Ombudsman Scheme
Hon	Honorary		

IHSM	Institute of Health Services Management	JCC	Joint Consultative Committee with the Liberal Democrat Party
IIC	International Institute for Conservation of Historic and Artistic Works	JNCC	Joint Nature Conservation Committee
		JP	Justice of the Peace
IiP	Investor in People	JSB	Judicial Studies Board
ILEX	Institute of Legal Executives	JSD	Doctor of Juristic Science
ILO	International Labour Office (or Organization)	KAR	King's African Rifles
		KBE	Knight Commander of the Order of the British Empire
ILT	Institute of Logistics and Transport		
IM	Institute of Management	KCB	Knight Commander of the Order of the Bath
IMF	International Monetary Fund (UN)		
IMO	International Maritime Organization (UN)	KCIE	Knight Commander of the Order of the Indian Empire
IMRO	Investment Management Regulatory Organisation	KCMG	Knight Commander of the Order of St Michael and St George
IN	Northern Ireland	KCSI	Knight Commander of the Order of the Star of India
Ind	Independent		
INSEAD	Institut Europe{a}en d'Administration des Affaires	KCVO	Knight Commander of the Royal Victorian Order
INSTRAW	International Research and Training Institute for the Advancement of Women (UN)	KG	Knight of the Order of the Garter
		KM	Knight of Malta
		KP	Knight, Order of St Patrick
INTELSAT	International Telecommunications Satellite Organization	KRRC	King's Royal Rifle Corps
		KStJ	Knight of the Most Venerable Order of the Hospital of St John of Jerusalem
INTERPOL	International Criminal Police Organization		
IOCA	Interception of Communications Act	KT	Knight of the Order of the Thistle
IOD	Institute of Directors	Kt	Knight Bachelor
IOM	International Organization for Migration	Kt	knighted
		Lab	Labour
IPT	Integrated Project Team	Lab Co-op	Labour Co-operative
IPU	Inter-Parliamentary Union	LACOTS	Local Authorities Co-Ordinating Body on Food and Trading Standards
IR	Inland Revenue		
IRS	Independent Review Service for The Social Fund		
		LAO	Lord of Appeal in Ordinary
IRTU	Industrial Research and Technology Unit	LAPADA	London and Provincial Dealers' Association
IS	Information Systems	LCC	London County Council (Later GLC)
ISC	Independent Schools Council		
ISIS	Independent Schools Information Service	LCCI	London Chamber of Commerce and Industry
ISO	Imperial Service Order	LDS	Licentiate in Dental Surgery
IT	Information Technology	LEA	Local Education Authority
ITC	Independent Television Commission	LEDU	Local Enterprise Development Unit
ITSA	Information Technology Services Agency	LEG	Legislation
		LG	Lady Companion, Order of the Garter
ITU	International Telecommunication Union (UN)		
		LGA	Local Government Association
IUA	International Underwriting Association	LGSM&D	Licentiate, Guildhall School of Music and Drama
IVF	*In Vitro* Fertilisation	LHS	Local Management of Schools
IWAAC	Inland Waterways Amenity Advisory Council	Lib Dem	Liberal Democrat
		LIBERTY	National Council for Civil Liberties
JARIC	Joint Air Reconnaissance Intelligence Centre	LIBiol	Licentiate, Institute of Biology

LISA	Logistic Information Systems Agency	MP	Member of Parliament
		MPH	Master of Public Health
LLB	Bachelor of Laws	MPhil	Master of Philosophy
LLD	Doctor of Laws	MRC	Medical Research Council
LLM	Master of Laws	MRCGP	Member, Royal College of General Practitioners
LRAM	Licentiate, Royal Academy of Music		
LRCP	Licentiate, Royal College of Physicians, London	MS	Master of Surgery
		MSA	Medical Supplies Agency
LRPC	London Regional Passengers' Committee	MSAE	Member, Society of Automotive Engineers (USA)
LRT	London Regional Transport	MSc	Master of Science
LSE	London School of Economics	MSC	Manpower Services Commission
LSS	RAF Logistics Support Services	MSDA	Military Survey Defence Agency
LT	London Transport	MSF	Manufacturing Science Finance Union
LTS	Lands Tribunal for Scotland		
LVO	Lieutenant of the Royal Victorian Order	MSP	Member of Scottish Parliament
		MSPFW	MSP for Falkirk West
LWT	London Weekend Television	MVO	Member of the Royal Victorian Order
MA	Master of Arts		
MAFF	Ministry of Agriculture, Fisheries and Food	NA	National Academician (USA)
		NAC	National Agriculture Centre
MB	Bachelor of Medicine	NACAB	National Association of Citizens' Advice Bureaux
MBA	Master of Business Administration		
MBC	Metropolitan Borough Council	NACRO	National Association for the Care and Resettlement of Offenders
MBE	Member of the Order of the British Empire		
		NALGO	National and Local Government Officers' Association (see Unison)
MC	Military Cross		
MCA	Maritime and Coastguard Agency		
MCA	Medicines Control Agency	NAO	National Audit Office
MD	Doctor of Medicine	NAPRB	Review Body for Nursing Staff, Midwives, Health Visitors and Professions Allied to Medicine
mda	Museum Documentation Association		
MDA	Medical Devices Agency		
MDC	Metropolitan District Council	NARO	Naval Aircraft Repair Organisation
MDP	Ministry of Defence Police Agency		
ME	Myalgic Encephalomyelitis	NAS	National Academy of Sciences
MEd	Master of Education	NAS	National Archives of Scotland
MELF	Middle East Land Forces	NATFHE	National Association of Teachers in Further and Higher Education
MEP	Member of the European Parliament		
MFCM	Member, Faculty of Community Medicine	NATO	North Atlantic Treaty Organization
		NATS	National Air Traffic Services
MGC	Museums and Galleries Commission	NBA	National Blood Authority
MHS	Meat Hygiene Service	NBSA	Naval Bases and Supply Agency
MIBiol	Member, Institute of Biology	NCB	National Coal Board
MICE	Member, Institution of Civil Engineers	NCC	National Consumer Council
		NCVO	National Council for Voluntary Organisations
MIMechE	Member, Institution of Mechanical Engineers		
		NCVQ	National Council for Vocational Qualifications
MIMinE	Member, Institution of Mining Engineers		
		NDPB	Non-Departmental Public Body
MISC	Miscellaneous	NEC	National Executive Committee
MLA	Member of Legislative Assembly	NECC	National Electricity Consumers' Council
MM	Military Medal		
MN	Merchant Navy	NEDC	National Economic Development Council
MO	Medical Officer		
MO	Military Operations	NERC	Natural Environment Research Council
MoD	Ministry of Defence		

NFCG	National Federation of Consumer Groups	NY	New York
NFER	National Foundation for Educational Research	OAU	Organisation for African Unity
		OBE	Officer of the Order of the British Empire
NFU	National Farmers' Union	OC	Officer Commanding
NGO	Non-governmental Organisation	OC	Officer, Order of Canada
NHBC	National House-Building Council	ODI	Overseas Development Institute
NHS	National Health Service	OECD	Organisation for Economic Co-Operation and Development
NIACAB	Northern Ireland Association of Citizens Advice Bureaux		
		OFFER	Office of Electricity Regulation
NIACT	Northern Ireland Advisory Committee on Telecommunications	OFGAS	Office of Gas Supply
		OFGEM	Office of Gas and Electricity Markets
NIAO	Northern Ireland Audit Office	OFLOT	Office of the National Lottery
NIBSC	National Institute for Biological Standards and Control	OFREG	Office for the Regulation of Electricity and Gas
NICO	National Insurance Contributions Office	OFSTED	Office for Standards in Education
		OFT	Office of Fair Trading
NICO	Northern Ireland Company Overseas	OFTEL	Office of Telecommunications
NIH	North Irish Horse	OFWAT	Office of Water Services
NILO	National Investment and Loans Office	OGD	Other Government Departments
		OHMCI W	HM Chief Inspector of Schools, Wales
NIO	Northern Ireland Office		
NIPS	Northern Ireland Prison Service	OLA	Other Lords of Appeal
NISRA	Northern Ireland Statistics and Research Agency	O & M	organisation and method
		OM	Order of Merit
NITB	Northern Ireland Tourist Board	OME	Office of Manpower Economics
NLCB	National Lottery Charities Board	ONS	Office for National Statistics
NLP	Natural Law Party	OP	Organo Phosphate Group
NMA	Naval Manning Agency	OPA	Oil and Pipelines Agency
NMEC	New Millennium Experience Company	OPEC	Organization of the Petroleum Exporting Countries
NMGM	National Museums and Galleries on Merseyside	OPRA	Occupational Pensions Regulatory Authority
NMS	National Museums of Scotland	OPRAF	Office of Passenger Rail Franchising
NPFA	National Playing Fields Association	OPS	Office of Public Service
NRA	National Rifle Association	ORR	Office of the Rail Regulator
NRA	National Rivers Authority	OS	Ordnance Survey
NRPB	National Radiological Protection Board	OSA	Office of the Subsidence Adviser
		OSCE	Organisation on Security and Co-operation in Europe
NRTA	Naval Recruiting and Training Agency		
		OSNI	Ordnance Survey of Northern Ireland
NS	National Savings		
NS	Nova Scotia	OSS	Office for the Supervision of Solicitors
NSMC	North-South Ministerial Council		
NSPCC	National Society for Prevention of Cruelty to Children	OSSW	Office of the Secretary of State for Wales
NUJ	National Union of Journalists	OStJ	Officer of the Most Venerable Order of the Hospital of St John of Jerusalem
NUM	National Union of Mineworkers		
NUPE	National Union of Public Employees (see Unison)		
		OTC	Officers' Training Corps
NUR	National Union of Railwaymen	OU	Open University
NUT	National Union of Teachers	OU	Oxford University
NVQ	National Vocational Qualification	PA	Personal Assistant
NWML	National Weights and Measures Laboratory	PAC	Public Accounts Committee
		PACE	Property Advisers to the Civil Estate

PACTS	Parliamentary Advisory Council for Transport Safety	PSX	Public Services and Public Expenditure
PAM	Professions Allied to Medicine	PTO	Public Trust Office
PAO	Prince Albert's Own	PWO	Prince of Wales's Own
PASEG	Parliamentary Astronomy and Space Environment Group	QAA	Quality Assurance Agency for Higher Education
PC	Privy Counsellor	QC	Queen's Counsel
PC	Productivity and Competitiveness	QCA	Qualifications and Curriculum Authority
PC	Plaid Cymru	QFL	Queen's Speeches and Future Legislation
PCA	Police Complaints Authority		
PCC	Press Complaints Commission	QMG	Quartermaster General
PE	Procurement Executive	QPM	Queen's Police Medal
PES	Public Expenditure Survey	QSO	Queen's Service Order (New Zealand)
PGCE	Post Graduage Certificate of Education	QUB	Queen's University, Belfast
PHAB	Physically Handicapped and Able-bodied	qv	quod vide (which see)
		QVS	Queen Victoria School
PhD	Doctor of Philosophy	RA	Radiocommunications Agency
PHLS	Public Health Laboratory Service Board	RA	Royal Academician
		RA	Royal Regiment of Artillery
PIA	Personal Investment Authority	RAC	Royal Agricultural College
PINS	Planning Inspectorate	RAC	Royal Automobile Club
PITCOM	Parliamentary Information Technology Committee	RACS	Royal Arsenal Co-operative Society
		RAF	Royal Air Force
PIU	Performance and Innovation Unit	RAFMGDA	RAF Maintenance Group Defence Agency
PLA	Port of London Authority		
Pl C	Plaid Cymru	RAFPMA	RAF Personnel Management Agency
plc	Public Limited Company		
PLP	Parliamentary Labour Party	RAFSEE	RAF Signals Engineering Establishment
PMB	Private Member's Bill		
PMPA	Public Management and Policy Association	RAF TGDA	RAF Training Group Defence Agency
PO	Post Office	RAFVR	Royal Air Force Volunteer Reserve
POEU	Post Office Engineering Union	RAMC	Royal Army Medical Corps
POST	Parliamentary Office of Science and Technology	RAPC	Royal Army Pay Corps
		RAPS	Rent Assessment Panels
POUNC	Post Office Users' National Council	RARO	Regular Army Reserve of Officers
PoW	Prisoner of War	RASC	Royal Army Service Corps
PPA	Pay and Personnel Agency	RASE	Royal Agricultural Society of England
PPARC	Particle Physics and Astronomy Research Council		
		RAuxAF	Royal Auxiliary Air Force
PPE	Philosophy, Politics and Economics	RC	Roman Catholic
PPS	Parliamentary Private Secretary	RCA	Rate Collection Agency
PPS	Political Planning Services	RCAC	Royal Canadian Armoured Corps
PR	Proportional Representation	RCAHMS	Royal Commission on the Ancient and Historical Monuments of Scotland
PR	Public Relations		
PRASEG	Parliamentary Renewable and Sustainable Energy Group		
		RCAHMW	Royal Commission on the Ancient and Historical Monuments of Wales
PRO	Public Record Office		
PRONI	Public Record Office of Northern Ireland		
		RCT	Royal Corps of Transport
PSA	Public Services Agreement	RCVS	Royal College of Veterinary Surgeons
psc	Graduate of Staff College		
PSD	Pesticides Safety Directorate	RD	Royal Naval and Royal Marine Forces Reserve Decoration
PSI	Policy Studies Institute		

RDA	Regional Development Agency	SAIF	National Society of Allied and Independent Funeral Directors
RDC	Rural Development Commission		
RDC	Rural District Council	SASA	Scottish Agricultural Science Agency
RE	Royal Engineers		
REME	Royal Electrical and Mechanical Engineers	SBAC	Society of British Aerospace Companies
Retd LAO	Retired Lord of Appeal in Ordinary	SCAA	School Curriculum and Assessment Authority
Rev	Reverend	SCC	Scottish Consumer Council
RFAC	Royal Fine Art Commission	SCE	Service Children's Education
RFC	Royal Flying Corps	SCET	Scottish Council for Educational Technology
RFC	Rugby Football Club		
RGN	Registered General Nurse	SCS	Senior Civil Servant
RGS	Royal Geographical Society	SDLP	Social Democratic and Labour Party
RHG	Royal Horse Guards		
RI	Rhode Island	SDP	Social Democratic Party
RICS	Royal Institution of Chartered Surveyors	SECS	Scottish Executive Corporate Services
RIIA	Royal Institute of International Affairs	SEDD	Scottish Executive Development Department
RLC	Royal Logistics Corps	SEED	Scottish Executive Education Department
RMC	Royal Military College (now RMA)		
RMN	Registered Mental Nurse	SEEDA	South East of England Development Agency
RMT	Rail, Maritime and Transport Union		
RN	Royal Navy	SEELLD	Scottish Executive Enterprise and Lifelong Learning Department
RNIB	Royal National Institute for the Blind		
		SEF	Scottish Executive Finance
RNLI	Royal National Lifeboat Institution	SEHD	Scottish Executive Health Department
RNR	Royal Navy Reserve		
RNVR	Royal Naval Volunteer Reserve	SEJD	Scottish Executive Justice Department
ROSA	Rent Office Service Agreements		
RPMS	Royal Postgraduate Medical School	SEO	Society of Education Officers
RPSGB	Royal Pharmaceutical Society of Great Britain	SEPA	Scottish Environment Protection Agency
RSA	Royal Society for the Encouragement of Arts, Manufactures and Commerce	SERAD	Scottish Executive Rural Affairs Department
		SERC	Science and Engineering Research Council
RSC	Royal Society of Chemistry		
RSO	Resident Surgical Officer	SES	Scottish Executive Secretariat
RSPB	Royal Society for the Protection of Birds	SF	Sinn Fein
		SFEFC	Scottish Further Education Funding Council
RSPCA	Royal Society for the Prevention of Cruelty to Animals		
		SFO	Serious Fraud Office
Rt Hon	The Right Honourable	SFPA	Scottish Fisheries Protection Agency
Rt Rev	The Right Reverend	SHAC	London Housing Aid Centre
RUCC	Rail Users' Consultative Committee	SHAEF	Supreme Headquarters, Allied Expeditionary Force
RUR	Royal Ulster Regiment		
RUSI	Royal United Services Institute	SHAPE	Supreme Headquarters, Allied Powers, Europe
RYS	Royal Yacht Squadron		
S	Scotland	SHEFC	Scottish Higher Education Funding Council
SA	South Africa		
SA	South Australia	SIs	Statutory Instruments
SAAS	Student Awards Agency for Scotland	SITPRO	Simpler Trade Procedures Board
SAC	Scottish Arts Council	SLC	Student Loans Company
SACOT	Scottish Advisory Committee on Telecommunications	SLD	Scottish Liberal Democrats
		SLD	Social and Liberal Democrats

SMMT	Society of Motor Manufacturers and Traders Ltd
SNH	Scottish Natural Heritage
SNP	Scottish National Party
SOGAT	Society of Graphical and Allied Trades
SOLACE	Society of Local Authority Chief Executives
SP	Scottish Parliament
SPCB	Scottish Parliament Corporate Body
SPPA	Scottish Public Pensions Agency
SPS	Scottish Prison Service
SPS	Specialist Procurement Services
SPUC	Society for the Protection of the Unborn Child
SQA	Scottish Qualifications Authority
SRB	Single Regeneration Budget
SRC	Science Research Council
SRC	Students' Representative Council
SRN	State Registered Nurse
SRO	Supplementary Reserve of Officers
SS	Saints
SSA	Ships Support Agency
SSA	Social Security Agency
SSAC	Social Security Advisory Committee
SSAFA	Soldiers', Sailors' and Airmen's Families Association
SSC	Solicitor before Supreme Court (Scotland)
SSEB	South of Scotland Electricity Board
SSP	Scottish Socialist Party
SSRA	Shadow Strategic Rail Authority
SSRB	Review Body on Senior Salaries
SSRC	Social Science Research Council
SSSI	Sites of Special Scientific Interest
STRB	School Teachers' Review Body
STV	Single Transferable Vote
SVQ	Scottish Vocational Qualification
T&AF	Territorial and Auxiliary Forces
TA	Territorial Army
TARO	Territorial Army Reserve of Officers
TASS	Technical Administrative and Supervisory Section of MSF (qv)
TAVRA	Territorial Auxiliary and Volunteer Reserve Association
TBA	The Buying Agency
TCPA	Town and Country Planning Association
TD	Territorial Efficiency Decoration
TEA	Training and Employment Agency
TEC	Training and Enterprise Council
TGO	Timber Growers' Association
TGWU	Transport and General Workers Union
TL	Team Leader
TOTE	Horserace Totalisator Board

TTA	Teacher Training Agency
TU	Trade Union
TUC	Trades Union Congress
TUPE	Transfer of Undertakings (Protection of Employment Regulation)
TV	Television
UC	University College
UCATT	Union of Construction, Allied Trades and Technicians
UCH	University College Hospital (London)
UCL	University College London
UDC	Urban Development Corporation
UDC	Urban District Council
UDUP	Ulster Democratic Unionist Party
UGC	University Grants Committee
UK	United Kingdom
UKAEA	United Kingdom Atomic Energy Authority
UKCC	United Kingdom Central Council for Nursing, Midwifery and Health Visiting
UKHO	United Kingdom Hydrographic Office
UK Sport	United Kingdom Sports Council
UKU	United Kingdom Unionist
UKUP	United Kingdom Unionist Party
ULTRA	Unrelated Live Transplant Regulatory Authority
UMIST	University of Manchester Institute of Science and Technology
UN	United Nations
UNCTAD	United Nations Conference on Trade and Development
UNDCP	United Nations International Drug Control Programme
UNDP	United Nations Development Programme
UNEP	United Nations Environment Programme
UNESCO	United Nations Educational, Scientific and Cultural Organization
UNFICYP	United Nations Force in Cyprus
UNFPA	United Nations Population Fund
UNHCR	United Nations High Commissioner for Refugees
UNICEF	United Nations Children's Fund
UNICRI	United Nations Inter-Regional Crime and Justice Research Institute
UNIDIR	United Nations Institute for Disarmament Research
UNIDO	United Nations Industrial Development Organization

UNISON	(an amalgamation of COHSE, NALGO and NUPE)	VMD	Veterinary Medicines Directorate
		VR	Volunteer Reserve
UNITAR	United Nations Institute for Training and Research	VRD	Royal Naval Volunteer Reserve Officers' Decoration
UNOG	United Nations Office at Geneva	WAAF	Women's Auxiliary Air Force
UNRISD	United Nations Research Institute for Social Development	WCL	Wildlife and Countryside Link
		WDA	Welsh Development Agency
UNRWA	United Nations Relief and Works Agency for Palestine Refugees in the Near East	WEA	Workers' Educational Association
		WEU	Western European Union
		WFP	World Food Programme (UN)
UNU	United Nations University	WFTU	World Federation of Trade Unions
UPU	Universal Postal Union (UN)	WHO	World Health Organization (UN)
URA	Urban Regeneration Agency	WIPO	World Intellectual Property Organization (UN)
US	United States		
USA	United States of America	WLGA	Welsh Local Government Association
USDAW	Union of Shop Distributive and Allied Workers	WMO	World Meteorological Organization (UN)
UUP	Ulster Unionist Party		
UUUC	United Ulster Unionist Coalition	WNC	Women's National Commission
VC	Victoria Cross	WS	Writer to the Signet
VCA	Vehicle Certification Agency	WTO	World Tourism Organization (UN)
VI	Vehicle Inspectorate	WTO	World Trade Organization
VLA	Valuation and Lands Agency	WW	Welfare to Work
VLA	Veterinary Laboratories Agency	YC	Young Conservative

Government Relations
and
Parliamentary Consultants'
Directory

Vacher Dod Publishing Limited
PO Box 3700, Westminster
London, SW1E 5NP
Tel: 020 7828 7256
Fax: 020 7828 7269
E-mail: politics@vacherdod.co.uk
Websites: www.vacherdod.co.uk
www.politicallinks.co.uk

GOVERNMENT RELATIONS AND PARLIAMENTARY CONSULTANTS

ADVANCE COMMUNICATIONS

Advance Communications offers monitoring, counselling and strategic planning services relating to all aspects of the political and government system in the UK and Europe. The company has particular specialisation in the healthcare field.

The company operates from its London base office using affiliates in Strasbourg and Brussels.

A range of businesses and charities of all sizes benefit from the company's many combined years of experience in this field.

For further information please contact:

Berkeley Greenwood

Advance Communications
3/19 Holmbush Road, Putney
London SW15 3LE
Tel: 020 8780 9110
Fax: 020 8789 0795
E-mail:
advance@portcullisresearch.com

Advocacy

Advocacy is an independent public affairs consultancy with high professional standards and a record of success.

It develops and executes public affairs strategies for national and international companies; local authorities and public bodies; professional, trade and voluntary associations and trade unions.

For information please contact:

Fred Silvester
Managing Director

Advocacy Limited
1 Queen Anne's Gate
London
SW1H 9BT

Tel: 020 7233 1066
Fax: 020 7233 1067
E-mail: lobby@advocacy.co.uk

APCO UK
Public Affairs and Strategic Communications

APCO UK, a London based strategic communications and public affairs consultancy is part of the APCO Worldwide network, which provides support to clients whose operating environment is affected by political, regulatory and communications issues. Our expertise includes: Political monitoring, government and media relations, coalition building, grassroots campaigning, corporate positioning, community relations, corporate citizenship, internal communications and technology services.

Number of UK staff: 38

Senior Directors:
Rosemary Grogan, Simon Milton, Nick DeLuca.

For further information please contact:

Managing Director: Nick DeLuca
APCO UK
95 New Cavendish Street
London W1M 7FR
Tel: 020 7526 3600
Fax: 020 7526 3699
E-mail: ndeluca@apcouk.com
Home Page: http://www.apco.net

APCO Europe
Joint Managing Directors:
Mark Dober, Brad Staples
Tel: 00 32 2 282 4848
Fax: 00 32 2 282 4849
E-mail:
bstaples@apco-europe.com
Home Page:
http://www.apcoassoc.com

APCO France
Managing Director:
Claire Boussagol
Tel: 00 33 1 44 94 86 66
Fax: 00 33 1 44 94 86 68
E-mail: mail@apco-fr.com
Home Page: www.apco.co.uk

APCO Geneva
Managing Director: John Weekes
Tel: 00 41 22 747 78 66
Fax: 00 41 22 747 79 66
E-mail: jweekes@apco-europe.com
Home Page: http://www.apco.net

BEAUMARK
LONDON • BRUSSELS

Beaumark provides expert public affairs guidance on Westminster, Whitehall and the institutions of the European Union. Beaumark consultants have proven expertise across the political parties and can demonstrate in-depth knowledge of the political process and parliamentary procedure

Consultancy services range from political research and strategic advice through to full political representation and advocacy.

Contact: David Bennett,
Managing Director,
Beaumark Ltd,
14 Great College Street,
London SW1P 3RX
Tel: 020 7222-1371
Fax: 020 7222-1440
E-mail:
info@beaumark.ndirect.co.uk
Website: www.beaumark.com

Europe Analytica
Av. Livingstone 26 (Bte 3)
B-1000 Brussels, Belgium
Tel: 0032-2-231-1299

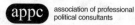
appc association of professional political consultants

B·K·S·H
Government Relations Worldwide

BKSH offers a seamless government relations service across Europe and the US. We give clients the total political picture and deliver measurable results.

BKSH is the government relations arm of **Burson-Marsteller**'s Public Affairs Practice, which offers full public issues campaign management and strategy, grassroots mobilisation, advocacy advertising, media relations, NGO dialogue and internet campaigning.

Contact:

Ian Lindsley
Director, UK
BKSH
24-28 Bloomsbury Way
London WC1A 2PX
Tel: 020 7300 6160
Fax: 020 7404 2360

CENTRAL LOBBY CONSULTANTS

CLC is a well-established independent consultancy, specialising in Government and political analysis in the UK and within the EU. CLC offers clients a comprehensive public affairs support service including:
· Political monitoring
· Policy analysis
· Legislative interpretation
· Strategic advice
· Campaign planning.
CLC has over 12 years' experience advising a broad range of clients about the political environment.

For further advice and information please contact:
Heather Cantley
Central Lobby Consultants
12 Little College Street
London SW1P 3SH
Tel: 020 7222 1265
Fax: 020 7222 1250

Citigate Public Affairs

The Strategic Public Policy Advisers

Citigate Public Affairs provides the full range of public affairs support – intelligence gathering, opinion forming, profile building and strategic advice. The consultancy is based in Westminster, and has offices in Brussels, Edinburgh and Cardiff. It is a member of the APPC and the PRCA. Members of the consultancy have extensive professional experience within each of the main UK political parties, the civil service and the voluntary sector. Political monitoring is provided by a specialist in-house team.

For more information about how we might help you, please contact:
Warwick Smith
Managing Director
Citigate Public Affairs
26 Grosvenor Gardens
London SW1W 0GT
Tel: 020 7838 4800
Fax: 020 7838 4801
Email: info@citigatepa.co.uk

The Communication Group plc

The Government and Political Affairs Division of the Communication Group implements results-driven, coherent and effective public affairs strategies. It is also able to offer integrated expertise across the spectrum of corporate, financial and consumer public relations. The company has offices in London, Edinburgh and Brussels and is a shareholder in Entente with offices across Europe.

For further information please contact:
Mark Adams
Managing Director
Political Division
The Communication Group plc
19 Buckingham Gate
London SW1E 6LB
Tel: 020 7630 1411
Fax: 020 7931 7800
E-mail: political@tcg-pr.co.uk
Website: www.tcg-pr.co.uk
Entente International
Communication SA
7 Rue Theresienne
1000 Bruxelles
Tel: 00 32 2/502 15 58
Fax: 00 32 2/502 48 69

CSM PARLIAMENTARY CONSULTANTS LTD

Founded in 1974, CSM is a small and independent consultancy with an all-graduate staff. No payments have ever been made to MPs or Peers. Services include monitoring, research, counselling and the handling of specific problems in the UK and EU institutions.

Associate company in Washington DC.

For further information please contact:
Christine Stewart Munro

Appleby House
46 St James's Place
London SW1A 1NS
Tel: 020 7355 3222
Fax: 020 7355 4774
E-mail: info@csm.prestel.co.uk

DECISION MAKERS LTD

Make your voice heard

International experts in anticipating and acting upon legislative proposals from Brussels, Westminster, Central and Eastern Europe.

Specialist areas of expertise: Funding, Project Management, Strategic Thinking, Change/Crisis Management, Transport, IT, Environment, Health, Local Government.

For further information contact:
Maureen Tomison (European Woman of Achievement)

Decision Makers Ltd
UK T +44 20 7233 9988
**   F +44 20 7233 9977**
politics@decisionmakers.co.uk

Brussels T +32 2 227 1178
**   F +32 2 218 3141**

France   T +33 6 09 31 94 51

www.decisionmakers.co.uk

Dod *on* Disk

The Vacher Dod

Parliamentary Database

that will run

on your PC

or Network

For further details

please telephone

the Westminster Office

020 7828 7256

GOVERNMENT RELATIONS AND PARLIAMENTARY CONSULTANTS (cont)

DYSON BELL MARTIN

PARLIAMENTARY AND PUBLIC AFFAIRS

The specialist law firm for Parliamentary and Public Affairs

We provide cost-effective, professional advice and support on all aspects of the governmental, policy-making, legislative and regulatory processes of the United Kingdom and the European Union.

Our services include: Constitutional and procedural advice; Policy research and analysis; Legislative drafting.

For further information, please contact:

Westminster – Jonathan Bracken
1 Dean Farrar Street
Westminster, London SW1H 0DY
Tel: +44 (0)20 7222 9458
Fax: +44 (0)20 7222 0650

Edinburgh – Ian McCulloch
1-3 St. Colme Street
Edinburgh EH3 6AA
Tel: +44 (0)131 220 8294
Fax: +44 (0)131 220 8394

Cardiff – Robert Owen
Temple Court, Cathedral Road
Cardiff CF11 9HA
Tel: +44 (0)29 2078 6574
Fax: +44 (0)29 2078 6573

Brussels – David Mundy
Rue Philippe Le Bon, 26 – Bte. 1
B-1000 Brussels
Tel: +322 280 1292
Fax: +322 280 1292

e-mail: dysonbell@bircham.co.uk

GJW GOVERNMENT RELATIONS LTD

GJW is Europe's largest specialist public affairs consultancy with offices in London, Edinburgh, Cardiff, Dublin, Brussels, and throughout Central and Eastern Europe. Since its formation in 1980, GJW has maintained strong cross-party representation, recruiting from all of the major parties as well as from the civil service.

GJW has developed specialities in a range of areas, in particular defence, healthcare, competition and regulation issues, planning and local government, construction and transport, and national heritage.

GJW is a founding member of the Association of Professional Political Consultants.

For further information contact:
Paul Barnes at
GJW London
2 Little Smith Street
London
SW1P 3DH
England
Tel: 020 7227 8900
Fax: 020 7227 8901
e-mail: londinfo@gjw.co.uk

GJW Edinburgh • GJW Cardiff
GJW Dublin • GJW Brussels
GJW Budapest • GJW Prague
GJW Warsaw

GPC Government Policy Consultants

Europe's leading Public Affairs consultancy, advising private, public and voluntary organisations on all aspects of public policy communications. Our consultants are organised in specialist units servicing the transport, health, environmental, local government, IT, energy, retailing, broadcast and defence sectors amongst others.

Based in London, Edinburgh, Berlin, Brussels, Paris and with a global network of affiliates including North America, our staff are drawn from a wide range of political, civil service, European Commission, academic and commercial backgrounds.

As part of the world-wide Omnicom group of companies, we manage strategic communications issues management and crises programmes.

For information please contact:

Peter Bingle
Managing Director
E-mail: peter.bingle@gpcma.com

GPC London
7 The Sanctuary
Parliament Square
London SW1P 3JS
Tel: 020 7799 1500
Fax: 020 7222 5872
Website:
www.gpcinternational.com

Caroline Wunnerlich
Managing Director
GPC Brussels
Rue d'Arlon 50
B-1000 Brussels
Tel: (00) 322 285 4604
Fax: (00) 322 230 3165

Jane Saren
Managing Director
GPC Edinburgh
14 Charlotte Square
Edinburgh EH2 4DJ
Tel: 0131-226 2102
Fax: 0131-225 9859

**GRANT BUTLER COOMBER
PUBLIC AFFAIRS**

The Award Winning
Results Orientated
Political and Public
Relations Agency

Carl Gibson
Grant Butler Coomber
Westminster House
Kew Road
Richmond
TW9 2ND
t: 020 8322 1922
f: 020 8322 1923
e: carlg@GBC.co.uk
w: grantbutlercoomber.com

HILL & KNOWLTON

H & K's Public and Corporate Affairs Division offers the full range of political consultancy services covering Whitehall, Westminster and Brussels. It develops strategies to manage issues and to influence policy through the full range of 'opinion formers' including regulators, the media, pressure and interest groups and think tanks.

H & K's services are designed to meet three fundamental client needs: to anticipate policy change; to influence the policy process; and to help clients protect their corporate reputation.

H & K offers a full international public affairs service.

For further information please contact:
Edward Bickham
Deputy Chairman
Hill & Knowlton (UK) Ltd
35 Red Lion Square
London WC1R 4SG
Tel: 020 7413 3000
Fax: 020 7413 3113
E-mail:
Ebickham@hillandknowlton.com

KEENE
PUBLIC AFFAIRS
CONSULTANTS LIMITED

Established in 1986 as an independent consultancy, we specialise in government relations and public affairs in the UK and Europe.

Through our London office and our European associates we offer a professional, cost-effective service based on a thorough analysis of our clients' needs.

Our services include: Monitoring, research and strategic advice; Assistance in contact-making and campaigning; Government marketing; Public and media relations; Crisis communications and media training; Speech writing; Event and conference organisation.

For further information please contact:
Tony Richards
Managing Director
Keene Public Affairs Consultants
Victory House
99-101 Regent Street
London W1R 7HB
Tel: 020 7287 0652
Fax: 020 7494 0493
E-mail:
kpac@keenepa.demon.co.uk

Dod *on* Disk

The Vacher Dod
Parliamentary Database
that will run
on your PC
or Network

For further details
please telephone
the Westminster Office

020 7828 7256

The PPS Group

The PPS Group comprises 40 public affairs professionals in two companies:
• PPS (Local and Regional) Ltd advises on presenting to local and regional government and community campaigning. Specialist areas include planning and the environment.
• PPS (Public Affairs) Ltd specialises in strategic advice, e-campaigning and public policy analysis in Westminster, Whitehall, Holyrood, Cardiff and Brussels.

For further information see our website www.ppsgroup.co.uk then contact:

Stephen Byfield
Director
PPS (Local and Regional) Ltd
or
Mark Pendlington
Managing Director
PPS (Public Affairs) Ltd

at
69 Grosvenor Street
London W1X 9DB
020 7629 7377

Craig Harrow
Associate Director
PPS Edinburgh
12 Alva Street
Edinburgh EH2 4QG
0131-226 1951

Jane Blower
Associate Director
PPS North
66/67 Barton Arcade Chambers
Deansgate
Manchester M3 2BJ
0161-832 2139

Fiona MacIntosh
Associate Director
PPS South West
Aztec Centre
Aztec West
Almondsbury
Bristol BS32 4TD
01454 203760

GOVERNMENT RELATIONS AND PARLIAMENTARY CONSULTANTS (cont)

Founded in 1991, Politics International now has over thirty staff working from our offices in London, Edinburgh, Cardiff, Belfast and Brussels. Our specialist local solutions network, and community relations advisors, provide grass-roots, local and regional support.

We offer the full range of public affairs and related services and provide a one-stop shop for strategic advice and practical support at all levels. The principles upon which the company was founded include a rigorously ethical approach; in-depth understanding of clients and their priorities; acute awareness of the commercial implications of political and public policy decisions and professionalism.

For more information about how we can help your business please contact:

Andrew Dunlop
Managing Director
Politics International
Greencoat House
Francis Street
London SW1P 1DH
Tel: 020 7592 3800
Fax: 020 7630 7283
E-mail: pi@politicsint.co.uk
Website: www.politicsint.co.uk

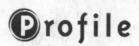

getting it right

Through the provision of accurate and timely political intelligence and the development of reality based strategies, Profile provides sound political relations and corporate communications advice and undertakes implementation of that advice for companies, organisations and overseas governments.

We work with our clients in establishing coalitions of support for their political message and then advise on the communicating of that message to a political audience. We particularly specialise in community relations, legislative support and campaign and issue management.

Our work covers local and national issues in the UK with our associate in Edinburgh. In addition, we have associates in Brussels, Washington DC, New York and Los Angeles.

For further information please contact:
Susan Eastoe
Director

Profile
31 Great Peter Street
London SW1P 3LR
Tel: 020 7654 5600
Fax: 020 7222 2030
E-mail: eastoes@profilecc.com

Understanding Government, informing policy – the true public private partnership

Sound advice depends on good information. Our clients reach better informed business decisions, because they get the best political intelligence.

By understanding and informing the public policy process, clients are enabled to influence outcomes. We aim to achieve clients' commercial objectives through high quality work, ethically conducted.

Advising multi-nationals, blue-chips, Government institutions, trade associations and charities, we provide a full range of Government relations services and skills, including monitoring, research and advocacy in the UK and EU political institutions.

Our clients benefit from a record of solid success across a comprehensive range of policy areas, including:

- financial services
- food & drink
- healthcare & pharmaceuticals
- industrial/environmental
- telecoms
- transport

Contact: **Charles Cockburn**

Portcullis Research
3/19 Holmbush Road
London SW15 3LE
Tel: 020•8789 2798
Fax: 020•8789 0795
E-mail:
info@portcullisresearch.com

The WATERFRONT
PARTNERSHIP

The Waterfront Partnership is a public affairs, strategic and media consultancy giving advice on Westminster, Whitehall and the European institutions.

Waterfront has a highly developed specialism in transport, local government, fiscal, food and drink and regulatory policy issues. The Waterfront Partnership's staff in London and Brussels advise a wide variety of corporate and public sector clients.

The Waterfront Partnership is a member of the Association of Professional Political Consultants.

For further information please contact:

Stephen Bramall
Deputy Managing Director

The Waterfront Partnership
9 Grosvenor Gardens
London SW1W 0BD
Tel: 020 7233 7500
Fax: 020 7233 7511

ADVERTISERS

The Voice of British Advertisers

ISBA is the authoritative source on all advertising matters from the advertiser's perspective. The economic contribution of our members makes us a crucial reference point for you on advertising and commercial communication issues.

For further details, contact:
John Hooper CBE
Director General
or
Ian Twinn
Director of Public Affairs
Tel: 020 7499 7502
Fax: 020 7629 5355
E-mail: info@isba.org.uk
44 Hertford Street
London W1Y 8AE

ANIMAL WELFARE

ANIMAL DEFENDERS

Educates, creates awareness, and promotes interest in the cause of justice and the suppression of all forms of cruelty to animals; to alleviate suffering, to conserve and protect animals and the environment.

Initiatives include a campaign against use of animals in circuses; to bring permanent circus quarters under regulation such as the Zoo Licensing Act.

Contact Jan Creamer, Director
Animal Defenders
261 Goldhawk Road
London W12 9PE
Tel: 020 8846 9777
Fax: 020 8846 9712
E-mail:
info@animaldefenders.org.uk
Web:
http://www.cygnet.co.uk/ad

NATIONAL ANTI-VIVISECTION SOCIETY

Provides scientific reports, briefing papers, video and photos from investigations of use of animals in experiments.

Currently campaigning on excessive secrecy of animal research licensing process.

We also fund sophisticated non-animal techniques; projects include breast and lung cancer, cataracts, dental filling toxicity, drugs, cot deaths, safety testing.

Contact Jan Creamer, Director,
National Anti-Vivisection Society
261 Goldhawk Road
London W12 9PE
Tel: 020 8846 9777
Fax: 020 8846 9712
E-mail: info@navs.org.uk
Web:
http://www.cygnet.co.uk/navs

ARCHITECTS

The Architects Registration Board was established by statute in 1997. As an independent body the aim is to protect consumers and safeguard the reputation of architects by

• maintaining an accurate register of all those entitled to use the term 'architect'
• maintaining and improving standards for education and practice
• taking action if we think somebody should not be on the register
• operating an efficient and effective complaints handling and information service.

Architects Registration Board
8 Weymouth Street
London W1N 3FB
Tel 020 7580 5861
Fax 020 7436 5269

BANKING AND FINANCE

BRITISH BANKERS' ASSOCIATION

105-108 Old Broad Street
London EC2N 1EX
The British Bankers' Association is the principal trade association for over 300 member banks from more than sixty countries doing banking business in the UK. We provide information on banking matters in the UK, EU and the World.

Press and General Information
Brian Capon 020 7216 8810

Director of Communications
Simon Pitkeathley 020 7216 8906
simonp@bba.org.uk

Banks & Building Societies
National Training Organisation
Liz Chiswell 020 7216 8900

BUSINESS REPRESENTATION

The Institute of Directors is a non-political business organisation, with 50,000 members worldwide. It helps directors to carry out their leadership responsibilities in creating wealth for the benefit of business and society. The IoD represents members' interests to government and opinion formers, in the areas of small business policy, corporate governance, employment, education and training, taxation, economic policy, environment and regulation.

Contact: Nina Wilkins
Policy Unit,
IoD,
116 Pall Mall,
London SW1Y 5ED
Tel: 020 7451 3280
Fax: 020 7839 2337
E-mail: policy-unit@iod.co.uk

CABLE COMMUNICATIONS

Telewest Communications plc is the UK's leading cable operator. The company has the potential to serve approximately 6 million homes and businesses throughout the country. Telewest's 1.5 million customers have access to multi-channel television, residential and business telephony, Internet and related services.

For further information and/or advice on policy issues contact:

Malcolm Taylor
Director of Public Policy:
Tel 01483 295117

Tim Brill
Director of Public Relations:
Tel 01483 295184

CONSTRUCTION

NATIONAL HOUSE-BUILDING COUNCIL
Buildmark House,
Chiltern Avenue, Chesham,
Bucks HP6 5AP

NHBC is the standard setting and independent regulatory body for the UK house-building industry. It has around 18,000 registered house builders and developers on its register and approximately 1.7 million homes under its Buildmark warranty and insurance cover. It has enjoyed 60 years at the heart of the house-building industry, and is a highly respected authority on housing construction and home buyer protection.

NHBC sets the standards for house-building, monitors homes built to those standards, and then provides its 'Buildmark' cover on around 90 per cent of private sector new homes in the UK. Independent actuaries have confirmed that housing defects are now less than half what they otherwise would have been without NHBC's insistence on raising standards.

Independent of Government, the Governing Council of NHBC represents all those interested in improving the standard of new home construction.
Contact: Derek Hamilton-Knight, Public Affairs Manager
Tel: 01494 434477
Fax: 01494 735201

EMPLOYMENT

Recruitment & Employment Confederation

The REC is the association for the recruitment and employment services industry, which has an annual turnover of £16 billion and finds work for over 900,000 temporary workers each day. In addition the industry places around 450,000 permanent staff each year. The REC was formed from the merger of FRES and the IEC.

REC members comply with a Code of Practice and are subject to our complaints and disciplinary procedures. The REC has 5,500 corporate members and 7,500 individual members.

For advice and information on the recruitment and employment sector contact Christine Little, Director, REC, 36-38 Mortimer Street London W1N 7RB
Tel: 020 7323 4300
Fax: 020 7637 7914
E-mail: info@rec.uk.com
Website: www.rec.uk.com

ENGINEERING

National Training Organisation for Engineering Manufacture

EMTA's mission is to raise the level of skills in the British engineering industry to world-class standards.

Contact us for information as follows:

EMTA
Tel: 020 7222 0464
Fax: 020 7222 3004

NVQs
Tel: 0345 581207

Engineering Careers
Tel: 0800 282167

Visit EMTA on the internet:
http://www.emta.org.uk

EMTA
2 Queen Anne's Gate Buildings
Dartmouth Street
London SW1H 9BP

ENERGY

BG Group

BG Group's widely recognised expertise spans the entire gas chain from exploration and production, through transportation and distribution, to power generation and market development. The Company also aims to be at the forefront of gas engineering and related technological innovation.

Via its Transco business, BG Group also owns and operates the extensive gas pipeline system in Great Britain. Transco provides an integrated gas transportation and distribution service for competing shippers and suppliers. It is also responsible for system safety and runs the national emergency number – 0800 111999.

For information on BG Group's activities, please contact:

Ian Priestner
Head of Government Relations and Public Policy (UK & International)

BG Group
100 Thames Valley Park
Reading, Berkshire RG6 1PT
Tel: 01189 293026
Fax: 01189 293397

National Grid Group
Government and European Relations
185 Park Street
London SE1 9DY

National Grid owns and operates the electricity transmission system in England and Wales. National Grid also has interests in electricity in USA, Argentina, Zambia, India and Brazil, and has developed a reputation for innovation and the use of hi-tech solutions to increase its business efficiency.

National Grid has also developed Energis, a major telecoms business, in which it retains a significant share and is part of a consortium developing a national telecoms network in Brazil.

Chief Executive: David Jones
Managing Director, Transmission: Roger Urwin

For further information on National Grid's role in managing the electricity system and on our business activities, please contact our Government and European Relations Team:

Judith Ward
Tel: 020 7620 8604
Fax: 020 7620 8879

Jane Smith
Tel: 020 7620 8252
Fax: 020 7620 8879
E-mail: govt.relations@ngc.co.uk

THE ELECTRICITY ASSOCIATION

Roger Pope
Head of Public Relations
020 7963 5881

Simon Gordon
Public Affairs Manager
020 7963 5786

Neil Williams
Public Affairs Officer
020 7963 5828
Fax: 020 7963 5967

THE ELECTRICITY ASSOCIATION
30 Millbank
SW1P 4RD

ScottishPower

Mike Watson
Government Relations Manager
Scottish Power plc
5th Floor
30 Cannon Street
London EC4M 6XH
Tel: 020 7651 2060
Fax: 020 7651 2062

Jamie Maxton
Parliamentary Liaison Officer
Scottish Power plc
1 Atlantic Quay
Glasgow G2 8SP
Tel: 0141 636 4563
Fax: 0141 636 4566

www.politicallinks.co.uk

INSURANCE

ASSOCIATION OF BRITISH INSURERS

ABI is the trade association for insurance companies and represents virtually the whole of the UK insurance company market. The Association represents insurers to Government, Parliament, civil servants and regulatory bodies.

The Association maintains close links with Westminster and Whitehall.

For briefings, information sheets, or help with constituents' queries, contact:

Mary Francis, Director General
Tel: 020 7216 7300
or
Tony Baker,
Deputy Director General
Tel: 020 7216 7400
Fax: 020 7696 8996
Internet: http://www.abi.org.uk

Association of British Insurers
51 Gresham Street
London
EC2V 7HQ

The **International Underwriting Association of London** is the research and representational association for companies operating in the wholesale international insurance and reinsurance market centred on London.

For news and information about our members' contribution to UK inward investment and invisible exports, contact:

Marie-Louise Rossi
Chief Executive
Nick Lowe
Government Affairs
Tel: 020 7617 4444
Fax: 020 7617 4440
Website: www.iua.co.uk

LEGAL RESEARCH

MANORIAL SOCIETY OF GREAT BRITAIN

Research into legal title, history, and the holding of auction sales and of Manors and Feudal Baronies. Publishers of *The House of Lords, a thousand years of British tradition*, *The House of Commons, 700 years of British tradition*, *The Monarchy, 1500 Years of British tradition*, and other historical and constitutional books.

Manorial Society of Great Britain
104 Kennington Road
London SE11 6RE

Tel: 020 7735 6633
Fax: 020 7582 7022

MORTGAGE LENDERS

Council of Mortgage Lenders

Representative body for mortgage lenders, covering 98% of the market.

3 Savile Row
London W1X 1AF
tel: 020 7437 0075
fax: 020 7734 6317

Director-General:
Michael Coogan
Deputy Director-General:
Peter Williams
Head of External Affairs:
Sue Anderson

POLICE

 POLICE FEDERATION OF ENGLAND AND WALES

15-17 Langley Road,
Surbiton, Surrey, KT6 6LP
Tel: 020 8335 1000
Fax: 020 8390 2249
Website: www.polfed.org.uk
E-mail: press.office@polfed.org.uk

The Police Federation is a non political organisation representing 126,000 police officers. It is concerned with issues of integrity, professionalism, training and efficiency across the police service. It advises on all matters affecting operational effectiveness, legislation, training, equipment, welfare, pay and conditions. The Federation publishes the monthly magazine *POLICE*.

POST OFFICE

THE POST OFFICE

The Post Office is a leading business, a significant player in the rapidly changing communications market. It delivers 75 million letters and parcels every working day to all 26 million UK addresses, and operates almost 19,000 post offices, the largest retail chain in the country. It also runs one of the country's biggest tele-management companies.

For further information please contact:

James Lindsay
Head of Political Communications Policy
Tel: 020 7250 2693

Mick Fisher
Head of Westminster Affairs
Tel: 020 7250 2446

Martin Walsh
Head of EU Affairs
Tel: 020 7250 2857/
00 322 280 2820

RETAIL

The Voice of British Retailing

Through its company and trade association membership, BRC represents the interests of 90% of the retail industry.

For information on retail issues please contact:

Leigh Tomkins
Parliamentary Officer
Mark Bradshaw
Acting Director-General

British Retail Consortium
5 Grafton Street
London
W1X 3LB
Tel: 020 7647 1500
Fax: 020 7647 1599

PARLIAMENTARY AGENTS

DYSON BELL MARTIN –
*see entry under Government
Relations and Parliamentary
Consultants on page 1190*

TELECOMMUNICATIONS

For advice on enquiries from
constituents and for guidance on
national and international telecommunications policy issues,
please contact:

**Christine Moore
Head of Public Policy
Tel: 020 7356 5353
Or call the MP Helpline
on 0800 200 789
(Monday–Friday 8am–6pm)**

**BT Public Affairs
BT Centre
81 Newgate Street
London
EC1A 7AJ
Fax: 020 7356 6583**

TRANSPORT

ARRIVA is one of Europe's leading passenger services groups with
an annual turnover of £1.5 billion.
We have 25,000 employees, running 9,000 buses from over 200
locations, serving over 600 million
passengers a year.

We are also a major motor
retailer in the UK with some 40
dealerships and nearly 60 vehicle
rental outlets, as well as a bus and
coach distributor.

Our aim is to provide bus and
rail transport that is efficient, customer friendly, innovative, safe and
environmentally responsible, as
well as delivering responsive, high
quality motor services.

To find out more, please visit our
website at **www.arriva.co.uk** or
contact:

Bob Davies
Chief Executive
Julian Evans
*Director of Corporate
Communications*
**ARRIVA plc
Tel: 0191-520 4000
Fax: 0191-520 4115**

SPT is Scotland's only
passenger transport authority
and executive, investing in rail,
bus, underground and ferry
services for 42 per cent of the
nation's population.

To find out more about SPT and
how we're shaping a future for
public transport, write to:

Strathclyde Passenger Transport
Consort House
12 West George Street
Glasgow G2 1HN
Tel: 0141 332 6811

WATER UTILITIES

SEVERN TRENT

ENVIRONMENTAL LEADERSHIP

**Severn Trent Plc includes Severn
Trent Water, Biffa Waste Services
and Severn Trent Services.**

To us, environmental leadership
and commercial success go hand
in hand. As a leading provider of
water, waste and utility services
around the world, we now employ
12,500 people in the UK, North
America and Europe, generating
sales last year of more than £1.3
billion. As individuals, we can all
work to improve the environment.
But a company the size of Severn
Trent can really make an impact.

**For further information contact:
David Daw 0121 722 4310
Corporate Marketing Director
Fax 0121 722 4242
E-mail:
david.daw@severntrent.co.uk
James Sheward 0121 722 4857
Corporate Government Relations
Manager
Fax 0121 722 4534
E-mail:
james.sheward@severntrent.co.uk
Severn Trent Plc
2297 Coventry Road
Birmingham B26 3PU
www.severn-trent.com
Severn Trent Water MPs' hotline
0121 722 4555**

INDEX OF ADVERTISERS

VACHER'S EUROPEAN COMPANION

The UK's definitive quarterly guide to
EUROPE

A wide-ranging reference book covering all the important EU institutions and other European organisations, history, new appointments, and national sections for East and West European countries.

- European Parliament election results June 1999

- EU Institutions – How the institution works, details of committees, full listing of personnel and how to make contact

- European Organisations – Professional, trade associations, pressure groups, research and educational bodies

- European Countries – Information on governments, elections, political structure, economic and trade activities, and general and public holidays etc

Vacher Dod Publishing Limited
PO Box 3700, Westminster, London SW1E 5NP
Tel: 020 7828 7256   Fax: 020 7828 7269
E-mail: politics@vacherdod.co.uk
Websites: www.vacherdod.co.uk   www.politicallinks.co.uk

INDEX